THE GREAT WORLD ATLAS

American Map Corporation

New York, N.Y.

ATTRIBUTION

Publisher:

American Map Corporation, New York, N.Y.

Editorial:

Vera Benson, Director of Cartography,
American Map Corporation, in cooperation
with Kartographisches Institut Bertelsmann

Art and Design:

Vera Benson, American Map Corporation and
Kartographisches Institut Bertelsmann

Cartography:

Verlagsgruppe Bertelsmann GmbH,
Kartographisches Institut Bertelsmann, Gütersloh

Satellite Photos:

Photos: Deutsche Forschungs- und Versuchsanstalt für Luft- und Raumfahrt e.V., Oberpfaffenhofen, p. 9, 10; Map of Ptolemy, Staatsbibliothek, Preußischer Kulturbesitz, Berlin, Signatur Inc. 2640, p. 10; European Space Agency (ESA), Paris, and National Aeronautics and Space Administration (NASA), Washington, D.C.

Satellite Picture Processing: Dr. Rupert Haydn, Gesellschaft für Angewandte Fernerkundung mbH, Munich

Design: topic GmbH, Munich

Statistical Maps and Charts:

Design: Josef Toman, Gütersloh, and Karl-Heinz Wirth, Bielefeld.

The Nature of Our Planet:

Photos: Buxton/Survival Anglia (2); Everts/Zefa (1); Geoscience Features (1); Heather Angel (3); Hutchison Picture Library (3); NASA/Science Photo Library (1); Photri/Zefa (1); Regent/Hutchison Picture Library (1); Schneiders/Zefa (1); Schumacher/Zefa (1); Spectrum Colour Library (3); Steemans/Zefa (1); Swiss Tourist Office (2); van Grulsen (1); Willock/Survival Anglia (1).

Layout: Hubert Hepfinger, Freising

© Verlagsgruppe Bertelsmann International GmbH, Munich.

The Nature of Our Universe:

Arbeitsgemeinschaft Astrofotografie, Neustadt (4);
Joachim Herrmann, Recklinghausen (2);
Kartographisches Institut Bertelsmann, Gütersloh (6);
Barbara Michael, Hamburg (4);
Mount Wilson and Palomar Observatories (2);
NASA, Washington (1);
Günter Radtke, Uetze (1).

Text:

For Satellite Photos: Dr. Konrad Hiller,
Deutsche Forschungs- und Versuchsanstalt für Luft- und Raumfahrt e.V., Oberpfaffenhofen and Ulrich Münzer, University of Munich.

For Introduction and Statistical Maps and Charts: Helmut Schaub, Stuttgart.

For The Nature of Our Planet:
© Verlagsgruppe Bertelsmann International GmbH, Munich.

For The Nature of Our Universe: Joachim Herrmann, Recklinghausen.

Translations: Introduction Joseph Butler, Munich,
Satellite part Deirdre Hiller, Steinebach,
Statistical Maps and Charts, Berlitz School, Stuttgart,
The Nature of Our Universe, Ann Hirst for German Language Services, New York.

Library of Congress Card Number 86-71065

© 1989 RV Reise- und Verkehrsverlag GmbH,
Munich, Berlin, Gütersloh, Stuttgart.

Printed and bound in W. Germany by Mohndruck Graphische Betriebe GmbH, Gütersloh.

ISBN 0-8416-2003-2

Second Edition

Printed in W. Germany

THE
GREAT
WORLD
ATLAS

INTRODUCTION

A world atlas is a condensed and systematic representation of human knowledge of the earth. The atlas, thus, fulfills two essential functions: first, it is a reference work of individual geographic facts; second, it sums up and comments upon our knowledge of various regions of the earth.

The means of cartographic representation are point, line and surface area, realized in color or pattern, and complemented by the written word, the explanatory element. Cartographers thus avail themselves of the same visual means of expression as graphic artists. Maps are scaled down, simplified, and annotated pictures of the earth and its regions. Cartographic representations number among the oldest cultural and artistic expressions of mankind. Maps are documents of man's contemplation of his environment and, as such, reveal his level of knowledge of his surroundings.

Like specialists in other areas, cartographers of today are faced with the difficult task of reducing a great diversity of complex information about the earth to a simplified, easy-to-understand form. The purpose of a world atlas is to present, clearly and concisely, those factors that shape the character of the whole earth or its regions – geofactors such as topography, climate, and vegetation; or the characteristics that result from the activities of mankind such as land use, economy, transportation, education, etc. In order to gain this comprehensive world picture, "The Great World Atlas" employs satellite photographs, topographic (physical) maps, thematic maps, as well as charts, illustrations, and text describing our world and universe.

"The Great World Atlas" is further distinguished by its clearly arranged sequence of maps, from north to south and from west to east, within the different continents, as well as by a unique system that uses fewer, chiefly true-to-area projections, and fewer scales. This facilitates the use of the atlas and the comparison of individual regions. Special attention has been paid to the United States by using the scale 1:3,750,000. This scale makes possible the complete reproduction of each individual state on one map. Continents are uniformly portrayed at a scale of 1:13,500,000. Numerous maps at a scale of 1:4,500,000 or 1:6,750,000 are devoted to countries and to important political, economic, and tourist regions. The worldwide phenomenon of the concentration of population in urban areas is taken into account by maps of major metropolitan centers (scale 1:225,000).

Satellite Photos: "The Great World Atlas" is unparalleled in its presentation of large regions of the earth through satellite photos. Satellite photos are "snapshots" of the surface of the earth. With the help of the topographic maps you can orient yourself in these landscapelike images. While topographic maps focus on the relief of the earth, satellite photos may emphasize the presence or absence of plant growth, or specific qualities of vegetation. The thematic maps, on the other hand, provide the facts behind the details in the images; e. g. climate maps may explain the reasons for the presence or absence of vegetation.

Satellite pictures and maps complement each other, neither one could replace the other. A separate chapter of this atlas looks into the technology of expensive high-tech satellite information gathering systems used to generate satellite imagery.

Topographic or physical maps: These constitute the major part of the atlas. The use of color and shading provide the impression of height and depth necessary to visualize various surface configurations of the earth. A great number of map symbols denote specific topographic forms such as deserts, swamps, glaciers and the like, but above all, the man-made topographic elements such as population centers, transportation routes or political borders. An additional characteristic of these topographic maps is the use of highly detailed nomenclature to identify the broad variety of geographic features.

Thematic maps: These maps either focus on single topics or form thematic groups, including precipitation or climate, soil, vegetation, population density, economy, nutrition, etc. Thematic data are built on simplified base maps containing major geographic features such as coast lines, waterways, political borders and important cities to assure spacial orientation and easy reference to the topographic maps. By comparing the topographic and thematic maps, the geographic forces, correlationships and interdependencies in the political, strategic, economic, and cultural spheres become evident.

Facts of general interest from the realms of population, economics, and politics become easy to grasp through vivid diagrams, graphs, and maps based on the latest figures in the section "Statistical Maps and Charts." In this way, special regional features emerge that complement the thematic maps.

Two sections new to this edition cover the topics of Earth Science and Astronomy. In The Nature of Our Planet we learn about the physical history and composition of our planet, and the processes of change it has undergone and continues to undergo. We can appreciate, for instance, that what transpires on a large scale over aeons – the destruction and creation of landforms – finds its counterpart, on a small scale, in the common, observable events of erosion by weathering, and deposition of eroded particles. Based on the latest scientific observations, The Nature of Our Universe offers insights into the structure and development of our solar system, our galaxy, and our ever-expanding universe.

"The Great World Atlas" makes a strong case for its claim as a special reference work with its extensive index of place names. It contains, in unabbreviated form, all the names that appear on the maps; in all, more than 100,000 entries.

All maps are up to date and reflect current scholarship and cartographic technology. Thus, "The Great World Atlas" meets the demands placed upon a modern map work with respect to both content and execution. For this achievement we extend our gratitude to all contributors, advisers, and institutions that have assisted us.

The Publisher

THE GREAT WORLD ATLAS

CONTENTS OVERVIEW

TABLE OF CONTENTS

PHOTO SECTION

SATELLITE PHOTOS

MAP SECTION

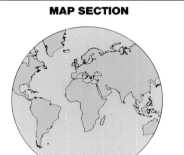

THE WORLD

TABLE OF CONTENTS

TABLE OF CONTENTS

THE GREAT WORLD ATLAS

TABLE OF CONTENTS

EARTH FROM OUTER SPACE

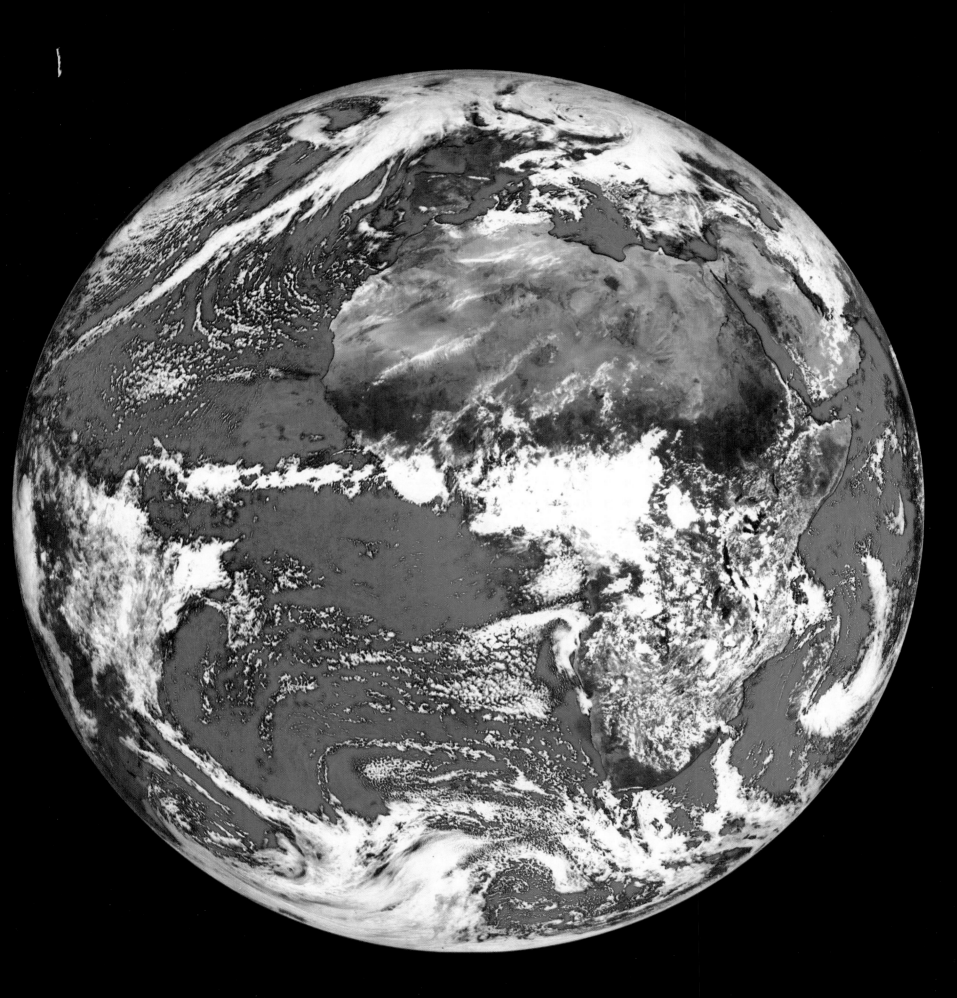

From Maps to Satellite Photos

Since early times man has tried to represent his environment pictorially. Today's familiar topographical maps are based on the concepts of the Greek natural scientist, Claudius Ptolemy. He first developed these during the second century in Alexandria, Egypt. Although his maps have not survived, his extant treatise, entitled "Geography", asserted great influence for centuries. It gives directions for presenting the spherical surface of the earth on a plane and for locating places on earth, using a grid with longitude and latitude lines. Ptolemy's directions reflect the knowledge of his time, yet maps reconstructed accordingly, around 1480, influenced official maps and geographical thinking for centuries thereafter. The world map below, printed in the 15th century, was drawn based upon Ptolemy's concept. It shows severe distortions in the proportions of some areas. The Black Sea, the Caspian Sea, and the Persian Gulf are each shown to be approximately the same size as the eastern Mediterranean. Geographers of that time had little reliable information and their ideas of the physical world were often influenced by imagination and legends. This accounts for non-existent mountain ranges and rivers in inner Africa and in the whole of eastern Asia. The distortion of features in the west-east direction caused Columbus to underestimate his western route to India by half of the real distance. Although he knew the correct circumference of the earth, his concept of geography was formed by such distorted maps. Fortunately, he reached land just as his supplies were running out. Thinking he was in India, he did not realize, at first, that he had discovered a new continent.

To satisfy the needs of the seafaring nations, coasts of newly discovered regions had priority over interior areas and were explored and surveyed first. The Englishman, Captain James Cook, made decisive contributions to coastal exploration, and geographical knowledge in general, during his three journeys between 1768 and 1779. He proved that no southern continent existed in the moderate climatic zone; discovered New Zealand and several other islands in the Pacific; and confirmed that Australia was a separate continent.

In the 18th and 19th centuries, the consequent seizure and division of newly discovered territories amongst the European powers stimulated detailed exploration, particularly of economically and strategically important areas. The publishing of larger-scaled maps and the introduction of thematic maps followed.

The development of a completely new dimension in cartography began with aerial photography. In 1858, the Parisian photographer, Nadar, working from a captive balloon, took the first aerial photo of the village of Bicètre, near Paris. Further developments followed fast, based upon developments in aviation. With the increasing distance and altitude capabilities of airplanes, larger and remoter areas could be surveyed (also see diagram p. 13). Concurrent advances in photography resulted in distortion-free lenses, precise shutters, and the use of a vacuum to keep film completely flat and in position. Progress in the development of materials resulted in a special fine-grained film, larger film formats, and the introduction of color film. The advanced state of this technology (at least militarily) was spotlighted in 1960 when the American U2-Pilot, Powers, was shot down over Russia. Films found in the wreck were published by the Soviet Union for propaganda purposes. These pictures, taken at a height of 15.5 mi., were able to distinguish a cyclist from a pedestrian!

In addition to maximum resolution, aerial photographs must meet other requirements. Minimum lens distortion is particularly important. This requires the lens to be calculated precisely and ground so that photographed landmarks do not appear displaced in the image. Distortions caused by imprecise lenses become immediately obvious during processing of the images by modern photogrammetric analyzing instruments. When viewing overlapping aerial photos through a stereoscope, a three-dimensional impression of the earth's surface is obtained. Such stereoscopic models may be used to derive exact locations and measurements of clearly defined points on the earth, and to determine topographic contour lines.

To obtain the overlapping aerial photos needed to produce a map, an airplane must fly on parallel courses, as many times as necessary, over the entire area. For control purposes, the position of the mid-point of each image is recorded on a small-scale diagram of the area. This pictorial information, together with data derived through the classic methods of photogrammetry, forms the basis for the production of topographical maps. First, the available image information is reduced according to the scale of the planned map and then it is transformed into drawings containing the familiar map symbols. Finally, color, shading, feature names, and explanatory technical notes are added.

Although generally unknown to the public, aerial photography is used in fields other than cartography. It aids in the planning of new highways and railway lines; redistribution of agricultural land; siting of landfill areas; expansion of suburbs; surveying of waste dumps; and damage to crops. Nevertheless, aerial photographs cannot meet several requirements. It is impossible to photograph large areas, for example, the state of New York, in a short time and at a reasonable cost. Such a project would take days or weeks, during which time weather and lighting conditions would constantly change. The only solution to this problem is the use of satellites, flying high above the earth's surface. Satellite images of areas as large as 112 x 122 mi. can be taken in a few minutes, under constant lighting and weather conditions. The area photographed is large enough to carry out extensive, comparative investigations of vegetative or geological phenomena. In extreme cases, the whole of Europe, as on the weather satellite image opposite, or even an earth hemisphere, as on the Meteosat-Image (title page), can be covered by a single picture. With the aid of satellite photography, it is possible to record completely the earth's surface and to almost continually observe it. Current technology, methods, and applications of satellite photography are described on the following pages.

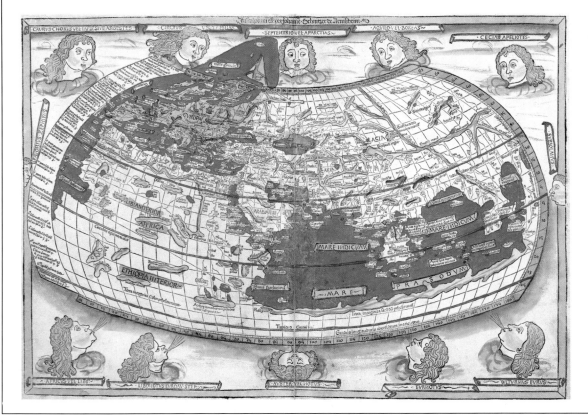

▷ Europe
Central Europe taken from the weather satellite NOAA – 7. Colors represent various surface temperatures. Blue represents low, yellow to red higher temperatures.

◁ Map of Ptolemy
During the Renaissance, maps drawn according to Claudius Ptolemy's concepts were widely used and influential. The one shown was published in 1482 in the "Cosmographia" by Linhart Holl in Ulm, Germany.

Distant Reconnaissance of the Earth
Techniques — Methods — Applications

In the last few years satellite images have become a common sight. Every evening television meteorologists use up-to-the-minute satellite maps to depict weather conditions across the continent. Reference books and magazines display satellite images of our cities or regional areas of interest. With few exceptions, these photos show strange, artificial red and gray tones dominating at our latitudes. The satellite imaging systems and the human eye obviously "see" things differently.

All substances whose temperatures register above absolute zero emit electromagnetic radiation. The higher the temperature, the shorter the emitted wavelength. Because the surface temperature of the sun averages 10,800°F, it radiates predominantly in the shorter wavelengths from ultraviolet to infrared. The human eye is adapted to a small portion of this radiation, which we sense as light.

Light coming directly from the sun appears colorless. Nevertheless when it strikes a body, some wavelengths are absorbed and others are reflected, resulting in color. The various characteristics of that body will determine the specific colors we see. A diagram of the range of electromagnetic radiation used in remote sensing from space is given opposite.

The earth's atmosphere strongly scatters and absorbs the blue part of the visible light. Therefore, remote sensing instruments do not register blue. They register the primary colors green and red, and a third component, shortwave infrared, which lies next to red in the spectrum, but is not visible to the eye.

Radiation from all three wavelengths is recorded separately in black and white. To reconstruct an image, the color blue is used to represent green light, green for red light, and red for infrared radia-

tion. This results in the false color images previously mentioned. Fresh vegetation, for example, appears red because the chlorophyll in the leaves strongly reflects infrared wavelengths. Damaged vegetation loses this characteristic, causing the green band to predominate, thus, transitional colors from red to violet and blue are obtained.

In contrast, optoelectronic instruments operate without film. Light reflected from an object is recorded by a sensor and then transformed into electric signals. These are amplified and transmitted, in digital form, to a receiving station on the earth and are stored on magnetic tape. The conversion to a false color image can take place either directly on a computer screen or through point by point exposure of data on film.

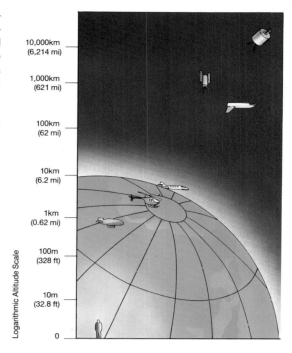

In contrast to a conventional camera, which takes a photograph in a single exposure, an electronic sensor receives only one image point, that is, light from a small part of the earth's surface. Light from subsequent surface points is conducted point by point to the sensor by a rotating mirror (mirror scanner). Filters, placed in the path of light, or diverse sensors split the light into separate bands of the electromagnetic spectrum. The American Landsat and weather satellites use this type of scanning instrument.

The future of this field lies in the Charge Coupled Device scanners. In these CCDs, up to 4000 sensors are mounted in a single row. Each sensor measures about 16 thousandths of a millimeter and the complete chip about 5 cm. The chip is installed with the row of sensors perpendicular to the flight path of the satellite. The image is created by recording information point by point and row by row, with each scanning point corresponding to one of the sensors. An advantage of this system is that no moving mechanical parts are necessary. This greatly increases the reliability of such instruments, particularly important for long missions in outer space.

Scanner systems have several basic advantages over conventional film cameras. The signals are recorded in digital form and can be processed by a computer; also, wavelength which lie outside the sensitivity range of film can be registered. For example, rays in the thermal region, that is, warmth emitted from a body, can be recorded. The image of Central Europe, page 11, was recorded in this way. To make the temperature differences of the various surface types visible, the colors blue, green and red are used for the lowest to highest temperatures respectively. Water bodies and pine forests are relatively cold (dark blue), agricultural areas cool (green) to warm (yellow to orange), and urban areas are very warm (red). Clouds and snow in the alpine regions are extremely cold hence, pale blue.

The production and processing of modern satellite images would be impossible without high capacity computers. Each Landsat image contains 32 million pieces of information! The standard processing of this information results in the strangely colored images already discussed.

Nevertheless, sophisticated computer programs now make it possible to simulate the scattered blue not recorded by sensing instruments. A combination of the simulated blue and the original signals from the green and red bands results in an image with more or less natural colors, depending upon the quality of the processing. The examples on the opposite page clearly illustrate the difference between the false color image and its corresponding natural color image. The area pictured is San Francisco Bay and its surroundings. The most noticeable contrasts are that the green areas of vegetation appear red in the original image and the brown unforested mountains appear yellow.

All the previously described remote sensing techniques are based on "passive" methods — they record reflected (from light) or radiated (from warmth) electromagnetic waves from the observed object. In addition, various "active" procedures are used in remote sensing. Various wavelengths from the radar band (see the "Electromagnetic Spectrum" diagram below) are emitted from a transmitter, on board an airplane or satellite, via an antenna. The time the signal takes to travel from the transmitter to the object and back again is recorded and, following several intermediate steps, converted into an image. The advantage of this method is that the relatively longwave radar radiation travels through the atmosphere, practically without interference, so that one can "see" through clouds. This technique is very useful in areas such as the Amazon Basin, where year-round cloud cover makes conventional photography useless.

The equipment and methods of analysis described above could, in principle, be used at all altitudes. In fact, the equipment and the altitude selected are based upon the particular task requirements and environmental considerations such as image size, ground resolution, spectral range, probability of cloud coverage, etc. Dirigibles and helicopters fly at the lowest altitudes — from 3 to 5mi. Airplanes usually fly between 2 and 9 mi., and military spy planes up to 19 mi. high. Above the earth's atmosphere the space shuttle orbits at an altitude of 125 to 188 mi. and the earth observation satellites at 438 to 563 mi. They take about 90 minutes for one revolution around the earth. The meteorological and communication satellites appear fixed above a point over the equator, because at 22,400 mi. altitude, they orbit at exactly the same speed as the earth rotates at the equator. From this orbit, an overall view of half of the earth's sphere is possible.

Satellite images have multiple uses. Weather satellites, located above a fixed point on the earth's surface, transmit an image every half an hour, day and night, providing data on cloud type, altitude, and direction of movement, as well as air temperature. Satellite and aerial photographs have become indispensable to cartographers, particularly for recording inaccessible or quickly changing phenomena. Extensive areas can be economically, precisely and, if necessary, repeatedly recorded. Producing maps and monitoring icebergs are specific examples of this use.

Multispectral analysis is used to distinguish between different materials. This is achieved by analyzing the different reflection characteristics of materials in the various wavelength ranges. It is mainly used in geology, forestry, and agriculture. In geology research is being carried out to determine the composition of rock and its tectonics through its spectral behavior. This can result in finding unknown ore deposits. The main applications in forestry and agriculture are the assessment of damage to forests and the estimation of expected harvest yields. In both cases periodically repeated surveys at different times of the year are necessary for accurate assessments. Important future applications will be in the field of environmental protection. Illegal discharges of oil from ships into the ocean or the release of toxic substance into rivers and lakes can be detected, and the responsible parties identified.

The images in this atlas were taken from the American satellites Landsat 1 to 4. The scales are 1:710,000 and 1:450,000. The orientation is north-northwest, picture size 112 x 112 mi. and 112 x 81 mi. respectively, and the ground resolution is 263 ft.

◁ *San Francisco*
Bay of San Francisco computer processed in two different ways: left false color image, right natural color version (see text).

△ *Remote sensing platforms*
The diagram displays the flight altitudes most commonly used for remote sensing platforms.

▷ *Electromagnetic spectrum*
Only part of the electromagnetic spectrum is used for remote sensing. It ranges from ultraviolet to the radar wavelengths, with visible light and short wave infrared being of particular importance.

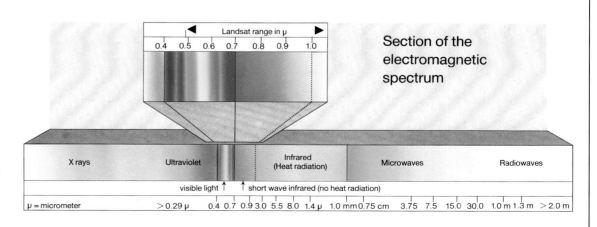

Section of the electromagnetic spectrum

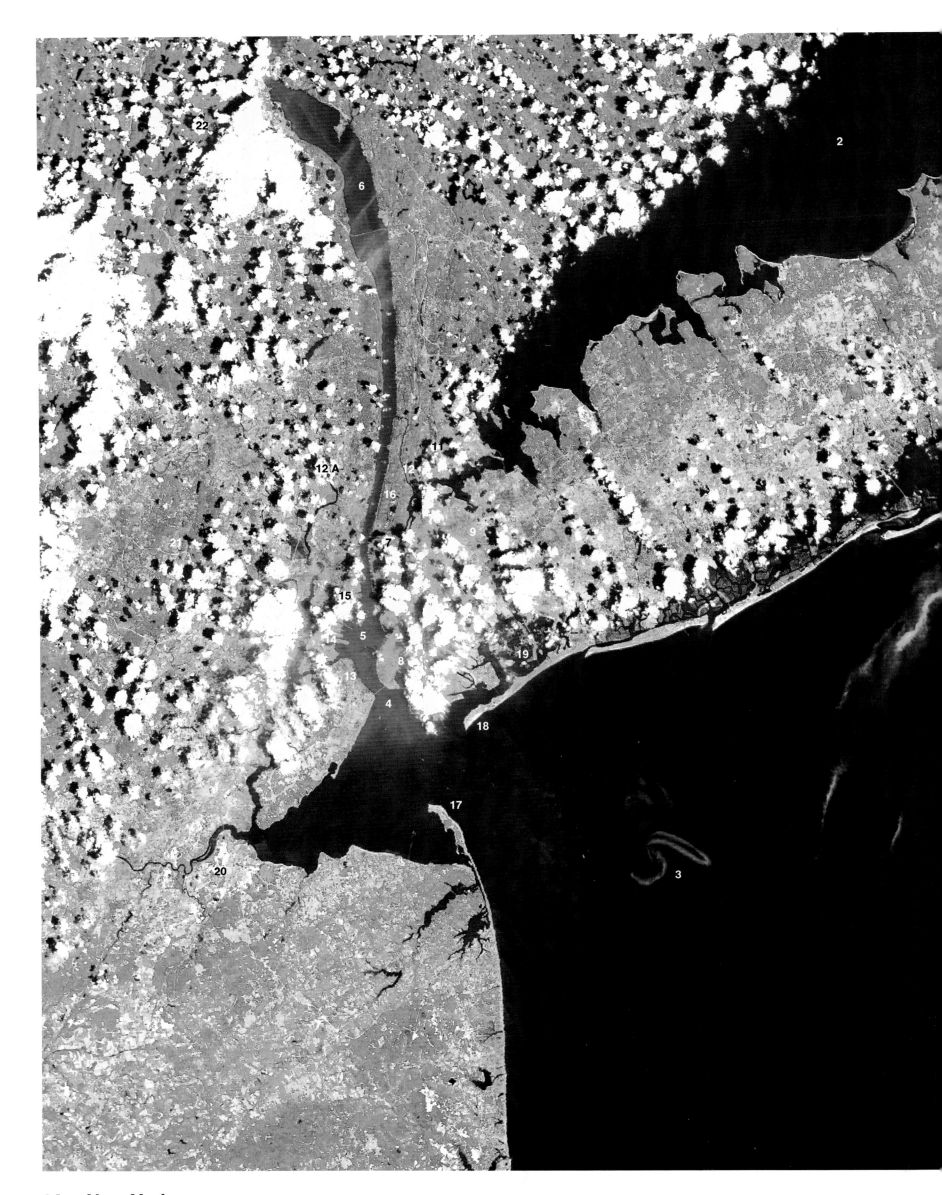

Hub of Commerce and Culture

The New York City Metropolitan Area is the focal point of this satellite image. Its urban areas are characterized by gray; agricultural regions form a mosaic of browns and greens; while forests and meadows appear in gradations of green.

Long Island (1) is separated from the mainland by Long Island Sound (2). Above the ocean, the wind forms ribbons from vapor trails of high-flying jets (3). The Verrazano Narrows Bridge (4) appears as a thin line crossing the Narrows and marks the entrance to Upper New York Bay (5). The Hudson River (6) – the lower part of which is actually a fjord – is navigable by ocean-going vessels as far as Albany, the state capital, 150 miles upstream. In the photograph, the five boroughs of New York City are partially obscured by clouds. The island of Manhattan (7) is separated from Brooklyn (8) and Queens (9) by the East River, from the Bronx (11) – and the New York mainland – by the Harlem River (12), and from New Jersey (12 A) by the Hudson River. Manhattan is separated from Staten Island (13) by Upper New York Bay. The Staten Island ferry crosses the bay and provides a link for thousands of Staten Island residents who work in Manhattan. The densely populated areas west of the Hudson in New Jersey are Jersey City (14) and Hoboken (15).

The cultural and commercial center of the New York Metropolitan Area is the island of Manhattan (7). New York's famous Museum Mile – including the Metropolitan Museum, the Guggenheim Museum, and several others – runs along Fifth Avenue. This forms the eastern edge of Central Park (16) which is visible as a green rectangle. Complementing the fine arts are the performing arts, with a dazzling array of live theater staged in the Theater District, as well as other parts of the city. Broadway, Off Broadway, and Off-Off Broadway performances offer visitors and residents the widest range of entertainment possibilities found anywhere. The Wall Street area is the home of the New York Stock Exchange and contains the highest concentration of commercial and financial concerns in the world.

Because of the high contrast between the dark blue color of the sea and the gray of the building complexes, numerous details along the shore lines can be observed. A filigree of 3000 docks and piers – about 100 miles long – can be followed in New York City as well as in New Jersey. The shores toward the Atlantic are characterized by offshore barrier beaches including Sandy Hook (17) and Breezy Point (18). East of these, the wildlife refuge of Jamaica Bay (19) appears as brown lagoons. The mosaic of green and gray in New Jersey's Middlesex County (20) indicates its diverse composition of towns, suburbs, parks, and industrial areas. Further west and north, the forests of the Watchung Mountains (21) and Hudson Highlands (22) form swatches of deep green.

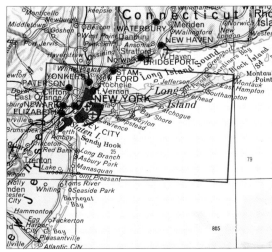

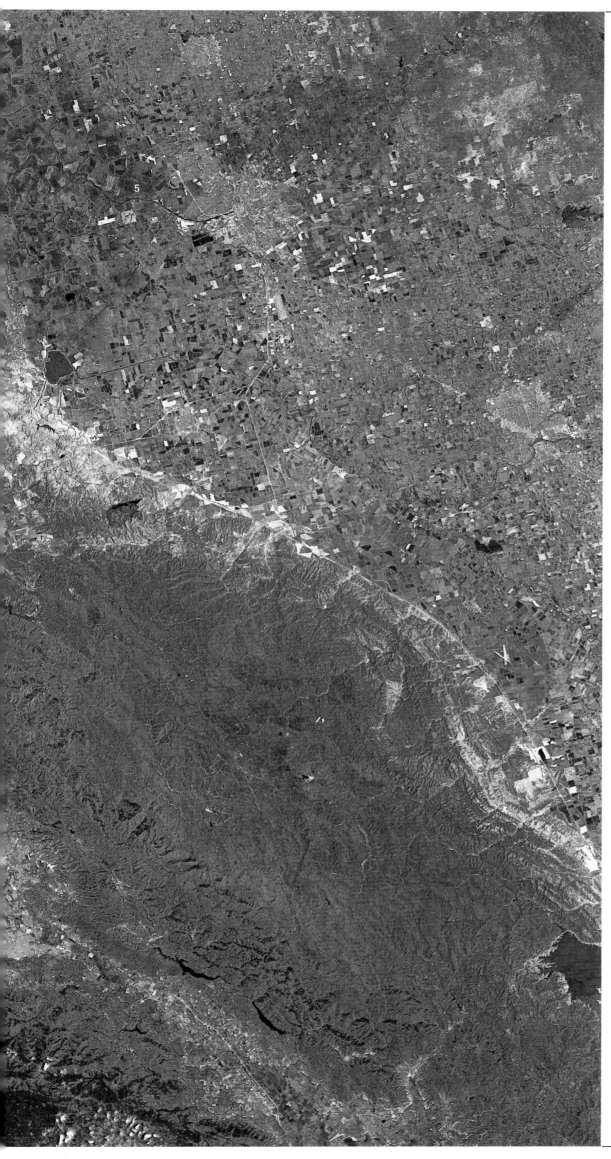

The City on the Bay

Founded in 1779 by Spanish missionaries, San Francisco is known as the romantic city of the gold rush, sailing ships, and cable cars, but also as the center of a devastating earthquake. Overlooking the best natural harbor of the Pacific coast, the city is the center of a huge megalopolis. Surrounding the bay, residential areas, port facilities, military installations, and industrial complexes lie side by side to form the "Bay Area".

This satellite image shows the Pacific coast (1), the Bay Area (2) with the coastal ranges in the west (3) and the valleys of the Sacramento (4) and San Joaquin (5) rivers to the north-east.

Golden Gate (6), the strait which links the open waters of the Pacific Ocean with the bay, is easy to recognize. Measuring only 5 mi. long by 2 mi. wide, this gap experiences tidal changes of up to 7 ft. The severe currents caused by these tidal changes acted as a major deterrent to escape for the prisoners of the former jail on Alcatraz Island (7). The water of the bay is heavily polluted from industrial and agricultural waste and, therefore, appears gray. This image, taken at low tide, shows the contaminated water flowing out to the ocean, mixing with dark, clear water, and drifting south.

The Golden Gate Bridge, supported by 745 ft high piers, spans the Golden Gate and is clearly visible as a white line (8). Within San Francisco city limits some landmarks are distinguishable: Golden Gate Park (9), the harbor docks (10), and just south of the city, the airport runways (11).

The bay of San Francisco is a geological syncline that forms part of the great San Andreas Fault system. Two continental plates are moving in opposite directions, one to the north-west (Pacific Plate), and the other south-east (North-American Plate). Over decades stress builds up along this 18 mi. deep fault until, at a critical point, pressure is released all at once. In 1906 an earthquake of this origin destroyed much of the city of San Francisco. Over a length of 125 mi. the western plate (Pacific Plate) moved 23 feet to the northwest. The San Andreas Fault (12) as well as other tectonic structures such as the Calaveras (13) and Hayward faults (14) show up as lines in the picture.

Bordering the bay and bounded by the Diablo (15) and Santa Cruz Mountains (16), flat alluvial land offers ideal conditions for settlement. Approximate - ly 10 million people live in this area, shown here in gray tones. Because of their coarser pattern one is able to distinguish the city centers of Oakland (17) and San Jose (18) from their suburbs. On the southern end of the bay, rice fields, planted on recently drained marshes, are highlighted by a dense green color and enclosed by white borders (19). The deep brown patches in the same area are basins where sea water is evaporated to win salt (20).

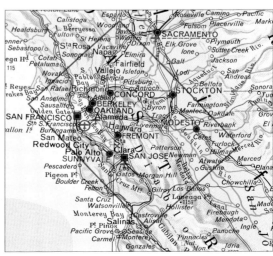

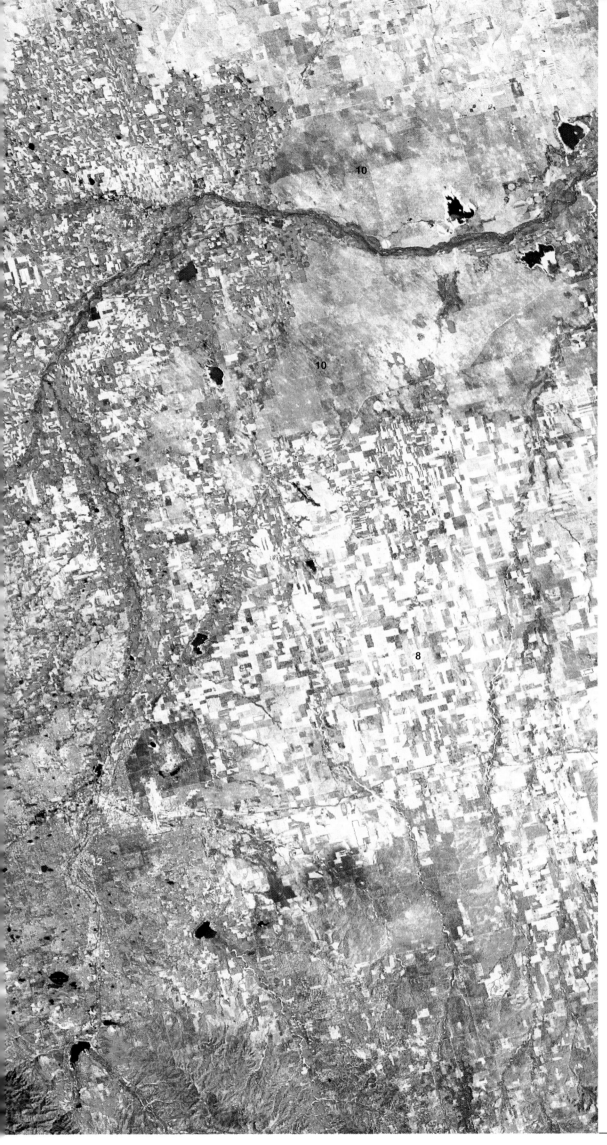

Mountains and Plains

The Front Ranges of the Rocky Mountains must have been an alarming sight for the early settlers traveling across the Great Plains. They rise up from the plains as a natural, seemingly insurmountable barrier, blocking the way west. Since there are no wide valleys, the few roads crossing the mountains have been constructed along deeply carved rivers and over high passes. Highway No. 40 (1), for example, follows Clear Creek (2) up to the 11,314 ft high Berthoud Pass (3) which is part of the continental divide. The continental divide runs from north to south and is roughly marked by the snowy peaks in the image. It separates water running west to the Colorado River (4), and eventually the Pacific Ocean, from that running east to the South Platte River (5) and the Gulf of Mexico. Aspen and coniferous trees, like Ponderosa pine, Douglas fir, and Rocky Mountain red cedar cover the mountains up to an altitude of 11,000 ft. Above this green zone brown meadows are found. High peaks such as Long's Peak rising to 14, 255 ft (6) and Hagues Peak (13,563 ft) (7), are covered with snow. Both are within the Rocky Mountain National Park.

In contrast to the dark green forests of the Rocky Mountains, one can see the multicolor checkered pattern of the Great Plains. This whole area is intensively farmed. The different types of land use can be recognized by the colors and sizes of the fields: yellow and brown represent winter wheat (8); green marks corn, beans and potatoes (9); and yellowish-brown indicates fallow land. Here the old field boundaries can barely be traced (10). The position of cultivated land along the South Platte River and its tributaries shows the area's dependence on the run-off water from the highlands. In fact, a substantial part of the irrigation water has to be diverted from the mountains east of the continental divide to the Great Plains by tunnel systems.

In 1858, a party of prospectors led by William Green Russell, discovered gold near Cherry Creek (11). This caused the Pikes Peak gold rush, during which about 50,000 people poured into the area. Cities such as Denver the capital of Colorado (12), Boulder (13), and Greeley (14) were founded during the late 19th century. Mining for gold was followed by mining for silver, but all these activities were short-lived, and by the end of the century the mountains were deserted, except for the operations of a few uranium and molybdenum mines.

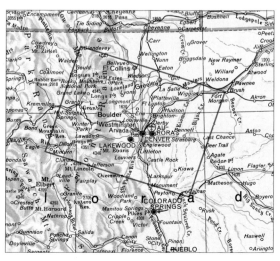

Denver 19

Frontier in the Desert

This satellite photo shows part of the Sonora Desert at the northern end of the Gulf of California. The political boundary between Sonora, Mexico, in the south, and Yuma County, Arizona, in the north, is visible as a fine, pale diagonal line through the upper third of the picture (1). It consists of a fence, erected to prevent illegal immigration into the U.S.A.

In this desert and semi-desert landscape of white, beige, red and brown tones, little green is to be found as an indicator of vegetation. Irrigated crop cultivation (2) is only possible in the area on the lower edge of this image, where the Rio Concepcion flows into the Gulf. Also the upper course of the Rio Sonoita (3) creates, in places, green river oases. Other signs of vegetation appear only during a few months, in spring when torrential rain falls cause the desert to turn green and burst into blossom overnight. The giant saguaro cactuses (organ pipe cactuses) can also be found here. They grow up to 50 feet high and live for 150 to 200 years. Their white, wax-like flower is the state flower of Arizona. Organ Pipe Cactus National Monument (4), just north of the border, was established to protect these plants.

The coastal region is, in comparison, total desert. The people in the small towns of Porto Penasco (5) and La Salina (6) make their living from fishing. The form and location of the sandbanks in Bahia de Adair (7) and Bahia de San Jorge (8) show the existence of currents running parallel to the coast. These are influenced by the debouchment of the Colorado River which lies to the northwest, outside the boundary of the image. The fringes of the Gran Desierto, which stretches as far as the Colorado River, reach into this photo (9). Its sand fields, containing huge star dunes (10), can be clearly seen. White patches in the region of the dark brown shore marshlands (11), arise from the efflorescence of salt through evaporation of sea water. The most conspicuous formation is that of the Pinacate volcano field. The highest peak (12) reaches 4,560 ft. The volcanic activity in this area is relatively young. Some of the volcanoes, recognizable by their dark more or less circular forms, first erupted during the last 1000 years. The youngest lava fields are represented by very dark, almost black colors (13) which indicate a basaltic composition. In addition to the more common basaltic volcanism, explosive volcanism also occurs here. In the latter case lava, very rich in gas, explodes in the deep layers of the earth. On the surface it produces the familiar, usually circular conal structures (14). Black dots, indicating young volcanic activity, are also apparent in the Gila (15) and Coyote (16) Mountains.

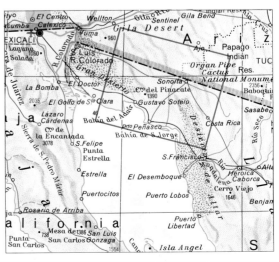

No Man's Land on the Pacific

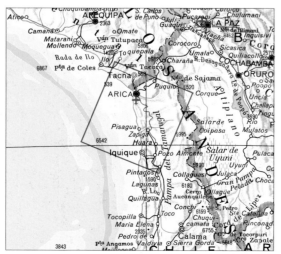

Like a string of pearls, the surf separates the deep blue waters of the Pacific Ocean from the cliffs of Peru and Chile. This image depicts one of the driest areas on earth. In some parts of the Atacama Desert (1) it has never been known to rain. Annual rainfall of under 3 mm is measured in the town of Arica (2), on the coast. The main part of Bolivia's foreign trade is transacted in this Chilean port city. The piers (3) are just visible. The Atacama, also known as Pampa del Tamarugal, lies on a high plateau between two mountain ranges: the Cordillera de la Costa (4) to the west, recognizable by its hills and typical fault systems, and the Cordillera Occidental (5) to the east. The ground varies between pale yellow and rust brown. It consists mainly of rubble which has been washed down from the steep slopes of the volcanoes (6) in the Cordillera Occidental. Gravel slopes stand out as white threads in various places (7). Rivers, such as the Rio Azapa (8) and the Rio Camarones (9) have carved deeply into the land. Their tributaries (10) run parallel to each other which indicates that the land drops evenly but very steeply. Bright green, representing plant growth, is only apparent near the town of Tacna (11) and along a few river beds.

The Chilean province of Tarapacá is economically important because of its sodium nitrate (saltpeter) deposits. They appear as white salt pans (12) at the foot of the coastal cordillera.

Country of Fire and Ice

This natural color satellite image shows the southeastern part of Iceland. It is easy to recognize the glacial areas: the Vatnajökull or Water Glacier (1), the Myrdalsjökull (2), the Hofsjökull (3), and the Tungnafellsjökull (4). Black glacial outwash plains on the Atlantic coast and green, moss covered infertile land characterize this region.

With an area of approximately 3,205 sq.mi., the plateau glacier Vatnajökull forms Europe's largest ice sheet. The neovolcanic zone of the Mid-Atlantic Ridge stretches through Iceland as an active volcanic zone. It runs in a northeasterly direction in the south, and in a northerly direction in the north. This pattern is reflected by the location and orientation of river systems, lakes, craters, and volcanoes in the area. The chain of volcanic craters of the Eldgja fissure (5) and that of the Laki fissure (6) stretch over almost 25 mi.. In 1783 the Laki fissure (Lakagigar) erupted, emitting approximately 450,000 million cu.ft. of lava, one of the largest discharges ever recorded.

Two especially dangerous volcanic centers can be found within the boundaries of this image: Katla (7) lying underneath the Myrdalsjökull plateau glacier and Grimsvötn (8), under the Vatnajökull. Powerfull subglacial volcanic eruptions lead to the dreaded Jökullhlaup — an enormous outpour of melted ice, triggered by heat from lava and volcanic gases. Such an eruption occurred from Grimsvötn in 1934, when an estimated 247,000 million cu.ft. of melted ice thundered down at 13,200,000 gal. per second, flooding the Skeidararsandur (9). During the last eruption of the Katla in 1918 an even higher record discharge speed of 52,000,000 gal./s was reached.

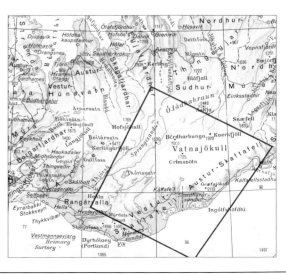

Old World Capital

Nestling in the hilly green countryside of south-east England, yet linked to the ocean by the Thames — the unique location of this metropolis is clearly reflected in our Landsat photograph.

Since 1884, London has been the hub of the world, both geographically and timewise. The old Royal Observatory in Greenwich (4) defines the geographical Prime Meridian. Times of the day throughout the world are determined by the Greenwich Mean Time (GMT), the time when the sun reaches its highest point at Greenwich.

Due to an image resolution of 80 m, and the presence of a thin veil of haze, the city center appears as a blue, more or less amorphous mass. Battersea Park (1), Hyde Park (2), and St. James Park (3) with Buckingham Palace, stand out as brown-green spots. Richmond Park and Wimbledon Common (5) together form a large forest area which is cut by a single road. The turns of the Thames, accentuated by light blue, and its harbor and docks are also easy to recognize: West India Docks (7), Victoria Dock (8), Royal Albert Dock (9) and King George Dock (10).

On the western perimeter of the city are several artificial and natural lakes. Among them are the reservoirs of King George VI (11), Queen Mary (12), and Queen Elizabeth (13). The dark blue color indicates that their water is relatively clear. In contrast, the light blue color of the Thames shows that it is heavily polluted and that it carries a high load of debris.

To the north of the King George VI Reservoir, London's international airport, Heathrow (14), can be seen in white and pale blue. Its runways and buildings cover an area of approx. 4.6 square miles.

Looking at the mouth of the Thames in the English Channel at Southend-on-Sea (15), different color shades are evident. Dark blue represents open, relatively clear water, and streaky light blue heavily polluted water. The even light blue marks the shallow water over the sand banks along the coast. When easterly winds cause a storm tide, the mouth of the Thames acts like a funnel through which water is pushed up the Thames. Hence, the center of London has been repeatedly flooded through the centuries.

In the surroundings of London one can distinguish several different types of land use: in the north, in Essex (16) and Buckingham (17) crops are grown; and in the south, in Sussex (18) and Kent (19), there are meadows and forests.

On the southern coast one can recognize the famous seaside resorts of Hastings (20) and Brighton (21). They show up as blue dots flanked by long white beaches reaching up and down the coast.

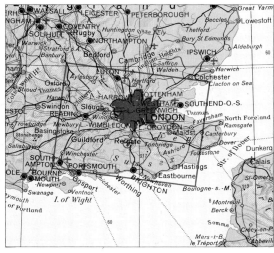

Mediterranean Landscapes

This image shows the French Riviera, from the mouth of the Rhone (1) to Béziers (2), the Rhone Valley (3) and its delta, as well as the Cévennes mountains (4). The foothills of the Maritime Alps are visible to the east (5).

The area of land which includes the coastal plains of Languedoc, as well as the Rhone Valley and Provence to the east, has been cultivated for centuries. Famous cities such as Avignon (6), Nîmes (7), and Arles (8) lie in the vast Rhone Valley. The river flows in a north-south direction and its winding path can easily be traced. Its waters are increased by the Durance (9), a main tributary coming from the Alps, which appears bright blue in its wide riverbed. This water is the lifeblood of the whole region. Through an extensive canal system, it irrigates this practically monocultural wine growing land. A recognizable example is the Bas-Rhone-Languedoc Canal which begins in Beaucaire (10) and ends in Montpellier (11). The rivers Hérault (12) and Orb (13), whose headwaters reach far into the Cévennes mountains, irrigate the southern Languedoc.

The coastline stands out through its almost continuous white fringe of sandy beaches. Étang de Thau (14), with the Port of Sète (15) and Étang de Mauguio (16) are the most important. In separated basins (17), recognizable by their slate gray color, water from the Mediterranean is evaporated to win salt.

Between the Grand Rhone (18), a branch of the Rhone delta which carries 85 percent of the water from the Rhone to the sea, and the Petit Rhone (19), and somewhat beyond it to the west, lies a unique area called the Camargue. Its landscape is characterized by numerous shallow lagoons. The largest of these is the Étang de Vaccàres (20). Because of their shallowness, the lagoons appear from pale to gray blue in the satellite photo. The large evaporation ponds of Salin-de-Giraud (21) can be recognized by their bordering dams. Further inland the yellow, brown and green shades represent a swamp and alluvial zone. Scrub land occurs in other parts of the Camargue due to the high salt content of the soil. These areas are used for the breeding of horses and fighting bulls.

To the east of the mouth of the Grand Rhone is the site of Fos-sur-Mer (22), an oil port that is still under construction.

The region to the west of the Rhone is conspicuous because of its unique green, wavy form (23). Rock folds have been exposed to the atmosphere through weathering. Plant growth, which differs in denseness according to the rock type, highlights the structure of the folding.

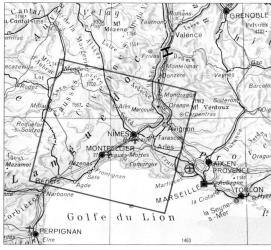

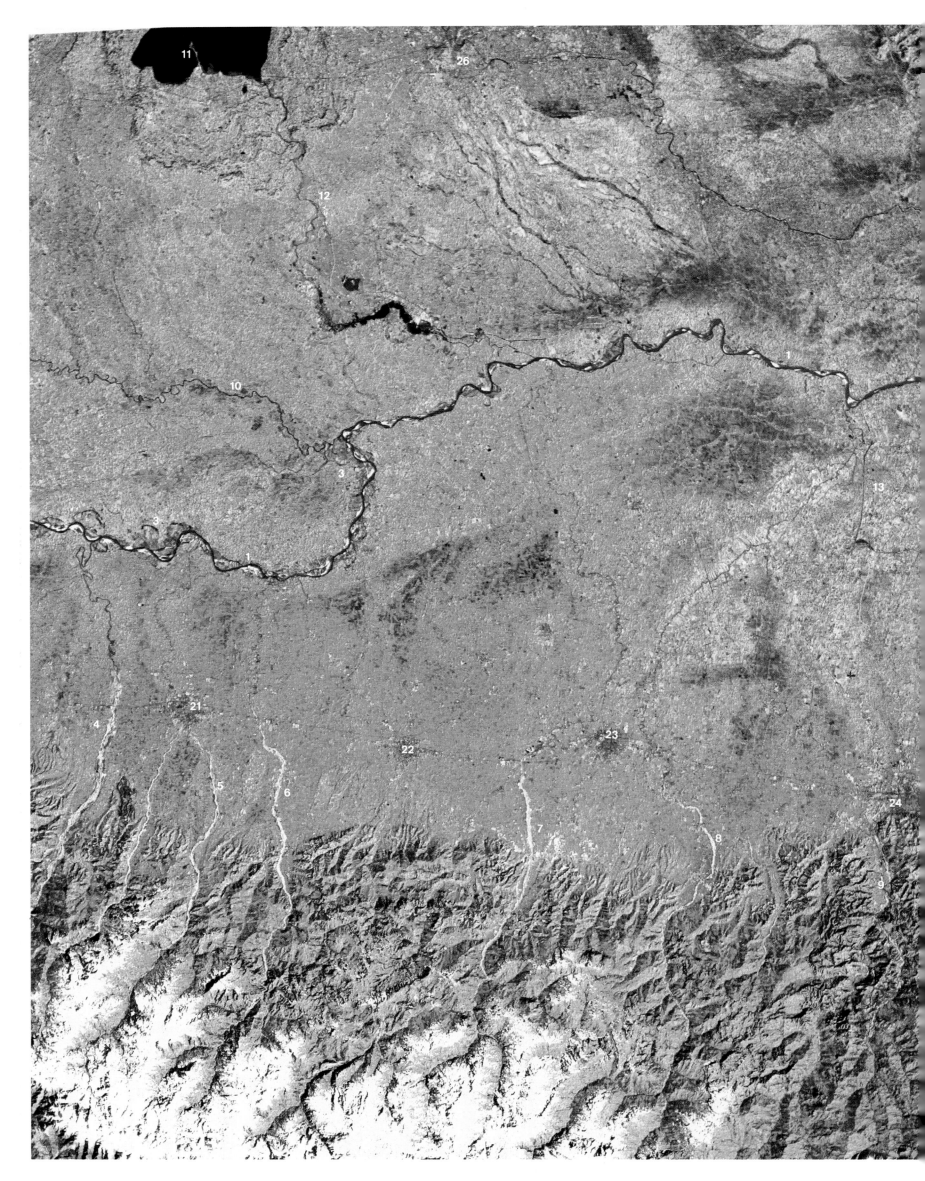

Farmland and Industrial Centers

The Po Valley, an alluvial plain, forms one of the largest natural complexes in Italy. It covers an area of approximately 19,300 sq.mi., one sixth of the total area of Italy. The valley is 310 mi. long and varies from 31 to 75 mi. in width. It stretches in a west–east direction, bordered in the north by the southern Alps, in the south by the Apennine Range, and in the east by the Adriatic Sea.

This satellite image covers the eastern part of the Po Valley with the Po delta (1) reaching into the Adriatic Sea (2). The river stands out against its surroundings like a black snake. The meandering nature of the river, and the numerous dark back-water curves (3) that were once part of the river-bed are sure signs of a slow-moving current, due to an extremely small gradient. The river descends only 1,312 ft over a length of 373 mi. The white sand banks in the river bed are quite conspicuous. Because these are continually changing, only small boats can navigate the river. The amount of water in the Po is determined by its tributaries from the Apennines, such as the Taro (4), Parma (5), Enza (6), Secchia (7), Panaro (8) and Setta (9); from the alpine rivers such as the Oglio (10); and from the river flowing out of Lake Garda (11), the Mincio (12). Artificial canals such as the Cavo Napoleonica (13) or the Canale Bianco (14) connect the tributaries of the Po and also form a link with the Adige River (15), to the north. They were built for irrigation purposes.

In the delta region, the Po divides into 14 branches of which the Po di Goro (16) and the Po di Gnocca (17) are the most significant. The delta consists of shallow lagoons which are separated from the Adriatic by a chain of white sand banks (18). Because of considerable debris, deposits, particularly from the Apennine rivers, the delta is growing out into the Adriatic Sea at a rate of about 230 to 260 ft annually. The coast lines from earlier centuries remain visible as prominent lines (19) on the mainland of today.

The intensive agricultural use of the land is apparent by the dense network of fields and meadows. Green tones in the west indicate orchards, vineyards and pastures; gray and red tones in the east are typical of crop growing areas. The land near the coast is predominantly used for the cultivation of rice. The noticeably large fields are surrounded by dams (20).

Industry is concentrated in a belt just north of the Apennines, including the cities of Parma (21), Reggio nell'Emilia (22), Modena (23), and Bologna (24). The road and railway track linking them is visible as a thin dark line. Ferrara (25) and Verona (26) are also of industrial importance.

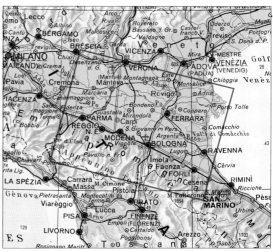

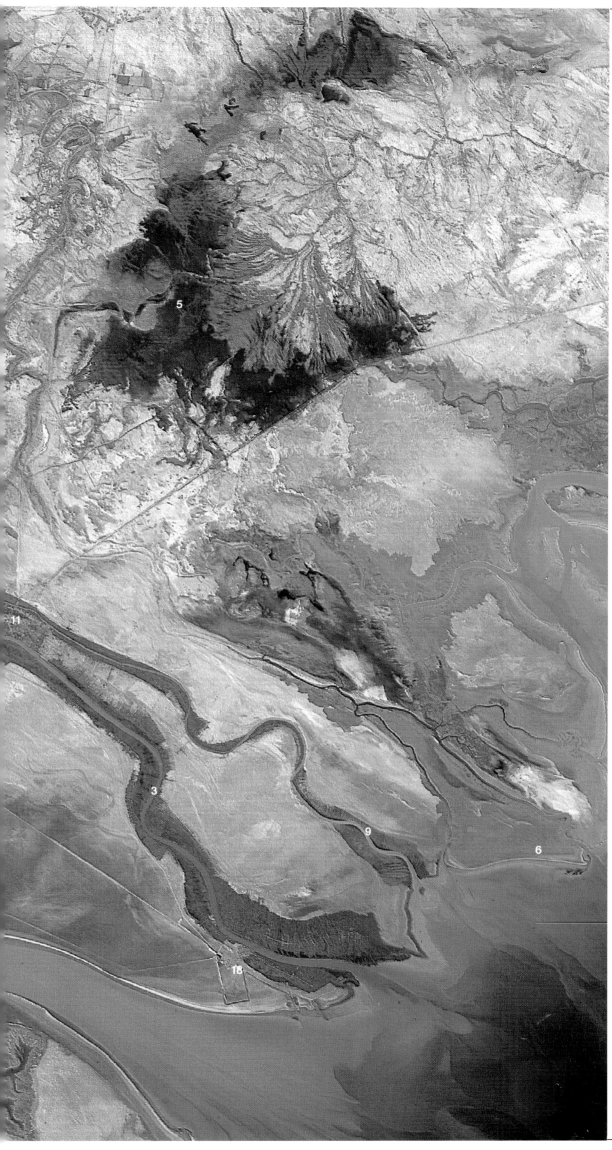

Swamps, Islands and Oil Fields

In ancient times, the Euphrates (1) and Tigris (2) rivers flowed independently into the Persian Gulf. Over the ages their estuaries have grown together forming the Shatt-al-Arab (3), whose river mouth is now approximately 106 miles from their confluence. With exception of the area on the lower left, the region shown in this image consists mainly of alluvial land, swamps and marshes.

In swamps, such as the Hawr-al-Hamar (4) or those in the region of the Jarrahi River (5), the black color shows clear, still water, and pale green represents polluted water. Young vegetation can be recognized by the bright green color, while darker green indicates older growth. The marshes (6) have gray tones and are covered by a multitude of dendritical rivers, which slowly meander over the flat land. The building of dams, artificial lakes, and irrigation plants in the upper Euphrates and Tigris rivers has heavily reduced the water volume and floating sediment in the Shatt-al-Arab. Hence, the first half of this river is a dark blue. The yellowish green, indicating sediment, first appears at the confluence of the Rud e-Karun River (7), which joins the Shatt-al-Arab near the city of Khorramshahr (8). Sediment from the other heavily loaded rivers such as the Khawr e-Bahmarshir (9) or Khawr-az-Zubayr (10) can be seen stretching far into the gulf. The huge amounts of mud which have been deposited can be understood if one considers that the city of Abadan (11) was an important port on the Persian Gulf during the tenth century. Today it lies 31 miles away from the coast.

Areas from three different countries appear in this image: Kuwait, Iraq, and the Iranian province of Khuzestan. A considerable part of the world's oil reserves are located in this region. The oil fields of Al-Rumaylah (12) in Iraq and As-Sabiriyah (13) in Kuwait are situated on the flat, loamy semi-desert of Ab-Dibdibah (14). Their platforms can be traced by following the black smoke trails which have been blown in a southeasterly direction. The drilling rigs and oil wells are linked by a network of streets (15) and pipelines (16). The latter run in straight lines and are mostly underground. Because of the closing of the ports of Al-Basrah (17) and Abadan on the Iraqi side, the loading of oil now takes place at the terminal of Khawr-al-Arnaiyah. This lies offshore and is not visible in the image. Before being shipped, the oil is stored in large tanks at Al-Faw (18). These tanks appear as orderly rows of pale dots.

The green area along both sides of the Shatt-al-Arab river marks the world's largest date producing area. Several hundred thousand tons of dates are harvested here annually.

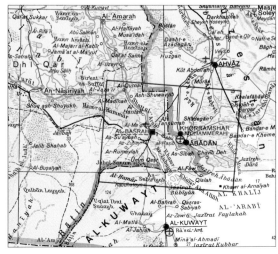

Persian Gulf   31

32 Philippines

Tropical Archipelago

Only a few of the 7107 islands, which comprise the Philippine archipelago are visible in this image. The eleven largest islands including Luzon (1) in the north, and Mindanao (not visible in photo) in the south, make up 96 percent of the total land area. Mindoro (2), the round island of Marinduque (3) and other, smaller islands seen as green spots, make up the remaining four percent.

The archipelago was first formed in the tertiary period, some 50 million years ago, when numerous volcanoes erupted through the ocean floor on the edge of the Pacific. Some of these can be recognized by their circular craters and radiating erosion grooves (4, 5).

Today there are twelve active volcanoes in the Philippines. These and frequent earthquakes show that the earth's crust in this region is not yet at rest. Consequently, the population is at times endangered by phenomena such as seismic sea waves, glowing clouds, ash rain, and lava flows.

As the Philippines are situated just north of the equator, they belong to the tropical climatic zone. Because of high temperatures throughout the year and substantial rainfall, the vegetation is lush. Hence, it is visible as deep dark green. Depending upon the altitude and respective rainfall, different types of forests are apparent: rain, monsoon and evergreen oak forest. However, due to the high monetary value of the timber, some areas have been completely deforested. This has led to erosion of the humus layer and the resulting barren mountainsides and deep ravines (6) can be seen on the island of Mindoro. The pale blue rivers (7) are also a part of this process. Their color indicates the presence of sediment that is transported from the eroded land into the sea.

The city of Calapan (8) is situated in the fertile lowlands to the east. Although these are partly covered by clouds, the settlements can be recognized by their purple-grey color. This is an intensively cultivated area where rice, pineapples, and coconut palms predominate.

Tourism is becoming an increasingly important economic factor here. The most popular attractions are the coral reefs just off the coast (9). The coral builds colonies of pipe-shaped lime secretions, which altogether form the coral reef. The animal requires clean, well-aerated saltwater at a temperature of 64 to 68°F, ample nourishment and a high intensity of light. As the reefs are aglow with a spectrum of colors, and provide shelter for many species of exotic fish, they are a favorite goal for scuba divers.

Philippines   33

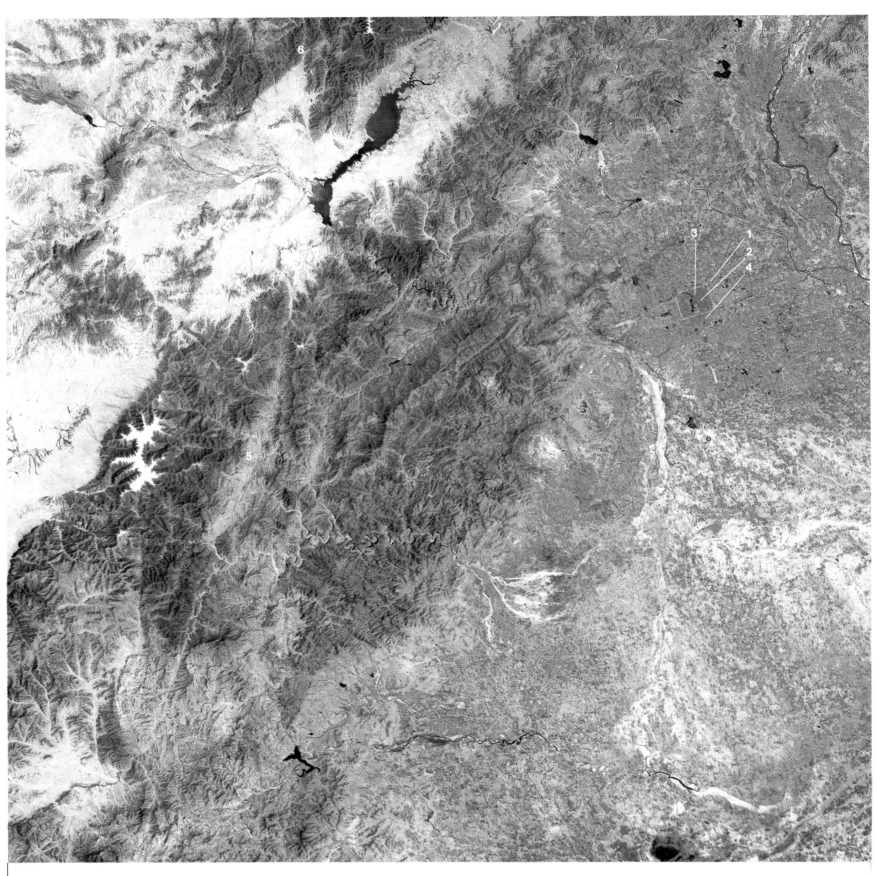

Civilization on Fertile Soil

One of the most noticeable features of this image is the center of the city of Beijing, which appears as a large gray spot. Its layout, based on a grid pattern, dates back to 1260. The white rectangle is the wall of the "Inner" or "Mongol" City (1). The dark, barely visible rectangle is the King's City with the "Forbidden City", the seat of the Chinese God-Emperors (2). The small black dots (3) are artificial lakes. The rectangle of the old "Chinese City" to the south is also just visible as its walls have been removed in recent times. The green patch inside the rectangle is the park of the Temple of Heaven (4).

Today, with a population of 8.7 million, the city of Beijing has extended well outside its old walls. The multicolored mosaic appearance of the fields in-

dicates intensive agricultural use. The high fertility of the "Great Plain" is due to its loess soil which has been deposited through flooding of the numerous rivers coming from the surrounding mountains.

The mountain range, lying on the diagonal of this image, is part of the larger Khingan Range. It consists of granite and basalt and is intersected by distinct faults (5). In one place (6), the left mountain block has been pushed southwards with respect to the right block. Although difficult to recognize at ground level, such large structures stand out well in satellite photographs.

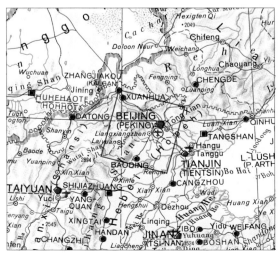

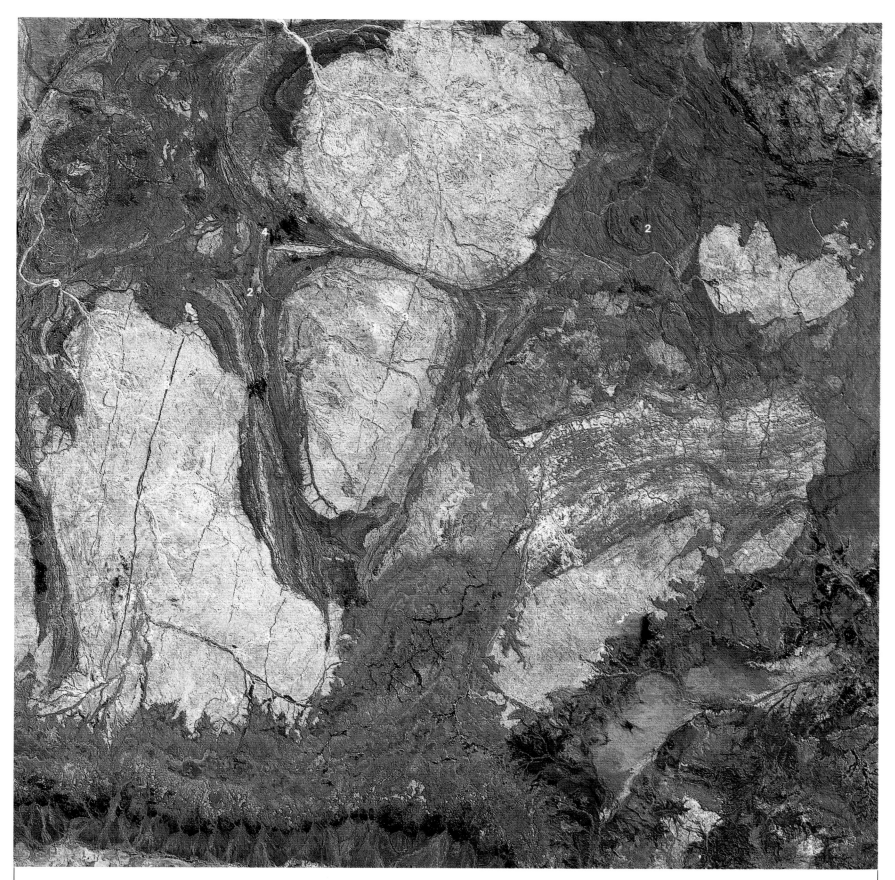

Archaic Rock Formations

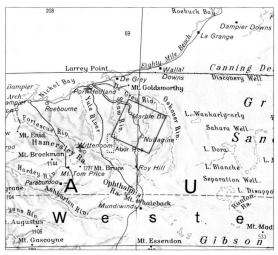

Lacking vegetation, this region reveals a part of the earth's early history. The rocks visible here were formed 2.5 to 3.5 billion years ago and belong to the oldest known formations on earth. At that time massive mountains reached heights of 12.5 miles. Over the ages the powers of erosion have reduced them to the truncated landscape of today.

Huge granite domes, called Plutons (1), were forced out of the deep layers of the earth's crust. Their bright yellow colors stand out well against the dark grayish-brown tones of the surrounding rocks (2). These belong to a so-called "mobile belt", a zone made up of gneisses, volcanic rock, and sedimentation, which were converted into metamorphic rock through heat and pressure.

The original stratification can still be recognized from the bands of differing shades of color. The brown tones indicate the high iron content of the crusty surface layer.

Dark veins (3), up to 60 miles long, were created by basaltic lava which forced its way into the fissures formed during the cooling period of the granite.

The Pilbara District is a highly important economic region in Western Australia. The gold mining cities of Marble Bar (4) and Nullagine (5) were built in the 1920's. By 1972 a total of 11 tons of gold and 1041 tons of silver had been mined here.

Seam of two Continents

At its northern end, the Red Sea is divided into two branches: the Gulf of Akaba or Khalij al-Aqabah in Arabic, and the Gulf of Suez or Khalij as-Suways. This image shows the middle section of the latter. It is named after the Port of Suez or As-Suways which lies at the northern end.

The Gulf of Suez is part of a geological structure which has been intensively investigated for decades. A zone of weakness in the earth's crust stretches from Zimbabwe, over the long lakes of East Africa, the Rift valley in Kenya, and through the valley of Danikil in Ethiopia. Close to Djibouti this zone splits into three branches: in the east, the Gulf of Aden; in the north, the Red Sea with the Gulf of Suez; the third branch runs from the Gulf of Akaba through the Dead Sea as far the Jordan valley. Along this structure, the crust of the earth is broken apart by movements of the earth's mantle. This process, called plate tectonics, is basically a shifting apart of the two rock shelves. The drift rate has been measured by laser beam and amounts to 2 to 5 cm per year. Approximately one million years ago the two coasts seen in the photograph were joined together. Today, these two parts of Egypt belong to two different continents which continue to move away from each other.

Due to the lack of vegetation and variety of colors, the different types of rock can easily be determined from this image. Granite and gneiss are indicated by dark areas (1) with prominent fractures cutting through the rock. The light gray rock embedded in circular forms (2) is older, paler granite. The remaining red and gray toned rock (3) consists mainly of different types of old limestone. The way in which the limestone is deposited in layers can be seen on the edges of eroded areas (4) and in dry river beds (5). These rivers are characterized by several arms and branches, and form, in geological terms, a dendritical net. The highest mountains in the region are of granite which best withstands erosion. To name a few: the Jabal Kathrinah (8,652 ft) (6), named after the legend of the Moses mountain and on whose slopes the famous Katherine Monastery (Dayr Katrinah) lies; the Jabal Mosá (7,497 ft) (7); and the Jabal Gharib (5,145 ft) (8).

The region has recently gained industrial importance through the oil fields near Ra's Gharib (9) and Abu Darbah (10). These fields stretch out partly under the seabed. Recently, tourism has also become an important industry. The prominent attractions are the coral reefs (11) which appear light blue in the image.

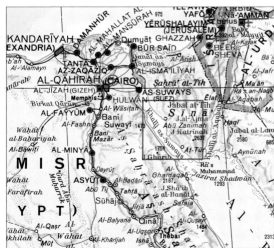

Diamond Deposits on the Shore

Namibia is a protectorate of the United Nations but is actually governed by the Republic of South Africa. The climate of the region shown is extremely inhospitable.

The gray, yellow, and brown colors, and especially the complete lack of green tones, show that this area is total desert land. In spite of this however, the region is geologically and particularly economically interesting. The sand dunes, bordered by the sea and the mountains, contain the largest diamond deposits in the world. They stretch along the coast from Oranjerivier in the south, to Walvisbaai in the north, and are an average of 75 miles wide. The actual origin of the diamonds is still unknown. They probably originate from the Kimberlit rocks, which are located further inland. For a period of several million years, erosion debris from these rocks has moved to the coast. The hard diamonds withstood this movement while the rest of the material, being softer, was gradually ground up. The original deposit contained very few diamonds per cubic foot. The redeposition produced a diamond-rich secondary deposit which consists essentially of a lightly bound mixture of sand and pebbles.

To extract the diamonds, the wind-blown layer of the sand dunes is cleared away and then the diamond containing layers are washed. The yield of diamonds in 1978 was approximately 1.9 million carats (at approx. 0.2 g ea.). Ninety percent of this was of gemstone quality. Along with diamonds, lead, zinc, and copper (Sinclair coppermine) (1) are also mined in certain areas.

The fishing industry is of little importance, despite the fact that the cold Benguela current is rich in nutriments and hence rich in fish. Spencer Bay (2) and Hottentot Bay (3) are not suitable for the building of ports. The port town of Lüderitz (approx. 6,000 citizens) is the only one which has been able to develop in this region. It is situated on Lüderitz Bay (Angra Pequena) (4) which lies just below the lower part of this image. Roads and railway lines (5) end there.

The variety of forms and colors of the sand dunes are particularly fascinating. The longitudinal dunes (6) are clearly separated from each other and stretch out up to 30 miles. They mark the general wind direction north-north-east. The ripple dunes (7) are closer to each other and are aligned crosswise to the others. The star dunes (8) can be several hundred yards high. They extend far into the high country in the area of the Tirasduines (9). In the midst of this sea of sand, isolated mountains such as Hauchab (3,280 ft) (10) appear as islands.

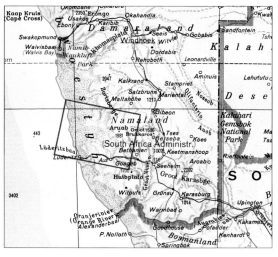

Volcanoes in the Sahara Desert

This image covers an area in the north of the Chad republic. The Tibesti Mountains, lying in the central Sahara, are "drowned" here in the adjoining gravel desert, the Serir de Tibesti (1). Different shades of yellow (2) represent parallel longitudinal sand dunes.

The Tibesti Mountains consist essentially of Precambrian rock, which was formed more than 600 million years ago. Over the ages the mountain tops of schist, phyllite and granite have been eroded, leaving the truncated forms of today. Most conspicuous are the faults (3) which run mainly in a north to northeasterly direction. They are accented by their light colored sand filling. The lengths and orientations of these faults have enabled researchers to draw conclusions about the powers which deformed the mountains. The angles at which the faults intersect each other (4) are also of particular significance to scientists.

In the Tertiary Age, about 50 million years ago, volcanoes erupted through the old rock. Their craters (5, 6, 7), in the lower part of the image, are easy to recognize by their circular shapes. The dark purple-gray of the volcanoes is typical of lava flows and volcanic ash. The age of the lava can be determined by the intensity of the color: the richer the color, the younger the lava. For example, relatively recent activity is indicated by the deep color of the Pic Toussidé volcano (8), the second highest mountain in the Sahara (10,712 ft). A small, strongly reflecting salt lake can be seen in the crater of Trou au Natron (9) nearby.

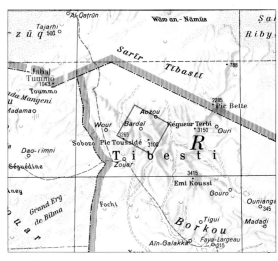

Key to Map Coverage

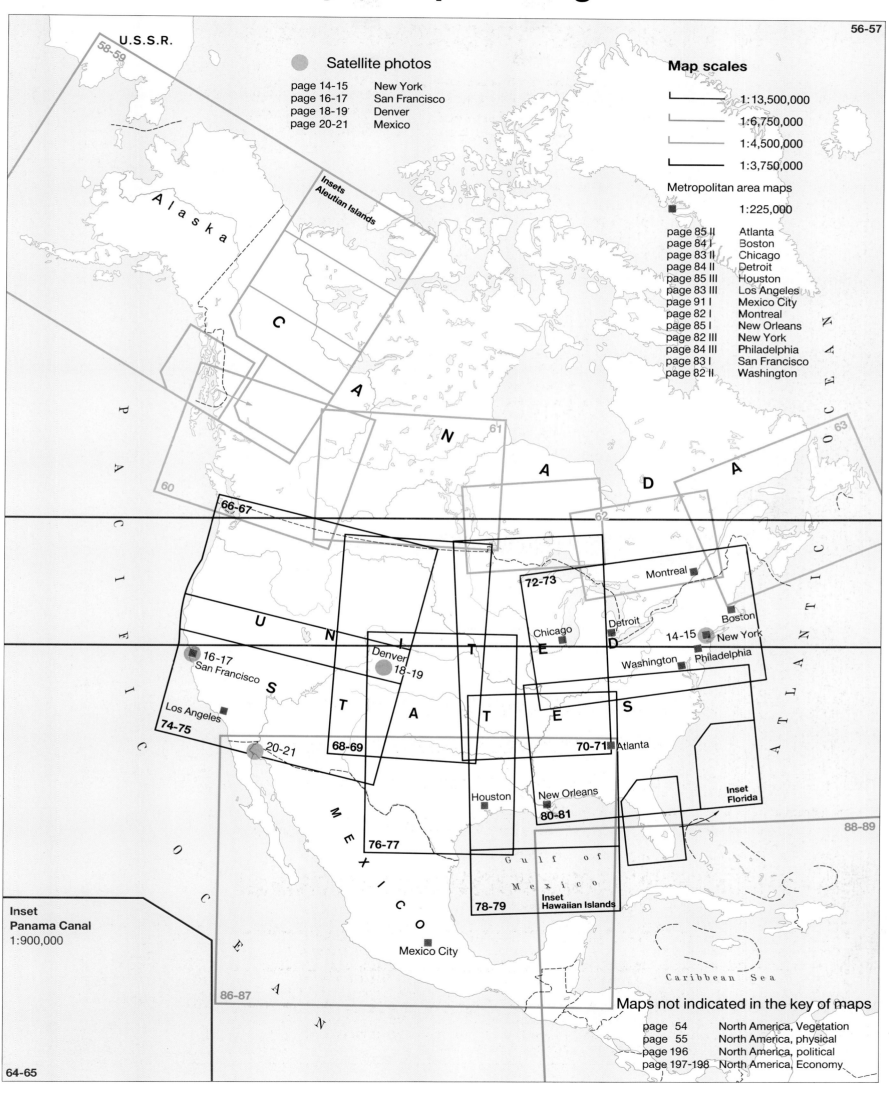

U.S.S.R.

58-59

Satellite photos

page 14-15	New York
page 16-17	San Francisco
page 18-19	Denver
page 20-21	Mexico

Map scales

1:13,500,000
1:6,750,000
1:4,500,000
1:3,750,000

Metropolitan area maps

1:225,000

page 85 II	Atlanta
page 84 I	Boston
page 83 II	Chicago
page 84 II	Detroit
page 85 III	Houston
page 83 III	Los Angeles
page 91 I	Mexico City
page 82 I	Montreal
page 85 I	New Orleans
page 82 III	New York
page 84 III	Philadelphia
page 83 I	San Francisco
page 82 II	Washington

Alaska

Insets
Aleutian Islands

C A N A D A

PACIFIC OCEAN

ATLANTIC OCEAN

61

62

63

60

66-67

72-73

Montreal

Detroit   Boston

Chicago

14-15   New York

UNITED STATES

Washington   Philadelphia

16-17
San Francisco

Denver
18-19

Los Angeles

74-75

20-21

68-69

70-71 Atlanta

Inset
Florida

MEXICO

Houston

New Orleans

80-81

76-77

88-89

Inset
Panama Canal
1:900,000

Gulf of Mexico

78-79

Inset
Hawaiian Islands

Mexico City

Caribbean Sea

86-87

Maps not indicated in the key of maps

page 54	North America, Vegetation
page 55	North America, physical
page 196	North America, political
page 197-198	North America, Economy

64-65

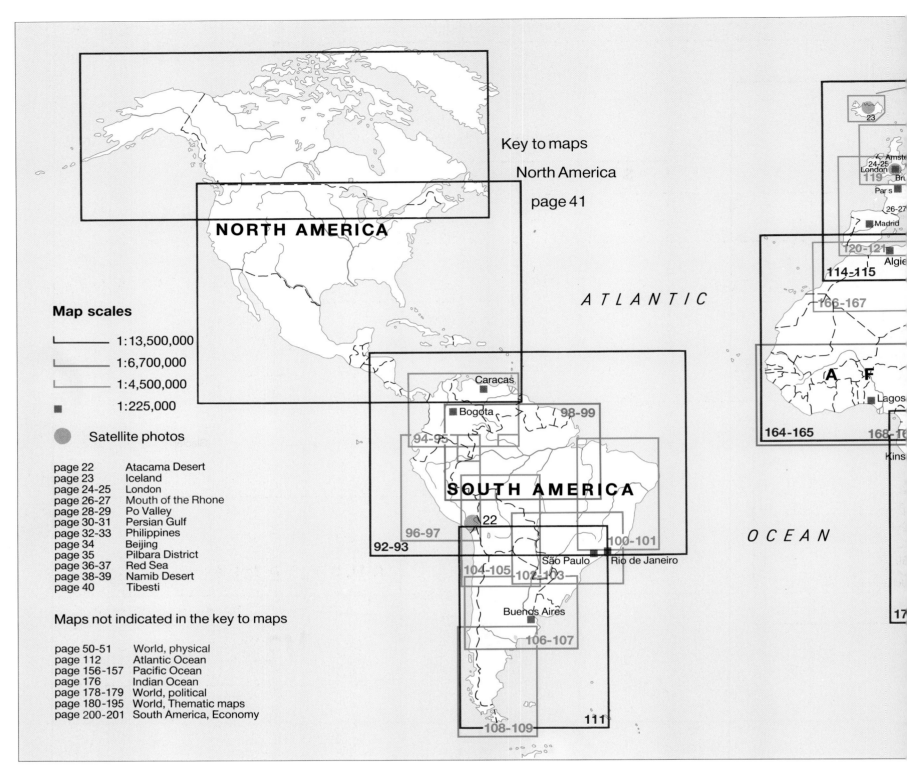

Key to maps
North America
page 41

NORTH AMERICA

A T L A N T I C

Map scales

└───── 1:13,500,000

└─── 1:6,700,000

└── 1:4,500,000

■ 1:225,000

● Satellite photos

page 22   Atacama Desert
page 23   Iceland
page 24-25   London
page 26-27   Mouth of the Rhone
page 28-29   Po Valley
page 30-31   Persian Gulf
page 32-33   Philippines
page 34   Beijing
page 35   Pilbara District
page 36-37   Red Sea
page 38-39   Namib Desert
page 40   Tibesti

Maps not indicated in the key to maps

page 50-51   World, physical
page 112   Atlantic Ocean
page 156-157   Pacific Ocean
page 176   Indian Ocean
page 178-179   World, political
page 180-195   World, Thematic maps
page 200-201   South America, Economy

Caracas

■ Bogota   98-99

94-95

SOUTH AMERICA

96-97 ● 22

92-93   100-101

O C E A N

São Paulo ■ ■ Rio de Janeiro

104-105   102-103

■ Buenos Aires

106-107

108-109   111

23

24-25 Amst
London 119   Bru
Paris ■
26-27
■ Madrid
120-121
114-115   Algie
166-167
A   F
■ Lagos
164-165   168-1
Kins
17

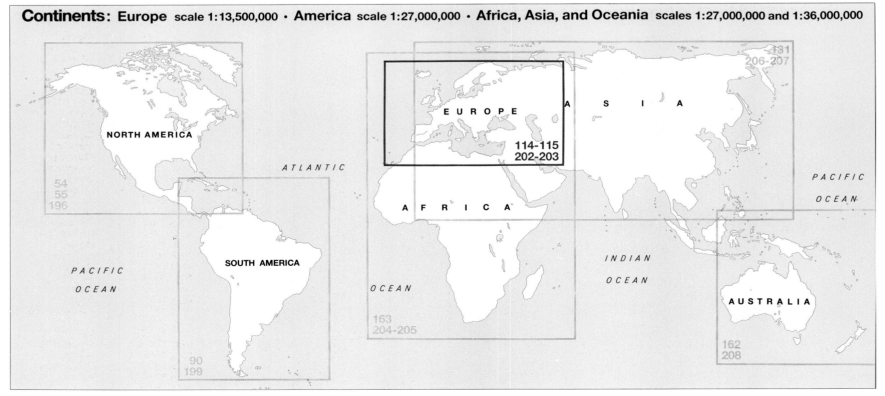

Continents: Europe scale 1:13,500,000 · **America** scale 1:27,000,000 · **Africa, Asia, and Oceania** scales 1:27,000,000 and 1:36,000,000

NORTH AMERICA

ATLANTIC

54
55
196

SOUTH AMERICA

PACIFIC

OCEAN

90
199

131
206-207

E U R O P E   A S I A

114-115
202-203

A F R I C A

OCEAN

163
204-205

PACIFIC

OCEAN

INDIAN

OCEAN

AUSTRALIA

162
208

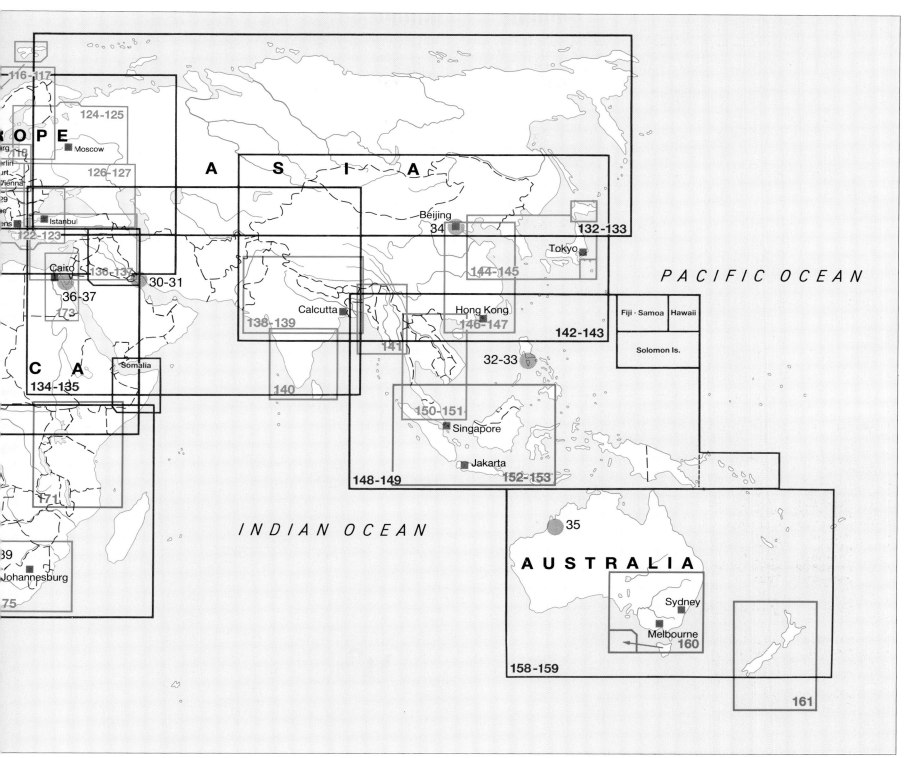

ROPE

124-125

Moscow

126-127

A S I A

Istanbul

122-123

Beijing

34

Tokyo

132-133

144-145

PACIFIC OCEAN

Cairo

136-137

30-31

36-37

173

Calcutta

138-139

Hong Kong

146-147

142-143

141

Fiji · Samoa   Hawaii

Solomon Is.

C A

Somalia

134-135

32-33

140

150-151

Singapore

148-149

Jakarta

152-153

INDIAN OCEAN

171

AUSTRALIA

35

39

Johannesburg

Sydney

75

Melbourne

160

158-159

161

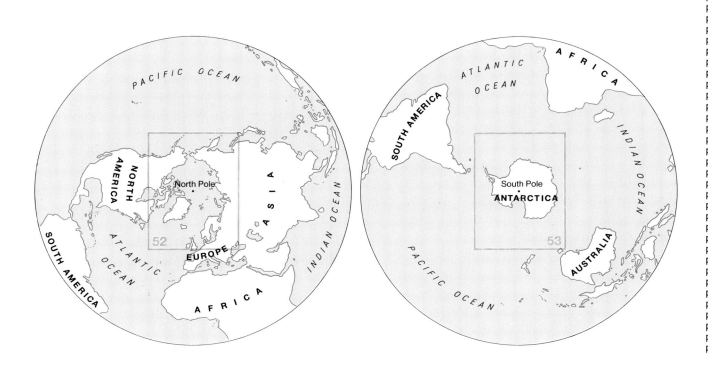

Arctic Region · Antarctic Region   scale 1:27,000,000

PACIFIC OCEAN

NORTH AMERICA

North Pole

ASIA

52

EUROPE

SOUTH AMERICA

ATLANTIC OCEAN

INDIAN OCEAN

AFRICA

ATLANTIC OCEAN

AFRICA

SOUTH AMERICA

South Pole

ANTARCTICA

53

INDIAN OCEAN

AUSTRALIA

PACIFIC OCEAN

Description of Map Types and Scales

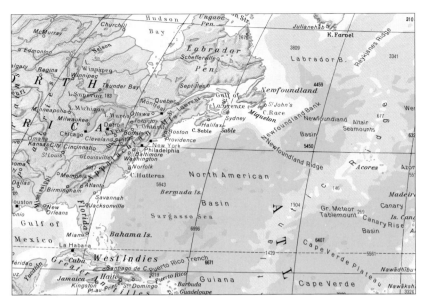

Scale 1:67,500,000 ≙ One inch to 1,065 miles
Scale 1:60,000,000 ≙ One inch to 947 miles

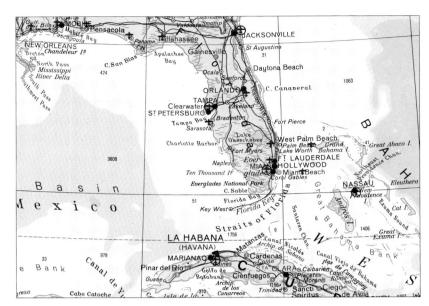

Scale 1:13,500,000 ≙ One inch to 213 miles

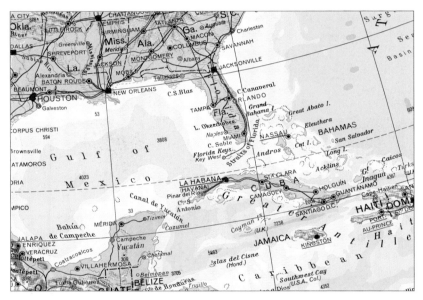

Scale 1:36,000,000 ≙ One inch to 568 miles
Scale 1:27,000,000 ≙ One inch to 426 miles

Scale 1:6,750,000 ≙ One inch to 107 miles
Scale 1:4,500,000 ≙ One inch to 71 miles
Scale 1:3,750,000 ≙ One inch to 59 miles

Topographic (Physical) Maps

Topographic maps combine natural (physical) features of the earth's surface with various man-made or "cultural" features.

The scale and coverage of a topographic map may depend on the need to depict features on a specific level of detail. For example, large-scale topographic maps may take into account the bridge, individual house, church, factory, a two-track railroad, footpath and copse of trees. Small-scale maps sketch a region in such comprehensive terms as coastlines, waterway networks, mountain ranges, towns and metropolises, railroad lines, or major roadways. On a relatively large-scale topographic map with a scale of 1:125,000, the District of Columbia occupies an area of 4 x 4 inches. At a much smaller scale of 1:60,000,000, the entire U.S. can be depicted in approximately the same space.

The term "physical" map commonly applied to topographic maps, although generally useful and descriptive, is not fully comprehensive. Topographic maps have two levels of presentation. The primary level depicts the "physis", i.e. the natural features of the earth, including coastlines, waterways, land elevation, sea depth, etc. The secondary level shows the effects of man: political borders, communities, transportation routes, and other elements of the civilized landscape. Language is an additional cultural feature which finds its expression in the geographic names and written comments on the map.

The map scale expresses the relationship between a certain distance in nature and the corresponding span on the map. The smaller the scale, the more cartographers

are forced to simplify and to restrict themselves to the essentials. Cartography is an art of intelligent omission. The map user must be aware of this important fact when comparing maps of different scales, otherwise he or she runs the risk of obtaining a false picture of the world. Not a few misjudgements in history can be traced, in part, to distorted geographic conceptions.

In "The Great World Atlas", the continents, with the exception of the polar regions, are pictured at a scale of 1:13,500,000. This uniformity in scale, together with uniformity in map projections, enables easy comparisions between all continents.

For the United States 1:3,750,000 is the primary scale. Only for Alaska was it necessary to choose the scale of 1:4,500,000 in order to be able to depict the mainland on one double page.

For regions outside the United States, the scales of 1:4,500,000 and 1:6,750,000 were chosen based upon the criteria of population density, as well as political, economic and touristic significance. The key to map coverage, pp. 41-43, presents this regional division according to map pages and scales in an easy-to-understand manner.

The explanation of symbols on page 48 is the cartographic alphabet for understanding the contents of the maps; the index of names is the key to the geographic inventory of the atlas. The index of names and the number of entries are marks of quality of any atlas. The index of "The Great World Atlas" contains about 110,000 items.

Description of Map Types and Scales

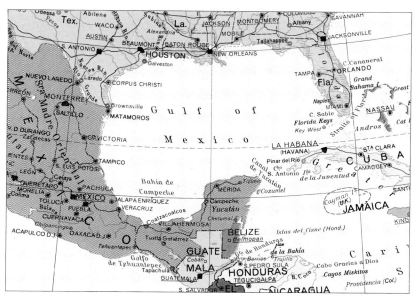

Scale 1:27,000,000 ≙ One inch to 426 miles
Scale 1:13,500,000 ≙ One inch to 213 miles

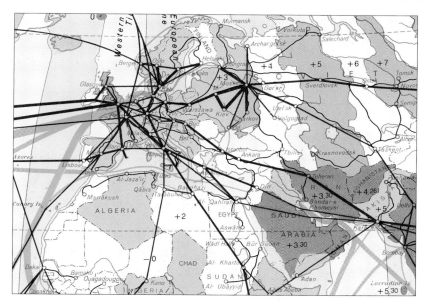

Scale 1:90,000,000 ≙ One inch to 1,420 miles
Scale 1:67,500,000 ≙ One inch to 1,065 miles

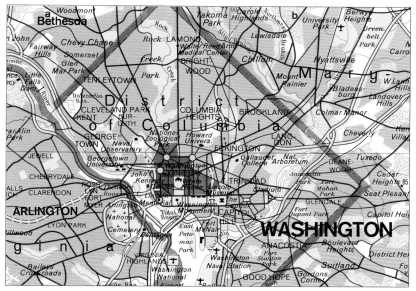

Scale 1:225,000 ≙ One inch to 3.6 miles

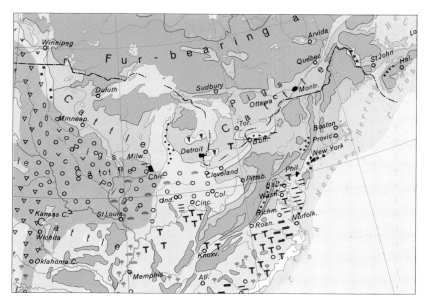

Scale 1:27,000,000 ≙ One inch to 426 miles

Political Maps

The geographic location, the extension of the land area, and the interrelationships resulting from the relative locations of political powers, find their unique cartographic expression in political maps. By means of colored areas, the divisions of the earth into sovereign states and their dependent territories become apparent. In "The Great World Atlas" these political maps are placed, for easy orientation, in front of the maps of the individual continents. The assignment of a certain color to each state is maintained throughout. The political power of the individual states cannot be deduced from these maps. Deductions about the political and economic behavior of the various states can be made, however, by comparing maps of climate, density, and distribution of population, economy, and transportation.

Metropolitan Area Maps

The increasing concentration of population in urban centers is a global phenomenon. While the population of the world has approximately doubled in the last 100 years, the number of people living in cities has increased fivefold. In the year 2000 more than half of the population of the world is expected to be living in cities. "The Great World Atlas" shows a selection of important metropolises from every corner of the world. All these maps make use of the same scale, 1:225,000, and the same legend, which makes possible immediate and global comparisons. The colored differentiation of built-up metropolitan areas, city centers and sprawling industrial parks, when viewed in conjunction with the scheme of the transportation network, allows conclusions to be drawn about the functional division of the cities and their surrounding area.

Thematic Maps

On thematic maps global phenomena and conditions are depicted. A distinction should be made between two groups of thematic maps: First, those maps whose topics are naturally occuring conditions such as geology, climate, and vegetation; second, those maps that deal with structures that have been created by man such as distribution of population, religion or the economy. These various aspects are transformed by cartographers into graphic representations. Not only the distribution of soil types, for example, or the occurence of petroleum are thus depicted, but bold or lightface arrows express the speed of ocean currents; shades of blue, the average temperature in January; the size of the symbol, the volume of production, and much more. Dynamic processes become apparent with regards to strength, direction, etc., as do differences in order of magnitude and, thus, in significance.

The study of geographic and thematic maps gives insight into the diverse relationships between mankind and his surroundings. Such study makes plain, furthermore, the connections and interdependencies among the different continents and regions and imparts understanding of the behavior of human groups, and of political and economic powers.

"The Great World Atlas" takes this into account with a series of thematic world maps, as well as economic maps of North and South America (pp. 197-198 and 200, 201), at the end of the topographical map section.

45

Projections

It is fundamentally impossible to depict without distortion the spherical surface of the earth on a flat surface. The curvature of the earth's surface can only be presented undistorted — that is, preserving areas, shapes, and angles — on a globe. In the three basic types of map projections, the parallels and meridians are projected onto a plane, or onto a cone or a cylinder which is subsequently cut and layed flat. In the first type, also known as an azimuthal projection, the earth's surface is projected onto a plane touching the globe at an arbitrary point. Distortion increases with distance from the point of contact. In the conical projection, the surface is projected onto an imaginary cone placed over the globe, usually so

that it touches the parallel running through the center of the area to be depicted. In this case, distortion increases with distance from the line of contact. In the cylindrical projection, the cone is replaced by a cylinder surrounding the earth, normally touching the equator. Distortion here increases with distance from the equator. In the cylindrical projection, all parallels and meridians become straight lines. One example of this type is the Mercator projection, which preserves angle and is, accordingly, used for marine charts. On a Mercator map, the line connecting two points (the "loxodrome") is a straight line following the correct compass direction.

This atlas uses the following projections:
1 Polar projections for polar maps, scale 1:27,000,000
2 Azimuthal projections for all maps to scales 1:13,500,000 and 1:27,000,000, with the exception of the 1:27,000,000 maps of Asia and the polar regions
3 Conical projections (Albers) for all maps to scales 1:3,750,000, 1:4,500,000 and 1:6,750,000
4 Bonne equal-area projection for the map of Asia 1:27,000,000
5 Winkel triple projection has been used for all maps of the world

Polar projection

With this method, the earth's surface is projected onto a plane touching the globe at the pole, which is at the centre of the map. Meridians are shown as straight lines intersecting at the centre of the map. Parallels are concentric circles around the center of the map. This projection preserves areas.

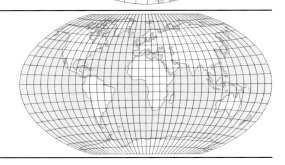

Equal-area azimuthal projection

With this method, the point of contact of the surface of projection is the equator (Africa 1:13 500 000) or an arbitrary latitude passing through the center of the area to be depicted.
These projections also approximately preserve angles, which is why they are called "azimuthal". Parallels and meridians are shown as curves generated from the combination of calculated and plotted coordinates.

The azimuthal projection is particularly suitable for depicting large regions. In the map of Asia, however, the distortions at the edges would be too great, therefore the Bonne Projection was preferred in this case.

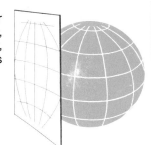 

Conical projection (Albers)

In the conical projection, circles of longitude are depicted as straight lines. Parallels are concentric circles whose center is the point of intersection of the meridians, which lies outside the map's borders. Two of the parallels preserve distance, and the pair is selected for the individual maps to minimize overall distortion of distance and direction.
This relatively simple method is used for large scale maps, which show only a small section of the globe and involve correspondingly small distortion.

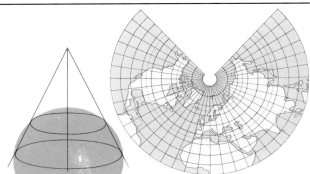

Bonne projection

This is also an equal-area method, based on a conical projection. The center meridian is shown as a straight line and divided to preserve lenght. One parallel is selected as a line of contact, and the other parallels are concentric circles, equally divided from the center meridian. The curves connecting corresponding segments generate the meridians. This method is particularly suitable for depicting large areas of the earth.

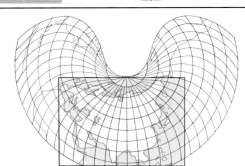

Winkel triple projection

This was used for world maps. The projection is based on Aitoff's method, which shows the poles as straight lines, with all meridians and parallels slightly curved.
While this projection does not preserve any attributes, it conveys an approximately equal-area impression of the earth's surface, particularly in the middle latitudes.

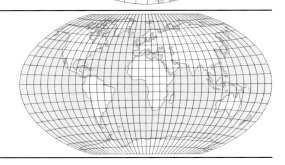

Abbreviations of Geographical Names and Terms

General

Bel.	Belyj, -aja -oje,yje	Mal.	Malyj, -aja, -oje	Sred.	Sredne, -ij, -'aja,-eje
Bol.	Bol'šoj, -aja, -oje, ije	Mc	Mac	St.	Sankt
Č.	Český, -á, -é	Nat.	National	St	Saint
Ea.	East	nat.	national	Sta	Santa
$G^{d(e)}$	Grand(e)	$N^{do(s)}$	Nevado(s)	Star.	Staryj, -aja -oje, -yje
G^{des}	Grandes	Niž.	Nižnij, -'aja, -eje, -ije	S^{te}	Sainte
Gr.	Groß, -er, -e, -es	N^{o}	Numero	S^{th}	South
G^{ral}	General	Nov.	Novo, -yj, -aja -oje	S^{to}	Santo
G^{t}	Great	N^{th}	North	Sv.	Sveti, -a, Svätý
Hag.	Hagia	N^{va}	Nueva	Upp.	Upper
Hág.	Hágios	N^{vo}	Nuevo	V.	Veliki, -a, -o
H^{te}	Haute	$P^{it(e)}$	Petit(e)	Vel.	Velikij, -aja, -oje
Juž.	Južnyj, -aja, -oje	Pr.	Prince	Vel.'	Vel'ká
Kr.	Krasno, -yj, -aja, oje, -yje	Pres.	Presidente	Verch.	Verchne, -ij, -'aja, -eje, -ije
L^{le}	Little	Prov.	Provincial	W....	West; Zapadnaja
		S....	San	Zap.	Zapadnaja
		Sev.	Severnyj, -aja -oje		

Islands, Landscapes

ad.	adasi	$\hat{I}^{e}$	Îsole	o-va	ostrova
Arch.	Archipelago	$I^{la(s)}$	Isla(s)	P.	Pulau
arch.	archipelag	$(-)I^{n}$	(-)Inseln, (-inseln)	Pen.	Peninsula
Archip.	Archipiélago	I^{s}	Islands	Poj.	Pojezierze
(-)I.	(-)Insel, (-insel)	$\hat{I}^{s}$	Îles	p-ov.	poluostrov
I....	Isle	k.	kosa	P.-p.	Pulau-pulau
....I.	Island	Kep.	Kepulauan	Res.	Reservation,-e
$\hat{I}$.	Île	L^{d}	Land	Rés.	Réservation
I^{a}	Ilha	$(-)I^{d(e)}$	(-)land(e)	s.	sima
I^{a}	Isola	Mon.	Monument	V^{ey}	Valley
I^{as}	Ilhas	o.	ostrov	y.ad.	yarimada, -si
				zapov.	zapovednik

Hydrography

Arr.	Arroio, Arroyo	j.	joki	$R^{ão}$	Ribeirão
B.	Basin, Bay	Jez.	Jezioro	$R^{ère}$	Rivière
(-)B.	(-)Bucht, (-Bucht)	j:vi	järvi	Res.	Reservoir
Bat.	Batang	Kan.	Kanal; Kanaal	Rib^{a}	Ribeira
Can.	Canal	(-)kan.	(-)kanal; -kanaal	Riv.	River
Chan.	Channel	kör.	körfezi, -i	-riv.	-rivier
Cr.	Creek	L.	Lago, Lake	...(-)S.	(-)See, (-see)
D.	Danau	Lim.	Limne	S^{ai}	Sungai
Est.	Estero	$L^{o(a)}$	Lago(a)	S^{d}	Sound
Est^{o}	Estrecho	$L^{una(s)}$	Laguna(s)	S^{ei}	Sungei
Fj.; -fj.	Fjord; -fjord	n.	nehir, nehri	Sel.	Selat
G.	Gulf	Ou.	Ouèd	Str.	Strait
g.	gawa	oz.	ozero	Tel.	Teluk
G^{fe}	Golfe	Pass.	Passage	vdchr.	vodochra-nilišče
G^{fo}	Golfo	prol.	proliv	W^{di}	Wadî
$g^{ü}$	gölü	R.	rio	zal.	zaliv

Mountains

A....	Alpes; Alpi	g.	gora	M^{ts}	Monts
...A.	Alpen	G^{a}	Góra	n.	nos
$Aig^{lle(s)}$	Aiguille(s)	Geb.	Gebirge	N^{do}	Nevado
Akr.	Akrotérion	-geb.	-gebirge	Ór.	Óros
App.	Appennino	Gl.	Glacier	P.,	
Bg.; -bg.	Berg; -berg	G^{ng}	Gunung	$P^{c(o)}$	Pic(o)
Bge.; -bge.	Berge; -berge	H.	Hill	Peg.	Pegunungan
B^{t}	Bukit	h.	hory	per.	pereval
C.	Cape	H^{d}	Head	$P^{k(s)}$	Peak(s)
C^{bc}	Cabo	H^{s}	Hills	pl^{a}	planina
chr.	chrebet	J.	Jabal	Pl^{au}	Plateau
$C^{l(e)}$	Col(le)	K	Kap	pl^{e}	planine
C^{ma}	Cima	M.	Monte	pr.	prusmyk
C^{no}	Corno	m.	mys	P^{rto}	Puerto
$Coll^{s}$	Collines	M^{as}	Montanhas	Prz.	Przelecz
Cord.	Cordillera	$M^{gne(s)}$	Montagne(s)	P^{so}	Passo
C^{po}	Capo	Mt.	Mount	$P^{t(e)}$	Point(e)
$C^{ro(s)}$	Cerro(s)	$M^{t(i)}$	Mont(i)	P^{ta}	Punta
Cuch.	Cuchilla	Mt^{n}	Mountain	P^{zo}	Pizzo
dağl.	dağlar, -i	Mts.	Mounts	$Ra^{(s)}$	Range(s)
$F^{êt}$	Forêt	Mt^{s}	Mountains	R^{ca}	Rocca

Mountains

Abbr.	Term	Abbr.	Term	Abbr.	Term
Ri.	Ridge	T^{ng}	Tanjung	-w.	-wald
S^{nia}	Serranía	$V^{än}$	Volcán	y.	yama
$S^{ra(s)}$	Sierra(s)	Vol.	Volcano		
S^{rra}	Serra	vozvyš.	vozvyšenn-ost'		

Places

Abbr.	Term	Abbr.	Term	Abbr.	Term
Arr.	Arroio, Arroyo	Hist.	Historical	P.	Port; Pulau
B.	Bad; Ban	-hm.	-heim	Pdg.	Padang
-bg.	-berg	Hqrs.	Headquarters	Ph.	Phum
$-b^{u}g.$	-burg	Hs.	House	P^{nte}	Puente
-bge.'	-berge	-hsn.	-hausen	P^{rto}	Puerto
B^{io}	Balneario	Hts.	Heights	P^{so}	Passo
-br(n).	-brück(en)	J^{n}	Junktion	P^{t}	Point
Build.	Building	K.	Kuala	P^{ta}	Punta
C^{d}	Ciudad	-kchn.	-kirchen	P^{te}	Pointe
Ch^{au}	Château	Km	Kilómetro	P^{to}	Porto
C^{le}	Castle	K^{ng}	Kampung	R.	Rio
Co.	Country	Kp.	Kompong	Rec.	Recreation
Coll.	College	K^{r}	Kangkar	S^{t}	Sidi
Cor.	Coronel	-lbn.	-leben	-st.	-stadt
Cr.	Creek	M.	Monte; Mu'o'ng	Stat.	Státion
-df.	-dorf	Mem.	Memorial	Tech.	Technical
$E^{ción}$	Estación	M^{gne}	Montagne	Univ.	University
$-f^{d}$	-field	Mt.	Mount	V^{a}	Vila
F^{rte}	Fuerte	$M^{t(s)}$	Mont(s)	V^{la}	Villa
F^{s}	Falls	Mt^{n}	Mountain	-wd.(e).	-wald(e)
$F^{t(e)}$	Fort(e)	Mt^{s}	Mountains		
F^{tin}	Fortin	Mus.	Museum		
-gn.	-ingen				

Administration

AK	Alaska	IL	Illinois	OR	Oregon
AL	Alabama	IN	Indiana	PA	Pennsylvania
A(O)	Autonomous (Oblast)	Ind.	India	P.D.R.	People's Democratic Republic
AR	Arkansas	Jap.	Japan	Port.	Portugal
Austr.	Australia	KS	Kansas	Reg.	Region
Aut.	Autonomous	KY	Kentucky	Rep.	Republic
AZ	Arizona	LA	Louisiana	RI	Rhode Island
Braz.	Brazil	MA	Massachusetts	S. Afr.	South Africa
CA	California	MD	Maryland	SC	South Carolina
CO	Colorado	ME	Maine	SD	South Dakota
Col.	Colombia	Mex.	Mexico	S.S.R.	Soviet Socialist Republic
C.Rica	Costa Rica	MI	Michigan	Terr.	Territory, -y, -ies
CT	Connecticut	MN	Minnesota	TN	Tennessee
DC	District of Columbia	MO	Missouri	TX	Texas
DE	Delaware	MS	Mississippi	U.K.	United Kingdom
Den.	Denmark	MT	Montana	U.S.A.	United States
Dist.	District	NC	North Carolina	U.S.S.R.	Soviet Union
Ec.	Ecuador	ND	North Dakota	UT	Utah
E.G.	Equatorial Guinea	NE	Nebraska	VA	Virginia
Fed.	Federal; Federated	NH	New Hampshire	Vietn.	Vietnam
FL	Florida	Nic.	Nicaragua	VT	Vermont
Fr.	France, French	NJ	New Jersey	WA	Washington
GA	Georgia	NM	New Mexico	WI	Wisconsin
HI	Hawai	Norw.	Norway	WV	West Virginia
Hond.	Honduras	NV	Nevada	WY	Wyoming
IA	Iowa	NY	New York		
ID	Idaho	N.Z.	New Zealand		
		OH	Ohio		
		OK	Oklahoma		

Organizations

ANZUS	Australia-New Zealand-U.S.A. (Tripartite Security Treaty)	NATO	North Atlantic Treaty Organization
ASEAN	Association of South East Asian Nations	OAS	Organization of American States
COMECON	Council of Mutual Economic Aid	OAU	Organization of African Unity
EC	European Community	OPEC	Organization of Petroleum Exporting Countries
EEC	European Economic Community	UNHCR	United Nations High Commissioner for Refugees
EFTA	European Free Trade Association	UNICEF	United Nations Children's Emergency Fund
FAO	Food and Agriculture Organization	UNO	United Nations Organization

Explanation of Symbols

Symbols

River, stream		Railroad		Place	Locality
Drying river, stream		Primary railroad } on larger scale maps		LOS ANGELES over – 1,000,000 Inhabitants	L.-A.-HOLLYWOOD
Intermittent river, stream		Secondary railroad		BOSTON 500,000 – 1,000,000 Inhabitants	B.-DORCHESTER

River, stream
Drying river, stream
Intermittent river, stream
Canal
Canal under construction
Waterfall, rapids
Dam
Fresh-water or salt-water lake with permanent shore line
Fresh-water or salt-water lake with variable or undefined shore line
Intermittent lake
Well in dry area
Swamp, Bog
Salt marsh
Flood area
Mud flat
Reef, Coral reef
Glacier
Average pack ice limit in summer
Average pack ice limit in winter
Shelf ice
Sand desert, gravel desert, etc.
Inhabited spot, station
Ruins
Lighthouse

Railroad
Primary railroad } on larger scale maps
Secondary railroad }
Suspended cable car
Railroad under construction
Train ferry
Tunnel
Major highway
Expressway } on larger scale maps
Expressway under construction }
Caravan route, path, track
Ferry
Pass
Airport, Airfield
International boundary
Boundary of autonomous area
Boundary of subsidiary administrative unit
WASHINGTON National capital
Harrisburg Principal cities of subsidiary administrative units
Nachičevan'
Castle or fort
Nature reserve

Place
LOS ANGELES over – 1,000,000 Inhabitants
BOSTON 500,000 – 1,000,000 Inhabitants
ATLANTA 100,000 – 500,000 Inhabitants
Malden 50,000 – 100,000 Inhabitants
Jefferson 10,000 – 50,000 Inhabitants
Cleveland under – 10,000 Inhabitants

Locality
L.-A.-HOLLYWOOD
B.-DORCHESTER
A.-BOLTON
Edgeworth

Supplemental symbols of Metropolitan area maps

City center, Old town
Residential area
Industrial area, Waterfront
Park
Christian cemetery
Moslem cemetery
Forest (partly scrub)
Expressway
Main road, Secondary road
Railroad with station
Airport, Airfield
Important building, Point of interest
Municipal boundary   Church
Town wall   Temple
Tower   ☆ Fort   Mosque

Type Styles

CANADA	Independent country	COAST RANGE / Colorado Plateau	Mountain	OCEAN / Gulf of Mexico / Mississippi River	Hydrography
Texas	Subordinate administrative unit	Mt. Shasta	Mountain, cape, pass, glacier	Cayman Trench	Ocean basin, trench, ridge etc.
(U.S.A.) (U.S.A.)	Political affiliation			2789	Altitude and depth in meters
DENVER / Columbia / Augusta	Places	MIDDLE WEST / Gila Desert / Isle Royale	Physical regions and islands	164	Depth of lakes below surface

Altitudes and depths

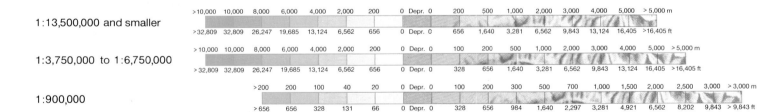

| 1:13,500,000 and smaller | >10,000 10,000 8,000 6,000 4,000 2,000 200 0 Depr. 0 200 500 1,000 2,000 3,000 4,000 5,000 >5,000 m |
| >32,809 32,809 26,247 19,685 13,124 6,562 656 0 Depr. 0 656 1,640 3,281 6,562 9,843 13,124 16,405 >16,405 ft |
| 1:3,750,000 to 1:6,750,000 | >10,000 10,000 8,000 6,000 4,000 2,000 200 0 Depr. 0 100 200 500 1,000 2,000 3,000 4,000 5,000 >5,000 m |
| >32,809 32,809 26,247 19,685 13,124 6,562 656 0 Depr. 0 328 656 1,640 3,281 6,562 9,843 13,124 16,405 >16,405 ft |
| 1:900,000 | >200 200 100 40 20 0 Depr. 0 100 200 300 500 700 1,000 1,500 2,000 2,500 3,000 >3,000 m |
| >656 656 328 131 66 0 Depr. 0 328 656 984 1,640 2,297 3,281 4,921 6,562 8,202 9,843 >9,843 ft |

Conversion diagram

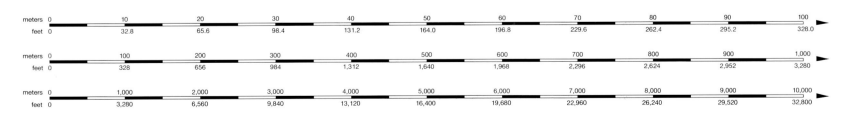

meters	0	10	20	30	40	50	60	70	80	90	100
feet	0	32.8	65.6	98.4	131.2	164.0	196.8	229.6	262.4	295.2	328.0
meters	0	100	200	300	400	500	600	700	800	900	1,000
feet	0	328	656	984	1,312	1,640	1,968	2,296	2,624	2,952	3,280
meters	0	1,000	2,000	3,000	4,000	5,000	6,000	7,000	8,000	9,000	10,000
feet	0	3,280	6,560	9,840	13,120	16,400	19,680	22,960	26,240	29,520	32,800

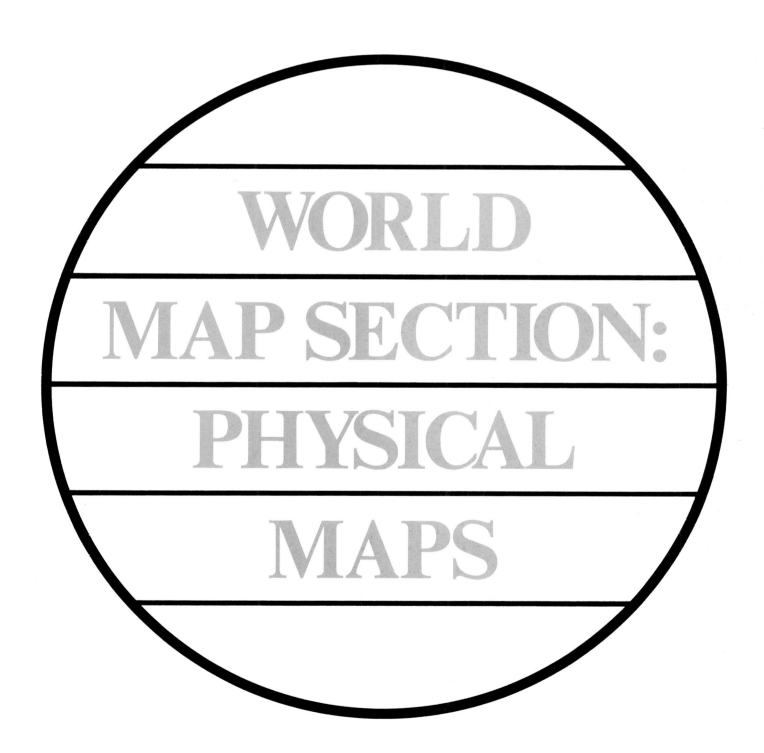

WORLD
MAP SECTION:
PHYSICAL
MAPS

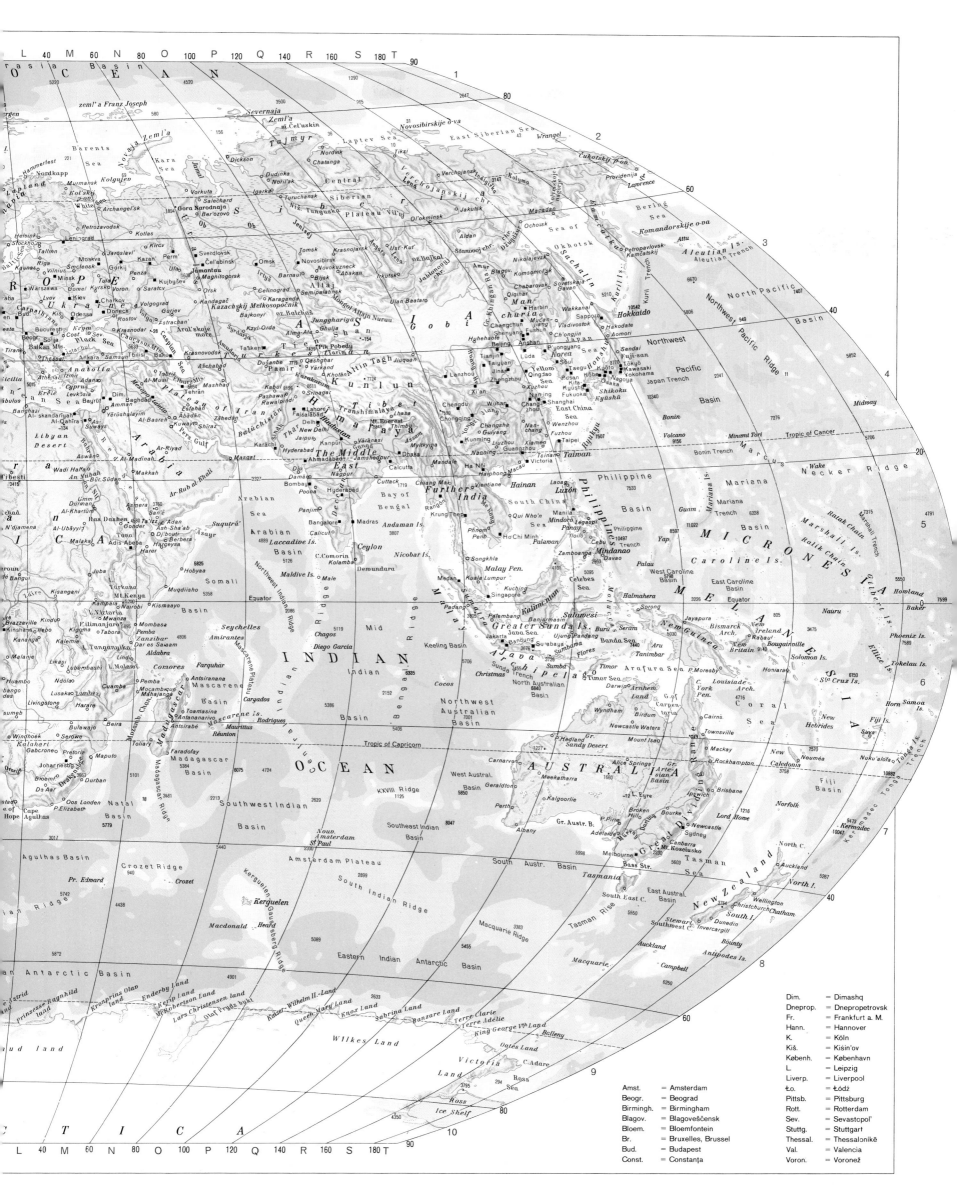

Dim. = Dimashq
Dneprop. = Dnepropetrovsk
Fr. = Frankfurt a. M.
Hann. = Hannover
K. = Köln
Kiš. = Kišin'ov
København. = København
L. = Leipzig
Liverp. = Liverpool
Ło. = Łódź
Pittsb. = Pittsburg
Rott. = Rotterdam
Sev. = Sevastopol'
Stuttg. = Stuttgart
Thessal. = Thessaloníkē
Val. = Valencia
Voron. = Voronež

Amst. = Amsterdam
Beogr. = Beograd
Birmingh. = Birmingham
Blagov. = Blagoveščensk
Bloem. = Bloemfontein
Br. = Bruxelles, Brussel
Bud. = Budapest
Const. = Constanța

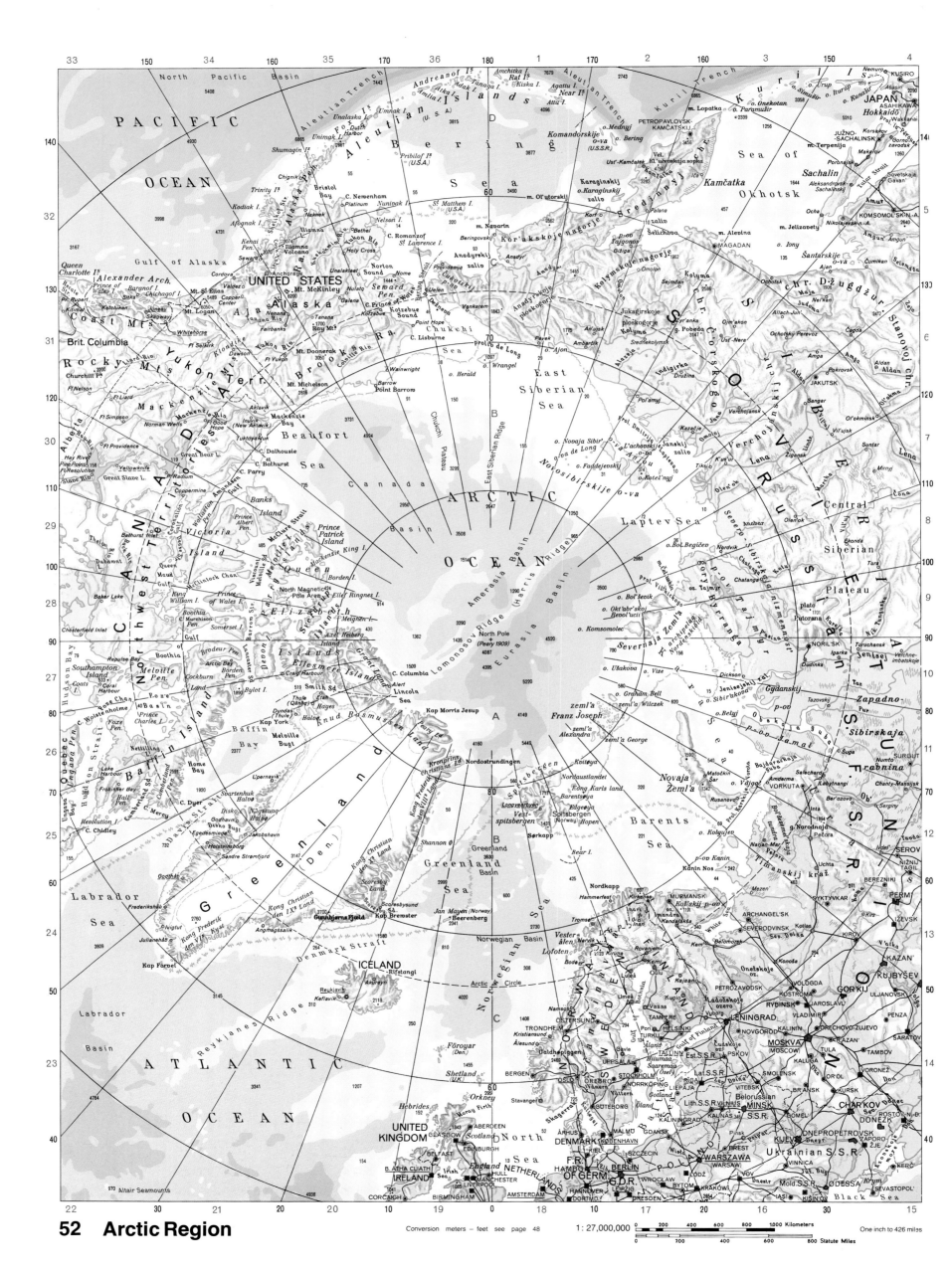

Conversion meters – feet see page 48

1 : 27,000,000

0 200 400 600 800 1000 Kilometers

One inch to 426 miles

0 200 400 600 800 Statute Miles

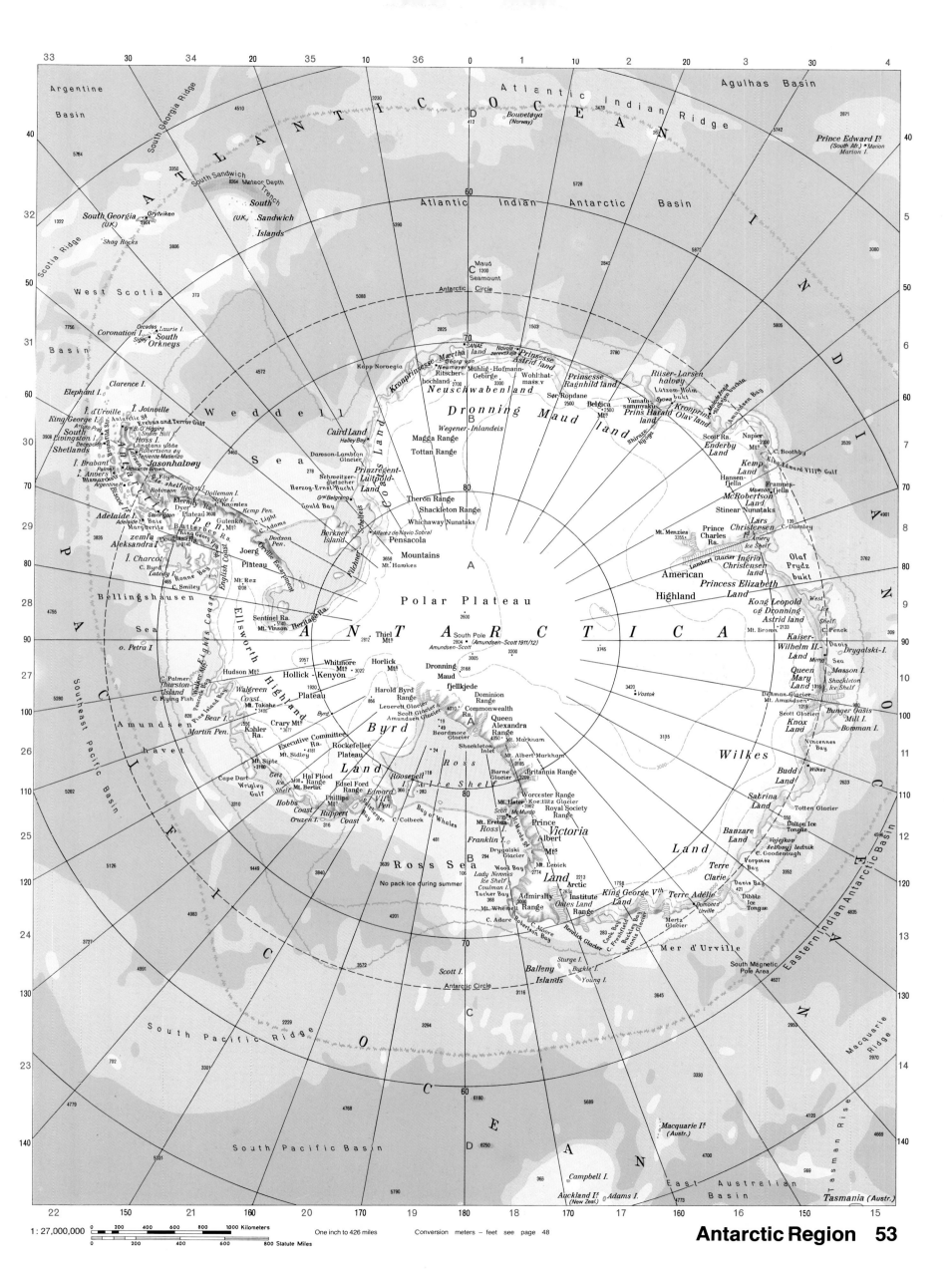

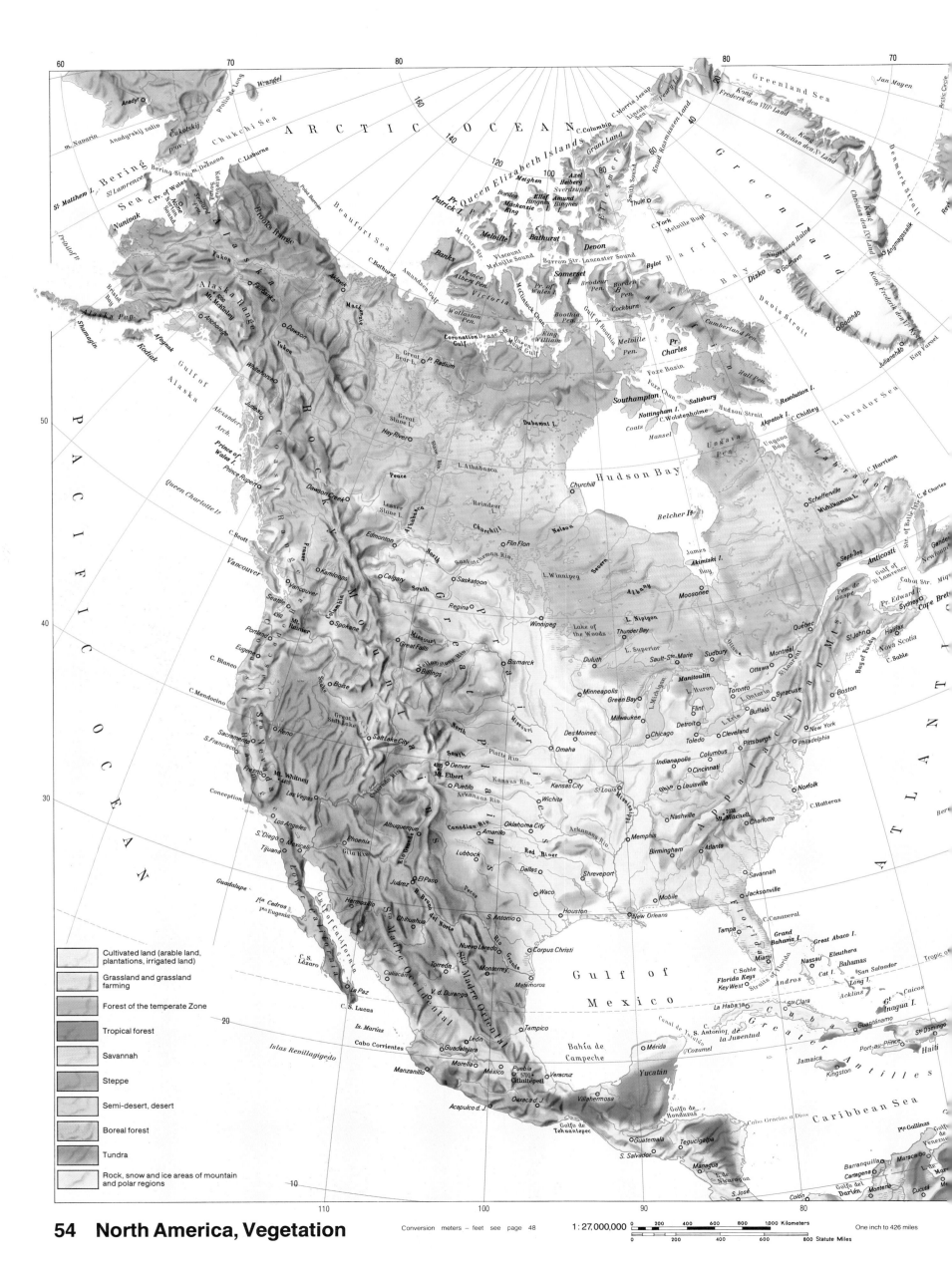

Conversion meters – feet see page 48

1 : 27,000,000

Legend:
- Cultivated land (arable land, plantations, irrigated land)
- Grassland and grassland farming
- Forest of the temperate Zone
- Tropical forest
- Savannah
- Steppe
- Semi-desert, desert
- Boreal forest
- Tundra
- Rock, snow and ice areas of mountain and polar regions

0 200 400 600 800 1,000 Kilometers

0 200 400 600 800 Statute Miles

One inch to 426 miles

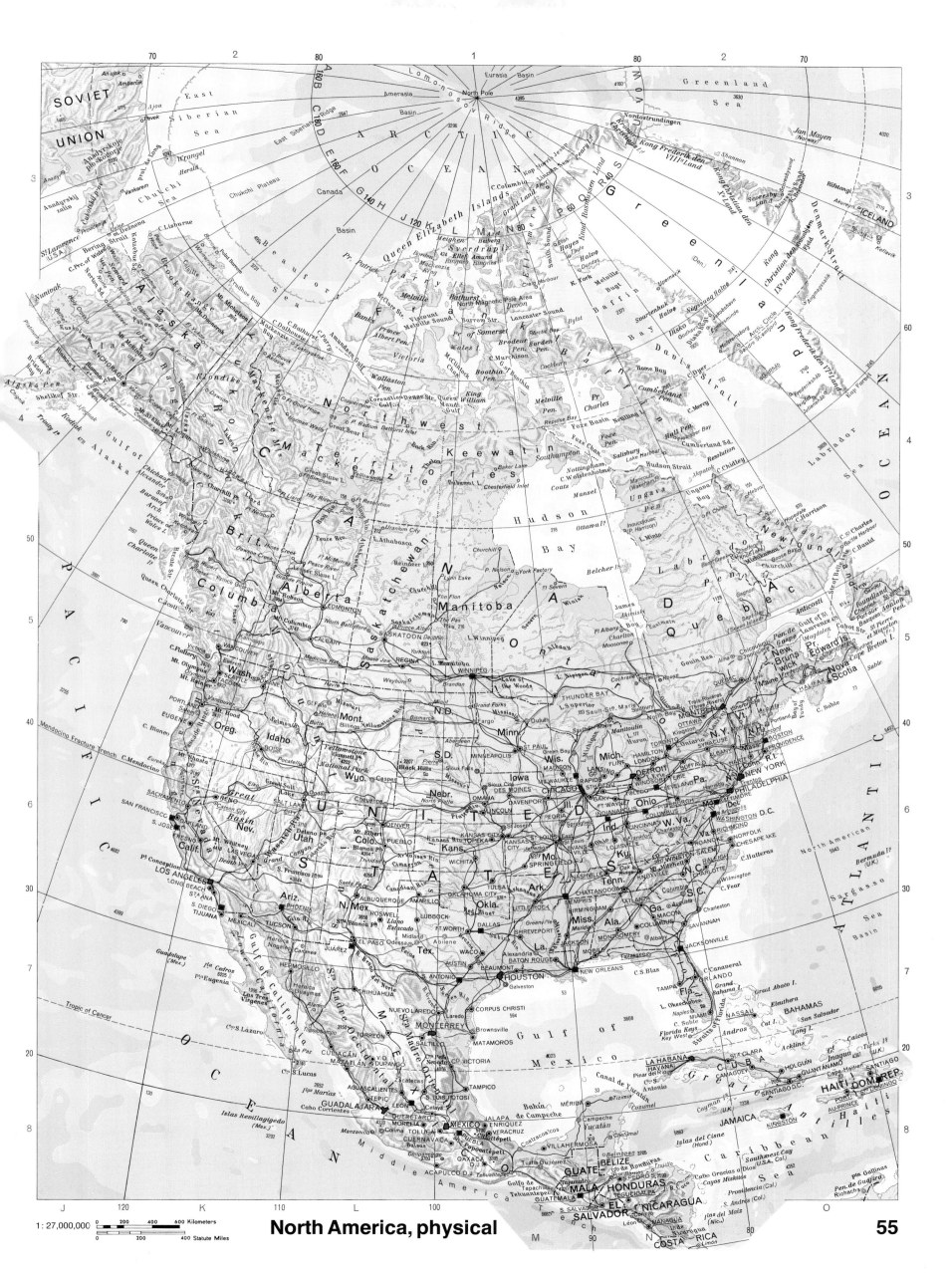

North America, physical

55

1 : 13,500,000

100   200   300   400   500 Kilometers

100   200   300   400

One inch to 213 miles   Conversion meters – feet see page 48

400 Statute Miles

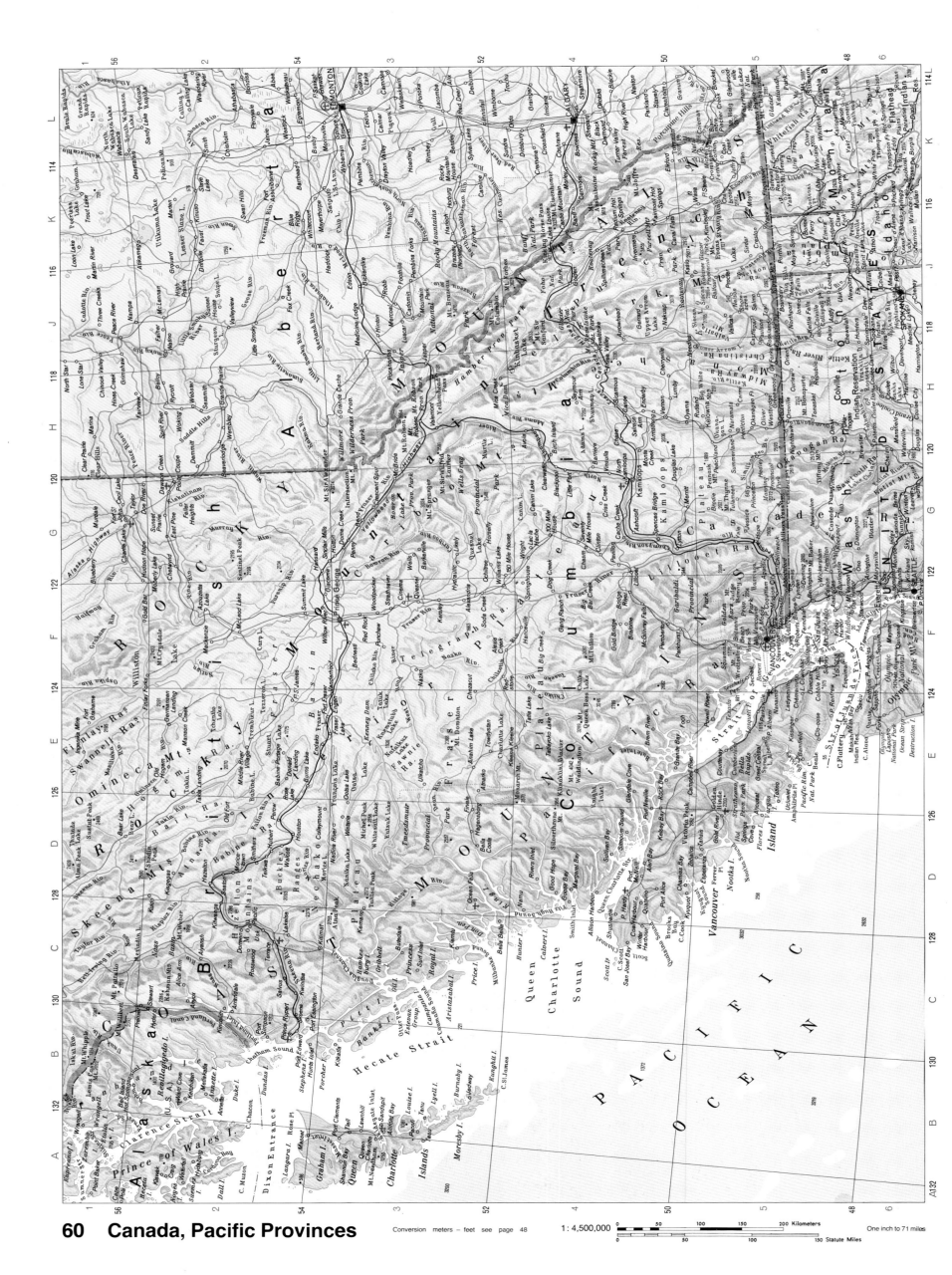

60   Canada, Pacific Provinces

Conversion meters – feet see page 48

1 : 4,500,000

One inch to 71 miles

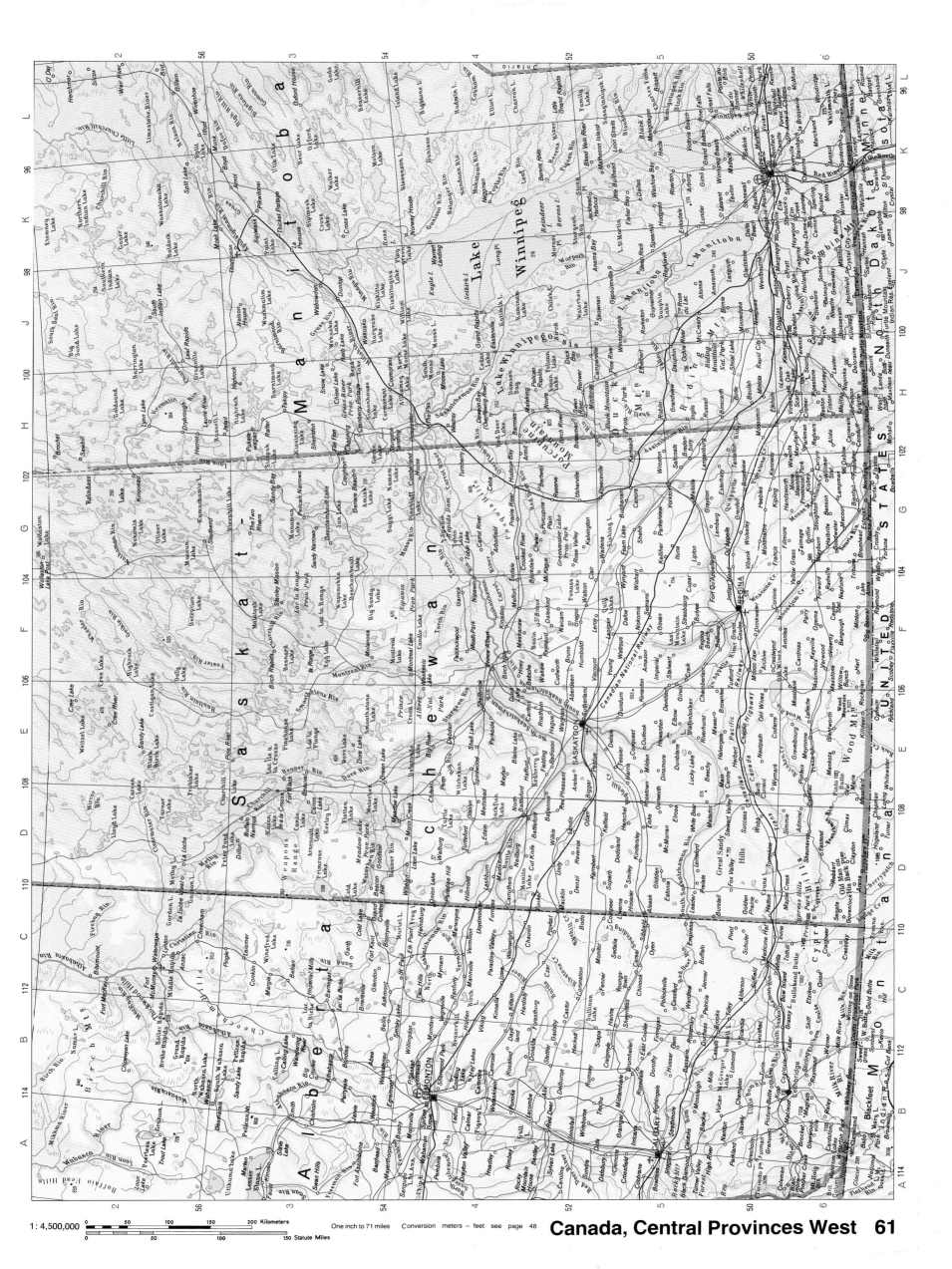

1 : 4,500,000

0   50   100   150   200 Kilometers

0   50   100   150 Statute Miles

One inch to 71 miles   Conversion meters – feet see page 48

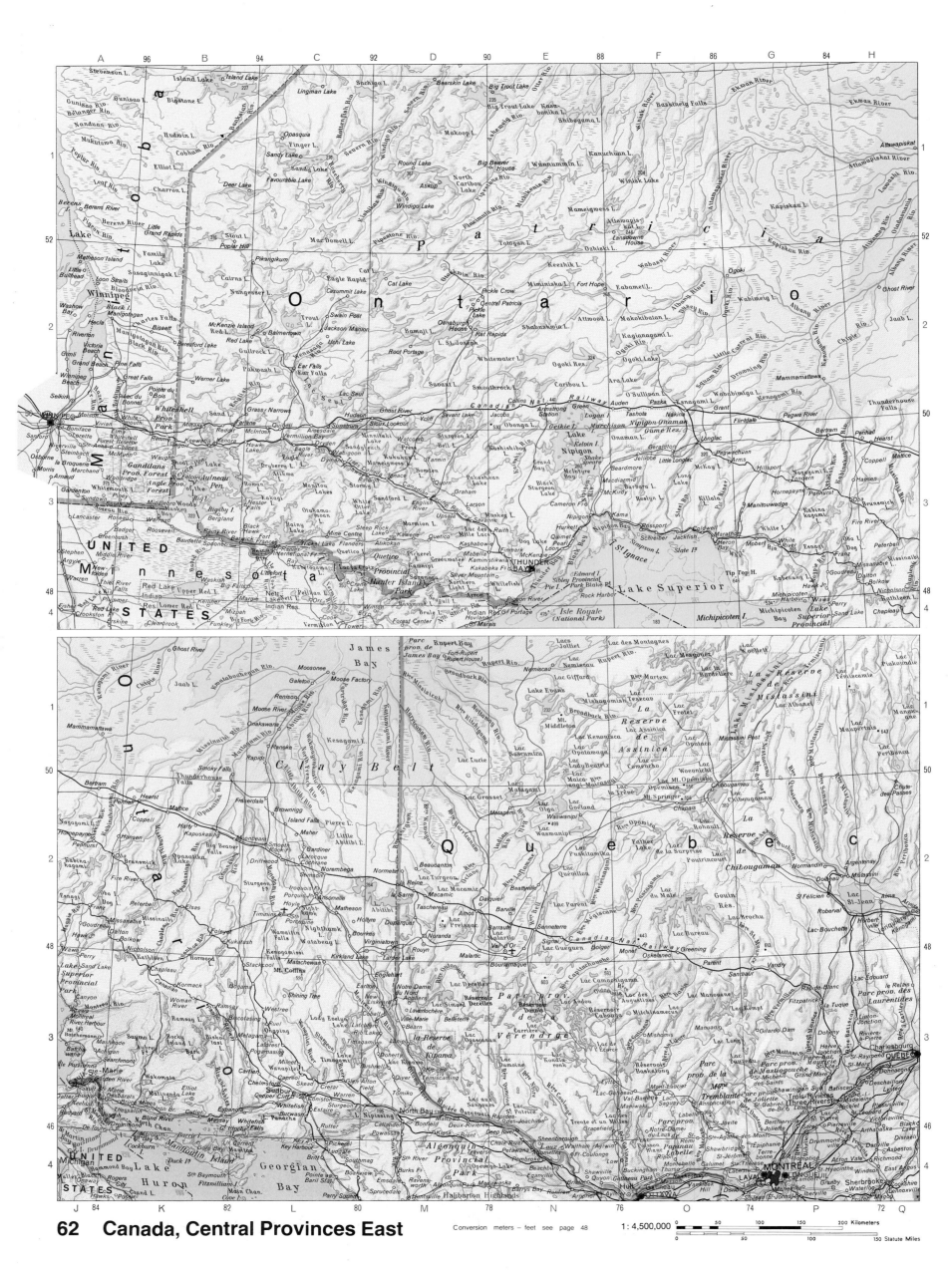

Conversion meters – feet see page 48

1 : 4,500,000

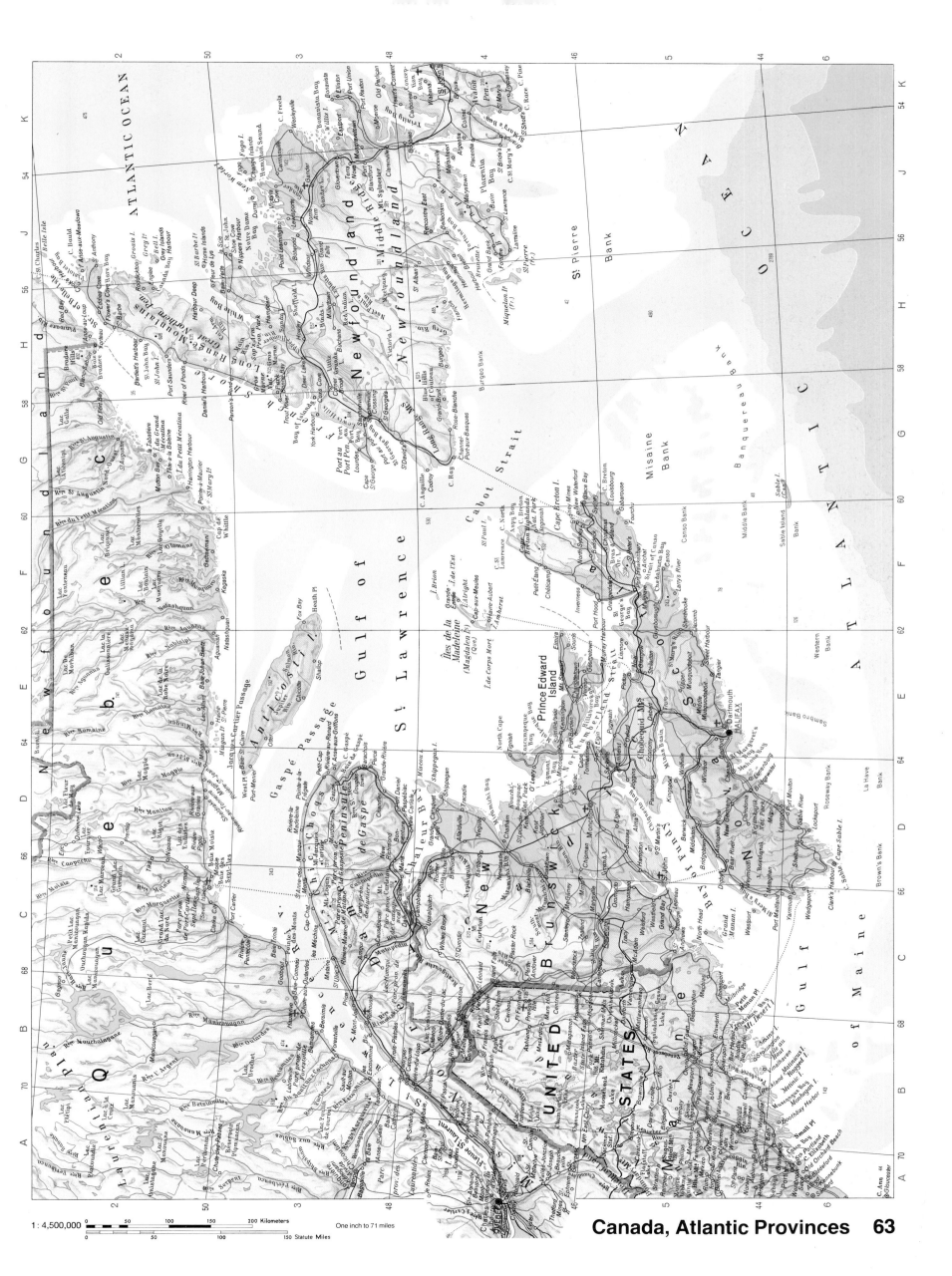

Canada, Atlantic Provinces 63

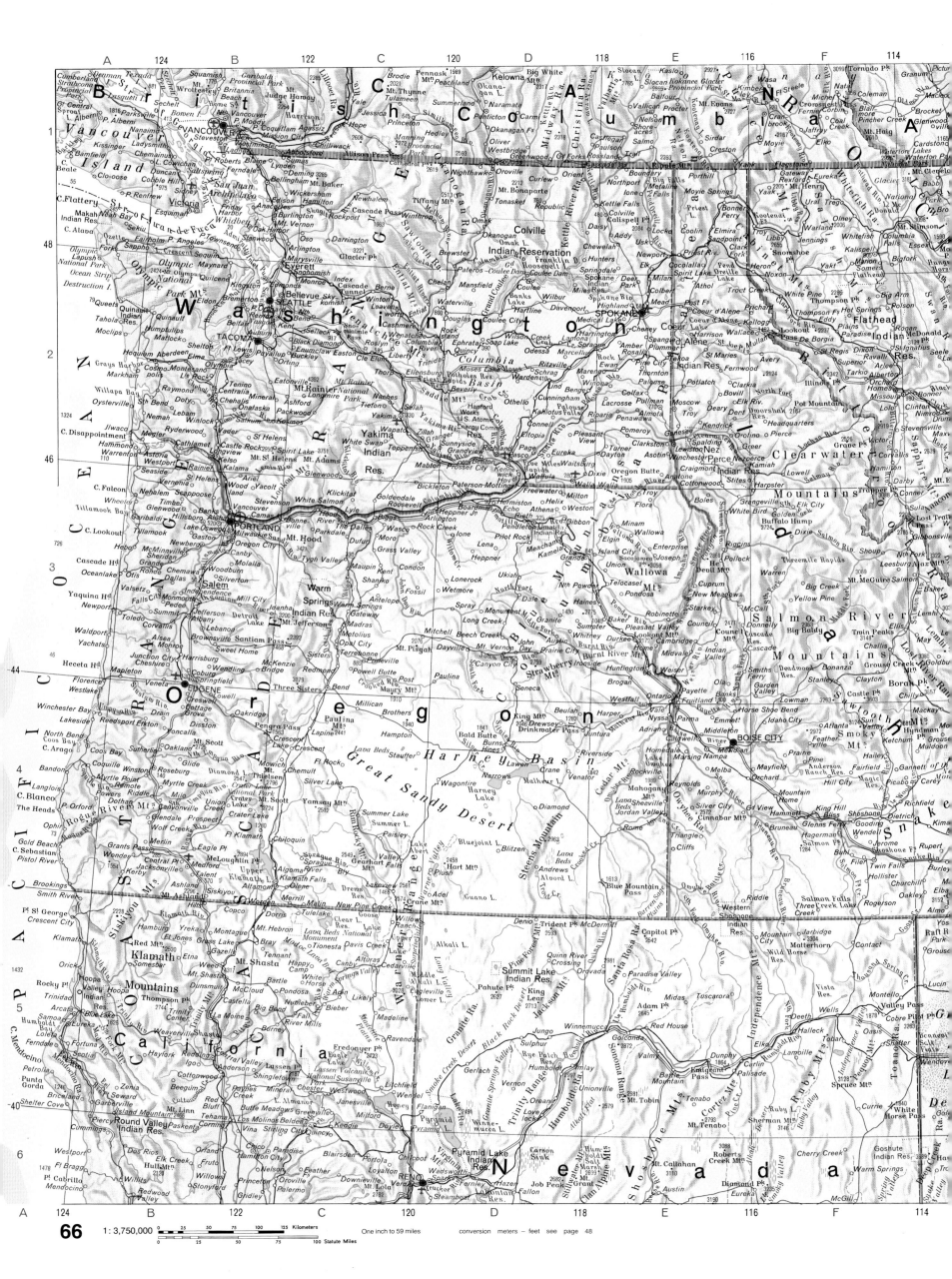

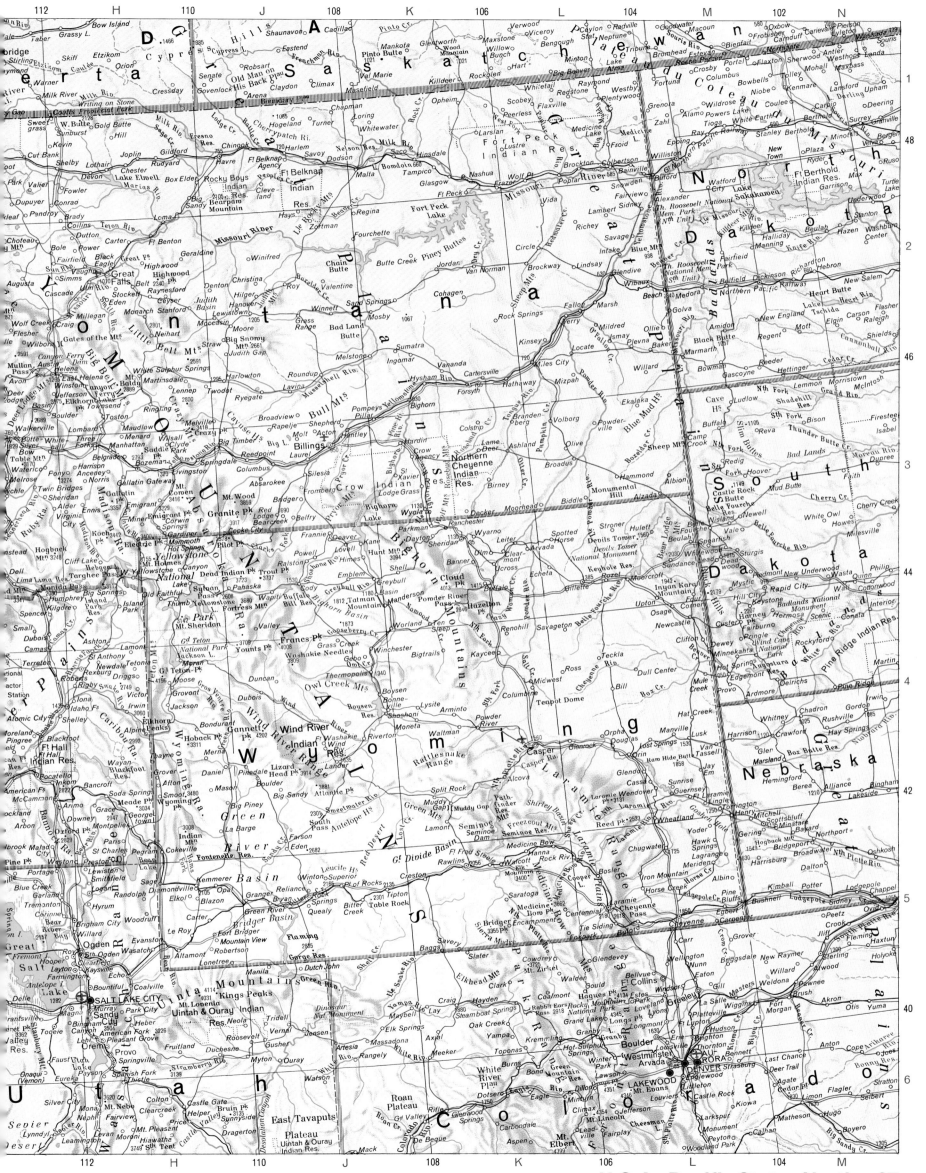

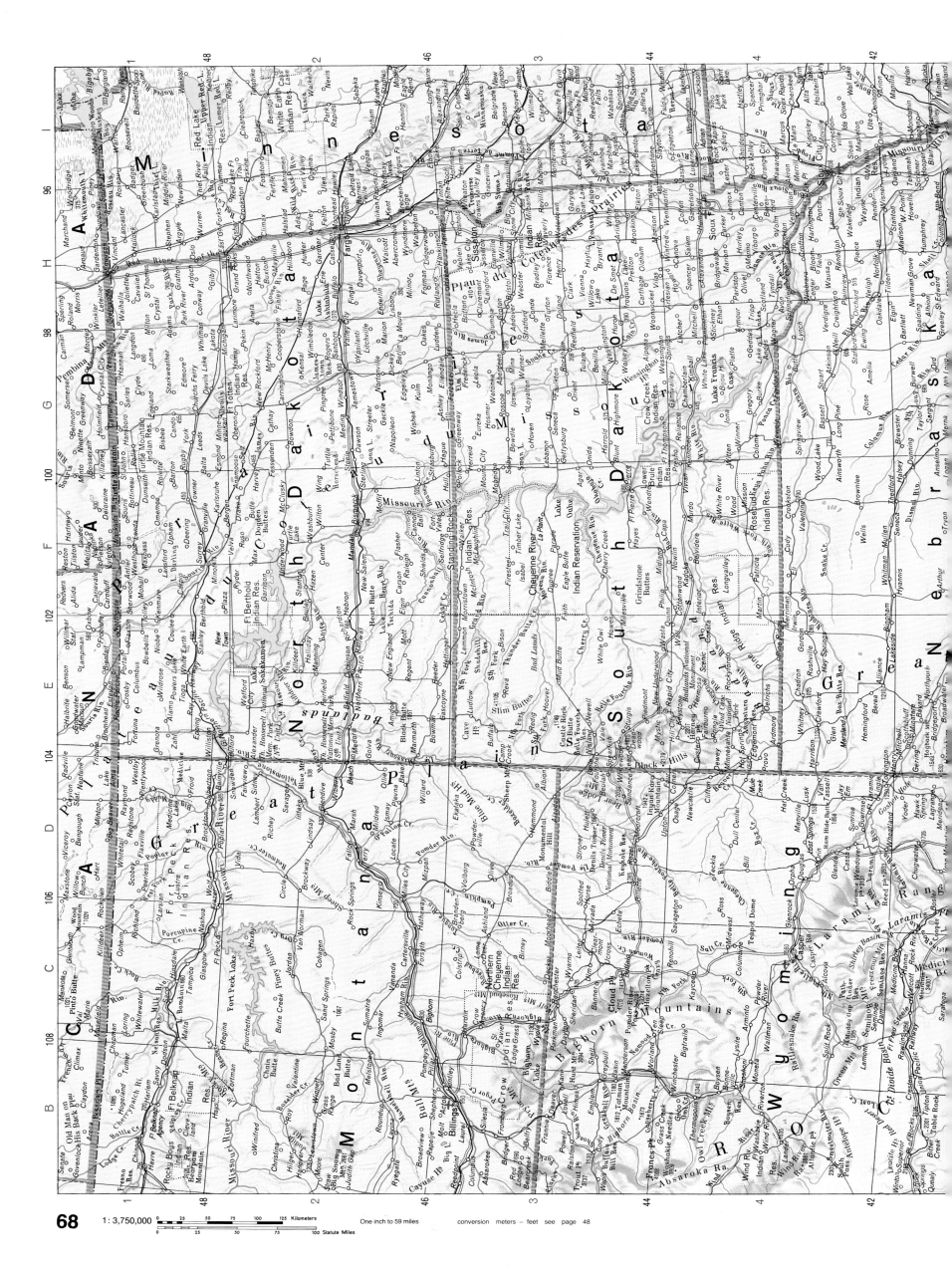

1 : 3,750,000

0 25 50 75 100 125 Kilometers

One inch to 59 miles

conversion meters - feet see page 48

0 25 50 75

100 Statute Miles

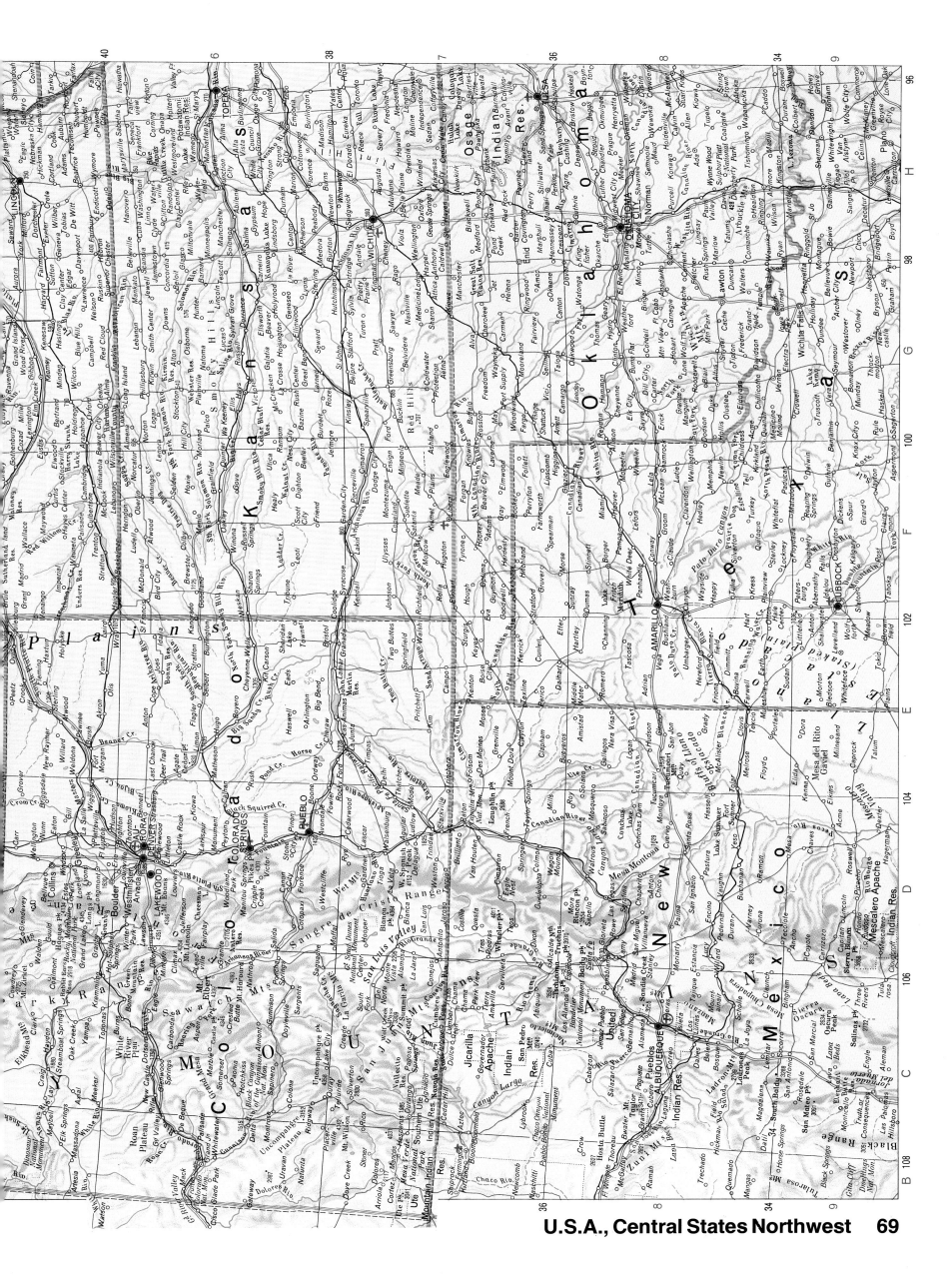

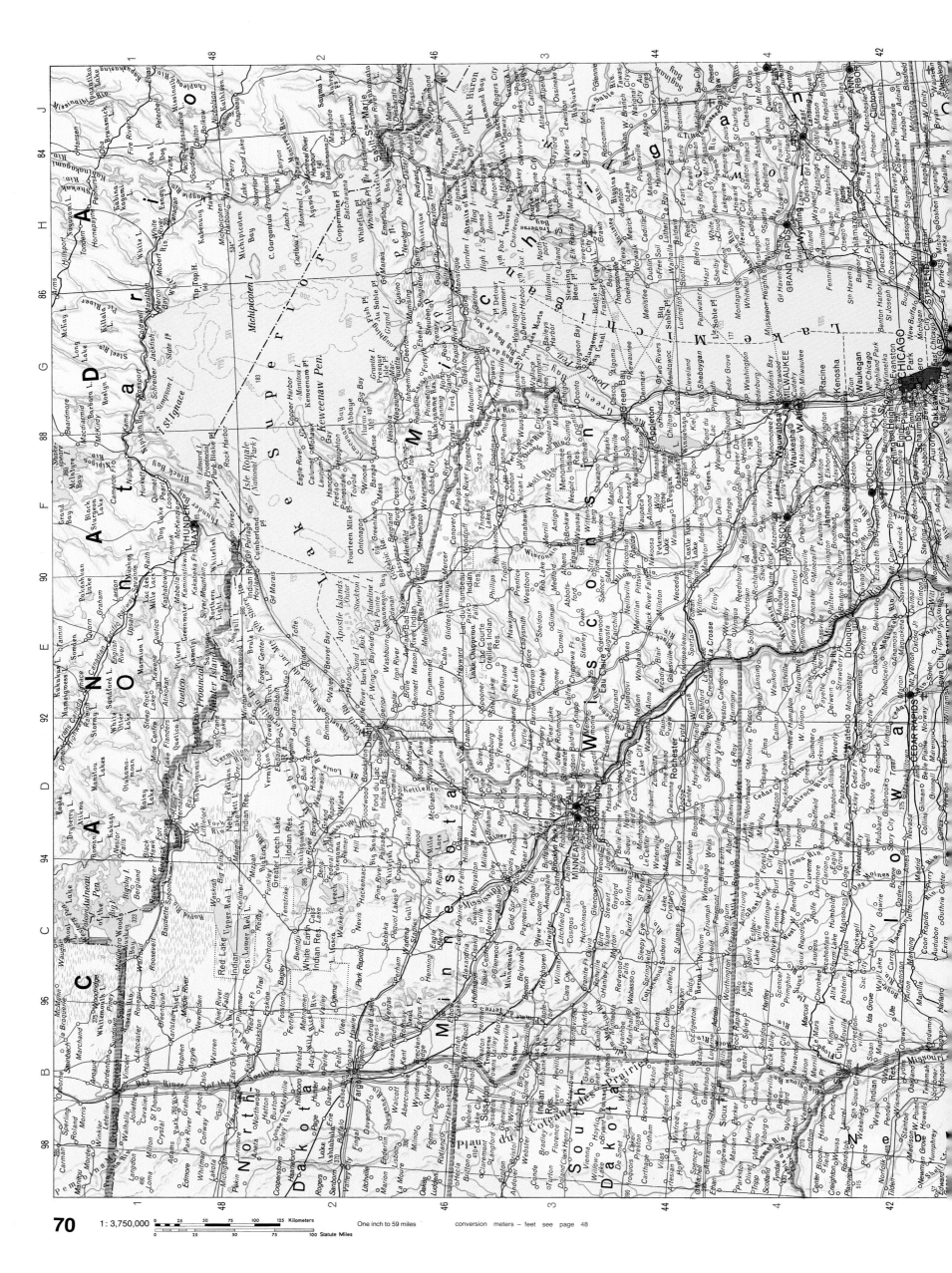

1 : 3,750,000

0 25 50 75 100 125 Kilometers

0 25 50 75 100 Statute Miles

One inch to 59 miles   conversion meters – feet see page 48

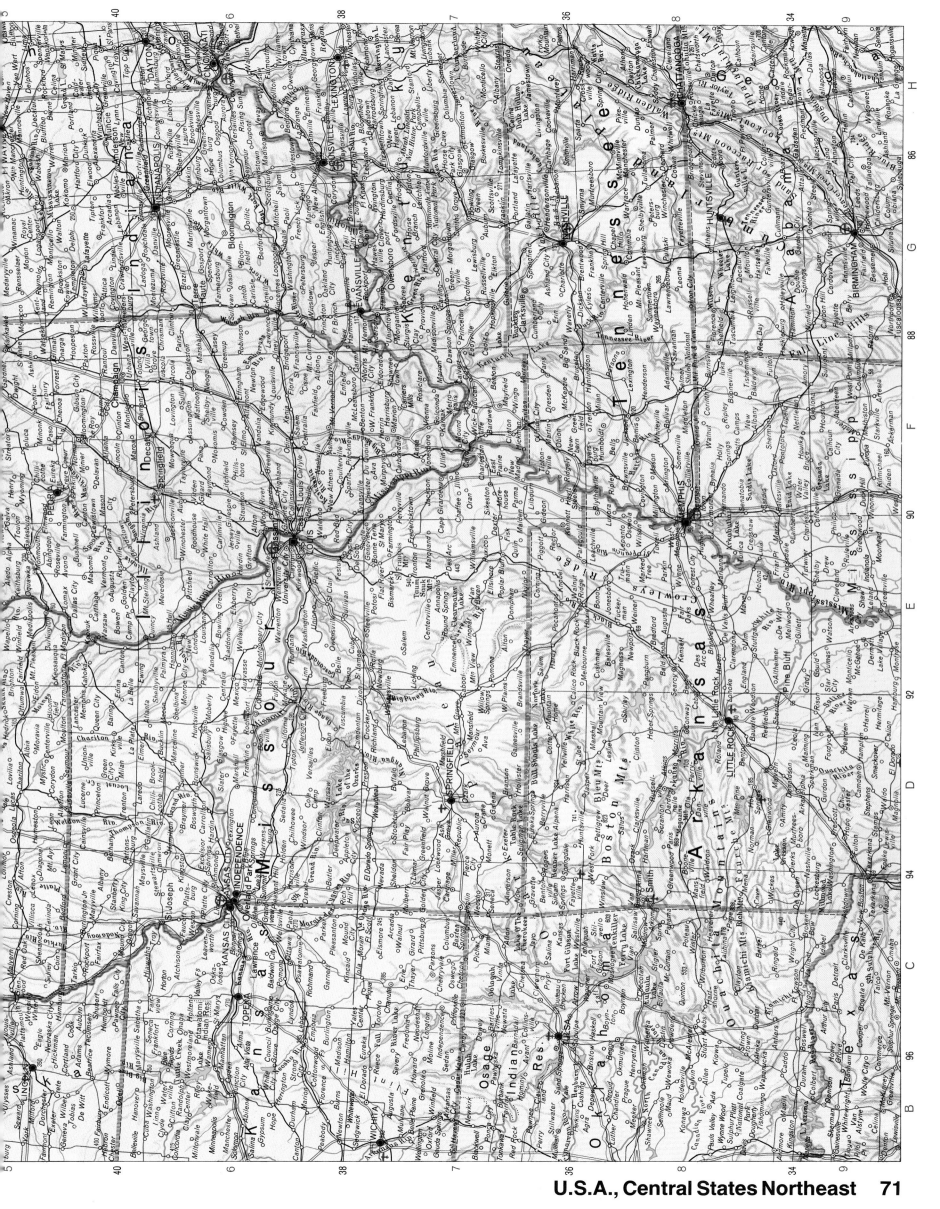

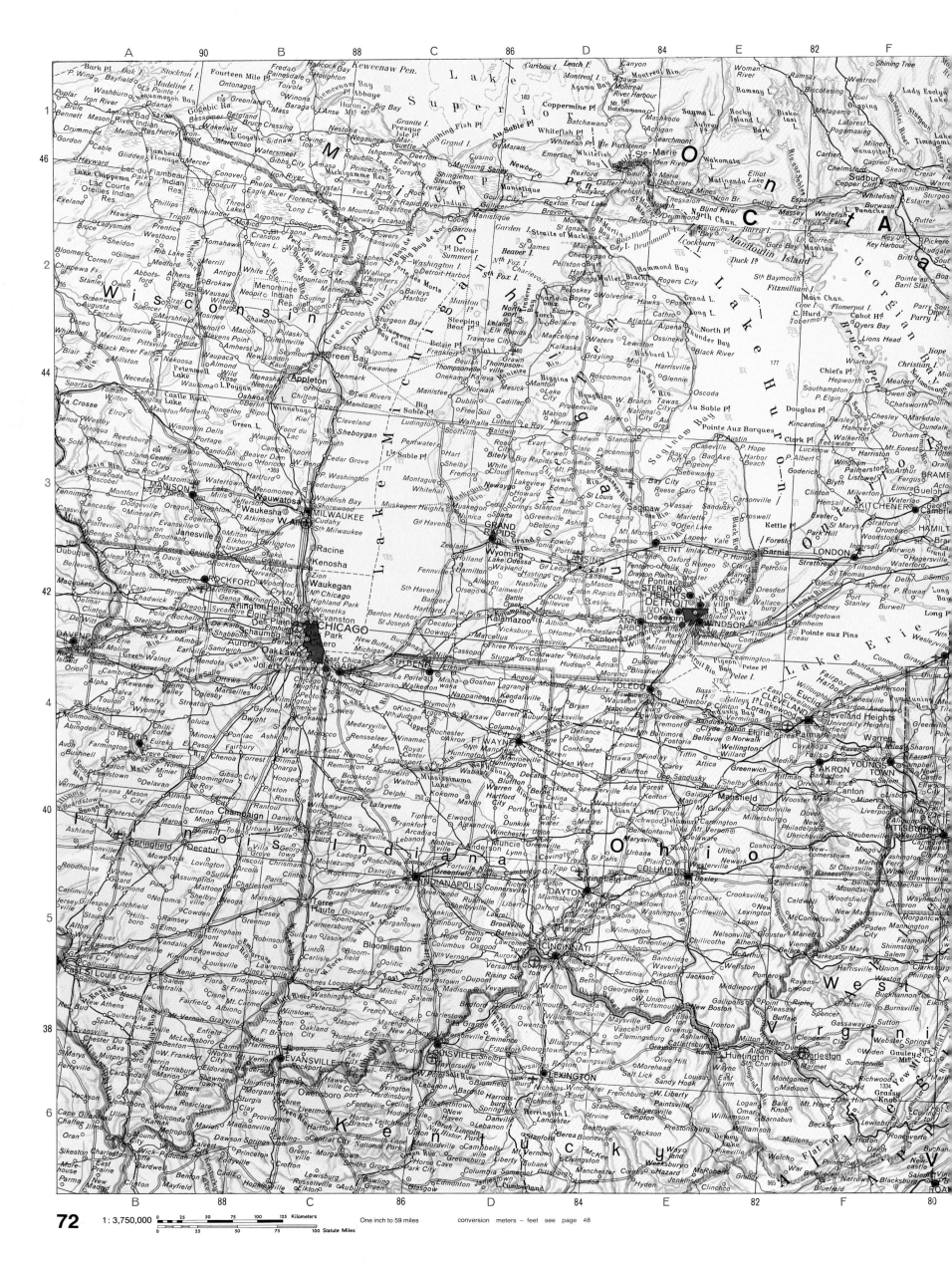

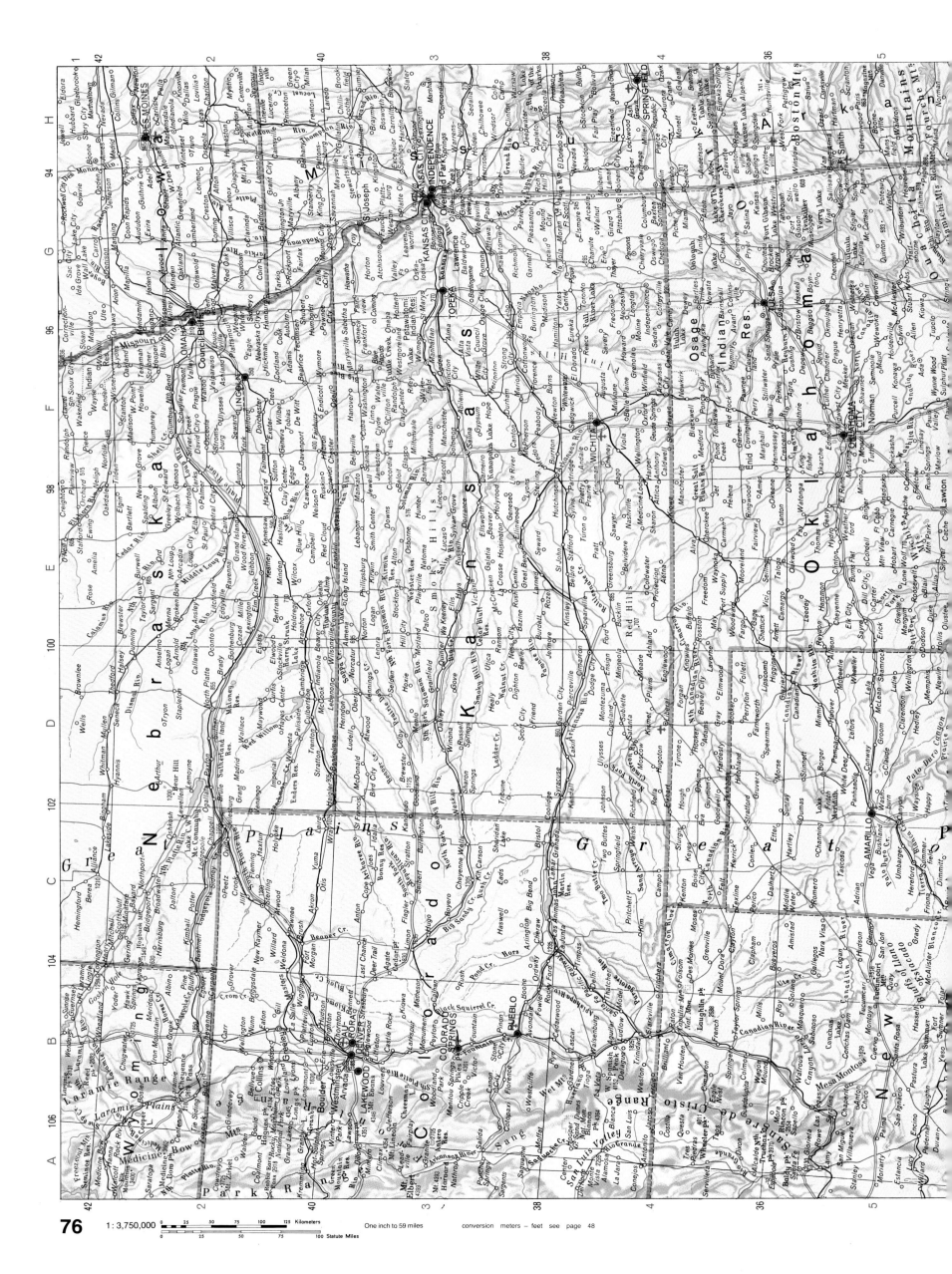

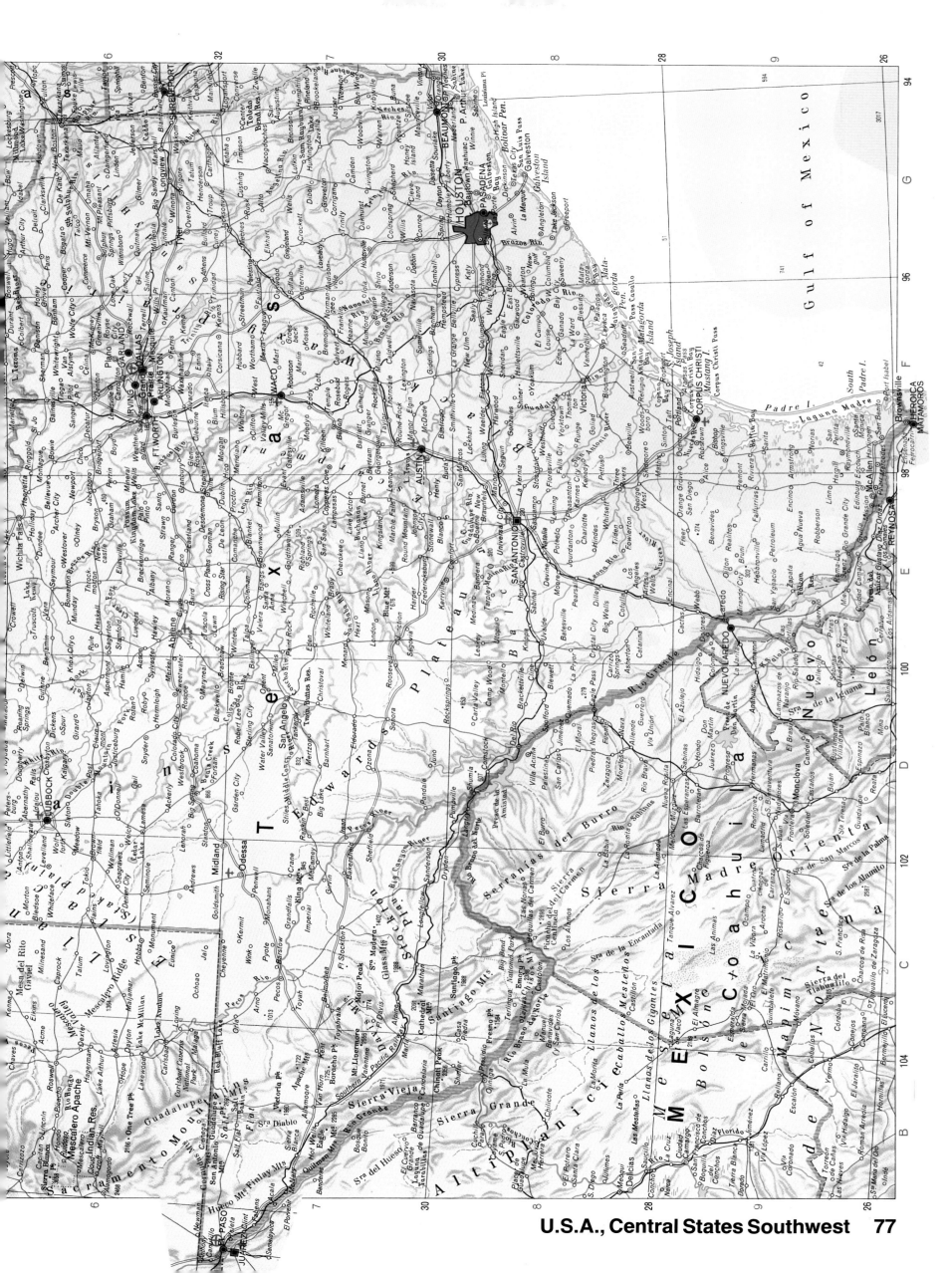

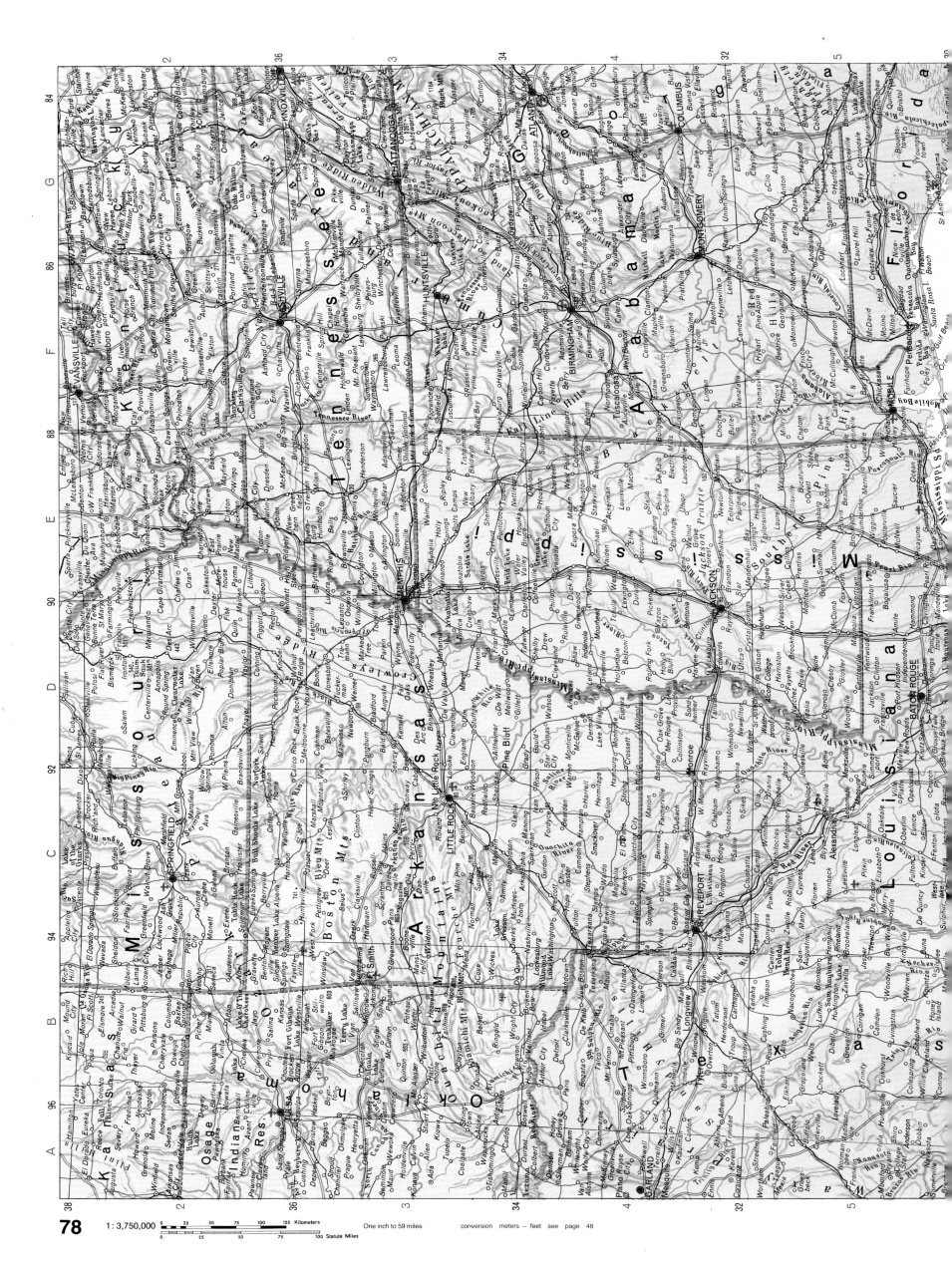

1 : 3,750,000

One inch to 59 miles   conversion meters — feet see page 48

0   25   50   75   100   125 Kilometers

0   25   50   75   100 Statute Miles

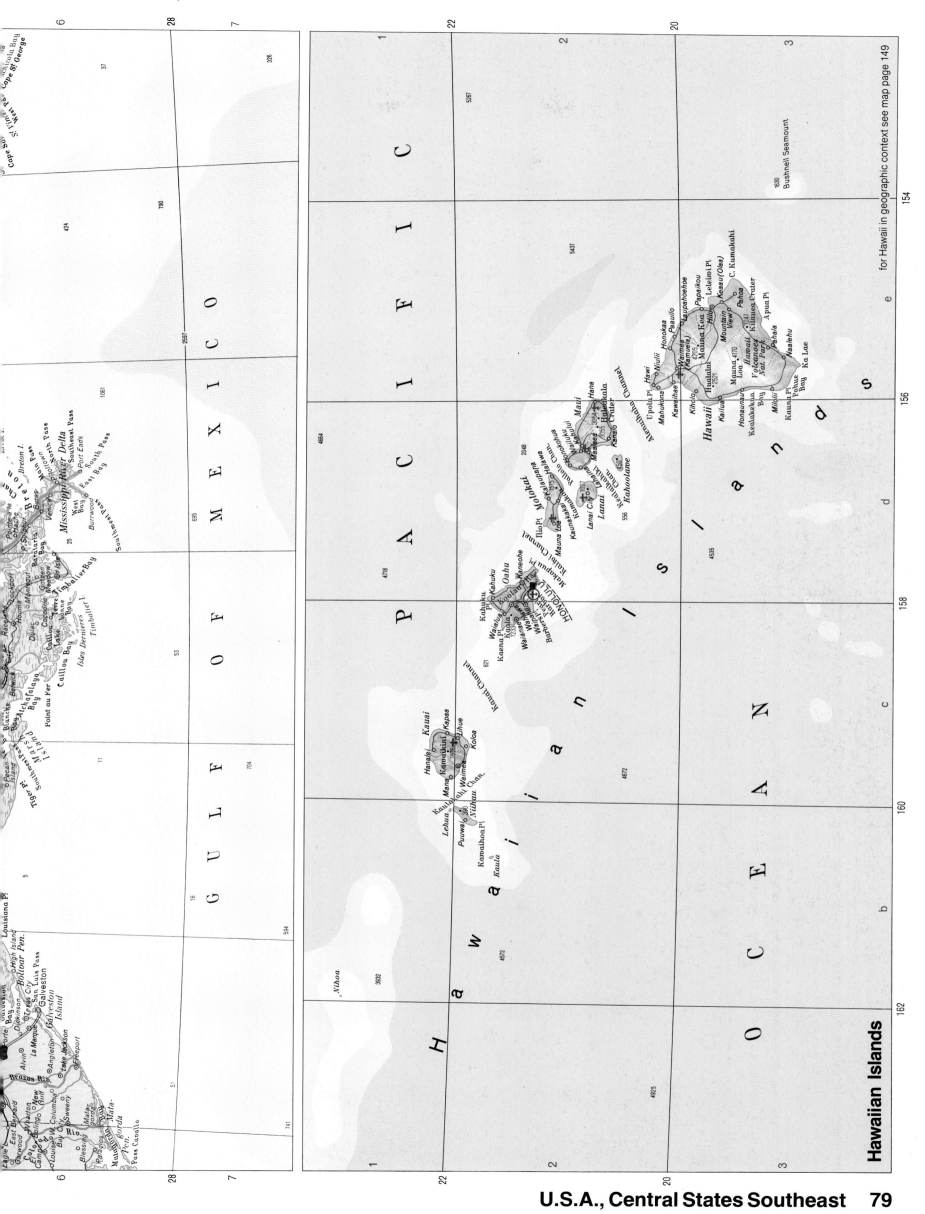

U.S.A., Central States Southeast   79

for Hawaii in geographic context see map page 149

Hawaiian Islands

Florida

82 Montreal·Washington·New York

Conversion meters – feet see page 48

1:225,000

0   2.5   5   7.5   10 Kilometers

0   2.5   5   7.5 Statute Miles

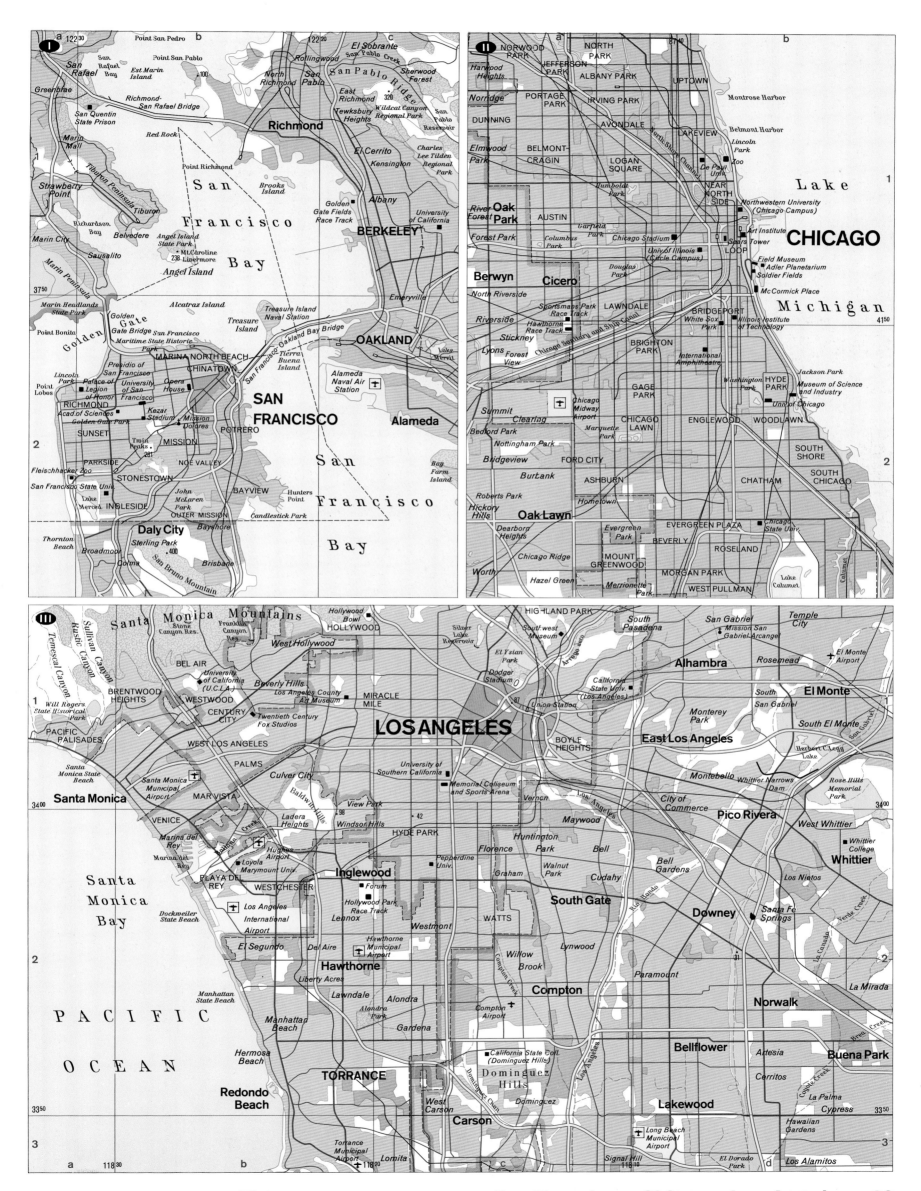

San Francisco · Chicago · Los Angeles　83

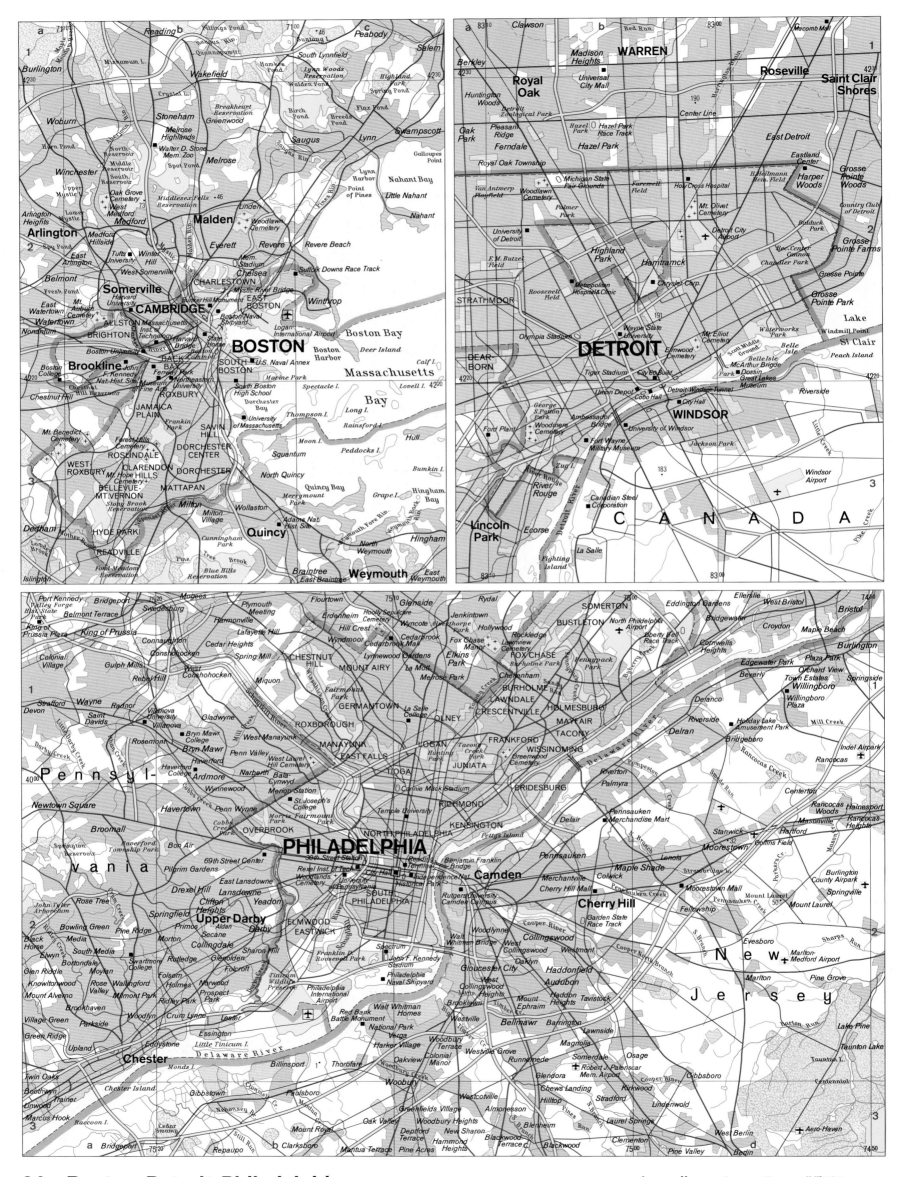

Conversion meters – feet see page 48

1 : 225,000

| 0 | 2.5 | 5 | 7.5 | 10 Kilometers |
| 0 | | 2.5 | 5 | 7.5 Statute Miles |

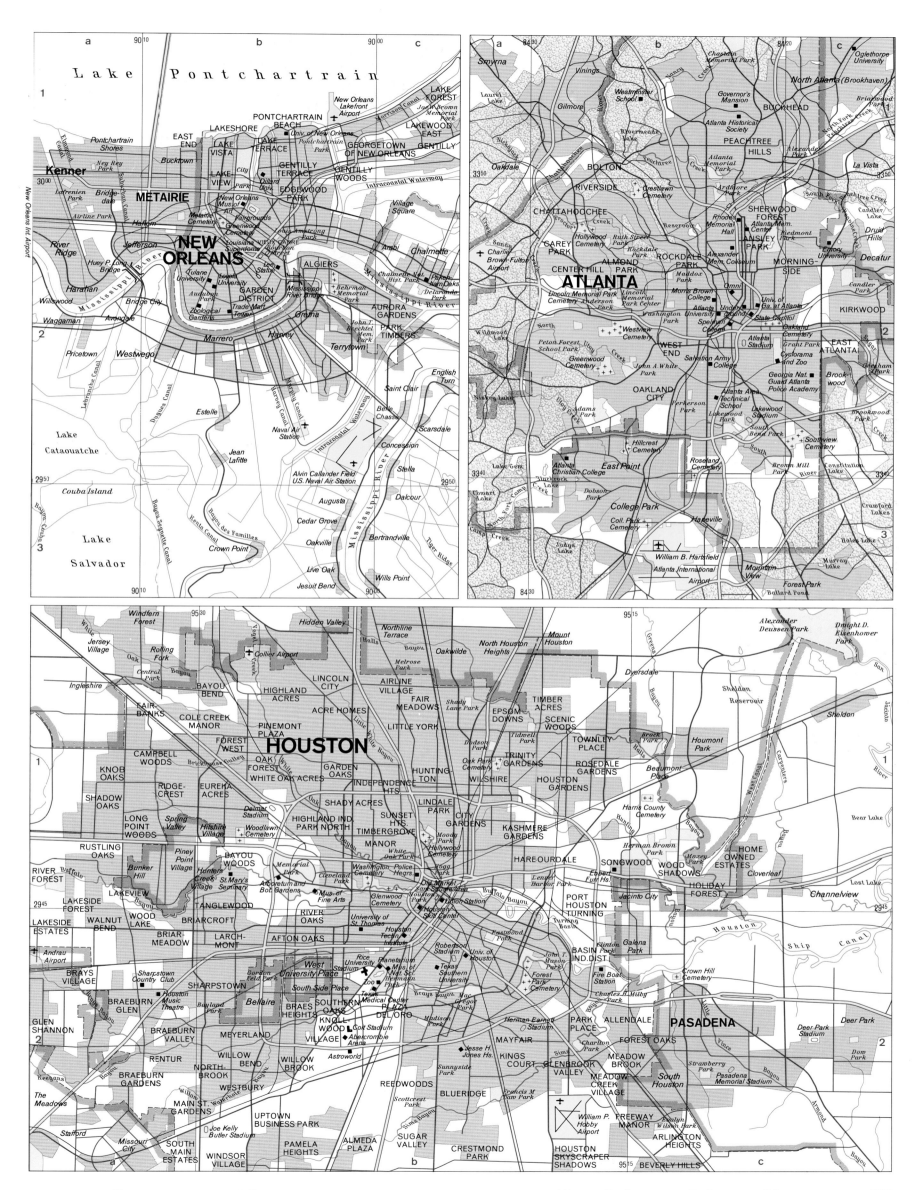

1 : 225,000

0   2.5   5   7.5   10 Kilometers

0   2.5   5   7.5 Statute Miles

One inch to 3.6 miles

Mexico 87

Conversion meters – feet see page 48

1 : 27,000,000

One inch to 426 miles

0   200   400   600   800   1000 Kilometers

0   200   400   600

800 Statute Miles

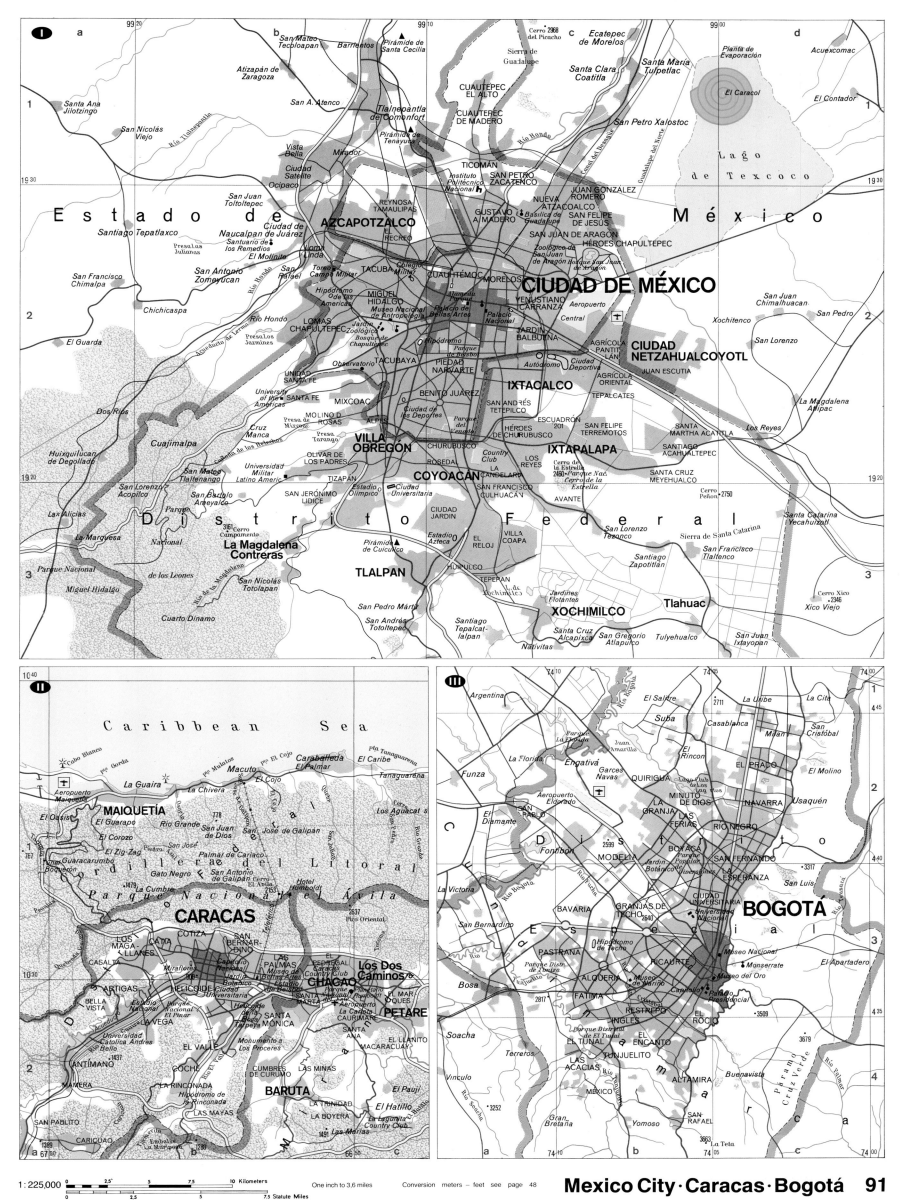

I

a   99 20   b   99 10   c   Cerro 2968 del Picacho   99 00   d

San Mateo Tecoloapan   Barrientos   Pirámide de Santa Cecilia   Ecatepec de Morelos   Planta de Evaporación   Acuexcomac

Santa María Tulpetlac   El Caracol   El Contador

1   Santa Ana Jilotzingo   Atizapán de Zaragoza   Sierra de Guadalupe   Santa Clara Coatitla   San Petro Xalostoc   1

San Nicolás Viejo   San A. Atenco   Río Tlalnepantla   Tlalnepantla de Comonfort   CUAUTEPEC EL ALTO   CUAUTEPEC DE MADERO   Río Hondo   Lago de Texcoco

Vista Bella   Pirámide de Tenayuca   Mirador   TICOMÁN   Canal del Desagüe   Guadalupe del Norte   19 30

19 30   Ciudad Satélite   Ocipaco   Instituto Politécnico Nacional   SAN PETRO ZACATENCO   JUAN GONZÁLEZ ROMERO

San Juan Toltoltepec   REYNOSA TAMAULIPAS   NUEVA ATZACOALCO   SAN FELIPE DE JESÚS

E s t a d o   d e   Santiago Tepatlaxco   Ciudad de Naucalpan de Juárez   **AZCAPOTZALCO**   EL RECREO   GUSTAVO A. MADERO   Basílica de Guadalupe   SAN JUAN DE ARAGÓN   **M é x i c o**

San Antonio Zomeyucan   Santuario de los Remedios   El Molinito   Loma Linda   Toreo Campo Militar   Colegio Militar   **CUAUHTÉMOC**   **MORELOS**   HÉROES CHAPULTEPEC   Zoológico de San Juan de Aragón   Bosque San Juan de Aragón   San Juan Chimalhuacan

2   Presas Julianas   San Rafael   TACUBA   MIGUEL HIDALGO   Museo Nacional de Antropología   Alameda Parque   **CIUDAD DE MÉXICO**   VENUSTIANO CARRANZA   Aeropuerto   San Juan Chimalhuacan   San Pedro   2

Chichicaspa   Hipódromo de las Américas   LOMAS CHAPULTEPEC   Jardín Zoológico   Palacio de Bellas Artes   Palacio Nacional   Central   Xochitenco

El Guarda   Presa Los Jazmines   Bosque de Chapultepec   Hipódromo   JARDÍN BALBUENA   AGRÍCOLA PANTITLÁN   **CIUDAD NETZAHUALCOYOTL**   San Lorenzo

San Francisco Chimalpa   Río Hondo   Presa de Mixcoac   Observatorio   TACUBAYA   Parque de Tlalco   Ciudad Deportiva   Autódromo   AGRÍCOLA ORIENTAL   JUAN ESCUTIA

Dos Ríos   UNIDAD SANTA FE   PIEDAD NARVARTE   TEPALCATES   La Magdalena Atlipac

University of the Americas   SANTA FE   MIXCOAC   BENITO JUÁREZ   Ciudad de los Deportes   SAN ANDRÉS TETEPILCO   **IXTACALCO**   SAN FELIPE TERREMOTOS   SANTA MARTHA ACATLA   Los Reyes

Cruz Manca   MOLINO D ROSAS   ALPES   Parque del Venado   ESCUADRÓN 201   HÉROES DE CHURUBUSCO   SANTIAGO ACAHUALTEPEC

Cuajimalpa   Presa Tarango   **VILLA OBREGÓN**   CHURUBUSCO   Country Club   **IXTAPALAPA**   SANTA CRUZ MEYEHUALCO

Huixquilucan de Degollado   Cañada de los Helechos   OLIVAR DE LOS PADRES   ROSEDAL   **COYOACÁN**   LA CANDELARIA   LOS REYES   Cerro de la Estrella 2460   Parque Nac. Cerro de la Estrella   Cerro Peñón 2750

19 20   San Mateo Tlaltenango   Universidad Militar Latino Americ   TIZAPÁN   SAN FRANCISCO CULHUACÁN   AVANTE   San Lorenzo Tezonco   Sierra de Santa Catarina   19 20

San Lorenzo Acopilco   San Bartolo Ameyalco   SAN JERÓNIMO LIDICE   Estadio Olímpico   Ciudad Universitaria   CIUDAD JARDÍN   Santa Catarina Yecahuizotl

Las Alicias   Parque Nacional   **D** i s t r i t o   **F** e d e r a l   Santa Cruz Meyehualco

La Marquesa   Cerro Campamento 3161   Estadio Azteca   EL RELOJ   VILLA COAPA   Santiago Zapotitlán   San Francisco Tlaltenco

3   Parque Nacional   de los Leones   **La Magdalena Contreras**   Pirámide de Cuicuilco   HUIPULCO   Cerro Xico 2346   Xico Viejo   3

Miguel Hidalgo   San Nicolás Totolapan   **TLALPAN**   TEPEPAN   Jardines Flotantes   Santiago Tepalcatlalpan   **XOCHIMILCO**   **Tlahuac**   San Juan Ixtayopan

Cuarto Dínamo   Río de la Magdalena   San Pedro Mártir   San Andrés Totoltepec   Santa Cruz Alcapixca   San Gregorio Atlapulco   Tulyehualco

Natívitas

II

a   10 40   b

C a r i b b e a n   S e a

Cabo Blanco   Pta Gorda   Pta El Cojo   Pta Tanaguarena   Caraballeda   El Caribe

Aeropuerto Maiquetía   La Guaira   La Chivera   Macuto   El Cojo   El Palmar   Tanaguarena

El Oasis   **MAIQUETÍA**   778   Los Aguacat s

El Guarapo   Río Grande   San Juan de Dios   José de Galipán   Cerro

El Corozo   San José   C o r d i l l e r a   d e l   L i t o r a l

767   El Zig-Zag   Palmar de Cariaco

Guacarumbo   Gato Negro   San Antonio de Galipán   Cerro El Ávila   Hotel Humboldt

Boquerón   1479   La Cumbre   **P a r q u e   N a c i o n a l   d e l   Á v i l a**

2753   2637   Pico Oriental

CARACAS   Teleférico   Pico

10 30   LOS MAGA-LLANES   CATIA   COTIZA   SAN BERNARDINO   10 30

CASALTA   Miraflores   Capitolio Nacional   LAS PALMAS   EL PEDREGAL   Caracas Country Club   **Los Dos Caminos**

ARTIGAS   HELICOIDE   Jardín Botánico   Museo de Bellas Artes   Estadio   **CHACAO**   EL MARQUES

BELLA VISTA   Estadio Nacional   Parque Nacional El Pinar   Ciudad Universitaria   Aeropuerto   La Carlota   CAURIMARE   **PETARE**

LA VEGA   SANTA MÓNICA   SANTA MARTA   EL LLANITO

Universidad Católica Andrés Bello   SANTA ANA   MACARACUAY

2   ANTÍMANO   1437   **EL VALLE**   Monumento a Los Próceres   2

MAMERA   COCHE   CUMBRES DE CURUMO   LAS MINAS   El Pauji

SAN PABLITO   LA RINCONADA   Hipódromo de la Rinconada   **BARUTA**   LA TRINIDAD   El Hatillo

1389   Embalse La Mariposa   LAS MAYAS   LA BOYERA   La Lagunita Country Club   1491   Las Marías

a   67 00   1280   66 50   b

CARICUAO

III

a   74 10   b   74 05   c   74 00   1

Argentina   El Salitre   La Uribe   La Cita   4 45

Río Bogotá   2711   Suba   Casablanca   Milán   San Cristóbal

Parque La Florida   Juan Amarillo   El Rincón   EL PRADO   El Molino

La Florida   Engativá   Garces Navas   QUIRIGUA   Lago Club de Los Lagos   Usaquén   2

Funza   Aeropuerto Eldorado   MINUTO DE DIOS   NAVARRA

El Diamante   SAN PABLO   LA GRANJA   LAS FERIAS   RÍO NEGRO

D i s   t   r   i   t   o

Fontibón   2599   MODELIA   BOYACÁ   Parque Popular   SAN FERNANDO   4 40

Jardín Botánico   LA ESPERANZA   3317   San Luis

La Victoria   Río Fucha   CIUDAD UNIVERSITARIA   Universidad Nacional   **BOGOTÁ**   E s p

BAVARIA   GRANJAS DE TECHO   2640

San Bernardino   Río Bogotá   Hipódromo de Techo   Museo Nacional   Monserrate   El Apartadero   3

PASTRANA   RICAURTE   Museo del Oro   i   a   l

Bosa   ALQUERÍA   Museo de Mariño   Castillo   Palacio Presidencial

2817   FATIMA   Cristóbal   3509

Soacha   INGLES   **RESTREPO**   EL ROCÍO   4 35

Parque Distrital de El Tunal   EL ENCANTO   3679

Terreros   EL TUNAL   3663   La Teta

Vínculo   LAS ACACIAS   TUNJUELITO   ALTAMIRA   Buenavista   4

3252   MEXICO   Río Tunjuelito   SAN RAFAEL

Río Soacha   Gran Bretaña   Yomoso   Páramo Cruz Verde

a   74 10   b   74 05   c   74 00

1 : 225,000   0   2.5   5   7.5   10 Kilometers   0   2.5   5   7.5 Statute Miles

One inch to 3,6 miles   Conversion meters – feet see page 48

Mexico City · Caracas · Bogotá   91

Northern South America 93

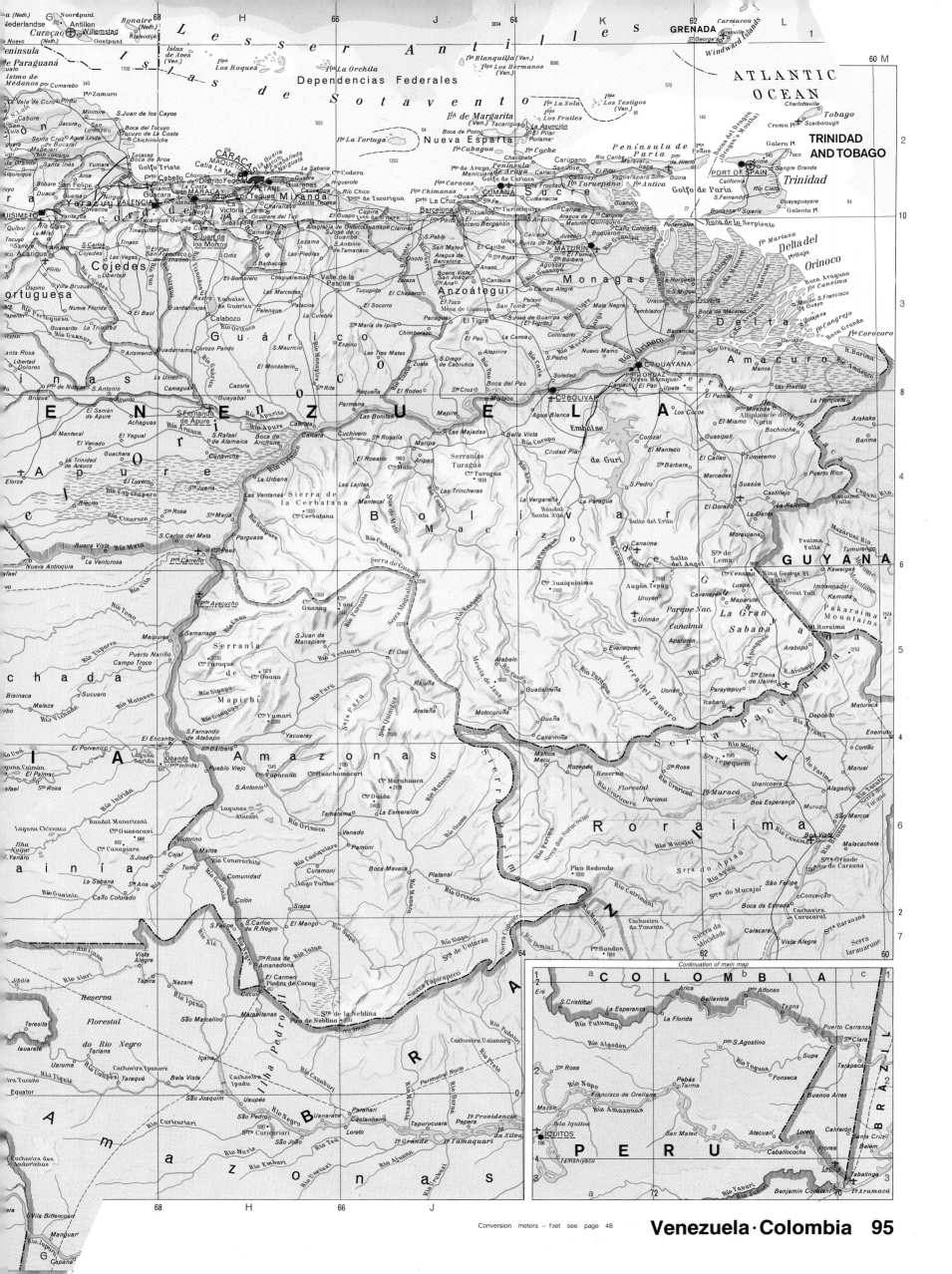

Venezuela · Colombia **95**

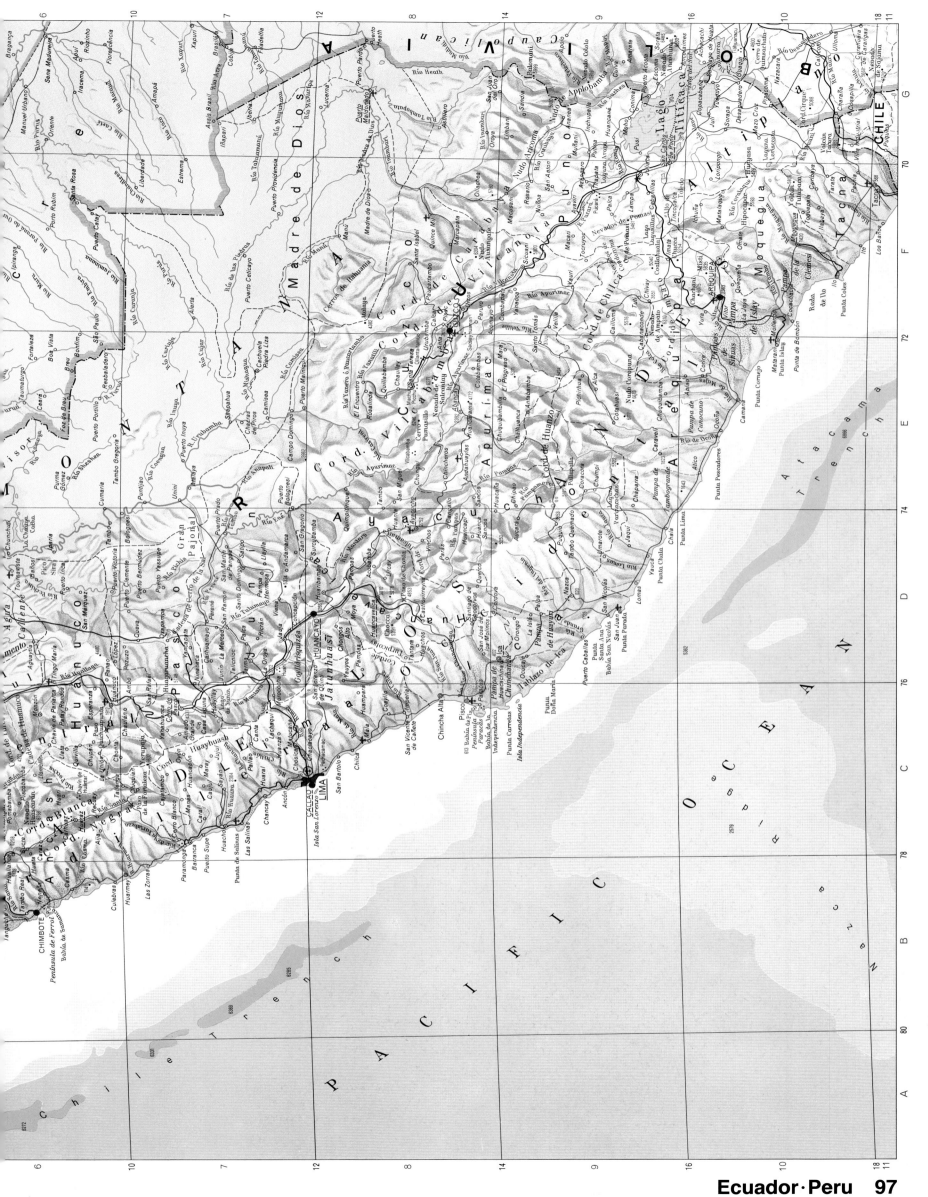

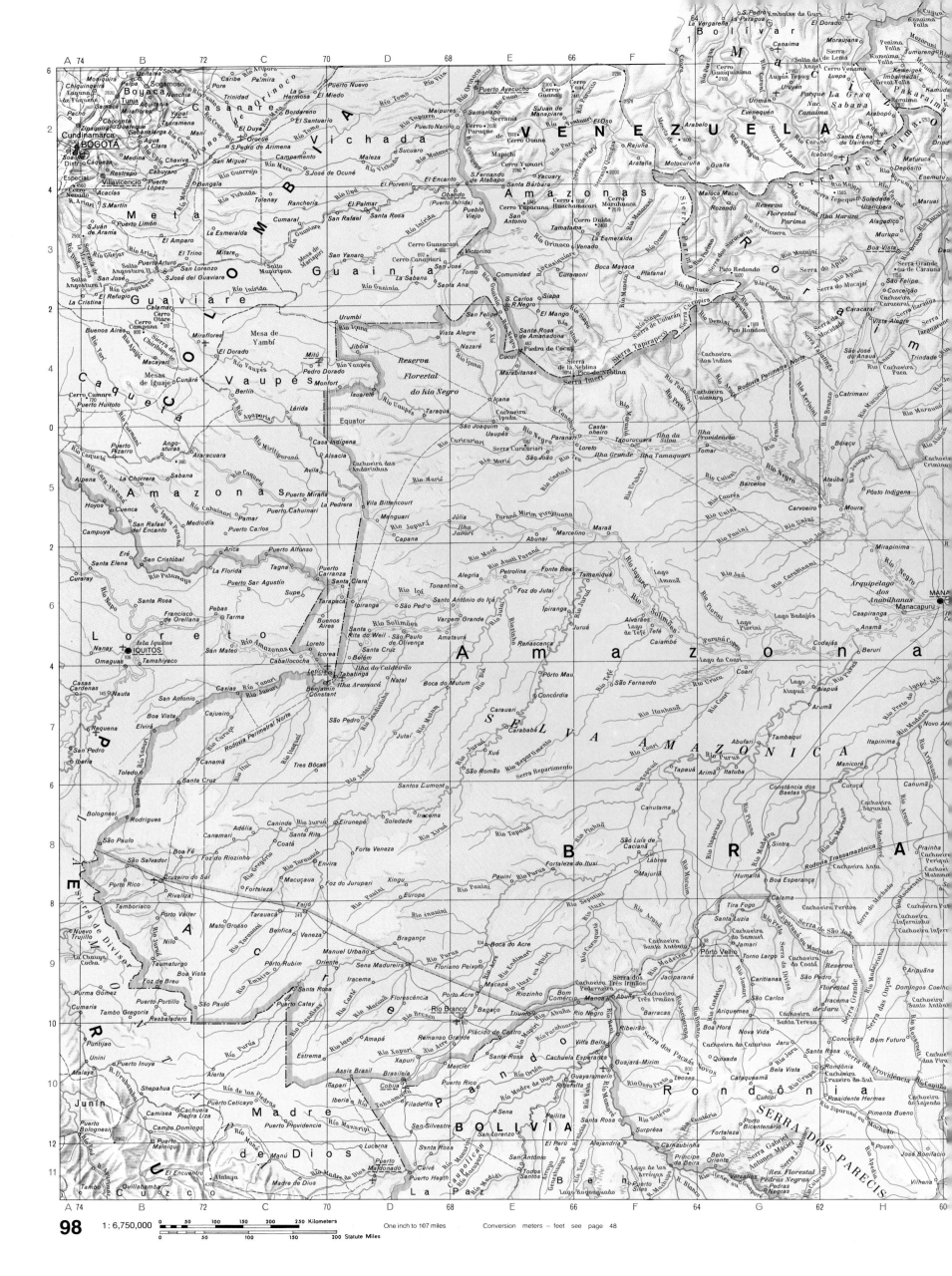

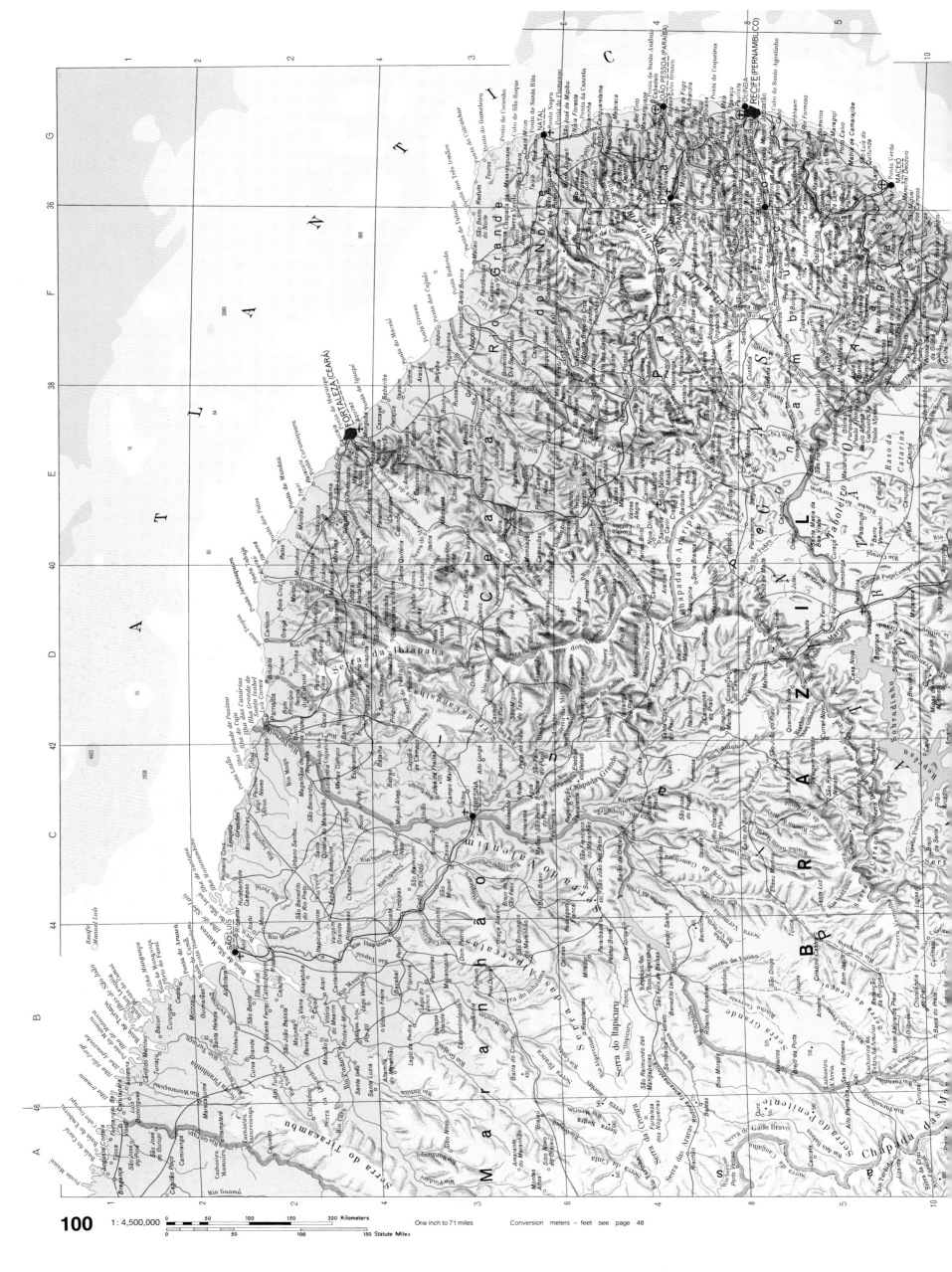

1 : 4,500,000

0   50   100   150   200 Kilometers

0   50   100   150 Statute Miles

One inch to 71 miles   Conversion meters – feet see page 48

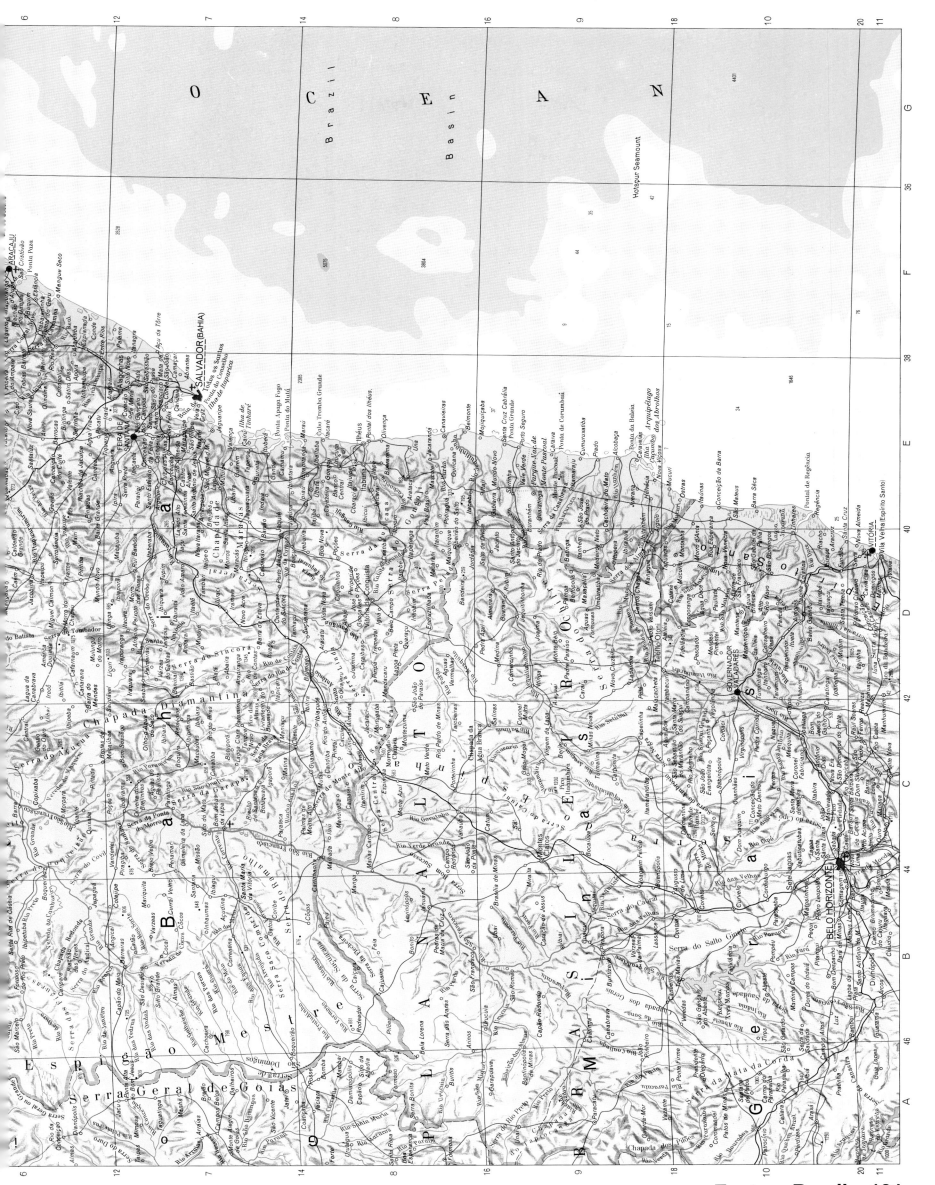

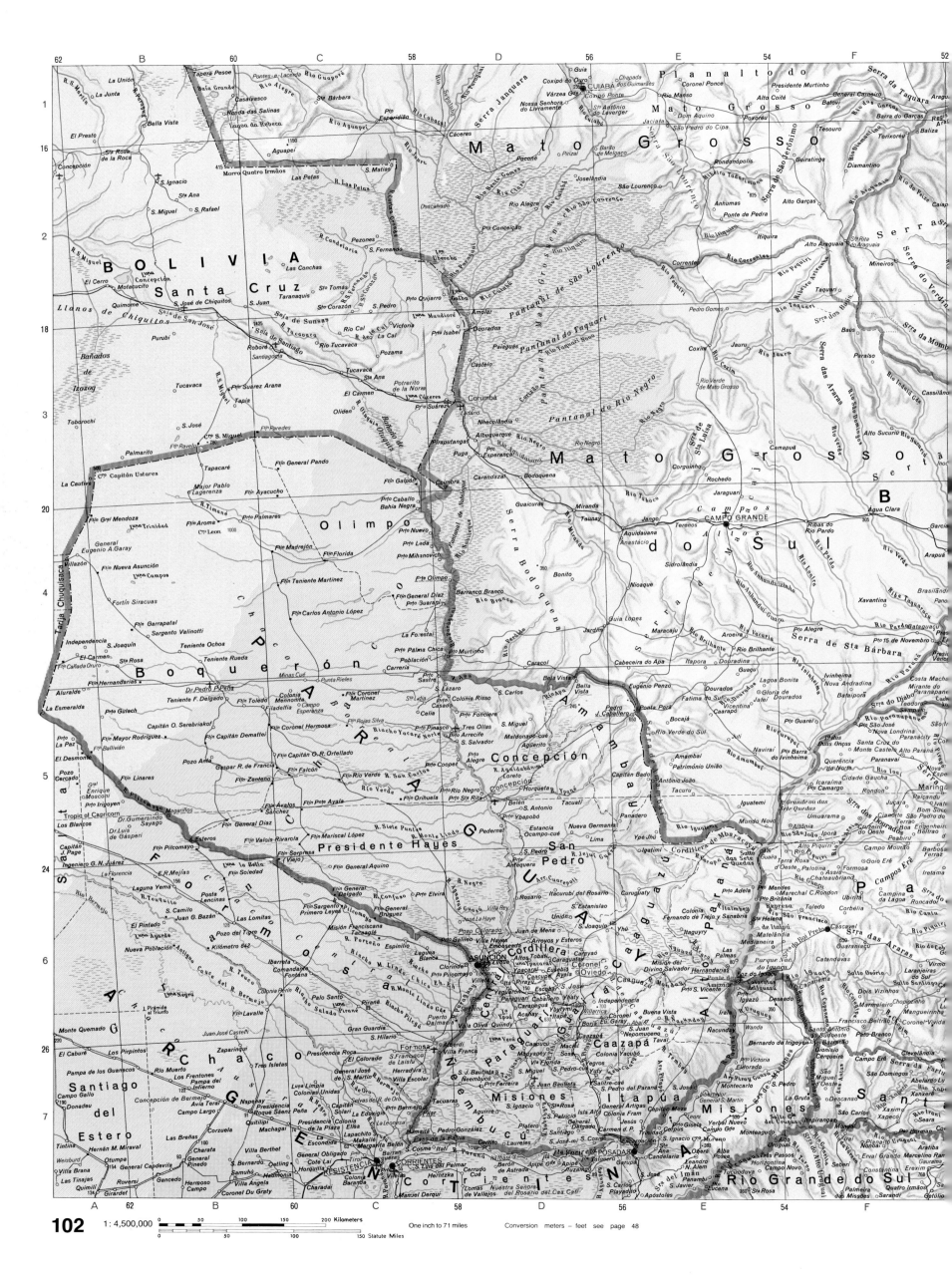

ATLANTIC

OCEAN

Tropic of Capricorn

PLANALTO

BRASÍLIA
Distrito Federal

GOIÂNIA

UBERLÂNDIA

UBERABA

BELO HORIZONTE

GOVERNADOR VALADARES

SÃO JOSÉ DO RIO PRETO

RIBEIRÃO PRETO

CAMPINAS

SÃO PAULO

SANTOS

RIO DE JANEIRO

NITERÓI

VOLTA REDONDA

PETRÓPOLIS

JUIZ DE FORA

CAMPOS

LONDRINA

PONTA GROSSA

CURITIBA

PARANAGUÁ

JOINVILE

BLUMENAU

FLORIANÓPOLIS
Ilha de Santa Catarina

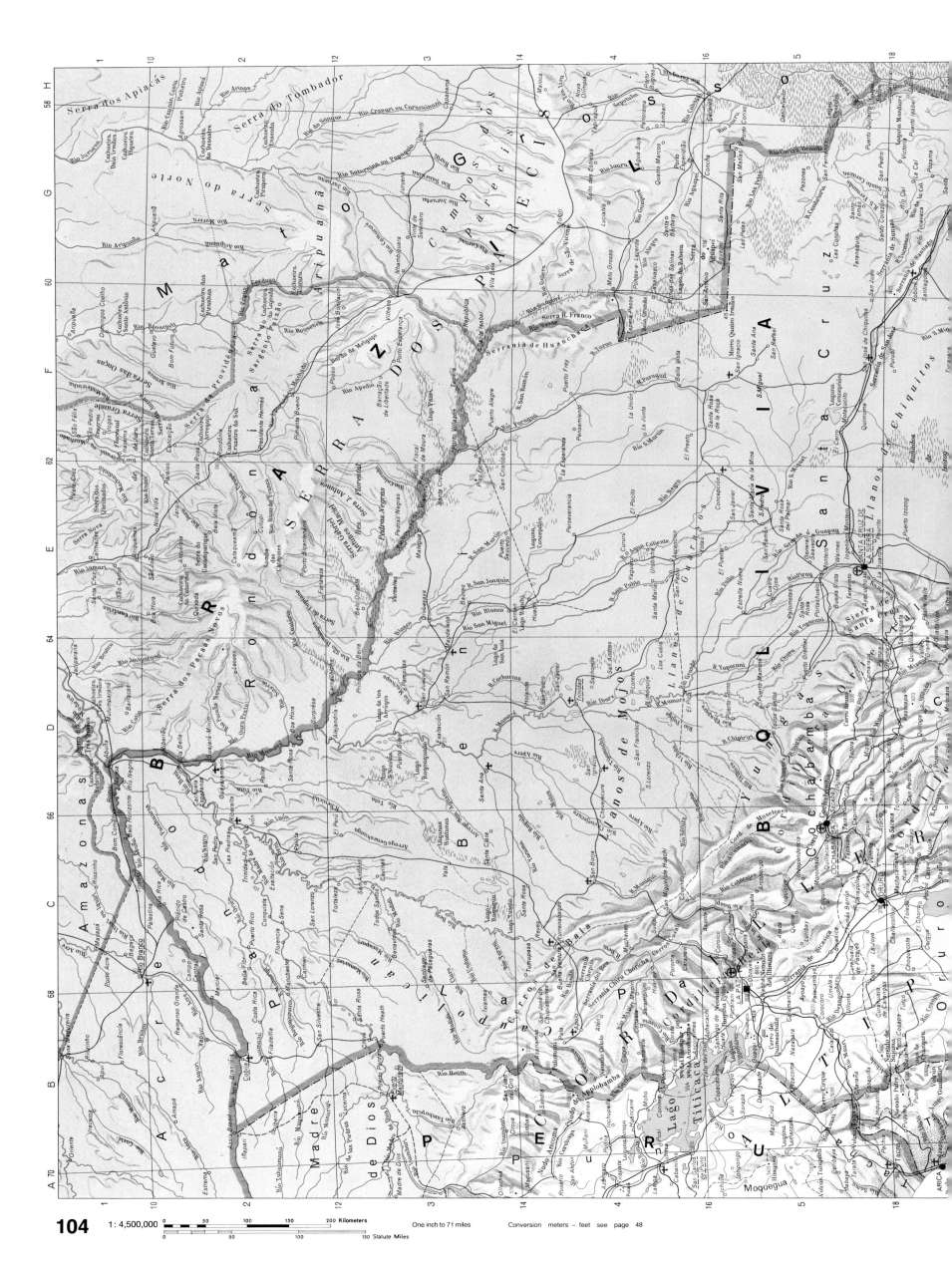

Bolivia 105

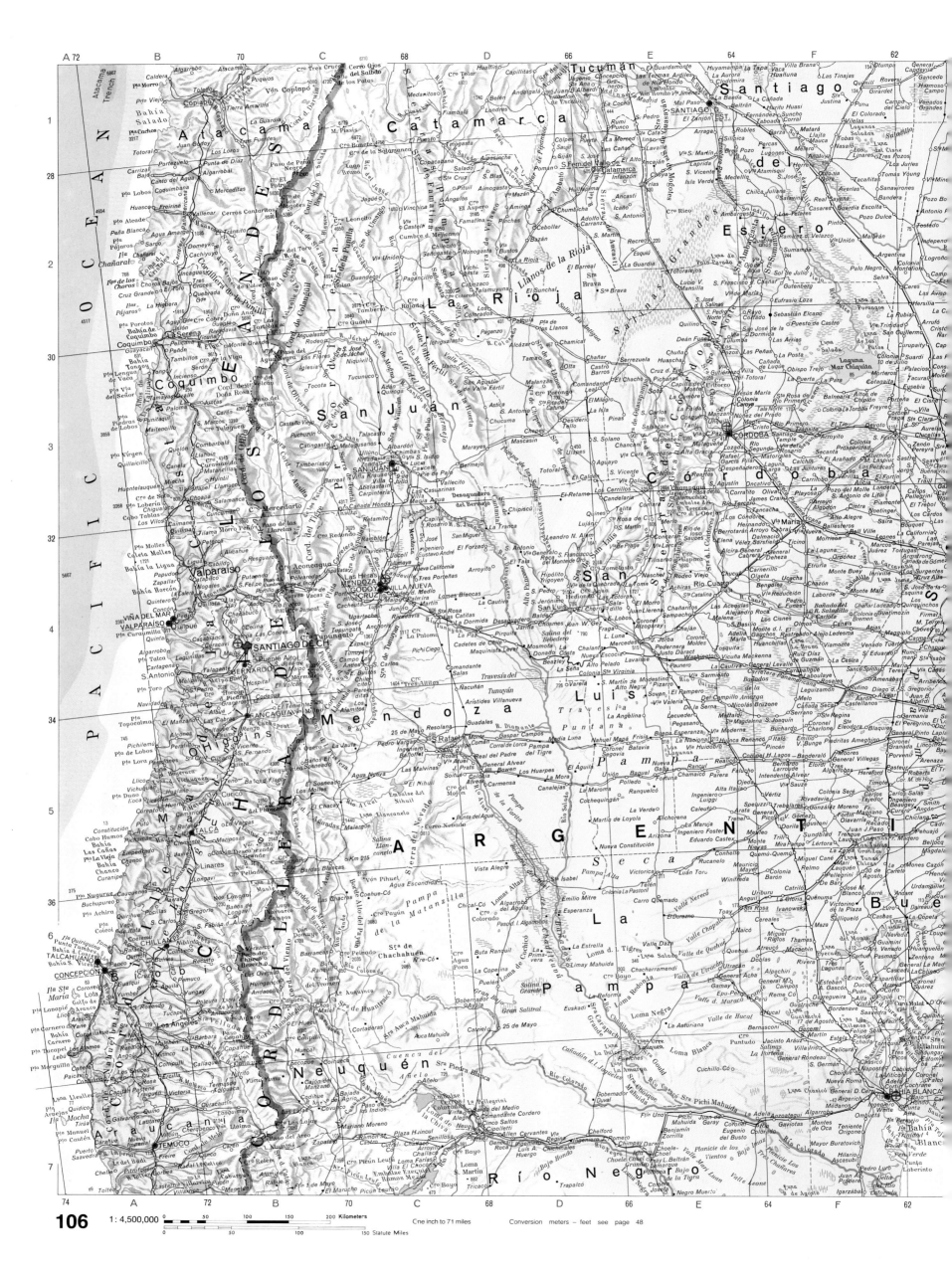

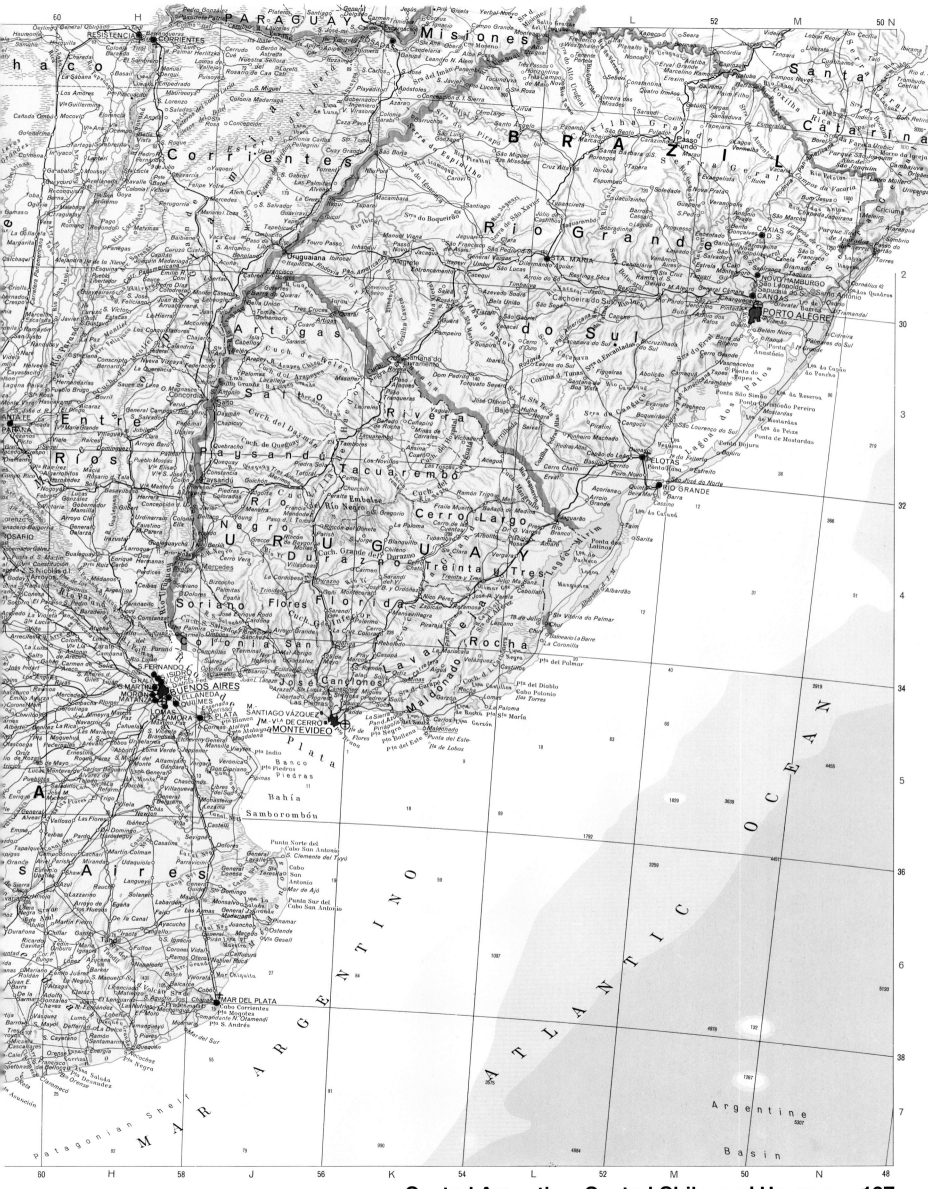

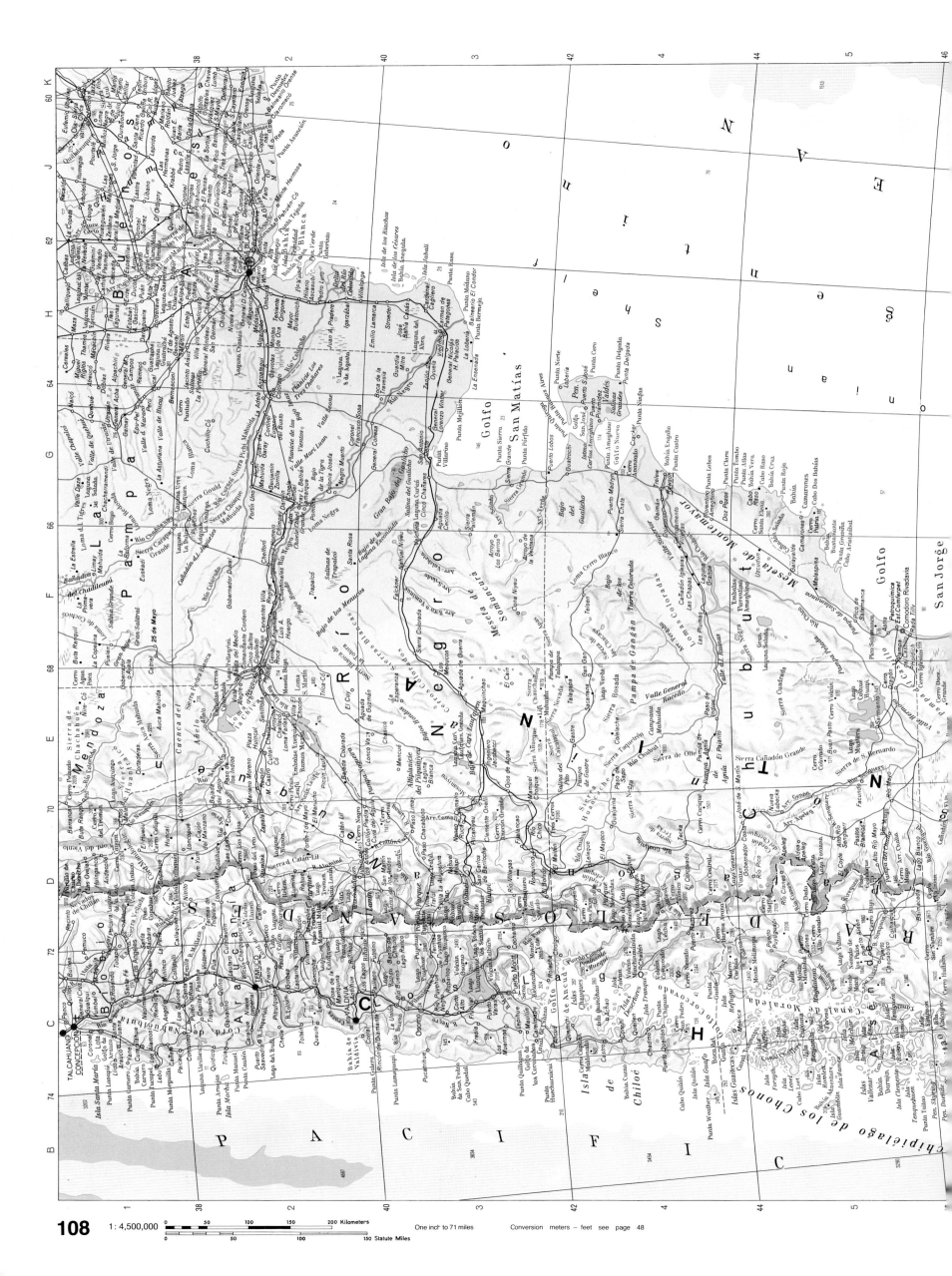

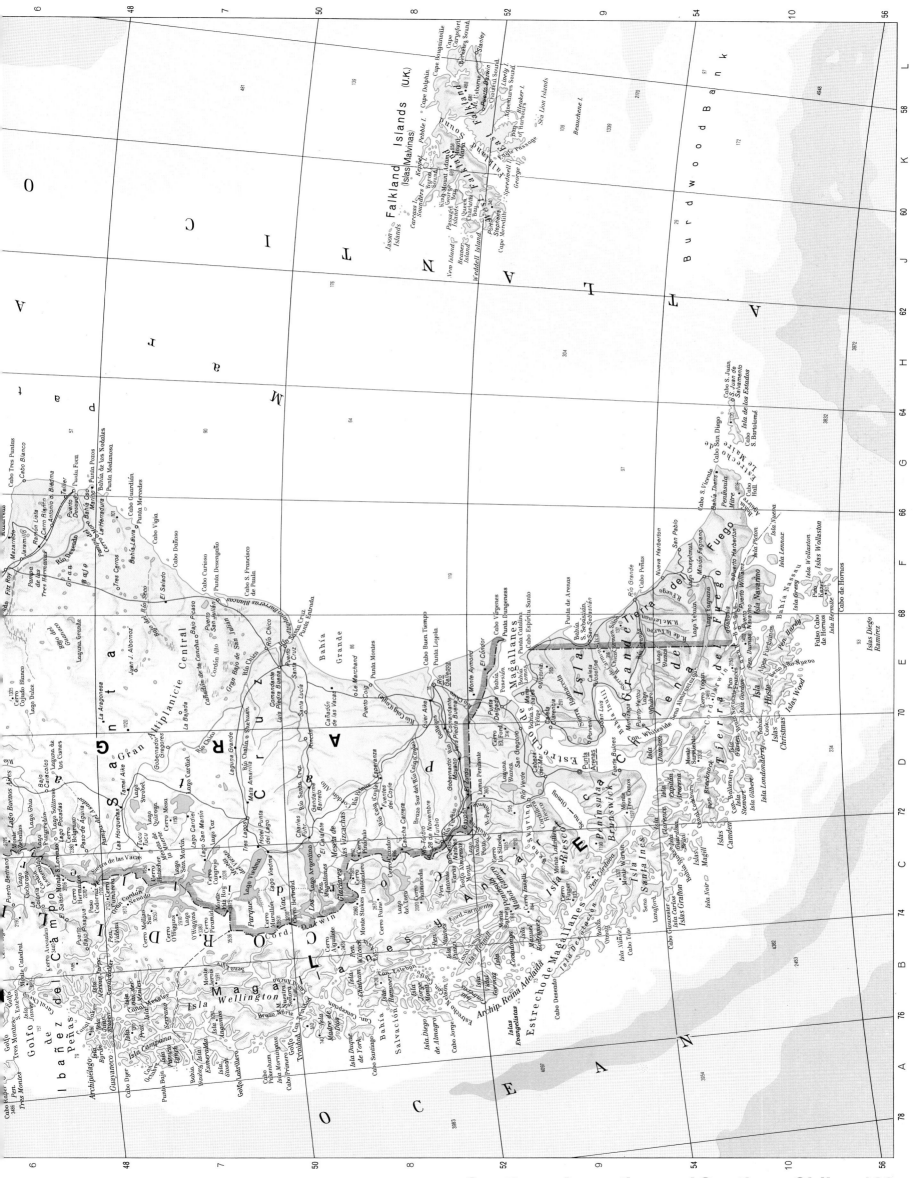

Southern Argentina and Southern Chile   109

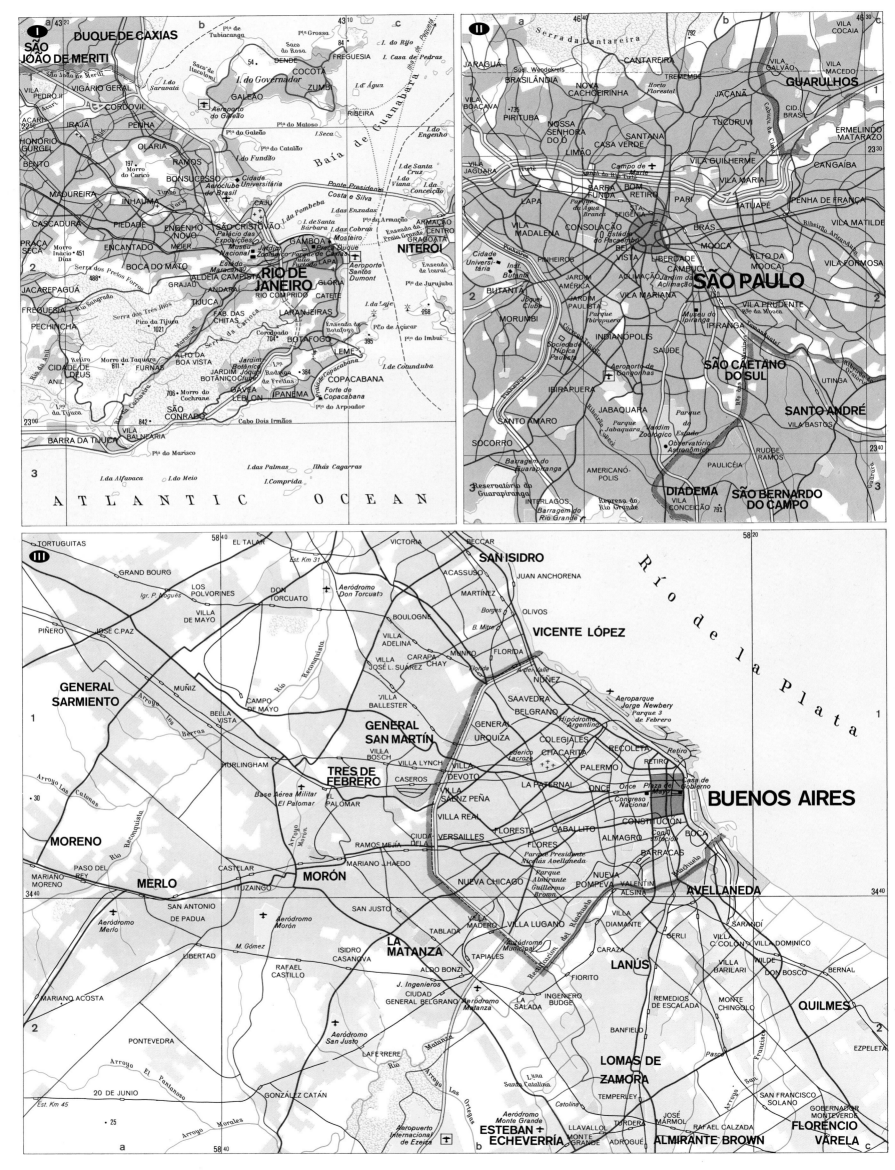

1 : 225,000

0   2.5   5   7.5   10 Kilometers

0   2.5   5   7.5 Statute Miles

One inch to 3.6 miles

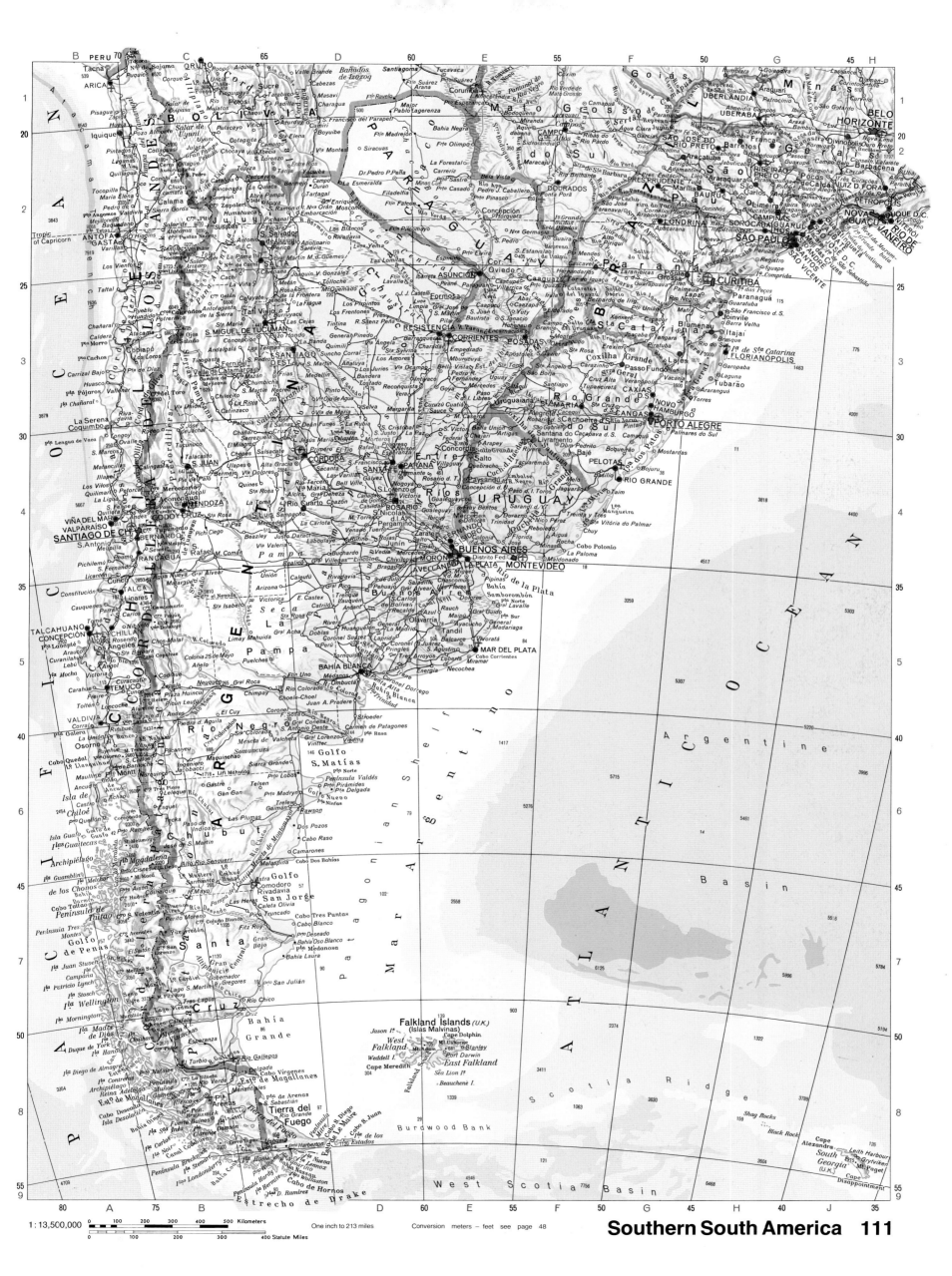

Southern South America 111

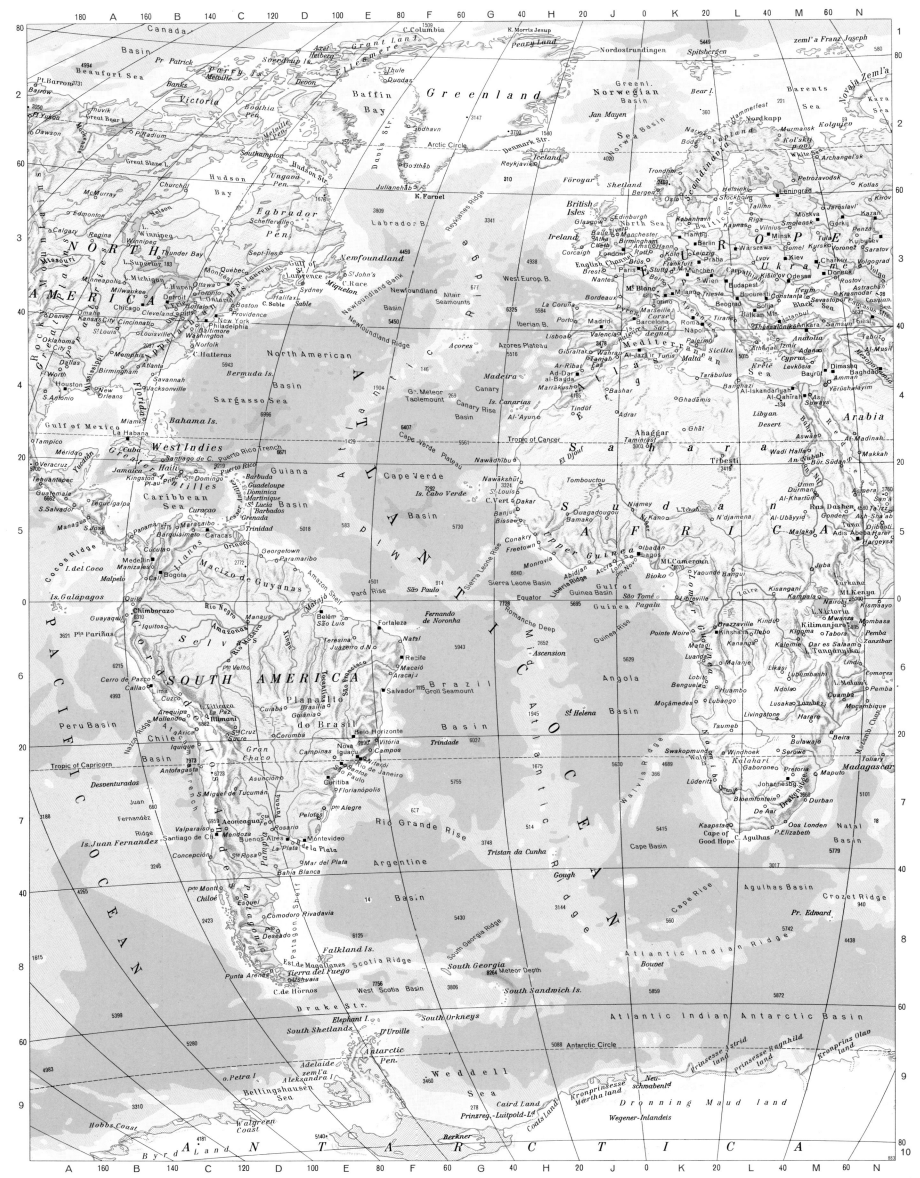

Conversion meters – feet see page 48

Scale at the center meridian 1 : 60,000,000   One inch to 947 miles

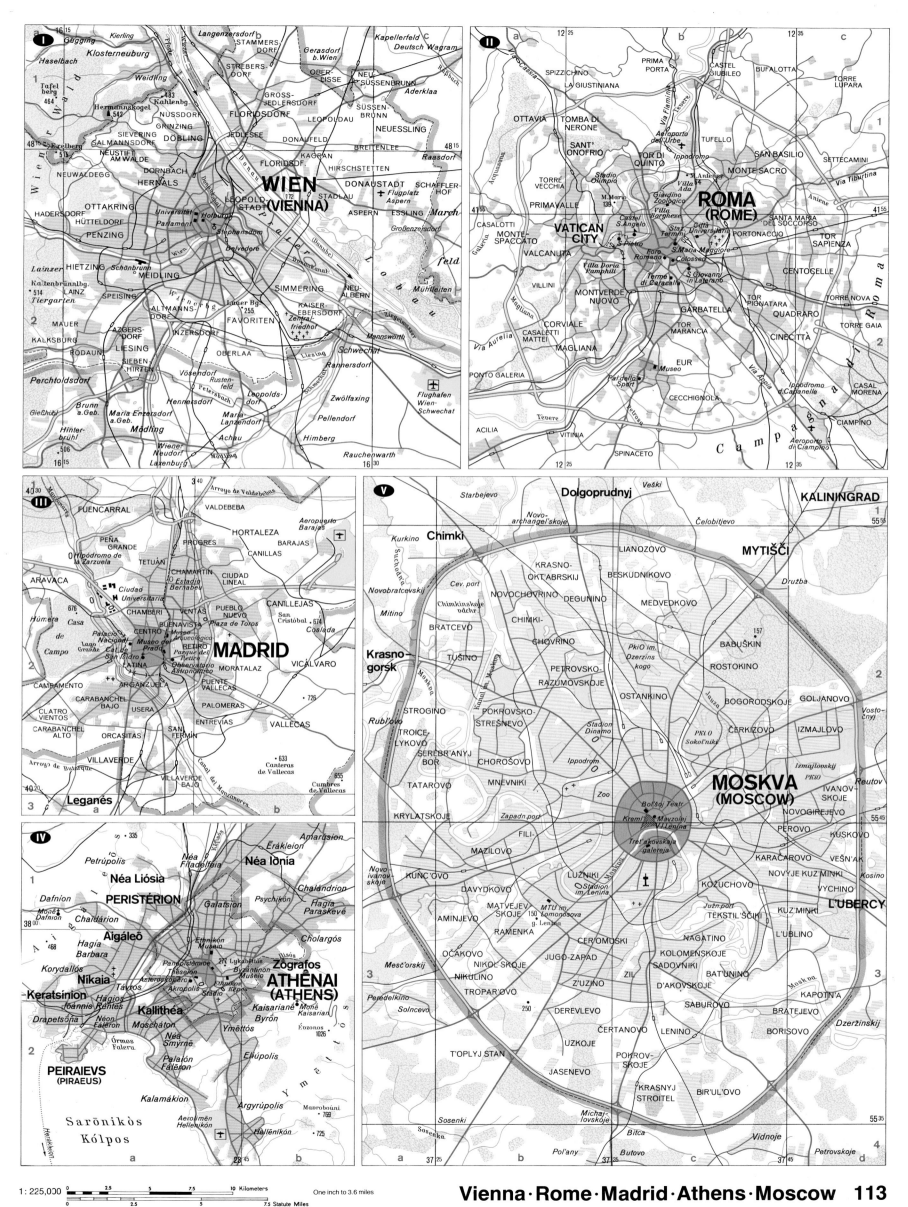

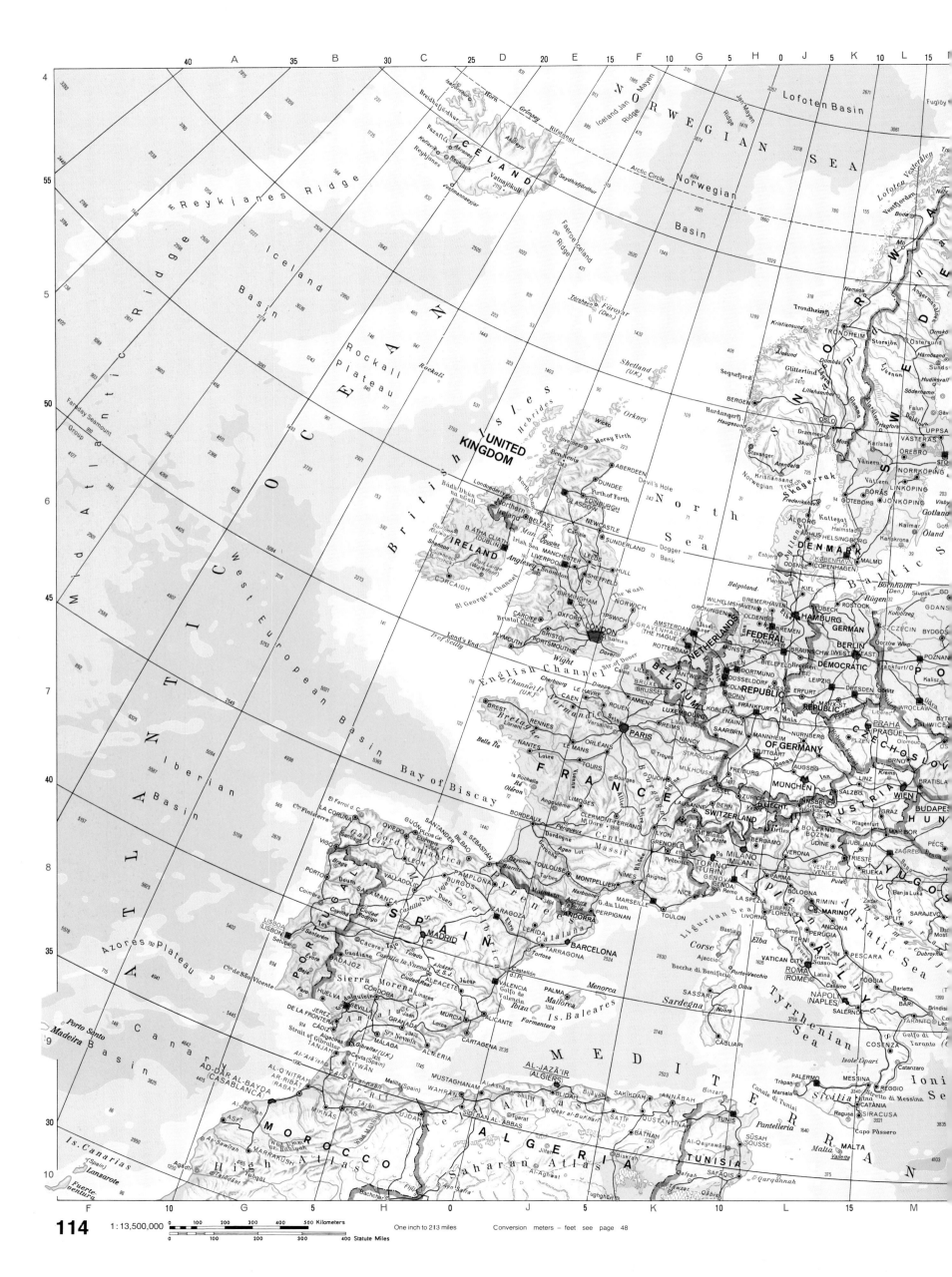

1 : 13,500,000

One inch to 213 miles   Conversion meters – feet see page 48

500 Kilometers

400 Statute Miles

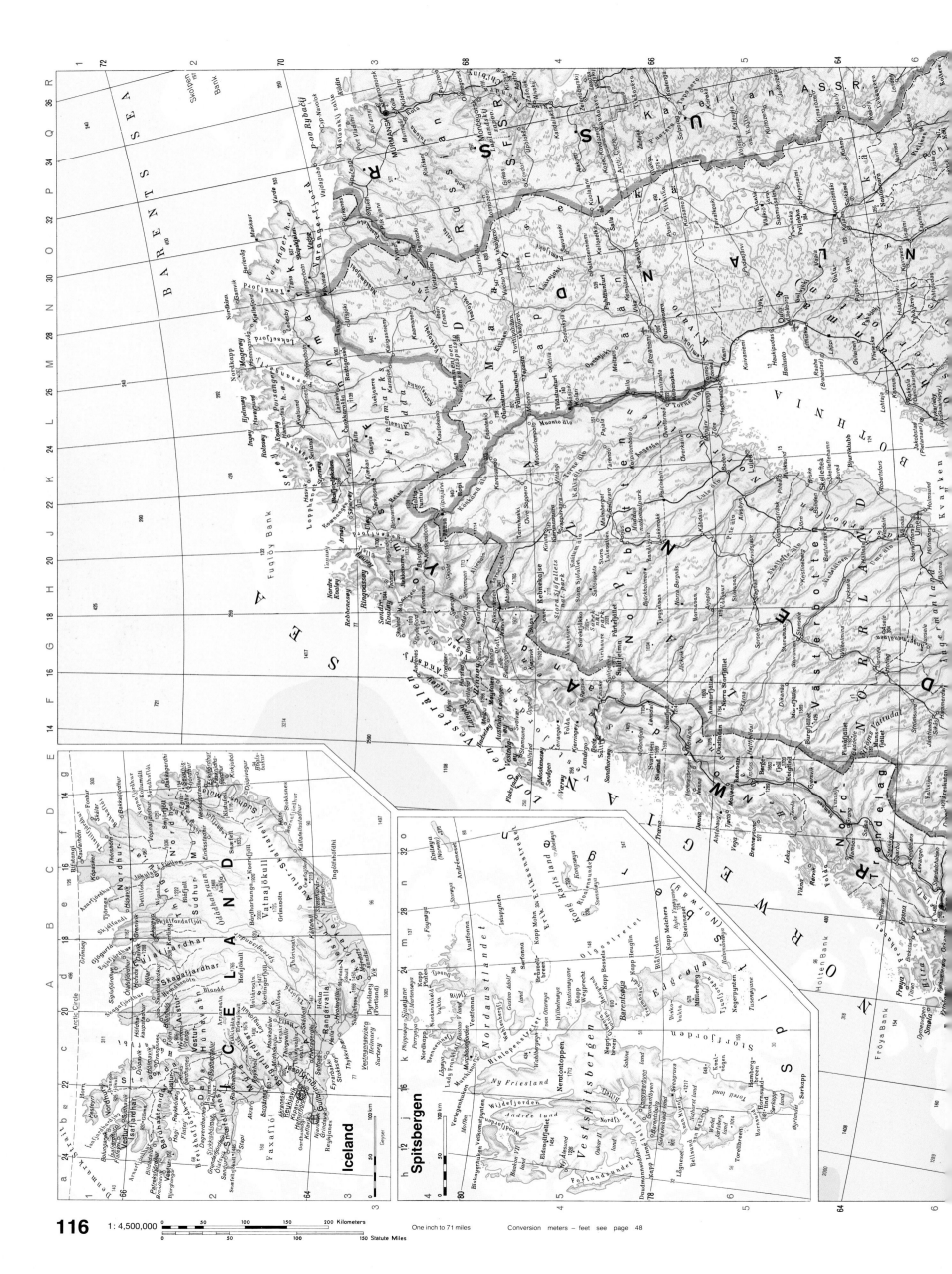

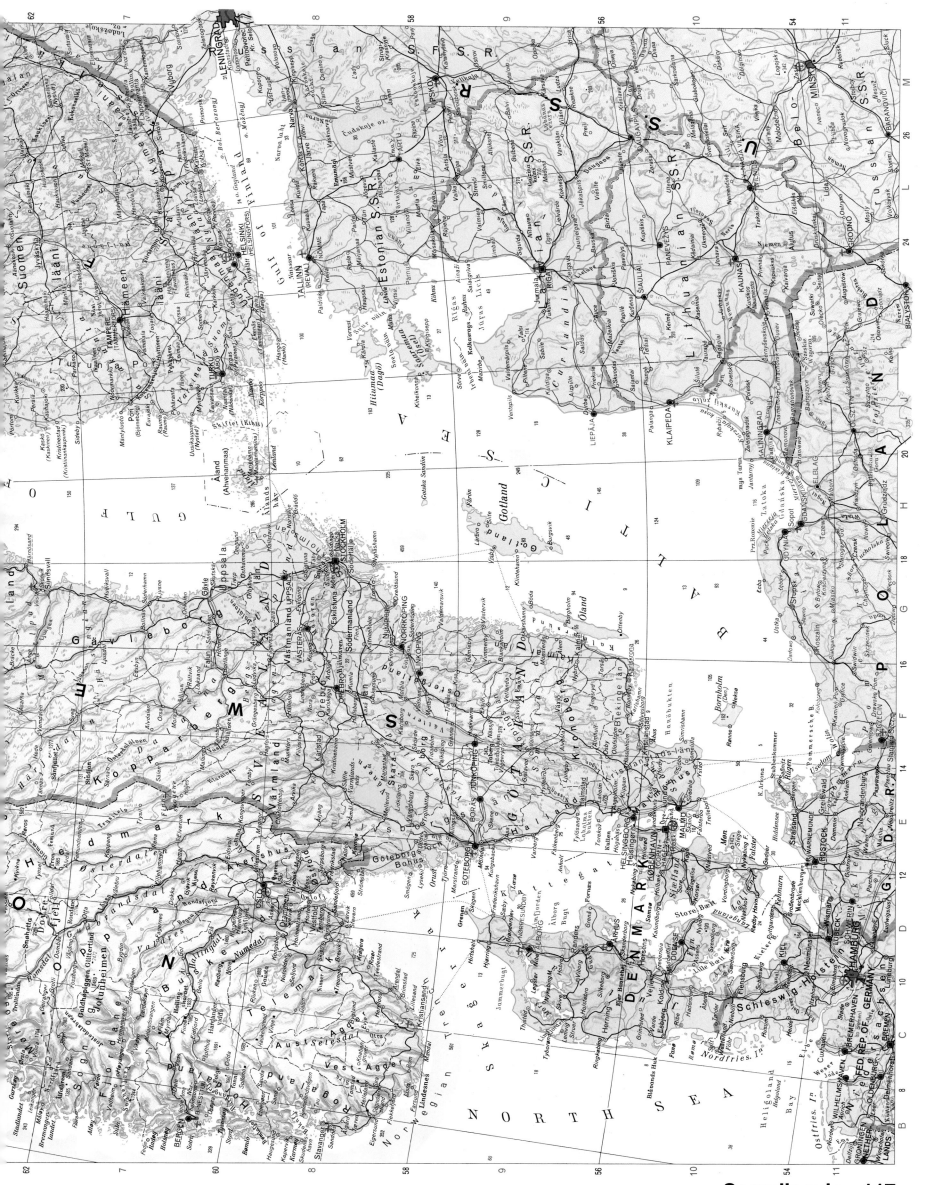

Scandinavia   117

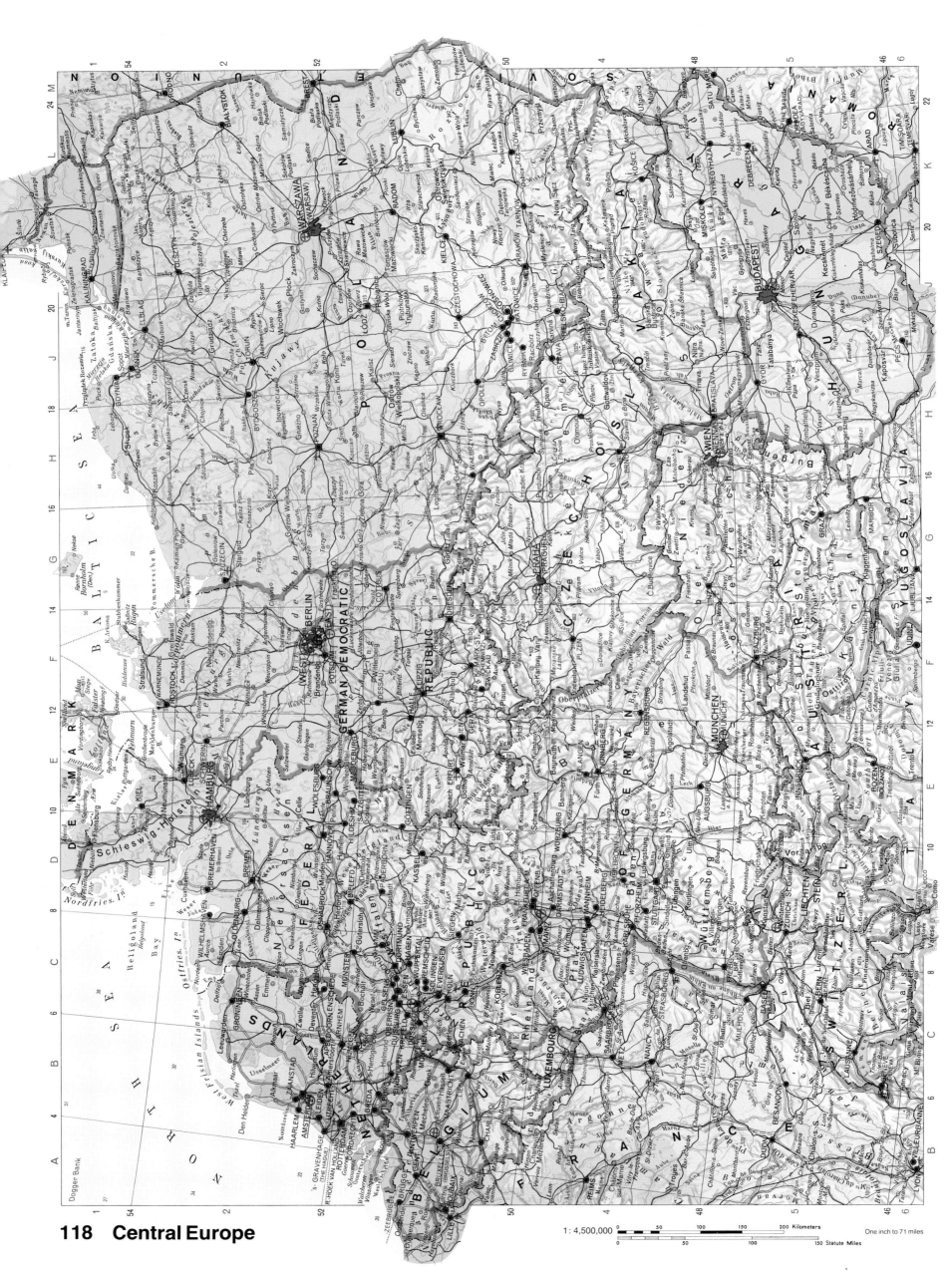

118   Central Europe

1 : 4,500,000

One inch to 71 miles

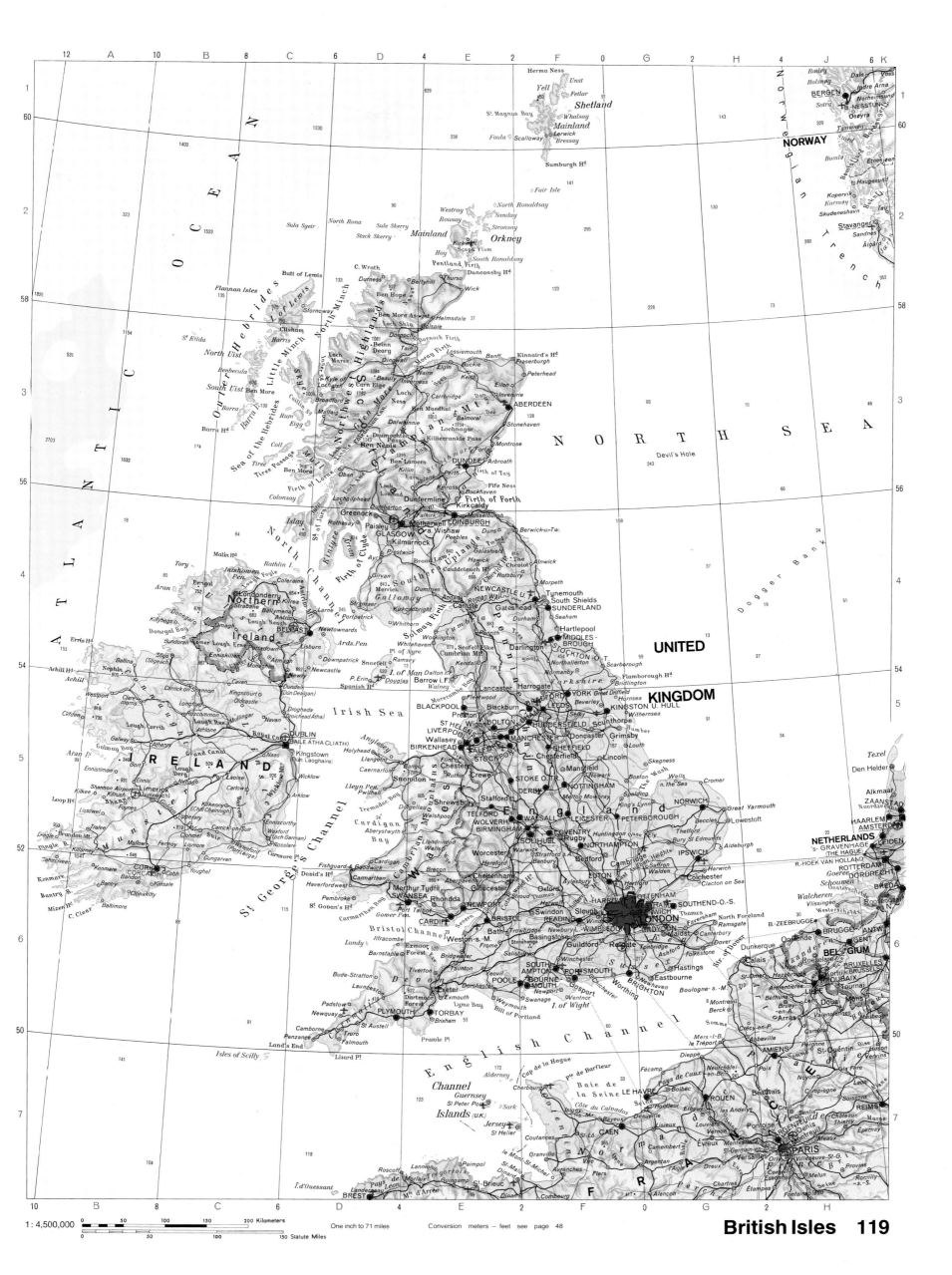

British Isles 119

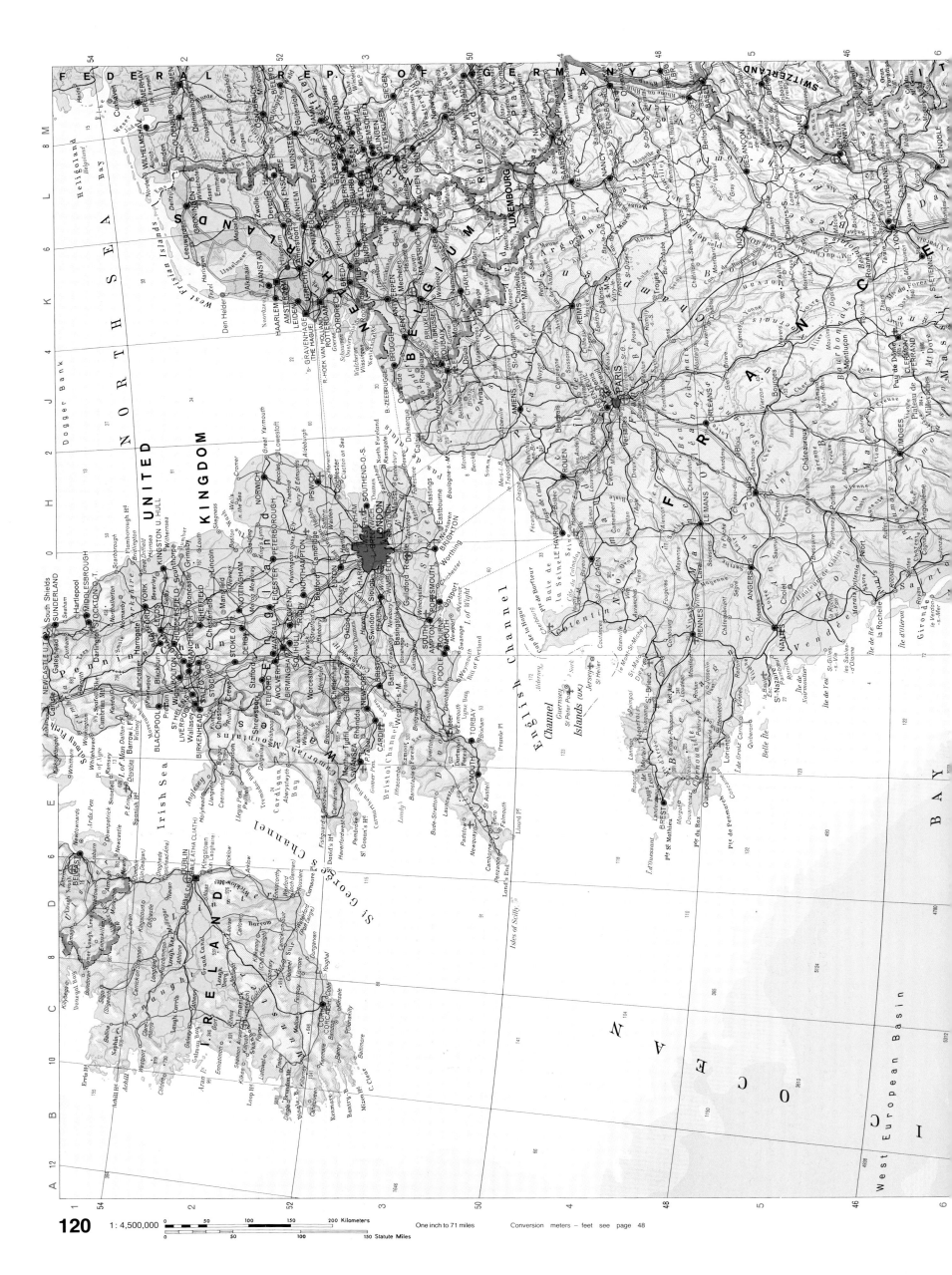

1 : 4 500 000

One inch to 71 miles   Conversion meters – feet see page 48

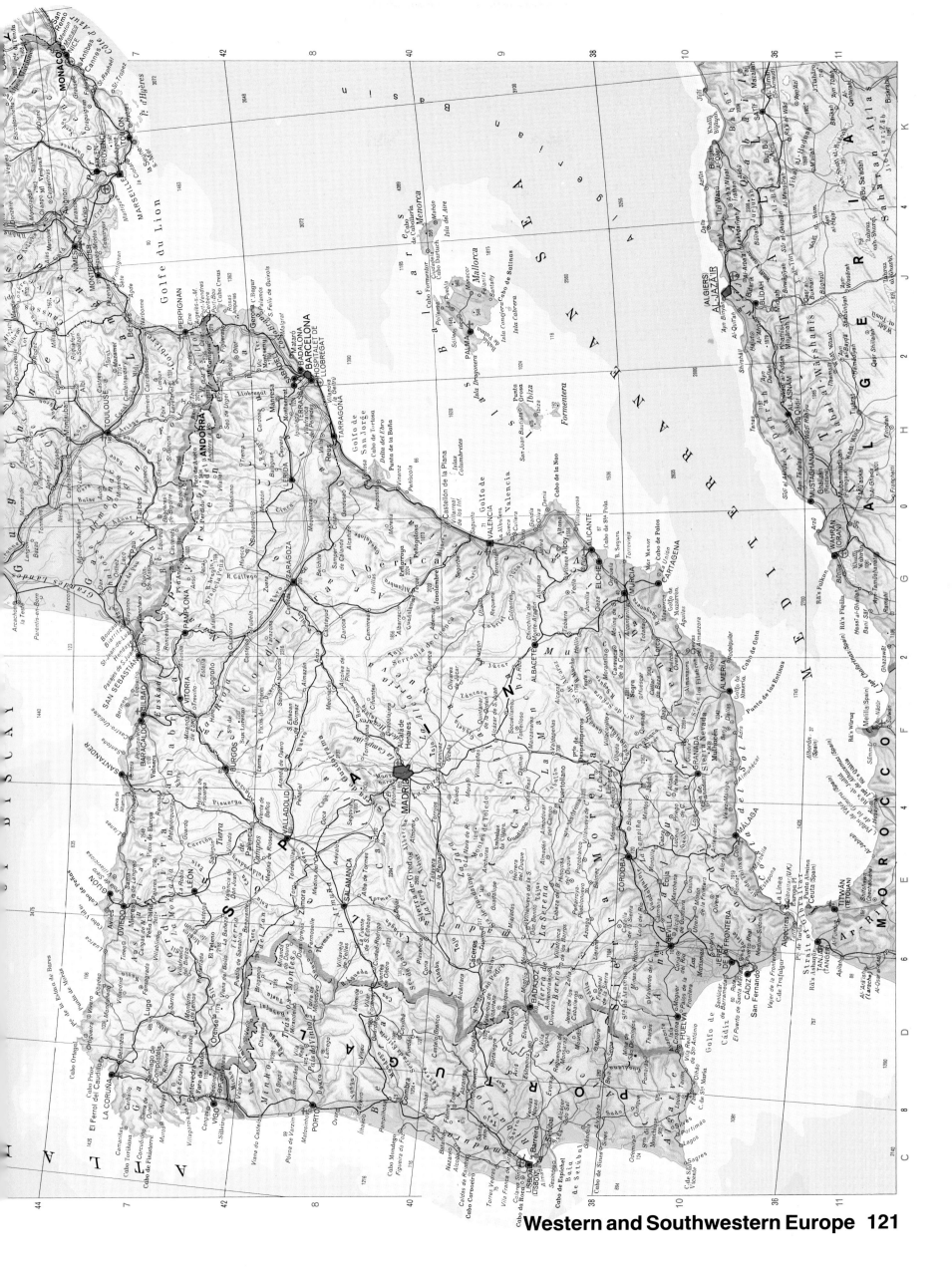

1 : 4,500,000

0   50   100   150   200 Kilometers

0   50   100
150 Statute Miles

One inch to 71 miles

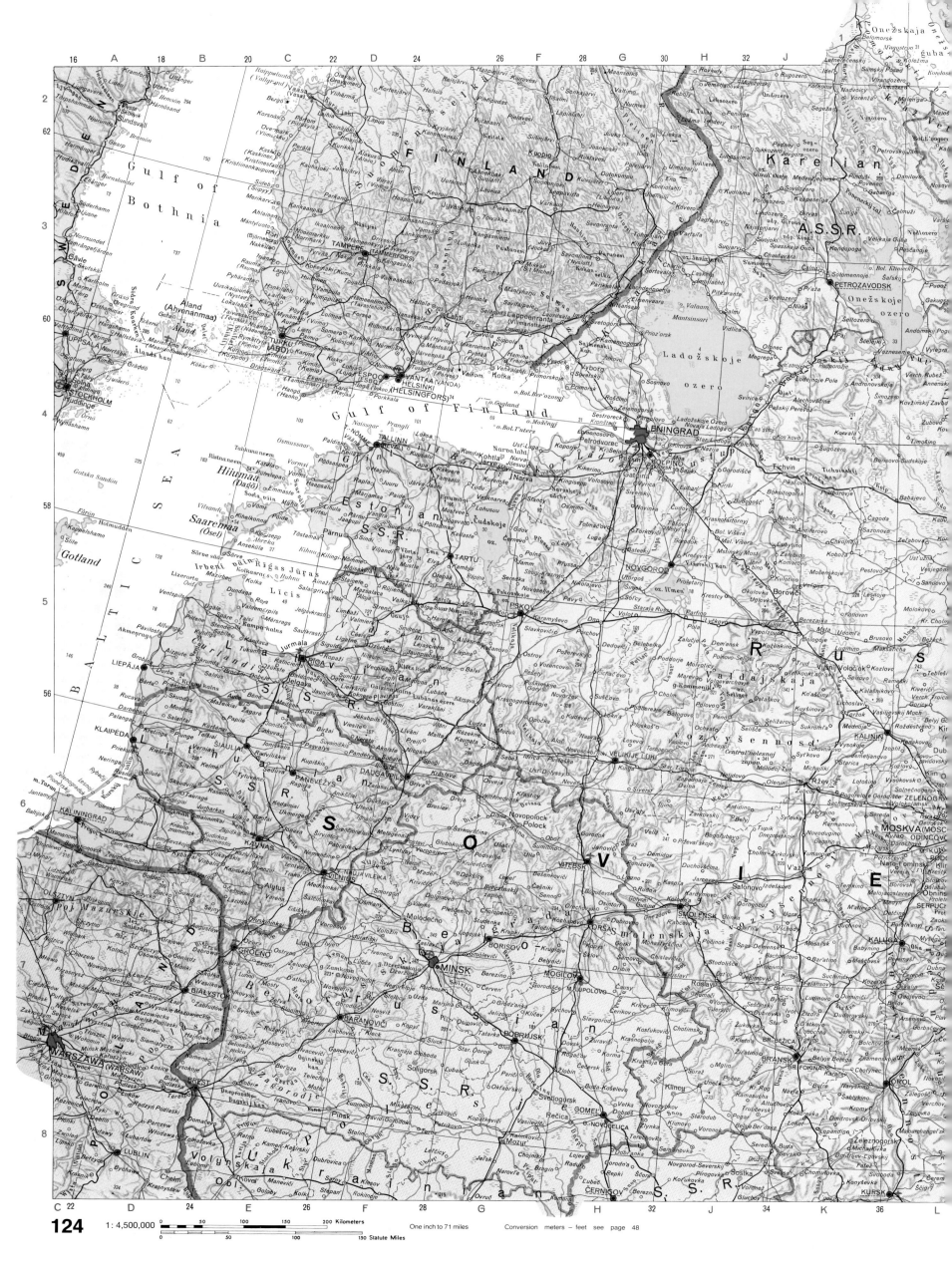

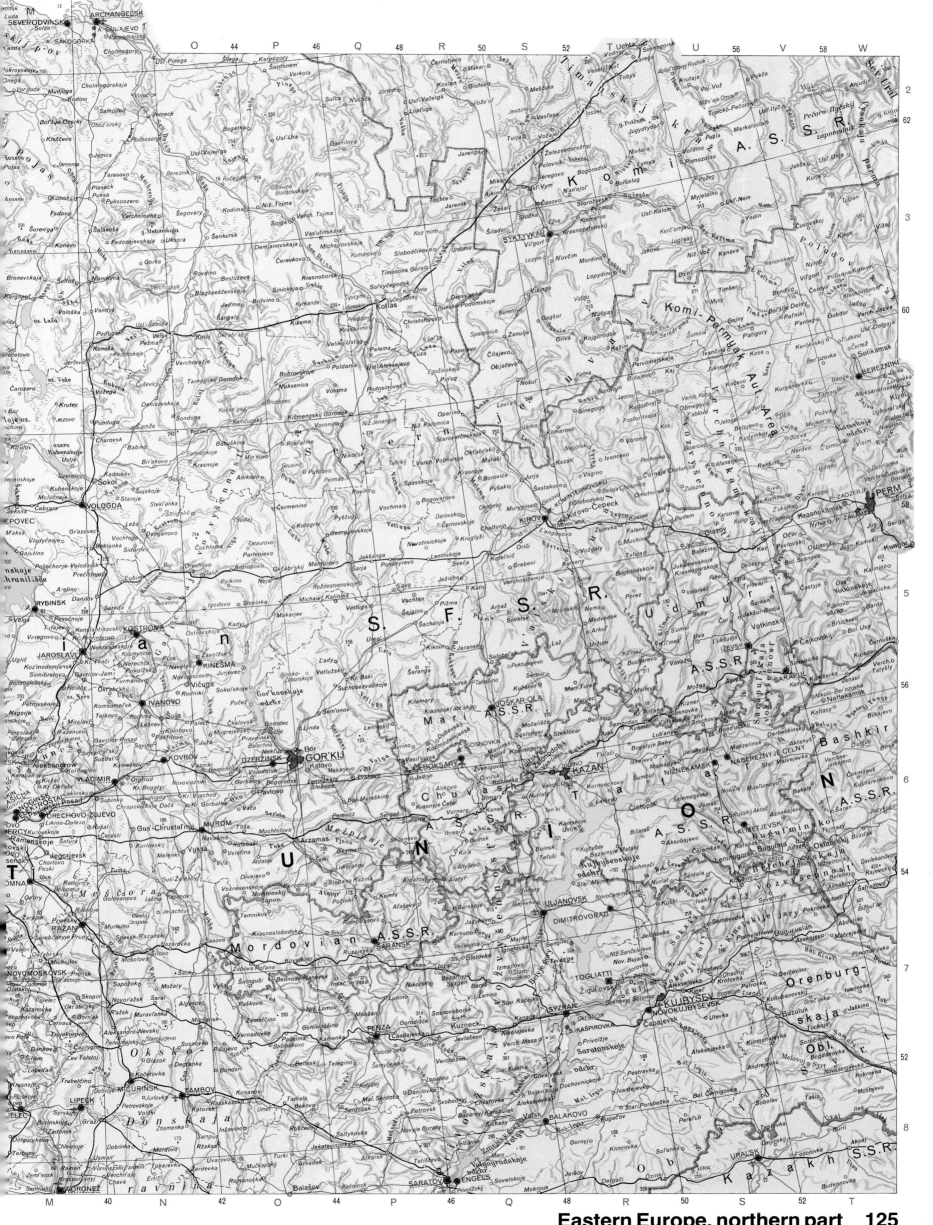

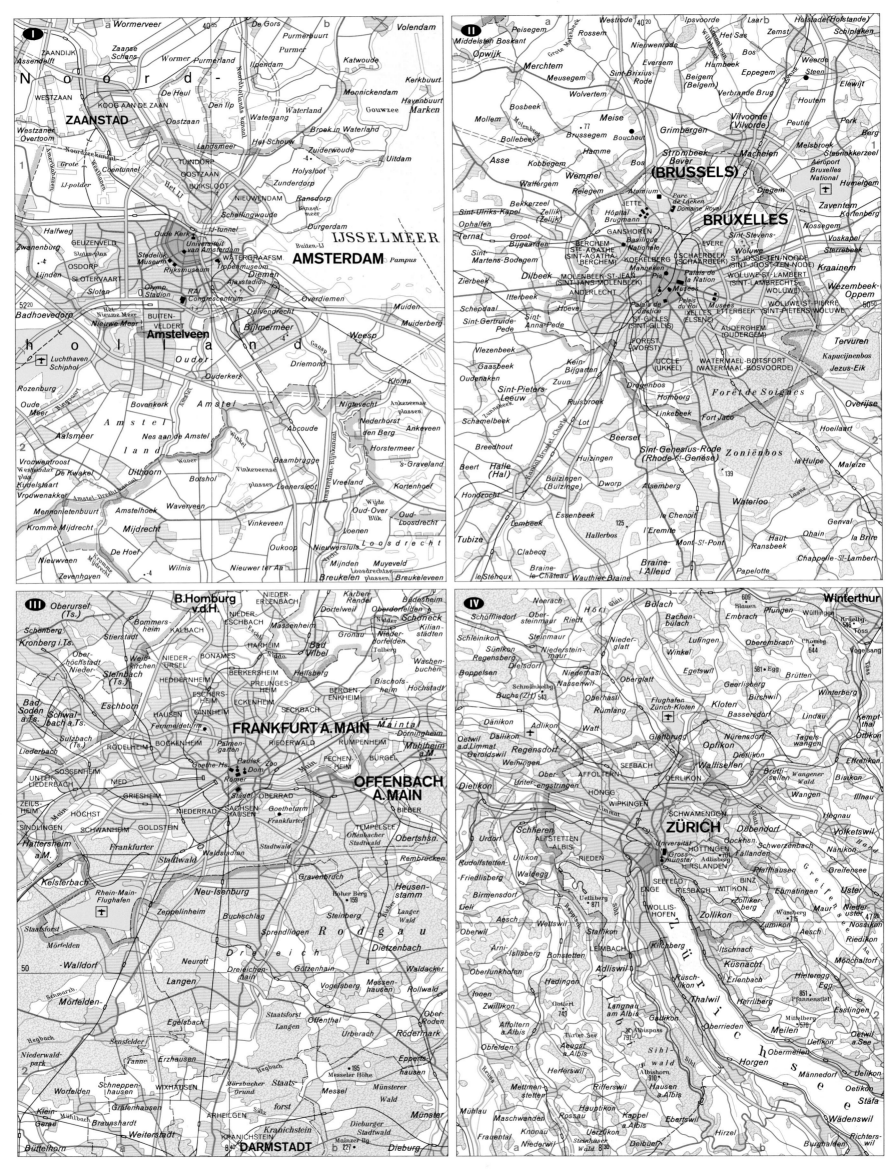

Conversion meters – feet see page 48

1 : 225,000

7.5 Kilometers

5 Statute Miles

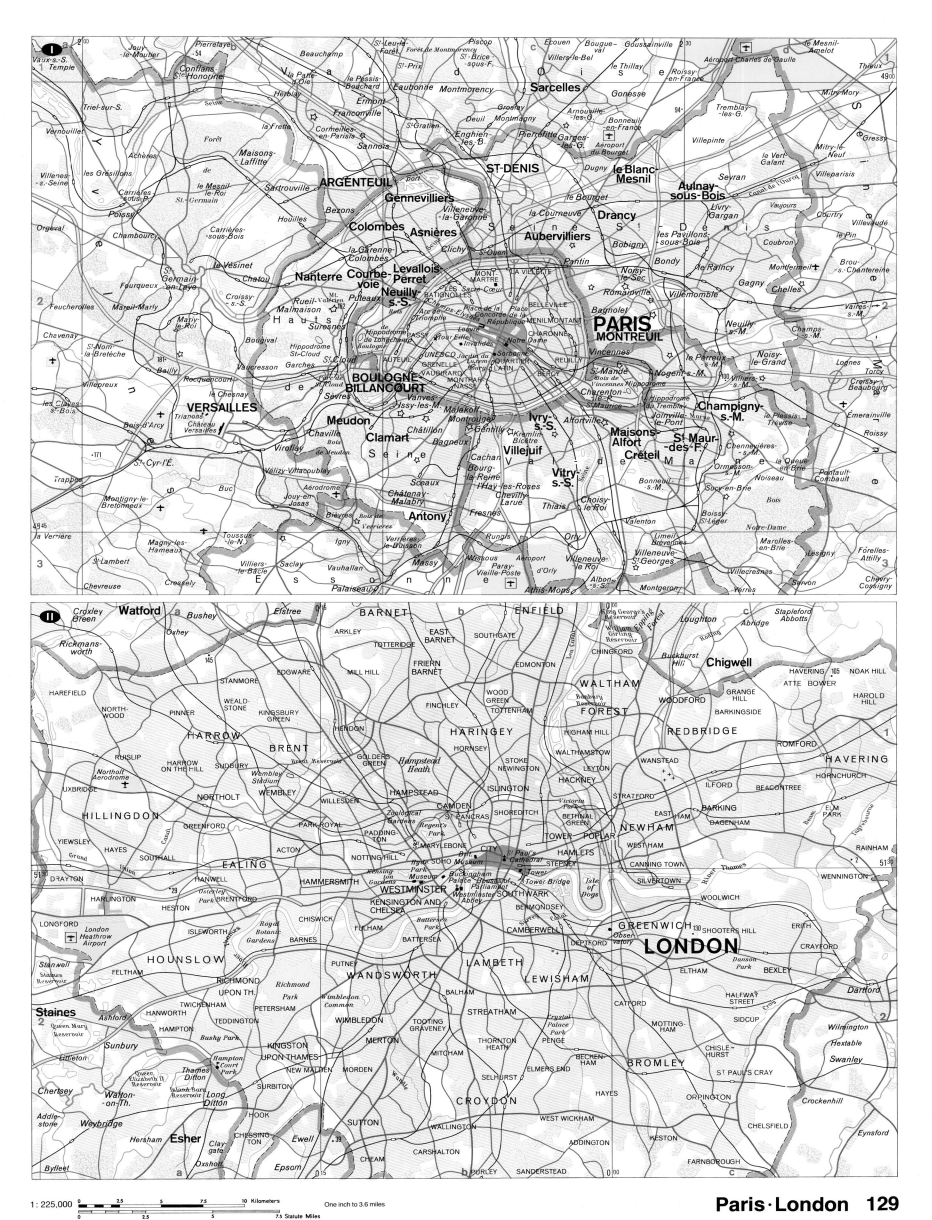

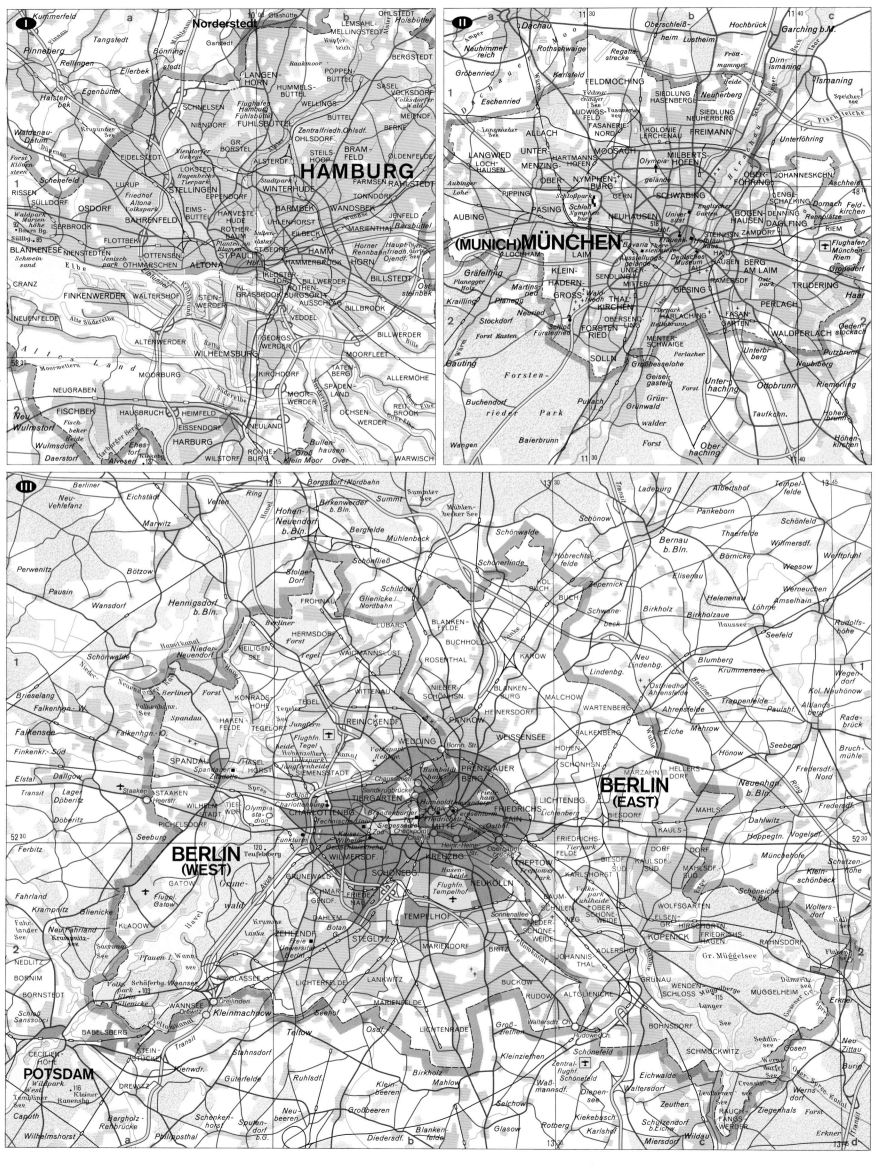

Conversion meters – feet see page 48

1 : 225,000

0   2.5   5   7.5   10 Kilometers

0   2.5   5   7.5 Statute Miles

One inch to 3.6 miles

1 : 36,000,000

Conversion meters – feet see page 48

Administrative units in the Soviet Union:
1 Komi- Permyak Aut. Area
2 Udmurt A.S.S.R.
3 Mari A.S.S.R.
4 Chuvash A.S.S.R.
5 Mordovian A.S.S.R.
6 Tatar A.S.S.R.
7 Bashkir A.S.S.R.
8 Kirghiz S.S.R.
9 Gorno- Altai Aut. Reg.
10 Khakass Aut. Reg.
11 Ust- Ordynsky- Buryat Aut. Area
12 Aginsky-Buryat Aut. Area
13 Jewish Aut. Reg.

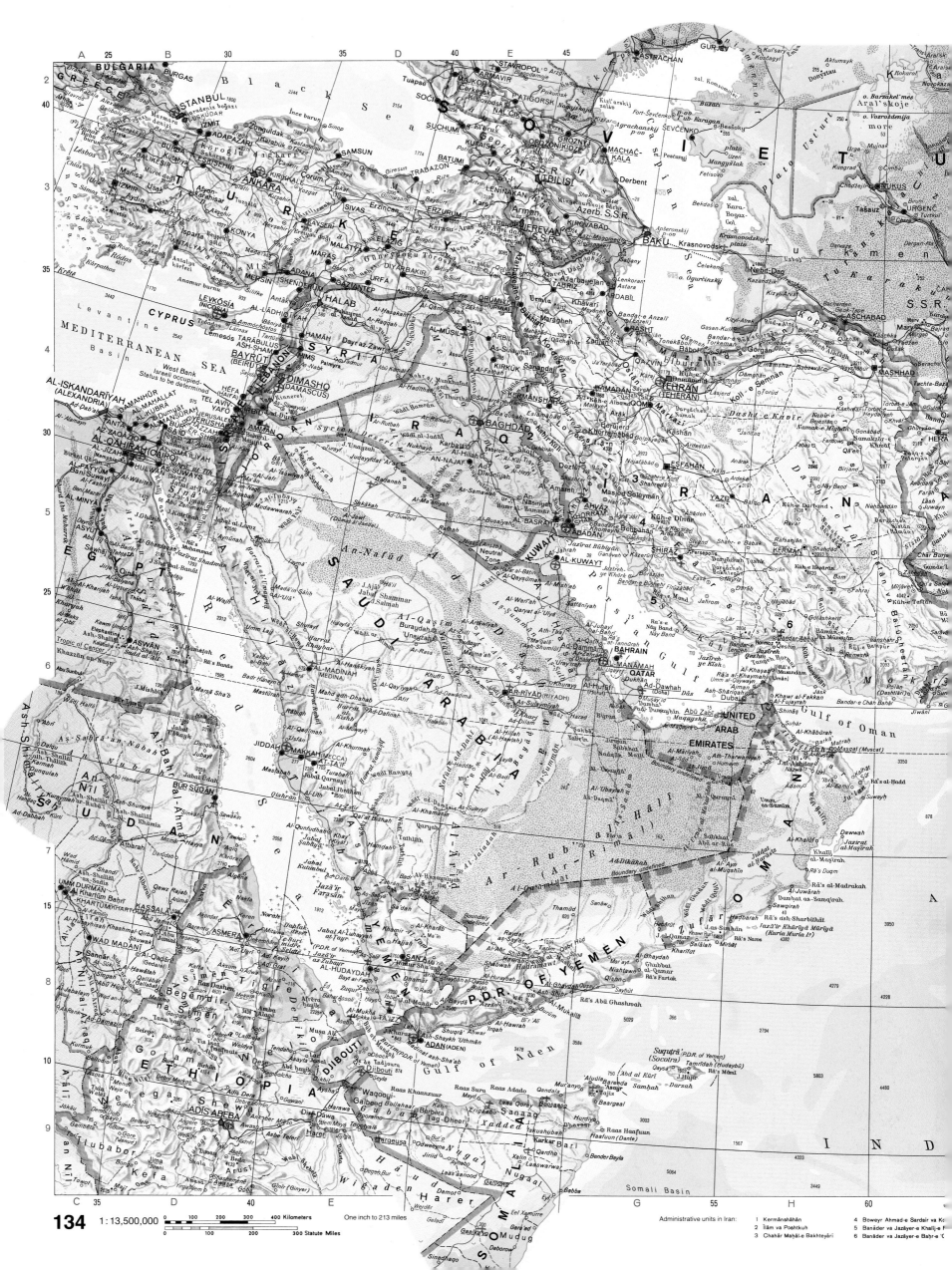

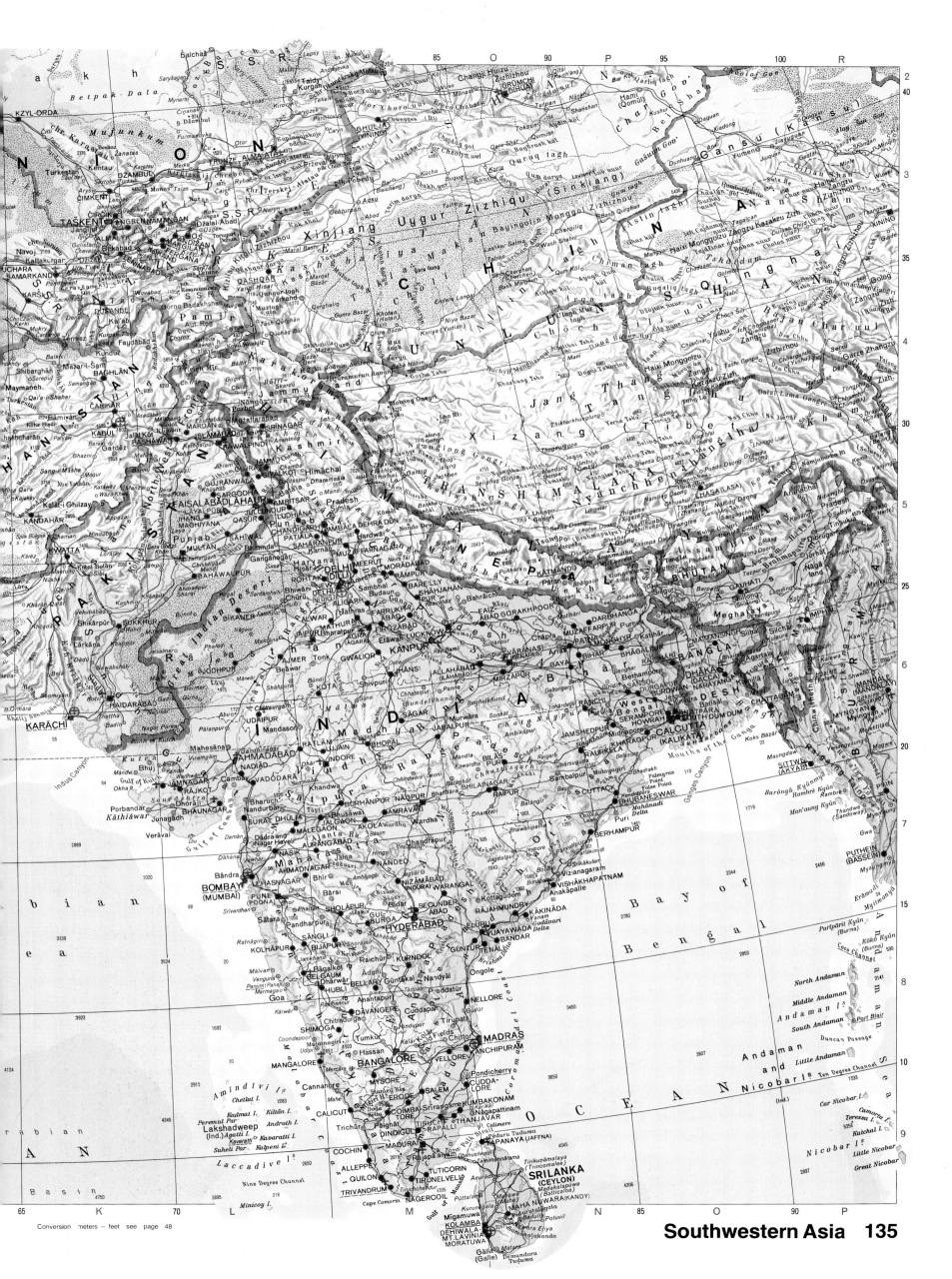

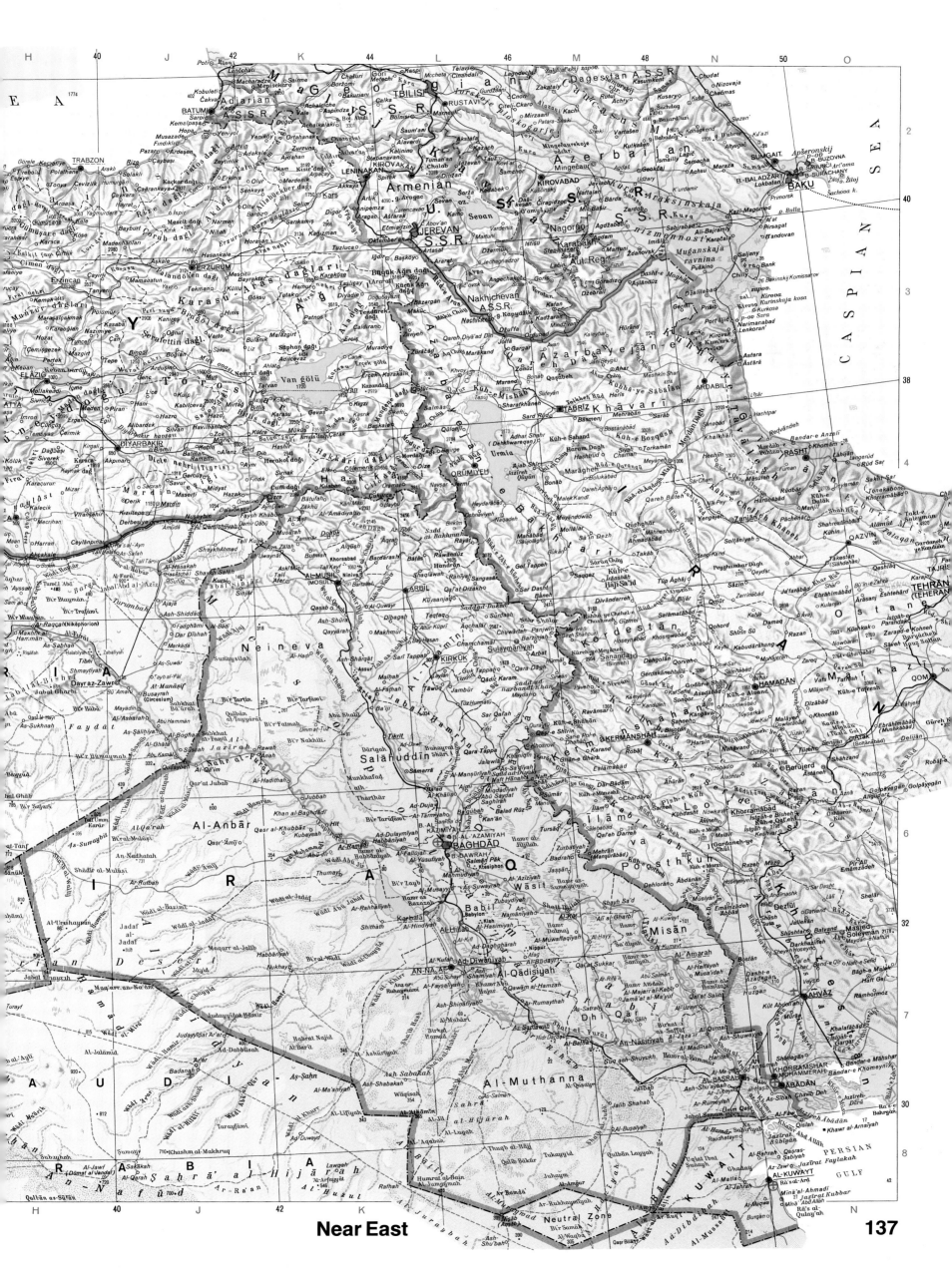

Near East   **137**

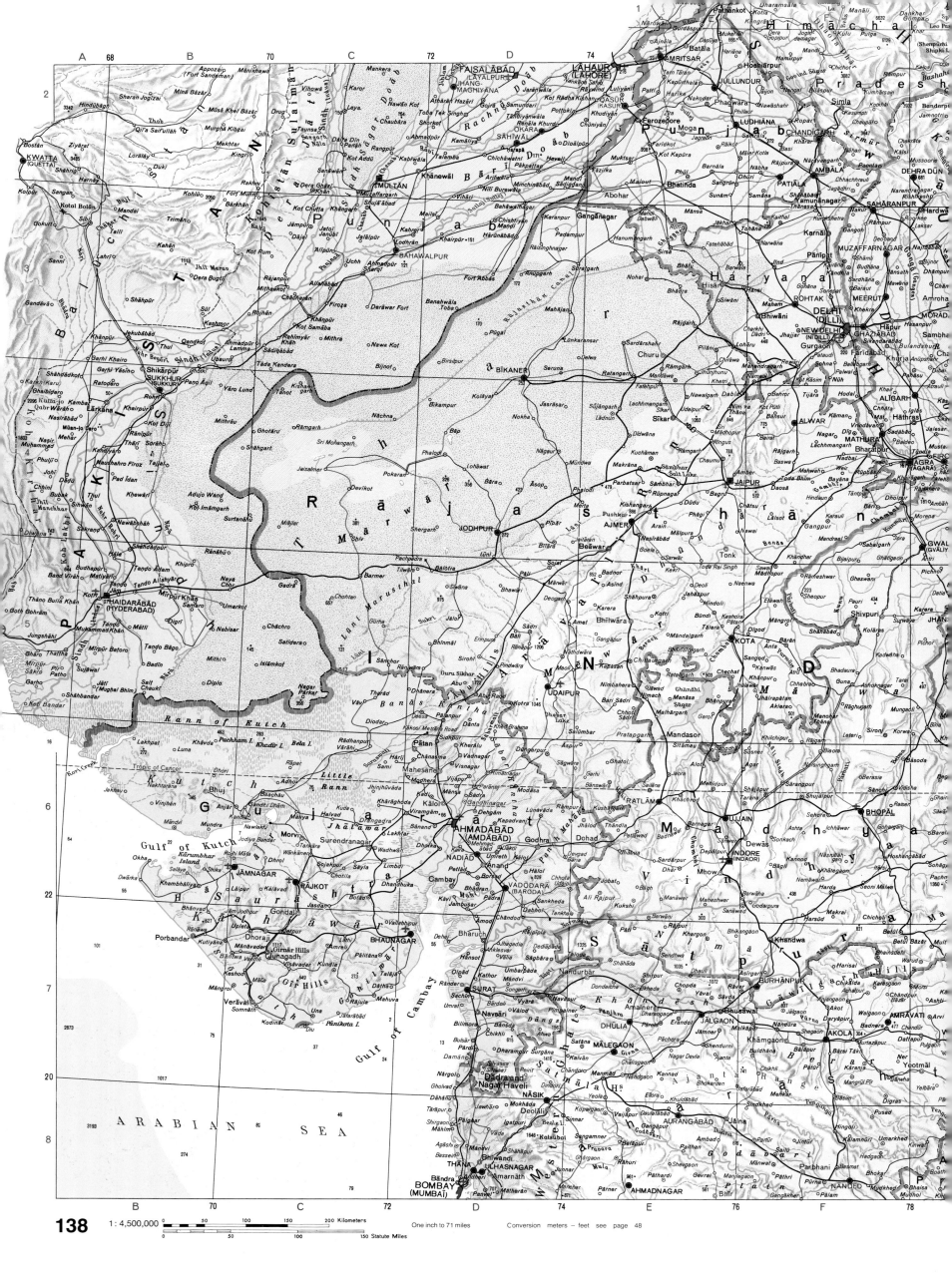

1 : 4,500,000   0   50   100   150   200 Kilometers

0   50   100   150 Statute Miles

One inch to 71 miles   Conversion meters – feet see page 48

Administrative units in Sri Lanka:
1 Uturè Palāna
2 Uturè Mèda Palāna
3 Vayamba Palāna
4 Madhyama Palāna
5 Nègenagira Palāna
6 Basnāngira Palāna
7 Sabaragamū Palāna
8 Ūva Palāna
9 Dakunu Palāna

Burma 141

1:13,500,000

Administrative units in China:

A Linxia Huizu Zizhizhou   D Dehong Daizu Zizhizhou
B Dêqên Zangzu Zizhizhou   E Xishuangbanna Daizu Zizhizhou
C Nujiang Lisuzu Zizhizhou   F Bortala Monggol Zizhizhou

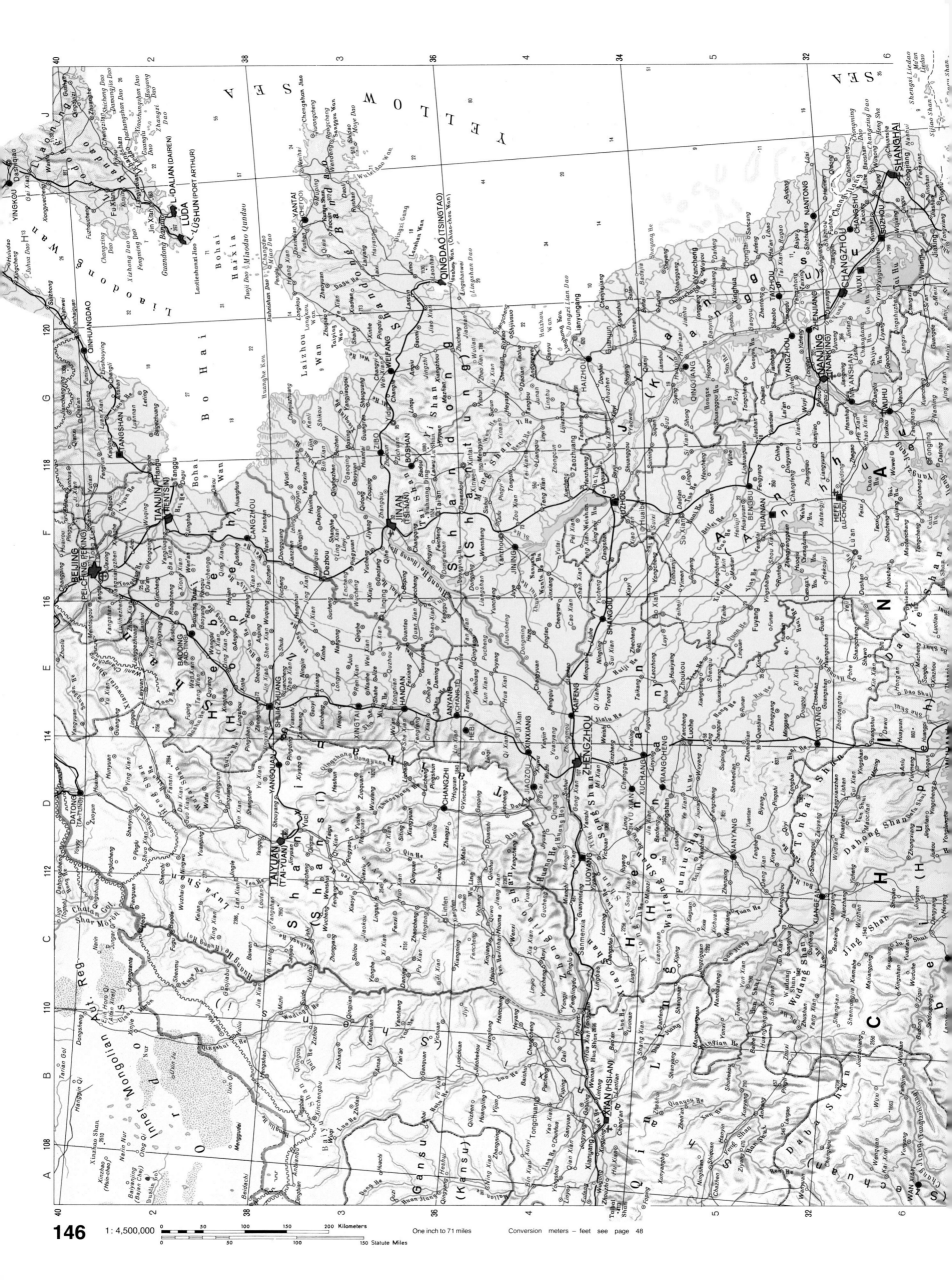

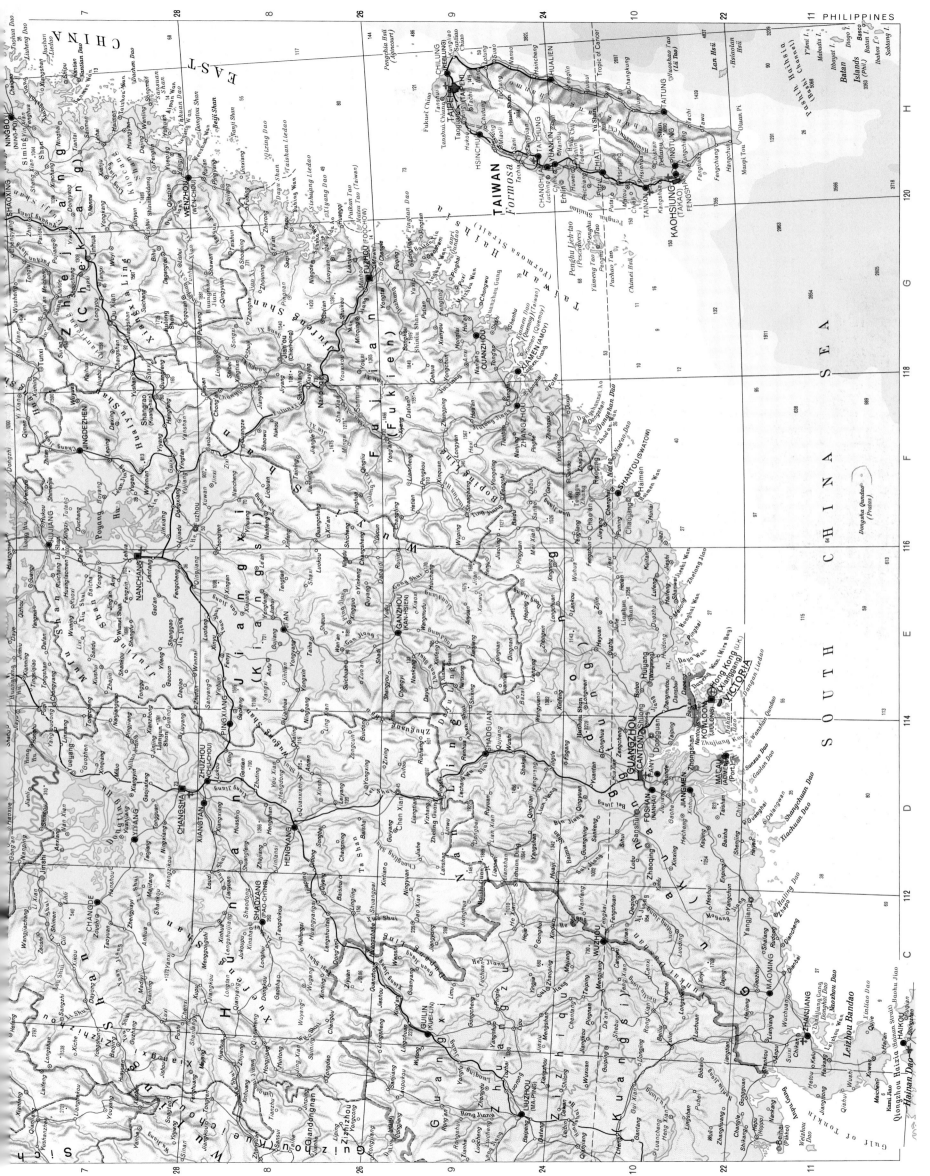

Eastern China · Taiwan 147

Fiji – Samoa

Hawaii

Solomon Islands

13 Yogyakarta
14 Jawa Timur
15 Bali
16 Nusa Tenggara Barat
17 Nusa Tenggara Timur
18 Sulawesi Utara
19 Sulawesi Tengah
20 Sulawesi Tenggara
21 Sulawesi Selatan
22 Maluku
23 Timor Timur

Conversion meters – feet see page 48

150 1 : 4,500,000

One inch to 71 miles   Conversion meters – feet see page 48

150 Statute Miles

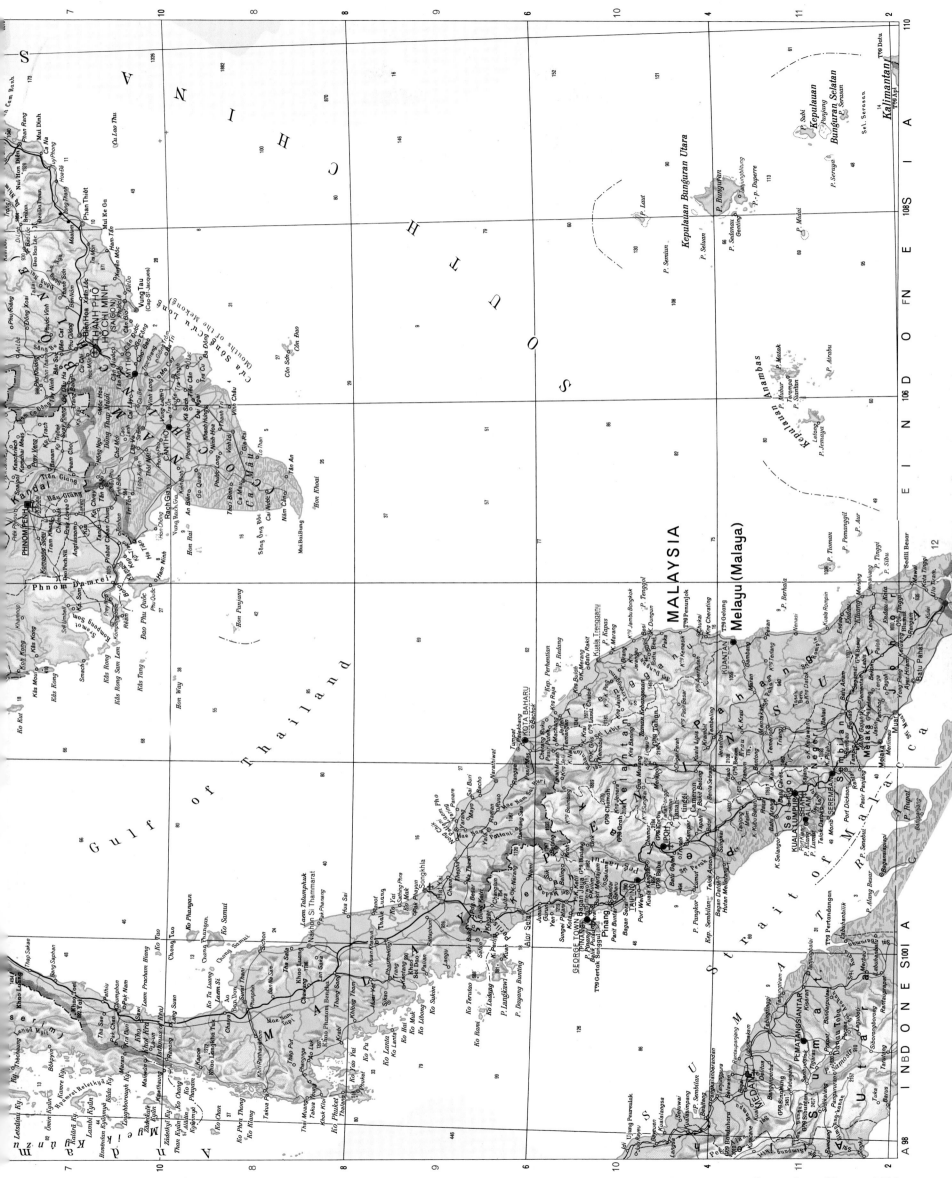

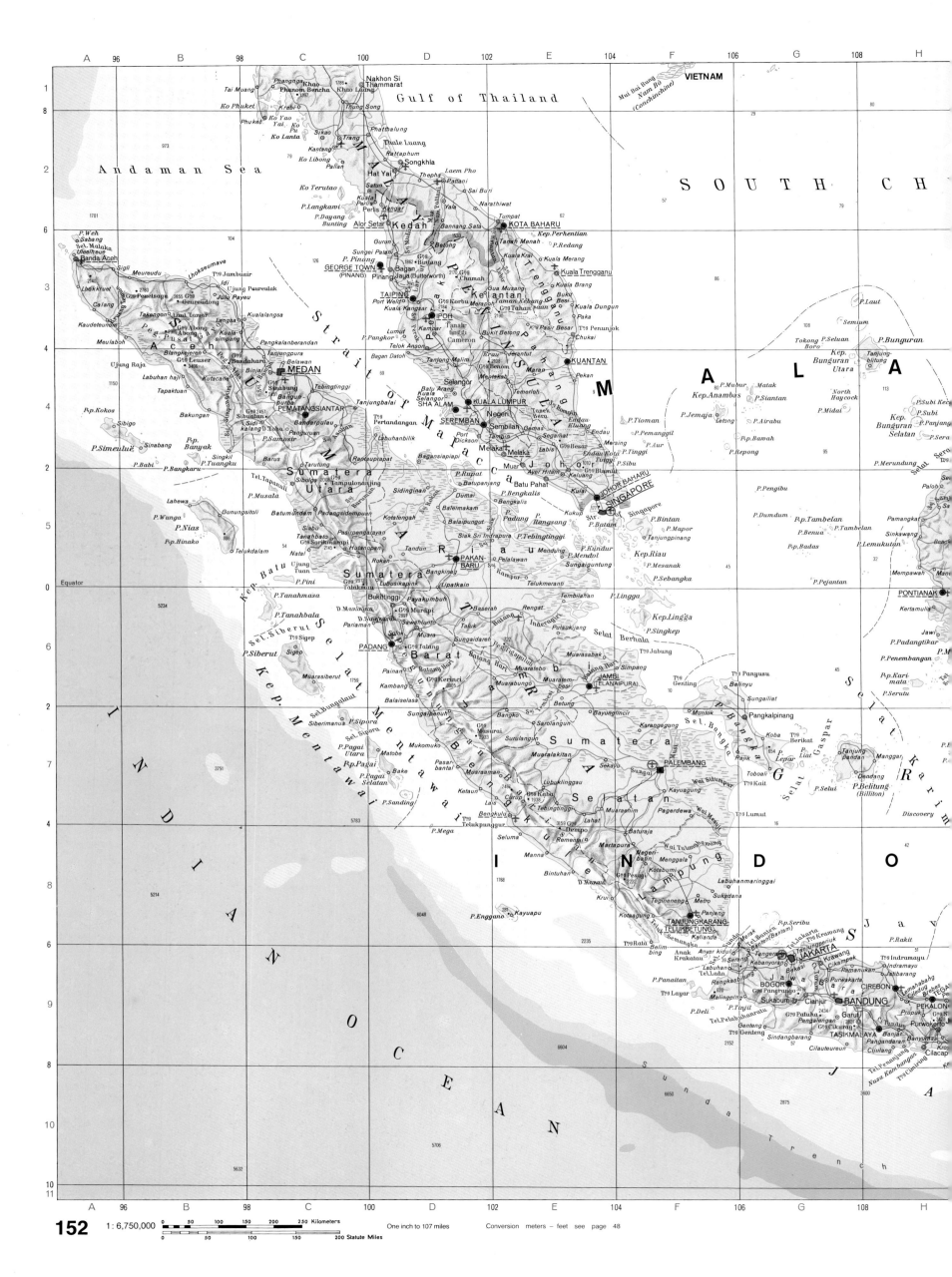

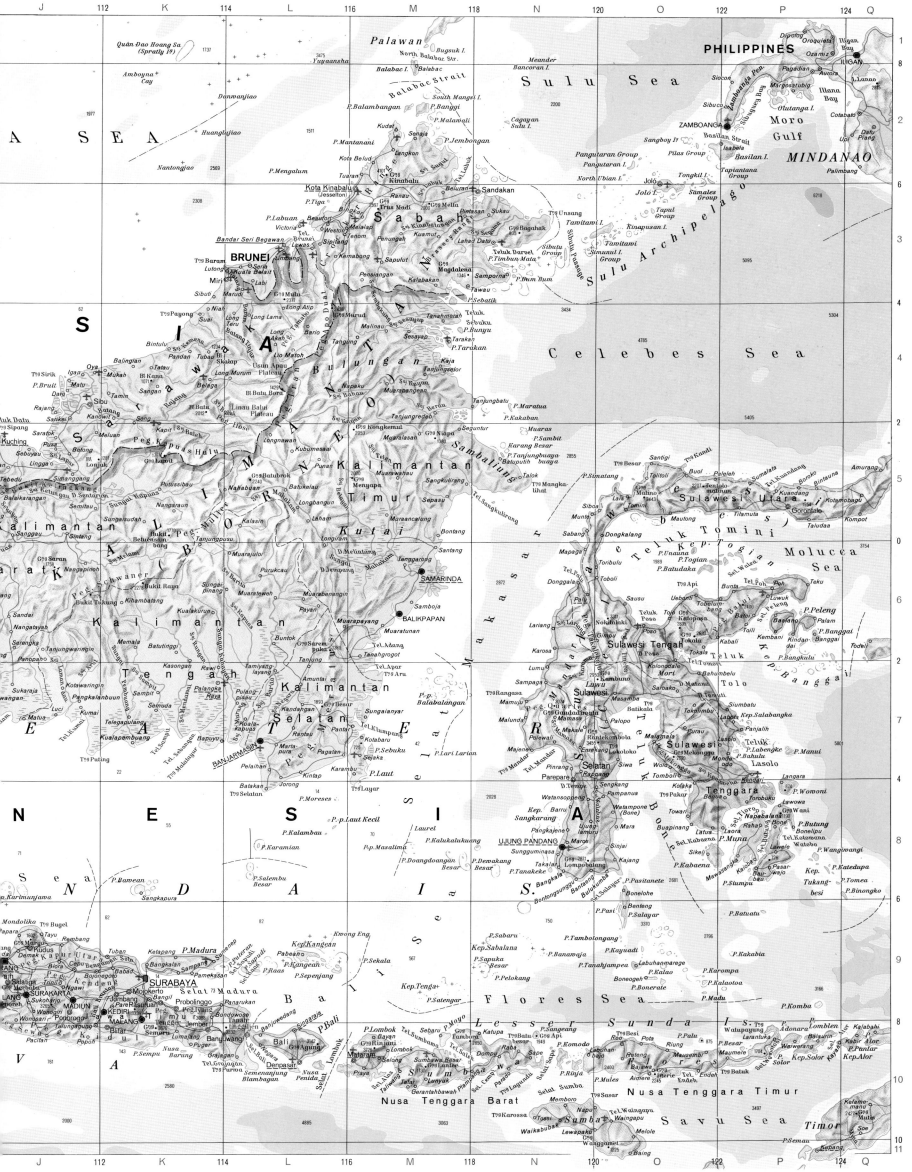

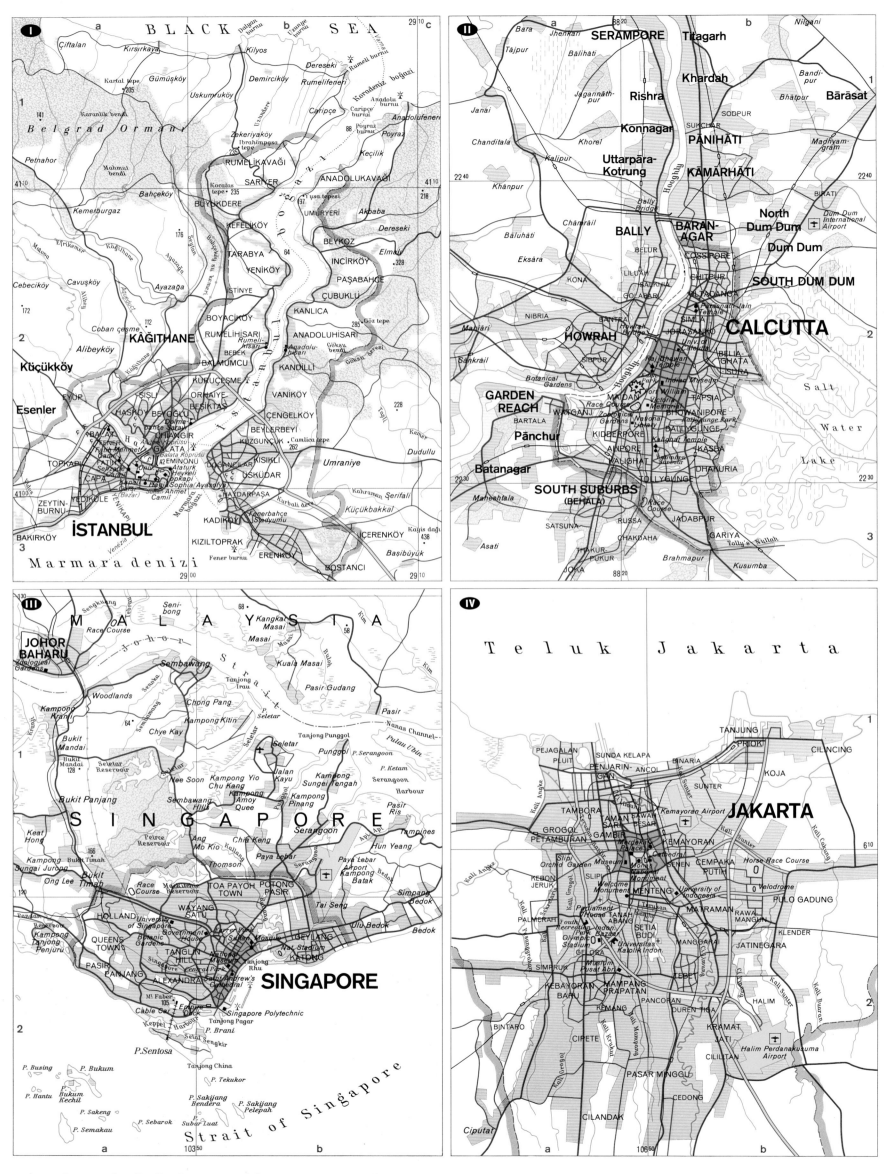

Conversion meters – feet see page 48   1 : 225,000

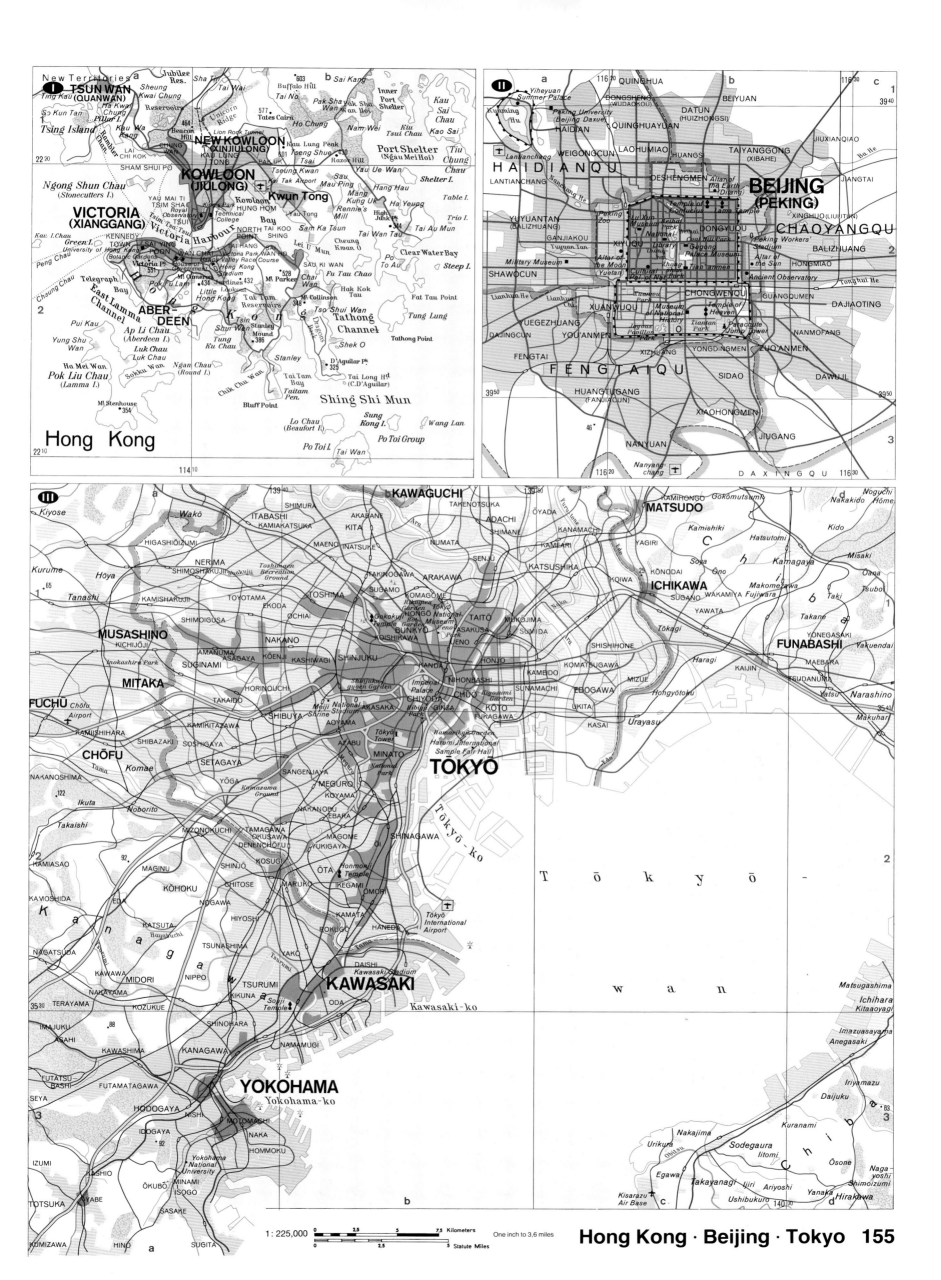

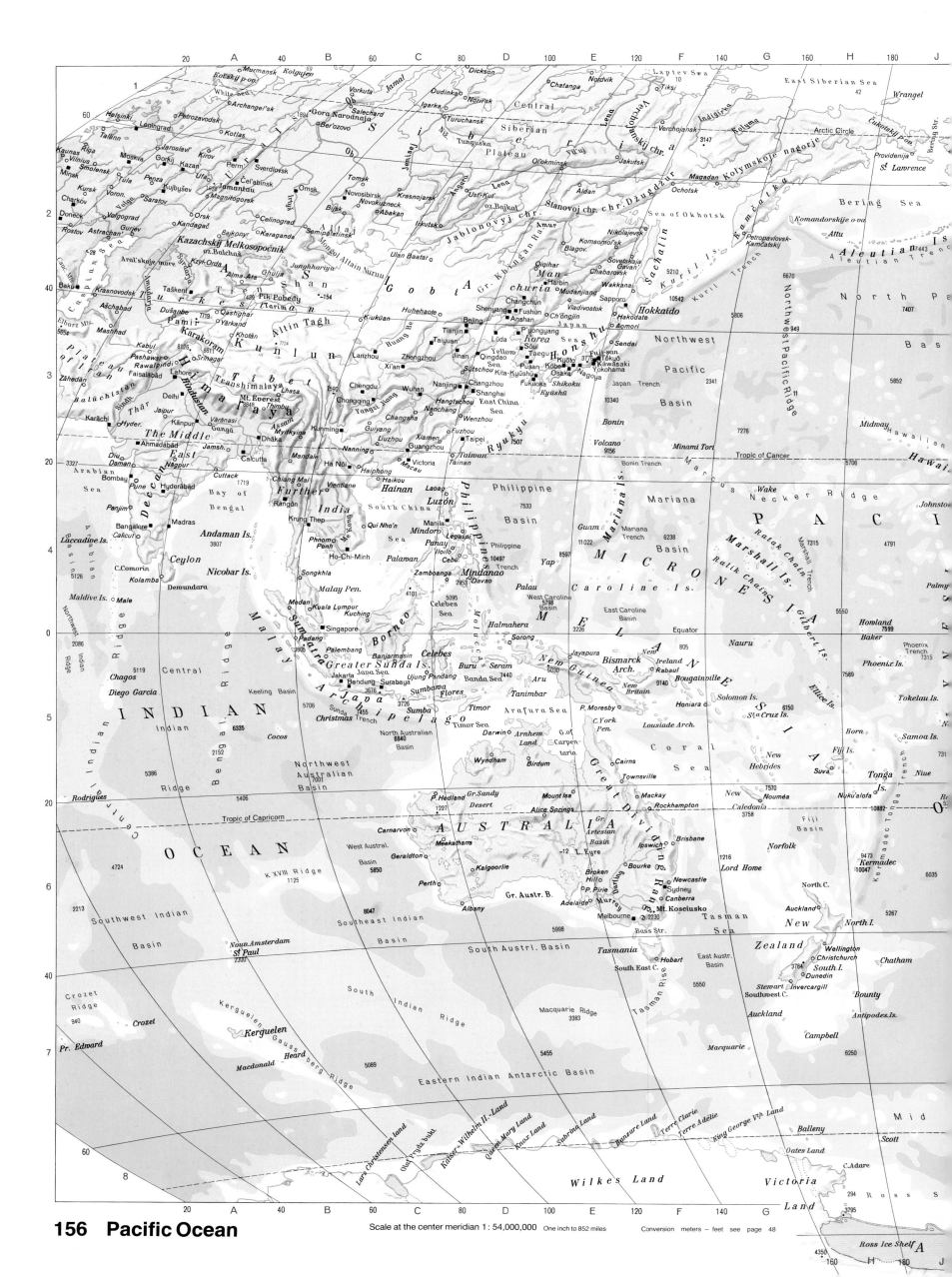

Scale at the center meridian 1 : 54,000,000   One inch to 852 miles   Conversion meters – feet see page 48

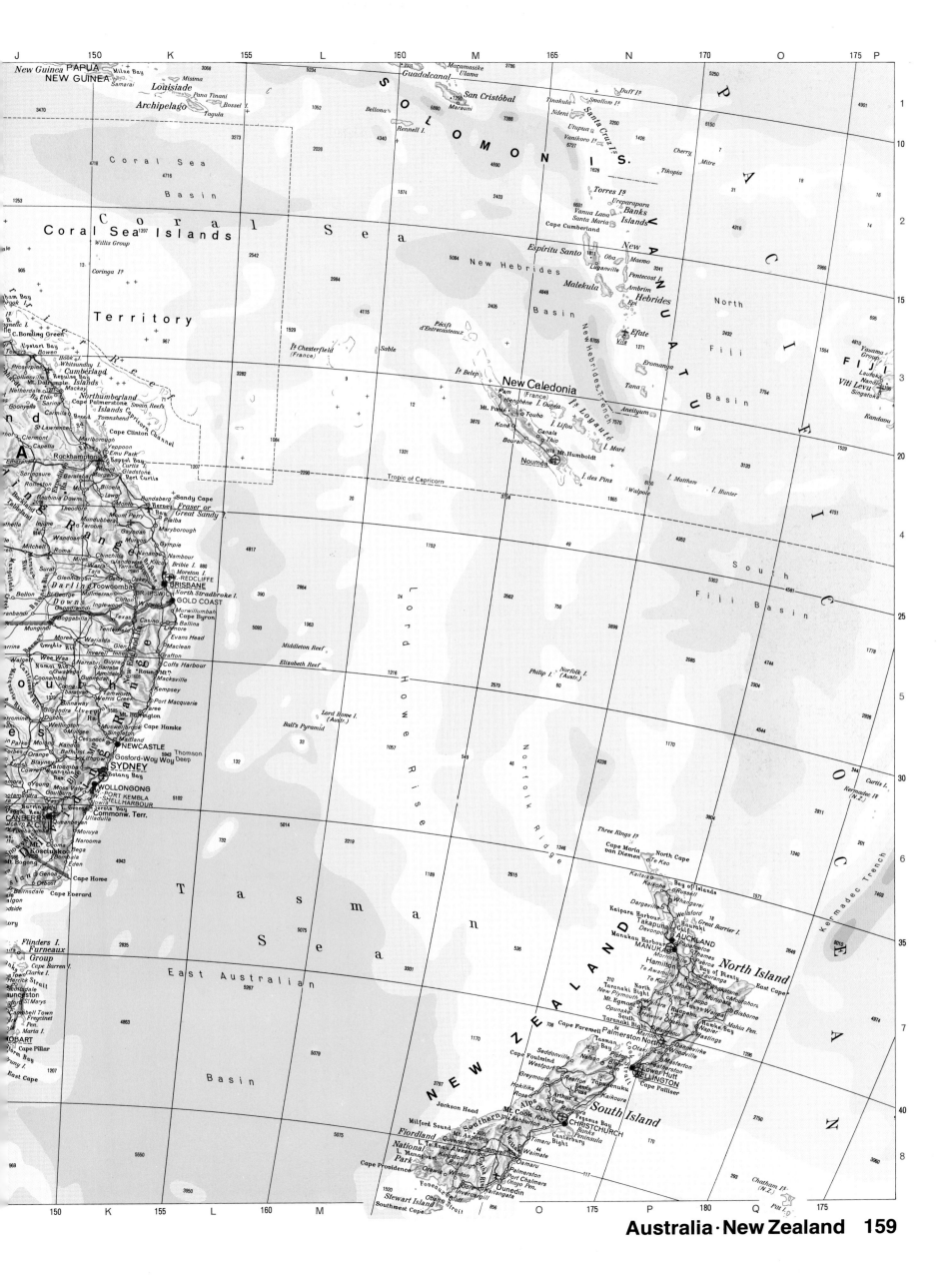

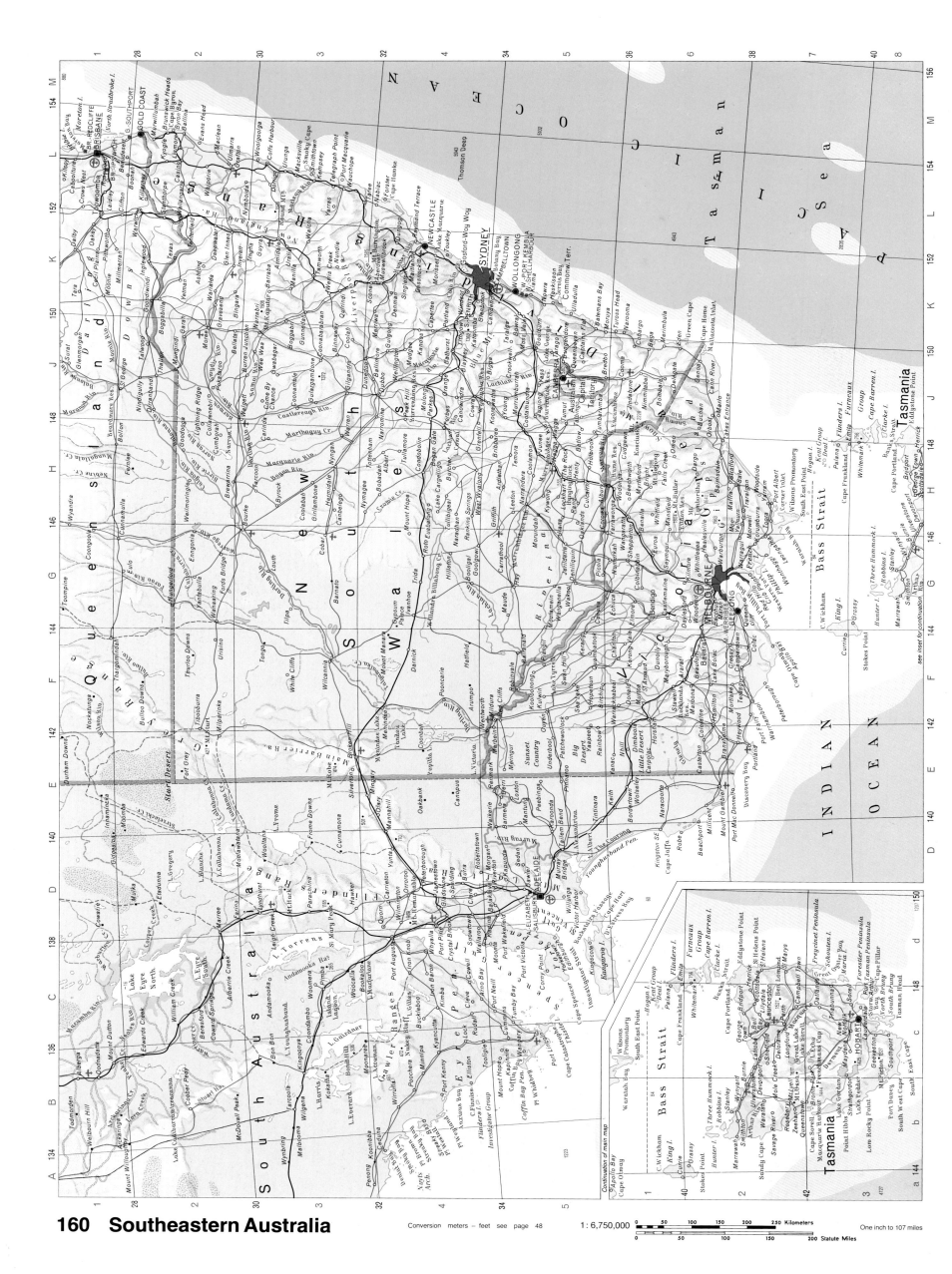

160   Southeastern Australia

Conversion meters — feet see page 48   1 : 6,750,000

One inch to 107 miles

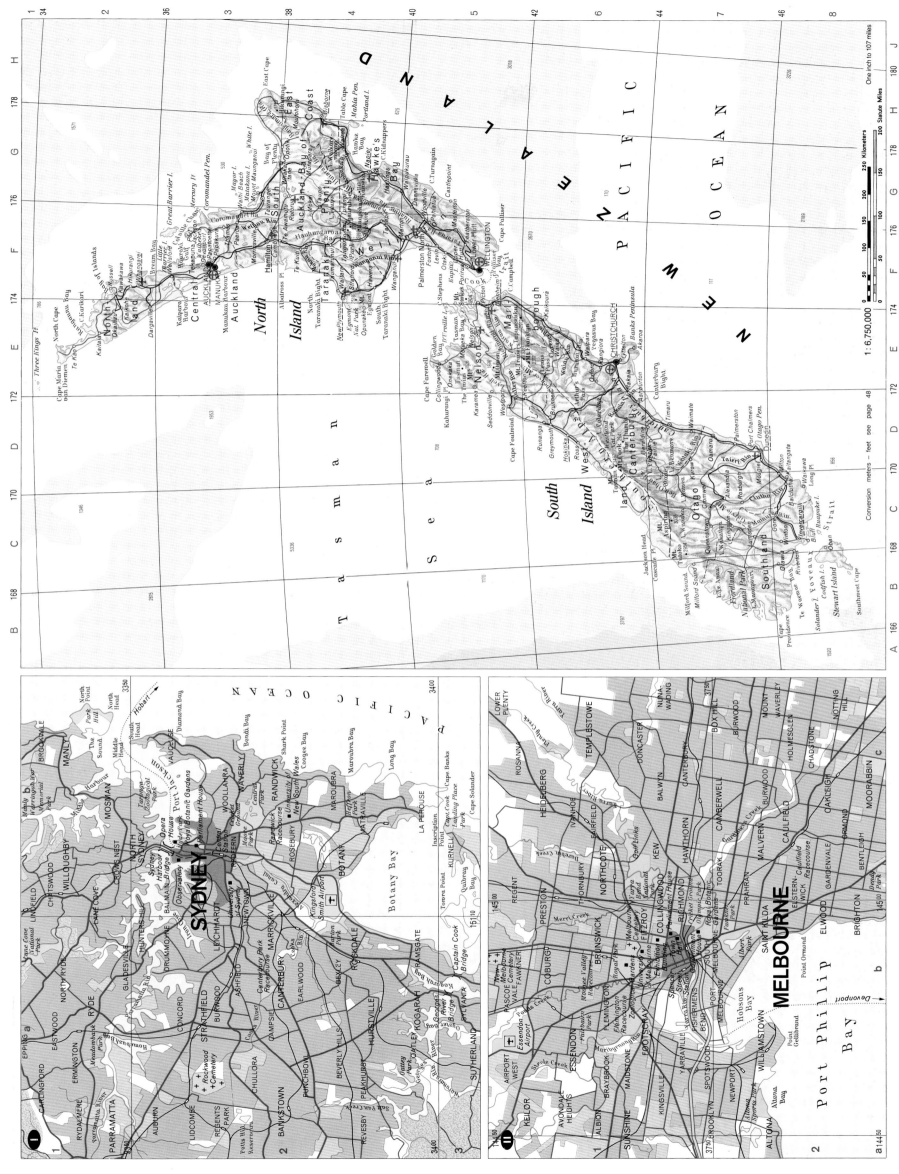

Sydney·Melbourne New Zealand **161**

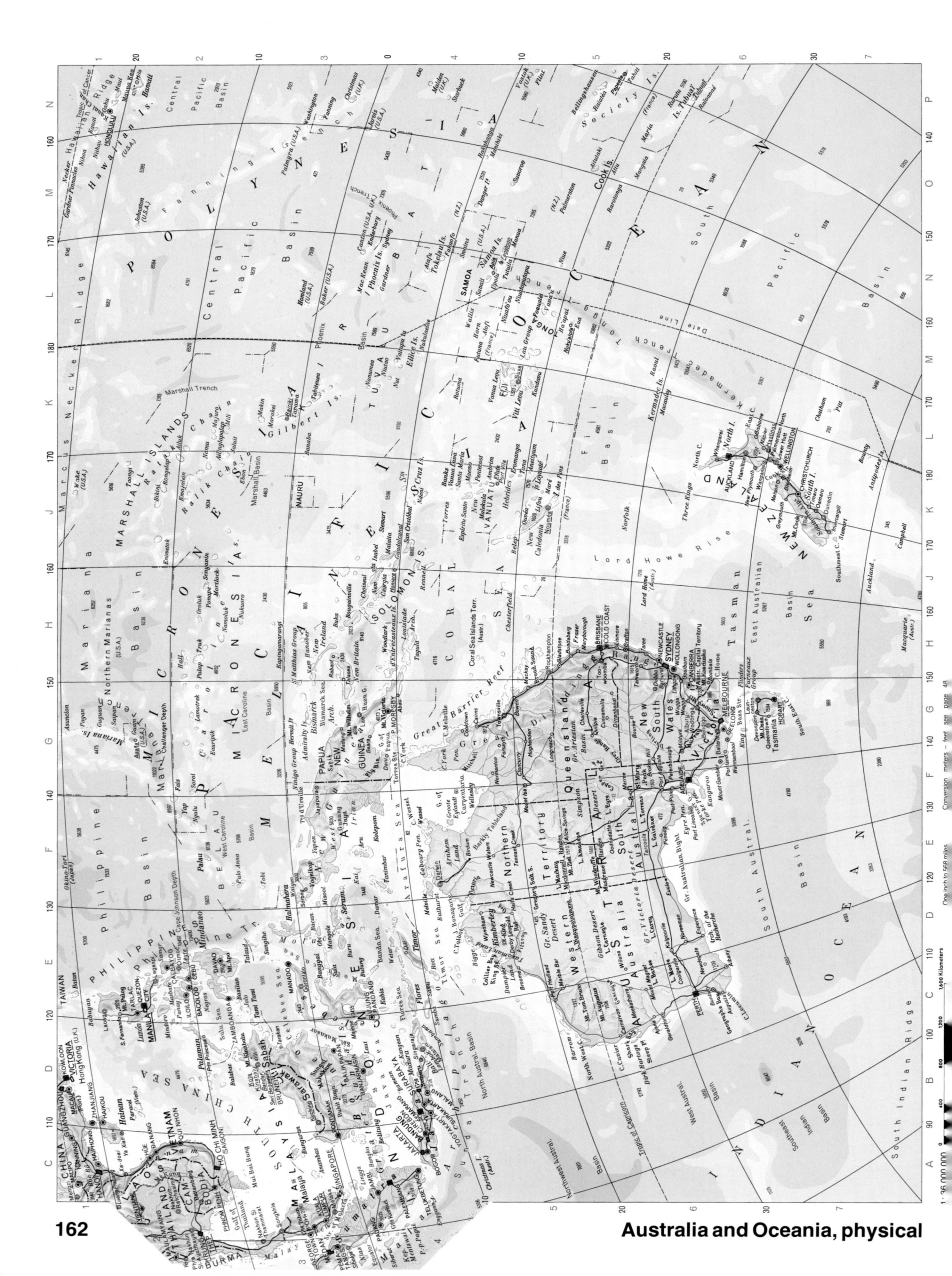

Australia and Oceania, physical

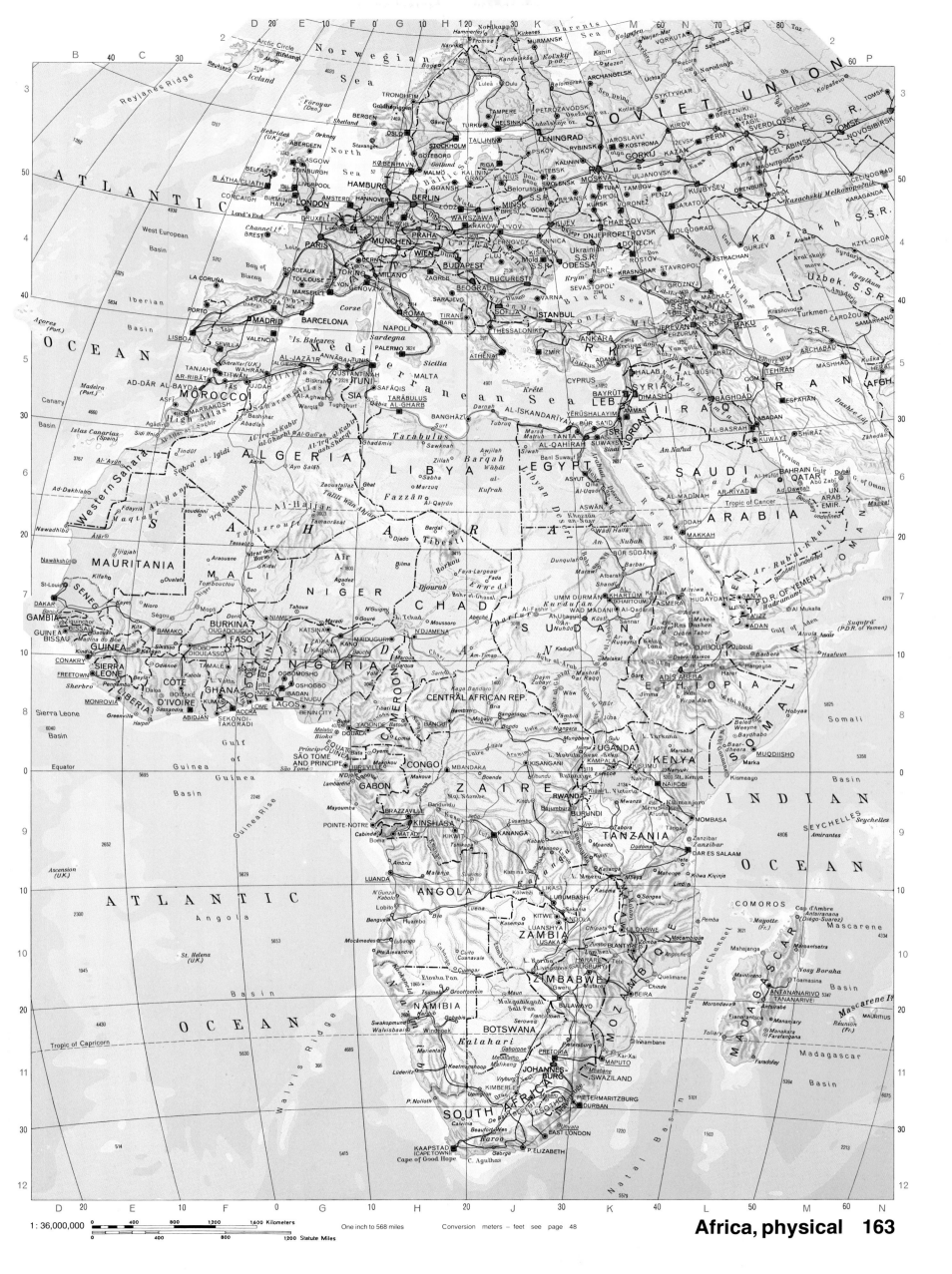

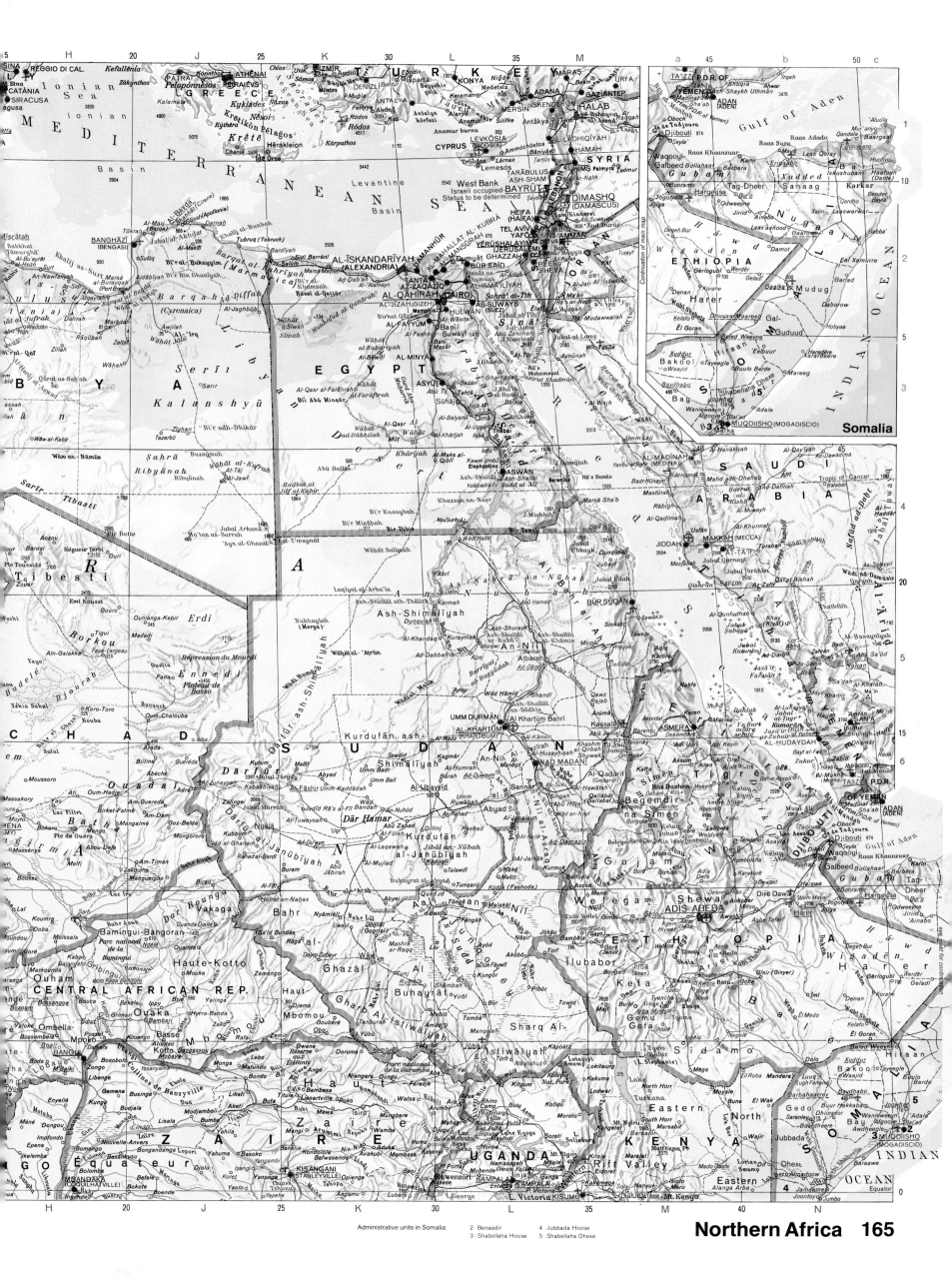

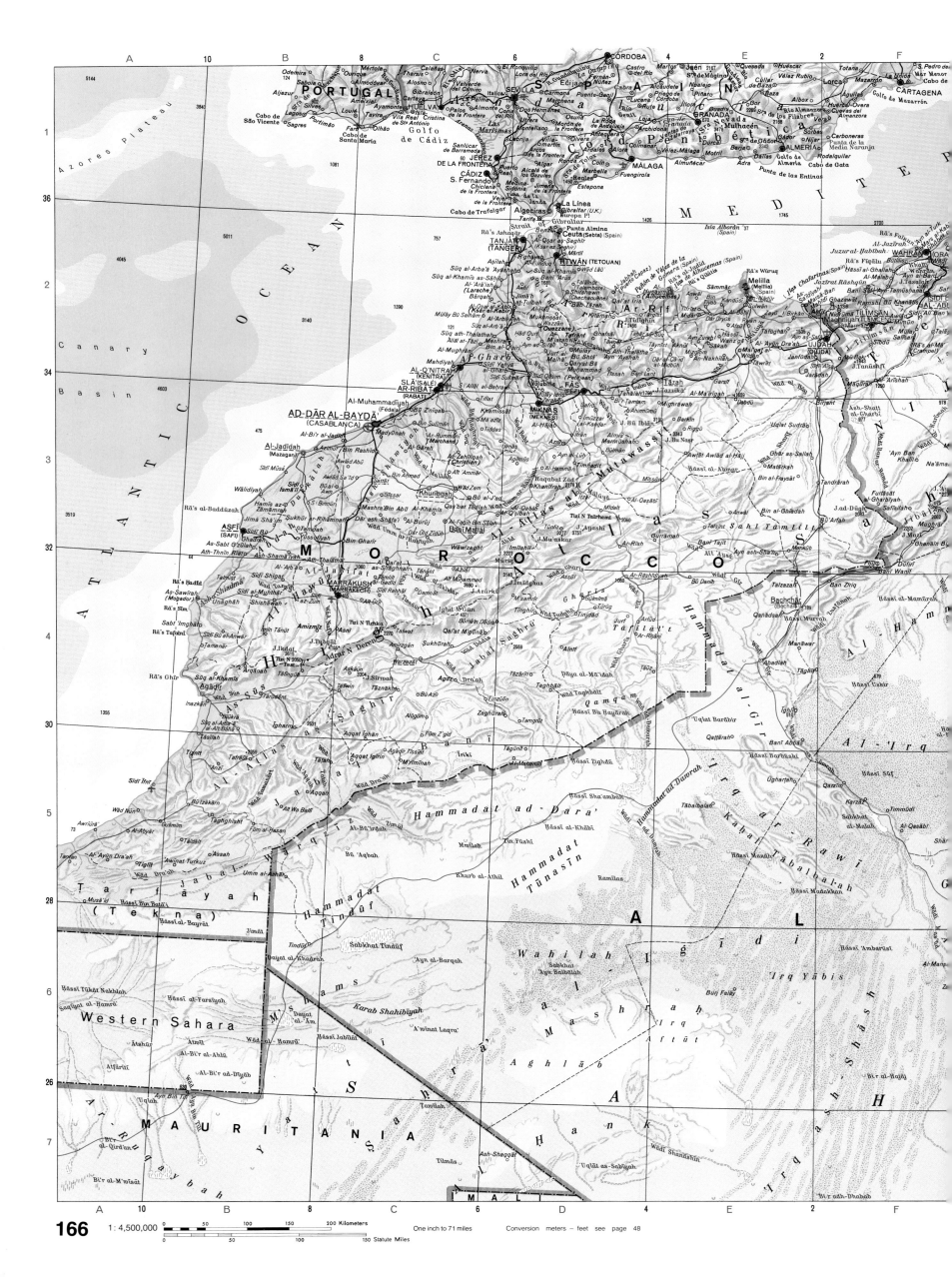

1 : 4,500,000

0 50 100 150 200 Kilometers
0 50 100 150 Statute Miles

One inch to 71 miles   Conversion meters — feet see page 48

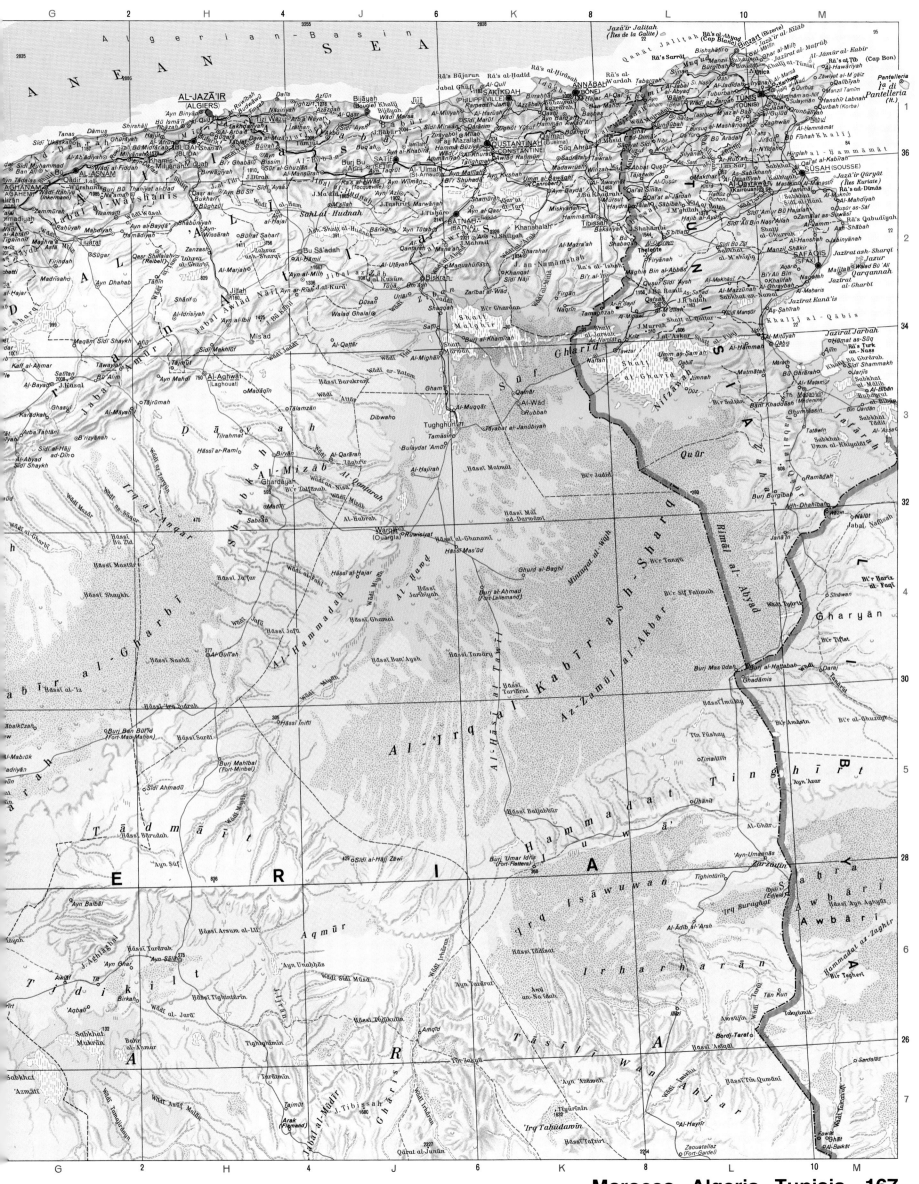

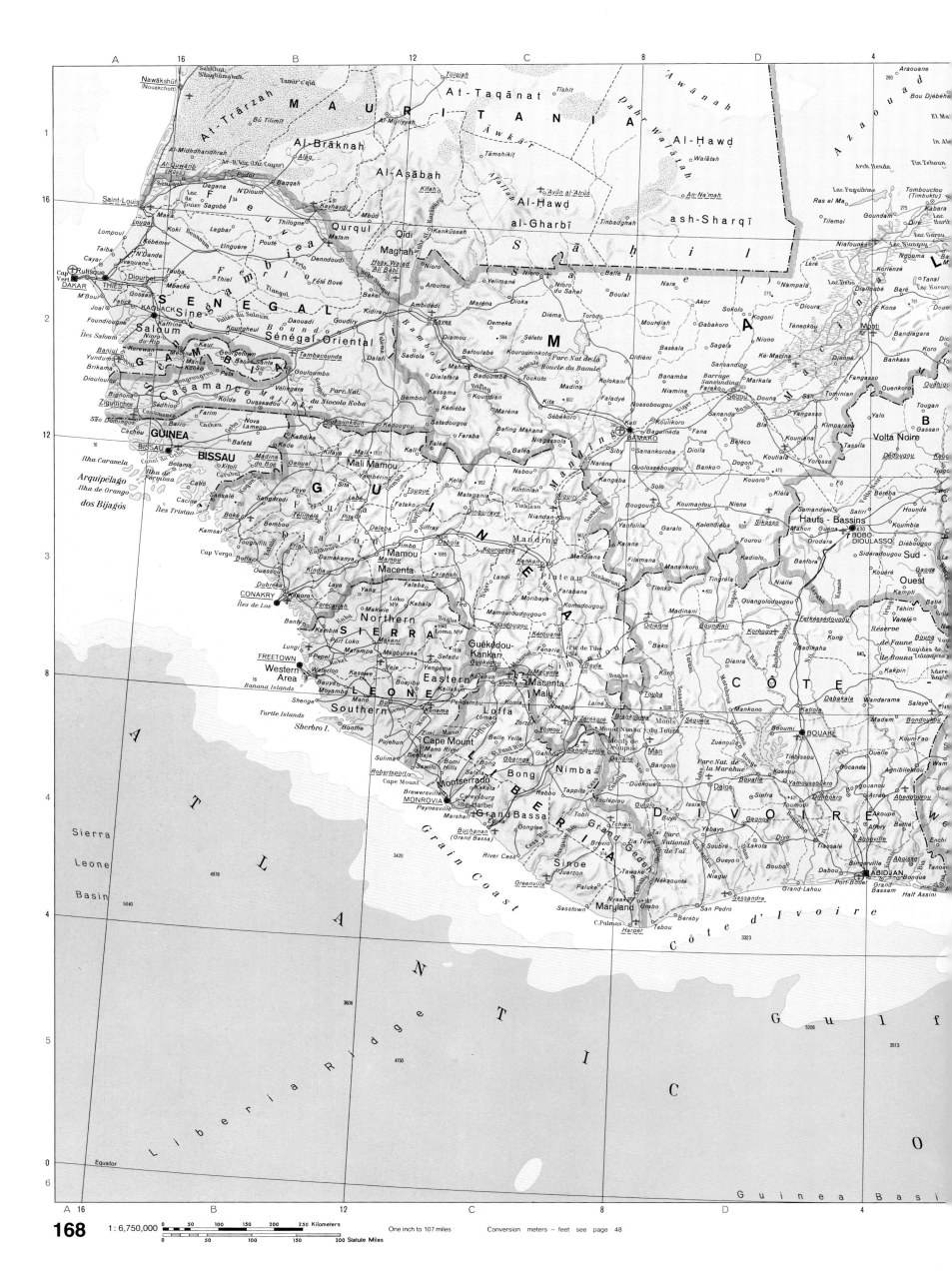

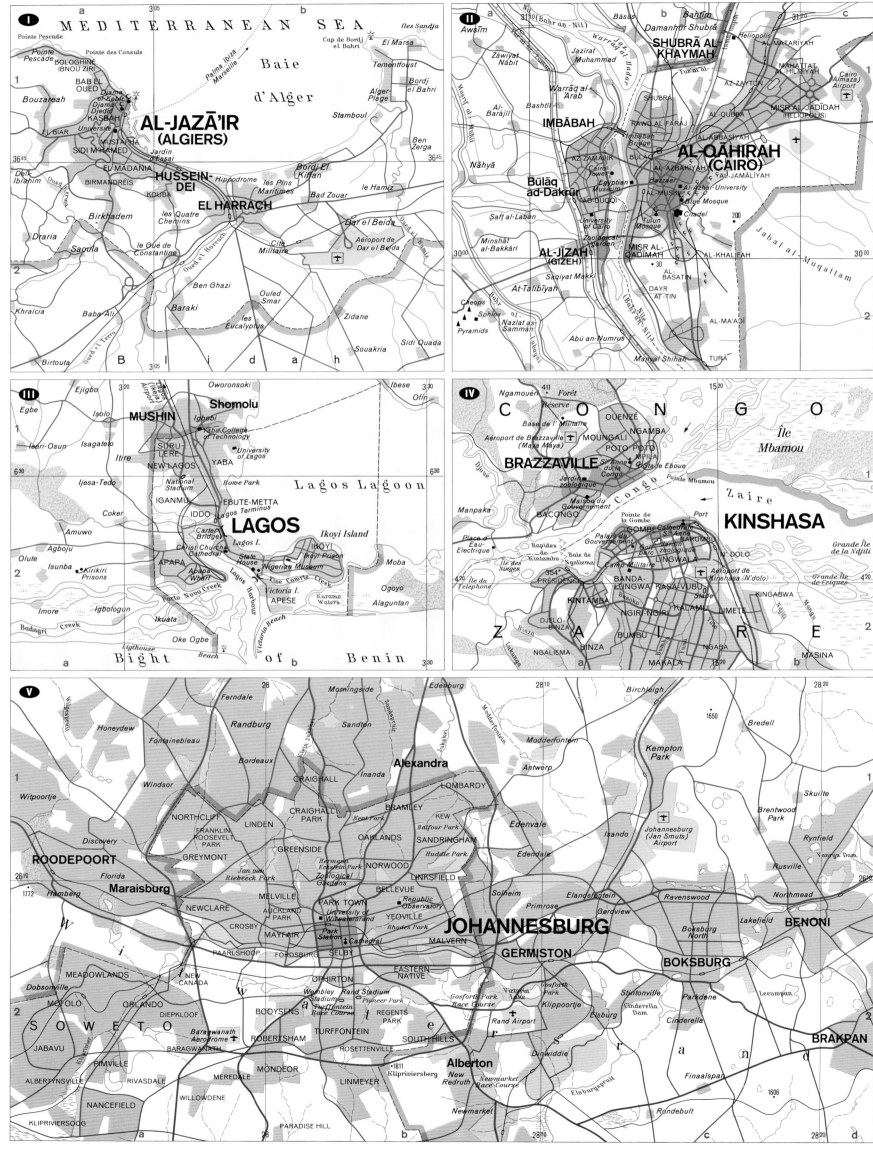

1 : 225,000

0   2.5   5   7.5 Kilometers

0   2.5   5 Statute Miles

One inch to 3.6 miles

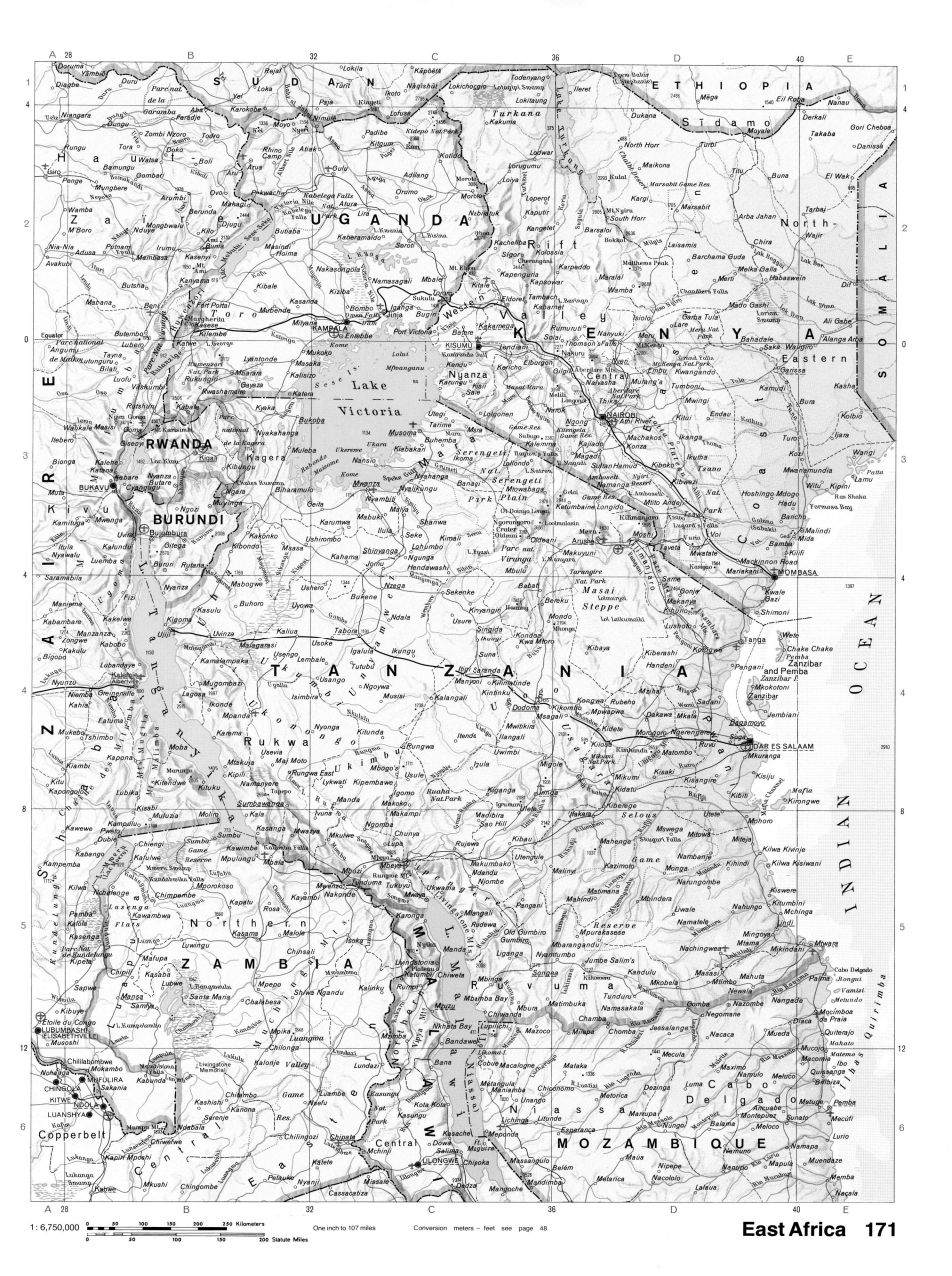

East Africa 171

172 Southern Africa

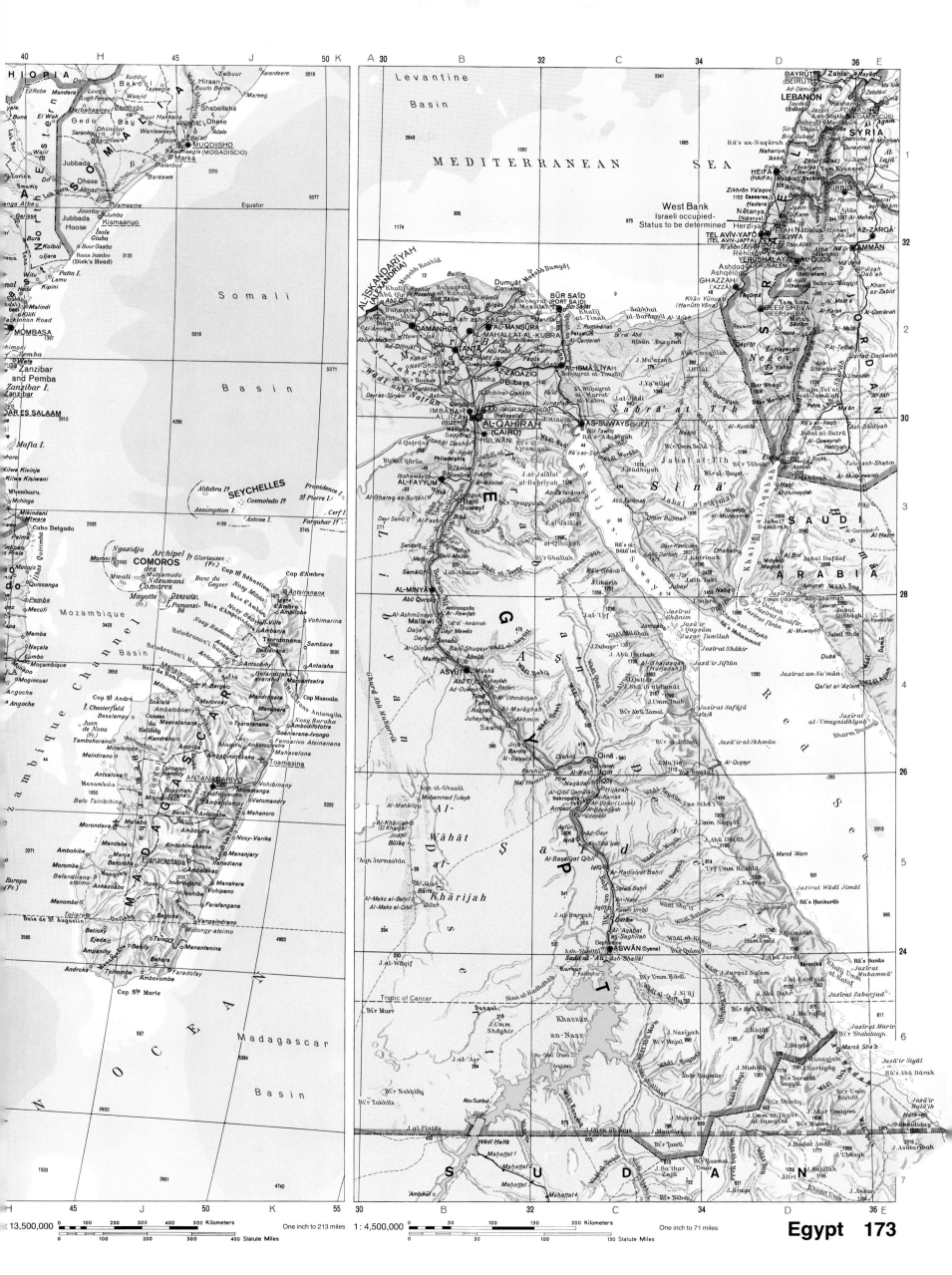

Egypt 173

1 : 4,500,000

0   50   100   150   200 Kilometers

0   50   100   150 Statute Miles

One inch to 71 miles   Conversion meters – feet see page 48

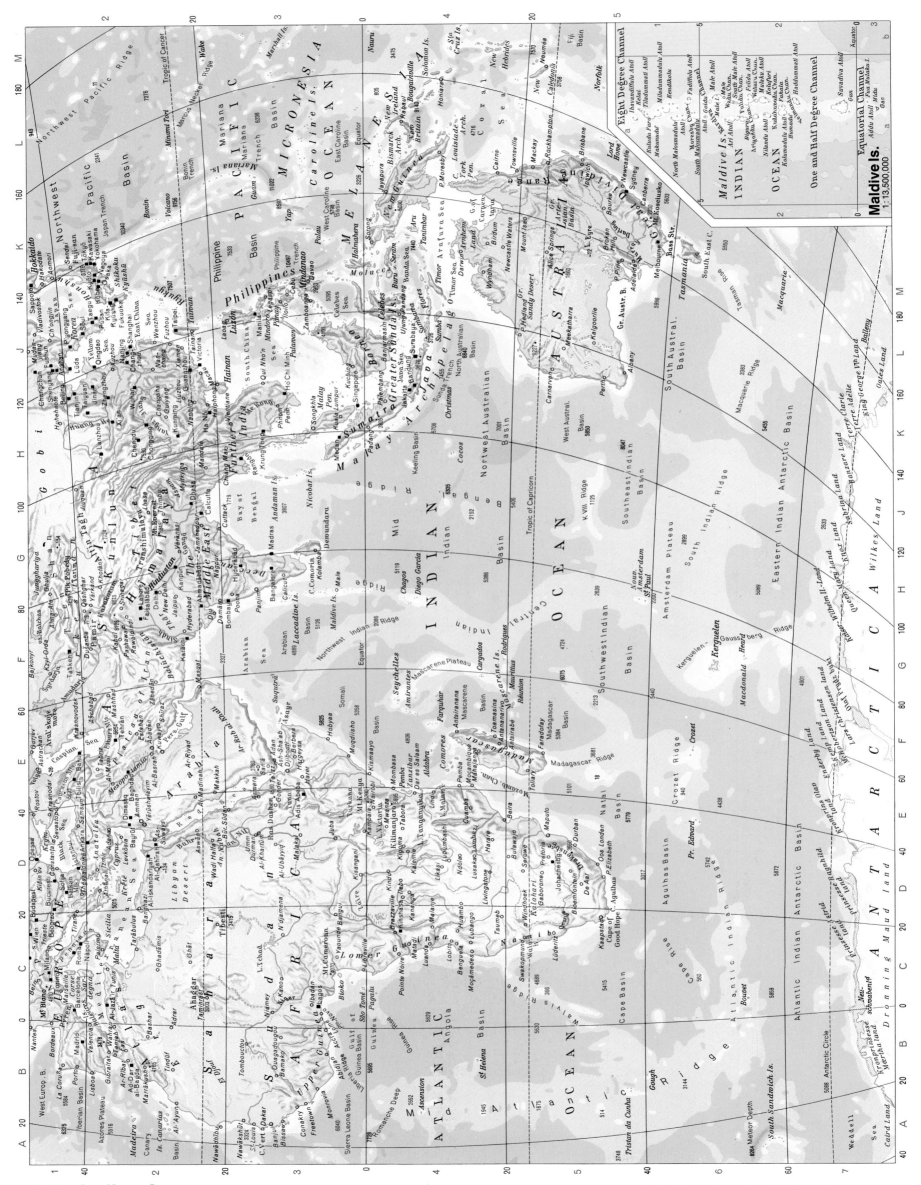

Conversion meters – feet see page 48

Scale at the center meridian 1 : 60,000,000   One inch to 947 miles

Maldive Is.
1 : 13,500,000

Eight Degree Channel

Maldive Is.
INDIAN
OCEAN

One and Half Degree Channel

Equatorial Channel

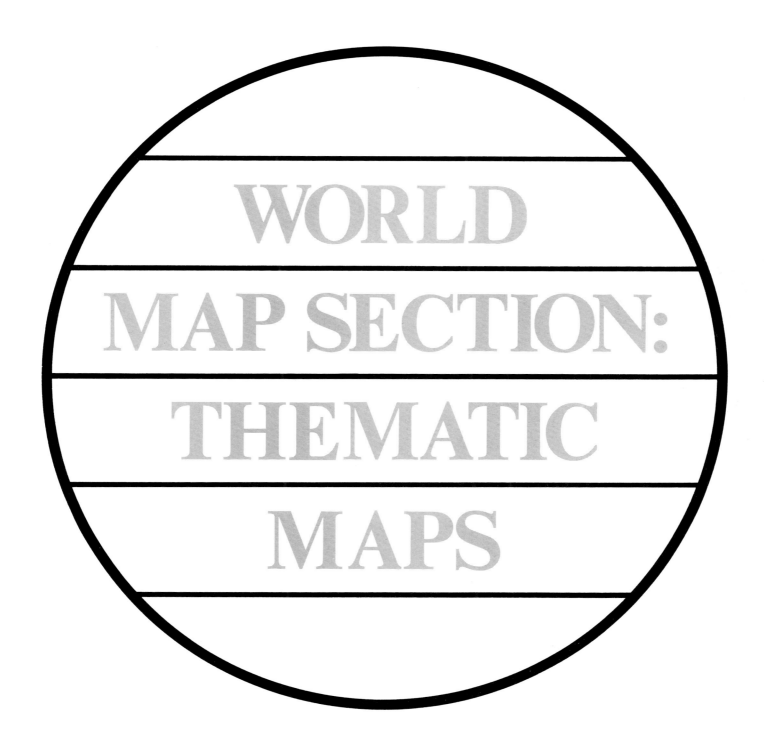

WORLD MAP SECTION: THEMATIC MAPS

A. = Andorra
ALB. = Albania
AU. = Austria
B. = Belgium
BA. = Bangladesh
BH. = Bhutan
BULG. = Bulgaria
CAM. = Cameroon
CAMB. = Cambodia
CZECH. = Czechoslovakia
DEN. = Denmark
DJ. = Djibouti
DOM. REP. = Dominican Republic

· Cities over 1,000,000 Population
○ Cities under 1,000,000 Population
— Shipping trade routes

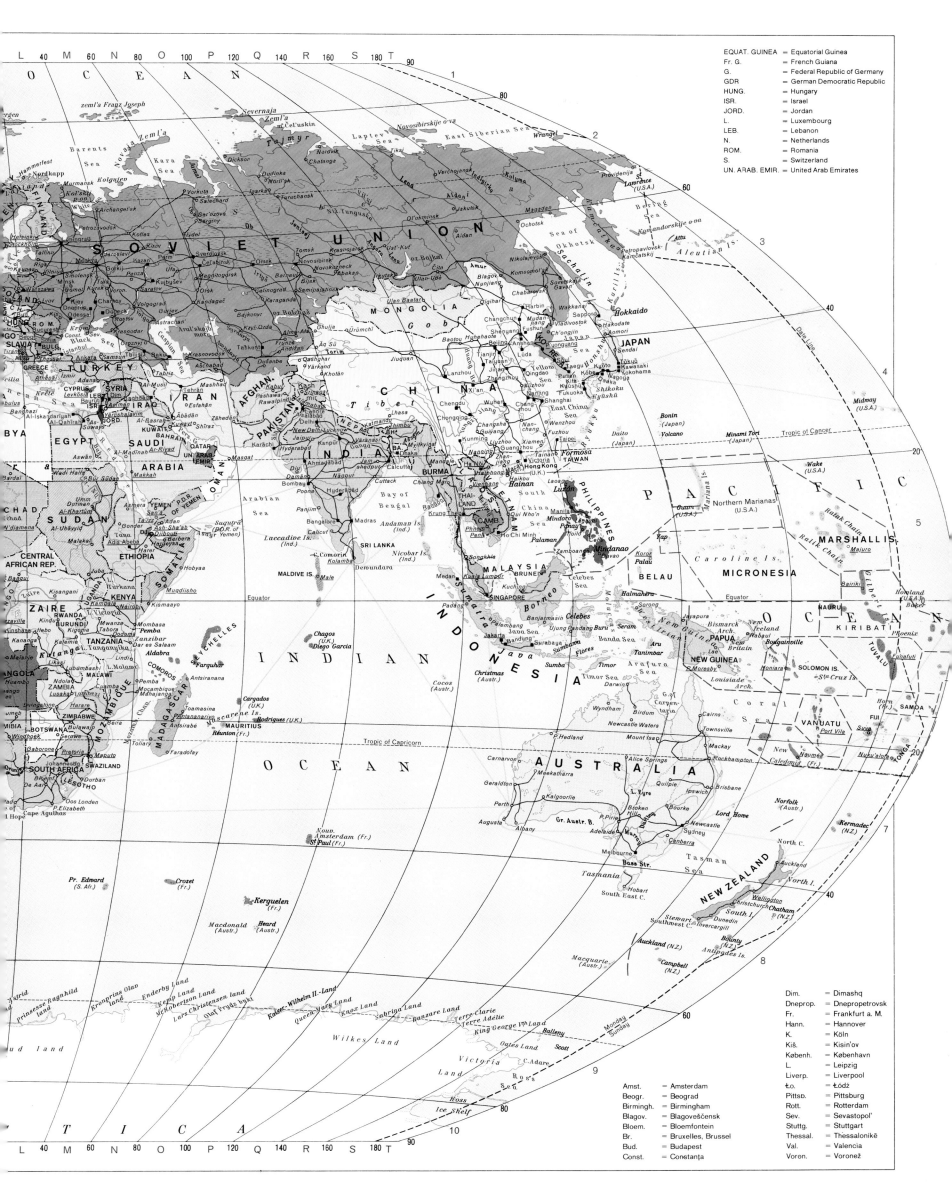

World, political 179

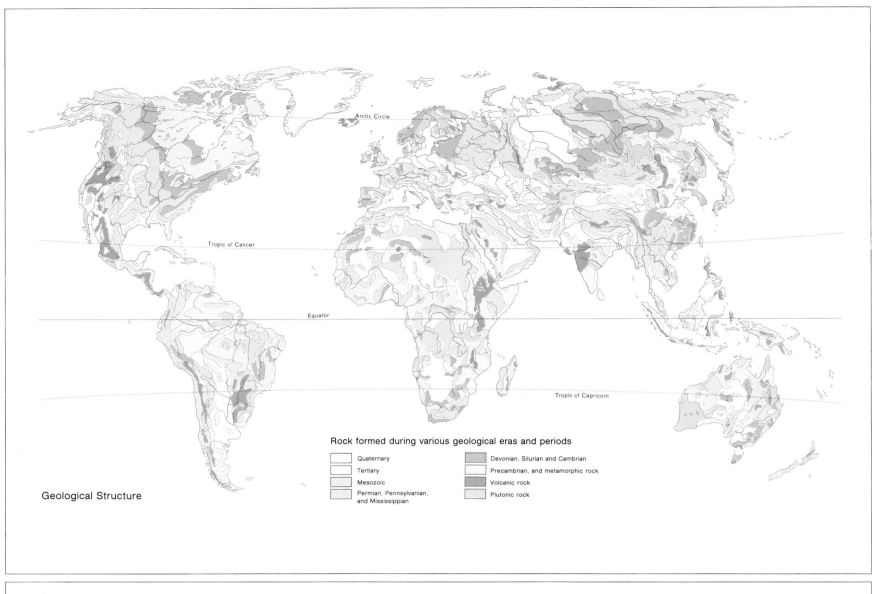

Rock formed during various geological eras and periods

	Quaternary		Devonian, Silurian and Cambrian
	Tertiary		Precambrian, and metamorphic rock
	Mesozoic		Volcanic rock
	Permian, Pennsylvanian, and Mississippian		Plutonic rock

Geological Structure

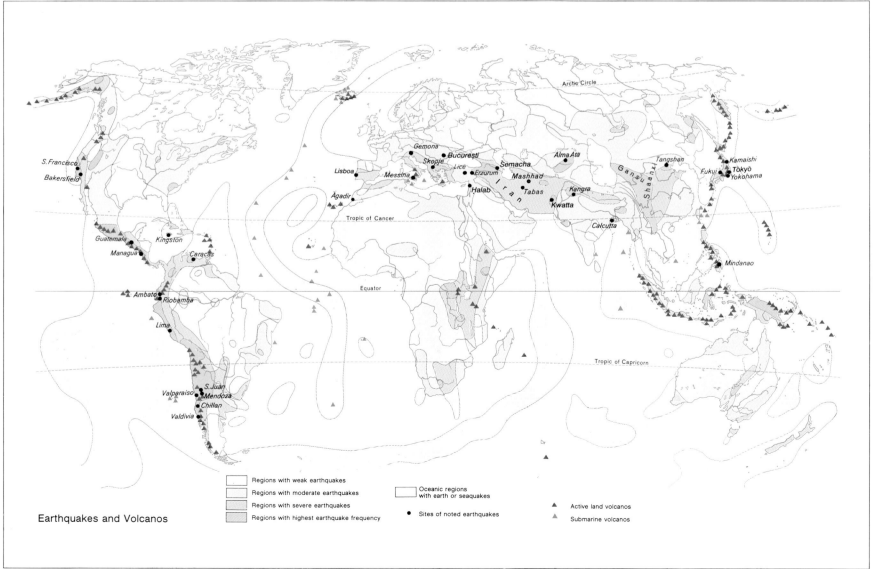

Earthquakes and Volcanos

	Regions with weak earthquakes		Oceanic regions with earth or seaquakes		Active land volcanos
	Regions with moderate earthquakes				Submarine volcanos
	Regions with severe earthquakes				
	Regions with highest earthquake frequency		Sites of noted earthquakes		

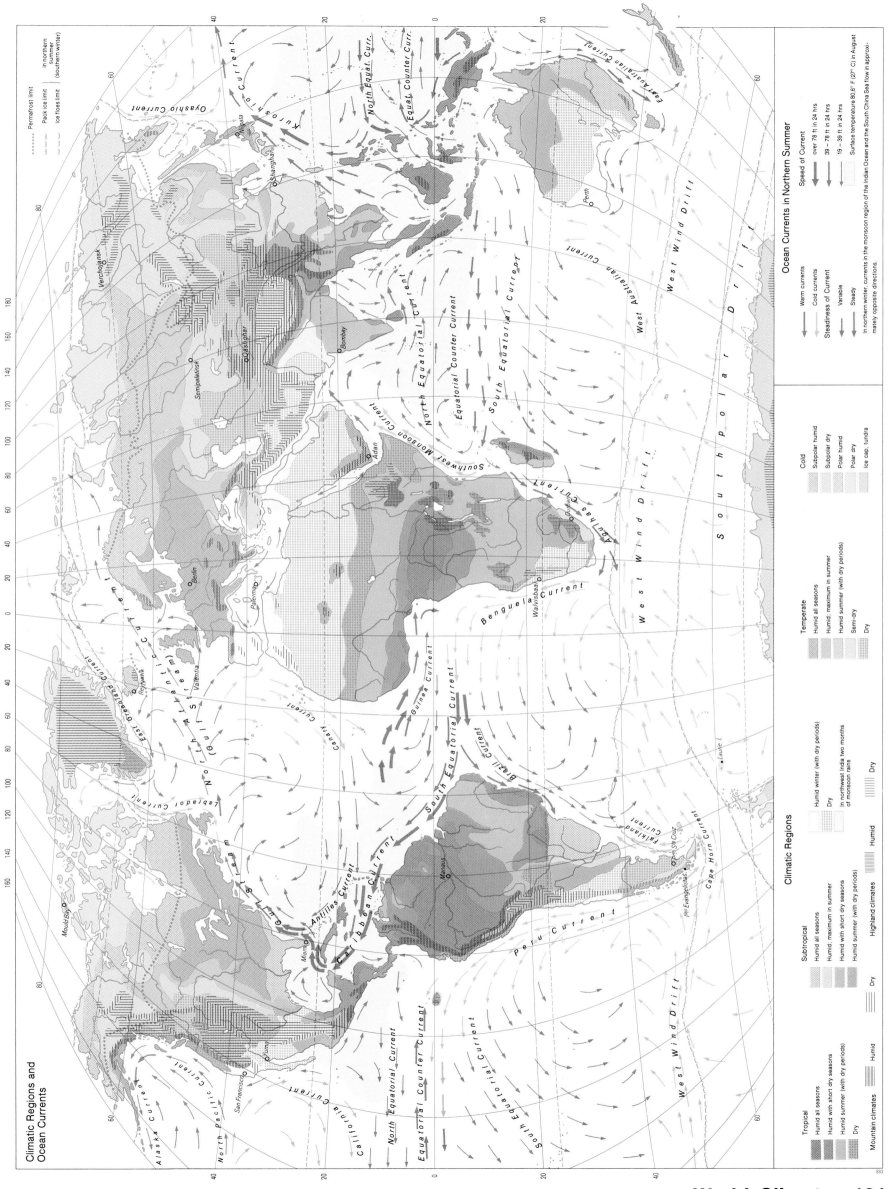

Climatic Regions and Ocean Currents

Scale at the center meridian 1 : 90,000,000   One inch to 1,420 miles

Climatic Regions

Tropical
Humid all seasons
Humid; maximum in summer
Humid with short dry seasons
Humid summer (with dry periods)
Dry
Humid
Mountain climates

Highland climates
Humid
Dry

Subtropical
Humid all seasons
Humid; maximum in summer
Humid with short dry seasons
Humid summer (with dry periods)
Dry
Humid winter (with dry periods)
Dry

In northwest India two months of monsoon rains

Temperate
Humid all seasons
Humid; maximum in summer
Humid summer (with dry periods)
Semi-dry
Dry

Cold
Subpolar humid
Subpolar dry
Polar humid
Polar dry
Ice cap, tundra

Ocean Currents in Northern Summer

Speed of Current
over 78 ft in 24 hrs
39 – 78 ft in 24 hrs
19 – 39 ft in 24 hrs

Surface temperature 80.6° F (27° C) in August

Warm currents
Cold currents

Steadiness of Current
Variable
Steady

In northern winter, currents in the monsoon region of the Indian Ocean and the South China Sea flow in approximately opposite directions.

Permafrost limit
Pack ice limit   in northern summer
Ice floes limit   (southern winter)

World, Climate 181

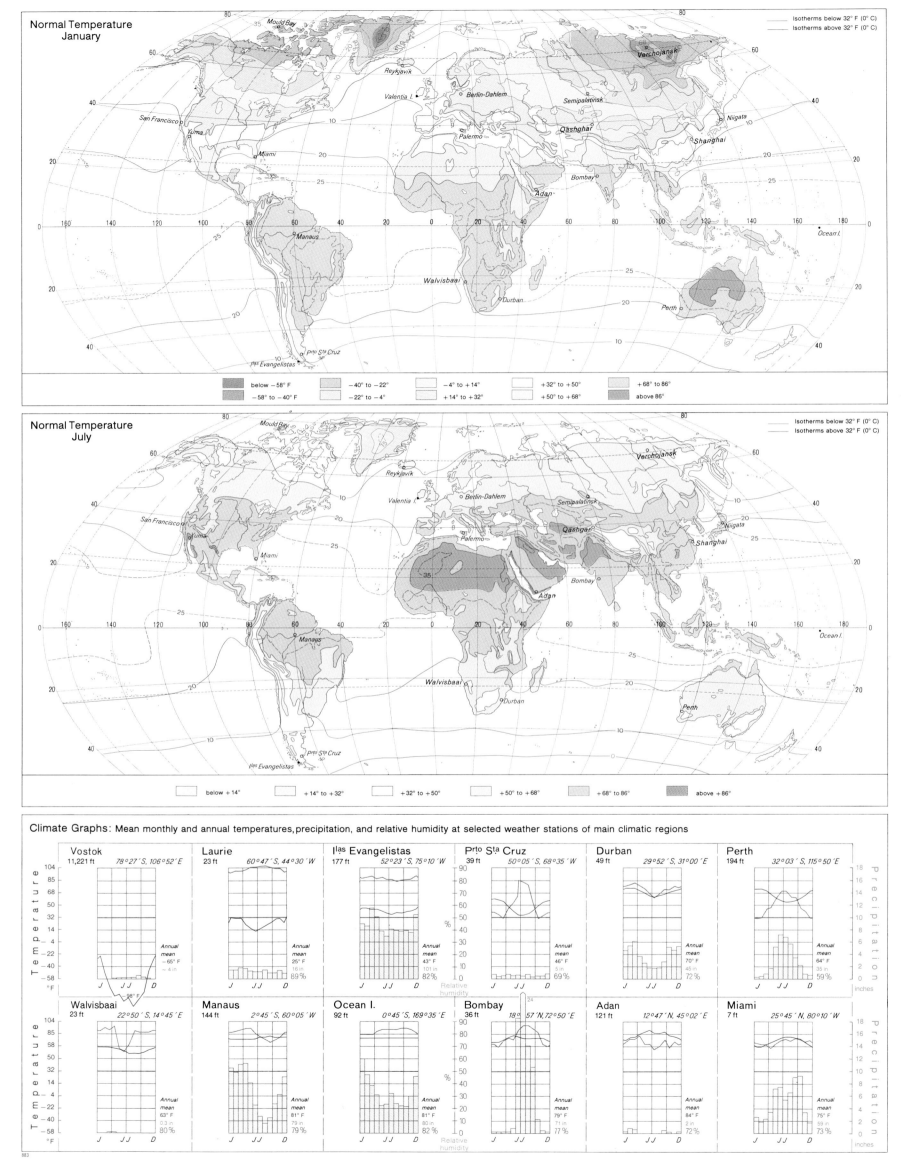

Normal Temperature
January

Isotherms below 32° F (0° C)
Isotherms above 32° F (0° C)

| below −58° F | −40° to −22° | −4° to +14° | +32° to +50° | +68° to 86° |
| −58° to −40° F | −22° to −4° | +14° to +32° | +50° to +68° | above 86° |

Normal Temperature
July

Isotherms below 32° F (0° C)
Isotherms above 32° F (0° C)

| below +14° | +14° to +32° | +32° to +50° | +50° to +68° | +68° to 86° | above +86° |

Climate Graphs: Mean monthly and annual temperatures, precipitation, and relative humidity at selected weather stations of main climatic regions

Vostok
11,221 ft   78°27′ S, 106°52′ E
Annual mean −65° F −4 in 89%

Laurie
23 ft   60°47′ S, 44°30′ W
Annual mean 25° F 16 in 89%

Ilas Evangelistas
177 ft   52°23′ S, 75°10′ W
Annual mean 43° F 101 in 82%

Prto Sta Cruz
39 ft   50°05′ S, 68°35′ W
Annual mean 46° F 5 in 69%

Durban
49 ft   29°52′ S, 31°00′ E
Annual mean 70° F 41 in 72%

Perth
194 ft   32°03′ S, 115°50′ E
Annual mean 64° F 35 in 59%

Walvisbaai
23 ft   22°50′ S, 14°45′ E
Annual mean 63° F 0.3 in 80%

Manaus
144 ft   2°45′ S, 60°05′ W
Annual mean 81° F 79 in 79%

Ocean I.
92 ft   0°45′ S, 169°35′ E
Annual mean 81° F 80 in 82%

Bombay
36 ft   18°57′ N, 72°50′ E
Annual mean 79° F 71 in 77%

Adan
121 ft   12°47′ N, 45°02′ E
Annual mean 84° F 2 in 72%

Miami
7 ft   25°45′ N, 80°10′ W
Annual mean 75° F 59 in 73%

Scale at the center meridian 1 : 162,000,000   One inch to 2.558 miles

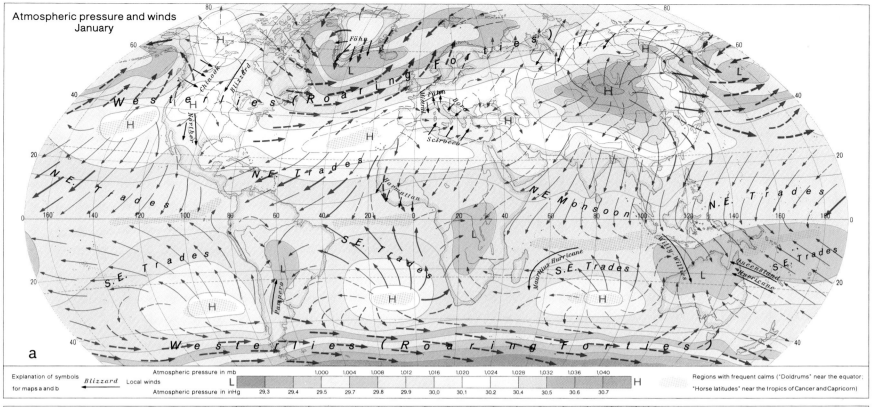

Atmospheric pressure and winds
January

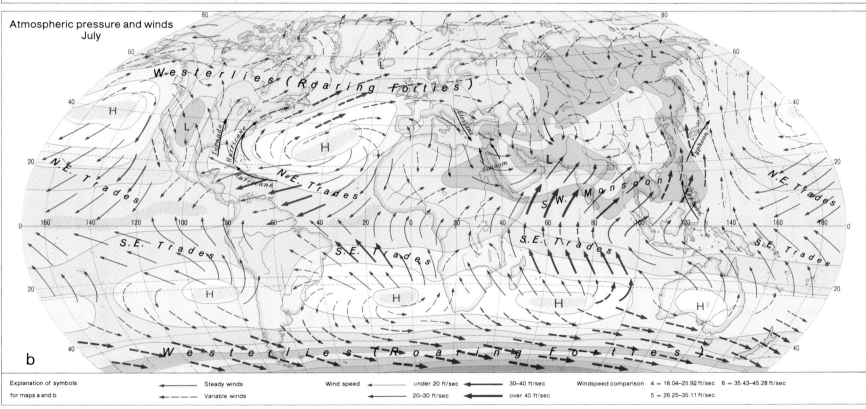

Atmospheric pressure and winds
July

Climate Graphs: Mean monthly and annual temperatures, precipitation, and relative humidity at selected weather stations of main climatic regions

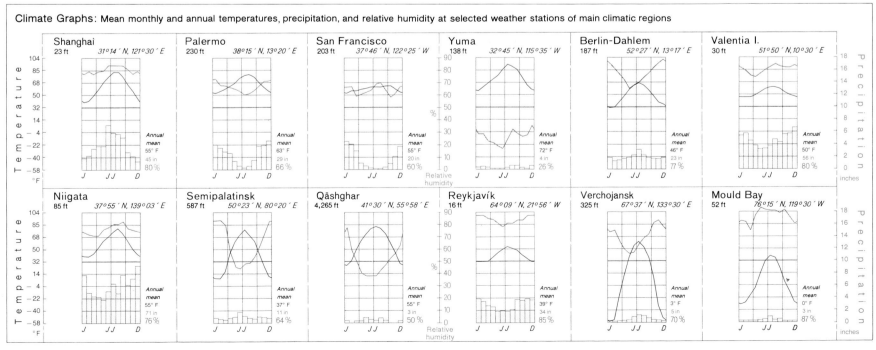

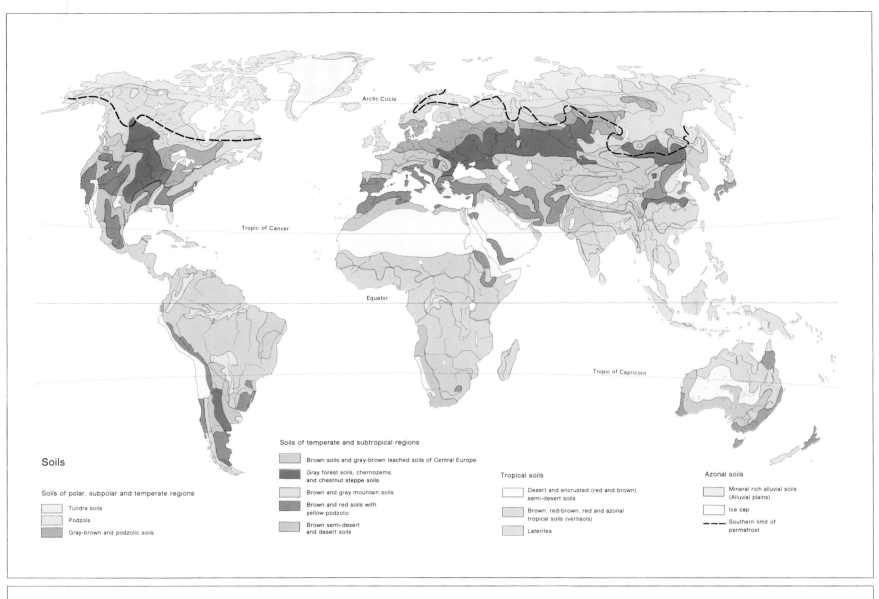

Soils

Soils of polar, subpolar and temperate regions

- Tundra soils
- Podzols
- Gray-brown and podzolic soils

Soils of temperate and subtropical regions

- Brown soils and gray-brown leached soils of Central Europe
- Gray forest soils, chernozems, and chestnut steppe soils
- Brown and gray mountain soils
- Brown and red soils with yellow podzolic
- Brown semi-desert and desert soils

Tropical soils

- Desert and encrusted (red and brown) semi-desert soils
- Brown, red-brown, red and azonal tropical soils (vertisols)
- Laterites

Azonal soils

- Mineral rich alluvial soils (Alluvial plains)
- Ice cap
- Southern limit of permafrost

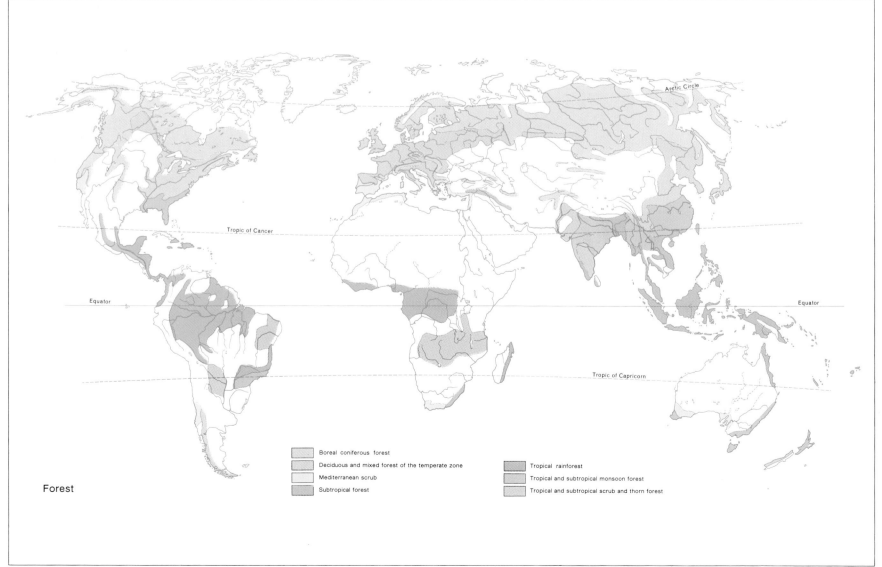

Forest

- Boreal coniferous forest
- Deciduous and mixed forest of the temperate zone
- Mediterranean scrub
- Subtropical forest
- Tropical rainforest
- Tropical and subtropical monsoon forest
- Tropical and subtropical scrub and thorn forest

Scale at the center meridian 1 : 135,000,000   One inch to 2,131 miles

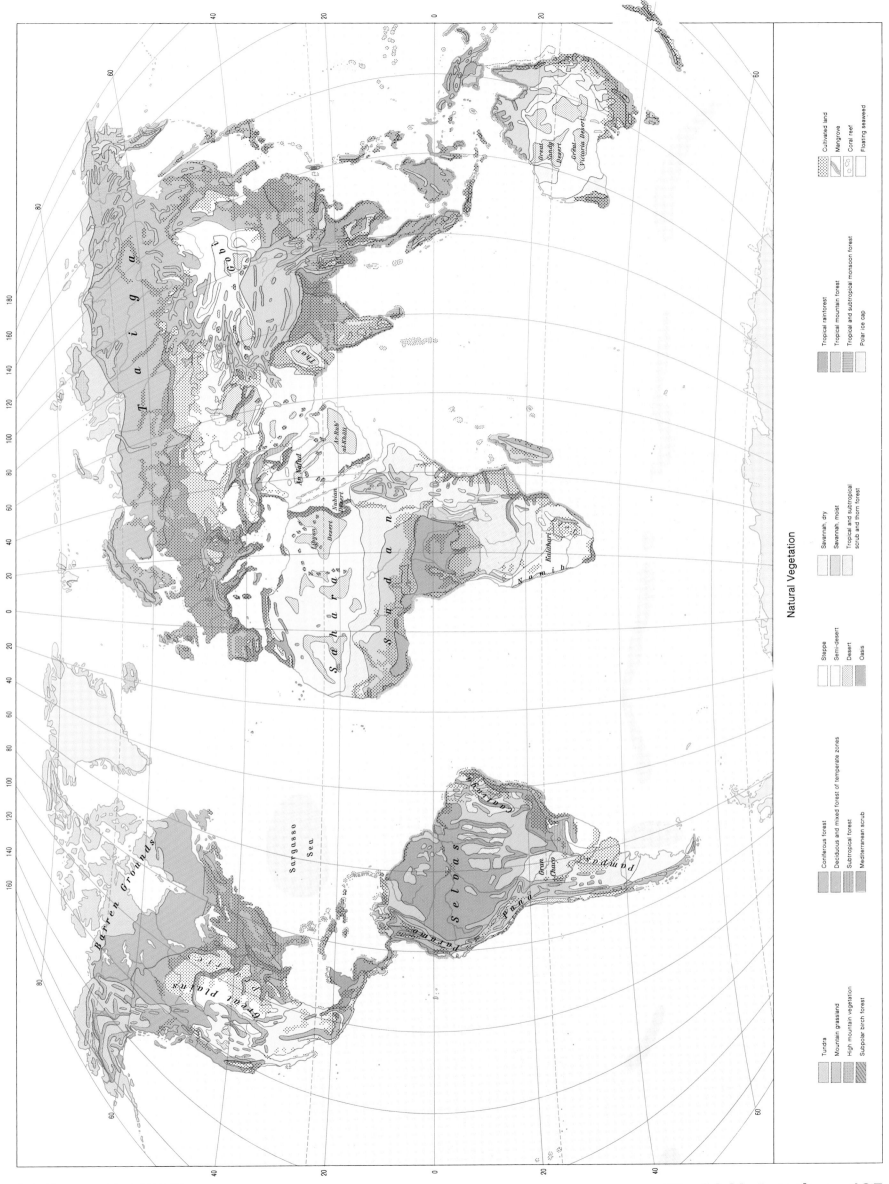

Natural Vegetation

Tundra
Mountain grassland
High mountain vegetation
Subpolar birch forest

Coniferous forest
Deciduous and mixed forest of temperate zones
Subtropical forest
Mediterranean scrub

Steppe
Semi-desert
Desert
Oasis

Savannah, dry
Savannah, moist
Tropical and subtropical scrub and thorn forest

Tropical rainforest
Tropical mountain forest
Tropical and subtropical monsoon forest
Polar ice cap

Cultivated land
Mangrove
Coral reef
Floating seaweed

Scale at the center meridian 1 : 90,000,000   One inch to 1,420 miles

World, Vegetation   185

Agricultural Resources

Grain

////// Wheat

≡≡≡ Rice

\\\\\ Maize (corn)

········· Polar limit of grain cultivation

✓✓✓ Limit of tropical and subtropical millet cultivation in Asia and Africa

Oil Plants

•—•—• Oil palm distribution

—·—·— Coconut tree distribution

◊ Peanuts

∪ Soy beans

Economy and Population Distribution

Industrial areas
over 500 pop./sq. mile

Predominantly agrarian areas
over 500 pop./sq. mile

Areas with 125–500 pop./sq. mile

Areas with 25–125 pop./sq. mile

Sparsely populated areas with 2–25 pop./sq. mile

Uninhabited or sparsely populated areas (steppes, savannahs, deserts and tundras)

Uninhabited or sparsely populated forest areas

Major fishing areas

Scale at the center meridian 1 : 67,500,000   One inch to 1,065 miles

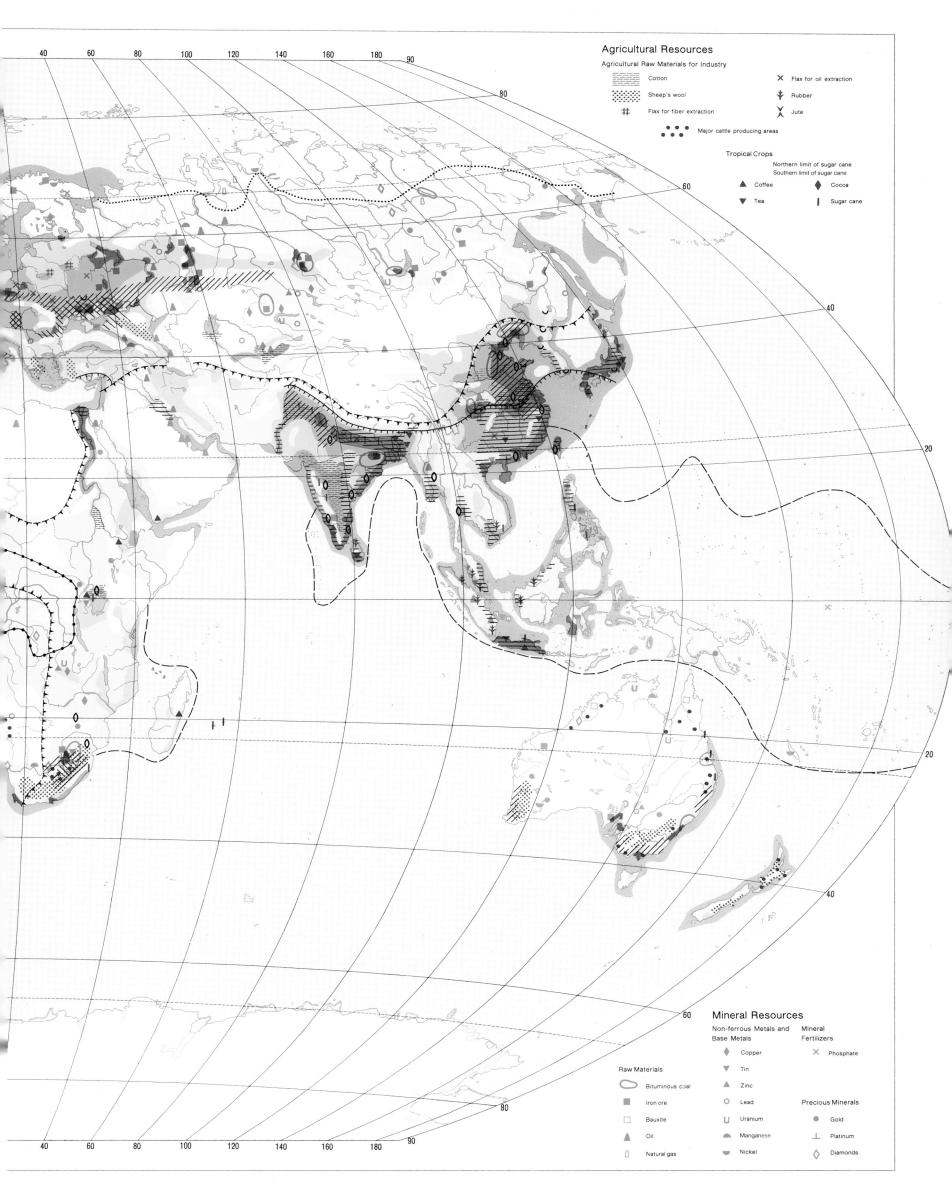

Agricultural Resources

Agricultural Raw Materials for Industry

≡ Cotton		✕ Flax for oil extraction	
⠿ Sheep's wool		↓ Rubber	
⌗ Flax for fiber extraction		⅄ Jute	
⣿ Major cattle producing areas			

Tropical Crops

Northern limit of sugar cane
Southern limit of sugar cane

▲ Coffee	◆ Cocoa
▼ Tea	▮ Sugar cane

Mineral Resources

Non-ferrous Metals and Base Metals	Mineral Fertilizers
◆ Copper	✕ Phosphate
▼ Tin	
▲ Zinc	
○ Lead	Precious Minerals
U Uranium	● Gold
⬓ Manganese	⊥ Platinum
▽ Nickel	◇ Diamonds

Raw Materials

| ⬭ Bituminous coal |
| ▪ Iron ore |
| ▫ Bauxite |
| ▲ Oil |
| ⬠ Natural gas |

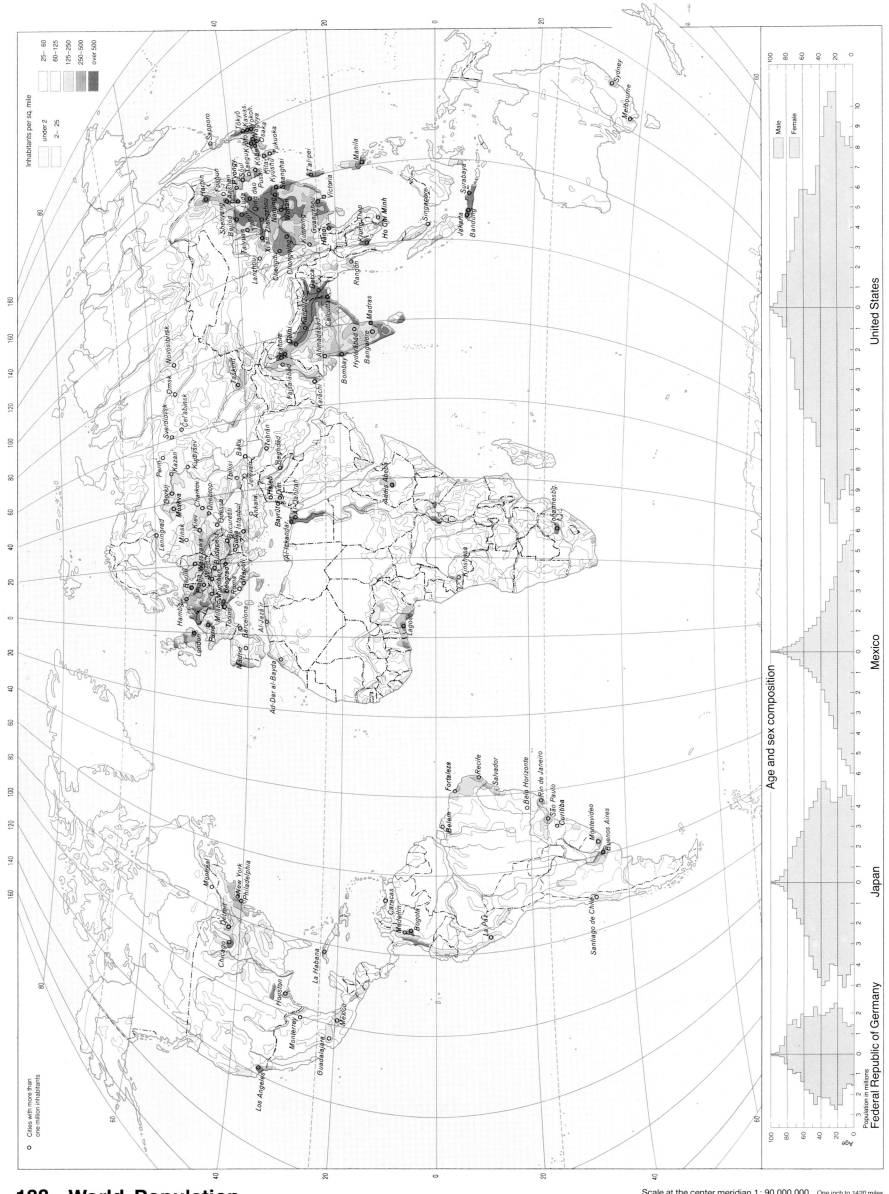

Inhabitants per sq. mile

under 2
2– 25
25– 60
60–125
125–250
250–500
over 500

○ Cities with more than
one million inhabitants

Age and sex composition

Male
Female

United States

Mexico

Japan

Federal Republic of Germany

Population in millions

Sydney

Melbourne

Sapporo
Tōkyō
Kawas.
Kyōto Nagoya
Ōsaka
Kōbe Yokoh.
Kita-kyūshū
Kyūshū
Fukuoka
Harbin
Fushun
Anshan
P'yōngyang
Sōul
Pusan
Ta'i-pei
Shenyang
Beijing
Taiyuan
Tianjin
Dalian
Qing'dao
Jinan
Lanzhou
Zhengzhou
Nanjing
Nantong
Shanghai
Chengdu
Chongqing
Wuhan
Kunming
Guangzhou
Guiyang
Victoria
Hanoi
Manila
Rangon
Krung Thep
Ho Chi Minh
Singapore
Jakarta
Surabaya
Bandung
Dacca
Calcutta
Kanpur
Delhi
Lahore
Faisalabad
Madras
Bombay
Hyderābād
Bangalore
Karāchi
Novosibirsk
Omsk
Sverdlovsk
Chelabinsk
Taskent
Baku
Tbilisi
Tehrān
Baghdad
Yerevan
Aleppo
Al-Qāhirah
Al-Iskandar.
Bayrūt
Dim.
Ankara
Istanbul
Addis Abeba
Kazan
Perm'
Gorkiy
Kuybyšev
Kharkov
Dnepropr
Odessa
Kiev
Moskva
Minsk
Leningrad
Bucureşti
Sofija
Beograd
Budapest
Warszawa
Praha
Wien
Roma
Napoli
München
Berlin
Hamburg
Paris
London
Madrid
Barcelona
Al-Jazā'ir
Ad-Dar al-Bayda
Lagos
Kinshasa
Johannesbg.

Montreal
New York
Philadelphia
Chicago
Detroit
Houston
La Habana
Caracas
Medellín
Bogotá
Paz
Los Angeles
Monterrey
Guadalajara
Mexico
Santiago de Chile
Montevideo
Buenos Aires
Curitiba
São Paulo
Rio de Janeiro
Belo Horizonte
Salvador
Recife
Fortaleza
Belém

Scale at the center meridian 1 : 90,000,000   One inch to 1,420 miles

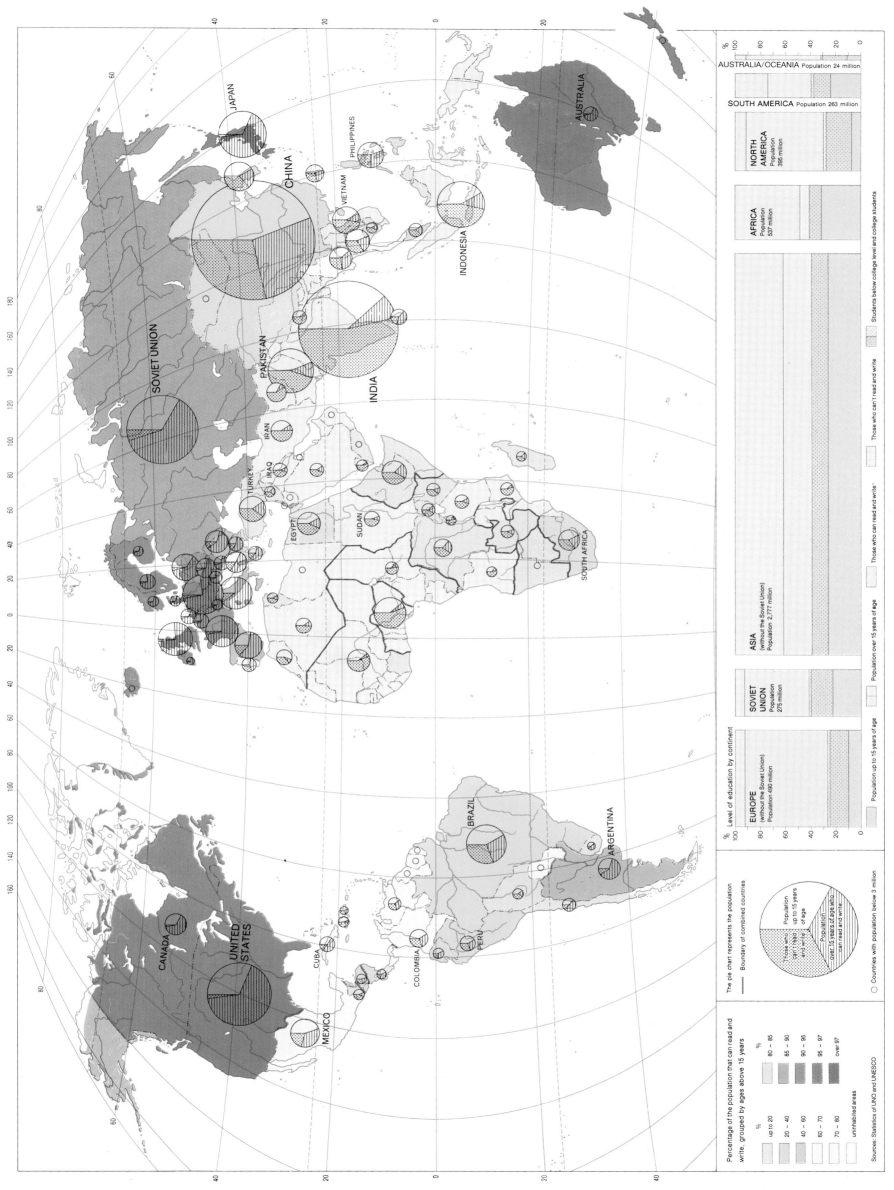

JAPAN

CHINA

PHILIPPINES

VIETNAM

INDONESIA

SOVIET UNION

PAKISTAN

INDIA

IRAN

TURKEY

IRAQ

EGYPT

SUDAN

SOUTH AFRICA

AUSTRALIA

BRAZIL

ARGENTINA

PERU

COLOMBIA

CUBA

MEXICO

UNITED STATES

CANADA

Scale at the center meridian 1 : 90,000,000   One inch to 1420 miles

Level of education by continent

AUSTRALIA/OCEANIA Population 24 million

SOUTH AMERICA Population 263 million

NORTH AMERICA Population 395 million

AFRICA Population 537 million

ASIA (without the Soviet Union) Population 2,777 million

SOVIET UNION Population 275 million

EUROPE (without the Soviet Union) Population 490 million

Population up to 15 years of age

Population over 15 years of age

Those who can read and write

Those who can't read and write

Students below college level and college students

The pie chart represents the population

Boundary of combined countries

Population up to 15 years of age

Population over 15 years of age who can read and write

Those who can't read and write

Countries with population below 3 million

Percentage of the population that can read and write, grouped by ages above 15 years

%
80 – 85
85 – 90
90 – 95
95 – 97
over 97

%
up to 20
20 – 40
40 – 60
60 – 70
70 – 80
uninhabited areas

Sources: Statistics of UNO and UNESCO

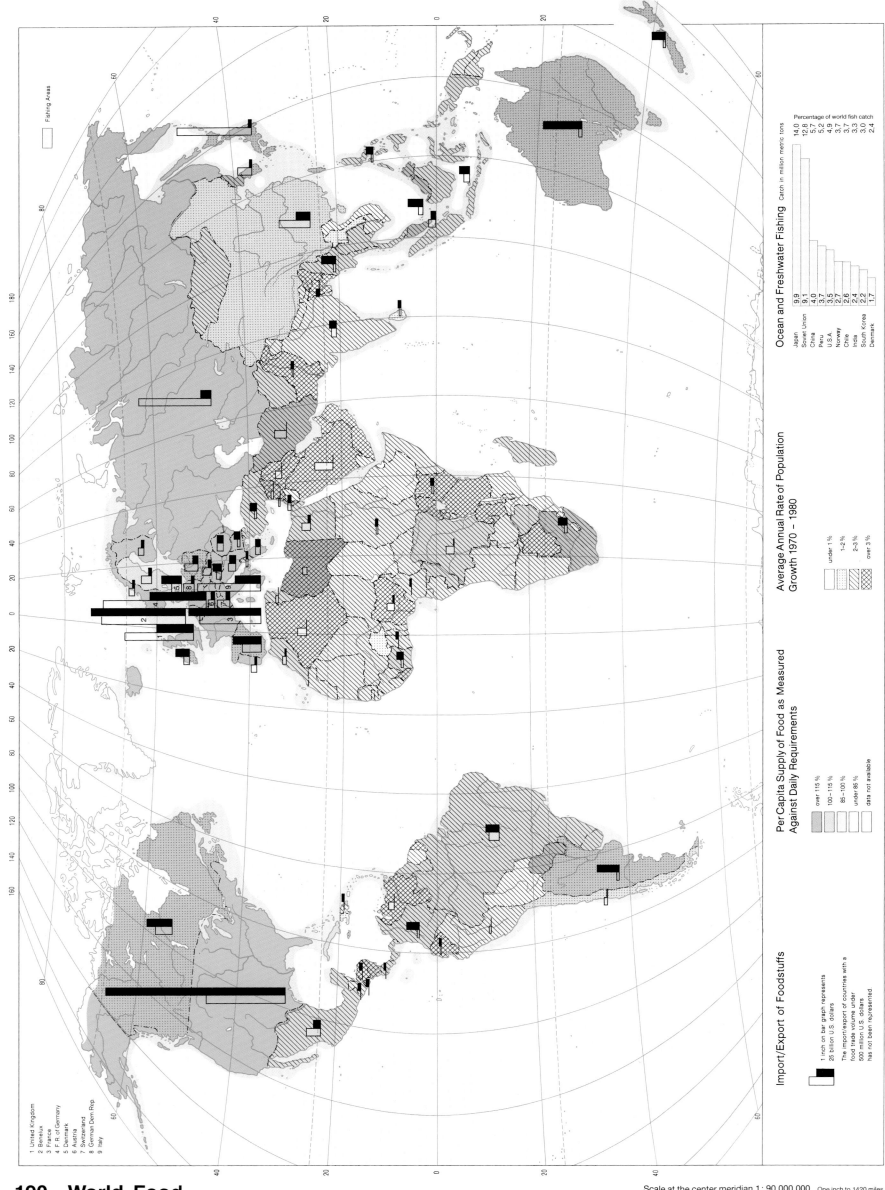

1 United Kingdom
2 Benelux
3 France
4 F R of Germany
5 Denmark
6 Austria
7 Switzerland
8 German Dem Rep
9 Italy

Fishing Areas

Import/Export of Foodstuffs

1 inch on bar graph represents
25 billion U.S. dollars

The import/export of countries with a
food trade volume under
500 million U.S. dollars
has not been represented

**Per Capita Supply of Food as Measured
Against Daily Requirements**

over 115 %
100–115 %
85–100 %
under 85 %
data not available

**Average Annual Rate of Population
Growth 1970 – 1980**

under 1 %
1–2 %
2–3 %
over 3 %

Ocean and Freshwater Fishing Catch in million metric tons

Percentage of world fish catch

Japan	9.9	14.0
Soviet Union	9.1	12.8
China	4.0	5.7
Peru	3.7	5.2
U.S.A.	3.5	4.9
Norway	2.7	3.7
Chile	2.6	3.7
India	2.4	3.3
South Korea	2.2	3.0
Denmark	1.7	2.4

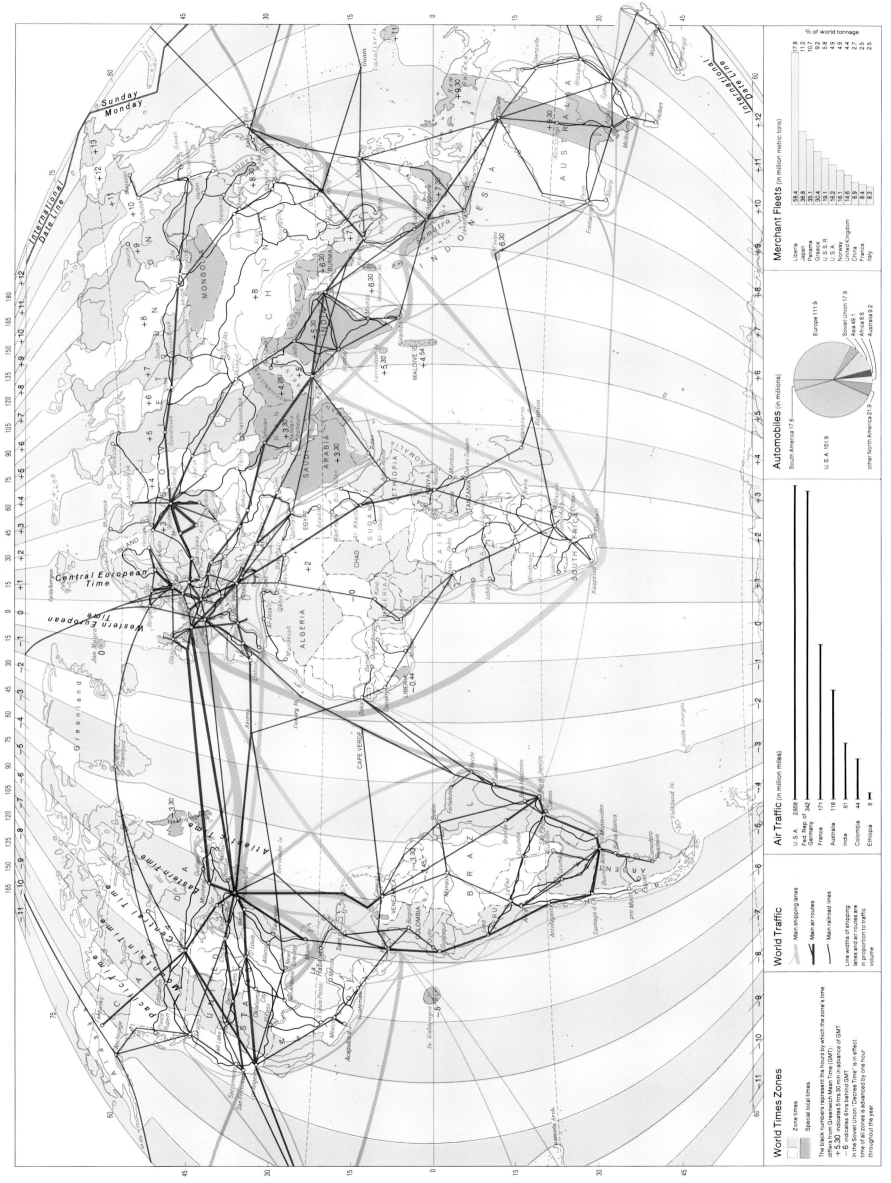

Scale at the center meridian 1 : 90,000,000 One inch to 1,420 miles

World Times Zones

Zone times

Special local times

The black numbers represent the hours by which the zone's time differs from Greenwich Mean Time (GMT).

+5.30 indicates 5 hrs 30 min in advance of GMT

−6 indicates 6 hrs behind GMT

In the Soviet Union "Decree Time" is in effect, time of all zones is advanced by one hour throughout the year

World Traffic

Main shipping lanes

Main air routes

Main railroad lines

Line widths of shipping lanes and air routes are in proportion to traffic volume

Air Traffic (in million miles)

U.S.A.	2,668
Fed. Rep. of	342
Germany	
France	171
Australia	118
India	61
Colombia	44
Ethiopia	8

Automobiles (in millions)

South America 17.6

U.S.A. 151.9

Europe 111.9

Soviet Union 17.9

Asia 49.1

Africa 8.6

Australia 9.2

other North America 21.9

Merchant Fleets (in million metric tons)

		% of world tonnage
Liberia	58.4	17.8
Japan	36.8	11.2
Panama	35.1	10.7
Greece	30.4	9.2
U.S.S.R.	19.1	5.9
U.S.A.	16.2	4.9
Norway	16.1	4.9
United Kingdom	14.6	4.4
China	8.9	2.7
France	8.4	2.5
Italy	8.3	2.5

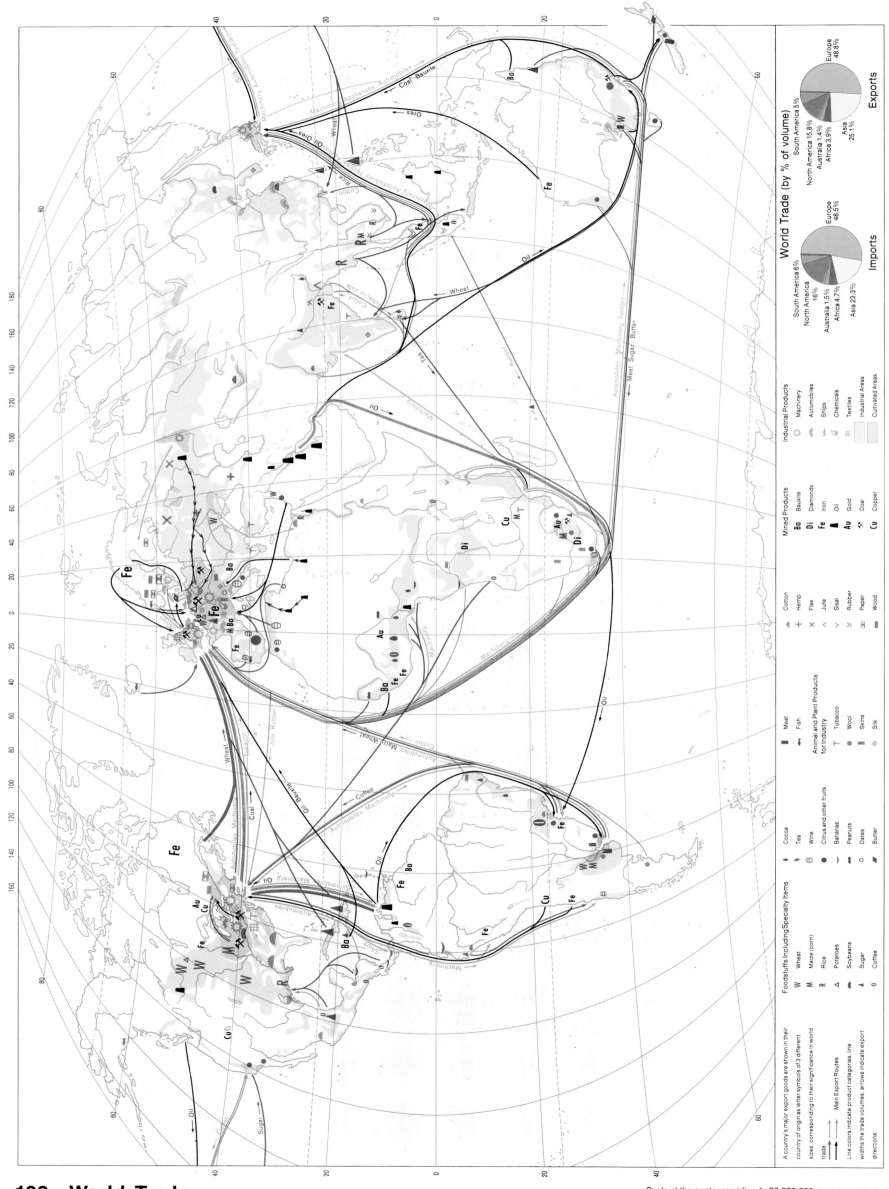

Scale at the center meridian 1 : 90,000,000   One inch to 1,420 miles

A country's major export goods are shown in their
country of origin as letter symbols of 3 different
sizes, corresponding to their significance in world
trade.

Line colors indicate product categories, line
widths the trade volumes, arrows indicate export
directions.

→ trade   ← Main Export Routes

Foodstuffs Including Specialty Items

W   Wheat
M   Maize (corn)
R   Rice
△   Potatoes
▲   Soybeans
◣   Sugar
O   Coffee

◆   Cocoa
◖   Tea
◐   Wine
●   Citrus and other fruits
)   Bananas
○   Peanuts
◢   Dates
◪   Butter

Mined Products

Ba   Bauxite
Di   Diamonds
Fe   Iron
◤   Oil
Au   Gold
Cu   Copper

Industrial Products

✿   Machinery
✕   Automobiles
⚓   Ships
⚙   Chemicals
▦   Textiles

▨   Industrial Areas
░   Cultivated Areas

Animal and Plant Products for Industry

+   Hemp
✕   Flax
<   Jute
>   Sisal
◇   Rubber
▦   Paper
▬   Wood

◼   Meat
➤   Fish
T   Tobacco
●   Wool
▮   Skins
✳   Silk

| Cotton |

World Trade (by % of volume)

Imports

Europe 48.5%
Asia 23.3%
Africa 4.7%
Australia 1.5%
North America 16%
South America 6%

Exports

Europe 48.8%
Asia 25.1%
Africa 3.9%
Australia 1.4%
South America 5%
North America 15.8%

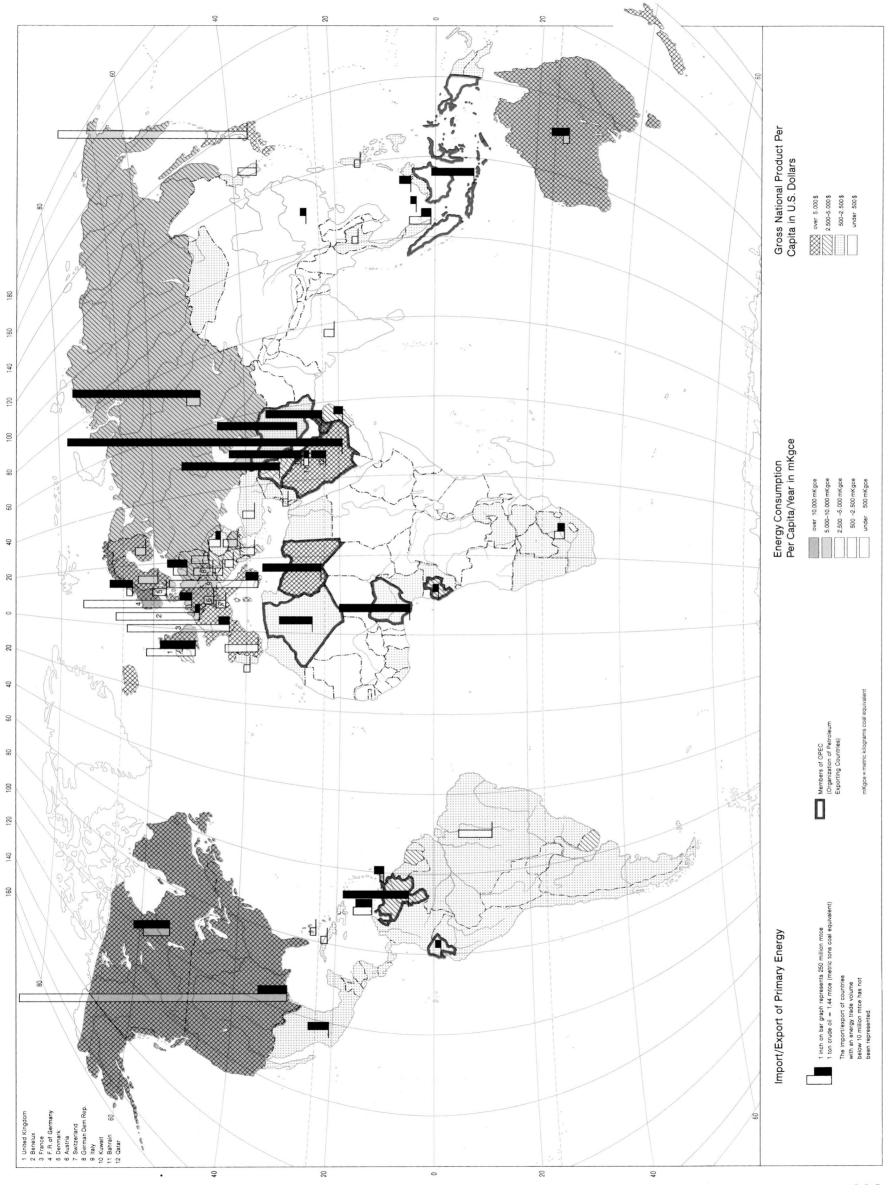

Gross National Product Per
Capita in U.S. Dollars

over 5,000 $		2,500–5,000 $
500–2,500 $		under 500 $

Energy Consumption
Per Capita/Year in mKgce

over 10,000 mKgce		5,000–10,000 mKgce
2,500–5,000 mKgce		500–2,500 mKgce
under 500 mKgce		

Members of OPEC
(Organization of Petroleum
Exporting Countries)

mKgce = metric kilograms coal equivalent

Import/Export of Primary Energy

1 inch on bar graph represents 250 million mtce
1 ton crude oil = 1.44 mtce (metric tons coal equivalent)

The import/export of countries
with an energy trade volume
below 10 million mtce has not
been represented.

1 United Kingdom
2 Benelux
3 France
4 F R of Germany
5 Denmark
6 Austria
7 Switzerland
8 German Dem. Rep.
9 Italy
10 Kuwait
11 Bahrain
12 Qatar

Scale at the center meridian 1 : 90,000,000   One inch to 1,420 miles

World, Energy   193

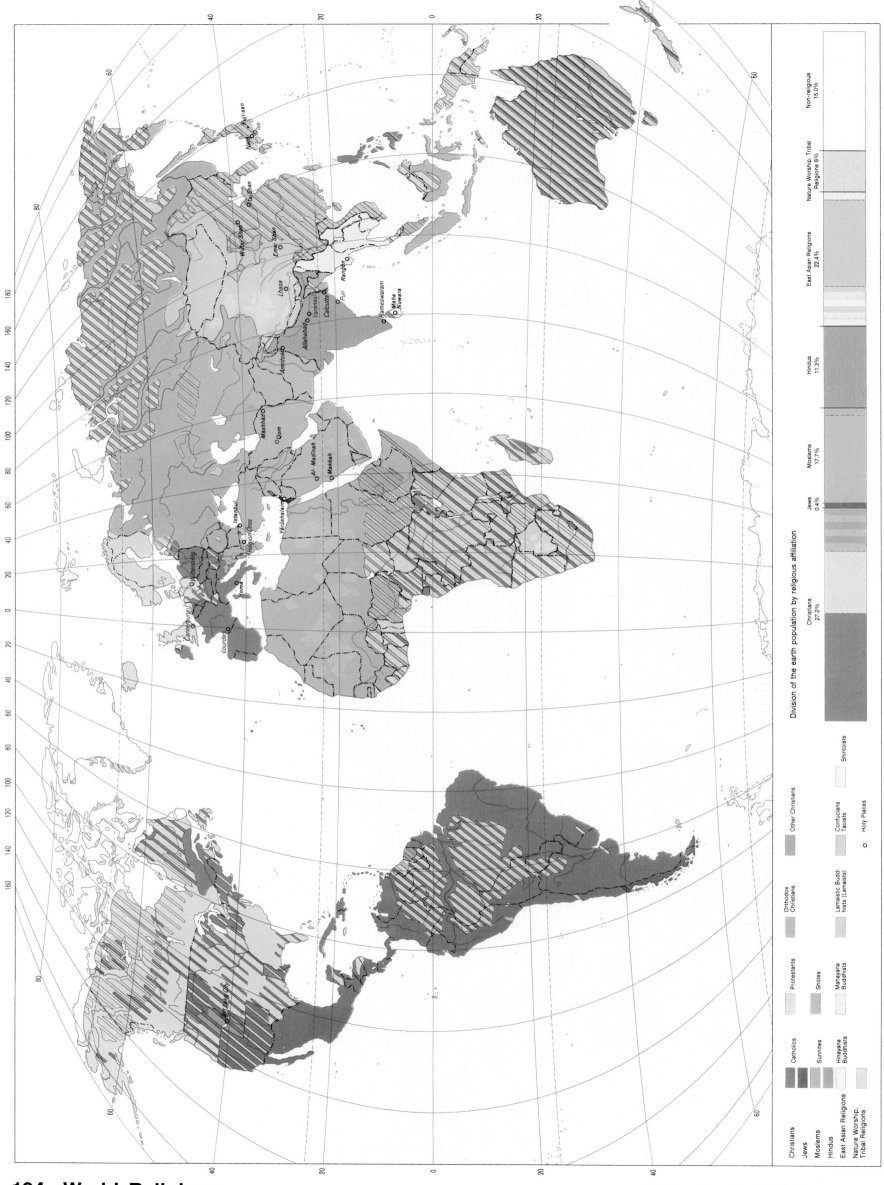

Division of the earth population by religious affiliation

| Christians 27.2% | Jews 0.4% | Moslems 17.7% | Hindus 11.3% | East Asian Religions 22.4% | Nature Worship, Tribal Religions 6% | Non-religious 15.0% |

Christians
  Catholics
  Protestants
  Orthodox Christians
  Other Christians

Jews

Moslems
  Sunnites
  Shiites

Hindus

East Asian Religions
  Hinayana Buddhists
  Mahayana Buddhists
  Lamaistic Buddhists (Lamaists)
  Confucians Taoists
  Shintoists

Nature Worship, Tribal Religions

○ Holy Places

Scale at the center meridian 1 : 90,000,000   One inch to 1,420 miles

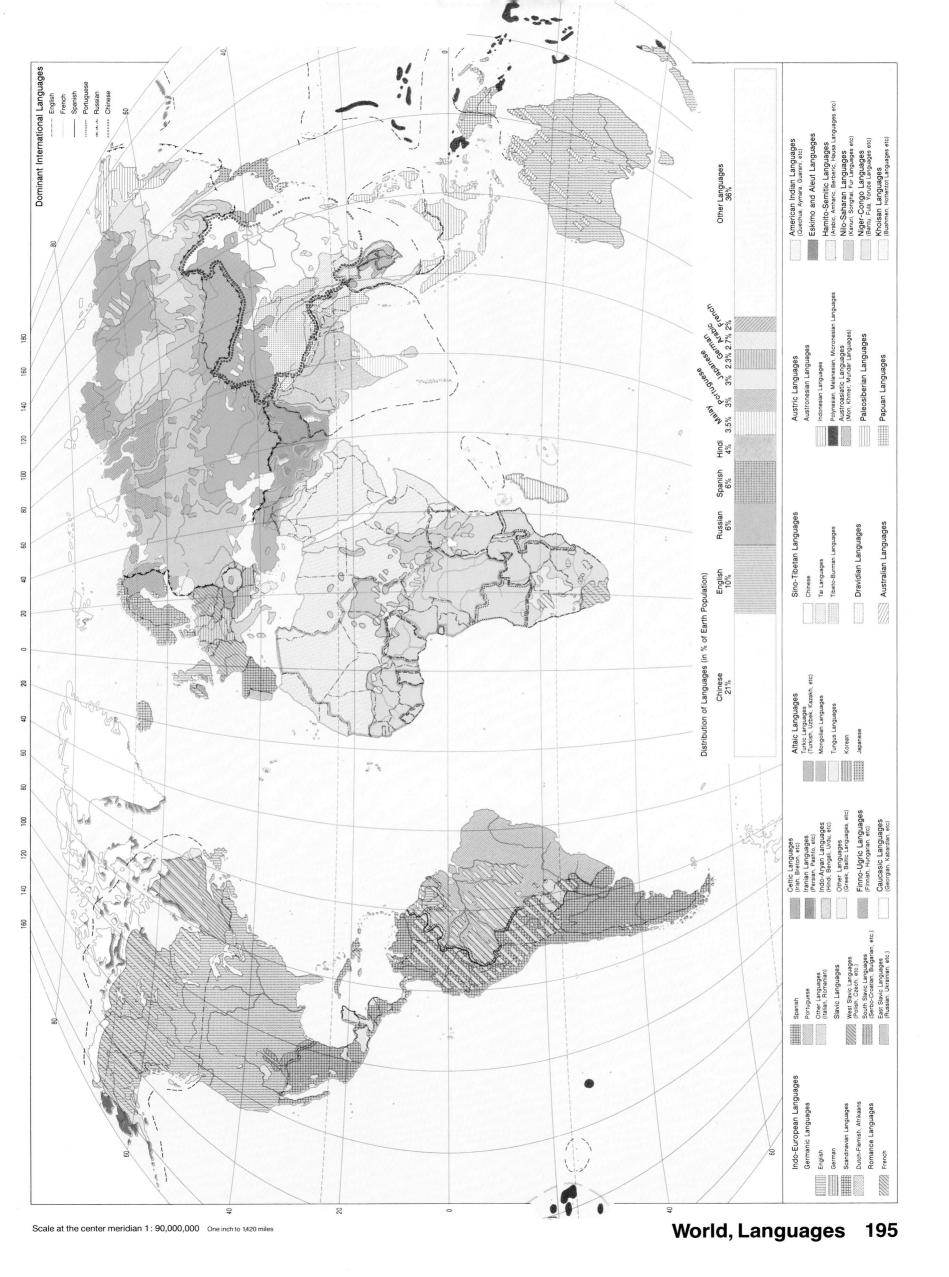

Dominant International Languages

English
French
Spanish
Portuguese
Russian
Chinese

Distribution of Languages (in % of Earth Population)

Chinese 21%
English 10%
Russian 6%
Spanish 6%
Hindi 4%
Malay 3.5%
Portuguese 3%
Japanese 3%
German 2.3%
Arabic 2.7%
French 2%
Other Languages 36%

Indo-European Languages

Germanic Languages
English
German
Scandinavian Languages
Dutch-Flemish, Afrikaans
Romance Languages
French

Spanish
Portuguese
Other Languages
(Italian, Romanian)
Slavic Languages
West Slavic Languages
(Polish, Czech, etc)
South Slavic Languages
(Serbo-Croatian, Bulgarian, etc)
East Slavic Languages
(Russian, Ukrainian, etc)

Celtic Languages
(Irish, Breton, etc)
Iranian Languages
(Persian, Pashto, etc)
Indo-Aryan Languages
(Hindi, Bengali, Urdu, etc)
Other Languages
(Greek, Baltic Languages, etc)
Finno-Ugric Languages
(Finnish, Hungarian, etc)
Caucasic Languages
(Georgian, Kabardian, etc)

Altaic Languages
Turkic Languages
(Turkish, Uzbek, Kazakh, etc)
Mongolian Languages
Tungus Languages
Korean
Japanese

Sino-Tibetan Languages
Chinese
Tai Languages
Tibeto-Burman Languages
Dravidian Languages
Australian Languages

Austric Languages
Austronesian Languages
Indonesian Languages
Polynesian, Melanesian, Micronesian Languages
Austroasiatic Languages
(Mon, Khmer, Munda Languages)
Paleosiberian Languages
Papuan Languages

American Indian Languages
(Quechua, Aymara, Guaraní, etc)
Eskimo and Aleut Languages
Hamito-Semitic Languages
(Arabic, Amharic, Berberic, Hausa Languages etc)
Nilo-Saharan Languages
(Kanuri, Songhai, Fur Languages etc)
Niger-Congo Languages
(Bantu, Fula, Yoruba Languages etc)
Khoisan Languages
(Bushmen, Hottentot Languages etc)

Scale at the center meridian 1 : 90,000,000   One inch to 1,420 miles

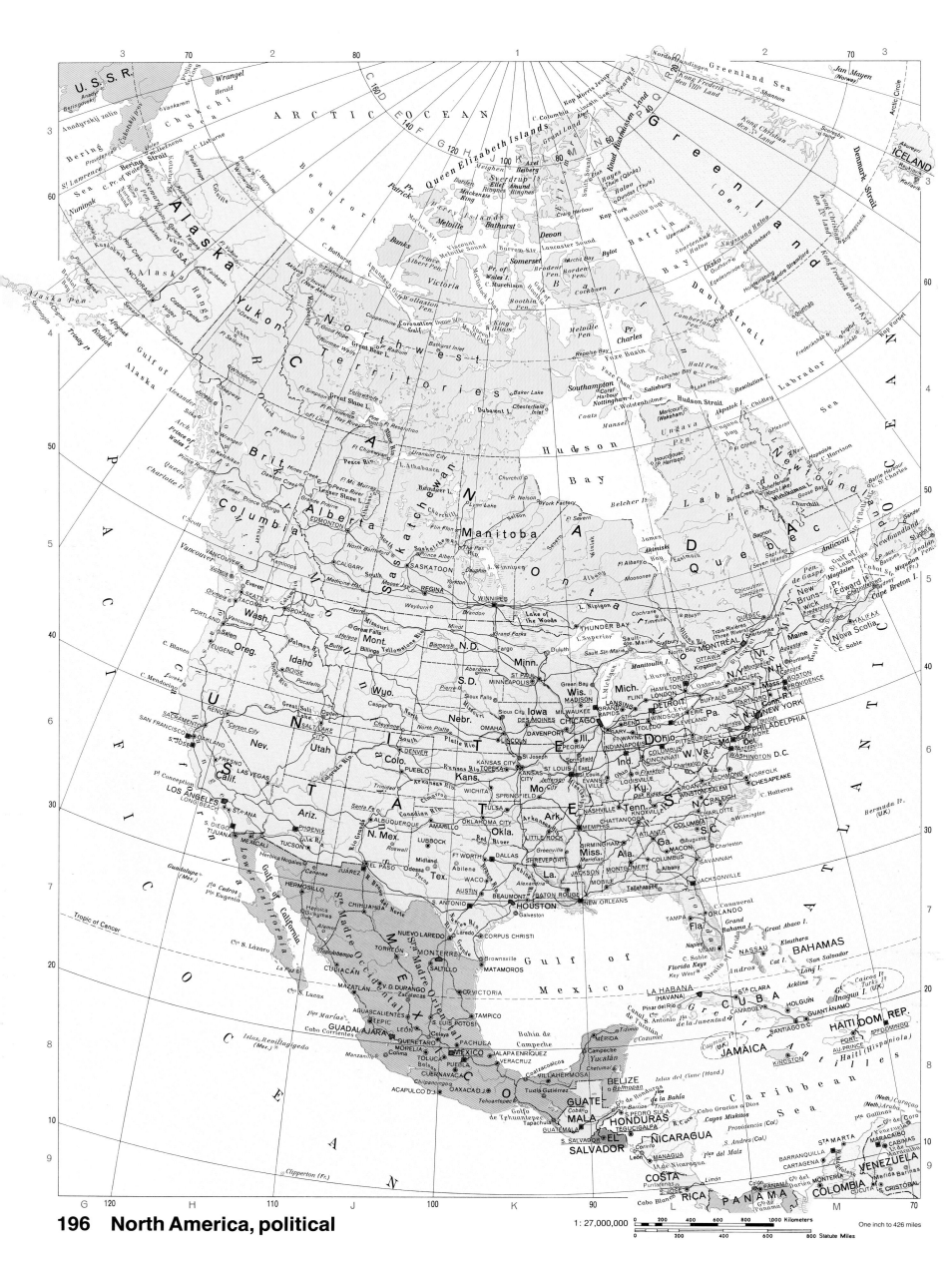

196 North America, political

1 : 27,000,000

One inch to 426 miles

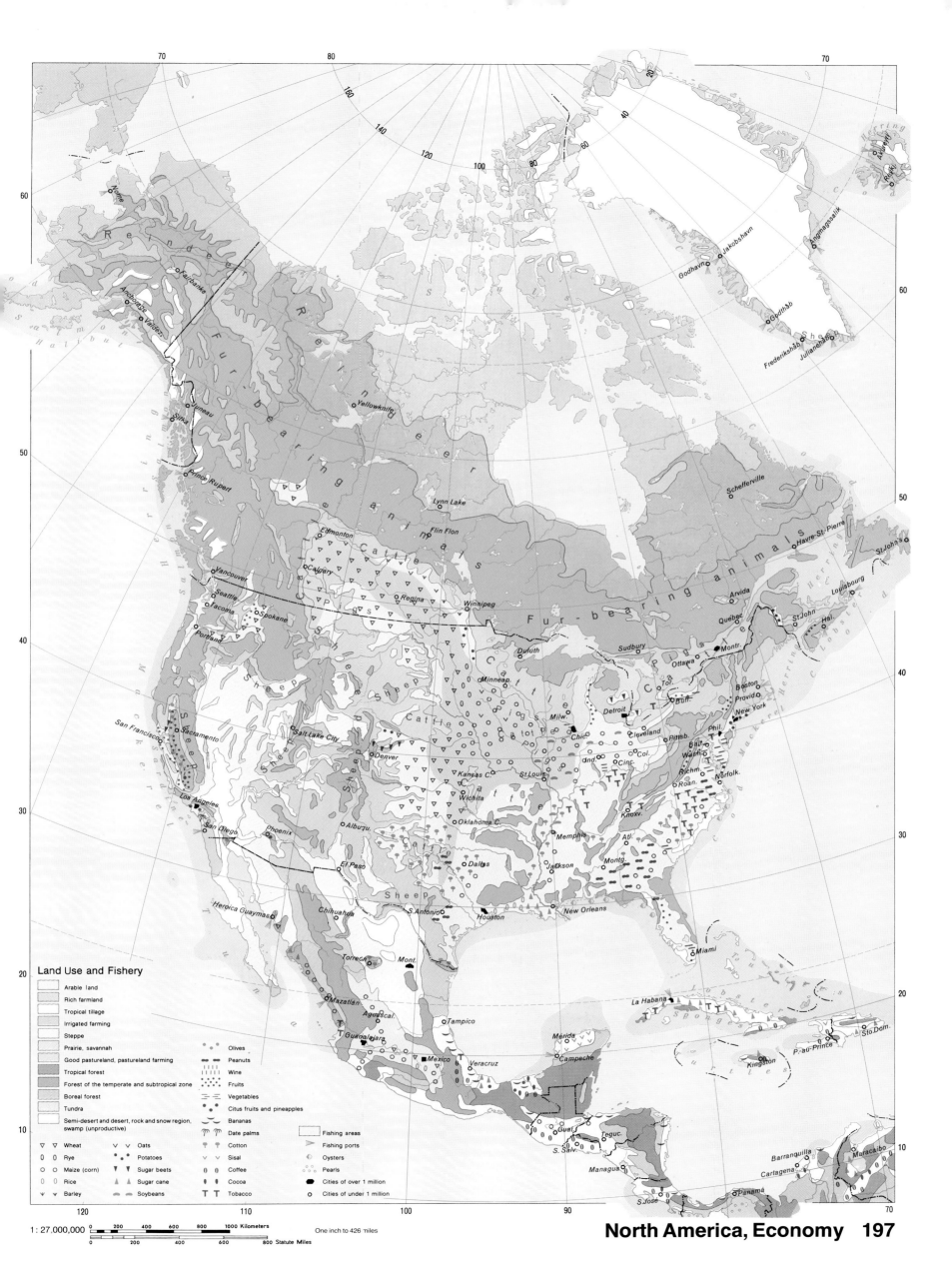

Land Use and Fishery

Arable land
Rich farmland
Tropical tillage
Irrigated farming
Steppe
Prairie, savannah
Good pastureland, pastureland farming
Tropical forest
Forest of the temperate and subtropical zone
Boreal forest
Tundra
Semi-desert and desert, rock and snow region, swamp (unproductive)

▽ ▽ Wheat
0 0 Rye
○ ○ Maize (corn)
0 0 Rice
↓ ↓ Barley

∨ ∨ Oats
•• •• Potatoes
▼ ▼ Sugar beets
▲ ▲ Sugar cane
⌒ ⌒ Soybeans

•• •• Olives
— — Peanuts
||||| Wine
⌇ ⌇ Fruits
∨ ∨ Vegetables
•• •• Citus fruits and pineapples
⌒⌒ Bananas
⋔⋔ ⋔⋔ Date palms
⊤ ⊤ Cotton
∨ ∨ Sisal
0 0 Coffee
♦ ♦ Cocoa
T T Tobacco

☐ Fishing areas
➤ Fishing ports
◇ Oysters
∴ Pearls
■ Cities of over 1 million
○ Cities of under 1 million

1 : 27,000,000
200 400 600 800 1000 Kilometers
0   200   400   600   800 Statute Miles
One inch to 426 miles

North America, Economy   197

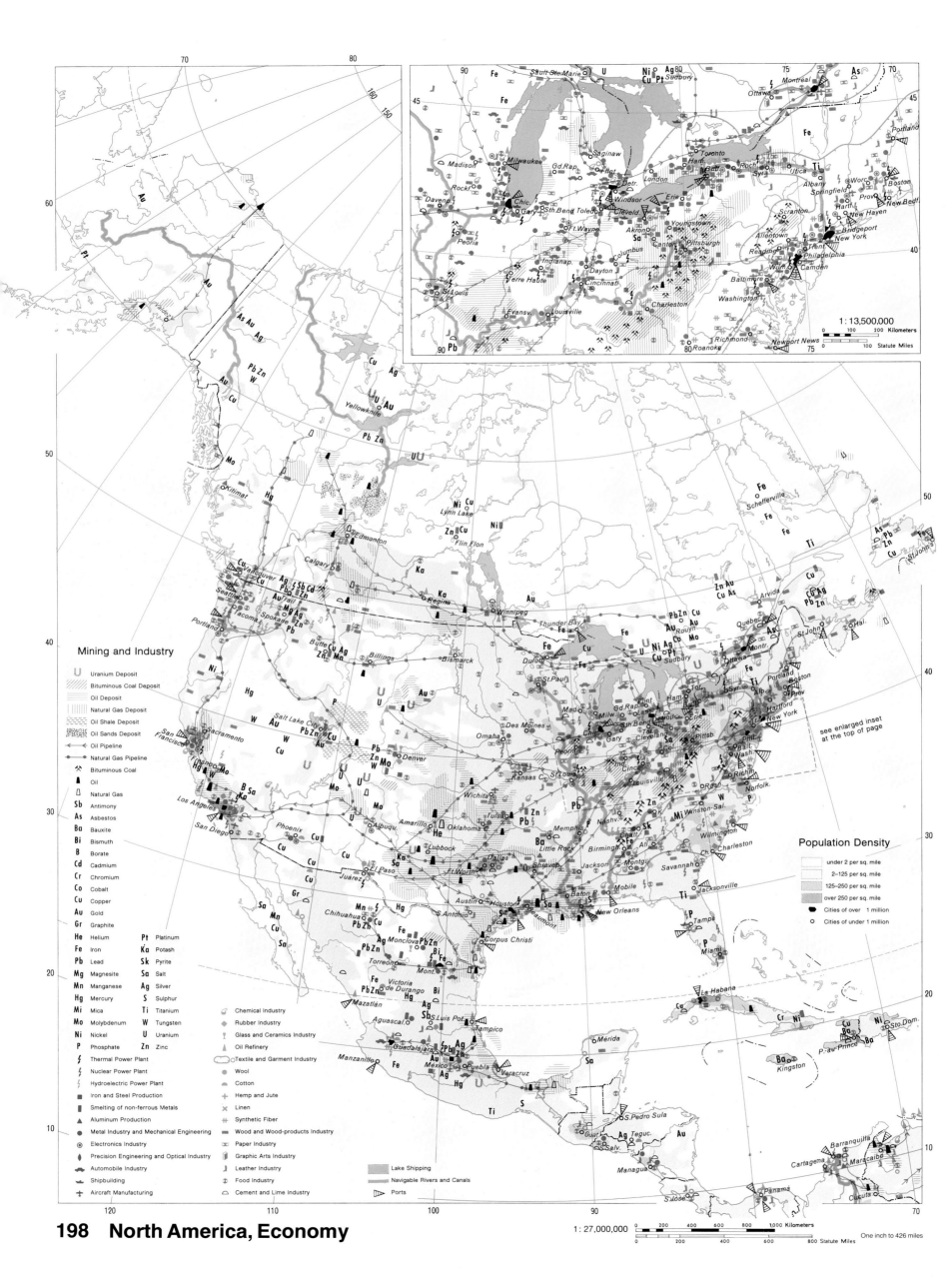

198 North America, Economy

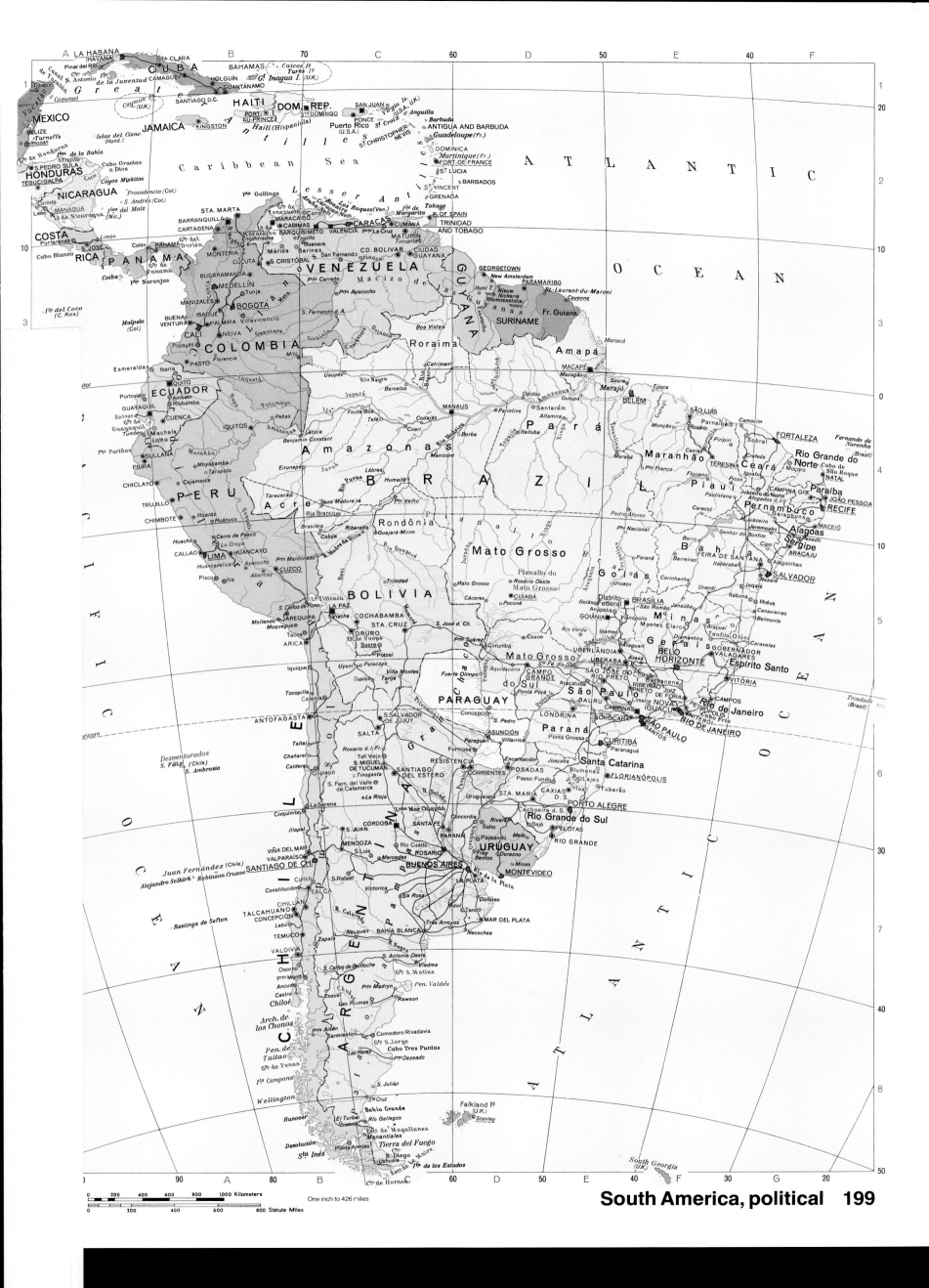

South America, political 199

Land Use and Fishery

Arable land
Rich farmland
Tropical tillage
Irrigated farming
Steppe (Monte)
Alpine steppe (Puma, Paramo), Tundra
Poor pastureland (Llanos, Campos)
Good pastureland (Pampa)
Tropical rainforest
Forest of the temperate and subtropical zone
Savannah (Chaco, Caatinga)
Semi-desert and desert, swamp, rock an snow region (unproductive)

▽ ▽ Wheat
○ ○ Maize
◦ ◦ Rice
Sweet potatoes, Maniok
Sugar cane
Wine
Fruits
Citrus fruits
Bananas
Cotton

∨ ∨ Sisal
0 0 Coffee
Cocoa
T T Tobacco
Fishing areas
Fishing ports
Oysters
Pearls
Cities of over 1 million
○ Cities of under 1 million

1 : 27,000,000

0 200 400 600 800 1000 Kilometers

0 200 400 600 800 Statute Miles

One inch to 426 miles

Mining and Industry

U	Uranium Deposit
	Bituminous Deposit
	Lignite Deposit
	Oil Deposit
	Natural Gas Deposit
	Oil Sands Deposit
	Oil Pipeline
	Natural Gas Pipeline
	Bituminous Coal
	Lignite
▲	Oil
	Natural Gas
Sb	Antimony
As	Asbestos
A	Asphalt
Ba	Bauxite
Bi	Bismuth
Cd	Cadmium
Cr	Chromium
Co	Cobalt
Cu	Copper
Di	Diamonds
Au	Gold

Gr	Graphite
Fe	Iron
Pb	Lead
Mg	Magnesit
Mn	Manganese
Hg	Mercury
Mi	Mica
Mo	Molybdenum
Ni	Nickel
Pt	Platinum
Sp	Salpeter
Sa	Salt
Ag	Silver
S	Sulphur
Ta	Tantalum
Zn	Tin
Ti	Titanium
W	Tungsten
Sn	Zinc

𝟇	Thermal Power Plant
𝟇	Nuclear Power Plant
𝟇	Hydroelectric Power Plant

■	Iron and Steel Production
▌	Smelting of non-ferrous Metals
▲	Aluminum Production
	Metal Industry and Mechanical Engineering
	Electronics Industry
	Automobile Industry
	Shipbuilding
	Aircraft Manufacturing
	Chemical Industry
	Rubber Industry
	Glass and Ceramics Industry
	Leather Industry
	Textile and Garment Industry
	Wood and Wood-products Industry
	Paper Industry
	Graphic Arts Industry
	Leather Industry
	Food Industry
	Cement and Lime Industry
	Navigable Rivers and Canals
	Ports

Population Density

	under 2 per sq. mile
	2–125 per sq. mile
	125–250 per sq. mile
	over 250 per sq. mile
	Cities of over 1 million
	Cities of under 1 million

1:27,000,000

| 0 | 200 | 400 | 600 | 800 | 1,000 Kilometers |

One inch to 426 miles

| 0 | 200 | 400 | 600 | 800 Statute Miles |

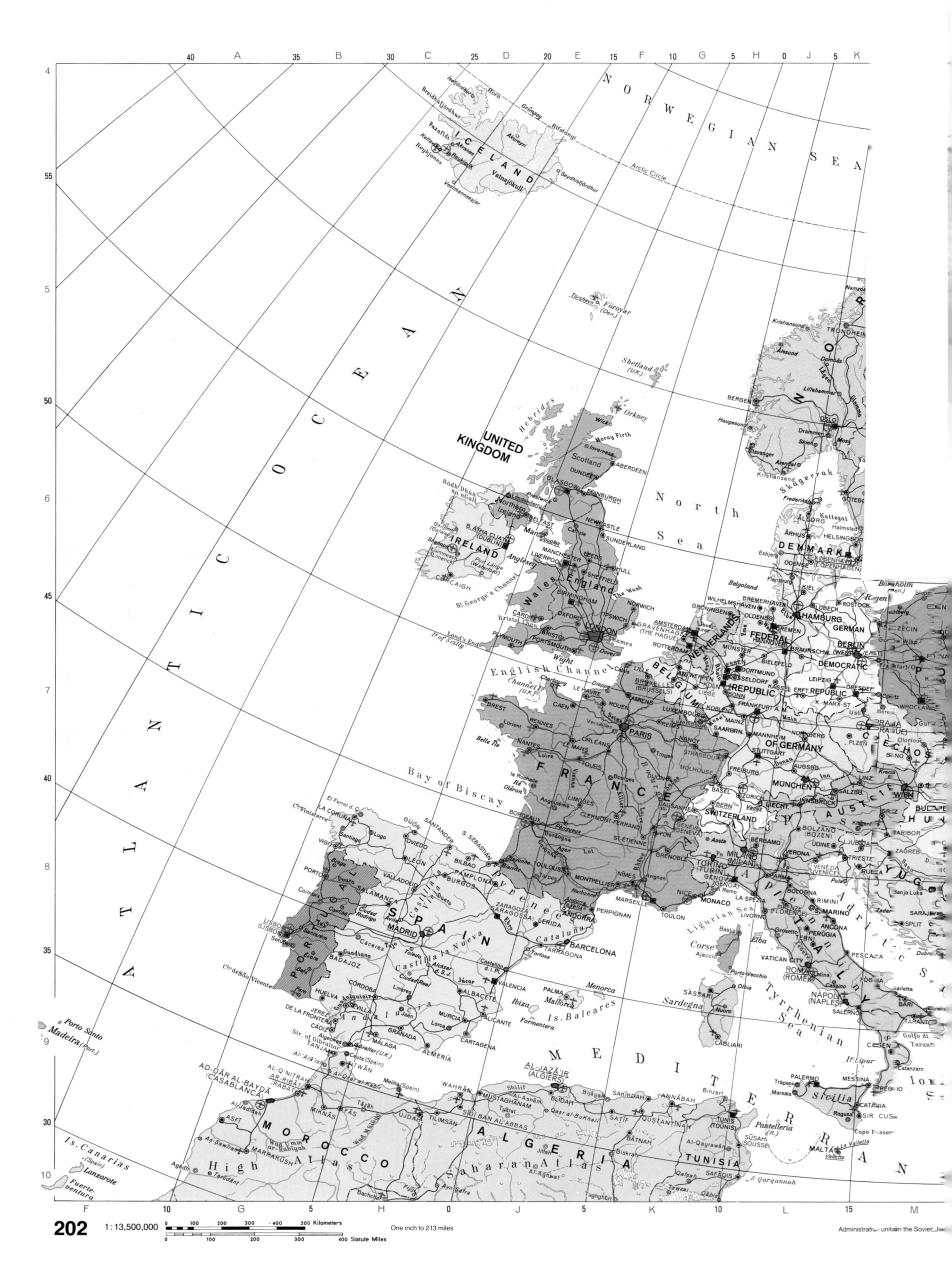

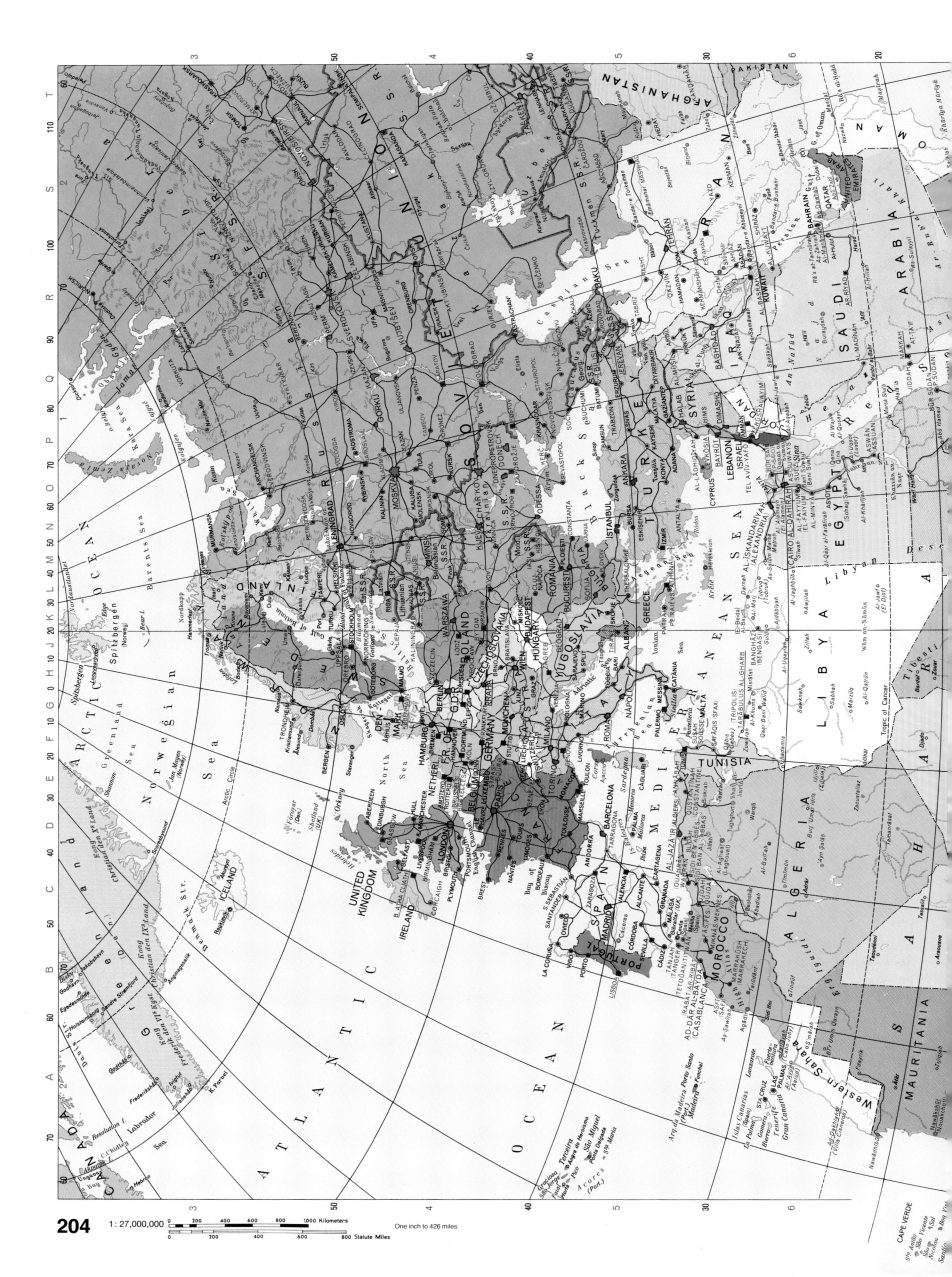

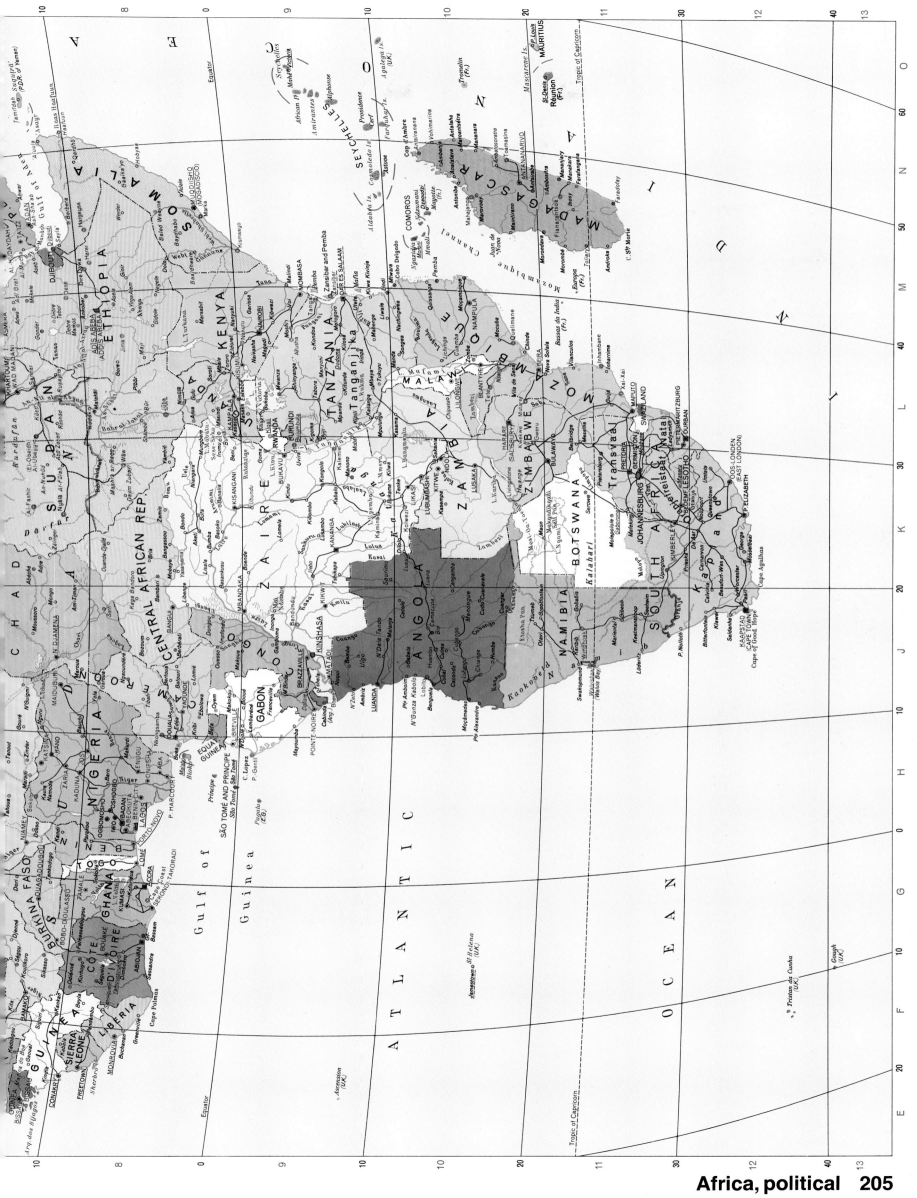

1 : 27,000,000

0   200   400   600   800   1000 Kilometers

0   200   400   600   800 Statute Miles

One inch to 426 miles   Conversion meters – feet see page 48

ATLANTIC OCEAN

Norwegian Sea

ICELAND

UNITED KINGDOM

IRELAND

PORTUGAL

SPAIN

MOROCCO

ALGERIA

TUNISIA

LIBYA

NIGER

CHAD

SUDAN

CENTRAL AFRIC. REP.

ZAIRE

UGANDA

KENYA

TANZANIA

BURUNDI

RWANDA

ANGOLA

SOMALIA

ETHIOPIA

DJIBOUTI

YEMEN

P.D.R. OF YEMEN

SAUDI ARABIA

EGYPT

ISRAEL

JORDAN

LEBANON

SYRIA

IRAQ

KUWAIT

BAHRAIN

QATAR

UNITED ARAB EMIRATES

OMAN

IRAN

AFGHANISTAN

PAKISTAN

INDIA

FRANCE

BELGIUM

NETHERL.

GERMANY

SWITZERL.

ITALY

SAN MARINO

ANDORRA

LUXEMB.

DEN MARK

POLAND

CZECHOSLOVAKIA

HUNGARY

YUGOSLAVIA

ROMÂNIA

BULGARIA

ALBANIA

GREECE

TURKEY

CYPRUS

NORWAY

SWEDEN

FINLAND

U.S.S.R.

R O S S I J A

MADRID

LISBOA

PARIS

LONDON

BERLIN

MOSKVA (MOSCOW)

LENINGRAD

WARSZAWA

BUDAPEST

BUCUREŞTI

SOFIA

ANKARA

ISTANBUL

BAGDAD

TEHRAN (TEHERAN)

KABUL

RIYAD (RIYADH)

AL-QAHIRAH

KHARTÛM

NAIROBI

ADIS ABEBA

Black Sea

MEDITERRANEAN Sea

Red Sea

Gulf of Aden

Arabian Sea

Baltic Sea

North Sea

Tropic of Cancer

Equator

Arctic Circle

INDIAN

BOMBAY

HYDERABAD

BANGALORE

NEW DELHI

KARACHI

TAŠKENT

SAMARKAND

BAKU

TBILISI

JEREVAN

DELHI

Asia, political   207

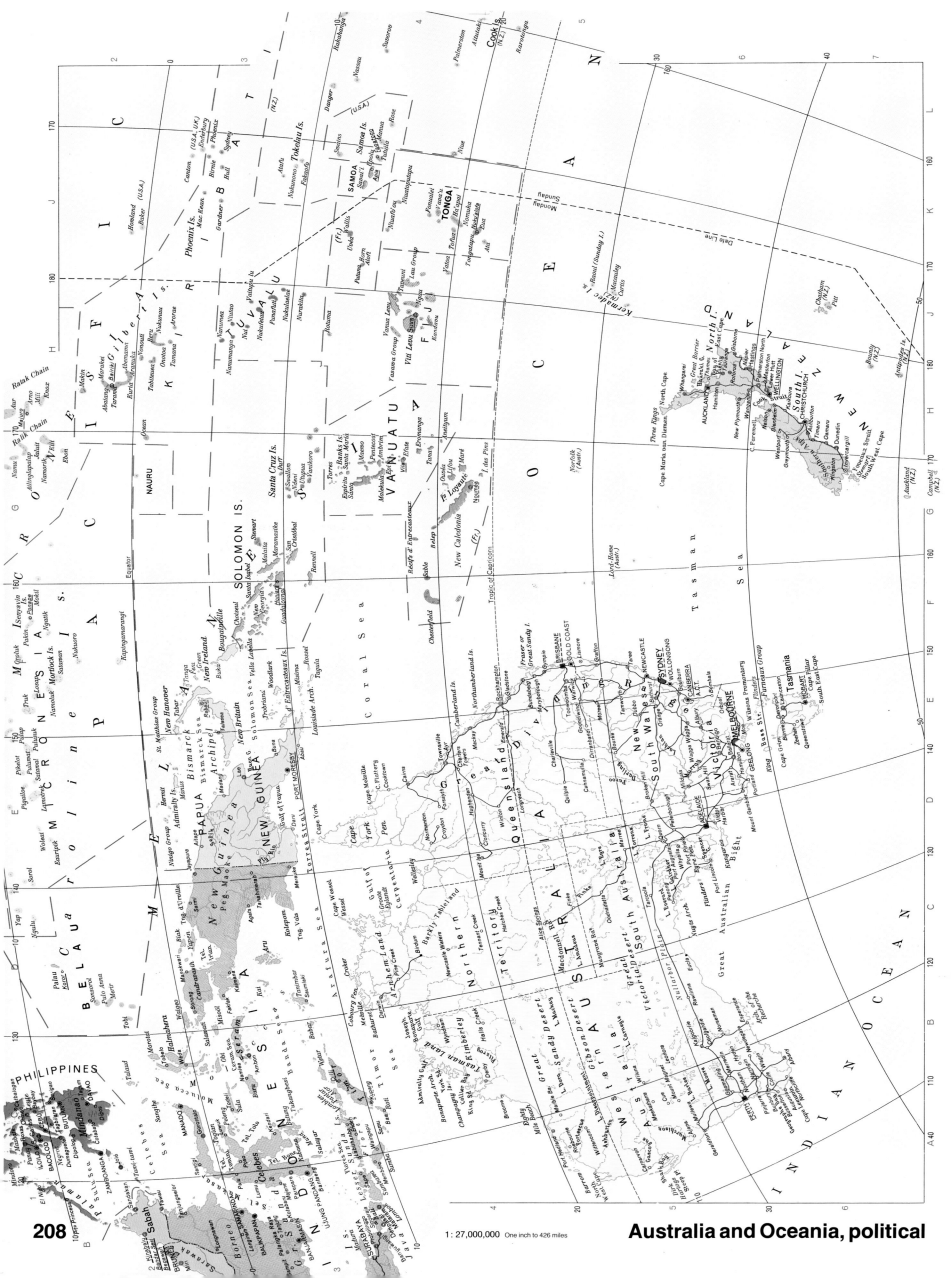

1 : 27,000,000   One inch to 426 miles

Australia and Oceania, political

STATISTICAL MAPS AND CHARTS

Population of the Earth

The Explosion of World Population

In 700 years, from 1000 to 1700, the population of the world more than doubled to just short of 600 million. Only 150 years later it had doubled again to around 1.2 billion, and from the beginning of the century to the present day, it has more than tripled to 4.8 billion. The world population in the year 2000 is estimated to be 6.2 billion.

What makes this population explosion a problem is the fact that the fastest growth is concentrated in the developing countries, and particularly in Africa and Latin America. By 2000, some four-fifths of humanity will live in developing countries.

The world population is very unevenly distributed, with some 70 percent living on 7 percent of the earth's surface. The increase in population in the twentieth century has been accompanied by migra-tion, mostly within national frontiers, towards urban centers. People are clustering in huge conurba-tions, whose populations are growing 4-6 percent a year, twice as fast as the total population. In the poorer countries in particular, the cities have tre-mendous attraction for the rural population, but the lack of jobs results in the growth of slums and in-crease in poverty.

The "Age Pyramid"

The age structure of a country's population has far-reaching social, economic and political consequen-ces. The "age pyramid" shows a national population by age and sex, and distinguishes between young, stagnating and shrinking populations. Young popu-lations, which include most developing countries, are distinguished by a particularly high proportion of younger generations in the total population. In Zim-babwe, for example, 50 percent of the population are young people below 15! These countries are faced with the difficult problems of ensuring ade-quate nutrition, providing education and creating sufficient jobs. Aging populations, due to increased life expectancy and falling birth rates, have a larger proportion of middle-aged and older generations in the general population; many European countries come under this heading. Here, the static or even declining numbers of younger people who are eco-nomically active have to help maintain increasing numbers of older people who have partly or com-pletely withdrawn from employment.

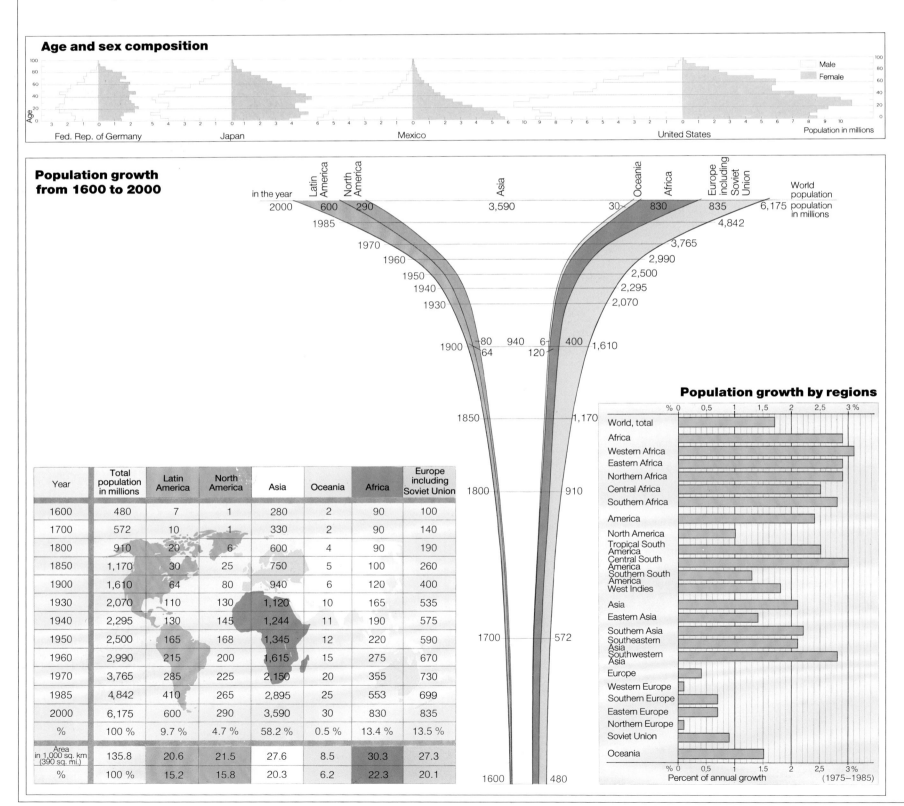

Age and sex composition — Male / Female. Age / Population in millions. Fed. Rep. of Germany, Japan, Mexico, United States.

Population growth from 1600 to 2000

Year	Total population in millions	Latin America	North America	Asia	Oceania	Africa	Europe including Soviet Union
1600	480	7	1	280	2	90	100
1700	572	10	1	330	2	90	140
1800	910	20	6	600	4	90	190
1850	1,170	30	25	750	5	100	260
1900	1,610	64	80	940	6	120	400
1930	2,070	110	130	1,120	10	165	535
1940	2,295	130	145	1,244	11	190	575
1950	2,500	165	168	1,345	12	220	590
1960	2,990	215	200	1,615	15	275	670
1970	3,765	285	225	2,150	20	355	730
1985	4,842	410	265	2,895	25	553	699
2000	6,175	600	290	3,590	30	830	835
%	100 %	9.7 %	4.7 %	58.2 %	0.5 %	13.4 %	13.5 %
Area in 1,000 sq. km (390 sq. mi.)	135.8	20.6	21.5	27.6	8.5	30.3	27.3
%	100 %	15.2	15.8	20.3	6.2	22.3	20.1

Population growth from 1600 to 2000, in the year:

Year	Latin America	North America	Asia	Oceania	Africa	Europe including Soviet Union	World population in millions
2000	600	290	3,590	30	830	835	6,175
1985							4,842
1970							3,765
1960							2,990
1950							2,500
1940							2,295
1930							2,070
1900	80 / 64		940	6 / 120	400		1,610
1850							1,170
1800							910
1700							572
1600							480

Population growth by regions

% 0   0,5   1   1,5   2   2,5   3 %

- World, total
- Africa
- Western Africa
- Eastern Africa
- Northern Africa
- Central Africa
- Southern Africa
- America
- North America
- Tropical South America
- Central South America
- Southern South America
- West Indies
- Asia
- Eastern Asia
- Southern Asia
- Southeastern Asia
- Southwestern Asia
- Europe
- Western Europe
- Southern Europe
- Eastern Europe
- Northern Europe
- Soviet Union
- Oceania

% 0   0,5   1   1,5   2   2,5   3 %
Percent of annual growth   (1975–1985)

Young and old countries

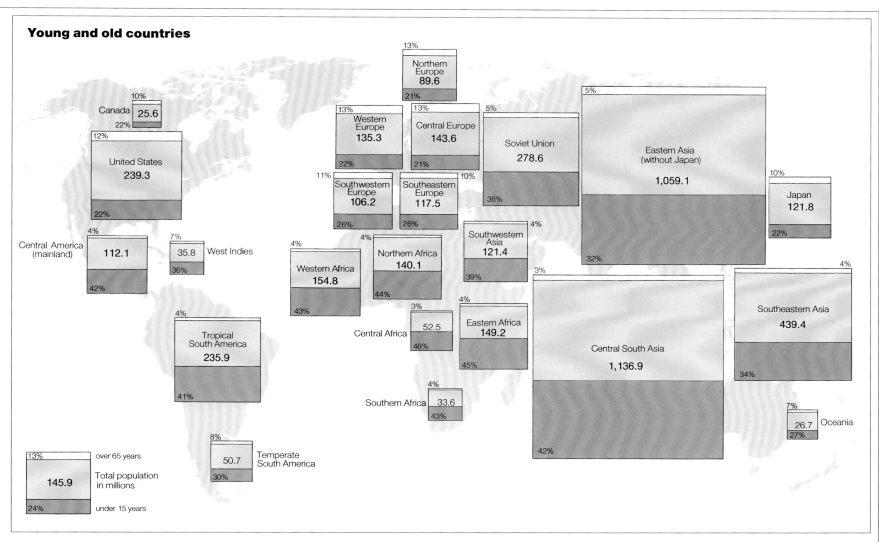

Northern Europe
89.6
13%
21%

Canada
25.6
10%
22%

Western Europe
135.3
13%
22%

Central Europe
143.6
13%
21%

Soviet Union
278.6
5%
36%

Eastern Asia (without Japan)
1,059.1
5%
32%

United States
239.3
12%
22%

Southwestern Europe
106.2
11%
26%

Southeastern Europe
117.5
10%
26%

Southwestern Asia
121.4
4%
39%

Japan
121.8
10%
22%

Central America (mainland)
112.1
4%
42%

West Indies
35.8
7%
36%

Western Africa
154.8
4%
43%

Northern Africa
140.1
4%
44%

Central Africa
52.5
3%
46%

Eastern Africa
149.2
4%
45%

Central South Asia
1,136.9
3%
42%

Southeastern Asia
439.4
4%
34%

Tropical South America
235.9
4%
41%

Southern Africa
33.6
4%
43%

Oceania
26.7
7%
27%

over 65 years
13%
Total population in millions
145.9
24%
under 15 years

Temperate South America
50.7
8%
30%

World urbanization

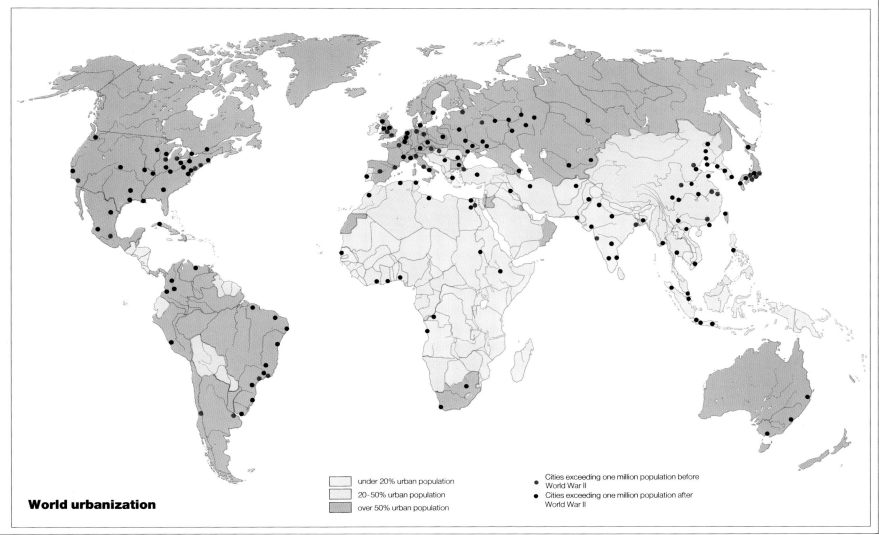

under 20% urban population
20-50% urban population
over 50% urban population

● Cities exceeding one million population before World War II
• Cities exceeding one million population after World War II

Population of the Earth   211

Food Production and Hunger

The Sources of Food

Of the approximately 136 million square kilometers of land on earth, some 11 percent is under cultivation. Experts estimate that up to 30 percent could be utilized. Aridity and cold set climatic limits to cultivation, with 28 percent of the land too dry, 6 percent too cold (excluding the ice-covered land surfaces of Greenland and the Antarctic); the remaining 55 percent of barren areas too rocky, too low in nutrients, or too wet.

In global terms, the world produces sufficient food to nourish the entire world population, according to a 1984 UNO study. Food production is, however, very unevenly distributed: in most developing countries, agricultural productivity is too low, and some 450 million people in these countries suffer from hunger or nutritional deficiency diseases, while surpluses increase in the industrialized nations.

Twenty years ago, the oceans were viewed as inexhaustible sources of food for humanity. At the beginning of the Seventies, the fish catch topped 70 million tons for the first time. At this point overfishing resulted in severe, localized declines in catches. In the North Atlantic, the herring population dropped by some 40 percent, the halibut population by 90 percent, and some species of whale have become extinct. Catches have recently recovered, reaching over 76 million tons in 1982.

Agriculture in the European Community (EC) is distinguished by high surpluses. The problem here is how to finance the surpluses produced under existing market structures with volume and price guarantees. The EC's main competitor on the world market for agricultural products is the U.S.A., without which the EC would be able to dispose of its huge surpluses.

According to 1981 FAO estimates, some 2.1 billion people earn their living from agriculture. Employment in agriculture is an effective indicator of the degree of industrialization. In the industrialized nations agriculture accounts for significantly less than 10 percent of total employment, while the picture is reversed in the developing countries where the share is well over 60 percent — in Mali, for example, it is over 90 percent.

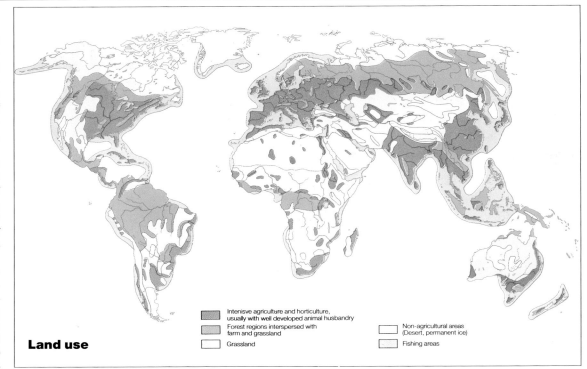

Land use

Intenisve agriculture and horticulture, usually with well developed animal husbandry

Forest regions interspersed with farm and grassland

Grassland

Non-agricultural areas (Desert, permanent ice)

Fishing areas

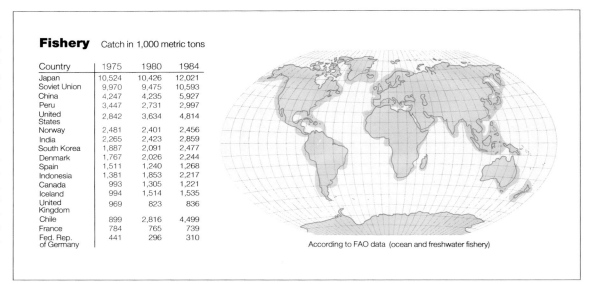

Fishery Catch in 1,000 metric tons

Country	1975	1980	1984
Japan	10,524	10,426	12,021
Soviet Union	9,970	9,475	10,593
China	4,247	4,235	5,927
Peru	3,447	2,731	2,997
United States	2,842	3,634	4,814
Norway	2,481	2,401	2,456
India	2,265	2,423	2,859
South Korea	1,887	2,091	2,477
Denmark	1,767	2,026	2,244
Spain	1,511	1,240	1,268
Indonesia	1,381	1,853	2,217
Canada	993	1,305	1,221
Iceland	994	1,514	1,535
United Kingdom	969	823	836
Chile	899	2,816	4,499
France	784	765	739
Fed. Rep. of Germany	441	296	310

According to FAO data (ocean and freshwater fishery)

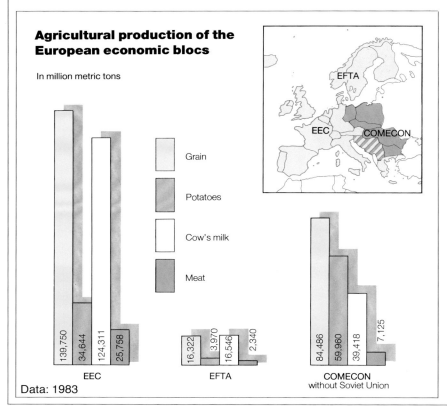

Agricultural production of the European economic blocs

In million metric tons

Grain

Potatoes

Cow's milk

Meat

EEC: 139,750 | 34,644 | 124,311 | 25,758

EFTA: 16,322 | 3,970 | 16,546 | 2,340

COMECON without Soviet Union: 84,486 | 59,960 | 39,418 | 7,125

Data: 1983

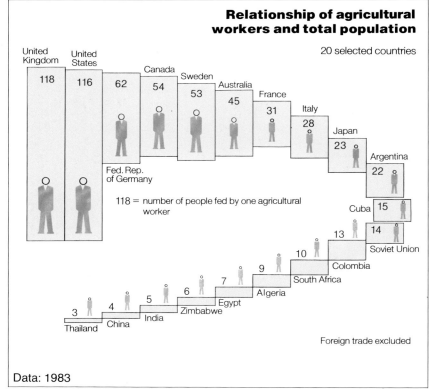

Relationship of agricultural workers and total population

20 selected countries

United Kingdom 118
United States 116
Canada 62
Sweden 54
Australia 53
France 45
Italy 31
Japan 28
Argentina 23
Cuba 22
Soviet Union 15
Colombia 14
South Africa 13
Algeria 10
Egypt 9
Zimbabwe 7
India 6
China 5
Thailand 4
3

Fed. Rep. of Germany

118 = number of people fed by one agricultural worker

Foreign trade excluded

Data: 1983

Food Production and Hunger

Hunger is an endemic problem in most developing countries. Years of drought caused hunger epidemics in the Sahel, and in Ethiopia; in Bangladesh it was catastrophic floods. Besides natural disasters like these, however, inadequate food production is a major reason for Third World hunger. Although world food production rose more than 10 percent from 1972 to 1982, more than half the population of Africa today has less to eat than ten years ago. The proportion of subsistence farming — farms which produce only enough food for the family with occasional surpluses for the market — is high in developing countries. Incentives to grow market crops for the domestic market — or even world market — are often eroded by low prices imposed by governments. On the other hand, there are examples of countries where large plantations produce for the world market, and not enough arable land is left to feed a growing population.

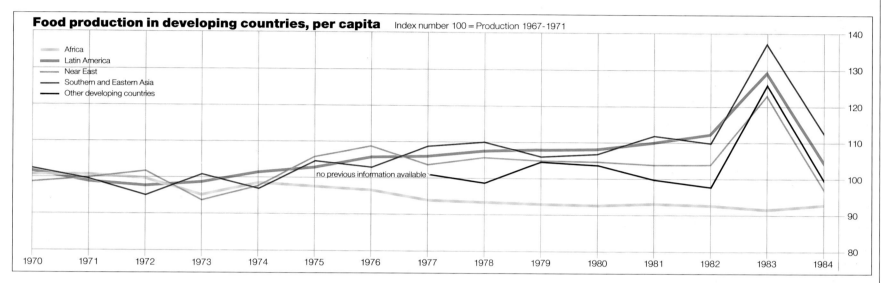

Food production in developing countries, per capita Index number 100 = Production 1967-1971

Africa
Latin America
Near East
Southern and Eastern Asia
Other developing countries

no previous information available

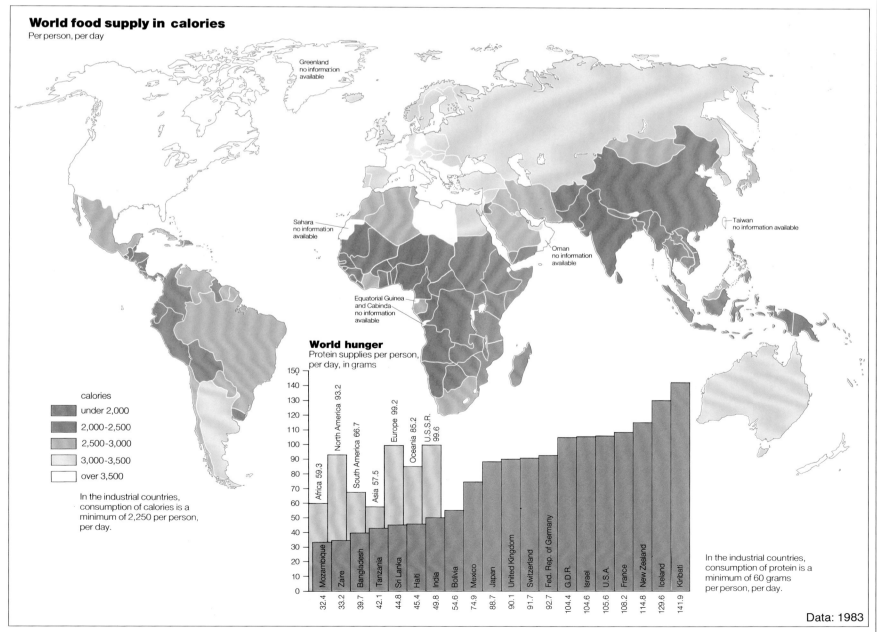

World food supply in calories
Per person, per day

Greenland
no information available

Sahara
no information available

Equatorial Guinea and Cabinda
no information available

Oman
no information available

Taiwan
no information available

calories
under 2,000
2,000-2,500
2,500-3,000
3,000-3,500
over 3,500

In the industrial countries, consumption of calories is a minimum of 2,250 per person, per day.

World hunger
Protein supplies per person, per day, in grams

Africa 59.3
North America 93.2
South America 66.7
Asia 57.5
Europe 99.2
Oceania 85.2
U.S.S.R. 99.6

Mozambique 32.4
Zaire 33.2
Bangladesh 39.7
Tanzania 42.1
Sri Lanka 44.8
Haiti 45.4
India 49.8
Bolivia 54.6
Mexico 74.9
Japan 88.7
United Kingdom 90.1
Switzerland 91.7
Fed. Rep. of Germany 92.7
G.D.R. 104.4
Israel 104.6
U.S.A. 105.6
France 108.2
New Zealand 114.8
Iceland 129.6
Kiribati 141.9

In the industrial countries, consumption of protein is a minimum of 60 grams per person, per day.

Data: 1983

Mineral Resources and Energy

Raw Materials

Industrial output today centers on about 80 important minerals. Of the deposits currently known only some will suffice well into the twenty-first century. Iron ore will last for another 400 years, aluminum around 260 years, copper 65 years. Reserves which will probably be exhausted in the near future include lead, tin and tungsten. Reprocessing makes possible recovery of raw materials from scrap, yielding some 30 percent of iron, and 20 percent of aluminum produced with a fraction of the energy originally used to mine and process the metal. Sales — and thus prices — of minerals depend heavily on the state of the industrialized economies, and the political situation. Many deposits are located in developing countries, in the southern hemisphere, which are interested in stable exports because of the resulting foreign currency revenue. In order to ensure reasonable prices, primary commodity agreements have become a necessity of world trade.

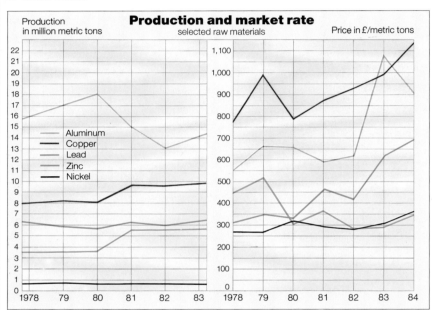

Production and market rate — selected raw materials

Production in million metric tons — Price in £/metric tons

Aluminum, Copper, Lead, Zinc, Nickel

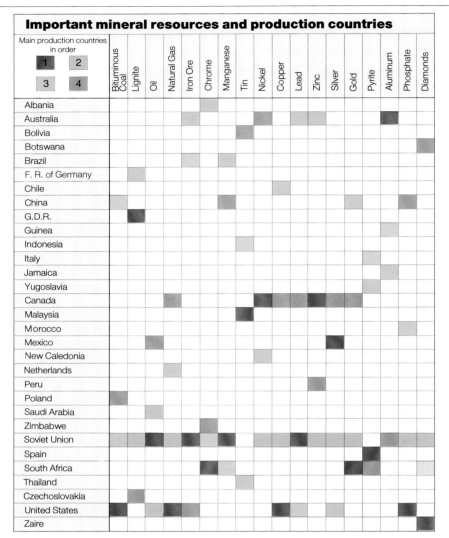

Important mineral resources and production countries

Main production countries in order: 1, 2, 3, 4

Country	Bituminous Coal	Lignite	Oil	Natural Gas	Iron Ore	Chrome	Manganese	Tin	Nickel	Copper	Lead	Zinc	Silver	Gold	Pyrite	Aluminum	Phosphate	Diamonds
Albania																		
Australia																		
Bolivia																		
Botswana																		
Brazil																		
F. R. of Germany																		
Chile																		
China																		
G.D.R.																		
Guinea																		
Indonesia																		
Italy																		
Jamaica																		
Yugoslavia																		
Canada																		
Malaysia																		
Morocco																		
Mexico																		
New Caledonia																		
Netherlands																		
Peru																		
Poland																		
Saudi Arabia																		
Zimbabwe																		
Soviet Union																		
Spain																		
South Africa																		
Thailand																		
Czechoslovakia																		
United States																		
Zaire																		

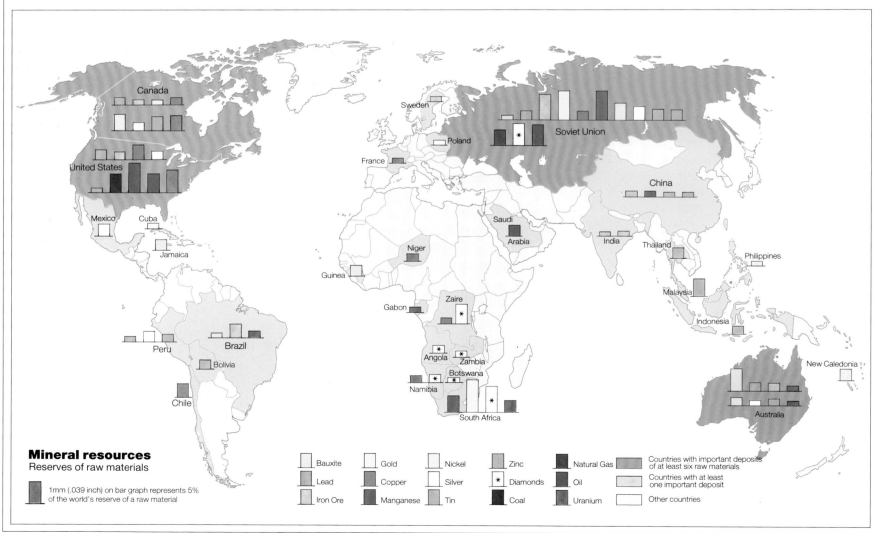

Mineral resources
Reserves of raw materials

1mm (.039 inch) on bar graph represents 5% of the world's reserve of a raw material

Bauxite · Gold · Nickel · Zinc · Natural Gas — Countries with important deposits of at least six raw materials

Lead · Copper · Silver · Diamonds (*) · Oil — Countries with at least one important deposit

Iron Ore · Manganese · Tin · Coal · Uranium — Other countries

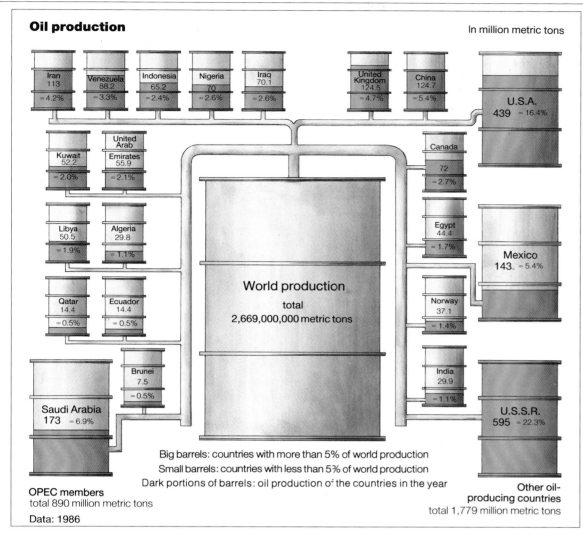

Oil production

In million metric tons

Iran 113 = 4.2%
Venezuela 88.2 = 3.3%
Indonesia 65.2 = 2.4%
Nigeria 70 = 2.6%
Iraq 70.1 = 2.6%
United Kingdom 124.5 = 4.7%
China 124.7 = 5.4%
U.S.A. 439 = 16.4%

Kuwait 52.2 = 2.0%
United Arab Emirates 55.9 = 2.1%
Canada 72 = 2.7%

Libya 50.5 = 1.9%
Algeria 29.8 = 1.1%
Egypt 44.4 = 1.7%

Mexico 143 = 5.4%

Qatar 14.4 = 0.5%
Ecuador 14.4 = 0.5%

World production
total
2,669,000,000 metric tons

Norway 37.1 = 1.4%

Brunei 7.5 = 0.5%

India 29.9 = 1.1%

Saudi Arabia 173 = 6.9%

U.S.S.R. 595 = 22.3%

Big barrels: countries with more than 5% of world production
Small barrels: countries with less than 5% of world production
Dark portions of barrels: oil production of the countries in the year

OPEC members
total 890 million metric tons

Data: 1986

Other oil-producing countries
total 1,779 million metric tons

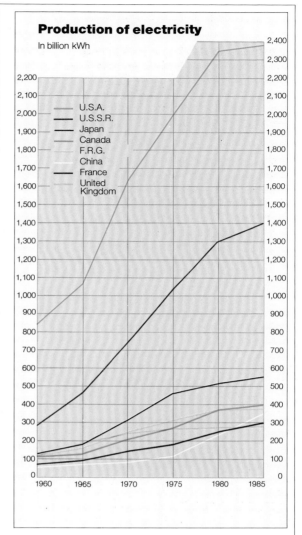

Production of electricity

In billion kWh

U.S.A.
U.S.S.R.
Japan
Canada
F.R.G.
China
France
United Kingdom

1960 1965 1970 1975 1980 1985

Energy

The key to industrial production and general prosperity is an adequate, secure supply of reasonably priced fuel. Until the mid-twentieth century, coal was the most important fuel, but hydroelectricity and subsequently crude oil and natural gas quickly gained in importance, with oil becoming the number one fuel. The first oil crisis — in 1973/74 when oil prices quadrupled in seven months — initiated a feverish search for new energy sources. Crude oil has nevertheless remained the number one fuel with a share of around 43 percent, followed by coal 31.7 percent, natural gas 21.5 percent, hydropower 2.7 percent and nuclear energy 1.3 percent. Energy consumption is rising much faster than world population, which grew 60 percent between 1950 and 1975, while energy consumption rose 330 percent over the same period. Energy consumption per capita reflects the difference in the technological and economic status of countries and regions. North America and western Europe consume some 45 percent of the total (share in world population: 16 percent), the East Bloc with China 33 percent (30 percent), Central and South America 5.2 percent (8 percent), and Africa 2.5 percent (8 percent). Fossil fuels (coal, crude oil and natural gas) are being exhausted. It will not be possible to replace them in the foreseeable future by other technically feasible and economically viable fuels. Although present figures indicate that reserves of coal and uranium will last several more generations, reserves of crude oil and natural gas could be exhausted in 35 to 60 years. They will probably be replaced by coal and nuclear energy.

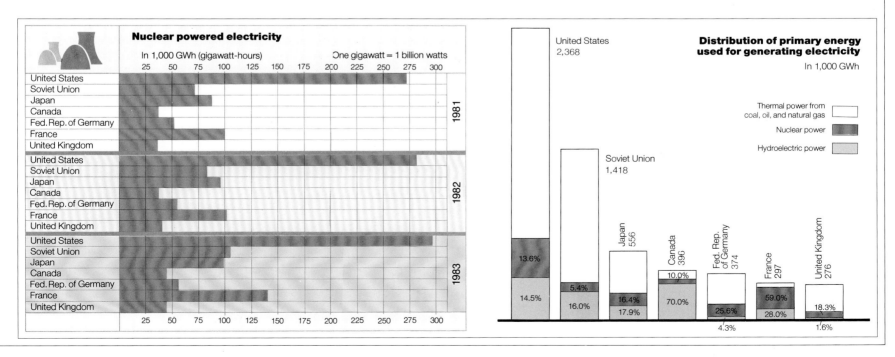

Nuclear powered electricity

In 1,000 GWh (gigawatt-hours)   One gigawatt = 1 billion watts

United States
Soviet Union
Japan
Canada
Fed. Rep. of Germany
France
United Kingdom — 1981

United States
Soviet Union
Japan
Canada
Fed. Rep. of Germany
France
United Kingdom — 1982

United States
Soviet Union
Japan
Canada
Fed. Rep. of Germany
France
United Kingdom — 1983

Distribution of primary energy used for generating electricity

In 1,000 GWh

United States 2,368
Soviet Union 1,418
Japan 556
Canada 390
Fed. Rep. of Germany 374
France 297
United Kingdom 276

Thermal power from coal, oil, and natural gas
Nuclear power
Hydroelectric power

13.6% / 14.5%
5.4% / 16.0%
16.4% / 17.9%
10.0% / 70.0%
25.6% / 4.3%
59.0% / 28.0%
18.3% / 1.6%

Economy and Trade

Industrial Areas and World Trade

The industrial revolution began in Europe in the eighteenth century, but the worldwide process of industrialization did not begin until the Second World War. The less developed countries (LDC's) regard industrialization as the only hope for increasing their standard of living significantly, and achieving genuine independence.

The major industrial areas are concentrated in the northern hemisphere, with only a few isolated industrial centers in the southern hemisphere. The heavy dominance of the north is reflected in the fact that the U.S.A., the European Community (EC) and Japan together account for some 50 percent of the total industrial output.

Besides industrial output, the industrialized nations also dominate world trade. UNO statistics for 1984 show that western industrialized nations accounted for 63 percent in value terms of total world exports of $ 1,235 billion, compared with COMECON's 11 percent and the developing countries' 23 percent. Another feature of the structure of world trade is that trade in commodities between the western industrialized nations far exceeds their trade with the LDCs, which consists mainly of exports of industrial products and imports of primary commodities.

In recent years, total imports of western industrialized nations and developing countries have been higher than their exports. The main reason for this was the rise in prices of crude oil and natural gas. Industrialized nations attempted to compensate for this by increasing their exports of industrial products. Shortages of foreign exchange forced developing countries to restrict oil imports, forcing limitation of production even of goods which could have been exported to generate desperately needed foreign currency earnings.

Ethiopia is an example of a situation that can arise. Only by exporting agricultural products can the country even approximately balance imports of essential fuels and industrial products. However, sited in Africa's dry belt, and plagued by epidemics and hunger, Ethiopia also desperately needs food. Among the countries with clear export surpluses are Japan, and several crude oil exporting countries. In some OPEC member countries, however, oil represents up to 85% of export revenues. This involves high macroeconomic and political risks.

World Industrial areas

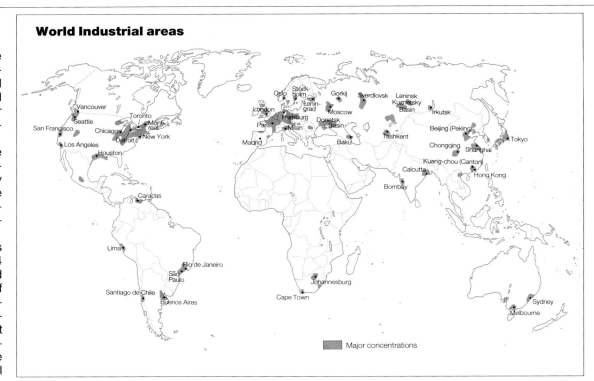

Major concentrations

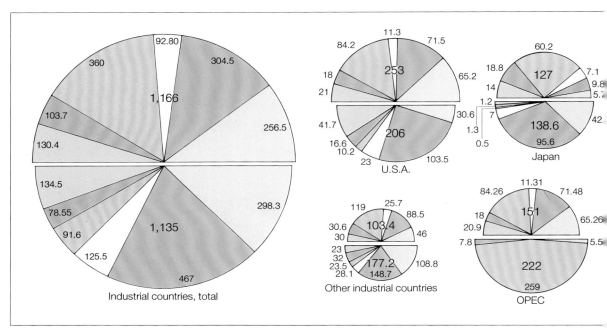

Industrial countries, total

U.S.A.

Japan

Other industrial countries

OPEC

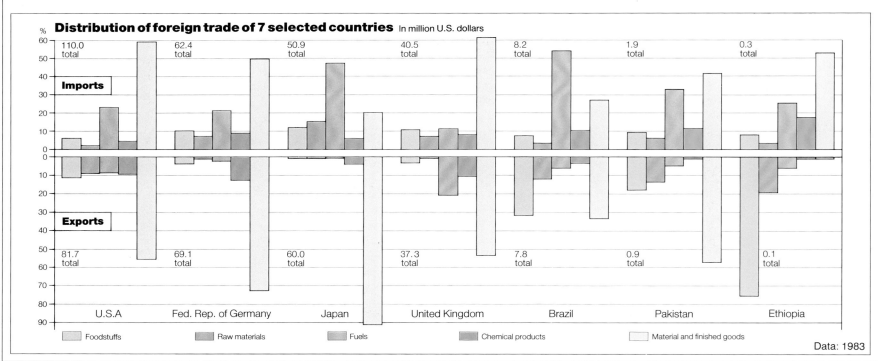

Distribution of foreign trade of 7 selected countries In million U.S. dollars

| | Foodstuffs | Raw materials | Fuels | Chemical products | Material and finished goods |

U.S.A   Fed. Rep. of Germany   Japan   United Kingdom   Brazil   Pakistan   Ethiopia

Data: 1983

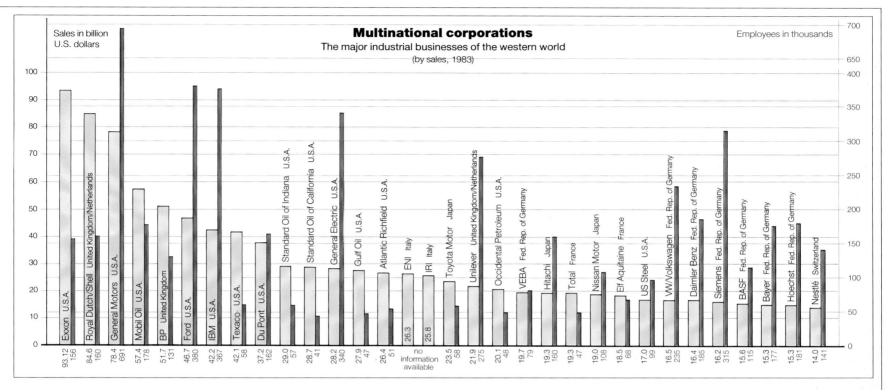

Multinational corporations
The major industrial businesses of the western world
(by sales, 1983)

Sales in billion U.S. dollars

Employees in thousands

Company	Country	Sales	Employees
Exxon	U.S.A.	93.12	156
Royal Dutch/Shell	United Kingdom/Netherlands	84.6	160
General Motors	U.S.A.	78.4	691
Mobil Oil	U.S.A.	57.4	178
BP	United Kingdom	51.7	131
Ford	U.S.A.	46.7	380
IBM	U.S.A.	42.2	367
Texaco	U.S.A.	42.1	58
Du Pont	U.S.A.	37.2	162
Standard Oil of Indiana	U.S.A.	29.0	57
Standard Oil of California	U.S.A.	28.7	41
General Electric	U.S.A.	28.2	340
Gulf Oil	U.S.A.	27.9	47
Atlantic Richfield	U.S.A.	26.4	51
ENI	Italy	26.3	no information available
IRI	Italy	25.8	no information available
Toyota Motor	Japan	23.5	58
Unilever	United Kingdom/Netherlands	21.9	275
Occidental Petroleum	U.S.A.	20.1	48
VEBA	Fed. Rep. of Germany	19.7	79
Hitachi	Japan	19.3	160
Total	France	19.3	47
Nissan Motor	Japan	19.0	108
Elf Aquitaine	France	18.5	68
US Steel	U.S.A.	17.0	99
VW/Volkswagen	Fed. Rep. of Germany	16.5	235
Daimler Benz	Fed. Rep. of Germany	16.4	185
Siemens	Fed. Rep. of Germany	16.2	315
BASF	Fed. Rep. of Germany	15.6	115
Bayer	Fed. Rep. of Germany	15.3	177
Hoechst	Fed. Rep. of Germany	15.3	181
Nestlé	Switzerland	14.0	141

World trade by countries and groups of countries
In billion U.S. dollars

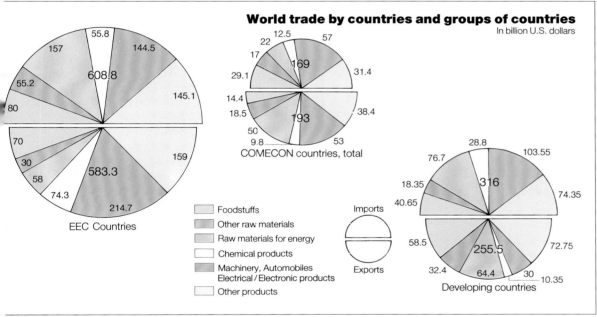

EEC Countries

COMECON countries, total

Developing countries

Legend:
- Foodstuffs
- Other raw materials
- Raw materials for energy
- Chemical products
- Machinery, Automobiles Electrical / Electronic products
- Other products

Imports

Exports

One sign of the advancing world economic integration is the activity of transnational business groups, the so-called "multis". These are involved in production of agricultural products like bananas, rubber or beef. They invest huge sums in prospecting and mining mineral resources, and in this way influence national economies and world trade. Another form of economic integration is the relocation of production facilities of major multinational companies to Third World countries.

The European Community (EC)

The European Community now has 12 member countries, and, regarded as a single economic area, forms the largest international unit, with a share of some 20 percent in world trade. There are, however, still obstacles to trade within the EC, and national interests are often pursued in external trade. More than 65 percent of the EC budget goes to the "European Agricultural Guideance and Guarantee Fund", which adjusts market prices of agricultural products to ensure that farmers enjoy a reasonable income.

Income of the EEC in %
Basket of EEC

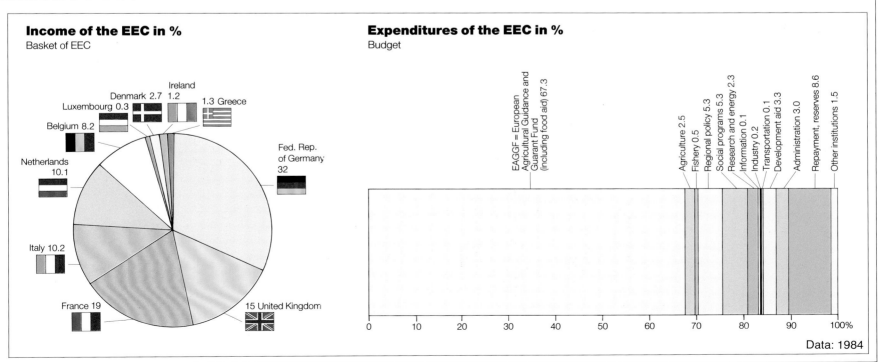

Country	%
Fed. Rep. of Germany	32
United Kingdom	15
France	19
Italy	10.2
Netherlands	10.1
Belgium	8.2
Denmark	2.7
Ireland	1.2
Greece	1.3
Luxembourg	0.3

Expenditures of the EEC in %
Budget

Category	%
EAGGF = European Agricultural Guidance and Guarant Fund (including food aid)	67.3
Agriculture	2.5
Fishery	0.5
Regional policy	5.3
Social programs	5.3
Research and energy	2.3
Information	0.1
Industry	0.2
Transportation	0.1
Development aid	3.3
Administration	3.0
Repayment, reserves	8.6
Other institutions	1.5

Data: 1984

Education and Information

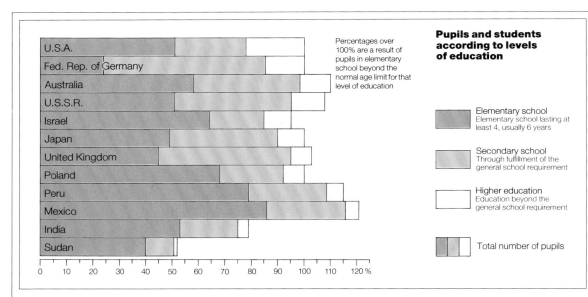

Pupils and students according to levels of education

Percentages over 100% are a result of pupils in elementary school beyond the normal age limit for that level of education

Elementary school
Elementary school lasting at least 4, usually 6 years

Secondary school
Through fulfillment of the general school requirement

Higher education
Education beyond the general school requirement

Total number of pupils

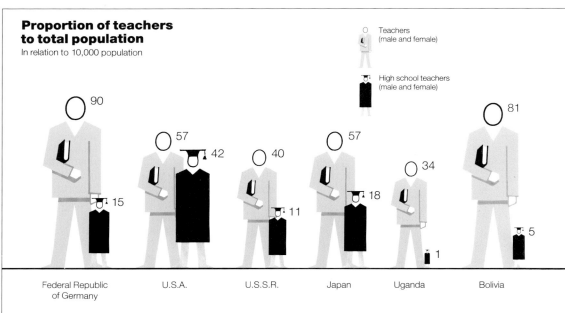

Proportion of teachers to total population
In relation to 10,000 population

Teachers (male and female)

High school teachers (male and female)

Federal Republic of Germany — 90, 15
U.S.A. — 57, 42, 11
U.S.S.R. — 40
Japan — 57, 18
Uganda — 34, 1
Bolivia — 81, 5

Literacy — Illiteracy and Education

Key measuring factors such as literacy, illiteracy, higher education, educational expenditure as a percentage of gross national product, as well as the level and penetration of modern communications indicate that the globe is unequally divided between the developed and developing nations.

At present, the U.S.A., Canada, nearly all of Europe, Argentina, the Soviet Union, Japan, Australia and New Zealand have illiteracy rates under 10 percent. In contrast, illiteracy is measured at 50 percent or greater for all of Africa, most of the Middle East, and throughout the Indian sub-continent. The East-African nations of Ethiopia and Somalia have staggering illiteracy rates of more than 90 percent.

The total number of illiterate people is estimated at around 825 million, or just under 30 percent of the world's population. Some 800 million of these live in developing nations. Currently, literacy rates are estimated at 26 percent in Africa, 53 percent in Asia, and 76 percent in Latin America. In these regions, female literacy is generally about 20 percent lower than male literacy, and is particularly low in islamic countries.

While many Third World countries have made tremendous gains in educational levels and opportunities since mid-century, they have not been able to keep pace with growing educational needs. Modern medicine and lower infant mortality rates have caused rapid increases in the school-age population, thereby placing greater demand on the already limited and strained educational resources of these developing countries. As a result, the total number of illiterates continues to grow; in fact, it increased by approximately 65 million since the last decade.

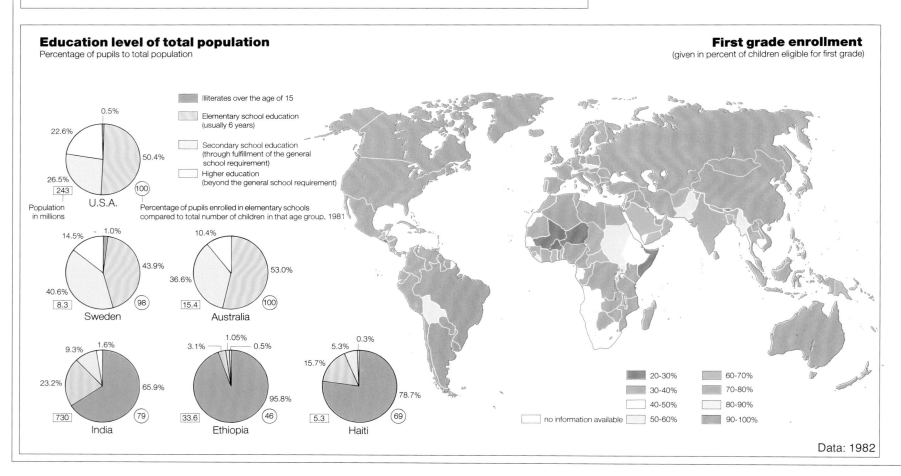

Education level of total population
Percentage of pupils to total population

Illiterates over the age of 15

Elementary school education (usually 6 years)

Secondary school education (through fulfillment of the general school requirement)

Higher education (beyond the general school requirement)

Population in millions

Percentage of pupils enrolled in elementary schools compared to total number of children in that age group, 1981

U.S.A. — 0.5%, 22.6%, 50.4%, 26.5%, 243, 100
Sweden — 1.0%, 14.5%, 43.9%, 40.6%, 8.3, 98
Australia — 10.4%, 53.0%, 36.6%, 15.4, 100
India — 1.6%, 9.3%, 65.9%, 23.2%, 730, 79
Ethiopia — 1.05%, 3.1%, 0.5%, 95.8%, 33.6, 46
Haiti — 5.3%, 0.3%, 15.7%, 78.7%, 5.3, 69

First grade enrollment
(given in percent of children eligible for first grade)

20-30%
30-40%
40-50%
50-60%
60-70%
70-80%
80-90%
90-100%
no information available

Data: 1982

As illiteracy rates fall, higher education rates rise. For example, Sweden and the U.S.A. have illiteracy rates of 1 percent and 0.5 percent respectively; and higher education rates of 14.5 percent and 22.6 percent. The converse of this relationship is made abundantly clear in countries such as Ethiopia and India where illiteracy rates are 95.8 percent and 65.9 percent respectively; while higher education rates stand at a miniscule 0.5 percent and 1.6. percent. Consequently, there is a critical shortage of skilled native workers, technicians, teachers, managerial professionals, and scientists in those areas of the world where they are needed most.

Modern Communications

Telephones, radios, television sets, printed matter, all modern communications are visible indicators of the current level of development in a specific country or region.

The number of telephones worldwide has increased dramatically in the last ten years from 273 million to 510 million. In the U.S.A. there are 84 telephones for every 100 inhabitants; in Africa there is an average of 2.5 telephones for every 100 inhabitants. In Zaire there are approximately 5 radios for every 1000 inhabitants; in the U.S.A. there are over 2000 radios for every 1000 inhabitants. The comparisons are even more lopsided for television sets. And, given the distribution pattern of illiteracy among the developed and the developing nations, it is not surprising that those countries with illiteracy rates of under 10 percent produce more than three-quarters of all book titles published in a single year.

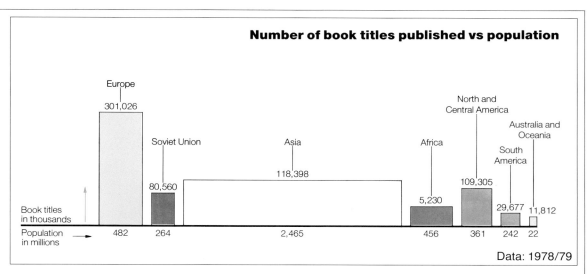

Number of book titles published vs population

Data: 1978/79

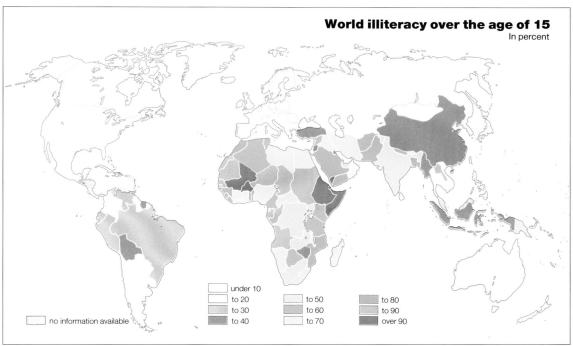

World illiteracy over the age of 15
In percent

under 10
to 20
to 30
to 40
to 50
to 60
to 70
to 80
to 90
over 90
no information available

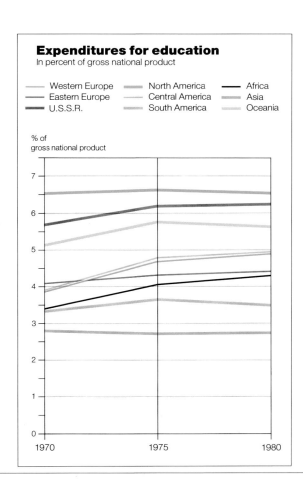

Expenditures for education
In percent of gross national product

— Western Europe
— Eastern Europe
— U.S.S.R.
— North America
— Central America
— South America
— Africa
— Asia
— Oceania

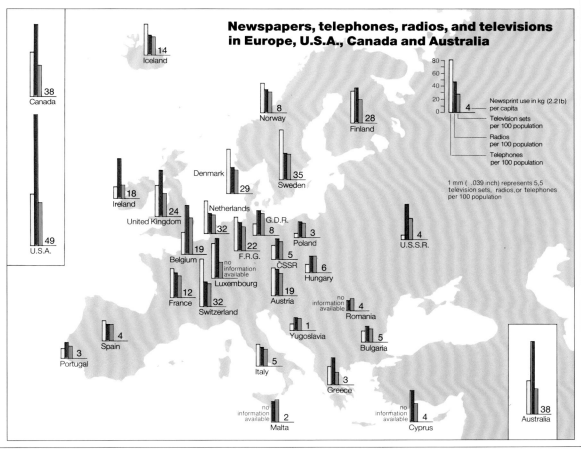

Newspapers, telephones, radios, and televisions in Europe, U.S.A., Canada and Australia

Newsprint use in kg (2.2 lb) per capita
Television sets per 100 population
Radios per 100 population
Telephones per 100 population

1 mm (.039 inch) represents 5,5 television sets, radios, or telephones per 100 population

Poor and Rich

Gross National Product and Income

Gross national product (gnp) is the expression of an economy's capacity and well-being. It represents the monetary value of all the goods and services produced during a year.

The following table shows the approximate distribution of world gnp among the world population.

	Share in total world gnp	Share in world population
Industrialized nations	81 %	28 %
Threshold countries with average level of development	11 %	30 %
Developing countries	8 %	42 %

Whereas average per capita income in the richer industrialized nations exceeds US$ 10,000 (Switzerland: US$ 16,500), it falls below US$ 300 in many developing countries – in Bangladesh, for example, it is around US$ 130, and in Chad US$ 120. Per capita income is extremely high in the United Arab Emirates at around US$ 26,860.

Development aid
In million U.S. dollars, converted to % of gross national product

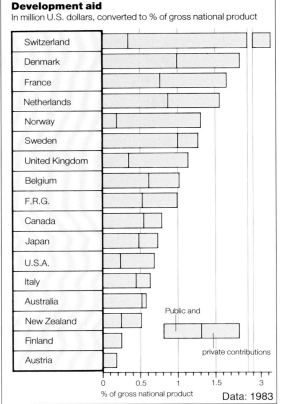

Switzerland
Denmark
France
Netherlands
Norway
Sweden
United Kingdom
Belgium
F.R.G.
Canada
Japan
U.S.A.
Italy
Australia
New Zealand
Finland
Austria

Public and
private contributions

% of gross national product

Data: 1983

Development Aid — Sovereign Debt

The unequal distribution of goods in the world, the contrast between riches and poverty, is a source of growing political and international tension, to the point of danger of armed conflict. Development aid from the industrialized nations, religious institutions, and international organizations aims to raise the industrial strength and standard of living in the Third World. The UN recommended that industrialized nations should contribute 0.7 percent of gnp in aid. Only a few countries, however, are providing aid on this scale, and the average is only 0.3 percent. From 1956 to 1985, 17 western nations contributed some US$ 950 billion in the form of loans, aid in kind and technical assistance – without, however, the hoped-for success. Valuable resources were lost as a result of mistakes in planning and waste, and others had to be devoted to relieving acute need (hunger and natural catastrophes). Generally, there has been no growth in gnp, and some countries have even seen a decline.

Another problem of the Third World is debt, partly due to the recent world economic recession and sharp drop in primary commodity prices. In some cases, sovereign debt has risen to the point where revenues are scarcely sufficient to service interest. Peru's foreign debt represents around 77 percent of its gnp, and 20 percent of this debt is due to arms purchases from the USSR.

Comparison of selected countries

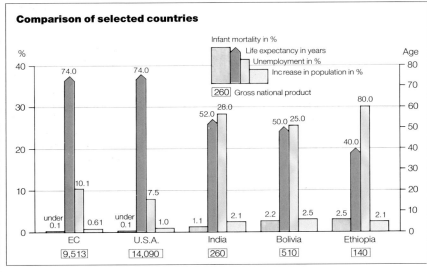

Infant mortality in %
Life expectancy in years
Unemployment in %
Increase in population in %
260 Gross national product

EC 9,513
U.S.A. 14,090
India 260
Bolivia 510
Ethiopia 140

Median annual increase of gross national product
Per capita in %

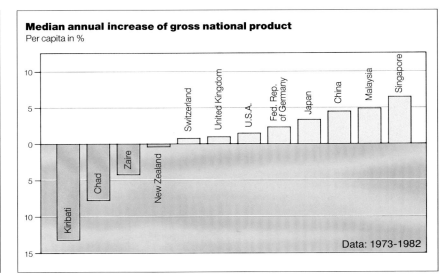

Kiribati
Chad
Zaire
New Zealand
Switzerland
United Kingdom
U.S.A.
Fed. Rep. of Germany
Japan
China
Malaysia
Singapore

Data: 1973-1982

Infant mortality vs gross national product, per capita

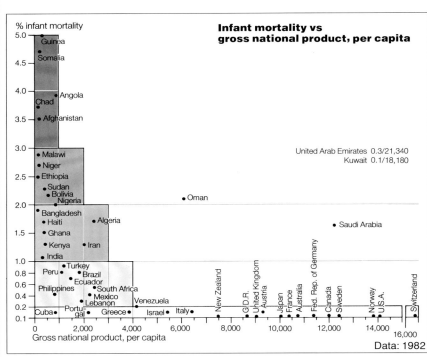

% infant mortality

Guinea
Somalia
Angola
Chad
Afghanistan
Malawi
Niger
Ethiopia
Sudan
Bolivia
Nigeria
Bangladesh
Haiti
Algeria
Ghana
Kenya
Iran
India
Turkey
Peru
Brazil
Ecuador
Philippines
South Africa
Mexico
Lebanon
Cuba
Portugal
Venezuela
Greece
Israel
Italy
Oman
Saudi Arabia

United Arab Emirates 0.3/21,340
Kuwait 0.1/18,180

New Zealand
G.D.R.
United Kingdom
Austria
Japan
France
Australia
Fed. Rep. of Germany
Canada
Sweden
Norway
U.S.A.
Switzerland

Gross national product, per capita

Data: 1982

Third World debt
Debt service in % of gross national product

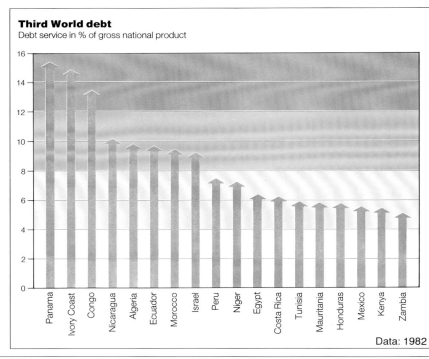

Panama
Ivory Coast
Congo
Nicaragua
Algeria
Ecuador
Morocco
Israel
Peru
Niger
Egypt
Costa Rica
Tunisia
Mauritania
Honduras
Mexico
Kenya
Zambia

Data: 1982

Health

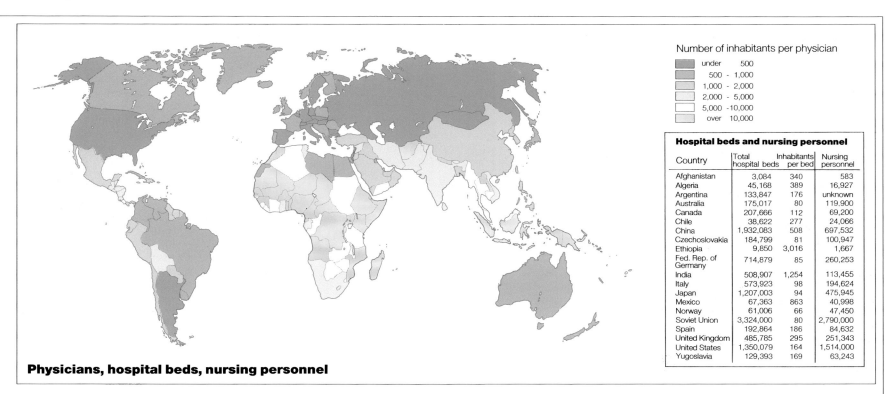

Physicians, hospital beds, nursing personnel

Number of inhabitants per physician

	under 500
	500 - 1,000
	1,000 - 2,000
	2,000 - 5,000
	5,000 -10,000
	over 10,000

Hospital beds and nursing personnel

Country	Total hospital beds	Inhabitants per bed	Nursing personnel
Afghanistan	3,084	340	583
Algeria	45,168	389	16,927
Argentina	133,847	176	unknown
Australia	175,017	80	119,900
Canada	207,666	112	69,200
Chile	38,622	277	24,066
China	1,932,083	508	697,532
Czechoslovakia	184,799	81	100,947
Ethiopia	9,850	3,016	1,667
Fed. Rep. of Germany	714,879	85	260,253
India	508,907	1,254	113,455
Italy	573,923	98	194,624
Japan	1,207,003	94	475,945
Mexico	67,363	863	40,998
Norway	61,006	66	47,450
Soviet Union	3,324,000	80	2,790,000
Spain	192,864	186	84,632
United Kingdom	485,785	295	251,343
United States	1,350,079	164	1,514,000
Yugoslavia	129,393	169	63,243

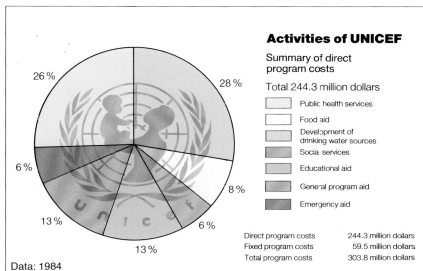

Activities of UNICEF

Summary of direct program costs

Total 244.3 million dollars

	Public health services
	Food aid
	Development of drinking water sources
	Social services
	Educational aid
	General program aid
	Emergency aid

Direct program costs	244.3 million dollars
Fixed program costs	59.5 million dollars
Total program costs	303.8 million dollars

Data: 1984

Health and Medical Care

Medical advances over the past hundred years — the decline in infant mortality, extensive vaccination, treatment of infectious diseases — have brought higher life expectancy and accompanying population growth. In 1955, life expectancy in the developed countries was 65.1 years; currently, this has reached 73 years, and will rise to 74.4 years by the year 2000. The comparable figures for the developing countries are 41, 56.6 and 61.8 years respectively.

These statistical averages should not, however, be allowed to obscure the fact that medical services in the developing countries are often totally inadequate, particularly in rural areas. It is estimated that only four out of every five African children live past the first year, and that vitamin A deficiency causes blindness in over 200,000 children a year. Overindulgence can also result in diseases and deaths. In developed countries, circulatory disorders cause 50 percent, and cancer 20 percent of the deaths. Around one third of cancer cases affect the respiratory system, and some 80 percent of these cases are causally related to smoking.

Causes of death (selection) per 100,000 population

In 15 countries

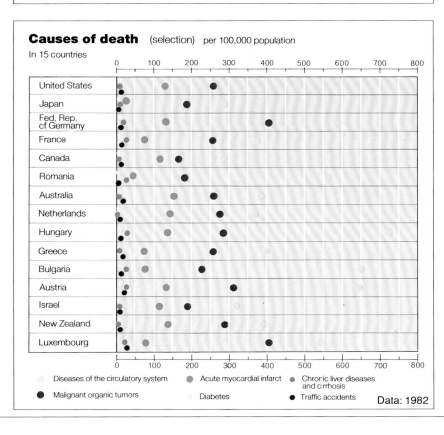

United States, Japan, Fed. Rep. of Germany, France, Canada, Romania, Australia, Netherlands, Hungary, Greece, Bulgaria, Austria, Israel, New Zealand, Luxembourg

- Diseases of the circulatory system
- Acute myocardial infarct
- Chronic liver diseases and cirrhosis
- Malignant organic tumors
- Diabetes
- Traffic accidents

Data: 1982

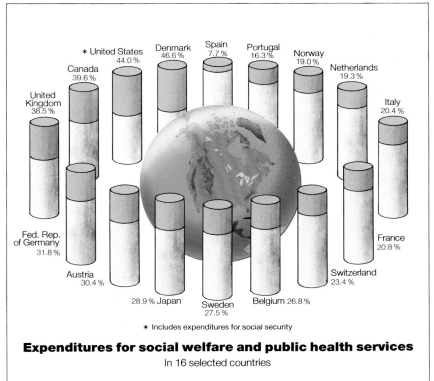

* Includes expenditures for social security

Expenditures for social welfare and public health services

In 16 selected countries

* United States 44.0%
Denmark 46.6%
Spain 7.7%
Portugal 16.3%
Norway 19.0%
Netherlands 19.3%
Canada 39.6%
United Kingdom 38.5%
Italy 20.4%
Fed. Rep. of Germany 31.8%
France 20.8%
Austria 30.4%
Switzerland 23.4%
28.9% Japan
Sweden 27.5%
Belgium 26.8%

Migration and Work

Man and Migration

Migration is part of the human condition. Hunger, war, persecution under national, racial, and religious intolerance, the search for a better life or income, and even the search for adventure may cause people to leave their homes. 1500 years ago, the movement of peoples in the age of migration formed the outlines of European nations. The European emigration to North America that began in the seventeenth century resulted in the formation of the U.S.A. Exiles, refugees, and people looking for food and work remain a feature of today's world.

According to the UNHCR the number of refugees in various host countries today breaks down into Europe 550,000; Middle East and Near East 3.7 million; Africa 2.7 million; Asia 3.8 million; North America 1.8 million; Latin America 850,000; and Oceania 330,000. The situation is particularly difficult where the host countries are also economically weak, such as Pakistan with its 3 million refugees from Afghanistan.

There is also a larger number of so-called expatriate workers, living abroad because of better earning possibilities, but intending to return to their homeland. Political and social problems also arise here, family ties are loosened, and expatriate workers are expelled at times of political tension or economic crisis. In 1983, for example, 2 million foreigners living illegally in Nigeria had to leave the country.

The proportion of foreign workers in the Arab oil states is extremely high. In Kuwait, 80 percent of workers are foreign, in the United Arab Emirates the figure is 88 percent — mostly Indians and Pakistanis. Opportunities for employment in the industrialized countries are relatively good. Switzerland, for example, employs some 700,000 foreign workers. A different form of migration involves migrant workers, who maintain a fixed residence and cross national borders at regular seasons; an example of these are the Mexicans who travel to California for particular harvest seasons.

Employment — Unemployment

There is not enough work in the world to provide all the people of employable age with jobs that pay an adequate wage. Recent years have seen unemployment increase worldwide. Full employment is a thing of the past, even in the East Bloc, where statistics showing full employment conceal a large number of underemployed people and low productivity. In 1984, unemployment in the Northern Hemisphere was around 10 percent, and in the South around 30-40 percent. In the North, unemployment only partly reflects a slowdown in economic growth; another factor is structural, the result of the introduction of new technologies that make it possible to dispense with human workers.

Worldwide, working conditions vary as much as working hours, which differ even within the EC. Total annual hours actually worked per employee topped 2,000 in Japan, and reached 1,860 in the U.S.A. and 1,650 in the Federal Republic of Germany. In Third World countries, a working day in excess of 10 hours is the rule rather than the exception.

A breakdown by industry of employment shows that a rising level of industrialization is accompanied by a decrease in employment in agriculture and an increase in the industrial and service sectors. In highly developed industrialized nations, employment in industry also declines, and the majority of the labor force is employed in the service sector.

Population shifts in Europe after 1939

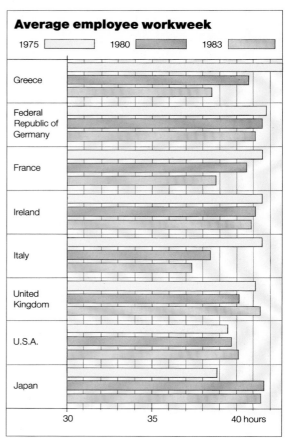

Average employee workweek

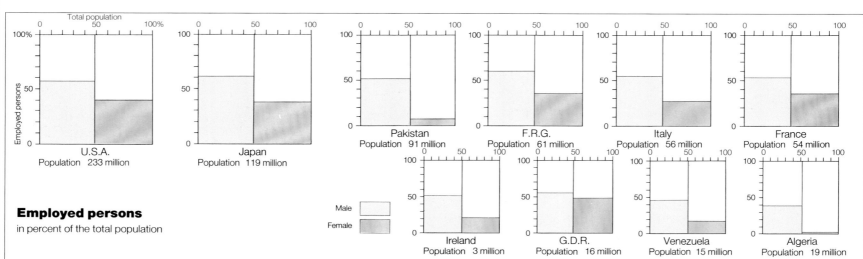

Employed persons
in percent of the total population

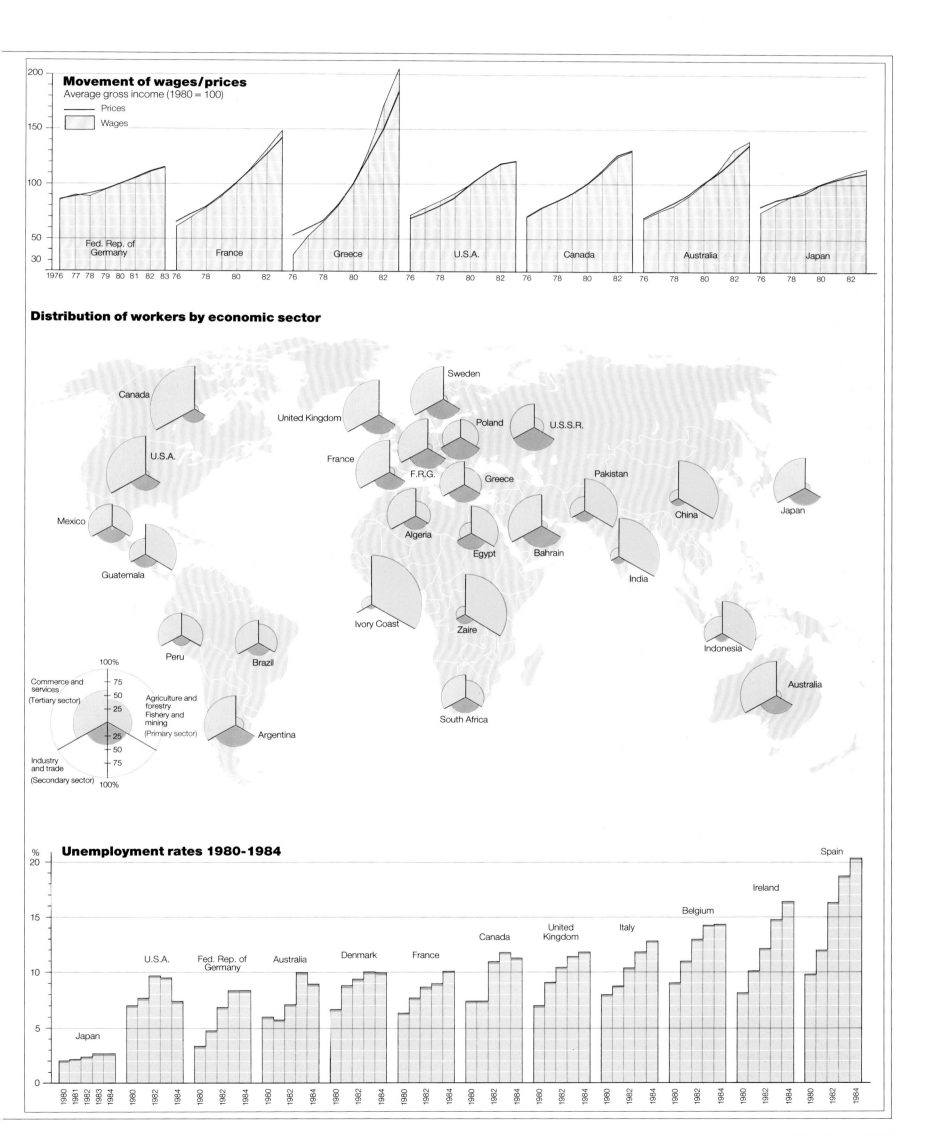

Movement of wages/prices
Average gross income (1980 = 100)

— Prices
▨ Wages

Fed. Rep. of Germany · France · Greece · U.S.A. · Canada · Australia · Japan

Distribution of workers by economic sector

Commerce and services
(Tertiary sector)

Agriculture and forestry
Fishery and mining
(Primary sector)

Industry and trade
(Secondary sector)

Canada · Sweden · United Kingdom · Poland · U.S.S.R. · France · F.R.G. · Greece · Pakistan · Japan · U.S.A. · Algeria · China · Mexico · Egypt · Bahrain · Guatemala · India · Ivory Coast · Zaire · Indonesia · Peru · Brazil · South Africa · Australia · Argentina

Unemployment rates 1980-1984

Japan · U.S.A. · Fed. Rep. of Germany · Australia · Denmark · France · Canada · United Kingdom · Italy · Belgium · Ireland · Spain

Alliances and Politics

The United Nations

In 1945, 51 countries founded the United Nations as a successor to the League of Nations. Today, this body has 159 members. Under the UN Charter, member states pledge inter alia to refrain from the use of force in international relationships, to seek peaceful resolutions of disputes, and to protect human rights. Specialist organizations have specific functions.

Military Pacts

Europe is the meeting point for the two major military organisations, the North Atlantic Treaty Organization (NATO) and the Warsaw Pact, which divide the continent. The two superpowers — the U.S.A. and the USSR — occupy the key positions within these organizations. Their allies generally share their respective political, social and economic convictions. ANZUS, by contrast, is a loose defensive alliance between the U.S.A., Australia, and New Zealand. Many Third World countries follow a policy of deliberate nonalignment with these systems.

Economic and Political Groupings

The most closely linked supranational economic grouping is the European Economic Community ("Common Market"). Its objectives go beyond a common European market to a political community of European states. Its counterpart in the East Bloc is COMECON, which is, however, limited to coordinating economic planning and expanding the transport systems. EFTA countries are seeking to remove trade barriers between members and promote economic growth.

Regional and continental national groupings, such as the OAS (Organization of American States), and the OAU (Organization of African Unity), are based on commitments by members to cooperation and solidarity in the political, economic, and cultural spheres.

Economic communities

- EC European Community
- associated with EC
- COMECON Council for Mutual Economic Assistance
- associated with COMECON
- Membership not claimed of COMECON
- EFTA European Free Trade Association
- associated with EFTA

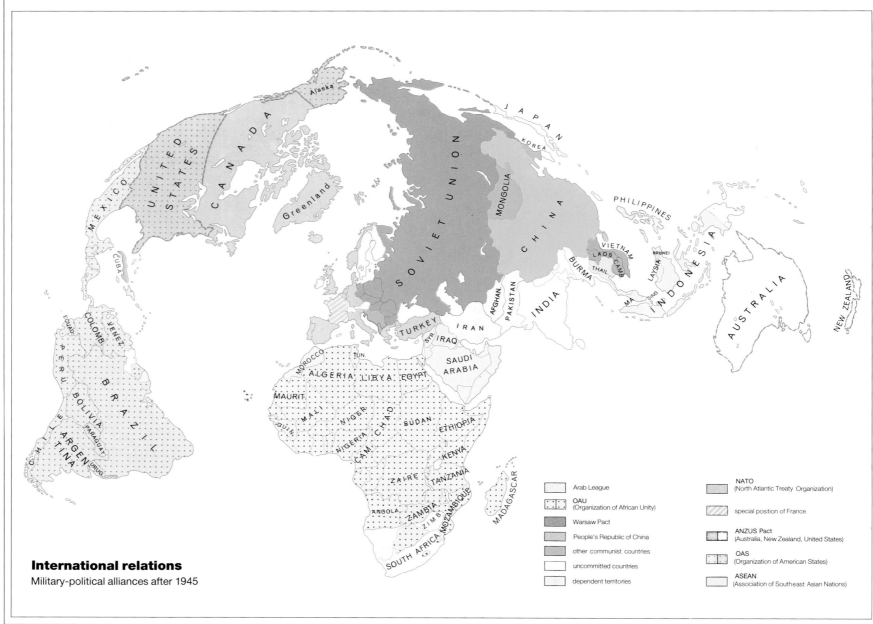

International relations
Military-political alliances after 1945

- Arab League
- OAU (Organization of African Unity)
- Warsaw Pact
- People's Republic of China
- other communist countries
- uncommitted countries
- dependent territories
- NATO (North Atlantic Treaty Organization)
- special position of France
- ANZUS Pact (Australia, New Zealand, United States)
- OAS (Organization of American States)
- ASEAN (Association of Southeast Asian Nations)

THE
NATURE
OF OUR
PLANET

Structure and surface of the Earth

The crust, the uppermost layer of the solid Earth, is a region of interaction between surface processes brought about by the heat of radioactive reactions deep in the Earth. Physically and chemically it is the most complex layer of the lithosphere. The Earth's crust contains a wide variety of rock types, ranging from sedimentary rocks dominated by single minerals, such as sandstone (which is mainly silica) and limestone (which is mainly calcite), to the mineral-chemical mixture igneous rocks such as basalt lavas and granite intrusions.

The crust is divided into ocean crust and continental crust. The average height of the two differs by about 2.8 mi. and the difference in their average total thickness is more exaggerated (continental crust is about 25 mi. thick, and oceanic crust about 4.4 mi.). The boundary between the crusts and the mantle is almost everywhere defined sharply by the Mohorovičić seismic discontinuity. There are further differences between the oceanic and continental crusts: They contrast strongly in structure, composition, average age, origin, and evolution. Vertical sections of both types of crust have been studied in zones of uplift caused by colliding tectonic plates. Combined with seismic evidence, these sections provide a unified view of crustal structure and composition.

Oceanic crust

Seismic studies of the ocean crust and upper mantle have identified four separate layers characterized by downward increases in wave propagation velocity, density, and thickness. The upper two layers were studied by the Deep Sea Drilling Project in 1968, whereas all that is known about the third and fourth layers has come only from ophiolites – uplifted ocean crust sections that are exposed on the Earth's surface. The top layer of the ocean crust, with an average thickness of nearly one third mile, comprises sedimentary muds (pelagic clays). They include the finest particles that were eroded from continents, and biochemically precipitated carbonate and siliceous deposits. The bottom three layers are made up of igneous materials formed during ocean-ridge processes. The chemical composition of these layers is that of basic igneous rocks, but their physical characteristics vary. The second layer, with an average thickness of one mile consists of basalt pillow lavas that were originally quenched by seawater when they erupted onto the sea floor. At the boundary between the second and third layers stratified lava is found that is interspersed with vertical dykes through which, originally, the pillow lava was ejected. These dykes lead to the third layer, a 2 mi. thick sequence of layered, coarse-grained, intrusive gabbros that must have cooled and crystallized slowly, with early formed crystals segregating into layers. The bottom layers includes layered peridotite which grades downwards into unlayered mantle peridotite.

The Earth has four main structural components, namely the crust, the mantle and the outer and inner cores. The crust extends down to about 25 mi. and consists of rocks with a density of less than 190 lb./cu. ft. The mantle, divided by a transition zone, is made up of denser rocks than the crust. The temperature in this region rises rapidly, particularly between 62 and 124 mi. below the surface, where it reaches more than 1,800° F. At the core-mantle boundary (the Gutenberg discontinuity), 1,800 mi. below the surface, the pressure suddenly increases, as does the density (from 340 lb./cu. ft. to 620 lb./cu. ft.). The outer core is completely liquid, but the inner core is solid with an average density of 690 lb./cu. ft.

Both layered perdotites and gabbros probably represent a fossilized magma chamber, which was originally created by the partial melting of the mantle beneath an ocean ridge. Molten material was probably ejected from the chamber roof, forming dykes that fed the pillow lava eruptions of the second layer. The Mohorovičić discontinuity lies between the two deepest layers.

Continental crust

In terms of seismic structure, the Earth's continental crust is much less regular than the ocean crust. A diffuse boundary called the Conrad discontinuity

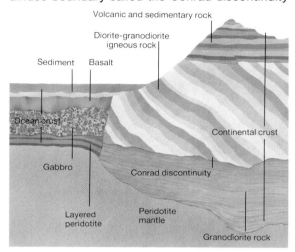

occurs between the upper and lower continental crusts at a depth of between 9 and 16 mi. The upper continental crust has a highly variable top layer which is a few miles thick and comprises relatively unmetamorphosed volcanic and sedimentary rocks. Most of the sedimentary rocks were laid down in shallow marine environments and subsequently uplifted. Beneath this superficial layer of the upper crust, most of the rock is similar in composition to granodiorite or diorite and is made up of intermediate, coarse-grained intrusive, igneous rocks. The total thickness of the upper continental crust reaches a maximum of about 16 mi. in zones of recent crustal thickening caused by igneous activity (as in the Andes mountain range in South America) and by tectonic overthrusting during collision (as in the Alps and Himalayas). This crust is of minimum thickness (about 9 mi.) in the ancient continental cratonic shield areas, where igneous rocks have been metamorphosed to form granite gneisses.

The lower continental crust extends down to the Mohorovičić discontinuity and comprises denser rocks that are only in their chemical composition similar to that of the upper crust. They include intermediate igneous rocks that have suffered intense metamorphism at high pressures, resulting in the growth of dense minerals; and basic igneous, less metamorphosed rocks. This region is the least well-known, most inaccessible part of the Earth's crust.

The Earth's interior

Despite the information available about the surface of our planet, comparatively little is known about the state and composition of its inaccessible interior. The deepest boreholes (about 6 mi.) hardly scratch the Earth's outer skin and the deepest known samples of rock, nodules of unmolten material brought up in volcanic lavas, come from a depth of only about 60 mi., just 1.5 per cent of the distance to the center.

Our knowledge of the deeper interior relies on indirect evidence from physical measurements of the Earth's mass, volume and mean density, observations of seismic waves that have passed through the deep interior, observations of meteorites and

The Earth's crust is divided into oceanic and continental crust. Oceanic crust is about 2.5 mi. lower than continental crust and is about 20 per cent of its thickness. The structure of oceanic crust is uniform: a layer of sediment covers three layers of igneous rock of which the thickest is the layer of gabbro. These layers form from the partial melting of the underlying peridotite mantle. In contrast to the uniformity of oceanic crust, the structure of continental crust is varied and changes over short distances.

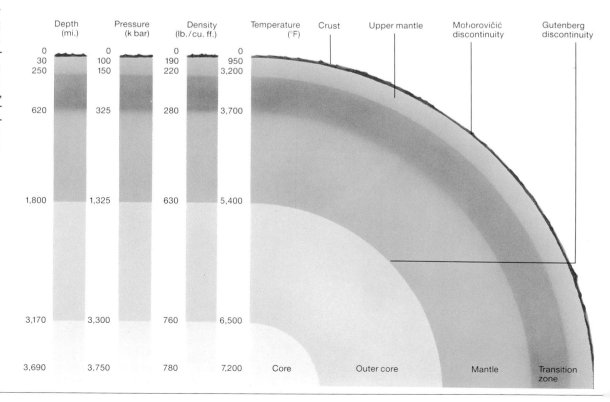

other bodies in the Solar System, experimental studies of natural materials at the high pressures and temperatures of the Earth's interior, and studies of the Earth's magnetic field.

Seismic waves passing through the Earth's interior have revealed two major and three relatively minor discontinuities where changes in chemical and physical states occur. These data also help to determine the density and elastic properties of the materials through which the waves pass, since these properties govern wave velocities.

The seismic discontinuities are broadly concentric with the Earth's surface. Therefore, they mark the boundaries of spherical shells with successively greater density – the major subdivisions into crust, mantle, and core occur at the Mohorovičić and Gutenberg discontinuities.

The crust varies in thickness from about 4 mi. in oceanic areas to about 25 mi. under the continents and the mantle extends down to 1,800 mi. It contains a low-velocity layer which lies between 30 and 125 mi. below the surface, where seismic wave velocities are reduced by a few per cent, and it is most prominent and shallow beneath oceanic areas. The mantle also has a transition zone (from 250 to about 620 mi. under the surface), which is characterized by several sharp increases in wave velocity that are concurrent with an increase in density. The Earth's core is subdivided into outer and inner regions by a minor discontinuity at a depth of about 3,200 mi. The outer core does not transmit seismic shear waves and is the only totally fluid layer in the Earth.

The mantle

The combined evidence from volcanic nodules, exposed thrust slices of possible mantle rocks, physical data and meteorite studies, indicates that the upper mantle is made of silicate minerals. Among these minerals dark green olivine predominates, together with lesser amounts of black pyroxene, iron silicates and calcium aluminum silicates in a rock type known as peridotite.

Because temperature increases rapidly with depth in the outer 60 to 125 mi. of the Earth, there comes a point (at about 2,700° F) at which peridotite starts to melt. The presence of partial melt accounts

for the low-velocity layer and basalt magmas that erupt, particularly from oceanic volcanoes. Because olivine has the highest melting temperature of the silicate minerals in peridotite it remains solid, while other, less abundant minerals contribute to the melt.

Temperature increases less rapidly with greater depth than does the melting point, so no further melting occurs at extreme depth although the hot, solid material is susceptible to plastic deformation and convects very slowly. This part of the mantle is

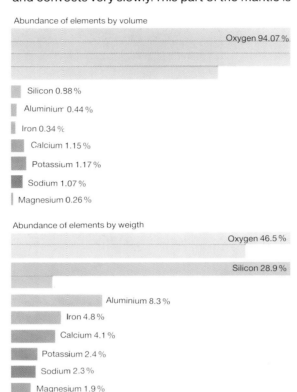

Abundance of elements by volume

	Oxygen 94.07 %

Silicon 0.98 %

Aluminium 0.44 %

Iron 0.34 %

Calcium 1.15 %

Potassium 1.17 %

Sodium 1.07 %

Magnesium 0.26 %

Abundance of elements by weigth

	Oxygen 46.5 %
	Silicon 28.9 %

Aluminium 8.3 %

Iron 4.8 %

Calcium 4.1 %

Potassium 2.4 %

Sodium 2.3 %

Magnesium 1.9 %

The chemical composition of the Earth's crust is dominated by eight elements, which together make up more than 99 per cent by weight and by volume of the crust. Of these elements, oxygen is the most abundant, followed by silicon; most of the rock forming minerals of the crust are therefore silicates.

the asthenosphere, or weak layer, which is distinct from the rigid uppermost mantle and crust, or lithosphere.

Increasing pressure is responsible for the transition zone where several rapid increases in density are probably caused by changes in the structure of the solids. In this zone the atomic structure of the compressed silicate minerals change to new forms in which the atoms are packed together more closely to occupy less volume. These new forms are thought to persist down to 1,800 mi.

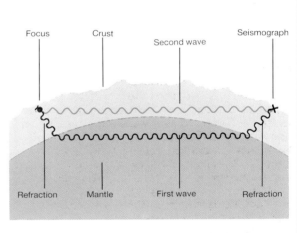

A seismic wave moving through the crust arrives at a point on the surface later than a wave that has travelled farther but that has been refracted into the denser mantle and then refracted back to the surface. This phenomenon occurs because the denser the rock the faster the wave travels.

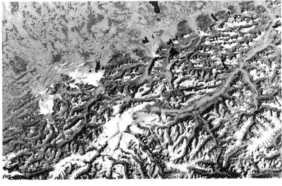

The Alps are a typical example of a mountain chain formed by tectonic overthrusting. At some stage the strata of the Alpine region were subjected to compressive deformation from opposing plates which resulted in extensive faulting and elevation.

Gneiss, visible in the foreground and in the middle distance bordering the bay, is an igneous rock that is formed under intense metamorphism deep in the crust. It is exposed over time by uplift and erosion.

Structure and surface of the Earth   227

Plate tectonics

On the human timescale most of the Earth seems passive and unchanging. But in some places – California, Italy, Turkey and Japan, for example – the Earth's crust is active and liable to move, producing earthquakes or volcanic eruptions. These and other dynamic areas lie on the major earthquake belts, most of which run along the middle of the ocean basins, although some are situated on the edges of oceans (around the Pacific Ocean, for instance) or pass across continental land masses (as along the Alpine-Himalayan belt).

It is this observation that there are several, relatively well-defined dynamic zones in the Earth's crust which forms the basis of plate tectonics. According to this theory, the crust consists of several large, rigid plates and the movements of the plates produce the Earth's major structural features, such as mountain ranges, mid-ocean ridges, ocean trenches and large faults. Stable areas with few or no earthquakes or active volcanoes lie in the middle of a plate, whereas active areas – where major structures are constantly being destroyed created – are situated along the plate boundaries.

The extent and nature of crustal plates

The positions and sizes of the crustal plates can be determined by studying the paths of seismic waves (shock waves produced by earthquakes) that travel around and through the Earth. Such studies have also made it possible to estimate the thickness of the plates. Geologists have found that seismic waves tend to slow down and become less intense between about 60 and 250 mi. below the surface. From this observation they suggest that the solid lithosphere (which consists of the Earth's outermost layer, the crust, and the top part of the mantle, the layer below the crust) "floats" on a less rigid layer (the asthenosphere) which, because it is plastic, allows vertical and horizontal movements of the rigid lithospheric plates.

By collating the findings from various seismological studies, geologists have discovered that the lithosphere is divided into a relatively small number of plates. Most of them are very large – covering millions of square miles – but are less than about 60 mi. thick.

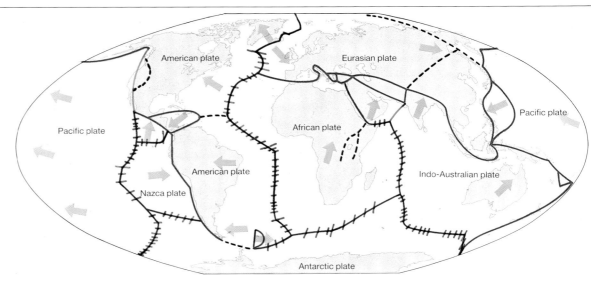

The main plates and their boundaries: Constructive boundaries are dark purple, destructive boundaries red, and transform faults green; broken black lines mark uncertain boundaries. Plate movements are shown with blue arrows.

Plate movements

The landforms, earthquake activity and vulcanism that characterize plate boundaries are caused by movements of the plates. There are three principal motions: the plates may move apart, collide or slide past each other.

Plate separation entails the formation of new lithosphere between the plates involved. This process occurs at constructive plate boundaries along the crests of mid-ocean ridges (and is therefore termed sea-floor spreading), where material from the mantle wells up to create the new crust.

Plate collision, on the other hand, necessitates the destruction of lithosphere at a plate boundary. Ocean trenches mark destructive plate boundaries, and at these sites the lithosphere of one plate is thrust beneath an overriding plate and resorbed into the mantle; this process is called subduction.

Ultimately, continued subduction of an ocean basin can lead to the complete disappearance of the basin and collision of the continents at its edges. In such collisions, mountain belts may be formed as the continents push against each other and force the intervening land upwards – as occurred when India collided with Asia some 50 million years ago, creating the Himalayas.

After a continental collision, the momentum of the plates is initially absorbed by thickening and overthrusting of the continental crust. But there is a limit to which this process can occur and, because the continental crust is too buoyant to be subducted, the momentum must be dissipated in other ways – by the sideways movements of small plates that form within the newly-created mountain belt or by a more general, probably world-wide, change in the boundaries and movements of the plates.

The other principal type of plate movement occurs when plates slide past each other (at what are called sites of transform faulting) which, unlike the first two types of movement, involves neither creation nor destruction of the intervening lithosphere. often major faults, such as the San Andreas fault in California, mark these plate boundaries (which are called conservative plate boundaries).

Rates of plate movements

Most of our knowledge about the very slow rates of plate movements has come from studies of the Earth's magnetic field. In the past the magnetic field has repeatedly reversed direction (a phenomenon called polarity reversal). A record of the changing magnetic field has been preserved in the permanent "fossil" magnetism of the basalt rocks that form the ocean floor.

Around sites of sea-floor spreading, bands of rocks with normal polarity alternate with bands having a reversed polarity. By dating these different bands, the rate of spreading can be deduced. Using this method it has been found that the rates of plate separation vary from about 9 mm a year in the northern Atlantic Ocean to 90 mm a year in the Pacific Ocean. From these determinations of separation rates geologists have calculated the relative motions of plates that are moving together or sliding past each other. They have thus determined the movements of almost all the plates on the surface of the Earth.

A spectacular demonstration of the activity at a constructive plate boundary occurred in November 1963 when the volcanic island of Surtsey emerged from the sea, erupting lava and emitting large amounts of gas and dust. Situated off southern Iceland, Surtsey stands on the Mid-Atlantic Ridge, which marks the boundary between the slowly-separating Eurasian and American plates.

The Pyrenees extend along the border between France and Spain. They were formed as a result of tectonic movements (which produced folding of the rock strata) during the Eocene and Oligocene periods (which together lasted from 54 to 26 million years ago).

Structure of continents

The continents are large areas of crust that make up the solid surface of the Earth. They consist of comparatively low-density material called sial, and hence tend to float above other crustal material – the sima – in which they are embedded.

On a map of the globe each continent has a very different shape and appearance from the others, and each has its own climate zones and animal life. The geological structure of each one is, however, very much the same.

The simple continent

In its simplest form, a continent is older at the center than at the edges. The old center is known as a craton and is made up of rocks that were formed several billion years ago when the Earth's crust was thinner than it now is. The craton is not involved in any mountain building activity because it is already compact and tightly deformed by ancient mountain building, although the mountains that had been found on it have long since been worn away by the processes of erosion. Typical cratons include the Canadian Shield, covering northern and central Europa and the Siberian Shield in northern Asia. Several smaller cratons exist in South America, India, Africa, Antarctia and Australia.

The craton is the nucleus of the continent. It is flanked by belts of fold mountains, the oldest being nearer the craton and the youngest farther away. North America provides an excellent example, consisting of the Canadian Shield flanked in the east by the Appalachians and in the west by the Rockies. Close to the shield the Appalachians were formed about 400 million years ago, whereas farther east they were formed about 300 million years ago. The same is true of the mountains to the west, with the main part of the Rockies being about 200 million years old, whereas the coastal ranges are still geologically active today.

The reason for this structure is that when a continent lies at a subduction zone at the boundary between two crustal plates, its mass cannot be drawn down into the higher-density mantle. Instead it crumples up at the edge, the sedimentary areas around the coast being forced up into mountain chains which may be laced through with volcanic

material from the plate tectonic activity. These movements may take place several times during a continent's history, with each subsequent mountain chain being attached to the one that was formed previously.

Supercontinents

In reality the situation is much more complicated. As the continents move about on the Earth's surface, two may collide with each other and become welded into a single mass. The result is a supercontinent, which has two or more cratons. The weld line between the two original continents is marked by a mountain range that was formed as their coastal ranges came together and crushed up any sediments that may have been between them. Europe and Asia together constitute such a supercontinent, the Urals having been formed when the two main masses came together about 30 million years ago.

On the other hand, a single continental mass may split, becoming two or more smaller continents. This has happened on a grand scale within the last 200 million years. Just before that thime all the continents of the Earth's crust had come together, forming one vast temporary supercontinent, known to geologists as Pangaea. Since then the single mass has fragmented into the distribution of continents we know today. Indeed the process is still continuing. The great Rift Valley of eastern Africa represents the first stage of a movement in which eastern Africa is breaking away from the main African landmass. The slumping structures found at the sides of a rift valley are also seen at the margins of the continents that are known to have split away and have not yet been subjected to any marginal mountain-building activity. The eastern coast of South America and the western coast of Africa show such features.

Not all continental masses are above sea level. The Indian Ocean contains many small continental fragments that have sheared off, just as India and Antarctica split away from Africa 200 million years ago. Such fragments include the Agulhas Plateau off South Africa, and the Seychelles and Kerguelen plateaux, each with islands representing their highest portions.

Areas of sedimentation

Another significant feature around the continents is their depositional basins. These are areas that have subsided and may even be below sea level. Because rivers tend to flow into such areas, the basins soon become thickly covered by sediments. The North Sea is an example of a sedimentary basin in northern Europe.

The Alps are comparatively young mountains, in geological terms, in which the rock strata form complex patterns because of the folding and faulting that accompanied their formations.

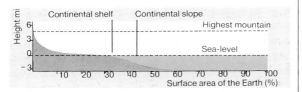

The continents – the land areas of the world – cover only about 30 per cent of the Earth's surface, and little of it rises to more than one half mile above sea-level.

In some areas of the continental margin a large river may flow over the continental shelf and deposit its sediments in the ocean beyond. In such areas the edge of the continental shelf becomes extended beyond that of the rest of the area. The rivers Indus and Ganges produce shelf sediments in the Indian Ocean, and the Amazon and Zaire do the same on opposite sides of the Atlantic.

The actual land area of a continent may also be increased by these means, if the river builds up an extensive delta at its mouth. Considerable land areas have been built up in this way at the mouths of the rivers Mississippi and Niger.

At the edge of a continent (below), where the continental crustal plate is riding over an oceanic plate, typical features include offshore island arcs (such as the Japanese islands) and relatively young mountain chains (such as the Andes). Farther inland a sedimentary basin (such as the North Sea), may form on tops of the older rocks of a craton. Rift valleys form in mid-continent.

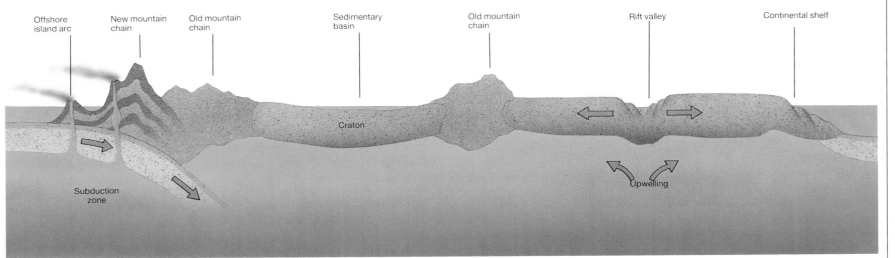

Continental drift

The continental masses that stand proud of their surrounding oceanic crust have never occupied fixed positions on the Earth's surface. They are constantly carried around on the tectonic plates rather like logs embedded in the ice-floes of a partly frozen river. The movement is going on at the present day, with North America moving away from Europe at a rate of about one inch per year. The movement of Africa against Europe is made evident by the intensity of earthquake activity and the presence of active volcanoes in the Mediterranean area.

The proof that this has been happening throughout geological time takes a number of forms.

Physical proof

The first line of evidence – in fact the first observation that suggested that the continents are in motion – is the apparent fit of one continental coastline with another. The eastern coast of South America and the western coast of Africa are so similar in shape that it seems quite obvious that the two once fitted together like the pieces of a jigsaw puzzle. The other continents can also be pieced together in a similar way, but usually the fit is not so obvious; for example, Africa, India, Antarctica and Australia would also mate together. It is the edges of the continental shelves, rather than the actual coastlines that provide the neat fit.

If the continents were placed together, certain physical features could be seen to be continuous from one to another across the joints. Mountains formed 400 million years ago and now found in south-eastern Canada and eastern Greenland would be continuous with those of the same age now found in Scotland and Norway, if North America and Europe were placed together. Mountain ranges in Brazil would be continuous with those in Nigeria if South America and Africa were brought together.

Evidence for ancient climates is also a good indicator of continental drift. Northern Europe went through a phase of desert conditions about 400 million years ago, followed by a phase of tropical forest 300 million years ago, and then another desert phase 200 million years ago. This is consistent with the movement of that area from the southern desert climate zone of the Earth, through the equatorial forest zone and into the northern desert zone.

About 280 million years ago an ice age gripped the Southern Hemisphere. The evidence for this includes ice-formed deposits and glacier marks from that period found in South America, southern Africa, Australia and, significantly, India – which is now in the Northern Hemisphere. If the continents were reassembled and the directions of ice movements analyzed, they would point to an ice cap with its center in Antarctica.

Biological proof

The evidence from fossils is just as spectacular. Fossils of the same land animals and plants have been found on all the southern continents in rocks dating from about 250 million years ago. These are creatures that could not have evolved independently on separate continents. *Mesosaurus* was a freshwater reptile, resembling a small crocodile, and its remains have been found both in South America and South Africa. *Lystrosaurus* was like a reptilian hippopotamus and its remains have been found in India, Africa and Antarctica. The fernlike plant *Glossopteris* is typical of the plants that lived at the same time as these creatures and its remains have been found in South America, Africa, India and Australia.

Similar biological evidence is found in the Northern Hemisphere where the dinosaurs of Europe, 150 million years ago, were similar to those of North America.

The mammals that developed in various parts of the world during the last 65 million years also reveal evidence of the movements of the continents. Up to about 10 million years ago the dominant mammals of South America were the pouched marsupials, similar to those of Australia today. This suggests that their origin lies in a single southern continent. Later, most of the South American marsupials became extinct after a sudden influx of more advanced placental mammals from North America, suggesting that South and North America became attached to one another about 10 million years ago. India was a similar isolated continent, broken away from the southern landmass, until it collided with Asia about 50 million years ago. It would be interesting to see if the mammals of India before this date were marsupials or not, but no Indian mammal fossils have been found for the relevant period. In 1980 a fossil maruspial was found in Antarctica, helping to substantiate the theories.

Magnetic proof

The positions of the Earth's magnetic poles change over a long period of time. Clues to their location in any particular geological period lie in the way in which particles in the rocks that formed in that period have been magnetized. As rocks are formed, the magnetic particles in them line up with the prevailing magnetic field of the Earth, and are then locked in position when the rock solidifies. This phenomenon is sometimes known as remanent magnetism and it has been actively studied since the 1960s. It has been found that the remanent magnetism for different periods in each of the continents point to a single north pole only if the continents are "moved" in relation to each other.

Nearly 200 million years ago, the landmasses of the Earth were concentrated into one supercontinent, called Pangaea (A). Some geologists propose that, at that time, the Earth was only four-fifths its present size, and computer-plotted maps seem to support this view. Then, as Pangaea broke up and the continents began to move apart, the Earth as a whole gradually became larger. Map B is a reconstruction of the Earth of about 120 million years ago. By about 55 million years ago (C), the Atlantic Ocean had widened, India was on a collision course with Asia, and Australia was beginning to become detached from Antarctica. Map D shows the Earth as it is now, but even today the crustal plates are not static. Sea-floor spreading will continue to widen the Atlantic and Indian oceans, and Australia will continue on its north-easterly course. Seismic and volcanic activity, as along the eastern seaboard of the Pacific Ocean, result from subduction of the Pacific plate as it is being overridden by the westward-moving Americas. In northeastern Africa, there is evidence that Arabia is splitting off from the rest of the continent.

The mountains of the Himalayan range were uplifted as a result of the impact between the Indian subcontinent and the Asian crustal plate about 50 million years ago.

Sedimentary rocks

Sedimentary rocks are the most common types on the Earth's surface. In general, they were all formed in a similar way – by the deposition, compression and cementing together of numerous small particles of mineral, animal or plant origin. The details of these processes are best exemplified by clastic sedimentary rocks, which consist of mineral fragments derived from pre-existing rocks.

As soon as rocks are exposed on the Earth's surface they begin to be broken down by the forces of erosion. The rock fragments, and the minerals washed out of them, are carried by the wind, by streams or the sea, and finally come to rest as sediment. Eventually it becomes covered with more sediment, and the underlying layers are compressed and cemented together to form sedimentary rock – a process called lithification. After millions of years, this rock may be uplifted by Earth movements – thereby again exposed to the forces of erosion – and the entire process is repeated. This cycle of erosion, transportation, deposition, lithification and uplift is known as the sedimentary cycle.

Erosion, transportation and deposition

By studying the various features of a sedimentary rock, geologists can deduce a great deal about the conditions prevalent at the time of its formation. Sedimentary rocks typically occur as separate horizontal layers called beds, each formed as a result of fairly frequent changes in the sedimentation conditions. When sedimentation stops, the sediments settle; when it resumes, a new layer begins to form on top of the previous one. Unlayered sedimentary rocks – described as massive – therefore reflect long periods of unchanging conditions. Analysis of the grains that make up the rocks may reveal the composition of those from which the fragments originated. In some, the minerals are the same as those in the original rock, but more commonly they have been altered by reactions with water and chemicals in the atmosphere.

The sizes and shapes of the constituent particles reflect the distance they have travelled and the current conditions they encountered. For instance, the faster a current of water, the larger are the rock fragments that can be carried by it. Thus, large-grained sedimentary rocks were originally formed from large pebbles and boulders deposited by fast-flowing rivers or by the sea. Such rocks are called conglomerates if their fragments are rounded, or breccias if they are jagged and angular. Sandstones consist of their sediments that were laid down by weaker currents. Extremely small particles can be carried long distances by even very slow-moving water. The sediments that result are silts and muds, which occur in slow-flowing rivers or on the sea floor far away from a turbulent shoreline. When lithified, these very fine sediments form siltstones, mudstones or shales.

A mixture of different sized grains in the same rock may indicate that the current stopped abruptly, thereby suddenly depositing all of the various sized particles it was carrying. Such a sedimentary bed is

The sedimentary cycle is the process that produces sedimentary rocks. Exposed rocks are broken down by the forces of weathering and erosion. The fragments are carried away by wind, rivers or sea currents and are then deposited as beds of sediment. Eventually these beds are buried and turned to rock (lithification). At a later time the beds of sedimentary rock are pushed upwards and exposed by mountain-building activity. The exposed rocks are then eroded and the cycle begins again.

Millions of years of erosion have exposed the layers of sedimentary rocks in the Grand Canyon (in Arizona, USA), thereby providing a superb record of the area's geological history. The Grand Canyon is about 5,500 ft. deep at its deepest point, where the rocks are some 1.8 billion years old. Its walls consist chiefly of limestones, shales and sandstones.

termed poorly sorted. Well-sorted beds, in which all the particles are of approximately the same size, result from stable current conditions.

The shape of the particles in a sedimentary rock indicates the distance the eroded fragments travelled before being deposited and lithified. The farther the fragments travelled, the rounder they are because of the greater amount of abrasion from rubbing against other particles.

Rocks from sediment

It takes millions of years for a sediment to become rock. After deposition, the sediments are compressed beneath further layers that accumulate on top of them. The weight of the upper layers forces the underlying particles closer together, causing them to interlock and form a solid mass, but the mass is not yet rock at this stage, because the particles – although tightly packed together – are still separate. In the next phase – cementation – the particles are bonded together to form rock. Groundwater percolating through rock and sediment often has calcite

dissolved in it, leached out of lime-rich rocks by the weak carbonic acid formed when carbon dioxide in the air reacts with water in rain. The dissolved calcite then precipitates in the minute spaces between grains, thereby cementing them together. The resulting compressed and cemented mass is the sedimentary rock.

Types of sedimentary rocks

In addition to clastic rocks, there are two other principal types of sedimentary rocks: chemical and organic (or biogenic). Chemical sedimentary rocks are formed when dissolved material precipitates out of water. For example, a bed of salt may be formed when part of the sea becomes cut off from the main body of water and eventually evaporates, leaving a deposit of salt, which may later be overlaid and compressed.

Organic sedimentary rocks are formed from the remains of animals or plants. One of the most common is limestone, which consists of the remains of small marine shellfish. When these creatures die, they sink to the sea bed, where their shells are broken up and then compressed and cemented together in the same way as clastic rocks.

Coal is probably the most familiar example of an organic sedimentary rock. It consists mainly of carbon, derived from masses of plant matter that accumulated in forested swamps aeons ago. Because of the lack of oxygen in the swamp water, the plants did not decompose; instead they became compressed and lithified into coal.

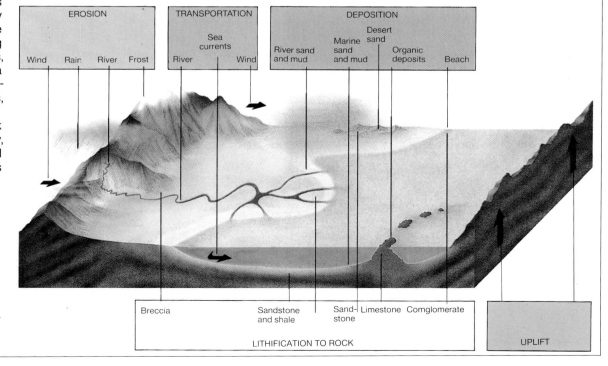

Igneous rocks

Igneous rocks orginate in masses of hot fluid that circulate deep within the Earth. This molten rock, called magma, may consist of part of the Earth's crust that has melted as a result of tectonic or mountain-building activity, or it may arise from the mantle (the layer immediately below the crust).

Rocks from magma

Igneous rocks are formed when molten magma cools and solidifies. Different types of igneous rocks may be produced out of the same mass of magma. As the magma cools, its components solidify in a set sequence. The first minerals to crystalize out of the melt are the high-temperature minerals – the olivines and pyroxenes, which are silicates of magnesium and iron. They tend to be the denser components and so they sink, leaving the remaining fluid deficient in magnesium and iron. The next group of minerals to solidify are the feldspars (silicate minerals of potassium, sodium, calcium and aluminum – the lighter metallic elements); the magma thus loses its metallic constituents first. Finally, any remaining silica crystallizes out as quartz. The entire solidification process, or differentation as it is called, therefore results in dense iron- and magnesium-rich rocks and less dense silica-rich rocks from the same original fluid. This is dramatically exemplified in the rare outcrops in which the different types of rock can be seen as layers in the same rock mass – as occurs in the approximately 980 ft. thick Palisade Sill in New Jersey in the United States, which has an olivine-rich layer at the bottom, and rocks with progressively less olivine above. Usually, however, an outcrop consists of only one type of igneous rock.

Geologists classify igneous rocks according to their composition. Those that have a low silica content (and are also usually rich in iron and magnesium) are called basic rocks; those with a high silica content are termed acid rocks. Basic rocks, such as gabbro, tend to be dark in colour because their constituent minerals are dark, whereas acid rocks (such as granite) are light in colour because they contain white and pink feldspars and glassy quartz. Igneous rocks are also categorized according to their origin: intrusive rocks, formed from magma that solidified beneath the surface, and extrusive rocks, from magma that solidified above the surface.

Magma that cools quickly, as in a lava flow, forms a very fine-grained rock, such as basalt. Contraction of the cooling rock may cause it to crack and form a series of hexagonal columns that stand perpendicular to the lava surface. The classic example of this phenomenon is the Giant's Causeway on the north-eastern coast of Northern Ireland.

Igneous textures

When hot magma cools slowly, the minerals in it have sufficient time to grow large crystals and hence, form coarse rock. The mineral crystals in rocks that have cooled quickly, on the other hand, are often too small to be seen with the naked eye. The coarseness of a rock depends on where it was formed. Very coarse-grained rocks, such as the gabbros and granites, solidified deep underground and therefore cooled slowly. Volcanic rocks, such as basalts and trachites, were formed from magma that cooled rapidly on the surface of the Earth and are therefore fine-grained. The finest-grained igneous rocks originated from volcanoes that erupted underwater or beneath glaciers, as a result of which the lava (magma ejected by a volcano) cooled extremely rapidly.

Occasionally, such igneous rocks are so fine-grained that no crystalline structure is visible, resulting in a natural glass called obsidian.

Sometimes an igneous rock has two textures. It may have large crystals (called phenocrysts) embedded in a matrix of very small ones. This type of two-textured rock forms when magma begins to differentiate slowly then, when some of the crystals have formed, solidifies much more rapidly – probably because it was forced into a cooler location. This texture is known as porphyritic, and the rock is called a porphyry.

The texture and composition of a rock can be studied by cutting a sample into thin transparent slices and examining them with a microscope. The rock's constituents can then be determined by viewing the sections using polarized light, a technique that causes each mineral crystal to appear as a different colour. This method reveals that the minerals which formed first have well-defined crystal shapes, whereas those that grew later tend to be distorted.

Igneous structures

It is not possible to observe igneous rocks while they form (except volcanic rocks, in which the crystallization and solidification can be particularly spectacular) because most igneous rocks form deep under the surface of the Earth in structures called intrusions. From these intrusions the magma can push its way through cracks, forcing aside or melting the surrounding rocks, and the resultant structures reflect this action.

The largest igneous intrusions are called batholiths and they form deep below the surface in active mountain chains. They may extend over hundreds of square miles. Underground cracks may fill with magma, forming sheets of igneous rock when the magma solidifies. The sheets are known as sills if they lie parallel to the strata of the surrounding rocks, or dykes if they cut across the strata. Igneous rocks may also form cylindrical structures – called stocks if they are broad and necks if they are narrow – which may once have led to volcanoes on the surface.

Igneous rocks (and metamorphic rocks) tend to be harder than any surrounding sedimentary formations. As a result, when a mass of rock containing both igneous and sedimentary types is eroded, the softer sedimentary rocks usually wear away first, leaving the igneous masses as hills and other landscape features that reflect their original shapes.

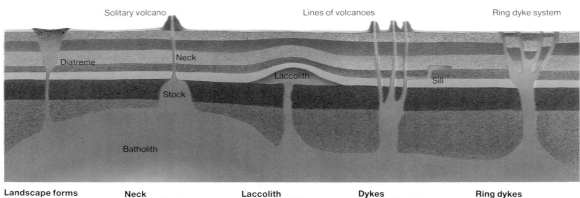

Solitary volcano — Diatreme — Neck — Stock — Batholith — Laccolith — Lines of volcanoes — Sill — Ring dyke system

Landscape forms

Diatreme
A diatreme is a funnel-shaped structure formed by the explosive expansion of magma as it rises through areas of lower pressure.

Neck
Erosion of the terrain down to a volcano's neck produces an isolated cylindrical hill, such as Devil's Tower in Wyoming, USA.

Laccolith
When a laccolith is exposed by erosion, it produces a rounded hill surrounded by circular scarps.

Dykes
A longitudinal dyke system results from erosion of a line of volcanoes.

Ring dykes
Ring dykes are concentric ridges of igneous rock that are formed when the land around a circular dyke system subsides.

Magma from a batholith pushes its way through the overlying rocks and forms igneous intrusions (stocks, laccoliths and sills, for example) as it solidifies. Igneous rocks tend to be harder than the rocks surrounding them, and so, after the softer rocks have been eroded away, various igneous structures are exposed and form characteristic landscape features, some of which are illustrated on the left.

Metamorphic rocks

When rocks are subjected to different conditions from those under which they originally formed, their minerals change. This alteration can happen when rocks are exposed at the Earth's surface and their minerals react with various chemicals in the atmosphere. Much more marked effects occur when rocks are buried deep in an emerging mountain range and subjected to very high temperatures and pressures. Under these conditions the rocks alter completely, becoming entirely different types of rocks with different mineral compositions. Such transformed rocks are called metamorphic rocks. The characteristic feature of a metamorphic rock is that its mineral composition changes without the rock itself melting. If the rock does melt and then solidify again, the result is an igneous not a metamorphic rock.

Regional metamorphism

Regional (or dynamic) metamorphic rocks – one of the two main types – are those that have been altered by great pressure but low temperature – as occurs, for example, in the heart of a fold mountain belt while it is being compressed between moving crustal plates. The efforts of such a movement are usually extensive, hence regional metamorphic rocks tend to occupy large areas.

At depths in the order of tens of miles the weight of the overlying rocks produces sufficiently high pressures to alter the mineral structure of the rocks beneath. For example, the minerals in shale (the black, flaky sedimentary rock that is produced by the lithification of mud) recrystallize into the mineral mica as a result of great pressure. The flat, leaf-like mica crystals form in parallel bands (known as the rock's foliation). Earth movements associated with metamorphic processes may then deform the mica, forcing it to distort along the lines of foliation and producing, in turn, a schist, a typical regional metamorphic rock. The mineral bands in schist are very pronounced and are often distorted and jagged in appearance – evidence of the great stresses involved in their formation. A schist can usually be easily split along its foliation lines; this tendency to split along certain planes of weakness is called cleavage.

The cleavage of a regional metamorphic rock is exploited commercially in the quarrying and work-ing of slate. Like schist, slate is formed by the metamorphism of shale, but under less extreme pressure. Compared with shale, the minerals in slate are small and are often invisible to the naked eye.

It is sometimes assumed – erroneously – that the cleavage of slate corresponds to the lines of the thin bedding in the shale from which it was originally formed. In fact the cleavage reflects the direction of the pressure to which the shale was subjected during its metamorphism rather than the original structure of the rock.

Thermal metamorphism

In the other main type of metamorphism – thermal (or contact) metamorphism – rocks are changed by the effects of great heat but low pressure. Thermal metamorphic rocks are formed when a hot igneous mass of magma forces its way through the Earth's crust, literally baking the rock surrounding it. In comparison with regional metamorphism, the volume of rock affected by thermal metamorphic processes is very small; the newly-formed thermal metamorphic rock may extend for only a few inches around the igneous intrusion (the affected area is called an aureole) or, occasionally, the new rock may be about one half mile wide around a very large batholith. There is usually a gradation of thermal metamorphic rocks around large intrusions; near such an intrusion there are high-temperature rocks, which gradually give way with increasing distance from the intrusion to low-temperature then unmetamorphosed rocks.

Probably the most familiar thermal metamorphic rock is marble, which is produced by the metamorphism of limestone, a sedimentary rock consisting almost entirely of calcite (calcium carbonate). When the calcite is subjected to great heat from a nearby igneous intrusion, it first gives off carbon dioxide then recombines with this gas, thereby reforming new calcite crystals and transforming the limestone to marble. The newly-formed crystals have a regular form and grain size (as opposed to the random collection of fragments in the original limestone) which gives the marble strength and an even texture.

Usually, however, the elements in the minerals of the original rock recombine during metamorphism to form completely different minerals, as occurs in

Vast slate quarries *illustrate the great quantities of rock that can be altered by regional metamorphism. Slate, which is produced by the metamorphism of shale, is used to make roofing tiles and is one of the few metamorphic rocks of significant commercial importance.*

the formation of hornfels, which often contains cordierite (a silicate mineral found only in thermal metamorphic rocks).

Other types of metamorphism

Dislocation metamorphism is a relatively rare type that occurs when the rocks on each side of a major fault move against each other as the fault slips. In this situation the stresses can be so great that the minerals in the rocks at the fault break down and recrystallize, thereby giving rise to a hard, flinty metamorphic rock called mylonite.

Metasomatism is similar to – and often associated with – thermal metamorphism. As an igneous mass cools, it gives off hot liquids and gases, which may percolate through cracks and cavities in the surrounding rock. The hot fluids may then alter the surrounding rock by a combination of heat and deposition of minerals dissolved in the fluids. Many of the most productive deposits of metal ores are from veins that have been emplaced by metasomatic activity.

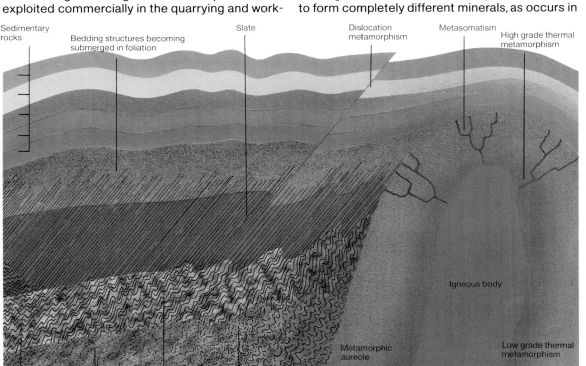

Sedimentary rocks · Bedding structures becoming submerged in foliation · Slate · Dislocation metamorphism · Metasomatism · High grade thermal metamorphism · Igneous body · Metamorphic aureole · Low grade thermal metamorphism · Contorted foliation · Coarse-grained foliation · Schist · Gneiss

Regional metamorphism *takes place deep underground where the pressure is great. The other main type – thermal metamorphism – occurs among the rocks "cooked" by the intrusion of a hot igneous body. Of the minor types, dislocation metamorphism occurs when a major fault slips, whereas metasomatism is caused by seepage of hot fluids (liquids and gases) from a igneous body into the surrounding rock.*

Volcanoes

Volcanoes are holes or cracks in the Earth's crust through which molten rock erupts. They usually occur at structural weaknesses in the crust, often in regions of geological instability, such as the edges of crustal plates. Volcanoes are important to Man because they provide information about the Earth's interior, and because volcanically-formed soils are highly fertile and good for growing crops. Violent eruptions, however, can devastate huge areas, and accurate techniques for predicting eruptions are essential if major disasters are to be avoided.

Formation of volcanoes

Scientists do not fully understand the process by which volcanoes are formed. It seems that at points where the Earth's mantle (the layer immediately beneath the crust) is particularly hot (hot spots), or where part of the crust is being forced down into the mantle (e. g. where two crustal plates meet and one is forced down under the other), the heat causes the lower part of the crust or upper part of the mantle to melt. The molten rock – called magma – is under pressure as more magma forms and, being less dense than the surrounding rock, it rises, often along lines of weakness such as faults or joints in the crust. As the magma rises, it melts a channel for itself in the rock and accumulates, together with gases released from the melting rock, in a magma chamber a few miles below the Earth's surface.

Eventually the pressure from the magma and gas builds up to such an extent that an eruption occurs, blasting a vent through the surface rocks. Lava (magma after emission) piles up around the vent to form a volcanic mountain or, if the eruption is from a fissure, a lava plateau. The volcano then undergoes

A composite illustration shows a section through a typical continental volcano (not to scale) and many features found in volcanic regions. Pahoehoe and aa are the two main types of lava; the former is relatively fluid, whereas the latter is more viscous and solidifies to form a rough surface. A tree mould is formed when a tree is covered with lava, which burns away the tree as the lava solidifies, leaving a mound of solid lava with a tree-shaped hole in the middle. Geysers periodically emit powerful jets of hot water. Fumaroles and solfataras give off steam and sulphurous gases. Other volcanic topographical features include crater lakes, hot springs, mud pools and mud pots.

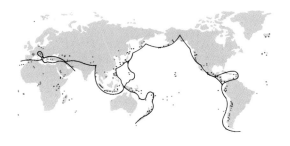

In the map of volcano distribution active volcanoes are marked by red dots, extinct ones by blue dots. Most volcanoes are located at the edges of crustal plates (shown as black lines), where earthquakes and mountain building also take place. Some extinct volcanoes mark areas of former crustal instability, such as the Great Riff Valley in East Africa.

periodic eruptions of gases, lava and rock fragments. It is termed active, dormant or extinct, according to the frequency with which it erupts.

Vents associated with declining volcanic activity and the cooling of lava periodically emit steam or hot water, and are often valuable sources of energy or minerals: solfataras (which are rich in sulphur) and fumaroles give out steam and gas; geysers are hot springs that eject jets of hot water or steam at regular intervals as underground water is heated to the boiling point by the magma.

The characteristics of eruptions vary greatly from volcano to volcano, and those typical of any one volcano change over the years. Eruptions are classified according to their explosiveness, which depends on the composition (especially the gas content) and viscosity of the magma involved, which in turn depends largely on the depth at which the rock becomes molten. Relatively viscous magma causes explosive eruptions; sticky magma often forms a plug in the neck of the volcano, blocking further eruptions until enough magma and gas have accumulated for their pressure to blast away the plug and allow the emission of gas, lava and fragmented magma (tephra). This accumulation may take several decades, or even centuries. Some explosive eruptions are quite small, but others (those in which large amounts of gas are trapped in the magma) are so violent that they blast away a large part of a mountain or a whole island.

Volcanoes formed mainly of rock fragments are generally steep-sided cones (with slopes of between 20° and 40° to the horizontal), because any fragments blasted into the air fall back near the vent. Those formed chiefly of viscous lava are usually highly convex domes (typically about 500 ft. high and 1,300 ft. across), because the lava is too thick to flow far before solidifying. Exceptionally viscous lava may solidify in the vent. The solid mass may then be forced slowly upwards, forming a spine that rises several hundred feet above the summit. This movement usually precedes a particularly violent eruption, caused by the sudden release of the accumulated pressure of the magma and gas. In 1902, such an event accompanied the destructive eruption of Mont Pelée on the island of Martinique in the West Indies.

At the other extreme, relatively fluid magma is extruded quite freely and quietly, with small eruptions that occur at frequent intervals or even continuously. The lava flows for long distances before it solidifies, and therefore forms a low, broad dome, or shield volcano (usually with slopes of less than about 10°), such as Mauna Loa on Hawaii; the island rises about 32,800 ft. from a seafloor base 360 ft. in diameter.

Submarine volcanoes

Submarine volcanoes are particularly common near oceanic ridges, where magma is constantly extruded as the continental plates drift apart. Many also form over hot spots. As the crust moves, the volcano also moves away from the hot spot and becomes extinct; a new volcano forms directly over the original hot spot, and a chain of volcanoes gradually forms.

In oceanic ridges and hot spots the lava is formed from mantle material that is forced up by deep convection currents. This lava is dense but fluid, unlike the silica-rich lava produced by melting crustal material, found in continental areas and offshore island chains. Where it appears above the water surface – in Iceland and Hawaii, for example – it forms flat lava plateaux or shield volcanoes.

Marine volcanic activity may lead to the sudden creation of islands (e. g. Surtsey, off Iceland, in 1963). Volcanic islands are subject to severe erosion by the sea, and may also subside when they move away from a ridge or hot spot and cease to be active. There are more than 2,000 submerged – usually extinct – volcanoes (seamounts) in the world; those that have been eroded nearly to sea

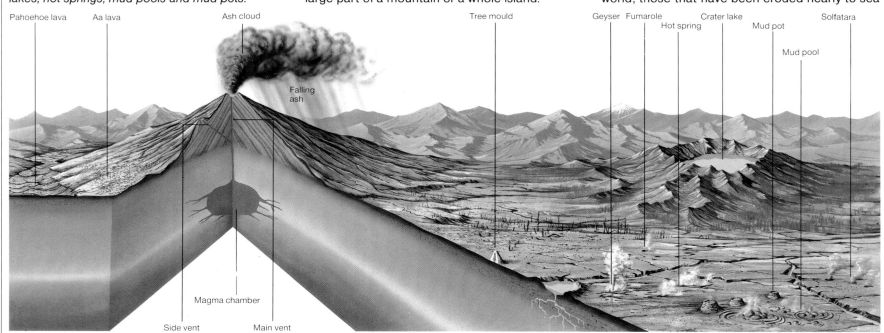

Pahoehoe lava   Aa lava   Ash cloud   Tree mould   Geyser Fumarole   Crater lake   Solfatara

Hot spring   Mud pot

Mud pool

Falling ash

Magma chamber

Side vent   Main vent

The section, right, *depicts Mount St. Helens before it erupted on May 18, 1980. On the far right is the volcano during the first eruption, when the north slope collapsed and hot volcanic gases, steam and dust* (a nuée ardente) *were blasted out sideways with explosive force. Simultaneously, a cloud of ash and dust was blown upwards.*

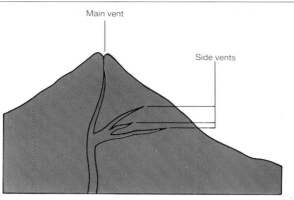

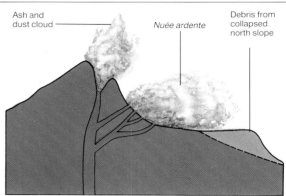

level and then subsequently submerged, which are known as guyots, are also common.

Predicting volcanic eruptions

Prediction of eruptions is of great importance because of the extensive damage they can cause to surrounding areas, which are often fertile and densely populated. Volcanic activity used to be assessed in terms of temperature and pressure, measured by means of borings into the sides of the vent. Recently, however, geologists have come to rely instead on seismography, on measurements of changes in emissions of gas and its sulphur dioxide content, and on detecting activity inside the crater (monitored with mirrors). Most of all, they look for changes in the angle of the mountainside (measured with tiltmeters): any expansion in one part of the mountain indicates that an eruption there is likely. Further information is obtained from analyses of the mineral content of the local water, recordings of vertical ground swelling, and readings from geodimeters, which use lasers to measure minute swellings in the ground.

These techniques are, however, by no means perfect. They were in use on Mount St. Helens in the State of Washington, when it erupted in May 1980 but, despite the fact that scientists were aware that an eruption was imminent, they were not able to anticipate the time, force or exact direction of the blast.

The Mount St. Helens eruption

Mount St. Helens is one of a chain of continental volcanoes in the Cascade Range in the northwestern United States. All the volcanoes in this mountain range are the result of the Pacific oceanic crustal plate being forced down into the mantle by the North American continental plate riding over it. The molten parts of the oceanic plate then rise through the crustal material, forming volcanoes. Normally an eruptive phase involves several of the Cascade Range volcanoes. During the nineteenth century, for example, Mount St. Helens erupted three times, simultaneously with nearby Mount Baker. Because of these coincident eruptions, some scientists believe that the two volcanoes may have a common origin where, at a depth of about 125 mi. below the surface, the Pacific crustal plate is being overridden by the North American plate.

After 123 years of dormancy, Mount St. Helens erupted in May 1980 – one of the most violent (and closely-monitored) eruptions in recent times. Volcanic activity was first noticed on March 20, when small tremors began and the mountain top started to bulge; about a week later fissures in the flank of the volcano emitted steam.

The first violent eruption occurred on May 18, when the slow accumulation of pressure within the volcano was released with explosive force. The north flank of the mountain collapsed and the contents of the vent were blasted out. The abrupt release of pressure caused the gas dissolved in the magma to come out of solution suddenly, forming bubbles throughout the hot mass – rather like the sudden formation of bubbles in champagne when the bottle is uncorked. A white-hot cloud of gas and pul-

The most devastating of Mount St. Helens' recent eruptions occurred in May 1980, but volcanic activity continued and there were several smaler eruptions during the later part of the year. The main explosion was estimated to have had the force of 500 Hiroshima atom bombs and was heard more than 185 mi. away.

verized magma (called a nuée ardente) then swept over the surrounding countryside, engulfing everything within a distance of about 5 mi. from the peak. (This phenomenon also occurred when Mont Pelée erupted in 1902; within a few minutes of the eruption the cloud had covered Saint-Pierre, then the capital of Martinique, killing its 30,000 inhabitants). At the same time, a vertical column of dust and ash was blown upwards. These two major effects were accompanied by a blast of air caused by the sudden expansion of the freed gases; the blast was so powerful that it flattened all trees near the volcano and knocked down some as far as 16 mi. away.

The nuée ardente and the vertical ash column produced cauliflower-shaped clouds 20 mi. wide that eventually reached a height of 15 mi. The ash in this cloud consisted mainly of silica, a reflection of the high silica content of the material emitted by continental volcanoes.

The ash falling back to earth and the debris of the collapsed flank (which amounted to about one cubic mile) combined with the water of nearby rivers and the meltwater of the mountain snows to form a mudflow (called a lahar). The mudflow plunged along the river valleys at speeds of up to about 50 m. p. h., destroying bridges and settle-

ments as far as 12 mi. downstream; in some places, the mud deposited by this flow was as much as 425 ft. deep.

Although the May eruption is perhaps the best known, Mount St. Helens erupted several times during the later part of the year. Each eruption was preceded by the growth of a dome of volcanic material in the crater left by the initial explosion, and the general pattern of the subsequent eruptions resembled that of the first.

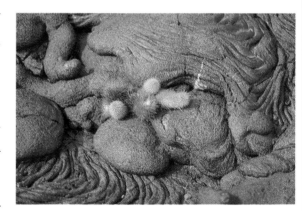

Pahoehoe-lava solidifies into characteristic ropy-textured folded sheets. In contrast, aa-lava – the other main type – is rough textured. The two types often have identical chemical compositions, and it is quite common for a lava flow that leaves a vent as pahoehoe to change to aa-lava as it progresses down a volcano's slopes.

Geology and landscape

Most people consider the landscape to be unchanging whereas in fact our planet is a dynamic body and its surface is continually altering – slowly on the human timescale, but relatively rapidly when compared to the great age of the Earth (about 4,500 million years). There are two principal influences that shape the terrain: constructive processes such as uplift, which create new landscape features, and destructive forced such as erosion, which gradually wear away exposed landforms.

Hills and mountains are often regarded as the epitome of permanence, successfully resisting the destructive forces of nature, but in fact they tend to be relatively short-lived in geological terms. As a general rule, the higher a mountain is, the more recently it was formed; for example, the high mountains of the Himalayas, situated between the Indian subcontinent and the rest of Asia, are only about 50 million years old. Lower mountains tend to be older, and are often the eroded relics of much higher mountain chains. About 400 million years ago, when the present-day continents of North America and Europe were joined, the Caledonian mountain chain was the same size as the modern Himalayas. Today, however, the relics of the Caledonian orogeny (mountain-building period) exist as the comparatively low mountains of Greenland, the northern Appalachians in the United States, the Scottish Highlands, and the Norwegian coastal plateau.

Some mountains were formed as a result of the Earth's crustal plates moving together and forcing up the rock at the plate margins. In this process, sedimentary rocks that originally formed on the sea bed may be folded upwards to altitudes of more than 26,000 ft. Other mountains may be raised by faulting, which produces block mountains, such as the Ruwenzori Mountains on the border of Uganda and Zaire in Africa. A third type of mountain may be formed as a result of volcanic activity; these tend to occur in the regions of active fold mountain belts, such as the Cascade range of western North America, which contains Mount St Helens, Mount Rainier and Mount Hood. The other principal type of mountain is one that has been pushed up by the em-

In deserts and other arid regions the wind is the main erosive agent. It carries small particles that wear away any exposed landforms, thereby creating yet more material to bombard the rocks.

placement of an intrusion below the surface; the Black Hills in South Dakota were formed in this way. As soon as land rises above sea level it is subjected to the destructive forces of denudation. The exposed rocks are attacked by the various weather processes and gradually broken down into fragments, which are then carried away and later deposited as sediments. Thus, any landscape represents only a temporary stage in the continuous battle between the forces of uplift (or of subsidence) and those of erosion.

The weather, in any of its forms, is the main agent of erosion. Rain washes away loose soil and penetrates cracks in the rocks. Carbon dioxide in the air reacts with the rainwater, forming a weak acid (carbonic acid) that may chemically attack the rocks. The rain seeps underground and the water may reappear later as springs. These springs are the sources of streams and rivers, which cut through

the rocks and carry away debris from the mountains to the lowlands.

Under very cold conditions, rocks can be shattered by ice and frost. Glaciers may form in permanently cold areas, and these slowly-moving masses of ice scour out valleys, carrying with them huge quantities of eroded rock debris.

In dry areas the wind is the principal agent of erosion. It carries fine particles of sand, which bombard the exposed rock surfaces, thereby wearing them into yet more sand.

Even living things contribute to the formation of landscapes. Tree roots force their way into cracks in rocks and, in so doing, speed their splitting. In contrast, the roots of grasses and other small plants may help to hold loose soil fragments together, thereby helping to prevent erosion by the wind.

The nature of the rocks themselves determines how quickly they are affected by the various processes of erosion. The minerals in limestone and granite react with the carbonic acid in rain, and these rocks are therefore more susceptible to chemical breakdown than are other types of rocks containing minerals that are less easily affected by acidic rainwater. Sandstone tends to be harder than shale, and so where both are exposed in alternating beds, the shale erodes more quickly than the sandstone, giving the outcrop a corrugated or stepped appearance. Waterfalls and rapids occur where rivers pass over beds or intrusions of hard igneous rock which overlie softer rocks.

The erosional forces of the weather, glaciers, rivers, and also the waves and currents of the sea, are essentially destructive processes. But they also have a constructive effect by carrying the eroded debris to a new area and depositing it as sediment. Particles eroded by rivers may be deposited as beds of mud and sand in deltas and shallow seas; wind-borne particles in arid areas come to rest as desert sands; and the massive boulders and tiny clay particles produced and transported by glaciers give rise to spectacular landforms (terminal moraines, for example) after the glaciers have melted.

The Himalayan range contains some of the world's highest mountains, with more than 30 peaks rising to over 22,900 ft. above sea level – including Mount Everest (29,029 ft.). Situated along the northern border of India, the Himalayas were uplifted when a plate bearing the once-separate Indian landmass collided with Asia. This occurred comparatively recently in geological terms (about 50 million years ago) and so there has been relatively little time for the peaks to be eroded.

Caves and their formation

As rainwater falls, it dissolves carbon dioxide from the air forming carbonic acid. This weak acid corrodes calcite (calcium carbonate), the main mineral component of limestone rocks. The acid dissolves the limestone and sculpts the rock, especially along joints and lines of weakness in the strata. Flowing rainwater makes its way through the dissolved gaps and holes and erodes caverns underground along the level of the water table. Where the water table reaches the surface, as on a slope, a spring forms and drainage is established. The place where the spring emerges is called the resurgence. At the level of the water table the pattern of linked caves is similar to that of a river, with converging branches and meanders formed by the flow of the water. Below the water table other caves are formed by solution effects, without current-formed features. These caves are full of water, joined to blind tunnels and hollows.

The cave system

When the water table drops, the current-formed cave system is left empty. Continuing solution effects undermine the rock and ceilings fall in, producing spacious caverns deep underground. Where a stream of water enters the caves, sink holes (also called potholes or swallow holes) form as the sides of the original gap are eroded and fall away.

Stalactites and stalagmites

When ground water, carrying dissolved calcite leached out of the rocks, seeps through to the ceiling of a cave it may hang there as a drip. Through loss of carbon dioxide the dissolved calcite is deposited on the ceiling as a minute mineral particle. This process happens also to the next and subsequent drips and over the years the accumulated particles produce a hanging icicle-like structure. It may take more than a thousand years to deposit one third inch of stalactite. The shapes of stalactites vary. Some are long and thin; others form curtain-like structures where the seeping water trickles down a sloping ceiling. A constant wind blowing through the cave may cause the stalactite to be crooked or eccentric.

Water from the stalactites drips to the floor. There the shock of the impact causes the calcite to separate from the water, which either flows away or evaporates. Constantly repeated, the result is the upward-growing equivalent of a stalactite – a stalagmite. Stalagmites also vary in shape; some resemble stacks of plates, whereas others have ledges and flutes that make them look like gigantic pine cones. Occasionally a stalactite and a stalagmite meet and grow into each other, producing a column. At times the calcite-rich water seeps through the wall into the cave, usually along a bedding plane, and

Stalactites and stalagmites develop in a variety of forms. The most common types are the thin straw stalactites and the broader icicle stalactites. Stalagmites, curtains, columns and gours (also called rimstone pools) are rarer. In the cave above are some fine examples of delicately-colored stalactites – and of a column. The red color of many of these is caused by iron impurities in the calcite; manganese impurities – the other main type – stain stalactites and stalagmites various shades of yellow.

gives rise to a cascade-like structure called a balcony, with stalactites and stalagmites that seem to flow over each other.

In the bed of an underground stream the calcite-rich water inevitably passes over ridges in the bed. A slight turbulence results and a particle of calcium carbonate is deposited on the ridge. This action is self-sustaining, because the more calcium carbonate there is deposited on an obstruction, the larger the obstruction becomes and the greater the turbulence. The result is a series of stalagmite ridges with horizontal crests, which act like dams that hold back the water in pools. These little dams are called gours, or rimstone pools.

The calcite that forms these features is a colorless mineral but impurities (mostly iron and manganese salts) stain the stalactites and stalagmites delicate shades of pink and yellow. The staining varies according to the composition of the rocks that the seeping water has passed through and it produces concentric patterns in the icicle-like stalactites, and bands of color on the curtain type.

Caves and Man

Caves were the traditional homes of early Man; his artefacts have been found buried in floor debris, and his paintings have been found on walls. The most important of such sites are in the Spanish Pyrenees and the Dordogne valley in France, which have caves that were inhabited about 25,000 or 30,000 years ago.

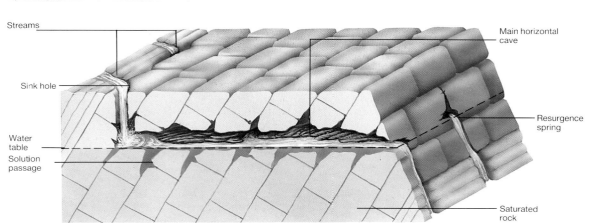

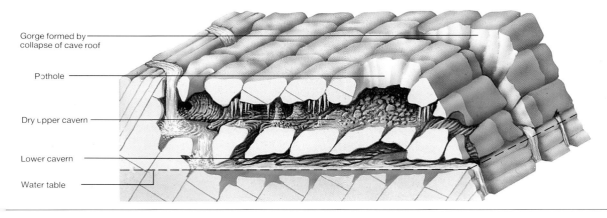

The horizontal network of a cave system forms along joints and weakness in the rock. Carbonic acid (formed by carbon dioxide dissolving in rainwater) attacks the calcite in limestone rocks, eventually dissolving the rock. The rainwater then flows underground through dissolved sink holes and corrodes a horizontal cavern system at the level of the water table. Drainage is established when the water breaks through to the surface, forming a resurgence spring. Meanwhile, rainwater continues to flow into the cave system and eventually corrodes a second, lower cavern. Thus the upper caves become dry whereas the lower, more recent, caves are water-filled.

The weather

The circulation of the atmosphere is essentially a gigantic heat exchange system, a consequence of the unequal heating of the Earth's surface by the Sun. The intensity of solar radiation is greatest around the equator and least near the poles. Thus the equator is the hottest region and, to balance the unequal heating, heat flows from the tropics to the poles.

Prevailing winds

Around the equator, radiation from the Earth's surface heats the lower layers of the atmosphere, causing them to expand and rise. This effect creates a permanent low-pressure zone (called the doldrums), with light to non-existent winds.

The light, warm air rises and eventually cools, spreading north and south to form convection currents. At around latitudes 30° North and 30° South the air in these current sinks, creating two belts of high pressure, called the horse latitudes. Like the doldrums, the horse latitudes are regions of light winds and calms. The dry, subsiding air and therefore stable atmospheric conditions of the horse latitudes tend to give rise to huge deserts on the Earth's surface – the Sahara, for example. From the horse latitudes, air currents (winds) flow outwards across the Earth's surface. Those that flow towards the equator are the Trade Winds, and those moving towards the poles are the Westerlies. The Westerlies eventually meet cold air currents (the Polar Easterlies) flowing from the poles – areas of high atmospheric pressure caused by the sinking of cold, dense air. The regions between 30° and 65° North and South are transition zones with changeable weather, contrasting with the stable conditions in the tropics. The weather in these transition zones is influenced by the formation of large depressions, or cyclones, which result from the intermingling of polar and subtropical air.

Complicating factors

Although there is a continual heat exchange between the tropics and the poles, winds do not blow directly north-south. The Coriolis effect, caused by the rotation of the Earth on its axis, deflects winds to the right of their natural direction in the Northern Hemisphere, and to the left in the Southern Hemisphere. (The Coriolis effect also deflects ocean currents in a similar way.)

The paths of winds and the positions of the dominant low- and high-pressure systems also undergo seasonal changes. These result from the 23½° tilt of the Earth's axis, which causes the Sun to move northwards and southwards (as seen from the Earth) during the year. At the equinoxes (on about March 21 and September 23) the Sun is overhead at the equator, and solar radiation is equally balanced between the two hemispheres. But on about June 21, the summer solstice in the Northern Hemisphere, the Sun is overhead at the Tropic of Cancer (23½° North), and on December 21, the winter

A depression consists of a wedge of warm air between masses of cold air. At the front edge of a depression is a warm front; a cold front marks the back edge. The approach of a depression is usually indicated by the appearance of high cirrus clouds, followed successively by cirrostratus, altrostratus, nimbostratus and stratus clouds, these last often bringing rain. When the warm front has passed, temperatures increase but thunderstorms often occur. The cold front is frequently marked by rain-bearing cumulonimbus clouds.

solstice in the Northern Hemisphere, the Sun is overhead at the Tropic of Capricorn (23½° South). The overall effect of these changes in heating is that the wind and pressure belts move north and south throughout the year. For example, Mediterranean regions come under the influence of the stable atmospheric conditions of the horse latitudes in summer, giving them hot, dry weather, but in winter the southward shift of wind belts brings cooler weather and cyclonic rain to Mediterranean lands. The astronomical dates pertaining to seasons do not coincide exactly with the actual seasons, however, because the Earth's surface is slow to

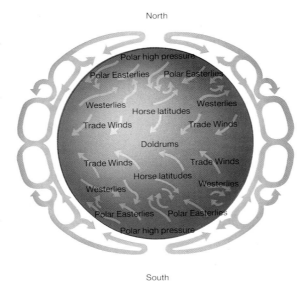

The atmosphere circulates because of unequal heating of the Earth by the Sun. At the equator air is heated, rises and then flows towards the poles, creating a permanent low-pressure area (the doldrums) around the equator. At about 30° N and 30° S some of the air sinks, giving rise to the zones of high pressure called the horse latitudes. Continuing to move away from the equator, the air cools and sinks (creating high pressure) over the poles. It then flows back towards the equator. The overall effect of the atmosphere's circulation is to create a pattern of prevailing winds (grey arrows in the illustration) that blow from high- to low-pressure areas.

warm up and cool down. As a result the summer months in the middle latitudes are June, July and August. Similarly, winter in the Northern Hemisphere occurs in December, January and February. Winds are also affected by the fact that land heats up and cools faster than water. Rapid heating of coastal regions during the day creates an area relatively low air pressure on land, into which cooler air from the sea is drawn. At night, the land cools rapidly and cold air flows from the land towards the relatively warmer sea.

Differential heating of the land and seal also leads to the development of huge air masses over the continents and oceans. There are four main types of air masses. Polar maritime air is relatively warm and moist, because it is heated from below by the water. Polar continental air, by contrast, is cold and mainly dry in winter, but warm in summer when the land heats quickly. Tropical maritime air is warm and moist, whereas tropical continental air, such as that over the Sahara Desert, is warm and dry. The movements of these air masses and their interaction with adjacent masses along boundaries called fronts have important effects on the weather in transitional areas.

Depressions

Depressions form along the polar front, the boundary between the polar and tropical air masses in the middle latitudes. They begin when undulations or waves develop in the front; warm air then flows into pronounced undulations, thereby forming depressions. The forward arc of the undulation is called the warm front, and the following arc is the cold front. Depressions are low-pressure air systems, and winds are therefore drawn towards their centers. But the deflection caused by the Coriolis effect makes winds circulate around rather than blow directly into the center of a depression. The wind circulation in depressions (cyclones) is in an anticlockwise direction in the Northern Hemisphere and clockwise in the Southern Hemisphere.

On weather maps depressions appear as a series of concentric isobars (lines joining places with equal atmospheric pressure – analogous to contour lines of height on land maps), with the lowest pressure at the center. When the isobars are close together the pressure gradient is steep, and the steeper the

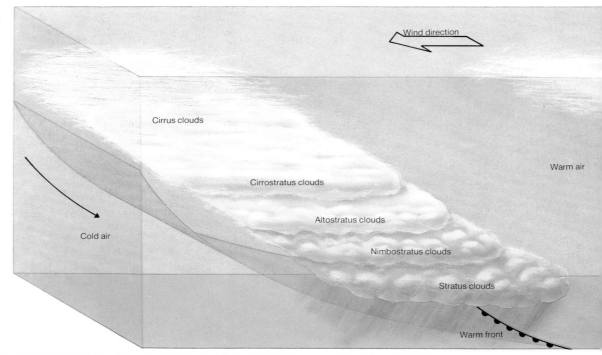

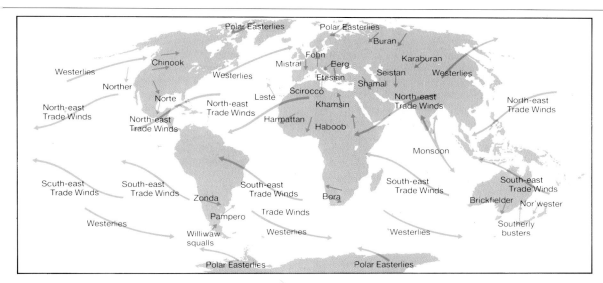

The map (above) shows the principal prevailing winds (large arrows) and various local winds (small arrows).

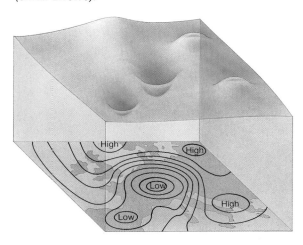

Air pressure is represented on weather maps by isobars – lines joining points of equal pressure. Depressions (or cyclones) are regions of low pressure, whereas anticyclones are high-pressure areas – as can be seen above where, on the graphical representation above the conventional isobar chart, depressions appear as troughs and anticyclones as mounds.

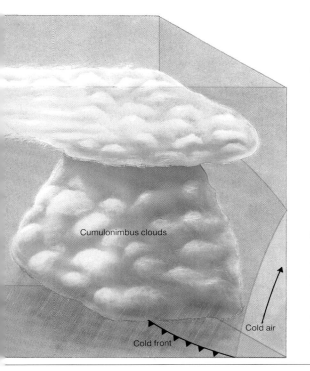

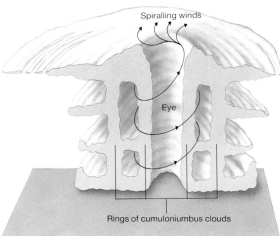

A hurricane is a large, intense low-pressure system consisting of concentric rings of mainly cumulonimbus clouds spiralling around a calm centre – the eye. Moist air circles and rises rapidly round the eye, generating winds that may reach speeds of 185 m. p. h. Within the eye, however, the sky is usually clear and the air almost stationary.

pressure gradient, the stronger are the winds, which tend to blow parallel to the isobars.

The formation of depressions is closely related to the paths of the jet streams in the upper atmosphere. On charts of the higher atmospheric layers, a poleward ripple in the westward-flowing jet stream usually indicates a depression below. The flow of the jet streams affects the development of depressions. When a jet stream broadens, it tends to suck air upwards, intensifying the low pressure below and causing wet, windy weather. When a jet stream narrows, it tends to push air down, thereby raising the pressure below. The jet streams are strongest in winter, when the temperature difference between polar and tropical regions is greatest; therefore the pressure gradient between these two regions is also steepest in winter. When a jet stream becomes strongly twisted, waves may break away. The jet stream soon connects up again, however, cutting off blocks of cold or warm air from the main flow. Such stationary blocks can bring spells of unseasonal weather, such as the so-called "Indian summer."

Within a depression warm air flows upwards over cold air along the warm front. Because the gradient is gradual, the clouds ahead of the warm front are usually stratiform in type. Along the cold front cold air undercuts the warm air, causing it to rise steeply; as a result, towering cumulonimbus clouds often form behind the cold front. Because the cold front moves faster than the warm front, the warm air is gradually pushed upwards, or occluded. Bands of cloud linger for some time above occluded fronts, but the depression soon weakens or is replaced by another.

Weather conditions in depressions

No two depressions bring exactly the same weather, but a knowledge of the general sequence of weather associated with these phenomena is an aid to forecasting. A depression is often heralded by the appearance of high cirrus clouds, usually drawn into long, hooked bands by the jet stream. As the warm front approaches, cloud cover increases as progressively lower clouds arrive: cirrostratus, altostratus, nimbostratus and stratus. The advance of the warm front is usually marked by increasingly heavy rain. After it has passed, air pressure stops falling and temperatures increase. After a few hours, however, thunderstorms often occur, associated with a narrow belt of squally weather along the cold front. After this belt has passed, the skies clear, pressure rises and humidity diminishes.

Anticyclones

Adding to the variety of weather conditions in the middle latitudes are anticyclones, or high-pressure air systems. Anticyclones appear on weather maps as a series of concentric isobars with the highest pressure at the center. Winds tend to blow outwards from the center of anticyclones (although not as strongly as winds blow into depressions) but are deflected by the Coriolis effect. As a result, the winds circulate around the center of an anticyclone in a clockwise direction in the Northern Hemisphere and in an anticlockwise direction in the Southern Hemisphere.

Anticyclones generally bring settled weather; warm weather with clear skies is typical in summer, whereas cold weather, frost and fogs are associated with anticyclones in winter.

Storms

The most common storms are thunderstorms, about 45,000 of which occur every day.

Thunderstorms, which are associated with cumulonimbus clouds formed in fast-rising air, are commonly accompanied by lightning, caused by the sudden release of accumulated static electricity in the clouds. The mechanisms by which static electricity forms in clouds is not known but, according to one popular theory, electrical charge is produced as a result of the freezing of supercooled droplets in clouds. The outer layers of these droplets freeze first and, in so doing, become positively charged (a phenomenon that has been observed in laboratory conditions); the warmer, still unfrozen cores acquire a negative charge. A fraction of a second later the cores freeze and expand, thus shattering the outer layers. Positively-charged fragments of the outer layers are then swept upwards to the top of the cloud while the still intact, negatively-charged cores remain in the cloud's lower levels. Eventually the total amount of charge in the cloud builds up sufficiently to overcome the electrical resistance of the air between the cloud and the ground, and the charge in the cloud is discharged as a huge electric spark – a flash of lightning. The violent expansion of the air molecules along the path of the lightning generates an intense sound wave, which is heard as thunder. Lightning is seen before thunder is heard because light travels faster than sound.

Weathering

As soon as any rock is exposed at the surface of the earth it is subjected to various forces of erosion, which reduce the rock to fragments and carry the resulting debris to areas of deposition. The weather is the most significant agent of this erosion and can act in one of two ways. It can produce physical changes in which the rocks are broken down by the force of rain, wind or frost; or it can produce chemical changes in which the minerals of the rocks are altered and the new substances formed dissolve in water or crumble away from the main rock mass. The different processes involved do not act independently of each other; the resulting erosion is caused by a combination of physical and chemical effects, although in some areas one erosive force tends to predominate.

Effects of rain

The effects of rain erosion of the landscape are best seen in areas of loose topsoil. Rock or soil that is already loose is easily dislodged and washed away in heavy rainstorms. The most spectacular examples of this type of rain erosion occur in volcanic areas, where the soil consists of deep layers of volcanic ash deposited by recent eruptions. Streams of rainwater running down the slopes carry away fragments of the exposed volcanic topsoil, and the force of these moving fragments dislodges other fragments. As a result, the slopes become scarred with converging gullies and small gorges that form where the erosion is greatest. In some places, the lower slopes are worn away so rapidly that the higher ground is undercut, resulting in a landslip.

In regions that have a deep topsoil, small areas may be protected from rain erosion by the presence of large rocks on the surface. The soil around these rocks may be worn away, leaving the rocks supported on pedestals of undisturbed material.

Rain falling on grassy slopes may cause soil creep. The soil tends to be washed down the slope, but the interlocking roots of the grass prevent it from moving far, leading to the formation of a series of steps in the hillside where bands of turf have moved slowly downwards. (Soil creeps in bands because the force of gravity overcomes the roots' cohesion in the downwards direction whereas the root network remains strong in the sideways direction.)

The chemical effect of rain depends on the fact that carbon dioxide in the atmosphere dissolves in the rain, forming weak carbonic acid. The acid reacts with the calcite (a crystalline form of calcium carbonate, the substance responsible for "hardness" in water) in limestone and with certain other minerals, thereby dissolving them. This erosive effect may give rise to any of several geological features, such as grikes, which are widened cracks in the exposed rock, and swallow holes, where streams disappear underground – features that are particularly common in limestone areas, such as northwestern Yugoslavia and the county of Yorkshire in Britain.

In arid regions temperature changes and the wind are the strongest weathering forces. Chemical action may also affect the surface of exposed rock, although its effect is relatively minor. Temperature changes cause rapid expansion (during the day) and contraction (at night) of the rock surface, as a result of which fragments of rock break off. These fragments are then further eroded into small particles while they are being carried by the wind (a process called attrition). The various weathering processes in dry regions produce characteristic landscape features, such as pedestal rocks, rounded hills (inselbergs), dreikanters and, in hot areas, sun-shattered rocks.

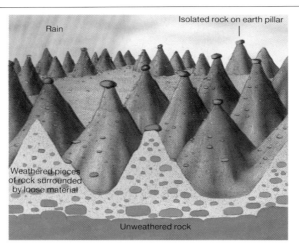

Earth pillars are unusual landscape features produced by rain erosion. In wet areas the rain is the principal agent of weathering. The chemical breakdown of the rock, helped by the action of vegetation, produces deep soil. Rain then washes the soil away, especially in areas where the vegetation has been removed. Where the soil has been protected by rocks resting on the surface, earth pillars may form as the surrounding soil is washed away.

Effects of temperature

Temperature changes are an important part of the weathering process, particularly in arid areas where the air is so dry that its insulating effect is negligible; the lack of insulation results in a large daily range of temperature.

Repeated heating and cooling of the surface of a rock while the interior remains at a constant temperature weakens the rock's outer layers. When this effect is combined with the chemical action that takes place after the infrequent desert downpours, the outer layers of the rock peel off – a process called exfoliation. Exfoliation may occur on only a small scale, affecting individual rocks, or it may affect whole mountainsides, especially those in which the bedding planes of the rock are parallel to the surface. Exfoliation of entire mountains typi-

cally produces prominent, rounded hills called inselbergs, a well-known example of which is Ayers Rock in central Australia.

Effects of wind

As with heat, the weathering effects of the wind are also greatest in arid regions, because the soil particles are not stuck together or weighed down with water and are therefore light and easily dislodged. Coarser soil particles blown by the wind bounce along close to the ground, (a mode of travel called saltation), rarely rising more than 3 ft. above groundlevel. These moving particles can be highly abrasive and, where the top of an exposed rock is above the zone of attrition, can erode the rock into a pedestal shape. Stones and small boulders on the ground may be worn smooth on the side facing the prevailing wind, eventually becoming so eroded that they overbalance and present a new face to the wind. This process then repeats itself, resulting in the formation of dreikanters – stones with three or more sides that have been worn smooth.

The effect of the various abrasive processes is cumulative: particles that have been abraded from the surfaces of exposed rocks and stones further abrade the landscape features (thereby increasing the rate of erosion), eventually giving rise to a typical desert landscape.

Human influence and weathering

A natural landscape is a balance between the forces of uplift, which produce new topographical features, and erosion, which gradually wears away exposed surface features. Man's activities, especially farming, may alter this balance – sometimes with far-reaching effects. The removal of natural vegetation may weaken the topsoil, and when the soil particles are no longer held together by extensive root systems they can be washed away easily by the rain. This process may result in a "badlands" topography: initially, fields of deep, fertile soil are cut with gullies then, as erosion continues, the soil is gradually broken down into small particles that are eventually washed away by rain or blown away as dust.

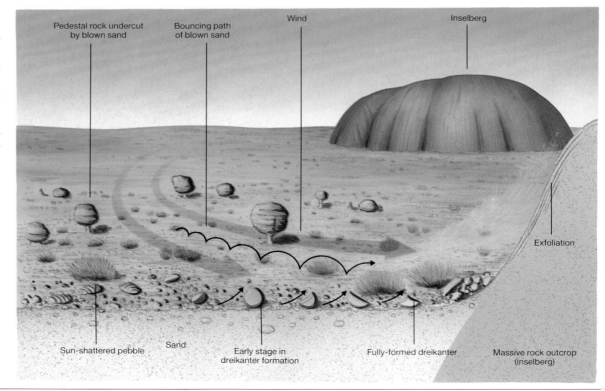

Frost erosion

Of all the forces of weathering that act on a landscape, water – particularly frozen water – produces the most dramatic topographical features. Water expands when it freezes, the expansion being accompanied by great outward pressure (it is this pressure that bursts pipes when the water in them freezes). This expansive force of frost can affect exposed terrain in two ways: rock may be broken into smaller fragments by freezing water expanding in its joints (a process called frost shattering), or the ground may be caused to expand and contract alternatively, known as frost heaving.

In order to be effective, the action of frost erosion must be strong enough to overcome the elasticity of the rock. The breakdown process starts when water seeps into pores or tiny cracks and joints in the rock. Then, when the water freezes, it forces the walls of the pores and joints further apart. On thawing, a slightly greater volume of water is able to enter the enlarged hole, and so a correspondingly stronger force is applied during the next freezing. Successive repetitions of this frost wedging process lead eventually to the shattering of a solid mass of rock into fragments.

Mountain landscapes

Frost erosion is particularly effective in mountainous areas, because temperatures are low and there is a wide daily variation in temperature. In some places, the eroded debris falls and collects in great quantities at the base of steep mountain slopes. Mountains with needle-like peaks formed by frost action are known as "aiguilles" (meaning needles); they are often further worn away to a pyramidal "horn" by the erosive effect of frost and glaciers on the flanks. Material broken off the side of a mountain gathers towards the foot of the slopes, to form a scree (or talus) slope. Fragments of scree are always angular and the scree slopes are steep; the larger the fragments, the greater the erosion has been, and the steeper the slope. If the falling debris is guided by natural gullies and channels in the mountain, it comes to rest in a scree slope that resembles the rounded side of a cone as it fans out from its channel. Since they are forming continuously, scree slopes tend to have no soil or vegetation.

Mountain sculpting

Above the snowline any hollow in a mountainside is permanently occupied by snow. The steady accumulation and compression of the snow into ice in the bottom of the hollow eventually gives rise to a glacier. The erosive effect of the compressed snow in such a hollow acts in all directions at the same rate and, combined with the downward movement of the glacier, lowers the floor and cuts back the walls so that the hollow becomes a steep-sided, flat-bottomed feature called a cirque. Neighbour-

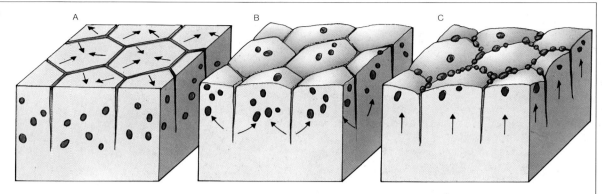

Polygonal shrinking in tundra occurs when the permafrost contracts and produces a series of interconnecting cracks in the soil surface. It is similar to the cracking that occurs in drying mud or cooling basalt, because when a homogeneous surface contracts, it does so towards a number of equally spaced centres on the surface. Cracks tend to appear at right angles to the forces (depicted by arrows) that act between each center (A). Expanding ice crystals under buried stones gradually push them to the surface (B), where they accumulate at the cracks (C).

The Matterhorn (14,691 ft.) on the Swiss-Italian border shows the classic features of a frost-eroded mountain. Its peak is sharp; it has straight, steeply-sloping walls; and it has been carved into a pyramid shape by the development of cirques on its flanks.

ing cirques on the flanks of a mountain are divided by a ridge. As the cirque walls are cut back the ridge becomes steep and sharp-crested and forms an arête, several of which may radiate from all sides of a mountain – by now a pyramidal horn mountain.

Above a glacier the falling frost-shattered rocks do not form a scree. The blocks that land on the moving ice are carried away and eventually dumped as moraines, which are a significant feature of glacial action.

Layers of snow on the higher areas of mountains may occasionally tumble down steep eroded slopes in avalanches. They usually occur when the lower slopes of snow have melted or been blown away, leaving the top unsupported. The falling snow compacts to ice as soon as it hits anything and the great weights involved can tear away vast quantities of forest and rock from the lower slopes.

Frost effects on flat land

The more complex effects of frost erosion are seen in areas such as the tundra, where temperatures are below the freezing point for most of the year and nearly all the visible landscape features have been produced by frost action. The frost heaving that takes place does not break down the rocks, but moves and mixes the soil particles.

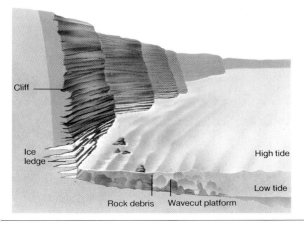

A strandflat is a coastal feature that results from a combination of wave and frost action. A ledge of ice forms as a semi-permanent feature on a cliff just above the high tide level. Frost shattering takes place along this ledge, its effect accentuated by the lower temperatures of the salt water ice, and the cliff becomes undercut. In this way the cliff is worn back and the wavecut platform is extended.

Cliff
Ice ledge
High tide
Low tide
Rock debris   Wavecut platform

As the temperature drops from 32° F to −4° F, the already expanded ice begins to contract. When this occurs on the surface of the earth the result is a general shrinkage of soil in which the surface cracks up into polygonal sections. These sections may be about 33 ft. across and are bounded by deep cracks. During thaws, water enters the cracks and ice wedging takes place when the next freeze occurs. The expansion pressure of the surrounding ice causes the centre of the polygon to rise in the shape of a shallow dome.

A stone buried in the soil cools more quickly than the surrounding damp soil because it is a better conductor of heat. The first place in which ice forms during a freeze is therefore directly under any buried stone. The crystals of ice below the stone push it upwards slightly as they expand. Over a period of several years this process brings the stone to the surface. (This frost heaving effect is particularly noted by gardeners in cold weather.) In polygonally cracked ground, the stones are ultimately brought to the surface of the polygons. From there they move down the slopes of the domes and gather in the surrounding cracks.

The force of frost

Most of the effects of frost erosion derive from the peculiar behavior of water at temperatures near its freezing point, and from the unique properties of ice. Water contracts as it cools, reaching its maximum density at 39.2° F. On further cooling it expands and, as it freezes at 32° F, it reaches a volume greater than water. As the temperature falls even lower, ice expands further and can exert enormous pressure (a familiar example of the effect of this force is the bursting of frozen water pipes in winter). Then, well below the freezing point, at around −8° F, ice contracts again – to a volume less than water.

River action

Most streams are formed in mountains and hills from surface run-off, by the emergence of absorbed rainwater from the ground (as springs), or from melting glaciers. Over many years a stream becomes a river by eroding its bed. The course of a river can be divided into three sections: the upper course, where erosion is predominant mainly because the steep slopes increase the velocity of the water; the middle course, where most of the transportation of the eroded material occurs; and the lower course, where deposition is the major feature because the gentler slopes reduce the speed of the water so that it is not able to carry the debris any farther.

The processes of erosion

The force of flowing water, known as hydraulic action, removes loose material from the surface and forces apart cracks in rocks. Boulders and pebbles carried by the current scour and excavate the bed by corrasion. The rocks carried by the river are themselves worn down by abrasion as they collide with and rub against each other, so that abrasion of the boulders in the upper course provides the fine particles in the lower course. Fine particles are transported in suspension by the water. Rocks that are too large to be suspended are picked up from the bed of the river by the turbulence, only to be dropped again. This bouncing action is called saltation. Boulders are rolled along the river bed by traction.

Solution action is another form of weathering performed by a river. Weak acids in the water, such as carbonic acid, may dissolve the rocks over which the water passes. Most erosion occurs when the river is in spate, when its movement is most turbulent and its speed increases.

Gorges and canyons

In the upper part of its course a river erodes chiefly by vertical corrasion, cutting a steep V-shaped valley that winds between interlocking spurs of high land. The level of a river is changed when there is either an isostatic lift in the land or an eustatic fall in the sea level. In both cases the river is forced to regrade its course to a new base level and in so doing cuts a new valley in the original floodplain. This rejuvenated erosion results in the formation of river terraces.

Incised meanders occur with renewed downcutting so that bends in a river are etched into the bedrock. In some cases an asymmetrical valley is formed where lateral erosion on the outside of a

bend produces river cliffs and a more gentle slip-off slope develops on the inside bend. If erosion is mainly vertical, then symmetrical valleys are formed. Localized undercutting by lateral erosion on both sides of the narrow neck of an incised meander can produce a natural bridge. When a passage is eventually excavated, the river bypasses the meander, leaving an abandoned meander loop beyond the bridge.

The Grand Canyon, one of the world's scenic wonders, was first cut in Miocene times (about 26 million years ago) as the Colorado Plateau was slowly uplifted by earth movements. The canyon has a maximum depth of about 5,500 ft. from the plateau top to the Colorado river. Differential erosion of the horizontal strata of sandstone, limestone and shales has formed a spectacular terraced valley up to 15 mi. wide.

River capture, which sometimes occurs in the upper course, results in an elbow-bend in the river and an H-shaped gorge. This happens when a stream erodes the land at its source until it breaks into the valley of another stream, and the adjacent stream is diverted into the new gorge.

Rapids and waterfalls

In the torrent stage of a stream, resistant bands of rock sometimes project transversely across the valley. If the hard band of rock dips gently downstream, then a series of rapids develop, as in the River Nile cataracts, where hard crystalline bands of rock cut across the rivers as it flows through the Nubian desert north of Khartoum. If the resistant layer is horizontal or dips upstream and covers a softer rock, then a waterfall may eventually result. In its outlet from Lake Erie, the Niagara River plunges 167 ft. over a hard dolomitic limestone ledge. The less resistant shales and sandstone beneath have been eroded by eddying in the plunge pool and by water dripping back under the ledge, leaving the limestone unsupported. This process of headward erosion has resulted in the formation of a receding gorge about 7 mi. long, downstream from the falls.

Waterfalls are not only produced by erosion of softer layers of rock, but also by glacial action where, due to the gouging of the main valley by ice, the valleys of tributary streams are left hanging high above the main valley floor. These hanging valleys often produce magnificent falls which plunge down the side of the main glacial trough.

Potholes are also a feature of the upper course of a river. They are formed when eddies whirl around pebbles, causing them to spin and act as grinding tools on the rock below.

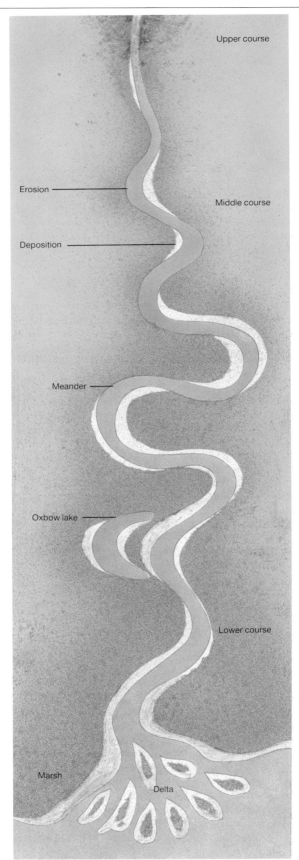

In its upper course, particularly if the gradient is steep, a river channel is straight and narrow, and the river runs rapidly. But when the slope is reduced, the river slows down and moves around obstacles. In addition, the wave motion of the water moves the river from side to side. Eventually, the river erodes the outer bank of a slight bend and deposits material on the inner bank. The river channel is deepened towards the outer side of the bend and is widened at the same time by lateral erosion. As this process continues, the river widens the valley floor and the bends migrate downstream. When the river meets the sea or a lake, the reduction in velocity causes it to deposit sediment and a delta develops.

The river terrace of the Taramakau River on South Island in New Zealand probably resulted from a drop in the sea level, which caused the river to renew its downcutting. The step along the side of the valley marks the former level of the valley floor. The broad plains of gravel alluvium represent the floodplain as it is today.

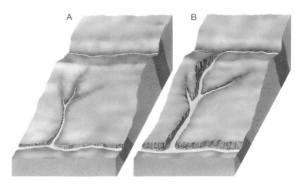

River capture occurs when a major river and its tributaries (A) become so entrenched that they wear through a divide and intercept another river so that its course is diverted (B). When the gorge of the captured river beyond the bend at the point of diversion (elbow of capture) is completely drained, it becomes a wind gap.

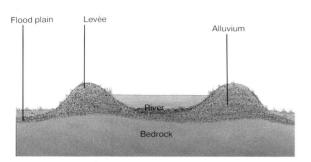

A **levée**, a raised bank found on both sides of a meandering river, forms from the accumulation of sediment that the river deposits when it overflows its banks. The river bed is raised by deposited sediment until it is higher than the floodplain.

River meanders

In the middle course of a river, most outcrops and formations are worn away and the bed is fairly flat. The current is just strong enough to carry debris from the upper course. But as a river flows onto flatter slopes it slows down and the coarsest debris is deposited. This debris may form sand and gravel bars around which the river is forced to flow. These deflections in its course develop into bends as the outer edges are eroded and as bars of sediment are deposited on the inner edges. In time, the curves become increasingly exaggerated and the river meanders.

The curves of a meandering river that flows across a wide flood plain slowly migrate downstream as erosion occurs on the outer bank of the bends and as sediments are deposited on the inner banks. The changing shape of the bends is due to the current, which usually follows a helical or corkscrew pattern as it goes downstream, flowing faster on the outer bank and sweeping more slowly towards the inner bank where it deposits a series of point bar sediments.

When a river is in spate, silt or alluvium may be spread over the floodplain. The river bed is raised higher than the surrounding land by deposition, while the river itself is contained by embankments, or levées, which are formed from the deposition of silt. Levées may break when the river is swollen and large areas of the floodplain may be inundated. At this time a river may alter its course, as did the Hwang Ho in China in 1852, when it shifted its mouth 300 mi. to the north of the Shantung Peninsula. On a smaller scale, individual meanders may be cut off if the river breaks through the narrow neck of land separating a meander loop. The river straightens its course at this point and the abandoned loop is left as an oxbow lake which gradually degenerates into a swamp as it is silted up by later floods.

A river is described as braided when it becomes wide and shallow and is split into several streams separated by mid-channels, bars of sand and shingle. Braiding often develops where a river emerges from a mountain region onto a bordering

A river delta in cross-section can be seen to be composed of several layers of material. The bottom set beds are made up of the finest particles which are carried out farthest; the foreset beds comprise coarser material and the topset beds consist of the heaviest sediment that is deposited at an early stage as the river meets the sea. These layers form a sloping fan under water that gradually extends along the sea floor as more material accumulates.

plain. The sudden flattening of the slope checks the velocity of the stream and sediment is deposited.

Deltas

Deposition is concentrated where a river is slowed on entering a lake or the sea. A delta forms at this point as long as no strong currents or tides prevent silt from settling. A typical cross-section through a delta shows a regular succession of beds in which fine particles of material – which are carried out farthest – create the bottom beds, whereas coarser material is deposited in a series of steep, angled wedges known as the foreset beds. As the delta progrades into the water, the coarsest sediment is carried through the river channel and laid down on the delta surface to form the top beds.

A good example of a lacustrine delta is found where the River Rhône enters Lake Geneva. The river is milky grey in colour because it is heavily charged with sediment acquired from its passage through the Bernese Oberland. The river plunges into the clear waters of the lake and slows down immediately, leaving the material it has transported to contribute to the outgrowth of the delta. Ultimately the lake may become completely silted up, although some lakes are initially divided by deltaic outgrowth. Derwentwater and Bassenthwaite in the English Lake District were originally one lake but are now separated by delta flats that were produced by the River Derwent.

Marine deltas are formed when the ocean currents at the river mouth are negligible, as in partially enclosed seas such as the Mediterranean and the Gulf of Mexico. The classic marine delta is exemplified by the arcuate type of the River Nile. Sediment is deposited in a broad arc surrounding the mouth of the river, which is made up of a series of distributary channels crossing the delta. Lagoons, marshes and coastal sand spits are also characteristic features of most deltas. The Mississippi delta has most of these features including levées, bayous (distributaries) and etangs (lagoons). The delta progrades seawards by way of several major channels which resemble outstretched fingers.

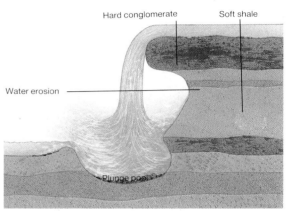

The Kaieteur Falls in Guyana (above) are typical of receding waterfalls. Splashing water from the plunge pool erodes the soft shale as does water dripping back under the hard conglomerate and sandstone ledge which, unsupported, eventually falls away.

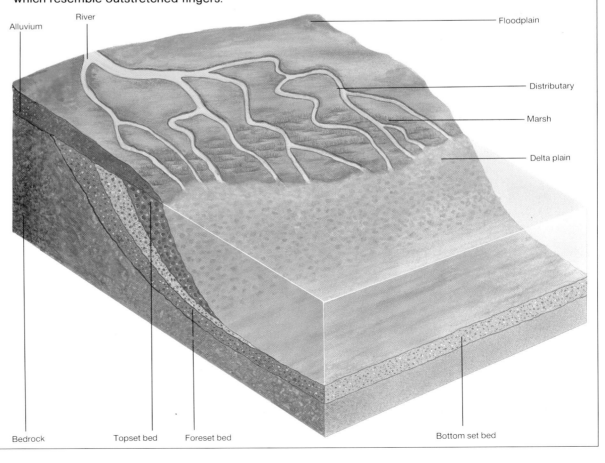

Coral reefs and islands

Not all rocks were formed hundreds of thousands of years ago. Enormous masses of limestone are being formed today in the warmer parts of the Indian and Pacific oceans, built up particle by particle through the activities of corals.

Corals are animals, relatives of the sea anemone that remain fixed to the same spot throughout life, feeding on organic material that drifts past in the water. They have a hard shell of calcite, formed by the extraction of calcium carbonate from sea water. A coral organism, called a polyp, can reproduce by budding and the result is a branching colony of thousands of individual creatures. Each colony is usually built up on the rocky skeletons of dead polyps, and in this way the coral mass can grow and spread to form a reef.

Corals flourish only in certain conditions. They live in sea water and grow best if the water is clear and silt-free, and at a temperature of between 73 and 77° F. Their tissues contain single-celled plants that help them to extract the calcite from water, and the plants must have sunlight to survive – in water less than 165 ft. deep. For these reasons, coral reefs are found in clear, shallow tropical seas.

Types of reefs

Most reefs tend to grow around islands. There are three main types of reefs. A fringing reef forms a shelf around an island, just below sea level. A barrier reef lies at a distance from the island, forming a rough ring around it and separated from it by a shallow lagoon. The third type of reef is the atoll, which is merely a ring of reef material without a central island. The three types can be considered as three stages in a single process.

Usually the island is volcanic, part of an island arc that rises from the sea floor where two crustal plates are converging. Once the island has appeared, corals begin to grow on its flanks, just below sea level. The outer limit of reef growth is defined by the depth (165 ft.) below which corals cannot grow. The result is a fringing reef.

As time passes the island may sink, possibly because, attached to its tectonic plate, it moves from a relatively shallow active area (such as an ocean ridge) towards deeper waters. Alternatively the "sinking" may be due to a rise in sea level caused by the melting of polar icecaps at the end of an ice age. As this occurs, the exposed part of the island – which is roughly conical in shape – becomes smaller. But the reef continues to build upwards from its original position. Sooner or later the island and reef become separated at the sur-

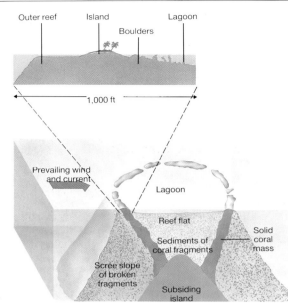

An atoll is a chain of coral islands, the remnants of a reef that once surrounded a volcanic island. Atolls are usually asymmetrical, growing more rapidly on the side to which the prevailing currents bring most nutrients.

face of the sea, producing a barrier reef. Eventually the island sinks completely, although the reef continues to grow and form the characteristic ring of an atoll.

If the atoll continues to sink and does so at such a rate that the growth of coral cannot keep ahead of it, then the coral dies and the whole reef is carried into depper water. This may account for the existence of guyots – flat-topped underwater hills whose summits may be 6,500 ft. below the surface of the sea.

The structure of a reef

A living reef forms a narrow plateau just below the surface of the water, producing an area of shallows that can be treacherous for swimmers and small craft. Where the reef crest is above the water it forms a small flat island, often crowned with coconut palms. The island is usually covered with white sand, made from the eroded fragments of coral skeletons. In the lagoon behind the reef there may be boulders of coral material that have been torn off the reef during storms and deposited in the calmer water. In the sheltered water of a lagoon,

Colorful damsel fish seek shelter among the finger-like growth of coral. The reefs support a wide variety of marine life, from the coral polyps themselves, through numerous species of molluscs and crustaceans, to the predatory fish that feed on them.

coral may grow into remarkable mushroom shapes and pinnacles and support a varied community of marine life.

The water in a lagoon is shallow, although not as shallow as over the reef itself. Its floor is covered by sediments of broken coral; this region is known as a flat reef. On the seaward side of the reef its edge may be composed of the skeletons of calcite-secreting algae, because these plants are better than corals at withstanding the rougher conditions. The outer edge forms a scree slope of fragments broken from the reef.

Fossil reefs

Geologically a reef is a mass of biogenic limestone, whose porous nature makes it a good reservoir rock for oil and natural gas. In early times the reef organisms were very different from today's. Modern corals did not evolve until about 200 million years ago (in the Triassic period), yet the first reefs date from the Cambrian of 570 million years ago. Many of the early reefs were built by calcite-producing algae, or by shellfish that existed on the heaps of shells left by their ancestors.

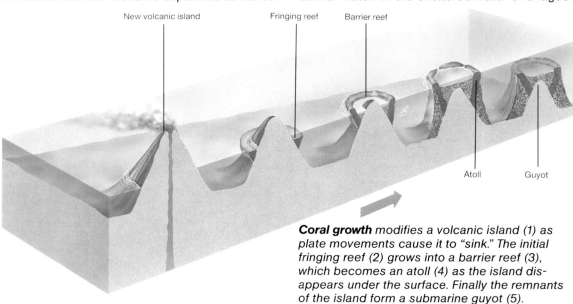

Coral growth modifies a volcanic island (1) as plate movements cause it to "sink." The initial fringing reef (2) grows into a barrier reef (3), which becomes an atoll (4) as the island disappears under the surface. Finally the remnants of the island form a submarine guyot (5).

Turbulent shallow water foams over the reef that fringes a small coral island in the Seychelles. Corals flourish in the warm waters of this part of the Indian Ocean.

The continental shelf

A continental shelf is a submerged, gently-sloping ledge that surrounds the edge of a continent. On the landward side it is bordered by the coastal plain and on the seaward side by the shelf break, where the continental shelf gives way to the steeper continental slope. The coastal plain, continental shelf and continental slope together comprise what is caled the continental terrace. Farther out to sea beyond the continental slope is the continental rise and then the abyssal plain – the sea floor of the deep ocean.

Knowledge of the continental shelf has increased greatly since the 1950s, helped by geophysical techniques originally developed to prospect for offshore oil and gas reserves. Particularly valuable have been the various sonar mapping methods, which use ultrasonic sound to penetrate the sea water. The depth of the sea-bed can be measured using echo-sounders, and lateral sonar beams can be used to obtain pictorial views of the sea-bed that are similar to aerial photographs of the land.

Size and depth of the continental shelf

The continental shelf constitutes 7 to 8 per cent of the total area of the sea floor, forming the bottom of most of the world's shallow seas. The width of the shelf varies from place to place; off the coast of southern California, for example, the shelf is less than two thirds of a mile wide, whereas off South America, between Argentina and the Falkland Islands, it is more than 300 mi. wide. It is narrowest on active crustal-plate margins bordering young mountain ranges, such as those around the Pacific Ocean and Mediterranean Sea, and broadest on passive margins – around the Atlantic Ocean, for example.

The shelf slopes gradually (at an average of only 0.1° to the horizontal) down to the shelf break, the mean depth of which is 425 ft. below sea level. The continental slope, the other main part of the continental terrace, begins at the shelf break and extends to a depth of between one and two miles. The slope varies from about 12 to 60 mi. wide and is much steeper than the shelf, having an average inclination of 4°, although in some places it is as steep as 20°.

Influences on the continental shelf

The continental shelf is affected by two main factors: earth movements and sea-level changes. On passive crustal-plate margins the shelf subsides as the Earth's crust gradually cools after rifting and becomes thinner through stretching. These processes are often accompanied by infilling with sediments, the weight of which adds to the subsidence of the shelf. And in polar regions the weight of ice depresses the continents by a considerable amount, with the result that the shelf break may be more than 1,970 ft. below sea level.

Superimposed on the results of subsidence is the effect of worldwide changes in sea level which, during the Earth's history, have repeatedly led to drowning of the continental margins. During the last few million years, sea-level changes were caused mainly by the freezing of the seas in the ice ages. The last major change, the melting of ice at the end of the Pleistocene Ice Age several thousand years ago, released water into the oceans and submerged the shelf. Since then shorelines have remained comparatively unchanged.

Many of the earlier changes in sea level, however, were related to the Earth's activity. During quiescent phases, when the Earth's surface is being eroded and the resultant debris deposited in the seas, the sea level rises as water is displaced by the accumulating debris. During active mountain-building phases, on the other hand, the sea level falls. Changes in the rate at which the continents move apart also cause fluctuations in sea level. During times of rapid separation, the rocks near the center of spreading of the ocean floor (from where the continental movements originate) become hot and expand, thereby displacing sea water, which drowns the edges of the continents.

Topography of the continental shelf

The continental shelf has a varied relief. Drowned river valleys, cliffs and beaches – submerged by the recent (in geological terms) sea-level rise – are common, and in northern latitudes the characteristic features left by retreating ice sheets and glaciers (U-shaped valleys and moraines, for example) are apparent.

Furthermore the shelf is not unchanging even today. It is being altered by numerous influences that affect the sediments left behind by the sea-level rise at the end of the Pleistocene Ice Age. In strongly tidal areas, such as the Yellow Sea and the North Sea, currents sweep sand deposits into wave-like patterns that resemble the wind-blown dunes in deserts.

Earth movements *and sea-level changes can affect the continental shelf, as shown by the cliff (above) which was originally an off-shore coral reef but was raised by earth movements and became part of the land.*

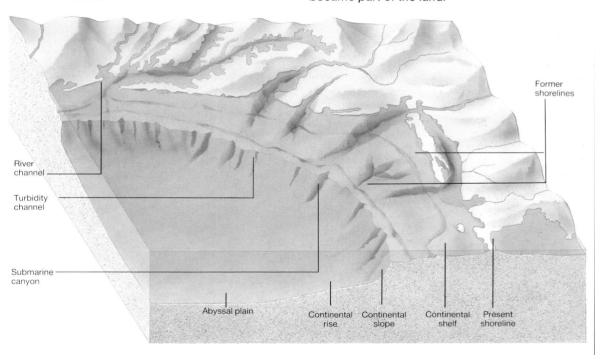

The narrow margins of the continents slope gradually before descending to the abyssal plain (the floor of the deep ocean). In the profile of the continental margin (below) the vertical scale has been exaggerated to enable the main zones to be clearly distinguishable.

The continental margin has a varied relief, with such features as submarine canyons and smaller turbidity and river channels. In some areas the former shorelines can also be seen.

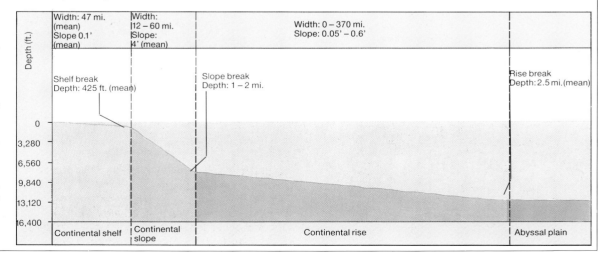

Ice caps

Within the last 1.6 million years the Earth has experienced an ice age during which almost one third of the land surface – about 11,600,000 sq. mi. – was covered by ice. Today the area of ice-covered land has dwindled to about 6,020,000 sq. mi., and continental ice sheets, such as those that were widespread during the last ice age, cover only Greenland and Antarctica. Smaller ice sheets, known as ice caps, occur in such northern landmasses as Iceland, Spitzbergen and the Canadian Islands. Valley glaciers that flow out over a plain and coalesce with others to form a broad sheet of ice are called piedmont glaciers; the classic examples of these are found along the southern coast of Alaska.

Ice movement

In very cold latitudes there is no summer thaw, and the snow that falls in winter is covered and compressed by snow in subsequent falls. The compressed snow eventually becomes glacier ice 2 to 2.5 mi. thick. The great pressure that builds up underneath the ice makes the ice crystals slide over each other and, because the pressure lowers the melting point of the ice, water is released which lubricates the mass. In addition, glacier ice under pressure can deform elastically like putty. As a result the ice sheet moves outwards, away from the build-up of pressure at the center. In Greenland the movement may be as great as 65 ft. per day, whereas in Antarctica it may only be 3 ft. per year. The bottom layers of the ice move and are deformed, but the top layers remain rigid and are carried along by them, cracking and splitting as they move.

The weight of a continental ice sheet depresses the land beneath it, so that a large percentage of the land surface of Greenland and Antarctica is below sea level. If these ice sheets were to melt, the level of the land below them would rise due to isostasy, as is happening in the areas of the Baltic Sea where the land is still recovering its isostatic balance after having lost the continental ice sheet that covered it during the last ice age. The restoration of balance

Nunataks, individual mountains that are completely surrounded by ice, occasionally protrude through the surface of an ice sheet. Lower mountains tend to be wholly engulfed and in such cases ice moving towards the sea can flow uphill.

does not just involve a simple raising of the land level; before this occurs the melting ice increases the volume of water in the oceans and raises the sea level at the same time.

When ice sheets pass over or through a mountain range and descend to a lower altitude, as they do in Iceland and the Canadian Islands, they squeeze through the passes and cols between the mountains in the form of lobes that may then become valley glaciers.

The various layers in an ice sheet can be detected by echo sounding, in which pulses of radio waves are sent down into the ice and the resulting echos analyzed. Reflections from different layers may

come from thin layers of dirt, which are probably deposits of volcanic ash that may have periodically drifted into and fallen on the area.

Ice ages

The Earth has had a number of ice ages. The area covered by them can be mapped by the distribution of rocks, called tillites, which consist of the same type of material found in glacial deposition. At least three ice ages are known to have occurred in Precambrian times and one in the Upper Ordovician or Lower Silurian period – 430 million years ago – evidence of which has been found in South Africa. A particularly important one occurred in Carboniferous and Permian times – 280 million years ago – and the evidence for this has been found in South America, central and southern Africa, India and Australia. It therefore provides substance for the theory of continental drift and the break-up of Gondwanaland – the great southern continent that existed then.

The most recent ice age was during the Pleistocene era. It began 1,600,000 years ago and ended a mere 11,000 years ago. It consisted of about 18 different advances and retreats of the ice sheets, each one separated by a warm interglacial period during which the climate in the temperate latitudes was at times warmer than it is now. It is possible that the glacial advances are not over yet and that we are experiencing another interglacial period before the advance of the next ice sheet.

Causes of ice ages

Many theories have been proposed. It has been suggested that the distribution of continental masses may be responsible, for example by preventing the warm oceanic water from reaching the poles. Or the albedo of ice sheets reflects a high percentage of solar radiation and so reduces temperatures sufficiently to affect the world climate. Or there may be fluctuations in the proportion of carbon dioxide or dust particles in the atmosphere; a reduction in carbon dioxide or an increase in dust would allow more heat to be lost from the Earth and so result in lower temperatures. Others suggest that the reason must be found in space, such as in a fluctuation of the Sun's energy output or the presence of a cloud of dust between the Earth and the Sun.

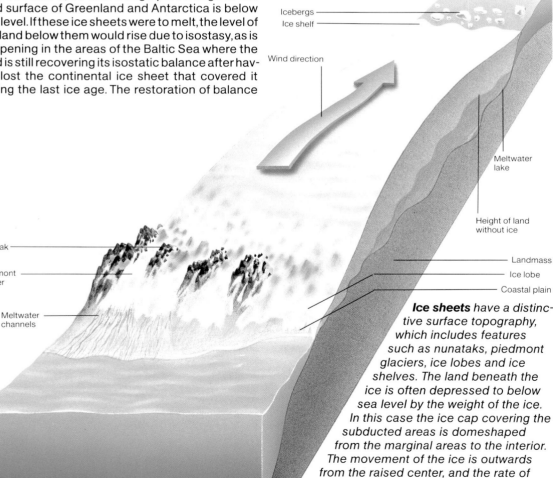

Icebergs
Ice shelf
Wind direction
Meltwater lake
Height of land without ice
Landmass
Ice lobe
Coastal plain
Nunatak
Piedmont glacier
Meltwater channels

Ice sheets have a distinctive surface topography, which includes features such as nunataks, piedmont glaciers, ice lobes and ice shelves. The land beneath the ice is often depressed to below sea level by the weight of the ice. In this case the ice cap covering the subducted areas is domeshaped from the marginal areas to the interior. The movement of the ice is outwards from the raised center, and the rate of flow increases as the ice flows down to the sea and through mountain valleys. The ice moves either as lobes through valleys or as part of the ice shelf into the sea where it melts or calves into icebergs.

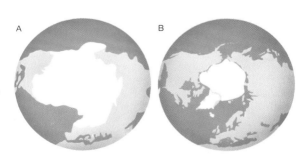

A   B

During the Pleistocene Ice Age, about 18,000 years ago (A), two ice sheets covered land in the Northern Hemisphere; one had as its center Scandinavia, and covered the North Sea, most of Britain, the Netherlands, northern Germany and Russia; the other spread over the North American continent as far down as Illinois. These ice sheets froze enough water to reduce the sea level to about 250 ft. lower than it is at present. Today in the Northern Hemisphere (B), only Greenland is covered by an ice sheet, and ice caps lie over Iceland, parts of Scandinavia and the Canadian Islands.

Mountain glaciers

The snowfields on mountain regions are constantly being replenished with fresh falls of snow, the weight of which compresses the underlying material into firn, or nevé. This material is composed of ice crystals separated from each other by small air spaces. With increasing depth and pressure, the firn gradually changes into much denser glacier ice which moves slowly out from the snowfields down existing valleys. The glacier becomes a river of moving ice, its surface marked by a series of deep cracks or crevasses. The cracks result from the fact that ice under pressure deforms and moves plastically, whereas the upper layers remain rigid and are therefore under tension and eventually shear. Transverse crevasses often occur where the slope of the glacier increases; these may be intersected by longitudinal crevasses, creating ice pinnacles, or seracs, between them. A large crevasse, known as a bergschrund, may also form near the head of a glacier in the firn zone where the ice pulls away from the mountain wall.

Glacial abrasion and plucking

Als a glacier moves it erodes the underlying rocks, mainly by abrasion and by plucking. Abrasion involves rock debris frozen into the sole of the glacier acting on the rocks underneath like coarse sandpaper. Plucking happens when the ice freezes onto rock projections, particularly in well-jointed rocks, and tears the blocks out as it moves.
Considerable evidence exists of glacial erosion having taken place during the Pleistocene Ice Age, when glaciers and ice sheets extended over much of northern Europe and North America. At that time, ice moved out of the high mountains and spread over the surrounding lowlands. It modified the shape of the land and left various distinctive landforms that can be seen today, long after the ice has receded.
In most glaciated valleys it is possible to find rock surfaces that have been grooved and scratched. These striations were caused by angular rock fragments frozen into the sole of a moving glacier. The marks give some indication of the direction of ice movement. Where a more resistant rock projects out of a valley floor it may have been moulded by the passage of ice so that it has a gentle slope on the upstream side (which is planed smooth by the glacier) and a steep ragged slope on the lee

side (a result of ice plucking). Seen from a distance these rocks were thought to resemble the sheepskin wigs fashionable in early nineteenth-century Europe, and so were named roches moutonnées.

Corries

An aerial view of a glaciated highland reveals large amphitheater-like hollows arranged around the mountain peaks. These great hollows are called corries (cirques in France, and cwms in Wales) and are the point at which glaciers were first formed during an ice age, or where present-day glaciers start in areas such as the Alps or the Rockies. The Aletsch glacier, for example, begins on the southeastern slopes of the Jungfrau in Switzerland and is fed by several tributary glaciers, each emerging from a corrie. Frost-shattering of the exposed walls of the corries results in their gradual enlargement; this process is accelerated by subglacial disintegration of the rock, which occurs when water reaches the rock floor through the bergschrund crevasse at the head of the glacier.
During an ice age most corries were probably filled to overflowing with glacier ice, and their walls and floors were subject to vigorous abrasion. When the ice melted, a corrie often became the site of a mountain lake, or tarn, with morainic material forming a dam at the outflow lip.
Corries are bordered by several precipitous knife-edged ridges known as arêtes. These develop when the walls of two adjoining corries meet after glacial erosion has taken place from both sides. When the arêtes themselves are worn back, the central mass may remain as an isolated peak where the heads of several corries meet. The Matterhorn in the Swiss Alps is a peak that was produced in this way.

Glacial valleys

When a glacier passes through a pre-existing river valley it actively erodes the valley to a characteristic U-shaped profile. The original interlocking spurs through which the former river wound are worn back and truncated. In this way the valley is straightened, widened and deepened, and its tributary valleys are left high above the main trough as hanging valleys. The streams in them often plunge down

A melting glacier in the Himalayas, near Sonamarg in Kashmir, lies in the U-shaped valley it has created. The typical rate of flow of a glacier is about 3 ft. a day and movement is due to slope and the plastic distortion of ice. Rock fragments that the glacier has plucked from the slopes of the valley can be seen littering the valley floor. They form the lateral moraine of the glacier and, at an earlier stage of glaciation, probably cut in and abraded the valley floor and sides as they were dragged along by the moving ice.

the valley side as spectacular waterfalls, as in the Lauterbrunnen valley between Interlaken and the Jungfrau in the Swiss Alps.
Where several tributary glaciers join the head of a major valley, the increased gouging by the extra ice flow results in the formation of a trough end, or steep step in the U-shaped trough. The floor of a glaciated valley is often eroded very unevenly and elongated depressions may become the sites of long, narrow, ribbon lakes. Some of the deeper ribbon lakes are dammed by morainic material at their outlets, as in lakes Como and Maggiore in northern Italy.
In mountainous regions glacial troughs may extend down to the coast where they form long steep-sided inlets, or fjords. The classic fjords of Norway, Scotland and British Columbia all result from intense glaciation, followed by a eustatic rise in sea level at the end of the Ice Age that flooded the lower ends of the U-shaped valleys.

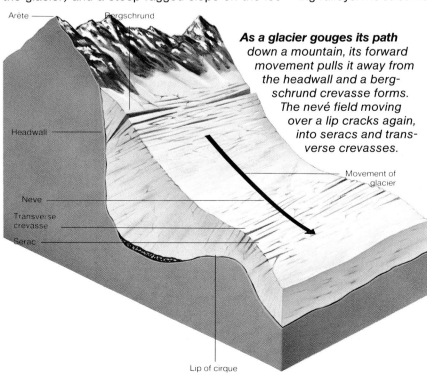

As a glacier gouges its path down a mountain, its forward movement pulls it away from the headwall and a bergschrund crevasse forms. The nevé field moving over a lip cracks again, into seracs and transverse crevasses.

Arète — Bergschrund
Headwall
Neve
Transverse crevasse
Serac
Lip of cirque
Movement of glacier

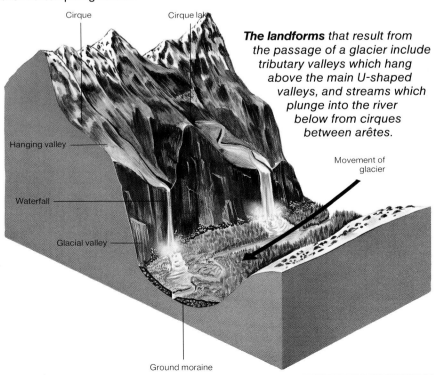

The landforms that result from the passage of a glacier include tributary valleys which hang above the main U-shaped valleys, and streams which plunge into the river below from cirques between arêtes.

Cirque   Cirque lake
Hanging valley
Waterfall
Glacial valley
Ground moraine
Movement of glacier

Post-glaciation

When a glacier emerges from its U-shaped valley, it spreads out over the surrounding lowlands as an ice sheet. Much of the surface material eroded by the glacier and carried by it to the plains is deposited when the ice starts to melt. The pre-glacial lowland landscape is therefore often markedly modified by various deposits left behind by the ice.

Surface deposits

When the great northern continental ice sheets reached their most southerly extent, they deposited a ridge-like terminal moraine. Similar ridges, known as recessional moraines, have resulted from pauses during the retreat of the ice sheet. The North German Plain is traversed by a series of parallel crescent-shaped (arcuate) moraines which were formed as the Scandinavian ice sheet advanced across the Baltic. The main line of low morainic hills can be traced southwards through the Jutland peninsula, and then eastwards through northern Germany and Poland. The Baltic Heights represent the most clearly defined moraine, reaching more than 1,180 ft. in height near Gdańsk. Similarly, a series of moraines cross the plains to the south of the Great Lakes, marking the various halts in the recession of the North American ice sheet.

Behind each terminal moraine, groups of low, hummocky hills known as drumlins often occur. These hills were formed as the ice sheet retreated and most are elliptical mounds of sand and clay, sometimes up to 200 ft. high, and elongated in the direction of the ice movement. How they were formed is not known but it is thought that they were caused by the overriding of previous ground moraine. Drumlins are arranged in an echelon, or belt, and form a distinctive drumlin topography. A drumlin field may contain as many as 10,000 drumlins – one of the largest known is on the north-western plains of Canada. Around Strangford Lough in County Down, Ireland, drumlins form islands within the lough itself. Winding across glaciated lowlands, there are often long, sinuous gravel ridges called eskers. They are thought to be deposits formed by subglacial streams at the mouths of the tunnels through which they flowed beneath the ice. Eskers are common in Finland and Sweden, where they run across the country between lakes and marshes.

When a delta is formed by meltwater seeping out from beneath the ice front, it develops into a mound of bedded sand and gravel known as a kame. In some areas kames are separated by water-filled depressions called kettle holes, formed originally as sediment piled up around patches of stranded ice which melted after the recession of the ice sheet. The chief product of glacial deposition is boulder clay, which is the ground moraine of an ice sheet. It comprises an unstratified mixture of sand and clay particles of various sizes and origins. For example, deposits in south-eastern England contain both

Erratics, blocks of till or bedrock, have been known to be carried for more than 500 mi. by a glacier. They are prominent on glacial landscapes and their position often suggest the direction of the ice movement.

chalk boulders of local derivation and igneous rock from Scandinavia. Blocks of rock that are transported far from their parent outcrop are known as erratics. The largest blocks are commonly seen resting on the boulder clay surface or even perched on exposed rock platforms.

The unsorted ground moraine behind the ice front contrasts strongly with the stratified drift of the outwash plain beyond. Meltwater streams deposit sand and gravel on the outwash plains, to form the undulating topography so typical of the Luneburg Heath of West Germany or the Geest of the Netherlands.

Proglacial lakes

At the end of the Ice Age, many rivers were dammed by ice and their waters formed proglacial lakes. During the retreat of the North American ice sheet, for example, a large lake – Lake Agassiz – was dammed up between the ice to the north and the continental watershed to the south. The remnants of this damming can be seen in Lake Winnipeg, which is now surrounded by lacustrine silts that were deposited on the floor of the ancient Lake Agassiz.

Beach strand lines are sometimes visible, which indicate the water levels at various stages in the draining of a lake. This probably occurred when the proglacial lake overflowed through spillways at successively lower levels, as the ice began to recede. In north-eastern England there is striking evidence of the diversion of drainage by ice. Preglacial rivers flowed eastwards into the North Sea, but were blocked by the Scandinavian ice front as it approached the base of the North York Moors. The Eskdale valley in the moors was turned into a lake which overflowed southwards via a spillway into Lake Pickering, about 16 mi. distant. This lake in turn drained through the Kirkham Abbey Gorge about 6 mi. away, and today the River Derwent still follows the southward route to the River Humber, having been diverted by ice from its pre-glacial eastwards course.

Periglacial features

Beyond the ice sheet margin lies the periglacial zone of permafrost, in which repeated freeze and thaw cycles result in the breaking of the soil surface and the differential sorting of loose fragments of rock, so that a pattern is produced. On flat surfaces, polygonal arrangements of stones occur, whereas on sloping surfaces, parallel lines are formed. Another periglacial landform is the pingo, or ice mound, created when a body of water freezes below ground and produces an ice core which raises the surface into a low hillock.

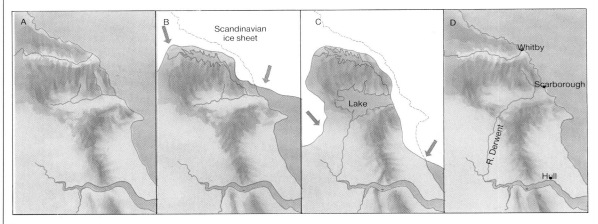

During the Ice Age, encroaching ice sometimes diverted a river. In north-eastern England, originally (A) the land was drained by rivers flowing eastwards. The advancing Scandinavian ice cap dammed a river (B), creating a lake which overspilled southwards. Further ice movement created another lake (C), forcing the river further south. (D) The River Derwent still follows the diverted course.

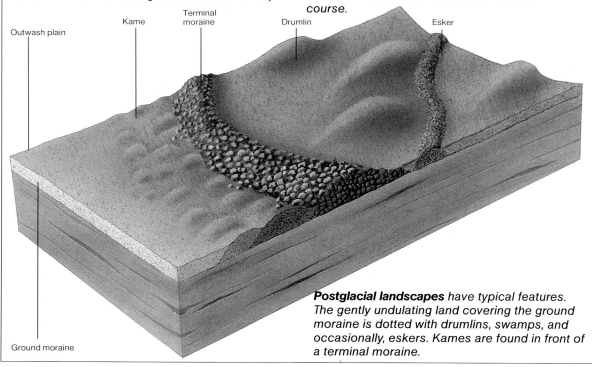

Postglacial landscapes have typical features. The gently undulating land covering the ground moraine is dotted with drumlins, swamps, and occasionally, eskers. Kames are found in front of a terminal moraine.

THE
NATURE
OF OUR
UNIVERSE

The Solar System

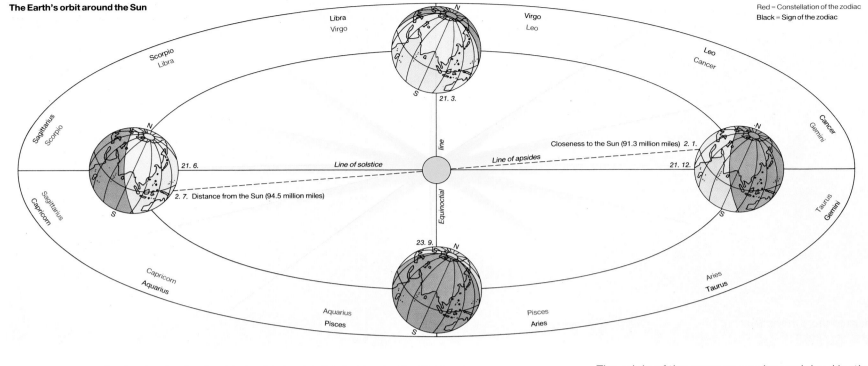

Red = Constellation of the zodiac
Black = Sign of the zodiac

Closeness to the Sun (91.3 million miles) 2. 1.
Line of apsides
Line of solstice
2. 7. Distance from the Sun (94.5 million miles)
Equinoctial line

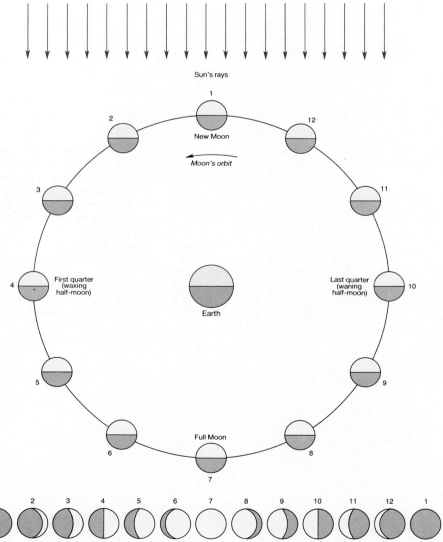

Sun's rays

New Moon

Moon's orbit

First quarter
(waxing
half-moon)

Earth

Last quarter
(waning
half-moon)

Full Moon

How the phases of the Moon occur

The origin of the seasons can be explained by the fact that on its orbit the Earth's axis is not vertical, but is tilted 23 ½ degrees from the vertical. Therefore, on June 21, our Earth's northern hemisphere is inclined slightly toward the Sun and is struck more directly by the rays of the Sun than the southern hemisphere. On December 21, the Earth's northern hemisphere is inclined slightly away from the Sun and is struck more obliquely by the Sun's rays than the southern hemisphere. It is then that winter begins in the northern hemisphere and summer in the southern hemisphere. Viewed from the perspective of the Earth rotating around the Sun, in the course of one year the Sun seems to pass before the backdrop of the twelve constellations of the zodiac.

For one revolution relative to the Sun, the Moon needs 29,531 days (the synodical month). During this time, the separate phases of the Moon also change. The waxing Moon can be observed more in the evening hours, the waning Moon after midnight and in the morning hours. At new Moon our satellite is invisible. The full Moon can be observed throughout the night. For one revolution relative to the stars, the Moon needs 27,322 days (the sidereal month). The average distance of the Moon from the Earth is 238,869 miles. This is only $\frac{1}{389}$th of the distance of the Sun from the Earth (92,960,000 miles). Therefore, in a scaled diagram of the Earth's orbit and of the Moon around our Sun, the orbit of the Moon is always bent concavely opposite the Sun.

The movement of the Earth around the Sun *at an angle to the orbit of the Earth is shown above. The middle illustration shows the movement of the Moon around our Earth; the numbered row shows the phases of the Moon in its different positions. The bottom illustration shows the monthly orbit of the Moon.*

The monthly orbit of the Moon

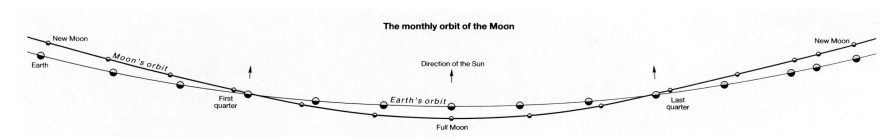

New Moon
Earth
Moon's orbit
First quarter
Direction of the Sun
Earth's orbit
Full Moon
Last quarter
New Moon

The Planetary System

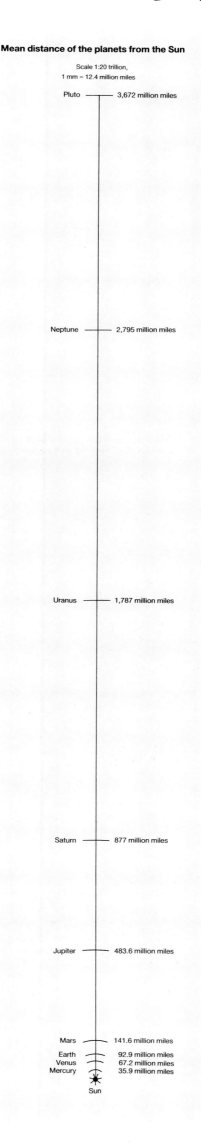

Mean distance of the planets from the Sun

Scale 1:20 trillion,
1 mm = 12.4 million miles

Pluto	— 3,672 million miles
Neptune	— 2,795 million miles
Uranus	— 1,787 million miles
Saturn	— 877 million miles
Jupiter	— 483.6 million miles
Mars	— 141.6 million miles
Earth	— 92.9 million miles
Venus	— 67.2 million miles
Mercury	— 35.9 million miles
Sun	

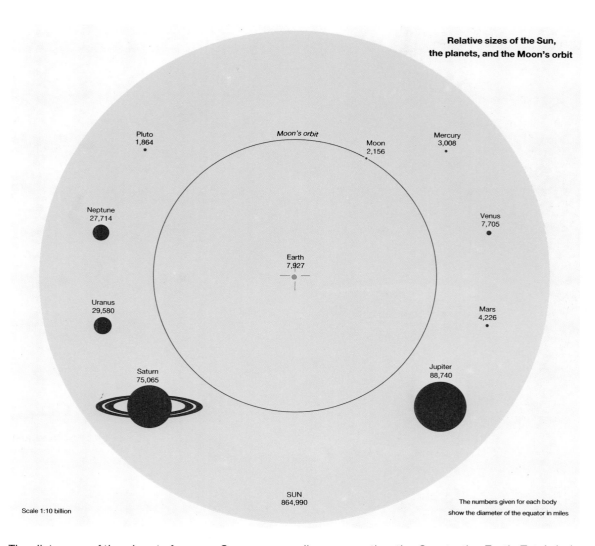

**Relative sizes of the Sun,
the planets, and the Moon's orbit**

Pluto 1,864
Moon's orbit
Moon 2,156
Mercury 3,008
Neptune 27,714
Venus 7,705
Earth 7,927
Uranus 29,580
Mars 4,226
Saturn 75,065
Jupiter 88,740
SUN 864,990

Scale 1:10 billion

The numbers given for each body
show the diameter of the equator in miles

The distances of the planets from our Sun vary so much that they can only be depicted accurately when drawn to scale. Using a scale of 1:20 trillion, the Sun, with a total diameter of 865,000,000 miles, shrinks to only 0.07 mm. The Earth then measures only 0.00068 mm and the largest planet, Jupiter, 0.007 mm. Nevertheless, one small part of Pluto's highly eccentric orbit still projects into Neptune's orbit. Pluto is the smallest of the nine large planets, measuring approximately 1,800 miles in diameter or 0.0002 mm on the aforementioned scale. The zone of the minor planets (asteroids and planetoids) lies between the planets Mars and Jupiter. Although almost 3,000 of these have been accurately identified, it is estimated that altogether they number 50,000, or more. Some of these minor planets rotate outside the main zone, deep within our planetary system, while others are in the outer regions.

Solar eclipses occur each time there is a new Moon, when the Moon is exactly incident with the line connecting the Sun to the Earth. Total darkness is observed within the umbra that the Moon casts on the Earth, while a partial solar eclipse is visible within the penumbra. A ring-shaped solar eclipse occurs when the Moon on its elliptical orbit is so far from the Earth that the point of the umbra no longer reaches the Earth's surface. As a result, the disc of the Moon appears to be slightly smaller than that of the Sun. An eclipse of the Moon takes place when the Moon enters into the shadow of the Earth. If the Moon passes completely through the Earth's umbra, then a total eclipse of the Moon occurs. A partial eclipse occurs when the Moon enters just slightly into the umbra. The Earth's penumbra has no significant effect.

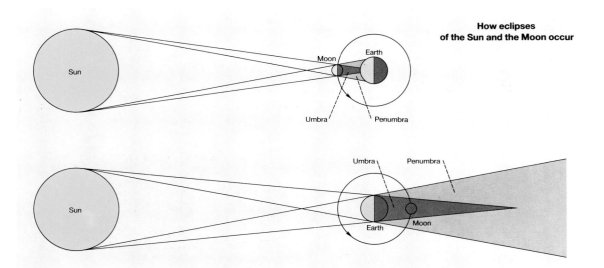

**How eclipses
of the Sun and the Moon occur**

Sun
Moon
Earth
Umbra
Penumbra

Umbra
Penumbra
Sun
Earth
Moon

The Sun

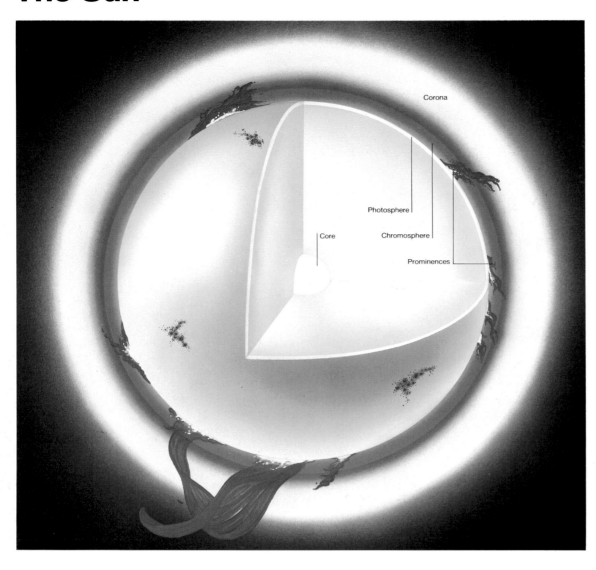

The central star of our planet, the Sun, is an ordinary star, like other fixed stars we call suns. It is a globe of gases, made up of 75% hydrogen, 23% helium, and 2% heavy elements. We can directly observe and measure its surface, which has a temperature of about 9,900 °F. The interior of the Sun, however, can only be deduced mathematically, using the theory of stellar evolution. At high temperatures in the core of the Sun (up to a maximum of 27,000,000 °F), four hydrogen nuclei (protons) at a time fuse to form one helium nucleus consisting of two protons and two neutrons. During this nuclear merging (nuclear fusion), mass is transformed into energy. This process is the source of our Sun's energy, which can maintain its present state of equilibrium for a total of approximately 8 billion years. Now the Sun is just 5 billion years old. About

3 billion years from now the Sun will expand to a giant red star, and still later collapse to a compact white dwarf star.

The Sun requires 25 days at its equator to rotate on its axis. In medium and high latitudes, rotation time increases by a few days. Sunspots appear in the Sun's equatorial zone. The number of sunspots fluctuates, approximately on an eleven-year cycle. They generally occur more or less in large groups and last anywhere from a few days to several months. Their temperature is approximately 7,200 °F. Sunspots are caused by strong magnetic fields that penetrate and cool a region of the Sun's surface. Consequently, they appear to be darker than the rest of the surface. Near the sunspots' brighter spots, Sun flares, with a temperature of approximately 11,700 °F appear. As a result, a large

number of sunspots does not alter the total intensity of our Sun.

The layer of the Sun visible with the naked eye or using a normal telescope is called the photosphere. The chromosphere that envelopes it can only be investigated using specialized instruments. Research reveals occasional powerful eruptions, especially in areas near active groups of sunspots. These are bright eruptions of light, accompanied by streams of particles, and they generally last only a few minutes or hours. Prominences are another form of ejection of matter, or movement above the Sun's surface. Caused by the structure of regional magnetic fields, these gas clouds often circulate in large swirls over the Sun's surface. Occasionally, too, eruptive prominences occur that flare up at great speed like flaming streamers into the Sun's upper atmosphere. During total solar eclipses a halo of light, the Sun's corona, can be discerned surrounding the disc of the Sun covered by the new Moon. This corona can be studied with specialized instruments. The temperature in the corona ranges from 1.8 to 5.4 million °F. It is from the corona that the Sun's X-rays radiate, a process that has been investigated in recent years using satellites. The Sun is also a powerful source of radio waves. Outbursts of radio waves often occur in conjunction with eruptions of the Sun.

Magnetosphere
An invisible shell of atomic particles formed by the Earth's magnetism; extends at least 40,390 miles into space

Van Allen Belt I
First protective shell of atomic particles; approx. 3,100 miles from Earth

Earth's atmosphere
A protective shell of air, approx. 310 miles wide

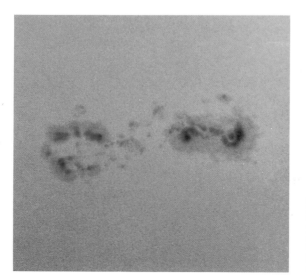

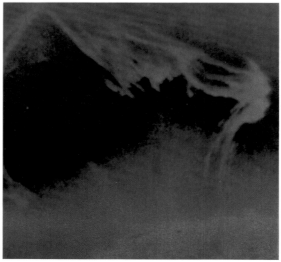

The Sun interacts strongly with our Earth. The seasons are, of course, the most obvious manifestation of this connection. Sun activities such as sunspots, flares, and eruptions also give rise to certain events on Earth. For example, the Sun's X-ray radiation creates, in the Earth's atmosphere at a height of between 50 and 155 miles, several electrically charged layers – the ionosphere. The Sun is also able to reflect, and thereby transmit, short waves. Disturbances on our Sun cause disturbances in radio communications.

Our Earth is surrounded by a magnetic field extending far out into space. This magnetosphere is slightly indented on the side facing the Sun. On the side facing away from the Sun, a long tail of the Earth's magnetic field appears. The Van Allen Belts are found within the magnetosphere at heights of about 3,100 and 12,400 miles. Electrically charged particles that fly quickly back and forth between the magnetic north and south poles are trapped in them. Essentially, these particles were originally ejected from the Sun. The Sun radiates more than electromagnetic waves such as light or radio waves. It also emits the Sun's "wind," a fine stream of other electrically charged particles. These particles are generally so low in energy that they cannot penetrate the magnetosphere on the side facing the Sun. Instead, they are deflected sideways and gradually infiltrate the magnetosphere from the side facing away from the Sun. Higher energy particles ejected during eruptions of the Sun cause such enormous confusion in this system that the particles in the Van Allen Belts are "shaken out" and penetrate into the Earth's atmosphere, especially in the polar regions. There, they collide with the atoms of the atmosphere, causing them to glow. These polar lights (the northern and southern lights) appear most often at a height of between 56 and 80 miles. The lowest polar lights have been detected at 43 miles, the highest at about 620 miles.

Magnetic storms, disturbances of the Earth's magnetic field, occur simultaneously with these other phenomena. Additional connections between the Sun's activity and our Earth – especially concerning the influence of the Sun on our weather – are still hotly debated. To date it has not been possible to determine whether or not dry summers or cold winters can be predicted on the basis of the Sun's prevailing activity. It is clear that the Sun's activity is only one among numerous factors that determine the behavior of the weather.

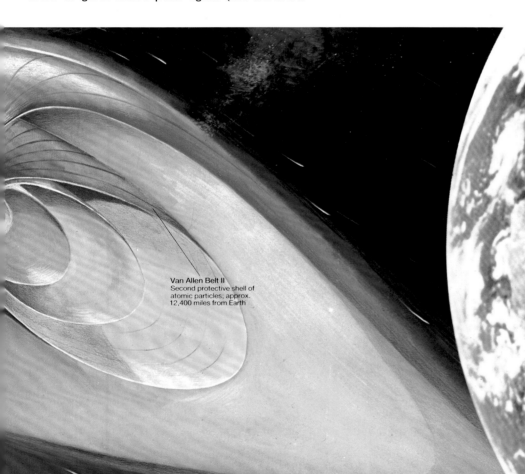

Van Allen Belt II
Second protective shell of
atomic particles; approx.
12,400 miles from Earth

The temperature of our Sun *increases markedly from the outside to the inside (see above left). Two photos on this page show a group of sunspots and a prominence (see below left). In the middle illustration, the Earth is shown surrounded by its magnetosphere, as well as the Van Allen Belts. Note the asymmetrical shape of the magnetosphere, with its geomagnetic tail on the side facing away from the Sun. On the right is a photo of the Earth, taken about halfway between the Earth and the Moon by Apollo II. In the middle is Africa, above right Arabia, and at the very top (under clouds) Europe. The yellow and reddish tones of the desert regions are particularly striking.*

The Milky Way

Stars are not randomly distributed, but often form groups or stellar clusters. The best-known are the two clusters in Taurus that can be seen with the naked eye: Hyades (the Rain Star) and Pleiades (the Seven Sisters). These are 130 to 410 light-years away from us and belong to the group of "open clusters." Open clusters generally consist of a few dozen to a few thousand stars clustered together so loosely that we can resolve them into individual stars through a telescope. They are relatively young collections of stars, up to a maximum of one billion years old. The globular clusters are considerably older. They contain 100,000 to 1 million stars and are arranged symmetrically, with stars strongly concentrated in the center. The brightest globular cluster, Omega Centauri, is found in the southern sky and is 17,000 light-years away. Globular clusters are approximately 12 billion years old.

The space between the stars is not completely empty. This is where the so-called interstellar matter (gas and dust) is found. As a rule, it contains only about 1 atom per cubic centimeter. In the bright and dark nebulae, visible through telescopes, the matter can, however, be concentrated to 100 to 10,000 atoms per cubic centimeter. Interstellar matter is the raw material for the creation of new stars. Phenomena like the Orion nebula of the Orion, the Rosette nebula of Monoceros, and the Omega nebula of Sagittarius are typical examples of such stellar birthplaces in the universe. So far, though, the causes of the compressions that lead to the creation of stars have not been completely explored. They may be gravitational waves of our Milky Way, or shock waves that emanate from supernova explosions and compress nearby interstellar dust. Our solar system may have originated in this way barely 5 billion years ago. Stars that can be seen today in the bright nebulae are especially young phenomena, between 10,000 and 1 million years old. A few infrared nebulae and infrared stars can even be regarded as stars in the process of creation. Such phenomena are often surrounded by thick cocoons of dust that may give rise to planetary systems. After a star compresses, the temperature inside increases causing atomic nuclear reactions, in particular the transformation of hydrogen into helium. An automatic balance is achieved: gravity, which might let the star collapse further, is counterbalanced by gas pressure operating from the inside out. If the generation of energy in the core of the star decreases as the hydrogen content decreases, gas pressure weakens simultaneously. The automatic balance is disturbed and gravity causes the core of the star to shrink. As a result the temperature rises. At present our Sun has a core temperature of 27 million °F. In about 3 billion years this will increase to between 90 and 180 million °F. At the same time, a new "ignition temperature" will be reached at which helium can transform into carbon. Then, even more energy will be produced in the core of the star. The gas pressure inside the star will cause it to expand into a red giant star. As the core temperature gradually rises, heavier and heavier elements, even iron, are formed. Then the star reaches the limits of its ability to maintain a stable balance and it collapses upon itself leaving a dense white dwarf star in its place. Stars with more than about 1.4 sun masses collapse into neutron stars. These measure approximately 12.5 miles in diameter and have a density of 10 trillion g/cm^3. Moreover, stars over 3 to 5 sun masses collapse into so-called black holes which can no longer be seen from the outside. The prevailing density inside these phenomena is up to 100,000 trillion g/cm^3.

The collapse of a star into a neutron star or a black hole is accompanied by a supernova explosion whereby the star's outer layers may be discarded. In this way, heavier elements formed earlier inside the star reach interstellar space. Stars that develop later from this substance will already contain a certain percentage of heavy elements.

All the stars visible to the naked eye (and most of those visible using a telescope) belong to our Milky Way or Galaxy. This is a flat spiral, 100,000 light-years in diameter. If we could view our Milky Way from the outside, it would look like a enormous Catherine wheel from above and like a flat disc from the side. The Sun and the planets lie about 30,000 light-years from the center of the Milky Way which, viewed from our perspective, is situated in the direction of Sagittarius. If we observe the sky from the Earth at the equatorial level of our Milky Way, we see a particularly large number of stars, and we can identify the band of the Milky Way with its myriad of stars. We can also see that the Milky Way (Galaxy) is clearly asymmetrical. It is brightest toward Sagittarius and weakest in the opposite direction (constellations Taurus and Auriga). With the aid of radio astronomy, it has been possible to detect a few spiral arms in the vicinity of the Sun; in particular the Perseus, Orion, and Sagittarius arms. Using techniques of radio astronomy, it has also been possible to explore the core of our Milky Way, which lies behind dark, light-absorbing clouds of interstellar

Two examples of stellar clusters: *the Pleiades or Seven Sisters in Taurus and the globular Omega Centauri cluster. The Rosette nebula of the constellation Monoceros and the Omega nebula of Sagittarius are examples of stellar birthplaces. We can clearly see bright young stars in them.*

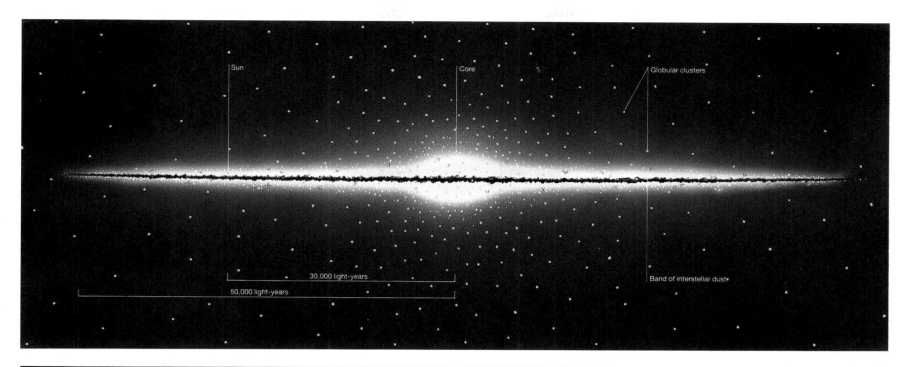

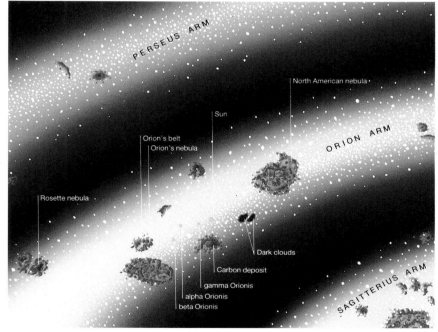

Labels on side-view diagram: Sun, Core, Globular clusters, 30,000 light-years, 50,000 light-years, Band of interstellar dust

Labels on top-view diagram: PERSEUS ARM, North American nebula, Sun, Orion's belt, Orion's nebula, ORION ARM, Rosette nebula, Dark clouds, Carbon deposit, gamma Orionis, alpha Orionis, beta Orionis, SAGITTERIUS ARM

matter. We know that a large mass is concentrated there in a relatively confined space. The exact structure of the Milky Way's core has, however, not yet been deciphered. Some researchers suspect it would reveal an enormous black hole.

Surrounding our own flat Milky Way is the galactic halo, where mainly globular stellar clusters are found. This halo extends far beyond the narrow confines of the Milky Way. If we include it, our galactic system might be 200,000 to 300,000 light-years in diameter. All stars rotate around the center of the galactic system. At an orbiting speed of about 155 miles per second, our Sun requires approximately 220 million years for this journey.

*Two diagrams on this page show the **structure of our Milky Way** system from above and from the side. Much of this information could only be obtained with the aid of radio astronomy and infrared astronomy. Our photo shows part of the Milky Way, with numerous stars, dark clouds, and bright nebulae. To the left is Sagittarius, to the right Cassiopeia.*

The Milky Way   255

Galaxies

A large number of "nebulae" that can be observed in the sky using telescopes are not true nebulae (like the Orion and Rosette nebulae for example), but independent stellar systems – galaxies – lying outside our own Milky Way. The best-known galaxy is the Andromeda Spiral. On a clear night it is visible to the naked eye as a pale nebula patch in the constellation Andromeda. However, it has only been possible to resolve its individual stars with the aid of the largest telescopes and long-exposure photographs. The Andromeda Spiral is 2.3 million light-years away and similar in size to our own Milky Way: it is 150,000 light-years in diameter and consists of 200 billion sun masses. It contains practically the same phenomena as our system, e. g., open clusters, globular clusters, variable stars, bright nebulae, etc. The stars in the Andromeda Spiral rotate at speeds similar to stars in our galactic system. Andromeda is a spiral nebula. There are also elliptical and irregular nebulae. Our own Milky Way contains two irregular nebulae as satellites, the Large and Small Magellanic Clouds. These are visible virtually only from our Earth's southern hemisphere and are about 165,000 light-years away.

Galaxies often occur in clusters containing anywhere from several dozen to 10,000 galaxies. Our Milky Way belongs to the so-called local nebula group that includes 20 to 30 galaxies. There is also a large number of tiny dwarf galaxies, only a few of which are 1,000 light-years in diameter. Most of these are elliptical or irregular.

Another famous galaxy cluster – the Virgo cluster – lies in the direction of the constellation Virgo. There are several indications that many galaxy clusters recombine to form super clusters. Some galaxies emit very strong radio waves that indicate intense activity in the cores of the galaxies (radio galaxies). In addition, the quasars – dot-shaped phenomena that look like stars – and Seyfert galaxies are most likely extremely active galaxies. Quasars occur only at great distances from Earth. The most remote ordinary galaxies that can be captured on long-exposure photos are about 3 to 4 billion light-years away. The quasars are up to 15 billion light-years away.

As a result of extensive expansion of the universe, the galaxies are receding from us. The further away they are, the faster they recede. Nevertheless, we only seem to be in the center of this movement of flight. One would have the same impression from every other position in the universe. The universe has no center. Its curved, expanding space probably originated somewhat more that 15 billion years ago from a small, immensely dense mass of material in a process called the "big bang." This assumption has been supported by the discovery of so-called cosmic background radiation falling on us equally from all parts of the universe. Most of this radiation is found at a wavelength of approximately 4 mm, but some is also present in the centimeter range of radio wave radiation. It is believed to be residual radiation from the big bang. The quarks and the first elementary particles must have come into being just fractions of a second after the big bang. Shortly afterward, hydrogen atoms formed in addition to the atomic nuclei of deuterium and helium. There were no elements heavier than helium during this early phase of the universe. These elements formed inside the stars much later. We cannot construct a model of our universe as a finite, boundless, and curved space. At best, we can get some idea of the structure of the universe by picturing the surface of a sphere. Just as a sphere is curved two-dimensionally and turns back on itself, so is three-dimensional space – that is, the universe is curved and turns back on itself. There are no solid boundaries. The question of whether the expansion of the universe as observed today will continue for all time still remains to be answered. It is, to a large extent, dependent on the mass present in the universe. If this mass is large enough, then the expansion can later be transformed into a contraction. The universe would once more be a dense mass of material and then, perhaps, recreate itself with a big bang. To date however, the material found in the universe represents little more than one hundreth of the mass required to cause the expansion to eventually change to a contraction. It is possible though, that there is as yet unknown matter – in the form of black holes, for example. Some researchers suspect that neutrinos – particles that exist in huge numbers in the universe as a result of atomic nuclear reactions – are not completely massless, as was earlier thought, but rather possess a tiny mass. This may strongly contribute to the overall mass of the universe.

The Andromeda nebula is a typical example of a close, spiral galaxy. It is 2.3 million light-years away, is 150,000 light-years in diameter, and contains approximately 200 billion sun masses. Our own Milky Way is quite similar in structure. Nearby, as satellites of the Andromeda nebula, we see two elliptical nebulae 2,300 and 7,800 light-years in diameter, respectively.

Index

The index contains all the names that appear on the metropolitan area, country, regional, and world maps. It is ordered alphabetically. The umlauts ä, ö, and ü have been treated as the letters a, o, and u, and the ligatures æ and œ as ae and oe, while the German ß is alphabetized as ss.

The first number after the name entry indicates the page or double page where the name being looked up is to be found. The letters and numbers after the page reference designate the grid in which the name is located or those grids through which the name extends.

The names that have been abbreviated on the maps are listed unabbreviated in the index. Only with U.S. place names have the official abbreviations been inserted according to common U.S. practice, e.g. Washington, D.C. The alphabetic sequence includes the prefix, e.g. Fort, Saint.

In order to facilitate the search for names consisting of more than one element, these have consistently been given double entries in the index, e.g. Isle of Wight, and Wight, Isle of —; Le Havre, and Havre, Le-.

To a large extent official second forms, language variants, renamings, and other secondary designations are recorded in the index, followed by the names as they appear on the map, e.g. Persia = Iran, Venice = Venézia, Moscow = Moskva.

To differentiate identical names of features located in various countries, motor vehicle nationality letters for the respective countries have been added in brackets following these names. A complete listing of abbreviations is shown below.

A	Austria	H	Hungary	RIM	Mauritania
ADN	People's Democratic Republic of Yemen	HK	Hong Kong	RL	Lebanon
		HV	Burkina Faso	RM	Madagascar
AFG	Afghanistan	I	Italy	RMM	Mali
AL	Albania	IL	Israel	RN	Niger
AND	Andorra	IND	India	RO	Romania
AUS	Australia	IR	Iran	ROK	South Korea
B	Belgium	IRL	Ireland	ROU	Uruguay
BD	Bangladesh	IRQ	Iraq	RP	Philippines
BDS	Barbados	IS	Iceland	RSM	San Marino
BG	Bulgaria	J	Japan	RU	Burundi
BH	Belize	JA	Jamaica	RWA	Rwanda
BOL	Bolivia	JOR	Jordan	S	Sweden
BR	Brazil	K	Cambodia	SD	Swaziland
BRN	Bahrain	KWT	Kuwait	SF	Finland
BRU	Brunei	L	Luxembourg	SGP	Singapore
BS	Bahamas	LAO	Laos	SME	Suriname
BUR	Burma	LAR	Libya	SN	Senegal
C	Cuba	LB	Liberia	SP	Somalia
CDN	Canada	LS	Lesotho	SU	Soviet Union
CH	Switzerland	M	Malta	SUDAN	Sudan
CI	Ivory Coast	MA	Morocco	SY	Seychelles
CL	Sri Lanka	MAL	Malaysia	SYR	Syria
CO	Colombia	MC	Monaco	T	Thailand
CR	Costa Rica	MEX	Mexico	TG	Togo
CS	Czechoslovakia	MS	Mauritius	TJ	China
CY	Cyprus	MW	Malawi	TN	Tunisia
D	Federal Republic of Germany	N	Norway	TR	Turkey
DDR	German Democratic Republic	NA	Netherlands Antilles	TT	Trinidad and Tobago
DK	Denmark	NIC	Nicaragua	USA	United States
DOM	Dominican Republic	NL	Netherlands	V	Vatican City
DY	Benin	NZ	New Zealand	VN	Vietnam
DZ	Algeria	P	Portugal	WAG	Gambia
E	Spain	PA	Panama	WAL	Sierra Leone
EAK	Kenya	PAK	Pakistan	WAN	Nigeria
EAT	Tanzania	PE	Peru	WD	Dominica
EAU	Uganda	PL	Poland	WG	Grenada
EC	Ecuador	PNG	Papua New Guinea	WL	Saint Lucia
ES	El Salvador	PY	Paraguay	WS	Samoa
ET	Egypt	Q	Qatar	WV	Saint Vincent
ETH	Ethiopia	RA	Argentina	Y	Yemen
F	France	RB	Botswana	YU	Yugoslavia
FJI	Fiji	RC	Taiwan	YV	Venezuela
FL	Liechtenstein	RCA	Central African Republic	Z	Zambia
GB	United Kingdom	RCB	Congo	ZA	South Africa
GCA	Guatemala	RCH	Chile	ZRE	Zaire
GH	Ghana	RFC	Cameroon	ZW	Zimbabwe
GR	Greece	RH	Haiti		
GUY	Guyana	RI	Indonesia		

A

Aachen 118 C 3
Aalen 118 E 4
Aalesund = Ålesund 116-117 AB 6
A'alī an-Nīl 164-165 KL 7
Aam, Daïa el — = Dayaṭ 'al-'Ām 166-167 B 6
Äänekoski 116-117 L 6
Aansluit 174-175 E 4
Aar, De — 172 D 8
Aarau 118 D 5
Aare 118 D 5
Aarón Castellanos 106-107 F 5
Aavasaksa 116-117 KL 4

Aba [WAN] 164-165 F 7
Aba [ZRE] 172 F 1
Abā' al-Qūr, Wādī — 136-137 J 7
Abā ar Rūs, Sabkhat — 134-135 GH 6
Abacaxis, Rio — 98-99 J 7
Abaco Island, Great — 64-65 L 6
Abad 142-143 E 3
Ābādān 134-135 F 4
Ābādān, Jazīreh — 136-137 N 7-8
Ābādeh 134-135 G 4
Abadia, El — = Al Ab'ādīyah 166-167 G 1
Abadiânia 102-103 H 2
Ab'ādīyah, Al- 166-167 G 1
Abadlah 164-165 D 2
Abaeté 102-103 K 3
Abaeté, Rio — 102-103 K 3
Abaetetuba 98-99 O 5
Abagnar Qi = Xilin Hot 142-143 M 3
Abai 111 E 3
Abaiang 208 H 2
Abaira 100-101 D 7
Abaji 168-169 G 3
Abajo Peak 74-75 J 4
Abakaliki 168-169 H 4
Abakan 132-133 R 7
Abalak 168-169 G 2
Aban 132-133 S 6
Abancay 92-93 E 7
Abanga 168-169 H 5
Abangarit, In — 164-165 F 5
Abapó 104-105 E 6
Ābār Ḥaymūr 173 CD 6
Abā Sa'ūd 134-135 EF 7
Abashiri 142-143 RS 3
Abashiriwan 144-145 d 1-2
Abasiri = Abashiri 142-143 RS 3
Abasolo 86-87 K 7
Abau 148-149 N 9
Abaung Bûm 141 F 2
Abay 164-165 M 6
Abaya 164-165 M 7
Abaza 132-133 R 7
Aba Zangu Zizhizhou 142-143 J 5
Abbabis 174-175 B 2
Abbāsīyah, Al-Qāhirah-al- 170 II b 1
Abbat Quṣūr 166-167 L 1-2
Abbeville 120-121 HJ 3
Abbeville, AL 78-79 G 5
Abbeville, GA 80-81 E 4-5
Abbeville, LA 78-79 CD 5
Abbeville, SC 80-81 E 3
Abbey Peak 158-159 HJ 2
Abbotsford 66-67 BC 1
Abbotsford, WI 70-71 E 3
Abbott 106-107 H 5
Abbottabad = Ebuṭṭābād 134-135 L 4
'Abdah 166-167 B 3
'Abd al-'Azīz, Jabal — 136-137 HJ 4
'Abd al Kūrī 134-135 G 8
'Abd Allāh, Khawr — 136-137 N 8
Ābdānān 136-137 M 6
Ābdānān, Rūdkhāneh-ye — 136-137 M 6
'Abd an-Nabī, Bi'r — 136-137 B 8
Abdulino 132-133 J 7
'Abdullah = Minā' 'Abd Allāh 136-137 N 8
Abe, Kelay — 164-165 N 6
Āb-e Bahreh 136-137 N 7
Abéché 164-165 J 6
Abécher = Abéché 164-165 J 6
Abed-Larache, El — = Al-'Ādib al-'Arsh 164-165 F 3
Abee 60 L 2
Ābe Estāda 134-135 K 4
Abeg, In- 164-165 D 4
Ab-e-Istādah = Ābe Estāda 134-135 K 4
Abejorral 94-95 D 5
Abelardo Luz 102-103 F 7
Abeløya 116-117 n 5
Abemama 208 H 2
Abengourou 164-165 D 7
Åbenrå 116-117 C 10
Abeokuta 164-165 E 7
Āb-e Raḥmat 136-137 N 6
Abercorn = Mbala 172 F 3
Abercrombie, ND 68-69 H 2
Abercrombie Arena 85 III b 2
Aberdare Mountains 172 G 1-2
Aberdare National Park 171 D 3
Aberdeen, ID 66-67 G 4
Aberdeen, MD 72-73 H 5
Aberdeen, MS 78-79 E 4
Aberdeen, NC 80-81 G 3
Aberdeen, SD 64-65 G 2
Aberdeen, WA 64-65 B 2
Aberdeen [AUS] 160 K 4
Aberdeen [CDN] 61 EF 4
Aberdeen [GB] 119 EF 3
Aberdeen [HK] 155 I a 2
Aberdeen [ZA] 172 D 8
Aberdeen Island = Ap Li Chau 155 I a 2
Aberdeen Lake 56-57 R 5
Aberfeldy [ZA] 174-175 H 5
Abergavenny 119 E 6
Aberjona River 84 I b 2
Abernathy, TX 76-77 D 6
Abert, Lake — 66-67 CD 4
Abertawe = Swansea 119 DE 6
Aberystwyth 119 D 5
Āb-e Shūr 136-137 N 7
Abez' 132-133 L 4
Āb-e Zimkān 136-137 LM 5
Abhā 134-135 E 7
Abhānpur 138-139 H 7
Ābhār 136-137 N 4
Abiad, Râss el — = Rā's al-Abyaḍ 164-165 FG 1
Abibe, Serranía de — 94-95 C 3-4
'Abīd, Umm al- 164-165 H 3
'Abīd, Wād al- 166-167 CD 3-4
Abīd al-'Arsh, Al- 164-165 F 3
Abidjan 164-165 CD 7
Abiekwasputs 174-175 D 4
Abi Hill 168-169 G 3
Abijan = Abidjan 164-165 CD 7
Abilene, KS 68-69 H 6
Abilene, TX 64-65 FG 5
Āb i Naft 136-137 L 6
Abingdon, IL 70-71 E 5
Abingdon, VA 80-81 EF 2
Abingdon = Isla Pinta 92-93 A 4
Abinsk 126-127 J 4
Abiod, Oued el — = Wādī al-Abyaḍ 166-167 JK 2
Abiod-Sidi-Cheikh, El- = Al-Abyaḍ 166-167 G 3
Abiquiu, NM 76-77 A 4
Abiseo, Río — 96-97 C 5
Ābi Sirwān 136-137 L 5
Abisko 116-117 H 3
Abitibi, Lake — 56-57 UV 8
Abitibi River 56-57 U 7-8
Abkhaz Autonomous Soviet Socialist Republic 126-127 K 5
Ābnāi Sandīp 141 B 4
Abnūb 173 B 4
Abo 144-145 H 1
Åbo = Turku 116-117 K 7
Abohar 138-139 E 2
Aboisso 164-165 D 7
Abolição 106-107 L 3
Abomé = Abomey 164-165 E 7
Abomey 164-165 E 7
Abong-Abong, Gunung — 152-153 B 3
Abong-Mbang 164-165 G 8
Abonnema 168-169 G 4
Aborigen, pik — 132-133 cd 5
Aboso 168-169 E 4
Abou-Deïa 164-165 H 6
Aboû eḍ Douhoûr = Abū aẓ-Ẓuhūr 136-137 G 6
Abov'an 126-127 M 6
'Abr, Al — 134-135 F 7
Abra, Laguna del — 108-109 H 3
Abraham Bay 58-59 p 6
Abraham Lincoln National Historical Park 70-71 H 7
Abra la Cruz Chica 104-105 D 7
Abrantes [BR] 100-101 E 7
Abrantes [P] 120-121 CD 9
Abra Pampa 111 CD 2
Abrego 94-95 E 3
Abreojos, Punta — 64-65 CD 6
'Abrī 164-165 L 4
Abridge 129 II c 1
Abrigos, Bahía de los — = Bay of Harbours 108-109 K 9
Abrolhos, Arquipélago dos — 92-93 M 8
Abruka 124-125 D 4
Abruzzi 122-123 EF 4
Absaroka Range 64-65 D 2-E 3
Absarokee, MT 68-69 B 3
Abu 134-135 L 6
Abū 'Ajāj = Jalib Shahab 136-137 M 7
Abū al-Ḥaṣīb 136-137 MN 7
Abū al-Maṭāmīr 173 AB 2
Abū an-Numrus 170 II b 2
Abū 'Aweiqîla = Abū 'Uwayjīlah 173 CD 2
Abū aẓ-Ẓuhūr 136-137 G 5
Abū Bakr 166-167 F 2
Abū Ballāṣ 164-165 K 4
Abū Ḍahr, Jabal — 173 D 6
Abū Dārah, Rā's — 173 E 6
Abū Darbah 173 C 3
Abū Dhi'āb, Jabal — 173 D 5
Abū Durba = Abū Darbah 173 C 3
Abufari 98-99 G 7
Abū Gashwah, Rā's — 134-135 G 8
Abū Gharādiq, Bi'r — 136-137 C 7
Abū Ḥadd, Wādī — 173 D 7
Abū Ḥaggâg = Rā's al-Ḥikmah 136-137 BC 7
Abū Ḥajār, Khawr — 136-137 L 7
Abū Ḥamad 164-165 L 5
Abū Ḥamāmid, Jabal — 173 D 5
Abū Ḥammān 136-137 J 5
Abū Ḥarbah, Jabal — 173 C 4
Abū Ḥashū'ifah, Khalīj — 136-137 BC 7
Abu Hills 138-139 D 5
Abū Ḥjār, Hôr — = Khawr Abū Ḥajār 136-137 L 7
Abū Hujar 164-165 LM 6
Abuja 164-165 F 7
Abū Jābirah 164-165 K 6
Abū Jahaf, Wādī — 136-137 K 6
Abū Jamal 164-165 M 5
Abū Jamal, Jabal — 164-165 M 6
Abū Jīr 136-137 K 6
Abū Jīr, Wādī — 136-137 K 6
Abū Jurdī, Jabal — 173 D 6
Abū Kabīr 173 B 2
Abū Kamāl 134-135 DE 4
Abū Khârga, Wādī — = Wādī Abū Kharjah 173 BC 3
Abū Kharjah, Wādī — 173 BC 3
Abukuma-sammyaku 144-145 N 4
Abū Marīs, Sha'īb — 136-137 L 7
Abū Marw, Wādī — 173 C 6
Abū Minqār, Bi'r — 164-165 K 3
Abū Muḥarrik, Ghurd — 164-165 KL 3
Abu Mukharik Dunes = Gurd Abu Muḥarik 164-165 KL 3
Abunã 92-93 FG 6
Abunã, Rio — 92-93 F 7
Abunai 98-99 E 5
Abū Qīr 173 B 2
Abū Qīr, Khalīj — 173 B 2
Abū Qurqāṣ 173 B 4
Abū Rijmayn, Jabal — 136-137 H 5
Abu Road 138-139 D 5
Abū Sa'fah, Bi'r — 173 D 6
Abū Ṣaida = Abū Ṣaydat Ṣaghīrah 136-137 L 6
Abū Salmān 136-137 M 7
Abū Ṣaydat Ṣaghīrah 136-137 L 6
Abū Shafil 136-137 K 5
Abū Shīl = Abū Shafil 136-137 K 5
Abu Simbil = Abu Sunbul 164-165 L 4
Abū Sinbil = Abu Sunbul 164-165 L 4
Abū Ṣkhair = Abū Ṣuhayr 136-137 L 7
Abū Ṣuhayr 136-137 L 7
Abu Sunbul 164-165 L 4
Abū Tīj 164-165 L 3
Abū 'Uwayjīlah 173 CD 2
Abū Zabad 164-165 K 6
Abū Ẓabī 134-135 G 6
Abū Zanīmah 164-165 L 3
Abū Zawal, Bi'r — 173 C 4
Abū Zenīma = Abū Zanīmah 164-165 L 3
Abyad 164-165 K 6
Abyaḍ, Ar-Rā's al- 164-165 A 4
Abyaḍ, Rā's al- 164-165 FG 1
Abyaḍ, Rimāl al- 166-167 L 4
Abyaḍ, Wādī al- 166-167 JK 2
Abyad Sīdī Shaykh, Al- 166-167 G 3
Abyār, Al- 166-167 A 5
Abyei 164-165 K 7
Abymes, les — 64-65 O 8
Abyssinia = Ethiopia 164-165 MN 7

Acacías 94-95 E 6
Acacias, Bogotá-Las — 91 III b 4
Acacio 104-105 C 5-6
Academy of Sciences 83 I ab 2
Acadia National Park 72-73 M 2
Acadie 56-57 XY 8
Acahay 102-103 D 6
Açaí 102-103 G 5
Acailândia 98-99 P 7
Acajutiba 100-101 EF 6
Acajutla 64-65 HJ 9
Acala, TX 76-77 B 7
Acámbaro 64-65 FG 7
Acampamento Grande 98-99 M 4
Acandí 92-93 D 3
Acapetagua 86-87 O 10
Acaponeta 64-65 EF 7
Acapulco de Juárez 64-65 FG 8
Acapuzal, Serra do — 98-99 MN 5
Acará 92-93 K 5
Acará, Cachoeira — 98-99 J 7
Acaraí, Serra — 92-93 H 4
Acaraú 92-93 LM 5
Acaraú, Rio — 100-101 D 2
Acaray, Río — 102-103 E 6
Açaré 100-101 E 4
Acari [BR, place] 100-101 F 4
Acari [BR, river] 110 I a 1
Acari, Rio — 98-99 J 7-8
Acari, Rio de Janeiro- 110 I a 1
Acarigua 92-93 F 3
Acassuso, San Isidro- 110 III b 1
Acay, Nevado de — 104-105 C 9
Acayucan 86-87 N 8-9
Acchila 104-105 D 7
Accomac, VA 80-81 J 2
Accra 164-165 DE 7
Acebal 106-107 G 4
Aceguá 106-107 K 3
Aceh = 1 ◁ 148-149 C 6
Acequias, Las — 106-107 EF 4
Acevedo 106-107 G 4
Achacachi 92-93 F 8
Achaguas 92-93 F 3
Achaïa 122-123 JK 6
Achalciche 126-127 L 6
Achalkalaki 126-127 L 6
Achalpur 138-139 F 7
Achampet 140 D 2
Achao 111 B 6
'Achârâ, El — = Al-'Asharah 136-137 J 5
Acharnaí 122-123 K 6
Achau 113 I b 2
Achegour 164-165 G 5
Achelōos 122-123 J 6
Acheng 142-143 O 2
Achères 129 I b 2
Acherusia = Zonguldak 134-135 C 2
Achigan 70-71 HJ 2
Achigh Köl 142-143 F 4
Achill 119 A 5
Achill Head 119 A 4-5
Achira, Pampa — 106-107 A 6
Achiras 106-107 E 4
Achōhampēṭa = Achampet 140 D 2
Achsu 126-127 O 6
Achter Roggeveld = Agter Roggeveld 174-175 D 6
Achtuba 126-127 N 3
Achtubinsk 126-127 MN 2
Achty 126-127 N 6
Achtyrka 126-127 G 1
Achur = Ātshūr 166-167 AB 6
Achur'an 126-127 L 6
Achuta, Río — 104-105 B 5
Acı göl 136-137 CD 4
Acilia, Roma- 113 II a 2
Ačinsk 132-133 R 6
Acıpayam 136-137 C 4
Acireale 122-123 F 7
Ačisu 126-127 N 5
Ackerly, TX 76-77 D 6
Ackerman, MS 78-79 E 4
Ackley, IA 70-71 D 4
Acklins Island 64-65 LM 7
Aclimação, São Paulo- 110 II b 2
Acme, LA 78-79 D 5
Acme, NM 76-77 B 6
Acme, TX 76-77 E 5
Acobambo 96-97 D 8
Acomayo 92-93 E 7
Aconcagua 111 C 4
Aconcagua, Río — 106-107 B 4
Aconquija, Sierra del — 104-105 CD 10
Acopiara 92-93 M 6
Açores 50-51 H 4
Açoriana 106-107 L 4
Acornhoek 174-175 J 3
Acotipa 98-99 L 4
Acoyapa 88-89 D 9
Àcqui Terme 122-123 C 3
Acraman, Lake — 158-159 FG 6
Acre 92-93 EF 6
Acre = 'Akkō 136-137 F 6
Acre, Rio — 92-93 F 6
Acre Homes, Houston-, TX 85 III b 1
Acri 122-123 G 6
Actatlán de Osorio 86-87 LM 8
Acton 72-73 F 3
Acton, CA 74-75 D 5
Acton, MT 68-69 B 3
Acton, London- 129 II a 1
Acton Vale 72-73 K 2
Actopan 86-87 KL 6-7
Açu 100-101 F 3
Açu, Lagoa — 100-101 B 2
Açu, Rio — 100-101 F 3
Açú, Rio — = Rio Piranhas 92-93 M 6
Açúcar, Pão de — 110 I c 2
Açu da Tôrre 100-101 EF 7
Açude Aracatiaçu 100-101 DE 2-3
Açude Araras 100-101 D 3
Açude Coremas 100-101 F 4
Açude de Banabuiú 100-101 E 3
Açude de Orós 100-101 E 4
Açude Pentecoste 100-101 E 2
Açudina 100-101 B 7
Acueducto 91 II b 2
Acueducto de Lerma 91 I b 2
Acuexcomac 91 I d 1
Acuña 106-107 J 2
Acuña, Villa — 76-77 D 8
Açungui 102-103 H 6
Acuruá, Rio — 96-97 F 6
Açuruá, Serra do — 100-101 C 6
Acworth, GA 80-81 D 3

Ada, MN 68-69 H 2
Ada, OH 72-73 E 4
Ada, OK 64-65 G 5
Ada [GH] 164-165 E 7
Ada, Villa — 113 II b 1
'Adabīyah, Rā's — 173 C 3
Adachi, Tōkyō- 155 III b 1
Adado, Raas — 164-165 b 1
Adafir 164-165 BC 5
Adair, Bahía del — 86-87 CD 2
Adairsville, GA 78-79 G 3
Adak, AK 58-59 u 7
Adakale 136-137 K 2
Adak Island 52 D 36
Adak Strait 58-59 u 7
Adale 164-165 b 3
Adalia = Antalya 134-135 C 3
Ādam 134-135 H 6
Adam, Monte — = Mount Adam 111 DE 8
Adam, Mount — 111 DE 8
Adama = Nazrēt 164-165 M 7
Adamana, AZ 74-75 HJ 5
Adamantina 92-93 JK 9
Adamaoua 164-165 G 7
Adamaua = Adamaoua 164-165 G 7
Adamello 122-123 D 2
Adam Peak 66-67 E 5
Adams, MA 72-73 K 3
Adams, ND 68-69 GH 1
Adams, NE 68-69 H 5
Adams, NY 72-73 HJ 3
Adams, OK 76-77 D 4
Adams, WI 70-71 F 4
Adams, Cape — 53 B 30-31
Adams, Mount — 64-65 B 2
Adam's Bridge 140 D 6
Adams Island 53 D 17
Adams Lake 60 H 4
Adams National Historical Site 84 I bc 3
Adams Park 85 II b 2
Adam's Peak = Samanalakanda 134-135 N 9
Adams River 60 H 4
Adamsville, AL 78-79 F 4
Adamsville, TN 78-79 E 3
Adamsville, TX 76-77 E 7
'Adan 134-135 F 8
Adana 136-137 F 4
Adang, Teluk — 152-153 M 6
Adán Quiroga 106-107 C 3
Adapazarı 134-135 C 2
Ādaraw Taungdan 141 C 5
Adare, Cape — 53 B 18
Adavale 158-159 HJ 5
Adda 122-123 C 3
Aḍ-Ḍab'ah 164-165 K 2
Ad-Dabbah 164-165 KL 5
Ad-Dabbūsah 136-137 J 7
Ad-Dafīnah 134-135 E 6
Ad-Daghgharah 136-137 L 6
Ad-Dahībah = Adh-Dhahībah 166-167 M 3
Ad-Dahnā' 134-135 E 5-F 6
Aḍ-Ḍahrah 166-167 G 1
Ad-Dakhlah 164-165 A 4
Ad-Damazīn 164-165 LM 6
Ad-Dāmir 164-165 L 5
Ad-Dammām 132-133 FG 5
Ad-Dāmūr 136-137 F 6
Addanki 140 D 3
Ad-Daqmā' 134-135 FG 6
Addâr, Râss — = Rā's aṭ-Ṭīb 164-165 G 1
Ad-Dār al-Bayḍā' 164-165 BC 2
Ad-Darb 134-135 E 7
Addatīgala 140 EF 2
Aḍ-Ḍaw 136-137 G 5
Ad-Dawādimā 134-135 EF 6
Ad-Dawḥah 134-135 G 5
Ad-Dawr 136-137 KL 5
Ad-Dayr 173 C 5
Ad-Delaimiya = Ad-Dulaymīyah 136-137 K 6
Ad-Dibdibah 136-137 M 8
Aḍ-Ḍiffah 164-165 J 2
Ad-Dikākah 134-135 G 7
Ad-Dilam 134-135 F 6
Ad-Dilinjāt 173 B 2
Addington, London- 129 II b 2
Addis Alem = Alem Gena 164-165 M 7
Addison, NY 72-73 H 3
Addison = Webster Springs, WV 72-73 F 5
Ad-Dīwānīyah 134-135 EF 4
Addlestone 129 II a 2
Addo 174-175 F 7
Ad-Dôr = Ad-Dawr 136-137 KL 5
Addu Atoll 176 a 3
Ad-Du'ayn 164-165 K 6
Ad-Dujayl 136-137 KL 6
Ad-Dulaymīyah 136-137 K 6
Ad-Duwayd 134-135 E 4
Ad-Duwaym 164-165 L 6
Ad-Duwayr 173 B 4
Addy, WA 66-67 E 1
Adel, GA 80-81 E 5
Adel, IA 70-71 C 5
Adel, OR 66-67 D 4
Adela Corti 106-107 F 7
Adelaide [AUS] 158-159 GH 6-7
Adelaide [ZA] 174-175 G 7
Adelaide-Elizabeth 158-159 G 6
Adelaide Island 53 C 29-30
Adelaide Peninsula 56-57 R 4
Adelaide River 158-159 F 2
Adelanto, CA 74-75 E 5
Adélia 98-99 C 8
Adelia, La — 106-107 E 7
Adelia María 106-107 E 4
Adélie, Terre — 53 C 14-15
Adélie Land = Terre Adélie 53 C 14-15
Ademuz 120-121 G 8
Aden, NM 76-77 A 6
Aden = 'Adan 134-135 EF 8
Aden, Gulf of — 134-135 F 8
Adendorp 174-175 F 7
Aderesso Rapides 168-169 E 3
Adghar = Adrār 164-165 DE 3
Adhaorā = Adhaura 138-139 J 5
Adhaura 138-139 J 5
Adh-Dhahībah 166-167 M 3
Adhibat, Sebkha el — = Sabkhat Tādit 166-167 M 3
Adhōi 138-139 C 6
Adi, Pulau — 148-149 K 7
Adib al-'Arsh, Al- 164-165 F 3
Adícora 94-95 FG 2
Adige 122-123 D 3
'Adi Grat 164-165 MN 6
Adi Kaye = Adi Keyih 164-165 MN 6
Adi Keyih 164-165 MN 6
Ādilābād 138-139 G 8
Adilang 171 C 2
Adilcevaz 136-137 K 3
Adin, CA 66-67 C 5
Adirāmpattinam 140 D 5
Adīrīyāt, Jabal al- 136-137 G 7
Adirondack Mountains 64-65 M 3
Adīs Abeba 164-165 M 7
Adīs Dera 164-165 M 6
'Adī Ugrī 164-165 M 6
Adıyaman 136-137 H 4
Adjai = Ajay 138-139 L 6
Adjaria = Adjarian Autonomous Soviet Socialist Republic 126-127 KL 6
Adjarian Autonomous Soviet Socialist Republic 126-127 KL 6
Adjim = Ajīm 166-167 M 3
Adjuntas, Presa de las — 86-87 LM 6
Adler, Soči- 126-127 J 5
Adler Planetarium 83 II b 1
Adlershof, Berlin- 130 III c 2
Adlikon 128 IV a 1
Adlisberg 128 IV b 1
Adliswil 128 IV ab 2
Admar, Irq — 164-165 F 4
Admiral 61 D 6
Admiralty Gulf 158-159 DE 2
Admiralty Inlet [CDN] 56-57 TU 3
Admiralty Inlet [USA] 66-67 B 1-2
Admiralty Island 56-57 K 6
Admiralty Islands 148-149 N 7
Admiralty Range 53 B 17
Admont 118 G 5
Ado-Ekiti 168-169 G 4
Adolfo E. Carranza 106-107 E 2
Adolfo Gonzales Chaves 106-107 GH 6-7
Adomi 168-169 EF 4
Adonara, Pulau — 148-149 H 8
Ādoni 134-135 M 7
Adour 120-121 G 7
Adra [E] 120-121 F 10
Ādra [IND] 138-139 L 6
Adramúttion = Edremit 134-135 B 3
Adrār 164-165 DE 3
Adrar des Iforas 164-165 E 4-5
Adrar N Deren 166-167 BC 4
Adraskan, Daryā-ye — = Hārūt Rōd 134-135 J 4
Adré 164-165 J 6
Adrī 164-165 G 3
Àdria 122-123 E 3
Adrian, MI 70-71 H 5
Adrian, MN 70-71 C 4
Adrian, OR 66-67 E 4
Adrian, TX 76-77 C 5
Adrianopel = Edirne 134-135 B 2
Adriatic Sea 114-115 LM 7
Adrogué, Almirante Brown- 110 III b 2
Adua 148-149 J 7
Adua = Adwa 164-165 M 6
Adujo Waṇḍ 138-139 B 4
Aduma 168-169 GH 3
Adūr 140 C 6
Adusa 172 E 1
Aduwa = Adwa 164-165 M 6
Advance 174-175 D 6
Adventure, Bahía — 108-109 B 5
Adventure Bank 122-123 DE 7
Adventures Sound 108-109 K 9
Adwa 164-165 M 6
Adyča 132-133 a 4
Adygei Autonomous Region 126-127 JK 4
Adyk 126-127 M 4
Adžamka 126-127 F 2
Adž Bogd uul 142-143 GH 3

Aegean Sea 114-115 NO 8
Aegina, Gulf of — = Sarōnikòs Kólpos 122-123 K 7
Ærø 116-117 D 10
Aeroclube do Brasil 110 I b 2
Aerodromo Don Torcuato 110 III b 1
Aeródromo Matanza 110 III b 2
Aeródromo Merlo 110 III a 2
Aeródromo Monte Grande 110 III b 2
Aeródromo Morón 110 III b 2
Aeródromo San Justo 110 III b 2
Aero-Haven 84 III d 3
Aerolimèn Hellenikón 113 IV a 2
Aeroparque Jorge Newbery 110 III b 1
Aéroport Bruxelles National 128 II b 1
Aéroport Charles de Gaulle 129 I d 1
Aéroport de Brazzaville 170 IV a 1
Aéroport de Cartierville 82 I a 1
Aéroport de Dar el Beida 170 I b 2
Aéroport de Kinshasa 170 IV ab 1
Aeroport d'Orly 129 I c 3
Aéroport du Bourget 129 I c 2
Aeroporto de Congonhas 110 II b 2
Aeroporto di Ciampino 113 II bc 2
Aeroporto do Galeão 110 I b 1
Aeroporto Santos Dumont 110 I c 2
Aeropuerto Barajas 113 III b 2
Aeropuerto Central 91 I c 2
Aeropuerto Eldorado 91 III ab 2
Aeropuerto Internacional de Ezeiza 110 III b 2
Aeropuerto La Carlota 91 II bc
Aeropuerto Maiquetía 91 II b 1
Aesch [CH ↘ Zürich] 128 IV b 2
Aesch [CH ↙ Zürich] 128 IV a 1
Aetna, KS 76-77 E 4
Aeugst am Albis 128 IV ab 2

'Afag 136-137 L 6
Afal, Wādī al- = Wādī al-'Ifāl 173 D 3
Afallah 164-165 B 5
Afam Uko 168-169 G 4
Afanasjevo 124-125 T 4
Afántu 122-123 N 7
Afars et Issas = Djibouti 164-165 N 6
Afasto 168-169 G 1
Affery 168-169 DE 4
Affoltern, Zürich- 128 IV ab 1
Affreville = Khamīs-Milyānah 166-167 H 1
Affroun, El- = Al-'Afrūn 166-167 H 1
Afghānestān 134-135 J 4-L 3
Afgooye 164-165 ab 3
Afhjalar = Āqchalar 136-137 L 5
'Afif 134-135 E 6
Afikpo 164-165 F 7
Aflāj, Al — 134-135 F 6
Aflou 166-167 H 2
Aflū 166-167 H 2
Afmadow 164-165 N 8
Afogados da Ingàzeira 92-93 M 6
Afognak, AK 58-59 L 7
Afognak Island 56-57 F 6
Afonso Bezerra 100-101 F 3
Afonso Cláudio 100-101 D 11
Afram 168-169 E 4
Afrânio 100-101 D 5
Afrânio Peixoto 100-101 D 7
Africa 50-51 J-L 5
African Islands 204-205 N 9
'Afrīn 136-137 G 4
Afrīneh 136-137 M 6
'Afrūn, Al- 166-167 H 1
Afşin 136-137 G 3
'Afsô = 'Afsū 166-167 E 2
'Afsū 166-167 E 2
Afton, IA 70-71 C 5
Afton, OK 76-77 G 4
Afton, WY 66-67 H 4
Afton Oaks, Houston-, TX 85 III b 2
Aftout, Reg — = 'Irq Aflūt 166-167 DE 6
Aftūt, Irq — 166-167 DE 6
Afuá 92-93 J 5
'Afūla 136-137 F 6
Afyonkarahisar 134-135 C 3
Afzalpur 140 C 2

Aga = Aginskoje 132-133 VW 7
Agadem 164-165 G 5
Agades = Agadèz 164-165 F 5
Agadèz 164-165 F 5
Agādīr 164-165 BC 2
Agādīr Tissīnt 166-167 C 5
Agadji 168-169 F 4
Agadyr' 132-133 N 8
Agaie 164-165 F 7
Agalega Islands 204-205 N 10
Agalta, Sierra de — 64-65 J 8-9
Agamor 168-169 F 1
Agan 132-133 O 5
Agapa 132-133 Q 3
Agar 138-139 F 6
Agar, SD 68-69 F 3
Agarā = Agra 134-135 M 5
Agareb = 'Aqārib 166-167 M 2
Agartala 134-135 P 6
Agāshi 138-139 D 8
Agassiz 66-67 BC 1
Agastīswaram 140 C 6-7
Agata, ozero — 132-133 R 4
Agate, CO 68-69 E 6
Agathonēsion 122-123 M 7
Agats 148-149 L 8
Agatti Island 134-135 L 8
Agattu Island 52 D 1
Agattu Strait 58-59 p 6
Agawa 70-71 H 2
Agawa Bay 70-71 H 2
Agbélouvé 168-169 F 4
Agboju 170 III a 2
Agboville 164-165 D 7
Agdam 126-127 N 7
Agdaš 126-127 N 6
Agde 120-121 J 7
Agdz 166-167 C 4
Agdžabedi 126-127 N 6
Agen 120-121 H 6
Agere Ḥiywer 164-165 M 7
Āghā Jarī 134-135 FG 4
Aghiyuk Island 58-59 e 1
Aghlāghal, Jabal — 166-167 G 6
Aghwāt, Al- 164-165 E 2
Agiapuk River 58-59 DE 4
Agilmūs 166-167 D 3
Ağın 136-137 H 3
Agincourt = Penchia Hsü 146-147 HJ 9
Aginskoje 132-133 VW 7
Aginskoje = Aginskoje 132-133 VW 7
Aginsky-Buryat Autonomous Area = 12 ◁ 132-133 V 7
Aglagal, Djebel — = Jabal Aghlāghal 166-167 G 6
Ağlasun 136-137 D 4
Agnew 158-159 D 5
Agnía, Pampa de — 108-109 E 4
Agnibilekrou 168-169 E 4
Agnone 122-123 F 5
Agochi = Aoji 144-145 H 1
Agoj, gora — 126-127 J 4
8 de Agosto, Laguna — 108-109 H 2
Agosto, Laguna 8 de — 106-107 F 7
Agout 120-121 J 7
Āgra 134-135 M 5
Agra, OK 76-77 F 5
Agrachanskij poluostrov 126-127 NO 5
Agrado 94-95 D 6
Agrestina 100-101 G 5
Ağrı [TR] 136-137 K 3
Agrícola Oriental, Ixtacalco- 91 I c 2
Agrícola Pantitlán, Ixtacalco- 91 I c 2
Agrigento 122-123 E 7
Agrihan 206-207 S 8
Agrínion 122-123 J 6
Agrio, Río — 106-107 B 7
Agrópoli 122-123 F 5
Agrossam 98-99 JK 10
Agryz 132-133 J 6
Agter Roggeveld 174-175 D 6
Água, Ilha d' 110 I c 1
Agua Amarga 106-107 B 2
Agua Blanca [BOL] 104-105 E 7
Agua Blanca [RA] 104-105 D 8
Agua Blanca [YV] 94-95 K 4
Água Boa 102-103 L 2-3
Água Branca [BR, Alagoas] 100-101 F 5
Água Branca [BR, Piauí] 100-101 C 3
Água Branca, Chapada da — 102-103 L 1-2
Água Branca, Parque da — 110 II ab 2
Agua Brava, Laguna de — 86-87 GH 6

258 Aachen

Albertville = Kalemie 172 E 3
Albertynsville, Johannesburg- 170 V a 2
Albi 120-121 J 7
Albia, IA 70-71 D 5
Al-Bībān [DZ] 166-167 J 1
Al-Bībān [TN] 166-167 M 3
Al-Bid' 173 D 3
Albin, WY 68-69 D 5
Albina 92-93 J 3
Albino 122-123 CD 3
Albion, IL 70-71 F 6
Albion, IN 70-71 H 5
Albion, MI 70-71 H 4
Albion, MT 68-69 D 3
Albion, NE 68-69 GH 5
Albion, NY 72-73 GH 3
Albion, Melbourne- 161 II b 1
Al-Biqā' 136-137 FG 5-6
Al-Bi'r ad-Diyāb 166-167 B 6
Al-Bi'r al-Ahlū 166-167 B 6
Al-Bi'r al-Jadīd 166-167 B 3
Albishorn 128 IV b 2
Albispass 128 IV b 2
Albisrieden, Zürich- 128 IV ab 1
Al-Biyāḍ = Al-Bayāḍ 134-135 F 6
Al-Bogham 136-137 J 5
Albon-sur-Seine 129 I c 3
Alborán 120-121 F 11
Ålborg 116-117 CD 9
Ålborg Bugt 116-117 D 9
Ålborg-Nørresundby 116-117 CD 9
Alborz, Reshteh Kūhhā-ye — 134-135 G 3
Al-Brāknah 168-169 B 1
Al-Bṣaiya = Al-Buṣaiyah 134-135 EF 4
Al-Bu'ayrāt al-Ḥsūn 164-165 H 2
Al-Budayr 136-137 L 7
Albué 106-107 B 5
Albufera, La — 120-121 GH 9
Al-Buhayrāt 164-165 KL 7
Al-Buḥayrat al-Murrat al-Kubrá 173 C 2
Al-Bū'irḍah 166-167 C 5
Albuquerque 102-103 D 3
Albuquerque, NM 64-65 EF 4
Albuquerque, Cayos de — 88-89 F 8
Al-Buraymī 134-135 H 6
Alburquerque 120-121 D 9
Al-Burūj 166-167 C 3
Albury 158-159 J 7
Al-Buṣaiyah 134-135 EF 4
Al-Busayṭā' 136-137 G 7-H 8
Alca 96-97 E 9
Alcácer do Sal 120-121 C 9
Alcade, Punta — 106-107 B 2
Alcalá de Guadaira 120-121 E 10
Alcalá de Henares 120-121 F 8
Alcalá la Real 120-121 F 10
Alcalde, NM 76-77 AB 4
Alcamo 122-123 E 7
Alcañiz 120-121 G 8
Alcântara [BR] 92-93 L 5
Alcántara [E] 120-121 D 9
Alcântaras 100-101 D 2
Alcantarilla 120-121 G 10
Alcantil 100-101 F 4
Alcaparra 76-77 AB 7
Alcaraz [E] 120-121 F 9
Alcaraz [RA] 106-107 H 3
Alcaraz, Sierra de — 120-121 F 9
Alcarria, La — 120-121 F 8
Alcatrazes, Ilha dos — 102-103 K 6
Alcatraz Island 83 I b 2
Alcázar 106-107 D 3
Alcázar de San Juan 120-121 F 9
Alcázarquivir = Al-Qṣar al-Kabīr 164-165 C 1
Alcazarseguer = Al-Qṣar aṣ-Ṣaghīr 166-167 D 2
Alcester Island 148-149 h 6
Al-Chebāyesh = Al-Jaza'ir 136-137 M 7
Alcira [E] 120-121 G 9
Alcira [RA] 111 D 4
Alcoa, TN 80-81 E 3
Alcobaça [BR] 92-93 M 8
Alcobaça [P] 120-121 C 9
Alcolea del Pinar 120-121 FG 8
Alcones 106-107 B 5
Alcoota 158-159 F 4
Alcorn College, MS 78-79 D 5
Alcorta 106-107 G 4
Alcova, WY 68-69 C 4
Alcoy 120-121 G 9
Aldabra Islands 172 J 3
Aldama [MEX, Chihuahua] 86-87 H 3
Aldama [MEX, Tamaulipas] 86-87 LM 6
Aldamas, Los — 76-77 E 9
Aldan, PA 84 III b 2
Aldan [SU, place] 132-133 XY 6
Aldan [SU, river] 132-133 Z 6
Aldana 94-95 C 7
Aldan Plateau = Aldanskoje nagorje 132-133 X-Z 6
Aldanskoje nagorje 132-133 X-Z 6
Aldea Apeleg 108-109 D 5
Aldeburgh 119 GH 5
Aldeia Campista, Rio de Janeiro- 110 I b 2
Alder, MT 66-67 GH 3
Alderney 119 E 7
Alder Peak 74-75 C 5
Alderson 61 C 5
Aldo Bonzi, La Matanza- 110 III b 2
Alduş = Temsiyas 136-137 H 3
Alechovščina 124-125 JK 3
Aledo, IL 70-71 E 5
Aleg = Alaq 164-165 B 5
Alegre 102-103 M 4
Alegrete 111 E 3-4
Alegria 98-99 E 6
Alejandra 106-107 H 2
Alejandra, Cabo — = Cape Alexandra 111 J 8
Alejandría 104-105 D 3
Alejandro Roca 106-107 EF 4
Alejandro Selkirk 199 A 7
Alejo Ledesma 106-107 F 4
Alejsk 132-133 P 7
Aleknagik, AK 58-59 HJ 7
Aleknagik, Lake — 58-59 H 7
Aleksandra, mys — 132-133 ab 7
Aleksandrija 126-127 F 2
Aleksandro-Nevskij 124-125 N 7
Aleksandrov 124-125 M 5
Aleksandrov Gaj 126-127 O 1
Aleksandrovka [SU, Rostovskaja Oblast'] 126-127 J 3
Aleksandrovsk [SU, Rossijskaja SFSR] 124-125 V 4
Aleksandrovsk = Belogorsk 132-133 YZ 7
Aleksandrovsk-Gruševskij = Šachty 126-127 K 3
Aleksandrovskoje [SU, Stavropol'skaja Oblast'] 126-127 L 4
Aleksandrovskoje [SU, Zapadno-Sibirskaja nizmennost'] 132-133 OP 5
Aleksandrovsk-Sachalinskij 132-133 bc 7
Aleksandrów Kujawski 118 J 2
Alekseјevka [SU, Kazachskaja SSR] 132-133 N 7
Alekseјevka [SU, Rossijskaja SFSR → Kujbyšev] 124-125 S 7
Alekseјevka [SU, Rossijskaja SFSR ↘ Kujbyšev] 124-125 S 7
Alekseјevka [SU, Rossijskaja SFSR Belgorodskaja Oblast'] 126-127 J 1
Alekseјevka [SU, Rossijskaja SFSR Saratovskaja Oblast'] 124-125 QR 7
Alekseјevka [SU, Ukrainskaja SSR] 126-127 GH 2
Alekseјevo-Lozovskoje 126-127 K 2
Aleksejevsk = Svobodnyj 132-133 YZ 7
Aleksin 124-125 L 6
Aleksinac 122-123 JK 4
Ålem 116-117 G 9
Alemán 96-97 D 3
Aleman, NM 76-77 A 6
Alemania 104-105 D 9
Alem Cué 106-107 J 2
Alem Gena 164-165 M 7
'Alem Maya 164-165 N 7
Além Paraíba 92-93 L 9
Alençon 120-121 H 4
Alenquer [BR] 92-93 HJ 5
Alentejo 120-121 C 10-D 9
Alenuihaha Channel 148-149 ef 3
Alenz 136-137 J 4
Aleppo = Halab 134-135 D 3
Alert 52 A 25
Alerta 92-93 E 7
Alert Bay 60 D 4
Åleru 140 D 2
Alès 120-121 K 6
Alessandria 122-123 C 3
Ålesund 116-117 AB 6
Aleutian Islands 52 D 35-1
Aleutian Range 56-57 E 6-F 5
Aleutian Trench 156-157 HJ 2
Aleutka 142-143 T 2
Alevina, mys — 132-133 cd 6
Alevisik = Samandağ 136-137 F 4
Alexander, ND 68-69 E 2
Alexander, Kap — 56-57 WX 2
Alexander, Point — 158-159 G 2
Alexander Archipelago 56-57 J 6-K 7
Alexanderbaai 172 BC 7
Alexander City, AL 78-79 FG 4
Alexander Deussen Park 85 III c 1
Alexander Ist Island = zemľa Aleksandra I 53 C 29
Alexander Memorial Coliseum 85 II b 2
Alexander Park 85 II c 1
Alexanderplatz 130 III b 1
Alexandra [NZ] 158-159 N 9
Alexandra [ZA] 170 V b 1
Alexandra = Umzinto 174-175 J 6
Alexandra, Cape — 111 J 8
Alexandra, Singapore- 154 III ab 2
Alexandra, zemľa — 132-133 FG 1
Alexandra Canal 161 I b 2
Alexandra Fiord 56-57 VW 2
Alexandra land = zemľa Alexandra 132-133 FG 1
Alexandretta = İskenderun 134-135 D 3
Alexandrette = İskenderun 134-135 D 3
Alexandria, IN 70-71 H 5
Alexandria, LA 64-65 H 5
Alexandria, MN 70-71 C 3
Alexandria, SD 68-69 H 4
Alexandria, VA 64-65 L 4
Alexandria [AUS] 158-159 G 3
Alexandria [BR] 92-93 M 6
Alexandria [CDN] 60 F 3
Alexandria [RO] 122-123 L 4
Alexandria [ZA] 172 E 8
Alexandria = Al-Iskandarīyah 164-165 KL 2
Alexandria-Braddock, VA 82 II a 2
Alexandrina, Lake — 158-159 GH 7
Alexandrovsk = Poľarnyj 116-117 P 3
Alexandrúpolis 122-123 L 5
Alexis Creek 60 F 3
Al-Faḥṣ 166-167 LM 1
Al-Fallūjah 136-137 JK 6
Alfambra 120-121 G 8
Al-Fant 173 B 3
Al-Faqīh Bin Ṣālaḥ 166-167 C 3
Al-Farā' 136-137 J 4
Alfarez de Navio Sobral 53 A 32-35
Al-Fāshir 164-165 K 6
Al-Fashn 164-165 KL 3
Alfatar 122-123 M 4
Al-Fatḥa = Al-Fatḥah 134-135 E 3
Alfavaca, Ilha da — 110 I b 3
Alfaville 166-167 G 3
Al-Fāw 136-137 N 7-8
Al-Fayṣalīyah 136-137 KL 7
Al-Fayyūm 164-165 KL 3
Alfeiós 122-123 J 7
Alfenas 102-103 JK 4
Alférez, Sierra de — 106-107 KL 4
Al-Fīfī 164-165 J 6
Alföld 118 J 5-L 4
Alfortville 129 I c 2
Ålfotbreen 116-117 A 7
Alfred, ME 72-73 L 3
Alfredo Chaves 102-103 M 4
Al-Fujairah = Al-Fujayrah 134-135 H 5
Al-Fujayrah 134-135 H 5
Al-Fūlah 164-165 K 6
Al-Funduq 166-167 D 2
Al-Furāt 134-135 DE 3
Alga 132-133 K 8
Algabas 126-127 Q 1
Al-Gadīdah = Al-Jadīdah [MA] 164-165 C 2
Al-Gadīdah = Al-Jadīdah [TN] 166-167 L 1
Al-Gamm = Al-Jamm 166-167 M 2
Al-Gāmūr al-Kabīr = Al-Jāmūr al-Kabīr 166-167 M 1
Al-Gārah 166-167 C 3
Ålgård 116-117 A 8
Algarrobal 106-107 B 2
Algarrobitos 106-107 GH 4
Algarrobo [RA] 106-107 F 7
Algarrobo [RCH, administrative unit] 106-107 AB 4
Algarrobo [RCH, place] 106-107 B 1
Algarrobo del Águila 106-107 D 6
Algarve 120-121 CD 10
Algasovo 124-125 N 7
Algeciras 120-121 E 10
Algēna 164-165 M 5
Alger, MI 70-71 H 3
Alger, Baie d' 170 I b 1
Algeria 164-165 D-F 3
Algerian Basin 120-121 J 10-L 8
Alger-Plage 170 I b 1
Al-Ghāb 136-137 G 5
Al-Ghār 166-167 L 5
Alghar = Al-Ghār 166-167 L 5
Al-Gharaq as-Sulṭānī 173 AB 3
Al-Gharb 166-167 C 2
Al-Ghardaqah 164-165 L 3
Al-Gharīs 166-167 G 2
Al-Ghāṭ' 136-137 J 5
Al-Ghaydah [ADN ← Sayḥūt] 134-135 FG 7-8
Al-Ghaydah [ADN ↗ Sayḥūt] 134-135 G 7
Alghero 122-123 C 5
Al-Ghraybah 166-167 LM 2
Al-Ghūr 136-137 F 7
Algiers = Al-Jazā'ir 164-165 E 1
Algiers, New Orleans-, LA 85 I b 2
Algoabaai 172 E 8
Algoa Bay = Algoabaai 172 E 8
Algodón, Río — 96-97 E 3
Algodones 74-75 F 6
Algoma, OR 66-67 C 4
Algoma, WI 70-71 G 3
Algona, IA 70-71 CD 4
Algonquin Park 72-73 G 2
Algonquin Provincial Park 56-57 V 8
Algorte 106-107 J 4
Alguada Reef = Agū'ādā Kyauktan 141 CD 8
Al-Habrah 166-167 J 3
Al-Ḥad 166-167 D 2
Al-Haddār 134-135 EF 6
Al-Ḥadītah 134-135 F 4
Al-Ḥaḍr 136-137 K 5
Al-Ḥafar al-Bāṭin 134-135 F 5
Al-Ḥājab 166-167 D 3
Al-Ḥajar [DZ] 166-167 KL 1
Al-Ḥajar [Oman] 134-135 H 6
Al-Hajara = Ṣaḥrā' al-Hijārah 136-137 JK 8
Al-Ḥajīrah 166-167 J 3
Al-Ḥajjār 164-165 EF 4
Al-Halfāyah 136-137 M 7
Al-Ḥalīl 136-137 F 7
Al-Ḥamād 136-137 H 6-J 7
Al-Ḥamār 136-137 M 8
Alhambra, CA 74-75 DE 5
Al-Ḥamdānīyah 136-137 G 5
Al-Hāmil 166-167 J 2
Al-Hamīs = Al-Khamīs 166-167 C 3
Al-Hammadah [DZ → Ghardāyah] 166-167 FG 4
Al-Hammadah [DZ ← Ghardāyah] 166-167 HJ 4
Al-Ḥammādat al-Ḥamrā' 164-165 G 2-3
Al-Ḥāmmah 166-167 L 3
Al-Ḥammām 136-137 C 7
Al-Ḥammāmāt 166-167 M 1
Al-Ḥammān 166-167 D 3
Al-Ḥamrā' [Saudi Arabia] 134-135 D 6
Al-Ḥamrā' [SYR] 136-137 G 5
Al-Ḥāmūl 173 B 2
Al Hamza = Qawām al-Ḥamzah 136-137 L 7
Al Ḥanākīyah 134-135 E 6
Al-Handaq = Al-Khandaq 164-165 KL 5
Alhandra 100-101 G 4
Al-Ḥanīyah 136-137 LM 8
Al-Ḥank 164-165 C 3-4
Al-Hanshah 166-167 M 2
Al-Haqūnīyah 164-165 B 3
Al-Hāritah 136-137 M 7
Al-Harmal 136-137 G 5
Al Ḥarrah 134-135 D 4
Al-Harūj al-Aswad 164-165 H 3
Al-Harūsh 166-167 K 1
Al 'Ḥasā' 134-135 F 5
Al-Ḥasakah 134-135 D 3
Al Hashemiya = Al-Hāshimīyah 136-137 L 6
Al-Hāshimīyah 136-137 L 6
Al-Ḥāsī aṭ-Ṭawīl 166-167 K 4-5
Al-Ḥaṭāṭibah 173 B 2
Al Ḥaurā = Al-Ḥawrah 134-135 F 8
Al-Hawārīyah 166-167 M 1
Al-Ḥawātah 164-165 LM 6
Al-Ḥawḍ [DZ] 166-167 J 4
Al-Ḥawḍ [RIM] 164-165 C 5
Al-Ḥawḍ al-Gharbī 168-169 C 1
Al-Ḥawḍ ash-Sharqī 168-169 D 1
Al-Ḥawrah 134-135 F 8
Al-Ḥawṭah = Al-Ḥillah 134-135 F 6
Al-Ḥawūz 166-167 B 4
Al-Hayrīr 166-167 L 7
Al-Ḥayy 134-135 F 4
Al-Hazīm 136-137 G 7
Al-Ḥazm 173 E 3
Al-Hazul = Al-Huzul 136-137 K 8
Al-Ḥijāz 134-135 D 5-6
Al-Hillah [IRQ] 134-135 E 4
Al-Ḥillah [Saudi Arabia] 134-135 F 6
Al-Hindīyah 136-137 KL 6
Al-Ḥomra = Al-Ḥumrah 164-165 L 6
Alhucemas = Al-Ḥusaymah 164-165 D 1
Alhucemas, Islas de — 166-167 E 2
Al-Ḥudaydah 134-135 E 8
Al-Hufūf 134-135 FG 5
Al-Ḥumaydah 173 D 3
Al-Ḥumrah 164-165 L 6
Al-Hums = Al-Khums 164-165 GH 2
Al-Huraybah 134-135 F 7
Al-Ḥuṣayḥīṣah 164-165 L 6
Al-Ḥusaymah 164-165 D 1
Al-Ḥusaynīyah 134-135 EF 7
Al-Huzul 136-137 K 8
'Alī = Ngarikorsum 138-139 HJ 2
'Alī, Sadd al- 164-165 L 5
Aliákmon 122-123 JK 5
'Alī al-Garbī 136-137 M 6
Alianca 100-101 G 4
Alianza 96-97 D 5
Alībāg 140 A 1
Ali-Bajramly 126-127 O 7
Alibardak 136-137 J 3
Alibej, ozero — 126-127 E 4
Alibey 154 I a 2
Alibey adasi 136-137 B 3
Alibeyköy 154 I a 2
Alibori 168-169 F 3
Alibunar 122-123 J 3
Alicahue 106-107 B 4
Alicante 120-121 GH 9
Alice 174-175 G 7
Alice, TX 64-65 G 6
Alice, Punta — 122-123 G 6
Alice Arm 60 C 2
Alicedale 174-175 G 7
Alice Springs 158-159 FG 4
Aliceville, AL 78-79 EF 4
Alicia 106-107 F 3
Alicias, Las — 91 I a 3
Alicudi 122-123 F 6
Alida 68-69 F 1
Al-'Idd 134-135 G 6
Al-Idrīsīyah 166-167 H 2
Ali Gabe 171 E 2
Alīganj 138-139 G 4
Aligar = Alīgarh 134-135 M 5
Alīgarh 134-135 M 5
Alīgūdarz 136-137 NO 6
Alihe 142-143 N 1
Alijos, Rocas — 86-87 C 5
Alikovo 124-125 Q 6
Alima 172 BC 2
Alindao 164-165 J 7-8
Alingsås 116-117 E 9
Alipore, Calcutta- 154 II ab 2
'Alīpur 138-139 CD 3
Alīpur Duār 134-135 M 5
Aliquippa, PA 72-73 F 4
Alī Rājpur 138-139 E 6
Al-'Irq 164-165 J 3
Al-'Irq al-Kabīr al-Gharbī 164-165 D 3-E 2
Al-'Irq al-Kabīr ash-Sharqī 164-165 F 2-3
Alisal, CA 74-75 C 4
Al-'Isāwīyah 134-135 D 4
Al-Iskandarīyah 164-165 KL 2
Al-Ismā'īlīyah 164-165 L 2
Alisos, Río — 86-87 E 2
Alitak Bay 58-59 f 1
Alitus = Alytus 124-125 E 6
Aliwal-Noord 172 E 8
Aliwal Suid = Mosselbaai 172 D 8
Alix 60 L 3
Al-Jabal al-Abyaḍ 166-167 L 1
Al-Jabalayn 164-165 L 6
Al-Jabīlat 166-167 BC 4
Al-Jadīdah [MA] 164-165 G 2
Al-Jadīdah [TN] 166-167 L 1
Al-Jafr [JOR, place] 134-135 D 4
Al-Jafr [JOR, river] 136-137 G 7
Al-Jaghbūb 164-165 J 3
Al-Jahrah 134-135 F 5
Al-Jajah 173 B 5
Al-Jaladah 134-135 F 7
Al-Jalāmīd 136-137 HJ 7
Al-Jalhāk 164-165 L 6
Al-Jamm 166-167 M 2
Al-Jāmūr al-Kabīr 166-167 M 1
Al-Jarāwī 136-137 H 7
Al-Jauf = Al-Jawf 134-135 DE 5
Al-Jawf [LAR] 164-165 J 4
Al-Jawf [Saudi Arabia] 134-135 DE 5
Al-Jawf [Y] 134-135 EF 7
Al-Jaza'ir [DZ] 164-165 E 1
Al-Jaza'ir [IRQ] 136-137 M 7
Al-Jazā'ir-Bab el Oued 170 I a 1
Al-Jazā'ir-Birmandréis 170 I a 2
Al-Jazā'ir-Bologhine Ibnou Ziri 170 I a 1
Al-Jazā'ir-El Biar 170 I a 1
Al-Jazā'ir-El Madania 170 I a 2
Al-Jazā'ir-Kasbah 170 I a 1
Al-Jazā'ir-Kouba 170 I ab 2
Al-Jazā'ir-Mustapha 170 I a 1
Al-Jazā'ir-Sidi M'Hamed 170 I a 1
Al-Jazīra = Arḍ al-Jazīrah 134-135 E 3-F 4
Al-Jazīrah [DZ] 166-167 F 2
Al-Jazīrah [IRQ] 136-137 J 5
Al-Jazīrah [Sudan] 164-165 L 6
Al-Jil 136-137 KL 7
Al-Jilidah = Al-Jaladah 134-135 F 6-7
Al-Jill = Al-Jil 136-137 KL 7
Al-Jiwā' 134-135 G 6
Al-Jīzah [ET] 164-165 KL 3
Al-Jīzah [JOR] 136-137 FG 7
Al-Jubail = Al-Jubayl al-Baḥrī 134-135 FG 5
Al-Jubayl al-Baḥrī 134-135 FG 5
Al Jumaima = Al-Jumaymah 136-137 KL 8
Al-Jumaymah 136-137 KL 8
Al-Junaynah 164-165 J 6
Al Juraiba = Al-Jurāybah 136-137 KL 8
Al-Jurāybah 136-137 KL 8
Al-Juwārah 134-135 H 7
Al-Kāf 164-165 F 1
Alkali Desert 66-67 EF 5
Alkali Flat 66-67 DE 5
Alkali Lake 66-67 D 5
Alkamari 168-169 H 2
Al-Kāmil 134-135 H 6
Al-Kamilīn 164-165 L 5
Al-Karak 134-135 D 4
Al-Karnak 173 C 5
Al-Kefil = Al-Kifl 136-137 L 6
Al-Khābūrah 134-135 H 6
Al-Khaīj as-Sintirā' 164-165 A 4
Al-Khalīj al-'Arabī 136-137 N 8
Al-Khāliṣ 136-137 L 6
Al-Khalūf 134-135 H 6
Al-Khamāsīn 134-135 EF 6
Al-Khamīs 166-167 C 3
Al-Khandaq 164-165 KL 5
Al-Kharāb 134-135 EF 7
Al-Khārījah 164-165 L 3
Al-Kharj 134-135 F 6
Al-Khartūm 164-165 L 5
Al-Khartūm Baḥrī 164-165 L 5
Al-Khaṣab 134-135 H 5
Al Khedir = Khiḍr Dardash 136-137 L 7
Al-Khums 164-165 GH 2
Al-Khurmah 134-135 E 6
Al-Khurub 166-167 K 1
Al-Kifl 136-137 L 6
Alkmaar 120-121 K 2
Al-Kūfah 136-137 L 6
Al-Kumayt 136-137 M 6
Al-Kunayt 136-137 M 6
Al-Kuntillā 173 D 3
Al Kūt 134-135 F 4
Al-Kuwayt 134-135 F 5
Al Kwair = Al-Quwayr 136-137 K 4
Al-La'ā' = Al-Lu'ā'ah 136-137 L 7
Allach, München- 130 II a 1
Allach-Jun' 132-133 a 5
Allada 164-165 E 7
Al-Lādhiqīyah 134-135 CD 3
Ållagaḍa = Allagadda 140 D 3
Allagadda 140 D 3
Allagash, ME 72-73 M 1
Allagash River 72-73 M 1
Allāhābād [IND] 134-135 N 5
Allāhābād [PAK] 138-139 C 3
Al-Lajā' 136-137 G 6
Allakaket, AK 56-57 F 4
Allaküekber dağı 136-137 K 2
'Allāl at-Tāzī 166-167 C 2
Allal Tazi = 'Allāl at-Tāzī 166-167 C 2
Allamoore, TX 76-77 B 7
Allampur = Ālampur 140 CD 3
Allanmyo = Ālanmyō 148-149 C 3
Allanridge 174-175 G 4
Allāpalli 138-139 H 8
Al-Laqawah 164-165 K 6
'Allāqī, Wadī al- 173 C 6
Allardville 63 D 4
Alldays 174-175 H 2
Allegan, MI 70-71 H 4
Alleghenies = Allegheny Mountains 64-65 K 4-L 3
Allegheny Mountains 64-65 K 4-L 3
Allegheny Plateau 72-73 F 5
Allegheny River 72-73 G 4
Allemanskraaldam 174-175 G 5
Allemorgens 174-175 D 7
Allen 106-107 D 7
Allen, OK 76-77 F 5
Allen, Mount — 58-59 QR 5
Allendale, SC 80-81 F 4
Allendale, Houston-, TX 85 III bc 2
Allende [MEX, Coahuila] 86-87 K 3
Allende [MEX, León] 86-87 KL 5
Allen Park, MI 72-73 E 3
Allen River 58-59 LM 3
Allentown, PA 64-65 L 3
Alleppey 134-135 M 9
Aller 118 D 2
Allermöhe, Hamburg- 130 I b 2
Allerton, IA 70-71 D 5
Alley Park 82 III d 2
Alliance, NE 64-65 F 3
Alliance, OH 72-73 F 4
Al-Lidām = Al-Khamāsīn 134-135 EF 6
Allier 120-121 J 6
Al-Līfīyah 136-137 K 7
Alliford Bay 60 B 3
Alligator Sound 80-81 HJ 3
Allison, IA 70-71 D 4
Allison, TX 76-77 DE 5
Allison Harbour 60 CD 4
Allison Pass 66-67 C 1
Alliston 72-73 G 2
Al-Līth 134-135 E 6
Allston, Boston-, MA 84 I b 2
Al-Lu'ā'ah 136-137 L 7
Al-Luhayyah 134-135 E 7
Allumettes, Île aux — 72-73 H 2
Allūr 140 E 3
Allūru Kottapatnam 140 E 3
Alma, AR 76-77 G 5
Alma, GA 80-81 E 5
Alma, KS 68-69 H 6
Alma, MI 70-71 H 4
Alma, NE 68-69 G 5
Alma, WI 70-71 E 3
Alma [CDN, New Brunswick] 63 D 5
Alma [CDN, Quebec] 56-57 W 8
Al'ma [SU] 126-127 F 4
Alma = Budwāwū 166-167 H 1
Alma, Lake — = Harlan County Reservoir 68-69 G 5-6
Al-Ma'anīyah 134-135 E 4
Al-Ma'arrah 136-137 G 4
Alma-Ata 132-133 O 9
Al-Mabrūk 166-167 G 5
Almada 120-121 C 9
Almadén 120-121 E 9
Al-Madīnah [IRQ] 136-137 M 7
Al-Madīnah [Saudi Arabia] 134-135 DE 6
Al-Mafraq 136-137 G 6
Al-Maghayrā' 134-135 G 6
Al-Māghrah 136-137 C 7
Almagre, El — 86-87 J 4
Almagro, Buenos Aires- 110 III b 1
Almaguer 94-95 C 7
Al-Maḥallat al-Kubra 164-165 L 2
Al-Maḥamīd 166-167 E 3
Al-Mahārī = Al-Muhārī 136-137 L 7
Al-Maḥārīq 173 B 5
Al-Maḥaris 166-167 M 2
Al-Mahdīyah 164-165 G 1
Al-Maḥmūdīyah 136-137 L 6
Al-Ma'īrījah 166-167 E 2-3
Al-Maisarī = Al-Maysarī 136-137 H 7
Al-Majarr al-Kabīr 136-137 M 7
Al-Makīlī 164-165 J 2
Al-Maknāsī 166-167 L 2
Al-Maks al-Baḥrī 173 AB 5
Al-Maks al-Qiblī 164-165 L 4
Al-Malaḥ 166-167 F 2
Almalyk 134-135 KL 2
Al-Manāmah 134-135 G 5
Al-Manāqil 164-165 L 6
Al-Manāṣif 136-137 J 5
Al-Manastīr 166-167 M 2
Al Man'nīyah = Al-Ma'anīyah 134-135 E 4
Almanor, Lake — 66-67 C 5
Almansa 120-121 G 9
Al-Manṣūr 166-167 F 6
Al-Manṣūrah [DZ] 166-167 HJ 1
Al-Manṣūrah [ET] 164-165 L 2
Al-Manṣūrīyah 136-137 L 5
Al-Manzilah 173 BC 2
Almanzora 120-121 F 10
Alma Peak 60 D 1
Al-Ma'qil 136-137 M 7
Al-Maqwa' 136-137 M 8
Al-Marāghah 173 B 4
Al-Marfa' = Al-Maghayrā' 134-135 G 6
Al-Marīyah 134-135 G 6
Al-Marj 164-165 J 2
Al-Marjah 166-167 H 2
Al-Marsā 166-167 M 1
Almas [BR, Bahia] 100-101 B 7
Almas [BR, Goiás] 100-101 A 6
Almas, Pico das — 100-101 CD 7
Almas, Ribeirão das — 102-103 JK 2
Almas, Serra das — 100-101 D 4
Al-Maṭāmīr 166-167 M 3
Al-Maṭlā' 136-137 M 8
Al-Mātlīn 166-167 M 1
Al-Māyah 166-167 G 3
Al-Mayāmsī 136-137 H 7
Almaza = Cairo Airport 170 II c 1
Almazán 120-121 F 8
Al-Mazār 136-137 F 7
Al-Mazr'a 136-137 F 7
Al-Mazra'ah 166-167 K 2
Al-Mazzūnah 166-167 L 2
Al-Mdaina = Al-Madīnah 136-137 M 7
Al-M'dīlah 166-167 L 2
Almeda, Houston-, TX 85 III b 2
Almeida 120-121 D 8
Almeidia Campos 92-93 K 8
Almeirim [BR] 92-93 J 5
Almeirim, Serra do — 98-99 M 5
Almena, KS 68-69 G 6
Almenara [BR] 92-93 LM 8
Almendralejo 120-121 D 9
Al-Meqdādiya = Al-Miqdādīyah 136-137 L 6
Almería 120-121 F 10
Almería, Golfo de — 120-121 F 10
Al'metjevsk 132-133 J 7
Älmhult 116-117 F 9
Al-Midhdharidhrah 164-165 A 5
Al-Mighāīr 166-167 J 3
Al-Mijrīyyah 164-165 B 5
Al-Milīyah 166-167 JK 1
Al-Minyā 164-165 KL 3
Almirantazgo, Seno — 108-109 DE 10
Almirante Brown [Antarctica] 53 C 30-31
Almirante Brown [RA] 110 III bc 2
Almirante Brown-Adrogué 110 III b 2
Almirante Brown-José Mármol 110 III b 2
Almirante Brown-Rafael Calzada 110 III b 2
Almirante Guillermo Brown, Parque — 110 III b 1
Almirante Montt, Golfo — 108-109 C 8
Al-Mish'āb 134-135 F 5
'Almis Marmūshah 166-167 D 3
Al-Mismīyah 136-137 G 6
Al-Miṣr 164-165 KL 3
Al-Mithūyah 166-167 LM 3
Al-Mitlawī 166-167 L 2
Al-Miṭūyah 166-167 LM 3
Al-Mizāb 166-167 J 3
Al-M'jārah 166-167 D 2
Almo, ID 66-67 G 4
Almodóvar del Campo 120-121 E 9
Al Moktar 168-169 G 2
Almond, WI 70-71 F 3
Almond Park, Atlanta-, GA 85 II b 2
Almonesson, NJ 84 III c 3
Almont, CO 68-69 C 6
Almonte [CDN] 72-73 H 2
Almora 138-139 G 3
Almorox 120-121 E 8
Almota, WA 66-67 E 2
Al-M'rāītī 164-165 C 4
Al-Mrayyah 164-165 C 5
Al-Mudawwarah 134-135 D 5
Al-Mughayrā' 136-137 G 8
Al-Mughrān 166-167 C 2
Al-Muḥammadīyah 166-167 C 3
Al-Muhārī 136-137 L 7
Al Mujlad 164-165 K 6
Al-Mukallā 134-135 FG 8
Al-Mukhā 134-135 E 8
Al-Muknīn 166-167 M 2
Almuñécar 120-121 F 10
Al-Muqayyar = Ur 134-135 F 4
Al-Muqqar 166-167 K 3
Al-Muraywad 136-137 L 8
Almus 136-137 G 2
Al-Musayyib 136-137 L 6
Al-Mūṣil 134-135 E 3
Al-Mussanāt 136-137 M 8
Al-Muthanna 136-137 L 7
Al-Muwaffaqīyah 136-137 L 6
Al-Muwayḥ 134-135 E 6
Al-Muwayliḥ 173 D 4
Alnaši 124-125 T 5
Alnavar 140 B 3
Alnīf 166-167 D 4
Alnwick 119 F 4
Alo Brasil 98-99 N 10-11
Alofi 148-149 b 1
Aloha, OR 66-67 B 3
Aloja 124-125 E 5
Al-'Ōja = Al-'Awjā 136-137 M 8
Alol' 124-125 G 5
Alondra, CA 83 III c 2
Alondra Park 83 III bc 2
Along, Baie d' = Vinh Ha Long 150-151 F 2
Alonsa 61 J 5
Alonso, Río — 102-103 G 6
Alor, Kepulauan — 152-153 Q 10
Alor, Pulau — 148-149 HJ 8
Alor, Selat — 152-153 PQ 10
Álora 120-121 E 10
Alor Gajah 150-151 D 11
Alor Setar 148-149 CD 5
Alot 138-139 E 6
Alota, Río — 104-105 C 7
Alotau 148-149 NO 9
Aloûgoûm = Alūgūm 166-167 C 4
Al-Ousseukh = 'Ayn Dhahab 166-167 G 2
Aloysius, Mount — 158-159 E 5
Alpachiri 106-107 F 6
Alpasinche 106-107 D 2
Alpena 94-95 DE 8
Alpena, AR 78-79 C 2
Alpena, MI 64-65 K 2
Alpena, SD 68-69 G 3
Alpercatas, Rio — 92-93 KL 6
Alpercatas, Serra das — 100-101 B 3-4
Alpes, Villa Obregón- 91 I b 2
Alpes Cottiennes 120-121 G 6
Alpes Fueguinos 108-109 E 10
Alpes Graies 120-121 L 6
Alpes Maritimes 120-121 L 6
Alpet e Shqipërisë 122-123 HJ 4
Alpha 158-159 J 4
Alpha, IL 70-71 E 5
Alphonse 204-205 N 9
Alpine, AZ 74-75 J 6
Alpine, ID 66-67 H 4
Alpine, TX 64-65 F 5
Alpinópolis 102-103 J 4
Alpi Transilvanici 122-123 KL 3
Alps 122-123 A 3-E 2
Alpu 136-137 D 3
Al-Qa'āmiyāt 134-135 F 7

260 Albertvi

Al-Qa'ara = Al-Qa'rah 136-137 J 6
Al-Qabāb 166-167 D 3
Al-Qabāil 166-167 HJ 1
Al-Qaḍārif 164-165 M 6
Al-Qaḍīmah 134-135 DE 6
Al-Qādisīyah 136-137 L 7
Al-Qāhirah 164-165 KL 2
Al-Qāhirah-ad-Duqqi 170 II b 1
Al-Qāhirah-al-Abbāsīyah 170 II b 1
Al-Qāhirah-al-Azbakīyah 170 II b 1
Al-Qāhirah-al-Basatin 170 II b 2
Al-Qāhirah-al-Jamālīyah 170 II b 1
Al-Qāhirah-al-Khalifah 170 II b 1
Al-Qāhirah-al-Ma'adī 170 II b 2
Al-Qāhirah-al-Matarīyah 170 II bc 1
Al-Qāhirah-al-Muski 170 II b 1
Al-Qāhirah-al-Qubba 170 II b 1
Al-Qāhirah-az-Zamālik 170 II b 1
Al-Qāhirah-az-Zaytun 170 II b 1
Al-Qāhirah-Būlāq 170 II b 1
Al-Qāhirah-Dayr at-Tin 170 II b 2
Al-Qāhirah-Maḥattat al-Hilmīyah 170 II bc 1
Al-Qāhirah-Miṣr al-Jadīdah 173 BC 2
Al-Qāhirah-Miṣr al-Qadīmah 170 II b 1
Al-Qāhirah-Rawḍ al-Faraj 170 II b 1
Al-Qāhirah-Shubrā 170 II b 1
Al-Qāhirah-Turā 170 II b 2
Al-Qā'im 136-137 J 5
Al-Qal'ah 164-165 F 1
Al-Qal'at al-Kabīrah 166-167 M 2
Al-Qal'at as-S'rāghnah 166-167 C 3-4
Al-Qāmishlīyah 134-135 E 3
Al-Qanṭarah [DZ, landscape] 166-167 J 3
Al-Qanṭarah [DZ, place] 166-167 J 2
Al-Qanṭarah [ET] 173 C 2
Al-Qa'rah [IRQ] 136-137 J 6
Al-Qārah [Saudi Arabia] 136-137 J 8
Al-Qarārah 166-167 J 3
Al-Qaryatayn 136-137 G 5
Al-Qaṣabah 136-137 B 7
Al-Qaṣābī 166-167 D 3
Al-Qaṣīm 134-135 E 5
Al-Qaṣr [DZ] 166-167 J 1
Al-Qaṣr [ET] 164-165 K 3
Al-Qaṣr al-Farāfirah 164-165 K 3
Al-Qaṣrayn 164-165 F 1-2
Al-Qaṭīf 134-135 F 5
Al-Qaṭrānah 136-137 FG 7
Al-Qaṭrūn 164-165 GH 4
Al-Qaṭṭār 166-167 J 2
Al-Qay'īyah 134-135 E 6
Al-Qayrawān 164-165 FG 1
Al-Qayṣūhmah 134-135 F 5
Al-Qiblī Qamūlā 173 C 5
Al-Q'nitrah 164-165 C 2
Al-Qōsh = Alqūsh 136-137 K 4
Al-Qṣar al-Kabīr 164-165 C 1
Al-Qṣar aṣ-Ṣaghīr 166-167 D 2
Al-Q'ṣībah 166-167 CD 3
Al-Qubayyāt 136-137 G 5
Al-Quds 136-137 F 7
Alqueria, Bogotá- 91 III b 3
Al-Qulī'ah 166-167 H 1
Al-Qull 166-167 K 1
Al-Qunfudhah 134-135 DE 7
Al-Qurayni 134-135 GH 6
Al-Qurayyah 173 DE 3
Al-Qurnah 136-137 M 7
Al-Quṣayr [ET] 164-165 L 3
Al-Quṣayr [IRQ] 136-137 L 7
Al-Quṣayr [SYR] 136-137 G 5
Alqūsh 136-137 K 4
Al-Qūṣīyah 173 B 4
Al-Quṣūr 166-167 L 2
Al-Quṭayfah 136-137 G 6
Al-Quwārib 164-165 A 5
Al-Quwaymāt 136-137 GH 6
Al-Quwayr 136-137 K 4
Al-Quwayrah 136-137 F 8
Alright, Île — 63 F 4
Alroy Downs 158-159 G 3
Als 116-117 C 10
Alsace 120-121 L 4-5
Alsacia 94-95 F 8
Alsask 61 D 5
Alsasua 120-121 FG 7
Alsea, OR 66-67 B 3
Alsek River 58-59 T 6-7
Alsemberg 128 II ab 2
Alsina, Laguna — 106-107 F 6
Alstahaug 116-117 DE 5
Alsterdorf, Hamburg- 130 I ab 1
Alšvanga 124-125 C 5
Alta 116-117 K 3
Alta, IA 70-71 C 4
Altaelv 116-117 K 3
Alta Gracia [RA] 111 CD 4
Altagracia [YV] 92-93 E 2
Altagracia de Orituco 94-95 HJ 3
Altair 102-103 H 4
Altair Seamounts 50-51 H 3
Alta Italia 106-107 E 5
Altaj [Mongolia, Altaj] 142-143 H 2
Altaj [Mongolia, Chovd] 142-143 G 2
Altaj [SU] 132-133 PQ 7
Altajn Nuruu = Mongol Altajn nuruu 142-143 F-H 2
Altamachi, Río — 104-105 C 5
Altamaha River 64-65 K 5
Altamira [BR] 92-93 J 5
Altamira [CO] 94-95 D 6
Altamira [CR] 88-89 DE 9
Altamira [RCH] 104-105 AB 9
Altamira, Bogotá 91 III b 4
Altamira, Cueva de — 120-121 EF 7
Altamira do Maranhão 100-101 B 3
Altamirano 106-107 H 5
Altamont, IL 70-71 F 6
Altamont, OR 66-67 BC 4
Altamont, WY 66-67 H 5
Altamura 122-123 G 5
Altamura, Isla — 86-87 F 5
Altanbulag 142-143 K 1-2
Altan Xiret = Ejin Horo Qi 146-147 BC 2
Altar 86-87 E 2
Altar, Desierto de — 86-87 D 2-3
Altar, Río — 86-87 E 2
Altar of the Earth 155 II b 2
Altar of the Moon 155 II ab 2
Altar of the Sun 155 II b 2
Altar Valley 74-75 H 7
Altata 86-87 FG 5
Alta Vista 106-107 F 6
Alta Vista, KS 68-69 H 6
Altavista, VA 80-81 G 2
Altay 142-143 F 2
Altay = Altaj 132-133 PQ 7
Altdorf 118 D 5
Altenburg 118 F 3
Altenwerder, Hamburg 130 I a 1
Alter do Chão [BR] 92-93 HJ 5
Alte Süderelbe 130 I a 1
Altevatn 116-117 H 3
Altglienicke, Berlin- 130 III c 2
Altheimer, AR 78-79 D 3
Altinho 100-101 F 5
Altinópolis 102-103 J 4
Altınözü = Fatikli 136-137 G 4
Altin Tagh 142-143 EF 4
Altintaş 136-137 CD 3
Altiplanicie del Pilquiniyeu 108-109 E 3
Altiplanicie de Nuria 94-95 L 4
Altiplanicie Mexicana 64-65 E 5-F 7
Altiplano 92-93 F 8
Altiplano Barreras Blancas 108-109 E 8-F 7
Altmannsdorf, Wien- 113 I b 2
Altmühl 118 E 4
Alto, TX 76-77 G 7
Alto, El — [PE] 96-97 A 4
Alto, El — [RA] 104-105 D 11
Alto Alegre 106-107 F 4
Alto Anapu, Rio — 92-93 J 5
Alto Araguaia 102-103 F 2
Alto Baudó 94-95 C 5
Alto Coité 102-103 EF 1
Alto da Boa Vista, Rio de Janeiro- 110 I b 2
Alto da Mooca, São Paulo — 110 II b 2
Alto de Carrizal 94-95 C 4
Alto del Buey 94-95 C 4
Alto de Quimar 94-95 C 3
Alto de Toledo 96-97 F 9
Alto Garças 92-93 J 8
Alto Grande, Chapada do — 100-101 EF 5
Alto Longá 92-93 L 6
Alto Molócuè = Molócuè 172 G 5
Alton, IL 64-65 HJ 4
Alton, KS 68-69 G 6
Alton, MO 78-79 D 2
Altona, Friedhof — 130 I a 1
Altona, Melbourne- 161 II ab 2
Altona Bay 161 II b 2
Altona Sports Park 161 II b 2
Alto Nevado, Cerro — 108-109 C 5
Altônia 102-103 F 5
Altoona, PA 64-65 L 3
Alto Paraná [BR] 102-103 F 5
Alto Paraná [PY] 102-103 E 6
Alto Parnaíba 92-93 K 6
Alto Pelado 106-107 DE 4
Alto Pencoso 106-107 D 4
Alto Piquiri 111 F 2
Alto Rio Doce 102-103 L 4
Alto Río Mayo 108-109 D 5
Alto Rio Novo 100-101 D 10
Alto Río Senguerr 111 BC 6-7
Altos [BR] 100-101 C 3
Altos [PY] 102-103 D 6
Alto Santo 100-101 E 3
Altos de Chipión 106-107 F 3
Altos de Maria Enrique 64-65 bc 2
Altos de Talinay 106-107 B 3
Altos de Tarahumar 86-87 G 4-5
Alto Sucuriú 102-103 F 3
Alto Tamar 94-95 D 4
Alto Turi 100-101 B 2
Alto Uruguai 106-107 K 1
Alto Uruguai, Serra do — 106-107 L 1
Altstetten, Zürich- 128 IV a 1
Altuchovo 124-125 JK 7
Altunhisar = Ortaköy 136-137 F 4
Āltūn Kūprī 136-137 L 5
Alturas, CA 66-67 C 5
Alturitas 94-95 E 3
Altus, OK 64-65 G 5
Altyagač 126-127 O 6
Altyn Tagh = Altin tagh 142-143 EF 4
Altyševo 124-125 Q 6
Al-'Ubaylah 134-135 G 6
Al-Ubayyiḍ 164-165 KL 6
Alucra 136-137 H 2
Al-'Udaysāt 173 C 5
Alūgūm 166-167 C 4
Alūksne 124-125 F 5
Al-'Ulā' 134-135 D 5
Al-'Ulmah 166-167 J 1
Aluminé 111 B 5
Aluminé, Lago — 106-107 B 7
Aluminé, Río — 108-109 D 2
Al-'Umshaymin 136-137 H 6
Alung Gangri 142-143 E 5
Alupka 126-127 G 4
Al-'Uqaylah 164-165 H 2
Al-'Uqayr 134-135 FG 5
Al-Uqṣur 164-165 L 3
Ālūr [IND, Andhra Pradesh] 140 C 3
Alūr [IND, Karnataka] 140 BC 4
Ālūra = Alūr 140 BC 4
Aluralde 102-103 A 5
Ālūru = Ālūr 140 C 3
Al-'Urūq al-Mu'tariḍah 134-135 G 6-7
Al-Ūssaltīyah 166-167 LM 2
Alušta 126-127 G 4
Al-Uṭāyah 166-167 J 2
Al-'Uthmānīyah 173 BC 4
Alut Oya 140 E 6
'Aluula 164-165 c 1
Al-'Uwayjā' 134-135 G 6
Al-'Uzayr 136-137 M 7
Alva, FL 80-81 c 3
Alva, OK 76-77 E 4
Alvalade 120-121 C 9-10
Alvand, Kūh-e — 134-135 FG 4
Alvar = Alwar 134-135 M 5
Alvarado 64-65 GH 8
Alvarado, TX 76-77 F 6
Alvarães 92-93 G 5
Álvares Machado 102-103 G 5
Álvarez do Toledo 106-107 H 5
Álvaro Obregón = Frontera 64-65 H 8
Alvaro Obregón, Presa — 86-87 F 4
Alvdal 116-117 D 6
Älvdalen 116-117 F 7
Alvear 106-107 J 2
Alverstone, Mount — 58-59 S 6
Alverthorpe Park 84 III c 1
Alvesen 130 I a 2
Alvesta 116-117 F 9
Alvin, TX 76-77 G 8
Alvin Callander Field United States Naval Air Station 85 I b 2
Alvord Lake 66-67 D 4
Älvsborgs län 116-117 E 8-9
Älvsbyn 116-117 J 5
Al-Wād 164-165 F 2
Al-Wadaḥ 173 D 6
Al-Wāḥāt al-Khārijah 164-165 KL 3-4
Al-Wajh 134-135 D 5
Al-Waqbá 136-137 L 8
Al-Waqf 173 C 4
Alwar 134-135 M 5
Al-Wari'ah 134-135 F 5
Al-Washm 134-135 EF 5-6
Al-Wāsiṭah 164-165 L 3
Alwaye 140 C 5
Al-Wazz 164-165 L 5
Al-Widyan 134-135 E 4
Al-Wūqbá = Al-Waqbá 136-137 L 8
Alys = Kızılırmak 134-135 D 3
Alytus 124-125 E 6
Al-Yūsufīyah 136-137 KL 6
Alzada, MT 68-69 D 3
Álzaga 106-107 H 6
Alzamaj 132-133 S 6

Amabele 174-175 G 7
Amacuro, Río — 94-95 L 3
Amada = 'Amādah 173 C 6
Amadabad = Ahmadābād 134-135 L 6
'Amādah 173 C 6
Amadeus, Lake — 158-159 F 4
Amādī 164-165 KL 7
'Amādīyah, Al- 136-137 K 4
Amadjuak Lake 56-57 W 4-5
Amado Grande 96-97 C 7
Amagá 94-95 D 4
Amagasaki 144-145 K 5
Amahai 148-149 J 7
Amaicha del Valle 110 III b 1
Amak Island 58-59 b 2
Amakusa nada 144-145 G 6
Amakusa-rettō 142-143 O 5
Amakusa syotō = Amakusa-rettō 142-143 O 5
Åmål 116-117 E 8
Amalfi [CO] 94-95 D 4
Amalfi [I] 122-123 F 5
Amaliás 122-123 J 7
Amalner 138-139 E 7
Amaluza 96-97 B 4
Amalyk 132-133 W 6
Amamá 104-105 E 10
Amambaí 102-103 E 5
Amambaí, Rio — 102-103 E 5
Amambaí, Serra de — 102-103 E 5
Amambay 102-103 DE 5
Amami-guntō 142-143 O 6
Amami-ō-shima 142-143 O 6
Amami-Ō sima = Amami-ō-shima 142-143 O 6
Amandola 122-123 E 4
Amangel'dy 132-133 M 7-8
Amaniú 100-101 CD 6
Amanos dağları = Nur dağları 136-137 G 4
Amantea 122-123 FG 6
Amanuma, Tōkyō- 155 III a 1
Amapá [BR, Acre] 98-99 D 10
Amapá [BR, Amapá administrative unit] 92-93 J 4
Amapá [BR, Amapá place] 92-93 J 4
Amapari, Rio — 98-99 M 4
Amar, Ḥāssī el — = Ḥāssī al-Aḥmar 166-167 E 3
Amara 164-165 M 6
Amarabūra 141 E 5
'Amarah, Al- 134-135 F 4
Amaraji 100-101 G 5
Amaramba, Lagoa — = Lagoa Chiuta 172 G 4
Amarante [BR] 92-93 L 6
Amarante do Maranhão 100-101 A 3
Amaranth 61 J 5
Amarapura = Amarabūra 141 E 5
Amarāvati [IND, Andhra Pradesh] 140 E 2
Amarāvati [IND, Tamil Nadu] 140 C 5
Amarāvatī = Amrāvati 134-135 M 6
Amarete 104-105 B 4
Amarga, Bañados de la — 106-107 EF 5
Amargo, CA 74-75 E 5
Amargosa 100-101 E 7
Amargosa Desert 74-75 E 4
Amargosa Range 74-75 E 4-5
Amargosa River 74-75 E 5
Amari, Laghi — = Al-Buḥayrat al-Murrat al-Kubrá 173 C 2
Amarillo, TX 64-65 F 4
'Amarina, Tel el- = Tall al-'Amārinah 173 B 4
'Amārinah, Tall al- 173 B 4
Amarkantak 138-139 HJ 6
Amarnāth 138-139 D 8
Amaro 106-107 L 4
Amaro Leite 92-93 JK 7
Amarpātan 138-139 H 5
Amarpatnam = Amarpātan 138-139 H 5
Amarpur 138-139 L 5
Amarpurá = Amrāpāra 138-139 L 5
Amarume 144-145 M 3
Amarúsion 122-123 KL 6-7
Amarvāŗā = Amarwāra 138-139 G 6
Amarwāra 138-139 G 6
Amasa, MI 70-71 F 2
Amāsīn, Bi'r — 166-167 LM 5
Amasra 136-137 E 2
Amasya 134-135 D 2
Amatān 86-87 O 9
Amataurá 98-99 DE 6
Amatignak Island 58-59 t 7
Amatique, Bahía de — 64-65 J 8
Amatonga 174-175 K 2
Amauã, Lago — 92-93 G 5
Amazon 61 F 5
Amazon = Amazonas 92-93 F-H 5
Amazon, Mouth of the — = Estuário do Rio Amazonas 92-93 JK 4
Amazonas [BR] 92-93 F-H 5
Amazonas [CO] 94-95 EF 8
Amazonas [EC] 96-97 B 3
Amazonas [PE] 96-97 B 4-C 5
Amazonas [YV] 94-95 HJ 6
Amazonas, Estuário do Rio — 92-93 JK 4
Amazonas, Rio — [BR] 92-93 HJ 5
Amazonas, Río — [PE] 92-93 E 5
Amazon Shelf 50-51 G 5-6
Āmbā = Ambāh 138-139 G 4
Amba Alage 164-165 MN 6
Amba Alaji = Amba Alage 164-165 MN 6
Ambābhona 138-139 J 7
Ambad 138-139 E 8
Āmbādalā = Ambodāla 138-139 J 8
Ambāh 138-139 G 4
Ambājogāi 134-135 M 7
Ambāla 134-135 M 4
Ambalamgoda 140 DE 7
Ambalamtota 140 E 7
Ambalapulai 140 C 6
Ambalavao 172 J 6
Ambalema 94-95 D 5
Ambam 164-165 G 8
Ambanja 172 J 4
Ambarčik 132-133 fg 4
Ambargasta 106-107 EF 2
Ambargasta, Sierra — 106-107 EF 2
Ambaro, Baie d' 172 J 4
'Ambarūsī, Ḥāssī — 166-167 F 6
Ambāsamudram 140 C 6
Ambassador Bridge 84 II b 3
Ambato 92-93 D 5
Ambato, Sierra de — 104-105 C 11
Ambatoboeny 172 J 5
Ambatolampy 172 J 5
Ambatondrazaka 172 J 5
Ambatosoratra 172 J 5
Ambelau, Pulau — 148-149 J 7
Ambepussa 140 DE 7
Amber 138-139 EF 4
Amber, WA 66-67 E 2
Amber Bay 58-59 e 1
Amberg 118 EF 4
Ambergris Cay 64-65 J 8
Ambidédi 168-169 C 2
Ambikāpur 134-135 N 6
'Ambikūl 173 B 7
Ambilobe 172 JK 4
Ambition, Mount — 58-59 W 8
Ambler River 58-59 J 3
Ambo 96-97 CD 7
Ambodāla 138-139 J 8
Ambodifototra 172 JK 5
Ambohibe 172 H 6
Ambohimahasoa 172 J 6
Amboim = Gabela 172 BC 4
Amboina = Pulau Ambon 148-149 J 7
Amboise 120-121 H 5
Amboland = Ovamboland 172 BC 5
Ambon 148-149 J 7
Ambon, Pulau — 148-149 J 7
Amboseli, Lake — 171 D 3
Amboseli Game Reserve 172 G 2
Ambositra 172 J 6
Ambovombe 172 J 7
Amboy, CA 74-75 F 5
Amboy, IL 70-71 F 5
Amboyna Cay 148-149 F 5
Ambrakikós Kólpos 122-123 J 6
Ambre, Cap d' 172 J 4
Ambre, Montagne d' 172 J 4
Ambridge, PA 72-73 FG 4
Ambrim 158-159 N 3
Ambriz 172 B 3
Ambrizete = N'Zeto 172 B 3
Ambrolauri 126-127 L 5
Ambrosini, Hassi — = Ḥāssī 'Ambarūsī 166-167 F 6
Ambrósio 100-101 B 4
Ambrósio, Serra do — 102-103 L 3
Āmbūr 140 D 4
Amchitka, AK 58-59 s 7
Amchitka Island 52 D 1
Amchitka Pass 58-59 t 7
Am-Dam 164-165 J 6
Amderma 132-133 L 4
Ameca 64-65 F 7
Ameca, Río — 86-87 H 7
Amedabad = Ahmadābād 134-135 L 6
Ameghino 106-107 F 5
Ameghino, Punta — 108-109 G 4
Amelia, NE 68-69 G 4
Amelia Court House, VA 80-81 GH 2
Amenábar 106-107 F 5
Aménas, In — = 'Ayn Umannās 164-165 F 3
Amenia, NY 72-73 K 4
Amer, Grand Lac — = Al-Buḥayrat al-Murrat al-Kubrá 173 C 2
Amerasia Basin 50-51 A-C 1
América Dourada 100-101 D 6
Americana 102-103 J 5
American Falls, ID 66-67 G 4
American Falls Reservoir 66-67 G 4
American Fork, UT 66-67 H 5
American Highland 53 B 8
Americanópolis, São Paulo — 110 II b 3
American River North Fork 74-75 C 3
Americas, Hipódromo de las — 91 I b 2
Americas, University of the — 91 I b 2
Americus, GA 64-65 K 5
Amerikahaven 128 I a 1
Amersfoort [NL] 120-121 K 2
Amersfoort [ZA] 174-175 HJ 4
Amery, WI 70-71 D 3
Amery Ice Shelf 53 BC 7-8
Amerzgân = Amirzgān 166-167 C 4
Ames, IA 64-65 H 3
Ames, OK 76-77 EF 4
Amesbury, MA 72-73 L 3
Amesdale 62 C 2-3
Ameṭ 138-139 DE 5
Amethi 138-139 H 4
Amfilochía 122-123 J 6
Ámfissa 122-123 K 6
Amga [SU, place] 132-133 Z 5
Amga [SU, river] 132-133 X 6
Āmgaon 138-139 H 7
Amgar, Al- 136-137 L 8
Amghar, Al — = Al-Amgar 136-137 L 8
Amgu 132-133 a 8
Amguema 132-133 k 4
Am-Guereda 164-165 J 6
Amguid = Amqīd 166-167 J 6
Amgun' [SU, place] 132-133 a 7
Amgun' [SU, river] 132-133 a 7
Āmguri 141 D 2
Amhara = Amara 164-165 M 6
Amherst 56-57 XY 8
Amherst, MA 72-73 K 3
Amherst, VA 80-81 G 2
Amherst = Kyaikhkamī 141 E 7
Amherst, Île — 63 F 4
Amherst, Mount — 158-159 E 3
Amherstburg 72-73 E 3
Amherst Junction, WI 70-71 F 3
Ami, Mont — 171 B 2
Amiata, Monte — 122-123 D 4
Amidon, ND 68-69 E 2
Amiens 120-121 J 4
'Amīj, Wādī — 136-137 J 6
Amik gölü 136-137 G 4
Amīndīvi Islands 134-135 L 8
Aminga 106-107 D 2
Aminjevo, Moskva- 113 V b 3
Amino 144-145 K 5
Aminuis 172 C 6
Aminuis Reserve 174-175 C 2
Amirantes 204-205 N 9
'Amīrīyah, Al- 173 AB 2
Amirzgān 166-167 C 4
Amisk Lake 61 G 3
Amisós = Samsun 134-135 D 2
Amistad, NM 76-77 C 5
Amistad, Presa de la — 86-87 JK 3
Amite, LA 78-79 D 5
Amity, AR 78-79 C 3
Amīzmīz 166-167 B 4
Amlekhganj 138-139 K 4
Amlia Island 52 D 36
'Ammān 134-135 D 4
Ammarfjället 116-117 FG 4
Ammerman Mount 58-59 RS 2
Ammersee 118 E 5
Ammóchōstos 134-135 CD 3
Ammochōstu, Kólpos — 136-137 EF 5
Amnat Charoen 150-151 E 5
Amnok-kang 142-143 O 3
Amnyemachhen Gangri 142-143 HJ 5
Āmod 138-139 D 6-7
Amolar 102-103 D 3
Amontada 100-101 DE 2
Amores, Los — 111 DE 3
Amorgós 122-123 LM 7
Amory, MS 78-79 E 3-4
Amos 56-57 V 8
Amos, CA 74-75 F 6
Amotape, Cerros de — 96-97 A 4
'Amoûdâ = 'Āmūdā 136-137 J 4
Amour, Djebel — = Jabal 'Amūr 166-167 G 3-H 2
Amoy = Xiamen 142-143 M 7
Ampanihy 172 H 6
Amparo 102-103 J 5
Amparo, El — 94-95 E 6
Amparo de Apure, El — 94-95 F 3
Ampasindava, Baie d' 172 J 4
Ampato, Cordillera de — 96-97 EF 9
Ampato, Nevado de — 92-93 E 8
Ampère = 'Ayn 'Azl 166-167 J 2
Amphípolis 122-123 K 5
Amphitrite Point 60 DE 5
Amposta 120-121 H 8
Ampurias 120-121 J 7
Amqīd 166-167 J 6
Amqui 63 C 3
Amrāpāra 138-139 L 5
Amrāvati 134-135 M 6
Amrawati = Amrāvati 134-135 M 6
Amreli 138-139 C 7
Amritsar 134-135 LM 4
Amroha 134-135 M 5
Amselhain 130 III c 1
Amsīd, Al- 164-165 B 3
Amstel 128 I a 2
Amstelhoek 128 I a 2
Amstelland 128 I a 2
Amsterdam, NY 72-73 JK 3
Amsterdam [NL] 120-121 K 2
Amsterdam [ZA] 174-175 J 4
Amsterdam, Universiteit van — 128 I ab 1
Amsterdam-Buiten Veldert 128 I a 2
Amsterdam-Geuzenveld 128 I a 1
Amsterdam Island = Nouvelle Amsterdam 204-205 NO 7
Amsterdam-Nieuwendam 128 I b 1
Amsterdam-Oostzaan 128 I ab 1
Amsterdam-Osdorp 128 I a 1
Amsterdam Plateau 50-51 NO 8
Amsterdam-Slotervaar 128 I a 1
Amsterdam-Tuindorp 128 I ab 1
Amstetten 118 G 4
Amt'ae-do 144-145 EF 5
Am-Timan 164-165 J 6
Amú, Río — 94-95 E 7
'Āmūdā 136-137 J 4
Amudarja 134-135 J 2
Amukta Island 58-59 l 4
Amukta Pass 58-59 kl 4
Amuku Mountains 98-99 J 3-4
Amund Ringnes Island 56-57 RS 2
Amundsen, Mount — 53 BC 11
Amundsen Bay 53 C 5
Amundsen Glacier 53 A 23-20
Amundsen Gulf 56-57 L-N 3
Amundsen havet 53 BC 25-26
Amundsen-Scott 53 A
Amuntai 152-153 L 7
Amur 132-133 Z 8
Amur = Heilong Jiang 142-143 P 2
Amurang 148-149 H 6
Amursk 132-133 a 7
Amurskij zaliv 144-145 H 1
Amuwo 170 III a 2
Amvrosijevka 126-127 HJ 3
Amyā Taunggyā 150-151 B 6

An 141 CD 6
Anabar 132-133 V 3
Anābib an-Nafṭ 134-135 DE 4
Ana Branch 158-159 H 6
Anabuki 144-145 K 5-6
Anacapa Island 74-75 D 6
Anaco 94-95 J 3
Anaconda, MT 64-65 D 2
Anaconda Range 66-67 G 2-3
Anacortes, WA 66-67 B 1
Anacostia, Washington-, DC 82 II b 2
Anacostia Park 82 II b 2
Anacostia River 82 II ab 2
Anadarko, OK 76-77 EF 5
Anadia [BR] 100-101 F 5
Anadolu burnu 154 I b 1
Anadolufeneri 154 I bc 1
Anadoluhisarı 154 I b 2
Anadoluhisarı, İstanbul- 154 I b 2
Anadolukavağı, İstanbul- 154 I b 1
Anadyr' [SU, place] 132-133 j 5
Anadyr' [SU, river] 132-133 hj 5
Anadyrskaja nizmennost' 132-133 j 4-5
Anadyrskij zaliv 132-133 j-l 5
Anadyrskoje ploskogorje 132-133 h 4
Anáfē 122-123 LM 7
Anagni 122-123 E 5
'Ānah 136-137 JK 5
Anaheim, CA 74-75 DE 6
Aṇahilvāḍ-Pātan = Pātan 138-139 D 6
Anahim Lake 60 E 3
Anahuac, TX 76-77 G 8
Anáhuac [MEX, Nuevo León] 86-87 K 4
Anáhuac [MEX, Zacatecas] 86-87 K 5
Anáhuac, Mesa de — 64-65 FG 7-8
Ānai Malai 140 C 5
Ānai Mudi 140 C 5
Anaiza, Jebel — = Jabal Unayzah 134-135 DE 4
Anajás 92-93 JK 5
Anajás, Ilha — 98-99 N 5
Anajás, Rio — 98-99 N 5
Anajatuba 100-101 B 2
Anajé 100-101 D 8
Anak 144-145 E 3
Anakāpalle 134-135 N 7
Anakāpalli = Anakāpalle 134-135 N 7
Anak Krakatau 148-149 DE 8
Anaktuk, AK 58-59 H 1
Anaktuvuk Pass, AK 58-59 KL 2
Anaktuvuk River 58-59 M 2
Analalava 172 J 4
Anamã 92-93 G 5
Anama Bay 61 J 5
Ānamaḍuwa 140 DE 7
Ānamala = Ānai Malai 140 C 5
Anambas, Kepulauan — 148-149 E 6
Anambra [WAN, administrative unit] 164-165 F 7
Anambra [WAN, river] 168-169 G 4
Anamoose, ND 68-69 FG 2
Anamosa, IA 70-71 E 4
Anamu, Rio — 98-99 K 4
Anamur 134-135 C 3
Anamur burnu 134-135 C 3
Anan 144-145 K 6
Ananás, Cachoeira — 98-99 M 8
Ānand 138-139 D 6
Anandpur 138-139 L 7
Ananea 96-97 G 9
Ananjev 126-127 DE 3
Anantapur 134-135 M 8
Anantnāg 134-135 M 4
Anapa 126-127 H 4
Anapali, Río — 96-97 E 7
Anápolis 92-93 K 8
Anapurna = Annapūrna 138-139 JK 3
Anār 134-135 GH 4
Anārak 134-135 G 4
Anārdara 134-135 J 4
Anari, Rio — 104-105 E 2
Anastácio 102-103 E 4
Anastácio, Ponta — 106-107 M 3
Anastasia Island 80-81 c 2
Anatolia 134-135 CD 3
Anatone, WA 66-67 E 2
Añatuya 111 D 3
Anauá, Rio — 98-99 HJ 4
Anavilhanas, Arquipélago dos — 98-99 H 6
Ānayirāvu 140 E 6
Anaypazarı 136-137 E 4
Anbār, Al- 136-137 J 6
Anbianbu 146-147 AB 3
An Biên 150-151 E 8
Anbyŏn 144-145 F 3
Ancaján 106-107 E 2
Ancash 96-97 BC 6
Ancasti 104-105 D 11
Ancasti, Sierra de — 106-107 E 2
Ancenis 120-121 G 5
Anceny, MT 66-67 H 3
An Châu 150-151 F 2
An-chi = Anji 146-147 G 6
An-ch'i = Anxi 146-147 G 9
Anchieta 102-103 M 4
An-ching = Anqing 142-143 M 5
An-ch'iu = Anqiu 146-147 G 3
Ancho, NM 76-77 B 6
Ancho, Canal — 108-109 B 7-8
Anchorage, AK 56-57 FG 5
Anchorena 106-107 E 5
Anchoris 106-107 C 4
Anchor Point, AK 58-59 M 7
Anchuras 120-121 E 9
Anci 146-147 F 2
Ancient Observatory 155 II b 2
Anciferovo 124-125 JK 4
Anclote Keys 80-81 b 2
Ancober = Ankober 164-165 MN 7
Ancohuma, Nevado — 104-105 B 4
Ancol, Jakarta- 154 IV ab 1
Ancon [EC] 96-97 A 3
Ancón [PE] 96-97 C 7
Ancón [RA] 106-107 G 5
Ancona 122-123 E 4
Ancon de Sardinas, Bahía de — 96-97 B 1
Âncora, Ilha da — 102-103 M 5
Ancoraimes 104-105 B 4
Ancos 96-97 BC 6
Ancuabe 172 G 4
Ancud 111 B 6
Ancud, Golfo de — 111 B 6
Ancyra = Ankara 134-135 C 3
Anda 142-143 NO 2
Andacollo 106-107 B 6
Andahuaylas 96-97 E 8
Andale, KS 68-69 H 7
Andalgalá 111 C 3
Åndalsnes 116-117 BC 6
Andalucía [CO] 94-95 CD 5
Andalucía [E] 120-121 D-F 10
Andalusia, AL 78-79 F 5
Andalusia = Andalucía 120-121 D-F 10
Andalusia = Jan Kemp 174-175 F 4
Andaman and Nicobar Islands 134-135 OP 8
Andaman Basin 148-149 BC 4-5
Andamān Dvīp = Andaman Islands 134-135 P 8
Andamanensee 148-149 C 4-5
Andaman Islands 134-135 P 8
Andaman Sea 148-149 C 4-5
Andamarca [BOL] 104-105 C 6
Andamarca [PE] 96-97 D 7
Andamooka 158-159 G 6
Andamooka Ranges 160 C 3
Andant 111 D 5
Andara 172 D 5
Andaraí 100-101 D 7
Andaraí, Rio de Janeiro- 110 I b 2
Andarin, Al- 136-137 G 5
Andelys, les — 120-121 H 4
Andenes 116-117 G 3
Andéramboukane 168-169 F 2
Andermatt 118 D 5
Anderson, CA 66-67 BC 5
Anderson, IN 64-65 J 3
Anderson, MO 76-77 G 4

Anderson 261

Anderson, SC 64-65 K 5
Anderson, TX 76-77 FG 7
Andersonkop 174-175 J 3
Anderson Park 85 II b 2
Anderson Ranch Reservoir 66-67 F 4
Anderson River 56-57 L 4
Andes 92-93 D 3
Andes, Cordillera de los — 92-93 E 3-F 9
Andes, Lake — 68-69 G 4
Andes, Los — 111 B 4
Andheri 138-139 D 8
Andhra 134-135 M 8-N 7
Andhra Pradesh 134-135 M 8-N 7
Andidanob, Jebel — = Jabal Asūtarībah 173 E 7
Andijskij chrebet 126-127 MN 5
Andijskoje Kojsu 126-127 MN 5
Andīmashk 136-137 N 6
Andırın 136-137 G 4
Andižan 134-135 L 2
Andizhan = Andižan 134-135 L 2
Andkhoy 134-135 JK 3
Andoas 92-93 D 5
Andoga 124-125 L 4
Āndol 140 D 2
Āndola 140 C 2
Āndōlā = Āndola 140 C 2
Andomskij Pogost 124-125 L 3
Andong 142-143 O 4
Andong = Dandong 142-143 N 3
Andongwei 146-147 G 4
Andorinha 100-101 DE 6
Andorinhas, Cachoeira das — 94-95 G 8
Andørja 116-117 GH 3
Andorra 120-121 H 7
Andorra la Vella 120-121 H 7
Andou, Lac — 72-73 H 1
Andover, OH 72-73 F 4
Andover, SD 68-69 GH 3
Andøy 116-117 FG 3
Andra = Āndhra 134-135 M 8-N 7
Andradina 92-93 J 9
Andrau Airport 85 III a 2
Andreafsky = Saint Marys, AK 58-59 F 5
Andreafsky, East Fork — 58-59 FG 5
Andreafsky River 58-59 F 5
Andreanof Islands 52 D 36
Andreapol' 124-125 J 5
Andreas, Cape — = Akrōthērion Hágios Andréa 136-137 F 5
Andréba = Ambatosoratra 172 J 5
Andrée land 116-117 j 5
Andréeneset 116-117 n 4
Andrejevka [SU, Kazachskaja SSR] 132-133 OP 8
Andrejevka [SU, Rossijskaja SFSR] 124-125 ST 7
Andrejevka [SU, Ukrainskaja SSR] 126-127 H 3
Andrelândia 102-103 KL 4
Andrés Bello, Universidad Catolica — 91 II b 2
Andréville 63 B 4
Andrew Au 141 CD 6
Andrews, NC 80-81 E 3
Andrews, OR 66-67 D 4
Andrews, SC 80-81 G 4
Andrews, TN 80-81 E 3
Andrews, TX 76-77 C 6
Andrews Air Force Base 82 II b 2
Ándria 122-123 FG 5
Andriba 172 J 5
Andringitra 172 J 6
Androka 172 H 7
Andronica Island 58-59 cd 2
Andronovskoje 124-125 K 3
Ándros 122-123 L 7
Androscoggin River 72-73 L 2
Andros Island 64-65 L 7
Andros Town 88-89 H 2
Andròth Island 134-135 L 8
Andruševka 126-127 D 1
Andr'uškino 132-133 de 4
Andsfjord 116-117 G 3
Andújar 120-121 EF 9
Andulo 172 C 4
Anecón Grande, Cerro — 108-109 D 3
Anéfis 168-169 F 1
Anegada 64-65 O 8
Anegada, Bahía — 108-109 HJ 3
Anegada Passage 64-65 O 8
Anegasaki 155 III d 3
Anécho 164-165 E 7
Aneityum 158-159 N 4
Anekal 140 C 4
Añelo 111 C 5
Añelo, Cuenca del — 106-107 C 7
Anenous 174-175 B 5
Anes Baraka 168-169 G 1
Aneta, ND 68-69 GH 2
Aneto, Pico de — 120-121 H 7
Aney 164-165 G 5
Anezī = 'Anzī 166-167 B 5
Anfeng 146-147 H 5
Anfu 146-147 E 8
An-fu = Linli 142-143 L 6
Angādippuram 140 BC 5
Angamāli 140 C 5
Angamos, Isla — 108-109 B 7
Angamos, Punta — 111 B 2
Ang-ang-ch'i = Ang'angxi 142-143 N 2
Ang'angxi 142-143 N 2
Angara 132-133 S 6
Angarsk 132-133 T 7
Angarskij kr'až 132-133 S-U 6
Angatuba 102-103 H 5
Angchhen Gonpa 138-139 N 2-3
Ånge 116-117 F 6
Angechakot 126-127 M 7
Angel, El — 96-97 C 1
Angel, Salto del — 92-93 G 3
Ángel de la Guarda, Isla — 64-65 D 6
Ángeles, Los — [RA] 106-107 GH 5
Ángeles, Los — [RCH] 111 B 5
Ángel Etcheverry 106-107 HJ 5
Ängelholm 116-117 E 9
Angelina 102-103 H 7
Angelina, La — 106-107 E 5
Angelina River 76-77 G 7
Angel Island 83 I b 1
Angel Island State Park 83 I b 1
Angel Provincial Forest 62 B 3
Ångermanälven 116-117 G 5-6
Ångermanland 116-117 GH 6
Angermünde 118 FG 2
Angers 120-121 G 5
Ängesån 116-117 K 4
Angical 100-101 B 6-7
Angical, Serra do — 100-101 B 6
Angicos 100-101 F 3
Angka, Doi — = Doi Inthanon 148-149 C 3
Angke, Kali — 154 IV a 1
Angkor 148-149 D 4
Angkor Thom 150-151 D 6
Angkor Vat 150-151 DE 6
Anglesey 119 D 5
Angleton, TX 76-77 G 8
Anglialing Hu = Ngangiha Ringtsho 138-139 J 2
Angliers 72-73 G 1
Angmagssalik = Angmagssaliq 56-57 de 4
Angmagssaliq 56-57 de 4
Ang Mo Kio 154 III ab 1
Ango 172 E 1
Angoche 172 GH 5
Angoche, Ilhas — 172 GH 5
Angol 111 B 5
Angola 172 CD 4
Angola, IN 70-71 H 5
Angola, NY 72-73 G 3
Angola Basin 50-51 JK 6
Angoon, AK 58-59 U 8
Angoon, AK 58-59 v 8
Angora = Ankara 134-135 C 3
Angostura = Ciudad Bolívar 92-93 G 3
Angostura I, Salto de — 92-93 E 4
Angostura II, Salto de — 92-93 E 4
Angostura Reservoir 68-69 E 4
Angosturas 92-93 E 5
Angoulême 120-121 H 6
Angoumois 120-121 GH 6
Angra do Heroismo 204-205 E 5
Angra dos Reis 102-103 K 5
Angrapa 118 KL 1
Angra Pequena = Lüderitzbaai 172 BC 7
Angren 134-135 KL 2
Angrenšachtstroj = Angren 134-135 KL 2
Angrigon, Jardin zoologique — 82 I b 2
Angtassom 150-151 E 7
Angteng La 138-139 L 3
Ang Thong 150-151 C 5
Anguá 106-107 H 2
Angualasto 106-107 C 3
Anguellou = 'Anqallaw 166-167 G 5
Anguera 100-101 E 7
Anguil 106-107 E 6
Anguila = Anguilla 64-65 O 8
Anguilla 64-65 O 8
Anguilla Cays 88-89 G 3
Anguille, Cape — 63 G 4
Anguj 138-139 K 7
Ángulos 106-107 D 2
Angumu 172 E 2
Anguo 146-147 E 2
Angustora, Presa de la — 86-87 O 9-10
Anhanduí-Guaçu, Rio — 102-103 EF 4
Anhanduízinho, Rio — 102-103 EF 4
Anholt 116-117 D 9
An-hsi = Anxi 142-143 H 3
An-hsiang = Anxiang 146-147 D 7
Anhua 146-147 C 7
An-Huei = Anhui 142-143 M 5
Anhuei = Anhui 142-143 M 5
Anhui 142-143 M 5
Anhumas 92-93 HJ 8
Ani 144-145 N 2-3
An-i = Anyi [TJ, Jiangxi] 146-147 E 7
An-i = Anyi [TJ, Shanxi] 146-147 C 4
Aniaī = Ani 144-145 N 2-3
Aniak, AK 58-59 H 6
Aniakchak Volcano 58-59 de 1
Aniak River 58-59 H 6
Aníbal Pinto, Lago — 108-109 C 8-9
Anicuns 102-103 GH 2
Anié 168-169 F 4
Anie, Pic d' 120-121 G 7
Anikovo 124-125 O 4
Anikščiai 124-125 E 6
Anil 100-101 B 2
Anil, Rio de Janeiro- 110 I a 2
Anil, Rio do — 110 I a 2
Animas, NM 74-75 J 7
Animas, Las — 76-77 C 9
Animas, Punta — 104-105 A 10
Animas Peak 74-75 J 7
Anin 141 E 8
Anina 122-123 JK 3
Anipemza 126-127 LM 6
Anita, AZ 74-75 G 5
Anita, IA 70-71 C 5
Anitápolis 102-103 H 7
Aniuk River 58-59 J 2
Aniva, mys — 132-133 b 8
Aniva, zaliv — 132-133 b 8
Aniva Bay = zaliv Aniva 132-133 b 8
Anjangāňv = Anjangaon 138-139 F 7
Anjangaon 138-139 F 7
Añjankōḍ = Anjengo 140 C 6
Anjār 134-135 KL 6
An-jên = Anren 146-147 D 8
Anjengo 140 C 6
Anjer = Anyerkidul 152-153 F 9
Anji 146-147 G 6
Anjou [CDN] 82 I b 1
Anjou [F] 120-121 G 5
Anjou, Les Galleries d' 82 I b 1
Anjou, ostrova — 52 B 4-5
Anjouan = Ndzuwani 172 HJ 4
Anju 142-143 O 4
Anjudin 124-125 W 2
Anka 168-169 G 2
Aṅkalēshvar = Anklesvar 138-139 D 7
Ankang 146-147 B 5
Ankara 134-135 C 3
Ankara suyu 136-137 DE 3
Ankaratra 172 J 5
Ankara-Yenidoğan 136-137 E 2
Ankara-Yenişehir 136-137 E 3
Ankazoabo 172 H 6
Ankeveen 128 I b 2
Ankeveense plassen 128 I b 2
An Khe 148-149 E 4
Anki = Anxi 146-147 G 9
Anking = Anqing 142-143 M 5
Ankiu = Anqiu 146-147 G 3
Anklam 118 F 2
Anklesvar 138-139 D 7
Ankober 164-165 MN 7
Ankola 140 B 3
Ankūr, Jabal — 173 DE 7
Ankwe 168-169 H 3
An Lao 150-151 G 5
An Lôc 150-151 F 7
Anlong 142-143 JK 6
Anlong Veng 150-151 E 5
Anlu 146-147 D 6
An-lu = Zhongxiang 146-147 D 6
Anlung = Anlong 142-143 JK 6
Anma-do 144-145 E 5
Ann, Cape — 72-73 L 3
Anna 126-127 K 1
Anna, IL 70-71 F 7
Annaba = Annābah 164-165 F 1
Annābah 164-165 F 1
An-Nabk [Saudi Arabia] 136-137 G 7
An-Nabk [SYR] 134-135 D 4
An-Nadhatah 136-137 J 6
An-Nadjaf = An-Najaf 134-135 E 4
An-Nāḍūr 166-167 E 2
An-Nafūd 134-135 E 5
An-Nahīlah = An-Nakhīlah 166-167 E 2
Annai 92-93 H 4
An-Najaf 134-135 E 4
An-Nakhīlah 166-167 E 2
Annalee Heights, VA 82 II a 2
Annam = Trung Bô 148-149 D 3-E 4
Annam, Porte d' = Đeo Ngang 150-151 F 3-4
An-Na'mah 164-165 C 5
An-Na'mānīyah 136-137 L 6
Anna Maria Key 80-81 b 3
An-Namlāt 166-167 KL 2
Annan 119 E 4
Annandale, MN 70-71 C 3
Annandale, VA 82 II a 2
Annapareddipalle 140 E 2
Annapolis, MD 64-65 L 4
Annapolis, MO 70-71 E 7
Annapolis Royal 56-57 XY 9
Annapūrna 138-139 JK 3
Ann Arbor, MI 64-65 K 3
An-Nāsirīyah 134-135 F 4
An-Naṣr 173 C 5
An-Nawfaliyah 164-165 H 2
Annecy 120-121 L 6
An Ne'māniya = An-Na'mānīyah 136-137 L 6
Annenskij Most 124-125 L 3
Annette, AK 58-59 x 8
Annette Island 58-59 x 9
An-N'fīdah 166-167 M 1
Angueur, Erg el — = 'Irq al-'Anqar 166-167 G 3-H 4
An Nho'n 148-149 E 4
Annigeri 140 B 3
An-Nikhaib = Nukhayb 134-135 E 4
An-Nīl 164-165 L 5
An-Nīl al-Abyaḍ 164-165 L 6
An-Nīl al-Azraq [Sudan, administrative unit] 164-165 L 6
An-Nīl al-Azraq [Sudan, river] 164-165 L 6
An Niṣāb = Anṣāb 134-135 F 8
Anniston, AL 64-65 JK 5
Annobón = Pagalu 204-205 H 9
Annonciation, l' 72-73 J 1
Annotto Bay 88-89 H 5
Annu 168-169 H 3
An-Nubah 164-165 K-M 4-5
An-Nuhaylah 173 B 4
An-Nuhūd 164-165 K 6
Anoka, MN 70-71 D 3
Año Nuevo, Seno — 108-109 E 10
Anoual = Anwāl [MA, An-Nāḍūr] 166-167 E 2
Anoual = Anwāl [MA, Ar-Rashidīyah] 166-167 E 3
Anou Mellene 168-169 F 1
An-pien-pao = Anbianbu 146-147 AB 3
Anping 146-147 E 2
Anpu 146-147 C 11
Anpu Gang 146-147 B 11
Anqallaw 166-167 G 5
'Anqar, 'Irq al- 166-167 G 3-H 4
Anqing 142-143 M 5
Anqiu 146-147 G 3
Anren 146-147 D 8
Anṣāb 134-135 F 8
Anṣāb = Niṣāb 134-135 EF 5
Ansai 146-147 B 3
Anṣārīyah, Jabal al- 136-137 G 5
Ansbach 118 E 4
Anse-au-Loup, l' 63 H 2
Anse-aux-Griffons, l' 63 DE 3
Anse-aux-Meadows, l' 63 J 2
Ansekūla 124-125 D 4
Anselmo, NE 68-69 FG 5
Anserma 94-95 CD 5
Anse-Saint-Jean, l' 63 A 3
Anshan 146-147 G 2
Anshun 142-143 K 6
Ansiang = Anxiang 146-147 D 7
Ansilta, Cerro — 106-107 C 3-4
Ansilta, Cordillera de — 106-107 C 3
Ansina 106-107 K 3
Ansley, NE 68-69 G 5
Ansley Park, Atlanta-, GA 85 II b 2
Ansó 120-121 G 7
Anson, TX 76-77 DE 6
Anson Bay 158-159 EF 2
Ansongo 164-165 E 5
Ansonia, CT 72-73 K 4
Ansonville 62 L 2
Ansŏng 144-145 F 4
Ansted, WV 72-73 F 5
Anta [IND] 138-139 F 5
Anta [PE] 92-93 E 7
An-ta = Anda 142-143 NO 2
Anta, Cachoeira — [BR, Amazonas] 98-99 H 8
Anta, Cachoeira — [BR, Pará] 98-99 O 7
Antabamba 92-93 E 7
Antāgarh 138-139 H 7
Antah = Anta 138-139 F 5
Antakya 134-135 D 3
Antalaha 172 K 4
Antália = Antalya 134-135 C 3
Antalya 134-135 C 3
Antalya körfezi 134-135 C 3
Antananarivo 172 J 5
Antarctica 53 B 28-9
Antarctic Peninsula 53 BC 30-31
Antarctic Sound 53 C 31
Antarī = Antri 138-139 G 4
Antarktika 53 B 28-9
Antártica Chilena, Magallanes y — 108-109 B 7-E 10
Antas 100-101 E 6
Antas, Rio das — [BR, Rio Grande do Sul] 106-107 M 2
Antas, Rio das — [BR, Santa Catarina] 102-103 F 7
Antēgiri = Annigeri 140 B 3
Antelope, OR 66-67 C 3
Antelope Hills 66-67 J 4
Antelope Island 66-67 G 5
Antelope Range 74-75 E 3
Antenne, Monte — 113 II b 1
Antenor Navarro 100-101 E 4
Antequera 120-121 E 10
Antero Reservoir 68-69 CD 6
Anthony, KS 76-77 EF 4
Anthony, NM 76-77 A 7
Anthony Lagoon 158-159 FG 3
Anti Atlas = Al-Aṭlas aṣ-Ṣaghīr 164-165 C 2-3
Antibes 120-121 L 7
Anticosti Island 56-57 Y 8
Antigo, WI 70-71 F 3
Antigua 64-65 O 8
Antigua and Barbuda 64-65 OP 8
Antigua Guatemala 64-65 H 9
Antiguo Cauce del Río Bermejo 104-105 F 9
Antiguo Morelos 86-87 L 6
Antiguos, Los — 108-109 D 6
Antikýthēra 122-123 K 8
Anti Lebanon = Jabal Lubnān ash-Sharqī 136-137 G 5-6
Antilhue 108-109 C 2
Antilla 104-105 D 10
Antímano, Caracas- 91 II b 2
Antimēlos 122-123 KL 7
Antimony, UT 74-75 H 3
Antinopolis 173 B 4
Antioch, CA 74-75 C 3-4
Antioch, IL 70-71 F 4
Antioch = Antakya 134-135 D 3
Antiócheia = Antakya 136-137 FG 4
Antiokia = Antakya 136-137 FG 4
Antiquia Pini 106-107 G 2
Antioquia [CO, administrative unit] 94-95 CD 4
Antioquia [CO, place] 92-93 D 3
Antíparos 122-123 L 7
Antipino 124-125 J 6
Antipodes Islands 156-157 HJ 7
Antisana 96-97 B 2
Antler, ND 68-69 F 1
Antlers, OK 76-77 G 5
Antofagasta [RCH, administrative unit] 104-105 BC 8
Antofagasta [RCH, place] 111 B 2
Antofagasta de la Sierra 111 C 3
Antofalla, Salar de — 104-105 C 9-10
Antofalla, Volcán — 104-105 BC 9
Antón 88-89 F 10
Anton, CO 68-69 E 6
Anton, TX 76-77 C 6
Anton Chico, NM 76-77 B 5
Antongila, Helodrona — 172 JK 5
Antonibe 172 J 4-5
Antonina 102-103 H 6
António Carlos 102-103 L 4
Antonio de Biedma 108-109 FG 6
Antônio Dias 102-103 L 3
Antônio João 102-103 E 5
Antônio Lemos 98-99 N 5
Antônio Prado 106-107 M 2
Antonio Varas, Península — 108-109 C 8
Antonito, CO 68-69 CD 7
Anton Lizardo, Punta — 86-87 N 8
Antony 129 I c 2
Antri 138-139 G 4
Antrim 119 C 4
Antrim Mountains 119 CD 4
Antropologia, Museo Nacional de — 91 I b 2
Antropovo 124-125 O 4
Antsalova 172 H 5
Antseh = Anze 146-147 D 3
Antsirabé 172 J 5
Antsiranana 172 JK 4
Antsla 124-125 F 5
Antsohihy 172 J 4
An Tuc = An Khe 148-149 E 4
Antuco 106-107 B 7
Antuco, Volcán — 106-107 B 6
Antuérpia 104-105 E 2
Antung = Dandong 142-143 N 3
An-tung = Lianshui 146-147 G 5
An-tung-wei = Andongwei 146-147 G 4
Antuševo 124-125 L 4
Antwerp 170 V bc 1
Antwerp = Antwerpen 120-121 K 3
Antwerpen 120-121 J 3
'Anu an-Na'idah 166-167 K 6
Añueque, Sierra — 108-109 E 3
Anugula = Angul 138-139 K 7
Anūi 144-145 F 5
An'ujsk 132-133 f 4
An'ujskij chrebet 132-133 fg 4
Anunciación, Bahía de la — = Berkeley Sound 108-109 KL 8
Anūpgarh 138-139 D 3
Anupshahar = Anūpshar 138-139 FG 3
Anūpshahr 138-139 FG 3
Anuradhapura = Anurādhapūraya 134-135 MN 9
Anurādhapūraya 134-135 MN 9
Āṅvalā = Aonla 138-139 G 3
Anvers = Antwerpen 120-121 J 3
Anvers, Île — 53 C 30
Anvik, AK 58-59 G 5
Anvik River 58-59 G 5
Anvil Peak 58-59 st 7
Anwāl [MA, An-Nāḍūr] 166-167 E 2
Anwāl [MA, Ar-Rashidīyah] 166-167 E 3
Anxi [TJ, Fujian] 146-147 G 9
Anxi [TJ, Gansu] 142-143 H 3
Anxiang 146-147 D 7
Anxious Bay 158-159 F 6
Anyang [ROK] 144-145 F 4
Anyang [TJ] 142-143 LM 4
Anyerkidul 152-153 F 9
Anyi [TJ, Jiangxi] 146-147 E 7
Anyi [TJ, Shanxi] 146-147 C 4
Anyox 60 C 2
Anyuan 146-147 E 9
Anzá [CO] 92-93 D 3
Anzac 61 C 2
Anzaldo 104-105 D 5
Anzarān, Bi'r — 164-165 B 4
'Anz ar-Ruḥaymāwī 136-137 K 7
Anze 146-147 D 3
Anžero-Sudžensk 132-133 PQ 6
Anzhero Sudzhensk = Anžero-Sudžensk 132-133 PQ 6
Anzhu = ostrova Anjou 132-133 a-d 2
'Anzī 166-167 B 5
Ánzio 122-123 E 5
Anzoategui 106-107 F 7
Anzoátegui 94-95 J 3
Aoba = Oba 158-159 N 3
Ao Ban Don 150-151 B 8
Aoga-shima 142-143 Q 5
Aoga sima = Aoga-shima 142-143 Q 5
Aoji 144-145 H 1
Aojiang 146-147 H 8
Ao Krung Thep 150-151 C 6
Ao Luk 150-151 B 8
Aomen = Macau 142-143 L 7
Aomori 142-143 QR 3
Aonae 144-145 a 2
Aonla 138-139 G 3
Aoraiyyā = Auraiya 138-139 G 4
Aoraṅgābād = Aurangābād [IND, Bihār] 138-139 K 5
Aoraṅgābād = Aurangābād [IND, Mahārāshtra] 138-139 E 8
Aoreora = Awrīūrā' 166-167 A 5
Aosta 122-123 B 3
Aougesses 168-169 G 1
Aouinet, El — = Al-Awaynāt 166-167 KL 2
Aouinet Legraa = 'Awīnat Laqra' 166-167 C 6
'Aouînet Torkoz = 'Awīnat Turkuz 166-167 B 5
Aouk, Bahr — 164-165 HJ 7
Aouker = Āwkār 164-165 BC 5
Âoulef = Awlīf 166-167 D 2
Aoulef-el Arab = Awlīf 166-167 G 6
Aouriôra = Awrīūrā' 166-167 A 5
Aoussedjine = Awsūjīn 166-167 L 6
Aoya 144-145 JK 5
Aoyama, Tōkyō- 155 III b 2
Aozou 164-165 H 4
Apa, Río — 111 E 2
Apache, AZ 74-75 J 7
Apache, OK 76-77 E 5
Apache Mountains 76-77 B 7
Apacheta Cruz Grande 104-105 D 7
Apagado, Volcán — 104-105 BC 8
Apaga Fogo, Ponta — 100-101 E 7
Apalachee Bay 64-65 K 6
Apalachicola, FL 78-79 G 6
Apalachicola Bay 78-79 G 6
Apalachicola River 78-79 G 5
Apan 86-87 L 8
Apapa, Lagos- 170 III b 2
Apapa Wharf 170 III b 2
Apaporis, Río — 92-93 EF 5
Apar, Teluk — 152-153 M 7
Aparado, Salto do — 102-103 G 6
Aparados da Serra, Parque Nacional de — 106-107 MN 2
Aparecida 102-103 K 5
Aparecida do Taboado 102-103 G 4
Aparicio 106-107 G 7
Aparri 148-149 H 3
Apartadero, El — 91 III c 3
Apararén 94-95 K 5
Apas, Sierra — 108-109 F 3-4
Apat 56-57 ab 4
Apatity 132-133 EF 4
Apatzingan de la Constitución 64-65 F 8
Ape 124-125 F 5
Apedia, Rio — 98-99 H 11
Apeldoorn 120-121 KL 2
Apeleg 108-109 D 5
Apeleg, Aldea — 108-109 D 5
Apeleg, Arroyo — 108-109 D 5
Apennines 122-123 C 3-G 5
Apere, Río — 104-105 D 4
Apese, Lagos- 170 III b 2
Apeuzinho, Ilha — 100-101 B 1
Apex, NC 80-81 G 3
Aphajalapura = Afzalpur 140 C 2
Api [Nepal] 138-139 H 2-3
Api [ZRE] 172 E 1
Api, Gunung — 152-153 N 10
Api, Tanjung — 152-153 O 6
Apia 148-149 c 1
Apiacá, Rio — 98-99 K 9
Apiacás, Serra dos — 92-93 H 6-7
Apiaí 111 G 3
Apiaí, Rio — 102-103 H 5
Api Api 154 III b 1
Apiaú, Rio — 94-95 L 6
Apiaú, Serra do — 92-93 G 4
Api Passage = Selat Serasan 150-151 G 11
Apipé 106-107 J 1
Apipé Grande, Isla — 106-107 J 1
Apishapa River 68-69 D 7
Apiúna 102-103 H 7
Ap Iwan, Cerro — 108-109 D 6
Apizaco 86-87 LM 8
Aplao 96-97 E 10
Ap Li Chau 155 I a 2
Apo, Mount — 148-149 HJ 5
Apodi 100-101 F 3
Apodi, Chapada do- 92-93 M 6
Apo Duat, Pegunungan — 152-153 L 3-4
Apolda 118 E 3
Apolinario Saravia 111 D 2
Apollo Bay 160 F 7
Apollonia = Sūsah 164-165 J 2
Apolo 92-93 F 7
Apolyont gölü 136-137 C 2
Apongüao, Río — 98-99 H 3
Apopka, FL 80-81 c 2
Aporá 100-101 E 6
Aporé, Rio — 92-93 J 8
Aporema 98-99 N 4
Apostle Islands 64-65 HJ 2
Apóstoles 111 E 3
Apostolovo 126-127 FG 3
Apoteri 92-93 H 4
Appalachia, VA 80-81 E 2
Appalachian Mountains 64-65 K 5-N 2
Appennino Abruzzese 122-123 E 4-F 5
Appennino Toscano 122-123 D 3-4
Appennino Umbro-Marchigiano 122-123 E 4
Appia, Via — 113 II b 2
Appleton, MN 70-71 BC 3
Appleton, WI 64-65 J 3
Appleton City, MO 70-71 CD 6
Applobamba, Nudo de — 104-105 B 4
Appomattox, VA 80-81 G 2
Appozai 134-135 K 4
Approuague 98-99 MN 2
Apšeronsk 126-127 JK 4
Apšeronskij poluostrov 126-127 OP 6
Apsheron Peninsula = Apšeronskij poluostrov 126-127 OP 6
Apsley Strait 158-159 EF 2
Apua Point 78-79 e 3
Apucarana 111 F 2
Apucarana, Serra de — 111 F 2
Apuí 104-105 B 1
Apuiarés 100-101 E 2
Apulia = Púglia 122-123 FG 5
Apure 94-95 GH 4
Apure, Río — 92-93 F 3
Apurímac 96-97 E 8
Apurimac, Río — 92-93 E 7
Apurito 94-95 G 4
Apurito, Río — 94-95 H 4
Apurlec 96-97 B 5
Apussigamasi River 61 K 3
Apyi = Api 138-139 H 2-3
'Aqabah, Al- [IRQ] 136-137 KL 7
'Aqabah, Al- [JOR] 134-135 CD 5
'Aqabah, Khalīj al- 134-135 C 5
'Aqabah, Wādī al- 173 CD 2-3
'Aqabat aṣ-Ṣaghīrah, Al- 173 C 5
Āqā Jarī = Āghā Jarī 134-135 FG 4
'Aqārib 166-167 M 2
'Aqbah, Bū — 166-167 C 5
'Aqbalī 166-167 G 6
Āqchalar 136-137 L 5
Āq Chāy 136-137 L 3
Āqdogh Mīsh, Rūd-e — 136-137 M 4
'Aqeila, el — = Al-'Uqaylah 164-165 H 2
'Aqīq 164-165 M 5
Aqjawajat 164-165 B 5
Aqmūr 166-167 HJ 6
'Aqqah 166-167 B 5
'Aqqah, Wād — 166-167 B 5
'Aqqa Îkirhene = 'Aqqat Igīrin 166-167 C 5
'Aqqa Îrhane = 'Aqqat Īghān 166-167 C 4
'Aqqat Īghān 166-167 C 4
'Aqqat Igīrin 166-167 C 5
'Aqrah 136-137 K 4
Aqshār 164-165 B 4
Āq Sū [IRQ] 136-137 L 5
Aqsu [TJ] 142-143 E 3
Aq Tagh Altai = Mongol Altajn Nuruu 142-143 F-H 2
Aquadas 94-95 D 5
Aquarius Plateau 74-75 H 3-4
Āquatorial-Guinea 164-165 FG 8
Aqueduc 82 I b 2
Aqueduct 154 I a 2
Aquidabã 100-101 F 6
Aquidabán-mi, Río — 102-103 D 5
Aquidauana 92-93 H 9
Aquidauana, Rio — 102-103 D 3
Aquila, L' 122-123 E 4
Aquiles Serdán 76-77 B 8
Aquio, Río — 94-95 GH 6
Aquiraz 100-101 E 2
Aquitania 94-95 E 5
Ara 155 III c 1
Ārā = Arrah 134-135 N 5
'Arab, Baḥr al- 164-165 K 6-7
'Arab, Khalīj al- 136-137 C 7
'Arab, Shaṭṭ al- 134-135 F 4
'Arab, Wādī al- 166-167 K 2
'Arabah, Wādī — 173 C 3
'Arabah, Wādī al- 136-137 F 7
Araban 136-137 G 4
Arabatskaja Strelka, kosa — 126-127 G 3-4
Arabela, Río — 96-97 D 2-3
Arabelo 94-95 J 5
'Arabestān = Khūzestān 134-135 F 4
Arabi, GA 80-81 E 5
Arabi, LA 85 I c 2
'Arabī, Al-Khalīj al- 136-137 N 8
Arabia 50-51 LM 4
Arabian Basin 50-51 N 5
Arabian Desert 164-165 L 3-4
Arabian Sea 134-135 JK 7
Arabistan = Khūzestān 134-135 F 4
Arabopó 94-95 L 5
Arabopó, Río — 94-95 L 5
Arabre 94-95 G 3
Araç 136-137 E 2
Araca 104-105 C 5
Araçá, Rio — 98-99 G 4
Aracaju 92-93 M 7
Aracataca 94-95 BE 2
Aracati 92-93 M 5
Aracatiaçu 100-101 D 2
Aracatiaçu, Açude — 100-101 DE 2-3
Aracatu 100-101 D 8
Araçatuba 92-93 JK 9
Araceli = Dumaran Island 148-149 GH 4
Aracena, Sierra de — 120-121 D 10
Arachthós 122-123 J 6
Araci 100-101 E 6
Aracoiaba 100-101 E 3
Aracruz 100-101 DE 10
Araçuaí 92-93 L 8
Araçuaí, Rio — 102-103 L 2
Arad 122-123 J 2
Arada 164-165 J 5-6
Arafura Sea 158-159 FG 2
Aragac 126-127 L 6
Aragac, gora — 126-127 M 6
Arago, Cape — 66-67 A 4
Aragón 120-121 G 7-8
Aragón, Río — 120-121 G 7
Aragonesa, La — 108-109 E 7
Aragua 94-95 H 2-3
Araguacema 92-93 K 6
Araguaçu 98-99 NO 11
Aragua de Barcelona 92-93 G 3
Aragua de Maturín 94-95 K 2-3
Araguaia, Parque Nacional do — 98-99 NO 10
Araguaia, Rio — 92-93 J 7
Araguaiana 102-103 FG 1
Araguaína 98-99 O 8
Araguao, Boca — 94-95 L 3
Araguao, Caño — 94-95 L 3
Araguari 92-93 K 8
Araguari, Rio — [BR, Amapá] 92-93 J 4
Araguari, Rio — [BR, Minas Gerais] 102-103 H 3
Araguatins 92-93 K 6
Arahoab = Aranos 174-175 C 3
Arai 144-145 M 4
'Araîch, el — = Al-'Arā'ish 164-165 C 1

262 Anderson

Baie de Ngaliema 170 IV a 1
Baie de Saint Augustin 172 H 6
Baie des Sept-Îles 63 CD 2-3
Baie-Johan-Beetz 63 E 2
Baie Marguerite 53 C 29-30
Baie Moisie 63 D 2
Baierbrunn 130 II a 2
Baie-Sainte-Catherine 63 AB 2-3
Baie-Sainte-Claire 63 DE 3
Baie-Saint-Paul 63 A 4
Baie-Trinité 63 C 3
Baie Verte 63 HJ 2-3
Baigezhuang 146-147 G 2
Baihar 138-139 H 6
Baihe [TJ, place] 142-143 KL 5
Bai He [TJ, river] 146-147 D 5
Bai Hu 146-147 F 6
Ba'ījī 136-137 K 5
Baiju 146-147 H 5
Baikunthpur 138-139 J 6
Baile Átha Cliath = Dublin 119 CD 5
Băileşti 122-123 K 3
Bailey 174-175 G 6
Baileys Crossroads, VA 82 II a 2
Baileys Harbor, WI 70-71 G 3
Bailique, Ilha — 98-99 O 4
Bailly 129 I b 2
Bailundo 172 C 4
Baima Shan 146-147 D 9-10
Bainbridge, OH 72-73 E 5
Baindbridge, GA 78-79 G 5
Baindūru 140 B 4
Baing 148-149 H 9
Bain-Tumen = Čojbalsan 142-143 L 2
Bainville, MT 68-69 D 1
Baipeng 146-147 B 9
Baipu 146-147 H 5
Baiqibao = Baiqipu 144-145 D 2
Baiqipu 144-145 D 2
Bā'ir 134-135 D 4
Bā'ir, Wādī — 136-137 G 7
Bairat 138-139 F 4
Bairath = Bairat 138-139 F 4
Baird, TX 76-77 E 6
Baird Inlet 58-59 EF 6
Baird Mountains 56-57 DE 4
Bairiki 208 H 2
Bairnsdale 158-159 J 7
Baïse 120-121 H 7
Baisha [TJ, Guangdong ↙ Haikou] 150-151 G 3
Baisha [TJ, Guangdong ← Macau] 146-147 D 10
Baisha [TJ, Hunan] 146-147 D 8
Baishi Guan 146-147 CD 9
Baishui [TJ, Hunan] 146-147 C 8
Baishui [TJ, Shaanxi] 146-147 B 4
Baitadi 138-139 H 3
Baitarani 138-139 KL 7
Bai Thu'o'ng 150-151 E 3
Baiti 138-139 N 3
Baitou Shan 144-145 FG 2
Baitou Shan = Changbai Shan 142-143 O 3
Bait Range 60 D 2
Baituchangmen 144-145 CD 2
Baitul = Bētūl 138-139 F 7
Baiwen 146-147 C 2
Baixa Grande 100-101 DE 6
Baixão 100-101 DE 7
Baixiang 146-147 E 3
Baixo Guandu 100-101 D 10
Baiyang Dian 146-147 EF 2
Baiyanjing 146-147 A 2
Baiyu Shan 146-147 B 3
Baja 118 J 5
Baja California Norte 64-65 CD 6
Baja California Sur 64-65 D 6
Bajada, La — 108-109 E 7
Bajada Colarada 108-109 E 2
Bajada del Agrio 106-107 BC 7
Bājah 164-165 F 1
Baján [MEX] 76-77 D 9
Bajan [Mongolia] 142-143 K 2
Bajan Adraga 142-143 KL 2
Bajanaul 132-133 O 7
Bajan Char uuul 142-143 H 5
Bajan Chej = Baiyanjing 146-147 A 2
Bajanchongor 142-143 HJ 2
Bajan Choto 142-143 JK 4
Bajandaj 132-133 U 7
Bajandalaj 142-143 J 3
Bajangol [Mongolia] 142-143 K 2
Bajan Gol [TJ] 142-143 K 3
Bajan Obo 142-143 K 3
Bajan Olgi 142-143 FG 2
Bajan Öndör 142-143 H 3
Bajan Sum = Bajan 142-143 K 2
Bajanteeg 142-143 J 2
Bajan Tümen = Čojbalsan 142-143 L 2
Bajan Ulaa = Bajan Uul 142-143 H 2
Bajan Ülegei = Ölgij 142-143 FG 2
Bajan Uul [Mongolia, Dornod] 142-143 L 2
Bajan Uul [Mongolia, Dzavchan] 142-143 H 2
Bajawa 148-149 GH 8
Baj-Baj = Budge-Budge 138-139 LM 6
Bajdarackaja guba 132-133 M 4
Bajé 111 F 4
Bajeuen 150-151 AB 10
Bajī 138-139 B 3
Bajío, El — 64-65 F 7
Bajirge 136-137 L 4
Bājitpūr 141 B 3
Bajkal, ozero — 132-133 U 7
Bajkal'skij chrebet 132-133 U 6-7
Bajkal'skoje 132-133 UV 6
Bajkit 132-133 S 5
Bajkonyr 132-133 M 8
Bajmak 132-133 K 7
Bajo Baudo 92-93 D 3
Bajo Caracoles 108-109 D 6
Bajo de Cari Laufquen 108-109 E 3
Bajo de la Laguna Escondida 108-109 F 2-G 3
Bajo de la Tigra 106-107 E 7
Bajo del Gualicho 108-109 G 4
Bajo del Guanaco 108-109 E 6
Bajo de los Menucos 108-109 F 2-3
Bajo de los Tierra Colorada 108-109 F 4
Bajo del Río Seco 108-109 EF 7
Bajo Hondo [RA, Buenos Aires] 106-107 G 7
Bajo Hondo [RA, Río Negro] 106-107 D 7
Bajo Imaz 106-107 E 7
Bajo Picaso 108-109 EF 7
Bajos Hondos 108-109 E 3
Bajram-Ali 134-135 J 3
Bajšint = Chongor 142-143 L 2
Baj-Sot 132-133 S 7
Bajtag Bogd uul 142-143 G 2-3
Bakal 132-133 K 6-7
Bakala 164-165 HJ 7
Bakal'skaja kosa 126-127 F 4
Bakaly 124-125 TU 6
Bakanas 132-133 O 8-9
Bakarganj = Bāqarganj 141 B 4
Bakāriyah 166-167 KL 2
Bakčar 132-133 P 6
Bake 152-153 D 7
Bakel [SN] 164-165 B 6
Baker 50-51 T 6
Baker, CA 74-75 E 5
Baker, ID 66-67 G 3
Baker, MT 68-69 D 2
Baker, NV 74-75 FG 3
Baker, OR 64-65 C 3
Baker, Canal — 111 B 7
Baker, Mount — 66-67 C 1
Baker Foreland 56-57 ST 5
Baker Island 58-59 vw 9
Baker Lake [CDN, lake] 56-57 R 5
Baker Lake [CDN, place] 56-57 R 5
Bakersfield, CA 64-65 C 4
Bakersfield, TX 76-77 CD 7
Bakerville 174-175 G 3-4
Bakhmah, Sadd al- 136-137 L 4
Bākhtarī, Āžarbayejān-e — 134-135 EF 3
Bakhtegān, Daryācheh — 134-135 G 5
Bakhuis Gebergte 98-99 K 2
26 Bakinskij Komissarov 126-127 OP 7
Bakır çayı 136-137 B 3
Bakırdağı = Taşçı 136-137 F 3
Bakırköy, İstanbul- 136-137 C 2
Bakkafjördhur 116-117 fg 1
Bakkaflói 116-117 f 1
Bakkagerdhi 116-117 g 2
Baklanka 124-125 N 4
Bako 168-169 D 3
Bakony 118 HJ 5
Bakool 164-165 a 3
Bakres 126-127 M 4
Baksan [SU, place] 126-127 L 5
Baksan [SU, river] 126-127 L 5
Baksar = Buxar 138-139 JK 5
Baku 126-127 OP 6
Baku-Baladžary 126-127 O 6
Baku-Buzovna 126-127 P 6
Bakungan 148-149 C 6
Bakuriani 126-127 L 6
Baku-Sabunči 126-127 OP 6
Baku-Surachany 126-127 P 6
Bakwanga = Mbuji-Mayi 172 D 3
B'ala [BG] 122-123 L 4
Bala [CDN] 72-73 G 2
Bālā [TR] 136-137 E 3
Bala, Cerros de — 92-93 F 7-8
Balabac 152-153 M 2
Balabac Island 148-149 G 5
Balabac Strait 148-149 G 5
Balabaia 172 B 4
Ba'labakk 136-137 G 5-6
Balabalangan, Pulau-pulau — 148-149 G 7
Balabanovo 124-125 L 6
Balabino 126-127 G 3
Balachna 124-125 O 5
Bala-Cynwyd, PA 84 III b 1
Balad [IRQ] 136-137 L 5-6
Bal'ad [SP] 164-165 b 3
Balad'ok 132-133 Z 7
Balad Rūz 136-137 L 6
Baladžary, Baku- 126-127 O 6
Balagansk 132-133 T 7
Bālāghāt 134-135 N 6
Bālāghāt Range 140 BC 1
Bālāgī = Bhālki 140 C 1
Balaguer 120-121 H 8
Balaikarangan 152-153 J 5
Balā'im, Rā's al- 173 C 3
Balaipungut 152-153 D 5
Balaiselasa 148-149 CD 7
Balaklava [AUS] 158-159 G 6
Balaklava [SU] 126-127 F 4
Balakleja [SU, Čerkasskaja Oblast'] 126-127 H 2
Balakleja [SU, Char'kovskaja Oblast'] 126-127 H 2
Balakovo 132-133 HJ 7
Balama 171 D 6
Balambangan, Pulau — 148-149 G 5
Bālānagar 140 D 2
Balança, Serra da — 100-101 E 4
Balancán de Domínguez 86-87 P 9
Balanças, Serra das — 100-101 DE 3
Balanda 126-127 M 1
Balangan, Kepulauan — = Pulau-pulau Balabalangan 148-149 G 7
Ba Lang An, Mui — = Mui Batangan 148-149 EF 3
Balangoḍa 140 E 7
Balāngīr 134-135 N 6
Balanka 168-169 F 3
Balankanche 86-87 QR 7
Balao 96-97 B 3
Bāļāpur 138-139 F 7
Balarāmpur 138-139 L 6
Balashov = Balašov 126-127 L 1
Balašicha 124-125 LM 5-6
B'ala Slatina 122-123 K 4
Balasore 134-135 O 6
Balašov 126-127 L 1
Balat, İstanbul- 154 I a 2
Balaton 118 HJ 5
Balaurin 152-153 P 10
Balboa 64-65 b 3
Balboa Heights 64-65 b 3
Balcarce 111 E 5
Bal'cer = Krasnoarmejsk 126-127 M 1
Balchari 138-139 M 7
Balchaš 132-133 N 8
Balchaš, ozero — 132-133 NO 8
Balčik 122-123 MN 4
Balclutha 161 C 8
Balcones Escarpment 64-65 F 6-G 5
Bald Butte 66-67 D 4
Balde 106-107 D 4
Baldeo 138-139 FG 4
Bald Head 158-159 C 7
Baldhill Reservoir 68-69 GH 2
Bald Knob, AR 78-79 D 3
Bald Knob, WV 80-81 F 2
Bald Mountain 74-75 F 4
Baldock Lake 61 K 2
Baldone 124-125 DE 5
Balduck Park 84 II c 2
Baldwin, MI 70-71 H 4
Baldwin, WI 70-71 D 3
Baldwin City, KS 70-71 C 6
Baldwin Hills 83 III b 1-2
Baldwin Peninsula 58-59 F 3
Baldwinsville, NY 72-73 H 3
Baldwyn, MS 78-79 E 3
Baldy, Mount — 66-67 H 2
Baldy Peak [USA, Arizona] 64-65 DE 5
Baldy Peak [USA, New Mexico] 76-77 AB 5
Balē 164-165 N 7-8
Bâle = Basel 118 C 5
Baléa 168-169 C 2
Baleares, Islas — 120-121 H 9-K 8
Balearic Islands = Islas Baleares 120-121 H 9-K 8
Baleh, Sungei — 152-153 K 5
Baleia, Ponta da — 100-101 E 9
Baleimakam 152-153 D 7
Balej 132-133 W 7
Bāleshvara = Balasore 134-135 O 6
Balezino 124-125 T 5
Balfour [CDN] 66-67 E 1
Balfour [ZA, Kaapland] 174-175 G 7
Balfour [ZA, Transvaal] 174-175 H 4
Balfour North = Balfour 174-175 H 4
Balfour Park 170 V b 1
Balḥāf 134-135 F 8
Balham, London- 129 II b 2
Balharshāh 138-139 G 8
Bāli [IND] 138-139 D 5
Bali [RI = 15 ◁] 148-149 F 8
Bālī = Bally 138-139 M 6
Bali, Pulau — 148-149 FG 8
Bali, Selat — 152-153 L 10
Bāliguda 138-139 J 7
Baligura = Bāliguda 138-139 J 7
Balīh, Nahr — 136-137 H 4
Bālihāti 154 II a 1
Balıkesir 134-135 B 3
Balikpapan 148-149 G 7
Balik Pulau 150-151 BC 10
Baling 150-151 C 10
Balingian 152-153 K 4
Balintang Channel 148-149 H 3
Bali Sea 148-149 FG 8
Baliyā = Ballia 138-139 K 5
Baliza 102-103 F 2
Balizhuang = Beijing-Yuyuantan 155 II a 2
Balizhuang, Beijing- 155 II bc 2
Baljabbūr, Ḥāssī — 166-167 K 5
Baljennie 61 DE 4
Balkan = Dedeköy 136-137 C 3-4
Balkan Mountains 122-123 K-M 4
Balkh 134-135 K 3
Balkh Āb 134-135 K 3
Balkhash, Lake — = ozero Balchaš 132-133 NO 8
Bālkonda 140 D 1
Ballā 141 B 3
Balla Balla = Mbalabala 172 EF 6
Ballabgarh 138-139 F 3
Balladonia 158-159 D 6
Ballarat 158-159 H 7
Ballard, Lake — 158-159 D 5
Ballard Pond 85 II b 3
Baḷḷāri = Bellary 134-135 M 7
Ballé 164-165 C 5
Ballena, Punta — 106-107 K 5
Ballenas, Canal de — 86-87 D 3
Ballenero, Canal 108-109 D 10
Balleny Islands 53 C 17
Ballesteros 106-107 F 4
Ballia 138-139 K 5
Balliguda = Bāliguda 138-139 J 7
Ballimore 160 J 4
Ballina [AUS] 158-159 K 5
Ballina [IRL] 119 B 4
Ballinger, TX 76-77 DE 7
Ballivián = Fortín Ballivián 102-103 AB 5
Ballona Creek 83 III b 2
Ball's Pyramid 158-159 L 6
Ballstad 116-117 EF 3
Bally 138-139 M 6
Bally Bridge 154 II b 2
Ballygunge, Calcutta- 154 II b 2
Ballygunge Park 154 II b 2
Ballymena 119 C 4
Balmaceda 108-109 CD 5
Balmaceda, Cerro — 108-109 C 8
Balmaceda, Sierra — 108-109 DE 9
Balmain, Sydney- 161 I b 2
Balmertown 62 C 2
Balmoral [GB] 119 E 3
Balmoral [ZA] 174-175 H 3
Balmorhea, TX 76-77 C 7
Balmumcu, İstanbul- 154 I b 2
Balnearia 106-107 F 3
Balneario El Condor 108-109 H 3
Balneario La Barre 106-107 L 4
Balneario Orense 106-107 H 7
Balod 138-139 H 7
Baloda Bāzār 138-139 J 7
Balōdbāzār = Baloda Bāzār 138-139 J 7
Balombo 172 B 4
Balonne River 158-159 J 5
Bālōtra 138-139 D 5
Balovale 172 D 4
Balqā, Al- 136-137 F 6-7
Balrāmpur 138-139 HJ 4
Balrāmpur = Balarāmpur 138-139 L 6
Balranald 158-159 H 6
Balsa 106-107 G 5
Balsāḍ = Bulsār 138-139 D 7
Balsar = Bulsār 138-139 D 7
Balsas [BR] 92-93 K 6
Balsas [MEX] 86-87 KL 8-9
Balsas [PE] 96-97 BC 5
Balsas, Rio — 64-65 F 8
Balsas, Rio das — 100-101 B 4
Balsas ó Mezcala, Río — 86-87 KL 8-9
Balsfjord 116-117 HJ 3
Balta, ND 68-69 FG 1
Balta [RO] 122-123 MN 3
Balta [SU] 126-127 D 3
Baltasi 124-125 RS 5
Bălți = Bel'cy 126-127 CD 3
Baltic Port = Paldiski 124-125 DE 4
Baltic Sea 114-115 L 5-M 4
Baltijsk 118 J 1
Baltijskoje more 124-125 B 6-C 4
Baltijsko-Ladožskij ustup 124-125 E-J 4
Balṭīm 173 B 2
Baltimore, MD 64-65 L 4
Baltimore [GB] 119 B 6
Baltimore [ZA] 174-175 H 2
Baltistān 134-135 M 3-4
Bāltīt 134-135 L 3
Balūchestān, Sīstān va — 134-135 H 4-J 5
Balūchistān 134-135 J 5-K 4
Bāluhāti 154 II a 2
Balui, Sungei — 152-153 KL 4
Bālumāth 138-139 K 6
Balurghāt 138-139 M 5
Balvi 124-125 F 5
Balwyn, Melbourne- 161 II c 1
Balya 136-137 B 3
Balyanā, Al- 164-165 L 3
Balygyčan 132-133 d 5
Balykši 126-127 PQ 3
Balyul = Nēpāl 134-135 NO 5
Balzar 96-97 B 2
Bam 134-135 H 5
Bama 164-165 G 6
Bamaco = Bamako 164-165 C 6
Bamaji Lake 62 D 2
Bamako 164-165 C 6
Bamba [EAK] 171 D 3
Bamba [RMM] 164-165 D 5
Bamba [ZRE] 172 C 3
Bambamarca 96-97 B 5
Bambara-Maoundé 168-169 E 2
Bambari 164-165 J 7
Bamberg 118 E 4
Bamberg, SC 80-81 F 4
Bambesa 172 E 1
Bambinga 172 C 2
Bamboesbaai 174-175 BC 6
Bamboi 168-169 E 3
Bambouk 164-165 B 6
Bamboulos, Mount — 168-169 H 4
Bambuí 92-93 K 8-9
Bamenda 164-165 G 7
Bamenda Highlands 168-169 H 4
Bamfield 66-67 A 1
Bamingui 164-165 HJ 7
Bamingui, Parc national de la — 164-165 HJ 7
Bamingui-Bangoran 164-165 HJ 7
Bāmiyān 134-135 K 4
Bamnet Narung 150-151 C 5
Bampu, Sungai — 152-153 C 4
Bampūr, Rūd-e 134-135 HJ 5
Ba mTsho 142-143 G 5
Bamūdā = Garhākota 138-139 G 6
Bamum = Foumban 164-165 G 7
Bamungu 171 B 2
Bana [MW] 171 C 6
Ba Na [VN] 150-151 FG 5
Baña, Punta de la — 120-121 H 8
Banabuiú, Açude de — 100-101 E 3
Banabuiú, Rio — 100-101 E 3
Banāder va Jazāyer-e Baḥr-e 'Omān = 6 ◁ 134-135 H 5
Banāder va Jazāyer-e Khalīj-e Fārs = 5 ◁ 134-135 G 5
Banadia 92-93 E 3
Bañado del Río Saladillo 106-107 F 4
Bañado de Medina 106-107 KL 4
Bañado de Rocha 106-107 K 3
Bañados de Izozog 92-93 G 8
Bañados de la Amarga 106-107 EF 5
Bañados del Atuel 106-107 D 5-6
Bañados del Chadileuvú 106-107 D 6
Bañados del Viñalito 104-105 E 9
Bañados Otuquis 104-105 G 6
Banagi 171 C 3
Banahwāla Ṭoba 138-139 D 3
Banāi 138-139 K 7
Baṇāīgaḍa = Bonaigarh 138-139 K 7
Banalia 172 DE 1
Banam 150-151 E 7
Banamana, Lago — 174-175 KL 2
Banamba 168-169 D 2
Banana 172 B 3
Banana Islands 168-169 B 3
Bananal 102-103 K 5
Bananal, Ilha do — 92-93 J 7
Bananeiras 92-93 M 6
Bāṇapura = Bānpur 138-139 K 8
Ban ar-Ramād, Wādī — 166-167 F 3
Banās 138-139 F 4
Banās Kāntha 138-139 CD 5
Banat 122-123 J 3
Bānatmyô 141 E 4
Banatului, Munții — 122-123 JK 3
Banawaja, Pulau — 152-153 N 9
Ban 'Aysh, Ḥāssī — 166-167 J 4
Banaz 136-137 C 3
Banaz çayı 136-137 C 3
Ban Ban 150-151 D 3
Ban Bat = Buôn Bat 150-151 G 6
Ban Bu 150-151 E 2
Ban Bung 150-151 C 6
Ban Bu'ng Sai 150-151 F 5
Banbury 119 F 5
Banbury Reservoir 129 II b 1
Banc du Geyser 172 J 4
Banco, El — 92-93 E 3
Banco Central 100-101 E 8
Banco Chinchorro 64-65 J 8
Banco Piedras 106-107 J 5
Bancoran Island 152-153 N 2
Bancroft 72-73 H 2
Bancroft, ID 66-67 H 4
Banḍā [IND, Madhya Pradesh] 138-139 G 5-6
Bānda [IND, Uttar Pradesh] 138-139 H 5
Banda = Sainte-Marie 172 B 2
Banda, Kepulauan — 148-149 J 7
Banda, La — 111 D 3
Banda, Punta — 64-65 C 5
Banda Aceh 148-149 BC 5
Bandahara, Gunung — 152-153 BC 4
Banda-Lungwa, Kinshasa- 170 IV a 1-2
Bandama 164-165 CD 7
Bandama Blanc 168-169 D 3
Bandama Rouge 168-169 D 4
Bandamūrlangkā = Bandamūrlanka 140 EF 2
Bandamūrlanka 140 EF 2
Ban Dan Na Lao 150-151 EF 5
Bandar [IND] 134-135 N 7
Bandar [Nēpāl] 138-139 H 3
Bandāra = Bandar 134-135 N 7
Bandar 'Abbās 134-135 H 5
Bandārawela 140 E 7
Bandar Baharu 150-151 C 10
Bāndarban 141 C 4
Bandar Banhā = Banhā 173 B 2
Bandar-e Anzalī 134-135 FG 3
Bandar-e Būshehr 134-135 G 5
Bandar-e Chāh Bahār 134-135 HJ 5
Bandar-e Khomeynī 134-135 FG 4
Bandar-e Lengeh 134-135 GH 5
Bandar-e Māhshar 136-137 N 7
Bandar-e Shāh 134-135 G 3
Bandar Maharani = Muar 148-149 D 6
Bandar Penggaram = Batu Pahat 148-149 D 6
Bandarpulau 152-153 C 4
Bandarpūnch 138-139 G 2
Bandar Rompin = Kuala Rompin 150-151 D 11
Bandar Seri Begawan 148-149 FG 5-6
Banda Sea 148-149 JK 8
Bandawe 172 F 4
Bande Bābā 134-135 J 4
Bandeira 100-101 D 8
Bandeira, Pico da — 92-93 L 9
Bandeirante 92-93 JK 7
Bandeirantes 102-103 GH 5
Bandelierkop 174-175 H 2
Bandelier National Monument 76-77 A 5
Band-e Qir 136-137 N 7
Bandera 111 D 3
Bandera, TX 76-77 E 8
Banderaló 106-107 F 5
Banderas 76-77 B 7
Banderas, Bahía de — 64-65 E 7
Bānd-e Turkestān = Tirbande Turkestān 134-135 JK 3
Bandiagara 164-165 D 6
Bandipur [IND, Karnataka] 140 C 5
Bandipur [IND, West Bengal] 154 II b 1
Bandırma 134-135 B 2
Bandjarmasin = Banjarmasin 148-149 F 7
Bandjermassin = Banjarmasin 148-149 F 7
Bandon, OR 66-67 A 4
Bandon [IRL] 119 B 6
Ban Đôn [VN] 150-151 FG 6
Ban Don, Ao — 150-151 B 8
Ban Dong Khaang 150-151 E 4
B'andovan 126-127 O 7
Bāndra 134-135 L 7
Bānduān 138-139 L 6
Bandundu [ZRE, administrative unit] 172 C 2-3
Bandundu [ZRE, place] 172 C 2
Bandung 148-149 E 8
Band Vīrāh 138-139 AB 5
Bāneh 136-137 L 4-5
Banes 64-65 L 7
Bañeza, La — 120-121 DE 7
Banff [CDN] 56-57 NO 7
Banff [GB] 119 E 3
Banff National Park 56-57 NO 7
Banfield, Lomas de Zamora- 110 III b 2
Banfora 164-165 D 6
Bang, Kompong — 150-151 E 6
Banga 168-169 H 3
Bāngaduni Island 138-139 M 7
Bangāl Khāṛī = Bay of Bengal 134-135 N-P 7
Bangalore 134-135 M 8
Banganapalle 140 D 3
Baṅganāpalli = Banganapalle 140 D 3
Bangangté 168-169 H 4
Bangaon 138-139 M 6
Bangap, Lau — 150-151 AB 11
Bangārapet 140 D 4
Bangarmaū 138-139 H 4
Bangarpet = Bangārapet 140 D 4
Bangassou 164-165 J 8
Bangassu = Bangassou 164-165 J 8
Bang Fai, Se — 150-151 E 4
Bangfou = Bengbu 142-143 M 5
Banggadeṇiya 140 D 7
Banggai 148-149 H 7
Banggai, Kepulauan — 148-149 H 7
Banggai, Pulau — 148-149 H 7
Banggala Au = Bay of Bengal 134-135 N-P 7
Banggi, Pulau — 148-149 G 5
Banghāzī 164-165 HJ 2
Bang Hieng, Se — 150-151 E 4
Bangil 152-153 K 9
Bangka, Pulau — 148-149 E 7
Bangka, Selat — 148-149 E 7
Bangkalan 152-153 N 8
Bangkaru, Pulau — 152-153 B 4-5
Bang Khonthi 150-151 B 6
Bangkinang 148-149 D 6
Bangko 148-149 D 7
Bangkok = Krung Thep 148-149 D 4
Bangkok, Bay of — = Ao Krung Thep 150-151 C 6
Bangkulu, Pulau — 152-153 P 6
Bangladesh 134-135 OP 6
Bang Lamung 150-151 C 6
Bang Len 150-151 BC 5-6
Bang Mun Nak 150-151 C 4
Bangolo 168-169 D 4
Bangor 119 DE 5
Bangor, ME 64-65 N 3
Bangor, MI 70-71 G 4
Bangor, PA 72-73 J 4
Bang Pahan = Phachi 150-151 C 5
Bang Pa-in 150-151 C 5
Bang Pakong 150-151 C 6
Bang Pakong, Mae Nam — 150-151 C 6
Bāngriposi 138-139 L 6
Bangs, TX 76-77 E 7
Bang Saphan 150-151 B 7
Bangu, Rio de Janeiro- 102-103 L 5
Bangui [RCA] 164-165 H 8
Bangui [RP] 148-149 GH 3
Bangunpurba 152-153 C 4
Bangweulu, Lake — 172 EF 4
Banhā 173 B 2
Ban Hin Heup 150-151 D 3
Ban Hong 150-151 B 3
Ban Huei Sai 150-151 C 2
Banī [DOM] 64-65 M 8
Bani [HV] 168-169 E 2
Bani [RMM] 164-165 C 6
Banī, Jabal — 164-165 C 2-3
Banī Abbās 164-165 D 2
Baniara 148-149 NO 8
Banī Khaddāsh 166-167 LM 3
Banī Lant 166-167 D 2
Banilouli 168-169 F 2
Banī Mallāl 164-165 C 2
Banī Mazār 164-165 L 3
Baning, Kampung — 150-151 D 10
Banī Sa 'd 136-137 L 6
Banī Ṣāf 166-167 F 2
Banī Shuqayr 173 B 4
Ban Island 58-59 L 7
Banī Suwayf 164-165 L 3
Banī Tajīt 166-167 E 3
Banī Wanīf 164-165 D 2
Bāniyāchung 141 B 3
Bāniyās [SYR, Al-Lādiqīyah] 134-135 D 3
Bāniyās [SYR, Dimashq] 136-137 FG 6
Banja Luka 122-123 G 3
Banjar 148-149 E 8
Banjarmasin 148-149 F 7
Banjermassin = Banjarmasin 148-149 F 7
Banjia 141 F 4
Banjo = Banyo 164-165 G 7
Banjul 164-165 A 6
Banjuwangi = Banyuwangi 148-149 F 8
Banjuwedang 152-153 L 9-10
Bank 126-127 O 7
Bānka [IND] 138-139 L 5
Banka = Pulau Bangka 148-149 E 7
Banka Banka 158-159 F 3
Bankaner = Wānkāner 138-139 C 6
Ban Karai 150-151 F 4
Bankass 168-169 E 2
Ban Ken = Ban Kheun 150-151 C 2
Ban Keng That Hai 150-151 EF 4
Ban Khai 150-151 C 6
Ban Khamphô 150-151 F 5
Ban Kha Panang 150-151 F 6
Ban Kheng = Ban Na Kheng 150-151 EF 4
Ban Kheun 150-151 C 2
Ban Khôk Kong 150-151 E 5
Bānki 138-139 K 6
Banko 168-169 D 2
Ban Kruat 150-151 D 5
Banks, ID 66-67 E 3
Banks, OR 66-67 B 3
Banks, Cape — 161 I b 3
Banksian River 62 B 1
Banks Island [AUS] 158-159 H 2
Banks Island [CDN, British Columbia] 56-57 KL 7
Banks Island [CDN, District of Franklin] 56-57 MN 3
Banks Islands 158-159 N 2
Banks Lake 66-67 D 2
Banks Peninsula 158-159 O 8
Banks Strait 158-159 J 8
Banks Strait = MacClure Strait 56-57 MN 2-3
Bankstown, Sydney- 161 I a 2
Bānkura 138-139 L 6
Ban Laem 150-151 BC 6
Ban Lat Hane 150-151 CD 2
Ban Mae = Mae Sariang 150-151 AB 3
Ban Mahdī 166-167 KL 1
Banmau 148-149 C 2
Banmauk 141 D 3
Ban Me Thuôt 148-149 E 4
Ban Mi 150-151 C 5
Ban Mo 150-151 C 5
Ban Mouong = Ban Muong 150-151 C 3
Ban Muang 150-151 D 4
Ban Muang = Pong 148-149 CD 3
Ban Mu'ang Ba 150-151 E 4
Ban Muong 150-151 C 3
Bannack, MT 66-67 G 3
Ban Na Kheng 150-151 EF 4
Ban Na Le 150-151 C 3
Ban Na Lu'ong 150-151 E 4
Ban Nam Bac 150-151 D 2
Ban Namone 150-151 D 3
Ban Nam Phao 150-151 C 3
Ban Nam Tao 150-151 C 4
Ban Nam Tia 150-151 D 3
Bannang Sata 150-151 C 9
Bannang Star = Bannang Sata 150-151 C 9
Ban Na Phao 150-151 E 4
Ban Na San 150-151 B 8
Ban Na Song 150-151 E 4
Ban Nathon 150-151 F 4
Banner, WY 68-69 C 3
Bannerman Town 88-89 HJ 2
Banning, CA 74-75 E 6
Banningville = Bandundu 172 C 2
Ban Nin Lan 150-151 E 3
Bannockburn [CDN] 72-73 GH 2
Bannockburn [ZW] 172 EF 6
Bannock Range 66-67 G 4
Ban Nong Kheun 150-151 D 3
Bannū 134-135 KL 4
Bano 138-139 K 6
Baños [EC] 96-97 B 2
Baños [PE] 96-97 D 6
Baños, Los — 96-97 F 11
Baños de Chihuio 108-109 CD 3
Baños del Flaco 106-107 B 5
Baños de Longaví 106-107 B 6
Baños El Sosneado 106-107 BC 5
Ban Pa Kha 150-151 F 5
Ban Pak Hop 150-151 C 3
Ban Pak Sang 150-151 D 3
Ban Pak Thone 150-151 F 5
Ban Phai 148-149 D 3
Ban Pho 150-151 C 6
Banphot Phisai 150-151 B 5
Ban Phu 150-151 D 4
Ban Phya Lat 150-151 D 2
Ban Pong 150-151 B 6
Ban Poung 150-151 E 4
Bānpur 138-139 K 8
Banquereau Bank 63 GH 5
Ban Rai 150-151 B 5
Ban Sa Ang 150-151 EF 4
Ban Sa Pout 150-151 C 2
Bańsavāḍā = Bānswāda 140 CD 1
Bānsbāria 138-139 LM 6
Bānsda 138-139 D 7
Bansdīh 138-139 JK 5
Ban Se Mat 150-151 F 6
Bānsgāñv = Bānsgaon 138-139 J 4
Bānsgaon 138-139 J 4
Bānsi [IND → Gonda] 138-139 J 4
Bānsi [IND ↓ Jhānsi] 138-139 G 5
Bansihāri 138-139 M 5
Ban Si Nhô 150-151 E 4
Banská Bystrica 118 J 4
Banská Štiavnica 118 J 4
Ban Sông Khôn 150-151 E 3
Ban Sot 150-151 E 3
Ban Soukhouma 150-151 E 5
Bānsur 138-139 F 4
Bāṅsvāṛā = Bānswāra 138-139 E 6
Bānswāda 140 CD 1
Bānswāra 138-139 E 6
Banta 138-139 L 7

266 Baie

Bantaeng 148-149 GH 8
Ban Tak 150-151 B 4
Bantam = Banten 148-149 E 8
Ban Taphane 150-151 E 5
Ban Ta Viang 150-151 D 3
Banteai Srei 150-151 D 6
Banten 148-149 E 8
Banten, Teluk — 152-153 G 8
Ban Thac Du'ot 150-151 F 5
Banthali = Vanthli 138-139 C 7
Ban Thieng 150-151 CD 3
Bāntra, Howrah- 154 II ab 2
Ban Tring = Buôn Hô 150-151 G 6
Bantry 119 B 6
Bantry Bay 119 AB 6
Bantul 152-153 J 9-10
Bāntva = Bāntwa 138-139 BC 7
Bāntwa 138-139 BC 7
Banūd 166-167 G 3
Ban Vang 150-151 C 3
Ban Waeng = Phong Thong 150-151 DE 4
Ban Xiêng Kok 150-151 C 2
Banyak, Pulau-pulau — 148-149 C 6
Banyak Islands = Pulau-pulau Banyak 148-149 C 6
Ban Yen Nhân 150-151 EF 2
Banyin 141 E 5
Banyo 164-165 G 7
Banyumas 152-153 H 9
Banyuwangi 148-149 F 8
Banzaburō-dake 144-145 M 5
Banzare Land 53 C 13
Ban Zīriq 166-167 F 4
Banzystad = Yasanyama 172 D 1
Banzyville = Yasanyama 172 D 1
Banzyville, Collines des — 172 D 1
Bao'an [TJ, Guangdong] 146-147 DE 10
Bao'an [TJ, Shaanxi] 146-147 BC 4
Baode 146-147 L 4
Baodi 146-147 F 2
Baoding 142-143 LM 4
Baofeng 146-147 D 5
Bao Ha 150-151 E 1
Baohe = Mengla 150-151 C 2
Baohu Jiao 146-147 C 11
Baoji 142-143 K 5
Baojidun = Badajia 146-147 H 5
Baojing 142-143 K 6
Baokang 146-147 C 6
Bao Lôc 150-151 FG 7
Bao Lôc, Đeo — 150-151 F 7
Baoqing 142-143 P 2
Baoshan [TJ, Shanghai] 146-147 H 6
Baoshan [TJ, Yunnan] 142-143 HJ 6
Baoting 150-151 G 3
Baotou 142-143 KL 3
Baoulé 164-165 C 6
Baoying 142-143 M 5
Bāp 138-139 D 4
Bapatlā 140 E 3
Baptai 124-125 DE 6
Baptiste 72-73 GH 2
Bapuyu 152-153 KL 7
Bāqarganj 141 B 4
Bāqīr, Jabal — 136-137 F 8
Baqqah 168-169 B 1
Ba'qūbah 134-135 EF 4
Baquedano 111 BC 2
Bar [SU] 126-127 C 2
Bar [YU] 122-123 H 4
Bara [IND, Rājasthān] 138-139 D 4
Bāra [IND, Uttar Pradesh] 138-139 H 5
Bara [IND, West Bengal] 154 II a 1
Bara [WAN] 168-169 H 3
Baraawe 164-165 N 8
Bāra Banki 138-139 H 4
Barabinsk 132-133 OP 6
Barabinskaja step' 132-133 O 6-7
Barābir, 'Uqlat — 166-167 E 4
Baraboo, WI 70-71 F 4
Baracaldo 120-121 F 7
Barachois 63 DE 3
Baracoa 88-89 J 4
Baradero 106-107 H 4
Baraga, MI 70-71 F 2
Baragaḍa = Bargarh 138-139 J 7
Bārāganul 122-123 M 3
Baragwanath, Johannesburg- 170 V a 2
Baragwanath Aerodrome 170 V a 2
Bārah 164-165 L 6
Baraḥānuddīn 141 B 4
Barahī = Barhi 134-135 O 6
Barahona [DOM] 64-65 M 8
Barai 150-151 E 6
Barāīj, Al- 136-137 G 5
Barail Range 141 C 3
Baraily = Bareli 138-139 G 6
Barajas, Aeropuerto — 113 III b 2
Barajas, Madrid- 113 III b 2
Barājīl, Al- 170 II a 1
Barāk 141 C 3
Barak = Karkamış 136-137 G 4
Baraka = Barka 164-165 M 5
Barākar 138-139 L 5
Baraki [AFG] 134-135 K 4
Baraki [ET] 170 I b 2
Barakram, Ḥāssī — 166-167 J 3
Baralaba 158-159 JK 4
Baram, Batang — 152-153 L 3-4
Barama 141 B 2
Bārāmati 140 B 1
Barāmba 138-139 K 7
Bārāmūlā 134-135 L 4
Bārān 138-139 F 5
Baranagar 154 II b 2
Barā Nikōbār = Great Nicobar 134-135 P 9
Barā Nikōbār = Little Nicobar 134-135 P 9
Baranoa 94-95 D 2
Baranof, AK 58-59 v 8
Baranof Island 56-57 JK 6
Baranoviči 124-125 EF 7
Barão de Cocais 102-103 L 3-4
Barão de Grajaú 92-93 L 6
Barão de Melgaço 104-105 F 3
Barão de Melgaço [BR, place] 102-103 E 2
Baraot = Baraut 138-139 F 3
Baraqua, Sierra de — 94-95 FG 2
Barārī = Borāri 138-139 L 5
Barāsat 154 II b 1
Barāsiā = Berasia 138-139 F 6
Barataria Bay 78-79 DE 6
Bar'atino 124-125 K 6
Barauaná, Serra — 98-99 H 3-4
Baraut 138-139 F 3
Baraya 94-95 D 6
Barbacena 92-93 L 9
Barbacoas [CO, Guajira] 94-95 E 2
Barbacoas [CO, Nariño] 94-95 B 7
Barbacoas [YV] 94-95 H 3
Barbados 64-65 OP 9
Barbalha 100-101 E 4
Barbar 164-165 L 5
Barbara Lake 70-71 G 1
Barbastro 120-121 GH 7
Barberspan 174-175 F 4
Barbers Point 78-79 c 2
Barberton 172 F 7
Barberton, OH 72-73 F 4
Barborā = Berbera 164-165 O 6
Barbosa [CO, Antioquia] 94-95 D 4
Barbosa [CO, Boyacá] 92-93 E 3
Barbosa Ferraz 102-103 F 6
Barbourville, KY 72-73 DE 6
Barbūshī, Ḥāssī — 166-167 E 5
Barca = Al-Marj 164-165 J 2
Barca, La — 86-87 J 7
Barcaldine 158-159 HJ 4
Barce = Al-Marj 164-165 J 2
Barcellona Pozzo di Gotto 122-123 F 6
Barcelona [E] 120-121 J 8
Barcelona [YV] 92-93 G 2
Barcelonnette 120-121 L 6
Barcelos [BR] 92-93 G 5
Barchama Guda 171 D 2
Barchöl Choto = Bar köl 142-143 G 3
Barco 94-95 E 3
Barco, El — [PE] 96-97 A 4
Barcoo River 158-159 H 4-5
Barcroft, Lake — 82 II a 2
Barda [SU, Azerbajdžanskaja SSR] 126-127 N 6
Barda [SU, Rossijskaja SFSR] 124-125 U 5
Barda del Medio 106-107 CD 7
Bardaï 164-165 H 4
Bardarash 136-137 K 4
Bardas Blancas 106-107 BC 5
Bardawīl, Sabkhat al- 173 C 2
Barddhāmān = Burdwān 134-135 O 6
Bardejov 118 K 4
Bardeliere, Lac la — 62 OP 1
Bárdharbunga 116-117 e 2
Bardīs 173 B 4
Bardīyah 164-165 K 2
Bardiz 136-137 K 2
Bārdoli 138-139 D 7
Bardstown, KY 70-71 H 7
Barduba 64-65 O 8
Bardwell, KY 78-79 E 2
Baré 168-169 E 2
Bareilly 134-135 MN 5
Barela 138-139 GH 6
Bareli 138-139 G 6
Barēlī = Bareilly 134-135 MN 5
Barentsburg 116-117 jk 5
Barents Island = Barentsøya 116-117 l 5
Barentsøya 116-117 l 5
Barents Sea 132-133 D-J 2-3
Barentu 164-165 M 5
Barfleur, Pointe de — 120-121 G 4
Barga [TJ] 142-143 M 2
Bargaon 138-139 K 6
Bargarh 138-139 J 7
Barguzin 132-133 UV 7
Barguzinskij chrebet 132-133 U 7-V 6
Bārh 138-139 K 5
Barhaḍ = Berar 138-139 F 7
Barhaj 138-139 J 4
Barhampura = Berhampur 134-135 NO 7
Barhār = Berar 138-139 F 7
Bar Harbor, ME 72-73 M 2
Barhi [IND, Bihār] 134-135 O 6
Bārhi [IND, Madhya Pradesh] 138-139 H 6
Bari [I] 122-123 G 5
Bāri [IND] 138-139 F 4
Bari [SP] 164-165 bc 1
Baria = Devgad Bāria 138-139 DE 6
Baricho 171 DE 3
Barī Dihing = Burhi Dihing 141 D 2
Bārī Doāb 138-139 D 2
Barika = Bārīkah 166-167 J 2
Bārīkah 166-167 J 2
Barīkot 138-139 J 3
Barillas 86-87 P 10
Bariloche, San Carlos de — 111 B 6
Barīm 134-135 E 8
Barima 94-95 L 4
Barima, Río — 94-95 L 3
Barinas [YV, administrative unit] 94-95 FG 3
Barinas [YV, place] 92-93 EF 3
Bārind 138-139 M 5
Baring, IA 70-71 D 5
Baring, Cape — 56-57 MN 3
Baringo, Lake — 171 D 2
Barinitas 94-95 F 3
Bario 152-153 L 4
Baripāda 138-139 L 6-7
Bariri 102-103 H 5
Bārīs 173 B 5
Bari Sādri 138-139 E 5
Barisāl 134-135 OP 6
Barisan, Pegunungan — 152-153 D 6-E 8
Barīt, Al- 136-137 K 7
Barito 148-149 F 7
Bāriyā = Devgad Bāria 138-139 DE 6
Barka [ETH] 164-165 M 5
Barkā' [Oman] 134-135 H 6
Barka = Al-Marj 164-165 J 2
Barka, Ain el — = 'Ayn al-Barqah 166-167 C 6
Barkāgāṅv = Barkāgaon 138-139 K 6
Barkāgaon 138-139 K 6
Barkaïna 168-169 E 1
Barkal 141 C 4
Barkan, Râs-e — = Ra's-e Bahrgān 136-137 N 7-8
Barkāt, Al- 166-167 M 7
Barke = Barkha 138-139 H 2
Barker 106-107 H 6
Barkerville 60 G 3
Barkha 138-139 H 2
Barkhān 138-139 B 3
Barkīn 166-167 E 3
Barking, London- 129 II c 1
Barkingside, London- 129 II c 1
Bark Lake 62 K 3
Barkley, Lake — 78-79 EF 2
Barkley Sound 66-67 A 1
Barkly East = Barkly-Oos 174-175 G 6
Barkly-Oos 174-175 G 6
Barkly-Pas 174-175 G 6
Barkly Pass = Barkly-Pas 174-175 G 6
Barkly Tableland 158-159 FG 3
Barkly-Wes 174-175 F 5
Barkly West = Barkly-Wes 174-175 F 5
Bar köl [TJ, lake] 142-143 G 3
Bar Köl [TJ, place] 142-143 G 3
Bark Point 70-71 E 2
Barla dağı 136-137 D 3-4
Bar-le-Duc 120-121 K 4
Barlee, Lake — 158-159 C 5
Barletta 122-123 G 5
Barlovento, Islas de — 64-65 OP 8-9
Barmbek, Hamburg- 130 I b 1
Bāṛmēr 134-135 L 5
Barmera 158-159 H 6
Barmhān 138-139 G 6
Barnabus, WV 80-81 EF 2
Barnagar 138-139 E 6
Barnāla 138-139 E 2
Barnard, KS 68-69 GH 6
Barnato 160 G 3
Barnaul 132-133 P 7
Barnegat 61 C 3
Barnegat Bay 72-73 JK 5
Barne Glacier 53 A 17-18
Barnes, London- 129 II a 2
Barnesville, GA 80-81 DE 4
Barnesville, MN 68-69 H 2
Barnesville, OH 72-73 F 4-5
Barnet, London- 129 II b 1
Barney Top 74-75 GH 4
Barnhart, TX 76-77 D 7
Barnsdall, OK 76-77 FG 4
Barnstable, MA 72-73 L 4
Barnstaple 119 D 6
Barnwell, SC 80-81 F 4
Baro 164-165 F 7
Baroda 174-175 F 7
Baroda = Vadōdarā 134-135 L 6
Baroe 174-175 F 7
Barōṅgā Kyūnmya 148-149 B 3
Barotirê, Reserva Florestal — 98-99 MN 8
Barouda, Hassi — = Ḥāssī Bārudah 166-167 GH 5
Barpeta 134-135 P 5
Barqa = Al-Marj 164-165 J 2
Bārqa = Bārqah 166-167 C 2
Barqah [LAR] 164-165 J 2
Bārqah [MA] 166-167 C 2
Barqah, 'Ain al- 166-167 M 7
Barqah, Jabal al- 173 C 5
Barqat al-Baḥrīyah 164-165 JK 2
Barqat al-Bayḍā' 164-165 HJ 2-3
Barquisimeto 92-93 EF 2-3
Barra [BR, Bahia] 92-93 L 7
Barra [BR, Piauí] 100-101 D 2
Barra [BR, Rio Grande do Sul] 106-107 LM 4
Barra [GB] 119 C 3
Barra, Ponta da — 174-175 L 2
Barraba 158-159 K 6
Barra Bonita 102-103 H 5
Barraca da Boca 98-99 MN 5
Barracão [BR, Rio Grande do Sul] 106-107 M 1
Barracão [BR, Santa Catarina] 102-103 F 7
Barragão de Libertade 104-105 F 3
Barracão do Barreto 92-93 H 6
Barracão São José 98-99 K 9
Barracas [BR] 98-99 F 9
Barracas, Buenos Aires- 110 III b 1
Barra da Estiva 100-101 D 7
Barra da Tijuca, Rio de Janeiro- 110 I ab 3
Barra de Icaparra 102-103 J 6
Barra de Santa Rosa 100-101 FG 4
Barra de São Francisco 100-101 D 10
Barra de São João 102-103 LM 5
Barra do Bugres 92-93 H 7-8
Barra do Corda 92-93 KL 6
Barra do Garças 92-93 J 8
Barra do Mendes 100-101 CD 6
Barra do Piraí 102-103 KL 5
Barra do Prata 100-101 B 6
Barra do Quaraí 106-107 J 3
Barra do Ribeiro 106-107 M 3
Barra do São Manuel 92-93 H 6
Barra Falsa, Ponta da — 174-175 L 2
Barra Funda, São Paulo- 110 II b 2
Barrage 164-165 C 6
Barrage de Gatun = Presa de Gatún 64-65 ab 2
Barragem do Guarapiranga 110 II a 3
Barragem do Rio Grande 110 II a 3
Barrage Sansanding 168-169 D 2
Barra Head 119 BC 3
Barra Islands 119 C 3
Barra Longa 102-103 L 4
Barra Mansa 102-103 KL 5
Barranca [PE] 92-93 D 5
Barranca [RCH] 96-97 BC 7
Barrancabermeja 92-93 E 3
Barrancas [RA, Neuquén] 106-107 BC 6
Barrancas [RA, Santa Fe] 106-107 G 4
Barrancas [YV, Barinas] 94-95 F 3
Barrancas [YV, Monagas] 92-93 G 3
Barrancas, Río — 106-107 BC 6
Barrancas Santa Rita 94-95 F 2
Barranco Branco 102-103 D 4
Barranco de Guadalupe 86-87 H 2
Barranco de Loba 94-95 DE 3
Barrancoso, Arroyo — 106-107 G 4
Barranqueras 111 DE 3
Barranquilla 92-93 DE 2
Barranquitas 94-95 E 3
Barras 100-101 C 3
Barra Seca 100-101 E 10
Barraute 62 N 2
Barra Velha 111 G 3
Barre, VT 72-73 K 2
Barre, Wilkes —, PA 64-65 L 3
Barreal 106-107 C 3
Barreal, El — 106-107 DE 2
Barreiras 92-93 KL 7
Barreirinha 92-93 H 5
Barreirinhas 92-93 L 5
Barreiro 120-121 C 9
Barreiros 92-93 MN 6
Barren Grounds 56-57 O 4-S 5
Barren Islands 58-59 LM 7
Barrenland = Barren Grounds 56-57 O 4-S 5
Barren Sage Plains 66-67 E 4
Barreras Blancas, Altiplano — 108-109 E 8-F 7
Barretos 92-93 K 9
Barrhead 60 K 2
Barrie 56-57 UV 9
Barrie Island 62 K 3
Barrientos 91 I b 1
Barrière 60 GH 4
Barrington, IL 70-71 F 4
Barrington, NJ 84 III c 2
Barrington, Mount — 158-159 K 6
Barrington Lake 61 HJ 2
Barro [BR] 100-101 E 4
Barro [Guinea Bissau] 168-169 B 2
Barrocas 100-101 E 6
Barro Colorado, Isla — 64-65 b 2
Barron, WI 70-71 DE 3
Barros, Lagoa dos — 106-107 M 2
Barros, Tierra de — 120-121 D 9
Barros Arana, Cerro — 108-109 CD 4
Barros Cassal 106-107 L 2
Barroterán 76-77 D 9
Barro Vermelho 100-101 E 5
Barrow, AK 56-57 E 3
Barrow [IRL] 119 C 5
Barrow [RA] 106-107 G 7
Barrow, Point — 56-57 EF 3
Barrow Creek 158-159 FG 4
Barrow in Furness 119 E 4
Barrow Island 158-159 BC 4
Barrows 61 H 4
Barrow Strait 56-57 RS 3
Barru 152-153 N 8
Barrudugsum 138-139 K 3
Barrydale 174-175 D 7
Barrys Bay 62 N 4
Barşā' 136-137 H 4
Barsakel mes, ostrov — 132-133 KL 8
Barsaloi 172 G 1
Barsalpur = Birsilpur 138-139 D 3
Barşatas 132-133 O 8
Bārshī = Bārsi 134-135 M 7
Bārsi 134-135 M 7
Bārsi Tākli 138-139 F 7
Barstow, CA 64-65 C 4-5
Barstow, TX 76-77 C 7
Bārsua 138-139 K 7
Bārsūr 138-139 H 8
Bar-sur-Aube 120-121 K 4
Bārta [SU, place] 124-125 C 5
Bartala, Garden Reach- 154 II a 2
Bartallah 136-137 K 4
Bartau = Bārta 124-125 C 5
Barter Island 58-59 Q 1
Bartibog 63 CD 4
Bartica 92-93 H 3
Bartın [TR] 136-137 E 2
Bartın çayı = Koca ırmak 136-137 E 2
Bartle, CA 66-67 C 5
Bartlesville, OK 64-65 G 4
Bartlett, NE 68-69 G 5
Bartlett, TX 76-77 F 7
Bartlett's Harbour 63 H 2
Bartolome Mitre 110 III b 1
Bartolomeu Dias 172 G 6
Barton, ND 68-69 FG 1
Barton Park 161 I a 2
Barton Run 84 III d 2
Bartoszyce 118 K 1
Bartow, FL 80-81 bc 3
Barú, Volcán — 64-65 K 10
Bārudah, Ḥāssī — 166-167 GH 5
Barumbu, Kinshasa- 170 IV a 1
Barumun, Sungai — 152-153 CD 5
Barung, Nusa — 152-153 K 10
Barus 152-153 C 4
Baruta 91 II b 2
Baruta-Cumbres de Curumo 91 II b 2
Baruta-La Boyera 91 II b 2
Baruta-Las Minas 91 II b 2
Baruta-La Trinidad 91 II b 2
Baruta-Santa Marta 91 II b 2
Baruun Urt 142-143 L 2
Bāruva 138-139 K 8
Barvāḍīh = Barwādih 138-139 K 6
Barvāhā = Barwāha 138-139 F 6
Barvālā = Barwāla 138-139 E 3
Barvānī = Barwāni 138-139 E 6
Barvenkovo 126-127 H 2
Barville 62 N 2
Barwādih 138-139 K 6
Barwāha 138-139 F 6
Barwāla 138-139 E 3
Barwāni 138-139 E 6
Barwick 62 BC 3
Barwon River 158-159 J 5
Barwon River = Darling River 158-159 H 6
Bary, De — 106-107 F 6
Barykova, mys — 132-133 jk 5
Barylas 132-133 Z 4
Baryš [SU, place] 124-125 Q 7
Baryš [SU, river] 124-125 Q 6
Barzanja = Barzinjah 136-137 L 5
Barzas 132-133 Q 6
Barzhung 138-139 M 4
Barzinjah 136-137 L 5
Basail 104-105 G 10
Başalīyat Qiblī, Al- 173 C 5
Basankusu 172 CD 1
Bašanta 126-127 K 3
Bāsar 140 CD 1
Basatin, Al-Qāhirah-al- 170 II b 2
Basavilbaso 106-107 H 4
Başbaş 166-167 KL 1
Basco 142-143 N 7
Base Aérea Militar El Palomar 110 III b 1
Base de l'Militaire 170 IV a 1
Basel 118 C 5
Baserah 152-153 DE 6
Basha 138-139 G 2
Bashahr = Bashahar 138-139 G 2
Basharrī 136-137 G 5
Basheerivier 174-175 H 7
Bashi Heixia = Pashih Haihsia 142-143 N 7
Bāshim = Bāsim 134-135 M 5
Bashkir Autonomous Soviet Socialist Republic = 7 ◁ 132-133 K 6
Bash Kurghan = Bash Qurghan 142-143 G 4
Bash Malghun 142-143 F 4
Bash Qurghan 142-143 G 4
Bashshār 164-165 D 2
Bashtīl 170 II ab 1
Ba Shui 146-147 E 6
Basi 138-139 F 2
Basia 138-139 K 6
Basiano 148-149 H 7
Başibüyük 154 I bc 3
Basilan Island 148-149 H 5
Basilan Strait 148-149 H 5
Basilica de Guadalupe 91 I c 2
Basilicata 122-123 FG 5
Basilio 111 F 4
Basilique Nationale 128 II ab 1
Basim 134-135 M 6
Basin, MT 66-67 G 2
Basin, WY 68-69 BC 3
Basin, Rivière — 62 O 3
Basingstoke 119 F 6
Basin Ind Dist, Houston-, TX 85 III b 2
Basin Lake 61 F 4
Basīt, Rā's al- 136-137 F 5
Basiyā = Basia 138-139 K 6
Başkale 136-137 KL 3
Baskatong, Réservoir — 72-73 J 1
Baskineig Falls 62 F 1
Baškirskaja Avtonomnaja Sovetskaja Socialističeskaja Respublika = Bashkir Autonomous Soviet Socialist Republic 132-133 K 7
Başköy 136-137 L 3
Baskunčak, ozero — 126-127 N 2
Basle = Basel 118 C 5
Bašmakovo 124-125 O 7
Basmat 138-139 F 8
Bāsmenj 136-137 M 4
Basna 138-139 J 7
Basnāngira Palāna ◁ 140 E 7
Bāsoda 138-139 FG 6
Basoko [ZRE, Haute Zaïre] 172 D 1
Basoko [ZRE, Kinshasa] 170 IV a 2
Basra = Al-Başrah 134-135 F 4
Başrah, Al- 134-135 F 4
Bassac = Champassak 148-149 DE 4
Bassain 138-139 D 8
Bassala 168-169 D 2
Bassano 61 B 5
Bassano del Grappa 122-123 D 3
Bassari 168-169 F 3
Bassas da India 172 GH 6
Bassein 138-139 D 8
Bassein = Puthein 148-149 B 3
Bassein = Puthein Myit 141 D 7
Basse Kotto 164-165 J 7-8
Bassersdorf 128 IV b 1
Basse Santa Su 168-169 B 2
Basse-Terre [Guadeloupe, island] 88-89 PQ 6
Basse-Terre [Guadeloupe, place] 64-65 O 8
Basseterre [Saint Christopher-Nevis] 64-65 O 8
Bassett, NE 68-69 G 4
Bassett, VA 80-81 F 2
Bass Islands 72-73 E 4
Basso, Plateau de — 164-165 J 5
Bass Strait 158-159 HJ 7
Basswood Lake 70-71 E 1
Basta 138-139 L 7
Bastar [IND, landscape] 138-139 H 8
Bastar [IND, place] 138-139 HJ 8
Bastī 138-139 J 4
Bastia 122-123 C 4
Bastianøyane 116-117 l 5
Bastião 100-101 D 7
Bastioes, Serra dos — 100-101 DE 4
Bastogne 120-121 KL 3-4
Bastos 102-103 G 4
Bastrop, LA 64-65 H 5
Bastrop, TX 76-77 F 7
Bastuträsk 116-117 HJ 5
Bāsūs 170 II b 1
Basutoland = Lesotho 172 E 7
Basutos 172 E 5
Basvā = Baswa 138-139 F 4
Baswa 138-139 F 4
Bas-Zaïre 172 BC 3
Bata [CO] 94-95 E 4
Bata [Equatorial Guinea] 164-165 F 8
Batabanó, Golfo de — 64-65 K 7
Batac 148-149 GH 3
Batagaj 132-133 Za 4
Batagaj-Alyta 132-133 YZ 4
Bataguaçu 102-103 F 4
Bataiporã 102-103 F 5
Batajsk 126-127 JK 3
Batakan 152-153 L 8
Bataklik 136-137 E 4
Batāla 134-135 M 4
Batalha [BR] 100-101 C 2-3
Batalha [P] 120-121 C 9
Batam, Pulau — 148-149 D 6
Batamaj 132-133 YZ 5
Batan 146-147 GH 4
Batanagar 154 II a 2
Batang [RI] 152-153 JK 4
Batang [TJ] 142-143 H 6
Batanga 168-169 H 6
Batangafo 164-165 H 7
Batangan, Mui — 148-149 EF 3
Batangas 148-149 H 4
Batang Baram 152-153 L 3-4
Batang Hari 148-149 D 7
Batang Inderagiri 148-149 D 7
Batang Kuantan = Batang Inderagiri 148-149 D 7
Batang Tinjar 152-153 L 4
Batan Island 142-143 N 7
Batan Islands 142-143 N 7
Batanta, Pulau — 148-149 JK 7
Batao = Batan 146-147 GH 4
Bāṭās 136-137 L 4
Batatais 102-103 J 4
Batatchatu = Chulaq Aqqan Su 142-143 G 4
Batavia, NY 72-73 GH 3
Batavia, OH 72-73 DE 5
Batavia [RA] 106-107 E 5
Batavia = Jakarta 148-149 E 8
Batbakkara = Amangel'dy 132-133 M 7
Batchawana 62 J 3
Batchawana, Mount — 70-71 H 2
Bateckij 124-125 H 4
Bāṭel = Al-Bāṭil 166-167 E 2
Batel, Esteros del — 106-107 HJ 2
Batemans Bay 160 K 5
Batesburg, SC 80-81 F 4
Batesville, AR 78-79 D 3
Batesville, IN 70-71 H 6
Batesville, MS 78-79 E 3
Batesville, OH 72-73 D 5
Batesville, TX 76-77 E 8
Bath 119 E 6
Bath, ME 72-73 M 3
Bath, NY 72-73 H 3
Batha 164-165 H 6
Baṭḥa, Al- 136-137 L 7
B'athar Zajū, Jabal — 173 C 7
Bathéay 150-151 E 6-7
Bathurst [AUS] 158-159 JK 6
Bathurst [CDN] 56-57 XY 8
Bathurst [ZA] 174-175 G 7
Bathurst = Banjul 164-165 A 6
Bathurst, Cape — 56-57 KL 3
Bathurst Inlet [CDN, bay] 56-57 P 4
Bathurst Inlet [CDN, place] 56-57 P 4
Bathurst Island [AUS] 158-159 EF 2
Bathurst Island [CDN] 56-57 R 2
Batié 164-165 D 6-7
Batignolles, Paris-les — 129 I c 2
Batikala, Tanjung — 152-153 O 7
Bāṭil, Al- 166-167 E 2
Bāṭin, Al- [IRQ ↙ As-Salmān] 136-137 K 7-L 8
Bāṭin, Al- [IRQ ↘ As-Salmān] 136-137 M 8
Baṭin, Humrat al- 136-137 KL 8
Bāṭin, Wādī al- 134-135 F 5
Bāṭinah, Al — 134-135 H 6
Batinga 100-101 D 3
Batiscan 72-73 K 1
Batiscan, Rivière — 72-73 K 1
Batista, Serra do — [BR, Bahia] 100-101 D 6
Batista, Serra do — [BR, Piauí] 100-101 D 4
Batlow 160 HJ 5
Batman 134-135 E 3
Batna = Batnah 164-165 F 1
Batnah 164-165 F 1
Ba To' 150-151 G 5
Batoche 56-57 PQ 7
Baton Rouge, LA 64-65 H 5
Batouri 164-165 G 8
Batovi 102-103 F 1
Batovi, Coxilha do — 106-107 K 3
Batrā, Jabal al- 136-137 F 8
Ba Tri 150-151 F 7-8
Batrūn, Al- 136-137 F 5
Battambang 148-149 D 4
Battambang, Stung — = Stung Sangker 150-151 D 6
Batterbee Range 53 BC 30
Battersea, London- 129 II b 2
Battersea Park 129 II b 2
Batticaloa = Maḍakalapūwa 134-135 N 9
Battle Creek, MI 64-65 J 3
Battle Creek [USA ◁ Milk River] 68-69 B 1
Battle Creek [USA ◁ Owyhee River] 66-67 E 4
Battle Harbour 56-57 Za 7
Battle Mountain, NV 66-67 E 5
Battle River 56-57 OP 7
Battonya 118 K 5
Batu 164-165 M 7
Batu, Bukit — 152-153 K 4
Batu, Kepulauan — 148-149 C 7
Batu Anam 150-151 D 11
Batu Arang 148-149 D 6
Batuatu, Pulau — 152-153 P 8
Batubesar, Tanjung — 152-153 N 10
Batu Besi 150-151 D 10
Batu Bora, Bukit — 152-153 L 4
Batubrok, Gunung — 152-153 L 5
Batu Caves 150-151 C 11
Batudaka, Pulau — 152-153 O 6
Bāṭūfah 136-137 K 4
Batu Gajah 150-151 C 10
Batui 152-153 P 6
Batui, Pegunungan — 152-153 OP 6
Batuk, Tanjung — 152-153 P 10
Batukelau 152-153 L 5
Batumi 126-127 K 6
Batumundam 152-153 C 5
Bat'unino, Moskva- 113 V c 3
Batu Pahat 148-149 D 6
Batupanjang 152-153 D 5
Batuputih 152-153 N 5
Baturaja 148-149 D 7
Batu Rakit 150-151 D 10
Baturi = Batouri 164-165 G 8
Baturino 132-133 Q 6
Baturité 92-93 M 5
Baturité, Serra do — 100-101 E 3
Batutinggi 148-149 F 7
Batvand 136-137 N 6-7
Bau [MAL] 152-153 J 5
Baú, Pico — 102-103 K 5
Baubau 148-149 H 8
Baucau 148-149 J 8
Bauchi [WAN, administrative unit] 168-169 H 3
Bauchi [WAN, place] 164-165 FG 6
Baudette, MN 70-71 C 1
Baudh 134-135 N 6
Baudó, Río — 94-95 C 5
Baudó, Serranía de — 94-95 C 4-5
Baudouinville = Moba 172 E 3
Baudwin 148-149 C 2
Bauhinia 158-159 J 4
Baûl, El — 92-93 F 3
Bauld, Cape — 56-57 Za 7
Baule = Baoulé 164-165 C 6
Baule-Escoublac, la — 120-121 F 5
Baumann, Pic — 168-169 F 4
Baumschulenweg, Berlin- 130 III bc 2
Baura [BD] 138-139 M 4
Baura [IND] 140 A 7
Bā'ūrah, Sabkhat — 136-137 J 5
Baures 92-93 G 7
Baurs Berg 130 I a 1
Bauru 92-93 K 9
Baús 102-103 F 3
Bauska 124-125 E 5
Bauske = Bauska 124-125 E 5
Bautino 126-127 OP 4
Bautzen 118 G 3
Bauxite, AR 78-79 C 3
Bauya 164-165 B 7
Bavaria 130 II b 2
Bavaria = Bayern 118 E 4
Bavaria, Bogotá- 91 III b 3
Bavarian Forest = Bayerischer Wald 118 F 4
Ba Vi 150-151 E 2
Bavispe 86-87 F 2
Bavispe, Río — 86-87 F 2-3
Bavispe, Río de — 74-75 J 7
Bavly 124-125 T 6
Bawah, Pulau-pulau — 152-153 G 4
Bawal, Pulau — 152-153 H 7
Bawean, Pulau — 148-149 F 8
Bāwīṭī, Al- 164-165 K 3
Bawku 164-165 D 6
Bawlagè 148-149 C 3
Bawlei Myit 141 DE 7
Bawmi Au 141 D 7
Ba Xian 146-147 F 2
Baxten Springs 76-77 G 4
Baxter State Park 72-73 M 1-2
Bay 164-165 a 3

Benithora 140 C 2
Benito Juárez 111 DE 5
Benito Juárez, Ciudad de México- 91 I bc 2
Benjamim Constant 92-93 EF 5
Benjamin, TX 76-77 DE 6
Benjamin, Isla — 108-109 BC 5
Benjamin Franklin Bridge 84 III c 2
Benjamin Hill 86-87 E 2
Benjamín Zorrilla 106-107 E 7
Benkelman, NE 68-69 F 5
Benkulen = Bengkulu 148-149 D 7
Ben Lawers 119 DE 3
Ben Lomond [AUS] 160 cd 2
Ben Macdhui [GB] 119 DE 3
Ben Macdhui [LS] 174-175 GH 6
Ben-Mehidi = Ban Mahdī 166-167 KL 1
Ben More [GB, Mull] 119 C 3
Ben More [GB, Outer Hebrides] 119 C 3
Benmore, Lake — 161 D 7
Ben More Assynt 119 DE 2
Bennett 58-59 U 7
Bennett, CO 68-69 D 6
Bennett, WI 70-71 E 2
Bennett, ostrov — 132-133 cd 2
Bennett's Harbour 88-89 J 2
Bennettsville, SC 80-81 G 3
Ben Nevis 119 D 3
Bennington, VT 72-73 K 3
Bên Nôm 150-151 F 7
Ben Ohau Range 161 C 7-D 6
Benom = Gunung Benom 150-151 CD 11
Benom, Gunung — 150-151 CD 11
Benoni 174-175 H 4
Benoud = Banūd 166-167 G 3
Bénoué 164-165 G 7
Benqi = Benxi 142-143 N 3
Bensheim 118 D 4
'Ben Slîmân = Bin Sulīmān 166-167 C 3
Benson 68-69 E 1
Benson, AZ 74-75 H 7
Benson, MN 70-71 C 3
Bên Suc 150-151 F 7
Benta Sebrang 150-151 CD 10
Benteng 152-153 O 9
Bên Thuy 150-151 EF 3
'Ben Tieb = Bin Ţiyab 166-167 E 2
Bentinck Island 158-159 GH 3
Bentinck Island = Pyinzabu Kyûn 150-151 A 7
Bentiū 164-165 KL 7
Bent Jebaïl = Bint Jubayl 136-137 F 6
Bentleigh, Melbourne- 161 II c 2
Bentley 60 K 3
Bento, Rio de Janeiro- 110 I a 2
Bento Gomes, Rio — 102-103 D 2
Bento Gonçalves 106-107 M 2
Benton, AL 78-79 F 4
Benton, AR 78-79 C 3
Benton, CA 74-75 D 4
Benton, IL 70-71 F 6-7
Benton, KY 78-79 E 2
Benton, LA 78-79 C 4
Benton, WI 70-71 E 4
Benton City, WA 66-67 D 2
Bentong 150-151 CD 11
Benton Harbor, MI 70-71 G 4
Bentonia, MS 78-79 D 4
Bentonville, AR 76-77 G 4
Bentota 140 DE 7
Benty 168-169 B 3
Benua 152-153 OP 8
Benua, Pulau — 152-153 G 5
Benue 164-165 F 7
Benué = Benue 164-165 F 7
Benue Plateau 164-165 F 7
Benxi 142-143 N 3
ben Yaïch, Hassi — = Ḥāssī Ban 'Aysh 166-167 J 4
Ben Zerga 170 I b 1
Ben-Zireg = Ban Zīriq 166-167 F 4
Benzoû = Benzú 166-167 D 2
Benzú 166-167 D 2
Beograd 122-123 J 3
Beograd-Zemun 122-123 HJ 3
Beohāri 138-139 H 5
Béoumi 168-169 D 4
Beppu 144-145 H 6
Bēppūr = Beypore 140 BC 5
Beqā', El — = Al-Biqā' 136-137 FG 5-6
Bequia 88-89 Q 8
Bera 138-139 M 5
Beraber, Oglat — = 'Uqlat Barābir 166-167 E 4
Berach 138-139 E 5
Beraïje = Al-Barāij 136-137 G 5
Beram, Tanjung — 152-153 KL 3
Berar 138-139 F 7
Berasia 138-139 F 6
Berat 122-123 H 5
Berau, Sungai — 152-153 M 4
Berau, Teluk — 148-149 K 7
Berau Gulf = Teluk Berau 148-149 K 7
Berber = Barbar 164-165 L 5
Berbera 164-165 b 1
Berbérati 164-165 a 1
Berbice 98-99 J 2-K 3
Berbice River 98-99 JK 3
Berbouchi, Hassi — = Ḥāssī Barbūshī 166-167 E 5
Berch 142-143 L 2
Berchem-Sainte-Agathe 128 II a 1
Berchtesgaden 118 F 5
Berck 120-121 H 3
Bercy, Paris- 129 I c 2
Berd'ansk 126-127 H 3
Berd'anskaja kosa 126-127 H 3
Berd'anskij zaliv 126-127 H 3
Berdičev 126-127 D 2
Berdichev = Berdičev 126-127 D 2
Berdigest'ach 132-133 XY 5
Berdjansk = Berd'ansk 126-127 H 3
Berea, KY 70-71 H 7
Berea, NE 68-69 E 4
Berea, OH 72-73 F 4
Béréba 168-169 E 3
Béréby 168-169 D 4
Bereg [SU, Vologodskaja Oblast'] 124-125 LM 4
bereg Charitona Lapteva 132-133 Q 3-R 2
Beregomet 126-127 B 2
Beregovo 126-127 A 2
bereg Prončiščeva 132-133 UV 2-3
Bereku 171 CD 4
Berenda, CA 74-75 CD 4
Berendejevo 124-125 M 5
Berenike 164-165 LM 4
Berens Island 61 K 4
Berens River [CDN, place] 56-57 R 7
Berens River [CDN, river] 56-57 R 7
Beresford 160 C 2
Beresford, SD 68-69 H 4
Beresford Lake 62 B 2
Beresina = Berezina 124-125 G 6-7
Beresniki = Berezniki 132-133 JK 6
Berestečko 126-127 B 1
Beretău 122-123 JK 2
Berezajka [SU, place] 124-125 JK 4-5
Berežany 126-127 B 2
Berezina 124-125 G 6-7
Berezino [SU, Kazachskaja SSR] 126-127 O 1
Berezino [SU, Rossijskaja SFSR] 124-125 G 7
Berezinskij zapovednik 124-125 G 6
Berezna 124-125 HJ 8
Bereznik 124-125 O 2
Berezniki [SU, Perm'skaja Oblast'] 132-133 JK 6
Berezno 126-127 C 1
Berezovka = Ber'ozovka [SU, Odesskaja SSR] 126-127 E 3
Berezovka = Ber'ozovka [SU, Perm'skaja Oblast'] 124-125 UV 4
Berg [B] 128 II b 1
Berga = Birkah 166-167 G 6
Bergama 134-135 B 3
Berg am Laim, München- 130 II b 2
Bèrgamo 122-123 CD 3
Bergantín 94-95 J 2-3
Bergen, ND 68-69 F 1-2
Bergen [DDR] 118 F 1
Bergen [N] 116-117 A 7
Bergen Beach, New York-, NY 82 III c 3
Bergenfield, NJ 82 III c 1
Bergen-Nesttun 116-117 AB 7
Bergen Point 82 III b 3
Bergerac 120-121 H 6
Bergfelde 130 III b 1
Bergholz-Rehbrücke 130 III a 2
Bergland, MI 70-71 F 2
Bergland [CDN] 70-71 C 1
Bergland [Namibia] 174-175 B 2
Bergslagen 116-117 F 7-8
Bergstedt, Hamburg- 130 I b 1
Berguennt = Birjant 166-167 EF 2-3
Bergville 174-175 H 5
Berhala, Pulau — 150-151 DE 11
Berhala, Selat — 152-153 EF 6
Berhampore 134-135 O 6
Berhampur 134-135 NO 7
Berhampur = Berhampore 134-135 O 6
Berikat, Tanjung — 152-153 G 7
Berilo 102-103 L 2
Bering, mys — 132-133 k 5
Bering, ostrov — 132-133 fg 7
Bering Glacier 56-57 H 5
Bering Lake 58-59 P 6
Beringovskij 132-133 j 5
Bering Sea 132-133 k 5-g 6
Bering Strait 56-57 B 5-C 4
Beris = Bāris 173 B 5
Berisso 106-107 J 5
Beristain 86-87 LM 7
Berja 120-121 F 10
Berjozovo = Ber'ozovo 132-133 LM 5
Berkan = Birkān 166-167 E 2
Berkeley, CA 64-65 B 4
Berkeley Sound 108-109 KL 8
Berkersheim, Frankfurt am Main- 128 III b 1
Berkîn = Barkīn 166-167 E 3
Berkley, MI 84 II ab 1
Berkner Island 53 B 31-32
Berkovica 122-123 K 4
Berland River 60 J 2
Berlengas, Rio — 100-101 C 4-5
Berlevåg 116-117 N 2
Berlin, MD 72-73 J 5
Berlin, ND 68-69 G 2
Berlin, NH 64-65 M 3
Berlin, NJ 84 III d 3
Berlin, WI 70-71 F 4
Berlin [CO] 94-95 F 7
Berlin [D] 118 FG 2
Berlin [ZA] 174-175 G 7
Berlin, Mount — 53 B 23
Berlin-Adlershof 130 III c 2
Berlin-Altglienicke 130 III c 2
Berlin-Baumschulenweg 130 III bc 2
Berlin-Biesdorf 130 III c 1
Berlin-Biesdorf-Süd 130 III c 2
Berlin-Blankenburg 130 III b 1
Berlin-Blankenfelde 130 III b 1
Berlin-Bohnsdorf 130 III c 2
Berlin-Britz 130 III b 2
Berlin-Buchholz 130 III b 1
Berlin-Buckow 130 III b 2
Berlin-Dahlem 130 III b 2
Berlin-Elsengrund 130 III c 2
Berliner Forst Spandau 130 III a 1
Berliner Forst Tegel 130 III ab 1
Berliner Ring 130 III c 1
Berlin-Falkenberg 130 III c 1
Berlin-Friedenau 130 III b 2
Berlin-Friedrichsfelde 130 III c 1-2
Berlin-Friedrichshain 130 III b 1
Berlin-Frohnau 130 III b 1
Berlin-Grunewald 130 III b 2
Berlin-Hakenfelde 130 III a 1
Berlin-Haselhorst 130 III a 1
Berlin-Heiligensee 130 III a 1
Berlin-Heinersdorf 130 III b 1
Berlin-Hellersdorf 130 III c 1
Berlin-Hirschgarten 130 III c 2
Berlin-Hohenschönhausen 130 III c 1
Berlin-Johannisthal 130 III c 2
Berlin-Karow 130 III b 1
Berlin-Kaulsdorf 130 III c 1-2
Berlin-Kaulsdorf-Süd 130 III c 2
Berlin-Kladow 130 III a 2
Berlin-Kolonie Buch 130 III b 1
Berlin-Konradshöhe 130 III a 1
Berlin-Kreuzberg 130 III b 2
Berlin-Lankwitz 130 III b 2
Berlin-Lübars 130 III b 1
Berlin-Mahlsdorf-Süd 130 III c 2
Berlin-Malchow 130 III bc 1
Berlin-Mariendorf 130 III b 2
Berlin-Marienfelde 130 III b 2
Berlin-Marzahn 130 III c 1
Berlin-Müggelheim 130 III c 2
Berlin-Niederschöneweide 130 III b 2
Berlin-Niederschönhausen 130 III b 1
Berlin-Nikolassee 130 III a 2
Berlin-Oberschöneweide 130 III c 2
Berlin-Prenzlauer Berg 130 III b 1
Berlin-Rahnsdorf 130 III c 2
Berlin-Rauchfangswerder 130 III c 2
Berlin-Rosenthal 130 III b 1
Berlin-Rudow 130 III b 2
Berlin-Schmargendorf 130 III b 2
Berlin-Siemensstadt 130 III b 1
Berlin-Staaken 130 III a 1
Berlin-Steinstücken 130 III a 2
Berlin-Tegelort 130 III ab 1
Berlin-Tiefwerder 130 III a 1
Berlin-Tiergarten 130 III b 1
Berlin-Treptow 130 III b 2
Berlin-Waidmannslust 130 III b 1
Berlin-Wannsee 130 III a 2
Berlin-Wartenberg 130 III c 1
Berlin-Wedding 130 III b 1
Berlin-Wendenschloss 130 III c 2
Berlin-Wilhelmstadt 130 III a 1
Berlin-Wilmersdorf 130 III b 2
Berlin-Wittenau 130 III b 1
Berlin-Wolfsgarten 130 III c 2
Bermejillo 86-87 J 5
Bermejo [BOL] 92-93 G 9
Bermejo [RA] 111 C 4
Bermejo, Desaguadera del — 106-107 D 3-4
Bermejo, Isla — 106-107 FG 7
Bermejo, Río — [RA ◁ Río Desaguadero] 106-107 C 3
Bermejo, Río — [RA ◁ Río Paraguay] 111 D 2
Bermejo, Río — = Río Colorado 106-107 D 2
Bermejos 96-97 B 3
Bermeo 120-121 F 7
Bermondsey, London- 129 II b 2
Bermuda Islands 64-65 NO 5
Bermudas = Bermuda Islands 64-65 NO 5
Bern 118 C 5
Berna 106-107 GH 2
Bernabeu, Estadio — 113 III ab 2
Bernal, Quilmes- 110 III c 2
Bernalillo, NM 76-77 A 5
Bernardino de Campos 102-103 H 5
Bernardo de Irigoyen 111 F 3
Bernardo Larroude 106-107 F 5
Bernasconi 106-107 EF 6
Bernburg 118 EF 3
Berne, IN 70-71 H 5
Berne, WA 66-67 C 2
Berne = Bern 118 C 5
Berne, Hamburg- 130 I b 1
Berner Alpen 118 C 5
Bernese Alps = Berner Alpen 118 C 5
Bernhardina 174-175 H 4
Bernice, LA 78-79 C 4
Bernier Bay 56-57 ST 3
Bernier Island 158-159 B 4
Bernina 118 D 5
Bèroia 122-123 JK 5
Berón de Astrada 106-107 J 1
Beroroha 172 HJ 6
Béroubouaye 168-169 F 3
Beroun 118 FG 4
Berounka 118 F 4
Ber'oza 124-125 E 7
Ber'ozovka [SU, Odesskaja SSR] 126-127 E 3
Ber'ozovka [SU, Perm'skaja Oblast'] 124-125 UV 4
Ber'ozovo 132-133 LM 5
Ber'ozovskaja 126-127 LM 1
Berrahal = Birrahhāl 166-167 K 1
Berras, Arroyo los — 110 III a 1
Ber Rechid = Bin Rashīd 166-167 BC 3
Berrekrem, Hassi — = Ḥāssī Barakram 166-167 J 3
Berri 160 E 5
Berriane = Biryān 166-167 HJ 3
Berrotarán 106-107 EF 4
Berrouaghia = Birwāgīyah 166-167 H 1
Berry 120-121 HJ 5
Berry, AL 78-79 F 4
Berryessa, Lake — 74-75 B 3
Berry Islands 88-89 GH 2
Berryville, AR 78-79 C 2
Berryville, VA 72-73 GH 5
Bersâ' = Barşā' 136-137 H 4
Bersabee = Bĕer Shevaʻ 134-135 C 4
Beršad' 126-127 D 2
Berseba 172 C 7
Bersimis 63 B 3
Berté, Lac — 63 BC 2
Berthierville 72-73 K 1
Berthold, ND 68-69 EF 1
Bertioga 102-103 J 5
Bertiskos 122-123 K 5
Bertolínia 92-93 L 6
Bertópolis 100-101 D 3
Bertoua 164-165 G 8
Bertram 62 G 3
Bertram, TX 76-77 EF 7
Bertrand, NE 68-69 G 5
Bertrand, Cerro — 108-109 C 8
Bertrandville, LA 85 I bc 3
Bertua = Bertoua 164-165 G 8
Bertwell 61 G 4
Beru 208 H 3
Berunda 171 B 2
Beruri 92-93 G 5
Berwick, LA 78-79 D 6
Berwick, PA 72-73 H 4
Berwick [CDN] 63 D 5
Berwick-upon-Tweed 119 EF 4
Berwyn, IL 70-71 FG 5
Berwyn Heights, MD 82 II b 1
Beryl, UT 74-75 G 4
Berytus = Bayrūt 134-135 CD 4
Berzekh el Jadîd = Rā's al-Jadīd 166-167 E 2
Berzekh el Kîlâtes = Rā's Qilātis 166-167 E 2
Berzekh Rhîr = Rā's Ghīr 166-167 AB 4
Berzekh Sbartel = Rā's Ashaqār 166-167 CD 2
Berzekh Thlèta Madârî = Rā's Wūruq 164-165 D 1
Besalampy 172 H 5
Besançon 120-121 L 5
Besar, Gunung — [MAL] 150-151 D 11
Besar, Gunung — [RI] 152-153 LM 7
Besar, Pulau — 152-153 P 10
Besar, Tanjung — 152-153 O 5
Besbes = Başbaş 166-167 KL 1
Besboro Island 58-59 G 4
Besed' 124-125 H 7
Bešenkoviči 124-125 G 6
Besi, Tanjung — 152-153 O 10
Beşiktaş, İstanbul- 154 I b 2
Beşîrê, El — = Buşayrah 136-137 J 5
Beşiri = Kobin 136-137 J 4
Besitang 150-151 B 10
Beskids = Beskidy 118 JK 4
Beskidy 118 JK 4
Beşkonak = Bozyaka 136-137 D 4
Beskudnikovo, Moskva- 113 V bc 2
Beslan 126-127 M 5
Besna Kobila 122-123 K 4
Besnard Lake 61 F 3
Besni 134-135 D 3
Beşparmak dağı 136-137 BC 4
Bessa Monteiro 172 B 3
Bessarabia = Bessarabija 126-127 C 2-D 3
Bessarabija 126-127 C 2-D 3
Bessarabka 126-127 D 3
Bessaz gora 132-133 M 9
Bessels, Kapp — 116-117 lm 5
Bessemer, AL 64-65 J 5
Bessemer, MI 70-71 EF 2
Bessemer City, NC 80-81 F 3
Besshi 144-145 J 6
Bessoky, gora — 134-135 G 2
Best, TX 76-77 D 7
Bestobe 132-133 N 7
Bestuževo [SU, Archangel'skaja Oblast'] 124-125 O 3
Bět = Okha 134-135 K 6
Betaf 148-149 L 7
Betafo 172 J 5
Betânia [BR] 100-101 EF 5
Betania [RA] 104-105 D 9
Betanzos [BOL] 104-105 D 6
Betanzos [E] 120-121 CD 7
Bétaré-Oya 164-165 G 7
Bethal 172 F 7
Bethanië = Bethanien 172 C 7
Bethanien 172 C 7
Bethany, MO 70-71 CD 5
Bethel, AK 56-57 D 5
Bethel, ME 72-73 L 2
Bethel, MN 70-71 D 3
Bethel, NC 80-81 H 3
Bethel, OH 72-73 DE 5
Bethel, OK 76-77 G 5
Bethel, VT 72-73 K 3
Bethesda, MD 82 II a 1
Bethlehem 172 E 7
Bethlehem, PA 72-73 J 4
Bethnal Green, London- 129 II b 1
Beth Shaan = Bēt Shě'ān 134-135 F 6
Bethulie 172 E 8
Bethune [CDN] 61 F 5
Béthune [F] 120-121 J 3
Betijoque 94-95 F 3
Betim 102-103 K 3-4
Betioky 172 H 6
Betiyā = Bettiah 138-139 K 4
Betlehem = Bayt Lahm 136-137 F 7
Betlica 124-125 JK 6-7
Betling Sib 141 BC 4
Betnoti 138-139 L 7
Betong 150-151 C 10
Betoota 158-159 H 5
Betpak-Dala 132-133 MN 8
Betroka 172 J 6
Bēt Shě'ān 134-135 F 6
Betsiamites 63 B 3
Betsiamites, Rivière — 63 B 3
Betsiboka 172 J 5
Betsie Point 70-71 G 3
Betsjoeanaland 172 D 7
Bette, Pic — 164-165 HJ 4
Bettiah 138-139 K 4
Bettiè 168-169 E 4
Bettles, AK 58-59 M 3
Bettles Field = Evansville, AK 58-59 LM 3
Bettyhill 119 DE 2
Betuensambang, Bukit — 152-153 K 5-6
Betūl 138-139 F 7
Betūl Bāzār 138-139 FG 7
Betung 152-153 E 6
Betwā = Betwa 134-135 M 6
Betwa 134-135 M 6
Beu, Serranía del — 104-105 BC 4
Beuharī = Beohāri 138-139 H 5
Beulah 61 H 5
Beulah, MI 70-71 G 3
Beulah, ND 68-69 EF 2
Beulah, OR 66-67 D 4
Beulah, WY 68-69 D 3
Beurkot 168-169 H 1
Beverley 119 F 5
Beverley, Lake — 58-59 H 7
Beverly, MA 72-73 L 3
Beverly, NJ 84 III d 1
Beverly, WA 66-67 D 2
Beverly, Chicago-, IL 83 II ab 2
Beverly Hills, CA 83 III b 1
Beverly Hills, Houston-, TX 85 III c 2
Beverly Hills, Sydney- 161 I a 2
Bexiga 106-107 L 2
Bexley, OH 72-73 E 4-5
Bexley, London- 129 II c 2
Bexley, Sydney- 161 I a 2
Beyābān, Kūh-e — 134-135 H 5
Beyce 136-137 C 3
Bey dağları 136-137 D 4
Beydili = Gerede 136-137 D 2
Bey el Kebir, Wadi — = Wādī Bey al-Kabīr 164-165 GH 2
Beykoz, İstanbul- 136-137 C 2
Beyla 164-165 C 7
Beylerbeyi, İstanbul- 154 I b 2
Beylikahır 136-137 D 3
Beyoğlu, İstanbul- 154 I a 2
Beypazarı 136-137 DE 2
Beypore [IND, place] 140 B 5
Beypore [IND, river] 140 BC 5
Beyrouth = Bayrūth 134-135 CD 4
Beyşehir 136-137 DE 4
Beyşehir gölü 134-135 C 3
Beyt = Okhā 134-135 K 6
Beytişebap = Elki 136-137 K 4
Bežeck 124-125 L 5
Bezerra, Rio — 100-101 A 7
Bezerros 100-101 G 5
Bežica, Br'ansk- 124-125 JK 7
Beziers 120-121 J 7
Bezons 129 I b 2
Bezwada = Vijayavāḍā 134-135 N 7

Bhabua 138-139 J 5
Bhachāu 138-139 C 6
Bhadaurā = Bhadaura 138-139 F 5
Bhadaura 138-139 F 5
Bhadohi 138-139 J 5
Bhādra [IND] 138-139 E 3
Bhādra [PAK] 138-139 A 3
Bhadrāchalam 140 E 2
Bhadrakh 134-135 O 6
Bhādran 138-139 D 6
Bhadra Reservoir 140 B 4
Bhadrāvati 140 B 4
Bhaensdehi = Bhainsdehi 138-139 F 7
Bhāgalpur 134-135 O 5-6
Bhāgīrathi [IND, Uttar Pradesh] 138-139 G 2
Bhāgīrathi [IND, West Bengal] 138-139 M 5-6
Bhainsdehi 138-139 F 7
Bhainsrorgarh 138-139 E 5
Bhairabasingapura 138-139 J 8
Bhairab Bāzār 134-135 P 6
Bhaisa 138-139 FG 8
Bhālki 140 C 1
Bhamangarh 138-139 HJ 6
Bhamo = Banmau 148-149 C 2
Bhānbarāya 138-139 N 4
Bhandāra 134-135 MN 6
Bhandaria 138-139 JK 6
Bhānder 138-139 G 5
Bhānga 138-139 MN 6
Bhānpura 138-139 E 5
Bhānrer Range 138-139 GH 6
Bhānurpratāppur 138-139 H 7
Bhānvad 138-139 B 7
Bhaoṅgāṅv = Bhongaon 138-139 G 4
Bharatpur [IND, Madhya Pradesh] 138-139 H 6
Bharatpur [IND, Rājasthān] 134-135 M 5
Bhāreli 141 C 2
Bharthana 138-139 G 4
Bharuch 134-135 L 6
Bhaṭakal = Bhatkal 140 B 4
Bhātapāra 138-139 HJ 7
Bhātār 138-139 L 6
Bhātgāṅv = Bhātgaon 134-135 O 5
Bhatgaon 134-135 O 5
Bhatiapara Ghat = Bhātiyāpārā Ghāṭ 138-139 MN 6
Bhatinda 134-135 L 4
Bhātiyāpārā Ghāṭ 138-139 MN 6
Bhatkal 140 B 4
Bhātpāra 134-135 O 6
Bhātpur 154 II b 1
Bhattiprolu 140 E 2
Bhatu 138-139 E 3
Bhaunagar 134-135 L 6
Bhavāni [IND, place] 140 C 5
Bhavānī [IND, river] 140 C 5
Bhavānīpāṭṇā = Bhawānipatna 134-135 N 7
Bhāvarī = Bhawāri 138-139 D 5
Bhawānipatna 134-135 N 7
Bhawāri 138-139 D 5
Bhelsā = Vidisha 134-135 M 6
Bheri 138-139 J 3
Bheri, Sāni — 138-139 J 3
Bhikangāṅv = Bhikangaon 138-139 EF 7
Bhikangaon 138-139 EF 7
Bhiker = Bhōkar 138-139 F 8
Bhikhna 138-139 K 4
Bhilainagar 134-135 N 6
Bhilsa = Vidisha 134-135 M 6
Bhīlvāṛā = Bhīlwāra 138-139 E 5
Bhīlwāra 138-139 E 5
Bhīma 134-135 M 7
Bhīmāvaram 140 E 2
Bhind 138-139 G 4
Bhīnmāl 138-139 D 5
Bhīr 134-135 M 7
Bhivānī = Bhiwāni 134-135 M 5
Bhiwandi 138-139 D 8
Bhiwani 134-135 M 5
Bhognīpur 138-139 G 4
Bhograi 138-139 L 7
Bhojpur 138-139 L 4
Bhokar 138-139 F 8
Bhokardan 138-139 E 7
Bhokardhan = Bhokardan 138-139 E 7
Bhoker = Bhokar 138-139 F 8
Bholā 141 B 4
Bhongaon 138-139 G 4
Bhongir 140 D 2
Bhopāl 134-135 M 6
Bhor 134-135 L 7
Bhore 138-139 K 4
Bhowanipore, Calcutta- 154 II b 2
Bhuban 138-139 KL 7
Bhubana = Bhuban 138-139 KL 7
Bhubanēshvara = Bhubaneswar 134-135 O 6
Bhubeneswar 134-135 O 6
Bhuj 134-135 KL 6
Bhūm 140 B 1
Bhūrgāṅv 141 B 2
Bhurgaon = Bhūrgāṅv 141 B 2
Bhusāval = Bhusāwal 134-135 M 6
Bhusāwal 134-135 M 6
Bhutan 134-135 OP 5
Bhuvanāgiri 140 DE 5

Bia [CI] 168-169 E 4
Bia, Phou — 150-151 D 3
Bia, Pu — = Phou Bia 150-151 D 3
Biá, Rio — 98-99 E 7
Biābān, Kūh-e = Kūh-e Beyābān 134-135 H 5
Biafra 164-165 F 7
Biak, Pulau — 148-149 L 7
Biała Podlaska 118 L 2-3
Białobrzegi 118 K 3
Białogard 118 GH 1-2
Białystok 118 L 2
Biankouma 168-169 CD 4
Biaora 138-139 F 6
Biar = Bihār 134-135 NO 6
Biar, Al-Jazā'ir-El — 170 I a 1
Biaro, Pulau — 148-149 J 6
Biarritz 120-121 G 7
Bias Bay = Daya Wan 146-147 E 10
Bias Fortes 102-103 KL 4
Biasso = Bissau 164-165 A 6
Bibā 173 B 3
Bibai 144-145 bc 2
Bibala 172 B 4
Bībān, Al- [DZ] 166-167 J 1
Bībān, Al- [TN] 166-167 M 3
Bībān, Bouḥeïret el — = Buḥayrat al-Bībān 166-167 M 3
Bībān, Buḥayrat al- 166-167 M 3
Bibans = Al-Bībān 166-167 J 1
Biberach 118 D 4
Bibiani 168-169 E 4
Bibile 140 E 7
Biblián 96-97 B 3
Bic 63 B 3
Bicaner = Bīkaner 134-135 L 5
Bicas 102-103 L 4
Biche, Lac la — 61 BC 3
Bichhia 138-139 H 6
Bichi 168-169 H 2
Bickerdike 60 J 3
Bickerton Island 158-159 G 2
Bickleton, WA 66-67 CD 2
Bicknell, IN 70-71 G 6
Bicknell, UT 74-75 H 3
Biḍ = Bhīr 134-135 M 7
Bid', Al- 173 D 3
Bida 164-165 F 7
Bīdar 134-135 M 7
Bidara = Bīdar 134-135 M 7
Biddeford, ME 64-65 MN 3
Biddle, MT 68-69 D 3
Bidele Depression = Djourab 164-165 H 5
Bidhūna 138-139 G 4
Bidor 150-151 C 10
Bi Doup 150-151 G 6
Bi Dup = Bi Doup 150-151 G 6
Bié = Kuito 172 C 4
Bieber 128 III b 1
Bieber, CA 66-67 C 5
Bieber, Offenbach- 128 III b 1
Biebrza 118 L 2
Biel 118 C 5
Bielawa 118 H 3
Bielefeld 118 D 2
Biele Karpaty 118 HJ 4
Biella 122-123 BC 3
Bielsko-Biała 118 J 4
Bielsk Podlaski 118 L 2
Bienfait 68-69 E 1
Biên Hoa 148-149 E 4
Bienne = Biel 118 C 5
Bienville, LA 78-79 C 4
Bienville, Lac — 56-57 W 6
Biesdorf, Berlin- 130 III c 1
Biesdorf-Süd, Berlin- 130 III c 2
Biesiesfontein 174-175 B 6
Biesiespoort 174-175 E 6
Biesjespoort = Biesiespoort 174-175 E 6
Bièvres 129 I b 2
Bifuka 144-145 c 1
Biğa 136-137 B 2
Bigadiç 136-137 C 3
Bigand 106-107 G 4
Big Arm, MT 66-67 FG 2
Big Baldy 66-67 F 3
Big Bar Creek 60 FG 4
Big Bay, MI 70-71 G 2
Big Bay de Noc 70-71 G 3
Big Beaver 68-69 D 1
Big Beaver Falls 62 K 2
Big Beaver House 62 DE 1
Big Bell 158-159 C 5
Big Belt Mountains 66-67 H 2
Big Bend, CA 66-67 C 5
Big Bend, CO 68-69 E 6
Big Bend National Park 64-65 F 6
Big Black River 78-79 D 4
Big Blue River 68-69 H 5-6
Big Canyon River 76-77 CD 7
Big Chino Wash 74-75 G 5
Big Coulee 61 B 3
Big Creek, ID 66-67 F 3
Big Creek [CDN] 60 F 4
Big Creek [USA] 68-69 FG 6
Big Cypress Indian Reservation 80-81 c 3
Big Cypress Swamp 80-81 c 3-4
Big Delta, AK 56-57 GH 5
Big Desert 160 E 5
Big Falls 66-67 E 1
Big Falls, MN 70-71 CD 1
Bigfork, MT 66-67 FG 1
Big Fork River 70-71 CD 2
Bigga 160 J 5
Biggar [CDN] 56-57 P 7
Bigge Island 158-159 DE 2
Biggs, OR 66-67 C 3
Bigha = Biğa 136-137 B 2
Big Hole River 66-67 G 3
Bighorn, MT 68-69 C 2
Bighorn Basin 68-69 B 3
Bighorn Lake 68-69 BC 3
Bighorn Mountains 64-65 E 2-3
Bighorn River 68-69 C 3
Bight of Benin 164-165 E 7-8
Big Island [CDN, Hudson Strait] 56-57 WX 5
Big Island [CDN, Lake of the Woods] 70-71 C 1
Big Koniuji Island 58-59 d 2
Big Lake 68-69 B 3
Big Lake, AK 58-59 N 3
Big Lake, TX 76-77 D 7
Big Lost River 66-67 G 4
Big Muddy Creek 68-69 D 1
Big Muddy River 70-71 F 6-7
Bignona 168-169 A 2
Bigobo 171 A 4
Bigot, Lac — 63 D 2
Bigou 168-169 F 3
Big Pine, CA 74-75 DE 4
Big Pine Key, FL 80-81 c 4
Big Piney, WY 66-67 HJ 4
Big Piney River 70-71 DE 7
Big Port Walter, AK 58-59 v 8
Biğrān 134-135 G 6
Big Rapids, MI 70-71 H 4
Big River [CDN, place] 61 E 4
Big River [CDN, river] 61 E 4
Big River [USA] 58-59 K 5
Big Sable Point 70-71 G 3
Big Salmon Range 56-57 K 5
Big Salmon River 58-59 U 6
Big Sand Lake 61 J 2
Big Sandy, MT 68-69 AB 1
Big Sandy, TN 78-79 EF 2
Big Sandy, TX 76-77 G 6
Big Sandy, WY 66-67 J 4
Big Sandy Creek 68-69 E 6
Big Sandy Lake [CDN] 61 F 3
Big Sandy Lake [USA] 70-71 D 2
Big Sandy River 74-75 G 5
Bigsby Island 70-71 C 1
Big Sioux River 68-69 H 4
Big Smoky Valley 74-75 E 3
Big Snowy Mountain 68-69 B 2
Big Spring, TX 64-65 F 5
Big Springs, ID 66-67 H 3
Big Squaw Lake = Chandalar, AK 58-59 NO 3
Big Stone City, SD 68-69 H 3
Big Stone Gap, VA 80-81 E 2
Bigstone Lake [CDN] 62 B 1
Big Stone Lake [USA] 68-69 H 3
Bigstone River 61 L 3

Bigstone 269

Big Sur, CA 74-75 BC 4
Big Timber, MT 66-67 J 3
Big Timber Creek 84 III c 2
Big Timber Creek South Branch 84 III c 3
Bigtrails, WY 68-69 C 4
Big Trout Lake [CDN, lake] 56-57 T 7
Big Trout Lake [CDN, place] 62 E 1
Biguaçu 102-103 H 7
Big Wells, TX 76-77 E 8
Big White Mountain 66-67 D 1
Big Wood River 66-67 F 4
Bihać 122-123 F 3
Bihār [IND, administrative unit] 134-135 NO 6
Bihār [IND, place] 134-135 O 6
Biharamulo 172 F 2
Bihāriganj 138-139 L 5
Bihor 122-123 K 2
Bihor, Munții — 122-123 K 2
Bihoro 144-145 d 2
Bihta 138-139 K 5
Bihu 146-147 G 7
Bijagós, Arquipélago dos — 164-165 A 6
Bijaipur 138-139 F 4
Bijang 141 F 2
Bijaorī = Bijauri 138-139 J 3
Bijāpur [IND, Karnataka] 134-135 LM 7
Bijāpur [IND, Madhya Pradesh] 140 E 1
Bijāpura = Bijāpur 134-135 LM 7
Bijār 134-135 F 3
Bijauri 138-139 J 3
Bijāvar = Bijāwar 138-139 G 5
Bijāwar 138-139 G 5
Bijāyah, Khalīj — 166-167 J 1
Bij-Chem = Bol'šoj Jenisej 132-133 S 7
Bijie 142-143 K 6
Bijistān = Bejestān 134-135 H 4
Bijlmermeer 128 I b 2
Bijnaor = Bijnor 138-139 G 3
Bijni 141 B 2
Bijnor 138-139 G 3
Bijnoṭ 134-135 L 5
Bijou Creek 68-69 D 5-6
Bijou Hills, SD 68-69 G 4
Bijrān 134-135 G 6
Bijsk 132-133 Q 7
Bikampur 138-139 D 4
Bīkaner 134-135 L 5
Bīkāpur 138-139 HJ 4
Bikin [SU, place] 132-133 Za 8
Bikin [SU, river] 132-133 a 8
Bikkavolu 140 EF 2
Bikkevels Mountains = Bokkeveldberge 174-175 C 6
Bikoro 172 C 2
Bikram 138-139 K 5
Bikramganj 138-139 K 5
Bilac 102-103 G 4
Biḷagī = Bilgi 140 B 2
Bilāra 138-139 D 4
Bilāri 138-139 G 3
Bil'arsk 124-125 S 6
Bilāspur [IND, Himāchal Pradesh] 138-139 F 2
Bilāspur [IND, Madhya Pradesh] 134-135 N 6
Bilāspur [IND, Uttar Pradesh] 138-139 G 3
Bilati 171 B 3
Bilauktaung Range = Tanintharī Taungdan 150-151 B 5-6
Bilauri 138-139 H 3
Bilbao 120-121 F 7
Bilbays 173 B 2
Bildudalur 116-117 ab 2
Bileća 122-123 H 4
Bilecik 136-137 C 2
Bilgi 140 B 2
Bilgrām 138-139 H 4
Bilhaor = Bilhaur 138-139 GH 4
Bilhaur 138-139 GH 4
Bili [ZRE, place] 172 DE 1
Bili [ZRE, river] 172 DE 1
Bilibiza 171 E 6
Bilimora 138-139 D 7
Bilin [BUR] 141 E 7
Bilin Myit 141 E 7
Biliran Island 148-149 H 4
Bill, WY 68-69 D 4
Billbrook, Hamburg- 130 I b 1
Billefjord 116-117 k 5
Billings, MT 64-65 E 2
Billinsport, NJ 84 III b 2
Billiton = Pulau Belitung 148-149 E 7
Bill of Portland 119 EF 6
Billstedt, Hamburg- 130 I b 1
Billwerder Ausschlag, Hamburg- 130 I b 1
Bill Williams River 74-75 FG 5
Bilma 164-165 G 5
Bilma, Grand Erg de — 164-165 G 5
Biloela 158-159 K 4
Bilo gora 122-123 G 2-3
Biloli 140 C 1
Biloxi, MS 64-65 J 5
Bilqās 173 B 2
Bilqas Qism Auwal = Bilqās 173 B 2
Biltine 164-165 J 6
Bilugyn = Bīlū Kyūn 148-149 C 3
Bīlū Kyūn 148-149 C 3
Bimbéréké 164-165 E 6
Bimbila 168-169 F 3
Bimlipatam 134-135 M 7
Bīna [IND] 138-139 G 5
Bin Aḥmad 166-167 C 3
Binakā = Binka 138-139 J 7
Binalbagan 148-149 H 4
Bin al-Fraysāt 166-167 E 3
Bin al-Ghīadah 166-167 E 3
Binaria, Jakarta- 154 IV b 1
Bin Baṭāʾī = Ḥāssī Bin Baṭāʾī 166-167 AB 5
Bin Baṭāʾī, Ḥāssī — 166-167 AB 5
Binboğa 136-137 G 3
Bindki 138-139 H 4-5
Bindloe = Isla Marchena 92-93 AB 4
Binga, Mount — 172 F 5
Bin Ganīyah, Bi'r — 164-165 J 2
Bingara 160 K 2
Bingen 118 C 4
Binger, OK 76-77 E 5
Bingerville 168-169 DE 4
Bingham, ME 72-73 M 2
Bingham, NE 68-69 EF 4
Bingham, NM 76-77 A 6
Bingham Canyon, UT 66-67 GH 5
Binghamton, NY 64-65 LM 3
Bin Gharīr 164-165 C 2
Binghui = Tianchang 146-147 G 5
Bingkor 152-153 LM 3
Bingo Bay = Hiuchi-nada 144-145 J 5
Bingöl 134-135 E 3
Bingöl dağları 136-137 J 3
Bingwang 150-151 G 3
Binhai 146-147 GH 4-5
Binh Khê 150-151 G 6
Binh Liêu 150-151 F 2
Bin Ho'p = Ban Hin Heup 150-151 D 3
Binh So'n 150-151 G 5
Binh Thanh 150-151 G 6
Binī 141 D 2
Binjai 148-149 C 6
Binjharpur 138-139 L 7
Binjhārpura = Binjharpur 138-139 L 7
Bin Jiang 146-147 D 9-10
Binka 138-139 J 7
Binnaway 158-159 JK 6
Binongko, Pulau — 152-153 Q 8
Bin Qardān 166-167 M 3
Bin Rashīd 166-167 BC 3
Binscarth 61 H 5
Bin Sulīmān 166-167 C 3
Bintan, Pulau — 148-149 DE 6
Bintang, Gunung — 150-151 C 10
Bintaro, Jakarta- 154 IV a 2
Bintauna 152-153 P 5
Bin Ṭiyab 166-167 E 2
Bint Jubayl 136-137 F 6
Bintuhan 148-149 D 7
Bintulu 148-149 F 6
Bin Xian [TJ, Shaanxi] 146-147 AB 4
Bin Xian [TJ, Shandong] 146-147 FG 3
Binz, Zürich- 128 IV b 1
Binza 170 IV a 2
Binza, Kinshasa- 170 IV a 2
Binzart 164-165 FG 1
Binzart, Buḥayrat — 166-167 LM 1
Binzert = Binzart 164-165 FG 1
Bíobío 106-107 AB 6
Bío Bío, Río — 111 B 5
Biograd 122-123 F 4
Bioko 164-165 F 8
Biola, CA 74-75 CD 4
Bionga 171 AB 3
Biorka, AK 58-59 no 4
Bioûgra = Bīūkrā 166-167 B 4
Bīpūr = Beypore 140 B 5
Biqā', Al- 136-137 FG 5-6
Bīr = Bhīr 134-135 M 7
Bira 132-133 Z 8
Bi'r 'Abd an-Nabī 136-137 B 8
Bi'r Abū Gharādiq 136-137 C 7
Bi'r Abū Minqār 164-165 K 3
Bi'r Abū Sa'fah 173 D 6
Bi'r Abū Zawal 173 C 4
Bi'r ad-Dīyāb, Al- 166-167 B 6
Bi'r adh-Dhahab 166-167 F 7
Bi'r adh-Dhikār 164-165 J 3
Birāk 164-165 G 3
Bir'akovo 124-125 N 4
Bi'r al-Abd 173 C 2
Bi'r al-'Ajramīyah 173 BC 3
Bi'r al-Bayyūḍ 136-137 H 5
Bi'r al-Ghuzayl 166-167 M 5
Bi'r al-Hajāj 166-167 F 6
Bi'r al-Hamsah = Bi'r al-Khamsah 164-165 K 2
Bi'r al-Ḥaysī 173 D 3
Bi'r al-Ḥukayyim 164-165 J 2
Bi'r 'Alī 134-135 F 8
Bi'r 'Alī Bin Khalīfah 166-167 M 2
Bi'r al-'Itir 166-167 KL 2
Bi'r al-Jidāmī 173 C 4
Bi'r al-Khamsah 164-165 K 2
Bi'r al-Khamsha 164-165 K 2
Bi'r al-Mashāriqah 166-167 L 1
Bi'r al-Mulūṣī 136-137 J 6
Bi'r al-M'wisāt 166-167 A 7
Bi'r al-Qaf 164-165 H 3
Bi'r al-Qird'an 166-167 A 7
Bi'r al Wādī 136-137 K 6
Bi'r Amāsīn 166-167 LM 5
Bi'r an-Na'ām 136-137 G 7
Bi'r Anzarān 164-165 B 4
Birao 164-165 J 6
Bi'r 'Araiyida = Bi'r 'Urayyiḍah 173 BC 3
Birati, Dum Dum- 154 II b 2
Birāṭnagar 138-139 L 4
Bi'r Bayḍā' 173 CD 4
Bi'r Beida = Bi'r Bayḍā' 173 CD 4
Bi'r Ben Gania = Bi'r Bin Ganīyah 164-165 J 2
Birbhūm 138-139 L 6
Bi'r Bin Ganīyah 164-165 J 2
Bi'r Btaymān 136-137 H 4
Birch Creek 58-59 P 3
Birch Creek, AK 58-59 P 3
Birches, AK 58-59 L 4
Birch Hills 61 F 4
Birchip 160 F 5
Birch Island [CDN, island] 61 J 4
Birch Island [CDN, place] 60 H 4
Birch Lake [CDN] 61 C 4
Birch Lake [USA] 70-71 E 2
Birchleigh 170 V c 1
Birch Mountains 56-57 O 6
Bir-Chouhada = Bi'r Shuhadā' 166-167 K 2
Birch Pond 84 I c 2
Birch Rapids 61 EF 3
Birch River [CDN, place] 61 H 4
Birch River [CDN, river] 61 B 2
Birchwil 128 IV b 1
Bird 61 L 2
Bird Cape 58-59 s 7
Bird City, KS 68-69 F 6
Bir Diab = Al-Bi'r ad-Dīyāb 166-167 B 6
Bi'r Dibis 164-165 K 4
Bird Island 58-59 cd 2
Bird Island, MN 70-71 C 3
Bird Island = Voëleiland 174-175 G 7
Bir Djedid = Bi'r Jadīd 166-167 K 3
Bir Djenêien = Janā'in 166-167 LM 4
Birdsville 158-159 G 5
Birdum 158-159 F 3
Birecik 136-137 GH 4
Bir ed Dacar = Bi'r ad-Dhikār 164-165 J 3
Bir ed Deheb = Bi'r adh-Dhahab 166-167 F 7
Bir-el-Ater = Bi'r al-'Itir 166-167 KL 2
Bir el Gar = Bi'r al-Qaf 164-165 H 3
Bir el Ghazeil = Bi'r al-Ghuzayl 166-167 M 5
Bir el Hadjaj = Bi'r al-Hajāj 166-167 F 6
Bi'r el-Ḥeisī = Bi'r al-Ḥaysī 173 D 3
Bi'r el-Khamsa = Bi'r al-Khamsah 164-165 K 2
Birestik 136-137 GH 3
Bi'r Fatmah 136-137 K 5
Birganj 134-135 NO 5
Bi'r Ghabālū 166-167 H 1
Bi'r Ghallah 173 C 3
Bi'r Ghardan 166-167 K 2
Bir-Ghbalou = Bi'r Ghabālū 166-167 H 1
Bir Guerdane = Bi'r Ghardan 166-167 K 2
Bi'r Gulbān aṭ-Ṭaiyārāt = Qulbān aṭ-Ṭayyārāt 136-137 JK 5
Bi'r Hābā 136-137 H 5
Bir Hacheim = Bi'r al-Ḥukayyim 164-165 J 2
Bi'r Hālidah 136-137 B 7
Birhan 164-165 M 6
Bi'r Ḥariz al-Faqī 166-167 M 4
Bi'r Ḥasmat 'Umar 173 CD 7
Bi'r Hismet 'Umar = Bi'r Ḥasmat 'Umar 173 CD 7
Bi'r Hooker 173 B 2
Bi'r Houmaïmâ = Bi'r Ḥumaymah 136-137 HJ 5
Bi'r Hûker = Bi'r Hooker 173 B 2
Bi'r Ḥumaymah 136-137 HJ 5
Birigui 92-93 J 9
Biril'ussy 132-133 QR 6
Birimşe 136-137 H 3
Biritinga 100-101 E 6
Bi'r Jadīd 166-167 K 3
Birjand 134-135 H 4
Birjant 166-167 EF 2-3
Bir Jdid Chavent = Al-Bi'r al-Jadīd 166-167 B 3
Birkah 166-167 G 6
Birkān 166-167 E 2
Birkat as-Saffāf 136-137 M 7
Birkat Hamad 136-137 KL 7
Birkat Qārūn 164-165 KL 3
Birkenhead 119 E 5
Birket-Fatmé 164-165 HJ 6
Birkhadem 170 I a 2
Bi'r Khālda = Bi'r Hālidah 136-137 B 7
Birkholz [DDR, Frankfurt] 130 III c 1
Birkholz [DDR, Potsdam] 130 III b 2
Birkholzaue 130 III c 1
Birkīm 136-137 L 4
Bi'r Kusaybah 164-165 K 4
Bîrlad [RO, place] 122-123 M 2
Bîrlad [RO, river] 122-123 M 2-3
Bir Lehlū = Al-Bi'r al-Ahlū 166-167 B 6
Bir Lemouissate = Bi'r al-M'wisāt 166-167 A 7
Birma 148-149 BC 2
Bi'r Majal 173 C 6
Birmandréïs, Al-Jazā'ir- 170 I a 2
Bi'r Mashash = Bi'r Mushāsh 136-137 G 7
Bir Mcherga = Bi'r al-Mashāriqah 166-167 L 1
Birmensdorf 128 IV a 1
Bi'r Miaws 173 D 6
Bi'r Mineiga = Bi'r Munayjah 173 D 6
Birmingham, AL 64-65 J 5
Birmingham [GB] 119 EF 5
Bi'r Misāhah 164-165 K 4
Bi'r Mlayḥān 136-137 H 4
Bi'r Munayjah 173 D 6
Bi'r Murr 173 B 6
Bi'r Mushāsh 136-137 G 7
Bi'r Nābah 173 C 7
Bi'r Nāhid 136-137 C 7
Bi'r Nakhīlī 136-137 K 5
Bi'r Nakhlāy 173 B 6
Birney, MT 68-69 C 3
Birnie [CDN] 61 J 5
Birnie [Kiribati] 208 J 3
Birnin Gwari 168-169 G 3
Birnin Kebbi 164-165 EF 6
Birni-n'Konni 164-165 EF 6
Birnin Kudu 168-169 H 3
Bi'r Nukheila = Nukhaylah 164-165 K 5
Birobidžan 132-133 Z 8
Birpur 138-139 L 4
Bi'r Qulayb 173 CD 5
Bi'r Quleib = Bi'r Qulayb 173 CD 5
Birraḥḥāl 166-167 K 1
Birrie River 160 H 2
Birrindudu 158-159 EF 3
Bi'r Sajarī 136-137 H 6
Bi'r Samāh 136-137 L 8
Bi'r Sararāt Sayyāl 173 D 6
Bi'r Sejrī = Bi'r Sajarī 136-137 H 6
Bi'r Shināy 173 D 6
Bi'r Shuhadā' 166-167 K 2
Bi'r Sīf Fatimah 166-167 L 4
Birsilpur 138-139 D 3
Birsk 132-133 K 6
Birskij = Obluč'e 132-133 Z 8
Bir Soltân = Bi'r Sulṭān 166-167 L 3
Bir Soltane = Bi'r Soltân 166-167 L 3
Bi'r Sulṭān 166-167 L 3
Bi'r Tābah 173 D 3
Bi'r Takhfīs 173 AB 6
Bi'r Ṭamṭam 166-167 D 3
Bir Tangueur = Bi'r Tanqūr 166-167 L 4
Bi'r Tanqūr 166-167 L 4
Bi'r Ṭarfāwī 136-137 K 5
Bi'r Ṭarṭīn 136-137 J 5
Bi'r Tarūfāwī 136-137 K 6
Birtavarre 116-117 J 3
Bi'r Ṭawīl 164-165 L 4
Bi'r Tegherī 166-167 M 6
Bi'r Ṭifist 166-167 M 4
Birtle 61 H 5
Birtouta 170 I a 2
Bi'r Trafāwī 136-137 H 4
Bi'r Trefâouî = Bi'r Trafāwī 136-137 H 4
Bir'učij ostrov 126-127 G 3
Bir'ulovo, Moskva- 124-125 LM 6
Bi'r Umm Bishtīt 173 DE 6
Bi'r Umm Ḥibāl 173 C 6
Bi'r Umm Qarayn 164-165 B 3
Bi'r Umm Sa'īd 173 CD 3
Biruni 132-133 L 9
Birūr 140 B 4
Bi'r 'Urayyiḍah 173 BC 3
Birūru = Birūr 140 B 4
Bir'usa 132-133 S 6
Birwāgīyah 166-167 H 1
Biryān 166-167 HJ 3
Biržai 124-125 E 5
Bi'r Zalfānah 166-167 HJ 3
Bi'r Zayb 136-137 K 6
Bir Zelfana = Bi'r Zalfānah 166-167 HJ 3
Bisa, Pulau — 148-149 J 7
Bisaliya, El — = Al-Baṣalīyat Qiblī 173 C 5
Bisaolī = Bisauli 138-139 G 3
Bisauli 138-139 G 3
Bisbee, AZ 74-75 HJ 7
Bisbee, ND 68-69 G 1
Biscay, Bay of — 114-115 GH 6
Biscayne Bay 80-81 c 4
Biscéglie 122-123 G 5
Bischofsheim 128 III b 1
Bischofshofen 118 F 5
Biscoe Islands 53 C 30
Biscotasing 62 KL 3
Biscra = Biskrah 164-165 F 2
Biscucuy 94-95 G 3
Biserovo 124-125 T 4
Biševo 122-123 F 4
Bīshah, Wādī — 134-135 E 6-7
Bishamkaṭaka = Bissamcuttack 138-139 J 8
Bīsheh, Īstgah-e — 136-137 N 6
Bishenpur 134-135 P 6
Bishnāth 141 C 2
Bishnupur 138-139 L 6
Bishop, CA 74-75 D 4
Bishop, TX 76-77 F 9
Bishopville, SC 80-81 F 3
Bishrī, Jabal al- 136-137 H 5
Bishshāṭir 166-167 L 1
Bisikon 128 IV b 1
Bisinaca 94-95 G 5
Biskayerhuken 116-117 hj 5
Biskotasi Lake 62 K 3
Biskrah 164-165 F 2
Bisling 148-149 J 5
Bismagar = Visnagar 138-139 D 6
Bismarck, MO 70-71 E 7
Bismarck, ND 64-65 F 2
Bismarck Archipelago 148-149 gh 5
Bismarckburg = Kasanga 172 F 3
Bismarck Range 148-149 M 7-N 8
Bismarck Sea 148-149 gh 5
Bismil 136-137 J 4
Bison, SD 68-69 E 3
Bīsotūn 136-137 M 5
Bissagos Islands = Arquipélago dos Bijagós 164-165 A 6
Bissamcuttack 138-139 J 8
Bissau 164-165 A 6
Bissett 62 B 2
Bistcho Lake 56-57 N 6
Bistineau, Lake — 78-79 C 4
Bistōnis, Límnē — 122-123 L 5
Bistriṭa [RO, place] 122-123 L 2
Bistriṭa [RO, river] 122-123 M 2
Bisvān = Biswān 138-139 H 4
Biswān 138-139 H 4
Bitam 172 B 1
Bitca 113 V c 4
Bitely, MI 70-71 GH 4
Bitik 126-127 P 1
Bitlis 134-135 E 3
Bitlis dağları 136-137 JK 3
Bitola 122-123 J 5
Bitonto 122-123 G 5
Bitter Creek 66-67 J 5
Bitter Creek, WY 68-69 B 5
Bitterfeld 118 F 3
Bitterfontein 172 C 8
Bitterroot Range 64-65 C 2-D 3
Bitterroot River 66-67 F 2
Bittou 168-169 E 3
Bit'ug 126-127 K 1
Bitumount 61 C 2
Bitung 148-149 J 6
Bitupitá 100-101 D 2
Bituruna 102-103 G 7
Biu 164-165 G 6
Bīūkrā 166-167 B 4
Biu Plateau 168-169 HJ 3
Biviraka 148-149 M 8
Biwa-ko 142-143 Q 4
Biyāḍ, Al- = Al-Bayāḍ 134-135 F 6
Biyalā 173 B 2
Biyang 146-147 D 5
Biysk = Bijsk 132-133 Q 7
Bizana 174-175 HJ 6
Bižbul'ak 124-125 U 7
Bizcocho 106-107 J 4
Bizerta = Binzart 164-165 FG 1
Bizerte = Binzart 164-165 FG 1

Bjargtangar 116-117 a 2
Bjelovar 122-123 G 3
Bjelowo = Belovo 132-133 Q 7
Bjelucha = gora Belucha 132-133 Q 8
Bjorkdale 61 FG 4
Björkholmen 116-117 H 4
Bjórko = Bol'šoj Ver'ozovyj ostrov 124-125 FG 3
Björkö = Primorsk 124-125 G 3
Björna 116-117 H 6
Björneborg = Pori 116-117 J 7
Bjuröklubb 116-117 JK 5

Bla 168-169 D 2
Blaauwberg = Blouberg 174-175 H 2
Blaauwkop = Bloukop 174-175 H 4
Blaauwpan 174-175 D 4
Black, AK 58-59 E 5
Blackall 158-159 HJ 4
Black Bay 70-71 F 1
Black Belt 64-65 J 5
Black Birch Lake 61 E 2
Blackburn 119 EF 5
Blackburn, Mount — 56-57 H 5
Black Butte 68-69 E 2
Black Canyon 74-75 F 5
Black Canyon of the Gunnison National Monument 68-69 C 6
Black Diamond 60 K 4
Black Diamond, WA 66-67 BC 2
Black Duck 56-57 ST 6
Black Eagle, MT 66-67 H 2
Blackfeet Indian Reservation 66-67 G 1
Blackfoot, ID 66-67 GH 4
Blackfoot, MT 66-67 G 1
Blackfoot Reservoir 66-67 H 4
Blackfoot River 66-67 G 2
Black Forest = Schwarzwald 118 D 4-5
Black Gobi = Char Gov' 142-143 GH 3
Black Hawk 62 C 3
Black Hills 64-65 F 3
Black Horse, PA 84 III a 2
Blackie 60 L 4
Black Island 62 A 2
Black Lake [CDN] 72-73 L 1-2
Black Lake [USA] 70-71 HJ 3
Black Lake [USA, Alaska] 58-59 d 1
Blackleaf, MT 66-67 G 1
Black Mbuluzi 174-175 J 4
Black Mesa 74-75 H 4
Black Mountain, NC 80-81 EF 3
Black Mountain [USA] 78-79 G 3
Black Mountains [USA] 64-65 D 4-5
Black Nossob = Swart Nossob 174-175 C 2
Black Pine Peak 66-67 G 4
Black Point 58-59 g 1
Blackpool [CDN] 60 G 4
Blackpool [GB] 119 E 5
Black Range 76-77 A 6
Black Rapids, AK 58-59 P 5
Black River, MI 72-73 E 2
Black River [CDN] 62 AB 2
Black River [USA ◁ Henderson Bay] 72-73 J 3
Black River [USA ◁ Mississippi River] 70-71 E 3
Black River [USA ◁ Porcupine River] 58-59 Q 3
Black River [USA ◁ Saint Clair River] 72-73 E 3
Black River [USA ◁ Salt River] 74-75 HJ 6
Black River [USA ◁ White River] 78-79 D 2-3
Black River = Sông Đa 148-149 D 2
Black River Falls, WI 70-71 E 3
Black Rock 56-57 N 6
Black Rock, AR 78-79 D 2
Black Rock, UT 74-75 G 3
Black Rock Desert 64-65 C 3
Blackrock Lake 85 II b 3
Blacksburg, VA 80-81 F 2
Black Sea 114-115 PQ 7
Blackshear, GA 80-81 EF 5
Black Springs, NM 74-75 J 6
Black Squirrel Creek 68-69 D 6
Blackstone, VA 80-81 GH 2
Black Sturgeon Lake 70-71 F 1
Black Umfolozi = Swart Umfolozi 174-175 J 4-5
Blackville 63 CD 4
Blackville, SC 80-81 F 4
Black Volta 164-165 D 7
Black Waxy Prairie 64-65 G 5
Blackwell, OK 76-77 F 4
Blackwell, TX 76-77 D 6
Blackwood, NJ 84 III c 3
Blackwood Terrace, NJ 84 III c 3
Bladensburg, MD 82 II b 1
Bladgrond 174-175 CD 5
Bláfjall 116-117 e 2
Blåfjorden 116-117 lm 5
Blagodarnoje 126-127 L 4
Blagodatnoje 126-127 G 3
Blagoevgrad 122-123 K 4-5
Blagoveščensk 132-133 YZ 7
Blagoveščenskij proliv 132-133 c 2-d 3
Blagoveščenskoje 124-125 O 3
Blagoveshchensk = Blagoveščensk 132-133 YZ 7
Blaine, WA 66-67 B 1
Blaine Lake 61 E 4
Blair, NE 68-69 H 5
Blair, OK 76-77 E 5
Blair, WI 70-71 E 3
Blair Athol 158-159 J 4
Blairbeth 174-175 G 3
Blairmore 66-67 F 1
Blairsden, CA 74-75 C 3
Blairsville, GA 80-81 DE 3
Blairsville, PA 72-73 G 4
Blakely, GA 78-79 G 5
Blake Point 70-71 F 1
Blambagan = Semenanjung Blambagan 152-153 L 10
Blanca, CO 68-69 D 7
Blanca Grande 106-107 G 6
Blanca Peak 64-65 E 4
Blanchard, LA 76-77 GH 6
Blanche, Lake — [AUS, South Australia] 158-159 GH 5
Blanche, Lake — [AUS, Western Australia] 158-159 D 4
Blanc-Mesnil, le — 129 I c 2
Blanco 174-175 E 7-8
Blanco, TX 76-77 E 7
Blanco Creek 76-77 C 5
Blancos, Los — [RA] 111 D 2
Blanc-Sablon 63 H 2
Blandá 116-117 d 2
Blanding, UT 74-75 J 4
Blaney 174-175 G 7
Blangkejeren 152-153 B 4
Blankaholm 116-117 FG 9
Blankenburg, Berlin- 130 III b 1
Blankenfelde, Berlin- 130 III b 1
Blanket, TX 76-77 E 7
Blanquillo 106-107 K 4
Blantyre 172 FG 5
Blao, Đeo- = Đeo Bao Lôc 150-151 F 7
Blaquier 106-107 F 5
Blauen [CH] 128 IV b 1
Blåvands Huk 116-117 BC 10
Blavet 120-121 F 4-5
Blaye 120-121 G 6
Blayney 158-159 J 6
Blaze, Point — 158-159 EF 2
Blazon, WY 66-67 H 5
Bleaker Island 108-109 K 9
Blednaja, gora — 132-133 M 2
Bledsoe, TX 76-77 C 6
Blejeşti 122-123 L 3
Blekinge län 116-117 F 9
Blenheim, NJ 84 III c 3
Blenheim [CDN] 72-73 F 3
Blenheim [NZ] 158-159 O 8
Blenque, Río — 96-97 B 2
Blessing, TX 76-77 F 8
Bleu Mountains 78-79 C 3
Blewett, TX 76-77 D 8
Blida = Blīdah 164-165 E 1
Blīdah [DZ, administrative unit] 170 I ab 2
Blīdah [DZ, place] 164-165 E 1
Blidet-Amor = Bulaydat 'Amūr 166-167 J 3
Blikana 174-175 G 6
Blind River 62 K 3
Bliss, ID 66-67 F 4
Blissfield, MI 72-73 E 4
Blitar 148-149 F 8
Blitong = Pulau Belitung 148-149 E 7
Blitta 164-165 E 7
Blitzen, OR 66-67 D 4
Block Island 72-73 L 4
Block Island Sound 72-73 KL 4
Bloedrivier [ZA, place] 174-175 J 4
Bloedrivier [ZA, river] 174-175 J 4-5
Bloemfontein 172 E 7
Bloemhof 174-175 F 4
Bloemspruitrivier 174-175 G 4-5
Blois 120-121 H 5
Blomspruit = Bloemspruitrivier 174-175 G 4-5
Blönduós 116-117 cd 2
Blood Vein River [CDN, place] 61 K 5
Bloodvein River [CDN, river] 62 AB 2
Bloody Falls 56-57 NO 4
Bloomer, WI 70-71 E 3
Bloomfield, IA 70-71 D 5
Bloomfield, IN 70-71 G 6
Bloomfield, KY 70-71 H 7
Bloomfield, NE 68-69 H 4
Bloomfield, NJ 82 III a 2
Bloomfield, NM 74-75 JK 4
Bloomfield, New York-, NY 82 III ab 3
Blooming Prairie, MN 70-71 D 4
Bloomington, IL 64-65 HJ 3
Bloomington, IN 64-65 J 4
Bloomington, MN 70-71 D 3
Bloomington, TX 76-77 F 8
Bloomsburg, PA 72-73 H 4
Blora 152-153 J 9
Blosseville Kyst 56-57 ef 4
Blossom, mys — 132-133 jk 3
Blouberg [ZA, mountain] 174-175 H 2
Blouberg [ZA, place] 174-175 H 2
Bloukop 174-175 H 4
Blountstown, FL 78-79 G 5
Bloupan 174-175 C 6
Bloupan = Blaauwpan 174-175 D 4
Blouwberg = Blouberg 174-175 H 2
Bloxom, VA 80-81 J 2
Blūdān 136-137 G 6
Blue Bell Knoll 74-75 H 3
Blueberry 60 G 1
Blue Bonnets, Champ de Course — 82 I b 2
Bluecliff 174-175 F 7
Blue Creek, UT 66-67 G 5
Blue Earth, MN 70-71 CD 4
Bluefield, VA 80-81 F 2
Bluefield, WV 80-81 F 2
Bluefields 64-65 K 9
Bluefields, Bahía de — 88-89 E 8
Bluegrass Region 70-71 H 6
Blue Hill, NE 68-69 G 5
Blue Hills of Couteau 63 GH 4
Blue Hills Reservation 84 I b 3
Blue Island, IL 70-71 FG 5
Bluejoint Lake 66-67 D 4
Blue Knob 72-73 G 4
Blue Lake, CA 66-67 B 5
Blue Mosque 170 II b 1
Blue Mountain [BUR] 141 C 4
Blue Mountain [USA, Montana] 68-69 DE 2
Blue Mountain [USA, Pennsylvania] 72-73 HJ 4
Blue Mountain Pass 66-67 E 4
Blue Mountains [JA] 64-65 L 8
Blue Mountains [USA, Maine] 72-73 L 2
Blue Mountains [USA, Oregon] 64-65 C 2-3
Blue Mountains [USA, Texas] 76-77 E 7
Blue Mud Bay 158-159 G 2
Blue Mud Hills 68-69 D 3
Blue Nile = An-Nīl al-Azraq 164-165 L 6
Bluenose Lake 56-57 N 4
Blue Rapids, KS 68-69 H 6
Blue Ridge, GA 80-81 D 3
Blue Ridge [CDN] 60 K 2
Blue Ridge [USA, Alabama] 78-79 FG 4
Blue Ridge [USA, New York] 72-73 J 3
Blue Ridge [USA, North Carolina] 64-65 KL 4
Blueridge, Houston-, TX 85 III b 2
Blue River 74-75 J 6
Blue Springs, MO 70-71 CD 6
Bluewater, NM 74-75 JK 5
Bluff 158-159 N 9
Bluff, AK 58-59 F 4
Bluff, UT 74-75 J 4
Bluff, The — 88-89 H 2
Bluff Point 155 I b 2
Bluffs of Llano Estacado 76-77 C 5
Bluffton, IN 72-73 D 4
Bluffton, OH 72-73 E 4
Blufton, IN 70-71 H 5
Blum, TX 76-77 F 6
Blumenau [BR] 111 FG 3
Blumut, Gunung — 148-149 D 6
Blunt, SD 68-69 FG 3
Bly, OR 66-67 C 4
Blying Sound 58-59 N 7
Blyth [CDN] 72-73 F 3
Blythe, CA 74-75 F 6
Blytheville, AR 64-65 HJ 4

B. Mitre 110 III b 1

Bo [WAL] 164-165 B 7
Boa Água 100-101 E 3
Boaco 88-89 D 8
Boaçu 100-101 D 8
Boa Esperança [BR, Amazonas] 98-99 G 8
Boa Esperança [BR, Ceará] 100-101 D 3
Boa Esperança [BR, Espírito Santo] 100-101 DE 10
Boa Esperança [BR, Goiás] 100-101 A 8
Boa Esperança [BR, Minas Gerais] 102-103 K 4
Boa Esperança [BR, Piauí] 100-101 C 5
Boa Esperança [BR, Roraima] 94-95 L 6
Boa Esperança, Represa da — 100-101 B 4
Boa Esperança do Sul 102-103 H 4
Boa Fé 98-99 B 8
Boa Hora 98-99 G 10
Bo 'ai 146-147 D 4
Boajibu 168-169 C 3
Boakview 72-73 FG 2
Boali 164-165 H 8
Boame 174-175 K 4

Boa Morada 100-101 B 4
Boa Nova [BR, Bahia] 92-93 LM 7
Boa Nova [BR, Pará] 98-99 J 9
Boardman, OR 66-67 D 3
Boa Sorte, Rio — 100-101 B 7
Boath 138-139 G 8
Boa Viagem 100-101 E 3
Boa Vista [BR, Acre] 98-99 BC 9
Boa Vista [BR, Amazonas] 98-99 B 7
Boa Vista [BR, Roraima] 92-93 G 4
Boa Vista [Cape Verde] 204-205 E 7
Boa Vista, Morro da — 102-103 K 5
Boa Vista, Serra da — 100-101 EF 4
Boaz, AL 78-79 FG 3
Bobadah 160 H 4
Bobai 146-147 BC 10
Bobare 94-95 G 2
Bobbejaanskloofberge 174-175 EF 7
Bobbili 134-135 N 7
Bòbbio 122-123 C 3
Bobigny 129 I c 2
Bobo-Dioulasso 164-165 D 6
Bobo-Diulasso = Bobo-Dioulasso 164-165 D 6
Bobonaza, Río — 96-97 C 2
Bobonong 172 E 6
Bóbr 118 G 3
Bobrik 124-125 F 7
Bobriki = Novomoskovsk 124-125 M 6
Bobrinec 126-127 F 2
Bobrka 126-127 B 2
Bobrof Island 58-59 u 6-7
Bobrov 126-127 J 1
Bobrovica 126-127 E 1
Bobrovskoje 124-125 P 3
Bobrujsk 124-125 G 7
Bobures 94-95 F 3
Bocá, Buenos Aires- 110 III b 1
Boca, Cachoeira da — 98-99 L 7
Boca, La — 64-65 b 3
Boca Araguao 94-95 L 3
Boca da Estrada 94-95 L 6
Boca de Arichuna 94-95 H 4
Boca de Aroa 94-95 GH 2
Boca de Jesus María 86-87 M 5
Boca de la Serpiente 92-93 G 2-3
Boca de la Travesía 108-109 GH 3
Boca del Pao 92-93 FG 3
Boca del Río 86-87 MN 8
Boca del Tocuyo 94-95 GH 2
Boca de Macareo 94-95 L 3
Boca de Pozo 94-95 J 2
Boca do Acre 92-93 F 6
Boca do Jari 92-93 J 5
Boca do Mato, Rio de Janeiro- 110 I b 2
Boca do Mutum 98-99 DE 7
Boca do Tapauá = Tapauá 92-93 FG 6
Boca Grande 94-95 L 3
Boca Grande, FL 80-81 b 3
Bocaina 102-103 H 5
Bocaina, Serra da — 102-103 GH 7-8
Bocaiuva 92-93 L 8
Bocaiuva do Sul 102-103 H 6
Bocajá 102-103 E 5
Boca Mavaca 94-95 J 6
Bocanda 168-169 DE 4
Bocaranga 164-165 H 7
Boca Raton, FL 80-81 cd 3
Bocas 86-87 K 6
Boca Santa María 86-87 M 5
Bocas de Caraparaná 94-95 E 8
Bocas del Dragon 94-95 L 2
Bocas del Toro 88-89 E 10
Bocas del Toro, Archipiélago de — 88-89 EF 10
Bocche di Bonifàcio 122-123 C 5
Bochina 118 K 4
Bochinche 94-95 L 4
Bocholt 118 C 3
Bochum 118 C 3
Bockenheim, Frankfurt am Main- 128 III a 1
Boconito 94-95 FG 3
Bocono 94-95 F 3
Boconó, Río — 94-95 G 3
Boçoroca 100-101 D 5
Boda [RCA] 164-165 H 8
Böda [S] 116-117 G 9
Bodajbo 132-133 VW 6
Bodega Head 74-75 B 3
Bodelé 164-165 H 5
Boden 116-117 JK 5
Bodensee 118 D 5
Bodhan 140 CD 1
Bodināyakkanūr 140 C 6
Bodo [CDN] 61 C 4
Bodø [N] 116-117 EF 4
Bodocó 100-101 E 4
Bodogodo = Badagada 138-139 K 8
Bodoquena 92-93 H 8
Bodoquena, Serra — 92-93 H 9
Bodrum 136-137 B 4
Bô Đu'c 150-151 F 6-7
Bod Zizhiqu 141 BC 1
Boekittingi = Bukittingi 148-149 CD 7
Boende 172 D 2
Boerne, TX 76-77 E 8
Boesakrivier 174-175 E 6
Boesakspruit = Boesakrivier 174-175 E 6
Boezak River = Boesakrivier 174-175 E 6
Bofete 102-103 H 5
Boffa 164-165 B 6
Bōfu = Hōfu 144-145 H 5-6
Bogale 141 D 7
Bogalusa, LA 64-65 HJ 5
Bogandé 164-165 DE 6
Bogan Gate 160 H 4
Bogan River 158-159 J 6
Bogarnes 116-117 bc 2
Bogata, TX 76-77 G 6
Bogatka 124-125 OP 2
Bogatoje 124-125 S 7
Bogatyje Saby 124-125 S 6
Boğazkale 136-137 F 2-3
Boğazköprü 136-137 F 3
Boğazlıyan 136-137 F 3
Bogd 142-143 J 2
Bogdanovka 124-125 T 7
Bogdo uul 142-143 FG 3
Bogenfels 174-175 A 4
Bogenhausen, München- 130 II b 2
Boget 126-127 NO 2
Boggabilla 158-159 JK 5
Boggabri 160 JK 3
Boggai, Lak — 171 D 2
Bogham, Al- 136-137 J 5
Boghari = Qasr al-Bukharī 164-165 E 1
Bogia 148-149 MN 7
Boğlan 136-137 J 3
Bogo [RP] 148-149 H 4
Bogoduchov 126-127 G 1
Bogol'ubovo [SU, Smolenskaja Oblast'] 124-125 J 6
Bogong, Mount — 158-159 J 7
Bogor 148-149 E 8
Bogorā 138-139 M 5
Bogorodick 124-125 LM 7
Bogorodsk [SU, Gor'kovskaja Oblast'] 124-125 O 5
Bogorodsk [SU, Komi ASSR] 124-125 ST 2
Bogorodskoje [SU, Kirovskaja Oblast'] 124-125 S 5
Bogorodskoje, Moskva- 113 V cd 2
Bogoslof Island 58-59 m 4
Bogotá 92-93 E 4
Bogota, NJ 82 III b 1
Bogotá, Río — 91 III b 1
Bogotá-Alqueria 91 III b 3
Bogotá-Bavaria 91 III b 3
Bogotá-Boyaca 91 III b 2
Bogotá-Ciudad Universitaria 91 III bc 3
Bogotá-El Encanto 91 III b 4
Bogotá-El Prado 91 III c 2
Bogotá-El Rocio 91 III bc 3-4
Bogotá-El Tunal 91 III b 4
Bogotá-Fatima 91 III b 3
Bogotá-Granjas de Techo 91 III b 3
Bogotá-Ingles 91 III b 4
Bogotá-La Esperanza 91 III c 3
Bogotá-La Granja 91 III b 2
Bogotá-Las Acacias 91 III b 4
Bogotá-Las Ferias 91 III b 2
Bogotá-México 91 III b 4
Bogotá-Minuto de Dios 91 III b 2
Bogotá-Navarra 91 III c 2
Bogotá-Pastrana 91 III ab 3
Bogotá-Quirigua 91 III b 2
Bogotá-Restrepo 91 III b 3
Bogotá-Ricaurte 91 III b 3
Bogotá-San Fernando 91 III c 2
Bogotá-San Pablo 91 III a 2
Bogotá-San Rafael 91 III b 4
Bogotá-Tunjuelito 91 III b 4
Bogotol 132-133 Q 6
Bogou 168-169 F 3
Bogovarovo 124-125 Q 4
Bogra = Bogorā 138-139 M 5
Bogučany 132-133 S 6
Bogučar 126-127 K 2
Boguševsk 124-125 H 6
Boguslav 126-127 E 2
Bogyi Ywa = Bôlkyīywā 150-151 A 5
Bo Hai 142-143 M 4
Bohai Haixia 142-143 N 4
Bohai Wan 146-147 FG 2
Bohemian Forest 118 F 4
Bohemian Forest = Böhmerwald 118 FG 4
Bohemian-Moravian Height = Českomoravská vrchovina 118 GH 4
Bohnsdorf, Berlin- 130 III c 2
Bohol 148-149 H 5
Bo Hu = Po Hu 146-147 F 6
Boi, Ponta do — 102-103 K 6
Boiaçu 98-99 H 5
Boibeīs, Límnē — 122-123 K 6
Boicovo 104-105 E 7
Boigu Island 148-149 M 8
Boim 92-93 H 5
Boipārīguḍā 140 F 1
Boi Preto, Serra do — 102-103 F 6
Bois, Lac des — 56-57 M 4
Bois, Rio dos — 102-103 G 3
Bois Blanc Island 70-71 HJ 3
Bois-d'Arcy 129 I b 2
Boise City, ID 64-65 G 3
Boise City, OK 76-77 C 4
Boise River 66-67 E 4
Bois le Duc = 's-Hertogenbosch 120-121 KL 3
Bois Notre-Dame 129 I d 2
Boissevain 68-69 FG 1
Boissy-Saint-Léger 129 I d 2
Boituva 102-103 J 5
Bojador, Cabo — = Rā's Bujdūr 164-165 AB 3
Bojarka 132-133 S 3
Bojnūrd 134-135 H 3
Bojonegoro 152-153 JK 9
Boju = Baiju 146-147 H 5
Bojuru 111 F 4
Bojuru, Ponta — 106-107 M 3
Bokani 168-169 G 3
Bokāro 138-139 K 6
Boké 164-165 B 6
Bo Kham 150-151 F 6
Bô Kheo 150-151 F 6
Bokkeveldberge 174-175 C 6
Bokkol 171 D 2
Bokkraal 174-175 C 6
Boknfjord 116-117 A 8
Bolukābād 136-137 M 4
Boko 141 B 3
Bokong 174-175 H 5
Bokor 150-151 DE 7
Bokoro 164-165 H 6
Bokote 172 D 1-2
Bokoto 168-169 F 3
Bokovskaja 126-127 K 2
Bōkpyin 150-151 B 7
Boksburg 174-175 H 4
Boksburg North 170 V c 2
Boksitogorsk 124-125 J 4
Bokungu 172 D 2
Bolaiti 172 DE 2
Bolama 164-165 A 6
Bolān, Kotal — 134-135 K 5
Bolangir = Balāngīr 134-135 N 6
Bolan Pass = Kotal Bolān 134-135 K 5
Bólbē, Límnē — 122-123 K 6
Bolbec 120-121 H 4
Bolchov 124-125 KL 7
Bole 164-165 D 7
Bole, MT 66-67 GH 2
Bolechov 126-127 AB 2
Boles, ID 66-67 E 3
Bolesławiec 118 GH 3
Bolgatanga 164-165 D 6
Bolger 62 N 2
Bolgrad 126-127 D 4
Boli [TJ] 142-143 P 2
Boli [ZRE] 171 B 2
Boliden 116-117 J 5
Boligee, AL 78-79 E 4
Boling, TX 76-77 FG 8
Bolissós 122-123 L 6
Bolivar, MO 70-71 D 7
Bolivar, TN 78-79 E 3
Bolívar [CO, Antioquia] 94-95 CD 5
Bolívar [CO, Armenia] 94-95 C 5
Bolívar [CO, Bolívar] 94-95 D 3
Bolívar [CO, Popayán] 94-95 C 7
Bolívar [EC] 96-97 B 2
Bolívar [PE] 92-93 D 6
Bolívar [YV] 94-95 JK 4
Bolívar, Pico — 92-93 E 3
Bolívar Peninsula 76-77 G 8
Bolivia 92-93 F-H 8
Bolkar dağları 136-137 F 4
Bolkow [CDN] 70-71 J 1
Bōlkyīywā 150-151 A 5
Bollebeek 128 II a 1
Bolling Air Force Base 82 II ab 2
Bollnäs 116-117 G 7
Bollon 158-159 J 5
Bolnisi 126-127 M 6
Bolobo 172 C 2
Bolochovo 124-125 LM 6
Bologhine Ibnou Ziri, Al-Jazā'ir- 170 I a 1
Bologna 122-123 D 3
Bolognesi [BR] 96-97 E 5
Bolognesi [PE] 96-97 D 7
Bologoje 132-133 EF 6
Bologovo 124-125 H 5
Bolomba 172 C 1
Bolor = Bāltistān 134-135 M 3-4
Bolo-retto = Penghu Lieh-tao 142-143 M 7
Bólos 122-123 K 6
Bolotnoje 132-133 P 6
Boloven, Cao Nguyên — 148-149 E 3-4
Bolpur 138-139 L 6
Bolsa, Cerro — 106-107 C 2
Boľšaja = Velikaja 132-133 h 5
Boľšaja Černigovka 124-125 S 7
Boľšaja Kinel' 124-125 T 7
Boľšaja Kokšaga 124-125 Q 5
Boľšaja L'vogora 124-125 L 2
Boľšaja Martynovka 126-127 KL 3
Boľšaja Orlovka 126-127 K 3
Boľšaja Sosnova 124-125 U 5
Boľšaja Usa 124-125 U 5
Boľšaja Višera 124-125 J 4
Boľšaja Vys' 126-127 E 2
Boľšekrepinskaja 126-127 JK 3
Boľšelug 124-125 T 2
Bolsena, Lago di — 122-123 DE 4
Boľševik, ostrov — 132-133 T-V 2
Boľšezemeľskaja tundra 132-133 JK 4
Bolshevik = ostrov Boľševik 132-133 T-V 2
Boľšije Abuli, gora — 126-127 LM 6
Boľšije Doldy 124-125 UV 3
Boľšije Ozerki [SU, Archangeľskaja Oblast'] 124-125 MN 2
Boľšije Uki 132-133 N 6
Boľšinka 126-127 K 2
Boľšoj An'uj 132-133 fg 4
Boľšoj Čeremšan 124-125 S 6
Boľšoj Muraškino 124-125 P 6
Boľšoj Irgiz 124-125 R 8
Boľšoj Jenisej 132-133 S 7
Boľšoj Klimeckij, ostrov — 124-125 KL 3
Boľšoj Oloj = Oloj 132-133 f 4
Boľšoj Šantar, ostrov — 132-133 ab 7
Boľšoj Teatr 113 V c 2
Boľšoj T'uters, ostrov — 124-125 FG 4
Boľšoj Uluj 132-133 R 6
Boľšoj Uzen' 126-127 O 2
Boľšoj Ver'ozovyj, ostrov — 124-125 FG 3
Bolsón, El — 108-109 D 3
Bolsón de Mapimí 64-65 F 6
Bolton 119 E 5
Bolton, NC 80-81 G 3
Bolton, Atlanta-, GA 85 II b 1
Bolu 136-137 D 2
Bo Luang 150-151 B 3
Bolukābād 136-137 M 4
Bolungarvík 116-117 ab 1
Boluo 146-147 E 10
Bolvadin 136-137 D 3
Bolzano 122-123 D 2
Boma 172 B 3
Boma, Gulf of — = Khalīj al-Bunbah 164-165 JK 2
Bomadi 168-169 G 4
Bomarton, TX 76-77 E 6
Bomba 100-101 A 8
Bómba, Khalig — = Khalīj al-Bunbah 164-165 J 2
Bomba, La — 86-87 C 2
Bombaim = Bombay 134-135 L 7
Bombala 158-159 JK 7
Bombarai 148-149 K 7
Bombay 134-135 L 7
Bombetoka, Baie de — 172 HJ 5
Bombo 171 C 2
Bom Comércio 92-93 F 6
Bom Conselho 100-101 F 5
Bom Despacho 92-93 KL 8
Bomdila 141 C 2
Bom Futuro 98-99 H 10
Bomi Hills 164-165 B 7
Bom Jesus [BR, Piauí] 92-93 L 6
Bom Jesus [BR, Rio Grande do Sul] 106-107 M 2
Bom Jesus da Gurguéia, Serra — 92-93 L 6-7
Bom Jesus da Lapa 92-93 L 7
Bom Jesus do Galho 102-103 LM 3
Bom Jesus do Norte 102-103 M 4
Bømlafjord 116-117 A 8
Bømlo 116-117 A 8
Bommersheim 128 III a 1
Bomokandi 172 E 1
Bomongo 172 C 1
Bom Princípio 100-101 D 2
Bom Retiro 102-103 H 7
Bom Rétiro, São Paulo- 110 II b 2
Bom Sossêgo 100-101 C 7
Bom Sucesso 102-103 K 4
Bom Sucesso, Serra — 102-103 KL 1
Bom Sucessu 102-103 FG 5
Bomu 172 D 1
Bon, Cap — = Rā' aṭ-Ṭīh 164-165 G 1
Bona = Annābah 164-165 F 1
Bona, Mount — 58-59 QR 6
Bonāb [IR ↖ Tabrīz] 136-137 LM 3
Bonāb [IR ↙ Tabrīz] 136-137 M 4
Bon Accord 174-175 H 3
Bonai = Banāī 138-139 K 7
Bonaigarh 138-139 K 7
Bon Air, PA 84 III b 2
Bonaire 64-65 N 9
Bonames, Frankfurt am Main- 128 III ab 1
Bonampak 86-87 P 9
Bonanza 88-89 D 8
Bonanza, ID 66-67 F 3
Bonaparte 96-97 D 5
Bonaparte, Mount — 66-67 D 1
Bonaparte Archipelago 158-159 DE 2
Bonasila Dome 58-59 G 5
Bonasse 94-95 L 2
Bonaventura 63 D 3
Bonavista 56-57 a 8
Bonavista Bay 63 K 3
Bon Bon 160 BC 3
Bond, CO 68-69 C 6
Bondari 124-125 O 7
Bondelswarts Reserve 174-175 C 4-5
Bondeno 122-123 D 3
Bond Hill 160 B 3
Bondi Bay 161 I b 2
Bondiss 60 L 2
Bondo [ZRE] 172 D 1
Bondoc Peninsula 148-149 H 4
Bondoukou 164-165 D 7
Bondowoso 152-153 KL 9
Bond'ug 124-125 U 3
Bondurant, WY 66-67 HJ 4
Bond'užskij 124-125 T 6
Bondy 129 I c 2
Bone 152-153 P 8
Bône = Annābah 164-165 F 1
Bone = Watampone 148-149 GH 7
Bone, Teluk — 148-149 H 7
Bonelipu 152-153 P 8
Bonelohe 152-153 O 8
Boneogeh 152-153 O 9
Bonerate, Pulau — 152-153 O 9
Bonete, Cerro — 106-107 C 1
Bonfield 72-73 G 1
Bonfim [BR, Amazonas] 96-97 E 6
Bonfim [BR, Gerais] 102-103 K 4
Bonfinópolis de Minas 102-103 JK 2
Bong [LB, administrative unit] 168-169 C 4
Bong [LB, place] 168-169 C 4
Bonga 164-165 M 7
Bongandanga 172 D 1
Bongāñv = Bangaon 138-139 M 6
Bongaon = Bangaon 138-139 M 6
Bongchhung 138-139 L 3
Bongo 172 AB 2
Bongolave 172 J 5
Bongor 164-165 H 6
Bongouanou 168-169 DE 4
Bongtol 138-139 HJ 2
Bonham, TX 76-77 F 6
Bonhu 100-101 E 3
Boni, Gulf of — = Teluk Bone 148-149 H 7
Bonibaou 168-169 J 4
Bonifacio 122-123 C 5
Bonifàcio, Bocche di — 122-123 C 5
Bonifay, FL 78-79 G 5
Bonilla, SD 68-69 G 3
Bonin 206-207 RS 7
Boninal 100-101 D 7
Bonin Trench 156-157 G 3
Bonita, AZ 74-75 HJ 6
Bonita, La — 96-97 C 1
Bonita, Point — 83 I a 2
Bonitas, Las — 92-93 FG 3
Bonito [BR, Mato Grosso do Sul] 102-103 D 4
Bonito [BR, Minas Gerais] 102-103 K 1
Bonito [BR, Pernambuco] 100-101 G 5
Bonn 118 C 3
Bonne Bay 63 H 2
Bonner, MT 66-67 G 2
Bonners Ferry, ID 66-67 E 1
Bonner Springs, KS 70-71 C 6
Bonne Terre, MO 70-71 E 7
Bonneuil-en-France 129 I c 2
Bonneuil-sur-Marne 129 I c 2
Bonneville, OR 66-67 C 3
Bonneville, WY 68-69 BC 4
Bonneville Salt Flats 66-67 G 5
Bonnie Rock 158-159 C 6
Bonnievale 174-175 CD 7
Bönningstedt 130 I a 1
Bonny 164-165 F 8
Bonny, Golfe de — 164-165 F 8
Bonny Reservoir 68-69 E 6
Bonnyville 56-57 O 7
Bono, AR 78-79 D 3
Bō-no misaki 144-145 GH 7
Bonoua 168-169 E 4
Bonpland 106-107 J 2
Bonstetten 128 IV a 2
Bonsucesso, Rio de Janeiro- 110 I b 2
Bont = Banta 138-139 L 7
Bontang 152-153 M 5
Bonthe 164-165 B 7
Bontongssunggu 148-149 G 8
Bontongsunggu 152-153 N 8-9
Bon Wier, TX 78-79 C 5
Bookabie 158-159 F 6
Bookaloo 158-159 G 6
Booker, TX 76-77 D 4
Book Plateau = Roan Plateau 68-69 B 6
Booligal 158-159 H 6
Boomrivier 174-175 D 5
Boonah 160 L 1-2
Böön Cagaan nuur 142-143 HJ 2
Boone, CO 68-69 D 6
Boone, IA 70-71 CD 4
Boone, NC 80-81 F 2
Booneville, AR 76-77 GH 5
Booneville, KY 72-73 E 6
Booneville, MS 78-79 E 3
Boons 174-175 G 3
Boonville, IN 70-71 G 6
Boonville, MO 70-71 D 6
Boonville, NY 72-73 J 3
Boopi, Río — 104-105 C 5
Booramo 164-165 a 2
Boosaaso 164-165 bc 1
Boothbay Harbor, ME 72-73 M 3
Boothby, Cape — 53 C 6-7
Boothia, Gulf of — 56-57 ST 3-4
Boothia Isthmus 56-57 S 4
Boothia Peninsula 56-57 RS 3
Boothwyn, PA 84 III a 3
Booué 172 B 1-2
Boowagendrift = Bo-Wadrif 174-175 CD 7
Booysens, Johannesburg- 170 V ab 2
Boping 146-147 F 3
Boping Ling 146-147 F 9
Boppelsen 128 IV a 1
Boqueirão [BR, Bahia ↘ Jataí] 100-101 AB 7
Boqueirão [BR, Bahia ↙ Xiquexique] 100-101 BC 6
Boqueirão [BR, Rio Grande do Sul] 111 F 4
Boqueirão, Serra do — [BR, Bahia] 92-93 L 7
Boqueirão, Serra do — [BR, Pernambuco] 100-101 F 5
Boqueirão, Serra do — [BR, Piauí] 100-101 C 4
Boqueirão, Serra do — [BR, Rio Grande do Sul] 106-107 K 2
Boqueirão dos Cochos 100-101 E 4
Boquerón [PY] 102-103 BC 4
Boquerón [YV] 94-95 K 3
Boquerón, Túnel — 91 II ab 1
Boquilla del Conchos 86-87 H 4
Boquillas del Carmen 86-87 J 3
Boquira 100-101 C 7
Bor [SU] 124-125 P 5
Bor [TR] 136-137 F 4
Bor [YU] 122-123 JK 3
Bōr = Būr 164-165 L 7
Bor, Lak — 172 G 1
Borabu 150-151 D 4-5
Boracho Peak 76-77 B 7
Borah Peak 64-65 D 3
Borai 138-139 HJ 7
Borāri 138-139 L 5
Borås 116-117 E 9
Borāzjān 134-135 G 5
Borba [BR] 92-93 H 5
Borbón, Isla de — = Pebble Island 108-109 K 8
Borborema 102-103 H 4
Borborema, Planalto da — 92-93 M 6
Bor Chadyn uul 142-143 EF 3
Bor Choro uul 142-143 E 3
Borçka = Yeniyol 136-137 JK 2
Borcu = Borkou 164-165 H 5
Borda da Mata 102-103 JK 5
Bordareno 94-95 F 5
Borde Alto del Payún 106-107 C 6
Bordeaux [F] 120-121 G 6
Bordeaux [ZA] 170 V ab 1
Bordeaux, Montréal- 82 I ab 1
Bordenave 106-107 F 6
Borden Island 56-57 NO 2
Borden Peninsula 56-57 U 3
Border 174-175 F 4
Bordertown 160 E 6
Bordighera 122-123 BC 4
Bordj-bou-Arréridj = Burj Bū 'Arīrij 166-167 J 1
Bordj Boûrguîba = Burj Būrgībah 166-167 LM 3
Bordj-de-Chegga = Shaqqah 166-167 JK 2
Bordj-de-Stil = Saṭīl 166-167 J 2
Bordj el Bahri 170 I b 1
Bordj el Bahri, Cap de — 170 I b 1
Bordj-el-Hamraïa = Burj al-Khamīrah 166-167 K 2
Bordj el Kiffan 170 I b 2
Bordj-Flye-Sainte-Marie = Burj Falāy 166-167 E 6
Bordj-Maïa = Al-Māyah 166-167 G 3
Bordj-Messouda = Burj Mas'ūdah 166-167 L 4
Bordj-Taguine = Tāḥīn 166-167 H 2
Bordj-Tarat 166-167 L 6
Bordj-Welvert = 'Ayn al-Ḥajal 166-167 H 2
Bordo, El — = Patía 94-95 C 6
Bordzongijn Gov' 142-143 K 3
Bóreioi Sporádes 122-123 KL 6
Bóreiron Stenōn Kerkýras 122-123 HJ 6
Borel 102-103 G 8
Borgå 116-117 LM 7
Borgampād 140 E 2
Borgarfjardhar 116-117 c 2
Børgefjell 116-117 EF 5
Borger, TX 64-65 F 4
Borges 110 III b 1
Borghese, Villa — 113 II b 1-2
Borgholm 116-117 G 9
Borgne, Lake — 78-79 E 5-6
Borgomanero 122-123 BC 3
Borgou 168-169 F 3
Borgsdorf/Nordbahn 130 III b 1
Borgu 168-169 FG 3
Bôrhâz Jbel Târoq = Bughāz Jabal Ṭāriq 164-165 CD 1
Bori 138-139 G 7
Borikhane 150-151 DE 3
Borinskoje 124-125 M 7
Borio 138-139 L 5
Borislav 126-127 A 2
Borisoglebsk 126-127 KL 1
Borisoglebskij 124-125 M 5
Borisov 124-125 G 6
Borisova, mys — 132-133 a 6
Borisovka 126-127 GH 1
Borisovo, Moskva- 113 V cd 3
Borisovo-Sudskoje 124-125 KL 4
Borispol' 126-127 E 1
Bōriyō = Borio 138-139 L 5
Borja [PE] 92-93 D 5
Borja [PY] 102-103 D 6
Borj es Sedra = 'Uqlat Ṣudrā' 166-167 E 3
Borkhaya Bay = guba Buor-Chaja 132-133 Z 3
B'ork'o = Primorsk 124-125 G 3
Borkou 164-165 H 5
Borku = Borkou 164-165 H 5
Borlänge 116-117 FG 7
Borlu 136-137 C 3
Bòrmida 122-123 C 3
Bornemouth 119 F 6
Borneo = Kalimantan 148-149 F 7-G 6
Bornholm 116-117 F 10
Börnicke [DDR, Frankfurt] 130 III c 1
Bornim, Potsdam- 130 III a 2
Borno [WAN] 164-165 G 6
Bornou = Borno 164-165 G 6
Bornstedt, Potsdam- 130 III a 2
Bornu = Borno 164-165 G 6
Borogoncy 132-133 Z 5
Borojó 94-95 F 2
Boroko 152-153 P 5
B'or'ol'och = Susuman 132-133 cd 5
Boromo 168-169 E 3
Boron, CA 74-75 E 5
Borough Park, New York-, NY 82 III bc 3
Boroūj, el — = Al-Burūj 166-167 C 3
Borovaja 126-127 HJ 2
Borovica 124-125 R 4
Borovići 132-133 EF 6
Borovl'anka 132-133 P 7
Borovoj 124-125 S 4
Borovsk 124-125 L 6
Borovskoj 132-133 LM 7
Borrazópolis 102-103 G 5
Borroloola 158-159 G 3
Borşa 122-123 L 2
Borsad 138-139 D 6
Boršč'ov 126-127 C 2
Borščovočnyj chrebet 132-133 W 7
Bortala Monggol Zizhizhou 142-143 E 2-3
Bor Talijn gol 142-143 E 3
Borto 132-133 V 7
Bortondale, PA 84 III a 2
Borūjerd 134-135 FG 4
Borusa Strait = proliv Vil'kickogo 132-133 S-U 2
Boryo = Fangliao 146-147 H 10
Bory Tucholskie 118 HJ 2
Borz'a 132-133 W 7
Borzna 126-127 F 1
Boržomi 126-127 L 6
Borzya = Borz'a 132-133 W 7
Bos [B ↖ Bruxelles] 128 II a 1
Bos [B ↗ Bruxelles] 128 II b 1
Bosa [CO] 94-95 D 5
Bosa [I] 122-123 C 5
Bosanska Gradiška 122-123 G 3
Bosanska Krupa 122-123 G 3
Bosanski Novi 122-123 FG 3
Bosanski Petrovac 122-123 G 3
Bosbeek [B, place] 128 II a 1
Bosbulten, De — 174-175 DE 5
Bosch 106-107 H 6
Bosch Bulten, De — = De Bosbulten 174-175 DE 5
Boschpoort 174-175 G 4
Boscobel, WI 70-71 E 4
Bosconia 94-95 E 2
Bose 142-143 K 7
Boshan 142-143 M 4
Bosho Boholu 174-175 E 3
Boshoek 174-175 G 3
Boshof 174-175 F 5
Boskamp 98-99 L 1-2
Bosler, WY 68-69 D 5
Bosluissoutpan 174-175 C 5
Bosmanland 172 C 7
Bosmanland, Groot — 174-175 CD 5
Bosmanland, Klein — 174-175 C 5
Bosmanskop 174-175 G 6
Bosmansriviermond 174-175 G 7
Bosna [BG] 122-123 M 4
Bosna [YU] 122-123 GH 3
Bosna i Hercegovina 122-123 GH 3-4
Bosobolo 172 C 1
Bōsō hantō 144-145 N 5
Bosporus = Karadeniz boğazı 134-135 BC 2
Bosque, NM 76-77 A 5
Bosque Bonito 76-77 B 7
Bosque de Chapultepec 91 I b 2
Bosque San Juan de Aragón 91 I c 2
Bossangoa 164-165 H 7
Bossembélé 164-165 H 7
Bossier City, LA 64-65 H 5
Bosso 164-165 G 6
Bostān [IR] 136-137 MN 7
Bostān [PAK] 138-139 A 2
Bostānābād 136-137 M 4
Bostancı, İstanbul- 154 I b 3
Boston, GA 80-81 E 5
Boston, MA 64-65 MN 3
Boston [GB] 119 FG 5
Boston-Allston, MA 84 I b 2
Boston-Back Bay, MA 84 I b 2
Boston Bay 84 I c 2
Boston-Bellevue-Mount Vernon, MA 84 I b 3
Boston-Brighton, MA 84 I b 2
Boston-Charlestown, MA 84 I b 2
Boston-Clarendon Hills, MA 84 I b 3
Boston College 84 I a 3
Boston Common 84 I b 2
Boston-Dorchester, MA 84 I b 3
Boston-Dorchester Center, MA 84 I b 3
Boston-East Boston, MA 84 I b 2
Boston Harbor 84 I c 2
Boston-Hyde Park, MA 84 I b 3
Boston-Jamaica Plain, MA 84 I b 3
Boston-Mattapan, MA 84 I b 3
Boston Mountains 64-65 H 4
Boston Naval Shipyard U.S.S. Constitution 84 I b 2
Boston-Readville, MA 84 I b 3
Boston-Roslindale, MA 84 I b 3
Boston-Roxbury, MA 84 I b 3
Boston-Savin Hill, MA 84 I b 3
Boston-South Boston, MA 84 I b 2
Boston Tea Party Ship 84 I b 2
Boston University 84 I b 2
Boston-West Roxbury, MA 84 I b 3
Bosveld 172 E 6
Boswell, OK 76-77 G 5-6
Bosworth, MO 70-71 D 6
Bōta = Boath 138-139 G 8
Botād 138-139 C 6
Botafogo, Enseada de — 110 I bc 2
Botafogo, Rio de Janeiro- 110 I b 2
Botan çayı 136-137 K 4
Botanical Gardens 154 II a 2
Botanic Garden of Tōkyō 155 III b 1
Botanic Gardens of Singapore 154 III a 2
Botanic Gardens of Victoria 155 I a 2
Botanischer Garten Berlin 130 III b 2
Botany, Sydney- 161 I b 2
Botany Bay 158-159 K 6
Botar = Botād 138-139 C 6
Botejevo 126-127 G 3
Botelhos 102-103 J 4
Botersleegte 174-175 D 6
Botev 122-123 L 4
Bothasberg 174-175 H 4
Bothaspas 174-175 H 4
Bothaville 174-175 G 4
Bothnia, Gulf of — 114-115 MN 3
Botkuľ, ozero — 126-127 N 2
Botletle 172 D 6
Botlich 126-127 N 5
Botoşani 122-123 M 2
Botou = Bozhen 146-147 F 2
Bô Trach 150-151 F 4

Botshol 128 I ab 2
Botswana 172 DE 6
Botte Donato 122-123 G 6
Bottineau, ND 68-69 F 1
Botucaraí, Serra — 106-107 L 2
Botucatu 92-93 K 9
Botulu 132-133 W 5
Botuporã 100-101 C 7
Botuquara 100-101 C 7
Botwood 63 J 3
Bou 168-169 D 3
Bouaflé 164-165 C 7
Bou Akba = Bū 'Aqbah 166-167 C 5
Bouaké 164-165 CD 7
Boualem = Bū 'Alim 166-167 G 3
Bou-Ali = Bū 'Alī 166-167 F 6
Boû 'Amaroû = Bu 'Amarū 136-137 HJ 5
Bouar 164-165 H 7
Boû 'Arâda = Bū 'Arādah 166-167 L 1
Boû 'Arfa = Bū 'Arfah 166-167 F 3
Boû 'Azzer = Bū Azīr 166-167 C 4
Boubker = Abū Bakr 166-167 F 2
Boubo 168-169 D 4
Bouca 164-165 H 7
Boucau 120-121 G 7
Bou-Chebka = Bū Shabaqah 166-167 L 2
Bouchegouf = Būshqūf 166-167 K 1
Boucheron = Al-Gārah 166-167 C 3
Boucherville, Îles de — 82 I bc 1
Boucle du Baoulé, Parc National de la — 168-169 C 2
Boûdenîb = Bū Danīb 166-167 E 4
Boudewijnstad = Moba 172 E 3
Bou Djébéha 164-165 D 5
Boudouaou = Budwāwū 166-167 H 1
Boû el Ja'd = Bū al-J'ad 166-167 CD 3
Boû el Louân = Bū al-'Awn 166-167 B 3
Bouerda, El — = Al-Bū'irḍah 166-167 C 5
Boufarik = Būfarīk 166-167 H 1
Boû Fîcha = Bū Fīshah 166-167 M 1
Bougaa = Buq'ah 166-167 J 1
Bougainville 148-149 j 6
Bougainville, Cape — 108-109 KL 8
Bougainville, Isla — = Lively Island 108-109 KL 9
Bougaroun, Cap — = Rā's Būjarun 166-167 JK 1
Bou-Ghezoul = Būghzūl 166-167 H 2
Bougie = Bijāyah 164-165 EF 1
Bougie, Golfe de — = Khalīj Bijāyah 166-167 J 1
Bougival 129 I b 2
Bougouni 164-165 C 6
Bou Grara = Bū Ghrārah 166-167 M 3
Bou Grara, Golfe de — = Khalīj Bū Ghrārah 166-167 M 3
Bougtenga 168-169 E 2
Bougtob = Bū Kutub 164-165 E 2
Bouguerra = Būgarā 166-167 H 1
Bougueval 129 I c 1
Boû Haïâra, Hâssî — = Ḥāssī Bū Ḥayārah 166-167 D 4
Bouheïret el Bîbân = Buḥayrat al-Bībān 166-167 M 3
Bouïra = Būirah 166-167 H 1
Bouira-Sakary = Būirat Ṣaḥarī 166-167 H 2
Bou-Ismaïl = Bū Ismā'īl 166-167 H 1
Boû Izakârn = Bū Izākārn 166-167 B 5
Boujad = Bū al-J'ad 166-167 C 3
Bou-Kadir = Bū Qādir 166-167 G 1
Bou Kadra, Djebel — = Jabal Bū Khaḍrah 166-167 KL 2
Bou Kahil, Djebel — = Jabal Bū Kāhil 166-167 HJ 2
Boukān = Būkān 136-137 LM 4
Boukhanefis = Bū Khanāfis 166-167 F 2
Bou Khelala, Hassi — = Ḥāssī Bū al-Khallalah 166-167 F 4
Bou-Ktoub = Bū Kutub 164-165 E 2
Boulain, Lac — 63 F 2
Boulal 168-169 C 2
Boulaouane = Bū al-'Awn 166-167 B 3
Boulder 158-159 D 6
Boulder, CO 64-65 EF 3-4
Boulder, MT 66-67 GH 2
Boulder, WY 66-67 HJ 4
Boulder City, NV 64-65 CD 4
Boulder Creek, CA 74-75 B 4
Boulder Dam = Hoover Dam 64-65 D 4
Boulevard Heights, MD 82 II b 2
Boulhaut = Bin Sulīmān 166-167 C 3
Bouli 168-169 E 2
Boulia 158-159 G 4
Boûlmân = Būlmān 166-167 D 3
Boulogne, San Isidro- 110 III b 1
Boulogne-sur-Mer 120-121 H 3
Boulsa 168-169 E 2
Boultoum 168-169 H 2
Boûmâln = Būmāln Dādis 166-167 CD 4
Boumba 164-165 H 8
Bou-Medfaa = Bū Midfār'ah 166-167 H 1
Bouna 164-165 D 7
Bouna, Réserve de Faune de — 164-165 D 7
Boû Naṣr, Jbel — = Jabal Bū Naṣr 166-167 E 3
Boundary, AK 58-59 R 4
Boundary Mountains 72-73 L 2
Boundary Peak 64-65 C 4
Boundary Plateau 66-67 J 1
Boundary, WA 66-67 E 1
Boundiali 164-165 C 7
Boundji 172 C 2
Boundou 164-165 B 6
Boung, Sông — 150-151 F 5
Boun Neua 150-151 CD 2
Bounoum 168-169 B 2
Bountiful, UT 66-67 H 5
Bounty 156-157 HJ 7
Bouquet 106-107 G 4
Bouraghet, Erg — = 'Irq Buraghat 166-167 L 6
Bourail 158-159 MN 4
Bourbonnais 120-121 J 5
Bourbon Street 85 I b 2
Bourem 164-165 DE 5
Bourg-en-Bresse 120-121 K 5
Bourges 120-121 J 5
Bourg-la-Reine 129 I c 2
Bourgogne 120-121 K 5-6
Bourgogne, Canal de — 120-121 K 5
Boû Rhrâra = Bū Ghrārah 166-167 M 3
Bourke 158-159 J 6
Bourkes 62 LM 2
Bourlamaque 62 N 2-3
Bou-Saâda = Bū Sa'ādah 166-167 J 2
Boû Salem = Bū Sālim 166-167 L 1
Bouse, AZ 74-75 FG 6
Bouşrá ech Châm = Buṣrat ash-Shām 136-137 G 6
Bousso 164-165 H 6
Boussougou 168-169 E 3
Boutilimit = Bū Tilimīt 164-165 B 5
Bou-Tlelis = Būtlīlis 166-167 F 2
Bouvard, Cape — 158-159 BC 6
Bouvet 50-51 K 8
Bouvetøya 53 D 1
Bouzareah 170 I a 1
Bou Zid, Hassi — = Ḥāssī Bū Zīd 166-167 G 4
Boûznîqa = Bū Z'nīqah 166-167 C 3
Bovenkerk 128 I a 2
Bovey, MN 70-71 D 2
Boviaanskloof Mountains = Bobbejaans-kloofberge 174-175 EF 7
Bovill, ID 66-67 E 2
Bovina, TX 76-77 C 5
Bovril 106-107 H 3
Bo-Wadrif 174-175 CD 7
Bowbells, ND 68-69 E 1
Bowdle, SD 68-69 G 3
Bowdoin, Lake — 68-69 C 1
Bowdon, ND 68-69 G 2
Bowen, IL 70-71 E 5
Bowen [AUS] 158-159 J 3-4
Bowen [RA] 106-107 D 5
Bowen Island 66-67 B 1
Boweyr Ahmad-e Sardsīr va Kohkīlūyeh = 4 ◁ 134-135 G 4
Bowie, AZ 74-75 J 6
Bowie, TX 76-77 F 6
Bow Island 66-67 H 1
Bowker's Park 174-175 G 6
Bowling Green, KY 64-65 J 4
Bowling Green, MO 70-71 E 6
Bowling Green, OH 72-73 E 4
Bowling Green, PA 84 III a 2
Bowling Green, VA 72-73 H 5-6
Bowling Green, Cape — 158-159 J 3
Bowman, ND 68-69 E 2
Bowman Island 53 C 11
Bowmanville 72-73 G 3
Bowness 60 K 4
Bowral 160 JK 5
Bowron Lake Provincial Park 60 G 3
Bowron River 60 G 3
Bow River 56-57 O 7
Bowsman 61 H 4
Box Butte Reservoir 68-69 E 4
Box Creek 68-69 D 4
Box Elder, MT 68-69 A 1
Boxelder Creek [USA ◁ Little Missouri River] 68-69 D 3
Boxelder Creek [USA ◁ Musselshell River] 68-69 B 2
Box Hill, Melbourne- 161 II c 1-2
Bo Xian 142-143 LM 5
Boxing 146-147 G 3
Boyabat 136-137 F 2
Boyacá 94-95 E 5
Boyacá, Bogotá- 91 III b 2
Boyacıköy, İstanbul- 154 I b 2
Boyalık = Çiçekdağı 136-137 F 3
Boyang 146-147 F 7
Boyce, LA 78-79 C 5
Boyd 61 K 3
Boyd, TX 76-77 F 6
Boydton, VA 80-81 G 2
Boyera, Baruta-La — 91 II b 2
Boyero, CO 68-69 E 6
Boyer River 70-71 C 4
Boyeruca, Laguna de — 106-107 AB 5
Boykins, VA 80-81 H 2
Boyle Heights, Los Angeles-, CA 83 III c 1
Boyne City, MI 70-71 H 3
Boynton, OK 76-77 G 5
Boynton Beach, FL 80-81 cd 3
Boysen, WY 68-69 BC 4
Boysen Reservoir 68-69 B 4
Boyuibe 92-93 G 9
Boyuyumanu, Río — 104-105 B 2
Bozburun 136-137 C 4
Bozca ada [TR, island] 136-137 AB 3
Bozdağ [TR, mountains] 136-137 D 2-3
Boz Dağı 136-137 C 4
Boz dağlar 136-137 C 3
Bozdoğan 136-137 C 4
Bozeman, MT 64-65 D 2
Bozen = Bolzano 122-123 D 2
Bozhen 146-147 F 2
Bozkır 136-137 E 4
Bozkurt 136-137 F 1-2
Bozok yaylâsı 136-137 F 2-3
Bozoum 164-165 H 7
Bozova = Hüvek 136-137 H 4
Bozqūsh, Kūh-e — 136-137 M 4
Bozüyük 136-137 CD 3

Bra 122-123 B 3
Brabant, Île — 53 C 30
Brac [RCH] 104-105 B 7
Brač [YU] 122-123 G 4
Bracciano, Lago di — 122-123 DE 4
Bracebridge 72-73 G 2
Bräcke 116-117 F 6
Brackettville, TX 76-77 D 8
Brackwater = Brakwater 174-175 B 2
Braclav 126-127 D 2
Braço do Norte, Rio — 102-103 H 7-8
Braço Menor de Araguia 92-93 JK 7
Brad 122-123 K 2
Brădano 122-123 G 5
Braddock, Alexandria-, VA 82 II a 2
Bradenton, FL 64-65 K 6
Bradford, AR 78-79 D 3
Bradford, PA 72-73 G 4
Bradford [CDN] 72-73 G 2
Bradford [GB] 119 F 5
Bradley, CA 74-75 C 5
Bradley, SD 68-69 H 3
Bradore, Baie — 63 H 2
Bradore Hills 63 H 2
Bradshaw, TX 76-77 DE 6
Brady, MT 66-67 H 1-2
Brady, NE 68-69 F 5
Brady, TX 76-77 E 7
Brady Glacier 58-59 T 7
Braeburn Gardens, Houston-, TX 85 III a 2
Braeburn Glen, Houston-, TX 85 III a 2
Braeburn Valley, Houston-, TX 85 III a 2
Braes Heights, Houston-, TX 85 III b 2
Braga 120-121 C 8
Braga, Serra do — 100-101 E 4
Bragado 111 D 5
Bragança 120-121 D 8
Bragança [BR, Amazonas] 98-99 D 9
Bragança [BR, Pará] 92-93 K 5
Bragança Paulista 92-93 K 9
Bragin 124-125 GH 8
Braham, MN 70-71 D 3
Brahestad = Raahe 116-117 L 5
Brahmanbaria = Brahmanbāriyā 141 B 4
Brahmanbāriyā 141 B 4
Brâhmani 134-135 O 6
Brahmapur 154 II b 3
Brahmapurī = Bramhapuri 138-139 G 7
Brahmaputra 134-135 P 5
Brahmaputra = Matsang Tsangpo 138-139 J 2-3
Brahmaputra = Tamchhog Khamba 138-139 J 2
Brahmaputra = Tsangpo 138-139 L 3
Brah Yang = Bralan 150-151 G 7
Brăila 122-123 M 3
Brainerd, MN 64-65 H 2
Braintree, MA 84 I bc 3
Brak = Birāk 164-165 G 3
Brâknah, Al- 168-169 B 1
Brakpan 174-175 H 4
Brakpoort 174-175 E 6
Brakrivier [ZA, Kaapland] 174-175 E 5
Brakrivier [ZA, Transvaal] 174-175 H 2
Brakwater 174-175 B 2
Bralan 150-151 G 7
Bralorne 60 F 4
Bramaputra = Brahmaputra 134-135 P 5
Bramaputra = Tsangpo 138-139 L 3
Bramfeld, Hamburg- 130 I b 1
Bramhapuri 138-139 G 7
Bramley, Johannesburg- 170 V b 1
Brampton 72-73 FG 3
Branch 63 JK 4
Branchville, SC 80-81 F 4
Brandberg 172 B 6
Brandenberg, MT 68-69 CD 3
Brandenburg, KY 70-71 G 6-7
Brandenburg [DDR, landscape] 118 FG 2
Brandenburg [DDR, place] 118 F 2
Brandenburger Tor 130 III b 1
Brandfort 174-175 G 5
Brandon, FL 80-81 b 3
Brandon, MS 78-79 DE 4
Brandon, VT 72-73 K 3
Brandon [CDN] 56-57 Q 8
Brandon Mount 119 AB 5
Brandsen 106-107 H 5
Brandsville, MO 78-79 CD 2
Brandvlei 174-175 D 6
Brandywine, MD 72-73 H 5
Branford, FL 80-81 b 1-2
Brang, Kuala — 148-149 D 5-6
Brani, Pulau — 154 III b 2
Braniewo 118 JK 1
Bransfield Strait 53 C 30-31
Br'ansk [SU] 124-125 JK 7
Br'ansk-Bežica 124-125 JK 7
Branson, MO 78-79 C 2
Brantas, Kali — 152-153 JK 9
Brantford 72-73 FG 3
Brantley, AL 78-79 FG 5
Branxholme 160 EF 6
Brás [BR] 98-99 JK 6
Brás, São Paulo- 110 II b 2
Brásc = Birāk 164-165 G 3
Bras d'Or Lake 56-57 YZ 8
Brasil, El — 76-77 D 9
Brasilândia 102-103 FG 4
Brasilândia, São Paulo- 110 II a 1
Brasiléia 92-93 F 7
Brasília 92-93 K 8
Brasília de Minas 102-103 KL 2
Brasília Legal 92-93 H 5
Braslav 124-125 F 6
Brașov 122-123 L 3
Brassey Range 152-153 MN 3
Bråsvellbreen 116-117 lm 5
Bratcevo, Moskva- 113 V ab 2
Bratejevo, Moskva- 113 V cd 3
Bratislava 118 H 4
Bratsk 132-133 T 6
Bratskoje 126-127 E 3
Bratskoje vodochranilišče 132-133 T 6
Brattleboro, VT 72-73 K 3
Brațul Chilia 122-123 N 3
Brațul Sfîntu Gheorghe 122-123 N 3
Brațul Sulina 122-123 N 3
Braunau 118 F 4
Braunschweig 118 E 2
Braunshardt 128 III a 2
Brava 204-205 E 7
Brava = Baraawe 172 H 1
Brawley, CA 64-65 C 5
Bray, CA 66-67 C 5
Braybrook, Melbourne- 161 II b 1
Bray Island 56-57 V 4
Braymer, MO 70-71 D 6
Brays Bayou 85 III a 2
Brays Village, Houston-, TX 85 III a 2
Brazeau 60 J 3
Brazeau, Mount — 60 J 3
Brazeau River 60 K 3
Brazil 92-93 F-M 6
Brazil, IN 70-71 G 6
Brazil Basin 50-51 H 6
Brazilian Plateau = Planalto Brasileiro 92-93 KL 8
Brazlândia 102-103 H 1
Brazo de Gatún 64-65 b 2
Brazo del Chagres 64-65 b 2
Brazo de Loba 94-95 D 3
Brazo Noroeste 108-109 DE 10
Brazo Norte 108-109 B 7
Brazos River 64-65 G 5-6
Brazos River, Clear Fork — 76-77 E 6
Brazos River, Salt Fork — 76-77 D 6
Brazo Sur del Río Coig 108-109 D 8
Brazza = Brač 122-123 G 4
Brazzaville 172 BC 2
Brazzaville, Aéroport de — 170 IV a 1
Brazzaville-Bacongo 170 IV a 1
Brazzaville-Moungali 170 IV a 1
Brazzaville-Mpila 170 IV a 1
Brazzaville-Ngamba 170 IV a 1
Brazzaville-Ouenzé 170 IV a 1
Brazzaville-Poto Poto 170 IV a 1
Brčko 122-123 H 3
Brdy 118 FG 4
Brea, Cordillera de la — 106-107 C 2
Brea Creek 83 III d 2
Breakheart Reservation 84 I b 2
Bream Bay 161 F 2
Brea Pozo 106-107 EF 2
Breas 104-105 A 9
Breaux Bridge, LA 78-79 D 5
Brebes 152-153 H 9
Brechin [CDN] 72-73 G 2
Breckenridge, MN 68-69 H 2
Breckenridge, TX 76-77 E 6
Brecknock, Peninsula — 111 B 8-9
Břeclav 118 H 4
Brecon 119 E 5-6
Breda 120-121 K 3
Bredasdorp 172 D 8
Bredbo 160 J 5
Bredell 170 V c 1
Bredenbury 61 H 5
Bredy 132-133 KL 7
Breedhout 128 II a 2
Breeds Pond 84 I c 2
Breërivier 174-175 D 8
Breezy Point, New York-, NY 82 III c 3
Bregalnica 122-123 K 5
Bregenz 118 DE 5
Bregovo 122-123 K 3
Breidhafjördhur 116-117 ab 2
Breidhavík 116-117 a 2
Breidi Fjord = Breidhafjördhur 116-117 ab 2
Breipaal 174-175 G 6
Breitenlee, Wien- 113 I bc 1
Brejão [BR, Goiás] 100-101 A 7
Brejão [BR, Pernambuco] 100-101 F 5
Brejinho 100-101 D 5
Brejinho do Nazaré 92-93 K 7
Brejo 100-101 C 2
Brejo, Riacho do — 100-101 C 5
Brejo da Madre de Deus 100-101 F 5
Brejo da Porta 100-101 B 5
Brejo da Serra 100-101 C 6
Brejo de São Félix 100-101 C 3
Brejo do Cruz 100-101 F 4
Brejões 100-101 E 7
Brejo Santo 100-101 E 4
Brejo Velho 100-101 C 7
Brejtovo 124-125 LM 4
Brekstad 116-117 C 6
Bremangerlandet 116-117 A 7
Bremen 118 D 2
Bremen, GA 78-79 G 4
Bremen, Colonia — 106-107 F 4
Bremerhaven 118 D 2
Bremerton, WA 64-65 B 2
Bremond, TX 76-77 F 7
Brem River 60 E 4
Breñas, Las — 104-105 F 10
Brenham, TX 76-77 F 7
Brenne 120-121 H 5
Brenner 118 E 5
Brennero = Brenner 118 E 5
Brennevinsfjord 116-117 k 4
Brent 72-73 G 1
Brent, London- 129 II a 1
Brentford, London- 129 II a 2
Brentwood, TN 78-79 F 2-3
Brentwood Heights, Los Angeles-, CA 83 III ab 1
Brentwood Park 170 V c 1
Brèscia 122-123 D 3
Bressanone 122-123 DE 2
Bressay 119 F 1
Bresse 120-121 K 5
Bressuire 120-121 G 5
Brest [F] 120-121 E 4
Brest [SU] 124-125 D 7
Bretagne 120-121 F 4-G 5
Breton, Cape — 56-57 Z 8
Breton Island 78-79 E 6
Breton Sound 64-65 J 6
Breu 96-97 E 6
Breueh, Pulau — 148-149 B 5
Breukeleveen 128 I b 2
Brevard, NC 80-81 E 3
Breves 92-93 J 5
Brevik 116-117 C 8
Brevort, MI 70-71 H 2
Brewarrina 158-159 J 5
Brewer, ME 72-73 M 2
Brewersville 168-169 C 4
Brewster, KS 68-69 F 6
Brewster, NE 68-69 G 4
Brewster, WA 66-67 CD 1
Brewster, Kap — 52 BC 20-21
Brewton, AL 78-79 F 5
Breyten 174-175 H 4
Brezina = B'rizyānah 166-167 G 3
Bria 164-165 J 7
Briançon 120-121 L 6
Brian Head 74-75 G 4
Briarcroft, Houston-, TX 85 III b 2
Briare 120-121 J 5
Briarmeadow, Houston-, TX 85 III a 2
Briarwood Park 85 II c 1
Bribbaree 160 HJ 5
Bribie Island 158-159 K 5
Bričany 126-127 C 2
Briceland, CA 66-67 AB 5
Bricelyn, MN 70-71 CD 4
Brickaville = Vohibinany 172 JK 5
Brickhouse Gulley 85 III b 1
Briconnet, Lac — 63 F 2
Bridesburg, Philadelphia-, PA 84 III c 2
Bridge, ID 66-67 G 4
Bridgeboro, GA 80-81 DE 5
Bridgeboro, NJ 84 III d 1
Bridge City, LA 85 I ab 2
Bridgedale, LA 85 I a 2
Bridgeport, AL 78-79 FG 3
Bridgeport, CA 74-75 D 3
Bridgeport, CT 64-65 M 3
Bridgeport, IL 70-71 FG 6
Bridgeport, NE 68-69 E 5
Bridgeport, NJ 84 III b 3
Bridgeport, PA 84 III a 1
Bridgeport, TX 76-77 F 6
Bridgeport, Chicago-, IL 83 II b 1
Bridger, MT 68-69 B 3
Bridger Basin 66-67 HJ 5
Bridge River 60 F 4
Bridger Peak 68-69 C 5
Bridgeton, NC 80-81 H 3
Bridgeton, NJ 72-73 J 5
Bridgetown [AUS] 158-159 C 6
Bridgetown [BDS] 64-65 OP 9
Bridgetown [CDN] 63 D 5
Bridgeview, IL 83 II a 2
Bridgewater 63 D 5
Bridgewater, PA 84 III d 1
Bridgewater, SD 68-69 H 4
Bridgton, ME 72-73 L 2
Bridgwater 119 E 6
Bridlington 119 FG 4
Bridport [AUS] 160 c 2
Brie 120-121 J 4
Briereville 61 C 3
Brig 118 CD 5
Briggsdale, CO 68-69 DE 5
Brigham City, UT 64-65 D 3
Bright 160 H 6
Brighton, IA 70-71 DE 5
Brighton, MI 70-71 HJ 4
Brighton, NY 72-73 H 3
Brighton [CDN] 72-73 GH 2
Brighton [GB] 119 FG 6
Brighton, Boston-, MA 84 I b 2
Brighton, Melbourne- 161 II bc 2
Brighton Indian Reservation 80-81 c 3
Brighton Park, Chicago-, IL 83 II a 2
Brightwood, Washington-, DC 82 II a 1
Brigthon, CO 68-69 D 5-6
Brigue = Brig 118 CD 5
Brigus 63 K 4
Brijnagar = Jhālawār 138-139 EF 5
Brijuni 122-123 E 3
Brikama 168-169 A 2
Brilhante, Rio — 102-103 E 4
Brilliant, NM 76-77 B 4
Brilon 118 D 3
Brimson, MN 70-71 DE 2
Brindaban = Vrindāvan 138-139 F 4
Brindakit 132-133 a 5-6
Brìndisi 122-123 GH 5
Brinkley, AR 78-79 D 3
Brinkspan 174-175 E 6
Brion, Île — 63 F 4
Brisbane 158-159 K 5
Brisbane, CA 83 I b 2
Brisbane-Ipswich 158-159 K 5
Brisbane-Redcliffe 158-159 K 5
Brisbane River 158-159 K 5
Bristol, CO 68-69 E 6
Bristol, FL 78-79 G 5
Bristol, PA 84 III d 1
Bristol, RI 72-73 L 4
Bristol, SD 68-69 H 3
Bristol, TN 80-81 E 2
Bristol, VA 64-65 K 4
Bristol [CDN] 72-73 H 2
Bristol [GB] 119 EF 6
Bristol Bay 56-57 DE 6
Bristol Channel 119 DE 6
Bristol Lake 74-75 EF 5
Bristow, OK 76-77 F 5
Britannia Beach 66-67 B 1
Britannia Range 53 AB 15-16
British Columbia 56-57 L 6-N 7
British Isles 114-115 F 5-G 4
British Mountains 56-57 HJ 4
British Museum 129 II b 1
Brits 174-175 G 3
Britstown 172 D 8
Britt 72-73 F 2
Britt, IA 70-71 D 4
Brittany = Bretagne 120-121 F 4-G 5
Britton, SD 68-69 GH 3
Britvino 124-125 OP 3
Britz, Berlin- 130 III b 2
Brive, la — 128 II b 2
Brive-la-Gaillarde 120-121 H 6
Brixen = Bressanone 122-123 DE 2
Brixham 119 E 6
B'rizyānah 166-167 G 3
Brjansk = Br'ansk [SU] 124-125 JK 7
Brno 118 H 4
Broa, Ensenada de la — 88-89 EF 3
Broach = Bharuch 134-135 L 6
Broadback, Rivière — 62 MN 1
Broadford 119 CD 3
Broad Law 119 E 4
Broadmoor, CA 83 I b 2
Broad Pass, AK 58-59 N 5
Broad River 80-81 F 3
Broad Sound 158-159 JK 4
Broadus, MT 68-69 D 3
Broadview 61 GH 5
Broadview, MT 68-69 B 2
Broadwater, NE 68-69 E 5
Broceni 124-125 D 5
Brochet 56-57 Q 6
Brochet, Lac — 63 B 3
Brochu, Lac — 62 OP 2
Brocken 118 E 3
Brock 60 L 5
Brock Island 56-57 N 2
Brocklyn Marine Park 82 III c 3
Brockman, Mount — 158-159 C 4
Brock Park 85 III c 1
Brockport, NY 72-73 GH 3
Brockton, MA 72-73 L 3
Brockton, MT 68-69 D 1
Brockville 56-57 V 9
Brockway, MT 68-69 D 2
Brockway, PA 72-73 G 4
Brodeur Peninsula 56-57 T 3
Brodhead, WI 70-71 F 4
Brodie 66-67 C 1
Brodnax, VA 80-81 GH 2
Brodnica 118 J 2
Brodósqui 102-103 J 4
Brody [SU, Ukrainskaja SSR] 126-127 B 1
Brogan, OR 66-67 E 3
Brokaw, WI 70-71 F 3
Broken Arrow, OK 76-77 G 4
Broken Bow, NE 68-69 G 5
Broken Bow, OK 76-77 G 5-6
Broken Hill 158-159 H 6
Broken Hill = Kabwe 172 E 4
Brokopondo 92-93 HJ 3
Bromhead 68-69 E 1
Brønderslev 116-117 CD 9
Bronevskaja 124-125 M 3
Brong-Ahafo 168-169 E 4
Bronkhorstspruit 174-175 H 3
Brønnøysund 116-117 DE 5
Bronson, FL 80-81 b 2
Bronson, MI 70-71 H 5
Bronson, TX 76-77 G 7
Bronte 122-123 F 7
Bronte, TX 76-77 D 7
Bronte Park 158-159 J 8
Bronx, New York-, NY 82 III c 1
Broodsnyersplaas 174-175 H 4
Brookeland, TX 76-77 GH 7
Brookfield, MO 70-71 D 6
Brookhaven, MS 78-79 D 5
Brookhaven, PA 84 III a 2
Brookhaven = North Atlanta, GA 85 II c 1
Brookings, OR 66-67 A 4
Brookings, SD 64-65 G 3
Brookland, Washington-, DC 82 II b 1
Brooklawn, NJ 84 III c 2
Brookline, MA 72-73 L 3
Brooklyn, IA 70-71 D 5
Brooklyn, MS 78-79 E 5
Brooklyn, Melbourne- 161 II ab 1-2
Brooklyn, New York-, NY 82 III bc 3
Brooklyn Park, MN 70-71 D 3
Brookneal, VA 80-81 G 2
Brooks 61 C 5
Brooks, Lake — 58-59 K 7
Brooks, Mount — 58-59 MN 5
Brooks Bay 60 CD 4
Brooks Island 83 I b 1
Brooks Mount 58-59 D 4
Brooks Range 56-57 E-H 4
Brookston, IN 70-71 G 5
Brookston, MN 70-71 D 2
Brooksville, FL 80-81 b 2
Brooksville, KY 72-73 DE 5
Brookton 158-159 C 6
Brookvale, Sydney- 161 I b 1
Brookville, IN 70-71 H 6
Brookville, OH 72-73 D 5
Brookville, PA 72-73 G 4
Brookwood, GA 85 II c 2
Brookwood Park 85 II c 2
Broomall, PA 84 III a 2
Broome 158-159 D 3
Broquerie, la — 61 KL 6
Brossard 82 I bc 2
Brotas 102-103 H 5
Brotas de Macaúbas 92-93 L 7
Brothers, OR 66-67 C 4
Brothers, The — = Jazā'ir al-Ikhwān 173 D 4
Brothers, The — = Samḥah, Darsah 134-135 G 8
Brou-sur-Chantereine 129 I d 2
Brovary 126-127 E 1
Brovio 168-169 C 4
Brovki 126-127 D 2
Brown, Mount — 53 BC 9
Brown, Point — 160 A 4
Brownfield, TX 76-77 CD 6
Browning, MT 66-67 G 1
Brownlee 61 E 5
Brownlee, NE 68-69 F 4
Brownlow Point 58-59 P 1
Brown Mill Park 85 II bc 2
Brownrigg 62 L 2
Brown's Bank 63 D 6
Brownstown, IN 70-71 GH 6
Browns Valley, MN 68-69 H 3
Brownsville, OR 66-67 B 3
Brownsville, PA 72-73 FG 4
Brownsville, TN 78-79 E 3
Brownsville, TX 64-65 G 6
Brownsweg 92-93 H 3-4
Brownville Junction, ME 72-73 M 2
Brownwood, TX 64-65 G 5
Broxton, GA 80-81 E 5
Bruay-en-Artois 120-121 J 3
Bruce, MS 78-79 E 3-4
Bruce, WI 70-71 E 3
Bruce, Mount — 158-159 C 4
Bruce Crossing, MI 70-71 F 2
Bruce Mines 70-71 J 2
Bruce Peninsula 72-73 F 2
Bruce Rock 158-159 C 6
Bruceton, TN 78-79 E 2
Bruchmühle 130 III d 1
Br'uchoveckaja 126-127 J 4
Br'uchovo 124-125 U 5
Bruchsal 118 D 4
Bruck an der Leitha 118 H 4
Bruck an der Mur 118 G 5
Brüelberg 128 IV b 1
Brug, De — 174-175 F 5
Bruges = Brugge 120-121 J 3
Brugge 120-121 J 3
Brugge-Zeebrugge 120-121 J 3
Brugmann, Hôpital — 128 II a 1
Bruin Peak 74-75 H 3
Bruit, Pulau — 152-153 J 4
Bruja, Cerro — 64-65 b 2
Brukkaros, Mount — = Groot Brukkaros 172 C 7
Brule, NE 68-69 F 5
Brule, WI 70-71 E 2
Brule Lake 70-71 E 2
Brule Rapids 60 L 1
Brumadinho 102-103 K 4
Brumado 92-93 L 7
Brundidge, AL 78-79 FG 5
Bruneau, ID 66-67 F 4
Bruneau River 66-67 F 4
Brunei 148-149 F 6
Brunei = Bandar Seri Begawan 148-149 FG 5-6
Brunei, Teluk — 152-153 L 3
Bruni, TX 76-77 E 9
Brunner 161 DE 6
Bruno 61 F 4
Brunswick, GA 64-65 K 5
Brunswick, MD 72-73 H 5
Brunswick, ME 72-73 LM 3
Brunswick, MO 70-71 D 6
Brunswick = Braunschweig 118 E 2
Brunswick, Melbourne- 161 II b 1
Brunswick, Peninsula — 111 B 8
Brunswick Bay 158-159 D 3
Brunswick Heads 160 LM 2
Brunswick Lake 70-71 D 1
Bruny Island 158-159 J 8
Brusenec 124-125 OP 3
Brush, CO 68-69 E 5
Brushy Mountains 80-81 F 2-3
Brus Laguna 88-89 DE 7

272 Botshol

Brusovo 124-125 K 5
Brusque 111 G 3
Brussegem 128 II a 1
Brussel = Bruxelles 120-121 JK 3
Brussel-Charleroi, Kanaal —
128 II a 2
Brussels 174-175 F 4
Brussels = Bruxelles 120-121 JK 3
Brütten 128 IV b 1
Brüttisellen 128 IV b 1
Bruxelles 120-121 JK 3
Bruxelles National, Aéroport —
128 II b 1
Bruyns Hill 174-175 J 5
Bruzual 94-95 G 3-4
Bryan, OH 70-71 H 5
Bryan, TX 64-65 G 5
Bryan, WY 66-67 J 5
Bryansk = Br'ansk 124-125 JK 7
Bryant, SD 68-69 H 3
Bryce Canyon National Park
74-75 GH 4
Bryn Mawr, PA 84 III b 1
Bryn Mawr College 84 III b 1
Bryson, TX 76-77 E 6
Bryson City, NC 80-81 E 3
Bryson City, TN 80-81 E 3
Brzeg 118 H 3
Bşaiya, Al- = Al-Buşaiyah
134-135 EF 4
Bsharri = Basharrī 136-137 G 5
Btaymān, Bi'r — 136-137 H 4
Bua 171 C 6
Bua Chum 150-151 C 5
Buake = Bouaké 164-165 CD 7
Buala 148-149 jk 6
Bū al-'Awn 166-167 B 3
Bū 'Alī 166-167 F 6
Bū 'Alim 166-167 G 3
Bū al-J'ad 166-167 CD 3
Bū al-Khallalah, Ḥāssī —
166-167 G 2-3
Bū'Amarū 136-137 HJ 5
Buapinang 152-153 O 8
Bū 'Aqbah 166-167 C 5
Bū 'Arādah 166-167 L 1
Buaran, Kali — 154 IV b 2
Bū 'Arfah 166-167 F 3
Bua Yai 150-151 D 5
Bu'ayrāt al-Ḥsūn, Al- 164-165 H 2
Bū Azīr 166-167 C 4
Bubak 138-139 A 4
Bub Chhu 138-139 LM 3
Būbīyan, Jazīrat — 134-135 FG 5
Bubtsang Tsangpo 138-139 K 2
Bubu 171 C 4
Bubu, Gunung — 150-151 C 10
Buc 129 I b 2
Bučač 126-127 B 2
Bucak 136-137 D 4
Bucakkışla 136-137 E 4
Bucaramanga 92-93 E 3
Bucatunna, MS 78-79 E 5
Buccaneer Archipelago 158-159 D 3
Buchan [AUS] 160 J 6
Buchanan, MI 70-71 G 5
Buchanan, NM 76-77 B 5
Buchanan, VA 80-81 FG 2
Buchanan [CDN] 61 G 5
Buchanan [LB] 164-165 B 7
Buchanan Lake 76-77 E 7
Buchans 56-57 Z 8
Buchara 134-135 JK 3
Buchardo 111 D 4
Bucharest = Bucureşti 122-123 L 3
Bucharevo 124-125 S 5
Buchendorf 130 III a 2
Buchholz, Berlin- 130 III b 1
Buchon, Point — 74-75 C 5
Buchschlag 128 III ab 1
Buchs (Zürich) 128 IV a 1
buchta Marii Prončiščevoj
132-133 VW 2
Buchtarma 132-133 Q 8
Buchtarminskoje vodochranilišče
132-133 PQ 8
Buchupureo 106-107 A 6
Buchyn Mangnaj uul 142-143 EF 4-5
Buckeye, AZ 74-75 G 6
Buckhannon, WV 72-73 F 5
Buckhaven 119 E 3
Buckhead, Atlanta-, GA 85 II bc 1
Buckhorn Lake 72-73 G 2
Buckhurst Hill 129 II c 1
Buckie 119 E 3
Buckingham [CDN] 72-73 J 2
Buckingham Palace 129 II b 2
Buckland, AK 58-59 G 4
Buckland River 58-59 G 4
Buckland Tableland 158-159 J 4-5
Buckleboo 158-159 G 6
Buckle Island 53 C 16-17
Buckley, WA 66-67 BC 2
Buckley Bay 53 C 15-16
Buckley Ranges 60 D 2
Bucklin, KS 68-69 G 7
Bucklin, MO 70-71 D 6
Buckow, Berlin- 130 III b 2
Bucksport, ME 72-73 M 2
Bucktown, LA 85 I b 1
Bucovina 122-123 LM 2
Buco Zau 172 B 2
Buctouche 63 D 4
Bucureşti 122-123 LM 3
Bucureşti-Jilava 122-123 M 5
Bucyrus, OH 72-73 E 4
Buda, TX 76-77 EF 7
Budai = Putai 146-147 GH 10
Buda-Koševo 124-125 H 7
Budakskij liman 126-127 E 4
Budalin 141 D 4
Bū Danīb 166-167 E 4
Budapest 118 J 5
Budarino 126-127 P 1
Budaun 134-135 M 5
Budayr, Al- 136-137 L 7
Buddh Gaya 138-139 K 5
Budd Land 53 C 12
Bude, MS 78-79 D 5
Budennovka 124-125 T 8
Büdesheim 128 III b 1
Bude-Stratton 119 D 6
Budge-Budge 138-139 LM 6
Budhāna 138-139 F 3
Budhapūr 138-139 AB 5
Búdhardalur 116-117 c 2
Būdhīyah, Jabal — 173 C 3
Budi, Lago del — 106-107 A 7
Budjala 172 CD 1
Budogošč' 124-125 J 4
Bud'onnovskaja 126-127 KL 3
Budop = Bô Đu'c 150-151 F 6-7
Budua 168-169 H 2
Budva 122-123 H 4
Budwāwū 166-167 H 1
Buea 164-165 F 8
Buena Esperanza 106-107 E 5
Buena Park, CA 83 III d 2
Buenaventura [CO] 92-93 D 4
Buenaventura [MEX] 86-87 G 3
Buenaventura, Bahía de —
92-93 D 4
Buena Vista, GA 78-79 G 4
Buena Vista, VA 80-81 G 2
Buena Vista [BOL] 104-105 E 5
Buenavista [CO] 91 III c 4
Buena Vista [PE] 96-97 B 6
Buena Vista [PY] 102-103 E 6
Buena Vista [YV, Anzoátegui]
94-95 J 3
Buena Vista [YV, Apure] 94-95 G 4
Buena Vista, Cordillera de —
94-95 FG 2
Buenavista, Madrid- 113 III ab 2
Buenavista, San José de —
148-149 H 4
Buena Vista Lake Bed 74-75 D 5
Buenolândia 102-103 GH 1
Buenópolis 102-103 KL 2
Buenos Aires [CO, administrative unit]
94-95 E 7
Buenos Aires [CO, place] 94-95 bc 2
Buenos Aires [PA] 64-65 b 2
Buenos Aires [RA, administrative unit]
111 DE 5
Buenos Aires [RA, place] 111 E 4
Buenos Aires, Lago — 111 B 7
Buenos Aires, Punta —
108-109 G 4-H 3
Buenos Aires-Almagro 110 III b 1
Buenos Aires-Barracas 110 III b 1
Buenos Aires-Belgrano 110 III b 1
Buenos Aires-Bocá 110 III b 1
Buenos Aires-Caballito 110 III b 1
Buenos Aires-Chacarita 110 III b 1
Buenos Aires-Colegiales 110 III b 1
Buenos Aires-Constitución
110 III b 1
Buenos Aires-Flores 110 III b 1
Buenos Aires-Floresta 110 III b 1
Buenos Aires-General Urquiza
110 III b 1
Buenos Aires-La Paternal 110 III b 1
Buenos Aires-Nueva Chicago
110 III b 1
Buenos Aires-Nueva Pompeya
110 III b 1
Buenos Aires-Núñez 110 III b 1
Buenos Aires-Once 110 III b 1
Buenos Aires-Palermo 110 III b 1
Buenos Aires-Recoleta 110 III b 1
Buenos Aires-Retiro 110 III b 1
Buenos Aires-Saavedra 110 III b 1
Buenos Aires-Versailles 110 III b 1
Buenos Aires-Villa Devoto 110 III b 1
Buenos Aires-Villa Lugano 110 III b 2
Buenos Aires-Villa Real 110 III b 1
Buenos Aires-Villa Sáenz Peña
110 III b 1
Buen Pasto 108-109 E 5
Buen Retiro 64-65 b 3
Buen Tiempo, Cabo —
108-109 EF 8
Buerarema 100-101 E 8
Buey, Alto del — 94-95 C 4
Bueyeros, NM 76-77 C 4-5
Bufalotta, Roma- 113 II b 1
Būfarīk 166-167 H 1
Buffalo 61 C 5
Buffalo, MN 70-71 D 3
Buffalo, MO 70-71 D 7
Buffalo, ND 68-69 H 2
Buffalo, NY 64-65 L 3
Buffalo, OK 76-77 E 4
Buffalo, SD 68-69 E 3
Buffalo, TX 76-77 FG 7
Buffalo, WV 72-73 F 5
Buffalo, WY 68-69 C 3
Buffalo Bayou 85 III b 1
Buffalo Bill Reservoir 68-69 B 3
Buffalo Head Hills 61 A 2
Buffalo Hill 155 I b 1
Buffalo Hump 66-67 F 3
Buffalo Lake 56-57 NO 5
Buffalo Narrows 61 D 3
Buffalo River = Bloedrivier
174-175 J 4-5
Buffalorivier = Buffelsrivier
174-175 J 4
Buffelsrivier [ZA, Drakensberge]
174-175 J 4
Buffelsrivier [ZA, Groot Karoo]
174-175 D 7
Buffelsrivier [ZA, Namakwaland]
174-175 C 6
Bū Fīshah 166-167 M 1
Buford, GA 80-81 DE 3
Buford, ND 68-69 E 1-2
Buford, WY 68-69 D 5
Buford Reservoir = Lake Sidney
Lanier 80-81 DE 3
Bug 118 L 2
Bug = Južnyj Bug 126-127 E 2
Bug, Južnyj — 126-127 E 3
Buga 92-93 D 4
Bugalagrande 94-95 CD 5
Bugant 142-143 K 2
Būgarā 166-167 H 1
Bugel, Tanjung — 152-153 J 9
Bughāz Jabal Tāriq 164-165 CD 1
Bū Ghrārah 166-167 M 3
Bū Ghrārah, Khalīj — 166-167 M 3
Būghzūl 166-167 H 2
Bugiri 171 C 2
Bugorkan 132-133 U 5
Bugrino 132-133 H 4
Bugsuk Island 152-153 M 1
Bugt 142-143 N 2
Bugul'ma 132-133 J 7
Bugul'minsko-Belebejevskaja
vozvyšennosť 124-125 TU 6
Buguruslan 132-133 J 7
Buhāeşti 122-123 M 2
Bū Ḥayārah, Ḥāssī — 166-167 D 4
Buhayrāt, Al- 164-165 KL 7
Buḥayrat al-Abyaḍ 164-165 KL 6
Buhayrat al-Assad 134-135 D 3
Buḥayrat al-Bībān 166-167 M 3
Buḥayrat al-Burullus 173 B 2
Buḥayrat al-Manzilah 173 BC 2
Buḥayrat at-Timsāḥ 173 C 2
Buḥayrat Binzart 166-167 LM 1
Buḥayrat Fazrārah 166-167 K 1
Buḥayrat Idkū 173 B 2
Buḥayrat Maryūṭ 173 AB 2
Buhayrat Shārī 136-137 L 5
Buheiret el Murrat el-Kubrâ = Al-
Buḥayrat al-Murrat al-Kubrá
173 C 2
Buhemba 171 C 3
Buhl, ID 66-67 F 4
Buhl, MN 70-71 D 2
Buhoro 171 B 4
Bū Iblān, Jabal — 166-167 D 3
Bui Chu 150-151 F 2
Bui Dam 168-169 E 3
Buin [PNG] 148-149 j 6
Buín [RCH] 106-107 B 4
Bū'īn-e Zahrā' 136-137 O 5
Buinsk [SU, Čuvašskaja ASSR]
124-125 Q 6
Buinsk [SU, Tatarskaja ASSR]
124-125 R 6
Buíque 100-101 F 5
Būīrah 166-167 H 1
Būīrat Şaḥarī 166-167 H 2
Bū'irḍah, Al- 166-167 C 5
Buir Nur 142-143 M 2
Bū Ismā'īl 166-167 H 1
Buiten-IJ 128 I b 1
Buiten Veldert, Amsterdam- 128 I a 2
Buitenzorg = Bogor 148-149 E 8
Bū Izākārn 166-167 B 5
Buizinge = Buizingen 128 II a 2
Buizingen 128 II a 2
Buj 132-133 G 6
Bujalance 120-121 EF 10
Būjarun, Ra's — 166-167 JK 1
Bū Jaydūr, Ra's — 164-165 AB 3
Buji 148-149 M 8
Bujnaksk 126-127 N 5
Bujumbura 172 EF 2
Bukačača 132-133 W 7
Bū Kāhil, Jabal — 166-167 HJ 2
Buka Island 148-149 hj 6
Bukama 172 E 3
Būkān 136-137 LM 4
Bukavu 172 E 2
Bukene 172 F 2
Bū Khaḍrah, Jabal — 166-167 KL 2
Bū Khanāfis 166-167 F 2
Bukit Batu 152-153 K 4
Bukit Batu Bora 152-153 L 4
Bukit Besi 148-149 D 6
Bukit Betong 148-149 D 6
Bukit Betuensambang
152-153 K 5-6
Bukit Kana 152-153 K 4
Bukit Kelingkang 152-153 J 5
Bukit Ketri 150-151 C 9
Bukit Lonjak 152-153 JK 5
Bukit Mandai 154 III a 1
Bukit Mandai [SGP, place] 154 III a 1
Bukit Mertajam 150-151 C 10
Bukit Panjang 154 III a 1
Bukit Raya 148-149 F 7
Bukit Skalap 152-153 KL 4
Bukit Timah 154 III a 1
Bukit Timah [SGP, place] 154 III a 1
Bukittinggi 148-149 CD 7
Bukit Tukung 152-153 JK 6
Bükk 118 K 4-5
Bukkapatnam 140 CD 3
Bukoba 172 F 2
Bukum, Pulau — 154 III a 2
Bukum Kechil, Pulau — 154 III a 2
Bū Kutub 164-165 E 2
Bula [RI] 148-149 K 7
Bula [SU] 124-125 R 6
Bulagan = Bulgan 142-143 J 2
Bulan 148-149 H 4
Bulancak 136-137 GH 2
Bulandshahar = Bulandshur
138-139 FG 3
Bulandshur 138-139 FG 3
Bulangu 168-169 H 2
Bulanık 136-137 K 3
Būlāq 173 B 5
Būlāq, Al-Qāhirah- 170 II b 1
Būlāq ad-Dakrūr 170 II ab 1
Bulawayo 172 E 6
Bulaydat 'Amūr 166-167 J 3
Buldan 136-137 C 3
Buldhāna 138-139 F 7
Bulḍhāṇā = Buldhāna 138-139 F 7
Buldir Island 58-59 r 6
Bulgan [Mongolia, administrative unit
= 9 ◁ 1] 142-143 J 2
Bulgan [Mongolia, place Bulgan]
142-143 J 2
Bulgan [Mongolia, place Chovd]
142-143 G 2
Bulgaria 122-123 K-M 4
Buli = Puli 146-147 H 10
Buli, Teluk — 148-149 J 6
Bulkī 164-165 M 7
Bulla, ostrov — 126-127 O 6
Bullahaar 164-165 a 1
Bullard, TX 76-77 G 6
Bullenhausen 130 I b 2
Buller, Mount — 160 H 6
Buller River 161 DE 5
Bullfinch 158-159 C 6
Bull Mountains 68-69 B 2
Bulloo Downs 158-159 H 5
Bulloo River 158-159 H 5
Bulls Bay 80-81 G 4
Bullshead Butte 61 C 6
Bull Shoals Lake 78-79 C 2
Būlmān 166-167 D 3
Bulnes 106-107 A 6
Buloh 154 III b 1
Buloh, Kampung — 150-151 D 10
Bulsār 138-139 D 7
Bultfontein 174-175 FG 5
Bulu 148-149 J 6
Buluan 148-149 H 5
Bulucan = Emirhan 136-137 GH 3
Bulukumba 148-149 GH 8
Bulungan 148-149 G 6
Buluntou Hai = Ojorong nuur
142-143 F 2
Bulwater 174-175 D 7
Bulwer 174-175 H 5
Bulyea 61 F 5
Bum, Mu'o'ng — = Mu'o'ng Boum
150-151 D 1
Būmāln Dādis 166-167 CD 4
Bumba [ZRE, Bandundu] 172 C 3
Bumba [ZRE, Équateur] 172 D 1
Bumba = Boumba 164-165 H 8
Bûmba Bûm 141 E 2
Bumbeni 174-175 K 4
Bumbu 170 IV a 2
Bumbu, Kinshasa- 170 IV a 2
Bum Bum, Pulau — 152-153 N 3
Bū Midfār'ah 166-167 H 1
Bumkin Island 84 I c 3
Bumthang 141 B 2
Bumthang Chhu 141 B 2
Buna, TX 78-79 C 5
Buna [EAK] 172 G 1
Buna [PNG] 148-149 N 8
Bū Naṣr, Jabal — 166-167 E 3
Bunbah, Khalīj al- 164-165 J 2
Bunbury 158-159 BC 6
Bundaberg 158-159 K 4
Bundelkhand 134-135 MN 6
Bündi 134-135 M 5
Bundooma 158-159 FG 4
Bundoran 119 B 4
Bündu 138-139 K 6
Bung, Sông — = Sông Boung
150-151 F 5
Bunga 168-169 H 4
Bungalaut, Selat — 152-153 C 6-7
Bunge, zemľa — 132-133 b 2-3
Bungendore 160 JK 5
Bunger Oasis 53 C 11
Bungku 148-149 H 7
Bung Kan 150-151 D 3
Bungo-suidō 142-143 P 5
Bungotakada 144-145 H 6
Bu'ng Sai = Ban Bu'ng Sai
150-151 F 5
Bunguran, Pulau — 148-149 E 6
Bunguran Selatan, Kepulauan —
148-149 E 6
Bunguran Utara, Kepulauan —
148-149 E 6
Buni 168-169 HJ 3
Bunia 172 F 1
Bunker Hill, AK 58-59 E 4
Bunker Hill, TX 85 III a 2
Bunker Hill Monument 84 I b 2
Bunkeya 172 E 4
Bunkie, LA 78-79 CD 5
Bunkyō, Tōkyō- 155 III b 1
Bunnell, FL 80-81 c 2
Bun No'a = Boun Neua
150-151 CD 2
Bunsuru 168-169 G 2
Bunta 148-149 H 7
Buntharik 150-151 E 5
Buntok 148-149 FG 7
Bunya 168-169 EF 3
Bünyan 136-137 F 3
Bunyu, Pulau — 148-149 G 6
Buol 148-149 H 6
Buolkalach 132-133 W 3
Buôn Bat 150-151 G 6
Buôn Hô 150-151 G 6
Buôn Ma Thuôt = Ban Mê Thuôt
148-149 E 4
Buôn Plao Sieng 150-151 FG 6
Buor-Chaja, guba — 132-133 Z 3
Buor-Chaja, mys — 132-133 Z 3
Bū Qadīr 166-167 G 1
Buq'ah 166-167 J 1
Buqaliq tagh 142-143 G 4
Buqian = Puqian 146-147 C 11
Buquim 100-101 F 6
Buquq 142-143 E 3
Būr 164-165 L 7
Bura 172 GH 2
Bur Acaba = Buur Hakkaba
164-165 N 8
Buraghat, 'Irq — 166-167 L 6
Bū Raghragh, Wād — 166-167 C 3
Burāgyī 141 E 7
Burajevo 124-125 U 6
Buram 164-165 K 6
Bū Ramlī, Jabal — 166-167 L 2
Buranhém 100-101 DE 9
Buranhém, Rio — 100-101 DE 9
Burao = Bur'o 164-165 O 7
Buras, LA 78-79 E 6
Burāthônzū Taunggyā 141 EF 8
Burathum 138-139 K 3
Bur'atskaja Avtonomnaja Sovetskaja
Socialističeskaja Respublika =
Buryat Autonomous Soviet
Socialist Republic
132-133 T 7-V 6
Būr Atyan = Nawādhību
164-165 A 4
Buraydah 134-135 E 5
Buraymī, Al- 134-135 H 6
Burbank, CA 74-75 DE 5
Burbank, IL 83 II a 2
Burbank, OK 76-77 F 4
Burchanbuudaj 142-143 H 2
Burcher 160 H 4
Burchun 142-143 F 2
Burdeau = Mahdīyah 164-165 E 1
Burdekin River 158-159 J 4
Burdett, KS 68-69 G 6
Burdur 134-135 BC 3
Burdur gölü 136-137 CD 4
Burdwān 134-135 O 6
Burdwood Bank 111 DE 8
Burē [ETH, Gojam] 164-165 M 6
Bure [ETH, Īlubabor] 164-165 M 7
Bureå 116-117 J 5
Bureau, Lac — 62 O 2
Büreen = Bürēn 142-143 K 2
Bureinskij chrebet 132-133 Z 7-8
Bureja 132-133 Z 7
Büren [Mongolia] 142-143 K 2
Burenchaan [Mongolia, Chentij]
142-143 L 2
Burenchaan [Mongolia, Chövsgöl]
142-143 H 2
Bürencogt 142-143 L 2
Būr Fu'ād = Būr Sādāt 173 C 2
Burg 118 EF 2
Būr Gābo = Buur Gaabo 172 H 2
Burgampahāḍ = Borgampād
140 E 2
Bur Gao = Buur Gaabo 172 H 2
Burgas 122-123 M 4
Burgaski zaliv 122-123 MN 4
Burgaw, NC 80-81 GH 3
Bürgel, Offenbach- 128 III b 1
Burg el-'Arab = Burj al-'Arab
136-137 C 7
Burgenland 118 H 5
Burgeo 63 H 4
Burgeo Bank 63 GH 4
Burgersdorp 172 E 8
Burgersfort 174-175 J 3
Burgerville 174-175 F 4
Burgess, Mount — 58-59 S 3
Burgfjället 116-117 F 5
Burghalden 128 IV b 2
Burghersdorp = Burgersdrop
172 E 8
Burgio 122-123 E 7
Burgos 120-121 F 7
Burgsvik 116-117 H 9
Būr Hakkaba 172 H 1
Burḥānā = Budhāna 138-139 F 3
Burhaniye 136-137 B 3
Burhānpur 134-135 M 6
Burhi Dihing 141 D 2
Burhi Gandak 138-139 K 4-5
Būrhi Gandaki 138-139 K 3-4
Burholme, Philadelphia-, PA 84 III c 1
Burholme Park 84 III c 1
Buri 102-103 H 5
Buria Gandak = Burhi Gandak
138-139 K 4-5
Burias Island 148-149 H 4
Burica, Punta — 64-65 K 10
Burietá 100-101 E 7
Burig 130 III d 2
Burin 63 J 4
Burin Peninsula 56-57 Z 8
Buri Ram 148-149 D 3-4
Buriti [BR, Maranhão] 92-93 L 5
Buriti [BR, Minas Gerais]
102-103 HJ 3
Buriti, Rio — 104-105 G 3
Buriti Alegre 102-103 H 3
Buriti Bravo 92-93 L 6
Buriticupu, Rio — 100-101 A 3
Buriti dos Lopes 92-93 L 5
Buritirama 100-101 C 6
Buritis 102-103 J 1
Buritizeiro 102-103 K 2
Burj al-Ahmad 166-167 K 4
Burj al-'Arab 136-137 C 7
Burj al-Haṭṭabah 164-165 F 2
Burj al-Khamīrah 166-167 K 2
Burj Ban Būl'īd 164-165 E 3
Burj Bu 'Arīrij 166-167 J 1
Burj Bū Na'amah 166-167 G 2
Burj Būrgībah 166-167 LM 3
Burj Falāy 166-167 E 6
Burjing = Burchun 142-143 F 2
Burj Luṭfī 164-165 F 3-4
Burj Marhūl 166-167 H 5
Burj Mas'ūdah 166-167 L 4
Burj 'Umar Idrīs 164-165 EF 3
Burkburnett, TX 76-77 E 5
Burke, SD 68-69 G 4
Burkesville, KY 78-79 G 2
Burketown 158-159 GH 3
Burkeville, VA 80-81 GH 2
Burkina Faso 164-165 D 6
Burks Falls 72-73 G 2
Burleith, Washington-, DC 82 II a 1
Burleson, TX 76-77 F 6
Burley, ID 66-67 G 4
Burli 124-125 T 8
Burlingame, CA 74-75 B 4
Burlingame, KS 70-71 BC 6
Burlington 72-73 G 3
Burlington, CO 68-69 E 6
Burlington, IA 64-65 H 3
Burlington, KS 70-71 BC 6
Burlington, MA 84 I a 1
Burlington, NC 80-81 G 2
Burlington, NJ 84 III d 1
Burlington, VT 64-65 M 3
Burlington, WA 66-67 BC 1
Burlington, WI 70-71 F 4
Burlington County Airpark 84 III de 2
Burlington Junction, MO 70-71 C 5
Burma 148-149 BC 2
Burma = Birma 148-149 BC 2
Burma Road 141 F 3
Burnaby Island 60 B 3
Burnet, TX 76-77 E 7
Burney, CA 66-67 C 5
Burney, Monte — 108-109 C 9
Burnie 158-159 HJ 8
Burns, CO 68-69 C 6
Burns, KS 68-69 H 6
Burns, OR 66-67 D 4
Burns Flat, OK 76-77 E 5
Burnside, KY 70-71 H 7
Burns Lake 56-57 LM 7
Burnsville, MS 78-79 E 3
Burnsville, WV 72-73 F 5
Burnt Creek 56-57 X 6-7
Burnt Ground 88-89 J 3
Burnt Lake 63 E 1
Burntop 174-175 J 4
Burnt Paw, AK 58-59 QR 3
Burnt River 66-67 DE 3
Burnt River Mountains 66-67 DE 3
Burntwood Lake 61 H 3
Burntwood River 61 J 3
Bur'o 164-165 b 2
Buron [SU] 126-127 M 5
Burqah, Khabrat — 136-137 GH 6
Burqān 136-137 M 8
Burra 158-159 G 6
Burra, Cape — = Ponta da Barra
174-175 L 3
Burra Falsa, Cape — = Ponta da
Barra Falsa 174-175 L 2
Burrendong Reservoir 160 J 4
Burren Junction 160 J 3
Burrinjuck Reservoir 158-159 J 7
Burro, El- 76-77 D 8
Burro, Serranías del — 64-65 F 6
Burrton, KS 68-69 H 6
Burruyacú 111 CD 3
Burrwood, LA 78-79 E 6
Bursa 134-135 B 2-3
Būr Sādāt 173 C 2
Būr Safāga = Safājah 164-165 L 3
Būr Sa'īd 164-165 L 2
Burstall 61 D 5
Burštyn 126-127 B 2
Būr Sūdān 164-165 M 5
Burt, IA 70-71 C 4
Būr Tawfīq 173 C 3
Burt Lake 70-71 H 3
Buru, Pulau — 148-149 J 7
Burūj, Al- 166-167 C 3
Burullus, Buḥayrat al- 173 B 2
Burūm 134-135 F 8
Burundi 172 EF 2
Burun-Šibertuj, gora —
132-133 UV 8
Bururi 172 E 2
Burutu 168-169 G 4
Burwash 72-73 F 1
Burwash Landing 58-59 RS 6
Burwell, NE 68-69 G 5
Burwood, Sydney- 161 I a 2
Buryat Autonomous Soviet Socialist
Republic 132-133 T 7-V 6
Burye = Burē 164-165 M 6
Buryn' 126-127 F 1
Buryńšik 126-127 P 4
Bury Saint Edmunds 119 G 5
Busa, Cape — = Akrotḗrion
Grambûsa 122-123 K 8
Bū Sa'ādah 166-167 J 2
Buşaiyah, Al- 134-135 EF 4
Bū Sālim 166-167 L 1
Buşayrah 136-137 J 5
Busayṭā', Al- 136-137 G 7-H 8
Busby 60 KL 3
Büs Cagaan Nuur = Böön Cagaan
nuur 142-143 HJ 2
Būsh 173 B 3
Bū Shabaqah 166-167 L 2
Būshehr = Bandar-e Būshehr
134-135 G 5
Bushey 129 II a 1
Bushire = Bandar-e Būshehr
134-135 G 5
Bushland, TX 76-77 CD 5
Bushnell 72-73 FG 1
Bushnell, IL 70-71 E 5
Bushnell, NE 68-69 E 5
Bushnell Seamount 78-79 f 3
Būshqūf 166-167 K 1
Bushy Park 129 II a 2
Busing, Pulau — 154 III a 2
Businga 172 D 1
Busira 172 C 1-2
Buskerud 116-117 C 7-D 8
Buşrat ash-Shām 136-137 G 6
Bussa 168-169 G 3
Busselton 158-159 BC 6
Bustamante 76-77 D 9
Bustamante, Bahía — 108-109 FG 5
Bustleton, Philadelphia-, PA 84 III c 1
Busto Arsizio 122-123 C 3
Busuanga Island 148-149 G 4
Busuluk = Buzuluk 132-133 J 7
Buta 172 D 1
Butantã, São Paulo- 110 II a 2
Buta Ranquil [RA, La Pampa]
106-107 D 6
Buta Ranquil [RA, Mendoza]
106-107 BC 6
Butare 171 B 3
Butarque, Arroyo de — 113 III a 2
Butedale 60 C 3
Bute Inlet 60 E 4
Butembo 171 B 2
Butere 171 C 2
Butha Buthe 174-175 H 5
Butha Qi 142-143 N 2
Būthīdaung 141 C 5
Bū Th'rārah, Khalīj — 166-167 M 3
Butiaba 172 F 1
Bū Tilimīt 164-165 B 5
Butler, AL 78-79 E 4
Butler, GA 78-79 G 4
Butler, IN 70-71 H 5
Butler, MO 70-71 C 6
Butler, PA 72-73 G 4
Būtīlīs 166-167 F 2
Buṭmah 136-137 K 4
Butovo 113 V c 4
Bu Toy 150-151 F 6
Butre 124-125 S 7
Butsha 171 B 2
Butsikáki 122-123 J 6
Butte, MT 64-65 D 2
Butte, NE 68-69 G 4
Butte Creek, MT 68-69 C 2
Büttelhorn 128 III a 2
Butte Meadows, CA 66-67 BC 5
Butterworth = Bagan Jaya
148-149 D 5
Butterworth = Gcuwa 172 E 8
Butt of Lewis 119 C 2
Butuan 148-149 HJ 5
Butung, Pulau — 148-149 H 7-8
Butung, Selat — 152-153 P 8
Buturlinovka 126-127 K 1
Buṭwāl = Butwāl 138-139 J 4
Butwāl 138-139 J 4
Buulo Berde 164-165 b 3
Buwārah, Jabal — 173 D 3
Buxar 138-139 JK 5
Buxton, ND 68-69 H 2
Buxton [GUY] 98-99 JK 1
Buxton [ZA] 174-175 F 4
Buyo 168-169 D 4
Buyr Nur = Buir Nur 142-143 M 2
Büyükada, İstanbul- 136-137 C 2
Büyük Ağrı dağı 134-135 E 2-3
Büyükdere, İstanbul- 154 I b 2
Büyük Doğanca 136-137 B 2
Büyük Köhne 136-137 F 3
Büyük Mahya 136-137 B 2
Büyük Menderes nehri 134-135 B 3
Buzači 134-135 G 1-2
Buzău [RO, place] 122-123 M 3
Buzău [RO, river] 122-123 M 3
Buzaymah 164-165 J 4
Buzd'ak 124-125 U 6
Buzi 146-147 G 5
Buzi = Potzu 146-147 H 10
Bū Zīd, Ḥāssī — 166-167 GH 4
Búzios, Cabo dos — 102-103 M 5
Búzios, Ilha dos — 102-103 K 5
Bū Z'nīqah 166-167 C 3
Bužory 126-127 D 3
Buzuluk 132-133 J 7
Buzzards Bay 72-73 L 4
Byādagī = Byādgi 140 B 3
Byādgi 140 B 3
Byam Martin Channel 56-57 PQ 2
Byam Martin Island 56-57 Q 2-3
Byar 138-139 G 2
Byārmā = Beārma 138-139 G 6
Byās = Beās 138-139 E 4
Byāurā = Biaora 138-139 F 6
Byāvar = Beāwar 134-135 LM 5
Byawar = Beāwar 134-135 LM 5
Byberry Creek 84 III cd 1
Byblos = Jubayl 136-137 F 5
Bychawa 118 L 3
Bychov 124-125 GH 7
Bydgoszcz 118 HJ 2
Byely Island = Belyj ostrov
132-133 MN 3
Byfleet 129 II a 2
Bygdin 116-117 C 7
Bygland 116-117 BC 8
Byhalia, MS 78-79 E 3
Byk 126-127 D 3
Bykovo [SU, Volgogradskaja Oblast']
126-127 M 2
Bylot Island 56-57 V 3
Byōhyī = Beohāri 138-139 H 5
Byoritsu = Miaoli 146-147 H 9
Byrd 53 AB 25
Byrd, Cape — 53 C 29
Byrd Land 53 AB 23-22
Byrock 158-159 J 6
Byrōn 113 IV b 2
Byron, CA 74-75 C 4
Byron, IL 70-71 F 4
Byron, Cape — 158-159 K 5
Byrón, Isla — 108-109 B 6
Byron Bay 160 LM 2
Byron Sound 108-109 J 8
Byrranga, gory — 132-133 Q 3-V 2
Byske 116-117 J 5
Byssa 132-133 Z 7
Bystrica 124-125 R 4
Bystryj Tanyp 124-125 U 6
Bytom 118 J 3

Bytom 273

Bytoš' 124-125 JK 7
Bytów 118 H 1
Byzantinon Museio 113 IV ab 2

Bzémá = Buzaymah 164-165 J 4
Bzura 118 J 2
Bzyp 126-127 K 5

C

Ca, Sông — 150-151 E 3
Caacupé 111 E 3
Čaadajevka 124-125 P 7
Caaguazú [PY, administrative unit] 102-103 DE 6
Caaguazú [PY, place] 111 EF 3
Caaguazú, Cordillera de — 111 E 3
Caála 172 BC 4
Caamaño Sound 60 BC 3
Caapiranga 98-99 H 6
Caapucú 111 E 3
Caarapó 102-103 E 5
Caatiba 100-101 D 8
Caatinga 92-93 K 8
Caatinga, Rio — 102-103 JK 2
Caatinga, Serra da — 100-101 EF 3
Caatingas 92-93 L 7-M 6
Caazapá [PY, administrative unit] 102-103 DE 7
Caazapá [PY, place] 111 E 3
Cabaçal, Rio — 102-103 CD 1
Cabaiguán 88-89 G 3
Caballería, Cabo de — 120-121 K 8
Caballero 102-103 D 6
Cáballito, Buenos Aires- 110 III b 1
Caballococha 92-93 E 5
Caballo Reservoir 76-77 A 6
Caballos Mesteños, Llanos de los — 76-77 BC 8
Cabana 96-97 BC 6
Cabanaconde 96-97 EF 9
Cabanatuan 148-149 H 3
Cabanillas 96-97 F 9
Cabano 63 B 4
Cabecão 102-103 L 5
Cabeceira do Apa 102-103 E 4-5
Cabeceras 94-95 C 5
Cabedelo 92-93 N 6
Cabeza del Buey 120-121 E 9
Cabeza del Mar 108-109 D 9
Cabeza de Vaca, Punta — 104-105 A 10
Cabeza Negra 86-87 HJ 8
Cabezas 92-93 G 8
Cabezon, NM 76-77 A 5
Cabildo [RA] 106-107 FG 7
Cabildo [RCH] 106-107 B 4
Cabimas 92-93 E 2
Cabinda [Angola, administrative unit] 172 B 3
Cabinda [Angola, place] 172 B 3
Cabinet Mountains 66-67 E 1
Cabin John, MD 82 II a 1
Cable, WI 70-71 E 2
Cable Car of Singapore 154 III a 2
Cabo Alejandra = Cape Alexandra 111 J 8
Cabo Alto = Cape Bougainville 108-109 KL 8
Cabo Alto = Cape Dolphin 111 E 8
Cabo Aristizábal 108-109 FG 5
Cabo Bagur 120-121 J 8
Cabo Beata 88-89 L 6
Cabo Blanco [CR] 64-65 J 10
Cabo Blanco [RA] 111 CD 7
Cabo Blanco [YV] 91 II b 1
Cabo Bojador = Rā's Bujdūr 164-165 AB 3
Cabo Branco 92-93 N 6
Cabo Buen Tiempo 108-109 EF 8
Cabo Cabrón 88-89 M 5
Cabo Caçiporé 92-93 JK 4
Cabo Camarón 88-89 D 6
Cabo Carvoeiro 120-121 C 9
Cabo Castro 108-109 B 8
Cabo Catoche 64-65 J 7
Cabo Codera 92-93 F 2
Cabo Colnett 86-87 B 2
Cabo Corrientes [C] 88-89 DE 4
Cabo Corrientes [CO] 92-93 D 3
Cabo Corrientes [MEX] 64-65 E 7
Cabo Corrientes [RA] 111 E 5
Cabo Corrientes = Cape Carysfort 108-109 L 8
Cabo Creus 120-121 J 7
Cabo Cruz 64-65 L 8
Cabo Curioso 108-109 F 7
Cabo Dañoso 108-109 F 7
Cabo da Roca 120-121 C 9
Cabo Dartuch 120-121 J 9
Cabo de Caballería 120-121 K 8
Cabo Decepción = Cape Disappointment 111 J 8-9
Cabo de Espichel 120-121 C 9
Cabo de Finisterre 120-121 BC 7
Cabo de Gata 120-121 FG 10
Cabo de Honduras 64-65 JK 8
Cabo de Hornos 111 CD 9
Cabo de la Aguja 94-95 D 2
Cabo de la Nao 120-121 H 9
Cabo de la Vela 92-93 E 2
Cabo Delgado [Mozambique, administrative unit] 172 GH 4
Cabo Delgado [Mozambique, cape] 172 H 4
Cabo de Palos 120-121 G 10
Cabo de Peñas 120-121 E 7
Cabo de Salinas 120-121 J 9
Cabo de San Juan de Guía 92-93 DE 2
Cabo de San Lorenzo 92-93 C 5
Cabo de Santa Maria 120-121 CD 10
Cabo de Santa Maria = Cap Sainte-Marie 172 J 7
Cabo de Santa Pola 120-121 GH 9
Cabo de Santo Agostinho 100-101 G 5
Cabo de São Roque 92-93 MN 6
Cabo de São Tomé 92-93 LM 9
Cabo de São Vicente 120-121 C 10
Cabo Deseado 111 AB 8
Cabo de Sines 120-121 C 10
Cabo de Tortosa 120-121 H 8
Cabo de Trafalgar 120-121 D 10
Cabo Dois Irmãos 110 I b 2
Cabo Dos Bahías 111 CD 7
Cabo dos Búzios 102-103 M 5
Cabo Dyer 108-109 AB 7
Cabo Engaño 88-89 MN 5
Cabo Espíritu Santo 108-109 EF 9
Cabo Esteban 108-109 B 8
Cabo Falso [Honduras] 88-89 E 7
Cabo Falso [MEX] 64-65 D 7
Cabo Farallón = Cabo Santa Elena 64-65 J 9
Cabo Formentor 120-121 J 8
Cabo Frio [BR, cape] 92-93 L 9
Cabo Frio [BR, place] 92-93 L 9
Cabo Glouster 108-109 BC 10
Cabo Gracias a Dios 64-65 K 8
Cabo Guardián 108-109 FG 7
Cabo Gurupi 98-99 PQ 5
Cabo Hall 108-109 G 10
Cabo Haro 64-65 D 6
Cabo Humos 106-107 A 5
Cabo Jorge 108-109 B 8
Cabo Lort 108-109 B 5
Cabo Lucrecia 88-89 J 4
Cabo Maguari 92-93 K 4-5
Cabo Maisí 64-65 M 7
Cabo Manglares 92-93 CD 4
Cabo Marzo 92-93 D 3
Cabo Matapalo 64-65 K 10
Cabo Meredit = Cape Meredith 111 D 8
Cabo Mondego 120-121 C 8
Cabonga, Réservoir — 72-73 HJ 1
Cabo Norte 92-93 K 4
Cabo Nuevo = Rā's al-Jadīd 166-167 E 2
Cabool, MO 78-79 CD 2
Caboolture 160 L 1
Cabo Orange 92-93 J 4
Cabo Ortegal 120-121 CD 7
Cabo Pakenham 108-109 AB 7
Cabo Pantoja = Pantoja 92-93 DE 5
Cabo Paquica 104-105 A 7
Cabo Pasado 92-93 C 5
Cabo Peñas 108-109 F 9
Cabo Polonio 111 F 4
Cabo Primero 108-109 AB 7
Cabo Prior 120-121 C 7
Cabo Quedal 111 AB 6
Cabo Quilán 108-109 B 4
Cabora Bassa 172 F 5
Cabo Raper 108-109 AB 6
Cabo Raso [RA, cape] 108-109 G 5
Cabo Raso [RA, place] 111 CD 6
Cabo Raso = Cabo Norte 92-93 K 4
Cabo Reyes 96-97 BC 3
Cabo Rizzuto 122-123 G 6
Cabo Rojo [MEX] 64-65 G 7
Cabo Rojo [Puerto Rico] 88-89 N 6
Cabo Samaná 88-89 M 5
Cabo San Antonio [C] 64-65 K 7
Cabo San Antonio [RA] 106-107 J 6
Cabo San Bartolomé 108-109 G 10
Cabo San Diego 111 CD 8
Cabo San Francisco de Paula 108-109 F 7
Cabo San Juan [Equatorial Guinea] 164-165 F 8
Cabo San Juan [RA] 111 D 8
Cabo San Lázaro 64-65 D 7
Cabo San Lucas 64-65 E 7
Cabo San Quintín 64-65 C 5
Cabo San Román 92-93 EF 2
Cabo Santa Elena 64-65 J 9
Cabo Santa Marta Grande 102-103 H 8
Cabo Santiago 108-109 AB 8
Cabo San Vicente 108-109 FG 10
Cabo Silleiro 120-121 C 7
Cabot, AR 78-79 CD 3
Cabo Tablas 106-107 AB 3
Cabo Taitao 111 A 7
Cabo Tate 108-109 BC 9
Cabot Head 72-73 F 2
Cabo Toriñana 120-121 C 7
Cabo Tres Puntas 111 CD 7
Cabo Tromba Grande 100-101 E 8
Cabot Strait 56-57 YZ 8
Cabo Verde, Islas — 50-51 H 5
Cabo Vidio 120-121 DE 7
Cabo Vigia 108-109 F 7
Cabo Vírgenes 111 C 8
Cabra 120-121 E 10
Cabra, Monte — 64-65 b 3
Cabra Corral, Embalse — 104-105 D 9
Cabral, La — 106-107 G 3
Cabral, Serra do — 102-103 K 2
Cabras [BR] 102-103 J 5
Cabras, Las — 106-107 B 5
Cabred 106-107 J 3
Cabrera 88-89 M 5
Cabrera, Isla — 120-121 J 9
Cabrel 120-121 G 9
Cabrillo, Point — 74-75 AB 3
Cabrobó 100-101 E 5
Cabrón, Cabo — 88-89 M 5
Cabruta 94-95 H 4
Cabuçu de Cima 110 II b 1
Cabul = Kabul 134-135 K 4
Cabure 94-95 G 2
Caburé, El — 104-105 E 10
Caburgua, Laguna — 108-109 D 2
Cabusa Island = Kabūzā Kyūn 150-151 AB 6
Cabuyaro 94-95 E 5
Caca 126-127 M 2
Caçador 111 F 3
Cacahual, Isla — 94-95 BC 5
Čačak 122-123 J 4
Cacaoui, Lac — 63 C 2
Caçapava 102-103 K 5
Caçapava, Serra de — 106-107 L 3
Caçapava do Sul 111 F 4
Càccia, Capo — 122-123 BC 5
Cacequi 111 F 3
Cáceres [BR] 92-93 H 8
Cáceres [CO] 92-93 D 3
Cáceres [E] 120-121 D 9
Cáceres, Laguna — 104-105 GH 6
Cachan 129 I c 2
Cachapoal, Río — 106-107 B 5
Cāchār [IND] 141 C 3
Cachar [TJ] 142-143 M 3
Cacharí 106-107 H 6
Cache, OK 76-77 E 5
Cache Creek 60 G 4
Cachegar = Qāshqār 142-143 CD 4
Cachemire = Kashmīr 134-135 LM 4
Cache Peak 66-67 G 4
Cacheu [Guinea Bissau, place] 164-165 A 6
Cacheu [Guinea Bissau, river] 168-169 B 2
Cacheuta 106-107 C 4
Cachi 111 C 3
Cachí, Nevado de — 111 C 2
Cachimbo, Parque Nacional do — 98-99 K 8-9
Cachimbo, Serra do — 92-93 HJ 6
Cachimo 172 D 3
Cachinal 104-105 B 9
Cáchira 94-95 E 4
Cachiyuyo 106-107 B 2
Cachoeira [BR ↙ Barreiras] 100-101 B 7
Cachoeira [BR ↓ Feira de Santana] 92-93 M 7
Cachoeira, Rio — 100-101 E 8
Cachoeira, Rio da — 110 I b 2
Cachoeira Acará 98-99 J 7
Cachoeira Alta [BR, Goias] 98-99 NO 7
Cachoeira Alta [BR, Paraná] 102-103 G 3
Cachoeira Ananás 98-99 M 8
Cachoeira Anta [BR, Amazonas] 98-99 H 8
Cachoeira Anta [BR, Pará] 98-99 O 7
Cachoeira Araras 98-99 M 8
Cachoeira Arregaço 104-105 F 2
Cachoeira Bela Vista 92-93 J 5
Cachoeira Benfica 98-99 L 5
Cachoeira Caiabi 98-99 L 10
Cachoeira Capinzal 98-99 JK 9
Cachoeira Capivara 92-93 J 6
Cachoeira Caracaraí 92-93 G 4
Cachoeira Cerreira Comprida 94-95 OP 10
Cachoeira Chapéu 98-99 K 7-8
Cachoeira Cinco de Maio 98-99 L 11
Cachoeira Comprida = Treze Quedas 92-93 H 4
Cachoeira Criminosa 98-99 HJ 5
Cachoeira Cruzeiro do Sul 98-99 H 10
Cachoeira da Boca 98-99 L 7
Cachoeira da Laje 98-99 L 5
Cachoeira da Pedra da Amolar 100-101 B 5
Cachoeira da Pedra Sêca 98-99 M 9
Cachoeira das Andorinhas 94-95 G 8
Cachoeira da Saudade 98-99 M 8
Cachoeira das Capoeiras 92-93 H 6
Cachoeira das Piranhas 98-99 HJ 10
Cachoeira de Paulo Afonso 92-93 M 6
Cachoeira de Rebojo 98-99 J 9
Cachoeira de Santa Isabel 98-99 OP 8
Cachoeira de São Lucas 98-99 J 9
Cachoeira de Tropêço Grande 98-99 OP 11
Cachoeira do Arari 92-93 K 5
Cachoeira do Catarino 98-99 G 10
Cachoeira Doce Ilusão 98-99 L 9
Cachoeira do Coatá 92-93 G 6
Cachoeira do Desastre 98-99 J 10
Cachoeira do Inferno 92-93 G 6
Cachoeira Dois Irmãos 98-99 J 9
Cachoeira do Jaú 98-99 OP 10
Cachoeira do Javari 98-99 LM 5
Cachoeira do Lajeado 98-99 H 10
Cachoeira do Limão 92-93 J 6
Cachoeira do Maribondo 102-103 H 4
Cachoeira do Mato 100-101 DE 9
Cachoeira do Pacu 92-93 J 9
Cachoeira do Periquito 92-93 G 6
Cachoeira do Pimenta 94-95 K 7
Cachoeira do Praião 92-93 K 8
Cachoeira do Samuel 98-99 G 9
Cachoeira do Sangue 98-99 L 7
Cachoeira do Sapateiro 92-93 H 5
Cachoeira dos Índios 92-93 G 4
Cachoeira dos Pilões 98-99 OP 9
Cachoeira do Sul 111 F 4
Cachoeira do Uba 98-99 MN 9
Cachoeira Dourada 102-103 H 3
Cachoeira do Urubu 98-99 OP 11
Cachoeira Figueira 98-99 J 9
Cachoeira Ilhas 98-99 JK 5
Cachoeira Ilhinha 98-99 K 5
Cachoeira Ipadu 92-93 F 4
Cachoeira Ipanoré 94-95 GH 7
Cachoeira Itaipava [BR, Rio Araguaia] 92-93 K 6
Cachoeira Itaipava [BR, Rio Xingu] 92-93 J 5
Cachoeira Jacureconga 100-101 A 2
Cachoeira Jaianary 94-95 J 7
Cachoeira Jararaca 102-103 G 6
Cachoeira Macaquara 98-99 M 4
Cachoeira Maçaranduba 92-93 J 4-5
Cachoeira Macuco 102-103 GH 4
Cachoeira Mamuíra 98-99 P 6
Cachoeira Manuel Jorge 98-99 LM 7
Cachoeira Maria Velha 98-99 K 7
Cachoeira Marmelão 98-99 KL 7
Cachoeira Matamatá 98-99 HJ 8
Cachoeira Miriti 98-99 J 8
Cachoeira Mortandade 98-99 P 8
Cachoeira Paca 98-99 H 4
Cachoeira Paiçandu 92-93 J 5
Cachoeira Pariaxá 98-99 N 6
Cachoeira Patauá 98-99 HJ 9
Cachoeira Paulista 102-103 K 5
Cachoeira Pederneira 92-93 FG 6
Cachoeira Pereira 98-99 KL 7
Cachoeira Peritos 98-99 GH 9
Cachoeira Pirapora 104-105 G 2
Cachoeira Pirarara 98-99 KL 5
Cachoeira Porto Seguro 98-99 MN 8
Cachoeira Querero 98-99 K 4-5
Cachoeira Regresso 92-93 HJ 5
Cachoeira Santa Teresa 98-99 G 9-10
Cachoeira Santo Antônio [BR, Rio Madeira] 92-93 FG 6
Cachoeira Santo Antônio [BR, Rio Roosevelt] 98-99 HJ 9
Cachoeira São Francisco 98-99 LM 7
Cachoeira Saranzal 98-99 H 8
Cachoeiras de Macacu 102-103 LM 5
Cachoeira Sêca 98-99 L 7
Cachoeira Soledade 98-99 LM 7
Cachoeira Tareraimbu 92-93 J 6
Cachoeira Temporal 92-93 J 7
Cachoeira Trava 92-93 H 5
Cachoeira Tucano 94-95 G 7
Cachoeira Uacuru 98-99 HJ 10
Cachoeira Uaianary 98-99 FG 4
Cachoeira Xateturu 98-99 MN 8
Cachoeiro de Itapemirim 92-93 LM 9
Cachoeiro do Canoeiro 98-99 OP 10
Cachoeiro Enseada 98-99 J 10
Cachoeiro Jacuzão 98-99 O 8
Cachoeiro Pereira 92-93 H 5
Cachos, Punta — 111 B 3
Cachuela Esperanza 104-105 D 2
Cachuela Piedra Liza 96-97 E 7
Cacimba de Dentro 100-101 G 4
Cacine 168-169 B 3
Caçiporé, Cabo — 92-93 JK 4
Caçiporé, Rio — 92-93 J 4
Cacique, Cerro — 108-109 D 4
Cacitúa, Morro — 108-109 C 4
Çaçmak 136-137 F 4
Cacolo 172 C 3-4
Caconda 172 BC 4
Cácota 94-95 E 4
Cactus, TX 76-77 E 9
Cactus Range 74-75 E 4
Caçu 102-103 G 3
Caculé 92-93 L 7
Caçumba, Ilha — 100-101 E 9
Cacuso 172 C 3
Čadan 132-133 R 7
Caddo, OK 76-77 F 5
Caddo Lake 76-77 GH 6
Cadena de Cerro de la Sal 96-97 D 7
Cadena de Huamuco 96-97 C 6
Cadereyta Jiménez 86-87 KL 5
Cadetes de Chile 106-107 D 4
Cadibarrawirracanna, Lake — 160 AB 2
Cadillac, MI 70-71 H 3
Cadillac [CDN] 66-67 JK 1
CaĐinh, Nam — = Nam Theun 150-151 E 3
Cádiz 120-121 D 10
Cadiz, CA 74-75 F 5
Cadiz, KY 78-79 EF 2
Cádiz, Golfo de — 120-121 D 10
Čadobec [SU, place] 132-133 S 6
Čadobec [SU, river] 132-133 S 6
Cadomin 60 J 3
Cadotte River 60 J 1
Cadret 106-107 G 5
Čadyr-Lunga 126-127 D 3
Caém 100-101 D 6
Caen 120-121 G 4
Caerdydd = Cardiff 119 E 6
Caerfyrddin = Carmarthen 119 D 6
Caernarfon 119 D 5
Caesarea 136-137 F 6
Caesarea = Kayseri 134-135 D 3
Caesarea Philippi = Bāniyās 136-137 FG 6
Caetê, Baía do — 100-101 A 1
Caeté, Rio — 98-99 D 9
Caetés 100-101 F 5
Caetité 92-93 L 7
Cafarnaum 100-101 D 6
Cafayate 111 C 3
Café, Serra do — 100-101 G 6
Cafelândia 102-103 H 4
Cafta = Kafta 164-165 M 6
Cagaan Cherem = Wanli Changcheng 142-143 K 4
Cagarras, Ilhas — 110 I b 3
Cagayan de Oro 148-149 HJ 5
Cagayan Islands 148-149 H 5
Cagayan Sulu Island 148-149 GH 5
Čagda 132-133 Z 6
Cageri 126-127 L 5
Caggan nuur 142-143 FG 2
Cagliari 122-123 C 6
Cagliari, Golfo di — 122-123 C 6
Čagoda [SU, place] 132-133 EF 6
Čagoda [SU, river] 124-125 K 4
Çağrankaya 136-137 J 2
Cag Sum = Dzag 142-143 H 2
Caguán, Río — 92-93 E 4
Caguas 64-65 N 8
Cahama 172 BC 5
Cahirciveen 119 AB 6
Cahors 120-121 H 6
Cahuapanas 92-93 D 6
Cahuapanas, Río — 96-97 C 4
Cahuilla Indian Reservation 74-75 E 6
Cahuinari, Río — 94-95 EF 8
Cahungula = Caungula 172 C 3
Caí 106-107 M 2
Caia [Mozambique] 172 G 5
Caiabi, Cachoeira — 98-99 L 10
Caiabis, Serra dos — 92-93 H 7
Caiambé 92-93 FG 5
Caiapó, Rio — 102-103 G 2
Caiapó, Serra do — 102-103 FG 2
Caiapônia 102-103 FG 2
Cai Ban, Đao — 148-149 E 2
Caibarién 64-65 L 7
Cai Bau 150-151 F 2
Cai Be 150-151 EF 7
Caiçara [BR, Bahia] 100-101 B 8
Caiçara [BR, Paraíba] 100-101 G 4
Caicara [YV] 92-93 F 3
Caicaral 94-95 K 3
Caicedonia 94-95 CD 5
Caicó 100-101 F 4
Caicos Islands 64-65 M 7
Caicos Passage 64-65 M 7
Cai Lây 150-151 EF 7
Cailloma 96-97 F 9
Caillou Bay 78-79 D 6
Caillou Lake 78-79 D 6
Caimán, Laguna — 94-95 G 6
Caimanero, Laguna del — 86-87 G 6
Caimanes 106-107 B 3-4
Caimito 64-65 b 3
Caimito, Río — 64-65 b 3
Caín, El — 108-109 E 3
Cain Creek 68-69 G 3
Caine, Río — 104-105 D 6
Cainsville, MO 70-71 D 5
Cai Nu'o'c 150-151 E 8
Cairari 92-93 K 5
Caird Land 53 B 33-34
Cairn Mount 58-59 K 6
Cairns 158-159 J 3
Cairns Lake 62 B 2
Cairo, GA 80-81 D 5
Cairo, IL 64-65 J 4
Cairo, NE 68-69 G 5
Cairo = Al-Qāhira 164-165 KL 2
Cairo Airport 170 II c 1
Cairo Tower 170 II b 1
Cairú 100-101 E 7
Cais, Rio — 100-101 D 3
Caiundo 172 C 5
Caiuvá, Lagoa do — 106-107 LM 4
Caiza 104-105 D 7
Caizi Hu 146-147 F 6
Cajabamba 92-93 D 6
Cajamar 102-103 J 5
Cajamarca [PE, administrative unit] 96-97 B 4-5
Cajamarca [PE, place] 92-93 D 6
Cajapió 92-93 KL 5
Cajarí 100-101 B 2
Cajatambo 92-93 D 7
Cajàzeira 100-101 E 8
Cajazeiras 100-101 E 4
Cajdam nuur 142-143 M 2
Cajdamyn nuur, Ich — 142-143 GH 4
Čajek 134-135 L 2
Čajkovskij 124-125 U 5
Cajón del Manzano 106-107 B 7
Cajon Pass 74-75 E 5
Caju, Ilha do — 100-101 CD 2
Caju, Rio de Janeiro- 110 I b 2
Cajuás, Ponta dos — 92-93 M 5
Cajueiro [BR, Amazonas] 98-99 C 7
Cajueiro [BR, Maranhão] 100-101 A 2
Cajueiros, Lago dos — 100-101 CD 2
Cajuí 100-101 CD 6
Cajuru 102-103 J 4
Çakıralan 136-137 F 2
Cakung, Kali — 154 IV b 1-2
Čakva 126-127 K 6
Çal = Demirciköy 136-137 C 3
Cal, La — 104-105 G 6
Cal, Río de la — 104-105 G 6
Cala [ZA] 174-175 G 6
Calabar 164-165 F 7-8
Calabogie 72-73 H 2
Calabozo 92-93 F 3
Calabozo, Ensenada de — 94-95 F 2
Calàbria 122-123 FG 6
Calacoto 104-105 B 5
Calada, CA 74-75 F 5
Calafat 122-123 K 3-4
Calafate 111 B 8
Calafquen, Lago — 108-109 C 2
Calagua Islands 148-149 H 4
Calahari = Kalahari Desert 172 CD 6
Calahorra 120-121 G 7
Calais 120-121 H 3
Calais, Pas de — 120-121 HJ 3
Calakmul 86-87 Q 9
Calalaste, Sierra de — 111 C 2-3
Calama [BR] 92-93 G 6
Calama [RCH] 111 C 2
Calamar [CO ↘ Bogotá] 92-93 E 4
Calamar [CO ↘ Cartagena] 94-95 D 2
Calamarca 104-105 B 5
Calamian Group 148-149 G 4
Calamus River 68-69 G 4
Calandria, La — 106-107 H 3
Calang 148-149 C 6
Calansho Sand Sea = Serīr Kalanshyū 164-165 J 3
Calapan 148-149 H 4
Călăraşi 122-123 M 3
Calarcá 94-95 D 5
Cala Road = Calaweg 174-175 G 6
Calatayud 120-121 G 8
Calate = Qalāt 134-135 K 5
Călăţele 122-123 K 2
Calaweg 174-175 G 6
Calayan Island 148-149 H 3
Calbayog 148-149 HJ 4
Calbuco, Volcán — 108-109 C 3
Calca 92-93 E 7
Calcanhar, Ponta do — 92-93 M 6-N 5
Calcasieu Lake 78-79 C 6
Calcasieu River 78-79 C 5
Calcatapul, Sierra — 108-109 E 4
Calceta 96-97 AB 2
Calcha 104-105 D 7
Calchaquí 106-107 G 2
Calchaquíes, Cumbres — 104-105 D 10
Calchaquíes, Valles — 104-105 CD 9
Calchín 106-107 F 3
Calçoene 92-93 J 4
Calçoene, Rio — 98-99 N 3-4
Calcutta 134-135 O 6
Calcutta-Alipore 154 II ab 2
Calcutta-Ballygunge 154 II b 2
Calcutta-Beliaghata 154 II b 2
Calcutta-Bhowanipore 154 II b 2
Calcutta-Chitpur 154 II b 2
Calcutta-Cossipore 154 II b 2
Calcutta-Dhakuria 154 II b 2
Calcutta-Gariya 154 II b 3
Calcutta-Jadabpur 154 II b 3
Calcutta-Jorasanko 154 II b 2
Calcutta-Kalighat 154 II ab 2
Calcutta-Kasba 154 II b 2
Calcutta-Kidderpore 154 II ab 2
Calcutta-Maidan 154 II ab 2
Calcutta-Simla 154 II b 2
Calcutta-Sura 154 II b 2
Calcutta-Tapsia 154 II b 2
Calcutta-Ultadanga 154 II b 2
Calcutta-Watganj 154 II a 2
Caldas [BR] 102-103 J 4
Caldas [CO, administrative unit] 94-95 D 5
Caldas [CO, place] 94-95 D 4
Caldas da Rainha 120-121 C 9
Caldas Novas 102-103 H 2
Caldeirão 100-101 D 7
Caldeirão, Ilha do — 98-99 D 7
Caldeirão Grande 100-101 D 6
Caldén, El — 106-107 DE 3
Caldera 111 B 3
Caldera, La — 104-105 D 9
Çaldere 136-137 G 2
Calderón 94-95 bc 2
Çaldıran 136-137 K 3
Caldono 94-95 C 6
Caldwell, ID 66-67 E 4
Caldwell, KS 76-77 F 4
Caldwell, OH 72-73 F 5
Caldwell, TX 76-77 F 7
Calecute = Calicut 134-135 LM 8
Caledon 172 CD 8
Caledon Bay 158-159 G 2
Caledonia, MN 70-71 E 4
Caledonia [CDN, Nova Scotia] 63 D 5
Caledonia [CDN, Ontario] 72-73 G 3
Caledonian Canal 119 D 3
Caledonrivier 172 E 7-8
Calemar 96-97 C 5
Calera 104-105 C 7
Calera, AL 78-79 F 4
Calera, La — 106-107 B 4
Caleta Buena 104-105 A 6
Caleta Clarencia 108-109 DE 9
Caleta de Vique 64-65 b 3
Caleta Guanilla del Norte 104-105 A 7
Caleta Josefina 108-109 E 9
Caleta Loa 104-105 A 7
Caleta Molles 106-107 AB 4
Caleta Olivia 111 C 7
Caleufú 111 D 5
Caleufú, Río — 108-109 D 3
Calexico, CA 74-75 F 6
Calf Island 84 I c 2
Calfucurá 106-107 J 6
Çalgan 136-137 H 4
Calgary 56-57 O 7
Calhan, CO 68-69 D 6
Calhoun, GA 78-79 G 3
Calhoun, LA 78-79 C 4
Calhoun, TN 80-81 D 3
Calhoun City, MS 78-79 E 4
Calhoun Falls, SC 80-81 E 3
Cali 92-93 D 4
Calico Rock, AR 78-79 CD 2
Calicut 134-135 LM 8
Caliente, CA 74-75 D 5
Caliente, NV 64-65 CD 4
California, MO 70-71 D 6
Califórnia [BR] 102-103 G 6
California [TT] 94-95 L 2
California [USA, administrative unit] 64-65 B 3-C 5
California [USA, landscape] 196 G 5-H 7
California, Gulf of — 64-65 D 5-E 7
California, La — 106-107 FG 4
California, University of — [USA, Los Angeles] 83 III b 1
California, University of — [USA, San Francisco] 83 I c 1
California State College 83 III c 2
California State University 83 III c 1
Căliman, Munţii — 122-123 L 2
Calimere, Point — 134-135 MN 8
Călineşti 122-123 L 3
Calingasta 111 BC 4
Calion, AR 78-79 C 4
Calipatria, CA 74-75 F 6
Calispell Peak 66-67 E 1
Calistoga, CA 74-75 B 3
Calitzdorp 174-175 D 7
Calka 126-127 M 6
Calkini 64-65 H 7
Callabonna, Lake — 158-159 G 5
Callabonna Creek 160 E 2
Calla-Calla, Cerros de — 96-97 BC 5
Callafo = Kelafo 164-165 N 7
Callahan, FL 80-81 c 1
Callahan, Mount — 74-75 E 3
Callander [CDN] 72-73 G 1
Callao 92-93 D 7
Callao, El — 94-95 L 4
Callaquén 106-107 B 6
Callaquén, Volcán — 106-107 B 6
Callaway, NE 68-69 FG 5
Calle Larga 94-95 E 3
Calling Lake [CDN, lake] 60 L 2
Calling Lake [CDN, place] 60 L 2
Callison Ranch 58-59 W 7
Calmar 60 L 3
Calmar, IA 70-71 DE 4
Calmon 102-103 G 7
Čalna 124-125 JK 3
Calógeras 102-103 GH 5
Caloosahatchee River 80-81 c 3
Calotmul 86-87 QR 7
Caltagirone 122-123 F 7
Caltama, Cerro — 104-105 BC 7
Caltanissetta 122-123 EF 7
Calulo 172 BC 3-4
Calumet, MI 70-71 F 2
Calumet [CDN] 72-73 J 2
Calumet [USA] 83 II b 2
Calumet, Lake — 83 II b 2
Calva, AZ 74-75 HJ 6
Calvados, Côte du — 120-121 G 4
Calvas, Río — 96-97 B 4
Calve 106-107 G 7
Calvert, AL 78-79 EF 5
Calvert, TX 76-77 F 7
Calvert City, KY 78-79 E 2
Calvert Island 60 C 4
Calvi 122-123 C 4
Calvin, OK 76-77 F 5
Calvinia 172 CD 8
Camabatela 172 C 3
Camaçari 100-101 E 7
Camachigama, Lac — 62 NO 3
Camacho [BOL] 104-105 D 7
Camacho [MEX] 86-87 JK 5
Camacupa 172 C 4
Camaguán 94-95 H 3
Camagüey 64-65 L 7
Camagüey, Archipiélago de — 64-65 L 7
Camajuaní 88-89 G 3
Çamalan 136-137 F 4
Camalaú 100-101 F 4
Camamu 100-101 E 7
Camaná 92-93 E 8
Camapuã 92-93 J 8
Camapuã, Sertão de — 92-93 J 8-9
Camaquã 111 F 4
Camaquã, Rio — 106-107 L 3
Camararé, Rio — 98-99 J 11
Çamardı 136-137 F 4
Camargo, OK 76-77 E 4-5
Camargo [BOL] 92-93 FG 9
Camargo [MEX] 64-65 E 6
Camargo, Ciudad — 76-77 E 9
Camargue 120-121 K 7
Camarico 106-107 B 5
Camarillo, CA 74-75 D 5
Camariñas 120-121 C 7
Camarón [MEX] 76-77 DE 9
Camarón [PA] 64-65 b 3
Camarón, Cabo — 88-89 D 6
Camarones 111 CD 6
Camarones, Bahía — 108-109 G 5
Camarones, Río — 104-105 AB 6
Camas, ID 66-67 G 3
Camas, WA 66-67 B 3
Camas Creek 66-67 GH 3
Camataquí = Villa Abecia 92-93 FG 9
Camatei 100-101 C 8
Ca Mâu 148-149 DE 5
Ca Mau = Quan Long 148-149 DE 5
Ca Mau, Mui — = Mui Bai Bung 148-149 D 5
Cambaia = Cambay 134-135 L 6
Cambajuva 106-107 N 2
Cambará 102-103 G 5
Cambay 134-135 L 6
Cambay, Gulf of — 134-135 L 6
Cambé 102-103 G 5
Camberwell, London- 129 II b 2
Camberwell, Melbourne- 161 II c 2
Cambing = Ilha de Ataúro 148-149 J 8
Cambodia 148-149 DE 4
Camboriú 102-103 H 7
Camborne 119 D 6
Cambrai 120-121 J 3
Cambray, NM 76-77 A 6
Cambria, CA 74-75 C 5
Cambrian Mountains 119 D 5-E 6
Cambridge, ID 66-67 E 3
Cambridge, IL 70-71 EF 5

274 Bytoš'

Cape Negrais = Nagare Angū 141 CD 7
Cape Newenham 56-57 D 6
Cape Nome 58-59 E 4
Cape North 56-57 YZ 8
Cape Oksenof 58-59 a 2
Cape Ommaney 58-59 v 8
Cape Otway 158-159 H 7
Cape Palliser 158-159 P 8
Cape Palmas 164-165 C 8
Cape Palmer 58-59 B 27
Cape Palmerston 158-159 JK 4
Cape Pankof 58-59 b 2
Cape Parry 56-57 M 3
Cape Pasley 158-159 D 6
Cape Peirce 58-59 FG 7
Cape Penck 53 C 9
Cape Pillar 158-159 J 8
Cape Pine 63 K 4
Cape Pingmar = Lingao Jiao 150-151 G 3
Cape Pole, AK 58-59 vw 9
Cape Portland 160 c 2
Cape Prince Alfred 56-57 KL 3
Cape Prince of Wales 56-57 C 4-5
Cape Providence [NZ] 158-159 MN 9
Cape Providence [USA] 58-59 ef 1
Cape Province = Kaapland — 172 DE 8
Cape Race 56-57 a 8
Cape Raper 56-57 XY 4
Cape Ray 56-57 Z 8
Cape Recife = Kaap Recife 174-175 FG 8
Cape Rise 50-51 K 8
Cape Rodney 58-59 D 4
Cape Romain 80-81 G 4
Cape Romano 80-81 bc 4
Cape Romanzof 56-57 C 5
Capertee 160 JK 4
Cape Sabak 58-59 pq 6
Cape Sable [CDN] 56-57 XY 9
Cape Sable [USA] 64-65 K 6
Cape Sable Island 63 D 6
Cape Saint-Blaize = Kaap Sint Blaize 174-175 E 8
Cape Saint Charles 56-57 Za 7
Cape Saint Elias 58-59 P 7
Cape Saint Francis = Sealpunt 174-175 F 8
Cape Saint George 78-79 G 5
Cape Saint George [CDN] 63 G 3
Cape Saint James 56-57 K 7
Cape Saint John 63 J 3
Cape Saint Lawrence 63 F 4
Cape Saint Martin = Kaap Sint Martin 174-175 B 7
Cape Saint Mary's 63 J 4
Cape Saint Paul 168-169 F 4
Cape Salatan = Tanjung Selatan 148-149 F 7
Cape San Agustin 148-149 J 5
Cape San Blas 64-65 J 6
Cape Sasmik 58-59 u 7
Cape Scott 56-57 L 7
Cape Seal = Kaap Seal 174-175 E 8
Cape Sebastian 66-67 A 4
Cape Sifa = Dahua Jiao 150-151 H 3
Cape Simpson 58-59 KL 1
Cape Smiley 53 B 29
Cape Smith 56-57 UV 5
Cape Solander 161 I b 3
Cape Sorell 158-159 HJ 8
Cape Spencer [AUS] 158-159 G 7
Cape Spencer [USA] 58-59 T 7
Cape Stephens 161 EF 5
Cape Suckling 58-59 Q 7
Cape Talbot 158-159 E 2
Cape Tanak 58-59 m 4
Cape Tatnam 56-57 ST 6
Cape Tavoy = Shinmau Sūn 150-151 AB 6
Cape Thompson 58-59 D 2
Cape Three Points 164-165 D 8
Cape Tormentine 63 DE 4
Cape Town = Kaapstad 172 C 8
Cape Turnagain 161 G 5
Cape Van Diemen 158-159 EF 2
Cape Verde 178-179 H 5
Cape Verde = Cap Vert 164-165 A 6
Cape Verde Basin 50-51 GH 4-5
Cape Verde Plateau 50-51 H 4-5
Cape Vincent, NY 72-73 HJ 2
Cape Ward Hunt 148-149 N 8
Cape Wessel 158-159 G 2
Cape Weymouth 158-159 HJ 2
Cape Wickham 160 b 1
Cape Wolstenholme 56-57 VW 5
Cape Wrath 119 D 2
Cape Yakak 58-59 u 7
Cape Yakataga, AK 58-59 QR 6
Cape York 158-159 H 2
Cape York Peninsula 158-159 H 2
Cap Falaise = Mui Đa Dựng 150-151 J 4
Cap Falcon = Rã's Falkun 166-167 F 2
Cap Figalo = Rã's Fiqãlu 166-167 F 2
Cap Ghir = Rã's Ghīr 166-167 AB 4
Cap-Haïtien 64-65 M 8
Capibara 92-93 F 4
Capilla, La — 96-97 B 4
Capilla del Monte 106-107 E 3
Capilla del Rosario 106-107 CD 4
Capillitas 104-105 C 10
Capim 98-99 OP 5
Capim, Rio — 92-93 K 5
Capinota 104-105 CD 5

Capinzal 102-103 G 7
Capinzal, Cachoeira — 98-99 JK 9
Capira 94-95 B 3
Capirona 96-97 CD 3
Capistrano 100-101 E 3
Capitachouahe, Rivière — 62 N 2-3
Capital Territory, Australian — 158-159 J 7
Capitan, NM 76-77 B 6
Capitán Aracena, Isla — 108-109 D 10
Capitán Bado 102-103 E 5
Capitán Costa Pinheiro, Rio — 104-105 CD 2
Capitan Grande Indian Reservation 74-75 E 6
Capitán Joaquín Madariaga 106-107 H 2
Capitán Maldonado, Cerro — 108-109 BC 4
Capitán Meza 102-103 E 5
Capitán O. Serebriakof 102-103 B 5
Capitán Pastene 106-107 A 7
Capitán Solari 104-105 G 10
Capitán Ustares, Cerro — 102-103 B 3
Capitão Cardoso, Rio — 98-99 HJ 10
Capitão de Campos 100-101 CD 3
Capitão-Mór, Serra do — 100-101 F 4-5
Capitão Poço 98-99 P 5
Capitol, The — 82 II ab 2
Capitol Heights, MD 82 II b 2
Capitol Hill, Washington-, DC 82 II ab 2
Capitólio 91 III b 3
Capitolio Nacional 91 II b 1
Capitol Peak 66-67 E 5
Capitol Reef National Monument 74-75 H 3
Capivara 100-101 G 3
Capivara, Cachoeira — 92-93 J 6
Capivara, Represa de — 102-103 G 5
Capivari 102-103 J 5
Capiz = Roxas 148-149 H 4
Čaplino 126-127 GH 2
Cap Lopez 172 A 2
Cap Masoala 172 K 5
Cap Nuevo = Rã's al-Jadīd 166-167 E 2
Capo Càccia 122-123 BC 5
Capo Carbonara 122-123 CD 6
Capo Comino 122-123 CD 5
Capo di Frasca 122-123 BC 6
Capo delle Colonne 122-123 G 6
CApodí, Chapada do — 92-93 M 6
Capo di Muro 122-123 C 5
Capoeira 98-99 P 7
Capoeiras 100-101 F 5
Capoeiras, Cachoeira das — 92-93 H 6
Capo Falcone 122-123 BC 5
Capo Pàssero 122-123 F 7
Capo San Marco 122-123 BC 6
Capo Santa Maria di Leuca 122-123 H 6
Capo San Vito 122-123 E 6
Capo Spartivento [I, Calàbria] 122-123 G 7
Capo Spartivento [I, Sardegna] 122-123 G 6
Cappari = Psérimos 122-123 M 7
Capràia 122-123 CD 4
Capreol 72-73 F 1
Caprera 122-123 C 5
Capri 122-123 EF 5
Capricorn Channel 158-159 K 4
Caprivistrook 172 D 5
Caprock, NM 76-77 C 6
Cap Rosa = Rã's al-Wardah 166-167 L 1
Cap Saint-André 172 H 5
Cap Sainte-Marie 172 J 7
Cap-Saint-Jacques = Vung Tau 150-151 F 7
Cap Saint-Sebastien 172 J 4
Cap Spartel = Rã's Ashaqãr 166-167 CD 2
Cap Tafelney = Rã's Tafalnī 166-167 AB 4
Captain Cook Bridge 161 I a 3
Captain Cook Landing Place Park 161 I b 3
Captains Flat 160 JK 5
Captiva, FL 80-81 b 3
Cap Tourane = Mui Đa Nãng 150-151 G 4
Cap Tres Forcas = Rã's Wūruq 164-165 D 1
Câpua 122-123 EF 5
Capulin Mountain National Monument 76-77 BC 4
Capunda 172 C 4
Cap Varella = Mui Điêu 148-149 EF 4
Cap Vert 164-165 A 6
Caquetá, Río — 92-93 E 5
Cáqueza 94-95 E 5
Čara [SU, place] 132-133 W 6
Čara [SU, river] 132-133 W 6
Carababã 98-99 J 7
Caraballeda 94-95 H 2
Carabanchel Alto, Madrid- 113 III a 2
Carabanchel Bajo, Madrid- 113 III a 2
Carabaya, Cordillera de — 92-93 F 7
Carabaya, Río — 96-97 FG 9

Carabinami, Rio — 98-99 G 6
Caracal 122-123 KL 3
Caracalla, Terme di — 113 II b 2
Caracaraí 92-93 G 4
Caracaraí, Cachoeira — 92-93 G 4
Caracas 92-93 F 2
Caracas, Islas — 94-95 J 2
Caracas-Antímano 91 II b 2
Caracas-Artigas 91 II b 2
Caracas-Caricuao 91 II b 2
Caracas-Catia 91 II b 1
Caracas-Coche 91 II b 2
Caracas-Cotiza 91 II b 1
Caracas Country Club 91 II b 1
Caracas-El Pedregal 91 II b 1
Caracas-El Valle 91 II b 2
Caracas-Helicoide 91 II b 2
Caracas-La Rinconada 91 II b 2
Caracas-Las Mayas 91 II b 1
Caracas-Las Palmas 91 II b 1
Caracas-La Vega 91 II b 2
Caracas-Los Magallanes 91 II b 1
Caracas-Mamera 91 II b 2
Caracas-San Bernardino 91 II b 1
Caracas-San Pablito 91 II ab 2
Caracas-Santa Mónica 91 II b 2
Carache 94-95 F 3
Caracol [BR, Mato Grosso do Sul] 102-103 M 4
Caracol [BR, Piauí] 92-93 L 6
Caracol, El — 91 I d 1
Caracol, Río — 100-101 A 5-6
Caracol, Serra do — 100-101 C 5
Caracoles, Punta — 88-89 G 11
Caracoli 94-95 E 2
Caracollo 104-105 C 5
Caracórum = Karakoram 134-135 L 3-4
Caraguatá, Cuchilla del — 106-107 K 3-4
Caraguatatuba 102-103 K 5
Caraguatay [PY] 102-103 D 6
Caraguatay [RA] 106-107 GH 2
Carahue 111 B 5
Caraí 102-103 M 2
Caraíbas 100-101 D 8
Caraíva 100-101 E 9
Carajás, Serra dos — 92-93 J 5-6
Caramanta 94-95 CD 5
Caraná, Rio — 104-105 G 3
Caranavi 104-105 C 4
Carandaí 102-103 L 4
Carandazal 102-103 G 4
Carangas 104-105 B 6
Carangola 102-103 L 4
Caranguejos, Ilha dos — 100-101 B 2
Caransebeş 122-123 K 3
Carapa, Río — 102-103 E 6
Carapacha Grande, Sierra — 106-107 DE 6-7
Carapachay, Vicente López- 110 III b 1
Cara-Paraná, Río — 94-95 E 8
Carapè, Serra do — 94-95 K 4
Carapebus, Lagoa — 102-103 M 5
Carapeguá 102-103 D 6
Carapicuíba 102-103 J 5
Carapo, Río — 94-95 K 4
Caraquet 63 D 4
Carata 88-89 J 7
Caratasca, Laguna de — 64-65 K 8
Caratinga 92-93 L 8
Carauari 92-93 F 5
Caraúbas [BR, Ceara] 92-93 M 6
Caraúbas [BR, Paraíba] 100-101 F 4
Carauna, Serra de — 98-99 H 3
Caravaca de la Cruz 120-121 FG 9
Caravela, Ilha — 168-169 A 3
Caravelas 92-93 M 8
Caravelí 92-93 E 8
Carayaó 102-103 D 6
Caraz 96-97 C 6
Caraza, Lanús- 110 III b 2
Carazinho 111 F 3
Carballo 120-121 C 7
Carberry 61 J 6
Carbonara, Capo — 122-123 CD 6
Carbon Creek 58-59 H 2
Carbondale, CO 68-69 C 6
Carbondale, IL 70-71 F 7
Carbondale, PA 72-73 J 4
Carbonear 56-57 a 8
Carbonera, Cuchilla de la — 106-107 K 4-5
Carbon Hill, AL 78-79 F 4
Carbônia 122-123 C 6
Carcajou Mountains 56-57 L 4-5
Carcar 148-149 H 4-5
Carcaraña 106-107 G 4
Carcaranã, Río — 106-107 FG 4
Carcassonne 120-121 J 7
Carchi 96-97 BC 1
Carcross 104-105 C 10
Carcote 104-105 B 7
Čardak 132-133 C 4
Cardamom Hills 141 C 5-6
Cardamom Island = Kadmat Island 134-135 L 8
Cárdenas 108-109 H 3
Cárdenas [C] 64-65 K 7
Cárdenas [MEX] 64-65 G 7
Cardı 136-137 C 3
Cardiff 119 E 6
Cardigan 119 D 5
Cardigan Bay 119 D 5

Cardington, OH 72-73 E 4
Cardona [E] 120-121 J 8
Cardona [ROU] 106-107 J 4
Cardos, Los — 106-107 G 4
Cardoso, Ilha do — 102-103 J 6
Cardross 61 F 6
Cardston 56-57 O 8
Careen Lake 61 DE 2
Carei 122-123 K 2
Careiro 92-93 H 5
Careiro, Ilha do — 98-99 J 6
Carelmapu 108-109 C 3
Carén [RCH, La Serena] 106-107 B 3
Carén [RCH, Temuco] 106-107 B 7
Čarencavan 126-127 M 6
Carey, ID 66-67 G 4
Carey, OH 72-73 E 4
Carey, Lake — 158-159 D 5
Carey Park, Atlanta-, GA 85 II b 2
Careysburg 164-165 BC 7
Cargados 50-51 N 6
Carhaix-Plouguer 120-121 F 4
Carhuamayo 96-97 D 7
Carhuaz 96-97 C 6
Cariacica 100-101 D 11
Cariaco 92-93 G 2
Cariaco, Golfo de — 94-95 JK 2
Cariamanga 96-97 B 4
Caribana, Punta — 92-93 D 3
Caribbean Basin 64-65 MN 8
Caribbean Sea 64-65 K-N 8
Caribe 94-95 F 5
Caribe, El — [YV, Anzoátegui] 94-95 J 3
Caribe, El — [YV, Distrito Federal] 91 II c 1
Caribe, Río — 86-87 P 8
Cariboo Mountains 56-57 M 7
Cariboo River 60 G 3
Caribou 158-159 J 4
Caribou, Lac — 56-57 M 7
Caribou, Mount — 60 G 3
Caribou Hide 58-59 XY 8
Caribou Lake 62 E 2
Caribou Mountains 56-57 NO 6
Caribou Range 66-67 H 4
Caribou River 58-59 c 2
Caricó, Morro do — 110 I b 2
Caricuao 91 II b 2
Caridade 100-101 E 3
Carievale 68-69 F 1
Cari Laufquen, Bajo de — 108-109 E 3
Cari Laufquen Grande, Laguna — 108-109 E 3
Carinda 160 H 4
Carinhanha 92-93 L 7
Carinhanha, Río — 92-93 L 7-8
Carinthia = Kärnten 118 FG 5
Carioca, Serra da — 110 I b 2
Caripare 100-101 B 6
Caripe 94-95 J 2
Caripito 92-93 G 2
Cariquima 104-105 B 6
Carira 100-101 F 6
Cariré 100-101 D 2
Caririaçu 100-101 E 4
Cariris Novos, Serra dos — 100-101 D 3-4
Carirubana 94-95 F 2
Caris, Río — 94-95 K 3
Caritianas 98-99 G 9
Carius 100-101 E 4
Carius, Riacho — 100-101 E 4
Carleton, Mount — 63 C 4
Carleton Place 72-73 HJ 2
Carletonville 174-175 G 4
Carlin, NV 66-67 F 5
Carlinville, IL 70-71 F 6
Carlingford, Sydney- 161 I a 1
Carlisle 119 E 4
Carlisle, IA 70-71 D 5
Carlisle, IN 70-71 G 6
Carlisle, KY 72-73 DE 5
Carlisle, PA 72-73 H 4
Carlisle, SC 80-81 F 3
Carlisle Island 58-59 l 4
Carlo, AK 58-59 N 5
Carlópolis 102-103 H 5
Carlos, Isla — 111 B 8
Carlos Ameghino, Istmo — 108-109 G 4
Carlos Beguerie 106-107 H 5
Carlos Casares 106-107 G 5
Carlos Chagas 92-93 LM 8
Carlos Pellegrini 106-107 G 4
Carlos Salas 106-107 FG 5
Carlos Tejedor 106-107 F 5
Carlota, La — [RA] 111 D 4
Carlow 119 C 5
Carlsbad, CA 74-75 E 6
Carlsbad, NM 64-65 F 5
Carlsbad Caverns National Park 76-77 B 6
Carlsruhe = Karlsruhe 118 D 4
Carlton, MN 70-71 D 2
Carlton [CDN] 61 E 4
Carlton [ZA] 174-175 F 6
Carlyle 61 G 6
Carlyle, IL 70-71 F 6
Carmacks 56-57 J 4
Carmagnola 122-123 BC 3
Carman 68-69 GH 1

Carmânia = Kermān 134-135 H 4
Carmanville 63 JK 3
Carmarthen 119 D 6
Carmarthen Bay 119 D 6
Carmaux 120-121 J 6
Carmel, CA 74-75 BC 4
Carmel 106-107 HJ 4-5
Carmelo, El — 94-95 EF 2
Carmen, AK 76-77 E 4
Carmen [BOL] 104-105 C 2
Carmen [BR] 98-99 L 11
Carmen [RA, Jujuy] 104-105 D 9
Carmen [RA, Santa Fe] 106-107 G 4
Carmen [ROU] 106-107 JK 4
Carmen, Ciudad del — 64-65 H 8
Carmen, El — [BOL, Beni] 104-105 E 3-4
Carmen, El — [BOL, Santa Cruz] 104-105 G 6
Carmen, El — [CO, Amazonas] 94-95 H 7
Carmen, El — [CO, Chocó] 94-95 C 5
Carmen, El — [CO, Norte de Santander] 94-95 E 3
Carmen, El — [EC] 96-97 B 2
Carmen, El — [PY] 102-103 AB 4
Carmen, Isla — 64-65 E 6
Carmen, Isla del — 86-87 OP 8
Carmen, Río del — [MEX] 86-87 J 3
Carmen, Río del — [RCH] 106-107 B 2
Carmen, Sierra del — 86-87 J 3
Carmen de Areco 106-107 H 5
Carmen de Bolívar, El — 92-93 D 3
Carmen del Paraná 102-103 DE 7
Carmen de Patagones 111 D 6
Carmensa 106-107 D 5
Carmen Silva, Río Chico — 108-109 E 9
Carmen Silva, Sierra de — 108-109 E 9
Carmi 86-87 D 6
Carmi, IL 70-71 F 6
Carmila 158-159 J 4
Carmo 102-103 L 5
Carmo da Cachoeira 102-103 K 4
Carmo da Mata 102-103 K 4
Carmo do Cajuru 102-103 K 4
Carmo do Paranaíba 102-103 J 3
Carmo do Rio Claro 102-103 JK 4
Carmona [Angola] 172 BC 3
Carmona [E] 120-121 E 10
Carmópolis 100-101 F 6
Carnac 120-121 F 5
Carnaíba 100-101 EF 4
Carnamah 158-159 C 5
Carnarvon [AUS] 158-159 B 4
Carnarvon [ZA] 172 D 8
Carnarvon Range 158-159 CD 5
Carnatic 134-135 M 8-9
Carnaubais 100-101 F 3
Carnaubal 100-101 D 3
Carnaubas 100-101 E 3
Carnaubinha 98-99 FG 11
Carndonagh 119 C 4
Carnduff 68-69 F 1
Carnegie, KS 68-69 GH 6
Carnegie, PA 72-73 F 4
Carnegie, Lake — 158-159 D 5
Carn Eige 119 D 3
Carneiro, KS 68-69 GH 6
Carnerillo 106-107 F 4
Carnero, Bahía — 106-107 A 6
Carnero, Punta — 106-107 A 6
Carnic Alps 122-123 E 2
Car Nicobar Island 134-135 P 9
Carnjoið 100-101 FG 4
Carnot 164-165 H 8
Carnot = Al-Abādiyah 166-167 G 1
Carnot Bay 158-159 D 3
Carnsore Point 119 CD 5
Caro, AK 58-59 NO 3
Caro, MI 72-73 E 3
Carole Highlands, MD 82 II b 1
Carolina 92-93 K 6
Carolina [CO] 94-95 D 4
Carolina [Puerto Rico] 88-89 O 5
Carolina [ZA] 172 EF 7
Carolina, La — [E] 120-121 F 9
Carolina, La — [RA] 106-107 G 4
Carolina, North — 64-65 KL 4
Carolina, South — 64-65 K 5
Caroline 60 K 3
Caroline Islands 206-207 RS 9
Caroline Livermore, Mount — 83 I b 1
Carol Springs, FL 80-81 c 3
Caroní, Río — 92-93 G 3
Carora 92-93 EF 2
Carovi 106-107 K 2
Carozero 122-123 M 3
Carp 72-73 HJ 2
Carp, NV 74-75 F 4
Carpathians 122-123 L 2-M 3
Carpentaria, Gulf of — 158-159 GH 2
Carpenter, WY 68-69 DE 5
Carpenters Bayou 85 III c 1
Carpentras 120-121 K 6
Carpi 122-123 D 3
Carpina 92-93 M 6
Carpinteria 106-107 C 3
Carpintería, CA 74-75 D 5
Cerpio, ND 68-69 F 1
Carp Lake 60 F 2
Cerpolac 158-159 H 7
Cerr, CO 68-69 D 5
Cerrabelle, FL 78-79 G 6
Cerrao, Río — 94-95 K 4
Cerrapateiro 100-101 D 3
Cerrara 122-123 D 3
Cerrasquero 94-95 BF 2
Cerrathool 160 G 5
Cerrbridge 119 E 3

Carreria 111 E 2
Carreta, La — 106-107 FG 6
Carretas, Punta — 96-97 C 9
Carretera Interamericana 88-89 E 10
Carretera Panamericana 106-107 B 2
Carriacou 94-95 L 1
Carrick on Shannon 119 BC 5
Carrick-on-Suir 119 C 5
Carrière, Lac — 72-73 H 1
Carriers Mills, IL 70-71 F 7
Carrieton 160 D 4
Carrillo 76-77 BC 9
Carrilobo 106-107 F 3
Carrington, ND 68-69 G 2
Carrión 120-121 E 7
Carrizal 94-95 E 1
Carrizal, Alto de — 94-95 C 4
Carrizal, Laguna de — 106-107 H 7
Carrizal Bajo 111 B 3
Carrizo Springs, TX 76-77 DE 8
Carrizozo, NM 76-77 B 6
Carroll 61 HJ 6
Carroll, IA 70-71 C 4
Carrollton, GA 78-79 G 4
Carrollton, IL 70-71 F 6
Carrollton, KY 70-71 H 6
Carrollton, MO 70-71 D 6
Carrollton, TX 76-77 F 6
Carro Quemado 106-107 E 6
Carrot River [CDN, place] 61 G 4
Carrot River [CDN, river] 61 GH 4
Carruthers 61 D 4
Çarşamba 136-137 G 2
Çarşamba suyu 136-137 DE 4
Çarşanga 134-135 K 4
Carshalton, London- 129 II b 2
Čarsk 132-133 P 8
Carson, CA 83 III c 3
Carson, ND 68-69 F 2
Carson City, NV 64-65 C 4
Carson Sink 64-75 D 5
Carstairs 60 K 3
Carstensz, Puncak = Jaya, Puncak — 148-149 LM 7
Cartagena [CO, Bolívar] 92-93 D 2
Cartagena [CO, Caquetá] 94-95 D 7
Cartagena [E] 120-121 G 10
Cartagena [RCH] 106-107 B 4
Cartago, CA 74-75 D 4
Cartago [CO] 92-93 D 4
Cartago [CR] 64-65 K 10
Carta Valley, TX 76-77 D 8
Carter, OK 76-77 E 5
Carter, WY 66-67 H 5
Carter Bridge 170 III b 2
Cartersville, GA 78-79 G 3
Cartersville, MT 68-69 C 2
Carthage, IL 70-71 E 5
Carthage, MO 64-65 H 4
Carthage, MS 78-79 E 4
Carthage, NC 80-81 G 3
Carthage, NY 72-73 J 2-3
Carthage, SD 68-69 H 3
Carthage, TN 78-79 G 2
Carthage, TX 76-77 G 6
Carthago 164-165 G 1
Cartier 62 L 3
Cartier Island 158-159 D 2
Cartierville, Aéroport de — 82 I a 1
Cartierville, Montréal- 82 I a 1
Cartum = Al Khartūm 164-165 L 5
Cartwright [CDN, Manitoba] 68-69 G 1
Cartwright [CDN, Newfoundland] 56-57 Z 7
Caru, Rio — 100-101 A 2
Caruachi 94-95 K 3
Caruaru 92-93 M 6
Carúpano 92-93 G 2
Carutapera 92-93 K 5
Carvalho 98-99 K 8
Carvoeiro 98-99 GH 5
Carvoeiro, Cabo — 120-121 C 9
Cary, NC 80-81 G 3
Čaryš 132-133 P 8
Čaryš 132-133 P 7
Carysfort, Cape — 108-109 L 8
Casabe [CO, landscape] 94-95 D 4
Casabe [CO, place] 94-95 D 4
Casablanca [CO] 91 III bc 2
Casablanca [RCH] 106-107 B 4
Casablanca = Ad-Dãr al-Baydã' 164-165 BC 2
Casa Branca [BR] 102-103 J 4
Casacajal, Punta — 94-95 B 6
Casa de Campo 113 III a 2
Casa de Gobierno 110 III b 1
Casa de Janos 86-87 F 2
Casadepaga, AK 58-59 EF 4
Casa de Pedras, Ilha — 110 I c 1
Casa Grande, AZ 74-75 H 6
Casa Indígena 94-95 F 8
Casa Laguna 96-97 C 7
Casal di Principe 122-123 EF 5
Casale Monferrato 122-123 C 3
Casaletti Mattei, Roma- 113 II a 2
Casalins 106-107 H 6
Casalmaggiore 122-123 CD 3
Casal Morena, Roma- 113 II c 2
Casalotti, Roma- 113 II a 1
Casalvasco 102-103 BC 1
Casamance [SN, administrative unit] 168-169 B 2
Casamance [SN, river] 168-169 AB 2
Casanare 94-95 EF 5
Casanare, Río — 92-93 E 3
Casanay 94-95 K 2
Casa Nova 92-93 L 6
Casa Piedra, TX 76-77 BC 8
Casares [RA] 106-107 F 2

Casas Cardenas 96-97 DE 4
Casas Grandes, Río — 64-65 E 5-6
Casa Verde, São Paulo- 110 II b 1
Cascada 106-107 FG 6
Cascadas, Las — 64-65 b 2
Cascade 66-67 DE 1
Cascade, IA 70-71 E 4
Cascade, ID 66-67 EF 3
Cascade, MT 66-67 GH 2
Cascade de Sica 168-169 F 3
Cascade Head 66-67 A 3
Cascade Pass 66-67 C 1
Cascade Point 161 BC 7
Cascade Range 64-65 B 2-3
Cascade Reservoir 66-67 EF 3
Cascade Tunnel 66-67 C 2
Cascadura, Rio de Janeiro- 110 I ab 2
Cascapèdia, Rivière — 63 C 3
Cascata 100-101 A 5
Cascatinha 102-103 L 5
Cascavel [BR, Ceará] 100-101 E 3
Cascavel [BR, Paraná] 111 F 2
Casco, WI 70-71 G 3
Casco Bay 72-73 LM 3
Cascumpeque Bay 63 DE 4
Čase'lka 132-133 P 4-5
Caseros, General San Martin- 110 III b 1
Caserta 122-123 F 5
Casetas 120-121 G 8
Caseville, MI 72-73 E 3
Casey, IL 70-71 FG 6
Cashmere, WA 66-67 C 2
Casigua [YV, Falcón] 94-95 F 2
Casigua [YV, Zuila] 94-95 E 3
Casilda 111 D 4
Casimiro de Abreu 102-103 L 5
Casino 158-159 K 5
Casiquiare, Río — 92-93 F 4
Casirieni, Río — 96-97 E 8
Casma 96-97 BC 6
Casma, Río — 96-97 BC 6
Casmalia, CA 74-75 C 5
Čašniki 124-125 G 6
Časovo 124-125 S 2
Caspe 120-121 GH 8
Casper, WY 64-65 E 3
Casper Range 68-69 C 4
Caspiana, LA 78-79 C 4
Caspian Sea 134-135 F 1-G 3
Cass, WV 72-73 FG 5
Cassa, WY 68-69 D 4
Cassacatiza 171 C 6
Cassai = Kasai 172 C 2
Cassai, Rio — 172 CD 4
Cassamba 172 D 4
Cass City, MI 72-73 E 3
Cassel = Kassel 118 D 3
Casselton, ND 68-69 H 2
Càssia 102-103 J 4
Cassia, Via — 113 II a 1
Cassiar Mountains 56-57 KL 6
Cassilândia 102-103 FG 3
Cassils 61 B 5
Cassinga = Kassinga 172 C 5
Cassino [BR] 106-107 LM 4
Cassino [I] 122-123 EF 5
Cass Lake, MN 70-71 C 2
Cassopolis, MI 70-71 GH 5
Cass River 70-71 J 4
Cassville, WI 70-71 F 4
Castaic, CA 74-75 D 5
Castanhal [BR, Amazonas] 98-99 K 9
Castanhal [BR, Pará] 92-93 K 5
Castanheiro 92-93 F 5
Castanõs 76-77 D 9
Castejón 120-121 FG 7
Castelar, Morón- 110 III ab 1
Castelfranco Veneto 122-123 DE 3
Castel Giubileo, Roma- 113 II b 1
Castella, CA 66-67 B 5
Castellammare, Golfo di — 122-123 E 6
Castellammare del Golfo 122-123 E 6
Castellammare di Stàbia 122-123 EF 5
Castellana Grotte 122-123 G 5
Castelli 106-107 C 1
Castelli = Juan José Castelli 111 DE 3
Castellón de la Plana 120-121 GH 9
Castelnaudary 120-121 HJ 7
Castelo [BR, Espírito Santo] 102-103 M 4
Castelo [BR, Mato Grosso do Sul] 102-103 D 3
Castelo, Serra do — 100-101 D 11
Castelo Branco 120-121 D 9
Castelo do Piauí 100-101 D 3
Castelrosso = Mégiste 136-137 C 4
Castel Sant'Angelo 113 II b 2
Castelsarrasin 120-121 H 6
Castelvetrano 122-123 E 7
Casterton 158-159 H 7
Castilla [PE, Loreto] 96-97 D 5
Castilla [PE, Piura] 96-97 A 4
Castilla la Nueva 120-121 E 9-F 8
Castilla la Vieja 120-121 E 8-F 7
Castilletes 92-93 E 1
Castillo, Pampa del — 111 C 7
Castillo de San Marcos National Monument 80-81 c 1
Castillón 86-87 J 3
Castillos 106-107 L 5
Castillos, Laguna — 106-107 KL 5
Castle Dale, UT 74-75 H 3
Castle Dome Mountains 74-75 FG 6
Castlegar 66-67 H 1
Castle Gate, UT 74-75 H 3

Castle Hayne, NC 80-81 H 3
Castlemaine 158-159 HJ 7
Castle Mount 58-59 LM 2
Castle Mountain 60 K 4
Castle Peak [USA, Colorado] 68-69 C 6
Castle Peak [USA, Idaho] 66-67 F 3
Castlepoint 161 G 5
Castlereagh Bay 158-159 FG 2
Castlereagh River 158-159 J 6
Castle Rock, CO 68-69 D 6
Castle Rock, WA 66-67 B 2
Castle Rock Butte 68-69 E 3
Castle Rock Lake 70-71 F 4
Castleton Corners, New York-, NY 82 III b 3
Castle Valley 74-75 H 3
Castolon, TX 76-77 C 8
Castor 61 C 4
Castres 120-121 J 7
Castries 64-65 O 9
Castro [BR] 111 F 2
Castro [RCH] 111 B 6
Castro, Cabo — 108-109 B 8
Castro, Punta — 108-109 G 4
Castro Alves 100-101 E 7
Castro Barros 106-107 E 3
Castro-Urdiales 120-121 F 7
Castrovillari 122-123 G 6
Castroville, CA 74-75 C 4
Castroville, TX 76-77 E 8
Castrovirreyna 92-93 DE 7
Častyje 124-125 U 5
Casuarinas, Las — 106-107 CD 3
Casuarinenkust 148-149 L 8
Casummit Lake 62 C 2
Casupá 106-107 K 5
Caswell, AK 58-59 MN 6
Çat = Yavı 136-137 J 3
Catacamas 88-89 D 7
Catacaos 96-97 A 4
Catacocha 96-97 B 3-4
Cataguases 102-103 L 4
Çatak 136-137 K 3-4
Catalão 102-103 J 3
Catalão, Punta do — 110 I b 2
Çatalca 136-137 C 2
Catalina 111 C 3
Catalina, Punta — 108-109 EF 9
Catalonia = Cataluña 120-121 H 8-J 9
Cataluña 120-121 H 8-J 7
Çatalzeytin 136-137 F 1-2
Catamarca 104-105 B 9-C 11
Catamarca = San Fernando del Valle de Catamarca 111 C 3
Catamayo, Río — 96-97 AB 4
Catandica 172 F 5
Catanduanes Island 148-149 HJ 4
Catanduva 92-93 K 9
Catanduvas 102-103 F 6
Catània 122-123 F 7
Catán Lil 108-109 D 2
Catán-Lil, Sierra de — 106-107 B 7
Catanzaro 122-123 G 6
Catão 100-101 B 7
Cataouatche, Lake — 85 I a 2
Catapilco 106-107 B 4
Cataqueamã 98-99 G 10
Catar = Qaṭar 134-135 G 5
Cataratas del Iguazú 111 F 3
Catarina 100-101 DE 4
Catarina, TX 76-77 E 8
Catarina, Gebel — = Jabal Katrīnah 164-165 L 3
Catarina, Raso da — 100-101 E 5
Catarino, Cachoeira do — 98-99 G 10
Catarman 148-149 HJ 4
Cat Arm River 63 H 2
Catastrophe, Cape — 158-159 F 7-G 6
Catatumbo, Río — 94-95 EF 3
Catavi 104-105 C 6
Cat Ba, Đao — 150-151 F 2
Catbalogan 148-149 HJ 4
Catedral, Monte — 108-109 BC 6
Catedral de San Isidro 113 III a 2
Catemaco 86-87 N 8
Catena Costiera = Coast Mountains 56-57 K 6-M 7
Catende 100-101 G 5
Catete 172 B 3
Catete, Rio — 98-99 LM 8
Catete, Rio de Janeiro- 110 I b 2
Catford, London- 129 II c 2
Cathay, ND 68-69 G 2
Cathcart 174-175 G 7
Cathedrale Sainte Anne 170 IV a 1
Cathedral Mountain 76-77 C 7
Cathedral of Jakarta 154 IV b 2
Cathedral of Johannesburg 170 V b 2
Cathedral Peak [LS] 174-175 H 5
Cathedral Peak [USA] 64-65 B 2-3
Cathkin Peak 172 EF 7
Cathlemat, WA 66-67 B 2
Cathro, MI 70-71 J 3
Catia, Caracas- 91 II b 1
Catiaeum = Kütahya 134-135 BC 3
Catia La Mar 94-95 H 2
Catiara 102-103 J 3
Catinzaco 111 C 3
Catió 164-165 AB 6
Catisimiña 94-95 K 5
Cat Island [BS] 64-65 L 7
Cat Island [USA] 78-79 E 5
Catitas, Las — 106-107 CD 4
Cativá 64-65 b 2
Cat Lake [CDN, lake] 62 CD 2
Cat Lake [CDN, place] 62 D 2
Catlettsburg, KY 72-73 E 5
Catmandu = Katmāndū 134-135 NO 5
Catoche, Cabo — 64-65 J 7
Catolé Grande, Rio — 100-101 D 8
Catolina 110 III b 2
Catramba, Serra do — 100-101 F 6
Catriel 106-107 CD 6
Catriló 111 D 5
Catrimani 92-93 G 4
Catrimani, Rio — 92-93 G 4
Catskill, NY 72-73 JK 3
Catskill Mountains 72-73 J 3
Cattaraugus, NY 72-73 G 3
Catu 100-101 E 7
Catuane 174-175 K 4
Catulé do Rocha 100-101 F 4
Catumbela 172 B 4
Catunda 100-101 DE 3
Catuni 102-103 L 2
Catuni, Serra do — 102-103 L 2
Caturaí 102-103 H 2
Câu, Sông — 150-151 E 2
Cauaburi, Rio — 98-99 E 4-F 5
Cauamé, Rio — 94-95 L 6
Cauaxi, Rio — 98-99 O 7
Cauca 94-95 C 6
Cauca, Río — 92-93 E 3
Caucagua 94-95 H 2
Caucaia 92-93 M 5
Caucasia 92-93 D 3
Caucasus Mountains 134-135 EF 2
Cauchari, Salar de — 104-105 C 8
Caughnawage 82 I ab 2
Câu Giat 150-151 E 3
Caujul 96-97 C 7
Câu Ke 150-151 EF 8
Cauldcleuch Head 119 E 4
Caulfield, Melbourne- 161 II c 2
Caulfield Racecourse 161 II c 1
Caungula 172 C 3
Caunpore = Kānpur 134-135 MN 5
Čaunskaja guba 132-133 gh 4
Caupolicán 92-93 F 7
Cauquenes 111 B 5
Caura, Río — 92-93 G 3
Caurés, Rio — 98-99 G 5
Caurimare, Petare- 91 II bc 2
Causapscal 63 C 3
Causapscal, Parc provincial de — 63 C 3
Causse du Kelifely 172 HJ 5
Causses 120-121 J 6
Čausy 124-125 H 7
Cautário, Rio — 98-99 FG 10
Cautén, Punta — 106-107 A 7
Cauterets 120-121 G 7
Cautiva, La — [BOL] 104-105 EF 6
Cautiva, La — [RA, Córdoba] 106-107 E 4
Cautiva, La — [RA, San Luis] 106-107 D 4
Cauvery 140 C 5
Cauvery Delta 140 D 5
Cauvery Falls 140 C 4
Caux, Pays de — 120-121 H 4
Cavalcante 92-93 K 7
Cavalheiros 102-103 HJ 2
Cavalier, ND 68-69 H 1
Cavally 164-165 C 7-8
Cavalonga, Sierra — 104-105 C 8
Cavan 119 C 4-5
Cavanayén 94-95 KL 5
Cave Hills 68-69 E 3
Caveiras, Rio — 102-103 G 7
Caverá, Coxilha — 106-107 K 3
Caviana, Ilha — 92-93 K 4
Cavinas 104-105 C 3
Cavite 148-149 H 4
Cavtat 122-123 GH 4
Çavuşçu gölü 136-137 DE 3
Çavuşköy 154 I a 2
Cawnpore = Kānpur 134-135 MN 5
Caxambu 102-103 K 4
Caxiabatay, Río — 96-97 D 5
Caxias [BR, Amazonas] 98-99 C 7
Caxias [BR, Maranhão] 92-93 L 5
Caxias do Sul 111 F 3
Caxito 172 B 3
Caxiuana, Baía de — 92-93 J 5
Çay 136-137 D 3
Çay = Okam 136-137 K 2
Cayaca, Cerro — 106-107 B 6
Cayambe [EC, mountain] 92-93 D 5
Cayambe [EC, place] 92-93 D 4
Cayar 168-169 A 2
Cayar, Lac — = Ar-R'kīz 164-165 AB 5
Cayastacito 106-107 G 3
Çaybaşı 136-137 J 2
Çaycuma 136-137 E 2
Çayeli = Çaybaşı 136-137 J 2
Cayenne [French Guiana, administrative unit] 98-99 M 3
Cayenne [French Guiana, place] 92-93 J 3-4
Cayes, Les — 64-65 M 8
Cayey 88-89 N 5
Çayıralan = Çayırşehri 136-137 F 3
Çayırhan 136-137 DE 2
Çayırlı 136-137 HJ 3
Çayırlıahmetçiler 136-137 D 2
Çayırşehri 136-137 F 3
Çaykara 136-137 J 2
Cayman Brac 64-65 L 8
Cayman Islands 64-65 KL 8
Cayman Trench 64-65 KL 8
Cayo Arenas 86-87 P 6
Cayo Centro 86-87 R 8
Cayo Coco 88-89 G 3
Cayo Guajaba 88-89 H 4
Cayo Lobos 86-87 R 8
Cayo Nuevo 86-87 O 7
Cayo Romano 64-65 L 7
Cayo Sabinal 88-89 H 4
Cayos Arcas 86-87 P 7
Cayos de Albuquerque 88-89 F 8
Cayos Miskito 64-65 K 9
Cay Sal 88-89 F 3
Cayucos, CA 74-75 C 5
Cayuga Lake 72-73 H 3
Cayungo = Nana Candundo 172 D 4
Cayuse Hills 68-69 B 2-3
Cazador, Cerro — 108-109 CD 8
Cazalla de la Sierra 120-121 E 10
Caza Pava 106-107 J 2
Cazombo 172 D 4
Cazorla [YV] 94-95 H 3

Cchaltubo 126-127 L 5

Cea 120-121 E 7
Ceahlău, Muntele — 122-123 LM 2
Ceará [BR, administrative unit] 92-93 LM 6
Ceará [BR, place] 96-97 E 6
Ceará = Fortaleza 92-93 M 5
Ceará-Mirim 100-101 G 3
Ceba 61 G 4
Ceballos 86-87 HJ 4
Cebeciköy 154 I a 2
Čeboksary 132-133 H 6
Čeboksary-Sosnovka 124-125 QR 5
Cebollar 106-107 D 2
Cebollatí 106-107 L 4
Cebollatí, Río — 106-107 K 4
Cebrikovo 126-127 E 3
Čebsara 124-125 M 4
Cebú [RP, island] 148-149 H 4
Cebú [RP, place] 148-149 H 4
Cecchignola, Roma- 113 II b 2
Çeceli 136-137 F 4
Čečel'nik 126-127 D 2
Čečen', ostrov — 126-127 N 4
Čečeno-Ingušskaja Avtonomnaja Sovetskaja Socialističeskaja Respublika = Checheno-Ingush Autonomous Soviet Socialist Republic 126-127 MN 5
Cecen Uul 142-143 H 2
Cecerleg 142-143 J 2
Čečersk 124-125 H 7
Čechov [SU, Sachalin] 132-133 b 8
Cecilia, KY 70-71 GH 7
Cecilienhöhe, Potsdam- 130 III a 2
Cecil Lake 60 GH 1
Cecil Plains 160 K 1
Cècina 122-123 D 4
Čečujsk 132-133 U 6
Cedar Bluff Reservoir 68-69 G 6
Cedar Breaks National Monument 74-75 G 4
Cedarbrook, PA 84 III c 1
Cedarbrook Mall 84 III bc 1
Cedarburg, WI 70-71 FG 4
Cedar City, UT 64-65 D 4
Cedar Creek [USA, North Dakota] 68-69 EF 2
Cedar Creek [USA, Virginia] 72-73 G 5
Cedar Falls, IA 70-71 D 4
Cedar Grove, LA 85 I b 3
Cedar Grove, NJ 82 III a 1
Cedar Grove, WI 70-71 G 4
Cedar Heights, MD 82 II b 2
Cedar Heights, PA 84 III b 1
Cedar Hill, NM 68-69 C 7
Cedar Island [USA, North Carolina] 80-81 H 3
Cedar Island [USA, Virginia] 80-81 J 2
Cedar Key, FL 80-81 b 2
Cedar Lake [CDN] 56-57 Q 7
Cedar Lake [USA] 76-77 C 6
Cedar Mountains [USA, Nevada] 74-75 E 3
Cedar Mountains [USA, Oregon] 66-67 E 4
Cedar Point 68-69 E 6
Cedar Rapids, IA 64-65 H 3
Cedar River [USA ⊲ Iowa River] 70-71 E 4-5
Cedar River [USA ⊲ Loup River] 68-69 G 5
Cedar Springs, MI 70-71 H 4
Cedar Swamp 84 III ab 3
Cedartown, GA 78-79 G 3-4
Cedar Vale, KS 76-77 F 4
Cedarville 174-175 H 6
Cedarville, CA 66-67 C 5
Cedarwood, CO 68-69 D 7
Cedong, Jakarta- 154 IV b 2
Cedral [BR, Maranhão] 100-101 B 1
Cedral [BR, São Paulo] 102-103 H 4
Cedro 92-93 M 6
Cedro Playa 96-97 E 4
Cedros, Isla — 64-65 C 6
Ceduna 158-159 F 6
Ceel 142-143 H 2
Cefalù 122-123 F 6
Cega 120-121 E 8
Čegdomyn 132-133 Z 7
Čegitun 58-59 B 3
Cegléd 118 J 5
Ceiba, La — [Honduras] 64-65 J 8
Ceiba, La — [YV] 92-93 E 3
Ceiba Grande 86-87 O 9
Ceibal, El — 104-105 E 10
Ceibas 106-107 H 4
Ceja, La — 94-95 D 5
Cejal 94-95 H 6
Cejas, Las — 111 D 3
Čekalin 124-125 L 6
Čekanovskogo, kr'až — 132-133 XY 3
Çekerek = Haciköy 136-137 F 2
Çekerekırmağı 136-137 F 3-G 2
Čekmaguš 124-125 U 6
Cela = Uaco Cungo 172 C 4
Čel'abinsk 132-133 L 6
Celaya 64-65 F 7
Čelbas 126-127 J 3
Celebes = Sulawesi 148-149 G 7-H 6
Celebes Sea 148-149 GH 6
Celebessee 148-149 GH 6
Çelebiler 136-137 E 2
Celedin 96-97 B 5
Čeleken 134-135 G 3
Celestún 86-87 P 7
Celia 102-103 C 5
Celikan 136-137 GH 4
Celina, OH 70-71 H 5
Celina, TN 78-79 G 2
Celina, TX 76-77 F 6
Celinograd 132-133 MN 7
Celje 122-123 F 2
Čelkar 132-133 KL 8
Celle 118 E 2
Čelmuži 124-125 KL 2
Čelobitjevo 113 V c 1
Çeltik 136-137 DE 3
Çeltikçi = Aziziye 136-137 D 4
Celuo = Chira Bazar 142-143 DE 4
Čel'uskin, mys — 132-133 T-V 2
Cement, OK 76-77 EF 5
Çemişgezek 136-137 H 3
Çemlidere = Mecrihan 136-137 H 4
Cempaka Putih, Jakarta- 154 IV b 2
Cempi, Selat — 152-153 N 10
Cenad 122-123 J 2
Cencia = Tyencha 164-165 M 7
Cenepa, Río — 96-97 B 4
Çengelköy, İstanbul- 154 I b 2
Centane 174-175 H 7
Centennial 84 III de 2
Centennial, WY 68-69 CD 5
Centeno 106-107 G 4
Center, CO 68-69 C 7
Center, ND 68-69 F 2
Center, NE 68-69 GH 4
Center, TX 76-77 GH 7
Centerfield, UT 74-75 H 3
Center Hill, Atlanta-, GA 85 II b 2
Center Line, MI 84 II b 2
Centerton, NJ 84 III d 2
Centerville, AL 78-79 F 4
Centerville, IA 70-71 D 5
Centerville, MO 70-71 E 7
Centerville, SD 68-69 H 4
Centerville, TN 78-79 F 3
Centerville, TX 76-77 FG 7
Centinela, Picacho del — 64-65 F 6
Centinela, Sierra del — 104-105 D 8-9
Centocelle, Roma- 113 II bc 2
Central, AK 58-59 P 4
Central, NM 74-75 JK 6
Central [BR] 100-101 C 6
Central [EAK] 172 G 2
Central [GH] 168-169 E 4
Central [MW] 171 C 6
Central [PY] 102-103 D 6
Central [Z] 172 E 4
Central, Plateau — = Cao Nguyên Trung Phân 148-149 E 4
Central African Republic 164-165 HJ 7
Central Auckland 161 EF 3
Central City, KY 70-71 G 7
Central City, NE 68-69 GH 5
Centrale 168-169 F 3
Central Falls, RI 72-73 L 4
Centralia, IL 64-65 J 4
Centralia, MO 70-71 DE 6
Centralia, WA 66-67 B 2
Central Indian Ridge 50-51 N 5-7
Central Intelligence Agency 82 II a 1
Central Karroo = Groot Karoo 172 D 8
Central Mount Stuart 158-159 F 4
Central'nojakutskaja ravnina 132-133 WX 5
Central'nolesnoj zapovednik 124-125 J 5
Central Pacific Basin 156-157 KL 4
Central Park [AUS] 161 I b 2
Central Park [USA, New York] 82 III c 2
Central Park [USA, Philadelphia] 85 III a 1
Central Park of Singapore 154 III ab 2
Central Patricia 62 DE 2
Central Point, OR 66-67 B 4
Central Province = Madhyama Palāna = 4 ⊲ 140 E 7
Central Range 174-175 H 5
Central Siberian Plateau 132-133 R-X 4-5
Central Station [AUS] 161 I b 2
Central Valley, CA 66-67 BC 5
Centre 168-169 E 2-3
Centre-Est 168-169 E 2-3
Centre-Ouest 168-169 E 3
Centreville 63 BC 4
Centreville, MD 72-73 HJ 5
Centreville, MS 78-79 D 5
Centro, El — 94-95 E 4
Centro, Niterói- 110 I c 2
Century City, Los Angeles-, CA 83 III b 1
Cenxi 146-147 C 10
Čepca 124-125 S 4
Cepeda [RA] 106-107 G 4
Cephalonia = Kefallēnia 122-123 J 6
Cepu 152-153 J 9
Ceram = Seram 148-149 JK 7
Ceram Sea 148-149 JK 7
Cerbatana, Serranía de la — 92-93 F 3
Cerbatano, Cerro — 94-95 H 4
Cerbère 120-121 J 7
Cercen = Chārchān 142-143 F 4
Čerdyn' 124-125 V 3
Cereal 61 C 5
Cereales 106-107 EF 6
Čeremchovo 132-133 T 7
Čeremisinovo 124-125 L 8
Čeremšan 124-125 S 6
Čerepanovo 132-133 P 7
Čerepet' 124-125 L 6
Čerepovec 132-133 F 6
Ceres, CA 74-75 C 4
Ceres [RA] 106-107 G 2
Ceres [ZA] 172 C 8
Céret 120-121 J 7
Ceretè 94-95 CD 3
Čerevkovo 124-125 P 3
Cerf Island 172 K 3
Cerignola 122-123 F 5
Cerigo = Kýthēra 122-123 K 7
Cerigotto = Antikýthēra 122-123 K 8
Čerikov 124-125 H 7
Cerillos 86-87 P 8
Cerillos, Los — 106-107 E 3
Čerkassy 126-127 EF 2
Çerkeş 136-137 E 2
Čerkessk 126-127 L 4
Čerkizovo, Moskva- 113 V c 2
Čerlak 132-133 N 7
Čermenino 124-125 OP 4
Çermik 136-137 H 3
Čern' 124-125 L 7
Čern'achov 126-127 D 1
Čern'achovsk 118 K 1
Čern'anka 126-127 HJ 1
Černatica 122-123 L 4-5
Černăuţi = Černovcy 126-127 B 2
Černava 124-125 M 7
Cernavodă 122-123 MN 3
Černevo 124-125 FG 4
Černigov 126-127 E 1
Černigovka 132-133 Z 9
Černobyl' 126-127 DE 1
Černogorsk 132-133 R 7
Černomorskoje 126-127 F 4
Černorečje = Dzeržinsk 132-133 GH 6
Černovcy 126-127 B 2
Černovskije Kopi, Čita- 132-133 V 7
Černuška 124-125 UV 5
Černutjevo 124-125 R 2
Černyševskij 132-133 V 5
Černyševskoje 118 KL 1
Černyškovskij 126-127 KL 2
Cero, Punta — 108-109 H 4
Cer'omuski, Moskva- 113 V bc 3
Cerralvo [MEX, island] 76-77 E 9
Cerralvo [MEX, place] 86-87 KL 4
Cerralvo, Isla — 64-65 E 7
Cerreira Comprida, Cachoeira — 98-99 OP 10
Cerrillos 104-105 D 9
Cerrito [BR] 106-107 L 3
Cerrito [CO] 94-95 E 4
Cerrito [PY] 102-103 D 7
Cerrito, El — 94-95 CD 6
Cerritos 64-65 FG 7
Cerritos, CA 83 III d 2
Cerritos Bayos 104-105 B 8
Cerro, El — 92-93 G 8
Cerro Agua Hedionda 106-107 DE 4
Cerro Agua Poca 106-107 C 6
Cerro Aguas Blancas 104-105 B 9
Cerro Aiguilete 108-109 C 8
Cerro Alto Nevado 108-109 C 5
Cerro Anecón Grande 108-109 D 3
Cerro Ansilta 106-107 C 3-4
Cerro Ap Iwan 108-109 D 6
Cerro Arenales 111 B 7
Cerro Aucanquilcha 111 C 2
Cerro Avanzado 108-109 G 4
Cerro Azul [BR] 102-103 H 6
Cerro Azul [MEX] 86-87 M 7
Cerro Balmaceda 108-109 C 8
Cerro Barros Arana 108-109 CD 4
Cerro Bayo [RA, La Pampa] 106-107 DE 6
Cerro Bayo [RA, Río Negro ↑ Loma San Martín] 106-107 C 7
Cerro Bayo [RA, Río Negro ← Loma San Martín] 106-107 C 7
Cerro Bayo [RCH] 108-109 CD 5
Cerro Belgrano 108-109 D 6
Cerro Bertrand 108-109 C 8
Cerro Blanco [PE] 96-97 C 7
Cerro Blanco [RA] 108-109 F 6
Cerro Blanco, Loma — 108-109 F 4
Cerro Bolsa 106-107 C 2
Cerro Bonete 106-107 C 1
Cerro Bravo [BOL] 104-105 D 5
Cerro Bravo [PE] 96-97 B 4
Cerro Bruja 64-65 b 2
Cerro Cacique 108-109 D 4
Cerro Caltama 104-105 BC 7
Cerro Campamento 91 I b 3
Cerro Campana 94-95 E 7
Cerro Campanario 111 BC 5
Cerro Canapiare 94-95 G 6
Cerro Cangrejo 108-109 C 7
Cerro Capitán Maldonado 108-109 BC 4
Cerro Capitán Ustares 102-103 B 3
Cerro Cayaca 106-107 B 6
Cerro Cazador 108-109 CD 8
Cerro Central 108-109 D 4
Cerro Cerbatano 94-95 H 4
Cerro Cerrón 94-95 F 2
Cerro Champaquí 106-107 E 3
Cerro Chato [BR] 106-107 L 3
Cerro Chato [ROU] 106-107 K 4
Cerro Chirripó Grande 64-65 K 10
Cerro Chorreras 86-87 GH 4
Cerro Cirque 104-105 B 5
Cerro Coan 96-97 B 5
Cerro Cobre 106-107 B 2
Cerro Coipasa 104-105 B 6
Cerro Cojudo Blanco 111 BC 7
Cerro Colipilli 106-107 B 6
Cerro Colorado [RA, Chubut] 108-109 E 5
Cerro Colorado [RA, La Pampa] 106-107 D 6
Cerro Colorado [RA, La Rioja] 106-107 D 2
Cerro Colorado [ROU] 106-107 K 4
Cerro Colupo 104-105 AB 8
Cerro Cónico 108-109 D 4
Cerro Copa 104-105 B 7
Cerro Corá 100-101 F 4
Cerro Corona 108-109 D 3
Cerro Crucero 86-87 H 7
Cerro Cuanacorral 96-97 B 5
Cerro Cumare 94-95 E 7
Cerro Cumbrera 108-109 C 7
Cerro Curamalal Grande 106-107 FG 6
Cerro Curamavida 106-107 B 3
Cerro Dedo 111 B 6
Cerro de la Encantada 64-65 C 5
Cerro de la Estrella 91 I c 2
Cerro de la Estrella, Parque Nacional — 91 I c 2-3
Cerro de la Sal, Cadena de — 96-97 D 7
Cerro de la Salamanca 106-107 C 2
Cerro de las Cuentas 106-107 K 4
Cerro de las Ovejas 106-107 E 4
Cerro de la Viga 106-107 B 3
Cerro del Inca 104-105 BC 7
Cerro del León 64-65 G 8
Cerro del Mojón 106-107 CD 5
Cerro de los Mogotes 106-107 C 2
Cerro del Picacho 91 I c 1
Cerro del Pinacate 86-87 D 2
Cerro del Toro 111 C 3
Cerro del Tromen 106-107 B 6
Cerro del Volcán 106-107 BC 3
Cerro de Pasco 92-93 D 7
Cerro de Pomasi 92-93 E 8
Cerro de Quimsachota 104-105 B 5
Cerro de San Antonio 94-95 D 2
Cerro de Soto 106-107 B 3
Cerro de Tocorpuri 92-93 F 9
Cerro Divisadero 108-109 C 8
Cerro Doce Grande 108-109 E 6
Cerro Doña Ana 106-107 B 2
Cerro Doña Ines 104-105 B 10
Cerro d'Ouro 106-107 KL 3
Cerro Dragón 108-109 E 5
Cerro Duida 94-95 J 6
Cerro El Aspero 106-107 D 2
Cerro El Avila 91 II b 1
Cerro El Ford 108-109 D 9
Cerro El Nevado 92-93 E 4
Cerro el Nevado [RA, mountain] 111 C 5
Cerro El Potro 106-107 C 2
Cerro El Viejo 94-95 E 4
Cerro Finger 108-109 C 9
Cerro Galán 111 C 3
Cerro Grande [BR] 106-107 M 3
Cerro Grande [MEX] 86-87 K 8-9
Cerro Guachi 106-107 C 2
Cerro Guaiquinima 92-93 G 3
Cerro Guanay 94-95 H 5
Cerro Guasacavi 94-95 G 6
Cerro Hatscher 108-109 C 7
Cerro Hermanos 108-109 C 6
Cerro Horcón de Piedra 106-107 B 4
Cerro Huachamacari 94-95 HJ 6
Cerro Huanchaca 104-105 C 7
Cerro Huchuento 64-65 E 7
Cerro Hudson 111 B 7
Cerro Hyades 108-109 C 6
Cerro Iglesias 108-109 EF 6
Cerro Illesca 96-97 A 4-5
Cerro Jeinemeni 108-109 C 6
Cerro Juncal 106-107 BC 4
Cerro Kilambé 88-89 CD 8
Cerro La Paloma 106-107 C 4
Cerro Largo [BR] 106-107 K 2
Cerro Largo [ROU] 106-107 KL 4
Cerro las Casitas 64-65 E 7
Cerro La Silveta 111 B 8
Cerro Las Lajas 106-107 B 7
Cerro Las Tórtolas 106-107 BC 2
Cerro Leiva 94-95 D 6
Cerro Leon 102-103 B 4
Cerro Leoncito 106-107 C 2
Cerro Limón Verde 104-105 B 8
Cerro Lloron 86-87 H 7
Cerro los Gigantes 106-107 E 3
Cerro los Hijos 96-97 B 5
Cerro Malcanio 104-105 CD 9
Cerro Marahuaca 92-93 FG 4
Cerro Marmolejo 106-107 BC 4
Cerro Mato 94-95 J 4
Cerro Mayo 108-109 D 5
Cerro Mellizo Sur 111 B 7
Cerro Mercedario 111 BC 4
Cerro Mesa 108-109 D 7
Cerro Mogotón 88-89 C 8
Cerro Mora 106-107 B 5
Cerro Moreno 106-107 K 1
Cerro Moro, Pampa del — 108-109 F 6-7
Cerro Munchique 94-95 C 6
Cerro Murallón 111 B 7
Cerrón, Cerro — 94-95 F 2
Cerro Negro 108-109 D 2
Cerro Nevado 108-109 C 4
Cerro Osborne = Mount Usborne 111 E 8
Cerro Otare 92-93 E 4
Cerro Otatal 86-87 E 3
Cerro Ovana 94-95 H 5
Cerro Paine 111 B 8
Cerro Pajonal 104-105 B 7
Cerro Paraque 94-95 H 5
Cerro Pata de Gallo 96-97 B 6
Cerro Patria 108-109 G 5
Cerro Payún 111 BC 5
Cerro Peinado 106-107 C 6
Cerro Pellado 106-107 B 5
Cerro Peña Nevada 64-65 FG 7
Cerro Peñon 91 I c 3
Cerro Picún Leufú 106-107 C 7
Cerro Pináculo 108-109 CD 8
Cerro Piramide 108-109 C 7
Cerro Pirre 94-95 C 4
Cerro Piti 111 C 2
Cerro Porongo 106-107 D 3
Cerro Pumasillo 96-97 E 8
Cerro Puntas Negras 111 C 2
Cerro Puntodo 106-107 E 7
Cerro Quimal 104-105 B 8
Cerro Rajado 106-107 C 2
Cerro Redondo 106-107 C 4
Cerro Relem 111 B 5
Cerro Rico 106-107 E 2
Cerro Río Grande 91 II c 1
Cerro San Lorenzo 111 B 7
Cerro San Miguel 104-105 F 6
Cerro San Pedro 108-109 C 4
Cerro Santa Elena 108-109 G 5
Cerro Santiago 88-89 EF 10
Cerro San Valentín 111 B 7
Cerros Bravos 104-105 B 10
Cerros Cantaritos 106-107 BC 2
Cerros Colorados [RA] 111 C 6
Cerros Colorados [RCH] 111 C 3
Cerros Colorados, Embalse — 106-107 C 7
Cerros Cusali 104-105 C 4
Cerros de Amotape 96-97 A 4
Cerros de Araracuara 94-95 EF 7
Cerros de Bala 92-93 F 7-8
Cerros de Calla-Calla 96-97 BC 5
Cerros de Campanquiz 92-93 D 5-6
Cerros de Canthyuaya 96-97 D 5
Cerros de Itahuania 96-97 F 8
Cerros de Quimurcu 104-105 AB 8
Cerro Sin Nombre 108-109 C 5-6
Cerro Steffen 108-109 D 5
Cerro Tacarcuna 94-95 C 3
Cerro Tamaná 94-95 CD 5
Cerro Tambería 106-107 C 2
Cerro Teotepec 64-65 FG 8
Cerro Tolar 104-105 C 10
Cerro Tomolasta 106-107 DE 4
Cerro Tres Altitos 106-107 C 4
Cerro Tres Cruces 106-107 C 1
Cerro Tres Picos 111 B 6
Cerro Tulaguen 106-107 B 3
Cerro Tunupa 104-105 C 6
Cerro Tupungato 111 BC 4
Cerro Turagua 94-95 J 4
Cerro Turimiquire 94-95 JK 2
Cerro Uritorco 106-107 E 3
Cerro Uspara 106-107 E 4
Cerro Velucá 88-89 D 7
Cerro Venamo 94-95 L 5
Cerro Ventisquero 108-109 D 3
Cerro Vera 106-107 J 4
Cerro Viejo 86-87 DE 2
Cerro Volcán 108-109 E 5
Cerro Xico 91 I d 3
Cerro Yapacana 94-95 H 6
Cerro Yarvicoya 104-105 B 6-7
Cerro Yaví 92-93 F 3
Cerro Yogan 111 BC 8
Cerro Yumari 92-93 F 4
Cerro Zanelli 108-109 C 9
Cerro Zapaleri 111 C 2
Cerro Zempoaltepec 64-65 GH 8
Cerrudo Cué 106-107 J 1
Čerskij 132-133 f 4
Certaldo 122-123 D 4
Čertanovo, Moskva- 113 V bc 3
Čertež 124-125 V 4
Čertkovo 126-127 K 2
Čerusti 124-125 N 6
Cervantes 106-107 D 7
Cervati, Monte — 122-123 F 5
Červen' 124-125 G 7
Červen br'ag 122-123 KL 4
Cervera 120-121 H 8
Cerveteri 122-123 E 4
Cèrvia 122-123 E 3
Červonoarmejskoje [SU, Zaparožskaja Oblast'] 126-127 GH 3
Červonograd 126-127 B 1
Červonozavodskoje 126-127 FG 1
Cesar 94-95 E 3
César, Río — 94-95 E 2
Cesareia = Caesarea 136-137 F 6
Césares, Isla de los — 108-109 HJ 3
Cesena 122-123 DE 3
Cesira, La — 106-107 F 4
Cēsis 124-125 E 5
Česká Třebova 118 G 4
České Budějovice 118 G 4
České zemĕ 118 F-H 4
Českomoravská vrchovina 118 GH 4
Çeşme 136-137 B 3
Cessford 56-57 O 7
Cessnock 158-159 K 6
Cess River 164-165 C 7
Cetinje 122-123 H 4
Çetinkaya 136-137 GH 3
Cetraro 122-123 F 6
Ceuta 164-165 CD 1
Cevennes 120-121 JK 6
Cevernyj port 113 V b 2
Cevizlik 136-137 H 2
Ceyhan 136-137 FG 4
Ceyhan nehri 136-137 G 4
Ceylânpınar 136-137 HJ 4
Ceylon = Srī Laṅkā 134-135 N 9
Ceylon Station 61 F 6

Chaaltyn gol 142-143 GH 4

Chaaltyn 277

Cha-am [T] 148-149 CD 4
Chaamba, Hassi — = Ḥāssī Sha'ambah 166-167 D 5
Chaapsalu = Haapsalu 124-125 D 4
Chaba 142-143 F 2
Chabar = Bandar-e Chah Bahār 134-135 HJ 5
Chabarovo 132-133 L 4
Chabarovsk 132-133 a 8
Chabás 106-107 G 4
Chab Chhu 138-139 M 3
Chablis 120-121 J 5
Chaca 104-105 AB 6
Chacabuco [RA] 106-107 G 5
Chacabuco [RCH] 106-107 B 4
Chacao 91 II bc 1-2
Chacao, Canal de — 108-109 C 3
Chacarita, Buenos Aires- 110 III b 1
Chacay, El — 106-107 BC 5
Chacays, Sierra de los — 108-109 F 4
Chachahuen, Sierra de — 106-107 C 6
Chachani 96-97 F 10
Chachapoyas 92-93 D 6
Chācharān 64-65 K 4
Chacharramendi 106-107 E 6
Ch'a-chên = Chazhen 146-147 B 5
Cha-chiang = Zhajiang 146-147 D 8
Cha-ching = Zhajin 146-147 E 7
Chacho, El — 106-107 E 3
Chāchro 138-139 C 5
Chachyoṭ = Chichot 138-139 F 2
Chaclacayo 96-97 C 7-8
Chaĉmas 126-127 O 6
Chaco 111 D 3
Chaco, El — 96-97 C 2
Chaco Austral 111 DE 3
Chaco Boreal 111 DE 2
Chaco Canyon National Monument 74-75 JK 4-5
Chaco Central 111 D 2-E 3
Chacon, Cape — 58-59 wx 9
Chacopata 94-95 JK 2
Chaco River 74-75 J 4
Chacras, Las — 106-107 BC 6
Chacras de Piros 96-97 E 7
Chad 164-165 HJ 5
Chad, Lake — = Lac Tchad 164-165 G 6
Chadasan 142-143 J 2
Chadchal = Chatgal 142-143 HJ 1
Chadileuvú, Bañados del — 106-107 D 6
Chadileuvú, Río — 106-107 DE 6
Chadmó 108-109 BC 4
Chadron, NE 68-69 E 4
Chadstone, Melbourne- 161 II c 2
Chadum 172 D 5
Chadwick, IL 70-71 F 4
Chadzaar 142-143 G 4
Chae Hom 150-151 B 3
Chaem, Nam Mae — 150-151 B 3
Chaenpur = Chainpur 138-139 K 6
Chaeryŏng 144-145 EF 3
Chafarinas, Islas — 166-167 EF 2
Chaffee, MO 78-79 DE 2
Chaffers, Canal — 108-109 B 5
Chaffers, Isla — 108-109 BC 5
Chāgalamarri 140 D 3
Chagang-do 144-145 EF 2
Chagan nuur 142-143 L 3
Chagas 102-103 H 1
Chageri = Hageri 124-125 E 4
Chagny 120-121 K 5
Cha Gonpa = Chhōra Gonpa 138-139 M 2
Chagos 50-51 N 6
Chagres [PA, place] 64-65 b 2
Chagres [PA, river] 64-65 ab 2
Chagres, Brazo del — 64-65 b 2
Chagres, Río — 64-65 bc 2
Chagres Arm = Brazo del Chagres 64-65 b 2
Chagual 96-97 C 5
Chaguaramas 94-95 H 3
Chagulak Island 58-59 l 4
Chāgwādam 141 F 2
Chāhār Burjak = Chār Burjak 134-135 J 4
Chahār Maḥāl-e Bakhteyārī = 3 ◁ 134-135 G 4
Chahbā = Shahbā' 136-137 G 6
Chāh Bāhār = Bandar-e Chāh Bahār 134-135 HJ 5
Chahbounia = Shābūnīyah 166-167 H 2
Ch'aho 144-145 G 2
Chai Badan 150-151 C 5
Chaibāsa 138-139 K 6
Chaidamu Pendi = Tsaidam 142-143 GH 4
Chaïdárion 113 IV a 1
Chailar = Hailar 142-143 M 2
Ch'ail-bong 144-145 F 2
Chai Nat 148-149 D 3
Chain Butte 68-69 B 2
Chaîne des Mitumba 172 E 3-4
Chainpur [IND] 138-139 K 6
Chainpur [Nepal] 138-139 L 4
Chaiqiao 146-147 HJ 7
Chaira, Laguna — 94-95 D 7
Chaitén 108-109 C 4
Chai Wan 155 I b 2
Chaiya 148-149 C 5
Chaiyaphum 150-151 CD 5
Chaiyeru = Punchu 140 D 4
Chaiyo 150-151 C 5
Chaiyyār = Cheyyar 140 D 4
Chaján 106-107 E 4
Chajarí 111 E 4
Chajdag gol 142-143 EF 3
Chajian 146-147 G 5
Chajlar 142-143 M 2
Chajlar = Hailar 142-143 M 2
Chajlar gol = Hailar He 142-143 MN 2
Chajrchan 142-143 J 2
Chajr'uzovo 132-133 e 6
Chakachamna Lake 58-59 L 6
Chakaktolik, AK 58-59 F 6
Chaka Nor = Chöch nuur 142-143 H 4
Chākar 138-139 AB 3
Chakaria = Chakariya 141 C 5
Chakariya 141 C 5
Chakdaha, South Suburbs- 154 II ab 3
Chake Chake 171 DE 4
Chakhcharān 134-135 K 4
Chakia 138-139 J 5
Chakkarat 150-151 D 5
Chakkra Rat = Chakkarat 150-151 D 5
Chakradharpur 138-139 K 6
Chakraotā = Chakrāta 138-139 FG 2
Chakrāta 138-139 FG 2
Chaksu = Chātsu 138-139 EF 4
Chākuliā 138-139 L 6
Chakwaktolik, AK 58-59 EF 6
Chāl = Shāl 136-137 N 5
Chala 92-93 E 8
Chala, Punta — 96-97 D 9
Chalab, gora — 126-127 M 6
Chalabesa 171 B 5
Chalakudi 140 C 5
Chalanta 106-107 DE 4
Cha-lan-tun = Yalu 142-143 N 2
Chalatenango 88-89 B 7-8
Chalbi Desert 171 D 2
Chalchuapa 88-89 B 8
Chalchyn gol 142-143 M 2
Chalcidice = Chalkidikē 122-123 K 5
Chaleur Bay 56-57 XY 8
Chalhuanca 92-93 E 7
Chalia, Arroyo — 108-109 D 5
Chalia, Pampa del — 108-109 D 5
Chalía, Río — 108-109 DE 7
Chalicán 104-105 D 9
Chaling 146-147 D 8
Cha-ling Hu = Kyaring Tsho 142-143 H 5
Chāḷīsgāñv = Chālisgaon 138-139 E 7
Chālisgaon 138-139 E 7
Chalkē 122-123 M 7
Chalkidikē 122-123 K 3
Chalkís 122-123 K 6
Chalk River 72-73 H 1-2
Chalkyitsik, AK 58-59 PQ 3
Challa 104-105 C 7
Challacó 106-107 C 7
Challacollo 104-105 C 6
Challacota 104-105 C 6
Challakere 140 C 3
Challapata 92-93 F 8
Challawa 168-169 G 3
Challis, ID 66-67 F 3
Chal'mer-Ju 132-133 L 4
Chalmer-Sede = Tazovskij 132-133 OP 4
Chalmette, LA 85 I c 2
Chalmette Natural Historical Park 85 I c 2
Chālna 138-139 M 6
Chalok 150-151 D 10
Châlons-sur-Marne 120-121 JK 4
Chalon-sur-Saône 120-121 K 5
Chalosse 120-121 G 7
Chalturin 132-133 H 6
Chalviri, Salar de — 104-105 C 8
Cham 118 F 4
Cham, Cu Lao — 150-151 G 5
Chama 168-169 E 3
Chama, NM 68-69 C 7
Chama, Rio — 76-77 A 4
Chamah, Gunung — 150-151 C 10
Chamaicó 106-107 E 5
Chamaites 174-175 B 4
Chaman 134-135 K 4
Chamao, Khao — 150-151 C 6
Chāmarājanagara = Chāmrājnagar 140 C 5
Chamartin, Madrid- 113 III ab 2
Chamaya, Río — 96-97 B 4-5
Chamba [EAT] 171 D 5
Chamba [IND] 134-135 M 4
Chambak 150-151 E 7
Chambal [IND ◁ Kālī Sindh] 134-135 M 5-6
Chambal [IND ◁ Yamunā] 134-135 M 5-6
Chambas 88-89 G 3
Chamberí, Madrid- 113 III a 2
Chamberlain 61 EF 5
Chamberlain, SD 68-69 G 4
Chamberlain Lake 72-73 M 1
Chamberlain River 158-159 E 3
Chamberlin, Mount — 58-59 P 2
Chambersburg, PA 72-73 GH 4
Chambers Island 70-71 G 3
Chambéry 120-121 K 6
Chambeshi 172 F 4
Chambī, Djebel — = Jabal Shaḥāmbī 166-167 L 2
Chambira, Río — 96-97 D 3
Chambourcy 129 I b 2
Chambres Pass = Cumbres Pass 68-69 C 7
Chambria, Río — 96-97 D 4
Chamchamāl 136-137 L 5
Chamdo = Chhamdo 142-143 H 5
Chame 88-89 G 10
Chamela 86-87 H 8
Chamical 106-107 DE 3
Chami Choto = Hami 142-143 G 3
Chamiss Bay 60 D 4
Chamo, Lake — = Tyamo 164-165 M 7
Chamōlī 138-139 G 2
Chāmpa [IND] 134-135 N 6
Champa [SU] 132-133 X 5
Champagne [CDN] 58-59 TU 6
Champagne [F] 120-121 J 5-K 4
Champagne Castle 174-175 H 5
Champagny Islands 158-159 D 3
Champaign, IL 64-65 J 3-4
Champaquí, Cerro — 106-107 E 3
Champara, Nevado de — 96-97 C 6
Champāran = Mōtihārī 134-135 NO 5
Champassak 148-149 DE 4
Champāvat = Champāwat 138-139 H 3
Champāwat 138-139 H 3
Champ de Course Blue Bonnets 82 I b 2
Champigny-sur-Marne 129 I d 2
Champion 61 B 5
Champlain, Lake — 64-65 LM 3
Champlain, Pont — 82 I b 2
Champotón 64-65 H 8
Champotón, Río — 86-87 P 8
Champs-Elysées 129 I c 2
Champs-sur-Marne 129 I d 2
Champur = Chainpur 138-139 L 4
Chāmrāl 154 II a 2
Chāmrājnagar 140 C 5
Chāmursi 138-139 GH 8
Chan, Ko — 150-151 AB 8
Chana 150-151 C 9
Chanāb 138-139 C 3
Chanāb = Chenāb 134-135 M 4
Chanak Kalesi = Çanakkale 134-135 B 2
Chañar 111 C 4
Chañaral [RCH ↖ Copiapó] 111 B 3
Chañaral [RCH ↙ Copiapó] 106-107 B 2
Chañaral, Isla — 111 B 3
Chañaritos 106-107 E 4
Chānasma 138-139 D 6
Chan Bogd 142-143 K 3
Chancaní 106-107 E 3
Chancay 92-93 D 7
Chancay, Río — 96-97 C 7
Chance Island = Ko Chan 150-151 AB 8
Chanch 142-143 J 1
Chan Chan 96-97 B 6
Chan-chiang = Zhanjiang 142-143 L 7
Chanchoengsao 148-149 D 4
Chanco 106-107 A 5
Chanco, Bahía — 106-107 A 5
Chānd 138-139 G 7
Chānda = Chandrapur 134-135 M 7
Chandaka 138-139 K 7
Chandalar, AK 58-59 NO 3
Chandalar, East Fork — 58-59 P 2
Chandalar, Middle Fork — 58-59 O 2-3
Chandalar, North Fork — 58-59 N 2-3
Chandalar Lake 58-59 NO 3
Chandalar River 56-57 G 4
Chandannagar = Mangalkōṭ 138-139 LM 6
Chandaolī = Chandauli 138-139 J 5
Chandaosī = Chandausi 138-139 G 3
Chandarpur 138-139 J 7
Chandauli 138-139 J 5
Chandausi 138-139 G 3
Chāndbāli 138-139 L 7
Chandeleur Islands 64-65 J 6
Chandeleur Sound 78-79 E 5-6
Chandernagore 138-139 LM 6
Chāndgad 140 AB 3
Chandīgarh 134-135 LM 4
Chāndil 138-139 L 6
Chanditala 154 II a 1
Chandler 56-57 Y 8
Chandler, AZ 74-75 H 6
Chandler, OK 76-77 F 5
Chandler Lake 58-59 LM 2
Chandler Park 84 II c 2
Chandler River 58-59 L 2
Chandlers Falls 171 D 2
Chandless, Rio — 98-99 C 9-10
Chāndod 138-139 D 6-7
Chāndor 138-139 DE 7
Chāndpur [BD] 141 B 4
Chāndpur [IND] 138-139 G 3
Chāndpur = Chāndpur Bāzār 138-139 FG 7
Chāndpur Bāzār 138-139 FG 7
Chandrā 138-139 F 1
Chandragiri 140 D 4
Chandrakona 138-139 L 6
Chandranagar = Chandernagore 138-139 LM 6
Chandrapur 134-135 M 7
Chāndūr 138-139 FG 7
Chāndūr = Chāndor 138-139 DE 7
Chanduy 96-97 A 3
Chandyga 132-133 a 5
Chang, Ko — [T, Andaman Sea] 150-151 B 8
Chang, Ko — [T, Gulf of Thailand] 148-149 D 4
Changai = Shanghai 142-143 N 5
Changaj 142-143 H 2
Changajn Nuruu 142-143 HJ 2
Changalane 174-175 K 4
Changam = Chengam 140 D 4
Chang'an 146-147 B 4
Ch'ang-an = Xi'an 142-143 K 5
Changanācheri 140 C 6
Changane, Rio — 172 F 6
Chang'ankou = Laopukou 146-147 B 9
Chang'anzhen = Rong'an 146-147 B 9
Changara 172 F 5
Changbai 144-145 FG 2
Changbai Shan 142-143 O 3
Changcheng 150-151 G 3
Changchhab 138-139 K 3
Chang-chia-k'ou = Zhangjiakou 142-143 L 3
Ch'ang Chiang = Changhua Jiang 150-151 G 3
Ch'ang Chiang = Chang Jiang 146-147 F 7
Chang-chia-p'ang = Zhangjiapang 146-147 E 6
Changchih = Changzhi 142-143 L 4
Ch'ang-chih = Changzhi 142-143 L 4
Ch'ang-ch'ing = Changqing 146-147 F 3
Chang-ch'iu = Zhangqiu 146-147 F 3
Changchow = Zhangzhou 142-143 M 7
Changchun 142-143 NO 3
Changdang Hu 146-147 G 6
Changdao 146-147 H 3
Changde 142-143 L 6
Changdu = Chhamdo 142-143 H 5
Change Islands 63 JK 3
Changfeng 146-147 F 5
Changge 146-147 D 4
Chang-hai = Shanghai 142-143 N 5
Changhang 144-145 F 4-5
Chang Ho = Zhang He 146-147 E 3
Changhowŏn 144-145 F 4
Ch'ang-hsing = Changxing 146-147 G 6
Ch'ang-hsing Tao = Changxing Dao 144-145 C 3
Chang Hu 146-147 D 6
Changhua [RC] 146-147 H 9
Changhua [TJ] 146-147 G 6
Changhua Jiang 150-151 G 3
Chang-huang = Zhanghuang 146-147 B 10
Changhŭng 144-145 F 5
Changhŭng-ni 144-145 FG 2
Changhwa = Changhua 146-147 H 9
Ch'ang-i = Changyi 146-147 G 3
Changjiang [TJ, place] 150-151 G 3
Chang Jiang [TJ, river ◁ Dong Hai] 142-143 K 5-6
Chang Jiang [TJ, river ◁ Poyang Hu] 146-147 F 7
Changji Huizu Zizhizhou 142-143 FG 3
Changjin 144-145 F 2
Changjin-gang 144-145 F 2
Changjin-ho 144-145 F 2
Changjŏn 144-145 G 3
Changkar Ri 138-139 L 2
Changkiakow = Zhangjiakou 142-143 L 3
Changkou = Zhangqiu 146-147 F 3
Chang-kuang-ts'ai Ling = Zhangguangcai Ling 142-143 O 2-3
Changkung 146-147 H 10
Changle [TJ, Fujian] 146-147 G 9
Changle [TJ, Guangdong] 146-147 B 11
Changle [TJ, Shandong] 146-147 G 3
Changli 146-147 G 2
Ch'ang-lo = Changle [TJ, Guangdong] 146-147 B 11
Ch'ang-lo = Changle [TJ, Shandong] 146-147 G 3
Changlun 150-151 C 9
Changluo = Changle 146-147 G 9
Changngananshēri = Changanācheri 140 C 6
Changngāṭ = Manattala 140 BC 5
Changnim-ni 144-145 F 3
Changning 146-147 D 8
Ch'angnyŏng 144-145 G 5
Ch'ang-pai = Changbai 144-145 FG 2
Ch'ang-pai Shan = Changbai Shan 142-143 O 3
Changping 146-147 F 1
Changping = Zhangping 146-147 F 9
Changpu = Zhangpu 146-147 F 9
Chang-p'u = Zhangpu 146-147 F 9
Changqing 146-147 F 3
Changsa 150-151 H 3
Chang-san-ying = Zhangsanying 144-145 AB 2
Changsha 142-143 L 6
Changshan 146-147 G 7
Changshan Dao = Miao Dao 146-147 H 3
Changsheng 146-147 EF 8
Changshu 142-143 N 5
Changshui 146-147 C 4
Chang Shui = Zhang Shui 146-147 E 9
Ch'angsŏng = Chongsŏng 144-145 GH 1
Changtai 146-147 F 9
Chang Tang = Jang Thang 142-143 E-G 5
Ch'ang-tê = Anyang 142-143 LM 4
Ch'ang-tê = Changde 142-143 L 6
Changteh = Changde 142-143 L 6
Changting 142-143 M 6
Changtsing = Changqing 146-147 F 3
Ch'ang-tu = Chhamdo 142-143 H 5
Changtutsung = Chhamdo 142-143 H 5
Chang-tzŭ = Zhangzi 146-147 D 3
Ch'angwŏn 144-145 G 5
Changxi = Changsa 150-151 H 3
Changxing 146-147 G 6
Changxing Dao [TJ, Dong Hai] 146-147 HJ 6
Changxing Dao [TJ, Liaodong Wan] 144-145 C 3
Changyang 146-147 C 6
Changyeh = Zhangye 142-143 J 4
Changyi 146-147 G 3
Changyŏn 142-143 NO 4
Changyuan 146-147 E 4
Changzhi 142-143 L 4
Changzhou 142-143 M 5
Chan-hua = Zhanhua 146-147 FG 3
Chañi, Sierra de — 104-105 D 8-9
Chaniá 122-123 KL 8
Chaniṓn, Kólpos — 122-123 KL 8
Chanka, ozero — 132-133 Z 9
Chañkam = Chengam 140 D 4
Chankiang = Zhanjiang 142-143 L 7
Chankliut Island 58-59 de 1
Channāb = Chenāb 134-135 M 4
Channagiri 140 BC 3-4
Channapatna 140 C 4
Channapattana = Channapatna 140 C 4
Channarāyapatna 140 C 4
Chañar Ladeado 106-107 F 4
Channel Islands [GB] 119 E 7
Channel Islands [USA] 74-75 CD 6
Channel Islands National Monument = Anacapa Island, Santa Barbara Island 74-75 D 6
Channel-Port-aux-Basques 56-57 Z 8
Channelview, TX 85 III c 1
Channing 61 H 3
Channing, MI 70-71 FG 2
Channing, TX 76-77 CD 5
Chansi = Shanxi 142-143 L 4
Chanskoje, ozero — 126-127 J 3
Chantaburi = Chanthaburi 148-149 D 4
Chantada 120-121 CD 7
Chantajka 132-133 PQ 4
Chantajskoje, ozero — 132-133 QR 4
Chantanika River 58-59 O 4
Chan Tengri, pik — 134-135 MN 2
Chanthaburi 148-149 D 4
Chantong = Shandong 142-143 M 4
Chantrey Inlet 56-57 RS 4
Chanty-Mansijsk 132-133 M 5
Chanty-Mansijskij Nacional'nyj Okrug = Khanty-Mansi Autonomous Area 132-133 L-P 5
Chanuman 150-151 E 4
Chanute, KS 70-71 C 7
Chanzy = Sīdī 'Alī Ban Yūb 166-167 F 2
Chao 96-97 B 6
Chao'an 142-143 M 7
Chao-an = Zhao'an 146-147 F 10
Chao-an Wan = Zhao'an Wan 146-147 F 10
Chao-ch'êng = Jiaocheng 146-147 CD 3
Chaochow = Chao'an 142-143 M 7
Chaohsien = Zhao Xian 146-147 E 3
Chao-hsien = Zhao Xian 146-147 G 4
Chao Hu 142-143 M 5
Chao-i = Chaoyi 146-147 BC 4
Chao Phraya, Mae Nam — 148-149 CD 3-4
Chaoping = Zhaoping 146-147 C 9
Chaor He 142-143 N 2
Chaosā = Chausa 138-139 JK 5
Chaotarā = Chautara 138-139 KL 4
Chaotung = Zhaotong 142-143 J 6
Chao-t'ung = Zhaotong 142-143 J 6
Chao Xian 146-147 FG 6
Chaoyang [TJ, Guangdong] 142-143 M 7
Chaoyang [TJ, Liaoning] 142-143 MN 3
Ch'ao-yang-chên = Huinan 142-143 O 3
Chaoyangqu, Beijing- 155 II bc 2
Chaoyi 146-147 BC 4
Chao-yüan = Zhaoyuan 146-147 H 3
Cha Pa 150-151 DE 1
Chapada 106-107 M 2
Chapada da Água Branca 102-103 L 1-2
Chapada da Serra Verde 100-101 FG 3
Chapada das Mangabeiras 92-93 K 6-L 7
Chapada de Maracás 100-101 DE 7
Chapada Diamantina 92-93 L 7
Chapada do Alto Grande 100-101 EF 5
Chapada do-Apodí 92-93 M 6
Chapada do Araripe 92-93 LM 6
Chapada do CApodí 92-93 M 6
Chapada dos Guimarães 102-103 E 1
Chapada dos Parecis 92-93 GH 7
Chapada dos Pilões 102-103 J 2-3
Chapada dos Veadeiros 92-93 K 7-8
Chapada do Tapiocanga 102-103 J 2
Chapada Grande 100-101 C 4
Chapada Redonda 100-101 B 6
Chapadinha 92-93 L 5
Chapadmalal 106-107 J 6-7
Chapado dos Gerais 92-93 K 8
Chapais 62 O 2
Chapala 86-87 J 7
Chapala, Lago de — 64-65 F 7
Chapalcó, Valle — 106-107 E 6
Chapare, Río — 104-105 D 5
Chāparmukh 141 C 2
Chāparra 96-97 E 9
Chaparral 94-95 D 6
Chaparro, El — 94-95 J 3
Chapas, Las — 108-109 F 4
Chapčeranga 132-133 V 8
Chapel Hill, NC 80-81 G 3
Chapel Hill, TN 78-79 F 3
Chaperito, NM 76-77 B 5
Chapéu, Cachoeira — 98-99 K 7-8
Chapéu, Morro do — 100-101 C 8
Chapicuy 106-107 J 3
Chapleau 62 H 4
Chapleau River 62 H 3
Chaplin 61 E 5
Chapman, MT 68-69 BC 1
Cha-p'o = Zhapo 146-147 C 11
Chappell, NE 68-69 E 5
Chappelle-Saint-Lambert 128 II b 2
Chāpra 134-135 N 5
Chā Preta 100-101 F 5
Chapultepec, Bosque de — 91 I b 2
Chapuy 106-107 G 4
Chaqui 92-93 F 8
Chā'r, Jebel — = Jabal Shā'r 136-137 GH 5
Charabali 126-127 N 3
Charadai 111 E 3
Charagua 92-93 G 8
Charagua, Cordillera de — 92-93 G 8-9
Char Ajrag 142-143 KL 2
Charalá 94-95 E 4
Charallave 94-95 H 2
Charaña 92-93 F 8
Charata 104-105 F 10
Charbin = Harbin 142-143 O 2
Chār Burjak 134-135 J 4
Charcas 64-65 F 7
Chārchān 142-143 F 4
Chārchān Darya 142-143 F 4
Char Chorin 142-143 J 2
Char Choto 142-143 J 3
Charcos de Figueroa 76-77 CD 9
Charcos de Risa 76-77 C 9
Charcot, Île — 53 C 29
Chardāvol 136-137 M 6
Chardon, OH 72-73 F 4
Charef = Shārif 166-167 H 2
Chāref, Ouèd — = Wād Shārif 166-167 E 3
Charente 120-121 G 6
Charenton-le-Pont 129 I c 2
Chargla = Hargla 124-125 F 5
Char Gov' 142-143 GH 3
Chari 164-165 H 6
Chārikār 134-135 K 3-4
Char Irčis 142-143 F 2
Chariton, IA 70-71 D 5
Charitona Lapteva, bereg — 132-133 Q 3-R 2
Chariton River 70-71 D 5-6
Charity 92-93 H 3
Charkhāri 138-139 G 5
Charkhi Dādri 138-139 EF 3
Charkhilik = Charqiliq 142-143 F 4
Char'kov 126-127 H 1-2
Charleroi 120-121 K 3
Charles, Cape — 64-65 LM 4
Charlesbourg 63 A 4
Charles City, IA 70-71 D 4
Charles de Gaulle, Aéroport — 129 I d 1
Charles Falls 62 B 2
Charles Fuhr 108-109 D 8
Charles H. Milby Park 85 III b 2
Charles Island 56-57 VW 5
Charles Lee Tilden Regional Park 83 I c 1
Charles River 84 I b 2
Charles River Basin 84 I b 2
Charleston, IL 70-71 FG 6
Charleston, MO 78-79 E 2
Charleston, MS 78-79 DE 3
Charleston, SC 64-65 KL 5
Charleston, TN 78-79 G 3
Charleston, WV 64-65 K 4
Charleston Peak 74-75 F 4
Charlestown, IN 70-71 H 6
Charlestown [Saint Christopher-Nevis] 64-65 O 8
Charlestown [ZA] 174-175 HJ 4
Charlestown, Boston-, MA 84 I b 2
Charleville 172 D 3
Charleville [AUS] 158-159 J 5
Charleville-Mézières 120-121 K 4
Charlevoix, MI 70-71 H 3
Charlevoix, Lake — 70-71 H 3
Charley River 58-59 Q 4
Charlie Brown-Fulton Airport 85 II a 2
Charlie Lake 60 G 1
Charlotte, MI 70-71 H 4
Charlotte, NC 64-65 KL 4-5
Charlotte, TN 78-79 F 2
Charlotte, TX 76-77 E 8
Charlotte Amalie 64-65 O 8
Charlotte Harbor 64-65 K 6
Charlotte Lake 60 E 3
Charlottenberg 116-117 E 8
Charlottenburg, Schloss — 130 III b 1
Charlottesville, VA 64-65 L 4
Charlottetown 56-57 Y 8
Charlottetown = Roseau 64-65 O 8
Charlotteville 94-95 L 2
Charlton 160 F 6
Charlton Island 56-57 UV 7
Charlton Park 85 III b 2
Charlu 124-125 H 3
Char Narijn uul 142-143 K 3
Char nuur [Mongolia] 142-143 G 2
Char nuur [TJ] 142-143 H 4
Charny [CDN] 63 A 4
Charolais, Monts du — 120-121 K 5
Charon = Bū Qādir 166-167 G 1
Charonne, Paris- 129 I c 2
Charouïne = Shārwīn 166-167 F 5
Charovsk 132-133 G 6
Charqī, Jebel ech — = Jabal ar-Ruwāq 136-137 G 5-6
Charqiliq 142-143 F 4
Charquecada 106-107 M 2
Charron Lake 62 B 1
Charters Towers 158-159 J 3-4
Chartres 120-121 H 4
Char us nuur 142-143 G 2
Chās [IND] 138-139 L 6
Chás [RA] 106-107 H 5
Chasan 144-145 H 1
Chasavjurt 126-127 N 5
Chaschuil, Río — 104-105 B 10
Chascomús 111 E 5
Chase 60 H 4
Chase City, VA 80-81 G 2
Chasicó [RA, Buenos Aires] 106-107 F 7
Chasicó [RA, Río Negro] 108-109 E 3
Chasicó, Laguna — 106-107 F 7
Chasm 60 G 4
Chasŏng 144-145 F 2
Chassahowitzka Bay 80-81 b 2
Chastain Memorial Park 85 II b 1
Chašuri 126-127 L 5-6
Chatanga 132-133 TU 3
Chatan gol 142-143 K 3
Chatangskij zaliv 132-133 UV 3
Chatanika, AK 58-59 O 4
Châteaubriant 120-121 G 5
Château-du-Loir 120-121 H 5
Châteaudun 120-121 H 4
Châteaulin 120-121 EF 4
Châteauroux 120-121 H 5
Château-Thierry 120-121 J 4
Château Versailles 129 I b 2
Châtellerault 120-121 H 5
Châtenay-Malabry 129 I c 2
Chatfield, MN 70-71 D 4
Chatgal 142-143 HJ 1
Chatham, AK 58-59 U 8
Chatham, LA 78-79 C 4
Chatham, NY 72-73 K 3
Chatham, VA 80-81 G 2
Chatham [CDN, New Brunswick] 56-57 XY 8
Chatham [CDN, Ontario] 56-57 U 9
Chatham = Isla San Cristóbal 92-93 B 5
Chatham, Chicago-, IL 83 II b 2
Chatham, Isla — 111 B 8
Chatham Islands 158-159 Q 8
Chatham Sound 60 B 2
Chatham Strait 56-57 K 6
Cha Thing Phra = Sathing Phra 150-151 C 9
Châtillon [F] 129 I c 2
Châtillon [I] 122-123 B 3
Châtillon-sur-Seine 120-121 K 5
Chātmohar 138-139 M 5
Chatom, AL 78-79 E 5
Chatou 129 I b 2
Chatra 138-139 K 5
Chatrapur 138-139 K 8
Chātsu 138-139 EF 4
Chatswood, Sydney- 161 I b 1
Chatsworth 72-73 F 2
Chatsworth, GA 78-79 G 3
Chaṭṭagām 134-135 P 6
Chaṭṭagām Pahāṛī 'Alāqa 141 C 4-5
Chattahoochee, FL 78-79 G 5
Chattahoochee, Atlanta-, GA 85 II b 2
Chattahoochee River 64-65 JK 5
Chattanooga, TN 64-65 J 4
Chattarpur = Chhatarpur 134-135 M 6
Chatturat 150-151 CD 5
Chaubāra 138-139 C 2
Chaucha 96-97 B 3
Chauchaiñeu, Sierra — 108-109 E 3
Chaudière, Rivière — 63 A 4-5
Châu Đôc = Châu Phu 148-149 E 4
Chauekuktuli Lake 58-59 HJ 6
Chauk 141 D 5
Chaulán 96-97 C 7
Chaullay 96-97 E 8
Chaumont 120-121 K 4
Chaumu 138-139 E 4
Chaŭn-do 144-145 EF 5
Chaungan Taunggya 141 E 2
Chaungʻū 141 D 5
Chaungzôn 141 E 7
Chaupāl 138-139 F 2
Châu Phu 148-149 E 4
Chauques, Islas — 108-109 C 4
Chausa 138-139 JK 5
Chautara 138-139 KL 4
Chautauqua Lake 72-73 G 3
Chautavara 124-125 J 2
Chauvin 61 C 4
Chauwis-Parganā = 24-Parganas 138-139 M 6-7
Chaux-de-Fonds, La — 118 C 5
Chauya Cocha, La — 96-97 D 6
Chāvākachchēri 140 E 6
Chaval 100-101 D 2
Chavarria 106-107 H 2
Chavast 134-135 K 2
Chavenay 129 I a 2
Chaves, NM 76-77 B 6

278 Cha

Chaves [BR] 92-93 K 5
Chaves [P] 120-121 D 8
Chaves, Isla — = Isla Santa Cruz 92-93 AB 5
Chavīb Deh 136-137 N 7
Chaville 129 I b 2
Chavín de Huántar 96-97 C 6
Chavín de Pariarca 96-97 C 6
Chaviva 92-93 E 4
Chawang 150-151 B 8
Chây, Sông — 150-151 E 1
Chaya = Drayā 142-143 H 5
Chayanta, Río — 104-105 CD 6
Chaynpur = Chainpur 138-139 L 4
Ch'a-yü = Dsayul 142-143 H 6
Chazhen 146-147 B 5
Chazón 111 D 4
Chbar, Prêk — 150-151 F 6
Cheam, London- 129 II b 2
Cheap, Canal — 108-109 B 6
Cheat Mountain 72-73 FG 5
Cheat River 72-73 G 5
Cheb 118 F 3
Chebāyesh, Al- = Al-Jaza'ir 136-137 M 7
Chèbba, Ech — = Ash-Shābah 166-167 M 2
Chebii, Uáu el — = Wādī Bay al-Kabīr 164-165 GH 2
Chebka, Région de la — = Shabkah 166-167 H 3-4
Cheboksary = Čeboksar 132-133 H 6
Cheboygan, MI 64-65 K 2
Chech, Erg — = Irq ash-Shāsh 164-165 D 3-4
Chechaouène = Shifshawn 164-165 CD 1
Chechat 138-139 E 5
Checheng = Zhecheng 146-147 E 4
Checheno-Ingush Autonomous Soviet Socialist Republic 126-127 MN 5
Chech'on 144-145 G 4
Checotah, OK 76-77 G 5
Chedabucto Bay 63 F 5
Chedādī, El- = Ash-Shiddādī 136-137 J 4
Cheduba = Man'aung 141 C 6
Cheduba Strait = Man'aung Reletkyā 141 CD 6
Cheecham 61 C 2
Cheecham Hills 61 B 3-C 2
Cheeching, AK 58-59 E 6
Cheektowaga, NY 72-73 GH 3
Cheepie 158-159 HJ 5
Cheesman Lake 68-69 D 6
Chef, Rivière du — 62 P 1-2
Chefoo = Yantai 142-143 N 4
Chefornak, AK 58-59 E 6
Chefu = Yantai 142-143 N 4
Chegar Prah = Chigar Perah 150-151 CD 10
Chegga = Ash-Shaqqāt 164-165 C 3
Chegga = Shaqqah 166-167 JK 2
Chegutu 172 EF 6
Chehalis, WA 66-67 B 2
Chehalis River 66-67 B 2
Chehel-e Chashmeh, Kūhhā-ye — 136-137 M 5
Cheikh, Hassi — = Ḥāssī Shaykh 166-167 G 4
Cheikh Aḥmed = Shaykh Ahmad 136-137 J 4
Cheikh Hlâl = Shaykh Hilāl 136-137 G 5
Cheikh Ṣalâḥ = Shaykh Salāh 136-137 J 4
Cheikh Zerâfâ = Zilāf 136-137 G 6
Chējarḷā = Mellavāgu 140 D 2
Cheju 142-143 O 5
Cheju-do 142-143 NO 5
Cheju-haehyŏp 142-143 O 5
Chê-jung = Zherong 146-147 GH 8
Chekiang = Zhejiang 142-143 MN 6
Chekkā, Râs — = Rā's ash-Shikk'ah 136-137 F 5
Chela, Serra da — 172 B 5
Chelan 61 G 4
Chelan, WA 66-67 CD 2
Chelan, Lake — 66-67 C 1
Chê-lang Chiao = Zhelang Jiao 146-147 E 10
Chelforó 106-107 D 7
Cheli = Jinghong 150-151 C 2
Chélia, Djebel — = Jabal Shīlyah 164-165 F 1
Chéliff, Oued — = Shilif 166-167 G 1
Cheline 174-175 L 2
Chê-ling Kuan = Zheling Guan 142-143 L 6
Chellala = Qaṣr Shillalah 166-167 H 2
Chellala-Dahrania = Shallālāt Ḍahrāniyah 166-167 G 3
Chelle 106-107 A 7
Chelleh Khāneh, Kūh-e — 136-137 N 4
Chelles 129 I d 2
Chełm 118 L 3
Chełmińskre, Pojezierze — 118 J 2
Chelmsford [CDN] 62 L 3
Chełmża 118 J 2
Chelsea, MA 84 I b 2
Chelsea, MI 70-71 HJ 4
Chelsea, OK 76-77 G 4
Chelsea, VT 72-73 K 2-3
Chelsfield, London- 129 II c 2
Cheltenham 119 EF 6
Cheltenham, PA 72-73 J 4
Chelyabinsk = Čel'abinsk 132-133 L 6
Chema'ia, ech — = Ash-Shamā'iyah 166-167 B 3
Chemainus 66-67 AB 1
Chemawa, OR 66-67 B 3
Chemba 172 F 5
Chemehuevi Valley Indian Reservation 74-75 F 5
Chemmora = Shamūrah 166-167 K 2
Chemnitz = Karl-Marx-Stadt 118 F 3
Chemor 150-151 C 10
Chemulpo = Inch'ŏn 142-143 O 4
Chemult, OR 66-67 C 4
Chenāb 134-135 M 4
Chenab = Chanāb 138-139 C 3
Chenachane, Oued — = Wādī Shanāshīn 166-167 E 7
Chena Hot Springs, AK 58-59 OP 4
Chên-an = Zhen'an 146-147 B 5
Chena River 58-59 OP 4
Ch'ên-ch'i = Chenxi 142-143 L 6
Ch'ên-chia-chiang = Chenjiajiang 146-147 GH 4
Chên-chiang = Zhenjiang 142-143 M 5
Ch'ên-chou = Yuanling 142-143 L 6
Chencoyi 86-87 PQ 8
Chenega, AK 58-59 NO 6
Cheney, KS 68-69 H 7
Cheney, WA 66-67 E 2
Chên-fan = Minqin 142-143 J 4
Cheṅgalpeṭṭai = Chingleput 140 DE 4
Chengam 140 D 4
Chengbu 146-147 C 8
Chengcheng 146-147 BC 4
Chêng-chia-i = Zhengjiayi 146-147 C 7
Ch'êng-chiang = Chengjiang 142-143 J 7
Chengde 142-143 M 3
Chengdong Hu 146-147 F 5
Chengdu 142-143 J 5
Chenghai 146-147 F 10
Chengjiang 142-143 J 7
Chengkiang = Chengjiang 142-143 J 7
Chengkou 142-143 K 5
Chengmai 142-143 KL 8
Chêng-ning = Zhengning 146-147 B 4
Chêng-pu = Chengbu 146-147 C 8
Ch'êng-shan Chiao = Chengshan Jiao 146-147 J 3
Chengshan Jiao 146-147 J 3
Chengteh = Chengde 142-143 M 3
Chengting = Zhengding 146-147 E 2
Chengtu = Chengdu 142-143 J 5
Chengwu 146-147 E 4
Cheng-Xian = Sheng Xian 142-143 N 6
Chengxi Hu 146-147 EF 5
Chengyang 146-147 GH 7
Chengyang = Zhengyang 146-147 E 5
Chêng-yang-kuan = Zhengyangguan 146-147 F 5
Chengzitan 144-145 D 3
Chenhai = Zhenhai 146-147 H 6-7
Chên-hsi = Bar Köl 142-143 G 3
Chenik, AK 58-59 KL 7
Chenjiajiang 146-147 GH 4
Chenjiazhuang 146-147 G 3
Chenkalādi 140 E 7
Cheṅkam = Chengam 140 D 4
Chenkiang = Zhenjiang 142-143 M 5
Chennagiri = Channagiri 140 BC 3-4
Chennapaṭṭaṇam = Madras 134-135 N 8
Chennarāyapaṭṭaṇā = Channarāyapatna 140 C 4
Chennevières-sur-Marne 129 I d 2
Chêng-ho = Zhenghe 146-147 G 8
Chenoa, IL 70-71 F 5
Chenoit, le — 128 II b 2
Chenping = Zhenping 146-147 D 5
Chensi = Bar Köl 142-143 G 3
Chensi = Shanxi 142-143 L 4
Chentiin Nuruu 142-143 K 2
Chentij 142-143 L 2
Chên-t'ung = Zhentong 146-147 GH 5
Chenxi 142-143 L 6
Chen Xian 142-143 L 6
Chenyang = Shenyang 142-143 NO 3
Chenyuan = Zhenyuan [TJ, Guizhou] 146-147 B 8
Chenyuan = Zhenyuan [TJ, Yunnan] 142-143 J 7
Chên-yüan = Zhenyuan [TJ, Yunnan] 142-143 J 7
Chên-yüeh = Yiwu 150-151 C 2
Chéom Ksan 150-151 E 5
Cheops Pyramids 170 II a 2
Cheo Reo 150-151 G 6
Chepan 146-147 FG 8
Chepelmut, Lago — 108-109 F 10
Chepén 96-97 B 5
Chepes 111 C 4
Chepes, Sierra de — 106-107 D 3
Chepite, Serrania — 104-105 BC 4
Chepo 88-89 G 10
Chequamegon Bay 70-71 E 2
Cher 120-121 J 5
Chĕrammādēvī = Sermādevi 140 C 6
Cherangani 171 C 2
Cherang Ruku 150-151 D 10
Cherating, Kampung — 150-151 D 10
Cheraw, CO 68-69 E 6
Cheraw, SC 80-81 FG 3
Cherbourg 120-121 G 4
Cherchar = Sharshar 166-167 K 2
Cherchell = Shirshāll 166-167 GH 1
Cherchen = Chārchān 142-143 F 4
Cheremkhovo = Čeremchovo 132-133 T 7
Cheren = Keren 164-165 M 5
Cherepon 168-169 EF 3
Chergui, Chott ech — = Ash-Shaṭṭ ash-Sharqī 164-165 DE 2
Chergui, Île — = Jazīrat ash-Sharqī 166-167 M 2
Cheribon = Cirebon 148-149 E 8
Cheriyam Island 140 AB 5
Cherkassi = Čerkassy 126-127 EF 2
Cherlen gol 142-143 KL 2
Cherlen gol = Herlen He 142-143 M 2
Chernabura Island 58-59 d 2
Chernigov = Černigov 126-127 E 1
Chernogorsk = Černogorsk 132-133 R 7
Chernovtsy = Černovcy 126-127 B 2
Cherokee, IA 70-71 C 4
Cherokee, OK 76-77 E 4
Cherokee, TX 76-77 E 7
Cherokee Lake 80-81 E 2
Cherque, Cordón del — 108-109 D 5
Cherquenco 106-107 AB 7
Cherrapunj = Cherrāpuṅji 134-135 P 5
Cherrapunji 134-135 P 5
Cherry 158-159 N 2
Cherry Creek 68-69 E 3
Cherry Creek, NV 74-75 F 3
Cherry Creek, SD 68-69 F 3
Cherrydale, Arlington-, VA 82 II a 2
Cherry Hill, NJ 84 III c 2
Cherry Hill Mall 84 III c 2
Cherrypatch Ridge 68-69 B 1
Cherryvale, KS 76-77 G 4
Cherryville 60 H 4
Cherskogo Mountains = chrebet Čerskogo 132-133 a 4-c 5
Cherso = Cres 122-123 F 3
Cherson [SU] 126-127 F 3
Chersonesskij, mys — 126-127 F 4
Chertsey 129 II a 2
Chesaning, MI 70-71 HJ 4
Chesapeake, VA 64-65 LM 4
Chesapeake Bay 64-65 L 4
Cheshire, OR 66-67 B 3
Cheshskaya Bay = Čošskaja guba 132-133 H 4
Chesley 72-73 F 2
Chesnay, le — 129 I b 2
Chessington, London- 129 II a 2
Chester, CA 66-67 C 5
Chester, IL 70-71 F 7
Chester, MT 66-67 H 1
Chester, NE 68-69 H 5
Chester, PA 72-73 J 5
Chester, SC 80-81 F 3
Chester [CDN] 63 D 5
Chester [GB] 119 E 5
Chesterbrook, VA 82 II a 2
Chesterfield 119 F 5
Chesterfield, Île — 172 H 5
Chesterfield, Îles — 158-159 L 3
Chesterfield Inlet [CDN, bay] 56-57 ST 5
Chesterfield Inlet [CDN, place] 56-57 ST 5
Chester Island 84 III a 3
Chestertown, MD 72-73 HJ 5
Chestnut Hill, MA 84 I ab 3
Chestnut Hill, Philadelphia-, PA 84 III b 1
Chestnut Hill Reservoir 84 I a 2
Chesuncook Lake 72-73 LM 1
Cheta [SU, place] 132-133 S 3
Cheta [SU, river] 132-133 S 3
Chetek, WI 70-71 E 3
Chéticamp 63 F 4
Chetlat Island 134-135 L 8
Chetopa, KS 76-77 G 4
Chetput 140 D 4
Chetumal 64-65 J 8
Chetumal, Bahía de — 64-65 J 8
Chetwynd 60 FG 2
Cheung Chau 155 I a 2
Cheung Kwan O 155 I b 2
Chevak, AK 58-59 E 6
Chevejecure 104-105 CD 4
Chevejecure, Río — 104-105 C 4
Cheverly, MD 82 II b 1
Chevilly-Larue 129 I c 2
Cheviot, The — 119 EF 4
Cheviot Hills 119 E 4
Chevreuse 129 I b 3
Chevry-Cossigny 129 I d 3
Chevy Chase, MD 82 II a 1
Chewelah, WA 66-67 DE 1
Chews Landing, NJ 84 III c 3
Chê-yang = Zherong 146-147 GH 8
Cheyenne, OK 76-77 E 5
Cheyenne, TX 76-77 C 7
Cheyenne, WY 64-65 F 3
Cheyenne Pass 68-69 D 5
Cheyenne River 64-65 F 3
Cheyenne River Indian Reservation 68-69 F 3
Cheyenne Wells, CO 68-69 E 6
Cheyūr 140 E 4
Cheyyar 140 D 4
Cheyyūr = Cheyūr 140 E 4
Chezacut 60 EF 3
Chhabaṛā = Chhabra 138-139 F 5
Chhabra 138-139 F 5
Chhachhrauli 138-139 F 2
Chhagtag Tsangpo 138-139 K 3
Chhamārchī 138-139 M 4
Chhamdo 142-143 H 5
Chhaprā = Chāpra 134-135 N 5
Chhārīkār = Chārikār 134-135 K 3-4
Chharpa Gonpa 138-139 H 2
Chhāta 138-139 F 4
Chhātak 141 B 3
Chhatarpur [IND, Bihār] 138-139 K 5
Chhatarpur [IND, Madhya Pradesh] 134-135 M 6
Chhatrapura = Chatrapur 138-139 K 8
Chhattīsgarh 134-135 N 6
Chhep 150-151 E 6
Chherang 138-139 N 4
Chherchhen 138-139 H 2
Chhergo La 138-139 H 2
Chhergundo 142-143 H 5
Chhergundo Zhou = Yushu Zangzu Zizhizhou 142-143 GH 5
Chhibchang Tsho 142-143 G 5
Chhibrāmau 138-139 G 4
Chhibro 138-139 HJ 3
Chhikhum 138-139 J 3
Chhindvāṛā = Chhindwāra [IND ↙ Jabalpur] 138-139 G 6
Chhindvāṛā = Chhindwāra [IND ← Seoni] 134-135 M 6
Chhindwāra [IND ↙ Jabalpur] 138-139 G 6
Chhindwāra [IND ← Seoni] 134-135 M 6
Chhinī 138-139 A 4
Chhinnamanūr = Chinnamanūr 140 C 6
Chhinnasēlam = Chinna Salem 140 D 5
Chhitāuni 138-139 J 4
Chhlong 150-151 EF 6
Chhōra Gonpa 138-139 M 2
Chhōṭā Andamān = Little Andaman 134-135 P 8
Chhōṭā Nikōbār = Little Nicobar 134-135 P 9
Chhota Udaipur 138-139 DE 6
Chhōṭā Udaypur = Chhota Udaipur 138-139 DE 6
Chhotī Sādri 138-139 E 5
Chhudrari 138-139 L 2
Chhudun Tsho 138-139 MN 2
Chhuīkhadān 138-139 H 7
Chhukor 138-139 L 3
Chhumar 142-143 G 4-5
Chhumbi 138-139 M 4
Chhumbong 138-139 L 3
Chhundu 138-139 L 3
Chhushul 142-143 FG 6
Chi, Lam — 150-151 D 5
Chi, Nam — 150-151 DE 5
Chía 94-95 DE 5
Chiachi Island 58-59 d 2
Chiadma, ech — = Ash-Shiādmā' 166-167 B 4
Chia-ho = Jiahe 146-147 D 9
Chia-hsien = Jia Xian [TJ, Henan] 146-147 D 5
Chia-hsien = Jia Xian [TJ, Shanxi] 146-147 C 2
Chia-hsing = Jiaxing 142-143 N 5
Chia-i 142-143 MN 7
Chia Keng 154 III b 1
Chiali 146-147 GH 10
Chia-li = Lharugö 142-143 G 5
Chia-li-chuang = Chiali 146-147 GH 10
Chia-ling Chiang = Jialing Jiang 142-143 K 5
Chia-lu Ho = Jialu He 146-147 E 4
Chia-mu-szŭ = Jiamusi 142-143 P 2
Chi-an = Ji'an [TJ, Jiangxi] 142-143 LM 6
Chi-an = Ji'an [TJ, Jilin] 144-145 EF 2
Chiang-chou = Xinjiang 142-143 L 4
Chiang Dao 148-149 CD 3
Chiange 172 B 5
Chiang-hsi = Jiangxi 142-143 LM 6
Chiang-hung = Jianghong 146-147 B 11
Chiangir, İstanbul- 154 I ab 2
Chiang Kham 150-151 BC 3
Chiang Khan 148-149 D 3
Chiang Khong 150-151 C 2
Chiang-k'ou = Jiangkou [TJ, Guangxi Zhuangzu Zizhiqu] 146-147 C 10
Chiang-k'ou = Jiangkou [TJ, Guizhou] 146-147 B 8
Chiang Krai, Lam — 150-151 C 5
Chiang-ling = Jiangling 146-147 CD 6
Chiang-lo = Jiangle 146-147 F 8
Chiang Mai 148-149 C 3
Chiang-mên = Xinhui 146-147 D 10
Chiang Muan 150-151 C 3
Chiang-ning-chên = Jiangning 146-147 G 6
Chiang-p'u = Jiangpu 146-147 G 5
Chiang Rai 148-149 CD 3
Chiang Saen 150-151 BC 2
Chiang-shan = Jiangshan 146-147 G 7
Chiang-su = Jiangsu 142-143 MN 5
Chiang-yin = Jiangyin 146-147 H 6
Chiao-chou Wan = Jiaozhou Wan 146-147 H 3-4
Chiao-ho-k'ou = Jiaohekou 146-147 B 4
Chiao-ling = Jiaoling 146-147 EF 9
Chiapa, Río — = Río Grande 64-65 H 8
Chiapas 64-65 H 8
Chiari 122-123 CD 3
Chia-shan = Jiashan [TJ, Anhui] 146-147 G 5
Chia-shan = Jiashan [TJ, Zhejiang] 146-147 H 6
Chia-ting = Jiading 146-147 H 6
Chiau 174-175 K 3
Chi-aün Ho = Jiyun He 146-147 F 2
Chiàvari 122-123 C 3
Chiavenna 122-123 C 2
Chiayi 142-143 MN 7
Chia-yü = Jiayu 146-147 D 6-7
Chiba 144-145 N 5
Chibabava 172 F 6
Chibata, Serra da — 100-101 D 10-11
Chibemba 172 BC 5
Chibia 172 B 5
Chibinogorsk = Kirovsk 132-133 EF 4
Chibougamau 56-57 VW 7-8
Chibougamau, Lac — 62 OP 2
Chibougamau, la Réserve de — 62 OP 2
Chiburi-jima 144-145 J 5
Chibuto 172 F 6
Chica, Costa — 86-87 L 9
Chicacole = Shrīkākulam 134-135 N 7
Chicago, IL 64-65 J 3
Chicago, University of — 83 II b 2
Chicago-Albany Park, IL 83 II a 1
Chicago-Ashburn, IL 83 II a 2
Chicago-Austin, IL 83 II a 1
Chicago-Avondale, IL 83 II b 1
Chicago-Belmont Cragin, IL 83 II a 1
Chicago-Beverly, IL 83 II ab 2
Chicago-Bridgeport, IL 83 II b 1
Chicago-Brighton Park, IL 83 II a 2
Chicago Campus = Northwestern University 83 II b 1
Chicago-Chatham, IL 83 II b 2
Chicago-Chicago Lawn, IL 83 II a 2
Chicago-Dunning, IL 83 II b 1
Chicago-Englewood, IL 83 II b 2
Chicago-Evergreen Plaza, IL 83 II ab 2
Chicago-Ford City, IL 83 II a 2
Chicago-Gage Park, IL 83 II a 2
Chicago Heights, IL 70-71 G 5
Chicago-Hyde Park, IL 83 II b 2
Chicago-Irving Park, IL 83 II b 1
Chicago-Jefferson Park, IL 83 II a 1
Chicago-Lakeview, IL 83 II ab 1
Chicago Lawn, Chicago-, IL 83 II a 2
Chicago-Lawndale, IL 83 II a 1
Chicago-Logan Square, IL 83 II a 1
Chicago-Loop, IL 83 II b 1
Chicago Midway Airport 83 II a 2
Chicago-Morgan Park, IL 83 II ab 2
Chicago-Mount Greenwood, IL 83 II a 2
Chicago-Near North Side, IL 83 II b 1
Chicago-North Park, IL 83 II a 1
Chicago-Norwood Park, IL 83 II a 1
Chicago-Portage Park, IL 83 II b 1
Chicago Ridge, IL 83 II a 2
Chicago-Roseland, IL 83 II b 2
Chicago Sanitary and Ship Canal 83 II a 1-2
Chicago-South Chicago, IL 83 II b 2
Chicago-South Shore, IL 83 II b 2
Chicago Stadium 83 II a 1
Chicago State University 83 II b 2
Chicago-Uptown, IL 83 II ab 1
Chicago-West Pullman, IL 83 II b 2
Chicago-Woodlawn, IL 83 II b 2
Chical-Có 106-107 CD 6
Chicama 96-97 B 5
Chicama, Río — 96-97 B 5
Chicapa, Rio — 172 D 3
Chic-Choqs, Monts — 56-57 X 8
Ch'i-ch = Qiqihar 142-143 N 2
Chichagof, AK 58-59 T 8
Chichagof, Cape — 58-59 HJ 7
Chichagof Island 56-57 J 6
Chichancanab, Laguna — 86-87 Q 8
Chīchāoua = Shishāwah 166-167 B 4
Chīchāwatnī 138-139 D 2
Chiché, Rio — 98-99 LM 9
Chichén Itzá 64-65 J 7
Chichester 119 F 6
Chi-ch'i = Jixi 146-147 G 6
Chichicaspa 91 I b 2
Chichinales 106-107 D 7
Chichiriviche 94-95 GH 2
Chichocane 174-175 L 2
Chichola 138-139 H 7
Chicholi 138-139 F 6
Chichot 138-139 F 2
Ch'i-chou Tao = Qizhou Liedao 150-151 H 3
Chickaloon, AK 58-59 NO 6
Chickamauga, GA 78-79 G 3
Chickamauga Lake 78-79 G 3
Chickasaw, AL 78-79 EF 5
Chickasha, OK 64-65 G 4-5
Chicken, AK 58-59 QR 4
Chiclana 106-107 G 5
Chiclayo 92-93 CD 6
Chico, CA 64-65 B 4
Chico, TX 76-77 F 6
Chico, Río — [RA, Chubut] 111 C 6
Chico, Río — [RA, Santa Cruz ◁ Bahía Grande] 111 C 7
Chico, Río — [RA, Santa Cruz ◁ Río Gallegos] 111 C 7
Chico, Río — [YV] 92-93 F 2
Chicoa 172 F 5
Chicoana 111 CD 3
Chicoma Peak = Tschicoma Peak 76-77 AB 4
Chicomo 174-175 KL 3
Chiconomo 171 CD 6
Chicontepec de Tejeda 86-87 LM 7
Chicopee, MA 72-73 K 3
Chicotte 63 E 3
Chicoutimi 56-57 WX 8
Chicuaco, Laguna — 94-95 G 6
Chicualacuala 174-175 JK 2
Chidambaram 140 DE 5
Chidenguele 174-175 L 3
Chidester, AR 78-79 C 4
Chidley, Cape — 56-57 Y 5
Chi-do 144-145 EF 5
Chiefland, FL 80-81 b 2
Chiefs Point 72-73 F 2
Chieh-hsiu = Jiexiu 146-147 CD 3
Chiehmo = Chārchān 142-143 F 4
Chieh-shih = Jieshi 146-147 E 10
Chieh-shih Wan = Jieshi Wan 146-147 E 10
Chieh-shou = Jieshou 146-147 E 5
Chieh-yang = Jieyang 146-147 F 10
Chiêm Hoa 150-151 E 1
Chiemsee 118 F 5
Ch'i en-an = Qian'an 146-147 G 1
Chien-ch'ang = Jianchang [TJ → Benxi] 144-145 E 2
Chien-ch'ang = Jianchang [TJ ↙ Jinzhou] 144-145 B 2
Chien-ch'ang = Nancheng 146-147 F 8
Chien-ch'ang-ying = Jianchangying 146-147 G 1
Ch'ien-chi = Qianji 146-147 G 4-5
Ch'ien-chiang = Qianjiang [TJ, Guangxi Zhuangzu Zizhiqu] 146-147 B 10
Ch'ien-chiang = Qianjiang [TJ, Hubei] 142-143 L 5
Ch'ien-chiang = Qianjiang [TJ, Sichuan] 146-147 B 7
Chiengi 172 E 3
Chieng Kong = Chiang Khong 150-151 C 2
Chiengmai = Chiang Mai 148-149 C 3
Chien-ho = Jianhe [TJ, place] 146-147 B 8
Chien-Ho = Jian He [TJ, river] 144-145 D 2
Ch'ien-hsi = Qianxi 146-147 G 1
Ch'ien-hsien = Qian Xian 146-147 B 4
Chien-ko = Jiange 142-143 JK 5
Chien-li = Jianli 146-147 D 7
Chien-ning = Jianning 146-147 F 8
Chien-ning = Jian'ou 142-143 M 6
Chien-ou = Jian'ou 142-143 M 6
Chien-p'ing = Jianping 144-145 B 2
Chien-p'ing = Langxi 146-147 G 6
Ch'ien-shan = Qianshan 146-147 F 6
Chien-shui = Jianshui 142-143 J 7
Chien-tê = Jiande 146-147 G 7
Ch'ien-wei = Qianwei 144-145 C 2
Chien-yang = Jianyang [TJ, Fujian] 146-147 FG 8
Chien-yang = Jianyang [TJ, Sichuan] 142-143 JK 5
Ch'ien-yang = Qianyang 146-147 C 8
Ch'ien-yu Ho = Qianyou He 146-147 B 5
Chieti 122-123 F 4
Chifeng 142-143 M 3
Chifre, Serra do — 92-93 L 8
Chiftak, AK 58-59 EF 6
Chigar Perah 150-151 CD 10
Chiginagak, Mount — 58-59 e 1
Chigmit Mountains 58-59 L 6
Chignecto Bay 63 D 5
Chignik, AK 56-57 E 6
Chignik Lake 58-59 de 1
Chigorodó 94-95 C 4
Chigu 138-139 L 3
Chigualoco 106-107 B 3
Chiguana 104-105 BC 7
Chiguana, Salar de — 104-105 C 7
Chiguao, Punta — 108-109 C 4
Chiguaza 96-97 C 2
Chigubo 174-175 K 2
Chigwell 129 II c 1
Chigyŏng 144-145 F 3
Ch'ih-ch'i = Chixi 146-147 D 10-11
Chih-chiang = Zhijiang [TJ, Hubei] 146-147 C 6
Chih-chiang = Zhijiang [TJ, Hunan] 142-143 KL 6
Chihe 146-147 FG 5
Ch'ih-fêng = Chifeng 142-143 M 3
Chih-fu = Yantai 142-143 N 4
Ch'ih-ho = Chihe 146-147 FG 5
Ch'ih-k'an = Chikan 146-147 C 11
Chihkiang = Zhijiang 142-143 KL 6
Chih-li Wan = Bo Hai 142-143 M 4
Chi-hsi = Jixi 142-143 P 2
Chi-hsien = Ji Xian [TJ, Hebei → Beijing] 146-147 F 1
Chi-hsien = Ji Xian [TJ, Hebei ↘ Shijiazhuang] 146-147 E 3
Chi-hsien = Ji Xian [TJ, Henan] 146-147 E 4
Chi-hsien = Ji Xian [TJ, Shanxi] 146-147 C 3
Ch'i-hsien = Qi Xian [TJ, Henan ↘ Kaifeng] 146-147 E 4
Ch'i-hsien = Qi Xian [TJ, Henan ↗ Xinxiang] 146-147 DE 4
Ch'i-hsien = Qi Xian [TJ, Shanxi] 146-147 D 3
Chihtan = Zhidan 146-147 B 3
Chihu 146-147 H 9-10
Chihuahua 64-65 E 6
Ch'i-i = Qiyi 146-147 D 5
Chiingij gol 142-143 GH 2
Chii-san = Chiri-san 144-145 F 5
Chikalda 138-139 F 7
Chikan 146-147 C 11
Chik Chu Wan 155 I b 2
Chike = Xunke 142-143 O 2
Chikhalī = Chikhli 138-139 F 7
Chikhli [IND, Gujarāt] 138-139 D 7
Chikhli [IND, Mahārāshtra] 138-139 F 7
Chikjājūr 140 BC 3
Chikkai = Chixi 146-147 D 10-11
Chikkamagaḷūru = Chikmagalūr 140 B 4
Chikkanāyakanahaḷḷi = Chiknayakanhalli 140 C 4
Chikmagalūr 140 B 4
Chiknayakanhalli 140 C 4
Chikodi 140 B 2
Chikrang, Stung — 150-151 E 6
Chikreng = Kompong Chikreng 150-151 E 6
Chikugo 144-145 H 6
Chikuminuk Lake 58-59 HJ 6
Chikwawa 172 FG 5
Chilako River 60 F 3
Chilapa de Alvarez 64-65 G 8
Chilās 134-135 L 3
Chilaw = Halāwata 140 D 7
Chilca 92-93 D 7
Chilca, Cordillera de — 96-97 EF 9
Chilca Juliana 106-107 F 2
Chilcoot, CA 74-75 CD 3
Chilcotin River 60 F 3-4
Childersburg, AL 78-79 F 4
Childress, TX 76-77 DE 5
Chile 111 B 5-C 2
Chile Basin 156-157 O 5-6
Chile Chico 108-109 D 6
Chilecito [RA, La Rioja] 111 C 3
Chilecito [RA, Mendoza] 106-107 C 4
Chileno 106-107 K 4
Chilete 92-93 D 6
Chilete, Río — 96-97 B 5
Chilhowee, MO 70-71 D 6
Chilia, Bratul — 122-123 N 3
Chilibre 64-65 b 2
Ch'i-li-chên = Qilizhen 146-147 B 4
Chilicote 76-77 B 8
Ch'i-lien Shan = Qilian Shan 142-143 HJ 4
Chilikadrotna River 58-59 K 6
Chilikā Hrada = Chilka Lake 134-135 NO 7
Chililabombwe 172 E 4
Chi-lin = Jilin [TJ, administrative unit] 142-143 N 2-O 3
Chi-lin = Jilin [TJ, place] 142-143 O 3
Chilivani 122-123 C 5
Chilka Lake 134-135 NO 7
Chilk Ballāpur 140 CD 4
Chilko Lake 56-57 M 7
Chillán 111 B 5
Chillán, Nevados de — 106-107 B 6
Chillanes 96-97 B 2
Chillar 106-107 H 6
Chill Chainnigh = Kilkenny 119 C 5
Chillicothe, IL 70-71 F 5
Chillicothe, MO 64-65 H 3-4
Chillicothe, OH 64-65 K 4
Chillicothe, TX 76-77 E 5
Chilliwack 66-67 C 1
Chillón, Río — 96-97 C 7
Chillum, MD 82 II b 1
Chilly 126-127 O 7
Chilly, ID 66-67 FG 3
Chiloé, Isla de — 111 AB 6
Chilok 132-133 UV 7
Chilonga 171 B 5-6
Chilongozi 171 BC 6
Chiloquin, OR 66-67 C 4
Chilpancingo de los Bravos 64-65 G 8
Chilpi 138-139 H 6
Chiltern Hills 119 F 6
Chilton, WI 70-71 F 3
Chilung 142-143 N 6
Chilwa, Lake — 172 G 5
Chima 94-95 E 4
Chiman 88-89 G 10
Chimanas, Islas — 94-95 J 2
Chiman tagh 142-143 FG 4
Chimbas 106-107 C 3
Chimbero 104-105 AB 10
Chimborazo [EC, administrative unit] 96-97 B 2-3
Chimborazo [EC, mountain] 92-93 D 5
Chimborazo [YV] 94-95 J 3
Chimbote 92-93 D 6
Chimei Hsü 146-147 G 10
Ch'i-mên = Qimen 146-147 F 7
Chimeo 104-105 E 7
Chimichagua 94-95 DE 3
Chi-ming-ho = Jiminghe 146-147 E 6
Chimkent = Čimkent 132-133 M 9
Chimki 124-125 L 5-6
Chimki-Chovrino, Moskva- 113 V b 2
Chimkinskoje vodochranilišče 113 V b 2
Chimney Peak = One Tree Peak 76-77 B 6
Chi-mo = Jimo 146-147 H 3
Chimoio 172 F 5
Chimpay 111 C 5
Chimpembe 171 B 5

Chimpemb 279

Chung-hsin-hsü = Zhongxin 146-147 E 9
Chunghwa 144-145 EF 3
Ch'ung-i = Chongyi 146-147 E 9
Ch'ung-jên = Chongren 146-147 EF 8
Ch'ungju 144-145 FG 4
Chungking = Chongqing 142-143 K 6
Chungli 146-147 H 9
Ch'ung-ming = Chongming 142-143 N 5
Ch'ung-ming Tao = Chongming Dao 146-147 HJ 6
Chung-mou = Zhongmou 146-147 DE 4
Ch'ungmu 144-145 G 5
Chung-pu = Huangling 146-147 B 4
Chŭngsan 144-145 E 3
Chungshan = Zhongshan 142-143 L 7
Chungsiang = Zhongxiang 146-147 D 6
Chung-t'iao Shan = Zhongtiao Shan 146-147 CD 4
Chung-tien = Zhongdian 142-143 HJ 6
Chung-tu = Zhongdu 146-147 B 9
Chungui 96-97 E 8
Chŭngŭj gol 142-143 GH 2
Chung Wan, Kowloon- 155 I a 1
Chung-wei = Zhongwei 142-143 JK 4
Ch'ung-wu = Chongwu 146-147 G 9
Chungyang = Chongyang 146-147 E 7
Chungyang Shanmo 142-143 N 7
Chün-hsien = Jun Xian 146-147 C 5
Chunhua 146-147 B 4
Chunian = Chūniyān 138-139 DE 2
Chūniyān 138-139 DE 2
Chunu, Cape — 58-59 u 7
Chunya 172 F 3
Chunzach 126-127 N 5
Chūō, Tōkyō- 155 III b 1
Chupadera, Mesa — 76-77 A 5-6
Chupán 96-97 C 6
Ch'ü-qu = Quwo 146-147 C 4
Chuquibamba 92-93 E 8
Chuquibambilla 96-97 E 9
Chuquicamata 111 C 2
Chuquichuqui 104-105 D 6
Chuquisaca 104-105 D 6-E 7
Chuquisaca = Sucre 92-93 FG 8
Chur 118 D 5
Churāchāndpur 141 C 3
Churchill, ID 66-67 FG 4
Churchill [CDN] 56-57 RS 6
Churchill [ROU] 106-107 JK 4
Churchill, Cape — 56-57 S 6
Churchill Falls 56-57 XY 7
Churchill Lake 61 DE 2-3
Churchill Peak 56-57 LM 6
Churchill River [CDN ◁ Hamilton Inlet] 56-57 Y 7
Churchill River [CDN ◁ Hudson Bay] 56-57 RS 6
Church Point, LA 78-79 CD 5
Churchs Ferry, ND 68-69 G 1
Chureo, Paso de — 106-107 B 6
Churk 138-139 J 5
Churu 134-135 LM 5
Churubusco, Coyoacán- 91 I c 2
Churuguara 94-95 G 2
Chusei-hokudō = Ch'ungch'ŏng-pukto 144-145 FG 4
Chusei-nandō = Ch'ungch'ŏng-namdo 144-145 F 4
Ch'ü Shan = Daqu Shan 146-147 J 6
Chu-shan = Zhushan 142-143 KL 5
Chusistan = Khūzestān 134-135 F 4
Chuska Mountains 74-75 J 4-5
Chusmisa 104-105 B 6
Chust 126-127 A 2
Chutag 142-143 J 2
Chu-t'an = Zhutan 146-147 E 7
Chute-aux-Outardes 63 BC 3
Chute-des-Passes 63 A 3
Chutes François Joseph 172 C 3
Chutes Rusumu 171 B 3
Chutes Tshungu 172 DE 1
Chutes Wissmann 172 CD 3
Chutes Wolff 172 D 3
Chu-t'ing = Zhuting 146-147 D 8
Chutorskoj 126-127 L 5
Chutung 146-147 H 9
Ch'ü-tzŭ-chên = Quzi 146-147 A 3
Chuučnar 142-143 G 5
Chuŭronjang 144-145 GH 2
Chuvash Autonomous Soviet Socialist Republic = 4 ◁ 132-133 H 6
Chuwārtah 136-137 L 5
Chu Xian 146-147 FG 5
Chuxiong 142-143 J 7
Chuxiong Yizu Zizhizhou 142-143 J 6
Chuxiong Zizhizhou 142-143 J 6
Chuy 111 F 4
Ch'ü-yang = Quyang [TJ, Hebei] 146-147 E 2
Ch'ü-yang = Quyang [TJ, Jiangxi] 146-147 E 8
Chu Yang Sin 148-149 E 4
Chü-yeh = Juye 146-147 F 4
Chužir 132-133 U 7
Chvalynsk 124-125 QR 7
Chvatovka 124-125 Q 7
Chvojnaja 124-125 K 4
Chwansha = Chuansha 146-147 HJ 6
Chwārta = Chuwārtah 136-137 L 5
Chye Kay 154 III a 1
Ciampino, Aeroporto di — 113 II bc 2
Ciampino, Roma- 113 II c 2
Cianjur 152-153 G 9
Cianorte 102-103 F 5
Čiatura 126-127 L 5
Čibit 132-133 Q 7
Čibju = Uchta 124-125 T 2
Cibola, AZ 74-75 F 6
Cibuta 74-75 H 7
Çiçekdağı 136-137 F 3
Cicero, IL 70-71 G 5
Cícero Dantas 92-93 M 7
Čichač'ovo 124-125 GH 5
Čičikleja 126-127 E 3
Cidade Brasil, Guarulhos- 110 II b 1
Cidade de Deus, Rio de Janeiro- 110 I ab 2
Cidade Universitária [BR, Rio de Janeiro] 110 I b 2
Cidade Universitária [BR, São Paulo] 110 II a 2
Cide 136-137 E 2
Cidreira 106-107 MN 3
Ciechanów 118 K 2
Ciego de Ávila 64-65 L 7
Ciénaga 92-93 DE 2
Ciénaga de Ayapel 94-95 D 3
Ciénaga de Oro 94-95 D 3
Ciénaga de Zapatosa 94-95 E 3
Ciénaga Grande 94-95 D 3
Ciénaga Grande de Santa Marta 94-95 DE 2
Ciénage La Raya 94-95 D 3
Cienega, NM 76-77 B 6
Cienfuegos 64-65 K 7
Cieza 120-121 G 9
Çiftalan 154 I a 1
Çifteler 136-137 D 3
Çiftlik [TR, Gümüşane] 136-137 H 2
Çiftlik [TR, Sivas] 136-137 G 2
Cifuentes 120-121 F 8
Čiganak 132-133 N 8-9
Çiğli 136-137 K 4
Cihanbeyli = İnevi 136-137 E 3
Cihanbeyli yaylâsı 136-137 E 3
Cihuatlán 86-87 H 8
Čiili 132-133 M 9
Cijara, Embalse de — 120-121 E 9
Cijulang 152-153 H 9
Cikampek 152-153 G 9
Čikola 126-127 L 5
Cikuray, Gunung — 152-153 G 9
Cilacap 148-149 E 8
Cilandak, Jakarta- 154 IV a 2
Cilauteureun 152-153 G 9
Çıldır = Zurzuna 136-137 K 2
Çıldır gölü 136-137 K 2
Ciledug 152-153 H 9
Cili 146-147 C 7
Cililitan, Jakarta- 154 IV b 2
Cilincing, Jakarta- 154 IV b 1
Ci Liwung 154 IV a 1
Cilo dağı 136-137 KL 4
Cima, CA 74-75 F 5
Cima da Serra, Campos de — 106-107 M 2
Cimaltepec 64-65 G 8
Cimarron, KS 68-69 FG 7
Cimarron, NM 76-77 B 4
Cimarron River, North Fork — 76-77 D 4
Čimbaj 132-133 KL 9
Çimen dağı 136-137 H 3
Cimiring, Tanjung — 152-153 H 9-10
Čimkent 132-133 M 9
Ciml'ansk 126-127 KL 3
Ciml'anskoje vodochranilišče 126-127 L 2-3
Cimmarron River 64-65 F 4
Cimone, Monte — 122-123 D 3
Cîmpina 122-123 LM 3
Cîmpulung 122-123 L 3
Cîmpulung Moldovenesc 122-123 LM 2
Cinandali 126-127 M 6
Çınar = Akpınar 136-137 J 4
Cinaruco, Río — 94-95 G 4
Cinca 120-121 H 8
Cincinnati, OH 64-65 K 4
Cinco Chañares 108-109 G 3
Cinco de Maio, Cachoeira — 98-99 L 11
Cinco Saltos 106-107 CD 7
Cinderella 170 V c 2
Cinderella Dam 170 V c 2
Cinder River 58-59 de 1
Çine 136-137 BC 4
Cinecittà, Roma- 113 II bc 2
Cinema 60 FG 3
Cingaly 132-133 MN 5
Cinnabar Mountain 66-67 E 4
Cinta, Serra da — 92-93 K 6
Cintalapa de Figueroa 86-87 NO 9
Cinto, Mont — 122-123 C 4
Cintra 106-107 F 4
Cintra = Sintra [BR] 92-93 G 6
Ciotat, la — 120-121 K 7
Čiovo 122-123 G 4
Cipete, Jakarta- 154 IV a 2
Cipikan 132-133 V 7
Ci Pinang 154 IV b 2
Cipó 92-93 M 7
Cipó, Rio — 102-103 L 3
Cipó, Serra do — 102-103 L 3
Cipolletti 106-107 D 7
Ciputat 154 IV a 2
Čir 126-127 L 2
Ciragidzor 126-127 N 6
Circel Campus = University of Illinois 83 II ab 1
Circeo, Monte — 122-123 E 5
Čirčik 132-133 M 9
Circle, AK 56-57 H 4
Circle, MT 68-69 D 2
Circle Cliffs 74-75 H 4
Circle Hot Springs, AK 58-59 PQ 4
Circleville, OH 72-73 E 5
Circleville, UT 74-75 G 3
Circuata 104-105 C 5
Cirebon 148-149 E 8
Cirenaica = Barqah 164-165 J 2
Cirene = Shaḥḥāt 164-165 J 2
Cirí, Río — 64-65 a 3
Cirò Marina 122-123 G 6
Čirpan 122-123 L 4
Cirque, Cerro — 104-105 B 5
Cisa, Passo della — 122-123 CD 3
Cisco, TX 76-77 E 6
Cisco, UT 74-75 J 3
Cisne, IL 70-71 F 6
Cisne, El — 106-107 G 3
Cisne, Ilhas del — = Swan Islands 64-65 K 8
Cisne, Laguna del — 106-107 FG 2
Cisneros 92-93 DE 3
Cisnes, Laguna de los — 108-109 D 6
Cisnes, Los — 106-107 F 4
Cisnes, Río — 108-109 D 5
Čist'akovo = Thorez 126-127 J 2-3
Cisterna di Latina 122-123 E 5
Cisternino 122-123 G 5
Čistopol' 132-133 HJ 6
Čita 132-133 V 7
Cita, La — 91 III c 1
Čita-Černovskije Kopi 132-133 V 7
Citadelle, La — 88-89 K 5
Citadel of Cairo 170 II b 1
Čitajevo 124-125 R 3
Ci Tanduy 152-153 H 9
Citaré, Rio — 98-99 L 4
Ci Tarum 152-153 G 9
Citeli-Ckaro 126-127 MN 6
Cité Militaire 170 I b 2
Citlaltépetl 64-65 G 8
Citra, FL 80-81 bc 2
Citronelle, AL 78-79 E 5
Citrusdal 172 CD 8
Citrus Height, CA 74-75 C 3
Citrus Heights, CA 64-65 B 4
Cittanova 122-123 FG 6
Città Universitaria 113 II b 2
City County Building 84 II b 2
City Gardens, Houston-, TX 85 III b 1
City Hall [CDN] 84 II b 3
City Hall [USA] 84 III bc 2
City Island 82 III d 1
City of Commerce, CA 83 III d 1-2
City Park 85 I b 1-2
Ciucaş 122-123 LM 3
Ciuciulco, Pirámide de — 91 I b 3
Ciudad Altamirano 86-87 K 8
Ciudad Bolívar 92-93 G 3
Ciudad Bolivia 92-93 E 3
Ciudad Camargo 76-77 E 9
Ciudad Camargo = Camargo 64-65 E 6
Ciudad Cancún 86-87 R 7
Ciudad del Carmen 64-65 H 8
Ciudad Delicias = Delicias 64-65 E 6
Ciudad del Maíz 86-87 L 6
Ciudad de los Deportes 91 I bc 2
Ciudad de México-Benito Juárez 91 I bc 2
Ciudad de México-Cuauhtémoc 91 I c 2
Ciudad de México-Cuautepec de Madero 91 I c 1
Ciudad de México-Cuautepec el Alto 91 I c 1
Ciudad de México-Gustavo A. Madero 91 I c 2
Ciudad de México-Héroes Chapultepec 91 I c 2
Ciudad de México-Jardín Balbuena 91 I c 2
Ciudad de México-Juan González Romero 91 I c 2
Ciudad de México-Lomas Chapultepec 91 I b 2
Ciudad de México-Miguel Hidalgo 91 I b 2
Ciudad de México-Morelos 91 I c 2
Ciudad de México-Nueva Atzacoalco 91 I c 2
Ciudad de México-Piedad Narvarte 91 I c 2
Ciudad de México-San Felipe de Jesús 91 I c 2
Ciudad de México-San Juan de Aragón 91 I c 2
Ciudad de México-San Petro Zacatenco 91 I c 1
Ciudad de México-Tacuba 91 I b 2
Ciudad de México-Tacubaya 91 I b 2
Ciudad de México-Ticomán 91 I c 1
Ciudad de México-Venustiano Carranza 91 I c 2
Ciudad de Naucalpan de Juárez 91 I b 2
Ciudad Deportiva 91 I c 2
Ciudadela 120-121 J 8-9
Ciudadela, Tres de Febrero- 110 III b 1
Ciudad General Belgrano, La Matanza- 110 III b 2
Ciudad Guayana 92-93 G 3
Ciudad Guayana-Puerto Ordaz 92-93 G 3
Ciudad Guerrero 86-87 G 3
Ciudad Guzmán 64-65 F 8
Ciudad Hidalgo 86-87 K 8
Ciudad Jardín, Coyoacán- 91 I c 3
Ciudad Juárez = Juárez 64-65 E 5
Ciudad Lerdo 64-65 EF 6
Ciudad Linares = Linares 64-65 G 7
Ciudad Lineal, Madrid- 113 III b 2
Ciudad Madero 64-65 G 7
Ciudad Mante 64-65 G 7
Ciudad Mendoza 86-87 M 8
Ciudad Mier 86-87 L 4
Ciudad Netzahualcóyotl 86-87 L 8
Ciudad Netzahualcoyotl-Juan Escutia 91 I C 2
Ciudad Obregón 64-65 DE 6
Ciudad Ojeda 92-93 E 2-3
Ciudad Pemex 86-87 O 9-P 8
Ciudad Piar 92-93 G 3
Ciudad Real 120-121 EF 9
Ciudad Río Bravo 86-87 LM 5
Ciudad Río Grande 86-87 J 6
Ciudad-Rodrigo 120-121 DE 8
Ciudad Satelite 91 I b 1
Ciudad Serdán 86-87 LM 8
Ciudad Trujillo = Santo Domingo 64-65 MN 8
Ciudad Universitaria [E] 113 III a 2
Ciudad Universitaria [MEX] 91 I bc 3
Ciudad Universitaria [YV] 91 II b 2
Ciudad Universitaria, Bogotá- 91 III bc 3
Ciudad Valles 64-65 G 7
Ciudad Victoria 64-65 G 7
Civa burnu 136-137 G 2
Civil'sk 124-125 Q 6
Cìvita Castellana 122-123 E 4
Civitanova Marche 122-123 EF 4
Civitavècchia 122-123 D 4
Çivril 136-137 C 3
Cixi 146-147 H 6
Ci Xian 146-147 E 3
Čiža 132-133 G 4
Čiža II 126-127 OP 1
Cizre 134-135 E 3

Čkalov = Orenburg 132-133 JK 7
Čkalovsk 124-125 O 5

Clacton on Sea 119 G 6
Clain 120-121 H 5
Clair 61 FG 4
Claire, Lake — 56-57 O 6
Clairefontaine = Al-Awaynāt 166-167 KL 2
Clairemont, TX 76-77 D 6
Clairton, PA 72-73 FG 4
Clamart 129 I bc 2
Clamecy 120-121 J 5
Clan Alpine Mountains 74-75 DE 3
Clanton, AL 78-79 F 4
Clanwilliam 172 C 8
Clanwilliamdam 174-175 C 7
Clapham, NM 76-77 C 4
Clara [BR] 106-107 K 2
Clara [RA] 106-107 H 3
Clara City, MN 70-71 C 3
Clara Island = Kalārā Kyûn 150-151 AB 7
Clara River 158-159 H 3
Claraz 106-107 H 6
Clare, MI 70-71 H 4
Clare [AUS] 158-159 G 6
Claremont, NH 72-73 KL 3
Claremont, SD 68-69 GH 3
Claremore, OK 76-77 G 4
Claremorris 119 B 5
Clarence, Cape — 56-57 S 3
Clarence, Isla — 111 B 8
Clarence Island 53 C 31
Clarence River 161 E 6
Clarence Strait [AUS] 158-159 F 2
Clarence Strait [USA] 58-59 w 8-x 9
Clarendon, AR 78-79 D 3
Clarendon, TX 76-77 D 5
Clarendon, Arlington-, VA 82 II a 2
Clarendon Hills, Boston-, MA 84 I b 3
Clarenville 63 J 3
Claresholm 60 KL 4
Clarinda, IA 70-71 C 5
Clarines 94-95 J 3
Clarion, IA 70-71 CD 4
Clarion, PA 72-73 G 4
Clarión, Isla — 86-87 C 8
Clarion Fracture Zone 156-157 KL 4
Clark, CO 68-69 C 5
Clark, SD 68-69 H 3
Clark, Lake — 58-59 K 6
Clarkdale, AZ 74-75 G 5
Clarke 106-107 G 4
Clarkebury 174-175 H 6
Clarke City 56-57 X 7
Clarke Island 158-159 J 8
Clarke River 158-159 HJ 3
Clarkfield, MN 70-71 BC 3
Clark Fork, ID 66-67 E 1
Clark Fork River 64-65 CD 2
Clark Hill Lake 80-81 E 4
Clarkia, ID 66-67 EF 2
Clark Mountain 74-75 F 5
Clark Point 72-73 EF 2
Clarks, NE 68-69 GH 5
Clarksboro, NJ 84 III b 3
Clarksburg, WV 64-65 K 4
Clarksdale, MS 64-65 HJ 5
Clarks Fork 68-69 B 3
Clarks Fork Yellowstone River 68-69 B 3
Clark's Harbour 63 CD 6
Clarkson 174-175 F 8
Clarks Point, AK 58-59 HJ 7
Clarkston, WA 66-67 E 2
Clarksville, AR 78-79 C 3
Clarksville, IA 70-71 D 4
Clarksville, TN 64-65 J 4
Clarksville, TX 76-77 G 6
Clarksville, VA 80-81 G 2
Claromecó 106-107 GH 7
Claromecó, Arroyo — 106-107 G 7
Claude, TX 76-77 D 5
Cláudio 102-103 K 4
Claudio Gay, Cordillera — 104-105 B 9-10
Claunch, NM 76-77 AB 5
Clawson, MI 84 II b 1
Claxton, GA 80-81 EF 4
Clay, KY 70-71 G 7
Clay, WV 72-73 F 5
Clay Belt 56-57 T-V 7
Clay Center, KS 68-69 H 6
Clay Center, NE 68-69 GH 5
Claydon 68-69 B 1
Clayes-sous-Bois, les — 129 I a 2
Claygate 129 II a 2
Claymont, DE 72-73 J 5
Claypool, AZ 74-75 H 6
Clayton, AL 78-79 G 5
Clayton, GA 80-81 E 3
Clayton, ID 66-67 F 3
Clayton, IL 70-71 E 5
Clayton, MO 70-71 E 6
Clayton, NC 80-81 G 3
Clayton, NM 76-77 C 4
Clayton, NY 72-73 HJ 2
Clayton, OK 76-77 G 5
Clearbrook, MN 70-71 C 2
Clear Creek 58-59 O 4
Clearcreek, UT 74-75 H 3
Cleare, Cape — 58-59 NO 7
Clearfield, PA 72-73 G 4
Clearfield, UT 66-67 GH 5
Clear Fork Brazos River 76-77 E 6
Clear Hills 56-57 N 6
Clearing, IL 83 II a 2
Clear Lake 74-75 B 3
Clear Lake, IA 70-71 D 4
Clear Lake, MN 70-71 D 3
Clear Lake, SD 68-69 H 3
Clear Lake, WI 70-71 DE 3
Clear Lake Reservoir 66-67 C 5
Clearmont, WY 68-69 C 3
Clear Prairie 60 H 1
Clearwater 60 G 4
Clearwater, FL 64-65 C 6
Clear Water Bay 155 I b 2
Clearwater Lake [CDN] 56-57 VW 6
Clearwater Lake [USA] 78-79 D 2
Clearwater Mountains 66-67 F 2-3
Clearwater River [CDN ◁ Athabasca River] 61 D 2
Clearwater River [CDN ◁ North Saskatchewan River] 60 K 3-4
Clearwater River [USA] 66-67 E 2
Clearwater River, North Fork — 66-67 F 2
Clearwater River, South Fork — 66-67 F 3
Cleburne, TX 64-65 G 3
Cle Elum, WA 66-67 C 2
Clemente, Isla — 108-109 B 5
Clemente Onelli 108-109 D 3
Clementon, NJ 84 III cd 3
Clemesi, Pampa de la — 96-97 F 10
Clen Cove, NY 82 III e 1
Clendenin, WV 72-73 F 5
Clermont, FL 80-81 bc 2
Clermont [AUS] 158-159 J 4
Clermont [CDN] 63 A 4
Clermont-Ferrand 120-121 J 6
Cleve 160 C 4
Cleveland, MS 78-79 D 4
Cleveland, MT 68-69 B 1
Cleveland, OH 64-65 K 3
Cleveland, OK 76-77 F 4
Cleveland, TN 64-65 K 4
Cleveland, TX 76-77 G 7
Cleveland, WI 70-71 G 4
Cleveland, Mount — 64-65 D 2
Cleveland Heights, OH 72-73 F 4
Clevelândia 102-103 F 7
Clevelândia do Norte 98-99 N 3
Cleveland Park 85 III b 1
Cleveland Park, Washington-, DC 82 II a 1
Clewiston, FL 80-81 c 3
Clichy 129 I c 2
Clifden 119 A 5
Cliff, NM 74-75 J 6
Cliff Lake, MT 66-67 H 3
Cliffs, ID 66-67 E 4
Clifton 158-159 K 5
Clifton, AZ 74-75 J 6
Clifton, KS 68-69 H 6
Clifton, NJ 72-73 J 4
Clifton, TX 76-77 F 7
Clifton, WY 68-69 D 4
Clifton Forge, VA 80-81 G 2
Clifton Heights, PA 84 III b 2
Clifton Hills 158-159 G 5
Climax 68-69 B 1
Climax, CO 68-69 C 6
Climax, GA 78-79 G 5
Climax, MN 68-69 H 2
Clinchco, VA 80-81 E 2
Clinch Mountain 80-81 E 2
Clinch Mountains 80-81 E 2
Clinch River 80-81 E 2
Cline 86-87 K 4
Cline, TX 76-77 D 8
Clint, TX 76-77 A 7
Clinton, AR 78-79 C 3
Clinton, IA 64-65 H 3
Clinton, IL 70-71 F 5
Clinton, IN 70-71 G 6
Clinton, KY 78-79 E 2
Clinton, LA 78-79 D 5
Clinton, MI 70-71 H 4
Clinton, MO 70-71 D 6
Clinton, MS 78-79 D 4
Clinton, MT 66-67 G 2
Clinton, NC 80-81 G 3
Clinton, OK 76-77 E 5
Clinton, SC 80-81 F 3
Clinton, TN 78-79 GH 2
Clinton, WI 70-71 F 4
Clinton [CDN, British Columbia] 60 G 4
Clinton [CDN, Ontario] 72-73 F 3
Clinton, Cape — 158-159 K 4
Clinton Creek 58-59 R 4
Clinton Park 85 III b 2
Clintonville, WI 70-71 F 3
Clio, AL 78-79 G 5
Clio, MI 70-71 J 4
Clipperton, Île — 64-65 E 9
Clipperton Fracture Zone 156-157 LM 4
Clisham 119 C 3
Cliza 104-105 D 5
Cloates, Point — 158-159 B 4
Clocolan 174-175 G 5
Clodomira 106-107 EF 1
Clonakilty 119 B 6
Cloncurry 158-159 H 4
Cloncurry River 158-159 H 3
Clonmel 119 BC 5
Clonmelt Creek 84 III b 2-3
Clo-oose 66-67 A 1
Cloppenburg 118 CD 2
Cloquet, MN 70-71 D 2
Cloquet River 70-71 DE 2
Clorinda 104-105 GH 9
Cloucester, VA 80-81 H 2
Cloudcroft, NM 76-77 B 6
Cloud Peak 64-65 E 3
Cloudy Mount 58-59 J 5
Clover, VA 80-81 G 2
Cloverdale, CA 74-75 B 3
Cloverdale, NM 74-75 J 7
Cloverleaf, TX 85 III c 1
Cloverport, KY 70-71 G 7
Clovis, CA 74-75 D 4
Clovis, NM 64-65 F 5
Clucellas 106-107 G 3
Cluj-Napoca 122-123 KL 2
Cluny 120-121 K 5
Clutha River 158-159 N 9
Clyde 56-57 X 3
Clyde, KS 68-69 H 6
Clyde, ND 68-69 G 1
Clyde, OH 72-73 E 4
Clyde, TX 76-77 E 6
Clyde, Firth of — 119 D 4
Clyde Park, MT 66-67 H 3
Clydesdale 174-175 GH 4
Clyo, GA 80-81 F 4

C. M. Naón 106-107 G 5

Cna [SU ◁ Mokša] 124-125 O 6
Cna [SU ◁ Prip'at'] 124-125 F 7
Cnori 126-127 MN 6
Cnossos = Knōssós 122-123 L 8

Coa 120-121 D 8
Coachella, CA 74-75 E 6
Coachella Canal 74-75 EF 6
Coahoma, TX 76-77 D 6
Coahuayutla de Guerrero 86-87 K 8
Coahuila 64-65 F 6
Coalbrook 174-175 GH 4
Coalcomán, Sierra de — 86-87 J 8
Coal Creek 66-67 F 1
Coal Creek, AK 58-59 PQ 4
Coaldale 66-67 G 1
Coaldale, NV 74-75 E 3
Coalgate, OK 76-77 F 5
Coal Harbour 60 CD 4
Coal Hill Park 155 II b 2
Coalinga, CA 74-75 C 4
Coallahuala 96-97 F 9
Coalmont, CO 68-69 C 5
Coalville, UT 66-67 H 5
Coamo 88-89 N 5-6
Coan, Cerro — 96-97 B 5
Coaraci 100-101 E 8
Coari 92-93 G 5
Coari, Lago do — 98-99 G 6-7
Coari, Rio — 92-93 G 5-6
Coast 172 GH 2
Coastal Cordillera = Cordillera de la Costa 111 B 4-5
Coast Mountains 56-57 K 6-M 7
Coast of Labrador 56-57 YZ 6-7
Coast Range 64-65 B 2-C 5
Coatá 98-99 C 8
Coatá, Cachoeira do — 92-93 G 6
Coatepec 64-65 G 8
Coatesville, PA 72-73 HJ 4
Coatiçaba 100-101 A 7-8
Coaticook 72-73 KL 2
Coats Island 56-57 U 5
Coats Land 53 B 33-34
Coatzacoalcos 64-65 H 8
Coayllo 96-97 C 8
Cobalt 72-73 G 1
Cobán 64-65 H 8
Coban çeşme 154 I a 2
Cobar 158-159 J 6
Cobargo 160 JK 6
Cobble Hill 66-67 AB 1
Cobbo = Kobo 164-165 MN 6
Cobbs Creek 84 III b 1-2
Cobbs Creek Park 84 III b 2
Cobe = Kōbe 142-143 PQ 5
Cobequid Mountains 63 DE 5
Cobh 119 B 6
Cobham River 62 B 1
Cobija 92-93 F 7
Cobija, Punta — 104-105 A 8
Coblence = Koblenz 118 C 3
Cobleskill, NY 72-73 J 3
Cobo 106-107 J 6
Coboconk 72-73 G 2
Cobo Hall 84 II b 3
Cobourg 72-73 GH 3
Cobourg Peninsula 158-159 F 2
Cobras, Ilha das — 110 I bc 2
Cobre, NV 66-67 F 5
Cobre, Cerro — 106-107 B 2
Cobre, Rio do — 102-103 FG 6
Cobre, Sierra del — 104-105 C 8-9
Cobres 104-105 C 8
Cobres, San Antonio de los — 111 C 2
Cobue 171 C 6
Coburg 118 E 3
Coburg, OR 66-67 B 3
Coburg, Melbourne- 161 II b 1
Coburg Island 56-57 V 2
Coca 120-121 E 8
Coca, Río — 96-97 C 2
Cocachacra 96-97 F 10
Cocal [BR, Bahia] 100-101 B 7
Cocal [BR, Piauí] 100-101 D 2
Cocalcomán de Matamoros 86-87 J 8
Cocalzinho, Serra do — 102-103 H 1
Cocanada = Kākināda 134-135 N 7
Cocha, La — 104-105 D 10
Cochabamba [BOL, administrative unit] 104-105 CD 5
Cochabamba [BOL, place] 92-93 F 8
Cochabamba, Cordillera de — 104-105 CD 5
Cochamal 96-97 C 5
Cochamó 108-109 CD 3
Cocharcas, Río — 104-105 D 3-4
Coche, Caracas- 91 II b 2
Coche, Isla — 94-95 K 2
Cochem 118 C 3
Cocheguingán 106-107 DE 5
Cochi = Kōchi 142-143 P 5
Cochicó, Loma de — 106-107 D 6
Cochim = Cochin 134-135 M 9
Cochin 134-135 M 9
Cochinchina = Nam Bô 148-149 DE 5
Cochin-Ernākulam 140 BC 5-6
Cochinoca, Sierra de — 104-105 D 8
Cochinos, Bahía de — 88-89 F 3-4
Cochise, AZ 74-75 J 6
Cochran, GA 80-81 E 4
Cochrane [CDN, Alberta] 60 K 4
Cochrane [CDN, Ontario] 56-57 U 8
Cochrane [RA] 106-107 FG 7
Cochrane, Lago — 108-109 C 6
Cochrane, Morro do — 110 I b 2
Cochrane River 56-57 Q 6
Cockburn, Canal — 111 B 8
Cockburn Island 62 K 4
Cockburn Land 56-57 UV 3
Cockeysville, MD 72-73 H 5
Coclé 88-89 F 10
Coco, Cayo — 88-89 G 3
Coco, El — 64-65 b 3
Coco, Isla del — 92-93 B 3
Coco, Punta — 94-95 C 6
Coco, Río — 64-65 K 9
Côco, Rio do — 98-99 O 9
Cocoa, FL 80-81 c 2
Coco Channel 148-149 B 4
Cocodrie, LA 78-79 D 6
Cocolalla, ID 66-67 E 1
Coconho, Ponta do — 100-101 G 3
Coconino Plateau 74-75 G 4-5
Cocos [AUS] 50-51 O 6
Côcos [BR, Bahia] 100-101 B 7
Côcos [BR, Minas Gerais] 100-101 B 8
Cocos = Isla del Coco 92-93 B 3
Cocos, Los — 94-95 KL 4
Côcos, Vereda de — 100-101 B 7
Coco Solo 64-65 b 2
Cocos Rise 156-157 N 4
Cocotá, Rio de Janeiro- 110 I b 1
Cocula 86-87 HJ 7
Cocuy, El — 92-93 E 3
Cocuy, Piedra de — 94-95 H 7
Cod, Cape — 64-65 N 3
Codajás 92-93 G 5
Codegua 106-107 B 4-5
Codera, Cabo — 92-93 F 2
Coderre 61 E 5
Codfish Island 161 B 8
Codihue 111 BC 5
Codó 92-93 L 5
Codorniz, Paso — 108-109 C 6
Codózinho 100-101 BC 3
Codózinho, Rio — 100-101 B 3
Codpa 104-105 B 6
Codroy 63 G 4
Cody, NE 68-69 F 4
Cody, WY 68-69 B 3
Coehue-Có 106-107 C 6
Coelemu 106-107 A 6
Coelho Neto 100-101 C 3
Coeli 172 C 4
Coello 94-95 D 5
Coen 158-159 H 2
Coengua, Río — 96-97 E 7
Coentunnel 128 I a 1
Coerney 174-175 F 7
Coeroeni 98-99 K 3
Coesfeld 118 C 3
Coeur d'Alene, ID 64-65 C 2
Coeur d'Alene Indian Reservation 66-67 E 2
Coeur d'Alene Lake 66-67 E 2
Coffee Bay 174-175 H 6
Coffee Creek 58-59 S 5
Coffeeville, MS 78-79 DE 4
Coffeyville, KS 64-65 G 4
Coffin Bay 158-159 FG 6
Coffin Bay Peninsula 158-159 FG 6
Coffs Harbour 158-159 K 6
Cofimvaba 174-175 G 7
Cofrentes 120-121 G 9
Cofu = Kōfu 142-143 Q 4

Cofuini, Río — 98-99 K 4
Cogealac 122-123 N 3
Cognac 120-121 G 6
Čogujev 126-127 H 2
Çoğun 136-137 F 3
Coguno 174-175 L 3
Cohagen, MT 68-69 C 2
Cohoes, NY 72-73 K 3
Cohuna 158-159 HJ 7
Cohutta Mountian 78-79 G 3
Coi, Sông = Sông Nhi Ha 148-149 D 2
Coiba, Isla — 64-65 K 10
Coicoi, Punta — 106-107 A 6
Coig, Río — 108-109 D 8
Coihaique 111 B 7
Coihaique Alto, Paso — 108-109 D 5
Coihueco [RA] 106-107 BC 7
Coihueco [RCH] 106-107 AB 6
Coimbatore 134-135 M 8
Coimbra [BR] 102-103 L 4
Coimbra [P] 120-121 C 8
Coin 120-121 E 10
Coin, IA 70-71 C 5
Coipasa, Cerro — 104-105 B 6
Coipasa, Lago de — 104-105 C 6
Coipasa, Salar de — 92-93 F 8
Coire = Chur 118 D 5
Coité, Río — 100-101 E 6
Čojbalsan 142-143 L 2
Čojbalsangijn Ajmag = Dornod ◁ 142-143 LM 2
Cojedes [YV, administrative unit] 94-95 G 3
Cojedes [YV, place] 94-95 G 3
Cojedes, Río — 94-95 G 3
Cojimies 92-93 C 4
Cojo, El — [YV, place] 91 II b 1
Cojo, El — [YV, river] 91 II b 1
Cojoro 94-95 F 2
Cojudo Blanco, Cerro — 111 BC 7
Cojutepeque 88-89 B 8
Çokak 136-137 G 4
Cokato, MN 70-71 C 3
Coker 170 III a 2
Cokeville, WY 66-67 H 4
Čokurdach 132-133 cd 3
Colac 158-159 H 7
Colachel = Kolachel 140 C 6
Colangüil, Cordillera de — 106-107 C 2-3
Colap dere 136-137 H 4
Colapur = Kōlhāpur 134-135 L 7
Cōlar = Kōlār Gold Fields 134-135 M 8
Colares 120-121 C 9
Colatina 100-101 D 10
Colbeck, Cape — 53 B 20-21
Colbert, OK 76-77 F 6
Colbert, WA 66-67 E 2
Colbert = 'Ayn Wilmān 166-167 J 2
Colbinabbin 160 G 6
Colbún 106-107 B 5
Colby, KS 68-69 F 6
Colca, Río — 92-93 E 8
Colcamar 96-97 BC 5
Colchester, VT 72-73 K 2
Colchester [GB] 119 G 6
Colchester [ZA] 174-175 FG 7
Cold Bay 58-59 b 2
Cold Bay, AK 58-59 b 2
Col des Nuages = Đeo Hai Van 150-151 G 4
Cold Lake [CDN, lake] 61 D 3
Cold Lake [CDN, place] 61 C 3
Cold Spring, MN 70-71 C 3
Coldspring, TX 76-77 G 7
Coldstream [ZA] 174-175 E 7-8
Col du Mont Cenis 120-121 L 6
Coldwater 72-73 G 2
Coldwater, KS 76-77 E 4
Coldwater, MI 70-71 H 5
Coldwater, OH 70-71 H 5
Coldwell 70-71 G 1
Colebrook, NH 72-73 L 2
Cole Camp, MO 70-71 D 6
Cole Creek Manor, Houston-, TX 85 III ab 1
Coleen Mount 58-59 Q 3
Coleen River 58-59 Q 2
Colegiales, Buenos Aires- 110 III b 1
Colégio = Porto Real do Colégio 92-93 M 6-7
Colegio Militar 91 I b 2
Colelache 108-109 E 4
Coleman 66-67 F 1
Coleman, MI 70-71 H 4
Coleman, TX 76-77 E 7
Coleman River 158-159 H 2-3
Çölemerik 136-137 K 4
Colenso 174-175 H 5
Coleraine [AUS] 160 EF 6
Coleraine [GB] 119 C 4
Coleridge, Lake — 161 D 6
Coleroon 140 D 5
Coles, Punta de — 92-93 E 8
Colesburg 172 DE 8
Colesville, CA 74-75 D 3
Colfax, CA 74-75 C 3
Colfax, IA 70-71 D 5
Colfax, LA 78-79 C 5
Colfax, WA 66-67 E 2
Colfax, WI 70-71 E 3
Colgong 138-139 L 5
Colhué Huapí, Lago — 111 C 7
Colico, Lago — 106-107 AB 7
Coligny 174-175 G 4
Colima 64-65 F 8
Colima, Nevado de — 64-65 EF 8
Colina [BR] 102-103 H 4
Colina [RCH] 106-107 B 4
Colina, La — 106-107 G 6
Colinas 92-93 L 6
Colinet 63 K 4
Colipilli, Cerro — 106-107 B 6
Coll 119 C 3
Collaguasi 111 C 2
Collarenebri 160 HJ 2
Colle di Tenda 122-123 B 3
College, AK 56-57 G 4-5
College Park, GA 80-81 DE 4
College Park Cemetery 85 II b 3
College Point, New York-, NY 82 III cd 2
College Station, TX 76-77 F 7
Colles 86-87 L 6
Colleymount 60 D 2
Collie 158-159 C 6
Collier Airport 85 III b 1
Collier Bay 158-159 D 3
Collierville, TN 78-79 E 3
Collines des Banzyville 172 D 1
Collingdale, PA 84 III b 2
Collingswood, NJ 84 III c 2
Collingwood [CDN] 72-73 FG 2
Collingwood [NZ] 161 DE 5
Collingwood, Melbourne- 161 II bc 1
Collins 62 E 2
Collins, IA 70-71 D 5
Collins, MS 78-79 E 5
Collins, MT 66-67 H 2
Collins, Mount — 62 L 3
Collins Field 84 III d 2
Collinson, Mount — 155 I b 2
Collinson Peninsula 56-57 Q 3-4
Collinston, LA 78-79 D 4
Collinsville 158-159 J 4
Collinsville, AL 78-79 FG 3
Collinsville, IL 70-71 F 6
Collinsville, OK 76-77 G 4
Collipulli 106-107 A 6
Collo = Al-Qull 166-167 K 1
Collón Curá 108-109 D 3
Collón Curá, Río — 108-109 D 3
Collpa 104-105 D 6
Colma, CA 83 I b 2
Colmar 120-121 L 4
Colmar Manor, MD 82 II b 1
Colmena 106-107 G 2
Colmor, NM 76-77 B 4
Colnett, Cabo — 86-87 B 2
Cologne = Köln 118 C 3
Cololo, Nevado — 92-93 F 7
Colomb-Béchar = Bashshār 164-165 D 2
Colombes 129 I bc 2
Colômbia [BR] 92-93 K 9
Colombia [CO] 92-93 D-F 4
Colombia [MEX] 76-77 DE 9
Colombine, Kaap — 174-175 B 7
Colombo 102-103 H 6
Colombo = Koḷamba 134-135 M 9
Colome, SD 68-69 G 4
Colón [C] 64-65 K 7
Colón [PA, administrative unit] 64-65 ab 2
Colón [PA, place] 64-65 b 2
Colón [RA, Buenos Aires] 106-107 G 4
Colón [RA, Entre Ríos] 106-107 H 4
Colón [YV] 94-95 H 6
Colón, Archipiélago de — 92-93 AB 5
Colona 158-159 F 6
Colona, CO 68-69 C 6
Colonche 96-97 A 2-3
Colonche, Cordillera de — 96-97 A 2-3
Colonia 106-107 HJ 5
Colonia, La — 108-109 C 6
Colonia Alvear 106-107 D 5
Colonia Baranda 104-105 G 10
Colonia Barón 106-107 F 6
Colonia Benjamín Aceval = Benjamín Aceval 102-103 D 6
Colonia Bremen 106-107 F 4
Colonia Cabildo = Cabildo 106-107 FG 7
Colonia Carlos Pellegrini 106-107 J 2
Colonia Caroya 106-107 EF 3
Colonia 10 de Julio 106-107 FG 3
Colonia del Sacramento 111 E 4
Colonia 25 de Mayo 111 C 5
Colonia Diez de Julio 106-107 FG 3
Colonia Dora 106-107 F 2
Colonia Elía 106-107 H 4
Colonia Elisa 104-105 G 10
Colonia Fernando de Trejo y Sanabria 102-103 E 6
Colonia Fram 102-103 DE 7
Colonia Garabí 106-107 JK 2
Colonia Isabel Victoria 106-107 H 2
Colonia Josefa 106-107 E 7
Colonia La Pastoril 106-107 DE 6
Colonia Las Heras = Las Heras 111 C 7
Colonia La Tordilla 106-107 F 3
Colonial Beach, VA 72-73 H 5
Colonial Heights, VA 80-81 H 2
Colonia Libertad = Libertad 106-107 HJ 3
Colonial Manor, NJ 84 III c 2
Colonial Village, PA 84 III a 1
Colonia Madariaga 106-107 J 2
Colonia Mennonita 102-103 C 5
Colonia Montefiore 106-107 FG 2
Colonia Osório 100-101 AB 2
Colonia Perín 104-105 FG 9
Colonia Prosperidad 106-107 F 3
Colonia Risso 102-103 D 5
Colonia Santa Virginia 106-107 DE 4-5
Colonia Seré 106-107 F 5
Colonias Unidas 104-105 G 10
Colonia Totorillas 104-105 E 10
Colonia Yacubó 102-103 DE 7
Colonia Yeruá = Yeruá 106-107 H 3
Colonne, Capo delle — 122-123 G 6
Colonsay 119 C 3
Colorada, La — 86-87 EF 3
Coloradito 94-95 K 3
Colorado [CR] 88-89 E 9
Colorado [USA] 64-65 EF 4
Colorado, El — [RA, Chaco] 104-105 G 10
Colorado, El — [RA, Santiago del Estero] 106-107 F 1
Colorado, Río — [RA, La Rioja] 106-107 D 2
Colorado, Río — [RA, Neuquén Río Negro] 111 D 5
Colorado City, TX 76-77 D 6
Colorado Desert 74-75 EF 6
Colorado National Monument 74-75 J 3
Colorado Plateau 64-65 DE 4
Colorado River [USA ◁ Gulf of California] 64-65 E 4
Colorado River [USA ◁ Gulf of Mexico] 64-65 G 5
Colorado River Aqueduct 74-75 F 5
Colorado River Indian Reservation 74-75 F 6
Colorados, Cerros — [RA] 111 C 6
Colorados, Cerros — [RCH] 111 C 3
Colorados, Los — 106-107 D 2
Colorado Springs, CO 64-65 F 4
Colo River 160 K 4
Colosseo 113 II b 2
Colotlán 86-87 J 6-7
Colpes 106-107 D 2
Colquechaca 104-105 CD 6
Colquiri 104-105 C 5
Colquitt, GA 78-79 G 5
Colstrip, MT 68-69 C 3
Coltauco 106-107 B 5
Colton, SD 68-69 H 4
Colton, UT 74-75 H 3
Colt Stadium 85 III b 2
Columbia, KY 70-71 H 7
Columbia, LA 78-79 CD 4
Columbia, MD 72-73 H 5
Columbia, MO 64-65 H 4
Columbia, MS 78-79 E 5
Columbia, NC 80-81 H 3
Columbia, PA 72-73 H 4
Columbia, SC 64-65 K 5
Columbia, SD 68-69 GH 3
Columbia, TN 78-79 F 3
Columbia, Cape — 52 A 25-26
Columbia, District of — 72-73 H 5
Columbia, Mount — 56-57 N 7
Columbia Basin 66-67 D 2
Columbia City, IN 70-71 H 5
Columbia Falls, MT 66-67 FG 1
Columbia Glacier 58-59 O 6
Columbia Heights, Washington-, DC 82 II a 1
Columbiana, AL 78-79 F 4
Columbia Plateau 64-65 C 2-3
Columbia River 64-65 BC 2
Columbia River, WA 66-67 C 2
Columbine, WY 68-69 C 4
Columbretes, Islas — 120-121 H 9
Columbus, GA 64-65 K 5
Columbus, IN 70-71 H 6
Columbus, KS 76-77 G 4
Columbus, MS 64-65 J 5
Columbus, MT 68-69 B 3
Columbus, ND 68-69 E 1
Columbus, NE 64-65 G 3
Columbus, NM 76-77 A 7
Columbus, OH 64-65 K 3-4
Columbus, TX 76-77 F 8
Columbus, WI 70-71 F 4
Columbus Junction, IA 70-71 E 5
Columbus Park 83 II a 1
Čolun-Chamur 126-127 M 4
Colupo, Cerro — 104-105 AB 8
Colusa, CA 74-75 BC 3
Colville, WA 66-67 E 1
Colville Bar, AK 58-59 K 2
Colville Channel 161 F 3
Colville Indian Reservation 66-67 D 1
Colville River 56-57 EF 4
Colwick, NJ 84 III c 2
Comàcchio 122-123 E 3
Comàcchio, Valli di — 122-123 E 3
Comalcalco 86-87 O 8
Comales, Los — 76-77 E 9
Comallo 108-109 DE 3
Comallo, Arroyo — 108-109 D 3
Comana 122-123 LM 3
Comanche, OK 76-77 F 5
Comanche, TX 76-77 E 7
Comandante Cordero 106-107 CD 7
Comandante Fontana 104-105 G 9
Comandante Leal 106-107 DE 3
Comandante Luis Piedra Buena [RA ← Río Gallegos] 108-109 DE 8
Comandante Luis Piedra Buena [RA ↑ Río Gallegos] 108-109 E 7
Comandante N. Otamendi 106-107 J 7
Comandante Salas 106-107 CD 4
Comarapa 104-105 D 5
Comau, Fiordo — 108-109 C 4
Comayagua 64-65 J 9
Combapata 96-97 F 9
Combarbalá 106-107 B 3
Comber 72-73 E 3
Combermere Bay = Combermere Pinleiau 141 C 6
Combermere Pinleiau 141 C 6
Combomune 174-175 K 2
Combourg 120-121 G 4
Combs, KY 72-73 E 6
Comeau, Baie — 56-57 X 8
Come By Chance 160 J 3
Comechingones, Sierra de — 106-107 E 4
Comencho, Lac — 62 O 1
Comer, GA 80-81 E 3
Comercinho 102-103 M 2
Cometela 174-175 L 1
Comfort, TX 76-77 E 7-8
Comilla = Komillā 134-135 P 6
Comino, Capo — 122-123 CD 5
Comiso 122-123 F 7
Comitán de Domínguez 64-65 H 8
Commadagga = Kommadagga 174-175 F 7
Commerce, GA 80-81 E 3
Commerce, TX 76-77 FG 6
Commewijne 98-99 L 2
Commissionerssoutpan 174-175 C 6
Committee Bay 56-57 T 4
Commonwealth Range 53 A
Commonwealth Territory 158-159 K 7
Como 122-123 C 3
Como, Lago di — 122-123 C 2-3
Comodoro Rivadavia 111 C 7
Comoé = Komoe 164-165 D 7
Comondú 86-87 DE 4
Comores, Archipel des — 172 HJ 4
Comorin, Cape — 134-135 M 9
Comoro Islands = Archipel des Comores 172 HJ 4
Comoros 172 HJ 4
Compeer 61 CD 5
Compiègne 120-121 J 4
Compostela 86-87 H 7
Comprida, Cachoeira — = Treze Quedas 92-93 H 4
Comprida, Ilha — [BR, Atlantic Ocean] 111 G 2-3
Comprida, Ilha — [BR, Rio de Janeiro] 110 I b 3
Comprida, Ilha — [BR, Rio Paraná] 102-103 G 4
Comprida, Lago — = Lagoa Nova 92-93 J 4
Compton, CA 74-75 DE 6
Comstock, TX 76-77 D 8
Comundú 86-87 DE 4
Comunidad 94-95 H 6
Čona 132-133 V 5
Conakry 164-165 B 7
Conambo 96-97 C 2
Conambo, Río — 96-97 C 2
Cona Niyeu 108-109 F 3
Conata, SD 68-69 E 4
Conca = Cuenca 92-93 D 5
Concarán 106-107 E 4
Concarneau 120-121 EF 5
Conceição [BR, Maranhão] 100-101 C 3
Conceição [BR, Mato Grosso] 92-93 H 6
Conceição [BR, Paraíba] 100-101 E 4
Conceição [BR, Rondônia] 98-99 H 10
Conceição [BR, Roraima] 98-99 H 3
Conceição, Ilha da — 110 I c 2
Conceição, Riacho — 100-101 D 4
Conceição, Rio — 100-101 A 7
Conceição da Barra 92-93 M 8
Conceição da Feira 100-101 E 7
Conceição das Alagoas 102-103 HJ 3
Conceição de Castelo 102-103 M 4
Conceição do Almeida 100-101 E 7
Conceição do Araguaia 92-93 JK 6
Conceição do Canindé 100-101 D 4
Conceição do Castelo 100-101 D 11
Conceição do Cuité 100-101 E 6
Conceição do Rio Verde 102-103 K 4
Concelho = Inhambane 172 G 6
Concepcion, CA 74-75 C 5
Concepción [BOL] 92-93 G 8
Concepción [CO, Putumayo] 92-93 DE 4
Concepcion [CO, Santander] 94-95 E 4
Concepción [EC] 96-97 B 1
Concepción [PE] 96-97 D 7
Concepción [PY, administrative unit] 102-103 D 5
Concepción [PY, place] 111 E 2
Concepción [RA, Corrientes] 106-107 J 2
Concepción [RA, Tucumán] 111 C 3
Concepción [RCH] 111 AB 5
Concepción, Bahía de — 106-107 A 6
Concepción, Bahía de la — 86-87 E 4
Concepción, Canal — 111 AB 8
Concepción, La — 92-93 E 2
Concepción, Laguna — [BOL → Santa Cruz de la Sierra] 104-105 F 5
Concepción, Laguna — [BOL ↑ Santa Cruz de la Sierra] 104-105 E 4
Concepción de Bermejo 104-105 F 10
Concepción de la Sierra 106-107 K 1
Concepción del Oro 64-65 F 7
Concepción del Uruguay 111 E 4
Conception, Point — 64-65 B 5
Conceptionbaai 174-175 A 2
Conception Bay 63 K 4
Conception Bay = Conceptionbaai 174-175 A 2
Concession, LA 85 I c 2
Concha 94-95 F 3
Conchas 102-103 J 5
Conchas, Las — 104-105 G 5
Conchas Dam, NM 76-77 B 5
Conchas Lake 76-77 B 5
Conchi [RCH, Antofagasta] 111 C 2
Conchi [RCH, Lagos] 108-109 C 4
Conchillas 106-107 HJ 5
Concho 76-77 B 9
Concho, AZ 74-75 J 5
Concho River 76-77 DE 7
Conchos, Río — 64-65 EF 6
Concón 106-107 B 4
Concord, CA 74-75 BC 4
Concord, NC 80-81 F 3
Concord, NH 64-65 M 3
Concord, Sydney- 161 I a 2
Concordia, KS 68-69 GH 6
Concordia, MO 70-71 D 6
Concórdia [BR, Amazonas] 98-99 E 7
Concórdia [BR, Santa Catarina] 102-103 FG 7
Concordia [CO] 94-95 CD 4
Concordia [PE] 96-97 D 4
Concordia [RA] 111 E 4
Concordia [ZA] 174-175 BC 5
Côn Cuông 150-151 E 3
Côn Đao 148-149 E 5
Conde 92-93 M 7
Conde, SD 68-69 GH 3
Conde de Araruama 102-103 M 5
Condes, Las — 106-107 B 4
Condé-Smedou = Zighūt Yūsuf 166-167 K 1
Condobolin 158-159 J 6
Condon, OR 66-67 C 3
Condor, Cordillera del — 96-97 B 3-4
Cóndor, El — 108-109 E 9
Cóndores, Los — 106-107 EF 4
Cóndores, Sierra de los — 106-107 E 4
Condoroma, Nevados de — 96-97 F 9
Condoto 94-95 C 5
Cône, Îlôt — = Kâs Moul 150-151 D 7
Conecuh River 78-79 F 5
Coneição do Mato Dentro 102-103 L 3
Conejera, Isla — 120-121 J 9
Conejos 76-77 C 9
Conejos, CO 68-69 C 7
Conejos River 68-69 C 7
Conesa 106-107 G 4
Coney Island 82 III c 3
Conflans-Sainte-Honorine 129 I b 1
Confucius, Temple of — 155 II b 2
Confusion Range 74-75 G 3
Confuso, Río — 102-103 C 6
Conghua 146-147 D 10
Congjiang 146-147 B 9
Congo 172 B 2-C 1
Congo = Zaïre 172 D 1
Congonhas, Aeroporto de — 110 II b 2
Congreso Nacional 110 III b 1
Congress, AZ 74-75 G 5
Congress Heights, Washington-, DC 82 II b 2
Conhello 106-107 E 5-6
Cónia = Konya 134-135 C 3
Conima 96-97 G 9
Coniston [CDN] 72-73 F 1
Conjeeveram = Kānchipuram 134-135 MN 8
Conklin 61 C 3
Conlara 106-107 E 4
Conlara, Río — 106-107 E 4
Conlen, TX 76-77 C 4
Connaught 119 B 4-5
Connaughton, PA 84 III ab 1
Conneaut, OH 72-73 F 3-4
Connecticut 64-65 M 3
Connecticut River 72-73 K 3-4
Connell, WA 66-67 D 2
Connellsville, PA 72-73 G 4
Conner, MT 66-67 FG 3
Conner, Mount — 158-159 F 5
Connersville, IN 70-71 H 6
Connersville, OH 72-73 D 5
Connie Mack Stadium 84 III c 2
Connors 63 B 4
Connors Pass 74-75 F 3
Cononaco 96-97 D 2
Cononaco, Río — 96-97 C 2
Conorochite, Río — 94-95 H 6
Conover, WI 70-71 F 2
Conquest 61 E 5
Conquista [BOL] 104-105 C 2
Conquista [BR] 102-103 J 3
Conquistadores, Los — 106-107 H 3
Conrad, MT 66-67 H 1
Conroe, TX 76-77 G 7
Consata 104-105 B 4
Consata, Río — 104-105 B 4
Conscripto Bernardi 106-107 H 3
Conselheiro Lafaiete 92-93 L 9
Conselheiro Pena 102-103 M 3
Conselho, Ponta do — 100-101 E 7
Conshohocken, PA 84 III ab 1
Consolação, São Paulo- 110 II ab 2
Côn So'n 150-151 F 8
Constable = Konstabel 174-175 CD 7
Constance = Konstanz 118 D 5
Constance, Lake — = Bodensee 118 D 5
Constancia [ROU] 106-107 HJ 4
Constância dos Baetas 92-93 G 6
Constanța 122-123 M 3
Constantina [BR] 106-107 L 1
Constantina = Qustantīnah 164-165 F 1
Constantine, Cape — 56-57 DE 6
Constantinople = İstanbul 134-135 BC 2
Constantinovka = Konstantinovka 126-127 H 2
Constanza 106-107 G 3
Constitución 111 B 5
Constitución, Buenos Aires- 110 III b 1
Constitution Lake 85 II c 2
Consuls, Pointe des — 170 I a 1
Contact, NV 66-67 F 5
Contador, El — 91 I d 1
Contagem 102-103 K 3
Contai 138-139 L 7
Contamana 92-93 DE 6
Contão 94-95 L 6
Contas, Rio de — 92-93 L 7
Contendas do Sincorá 100-101 D 7
Continental, AZ 74-75 H 7
Continental, OH 70-71 H 5
Con Tom = Kon Tom 150-151 F 4
Contoy, Isla — 86-87 R 7
Contratación 92-93 E 3
Contreras, Isla — 111 AB 8
Contria 102-103 K 3
Controller Bay 58-59 P 6
Contulmo 106-107 A 6
Contumazá 96-97 B 5
Contwoyto Lake 56-57 OP 4
Convención 94-95 E 3
Convento, Montañas de — 96-97 B 1-2
Converse, LA 78-79 C 5
Conway, AR 78-79 C 3
Conway, ND 68-69 H 1
Conway, NH 72-73 L 3
Conway, SC 80-81 G 4
Conway, TX 76-77 D 5
Conyers, GA 80-81 DE 4
Coober Pedy 158-159 F 5
Cooch Behār 138-139 M 4
Coogee Bay 161 I b 2
Cook 158-159 F 6
Cook, MN 70-71 D 2
Cook, NE 68-69 H 5
Cook, Bahía — 111 B 9
Cook, Cape — 60 CD 4
Cook, Mount — [NZ] 158-159 NO 8
Cook, Mount — [USA] 58-59 RS 6
Cook Bay 53 C 16
Cooke City, MT 66-67 J 3
Cookeville, TN 78-79 G 2
Cookhouse = Kookhuis 174-175 FG 7
Cooking Lake 60 L 3
Cook Inlet 56-57 F 5-6
Cook Islands 156-157 K 6
Cooks, MI 70-71 G 3
Cook's Harbour 63 HJ 2
Cookshire 62 Q 4
Cooks River 161 I a 2
Cook Strait 158-159 O 8
Cooktown 158-159 HJ 3
Coolabah 160 H 3
Coolah 160 J 3
Coolamon 160 H 5
Coolgardie 158-159 CD 6
Coolidge, AZ 74-75 H 6
Coolidge, KS 68-69 EF 6
Coolidge Dam 74-75 H 6
Coolin, ID 66-67 E 1
Cooma 158-159 J 7
Coonabarabran 158-159 JK 6
Coonamble 158-159 J 6
Coonana 158-159 D 6
Coonbah 160 EF 4
Coondambo 160 BC 3
Coondapoor 134-135 L 8
Coongoola 158-159 HJ 5
Coonor 140 C 5
Coon Rapids, IA 70-71 C 5
Cooper 174-175 DE 8
Cooper, TX 76-77 G 6
Cooper Creek 158-159 G 5
Cooper Lake 68-69 CD 5
Cooper Landing, AK 58-59 N 6
Cooper North Branch 84 III cd 2
Cooper River 84 III c 2
Cooper's Town 88-89 GH 1
Cooperstown, ND 68-69 GH 2
Cooperstown, NY 72-73 J 3
Coorg 140 BC 4
Coorong, The — 158-159 G 7
Coosa River 78-79 G 3
Coos Bay 66-67 A 4
Coos Bay, OR 64-65 AB 3
Cootamundra 158-159 J 6
Čop 126-127 A 2
Copa, Cerro — 104-105 B 7
Copacabana 104-105 B 5
Copacabana [CO] 94-95 D 4
Copacabana [RA] 104-105 C 11
Copacabana, Forte de — 110 I bc 2
Copacabana, Rio de Janeiro- 110 I bc 2
Copahue 106-107 B 6
Copahue, Paso — 111 BC 5
Copalyacu, Río — 96-97 D 3
Copán 64-65 J 9
Copán, Santa Rosa de — 64-65 J 9
Copano Bay 76-77 F 8
Copco, CA 66-67 B 4-5
Cope, CO 68-69 E 6
Copeland, KS 68-69 F 7
Copelina, La — 106-107 D 6
Copenhagen = København 116-117 DE 10
Copere 104-105 E 6
Copeta, La — 106-107 G 6
Copetonas 106-107 G 7
Copiapó 111 BC 3
Copiapó, Río — 106-107 B 1
Copiapó, Volcán — 106-107 C 1
Copixaba 100-101 C 6
Čopoviči 126-127 D 1
Copparo 122-123 DE 3
Coppell 62 K 2
Coppename 98-99 K 2
Copperas Cove, TX 76-77 EF 7
Copperbelt 172 E 4
Copper Center, AK 56-57 G 5
Copper Cliff 62 L 3
Copper Harbor, MI 70-71 G 2
Coppermine 56-57 N 4
Coppermine Point 70-71 H 2
Coppermine River 56-57 NO 4
Copper River 56-57 GH 5
Copșa Mică 122-123 L 2
Coqueiros, Ponta do — 100-101 G 4
Coquilhatville = Mbandaka 172 C 1-2
Coquille, OR 66-67 AB 4
Coquille River 66-67 AB 4
Coquimbana 106-107 B 2
Coquimbo [RCH, administrative unit] 106-107 B 3
Coquimbo [RCH, place] 111 B 2
Coquimbo, Bahía de — 106-107 B 2
Coquinhos 100-101 D 8
Corabia 122-123 L 4
Coração de Jesus 102-103 K 2
Coração de Maria 100-101 E 7
Coracora 92-93 E 7-8
Corais, Ilhas dos — 102-103 HJ 6
Coralaque, Río — 96-97 F 10
Coral Gables, FL 64-65 KL 6
Coral Harbour 56-57 U 5
Coral Sea 158-159 K-M 3
Coral Sea Basin 158-159 K 2
Coral Sea Islands Territory 158-159 JK 3
Corantijn 92-93 H 4
Corato 122-123 G 5
Corazón, El — 96-97 B 2
Corbeil-Essonnes 120-121 HJ 4
Corbélia 102-103 F 6
Corbières 120-121 J 7
Corbin 66-67 F 1
Corbin, KY 64-65 K 4
Corcaigh = Cork 119 B 6
Corcoran, CA 74-75 D 4
Corcovado 110 I b 2
Corcovado, El — 108-109 D 4
Corcovado, Volcán — 111 B 6
Corcubión 120-121 C 7
Corda, Rio — 100-101 B 3-4
Cordeiro 102-103 L 4-5
Cordele, GA 80-81 DE 4
Cordell, OK 76-77 E 5
Cordilheiras, Serra das — 98-99 OP 8
Cordillera 102-103 D 6
Cordillera Azul 92-93 D 6
Cordillera Blanca 92-93 D 6
Cordillera Cantábrica 120-121 D-F 7
Cordillera Central [BOL] 92-93 F 8-G 9
Cordillera Central [CO] 92-93 D 4-E 3
Cordillera Central [DOM] 64-65 M 8
Cordillera Central [PE] 92-93 D 6
Cordillera Central [RP] 148-149 H 3
Cordillera Claudio Gay 104-105 B 9-10
Cordillera Darwin [RCH, Cordillera Patagónica] 108-109 C 7-8
Cordillera Darwin [RCH, Tierra del Fuego] 108-109 DE 10
Cordillera de Aguaragüe 104-105 E 7
Cordillera de Ampato 96-97 EF 9
Cordillera de Ansilta 106-107 C 3
Cordillera de Buena Vista 94-95 FG 2
Cordillera de Caaguazú 111 E 3
Cordillera de Carabaya 92-93 EF 7
Cordillera de Charagua 92-93 G 8-9
Cordillera de Chilca 96-97 EF 9
Cordillera de Chocaya 104-105 C 7
Cordillera de Chugchilán 96-97 B 2
Cordillera de Cochabamba 104-105 CD 5
Cordillera de Colangüil 106-107 C 2-3
Cordillera de Colonche 96-97 A 2-3
Cordillera de Cumullca 96-97 B 5
Cordillera de Darién 88-89 D 8
Cordillera de Darwin 104-105 B 10
Cordillera de Doña Rosa 106-107 B 3
Cordillera de Guamani 96-97 AB 4
Cordillera de Huanzo 96-97 E 9
Cordillera de Julcamarca 96-97 D 8
Cordillera de la Brea 106-107 C 2
Cordillera de la Costa [RCH] 111 B 2-3
Cordillera de la Costa [YV] 92-93 FG 3
Cordillera de la Ortiga 106-107 BC 2
Cordillera de la Punilla 106-107 B 2
Cordillera de las Llarretas 106-107 C 4-5
Cordillera de la Totora 106-107 BC 3
Cordillera del Condor 96-97 B 3-4
Cordillera de Lípez 92-93 F 9
Cordillera del Litoral 91 II bc 1
Cordillera de los Andes 92-93 E 3-F 9
Cordillera de los Frailes 104-105 CD 6
Cordillera del Tigre 106-107 C 3-4
Cordillera del Viento 106-107 B 6
Cordillera de Mbaracayú 102-103 E 5-6
Cordillera de Melo 106-107 AB 7
Cordillera de Mérida 92-93 EF 3
Cordillera de Mochara 104-105 D 7
Cordillera de Mosetenes 104-105 C 5
Cordillera de Nahuelbuta 106-107 A 6-7
Cordillera de Oliva 111 BC 3
Cordillera de Olivares 106-107 C 3
Cordillera de Ollita 111 B 4
Cordillera de San Blas 64-65 L 10

282 Cofuini

Cordillera de San Buenaventura 104-105 BC 10
Cordillera de San Pablo de Balzar 96-97 AB 2
Cordillera de Santa Rosa 106-107 C 2
Cordillera de Suaruro 104-105 DE 7
Cordillera de Tajsara 104-105 D 7
Cordillera de Talamanca 88-89 E 10
Cordillera de Turco 96-97 C 6
Cordillera de Turpicotay 96-97 D 8
Cordillera de Vilcanota 96-97 E 8-F 9
Cordillera de Yolaina 88-89 D 9
Cordillera Domeyko 111 C 2-3
Cordillera Entre Rios 64-65 J 9
Cordillera Huayhuash 96-97 C 7
Cordillera Iberica 120-121 F 7-G 8
Cordillera Isabella 64-65 J 9
Cordillera Mandolegüe 106-107 B 6
Cordillera Negra 92-93 D 6
Cordillera Occidental [CO] 92-93 D 3-4
Cordillera Occidental [PE] 92-93 D 6-E 8
Cordillera Oriental [BOL] 92-93 FG 8
Cordillera Oriental [CO] 92-93 D 4-E 3
Cordillera Oriental [DOM] 64-65 N 8
Cordillera Oriental [PE] 92-93 D 5-E 7
Cordillera Patagónica 111 B 8-5
Cordillera Penibética 120-121 E 9-G 8
Cordillera Real [BOL] 104-105 B 4-C 5
Cordillera Real [EC] 92-93 D 5
Cordillera Riesco 108-109 D 9
Cordillera Sarmiento 108-109 C 8-9
Cordillera Sillajguai 104-105 B 6
Cordillera Vilcabamba 92-93 E 7
Cordisburgo 102-103 KL 3
Córdoba [CO] 94-95 D 3
Córdoba [E] 120-121 E 10
Córdoba [MEX, Durango] 76-77 C 9
Córdoba [MEX, Veracruz] 64-65 G 8
Córdoba [RA] 111 D 4
Córdoba, Sierra de — [RA] 111 C 4-D 3
Cordobesa, La — 106-107 J 4
Cordón Alto [RA ↙ Puerto Santa Cruz] 108-109 D 8
Cordón Alto [RA ↑ Puerto Santa Cruz] 108-109 E 7
Cordón del Cherque 108-109 D 5
Cordón de Mary 106-107 BC 6
Cordón de Plata 106-107 C 4
Cordón de Portillo 106-107 C 4
Cordón El Pluma 108-109 D 6
Cordón Esmeralda 108-109 C 6
Cordón Leleque 108-109 D 4
Cordón Nevado 108-109 D 3
Córdova 92-93 DE 7
Cordova, AK 56-57 G 5
Cordova, AL 78-79 F 4
Córdova, Península — 108-109 C 9
Cordova Bay 58-59 w 9
Cordova Peak 58-59 P 6
Cordovil, Rio de Janeiro- 110 I b 1
Coreaú 100-101 D 2
Coreaú, Rio — 100-101 D 2
Coremas 100-101 F 4
Coremas, Açude — 100-101 F 4
Core Sound 80-81 H 3
Corfield 158-159 H 4
Corfu = Kérkyra 122-123 H 6
Corguinho 102-103 E 3
Coria 120-121 D 8-9
Coria del Río 120-121 D 10
Coribe 100-101 B 7
Coringa Islands 158-159 K 3
Corinne 61 F 5
Corinne, UT 66-67 G 5
Corinth, MS 78-79 E 3
Corinth = Kórinthos 122-123 K 7
Corinth, Gulf of — = Korinthiakòs Kólpos 122-123 JK 6
Corinto [BR] 92-93 KL 8
Corinto [CO] 94-95 C 6
Corinto [NIC] 64-65 J 9
Coripata 104-105 C 5
Corire 96-97 E 10
Corisco, Isla de — 164-165 F 8
Corixa Grande, Rio — 102-103 C 2
Corixão 102-103 D 3
Cork 119 B 6
Corleone 122-123 E 7
Corleto Perticara 122-123 FG 5
Çorlu 136-137 B 2
Çorlu suyu 136-137 B 2
Cormeilles-en-Parisis 129 I b 2
Cormoranes, Rocas — = Shag Rocks 111 H 8
Cormorant 61 HJ 3
Cormorant Lake 61 H 3
Č'ormoz 124-125 UV 4
Cornaca 104-105 D 7
Čornaja [SU, Rossijskaja SFSR] 132-133 Q 3
Č'ornaja Cholunica 124-125 ST 4
Č'ornaja Sloboda 124-125 LM 3
Corneille = Marwānah 166-167 J 2
Cornejo, Punta — 96-97 E 10
Cornelia 174-175 H 4
Cornelia, GA 80-81 E 3
Cornélio Procópio 111 FG 2
Cornelius 106-107 MN 2
Cornell, WI 70-71 E 3
Corner Brook 56-57 Z 8
Corner Inlet 160 H 7
Corning, AR 78-79 D 2
Corning, CA 74-75 B 3
Corning, IA 70-71 C 5
Corning, KS 70-71 BC 6
Corning, NY 72-73 H 3
Cornish, Seno — 108-109 B 6
Corn Islands = Islas del Maíz 64-65 K 9
Cornouaille 120-121 EF 4
C'ornovskoje 124-125 QR 4
Cornudas Mountains 76-77 B 6-7
Cornwall [BS] 88-89 H 2
Cornwall [CDN] 56-57 VW 8
Cornwall [GB] 119 D 6
Cornwallis Island 56-57 RS 2-3
Cornwall Island 56-57 RS 2
Cornwells Heights, PA 84 III d 1
Č'ornyje zemli 126-127 N 3-4
Čornyj Jar 126-127 MN 2
Corny Point 160 C 5
Coro 92-93 EF 2
Coro, Golfete de — 94-95 F 2
Coroaci 102-103 L 3
Coroados 102-103 G 4
Coroatá 92-93 L 5
Corobamba, Pampas de — 96-97 B 4-C 5
Corocoro 92-93 F 8
Corocoro, Isla — 94-95 LM 3
Coroico 92-93 F 8
Coromandel 102-103 J 3
Coromandel Coast 134-135 N 7-8
Coromandel Peninsula 161 FG 3
Coromandel Range 161 F 3
Corona, CA 74-75 E 6
Corona, NM 76-77 B 5
Corona, Cerro — 108-109 D 3
Coronado, CA 74-75 E 6
Coronado, Bahía de — 64-65 K 10
Coronados, Golfo de los — 108-109 BC 3
Coronados, Islas de — 74-75 E 6
Coronation 61 C 4
Coronation Gulf 56-57 OP 4
Coronation Island [Orkney Is.] 53 CD 32
Coronation Island [USA] 58-59 v 9
Coronation Islands 158-159 D 2
Coronda 106-107 G 3
Coronda, Laguna — 106-107 G 3-4
Coronel 106-107 A 6
Coronel Alzogaray 106-107 E 4
Coronel Charlone 106-107 F 5
Coronel Cornejo 104-105 E 8
Coronel Dorrego 111 DE 5
Coronel Du Graty 104-105 F 10
Coronel Eugenio del Busto 106-107 E 7
Coronel Eugenio Garay 102-103 DE 6
Coronel Fabriciano 92-93 L 8
Coronel Falcón 106-107 G 7
Coronel Fraga 106-107 FG 3
Coronel Francisco Sosa 111 CD 5-6
Coronel Galvão = Rio Verde de Mato Grosso 92-93 HJ 8
Coronel Granada 106-107 FG 5
Coronel H. Lagos 106-107 EF 5
Coronel Martinez de Hoz 106-107 FG 5
Coronel Moldes 106-107 E 4
Coronel Mom 106-107 G 5
Coronel Murta 102-103 L 2
Coronel Oviedo 92-93 E 2-3
Coronel Ponce 102-103 E 1
Coronel Pringles 111 D 5
Coronel R. Bunge 106-107 GH 6
Coronel Segovia 106-107 DE 5
Coronel Suárez 111 D 5
Coronel Vidal 106-107 HJ 6
Coronel Vivida 102-103 F 6-7
Coronie 98-99 K 2
Coronilla, La — 106-107 L 4
Coropuna, Nudo — 92-93 E 8
Corowa 160 H 5-6
Corozal [BH] 64-65 J 8
Corozal [CO] 94-95 D 3
Corozal [YV] 94-95 K 4
Corozo, El — 91 II b 1
Corozo Pando 94-95 H 3
Corps Mort, Île de — 63 E 4
Corpus 106-107 K 1
Corpus Christi, TX 64-65 G 6
Corpus Christi Bay 76-77 F 9
Corpus Christi Pass 76-77 F 9
Corque 92-93 F 8
Corral [PE] 96-97 B 4
Corral [RCH] 111 B 5
Corral de Lorca 106-107 D 5
Corralito 106-107 EF 4
Correa 106-107 G 4
Correas, Los — 106-107 J 5
Correctionsville, IA 70-71 BC 4
Corregidor Island 148-149 GH 4
Córrego Bacuri-mirim 102-103 G 4
Córrego Traição 110 II ab 2
Corrente 92-93 KL 7
Corrente, Riacho — 100-101 B 4-5
Corrente, Rio — [BR, Bahia] 92-93 L 7
Corrente, Rio — [BR, Goiás ◁ Rio Paraná] 100-101 A 8
Corrente, Rio — [BR, Goiás ◁ Rio Paranaíba] 102-103 G 3
Corrente, Rio — [BR, Piauí] 100-101 D 3
Correntes [BR, Mato Grosso] 92-93 HJ 8
Correntes [BR, Pernambuco] 100-101 F 5
Correntes, Rio — 102-103 E 2
Correntina 92-93 KL 7
Correo, NM 76-77 A 5
Corrib, Lough — 119 B 5
Corrientes [PE] 96-97 D 4
Corrientes [RA, administrative unit] 106-107 HJ 2
Corrientes [RA, place] 106-107 H 1
Corrientes, Cabo — [C] 88-89 DE 4
Corrientes, Cabo — [CO] 92-93 D 3
Corrientes, Cabo — [MEX] 64-65 E 7
Corrientes, Cabo — [RA] 111 E 5
Corrientes, Cabo — = Cape Carysfort 108-109 L 8
Corrientes, Río — [EC] 96-97 C 3
Corrientes, Río — [RA] 106-107 H 2
Corrigan, TX 76-77 G 7
Corrigin 158-159 C 6
Corry, PA 72-73 G 4
Corse 122-123 C 4
Corse, Cap — 122-123 C 4
Corsica = Corse 122-123 C 4
Corsicana, TX 64-65 G 5
Č'orskogo, chrebet — 132-133 a 4-c 5
Cortaderas 106-107 C 6
Cortazar 86-87 K 7
Corte 122-123 C 4
Cortês [BR] 100-101 G 5
Cortés [C] 88-89 E 3
Cortez, CO 74-75 J 4
Cortez Mountains 66-67 E 5
Cortina d'Ampezzo 122-123 E 2
Čortkov 126-127 BC 2
Cortland, NE 68-69 H 5
Cortland, NY 72-73 HJ 3
Corto Alto 108-109 C 3
Cortona 122-123 D 4
Corubal 168-169 B 3
Çoruh = Artvin 134-135 E 2
Çoruh dağları 136-137 J 2
Çoruh nehri 136-137 J 2
Çorum 134-135 CD 2
Corumbá 92-93 H 8
Corumbá, Rio — 92-93 K 8
Corumbá de Goiás 102-103 H 1
Corumbaíba 102-103 H 3
Corumbataí, Rio — 102-103 G 6
Corumbaú, Ponta de — 100-101 E 9
Corumiquara, Ponta — 100-101 E 2
Coruña, La — 120-121 C 7
Corundum 174-175 J 3
Corunna, MI 70-71 H 4
Corunna = La Coruña 120-121 C 7
Corupá 102-103 H 7
Coruripe 100-101 F 6
Corvallis, MT 66-67 FG 2
Corvallis, OR 64-65 B 3
Corviale, Roma- 113 II ab 2
Corwin, AK 58-59 E 2
Corwin, Cape — 58-59 E 7
Corwin Springs, MT 66-67 H 3
Corydon, IA 70-71 D 5
Corydon, IN 70-71 GH 6
Corzuela 104-105 F 10
Cos = Kōs 122-123 M 7
Cosala 86-87 G 5
Cosamaloapan 86-87 MN 8
Cosapa 104-105 B 6
Cosapa, Río — 104-105 B 6
Cosapilla 104-105 B 5
Cosenza 122-123 FG 6
Coshocton, OH 72-73 EF 4
Cosigüina, Punta — 64-65 J 9
Cosigüina, Volcán — 64-65 J 9
Coslada 113 III b 2
Cosmoledo Islands 172 J 3
Cosmópolis 102-103 J 5
Cosmopolis, WA 66-67 B 2
Cosmos, MN 70-71 C 3
Cosna River 58-59 M 4
Cosquín 106-107 E 3
Cossipore, Calcutta- 154 II b 2
Č'osskaja guba 132-133 H 4
Costa 100-101 C 4
Costa, Canal — 108-109 C 5
Costa, Cordillera de la — [RCH] 111 B 2-3
Costa, Cordillera de la — [YV] 92-93 FG 3
Costa, La — 106-107 D 4
Costa Brava 120-121 J 8
Costa Chica 86-87 L 9
Costa del Sol 120-121 EF 10
Costa de Mosquitos 64-65 K 9
Costa Grande 64-65 F 8
Costa Machado 102-103 FG 5
Costa Rica [BOL] 104-105 B 2
Costa Rica [CR] 64-65 JK 9-10
Costa Rica [MEX, Sinaloa] 86-87 FG 5
Costa Rica [MEX, Sonora] 86-87 D 2
Costera del Golfo, Llanura — 86-87 L-N 5-8
Costera del Pacífico, Llanura — 86-87 E-H 2-7
Costermansville = Bukavu 172 E 2
Costigan Lake 61 EF 2
Costilla, NM 76-77 B 4
Cotabambas 96-97 E 8
Cotabato 148-149 H 5
Cotacachi 96-97 B 1
Cotacajes, Río — 104-105 C 5
Cotagaita [BOL] 92-93 F 9
Cotagaita [RA] 106-107 F 3
Cotahuasi 92-93 E 8
Cotati, CA 74-75 B 3
Cotaxé 100-101 D 10
Coteau des Prairies, Plateau du — 64-65 G 2-3
Coteau du Missouri, Plateau du — 64-65 FG 2
Côteau-Station 72-73 J 2
Cote Blanche Bay 78-79 D 6
Côte d'Azur 120-121 L 7
Côte du Calvados 120-121 G 4
Côte du Poivre = Malabar Coast 134-135 L 8-M 9
Cotegipe, Rio — 102-103 F 6
Cotejipe 100-101 B 7
Coté-Lai 104-105 G 10
Cotentin 120-121 G 4
Côte-Saint-Luc 82 I ab 2
Côte-Visitation, Montréal- 82 I b 1
Cotia 102-103 J 5
Cotia, Rio — 104-105 D 1
Cotiza, Caracas- 91 II b 1
Cotonou 164-165 E 7
Cotonu = Cotonou 164-165 E 7
Cotopaxi, CO 68-69 D 6
Cotopaxi [EC, administrative unit] 96-97 B 2
Cotopaxi [EC, mountain] 92-93 D 5
Cotswold Hills 119 EF 6
Cottage Grove, OR 66-67 B 4
Cottageville, SC 80-81 F 4
Cottbus 118 G 3
Cotter, AR 78-79 C 2
Cottian Alps = Alpes Cottiennes 120-121 L 6
Cottica 92-93 J 4
Cottondale, FL 78-79 G 5
Cotton Valley, LA 78-79 C 4
Cottonwood, AZ 74-75 GH 5
Cottonwood, CA 66-67 B 5
Cottonwood, ID 66-67 E 2
Cottonwood, SD 68-69 F 4
Cottonwood Creek 66-67 B 5
Cottonwood Falls, KS 68-69 H 6
Cottonwood River 70-71 C 3
Cottonwood Wash 74-75 HJ 5
Cotulla, TX 76-77 E 8
Cotunduba, Ilha de — 110 I c 2
Couba Island 85 I a 3
Coubron 129 I d 2
Coudersport, PA 72-73 GH 4
Coudres, Île aux — 63 A 4
Coulee, ND 68-69 EF 1
Coulee City, WA 66-67 D 2
Coulee Dam, WA 66-67 D 1-2
Coulman Island 53 B 18
Coulonge, Rivière — 72-73 H 1
Coulterville, IL 70-71 F 6
Council, AK 58-59 F 4
Council, ID 66-67 E 3
Council Bluffs, IA 64-65 GH 3
Council Grove, KS 68-69 H 6
Council Mountain 66-67 E 3
Country Club 91 I c 2
Country Club of Detroit 84 II c 2
Courantyne River 98-99 K 3
Courbevoie 129 I bc 2
Courland = Curlandia 124-125 CD 5
Courneuve, la — 129 I c 2
Courtenay [CDN] 56-57 LM 8
Courtrai = Kortrijk 120-121 J 3
Courtry 129 I d 2
Coushatta, LA 78-79 C 4
Coutances 120-121 G 4
Coutinho 100-101 D 3
Couto Magalhães 98-99 O 9
Coutts 66-67 H 1
Couves, Ilha das — 102-103 K 5
Covadonga, Isla — 108-109 BC 9
Cove, AR 76-77 G 5
Cove Island 62 KL 4
Coveñas 92-93 D 3
Covendo 104-105 C 4
Coventry 119 F 5
Covil, Serra do — 100-101 BC 6
Covilhã 120-121 D 8
Covington, GA 80-81 E 4
Covington, IN 70-71 G 5
Covington, KY 64-65 JK 4
Covington, LA 78-79 D 5
Covington, MI 70-71 F 2
Covington, OH 70-71 H 5
Covington, OK 76-77 F 4
Covington, TN 78-79 E 3
Covington, VA 80-81 FG 2
Covunco 106-107 BC 7
Covunco, Arroyo — 106-107 BC 7
Cowal, Lake — 158-159 J 6
Cowan, TN 78-79 FG 3
Cowan, Lake — 158-159 D 6
Cowansville 72-73 K 2
Coward Springs 158-159 G 5
Cowarie 158-159 G 5
Cowart Lake 85 II a 3
Cowden, IL 70-71 F 6
Cowdrey, CO 68-69 C 5
Cowell 160 C 4
Cowen, Mount — 66-67 H 3
Cowlitz River 66-67 B 2
Cowra 158-159 J 6
Coxilha 106-107 LM 2
Coxilha Caverá 106-107 K 3
Coxilha da Santana 111 E 3-F 4
Coxilha das Tunas 106-107 L 3
Coxilha do Batovi 106-107 K 3
Coxilha Geral 106-107 K 3
Coxilha Grande 111 F 3
Coxilha Pedras Altas 106-107 L 3
Coxilha Rica 102-103 G 7
Coxim 92-93 J 8
Coxim, Rio — 102-103 E 3
Coxipó do Ouro 102-103 D 1
Coxipó Ponte 102-103 DE 1
Cox River 158-159 FG 3
Cox's Bazar = Koks Bāzār 134-135 P 6
Cox's Cove 63 GH 3
Coyame 86-87 H 3
Coyle = Río Coig 108-109 D 8
Coyoacán 91 I bc 2
Coyoacán-Churubusco 91 I c 2
Coyoacán-Ciudad Jardin 91 I c 3
Coyoacán-la Candelaria 91 I c 2
Coyoacán-Rosedal 91 I c 2
Coyoacán-San Francisco Culhuacán 91 I c 3
Coyote, NM 76-77 B 6
Coyote Creek 83 III d 2
Coyotes Indian Reservation, Los — 74-75 E 6
Coyte, El — 108-109 D 5
Coyuca de Catalán 86-87 K 8
Cozad, NE 68-69 G 5
Cozumel 64-65 J 7
Cozumel, Isla de — 64-65 J 7
Cozzo Pellegrino 106-107 HJ 5
Crab Creek 66-67 D 2
Cracker 108-109 G 4
Cradock 172 E 8
Craig, CO 68-69 C 5
Craig, MT 66-67 GH 2
Craighall, Johannesburg- 170 V b 1
Craighall Park, Johannesburg- 170 V b 1
Craig Harbour 56-57 UV 2
Craigmont, ID 66-67 E 2
Craigmyle 61 B 5
Craigower 61 CD 6
Craik 61 F 5
Craiova 122-123 K 3
Crakow = Kraków 118 JK 3
Crampel = Ra's al-Mā' 164-165 D 2
Cranberry Portage 61 H 3
Cranbrock 56-57 NO 8
Cranbrook 60 JK 5
Crandon, WI 70-71 F 3
Crane, MO 78-79 C 2
Crane, OR 66-67 D 4
Crane, TX 76-77 C 7
Crane Lake 61 D 5
Crane Lake, MN 70-71 DE 1
Crane Mountain 66-67 CD 4
Cranston, RI 72-73 L 4
Cranz, Hamburg- 130 I a 1
Crary Mountains 53 B 25
Crasna [RO, place] 122-123 M 2
Crasna [RO, river] 122-123 K 2
Crater Lake 64-65 B 3
Crater Lake, OR 66-67 BC 4
Crater Lake National Park 66-67 BC 4
Craters of the Moon National Monument 66-67 G 4
Crateús 92-93 LM 6
Crato [BR] 92-93 M 6
Crau 120-121 K 7
Crauford, Cape — 56-57 TU 3
Cravari, Rio — 104-105 GH 3
Cravinhos 102-103 J 4
Cravo Norte 92-93 EF 3
Cravo Norte, Río — 94-95 F 4
Cravo Sur, Río — 94-95 EF 5
Crawford, GA 80-81 E 4
Crawford, NE 68-69 E 4
Crawford Lakes 85 II c 3
Crawfordsville, IN 70-71 G 5
Crawfordville, FL 80-81 DE 4
Cray 129 II c 2
Crayford, London- 129 II c 2
Crazy Mountains 66-67 H 2-3
Crazy Peak 66-67 HJ 3
Crazy Woman Creek 68-69 C 3
Crean Lake 61 E 3
Creciente, Isla — 86-87 DE 5
Creede, CO 68-69 C 7
Creedmoor, NC 80-81 G 2
Creel 86-87 G 4
Cree Lake [CDN, lake] 56-57 P 6
Cree Lake [CDN, place] 61 E 2
Cree River 61 E 2
Crefeld = Krefeld 118 BC 3
Creighton 61 GH 3
Creighton, NE 68-69 GH 4
Creil 120-121 J 4
Crema 122-123 C 3
Cremona [CDN] 61 A 5
Cremona [I] 122-123 CD 3
Crenshaw, MS 78-79 D 3
Creporí, Rio — 98-99 K 7
Crerar 72-73 F 1
Cres [YU, island] 122-123 F 3
Cres [YU, place] 122-123 F 3
Crescent, OK 76-77 F 4-5
Crescent, OR 66-67 C 4
Crescent, Lake — 66-67 B 1
Crescent City, CA 66-67 A 5
Crescent City, FL 80-81 c 2
Crescent Junction, UT 74-75 J 3
Crescent Lake, OR 66-67 C 4
Crescent Spur 60 GH 3
Crescentville, Philadelphia-, PA 84 III c 1
Cresciente, Isla — 86-87 DE 5
Cresco, IA 70-71 DE 4
Crespo 106-107 G 4
Cressday 68-69 A 1
Cressely 129 I b 3
Cressy 160 F 7
Crested Butte, CO 68-69 C 6
Crestlawn Cemetery 85 II b 2
Crestline, NV 74-75 F 4
Crestmond Park, Houston-, TX 85 III b 2
Creston 66-67 E 1
Creston, IA 70-71 C 5
Creston, WY 68-69 BC 5
Crestview, FL 78-79 F 5
Crestwynd 61 F 5
Creswell, OR 66-67 B 4
Crete, NE 68-69 H 5
Crete = Krētē 122-123 L 8
Créteil 129 I c 2
Crêtéville = Jabal al-Gulūd 166-167 M 1
Creus, Cabo — 120-121 J 7
Creuse 120-121 H 5
Creusot, le — 120-121 K 5
Creve Coeur, IL 70-71 F 5
Crevice Creek, AK 58-59 LM 3
Crewe 119 E 5
Crewe, VA 80-81 G 2
Cribi = Kribi 164-165 F 8
Crib Point 160 G 7
Crichna = Krishna 134-135 M 7
Criciúma 106-107 N 2
Cricket Ground [AUS, Melbourne] 161 II bc 1
Cricket Ground [AUS, Sydney] 161 I b 2
Crikvenica 122-123 F 3
Crillon, Mount — 58-59 T 7
Crillon, mys — 132-133 b 8
Crimea = Krym 126-127 FG 4
Criminosa, Cachoeira — 98-99 HJ 5
Criolla, La — 106-107 G 3
Cripple, AK 58-59 JK 5
Cripple Creek, CO 68-69 D 6
Criques, Grande Île de — 170 IV b 1-2
Crişana 122-123 JK 2
Crisfield, MD 72-73 J 5-6
Crisnejas, Río — 96-97 BC 5
Crisópolis 100-101 E 6
Criss Creek 60 G 4
Cristais, Serra dos — 102-103 J 2
Cristalândia 98-99 O 10
Cristalândia do Piauí 100-101 B 5-6
Cristales, Loma de los — 106-107 B 2
Cristalina 102-103 J 2
Cristina 102-103 K 5
Cristina, La — 94-95 E 4
Cristino Castro 100-101 B 5
Cristobal 64-65 b 2
Cristóbal Colón, Pico — 94-95 E 2
Crişul Alb 122-123 J 2
Crişul Negru 122-123 JK 2
Crivitz, WI 70-71 FG 3
Crna Reka 122-123 J 5
Croatia 122-123 F-H 3
Crockenhill 129 II c 2
Crocker, MO 70-71 D 7
Crocker Range 152-153 L 3-M 2
Crockett, TX 76-77 G 7
Crocodile Islands 158-159 FG 2
Croeira, Serra da — 100-101 A 4
Crofton, KY 78-79 F 2
Crofton, NE 68-69 H 4
Croissy-Beaubourg 129 I d 2
Croissy-sur-Seine 129 I b 2
Croix, Lac à la — 63 A 2
Croix, Lac la — 70-71 DE 1
Croker Island 158-159 F 2
Cromer [CDN] 61 H 6
Cromer [GB] 119 G 5
Cromwell 158-159 NO 8-9
Cromwell, MN 70-71 D 2
Crook, CO 68-69 E 5
Crooked Creek 66-67 DE 4
Crooked Creek, AK 58-59 QR 4
Crooked Creek, AK 58-59 H 6
Crooked Island 64-65 M 7
Crooked Island Passage 64-65 LM 7
Crooked River [CDN] 61 G 4
Crooked River [USA] 66-67 C 3
Crookes Point 82 III b 3
Crookston, MN 68-69 H 2
Crookston, NE 68-69 F 4
Crooksville, OH 72-73 E 5
Crookwell 160 J 5
Crosby, MN 70-71 CD 2
Crosby, MS 78-79 D 5
Crosby, ND 68-69 E 1
Crosby, Johannesburg- 170 V a 2
Crosbyton, TX 76-77 D 6
Cross 168-169 H 4
Cross, Cape — = Kaap Kruis 172 B 6
Cross City, FL 80-81 b 2
Crosse, La —, WI 64-65 H 3
Crossett, AR 78-79 D 4
Crossfield 60 K 4
Crossinsee 130 III c 2
Cross Lake [CDN, lake] 61 K 3
Cross Lake [CDN, place] 61 K 3
Crossman Peak 74-75 FG 5
Cross Plains, TX 76-77 E 6
Cross River 164-165 F 7-8
Cross Sound 56-57 J 6
Crossville, TN 78-79 G 3
Croswell, MI 72-73 E 3
Crotone 122-123 G 6
Crow Agency, MT 68-69 C 3
Crow Creek 68-69 D 5
Crow Creek Indian Reservation 68-69 G 3
Crowder, OK 76-77 FG 5
Crowell, TX 76-77 E 6
Crowie Creek 160 H 4
Crow Indian Reservation 68-69 BC 3
Crowley, LA 64-65 H 5-6
Crowley, Lake — 74-75 D 4
Crowleys Ridge 78-79 D 2-3
Crown Hill Cemetery 85 III c 2
Crown King, AZ 74-75 G 5
Crown Point 94-95 L 2
Crown Point, IN 70-71 G 5
Crown Point, LA 85 I b 3
Crownpoint, NM 74-75 JK 5
Crown Prince Christian Land = Kronprins Christians Land 52 AB 20-21
Crows Nest 160 L 1
Crows Nest, Sydney- 161 I b 1
Crowsnest Pass 66-67 F 1
Croxley Green 129 II a 1
Croydon 158-159 H 3
Croydon, PA 84 III d 1
Croydon, London- 119 FG 7
Crozet 50-51 M 8
Crozet Ridge 50-51 M 8
Crucero, CA 74-75 EF 5
Crucero, Cerro — 86-87 H 7
Crucero, El — 94-95 J 2-3
Cruces 88-89 FG 3
Cruces, Las — 64-65 b 2
Cruces, Las —, NM 64-65 E 5
Cruces, Punta — 94-95 C 4
Crum Creek 84 III a 2
Crum Lynne 84 III b 2
Cruxati, Rio — 100-101 E 2
Cruz, Bahía — 108-109 G 5
Cruz, Cabo — 64-65 L 8
Cruz, La — [CO] 94-95 C 7
Cruz, La — [CR] 88-89 CD 9
Cruz, La — [MEX] 76-77 B 9
Cruz, La — [RA] 106-107 J 2
Cruz, La — [ROU] 106-107 JK 4
Cruz, Serra da — 100-101 A 5
Cruz Alta [BR] 111 F 3
Cruz Alta [RA] 106-107 G 4
Cruz das Almas 100-101 E 7
Cruz del Eje 111 CD 4
Cruz de Malta 100-101 DE 5
Cruz de Taratara, La — 94-95 G 2
Cruz do Espírito Santo 100-101 G 4
Cruzeiro 92-93 L 9
Cruzeiro do Oeste 102-103 F 5
Cruzeiro do Sul 92-93 E 6
Cruzeiro do Sul, Cachoeira — 98-99 H 10
Cruzen Island 53 B 22-23
Cruzes, Rio — 108-109 C 2
Cruz Grande [MEX] 86-87 L 9
Cruz Grande [RCH] 106-107 B 2
Cruzília 102-103 K 4
Cruz Machado 102-103 G 6
Cruz Manca 91 I b 2
Cruz Ramos 96-97 C 5
Cruz Verde, Páramo — 91 III c 4
Crysdale, Mount — 60 F 2
Crystal, ND 68-69 H 1
Crystal Bay 80-81 b 2
Crystal Brook 160 CD 4
Crystal City 68-69 G 1
Crystal City, MO 70-71 E 6
Crystal City, TX 76-77 E 8
Crystal Falls, MI 70-71 F 2-3
Crystal Lake, IL 70-71 FG 4
Crystal Lake [CDN] 70-71 GH 3
Crystal Lake [USA] 84 I b 2
Crystal Palace Park 129 II b 2
Crystal River, FL 80-81 b 2
Crystal Springs, MS 78-79 D 4-5

Csongrád 118 K 5

Ctesiphon = Ktesiphon 136-137 L 6

Ču 132-133 N 9
Cúa 94-95 H 2
Cuadrada, Sierra — 108-109 E 5
Cuadrilla 104-105 C 7
Cuajimalpa 91 I b 2
Cuajinicuilapa 86-87 L 9
Cu'a Lo 150-151 E 3
Cuamba 172 G 4
Cuanacorral, Cerro — 96-97 B 5
Cuando, Rio — 172 D 5
Cuando-Cubango 172 C 4-D 5
Cuangar 172 C 5
Cuango 172 C 3
Cuango, Rio — 172 C 3
Cuanza Norte 172 BC 3-4
Cuanza Sul 172 BC 3-4
Cuao, Río — 94-95 H 5
Cu'a Rao 148-149 DE 3
Cuarein, Río — 106-107 J 3
Cuarepoti, Arroyo — 102-103 D 6
Cuaró [ROU, Artigas] 106-107 J 3
Cuaró [ROU, Tucuarembó] 106-107 K 3
Cuarto Dinamo 91 I b 3
Cu'a Sông Cu'u Long 148-149 E 5
Cuatro Ciénegas de Carranza 86-87 J 4
Cuatro Ojos 104-105 E 5
Cuatro Vientos, Madrid- 113 III a 2
Cu'a Tung 150-151 F 4
Cuauhtémoc 64-65 C 6
Cuauhtémoc, Ciudad de México- 91 I c 2
Cuautepec de Madero, Ciudad de México- 91 I c 1
Cuautepec el Alto, Ciudad de México- 91 I c 1
Cuay Grande 106-107 J 2
Cuba 64-65 KL 7
Cuba, KS 68-69 H 6
Cuba, MO 70-71 E 6
Cuba, NM 76-77 A 4
Cubagua, Isla — 94-95 J 2
Cubal 172 B 4
Cubango 172 C 4
Cubango, Rio — 172 C 5
Cubará 94-95 E 4
Čubartau = Baršatas 132-133 O 8
Cubatão 102-103 J 5
Cubero, NM 76-77 A 5
Cubo 174-175 K 2
Cubuk 136-137 E 2
Çubuklu, İstanbul- 154 I b 2
Cucao, Bahía — 108-109 B 4
Cu Chi 150-151 F 7
Cuchi, Rio — 172 C 4-5
Cuchilla de Belen 106-107 J 3
Cuchilla de Haedo 111 E 4
Cuchilla de la Carbonera 106-107 KL 4-5
Cuchilla de la Tristeza 106-107 C 5
Cuchilla del Caraguatá 106-107 K 3-4
Cuchilla del Daymán 106-107 J 3
Cuchilla del Hospital 106-107 K 3
Cuchilla de los Arapeyes 106-107 J 3
Cuchilla de Montiel 106-107 H 3
Cuchilla de Queguay 106-107 J 3
Cuchilla Grande [RA] 106-107 H 2-3
Cuchilla Grande [ROU] 111 EF 4
Cuchilla Grande del Durazno 106-107 JK 4
Cuchilla Grande Inferior 106-107 JK 4

Cuchilla 283

Cuchilla Mangrullo 106-107 KL 4
Cuchilla Negra 106-107 K 3
Cuchilla San Salvador 106-107 HJ 4
Cuchillo-Có 106-107 E 7
Cuchillo Parado 76-77 B 8
Cuchivero 94-95 J 4
Cuchivero, Río — 94-95 J 4
Čuchloma 124-125 O 4
Cucuí 92-93 F 4
Cucumbi 172 C 4
Cucunor = Chöch nuur 142-143 H 4
Cucurrupí 94-95 C 5
Cúcuta 92-93 E 3
Cudahy, CA 83 III c 2
Cudahy, WI 70-71 G 4
Cuddalore 134-135 MN 8
Cuddapah 134-135 M 8
Cudgewa 160 HJ 6
Cudi dağı 136-137 K 4
Cudinamarca 94-95 DE 5
Čudovo 132-133 E 6
Čudskoje ozero 132-133 O 6
Cudworth 61 EF 4
Cue 158-159 C 5
Cuello 86-87 Q 8
Cuemaní, Río — 94-95 E 7-8
Cuenca [CO] 94-95 E 8
Cuenca [E] 120-121 FG 8
Cuenca [EC] 92-93 D 5
Cuenca, Serranía de — 120-121 F 8-G 9
Cuenca del Añelo 106-107 C 7
Cuencamé de Ceniceros 86-87 J 5
Cuenlum = Kunlun Shan 142-143 D-H 4
Cuernavaca 64-65 FG 8
Cuero, TX 76-77 F 8
Cuervo, NM 76-77 B 5
Cuervo Grande, El — 76-77 B 7
Cuesta Pass 74-75 C 5
Cueva 96-97 D 7
Cueva, La — 94-95 E 2
Cueva de Altamira 120-121 EF 7
Cuevas, Las — 106-107 BC 4
Cuevas del Almanzora 120-121 G 10
Cuevitas 94-95 C 5
Cufra, Wāḥāt el — = Wāḥāt al-Kufrah 164-165 J 4
Čuguš, gora — 126-127 JK 5
Cuiabá [BR, Amazonas] 92-93 H 6
Cuiabá [BR, Mato Grosso] 92-93 H 8
Cuiabá, Rio — 92-93 H 8
Cuicas 94-95 F 3
Cuieté, Río — 102-103 M 3
Cuil, El — 94-95 B 6
Cuilapa 86-87 P 10
Cuillin Sound 119 C 3
Cuilo, Rio — 172 C 3
Cuíma 172 C 4
Cuipo 64-65 a 2
Cuité 100-101 F 4
Cuité, Serra do — 100-101 F 4
Cuito, Rio — 172 CD 5
Cuito Cuanavale 172 CD 5
Cuitzeo, Laguna de — 86-87 K 8
Cuiuni, Rio — 98-99 G 5
Cujar, Río — 96-97 E 7
Čukotskij, mys — 132-133 l 5
Čukotskij Nacional'nyj Okrug = Chukot Autonomous Area 132-133 g-k 4
Čukotskij poluostrov 132-133 kl 4
Çukurca 136-137 K 4
Çukurova 136-137 F 4
Cu Lao Cham 150-151 G 5
Cu Lao Hon = Cu Lao Thu 148-149 EF 4
Cu Lao Poulo Gambir 150-151 GH 6
Cu Lao Rê 150-151 G 5
Cu Lao Thu 148-149 EF 4
Cu Lao Xanh = Cu Lao Poulo Gambir 150-151 GH 6
Culbertson, MT 68-69 D 1
Culbertson, NE 68-69 F 5
Culcairn 158-159 J 7
Culebra [PA] 64-65 b 2
Culebra [Puerto Rico] 88-89 O 5
Culebra, La — 94-95 H 3
Culebras 96-97 B 6
Culgoa River 158-159 J 5
Culiacán 64-65 E 6-7
Culiacán Rosales = Culiacán 64-65 E 6-7
Culichucani 104-105 D 5
Culion Island 148-149 G 4
Čulkovo 132-133 Q 5
Cúllar de Baza 120-121 F 10
Cullera 120-121 GH 9
Cullinan 174-175 H 3
Cullman, AL 78-79 F 3
Čul'man 132-133 XY 6
Culpeper, VA 72-73 GH 5
Culpina 104-105 D 7
Culta 104-105 C 6
Cultural Palace of Nationalities 155 II b 2
Culuene, Rio — 92-93 J 7
Čuluut gol 142-143 J 2
Culver, Point — 158-159 DE 6
Culver City, CA 83 III b 1
Čulym [SU, place] 132-133 P 6
Čulym [SU, river] 132-133 Q 6
Cum = Qom 134-135 G 4
Cumã, Baía de — 100-101 B 1-2
Cumae 122-123 EF 5
Cumamoto = Kumamoto 142-143 P 5
Cumaná 92-93 G 2
Cumanacoa 94-95 K 2
Cumaral 94-95 F 6
Cumare, Cerro — 94-95 E 7
Cumari 102-103 HJ 3
Cumaria 96-97 DE 6
Cumaribo 94-95 G 5
Cumassia = Kumasi 164-165 D 7
Cumbal, Nevado de — 94-95 BC 7
Cumberland 66-67 A 1
Cumberland, IA 70-71 C 5
Cumberland, KY 80-81 E 2
Cumberland, MD 64-65 L 4
Cumberland, VA 80-81 GH 2
Cumberland, WI 70-71 DE 3
Cumberland, Cape — 158-159 N 2
Cumberland, Lake — 70-71 H 7
Cumberland City, TN 78-79 F 2
Cumberland House 61 GH 3-4
Cumberland Island 80-81 F 5
Cumberland Islands 158-159 JK 4
Cumberland Peninsula 56-57 XY 4
Cumberland Plateau 64-65 J 5-K 4
Cumberland Point 70-71 F 2
Cumberland River 64-65 J 4
Cumberland Sound [CDN] 56-57 X 4-Y 5
Cumberland Sound [USA] 80-81 c 1
Cumborah 160 H 2
Cumbre, La — [RA] 106-107 E 3
Cumbre, La — [YV] 91 II b 1
Cumbre, Paso de la — 111 BC 4
Cumbre del Laudo 104-105 B 10
Cumbre de Mejicana 111 C 3
Cumbrera, Cerro — 108-109 C 7
Cumbres Calchaquíes 104-105 D 10
Cumbres de Curumo, Baruta- 91 II b 2
Cumbres de Vallecas 113 III b 2
Cumbres Pass 68-69 C 7
Cumbria 119 F 4
Cumbrian Mountains 119 E 4
Cumbum = Kambam 140 C 6
Čumikan 132-133 Za 7
Cuminá, Rio — 92-93 H 5
Cuminapanema, Rio — 98-99 L 4-5
Cummings, CA 74-75 B 3
Cummins 158-159 G 6
Çumra 136-137 E 4
Cumullca, Cordillera de — 96-97 B 5
Cumuruxaiba 100-101 E 9
Čuna [SU ◁ Angara] 132-133 S 6
Čun'a [SU ◁ Podkamennaja Tunguska] 132-133 ST 5
Cunaco 106-107 B 5
Cunani 92-93 J 4
Cuñapirú 106-107 K 3
Cuñaré 94-95 E 7
Cunaviche 94-95 H 4
Cunco 111 B 5
Cuncumén 106-107 B 3
Cunene 172 C 5
Cunene, Rio — 172 B 5
Cúneo 122-123 B 3
Cuney, TX 76-77 G 6
Çüngüş 136-137 H 3
Cunha 102-103 K 5
Cunnamulla 158-159 HJ 5
Cunningham, WA 66-67 D 2
Cunningham Park [USA, Boston] 84 I b 3
Cunningham Park [USA, New York] 82 III d 2
Cunocuno, Pampa de — 96-97 E 10
Čuokkarašša 116-117 KL 2
Cupar 61 F 5
Cupecê, Ribeirão — 110 II b 2
Cupica 94-95 C 4
Cupica, Golfo de — 92-93 D 3
Cupira [BR] 100-101 G 5
Cúpira [YV] 94-95 J 2
Cuprum, ID 66-67 E 3
Cuptana, Isla — 108-109 C 5
Cupupira, Sierra — 94-95 J 6-7
Čur 124-125 T 5
Curaçá [BR, Amazonas] 92-93 G 6
Curaçá [BR, Bahia] 92-93 LM 6
Curaçá, Rio — 100-101 E 5
Curaçao 64-65 N 9
Curacautín 111 B 5
Curacaví 106-107 B 4
Curacó, Río — 106-107 E 7
Curahuara de Carangas 104-105 B 5
Curahuara de Pacajes 104-105 C 5
Cura Mala, Sierra de — 106-107 FG 6-7
Curamalal Grande, Cerro — 106-107 FG 6
Curamavida, Cerro — 106-107 B 3
Curamoni 94-95 H 6
Curanilahue 111 B 5
Curanipe 106-107 A 5
Curanja, Río — 96-97 F 7
Curapaligüe 106-107 F 5
Čurapča 132-133 Z 5
Curaray [EC] 96-97 C 2
Curaray [PE] 96-97 D 3
Curaray, Río — 92-93 D 5
Curarigua 94-95 FG 3
Curarú 106-107 FG 5
Curaumilla, Punta — 106-107 AB 4
Curdistān = Kordestān 134-135 F 3
Curepto 106-107 A 5
Curiapo 92-93 G 3
Curibaya 96-97 F 10
Curicó 111 B 4
Curicó, Laguna — 108-109 G 3
Curicuriari, Río — 98-99 DE 5
Curicuriari, Serra — 98-99 E 5
Curimatá 100-101 B 6
Curimatá, Rio — 100-101 B 5-6
Curioso, Cabo — 108-109 F 7
Curiplaya 94-95 D 7
Curitiba 111 G 3
Curitibanos 102-103 G 7
Curiuja, Río — 96-97 E 7
Curiúva 102-103 G 6
Curlandia 124-125 CD 5
Curlew, WA 66-67 D 1
Curnamona 158-159 GH 6
Currais Novos 92-93 M 6
Curralinho 98-99 NO 5
Curral Novo 100-101 CD 5
Curral Novo, Serra — 100-101 EF 6
Curral Velho 100-101 B 7
Currant, NV 74-75 F 3
Current River 78-79 D 2
Currie 158-159 H 7-8
Currie, MN 70-71 C 3
Currie, NV 66-67 F 5
Currituck Sound 80-81 J 2
Curry, AK 58-59 MN 5
Curtea-de-Argeş 122-123 L 3
Curtin Springs 158-159 F 5
Curtis, NE 68-69 F 5
Curtis Island [AUS] 158-159 K 4
Curtis Island [NZ] 158-159 Q 6
Curuá, Ilha — 98-99 NO 4
Curuá, Rio — [BR ◁ Rio Amazonas] 98-99 L 4-5
Curuá, Rio — [BR ◁ Rio Iriri] 92-93 J 6
Curuá do Sul, Rio — 98-99 LM 6
Curuaés, Rio — 98-99 L 9
Curuaí 92-93 H 5
Curuai, Lago Grande do — 98-99 L 6
Curuá Una, Rio — 98-99 L 6
Curuçá 92-93 K 5
Curuçá, Ponta — 98-99 P 5
Curuçá, Rio — 98-99 C 7
Curucuinazá, Rio — 104-105 GH 3
Curuguaty 102-103 E 6
Curumaní 94-95 E 3
Curumu 98-99 N 5
Cururuí, Serra do — 98-99 MN 4
Curup 148-149 D 7
Curupá 100-101 AB 5
Curupai, Rio — 102-103 EF 5
Curupaity 106-107 G 3
C'urupinsk 126-127 F 3
Curupira 100-101 E 3
Curuquetê, Rio — 98-99 F 9
Cururú 92-93 G 8
Cururu-Açu, Rio — 98-99 K 9
Cururupu 92-93 L 5
Curuzú Chalí, Isla — 106-107 H 3
Curuzú Cuatiá 111 E 3
Curva 104-105 B 4
Curva Grande 92-93 K 5
Curvelo 92-93 L 8
Curzola = Korčula 122-123 G 4
Cusali, Cerros — 104-105 C 4
Čuševicy 124-125 N 3
Cushing, OK 76-77 F 5
Cushing, TX 76-77 G 7
Cushman, AR 78-79 D 3
Cusiana, Río — 94-95 E 5
Cusino, MI 70-71 G 2
Cusis, Los — 104-105 D 4
Čusovoj 132-133 K 6
Čusovskoj 124-125 V 3
Cusseta, GA 78-79 G 4
Čust 134-135 L 2
Custer, SD 68-69 E 4
Custódia 100-101 F 5
Cutanga, Volcán — 94-95 C 7
Cutapines, Lomba das — 104-105 E 2
Cut Bank, MT 66-67 GH 1
Cutch = Kutch 134-135 K 6
Cutervo 92-93 D 6
Cuthbert, GA 78-79 G 5
Cut Knife 61 D 4
Cutler 62 K 3
Cutler, CA 74-75 D 4
Cutler River 58-59 HJ 3
Cutral-Có 106-107 C 7
Cuttaburra Creek 160 G 2
Cuttack 134-135 NO 6
Cutupí 98-99 G 10
Cutzamala, Río — 86-87 K 8
Cu'u Long, Cu'a Sông — 148-149 E 5
Čuvašskaja Avtonomnaja Sovetskaja Socialističeskaja Respublika = Chuvash Autonomous Soviet Socialist Republic 132-133 H 6
Cuvelai 172 C 5
Cuvier, Cape — 158-159 B 4
Cuvo, Rio — 172 B 4
Cuxhaven 118 D 2
Cuy, El — 111 C 5
Cuyabeno 96-97 D 2
Cuyahoga Falls, OH 72-73 F 4
Cuyama River 74-75 C 5
Cuyo Islands 148-149 H 4
Cuyuni River 92-93 G 3
Cuzco [PE, administrative unit] 96-97 EF 8
Cuzco [PE, place] 92-93 E 7
C. W. MacConaughy, Lake — 68-69 E 5
Cyangugu 171 B 3
Cybulev 126-127 DE 2
Cyclorama and Zoo 85 II bc 2
Cymru = Wales 119 E 5-6
Cynthiana, KY 72-73 DE 5
Cyphergat = Syfergat 174-175 G 6
Cyp-Navolok 116-117 PQ 3
Cypress, CA 83 III d 2
Cypress, LA 78-79 C 5
Cypress, TX 76-77 FG 8
Cypress Hills 56-57 OP 8
Cypress Hills Provincial Park 61 CD 6
Cypress Lake 66-67 J 1
Cyprus 134-135 C 4
Cyrenaica = Barqah 164-165 J 2
Cyrene = Shaḥḥat 164-165 J 2
Czar 61 C 4
Czechoslovakia 118 F-K 4
Czersk 118 J 2
Częstochowa 118 JK 3

D

Đa, Sông — 148-149 D 2
Da'an 146-147 C 10
Ḍab'ah 136-137 G 7
Ḍab'ah, Aḍ- 164-165 K 2
Ḍab'ah, Rā's, aḍ- 136-137 C 7
Dabaidi 146-147 E 8
Dabajuro 94-95 F 2
Dabakala 164-165 D 7
Daba Shan 142-143 KL 5
Dabas nuur 142-143 H 4
Dabat = Debark 164-165 MN 7
Dabbā = Jabal Jarbī 136-137 H 5
Dabbah, Ad- 164-165 KL 5
Dabbūsah, Ad- 136-137 J 7
Dabdū 166-167 E 3
Dabeiba 92-93 D 3
Dabhoi 138-139 D 6
Dābhol 140 A 2
Dabie Shan [TJ, mountain] 146-147 EF 6
Dabie Shan [TJ, mountains] 142-143 M 5
Dabla 138-139 E 4
Dabola 164-165 B 6
Daborow 164-165 b 2
Dabou 168-169 D 4
Daboya 168-169 E 3
Dąbrowa Tarnowska 118 K 3
Dabu 146-147 F 9
Dābugām 138-139 J 8
Dabul = Dābhol 140 A 2
Dabuxun Hu = Dabas nuur 142-143 H 4
Dacaidan = Tagalgan 142-143 H 4
Dacar = Dakar 164-165 A 6
Dacar, Bîr ed — = Bi'r ad-Dhikār 164-165 J 3
Dacca = Ḍhākā [BD, administrative unit] 138-139 N 5-6
Dacca = Ḍhākā [BD, place] 134-135 OP 6
Dachaidan = Tagalgan 142-143 H 4
Dachangshan Dao 144-145 D 3
Dachangtu Shan 146-147 J 6
Dachau 118 E 4
Dachen Dao 146-147 HJ 7
Dacheng = Daicheng 146-147 F 2
Dachepalle 140 DE 2
Dachovskaja 126-127 JK 4
Dachstein 118 F 5
Đạc Lắc, Cao Nguyên — 148-149 E 4
Dadache, Rio — 174-175 K 2
Dadaituan = Shentuan 146-147 G 4
Dadanawa 98-99 HJ 3
Daday 136-137 E 2
Dade City, FL 80-81 b 2
Dadeville, AL 78-79 FG 4
Dadian [TJ, Anhui] 146-147 F 5
Dadian [TJ, Shandong] 146-147 G 4
Dādis, Wād — 166-167 C 4
Dadra and Nagar Haveli 134-135 L 6
Dādrī = Charkhi Dādri 138-139 EF 3
Da Drin = Sông Tra 150-151 G 5
Dāḍū 134-135 K 5
Dadu He 142-143 J 5
Dadukou 146-147 F 6
Đa Dung 150-151 FG 7
Đa Du'ng, Mui — 150-151 EF 3
Daduru Oya 140 DE 7
Dadynskoje, ozero — 126-127 M 4
Daerstorf 130 I a 2
Daet 148-149 H 4
Dafan 146-147 E 7
Dafdaf, Jabal — 173 D 3
Dafeng 146-147 H 5
Dafeng Shan = Shinaibeidong 146-147 H 7
Dafinah, Ad- 134-135 E 6
Dafla Hills 141 C 2
Dafnion 113 IV a 1
Dafoe 61 F 5
Dafoe River 61 L 3
Dafou = Wangmudu 146-147 E 9
Dafter, MI 70-71 H 2
Dafu Shui 146-147 D 6
Dagabur = Degeh Bur 164-165 N 7
Daga Myit 141 D 7
Dagana 164-165 AB 5
Dagangtou 146-147 G 7
Dağbaşı 136-137 H 4
Dagda 124-125 F 5
Dagelet = Ullŭng-do 142-143 P 4
Dagenham, London- 129 II c 1
Dagestan Autonomous Soviet Socialist Republic 126-127 MN 5
Dagestanskije Ogni 126-127 O 5
Daggett, CA 74-75 E 5
Daghgharah, Ad- 136-137 L 6
Daglfing, München- 130 II bc 2
Dağlıca = Oramar 136-137 KL 4
Dagmar 138-139 MN 2
Dagö = Hiiumaa 124-125 CD 4
Dagomba 164-165 D 7
Dagomys, Soči- 126-127 J 5
Dagoum 168-169 J 2
Dagu 146-147 F 2
Dagua [CO] 94-95 C 6
Dagua [PNG] 148-149 M 7
Daguan 146-147 H 6
Dagu He 146-147 H 3
D'Aguilar, Cape — = Tai Long Head 155 I b 2
D'Aguilar Peak 155 I b 2
Dagujia 144-145 E 1
Dagverdharnes 116-117 b 2
Dāhānu 134-135 L 6-7
Dahao Dao 146-147 DE 10
Dahar = Ẓahar 166-167 LM 3
Daheishan Dao 146-147 GH 3
Dahej = Dehej 138-139 D 7
Dahī, Nafūd ad- 134-135 EF 6
Dahībah, Ad- = Adh-Dhahībah 166-167 M 3
Dahlak desēt 164-165 N 5
Dahlem, Berlin- 130 III b 2
Dahnā', Ad- 134-135 E 5-F 6
Dāhōd = Dohad 138-139 E 6
Dahomey = Benin 164-165 E 6-7
Dahongcheng 146-147 CD 1
Dahong Shan 146-147 D 6
Dahra = Aḍ-Ḍahrah 166-167 G 1
Ḍahrah 164-165 H 3
Ḍahrah, Aḍ- 166-167 G 1
Ḍahr Walātah 164-165 C 5
Dahshūr = Minshāt Dahshūr 173 B 3
Dahua Jiao 150-151 H 3
Dahūk 136-137 K 4
Dahushan 144-145 D 2
Daïa, Monts de — = Jabal aḍ-Ḍāyah 166-167 F 2
Daïa, Région des — = Ḍāyah 166-167 HJ 3
Daïa el Aam = Dayaṭ 'al-Ām 166-167 B 6
Daïa el Maïda = Ḍaya al-Mā'idah 166-167 D 4
Daibang Wand = Dapeng Wan 146-147 E 10
Daïet el Khadra = Ḍayat al-Khaḍrah 166-167 BC 6
Daijuku 155 III d 3
Daik'ū 141 E 7
Dailekh 138-139 H 3
Đai Lôc 150-151 G 5
Daimiel 120-121 F 9
Đai Ngai 150-151 EF 8
Daingerfield, TX 76-77 G 6
Daiō zaki 144-145 L 5
Daipingqiao = Taipingshao 144-145 E 2
Dāira Dīn Panāh 138-139 C 2
Daireaux 106-107 G 6
Dairen = Lüda-Dalian 142-143 N 4
Dairūṭ = Dayrūṭ 164-165 L 3
Dai-sen 144-145 J 5
Dai-Sengen dake 144-145 ab 3
Daisetta, TX 76-77 G 7
Dai Shan 146-147 HJ 6
Dai Shan = Taishan Liedao 146-147 H 8
Daishi, Kawasaki- 155 III b 2
Dais hōji = Kaga 144-145 L 4
Daisy, WA 66-67 DE 1
Daito-jima 142-143 P 6
Daitō-shima 142-143 P 6
Daitō sima = Daitō-shima 142-143 P 6
Dai Xian 146-147 D 2
Dājal 138-139 C 3
Dajarra 158-159 G 4
Dajiangkou = Jiangkou 146-147 C 8
Dajiangtou = Dagangtou 146-147 G 7
Dajiaoting, Beijing- 155 II bc 2
Dajing [TJ, Guangdong] 146-147 C 10
Dajing [TJ, Zhejiang] 146-147 H 7
Dajingcun, Beijing- 155 II a 2
Daka 168-169 E 3
Dakar 164-165 A 6
Dakawa 171 D 4
Dakaye 168-169 E 3
Daketa 164-165 N 7
Dakhan = Deccan 134-135 M 6-8
Dakhan Shāhbāzpūr Dīp 141 B 4
Dākhilah, Wāḥāt ad- 164-165 K 3
Dakhin Shahbazpur Island = Dakhan Shāhbāzpūr Dīp 141 B 4
Dakhlah, Ad- 164-165 A 4
Dakhla Oasis = Wāḥāt ad-Dākhilah 164-165 K 3
Dak Hon 150-151 F 5
Dakka = Ḍhāka 134-135 OP 6
Dākor 138-139 D 6
Dakoro 168-169 G 2
Dakota, North — 64-65 FG 2
Dakota, South — 64-65 FG 3
D'akovskoje, Moskva- 113 V c 3
Dak Po'kô 150-151 F 5
Dakshiṇ Andamān = South Andamān 134-135 P 8
Dakshiṇ Koīl = South Koel 138-139 K 6
Dakshiṇ Paṭhār = Deccan 134-135 M 6-8
Dakshiṇ Shālmārā = South Sālmāra 138-139 N 5
Dak Sut 150-151 F 5
Dak Tô 150-151 F 5
Dakunū Palāna ◁ 140 E 7
Dākur = Dākor 138-139 D 6
Dala 116-117 bc 2
Dalaba 164-165 B 6
Dalafi 168-169 B 2
Dalai 142-143 N 2
Dalai Lama Gangri 142-143 GH 5
Dalai Nur 142-143 M 2
Dalaj Nuur = Hulun Nur 142-143 M 2
Dalāk, Kūh-e — 136-137 N 4
Dalälven 116-117 G 7
Dalaman nehri 136-137 C 4
Dalandzadgad 142-143 JK 3
Dalangwan 146-147 D 11
Dalarna 116-117 EF 7
Da Lat 148-149 E 4
Dalavakasır 136-137 J 4
Dālbandīn 134-135 J 5
Dalby [AUS] 158-159 K 5
Dalcour, LA 85 I c 3
Dale 116-117 AB 7
Dale, OR 66-67 D 3
Dale, PA 72-73 G 4
Dalecarlia Reservoir 82 II a 1
Dale Hollow Lake 78-79 G 2
Dalen 116-117 C 8
Dalesford 61 F 4
Dalgaranger, Mount — 158-159 C 5
Dalhart, TX 76-77 C 4
Dalhauzī 138-139 M 7
Dalhousie 63 C 3
Dalhousie = Dalhauzī 138-139 M 7
Dalhousie, Cape — 56-57 KL 3
Dalhousie Island 138-139 M 7
Dali [TJ, Shaanxi] 146-147 B 4
Dali [TJ, Yunnan] 142-143 HJ 6
Dalian, Lüda- 142-143 N 4
Dalias 120-121 F 10
Dali Baizu Zizhizhou 142-143 HJ 6
Dalies, NM 76-77 A 5
Dali He 146-147 B 3
Daling He 144-145 C 2
Dalís 166-167 HJ 1
Daljā' 173 B 4
Ḍalkūt = Kharīfūt 134-135 G 7
Dall, Mount — 58-59 LM 5
Dallas 61 K 5
Dallas, GA 78-79 G 4
Dallas, IA 70-71 D 5
Dallas, OR 66-67 B 3
Dallas, TX 64-65 G 5
Dallas City, IL 70-71 E 5
Dällikon 128 IV a 1
Dalli Rājhara 138-139 H 7
Dall Island 56-57 K 7
Dall Lake 58-59 F 6
Dall Mount 58-59 N 3
Dallol Bosso 164-165 E 5-6
Dall River 58-59 N 3
Dalmacija 122-123 F 3-H 4
Dalmacio Vélez Sarsfield 106-107 EF 4
Dalmaj, Hawr — 136-137 L 6
Dalmatia = Dalmacija 122-123 F 3-H 4
Dalmau 138-139 H 4
Dalmiyapuram 140 D 5
Dalnegorsk 132-133 a 9
Dalnerečensk 132-133 Za 8
Dal'nij = Lüda-Dalian 142-143 N 4
Daloa 164-165 C 7
Dalqū 164-165 L 4-5
Dalquier 62 MN 2
Dalrymple, Mount — 158-159 J 4
Dalsingh Saraj 138-139 K 5
Dalton 70-71 HJ 1
Dalton, GA 64-65 JK 5
Dalton, MA 72-73 K 3
Dalton, NE 68-69 E 5
Daltonganj 134-135 N 6
Dalton Ice Tongue 53 C 12-13
Dalton in Furness 119 E 4
Dalvik 116-117 d 2
Dalwhinnie 119 D 3
Dalyan burnu 154 I b 1
Daly City, CA 74-75 B 4
Daly Lake 61 F 2
Daly River 158-159 F 2
Daly Waters 158-159 F 3
Damā, Wādī — 173 DE 4
Damakanya 168-169 B 3
Damān 134-135 L 6
Damanhūr 164-165 L 2
Damanhūr Shubrā 170 II b 1
Damão = Damān 134-135 L 6
Damaq 136-137 N 5
Damar, Pulau — 148-149 J 8
Damaraland 172 C 6
Damascus, VA 80-81 F 2
Damascus = Dimashq 134-135 D 4
Damaturu 164-165 G 6
Damāvand, Kūh-e — 134-135 G 3
Damazīn, Ad- 164-165 LM 6
Damba 172 BC 3
Dambuki 142-143 S 3-T 2
Dambulla 140 E 7
Dam Dam = South Dum Dum 134-135 OP 6
Damdek = Phum Damdek 150-151 DE 6
Dame Marie, Cap — 88-89 J 5
Damenglong 150-151 C 2
Dämeritzsee 130 III c 2
Dāmghān 134-135 GH 3
Đâm Ha 150-151 F 2
Damianópolis 100-101 A 8
Damiaoshan = Rongshui 146-147 B 9
Damietta = Dumyāṭ 164-165 L 2
Damietta Mouth = Maṣabb Dumyāṭ 173 BC 2
Daming 146-147 E 3
Dāmīr, Ad- 164-165 L 5
Damīr Qābū 136-137 JK 4
Dammām, Ad- 132-133 FG 5
Damnāt 166-167 C 4
Dāmodar 134-135 O 6
Damoh 138-139 G 6
Damongo 168-169 E 3
Damot 164-165 b 2
Damous = Dāmus 166-167 G 1
Dampier 158-159 C 4
Dampier, Selat — 148-149 K 7
Dampier Archipelago 158-159 C 4
Dampier Downs 158-159 D 3
Dampier Land 158-159 D 3
Damrei, Phnom — 150-151 DE 7
Dāmūr, Ad- 136-137 F 6
Dāmus 166-167 G 1
Dan, Kap — 56-57 d 4
Dana, Mount — 74-75 D 4
Danané 168-169 CD 4
Đa Năng 148-149 E 3
Đa Năng, Mui — 150-151 G 4
Dānāpur = Dinapore 138-139 K 5
Danau Jempang 152-153 LM 6
Danau Maninjau 152-153 CD 6
Danau Matana 152-153 O 7
Danau Melintang 152-153 LM 6
Danau Poso 152-153 O 6
Danau Ranau 152-153 E 8
Danau Sentarum 152-153 JK 5
Danau Singkarak 152-153 CD 6
Danau Tempe 148-149 GH 7
Danau Toba 148-149 C 6
Danau Towuti 148-149 H 7
Danau Wissel 148-149 L 7
Danbury, CT 72-73 K 4
Danbury, WI 70-71 D 2-3
Danby Lake 74-75 F 5
Dancharia 120-121 G 7
Dandarah 173 C 4
Danḍeldhurā 138-139 H 3
Dandeli 140 B 3
Dandelli = Dandeli 140 B 3
Dandolidhura = Danḍeldhurā 138-139 H 3
Dandong 142-143 N 3
Danfeng 146-147 C 5
Danforth, ME 72-73 MN 2
Danfu 148-149 h 5
Dang 98-99 L 2
Dangan Liedao 146-147 E 10-11
Ḍangaripalli = Dungripalli 138-139 J 7
Dange, Rio — 172 B 3
Danger 208 K 4
Dangpe La 138-139 M 3
Dang Raek, Phanom — 148-149 DE 4
Dangraek, Phnom — = Phanom Dong Raek 148-149 DE 4
Dāngs 138-139 D 7
Dangs, The — = Dāngs 138-139 D 7
Dangshan 146-147 F 4
Dangtu 146-147 G 6
Dan Gulbi 168-169 G 3
Danguno 164-165 F 6-7
Dangyang 146-147 CD 6
Danhao Dao 146-147 DE 10
Dan He 146-147 D 4
Da Nhim 150-151 G 7
Daniel, WY 66-67 H 4
Daniel's Harbour 63 GH 2
Dänikon 128 IV a 1
Danilov 132-133 G 6
Danilovka 124-125 P 7
Danilovo 124-125 KL 2
Daning 146-147 C 3
Danissa 171 E 2
Dan Jiang 146-147 C 5
Danjo-shotō 144-145 G 6
Ḍank 134-135 H 6
Dankana 168-169 GH 2
Dankhar Gömpa 138-139 G 1
Dan Khun Thot 150-151 CD 5
Dankov 124-125 M 7
Danlí 64-65 J 9
Dan Na Lao = Ban Dan Na Lao 150-151 EF 5
Dannemora, NY 72-73 JK 2
Dannevirke 158-159 P 8
Dannhauser 174-175 HJ 4-5
Dañoso, Cabo — 108-109 F 7
Dan River 80-81 FG 2
Dan Sai 150-151 C 4
Danshui 146-147 E 10
Danshui = Tanshui 142-143 N 6
Danshui He = Tanshui Chiang 146-147 H 9
Dansia 92-93 H 4
Danson Park 129 II c 2
Dansville, NY 72-73 H 3
Dānta 138-139 D 5
Danta, La — 94-95 L 4
Dāntan 138-139 L 7
Dānta Rāmgarh = Rāmgarh 138-139 E 4
Dante, VA 80-81 E 2
Dante = Haafuun 164-165 c 1
Dantewara 140 E 1
Dantyaorā = Dantewāra 140 E 1
Danube = Duna 118 J 5
Danubyū 141 D 7
Danushkodi 134-135 MN 9
Danville 72-73 KL 2
Danville, AR 78-79 C 3
Danville, IL 64-65 J 3
Danville, IN 70-71 G 6
Danville, KY 70-71 H 7
Danville, ME 72-73 L 2-3
Danville, VA 64-65 L 4
Danwanjiao 152-153 KL 2
Dan Xian 142-143 K 8
Danyang 146-147 G 6
Danzin Au 141 D 7
Đao Bach Long Vi 150-151 F 2
Đao Cai Ban 148-149 E 2
Đao Cat Ba 150-151 F 2
Đao Kersaint 150-151 FG 2
Daolatābād = Daulatābād 138-139 E 8
Daoli 146-147 H 3
Dao Ly So'n = Cu Lao Rê 150-151 G 5
Đao Phu Quôc 148-149 D 4
Daosā 138-139 F 4
Dao Shui 146-147 E 6
Đao Tching Lan Xan 150-151 FG 2
Dao-Timni 164-165 G 4
Ḍaou, Eḍ — = Aḍ-Ḍaw 136-137 G 5
Daouadi 168-169 B 2

284 Cuchilla

Daoura, Hamada de la — = Hammadat ad-Dawrah 166-167 DE 5
Daoura, Ouèd ed — = Wādī ad-Dawrah 166-167 DE 5
Đao Vinh Thu'c = Đao Kersaint 150-151 FG 2
Dao Xian 146-147 C 9
Dapango 168-169 F 3
Đap Câu 150-151 F 2
Dapchi 168-169 H 2
Dapeng 146-147 E 10
Dapeng Wan 146-147 E 10
Dapingzu = Huitongqiao 141 F 3
Dapna Bum 141 E 2
Dapodi = Dabaidi 146-147 E 8
Dāpoli 140 A 2
Dapsang = K2 134-135 M 3
Dapu = Dabu 146-147 F 9
Dāpung = Brāpung 138-139 N 3
Dapupan 148-149 GH 3
Daqi = Ta-ch'i [RC ✓ Taipei] 146-147 H 9
Daqi = Ta-ch'i [RC ✓ Taitung] 146-147 H 10
Daqiao 146-147 E 7
Daqing Shan 142-143 L 3
Daqmā', Ad- 134-135 FG 6
Daqq-e Patargān 134-135 J 4
Daquan 142-143 H 3
Daqu Shan 146-147 J 6
Dar'ā 136-137 G 6
Darā, Jazīreh — 136-137 N 7
Daraá, Rio — 94-95 J 7-8
Dara' al-Mizān 166-167 HJ 1
Dārāb 134-135 GH 5
Darabani 122-123 M 1
Darad = Dardistān 134-135 L 3
Darag = Legaspi 148-149 H 4
Daraj 164-165 G 2
Dār al-Bayḍā', Ad- 164-165 BC 2
Dār al-Qā'id al-Midbūh 166-167 DE 2
Darang = Dirang 141 C 2
Dār ash-Shāfa'ī 166-167 C 3
Darašun = Veršino-Darasunskij 132-133 VW 7
Darau = Darāw 173 C 5
Darāw 173 C 5
Darb, Ad- 134-135 E 7
Dār Bādām 136-137 M 6
Darband, Kūh-e — 134-135 H 4
Darbandī Khan, Sadd ad- 136-137 L 5
Darbanga = Darbhanga 134-135 O 5
Darbėnai 124-125 C 5
Darbhanga 134-135 O 5
Darbi = Darvi 142-143 G 2
Darby, MT 66-67 FG 2
Darby, PA 84 III b 2
Darby, Cape — 58-59 F 4
Darby Creek 84 III b 2
Darby Mountains 58-59 E 4
Dar Caid Medboh = Dār al-Qā'id al-Midbūh 166-167 DE 2
Dar Chafaï = Dār ash-Shāfa'ī 166-167 C 3
Darchan 142-143 K 2
Dardanelle, AR 78-79 C 3
Dardanelles = Çanakkale boğazı 134-135 B 2-3
Dār Dīshah 136-137 J 5
Dardo = Kangding 142-143 J 5-6
Dar Dryūs 166-167 E 2
Darebin Creek 161 II c 1
Dār ech Chāfaî = Dār ash-Shāfa'ī 166-167 C 3
Dar el Beida 170 I b 2
Dar el Beida, Aéroport de — 170 I b 2
Dâr el Beïḍā', ed — = Ad-Dār al-Bayḍā' 164-165 BC 2
Darende 136-137 G 3
Dar es Salaam 172 GH 3
Dārfūr 164-165 J 6
Dārfūr al-Janūbīyah 164-165 JK 6
Dārfūr ash-Shimālīyah 164-165 J 6-K 5
Dargagā, Jebel ed — = Jabal Ardar Gwagwa 173 D 6
Dargan-Ata 134-135 J 2
Dargaville 158-159 O 7
Dargo 160 H 6
Dargol 168-169 F 2
Dargyalükutong Gonpa 138-139 MN 2
Dār Ḥamar 164-165 K 6
Dar Hu = Dalaj Nur 142-143 M 3
Darien, GA 80-81 F 5
Darién [PA, landscape] 64-65 L 10
Darien [PA, place] 64-65 b 2
Darien = Lüda-Dalian 142-143 N 4
Darién, Cordillera de — 88-89 D 8
Darién, Golfo del — 92-93 D 3
Darién, Serranía del — 88-89 H 10
Dārigah 136-137 K 5
Dariganga 142-143 L 2
Daringbādi 138-139 JK 8
Darjeeling 134-135 O 5
Dārjiling = Darjeeling 134-135 O 5
Darjinskij 124-125 S 8
Darkhazīneh 136-137 N 7
Darling 174-175 C 7
Darling, Lake — 68-69 F 1
Darling Downs 158-159 JK 5
Darling Range 158-159 C 6
Darling River 158-159 H 6
Darlington 119 EF 4
Darlington, SC 80-81 FG 3
Darlington, WI 70-71 EF 4
Darlowo 118 H 1
Darmsāla 138-139 KL 7
Darmstadt 118 D 4
Darmstadt-Kranichstein 128 III b 2
Darnah 164-165 J 2
Darnall 174-175 J 5
Darnick 158-159 H 6
Darnley, Cape — 53 C 7-8
Daro 152-153 J 4
Daroca 120-121 G 8
Darovskoj 124-125 Q 4
Darregueira 106-107 F 6
Darrington, WA 66-67 C 1
Dar Rounga 164-165 J 6-7
Dar Runga = Dar Rounga 164-165 J 6-7
Darsah 134-135 G 8
Darshi = Darsi 140 D 3
Darsi 140 D 3
Dart, Cape — 53 B 24
Dartford 129 II c 2
Dartmoor Forest 119 E 6
Dartmouth [CDN] 56-57 Y 9
Dartuch, Cabo — 120-121 J 9
Daru 148-149 M 8
Darūdāb 164-165 M 5
Dārugiri 141 B 3
Dār Ūld Zīdūḥ 166-167 C 3
Daruvar 122-123 G 3
Darvaza 134-135 H 2
Darvel, Teluk — 152-153 N 3
Dārvhā = Dārwha 138-139 F 7
Darvi 142-143 G 2
Darwešān 134-135 JK 4
Dārwha 138-139 F 7
Darwin, CA 74-75 E 4
Darwin [AUS] 158-159 F 2
Darwin [RA] 106-107 E 7
Darwin, Bahía — 111 AB 7
Darwin, Canal — 108-109 B 5
Darwin, Cordillera — [RCH, Cordillera Patagónica] 108-109 C 7-8
Darwin, Cordillera — [RCH, Tierra del Fuego] 108-109 DE 10
Darwin, Cordillera de — 104-105 B 10
Darwin zapovednik 124-125 LM 4
Daryācheh Bakhtegān 134-135 G 5
Daryācheh Ḥowḍ Solṭān 136-137 O 5
Daryācheh i Niriz = Daryācheh Bakhtegān 134-135 G 5
Daryācheh Namak 134-135 G 4
Daryācheh Reḍā'īyeh = Daryācheh-ye Orūmīyeh 134-135 F 3
Daryācheh Sīstān 134-135 HJ 4
Daryācheh Ṭashk 134-135 GH 5
Daryācheh Urmia = Daryācheh Orūmīyeh 134-135 F 3
Daryācheh-ye Orūmīyeh 134-135 E 3
Daryāpur 138-139 F 7
Dāryā-ye Adraskan = Hārūt Rōd 134-135 J 4
Dārya-ye-Hilmānd = Helmand Rōd 134-135 K 4
Dāryā-ye 'Omān = Khalīj 'Umān 134-135 HJ 6
Dās 134-135 G 5
Dasamantapur 138-139 J 8
Dašava 126-127 AB 2
Dašev 126-127 D 2
Dasha He 146-147 E 2
Dashamantpura = Dasamantapur 138-139 J 8
Dashen, Ras — 164-165 M 6
Dashiqiao 144-145 D 2
Dasht 134-135 J 5
Dasht-e Āzādegān 136-137 N 7
Dasht-e Kavīr 134-135 GH 4
Dasht-e Lūṭ 134-135 H 4
Dasht-e Marg 134-135 J 4
Dasht-e Margoh = Dasht-e Marg 134-135 J 4
Dasht-e Moghān 134-135 F 3
Dashtīāri = Polān 134-135 J 5
Daškesan 126-127 MN 6
Daspalla 138-139 K 7
Dassa-Zoumé 168-169 F 4
Dassel, MN 70-71 C 3
Dasseneiland 174-175 BC 7
Dasūā = Dasūya 138-139 E 2
Dasūya 138-139 E 2
Dātāganj 138-139 G 3
Datang 146-147 B 9
Dataran Tinggi Cameron = Tanah-tinggi Cameron 148-149 D 6
Datça = Reşadiye 136-137 B 4
Đât Đo 150-151 F 7
Date 144-145 b 2
Dātha 138-139 C 7
Datia 134-135 M 5
Datian 146-147 F 9
Datil, NM 76-77 A 5
Datiyā = Datia 134-135 M 5
D'atkovo 124-125 K 7
D'atlovo 124-125 E 7
Datok, Kampung — 150-151 D 11
Datong [TJ, Anhui] 146-147 F 6
Datong [TJ, Shanxi] 142-143 L 3
Datong He 142-143 J 4
Datori 168-169 F 3
Da Troun, Đeo — 150-151 G 7
Da Trun, Đeo — = Đeo Da Troun 150-151 G 7
Dattapur 138-139 FG 7
Datu, Tanjung — 148-149 E 6
Datu, Teluk — 148-149 EF 6
Datun, Beijing- 155 II b 2
Datu Piang 148-149 H 5
Dau'an = Al-Hurayḍah 134-135 F 7
Daudkaṇḍī 141 B 4
Daudmannsodden 116-117 hj 5
Daudnagar 138-139 K 5
Daugava 124-125 E 5
Daugava = Severnaja Dvina 132-133 G 5
Daugavpils 124-125 EF 6
Daulagiri = Dhaulāgiri 134-135 N 5
Daulatābād 138-139 E 8
Daule 96-97 AB 2
Daule, Río — 92-93 CD 5
Dauna Parma = Dawa 164-165 M 7-8
Daun Tri, Stung — 150-151 D 6
Dauphin 56-57 QR 7
Dauphiné 120-121 KL 6
Dauphin Island 78-79 EF 5
Dauphin Lake 61 J 5
Daura 168-169 GH 2
Daura, Wed ed — = Wādī ad-Dawrah 166-167 DE 5
Daurskij chrebet 132-133 V 7
Dausā = Daosā 138-139 F 4
Dautlatābād = Malāyer 134-135 F 4
Davalguiri = Dhaulāgiri 134-135 N 5
Davalinskogo = Ararat 126-127 M 7
Dāvangere 140 BC 3
Davao 148-149 J 5
Davao Gulf 148-149 J 5
Dāvariyā = Deoria 138-139 J 4
Davel 174-175 H 4
Davenport, AK 58-59 JK 5
Davenport, IA 64-65 H 3
Davenport, ND 68-69 H 2
Davenport, NE 68-69 H 5
Davenport, WA 66-67 D 2
Davenport Downs 158-159 H 4
Davenport Range 158-159 FG 4
Davey, Port — 158-159 HJ 8
David 64-65 K 10
David City, NE 68-69 H 5
David-Gorodok 124-125 F 7
Davidof Island 58-59 s 6-7
Davids Island 82 III d 1
Davidson 61 E 5
Davidson, OK 76-77 E 5
Davidson Mountains 56-57 H 4
Daviesville 174-175 HJ 2
Davignab 174-175 C 4
Davis, CA 74-75 BC 3
Davis, IL 70-71 F 4
Davis, OK 76-77 F 5
Davis, WV 72-73 G 5
Davis Bay 53 C 14
Davis Creek, CA 66-67 C 5
Davis Dam, AZ 74-75 F 5
Davis Island = Than Kyûn 150-151 A 8
Davis Mountains 76-77 BC 7
Davis Sea 53 C 10
Davis Strait 56-57 Z 4-5
Davlekanovo 132-133 JK 7
Davo 168-169 D 4
Davos 118 DE 5
Davydkovo, Moskva- 113 V b 3
Davydovka 126-127 J 1
Ḍaw, Aḍ- 136-137 G 5
Dawa 164-165 M 7-8
Dawadawa 168-169 E 3
Dawādimā, Ad- 134-135 EF 6
Dawan 146-147 B 10
Dawangjia Dao 144-145 D 3
Dawanle = Dewelē 164-165 N 6
Dawarah, Wād ad- 166-167 D 4
Dawāsir, Wādī ad- 134-135 EF 6
Dawenkou 146-147 F 3-4
Dawḥah, Ad- 134-135 G 5
Dawhat aḍ-Ḍuwayḥin 134-135 G 6
Dawḥat as-Sawqirah 134-135 H 7
Dawingnab = Davignab 174-175 C 4
Dawna Taungdan 141 EF 7
Dawr, Ad- 136-137 KL 5
Dawrah, Baghdād- 136-137 L 6
Dawrah, Hammadat ad- 166-167 DE 5
Dawrah, Wādī ad- 166-167 DE 5
Dawson 56-57 J 5
Dawson, GA 78-79 G 5
Dawson, ND 68-69 G 2
Dawson, Isla — 111 BC 8
Dawson Bay [CDN, bay] 61 H 4
Dawson Bay [CDN, place] 61 H 4
Dawson Creek 56-57 M 6
Dawson-Lambton Glacier 53 B 33-34
Dawson Range 56-57 J 5
Dawson Springs, KY 70-71 FG 7
Dawu 146-147 E 6
Dawu = Tawu 146-147 H 10
Dawujì, Beijing- 155 II b 2
Dawwah 134-135 H 6
Dawwāya = Jamā'at al-Ma'yuf 136-137 M 7
Dax 120-121 G 7
Da Xi 146-147 G 7-8
Da Xi = Longquan Xi 146-147 G 7-8
Da Xian 142-143 K 5
Daxindian 146-147 H 3
Daxing 146-147 F 2
Daxinggu 155 II b 3
Daxue Shan 142-143 J 5-6
Day, FL 80-81 b 1
Ḍāya al-Mā'idah 166-167 D 4
Ḍāyah 166-167 HJ 3
Ḍāyah, Jabal aḍ- 166-167 F 2
Dayang Bunting, Pulau — 148-149 C 5
Dayang He 144-145 D 2
Dayat 'al-'Ām 166-167 B 6
Ḍayat al-Khadrah 166-167 BC 6
Daya Wan 146-147 E 10
Daye 146-147 E 6
Daying Jiang 141 EF 3
Daylesford 160 G 6
Daymān 106-107 J 3
Daymán, Cuchilla del — 106-107 J 3
Daym Zubayr 164-165 K 7
Day Nui Atouat 148-149 E 3
Dayong 142-143 L 6
Dayr, Ad- 173 C 5
Dayr as-Suryānī 173 AB 2
Dayr at-Tin, Al-Qāhirah- 170 II b 2
Dayr az-Zawr 134-135 DE 3
Dayr Ḥāfir 136-137 G 4
Dayr Katrīnah 173 C 3
Dayr Māghar 136-137 H 4
Dayr Mawās 173 B 4
Dayr Samū'īl 173 B 3
Dayrūṭ 164-165 L 3
Daysland 61 BC 4
Dayton, NM 76-77 B 6
Dayton, NV 74-75 D 3
Dayton, OH 64-65 K 4
Dayton, TN 78-79 G 3
Dayton, TX 76-77 G 7
Dayton, WA 66-67 E 2
Dayton, WY 68-69 C 3
Daytona Beach, FL 64-65 KL 6
Dayu 142-143 L 6
Dayu Ling 146-147 DE 9
Da Yunhe [TJ, Jiangsu] 142-143 M 5
Da Yunhe [TJ, Shandong] 146-147 EF 3
Dayu Shan 146-147 H 6
Dayville, OR 66-67 D 3
Dazhang Xi 146-147 G 9
Dazhou Dao 150-151 H 3
Dazkırı 136-137 CD 4
De Aar 172 D 8
Dead Indian Peak 66-67 HJ 3
Dead Lake 70-71 BC 2
Deadman Bay 80-81 b 2
Deadman Mount 58-59 NO 5
Dead Sea = Yām Hammelah 136-137 F 7
Deadwood, SD 68-69 E 3
Deadwood Reservoir 66-67 F 3
Dealesville 174-175 F 5
Deal Island 160 cd 1
De'an 146-147 EF 7
Deanewood, Washington-, DC 82 II b 2
Deán Funes 111 D 4
Dean River 56-57 L 7
Dearborn, MI 72-73 E 3
Dearborn Heights, IL 83 II a 2
Dearg, Beinn — 119 D 3
Deary, ID 66-67 E 2
Dease Arm 56-57 MN 4
Dease Inlet 58-59 K 1
Dease Lake 56-57 KL 6
Dease Strait 56-57 P 4
Death Valley 64-65 C 4
Death Valley, CA 74-75 E 4
Death Valley National Monument 74-75 E 4-5
Deauville 120-121 GH 4
Deaver, WY 68-69 B 3
Debal'cevo 126-127 J 2
Debar 122-123 J 5
Debark 164-165 M 6
De Bary 106-107 F 6
Debden 61 E 4
Debdoû = Dabdū 166-167 E 3
De Beers Mine 174-175 F 5
Debeeti 174-175 G 2
De Behagle = Laï 164-165 H 7
De Beque, CO 68-69 BC 6
Debert 63 E 5
Debesy 124-125 T 5
Dēbgada = Deogarh 138-139 K 7
Dębica 118 K 3-4
Dęblin 118 KL 3
Debo, Lac — 164-165 D 5
Deborah, Mount — 58-59 O 5
De Borgia, MT 66-67 F 2
De Bosbulten 174-175 DE 5
De Bosch Bulten = De Bosbulten 174-175 DE 5
Debra Birhan = Debre Birhan 164-165 MN 7
Debra Marcos = Debre Markos 164-165 M 6
Debre Birhan 164-165 MN 7
Debrecen 118 K 5
Debre Markos 164-165 M 6
Debre Tabor 164-165 M 6
De Brug 174-175 F 5
Decamere = Dekemḥarē 164-165 M 5
Decatur, AL 64-65 J 5
Decatur, GA 64-65 K 5
Decatur, IL 64-65 HJ 3-4
Decatur, IN 70-71 H 5
Decatur, MI 70-71 GH 4
Decatur, TX 76-77 F 6
Decazeville 120-121 J 6
Decelles, Lac — 62 M 3
Decelles, Réservoir — 72-73 GH 1
Decepción, Cabo — = Cape Disappointment 111 J 8-9
Deception 53 C 30
Deception Lake 61 F 2
Decherd, TN 78-79 FG 3
Děčín 118 G 3
Decker, MT 68-69 C 3
Declo, ID 66-67 G 4
Decorah, IA 70-71 E 4
Decoto, CA 74-75 BC 4
Décou-Décou, Massif — 98-99 LM 2
Deda 122-123 L 2
Dedaye 141 D 7
Dedeagach = Alexandrúpolis 122-123 L 5
Dedeköy 136-137 C 3-4
Dedham, MA 84 I a 3
Dediāpāda 138-139 D 7
Ḍēḍiyāpāḍā = Dediāpāda 138-139 D 7
Dedo, Cerro — 111 B 6
De Doorns 174-175 CD 7
Dédougou 164-165 D 6
Dedoviči 124-125 GH 5
Dedovsk 124-125 L 6
Dedza 172 F 4
Deeg = Dīg 138-139 F 4
Deelfontein 174-175 E 6
Deep Creek Range 74-75 G 2-3
Deep River [CDN] 72-73 GH 1
Deep River [USA] 80-81 G 3
Deepwater 160 K 2
Deepwater, MO 70-71 D 6
Deer, AR 78-79 C 3
Deerfield Beach, FL 80-81 cd 3
Deering, AK 58-59 F 3
Deering, ND 68-69 F 1
Deering, Mount — 158-159 E 5
Deer Island [USA, Boston Bay] 84 I c 2
Deer Island [USA, Pacific Ocean] 58-59 b 2
Deer Lake [CDN, Newfoundland] 63 H 3
Deer Lake [CDN, Ontario] 62 B 1
Deer Lodge, MT 66-67 G 2
Deer Lodge Mountains 66-67 G 2
Deer Lodge Pass 66-67 G 3
Deer Park, AL 78-79 E 5
Deer Park, TX 85 III c 2
Deer Park, WA 66-67 E 2
Deer Park Stadium 85 III c 2
Deer River, MN 70-71 CD 2
Deerton, MI 70-71 G 2
Deer Trail, CO 68-69 DE 6
Deerwood, MN 70-71 D 2
Deesa 138-139 D 5
Deeth, NV 66-67 F 5
Deffa, ed — = Aḍ-Ḍiffah 164-165 J 2
Defferrari 106-107 H 7
Defiance, OH 70-71 H 5
De Funiak Springs, FL 78-79 FG 5
Degaon = Dehgām 138-139 D 6
Dêge 142-143 H 5
Degeh Bur 164-165 N 7
Dégelis 63 B 4
Dêgên Zangzu Zizhizhou 142-143 H 6
Deggendorf 118 F 4
Deglūr 140 C 1
De Goede Hoop 98-99 K 2
De Goeje Gebergte 98-99 L 3
Degome 168-169 F 4
De Gors 128 I b 1
De Gouph = Die Koup 174-175 E 7
De Grey 158-159 CD 4
De Grey River 158-159 CD 4
Degt'anka 124-125 N 7
Degunino, Moskva- 113 V b 2
Dehbat = Adh-Dhahībah 166-167 M 3
Deheb, Bir ed — = Bi'r adh-Dhahab 166-167 H 4
Dehej 138-139 D 7
De Heul 128 I a 1
Dehgām 138-139 D 6
Dehgolān 136-137 M 5
Dehibat = Adh-Dhahībah 166-167 M 3
Dehiwala-Mount Lavinia 134-135 M 9
Dehkhwareqan = Āzar Shahr 136-137 LM 4
Dehlorān 134-135 F 4
Dehna = Ad Dahnā' 134-135 E 5-F 6
Dehna, Ed- = Ad-Dahnā' 134-135 E 5-F 6
De Hoef 128 I a 2
Dehōk = Dahūk 136-137 K 4
Dehong Daizu Zizhizhou 142-143 H 6-7
Dehra Dūn 134-135 M 4
Dēhrā Gōpīpur = Dera Gopipur 138-139 F 2
Dehri 138-139 JK 5
Dehua 146-147 G 9
Deibüel 128 IV b 2
Deir, Ed — = Ad-Dayr 173 C 5
Deir es-Suryānī = Dayr as-Suryānī 173 AB 2
Deir ez Zôr = Dayr az-Zawr 134-135 DE 3
Deir Ḥāfir = Dayr Ḥāfir 136-137 G 4
Deir Katerîna = Dayr Katrīnah 173 C 3
Deir Mâghar = Dayr Māghar 136-137 H 4
Deir Mawâs = Dayr Mawās 173 B 4
Deir Samweil = Dayr Samū'īl 173 B 3
Dej 122-123 K 2
De Jong, Tanjung — 148-149 L 8
De Kalb, IL 70-71 F 5
De Kalb, MS 78-79 E 4
De Kalb, TX 76-77 G 6
De-Kastri 132-133 ab 7
Dekemḥarē 164-165 M 5
Dekese 172 D 2
Dekoûa, Tell — = Tall adh-Dhakwah 136-137 G 6
De Kwakel 128 I a 2
De la Canal 106-107 H 6
De la Garma 106-107 G 6-7
Delagoa Bay = Baía do Maputo 172 F 7
Delagua, CO 68-69 D 7
Delaimiya, Ad- = Ad-Dulaymīyah 136-137 K 6
Delair, NJ 84 III c 2
Del Aire, CA 83 III b 2
Delanco, NJ 84 III d 1
De Land, FL 80-81 c 2
Delano, CA 74-75 D 5
Delano, MN 70-71 CD 3
Delano Peak 64-65 D 4
Delareyville 174-175 F 4
Delarof Islands 58-59 t 7
Delaronde Lake 61 E 3-4
Delarondeo Park 85 I c 2
De la Serna 106-107 E 5
Delavan, IL 70-71 F 5
Delavan, WI 70-71 F 4
Delaware 64-65 LM 4
Delaware, OH 72-73 E 4
Delaware Bay 64-65 LM 4
Delaware Lake 72-73 E 4
Delaware Reservoir 72-73 E 4
Delaware River 72-73 J 5
Delburne 60 L 3
Delcambre, LA 78-79 CD 6
Del Campillo 106-107 E 5
Delčevo 122-123 K 4-5
Delegate 160 J 6
De Leon, TX 76-77 E 6
Delfi = Delphoí 122-123 K 6
Delfim Moreira 102-103 K 5
Delfino 100-101 D 6
Delfinópolis 102-103 J 4
Dèlft [CL] 140 D 6
Delfzijl 120-121 L 2
Delgerchet 142-143 L 2
Delger mörön 142-143 H 1-2
Delgo = Delqū 164-165 L 4-5
Delhi, CO 68-69 DE 7
Delhi, LA 78-79 D 4
Delhi, NY 72-73 J 3
Delhi [CDN] 72-73 F 3
Delhi [IND] 134-135 M 5
Delhi = Dilli 148-149 J 8
Deli, Pulau — 148-149 DE 8
Delice 136-137 E 3
Delicermak 136-137 F 3
Délices 92-93 J 4
Delicias 64-65 E 6
Deli-Ibrahim 170 I a 2
Delījān 136-137 O 5-6
Delingde 132-133 VW 4
Delipuna Miao = Brāpung 138-139 N 3
Delisle 61 E 5
Delitua 150-151 B 11
Dell, MT 66-67 G 3
Della Rapids 60 DE 5
Delle, UT 66-67 G 5
Dellys = Dalīs 166-167 HJ 1
Del Mar, CA 74-75 E 6
Delmar, IA 70-71 E 4-5
Delmar Stadium 85 III b 1
Delmas 174-175 H 4
Delmenhorst 118 CD 2
Delmiro Gouveia 100-101 F 5
Del Norte, CO 68-69 C 7
Delong, proliv — 132-133 j 3-4
De Long Mountains 56-57 D 4
Deloraine [AUS] 160 c 2
Deloraine [CDN] 68-69 F 1
Dêlos 122-123 L 7
Delphi, IN 70-71 G 5
Delphoí 122-123 K 6
Delphos, OH 70-71 H 5
Delportshoop 174-175 EF 5
Delran, NJ 84 III d 1
Delray Beach, FL 80-81 cd 3
Del Rio, TX 64-65 F 6
Delta, CO 68-69 B 6
Delta, UT 74-75 G 3
Delta Amacuro 94-95 L 3
Delta Beach 61 JK 5
Delta del Ebro 120-121 H 8
Delta del Orinoco 92-93 G 3
Delta del Río Colorado 108-109 H 2
Delta del Río Paraná 106-107 H 4-5
Delta Dunarii 122-123 N 3
Delta Junction, AK 58-59 OP 4
Delta Mendota Canal 74-75 C 4
Delta River 58-59 OP 5
Delvā = Delwa 138-139 DE 3
Del Valle 106-107 G 5
Delvinë 122-123 HJ 6
Delwa 138-139 DE 3
Delwin, TX 76-77 D 6
Demachi = Tonami 144-145 L 4
Demāgiri 141 C 4
Demak 152-153 J 9
Dem'ansk 124-125 J 5
Demarcation Point 58-59 RS 2
Demarchi 106-107 G 5
De Mares 94-95 DE 4
Demavend = Kūh-e Damāvāvand 134-135 G 3
Demba 172 D 3
Dembī Dolo 164-165 LM 7
Demchhog 142-143 D 5
Ḍemeir = Ḍumayr 136-137 G 6
Demeke 168-169 C 2
Demer, Djebel — = Jabal al-Qṣūr 166-167 M 3
Demerara 98-99 J 1-2
Demerara = Georgetown 92-93 H 3
Demerara River 98-99 J 1-2
Demidov 124-125 H 6
Deming, WA 66-67 BC 1
Demini, Rio — 92-93 G 4-5
Demirci 136-137 C 3
Demirciköy [TR, Denizli] 136-137 C 3
Demirciköy [TR, İstanbul] 154 I b 1
Demirköprü barajı 136-137 C 3
Demirköy 136-137 BC 2
Demir Qâboû = Damir Qābū 136-137 JK 4
Demjanka 132-133 N 6
Demjanovo 124-125 N 4
Demjanovskaja 124-125 P 3
Demjanskoje 132-133 MN 6
Demmin 118 F 2
Demmitt 60 H 2
Demnate = Damnāt 166-167 C 4
Demopolis, AL 78-79 EF 4
De Morhiban, Lac — 63 E 2
Dempo, Gunung — 148-149 D 7
Demta 148-149 M 7
De Naauwte 174-175 DE 6
Denali, AK 58-59 O 5
Denan 164-165 N 7
Denare Beach 61 GH 3
Denau 134-135 K 3
Denbigh [CDN] 72-73 H 2
Denbigh, Cape — 58-59 FG 4
Dendang 148-149 E 7
Dende, Rio de Janeiro- 110 I b 1
Dendy Park 161 II c 2
Denenchōfu, Tōkyō- 155 III ab 2
Dengkou = Bajan Gol 142-143 K 3
Denglou Jiao = Kami Jiao 146-147 B 11
Deng Xian 146-147 D 5
Den Haag = 's-Gravenhage 120-121 JK 2
Denham 158-159 B 5
Denham Springs, LA 78-79 D 5
Den Helder 120-121 K 2
Denia 120-121 H 9
Denial Bay 160 A 4
Denikil 164-165 N 6
Deniliquin 158-159 HJ 7
Den Ilp 128 I ab 1
Denio, OR 66-67 D 5
Denison, IA 70-71 C 4-5
Denison, TX 64-65 G 5
Denison, Mount — 58-59 KL 7
Denisovskaja 124-125 NO 3
Deṇiyāya 140 E 7
Denizli 134-135 B 3
Denman 160 K 4
Denman Glacier 53 BC 10-11
Denman Island 66-67 A 1
Denmark, SC 80-81 F 4
Denmark, WI 70-71 G 3
Denmark [AUS] 158-159 C 6
Denmark [DK] 116-117 CD 10
Denmark Strait 56-57 f 4-e 5
Denndoudi 168-169 B 2
Denning, München- 130 II bc 2
Denpasar 148-149 FG 8
Dent, ID 66-67 E 2
Dent du Tigre = Dông Voi Mêp 148-149 F 4
Denton, MD 72-73 HJ 5
Denton, MT 68-69 B 2
Denton, NC 80-81 FG 3
Denton, TX 64-65 G 5
d'Entrecasteaux Islands 148-149 h 6
Denver, CO 64-65 EF 4
Denver City, TX 76-77 C 6
Denver Harbor Park 85 III b 1
Denzil 61 D 4
Đeo Ai Vân = Đeo Hai Van 150-151 G 4
Deoband 138-139 F 3
Đeo Bao Lôc 150-151 F 7
Deobhog 138-139 J 8
Đeo-Blao = Đeo Bao Lôc 150-151 F 7
Deodar = Diodar 138-139 C 5
Đeo Da Troun 150-151 G 7
Đeo Da Trun = Đeo Da Troun 150-151 G 7
Deodrug 140 C 2
Deogarh [IND, Orissa] 138-139 K 7
Deogarh [IND, Rājasthān] 138-139 D 5
Deogarh Peak 138-139 J 6
Deoghar 134-135 O 6
Đeo Hai Van 150-151 G 4
Đeo Keo Neua 150-151 E 3
Deolāli 138-139 D 8
Deoli [IND, Mahārāshtra] 138-139 G 7
Deoli [IND, Rājasthān] 138-139 E 5
Đeo Lô Qui Hô = Đeo Hai Yân 150-151 D 1
Đeo Mang Yang 150-151 G 5
Đeo Mu' Gia 150-151 E 4
Đeo Mu'o'ng Sen 148-149 DE 3
Đeo Ngang 150-151 F 3-4
Đeo Pech Nil 150-151 E 7
Deoprayag = Devaprayāg 138-139 G 2
Deori 138-139 G 6
Deoria 138-139 J 4
Depālpur 138-139 E 6
De Paul University 83 II b 1
Dependencias Federales 94-95 HJ 2
Depew, OK 76-77 F 5
Deping 146-147 F 3
Depósito 98-99 I 2
Deppegūda 138-139 JK 8
Dépression du Mourdi 164-165 J 5
Deptford, London- 129 II b 2
Deptford Terrace, NJ 84 III c 3
De Put = Die Put 174-175 E 6
Deqen 142-143 H 6
Deqen Zizhizhou = B ◁ 142-143 H 6
Deqing [TJ, Guangdong] 146-147 C 10
Deqing [TJ, Zhejiang] 146-147 GH 6
De Queen, AR 76-77 G 5
De Quincy, LA 78-79 C 5
Der'ā = Dar'ā 136-137 G 6
Dera, Lak — 172 H 1
Dērā Bassī = Basi 138-139 F 2
Ḍera Bugṭī 138-139 B 3
Dera Ghāzi Khān 134-135 L 4
Dera Gopipur 138-139 F 2
Dera Ismaīl Khān 134-135 L 4
Dera Jāt 138-139 C 2-3
Derajat = Ḍera Jāt 138-139 C 2-3
Derāpur 138-139 G 4
Derāwar Forṭ 138-139 C 3
Deraž'n'a 126-127 C 2
Derbent 126-127 O 5

Derbent 285

Derbesiye 136-137 J 4
Derbeškinskij 124-125 T 6
Derby [AUS] 158-159 D 3
Derby [GB] 119 F 5
Derby [ZA] 174-175 G 3
Derdepoort 174-175 G 3
Dereköy [TR, Sivas] 136-137 G 2
Dereli 136-137 H 2
Deren, Adrar N — 166-167 BC 4
Dereseki [TR ↑ İstanbul] 154 I b 1
Dereseki [TR ↗ İstanbul] 154 I b 2
Derevlevo, Moskva- 113 V b 3
Derg' = Daraj 164-165 G 2
Derg, Lough — 119 BC 5
Dergači [SU, Rossijskaja SFSR] 124-125 R 8
Dergači [SU, Ukrainskaja SSR] 126-127 H 1
Ḍergāňv = Dergaon 141 C 2
Dergaon 141 C 2
De Ridder, LA 78-79 C 5
Derik 136-137 J 4
Derinkuyu 136-137 F 3
Derj = Daraj 164-165 G 2
Derkali 171 E 2
Derm 174-175 C 2
Dermott, AR 78-79 D 4
Derna = Darnah 164-165 J 2
Derry, NH 72-73 L 3
Derūdēb = Darūdāb 164-165 M 5
De Rust 174-175 E 7
Derventa 122-123 G 3
Derwent [AUS] 160 c 3
Derwent [ZA] 174-175 H 3
Deržavino 124-125 T 7
Deržavinskij 132-133 M 7
Desaguadera del Bermejo 106-107 D 3-4
Desaguadero [PE] 96-97 G 10
Desaguadero [RA] 106-107 D 4
Desaguadero, Río — [BOL] 92-93 F 8
Desaguadero, Río — [RA] 106-107 D 4
Desagüe, Canal del — 91 I c 1
Des Arc, AR 78-79 D 3
Des Arc, MO 78-79 D 2
Desastre, Cachoeira do — 98-99 J 10
Desbarats 70-71 J 2
Descabezado Grande, Volcán — 106-107 B 5
Descalvado 102-103 D 2
Descanso 102-103 F 7
Descanso, El — 86-87 B 1
Descanso, Punta — 86-87 B 1
Deschaillons 72-73 KL 1
Deschambault Lake [CDN, lake] 61 FG 3
Deschambault Lake [CDN, place] 61 G 3
Deschutes River 66-67 C 3
Desdemona, TX 76-77 E 6
Desē 164-165 MN 6
Deseado 102-103 EF 6
Deseado = Puerto Deseado 111 CD 7
Deseado, Cabo — 111 AB 8
Deseado, Río — 111 BC 7
Desecho, Paso de — 106-107 B 6
Desemboque, El — 86-87 D 2
Desengaño, Punta — 108-109 F 7
Desenzano del Garda 122-123 D 3
Deseret Peak 66-67 G 5
Deseronto 72-73 H 2
Desertas, Ilhas — 164-165 A 2
Desert Center, CA 74-75 F 6
Desertores, Islas — 108-109 C 4
Deserto Salato = Dasht-e Kavīr 134-135 GH 4
Desful = Dezfūl 134-135 F 4
Deshengmen, Beijing- 155 II b 2
Deshler, OH 72-73 E 4
Deshu 134-135 J 4
Desiderio Tello 106-107 DE 3
Desierto, El — 104-105 B 8
Desierto de Altar 86-87 D 2-3
Desierto de Atacama 111 B 3-C 2
Desierto de Sechura 96-97 A 4-5
Desierto de Vizcaíno 86-87 CD 4
Desirade, La — 88-89 Q 6
Desmarais 60 KL 2
De Smet, SD 68-69 H 3
Des Moines, IA 64-65 GH 3
Des Moines, NM 76-77 C 4
Des Moines River 64-65 GH 3
Des Moines River, East Fork — 70-71 C 4
Des Moines River, West Fork — 70-71 C 4
Desmonte, El — 104-105 E 8
Desna 124-125 K 7
Desnudez, Punta — 106-107 H 7
Desolación, Isla — 111 AB 8
Desolation Canyon 74-75 J 3
Desordem, Serra da — 100-101 AB 2
De Soto, MO 70-71 E 6
De Soto, WI 70-71 E 4
Despatch 174-175 F 7
Despeñaderos 106-107 EF 3
Despeñaperros, Puerto de — 120-121 F 9
Des Plaines, IL 70-71 FG 4
Despoblado de Pabur 96-97 A 4
Dessau 118 F 3
Desterrada, Isla — 86-87 Q 6
Destêrro 100-101 F 4
D'Estrees Bay 160 CD 5-6
Destruction Bay 58-59 S 6
Destruction Island 66-67 A 2
Desventurados 199 AB 6
Desvio El Sombrero = El Sombrero 106-107 H 1
Detčino 124-125 KL 6
Dete 172 E 5
Detmold 118 D 3
De Tour, MI 70-71 HJ 2-3
Detrital Valley 74-75 F 4-5
Detroit, MI 64-65 K 3
Detroit, TX 76-77 G 6
Detroit, Country Club of — 84 II c 2
Detroit, University of — 84 II b 2
Detroit City Airport 84 II bc 2
Detroit Harbor, WI 70-71 G 3
Detroit Lake 66-67 B 3
Detroit Lakes, MN 70-71 BC 2
Detroit River 72-73 E 3-4
Detroit-Strathmoor, MI 84 II a 2
Detroit-Windsor Tunnel 84 II bc 3
Detroit Zoological Park 84 II ab 2
Dettifoss 116-117 e 2
Det Udom 150-151 E 5
Deuil 129 I c 2
Deutsches Museum 130 II b 2
Deux-Rivières 72-73 G 1
Deva 122-123 K 3
Devakottai 140 D 6
De Valls Bluff, AR 78-79 D 3
Devanahaḷḷi = Devanhalli 140 CD 4
Devanhalli 140 CD 4
Devaprayāg 138-139 G 2
Dēvarakoṇḍā = Devarkonda 140 D 2
Devarkonda 140 D 2
Dēvās = Dewās 138-139 F 6
Dévaványa 118 K 5
Dēvbālodā 138-139 H 7
Dēvband = Deoband 138-139 F 3
Deveci dağları 136-137 FG 2
Develi [TR, Kayseri] 136-137 F 3
Deventer 120-121 L 2
Devgad Bāria 138-139 DE 6
Devgarh 140 A 2
Devikolam 140 C 5
Devīkot 138-139 C 4
Devil Mount 58-59 E 3
Devils Elbow 58-59 JK 5
Devils Gate 74-75 D 3
Devil's Hole 114-115 HJ 4
Devils Lake 68-69 G 1
Devils Lake, ND 68-69 G 1
Devils Paw 58-59 UV 7
Devils Playground 74-75 EF 5
Devil's Point = Yak Tuḍuwa 140 DE 6
Devils Tower 68-69 D 3
Devils Tower National Monument 68-69 D 3
Devin 122-123 L 5
Devine, TX 76-77 E 8
Devipatam = Devipattanam 140 D 6
Devipattanam 140 D 6
Dēvlālī = Deolāli 138-139 D 8
Dēvlī = Deoli [IND, Mahārāshtra] 138-139 G 7
Dēvlī = Deoli [IND, Rājasthān] 138-139 E 5
Devodi Munda 140 F 1
Devoll 122-123 J 5
Devon, MT 66-67 H 1
Devon, PA 84 III a 1
Devon [GB] 119 DE 6
Devon Island 56-57 S-U 2
Devonport [AUS] 158-159 J 8
Devonport [NZ] 158-159 O 7
Devonshire = Devon 119 DE 6
Devoto 106-107 F 3
Devrek 136-137 DE 2
Devrekâni 136-137 EF 2
Devrez çayı 136-137 EF 2
de Vries, proliv — 142-143 S 2
Dēvrī-Khās = Deori 138-139 G 6
Dewakang Besar, Pulau — 152-153 N 8
Dewās 138-139 F 6
Dewdar = Diodar 138-139 C 5
Dewelē 164-165 N 6
Dewetsdorp 174-175 G 5
Dewey, OK 76-77 FG 4
Dewey, SD 68-69 DE 4
Dewey Lake 80-81 E 2
De Witt, AR 78-79 D 3
De Witt, IA 70-71 E 5
De Witt, NE 68-69 H 5
Dewli = Deoli 138-139 G 7
Dewundara Tuḍuwa 134-135 N 9
Dexian = Dezhou 142-143 M 4
Dexing 146-147 F 7
Dexter, ME 72-73 M 2
Dexter, MO 78-79 DE 2
Dexter, NM 76-77 B 6
Deyālā = Diyālā 134-135 EF 4
Dey Dey, Lake — 158-159 F 5
Deylamān 136-137 NO 4
Dez, Rūd-e — 136-137 N 6
Dezadeash Lake 58-59 T 6
Dezfūl 134-135 F 4
Dezhou 142-143 M 4
Dezh Shāhpur = Marīvān 136-137 M 5
Dezinga 171 D 6
Dežneva, mys — 132-133 lm 4
Dhahab 173 D 3
Dhahab, Bi'r adh- 166-167 F 7
Dhahar = Ẓahar 166-167 LM 3
Dhahībah, Adh- 166-167 M 3
Dhahran = Aẓ-Ẓahrān 134-135 FG 5
Ḍhāka 138-139 N 6
Ḍhākā = Ḍhāka [BD, administrative unit] 138-139 N 5-6
Ḍhākā = Ḍhāka [BD, place] 138-139 N 6
Dhakuria, Calcutta- 154 II b 2
Dhakwah, Tall adh- 136-137 G 6
Dhāma 138-139 JK 7
Dhamār 134-135 EF 8
Dhamda 138-139 H 7
Dhāmpur 138-139 G 3
Dhamtari 134-135 N 6
Dhānbād 138-139 L 6
Dhandhuka 138-139 CD 6
Dhānera 138-139 D 5
Dhangarhī 138-139 H 3
Dhankuta 134-135 O 5
Dhansiri 141 C 2
Dhanushkodi 134-135 MN 9
Dhanuṣhkōṭi = Dhanushkodi 134-135 MN 9
Dhanvār = Dhanwār 138-139 KL 5
Dhanwār 138-139 KL 5
Dhaola Dhār 138-139 F 1-2
Dhaolāgiri = Daulāgiri 134-135 N 5
Dhār 134-135 M 6
Dharampur 138-139 D 7
Dharamsālā 134-135 M 4
Dhārangāňv = Dharangaon 138-139 E 7
Dharangaon 138-139 E 7
Dhārāpuram 140 C 5
Dhārāshiva = Osmānābād 140 C 1
Dhāravāda = Dhārwār 134-135 LM 7
Dharlā 138-139 M 5
Dharmanagar 141 C 3
Dharmapuri 140 CD 4
Dharmavaram 140 C 3
Dharmjaygarh 138-139 J 6
Dharmsala = Dharamsālā 134-135 M 4
Dharmshala = Dharamsālā 134-135 M 4
Dharoor 164-165 c 1
Dhārūr 140 BC 1
Dhārvāḍ = Dhārwār 134-135 LM 7
Ḍhar Walātah 164-165 C 5
Dhārwār 134-135 LM 7
Dhasān 138-139 G 5
Dhāt al-Ḥājj = Ḥājj 173 DE 3
Dhāṭ yā Thar = Great Indian Desert 134-135 L 5
Dhauladhar = Dhaola Dhār 138-139 F 1-2
Dhaulāgiri 134-135 N 5
Dhauli 138-139 E 7
Dhāvan'gerē = Dāvangere 134-135 M 8
Dhawladhar = Dhaola Dhār 138-139 F 1-2
Dhebar Lake 138-139 D 5
Ḍhēṅkānal = Dhenkānāl 138-139 K 7
Dhenkānāl 138-139 K 7
Dhiinsoor 164-165 N 8
Dhikār, Bi'r adh- 164-165 J 3
Dhi-Oār 136-137 LM 7
Dholpur 138-139 F 4
Dhōnā = Dhone 140 C 3
Dhond 134-135 L 7
Dhone 140 C 3
Dhorāji 134-135 L 6
Dhori 138-139 B 6
Dhrāngadhra = Drangadra 138-139 C 6
Dhrangdhra = Drangadra 138-139 C 6
Dhrbarī = Dhubri 134-135 OP 5
Dhrol 138-139 C 6
Dhubri 134-135 OP 5
Dhufar = Ẓufār 134-135 G 7
Dhulēṅ = Dhūlia 134-135 L 6
Dhūlia 134-135 L 6
Dhūliyā = Dhūlia 134-135 L 6
Dhūndār 138-139 E 5-F 4
Dhūri 138-139 EF 2
Dhuusa Maareeb 164-165 b 2
Dia 122-123 L 8
Diable, Île du — 92-93 J 3
Diablo, Punta del — 106-107 L 5
Diablo, Sierra — 76-77 B 7
Diablo Heights 64-65 b 3
Diablo Range 64-65 BC 4
Diabo, Serra do — 102-103 F 5
Diaca 171 DE 5
Diadema 102-103 J 5
Diadema-Paulicéia 110 II b 3
Diadema-Vila Conceição 110 II b 3
Diagbe 171 AB 1
Diagonal, IA 70-71 CD 5
Dialafara 168-169 C 2
Dialloubé 168-169 DE 2
Diamante [RA] 111 DE 4
Diamante, El — 91 III a 2
Diamante, Río — 106-107 D 5
Diamantina 92-93 L 8
Diamantina River 158-159 H 4
Diamantino [BR ↗ Alto Garças] 102-103 F 2
Diamantino [BR ↖ Cuiabá] 92-93 H 7
Diamantino, Rio — 102-103 F 2
Diamond, OR 66-67 D 4
Diamond Bay 161 I b 2
Diamond Harbour 138-139 LM 6
Diamond Island = Leik Kyûn 141 CD 8
Diamond Lake 66-67 B 4
Diamond Peak 74-75 EF 3
Diamondville, WY 66-67 H 5
Diamou 168-169 C 2
Dianbai 146-147 C 11
Diancheng 142-143 L 7
Dian Chi 142-143 J 7
Dianfou = Feidong 146-147 F 6
Dianópolis 92-93 K 7
Dianra 168-169 D 3
Diaocha Hu 146-147 D 6
Diapaga 164-165 E 6
Diari 168-169 E 3
Díaz [MEX] 76-77 B 9
Díaz [RA] 106-107 G 4
Dībaga = Dībagah 136-137 KL 5
Dībagah 136-137 KL 5
Dibai 138-139 G 3
Dibaya 172 D 3
Dibbāgh, Jabal — 173 D 4
Dibble Ice Tongue 53 C 14
Dibdibah, Ad- 136-137 M 8
Dibele, Bena- 172 D 2
Dibella 164-165 G 5
Dibeng 174-175 E 4
Dibis, Bi'r — 164-165 K 4
Diboll, TX 76-77 G 7
Dibrugarh 134-135 PQ 5
Dibsah 136-137 GH 5
Dibulla 92-93 E 2
Dibwah 166-167 J 3
Dickens, TX 76-77 D 6
Dickey, ND 68-69 G 2
Dickinson, ND 64-65 F 2
Dickinson, TX 76-77 G 8
Dick's Head = Raas Jumbo 172 H 2
Dickson 132-133 P 3
Dickson, AK 58-59 E 4
Dickson, TN 78-79 F 2-3
Dickson City, PA 72-73 HJ 4
Dickson Harbour = P'asinskij zaliv 132-133 PQ 3
Dicle = Piran 136-137 J 3
Dicle nehri 136-137 J 4
Didiéni 164-165 C 6
Didirhine, Djebel — = Jabal Tidighin 166-167 D 2
Didsbury 60 K 4
Ḍīḍvānā = Dīdwāna 138-139 E 4
Dīdwāna 138-139 E 4
Didymóteichon 122-123 LM 5
Diébougou 168-169 E 3
Dieburger Stadtwald 128 III b 2
Dieciocho de Julio 106-107 L 4
Dieciséis de Julio 106-107 G 6
Diecisiete de Agosto 106-107 F 6
Diedersdorf 130 III b 2
Diefenbaker, Lake — 61 E 5
Diego de Alvear 106-107 F 5
Diego de Amagro, Isla — 111 A 8
Diego Garcia 50-51 N 6
Diego Ramírez, Islas — 111 C 9
Diégo-Suarez = Antsiranana 172 JK 4
Die Koup 174-175 E 7
Diéma 168-169 C 2
Diemen 128 I b 1
Diemensland, Van — = Tasmania 158-159 HJ 8
Điên Ban 150-151 G 5
Điên Biên Phu 148-149 D 2
Điên Khanh 150-151 G 6
Diepensee 130 III c 2
Diepholz 118 D 2
Diepkloof, Johannesburg- 170 V a 2
Dieppe 120-121 H 4
Die Put 174-175 E 6
Dierks, AR 76-77 GH 5
Dietlikon 128 IV b 1
Dietrich, ID 66-67 F 4
Dietrich River 58-59 N 3
Diêu, Mui — 148-149 EF 4
Diez de Julio, Colonia — 106-107 FG 3
Dif 172 H 1
Diffa 164-165 G 6
Ḍiffah, Aḍ- 164-165 J 2
Difícil, El — 92-93 E 3
Dīg 138-139 F 4
Digboi 141 D 2
Digby 63 CD 5
Digha 138-139 L 7
Dighton, KS 68-69 F 6
Digne 120-121 L 6
Digod 138-139 F 5
Digoin 120-121 JK 5
Digor 136-137 K 2
Digos 148-149 J 5
Digras 138-139 F 7
Digrī 138-139 B 5
Digul 148-149 M 8
Digurá 176 a 2
Dih 136-137 K 4
Dihang 134-135 PQ 5
Dihri = Dehri 138-139 JK 5
Dihua = Ürümchi 142-143 F 3
Dīˈīb, Wādī — 173 DE 6-7
Dijlah, Nahr — 134-135 E 3
Dijlah, Shaṭṭ — 134-135 F 4
Dijon 120-121 K 5
Dikabi 174-175 G 2
Dikākah, Ad- 134-135 G 7
Dikanäs 116-117 F 5
Dikeman, AK 58-59 J 5
Dikhil 164-165 N 6
Dikili 136-137 B 3
Dikoa = Dikwa 164-165 G 6
Díktē Óros 122-123 L 8
Dikwa 164-165 G 6
Dīla 164-165 M 7
Dilam, Ad- 134-135 F 6
Dilbeek 128 II a 1
Dilermando Aguiar 106-107 KL 2
Di Linh 148-149 E 4
Dilinjāt, Ad- 173 B 2
Diližan 126-127 M 6
Dillard University 85 I b 1
Dill City, OK 76-77 E 5
Dilley, TX 76-77 E 8
Dilli 148-149 J 8
Dillī = Delhi 134-135 M 5
Dillia 164-165 G 5-6
Dillingham, AK 56-57 DE 6
Dillinj 164-165 KL 6
Dillman = Shāhpūr 136-137 L 3
Dillon 61 D 3
Dillon, CO 68-69 C 6
Dillon, MT 66-67 G 3
Dillon, SC 80-81 G 3
Dillwyn, VA 80-81 G 2
Dilolo 172 D 4
Dima, Lak — 171 E 2
Dimāpur 141 C 3
Dimās, Rā's ad- 166-167 M 2
Dimashq 134-135 D 4
Dimbokro 164-165 D 7
Dimboola 160 EF 6
Dime Landing, AK 58-59 FG 4
Dimitrijevskoje = Talas 134-135 L 2
Dimitrovgrad [BG] 122-123 LM 4
Dimitrovgrad [SU] 132-133 HJ 7
Dimmitt, TX 76-77 C 5
Dīmōna 136-137 F 7
Dimpo 174-175 D 3
Dina 94-95 CD 6
Dinagat Island 148-149 J 4
Dinājpūr 138-139 M 5
Dinamo, Stadion — 113 V b 2
Dinan 120-121 F 4
Dinapore 138-139 K 5
Dinar 136-137 CD 3
Dīnār, Kūh-e — 134-135 G 4
Dinara 122-123 G 3-4
Dināra [IND] 138-139 K 5
Dinard 120-121 F 4
Dinaric Alps = Dinara 122-123 G 3-4
Dindi 140 D 2
Dindigul 134-135 M 8
Dindivanam = Tindivanam 140 DE 4
Dindori [IND, Madhya Pradesh] 138-139 H 6
Dindori [IND, Mahārāshtra] 138-139 D 7
Dinḍukkal = Dindigul 134-135 M 8
Dineley, Bahía — 108-109 AB 7
Ding 142-143 M 4
Ding'an 150-151 H 3
Dingbian 146-147 A 3
Ding Den, Phu — 150-151 F 5
Dinghai 146-147 J 6-7
Dingjiang = Qingjiang 146-147 E 7
Dingla 138-139 L 4
Dingle 119 A 5
Dingle Bay 119 A 5
Dingnan 146-147 E 9
Dingqiang = Dingxiang 146-147 D 2
Dingri Zong = Tingri Dsong 138-139 L 3
Dingshan = Qingshuzhen 146-147 G 6
Dingshuzhen 146-147 G 6
Dingtao 146-147 E 4
Dinguiraye 164-165 BC 6
Dingwall 119 D 3
Dingxi 142-143 J 4
Ding Xian 146-147 E 2
Dingxiang 146-147 D 2
Dingxin 142-143 H 3
Dingxing 146-147 E 2
Dingyuan 146-147 F 5
Dingzi Gang 146-147 H 3
Dingzi Wan = Dingzi Gang 146-147 H 3
Dinh, Mui — 148-149 E 4
Dinhāta 138-139 M 4
Đinh Lập 150-151 F 2
Dinkimo 168-169 G 2
Dinnebito Wash 74-75 H 5
Dinosaur National Monument 66-67 J 5
Dinsmore 61 E 5
Dinuba, CA 74-75 D 4
Dinwiddie 170 V bc 2
Diodar 138-139 C 5
Diogo Island 146-147 H 11
Dioïla 164-165 C 6
Dioka 168-169 C 2
Diomida, ostrova — 56-57 C 4-5
Dionísio Cerqueira 102-103 F 7
Diosig 122-123 JK 2
Diougani 168-169 E 2
Diouloulou 164-165 A 6
Dioura 168-169 D 2
Diourbel 164-165 A 6
Dipālpūr 138-139 D 2
Dipēyin 141 D 4
Dipfaryas = Rizokárpason 136-137 EF 5
Diphu 141 C 3
Diplo 138-139 B 5
Dipolog 148-149 H 5
Dipurdû 94-95 C 5
Dir 134-135 L 3
Dira, Djebel — = Jabal Dīrah 166-167 H 1
Diradawa = Dirē Dawa 164-165 N 7
Dīrah, Jabal — 166-167 H 1
Dirang 141 C 2
Dīrat at-Tulūl 136-137 G 6
Dirē 164-165 D 5
Dirē Dawa 164-165 N 7
Direkli 136-137 G 3
Dīret et Touloûl = Dīrat at-Tulūl 136-137 G 6
Dirfys 122-123 KL 6
Dirico 172 D 5
Dirk Hartogs Island 158-159 B 5
Dirkiesdorp 174-175 J 4
Dirkou 164-165 G 5
Dirnismaning 130 II bc 1
Dirranbandi 158-159 J 5
Dirty Devil River 74-75 H 3-4
Dīsā = Deesa 138-139 D 5
Disappointment, Cape — [Falkland Islands] 111 J 8-9
Disappointment, Cape — [USA] 66-67 A 2
Disappointment, Lake — 158-159 DE 4
Discovery [RI] 152-153 H 7
Discovery [ZA] 170 V a 1
Discovery Bay 158-159 GH 7
Discovery Well 158-159 D 4
Dishkakat, AK 58-59 J 5
Dishnā 173 C 4
Dishna River 58-59 J 5
Disko 56-57 a 4
Disko Bugt 56-57 a 4
Diskobukta 116-117 l 6
Dismal River 68-69 F 5
Dismal Swamp 80-81 H 2
Disna [SU, place] 124-125 G 6
Disna [SU, river] 124-125 FG 6
Disraëli 72-73 L 2
Disston, OR 66-67 B 4
District Heights, MD 82 II b 2
District of Columbia 72-73 H 5
District of Franklin 56-57 N-V 3
District of Keewatin 56-57 RS 4-5
District of Mackenzie 56-57 L-P 5
Distrito Especial 94-95 D 5
Distrito Federal [BR] 92-93 K 8
Distrito Federal [MEX] 86-87 L 8
Distrito Federal [RA] 111 E 4
Distrito Federal [YV] 94-95 H 2
Disūq 173 B 2
Ditang = Altar of the Earth 155 II b 2
Ditu, Mwene- 172 D 3
Diu 134-135 L 6
Dīvāndarreh 136-137 M 5
Divāngiri 134-135 P 5
Divejevo 124-125 O 6
Diver 72-73 G 1
Diversiones, Parque Popular de — 91 III bc 2-3
Diviči 126-127 O 6
Divide, MT 66-67 G 3
Dividive, El — 94-95 F 3
Divino 102-103 L 4
Divinópolis 92-93 KL 9
Divi Point 140 E 3
Divisa 88-89 F 10
Divisa, Monte da — 102-103 J 4
Divisa, Serra da — 98-99 G 9
Divisadero, Cerro — 108-109 C 8
Divisa Nova 102-103 J 4
Diviso, El — [CO, Nariño] 94-95 B 7
Diviso, El — [CO, Putumayo] 94-95 D 7
Divisões, Serra das — 92-93 JK 8
Divisor, Sierra de — 92-93 E 6
Divisorio, El — 106-107 G 7
Divnoje 126-127 L 4
Divo 168-169 D 4
Divriği 136-137 GH 3
Diwāna 138-139 A 4
Dīwānganj 134-135 OP 5
Dīwānīyah, Ad- 134-135 EF 4
Diweir, Ed — = Ad-Duwayr 173 B 4
Dixfield, ME 72-73 L 2
Dixie, ID 66-67 F 3
Dixie, WA 66-67 DE 2
Dixon, CA 74-75 C 3
Dixon, IL 70-71 F 5
Dixon, MO 70-71 DE 6
Dixon, MT 66-67 F 2
Dixon, NM 76-77 B 4
Dixon Entrance 56-57 K 7
Diyadin 136-137 K 3
Diyālā 134-135 EF 4
Diyālā, Nahr — 134-135 EF 4
Diyālā, Sadd ad- 136-137 L 5
Diyarbakır 134-135 DE 3
Diyarbakır havzası 136-137 J 3
Dīzābād 136-137 N 5
Dize 136-137 L 4
Dizful = Dezfūl 134-135 F 4
Dja 164-165 G 8
Djado 164-165 G 4
Djado, Plateau du — 164-165 G 4
Djafar, Hassi — = Ḥassī Ja'far 166-167 H 4
Djafou, Hassi — = Ḥāssī Jafū 164-165 E 2
Djafou, Ouèd — = Wādī Jafū 166-167 H 4
Djakarta = Jakarta 148-149 E 8
Djakovica 122-123 J 4
Djakovo 122-123 H 3
Djala 122-123 J 2
Djâliṭa, Djezîret — = Jazā'ir Jaliṭah 166-167 L 1
Djâliṭa, Qanât — = Qanāt Jaliṭah 166-167 L 1
Djamaa = Gham'ā 166-167 J 3
Djama Djedid 170 I a 1
Djama el-Kebir 170 I a 1
Djambala 172 BC 2
Djardjîr = Jarjīs 166-167 M 3
Djaret, Ouèd el — = Wādī al-Jarā' 166-167 H 6
Djebel Abiod = Al-Jabal al-Abyaḍ 166-167 L 1
Djebel Aglagal = Jabal Aghlāghal 166-167 G 6
Djebel Aïssa = Jabal 'Aysá 166-167 F 3
Djebel Amour = Jabal 'Amūr 166-167 G 3-H 2
Djebel Babor = Jabal Bābūr [DZ, mountain] 166-167 J 1
Djebel Babor = Jabal Bābūr [DZ, mountains] 166-167 J 1
Djebel Bou Kadra = Jabal Bū Khaḍrah 166-167 KL 2
Djebel Bou Kahil = Jabal Bū Kāhil 166-167 HJ 2
Djebel Chambi = Jabal Shaḥāmbī 166-167 L 2
Djebel Chélia = Jabal Shīlyah 164-165 F 1
Djebel Demér = Jabal al-Qṣūr 166-167 M 3
Djebel Didirhine = Jabal Tidighin 166-167 D 2
Djebel Dira = Jabal Dīrah 166-167 H 1
Djebel Dough = Jabal ad-Dūgh 166-167 F 3
Djebel el Abiad = Al-Jabal al-Abyaḍ 166-167 L 1
Djebel el Goufi = Jabal Ghūfī 166-167 KL 1
Djebel el Koraa = Jabal al-Kurā' 166-167 J 2
Djebel el Ksoum = Jabal al-Kusūm 166-167 J 2
Djebel es Serdj = Jabal as-Sarj 166-167 L 2
Djebel Idget = Jabal 'Ikdat 166-167 B 4
Djebel Idjerane = Jabal Ijrān 166-167 H 6
Djebel Ksel = Jabal Kasal 166-167 G 3
Djebel Maâdid = Jabal Ma'ḍīd 166-167 J 2
Djebel Morra = Jabal Murrah 166-167 L 2
Djebel Msid = Jabal Masīd 166-167 L 1
Djebel Mzi = Jabal Mazī 166-167 F 3
Djebel Nefoussa = Jabal Nafusah 164-165 G 2
Djebel Orbâṭa = Jabal R'bāṭah 166-167 L 2
Djebel Ouarsenis = Jabal al-Wārshanīs 166-167 GH 2
Djebel Sargho = Jabal Ṣaghrū' 164-165 C 2
Djebel Sarro = Jabal Ṣaghrū 164-165 C 2
Djebel Tachrirt = Jabal Tashrīrt 166-167 J 2
Djebel Tenouchfi = Jabal Tanūshfī 166-167 F 2
Djebel Tessala = Jabal Tasalah 166-167 F 2
Djebel Tichao = Jabal Tīshāro 166-167 JK 2
Djebilet = Al-Jabīlat 166-167 BC 4
Djebilet, Hassi — = Ḥassī Jabīlāt 166-167 BC 6
Djebiniâna = Jabinyānah 166-167 M 2
Djedeïda, El- = Al-Jadīdah 166-167 L 1
Djedi, Ouèd — = Wādī Jaddī 166-167 JK 2
Djedid, Bir — = Bi'r Jadīd 166-167 K 3
Djeffâra = Jafārah 166-167 M 3
Djelfa = Jilfah 164-165 E 2
Djelo-Binza, Kinshasa- 170 IV a 2
Djem, El — = Al-Jamm 166-167 M 2
Djema 164-165 K 7
Djemel, Hassi — = Ḥāssī Ghamal 166-167 J 4
Djemila = Jamīlah 166-167 J 1
Djemmâl = Jammāl 166-167 M 2
Djemna = Jimnah 166-167 L 3
Djeneïen = Janā'in 166-167 LM 4
Djenien-bou-Rezg = Ghanāin Bū Rizq 166-167 F 3
Djenné 164-165 D 6
Djenoun, Garet el — = Qārat al-Junūn 166-167 J 7
Djerâdoû = Jirādū 166-167 M 1
Djerba = Ḥūmat as-Sūq 166-167 M 3
Djerba, Djezîret — = Jazīrat Jarbah 166-167 M 3
Djérém 164-165 G 7
Djeribia, Hassi — = Ḥāssī Jarībīyah 166-167 J 4
Djerîd = Gharīd 166-167 K 3
Djerîd, Chott el — = Shaṭṭ al-Jarīd 164-165 F 2
Djezîra el Rharbî = Jazīrat al-Gharbī 166-167 M 2
Djezîrat el Maṭroûḥ = Jazīrat al-Maṭrūḥ 166-167 M 1
Djezîra Zembra = Al-Jāmūr al-Kabīr 164-165 M 1
Djezîret Djâliṭa = Jazā'ir Jaliṭah 166-167 L 1
Djezîret Djerba = Jazīrat Jarbah 166-167 M 3
Djezîret Qerqena = Jazur Qarqannah 166-167 M 2
Djezir Qoûriât = Jazā'ir Qūryāt 166-167 M 2
Djibhalanta = Uliastaj 142-143 H 2
Djibo 164-165 D 6
Djibouti [Djibouti, place] 164-165 N 6
Djibouti [Djibouti, state] 164-165 N 6
Djibuti = Djibouti 164-165 N 6
Djidda = Jiddah 134-135 D 6
Djidjelli = Jījili 164-165 F 1
Djiguina 168-169 G 2
Djiledug = Ciledug 152-153 H 9
Djilolo = Halmahera 148-149 JK 6
Djirgalanta = Chovd 142-143 G 2
Djokjakarta = Yogyakarta 148-149 EF 8
Djolu 172 D 1
Djoua = Juwā' 166-167 KL 5
Djouah 172 B 1
Djoué 170 IV a 1
Djougou 164-165 E 7
Djourab 164-165 H 5

286 Derbesiy

Djuba = Webi Ganaane 164-165 N 8
Djugu 172 EF 1
Djúpavík 116-117 c 2
Djúpivogur 116-117 fg 2
Djurdjura = Jurjurah 164-165 EF 1
Dmitrija Lapteva, proliv — 132-133 a-c 3
Dmitrijevka [SU, Černigov] 126-127 F 1
Dmitrijevka = Talas 134-135 L 2
Dmitrijev-L'govskij 124-125 KL 7
Dmitrov 132-133 F 6
Dmitrovsk-Orlovskij 124-125 KL 7
Dnepr 124-125 H 7
Dneprodzerzhinsk = Dneprodzeržinsk 126-127 FG 2
Dneprodzeržinsk 126-127 FG 2
Dneprodzeržinskoje vodochranilišče 126-127 F 2
Dnepropetrovsk 126-127 GH 2
Dneprorudnoje 126-127 G 3
Dneprovskij liman 126-127 EF 3
Dneprovsko-Bugskij kanal 124-125 E 7
Dneprovskoje 124-125 JK 6
Dnestr 126-127 D 2-3
Dnestrovskij liman 126-127 DE 3
Dnieper = Dnepr 124-125 H 7
Dniester = Dnestr 126-127 D 2-3
Dnjepr = Dnepr 124-125 H 7
Dnjestr = Dnestr 126-127 D 2-3
Dno 124-125 G 5
Doab 134-135 MN 5
Doaktown 63 CD 4
Doangdoangan Besar, Pulau — 152-153 M 8
Doba 164-165 H 7
Dobbiaco 122-123 E 2
Dobbin, TX 76-77 G 7
Dobbyn 158-159 GH 3
Dobele 124-125 D 5
Döberitz [DDR ← Berlin] 130 III a 1
Doblas 111 D 5
Dobo 148-149 K 8
Doboj 122-123 GH 3
Dobovka 126-127 M 2
Dobr'anka [SU, Rossijskaja SFSR] 124-125 V 4
Dobr'anka [SU, Ukrainskaja SSR] 124-125 H 7
Dobreta Turnu Severin 122-123 K 3
Dobrinka [SU] 124-125 N 7
Dobroje [SU, Rossijskaja SFSR] 124-125 MN 7
Dobroje [SU, Ukrainskaja SSR] 126-127 F 3
Dobropolje [SU] 126-127 H 2
Dobruja 122-123 M 4-N 3
Dobruš 124-125 H 7
Dobson Park 85 II b 3
Dobsonville 170 V a 2
Doč 126-127 F 1
Docampadó, Ensenada de — 94-95 C 5
Doce Grande, Cerro — 108-109 E 6
Doce Ilusão, Cachoeira — 98-99 L 9
Dockweiler State Beach 83 III b 2
Doctor, El — 86-87 C 2
Doctor Domingo Harósteguy 106-107 H 6
Doctor Gumersindo Sayago 102-103 B 5
Doctor Luis de Gásperi 102-103 B 5
Doctor Pedro P. Peña 111 D 2
Doda Betta 134-135 M 8
Dod Ballāpur 140 C 4
Dodecanese = Dōdekánēsos 122-123 M 7-8
Dōdekánēsos 122-123 M 7-8
Dodge Center, MN 70-71 D 3-4
Dodge City, KS 64-65 FG 4
Dodgeville, WI 70-71 EF 4
Dodoma 172 G 3
Do Doorns 174-175 CD 7
Dodsland 61 D 5
Dodson, MT 68-69 BC 1
Dodson, TX 76-77 DE 5
Dodson Park 85 III b 1
Dodson Peninsula 53 B 30-31
Dodurga 136-137 C 3
Doembang Nangbuat 150-151 BC 5
Doe River 60 G 1
Doerun, GA 80-81 E 5
Dofar = Ẓufār 134-135 G 7
Dogai Tshoring 142-143 F 5
Doğancılar, İstanbul- 154 I b 2
Doğanhisar 136-137 D 3
Doğanşehir 136-137 G 3
Dog Creek 60 FG 4
Dogden Buttes 68-69 F 2
Doger Stadium 83 III c 1
Dogger Bank 114-115 J 4-5
Dog Island 78-79 G 6
Dog Lake [CDN ↖ Missanabie] 70-71 HJ 1
Dog Lake [CDN ↖ Thunder Bay] 70-71 F 1
Dōgo 142-143 P 4
Dogondoutchi 164-165 E 6
Dogoni 168-169 D 2
Dōgo yama 144-145 J 5
Dogs, Isle of — 129 II b 2
Doğubayazıt 136-137 KL 3
Dogué 168-169 F 3
Doha = Ad-Dawhah 134-135 G 5
Dohad 138-139 E 6
Dohazārī 141 BC 4
Doheny 72-73 K 1
Doherty 72-73 G 1
Dohlka 138-139 D 6
Dohrīghāt 138-139 J 4
Doi Angka = Doi Inthanon 148-149 C 3
Doi Inthanon 148-149 C 3
Doi Lang Ka 150-151 B 3
Doi Pui = Doi Suthep 150-151 B 3
Dois Córregos 102-103 HJ 5
Dois Irmãos, Cabo — 110 I b 2
Dois Irmãos, Cachoeira — 98-99 J 9
Dois Irmãos, Serra — 92-93 L 6
Doi Suthep 150-151 B 3
Dois Vizinhos 102-103 F 6
Dokan, Sad ad- = Sadd ad-Dukān 136-137 L 4-5
Doka Tofa 168-169 H 3
Dokka 116-117 D 7
Doko 171 B 2
Dokós 122-123 K 7
Dokšicy 124-125 FG 6
Doland, SD 68-69 GH 3
Dolavon 108-109 FG 4
Dolbeau 56-57 W 8
Dôle 120-121 K 5
Dolgaja kosa 126-127 HJ 3
Dolgano-Nenets Autonomous Area 132-133 P-U 3
Dolgellau 119 DE 5
Dolgij, ostrov — 132-133 K 4
Dolgij ostrov [SU, Azovskoje more] 126-127 HJ 3
Dolgij'ostrov [SU, Black Sea] 126-127 E 3
Dolginovo 124-125 F 6
Dolgoi Island 58-59 c 2
Dolgoje [SU, Rossijskaja SFSR Orlovskaja Oblast'] 124-125 L 7
Dolgoprudnyj 113 V bc 1
Dolgorukovo 124-125 M 7
Dolhasca 122-123 M 2
Dolina 126-127 AB 2
Dolinsk 132-133 b 8
Dolinskaja 126-127 F 2
Dolinskoje 126-127 DE 3
Dolleman Island 53 B 30-31
Dolmabahçe Sarayi 154 I a 2
Dolmaithang Tsho 138-139 JK 2
Dolo 164-165 N 8
Dolomites = Dolomiti 122-123 DE 2
Dolomiti 122-123 DE 2
Doloon Choolojn Gobi = Zaaltajn Gov' 142-143 H 3
Doloon Nuur 142-143 LM 3
Dolores, CO 74-75 J 4
Dolores, TX 76-77 E 9
Dolores [CO] 94-95 D 6
Dolores [RA] 111 E 5
Dolores [ROU] 111 E 4
Dolores [YV] 94-95 G 3
Dolores Hidalgo 86-87 K 7
Dolores River 64-65 E 4
Doloroso, MS 78-79 D 5
Dolphin, Cape — 111 E 8
Dolphin and Union Strait 56-57 NO 4
Đô Lu'o'ng 150-151 E 3
Dolžanskaja 126-127 HJ 3
Dom [D] 128 III b 1
D'oma [SU] 124-125 U 7
Doma [WAN] 168-169 H 3
Domačevo 124-125 DE 8
Domaine Royale 128 II b 1
Domanevka 126-127 E 3
Dom Aquino 102-103 E 1
Domār 138-139 M 4
Domariāganj 138-139 J 4
Domazlice 118 F 4
Dombaj-Ul'gen, gora — 126-127 KL 5
Dombarovskij 132-133 K 7
Dombås 116-117 C 6
Dombe Grande 172 B 4
Dombóvár 118 HJ 5
Dome, AZ 74-75 F 6
Dôme, Puy de — 120-121 J 6
Dome Creek 60 G 3
Dōmēl = Muẓaffarābād 134-135 LM 4
Domel Island = Letsûtau Kyûn 150-151 AB 7
Dome Rock Mountains 74-75 F 6
Domesnäs = Kolkasrags 124-125 D 5
Domeyko 106-107 B 2
Domeyko, Cordillera — 111 C 2-3
Domingos Coelho 98-99 HJ 9
Domingos Martins 100-101 D 11
Domínguez 106-107 H 3
Dominguez, CA 83 III c 2
Dominguez Channel 83 III c 2
Dominguez Hills 83 III c 2
Dominica 64-65 O 8
Dominical 88-89 DE 10
Dominican Republic 64-65 MN 7-8
Dominica Passage 88-89 Q 7
Dominion Range 53 A 18-19
Dom Joaquim 102-103 L 3
Dom Noi, Lam — 150-151 E 5
Domodóssola 122-123 C 2
Dom Pedrito 111 F 4
Dom Pedro 100-101 B 3
Dompu 152-153 N 10
Dom Silverio 102-103 L 4
Domsjö 116-117 H 6
Domuyo, Volcán — 111 BC 5
Dom Yai, Lam — 150-151 E 5
Don [GB] 119 E 3
Don [IND] 140 BC 2
Don [SU] 124-125 M 7
Doña Ana, Cerro — 106-107 B 2
Donadeu 104-105 E 10
Donado 106-107 D 4
Doña Ines, Cerro — 104-105 B 10
Doña Inés Chica, Quebrada — 104-105 B 10
Donald 158-159 H 7
Donalda 61 B 4
Donald Landing 60 E 2
Donaldson, AR 78-79 C 3
Donaldsonville, LA 78-79 D 5
Donalsonville, GA 78-79 G 5
Doña María, Punta — 92-93 D 7
Doña Rosa, Cordillera de — 106-107 B 3
Donau 118 G 4
Donaueschingen 118 D 5
Donaufeld, Wien- 113 I b 1
Donaustadt, Wien- 113 I bc 2
Donauwörth 118 E 4
Donbei 146-147 D 9
Don Benito 120-121 E 9
Don Bosco, Quilmes- 110 III c 2
Doncaster 119 F 5
Doncaster, Melbourne- 161 II c 1
Don Cipriano 106-107 J 5
Dondaicha 138-139 E 7
Dondo [Angola] 172 BC 3
Dondo [Mozambique] 172 FG 5
Dondra Head = Dewundara Tuḍuwa 134-135 N 9
Đo'n Du'o'ng 150-151 G 7
Doneck 126-127 H 2-3
Doneckij kr'až 126-127 H-K 2
Donegal 119 B 4
Donegal Bay 119 B 4
Donets = Severnyj Donec 126-127 J 2
Donetsk = Doneck 126-127 H 2-3
Donez = Severnyj Donec 126-127 J 2
Donga 164-165 G 7
Dong'a = Dong'ezhen 146-147 F 3
Dong'an 146-147 C 8
Dongara 158-159 B 5
Dongargarh 138-139 H 7
Dongba 138-139 J 3
Dongbei 146-147 D 9
Dongbei = Xinfeng 146-147 EF 8
Dongbi = Dongbei 146-147 D 9
Dongbo = Dongbei 146-147 D 9
Đông Châu 150-151 F 2
Dongchuan 142-143 J 6
Đông Đăng 148-149 E 2
Dong'ezhen 146-147 F 3
Dongfang 142-143 K 8
Donggala 148-149 G 7
Donggou 144-145 DE 3
Dongguan 142-143 LM 7
Dongguang 146-147 F 3
Đông Ha 150-151 F 4
Donghai 146-147 G 4
Donghai Dao 146-147 C 11
Dong He 146-147 A 3
Đông Hene 150-151 E 4
Đông Ho'i 148-149 E 3
Dong Hu = Chengdong Hu 146-147 F 5
Dong Jiang 146-147 DE 10
Dongjiang = Congjiang 146-147 B 9
Dongjiang = Tungchiang 146-147 H 10
Dong Jiang = Xu Jiang 146-147 F 8
Dongjin = Dongjing 146-147 BC 10
Dongjing 146-147 BC 10
Dongjing Wan = Beibu Wan 142-143 K 7-8
Dongjinping = Zuo'an 146-147 E 8
Dongkalang 148-149 GH 6
Đông Khê 150-151 F 1
Dong Khiang = Ban Dong Khaang 150-151 E 4
Dong Khoang = Ban Dong Khaang 150-151 E 4
Dong Khuang = Ban Dong Khaang 150-151 E 4
Dongkou 146-147 C 8
Dongliu 146-147 F 6
Dongming 146-147 E 4
Đông Nai 150-151 F 7
Đông Ngai 150-151 F 4
Dongola = Dunqulah 164-165 KL 5
Dongou 172 C 1
Dong Phaya Yen 148-149 D 3
Dongping 146-147 F 4
Dongping = Anhua 146-147 C 7
Dongping Hu 146-147 F 3-4
Dong Qi = Songxi 146-147 G 8
Dongshan 146-147 F 10
Dongshan Dao 146-147 F 10
Dongshannei Ao 146-147 F 10
Dongsha Qundao 142-143 LM 7
Dongsheng 142-143 KL 4
Dongsheng, Beijing- 155 II ab 1
Dongtai 142-143 N 5
Dong Thap Mu'o'i 150-151 EF 7
Dongting Hu 142-143 L 6
Dongtou Shan 146-147 H 8
Đông Trang 150-151 G 6
Đông Triêu 150-151 F 2
Đông Voi Mệp 148-149 E 3
Dongxiang 146-147 F 7
Dongxi Lian Dao 146-147 GH 4
Dongxing 142-143 K 7
Đông Xoai 148-149 E 4
Đông Xuân 150-151 G 6
Dongyang 146-147 H 7
Dong Yunhe = Chuanchang He 146-147 GH 5
Dongyuqu, Beijing- 155 II b 2
Dongzhen = Xinyi 146-147 C 10
Dongzhi 146-147 F 6
Doniphan, MO 78-79 D 2
Donjek River 58-59 S 5
Donji Vakuf 122-123 G 3
Donkerpoort 174-175 F 6
Dôn Kyûn 150-151 AB 6
Don Martín 76-77 D 9
Dønna 116-117 DE 4
Donnacona 63 A 4
Donnely, ID 66-67 EF 3
Donner Pass 64-65 B 4
Donnybrook 174-175 H 5
Donoso 88-89 F 10
Don Peninsula 60 C 3
Donskoj 124-125 M 7
Donsol 148-149 H 4
Dônthami 141 E 7
Don Torcuato, Tigre- 110 III b 1
Donúsa 122-123 LM 7
Donuzlav, ozero — 126-127 F 4
Donyztau 132-133 K 8
Donzère 120-121 K 6
Doonerak, Mount — 56-57 FG 4
Doornbosch = Doringbos 174-175 C 6
Doornik = Tournai 120-121 J 3
Doornriver = Doringrivier 174-175 C 6
Doorns, De — 174-175 CD 7
Doorns, Do — 174-175 CD 7
Door Peninsula 70-71 G 3
Dōr, Ad- = Ad-Dawr 136-137 KL 5
Dora, NM 76-77 C 6
Dóra, Baghdād- = Baghdād-Dawrah 136-137 L 6
Dora, Lake — 158-159 D 4
Dora Bâltea 122-123 B 3
Dorada, La — 92-93 E 3
Dorado 76-77 B 9
Dorado, El —, AR 64-65 H 5
Dorado, El — [CO] 92-93 E 4
Dorado, El — [RA] 106-107 G 5
Dorado, El — [YV] 92-93 G 3
Doral 142-143 F 3
D'Orbigny [BOL] 104-105 E 7
D'Orbigny [RA] 106-107 G 6
Dorbjany = Darbėnai 124-125 C 5
Dörböt Dabaan 142-143 FG 2
Dorchester 119 E 6
Dorchester, NE 68-69 H 5
Dorchester, Boston-, MA 84 I b 3
Dorchester, Cape — 56-57 V 4
Dorchester Bay 84 I b 3
Dorchester Center, Boston-, MA 84 I b 3
Dordabis 172 C 6
Dordogne 120-121 GH 6
Dordrecht [NL] 120-121 JK 3
Dordrecht [ZA] 174-175 G 6
Dore 120-121 J 6
Dore, Mont — 120-121 J 6
Doré Lake [CDN, lake] 61 E 3
Doré Lake [CDN, place] 61 E 3
Dore River 61 E 3
Dores do Indaiá 102-103 K 3
Dorey 168-169 E 2
Dorgali 122-123 C 5
Dori 164-165 DE 6
Doria Pamphili, Villa — 113 II b 2
Dorila 106-107 F 5
Doringberge 174-175 E 5
Doringbos 174-175 C 6
Doringrivier 174-175 C 6
Dorion 72-73 J 2
Dormida, La — 106-107 D 4
Dornach [D, Oberbayern] 130 II c 2
Dornakal 140 E 2
Dornbach, Wien- 113 I b 2
Dörnigheim 128 III b 1
Dornoch 119 D 3
Dornoch Firth 119 E 3
Dornod ◁ 142-143 LM 2
Dornogov 142-143 K 3
Doro 168-169 E 1
Dorochovo 124-125 L 6
Dorofejevskaja 132-133 P 3
Dorogobuž 124-125 J 6
Dorohoi 122-123 M 2
Doronāgāñv 138-139 MN 4
Doronagaon = Doroņāgāñv 138-139 MN 4
Dörööneuur 142-143 GH 2
Dorotea 116-117 G 5
Dorothy 61 B 5
Dorrance, KS 68-69 G 6
Dorreen 60 C 2
Dorre Island 158-159 B 5
Dorrigo 160 L 3
Dorris, CA 66-67 C 5
Dortelweil 128 III b 1
Dortmund 118 CD 3
Dortmund-Ems-Kanal 118 C 2-3
Dörtyol 136-137 G 4
Dorūd 136-137 N 6
Doruma 172 E 1
Dorval 82 I a 2
Dorval, Île de — 82 I a 2
Dörvöldžin 142-143 GH 2
Dorya, Ganale — = Genale 164-165 N 7
Dorylaeum = Eskişehir 134-135 C 2-3
Dos Bahías, Cabo — 111 CD 7
Dos Caminos, Los — 91 II c 2
Dos de Mayo 92-93 DE 6
Dos Hermanas [RA] 106-107 H 4
Dos Lagunas 86-87 PQ 9
Đô So'n 150-151 F 2
Dos Pozos 111 CD 6
Dos Rios, CA 74-75 B 3
Dos Rios [MEX] 91 I a 2
Dossin Great Lakes Museum 84 II c 2-3
Dosso 164-165 E 6
Doswell, VA 80-81 H 2
Dothan, AL 64-65 J 5
Dothan, OR 66-67 B 4
Dot Lake, AK 58-59 PQ 5
Dotsero, CO 68-69 C 6
Doty, WA 66-67 B 2
Doua = Cavally 164-165 C 7-8
Douāb, Rūd-e — = Qareh Sū 134-135 FG 3-4
Douai 120-121 J 3
Douala 164-165 FG 8
Douarnenez 120-121 E 4
Double Mountain Fork 76-77 D 6
Double Peak 58-59 LM 6
Double Springs, AL 78-79 F 3-4
Doubs 120-121 L 5
Doucen = Dūsan 166-167 J 2
Doudaogoumen = Yayuan 144-145 F 2
Douentza 164-165 D 6
Dough, Djebel — = Jabal ad-Dūgh 166-167 F 3
Dougherty, OK 76-77 F 5
Dougherty, TX 76-77 D 6
Dougherty Plain 80-81 DE 5
Douglas, AK 58-59 UV 7
Douglas, AZ 64-65 E 5
Douglas, GA 80-81 E 5
Douglas, WA 66-67 CD 2
Douglas, WY 68-69 D 4
Douglas [CDN] 61 J 6
Douglas [GB] 119 D 4
Douglas [ZA] 172 D 7
Douglas, Cape — 58-59 L 7
Douglas, Mount — 58-59 KL 7
Douglas Channel 60 C 3
Douglas Lake [CDN] 60 GH 4
Douglas Lake [USA] 80-81 E 2-3
Douglas Park 83 II a 1
Douglas Point 72-73 EF 2
Douglas Range 53 BC 29-30
Douglastown 63 D 3
Dougou 146-147 F 3
Doûh, Jbel ed — = Jabal ad-Dūgh 166-167 F 3
Douhudi = Gong'an 146-147 D 6-7
Doûmâ = Dūmā 136-137 G 6
Doumé 164-165 G 8
Douna [HV] 168-169 D 2
Douna [RMM] 168-169 E 2
Dounan = Tounan 146-147 H 10
Dourada, Cachoeira — 102-103 H 3
Dourada, Serra — 92-93 K 7
Douradina 102-103 E 4
Dourado 102-103 H 4
Dourados [BR ↑ Corumbá] 102-103 D 3
Dourados [BR ↖ Ponta Porã] 92-93 J 9
Dourados, Rio — [BR, Mato Grosso do Sul] 102-103 E 5
Dourados, Rio — [BR, Minas Gerais] 102-103 J 3
Dourados, Serra dos — 111 F 2
Douro 120-121 C 8
Dou Rūd = Dorūd 136-137 N 6
Dou Sar = Dow Sar 136-137 N 5
Doûz = Dūz 166-167 L 3
Dovbyš 126-127 C 1
Dove Creek, CO 74-75 J 4
Dove Elbe 130 I b 2
Dover, DE 64-65 L 4
Dover, GA 80-81 F 4
Dover, NC 80-81 H 3
Dover, NH 72-73 L 3
Dover, NJ 72-73 J 4
Dover, OH 72-73 F 4
Dover, OK 76-77 EF 4
Dover [GB] 119 G 7
Dover [ZA] 174-175 G 4
Dover, Strait of — 119 GH 6
Dover-Foxcroft, ME 72-73 M 2
Doveyrīch, Rūd-e — 136-137 M 6
Dovrefjell 116-117 C 6
Dovsk 124-125 H 7
Dow, Lake — 172 D 6
Dowa 172 F 4
Dowagiac, MI 70-71 GH 4
Dowlatābād = Malāyer 134-135 F 4
Downey, CA 83 III d 2
Downey, ID 66-67 GH 4
Downieville, CA 74-75 C 3
Downpatrik 119 D 4
Downs, KS 68-69 G 6
Downton, Mount — 60 E 3
Dow Park 85 III c 2
Dows, IA 70-71 D 4
Dow Sar 136-137 N 5
Doyle, CA 66-67 C 5
Doyleville, CO 68-69 C 6
Dözen 142-143 P 4
Dozois, Réservoir — 72-73 H 1
Dozornoje 126-127 F 4
Dra, Hamada du — = Hammadat ad-Dara' 164-165 CD 3
Drâ, Ouèd ed — = Wad Dra'ah 164-165 BC 3
Draa, Oued — = Wād Dra'ah 166-167 C 5
Dra'ah, Wād — 164-165 BC 3
Dracena 102-103 G 4
Dra-el-Mizan = Dara' al-Mizān 166-167 HJ 1
Drăgăneşti-Vlaşca 122-123 L 3
Drăgăşani 122-123 L 3
Dragerton, UT 74-75 H 3
Draghoender 174-175 E 5
Dragon, Bocas del — 94-95 L 2
Dragonera, Isla — 120-121 HJ 9
Dragones 104-105 E 8
Dragons Back 155 I b 2
Dragon's Mouths = Bocas del Dragon 94-95 L 2
Dragoon, AZ 74-75 HJ 6
Draguignan 120-121 L 7
Drain, OR 66-67 B 4
Drake, AZ 74-75 G 5
Drake, ND 68-69 F 2
Drake, Estrecho de — 111 B-D 9
Drakensberge 172 E 8-F 7
Drakes Bay 74-75 B 4
Drākshārama 140 F 2
Dráma 122-123 KL 5
Drammen 116-117 CD 8
Dran = Đo'n Du'o'ng 150-151 G 7
Dranda 126-127 K 5
Drang, Ya — 150-151 F 6
Drangajökull 116-117 bc 1
Drangsnes 116-117 c 2
Draper, NC 80-81 G 2
Draper, Mount — 58-59 S 7
Drapetsŏna 113 IV a 2
Dräpung = Bräpung 138-139 N 3
Draria 170 I a 2
Drau 118 F 5
Drava 118 H 6
Drawa 118 G 2
Drawsko Pomorskie 118 GH 2
Drayā 142-143 H 5
Drayton Plains, MI 72-73 E 3
Drayton Valley 60 K 3
Dre Chhu = Mörönus 142-143 G 5
Dreieichenhain 128 III ab 1-2
Dreikikir 148-149 M 7
Drepung = Bräpung 138-139 N 3
Dresden, TN 78-79 E 2
Dresden [CDN] 72-73 E 3
Dresden [DDR] 118 FG 3
Dresv'anka 124-125 R 3
Dreunberg 174-175 FG 6
Dreux 120-121 H 4
Drew, MS 78-79 D 4
Drewitz, Potsdam- 130 III a 2
Drewsey, OR 66-67 D 4
Drews Reservoir 66-67 C 4
Drexel, MO 70-71 C 6
Drexel Hill, PA 84 III b 2
Dribin 124-125 H 6
Driemond 128 I b 2
Drifton, FL 80-81 DE 5
Driftpile 60 JK 2
Driggs, ID 66-67 H 4
Drin 122-123 J 4
Drina 122-123 H 3
Dring, Isla — 108-109 B 5
Drini i Bardhë 122-123 J 4
Drini i Zi 122-123 J 5
Drinit, Gjiri i — 122-123 H 5
Drinkwater 61 F 5
Drinkwater Pass 66-67 D 4
Drissa 124-125 G 6
Drøback 116-117 D 8
Drogenbos 128 II ab 2
Drogheda 119 CD 5
Drogobyč 126-127 AB 2
Droichead Átha = Drogheda 119 CD 5
Drôme 120-121 K 6
Dromo 138-139 M 4
Dronne 120-121 H 6
Dronning Maud fjellkjede 53 A
Dronning Maud land 53 B 36-4
Droupolé, Monts de — 168-169 CD 4
Drowning River 62 G 2
Drug 138-139 C 2
Drug = Durg 138-139 H 7
Druid Hills, GA 85 II c 2
Druja 124-125 F 6
Drumbo 72-73 F 3
Drumheller 56-57 O 7
Drummond, MI 70-71 J 2
Drummond, MT 66-67 G 2
Drummond, WI 70-71 E 2
Drummond Island 70-71 HJ 3
Drummondlea 174-175 H 3
Drummondville 56-57 W 8
Drummoyne, Sydney- 161 I a 2
Drumochter Pass 119 D 3
Drury Lake 58-59 U 5
Druskininkai 124-125 DE 6-7
Druskinınkaj = Druskininkai 124-125 DE 6-7
Druso, Gebel — = Jabal ad-Durūz 134-135 D 4
Družba [SU, Kazachskaja SSR] 132-133 P 8
Družba [SU, Moskva] 113 V cd 2
Družba [SU, Ukrainskaja SSR] 124-125 J 7
Družina 132-133 bc 4
Drvar 122-123 G 3
Dry Bay 58-59 S 7
Dryberry Lake 62 C 3
Drybrough 61 H 2
Dry Creek 68-69 C 2
Dryden 56-57 K 1
Dryden, TX 76-77 C 7-8
Drygalski Glacier 53 B 17-18
Drygalskiinsel 53 C 10
Dry Lake, NV 74-75 F 4
Drysdale River 158-159 E 2-3
Dry Tortugas 80-81 b 4
Dsayul 142-143 H 6
Dschang 164-165 G 7
Dua 172 D 1
Duaca 94-95 G 2
Duala = Douala 164-165 FG 8
Du'an 142-143 K 7
Duanshi 146-147 D 4
Duao, Punta — 106-107 A 5
Duarte, Pico — 64-65 M 8
Duartina 102-103 H 5
Duas Igrejas 120-121 DE 8
Duas Onças, Ilha das — 102-103 F 5
Du'ayn, Ad- 164-165 K 6
Ḍubā 173 D 4
Dubach, LA 78-79 C 4
Dubawnt Lake 56-57 Q 5
Dubawnt River 56-57 Q 5
Dubay 134-135 GH 5
Dubbo 158-159 J 6
Dubda 138-139 M 3
Dübendorf 128 IV b 1
Dubie 171 B 5
Dublin 119 CD 5
Dublin, GA 64-65 K 5
Dublin, MI 70-71 GH 3
Dublin, TX 76-77 E 6
Dubli River 58-59 JK 4
Dubna [SU, place Moskovskaja Oblast'] 124-125 L 5
Dubna [SU, place Tul'skaja Oblast'] 124-125 L 6
Dubna [SU, river] 124-125 M 5
Dubno 126-127 B 1
Dubois, ID 66-67 G 3
Du Bois, PA 72-73 G 4
Dubois, WY 66-67 J 4
Dubossary 126-127 D 3
Dubov'azovka 126-127 F 1
Dubovskij 124-125 Q 5
Dubovskoje 126-127 L 3
Dubovyj Ovrag 126-127 LM 2
Dubrājpur 138-139 L 6
D'ubrar, gora — 126-127 O 6
Dubréka 164-165 B 7
Dubrovica 124-125 EF 8
Dubrovka [SU, Br'anskaja Oblast'] 124-125 JK 7
Dubrovka [SU, Leningradskaja Oblast'] 124-125 H 4
Dubrovnik 122-123 GH 4
Dubrovno 124-125 H 6
Dubuque, IA 64-65 H 3
Dubysa 124-125 D 6
Duchang 146-147 F 7
Duchesne, UT 66-67 H 5
Duchess [AUS] 158-159 G 4
Duchess [CDN] 61 BC 5
Duchovnickoje 124-125 R 7
Duchovščina 124-125 J 6
Ducie [GH] 168-169 E 3
Ducie [Pitcairn] 156-157 L 6
Duck Bay 61 H 4
Duck Hill, MS 78-79 DE 4
Duck Islands 62 K 4
Duck Lake 61 EF 4
Duck Mountain 61 H 5
Duck Mountain Provincial Park 61 H 5
Duck River 78-79 F 2-3
Ducktown, TN 78-79 G 3
Duckwater Peak 74-75 F 3
Ducor, CA 74-75 D 5
Ducos 106-107 F 6
Đu'c Phô 150-151 G 5
Đu'c Trong 150-151 G 7
Duda, Río — 94-95 D 6
Dudčany 126-127 F 3
Duddhi = Dūdhi 138-139 J 5
Dūdhi 138-139 J 5
Dudh Kōsī 138-139 L 4
Dudhnā = Dudna 138-139 E 8
Dudhnai 141 B 3
Dudignac 106-107 G 5
Dudinka 132-133 PQ 4
Dudna 138-139 E 8
Dudnaī = Dudhnai 141 B 3
Dudorovskij 124-125 K 7
Dūdu 138-139 E 4
Dudullu 154 I bc 2
Duékoué 168-169 D 4
Duende, Península — 108-109 B 6
Dueré, Rio — 98-99 O 10
Duero 120-121 F 8
Duevé 98-99 O 10
Dufaur 106-107 F 6
Dufayt, Wādī — 173 D 6
Duff Islands 148-149 l 6
Dūfīri 166-167 F 3
Dufresne Lake 63 D 2
Dufur, OR 66-67 C 3
Duga-Zapadnaja, mys — 132-133 bc 6
Dugdown Mountain 78-79 G 3-4
Dūgh, Jabal ad- 166-167 F 3
Dugi Otok 122-123 F 4
Dugna 124-125 L 6
Dugny 129 I c 2
Dugo Selo 122-123 G 3
Dugues Canal 85 I b 2
Duğur 136-137 K 2
Du He 146-147 C 5
Duida, Cerro — 94-95 J 6
Duifken Point 158-159 H 2
Duisburg 118 C 3
Duitama 94-95 E 5
Duiwelskloof = Duiwelskloof 174-175 J 2
Duivendrecht 128 I b 2
Duiwelskloof 174-175 J 2
Dujail = Ad-Dujayl 136-137 KL 6
Dujayl, Ad- 136-137 KL 6
Dujiawobu = Ningcheng 144-145 B 2
Dukān, Sadd ad- 136-137 L 4-5
Dukana 171 D 2
Duk Ayod = Ayōd 164-165 L 7
Duke, OK 76-77 E 5
Duke Island 58-59 x 9
Dūk Fāywīl 164-165 L 7
Dukhān 134-135 G 5
Dukī 138-139 B 2
Dukielska, Przełęcz — 118 KL 4
Dukkālah 164-165 C 2
Dukla Pass = Dukelský průsmyk 118 KL 4
Dukou 142-143 J 6
Dūkštas 124-125 EF 6
Duku 168-169 H 3
Dulaanchaan 142-143 JK 1-2
Dulaan Chijd 142-143 H 4
Dulac, LA 78-79 D 6
Dulawan = Datu Piang 148-149 H 5
Dulaymīyah, Ad- 136-137 K 6
Dulce, NM 68-69 C 7

Dulce 287

Dulce, La — 106-107 H 7
Dulce, Río — 111 D 3-4
Dulgalach 132-133 Z 4
Duliu Jiang 146-147 B 9
Dullabchara 141 C 3
Dull Center, WY 68-69 D 4
Dullstroom 174-175 J 3
Dulovo 122-123 M 4
Duluth, MN 64-65 H 2
Dūmā 136-137 G 6
Dumaguete 148-149 H 5
Dumai 152-153 D 5
Dumaran Island 148-149 GH 4
Ḍumariyāganj = Domariāganj 138-139 J 4
Dumas, AR 78-79 D 4
Dumas, TX 76-77 D 5
Dumas, Peninsula — 108-109 E 10
Dūmat al-Jandal = Al-Jawf 134-135 DE 5
Dumayj, Sharm — 173 DE 4
Ḍumayr 136-137 G 6
Dumbarton 119 D 3-4
Dumboa 168-169 J 3
Dum Dum 154 II b 2
Dumdum, Pulau — 152-153 G 5
Dum Duma 141 D 2
Dumduma = Dum Duma 141 D 2
Dum Dum-Birati 154 II b 2
Dum Dum International Airport 154 II b 2
Dume = Doumé 164-165 G 8
Dumfries 119 E 4
Duminiči 124-125 K 7
Dumkā 138-139 L 5
Dumlu = Hinş 136-137 J 2
Dumlupınar 136-137 CD 3
Dumoine, Lac — 72-73 H 1
Dumoine, Rivière — 72-73 H 1
Dumont d'Urville 53 C 14-15
Dumra 138-139 K 4
Dumrāṅv = Dumraon 138-139 K 5
Dumraon 138-139 K 5
Ḍumrī 138-139 KL 6
Dumyāṭ 164-165 L 2
Dumyāṭ, Maṣabb — 173 BC 2
Duna [Bhutan] 138-139 M 4
Duna [H] 118 J 5
Dunaföldvár 118 J 5
Dunaj [SU] 144-145 J 1
Dunaj, ostrova — 132-133 XY 3
Dunajec 118 K 4
Dunajevcy 126-127 C 2
Dunareă 122-123 M 3
Dunarii, Delta — 122-123 N 3
Dunas 106-107 L 3
Dunaújváros 118 J 5
Dunav 122-123 J 3
Dunbar, AK 58-59 N 4
Dunbar, OK 76-77 G 5
Dunbar, WV 72-73 F 5
Dunblane [CDN] 61 E 5
Dunblane [GB] 119 DE 3
Duncan 66-67 AB 1
Duncan, AZ 74-75 J 6
Duncan, OK 64-65 G 5
Duncan, WY 66-67 J 4
Duncan Passage 134-135 P 8
Duncansby Head 119 E 2
Dundaga 124-125 D 5
Dund Ajmang = Töv ◁ 142-143 K 2
Dundalk, MD 72-73 H 5
Dundalk [CDN] 72-73 F 2
Dundalk [IRL] 119 CD 4-5
Dundas 56-57 X 2
Dundas, Lake — 158-159 D 6
Dundas Island 60 B 2
Dundas Peninsula 56-57 O 2-3
Dundas Strait 158-159 F 2
Dún Dealgan = Dundalk 119 CD 4-5
Dundee, MI 72-73 E 4
Dundee, TX 76-77 E 6
Dundee [GB] 119 E 3
Dundee [ZA] 172 F 7
Dundgov' ◁ 142-143 K 2
Dundurn 61 E 5
Dundwa Range 138-139 J 4
Dunedin 158-159 O 9
Dunedin, FL 80-81 b 2
Dunedoo 160 J 4
Dunfermline 119 DE 3
Dūngarpur 138-139 D 6
Dungarvan 119 C 5
Dung Büree uul 142-143 FG 4-5
Dungeness, Punta — 108-109 EF 9
Dungog 160 KL 4
Dungripalli 138-139 J 7
Dungtshākha 138-139 M 3
Dungu [ZRE, place] 172 E 1
Dungu [ZRE, river] 171 B 2
Dungun, Kuala — 148-149 D 6
Dungun, Sungei — 150-151 D 10
Dungunab = Dunqunāb 164-165 M 4
Dunhua 142-143 O 3
Dunhuang 142-143 GH 3
Dunière, Parc provincial de — 63 C 3
Dunkerque 120-121 HJ 3
Dunkirk, IN 70-71 H 5
Dunkirk, NY 72-73 G 3
Dunkirk = Dunkerque 120-121 HJ 3
Dunkwa 164-165 D 7
Dún Laoghaire = Kingstown 119 CD 5
Dunlap, TN 78-79 G 3
Dunlop 61 J 3
Dunmarra 158-159 F 3
Dunmore, PA 72-73 J 4
Dunn, NC 80-81 G 3
Dunnellon, FL 80-81 b 2
Dunning, NE 68-69 FG 5
Dunning, Chicago-, IL 83 II b 1
Dunnville 72-73 FG 3
Dunolly 160 F 6
Dunphy, NV 66-67 E 5
Dunqul 173 B 6
Dunqulah 164-165 KL 5
Dunqunāb 164-165 M 4
Duns 119 E 4
Dunseith, ND 68-69 F 1
Dunsmuir, CA 66-67 B 5
Duolun = Doloon Nuur 142-143 LM 3
Duong Đông = Phu Quôc 150-151 D 7
Duo Qi = Ting Jiang 146-147 F 9
Duozhu 146-147 E 10
Dupang Ling 146-147 C 9
Duparquet 62 M 2
Dūpenau 130 I a 1
Duperré = 'Ayn Daflah 166-167 GH 1
Duperre, Pulau-pulau 150-151 G 11
Dupleix = Dāmus 166-167 G 1
Dupleix Range = Tanglha 142-143 FG 5
Dupont, IN 70-71 H 6
Dupree, SD 68-69 F 3
Dupuyer, MT 66-67 G 1
Duqqi, Al-Qāhirah-ad- 170 II b 1
Duque de Bragança 172 C 3
Duque de Caxias 92-93 L 9
Duque de York, Isla — 111 A 8
Duquesne, PA 72-73 G 4
Du Quoin, IL 70-71 F 6-7
Durack Range 158-159 E 3
Duragan 136-137 F 2
Duran, NM 76-77 B 5
Durance 120-121 K 7
Durand, MI 72-73 E 3
Durand, WI 70-71 E 3
Durango, CO 64-65 E 4
Durango [MEX] 64-65 EF 6
Durango, Victoria de — 64-65 F 7
Durañona 106-107 G 6
Durant, MS 78-79 DE 4
Durant, OK 64-65 G 5
Durazno [ROU, administrative unit] 106-107 JK 4
Durazno [ROU, place] 111 E 4
Durazno, Cuchilla Grande del — 106-107 JK 4
Durazno, El — 106-107 E 6
Durazzo = Durrës 122-123 H 5
Durban 172 F 7
Durbanville 174-175 C 7
Durbe 124-125 C 5
Duren Tiga, Jakarta- 154 IV b 2
Durg 138-139 H 7
Durga nuur = Döröö nuur 142-143 GH 2
Durgapūr [BD] 141 B 3
Durgapur [IND] 134-135 O 6
Durgerdam 128 I b 1
Durham, KS 68-69 H 6
Durham, NC 64-65 L 4
Durham [CDN] 72-73 F 2
Durham [GB] 119 EF 4
Durham Downs 160 E 1
Dūrinzeik 141 E 7
Durkee, OR 66-67 E 3
Durmitor 122-123 H 4
Durness 119 D 2
Duro, Serra do — 98-99 P 10-11
Durrel 63 J 3
Durrës 122-123 H 5
Dur Sargon = Khorsabad 136-137 K 4
Dur Sharrukīn = Khorsabad 136-137 K 4
Dursunbey 136-137 C 3
Durt = Chanch 142-143 J 1
D'urt'uli 124-125 U 6
Duru [ZRE, place] 171 B 1
Duru [ZRE, river] 171 B 1
Durūz, Jabal ad- 134-135 D 4
D'Urville Island 161 E 5
Dušak 134-135 J 3
Dūsan 166-167 J 2
Dušanbe 134-135 K 3
Dušeti 126-127 M 5
Dusey River 62 F 2
Dūsh 173 B 5
Du Shan [TJ, mountain] 144-145 B 2
Dushan [TJ, place] 146-147 F 6
Du Shan = Lu Shan 146-147 FG 3
Dusheng 146-147 F 2
Du Shui = Du He 146-147 C 5
Düsseldorf 118 C 3
Dustin, OK 76-77 FG 5
Dustin Gol 146-147 A 2
Dutch Habor 52 D 35
Dutch John, UT 66-67 J 5
Dutou 146-147 D 9
Dutsen Wai 168-169 H 3
Dutton, MT 66-67 H 2
Dutton, Mount — 74-75 G 3-4
Duvan 132-133 K 6
Duved 116-117 E 6
Duvefjord 116-117 I 4
Duvernay 82 I a 1
Duveyrier = Dūfirī 166-167 F 3
Duvivier = Būshqūf 166-167 K 1
Duwayd, Ad- 134-135 E 5
Ḍuwayḥin, Dawhat aḍ- 134-135 G 6
Duwaym, Ad- 164-165 L 6
Duwayr, Ad- 173 B 4
Duxun 146-147 F 10
Duya, El — 94-95 F 5
Duyun 142-143 K 6
Duyūrah, Qaṭṭārat ad- 136-137 C 7
Dūz 166-167 L 3
Düzce 136-137 D 2
Duzerville = Al-Ḥajar 166-167 KL 1
Dvārka = Dwārka 138-139 B 6
Dvina, Severnaja — 132-133 G 5
Dvinsk = Daugavpils 124-125 EF 6
Dvinskaja guba 132-133 F 4-5
Dvorchangaj 142-143 J 2
Dvuch Cirkov, gora — 132-133 gh 4
Dwangwa 171 C 6
Dwārāhāt 138-139 G 3
Dwari Bay = Ise-wan 144-145 L 5
Dwārka 138-139 B 6
Dwarsberge 174-175 G 3
Dwarsrand 174-175 J 4
Dwarsrivier 174-175 H 2
Dwight, IL 70-71 F 5
Dwight D. Eisenhower Park 85 III c 1
Dworp 128 II a 2
Dworshak Reservoir 66-67 F 2
Dwyka 174-175 D 7
Dyaul Island 148-149 gh 5
Dychtau, gora — 126-127 L 5
Dyer, Cabo — 108-109 AB 7
Dyer, Cape — 56-57 YZ 4
Dyereiland 174-175 C 8
Dyer Island = Dyereiland 174-175 C 8
Dyer Plateau 53 BC 30
Dyers Bay 72-73 F 2
Dyersburg, TN 64-65 J 4
Dyersdale, TX 85 III bc 1
Dyersville, IA 70-71 E 4
Dyje 118 H 4
Dyker Beach Park 82 III b 3
Dylewska Gora 118 JK 2
Dyment 62 C 3
Dymer 126-127 E 1
Dyrhólaey 116-117 d 3
Dyrnesvågen 116-117 B 6
Dysselsdorp 174-175 E 7
Dzacha 142-143 H 4
Dza Chhu 142-143 H 5
Dzag 142-143 H 2
Džagdy, chrebet — 132-133 YZ 7
Dzahar es Soûq = Tahār as-Sūq 166-167 DE 2
Džalal-Abad 134-135 L 2
Džalilabad 126-127 O 7
Džalinda 132-133 XY 7
Džambajskij, ostrov — 126-127 OP 3
Džambejty 132-133 J 7
Džambul [SU ← Frunze] 132-133 MN 9
Džambul [SU ↖ Gurjev] 126-127 P 3
Džambul, gora — 132-133 N 9
Džangil'da = Turgaj 132-133 L 8
Džankoj 126-127 G 4
Džanybek 126-127 N 2
Dzaoudzi 172 J 4
Dzardžan 132-133 X 4
Dzargalant 142-143 LM 2
Dzargalant = Chovd 142-143 G 2
Džarkent = Panfilov 132-133 OP 9
Dzartaj Dabas nuur 142-143 JK 4
Džarylgač, ostrov — 126-127 F 3-4
Dzasag = Xinjie 146-147 B 2
Dzaudžikau = Ordžonikidze 126-127 M 5
Džava 126-127 LM 5
Dzavchan [Mongolia, administrative unit = 4 ◁] 142-143 H 2
Dzavchan [Mongolia, place] 142-143 G 2
Dzavchan gol 142-143 H 2
Džebrail 126-127 N 7
Dzedy 132-133 M 8
Dzei Chhu 142-143 H 5-6
Dzenzik, mys — 126-127 H 3
Džerbene 124-125 E 5
Džermuk 126-127 M 7
Dzerzhinsk = Dzeržinsk 124-125 O 5
Dzeržinsk [SU, Belorusskaja SSR] 124-125 F 7
Dzeržinsk [SU, Rossijskaja SFSR] 132-133 GH 6
Dzeržinsk [SU, Ukrainskaja SSR] 126-127 CD 1
Dzeržinskij 113 V d 3
Dzeržinskij = Narjan-Mar 132-133 JK 4
Dzeržinskogo, PkiO im. — 113 V c 2
Džetygara 132-133 L 7
Džezkazgan 132-133 M 8
Dzhambul = Džambul 132-133 MN 9
Dzhardzhan = Džardžan 132-133 X 4
Dzhargalantu = Chovd 142-143 G 2
Dzhugdzhur Mountains = chrebet Džugdžur 132-133 Z-b 6
Działdowo 118 K 2
Dzibchalantu = Uliastaj 142-143 H 2
Dzibgalantu = Uliastaj 142-143 H 2
Dziedzice 118 J 4
Džikimde 132-133 X 6
Dzilam de Bravo 86-87 Q 7
Dzioua = Dibwah 166-167 J 3
Dzirgalantu = Chovd 142-143 G 2
Dzitbalche 86-87 PQ 7
Džizak 134-135 K 2
Dzöjtön nuur 142-143 G 4
Dz'ol' 124-125 T 3
Dzübchulant = Uliastaj 142-143 H 2
Džugdžur, chrebet — 132-133 Z-b 6
Džūkste 124-125 D 5
Dzul'fa 126-127 M 7
Dzum Bulag = Džargalant 142-143 LM 2
Dzungaria = Junggariya 142-143 EF 2
Džungarskij Alatau, chrebet — 132-133 O 9-P 8
Džurin 126-127 D 2
Džusaly 132-133 L 8
Dzüsten Öls 142-143 F 2
Dzüünbajan 142-143 KL 3
Dzuunmod 142-143 K 2
Džvari 126-127 L 5

E

Eabamet Lake 62 F 2
Eads, CO 68-69 E 6
Eagar, AZ 74-75 J 5
Eagle, AK 58-59 R 4
Eagle, CO 68-69 C 6
Eagle, NE 68-69 H 5
Eagle Bend, MN 70-71 C 2
Eagle Butte, SD 68-69 F 3
Eagle Grove, IA 70-71 D 4
Eaglehill Creek 61 DE 5
Eagle Island 61 J 4
Eagle Lake, ME 72-73 M 1
Eagle Lake, TX 76-77 F 8
Eagle Lake [CDN] 62 C 3
Eagle Lake [USA, California] 66-67 C 5
Eagle Lake [USA, Maine] 72-73 M 1
Eagle Mountains 76-77 B 7
Eagle Nest, NM 76-77 B 4
Eagle Pass, TX 64-65 FG 6
Eagle Passage 108-109 K 9
Eagle Point, OR 66-67 B 4
Eagle Rapid 62 CD 2
Eagle River, AK 58-59 N 6
Eagle River, MI 70-71 F 2
Eagle River, WI 70-71 F 3
Eagle River [CDN] 62 C 3
Eagle Summit 58-59 P 4
Eagle Tail Mountains 74-75 G 6
Eagleville, CA 66-67 CD 5
Ea Hleo 150-151 F 6
Ea Krong 150-151 FG 6
Ealing, London- 129 II a 1
Ear Falls [CDN, place] 62 C 2
Ear Falls [CDN, river] 62 C 2
Earlimart, CA 74-75 D 5
Earlington, KY 70-71 G 7
Earlton 62 LM 3
Earlville, IL 70-71 F 5
Earlwood, Sydney- 161 I a 2
Early, IA 70-71 C 4
Earn 119 DE 3
Earn Lake 58-59 U 5
Earth, TX 76-77 C 5
Earth, Altar of the — 155 II b 2
Easley, SC 80-81 E 3
East Anglian Heights 119 F 6-G 5
East Angus 72-73 L 2
East Arlington, MA 84 I ab 2
East Atlanta, Atlanta-, GA 85 II c 2
East Australian Basin 156-157 GH 7
East Barnet, London- 129 II b 1
East Bay 78-79 E 6
East Bengal = Mashraqī Bangāl 134-135 O 5-P 6
East Bernard, TX 76-77 FG 8
Eastborne 119 G 6
East Boston, Boston-, MA 84 I b 2
East Brady, PA 72-73 G 4
East Braintree, MA 84 I c 3
East Broughton 72-73 L 1
East Caicos 88-89 L 4
East Cape [NZ] 158-159 P 7
East Cape [USA] 58-59 s 7
East Caroline Basin 156-157 G 4
East Chicago, IN 70-71 G 5
East China Sea 142-143 N 6-O 5
East Cleveland, OH 72-73 EF 4
East Coast 161 GH 4
East Coulée 61 BC 5
East Detroit, MI 84 II c 2
East Elmhurst, New York-, NY 82 III c 2
East Ely, NV 74-75 F 3
Eastend 66-67 J 1
East End, Metairie-, LA 85 I b 1
Easter Island 156-157 M 6
Eastern [EAK] 172 G 1-2
Eastern [GH] 168-169 E 4
Eastern [WAL] 168-169 C 3
Eastern [Z] 172 F 4
Eastern Ghats 134-135 M 8-N 7
Eastern Group = Lau Group 148-149 b 2
Eastern Indian Antarctic Basin 50-51 O-Q 8
Eastern Native, Johannesburg- 170 V b 2
Eastern Province = Nègenangira Palāna = 5 ◁ 140 E 6
Eastern Sayan Mountains = Vostočnyj Sajan 132-133 R 6-T 7
Eastern Sierra Madre = Sierra Madre Oriental 64-65 F 6-G 7
Easter Plateau 156-157 L-N 6
Easterville 61 J 4
East Falkland 111 E 8
East Falls, Philadelphia-, PA 84 III b 1
East Falls Church, Arlington-, VA 82 II a 2
East Fork Andreafsky 58-59 FG 5
East Fork Chandalar 58-59 P 2
East Fork Des Moines River 70-71 C 4
East Fork Sevier River 74-75 GH 4
East Fork White River 70-71 GH 6
East Frisian Islands = Ostfriesische Inseln 118 C 2
Eastgate, NV 74-75 DE 3
East Glacier Park, MT 66-67 G 1
East Grand Forks, MN 68-69 H 1-2
East Ham, London- 129 II c 1
East Hampton, NY 72-73 KL 4
East Helena, MT 66-67 H 2
East Island 148-149 h 7
East Lamma Channel 155 I a 2
Eastland, TX 76-77 E 6
Eastland Center 84 II c 2
East Lansdowne, PA 84 III b 2
East Lansing, MI 70-71 H 4
East Liverpool, OH 72-73 F 4
East London = Oos-Londen 172 EF 8
East Los Angeles, CA 83 III d 1
East Lynn, WV 72-73 E 5
East-Main 56-57 V 7
Eastmain River 56-57 VW 7
Eastman, GA 80-81 E 4
East Marin Island 83 I b 1
East Moline, IL 70-71 EF 5
East New York, New York-, NY 82 III c 2-3
Easton, MD 72-73 HJ 5
Easton, PA 72-73 J 4
Easton, WA 66-67 C 2
East Orange, NJ 72-73 J 4
Eastover, SC 80-81 F 4
East Pacific Ridge 156-157 M 5-6
East Palatka, FL 80-81 c 2
East Pass 78-79 G 6
East Pine 60 G 2
East Point, GA 64-65 K 5
Eastport 63 K 3
East Potomac Park 82 II a 2
East Prairie, MO 78-79 E 2
East Richmond, CA 83 I c 1
East River 82 III bc 2
East Saint Louis, IL 64-65 HJ 4
East Siberian Ridge 52 B 36-1
East Siberian Sea 132-133 d-h 3
East Tavaputs Plateau 74-75 J 3
East Watertown, MA 84 I ab 2
East Weymouth, MA 84 I c 3
Eastwick, Philadelphia-, PA 84 III b 2
Eastwood, Sydney- 161 I a 1
Eastwood Park 85 III b 2
Eaton, CO 68-69 D 5
Eaton, OH 70-71 H 6
Eaton, Lake — 158-159 EF 4
Eatonia 61 D 5
Eaton Rapids, MI 70-71 H 4
Eatonton, GA 80-81 E 4
Eatonville, WA 66-67 BC 2
Eaubonne 129 I c 2
Eau Claire, WI 64-65 H 3
Eauripik 148-149 M 5
Ébano 86-87 L 6
Ebara, Tōkyō- 155 III b 2
Ebba Ksoûr = Abbat Quṣūr 166-167 L 1-2
Ebbert Furr House 85 III b 1
Eben Junction, MI 70-71 G 2
Eber gölü 136-137 D 3
Eberswalde-Finow 118 F 2
Ebertswil 128 IV b 2
Ebetsu 144-145 b 2
Ebi nuur 142-143 E 3
Ebmatingen 128 IV b 1
Ebola 172 D 1
Eboli 122-123 F 5
Ebolowa 164-165 G 8
Ebon 208 G 2
Ebony 172 BC 6
Eboue, Stade — 170 IV a 1
Ebrāhīmābād [IR ↗ Arāk] 136-137 O 5
Ebrāhīmābād [IR ↓ Qazvīn] 136-137 N 5
Ebro 120-121 G 8
Ebro, Delta del — 120-121 H 8
E. Bustos 106-107 C 4
Ebute-Metta, Lagos- 170 III b 2
Ebuṭṭābād 134-135 L 4
Ecatepec de Morelos 91 I c 1
Ecbatana = Hamadān 134-135 F 3-4
Eceabat 136-137 AB 2
Ech Chèbba = Ash-Shābah 166-167 M 2
ech Chema'ia = Ash-Shamā'īyah 166-167 B 3
ech Chiadma = Ash-Shiādmā' 166-167 B 4
Echeng 146-147 E 6
Echeta, WY 68-69 CD 3
Echigo sammyaku 144-145 M 4-N 3
Echo, OR 66-67 D 3
Echo, UT 66-67 H 5
Echo, Lake — 160 c 3
Echo Bank 64-65 P 7
Echo Cliffs 74-75 H 4
Echuca 158-159 H 7
Écija 120-121 E 10
Ecilda Paullier 106-107 J 5
Eckenheim, Frankfurt am Main- 128 III b 1
Eckington, Washington-, DC 82 II ab 1
Eclipse Spund 56-57 UV 3
Ečmiadzin 126-127 M 6
Economy 63 DE 5
Ecoporanga 100-101 D 10
Écorce, Lac de l' 72-73 HJ 1
Ecorse, MI 84 II b 3
Écouen 129 I c 1
Ecuador 92-93 CD 5
Ecuador = Équateur 172 CD 1
Ed [ETH] 164-165 N 6
Eda, Yokohama- 155 III a 2
Edam 61 D 4
Edcouch, TX 76-77 EF 9
Ed Damur = Ad-Dāmūr 136-137 F 6
Eḍ Ḍaou = Aḍ-Ḍaw 136-137 G 5
ed Dâr el Beïḍâ' = Ad-Dār al-Bayḍā' 164-165 BC 2
ed Deffa = Aḍ-Ḍiffah 164-165 J 2
Ed Dehîbet = Adh-Dhahībah 166-167 M 3
Ed-Dehna = Ad-Dahnā' 134-135 E 5-F 6
Ed Deir = Ad-Dayr 173 C 5
Eddies Cove 63 HJ 2
Eddington Gardens, PA 84 III d 1
Ed Diweir = Ad-Duwayr 173 B 4
Eddy, MT 66-67 F 2
Eddy, TX 76-77 F 7
Eddystone, PA 84 III b 2
Eddystone Point 160 d 2
Eddyville, KY 78-79 EF 2
Eddyville, NE 68-69 G 5
Ede [WAN] 168-169 G 4
Edéa 164-165 G 8
Edeia 102-103 H 2
Edeien el-Murzûq = Ṣaḥrā' Marzūq 164-165 G 3-4
Edeien-'Ubâri = Ṣaḥrā' Awbārī 164-165 G 3
Eden 158-159 JK 7
Eden, MT 66-67 H 2
Eden, NC 80-81 G 2
Eden, TX 76-77 E 7
Eden, WY 66-67 J 4
Edenburg [ZA, Oranje-Vrystaat] 174-175 FG 5
Edenburg [ZA, Transvaal] 170 V b 1
Edendale [ZA, Natal] 174-175 HJ 5
Edendale [ZA, Transvaal] 170 V bc 1
Eden Park 154 II b 2
Edenton, NC 80-81 H 2
Edenvale 170 V bc 1
Edenville 174-175 G 4
Eder 118 D 3
Ederet 142-143 JK 2
Édessa 122-123 JK 5
Edessa = Urfa 134-135 D 3
Edeyin el Murzuq = Sahrā' Marzūq 164-165 G 3-4
Edeyin Ubari = Ṣaḥrā' Awbārī 164-165 G 3
Edgar, NE 68-69 H 5
Edgar, WI 70-71 EF 3
Edgard, LA 78-79 D 5-6
Edgartown, MA 72-73 L 4
Edgefield, SC 80-81 EF 4
Edge Island = Edgeøya 116-117 l 5-6
Edgeley, ND 68-69 G 2
Edgell Island 56-57 Y 5
Edgemont, SD 68-69 E 4
Edgeøya 116-117 l 5-6
Edgerton, MN 70-71 BC 4
Edgerton, WI 70-71 F 4
Edgewater Park, NJ 84 III d 1
Edgewood, IL 70-71 F 6
Edgewood Park, New Orleans-, LA 85 I b 2
Edgware, London- 129 II a 1
Edina 168-169 C 4
Edina, MO 70-71 DE 5
Edinburg, IN 70-71 H 6
Edinburg, MS 78-79 E 4
Edinburg, TX 64-65 G 6
Edinburgh 119 E 4
Edirne 134-135 B 2
Edison, GA 78-79 G 5
Edison, WA 66-67 B 1
Edisto Island, SC 80-81 FG 4
Edisto River 80-81 F 4
Edithburgh 160 C 5
Edjelé = Ibjīl 164-165 F 3
Edmond, OK 76-77 F 5
Edmonds, WA 66-67 BC 2
Edmonton 56-57 NO 7
Edmonton, KY 70-71 H 7
Edmonton, London- 129 II b 1
Edmore, MI 70-71 H 4
Edmore, ND 68-69 G 1
Edmundston 56-57 X 8
Edna, TX 76-77 F 8
Edna Bay, AK 58-59 w 9
Edo 155 III c 2
Edo = Tōkyō 142-143 QR 4
Edogawa, Tōkyō- 155 III c 1
Edough = Idūgh 166-167 K 1
Edremit 134-135 B 3
Edremit körfezi 136-137 B 3
Edrī = Adrī 164-165 G 3
Edsbyn 116-117 F 7
Edsel Ford Range 53 B 22-23
Edson 56-57 N 7
Eduardo Castex 111 D 5
Eduvigis, La — 104-105 G 10
Edward Island 70-71 F 1
Edwards, CA 74-75 E 5
Edwards, MS 78-79 D 4
Edwards Creek 158-159 G 5
Edwards Plateau 64-65 FG 5
Edwardsville, IL 70-71 F 6
Edward VIIth Peninsula 53 B 21-22
Edziza Peak 58-59 W 8
Edznā 86-87 PQ 8
Eek, AK 58-59 FG 6
Eek River 58-59 G 6
'Eelbuur 164-165 b 3
Eel River [USA, California] 66-67 AB 5
Eel River [USA, Indiana] 70-71 GH 5
Eel Xamurre 164-165 bc 2
Eensaamheidpan = Eenzamheidpan 174-175 D 4
Eenzamheidpan 174-175 D 4
Eesti = Estnische Sozialistische Sowjetrepublik 124-125 EF 4
Eesti = Estonian Soviet Socialist Republic 124-125 EF 4
Efate 158-159 N 3
Efes = Ephesos 136-137 B 4
Efeso = Ephesos 136-137 B 4
Effingham, IL 64-65 F 4
Efrichu = Evrýchu 136-137 E 5
Efrikemer 154 I a 2
Efu = Idfu 164-165 L 3
Égadi, Ìsole — 122-123 DE 6
Egaña [RA] 106-107 H 6
Egaña [ROU] 106-107 J 4
Eganville 72-73 H 2
Egawa 155 III c 3
Egbe [WAN, Kwara] 168-169 G 3
Egbe [WAN, Ogun] 170 III a 1
Egbert, WY 68-69 D 5
Ege denizi 134-135 A 2-B 3
Egedesminde = Auslait 56-57 Za 4
Egegik, AK 58-59 J 7
Egegik River 58-59 HJ 7
Egeland, ND 68-69 G 1
Egenbüttel 130 I a 1
Eger 118 K 5
Egetswil 128 IV b 1
Egg [CH, mountain] 128 IV b 1
Eggers Ø 56-57 bc 6
Egg Harbor City, NJ 72-73 J 5
Egg Island 58-59 G 5
Egg Lake [CDN, Quebec] 56-57 W 7
Egg Lake [CDN, Saskatchewan] 61 F 3
Egijin gol 142-143 J 1-2
Egil 136-137 HJ 3
Egilsstadhir 116-117 f 2
Eglab, El — = Aghlāb 164-165 CD 3
Eglinton Island 56-57 MN 2
Egmont, Mount — 158-159 O 7
Egmont Bay 63 D 4
Egmont National Park 161 E 4
Egoji, Kelay — 164-165 N 6
Egošinskaja 124-125 QR 3
Egrā 138-139 L 7
Egremont 60 L 2
Eğret 136-137 D 3
Eğridir 134-135 C 3
Eğridir gölü 136-137 D 4
Eğrigöz dağı 136-137 C 3
Éguas, Rio das — 100-101 B 7
Egypt 164-165 KL 3
Egyptian Museum 170 II b 1
Eha Amufu 168-169 G 4
Eh-Eh, Riacho — 104-105 GH 9
Ehestorf 130 I a 2
Ehime 144-145 J 6
Eiche 130 III c 1
Eichstätt 118 E 4
Eid 116-117 AB 7
Eidelstedt, Hamburg- 130 I a 1
Eidfjord 116-117 B 7
Eidsvåg 116-117 BC 6
Eidsvoll 116-117 D 7
Eidsvollfjellet 116-117 j 5
Eifel 118 C 3
Eiffel, Tour — 129 I c 2
Eige, Carn — 119 D 3
Eigersund 116-117 A 8
Eigg 119 C 3
Eight Degree Channel 176 ab 1
Eights Coast 53 B 27-28
Eighty Mile Beach 158-159 D 3
Eilat = Ėlat 134-135 C 5
Eilbeck, Hamburg- 130 I b 1
Eildon Reservoir 158-159 J 7
Eilerts de Haan Gebergte 92-93 H 4
Eil Roba 172 GH 1
Eimsbüttel, Hamburg- 130 I a 1
Einasleigh 158-159 HJ 3
Einasleigh River 158-159 H 3
Eindhoven 120-121 K 3
Eindpaal 174-175 C 3
Einmé 141 D 7
Eiríksjökull 116-117 cd 2
Eiríksstadhir 116-117 f 2
Eiru, Rio — 96-97 F 5
Eirunepé 92-93 EF 6
Eiseb 172 C 6
Eisenach 118 E 3
Eisenerz 118 G 5
Eisenhower, Mount — 60 K 4
Eisenhüttenstadt 118 FG 2
Eisenstadt 118 H 5
Eišiškės 124-125 E 6
Eisleben 118 E 3
Eissendorf, Hamburg- 130 I a 2
Eiwugen = Saint Lawrence Island 56-57 BC 5
Ejeda 172 H 6
Ejer Bavnehøj 116-117 C 9-10
Ejido 94-95 F 3
Ejigbo 170 III a 1
Ejin Horo Qi 146-147 BC 2
Ejura 168-169 E 4
Ekalaka, MT 68-69 D 3
Ekang 168-169 H 4
Ekbatana = Hamadān 134-135 F 3-4
Ekece = Liz 136-137 JK 3
Ekecek dağı 136-137 EF 3
Ekenäs 116-117 K 7-8
Ekenie 168-169 G 4
Eket 168-169 G 4
Ekiatapskij chrebet 132-133 jk 4
Ekibastuz 132-133 NO 7
Ekimčan 132-133 Z 7
Ekoda, Tōkyō- 155 III ab 1
Ekonda 132-133 TU 4
Eksåra 154 II a 2
Eksere 136-137 DE 4
Eksjö 116-117 F 9

288 Dulce

Ektagh Altai = Mongol Altajn nuruu 142-143 F-H 2
Ekwan River 56-57 U 7
Ekwok, AK 58-59 J 7

El Abadia = Al Ab'ādīyah 166-167 G 1
El Abed-Larache = Al-Ādib al-'Arsh 164-165 F 3
El-Abiod-Sidi-Cheikh = Al-Abyaḍ 166-167 G 3
El 'Achâra = Al-'Asharah 136-137 J 5
El-Affroun = Al-'Afrūn 166-167 H 1
Elafonēsu, Stenón — 122-123 K 7
El Águila 106-107 D 5
El Aguilar 104-105 D 8
el 'Aïoûn = Al-'Ayūn Dra'ah [MA, Agādīr] 166-167 A 5
el 'Aïoûn = Al-'Ayūn Dra'ah [MA, Ujdah] 166-167 E 2
el Aïoun du Draâ = Al-'Ayūn Dra'ah 166-167 A 5
El Aiun = Al-'Ayūn 164-165 B 3
El 'Ajam = Al-'Ajam 136-137 G 6
Ēlakkibeṭṭa = Cardamom Hills 140 C 5-6
El Álamo [MEX, Nuevo León] 76-77 E 9
El Almagre 86-87 J 4
El Alto [PE] 96-97 A 4
El Alto [RA] 104-105 D 11
Ēlāmala = Cardamom Hills 140 C 5-6
Ēlāmalai = Cardamom Hills 140 C 5-6
Elamanchili 140 F 2
Ela Medo = Ēl Medo 164-165 N 7
El Amparo 94-95 E 6
El Amparo de Apure 94-95 F 3
Elandsfontein 170 V c 2
Elands Height 174-175 H 6
Elandshoek 174-175 J 3
Elandsrivier [ZA ◁ Krokodilrivier] 174-175 G 3
Elandsrivier [ZA ◁ Olifantsrivier] 174-175 H 3
Elandsvlai 174-175 C 7
Elanga 174-175 H 6
El Angel 96-97 C 1
El Aouinet = Al-Awaynāt 166-167 KL 2
El Apartadero 91 III c 3
el 'Aqeila = Al-'Uqaylah 164-165 H 2
el 'Araîch = Al-'Arā'ish 164-165 C 1
El Arañado 106-107 F 3
el Arb'â' Amrân = Tamdah 166-167 B 3
El Arco 86-87 D 3
El-Aricha = Al-'Arīshah 166-167 F 2
El-Arrouch = Al-Harūsh 166-167 K 1
El Aspero, Cerro — 106-107 D 2
Elassôn 122-123 K 6
Ēlat 134-135 C 5
Elato 148-149 N 5
El-Auja = Qĕẕī'ōt 136-137 F 7
El Avila, Cerro — 91 II b 1
Elâzığ 134-135 D 3
El Azraq = Azraq ash-Shīshān 136-137 G 7
El Azulejo 76-77 D 9
Elba 122-123 D 4
Elba, AL 78-79 FG 5
Elba, ID 66-67 G 4
Elba, NE 68-69 G 5
El Bajío 64-65 F 7
El Banco 92-93 E 3
El Barco [PE] 96-97 A 4
El Barreal 106-107 DE 2
Elbasan 122-123 HJ 5
Elbaşı 136-137 FG 3
El Baúl 92-93 F 3
Elbe 118 D 1-2
El Beidâ' = Al-Bayḍā' 164-165 J 2
El Beqâ' = Al-Biqā' 136-137 FG 5-6
Elberton, GA 80-81 E 3
El Beşîrê = Buṣayrah 136-137 J 5
Elbeuf 120-121 H 4
El Bisaliya = Al-Baṣalīyat Qiblī 173 C 5
Elbistan 136-137 G 3
Elbląg 118 J 1
El Bolsón 108-109 D 3
El Bordo = Patía 94-95 C 6
el Boroûj = Al-Burūj 166-167 C 3
El Bouerda = Al-Bū'irdah 166-167 C 5
Elbow 61 E 5
Elbow Lake, MN 70-71 BC 2
El Brasil 76-77 D 9
El'brus, gora — 126-127 L 5
Elbtunnel 130 I a 1
Elbūr 172 J 1
Elburgon 171 C 3
El-Burro 76-77 D 8
Elburs = Reshteh Kūhhā-ye Alborz 134-135 G 3
Elburz = Reshteh Kūhhā-ye Alborz 134-135 G 3
Elburz Mountains 134-135 G 3
El Caburé 104-105 E 10
El Cadillal, Embalse — 104-105 D 10
El Caín 108-109 E 3
El Cajon, CA 74-75 E 6
El Caldén 106-107 DE 3
El Callao 94-95 L 4
El Campo, TX 76-77 F 8
El Cantón 94-95 F 4
El Caracol 91 I d 1
El Caribe [YV, Anzoátegui] 94-95 J 3
El Caribe [YV, Distrito Federal] 91 II c 1
El Carmelo 94-95 EF 2
El Carmen [BOL, Beni] 104-105 E 3-4
El Carmen [BOL, Santa Cruz] 104-105 G 6
El Carmen [CO, Amazonas] 94-95 H 7
El Carmen [CO, Chocó] 94-95 C 5
El Carmen [CO, Norte de Santander] 94-95 E 3
El Carmen [EC] 96-97 B 2
El Carmen [PY] 102-103 AB 4
El Carmen de Bolívar 92-93 DE 3
El Ceibal 104-105 E 10
El Centro 94-95 E 4
El Centro, CA 64-65 CD 5
El Cerrito 94-95 CD 6
El Cerrito, CA 83 I c 1
El Cerro 92-93 G 8
El Chacay 106-107 BC 5
El Chacho 106-107 E 3
El Chaco 96-97 C 2
El Chaparro 94-95 J 3
Elche 120-121 G 9
El-Chedâdî = Ash-Shiddādī 136-137 J 4
Elcho Island 158-159 G 2
El Chorillo 106-107 DE 4
El Chorro 104-105 C 6
El Cisne 106-107 G 3
El Coco 64-65 b 3
El Cocuy 92-93 E 3
El Cojo [YV, place] 91 II b 1
El Cojo [YV, river] 91 II b 1
El Cojo, Punta — 91 II b 1
El Colorado [RA, Chaco] 104-105 G 10
El Colorado [RA, Santiago del Estero] 106-107 F 1
El Cóndor 108-109 E 9
El Contador 91 I d 1
El Corazón 96-97 B 2
El Corcovado 108-109 D 4
El Corozo 91 II b 1
El Coyte 108-109 D 5
El Crucero 94-95 J 2-3
El Cuervo Grande 76-77 B 7
El Cuil 94-95 B 6
El Cuy 111 C 5
Elda 120-121 G 9
El Descanso 86-87 B 1
El Desemboque 86-87 D 2
El Desierto 104-105 B 8
El Desmonte 104-105 E 8
El Diamante 91 III a 2
El Difícil 92-93 E 3
El'dikan 132-133 a 5
El Dividive 94-95 F 3
El Diviso [CO, Nariño] 94-95 B 7
El Diviso [CO, Putumayo] 94-95 D 7
El Divisorio 106-107 G 7
El-Djedeïda = Al-Jadīdah 166-167 L 1
El Djem = Al-Jamm 166-167 M 2
El Doctor 86-87 C 2
Eldon, IA 70-71 DE 5
Eldon, MO 70-71 D 6
Eldon, WA 66-67 B 2
Eldora, IA 70-71 D 4
El Dorado, AR 64-65 H 5
El Dorado, AR 64-65 H 5
Eldorado, IL 70-71 F 7
El Dorado, KS 68-69 H 7
Eldorado, OK 76-77 E 5
Eldorado, TX 76-77 D 7
Eldorado [BR] 102-103 HJ 6
El Dorado [CO] 92-93 E 4
Eldorado [MEX] 86-87 G 5
El Dorado [RA] 106-107 G 5
Eldorado [RA, Misiones] 111 EF 3
El Dorado [YV] 92-93 G 3
Eldorado, Aeropuerto — 91 III ab 2
Eldorado Mountains 74-75 F 5
El Dorado Park 83 III d 3
El Dorado Springs, MO 70-71 CD 7
Eldoret 172 G 1
El Durazno 106-107 E 6
El Duya 94-95 F 5
Electra, TX 76-77 E 5
Electric Mills, MS 78-79 E 4
Electric Peak 66-67 H 3
Elefantes, Golfo — 108-109 BC 6
Elefantes, Rio dos — 174-175 K 2-3
Elefantina = Elephantine 164-165 L 4
Éléfants, Réserve aux — 172 E 1
El Eglab = Aghlāb 164-165 CD 3
Elei, Wādī — = Wādī Ilay 173 D 7
Elekmonar 132-133 Q 7
Elektrostal' 124-125 M 5-6
El Empedrado 94-95 FG 3
Elena [RA] 106-107 E 4
El Encanto 94-95 GH 5
El Encuentro 96-97 E 8
Eleodoro Lobos 106-107 E 4
Elephanta Island 140 A 1
Elephant Butte Reservoir 76-77 A 6
Elephantine 164-165 L 4
Elephant Island 53 CD 31
Elephant Pass = Āṇayirāvu 140 E 6
Elephant Point, AK 58-59 G 3
el 'Erg = Al-'Irq 164-165 J 3
El Ergh = Al-'Irq 164-165 J 3
Elesbão Veloso 100-101 C 4
El Escorial 120-121 EF 8
Eleşkirt = Zidikân 136-137 K 3
El Estor 86-87 Q 10
Elets = Jelec 124-125 M 7
El Eulma = Al-'Ulmah 166-167 J 1
Eleuthera Island 64-65 LM 6
Elevi = Görele 136-137 H 2
Elewijt 128 II b 1
El Faijum = Al-Fayyūm 164-165 KL 3
El-Fâsher = Al-Fāshir 164-165 K 6
El Fayum = Al-Fayyūm 164-165 KL 3
El Ferrol de Caudillo 120-121 C 7
Elfin Cove, AK 58-59 TU 7
El Ford, Cerro — 108-109 D 9
El Fortín 106-107 F 3
El Forzado 106-107 D 4
El-Fourât = Al-Furāt 136-137 H 5
El Fuerte 86-87 F 4
El Furrial 94-95 K 3
El Galpón 104-105 D 9
el Gâra = Al-Gārah 166-167 C 3
el-Gatrun = Al-Qaṭrūn 164-165 GH 4
el Gedid = Sabhah 164-165 G 3
El-Geneina = Al-Junaynah 164-165 J 6
El Gezira = Al-Jazīrah 164-165 L 6
El Ghâb = Al-Ghāb 136-137 G 5
Elghena = Algēna 164-165 M 5
El Ghōr = Al-Ghūr 136-137 F 7
El Ghurdaqa = Al-Ghardaqah 164-165 L 3
Elgin, IL 64-65 J 3
Elgin, ND 68-69 F 2
Elgin, NE 68-69 G 5
Elgin, NV 74-75 F 4
Elgin, OR 66-67 E 3
Elgin, TX 76-77 F 7
Elgin [CDN] 63 D 5
Elgin [GB] 119 E 3
El-Goléa = Al-Gulī'ah 164-165 E 2
El Golfo de Santa Clara 86-87 C 2
Elgon, Mount — 172 F 1
El Goran 164-165 N 7
El Grullo 86-87 H 8
El Guapo 94-95 HJ 2
El Guarapo 91 II b 1
El Guarda 91 I a 2
El Guardamonte 104-105 D 10
El Guayabo [CO] 94-95 E 4
El Guayabo [YV] 94-95 EF 3
El Guettar = Al-Qaṭṭār 166-167 J 2
El Hadjar = Al-Hajar 166-167 KL 1
El-Hadjira = Al-Ḥajīrah 166-167 J 3
El Hagunia = Al-Haqūnīyah 164-165 B 3
el Ḥâjeb = Al-Ḥājab 166-167 D 3
El Hamada = Al-Hammadah 166-167 FG 4
El-Hamel = Al-Hāmil 166-167 J 2
El Ḥammâmêt = Al-Ḥammāmāt 166-167 M 1
El Haouâria = Al-Hawārīyah 166-167 M 1
el Ḥaouz = Al-Ḥawūz 166-167 B 4
El Harrach 170 I b 2
El Ḥaṣâḥeïṣa = Al-Ḥuṣayḥiṣah 164-165 L 6
El-Hasetchê = Al-Hasakah 134-135 D 3
El Hatillo [YV, place] 91 II c 2
El Hatillo [YV, river] 91 II c 2
El-Heir = Qaṣr al-Ḥayr 136-137 H 5
El Ḥencha = Al-Hanshah 166-167 M 2
El Hermel = Al-Harmal 136-137 G 5
el Hobra = Al-Habrah 166-167 J 3
el Hoṣeima = Al-Ḥusaymah 164-165 D 1
Elhovo 122-123 M 4
El Huecu 106-107 B 6
Eli, NE 68-69 F 4
Eliasville, TX 76-77 E 6
Elida, NM 76-77 C 6
El 'Idîsât = Al-'Udaysāt 173 C 5
El Idrissia = Al-Idrīsīyah 166-167 H 2
Elie [CDN] 61 K 6
Elikí 164-165 F 6
Elila 172 E 2
Elim, AK 58-59 FG 4
Elim [ZA] 174-175 C 8
Eling Hu = Ngoring Tsho 142-143 H 4-5
Elisa 106-107 G 3
Elisabethbaai 174-175 A 4
Elisabeth Reef 158-159 L 5
Elisabethville = Lubumbashi 172 E 4
Elisenau 130 III c 1
Elisenvaara 124-125 GH 3
Elista 126-127 M 3
El-'Itmânîya = Al-'Uthmānīyah 173 BC 4
Eliúpolis 113 IV b 2
Elizabeth, IL 70-71 EF 4
Elizabeth, LA 78-79 C 5
Elizabeth, NJ 72-73 J 4
Elizabeth, Adelaide- 158-159 G 6
Elizabeth, Cape — 72-73 LM 3
Elizabeth, Cape — = Cape Pillar 158-159 J 8
Elizabeth Bay = Elisabethbaai 174-175 A 4
Elizabeth City, NC 80-81 H 2
Elizabeth-Port, NJ 82 III a 3
Elizabethton, TN 80-81 EF 2
Elizabethtown, KY 70-71 H 7
Elizabethtown, NC 80-81 G 3
Elizabethtown, NY 72-73 JK 2
Elizeu Martins 100-101 C 5
el Jadîda = Al-Jadīdah 164-165 C 2
El-Jafr = Al-Jafr 134-135 D 4
El Jaralito 76-77 B 9
El Jauf = Al-Jawf 164-165 J 4
El-Jebelein = Al-Jabalayn 164-165 L 6
el Jeblêt = Al-Jabilat 166-167 BC 4
El Jîzah = Al-Jīzah 136-137 FG 7
el Jofra Oasis = Wāḥāt al-Jufrah 164-165 GH 3
El Juile 86-87 N 9
Elk 118 L 2
Elk, CA 74-75 B 3
Elk, WA 66-67 E 1
Elkader, IA 70-71 E 4
El Kala = Al-Qal'ah 164-165 F 1
El-Kâmlîn = Al-Kamilīn 164-165 L 5
El-Kantara = Al-Qanṭarah 166-167 J 2
El-Katif = Al-Qaṭīf 134-135 F 5
el Kbab = Al-Qabāb 166-167 D 3
Elk City, ID 66-67 F 3
Elk City, OK 76-77 E 5
Elk Creek, CA 74-75 B 3
Elkedra 158-159 G 4
el Kelaa des Srarhna = Al-Qal'at as-S'rāghnah 166-167 C 3-4
Elkford 60 K 4
Elk Grove, CA 74-75 C 3
El-Khaḍl = Al-Haḍl 136-137 F 7
El-Khandaq = Al-Khandaq 164-165 KL 5
El-Khârga = Al-Khārijah 164-165 L 3
Elkhart, IN 70-71 GH 5
Elkhart, KS 76-77 D 4
Elkhart, TX 76-77 G 7
El-Kharṭūm Baḥrī = Al-Kharṭūm Baḥrī 164-165 L 5
El-Khaṭāṭba = Al-Haṭāṭibah 173 B 2
Elkhead Mountains 68-69 C 5
el Khemîs = Al-Khamīs 166-167 C 3
el Khemîs = Hamīs az-Zāmāmrah 166-167 B 3
el Khemîs = Sūq al-Khamīs as-Sāḥil 166-167 C 2
el Khemîs = Sūq al-Khamīs Banī 'Arūs 166-167 D 2
el Khemîssèt = Khamīssāt 166-167 CD 3
el Khemîs Zemâmra = Hamīs az-Zāmāmrah 166-167 B 3
El Khenachich 164-165 D 4
Elkhorn 61 H 5
Elkhorn, WI 70-71 F 4
Elkhorn Peak 66-67 H 2
Elkhorn Peaks 66-67 H 4
Elkhorn River 68-69 G 4
El Khroub = Al-Khurub 166-167 K 1
Elki 136-137 K 4
Elkin, NC 80-81 F 2
Elkins, NM 76-77 BC 6
Elkins, WV 72-73 FG 5
Elkins Park, PA 84 III c 1
Elk Mountain 68-69 C 5
Elko 66-67 F 1
Elko, NV 64-65 C 3
Elkol, WY 66-67 H 5
Elk Point 61 C 4
Elk Point, SD 68-69 H 4
Elk Rapids, MI 70-71 H 3
El Krenachich = El Khenachich 164-165 D 4
Elk Ridge 74-75 J 4
Elk River 66-67 F 1
Elk River, ID 66-67 EF 2
Elk River, MN 70-71 D 3
El Kseur = Al-Qaṣr 166-167 J 1
el Ksiba = Al-Q'ṣībah 166-167 CD 3
Elk Springs, CO 68-69 BC 5
Elkton, KY 78-79 F 2
Elkton, MD 72-73 HJ 5
Elkton, OR 66-67 B 4
Elkton, SD 68-69 H 3
Ella 140 E 7
El Ladiqiya = Al-Lādhiqīyah 134-135 CD 3
El-Lagodei = Qardho 134-135 F 9
El Lagowa = Al-Laqawah 164-165 K 6
Ellamar, AK 58-59 O 6
Ellāndu = Yellandu 140 E 2
Ellaville, GA 78-79 G 4
Ellef Ringnes Island 56-57 Q 2
El-Lejâà = Al-Lajā' 136-137 G 6
Ellen, Mount — 74-75 H 3
Ellendale, ND 68-69 G 2-3
El Lenguaraz 106-107 H 6-7
Ellensburg, WA 66-67 C 2
Ellenville, NY 72-73 J 4
Ellerbe, NC 80-81 G 3
Ellerbek 130 I a 1
Ellerslie, PA 84 III d 1
Ellesmere Island 52 B 27-A 26
Ellice Islands 156-157 H 5
Ellichpur = Achalpur 138-139 F 7
Ellijay, GA 78-79 G 3
Ellikane 168-169 H 2
Ellinwood, KS 68-69 G 6
Elliot 172 E 8
Elliotdale = Xhora 174-175 H 6
Elliot Lake [CDN, lake] 62 B 1
Elliot Lake [CDN, place] 56-57 U 8
Elliott 158-159 F 3
Elliott Knob 72-73 G 5
Ellis, ID 66-67 F 3
Ellis, KS 68-69 G 6
Ellis Land 82 III b 2
Elliston [AUS] 158-159 F 6
Elliston [CDN] 63 K 3
Ellisville, MS 78-79 E 5
El Lobo 96-97 A 4
Ellon 119 E 3
Ellora 138-139 E 7
Ellore = Elūru 134-135 N 7
Elloree, SC 80-81 F 4
Ellsinore, MO 78-79 D 2
Ellsworth, KS 68-69 G 6
Ellsworth, ME 72-73 M 2
Ellsworth, WI 70-71 D 3
Ellsworth Highland 53 B 28-25
El Lucero [MEX] 76-77 C 10
El Lucero [YV] 94-95 G 4
Ellwood City, PA 72-73 F 4
Elma 61 KL 6
Elma, IA 70-71 D 4
Elma, WA 66-67 B 2
El-Mabrouk = Al-Mabrūk 166-167 G 5
El Macao 88-89 M 5
Elma dağı [TR, mountain Ankara] 136-137 E 3
Elma dağı [TR, mountain Antalya] 136-137 CD 4
Elmadağı [TR, place] 136-137 E 3
El Maestro, Laguna — 106-107 J 6
El-Mahder = 'Ayn al-Qasr 166-167 K 2
El Mahia 164-165 D 4
El Maïa = Al-Māyah 166-167 G 3
El Maitén 108-109 D 4
Elmalı [TR, Antalya] 136-137 CD 4
Elmalı [TR, İstanbul] 154 I b 2
El Mamoun 168-169 E 1
El Mango 94-95 H 7
El-Mansour = Al-Manṣūr 166-167 F 6
El Manteco 92-93 G 3
El Manzano [RA] 106-107 E 3
El Manzano [RCH] 106-107 B 5
El Marsa 170 I b 1
El Marucho 106-107 BC 7
El Matrimonio 76-77 C 9
El Mayoco 108-109 D 4
El Mayor 74-75 F 6
Elm Creek 61 JK 6
Elm Creek, NE 68-69 G 5
El Medjdel = Ashqĕlōn 136-137 F 7
Ēl Medo 164-165 N 7
El Meghaier = Al-Mighāir 166-167 J 3
Elmer, MO 70-71 D 6
El Merdja = Al-Marjah 166-167 H 2
el-Merq = Al-Marj 164-165 J 2
Elmers End, London- 129 II b 2
El Metlaoui = Al-Mitlawī 164-165 F 2
El Mètlîn = Al-Māṭlīn 166-167 M 1
El Meṭoula = Al-Miṭūyah 166-167 LM 3
El Mezeraa = Al-Mazra'ah 166-167 K 2
el Mḥamîd = Al-Maḥamīd 166-167 D 5
Elmhurst, IL 70-71 FG 5
El Miamo 94-95 L 4
El Miedo 94-95 F 5
El Milagro 111 C 4
El Milia = Al-Mīlīyah 166-167 JK 1
Elmira, CA 74-75 C 3
Elmira, ID 66-67 E 1
Elmira, MI 70-71 H 3
Elmira, NY 64-65 L 3
Elmira [CDN, Ontario] 72-73 F 3
Elmira [CDN, Prince Edward I.] 63 E 4
El Mirador 86-87 P 9
el-Mja'ra = Al-M'jarah 166-167 D 2
Elm Lake 68-69 G 3
El Moknin = Al-Muknīn 166-167 M 2
El Molinito 91 I b 2
El Molino 91 III c 2
El Monasterio 94-95 H 3
El Monastîr = Al-Manastīr 166-167 M 2
Elmont, NY 82 III d 2
El Monte 104-105 D 7
El Monte, CA 83 III d 1
El Monte Airport 83 III d 1
El Moral 76-77 D 8
Elmore 160 G 6
el Morhân = Al-Mughrān 166-167 C 2
El Moro 106-107 H 7
El Morro 106-107 E 4
Elm Park, London- 129 II c 1
El Mreïti = Al-M'rāītī 164-165 C 4
Elmshorn 118 DE 2
Elmvale 72-73 G 2
Elmwood, IL 70-71 EF 5
Elmwood, OK 76-77 D 4
Elmwood, Philadelphia-, PA 84 III b 2
Elmwood Canal 85 I a 1
Elmwood Cemetery 84 II b 2
Elmwood Park 83 II a 1
Elne 120-121 J 7
El Nemlêt = An-Namlāt 166-167 KL 2
El Nido 148-149 G 4
El Nihuil 106-107 C 5
El Oasis 91 II ab 1
El-Obeidh = Al-Ubayyiḍ 164-165 KL 6
E. Lobos 106-107 E 4
Eloğlu 136-137 G 4
Elói Mendes 102-103 K 4
Elordi 106-107 F 5
el Ordi = Dunqulah 164-165 KL 5
El Oro [EC] 96-97 AB 3
El Oro [MEX, Coahuila] 76-77 C 9
El Oro [MEX, México] 86-87 K 8
Elorza 92-93 F 3
El Oso 94-95 J 5
El-Oued = Al-Wād 164-165 F 2
El Oûssel'tia = Al-Ūssaltīyah 166-167 LM 2
El-Oustaïa = Al-Uṭāyah 166-167 J 2
El-Outaïa = Al-Uṭāyah 166-167 J 2
Eloy, AZ 74-75 H 6
El Pacífico 94-95 C 4
El Pajarito 108-109 E 4
El Pájaro 94-95 E 2
El Palimito 86-87 H 5
El Palmar [BOL] 104-105 D 7
El Palmar [CO] 94-95 G 6
El Palmar [YV, Bolívar] 94-95 L 3-4
El Palmar [YV, Caracas] 91 II b 1
El Pampero 106-107 E 5
El Pantanoso, Arroyo — 110 III a 2
El Pao [YV, Anzoátegui] 94-95 J 3
El Pao [YV, Bolívar] 92-93 G 3
El Pao [YV, Cojedes] 94-95 GH 3
El Paraíso 106-107 GH 4
El Paso 92-93 E 3
El Paso, IL 70-71 F 5
El Paso, TX 64-65 E 5
El Paují 91 II c 2
El Pensamiento 106-107 G 7
El Peregrino 106-107 FG 5
El Perú 104-105 C 3
El Petén 64-65 H 8
Elphinstone Island 150-151 AB 6
Elphinstone Island = Pulau-pulau Duperre 150-151 G 11
Elphinstone Island = Tharawthèdangyī Kyûn 150-151 AB 6
El Pico 92-93 G 8
El Pilar 94-95 K 2
El Pinar, Parque Nacional — 91 II b 2
El Pingo 106-107 H 3
El Pintado 104-105 F 9
El Piquete 104-105 D 9
Ēlpiṭiya 140 E 7
El Pluma 108-109 DE 6
El Pluma, Cañadón — 108-109 D 6
El Pluma, Cordón — 108-109 D 6
El Pocito 104-105 E 4
El Portal, CA 74-75 CD 4
El Portugues 92-93 D 6
El Porvenir [CO] 94-95 G 6
El Porvenir [MEX] 76-77 AB 7
El Potosí 86-87 K 5
El Potossí 86-87 K 5
El Potrero 76-77 B 8
El Potro, Cerro — 106-107 C 2
El Pozo 86-87 F 2
El Presto 104-105 F 4
El Progreso [GCA] 86-87 P 10
El Progreso [Honduras] 64-65 J 8
El Progreso [PE] 96-97 E 9
El Puente [BOL, Santa Cruz] 104-105 E 5
El Puente [BOL, Tarija] 104-105 D 7
El Puerto de Santa Maria 120-121 D 10
El Puesto 104-105 C 10
El Qairouân = Al-Qayrawān 164-165 FG 1
El Qaṣṣerîn = Al-Qaṣrayn 164-165 F 1-2
el Qbâb = Al-Qabāb 166-167 D 3
El-Qedhâref = Al-Qaḍārif 164-165 M 6
el Qela'a es 'Srarhnâ = Al-Qal'at as-S'rāghnah 166-167 C 3-4
el Qenîtra = Al-Q'nitrah 164-165 C 2
El-Qoseir = Al-Quṣayr 164-165 L 3
El-Qoubayât = Al-Qubayyāt 136-137 G 5
El-Qouṣair = Al-Quṣayr 136-137 G 5
El Qsâbî = Al-Qaṣābī 166-167 D 3
El Qsour = Al-Quṣūr 166-167 L 2
El Quebrachal 104-105 DE 9
Elquí, Río — 106-107 B 3
El Rastreador 106-107 F 4
El Rastro 94-95 H 3
El Real 88-89 H 10
El Recado 106-107 FG 5
El Refugio 94-95 E 6
El Reno, OK 64-65 G 4
El Retamo 106-107 D 3-4
el Rharb = Al-Gharb 166-167 C 2
El Rhraïba = Al-Ghraybah 166-167 LM 2
El Rincon 91 II bb 2
El Rodeo 94-95 J 3
El Rosario [YV, Bolívar] 94-95 J 4
El Rosario [YV, Zulia] 94-95 E 3
Elrose 61 DE 5
El-Routbé = Ar-Ruṭbah 136-137 G 6
Elroy, WI 70-71 E 4
El Salado 108-109 F 7
El Salitre 91 III b 1
El Salto 64-65 E 7
El Saltón 111 B 7
El Salvador [ES] 64-65 J 9
El Salvador [RCH] 104-105 B 10
El Samán de Apure 94-95 G 4
El Santuario 94-95 F 5
Elsas 70-71 J 1
El Sauce 88-89 C 8
El Sauz 86-87 G 3
El Sauzal 74-75 E 7
Elsberry, MO 70-71 E 6
Elsburg 170 V c 2
Elsburgspruit 170 V c 2
El Segundo, CA 83 III b 2
Elsengrund, Berlin- 130 III c 2
Elsinore, CA 74-75 E 6
Elsmore, KS 70-71 C 7
El Sobrante, CA 83 I c 1
El Socorro [MEX] 76-77 C 9
El Socorro [RA] 106-107 G 4
El Socorro [YV] 94-95 J 3
El Sombrerito 106-107 H 2
El Sombrero [RA] 106-107 H 1
El Sombrero [YV] 92-93 F 3
El Sosneado 106-107 BC 5
Elstal 130 III a 1
Elsternwick, Melbourne- 161 II bc 2
Elstree 129 II a 1
El Sueco 86-87 GH 3
El Sunchal 106-107 D 2
El Tablazo 94-95 F 2
El Tablón [CO, Nariño] 94-95 C 7
El Tablón [CO, Sucre] 94-95 D 3
El Taj = At-Tāj 164-165 J 4
El Tajín 86-87 M 7
El Tala [RA, San Luis] 106-107 D 4
El Tala [RA, Tucumán] 104-105 D 9-10
El Tambo [CO, Cauca] 92-93 D 4
El Tambo [CO, Nariño] 94-95 C 7
El Tambo [EC] 96-97 B 3
El Tejar 106-107 G 5
El Teleno 120-121 D 7
El Temazcal 86-87 LM 5
El Teniente 111 BC 4
Eltham, London- 129 II c 2
El Tigre [CO] 94-95 F 4
El Tigre [YV] 92-93 G 3
Eltingville, New York-, NY 82 III ab 3
El Tío 111 D 4
El Toba, Arroyo — 106-107 GH 2
El Toco 94-95 J 3
El Tocuyo 92-93 F 3
El Tofo 106-107 B 2
El'ton 126-127 N 2
Elton, LA 78-79 C 5
El'ton, ozero — 126-127 N 2
Eltopia, WA 66-67 D 2
El Tránsito 106-107 B 2
El Trebol 106-107 G 4
El Trigo 106-107 H 5
El Trino 94-95 E 6
El Triunfo 106-107 G 5
El Tuito 86-87 H 7
El Tunal 104-105 D 9
El Tunal, Parque Distrital de — 91 III b 4
El Turbio 111 B 8
Eluan Bi = Oluan Pi 146-147 H 11
Elūru 134-135 N 7
Elva 124-125 F 4
El Valle 94-95 C 4
El Valle, Río — 91 II b 2
Elvanlar = Eşme 136-137 C 3
Elvas 120-121 D 9
El Venado 94-95 G 4
Elverum 116-117 DE 7
Elvesís 122-123 K 6
El Viejo, Cerro — 94-95 E 4
El Vigía 92-93 E 3
Elvira 92-93 E 6
Elvira, Cape — 56-57 P 3
El Volcán 106-107 BC 4
El Wak 172 H 1
Elwell Lake 66-67 H 1
Elwood, IN 70-71 H 5
Elwood, NE 68-69 FG 5
Elwood, Melbourne- 161 II b 2
El Wuz = Al-Wazz 164-165 L 5
Elwyn, PA 84 III a 2
Ely 119 G 5
Ely, MN 70-71 DE 2
Ely, NV 64-65 D 4
El Yagual 94-95 G 4
Elyria, OH 72-73 E 4
El Ysian Park 83 III c 1
El Zanjón 106-107 E 1
El Zig-Zag 91 II b 1
El Zurdo 108-109 D 8

Emagusheni = Magusheni 174-175 H 6
Ema jõgi 124-125 F 4
Emāmzādeh 'Abbās 136-137 MN 6
Emān 116-117 F 9
Emangak, AK 58-59 E 5
Emba [SU, place] 132-133 K 8
Emba [SU, river] 132-133 K 8
Embalse Cabra Corral 104-105 D 9
Embalse Cerros Colorados 106-107 C 7
Embalse de Cijara 120-121 E 9
Embalse de Escaba 106-107 DE 1
Embalse de Guárico 94-95 H 3
Embalse de Guri 94-95 K 4
Embalse del Nihuil 106-107 C 5
Embalse del Río Negro 111 E 4
Embalse del Río Tercero 106-107 E 4
Embalse El Cadillal 104-105 D 10
Embalse el Chocón 106-107 C 7
Embalse Escaba 104-105 CD 10
Embalse Ezequiel Ramos Mexia 106-107 C 7
Embalse Florentino Ameghino 108-109 F 5
Embalse La Mariposa 91 II b 2
Embalse Río Hondo 106-107 E 1
Embalse Salto Grande 111 E 4
Embarcación 111 D 2
Embarí, Rio — 94-95 H 8
Embarrass, MN 70-71 D 2
Embarrass River 70-71 FG 6
Embenčime 132-133 ST 4
Embetsu 144-145 b 1
Embira, Rio — 98-99 C 9
Emblem, WY 68-69 B 3
Emborai, Baía do — 100-101 AB 1
Emboscada 102-103 D 6
Embrach 128 IV b 1
Embu 172 G 2
Embuguaçu 102-103 J 5
Emden 118 C 2
Emei Shan 142-143 J 6
Emel gol 142-143 E 2
Émerainville 129 I d 2
Emerald 158-159 J 4
Emerson 68-69 H 1
Emerson, AR 78-79 C 4
Emerson, MI 70-71 H 2
Emery, UT 74-75 H 3
Emeryville, CA 83 I c 1-2
Emesa = Ḥimṣ 134-135 D 4
Emet 136-137 C 3
Emi 132-133 S 7
Emigrant, MT 66-67 H 3
Emigrant Gap, CA 74-75 C 3
Emigrant Pass 66-67 E 5

Emigrant 289

Evansville, IL 70-71 F 6
Evansville, IN 64-65 J 4
Evansville, WI 70-71 F 4
Evant, TX 76-77 EF 7
Evaporación, Planta de — 91 I d 1
Evaristo 106-107 L 3
Evart, MI 70-71 H 4
Evaton 174-175 G 4
Évboia, Kaí — 122-123 K 6-L 7
Evboïkós Kólpos 122-123 KL 6
Eveleth, MN 70-71 D 2
Evenequén 94-95 K 5
Evenki Autonomous Area 132-133 R-T 5
Evensk 132-133 e 5
Everard, Cape — 158-159 JK 7
Everard, Lake — 158-159 F 6
Everard Park 158-159 F 5
Everard Ranges 158-159 F 5
Everest, Mount — = Sagarmatha 142-143 F 6
Everett, GA 80-81 F 5
Everett, MA 84 I b 2
Everett, WA 64-65 B 2
Everett, Mount — 72-73 K 3
Everglades 64-65 K 6
Everglades, FL 80-81 c 4
Everglades National Park 64-65 K 6
Evergreen, AL 78-79 F 5
Evergreen Park, IL 83 II a 2
Evergreen Plaza, Chicago-, IL 83 II ab 2
Eversem 128 II ab 1
Evesboro, NJ 84 III d 2
Evinayong 164-165 G 8
Evje 116-117 BC 8
Évora 120-121 CD 9
Évreux 120-121 H 4
Evrýchu 136-137 E 5
Evrykhou = Evrýchu 136-137 E 5
Évzonos 113 IV b 2

Ewan, WA 66-67 E 2
Ewan Lake 58-59 P 5
Ewaso Ngiro 172 G 2
Ewell 129 II a 2
Ewing, KY 72-73 E 5
Ewing, MO 70-71 E 5-6
Ewing, NE 68-69 G 4
Ewing, VA 80-81 E 2
Ewo 172 BC 2

Exaltación [BOL] 92-93 F 7
Exaltación [BR] 104-105 C 2
Excelsior 174-175 G 5
Excelsior Mountains 74-75 D 3
Excelsior Springs, MO 70-71 CD 6
Excursion Inlet, AK 58-59 U 7
Exe 119 E 6
Executive Committee Range 53 B 24
Exeland, WI 70-71 E 3
Exelberg 113 I ab 1
Exeter, CA 74-75 D 4
Exeter, MO 78-79 C 2
Exeter, NE 68-69 H 5
Exeter, NH 72-73 L 3
Exeter [CDN] 72-73 F 3
Exeter [GB] 119 E 6
Exhibition Building 161 II b 1
Exira, IA 70-71 C 5
Exmoor Forest 119 E 6
Exmore, VA 80-81 HJ 2
Exmouth 119 E 6
Exmouth Gulf [AUS, bay] 158-159 B 4
Exmouth Gulf [AUS, place] 158-159 B 4
Expedition Range 158-159 J 4
Exploits River 63 HJ 3
Explorer Mount 58-59 FG 7
Extrema 102-103 JK 5
Extremadura 120-121 D 9-E 8
Exu 100-101 E 4
Exuma Island, Great — 64-65 L 7
Exuma Sound 64-65 L 7

Eyasi, Lake — 172 FG 2
Eyehill Creek 61 C 4
Eyjafjardhar 116-117 d 2
Eyjafjördhur 116-117 d 1
Eyl 164-165 b 2
Eynihal 136-137 CD 4
Eynsford 129 II c 2
Eyota, MN 70-71 D 3-4
Eyrarbakki 116-117 c 3
Eyre 158-159 E 6
Eyre, Lake — 158-159 G 5
Eyre, Seno — 111 B 7
Eyre North, Lake — 160 C 2
Eyre Peninsula 158-159 G 6
Eyre South, Lake — 160 C 2
Eyüp, İstanbul- 154 I a 2

Ezeiza, Aeropuerto Internacional de — 110 III b 2
Ezequiel Ramos Mejías 104-105 F 9
Ezequiel Ramos Mexía, Embalse — 106-107 C 7
Ezine 136-137 B 3
Ezinepazar = Zigala 136-137 G 2
Ezpeleta, Quilmes- 110 III c 2
Ezraa = Izra' 136-137 G 6
Ežva 124-125 S 3
Ez-Zagazig = Az-Zaqāzīq 164-165 KL 2
Ez Zemoul el Akbar = Az-Zamūl al-Akbar 166-167 K 5-L 4

F

Fáb. das Chitas, Rio de Janeiro- 110 I b 2
Fabens, TX 76-77 AB 7
Faber, Mount — 154 III a 2
Fabriano 122-123 E 4
Facatativá 94-95 D 5
Fachi 164-165 G 5
Facundo 108-109 DE 5
Fada 164-165 J 5
Fada-n'Gourma 164-165 DE 6
Faddeja, zaliv — 132-133 UV 2
Faddejevskij, ostrov — 132-133 b-d 2
Faddeyev Island = ostrov Faddejevskij 132-133 b-d 2
Fadghāmī 136-137 J 5
Fadiffolu Atoll 176 ab 1
Fadu N'Gurma = Fada-n'Gourma 164-165 DE 6
Faenza 122-123 D 3
Færingehavn 56-57 a 5
Faeroe Iceland Ridge 114-115 FG 3
Fafa 168-169 F 2
Fafan = Fafen 164-165 N 7
Fafanlap 148-149 K 7
Fafen 164-165 N 7
Faga 168-169 F 2
Făgăraş 122-123 L 3
Fagatoga 148-149 c 1
Fagernes 116-117 C 7
Fagersta 116-117 FG 7-8
Fagibin, Lake — = Lac Faguibine 164-165 CD 5
Fagnano, Lago — 108-109 EF 10
Faguibine, Lac — 164-165 CD 5
Fagundes [BR, Pará] 92-93 H 6
Fagundes [BR, Paraíba] 100-101 FG 4
Fahala 176 a 2
Fahl, Oued el — = Wādī al-Fahl 166-167 HJ 4
Fahl, Wādī al- 166-167 HJ 4
Fähna = Vääna 124-125 E 4
Fahraj 134-135 H 5
Fahrlander See 130 III a 2
Fahs, Al- 166-167 LM 1
Faial 204-205 DE 5
Fa'id 173 C 2
Faīdāt = Faydāt 136-137 HJ 5
Faifo = Hôi An 150-151 G 5
Faijum, El — = Al-Fayyūm 164-165 KL 3
Fair 106-107 H 6
Fairbairn Park 161 II b 1
Fairbank, AZ 74-75 H 7
Fairbanks, AK 56-57 G 5
Fairbanks, Houston-, TX 85 III a 1
Fairburn, GA 78-79 G 4
Fairburn, SD 68-69 E 4
Fairbury, IL 70-71 F 5
Fairbury, NE 64-65 G 3
Fairchild, WI 70-71 E 3
Fairfax, AL 78-79 G 4
Fairfax, MN 70-71 C 3
Fairfax, MO 70-71 C 5
Fairfax, OK 76-77 F 4
Fairfax, SC 80-81 F 4
Fairfax, SD 68-69 G 4
Fairfield, AL 78-79 F 4
Fairfield, CA 74-75 BC 3
Fairfield, IA 70-71 E 5
Fairfield, ID 66-67 F 4
Fairfield, IL 70-71 F 6
Fairfield, ME 72-73 M 2
Fairfield, MT 66-67 H 2
Fairfield, ND 68-69 E 2
Fairfield, TX 76-77 FG 7
Fairfield, Melbourne- 161 II c 1
Fairgrounds 85 I b 2
Fairholm, WA 66-67 AB 1
Fairhope, AL 78-79 F 5
Fair Isle 119 F 2
Fairlie 158-159 NO 8
Fair Meadows, Houston-, TX 85 III b 1
Fairmont, MN 70-71 C 4
Fairmont, NC 80-81 G 3
Fairmont, NE 68-69 H 5
Fairmont, WV 72-73 F 5
Fairmont Hot Springs 60 K 4
Fairmount, ND 68-69 H 2-3
Fairmount Park 84 III b 1-2
Fair Oaks, AR 78-79 D 3
Fairplay, CO 68-69 CD 6
Fair Play, MO 70-71 D 7
Fairport, NY 72-73 H 3
Fairport Harbor, OH 72-73 F 4
Fairview 60 H 1
Fairview, KS 70-71 C 6
Fairview, MT 68-69 D 2
Fairview, OK 76-77 E 4
Fairview, UT 74-75 H 3
Fairway Hills, MD 82 II a 1
Fairway Rock 58-59 C 4
Fairweather, Cape — 58-59 ST 7
Fairweather, Mount — 56-57 J 6
Fais 206-207 S 9
Faisalābād 134-135 L 4
Faith, SD 68-69 EF 3
Faizābād 134-135 N 5
Fajansovyj 124-125 K 6
Fajardo 88-89 O 5
Fajj Mazallah 166-167 JK 1
Fajr, Wādī — 134-135 D 5
Fakaofo 208 J 3
Fakel 124-125 T 5
Fakfak 148-149 K 7
Fakīragrām 138-139 MN 4
Fak Tha 150-151 C 3-4
Falaba 168-169 C 3
Faladyé 168-169 C 2
Falaise, Cap — = Mui Đa Du'ng 150-151 EF 3
Falaise de Tiguidit 168-169 GH 1
Fālākāta 138-139 M 4
Falam = Hpalam 148-149 B 2
Fălciu 122-123 MN 2
Falckner 108-109 F 3
Falcón 94-95 FG 2
Falcon, Cap — = Rā's Falkun 166-167 F 2
Falcon, Cape — 66-67 A 3
Falcone, Capo — 122-123 BC 5
Falcon Island 62 B 3
Falcon Reservoir 64-65 G 6
Falda, La — 106-107 E 3
Faléa 168-169 C 2
Falémé 164-165 B 6
Falemé = Falémé 164-165 B 6
Falenki 124-125 S 4
Faleru, Órmos — 113 IV a 2
Faleşty 126-127 C 3
Falfurrias, TX 76-77 E 9
Falher 60 J 2
Falkenberg [DDR] 118 F 3
Falkenberg [S] 116-117 DE 9
Falkenberg, Berlin- 130 III c 1
Falkenhagener See 130 III a 1
Falkenhagen-Ost 130 III a 1
Falkenhagen-West 130 III a 1
Falkirk 119 E 3-4
Falkland Islands 111 DE 8
Falkland Sound 111 DE 8
Falkonéra 122-123 KL 7
Falköping 116-117 EF 8
Falkun, Rā's — 166-167 F 2
Falkville, AL 78-79 F 3
Fällanden 128 IV b 1
Fallbrook, CA 74-75 E 6
Fall Line Hills [USA, Alabama] 78-79 E 3
Fall Line Hills [USA, Georgia] 80-81 D-F 4
Fallon, MT 68-69 D 2
Fallon, NV 64-65 C 4
Fall River, MA 64-65 MN 3
Fall River Lake 70-71 BC 7
Fall River Mills, CA 66-67 C 5
Falls Church, VA 82 II a 2
Falls City, NE 70-71 C 5
Falls City, OR 66-67 B 3
Falls City, TX 76-77 EF 8
Falls Creek 160 H 6
Fallūjah, Al- 136-137 JK 6
Falmouth 119 D 6
Falmouth, KY 70-71 H 6
Falmouth, MA 72-73 L 4
Falsa Chipana, Punta — 104-105 A 7
False Bay = Valsbaai [ZA, Kaapland] 172 C 8
False Bay = Valsbaai [ZA, Natal] 174-175 K 4
False Cabo de Hornos 108-109 E 10
False Cape 80-81 c 2
False Divi Point 140 E 3
False Pass, AK 58-59 ab 2
False Point 134-135 O 6
Falster 116-117 E 10
Falsterbo 116-117 E 10
Faltbush, New York-, NY 82 III c 3
Falterona, Monte — 122-123 DE 4
Fălticeni 122-123 M 2
Falucho 106-107 E 5
Falun 116-117 F 7
Famagusta = Ammóchōstos 134-135 CD 3
Famagusta Bay = Kólpos Ammochōstu 136-137 EF 5
Famatina 106-107 D 2
Famatina, Sierra de — 106-107 D 2
Family Lake 62 B 2
Fana 168-169 D 2
Fanchang 146-147 G 6
Fancheng = Xiangfan 142-143 L 5
Fanchih = Fanshi 146-147 D 2
Fanegas 106-107 H 2
Fang 150-151 B 3
Fāngāk 164-165 L 7
Fangasso 168-169 DE 2
Fangcheng [TJ, Guangdong] 150-151 G 2
Fangcheng [TJ, Henan] 142-143 L 5
Fang-ch'êng = Fangcheng 150-151 G 2
Fangfeng 146-147 E 3
Fanghsien = Fang Xian 146-147 C 5
Fanglan = Jiangcun 146-147 D 2
Fangliao 146-147 H 10
Fangshan [TJ, Beijing] 146-147 E 2
Fangshan [TJ, Shanxi] 146-147 C 3
Fang-shan = Fengchiang 146-147 H 10
Fang Shan = Huoshan 146-147 F 6
Fang Xian 146-147 C 5
Fan-hsien = Fan Xian 146-147 E 4
Fanjiacun = Beijing-Huangtugang 155 II ab 2
Fanning 156-157 K 4
Fanning Trench 156-157 J 4-K 5
Fanø [DK] 116-117 C 10
Fano [I] 122-123 E 4
Fanshan 146-147 C 3
Fanshi 146-147 D 2
Fan Si Pan 148-149 D 2
Fant, Al- 173 B 3
Fantās, Gebel el — = Jabal al-Fintās 173 B 6
Fan Xian 146-147 E 4
Fanyu = Panyu 146-147 D 10
Fanzhi = Fanshi 146-147 D 2
Faqīh Bin Şālah, Al- 166-167 C 3
Fāqūs 173 BC 2
Farā', Al- 136-137 J 4
Faraba 168-169 C 2
Farabana 168-169 C 3
Faraday Seamount Group 114-115 C 5-6
Faradje 172 E 1
Faradofay 172 J 7
Farafangana 172 J 6
Farāfirah, Al-Qaşr al- 164-165 K 3
Farāfirah, Wāhāt al- 164-165 K 3
Farāh 134-135 J 4
Farāh Rōd 134-135 J 4
Farako 168-169 D 2
Farallón, Cabo — = Cabo Santa Elena 64-65 J 9
Farallon de Pajaros 206-207 S 7
Farallon Islands 74-75 B 4
Faranah 164-165 BC 6
Farasān, Jazā'ir — 134-135 E 7
Faraulep 148-149 M 5
Farāyid, Jabal al- 173 D 6
Fārbisganj = Forbesganj 138-139 L 4
Farewell, AK 58-59 KL 5
Farewell, MI 72-73 D 3
Farewell, Cape — 158-159 O 8
Farewell, Cape — = Kap Farvel 56-57 c 6
Farewell Field 84 II b 2
Fargo, GA 80-81 E 5
Fargo, ND 64-65 G 2
Fargo, OK 76-77 E 4
Faria 110 I b 2
Farias Brito 100-101 E 4
Faribault, MN 70-71 D 3
Farīdābād 138-139 F 3
Farīdkot 138-139 E 2
Farīdpūr [BD] 138-139 M 6
Faridpur [IND] 138-139 G 3
Farīgh, Wādī al- 164-165 HJ 2-3
Farim 164-165 AB 6
Farina 158-159 G 6
Farinha, Rio — 100-101 A 4
Fāris 134-135 G 6
Farka 168-169 F 2
Farlane 62 BC 2
Farmer City, IL 70-71 F 5
Farmersburg, IN 70-71 G 6
Farmerville, LA 78-79 C 4
Farmington, CA 74-75 C 4
Farmington, IA 70-71 DE 5
Farmington, IL 70-71 EF 5
Farmington, ME 72-73 LM 2
Farmington, MN 70-71 D 3
Farmington, MO 70-71 EF 7
Farmington, NM 74-75 J 4
Farmington, UT 66-67 GH 5
Farmsen, Hamburg- 130 I b 1
Farmville, NC 80-81 H 3
Farmville, VA 80-81 G 2
Farnborough, London- 129 II c 2
Farnham [CDN] 72-73 K 2
Farnsworth, TX 76-77 D 4
Faro [BR] 92-93 H 5
Faro [P] 120-121 CD 10
Faro [RA] 106-107 G 7
Faro [RFC] 164-165 G 7
Faro, Punta di — 122-123 F 6
Faro de Avión 120-121 CD 7
Farofa, Serra da — 106-107 MN 2
Fårön 116-117 H 9
Farquhar Islands 172 JK 4
Farrars Creek 158-159 H 4-5
Farrell, PA 72-73 F 4
Farrer Park 154 III b 2
Far Rockawa, New York-, NY 82 III d 3
Farroupilha 106-107 M 2
Farrukhābād 134-135 M 5
Fārs 134-135 G 4-5
Fársala 122-123 K 6
Farshūṭ 173 BC 4
Farsia = Ḥāssī al-Farsīyah 166-167 B 6
Farsīyah, Ḥāssī al- 166-167 B 6
Farson, WY 66-67 J 4
Farsund 116-117 B 8
Fartak, Rā's — 134-135 G 7
Fartura 102-103 H 5
Fartura, Serra da — 102-103 FG 7
Farvel, Kap — 56-57 c 6
Farwell, MI 70-71 H 4
Farwell, TX 76-77 C 5
Fas 164-165 CD 2
Fasā 134-135 G 5
Fasanerie-Nord, München- 130 II b 1
Fasaneriesee 130 II b 1
Fasangarten, München- 130 II b 2
Fasano 122-123 G 5
Fāsher, El- = Al-Fāshir 164-165 K 6
Fāshir, Al- 164-165 K 6
Fashn, Al- 164-165 KL 3
Fashoda = Kūdūk 164-165 L 6-7
Fáskrúdhsfjördhur 116-117 fg 2
Fastov 126-127 D 1
Fatagar, Tanjung — 148-149 K 7
Fatahgarh = Fatehgarh 138-139 G 4
Fatahpur = Fatehpur [IND, Bihār] 138-139 K 5
Fatahpur = Fatehpur [IND, Rājasthān] 134-135 L 5
Fatahpur = Fatehpur [IND, Uttar Pradesh ↘ Kānpur] 138-139 H 5
Fatahpur = Fatehpur [IND, Uttar Pradesh ↗ Lucknow] 138-139 H 4
Fatako 168-169 C 3
Fatala 168-169 B 3
Fatehābād [IND, Haryana] 138-139 E 3
Fatehābād [IND, Uttar Pradesh] 138-139 G 4
Fatehgarh 138-139 G 4
Fatehpur [IND, Bihār] 138-139 K 5
Fatehpur [IND, Rājasthān] 134-135 L 5
Fatehpur [IND, Uttar Pradesh ↘ Kānpur] 138-139 H 5
Fatehpur [IND, Uttar Pradesh ↗ Lucknow] 138-139 H 4
Fatehpur [Nepal] 138-139 L 4
Fatež 124-125 K 7
Fatha, Al- = Al-Fatḥah 134-135 E 3
Father Lake 62 O 2
Fatick 168-169 A 2
Fatih, İstanbul- 154 I a 2
Fatih Mehmet Camii 154 I a 2
Fatikli 136-137 G 4
Fátima 120-121 C 9
Fatima, Bogotá- 91 III b 3
Fatima do Sul 102-103 E 5
Fatkong = Fogang 146-147 D 10
Fatmah, Bi'r — 136-137 K 5
Fatsa 136-137 G 2
Fat Tau Point 155 I b 2
Fatuma 171 B 4
Faucett, MO 70-71 C 6
Faucilles, Monts — 120-121 K 5-L 4
Faulkton, SD 68-69 G 3
Făurei 122-123 M 3
Fauresmith 174-175 F 5
Fauro 148-149 j 6
Fauske 116-117 F 4
Faust 60 K 2
Faust, UT 66-67 G 5
Faustino M. Parera 106-107 H 4
Faval, Porto do — 100-101 B 1
Fåvang 124-125 K 6
Favara 122-123 E 7
Faversham 119 G 6
Favignana 122-123 DE 7
Favoriten, Wien- 113 I b 2
Favourable Lake 62 C 1
Faw, Al- 136-137 N 7-8
Fawāt 166-167 M 7
Fawkner, Melbourne- 161 II b 1
Fawkner Park 161 II b 2
Fawnie Range 60 E 3
Fawn River 56-57 T 7
Faxaflói 116-117 b 2
Faxinal 102-103 G 5
Fay, OK 76-77 E 5
Faya = Largeau 164-165 HJ 5
Fayala 172 C 2
Faya-Largeau 164-165 H 5
Faydābād 134-135 KL 3
Faydāt 136-137 HJ 5
Fayette, AL 78-79 F 4
Fayette, IA 70-71 E 4
Fayette, MO 70-71 D 6
Fayette, MS 78-79 D 5
Fayetteville, AR 64-65 H 4
Fayetteville, NC 64-65 L 4-5
Fayetteville, OH 72-73 E 5
Fayetteville, TN 78-79 F 3
Fāyid = Fā'id 173 C 2
Faylakah, Jazīrat — 136-137 N 8
Faysalīyah, Al- 136-137 KL 7
Faysh Khābūr 136-137 JK 4
Fayum, El — = Al-Fayyūm 164-165 KL 3
Fayyūm, Al- 164-165 KL 3
Fayzabad = Faizābād 134-135 N 5
Fāzilka 138-139 E 2
Fazrārah, Buḥayrat — 166-167 K 1
Fazzān 164-165 GH 3

Fdayrik 164-165 B 4

Fear, Cape — 64-65 L 5
Feather Falls, CA 74-75 C 3
Feather River 74-75 C 3
Feather River, North Fork — 74-75 C 2-3
Featherston 158-159 P 8
Featherville, ID 66-67 F 4
Febre 106-107 GH 4
Febrero, Parque 3 de — 110 III b 1
Fécamp 120-121 H 4
Fechenheim, Frankfurt am Main- 128 III b 1
Fédala = Al-Muḥammadīyah 166-167 C 3
Federación 106-107 HJ 3
Federal 111 E 4
Federal Capital Territory = 1 ◁ 164-165 F 7
Federal Capital Territory = Australian Capital Territory 158-159 J 7
Federal Dam, MN 70-71 CD 2
Federick Hills 158-159 G 2
Federico Lacroze 110 III b 1
Fedje 116-117 A 7
Fedjedj, Chott el — = Shaṭṭ al-Fijāj 166-167 L 2-3
Fedj-M'zala = Fajj Mazallah 166-167 JK 1
Fedosejevskaja 124-125 N 2
Fedotova, kosa — 126-127 G 3
Fedovo 124-125 M 2
Fehmarn 118 E 1
Feia 100-101 B 8
Feia, Lagoa — 92-93 L 9
Feicheng 146-147 F 3
Feidong 146-147 F 6
Feiheji 146-147 E 5
Feihekou = Feiheji 146-147 E 5
Fei-hsi = Feixi 146-147 F 6
Feihsien = Fei Xian 146-147 FG 4
Feijó 92-93 E 6
Feira de Santana 92-93 LM 7
Feisabad = Faizābād 134-135 N 5
Feitoria, Ilha da — 106-107 LM 3
Feixi 146-147 F 6
Fei Xian 146-147 FG 4
Feixiang 146-147 E 3
Fei-yün Chiang = Feiyun Jiang 146-147 GH 8
Feiyun Jiang 146-147 GH 8
Feke = Asmaca 136-137 F 4
Felāhiye 136-137 F 3
Felanitx 120-121 J 9
Feldberg 118 C 5
Feldioara 122-123 L 3
Feldkirch 118 DE 5
Feldmochinger See 130 II ab 1
Feliciano, Arroyo — 106-107 H 3
Felidu Atoll 176 a 2
Felipe Carillo Puerto 64-65 J 8
Felipe Solá 106-107 F 6-7
Felipe Yofré 106-107 HJ 2
Felixlândia 102-103 K 3
Felixton 174-175 JK 5
Félix U. Gómez 86-87 H 2
Feller Heights 60 G 2
Fellowship, NJ 84 III d 2
Fellsmere, FL 80-81 c 3
Felt, OK 76-77 C 4
Feltham, London- 129 II a 2
Felton, CA 74-75 B 4
Felton, MN 68-69 H 2
Feltre 122-123 D 2
Femund 116-117 D 6
Femundsenden 116-117 D 7
Fenaria 168-169 C 3
Fencheng 146-147 C 4
Fenelon Falls 72-73 G 2
Fener, İstanbul- 154 I a 2
Fenerbahçe Stadyumu 154 I b 3
Fener burnu 154 I b 3
Fénérive = Fenoarivo Atsinanana 172 JK 5
Fengári 122-123 L 5
Fengcheng [TJ, Jiangxi] 146-147 E 7
Fengcheng [TJ, Liaoning] 142-143 N 3
Fengchiang 146-147 H 10
Fêng-chieh = Fengjie 142-143 K 5
Fêng-ch'iu = Fengqiu 146-147 E 4
Fengchuan 146-147 C 10
Fengdu 142-143 K 5-6
Fêng-fêng = Fengfeng 146-147 DE 3
Fêng-hsin = Fengxin 146-147 E 7
Fenghua 146-147 H 7
Fêng-hua = Fenghua 146-147 H 7
Fenghuang 146-147 B 8
Fengjie 142-143 K 5
Fengjun = Fengrun 146-147 FG 2
Fengkai 146-147 C 10
Fengkieh = Fengjie 142-143 K 5
Fengliang 146-147 F 10
Fenglin [RC] 146-147 H 10
Fenglin [TJ] 146-147 H 7
Fenglingdu 146-147 C 4
Fêng-ling-tu = Fenglingdu 146-147 C 4
Fengming Dao 144-145 C 3
Fêng-ming Tao = Fengming Dao 144-145 C 3
Fengning 142-143 M 3
Fengqiu 146-147 E 4
Fengrun 146-147 FG 2
Fengshan [RC] 146-147 GH 10
Feng Shan [TJ] 146-147 B 5
Fengshun 146-147 EF 10
Fengsien = Feng Xian 142-143 K 5
Fengtai 146-147 F 5
Fengtai, Beijing- 155 II a 2
Fengtaiqu, Beijing- 155 II ab 2
Fengting 146-147 G 9
Fengtu = Fengdu 142-143 K 5-6
Fengxian [TJ, Jiangsu ↓ Shanghai] 146-147 H 6
Feng Xian [TJ, Jiangsu ↖ Xuzhou] 146-147 F 4
Feng Xian [TJ, Shaanxi] 142-143 K 5
Fengxin 146-147 E 7
Fengyang 146-147 F 5
Fengyüan 146-147 H 9
Fen He 142-143 L 4
Fên Ho = Fen He 142-143 L 4
Fen-hsi = Fenxi 146-147 C 3
Feni 141 B 4
Feni = Fenyi 146-147 E 8
Feniak Lake 58-59 HJ 2
Feni Islands 148-149 h 5
Fênix Grande, Rio — 108-109 D 6
Fenner 61 C 5
Fennimore, WI 70-71 E 4
Fennville, MI 70-71 G 4
Fenoarivo Atsinanana 172 JK 5
Fenshui Ling 144-145 D 2-3
Fensi = Fenxi 146-147 C 3
Fenton, LA 78-79 C 5
Fenton, MI 70-71 J 4
Fenway Park 84 I b 2
Fenxi 146-147 C 3
Fenyang 142-143 L 4
Fenyi 146-147 E 8
Feodosija 126-127 G 4
Feou-ning = Funing 142-143 MN 5
Fer, Cap de — = Rā's al-Ḥadīd 166-167 K 1
Fer, Point au — 78-79 D 6
Férai 122-123 M 5
Ferbitz 130 III a 2
Ferdows 134-135 H 4
Fère, la — 120-121 J 4
Fergana 134-135 L 2-3
Ferganskaja dolina 134-135 L 2
Ferghana = Fergana 134-135 L 2-3
Fergus 72-73 F 3
Fergus Falls, MN 64-65 GH 2
Fergusson Island 148-149 h 6
Feriāna = Firyānah 166-167 L 2
Ferias, Bogotá-Las — 91 III b 2
Ferkane = Firgān 166-167 K 2
Ferkéssédougou 164-165 CD 7
Ferlo [SN, landscape] 164-165 AB 5
Ferlo [SN, river] 168-169 B 2
Fermo 122-123 E 4
Fermoselle 120-121 DE 8
Fermoy 119 B 5
Fernandes Belo 100-101 AB 1
Fernandes Pinheiro 102-103 G 6
Fernández 106-107 F 1
Fernandina, FL 80-81 c 1
Fernandina, Isla — 92-93 A 4-5
Fernando de Noronha 92-93 N 5
Fernando de Noronha, Ilha — 92-93 N 5
Fernando de Trejo y Sanabria, Colonia — 102-103 E 6
Fernandópolis 102-103 GH 4
Fernando Póo, Isla de — = Bioko 164-165 F 8
Ferndale 170 V a 1
Ferndale, CA 66-67 A 5
Ferndale, MI 84 II b 2
Ferndale, WA 66-67 B 1
Fernie 66-67 F 1
Fernlee 160 H 2
Fernley, NV 74-75 D 3
Fernmeldeturm Frankfurt 128 III a 1
Fernsehturm 130 II b 1
Fernwood, ID 66-67 EF 2
Ferokh 140 B 5
Ferozepore 138-139 E 2
Ferrara 122-123 DE 3
Ferré 106-107 G 5
Ferreira [ZA] 174-175 G 5
Ferreira Gomes 92-93 J 4
Ferreñafe 92-93 D 6
Ferrer Point 60 D 5
Ferriday, LA 78-79 D 5
Ferris, TX 76-77 F 6
Ferro = Hierro 164-165 A 3
Ferrol, Península de — 92-93 CD 6
Ferrol de Caudillo, El — 120-121 C 7
Ferros 102-103 L 3
Ferry, AK 58-59 N 4
Ferryville = Manzil Būrgībah 166-167 L 1
Fertile, MN 68-69 H 2
Fes = Fās 164-165 CD 2
Feshi 172 C 3
Fessenden, ND 68-69 FG 2
Festus, MO 70-71 E 6
Fête Bové 168-169 B 2
Feteşti 122-123 M 3
Fethiye 134-135 B 3
Fethiye körfezi 136-137 C 4
Fetisovo 134-135 G 2
Fetlar 119 F 1
Fetzara, Lac — = Buḥayrat Fazrārah 166-167 K 1
Feucherolles 129 I ab 2
Feuerland 111 C 8
Feuét = Fawāt 166-167 M 7
Fevat = Fawāt 166-167 M 7
Fevzipaşa 136-137 G 4
Fez = Fās 164-165 CD 2
Fezzan = Fazzān 164-165 GH 3

Fiambalá 104-105 C 10
Fiambalá, Río — 104-105 C 10
Fianarantsoa 172 J 6
Fichtelgebirge 118 EF 3
Ficksburg 174-175 GH 5
Ficuar 96-97 A 4
Fidalgo, Rio — 100-101 C 4
Fidelandia 100-101 D 10
Fidenza 122-123 D 3
Field 72-73 FG 1
Field, NM 76-77 A 5
Fielding 61 E 4
Field Museum 83 II b 1
Fier 122-123 H 5
Fier, Porţile de — 122-123 K 3
Fife Ness 119 E 3
Fīfī, Al- 164-165 J 6
Figalo, Cap — = Rā's Fīqālu 166-167 F 2
Figeac 120-121 J 6
Fighting Island 84 II b 3
Figig = Fijīj 164-165 D 2
Figueira, Cachoeira — 98-99 J 9
Figueira da Foz 120-121 C 8
Figueiras 106-107 L 3
Figueras 120-121 J 7
Figuig = Fijīj 164-165 D 2
Figuras, Serra das — 100-101 B 6
Fijāj, Shaṭṭ al- 166-167 L 2-3
Fiji 148-149 ab 2
Fiji Basin 156-157 H 6
Fiji Islands 148-149 ab 2
Fijīj 164-165 D 2
Fila = Vila 158-159 N 3
Filabres, Sierra de los — 120-121 F 10
Filadelfia [BR, Acre] 96-97 G 7
Filadélfia [BR, Goiás] 92-93 K 6
Filadelfia [PY] 111 D 2
Filadu 140 A 7
Filamana 168-169 CD 3
Filchner-Schelfeis 53 A 30-B 33
Filer, ID 66-67 F 4
Filiaşi 122-123 K 3
Filiátai 122-123 J 6
Filiatrá 122-123 J 7
Filicudi 122-123 F 6
Fili-Mazilovo, Moskva- 113 V b 3
Filingué 164-165 E 6
Filipevila = Sakīkdah 164-165 F 1
Filippiás 122-123 J 6
Filipstad 116-117 EF 8
Fillmore 61 G 6
Fillmore, CA 74-75 D 5
Fillmore, UT 74-75 G 3
Filyos çayı 136-137 E 2
Fimi 172 C 2
Finaalspan 170 V c 2

Finaalsp 291

Financial District, New York-, NY 82 III bc 3
Finch 72-73 J 2
Finchley, London- 129 II b 1
Fındık 136-137 JK 4
Fındıklı 136-137 J 2
Findlay, OH 64-65 K 3
Fine Arts, Museum of — [USA, Boston] 84 I b 2
Fine Arts, Museum of — [USA, Houston] 85 III b 1
Fingal, ND 68-69 H 2
Finger, Cerro — 108-109 C 9
Finger Lake 62 C 1
Finger Lakes 64-65 L 3
Fingoè 172 F 5
Fingoland 174-175 GH 7
Finike 136-137 D 4
Finisterre, Cabo de — 120-121 BC 7
Fink Creek, AK 58-59 F 4
Finke 158-159 FG 5
Finkenkrug-Süd 130 III a 1
Finke River 158-159 G 5
Finland 116-117 K 7-M 4
Finland, MN 70-71 E 2
Finland, Gulf of — 114-115 N 4-O 3
Finlay Forks 60 EF 1
Finlay Mountains 76-77 B 7
Finlay Ranges 60 E 1
Finlay River 56-57 LM 6
Finley, ND 68-69 H 2
Finmark 70-71 F 1
Finnegan 61 BC 5
Finnis, Cape — 160 B 4
Finnmark 116-117 K 3-N 2
Finnmarksvidda 116-117 KL 3
Finn Mount 58-59 J 6
Finnskogene 116-117 E 7
Finnsnes 116-117 GH 3
Finschhafen 148-149 N 8
Finse 116-117 B 7
Finspång 116-117 FG 8
Finsteraarhorn 118 CD 5
Finsterwalde 118 FG 3
Fintās, Jabal al- 173 B 6
Fiordland National Park 158-159 N 8-9
Fiordo Comau 108-109 C 4
Fiorito, Lomas de Zamora- 110 III b 2
Fiqālu, Rā's — 166-167 F 2
Fırat nehri 134-135 D 3
Firebag River 61 C 2
Firebaugh, CA 74-75 C 4
Fire Boat Station 85 III b 2
Fire Island 58-59 M 6
Firenze 122-123 D 4
Fire River 70-71 HJ 1
Firesteel, SD 68-69 F 3
Firgān 166-167 K 2
Firindah 166-167 G 2
Firkessedougou = Ferkéssédougou 164-165 CD 7
Firmat 106-107 G 4
Firminópolis 102-103 GH 2
Firovo 124-125 J 5
Firoza 138-139 C 3
Firozābād 134-135 M 5
Fīrōzpur = Ferozepore 138-139 E 2
Firth of Clyde 119 D 4
Firth of Forth 119 EF 3
Firth of Lorne 119 CD 3
Firth of Tay 119 E 3
Firth River 58-59 R 2
Fīrūzābād [IR, Fārs] 134-135 G 5
Fīrūzābād [IR, Lorestān] 136-137 MN 6
Firvale 60 DE 3
Firyānah 166-167 L 2
Fischbek, Hamburg- 130 I a 2
Fischbeker Heide 130 I a 2
Fischteiche 130 II c 1
Fish Creek 58-59 LM 1
Fisher, MN 68-69 H 2
Fisher Bay 61 K 5
Fishermans Island 80-81 J 2
Fishermens Bend, Melbourne- 161 II b 1
Fisher Strait 56-57 U 5
Fishguard & Goodwick 119 D 5-6
Fishing Lake 61 G 5
Fishing Point 80-81 J 2
Fish Lake Valley 74-75 DE 4
Fish River 58-59 F 4
Fish River = Visrivier 174-175 B 3
Fisk, MO 78-79 D 2
Fiskåfjället 116-117 F 5
Fiske 61 D 5
Fiskenæsset = Qeqertarssuatsiaq 56-57 a 5
Fiskivötn 116-117 c 2
Fišt, gora — 126-127 J 5
Fitalancao 108-109 D 3
Fitchburg, MA 72-73 KL 3
Fittri, Lac — 164-165 H 6
Fitzgerald, GA 80-81 E 5
Fitz Hugh Sound 60 D 4
Fitzmaurice River 158-159 EF 2
Fitzpatrick 72-73 K 1
Fitz Roy 111 C 7
Fitzroy, Melbourne- 161 II b 1
Fitz Roy, Monte — 111 B 7
Fitzroy Crossing 158-159 DE 3
Fitzroy River [AUS, Queensland] 158-159 JK 4
Fitzroy River [AUS, Western Australia] 158-159 DE 3
Fitzwilliam Island 62 KL 4
Fitzwilliam Strait 56-57 NO 2
Fiume = Rijeka 122-123 F 3
Five Cowrte Creek 170 III b 2
Five Dunes 174-175 D 4
Five Miles Rapids 66-67 D 2
Fizi 172 E 2
Fizuli 126-127 N 7
Fkih 'Ben Ṣālaḥ = Al-Faqīh Bin Ṣālaḥ 166-167 C 3
Flå 116-117 C 7
Fladelfia 104-105 B 2
Flagler, CO 68-69 E 6
Flagstaff, AZ 64-65 D 4
Flagstaff Lake 72-73 L 2
Flagstaff Siphaqeni 172 EF 8
Flagstone 66-67 F 1
Flaherty Island 56-57 U 6
Flakensee 130 III cd 2
Flakstadøy 116-117 E 3
Flåm 116-117 B 7
Flamand = Arak 164-165 E 3
Flambeau Flowage 70-71 E 2
Flamborough Head 119 FG 4
Flamenco 104-105 A 10
Flamengo, Ponta do — 100-101 G 3
Flamengo, Serra do — 100-101 E 4
Fläming 118 F 2-3
Flaming Gorge Reservoir 66-67 J 5
Flamingo, FL 80-81 c 4
Flamingo, Teluk — 148-149 L 8
Flaminia, Via — 113 II b 1
Flanders 62 C 3
Flanders = Vlaanderen 120-121 J 3
Flandes 94-95 D 5
Flandreau, SD 68-69 H 3
Flanigan, NV 66-67 D 5
Flannan Isles 119 BC 2
Flasher, ND 68-69 F 2
Flat, AK 58-59 HJ 5
Flatey 116-117 b 2
Flateyri 116-117 ab 1
Flathead Indian Reservation 66-67 FG 2
Flathead Lake 64-65 CD 2
Flathead Mountains = Salish Mountains 66-67 F 1-2
Flathead River 66-67 F 1
Flat Island = Pulau Subi 150-151 G 11
Flatonia, TX 76-77 F 8
Flat River, MO 70-71 E 7
Flattery, Cape — [AUS] 158-159 J 2
Flattery, Cape — [USA] 66-67 A 1
Flat Top Mountain 80-81 F 2
Flaxman Island 58-59 P 1
Flax Pond 84 I c 2
Flaxton, ND 68-69 E 1
Flaxville, MT 68-69 D 1
Flèche, la — 120-121 GH 5
Flecheira, Serra da — 100-101 B 8
Fleetwood 119 E 5
Fleischhacker Zoo 83 II ab 2
Flekkefjord 116-117 AB 8
Fleming, CO 68-69 E 5
Flemingsburg, KY 72-73 E 5
Flemington, Melbourne- 161 II b 1
Flemington Racecourse 161 II b 1
Flen 116-117 G 8
Flensburg 118 DE 1
Flers 120-121 G 4
Flesher, MT 66-67 G 2
Fletcher, OK 76-77 EF 5
Fleur de Lys 63 HJ 2
Fleur de May, Lac — 63 D 2
Fleuve 168-169 B 1-2
Fleuve Saint-Laurent 56-57 W 8-9
Flinders Bay 158-159 BC 6
Flinders Island [AUS, Bass Strait] 158-159 J 7
Flinders Island [AUS, Great Australian Bight] 158-159 F 6
Flinders Range 158-159 G 6
Flinders River 158-159 H 3-4
Flin Flon 56-57 Q 7
Flint, MI 64-65 K 3
Flint [GB] 119 E 5
Flint [island] 156-157 K 6
Flintdale 62 G 2
Flint Hills 68-69 H 6-7
Flint River [USA, Georgia] 78-79 G 5
Flint River [USA, Michigan] 72-73 E 3
Flomaton, AL 78-79 F 5
Floodwood, MN 70-71 D 2
Flora 116-117 A 7
Flora, IL 70-71 F 6
Flora, OR 66-67 E 3
Florala, AL 78-79 F 5
Floral Park, NY 82 III de 2
Florânia 100-101 F 4
Floreana 92-93 AB 5
Floreana, Isla — 92-93 A 5
Florence, AL 64-65 J 5
Florence, AZ 74-75 H 6
Florence, CA 83 III c 2
Florence, CO 68-69 D 6
Florence, KS 68-69 H 6
Florence, OR 66-67 A 4
Florence, SC 64-65 L 5
Florence, SD 68-69 H 3
Florence, WI 70-71 F 3
Florence = Firenze 122-123 D 4
Florence Junction, AZ 74-75 H 6
Florencia [BOL] 104-105 C 2
Florencia [CO] 92-93 DE 4
Florencia [RA] 106-107 H 2
Florencia, La — 104-105 EF 9
Florencio Sánchez 106-107 J 4-5
Florencio Varela 110 III c 2
Florencio Varela-Gobernador Monteverde 110 III c 2
Florentino Ameghino 108-109 G 4
Florentino Ameghino, Embalse — 108-109 F 5
Flôres [BR] 100-101 EF 4
Flores [GCA] 64-65 J 8
Flores [RI] 148-149 H 8
Flores [ROU] 106-107 J 4
Flores, Arroyo de las — 106-107 GH 5-6
Flores, Buenos Aires- 110 III b 1
Flores, Isla de — 106-107 K 5
Flores, Las — [RA, Buenos Aires] 111 E 5
Flores, Las — [RA, Salta] 104-105 E 9
Flores, Las — [RA, San Juan] 106-107 C 3
Florescência 98-99 D 9
Florescênia 96-97 G 6
Flores Island 60 D 5
Flores Sea 148-149 GH 8
Floressee 148-149 GH 8
Floresta, Buenos Aires- 110 III b 1
Floresta Amazônica 92-93 E-H 6
Florešty 126-127 CD 3
Floresville, TX 76-77 EF 8
Floriano 92-93 L 6
Floriano Peixoto 98-99 DE 9
Florianópolis 111 G 3
Florida, NM 76-77 A 6
Florida [C] 88-89 GH 4
Florida [CO] 94-95 C 6
Florida [ROU, administrative unit] 106-107 JK 4
Florida [ROU, place] 111 E 4
Florida [USA] 64-65 K 5-6
Florida [ZA] 170 V a 1
Florida, Cape — 80-81 cd 4
Florida, La — [CO, Cundinamarca] 91 III a 2
Florida, La — [CO, Nariño] 94-95 C 7
Florida, La — [PE] 96-97 F 3
Florida, Straits of — 64-65 K 7-L 6
Florida, Vicente López- 110 III b 1
Florida Bay 64-65 K 7
Floridablanca 94-95 E 4
Florida City, FL 80-81 c 4
Florida Island 148-149 jk 6
Florida Keys 64-65 K 6-7
Florido, Río — 76-77 B 8-9
Florien, LA 78-79 C 5
Flórina 122-123 J 5
Florissant, MO 70-71 EF 6
Flottbek, Hamburg- 130 I a 1
Flotten Lake 61 D 3
Flourtown, PA 84 III b 1
Flowerpot Island 72-73 F 2
Flower's Cove 63 HJ 2
Flower Station 72-73 H 2
Floyd, NM 76-77 C 5
Floyd, VA 80-81 F 2
Floyd, Mount — 74-75 G 5
Floydada, TX 76-77 D 5-6
Floyd River 70-71 BC 4
Flughafen Hamburg-Fuhlsbüttel 130 I ab 1
Flughafen München-Riem 130 II c 2
Flughafen Tegel 130 III b 1
Flughafen Tempelhof 130 III b 2
Flughafen Wien-Schwechat 113 I c 2
Flughafen Zürich-Kloten 128 IV b 1
Flugplatz Aspern 113 I c 2
Flugplatz Gatow 130 III a 2
Flume Creek, AK 58-59 Q 4
Flumendosa 122-123 C 6
Flushing = Vlissingen 120-121 J 3
Flushing, New York-, NY 82 III d 2
Flushing Airport 82 III d 2
Flushing Meadow Park 82 III c 2
Flying Fish, Cape — 53 BC 26
Fly River 148-149 M 8

F. M. Butzel Field 84 II ab 2

Fô 168-169 D 3
Foam Lake 61 G 5
Foça [TR] 136-137 B 3
Foča [YU] 122-123 H 4
Foca, Punta — 108-109 G 6
Foch 60 E 4
Fo-chan = Foshan 142-143 L 7
Fochi 164-165 H 5
Fochville 174-175 G 4
Focşani 122-123 M 3
F'odorovka [SU, Kazachskaja SSR] 124-125 ST 8
F'odorovka [SU, Rossijskaja SFSR] 124-125 RS 7
Fogang 146-147 D 10
Fòggia 122-123 F 5
Fogo [Cape Verde] 204-205 E 7
Fogo [CDN] 63 J 3
Fogo Island 56-57 a 8
Föhr 118 D 1
Foix [F, landscape] 120-121 H 7
Foix [F, place] 120-121 H 7
Fo-kang = Fogang 146-147 D 10
Fokino 124-125 K 7
Folcroft, PA 84 III b 2
Folda [N, Nordland] 116-117 F 4
Folda [N, Nord-Trøndelag] 116-117 D 5
Folégandros 122-123 L 7
Foley, AL 78-79 F 5
Foley, MN 70-71 CD 3
Foleyet 62 K 2
Foley Island 56-57 V 4
Folgefonni 116-117 B 7-8
Folger, AK 58-59 JK 5
Foligno 122-123 E 4
Folkestone 119 G 6
Folkston, GA 80-81 E 5
Folldal 116-117 CD 6
Follett, TX 76-77 D 4
Folsom, CA 74-75 C 3
Folsom, NM 76-77 C 4
Folsom, PA 84 III b 2
Folteşti 122-123 MN 3
Fombonou 168-169 F 2
Fominskoje [SU ↗ Vologda] 124-125 O 4
Fonda, IA 70-71 C 4
Fonda, NY 72-73 J 3
Fondaq = Al-Funduq 166-167 D 2
Fond-du-Lac 56-57 PQ 6
Fond du Lac, WI 64-65 J 3
Fond du Lac Indian Reservation 70-71 D 2
Fond du Lac Mountains 70-71 E 2
Fond du Lac River 56-57 Q 6
Fondeadero Mazarredo 108-109 F 6
Fondi 122-123 E 5
Fondouk = Lakhḍarīyah 166-167 H 1
Fonsagrada 120-121 D 7
Fonseca [CO] 94-95 E 2
Fonseca [PE] 96-97 F 3
Fonseca, Golfo de — 64-65 J 9
Fontainebleau [F] 120-121 J 4
Fontainebleau [ZA] 170 V a 1
Fontana, Lago — 108-109 D 5
Fonte Boa 92-93 F 5
Fonteneau, Lac — 63 F 2
Fontenelle Reservoir 66-67 HJ 4
Fontibón 91 III ab 2
Fontur 116-117 fg 1
Fonualei 148-149 c 2
Foochow = Fengdu 142-143 K 5-6
Foochow = Fujian 142-143 MN 6
Foochow = Fuzhou 142-143 MN 6
Foothills 60 J 3
Footscray, Melbourne- 161 II b 1
Foping 146-147 AB 5
Foraker, Mount — 56-57 F 5
Forbes 158-159 J 6
Forbes, ND 68-69 G 3
Forbes, Mount — 60 J 4
Forbesganj 138-139 L 4
Forbes Island = Kawre Kyūn 150-151 B 7
Ford, KS 68-69 G 7
Ford, KY 70-71 H 7
Ford, Cape — 158-159 E 2
Ford City, CA 74-75 D 5
Ford City, Chicago-, IL 83 II a 2
Førde 116-117 AB 7
Ford Lake 74-75 F 6
Ford Plant 84 II b 3
Ford River 70-71 G 2-3
Fords Bridge 158-159 HJ 5
Fordsburg, Johannesburg- 170 V b 2
Fordsville, KY 70-71 G 7
Fordyce, AR 78-79 C 4
Forécariah 164-165 B 7
Forel, Mont — 56-57 d 4
Fórelles-Attily 129 I d 3
Forest, MS 78-79 E 4
Forest, OH 72-73 E 4
Forest [CDN] 72-73 E 3
Foresta 100-101 E 5
Forestal, La — 111 E 2
Forestburg 61 BC 4
Forest Center, MN 70-71 E 2
Forest City, IA 70-71 D 4
Forest City, NC 80-81 EF 3
Forest Heights, MD 82 II ab 2
Forest Hills Cemetery 84 I b 3
Forestier Peninsula 160 d 3
Forest Lake, MN 70-71 D 3
Forest Oaks, Houston-, TX 85 III bc 2
Forest Park, GA 85 II bc 3
Forest Park [USA, New York] 82 III c 2
Forest Park [USA, San Francisco] 83 II a 1
Forest Park Cemetery 85 III b 2
Forest View, IL 83 II a 2
Forestville 63 B 3
Forestville, MD 82 II b 2
Forestville, Parc provincial de — 63 B 3
Forest West, Houston-, TX 85 III b 1
Forêt de Saint-Germain 129 I b 2
Fôret de Soignes 128 II b 2
Forêt Réserve 170 IV a 1
Forez, Monts du — 120-121 J 6
Forfar 119 E 3
Forgan, OK 76-77 D 4
Fork Mountain, TN 78-79 G 2
Forks, WA 66-67 A 1-2
Forlandsundet 116-117 hj 5
Forlì 122-123 DE 3
Forman, ND 68-69 H 2
Formentera 120-121 H 9
Formentor, Cabo — 120-121 J 8
Formiga 92-93 K 9
Formile Run 82 II a 2
Formosa [BR, Bahia] 100-101 E 5
Formosa [BR, Goiás] 92-93 K 8
Formosa [BR, Paraná] 102-103 F 6
Formosa [BR, Piauí] 100-101 C 4
Formosa [RA, administrative unit] 104-105 F 8-G 9
Formosa [RA, place] 111 E 3
Formosa = Taiwan 142-143 N 7
Formosa, Ilha de — 168-169 AB 3
Formosa, Serra — 92-93 HJ 7
Formosa Bay 171 E 3
Formosa Strait = Taiwan Haihsia 142-143 M 7-N 6
Formoso 98-99 O 10
Formoso, Rio — 100-101 B 7
Formoso de Rio Preto 100-101 B 6
Fornæs 116-117 D 9
Foro Romano 113 II b 2
Forqlôs = Furqlus 136-137 G 5
Forrest, IL 70-71 F 5
Forrest [AUS] 158-159 E 6
Forrest [CDN] 61 J 5
Forrest City, AR 78-79 D 3
Forrester Island 58-59 vw 9
Forsan, TX 76-77 D 6
Forsayth 158-159 H 3
Forsmo 116-117 G 6
Forssa 116-117 K 7
Forstenried, München- 130 II ab 2
Forstenrieder Park 130 II a 2
Forster 160 L 4
Forst Erkner 130 III c 2
Forst Kasten 130 II a 2
Forst Klövensteen 130 I a 1
Forsyth, GA 80-81 E 4
Forsyth, MI 70-71 G 2
Forsyth, MT 68-69 C 2
Forsyth, Isla — 108-109 B 5
Forṭ 'Abbās 138-139 D 3
Fort Albany 56-57 U 7
Fortaleza [BOL] 104-105 C 3
Fortaleza [BR, Acre] 96-97 E 6
Fortaleza [BR, Amazonas] 98-99 C 8
Fortaleza [BR, Ceará] 92-93 M 5
Fortaleza [BR, Rondônia] 98-99 G 10
Fortaleza, Paso de la — 96-97 C 7
Fortaleza, Río de la — 96-97 C 7
Fortaleza do Ituxi 98-99 EF 8
Fortaleza dos Nogueiras 100-101 A 4
Fort Apache Indian Reservation 74-75 HJ 5
Fort-Archambault = Sarh 164-165 H 7
Fort Assiniboine 60 K 2
Fort Atkinson, WI 70-71 F 4
Fort Bayard = Zhanjiang 142-143 L 7
Fort Beaufort 174-175 G 7
Fort Belknap Agency, MT 68-69 B 1
Fort Belknap Indian Reservation 68-69 B 1
Fort Benton, MT 66-67 H 2
Fort Berthold Indian Reservation 68-69 EF 2
Fort Black 61 DE 3
Fort Bragg, CA 74-75 AB 3
Fort Bragg, NC 80-81 G 3
Fort Branch, IN 70-71 G 6
Fort Bridger, WY 66-67 HJ 5
Fort Bruce = Pībōr 164-165 L 7
Fort Brussaux = Markounda 164-165 H 7
Fort-Charlet = Jannah 164-165 FG 4
Fort Chimo 56-57 X 6
Fort Chipewyan 56-57 OP 6
Fort Cobb, OK 76-77 E 5
Fort Collins, CO 64-65 EF 3
Fort-Coulonge 72-73 H 2
Fort-Crampel = Kaga Bandoro 164-165 HJ 7
Fort-Dauphin = Faradofay 172 J 7
Fort Davis, TX 76-77 C 7
Fort Defiance, AZ 74-75 J 5
Fort-de-France 64-65 O 9
Fort de Kock = Bukittinggi 148-149 CD 7
Fort-de-Polignac = Illizi 166-167 L 6
Fort Deposit, AL 78-79 F 4-5
Fort-de-Possel = Possel 164-165 H 7
Fort Dodge, IA 64-65 GH 3
Fort Dupont Park 82 II b 2
Fort Duquesne = Pittsburg, Pa. 64-65 KL 3
Forte 100-101 A 8
Forteau 63 H 2
Forte Coimbra = Coimbra 102-103 D 3
Forte de Copacabana 110 I bc 2
Fort Edward 174-175 HJ 2
Fort Edward, NY 72-73 K 3
Forte Lami = N'Djamena 164-165 GH 6
Fort Erie 72-73 G 3
Fortescue River 158-159 C 4
Forte Veneza 98-99 D 8
Fort Fairfield, ME 72-73 MN 1
Fort-Flatters = Burj 'Umar Idrīs 164-165 EF 3
Fort Frances 56-57 S 8
Fort Fraser 60 EF 2
Fort Fred Steele, WY 68-69 C 5
Fort Gaines, GA 78-79 G 5
Fort-Gardel = Zaouatallaz 164-165 F 3-4
Fort George River 56-57 V 7
Fort Gibson, OK 76-77 G 5
Fort Gibson Lake 76-77 G 4
Fort Glenn, AK 58-59 mn 4
Fort Good Hope 56-57 L 4
Fort Grahame 60 E 1
Fort Grey 158-159 H 5
Forth, Firth of — 119 EF 3
Fort Hall, ID 66-67 G 4
Fort Hall = Murang'a 172 G 2
Fort Hall Indian Reservation 66-67 GH 4
Fort Harrison = Hsadôn 141 EF 3
Forthassa-Rharbia = Furtāsāt al-Gharbīyah 166-167 F 3
Fort Hertz = Pūdāō 148-149 C 1
Fort Hope 62 E 2
Fort Huachuca, AZ 74-75 H 7
Fortim 100-101 EF 3
Fortín, El — 106-107 F 3
Fortín Aroma 102-103 B 4
Fortín Ávalos Sánchez 102-103 BC 5
Fortín Ayacucho 102-103 BC 3
Fortín Ballivián 102-103 AB 5
Fortín Capitán Demattei 102-103 B 5
Fortín Capitán O. R. Ortellado 102-103 C 5
Fortín Carlos Antonio López 102-103 C 4
Fortín Coronel Hermosa 102-103 BC 5
Fortín Coronel Martínez 102-103 C 5
Fortín 1 de Mayo 106-107 B 7
Fortín Falcón 111 DE 2
Fortín Florida 102-103 C 4
Fortín Galpón 102-103 C 3
Fortín Garrapatal 102-103 B 4
Fortín General Aquino 102-103 C 6
Fortín General Bruguez 102-103 C 6
Fortín General Delgado 102-103 C 6
Fortín General Díaz [PY, Boquerón] 102-103 B 5
Fortín General Díaz [PY, Olimpo] 102-103 CD 4
Fortín General Mendoza 102-103 B 4
Fortín General Pando 102-103 C 3
Fortín Hernandarías 102-103 AB 4
Fortín Lavalle 111 D 3
Fortín Linares 102-103 B 5
Fortín Madrejón 111 D 2
Fortín Mayor Rodríguez 102-103 B 5
Fortín Muariscal López 102-103 C 5
Fortín Nueva Asunción 102-103 B 4
Fortín Olavarría 106-107 F 5
Fortín Orihuela 102-103 C 5
Fortín Paredes 104-105 G 6
Fortín Pilcomayo 111 DE 2
Fortín Príncipe de Beira = Príncipe da Beira 92-93 G 7
Fortín Puente Ayala 102-103 C 5
Fortín Ravelo 92-93 G 8
Fortín Río Verde 102-103 C 5
Fortín Rojas Silva 102-103 C 5
Fortín Sargento Primero Leyes 104-105 G 9
Fortín Soledad 104-105 F 9
Fortín Sorpresa 102-103 C 5-6
Fortín Suárez Arana 92-93 G 8
Fortín Teniente Martínez 102-103 C 4
Fortín Toledo 102-103 B 5
Fortín Uno 111 CD 5
Fortín Valois Rivarola 102-103 BC 5
Fortín Zenteno 102-103 BC 5
Fort Jackson 174-175 GH 7
Fort Jaco 128 II b 2
Fort Jameson = Chipata 172 F 4
Fort Johnston = Mangoche 172 G 4
Fort Jones, CA 66-67 B 5
Fort Kent 61 C 3
Fort Kent, ME 72-73 M 1
Fort Klamath, OR 66-67 BC 4
Fort Knox, KY 64-65 J 4
Fort-Lallemend = Burj al-Aḥmad 166-167 K 4
Fort-Lamy = N'Djamena 164-165 GH 6
Fort-Laperrine = Tamanrâsat 164-165 EF 4
Fort Laramie, WY 68-69 D 4
Fort Lauderdale, FL 64-65 KL 6
Fort Lee, NJ 82 III c 1
Fort Lewis, WA 66-67 B 2
Fort Liard 56-57 M 5
Fort Liberté 88-89 KL 5
Fort Lupton, CO 68-69 D 5
Fort MacDowell Indian Reservation 74-75 H 6
Fort MacKay 61 BC 2
Fort-Mac-Mahon = Burj Ban Būl'īd 164-165 E 3
Fort MacMurray 56-57 O 6
Fort MacNair 82 II a 2
Fort MacPherson 56-57 JK 4
Fort Madison, IA 64-65 H 3
Fort Maguire 172 FG 4
Fort Mahan Park 82 II b 2
Fort Manning = Mchinji 172 F 4
Fort Meade, FL 80-81 bc 3
Fort Mill, SC 80-81 F 3
Fort-Miribel = Burj Maḥībal 166-167 H 5
Fort Mohave Indian Reservation 74-75 F 5
Fort Morgan, AL 78-79 EF 5
Fort Morgan, CO 68-69 E 5
Fort Munro 138-139 B 2-3
Fort Myer, Arlington-, VA 82 II a 2
Fort Myers, FL 64-65 K 6
Fort Nassau = Albany, NY 64-65 LM 3
Fort-National = Arb'ā Nāyat Īrāthan 166-167 J 1
Fort Nelson 56-57 M 6
Fort Nelson River 56-57 M 6
Fort Norman 56-57 L 4-5
Fort Ogden, FL 80-81 c 3
Fort Payne, AL 78-79 G 3
Fort Peck, MT 68-69 C 1
Fort Peck Indian Reservation 68-69 CD 1
Fort Peck Lake 64-65 E 2
Fort Pierce, FL 64-65 KL 6
Fort Pierre, SD 68-69 F 3
Fort Plain, NY 72-73 J 3
Fort Portal 172 F 1
Fort Providence 56-57 N 5
Fort Qu'Appelle 61 FG 5
Fort Randolph 64-65 b 2
Fort Reliance 56-57 P 5
Fort Resolution 56-57 O 5
Fortress Mountain 66-67 HJ 3
Fort Richardson, AK 58-59 N 6
Fort Ripley, MN 70-71 CD 2
Fort Rock, OR 66-67 C 4
Fort Rosebery = Mansa 172 E 4
Fort Ross, CA 74-75 B 3
Fort-Rousset = Owando 172 C 2
Fort Rupert 56-57 V 7
Fort-Saint = Burj al-Haṭṭabah 164-165 F 2
Fort Saint James 56-57 M 7
Fort Saint John 56-57 M 6
Fort Sandeman = Appozai 134-135 K 4
Fort Saskatchewan 56-57 NO 7
Fort Scott, KS 70-71 C 7
Fort Selkirk 56-57 JK 5
Forṭ Sendeman = Appozai 134-135 K 4
Fort-Ševčenko 126-127 OP 4
Fort Severn 56-57 T 6
Fort Seward, CA 66-67 B 5
Fort Sherman 64-65 ab 2
Fort Sibut = Sibut 164-165 H 7
Fort Simpson 56-57 M 5
Fort Smith 56-57 OP 5
Fort Smith, AR 64-65 H 4
Fort Stanton Park 82 II b 2
Fort Steele 60 K 5
Fort Stockton, TX 64-65 F 5
Fort Sumner, NM 76-77 B 5
Fort Supply, OK 76-77 E 4
Fort Thomas, AZ 74-75 HJ 6
Fort Thompson, SD 68-69 FG 3
Fort Totten Indian Reservation 68-69 G 2
Fort Towson, OK 76-77 G 5
Fort-Trinquet = Bīr Umm Qarayn 164-165 B 3
Fortuna 106-107 E 5
Fortuna, CA 66-67 AB 5
Fortuna, ND 68-69 E 1
Fortuna Lodge = Marshall, AK 58-59 FG 6
Fortune 63 HJ 4
Fortune Bay 56-57 Z 8
Fort Valley, GA 80-81 DE 4
Fort Vermilion 56-57 NO 6
Fort Victoria = Nyanda 172 F 5-6
Fortville, IN 70-71 H 6
Fort Walton Beach, FL 78-79 F 5
Fort Washakie, WY 68-69 B 4
Fort Wayne, IN 64-65 JK 3
Fort Wayne Military Museum 84 II b 3
Fort Wellington 98-99 K 1
Fort William [IND] 154 II b 2
Fort Wingate, NM 74-75 J 5
Fort Worth, TX 64-65 G 5
Fort Yates, ND 68-69 F 2
Fortymile 58-59 RS 4
Fortymile, Middle Fork — 58-59 Q 4
Fortymile, North Fork — 58-59 QR 4
Fortymile, West Fork — 58-59 Q 5
Fortymile River 58-59 R 4
Fort Yukon, AK 56-57 GH 4
Forum 83 III bc 2
Forward 61 F 6
Forzado, El — 106-107 D 4
Fosca 94-95 E 5
Fosforitnaja 124-125 ST 4
Foshan 142-143 L 7
Fosheim Peninsula 56-57 U 1-2
Fosna 116-117 CD 6
Foso 168-169 E 4
Fossano 122-123 BC 3
Fossberg 116-117 BC 7
Fossil, OR 66-67 C 3
Fosston, MN 70-71 BC 2
Foster 72-73 K 2
Foster River 61 F 2
Fostoria, OH 72-73 E 4
Fotan 146-147 FG 9
Foucauld = Awlād Abū 166-167 BC 3
Foucheng = Fucheng 146-147 F 3
Fougamou 172 B 2
Fougères 120-121 G 4
Fouke, AR 78-79 C 4
Foula 119 E 1
Foul Bay = Khalīj Umm al-Kataf 173 D 6
Foul Point = Pahan Tuḍuwa 140 E 6
Foulpointe = Mahavelona 172 JK 5
Foulwind, Cape — 158-159 NO 8
Fouman = Fūman 136-137 N 4
Foumban 164-165 G 7
Foum Taṭāouīn = Taṭāwīn 164-165 G 2
Foundiougne 164-165 A 6
Fountain, CO 68-69 D 6
Fountain Creek 68-69 D 6
Fouping = Fuping 146-147 E 2
Fourât, El- = Al-Furāt 136-137 H 5
Fourche Mountains 76-77 GH 5
Fourchette, MT 68-69 BC 2
Fourchu 63 FG 5
Four Corners, WY 68-69 D 3-4
Fourcroy, Cape — 158-159 E 2
Fouriesburg 174-175 H 5
Four Mountains, Islands of — 58-59 lm 4
Fournier, Lac — 63 D 2
Fourou 168-169 D 3
Fourqueux 129 I b 2
Fourteen Mile Point 70-71 F 2
Fourteen Streams = Veertien Strome 174-175 F 4-5
Foushan = Fushan 146-147 C 4
Fouta Djalon 164-165 B 6
Foux, Cap-à- 88-89 K 5
Foveaux Strait 158-159 N 9
Fowl Cay 88-89 H 2
Fowler, CO 68-69 D 6
Fowler, IN 70-71 G 5
Fowler, MI 70-71 H 4
Fowler, MT 66-67 H 1
Fowlers Bay 158-159 F 6
Fowlerton, TX 76-77 E 8
Fowling = Fengdu 142-143 K 5-6
Fowl Meadow Reservation 84 I b 3
Fowning = Funing 142-143 MN 5
Fox, AK 58-59 O 4
Fox Bay 63 F 3
Fox Chase, Philadelphia-, PA 84 III c 1
Fox Chase Manor, PA 84 III c 1
Fox Creek 60 J 2
Foxe Basin 56-57 UV 4
Foxe Channel 56-57 UV 4-5
Foxe Peninsula 56-57 V 5
Fox Islands 52 D 35
Foxpark, WY 68-69 CD 5

292 Financia

Geraldton [AUS] 158-159 B 5
Geraldton [CDN] 56-57 T 8
Gerantahbawah 152-153 M 10
Gērasappa = Gersoppa 140 B 3
Gerasdorf bei Wien 113 I b 1
Gerasimovka 132-133 N 6
Gercif = Garsīf 166-167 E 2
Gercüş 136-137 J 4
Gerdakānehbālā 136-137 M 5
Gerdine, Mount — 56-57 F 5
Gerdview 170 V c 2
Gerede [TR, Bolu] 136-137 E 2
Gerede [TR, Eskişehir] 136-137 D 2
Gerede çayı 136-137 E 2
Gergebil' 126-127 N 5
Gering, NE 68-69 E 5
Gerlach, NV 66-67 D 5
Gerlachovský štít 118 JK 4
Gerli, Avellaneda- 110 III b 2
Gērloqubī 164-165 NO 7
German Democratic Republic 118 E-G 2-3
Germania 106-107 FG 5
Germansen Landing 60 E 2
Germantown, TN 78-79 E 3
Germantown, Philadelphia-, PA 84 III b 1
Germany, Federal Republic of — 118 C-F 2-4
Germencik 136-137 B 4
Germī 136-137 N 3
Germiston 172 E 7
Gern, München- 130 II b 2
Ger'nsy = Goris 126-127 N 7
Geroldswil 128 IV a 1
Gerona 120-121 J 8
Gerrard 60 J 4
Gers 120-121 H 7
Gersoppa 140 B 3
Gerstle River 58-59 P 5
Gertak Sanggui, Tanjung — 150-151 BC 10
Géryville = Al-Bayadh 166-167 G 3
Gerze 136-137 F 2
Gethsémani 63 F 2
Gettysburg, PA 72-73 H 5
Gettysburg, SD 68-69 G 3
Getulina 102-103 GH 4
Getúlio Vargas 106-107 LM 1
Getz Ice Shelf 53 B 23-24
Geuda Springs, KS 76-77 F 4
Geureudong, Gunung — 152-153 B 3
Geuzenveld, Amsterdam- 128 I a 1
Gevar ovası 136-137 L 4
Gevaş 136-137 K 3
Gevgelija 122-123 K 5
Gevrai 138-139 E 8
Gewanī 164-165 N 6
Geyang = Guoyang 146-147 F 5
Geyik dağı 136-137 E 4
Geylang, Singapore- 154 III b 2
Geyser, MT 66-67 H 2
Geyser, Banc du — 172 J 4
Geysir 116-117 c 2
Geyve 136-137 D 2
Gezira, El — = Al-Jazīrah 164-165 L 6
Gezir el-Ikhwân = Jazā'ir al-Ikhwān 173 D 4
Gezîret Mirêar = Jazīrat Marīr 173 DE 6
Gezir Qeisûm = Jazā'ir Qaysūm 173 CD 4
Ghāb, Al- 136-137 G 5
Ghâb, El — = Al-Ghāb 136-137 G 5
Ghāb, Jabal — 136-137 H 5
Ghabāt al-Mushajjarīn 166-167 F 2-G 1
Ghadai = Ghaday 136-137 M 8
Ghadâmes = Ghadāmis 164-165 FG 2-3
Ghadāmis 164-165 FG 2-3
Ghaday 136-137 M 8
Ghadūn, Wādī — 134-135 G 7
Ghaeratganj = Ghairatganj 138-139 G 6
Ghafargāon 138-139 N 5
Ghafsāi 166-167 D 2
Ghaggar 138-139 E 3
Ghāghara 134-135 N 5
Ghaibīḍero 138-139 A 4
Ghairatganj 138-139 G 6
Ghallah, Bi'r — 173 C 3
Ghalvāḍ = Gholvad 138-139 D 7
Ghām'ā 166-167 J 3
Ghamal, Ḥāssī — 166-167 J 4
Ghana 164-165 DE 7
Ghanāīn Bū Rizq 166-167 F 3
Ghanamī, Ḥāssī al- 166-167 JK 4
Ghāndhi Sāgar 138-139 E 5
Ghānim, Jazīrat — 173 C 4
Ghanzi 172 D 6
Ghār, Al- 166-167 L 5
Ghār ad-Dimā' 166-167 L 1
Ghār al-Milḥ 166-167 M 1
Ghārāpuri = Elephanta Island 140 A 1
Gharaq as-Sulṭānī, Al- 173 AB 3
Ghār aṣ-Ṣallah 166-167 E 3
Gharb, Al- 166-167 C 2
Gharb al-Istiwāīyah 164-165 KL 7
Gharbī, Jabal — 136-137 H 5
Gharbī, Jazīrat al- 166-167 M 2
Gharbī, Wādī al- 166-167 G 3-4
Ghardan, Bi'r — 166-167 K 2
Ghardaqah, Al- 164-165 L 3
Ghardāyah 164-165 E 2
Ghardimaou = Ghār ad-Dimā' 166-167 L 1
Gharduār 141 C 2
Ghārgāñv = Ghārgaon 138-139 E 8
Ghārgaon 138-139 E 8
Ghargoda 138-139 J 6
Ghārib, Jabal — 164-165 L 3
Gharīd 166-167 K 3
Ghāris [DZ] 166-167 J 7
Ghāris [MA] 166-167 D 4
Ghāris, Al- 166-167 G 2
Ghāris, Wād — 166-167 D 3-4
Ghāro 138-139 A 5
Gharqābād 136-137 NO 5
Gharsa, Chott el — = Shaṭṭ al-Jarsah 166-167 KL 2
Gharyān 164-165 G 2
Ghassoul = Ghasul 166-167 G 3
Ghasul 166-167 G 3
Ghaswani 138-139 F 5
Ghat 164-165 G 3
Ghāṭ'ā, Al- 136-137 J 5
Ghātāl 138-139 L 6
Ghātampur 138-139 GH 4
Ghāṭīgāñv = Ghāṭīgaon 138-139 F 4
Ghāṭīgaon 138-139 F 4
Ghatol 138-139 E 6
Ghatprabha 140 B 2
Ghats, Eastern — 134-135 M 8-N 7
Ghats, Western — 134-135 L 6-M 8
Ghāṭshilā = Ghātsīla 138-139 L 6
Ghātsīla 138-139 L 6
Ghawdex 122-123 F 7
Ghayḍah, Al- [ADN ← Sayḥūt] 134-135 FG 7-8
Ghayḍah, Al- [ADN ↗ Sayḥūt] 134-135 G 7
Ghazāl, 'Ayn al- [ET] 173 B 5
Ghazal, 'Ayn al- [LAR] 164-165 J 4
Ghazawāt 164-165 D1
Ghazeil, Bîr el — = Bi'r al-Ghuzayl 166-167 M 5
Ghāziābād 138-139 F 3
Ghāzīpur 138-139 J 5
Ghazīr = Jazīr 136-137 F 5
Ghaz köl 142-143 G 4
Ghazni 134-135 K 4
Ghazzah 134-135 C 4
Ghedo = Gēdo 164-165 M 7
Ghent = Gent 120-121 JK 3
Gheorghe Gheorghiu-Dej 122-123 M 2
Gheorghieni 122-123 LM 2
Gheorghiu-Dej 126-127 JK 1
Gherāsahan 138-139 K 4
Gherdi 140 B 2
Gheris, Oued — = Wād Gharīs 166-167 D 3-4
Gherla 122-123 KL 2
Gherlogubi = Gerlogubī 164-165 NO 7
Ghiedo = Gēdo 164-165 M 7
Ghigner = Gīnīr 164-165 N 7
Ghimbi = Gimbī 164-165 M 7
Ghinah, Wādī al- 136-137 G 7-8
Ghio, Lago — 108-109 D 6
Ghir, Cap — = Rā's Ghīr 166-167 AB 4
Ghir, Cape — = Rā's Ghīr 166-167 AB 4
Ghīr, Rā's — 166-167 AB 4
Ghod 140 B 1
Gholvad 138-139 D 7
Ghōr, El — = Al-Ghūr 136-137 F 7
Ghōṛāsahan = Gherāsahan 138-139 K 4
Ghosi 138-139 J 4
Ghost River [CDN ↗ Dryden] 62 D 2
Ghost River [CDN ↑ Hearst] 62 H 2
Ghotāru 138-139 C 4
Ghotki 138-139 B 3-4
Ghoumerassen = Ghumrāssin 166-167 M 3
Ghraybah, Al- 166-167 LM 2
Ghriss = Al-Gharīs 166-167 G 2
Ghubbat al-Qamar 134-135 G 7
Ghubbat Ṣauqirah = Dawḥat as-Sawqirah 134-135 H 7
Ghughri 138-139 H 6
Ghugri 138-139 L 5
Ghūgus 138-139 G 8
Ghuja 142-143 E 3
Ghumrāssin 166-167 M 3
Ghūr, Al- 136-137 F 7
Ghurarah 166-167 FG 5
Ghūrāyah 166-167 GH 1
Ghurd Abū Muḥarrik 164-165 KL 3
Ghurd al-Baghl 166-167 K 4
Ghurdaqa, El — = Al-Ghardaqah 164-165 L 3
Ghurrah, Shaṭṭ al- 166-167 M 2
Ghūryān 134-135 J 4
Ghuzayl, Bi'r al- 166-167 M 5

Gia Lai, Cao Nguyên — 150-151 G 5
Gia Nghia 150-151 F 7
Giannitsá 122-123 K 5
Giannutri 122-123 D 4
Giant Mountains 118 GH 3
Giant's Castle 174-175 H 5
Giant's Castle National Park 174-175 H 5
Gia Rai 148-149 E 5
Giardino Zoologico 113 II b 1
Giarre 122-123 F 7
Gibara 88-89 HJ 4
Gibbon, NE 68-69 G 5
Gibbon, OR 66-67 D 3
Gibbonsville, ID 66-67 G 3
Gibbsboro, NJ 84 III d 2
Gibbs City, MI 70-71 F 2
Gibbs City, WI 70-71 F 2
Gibbstown, NJ 84 III b 3
Gibeil = Jubayl 173 C 3
Gibeon [Namibia, administrative unit] 174-175 C 3
Gibeon [Namibia, place] 172 C 7
Gibraltar 120-121 E 10
Gibraltar, Strait of — 120-121 DE 11
Gibsland, LA 78-79 C 4
Gibson City, IL 70-71 F 5
Gibson Desert 158-159 DE 4
Gidajevo 124-125 ST 4
Gidan Mountains = Kolymskij nagorje 132-133 g 4-e 5
Giddalūr 140 D 3
Giddalūru = Giddalūr 140 D 3
Giddings, TX 76-77 F 7
Gideon, MO 78-79 DE 2
Gidgealpa 160 DE 1
Gīdolē 164-165 M 7
Gien 120-121 J 5
Giesing, München- 130 II b 2
Giessen 118 D 3
Giesshübl 113 I a 2
Giffard, Lac — 62 N 1
Gifu 142-143 Q 4
Gigant 126-127 K 3
Giganta, Sierra de la — 64-65 D 6-7
Gigantes, Cerro los — 106-107 E 3
Gigantes, Llanos de los — 86-87 HJ 3
Giglio 122-123 D 4
Gigüela 120-121 F 9
Gihân, Râs — = Rā's al-Bālā'im 173 C 3
Giheina = Juhaynah 173 B 4
Gihu = Gifu 142-143 Q 4
Gijón 120-121 E 7
Gil [BR] 106-107 M 2
Gil [RA] 106-107 G 7
Gila Bend, AZ 74-75 G 6
Gila Cliff 74-75 J 6
Gila Cliff Dwellings National Monument 74-75 J 6
Gila Desert 64-65 D 5
Gilām = Jihlam 138-139 D 2
Gila Mountains 74-75 J 6
Gīlān 134-135 FG 3
Gīlān, Sārāb-e — 136-137 LM 5
Gīlān-e Gharb 136-137 LM 5
Gilardo Dam 72-73 K 1
Gila River 64-65 D 5
Gila River Indian Reservation 74-75 GH 6
Gilbert 106-107 H 4
Gilbert, Isla — 108-109 D 10
Gilbert, Mount — 58-59 o 3
Gilbert Islands 208 H 2-3
Gilbertown, AL 78-79 E 5
Gilbert River [AUS, place] 158-159 H 3
Gilbert River [AUS, river] 158-159 H 3
Gilbués 92-93 K 6
Gilby, ND 68-69 H 1
Gildford, MT 68-69 A 1
Gilead 174-175 H 2
Gilf Kebir Plateau = Haḍbat al-Jilf al-Kabīr 164-165 K 4
Gilgandra 158-159 J 6
Gilgat = Gilgit 134-135 L 3
Gilgil 171 CD 3
Gilgit 134-135 L 3
Gilindire 136-137 E 4
Gil Island 60 C 3
Gill, CO 68-69 D 5
Gillam 56-57 S 6
Gillen, Lake — 158-159 D 5
Gilles, Lake — 160 C 4
Gillespie, IL 70-71 EF 6
Gillett, AR 78-79 D 3
Gillett, WI 70-71 F 3
Gillette, WY 68-69 D 3
Gillon Point 58-59 p 6
Gilman, IA 70-71 D 5
Gilman, IL 70-71 FG 5
Gilman, WI 70-71 E 3
Gilmer, TX 76-77 G 6
Gilmore, GA 85 II b 1
Gilmore, ID 66-67 G 3
Gilolo = Halmahera 148-149 J 6
Gilroy, CA 74-75 G 4
Giluwe, Mount — 148-149 M 8
Gimbala, Jebel — = Jabal Marrah 164-165 JK 6
Gimbī 164-165 M 7
Gimli 62 A 2
Gimma = Jīma 164-165 M 7
Gimpu 148-149 GH 7
Gineifa = Junayfah 173 C 2
Ginevrabotnen 116-117 kl 5
Gin Ganga = Ging Ganga 140 E 7
Ginge 140 D 4
Ging Ganga 140 E 7
Gingindlovu 174-175 J 5
Gingiova 122-123 KL 4
Gīnīr 164-165 N 7
Ginnheim, Frankfurt am Main- 128 III a 1
Ginyer = Gīnīr 164-165 N 7
Ginza, Tōkyō- 155 III b 1
Giòia del Colle 122-123 G 5
Giông Riêng = Kiên Binh 150-151 E 8
Giông Trôm 150-151 F 7-8
Giovi, Passo dei — 122-123 C 3
Gippsland 158-159 J 7
Gīr, Hammadat al- 166-167 E 4
Gīr, Wādī — 166-167 E 4
Girard, IL 70-71 F 6
Girard, KS 70-71 C 7
Girard, OH 72-73 F 4
Girard, PA 72-73 F 3-4
Girard, TX 76-77 D 6
Girardet 106-107 F 1
Girardot 92-93 E 4
Girardota 94-95 D 4
Girawān = Girwān 138-139 H 5
Girdwood, AK 58-59 N 6
Giren = Jīma 164-165 M 7
Giresun 134-135 D 2
Giresun dağları 136-137 H 2
Girge = Jirjā 164-165 L 3
Gīr Hills 138-139 C 7
Giri 172 C 1
Giridih 134-135 O 6
Girilambone 160 H 3
Girishk 134-135 J 4
Girna 138-139 E 7
Girnār Hills 138-139 C 7
Girón [CO] 94-95 E 4
Girón [EC] 96-97 B 3
Gironde 120-121 G 6
Girsovo 124-125 RS 4
Girvan 119 D 4
Girvas [SU, Karel'skaja ASSR] 124-125 J 2
Girvas [SU, Rossijskaja SFSR] 116-117 O 4
Girvas, vodopad — 124-125 J 2
Girvin 61 E 5
Girvin, TX 76-77 C 7
Girwān 138-139 H 5
Gisasa River 58-59 H 4
Gisborne 158-159 P 7
Giscome 60 FG 2
Gisenyi 172 E 2
Gislaved 116-117 E 9
Gisr ash-Shughur 136-137 G 5
Giṣṣar 166-167 C 3
Gitega 172 EF 2
Giuba = Webi Ganaane 172 H 1
Giuba, Isole — 172 H 2
Giulianova 122-123 EF 4
Giumbo = Jumbo 172 H 2
Giūra 122-123 L 6
Giurgiu 122-123 L 4
Giustiniana, Roma-La — 113 II ab 1
Givet 120-121 K 3
Giyani 174-175 J 2
Giždúvan 132-133 L 9
Gizeh = Al-Jīzah 164-165 KL 3
Gizhigin Bay = Gižiginskaja guba 132-133 e 5
Gižiga 132-133 f 5
Gižiginskaja guba 132-133 e 5
Gizmel 136-137 M 5
Gizo 148-149 j 6
Giżycko 118 KL 1

Gjersvik 116-117 E 5
Gjiri i Drinit 122-123 H 5
Gjirokastër 122-123 HJ 5
Gjögurtá 116-117 d 1
Gjøvik 116-117 D 7
Gjuhës, Kepi i — 122-123 H 5

Glace Bay 56-57 YZ 8
Glacier Bay 58-59 TU 7
Glacier Bay National Monument 56-57 J 6
Glacier Mount 58-59 QR 4
Glacier National Park [CDN] 60 J 4
Glacier National Park [USA] 64-65 CD 2
Glacier Peak 66-67 C 1
Gladbrook, IA 70-71 D 4
Glade Park, CO 74-75 J 3
Gladesville, Sydney- 161 I a 1
Gladstone, MI 70-71 G 3
Gladstone [AUS, Queensland] 158-159 K 4
Gladstone [AUS, South Australia] 158-159 G 6
Gladstone [CDN] 61 J 5
Gladwin, MI 70-71 H 4
Gladwyne, PA 84 III b 1
Glady, WV 72-73 G 5
Glåma 116-117 D 7
Glamis, CA 74-75 F 6
Glasco, KS 68-69 H 6
Glasgow 119 DE 4
Glasgow, KY 70-71 H 7
Glasgow, MO 70-71 D 6
Glasgow, MT 68-69 C 1
Glaslyn 61 D 4
Glassboro, NJ 72-73 J 5
Glass Mountains 76-77 C 7
Glattbrugg 128 IV b 1
Glauchau 118 F 3
Glavnyj Kut 126-127 N 5
Glazier, TX 76-77 D 4
Glazok 124-125 N 7
Glazov 132-133 J 6
Gleeson, AZ 74-75 J 7
Gleisdorf 118 GH 5
Glen 174-175 G 5
Glen, NE 68-69 E 4
Glen Afton 72-73 FG 1
Glenboro 61 J 6
Glenbrook 160 K 4
Glenbrook Valley, Houston-, TX 85 III b 2
Glen Canyon 74-75 H 4
Glencoe, MN 70-71 C 3
Glencoe [CDN] 72-73 F 3
Glencoe [ZA] 174-175 HJ 5
Glendale, AZ 64-65 D 5
Glendale, CA 64-65 C 5
Glendale, NV 74-75 F 4
Glendale, OR 66-67 B 4
Glendale, Washington-, DC 82 II b 2
Glendale Cove 60 E 4
Glendevey, CO 68-69 D 5
Glendive, MT 68-69 D 2
Glendo, WY 68-69 D 4
Glendon 61 C 3
Glendora, NJ 84 III c 2
Glenelg 160 E 6
Glengyle 158-159 GH 4
Glen Innes 158-159 K 5
Glen Lyon, PA 72-73 HJ 4
Glen Mar Park, MD 82 II a 1
Glenmora, LA 78-79 C 5
Glen More 119 D 3
Glenmorgan 158-159 JK 5
Glennallen, AK 58-59 P 5
Glennie, MI 70-71 J 3
Glenns Ferry, ID 66-67 F 4
Glenolden, PA 84 III b 2
Glenora 58-59 W 8
Glenore 158-159 H 3
Glen Riddle, PA 84 III a 2
Glen Ridge, NJ 82 III a 2
Glenrio, NM 76-77 C 5
Glenrock, WY 68-69 D 4
Glen Rose, TX 76-77 F 6
Glens Falls, NY 72-73 K 3
Glen Shannon, Houston-, TX 85 III a 2
Glenside 174-175 J 5
Glenside, PA 84 III c 1
Glentworth 68-69 C 1
Glenville, MN 70-71 D 4
Glenwood, AR 78-79 C 3
Glenwood, IA 70-71 C 5
Glenwood, MN 70-71 C 3
Glenwood, OR 66-67 B 3
Glenwood, WA 66-67 C 2
Glenwood Cemetery 85 III b 1
Glenwood Springs, CO 68-69 C 6
Glenwoodville 60 L 5
Gleta, La — = Ḥalq al-Wad 166-167 M 1
Glicério 102-103 LM 5
Glidden 61 D 5
Glidden, WI 70-71 E 2
Glide, OR 66-67 B 4
Glienicke 130 III a 2
Glina 122-123 G 3
Glinka 124-125 J 6
Glint ustup 124-125 E-J 4
Glittertind 116-117 C 7
Gliwice 118 J 3
Globe, AZ 64-65 D 5
Globino 126-127 F 2
Gloggnitz 118 G 5
Głogów 118 GH 3
Glomfjord 116-117 EF 4
Glomma 116-117 D 7
Glommersträsk 116-117 HJ 5
Glória 92-93 M 6
Gloria, La — [CO] 92-93 E 3
Gloria, La — [RA] 106-107 F 6
Glória, Rio de Janeiro- 110 I b 2
Gloria de Dourados 102-103 EF 5
Glória do Goitá 100-101 G 4-5
Glorieta, NM 76-77 B 5
Glorieuses, Îles — 172 J 4
Glorioso Islands = Îles Glorieuses 172 J 4
Glosam 174-175 E 5
Gloster, MS 78-79 D 5
Glotovka 124-125 Q 7
Glotovo 124-125 RS 2
Gloucester, MA 72-73 L 3
Gloucester City, NJ 72-73 J 5
Glouchester 119 E 6
Glouster, OH 72-73 EF 5
Glouster, Cabo — 108-109 BC 10
Gloversville, NY 72-73 J 3
Glovertown 63 J 3
Glubacha 124-125 V 4
Glubokij 126-127 K 2
Glubokoje [SU, Belorusskaja SSR] 124-125 F 6
Glubokoje [SU, Kazachskaja SSR] 132-133 P 7
Gluchov 124-125 J 8
Gluša 124-125 G 7
Glusk 124-125 G 7
Glyndon, MN 68-69 H 2

Gmelinka 126-127 N 1
Gmünd 118 G 4
Gmunden 118 FG 5

Gnaday 136-137 M 8
Gnezdovo 124-125 H 6
Gniezno 118 H 2
Gniloj Tikič 126-127 E 2
Gnowangerup 158-159 C 6

Goa 134-135 L 7
Goageb [Namibia, place] 172 C 7
Goageb [Namibia, river] 174-175 B 4
Goālpara 141 B 2
Goanikontes 174-175 A 2
Goaso 164-165 D 7
Goba [ETH] 164-165 N 7
Goba [Mozambique] 174-175 K 4
Gobabis 172 C 6
Goba La 138-139 K 2
Gobas 174-175 C 4
Gobernador Ayala 106-107 CD 6
Gobernador Costa 108-109 D 5
Gobernador Crespo 106-107 G 3
Gobernador Duval 106-107 DE 7
Gobernador Gálvez 106-107 GH 4
Gobernador Gregores 111 BC 7
Gobernador Ingeniero Valentín Virasoro 106-107 J 2
Gobernador Mansilla 106-107 H 4
Gobernador Monteverde, Florencio Varela- 110 III c 2
Gobernador Moyano 108-109 D 8
Gobernador Piedra Buena 104-105 D 10
Gobi 142-143 H-L 3
Gobindganj 138-139 K 4
Gobindpur 138-139 K 6
Gobō 144-145 K 6
Gochas 174-175 C 3
Gockhausen 128 IV b 1
Go Công 150-151 F 7
Goḍāgāri 138-139 M 5
Godār-e Shāh 136-137 MN 5
Godarpura 138-139 F 6
Go Dâu Ha 150-151 F 7
Godāvari 134-135 N 7
Godāvari Delta 134-135 N 7
Godāvari Plain 138-139 EF 8
Godbout 63 C 3
Godda 138-139 L 5
Goddo 92-93 HJ 4
Godḍua = Ghuddawah 164-165 G 3
Goderich 72-73 EF 3
Godfrey's Tank 158-159 E 4
Godhavn = Qeqertarssuq 56-57 Za 4
Godhra 138-139 D 6
Godoy [RA] 106-107 G 4
Godoy Cruz 111 BC 4
Gods Lake [CDN, lake] 56-57 S 7
Gods Lake [CDN, place] 56-57 S 7
Godthåb = Nûk 56-57 a 5
Godwin Austen, Mount — = K2 134-135 M 3
Goede Hoop, De — 98-99 K 2
Goeje Gebergte, De — 98-99 L 3
Goela 138-139 E 4
Goëland, Lac — 62 N 2
Goeree 120-121 J 3
Goethehaus 128 III ab 1
Goetheturm 128 III b 1
Goffs, CA 74-75 F 5
Gogebic, Lake — 70-71 F 2
Gogebic Range 70-71 EF 2
Goggiam = Gojam 164-165 M 6
Gogland, ostrov — 124-125 F 3
Gogra = Ghāghara 134-135 N 5
Gogrial = Qūqriāl 164-165 K 7
Gohad 138-139 G 4
Gohāna 138-139 F 3
Goharganj 138-139 F 6
Gohilwār 138-139 C 7
Gohpur 141 C 2
Goiabal 96-97 F 4
Goiana 92-93 MN 6
Goiandira 92-93 K 8
Goiânia 92-93 JK 8
Goianinha 100-101 G 4
Goiás [BR, administrative unit] 92-93 J 8-K 7
Goiás [BR, place] 92-93 JK 8
Goiatuba 92-93 K 8
Goicoechea, Isla de — = New Island 108-109 J 8
Goidu 176 a 2
Goio Erê 102-103 F 6
Goioxim 102-103 FG 6
Gojam 164-165 M 6
Gojjam = Gojam 164-165 M 6
Gojrā 138-139 D 2
Gokāk 140 B 2
Gōkāka = Gokāk 140 B 2
Gökbel 136-137 C 4
Gökçe 136-137 A 2
Gökçe ada 136-137 AB 2
Gōkhteik 141 E 4
Gökırmak 136-137 F 2
Gokokuji Temple 155 III b 1
Gokōmutsumi 155 III c 1
Göksu [TR, place] 136-137 K 3
Göksu [TR, river] 136-137 FG 4
Göksu bendi 154 I b 2
Göksu deresi 154 I b 2
Göksun 136-137 G 3
Göksu nehir 134-135 C 3
Gök tepe 136-137 C 4
Gokurt 138-139 A 3
Gokwe 172 E 5
Gol 116-117 C 7
Gola 138-139 K 6
Golabari, Howrah- 154 II b 2
Golāghāt 141 CD 2
Golā Gokarannāth 138-139 H 3
Golaja Pristan' 126-127 F 3
Golakganj 138-139 MN 4
Golāshkerd 134-135 H 5
Gölbaşı [TR, Adıyaman] 136-137 G 4
Gölbaşı [TR, Ankara] 136-137 E 3
Golconda, IL 70-71 F 7
Golconda, NV 66-67 E 5
Gölcük [TR, Kocaeli] 136-137 CD 2
Goldap 118 L 1
Gold Bar 60 F 1
Gold Beach, OR 66-67 A 4
Gold Bridge 60 F 4
Goldburg, ID 66-67 G 3
Gold Butte, MT 66-67 H 1
Gold Coast [AUS] 158-159 K 5
Gold Coast [GH] 164-165 DE 8
Gold Coast-Southport 160 LM 1
Gold Creek, AK 58-59 N 5
Golden 60 J 4
Golden, ID 66-67 F 3
Golden, IL 70-71 E 5
Golden Bay 161 E 5
Golden City, MO 70-71 C 7
Goldendale, WA 66-67 C 3
Golden Ears Provincial Park 60 F 5
Golden Gate 64-65 B 4
Golden Gate Bridge 83 I b 2
Golden Gate Fields Race Track 83 I bc 1
Golden Gate Park 83 I ab 2
Golden Hinde 60 E 5
Golden Meadow, LA 78-79 D 6
Golden Prairie 61 D 5
Golden Vale 119 BC 5
Golders Green, London- 129 II b 1
Goldfield, NV 74-75 E 4
Gold Hill, UT 66-67 G 5
Goldküste 164-165 D 8-E 7
Gold Point, NV 74-75 E 4
Gold River 60 D 5
Goldsand Lake 61 H 2
Goldsboro, NC 64-65 L 4-5
Goldsmith, TX 76-77 C 6-7
Goldstein, Frankfurt am Main- 128 III a 1
Goldsworthy, Mount — 158-159 CD 4
Goldthwaite, TX 76-77 E 7
Göle = Merdenik 136-137 K 2
Goléa, El- = Al-Gulī'ah 164-165 E 2
Golec-In'aptuk, gora — = gora In'aptuk 132-133 UV 6
Golec-Longdor, gora — = gora Longdor 132-133 W 6
Golela 172 F 7
Goleniów 118 G 2
Goleta, CA 74-75 D 5
Golf du Lion 120-121 JK 7
Golfe de Bejaïa = Khalīj Bijāyah 166-167 1
Golfe de Bonny 164-165 F 8
Golfe de Bougie = Khalīj Bijāyah 166-167 J 1
Golfe de Bou Grara = Khalīj Bū Ghrārah 166-167 M 3
Golfe de Honduras 64-65 J 8
Golfe de la Gonâve 64-65 M 8
Golfe de los Mosquitos 64-65 K 10
Golfe de Tadjoura 164-165 N 6
Golfe du Saint-Laurent = Gulf of Saint Lawrence 56-57 Y 8
Golfe Nuevo 111 D 6
Golfete de Coro 94-95 F 2
Golfito 64-65 K 10
Golf Links 161 II c 1
Golfo Almirante Montt 108-109 C 8
Golfo Aranci 122-123 CD 5
Golfo Corcovado 108-109 C 4
Golfo de Almería 120-121 F 10
Golfo de Ancud 111 B 6
Golfo de Arauco 106-107 A 6
Golfo de Batabanó 64-65 K 7
Golfo de Cádiz 120-121 D 10
Golfo de Cariaco 94-95 JK 2
Golfo de Chiriquí 64-65 K 10
Golfo de Cupica 92-93 D 3
Golfo de Fonseca 64-65 J 9
Golfo de Guacanayabo 64-65 L 7
Golfo de Guafo 111 B 6
Golfo de Guayaquil 92-93 C 5
Golfo del Darién 92-93 D 3
Golfo de los Coronados 108-109 BC 3
Golfo del Papagayo 64-65 J 9
Golfo de Mazarrón 120-121 G 10
Golfo de Montijo 88-89 F 11
Golfo de Morrosquillo 92-93 D 2-3
Golfo de Nicoya 64-65 J 9
Golfo de Panamá 64-65 L 10
Golfo de Paria 92-93 G 2
Golfo de Parita 88-89 FG 10
Golfo de Penas 111 AB 7
Golfo de San Jorge 120-121 H 8
Golfo de San Miguel 88-89 G 10
Golfo de Santa Clara, El — 86-87 C 2
Golfo de Tehuantepec 64-65 GH 8
Golfo de Urabá 92-93 D 3
Golfo de Valencia 120-121 H 9
Golfo de Venezuela 92-93 E 2
Golfo di Cǎgliari 122-123 C 6
Golfo di Castellammare 122-123 E 6
Golfo di Gaeta 122-123 E 5
Golfo di Gènova 122-123 C 4
Golfo di Manfredònia 122-123 FG 5
Golfo di Nàpoli 122-123 EF 5
Golfo di Policastro 122-123 F 5-6
Golfo di Salerno 122-123 F 5
Golfo di Sant'Eufèmia 122-123 FG 6
Golfo di Squillace 122-123 G 6
Golfo di Tàranto 122-123 G 5
Golfo di Venèzia 122-123 E 3
Golfo Dulce 64-65 K 10
Golfo Elefantes 108-109 BC 6
Golfo Ladrillero 108-109 AB 7
Golfo San Esteban 108-109 B 6
Golfo San Jorge 111 CD 7
Golfo San José 108-109 G 4
Golfo San Matías 111 D 6
Golfo Tres Montes 108-109 B 6
Golfo Trinidad 108-109 B 7
Golfo Triste 94-95 GH 2
Golf parc 170 IV a 1
Gölhisar 136-137 C 4
Goliad, TX 76-77 F 8
Goljanovo, Moskva- 113 V d 2
Gölköy = Kuşluyan 136-137 G 2
Gollel 174-175 J 4
Göllü = Çoğun 136-137 F 3
Gölmarmara 136-137 BC 3
Golmo 142-143 GH 4
Goloby 124-125 E 8
Golodnaja step' = Betpak-Dala 132-133 MN 8
Golog Zangzu Zizhizhou 142-143 HJ 5
Golog Zizhizhou 142-143 HJ 5
Golondrina 106-107 G 2
Golondrinas, Arroyo — 106-107 G 2
Golovanovo 124-125 N 6
Golovinščino 124-125 OP 7
Golovnin, AK 58-59 F 4
Golovnin Bay 58-59 F 4
Golovnin Mission, AK 58-59 F 4
Golpāyegān 134-135 G 4
Gölpazarı 136-137 D 2
Golspie 119 E 2-3
Gol Tappeh 136-137 L 4
Golubi 124-125 NO 4
Golubovka 126-127 G 2
Golungo Alto 172 B 3
Golva, ND 68-69 E 2
Gölveren 136-137 E 4
Golynki 124-125 H 6
Golyšmanovo 132-133 MN 6
Goma 172 E 2
Gomang Tsho 138-139 M 2
Gomati 134-135 N 5
Gomba 171 D 5
Gombari 171 B 2
Gombe [EAT] 172 F 2
Gombe [WAN] 164-165 G 6
Gombe, Kinshasa- 170 IV a 1

Gombe 295

Great Karas Mountains = Groot Karasberge 172 C 7
Great Karoo = Groot Karoo 172 D 8
Great Kei = Kepulauan Kai 148-149 K 8
Great Kei River = Groot Keirivier 172 EF 8
Great Kills, New York-, NY 82 III b 3
Great Lake 158-159 J 8
Great Meteor Tablemount 50-51 H 4
Great Namaqua Land = Namaland 172 C 7
Great Natuna = Pulau Bunguran 148-149 E 6
Great Neck, NY 82 III d 2
Great Nicobar 134-135 P 9
Great Northern Pacific Railway 64-65 DE 2
Great Northern Peninsula 56-57 Z 7-8
Great Oasis = Al-Wāḥāt al-Khārīyah 164-165 KL 3-4
Great Oyster Bay 160 d 3
Great Peconic Bay 72-73 K 4
Great Plains 64-65 E 2-F 5
Great Ruaha 172 G 3
Great Sacandaga Lake 72-73 JK 3
Great Salt Desert = Dasht-e Kavīr 134-135 GH 3
Great Salt Lake 64-65 D 3
Great Salt Lake Desert 64-65 D 3
Great Salt Plains Reservoir 76-77 EF 4
Great Sand Dunes National Monument 68-69 CD 7
Great Sand Sea = Libysche Wüste 164-165 J 3-L 4
Great Sandy Desert [AUS] 158-159 DE 4
Great Sandy Desert [USA] 64-65 BC 3
Great Sandy Hills 61 D 5
Great Sandy Island 158-159 KL 4-5
Great Slave Lake 56-57 NO 5
Great Smoky Mountains 80-81 E 3
Great Smoky Mountains National Park 80-81 E 3
Great Swinton Island = Hswindan Kyûnmyâ 150-151 AB 7
Great Ums = Groot-Ums 174-175 C 2
Great Usutu 174-175 J 4
Great Valley 80-81 D 3
Great Victoria Desert 158-159 EF 5
Great Wall 142-143 K 4
Great Western Erg = Al-'Irq al-Kabīr al-Gharbī 164-165 D 3-E 2
Great Whale River 56-57 VW 6
Great Winterhoek = Groot Winterhoek 174-175 C 7
Great Yarmouth 119 GH 5
Grebenà 122-123 J 5
Grebeni 124-125 R 4
Greboun, Mont — 164-165 F 4-5
Grecco 106-107 J 4
Greco, Cape — = Akrōthḗrion Gréko 136-137 F 5
Gredos, Sierra de — 120-121 E 8
Greece 122-123 J 7-L 5
Greeley, CO 64-65 F 3
Greeley, NE 68-69 G 5
Greely Fiord 56-57 UV 1
Green 62 E 2
Green Bay 64-65 J 2-3
Green Bay, WI 64-65 J 3
Greenbelt Park 82 II b 1
Greenbrae, CA 83 I a 1
Greenbrier River 72-73 FG 5
Greenbush, MN 70-71 BC 1
Green Cape 160 K 6
Greencastle, IN 70-71 G 6
Greencastle, PA 72-73 GH 5
Green City, IA 70-71 D 5
Green Cove Springs, FL 80-81 bc 1
Greene, IA 70-71 D 4
Greeneville, TN 80-81 E 2
Greenfield, CA 74-75 C 4
Greenfield, IA 70-71 C 5
Greenfield, IN 70-71 H 6
Greenfield, MA 72-73 K 3
Greenfield, MO 70-71 CD 7
Greenfield, OH 72-73 E 5
Greenfield, TN 78-79 E 2
Greenfield Park 82 I c 2
Greenfields Village, NJ 84 III c 3
Greenford, London- 129 II a 1
Greenhorn Mountains 74-75 D 5
Greening 62 O 2
Green Island [AUS] 158-159 J 3
Green Island [HK] 155 I a 2
Green Island [USA] 58-59 O 6
Green Islands 148-149 hj 5
Green Lake [CDN] 61 E 3
Green Lake [USA] 70-71 F 4
Greenland 52 BC 23
Greenland, MI 70-71 F 2
Greenland Basin 50-51 JK 2
Greenland Sea 52 B 20-18
Green Mountain Reservoir 68-69 C 6
Green Mountains [USA, Vermont] 72-73 K 2-3
Green Mountains [USA, Wyoming] 68-69 C 4
Greenock 119 D 4
Green Pond, SC 80-81 F 4
Greenport, NY 72-73 K 4
Green Ridge, PA 84 III a 2
Green River, UT 74-75 H 3
Green River, WY 66-67 J 5
Green River [USA, Illinois] 70-71 F 5
Green River [USA, Kentucky] 70-71 G 7
Green River [USA, Wyoming] 64-65 E 3-4
Green River Basin 64-65 DE 3
Greens Bayou 85 III c 1
Greensboro, AL 78-79 F 4
Greensboro, GA 80-81 E 4
Greensboro, NC 64-65 L 4
Greensburg, IN 70-71 H 6
Greensburg, KS 68-69 G 7
Greensburg, KY 70-71 H 7
Greensburg, PA 72-73 G 4
Greenside, Johannesburg- 170 V b 1
Green Swamp 80-81 G 3
Greenup, IL 70-71 FG 6
Greenup, KY 72-73 E 5
Greenvale 158-159 HJ 3
Greenville 164-165 C 7-8
Greenville, AL 78-79 F 5
Greenville, CA 66-67 C 5
Greenville, FL 80-81 E 5
Greenville, IL 70-71 F 6
Greenville, IN 72-73 D 4
Greenville, KY 70-71 G 7
Greenville, ME 72-73 LM 2
Greenville, MI 70-71 H 4
Greenville, MS 64-65 HJ 5
Greenville, NC 64-65 L 4
Greenville, OH 70-71 H 5
Greenville, PA 72-73 F 4
Greenville, SC 64-65 K 5
Greenville, TX 64-65 GH 5
Greenwater Lake 70-71 E 1
Greenwater Lake Provincial Park 61 G 4
Greenway 68-69 G 1
Greenway, SD 68-69 G 3
Greenwich, OH 72-73 E 4
Greenwich, London- 119 FG 6
Greenwich Village, New York-, NY 82 III b 2
Greenwood 66-67 D 1
Greenwood, AR 76-77 GH 5
Greenwood, IN 70-71 GH 6
Greenwood, MA 84 I b 2
Greenwood, MS 64-65 HJ 5
Greenwood, SC 64-65 K 5
Greenwood, WI 70-71 E 3
Greenwood Cemetery [USA, Atlanta] 85 II b 2
Greenwood Cemetery [USA, New Orleans] 85 I b 2
Greenwood Cemetery [USA, Philadelphia] 84 III d 1
Greer, ID 66-67 EF 2
Greer, SC 80-81 E 3
Greeson, Lake — 78-79 C 3
Gregório, Rio — 98-99 C 8
Gregory, SD 68-69 G 4
Gregory, Lake — 158-159 GH 5
Gregory Downs 158-159 G 3
Gregory Range 158-159 H 3
Gregory River 158-159 G 3
Gregory Salt Lake 158-159 E 3-4
Greifswald 118 F 1
Grein 118 G 4
Greinerville 171 B 4
Greiz 118 EF 3
Grḗko, Akrōtḗrion — 136-137 F 5
Gremicha 132-133 F 4
Grenå 116-117 D 9
Grenada 64-65 O 9
Grenada, MS 78-79 E 4
Grenada Lake 78-79 E 4
Grenada Reservoir = Grenada Lake 78-79 E 4
Grenadines 64-65 O 9
Grenelle, Paris- 129 I c 2
Grenen 116-117 D 9
Grenfell [AUS] 160 HJ 4
Grenfell [CDN] 61 G 5
Grenivík 116-117 de 2
Grenoble 120-121 KL 6
Grenola, KS 76-77 F 4
Grenora, ND 68-69 E 1
Grenvill, Cape — 158-159 H 2
Grenville 94-95 L 1
Grenville, NM 76-77 C 4
Grenville, SD 68-69 H 3
Gresham Park 85 II c 2
Grésillons, les — 129 I b 2
Gressy 129 I d 2
Gretna 68-69 H 1
Gretna, LA 64-65 HJ 6
Grevy, Isla — 108-109 F 10
Grey, De — 158-159 CD 4
Greybull, WY 68-69 BC 3
Greybull River 68-69 B 3
Grey Islands 56-57 Za 7
Grey Islands Harbour 63 J 2
Greylingstad 174-175 H 4
Greylock, Mount — 72-73 K 3
Greymont, Johannesburg- 170 V a 1
Greymouth 158-159 O 8
Grey Range 158-159 H 5
Grey River 63 H 4
Grey River, De — 158-159 CD 4
Greytown 174-175 J 5
Greytown = Bluefields 64-65 K 9
Gribanovskij 126-127 KL 1
Gribbell Island 60 C 3
Gribingui 164-165 H 7
Gridley, CA 74-75 C 3
Griekwaland-Oos 174-175 H 6
Griekwaland-Wes 172 D 7
Griekwastad 174-175 E 5
Griesheim, Frankfurt am Main- 128 III a 1
Griffin 61 G 6
Griffin, GA 64-65 K 5
Griffin Point 58-59 QR 1
Griffith 158-159 J 6
Grigoriopol' 126-127 D 3
Grik 150-151 C 10
Grim, Cape — 158-159 H 8
Grimajlov 126-127 BC 2
Grimari 164-165 HJ 7
Grimes, CA 74-75 C 3
Grimma 118 F 3
Grimsby [CDN] 72-73 G 3
Grimsby [GB] 119 FG 5
Grímsey 116-117 d 1
Grimshaw 60 HJ 1
Grimstad 116-117 C 8
Grímsvötn 116-117 e 2
Grindavík 116-117 b 3
Grindsted 116-117 C 10
Grindstone Buttes 68-69 F 3
Grinnell, IA 70-71 D 5
Grinnell Land 56-57 UV 1-2
Grinnell Peninsula 56-57 RS 2
Grinzing, Wien- 113 I b 1
Griqualand East = Griekwaland-Oos 174-175 H 6
Griqualand West = Griekwaland-Wes 172 D 7
Griquatown = Griekwastad 174-175 E 5
Gris, Kuala — 150-151 D 10
Griswold, IA 70-71 C 5
Grita, La — 94-95 F 3
Grīva [SU, Lietuva] 124-125 F 6
Griva [SU, Rossijskaja SFSR] 124-125 S 3
Grīz = Krīz 166-167 L 2
Groais Island 63 J 2
Gröbenried 130 II a 1
Grobina 124-125 C 5
Groblersdal 174-175 H 3
Groblershoop 174-175 DE 5
Grodno 124-125 DE 7
Grodz'anka 124-125 G 7
Groenrivier [ZA ◁ Atlantic Ocean] 174-175 B 6
Groenrivier [ZA ◁ Ongersrivier] 174-175 E 6
Groenriviermond 174-175 B 6
Groenwaterrivier 174-175 E 5
Groesbeck, TX 76-77 F 7
Grœtavær 116-117 G 3
Grogol, Kali — 154 IV a 2
Grogol Petamburan, Jakarta- 154 IV a 1
Groix, Île de — 120-121 F 5
Groll Seamount 50-51 H 6
Grombalia = Qrunbālīyah 166-167 M 1
Gronau 128 III b 1
Gronbâlia = Qrunbālīyah 166-167 M 1
Grong 116-117 E 5
Groningen [NL] 120-121 L 2
Groningen [SME] 92-93 HJ 3
Gronsdorf 130 II c 2
Groom, TX 76-77 D 5
Groot Bergrivier 174-175 C 7
Groot-Bijgaarden 128 II a 1
Groot Bosmanland 174-175 CD 5
Groot-Brakrivier 174-175 E 8
Groot Brukkaros 172 C 7
Grootdoring 174-175 E 5
Grootdrink 174-175 D 5
Groote Eylandt 158-159 G 2
Groote River = Grootrivier [ZA ◁ Gourits] 174-175 D 7
Groote River = Grootrivier [ZA ◁ Sint Francisbaai] 174-175 F 7
Grootfontein 172 C 5
Groot Karasberge 172 C 7
Groot Karoo 172 D 8
Groot Keirivier 172 EF 8
Groot Letaba 174-175 J 2
Groot-Marico 174-175 G 3
Groot Rietrivier 174-175 D 6-7
Grootrivier [ZA ◁ Gourits] 174-175 D 7
Grootrivier [ZA ◁ Sint Francisbaai] 174-175 F 7
Grootrivierhoogte 174-175 EF 7
Groot Shingwedzi 174-175 J 2
Groot Shingwidzi = Groot Shingwedzi 174-175 J 2
Groot-Spelonke 174-175 HJ 2
Groot Swartberge 174-175 DE 7
Groot-Ums 174-175 C 2
Groot Visrivier 172 C 7
Grootvlei 174-175 H 4
Grootvloer 174-175 D 5
Groot Winterhoek 174-175 C 7
Grosa, Punta — 120-121 H 9
Groslay 129 I c 2
Gros Morne [CDN] 63 H 3
Gros-Morne [RH] 88-89 K 5
Gros Morne National Park 56-57 Za 8
Grosnyj = Groznyj 126-127 M 5
Gross Borstel, Hamburg- 130 I a 1
Grossenbrode 118 E 1
Grosse Pointe, MI 84 II c 2
Grosse Pointe Farms, MI 84 II c 2
Grosse Pointe Park, MI 84 II c 2
Grosse Pointe Woods, MI 84 II c 2
Grosser Arber 118 F 3
Grosser Beerberg 118 E 3
Grosse Tet, LA 78-79 D 5
Grosseto 122-123 D 4
Grossglockner 118 F 5
Grosshadern, München- 130 II a 2
Grosshesselohe 130 II b 2
Grossjedlersdorf, Wien- 113 I b 1
Gross Moor 130 I b 2
Grossmünster 128 IV b 1
Grossos 100-101 F 3
Grossziethen [DDR, Potsdam] 130 III b 2
Grosvenor, Lake — 58-59 K 7
Gros Ventre River 66-67 H 4
Grote IJ-polder 128 I a 1
Grote Molenbeek 128 II a 1
Grotli 116-117 BC 6
Groton, NY 72-73 H 3
Groton, SD 68-69 GH 3
Grottoes, VA 72-73 G 5
Grouard 60 JK 2
Groundhog River 62 K 2
Grouse, ID 66-67 G 4
Grouse Creek, UT 66-67 G 5
Grouse Creek Mountain 66-67 FG 3
Grove City, PA 72-73 FG 4
Grove Hill, AL 78-79 F 5
Groveland, CA 74-75 CD 4
Grover, CO 68-69 DE 5
Grover, WY 66-67 H 4
Grover City, CA 74-75 C 5
Groveton, TX 76-77 G 7
Grovont, WY 66-67 H 4
Growler, AZ 74-75 FG 6
Growler Mountains 74-75 G 6
Grozny = Groznyj 126-127 M 5
Groznyj 126-127 M 5
Grū', Wād — 166-167 C 3
Grudovo 122-123 M 4
Grudziądz 118 J 2
Gruesa, Punta — 104-105 A 7
Grulla, TX 76-77 E 9
Grullo, El — 86-87 H 8
Grumantbyen 116-117 jk 5
Grumeti 171 C 3
Grumo Appula 122-123 G 5
Grünau [Namibia] 172 C 7
Grundarfjördhur 116-117 ab 2
Grundy, VA 80-81 EF 2
Grundy Center, IA 70-71 D 4
Grunewald [D] 130 III a 2
Grunewald, Berlin- 130 III b 2
Grunidora, Llanos de la — 86-87 JK 5
Grünwalder Forst 130 II b 2
Grušino 124-125 P 4
Gruta, La — 102-103 F 7
Gruver, TX 76-77 D 4
Gryfice 118 G 2
Gryllefjord 116-117 G 3
Grymes Hill, New York-, NY 82 III b 3
Grytviken 111 J 8

Gşaiba = Quşaybah 136-137 J 5

Gua 138-139 K 6
Guacanayabo, Golfo de — 64-65 L 7
Guacang Shan = Kuocang Shan 146-147 H 7
Guacara 94-95 GH 2
Guacarí 94-95 C 6
Guacas 94-95 F 4
Guachaca 94-95 E 2
Guachara 94-95 G 4
Guácharos, Las Cuevas de los — 94-95 CD 7
Guachi, Cerro — 106-107 C 2
Guachipas 104-105 D 9
Guachiria, Río — 94-95 F 5
Guachochi 86-87 G 4
Guaçu 102-103 E 5
Guaçu, Rio — 102-103 F 6
Guaçuí 102-103 M 4
Guadalajara [E] 120-121 F 8
Guadalajara [MEX] 64-65 EF 7
Guadalaviar 120-121 G 8
Guadalcanal [Solomon Is.] 148-149 j 6
Guadalcanar Gela = Guadalcanal 148-149 j 6
Guadales 106-107 D 5
Guadalete 120-121 DE 10
Guadalimar 120-121 F 9
Guadalope 120-121 G 8
Guadalquivir 120-121 E 10
Guadalupe, CA 74-75 C 5
Guadalupe [BOL] 104-105 DE 6
Guadalupe [CO] 94-95 D 4
Guadalupe [E] 120-121 E 9
Guadalupe [MEX ↗ San Luis Potosí] 86-87 KL 6
Guadalupe [MEX ↑ San Luis Potosí] 86-87 K 6
Guadalupe [MEX, Baja California] 86-87 B 2
Guadalupe [MEX, Coahuila] 76-77 D 9
Guadalupe [MEX, Nuevo León] 64-65 FG 6
Guadalupe [MEX, Zacatecas] 86-87 JK 6
Guadalupe [PE] 96-97 B 5
Guadalupe, Basilica de — 91 I c 2
Guadalupe, Isla de — 64-65 C 6
Guadalupe, Sierra de — [E] 120-121 E 9
Guadalupe, Sierra de — [MEX] 91 I c 1
Guadalupe Bravos 86-87 G 2
Guadalupe del Norte 91 I c 1
Guadalupe Mountains [USA → El Paso] 76-77 B 6-7
Guadalupe Peak 64-65 F 5
Guadalupe River 76-77 F 8
Guadalupe Victoria 86-87 J 5
Guadalupe y Calvo 86-87 G 4
Guadalupita, NM 76-77 B 4
Guadarrama [YV] 94-95 GH 3
Guadarrama, Sierra de — 120-121 EF 8
Guadeloupe 64-65 O 8
Guadeloupe Passage 64-65 O 8
Guadiana 120-121 D 10
Guadiana Menor 120-121 F 10
Guadix 120-121 F 10
Guadur = Gwādar 134-135 J 5
Guafo, Golfo de — 111 B 6
Guafo, Isla — 111 AB 6
Guai 148-149 L 7
Guaíba 106-107 M 3
Guaíba, Rio — 106-107 M 3
Guaicui 102-103 K 2
Guaicuras 102-103 D 4
Guainía 94-95 FG 6
Guainía, Río — 92-93 F 4
Guaiquinima, Cerro — 92-93 G 3
Guaíra [BR, Paraná] 111 F 2
Guaíra [BR, São Paulo] 102-103 H 4
Guairá [PY] 102-103 D 6-7
Guaira, La — 94-95 H 2
Guaire, Río — 91 II b 2
Guaitecas, Islas — 111 AB 6
Guajaba, Cayo — 88-89 H 4
Guajará 98-99 J 7
Guajará-Mirim 92-93 FG 7
Guajeru 100-101 D 8
Guajira 94-95 E 2
Guajira, Península de — 92-93 E 2
Guala, Punta — 108-109 C 4
Gualaceo 96-97 B 3
Gualala, CA 74-75 B 3
Gualán 86-87 Q 10
Gualaquiza 92-93 D 5
Gualeguay 111 E 4
Gualeguay, Río — 106-107 H 4
Gualeguaychú 111 E 4
Gualicho, Bajo del — 108-109 G 4
Gualicho, Gran Bajo del — 108-109 G 3
Gualicho, Salina del — 108-109 G 3
Gualior = Gwalior 134-135 M 5
Gualjaina 108-109 D 4
Gualjaina, Río — 108-109 D 4
Guallatiri, Volcán — 104-105 B 6
Gualqui 106-107 A 6
Guam 206-207 S 8
Guamá [BR] 98-99 P 5
Guama [YV] 94-95 G 2
Guamá, Rio — 100-101 A 2
Guamal [CO, Magdalena] 94-95 DE 3
Guamal [CO, Meta] 94-95 E 5
Guamal, Quebrada — 91 II b 1
Guamani, Cordillera de — 96-97 AB 4
Guamblin, Isla — 111 A 6
Guamini 106-107 F 6
Guamo [CO] 94-95 D 5
Guamo [YV] 94-95 E 3
Guamote 96-97 B 2
Guampi, Serra de — 94-95 J 4-5
Guamúchil 86-87 FG 5
Guamués, Río — 94-95 C 7
Gua Musang 150-151 CD 10
Gu'an 146-147 F 2
Guaña 92-93 G 4
Guanabara, Baía de — 102-103 L 5
Guanacache, Lagunas de — 106-107 CD 4
Guanaco, Bajo del — 108-109 E 6
Guanahacabibes, Península de — 88-89 D 4
Guanahani = San Salvador 64-65 M 7
Guanaja 88-89 D 6
Guanajutao 64-65 F 7
Guanambi 100-101 C 8
Guanani 94-95 E 3
Guanape 94-95 J 3
Guanare 92-93 F 3
Guanare, Río — 94-95 G 3
Guanarito 92-93 F 3
Guanay, Cerro — 94-95 H 5
Guandacol 106-107 C 2
Guandacol, Río — 106-107 C 2
Guandian 146-147 G 5
Guandong Bandao 144-145 C 3
Guandu 146-147 DE 7
Guane 64-65 K 7
Guang'an 142-143 K 5
Guangchang 142-143 M 6
Guangde 146-147 G 6
Guangdong 142-143 L 7
Guangfeng 146-147 G 7
Guanghai 142-143 L 7
Guanghua 142-143 L 5
Guangji 142-143 M 6
Guangling 146-147 E 2
Guanglu Dao 144-145 D 3
Guangnan 142-143 JK 7
Guangning 146-147 D 10
Guangping 146-147 E 3
Guangrao 146-147 G 3
Guangshan 146-147 E 5
Guangshui 146-147 E 6
Guangxi Zhuangzu Zizhiqu 142-143 KL 7
Guangyuan 142-143 K 5
Guangze 146-147 F 8
Guangzhou 142-143 LM 7
Guangzhou Wan = Zhanjiang Gang 142-143 L 7
Guanhães 102-103 L 3
Guanipa, Mesa de — 94-95 J 3
Guanipa, Río — 94-95 K 3
Guan Jiang 146-147 C 9
Guankou = Minhou 146-147 G 8
Guannan 146-147 G 4
Guano 96-97 B 2
Guanoco 94-95 K 2
Guano Islands = Penguin Eilanden 174-175 A 3-5
Guano Lake 66-67 D 4
Guanqumen, Beijing- 155 II b 2
Guanshui 144-145 E 2
Guanta [RCH] 106-107 B 2
Guanta [YV] 94-95 J 2
Guantánamo 64-65 LM 7-8
Guantao 146-147 E 3
Guantou Jiao 150-151 G 2
Guan Xian 146-147 E 3
Guanyang 146-147 C 9
Guanyintang 146-147 CD 4
Guanyun 142-143 MN 5
Guapay, Río — 104-105 E 5
Guapé 102-103 K 4
Guapi 92-93 D 4
Guapiara 102-103 H 6
Guápiles 88-89 E 9
Guapó 102-103 H 2
Guapo, El — 94-95 HJ 2
Guaporé 106-107 LM 2
Guaporé = Rondônia 92-93 G 7
Guaporé, Rio — [BR ◁ Rio Mamoré] 92-93 G 7
Guaporé, Rio — [BR ◁ Rio Taquari] 106-107 L 2
Guaqui 92-93 F 8
Guará [BR, Rio Grande do Sul] 106-107 K 3
Guará [BR, São Paulo] 102-103 J 4
Guará, Rio — 100-101 B 7
Guarabira 92-93 MN 6
Guaraçaí 102-103 G 4
Guaracarumbo 91 II b 1
Guaraciaba do Norte 100-101 D 3
Guaraji 102-103 G 3
Guaramirim 102-103 H 7
Guaranda 92-93 D 5
Guaranésia 102-103 J 4
Guarani 102-103 L 4
Guaraniaçu 102-103 F 6
Guarantã 102-103 H 4
Guarapiranga, Barragem do — 110 II a 3
Guarapiranga, Reservatório de — 110 II a 3
Guarapo, El — 91 II b 1
Guarapuava 111 F 3
Guarapuavinha 102-103 G 6
Guaraqueçaba 102-103 HJ 6
Guarará 110 II c 3
Guararapes 102-103 G 4
Guararema 102-103 JK 5
Guaratinga 100-101 E 9
Guaratinguetá 92-93 KL 9
Guaratuba 111 G 3
Guaratuba, Baía de — 102-103 HJ 6
Guarayos, Llanos de — 92-93 G 8
Guarda 120-121 D 8
Guarda, El — 91 I a 2
Guardafui = 'Asayr 134-135 G 8
Guardamonte, El — 104-105 D 10
Guarda-Mor 102-103 J 2
Guardatinajas 94-95 H 3
Guardia, La — [BOL] 104-105 E 5
Guardia, La — [RA] 106-107 E 2
Guardia, La — [RCH] 106-107 C 1
Guardia Escolta 106-107 F 2
Guardia Mitre 108-109 H 3
Guardián, Cabo — 108-109 FG 7
Guardian Brito, Isla — 108-109 C 10
Guardo 120-121 E 7
Guarenas 94-95 H 2
Guariba 102-103 H 4
Guaricana, Pico — 102-103 H 6
Guarico 94-95 G 3
Guárico, Embalse de — 94-95 H 3
Guarico, Punta — 88-89 JK 4
Guárico, Río — 94-95 H 3
Guarita, Rio — 106-107 L 1
Guarrojo, Río — 94-95 F 5
Guarujá 102-103 JK 5-6
Guarulhos 92-93 K 9
Guarulhos-Cidade Brasil 110 II b 1
Guarulhos-Vila Cocaia 110 II b 1
Guarulhos-Vila Galvão 110 II b 1
Guarulhos-Vila Macedo 110 II b 1
Guasacavi, Cerro — 94-95 G 6
Guasapampa, Sierra de — 106-107 E 3
Guasave 64-65 E 6
Guasayán, Sierra de — 104-105 D 10-11
Guascama, Punta — 92-93 D 4
Guasdualito 92-93 EF 3
Guasipati 92-93 G 3
Guastalla 122-123 D 3
Guatapará 102-103 J 4
Guatavita 94-95 E 5
Guatemala [GCA, place] 64-65 HJ 9
Guatemala [GCA, state] 64-65 HJ 8
Guatemala Basin 156-157 N 4
Guateque 94-95 E 5
Guatimozín 106-107 FG 4
Guatire 94-95 H 2
Guatisiimiña 94-95 K 5
Guatraché 106-107 F 6
Guatraché, Laguna — 106-107 F 6
Guatrochi 108-109 G 4
Guavatayoc, Laguna de — 104-105 CD 8
Guaviare 94-95 EF 6
Guaviare, Río — 92-93 F 4
Guaviravi 106-107 J 2
Guaxupé 92-93 K 9
Guayabal [C] 88-89 H 4
Guayabal [YV] 94-95 H 4
Guayabero, Río — 94-95 E 6
Guayabo, El — [CO] 94-95 E 4
Guayabo, El — [YV] 94-95 EF 3
Guayabones 94-95 F 3
Guayacán 106-107 B 2-3
Guayaguayare 94-95 L 2
Guayama 88-89 N 6
Guayana = Guyana 92-93 H 3-4
Guayaneco, Archipiélago — 108-109 AB 6
Guayapo, Río — 94-95 H 5
Guayaquil 92-93 CD 5
Guayaquil, Golfo de — 92-93 C 5
Guayaramerín 92-93 F 7
Guayas 96-97 AB 3
Guayas, Río — [CO] 94-95 D 7
Guayas, Río — [EC] 96-97 B 3
Guaycurú 106-107 GH 2
Guaycurú, Rio — 102-103 C 7
Guayllabamba, Río — 94-95 B 1
Guaymas = Heroica Guaymas 64-65 D 6
Guayquiraró 106-107 H 3
Guayquiraró, Río — 106-107 H 3
Guazapares 86-87 G 4
Guba 172 E 4
guba Buor-Chaja 132-133 Z 3
Gubacha 132-133 K 6
guba Mašigina 132-133 HJ 3
Guban 164-165 ab 1
Gubanovo = Vereščagino 132-133 JK 6
Gubbi 140 C 4
Gùbbio 122-123 E 4
Gubdor 124-125 V 3
Guben 118 G 3
Gubio 168-169 J 2
Gubkin 126-127 H 1
Gucheng [TJ, Hebei] 146-147 EF 3
Gucheng [TJ, Hubei] 146-147 C 5
Gucheng [TJ, Shanxi] 146-147 CD 4
Gučin Us 142-143 J 2
Gucun 146-147 F 8
Gūdalūr [IND ↖ Coimbatore] 140 C 5
Gūdalūr [IND ↙ Madurai] 140 C 6
Gūḍalūr = Cuddalore 134-135 MN 8
Gūḍam = Gūdem 140 F 2
Gudāri 138-139 JK 8
Gudauta 126-127 K 5
Gudbrandsdal 116-117 CD 7
Gūdem 140 F 2
Gudenå 116-117 CD 9
Gudermes 126-127 N 5
Gudibanda 140 CD 4
Gudivāda 140 E 2
Gudiyāttam 140 D 4
Gudong 141 F 3
Güdül 136-137 E 2
Gūḍūr 134-135 MN 8
Gūḍūru = Gūḍūr 134-135 MN 8
Guéckédou 164-165 BC 7
Gué de Constantine, le — 170 I ab 2
Guéguen, Lac — 62 N 2
Guéjar, Río — 94-95 E 6
Guékédou-Kankan 168-169 C 3
Guelma = Qalmah 164-165 F 1
Guelph 56-57 UV 9
Guémar = Qamār 166-167 K 3
Guéna 168-169 D 3
Guéné 164-165 E 6
Guenfouda = Janfūdah 166-167 E 2
Guenguel, Río — 108-109 D 5-6
Guentras, Région des — = Al-Qanṭarah 166-167 J 3
Güeppí 96-97 D 2
Güepsa 94-95 E 4
Guéra, Pic de — 164-165 H 6
Güer Aike 108-109 DE 8
Guerara = Al-Qarārah 166-167 J 3
Guerdane, Bir — = Bi'r Ghardan 166-167 K 2
Güere, Río — 94-95 J 3
Guereda 164-165 J 6
Guerém 100-101 E 7
Guéret 120-121 H 5
Guernsey 119 E 7
Guernsey, WY 68-69 D 4
Guerrero [MEX, administrative unit] 64-65 FG 8
Guerrero [MEX, place Coahuila] 76-77 D 8
Guerrero [MEX, place Tamaulipas] 76-77 E 9
Guerrero Negro 86-87 CD 3-4
Guersīf = Garsīf 166-167 E 2
Guerzim = Qarzīm 166-167 F 5
G'uešero 122-123 K 4
Guettar, El — = Al-Qaṭṭār 166-167 J 2
Guettara = Qaṭṭārah 166-167 E 4
Guettara, Aïn El — 164-165 D 4
Guetter, Chott el — = Shaṭṭ al-Qaṭṭār 166-167 L 2
Gueydan, LA 78-79 C 5-6
Gueyo 168-169 D 4
Gugē 164-165 M 7
Gugging 113 I b 1
Gughe = Gugē 164-165 M 7
Gugong Palace Museum 155 II b 2
Gūha = Gua 138-139 K 6
Guhāgar 140 A 2
Guia 92-93 H 8
Guia Lopes 102-103 J 4
Guia Lopes da Laguna 102-103 DE 4
Guiana Basin 50-51 G 5
Guiana Brasileira 92-93 G-J 4-5
Guiana Highlands = Macizo de las Guyanas 92-93 F 3-J 4
Guibes 174-175 B 4
Guichi 142-143 M 5
Guichicovi 86-87 N 9
Guichón 106-107 J 4
Guidder = Guider 164-165 G 6-7
Guide 142-143 J 4
Guider 164-165 G 6-7
Guiding 142-143 K 6
Guidong 146-147 D 8
Guier, Lac de — 164-165 AB 5
Guiglo 164-165 C 7
Güigüe 94-95 H 2-3
Gui He = Kuai He 146-147 F 5
Guija 174-175 K 3
Gui Jiang 146-147 C 9-10
Guiji Shan 146-147 H 7
Guildford 119 F 6
Guilin 142-143 KL 6
Guimarães [BR] 92-93 L 5
Guimarães [P] 120-121 C 8
Guimaras Island 148-149 H 4
Guimbalete 76-77 C 9
Guinan Zhou = Qiannon Zizhizhou 142-143 K 6
Guinea 164-165 B 6-C 7
Guinea, Gulf of — 164-165 C-F 8

Guinea 297

Hatia = Hâtiya 141 B 4
Hatia Islands = Hâtiya Dīpsamuh 141 B 4
Ha Tiên 150-151 E 7
Hatillo, El — [YV, place] 91 II c 2
Hatillo, El — [YV, river] 91 II c 2
Haṭinā-Māḷiyā = Māḷia 138-139 C 7
Ha Tinh 150-151 EF 3
Hatinohe = Hachinohe 142-143 R 3
Hatip 136-137 E 4
Hâtiya 141 B 4
Hâtiya Dīpsamuh 141 B 4
Hatizyô zima = Hachijō-jima 142-143 Q 5
Hātkanagale 140 B 2
Hatkanangale = Hātkanagale 140 B 2
Hat Nhao 150-151 F 5
Hato Corozal 94-95 F 4
Ha-tongsan-ni 144-145 F 3
Hatscher, Cerro — 108-109 C 7
Hat Sieo = Si Satchanalai 150-151 B 4
Hatsutomi 155 III c 1
Hatta 138-139 G 5
Hatteras, NC 80-81 J 3
Hatteras, Cape — 64-65 LM 4
Hatteras Island 64-65 LM 4
Hattfjelldal 116-117 F 5
Hattiesburg, MS 64-65 J 5
Hattingspruit 174-175 HJ 5
Haṭṭīyah 136-137 F 8
Hatton 56-57 P 7
Hatton, ND 68-69 H 2
Hatton = Heṭan 140 E 7
Hatvan 118 JK 5
Hat Yai 148-149 D 5
Hauchab 174-175 A 3
Haud = Hâwd 164-165 NO 7
Hâu Du'c 150-151 G 5
Haugesund 116-117 A 8
Hâu Giang 150-151 E 7
Hauhungaroa Range 161 F 4
Haukadalur 116-117 c 2
Haukeligrend 116-117 B 8
Haukipudas 116-117 L 5
Haukivesi 116-117 N 6-7
Haukivuori 116-117 M 6-7
Haultain River 61 E 2
Haumonía 104-105 F 10
Haungtharaw Myit 150-151 B 4
Hauptbahnhof Hamburg 130 I ab 1
Hauptbahnhof München 130 II b 2
Hauptfriedhof Öjendorf 130 I b 1
Hauptikon 128 IV ab 2
Ḩaurā = Ḩawrah 134-135 F 7
Ḩāurā = Howrah 134-135 O 6
Ḩaurā, Al — = Al-Ḩawrah 134-135 F 8
Hauraki Gulf 158-159 OP 7
Ḩauşah = Ḩawşah 136-137 G 8
Hausbruch, Hamburg- 130 I a 2
Hausen, Frankfurt am Main- 128 III a 1
Hausen am Albis 128 IV b 2
Hausruck 118 F 4
Haussee 130 III c 1
Haussonvillers = Nāsirīyah 166-167 HJ 1
Hautavaara = Chautavara 124-125 J 2
Haute-Kotto 164-165 J 7
Hauterive 63 B 3
Haute-Sangha 164-165 H 8
Hautes Plateaux = Nijād al-'Ālī 164-165 D 2-E 1
Hauteurs de Gâtine 120-121 G 5
Haut-Mbomou 164-165 K 7
Haut-Ransbeek 128 II b 2
Hauts-Bassins 168-169 D 3
Haut-Zaïre 172 E 1
Hauz = Al-Ḩawūz 166-167 B 4
Havana, FL 78-79 G 5
Havana, IL 70-71 E 5
Havana, ND 68-69 H 3
Havana = La Habana 64-65 K 7
Havasu Lake 74-75 FG 5
Have Bank, La — 63 D 6
Havel 118 F 2
Ḩavelī 138-139 D 2
Havelock 72-73 GH 2
Havelock, NC 80-81 H 3
Havenbuurt 128 I b 1
Haverford, PA 84 III b 1
Haverford College 84 III b 1
Haverford Township Park 84 III a 2
Haverfordwest 119 D 6
Haverhill, MA 72-73 L 3
Haverhill, NH 72-73 KL 3
Hāveri 140 B 3
Havering, London- 129 II c 1
Haverstraw, NY 72-73 JK 4
Havertown, PA 84 III ab 2
Havilhanlan 136-137 J 3
Havlíčkův Brod 118 G 4
Havøysund 116-117 L 2
Havre, MT 64-65 DE 2
Havre, le — 120-121 GH 4
Havre-Aubert 63 F 4
Havre de Grace, MD 72-73 HJ 5
Havre-Saint-Pierre 56-57 Y 7
Havsa 136-137 B 2
Havza 136-137 F 2
Hawai = Hawaii 148-149 ef 4
Hawaii 148-149 ef 4
Hawaiian Gardens, CA 83 III d 3
Hawaiian Islands 148-149 d 3-e 4
Hawaiian Ridge 156-157 JK 3
Hawaii Volcanoes National Park 78-79 e 3
Hawal 168-169 J 3
Hawarden 61 E 5
Hawarden, IA 68-69 H 4
Hawārīyah, Al- 166-167 M 1
Hawash, Wadi — = Haouach 164-165 J 5
Ḩawashīyah, Wādī — 173 C 3
Ḩawātah, Al- 164-165 LM 6
Hâwd 164-165 NO 7
Ḩawḑ, Al- [DZ] 166-167 J 4
Ḩawḑ, Al- [RIM] 164-165 C 5
Ḩawḑ al-Gharbī, Al- 168-169 C 1
Ḩawḑ ash-Sharqī, Al- 168-169 D 1
Hawea, Lake — 161 C 7
Hawera 158-159 OP 7
Hawesville, KY 70-71 G 7
Hawi, HI 78-79 e 2
Hawick 119 E 4
Ḩawīzah, Hawr al- 136-137 M 7
Hawke, Cape — 158-159 K 6
Hawke Bay 158-159 P 7
Hawker 158-159 G 6
Hawkes, Mount — 53 A 32-33
Hawke's Bay 161 G 4
Hawkesbury 72-73 J 2
Hawkesbury Island 60 C 3
Hawkes Pond 84 I b 1
Hawk Inlet, AK 58-59 U 7
Hawkins, WI 70-71 E 3
Hawkinsville, GA 80-81 E 4
Hawk Junction 62 J 2
Hawk Lake 62 C 3
Hawks, MI 70-71 HJ 3
Hawksbill Cay 88-89 H 2
Hawk Springs, WY 68-69 D 5
Hawley, MN 70-71 BC 2
Hawley, TX 76-77 E 6
Ḩawrah 134-135 F 7
Ḩawrah, Al- 134-135 F 8
Hawr al-Ḩabbānīyah 136-137 K 6
Hawr al-Ḩammār 134-135 F 4
Hawr al-Ḩawīzah 136-137 M 7
Hawr al-Jiljilah 136-137 L 6
Ḩawrān, Wādī — 134-135 E 4
Hawr ar-Razazah 136-137 KL 6
Hawr as-Sa'dīyah 136-137 M 6
Hawr as-Sanīyah 136-137 M 7
Hawr as-Suwayqīyah 136-137 LM 6
Hawr Awdah 136-137 M 7
Hawr Dalmaj 136-137 L 6
Haw River 80-81 G 3
Ḩawşah 136-137 G 8
Ḩawsh 'Īsā 173 B 2
Hawston 174-175 C 8
Ḩawṭah, Al- = Al-Ḩillah 134-135 F 6
Hawthorn, FL 80-81 bc 2
Hawthorn, Melbourne- 161 II c 1
Hawthorne, CA 83 III b 2
Hawthorne, NV 74-75 D 3
Hawthorne Municipal Airport 83 III bc 2
Hawthorne Race Track 83 II a 1-2
Ḩawūz, Al- 166-167 B 4
Haxby, MT 68-69 C 2
Haxtun, CO 68-69 E 5
Hay [AUS] 158-159 HJ 6
Hay, Mount — 58-59 T 7
Ḩāy, Wād al- 166-167 E 2
Hayabuchi 155 III a 2
Hayang 144-145 G 5
Haycock, AK 58-59 G 4
Haydar dağı 136-137 DE 4
Haydarpaşa, İstanbul- 154 I b 3
Hayden, AZ 74-75 H 6
Hayden, CO 68-69 C 5
Haydrah 166-167 L 2
Hayes, LA 78-79 C 5
Hayes, SD 68-69 F 3
Hayes, London- [GB, Bromley] 129 II bc 2
Hayes, London- [GB, Hillingdon] 129 II a 1
Hayes, Mount — 56-57 G 5
Hayes Center, NE 68-69 F 5
Hayes Glacier 58-59 L 6
Hayes Halvø 56-57 XY 2
Hayes River 56-57 S 6
Ha Yeung 155 I b 2
Hayfield, MN 70-71 D 4
Hayfork, CA 66-67 B 5
Hay Lake = Habay 56-57 N 6
Hay Lakes 61 B 4
Hay-les-Roses, l' 129 I c 2
Haylow, GA 80-81 E 5
Haymana 136-137 E 3
Haymana yaylâsı 136-137 E 3
Ḩaymūr, Ābār — 173 CD 6
Ḩaymūr, Wādī — 173 C 6
Haynesville, LA 78-79 C 4
Hayneville, AL 78-79 F 4
Hayrabolu 136-137 B 2
Hayrabolu deresi 136-137 B 2
Hayrat 136-137 J 2
Hayrīr, Al- 166-167 L 7
Hay River [AUS] 158-159 G 4
Hay River [CDN, place] 56-57 NO 5
Hay River [CDN, river] 56-57 N 6
Ḩays 134-135 E 8
Hays, KS 64-65 G 4
Hays, MT 68-69 B 2
Ḩaysī, Bi'r al- 173 D 3
Hay Springs, NE 68-69 E 4
Haystack Mountain 72-73 K 3
Haystack Peak 74-75 G 3
Hayti, MO 78-79 E 2
Hayti, SD 68-69 H 3
Hayton's Falls 171 CD 3
Hayward, CA 74-75 BC 4
Hayward, WI 70-71 E 2
Haywood 61 J 6
Ḩayy, Al- 134-135 F 4
Ḩayyā 164-165 M 5
Hazak 136-137 J 4
Hazārān, Kūh-e — = Kūh-e Hezārān 134-135 H 5
Hazard, KY 64-65 K 4
Hazārībāgh 138-139 K 5-6
Hazārībāgh Range 138-139 JK 6
Ḩaẕawẓā' 136-137 GH 7
Hazebrouck 120-121 J 3
Hazel Creek River 62 A 2
Hazel Green, IL 83 II a 2
Hazel Park 84 II b 2
Hazel Park, MI 84 II b 2
Hazel Park Race Track 84 II b 2
Hazelton Mountains 60 CD 2
Hazelton Peak 68-69 C 3
Hazen, AR 78-79 D 3
Hazen, ND 68-69 F 2
Hazen, NV 74-75 D 3
Hazen Strait 56-57 OP 2
Hazīm, Al- 136-137 G 7
Ḩazimī, Wādī al- 136-137 J 6
Hazipur = Hājīpur 138-139 K 5
Hazlehurst, GA 80-81 E 5
Hazlehurst, MS 78-79 D 5
Hazleton, PA 72-73 J 4
Hazlett, Lake 158-159 E 4
Ḩazm, Al- 173 E 3
Hazo 136-137 J 3
Hazro 136-137 J 3
Hazul, Al- = Al-Huzul 136-137 K 8
Hazuur 174-175 C 4
Hazzān an-Naṣr 173 C 6
Headland, AL 78-79 G 5
Headquarters, ID 66-67 F 2
Heads, The — 66-67 A 4
Healdsburg, CA 74-75 B 3
Healdton, OK 76-77 F 5
Healesville 160 GH 6
Healy, AK 58-59 N 5
Healy, KS 68-69 F 6
Healy Lake 58-59 P 5
Healy River 58-59 P 4
Heard 50-51 N 8
Hearne, TX 76-77 F 7
Hearst 56-57 U 8
Hearst Island 53 BC 30-31
Heart Butte 68-69 EF 2
Heart Butte Reservoir = Lake Tschida 68-69 EF 2
Heart River 68-69 F 2
Heart's Content 63 K 4
Heath, Río — 96-97 G 8
Heath Point 63 F 3
Heaven, Temple of — 155 II b 2
Heavener, OK 76-77 G 5
Hebbronville, TX 76-77 E 9
Hebei 142-143 LM 4
Heber, UT 66-67 H 5
Heber Springs, AR 78-79 C 3
Hebgen Lake 66-67 H 3
Hebi 146-147 E 4
Hebo, OR 66-67 AB 3
Hebrides, Sea of the — 119 C 3
Hebron, ND 68-69 EF 2
Hebron, NE 68-69 H 5
Hebron [CDN] 56-57 Y 6
Hebron [ZA] 174-175 H 3
Hébron = Al-Halīl 136-137 F 7
Hebron = Windsorton 174-175 F 5
Hecate Strait 56-57 K 7
Heceta Head 66-67 A 3
Heceta Island 58-59 vw 9
Hecheng 146-147 D 10
Hechuan 142-143 JK 5
Hecla 62 A 2
Hecla, SD 68-69 GH 3
Hecla and Griper Bay 56-57 O 2
Hectorspruit 174-175 JK 3
Hede 116-117 E 6
He Devil Mountain 66-67 E 3
Hedien = Khotan 142-143 DE 4
Hedingen 128 IV a 2
Hedjas 134-135 D 5-6
Hedley 66-67 CD 1
Hedley, TX 76-77 D 5
Hedmark 116-117 D 6-E 7
Hedrick, IA 70-71 D 5
Heerlen 120-121 KL 3
Hefei 142-143 M 5
Hefeng 146-147 BC 7
Heffron Park 161 I b 2
Heflin, AL 78-79 G 4
Hegang 142-143 OP 2
Hegbach 128 III b 2
Hegnau 128 IV b 1
Hēgumenítsa 122-123 J 6
He Hu = Ge Hu 146-147 G 6
Heian-hokudō = P'yŏngan-pukto 144-145 E 2-3
Heian-nandō = P'yŏngan-namdo 144-145 EF 3
Ḩeidarābād = Ḩeydarābād 136-137 L 4
Heide [D] 118 D 1
Heide [Namibia] 174-175 B 2
Heidelberg, MS 78-79 E 5
Heidelberg [D] 118 D 4
Heidelberg [ZA, Kaapland] 174-175 D 8
Heidelberg [ZA, Transvaal] 174-175 H 4
Heidelberg, Melbourne- 161 II c 1
Heidoti 98-99 K 2
Ḩeifa 134-135 CD 4
Height of Land 63 A 5
Hei-ho = Aihui 142-143 O 1
Heijo = P'yŏngyang 142-143 NO 4
Heilar He = Chajlar gol 142-143 N 1-2
Heilbron 174-175 GH 4
Heilbronn 118 D 4
Heiligensee, Berlin- 130 III a 1
Heilongjiang [TJ, administrative unit] 142-143 M-P 2
Heilong Jiang [TJ, river] 142-143 O 1
Heilsberg 128 III b 1
Hei-lung Chiang = Heilong Jiang 142-143 O 1
Heilung Kiang = Heilong Jiang 142-143 O 1
Heimaey 116-117 c 3
Heimfeld, Hamburg- 130 I a 2
Heine Creek, AK 58-59 N 4
Heinersdorf, Berlin- 130 III b 1
Heinola 116-117 M 7
Heinsburg 61 C 4
Heinze Bay = Bōlkyīywā 150-151 A 5
Heir, El- = Qaşr al-Ḩayr 136-137 H 5
Heishan 144-145 CD 2
Ḩeisī, Bi'r el- = Bi'r al-Ḩaysī 173 D 3
Hejaz 131 G 7-8
Hejaz = Al-Hijaz 134-135 D 5-6
Hejian 146-147 EF 2
Hejiang [TJ, place] 146-147 C 11
He Jiang [TJ, river] 146-147 C 10
Hejie 146-147 C 9
Hejin 146-147 C 4
Hekimdağ = Taşköprü 136-137 D 3
Hekimhan 136-137 G 3
Hekla 116-117 d 3
Hekou = Hekouji 146-147 F 5
Hekouji 146-147 F 5
Hekpoort 174-175 G 3
Helagsfjället 116-117 E 6
Helder, Den — 120-121 K 2
Hele 150-151 H 3
Helechos, Cañada de los — 91 I b 2
Helem 141 C 2
Helen, Mount — 74-75 E 4
Helena, AR 64-65 H 5
Helena, GA 80-81 E 4
Helena, MT 64-65 D 2
Helena, OK 76-77 E 4
Helendale, CA 74-75 E 5
Helenenau 130 III c 1
Helen Reef 148-149 K 6
Heleysund 116-117 l 5
Helgeland 116-117 E 5-F 4
Helgoland 118 C 1
Helicoide, Caracas- 91 II b 2
Helicoide de la Roca Tarpeya 91 II b 2
Heligoland = Helgoland 118 C 1
Heligoland Bay 118 C 1
Helikōn 122-123 K 6
He Ling 150-151 G 3
Heliopolis 170 II b 1
Heliopolis = Al-Qahirah-Mişr al-Jadīdah 173 BC 2
Heliopolis = Ḩammān Awlād 'Alī 166-167 K 1
Heliqi = Helixi 146-147 G 6
Heliu = Heliuji 146-147 F 5
Heliuji 146-147 F 5
Helix, OR 66-67 D 3
Helixi 146-147 G 6
Hella 116-117 c 3
Hellabrunn, Tierpark — 130 II b 2
Helleland 116-117 B 8
Hellenikòn, Aerolimēn — 113 IV a 2
Hellepoort = Portes de l'Enfer 172 E 3
Hellersdorf, Berlin- 130 III c 1
Hellín 120-121 G 9
Hell-Ville 172 J 4
Helmand Rōd 134-135 K 4
Helmeringhausen 174-175 B 3-4
Helmet Mount 58-59 P 3
Helmond 120-121 KL 3
Helmsdale 119 E 2
Helmstedt 118 E 2
Helmville, MT 66-67 G 2
Helodranon'i Mahajamba 172 J 4-5
Helodranon'i Narinda 172 J 4
Helodrona Antongila 172 JK 5
Helong 142-143 O 3
Helper, UT 74-75 H 3
Helpmekaar 174-175 J 5
Helsingborg 116-117 DE 9
Helsingfors = Helsinki 116-117 L 7
Helsingør 116-117 DE 9
Helsinki 116-117 L 7
Helska, Mierzeja — 118 J 1
Heluo = Hele 150-151 H 3
Helvécia [BR] 100-101 E 9
Helvecia [RA] 106-107 G 3
Helvetia 174-175 G 5
Helwâk 140 A 2
Ḩelwân = Ḩulwān 164-165 L 3
Hemagiri 138-139 J 6-7
Hemāvati 140 B 4
Hemet, CA 74-75 E 6
Hemingford, NE 68-69 E 4
Hemphill, TX 78-79 C 5
Hempstead, NY 72-73 K 4
Hempstead, TX 76-77 F 7
Hempstead Harbor 82 III d 1-e 2
Hempstead Lake State Park 82 III de 2
Henan 142-143 L 5
Henares 120-121 F 8
Henashi-saki 144-145 M 2
Henbury 158-159 F 4
Ḩencha, El — = Al-Hanshah 166-167 M 2
Henchîr Lebna = Hanshīr Labnah 166-167 M 1
Henchow = Hengyang 142-143 L 6
Hendawashi 171 C 3
Hendaye 120-121 FG 7
Hendek 136-137 D 2
Henderson, KY 64-65 J 4
Henderson, NC 80-81 G 2
Henderson, NV 74-75 F 4
Henderson, TN 78-79 E 3
Henderson, TX 76-77 G 6
Henderson [RA] 106-107 G 6
Henderson Bay 72-73 H 2-3
Hendersonville, NC 80-81 E 3
Hendersonville, TN 78-79 F 2
Hendon, London- 129 II b 1
Hendriktop 98-99 K 2
Hendrik Verwoerd Dam 174-175 FG 6
Hendrina 174-175 HJ 4
Heng'ang = Hengyang 142-143 L 6
Heng-chan = Hengyang 142-143 L 6
Heng-chou = Heng Xian 142-143 K 7
Hengdong 146-147 D 8
Hengduan Shan 142-143 H 6
Hengelo 120-121 L 2
Hengfeng 146-147 F 7
Henghsien = Heng Xian 142-143 K 7
Heng Sha 146-147 HJ 6
Hengshan [TJ, Hunan] 142-143 L 6
Hengshan [TJ, Shaanxi] 146-147 B 3
Heng Shan [TJ, Shanxi] 146-147 D 2
Hengshan = Hengyang 142-143 L 6
Hengshui 142-143 LM 4
Heng Xian 142-143 K 7
Hengyang 142-143 L 6
Henik Lake = South Henik Lake 56-57 R 5
Henlopen, Cape — 72-73 J 5
Henly, TX 76-77 E 7
Hennebont 120-121 F 5
Hennenman 174-175 G 4
Hennersdorf [A] 113 I b 2
Hennesberget 116-117 E 4
Hennessey, OK 76-77 F 4
Henning, MN 70-71 C 2
Henrietta, TX 76-77 E 6
Henrietta Maria, Cape — 56-57 U 6
Henriette, ostrov — 132-133 ef 2
Henrique de Carvalho = Saurimo 172 D 3
Henry, IL 70-71 F 5
Henry, NE 68-69 DE 4
Henry, SD 68-69 H 3
Henry, Cape — 80-81 J 2
Henry, Mount — 66-67 F 1
Henryetta, OK 76-77 FG 5
Henry, Île aux — 82 I b 2
Henry Kater Peninsula 56-57 XY 4
Henry Mountains 74-75 H 3-4
Henrys Fork 66-67 H 3-4
Hensall 72-73 F 3
Henson Creek 82 II b 2
Henty 160 H 5
Henzada = Hinthâda 148-149 BC 3
Heping 146-147 E 9
Hepo = Jiexi 146-147 E 10
Heppner, OR 66-67 D 3
Heppner Junction, OR 66-67 CD 3
Hepu 142-143 K 7
Hepworth 72-73 F 2
Hequ 146-147 C 2
Heraclea 122-123 G 5
Heraclea = Ereğli 134-135 C 2
Héradhsflói 116-117 fg 2
Héradhsvötn 116-117 d 2
Herákleia 122-123 L 7
Herákleia = Ereğli 134-135 C 2
Hērákleion 122-123 L 8
Herakol dağı 136-137 K 4
Herald, ostrov — 52 B 36
Heras, Las — [RA, Mendoza] 106-107 C 4
Heras, Las — [RA, Santa Cruz] 111 C 7
Herāt 134-135 J 4
Herbert 61 E 5
Herbert C. Legg Lake 83 III d 1
Herbert Island 58-59 l 4
Herbertsdale 174-175 DE 8
Hèrbertville 62 PQ 2
Herb Lake 61 HJ 3
Herblay 129 I b 2
Hercegnovi 122-123 H 4
Herchmer 61 L 2
Hercilio, Rio — 102-103 GH 7
Heredia 88-89 DE 9
Hereford, TX 76-77 C 5
Hereford [GB] 119 E 5
Hereford [RA] 106-107 F 5
Herefoss 116-117 C 8
Herero 174-175 C 2
Hereroland 172 CD 6
Herferswil 128 IV a 2
Herford 118 D 2
Herglad = Hirglah 166-167 M 1
Herington, KS 68-69 H 6
Heri Rud = Harī Rūd 134-135 J 4
Herīs 136-137 M 3
Heritage Range 53 B 28-A 29
Herlen He 142-143 M 2
Herlitzka 106-107 H 1
Herman, MN 70-71 BC 3
Hermanas 86-87 K 4
Hermanas, NM 74-75 JK 7
Hermanas, Las — 106-107 G 6
Herman Barnett Stadium 85 III a 1
Herman Brown Park 85 III bc 1
Herma Ness 119 F 1
Hermann, MO 70-71 E 6
Hermann Eckstein Park 170 V b 1
Hermann Park 85 III b 2
Hermannsburg [AUS] 158-159 F 4
Hermannskogel 113 I b 1
Hermanos, Cerro — 108-109 C 6
Hermansverk 116-117 B 7
Hermansville, MI 70-71 G 3
Hermanus 174-175 C 8
Hermel, El — = Al-Harmal 136-137 G 5
Hermes, Cape — = Kaap Hermes 174-175 H 6
Hermes, Kaap — 174-175 H 6
Hermidale 160 H 3
Hermiston, OR 66-67 D 3
Hermitage 63 HJ 4
Hermitage, AR 78-79 C 4
Hermitage Bay 63 H 4
Hermite, Isla — 111 C 9
Hermit Islands 148-149 N 7
Hermleigh, TX 76-77 D 6
Hermôn = Jabal as-Sayḩ 136-137 FG 6
Hèrmos = Gediz çayı 136-137 C 3
Hermosa, SD 68-69 E 4
Hermosa, La — 94-95 F 5
Hermosa Beach, CA 83 III b 2
Hermosillo 64-65 D 6
Hermoso Campo 104-105 F 10
Hermúpolis 122-123 L 7
Hernals, Wien- 113 I b 2
Hernandarias 111 F 3
Hernández 106-107 GH 4
Hernando 106-107 EF 4
Hernando, MS 78-79 E 3
Herman M. Miraval 104-105 EF 10
Herndon, KS 68-69 F 6
Herning 116-117 C 9
Héroes Chapultepec, Ciudad de México- 91 I c 2
Héroes de Churubusco, Ixtapalapa- 91 I c 2
Heroica Alvarado = Alvarado 64-65 GH 8
Heroica Caborca 64-65 D 5
Heroica Cárdenas 86-87 O 8-9
Heroica Guaymas 64-65 D 6
Heroica Matamoros = Matamoros 64-65 G 6
Heroica Nogales 64-65 D 5
Heroica Puebla de Zaragoza = Puebla de Zaragoza 64-65 G 8
Heroica Tlapacoyan 86-87 M 7-8
Heroica Veracruz = Veracruz 64-65 GH 8
Heroica Zitácuaro 86-87 K 8
Heron, MT 66-67 F 1
Heron Bay 70-71 G 1
Herong 146-147 CD 6
Heron Lake 70-71 C 4
Herowabad = Khalkhāl 136-137 N 4
Herradura 104-105 G 10
Herradura, La — 108-109 F 7
Herreid, SD 68-69 FG 3
Herrera [E] 120-121 F 7
Herrera [PA] 88-89 F 10
Herrera [RA, Entre Ríos] 106-107 H 4
Herrera [RA, Santiago del Estero] 106-107 F 2
Herrera del Duque 120-121 E 9
Herrera de Pisuerga 120-121 EF 7
Herrera Vegas 106-107 G 6
Herrick 158-159 J 8
Herrin, IL 70-71 F 7
Herrington Island 72-73 DE 5
Herrington Lake 70-71 H 7
Herriot 61 H 2
Herrliberg 128 IV b 2
Herschel [CDN, island] 58-59 S 2
Herschel [CDN, place] 61 D 5
Herschel [ZA] 174-175 G 6
Herschel Island 56-57 J 3-4
Hersham 129 II a 2
Hersilia 106-107 G 2-3
Herson = Cherson 126-127 F 3
Hertford 119 FG 6
Hertford, NC 80-81 H 2
Hertogenbosch, 's- 120-121 KL 3
Hertzogville 174-175 F 5
Hervey Bay 158-159 K 4-5
Hervey-Jonction 72-73 K 1
Herẕliya 173 D 1
Herzog-Ernst-Bucht 53 B 32-33
Heshjīn 136-137 N 4
Heshui [TJ, Gansu] 146-147 B 4
Heshui [TJ, Guangdong] 146-147 CD 10
Heshun 146-147 D 3
Hesperia, CA 74-75 E 5
Hesperus, CO 68-69 BC 7
Hess Creek 58-59 N 4
Hesse = Hessen 118 D 3
Hessen 118 D 3
Hess Mount 58-59 O 5
Hesteyri 116-117 b 1
Heston, London- 129 II a 2
Heṭan 140 E 7
Hetian [TJ, Fujian] 146-147 F 9
Hetian [TJ, Guangdong] 146-147 E 10
Het IJ 128 I a 1
Het Nieuwe Meer 128 I a 1-2
Hetou 146-147 B 11
Het Sas 128 II b 1
Het Schouw 128 I b 1
Hettinger, ND 68-69 E 2-3
Hettipola 140 DE 7
Heuglin, Kapp — 116-117 lm 5
Heul, De — 128 I a 1
Heuningspruit 174-175 G 4
Heuningvleisoutpan 174-175 E 4
Heves 118 K 5
Hewlett, NY 82 III d 3
Hexi 146-147 F 9
He Xian [TJ, Anhui] 146-147 G 6
He Xian [TJ, Guangxi Zhuangzu Zizhiqu] 142-143 L 7
Hexigten Qi 142-143 M 3
Hexrivier 174-175 C 7
Hexrivierberge 174-175 C 7
Hext, TX 76-77 E 7
Hextable 129 II c 2
Hexue = Haoxue 146-147 D 6
Heyang [TJ, Shaanxi] 146-147 C 4
Heyang [TJ, Shandong] 146-147 G 4
Heyburn Lake 76-77 F 4-5
Ḩeydarābād 136-137 L 4
Heyuan 146-147 E 10
Heywood [AUS] 160 EF 7
Hezārān, Kūh-e- 134-135 H 5
Heze 142-143 M 4
Hezelton 56-57 L 6
Hialeah, FL 80-81 c 4
Hiawatha, KS 70-71 C 6
Hiawatha, UT 74-75 H 3
Hibbing, MN 64-65 H 2
Hibbs, Point — 160 b 3
Hibiya Park 155 III b 1-2
Hichiro-wan = zaliv Terpenija 132-133 b 8
Hickman, KY 78-79 E 2
Hickman, NE 68-69 H 5
Hickman, NM 74-75 JK 5
Hickman, Mount — 58-59 x 8
Hickmann 104-105 E 8
Hickory, NC 80-81 F 3
Hickory, Lake — 80-81 F 3
Hickory Hills, IL 83 II a 2
Hicksville, OH 70-71 H 5
Hico, TX 76-77 EF 6
Hidaka 144-145 c 2
Hidaka-sammyaku 144-145 c 2
Hidalgo [MEX, Coahuila] 76-77 DE 9
Hidalgo [MEX, Hidalgo] 64-65 G 7
Hidalgo [MEX, Tamaulipas] 86-87 L 5
Hidalgo, Ciudad — 86-87 K 8
Hidalgo, Salinas de — 86-87 JK 6
Hidalgo del Parral 64-65 E 6
Hida sammyaku 144-145 L 4-5
Hiddensee 118 F 1
Hidden Valley, TX 85 III b 1
Hidrolândia 102-103 H 2
Hiem, Mu'o'ng — 150-151 D 2
Hienghène 158-159 MN 4
Hiệp Đu'c 150-151 G 5
Hierápetra 122-123 L 8
Hierisós 122-123 KL 5
Hieropolis = Manbij 136-137 GH 4
Hierra, La — 106-107 H 3
Hierro 164-165 A 3
Hietzing, Wien- 113 I b 2
Higashiōizumi, Tōkyō- 155 III a 1
Higasiōsaka 144-145 KL 5
Higbee, MO 70-71 D 6
Higgins, TX 76-77 D 4
Higgins Lake 70-71 H 3
Higham Hill, London- 129 II b 1
High Atlas 164-165 CD 2
Highflats 174-175 J 6
High Hill River 61 L 3
High Island 70-71 GH 3
High Island, TX 76-77 GH 8
High Island = Pulau Serasan 150-151 G 11
High Junk Peak 155 I b 2
Highland, IL 70-71 F 6
Highland, WA 66-67 E 2
Highland Acres, Houston-, TX 85 III b 1
Highland Ind. Park North, Houston-, TX 85 III b 1
Highland Park 84 I c 1
Highland Park, IL 70-71 G 4
Highland Park, MI 72-73 E 3
Highland Park, Los Angeles-, CA 83 III c 1
Highland Peak 74-75 F 4
Highmore, SD 68-69 G 3
High Point, NC 64-65 KL 4
High Prairie 56-57 NO 6
High River 60 KL 4
Highrock 61 HJ 3
High Rock Lake 80-81 FG 3
Highrock Lake [CDN, Manitoba] 61 H 3
Highrock Lake [CDN, Saskatchewan] 61 F 2
High Springs, FL 80-81 b 2
Highwood, MT 66-67 H 2
Highwood Peak 66-67 H 2
Higuera, La — 106-107 B 2
Higuerote 94-95 HJ 2
Hiidenmaa = Hiiumaa 124-125 CD 4
Hiiumaa 124-125 CD 4
Ḩijārah, Şaḩrā' al- [IRQ] 136-137 L 7
Ḩijārah, Şaḩrā' al- [Saudi Arabia] 136-137 JK 8
Ḩijāz, Al- 134-135 D 5-6
Ḩijāzah 173 C 5
Hijo = Tagum 148-149 J 5
Hijos, Cerro los — 96-97 B 5
Hikari 144-145 H 6
Hikkaduwa 140 DE 7
Hiko, NV 74-75 F 4
Hikone 144-145 L 5
Hiko-san 144-145 H 6
Hikurangi [NZ, mountain] 161 H 3-4
Hikurangi [NZ, place] 161 F 2
Hilāl, Jabal — 173 CD 2
Hilālī, Wādī al- 136-137 J 7
Hilario Ascasubi 106-107 F 7
Hilbert, WI 70-71 FG 3
Hildesheim 118 DE 2
Hilger, MT 68-69 B 2
Hill, MT 66-67 H 1
Hillah, Al- [IRQ] 134-135 E 4
Ḩillah, Al- [Saudi Arabia] 134-135 F 6
Hill Bāndh = Panchêt Pahār Bāndh 138-139 L 6
Hill City, ID 66-67 F 4
Hill City, KS 68-69 G 6
Hill City, MN 70-71 D 2
Hill City, SD 68-69 E 3-4
Hill Crest, PA 84 III b 1
Hillcrest Cemetery 85 II b 2
Hillcrest Heights, MD 82 II b 2
Hillerød 116-117 DE 10
Hillī 138-139 M 5

300 Hatia

Hillman, MN 70-71 D 2-3
Hillmond 61 D 4
Hills, MN 68-69 H 4
Hillsboro, GA 80-81 E 4
Hillsboro, IL 70-71 F 6
Hillsboro, NC 80-81 G 2
Hillsboro, ND 68-69 H 2
Hillsboro, NH 72-73 L 3
Hillsboro, NM 76-77 A 6
Hillsboro, OH 72-73 E 5
Hillsboro, OR 66-67 B 3
Hillsboro, TX 76-77 F 6
Hillsboro Canal 80-81 c 3
Hillsborough Bay 63 E 4
Hillsdale, MI 70-71 H 5
Hillside, AZ 74-75 G 5
Hillside, NJ 82 III a 2
Hillsport 70-71 H 1
Hillston 158-159 HJ 6
Hillsville, VA 80-81 F 2
Hilltop 174-175 H 5
Hilltop, NJ 84 III c 3
Hillwood, VA 82 II a 2
Hilmānd, Dārya-ye- = Helmand Rōd 134-135 K 4
Hilmar, CA 74-75 C 4
Hilo, HI 148-149 ef 4
Hilsa 138-139 K 5
Hilshire Village, TX 85 III a 2
Hilton Head Island 80-81 F 4
Hilts, CA 66-67 B 5
Hilu-Babor = Ïlubabor 164-165 LM 7
Hilvan = Karaçurun 136-137 H 4
Hilversum 120-121 K 2
Himāchal Pradesh 134-135 M 4
Himālaya 134-135 L 4-P 5
Himālchūli 138-139 K 3
Himatnagar 138-139 D 6
Himeji 142-143 P 5
Himes, WY 68-69 B 3
Hime-saki 144-145 M 3
Himeville 174-175 H 5
Himezi = Himeji 142-143 P 5
Himi 144-145 L 4
Ḥimş 134-135 D 4
Hinai 144-145 N 2
Hinako, Pulau-pulau — 152-153 B 5
Hinche 88-89 KL 5
Hinchinbrook Entrance 58-59 OP 6
Hinchinbrook Island [AUS] 158-159 J 3
Hinchinbrook Island [USA] 58-59 OP 6
Hinckley, MN 70-71 D 2-3
Hinckley, UT 74-75 G 3
Hinḍaon = Hindaun 138-139 F 4
Hindaun 138-139 F 4
Hindes, TX 76-77 E 8
Hindi 138-139 K 4
Hindia, Lautan — 148-149 B 6-D 8
Hindīyah, Al- 136-137 KL 6
Hindoli 138-139 E 5
Hinds Lake 63 H 3
Hindūbāgh 134-135 K 4
Hindū Kush 134-135 KL 3
Hindupur 134-135 M 8
Hindupura = Hindupur 134-135 M 8
Hindustan 134-135 M 5-O 6
Hindusthān = Hindustan 134-135 M 5-O 6
Hines, FL 80-81 b 2
Hines, OR 66-67 D 4
Hines Creek 56-57 N 6
Hinesville, GA 80-81 F 5
Hingan = Ankang 146-147 B 5
Hinganghāt 138-139 G 7
Hingham, MA 84 I c 3
Hingham Bay 84 I c 3
Hinghsien = Xing Xian 146-147 C 2
Hinghwa = Xinghua 142-143 M 6
Hinghwa = Xinghua 146-147 GH 5
Hinghwa Wan = Xinghua Wan 146-147 G 5
Hingīr = Hemagiri 138-139 J 6-7
Hingjen = Xingren 142-143 K 6
Hingkwo = Xingguo 146-147 E 8
Hingol 134-135 K 5
Hingoli 134-135 M 7
Hingshan = Xingshan 146-147 C 6
Hingtang = Xingtang 146-147 E 2
Hingurakgoḍa 140 E 6-7
Hinis 136-137 J 3
Hinkley, CA 74-75 E 5
Hinlopenstretet 116-117 kl 5
Hinna = Ïmî 164-165 N 7
Hinnøy 116-117 FG 3
Hino, Yokohama- 155 III a 3
Hinojo 106-107 GH 6
Hinojosa del Duque 120-121 E 9
Hinomi-saki 144-145 J 5
Hinş 136-137 J 2
Hinsdale, MT 68-69 C 1
Hinterbrühl 113 I ab 2
Hinteregg 128 IV b 2
Hinterrhein 118 D 5
Hinthāda 148-149 BC 3
Hinw, WA 80-81 F 2
Hinton [CDN] 56-57 N 7
Hinzir burnu 136-137 F 4
Hinzir dağı 136-137 FG 3
Hipocapac 96-97 F 10
Hipódromo Argentino 110 III b 1
Hipódromo de la Rinconada 91 II b 2
Hipódromo de las Americas 91 I b 2
Hipódromo de la Zarzuela 113 III a 2
Hipódromo de México 91 I bc 2
Hipódromo de Techo 91 III b 3
Hipólito 86-87 K 5
Hippodrome de Al-Jazā'ir 170 I b 2
Hippodrome de Longchamp 129 I bc 2

Hippodrome de Tremblay 129 I cd 2
Hippodrome de Vincennes 129 I c 2
Hippodrome Saint-Cloud 129 I b 2
Hippo Regius = Annābah 164-165 F 1
Hiraan 164-165 ab 3
Hirado 144-145 G 6
Hirado-shima 144-145 G 6
Hirakawa 155 III d 3
Hirākūd Reservoir 138-139 J 7
Hiranghātā 138-139 M 6-N 7
Ḥirāpur 138-139 G 5
Ḥirāsah, Rā's al- 166-167 K 1
Hirata 144-145 J 5
Hirato shima = Hirado-shima 144-145 G 6
Hiratori 144-145 c 2
Hireimis, Qārat el — = Qārat Huraymis 136-137 B 7
Hirekerūr 140 B 3
Hirfanlı baraji 136-137 E 3
Hirglah 166-167 M 1
Ḥirlāu 122-123 M 2
Hirondelles, Cap des — = Mui Yên 150-151 G 6
Hirono 144-145 N 4
Hiroo 144-145 c 2
Hirosaki 142-143 QR 3
Hiroshima 142-143 P 5
Hirosima = Hiroshima 142-143 P 5
Hirota-wan 144-145 NO 3
Hirr, Wādī al- 136-137 K 7
Hirschau [D, Oberbayern] 130 II b 1
Hirschgarten, Berlin- 130 III c 2
Hirschstetten, Wien- 113 I bc 2
Hirslanden, Zürich- 128 IV b 1
Hirson 120-121 K 4
Hirtshals 116-117 C 9
Hirzel 128 IV b 2
Hisaka-jima 144-145 G 6
Hisār 134-135 M 5
Ḥiṣār, Kohe — 134-135 K 4
Hisarönü 136-137 DE 2
Ḥismā 173 DE 3
Ḥismet 'Umar, Bīr — = Bi'r Ḥasmat 'Umar 173 CD 7
Hispaniola 64-65 MN 8
Hissār = Hisār 134-135 M 5
Ḥiṣṣar, Kūh-e- = Kōhe Ḥiṣār 134-135 K 4
Histiaía 122-123 K 6
Hisua 138-139 K 5
Ḥit 136-137 K 6
Hita 144-145 H 6
Hitachi 142-143 R 4
Hitachi-Ōta = Hitati-Ōta 144-145 N 4
Hitati = Hitachi 142-143 R 4
Hitchland, TX 76-77 D 4
Hite, UT 74-75 H 4
Hitoyoshi 144-145 H 6
Hitra 116-117 C 6
Hitteren = Hitra 116-117 C 6
Hiuchi-dake 144-145 M 4
Hiuchi-nada 144-145 J 5
Hiw 173 C 4-5
Hiwasa 144-145 K 6
Hiyoshi, Yokohama- 155 III a 2
Hizan = Karasu 136-137 K 3

Hjälmaren 116-117 FG 8
Hjälmar Lake = Hjälmaren 116-117 FG 8
Hjelmelandsvågen 116-117 AB 8
Hjelmsøy 116-117 L 2
Hjørring 116-117 C 9

Hka, Nam — 141 F 5
Hkakabo Rāzī 141 EF 1
Hkamōwa 141 F 8
Hkaunglanbū 141 F 2
Hkaungzaunggwei 150-151 B 5
Hkaw, Lūy — 141 F 5
Hkayan 141 E 7
Hkin'ū 141 D 4
Hkweibūm 148-149 B 2

Hlabisa 174-175 JK 5
Hlaingbwè 148-149 C 3
Hlatikulu 174-175 J 4
Hlegu = Hīigū 141 E 7
Hleo, Ea — 150-151 F 6
Hīigū 141 E 7
Hlobane 174-175 J 4
Hlobyne = Globino 126-127 F 2
Hluhluwe 174-175 K 5
Hluhluwe Game Reserve 174-175 JK 4-5
Hluingbwe = Hlaingbwè 148-149 C 3
Hluti 174-175 J 4

Hmelnizkij = Chmeľnickij 126-127 C 2

Ho 164-165 E 7
Hoa Binh 148-149 DE 2
Hoachanas 174-175 C 2
Hoa Đa 150-151 G 7
Hoadley 60 K 3
Hoai Nho'n 148-149 E 4
Hoang = Huang He 142-143 L 4
Hoang Sa, Quân Đao —
Hoarusib 172 B 5
Hoback Peak 66-67 H 4
Hōban 141 F 4
Hobart, IN 70-71 G 5
Hobart, OK 76-77 E 5
Hobbs, NM 64-65 F 5
Hobbs Coast 53 B 23

Hobe Sound, FL 80-81 cd 3
Hobetsu 144-145 bc 2
Hobhouse 174-175 G 5
Hōbin 141 E 3
Hobo 94-95 D 6
Hoboken, NJ 82 III b 2
Hōbōn 141 E 5
Hobra, el — = Al-Habrah 166-167 J 3
Hobrechtsfelde 130 III c 1
Hobro 116-117 C 9
Höbsögöl Dalay = Chövsgöl nuur 142-143 J 1
Hobson's Bay 161 II b 2
Hobyas 164-165 b 2
Hochbrück 130 II b 1
Hochfeld = Hoëveld [ZA, Oranje-Vrystaat] 174-175 G 5-H 4
Hochfeld = Hoëveld [ZA, Transvaal] 174-175 HJ 4
Hochgolling 118 FG 5
Ho-chi'i = Hexi 146-147 F 9
Ho-chiang = Hejiang 146-147 C 11
Ho Chiang = He Jiang 146-147 C 10
Ho-chien = Hejian 146-147 EF 2
Hoching = Hejin 146-147 C 4
Hochow = Hechuan 142-143 K 5-6
Hochstadt [D] 128 III b 1
Ho-chi'ü = Hequ 146-147 C 2
Ho Chung 155 I b 1
Hochwan = Hechuan 142-143 K 5-6
Hodna, Chott el — = Ash-Shaṭṭ al-Hudnah 164-165 EF 1
Hodna, Monts du — = Jibal al-Hudnah 166-167 J 1-2
Hodna, Plaine du — = Sahl al-Hudnah 166-167 J 2
Hodogaya, Yokohama- 155 III a 3
Hodzana River 58-59 N 3
Hoef, De — 128 I a 2
Hoë Karoo 174-175 C-F 6
Hoek van Holland, Rotterdam-120-121 JK 3
Hoengsŏng 144-145 FG 4
Hoeryŏng 144-145 G 1
Hoeveld [ZA, Oranje-Vrystaat] 174-175 G 5-H 4
Hoëveld [ZA, Transvaal] 174-175 HJ 4
Hoey 61 F 4
Hoeyang 144-145 F 3
Hof 118 E 5
Hofbräuhaus 130 II b 2
Hofburg 113 I b 2
Höfdhakaupstadhur 116-117 cd 2
Hofei = Hefei 142-143 M 5
Hoffman, MN 70-71 BC 3
Hofmeyr [Namibia] 174-175 C 3
Hofmeyr [ZA] 174-175 FG 6
Höfn 116-117 f 2
Hofors 116-117 FG 7
Ḥofrat en Naḥās — = Ḥufrat an-Naḥās 164-165 JK 7
Hofsjökull 116-117 d 2
Hofsós 116-117 d 2
Hofstade 128 II b 1
Hofstande = Hofstade 128 II b 1
Hōfu 144-145 h 5-6
Hōganās 116-117 E 9
Hogan Island 160 c 1
Hogansville, GA 78-79 G 4
Hogatza River 58-59 K 3
Hogback Mountain [USA, Montana] 66-67 GH 3
Hogback Mountain [USA, Nebraska] 68-69 E 5
Hogeland, MT 68-69 B 1
Hogem Range 60 D 1-E 2
Hogg Park 85 II b 1
Hog Island [USA, Michigan] 70-71 H 3
Hog Island [USA, Virginia] 80-81 J 2
Hog River, AK 58-59 K 3
Hoha 174-175 H 6
Hohe Acht 118 C 3
Hohenschönhausen, Berlin-130 III c 1
Hohenwald, TN 78-79 F 3
Hohenzollernkanal 130 III b 1
Hoher Atlas 164-165 CD 2
Hoher Berg [D, Hessen] 128 III b 1
Hohe Tauern 118 F 5
Hohhot = Huhehaote 142-143 L 3
Hoh-kai = Ohōtsuku-kai 144-145 cd 1
Hoholitna River 58-59 J 6
Hohpi = Hebi 146-147 D 4
Ho-hsien = He Xian 146-147 C 9
Ho-hsüeh = Haoxue 146-147 D 6
Hōi An 150-151 G 5
Hoifung = Haifeng 142-143 M 7
Hoihong = Haikang 142-143 KL 7
Hoima 172 F 1
Hoion = Hai'an 142-143 KL 7

Hoisbüttel 130 I b 1
Hoisington, KS 68-69 G 6
Hŏi Xuân 150-151 E 2
Ho-jung = Herong 146-147 CD 6
Höketçe 136-137 G 3
Hokien = Hejian 146-147 EF 2
Hokitika 158-159 NO 8
Hokkaidō [J, administrative unit] 144-145 bc 2
Hokkaidō [J, island] 142-143 RS 3
Hokkō = Peichiang 146-147 H 10
Hoku = Hequ 146-147 C 2
Hokuriku 144-145 L 5-M 4
Holākēķērē = Holakere 140 C 3
Holakere 140 C 3
Holanda 104-105 D 4
Hōlar 116-117 d 2
Holbæk 116-117 D 10
Holbox, Isla — 86-87 R 7
Holbrook 160 H 5
Holbrook, AZ 74-75 HJ 5
Holbrook, ID 66-67 G 4
Holden 61 BC 4
Holden, MO 70-71 CD 6
Holden, UT 74-75 G 3
Holdenville, OK 76-77 F 5
Holdich 108-109 F 5
Holdrege, NE 68-69 G 5
Holē-Narasïpura = Hole Narsïpur 140 C 4
Hole Narsïpur 140 C 4
Holgate, OH 70-71 HJ 5
Holguín 64-65 L 7
Holiday Forest, Houston-, TX 85 III c 1
Holiday Lake Amusement Park 84 III d 1
Holikachuk, AK 58-59 H 5
Ho Ling = He Ling 150-151 G 3
Holitna River 58-59 J 6
Ho-liu = Heliuji 146-147 F 5
Höljes 116-117 E 7
Hollam's Bird Island = Hollams Voëleiland 174-175 A 3
Hollam's Bird Islands = Hollams Voëleilanden 174-175 H 3
Hollams Voëleiland 174-175 A 3
Holland, MI 70-71 GH 4
Holland, NM 76-77 B 6
Hollandale, MS 78-79 D 4
Hollandia = Jayapura 148-149 M 7
Hollick-Kenyon Plateau 53 AB 25-26
Holliday, TX 76-77 E 6
Hollidaysburg, PA 72-73 G 4
Hollis, OK 76-77 E 5
Hollis, New York-, NY 82 III d 2
Hollister, CA 74-75 C 4
Hollister, ID 66-67 F 4
Hollister, MO 78-79 C 2
Hollmann, Cape — 148-149 gh 5
Holly, MI 72-73 E 3
Holly Bluff, MS 78-79 D 4
Holly Hill, FL 80-81 c 2
Holly Hill, SC 80-81 F 4
Holly Ridge, NC 80-81 H 3
Holly Springs, MS 78-79 E 3
Hollywood, FL 64-65 KL 6
Hollywood, YOK-AA 84 III c 1
Hollywood, Los Angeles-, CA 64-65 BC 5
Hollywood Bowl 83 III b 1
Hollywood Cemetery [USA, Atlanta] 85 II b 2
Hollywood Cemetery [USA, Houston] 85 III b 1
Hollywood Park Race Track 83 III bc 2
Holman Island 56-57 NO 3
Hōlmavik 116-117 c 2
Holmdene 174-175 H 4
Holmes, PA 84 III b 2
Holmes, Mount — 66-67 H 3
Holmesburg, Philadelphia-, PA 84 III c 1
Holmes Run 82 II a 2
Holmestrand 116-117 CD 8
Holmfield 68-69 G 1
Holmsund 116-117 J 6
Holo Islands = Sulu Archipelago 148-149 H 5
Holoog 174-175 BC 4
Holopaw, FL 80-81 c 2
Holroyd River 158-159 H 2
Holsnøy 116-117 A 7
Holstebro 116-117 C 9
Holstein, IA 70-71 C 4
Holsteinsborg = Sisimiut 56-57 Za 4
Holston River 80-81 E 2
Holt, AL 78-79 F 4
Holt, FL 78-79 F 5
Holten, KS 70-71 C 6
Holten Bank 116-117 C 5
Holtville, CA 74-75 F 6
Holtyre 62 LM 2
Holung = Helong 144-145 G 1
Holy Cross, AK 56-57 DE 5
Hōnmalin 141 D 3
Hon Mê 150-151 EF 3
Honmoju Temple 155 III b 2
Honnāli 140 B 3
Honningsvåg 116-117 LM 2
Honokaa, HI 78-79 d 2
Honokohua, HI 78-79 d 2
Honório Gurgel, Rio de Janeiro-110 I a 2
Hōnow 130 III c 1
Hon Panjang 148-149 D 5
Hon'o Quan = An Lôc 150-151 F 7
Hon Rai 150-151 F 7
Hōnshū 142-143 PQ 4
Honsyū = Honshū 142-143 PQ 4

Hōme 155 III d 1
Home, OR 66-67 E 3
Home Bay 56-57 XY 4
Homebush Bay 161 I a 1-2
Homedale, ID 66-67 E 4
Homel = Gomel' 124-125 H 7
Home Owned Estates, Houston-, TX 85 III c 1
Homer, AK 56-57 F 6
Homer, LA 78-79 C 4
Homer, MI 70-71 H 4
Homer, NY 72-73 H 3
Homerville, GA 80-81 E 5
Homesglen, Melbourne- 161 II c 2
Homestead 158-159 HJ 4
Homestead, FL 80-81 c 4
Hometown, IL 83 II a 2
Homewood, AL 78-79 F 4
Hominy, OK 76-77 F 4
Hommoku, Yokohama- 155 III ab 3
Homnābād 140 C 2
Homoine 172 FG 6
Homoljske Planine 122-123 J 3
Ḥomra, Al- = Al-Humrah 164-165 L 6
Homra, Hamada el — — = Al-Ḥamādat al-Ḥamrā' 164-165 G 2-3
Ḥomş = Al-Khums 164-165 GH 2
Ḥims = Ḥimş 134-135 D 4
Hon, Cu Lao — = Cu Lao Thu 148-149 EF 4
Honan = Henan 142-143 L 5
Honanau, HI 78-79 de 3
Honāvar 140 B 3
Hōnavara = Honāvar 140 B 3
Honaz dağı 136-137 C 4
Honbetsu 144-145 cd 2
Hon Chông 150-151 E 7
Honda 92-93 E 3
Honda, Bahia — 94-95 EF 1
Honda, La — 94-95 C 4
Honda Bay 148-149 G 5
Hondeklipbaai [ZA, bay] 174-175 B 6
Hondeklipbaai [ZA, place] 174-175 B 6
Hondeklip Bay = Hondeklipbaai 174-175 B 6
Hondo, NM 76-77 B 6
Hondo, TX 76-77 E 8
Hondo [J] 144-145 H 6
Hondo [MEX] 86-87 Q 8
Hondo = Honshū 142-143 PQ 4
Honduras 64-65 J 9
Honduras, Cabo de — 64-65 JK 8
Honduras, Golfe de — 64-65 J 8
Hondzocht 128 II a 2
Honesdale, PA 72-73 J 4
Honeydew 170 V a 1
Honey Grove, TX 76-77 FG 6
Honey Island, TX 76-77 G 7
Honey Lake 66-67 C 5
Honfleur 120-121 H 4
Hồn Gai 150-151 F 2
Hong'an 146-147 E 6
Hongch'ŏn 144-145 FG 4
Hong-do 144-145 E 5
Hōngg, Zürich- 128 IV ab 1
Honghai Wan 146-147 E 10
Hong He [TJ, Henan] 146-147 E 5
Hong He [TJ, Inner Mongolian Aut. Reg.] 146-147 CD 1
Hong He [TJ, Yunnan] 142-143 J 7
Honghe Hanizu Yizu Zizhizhou 142-143 J 7
Hong Hu [TJ, lake] 146-147 D 7
Honghu [TJ, place] 142-143 KL 6
Hong Jiang = Wu Shui 146-147 BC 8
Hong Kong 142-143 LM 7
Hong Kong Stadium 155 I b 2
Honglai 146-147 G 5
Hongliu He 146-147 B 3
Hongluoxian 144-145 C 2
Hongmoxian = Hongluoxian 144-145 C 2
Hồng Ngu' 150-151 E 7
Hongo, Tōkyō- 155 III b 1
Hongqizhen 150-151 G 3
Hong Sa = Mu'o'ng Hong Sa 150-151 C 3
Hongshan = Maocifan 146-147 D 6
Hongshui He 142-143 K 6-7
Hongsŏng 144-145 F 4
Hongtong 146-147 C 3
Hongŭ 144-145 K 6
Hongwŏn 144-145 FG 2-3
Hongyŏtoku 155 III c 1
Hongze 146-147 G 5
Hongze Hu 146-147 G 5
Honiara 148-149 j 6
Honjo 144-145 MN 3
Honjo, Tōkyō- 155 III b 1
Hon Khoai, Vung — 150-151 G 8

Hōme 155 III d 1

Honai 144-145 J 6

Hon Tre 150-151 G 6
Hon Vong Phu = Nui Vong Phu 150-151 G 6
Hon Way 150-151 D 8
Honye 174-175 F 3
Hood = Isla Española 92-93 B 5
Hood, Mount — 64-65 B 2
Hood Canal 66-67 B 2
Hood Point 158-159 CD 6
Hood River, OR 66-67 C 3
Hooghly 138-139 LM 7
Hoogli = Hoogly 138-139 LM 7
Hoogte 174-175 H 4
Hook, London- 129 II a 2
Hooker, OK 76-77 D 4
Hooker, Bi'r — 173 B 2
Hooker Creek 158-159 F 3
Hook of Holland = Rotterdam-Hoek van Holland 120-121 JK 3
Hoonah, AK 56-57 JK 6
Hoopa, CA 66-67 B 5
Hoopa Valley Indian Reservation 66-67 AB 5
Hooper, CO 68-69 D 7
Hooper, NE 68-69 H 5
Hooper, UT 66-67 G 5
Hooper Bay 58-59 DE 6
Hooper Bay, AK 58-59 D 6
Hoopeston, IL 70-71 G 5
Hoopstad 174-175 F 4
Hoosier 61 CD 5
Hoover, SD 68-69 E 3
Hoover, TX 76-77 D 5
Hoover Dam 64-65 D 4
Hopa 136-137 J 2
Hope 66-67 C 1
Hope, AK 58-59 N 6
Hope, AR 64-65 H 5
Hope, AZ 74-75 G 6
Hope, IN 70-71 H 6
Hope, KS 68-69 H 6
Hope, NM 76-77 B 6
Hope, Ben — 119 D 2
Hopedale 56-57 YZ 6
Hopefield 174-175 C 7
Hope Island 72-73 F 2
Hopelchén 86-87 PQ 8
Hopen 52 B 16
Hopes Advance, Cape — 56-57 X 5
Hopetoun [AUS, Victoria] 158-159 H 7
Hopetoun [AUS, Western Australia] 158-159 D 6
Hopetown 172 D 7
Hopewell, VA 80-81 H 2
Ho-pi = Hebi 146-147 D 4
Hopi Indian Reservation 74-75 H 4-5
Hopin = Hōbin 141 E 3
Ho-p'ing = Heping 146-147 E 9
Hopkins, Lake — 158-159 E 4
Hopkinsville, KY 64-65 J 4
Hopland, CA 74-75 B 3
Ho-p'o-hsü = Jiexi 146-147 E 10
Hopong = Hōbōn 141 E 5
Hoppo = Hepu 142-143 K 7
Hopu = Hepu 142-143 K 7
Hō Qui'm 155 II b 2
Hor = Hebron 136-137 F 7
Hor, Cape — = Cabo de Hornos 111 C 9
Horana = Hosan 146-147 D 10
Horamavu 154 IV b 2
Hoře, Îles — 148-149 b 1
Hōn, Îles — 148-149 b 1
Hōnmalin 141 D 3
Hon Mê 150-151 EF 3
Honmoju Temple 155 III b 2
Honnāli 140 B 3
Honningsvåg 116-117 LM 2
Honokaa, HI 78-79 d 2
Honokohua, HI 78-79 d 2
Honório Gurgel, Rio de Janeiro-110 I a 2
Hōnow 130 III c 1
Hon Panjang 148-149 D 5
Hon'o Quan = An Lôc 150-151 F 7
Hon Rai 150-151 F 7
Hōnshū 142-143 PQ 4
Honsyū = Honshū 142-143 PQ 4

Horn Reefs = Blåvands Huk 116-117 BC 10
Hornsea 119 FG 5
Hornsey, London- 129 II b 1
Hornsund 116-117 jk 6
Hornsundtind 116-117 k 6
Horobetsu 144-145 b 2
Hōr Ôda = Hawr Awdah 136-137 M 7
Horodenka = Gorodenka 126-127 B 2
Hottingca = Gorodnica 126-127 C 1
Horodok = Gorodok [SU, Chmeľnickaja Oblast'] 126-127 B 2
Horodok = Gorodok [SU, L'vovskaja Oblast'] 126-127 AB 2
Horodyšče = Gorodišče 126-127 E 2
Horonobe 144-145 bc 1
Horowupotāna 140 E 6
Horqueta 111 E 2
Horqueta, La — [YV, Bolívar] 94-95 L 4
Horqueta, La — [YV, Monagas] 94-95 K 3
Horquetas, Las — 108-109 D 7
Horquilla 104-105 G 10
Horsburgh's Island = Zādetkale Kyūn 150-151 AB 7
Horse Branch, KY 70-71 G 7
Horse Cave, KY 70-71 H 7
Horse Creek, WY 68-69 D 5
Horse Creek [USA, Colorado] 68-69 E 6
Horse Creek [USA, Wyoming] 68-69 D 5
Horsefly 60 G 3
Horsehead Lake 68-69 FG 2
Horseheads, NY 72-73 H 3
Horse Islands 63 J 2
Horsens 116-117 CD 10
Horse Race Course of Jakarta 154 IV b 2
Horseshoe 158-159 C 5
Horse Springs, NM 74-75 JK 6
Horsham [AUS] 158-159 H 7
Horsham [Açores] 204-205 E 5
Horstermeer 128 I b 2
Hortaleza, Madrid- 113 III b 2
Horten 116-117 D 8
Hortensia 106-107 G 5
Horto Florestal 110 II b 1
Horton, KS 70-71 C 6
Horton River 56-57 M 4
Horzum-Armutlu = Gölhisar 136-137 C 4
Hosadurga = Hosdrug 140 B 4
Hosadurga = Hosdurga 140 C 4
Hōsakōṭṭē = Hoskote 140 C 3
Hosanagar = Hosanagara 140 B 4
Hosanagara 140 B 4
Hosapēṭa = Hospet 140 C 3
Hosdrug 140 B 4
Hosdurga 140 C 4
Hose, Pegunungan — 152-153 K 4-L 5
Hoşeima, el — = Al-Husaymah 164-165 D 1
Hoşeinābād = Īlām 134-135 F 4
Hoseynābād 136-137 MN 6
Hoseyniyeh 136-137 MN 6
Hoshan = Hecheng 146-147 D 10
Hoshangābād 138-139 FG 6
Hoshiārpur 138-139 EF 2
Hoshingo Mdogo 171 D 3
Hōsh 'Ïsā = Ḥawsh 'Ïsā 173 B 2
Hōshiyārpur = Hoshiārpur 138-139 EF 2
Ho-shui = Heshui [TJ, Gansu] 146-147 B 4
Ho-shui = Heshui [TJ, Guangdong] 146-147 CD 10
Hoshun = Heshun 146-147 D 3
Hoskote 140 C 3
Hosmer, SD 68-69 G 3
Hospet 140 C 3
Hospital 106-107 B 4
Hospital, Cuchilla del — 106-107 K 3
Hospitalet de Llobregat 120-121 J 8
Hosta Butte 74-75 JK 5
Hoste, Isla — 111 C 9
Hosūr 140 C 4
Hot 148-149 C 3
Hotan = Khotan 142-143 DE 4
Hotazel 174-175 E 4
Hotchkiss, CO 68-69 C 6
Hot Creek Valley 74-75 E 3
Hotel Humboldt 91 II b 1
Hotel Punta del Lago 108-109 CD 7
Hotham Inlet 58-59 FG 3
Hotien = Khotan 142-143 DE 4
Hot'ien-hsü = Hetian 146-147 E 10
Hoting 116-117 G 5
Hotong Qagan Nur 146-147 B 2
Hot Springs, AR 64-65 H 5
Hot Springs, MT 66-67 F 2
Hot Springs, NC 80-81 E 3
Hot Springs, SD 68-69 E 4
Hot Springs, VA 80-81 G 2
Hot Springs Cove 60 D 5
Hotspur Seamount 100-101 FG 9
Hottah Lake 56-57 N 4
Hotte, Massif de la — 88-89 JK 5
Hottentot Bay = Hottentotsbaai 174-175 A 4
Hottentot Reserve 174-175 B 3-4
Hottentotsbaai 174-175 A 4
Hottingen, Zürich- 128 IV b 1

I

Ilāhābād = Allahābād 134-135 N 5
Ilak Island 58-59 t 7
Ila La Tortuga 92-93 FG 2
Īlām [IR] 134-135 F 4
Ilam [Nepal] 138-139 L 4
Īlām va Poshtkuh = 2 ◁ 134-135 F 4
Ilan 146-147 H 9
Ilan = Yilan 142-143 OP 2
Ilangali 172 FG 3
Ilanskij 132-133 S 6
Ilaro 164-165 E 7
Ilatane 168-169 G 1
Ilave, Río — 96-97 G 10
Ilay, Wādī — 173 D 7
Ilayāngudi 140 D 6
Ilchuri Alin = Yilehuli Shan 142-143 NO 1
Île à la Crosse 61 D 3
Île à la Crosse, Lac — 61 E 3
Île Alright 63 F 4
Île Amherst 63 F 4
Île Anvers 53 C 30
Île aux Allumettes 72-73 H 2
Île aux Coudres 63 A 4
Île aux Hérons 82 I b 2
Ilebo 172 D 2
Île Brabant 53 C 30
Île Brion 63 F 4
Île Charcot 53 C 29
Île Chergui = Jazīrat ash-Sharqī 166-167 M 2
Île Chesterfield 172 H 5
Ileckaja Zaščita = Sol'-Ileck 132-133 JK 7
Île Clipperton 64-65 E 9
Île de Corps Mort 63 E 4
Île de Dorval 82 I a 2
Île-de-France 120-121 HJ 4
Île de Groix 120-121 F 5
Île de la Gonâve 64-65 M 8
Île de la Table = Đao Cai Ban 148-149 E 2
Île de la Tortue 64-65 M 7
Île de la Visitation 82 I b 1
Île de Montréal 82 I a 2-b 1
Île de Noirmoutier 120-121 F 5
Île de Ré 120-121 G 5
Île de Sainte Helène 82 I b 1
Île des Chins = Jazā'ir al-Kilāb 166-167 M 1
Île des Singes 170 IV a 1
Île des Sœurs 82 I b 2
Île de Verte 82 I bc 1
Île de Yeu 120-121 F 5
Île du Diable 92-93 J 3
Île du Grand Mécatina 63 G 2
Île du Petit Mécatina 63 G 2
Île du Teléphone 170 IV a 1-2
Île Europa 172 H 6
Île Hunter 158-159 O 4
Île Jésus 82 I a 1
Île Joinville 53 C 31
Ilek [SU, Kurskaja Oblast'] 126-127 G 1
Ilek [SU, Orenburgskaja Oblast' place] 124-125 T 8
Ilek [SU, Orenburgskaja Oblast' river] 124-125 T 8
Ileksa 124-125 L 2
Île Lifou 158-159 N 4
Île Maré 158-159 N 4
Île Marina = Espíritu Santo 158-159 MN 3
Île Matthew 158-159 O 4
Île Mbamou 170 IV b 1
Île Nightingale = Đao Bach Long Vi 150-151 F 2
Île Ouvéa 158-159 N 4
Île Pamanzi-Bé 172 J 4
Île Parisienne 72-73 D 1
Île Plane = Al-Jazīrah 166-167 F 2
Île Plane = Jazīrat al-Maṭrūḥ 166-167 M 1
Île Rachgoun = Jazīrat Rāshqūn 166-167 EF 2
Ileret 171 D 1
Île Royale = Cape Breton Island 56-57 X-Z 8
Île Sainte-Marie = Nosy Boraha 172 K 5
Île Saint-Ignace 70-71 FG 1
Îles Belep 158-159 M 3
Îles Cani = Jazā'ir al-Kilāb 166-167 M 1
Îles Chesterfield 158-159 L 3
Îles de Boucherville 82 I bc 1
Îles de la Galite = Jazā'ir Jaliṭah 166-167 L 1
Îles de la Madeleine 56-57 Y 8
Îles de Los 168-169 B 3
Îles de Pins 158-159 N 4
Îles des Saintes 88-89 PQ 7
Îles du Salut 98-99 MN 2
Îles Glorieuses 172 J 4
Ilesha 164-165 EF 7
Îles Habibas = Juzur al-Ḥabībah 166-167 F 2
Îles Horn 148-149 b 1
Îles Kerkenna = Jazur Qarqannah 164-165 G 2
Îles Kuriate = Jazā'ir Qūryāt 166-167 M 2
Îles Loyauté 158-159 N 4
Îles Marquises 156-157 L 5
Îles Paracels = Quần Đao Tây Sa 148-149 F 3
Îles Saloum 168-169 A 2
Îles Sandja 170 I b 1
Îles Toumotou 156-157 K 5-L 6
Îles Tristao 168-169 B 3
Îles Tuamotu 156-157 K 5-L 6
Îles Tubuaï 156-157 K 6
Îles Wallis 148-149 b 1
Ilet' = Krasnogorskij 124-125 R 5
Île Tidra 164-165 A 5
Île Vaté = Efate 158-159 N 3
Île Victoria = Victoria Island 56-57 O-Q 3
'Ilfag = 'Afag 136-137 L 6
Ilford 56-57 RS 6
Ilford, London- 129 II c 1
Ilfracombe 119 D 6
Ilgaz 136-137 E 2
Ilgaz dağlar 136-137 EF 2
Ilgin 136-137 DE 3
Ilha Anajás 98-99 N 5
Ilha Apeuzinho 100-101 B 1
Ilha Aramacá 94-95 c 3
Ilha Bailique 98-99 O 4
Ilhabela 102-103 K 5
Ilha Benguêrua 174-175 L 1
Ilha Caçumba 100-101 E 9
Ilha Caravela 168-169 A 3
Ilha Casa de Pedras 110 I c 1
Ilha Caviana 92-93 K 4
Ilha Comprida [BR, Atlantic Ocean] 111 G 2-3
Ilha Comprida [BR, Rio de Janeiro] 110 I b 3
Ilha Comprida [BR, Rio Paraná] 102-103 G 4
Ilha Curuá 98-99 NO 4
Ilha da Alfavaca 110 I b 3
Ilha da Âncora 102-103 M 5
Ilha da Conceição 110 I c 2
Ilha da Feitoria 106-107 LM 3
Ilha da Laguna 98-99 N 5
Ilha da Laje 110 I c 2
Ilha da Pombeba 110 I b 2
Ilha das Canárias 92-93 L 5
Ilha das Cobras 110 I bc 2
Ilha das Couves 102-103 K 5
Ilha das Duas Onças 102-103 F 5
Ilha das Enxadas 110 I bc 2
Ilha da Silva 98-99 F 5
Ilha das Onças 98-99 K 6
Ilha das Palmas 110 I b 3
Ilha das Peças 111 G 3
Ilha da Trindade 92-93 NO 9
Ilha da Vitória 102-103 K 5
Ilha de Ataúro 148-149 J 8
Ilha de Cananeia 102-103 J 6
Ilha de Cotunduba 110 I c 2
Ilha de Formosa 168-169 AB 3
Ilha de Itaparica 100-101 E 7
Ilha de Maracá 92-93 JK 4
Ilha de Marajó 92-93 JK 5
Ilha de Mutuoca 100-101 B 1
Ilha de Orango 164-165 A 6
Ilha de Santa Bárbara 110 I b 2
Ilha de Santa Catarina 111 G 3
Ilha de Santa Cruz 110 I c 2
Ilha de Santana 92-93 L 5
Ilha de Santo Amaro 102-103 JK 6
Ilha de São Francisco 102-103 HJ 7
Ilha de São Luís 100-101 BC 1-2
Ilha de São Sebastião 92-93 KL 9
Ilha de Tinharé 100-101 E 7
Ilha do Arvoredo 102-103 HJ 7
Ilha do Bananal 92-93 J 7
Ilha do Bazaruto 172 G 6
Ilha do Caju 100-101 CD 2
Ilha do Caldeirão 98-99 D 7
Ilha do Cardoso 102-103 J 6
Ilha do Careiro 98-99 J 6
Ilha do Engenho 110 I c 2
Ilha do Fundão 110 I b 2
Ilha do Gado Bravo 100-101 C 6
Ilha do Governador 110 I b 1
Ilha do Meio 110 I b 3
Ilha do Mel 102-103 H 6
Ilha do Pacoval 98-99 K 6
Ilha do Príncipe 164-165 F 8
Ilha do Rijo 110 I c 1
Ilha dos Alcatrazes 102-103 K 6
Ilha do Saravatá 110 I b 1
Ilha dos Búzios 102-103 K 5
Ilha dos Caranguejos 100-101 B 2
Ilha dos Macacos 98-99 N 5
Ilha dos Porcos 102-103 K 5
Ilha do Viana 110 I c 2
Ilha Fernando de Noronha 92-93 N 5
Ilha Grande [BR, Amazonas] 98-99 F 5
Ilha Grande [BR, Rio de Janeiro] 92-93 L 9
Ilha Grande [BR, Rio Grande do Sul] 106-107 M 3
Ilha Grande = Ilha das Sete Quedas 111 EF 2-3
Ilha Grande, Baía da — 102-103 K 5
Ilha Grande de Gurupá 92-93 J 5
Ilha Grande de Jutai 98-99 O 6
Ilha Grande de Paulino 100-101 CD 2
Ilha Grande de Santa Isabel 92-93 L 5
Ilha Grande ou das Sete Quedas 92-93 HJ 9
Ilha Inhaca 174-175 K 4
Ilha Irmãos 100-101 B 1
Ilha Janaucu 92-93 JK 4
Ilha Javari 98-99 E 5
Ilha Jurupari 98-99 NO 4
Ilha Mangunça 100-101 B 1
Ilha Maracá 92-93 G 4
Ilha Mariana 174-175 K 3
Ilha Mexiana 92-93 K 4-5
Ilha Mucunambiba 100-101 C 1-2
Ilha Mututi 98-99 N 5
Ilha Naipo 94-95 G 6
Ilha Pedro II 94-95 H 7
Ilha Providencia 94-95 J 8
Ilha Queimada 98-99 N 5
Ilha Queimada Grande 102-103 J 6
Ilha Rata 92-93 N 5
Ilhas, Cachoeira — 98-99 JK 5
Ilhas Angoche 172 GH 5
Ilha Santa Ana 102-103 M 5
Ilha São Jorge 100-101 B 1
Ilha São Tomé 164-165 F 8-9
Ilhas Cagarras 110 I b 3
Ilhas del Cisne = Swan Islands 64-65 K 8
Ilhas de Sao João 92-93 L 5
Ilhas Desertas 164-165 A 2
Ilhas dos Corais 102-103 HJ 6
Ilha Seca 110 I b 2
Ilhas Itacolomi 102-103 H 6
Ilhas Martim Vaz 92-93 O 9
Ilhas Quirimba 172 H 4
Ilhas Selvagens 164-165 A 2
Ilhas Três Irmãos 102-103 H 7
Ilha Tamaquari 98-99 F 5
Ilha Tupinambaranas 92-93 H 5
Īlhavo 120-121 C 8
Ilheo Bay, Port de — = Sandvisbai 174-175 A 2
Ilherir = Al-Hayrīr 166-167 L 7
Ilhéus 92-93 M 7
Ilhinha, Cachoeira — 98-99 K 5
Ili [SU] 132-133 O 8
Ili [TJ] 142-143 E 3
Ili = Gulja 142-143 E 3
Iliamna, AK 58-59 K 7
Iliamna Bay 58-59 L 7
Iliamna Lake 56-57 E 6
Iliamna Volcano 56-57 EF 5
Ilič 136-137 H 3
Iliff, CO 68-69 E 5
Iligan 148-149 H 5
Iligan Bay 152-153 PQ 1
Ilihuli Shan = Ilchuri Alin 142-143 NO 1
Ilion, NY 72-73 J 3
Ilion = Troia 134-135 B 3
Ilio Point 78-79 d 2
Ilisós 113 IV b 2
Ilivit Mountains 58-59 G 5
Iljič 132-133 M 9
Iljič'ovsk [SU, Nachičevanskaja ASSR] 126-127 M 7
Iljič'ovsk [SU, Ukrainskaja SSR] 126-127 E 3
Iljincy 126-127 D 2
Iljino 124-125 H 6
Iljinskij [SU ↑ Južno-Sachalinsk] 132-133 b 8
Iljinskij [SU ↖ Perm'] 124-125 U 4
Iljinsko-Podomskoje 124-125 QR 3
Iljinsko-Zaborskoje 124-125 OP 5
Ilkāl 140 C 3
Illampu, Nevado — 92-93 F 8
Illana Bay 152-153 P 2
Illapel 111 B 4
Illecas 86-87 JK 6
Illela 168-169 G 2
Iller 118 E 4
Illescas, Cerro — 96-97 A 4-5
Illimani, Nevado de — 92-93 F 8
Illinci = Iljincy 126-127 D 2
Illiniza 96-97 B 2
Illinois 64-65 HJ 3
Illinois, University of — 83 II ab 1
Illinois Institute of Technology 83 II b 1
Illinois Peak 66-67 F 2
Illinois River 64-65 HJ 3-4
Illizi 166-167 L 6
Illmo, MO 78-79 E 2
Illo 168-169 F 3
Illovo Beach 174-175 J 6
Illubabor = Īlubabor 164-165 LM 7
Il'men', ozero — 132-133 E 6
Ilnik, AK 58-59 cd 1
Ilo 92-93 E 8
Ilo, Rada de — 92-93 E 8
Iloca 106-107 A 5
Iloilo 148-149 H 4
Ilopango, Lago de — 88-89 B 8
Ilorin 164-165 E 7
Ilosva = Iršava 126-127 A 2
Ilôt Cône = Kâs Moul 150-151 D 7
Ilovajsk 126-127 J 3
Ilovatka 126-127 MN 1
Ilovatnyj = Ilovatka 126-127 MN 1
Ilovľa [SU, place] 126-127 LM 2
Ilovľa [SU, river] 126-127 M 1
Ilp, Den — 128 I ab 1
Il'pyrskij 132-133 f 5-6
Il'skij 126-127 J 4
Īlubabor 164-165 LM 7
Ilūkste 124-125 EF 6
Ilula 171 C 3
Iluyana Potosí, Nevado — 104-105 B 5
Ilwaco, WA 66-67 AB 2
Ilwaki 148-149 J 8
Ilyč 124-125 V 2
Ilža 118 K 3
Imabari 144-145 J 5-6
Imabetsu 144-145 N 2
Imabu, Rio — 98-99 K 5
Imaculda 100-101 H 4
Imagane 144-145 ab 2
Imaichi 144-145 M 4
Imajō 144-145 KL 5
Imajuku, Yokohama- 155 III a 3
Imāmganj = Chhatarpur 138-139 K 5
Imán, Sierra del — 106-107 K 1
Imandra, ozero — 132-133 E 4
Imari 144-145 GH 6
Imaruí 102-103 H 8
Imata 96-97 F 9
Imataca, Serranía de — 92-93 G 3
Imatra 116-117 N 7
Imatra vallinkoski 116-117 N 7
Imaz, Bajo — 106-107 E 7
Imazu 144-145 KL 5
Imazuasayama 155 III d 3
Imbābah 173 B 2
Imbābah Bridge 170 II b 1
Imbabura 96-97 B 1
Imbaimadai 92-93 G 3
Imbituba 102-103 H 8
Imbituva 102-103 G 6
Imbros = İmroz 136-137 A 2
Imbuí, Punta do — 110 I c 2
Imbuíra 100-101 D 8
Imedrhâs, Jbel — = Jabal Īmīdghās 166-167 D 4
I-mên = Yimen 146-147 F 5
Imeral, Adrâr n' = Jabal Mūriq 166-167 CD 3
Imeri, Serra — 92-93 F 4
Imfal = Imphāl 134-135 P 6
Īmī 164-165 N 7
Īmīdghās, Jabal — 166-167 D 4
Imilac 111 C 2
Imīlshīl 166-167 D 3
Īmīn Tānūt 166-167 B 4
Imirhou, Oued — = Wādī Īmirhu 166-167 L 7
Īmirhu, Wādī — 166-167 L 7
Imišli 126-127 NO 7
Imja-do 144-145 E 5
Imjin-gang 144-145 F 3
Imlay, NV 66-67 DE 5
Imlay City, MI 72-73 E 3
Immokalee, FL 80-81 c 3
Immyŏng-dong 144-145 G 2
Imnaha River 66-67 E 3
Imo 164-165 F 7
Imola 122-123 D 3
Imore 170 III a 2
Imotski 122-123 G 4
Imoulaye, Hassi — = Ḥāssī Īmūlāy 166-167 L 5
Imouzzer des Ida-Outanane = Sūq al-Khamīs 166-167 B 4
Imoûzzer Kandar = Īmūzzar al-Kandar 166-167 D 3
Impendhle = Impencle 174-175 HJ 5
Impendle 174-175 HJ 5
Imperatriz 92-93 K 6
Impéria 122-123 C 4
Imperial, CA 74-75 F 6
Imperial, NE 68-69 F 5
Imperial, TX 76-77 C 7
Imperial [CDN] 61 F 5
Imperial [PE] 96-97 C 8
Imperial, Río — 106-107 A 7
Imperial Dam 74-75 F 6
Imperial Mills 61 C 3
Imperial Palace 155 III b 1
Imperial Valley 64-65 CD 5
Impfondo 172 C 1
Imphāl 134-135 P 6
Impilachti 124-125 H 3
Imp'o 144-145 FG 5
İmralı 136-137 C 2
İmranlı 136-137 GH 3
İmron 136-137 H 3
Imthān 136-137 G 6
Īmūlāy, Ḥāssī — 166-167 L 5
Imuris 86-87 E 2
Imuruan Bay 148-149 G 4
Imuruk Basin 58-59 DE 4
Imuruk Lake 58-59 F 4
Īmūzzar al-Kandar 166-167 D 3
Imūzzar al-Kandar 166-167 D 3
Imvani 174-175 G 7
Imwŏnjin 144-145 G 4
Ina [J] 144-145 LM 5
In'a [SU, place] 132-133 b 6
In'a [SU, river] 132-133 c 5
In Abangarit 164-165 F 5
In-Abeg 164-165 D 4
Inácio Dias, Morro — 110 I ab 2
Inácio Martins 102-103 G 6
Inajá 100-101 F 5
Inajá, Rio — 98-99 N 9
Inajá, Serra do — 98-99 N 9
In Alay 164-165 D 5
In Aménas = 'Ayn Umannās 164-165 F 3
Inanda 170 V b 1
Inanudak Bay 58-59 m 4
Inanwatan 148-149 K 7
Inâouèn, Ouèd — = Wād Īnāwīn 166-167 D 2
Iñapari 92-93 EF 7
In'aptuk, gora — 132-133 UV 6
'In Aquiel, Hassi — = Ḥāssī 'Ayn Aghyūl 166-167 M 6
In Areï 168-169 F 1
Inari [SF, lake] 116-117 MN 3
Inari [SF, place] 116-117 M 3
Inaru River 58-59 J 1
Inatsuke, Tōkyō- 155 III b 1
Inauini, Rio — 98-99 D 9
Inawashiro 144-145 MN 4
Inawashiro ko 144-145 MN 4
Īnāwīn, Wād — 166-167 D 2
In Azaoua 164-165 F 4
In Azaoua = 'Ayn 'Azāwah 166-167 K 7
'In 'Azar = 'Ayn 'Azar 166-167 M 5
Inazkān 166-167 B 4
In-Belbel = 'Ayn Balbāl 166-167 G 6
Inca 120-121 J 9
Inca, Cerro del — 104-105 BC 7
Incaguasi 106-107 B 2
Incahuasi, Salina de — 104-105 C 9
İnce burun 134-135 C 2
İncekum burnu 136-137 EF 4
İncesu 136-137 F 3
Inch'ŏn 144-145 F 4
Inchupalla 96-97 G 9
Inchwe 174-175 G 2
Incienso 106-107 B 3
İncili 136-137 D 2
İncir burun 136-137 G 2
Incirköy, İstanbul- 154 I b 2
Incomáti, Rio — 174-175 K 3
Incoronata = Kornat 122-123 F 4
Incudine, l' 122-123 C 5
Indaiá 100-101 E 7
Indaia, Rio — 102-103 K 3
Indaiá Grande, Rio — 102-103 F 3
Indaial 102-103 H 7
Indaiatuba 102-103 J 5
Indaor = Indore 134-135 M 6
Indāpur 140 B 1
Indau 141 E 3
Indaugyī Aing 141 E 3
Indaur = Indore 134-135 M 6
Indaw 141 E 5
Indaw = Indau 141 D 4
Indawgyi, Lake — = Indaugyī Aing 141 E 3
Indé 76-77 B 10
Indel Airpark 84 III d 1
In Délimane 168-169 F 2
Independence, CA 74-75 D 4
Independence, IA 70-71 E 4
Independence, KS 76-77 FG 4
Independence, LA 78-79 D 5
Independence, MO 64-65 H 4
Independence, OR 66-67 B 3
Independence Heights, Houston-, TX 85 III b 1
Independence Mountains 66-67 EF 5
Independence National Historical Park 84 III c 2
Independence Valley 66-67 F 5
Independencia [BOL] 104-105 C 5
Independência [BR] 100-101 D 3
Independencia [MEX] 74-75 F 6
Independencia [PY, Boquerón] 102-103 AB 4
Independencia [PY, Guairá] 102-103 DE 6
Independencia [RA] 106-107 G 2
Independencia, Bahía de la — 96-97 C 8-9
Independencia, Islas — 92-93 D 7
Inder, ozero — 126-127 PQ 2
Inderagiri, Batang — 148-149 D 7
Inderborskij 126-127 P 2
Index, WA 66-67 C 2
Index Mount 58-59 PQ 2
Indi 140 BC 2
India 134-135 L-O 6
India, Bassas da — 172 GH 6
Indiana 64-65 J 3-4
Indiana, PA 72-73 G 4
Indianapolis, IN 64-65 J 4
Indian Head 61 FG 5
Indian Lake [USA, Michigan] 70-71 G 2-3
Indian Lake [USA, Ohio] 72-73 E 4
Indian Mountain 66-67 H 4
Indian Museum 154 II b 2
Indian Ocean 50-51 N-O 6-7
Indianola, IA 70-71 D 5
Indianola, MS 78-79 D 4
Indianola, NE 68-69 F 5
Indianópolis 102-103 J 3
Indianópolis, São Paulo- 110 II b 2
Indian Peak 74-75 G 3
Indian River [CDN] 62 N 2
Indian River [USA, Alaska] 58-59 KL 4
Indian River [USA, Florida] 64-65 K 6
Indian Springs, NV 74-75 F 4
Indian Springs, VA 82 II a 2
Indian Valley, ID 66-67 E 3
Indiga 132-133 HJ 4
Indigirka 132-133 bc 4
Indio, CA 74-75 E 6
Indio, Punta — 106-107 J 5
Indio, Río — 64-65 c 2
Indio Rico 106-107 G 7
Indios 102-103 G 7
Índios, Cachoeira dos — 92-93 G 4
Indispensable Strait 148-149 k 6
Indo = Sindh 134-135 L 4
Indonesia 148-149 D-K 7
Indonesian Bazaar 154 IV a 2
Indore 134-135 M 6
Indramaiu = Indramayu 148-149 E 8
Indramayu 148-149 E 8
Indramayu, Tanjung — 152-153 H 9
Indrāvati 134-135 N 7
Indre 120-121 H 5
Indre Arna 116-117 AB 7
Indura 124-125 DE 7
Indūra = Nizāmābād 134-135 M 7
Indus = Sengge Khamba 142-143 DE 5
Indus = Sindh 134-135 L 4
Indus Canyon 134-135 K 6
Indwe [ZA, place] 174-175 G 6
Indwe [ZA, river] 174-175 G 6
İnebolu 136-137 E 2
İnegöl 136-137 C 2
Inerie, Gunung — 148-149 H 8
Inés Indart 106-107 G 5
Ineul 122-123 L 2
İnevi 136-137 E 3
Inezgan = Inazkān 166-167 B 4
Inezgane = Inazkān 166-167 B 4
In-Ezzane = 'Ayn 'Azzān 166-167 G 4
Infanta, Cape — = Kaap Infanta 174-175 D 8
Infanta, Kaap — 174-175 D 8
Infantas 94-95 E 4
Infanzón 104-105 D 11
In Farghas 168-169 F 1
Infernão, Cachoeira do — 92-93 G 6
Infernínho, Caocheira — 98-99 H 9
Infiernillo, Presa del — 86-87 JK 8
Ing, Nam Mae — 150-151 C 2-3
Ingá [BR] 100-101 G 4
Ingabū 141 D 7
In-Gall 164-165 F 5
Ingapirca 96-97 B 3
Ingende 172 C 2
Ingeniero Balloffet 106-107 C 5
Ingeniero Beaugey 106-107 FG 5
Ingeniero Budge, Lomas de Zamora- 110 III b 2
Ingeniero Foster 106-107 E 5
Ingeniero Guillermo N. Juárez 104-105 EF 8
Ingeniero Gustavo André 106-107 CD 4
Ingeniero Jacobacci 111 BC 6
Ingeniero Julián Romero 106-107 DE 7
Ingeniero Luiggi 106-107 E 5
Ingeniero Luis A. Huergo 106-107 D 7
Ingeniero Montero 104-105 E 5
Ingeniero Pablo Nogues 110 III a 1
Ingeniero White 106-107 F 7
Ingenika Mine 60 E 1
Ingenio, Río del — 96-97 D 9
Ingenio Santa Ana 106-107 DE 1
Ingenstrem Rocks 58-59 q 6
Ingersoll 72-73 F 3
Ingham 158-159 J 3
Ingle, CA 74-75 C 4
Inglefield Bredning 56-57 XY 2
Inglefield Land 56-57 XY 2
Ingles, Bogotá- 91 III b 4
Ingleshire, TX 85 III a 1
Ingleside, San Francisco-, CA 83 I b 2
Inglewood 158-159 K 5
Inglewood, CA 74-75 D 6
Inglis 61 H 5
Inglutalik River 58-59 G 4
Ingōgā Būm 141 E 3
Ingogo 174-175 HJ 4
Ingolf 62 B 3
Ingólfshöfdhi 116-117 ef 3
Ingolstadt 118 EF 4
Ingomar, MT 68-69 C 2
Ingonisch 63 F 4
Ingøy 116-117 KL 2
Ingrebourne 129 II c 1
Ingrid Christensen land 53 BC 8
In Guezzam = 'Ayn Qazzān 164-165 EF 5
Ingul 126-127 F 3
Ingulec 126-127 F 2
Ingwavuma [ZA, place] 174-175 JK 4
Ingwavuma [ZA, river] 174-175 J 4
Inhaca, Ilha — 174-175 K 4
Inhaca, Península — 174-175 K 4
Inhambane [Mozambique, administrative unit] 172 FG 6
Inhambane [Mozambique, place] 172 G 6
Inhambane, Baía de — 174-175 L 2
Inhambupe 92-93 M 7
Inhambupe, Rio — 100-101 E 6
Inhaminga 172 FG 5
Inhamuns 100-101 DE 3
Inhanduí 106-107 JK 2
Inhapim 102-103 LM 3
Inharrime 172 G 6
Inharrime, Rio — 174-175 L 3
Inhas = 'Ayn Unaḥḥās 166-167 HJ 6
Inhaúma, Rio de Janeiro- 110 I b 2
Inhaúma, Serra do — 100-101 B 3
Inhaumas 100-101 B 7
Inhobim 100-101 D 8
Inhulec' = Ingulec' 126-127 F 3
Inhuma 100-101 D 4
Inhumas 102-103 H 2
Inhung-ni 144-145 F 3
Inírida, Río — 92-93 F 4
Inishowen Peninsula 119 C 4
Injune 158-159 J 5
Inkerman 158-159 H 3
Inkermann = Wādī Rāhīyu 166-167 G 2
Inklin 58-59 V 7
Inklin River 58-59 V 7
Inkom, ID 66-67 GH 4
Inland Lake 58-59 H 3
Inland Sea = Seto-naikai 142-143 P 5
Inle Aing 141 E 5
Inn 118 E 5
Innamincka 160 E 1
Inner Mongolian Autonomous Region 142-143 K 3-M 2
Inner Port Shelter 155 I b 1
Inner Sound 119 D 3
Innisfail [AUS] 158-159 J 3
Innisfail [CDN] 60 L 3
Innoko River 58-59 H 5
Innoshima 144-145 J 5
Innsbruck 118 E 5
Innymnej, gora — 132-133 kl 4
Ino 144-145 J 6
Inocência 102-103 FG 3
Inokashira Park 155 III a 1
Inomino-misaki 144-145 J 6
Inongo 172 C 2
İnönü 136-137 D 3
Inoucdjouac 56-57 V 6
Inowrocław 118 HJ 2
Inquisivi 92-93 F 8
In-Rhar = 'Ayn Ghar 166-167 G 6
Inriville 106-107 F 4
In-Salah = 'Ayn Ṣāliḥ 164-165 E 3
Insar 124-125 P 7
Inscription, Cape — 158-159 B 5
Inscription Point 161 I b 2-3
Insein = Inzein 148-149 C 3
Instituto Butantã 110 II a 2
Instituto Politécnico Nacional 91 I c 1-2
Inta 132-133 KL 4
Intake, MT 68-69 D 2
In Tallak 168-169 F 1
In Tebezas 168-169 F 1
In Tedeini = 'Ayn Tādīn 164-165 E 4
In Témégui 168-169 F 1
Intendente Alvear 106-107 F 5
Interamericana, Carretera — 88-89 E 10
Interior, SD 68-69 F 4
Interior Plateau 60 D 2-F 4
Interlagos, São Paulo- 110 II a 3
Interlaken 118 CD 5
International Amphitheatre 83 II b 2
International Falls, MN 70-71 D 1
Intersection, Mount — 60 G 3
Inthanon, Doi — 148-149 C 3
Intiyaco 111 DE 3
Intracoastal Waterway 78-79 C 6
Intuto 96-97 D 3
Inubō saki 144-145 N 5
Inútil, Bahía — 111 BC 8
Inuvik 56-57 K 4
Inuya, Río — 96-97 E 7
In'va 124-125 U 4
Invalides 129 I c 2
Inveja, Serra da — 100-101 F 5
Invercargill 158-159 NO 9
Inverell 158-159 K 5
Inverleigh 158-159 H 3
Invermere 60 J 4
Inverness, FL 80-81 b 2
Inverness [CDN] 63 F 4
Inverness [GB] 119 DE 3
Inverurie 119 EF 3
Inverway 158-159 EF 3
Investigator Group 160 AB 4
Investigator Strait 158-159 FG 7
Inwa 141 D 5
Inwood, NY 82 III d 3
Inxu 174-175 H 6
Inyak Island = Ilha Inhaca 174-175 K 4
Inyak Peninsula = Península Inhaca 174-175 K 4
Inyangani 172 F 5
Inyan Kara Mountain 68-69 D 3
Inyokern, CA 74-75 DE 5
Inyo Mountains 74-75 DE 4
Inza [SU, place] 132-133 H 7
Inza [SU, river] 124-125 PQ 7
Inžavino 124-125 O 7
Inzein 148-149 C 3
Inzersdorf, Wien- 113 I b 2
Inzia 172 C 3
Inzūtzūt 141 E 3
Iō 206-207 S 7
Iōánnina 122-123 J 6
Iō-jima 144-145 H 7
Iō-jima = Volcano Islands 206-207 S 7
Iola, KS 70-71 C 7
Iola, TX 76-77 FG 7
Iolotan' 134-135 J 3
Iona, ID 66-67 H 4
Iona, SD 68-69 G 4
Ione, CA 74-75 C 3
Ione, OR 66-67 D 3
Ione, WA 66-67 E 1
Ionen 128 IV a 2
Ionia, MI 70-71 H 4
Ionian Basin 164-165 HJ 1-2
Ionian Islands 122-123 H 6-J 7
Ionian Sea 114-115 M 8
Ionti = Joontoy 172 H 2
Iony, ostrov — 132-133 b 6
Iori 126-127 N 6
Iorskoje ploskogorje 126-127 MN 6
Íos 122-123 L 7
Iosser 124-125 T 2
Iota, LA 78-79 C 5
Iowa 64-65 H 3
Iowa, LA 78-79 C 5
Iowa City, IA 70-71 E 5
Iowa Falls, IA 70-71 D 4
Iowa Park, TX 76-77 E 5-6
Iowa River 70-71 E 5
Ipadu, Cachoeira — 92-93 F 4
Ipameri 92-93 K 8
Ipanema 102-103 M 3
Ipanema, Rio — 100-101 F 5
Ipanema, Rio de Janeiro- 110 I b 2
Ipanoré, Cachoeira — 94-95 GH 7
Ipaŕía 92-93 E 6
Ipatinga 100-101 C 10
Ipatovo 126-127 L 4
Ipauçu 102-103 H 5
Ipaumirim 100-101 E 4
Ipecaetá 100-101 E 7
Ipel' 118 J 4
Ipewik River 58-59 E 2
Ipiales 94-95 C 7
Ipiaú 92-93 M 7
Ipin = Yibin 142-143 JK 6
Ipirá 100-101 E 7
Ipiranga [BR, Acre] 96-97 F 6
Ipiranga [BR, Amazonas ↗ Benjamin Constant] 92-93 F 5
Ipiranga [BR, Amazonas ↑ Benjamin Constant] 98-99 D 6
Ipiranga [BR, Paraná] 102-103 G 6
Ipiranga, São Paulo- 110 II b 2
Ipiranga do Piauí 100-101 D 4
Ipixuna 92-93 KL 5
Ipixuna, Rio — [BR ◁ Rio Juruá] 96-97 E 5
Ipixuna, Rio — [BR ◁ Rio Purus] 92-93 G 6

304 Ilāhābād

Ipoh 148-149 D 6
Iporá [BR, Goiás] 92-93 J 8
Ipora [BR, Mato Grosso do Sul] 102-103 F 5
Iporanga 102-103 H 6
Ippodrom 113 V b
Ippodromo 113 II b 2
Ippodromo Capanelle 113 II bc 2
Ippy 164-165 J 7
İpsala 136-137 B 2
Ipsario = Hypsárion 122-123 L 5
Ipsvoorde 128 II b 1
Ipswich, SD 68-69 G 3
Ipswich [GB] 119 G 5
Ipswich, Brisbane- 158-159 K 5
Ipu 92-93 L 5
Ipubí 100-101 D 4
Ipueiras 92-93 L 5
Iput' 124-125 H 7

Iqfit 173 C 5
Iquique 111 B 2
Iquiri, Morro — 102-103 H 7
Iquiri, Rio — 98-99 E 9
Iquitos 92-93 E 5
Iquitos, Isla — 96-97 E 3

Iraan, TX 76-77 D 7
Iracema [BR, Acre] 98-99 D 9
Iracema [BR, Amazonas] 98-99 D 8
Iracema [BR, Ceará] 100-101 E 3
Iracema [BR, Rondônia] 98-99 H 9
Iracoubo 92-93 J 3
Irago-suidō 144-145 L 5
Irago-zaki 144-145 L 5
Irai 106-107 L 1
Irajá 110 I b 1-2
Irajá, Rio de Janeiro- 110 I b 1
Irak 134-135 D-F 4
Irak = Arāk 134-135 F 4
Iraklion = Hērákleion 122-123 L 8
Irala [PY] 111 EF 3
Irala [RA] 106-107 G 5
Iramaia 100-101 D 7
Iran 134-135 F-H 4
Iran = Ilan 146-147 H 9
Iran, Pegunungan — 152-153 L 4-5
Iran, Plateau of — 50-51 MN 4
Iranaitivu = Iraneitivu 140 DE 6
Iraneitivu 140 DE 6
Irani, Rio — 102-103 F 7
Īrānshāh 136-137 M 4
Īrānshahr 134-135 HJ 5
Iraola 106-107 H 6
Irapa 92-93 G 2
Iraporanga 100-101 D 7
Irapuato 64-65 F 7
'Irāq Arabī 136-137 L 6-M 7
Iraquara 100-101 D 7
Irará 100-101 E 6-7
Irarrarene = Irharharān 164-165 F 3
Irati 111 F 3
Irau, Tanjong — 154 III b 1
Irauçuba 100-101 E 2
Irawadi = Erāwadī Myit 148-149 C 2
Irazú, Volcán — 64-65 K 9
Irazusta 106-107 H 4
Irbeni väin 124-125 CD 5
Irbid 134-135 D 4
Irbit 132-133 L 6
Irecê 92-93 L 7
Ireland 119 BC 5
Irene 111 D 5
Iretama 102-103 F 6
Irgalem = Yirga 'Alem 164-165 M 7
Irgâřv = Kuru 138-139 K 6
Irgiz 132-133 L 8
Irharharān 164-165 F 3
Īrherm = Īgharm 166-167 B 4
Irhyang-dong 144-145 GH 2
Iri 144-145 F 4-5
Irian, Teluk — 148-149 KL 7
Iriba 164-165 J 5
Iricoumé, Serra — 98-99 K 4
Iriga 148-149 H 4
Īrīkī 166-167 C 5
Iringa 172 G 3
Iringo 168-169 E 3
Irinjālakuda 140 BC 5
Iriomote-jima 142-143 N 7
Iriomote zima = Iriomote-jima 142-143 N 7
Iriri, Rio — 92-93 J 5
Irish Sea 119 D 5
Irituia 92-93 K 5
Irivi Novo, Rio — 98-99 M 9
Iriyamazu 155 III d 3
Irkilev 126-127 EF 2
Irkutsk 132-133 TU 7
Irma 61 C 4
Irmak 136-137 E 3
Irmãos, Ilha — 100-101 B 1
Irmingersee 56-57 d-f 5
Iro, Lac — 164-165 HJ 7
Īrōḍ = Erode 134-135 M 8
Irona 88-89 D 7
Iron Baron 160 C 4
Iron Bridge 62 K 3
Iron City, TN 78-79 F 3
Iron Cove 161 I ab 2
Iron Creek, AK 58-59 E 4
Irondequoit, NY 72-73 H 3
Iron Gate = Porţile de Fier 122-123 K 3
Iron Knob 158-159 G 6
Iron Mountain 74-75 G 4
Iron Mountain, MI 70-71 FG 3
Iron Mountain, WY 68-69 D 5
Iron River, MI 70-71 F 2
Iron River, WI 70-71 E 2
Ironside, OR 66-67 DE 3
Ironton, MO 70-71 E 7
Ironton, OH 72-73 E 5
Ironwood, MI 64-65 HJ 2
Iroquois, SD 68-69 H 3
Iroquois Falls 56-57 U 8
Irō saki 144-145 M 5
Irpen' [SU, place] 126-127 E 1
Irpen' [SU, river] 126-127 DE 1
'Irq, Al- 164-165 J 3
Irq Admar 164-165 F 4
Irq Aftut 166-167 DE 6
'Irqah 134-135 F 8
'Irq al-'Anqar 166-167 G 3-H 4
'Irq al-Kabīr al-Gharbī, Al- 164-165 D 3-E 2
'Irq al-Kabīr ash-Sharqī, Al- 164-165 F 2-3
'Irq ar-Rawī 164-165 D 3
'Irq ash-Shāsh 164-165 D 3-4
'Irq Buraghat 166-167 L 6
'Irq Isāwuwan 164-165 F 3
'Irq Sidrah, Ḥāssī — 166-167 H 4
'Irq Tahūdawīn 166-167 K 7
'Irq Yābis 166-167 EF 6
Irrawaddy = Erāwadī Myit 148-149 C 2
Irricana 60 L 4
Irruputunco, Volcán — 104-105 B 7
Irša 126-127 D 1
Iršava 126-127 A 2
Irtyš 132-133 N 6
Irtyšskoje 132-133 NO 7
Irumu 172 E 1
Irún 120-121 G 7
Irupana 104-105 C 5
Iruya 111 CD 2
Iruya, Río — 104-105 D 8
Irvine 61 CD 6
Irvine, KY 72-73 E 6
Irving, TX 76-77 F 6
Irving Park, Chicago-, IL 83 II b 1
Irvington, KY 70-71 G 7
Irvington, NJ 82 III a 2
Irwin, ID 66-67 H 4
Irwin, NE 68-69 EF 4
Irwŏl-san 144-145 G 4
Iryānah 166-167 M 1

Īs, Jabal — 173 D 6
Isa 168-169 G 2
Isabel, SD 68-69 F 3
Isabela 148-149 H 5
Isabela, Isla — 92-93 A 5
Isabela, La — 88-89 FG 3
Isabella, CA 74-75 D 5
Isabella, MN 70-71 E 2
Isabella, Cordillera — 64-65 J 9
Isabella Lake 74-75 D 5
Isabel Victoria = Colonia Isabel Victoria 106-107 H 2
Isachsen 56-57 Q 2
Isachsen, Cape — 56-57 OP 2
Isafjardhardjúp 116-117 b 1
Isa Fjord = Ísafjardhadjúp 116-117 b 1
Ísafjördhur 116-117 b 1
Isagateto 170 III a 1
Isahara = Isahaya 144-145 GH 6
Isahaya 144-145 GH 6
Isakly 124-125 S 6
Isakogorka, Archangel'sk- 124-125 MN 1
Isan 138-139 G 4
Isana, Río — 94-95 F 7
Isando 170 V c 1
Isangi 172 D 1
Isar 118 F 4
'Isāwīyah, Al- 134-135 D 4
Isāwuwan, 'Irq — 164-165 F 3
Iscayachi 104-105 D 7
Isca Yacú 104-105 D 10
Ischia 122-123 E 5
Iscuandé 94-95 BC 6
Iscuandé, Río — 94-95 C 6
Ise [J] 144-145 L 5
Išejevka 124-125 QR 6
Iseo 122-123 D 3
Iserbrook, Hamburg- 130 I a 1
Isère 120-121 K 6
Isère, Pointe — 92-93 J 3
Išerim, gora — 132-133 K 5
Iseri-Osun 170 III a 1
Isèrnia 122-123 F 5
Iset' 132-133 L 6
Ise-wan 144-145 L 5
Iseyin 164-165 E 7
Isezaki 144-145 M 4
Isfahan = Eşfahān 134-135 G 4
Isfendiyar dağları 134-135 CD 2
Isfjorden 116-117 j 5
Ishakli 136-137 D 3
I-shan = Yishan 142-143 K 7
Isherton 98-99 J 3
Ishibashi 144-145 N 3
Ishigaki-shima 142-143 NO 7
Ishikari 144-145 b 2
Ishikari gawa 144-145 b 2
Ishikari-wan 144-145 b 2
Ishikawa 144-145 L 4
Ishinomaki 144-145 N 3
Ishinomaki wan 144-145 N 3
Ishioka 144-145 N 4
Ishizuchino san 144-145 J 6
Ishpeming, MI 70-71 G 2
'Ishsh, Ra's al- 166-167 KL 2
I-shui = Yishui 146-147 G 4
Ishurdi 138-139 M 5
Ishwaripur 138-139 M 6
Isiboro, Río — 104-105 D 5
Isidoro 100-101 E 4
Isidro Casanova, La Matanza- 110 III b 2
Isigaki sima = Ishigaki-shima 142-143 NO 7
Isigny-sur-Mer 120-121 G 4
Işık dağı 136-137 E 2
Isil'kul' 132-133 N 7
Išim [SU, place] 132-133 M 6
Išim [SU, river] 132-133 M 7
Išimbaj 132-133 K 7
Isimbira 171 BC 4
Išimskaja step' 132-133 N 6-7
Isiolo 172 G 1
Isipingo Beach 174-175 J 5-6
Isiro 172 E 1
Isisford 158-159 H 4
Isispynten 116-117 mn 5
Iskandar 132-133 M 9
Īskandarīyah, Al- 164-165 KL 2
Iskar 122-123 L 4
Iskardū = Skardū 134-135 M 3
Iškejevo 124-125 S 6
İskele 136-137 F 4
İskenderun 134-135 D 3
İskenderun körfezi 136-137 F 4
İskilip 136-137 F 2
Iskitim 132-133 P 7
Iskorost' = Korosten' 126-127 D 1
Iskushuban 164-165 bc 1
Iskut River 60 B 1
Isla 86-87 N 8
Islá, La — [PE] 96-97 D 9
Isla, La — [RA] 106-107 DE 3
Isla, Salar de la — 104-105 B 9
Isla Águila = Speedwell Island 108-109 JK 9
Isla Alta 102-103 D 7
Isla Altamura 86-87 F 5
Isla Angamos 108-109 B 7
Isla Ángel de la Guarda 64-65 D 6
Isla Antica 94-95 K 2
Isla Apipé Grande 106-107 J 1
Isla Barro Colorado 64-65 b 2
Isla Beata 64-65 M 8
Isla Benjamin 108-109 BC 5
Isla Bermejo 106-107 FG 7
Isla Blanca 86-87 R 7
Isla Bougainville = Lively Island 108-109 KL 9
Isla Byrón 108-109 B 6
Isla Cabellos 106-107 J 3
Isla Cabrera 120-121 J 9
Isla Cacahual 94-95 BC 5
Isla Campana 111 A 7
Isla Campo Rico 106-107 G 4
Isla Caneima 94-95 L 3
Isla Cangrejo 94-95 L 3
Isla Capitán Aracena 108-109 D 10
Isla Carlos 111 B 8
Isla Carmen 64-65 DE 6
Isla Cedros 64-65 C 6
Isla Cerralvo 64-65 E 7
Isla Chaffers 108-109 BC 5
Isla Chañaral 111 B 3
Isla Chatham 111 B 8
Isla Chaves = Isla Santa Cruz 92-93 AB 5
Isla Choele Choel Grande 106-107 DE 7
Isla Christmas 108-109 D 10
Isla Clarence 111 B 8
Isla Clarión 86-87 C 8
Isla Clemente 108-109 B 5
Isla Coche 94-95 K 2
Isla Coiba 64-65 K 10
Isla Conejera 120-121 J 9
Isla Contoy 86-87 R 7
Isla Contreras 111 AB 8
Isla Corocoro 94-95 LM 3
Isla Covadonga 108-109 BC 9
Isla Creciente 86-87 DE 5
Isla Cresciente 86-87 DE 5
Isla-Cristina 120-121 D 10
Isla Cubagua 94-95 J 2
Isla Cuptana 108-109 C 5
Isla Curuzú Chalí 106-107 H 3
Isla Dawson 111 BC 8
Isla de Borbón = Pebble Island 108-109 K 8
Isla de Chiloé 111 AB 6
Isla de Corisco 164-165 F 8
Isla de Cozumel 64-65 J 7
Isla de Fernando Póo = Bioko 164-165 F 8
Isla de Flores 106-107 K 5
Isla de Goicoechea = New Island 108-109 J 8
Isla de Guadalupe 64-65 C 6
Isla de la Bahía 64-65 J 8
Isla del Aire 120-121 K 9
Isla de la Juventud 64-65 K 7
Isla de la Nieve 106-107 H 2
Isla de la Plata 92-93 C 5
Isla del Caño 88-89 DE 10
Isla del Carmen 86-87 OP 8
Isla del Coco 92-93 B 3
Isla de Lobos 106-107 K 5
Isla de los Césares 108-109 HJ 3
Isla de los Estados 111 D 8
Isla de los Riachos 108-109 HJ 3
Isla del Pillo 106-107 G 4
Isla del Rey 64-65 L 10
Isla del Rosario 94-95 CD 2
Isla del Rosario = Carass Island 108-109 J 8
Isla del Sol 104-105 B 4-5
Isla de Margarita 92-93 G 2
Isla de Ometepe 64-65 J 9
Isla de Providencia 92-93 C 2
Isla de Roatán 64-65 J 8
Isla Desolación 111 AB 8
Isla Desterrada 86-87 Q 6
Isla Diego de Amagro 111 A 8
Isla Dragonera 120-121 HJ 9
Isla Dring 108-109 B 5
Isla Duque de York 111 A 8
Isla Esmeralda 108-109 B 7
Isla Española 92-93 B 5
Isla Espiritu Santo 86-87 EF 5
Isla Fernandina 92-93 A 4-5
Isla Floreana 92-93 A 5
Isla Forsyth 108-109 B 5
Isla Fuerte 94-95 C 3
Isla Galeta 64-65 b 2
Isla Genovesa 92-93 B 4
Isla Gilbert 108-109 D 10
Isla Gordon 108-109 E 10
Isla Gorgona 92-93 D 4
Isla Grande de Tierra del Fuego 108-109 D-F 9-10
Isla Grevy 108-109 F 10
Isla Guafo 111 AB 6
Isla Guamblin 111 A 6
Isla Guardian Brito 108-109 C 10
Isla Hanover 111 AB 8
Isla Hermite 111 C 9
Isla Holbox 86-87 R 7
Isla Hoste 111 C 9
Isla Humedad 64-65 a 2
Isla Humos 108-109 BC 5
Isla Iquitos 96-97 E 3
Isla Isabela 92-93 A 5
Isla Jabali 108-109 HJ 3
Isla James 108-109 B 5
Isla Javier 108-109 B 6
Isla Jorge = George Island 108-109 JK 9
Isla Jorge Montt 108-109 B 8
Isla Juan Gallegos 64-65 b 2
Isla Juan Stuven 111 A 7
Isla La Blanquilla 92-93 G 2
Isla Largo Remo 64-65 b 2
Isla La Sola 94-95 K 2
Isla Lennox 111 C 9
Isla Level 108-109 B 5
Isla Luz 108-109 BC 5
Islāmābād 134-135 L 4
Islāmābād = Anantnāg 134-135 M 4
Isla Madre de Dios 111 A 8
Isla Magdalena 111 B 6
Isla Malpelo 92-93 C 4
Isla Manuel Rodriguez 108-109 BC 9
Isla Marchena 92-93 AB 4
Isla Margarita 94-95 D 3
Isla María Cleofas 86-87 G 7
Isla María Madre 64-65 E 7
Isla María Magdalena 86-87 E 7
Isla Mariusa 94-95 L 3
Isla Melchor 111 AB 7
Isla Merino Jarpa 108-109 BC 6
Islāmkoṭ 138-139 C 5
Isla Mocha 111 B 5
Isla Monserrate 86-87 E 5
Islamorada, FL 80-81 c 4
Isla Mornington 111 A 7
Islāmpur 138-139 K 5
Islāmpur = Urun Islāmpur 140 B 2
Isla Mujeres 86-87 R 7
Isla Nalcayec 108-109 C 6
Isla Naos 64-65 bc 3
Isla Navarino 111 C 9
Island Barn Reservoir 129 II a 2
Island City, OR 66-67 E 3
Island Falls 62 L 2
Island Falls, ME 72-73 M 1-2
Island Lagoon 158-159 G 6
Island Lake [CDN, lake] 56-57 RS 7
Island Lake [CDN, place] 62 BC 1
Island Maria = Bleaker Island 108-109 K 9
Island Mountain, CA 66-67 B 5
Island Park, ID 66-67 H 3
Island Park Reservoir 66-67 H 3
Island Pond, VT 72-73 KL 2
Islands, Bay of — [CDN] 63 G 3
Islands, Bay of — [NZ] 158-159 OP 7
Islands of Four Mountains 58-59 lm 4
Isla Noir 111 B 8
Isla Nueva 111 C 9
Isla Núñez 108-109 BC 9
Isla O'Brien 108-109 D 10
Isla Orchila 92-93 F 2
Isla Patricio Lynch 111 A 7
Isla Pedro González 94-95 B 3
Isla Pérez 86-87 PQ 6
Isla Piazzi 108-109 BC 8
Isla Picton 108-109 F 10
Isla Pinta 92-93 A 4
Isla Prat 108-109 B 7
Isla Puná 92-93 C 5
Isla Quilán 108-109 B 4
Isla Quinchao 108-109 C 4
Isla Quiriquina 106-107 A 6
Isla Raya 88-89 FG 11
Isla Refugio 108-109 C 4
Isla Riesco 111 B 8
Isla Rivero 108-109 B 5
Isla Rojas 108-109 C 5
Isla Rowlett 108-109 B 5
Isla San Benedicto 64-65 DE 8
Isla San Benito 86-87 BC 3
Isla San Cristóbal 92-93 B 5
Isla San Jerónimo 106-107 H 2
Isla San José [MEX] 64-65 DE 6
Isla San José [PA] 88-89 G 10
Isla San José = Weddell Island 111 D 8
Isla San Juanico 86-87 G 7
Isla San Lorenzo [MEX] 86-87 D 3
Isla San Lorenzo [PE] 92-93 D 7
Isla San Marcos 86-87 DE 4
Isla San Rafael = Beaver Island 108-109 J 8
Isla San Salvador 92-93 A 5
Isla San Sebastian 86-87 DE 3
Isla Santa Catalina 86-87 EF 5
Isla Santa Cruz [EC] 92-93 AB 5
Isla Santa Cruz [MEX] 86-87 E 5
Isla Santa Inés 111 B 8
Isla Santa Magdalena 86-87 D 5
Isla Santa Margarita 64-65 D 7
Isla Santa María 106-107 A 6
Isla Saona 64-65 N 8
Islas Baleares 120-121 H 9-K 8
Islas Cabo Verde 50-51 H 5
Islas Camden 108-109 C 10
Islas Canarias 164-165 A 3
Islas Caracas 94-95 J 2
Islas Chafarinas 166-167 EF 2
Islas Chauques 108-109 C 4
Islas Chimanas 94-95 J 2
Islas Columbretes 120-121 H 9
Islas de Alhucemas 166-167 E 2
Islas de Barlovento 64-65 OP 8-9
Islas de Coronados 74-75 E 6
Islas de la Bahía 64-65 J 8
Islas de las Lechiguanas 106-107 H 4
Islas del Maíz 64-65 K 9
Islas de los Chonos 106-107 B 2
Islas del Pasaje = Passage Islands 108-109 J 8
Islas de Revillagigedo 64-65 D 8
Islas de San Bernardo 94-95 CD 3
Islas Desertores 108-109 C 4
Islas Diego Ramírez 111 C 9
Islas Serrano 108-109 B 7
Islas Escalante 96-97 AB 3
Islas Evangelistas 108-109 B 9
Islas Georgias del Sur = South Georgia 111 J 8
Islas Grafton 108-109 C 10
Islas Guaitecas 111 AB 6
Islas Simpson 108-109 C 5
Islas Independencia 92-93 D 7
Islas Las Aves 92-93 F 2
Islas Londonderry 111 B 9
Islas Los Frailes 94-95 K 2
Islas Los Hermanos 94-95 JK 2
Islas Los Monjes 92-93 EF 2
Islas Los Roques 92-93 F 2
Islas Los Testigos 92-93 G 2
Islas Magill 108-109 C 10
Islas Marías 64-65 E 7
Islas Socorro 64-65 DE 8
Islas Soledad = East Falkland 111 E 8
Islas Pájoros 106-107 B 2
Islas Rennell 108-109 B 8-C 9
Islas Revillagigedo 86-87 C-E 8
Islas Stewart 111 B 8-9
Islas Torres 106-107 L 5
Islas Stosch 111 A 7
Islas Vallenar 108-109 B 5
Islas Wollaston 111 C 9
Islas Wood 108-109 E 10
Isla Taboga 64-65 bc 3
Isla Taboguilla 64-65 bc 3
Isla Talavera 106-107 J 1
Isla Talcan 108-109 C 4
Isla Tenquehuen 108-109 B 5
Isla Teresa 108-109 C 5
Isla Tiburón 64-65 D 6
Isla Tortuguilla 94-95 C 3
Isla Traiguén 108-109 C 5
Isla Tranqui 108-109 C 4
Isla Trinidad 111 D 5
Isla Trinidad = Sounders Island 108-109 J 8
Isla Turuepano 94-95 K 2
Isla Urabá 64-65 bc 3
Isla van der Meulen 108-109 B 7
Isla Venado 64-65 b 3
Isla Verde [CO] 94-95 D 2
Isla Verde [RA] 106-107 E 2
Isla Vidal Gormaz 108-109 B 8-9
Isla Vigía = Keppel Island 108-109 K 8
Isla Wellington 111 AB 7
Isla Wollaston 108-109 F 10
Isla Wood 106-107 F 7
Islay 119 C 4
Islay, Pampa de — 96-97 F 10
Islay, Punta — 96-97 E 10
Isla Yaciretá 102-103 D 7
Isla Zorra 64-65 b 2
Isle 120-121 H 6
Isle au Haut 72-73 M 2-3
Isle of Dogs 129 II b 2
Isle of Lewis 119 C 2
Isle of Man 119 DE 4
Isle of Wight 119 F 6
Isle Royale 64-65 J 2
Isle Royale National Park 70-71 F 2
Isles Dernieres 78-79 D 6
Isles of Scilly 119 C 7
Isleta, NM 76-77 A 5
Isleton, CA 74-75 C 3
Isleworth, London- 129 II a 2
Islington, MA 84 I a 3
Islington, London- 129 II b 1
Islón 106-107 B 2
Ismailia = Al-Ismā'īlīyah 164-165 L 2
Ismā'īlīyah, Al- 164-165 L 2
Ismā'īlīyah, Tur'at al- 170 II b 1
Ismailly 126-127 O 6
Ismay, MT 68-69 D 2
Ismetpaşa 136-137 H 3
Isnā 164-165 L 3
Isnotú 94-95 F 3
Isogo, Yokohama- 155 III a 3
Isohama = Ōarai 144-145 N 4
Isoka 172 F 4
Ìsola Lampedusa 164-165 G 1
Ìsola Linosa 164-165 G 1
Ìsola Pianosa 122-123 D 4
Ìsola Salina 122-123 F 6
Ìsola Vulcano 122-123 F 6
Ìsole Ègadi 122-123 DE 6
Ìsole Eòlie o Lìpari 122-123 F 6
Ìsole Giuba 172 H 2
Ìsole Ponziane 122-123 E 5
Ìsole Trèmiti 122-123 F 4
Isolo 170 III a 1
Ispahan = Eşfahān 134-135 G 4
Isparta 134-135 C 3
Isperih 122-123 M 4
İspir 136-137 J 2
Israel 134-135 CD 4
Israelite Bay 158-159 DE 6
Issa 124-125 P 7
Issano 92-93 H 3
Issaouane, Erg — = 'Irq Isāwuwan 164-165 F 3
Issati 168-169 F 3
Isser, Ouèd — = Wādī Yassar 166-167 H 1
Issia 168-169 D 4
Issoudun 120-121 HJ 5
Issyk-Kul', ozero — 142-143 M 3
Istādah, Ab-e- = Ābe Estāda 134-135 K 4
İstanbul 134-135 BC 2
İstanbul-Anadoluhisarı 154 I b 2
İstanbul-Anadolukavağı 154 I b 1
İstanbul-Bakırköy 136-137 C 2
İstanbul-Balat 154 I a 2
İstanbul-Balmumcu 154 I b 2
İstanbul-Bebek 154 I b 2
İstanbul-Beşiktaş 154 I b 2
İstanbul-Beykoz 136-137 C 2
İstanbul-Beylerbeyi 154 I b 2
İstanbul-Beyoğlu 154 I a 2
İstanbul boğazı 154 I b 1-2
İstanbul-Bostancı 154 I b 3
İstanbul-Boyaciköy 154 I b 2
İstanbul-Büyükada 136-137 C 2
İstanbul-Büyükdere 154 I b 2
İstanbul-Çapa 154 I a 2
İstanbul-Çengelköy 154 I b 2
İstanbul-Chiangir 154 I ab 2
İstanbul-Çubuklu 154 I b 2
İstanbul-Doğancılar 154 I b 2
İstanbul-Eminönü 154 I ab 2
İstanbul-Erenköy 154 I b 3
İstanbul-Eyüp 154 I a 2
İstanbul-Fatih 154 I a 2
İstanbul-Fener 154 I a 2
İstanbul-Galata 154 I a 2
İstanbul-Hasköy 154 I a 2
İstanbul-Haydarpaşa 154 I b 3
İstanbul-İçerenköy 154 I b 3
İstanbul-İncirköy 154 I b 2
İstanbul-İstinye 154 I b 2
İstanbul-Kadıköy 136-137 C 2
İstanbul-Kandilli 154 I b 2
İstanbul-Kanlıca 154 I b 2
İstanbul-Kartal 136-137 C 2
İstanbul-Kefeliköy 154 I b 2
İstanbul-Kızıltoprak 154 I b 3
İstanbul-Kuruçeşme 154 I b 2
İstanbul-Kuzguncuk 154 I b 2
İstanbul-Orhaiye 154 I b 2
İstanbul-Paşabahce 154 I b 2
İstanbul-Rumelihisarı 154 I b 2
İstanbul-Rumelikavağı 154 I b 1
İstanbul-Sarıyer 136-137 C 3
İstanbul-Skutari = İstanbul-Üsküdar 134-135 BC 2
İstanbul-Tarabya 154 I b 2
İstanbul-Topkapı 154 I a 2
İstanbul-Umuryeri 154 I b 2
İstanbul-Üsküdar 134-135 BC 2
İstanbul-Vaniköy 154 I b 2
İstanbul-Yedikule 154 I a 3
İstanbul-Yenikapı 154 I a 3
İstanbul-Yeniköy 154 I b 2
İstanbul-Zeytinburnu 154 I a 3
Īstgāh-e Bīsheh 136-137 N 6
Īstgāh-e Gargar 136-137 N 7
Īstgāh-e Keshvar 136-137 N 6
Īstgāh-e Parandak 136-137 O 5
Isthilart 106-107 HJ 3
İstinye, İstanbul- 154 I b 2
Istisu 126-127 MN 7
Istmina 92-93 D 3
Istmo Carlos Ameghino 108-109 G 4
Istmo de Médanos 94-95 G 2
Istmo de Ofqui 108-109 B 6
Istmo de Panamá 64-65 L 9-10
Istmo de Tehuantepec 64-65 GH 8
Isto, Mount — 58-59 Q 2
Istra [SU] 124-125 L 6
Istranca dağları 136-137 B 1-C 2
Istria 122-123 EF 3
Isunba 170 III a 2
Isvestia Islands = ostrova Izvestij CIK 132-133 OP 2

Itá 102-103 D 6
Itabaiana 100-101 F 6
Itabaianinha 92-93 M 7
Itabaina 92-93 M 6
Itabapoana 102-103 M 4
Itabapoana, Rio — 102-103 M 4
Itabashi, Tōkyō- 155 III ab 1
Itaberá 102-103 H 5
Itaberaba 92-93 L 7
Itaberaí 92-93 JK 8
Itabira 102-103 L 3
Itabirito 102-103 L 4
Itaboraí 102-103 L 5
Itabuna 92-93 M 7
Itacaiúnas, Rio — 92-93 JK 6
Itacajá 98-99 P 9
Itacambira, Pico — 102-103 L 2
Itacambiruçu, Rio — 102-103 L 2
Itacaré 92-93 M 7
Itacira 100-101 D 7
Itacoatiara 92-93 H 5
Itacolomi, Ilhas — 102-103 H 6
Itacolomi, Pico — 92-93 L 9
Itacolomi, Ponta — 100-101 BC 1-2
Itacolomi, Saco de — 110 I b 1
Itacuaí, Rio — 96-97 F 5
Itacurubí del Rosario 102-103 D 6
Itaetê 92-93 L 7
Itaguá 100-101 D 4
Itaguaçu 100-101 D 10
Itaguaí 102-103 KL 5
Itaguara 102-103 K 4
Itaguari, Rio — 100-101 B 8
Itaguatins 92-93 K 6
Itagüí 94-95 D 4
Itaguyry 102-103 E 6
Itahuania, Cerros de — 96-97 F 8
Itaí 111 G 2
Itaíba 100-101 F 5
Itá Ibaté 106-107 J 1
Itaiçaba 100-101 F 3
Itaim, Rio — 100-101 D 4
Itaimbé 100-101 D 10
Itaimbey, Río — 102-103 E 6
Itainópolis 100-101 D 4
Itaiópolis 102-103 H 7
Itaipava, Cachoeira — [BR, Rio Araguaia] 92-93 K 6
Itaipava, Cachoeira — [BR, Rio Xingu] 92-93 J 5
Itaípe 100-101 D 7
Itaipu, Ponta — 102-103 J 6
Itaituba 92-93 H 5
Itajaí 111 G 3
Itajaí, Rio — 102-103 H 7
Itajaí do Sul, Rio — 102-103 H 7
Itajaí-Mirim, Rio — 102-103 H 7
Itají 100-101 E 9
Itajibá 100-101 E 8
Itajubá 92-93 K 9
Itajuípe 92-93 LM 7
Itaka 132-133 W 7
Ītal, Wādī — 166-167 J 2-3
Itala = 'Adale 172 J 1
Itala, Río — 106-107 A 6
Itálica 120-121 DE 10
Italó 106-107 F 5
Italy 122-123 C 3-F 5
Italy, TX 76-77 F 6
Itamaraju 100-101 E 9
Itamarandiba 102-103 L 2
Itamataré 100-101 A 2
Itambacuri 102-103 M 3
Itambacuri, Rio — 102-103 M 3
Itambé 92-93 L 8
Itambé, Pico de — 102-103 L 3
Itamirim 100-101 C 8
Itamoji 102-103 J 4
Itamotinga 100-101 DE 5
Itanagra 100-101 EF 7
Itanhaém 102-103 J 6
Itanhandu 102-103 K 5
Itanhauã, Rio — 98-99 F 7
Itanhém 100-101 D 3
Itanhém, Rio — 100-101 E 9
Itanhomi 102-103 M 3
Itany 92-93 J 4
Itaocara 92-93 L 9
Itapaci 92-93 JK 7
Itapagé 92-93 LM 5
Itaparaná, Rio — 98-99 G 8
Itaparica, Ilha de — 100-101 E 7
Itapé [BR] 100-101 E 8
Itapé [PY] 102-103 D 6
Itapebi 92-93 M 8
Itapeim 100-101 EF 3
Itapeipu 100-101 D 6
Itapemirim 92-93 LM 9
Itapercerica 102-103 K 4
Itaperuna 102-103 LM 4
Itapetim 100-101 F 4
Itapetinga 92-93 LM 8
Itapetininga 111 G 2
Itapeva 111 G 2
Itapeva, Lagoa — 106-107 MN 2
Itapevi 106-107 K 2
Itapicuru [BR ↑ Alagoinhas] 100-101 EF 6
Itapicuru [BR ← Jequié] 100-101 D 7
Itapicuru, Rio — [BR, Bahia] 92-93 M 7
Itapicuru, Rio — [BR, Maranhão] 92-93 L 5
Itapicuru, Serra — 92-93 KL 6
Itapicuru Açu, Rio — 100-101 DE 6
Itapicurumirim 92-93 L 5
Itapicuruzinho, Rio — 100-101 DE 6
Itapicuruzinho, Rio — 100-101 C 3
Itapina 100-101 D 10
Itapinima 98-99 H 7
Itapinima, Raudal — 94-95 F 7
Itapipoca 92-93 M 5
Itapira 92-93 K 9
Itapiranga 102-103 F 7
Itapirapuã, Pico — 102-103 H 6
Itapitocaí 106-107 J 2
Itapiúna 100-101 E 3
Itápolis 102-103 H 4
Itapora 102-103 E 4-5
Itaporanga [BR, Paraíba] 100-101 EF 4
Itaporanga [BR, São Paulo] 102-103 H 5
Itaporanga d'Ajuda 100-101 F 6
Itapuã [BR] 106-107 M 3
Itapúa [PY] 102-103 DE 7
Itapuí 102-103 H 5
Itapuí, Rio — 98-99 C 7
Itaquatiara, Riacho — 100-101 D 5
Itaqui 111 E 3
Itarantim 100-101 DE 8
Itararé 102-103 H 6
Itararé, Rio — 102-103 H 5
Itarema 100-101 E 2
Itariri 102-103 J 6
Itārsi 134-135 M 6
Itarumã 102-103 G 3
Itasca, TX 76-77 F 6
Itasca, Lake — 64-65 G 2
Itatí 106-107 H 1
Itatiba 102-103 J 5

Itatiba 305

Itatina, Serra dos — 102-103 J 6
Itatinga 102-103 H 5
Itatique 104-105 E 7
Itatira 100-101 E 3
Itatuba 92-93 G 6
Itauçu 102-103 H 2
Itaueira 100-101 C 4
Itaueira, Rio — 100-101 C 4-5
Itaúna 102-103 K 4
Itaúnas 100-101 E 10
Iṭāva = Bīna 138-139 G 5
Iṭāvā = Etāwah 138-139 F 5
Itawa = Etāwah 134-135 M 5
Itbayat Island 146-147 H 11
Ite 96-97 F 10
Itebero 171 AB 3
Itel, Ouèd — = Wādī Īṭal 166-167 J 2-3
Itende 171 C 4
Itenes, Rio — 104-105 E 3
Ithaca, MI 70-71 H 4
Ithaca, NY 64-65 L 3
Ithaca = Ithákē 122-123 J 6
Ithákē 122-123 J 6
Ithan Creek 84 III a 1
Ithrā = Itrah 136-137 G 7
Itigi 172 F 3
Itimbiri 172 D 1
Itinga [BR, Maranhão] 98-99 P 7
Itinga [BR, Minas Gerais] 102-103 M 2
Itinga da Serra 100-101 DE 6
Itinoseki = Ichinoseki 142-143 QR 4
Itiquira 92-93 J 8
Itiquira, Rio — 92-93 H 8
Itirapina 102-103 J 5
Itire 170 III ab 1
Itiruçu 92-93 L 7
Itiúba 92-93 M 7
Itkillik River 58-59 M 2
'Itmāniya, El- = Al-'Uthmānīyah 173 BC 4
Itō 144-145 M 5
Itoigawa 144-145 L 4
Itoikawa = Itoigawa 144-145 L 4
Itororó 100-101 DE 8
Itrah 136-137 G 7
Itrī, Jabal — 173 D 7
Iṭsā 173 B 3
Itschnach 128 IV b 2
Itsjang = Yichang 142-143 L 5
Itterbeek 128 II a 1
Itu [BR] 102-103 J 5
Itu [WAN] 168-169 G 4
I-tu = Yidu 142-143 M 4
Itu = Yidu 146-147 C 6
Ituaçu 92-93 L 7
Ituango 94-95 D 4
Ituberá 100-101 E 7
Itueta 102-103 M 3
Ituí, Rio — 92-93 E 6
Ituim 106-107 M 2
Ituiutaba 102-103 H 3
Itula 172 E 2
Itulilik, AK 58-59 J 6
Itumbiara 92-93 K 8
Itumbiara, Represa de — 102-103 H 3
Itumirim 102-103 K 4
Ituna 61 G 5
Ituni Township 92-93 H 3
Itupeva 100-101 D 3
Itupiranga 92-93 JK 6
Ituporanga 102-103 H 7
Iturama 102-103 GH 3
Ituri 172 E 1
Iturregui 106-107 G 6
Iturup, ostrov — 132-133 c 8
Ituverava 102-103 J 4
Ituxi, Rio — 92-93 F 6
Ituzaingó 106-107 J 1
Ituzaingó, Morón- 110 III b 1
Itzar 166-167 D 3
Itzawisis 174-175 C 4
Itzehoe 118 D 1-2

Iuiú 100-101 C 8
Iuka, MS 78-79 E 3
Iúna 100-101 D 11

Iva, SC 80-81 E 3
Ivaceviči 124-125 E 7
Ivaí, Rio — 111 F 2
Ivaiporã 102-103 G 6
Ivajlovgrad 122-123 M 5
Ivalo 116-117 M 3
Ivalojoki 116-117 M 3
Ivan, AR 78-79 C 4
Ivancevo 124-125 S 4
Ivančina 124-125 TU 3
Ivangorod 124-125 G 4
Ivanhoe 158-159 H 6
Ivanhoe, MN 70-71 BC 3
Ivanhoe, Melbourne- 161 II c 1
Ivanhoe River 62 K 2-3
Ivaniči 126-127 B 1
Ivankov 126-127 DE 1
Ivan'kovo [SU, Kalininskaja Oblast'] 124-125 L 5
Ivanof Bay, AK 58-59 cd 2
Ivano-Frankovsk 126-127 B 2
Ivanov 126-127 D 2
Ivanovka [SU, Rossijskaja SFSR] 124-125 T 7
Ivanovka [SU, Ukrainskaja SSR] 126-127 E 3
Ivanovo [SU, Belorusskaja SSR] 124-125 E 7
Ivanovo [SU, Rossijskaja SFSR] 132-133 FG 6
Ivanovo, Voznesensk- = Ivanovo 132-133 FG 6
Ivanovskaja 124-125 UV 3
Ivanovskoje, Moskva- 113 V d 2
Ivanowsky 106-107 F 6
Ivantejevka [SU, Saratovskaja Oblast'] 124-125 R 7
Ivanuškova 132-133 UV 6
Ivaščenkovo = Čapajevsk 132-133 HJ 7
Ivatuba 102-103 FG 5
Ivdel' 132-133 L 5
Ivenec 124-125 F 7
Ivigtût 56-57 b 5
Ivindo 172 B 1
Ivinheima 102-103 F 5
Ivinheima, Rio — 92-93 J 9
Ivisaruk River 58-59 G 1-2
Iviza = Ibiza 120-121 H 9
Ivje 124-125 E 7
Ivnica 126-127 D 1
Ivohibe 172 J 6
Ivón 104-105 C 2
Ivón, Río — 104-105 C 2
Ivory Coast [RI, landscape] 164-165 CD 8
Ivory Coast [RI, state] 164-165 CD 7
Ivot 124-125 K 7
Ivrea 122-123 B 3
İvrindi 136-137 B 3
Ivry-sur-Seine 129 I c 2
Ivuna 171 C 5

Iwadate 144-145 MN 2
Iwaizumi 144-145 NO 3
Iwaki 144-145 N 4
Iwaki yama 144-145 N 2
Iwakuni 144-145 J 5
Iwamizawa 142-143 R 3
Iwanai 144-145 b 2
Iwanowo = Ivanovo 132-133 FG 6
Iwanuma 144-145 N 3
Iwata 144-145 LM 5
Iwate [J, administrative unit] 144-145 N 2-3
Iwate [J, place] 144-145 N 3
Iwate-yama 144-145 N 3
Iwo 164-165 E 7
Iwō-jima = Iō-jima 144-145 H 7
Iwōn 144-145 G 2
Iwopin 168-169 G 4
Iwu = Yiwu 146-147 GH 7

Ixiamas 92-93 F 7
Ixopo 172 EF 8
Ixtacalco 91 I c 2
Ixtacalco-Agrícola Oriental 91 I c 2
Ixtacalco-Agrícola Pantitlán 91 I c 2
Ixtacalco-San Andrés Tetepilco 91 I c 2
Ixtapalapa 91 I c 2
Ixtapalapa-Avante 91 I c 3
Ixtapalapa-Escuadrón 201 91 I c 2
Ixtapalapa-Héroes de Churubusco 91 I c 2
Ixtapalapa-Los Reyes 91 I c 2
Ixtapalapa-San Felipe Terremotos 91 I c 2
Ixtapalapa-Santa Cruz Meyehualco 91 I c 2
Ixtapalapa-Santa Martha Acatitla 91 I cd 2
Ixtapalapa-Santiago Acahualtepec 91 I c 2
Ixtapalapa-Tepalcates 91 I c 2
Ixtayutla 86-87 M 9
Ixtepec 64-65 G 8
Ixtlán del Río 86-87 HJ 7

I-yang = Yiyang [TJ, Hunan] 142-143 L 6
Iyang = Yiyang [TJ, Jiangxi] 146-147 F 7
I-yang = Yiyang [TJ, Jiangxi] 146-147 F 7
Iyang, Pegunungan — 152-153 K 9
Iyo 144-145 J 6
Iyomishima 144-145 J 6
Iyonada 144-145 HJ 6
I-yüan = Yiyuan 146-147 G 3

Iž 124-125 T 5
'Iz, Ḥāssī al- 166-167 G 4
Izabal, Lago de — 64-65 HJ 8
Izalco 64-65 H 9
Izamal 86-87 Q 7
Izashiki = Sata 144-145 H 7
Iz'aslav 126-127 C 1
Izaviknek River 58-59 F 6
Izberbaš 126-127 NO 5
Izdeškovo 124-125 JK 6
Izembek Bay 58-59 b 2
Iževsk 132-133 J 6
Izhevsk = Iževsk 132-133 J 6
Izigan, Cape — 58-59 n 4
Izki 134-135 H 6
Ižma [SU, place] 132-133 J 4
Ižma [SU, river] 132-133 J 5
Izmail 126-127 D 4
Izmajlovo 124-125 Q 7
Izmajlovo, Moskva- 113 V d 2
Izmajlovskij PkiO 113 V d 2
Izmalkovo 124-125 LM 7
İzmir 134-135 B 3
İzmir körfezi 136-137 B 3
İzmit 134-135 BC 2
İzmit körfezi 136-137 C 2
İznik 136-137 C 2
İznik gölü 136-137 C 2
Izobil'nyj 126-127 KL 4
Izoplit 124-125 KL 5
Izozog 104-105 E 6
Izozog, Bañados de — 92-93 G 8
Izra' 136-137 G 6
Izúcar de Matamoros 86-87 LM 8
Izu hantō 144-145 M 5
Izuhara 144-145 G 5
Iz'um 126-127 H 2
Izumi 144-145 H 6
Izumi, Yokohama- 155 III a 3
Izumo 144-145 J 5
Izu-shotō 142-143 QR 5
Izu syotō = Izu-shotō 142-143 QR 5
Izvestij CIK, ostrova — 132-133 OP 2

J

Ja = Dja 164-165 G 8
Jaab Lake 62 K 1
Jaagupi 124-125 E 4
Jaani, Järva- 124-125 EF 4
Ja Ayun = Ya Ayun 150-151 G 6
Jāb, Tall — 136-137 G 6
Jabal, Baḥr al- 164-165 L 7
Jabalā 166-167 D 2
Jabal 'Abd al-'Azīz 136-137 HJ 4
Jabal Abū Ḍahr 173 D 6
Jabal Abū Dhi'āb 173 D 5
Jabal Abū Ḥamāmīd 173 D 5
Jabal Abū Ḥarbah 173 C 4
Jabal Abū Jamal 164-165 M 6
Jabal Abū Jurdī 173 D 6
Jabal Abū Rijmayn 136-137 H 5
Jabal aḍ-Ḍayah 166-167 F 2
Jabal ad-Dūgh 166-167 F 3
Jabal ad-Durūz 134-135 D 4
Jabal Aghlāghal 166-167 G 6
Jabal Ajā 134-135 E 5
Jabal 'Ajlūn 136-137 FG 6
Jabal al-Abyaḍ, Al- 166-167 L 1
Jabal al-Adirīyāt 136-137 G 7
Jabal al-Aḥmar 173 B 3
Jabal al-'Ajmah 164-165 L 3
Jabal al-Akhḍar [LAR] 164-165 J 2
Jabal al-Akhḍar [Oman] 134-135 H 6
Jabal al-Anṣārīyah 136-137 G 5
Jabal al-'Askar 166-167 L 2
Jabal al-Asīyah 173 C 4
Jabal al-'Aṣr 173 B 6
Jabal al-Awrās 166-167 JK 2
Jabal al-Barqah 173 C 5
Jabal al-Batrā 136-137 F 8
Jabal al-Bishrī 136-137 H 5
Jabal al-Farāyid 173 D 6
Jabal al-Finṭās 173 B 6
Jabal al-Gulūd 166-167 M 1
Jabal al-Ḥāṣ 136-137 G 5
Jabal al-Jalālat al-Baḥrīyah 173 BC 3
Jabal al-Jalālat al-Qiblīyah 173 C 3
Jabal al-Jaw'alīyāt 136-137 G 7
Jabal al-Jiddī 173 C 2
Jabal al-Julūd 166-167 M 1
Jabal al-Kurā' 166-167 J 2
Jabal al-Kusūm 166-167 J 2
Jabal al-Lawz 134-135 D 5
Jabal al-Majradah 166-167 KL 1
Jabal al-Manār 134-135 EF 8
Jabal al-Mūdīr 166-167 HJ 7
Jabal al-Muqattam 170 II b 1-c 2
Jabal al-Qamar 134-135 G 7
Jabal al-Qṣūr 166-167 M 3
Jabal al-Tīṭri 166-167 H 1-2
Jabal al-'Urf 173 C 4
Jabal al-'Uwaynāt 164-165 K 4
Jabal al-Wāqif 173 B 6
Jabal al-Wārshanīs [DZ, mountain] 166-167 G 1-2
Jabal al-Wārshanīs [DZ, mountains] 166-167 GH 2
Jabal Ankūr 173 DE 7
Jabal an-Namāshah 166-167 K 2
Jabal an-Nasir 164-165 F 4
Jabal Ardar Gwagwa 173 D 6
Jabal Arkanū 164-165 J 4
Jabal ar-Ruwāq 136-137 G 5-6
Jabal as-Sarj 166-167 L 2
Jabal as-Sawdā' 164-165 GH 3
Jabal aṣ-Ṣāyda' 166-167 G 2
Jabal as-Saykh 136-137 FG 6
Jabal as-Sibā'ī 173 CD 5
Jabal as-Simḥām 134-135 GH 7
Jabal Asūtarībah 173 E 7
Jabal 'Atāqah 173 C 2-3
Jabal ath-Thabt 173 CD 3
Jabal at-Tanf 136-137 H 6
Jabal aṭ-Ṭayr 134-135 E 7
Jabal at-Tīh 164-165 L 3
Jabal aṭ-Ṭubayq 134-135 D 5
Jabal Awlād Nāil 166-167 H 2
Jabal 'Ayashī 164-165 CD 2
Jabalayn, Al- 164-165 L 6
Jabal 'Aysa 166-167 F 3
Jabal Azūrkī 166-167 C 4
Jabal az-Zāb 166-167 J 2
Jabal az-Zāwīyah 136-137 G 5
Jabal az-Zūjitīn 166-167 L 1-2
Jabal Bābūr [DZ, mountain] 166-167 J 1
Jabal Bābūr [DZ, mountains] 166-167 J 1
Jabal Banī 164-165 C 2-3
Jabal Bāqīr 136-137 F 8
Jabal B'athar Zajū 173 C 7
Jabal Bayḍā' 173 D 6
Jabal Būdhīyah 173 C 3
Jabal Bū Iblān 166-167 D 3
Jabal Bū Kāhil 166-167 HJ 2
Jabal Bū Khaḍrah 166-167 KL 2
Jabal Bū Naṣr 166-167 E 3
Jabal Bū Ramlī 166-167 L 2
Jabal Buwārah 173 D 3
Jabal Dafdaf 173 D 3
Jabal Dibbāgh 173 D 4
Jabal Dīrah 166-167 H 1
Jabal Ghāb 136-137 H 5
Jabal Gharbī 136-137 H 5
Jabal Ghārib 164-165 L 3
Jabal Hadal 'Awāb 173 D 7
Jabal Hajīr 134-135 G 8
Jabal Ḥamātah 164-165 LM 4
Jabal Ḥamrīn 136-137 KL 5
Jabal Hilāl 173 CD 2
Jabali, Isla — 108-109 HJ 3
Jabal Ibrāhīm 134-135 E 6
Jabal Ijrān 166-167 H 6
Jabal 'Ikdat 166-167 B 4
Jabal Īmīdghās 166-167 D 4
Jabal Īs 173 D 6
Jabal Itrī 173 D 7
Jabal Jirays 173 D 7
Jabal Jūrgāy 164-165 JK 6
Jabal Kalāt 173 D 6
Jabal Kasal 166-167 G 3
Jabal Katrīnah 164-165 L 3
Jabal Kharaz 134-135 E 8
Jabal Korbiyāy 173 D 6
Jabal Kutunbul 134-135 E 7
Jabal Loubnān = Jabal Lubnān 136-137 FG 5-6
Jabal Lubnān 136-137 FG 5-6
Jabal Lubnān ash-Sharqī 136-137 G 5-6
Jabal Ma'azzah 173 C 2
Jabal Ma'dīd 166-167 J 2
Jabal Mahmil 166-167 K 2
Jabal Ma'rafāy 173 D 6
Jabal Marrah 164-165 JK 6
Jabal Mazhafah = Jabal Buwārah 173 D 3
Jabal Mazi 166-167 F 3
Jabal M'ghīlah 166-167 L 2
Jabal Mishbīh 164-165 L 4
Jabal Mōāb 136-137 F 7
Jabal Mu'askar 166-167 D 3
Jabal Mubārak 136-137 F 8
Jabal Mudaysīsāt 136-137 G 7
Jabal Muqsim 173 CD 6
Jabal Mūrig 166-167 CD 3
Jabal Murrah 166-167 L 2
Jabal Mu'tiq 173 C 4
Jabal Nafusah 164-165 G 2
Jabal Nasīyah 173 C 6
Jabal Nī'āj 173 C 6
Jabal Nuqruṣ 173 D 5
Jabalón 120-121 F 9
Jabalpur 134-135 MN 6
Jabal Qarn at-Tays 173 C 6
Jabal Qarnayt 134-135 E 6
Jabal Qaṭrānī 173 B 3
Jabal Qaṭṭār 173 C 4
Jabal Rām 136-137 F 8
Jabal R'bāṭah 166-167 L 2
Jabal Ṣabāyā 134-135 E 7
Jabal Ṣaghrū' 164-165 C 2
Jabal Ṣahrā 173 CD 4
Jabal Salālah 173 D 7
Jabal Salmah 134-135 E 5
Jabal Sanām 136-137 M 7
Jabal Shaḥāmbī 164-165 F 1-2
Jabal Shā'ib al-Banāt 164-165 L 3
Jabal Shammar 134-135 E 5
Jabal Shār [Saudi Arabia] 173 D 4
Jabal Shā'r [SYR] 136-137 GH 5
Jabal Shīlyah 164-165 F 1
Jabal Shindidāy 173 E 6
Jabal Sinjār 136-137 JK 4
Jabal Sīrwah 166-167 C 4
Jabal Talju 164-165 K 6
Jabal Tanūshfī 166-167 F 2
Jabal Ṭāriq, Bughāz — 164-165 CD 1
Jabal Tasasah 166-167 F 2
Jabal Tashrīrt 166-167 J 2
Jabal Tazzikā' 166-167 DE 2
Jabal Tibissah [DZ] 166-167 J 7
Jabal Tibissah [TN] 166-167 L 2
Jabal Tidighīn 166-167 D 2
Jabal Tilimsān 166-167 F 2
Jabal Tīshāro 166-167 JK 2
Jabal Tubqāl 164-165 C 2
Jabal Ṭummō 164-165 G 4
Jabal Ṭuwayq 134-135 F 6
Jabal 'Ubkayk 164-165 M 4
Jabal Ūdah 164-165 M 4
Jabal Umm aṭ-Ṭuyūr al-Fawqānī 173 D 6
Jabal Umm 'Inab 173 C 5
Jabal Umm Naqqāṭ 173 CD 5
Jabal Umm Shāghir 173 B 6
Jabal 'Unayzah 134-135 DE 4
Jabal Wārqzīz 164-165 C 3
Jabal Yu'alliq 173 C 2
Jabal Zubayr 173 C 4
Jabaquara, São Paulo- 110 II b 2
Jabavu, Johannesburg- 170 V a 2
Jabīlat, Al- 166-167 BC 4
Jabīlāt, Ḥāssī — 166-167 C 6
Jabinyānah 166-167 M 2
Jabjabah, Wādī — 173 C 7
Jablah 136-137 F 5
Jablanica [AL] 122-123 J 5
Jablanica [BG] 122-123 L 4
Jablanica [YU] 122-123 G 4
Jablunca Pass = Jablunkovsky průsmyk 118 J 4
Jablunkovský průsmyk 118 J 4
Jaboatão 100-101 G 5
Jabotablon 94-95 CD 4
Jabung, Tanjung — 148-149 DE 7
Jabuticabal 92-93 K 9
Jabuticatubas 102-103 L 3
Jaca 120-121 G 7
Jacaf, Canal — 108-109 C 5
Jaçanã, São Paulo- 110 II b 1
Jacaqua 106-107 K 2
Jacaraci 100-101 C 8
Jacaraí, Rio — 100-101 D 2
Jacarandá 100-101 E 8
Jacaraú 100-101 G 4
Jacaré, Rio — [BR, Bahia] 92-93 L 6-7
Jacaré, Rio — [BR, Minas Gerais] 102-103 K 4
Jacaré, Travessão — 98-99 O 10
Jacareacanga 98-99 JK 8
Jacareí 92-93 K 9
Jacarepaguá, Rio de Janeiro- 110 I ab 2
Jacaretinga 98-99 J 9
Jacarèzinho 102-103 H 5
Jáchal = San José de Jáchal 111 C 4
Jáchal, Río — 106-107 C 3
Jachhen 142-143 E 5
Jachroma 124-125 L 5
Jáchymov 118 F 3
Jaciara 102-103 E 1
Jacinto 100-101 D 3
Jacinto Aráuz 106-107 F 7
Jacinto City, TX 85 III bc 1
Jaciparaná 92-93 G 6
Jaciparana, Rio — 98-99 F 9-10
Jackfish 70-71 G 1
Jackfish Lake 61 DE 4
Jackhead Harbour 61 K 5
Jackman Station, ME 72-73 L 2
Jacksboro, TX 76-77 EF 6
Jackson, AL 78-79 F 5
Jackson, CA 74-75 C 3
Jackson, GA 80-81 DE 4
Jackson, KY 72-73 E 6
Jackson, LA 78-79 D 5
Jackson, MI 64-65 JK 3
Jackson, MN 70-71 C 4
Jackson, MO 70-71 F 7
Jackson, MS 64-65 HJ 5
Jackson, MT 66-67 G 3
Jackson, OH 72-73 E 5
Jackson, TN 64-65 J 4
Jackson, WY 66-67 H 4
Jackson, ostrov — 132-133 H-K 1
Jackson Head 158-159 N 8
Jackson Heights, New York-, NY 82 III c 2
Jackson Lake 66-67 H 4
Jackson Manion 62 CD 2
Jackson Mountains 66-67 D 5
Jackson Park [CDN] 84 II bc 3
Jackson Park [USA] 83 II b 2
Jackson Prairie 78-79 E 4
Jacksonville, AL 78-79 FG 4
Jacksonville, FL 64-65 KL 5
Jacksonville, IL 70-71 EF 6
Jacksonville, NC 80-81 H 3
Jacksonville, OR 66-67 B 4
Jacksonville, TX 76-77 G 6-7
Jacksonville Beach, FL 80-81 F 5
Jäckvik 116-117 G 4
Jacmel 64-65 M 8
Jacobina 92-93 L 7
Jacob Island 58-59 d 2
Jacob Lake, AZ 74-75 GH 4
Jacobs 62 E 2
Jacobsdal 174-175 F 5
Jaconda 86-87 J 8
Jacques Cartier 82 I bc 1
Jacques Cartier, Mount — 63 D 3
Jacques Cartier, Pont — 82 I b 1
Jacques Cartier, Rivière — 63 A 4
Jacques Cartier Passage 56-57 Y 7-8
Jacu 100-101 A 7
Jacu, Rio — 100-101 G 4
Jacuí [BR, Minas Gerais] 102-103 J 4
Jacuí [BR, Rio Grande do Sul] 106-107 L 2-3
Jacuí, Rio — 106-107 L 2
Jacuípe, Rio — 92-93 LM 7
Jacuizinho 106-107 L 2
Jacumba, CA 74-75 EF 6
Jacundá 92-93 K 5
Jacundá, Rio — 98-99 N 6
Jacupiranga 102-103 HJ 6
Jacura 94-95 G 2
Jacurecanga, Cachoeira — 100-101 A 2
Jacurici, Rio — 100-101 E 6
Jacutinga 102-103 J 5
Jacuzão, Cachoeiro — 98-99 O 8
Jadā, Sha'īb — = Sha'īb al-Judā' 136-137 LM 7-8
Jadabpur, Calcutta- 154 II b 3
Jadaf, Wādī al- 134-135 E 4
Jadaf al-Jadaf 136-137 J 6
Jaddangi 140 F 2
Jaddī 166-167 JK 2
Jaddī, Wādī — 164-165 E 2
Jade 118 D 2
Jadīd, Berzekh el — = Rā's al-Jadīd 166-167 E 2
Jadīd, Bi'r — 166-167 K 3
Jadīd, Rā's al- 166-167 E 2
Jadīda, el — = Al-Jadīdah 164-165 C 2
Jadīdah, Al- [MA] 164-165 G 2
Jadīdah, Al- [TN] 166-167 L 1
Jadīd Rā's al-Fīl 164-165 K 6
Jado = Jādū 164-165 G 2
Jadotville = Likasi 172 E 4
Jadrin 124-125 Q 6
Jādū 164-165 G 2
Jaen [E] 120-121 F 10
Jaen [PE] 96-97 B 4
Jaenagar = Jaynagar 138-139 L 4
Jæren 116-117 A 8
Jaesalmēr = Jaisalmer 134-135 KL 5
Jafa, Tel Avive — = Tel Avīv-Yafō 134-135 C 4
Ja'far, Ḥāssī — 166-167 H 4
Jāfarābād [IND, Gujarāt] 138-139 C 7
Jafarābād [IND, Mahārāshtra] 138-139 EF 7
Ja'farābād [IR] 134-135 F 3
Jāfarah 166-167 M 3
Jaffa, Cape — 160 D 6
Jaffatin = Jazā'ir Jiftūn 173 CD 4
Jaffna = Yāpanaya 134-135 MN 9
Jaffna Lagoon = Yāpanē Kalapuwa 140 E 6
Jaffray 66-67 F 1
Jafr, Al- [JOR, place] 134-135 D 4
Jafr, Al- [JOR, river] 136-137 G 7
Jafr, El- = Al-Jafr 134-135 D 4
Jāfrābād = Jāfarābād 138-139 C 7
Jafū, Ḥāssī — 164-165 E 2
Jafū, Wādī — 166-167 H 4
Jagādharī = Jagādhri 138-139 F 2
Jagādhri 138-139 F 2
Jagalūr 140 C 3
Jagaḷūru = Jagalūr 140 C 3
Jagannāthpur 154 II a 1
Jagatsingpur 138-139 KL 7
Jagatsiṅhpur = Jagatsingpur 138-139 KL 7
Jagdalpur 134-135 N 7
Jagdīspur 138-139 K 5
Jagersfontein 174-175 F 5
Jaggayyapeta 140 E 2
Jaghbūb, Al- 164-165 J 3
Jaghiagh, Wādī — 136-137 J 4
Jaghjagh, Ouādī — = Wādī Jaghiagh 136-137 J 4
Jagir = Yelandūr 140 C 4
Jagl'ajarvi 124-125 H 2
Jagodnoje 132-133 cd 5
Jagog Tsho 142-143 F 5
Jago River 58-59 Q 2
Jagotin 126-127 E 1
Jagraon 138-139 E 2
Jagst 118 DE 4
Jagtiāl 134-135 M 7
Jagua, La — 92-93 E 3
Jaguapitā 102-103 G 5
Jaguaquara 100-101 E 7
Jaguarão 111 F 4
Jaguarari 92-93 LM 7
Jaguaretama 100-101 E 3
Jaguari 106-107 K 2
Jaguari, Rio — 106-107 K 2
Jaguariaíva 102-103 H 6
Jaguaribe 100-101 E 3
Jaguaribe, Rio — 92-93 M 6
Jaguaripe 100-101 E 7
Jaguaruana 100-101 F 3
Jaguaruna 102-103 H 8
Jagüé 106-107 C 2
Jagüé, Río del — 111 C 3
Jagüeles, Cañadón de los — 106-107 D 7
Jagüey Grande 88-89 F 3
Jahānābād 138-139 K 5
Jahāzpur 138-139 E 5
Jahīrābād = Zahīrābād 140 C 2
Jahotyn = Jagotin 126-127 E 1
Jahrah, Al- 134-135 F 5
Jahrom 134-135 G 5
Jaianary, Cachoeira — 94-95 J 7
Jaicós 92-93 L 6
Jaijon 138-139 F 2
Jailolo 148-149 J 6
Jaime Prats 106-107 CD 5
Jaintgaḍa = Jaintgarh 138-139 K 6
Jaintgarh 138-139 K 6
Jaintiapur = Jaintiyāpūr 141 BC 3
Jaintiyāpūr 141 BC 3
Jaipur [IND, Assam] 141 D 2
Jaipur [IND, Rājasthān] 134-135 M 5
Jaipūr Hāṭ 138-139 M 5
Jaisalmer 134-135 KL 5
Jaitāran 138-139 DE 4
Jaja 132-133 Q 6
Jajah, Al- 173 B 5
Jājarkot 138-139 HJ 3
Jājarm 134-135 H 3
Jajce 122-123 G 3
Jajin, Kampung — 150-151 D 10
Jājpur 138-139 L 7
Jajva [SU, place] 124-125 V 4
Jajva [SU, river] 124-125 V 4
Jakan, mys — 132-133 j 4
Jakarta 148-149 E 8
Jakarta, Teluk — 152-153 G 8-9
Jakarta-Ancol 154 IV ab 1
Jakarta-Binaria 154 IV b 1
Jakarta-Bintaro 154 IV a 2
Jakarta-Cedong 154 IV b 2
Jakarta-Cempaka Putih 154 IV b 2
Jakarta-Cilandak 154 IV a 2
Jakarta-Cililitan 154 IV b 2
Jakarta-Cilincing 154 IV b 1
Jakarta-Cipete 154 IV a 2
Jakarta-Duren Tiga 154 IV b 2
Jakarta-Gambir 154 IV a 1
Jakarta-Gelora 154 IV a 2
Jakarta-Grogol Petamburan 154 IV a 1
Jakarta-Halim 154 IV b 2
Jakarta-Jatinegara 154 IV b 2
Jakarta-Kebayoran Baru 154 IV a 2
Jakarta-Kebon Jeruk 154 IV a 2
Jakarta-Kemang 154 IV a 2
Jakarta-Kemayoran 154 IV b 1
Jakarta-Klender 154 IV b 2
Jakarta-Koja 154 IV b 1
Jakarta-Kramat Jati 154 IV b 2
Jakarta-Mampang Prapatan 154 IV a 2
Jakarta-Manggarai 154 IV b 2
Jakarta-Matraman 154 IV b 2
Jakarta-Menteng 154 IV a 2
Jakarta-Palmerah 154 IV a 2
Jakarta-Pancoran 154 IV ab 2
Jakarta-Pasar Minggu 154 IV ab 2
Jakarta-Pejagalan 154 IV a 1
Jakarta-Penjaringan 154 IV a 1
Jakarta-Pluit 154 IV a 1
Jakarta-Pulo Gadung 154 IV b 2
Jakarta-Rawamangun 154 IV b 2
Jakarta-Sawa Besar 154 IV ab 1
Jakarta-Senen 154 IV b 2
Jakarta-Setia Budi 154 IV ab 2
Jakarta-Simpruk 154 IV a 2
Jakarta-Slipi 154 IV a 2
Jakarta-Sunda Kelapa 154 IV ab 1
Jakarta-Sunter 154 IV b 1
Jakarta-Taman Sari 154 IV a 1
Jakarta-Tambora 154 IV a 1
Jakarta-Tanah Abang 154 IV a 2
Jakarta-Tanjung Priok 154 IV b 1
Jakarta-Tebet 154 IV b 2
Jākhal 138-139 E 3
Jakhao = Jakhau 138-139 B 6
Jakhau 138-139 B 6
Jakima = Lachdenpochja 124-125 GH 3
Jakkalawater 174-175 A 2
Jakobsdal = Jacobsdal 174-175 F 5
Jakobshavn = Jlulissat 56-57 ab 4
Jakobstad 116-117 JK 6
Jakobstadt = Jēkabpils 124-125 E 5
Jakovlevo 126-127 H 1
Jakovo 124-125 T 3
Jakša 132-133 K 5
Jakšanga 124-125 PQ 4
Jakšur-Bodja 124-125 T 5
Jakutsk 132-133 Y 5
Jal, NM 76-77 C 6
Jaladah, Al- 134-135 F 7
Jalālābād 138-139 GH 4
Jālālābad = Jalāl Kōt 134-135 KL 4
Jalālat al-Baḥrīyah, Jabal al- 173 BC 3
Jalālat al-Qiblīyah, Jabal al- 173 C 3
Jalāl Kōt 134-135 KL 4
Jalālpur [IND] 138-139 J 4
Jalālpūr [PAK] 138-139 C 3
Jalama 126-127 O 6
Jalāmīd, Al- 136-137 HJ 7
Ja'lan 134-135 H 6
Jalandar = Jullundur 134-135 LM 4
Jalandhar = Jullundur 134-135 LM 4
Jalangi 138-139 M 5
Jalan Kayu 154 III b 1
Jalaon = Jalaun 138-139 G 4
Jalapa 86-87 Q 10
Jalapa Enríquez 64-65 GH 8
Jalārpet 140 D 4
Jalaun 138-139 G 4
Jalawlā' 136-137 L 5
Jalca, La — 96-97 C 5
Jāle 138-139 K 4
Jales 102-103 G 4
Jalesar 138-139 G 4
Jalēshvara = Jaleswar 138-139 L 7
Jaleswar [IND] 138-139 L 7
Jalēśwar [Nepal] 138-139 KL 4
Jalgāṅv = Jālgaon [IND ← Bhusāwal] 134-135 M 6
Jalgāṅv = Jālgaon [IND → Bhusāwal] 138-139 F 7
Jālgaon [IND ← Bhusāwal] 134-135 M 6
Jālgaon [IND → Bhusāwal] 138-139 F 7
Jalhāk, Al- 164-165 L 6
Jalīb, Maqarr al- 136-137 J 6
Jalībah 136-137 M 7
Jalib Shahab 136-137 M 7
Jalingo 164-165 G 7
Jalisco 64-65 EF 7
Jalitah, Jazā'ir — 166-167 L 1
Jaliṭah, Qanāt — 166-167 L 1
Jallekān 136-137 N 6
Jālna 134-135 M 7
Jalon = Jalaun 138-139 G 4
Jalón, Río — 120-121 G 8
Jalo Oasis = Wāḥāt Jālū 164-165 J 3
Jālor 138-139 D 5
Jalore = Jālor 138-139 D 5
Jalostotitlán 86-87 J 7
Jalpa 86-87 J 7
Jalpaiguri 138-139 M 4
Jalpan 86-87 KL 6-7
Jalpug 126-127 D 3-4
Jalpug, ozero — 126-127 D 4
Jalta 126-127 G 4
Jaltenango 86-87 O 10
Jaltuškov 126-127 C 2
Jalu = Yalu Jiang 144-145 EF 2
Jālū, Wāḥāt — 164-165 J 3
Jaluit 208 G 2
Jama [EC] 96-97 A 2
Jama = Silyānah 166-167 L 1
Jama, Salina de — 104-105 C 8
Jamaame 164-165 N 8
Jamaari 168-169 H 3
Jamaat 142-143 E 2
Jamā'at al-Ma'yuf 136-137 M 7
Jamaica 64-65 L 8
Jamaica, New York-, NY 82 III d 2
Jamaica Bay 82 III cd 3
Jamaica Channel 64-65 L 8
Jamaica Plain, Boston-, MA 84 I b 3
Jamaika 64-65 L 8
Jamakhaṇḍi = Jamkhandi 134-135 LM 7
Jamal, poluostrov — 132-133 MN 3
Jamālīyah, Al-Qāhirah-al- 170 II b 1
Jamalo-Neneckij Nacional'nyj Okrug = Yamalo-Nenets Autonomous Area 132-133 M-O 4-5
Jamālpur [BD] 138-139 M 5
Jamālpur [IND] 138-139 L 5
Jamantau, gora — 132-133 K 7
Jamanxim, Rio — 92-93 H 6
Jamari 98-99 G 9
Jamari, Rio — 92-93 G 6
Jamaši 124-125 S 6
Jambelí, Canal de — 96-97 AB 3

306 Itatina

Jambi [RI, administrative unit = 5 ◁] 148-149 D 7
Jambi [RI, place] 148-149 D 7
Jambol 122-123 M 4
Jambuair, Tanjung — 152-153 BC 3
Jambūr 136-137 L 5
Jambusar 138-139 D 6
Jamdena, Pulau — 148-149 K 8
James, Isla — 108-109 B 5
James Bay 56-57 UV 7
James Bay, Parc provincial de — 62 M 1
James Craik 106-107 F 4
James Island = Bāda Kyûn 150-151 B 7
James Range 158-159 F 4
James River [USA ◁ Chesapeake Bay] 64-65 L 4
James River [USA ◁ Missouri River] 64-65 G 2
Jamestown, KS 68-69 H 6
Jamestown, KY 70-71 H 7
Jamestown, ND 64-65 G 2
Jamestown, NY 64-65 L 3
Jamestown, OH 72-73 E 5
Jamestown, TN 78-79 G 2
Jamestown [AUS] 160 D 4
Jamestown [Saint Helena] 204-205 G 10
Jamestown [ZA] 174-175 G 6
Jamestown Reservoir 68-69 G 2
Jamikunta 140 D 1
Jamīlah 166-167 J 1
Jaminaua, Rio — 96-97 F 6
Jām Jodhpur 138-139 BC 7
Jamkhandi 134-135 LM 7
Jāmkhed 140 B 1
Jamm 124-125 G 4
Jamm, Al- 166-167 M 2
Jammāl 166-167 M 2
Jammalamadugu 140 D 3
Jammerbugt 116-117 C 9
Jammerdrif 174-175 G 5
Jammu 134-135 LM 4
Jammu and Kashmir 134-135 LM 3-4
Jamnā = Yamuna 134-135 MN 5
Jāmnagar 134-135 L 6
Jāmner 138-139 E 7
Jamnotri 138-139 G 2
Jampol' [SU, Chmel'nickaja Oblast'] 126-127 C 2
Jampol' [SU, Vinnickaja Oblast'] 126-127 D 2
Jāmpūr 134-135 KL 5
Jamsah 173 C 4
Jämsänkoski 116-117 L 7
Jamshedpur 134-135 NO 6
Jamsk 132-133 de 6
Jāmtāra 138-139 L 5-6
Jämtland 116-117 E-G 6
Jämtlands Sikås 116-117 F 6
Jamūi 138-139 L 5
Jamūnā [BD] 138-139 M 5
Jamuna [IND] 141 C 2
Jamundí 94-95 C 6
Jāmūr al-Kabīr, Al- 166-167 M 1
Jamursba, Tanjung — 148-149 K 7
Jana 132-133 Z 4
Janagāṅv = Jangaon 140 D 2
Janai 154 II a 1
Janā'in 166-167 LM 4
Janaperi, Rio — 92-93 G 4
Janaúba 92-93 L 8
Janaucu, Ilha — 92-93 JK 4
Janaul 132-133 JK 6
Jandaia 102-103 GH 2
Jandaia do Sul 102-103 G 5
Jandaq 134-135 GH 4
Jandiatuba, Rio — 92-93 F 5-6
Jandowae 158-159 K 5
Janeiro, Rio de — 100-101 B 6
Janemale 98-99 L 3
Janesville, CA 66-67 C 5
Janesville, WI 70-71 F 4
Jang 141 B 2
Jangada 102-103 G 7
Jangamo 174-175 L 3
Jangaon 140 D 2
Jangarej 132-133 L 4
Jangi 138-139 G 2
Jangijul' 132-133 M 9
Jangipur 138-139 LM 5
Janglung 138-139 H 2
Jangmu 138-139 LM 3
Jango 102-103 E 4
Jangory 124-125 LM 2
Jangri Tsho 138-139 JK 2
Jang Thang 142-143 E-G 5
Jangtse Chhu 138-139 J 2
Jangtsekiang = Chang Jiang 142-143 K 5-6
Jānī Beyglū 136-137 M 3
Janīn 136-137 F 6
Janisjarvi, ozero — 124-125 H 3
Janjgīr 138-139 J 6
Janji = Gingee 140 D 4
Jan Kemp 174-175 F 4
Jan Lake 61 G 3
Jan Mayen 52 B 19-20
Jan Mayen Ridge 114-115 H 1-2
Jannah 164-165 FG 4
Jano-Indigirskaja nizmennost' 132-133 Z-c 3
Jánoshalma 118 J 5
Janoviči 124-125 H 6
Janovka = Ivanovka 126-127 E 3
Janowo = Jonava 124-125 E 6
Jānsath 138-139 F 3
Jansenville 174-175 F 7
Janskij 132-133 Za 4
Janskij zaliv 132-133 Za 3
Jan Smuts = Johannesburg Airport 170 V c 1
Jantarnyj 118 J 1
Jantra 122-123 M 4
J. Antunes, Serra — 98-99 G 10-11
Januária 92-93 KL 8
Jan von Riebeeck Park 170 V ab 1
Jao-ho = Raohe 142-143 P 2
Jaonpur = Jaunpur 134-135 N 5
Jaoping = Raoping 146-147 F 10
Jaora 138-139 E 6
Jaorā = Jora 138-139 F 4
Jaoyang = Raoyang 146-147 EF 2
Jao-yang Ho = Raoyang He 144-145 D 2
Japan 142-143 P 5-R 3
Japan Sea 142-143 P 4-Q 3
Japan Trench 156-157 G 3
Japão, Serra do — 100-101 F 5-6
Japara 148-149 F 8
Jāpharābād = Jafarābād 138-139 EF 7
Japonskoje more 132-133 a 9
Japurá, Rio — 92-93 F 5
Jāpvo, Mount — 141 CD 3
Jaqué 94-95 B 4
Jaquí 96-97 D 9
Jaquirana 106-107 M 2
Jar 124-125 T 4
Jara, La — 120-121 E 9
Jarā', Wādī al- 166-167 H 6
Jarābulus 136-137 GH 4
Jarādah 164-165 D 2
Jaraguá 102-103 H 1
Jaraguá, São Paulo- 110 II a 1
Jaraguá, Serra do — 102-103 H 7
Jaraguá do Sul 102-103 H 7
Jaraguari 92-93 HJ 8-9
Jaralito, El — 76-77 B 9
Jaramillo 108-109 F 6
Jaranpada = Jarpara 138-139 K 7
Jaransk 132-133 H 6
Jarānwāla 138-139 D 2
Jararaca, Cachoeira — 102-103 G 6
Jarārah, Wādī — 173 D 6
Jarau 106-107 J 3
Jarauçu, Rio — 98-99 M 5-6
Jarāwī, Al- 136-137 H 7
Jarbah, Jazīrat — 164-165 G 2
Jarbidge, NV 66-67 F 5
Jarcevo [SU, Jenisej] 132-133 R 5
Jarcevo [SU, Smolenskaja Oblast'] 124-125 J 6
Jardim [BR, Ceará] 100-101 E 4
Jardim [BR, Mato Grosso do Sul] 102-103 D 4
Jardim América, São Paulo- 110 II ab 2
Jardim Botânico, Rio de Janeiro- 110 I b 2
Jardim Botânico do Rio de Janeiro 110 I b 2
Jardim da Aclimação 110 II b 2
Jardim de Piranhas 100-101 F 4
Jardim do Seridó 100-101 F 4
Jardim Paulista, São Paulo- 110 II ab 2
Jardim Zoológico do Rio de Janeiro 110 I b 2
Jardim Zoológico do São Paulo 110 II b 2
Jardín Balbuena, Ciudad de México- 91 I c 2
Jardín Botánico de Bogotá 91 III b 2-3
Jardín Botánico de Caracas 91 II b 1-2
Jardin botanique 82 I b 1
Jardin d'Essai 170 I ab 1
Jardin du Luxembourg 129 I c 2
Jardines de la Reina 64-65 L 7
Jardines Flotantes 91 I C 3
Jardinésia 102-103 H 3
Jardines Lookout 155 I b 2
Jardinópolis 102-103 J 4
Jardín Zoológico de México 91 I b 2
Jardin zoologique Angrignon 82 I b 2
Jardin zoologique de Brazzaville 170 IV a 1
Jardin zoologique de Kinshasa 170 IV a 1
Jarega 124-125 TU 2
Jarenga [SU, place] 124-125 R 2
Jarenga [SU, river] 124-125 R 2
Jarensk 132-133 H 5
Jares'ki 126-127 FG 2
Jari, Rio — 92-93 J 5
Jaria Jhangjail = Jariyā Jhanjāyl 141 B 3
Jarībīyah, Ḥāssī — 166-167 J 4
Jarīd, Shaṭṭ al- 164-165 F 2
Jarilla 106-107 D 4
Jarina, Rio — 98-99 M 10
Jarīr, Wādī — 134-135 E 5-6
Jarita, La — 86-87 KL 4
Jariyā Jhanjāyl 141 B 3
Jarjīs 166-167 M 3
Jarkand = Yarkand 142-143 D 4
Jarkovo 132-133 M 6
Jarmashīn, 'Ayn — 173 B 5
Jarnema 124-125 MN 2
Jarny 120-121 K 4
Jarocin 118 H 2-3
Jarok, ostrov — 132-133 a 3
Jaroslavl' 132-133 FG 6
Jarosław 118 L 3-4
Jaroso, CO 68-69 D 7
Jarpara 138-139 K 7
Järpen 116-117 E 6
Jarrāḥī, Rūd-e — 136-137 N 7
Jarry, Parc — 82 I b 1
Jarsah, Shaṭṭ al- 166-167 KL 2
Jar-Sale 132-133 MN 4
Jartum = Al-Kharṭūm 164-165 L 5
Jaru 92-93 G 7
Jaru, Reserva Florestal de — 98-99 GH 9
Jaru, Rio — 98-99 G 10
Järva-Jaani 124-125 EF 4
Järvenpää 116-117 L 7
Jarvie 60 L 2
Jarvis 156-157 J 5
Jarygino 124-125 K 6
Jasdan 138-139 C 6
Jasel'da 124-125 E 7
Jasenevo, Moskva- 113 V b 3
Jasenskaja kosa 126-127 HJ 3
Jashpurnagar 138-139 JK 6
Jasikan 168-169 F 4
Jasin 150-151 D 11
Jasinovataja 126-127 H 2
Jāsk 134-135 H 5
Jaškino 124-125 T 7
Jaškul' 126-127 M 3
Jasnogorsk 124-125 LM 6
Jasnyj 132-133 Y 7
Jasonhalvøy 53 C 30-31
Jason Islands 111 D 8
Jasonville, IN 70-71 G 6
Jasper, AL 78-79 F 4
Jasper, AR 78-79 C 2-3
Jasper, FL 80-81 b 1
Jasper, GA 78-79 G 3
Jasper, IN 70-71 G 6
Jasper, MN 68-69 H 4
Jasper, MO 76-77 G 4
Jasper, TX 76-77 GH 7
Jasper [CDN, Alberta] 56-57 N 7
Jasper [CDN, Ontario] 72-73 J 2
Jasper National Park 56-57 N 7
Jasrāsar 138-139 D 4
Jaṣṣān 136-137 L 6
Jassy = Iaşi 122-123 M 2
Jastrebac 122-123 J 4
Jastrebovka 126-127 H 1
Jászberény 118 JK 5
Jataí [BR ↘ Arrais] 100-101 A 7
Jataí [BR ↙ Rio Verde] 92-93 J 8
Jatapu, Rio — 92-93 H 5
Jatāra 138-139 G 5
Jataúba 100-101 F 4
Jatei 102-103 E 5
Jath 140 B 2
Jati [BR] 100-101 E 4
Jāti [PAK] 138-139 B 5
Jatibarang 152-153 H 9
Jatinegara, Jakarta- 154 IV b 2
Játiva 120-121 G 9
Jatni 138-139 K 7
Jatobá 92-93 JK 5
Jatoī Janūbī 138-139 C 3
Jat Potī = Kārēz 134-135 K 4
Jatunhuasi 96-97 CD 8
Jaú 92-93 K 9
Jaú, Cachoeira do — 98-99 OP 10
Jaú, Rio — 92-93 G 5
Jaua, Meseta de — 94-95 J 5
Jau'alīyat, Jebel el- = Jabal al-Aḍīriyāt 136-137 G 7
Jauari, Serra — 98-99 M 5
Jauf, Al- = Al-Jawf 134-135 DE 5
Jauf, El — = Al-Jawf 164-165 J 4
Jauja 92-93 DE 7
Jaula, La — 106-107 C 5
Jaumave 86-87 L 6
Jaunde = Yaoundé 164-165 G 8
Jaunjelgava 124-125 E 5
Jaunpiebalga 124-125 F 5
Jaunpur 134-135 N 5
Jaura = Jora 138-139 F 4
Jauru 102-103 E 3
Jauru, Rio — [BR ◁ Rio Coxim] 102-103 EF 3
Jauru, Rio — [BR ◁ Rio Paraguai] 102-103 CD 2
Jauza 113 V c 2
Java 98-99 L 2
Jāvad = Jāwad 138-139 E 5
Javādi Hills 140 D 4
Javaés, Serra dos — 98-99 O 10
Java Head = Tanjung Lajar 148-149 DE 8
Javaj, poluostrov — 132-133 NO 3
Javalambre 120-121 G 8
Javari, Cachoeira do — 98-99 LM 5
Javari, Ilha — 98-99 E 5
Javari, Rio — 92-93 E 6
Java Sea 148-149 EF 8
Javhār = Jawhār 134-135 L 7
Javier, Isla — 108-109 B 6
Javlenka 132-133 M 7
Javor 122-123 HJ 4
Javorov 126-127 A 2
Jāvrā = Jaora 138-139 E 6
Jawa = Java 148-149 EF 8
Jawa Barat = 11 ◁ 148-149 E 8
Jāwad 138-139 E 5
Jaw'alīyāt, Jabal al- 136-137 G 7
Jawa Tengah = 12 ◁ 148-149 E 8
Jawa Timur = 14 ◁ 148-149 F 8
Jawf, Al- [LAR] 164-165 J 4
Jawf, Al- [Saudi Arabia] 134-135 DE 5
Jawf, Al- [Y] 134-135 EF 7
Jawhār 134-135 L 7
Jawi 152-153 H 6
Jawor 118 H 3
Jaxartes = Syrdarja 134-135 K 2
Jay, OK 76-77 G 4
Jaya, Gunung — 148-149 L 7
Jayanca 96-97 B 5
Jayapatna 138-139 J 8
Jayapura 148-149 M 7
Jayawijaya, Pegunungan — 148-149 LM 7
Jaydebpūr 141 B 3
Jay Em, WY 68-69 D 4
Jaygaḍ = Jaygarh 140 A 2
Jaygarh 140 A 2
Jāyid 136-137 J 6
Jaynagar [IND, Bihār] 138-139 L 4
Jaynagar [IND, West Bengal] 138-139 M 6
Jaypur = Jaipur [IND, Assam] 141 D 2
Jaypur = Jaipur [IND, Rājasthān] 134-135 M 5
Jaypura = Jeypore 134-135 N 7
Jayton, TX 76-77 D 6
Jaza'ir, Al- [DZ] 164-165 E 1
Jaza'ir, Al- [IRQ] 136-137 M 7
Jazā'ir al-Ikhwān 173 D 4
Jazā'ir al-Kilāb 166-167 M 1
Jazā'ir az-Zubayr 134-135 E 7-8
Jazā'ir Farasān 134-135 E 7
Jazā'ir Ḥalāib 173 E 6
Jazā'ir Jalitah 166-167 L 1
Jazā'ir Jiftūn 173 CD 4
Jazā'ir Khūrīyā Mūrīyā 134-135 H 7
Jazā'ir Qaysūm 173 CD 4
Jazā'ir Qūryāt 166-167 M 2
Jazā'ir Siyāl 173 E 6
Jazīr 136-137 F 5
Jazīra, Al- = Arḍ al-Jazīrah 134-135 E 3-F 4
Jazīrah, Al- [DZ] 166-167 F 2
Jazīrah, Al- [IRQ] 136-137 J 5
Jazīrah, Al- [Sudan] 164-165 L 6
Jazīrah, Arḍ al- 134-135 E 3-F 4
Jazīrah Warraq al-Hadar 170 II b 1
Jazīrat al-Gharbī 166-167 M 2
Jazīrat al-Maṣīrah 134-135 HJ 6
Jazīrat al-Maṭrūḥ 166-167 M 1
Jazīrat al-'Uwaynidhīyah 173 DE 4
Jazīrat an Na'mān = Jazīrat an-Nu'mān 173 D 4
Jazīrat an-Nu'mān 173 D 4
Jazīrat ash-Sharqī 166-167 M 2
Jazīrat Būbīyan 134-135 FG 5
Jazīrat Faylakah 136-137 N 8
Jazīrat Fulaikā' = Jazīrat Faylakah 136-137 N 8
Jazīrat Ghānim 173 C 4
Jazīrat Jarbah 164-165 G 2
Jazīrat Kanā'is 166-167 M 2
Jazīrat Kubbar 136-137 N 8
Jazīrat Marīr 173 DE 6
Jazīrat Muhammad 170 II b 1
Jazīrat Mukawwa' 173 DE 6
Jazīrat Rāshqūn 166-167 EF 2
Jazīrat Safājā 173 D 4
Jazīrat Ṣanāfīr 173 D 4
Jazīrat Shakir 164-165 LM 3
Jazīrat Tīrān 173 D 4
Jazīrat Umm Quṣur 173 D 3-4
Jazīrat Wādī Jimāl 173 D 5
Jazīrat Zabarjad 173 DE 6
Jazīreh Ābādān 136-137 N 7-8
Jazīreh Darā 136-137 N 7
Jazīreh-Qeshm 134-135 H 5
Jazīreh Qūyūn 136-137 L 4
Jazīreh-ye Khārk 134-135 FG 5
Jazīreh-ye Kīsh 134-135 G 5
Jāz Mūreyān, Hāmūn-e — 134-135 H 5
Jazur Qarqannah 164-165 G 2
Jaz'va 124-125 V 3
Jazykovo [SU, Baškirskaja ASSR] 124-125 U 6
Jazykovo [SU, Uljanovskaja Oblast'] 124-125 Q 6
Jazzīn 136-137 F 6
Jbel Azoûrkî = Jabal Azūrkī 166-167 C 4
Jbel Boû Naṣr = Jabal Bū Naṣr 166-167 E 3
Jbel ed Doûh = Jabal ad-Dūgh 166-167 F 3
Jbel Imedrhâs = Jabal Imīdghās 166-167 D 4
Jbel Mâsker = Jabal Mu'askar 166-167 D 3
Jbel Ṣarhrô' = Jabal Ṣaghrū' 166-167 C 4
Jbel Ṭâroq, Bôrhâz — = Bughāz Jabal Ṭāriq 164-165 CD 1
Jbel Tazzeka = Jabal Tazzikā' 166-167 DE 2
Jbel Toubqâl = Jabal Tubqāl 164-165 C 2
Jean, NV 74-75 F 5
Jeanerette, LA 78-79 D 6
Jeanette, ostrov — 132-133 ef 2
Jean Lafitte, LA 85 I b 2
Jebāil = Jubayl 136-137 F 5
Jebalā = Jabalā' 166-167 D 2
Jebba 164-165 E 7
Jebba = Al-Jabhah 166-167 D 2
Jebel Anaiza = Jabal Unayzah 134-135 DE 4
Jebel Andidanob = Jabal Asūtarībah 173 E 7
Jebel Arkenu = Jabal Arkanū 164-165 J 4
Jebel Châ'r = Jabal Shā'r 136-137 GH 5
Jebel ech Charqî = Jabal ar-Ruwāq 136-137 G 5-6
Jebel ed Dargagâ = Jabal Ardar Gwagwa 173 D 6
Jebelein, El- = Al-Jabalayn 164-165 L 6
Jebel el-Jau'alīyāt = Jabal al-Aḍīriyāt 136-137 G 7
Jebel el Sauda = Jabal as-Sawdā' 164-165 GH 3
Jebel esh Sharqî = Jabal Lubnān ash-Sharqī 136-137 G 5-6
Jebel Etrī = Jabal Itrī 173 D 7
Jebel Gimbala = Jabal Marrah 164-165 JK 6
Jebel Obkeik = Jabal 'Ubkayk 164-165 M 4
Jebel 'Ōda = Jabal Ūdah 164-165 M 4
Jebel Teljō = Jabal Talju 164-165 K 6
Jebel Tenf = Jabal at-Tanf 136-137 H 6
Jebel Tisiten = Jabal Tīdīghīn 166-167 D 2
Jeberos 96-97 C 4
Jebīlēt, el — = Al-Jabīlat 166-167 BC 4
Jeblê = Jablah 136-137 F 5
Jechegnadzor 126-127 M 7
Jeddah = Jiddah 134-135 D 6
Jedincy 126-127 C 2
Jedlesee, Wien- 113 I b 1
Jed'ma 124-125 O 3
Jędrzejów 118 K 3
Jedway 60 B 3
Jefara = Az-Zāwīyah 164-165 G 2
Jeffara = Jafārah 166-167 M 3
Jeffers, MN 70-71 C 3
Jefferson, CO 68-69 D 6
Jefferson, GA 80-81 E 3
Jefferson, IA 70-71 C 4-5
Jefferson, LA 85 I ab 2
Jefferson, MT 66-67 GH 2
Jefferson, OH 72-73 F 4
Jefferson, OR 66-67 B 3
Jefferson, TX 76-77 G 6
Jefferson, WI 70-71 F 4
Jefferson, Mount — [USA, Nevada] 74-75 E 3
Jefferson, Mount — [USA, Oregon] 66-67 C 3
Jefferson, Village, VA 82 II a 2
Jefferson City, MO 64-65 H 4
Jefferson City, TN 80-81 E 2
Jefferson Park, Chicago-, IL 83 II a 1
Jeffersonville, GA 80-81 E 4
Jeffersonville, IN 70-71 H 6
Jeffrey Depth 158-159 F 7
Jefremov 124-125 LM 7
Jega 168-169 G 2-3
Jegorjevsk 132-133 FG 6
Jegorlyk 126-127 K 4
Jegorlykskaja 126-127 K 3
Jegyrjach 132-133 M 5
Jēhlam = Jhilam 134-135 L 4
Jehlum = Jhilam 134-135 L 4
Jehol = Chengde 142-143 M 3
Jeinemeni, Cerro — 108-109 C 6
Jeja 126-127 J 3
Jejsk 126-127 J 3
Jejuí Guazú, Río — 102-103 DE 6
Jejuri 140 B 1
Jēkabpils 124-125 E 5
Jekatarinburg = Sverdlovsk 132-133 L 6
Jekaterinfel'd = Bolnisi 126-127 M 6
Jekaterinodar = Krasnodar 126-127 J 4
Jekaterinoslav = Dnepropetrovsk 126-127 GH 2
Jekaterinovka [SU, Primorskij Kraj] 144-145 J 1
Jekaterinovka [SU, Saratovskaja Oblast'] 124-125 OP 7
Jekaterinštadt = Marx 124-125 Q 8
Jekimoviči 124-125 J 6
Jekubābād 134-135 K 5
Jekyakarta = Yogyakarta 148-149 EF 8
Jelan' [SU, place] 126-127 L 1
Jelan' [SU, river] 126-127 L 1
Jelanec 126-127 E 3
Jelan'-Kolenovskij 126-127 K 1
Jelchovka 124-125 S 7
Jelec 124-125 M 7
Jelenia Góra 118 GH 3
Jelenovka = Sevan 126-127 M 6
Jelenskij 124-125 K 7
Jelfa = Jilfah 164-165 E 2
Jelgava 124-125 DE 5
Jelgavkrasti 124-125 DE 5
Jeli, Kampung — 150-151 CD 10
Jelizavetgrad = Kirovograd 126-127 EF 2
Jelizavetpol' = Kirovabad 126-127 N 6
Jelizavety, mys — 132-133 b 7
Jelizovo [SU, Belorusskaja SSR] 124-125 G 7
Jelizovo [SU, Rossijskaja SFSR] 132-133 e 7
Jellico, TN 78-79 G 2
Jellicoe 62 F 3
Jel'n'a 124-125 J 6
Jeloga 124-125 T 4
Jelovo 124-125 U 5
Jelpačicha 124-125 UV 5
Jelšanka 124-125 Q 8
Jel'sk 124-125 G 8
Jelva 124-125 S 2
Jema = Djema 164-165 K 7
Jema Chhu 138-139 J 2
Jema eṭ Tolba = Jimā'h aṭ-Ṭulbah 166-167 D 2
Jemaja, Pulau — 148-149 DE 6
Jemaluang 150-151 DE 11
Jem'ā' Sha'îm Thlêthâ' = Jimā' 'Shā'im 166-167 B 3
Jemât = Jimāt 166-167 B 6
Jember 152-153 K 9-10
Jembiani 171 DE 4
Jembongan, Pulau — 148-149 G 5
Jemca [SU, place] 124-125 N 2
Jemca [SU, river] 124-125 N 2
Jemeck 132-133 G 5
Jemeljanovka 124-125 H 2
Jemeljanovo 124-125 K 5
Jemen 134-135 E 7-8
Jementah 150-151 D 11
Jementau 132-133 N 7
Jemez Pueblo, NM 76-77 A 5
Jemmapes = 'Azzābah 166-167 K 1
Jempang, Danau — 152-153 LM 6
Jena 118 E 3
Jena, LA 78-79 CD 5
Jenakijevo 126-127 J 2
Jenašimskij Polkan, gora — 132-133 RS 6
Jendoûba = Jundūbah 166-167 L 1
Jenera, Kampung — 150-151 C 10
Jenfeld, Hamburg- 130 I b 1
Jên Ho = Ren He 146-147 B 5
Jenhsien = Ren Xian 146-147 E 3
Jên-hua = Renhua 146-147 D 9
Jenischpark 130 I a 1
Jenisej 132-133 Q 4
Jenisej, Bol'šoj — 132-133 S 7
Jenisej, Malyj — 132-133 RS 7
Jenisejsk 132-133 R 6
Jenisejskij kr'až 132-133 R 5-6
Jenisejskij zaliv 132-133 OP 3
Jenkins, KY 80-81 E 2
Jenkins Corner, MD 82 II b 2
Jenkintown, PA 84 III c 1
Jenkiu = Renqiu 142-143 M 4
Jenner 61 C 5
Jenner, CA 74-75 B 3
Jennings, KS 68-69 F 6
Jennings, LA 78-79 C 5
Jennings, MT 66-67 F 1
Jenny Lind Island 56-57 Q 4
Jenotajevka 126-127 N 3
Jensen, UT 66-67 J 5
Jensen Beach, FL 80-81 cd 3
Jens Munk Island 56-57 UV 4
Jens Munks Ø 56-57 cd 5
Jenud = Gorē 164-165 M 7
Jen'uka 132-133 X 6
Jeol = Chengde 142-143 M 3
Jeppener 106-107 HJ 5
Jequeri 102-103 L 4
Jequié 92-93 L 7
Jequitaí 92-93 L 8
Jequitaí, Rio — 102-103 K 2
Jequitinhonha 100-101 D 3
Jequitinhonha, Rio — 92-93 L 8
Jerâblous = Jarābulus 136-137 GH 4
Jerachtur 124-125 N 6
Jerāda = Jarādah 164-165 D 2
Jerantut 148-149 D 6
Jerba = Jazīrat Jarbah 164-165 G 2
Jerbogač'on 132-133 U 5
Jerčevo 124-125 MN 3
Jeremejevo [SU, Komi ASSR] 124-125 V 2
Jérémie 64-65 M 8
Jeremoabo 92-93 M 6-7
Jerevan 126-127 M 6
Jerez de García Salinas 64-65 F 7
Jerez de la Frontera 120-121 DE 10
Jerez de los Caballeros 120-121 D 9
Jergeni 126-127 M 2-3
Jericho [AUS] 158-159 J 4
Jericho [ZA] 174-175 GH 3
Jericho = Arīḥa 136-137 F 7
Jericó 94-95 CD 5
Jeridoaquara, Ponta — 100-101 DE 2
Jerik = Ilovatka 126-127 MN 1
Jerilderie 160 G 5
Jermak 132-133 O 7
Jermakovskoje 132-133 R 7
Jermī 136-137 L 4
Jeroaquara 102-103 G 1
Jerofej Pavlovič 132-133 X 7
Jerome, AZ 74-75 G 5
Jerome, ID 66-67 F 4
Jeropol 132-133 g 4
Jersey 119 E 7
Jersey City, NJ 64-65 M 3-4
Jersey Shore, PA 72-73 H 4
Jersey Village, TX 85 III a 1
Jerseyville, IL 70-71 E 6
Jeršiči 124-125 J 7
Jerteh 150-151 D 10
Jerumenha 92-93 L 6
Jerusalem = Yĕrūshālayim 134-135 CD 4
Jeruslan 126-127 N 1
Jervis, Monte — 108-109 B 7
Jervis Bay 158-159 K 7
Jervois Range 158-159 G 4
Jerzovka 126-127 M 2
Jesenice 122-123 EF 2
Jeseník 118 H 3
Jesil' 132-133 M 7
Jessalange 171 D 5
Jessaur = Jessore 134-135 O 6
Jesse H. Jones House 85 III b 2
Jessej 132-133 T 4
Jesselton = Kota Kinabalu 148-149 FG 5
Jessentuki 126-127 L 4
Jessica 66-67 C 1
Jesso = Hokkaidō 142-143 RS 3
Jessore 134-135 O 6
Jestro, Webi — = Weyb 164-165 N 7
Jesuit Bend, LA 85 I b 3
Jesup, GA 80-81 EF 5
Jesup, IA 70-71 DE 4
Jesús 102-103 E 7
Jésus, Île — 82 I a 1
Jesús Carranza 86-87 N 9
Jesús María [CO] 94-95 E 5
Jesús María [MEX] 86-87 HJ 6
Jesús María [RA] 111 D 4
Jesus María, Boca de — 86-87 M 5
Jet, OK 76-77 E 4
Jetait 61 H 2
Jetmore, KS 68-69 FG 6
J. E. Torrent 106-107 J 2
Jetpur 138-139 C 7
Jevdino 124-125 S 2
Jevgora 124-125 J 2
Jevlach 126-127 N 6
Jevlaševo 124-125 Q 7
Jevpatorija 126-127 F 4
Jewell, IA 70-71 D 4
Jewell, KS 68-69 GH 6
Jewell, Arlington-, VA 82 II a 2
Jewish Autonomous Region = 13 ◁ 132-133 Z 8
Jeypore 134-135 N 7
Ježicha 124-125 Q 4
Jezioro Mamry 118 K 1
Jezioro Śniardwy 118 K 2
Jez'ovo [SU, Udmurtskaja ASSR] 124-125 T 4
Jezovo [SU, Vologodskaja Oblast'] 124-125 M 3
Jez'ovo-Čerkessk = Čerkessk 126-127 L 4
Jēzurī = Jejuri 140 B 1
Jezus-Eik 128 II b 2
Jezzīn = Jazzīn 136-137 F 6
Jhābua 138-139 E 6
Jhagadia 138-139 D 7
Jhagaḍiyā = Jhagadia 138-139 D 7
Jha Jha 138-139 L 5
Jhajjar 138-139 F 3
Jhalakāṭī 141 B 4
Jhālāvāṛ = Jhālawār 138-139 EF 5
Jhālāwār [IND, landscape] 138-139 C 6
Jhālawār [IND, place] 138-139 EF 5
Jhalidā 138-139 KL 6
Jhālod 138-139 E 6
Jhālrapātan 138-139 F 5
Jhang Maghiana = Jhang-Maghiyāna 134-135 L 4
Jhang-Maghiyāna 134-135 L 4
Jhanīdāh 138-139 M 6
Jhanjhārpur 138-139 L 4
Jhānsi 134-135 M 5
Jhāpa 138-139 L 4
Jhārgrām 138-139 L 6
Jharia 138-139 L 6
Jhārsuguda 134-135 NO 6
Jharsugura = Jhārsuguda 134-135 NO 6
Jhavānī = Jhawani 138-139 K 4
Jhawani 138-139 K 4
Jhelum = Jihlam 134-135 L 4
Jhenida = Jhanīdāh 138-139 M 6
Jhīl Manchhar 138-139 A 4
Jhīl Marav 138-139 B 3
Jhinjhūvāda 138-139 C 6
Jhorīgāṅ = Jorigām 138-139 J 8
Jhūnjhunu 138-139 E 3
Jhūṭhī Divi Antarīp = False Divi Point 140 E 3
Jiading 146-147 H 6
Jiaganj 138-139 M 5
Jiahe 146-147 D 9
Jiali = Lharugō 142-143 G 5
Jiali = Qionghai 142-143 L 8
Jialing Jiang 142-143 K 5
Jialu He 146-147 E 4
Jialuo Shankou = Kar La 138-139 MN 3
Jiamusi 142-143 P 2
Ji'an [TJ, Jiangxi] 142-143 LM 6
Ji'an [TJ, Jilin] 144-145 EF 2
Jianchang [TJ → Benxi] 144-145 E 2
Jianchang [TJ ← Jinzhou] 144-145 B 2
Jianchangying 146-147 G 1
Jiande 146-147 G 7
Jiangcun 146-147 D 2
Jiangdu 146-147 G 5
Jiangdu = Yangzhou 142-143 M 5
Jiange 142-143 JK 5
Jianghong 146-147 B 11
Jianghua 146-147 C 9
Jiangkou [TJ, Guangxi Zhuangzu Zizhiqu] 146-147 C 10
Jiangkou [TJ, Guizhou] 146-147 B 8
Jiangkou [TJ, Hubei] 146-147 C 6
Jiangkou [TJ, Hunan] 146-147 C 8
Jiangle 146-147 F 8
Jiangling 142-143 L 5
Jiangmen 142-143 L 7
Jiangnan = Shankou 146-147 C 7
Jiangning 146-147 G 6
Jiangpu 146-147 G 5
Jiangshan 146-147 G 7
Jiangsu 142-143 MN 5
Jiangtai, Beijing- 155 II bc 2
Jiangxi 142-143 LM 6
Jiang Xian 146-147 CD 4
Jiangyin 146-147 H 6
Jiangyong 146-147 C 9
Jianhe [TJ, place] 146-147 B 8
Jian He [TJ, river] 144-145 D 2
Jianhu 146-147 G 5
Jianli 146-147 D 7
Jianning 146-147 F 8
Jian'ou 142-143 M 6
Jianping 144-145 B 2
Jianqian He 146-147 BC 5
Jianshi 146-147 B 6
Jianshui 142-143 J 7
Jianyang [TJ, Fujian] 142-143 M 6
Jianyang [TJ, Sichuan] 142-143 JK 5
Jiaocheng 146-147 CD 3
Jiaohekou 146-147 B 4
Jiaokou 146-147 C 3
Jiaoling 146-147 EF 9
Jiaonan 146-147 G 4
Jiao Xi 146-147 G 8

Jiao Xian 142-143 M 4
Jiaozhou Wan 146-147 H 3-4
Jiaozou 142-143 L 4
Jia Qi = Jiao Xi 146-147 G 8
Jia Qi = Xiao Xi 146-147 GH 7-8
Jiaqian = Jia Xian 146-147 C 2
Jiashan [TJ, Anhui] 146-147 G 5
Jiashan [TJ, Zhejiang] 146-147 H 6
Jiāwān 138-139 J 5
Jia Xian [TJ, Henan] 146-147 D 5
Jia Xian [TJ, Shanxi] 146-147 C 2
Jiaxing 142-143 N 5
Jiayi = Chiayi 142-143 MN 7
Jiayu 146-147 D 6-7
Jiayuguan 142-143 H 4
Jiazi 146-147 F 10
Jibal al-Hudnah 166-167 J 1-2
Jibāl al-Quṣūr 166-167 FG 3
Jibāl an-Nūbah 164-165 KL 6
Jibhalanta = Uliastaj 142-143 H 2
Jibiya 168-169 G 2
Jibóia 98-99 D 4
Jibou 122-123 K 2
Jicarilla Apache Indian Reservation 76-77 A 4
Jičín 118 G 3
Jidaidat Ḥāmir = Judayyiat Ḥāmir 136-137 J 7
Jidāmī, Bi'r al- 173 C 4
Jiddah 134-135 D 6
Jiddat al Ḥarāsīs 134-135 H 6-7
Jiddī, Jabal al- 173 C 2
Jido 134-135 P 5
Jidole = Gīdolē 164-165 M 7
Jiekkevarre 116-117 H 3
Jie Shan = Wudang Shan 146-147 C 5
Jieshi 146-147 E 10
Jieshi Wan 146-147 E 10
Jieshou [TJ, Anhui] 146-147 E 5
Jieshou [TJ, Guangxi Zhuangzu Zizhiqu] 146-147 C 9
Jieshou [TJ, Jiangsi] 146-147 G 5
Jiešjavrre 116-117 L 3
Jiexi 146-147 E 10
Jiexiu 146-147 CD 3
Jieyang 146-147 F 10
Jiftūn, Jazā'ir — 173 CD 4
Jiggithai Tsho 142-143 F 4
Jih-chao = Rizhao 146-147 G 4
Jihlam [PAK, place] 134-135 L 4
Jihlam [PAK, river] 134-135 L 4
Jihlava 118 G 4
Jījiga 164-165 N 7
Jījili 164-165 F 1
Jil, Al- 136-137 KL 7
Jilava, București- 122-123 M 5
Jilemutu 142-143 N 1
Jilf al-Kabīr, Haḍbat al- 164-165 K 4
Jilib 164-165 N 8
Jilīb Bākūr = Qalīb Bākūr 136-137 L 8
Jilidah, Al- = Al-Jaladah 134-135 F 6-7
Jilin [TJ, administrative unit] 142-143 N 2-O 3
Jilin [TJ, place] 142-143 O 3
Jiljila, Hôr al- = Hawr al-Jiljilah 136-137 L 6
Jiljilah, Hawr al- 136-137 L 6
Jill, Al- = Al-Jil 136-137 KL 7
Jilong = Chilung 142-143 N 6
Jīma 164-165 M 7
Jimā'h aṭ-Ṭulbah 166-167 D 2
Jimaja = Pulau Jemaya 148-149 DE 6
Jimāl, Wādī — 173 D 5
Jimā 'Shā'im 166-167 B 3
Jimāt 166-167 B 6
Jimbolia 122-123 J 3
Jiménez [MEX, Chihuahua] 64-65 F 6
Jiménez [MEX, Coahuila] 76-77 D 8
Jimeta 168-169 J 3
Jiminghe 146-147 E 6
Jimma = Jīma 164-165 M 7
Jimnah 166-167 L 3
Jimo 146-147 H 3
Jim River 58-59 M 3
Jimulco 86-87 J 5
Jinah 173 B 5
Jinan 142-143 M 4
Jincheng 142-143 L 4
Jind 138-139 F 3
Jindabyne 160 J 6
Jing'an 146-147 E 7
Jing'anji 146-147 F 4
Jingbian 146-147 B 3
Jingbo Hu 142-143 O 3
Jingchuan 142-143 K 4
Jingde 146-147 G 6
Jingdezhen 142-143 M 6
Jingdong 142-143 J 7
J. Ingenieros 110 III b 2
Jinggu 142-143 J 7
Jinghai 146-147 F 2
Jinghe [TJ, place] 142-143 E 3
Jing He [TJ, river] 146-147 B 4
Jinghong 142-143 J 7
Jingji = Jingzhi 146-147 G 3
Jingjiang 146-147 H 5-6
Jingjiang = Tongguan 146-147 D 7
Jingle 146-147 CD 2
Jingmen 146-147 CD 6
Jingning 142-143 K 4
Jing Shan [TJ, mountains] 146-147 C 6
Jingshan [TJ, place] 146-147 D 6
Jingshi = Jinshi 142-143 L 6
Jingtai 142-143 J 4
Jingtian 146-147 E 8
Jing Xian [TJ, Anhui] 146-147 G 6
Jing Xian [TJ, Hebei] 146-147 EF 3
Jing Xian [TJ, Hunan] 146-147 B 8
Jingxing 146-147 DE 2
Jingyang 146-147 B 4
Jingyu 144-145 F 1
Jingyuan 142-143 JK 4
Jingzhen = Xinchengbu 142-143 K 4
Jingzheng = Jiyiz 146-147 C 4
Jingzhi 146-147 G 3
Jingziguan 146-147 C 5
Jinhua 142-143 MN 6
Jiniiang = Quanzhou 142-143 MN 6-7
Jining [TJ, Inner Mongolian Aut. Reg.] 142-143 L 3
Jining [TJ, Shandong] 142-143 M 4
Jinja 172 F 1
Jin Jiang [TJ ◁ Gan Jiang] 146-147 E 7
Jin Jiang [TJ ◁ Quanzhou Gang] 146-147 FG 9
Jinjing 146-147 D 7
Jinjing He = Jinqian He 146-147 BC 5
Jinkou 146-147 E 6
Jinlanshi = Jinlansi 146-147 D 8
Jinlansi 146-147 D 8
Jinmen = Kinmen Dao 142-143 M 7
Jinmu Jiao = Jintu Jiao 142-143 KL 8
Jinniu 146-147 E 6-7
Jinotega 64-65 J 9
Jinotepe 88-89 C 9
Jinping 146-147 B 8
Jinqi = Jinxi 146-147 F 8
Jin Qi = Jin Xi 146-147 F 8
Jinsen = Inch'ŏn 142-143 O 4
Jinsha Jiang 142-143 J 6
Jinshan 146-147 H 6
Jinshi 142-143 L 6
Jinshi = Jianshi 146-147 B 6
Jintan 146-147 G 6
Jintian 146-147 E 8
Jintu Jiao 142-143 KL 8
Jintūr 138-139 F 8
Jin Xi [TJ, Fujian] 146-147 F 8
Jinxi [TJ, Jiangsi] 146-147 F 8
Jinxi [TJ, Liaoning] 144-145 C 2
Jin Xian [TJ, Hebei] 146-147 E 2
Jinxian [TJ, Jiangxi] 146-147 F 7
Jin Xian [TJ, Liaoning ↗ Jinzhou] 144-145 C 2
Jin Xian [TJ, Liaoning ↑ Lüda] 142-143 N 4
Jinxiang [TJ, Shandong] 146-147 EF 4
Jinxiang [TJ, Zhejiang] 146-147 H 8
Jinxiu 146-147 C 9
Jinyuan 146-147 D 3
Jinyun 146-147 H 7
Jinzhai 146-147 E 6
Jinzhou 142-143 N 3
Jiparaná, Rio — 92-93 G 6-7
Jipijapa 92-93 C 5
Jiqi = Jixi 146-147 G 6
Jirādū 166-167 M 1
Jirays, Jabal — 173 D 7
Jiren = Jīma 164-165 M 7
Jirgalanta = Chovd 142-143 G 2
Jiriid 164-165 b 2
Jirijirimo, Raudal — 94-95 F 8
Jirira 104-105 B 6
Jirjā 164-165 L 3
Jīroft 134-135 H 5
Jiruá 106-107 K 1-2
Jirwān 134-135 G 6
Jishar 146-147 C 4
Jishi Shan = Amnyemachhen Gangri 142-143 HJ 5
Jishou 146-147 B 7
Jishui 146-147 E 8
Jisr ech Chaghoûr = Gisr ash-Shughūr 136-137 G 5
Jitan 146-147 E 9
Jitaúna 100-101 E 7-8
Jitra 150-151 C 9
Jiu 122-123 K 3
Jiuchangjiang = Changcheng 150-151 G 3
Jiuchaoxian = Chao Xian 146-147 FG 6
Jiudaoliang 146-147 BC 6
Jiufeng Shan 146-147 G 8
Jiugan'en = Gancheng 150-151 G 3
Jiugang, Beijing- 155 II b 3
Jiugong'an = Nanping 146-147 D 7
Jiugou = Jiukou 146-147 D 6
Jiuhe 146-147 E 10
Jiujiang [TJ, Guangdong] 146-147 D 10
Jiujiang [TJ, Jiangxi] 142-143 M 6
Jiukou 146-147 D 6
Jiuling Shan 146-147 E 7
Jiulong = Kowloon 142-143 LM 7
Jiulong Jiang 146-147 F 9
Jiulong Shan 146-147 G 7
Jiulong Xi 146-147 F 8
Jiunantian = Nantian 146-147 HJ 7
Jiuquan 142-143 H 4
Jiurongcheng 146-147 J 3
Jiushan Liedao 146-147 J 7
Jiusiyang = Siyang 146-147 G 5
Jiuxian 146-147 D 5
Jiuxiangcheng 146-147 E 5
Jiuxian He 146-147 F 9
Jiuxianqiao, Beijing- 155 II bc 2
Jiuyuhang 146-147 GH 6
Jiwā', Al- 134-135 G 6
Jiwānī 134-135 J 5-6
Jixi [TJ, Anhui] 146-147 G 6
Jixi [TJ, Heilongjiang] 142-143 P 2
Ji Xian [TJ, Hebei → Beijing] 146-147 F 1
Ji Xian [TJ, Hebei ↘ Shijiazhuang] 146-147 E 3
Ji Xian [TJ, Henan] 146-147 E 4
Ji Xian [TJ, Shanxi] 146-147 C 3
Jiyāganj = Jiaganj 138-139 M 5
Jiyang [TJ, Fujian] 146-147 FG 8
Jiyang [TJ, Shandong] 146-147 F 3
Jiyi 146-147 C 4
Jiyizhen = Jiyi 146-147 C 4
Jiyuan 146-147 D 4
Jiyun He 146-147 F 2
Jīzah, Al- [ET] 164-165 KL 3
Jīzah, Al- [JOR] 136-137 FG 7
Jīzah, El — = Al-Jīzah 136-137 FG 7
Jīzān 134-135 E 7
Jize 146-147 E 3
Jizl, Wādī al- 134-135 D 5
J. J. Almeyra 106-107 H 5
J. Jorba 106-107 E 4
Jlaiba = Jalībah 136-137 M 7
Jllovo Beach 174-175 J 6
Jlullssat 56-57 ab 4
Joaçaba 111 F 3
Jōāī = Jowai 141 C 3
Joaíma 100-101 D 3
Joal 168-169 A 2
Joana Peres 92-93 JK 5
Joanes 98-99 O 5
Joanina 100-101 D 8
Joaninha, Serra da — 100-101 D 3
Joanna Spring 158-159 DE 4
João 92-93 J 5
João Amaro 100-101 D 7
João Câmara 100-101 G 3
João de Almeida = Chibia 172 B 5
João do Vale, Serra — 100-101 F 3-4
João Lisboa 98-99 P 7
João Monlevale 102-103 L 3
João Pessoa 92-93 N 6
João Pinheiro 102-103 JK 2
Joaquim Felício 92-93 KL 8
Joaquim Murtinho 102-103 GH 6
Joaquim Távora 102-103 GH 5
Joaquín V. González 111 D 3
Jobal Island = Jazā'ir Qaysūm 173 CD 4
Jobat 138-139 E 6
Job Peak 74-75 D 3
Jo-ch'iang = Charqiliq 142-143 F 4
Jockey 88-89 DE 8
Jocolí 111 C 4
Jodhpur 134-135 L 5
Jodiya Bandar 138-139 C 6
Jodpur = Jodhpur 134-135 L 5
Joe Kelly Butler Stadium 85 III b 2
Joensuu 116-117 NO 6
Joerg Plateau 53 B 29-30
Joes, CO 68-69 E 6
Jõesuu, Narva- 124-125 FG 4
Joe W. Brown Memorial Park 85 I c 1
Jofane 172 F 6
Joffre, Mount — 60 K 4
Jofra Oasis, el — = Wāḥāt al-Jufrah 164-165 GH 3
Jogbani 138-139 L 4
Jõgeva 124-125 F 4
Jog Falls 140 B 3
Joggins 63 D 5
Jogighopa 141 B 2
Jogindamagar 138-139 F 1-2
Jogipet 140 CD 2
Jögödseer Chijd = Erdenecagaan 142-143 LM 2
Jogyakarta = Yogyakarta 148-149 EF 8
Jōhana 144-145 L 4
Johanna Island = Anjouan 172 HJ 4
Johannesburg 172 E 7
Johannesburg Airport 170 V c 1
Johannesburg-Albertynsville 170 V a 2
Johannesburg-Auckland Park 170 V ab 2
Johannesburg-Baragwanath 170 V a 2
Johannesburg-Bellevue 170 V b 2
Johannesburg-Booysens 170 V ab 2
Johannesburg-Bramley 170 V b 1
Johannesburg-Craighall 170 V b 1
Johannesburg-Craighall Park 170 V b 1
Johannesburg-Crosby 170 V a 2
Johannesburg-Diepkloof 170 V a 2
Johannesburg-Eastern Native 170 V b 2
Johannesburg-Franklin Roosevelt Park 170 V a 1
Johannesburg-Greenside 170 V b 1
Johannesburg-Greymont 170 V a 1
Johannesburg-Jabavu 170 V a 2
Johannesburg-Kew 170 V b 1
Johannesburg-Klipriviersoog 170 V a 2
Johannesburg-Linden 170 V ab 1
Johannesburg-Linksfield 170 V b 1
Johannesburg-Linmeyer 170 V b 2
Johannesburg-Lombardy 170 V b 1
Johannesburg-Malvern 170 V b 2
Johannesburg-Mayfair 170 V b 2
Johannesburg-Meadowlands 170 V a 2
Johannesburg-Melville 170 V ab 2
Johannesburg-Meredale 170 V a 2
Johannesburg-Mofolo 170 V a 2
Johannesburg-Mondeor 170 V ab 2
Johannesburg-Nancefield 170 V a 2
Johannesburg-New Canada 170 V a 2
Johannesburg-Newclare 170 V a 2
Johannesburg-Northcliff 170 V a 1
Johannesburg-Norwood 170 V b 1
Johannesburg-Oaklands 170 V b 1
Johannesburg-Ophirton 170 V b 2
Johannesburg-Orlando 170 V a 2
Johannesburg-Paarlshoop 170 V a 2
Johannesburg-Paradise Hill 170 V b 2
Johannesburg-Park Town 170 V b 2
Johannesburg-Pimville 170 V a 2
Johannesburg-Regents Park 170 V b 2
Johannesburg-Rivasdale 170 V a 2
Johannesburg-Robertsham 170 V ab 2
Johannesburg-Rosettenville 170 V b 2
Johannesburg-Sandringham 170 V b 1
Johannesburg-Selby 170 V b 2
Johannesburg-South Hills 170 V b 2
Johannesburg-Soweto 174-175 G 4
Johannesburg-Turffontein 170 V b 2
Johannesburg-Willowdene 170 V a 2
Johannesburg-Yeoville 170 V b 2
Johanneskirchen, München- 130 II bc 1
Johannisthal, Berlin- 130 III c 2
Johi [GUY] 92-93 H 4
Johī [PAK] 138-139 A 4
Johilla 138-139 H 6
John A. White Park 85 II b 2
John Day, OR 66-67 D 3
John Day River 66-67 C 3
John Day River, Middle Fork — 66-67 D 3
John Day River, North Fork — 66-67 D 3
John Day River, South Fork — 66-67 D 3
John F. Kennedy Center 82 II a 2
John F. Kennedy International Airport 82 III d 3
John F. Kennedy National Historical Site 84 I b 2
John F. Kennedy Stadium 84 III bc 2
John MacLaren Park 83 I b 2
John Martin Reservoir 68-69 E 6-7
John River 58-59 L 3
Johnson, KS 68-69 F 7
Johnson, Pico de — 86-87 DE 3
Johnsonburg, PA 72-73 G 4
Johnson City, NY 72-73 J 3
Johnson City, TN 64-65 K 4
Johnson City, TX 76-77 E 7
Johnsonville, SC 80-81 G 4
Johnston, SC 80-81 F 4
Johnston Lakes 158-159 D 6
Johnstown, NY 72-73 JK 3
Johnstown, PA 64-65 L 3-4
John T. Brechtel Memorial Park 85 I b 2
John T. Mason Park 85 III b 2
John Tyler Arboretum 84 III a 2
Johor 150-151 D 11
Johor Baharu 148-149 DE 6
Johor Strait 154 III ab 1
Jõhvi 124-125 F 4
Joinvile 111 G 3
Joinville, Île — 53 C 31
Joinville-le-Pont 129 I cd 2
Joka, South Suburbs- 154 II a 3
Jōkāu 164-165 L 7
Jokkmokk 116-117 HJ 4
Joko = Yoko 164-165 G 7
Jokohama = Yokohama 142-143 QR 4
Jökulsá á Brú 116-117 f 2
Jökulsá á Fjöllum 116-117 ef 2
Jolfā 134-135 F 3
Joliet, IL 64-65 J 3
Joliette 56-57 W 8
Joliette, ND 68-69 H 1
Joliette, Parc provincial de — 62 OP 3
Jolliet, Lacs — 62 N 1
Joló 148-149 H 5
Joló Island 148-149 H 5
Jombang 152-153 K 9
Jomo Gangkar 138-139 MN 3
Jomo Lhari 138-139 M 4
Jomotsering 134-135 O 5
Jomu 171 C 3
Jomuro 168-169 E 4
Jonava 124-125 E 6
Jones, Cape — 56-57 UV 7
Jonesboro, AR 64-65 H 4
Jonesboro, GA 78-79 G 4
Jonesboro, IL 70-71 F 7
Jonesboro, LA 78-79 C 4
Jones Islands 58-59 N 1
Jones Point 82 II a 2
Jonesport, ME 72-73 N 2
Jones Sound 56-57 TU 2
Jonesville, AK 58-59 N 6
Jonesville, LA 78-79 CD 5
Jonesville, MI 70-71 H 4-5
Jongkha 142-143 F 6
Joniškėlis 124-125 DE 5-6
Joniškis 124-125 DE 5
Jonkersberg 174-175 DE 7
Jonköping 116-117 EF 9
Jönköpings län 116-117 EF 9
Jonquière 56-57 WX 8
Jonzac 120-121 G 6
Joontoy 172 H 2
Joowhar 164-165 ab 3
Jo'öyu Ri 138-139 L 3
Joplin, MO 64-65 H 4
Joplin, MT 66-67 H 1
Jóquei Clube [BR, Rio de Janeiro] 110 I b 2
Jóquei Clube [BR, São Paulo] 110 II a 2
Jora 138-139 F 4
Jorasanko, Calcutta- 154 II b 2
Jordan 134-135 D 4
Jordan, MN 70-71 D 3
Jordan, MT 68-69 C 2
Jordan = Nahr ash-Sharī'ah 136-137 F 6-7
Jordan Creek 66-67 E 4
Jordânia 100-101 D 8
Jordan Valley, OR 66-67 E 4
Jordão, Rio — 102-103 G 6
Jorf = Jurf 166-167 D 4
Jorf el Mellâḥ = Jurf al-Malḥā' 166-167 D 2
Jorge, Cabo — 108-109 B 8
Jorge, Isla — = George Island 108-109 JK 9
Jorge Montt, Isla — 108-109 B 8
Jorge Newbery, Aeroparque — 110 III b 1
Jorhāt 134-135 PQ 5
Jorigām 138-139 J 8
Jörn 116-117 J 5
Jornada del Muerto 76-77 A 6
Jorong 152-153 L 7-8
Jortom 124-125 Q 2
Jos 164-165 F 7
José A. Guisasola 106-107 G 7
José Bahía Casás 108-109 H 3
José Battle y Ordóñez 106-107 K 4
José Bonifácio [BR, Rondônia] 98-99 H 11
José Bonifácio [BR, São Paulo] 102-103 H 4
Jośe C. Paz, Sarmiento- 110 III a 1
José de Freitas 100-101 C 3
José de San Martín 111 BC 6
José Enrique Rodó 106-107 J 4
José Gonçalves 100-101 D 8
José La Haye 102-103 D 6
Joselândia [BR, Maranhão] 100-101 B 3
Joselândia [BR, Mato Grosso] 102-103 DE 2
José María Blanco 106-107 F 6
José Mármol, Almirante Brown- 110 III b 2
José M. Micheo 106-107 H 5
José Otávio 106-107 K 3
José Pedro, Rio — 102-103 M 3-4
José Pedro Varela 106-107 KL 4
Joseph, OR 66-67 E 3
Joseph, Lac — 56-57 XY 7
Joseph, Lake — 72-73 G 2
Joseph Bonaparte Gulf 158-159 E 2
Joseph City, AZ 74-75 H 5
José S. Arévalo 106-107 H 5
Joshīmath 138-139 G 2
Joshīpur 138-139 L 7
Joshipura = Joshīpur 138-139 L 7
Joshua Tree, CA 74-75 E 5
Joshua Tree National Monument 64-65 CD 5
Joškar-Ola 132-133 H 6
Joson Bulag = Altaj 142-143 H 2
Jos Plateau 164-165 E 6-7
Josselin 120-121 F 5
Jostedalsbreen 116-117 B 7
Jotajana 94-95 L 3
Jotunheimen 116-117 BC 7
Joubertina 174-175 EF 7
Joûniyé = Jūnīyah 136-137 F 6
Jourdanton, TX 76-77 E 8
Joutsa 116-117 LM 7
Jouy-en-Josas 129 I b 3
Jouy-le-Moutier 129 I b 1
Jovellanos 88-89 F 3
Jowai 141 C 3
Jow Kār 136-137 N 5
Joya, La — [BOL] 104-105 C 5
Joya, La — [PE] 96-97 F 10
Joyous Pavillon Park 155 II b 2
Joypur = Jaipur 141 D 2
J. Prats 106-107 CD 5
J. S. Arévalo 106-107 H 5
Juaba 98-99 O 6
Juan Aldama 64-65 F 7
Juan Amarillo 91 III b 2
Juan Anchorena, San Isidro- 110 III b 1
Juan A. Pradere 111 D 5
Juan B. Alberdi 106-107 G 5
Juan B. Arruabarrena 106-107 H 3
Juan Bautista Alberdi 104-105 CD 10
Juan B. Molina 106-107 G 4
Juancheng 146-147 E 4
Juancho 106-107 J 6
Juan de Fuca, Strait of — 56-57 LM 8
Juan de Garay 106-107 E 7
Juan del Monte 96-97 C 5
Juan de Mena 102-103 D 6
Juan de Nova 172 H 5
Juan Díaz 64-65 c 2
Juan E. Barra 106-107 G 6
Juan Escutia, Ciudad Netzahualcoyotl- 91 I C 2
Juan Fernández Ridge 156-157 N 6
Juan Gallegos, Isla — 64-65 b 2
Juan G. Bazán 104-105 F 9
Juan Godoy 106-107 B 1
Juan González Romero, Ciudad de México- 91 I c 2
Juan Guerra 96-97 C 5
Juan J. Albornoz 108-109 E 7
Juan J. Almeyra 106-107 H 5
Juanjiang 146-147 D 7
Juan Jorba 106-107 E 4
Juan José Castelli 111 DE 3
Juan J. Paso 106-107 F 5
Juanjuí 92-93 D 6
Juankoski 116-117 N 6
Juan L. Lacaze 106-107 J 5
Juan Llerena 106-107 E 4
Juan N. Fernández 106-107 H 7
Juan Pujol 106-107 HJ 3
Juan Stuven, Isla — 111 A 7
Juan W. Gez 106-107 DE 4
Juarci 100-101 D 7
Juárez [MEX ↑ Chihuahua] 64-65 E 5
Juárez [MEX ↖ Chihuahua] 86-87 F 2
Juárez, Oaxaca de — 64-65 GH 8
Juárez, Sierra de — 64-65 C 5
Juarzon 168-169 C 4
Juatinga, Ponta do — 92-93 L 9
Juàzeirinho 100-101 F 4
Juazeiro 92-93 L 6
Juazeiro do Norte 92-93 M 6
Jūbā 164-165 L 8
Jubail, Al- = Al-Jubayl al-Baḥrī 134-135 FG 5
Jubal, Madiq — = Jazīrat Shadwan 164-165 LM 3
Jubayl [ET] 173 C 3
Jubayl [RL] 136-137 F 5
Jubayl al-Baḥrī, Al- 134-135 FG 5
Jubayt 164-165 M 4
Jubba = Jubbah 136-137 K 6
Jubbabe Hoose 172 H 2
Jubbada Hoose ◁ 4 164-165 N 8
Jubbade Dhexe 164-165 N 8
Jubbah 136-137 K 6
Jubbulpore = Jabalpur 134-135 MN 6
Jubeil = Jubayl 136-137 F 5
Jubilee Lake 158-159 E 5
Jubilee Reservoir 155 I a 1
Jubileo 106-107 H 3
Júcar 120-121 G 9
Juçara 102-103 F 5
Juçaral, Rio — 100-101 C 2
Júcaro 88-89 G 4
Jucás 92-93 LM 6
Juchitán de Zaragoza 64-65 GH 8
Juchmači 124-125 RS 6
Juchnov 124-125 K 6
Jucurucu, Rio — 100-101 DE 9
Jucurutu 100-101 F 3-4
Judā', Sha'īb al- 136-137 L 8-M 7
Judas, Punta — 88-89 D 10
Judayyidat-Ar'ar 134-135 DE 4
Judayyidat Ḥāmir 136-137 J 7
Judea 174-175 BC 2
Judenburg 118 G 5
Judge Haway, Mount — 66-67 BC 1
Judino = Petuchovo 132-133 M 6
Judino, Kazan'- 124-125 R 6
Judith, Point — 72-73 L 4
Judith Basin 68-69 AB 2
Judith Bassin 66-67 HJ 2
Judith Gap, MT 68-69 B 2
Judith Mountains 68-69 B 2
Judoma 132-133 a 6
Judys Lake 85 II b 3
Juejiang = Rudong 146-147 H 5
Juerana 100-101 E 9
Jufrah, Wāḥāt al- 164-165 GH 3
Jug [SU, place] 124-125 V 5
Jug [SU, river] 124-125 Q 3
Juggernaut = Purī 134-135 O 7
Jugiong 160 J 5
Jugo-Kamskij 124-125 UV 5
Jugorskij poluostrov 132-133 L 4
Jugorskij Šar, proliv — 132-133 L 4-M 3
Jugydtydor 124-125 T 2
Juhaym 136-137 L 8
Juhaynah 173 B 4
Ju He = Ju Shui 146-147 C 6
Juhua Dao 144-145 C 2
Juian = Rui'an 146-147 H 8
Juichang = Ruichang 146-147 E 7
Juigalpa 88-89 D 8
Juikin = Ruijin 142-143 M 6
Juile, El — 86-87 N 9
Juisui 146-147 H 10
Juiz de Fora 92-93 KL 9
Jujul 96-97 C 7
Jujuy 111 C 2
Jujuy = San Salvador de Jujuy 111 CD 2
Jujuy, San Salvador de — 111 CD 2
Jukagirskoje ploskogorje 132-133 de 4
Jukamenskoje 124-125 T 5
Jukao = Rugao 142-143 N 5
Jukoupu 146-147 C 8
Juksejevo 124-125 TU 4
Jukskei 170 V b 1
Jukte 132-133 TU 5
Jula 124-125 P 2
Julaca 92-93 F 9
Julcamarca, Cordillera de — 96-97 D 8
Julesburg, CO 68-69 EF 5
Juli 92-93 F 8
Júlia [BR] 98-99 DE 5
Juliaca 92-93 E 8
Julia Creek 158-159 H 4
Julian, CA 74-75 E 6
Julian Alps 122-123 EF 2
Julianatop 98-99 K 3
Julianehåb = Qaqortoq 56-57 b 5
Jülich 118 C 3
Julimes 76-77 B 8
9 de Julio, Bahía = King George Bay 108-109 J 8
Júlio de Castilhos 106-107 L 2
Júlio Furtado, Parque — 110 I b 2
Julio María Sanz 106-107 KL 4
Juliuhe 144-145 D 1
Julius, AK 58-59 N 4
Jullundur 134-135 LM 4
Julu 146-147 E 3
Julundur = Jullundur 134-135 LM 4
Julu Rayeu 152-153 BC 3
Jumaima, Al — = Al-Jumaymah 136-137 KL 8
Jumaymah, Al- 136-137 KL 8
Jumbe Salim's 171 D 5
Jumbilla 92-93 D 6
Jumbo 172 H 2
Jumbo, Raas — 172 H 2
Jume, Languna — 106-107 FG 4
Jumilla 120-121 G 9
Jumla 138-139 J 3
Jumna = Yamunā 134-135 MN 5
Jumnotri = Jamnotri 138-139 G 2
Jun = Jun Xian 146-147 C 5
Junāgaḍa = Jūnāgarh 138-139 J 8
Junagadh 134-135 KL 6
Jūnāgarh 138-139 J 8
Junagarh = Junagadh 134-135 KL 6
Junan 146-147 G 4
Junayfah 173 C 2
Junaynah, Al- 164-165 J 6
Juncal, Cerro — 106-107 BC 4
Junction, TX 76-77 E 7
Junction, UT 74-75 G 3
Junction City, AR 78-79 C 4
Junction City, KS 64-65 G 4
Jundah 158-159 H 4
Jundiaí 102-103 J 5
Jundtion City, OR 66-67 B 3
Juneau, AK 56-57 K 6
Juneau, WI 70-71 F 4
Junee 160 H 5
June Lake, CA 74-75 D 4
Jungar Qi 146-147 C 2
Jungcheng = Rongcheng 146-147 EF 2
Jungfernheide 130 III b 1
Jungfernheide, Volkspark — 130 III b 1
Jungghariyā 142-143 EF 2
Jung-hsien = Rong Xian 146-147 C 10
Jungo, NV 66-67 D 5
Jungshāhī 138-139 A 5
Jun-ho-chi = Runheji 146-147 F 5
Juniata, Philadelphia-, PA 84 III c 1
Juniata River 72-73 H 4
Junín [EC] 96-97 A 2
Junín [PE, administrative unit] 96-97 D 7
Junín [PE, place] 92-93 D 7
Junín [RA, Buenos Aires] 111 D 4
Junín [RA, Mendoza] 106-107 C 4
Junín, Lago de — 96-97 C 7
Junín de los Andes 111 BC 5
Junio, La Matanza-20 de — 110 III a 2
Juniper Mountains 74-75 G 5
Jūnīyah 136-137 F 6
Juniye = Jūnīyah 136-137 F 6
Junjik River 58-59 OP 2
Junnar 138-139 DE 8
Juno, TX 76-77 D 7
Junqolĕy 164-165 L 7
Junqueiro 100-101 F 5
Junsele 116-117 G 6
Junta, La — [BOL] 104-105 F 4
Junta, La — [MEX] 86-87 G 3
Juntas 106-107 B 3
Junten = Sunch'ŏn 142-143 O 4-5
Juntura, OR 66-67 DE 4
Junturas, Las — 106-107 F 3
Junun 150-151 C 10
Junxian = Xun Xian 146-147 E 4
Jupaguá 100-101 B 6
Juparanã, Lagoa — 100-101 DE 10
Jupiá, Represa de — 92-93 J 9
Jupiter River 63 E 3
Juquiá 102-103 J 6
Jūr, Nahr al- 164-165 K 7
Jūr, Nahr el — = Nahr al-Jūr 164-165 K 7
Jura [CH] 118 BC 5
Jura [GB] 119 D 3-4
Jura, Sound of — 119 D 4
Jurab = Djourab 164-165 H 5
Juradó 94-95 C 4
Juraiba, Al — = Al-Juraybah 136-137 KL 8
Juramento, Río — 104-105 D 9
Juratiški 124-125 EF 6
Juraybah, Al- 136-137 KL 8
Jurbarkas 124-125 D 6
Jurborg = Jurbarkas 124-125 D 6
Jurdī, Wādī — 173 C 4
Juréia, Praia da — 102-103 J 6
Jurema 100-101 F 5
Juremal 100-101 D 5
Jurf 166-167 D 4
Jurf ad-Darāwish 136-137 FG 7
Jurf al-Malḥā 166-167 D 2
Jurf ed Darāwish = Jurf ad-Darāwish 136-137 FG 7
Jurga 132-133 P 6
Jūrgāy, Jabal — 164-165 JK 6
Jurien Bay 158-159 B 6
Juríes, Los — 111 D 3
Jurino 124-125 PQ 5
Juriti 98-99 KL 6
Jurja 124-125 R 4
Jurjevec 132-133 G 6
Jurjev-Pol'skij 124-125 MN 5
Jurjurah 164-165 EF 1
Jurla 124-125 U 4
Jurlovka 124-125 N 7
Jurmala 124-125 DE 5
Jurong 146-147 G 6
Juruá 98-99 EF 6
Juruá, Rio — 92-93 F 6
Juruàzinho, Rio — 96-97 FG 5
Juruena 92-93 H 7
Juruena, Rio — 92-93 H 6-7
Jurujuba, Punta de — 110 I c 2

Jurumirim, Represa de —
102-103 H 5
Jurupari, Ilha — 98-99 NO 4
Jurupari, Rio — 96-97 F 5-G 6
Jusepín 94-95 K 3
Jushan = Rushan 146-147 H 3
Ju Shui 146-147 C 6
Juškozero 132-133 E 5
Jussey 120-121 K 5
Justa 126-127 N 3
Justice, Palais de — 128 II ab 1-2
Justiceburg, TX 76-77 D 6
Justo Daract 111 CD 4
Jus'va 124-125 U 4
Jutaí [BR, Amazonas] 98-99 D 7
Jutaí [BR, Pernambuco] 100-101 D 5
Jutaí, Ilha Grande de — 98-99 O 6
Jutaí, Rio — 92-93 F 5
Jutaí, Serra do — 98-99 M 5
Jutaza 124-125 T 6
Jüterbog 118 F 2-3
Jūṭhī Antarīp = False Point
134-135 O 6
Juti 102-103 E 5
Jutiapa 64-65 HJ 9
Juticalpa 64-65 J 9
Jutland 116-117 C 9-10
Ju-tung = Rudong 146-147 C 11
Juuka 116-117 N 6
Juuru 124-125 E 4
Juva 116-117 MN 7
Juventud, Isla de la — 64-65 K 7
Juwā' 166-167 KL 5
Juwārah, Al- 134-135 H 7
Ju Xian 142-143 M 4
Juye 146-147 F 4
Ju-yüan = Ruyuan 146-147 D 9
Juža 124-125 O 5
Jūzān 136-137 N 5
Južnaja Kel'tma 124-125 U 3
Južna Morava 122-123 JK 4
Južno-Kuril'sk 132-133 c 9
Južno-Sachalinsk 132-133 bc 8
Južnyj, mys — 132-133 e 6
Južnyj An'ujskij chrebet = An'ujskij
chrebet 132-133 fg 4
Južnyj Bug 126-127 E 3
Južnyj port 113 V c 3
Južnyj Ural 132-133 K 7-L 6
Juzovka = Doneck 126-127 H 2-3
Južsib 132-133 L 7
Juzur al-Ḥabībah 166-167 F 2
Juzur Ṭawīlah 173 CD 4

Jyäjpura = Jājpur 138-139 L 7
Jyavan = Jiāwān 138-139 J 5
Jyekunde = Chhergundo
142-143 H 5
Jyväskylä 116-117 L 6

K

K 2 134-135 M 3

Ka 164-165 F 6
Kaain Veld = Kaiingveld
174-175 D 6-E 5
Kaala 78-79 c 2
Kaalkaroo 174-175 C 6
Kaamanen 116-117 M 3
Kaap Colombine 174-175 B 7
Kaap Frio 172 B 5
Kaap Hangklip 174-175 C 8
Kaap Hermes 174-175 H 6
Kaap Infanta 174-175 D 8
Kaap Kruis 172 B 6
Kaapland 172 DE 8
Kaapmuiden 174-175 J 3
Kaapplato 172 D 7
Kaapprovinsie = Kaapland 172 DE 8
Kaap Recife 174-175 FG 8
Kaap Seal 174-175 E 8
Kaap Sint Blaize 174-175 E 8
Kaap Sint Martin 174-175 B 7
Kaapstad 172 C 8
Kaaschka 134-135 HJ 3
Kaba [WAL] 168-169 B 3
Kaba, Gunung — 152-153 E 7
Kabaena, Pulau — 148-149 H 8
Kabaena, Selat — 152-153 O 8
Kabahaydar = Kalecik 136-137 H 4
Kabāla [GR] 122-123 L 5
Kabala [WAL] 164-165 B 7
Kabale 172 EF 2
Kabali 152-153 OP 6
Kabalo 172 E 3
Kabambare 172 E 2
Kabango 171 B 5
Kabanjahe 150-151 B 11
Kabansk 132-133 U 7
Kabara 168-169 E 1
Kabardino-Balkar Autonomous Soviet
Socialist Republic 126-127 LM 5
Kabare [RCB] 172 E 2
Kabare [RI] 148-149 K 7
Kabarnet 171 CD 2
Kabarṭal 166-167 F 5
Kabba 164-165 F 7
Kabbani 140 C 4-5
Kåbdalis 116-117 J 4
Kabelega Falls 172 F 1
Kabelega Falls National Park 172 F 1
Kabenung Lake 70-71 H 1
Kaberamaido 171 C 2
Kabertene = Kabarṭal 166-167 F 5
Kabetogama Lake 70-71 D 1
Kabilcevaz 136-137 J 3
Kabinakagami Lake 70-71 H 1
Kabinakagami River 62 G 3
Kabin Buri 148-149 D 4
Kabinchaung 150-151 B 6
Kabinda 172 DE 3
Kabinda = Cabinda 172 B 3
Kabingyaung = Kabinchaung
150-151 B 6
Kabir 152-153 Q 10
Kabīr, Wāw al- 164-165 H 3
Kabīr, Zāb al- 136-137 K 4
Kabīr Kūh 134-135 F 4
Kabīwāla 138-139 C 2
Kabkābīyah 164-165 J 6
Kabo 164-165 H 7
Kabobo 171 B 4
Kabompo 172 D 4
Kabongo 172 DE 3
Kabosa Island = Kabūzā Kyûn
150-151 AB 6
Kaboûdia, Râss — = Rā's
Qabūdīyah 166-167 M 2
Kabudārāhang 136-137 N 5
Kābul 134-135 K 4
Kabunda 171 B 6
Kaburuang, Pulau — 148-149 J 6
Kabūzā Kyûn 150-151 AB 6
Kabwe 172 E 4
Kača 126-127 F 4
Kačalinskaja 126-127 M 2
Kačanovo 124-125 FG 5
K'achana = Kafan 126-127 N 7
Kachchh = Kutch 134-135 K 6
Kacheliba 171 C 2
Ka-Chem = Malyj Jenisej
132-133 RS 7
Kachemak Bay 58-59 M 7
Kachgar = Qāshqār 142-143 CD 4
Kachhār = Cāchār 141 C 3
Kachi 126-127 N 6
Kachia 168-169 G 3
Kachin Pyinnei 148-149 C 1-2
Kachkatt = Yūssufīyah 166-167 B 3
Kachovka 126-127 F 3
Kachovskoje vodochranilišče
126-127 F 3
K'achta 132-133 U 7
Kaçkar dağı 136-137 J 2
Kačug 132-133 U 7
Kadada 124-125 Q 7
Kadaingdi 148-149 C 3
Kadaingti = Kadaingdi 148-149 C 3
Kadaiyanallūr 140 C 6
Kadaiyyanallūr = Kadaiyanallūr
140 C 6
Kadan Kyûn 148-149 C 4
Kaḍappa = Cuddapah 134-135 M 8
Kādarī = Kadiri 140 D 3
Kade [GH] 164-165 D 7
Kade [Guinea] 168-169 B 2
Kadei 164-165 H 8
Kadgoron = Ardon 126-127 M 5
Kadhdhāb, Sinn al- 173 BC 6
Kadi 138-139 D 6
Kadievka = Stachanov 126-127 J 2
Kadıköy, İstanbul- 136-137 C 2
Kadina 160 CD 4-5
Kadınhanı 136-137 E 3
Kadiolo 168-169 D 3
Kādīpur 138-139 J 4
Kadiri 140 D 3
Kadirli 136-137 FG 4
Kadiyevka = Stachanov
126-127 J 2
Kadmat Island 134-135 L 8
Kadnikov 124-125 N 4
Ka-do 144-145 E 3
Kadoka, SD 68-69 F 4
Kadoma 172 E 5
Kadon 150-151 E 5
Kadugli = Kāduqlī 164-165 KL 6
Kaduj 124-125 L 4
Kaduna [WAN, administrative unit]
168-169 G 3
Kaduna [WAN, place] 164-165 F 6
Kāduqlī 164-165 KL 6
Kaḍūr 141 BC 4
Kaḍūru = Kaḍūr 140 BC 4
Kadwāha 138-139 F 5
Kadyj 124-125 O 5
Kadykčan 132-133 C 5
Kadžaran 126-127 N 7
Kaech'i-ri 144-145 G 2
Kaemōr = Kaimur Hills
138-139 HJ 5
Kaena Point 78-79 c 2
Kaeng Khoi 150-151 C 5
Kaerānā = Kairāna 138-139 F 3
Kaesarganj = Kaisarganj
138-139 H 4
Kaesŏng 142-143 O 4
Kaethal = Kaithal 138-139 F 3
Kāf 134-135 D 4
Kāf, Al- 164-165 F 1
Kafan 126-127 N 7
Kafanchan 164-165 F 7
Kaférévs, Akrōtērion — 122-123 L 6
Kafferrivier 174-175 FG 5
Kaffraria = Transkei 172 E 8
Kaffrine 164-165 AB 6
Kafr ash-Shaykh 173 B 2
Kafr az-Zayyāt 173 B 2
Kafta 164-165 M 6
Kafu 172 F 1
Kafue [Z, place] 172 E 5
Kafue [Z, river] 172 E 5
Kafue Flats 172 E 5
Kafue National Park 172 E 4-5
Kafulwa 171 B 5
Kaga 144-145 L 4
Kaga Bandoro 164-165 HJ 7
Kāgal 140 B 2
Kagamil Island 58-59 lm 4
Kagan 134-135 J 3
Kaganovič = Popasnaja
126-127 J 2
Kagarlyk 126-127 E 2
Kagati Lake 58-59 GH 7
Kagawa 144-145 JK 5
Kagera 172 F 2
Kagera, Parc national de la —
172 F 2
Kagera Magharibi 172 F 2
Kagi = Chiayi 142-143 MN 7
Kagianagami Lake 62 F 2
Kâğithane [TR, place] 154 I ab 2
Kâğithane [TR, river] 154 I a 2
Kağızman 136-137 K 2
Kagmār 164-165 L 6
Kāgna 140 C 2
Kagoro 164-165 F 7
Kagoshima 142-143 OP 5
Kagoshima wan 144-145 H 7
Kagosima = Kagoshima
142-143 OP 5
Kagran, Wien- 113 I b 2
Kagul [SU, place] 126-127 D 4
Kaguyak, AK 58-59 g 1
Kahā 138-139 BC 3
Kahalgāṅv = Colgong 138-139 L 5
Kahal Tābalbalah 166-167 EF 5
Kahal Tabelbala = Kaḥal Tābalbalah
166-167 EF 5
Kahama 172 F 2
Kahān 138-139 B 3
Kahayan, Sungai — 148-149 F 7
Kahemba 172 C 3
Kahia 172 E 3
Kahiltna Glacier 58-59 M 5
Kahlā [IR] 136-137 N 5
Kahlenberg 113 I b 1
Kahler Asten 118 D 3
Kahlotus, WA 66-67 D 2
Kahoka, MO 70-71 DE 5
Kahoku-gata 144-145 L 4
Kahoolawe 148-149 e 3
Kahraman 154 I b 3
Kahror 138-139 C 3
Kahta = Kölük 136-137 H 4
Kahuku, HI 78-79 d 2
Kahuku Point 78-79 cd 2
Kahului, HI 78-79 d 2
Kahurangi Point 161 DE 5
Kai, Kepulauan — 148-149 K 8
Kaiama 164-165 E 7
Kaiashk River 62 E 3
Kaibab Indian Reservation 74-75 G 4
Kaibab Plateau 74-75 G 4
Kai Besar, Pulau — 148-149 K 8
K'ai-chien = Nanfeng 146-147 C 10
Kaidong = Tongyu 142-143 N 3
Kaieteur Falls 92-93 GH 3
Kai Ēvboia 122-123 K 6-L 7
Kaifeng 142-143 LM 5
K'ai-fong = Kaifeng 142-143 LM 5
Kaihsien = Kai Xian 146-147 B 6
Kaihua 146-147 G 7
Kaihwa = Wenshan 142-143 JK 7
Kaiingveld 174-175 D 6-E 5
Kaijian = Nanfeng 146-147 C 10
Kaijin, Funabashi- 155 III c 1
Kaikalūr 140 E 2
Kaikalūru = Kaikalūr 140 E 2
Kai Kecil, Pulau — 148-149 K 8
Kaikohe 158-159 O 7
Kaikoura 158-159 O 8
Kaila Hu = Kalba Tsho
138-139 M 3
Kailahun 168-169 C 3
Kailasahar = Kailāshahar 141 C 3
Kailas Gangri = Kailash Gangri
142-143 E 5
Kailāsh = Gangrinpochhe
138-139 H 2
Kailāshahar 141 C 3
Kailash Gangri 142-143 E 5
Kailu 142-143 N 3
Kailua, HI 78-79 de 3
Kaimana 148-149 K 7
Kaimanawa Mountains 161 G 4
Kaimganj 138-139 G 4
Kaimon-dake 144-145 H 7
Kaimur Hills 138-139 HJ 5
Kainan 144-145 K 5
Kainantu 148-149 N 8
Kaining = Port Canning
138-139 M 6
Kainji Dam 164-165 EF 6-7
Kainji Reservoir 168-169 G 3
Kainoma Hill 168-169 G 2
Kainsk = Kujbyšev 132-133 O 6
Kaioba 152-153 P 8
Kaipara Harbour 158-159 O 7
Kaiparowits Plateau 74-75 H 4
Kaiping [TJ, Guangdong]
146-147 D 10
Kaiping [TJ, Hebei] 146-147 G 2
Kaira 138-139 D 6
Kairāna 138-139 F 3
Kairiru 148-149 M 7
Kairouan = Al-Qayrawān
164-165 FG 1
Kairuku 148-149 N 8
Kaisarganj 138-139 H 4
Kaisarianē 113 IV b 2
Kaisariyah = Caesarea 136-137 F 6
Kaiserebersdorf, Wien- 113 I b 2
Kaiser Peak 74-75 D 4
Kaiserslautern 118 CD 4
Kaiser-Wilhelm-Gedächtniskirche
130 III b 1-2
Kaiser-Wilhelm II.-Land 53 C 9-10
Kaishū = Haeju 142-143 O 4
Kait, Tanjung — 152-153 G 7
Kaitaia 158-159 O 7
Kai Tak Airport 155 I b 2
Kaitangata 158-159 NO 9
Kaithal 138-139 F 3
Kaitum älv 116-117 HJ 4
Kaiwi Channel 78-79 d 2
Kai Xian 146-147 B 6
Kaiyuh Mountains 58-59 H 5-J 4
Kaizanchin = Hyesanjin
142-143 O 3
Kaj 124-125 T 4
Kajaani 116-117 MN 5
Kajabbi 158-159 H 4
Kājakay 134-135 JK 4
Kajakent 126-127 N 5
Kajan 152-153 P 10
Kajang [MAL] 150-151 CD 11
Kajang [RI] 148-149 H 8
Kajasula 126-127 M 4
Kajiado 172 G 2
Kājīrangā = Kāziranga 141 C 2
Kajnar [SU, Kazachskaja SSR]
132-133 O 8
Kajsajmas 126-127 P 1
Kākā 164-165 L 6
Kakaban, Pulau — 152-153 N 4
Kakabeka Falls 70-71 EF 1
Kakabia, Pulau — 152-153 P 9
Kakagi Lake 62 C 3
Kakamas 172 D 7
Kakamega 172 FG 1
Kakarka = Sovetsk 132-133 H 6
Kakata 164-165 B 7
Kākatpur 138-139 L 7-8
Kākatpura = Kākatpur
138-139 L 7-8
Kakbil = Karaoğlan 136-137 H 3
Kākdwīp 138-139 LM 7
Kake 144-145 J 5
Kake, AK 58-59 w 8
Kakegawa 144-145 LM 5
Kakelwe 171 B 4
Kakhea = Kakia 174-175 E 3
Kakhonak, AK 58-59 K 7
Kakia 172 D 6-7
Kaki Bukit 150-151 BC 9
Kākināda 134-135 N 7
Käkisalmi = Prioz'orsk
132-133 DE 5
Kakogawa 144-145 K 5
Kakonko 171 B 3
Kākosi Metrāna Road 138-139 CD 5
Kakpin 168-169 E 3
Kaktovik, AK 58-59 Q 1
Kakuda 144-145 N 4
Kakuli 171 AB 4
Kakuma 172 FG 1
Kakunodate 144-145 N 3
Kakwa River 60 H 2
Kala 171 B 5
Kala, El — = Al-Qal'ah 164-165 F 1
Kalaa Djerda = Qal'at al-Jardah
166-167 L 2
Kalaa Kebira = Al-Qal'at al-Kabīrah
166-167 M 2
Kalaat es Senam = Qal'at Sinān
166-167 L 2
Kalabahi 148-149 H 8
Kalabakan 152-153 M 3
Kalabo 172 D 5
Kalábryta 122-123 K 6
Kalābsha 164-165 L 4
Kalač 126-127 K 1
Kalač-na-Donu 126-127 L 2
Kalādān 141 C 4
Kaladan = Kulādan Myit 141 C 5
Kaladar 72-73 H 2
Kalādgi 140 B 2
Ka Lae 148-149 e 4
Kalaghātagi = Kalghatgi 140 B 3
Kalagôk Kyûn 141 E 8
Kalāhāndi 138-139 J 8
Kalahari = Kalahari Desert 172 CD 6
Kalahari Desert 172 CD 6
Kalahari Gemsbok National Park
172 D 7
Kālahasti 140 D 4
Kalakan 132-133 W 6
Kalam 140 C 1
Kalama, WA 66-67 B 2-3
Kalamākion 113 IV a 2
Kalamáta 122-123 JK 7
Kalamazoo, MI 64-65 J 3
Kalamazoo River 70-71 H 4
Kaḷamba = Kaḷam 140 C 1
Kalamba La 138-139 M 2
Kalambau, Pulau — 152-153 L 8
Kalambo Falls 172 F 3
Kalamitskij zaliv 126-127 F 4
Kalamnūri 138-139 F 8
Kalampáka 122-123 JK 6
Kalamu, Kinshasa- 170 IV a 2
Kalana 168-169 CD 3
Kalančak 126-127 F 3
Kalang 141 C 2
Kalangali 171 C 4
Kalankpa, Mount — 168-169 F 3
Kalannie 158-159 C 6
Kalanshyū, Serīr — 164-165 J 3
Kalao, Pulau — 152-153 O 9
Kalaotoa, Pulau — 148-149 H 8
Kalā Oya 140 E 6
Kalar 132-133 W 6
Kalārā Kyûn 150-151 AB 7
Kalaraš 126-127 D 3
Kalasin [RI] 148-149 F 6
Kalasin [T] 148-149 D 3
Kalašnikovo 124-125 K 5
Kalat = Qalāt 134-135 K 5
Kalāt, Jabal — 173 D 6
Kalātdlit nunāt 56-57 b 2-c 5
Kalāt-i Ghilzay 134-135 K 4
Kalatrava 168-169 H 5
Kalāu = Lansdowne 138-139 G 3
Kalaupapa, HI 78-79 d 2
Kalaus 126-127 L 4
Kalāvad 138-139 C 6
Kal'azin 124-125 LM 5
Kalbach, Frankfurt am Main-
128 III a 1
Kalbashar 138-139 M 3
Kalba Tsho 138-139 M 3
Kalbīyah, Sabkhat — 166-167 M 2
Kaldıdağ 136-137 F 4
Kale [TR, Denizli] 136-137 C 4
Kale [TR, Gümüşane] 136-137 H 2
Kale = Eynihal 136-137 CD 4
Kalecik [TR, Ankara] 136-137 E 2
Kalecik [TR, Urfa] 136-137 H 4
Kalegauk Island = Kalagôk Kyûn
141 E 8
Kalegosilik River 58-59 N 2-O 1
Kalehe 172 E 2
Kalemie 172 E 3
Kalemma 171 CD 3
Kalemyō 141 D 4
Kalenyj 126-127 P 2
Kale Sultanie = Çanakkale
134-135 B 2
Kaletwa 148-149 B 2
Kaleva, MI 70-71 GH 3
Kalevala 132-133 E 4
Kalewa 148-149 BC 2
Kaleybar 136-137 M 3
Kálfafell 116-117 de 2-3
Kálfafellstadhur 116-117 f 2
Kalgačicha 124-125 L 2
Kalgan = Zhangjiakou 142-143 L 3
Kalgary, TX 76-77 D 6
Kalghatgi 140 B 3
Kalgin Island 58-59 M 6
Kalgoorlie 158-159 D 6
Kalhāt 134-135 H 6
Kali [Guinea] 168-169 C 2
Kāli [IND] 138-139 G 4
Kāli [Nepal] 138-139 H 3
Kali = Sangha 172 C 1-2
Kaliakra, nos — 122-123 N 4
Kalianda 152-153 F 8
Kali Angke 154 IV a 1
Kalibo 148-149 H 4
Kali Brantas 152-153 JK 9
Kali Buaran 154 IV b 2
Kali Cakung 154 IV b 1-2
Kāli Gaṇḍak 138-139 JK 4
Kālīganj [BD → Calcutta]
138-139 M 6
Kālīganj [BD ↑ Jessaur] 138-139 M 6
Kalighat, Calcutta- 154 II ab 2
Kalighat Temple 154 II b 2
Kali Grogol 154 IV a 2
Kalikātā = Calcutta 134-135 O 6
Kali Krukut 154 IV a 2
Kalima 172 E 2
Kalimalang 140 E 1
Kali Mampang 154 IV a 2
Kalimantan 148-149 F 7-G 6
Kalimantan Barat = 5 ◁
148-149 F 7
Kalimantan Selatan = 9 ◁
148-149 G 7
Kalimantan Tengah = 8 ◁
148-149 F 7
Kalimantan Timur = 10 ◁
148-149 G 6
Kālimpong 138-139 M 4
Kālimpōṅg = Kālimpong
138-139 M 4
Kālīnadi 140 B 3
Kālingia 138-139 K 7
Kalinin 132-133 EF 6
Kaliningrad 118 K 1
Kalinino [SU, Arm'anskaja SSR]
126-127 M 6
Kalinino [SU, Rossijskaja SFSR]
124-125 UV 5
Kalininsk [SU, Moldavskaja SSR]
126-127 C 2
Kalininsk [SU, Rossijskaja SFSR]
124-125 P 8
Kalininskoje 126-127 F 3
Kalinkoviči 124-125 G 7
Kalinku 171 C 5
Kalinovka 126-127 D 2
Kali Pesanggrahan 154 IV a 2
Kalipur 154 II a 1
Kali Sekretaris 154 IV a 2
Kāli Sindh 138-139 F 5-6
Kalisizo 171 BC 3
Kalispell, MT 64-65 CD 2
Kali Sunter 154 IV b 1
Kalisz 118 J 3
Kalisz Pomorski 118 GH 2
Kalitva 126-127 K 2
Kaliua 172 F 2-3
Kalix älv 116-117 JK 4
Kālīyāganj 138-139 M 5
Kalkāli Ghāt 141 C 3
Kalkan 136-137 C 4
Kalkaska, MI 70-71 H 3
Kalkfeld 172 C 6
Kalkfontein 174-175 C 5
Kalkfontein = Karasburg 172 C 7
Kalkfonteindam 174-175 F 5
Kalk Plateau = Kalkplato
174-175 C 3
Kalkplato 174-175 C 3
Kalkrand 172 C 6
Kalksburg, Wien- 113 I ab 2
Kalksee 130 III cd 2
Kalkuni 98-99 K 2
Kallafo = Ķelafo 164-165 N 7
Kallakkurichchi 140 D 5
Kallands, AK 58-59 L 4
Kallang 154 III b 2
Kallar 140 C 6
Kallaste 124-125 F 4
Kallidaikurichchi 140 C 6
Kallipolis = Gelibolu 134-135 B 2
Kallithéa [GR, Attikē] 113 IV a 2
Kallsjön 116-117 E 6
Kallūr 140 E 2
Kallūru = Kallūr 140 E 2
Kalmar 116-117 G 9
Kalmar län 116-117 FG 9
Kalmarsund 116-117 G 9
Kal'mius 126-127 HJ 3
Kalmunai = Galmūṇē 140 EF 7
Kalmyckaja Avtonomnaja Sovetskaja
Socialističeskaja Respublika =
Kalmyk Autonomous Soviet
Socialist Republic 126-127 MN 3
Kalmyckij Bazar = Privolžskij
126-127 NO 3
Kalmyk Autonomous Soviet Socialist
Republic 126-127 MN 3
Kalmykovo 132-133 J 8
Kalnai 138-139 J 6
Kalnciems 124-125 DE 5
Kalnī 141 B 3
Kalnibolotskaja 126-127 JK 3
Kaloko 172 E 3
Kālol 138-139 D 6
Kalola 171 B 5
Kalomo 172 E 5
Kalonje 171 B 6
Kalpa 138-139 G 2
Kalpeni Island 134-135 L 8
Kālpi 138-139 G 4
Kalpitiya 140 D 6
Kal Sefīd 136-137 M 5
Kālsi 138-139 F 2
Kalskag, AK 58-59 G 6
Kalsūbai 138-139 DE 8
Kaltag, AK 58-59 H 4
Kaltasy 124-125 U 6
Kaltenbrünnlberg 113 I ab 2
Kaluga 124-125 KL 6
Kalukalukuang, Pulau —
152-153 MN 8
Kalulaui = Kahoolawe 148-149 e 3
Kalundborg 116-117 D 10
Kalundu 171 B 3
Kalungwishi 171 B 5
Kaluš 126-127 B 2
Kalutara 134-135 MN 9
Kalvān 138-139 E 7
Kalvarija 124-125 D 6
Kalwad = Kālāvad 138-139 C 6
Kalwākurti 140 D 2
Kalwan = Kalvān 138-139 E 7
Kalyāṇadurga = Kalyāndrug 140 C 3
Kalyāndrug 140 C 3
Kalyāni 140 C 2
Kálymnos 122-123 M 7
Kam [WAN] 168-169 H 3
Kam, Nam — 150-151 E 4
Kāma [BUR] 141 D 6
Kama [CDN] 70-71 G 1
Kama [RCB] 172 E 2
Kama [SU, place] 124-125 TU 5
Kama [SU, river] 132-133 J 6
Kamae 144-145 HJ 6
Kamaeura = Kamae 144-145 HJ 6
Kamagaya 155 III cd 1
Kamaggas Mountains =
Komaggasberge 174-175 B 5-6
Kamaing 141 E 3
Kamaishi 142-143 R 4
Kamaishi wan 144-145 NO 3
Kamaisi = Kamaishi 142-143 R 4
Kamakou 78-79 d 2
Kamalampakea 171 B 4
Kamālāpuram 140 D 3
Kamalāpuramu = Kāmalāpuram
140 D 3
Kamalasai 150-151 D 4
Kamalia = Kamāliya 138-139 D 2
Kamāliya 138-139 D 2
Kamalpur 141 BC 3
Kamamaung 141 E 7
Kāman [IND] 138-139 F 4
Kaman [TR] 136-137 E 3
Kamane, Se — 150-151 F 5
Kamarān 134-135 E 7
Kamar Bay = Ghubbat al-Qamar
134-135 G 7
Kāmāreddi 140 CD 1
Kamareddy = Kāmāreddi 140 CD 1
Kamarhati 138-139 M 6
Kamar'u = Artašat 126-127 M 7
Kamata, Tōkyō- 155 III b 2
Kamba [WAN] 168-169 FG 3
Kamba [ZRE] 172 D 2
Kambakkoddai = Kambākōṭṭē
140 E 6
Kambākōṭṭē 140 E 6
Kambal'naja sopka = Velikaja
Kambalnaja sopka 132-133 e 7
Kambalnaja sopka, Velikaja —
132-133 e 7
Kambam 140 C 6
Kambang 152-153 D 6
Kambangan, Nusa —
152-153 H 9-10
Kambar 138-139 AB 4
Kambarka 124-125 U 5
Kambia 164-165 B 7
Kambing, Pulau — = Ilha de Ataúro
148-149 J 8
Kambja 124-125 F 4
Kambove 172 E 4
Kambuno, Gunung — 152-153 O 7
Kamčatka 132-133 e 6-7
Kamčatskij poluostrov 132-133 fg 6
Kamčatskij zaliv 132-133 f 6
Kamchatka = Kamčatka
132-133 e 6-7
Kamčija 122-123 M 4
Kamčugskij 124-125 O 3
Kameari, Tōkyō- 155 III c 1
Kameido, Tōkyō- 155 III bc 1
Kamela, OR 66-67 D 3
Kamenec 124-125 D 7
Kamenec-Podol'skij 126-127 C 2
Kāmeng 141 C 2
Kameng Frontier Division = Kāmeng
141 C 2
Kamenjak, Rt — 122-123 E 3
Kamenka [SU, Rossijskaja SFSR
Mezenskaja guba] 132-133 G 4
Kamenka [SU, Rossijskaja SFSR
Penzenskaja Oblast']
124-125 OP 7
Kamenka [SU, Rossijskaja SFSR
Voronežskaja Oblast'] 126-127 J 1
Kamenka-Bugskaja 126-127 B 1
Kamenka-Dneprovskaja 126-127 G 3
Kamen'-Kaširskij 124-125 E 8
Kamen'-na-Obi 132-133 OP 7
Kamennogorsk 124-125 GH 3
Kamennomostskij 126-127 K 4
Kamennomostskoje 126-127 L 5
Kamennyj Jar 126-127 M 2
Kamenskaya = Kamensk-Šachtinskij
126-127 K 2
Kamenskij 126-127 MN 1
Kamenskoje [SU, Rossijskaja SFSR]
132-133 fg 5
Kamenskoje = Dneprodzeržinsk
126-127 FG 2
Kamensk-Šachtinskij 126-127 K 2
Kamensk-Ural'skij 132-133 LM 6
Kamenz 118 FG 3
Kameoka 144-145 K 5
Kameshli = Al-Qāmishlīyah
134-135 E 3
Kameškovo 124-125 N 5
Kāmēt 134-135 M 4
Kamiah, ID 66-67 EF 2
Kamiakatsuka, Tōkyō- 155 III ab 1
Kamians'ke = Dneprodzeržinsk
126-127 FG 2
Kamiasao, Kawasaki- 155 III a 2
Kamień Pomorski 118 G 2
Kamiesberge 174-175 BC 6
Kamieskroon 174-175 B 6
Kamihongo, Matsudo- 155 III c 1
Kamiishihara, Chōfu- 155 III a 2
Kamiiso 144-145 b 3
Kami Jiao 146-147 B 11
Kamikawa 144-145 c 2
Kamikitazawa, Tōkyō- 155 III a 2
Kami-Koshiki-shima 144-145 G 7
Kāmil, Al- 134-135 H 6
Kamilīn, Al- 164-165 L 5
Kamina 172 DE 3
Kaministikwia 70-71 EF 1
Kaminokuni 144-145 ab 3
Kaminoshima 144-145 G 5
Kaminoyama 144-145 N 3
Kamishak Bay 58-59 KL 7
Kamishakujii, Tōkyō- 155 III a 1
Kamishiki 155 III c 1
Kami-Sihoro 144-145 c 2
Kamitsushima 144-145 G 5
Kamituga 171 AB 3
Kamiyaku 144-145 H 7
Kam Keut 150-151 E 3
Kam Ko't = Kam Keut 150-151 E 3
Kamla 138-139 L 4-5
Kāmlīn, El- = Al-Kamilīn
164-165 L 5
Kamliun, Cape — 58-59 e 1
Kamloops 56-57 MN 7
Kamloops Plateau 60 G 4-5
Kammanassierivier 174-175 E 7
Kammenik, gora — 124-125 HJ 5
Kammuri yama 144-145 HJ 5
Kamnasie River = Kammanassierivier
174-175 E 7
Kamniokan 132-133 V 6
Kamo [J] 144-145 M 4
Kamo [SU] 126-127 M 6
Kamoa Mountains 98-99 J 4
Kamoenai 144-145 ab 2
Kamortā Drīp = Camorta Island
134-135 P 9
Kamoshida, Yokohama- 155 III a 2
Kamp 118 G 4
Kampala 172 F 1
Kampar 148-149 D 6
Kampar, Sungai — 152-153 DE 5
Kamparkalns 124-125 D 5
Kampe 168-169 G 3
Kampemba 171 AB 5
Kamphaeng Phet 150-151 BC 4
Kampli 140 C 3
Kamp'o 144-145 G 5
Kampo = Campo 164-165 F 8
Kampolombo, Lake — 172 E 4
Kampong Amoy Quee 154 III b 1
Kampong Batak 154 III b 1
Kampong Kitin 154 III ab 1
Kampong Kranji 154 III a 1
Kampong Pinang 154 III b 1
Kampong Sungai Jurong 154 III a 1
Kampong Sungei Tengah 154 III b 1
Kampong Tanjong Penjuru 154 III a 2
Kampong Yio Chu Kang 154 III b 1
Kampot 148-149 D 4
Kāmptee 138-139 G 7
Kampti 168-169 E 3
Kampuchéa = Kambodscha
148-149 DE 4
Kampulu 171 B 5
Kampung Baning 150-151 D 10
Kampung Buloh 150-151 D 10
Kampung Cherating 150-151 D 10
Kampung Datok 150-151 D 11
Kampung Hantu = Kampung Limau
150-151 CD 10
Kampung Jajin 150-151 D 10
Kampung Jeli 150-151 CD 10
Kampung Jenera 150-151 C 10
Kampung Kuala Ping 150-151 D 10
Kampung Lenga = Lenga
150-151 D 11
Kampung Pasir Besar 148-149 D 6
Kampung Raja 150-151 D 10
Kāmrūp 141 B 2
Kamsack 61 GH 5
Kamsar 168-169 B 3

Kamsar 309

Kamskoje Ustje 124-125 R 6
Kamskoje vodochranilišče 132-133 K 6
Kamuchawie Lake 61 G 2
Kamuda 98-99 HJ 2
Kamudi [EAK] 171 D 3
Kamuḍi [IND] 140 D 6
Kamuela = Waimea, HI 78-79 e 2-3
Kamui-misaki 144-145 ab 2
Kamunars'ke = Kommunarsk 126-127 J 2
Kāmyārān 136-137 M 5
Kamyšin 126-127 M 1
Kamyšlov 132-133 L 6
Kamyš-Zar'a 126-127 H 3
Kamyz'ak 126-127 O 3
Kan [BUR] 141 D 4
Kan [SU] 132-133 S 6-7
Kana, Bukit — 152-153 K 4
Kanaal Brussel-Charleroi 128 II a 2
Kanaal van Willebroek 128 II b 1
Kanaaupscow River 56-57 VW 7
Kanab, UT 74-75 G 4
Kanab Creek 74-75 G 4
Kānad = Kannad 138-139 E 7
Kanada = Kannada Pathār 140 BC 3
Kanadej 124-125 Q 7
Kanaga Island 58-59 u 6-7
Kanaga Strait 58-59 u 7
Kanagawa 144-145 M 5
Kanagawa, Yokohama- 155 III a 3
Kanaima Falls 94-95 L 4
Kanaio, HI 78-79 d 2
Kanā'is, Jazīrat — 166-167 M 2
Kanā'is, Rā's al- 136-137 BC 7
Kanakanak, AK 58-59 H 7
Kanakapura 140 C 4
Kanala = Canala 158-159 N 4
Kanal im. Moskvy 113 V b 2
kanal Moskvy 124-125 L 5
Kanamachi, Tōkyō- 155 III c 1
Kan'ān 136-137 L 6
Kananga 172 D 3
Kanara = Kannada Pathār 140 BC 3
Kanarraville, UT 74-75 G 4
Kanaš 132-133 H 6
Kaṇasvā = Kanwās 138-139 F 5
Kanava 124-125 U 3
Kanawha River 72-73 EF 5
Kanazawa 142-143 Q 4
Kanbalū 141 D 4
Kanbauk 150-151 AB 5
Kanbetlet 141 CD 5
Kanchanaburi 148-149 C 4
Kancheepuram = Kānchipuram 134-135 MN 8
Kanchenjunga = Gangchhendsönga 134-135 O 5
Kan Chiang = Gan Jiang 146-147 E 8
Kanchibia 171 B 5
Kānchipuram 134-135 MN 8
Kanchor 150-151 DE 6
Kanchow = Zhangye 142-143 J 4
Kanchrāpāṛā 138-139 M 6
Kanchriech 150-151 E 7
Kanchuan = Ganquan 146-147 B 3
K'anda 124-125 M 1
Kanda, Tōkyō- 155 III b 1
Kandahār [AFG] 134-135 K 4
Kandahār [IND] 140 C 1
Kandal [K, administrative unit] 150-151 E 7
Kandal [K, place] 148-149 DE 4
Kandalakša 132-133 EF 4
Kandalakšskaja guba 132-133 EF 4
Kandangan 148-149 FG 7
Kandau = Kandava 124-125 D 5
Kandava 124-125 D 5
Kandavu 148-149 a 2
Kandé 168-169 F 3
Kandhla 138-139 F 3
Kandi [BUR] 141 E 6
Kandi [DY] 164-165 E 6
Kāndi [IND] 138-139 LM 6
Kandi, Tanjung — 152-153 O 5
Kandiaro = Kandiyāro 138-139 B 4
Kandika 168-169 B 2
Kandik River 58-59 R 4
Kandilli, İstanbul- 154 I b 2
Kandira 136-137 D 2
Kandiyāro 138-139 B 4
Kandla 134-135 L 6
Kandos 158-159 JK 6
Kandoūsī = Kandūsī 166-167 E 2
Kāndra 138-139 KL 6
Kandreho 172 J 5
Kandukūr 140 D 3
Kandukūru = Kandukūr 140 D 3
Kandūleh 136-137 M 5
Kandulu 171 D 5
Kandūsī 166-167 E 2
Kandy = Maha Nuwara 134-135 N 9
Kane, PA 72-73 G 4
Kane, WY 68-69 BC 3
Kane Basin 56-57 WX 2
Kanektok River 58-59 G 7
Kanem 164-165 H 6
Kaneohe, HI 78-79 d 2
Kanev 126-127 E 2
Kanevskaja 126-127 J 3
Kaneyama 144-145 M 4
Kang 172 D 6
Kangaba 168-169 CD 3
Kangal 136-137 G 3
Kangar 148-149 D 5
Kangaroo Island 158-159 G 7
Kangaruma 98-99 J 2
Kangāvar 136-137 M 5
Kāngayam 140 C 5
Kangding 142-143 J 5-6
Kangean, Pulau — 148-149 G 8
Kangerdlugssuaq [Greenland, bay] 56-57 ef 4
Kangerdlugssuaq [Greenland, place] 56-57 ab 4
Kangetet 172 G 1
Kanggye 142-143 O 3
Kanggyŏng 144-145 F 4
Kanghwa 144-145 F 4
Kanghwa-do 144-145 EF 4
Kanghwa-man 144-145 E 4
Kangik, AK 58-59 GH 1
Kangjin 144-145 F 5
Kangkar Jemaluang = Jemaluang 150-151 DE 11
Kangkar Lenggor = Lenggor 150-151 D 11
Kangkar Masai 154 III b 1
Kangnŭng 144-145 G 4
Kango 172 B 1
Kāngpokpi 141 C 3
Kāngra 138-139 F 1
Kāngsā 141 B 3
Kangsar, Kuala — 148-149 CD 6
Kangshan 146-147 GH 10
Kangsŏ 144-145 E 3
Kanhan 138-139 G 6-7
Kanhar 138-139 J 5-6
Kan Ho = Gan He 142-143 N 1
Kanī [BUR] 141 D 4
Kani [RB] 174-175 D 3
Kaniāh 138-139 K 7
Kaniama 172 DE 3
Kaniapiskau Lake 56-57 W 7
Kaniapiskau River 56-57 X 6
Kaniet Islands 148-149 N 7
Kanigiri 140 D 3
Kānī Masī 136-137 K 4
Kanin, poluostrov — 132-133 GH 4
Kanin Nos 132-133 G 4
Kanireş 136-137 J 3
Kanita 144-145 N 2
Kankakee, IL 64-65 J 3
Kankakee River 70-71 G 5
Kankan 164-165 C 6
Kankasanturē 140 E 6
Kankauli 140 A 2
Kānker 138-139 H 7
Kankesanturai = Kankasanturē 140 E 6
Kankō = Hamhŭng 142-143 O 3-4
Kankō = Hŭngnam 142-143 O 4
Kankossa = Kankūssah 164-165 B 5
Kan-kou-chên = Gango 144-145 B 2
Kānksā = Mānkur 138-139 L 6
Kankūssah 164-165 B 5
Kankwi 174-175 D 3
Kankyŏ-hokudō = Hamgyŏng-pukto 144-145 G 2-H 1
Kankyŏ-nandō = Hamgyŏng-namdo 144-145 FG 2-3
Kanlica, İstanbul- 154 I b 2
Kannad 138-139 E 7
Kannada Pathār 140 BC 3
Kannanūr = Cannanore 134-135 LM 8
Kannaoj = Kannauj 138-139 G 4
Kannapolis, NC 80-81 F 3
Kannaṛa = Kannada Pathār 140 BC 3
Kannauj 138-139 G 4
Kan-ngen = Gancheng 150-151 G 3
Kanniyākumāri 140 C 6-7
Kannod 138-139 F 6
Kannoj = Kannauj 138-139 G 4
Kannus 116-117 K 6
Kano [WAN, administrative unit] 168-169 H 3
Kano [WAN, place] 164-165 F 6
Kano [WAN, river] 168-169 H 3
Kanoji 144-145 J 5
Kanona 171 B 6
Kanopolis Lake 68-69 H 6
Kanorado, KS 68-69 EF 6
Kanosh, UT 74-75 G 3
Kanouri 164-165 G 6
Kanovlei 152-153 JK 4
Kanoya 144-145 H 7
Kānpur 134-135 MN 5
Kanṣāī = Kāsai 138-139 L 6
Kansas 64-65 FG 4
Kansas, OK 76-77 G 4
Kansas City, KS 64-65 GH 4
Kansas City, MO 64-65 H 4
Kansas River 64-65 G 4
Kansk 132-133 S 6
Kansŏng 144-145 G 3
Kansu = Gansu 142-143 G 3-J 4
Kantalahti = Kandalakša 132-133 EF 4
Kantalai = Gangtalē 140 E 6
Kantang 150-151 B 9
Kan-t'ang = Gantang 146-147 B 10
Kantani = Centane 174-175 H 7
Kantara = Al-Qanṭarah 173 C 2
Kantara, El- = Al-Qanṭarah 166-167 J 2
Kantchari 164-165 E 6
Kantemirovka 126-127 JK 2
Kanthāralak 150-151 E 5
Kantharārom 150-151 E 5
Kantharawichai 150-151 D 4
Kānthi = Contai 138-139 L 7
Kantishna, AK 58-59 M 5
Kantishna River 58-59 M 4
Kantō 144-145 MN 4
Kantō sammyaku 144-145 M 4-5
Kanuchuan Lake 62 EF 1
Kanukov = Privolžskij 126-127 NO 3
Kanuku Mountains 98-99 J 3
Kanuma 144-145 M 4
Kanuparti 140 E 3
Kanuri = Kanouri 164-165 G 6
Kanus 174-175 C 4
Kanuti River 58-59 L 3
Kanvās = Kanwās 138-139 F 5
Kanwās 138-139 F 5
Kanyākumārī Antarīp = Cape Comorin 134-135 M 9
Kanyama 171 B 2
Kanye 172 DE 6-7
Kanyu = Ganyu 146-147 G 4
Kan-yü = Ganyu 146-147 G 4
Kanzanlı 136-137 F 4
Kao-an = Gao'an 142-143 LM 6
Kao-chia-fang = Gaojiafang 146-147 D 7
Kaohsiung 142-143 MN 7
Kao-i = Gaoyi 146-147 E 3
Kaokoveld 172 B 5-6
Kaolack 164-165 A 6
Kaolak River 58-59 G 2
Kaolan = Lanzhou 142-143 JK 4
Kao-lan Tao = Gaolan Dao 146-147 D 11
Kao-li-kung Shan = Gaoligong Shan 142-143 H 6
Kaoling = Gaoling 146-147 B 4
Kaomi = Gaomi 146-147 G 3
Kaoping = Gaoping 146-147 D 4
Kao Sai 155 I b 1
Kao-sha = Gaosha 146-147 C 8
Kaosiung = Kaohsiung 142-143 MN 7
Kaotai = Gaotai 142-143 H 4
Kaotang = Gaotang 146-147 F 3
Kao-tien-tzŭ = Gaodianzi 146-147 BC 6
Kao-ts'un = Gaocun 146-147 E 7
Kaotwe 174-175 E 2
Kaouar 164-165 G 5
Kaoyang = Gaoyang 146-147 E 2
Kaoyu = Gaoyou 146-147 G 5
Kao-yüan = Gaoyuan 146-147 F 3
Kao-yu Hu = Gaoyou Hu 146-147 G 5
Kapaa, HI 78-79 c 1
Kap'a-do 144-145 F 6
Kapadvanj 138-139 D 6
Kapagere 148-149 N 8-9
Kap Alexander 56-57 WX 2
Kapalı Çarşı 154 I ab 2
Kapanga 172 D 3
Kap Arkona 118 F 1
Kapas, Pulau — 150-151 D 10
Kapāsan 138-139 E 5
Kapasin = Kapāsan 138-139 E 5
Kapatu 171 B 5
Kap Brewster 52 BC 20-21
Kapčagajskoje vodochranilišče 134-135 O 9
Kap Dan 56-57 d 4
Kapela 122-123 F 3
Kapellerfeld 113 I c 1
Kapenguria 171 C 2
Kap Farvel 56-57 c 6
Kapfenberg 118 G 5
Kapıdağı yarımadası 136-137 BC 2
Kapingamarangi 208 F 2
Kapinnie 160 B 5
Kapiri Mposhi 172 E 4
Kapiskau Lake 62 G 1
Kapiskau River 62 G 1-2
Kapit 148-149 F 6
Kapit Island 161 F 5
Kaplan, LA 78-79 C 5-6
Kaplanova = Babajurt 126-127 N 5
Kap Morris Jesup 52 A 19-23
Kapoe 150-151 B 8
Kāpōētā 164-165 L 8
Kapona 172 E 3
Kapongolo 171 AB 4
Kaporo 168-169 B 3
Kapos 118 J 5
Kaposvár 118 HJ 5
Kapotn'a, Moskva- 113 V d 3
Kapoudia, Ras — = Rā's Qabūdīyah 166-167 M 2
Kapp Bessels 116-117 lm 5
K'appesel'ga 124-125 JK 2
Kapp Heuglin 116-117 lm 5
Kapp Linné 116-117 j 5
Kapp Melchers 116-117 m 6
Kapp Mohn 116-117 m 5
Kapp Norvegia 53 B 34-35
Kapp Platen 116-117 lm 4
Kapp Weyprecht 116-117 l 5
Kapsan 144-145 FG 2
Kapsowar 171 CD 2
Kapsukas 124-125 D 6
Kapuas, Sungai — [RI, Kalimantan Barat] 148-149 F 6
Kapuas, Sungai — [RI, Kalimantan Tengah] 152-153 L 6
Kapuas Hulu, Pegunungan — 152-153 K 5
Kapucijnenbos 128 II b 2
Kapunda 160 D 5
Kapūrthala 138-139 E 2
Kapur Utara, Pegunungan — 152-153 JK 9
Kapuskasing 56-57 U 8
Kapuskasing River 62 FG 3
Kapustin Jar 126-127 MN 2
Kaputar, Mount — 160 JK 3
Kaputir 171 C 2
Kapvāhā = Kadwāha 138-139 F 5
Kapydžik, gora — 126-127 M 7
Kap York 56-57 X 2
Kara 132-133 LM 4
Kara = Karrā 138-139 K 6
Karaali 136-137 E 3
Karababa dağı 136-137 FG 3
Karabanovo 124-125 M 5
Karabaš 124-125 T 6
Karabekaul 134-135 JK 3
Karabiğa 136-137 B 2
Kara-Bogaz-Gol, zaliv — 134-135 G 2
Karab Shahibīyah 166-167 C 6
Karabük 134-135 C 2
Kara burun [TR] 136-137 AB 3
Karaburun = Ahırlı 136-137 B 3
Karabutak 132-133 L 8
Karaca 136-137 H 2
Karacabey 136-137 C 2
Karaca dağ [TR, Ankara] 136-137 E 3
Karaca dağ [TR, Konya] 136-137 E 4
Karacadağ [TR, Urfa] 136-137 H 4
Karaca dağ = Kaynak 136-137 H 4
Karačajevsk 126-127 KL 5
Karacaköy 136-137 C 2
Karačala 126-127 O 7
Karačarovo, Moskva- 113 V cd 3
Karacasu 136-137 C 4
Karačev 124-125 K 7
Karachayevo-Cherkess Autonomous Region 126-127 KL 5
Karāchī 134-135 K 6
Karaçurun 136-137 H 4
Karād 140 B 2
Karadağ 136-137 E 4
Kara deniz 134-135 B-D 2
Karadeniz boğazı 134-135 BC 2
Karādkah 166-167 G 3
Karadoğan 136-137 DE 2
Karafuto = Sachalin 132-133 b 7-8
Karagaj 124-125 U 4
Karagajly 132-133 NO 8
Karagan 126-127 P 4
Karaganda 132-133 NO 8
Kar'agino = Fizuli 126-127 N 7
Karaginskij, ostrov — 132-133 fg 6
Karaginskij zaliv 132-133 fg 6
Karagoua 164-165 G 6
Karahal = Karhal 138-139 G 4
Karahallı 134-135 C 3
Karahasanlı = Sadıkali 136-137 F 3
Karai = Ban Karai 150-151 F 4
Karaikkāl = Kārikāl 134-135 MN 8
Kāraikkudi 140 D 5
Kāraikuḍi = Kāraikkudi 140 D 5
Karaira = Karera 138-139 G 5
Karaisalı = Çeceli 136-137 F 4
Karaitivu = Kāreitivu 140 DE 6
Karaj 134-135 G 3
Karak 150-151 CD 11
Karak, Al- 134-135 D 4
Karakāla = Kārkal 140 B 4
Karakāla = Perdūru 140 B 4
Karakallı 136-137 KL 3
Kara-Kalpak Autonomous Soviet Socialist Republic 202-203 UV 7
Karakeçi = Mizar 136-137 H 4
Karakeçili 136-137 E 3
Karakelong, Pulau — 148-149 J 6
Karaklis = Kirovakan 126-127 LM 6
Karakoçan = Tepe 136-137 HJ 3
Karakoram 134-135 L 3-M 4
Karakoram Pass = Qaramurun davan 134-135 MN 3
Karakorē 164-165 MN 6
Karakorum = Char Chorin 142-143 J 2
Karaköse 134-135 E 3
Karakubstroj = Komsomol'skoje 126-127 HJ 3
Karakumskij kanal 134-135 J 3
Karakumy 134-135 HJ 3
Karakūrū, Nahr al- 168-169 C 1-2
Karalat 126-127 O 4
Karam = Karin 164-165 O 6
Karama, Sungai — 152-153 N 6-7
Karaman 134-135 C 3
Karaman = Çameli 136-137 C 4
Karambu 152-153 LM 7
Karamea 161 DE 5
Karami 168-169 H 3
Karamian, Pulau — 148-149 F 8
Karamürsel 136-137 C 2
Karamyševo 124-125 G 5
Karanambo 98-99 J 3
Karand 136-137 M 5
Karang = Gunung Chamah 150-151 C 10
Karangagung 152-153 F 7
Karangania 141 C 2
Karang Besar 152-153 N 5
Karanja 138-139 F 7
Karanjia 138-139 KL 7
Karanlık bendi 154 I a 1
Karaṇpur 138-139 D 3
Karantinmoje = Privolžskij 126-127 NO 3
Karaoğlan 136-137 H 3
Karaolī = Karauli 138-139 F 4
Karapınar 136-137 E 4
Karas, Pulau — 148-149 K 7
Karasaj 126-127 O 2
Karasberge, Groot — 172 C 7
Karasberge, Klein — 174-175 C 4
Karasburg 172 C 7
Kara Sea 132-133 L 3-Q 2
Karasgāṅv = Karasgaon 138-139 F 7
Karasgaon 138-139 F 7
Kara Shar = Qara Shahr 142-143 F 3
Kara Shar = Qara Shahr 142-143 F 3
Karasjok 116-117 L 3
Karasjokka 116-117 L 3
Karas Mountains, Great — = Groot Karasberge 172 C 7
Karas Mountains, Little — = Klein Karasberge 174-175 C 4
Kara Strait = proliv Karskije Vorota 132-133 J-L 3
Karasu [SU] 126-127 N 6
Karasu [TR, place] 136-137 K 3
Karasu [TR, river] 136-137 J 3
Karasu = İncili 136-137 D 2
Karasu = Salavat 136-137 F 2
Karasu-Aras dağları 134-135 E 2-3
Karasu-Bazar = Belogorsk 126-127 G 4
Karasuk 132-133 O 7
Karataş = İskele 136-137 F 4
Karataş burnu 136-137 F 4
Karatau 132-133 N 9
Karatau, chrebet — 132-133 MN 9
Karativu 140 D 6
Karatobe 132-133 J 8
Karatoya 138-139 M 5
Karatsu 144-145 G 6
Karaul 132-133 P 3
Karauli 138-139 F 4
Karaussa Nor = Char us nuur 142-143 G 2
Karavansaraj = Idževan 126-127 M 6
Karavānsarā-ye Ḥouz Solṭān = Daryācheh Ḥowḍ Solṭān 136-137 O 5
Karayazı = Bayraktar 136-137 JK 3
Karayün 136-137 G 3
Karažal 132-133 N 8
Karbalā' 134-135 E 4
Karben-Rendel 128 III b 1
Karcag 118 K 5
Kardeljevo 122-123 G 4
Kardítsa 122-123 JK 6
Kardiva Channel 176 a 1-2
Kärdla 124-125 D 4
Kardymovo 124-125 J 6
Kārdžali 122-123 L 5
Karee 174-175 G 5
Kareeberge 172 D 8
Kareima = Kuraymah 164-165 L 5
Kāreitivu 140 DE 6
Karelia 124-125 GH 2-3
Karelian Autonomous Soviet Socialist Republic 132-133 E 4-5
Karel'skaja Avtonomnaja Sovetskaja Socialističeskaja Respublika = Karelian Autonomous Soviet Socialist Republic 132-133 E 4-5
Karelstad = Charlesville 172 D 3
Karema 172 F 3
Karen = Karin Pyinnei 148-149 C 3
Karenni = Karin Pyinnei 148-149 C 3
Karera [IND ↓ Ajmer] 138-139 E 5
Karera [IND ← Jhānsi] 138-139 G 5
Karesuando 116-117 JK 3
Karet = Qārrāt 164-165 C 4
Kārēz 134-135 K 4
Kargalinskaja 126-127 MN 5
Kargat 132-133 P 6
Kargi [EAK] 171 D 2
Kargi [TR] 136-137 F 2
Kargopol' 132-133 F 5
Karhāḍ = Karād 140 B 2
Karhal 138-139 G 4
Karhula 116-117 M 7
Kari = Kadi 138-139 D 6
Karia ba Mohammed = Qaryat Bā Muḥammad 166-167 D 2
Kariba, Lake — 172 E 5
Kariba Dam 172 E 5
Kariba Gorge 172 EF 5
Kariba-yama 144-145 ab 2
Karibib 172 C 6
Kariega 174-175 E 7
Karigasniemi 116-117 LM 3
Kārikāl 134-135 MN 8
Karikari, Cape — 161 EF 1
Karima = Kuraymah 164-165 L 5
Karīmah, Wādī al- 166-167 F 3
Kārimangalam 140 D 4
Karimata, Pulau-pulau — 148-149 E 7
Karimata, Selat — 148-149 E 7
Karīmganj 141 C 3
Karīmnagara = Karīmnagar 140 D 1
Karimon Java Islands = Pulau-pulau Karimunjawa 148-149 EF 8
Karimunjawa, Pulau-pulau — 148-149 EF 8
Karin 164-165 O 6
Karin Pyinnei 148-149 C 3
Karis 116-117 KL 7-8
Karisimbi, Mont — 172 E 2
Kariya 144-145 L 5
Karjaa = Karis 116-117 KL 8
Karjat [IND → Bombay] 140 A 1
Karjat [IND ↖ Kurduvādi] 140 B 1
Kārkal 140 B 4
Karkamış 136-137 G 4
Karkar 164-165 b 2
Karkar Island 148-149 N 7
Karkh 138-139 A 4
Karkheh, Rūd-e — 136-137 N 6-7
Karkinitskij zaliv 126-127 F 4
Karkkila 116-117 KL 7
Karkūk = Kirkūk 134-135 EF 3
Kar La [TJ] 138-139 MN 3
Karl Alexander, ostrov — 132-133 H-K 1
Karliova = Kanireş 136-137 J 3
Karl-Marx-Stadt 118 F 3
Karlobag 122-123 F 3
Karlovac 122-123 F 3
Karlovka 126-127 G 2
Karlovy Vary 118 F 3
Karlsborg 116-117 F 8
Karlsfeld 130 II a 1
Karlshamn 116-117 F 9
Karlshof 130 III c 2
Karlskoga 116-117 F 8
Karlskrona 116-117 FG 9
Karlsruhe 118 D 4
Karlsruhe, ND 68-69 F 1
Karlstad 116-117 EF 8
Karlstad, MN 68-69 H 1
Karluk, AK 58-59 K 8
Karluk Lake 58-59 fg 7
Karmah 164-165 L 5
Karmāla 140 B 1
Karmāḷēṅ = Karmāla 140 B 1
Karmanovo [SU, Rossijskaja SFSR] 124-125 K 6
Karmøy 116-117 A 8
Karnak, IL 70-71 F 7
Karnak, Al- 173 C 5
Karnāl 134-135 M 5
Karnāli 138-139 H 3
Karnāli, Mūgu — 138-139 J 3
Karṇāphulī 141 BC 4
Karnaprayāg 138-139 G 2
Karnataka 134-135 M 7-8
Karṇāṭaka Paṭhār = Kannada Pathār 140 BC 3
Karnes City, TX 76-77 EF 8
Karnobat 122-123 M 4
Kärnten 118 FG 5
Karnūlu = Kurnool 134-135 M 7
Karoi 172 E 5
Karokobe 171 B 2
Karompa, Pulau — 152-153 OP 9
Karondh = Kalāhāndi 138-139 J 8
Karonga 172 F 3
Karoo, Groot — 172 D 8
Karoo, Hoë — 174-175 C-F 6
Karoo, Klein — 172 D 8
Karoonda 160 DE 5
Karor 138-139 C 2
Kārōra 164-165 M 5
Karossa 148-149 G 7
Karow, Berlin- 130 III b 1
Kárpas 136-137 EF 5
Kárpathos [GR, island] 122-123 M 8
Kárpathos [GR, place] 122-123 M 8
Karpeddo 171 D 2
Karpenḗsion 122-123 JK 6
Karpinsk = Krasnoturjinsk 132-133 L 5-6
Karpogory 124-125 P 1
Karrā 138-139 K 6
Karrats Fjord 56-57 Za 3
Karree = Karee 174-175 G 5
Kars 134-135 E 2
Karsakpaj 132-133 M 8
Karsantı 134-135 F 4
Kārsava 124-125 F 5
Kārši 134-135 K 3
Karşıyaka 136-137 B 3
Karsiyāng = Kurseong 138-139 LM 4
Karskije Vorota, proliv — 132-133 J-L 3
Karsovaj 124-125 T 4
Karsun 124-125 Q 6
Kartabu 98-99 J 1
Kartal, İstanbul- 136-137 C 2
Kartal tepe 154 I a 1
Kartaly 132-133 KL 7
Karti = Kadi 138-139 D 6
Kartlijskij chrebet 126-127 M 5-6
Karu = Karkh 138-139 A 4
Karumba 158-159 H 3
Karumbhar Island 138-139 B 6
Karumwa 171 C 3
Kārūn, Rūd-e — 134-135 FG 4
Karunāgapalli 140 C 6
Karunagapally = Karunāgapalli 140 C 6
Kāruṇḍa = Kalāhāndi 138-139 J 8
Karungi 116-117 K 4-5
Karungu 171 C 3
Karūr 140 CD 5
Karvai = Korwai 138-139 FG 5
Karvī = Karwi 138-139 H 5
Karviná 118 J 4
Kārwār 134-135 L 8
Karwi 138-139 H 5
Karyai 122-123 KL 5
Karzāz 166-167 F 5
Kaş 134-135 BC 3
Kasa = Ui-do 144-145 E 5
Kasaba [TR] 136-137 J 3
Kasaba [Z] 171 B 5
Kasaba = Turgutlu 136-137 BC 3
Kasabonika Lake 62 E 1
Kasache 171 C 6
Kāsai [IND] 138-139 L 6
Kasai [ZRE] 172 C 2
Kasai, Tōkyō- 155 III c 2
Kasai-Occidental 172 CD 2-3
Kasai-Oriental 172 DE 2-3
Kasaji 172 D 4
Kasal, Jabal — 166-167 G 3
Kasama 172 F 4
Kasan = Kazan' 132-133 HJ 6
Kasanda 171 BC 2
Kasane 172 DE 5
Kasanga 172 F 3
Kasaoka 144-145 J 5
Kāsaragod 140 B 4
Kasargōd = Kāsaragod 140 B 4
Kasary 126-127 K 2
Kasatochi Island 58-59 j 4
Kasa-Vubu, Kinshasa- 170 IV a 2
Kasba 138-139 L 5
Kasba, Calcutta- 154 II b 2
Kasbah, Al-Jazā'ir- 170 I a 1
Kasba Lake 56-57 Q 5
Kasba Paṭāspur 138-139 L 6
Kasba Tadla = Qaṣ'bat Tādlah 166-167 C 3
Kaseda 144-145 H 7
Kasegaluk Lagoon 58-59 EF 2
Kasempa 172 DE 4
Kasenga 172 E 4
Kasenyi 172 EF 1
Kasese 172 EF 1
Kaset Wisai 150-151 D 5
Kasewe 168-169 B 3
Kāsganj 138-139 G 4
Kasha 171 E 3
Kashabowie 70-71 EF 1
Kāshān 134-135 G 4
Kashega, AK 58-59 n 4
Kashegelok, AK 58-59 J 6
Kashgar = Qashqar 142-143 CD 4
Kashghariya 142-143 DE 4
Kashi 142-143 D 4
Kashi = Qāshqār 142-143 CD 4
Kashima 144-145 GH 6
Kashing = Jiaxing 142-143 N 5
Kashio, Yokohama- 155 III a 3
Kāshipur [IND, Orissa] 138-139 J 8
Kāshīpur [IND, Uttar Pradesh] 138-139 G 3
Kāshīpura = Kāshipur 138-139 J 8
Kashishi 171 B 6
Kashishibog Lake 62 E 3
Kashiwagi, Tōkyō- 155 III b 1
Kashiwazaki 144-145 LM 4
Kashkān, Rūdkhāneh-ye — 136-137 N 6
Kāshmar 134-135 H 3-4
Kashmere Gardens, Houston-, TX 85 III b 1
Kashmīr 134-135 LM 4
Kashmīr, Jammu and — 134-135 LM 3-4
Kashmor 134-135 O 5
Kashqar = Qāshqār 142-143 CD 4
Kash Rūd = Khāsh Rōd 134-135 J 4
Kasia 138-139 JK 4
Kasiāri 138-139 L 6
Kasigao 171 D 3
Kasigluk, AK 58-59 F 6
Kasilof, AK 58-59 M 6
Kasimov 132-133 G 7
Kašin 124-125 L 5
Kaširа 124-125 LM 6
Kasirota = Pulau Kasiruta 148-149 J 7
Kasiruta, Pulau — 148-149 J 7
Kasivobara = Severo-Kuril'sk 132-133 de 7
Kasiyā = Kasia 138-139 JK 4
Kaskaskia River 70-71 F 6
Kaskinen = Kaskö 116-117 J 6
Kaskö 116-117 J 6
Kâs Kong 150-151 D 7
Kaslo 60 J 5
Kâs Moul 150-151 D 7
Kasongan 152-153 K 6-7
Kasongo 172 E 2
Kasongo-Lunda 172 C 3
Kásos 122-123 M 8
Kasossa, Tanjung — 152-153 N 10
Kaspi 126-127 M 5-6
Kaspijsk 126-127 NO 5
Kaspijskij 126-127 N 4
Kašpirovka, Syzran'- 124-125 R 7
Kaspl'a 124-125 HJ 6
Kasrık 136-137 K 3
Kâs Rong 150-151 D 7
Kâs Rong Sam Lem 150-151 D 7
Kassai = Kasai 172 C 2
Kassalā 164-165 M 5
Kassama 168-169 C 2
Kassándra 122-123 K 5-6
Kassel 118 D 3
Kasserine = Al-Qaṣrayn 164-165 F 1-2
Kastamonu 134-135 CD 2
Kastamum = Kastamonu 134-135 CD 2
Kâs Tang 150-151 D 7
Kasteli Selianou = Palaiochṓra 122-123 KL 8
Kastéllion 122-123 K 8
Kastellórizon = Mégistē 136-137 C 4
Kasten, Forst — 130 II a 2
Kastoría 122-123 J 5
Kastornoje 124-125 LM 8
Kasulu 172 F 2
Kasumiga ura 144-145 N 5
Kasumkent 126-127 O 6
Kasumpti 138-139 F 2
Kasungu 172 F 4
Kasungu National Park 171 C 6
Kasur = Qaṣūr 134-135 L 4
Kasvā = Kasba 138-139 L 5
Kataba 172 DE 5
Katahdin, Mount — 64-65 MN 2
Kaṭaka = Cuttack 134-135 NO 6
Katako-Kombe 172 D 2
Katakturuk River 58-59 P 2
Katakumba 172 D 3
Katalla, AK 58-59 P 6
Katami sammyaku 144-145 c 1-2
Katana 171 B 3
Katanga 132-133 T 5-6
Katanga = Shaba 172 DE 3
Katāngi 138-139 G 7
Katangli 132-133 b 7
Katanning 158-159 C 6
Kātapuram 140 E 1
Katar 134-135 G 5
Katārniān Ghat 138-139 H 3
Katav-Ivanovsk 132-133 K 7
Katāwāz 134-135 K 4
Katberg 174-175 G 7
Katbergpas 174-175 G 7
Katchal Island 134-135 P 9
Katchall Island 148-149 B 5
Katedupa, Pulau — 152-153 PQ 8
Kateel River 58-59 H 4
Katenga 172 E 3
Katera 171 BC 3
Katerîna, Gebel — = Jabal Katrīnah 164-165 L 3
Katerínē 122-123 K 5
Katerynoslav = Dnepropetrovsk 126-127 GH 2

310 Kamskoje

Kates Needle 56-57 KL 6
Katete 172 F 4
Katghora 138-139 J 6
Kathā 148-149 C 2
Katherina, Gebel — = Jabal Katrīnah 164-165 L 3
Katherine 158-159 F 2
Kāthgodām 138-139 G 3
Kāthiāwār 134-135 K 6
Kathlambagebirge = Drakensberge 172 E 8-F 7
Kathleen Lake 70-71 J 2
Kathleen Lakes 58-59 T 6
Kathor 138-139 D 7
Kathua 171 D 3
Kati 164-165 C 6
Katif, El- = Al-Qaṭīf 134-135 F 5
Katihār 134-135 O 5
Katimik Lake 61 J 4
Katiola 164-165 CD 7
Katkop 174-175 D 6
Katkopberge 174-175 C 6-D 5
Katkop Hills = Katkopberge 174-175 C 6-D 5
Katmai, Mount — 56-57 F 6
Katmai Bay 58-59 K 8
Katmai National Monument 56-57 EF 6
Kātmāndu 134-135 NO 5
Katni [IND] 138-139 H 6
Katni [SU] 124-125 QR 5
Káto Achaïa 122-123 J 6
Kātol 138-139 G 7
Katomba 158-159 JK 6
Katong, Singapore- 154 III b 2
Katonga 171 B 2-3
Katoomba 160 JK 4
Katoomba = Blue Mountains 158-159 JK 6
Katopasa, Gunung — 152-153 O 6
Katowice 118 J 3
Katra 138-139 K 4
Katrancık dağı 136-137 D 4
Katrīnah, Jabal — 164-165 L 3
Katrineholm 116-117 G 8
Katsina 164-165 F 6
Katsina Ala [WAN, place] 164-165 F 7
Katsina Ala [WAN, river] 168-169 H 4
Katsuda 144-145 N 4
Katsumoto 144-145 G 6
Katsushika, Tōkyō- 155 III bc 1
Katsuta, Yokohama- 155 III a 2
Katsuura 144-145 N 5
Katsuyama 144-145 L 4
Katta = Katsuta 144-145 N 4
Kattakurgan 134-135 K 2-3
Kattegat 116-117 D 9
Katupa 152-153 N 10
Kātvā = Kātwa 138-139 LM 6
Kātwa 138-139 LM 6
Katwe 171 B 3
Katwoude 128 I b 1
Katy, TX 76-77 G 8
Kau, Teluk — 148-149 J 6
Kauai 148-149 e 3
Kauai Channel 148-149 e 3
Kaudeteunom 152-153 A 3
Kaufbeuren 118 E 5
Kaufman, TX 76-77 FG 6
Kaugama 168-169 H 2
Kauhajoki 116-117 JK 6
Kau I Chau 155 I a 2
Kaukasus Mountains 126-127 J 4-N 6
Kaukauna, WI 70-71 F 3
Kaukauveld 172 D 5
Kaukkwe Chaung 141 E 3
Kaukurus 174-175 C 2
Kaula 78-79 b 2
Kaulakahi Channel 78-79 b 1-c 2
Kauliranta 116-117 KL 4
Kaulsdorf, Berlin- 130 III c 1-2
Kaulsdorf-Süd, Berlin- 130 III c 2
Kaulun = Kowloon 142-143 LM 7
Kau Lung Peak 155 I b 1
Kau Lung Tong, Kowloon- 155 I b 1
Kau-mi = Gaomi 146-147 G 3
Kaunakakai, HI 78-79 d 2
Kauna Point 78-79 de 3
Kaunas 124-125 DE 6
Kaunata 124-125 F 5
Kaunch = Konch 138-139 G 4-5
Kaur 168-169 B 2
Kaura Namoda 164-165 F 6
Kauriāla Ghāt 138-139 H 3
Kau Sai Chau 155 I b 1
Kautokeino 116-117 KL 3
Kau Wa Kang 155 I a 1
Kavajë 122-123 H 5
Kavak [TR, Samsun] 136-137 FG 2
Kavak [TR, Sivas] 136-137 G 3
Kavalga Island 58-59 t 7
Kāvali 140 DE 3
Kaval'kan 132-133 a 6
Kavaratti 134-135 L 8
Kavaratti Island 134-135 L 8
Kavardhā = Kawardha 134-135 N 6
Kavarna 122-123 N 4
Kāveri = Cauvery 140 C 5
Kaveri Delta = Cauvery Delta 140 D 5
Kāvi 138-139 D 6
Kavieng 148-149 h 5
Kavik River 58-59 O 2
Kavīr, Dasht-e — 134-135 GH 4
Kavīr-e Khorāsān = Dasht-e Kavīr 134-135 GH 4
Kāvīr-e Khorāsān = Kavīr-e Namak-e Mīghān 134-135 H 4
Kavīr-e Lūt 132-133 J 5
Kavīr-e Mīghān 136-137 N 5
Kavīr-e Namak-e Mīghān 134-135 H 4
Kavirondo Gulf 171 C 3
Kavkaz 126-127 H 4
Kavkaz, Malyj — 126-127 L 5-N 7
Kavkazskij zapovednik 126-127 K 5
Kavu 171 B 4
Kaw 92-93 J 4
Kawa 141 E 7
Kawagoe 144-145 M 5
Kawaguchi 144-145 MN 4-5
Kawaharada = Sawata 144-145 M 3-4
Kawaihae, HI 148-149 e 3
Kawaihoa Point 78-79 b 2
Kawaikini 78-79 c 1
Kawakawa 161 F 2
Kawamata 144-145 N 4
Kawambwa 172 EF 3
Kawanoe 144-145 J 5-6
Kawardha 134-135 N 6
Kawasaki 142-143 QR 4
Kawasaki-Chitose 155 III a 2
Kawasaki-Daishi 155 III b 2
Kawasaki-Kamiasao 155 III a 2
Kawasaki-ko 155 III b 2
Kawasaki-Kosugi 155 III ab 2
Kawasaki-Maginu 155 III a 2
Kawasaki-Maruko 155 III b 2
Kawasaki-Mizonokuchi 155 III a 2
Kawasaki-Nakanoshima 155 III a 2
Kawasaki-Nogawa 155 III a 2
Kawasaki-Oda 155 III b 2
Kawasaki-Shinjō 155 III a 2
Kawasaki Stadium 155 III b 2
Kawashima, Yokohama- 155 III a 3
Kawashiri-misaki 144-145 H 5
Kawawa, Yokohama- 155 III a 2
Kaweka 161 G 4
Kawene 70-71 E 1
Kawewe 171 AB 5
Kawgareik 141 F 7
Kawich Range 74-75 E 3-4
Kawimbe 172 F 3
Kawinaw Lake 61 J 4
Kawkareik = Kawgareik 141 F 7
Kawlin 148-149 C 2
Kawm Umbū 164-165 L 4
Kawnipi Lake 70-71 E 1
Kawn Ken = Khon Kaen 148-149 D 3
Kawre Kyûn 150-151 B 7
Kawthaung 148-149 C 4
Kaya [HV] 164-165 D 6
Kaya [J] 144-145 K 5
Kaya [RI] 148-149 G 6
Kayadibi 136-137 F 3
Kayak Island 56-57 H 6
Kāyalpatnam 140 D 6
Kayambi 172 F 3
Kayamganj = Kaimganj 138-139 G 4
Kayan = Hkayan 141 E 7
Kayan, Sungai — 152-153 M 4
Kāyānakulam = Kāyankulam 140 C 6
Kāyankulam 140 C 6
Kayā Pyinnei 148-149 C 3
Kaya-san 144-145 G 5
Kaycee, WY 68-69 C 4
Kayenta, AZ 74-75 H 4
Kayes 164-165 B 6
Kayhaydi 164-165 B 5
Kayis dağı 154 I bc 3
Kaymas 136-137 D 2
Kaynak 136-137 H 4
Kaynar 136-137 G 3
Kaynaslı 136-137 D 2
Kayoa, Pulau — 148-149 J 6
Kaypak = Serdar 136-137 G 4
Kay Point 58-59 S 2
Kayser Gebergte 98-99 K 3
Kayseri 134-135 D 3
Kaysville, UT 66-67 GH 5
Kayuadi, Pulau — 152-153 O 9
Kayuagung 148-149 DE 7
Kayuapu 152-153 E 8
Kayville 61 F 6
Kazach 126-127 M 6
Kazachskaja Sovetskaja Socialističeskaja Respublika = Kazakh Soviet Socialist Republic 132-133 J-P 8
Kazachskij Melkosopočnik 132-133 M-P 7-8
Kazachstan = Aksaj 132-133 J 7
Kazačinskoje [SU, Jenisej] 132-133 R 6
Kazačinskoje [SU, Kirenga] 132-133 U 6
Kazačje 132-133 a 3
Kazakh Soviet Socialist Republic 132-133 J-P 8
Kazakhstan 114-115 T-V 6
Kazakhstan = Kazakh Soviet Socialist Republic 132-133 J-P 8
Kazakh Uplands = Kazachskij Melkosopočnik 132-133 M-P 7-8
Kazamoto = Katsumoto 144-145 G 6
Kazan' [SU, Kirovskaja Oblast'] 124-125 RS 4
Kazan' [SU, Tatarskaja ASSR] 132-133 HJ 6
Kazandağ 136-137 K 3
Kazandžik 134-135 GH 3
Kazan'-Judino 124-125 R 6
Kazanka [SU, Rossijskaja SFSR] 124-125 R 5-6
Kazanka [SU, Ukrainskaja SSR] 126-127 F 3
Kazanlak 122-123 L 4
Kazan Lake 61 D 3
Kazanovka 124-125 M 7
Kazan-rettō = Volcano Islands 206-207 RS 7
Kazan River 56-57 Q 5
Kazanskaja 126-127 K 2
Kazanskoje [SU, Zapadno-Sibirskaja nizmennost'] 132-133 M 6
Kazantip, mys — 126-127 G 4
Kazatin 126-127 D 2
Kazaure 168-169 GH 2
Kazbegi 126-127 M 5
Kazbek, gora — 126-127 M 5
Kazer, Pico — 108-109 F 10
Kāzerūn 134-135 G 5
Kažim 124-125 ST 3
Kazi-Magomed 126-127 O 6
Kāẓimīyah, Baghdād-Al- 136-137 L 6
Kazimoto 171 D 5
Kazincbarcika 118 K 4
Kāziranga 141 C 2
Kazly Rūda 124-125 DE 6
Kaztalovka 126-127 O 2
Kazū 141 E 3
Kazumba 172 D 3
Kazungula 172 E 5
Kazvin = Qazvīn 134-135 FG 3
Kazym 132-133 M 5

Kbab, el — = Al-Qabāb 166-167 D 3
Kbaisa = Kubaysah 136-137 K 6
Kbal Damrei 150-151 E 5
Kbīr Kūh 134-135 F 4

Kdey, Kompong — = Phum Kompong Kdey 150-151 E 6

Kea 122-123 L 7
Keaau, HI 78-79 e 3
Kealaikahiki Channel 78-79 d 2
Kealakekua Bay 78-79 de 3
Keams Canyon, AZ 74-75 H 5
Kê An = Kê Sach 150-151 EF 8
Kearney, NE 64-65 G 3
Kearny, NJ 82 III b 2
Keat Hong 154 III a 1
Keban 136-137 H 3
Keban barajı 136-137 H 3
Kebang 134-135 PQ 5
Kebanyoran 152-153 G 9
Kebayoran Baru, Jakarta- 154 IV a 2
Kebbi = Sokoto 164-165 EF 6
Kébémer 164-165 A 5
Kebili = Qabilī 166-167 L 3
Kebkābiya = Kabkābīyah 164-165 J 6
Kebnekajse 116-117 H 4
Kebon Jeruk, Jakarta- 154 IV a 2
Kebumen 148-149 E 8
Kebyang 138-139 JK 2
Keçiborlu 136-137 D 4
Keçilik 154 I b 1
Kecskemét 118 J 5
Keda 126-127 K 6
Kedabek 126-127 M 6
Kedah 150-151 C 9-10
Kėdainiai 124-125 DE 6
Kedārnāth 138-139 G 2
Keddie, CA 74-75 C 2-3
Kedia d'Idjil = Kidyat Ijjill 164-165 B 4
Kediri 148-149 F 8
Kédougou 164-165 B 6
Keegans Bayou 85 III a 2
Keele Peak 56-57 KL 5
Keeler, CA 74-75 E 4
Keele River 56-57 L 5
Keeley Lake 61 D 3
Keeling Basin 50-51 OP 6
Keelung = Chilung 142-143 N 6
Keene, NH 72-73 K 3
Keeseville, NY 72-73 K 2
Keetmanshoop 172 C 7
Keewatin 62 B 3
Keewatin, District of — 56-57 RS 4-5
Keewatin River 61 H 2
Keezhik Lake 62 E 2
Kefa 164-165 M 7
Kefallēnía 122-123 J 6
Kéfalos 122-123 M 7
Kefamenanu 148-149 HJ 8
Kef-el-Ahmar = Kaff al-Aḥmar 166-167 G 3
Kefeliköy, İstanbul- 154 I b 2
Keferdiz 136-137 G 4
Keffi 168-169 G 3
Kefil, Al- = Al-Kifl 136-137 L 6
Kéfisiá 122-123 KL 6
Kēfisós 113 IV a 1
Keflavík 116-117 b 2-3
Kef Mahmel = Jabal Mahmil 166-167 K 2
Ke Ga, Mui — 150-151 FG 7
Kégalla 140 E 7
Kegaska 63 F 2
Kegel = Keila 124-125 E 4
Kégueur Terbi 164-165 H 4
Kegul'ta 126-127 M 3
Kehl 118 CD 4
Kei 171 B 2
Kei Islands = Kepulauan Kai 148-149 K 8
Keiki-dô = Kyŏnggi-do 144-145 F 4
Keila 124-125 E 4
Keilor, Melbourne- 161 II b 1
Keimoes 174-175 D 5
Kei Mouth 174-175 H 7
Kein-Bijgarten 128 II a 2
Keishō-hokudō = Kyŏngsang-pukto 144-145 G 4
Keishō-nandō = Kyŏngsang-namdo 144-145 FG 5
Keiskamahoek = Keiskammahoek 174-175 G 7
Keiskammahoek 174-175 G 7
Keiskammarivier 174-175 G 7
Keitele 116-117 LM 6
Keith [AUS] 158-159 GH 7
Keith [GB] 119 E 3
Keith Arm 56-57 M 4
Keithsburg, IL 70-71 E 5
Keithville, LA 76-77 GH 6
Keitsaub 174-175 C 2
Keitū = Keytū 136-137 N 5
Kejimkujik National Park 63 D 5
Kēkarī = Kekri 138-139 E 5
Kekirāwa 140 E 6
Kekri 138-139 E 5
Kela 168-169 C 3
Kelaa des Mgouna = Qal'at M'gūnā' 166-167 C 4
Kelaa des Srarhna, el — = Al-Qal'at as-S'rāghnah 166-167 C 3-4
Kelafo 164-165 N 7
Kelai 140 A 7
Kelan 146-147 C 2
Kelantan 150-151 CD 10
Kelantan, Sungei — 150-151 CD 10
Kelay Abe 164-165 N 6
Kelay Egoji 164-165 N 6
Kelay Tana 164-165 M 6
Kelbia, Sebkhet — = Sabkhat Kalbīyah 166-167 M 2
Keles 136-137 C 3
Kelfield 61 D 5
Kelford, NC 80-81 H 2
Kelibia = Qalībīyah 166-167 M 1
Kelifely, Causse du — 172 HJ 5
Kelif'un, gora — 132-133 g 4
Kelingkang, Bukit — 152-153 J 5
Kelkit = Çiftlik 136-137 H 2
Kelkit çayı 136-137 G 2
Kellé 172 B 1-2
Keller Lake 56-57 M 5
Kellett, Cape — 56-57 L 3
Kelleys Island 72-73 E 4
Kelleys Islands 72-73 E 4
Kelliher 61 G 5
Kelliher, MN 70-71 C 1-2
Kellogg, ID 66-67 EF 2
Kelloselkä 116-117 N 4
Kelly, Mount — 58-59 EF 2
Kelly River 58-59 F 2
Kelm = Kelmė 124-125 D 6
Kelmė 124-125 D 6
Kélo 164-165 H 7
Kelowna 56-57 N 7-8
Kelsey Bay 60 D 4
Kelso, CA 74-75 F 5
Kelso, WA 66-67 B 2
Kelso [ZA] 172 F 8
Kelton Pass 66-67 G 5
Kelu 146-147 C 11
Keluang 150-151 D 11-12
Kelulun He = Herlen He 142-143 M 2
Kelushi = Kelu 146-147 C 11
Kelvin, AZ 74-75 H 6
Kelvington 61 G 4
Kelvin Island 62 E 3
Kem' [SU, place] 132-133 E 4
Kemā 142-143 H 6
Kemabong 152-153 LM 3
Kê-Macina 164-165 C 6
Kemah 136-137 H 3
Kemaliye [TR, Erzincan] 136-137 H 3
Kemaliye [TR, Trabzon] 136-137 H 2
Kemalpaşa [TR, Artvin] 136-137 J 2
Kemalpaşa [TR, İzmir] 136-137 B 3
Kemanai = Towada 144-145 N 2
Kemang, Jakarta- 154 IV a 2
Kemayoran, Jakarta- 154 IV b 1
Kemayoran Airport 154 IV b 1
Kembalpūr 134-135 L 4
Kembani 152-153 P 6
Kembolcha 164-165 MN 6
Kemena, Sungei — 152-153 K 4
Kemer [TR, İstanbul] 154 I bc 2
Kemer [TR, Muğla] 136-137 C 4
Kemer = Eskiköy 136-137 D 4
Kemerovo 132-133 PQ 6
Kemi 116-117 L 5
Kemijärvi [SF, lake] 116-117 MN 4
Kemijärvi [SF, place] 116-117 M 4
Kemijoki 116-117 L 4-5
Kemijoki = Kem' 132-133 E 4
Kem Kem = Qamqam 166-167 D 4
Keml'a 124-125 P 6
Kemmerer, WY 66-67 H 5
Kemnay 61 H 6
Kémo-Gribingui 164-165 H 7
Kemp, TX 76-77 F 6
Kemp, Lake — 76-77 E 6
Kemp Land 53 C 6
Kemp Peninsula 53 B 31
Kempsey 158-159 K 6
Kempt, Lac — 72-73 JK 1
Kempten 118 E 5
Kempton Park 170 V c 1
Kemptthal 128 IV b 1
Kemptville 72-73 HJ 2
Kemubu 150-151 D 10
Ken 138-139 H 5
Kena 124-125 M 2
Kena = Qinā 164-165 L 3
Kenadsa = Qanādsah 166-167 E 4
Kenai, AK 56-57 F 5
Kenai Lake 58-59 N 6
Kenai Mountains 56-57 F 6-G 5
Kenai Peninsula 56-57 FG 5
Kenamo 56-57 L 7
Kenansville, FL 80-81 c 3
Kenaston 61 EF 5
Kenbridge, VA 80-81 GH 2
Kendal [GB] 119 E 4
Kendal [RI] 152-153 J 9
Kendal [ZA] 174-175 H 4
Kendall, KS 68-69 F 7
Kendallville, IN 70-71 H 5
Kendari 148-149 H 7
Kendawangan 148-149 F 7
Kendeng, Pegunungan — 152-153 JK 9
Kendikolu 176 a 1
Kendong Si = Mendong Gonpa 138-139 K 2
Kēndrāpadā = Kendrāpāra 134-135 O 6
Kendrāpāra 134-135 O 6
Kendrew 174-175 F 7
Kendrick, ID 66-67 E 2
Kendu 171 C 3
Kēndujhar = Keonjhargar 138-139 KL 7
Kenedy, TX 76-77 EF 8
Kenega = Kenegha 174-175 H 6
Kenegha 174-175 H 6
Kenema 164-165 B 7
Kenesaw, NE 68-69 G 5
Kenge 172 C 2
Keng Kabao 150-151 E 4
Keng Kok 150-151 E 4
Keng Phao = Ban Keng Phao 150-151 F 5
Keng That Hai = Ban Keng That Hai 150-151 EF 4
Kengtung = Kyöngdôn 148-149 CD 2
Kenhardt 172 D 7
Kenia 172 G 1
Kenibuna Lake 58-59 L 6
Kéniéba 164-165 B 6
Kenitra = Al-Q'nitrah 164-165 C 2
Kenli 146-147 G 3
Kenmare, ND 68-69 EF 1
Kenmare [IRL, place] 119 B 6
Kenmare [IRL, river] 119 A 6
Kenmore, NY 72-73 G 3
Kenna, NM 76-77 BC 6
Kennebec, SC 68-69 FG 4
Kennebec River 72-73 LM 2
Kennebunk, ME 72-73 L 3
Kennedy 61 GH 5
Kennedy, Mount — 56-57 J 5
Kennedy Channel 56-57 WX 1-2
Kennedy Taungdeik 141 CD 4
Kennedy Town, Victoria- 155 I a 2
Kenner, LA 78-79 D 5-6
Kennett, MO 78-79 DE 2
Kennewick, WA 66-67 D 2
Kenney Dam 56-57 M 7
Kennicott, AK 58-59 Q 6
Kénogami 63 A 3
Kenogami River 62 G 2
Kenogamissi Falls 62 L 2-3
Keno Hill 56-57 JK 5
Kenonisca, Lac — 62 NO 1
Kenora 56-57 S 8
Kenosha, WI 64-65 J 3
Kenova, WV 72-73 E 5
Kenozero 124-125 M 2
Kensal, ND 68-69 G 2
Kensett, AR 78-79 D 3
Kensington 63 E 4
Kensington, CA 83 I c 1
Kensington, New York-, NY 82 III c 3
Kensington, Philadelphia-, PA 84 III c 2
Kensington and Chelsea, London- 129 II b 2
Kent 119 G 6
Kent, MN 68-69 H 2
Kent, OH 72-73 F 4
Kent, OR 66-67 C 3
Kent, TX 76-77 B 7
Kent, WA 66-67 B 2
Kent, Washington-, DC 82 II a 1
Kenta Canal 85 I b 3
Kentau 132-133 M 9
Kent Group 160 cd 1
Kent Junction 63 D 4
Kentland, IN 70-71 G 5
Kenton, OH 72-73 E 4
Kenton, OK 76-77 C 4
Kent Park 170 V b 1
Kent Peninsula 56-57 P 4
Kentucky 64-65 JK 4
Kentucky Lake 64-65 J 4
Kentucky River 70-71 H 6
Kent Village, MD 82 II b 1
Kentville 63 D 5
Kentwood, LA 78-79 D 5
Kenya 172 GH 1
Kenya, Mount — 172 G 1-2
Keokuk, IA 64-65 H 3
Keo Neua, Đeo — 150-151 E 3
Keonjhargar 138-139 KL 7
Keosauqua, IA 70-71 E 5
Kep 150-151 E 7
Kēpe = Quepem 140 B 3
Kepi i Gjuhës 122-123 H 5
Kępno 118 J 3
Keppel Bay 158-159 K 4
Keppel Harbour 154 III ab 2
Keppel Island 108-109 JK 8
Kepsut 136-137 C 3
Kepulauan Aju 148-149 K 6
Kepulauan Alor 152-153 Q 10
Kepulauan Anambas 148-149 E 6
Kepulauan Aru 148-149 KL 8
Kepulauan Asia 148-149 K 6
Kepulauan Babar 148-149 JK 8
Kepulauan Balangan = Pulau-pulau Balabalangan 148-149 G 7
Kepulauan Banda 148-149 J 7
Kepulauan Banggai 148-149 H 7
Kepulauan Batu 148-149 C 7
Kepulauan Bunguran Selatan 148-149 E 6
Kepulauan Bunguran Utara 148-149 E 6
Kepulauan Kai 148-149 K 8
Kepulauan Leti 148-149 J 8
Kepulauan Lingga 148-149 DE 7
Kepulauan Mapia 148-149 KL 6
Kepulauan Mentawai 148-149 CD 7
Kepulauan Perhentian 150-151 D 10
Kepulauan Riau 148-149 DE 6
Kepulauan Sabalana 152-153 N 9
Kepulauan Salabangka 152-153 P 7
Kepulauan Sangihe 148-149 J 6
Kepulauan Sangkarang 152-153 N 8
Kepulauan Sembilan 150-151 C 10
Kepulauan Seram-laut 148-149 K 7
Kepulauan Solor 152-153 P 10
Kepulauan Sula 148-149 HJ 7
Kepulauan Talaud 148-149 J 6
Kepulauan Tanimbar 148-149 K 8
Kepulauan Tenga 148-149 G 8
Kepulauan Togian 148-149 H 7
Kepulauan Tukangbesi 148-149 H 8
Kerākat = Kirākat 138-139 J 5
Kerakda = Kerrādkah 166-167 G 3
Kerala 134-135 M 8-9
Kerang 158-159 H 7
Kerasûs = Giresun 134-135 D 2
Keratsínion 113 IV a 2
Kerava 116-117 L 7
Kerbi = Poliny-Osipenko 132-133 a 7
Kerby, OR 66-67 B 4
Kerč' 126-127 H 4
Kerčenskij poluostrov 126-127 GH 4
Kerčenskij proliv 126-127 H 4
Kerčevskij 124-125 UV 4
Kerch = Kerč' 126-127 H 4
Kerč'omja 124-125 T 3
Kereda = Karera 138-139 E 5
Kerema 148-149 N 8
Kerempe burnu 136-137 E 1
Keren 164-165 M 5
Kerens, TX 76-77 EF 6
Kerewan 168-169 A 2
Kerga 124-125 PQ 2
Kerguelen 50-51 N 8
Kerguelen-Gaussberg Ridge 50-51 N 8-O 9
Kericho 171 C 3
Kerinci, Gunung — 148-149 D 7
Kerio 171 D 2
Keriske 132-133 Z 4
Keriya 142-143 E 4
Keriya Darya 142-143 E 4
Kerkbuurt 128 I b 1
Kerkenah Island = Juzur Qarqannah 164-165 G 2
Kerkenna, Îles — = Jazur Qarqannah 164-165 G 2
Kerkhoven, MN 70-71 C 3
Kerki 134-135 K 3
Kérkyra [GR, island] 122-123 H 6
Kérkyra [GR, place] 122-123 H 6
Kerling 116-117 d 2
Kerlingarfjöll 116-117 d 2
Kerma = Karmah 164-165 L 5
Kerma, Oued — 170 I a 2
Kermadec Islands 158-159 PQ 6
Kermadec Tonga Trench 156-157 J 5-6
Kermān 134-135 H 4
Kerman, CA 74-75 CD 4
Kermānshāh 134-135 F 4
Kermānshāhān = 1 ◁ 134-135 F 4
Kerme körfezi 136-137 B 4
Kermit, TX 76-77 C 7
Kernaka 168-169 G 2
Kern River 74-75 D 5
Kernville, CA 74-75 D 5
Kérouané 164-165 C 7
Kerpe burnu 136-137 D 2
Kerrick, TX 76-77 C 4
Kerrobert 61 D 4-5
Kerrville, TX 76-77 E 7
Kersaint, Đao — 150-151 FG 2
Kershaw, SC 80-81 F 3
Kersley 60 F 3
Kertamulia 152-153 H 6
Kerulen = Cherlen gol 142-143 L 2
Kerūr 140 B 3
Kerzaz = Karzāz 166-167 F 5
Kerženec 124-125 P 5
Kesabpūr 138-139 M 6
Kê Sach 150-151 EF 8
Kesagami Lake 62 L 1
Kesagami River 62 LM 1
Keşan 136-137 B 2
Kesānē = Keşan 136-137 B 2
Keşap 136-137 H 2
Kesariya 138-139 K 4
Ke Sắt 150-151 F 8
Kesennuma 144-145 NO 3
Keshan 142-143 O 2
Keshod 138-139 BC 7
Keshorai Pātan 138-139 EF 5
Keshvar, Īstgāh-e — 136-137 N 6
Kesinga 138-139 J 7
Kesiyārī = Kasiārī 138-139 L 6
Keskin 136-137 E 3
Keski-Suomen lääni 116-117 L 6
Kes'ma 124-125 L 4
Kesrā = Kisrā 166-167 L 2
Kestell 174-175 H 5
Kesten'ga 132-133 E 4
Kestenga 116-117 OP 5
Kestep 136-137 C 4
Keston, London- 129 II c 2
Keszthely 118 H 5
Ket' 132-133 P 6
Keta 164-165 E 7
Keta, ozero — 132-133 QR 4
Ketam, Pulau — 154 III b 1
Ketama = Kitāmah 166-167 D 2
Ketapang [RI, Java] 152-153 K 9
Ketapang [RI, Kalimantan] 148-149 F 7
Ketaun 152-153 D 7
Ketchikan, AK 56-57 K 6
Ketchum, ID 66-67 F 4
Kete Krachi 164-165 DE 7
Keṭī Bandar 138-139 A 5
Ketik River 58-59 H 2
Ketil, Kuala — 150-151 C 10
Ketok Mount 58-59 J 7
Ketou 168-169 F 4
Kętrzyn 118 K 1-2
Kettering, OH 72-73 DE 5
Kettharin Kyûn 148-149 C 4
Kettle Falls, WA 66-67 DE 1
Kettle Point 72-73 EF 3
Kettle River [CDN] 66-67 D 1
Kettle River [USA] 70-71 D 2
Kettle River Range 66-67 D 1
Ketumbaine 171 D 3
Ketungau, Sungai — 152-153 J 5
Kevin, MT 66-67 H 1
Kevir = Kavīr-e Namak-e Mīghān 134-135 GH 4
Kew 88-89 KL 4
Kew, Johannesburg- 170 V b 1
Kew, Melbourne- 161 II c 1
Kewanee, IL 70-71 F 5
Kewaunee, WI 70-71 G 3
Keweenaw Bay 70-71 FG 2
Keweenaw Peninsula 64-65 J 2
Keweenaw Point 70-71 G 2
Keweigek 98-99 H 2
Kewir = Kavīr-e Namak-e Mīghān 134-135 GH 4
Kexholm = Priozʼorsk 132-133 DE 5
Keyaluvik, AK 58-59 E 6
Keya Paha River 68-69 FG 4
Keyes, OK 76-77 C 4
Key Harbour 72-73 F 2
Keyhole Reservoir 68-69 D 3
Key Junction 72-73 F 2
Key Largo 80-81 cd 4
Key Largo, FL 80-81 c 4
Keyser, WV 72-73 G 5
Keystone, SD 68-69 E 4
Keysville, VA 80-81 G 2
Keytū 136-137 N 5
Key West, FL 64-65 K 7
Kez 124-125 T 5
Kezar Stadium 83 I b 2
Kežma 132-133 T 6
Kežmarok 118 K 4

Kgokgole 174-175 E 4
Kgokgolelaagte = Kgokgole 174-175 E 4
Kgun Lake 58-59 EF 6

Khaanzuur, Raas — 164-165 ab 1
Khabarovsk = Chabarovsk 132-133 a 8
Khābī, Ḥāssī al- 166-167 D 5
Khabīr, Zāb al- = Zāb al-Kabīr 136-137 K 4
Khabra Najid = Habrat Najid 136-137 K 7
Khābūr, Nahr al- 134-135 E 3
Khābūrah, Al- 134-135 H 6
Khachraud = Khāchrod 138-139 E 6
Khāchrod 138-139 E 6
Khadiāla = Khariār 138-139 J 7
Khādir Dvīp = Khadīr Island 138-139 C 6
Khadīr Island 138-139 C 6
Khadra, Daïet el — = Ḍayat al-Khaḍrah 166-167 BC 6
Khaḍrah, Ḍayat al- 166-167 BC 6
Kha Dsong 138-139 M 4
Khaer = Khair 138-139 F 4
Khāgā 138-139 H 5
Khagaria 138-139 L 5
Khahrat Burqah 136-137 GH 6
Khaibar = Shurayf 134-135 D 5
Khāibar, Kotal — 134-135 L 4
Khaīj as-Sīntirā', Al- 164-165 A 4
Khailung La 138-139 KL 2
Khair 138-139 F 4
Khairābād 134-135 N 5
Khairāgarh [IND, Madhya Pradesh] 138-139 H 7
Khairāgarh [IND, Uttar Pradesh] 138-139 FG 4
Khairpūr [PAK, Punjab] 134-135 K 5
Khairpūr [PAK, Sindh] 138-139 D 3
Khaitri = Khetri 138-139 E 3
Khajuha 138-139 H 4
Khakass Autonomous Region = 10 ◁ 132-133 R 7
Khalafābād 136-137 N 7
Khalaf al-Allāh 166-167 G 2
Khālāpur 140 A 1
Khālda, Bīr — = Bi'r Hālidah 136-137 B 7
Khalfallah = Khalaf al-Allāh 166-167 G 2
Khalīdj Toûnis = Khalīj at-Tūnisī 166-167 M 1
Khalīfah, Al-Qāhirah-al- 170 II b 1
Khalig Bômba = Khalīj al-Bunbah 164-165 J 2
Khalīg es Suweis = Khalīj as-Suways 164-165 L 3
Khalīg Sidra = Khalīj as-Surt 164-165 H 2
Khalīj Abū Hashū'ifah 136-137 BC 7
Khalīj Abū Qīr 173 B 2
Khalīj al-'Aqabah 134-135 C 5
Khalīj al-'Arab 136-137 C 7
Khalīj al-Bunbah 164-165 J 2
Khalīj al-Ḥammāmāt 164-165 G 1
Khalīj al-Maṣīrah 134-135 H 6-7
Khalīj al-Qābis 164-165 G 2
Khalīj as-Surt 164-165 H 2
Khalīj as-Suways 164-165 L 3
Khalīj aṭ-Ṭīnah 173 C 2
Khalīj at-Tūnisī 166-167 M 1

Khalīj 311

Khalīj Bijāyah 166-167 J 1
Khalīj Bū Ghrārah 166-167 M 3
Khalīj Bū Th'rārah 166-167 M 3
Khalīj Sonmiyānī 134-135 J 6-K 5
Khalīj Umm al-Kataf 173 D 6
Khalīj Wahrān 166-167 F 2
Khalīl, El- = Al-Halīl 136-137 F 7
Khalīlābād 138-139 J 4
Khaliq tau 142-143 E 3
Khāliṣ, Al- 136-137 L 6
Khalkhāl 136-137 N 4
Khalki = Chálkē 122-123 M 7
Khalūf, Al- 134-135 H 6
Kham 142-143 H 5
Khāmam = Khammam 140 E 2
Khamāsīn, Al- 134-135 EF 6
Khambat = Cambay 134-135 L 6
Khambhalia = Khambhāliya 138-139 B 6
Khambhāliya 138-139 B 6
Khambhāt = Cambay 134-135 L 6
Khambhāt nī Khāḍī = Gulf of Cambay 134-135 L 6
Khāmgāñv = Khāmgaon 138-139 F 7
Khāmgaon 138-139 F 7
Khamir 134-135 E 7
Khamīs, Al- 166-167 C 3
Khāmis, Ash-Shallāl al- 164-165 L 5
Khamīs-Milyānah 166-167 H 1
Khamīssāt 166-167 CD 3
Kham Khuan Kaeo 150-151 E 5
Khamlā Chhu = Subansiri 141 D 2
Khammam 140 E 2
Khammouane 150-151 E 3-4
Khamnop 150-151 D 7
Khampa Dsong 142-143 F 6
Khamphô = Ban Khamphô 150-151 F 5
Khamsa, Bīr el- = Bi'r al-Khamsah 164-165 K 2
Khamsha, Bi'r al- 164-165 K 2
Khan 174-175 A 2
Khan, Nam — 150-151 D 2-3
Khān al-Baghdādī 136-137 K 6
Khānāpur [IND, Karnataka] 140 B 3
Khānāpur [IND, Madhya Pradesh] 140 B 2
Khānāpura = Khānāpur 140 B 3
Khānaqīn = Khāniqīn 136-137 L 5
Khān az-Zabīb 136-137 G 7
Khand = Khanda 138-139 J 7
Khanda 138-139 J 7
Khandāla [IND ↓ Pune] 140 AB 1
Khandāla [IND ↖ Pune] 140 A 1
Khandaq, Al- 164-165 KL 5
Khandaq, El- = Al-Khandaq 164-165 KL 5
Khaṇḍavā = Khandwa 134-135 M 6
Khānderi Island 140 A 1
Khāndēsh 138-139 E 7
Khāndhar 138-139 F 4
Khandhkot = Qandkoṭ 138-139 B 3
Khands = Khanda 138-139 J 7
Khandwa 134-135 M 6
Khānewāl 138-139 CD 2
Khan ez Zābib = Khān az-Zabīb 136-137 G 7
Khangai = Changajn nuruu 142-143 HJ 2
Khāngarh 138-139 C 3
Khanga-Sidi-Nadji = Khanqat Sīdī Nājī 166-167 K 2
Khang Khay 150-151 D 3
Khangmar [TJ ↓ Gyangtse] 138-139 M 3
Khangmar [TJ ↘ Mendong Gonpa] 138-139 K 2
Khanh Hoa = Diên Khanh 150-151 G 6
Khanh Hu'ng 150-151 E 8
Khania = Chaniá 122-123 KL 8
Khanīfrah 166-167 D 3
Khanion Bay = Kólpos Chaniōn 122-123 KL 8
Khāniqīn 134-135 F 4
Khānpur [IND, Calcutta] 154 II a 2
Khānpur [IND, Rajasthān] 138-139 F 5
Khānpūr [PAK, Punjab] 138-139 AB 3
Khānpūr [PAK, Sindh] 134-135 KL 5
Khanqat Sīdī Nājī 166-167 K 2
Khanshalah 164-165 F 1
Khantan = Kuantan 148-149 D 6
Khanty-Mansi Autonomous Area 132-133 L-P 5
Khanty-Mansiysk = Chanty-Mansijsk 132-133 M 5
Khanu Woralaksaburi 150-151 B 4
Khān Yūnūs 173 CD 2
Khanzi 172 D 6
Khanzi = Ghanzi 172 D 6
Khanzūr, Ras — = Raas Khaanzuur 164-165 ab 1
Khao Chamao 150-151 C 6
Khao Khieo 150-151 C 6
Khao Laem 150-151 C 5
Khao Langkha Tuk 150-151 B 8
Khao Luang [T ← Nakhon Si Thammarat] 148-149 CD 5
Khao Luang [T ← Thap Sakae] 150-151 B 7
Khao Mokochu 150-151 B 5
Khao Pa Cho = Doi Lang Ka 150-151 B 3
Khao Pha Napo 150-151 BC 4
Khao Phanom Bencha 150-151 B 8
Khao Soi Dao 150-151 B 9
Khao Soi Dao Tai 150-151 CD 6
Khao Song Khwae = Khaungzaunggwei 150-151 B 5
Khao Toei Yai 150-151 B 7
Khao Yai 150-151 B 5
Khao Yoi 150-151 B 6
Kha Panang = Ban Kha Panang 150-151 F 6
Khar 138-139 G 1-2
Kharāb, Al- 134-135 EF 7
Khārāghoḍa 138-139 CD 6
Kharagpur [IND, Bihār] 138-139 L 5
Kharagpur [IND, West Bengal] 134-135 O 6
Kharan Kalat = Khārān Qalāt 134-135 K 5
Khārān Qalāt 134-135 K 5
Kharar 138-139 F 2
Kharār = Lādnun 138-139 E 4
Kharaz, Jabal — 134-135 E 8
Kharbin = Harbin 142-143 O 2
Khardah 154 II b 1
Khardam = Khar 138-139 H 2
Khārepātan 140 A 2
Khārga, El- = Al-Khārijah 164-165 L 3
Khārga, Wāḥāt el- = Al-Wāḥāt al-Khārijah 164-165 KL 3-4
Khargaon = Khargon 138-139 E 7
Khargon 138-139 E 7
Khargpur = Kharagpur 138-139 L 5
Khāri 138-139 E 5
Khariār 138-139 J 7
Kharībāṛi 138-139 M 4
Kharīfūt 134-135 G 7
Khārijah, Al- 164-165 L 3
Khārijah, Al-Wāḥāt al- 164-165 KL 3-4
Kharīṭ, Wādī al- 173 CD 5
Kharīṭ, Wādī el- = Wādī al-Kharīṭ 173 CD 5
Kharj, Al- 134-135 F 6
Khārk, Jazīreh-ye — 134-135 FG 5
Kharkheh, Rūd-e — 136-137 M 6
Kharkov = Char'kov 126-127 H 1-2
Kharora 138-139 HJ 7
Khar Rūd 136-137 N 5
Kharsāwān 138-139 K 6
Kharsūaṅ = Kharsāwān 138-139 K 6
Khartoum = Al-Kharṭum 164-165 L 5
Khartoum North = Al-Kharṭūm Baḥrī 164-165 L 5
Khartshang 138-139 M 2
Kharṭūm, Al- 164-165 L 5
Khartūm Baḥri, Al- 164-165 L 5
Kharṭūm Baḥrī, El- = Al-Kharṭūm Baḥrī 164-165 L 5
Khaṣab, Al- 134-135 H 5
Khashm al-Makhrūq 136-137 J 7
Khashm al-Qirbah 164-165 LM 6
Khāsh Rōd 134-135 J 4
Khāsi-Jaintia Hills 141 BC 3
Khaṭāṭba, El- = Al-Haṭāṭibah 173 B 2
Khātēgāñv = Khātegaon 138-139 F 6
Khātegaon 138-139 F 6
Khaṭṭ, Wād al- 164-165 B 3
Khāvarī, Āzarbayejān-e- 134-135 EF 3
Khāvda 138-139 B 6
Khawr 'Abd Allāh 136-137 N 8
Khawr Abū Ḥajār 136-137 L 7
Khawr al-Amaīyah 136-137 N 8
Khawr al-Fakkān 134-135 H 5
Khawr az-Zubayr 136-137 MN 7
Khawr Rūrī 134-135 G 7
Khawr Unib 173 D 7
Khay' 134-135 E 7
Khaybar, Ḥarrat — 134-135 DE 5
Khazhung Tsho 142-143 F 5
Khāzir, Nahr al- 136-137 K 4
Khazir Su = Nahr al-Khāzir 136-137 K 4
Khazzan an-Naṣr 164-165 L 4
Khebi, Hassi el — = Ḥāssī al-Khābī 166-167 D 5
Khê Bô 150-151 E 3
Khechmâ = Al-Bogham 136-137 J 5
Khed [IND ↑ Pune] 140 AB 1
Khed [IND ↙ Pune] 140 A 2
Khēḍā = Kaira 138-139 D 6
Khed Brahma 138-139 D 5
Khedir, Al — = Khiḍr Dardash 136-137 L 7
Khekra 138-139 F 3
Khemarat 148-149 DE 3
Khem Belder = Kyzyl 132-133 R 7
Khemīs, el — = Al-Khamīs 166-167 C 3
Khemīs, el — = Hamīs az-Zāmāmrah 166-167 B 3
Khemīs, el — = Sūq al-Khamīs as-Sāhil 166-167 C 2
Khemīs, el — = Sūq al-Khamīs Banī 'Arūs 166-167 D 2
Khemis-Milana = Khamīs Milyānah 166-167 H 1
Khemīssèt, el — = Khamīssāt 166-167 CD 3
Khemīs Zemāmra, el — = Hamīs az-Zāmāmrah 166-167 B 3
Khenachich, El — 164-165 D 4
Khenachich, Oglat — 164-165 D 4
Khenchela = Khanshalah 164-165 F 1
Khenīfra = Khanīfrah 166-167 D 3
Khentei Nuruu = Chentin nuruu 142-143 K 2
Khera = Kaira 138-139 D 6
Khērāgaṛh = Khairāgarh 138-139 FG 4
Kherālu 138-139 D 6
Kheri 138-139 H 4
Kherson = Cherson 126-127 F 3
Khētaṛī = Khetri 138-139 E 3
Khetri 138-139 E 3
Kḥewāṛī 138-139 B 4
Khiching 138-139 K 7
Khiḍr Dardash 136-137 L 7
Khiehshow = Jieshou 146-147 E 5
Khieo, Khao — 150-151 C 6
Khilchipur 138-139 F 5
Khios = Chios 122-123 L 6
Khipro 138-139 B 5
Khīrābād = Khairābād 134-135 N 5
Khirbat Kilwa 136-137 G 8
Khiri Ratthanikhom 150-151 B 8
Khirr, Wādī al- 134-135 E 4
Khlong Luang 150-151 C 5
Khlong Thom 150-151 B 9
Khlung 150-151 D 6
Khmel'nyc'kij = Chmel'nickij 126-127 C 2
Khoai, Hon — 150-151 E 8
Khobdo = Chovd 142-143 G 2
Khobso Gol = Chövsgöl nuur 142-143 J 1
Khökh Nuur = Chöch nuur 142-143 H 4
Kho Khot Kra 148-149 CD 4
Khok Kloi 150-151 AB 8
Khok Kong = Ban Khôk Kong 150-151 E 5
Kho Kong 150-151 D 7
Khok Samrong 150-151 C 5
Khomām 136-137 NO 4
Khomas Highland = Khomasplato 172 C 6
Khomasplato 172 C 6
Khomeyn 136-137 NO 6
Khomodimo 174-175 EF 2
Khon Buri 150-151 D 5
Khondāb 136-137 N 5
Khong [LAO] 150-151 EF 5
Khong [T] 150-151 D 5
Khong Chiam 150-151 E 5
Khong Sedone 148-149 E 3
Khon Kaen 148-149 D 3
Khon Sawan 150-151 CD 5
Khorāsān 134-135 H 3-4
Khorāsān, Kāvīr-e — = Kavīr-e Namak-e Mīghān 134-135 H 4
Khorat = Nakhon Ratchasima 148-149 D 3-4
Khorb el Ethel = Khurb al-Athil 166-167 CD 5
Khore 174-175 E 2
Khorel 154 II a 1
Khoribari = Kharībāṛi 138-139 M 4
Khōrmāl = Hūrmāl 136-137 LM 5
Khōr Onib = Khawr Unib 173 D 7
Khorramābād [IR, Lorestān] 134-135 FG 4
Khorramābād [IR, Māzandarān] 136-137 O 4
Khorramshahr 134-135 F 4
Khorsabad 136-137 K 4
Khosrovī 136-137 L 5
Khosrowābād [IR, Hamadān] 136-137 N 5
Khosrowābād [IR, Kordestan] 136-137 M 5
Khotan 142-143 DE 4
Khotan darya 142-143 E 3-4
Khoti 174-175 E 3
Khotol Mount 58-59 J 4
Khoumīr = Khumīr 166-167 L 1
Khourībga = Khurībgah 164-165 C 2
Khowai 141 B 3
Khraicia 170 I a 1
Khram Yai, Ko — 150-151 C 5
Khroub, El — = Al-Khurub 166-167 K 1
Khroumirie = Khumīr 166-167 L 1
Khrū 141 C 2
Khuan Khanun 150-151 BC 9
Khubai Gangri 138-139 J 3
Khudian = Khudiyān 138-139 E 2
Khudiyān 138-139 E 2
Khuff 134-135 E 6
Khuis 174-175 D 4
Khukhan 150-151 E 5
Khükhe Noor = Chöch nuur 142-143 H 4
Khuldābād 138-139 E 7-8
Khulnā 138-139 M 6
Khumīr 166-167 L 1
Khums, Al- 164-165 GH 2
Khungsharyar 138-139 K 2
Khunti 138-139 K 6
Khun Yuam 150-151 AB 3
Khurai 138-139 G 5
Khurasan = Khorāsān 134-135 H 3-4
Khurayṣ 134-135 F 5
Khurb al-Athil 166-167 CD 5
Khūr-e Mūsā 136-137 N 7-8
Khuria Tank 138-139 H 6
Khurībgah 164-165 C 2
Khūrīyā Mūrīyā, Jazā'ir — 134-135 H 7
Khurja 138-139 F 3
Khurmah, Al- 134-135 E 6
Khūrmāl 136-137 LM 5
Khurr, Wādī al- = Wādī al-Khirr 136-137 K 7
Khurub, Al- 166-167 K 1
Khushāb 134-135 L 4
Khūzdār 134-135 K 5
Khūzestān 134-135 F 4
Khuzistan = Khuzestan 134-135 F 4
Khvāf 134-135 J 4
Khvostof Island 58-59 s 6
Khvoy 134-135 EF 3
Khwae Noi, Mae Nam — 150-151 B 5-6
Khwāf = Khvāf 134-135 J 4
Khyatthin 141 D 4
Khyber Pass = Kotal Khāibar 134-135 L 4
Khyetentshering 142-143 G 5
Kiabakari 171 C 3
Kiama 160 K 5
Kiambi 172 E 3
Kiamichi Mountains 76-77 G 5
Kiamichi River 76-77 G 5-6
Kiamusze = Jiamusi 142-143 P 2
Kian = Ji'an 142-143 LM 6
Kiana, AK 58-59 G 3
Kiangling = Jiangling 146-147 CD 6
Kiangning = Nanjing 142-143 M 5
Kiangshan = Jiangshan 146-147 G 7
Kiangsi = Jiangxi 142-143 LM 6
Kiangsu = Jiangsu 142-143 MN 5
Kiangtu = Jiangdu 146-147 G 5
Kiangyin = Jiangyin 146-147 H 6
Kiantajärvi 116-117 N 5
Kiaohsien = Jiao Xian 142-143 M 4
Kiating = Jiading 146-147 H 6
Kiawah Island 80-81 FG 4
Kiayu = Jiayu 146-147 D 6-7
Kiayukwan = Jiuquan 142-143 H 4
Kibaha = Bagamoyo 172 G 3
Kibale 171 B 2
Kibali 172 EF 1
Kibamba 172 E 2
Kibangou 172 B 2
Kibarty = Kybartai 124-125 D 6
Kibau 172 FG 3
Kibaya 172 G 3
Kiberashi 171 D 4
Kiberege 172 G 3
Kibiti 171 D 4
Kiboko 171 D 3
Kibombo 172 E 2
Kibondo 172 F 2
Kıbrıscık = Karadoğan 136-137 DE 2
Kibungu 172 F 2
Kibuye 171 AB 5
Kibwezi 172 G 2
Kičevo 122-123 J 5
Kichčik 132-133 de 7
Kichha 138-139 G 3
Kichijōji, Musashino- 155 III a 1
Kichinev = Kišin'ov 126-127 D 3
Kicking Horse Pass 56-57 NO 7
Kičmengskij Gorodok 124-125 P 3
Kidal 164-165 E 5
Kidaroupérou 168-169 F 3
Kidatu 172 G 3
Kidderpore, Calcutta- 154 II ab 2
Kidd's Beach 174-175 GH 7
Kidepo National Park 172 F 1
Kidete 171 D 4
Kidira 164-165 B 6
Kidjaboun 168-169 EF 3
Kidnappers, Cape — 161 GH 4
Kido 155 III d 1
Kidston 158-159 H 3
Kidul, Pegunungan — 152-153 J 9-K 10
Kidyat Ijjill 164-165 B 4
Kiekeberg 130 I a 2
Kiekebusch 130 III c 2
Kiel 118 E 1
Kiel, WI 70-71 F 4
Kiel Canal = Nord-Ostsee-Kanal 118 D 1-2
Kielce 118 K 3
Kieler Bucht 118 E 1
Kiên An 150-151 F 2
Kienan = Qian'an 146-147 G 1
Kiên Binh 150-151 E 8
Kiên Hung = Go Quao 148-149 DE 5
Kienkiang = Qianjiang 146-147 B 7
Kienli = Jianli 146-147 D 7
Kienning = Jian'ou 142-143 M 6
Kienshih = Jianshi 146-147 B 6
Kienshui = Jianshui 142-143 J 7
Kienteh = Jiande 146-147 G 7
Kienwerder 130 III a 2
Kierling 113 I b 1
Kierunavaara 116-117 J 4
Kiestinki = Kesten'ga 132-133 E 4
Kieta 148-149 j 6
Kiewietskuil 174-175 E 7
Kīfah 164-165 B 5
Kifaya 168-169 B 2
Kiffa = Kīfah 164-165 B 5
Kifl, Al- 136-137 L 6
Kifrī 136-137 L 5
Kigali 172 F 2
Kigalik River 58-59 K 2
Kiganga 171 C 4
Kiğı = Kasaba 136-137 J 3
Kigluaik Mountains 58-59 DE 4
Kigoma 172 E 2
Kigosi 171 B 3
Kıgzı 136-137 K 3
Kiha = Kwiha 164-165 MN 6
Kihambatang 152-153 K 6
Kihelkonna 124-125 D 4
Kihindi 171 D 5
Kihnu 124-125 D 4
Kiholo, HI 78-79 e 3
Kihowera 171 D 5
Kihsien = Qi Xian [TJ, Henan] 146-147 E 4
Kihsien = Qi Xian [TJ, Shanxi] 146-147 D 3
Kihti = Skiftet 116-117 J 7
Kihurio 171 D 4
Kii hantō 142-143 Q 5
Kiik-Atlama, mys — 126-127 GH 4
Kii sammyaku 144-145 KL 5-6
Kii-suidō 142-143 PQ 5
Kijang 144-145 G 5
Kijev 126-127 DE 1
Kijevka [SU, Kazachskaja SSSR] 132-133 N 7
Kijevka [SU, Rossijskaja SFSR] 144-145 J 1
Kijevskoje vodochranilišče 126-127 E 1
Kijik, AK 58-59 K 6
Kikerino 124-125 G 4
Kikiakrorak River 58-59 L 2
Kikinda 122-123 J 3
Kiknur 124-125 Q 5
Kikombo 171 CD 4
Kikonai 144-145 B 3
Kikori 148-149 M 8
Kikuna, Yokohama- 155 III a 2
Kikus 124-125 V 3
Kikwit 172 C 3
Kil 116-117 E 8
Kilāb, Jazā'ir al- 166-167 M 1
Kilaban 136-137 K 4
Kilakkarai 140 D 6
Kilambé, Cerro — 88-89 CD 8
Kilātes, Berzekh el — = Rā's Qilātis 166-167 E 2
Kilauea Crater 148-149 ef 4
Kil'azi 126-127 O 6
Kilbuck Mountains 56-57 E 5-D 6
Kilchu 144-145 G 2
Kilcoy 158-159 K 5
Kildinstroj 116-117 PQ 3
Kildonan 172 F 5
Kilemary 124-125 Q 5
Kilembe 171 B 2
Kilemon 174-175 D 2
Kilgore, ID 66-67 GH 3
Kilgore, TX 76-77 G 6
Kili 208 G 2
Kilifi 172 GH 2
Kiligwa River 58-59 H 2
Kilija 126-127 D 4
Kilimanjaro [EAT, administrative unit] 172 G 2
Kilimanjaro [EAT, mountain] 172 G 2
Kilimatinde 172 FG 3
Kilin = Jilin 142-143 N 2-O 3
Kilingi-Nõmme 124-125 E 4
Kilinochchi 140 E 6
Kilis 136-137 G 4
Kiliuda Bay 58-59 g 1
Kiliyanūr 140 DE 4
Kilkee 119 AB 5
Kilkenny 119 C 5
Kilkis 122-123 K 5
Killala Lake 70-71 G 1
Killam 61 C 4
Killarney [AUS] 160 L 2
Killarney [CDN] 68-69 FG 1
Killarney [IRL] 119 B 5
Killdeer 68-69 C 1
Killdeer, ND 68-69 E 2
Killdeer Mountains 68-69 E 2
Killeen, TX 76-77 F 7
Killiecrankie Pass 119 E 3
Killik 136-137 G 3
Killik River 58-59 KL 2
Killin 119 D 3
Killinek Island 56-57 Y 5
Killington Peak 72-73 K 3
Kill van Kull 82 III b 3
Killybegs 119 B 4
Kilmarnock 119 DE 4
Kil'mez' [SU, place Kirovskaja Oblast'] 124-125 S 5
Kil'mez' [SU, place Udmurtskaja ASSR] 124-125 S 5
Kil'mez' [SU, river] 124-125 S 5
Kilmichael, MS 78-79 E 4
Kilmore 160 G 6
Kilo 171 B 2
Kilombero 172 G 3
Kilómetro 106-107 C 5
Kilómetro 31, Estación — 110 III b 1
Kilómetro 45, Estación — 110 III a 2
Kilómetro 642 104-105 F 9
Ki-long = Chilung 142-143 N 6
Kilosa 172 G 3
Kilossa = Kilosa 172 G 3
Kilpisjärvi 116-117 J 3
Kilrea 119 C 4
Kilrush 119 B 5
Kiltān Island 134-135 L 8
Kilunga 168-169 J 3
Kilwa 172 E 3
Kilwa, Khirbat — 136-137 G 8
Kilwa Kisiwani 172 GH 3
Kilwa-Kissiwni = Kilwa Kisiwani 172 GH 3
Kilwa Kivinje 172 GH 3
Kilwa-Kiwindje = Kilwa Kivinje 172 GH 3
Kim, CO 68-69 E 7
Kim [MAL] 154 III b 1
Kim [RFC] 168-169 H 4
Kimaam 148-149 L 8
Kimali 171 C 3
Kimama, ID 66-67 G 4
Kimasozero 116-117 O 5
Kimba 160 C 4
Kimball, MN 70-71 C 3
Kimball, NE 68-69 E 5
Kimball, SD 68-69 G 4
Kimball, Mount — 58-59 PQ 5
Kimbe 148-149 gh 6
Kimbe Bay 148-149 h 6
Kimberley [AUS] 158-159 E 3
Kimberley [CDN] 56-57 NO 8
Kimberley [ZA] 172 DE 7
Kimberly, NV 74-75 F 3
Kimchaek 142-143 OP 3
Kimch'ŏn 142-143 O 4
Kimen = Qimen 146-147 F 7
Kimhandu 171 D 4
Kimje 144-145 F 5
Kimkang = Chengmai 142-143 KL 8
Kimōlos 122-123 L 7
Kimparana 168-169 D 2
Kimpoku san 144-145 LM 3
Kimry 132-133 F 6
Kim So'n 150-151 F 2
Kimuenza 172 C 2
Kinabalu, Gunung — 148-149 G 5
Kinabatangan, Sungei — 152-153 M 3
Kinak Bay 58-59 F 7
Kinapusan Island 152-153 O 3
Kinārsāni 140 E 2
Kinaskan Lake 58-59 WX 8
Kinbasket Lake 60 HJ 4
Kincaid, KS 70-71 C 6
Kincardine [CDN] 72-73 F 2
Kinchinjunga = Gangchhendsönga 134-135 O 5
Kincolith 60 BC 2
Kinda = Kinh Đu'c 150-151 F 7
Kindan Bûm 141 E 2
Kindandai 152-153 P 6
Kindat = Kintat 141 D 4
Kinder, LA 78-79 C 5
Kindersley 56-57 P 7
Kindia 164-165 B 6
Kindu 172 E 2
Kinel' 132-133 J 7
Kinel'skije jary 124-125 ST 7
Kinešma 132-133 G 6
Kingabwa, Kinshasa- 170 IV b 2
King and Queen Court House, VA 80-81 H 2
King Charles Land = Kong Karsland 116-117 mn 5
Kingchow = Jiangling 142-143 L 5
King Christian IX Land = Kong Christian den IXs Land 52 C 22
Kingchwan = Jingchuan 142-143 K 4
King City, CA 74-75 C 4
King City, MO 70-71 C 5
King Cove, AK 58-59 bc 2
King Edward VIIIth Gulf 53 C 6-7
King Edward VIIth Land = Edward VIIth Peninsula 53 B 21-22
King Edward VIIth Plateau = Dronning Maud fjellkjede 53 A
Kingfisher, OK 76-77 F 5
King Frederik VIII Land = Kong Frederik den VIIIs Land 52 B 21
King Frederik VI Land = Kong Frederik den VIs Kyst 52 C 23
King George Bay 108-109 J 8
King George Island 53 CD 30-31
King George Sound 158-159 CD 7
King George's Reservoir 129 II bc 1
King George VI. Falls 94-95 L 5
King George VIth Sound 53 B 29-30
King George Vth, Taman Kebangsaan — 150-151 D 10
King George Vth Land 53 BC 15-16
King Hill, ID 66-67 F 4
Kinghsien = Jing Xian 146-147 G 6
Kingisepp [SU, Eesti] 124-125 D 4
Kingisepp [SU, Rossijskaja SFSR] 124-125 G 4
King Island [AUS] 158-159 H 7
King Island [CDN] 60 D 3
King Island [USA] 58-59 C 4
King Island = Kadan Kyûn 148-149 C 4
Kingku = Jinggu 142-143 J 7
King Lear 66-67 D 5
King Leopold Ranges 158-159 DE 3
Kingman, AZ 74-75 FG 5
Kingman, KS 68-69 GH 7
Kingmen = Jingmen 146-147 CD 6
King Mountain [USA, Oregon] 66-67 D 4
King Mountain [USA, Texas] 76-77 C 7
King of Prussia, PA 84 III a 1
King of Prussia Plaza 84 III a 1
Kingoonya 158-159 G 6
King Oscar Land 56-57 TU 2
Kingri 138-139 B 2
King Salmon, AK 58-59 JK 7
King Salmon River [CDN ⊲ Egegik Bay] 58-59 J 7
King Salmon River [CDN ⊲ Nushagak River] 58-59 HJ 6
Kingsbury Green, London- 129 II a 1
Kings Canyon National Park 74-75 D 4
Kingscote 158-159 G 7
Kingscourt 119 C 5
Kings Court, Houston-, TX 85 III b 2
Kingsford Smith Airport 161 I ab 2
Kingsland, GA 80-81 F 5
Kingsland, TX 76-77 E 7
Kingsley 174-175 J 4
Kingsley, IA 70-71 BC 4
King's Lynn 119 FG 5
Kings Mountain, NC 80-81 F 3
King Sound 158-159 D 3
King's Park 155 I b 2
Kings Peaks 64-65 DE 3
Kings Point, NY 82 III d 2
Kingsport 63 D 5
Kingsport, TN 80-81 E 2
Kings River 74-75 CD 4
Kingston, MO 70-71 C 6
Kingston, NY 72-73 JK 4
Kingston, OK 76-77 F 5-6
Kingston, PA 72-73 HJ 4
Kingston, WA 66-67 B 2
Kingston [CDN] 56-57 Y 9
Kingston [JA] 64-65 L 8
Kingston [NZ] 158-159 N 9
Kingston Peak 74-75 EF 5
Kingston SE 158-159 G 7
Kingston upon Hull 119 FG 5
Kingstown [IRL] 119 CD 5
Kingstown [West Indies] 64-65 O 9
Kingstree, SC 80-81 G 4
Kingsville, TX 64-65 G 6
Kingsville, Melbourne- 161 II b 1
Kingswood 174-175 F 4
King William Island 56-57 R 4
King William's Town 172 E 8
Kingwood, WV 72-73 G 5
Kingyang = Qingyang 142-143 K 4
Kingyuan = Yishan 142-143 K 7
Kingyun = Qingyun 146-147 F 3
Kinh Đu'c 150-151 F 7
Kinhwa = Jinhua 142-143 MN 6
Kinibalu = Mount Kinabalu 148-149 G 5
Kınık 136-137 B 3
Kinistino 61 F 4
Kinkala 172 B 2
Kinkazan tō 144-145 NO 3
Kinmen = Kinmen Dao 142-143 M 7
Kinmen Dao 142-143 M 7
Kinmount 72-73 G 2
Kinmundy, IL 70-71 F 6
Kinnaird's Head 119 F 3
Kinneret, Yam — 134-135 D 4
Kino kawa 144-145 K 5
Kinomoto = Kumano 144-145 L 6
Kinoosao 61 GH 2
Kinosaki 144-145 K 5
Kinross 119 E 3
Kinsale 119 B 6
Kinsella 61 BC 4
Kinselmeer 128 I b 1
Kinsey, MT 68-69 D 2
Kinshan = Jinshan 146-147 H 6
Kinshasa 172 C 2
Kinshasa, Aéroport de — 170 IV ab 1
Kinshasa-Banda-Lungwa 170 IV a 1-2
Kinshasa-Barumbu 170 IV a 1
Kinshasa-Binza 170 IV a 2
Kinshasa-Bumbu 170 IV a 2
Kinshasa-Djelo-Binza 170 IV a 2
Kinshasa-Gombe 170 IV a 1
Kinshasa-Kalamu 170 IV a 2
Kinshasa-Kasa-Vubu 170 IV a 2
Kinshasa-Kingabwa 170 IV b 2
Kinshasa-Kintambo 170 IV a 2
Kinshasa-Limete 170 IV b 2
Kinshasa-Lingwala 170 IV a 1
Kinshasa-Makala 170 IV a 2
Kinshasa-Masina 170 IV b 2
Kinshasa-N'dolo 170 IV b 1
Kinshasa-Ngaba 170 IV ab 2
Kinshasa-Ngaliema 170 IV a 2
Kinshasa-Ngiri-Ngiri 170 IV a 2
Kinshasa-Présidence 170 IV a 1
Kinsien = Jin Xian 142-143 N 4
Kinsley, KS 68-69 G 7
Kinston, NC 64-65 L 4
Kintamba, Kinshasa- 170 IV a 2
Kintambo, Rapides de — 170 IV a 1
Kintampo 164-165 D 7
Kintan = Jintan 146-147 G 6
Kintap 148-149 G 7
Kintat 141 D 4
Kin-tcheou = Jinzhou 142-143 N 3
Kintinian 168-169 C 3
Kintinku 171 C 4
Kintyre 119 D 4
Kinuso 60 K 2
Kinvat = Kinwat 138-139 FG 8
Kinwat 138-139 FG 8
Kinyangiri 171 C 4
Kinyeti 171 C 1
Kiokluk Mount 58-59 HJ 6
Kiokluk Mountains 58-59 H 6
Kíos = Gemlik 136-137 C 2
Kioshan = Queshan 142-143 L 5
Kiosk 72-73 G 1
Kioto = Kyōto 142-143 PQ 4
Kiowa, CO 68-69 D 6
Kiowa, KS 76-77 E 4
Kiowa, OK 76-77 FG 5
Kiowa Creek 68-69 D 5-6
Kipahigan Lake 61 H 3
Kipawa 72-73 G 1
Kipawa, Lac — 72-73 G 1
Kipawa, la Reserve de — 72-73 G 1
Kipembawe 172 F 3
Kipengere 171 C 5
Kipeta 171 B 5
Kipili 172 F 3
Kipini 172 H 2
Kipling 61 G 5
Kipnuk, AK 58-59 EF 7
Kipp 66-67 G 1
Kiptopeke, VA 80-81 J 2
Kipushi 172 E 4
Kir'a 124-125 Q 6
Kirākat 138-139 J 5
Kirakira 148-149 k 7
Kirandul 140 E 1
Kīranūr [IND ↑ Neyveli] 140 D 5
Kīranūr [IND ↙ Thanjāvar] 140 D 5
Kiraoli 138-139 F 4
Kirāvalī = Kiraoli 138-139 F 4
Kiraz 136-137 C 3
Kırbaşı 136-137 DE 2-3
Kirbyville, TX 76-77 GH 7
Kirchdorf, Hamburg- 130 I b 2
Kirenga 132-133 U 6
Kirensk 132-133 U 6
Kirgali 136-137 H 4
Kirghiz Soviet Socialist Republic 134-135 LM 2
Kirgis Nor = Chjargas nuur 142-143 GH 2
Kirgiz Kizilsu Zizhizhou 142-143 CD 3-4

312 Khalīj

Kirgizskaja Sovetskaja Socialističeskaja Respublika = Kirghiz Soviet Socialist Republic 134-135 LM 2
Kirgizskij chrebet 134-135 LM 2
Kiri 172 C 2
Kiribati 178-179 S 6
Kiries East = Kiries-Oos 174-175 C 4
Kiries-Oos 174-175 C 4
Kiries Wes = Kiries West 174-175 C 4
Kiries West 174-175 C 4
Kırık 136-137 J 2
Kırıkhan 136-137 G 4
Kirikiri Prisons 170 III a 2
Kırıkkale 134-135 C 2-3
Kirillov 132-133 F 6
Kirillovka 126-127 G 3
Kirin = Jilin [TJ, administrative unit] 142-143 N 2-O 3
Kirin = Jilin [TJ, place] 142-143 O 3
Kirindi Oya 140 E 7
Kirin-do 144-145 E 4
Kirishima-yama 144-145 H 7
Kiriši 124-125 J 4
Kiris-Ost = Kiries-Oos 174-175 C 4
Kiris-West = Kiries West 174-175 C 4
Kirit = Jiriid 164-165 O 7
Kiriwina Islands = Trobriand Islands 148-149 h 6
Kırka 136-137 D 3
Kırkağaç 136-137 BC 3
Kirkcaldy 119 E 3
Kirkcudbright 119 DE 4
Kirkenes 116-117 O 3
Kırkgeçit = Kasrık 136-137 K 3
Kirkjuból 116-117 g 2
Kirkland, TX 76-77 D 5
Kirkland Lake 56-57 U 8
Kırklareli 134-135 B 2
Kirksville, MO 64-65 H 3
Kirkūk 134-135 EF 3
Kirkwall 119 E 2
Kirkwood 172 DE 8
Kirkwood, MO 70-71 E 6
Kirkwood, NJ 84 III cd 3
Kirkwood, Atlanta-, GA 85 II c 2
Kirlangıç burnu = Gelidonya burnu 136-137 D 4
Kirman = Kermān 134-135 H 4
Kirmir çayı 136-137 E 2
Kırobası = Mağara 136-137 EF 4
Kirongwe 171 DE 4
Kirov [SU, Kalužskaja Oblasť] 124-125 K 6
Kirov [SU, Kirovskaja Oblasť] 132-133 HJ 6
Kirova, zaliv — 126-127 O 7
Kirova, zapovednik — 126-127 O 7
Kirovabad 126-127 N 6
Kirovakan 126-127 LM 6
Kirov-Kominternovskij 124-125 RS 4
Kirovo-Čepeck 124-125 S 4
Kirovograd 126-127 EF 2
Kirovsk [SU, Azerbajdžanskaja SSR] 126-127 O 7
Kirovsk [SU, Rossijskaja SFSR ↓ Murmansk] 132-133 EF 4
Kirovsk [SU, Rossijskaja SFSR Leningradskaja Oblasť] 124-125 H 4
Kirovskij [SU, Kazachskaja SSR] 132-133 O 9
Kirovskij [SU, Rossijskaja SFSR ↓ Astrachan'] 126-127 O 4
Kirovskij [SU, Rossijskaja SFSR ↖ Petropavlovsk-Kamčatskij] 132-133 de 7
Kirpil'skij liman 126-127 HJ 4
Kirs 132-133 J 6
Kirsanov 124-125 O 7
Kırşehir 134-135 C 3
Kırsırkaya 154 I a 1
Kirstonia 174-175 E 3
Kīrthar, Koh — 134-135 K 5
Kirthar Range = Koh Kīrthar 134-135 K 5
Kirtland, NM 74-75 J 4
Kiruna 116-117 HJ 4
Kiruru 148-149 KL 7
Kirwin, KS 68-69 G 6
Kirwin Reservoir 68-69 G 6
Kiryū 144-145 M 4
Kiržač 124-125 M 5
Kisa 116-117 F 8-9
Kisabi 171 B 4-5
Kisakata 144-145 M 3
Kisaki 171 D 4
Kisale, Lac — 172 E 3
Kisangani 172 E 1
Kisangire 172 G 3
Kisar, Pulau — 148-149 J 8
Kisaralik River 58-59 G 6
Kisaran 150-151 B 11
Kisarawe 172 G 3
Kisarazu 144-145 MN 5
Kisarazu Air Base 155 III c 3
Kisbey 61 G 6
Kisel'ovsk 132-133 Q 7
Kisen = Hŭich'ŏn 142-143 O 3
Kisengwa 172 E 3
Kišen'ki 126-127 G 2
Kisenyi = Gisenyi 172 E 2
Kisgegas 60 D 2
Kish 136-137 L 6
Kīsh, Jazīreh-ye — 134-135 G 5
Kishan = Ch'i-shhan 146-147 H 10
Kishanganj 138-139 LM 4-5
Kishangarh [IND ↗ Ajmer] 138-139 E 4
Kishangarh [IND ↑ Rāmgarh] 138-139 C 4
Kishb, Ḥarrat al- 134-135 E 6
Kishi 168-169 F 3
Kishikas River 62 CD 1
Kishinev = Kišin'ov 126-127 D 3
Kishiwada 144-145 K 5
Kishm = Qeshm [IR, landscape] 134-135 H 5
Kishm = Qeshm [IR, place] 134-135 H 5
Kishorganj 141 B 3
Kishui = Jishui 146-147 E 8
Kisigo 171 C 4
Kisii 172 F 2
Kisiju 171 D 4
Kısıklı 154 I b 2
Kišin'ov 126-127 D 3
Kısır dağı 136-137 K 2
Kiska Island 52 D 1
Kiskatinaw River 60 G 2
Kiska Volcano 58-59 r 6
Kiskittogisu Lake 61 J 3
Kiskitto Lake 61 J 3
Kiskunfélegyháza 118 JK 5
Kiskunhalas 118 J 5
Kislovodsk 126-127 L 5
Kismaanyo 172 H 2
Kismayu = Kismaanyo 172 H 2
Kismet, KS 76-77 D 4
Kiso gawa 144-145 L 5
Kiso sammyaku 144-145 L 5
Kispiox River 60 C 2
Kisrā 166-167 L 2
Kisreka 116-117 O 5
Kissangire = Kisangire 172 G 3
Kissaraing Island = Kettharin Kyūn 148-149 C 4
Kissenje = Gisenyi 172 E 2
Kissenji = Gisenyi 172 E 2
Kisserawe = Kisarawe 172 G 3
Kissidougou 164-165 BC 7
Kissimmee, FL 80-81 c 2
Kissimmee, Lake — 80-81 c 2-3
Kissimmee River 80-81 c 3
Kissinger 66-67 A 1
Kississing Lake 61 H 3
Kistna = Krishna 134-135 M 7
Kistufell 116-117 f 2
Kisumu 172 FG 2
Kisvárda 118 KL 4
Kiswere 171 D 5
Kita 164-165 C 6
Kita, Tōkyō- 155 III b 1
Kitaaoyagi 155 III d 2
Kita Daitō-jima 142-143 P 6
Kita-Daitō zima = Kita-Daitō-jima 142-143 P 6
Kitagō 144-145 H 7
Kitai = Qitai 142-143 FG 3
Kita-Ibaraki 144-145 N 4
Kita Iwojima = Kita-lo 206-207 S 7
Kitakami 144-145 N 3
Kitakami gawa 142-143 R 4
Kitakami kōti 144-145 N 2-3
Kitakata 144-145 MN 4
Kita-Kyūshū 142-143 OP 5
Kita-Kyūsyū = Kita-Kyūshū 142-143 OP 5
Kitale 172 G 1
Kita lo 206-207 S 7
Kitāmah 166-167 D 2
Kitami 142-143 R 3
Kita ura 144-145 N 4
Kitčan 132-133 Y 5
Kit Carson, CO 68-69 E 6
Kitchener 56-57 U 9
Kitchigama, Rivière — 62 M 1
Kitchioh = Jieshi 146-147 E 10
Kitchioh Wan = Jieshi Wan 146-147 E 10
Kitee 116-117 O 6
Kitega = Gitega 172 EF 2
Kitendwe 171 B 4
Kitengela Game Reserve 171 D 3
Kitgum 172 F 1
Kithāmah 166-167 D 2
Kitimat 56-57 L 7
Kitinen 116-117 LM 3
Kitkatla 60 B 3
Kitlope River 60 D 3
Kitsansara 124-125 GH 3
Kitseh = Jize 146-147 E 3
Kitsuki 144-145 H 6
Kittanning, PA 72-73 G 4
Kittery, ME 72-73 L 3
Kitthareng = Kettharin Kyūn 148-149 C 4
Kittilä 116-117 L 4
Kittūr 140 B 3
Kitty Hawk, NC 80-81 J 2
Kitu 171 A 4
Kitui 172 G 2
Kituku 171 B 4
Kitumbini 171 DE 5
Kitunda 172 F 3
Kitwanga 60 C 2
Kitwe 172 E 4
Kityang = Jieyang 146-147 F 10
Kitzbühel 118 EF 5
Kitzingen 118 E 4
Kiuchuan = Jiuquan 142-143 H 4
Kiuhsien = Qiu Xian 146-147 E 3
Kiukiang = Jiujiang 142-143 M 6
Kiulong Kiang = Jiulong Jiang 146-147 F 9
Kiunga 148-149 M 8
Kiung-chow = Qiongshan 142-143 L 8
Kiungchow Hai-hsia = Qiongzhou Haixia 142-143 KL 7
Kiuruvesi 116-117 M 6
Kiushiu = Kyūshū 142-143 P 5
Kiu Tsui Chau 155 I b 1
Kivač, vodopad — 124-125 J 2
Kivalina, AK 58-59 E 3
Kivalina River 58-59 E 2-3
Kivalo 116-117 L 5-M 4
Kivercy 126-127 B 1
Kiveriči 124-125 L 5
Kivu 172 E 2
Kivu, Lac — 172 EF 2
Kiwalik, AK 58-59 FG 3
Kiyang = Qiyang 146-147 CD 8
Kiyāt = Khay' 134-135 E 7
Kiyev = Kijev 126-127 DE 1
Kiyose 155 III a 1
Kiyosumi Garden 155 III b 1
Kizel 132-133 K 6
Kizema 124-125 P 3
Kiziba 171 C 2
Kızılcahamam 136-137 E 2
Kızılçakcak = Akkaya 136-137 K 2
Kızılırmak 134-135 D 3
Kızılırmak = Hüseyinli 136-137 EF 2
Kiziljurt 126-127 N 5
Kızılkaya 136-137 E 4
Kizil Khoto = Kyzyl 132-133 R 7
Kızılkoca = Şefaatli 136-137 F 3
Kizil Orda = Kzyl-Orda 132-133 M 9
Kizilsu Kirgiz Zizhizhou 142-143 C 4-D 3
Kiziltepe 136-137 J 4
Kızıltoprak, İstanbul- 154 I b 3
Kizilveran 136-137 F 2
Kizľar 126-127 N 5
Kizľarskij zaliv 126-127 N 4
Kizner 124-125 S 5
Kızören 136-137 E 3
Kizyl-Arvat 134-135 H 3
Kizyl-Atrek 134-135 G 3
Kjækan 116-117 K 3
Kjerringøy 116-117 EF 4
Kjøllefjord 116-117 MN 2
Kjøpsvik 116-117 G 3
Klaarstroom 174-175 E 7
Kladno 118 FG 3
Kladovo 122-123 K 3
Kladow, Berlin- 130 III a 2
Klaeng 150-151 C 6
Klagenfurt 118 G 5
Klaipėda 124-125 C 6
Klamath, CA 66-67 A 5
Klamath Falls, OR 64-65 B 3
Klamath Mountains 64-65 B 3
Klamath River 64-65 B 3
Klamono 148-149 K 7
Klang, Ko — 150-151 AB 8
Klang, Pulau — 150-151 C 11
Klappan River 58-59 X 8
Klapper = Pulau Deli 148-149 DE 8
Klarälven 116-117 E 7
Kľasticy 124-125 G 6
Klatovy 118 F 4
Klaver = Klawer 172 C 8
Kľavlino 124-125 ST 6
Klawer 172 C 8
Klawock, AK 58-59 w 9
Klay = Bomi Hills 164-165 B 7
Kľaz'ma 124-125 N 5
Kleck 124-125 F 7
Kleena Kleene 60 E 3
Kleides 136-137 F 5
Kleinbeeren 130 III b 2
Kleinbegin 174-175 D 5
Klein Bosmanland 174-175 C 5
Kleiner Ravensberg 130 III a 2
Klein Gerau 128 III a 2
Klein Glienicke, Volkspark — 130 III a 2
Klein Grasbrook, Hamburg- 130 I ab 1
Kleinhadern, München- 130 II a 2
Klein Jukskei 170 V b 1
Klein-Karas 174-175 C 4
Klein Karasberge 174-175 C 4
Klein Karoo 172 D 8
Klein Letaba 174-175 J 2
Klein Moor 130 I b 2
Klein Namakwaland 174-175 B 5
Kleinpoort 174-175 F 7
Klein Rietrivier 174-175 D 6-7
Klein Roggeveld 174-175 D 7
Kleinschönebeck 130 III c 2
Kleinsee 174-175 B 5
Klein Swartberge 174-175 D 7
Kleinziethen 130 III b 2
Klela 168-169 D 3
Klemtu 60 C 3
Klender, Jakarta- 154 IV b 2
Klerksdorp 172 E 7
Klery Creek, AK 58-59 GH 3
Kleščevo 124-125 M 2
Klesov 124-125 F 8
Klet'na 124-125 J 7
Klēts kalns 124-125 F 5
Kletskij 126-127 L 2
Klevan' 126-127 BC 1
Kleve 118 BC 3
Kleven' 126-127 F 1
Kličev 124-125 G 7
Klickitat, WA 66-67 C 3
Klickitat River 66-67 C 2-3
Klidhes Island = Kleides 136-137 F 5
Klimoviči 124-125 HJ 7
Klimovo 124-125 J 7
Klimovsk 124-125 L 6
Klin 132-133 F 6
Klinaklini Glacier 60 E 4
Klincovka 124-125 R 8
Klincy 124-125 J 7
Klinovec 118 F 3
Klintehamn 116-117 GH 9
Klipdale 174-175 C 8
Klipdam 174-175 C 4
Klipkrans 174-175 E 7
Klippan 116-117 E 9
Klippebjergene = Rocky Mountains 56-57 L 5-P 9
Klippiga bergen = Rocky Mountains 56-57 L 5-P 9
Klipplaat 174-175 F 7
Klippoortje 170 V c 2
Kliprivier [ZA, Drakensberge] 174-175 H 4
Kliprivier [ZA, Johannesburg] 170 V a 2
Kliprivierberg 170 V b 2
Kliprivierssoog, Johannesburg- 170 V a 2
Kliprugberg 174-175 C 6
Kliprug Kop = Kliprugberg 174-175 C 6
Kłodzko 118 H 3
Klomp 128 I b 2
Klondike 56-57 HJ 5
Klong, Mae — = Mae Nam Klong 150-151 CD 3-4
Klong, Nam Mae — = Nam Mae Ngat 150-151 B 3
Klosterneuburg 118 GH 4
Klostertor, Hamburg- 130 I b 1
Klotz, Mount — 58-59 R 4
Klövensteen, Forst — 130 I a 1
Kluane 58-59 ST 6
Kluane Lake 56-57 J 5
Kluane National Park 58-59 RS 6
Kľučevskaja sopka = Velikaja Kľučevskaja sopka 132-133 f 6
Kluchor = Karačajevsk 126-127 KL 5
Kluchorskij, pereval — 126-127 K 5
Kľuči 132-133 f 6
Kluczbork 118 HJ 3
Klukwan, AK 58-59 U 7
Klumpang, Teluk — 152-153 M 7
Klutina Lake 58-59 OP 6
Kmeit = Al-Kumayt 136-137 M 6
Knabengruver 116-117 B 8
Knapp, WI 70-71 DE 3
Kn'aščiny 124-125 K 5
Kneïss, Djezîret = Jazīrat Kanā'is 166-167 M 2
Knewstubb Lake 60 E 3
Kneža 122-123 L 4
Knife River 68-69 EF 2
Knife River, MN 70-71 DE 2
Knight Inlet 60 E 4
Knight Island 58-59 N 6
Knin 122-123 FG 3
Knippa, TX 76-77 E 8
Kn'aževac 122-123 K 4
Knobel, AR 78-79 D 2
Knob Lake = Schefferville 56-57 X 7
Knob Oaks, Houston-, TX 85 III a 1
Knolls, UT 66-67 G 5
Knollwood Village, Houston-, TX 85 III b 2
Knonau 128 IV a 2
Knōssós 122-123 L 8
Knowles, OK 76-77 DE 4
Knowles, Cape — 53 B 30-31
Knowltonwood, PA 84 III a 2
Knox 208 H 2
Knox, IN 70-71 G 5
Knox City, TX 76-77 DE 6
Knox Land 53 C 11
Knoxville, IA 70-71 D 5
Knoxville, TN 64-65 K 4
Knuckles 140 E 7
Knud Rasmussen Land 52 B 25-A 21
Knysna 172 D 8
Ko, gora — 132-133 a 8
Koba 152-153 G 7
Kob'aj 132-133 Y 5
Kobakof Bay 58-59 j 4-5
Kobayashi 144-145 H 6-7
Kobbegem 128 II a 1
Kobdo = Chovd 142-143 G 2
Kōbe 142-143 PQ 5
Kobeberge 174-175 C 6
Kobe Mountains = Kobeberge 174-175 C 6
København 116-117 DE 10
Koberivier 174-175 C 6
Kobin 136-137 J 4
Koblenz 118 C 3
Kobo 164-165 MN 6
Koboža [SU, place] 124-125 K 4
Kobra [SU, place] 124-125 S 3
Kobra [SU, river] 124-125 S 4
Kobrin 124-125 E 7
Kobroör, Pulau — 148-149 KL 8
Kobrur = Pulau Kobroör 148-149 KL 8
Kobuk, AK 58-59 J 3
Kobuk River 56-57 E 4
Kobuleti 126-127 K 6
Koca çay [TR ◁ Apolyont gölü] 136-137 C 3
Koca çay [TR ◁ Manyas gölü] 136-137 B 3
Koca çay [TR ◁ Mediterranean Sea] 136-137 C 4
Kocaeli 136-137 CD 2
Koca ırmak 136-137 E 2
Kočani 122-123 K 5
Kocapinar = Ömerin 136-137 JK 4
Koçarlı 136-137 B 4
Kocatas tepe 154 I b 1-2
Kočečum 132-133 ST 4
Kočen'ga 124-125 O 3
Kočetovka 124-125 N 7
Kočevje 122-123 F 3
Kočevo 124-125 TU 4
Ko Chan 150-151 AB 8
Kochana = Kočani 122-123 K 5
Kŏch'ang 144-145 F 5
Ko Chang [T, Andaman Sea] 150-151 B 8
Ko Chang [T, Gulf of Thailand] 148-149 D 4
Kochanovo 124-125 GH 6
Koch Bihār = Cooch Behār 138-139 M 4
Kochchi-Kaṇayannūr = Cochin 134-135 M 9
Kōchi 142-143 P 5
Kochig = Khiching 138-139 K 7
Kŏchiṅgā = Khiching 138-139 K 7
Koch Island 56-57 V 4
Ko-chiu = Gejiu 142-143 J 7
Kochma 124-125 N 5
Kochow = Maoming 142-143 L 7
Koch Peak 66-67 H 3
Kochtel = Kohtla 132-133 D 6
Kočki 132-133 P 7
Kočkoma 124-125 JK 1-2
Kočubej 126-127 N 4
Koḍagu = Coorg 140 BC 4
Kodaikānal 140 C 5
Kōḍaṅgala = Korangal 140 C 2
Kōdangauk 141 C 5
Kodār 140 DE 2
Kodarma 138-139 K 5
Koddiyar Bay = Koḍḍiyār Warāya 140 E 6
Koḍḍiyār Warāya 140 E 6
Kodiak, AK 56-57 F 6
Kodiak Island 56-57 F 6
Koḍikāmam 140 E 6
Kōdikkarai Antarīp = Point Calimere 134-135 MN 8
Kodima 124-125 O 2
Kodinār 138-139 C 7
Kodino 132-133 F 5
Kōdit Taung 141 D 6
Kodiyakkarai 140 DE 5
Kodŏk = Kŭdŭk 164-165 L 6-7
Kodomari-misaki 144-145 MN 2
Kodori 126-127 K 5
Kodorskij, pereval — 126-127 MN 5
Kodorskij chrebet 126-127 KL 5
Kodumūru 140 C 3
Kodyma [SU, river] 126-127 E 3
Koeberg 174-175 C 5
Koegas 174-175 E 5
Koegrabie 174-175 D 5
Koekenaap 174-175 C 6
Koel 138-139 J 5
Koel, North — = Koel 138-139 J 5
Koel, South — 138-139 K 6
Kōenji, Tōkyō- 155 III ab 1
Koes 172 C 7
Koesan 144-145 FG 4
Koettlitz Glacier 53 B 15-16
Kofa Mountains 74-75 FG 6
Koffiefontein 174-175 F 5
Kofiau, Pulau — 148-149 JK 7
Koforidua 164-165 DE 7
Kofouno 168-169 F 2
Kōfu 142-143 Q 4
Koga 144-145 M 4
Kogane-saki = Henashi-saki 144-145 M 2
Kogarah, Sydney- 161 I a 2
Kogarah Bay 161 I a 2-3
Køge 116-117 DE 10
Kŏgen-dō = Kangwŏn-do 144-145 F 3-G 4
Kogil'nik 126-127 D 3
Kogoluktuk River 58-59 J 3
Kogon 168-169 B 3
Kogoni 168-169 D 2
Kogota 144-145 N 3
Kogrukluk River 58-59 H 6
Kŏgŭm-do 144-145 F 5
Kogunsan-kundo 144-145 EF 5
Ko Hai 150-151 B 9
Kohāṭ 134-135 L 4
Kohe Ḥiṣār 134-135 K 4
Kohīma 134-135 P 5
Kohistān Sulaimān 134-135 KL 4-5
Koh Kīrthar 134-135 K 5
Koh Kong 148-149 D 4
Koh Lakḥī 138-139 A 4-5
Köhlbrand 130 I a 1
Kohler Range 53 B 25
Kohlū 138-139 B 3
Kōhoku, Yokohama- 155 III a 2
Kohtla-Järve 132-133 D 6
Kōhu = Kōfu 142-143 Q 4
Koichab 174-175 AB 4
Koichabpan 174-175 A 4
Koide 144-145 M 4
Koil, Dakshiṇī — = South Koel 138-139 K 6
Koil, Uttarī — = Koel 138-139 J 5
Koilkuntla 140 D 3
Kōisanjaq = Kūysanjaq 136-137 L 4
Koishikawa, Tōkyō- 155 III b 1
Koitere 116-117 O 6
Koivisto = ostrov Boľšoj Ber'ozovyj 124-125 FG 3
Koivisto = Primorsk 124-125 G 3
Koiwa, Tōkyō- 155 III c 1
Koja, Jakarta- 154 IV b 1
Kojdanov = Dzeržinsk 124-125 F 7
Kŏje 144-145 G 5
Kŏje-do 144-145 G 5
Kojgorodok 132-133 HJ 5
Kojp, gora — 124-125 W 2
Kojsug 126-127 JK 3
Kok, Nam — 150-151 B 2-3
Kŏkai = Kanggye 142-143 O 3
Kŏkai-hokudō = Hwanghae-pukto 144-145 EF 3
Kŏkai-nandō = Hwanghae-namdo 144-145 E 3-4
Kokand 134-135 L 2-3
Kokanee Glacier Provincial Park 66-67 E 1
Kokaral, ostrov — 132-133 L 8
Kokatha 160 B 3
Kokčetav 132-133 MN 7
Kŏk-dong = Irhyang-dong 144-145 GH 2
Kokechik Bay 58-59 D 6
Kokemäenjoki 116-117 JK 7
Ko Kha 150-151 B 3
Ko Khram Yai 150-151 C 5
Koki 168-169 AB 2
Kokiu = Gejiu 142-143 J 7
Kok-Jangak 134-135 L 2
Kokkaniseri = Kokkānisseri 140 B 4
Kokkānisseri 140 B 4
Kokkola 116-117 K 6
Ko Klang 150-151 AB 8
Koknese 124-125 E 5
Koko 168-169 G 3
Kokoda 148-149 N 8
Kŏkō Kyūn 148-149 B 4
Kokolik River 58-59 G 2
Kokomo, IN 64-65 JK 3
Kokonau 148-149 L 7
Koko Noor = Chŏch nuur 142-143 H 4
Koko Nor = Chŏch nuur 142-143 H 4
Kokonselkä 116-117 N 7
Kokorevka 124-125 K 7
Kokos, Pulau-pulau — 152-153 A 4
Koko Shili = Chŏch Šili uul 142-143 FG 4
Kokpekty 132-133 P 8
Kokrines, AK 58-59 K 4
Kokrines Hills 58-59 KL 4
Kokšaal-Tau, chrebet — 134-135 M 2
Koksan 144-145 F 5
Koks Bāzār 134-135 P 6
Kokšen'ga 124-125 O 3
Kŏk shal 142-143 D 3
Koksoak River 56-57 X 6
Koksŏng 144-145 F 5
Koksovyj 126-127 K 2
Kokstad 174-175 H 6
Kŏk Tappa = Gŭk Tappah 136-137 L 5
Kokubo = Kokubu 144-145 H 7
Kokubu 144-145 H 7
Ko Kut 148-149 D 4
Kokwok River 58-59 HJ 7
Kōl = Aligarh 134-135 M 5
Kola [SU, place] 132-133 E 4
Kola [SU, river] 116-117 P 3
Kola, Pulau — 148-149 KL 8
Kolachel 140 C 6
Kolachil = Kolachel 140 C 6
Ko Ladang 150-151 B 9
Kolahun 168-169 C 3
Kolaka 148-149 H 7
Koḷamba 134-135 MN 9
Ko Lamphuk, Laem — = Laem Talumphuk 150-151 C 8
Ko Lan 150-151 C 6
Kolan = Kelan 146-147 C 2
Kolanjin = Kulanjīn 136-137 N 5
Ko Lanta 150-151 B 9
Kōlāpura = Kolhāpur 140 D 2
Kolār 134-135 M 8
Kolāras 138-139 F 5
Kolār Gold Fields 134-135 M 8
Kolari 116-117 KL 4
Kōlāru = Kolār 134-135 M 8
Kolašin 122-123 H 4
Ko Latang = Ko Ladang 150-151 B 9
Kolāyat 138-139 D 4
Kolbio 172 H 2
Kolbuszowa 118 KL 3
Koľčugino 124-125 MN 5
Koľčugino = Leninsk-Kuzneckij 132-133 Q 6-7
Kolda 164-165 B 6
Kolding 116-117 C 10
Kole 172 D 2
Koléa = Al-Qulʻah 166-167 H 1
Kolebira 138-139 K 6
Kolepom, Pulau — 148-149 L 8
Koležma 124-125 KL 1
Kolgaon = Colgong 138-139 L 5
Kolguev Island = ostrov Kolgujev 132-133 GH 4
Kolgujev, ostrov — 132-133 GH 4
Kolhān 138-139 KL 6
Kolhāpur [IND, Andhra Pradesh] 140 D 2
Kolhāpur [IND, Mahārāshtra] 134-135 L 7
Koli 116-117 N 6
Ko Libong 150-151 B 9
Koliganek, AK 58-59 J 7
Kolín 118 G 3-4
Kolka 124-125 D 5
Kolkasrags 124-125 D 5
Kolki 126-127 B 1
Kollam = Quilon 134-135 M 9
Kollangod 140 C 5
Kollankōḍ = Kollangod 140 C 5
Kollegāl 140 C 4
Kolleru Lake 140 E 2
Koll-e Semnan 134-135 GH 3
Kolliṭam = Coleroon 140 D 5
Kollumúli 116-117 fg 2
Kolmanskop 174-175 A 4
Köln 118 C 3
Kolno 118 K 2
Koło 118 J 2
Koloa, HI 78-79 c 2
Kolobovo 124-125 N 5
Kołobrzeg 118 GH 1
Kolodn'a 124-125 HJ 6
Kologriv 132-133 G 6
Kolokani 164-165 C 6
Kolombangara 148-149 j 6
Kolombo = Koḷamba 134-135 MN 9
Kolomenskoje, Moskva- 113 V c 3
Kolomna 124-125 LM 6
Kolomyja 126-127 B 2
Kolondiéba 168-169 D 3
Kolonie Buch, Berlin- 130 III b 1
Kolonie Lerchenau, München- 130 II b 1
Kolonie Neuhönow 130 III cd 1
Kolonodale 148-149 H 7
Kolosib 141 C 3
Kolosovka 132-133 N 6
Kolossia 171 CD 2
Kolp' [SU ◁ Suda] 124-125 K 4
Kolpaševo 132-133 P 6
Kolpino 124-125 H 4
Kolpny 124-125 L 7
Kólpos Akrōtēríu 136-137 E 5
Kólpos Ammochōstu 136-137 EF 5
Kólpos Chaniṓn 122-123 KL 8
Kólpos Chrysochûs 136-137 E 5
Kólpos Episkopḗs 136-137 E 5
Kólpos Mirampéllu 122-123 LM 8
Kólpos Mórfu 136-137 E 5
Kólpos Orfánu 122-123 KL 5
Kólpos Petaliṓn 122-123 L 7
Kolpūr 138-139 A 3
Koľskij poluostrov 132-133 EF 4
Koltubanovskij 124-125 T 7
Koluel Kayke 108-109 EF 6
Kolufuri 176 a 2
Kölük 136-137 H 4
Kolumadulu Channel 176 a 2
Kolva 124-125 V 3
Kolwezi 172 DE 4
Kolyma 132-133 de 4
Kolymskaja nizmennosť 132-133 de 4
Kolymskoje nagorje 132-133 e 4-f 5
Kolyšlej 124-125 P 7
Kom 122-123 K 4
Komadugu Gana 164-165 G 6
Komadugu Yobe 164-165 G 6
Komae 155 III a 2
Komaga-dake 144-145 b 2
Komagane 144-145 LM 5
Komaga take 144-145 M 4
Komaggasberge 174-175 B 5-6
Komaggas Mountains = Komaggasberge 174-175 B 5-6
Komagome, Tōkyō- 155 III b 1
K'o-mai = Kemä 142-143 H 6
Ko Mak [T, Gulf of Thailand] 150-151 D 7
Ko Mak [T, Thale Luang] 150-151 C 9
Komandorskije ostrova 132-133 f 6-g 7
Komarin 124-125 H 8
Komarno [SU] 126-127 AB 2
Komárom 118 J 5
Komarovo [SU, Archangeľskaja Oblasť] 124-125 Q 3
Komarovo [SU, Kirovskaja Oblasť] 124-125 RS 4
Komarovo [SU, Novgorodskaja Oblasť] 124-125 JK 4
Komati 174-175 J 3-4
Komatipoort 172 F 7
Komatsu 144-145 L 4
Komatsugawa, Tōkyō- 155 III c 1
Komatsujima = Komatsushima 144-145 K 5-6
Komatsushima 144-145 K 5-6
Komazawa Ground 155 III a 2
Komba, Pulau — 152-153 P 9
Kombe, Katako- 172 D 2
Kombissiguiri 168-169 E 2
Kombol = Kompot 148-149 H 6
Kombolcha = Kembolcha 164-165 MN 6
Komchai Meas 150-151 E 7
Kome [EAT] 171 C 3
Kome [EAU] 171 C 3
Kome [RB] 174-175 E 3
Komga 174-175 GH 7
Komgha = Komga 174-175 GH 7
Komi Autonomous Soviet Socialist Republic 132-133 JK 5
Komi Avtonomnaja Sovetskaja Socialističeskaja Respublika = Komi Autonomous Soviet Socialist Republic 132-133 JK 5
Komillā 134-135 P 6
Kōminā = Kumund 138-139 J 7
Komine 168-169 H 4
Komintern = Marganec 126-127 G 3
Komintern = Novošachtinsk 126-127 J 3
Kominternovskij, Kirov- 124-125 RS 4
Kominternovskoje 126-127 E 3
Komi-Permyak Autonomous Area = 1 ◁ 132-133 J 6
Kommadagga 174-175 F 7
Kommunarsk 126-127 J 2
Kommunizma, pik — 134-135 L 3
Komodo, Pulau — 148-149 G 8
Komodougou 168-169 C 3
Komoe 164-165 D 7
Kôm Ombô = Kawm Umbū 164-165 L 4
Komono 172 B 2
Komoran, Pulau — 148-149 L 8
Komoro 144-145 M 4
Komotēnē 122-123 L 5
Kompasberg 174-175 F 6
Kompong Bang 150-151 E 6
Kompong Cham 148-149 E 4
Kompong Chhnang 148-149 D 4
Kompong Chikreng 150-151 E 6
Kompong Chrey 150-151 E 7

Kompong 313

Kompong Kdey = Phum Kompong Kdey 150-151 E 6
Kompong Kleang 148-149 DE 4
Kompong Prasath 150-151 E 6
Kompong Râu 150-151 EF 7
Kompong Som 148-149 D 4
Kompong Som, Sremot — 150-151 D 7
Kompong Speu 148-149 D 4
Kompong Sralao 150-151 E 5
Kompong Taches 150-151 E 6
Kompong Thmâr 150-151 E 6
Kompong Thom 148-149 DE 4
Kompong Trabek [K. Kompong Thom] 150-151 E 6
Kompong Trabek [K. Prey Veng] 150-151 E 7
Kompong Trach [K. Kampot] 150-151 E 7
Kompong Trach [K. Svay Rieng] 150-151 E 7
Kompot 148-149 H 6
Komrat 126-127 D 3
Komsa 132-133 Q 5
Komsberg 174-175 D 7
Komsberge 174-175 D 7
Komsomolec 132-133 L 7
Komsomolec = Džambul 126-127 P 3
Komsomolec, ostrov — 132-133 P-R 1
Komsomolec, zaliv — 134-135 G 1
Komsomolets = ostrov Komsomolec 132-133 P-R 2
Komsomol'sklvanovo 124-125 N 5
Komsomol'skij [SU, Kalmyckaja ASSR] 126-127 N 4
Komsomol'skij [SU, Neneckij NO] 132-133 KL 4
Komsomol'sk-na-Amure 132-133 a 7
Komsomol'skoje [SU, Rossijskaja SFSR] 126-127 N 1
Komsomol'skoje [SU, Ukrainskaja SSR] 126-127 HJ 3
Komsomol'skoj Pravdy, ostrova — 132-133 U-W 2
Ko Muk 150-151 B 9
Kōmun-do 144-145 F 5
Komusan 144-145 G 1
Kon 138-139 J 5
Kona 164-165 D 6
Kona, Howrah- 154 II a 2
Konagkend 126-127 O 6
Konakovo 124-125 L 5
Konārak 138-139 L 8
Konawa, OK 76-77 F 5
Konaweha, Sungai — 152-153 O 7-8
Konch 138-139 G 4-5
Koncha = Kontcha 164-165 G 7
Konche darya 142-143 F 3
Konda 132-133 M 6
Koṇḍāgāṅv = Kondagaon 138-139 H 8
Kondagaon 138-139 H 8
Kondalwādi 140 C 1
Kondapalle 140 E 2
Koṇḍapalli = Kondapalle 140 E 2
Kondhāli 138-139 G 7
Kondiaronk, Lac — 72-73 H 1
Kondinskoje = Okt'abr'skoje 132-133 M 5
Kondirskoje 132-133 M 6
Kondoa 172 G 2
Kondolole 172 E 1
Kondopoga 132-133 EF 5
Kondostrov 124-125 L 1
Kondurča 124-125 S 6
Koné 158-159 M 4
Konec-Kovdozero 116-117 O 4
Koness River 58-59 P 2
Konevo 124-125 M 2
Kong 168-169 D 3
Kong, Kâs — 150-151 D 7
Kong, Mae Nam — 148-149 D 3
Kong, Mé — 148-149 E 4
Kong, Nam — 150-151 F 5
Kong, Sé — [K] 150-151 F 5-6
Kong, Se — [LAO] 150-151 F 5
Kongakut River 58-59 QR 2
Kongcheng 146-147 F 6
Kong Christian den IX[s] Land 56-57 de 4
Kong Christian den X[s] Land 52 B 21-22
Kong Frederik den VIII[s] Land 52 B 21
Kong Frederik den VI[s] Kyst 56-57 c 5
Kongga Zong = Gongkar Dsong 138-139 N 3
Konghow = Jiangkou 146-147 C 10
Kongju 144-145 F 4
Kong Karls land 116-117 mn 5
Kongkemul, Gunung — 152-153 M 5
Kong Leopold og Dronning Astrid land 53 BC 9
Kongmoon = Xinhui 146-147 D 10
Kongolo 172 E 3
Kongōr 164-165 L 7
Kongoussi 168-169 E 2
Kongpo 142-143 G 6
Kongsberg 116-117 C 8
Kongsøya 116-117 n 5
Kongsvinger 116-117 DE 7
Kongwa 172 G 3
Kongyu Tsho 138-139 HJ 2
Kōnha-dong 144-145 F 2
Koni, poluostrov — 132-133 d 6
Konia 168-169 C 3-4
Konin 118 J 2
Koning 174-175 E 4
Konjic 122-123 GH 4
Könkämä älv 116-117 J 3
Konkan 140 A 1-3
Konken = Khon Kaen 148-149 D 3
Konkiep = Goageb 172 C 7
Konkobiri 168-169 F 3
Konkouré 168-169 B 3
Konna = Kona 164-165 D 6
Konnagar 154 II b 1
Kōnodai, Ichikawa- 155 III c 1
Konongo 168-169 E 4
Konoša 132-133 G 5
Konotop 126-127 F 1
Konpāra 138-139 J 6
Kon Plong 150-151 G 5
Konradshöhe, Berlin- 130 III a 1
Konstabel 174-175 CD 7
Konstantinograd = Krasnograd 126-127 G 2
Konstantinovka 126-127 H 2
Konstantinovsk 126-127 K 3
Konstantinovskij [SU, Moskovskaja Oblast'] 124-125 MN 5
Konstanz 118 D 5
Konta 140 E 2
Kontagora 164-165 F 6
Kontcha 164-165 G 7
Kontiomäki 116-117 N 5
Kon Tom 150-151 F 4
Kontrashibuna Lake 58-59 KL 6
Kontum 148-149 E 4
Konur = Sulakyurt 136-137 E 2
Konya 134-135 C 3
Konya ovası 136-137 E 4
Konyševka 124-125 K 8
Konza 171 D 3
Koog aan de Zaan, Zaanstad- 128 I a 1
Kooigoedvlaktes 174-175 C 6
Kookhuis 174-175 FG 7
Kookynie 158-159 D 5
Koolau Range 78-79 cd 2
Kooloonong 160 F 5
Koonap 174-175 G 7
Koonibba 160 AB 3
Koopmansfontein 174-175 EF 5
Koorawatha 160 J 5
Koosharem, UT 74-75 H 3
Kootenai = Kootenay 56-57 N 8
Kootenai Falls 66-67 F 1
Kootenai River 64-65 C 2
Kootenay 56-57 N 8
Kootenay Lake 60 J 4-5
Kootenay National Park 60 J 4
Kootenay River 66-67 E 1
Kootjieskolk 174-175 D 6
Kopaonik 122-123 J 4
Kōpargāṅv = Kopargaon 138-139 E 8
Kopargaon 138-139 E 8
Kópasker 116-117 ef 1
Kopatkeviči 124-125 G 7
Kópavogur 116-117 bc 2
Kopejsk 132-133 L 6-7
Koper 122-123 EF 3
Kopervik 116-117 A 8
Kopeysk = Kopejsk 132-133 L 6-7
Ko Phai 150-151 C 6
Ko Phangan 148-149 CD 5
Ko Phayam 150-151 B 8
Ko Phra Thong 150-151 AB 8
Ko Phuket 148-149 C 5
Köping 116-117 FG 8
Koporje 124-125 G 4
Koppa 140 B 4
Koppal 140 C 3
Koppang 116-117 D 7
Kopparberg 116-117 EF 7
Koppeh Dāgh 134-135 HJ 3
Kopperå 116-117 D 6
Koppies 174-175 G 4
Koprivnica 122-123 G 2
Köprürmağı 136-137 D 4
Köprülü = Tito Veles 122-123 JK 5
Ko Pu 150-151 B 9
Kopyčincy 126-127 B 2
Kopyl' 124-125 F 7
Kopys' 124-125 H 6
Kora 138-139 L 5
Koraa, Djebel el — = Jabal al-Kurā' 166-167 J 6
Korab 122-123 J 5
Korahe 164-165 NO 7
Koraka burnu 136-137 B 3
Kor'akskaja sopka = Velikaja Kor'akskaja sopka 132-133 ef 7
Kor'akskoje nagorje 132-133 j-f 5
Koram = Korem 164-165 M 6
Korangal 140 C 2
Korannaberge 174-175 E 4
Korapun 148-149 h 6
Koraput 140 F 1
Korarou, Lac — 164-165 D 5
Korat = Nakhon Ratchasima 148-149 D 3-4
Koratagere 140 C 4
Koratalā = Koratla 140 D 1
Koratla 140 D 1
Ko Rawi 150-151 B 9
Kor'ažma 124-125 Q 3
Korba 138-139 J 6
Korba = Qurbah 166-167 M 1
Korbiyāy, Jabal — 173 D 6
Korbous = Qurbūş 166-167 M 1
Korbu, Gunung — 148-149 D 5-6
Korçë 122-123 J 5
Korčino 132-133 P 7
Korčula 122-123 G 4
Kordestān 134-135 F 3
Kordofān = Kurdufān al-Janūbīyah 164-165 KL 6
Korea Bay = Sōhan-man 142-143 NO 4
Korea Strait = Chōsen-kaikyō 142-143 O 4-5
Korec 126-127 C 1
Kōrēgāṅv = Koregaon 140 B 2
Koregaon 140 B 2
Korein = Al-Kuwayt 134-135 F 5
Korem 164-165 M 6
Korenevo 126-127 G 1
Korenovsk 126-127 J 4
Koret 172 D 1
Korf 132-133 g 5
Korgu = Coorg 140 BC 4
Kōṛhā = Kora 138-139 L 5
Korhogo 164-165 C 7
Kori Creek 138-139 B 6
Korienzé 168-169 E 2
Kōrī Khāḍī = Kori Creek 138-139 B 6
Korima, Ouèd el — = Wādī al-Karīmah 166-167 F 3
Korinthiakòs Kólpos 122-123 JK 6
Kórinthos 122-123 K 7
Kori Nullah = Kori Creek 138-139 B 6
Kōrishegy 118 HJ 5
Kōriyama 142-143 QR 4
Korkino 132-133 L 7
Korkodon 132-133 de 5
Korkuteli 136-137 D 4
Korla 142-143 F 3
Korma 124-125 H 7
Kormack 62 K 3
Kormakitēs, Akrōtērion — 136-137 E 5
Kornat 122-123 F 4
Kornetspruit 174-175 G 5-6
Kornouchovo 124-125 RS 6
Kornsjø 116-117 DE 8
Koro [CI] 168-169 D 3
Koro [FJI] 148-149 a 2
Koro [HV] 168-169 E 2
Koroča 126-127 H 1
Köroğlu tepesi 136-137 DE 2
Korogwe 172 G 3
Koromo = Toyota 144-145 L 5
Korōneia, Límnē — 122-123 K 5
Korong Vale 160 F 6
Korop 126-127 F 1
Koror 148-149 KL 5
Körös 118 K 5
Koro Sea 148-149 ab 2
Korosko = Wādī Kuruskū 173 C 6
Korosten' 126-127 D 1
Korostyšev 126-127 D 1
Korotojak 126-127 J 1
Koro-Toro 164-165 H 5
Korotovo 124-125 L 4
Korovin Island 58-59 cd 2
Korovino 126-127 H 1
Korovinski, AK 58-59 j 4
Korovin Volcano 58-59 jk 4
Korowelang, Tanjung — 152-153 H 9
Korpilombolo 116-117 JK 4
Korppoo 116-117 JK 7
Korsakov 132-133 b 8
Korsakovo 124-125 L 7
Korsør 116-117 D 10
Kōrṭagērē = Koratagere 140 C 4
Kortenberg 128 II b 1
Kōrtī = Kūrtī 164-165 L 5
Korneros 124-125 ST 3
Kortrijk 120-121 J 3
Kor'ukovka 124-125 J 8
Korumburra 160 GH 7
Korvā = Korba 138-139 J 6
Korvala 124-125 K 3
Korwai 138-139 FG 5
Koryak Autonomous Area 132-133 g 5-e 6
Korydallós 113 IV a 2
Kōs [GR, island] 122-123 M 7
Kōs [GR, place] 122-123 M 7
Kosa [SU, place] 124-125 U 4
Kosa [SU, river] 124-125 U 4
kosa Arabatskaja Strelka 126-127 G 3-4
kosa Fedotova 126-127 G 3
Koš-Agač 132-133 Q 7-8
Kosaja Gora 124-125 L 6
Kosaka 144-145 N 2
Kō-saki 144-145 G 5
Ko Samae San 150-151 C 6
Ko Samaesan = Ko Samae San 150-151 C 6
Ko Samet 150-151 C 6
Ko Samui 148-149 D 5
Košary 126-127 F 1
Koščagyl 134-135 G 1
Koscian 118 H 2
Kościerzyna 118 HJ 1
Kosciusko, MS 78-79 E 4
Kosciusko, Mount — 158-159 J 7
Kosciusko Island 58-59 vw 9
Köse 136-137 H 2
Köse dağı 136-137 GH 2
Kosgi 140 C 2
Ko-shan = Keshan 142-143 O 2
Koshigi = Kosgi 140 C 2
Koshigi = Kosigi 140 C 3
K'o-shih = Qāshqār 142-143 CD 4
Koshiki-rettō 144-145 G 7
Kōshū = Kwangju 142-143 O 4
Kōsī = Aruṇ 134-135 O 5
Kōsī = Sapt Kosi 134-135 O 5
Kōsī, Dudh — 138-139 L 4
Kosi, Lake — = Kosimeer 174-175 K 4
Kōsī, Sūn — 134-135 O 5
Kōsī, Tambā — 138-139 L 4
Kosibaai 174-175 K 4
Košice 118 K 4
Ko Sichang 150-151 C 6
Kosigi 140 C 3
Kosimeer 174-175 K 4
Kosino [SU, Kirovskaja Oblast'] 124-125 S 4
Kosino [SU, Moskovskaja Oblast'] 113 V d 3
Kosi Reservoir 138-139 L 4
Kosju 132-133 KL 4
Koški [SU] 132-133 M 3
Kos'kovo 124-125 J 3
Koslan 132-133 H 5
Kosmos, WA 66-67 BC 2
Kosmynino 124-125 N 5
Koso Gol = Chövsgöl nuur 142-143 J 1
Kosŏng [North Korea] 142-143 O 4
Kŏsŏng [ROK] 144-145 G 5
Kosŏng-ni 144-145 F 6
Kosov 126-127 B 2
Kosovo 122-123 J 4
Kosovo polje 122-123 J 4
Kosovska Mitrovica 122-123 J 4
Kosse, TX 76-77 F 7
Kossou 168-169 D 4
Kossovo 124-125 E 7
Koster 174-175 G 3
Kōsti = Kūstī 164-165 L 6
Kostino [SU ↓ Igarka] 132-133 Q 4
Kostopol' 126-127 C 1
Kostroma [SU, place] 132-133 G 6
Kostroma [SU, river] 124-125 N 4
Kostrzyn 118 G 2
Kost'ukoviči 124-125 HJ 7
Kosugi, Kawasaki- 155 III ab 2
Ko Sukon 150-151 B 9
Kosum Phisai 150-151 D 4
Kos'va 124-125 V 4
Koszalin 118 H 1
Kőszeg 118 H 5
Kota [IND] 134-135 M 5
Kota [MAL] 150-151 C 10
Kotaagung 148-149 D 8
Kota Baharu 148-149 D 5
Kotabaru 148-149 G 7
Kotabaru = Jayapura 148-149 M 7
Kota Belud 148-149 G 5
Kotabumi 148-149 DE 7
Koṭ Addū 138-139 C 2
Kotah = Kota 134-135 M 5
Kot'ajevka 126-127 O 3
Kota Kinabalu 148-149 FG 5
Kota Kota 172 F 4
Kotal Bolān 134-135 K 5
Kotal Khāibar 134-135 L 4
Ko Ta Luang 150-151 B 8
Koṭal Wākhjīr 134-135 LM 3
Kotamobagu 148-149 HJ 6
Ko Tao 150-151 BC 7
Kotapāt 138-139 J 8
Kotatengah 148-149 D 6
Kotawaringin 152-153 JK 7
Koṭchāndpūr 138-139 M 6
Koṭ Chuṭṭa 138-139 C 3
Koṭ Dījī 138-139 B 4
Kōṭdvārā = Kotdwāra 138-139 G 3
Kotdwāra 138-139 G 3
Kotel 122-123 M 4
Koteľnič 132-133 H 6
Koteľnikovo 126-127 L 3
Koteľnyj, ostrov — 132-133 Za 2-3
Koteľva 126-127 G 1
Ko Terutao 148-149 C 5
Kothi 138-139 H 5
Kothráki = Kythréa 136-137 E 5
Kotido 172 F 1
Koṭ Imāmgaṛh 138-139 B 4
Kotjeskolk = Kootjieskolk 174-175 D 6
Kotka 116-117 M 7
Kot Kapūra 138-139 E 2
Kot Kāsim 138-139 F 3
Kotkhāi 138-139 F 2
Kotla 138-139 F 1
Kotl'arevskaja = Majskij 126-127 M 5
Kotlas 132-133 H 5
Kotlik, AK 58-59 F 5
Kotlovan 124-125 K 4
Kōto, Tōkyō- 155 III b 1
Kotolnoi Island = Koteľnyj ostrov 132-133 Za 2
Kotooka 144-145 N 2
Kotor 122-123 H 4
Kotor Varoš 122-123 G 3
Kotovo [SU, Saratovskaja Oblast'] 126-127 M 1
Kotovsk [SU, Rossijskaja SFSR] 124-125 N 7
Kotovsk [SU, Ukrainskaja SSR] 126-127 D 3
Kotowana Watobo, Teluk — 152-153 P 9
Kot Pūtli 138-139 F 4
Kotra 138-139 D 5
Kot Rādha Kishan 138-139 DE 2
Kotri [IND, place] 138-139 E 5
Kotri [IND, river] 138-139 H 8
Koṭrī [PAK] 134-135 K 5
Koṭ Rum 138-139 BC 3
Koṭ Samāba 138-139 C 3
Kotta = Kotla 138-139 F 1
Kottagūdem 134-135 N 7
Kottai Malai 140 C 6
Kōṭṭapaṭṭaṇam = Allūru Kottapatnam 140 E 3
Kottārakara 140 C 6
Kottātukuḷam = Kuttāttukulam 140 C 6
Koṭṭayādi = Kuttyādi 140 B 5
Kottayam 140 C 6
Kotte 140 DE 7
Kotto 164-165 J 7
Kottūru 140 BC 3
Kotuj 132-133 T 3
Kotujkan 132-133 U 3
Kotum 136-137 K 3
Kotzebue, AK 56-57 D 4
Kotzebue Sound 56-57 CD 4
Kouango 164-165 HJ 7
Kouara Débé 168-169 F 2
Kouba 164-165 H 5
Kouba, Al-Jazā'ir- 170 I ab 2
Kouchibouguac National Park 63 D 4
Koudougou 164-165 D 6
Kouéré 168-169 E 3
Koueveldberge 174-175 EF 7
Koufra, Oasis de — = Wāḥāt al-Kufrah 164-165 J 4
Kougaberge 174-175 EF 7
Kougarivier 174-175 F 7
Kougarok Mount 58-59 E 4
Kouilou 172 B 2
Koukdjuak River 56-57 W 4
Koula-Moutou 172 B 2
Koulen 148-149 DE 4
Koulikoro 164-165 C 6
Koumantou 168-169 D 3
Koumass = Kumasi 164-165 D 7
Koumbia 168-169 E 3
Koumra 164-165 H 7
Koundian 168-169 C 2
Koun-Fao 168-169 E 4
Koungheul 164-165 B 6
Kouniana 168-169 D 2
Kounradskij 132-133 O 8
Kountze, TX 76-77 G 7
Kouoro 168-169 D 3
Koup 174-175 D 7
Koup, Die — 174-175 E 7
Kou-pang-tzŭ = Goubangzi 144-145 CD 2
Koupéla 164-165 D 6
Kourba = Qurbah 166-167 M 1
Kourou 92-93 J 3
Kourouninkoto 168-169 C 2
Kouroussa 164-165 BC 6
Koutiala 164-165 C 6
Kouveld Berge = Koueveldberge 174-175 EF 7
Kouvola 116-117 M 7
Kouyou 172 BC 2
Kovdor 132-133 DE 4
Kovdozero 116-117 OP 4
Koveľ 124-125 E 8
Kovero 116-117 O 6
Kovik 56-57 V 5
Kovilpatti 140 C 6
Kovľar 126-127 M 6
Kovno = Kaunas 124-125 DE 6
Kovpyta 126-127 E 1
Kovrov 132-133 G 6
Kovūr 140 DE 3
Kovvūr 140 E 2
Kōvvūru = Kovūr 140 DE 3
Kovylkino 124-125 O 6
Kovža [SU, place] 124-125 L 3
Kovža [SU, river] 124-125 L 3
Kovžinskij Zavod 124-125 L 3
Kowas 174-175 BC 2
Kowloon 142-143 LM 7
Kowloon Bay 155 I b 2
Kowloon-Chung Wan 155 I a 1
Kowloon-Hung Hom 155 I b 2
Kowloon-Kau Lung Tong 155 I b 1
Kowloon-Pak Uk 155 I b 1
Kowloon-Sham Shui Po 155 I a 2
Kowloon-Tsim Sha Tsui 155 I a 2
Kowloon-Yau Mai Ti 155 I a 2
Kowŏn 142-143 O 4
Ko Yai 150-151 C 9
Kōyalkuṇṭalā = Koilkuntla 140 D 3
Koyama, Tōkyō- 155 III b 2
Kōyampattūr = Coimbatore 134-135 M 8
Ko Yao Yai 150-151 B 9
Köyceğiz = Yüksekkum 136-137 C 4
Kōyilpaṭṭi = Kovilpatti 140 C 6
Kōyikōṭa = Calicut 134-135 LM 8
Koyna 140 A 2
Koyuk, AK 58-59 G 4
Koyuk River 58-59 FG 4
Koyukuk, AK 58-59 HJ 4
Koyukuk, Middle Fork — 58-59 M 3
Koyukuk, North Fork — 58-59 M 3
Koyukuk, South Fork — 58-59 M 3
Koyukuk Island 58-59 J 4
Koyukuk River 56-57 EF 4
Koyulhisar 136-137 GH 2
Köyyeri 136-137 G 3
Koža [SU, river] 124-125 M 2
Kozan 136-137 F 4
Kozánē 122-123 J 5
Kozara 122-123 G 3
Kozelec 126-127 E 1
Kozel'ščina 126-127 F 2
Kozel'sk 124-125 K 6
Kozi 171 DE 3
Kožle 118 HJ 3
Kozloduj 122-123 K 4
Kozlovka [SU, Čuvašskaja ASSR] 124-125 QR 6
Kozlovka [SU, Voronežskaja Oblast'] 126-127 K 1
Kozlovo [SU ↘ Kalinin] 124-125 KL 5
Kozlovo [SU → Vyšnij Voloč'ok] 124-125 K 5
Kozluk = Hazo 136-137 J 3
Koz'mino [SU ↗ Kotlas] 124-125 QR 3
Koz'mino [SU ↘ Nachodka] 144-145 J 1
Koz'modemjansk [SU, Jaroslavskaja Oblast'] 124-125 M 5
Koz'modemjansk [SU, Marijskaja ASSR] 124-125 Q 5
Kožozero 124-125 M 2
Kožuchovo, Moskva- 113 V c 3
Kozukue, Yokohama- 155 III a 2
Kōzu-shima 144-145 M 5
Kožva 132-133 K 4
Kpalimé 164-165 E 7
Kpandu 164-165 DE 7
Kra, Isthmus of — = Kho Kot Kra 148-149 CD 4
Kra, Kho Khot — 148-149 CD 4
Kraainem 128 II b 1
Kraairivier 174-175 G 6
Kraankuil 174-175 F 5
Krabbé 106-107 G 6
Krabi 148-149 C 5
Kra Buri 148-149 C 4
Krachar 150-151 DE 6
Kragerø 116-117 C 8
Kragujevac 122-123 J 3
Krai, Kuala — 148-149 D 5
Krailling 130 II a 2
Krakatao = Anak Krakatau 148-149 DE 8
Krakatau, Anak — 148-149 DE 8
Krakor 150-151 DE 6
Kraków 118 JK 3
Kralanh 150-151 D 6
Kralendijk 64-65 N 9
Kraljevo 122-123 J 4
Kramat Jati, Jakarta- 154 IV b 2
Kramatorsk 126-127 H 2
Krambit 150-151 D 10
Kramfors 116-117 G 6
Krampnitz 130 III a 2
Krampnitzsee 130 III a 2
Kranichstein, Darmstadt- 128 III b 2
Kranichstein, Staatsforst — 128 III b 2
Kranídion 122-123 K 7
Kranj 122-123 F 2
Kranji 154 III a 1
Kransfontein 174-175 H 5
Kranskop [ZA, mountain] 174-175 H 4
Kranskop [ZA, place] 174-175 J 5
Kranzberg [Namibia] 174-175 A 1
Krapina 122-123 FG 2
Krapivna [SU, Smolenskaja Oblast'] 124-125 JK 6
Kras 122-123 EF 3
Krasavino 132-133 GH 5
Krasilov 126-127 C 2
Krasilovka 126-127 DE 1
Kraskino 144-145 H 1
Krāslava 124-125 F 6
Krasnaja Gora [SU, Br'anskaja Oblast'] 124-125 HJ 7
Krasnaja Gorbatka 124-125 NO 6
Krasnaja Pol'ana [SU Kirovskaja Oblast'] 124-125 S 5
Krasnaja Pol'ana [SU Krasnodarskaja Oblast'] 126-127 K 5
Krasnaja Sloboda 124-125 F 7
Kraśnik 118 KL 3
Krasnoarmejsk [SU, Kazachskaja SSR] 132-133 MN 7
Krasnoarmejsk [SU, Saratovskaja Oblast'] 126-127 M 1
Krasnoarmejsk, Volgograd- 126-127 M 2
Krasnoarmejskaja 126-127 J 4
Krasnoarmejskij 126-127 L 3
Krasnoarmejskoje = Červonoarmejskoje 126-127 GH 3
Krasnoborsk 124-125 P 3
Krasnodar 126-127 J 4
Krasnodon 126-127 JK 2
Krasnofarfornyj 124-125 HJ 4
Krasnogorodskoje 124-125 G 5
Krasnogorsk 124-125 L 5-6
Krasnogorskij 124-125 R 5
Krasnogorskoje 124-125 T 5
Krasnograd 126-127 G 2
Krasnogvardejsk 134-135 K 3
Krasnogvardejsk = Gatčina 132-133 DE 6
Krasnogvardejskoje [SU, Rossijskaja SFSR Stavropol'skaja Oblast'] 126-127 KL 4
Krasnogvardejskoje [SU, Rossijskaja SFSR Voronežskaja Oblast'] 126-127 HJ 1
Krasnogvardejskoje [SU, Ukrainskaja SSR] 126-127 G 4
Krasnoil's'ke = Mežirečje 126-127 B 2
Krasnoj Armii, proliv — 132-133 ST 1
Krasnojarsk 132-133 R 6
Krasnoje [SU, Rossijskaja SFSR Kirovskaja Oblast'] 124-125 QR 4
Krasnoje [SU, Rossijskaja SFSR Lipeckaja Oblast'] 124-125 M 7
Krasnoje [SU, Rossijskaja SFSR Vologodskaja Oblast'] 124-125 O 4
Krasnoje [SU, Ukrainskaja SSR] 126-127 B 2
Krasnoje Selo 124-125 GH 4
Krasnokamensk 132-133 W 7-8
Krasnokamsk 132-133 K 6
Krasnokutsk 126-127 G 1
Krasnolesnyj 124-125 M 8
Krasnonamenskij 132-133 M 7
Krasnookt'abr'skij [SU, Marijskaja ASSR] 124-125 Q 5
Krasnookt'abr'skij [SU, Volgogradskaja Oblast'] 126-127 M 2
Krasnookt'abrskij, Moskva- 113 V b 2
Krasnopavlovka 126-127 H 2
Krasnoperekopsk 126-127 FG 3-4
Krasnopolje [SU, Belorusskaja SSR] 124-125 H 7
Krasnopolje [SU, Ukrainskaja SSR] 126-127 G 1
Krasnosel'kup 132-133 OP 4
Krasnoslobodsk [SU, Mordovskaja ASSR] 124-125 O 6
Krasnoslobodsk [SU, Volgogradskaja Oblast'] 126-127 M 2
Krasnoturjinsk 132-133 L 5-6
Krasnoufimsk 132-133 K 6
Krasnoural'sk 132-133 L 6
Krasnovišersk 132-133 K 5
Krasnovodsk 134-135 G 2-3
Krasnovodskoje plato 134-135 G 2
Krasnoyarsk = Krasnojarsk 132-133 R 6
Krasnozatonskij 124-125 ST 3
Krasnozavodsk 124-125 LM 5
Krasnyj = Možga 132-133 J 6
Krasnyj Bogatyr' 124-125 N 5
Krasnyj Cholm 124-125 L 4
Krasnyj Čikoj 132-133 UV 7
Krasnyj Dolginec 126-127 P 4
Krasnyje Baki 124-125 P 5
Krasnyje Četai 124-125 Q 6
Krasnyje Okny 126-127 D 3
Krasnyje Tkači 124-125 MN 5
Krasnyj Jar [SU, Astrachanskaja Oblast'] 126-127 NO 3
Krasnyj Jar [SU, Kujbyševskaja Oblast'] 124-125 S 7
Krasnyj Jar [SU, Volgogradskaja Oblast'] 126-127 M 1
Krasnyj Kut 126-127 N 1
Krasnyj Liman 126-127 HJ 2
Krasnyj Luč 126-127 J 2
Krasnyj Okt'abr' [SU, Vladimirskaja Oblast'] 124-125 M 5
Krasnyj Okt'abr' [SU, Volgogradskaja Oblast'] 126-127 M 2
Krasnyj Profintern 124-125 MN 5
Krasnyj Rog 124-125 J 7
Krasnyj Steklovar 124-125 R 5
Krasnyj Stroitel, Moskva- 113 V c 3
Krasnyj Sulin 126-127 K 3
Krasnyj Tekstil'ščik 126-127 M 1
Krasnyj Voschod 124-125 NO 6
Krasnystaw 118 L 3
Kratié 148-149 E 4
Krau 150-151 D 11
Krau, Kuala — 150-151 D 11
Krauchmar 150-151 E 6
Kraulshavn = Nûgssuaq 56-57 YZ 3
Kravanh, Phnom — 150-151 D 6-7
Krawang 148-149 E 8
Krawang, Tanjung — 152-153 G 8
kr'až Čekanovskogo 132-133 XY 3
kr'až Vetrenyj Pojas 124-125 K-M 2
Kreb Chehiba = Karab Shahibīyah 166-167 C 6
Krebs, OK 76-77 G 5
Krebu = Kamparkalns 124-125 D 5
Krečetovo 124-125 M 3
Krečevicy 124-125 HJ 4
Kreefte Bay = Groenriviermond 174-175 B 6
Kreewu kalns = Krievu kalns 124-125 CD 5
Krefeld 118 BC 3
Kreider = Al-Khaydar 166-167 G 2
Krekatok Island 58-59 D 5
Kremenčug 126-127 F 2
Kremenčugskoje vodochranilišče 126-127 EF 2
Kremenec 126-127 BC 1
Kreml' 113 V c 2
Kremlin-Bicêtre 129 I c 2
Kremmling, CO 68-69 C 5
Kremnica 118 J 4
Krems 118 G 4
Krenachich, El — = El Khenachich 164-165 D 4
Krenachich, Oglat — = Oglat Khenachich 164-165 D 4
Krênê = Çeşme 136-137 B 3
Krenitzin Islands 58-59 no 3
Kress, TX 76-77 D 5
Kresta, zaliv — 132-133 k 4
Krestcy 124-125 HJ 4
Krestovaja guba 132-133 H-K 3
Krestovyj, pereval — 126-127 M 5
Kresty [SU, Moskovskaja Oblast'] 124-125 L 6
Krêtê 122-123 L 8
Kretinga 124-125 C 6
Kreuzberg, Berlin- 130 III b 2
Kribi 164-165 F 8
Kričev 124-125 H 7
KXVIII Ridge 50-51 O 7
Kriel 174-175 H 4
Krieng 150-151 F 6
Krievu kalns 124-125 CD 5
Krige 174-175 C 8
Kriós, Akrōtērion — 122-123 K 8
Krishna 134-135 M 7
Krishna Delta 134-135 N 7
Krishnagiri 140 D 4
Krishnanagar 138-139 M 6
Krishnapur 138-139 M 5
Krishnarāja Sāgara 140 BC 4
Krishnarjapet 140 C 4
Kristiansand 116-117 BC 8
Kristianstad 116-117 F 9-10
Kristianstads län 116-117 E 9-F 10
Kristiansund 116-117 B 6
Kristiinankaupunki = Kristinestad 116-117 J 6
Kristineberg 116-117 H 5
Kristinehamn 116-117 EF 8
Kristinestad 116-117 J 6
Krivaja kosa 126-127 HJ 3
Kriva Palanka 122-123 JK 4
Kriviči 124-125 F 6
Krivoi Rog = Krivoj Rog 126-127 F 3
Krivoj Pojas 124-125 LM 2
Krivoj Rog 126-127 F 3

314 Kompong

Krivoy Rog = Krivoj Rog 126-127 F 3
Kříž 166-167 L 2
Križevci [YU, Bilo gora] 122-123 G 2
Krk 122-123 F 3
Krnov 118 HJ 3
Krochino 124-125 M 3
Kroh 150-151 C 10
Krohnwodoke = Nyaake 164-165 C 8
Krokodilrivier [ZA ◁ Marico] 174-175 G 3
Krokodilrivier [ZA ◁ Rio Incomáti] 174-175 J 3
Krokodilsbrug 174-175 JK 3
Krok Phra 150-151 BC 5
Kroksfjardharnes 116-117 c 2
Krolevec 126-127 F 1
Kromdraai [ZA ↘ Standerton] 174-175 H 4
Kromdraai [ZA ↖ Witbank] 174-175 H 3
Kromme Mijdrecht [NL, place] 128 I a 2
Kromme Mijdrecht [NL, river] 128 I a 2
Kromme River = Kromrivier 174-175 C 6
Kromrivier [ZA, place] 174-175 E 6
Kromrivier [ZA, river] 174-175 C 6
Kromy 124-125 K 7
Krong Po'kô = Dak Po'kô 150-151 F 5
Kronoberg 116-117 EF 9
Kronockaja sopka = Velikaja Kronockaja sopka 132-133 ef 7
Kronockij, mys — 132-133 f 7
Kronockij zaliv 132-133 f 7
Kronoki 132-133 f 7
Kronprins Christians Land 52 AB 20-21
Kronprinsesse Mærtha land 53 B 35-1
Kronprins Frederiks Bjerge 56-57 de 4
Kronprins Olav land 53 C 5
Kronštadt 124-125 G 3-4
Kroonstad 172 E 7
Kropotkin 126-127 K 4
Krosno 118 K 4
Krosno Odrzańskie 118 G 2-3
Krotoszyn 118 H 3
Krotovka 124-125 S 7
Krottingen = Kretinga 124-125 C 6
Krotz Springs, LA 78-79 D 5
Kroya 152-153 H 9
Krueng Teunom 152-153 AB 3
Kruger National Park 172 F 6-7
Krugers 174-175 F 5
Krugersdorp 172 E 7
Krugloi Point 58-59 pq 6
Krugloje 124-125 G 6
Kruglyži 124-125 QR 4
Krui 148-149 D 8
Kruidfontein 174-175 D 7
Kruis, Kaap — 172 B 6
Krujë 122-123 HJ 5
Krukut, Kali — 154 IV a 2
Kruleváčina 124-125 FG 6
Krummensee [DDR] 130 III c 1
Krung Thep, Ao — 150-151 C 6
Krupki 124-125 G 6
Krupunder See 130 I a 1
Krusenstern, Cape — 58-59 EF 3
Kruševac 122-123 J 4
Kruševo 122-123 J 5
Krutaja 124-125 U 2
Krutec 124-125 M 3
Kruzof Island 58-59 v 8
Krylatskoje, Moskva- 113 V ab 2
Krylovskaja ↑ Tichoreck 126-127 JK 3
Krym 126-127 FG 4
Krymsk 126-127 HJ 4
Krymskaja Oblast' 126-127 FG 4
Krymskije gory 126-127 FG 4
Krymskij zapovednik 126-127 G 4
Krynica 118 K 4
Krzyż 118 H 2

Ksabi = Al-Qaṣābī [DZ] 166-167 F 5
Ksabi = Al-Qaṣābī [MA] 166-167 D 3
Ksar ben Khrdache = Banī Khaddāsh 166-167 LM 3
Ksar-Chellala = Qaṣr Shillalah 166-167 H 2
Ksar-el-Boukhari = Qaṣr al-Bukharī 164-165 E 1
Ksar el Kebir = Al-Qaṣr al-Kabīr 164-165 C 1
Ksar es Seghir = Al-Qaṣr aṣ-Ṣaghīr 164-165 D 2
Ksar es Souk = Al-Qaṣr as-Sūq 164-165 K 2
Ksel, Djebel — = Jabal Kasal 166-167 G 3
Ksenjevka 132-133 WX 7
Kseur, El — = Al-Qaṣr 166-167 J 1
Kshatrapur = Chatrapur 138-139 K 8
Kshwan Mountain 60 C 2
Ksiba, el — = Al-Q'sībah 166-167 CD 3
Ksoum, Djebel el — = Jabal al-Kusūm 166-167 J 2
Ksour = Al-Quṣūr 166-167 L 2
Ksour, Monts des — = Jibāl al-Quṣūr 166-167 FG 3
Ksour Essaf = Quṣūr as-Sāf 166-167 M 2
Ksour Sidi Aïch = Quṣūr Sīdī 'Aysh 166-167 L 2
Kstovo 124-125 P 5
Ksyl-Orda = Kzyl-Orda 132-133 M 8-9
Ktĕma 136-137 E 5
Ktesiphon 136-137 L 6
Ktima = Ktĕma 136-137 E 5

Kuah 150-151 BC 9
Kuai He 146-147 F 5
Kuaiji Shan = Guiji Shan 146-147 H 7
Kuala 150-151 B 11
Kuala Belait 148-149 F 6
Kuala Brang 148-149 D 5-6
Kuala Dungun 148-149 D 6
Kuala Gris 150-151 D 10
Kuala Kangsar 148-149 CD 6
Kualakapuas 148-149 F 7
Kuala Kelawang 150-151 D 11
Kuala Ketil 150-151 C 10
Kuala Krai 148-149 D 5
Kuala Krau 150-151 D 11
Kuala Kubu Baharu 150-151 C 11
Kualakurun 152-153 K 6
Kualalangsa 148-149 C 6
Kuala Lipis 150-151 D 10
Kuala Lumpur 148-149 D 6
Kuala Marang 150-151 D 10
Kuala Masai 154 III b 1
Kuala Merang 148-149 D 5
Kuala Nal 150-151 CD 10
Kuala Nerang 150-151 C 9
Kualapembuang 152-153 K 7
Kualaperbaungan = Rantaupanjang 150-151 B 11
Kuala Perlis 148-149 CD 5
Kuala Pilah 150-151 D 11
Kuala Rompin 150-151 D 11
Kuala Selangor 148-149 D 6
Kuala Setiu = Setiu 150-151 D 10
Kualasimpang 152-153 B 3
Kuala Trengganu 148-149 DE 5
Kualu, Sungai — 150-151 BC 11
Kuamut 152-153 M 3
Kuan = Gu'an 146-147 F 2
Kuancheng 144-145 B 2
Kuan Chiang = Guan Jiang 146-147 C 9
Kuandang 148-149 H 6
Kuandang, Teluk — 152-153 P 5
Kuandian 144-145 E 2
Kuang-an = Guang'an 142-143 K 5
Kuang-ch'ang = Guangchang 142-143 M 6
Kuangchou = Guangzhou 142-143 L 7
Kuang-chou Wan = Zhanjiang Gang 142-143 L 7
Kuang-fêng = Guangfeng 146-147 G 7
Kuang-hai = Guanghai 142-143 L 7
Kuang-hsi = Guangxi Zhuangzu Zizhiqu 142-143 KL 7
Kuang-hsin = Shangrao 142-143 M 6
Kuang-jao = Guangrao 146-147 G 3
Kuang-ling = Guangling 146-147 E 2
Kuang-lu Tao = Guanglu Dao 144-145 D 3
Kuang-nan = Guangnan 142-143 JK 7
Kuang-ning = Guangning 146-147 D 10
Kuango = Kwango 172 C 2-3
Kuang-p'ing = Guangping 146-147 E 3
Kuang-shan = Guangshan 146-147 E 5
Kuang-shui = Guangshui 146-147 E 6
Kuangsi = Guangxi Zhuangzu Zizhiqu 142-143 KL 7
Kuang-tê = Guangde 146-147 G 6
Kuang-tsê = Guangze 146-147 F 8
Kuangtung = Guangdong 142-143 L 7
Kuang-yüan = Guangyuan 142-143 K 5
Kuanhsien = Guan Xian 146-147 E 3
Kuan-shan = Lilung 146-147 H 10
Kuantan 148-149 D 6
Kuantan, Batang — = Batang Inderagiri 148-149 D 7
Kuan-t'ao = Guantao 146-147 E 3
K'uan-tien = Kuandian 144-145 E 2
Kuan-t'ou Chiao = Guantou Jiao 150-151 G 2
Kuan-tung Pan-tao = Guandong Bandao 144-145 C 3
Kuan-yang = Guanyang 146-147 C 9
Kuan-yin-t'ang = Guanyintang 146-147 CD 4
Kuan-yün = Guanyun 142-143 MN 5
Kub [SU] 124-125 V 4
Kub [ZA] 174-175 B 3
Kuba [C] 64-65 KL 7
Kuba [SU] 126-127 O 6
Kuban' 126-127 J 4
Kubango = Rio Cubango 172 C 5
Kubaysah 136-137 K 6
Kubbar, Jazīrat — 136-137 N 8
Kubbum 164-165 J 6
Kubena 124-125 N 3
Kubenskoje 124-125 M 4
Kubenskoje, ozero — 124-125 M 4
Kuberle 126-127 KL 3
Kubiskowberge 174-175 C 6
Kubli Hill 168-169 FG 3
Kubn'a 124-125 Q 6
Kubokawa 144-145 J 6
Kubolta 126-127 C 2
Kuboos = Richtersveld 174-175 B 5
Kubu Bahru = Kuala Kubu Baharu 150-151 C 11
Kubumesaai 152-153 L 5
Kučevo 122-123 J 3
Kucha 142-143 E 3
Kuchāman 138-139 E 4
Ku-chang = Guzhang 146-147 BC 7
Kuche = Kucha 142-143 E 3
Ku-chên = Guzhen 146-147 F 5
Kucheng = Gucheng 146-147 C 5
Ku-ch'êng = Gucheng 146-147 EF 3
Kuchengtze = Qitai 142-143 FG 3
Ku-chiang = Gujiang 146-147 E 8
Kuchinarai 150-151 E 4
Kuchinda 138-139 K 7
Kuching 148-149 F 6
Kuchinoerabu-jima 144-145 GH 7
Kuchino-shima 144-145 G 7
Kuchow = Quzhou 146-147 E 3
Ku-chu = Guzhu 146-147 E 10
Küçük Ağrı dağı 136-137 L 3
Küçükbakkal 154 I b 3
Küçükköy 154 I a 2
Küçüksu = Kotum 136-137 K 3
Küçükyozgat = Elma dağı 136-137 E 3
Kuda 138-139 C 6
Kūdachi 140 B 2
Kudahuvadu Channel 176 a 2
Kudāl 140 A 2-3
Kuḍaligi = Kūdligi 140 C 3
Kudamatsu 144-145 H 5-6
Kudat 148-149 G 5
Kuḍḍlā = Kandla 134-135 L 6
Kudelstaart 128 I a 2
Kudever' 124-125 G 5
Kudiakof Islands 58-59 b 2
Kudiraimukha = Kudremukh 140 B 4
Kūdligi 140 C 3
Kudō = Taisei 144-145 ab 2
Kudobin Islands 58-59 c 1
Kudremukh 140 B 4
Kūdūk 164-165 L 6-7
Kudumalapshwe 174-175 F 2
Kudus 152-153 J 9
Kudymkar 132-133 JK 6
Kuei-ch'i = Guixi 146-147 F 7
Kuei Chiang = Gui Jiang 146-147 C 9-10
Kuei-ch'ih = Guichi 142-143 M 5
Kueichou = Guizhou 142-143 JK 6
Kuei-chou = Zigui 146-147 C 6
Kuei-lin = Guilin 142-143 KL 6
Kuei-p'ing = Guiping 142-143 KL 7
K'uei-t'an = Kuitan 146-147 E 10
Kuei-tê = Guide 142-143 J 4
Kuei-ting = Guiding 142-143 K 6
Kuei-tung = Guidong 146-147 D 8
Kuei-yang = Guiyang [TJ, Guizhou] 142-143 K 6
Kuei-yang = Guiyang [TJ, Hunan] 142-143 L 6
Kuerhlei = Korla 142-143 F 3
Kūfah, Al- 136-137 L 6
Kufra = Wāḥāt al-Kufrah 164-165 J 4
Kufrah, Wāḥāt al- 164-165 J 4
Kufra Oasis = Wāḥāt al-Kufrah 164-165 J 4
Küfre 136-137 K 3
Kufstein 118 E 5
Kugruа River 58-59 H 1
Kugruk River 58-59 F 4
Kugururok River 58-59 G 2
Kūh, Pīsh-e — 136-137 M 6
Kūhak 134-135 J 5
Kuh dağı = Kazandağ 136-137 K 3
Kūhdasht 136-137 M 6
Kūh-e Alvand 134-135 FG 4
Kūh-e-Beyābān 134-135 H 5
Kūh-e Bozqūsh 136-137 M 4
Kūh-e Chelleh Khāneh 136-137 N 4
Kūh-e Dalāk 136-137 N 4
Kūh-e Damāvand 134-135 G 3
Kūh-e Darband 134-135 H 4
Kūh-e Dīnār 134-135 G 4
Kūh-e Ḥājī Sa'īd 136-137 M 4
Kūh-e Hazārān = Kūh-e Hezārān 134-135 H 5
Kūh-e-Hezārān 134-135 H 5
Kūh-e-Ḥiṣṣar = Kōhe Ḥiṣār 134-135 K 4
Kūh-e Māneshṭ 136-137 M 6
Kūh-e-Marzu 136-137 M 6
Kūh-e Mīleh 136-137 M 6
Kūh-e Mīshāb 136-137 L 3
Kūh-e Qal'eh 136-137 N 6
Kūh-e Qotbeh 136-137 M 6
Kūh-e Sāfīd = Kūh-e Sefīd 136-137 M 5-N 6
Kūh-e Sahand 136-137 M 4
Kūh-e Sefīd 136-137 M 5-N 6
Kūh-e Shāhān 136-137 LM 5
Kūh-e Sīāh = Kūh-e Marzu 136-137 M 6
Kūh-e Tafresh 136-137 NO 5
Kūh-e Taftān 134-135 J 5
Kūhhā-ye Chehel-e Chashmeh 136-137 M 5
Kūhhā-ye Sābālān 136-137 M 3
Kūhha-ye Ṭavālesh 136-137 MN 3
Kūhhā-ye Zāgros 134-135 F 3-4
Kūhīn 136-137 N 4
Kuhmo 116-117 NO 5
Kuibis = Guibes 174-175 B 4
Kuiepan 174-175 DE 4
Kuis 174-175 B 3
Kuiseb 174-175 B 2
Kuitan 146-147 E 10
Kuito 172 C 4
Kuitozero 116-117 O 5
Kuiu Island 56-57 K 6
Kuivaniemi 116-117 L 5
Kuja 132-133 G 4
Kujal'nickij liman 126-127 E 3
Kujang-dong 144-145 EF 3
Kujawy 118 J 2
Kujbyšev [SU, Kujbyševskaja Oblast'] 132-133 HJ 7
Kujbyšev [SU, Om'] 132-133 O 6
Kujbyšev [SU, Tatarskaja ASSR] 124-125 R 6
Kujbyševka-Vostočnaja = Belogorsk 132-133 YZ 7
Kujbyševo 126-127 J 3
Kujbyševskoje vodochranilišče 132-133 HJ 7
Kujeda 124-125 U 5
Kujgenkol' 126-127 NO 2
Kuji 142-143 R 3
Kujto, ozero — 132-133 E 5
Kujulik Bay 58-59 e 1
Kujumba 132-133 S 5
Kujū-san 144-145 H 6
Kuk 58-59 H 1
Kukaklek Lake 58-59 K 7
Kukami 174-175 E 3
Kukānār 140 E 1
Kukarka = Sovetsk 132-133 H 6
Kukatush 62 KL 2
Kukawa 164-165 G 6
Kuke 172 D 6
Kukiang = Qujiang 146-147 D 9
Kukkus = Privolžskoje 126-127 MN 1
Kukmor 124-125 S 5
Kukong 174-175 E 3
Kukpowruk River 58-59 F 2
Kukpuk River 58-59 DE 2
Kukshi 138-139 E 6
Kukukus Lake 70-71 E 1
Kukumane Kraal 174-175 F 2
Kuku Noor = Chŏch nuur 142-143 H 4
Kukup 152-153 E 5
Kula [BG] 122-123 K 4
Kula [TR] 136-137 C 3
Kula [YU] 122-123 H 3
Kul'ab 134-135 K 3
Kulādan 141 C 5
Kulādan Myit 141 C 5
Ku-la-gauk = Kalagôk Kyûn 141 E 8
Kulagino 126-127 P 2
Kulai 150-151 D 12
Kulaiburu 138-139 K 6
Kulal 171 D 2
Kulaly, ostrov — 126-127 O 4
Kulāma Taunggyā 150-151 B 7
Kulambangra = Kolombangara 148-149 j 6
Kulanjin 136-137 N 5
Kular, chrebet — 132-133 Z 4
Kulasekharapatnam 140 D 6
Kuḷashekharapaṭṭaṇam = Kulasekharapatnam 140 D 6
Kulaura 134-135 P 6
Kuldīga 124-125 CD 5
Kuldja = Gulja 142-143 E 3
Kuldo 60 CD 2
Kulebaki 124-125 O 6
Kulên, Phnom — 150-151 DE 6
Kulfo 168-169 G 3
Kulgera 158-159 F 5
Kulha Gangri 142-143 G 6
Kulhakangri = Kalha Gangri 138-139 N 3
Kulhakangri = Kulha Gangri 142-143 G 6
Kuligi 124-125 T 4
Kulik, Lake — [USA ↑ Kuskokwim River] 58-59 G 6
Kulik, Lake — [USA ↓ Kuskokwim River] 58-59 H 7
Kulikoro = Koulikoro 164-165 C 6
Kulikovka 126-127 E 1
Kulikovo Pole 124-125 LM 7
Kulim 150-151 C 10
Kulittalai 140 D 5
Kuliyāpiṭiya 140 DE 7
Kulja = Ghulja 142-143 E 3
Kullanchāvadi 140 DE 5
Kullen 116-117 E 9
Küllü 136-137 J 3
Kullū = Kulu 138-139 F 2
Küllük = Güllük 136-137 B 4
Kulm, ND 68-69 G 2
Kulmbach 118 E 3
Kuloj [SU, place] 124-125 O 3
Kuloj [SU, river] 124-125 O 3
Kulotino 124-125 J 4
Kulp 136-137 J 3
Kulpahār 138-139 G 5
Kulpawn 168-169 E 3
Kul'sary 132-133 J 8
Kulti 138-139 L 6
Kultuk 132-133 T 7
Kulu [IND] 138-139 F 2
Kulu [TR] 136-137 E 3
Kulu = Julu 146-147 E 3
Kuludu Faro 176 a 1
Kulukak Bay 58-59 H 7
Kulumadau 148-149 h 6
Kulunda 132-133 OP 7
Kulundinskaja step' 132-133 O 7
Kuḷuttalai = Kulittalai 140 D 5
Kulwin 160 F 5
Kum = Qom 134-135 G 4
Kuma [J] 144-145 J 6
Kuma [SU] 126-127 N 4
Kuma [TJ] 138-139 M 3
Kumagaya 144-145 M 4
Kumai 152-153 J 7
Kumai, Teluk — 148-149 F 7
Kumaishi 144-145 ab 2
Kumaka 98-99 J 3
Kumakahi, Cape — 78-79 e 3
Kumamba, Pulau-pulau — 148-149 LM 7
Kumamoto 142-143 P 5
Kumano 144-145 L 6
Kumano-nada 144-145 L 5-6
Kumanovo 122-123 JK 4
Kumārsaen = Kumhārsain 138-139 F 2
Kumasi 164-165 D 7
Kumaun 134-135 M 4
Kumayt, Al- 136-137 M 6
Kumba 164-165 F 8
Kumbakale 148-149 j 6
Kumbakonam 134-135 MN 8
Kumbe 148-149 LM 8
Kumbher 138-139 H 3
Kumbhir 141 C 3
Kumbukkan Oya 140 E 7
Kŭmch'on 144-145 F 3
Kŭmch'ŏn = Kimch'ŏn 142-143 O 4
Kŭmē [SU] 141 E 5
Kumeny 124-125 RS 4
Kumertau 132-133 K 7
Kŭm-gang 144-145 F 4
Kŭmgang-san 144-145 FG 3
Kumhārsain 138-139 F 2
Kŭmhwa 144-145 F 3
Kumini-dake 144-145 H 6
Kumizawa, Yokohama- 155 III a 3
Kŭmje = Kimje 144-145 F 5
Kumla 116-117 F 8
Kumluca 136-137 D 4
Kummerfeld 130 I a 1
Kŭmnyŏng 144-145 F 6
Kumo 168-169 H 3
Kŭmo-do 144-145 FG 5
Kumo-Manyčskaja vpadina 126-127 K 3-M 4
Kumon Range = Kŭmûn Taungdan 148-149 C 1
Kumphawapi 148-149 D 3
Kŭmsan 144-145 F 4
Kumta 140 B 3
Kumuch 126-127 N 5
Kumul = Hami 142-143 G 3
Kumund 138-139 J 7
Kŭmûn Taungdan 148-149 C 1
K'um'urk'oj, gora — 126-127 O 7
Kuna River 58-59 J 2
Kunašir, ostrov — 132-133 c 9
Kunatata Hill 168-169 H 4
Kūnavaram 140 E 2
Kunayt, Al- 136-137 M 6
Kuncevo, Moskva- 124-125 L 6
Kunda [IND] 138-139 H 5
Kunda [SU] 124-125 F 4
Kundabwika Falls 171 B 5
Kuṅḍāpura = Condapoor 134-135 L 8
Kundelungu 172 E 3-4
Kundelungu, Parc National de — 171 AB 5
Kundgol 140 B 3
Kundiawa 148-149 M 8
Kundla 138-139 C 7
Kunduk = ozero Sasyk 126-127 DE 4
Kundur, Pulau — 148-149 D 6
Kunduz 134-135 K 3
Kunene 172 B 5
Kungā 138-139 M 7
Kung-ch'êng = Gongcheng 146-147 C 9
K'ung-ch'êng = Kongcheng 146-147 F 6
Kungej-Alatau, chrebet — 132-133 O 9
Kunghit Island 60 B 3
Kung-hsien = Gong Xian 146-147 D 4
Kung-hui = Gonghui 146-147 C 9
Kung-kuan = Gongguan 146-147 B 11
Kungliao 146-147 HJ 9
Kungok River 58-59 H 1
Kungrad 132-133 K 9
Kungsbacka 116-117 DE 9
Kung-shan = Gongshan 141 F 2
Kung Shui = Gong Shui 146-147 E 9
Kungu 172 C 1
Kungur 132-133 K 6
Kŭngyangŏn 141 E 7
Kung-ying-tsŭ = Gongyingzi 144-145 BC 2
Kunie = Île des Pins 158-159 N 4
Kunigal 140 C 4
Kuṇigala = Kunigal 140 C 4
Kunja 124-125 H 5
Kŭnlôn 148-149 C 2
Kunlun Shan 142-143 D-H 4
Kunming 142-143 J 6
Kunming Hu 155 II a 2
Kunnamangalam 140 BC 5
Kunnamkulam 140 BC 5
Kunnūr = Coonor 140 C 5
Kunsan 142-143 O 4
Kunsan-man 144-145 F 5
Kunshan 146-147 H 6
Kŭnthī Kyûn 150-151 A 7
Kuntillā, Al- 173 D 3
Kunu 138-139 F 5
Kuṅvārī = Kunwāri 138-139 F 4
Kunwāri 138-139 F 4
K'ŭnyŏnp'yŏng-do = Tae-yŏnp'yŏng-do 144-145 E 4
Kunyu Shan 146-147 H 3
Kuocang Shan 146-147 H 7
Kuo Ho = Guo He 146-147 F 5
Kuo-hsien = Yuanping 146-147 D 2
Kuolisma 124-125 HJ 2
Kuopio 116-117 M 6
Kupa 122-123 FG 3
Kupang 148-149 H 9
Kup'ansk 126-127 H 2
Kupanskoje 124-125 M 5
Kup'ansk-Uzlovoj 126-127 HJ 2
Kuparuk River 58-59 N 1-2
Kupferteich 130 I b 1
Kupino 132-133 O 7
Kupiškis 124-125 E 6
Kuppili 140 FG 1
Kupreanof Island 56-57 K 6
Kupreanof Point 58-59 d 2
Kupreanof Strait 58-59 KL 7
Kura [SU ◁ Caspian Sea] 126-127 MN 6
Kura [SU ◁ Nogajskaja step'] 126-127 M 4
Kurā', Jabal al- 166-167 J 2
Kura-Araksinskaja nizmennost' 126-127 NO 6-7
Kurahashi-jima 144-145 J 5
Kuramo Waters 170 III b 2
Kuranami 155 III cd 3
Kurāndvād 140 B 2
Kurashiki 144-145 J 5
Kuratovo 124-125 R 3
Kuraymah 164-165 L 5
Kurayoshi 144-145 JK 5
Kurbali dere 154 I b 3
Kurchahan Hu = Chagan nuur 142-143 L 3
Kur Chhu 141 B 2
K'urdamir 126-127 O 6
Kurdeg 138-139 K 6
Kurdikos Naumiestis 124-125 D 6
Kurdistan = Kordestān 134-135 F 3
Kurdufān al-Janūbīyah 164-165 KL 6
Kurdufān ash-Shimālīyah 164-165 KL 5-6
Kurduvādi 140 B 1
Kure [J] 142-143 P 5
Küre [TR] 136-137 E 2
Kūreh-ye Meyāneh 136-137 M 5
Kurejka [SU, place] 132-133 PQ 4
Kurejka [SU, river] 132-133 QR 4
Kuremäe 124-125 F 4
Kuressaare = Kingisepp 124-125 D 4
Kurgan 132-133 M 6
Kurganinsk 126-127 K 4
Kurganovka 124-125 U 4
Kurgan-Tube 134-135 KL 3
Kuria 208 H 2
Kuria Muria Island = Jazā'ir Khūrīyā Mūrīyā 134-135 H 7
Kuriate, Îles — = Jazā'ir Qūryāt 166-167 M 2
Kuṛigrām 138-139 M 5
Kurikka 116-117 JK 6
Kurikoma yama 144-145 N 3
Kuril Islands 142-143 S 3-T 2
Kurilovka 126-127 O 1
Kuril'sk 132-133 c 8
Kuril'skije ostrova 142-143 S 3-T 2
Kuril Trench 156-157 GH 2
Kurinskaja kosa 126-127 O 7
Kurinskaja Kosa = Kurkosa 126-127 O 7
Kurja 124-125 V 3
Kürkcü 136-137 E 4
Kurkino [SU, Moskva] 113 V a 2
Kurkosa 126-127 O 7
Kurkur 173 C 6
Kurle = Korla 142-143 F 3
Kurleja 132-133 WX 7
Kurlovskij 124-125 N 6
Kurmanajevka 124-125 ST 7
Kurman-Kamel'či = Krasnogvardejskoje 126-127 G 4
Kurmuk 164-165 L 6
Kurnell, Sydney- 161 I b 3
Kurnool 134-135 M 7
Kurobe 144-145 L 4
Kuroishi 144-145 N 2
Kuromatsunai 144-145 b 2
Kurosawajiri = Kitakami 144-145 N 3
Kuro-shima 144-145 G 7
Kurovskoje 124-125 M 6
Kurow [NZ] 161 CD 7
Kursavka 126-127 L 4
Kuršėnai 124-125 D 5
Kurseong 138-139 LM 4
Kursī 136-137 J 4
Kursk 124-125 KL 8
Kurskaja kosa 118 K 1
Kurskij zaliv 118 K 1
Kuršumlija 122-123 J 4
Kurşunlu [TR, Çankırı] 136-137 E 2
Kurtalan = Misriç 136-137 J 4
Kurthasanlı 136-137 E 3
Kurtī 164-165 L 5
Kurtoğlu burnu 136-137 C 4
Kuru [IND] 138-139 K 6
Kurucaşile 136-137 E 2
Kuruçay 136-137 H 3
Kuruçeşme, İstanbul- 154 I b 2
Kurukkuchālai 140 D 6
Kurukshetra 138-139 F 3
Kuruman 172 D 7
Kuruman Heuvels 174-175 E 4
Kurume [J, Honshū] 155 III a 1
Kurume [J, Kyūshū] 144-145 H 6
Kurumkan 132-133 V 7
Kuruṇegala 134-135 MN 9
Kurung Tāl = Kurung Tank 138-139 J 6
Kurung Tank 138-139 J 6
Kurun-Ur'ach 132-133 a 6
Kurupa Lake 58-59 KL 2
Kurupa River 58-59 K 2
Kurupukari 92-93 H 4
Kuruskū, Wādī — 173 C 6
Kuryongp'o 144-145 G 5
Kus 150-151 E 4
Kuşadası 136-137 B 4
Kuşadası körfezi 136-137 B 4
Kusakaki-shima 144-145 G 7
Kusal = Kuusalu 124-125 E 4
Kusary 126-127 O 6
Kusatsu 144-145 KL 5
Kusawa Lake 58-59 T 6
Kusawa River 58-59 T 6
Kusaybah, Bi'r — 164-165 K 4
Kuščinskij 126-127 N 6
Kušč'ovskaja 126-127 JK 3
Kusgölü 136-137 BC 2
Kushālgarh 138-139 E 6
Ku-shan = Gushan 144-145 D 3
Kusheriki 168-169 G 3
Kushih = Gushi 142-143 M 5
Kushikino 144-145 GH 7
Kushima 144-145 H 7
Kushimoto 144-145 K 6
Kushiro 142-143 RS 3
Kūshkak 136-137 NO 5
Kushtagi 140 C 3
Kushtaka Lake 58-59 PQ 6
Kushtia = Kushṭiyā 138-139 M 6
Kushṭiyā 138-139 M 6
Kushui 142-143 G 3
Kusilvak Mount 58-59 EF 6
Kusiro = Kushiro 142-143 RS 3
Kusiyārā 141 BC 3
Kuška 134-135 J 3
Kuskokwim, North Fork — 58-59 KL 5
Kuskokwim, South Fork — 58-59 KL 5
Kuskokwim Bay 56-57 D 6
Kuskokwim Mountains 56-57 EF 5
Kuskokwim River 56-57 DE 5
Kuskovo, Moskva- 113 V d 3
Kušluyan 136-137 G 2
Kusmā 138-139 J 3
Kusmi 138-139 J 6
Kušmurun 132-133 LM 7
Kušnarenkovo 124-125 U 6
Kusnezk = Kuzneck 132-133 H 7
Kusŏng 144-145 E 2-3
Kustāgi = Kushtagi 140 C 3
Kustanaj 132-133 LM 7
Kustatan, AK 58-59 M 6
K'ustendil 122-123 K 4
Küstenkanal 118 CD 2
Kuštī 164-165 L 6
Kusu 144-145 H 6
Kušum 126-127 P 1
Kusūm, Jabal al- 166-167 J 2
Kusuman 150-151 E 4
Kusumba 154 II b 3
K'us'ur 132-133 Y 3
Kušva 132-133 K 6
Kūt, Al — 134-135 F 4
Kut, Ko — 148-149 D 4
Kūt 'Abdollāh 136-137 N 7
Kutacane 150-151 AB 11
Kütahya 134-135 BC 3
Kutai 148-149 G 6
Kutais 126-127 J 4
Kutaisi 126-127 L 5
Kut-al-Imara = Al-Kūt 134-135 F 4
Kutaradja = Banda Aceh 148-149 BC 5
Kutch 134-135 K 6
Kutch, Gulf of — 134-135 KL 6
Kutch, Rann of — 134-135 KL 6
Kutchan 144-145 b 2
Kutcharo-ko 144-145 d 2
Kutchi Hill 168-169 H 3
Kutien = Gutian 146-147 G 8
Kutina 122-123 G 3
Kutiyāna 138-139 BC 7
Kuṭiyāṭṭam = Gudiyāttam 140 D 4
Kutkašen 126-127 N 6
Kutno 118 J 2
Kutru 138-139 H 8
Kutsing = Qujing 142-143 J 6
Kutta-jo Qabr 138-139 A 4
Kuttāttukulam 140 C 6
Kuttuparamb = Kūttuparamba 140 B 5
Kūttuparamba 140 B 5
Kuttyādi 140 B 5
Kutu 172 C 2
Kutubdia Island = Kutubdiyā Dīp 141 B 5
Kutubdiyā Dīp 141 B 5
Kutum 164-165 J 6
Kutunbul, Jabal — 134-135 E 7
Kutuzof, Cape — 58-59 c 1
Kuusalu 124-125 E 4
Kuusamo 116-117 N 5
Kuusankoski 116-117 M 7
Kuvandyk 132-133 K 7
Kuvšinovo 124-125 K 5
Kuwaima Falls 98-99 H 1-2
Kuwait 134-135 F 5
Kuwana 144-145 L 5
Kuwayt, Al- 134-135 F 5
Kuwo = Quwo 146-147 C 4
Kuyang = Quyang 146-147 E 2
Kuyeh = Juye 146-147 F 4
Kuye He 146-147 C 2
K'u-yeh Ho = Kuye He 146-147 C 2
Kūysanjaq 136-137 L 4
Kuyucak 136-137 C 4
Kuyung = Jurong 146-147 G 6
Kuyuwini River 98-99 J 3
Kužener 124-125 R 5
Kuženkino 124-125 J 5
Kuzguncuk, İstanbul- 154 I b 2
Kuzitrin River 58-59 EF 4
Kuz'minki, Moskva- 113 V cd 3
Kuz'movka 132-133 QR 5
Kuzneck 132-133 H 7
Kuzneckij Alatau 132-133 Q 6-7

Kuznecki 315

Kuzneck-Sibirskij = Novokuzneck 132-133 Q 7
Kuznetsk = Kuzneck 132-133 H 7
Kuzomen' 132-133 F 4
Kuzucubelen 136-137 EF 4

Kvænangen 116-117 J 2
Kvailāṅgī = Quilāndi 140 B 5
Kvaløy 116-117 KL 2
Kvalsund 116-117 KL 2
Kvalvågen 116-117 k 6
Kvareli 126-127 MN 6
Kvarken 116-117 J 6
Kvarner 122-123 F 3
Kvarnerić 122-123 F 3
Kverkfjöll 116-117 ef 2
Kvichak, AK 58-59 J 7
Kvichak Bay 58-59 J 7
Kvichak River 58-59 J 7
Kvigtind 116-117 EF 5
Kvikne 116-117 D 6
Kvirily = Zestafoni 126-127 L 5
Kvitøya 116-117 no 4

Kwa 172 C 2
Kwabhaca 174-175 H 6
Kwaggablad 174-175 EF 4
Kwai 174-175 D 3
Kwair, Al — = Al-Quwayr 136-137 K 4
Kwakel, De — 128 I a 2
Kwakhanai 172 D 6
Kwakoegron 98-99 L 2
Kwakwani 98-99 JK 2
Kwakwasa 168-169 GH 3
Kwale 171 D 4
Kwa Mbonambi 174-175 K 5
Kwambonambi = Kwa Mbonambi 174-175 K 5
Kwamouth 172 C 2
Kwa Mtoro 171 CD 4
Kwangan = Guang'an 142-143 K 5
Kwangando 171 D 3
Kwangchang = Guangchang 142-143 M 6
Kwangch'on 144-145 F 4
Kwangchow = Guangzhou 142-143 L 7
Kwanghua = Guanghua 142-143 L 5
Kwangjao = Guangrao 146-147 G 3
Kwangju 142-143 O 4
Kwango 172 C 2-3
Kwangsi = Guangxi Zhuangzu Zizhiqu 142-143 KL 7
Kwangteh = Guangde 146-147 G 6
Kwangtseh = Guangze 146-147 F 8
Kwangtung = Guangdong 142-143 L 7
Kwangyuan = Guangyuan 142-143 K 5
Kwania, Lake — 171 C 2
Kwanmo-bong 144-145 G 2
Kwanto = Kantō 144-145 MN 4
Kwanyun = Guanyun 142-143 MN 5
Kwanza 172 C 3-4
Kwanza, Rio — 172 B 3
Kwara 164-165 E 6-F 7
Kwataboahegan River 62 KL 1
Kwatta 134-135 K 4
Kwazulu 172 F 7
Kwedia 174-175 F 3
Kweiang = Guiyang 142-143 K 6
Kweichih = Guichi 142-143 M 5
Kweichow = Fengjie 142-143 K 5
Kweichow = Guizhou 142-143 JK 6
Kweichow Island = Weizhou Dao 150-151 G 2
Kweichu = Guiyang 142-143 K 6
Kweilin = Guilin 142-143 KL 6
Kweiping = Guiping 142-143 KL 7
Kweiteh = Shangqiu 142-143 LM 5
Kweiyang = Guiyang 142-143 K 6
Kwekwe 172 E 5
Kwenge 172 C 3
Kwenlun = Kunlun Shan 142-143 D-H 4
Kwesang-bong 144-145 G 2
Kwethluk, AK 56-57 DE 5
Kwethluk River 58-59 G 6
Kwidzyn 118 J 2
Kwigillingok, AK 56-57 D 6
Kwigluk Island 58-59 E 7
Kwiguk, AK 58-59 E 5
Kwiha 164-165 MN 6
Kwikpak, AK 58-59 E 5
Kwilu 172 C 2
Kwinana 158-159 BC 6
Kwingauk 141 D 7
Kwinhagak = Quinhagak, AK 58-59 FG 7
Kwinitsa 60 C 2
Kwohsien = Juanping 146-147 D 2
Kwonai 168-169 G 3
Kwong Eng 152-153 LM 9
Kwonghoi = Guanghai 142-143 L 7
Kwun Tong 155 I b 2

Kyaikdōn 141 F 7-8
Kyaikhkamī 141 E 7
Kyaikhtau 141 DE 7
Kyaikhtīrō Burā 141 E 7
Kyaikkami = Kyaikhkamī 141 E 7
Kyaiklat 141 D 7
Kyaikmaraw 141 EF 7
Kyaiktō 148-149 C 3
Kya-in = Kyā'inzeikkyī 141 EF 7
Kyā'inzeikkyī 141 EF 7
Kyaka 171 B 3
Kyancutta 158-159 G 6
Kyangdam 138-139 L 2
Kyangin 141 D 6
Ky Anh 150-151 F 3
Kyaring Tsho [TJ, Qinghai] 142-143 H 5
Kyaring Tsho [TJ, Xizang Zizhiqu] 142-143 F 5
Kyaukhpyū 141 C 6
Kyaukhsī 148-149 C 2
Kyaukkyī 141 E 6
Kyaukmē 141 E 4
Kyaukpandaung [BUR, Magwe Taing] 141 D 6
Kyaukpandaung [BUR, Mandale Taing] 141 D 5
Kyaukse = Kyaukhsī 148-149 C 2
Kyauksit 141 E 5-6
Kyauktan 141 E 7
Kyauktan = Kyaikhtau 141 DE 7
Kyauktau 141 C 5
Kyauktaw = Kyauktau 141 C 5
Kyaunggōn 141 D 7
Kybartai 124-125 D 6
Kydōniai = Ayvacık 136-137 B 3
Kyebang-san 144-145 G 4
Kyeindalī 141 D 6-7
Kyeintali = Kyeindalī 141 D 6-7
Kyezimanzan 148-149 C 2
Kyid Chhu 138-139 N 3
Kyirong 138-139 K 3
Kyikaukpyu = Kyaukhpyū 141 C 6
Kylābyin 141 D 7
Kyle of Lochalsh 119 D 3
Kyllēnē 122-123 J 7
Kýmē 122-123 L 6
Kymen lääni 116-117 MN 7
Kymijoki 116-117 M 7
Kynö = Kihnu 124-125 D 4
Kynuna 158-159 H 4
Kyōbingauk 141 DE 6
Kyoga, Lake — 172 F 1
Kyogami, Cape — = Kyōga-saki 144-145 K 5
Kyōga-saki 144-145 K 5
Kyogle 160 L 2
Kyōmip'o = Songnim 142-143 O 4
Kyōn 141 E 5
Kyônbyau 141 D 7
Kyōndō 141 EF 7
Kyong = Kyōn 141 E 5
Kyōngadūn 141 D 7
Kyōngan-ni 144-145 F 4
Kyōngdōn 148-149 CD 2
Kyōnggi-do 144-145 F 4
Kyonghūng 144-145 H 1
Kyōngju 142-143 OP 4
Kyōnglaung 141 C 5
Kyōngnyōlbi-yōlto 144-145 E 4
Kyōngsan 144-145 G 5
Kyōngsang-pukto 144-145 G 4
Kyōngsan-namdo 144-145 FG 5
Kyōngsōng 144-145 GH 2
Kyōngsōng = Sōul 142-143 O 4
Kyōngwōn 144-145 H 1
Kyonpyaw = Kyōnbyau 141 D 7
Kyōto 142-143 PQ 4
Kyparissia 122-123 J 7
Kyparissiakòs Kólpos 122-123 J 7
Kyrá Panagía 122-123 KL 6
Kyrēneia 136-137 E 5
Kyrenia = Kyrēneia 136-137 E 5
Kyrkanda 124-125 P 3
Kyrksæterøra 116-117 C 6
Kyrkslätt 116-117 L 7
Kyrönjoki 116-117 K 6
Kyštovka 132-133 O 6
Kyštym 132-133 L 6
Kysykkamys 126-127 P 2
Kýthēra 122-123 K 7
Kythēron, Stenōn — 122-123 K 7-8
Kýthnos 122-123 L 7
Kythrēa 136-137 E 5
Kytyl-Žura 132-133 Y 5
Kyūgōk 148-149 C 2
Kyuguot Sound 60 D 5
Kyūndōn 141 DE 5
Kyūnhla 141 D 4
Kyuquot 60 D 4
Kyūshū 142-143 P 5
Kyushu Ridge 142-143 P 6-Q 7
Kyūshū sammyaku 144-145 H 6
Kyūsyū = Kyūshū 142-143 P 5
Kywèbwè 141 E 6
Kywong 160 H 5
Kyzyl 132-133 R 7
Kyzyl-Kija 134-135 L 2-3
Kyzylkum 132-133 LM 9
Kyzyl-Mažalyk 132-133 QR 7
Kyzylsu 134-135 L 3

Kzyl-Orda 132-133 M 9

L

Laa 118 H 4
La'ā', Al- = Al-Lu'ā'ah 136-137 L 7
La Adelia 106-107 EF 7
Laaer Berg 113 I b 2
La Alameda 76-77 CD 8
La Albufera 120-121 GH 9
La Alcarria 120-121 F 8
La Amarga, Laguna — 106-107 DE 7
La Angelina 106-107 E 5
La Antigua, Salina — 106-107 DE 2-3
Laar [B] 128 II b 1
La Aragonesa 108-109 E 7
La Argentina 106-107 H 4
La Armuña 120-121 DE 8
Laas'aanood 164-165 b 2
Laas Qoray 164-165 b 1
La Asturiana 106-107 E 6
La Asunción 92-93 G 2
Laaswarwar 164-165 bc 2
La Aurora 106-107 EF 1
Laba 168-169 G 2
La Babia 76-77 CD 8
la Baie 63 A 3
La Bajada 108-109 E 7
La Banda 111 D 3
La Bañeza 120-121 DE 7
La Barca 86-87 J 7
Labardén 106-107 H 6
La Barge, WY 66-67 HJ 4
La Barre, Balneario — 106-107 L 4
la Baule-Escoublac 120-121 F 5
Labbezanga 164-165 E 5-6
Labchhung Gangri 138-139 K 2
Labchhung Tsho 138-139 K 2
Labe [CS] 118 G 3
Labé [Guinea] 164-165 B 6
La Beba 106-107 G 5
Labelle 72-73 J 1
La Belle, FL 80-81 c 3
La Belle, MO 70-71 DE 5
Labengke, Pulau — 152-153 P 7
Laberge, Lake — 58-59 U 6
Laberinto, Punta — 106-107 FG 7
Labertino, Bahía del — = Adventures Sound 108-109 K 9
Labi 152-153 L 3
Labiar = Al Abyār 166-167 A 5
Labin 122-123 F 3
Labinsk 126-127 K 4
Labis 148-149 D 6
La Blanquilla, Isla — 92-93 G 2
La Boca 64-65 b 3
La Bomba 86-87 C 2
La Bonita 96-97 C 1
La Boquilla, Presa — 86-87 GH 4
Laborde 106-107 F 4
Labota 148-149 H 7
Labougle 106-107 HJ 3
Laboulaye 111 D 4
Labrador, Coast of — 56-57 YZ 6-7
Labrador Basin 50-51 G 3
Labrador City 56-57 X 7
Labrador Peninsula 56-57 V 6-Y 7
Labrador Sea 56-57 Y-a 5-6
La Brava, Laguna — 106-107 F 4
Lábrea 92-93 G 6
Labrieville 63 B 3
la Brive 128 II b 2
la Broquerie 61 KL 6
Labuan, Pulau — 148-149 FG 5
Labuha 148-149 J 7
Labuhan 148-149 E 8
Labuhanbajo 148-149 GH 8
Labuhanbatu 150-151 BC 11
Labuhanbilik 148-149 CD 6
Labuhan haji 152-153 B 4
Labuhanmarege 152-153 O 9
Labuk, Sungei — 152-153 M 2-3
Labuk, Teluk — 152-153 M 2
Labūttā 141 D 7
Labytnangi 132-133 M 4
Laċa, ozero — 124-125 M 3
La Cabral 106-107 G 3
La Cal 104-105 G 6
Lac à la Croix 63 A 2
La Calandria 106-107 H 3
Lac Alaotra 172 J 5
Lac Albanel 62 P 1
La Caldera 104-105 D 9
La Calera 106-107 B 4
La California 106-107 FG 4
Lac-Allard 63 E 2
La Campiña [E, Andalucia] 120-121 E 10
La Campiña del Henares 120-121 F 8
La Cañada 106-107 F 1
La Canada Verde Creek 83 III d 2
La Candelaria 104-105 D 10
Lac Andou 72-73 H 1
La Canoa 94-95 JK 3
La Capilla 96-97 B 4
Lácar, Lago — 108-109 D 3
La Carlota [RA] 111 D 4
La Carlota, Aeropuerto — 91 II bc
La Carolina [E] 120-121 F 9
La Carolina [RA] 106-107 G 4
La Carreta 106-107 FG 6
Lac Assal 164-165 N 6
Lac Assinica 62 O 1
Lac Aticonipi 63 G 2
La Cautiva [BOL] 104-105 EF 6
La Cautiva [RA, Córdoba] 106-107 E 4
La Cautiva [RA, San Luis] 106-107 D 4
Lac aux Sangsues 72-73 GH 1
Lac Berté 63 BC 2
Lac Bienville 56-57 W 6
Lac Bigot 63 D 2
Lac-Bouchette 62 P 2
Lac Boulain 63 F 2
Lac Briconnet 63 F 2
Lac Brochet 63 B 3
Lac Brochu 62 OP 2
Lac Bureau 62 O 2
Lac Cacaoui 63 C 2
Laccadive Islands 134-135 L 9
Lac Camachigama 62 NO 3
Lac Caribou = Rentiersee 56-57 Q 6
Lac Carrière 72-73 H 1
Lac Cayar = Ar-R'kiz 164-165 AB 5
Lac Chibougamau 62 OP 2
Lac Comencho 62 O 1
Lac Courte Oreilles Indian Reservation 70-71 E 3
Lac Debo 164-165 D 5
Lac Decelles 62 M 3
Lac de Guier 164-165 AB 5
Lac de la Robe Noir 63 E 2
Lac de la Surprise 62 O 2
Lac De Morhiban 63 E 2
Lac de Neuchâtel 118 C 5
Lac des Augustines 72-73 J 1
Lac des Bois 56-57 M 4
Lac des Eudistes 63 D 2
Lac des Mille Lacs 70-71 EF 1
Lac des Montagnes 62 O 1
Lac des Trente et un Milles 72-73 HJ 1
Lac du Bonnet 62 AB 2
Lac du Flambeau Indian Reservation 70-71 E 2-3
Lac du Male 62 O 2
Lac Dumoine 72-73 H 1
Lac-Édouard 62 PQ 3
La Ceiba [Honduras] 64-65 J 8
La Ceiba [YV] 92-93 E 3
La Ceja 94-95 D 5
Lacepede Islands 158-159 D 3
La Cesira 106-107 F 4
Lac Evans 62 N 1
Lacey, WA 66-67 B 2
Lac Faguibine 164-165 CD 5
Lac Fetzara = Buḥayrat Fazrārah 166-167 K 1
Lac Fittri 164-165 H 6
Lac Fleur de May 63 D 2
Lac Fonteneau 63 F 2
Lac Fournier 63 D 2
Lac-Frontiere 63 A 4
Lac Frotet 62 O 1
Lac Galle 63 G 2
Lac Garou 168-169 E 1
Lac-Gatineau 72-73 HJ 1
Lac Giffard 62 N 1
Lac Goéland 62 N 2
Lac Goyelle 63 F 2
Lac Grasset 62 MN 2
Lac Guéguen 62 N 2
Lachaqui 96-97 C 7
Lac Haribongo 168-169 E 1
La Chaux-de-Fonds 118 C 5
La Chauya Cocha 96-97 D 6
Lachdenpochja 124-125 GH 3
Lachhmangarh 138-139 F 4
Lachhmangarh Sīkar 138-139 E 4
Lachine 72-73 JK 2
Lachine, Canal — 82 I b 2
Lachine, Rapides de — 82 I b 2
La Chivera 91 II b 1
Lachlan River 158-159 HJ 6
La Chorrera [CO] 94-95 E 8
La Chorrera [PA] 64-65 b 3
L'achoviči 124-125 EF 7
Lac-Humqui 63 C 3
Lachute 72-73 JK 2
Lac Île à la Crosse 61 E 3
Lačin 126-127 N 7
la Ciotat 120-121 K 7
Lac Iro 164-165 HJ 7
La Cita 91 III c 1
La Citadelle 88-89 K 5
Lac Joseph 56-57 XY 7
Lackawanna, NY 72-73 G 3
Lac Kempt 72-73 JK 1
Lac Kenonisca 62 NO 1
Lac Kipawa 72-73 G 1
Lac Kisale 172 E 3
Lac Kivu 172 EF 2
Lac Kondiaronk 72-73 H 1
Lac Korarou 164-165 D 5
Lac la Bardeliere 62 OP 1
Lac la Biche 61 BC 3
Lac La Biche [CDN, place] 61 C 3
Lac la Croix 70-71 DE 1
Lac Lady Beatrix 62 N 1
Lac la Galissonnière 63 E 2
Lac la Hache 60 G 4
Lac la Martre 56-57 MN 5
Lac la Plonge 61 E 3
Lac la Ronge 56-57 Q 6
Lac la Ronge Provincial Park 61 F 3
Lac la Trêve 62 O 2
Lac Léopold II = Mai Ndombe 172 C 2
Lac Long 72-73 J 1
Lac Lucie 62 M 1
Lac Macamic 62 M 2
Lac Magpie 63 D 2
Lac Maicasagi 62 N 1
Lac Malartic 62 N 2
Lac Manicouagan 63 BC 2
Lac Manouane [CDN ↑ Québec] 63 A 2
Lac Manouane [CDN ← Québec] 72-73 J 1
Lac Manouanis 63 AB 2
Lac Marceau 63 CD 2
Lac Matagami 62 N 2
Lac Maunoir 56-57 M 4
Lac Maupertuis 62 PQ 1
Lac Memphremagog 72-73 KL 2
Lac Menaskwagama 63 EF 2
Lac Mesgouez 62 O 1
Lac Mishagomish 62 NO 1
Lac Mitchinamecus 72-73 J 1
Lac Mobutu-Sese-Seko 172 F 1
Lac Montcevelles 63 FG 2
Lac Musquaro 63 F 2
Lac Nemiscau 62 N 1
Lac Niangay 168-169 E 2
La Cocha 104-105 D 10
La Cocha, Laguna — 94-95 C 7
Lac Ogascanan 72-73 GH 1
Lac Olga 62 N 2
La Colina 106-107 G 6
Lacolle 72-73 K 2
La Colonia 108-109 C 6
La Colorada 86-87 EF 3
Lacombe 56-57 O 7
Lac Onangué 172 AB 2
La Concepción 92-93 E 2
Laconia, NH 72-73 L 3
Lac Onistagane 63 A 2
Lacoochee, FL 80-81 b 2
Lac Opataka 62 O 1
Lac Opatawaga 62 N 1
Lac Opémisca 62 O 1
La Copelina 106-107 D 6
La Copeta 106-107 G 6
La Cordobesa 106-107 J 4
La Coronilla 106-107 L 4
La Coruña 120-121 C 7
La Costa 106-107 D 4
la Courneuve 129 I c 2
Lac Parent 62 N 2
Lac Peribonca 63 A 2
Lac Piacouadie 63 A 2
Lac Plétipi 63 A 2
Lac Poisson Blanc 72-73 J 1-2
Lac Poulin de Courval 63 AB 3
Lac Poutrincourt 62 O 2
Lac Preissac 62 M 2
Lac Puskitamika 62 N 2
Lacq 120-121 G 7
Lac Quévillon 62 N 2
Lac qui Parle 68-69 H 3
La Crescent, MN 70-71 E 4
La Criolla 106-107 G 3
La Cristina 94-95 E 6
Lac R'kiz = Ar-R'kiz 164-165 AB 5
Lac Rohault 62 O 2
La Crosse, KS 68-69 G 6
Lacrosse, WA 66-67 E 2
La Crosse, WI 64-65 H 3
La Cruz [CO] 94-95 C 7
La Cruz [CR] 88-89 CD 9
La Cruz [MEX] 76-77 B 9
La Cruz [RA] 106-107 J 2
La Cruz [ROU] 106-107 JK 4
La Cruz de Taratara 94-95 G 2
Lac-Saguay 72-73 J 1
Lac Sainte-Louis 82 I a 2
Lac Saint François 72-73 L 2
Lac Saint-Jean 56-57 W 8
Lac Saint Patrice 72-73 H 1
Lac Saint-Pierre 72-73 K 1
Lac Seul 56-57 S 7
Lac Seul [CDN, place] 62 C 2
Lac Simard 72-73 G 1
Lacs Jolliet 62 N 1
Lac Soscumica 62 N 1
Lac Taureau 72-73 K 1
Lac Tauredu 62 OP 3
Lac Tchad 164-165 G 6
Lac Témiscamie 62 PQ 1
Lac Temiscouata 63 BC 4
Lac Tesecav 62 O 1
Lac Tumba 172 C 2
Lac Turgeon 62 M 2
La Cueva 94-95 E 2
La Culebra 94-95 H 3
Lacul Razelm 122-123 N 3
La Cumbre [RA] 106-107 E 3
La Cumbre [YV] 91 II b 1
Lac Upemba 172 E 3
Lac Waswanipi 62 N 2
Lac Woeonichi 62 O 1
Lac Woollett 62 P 1
Lada, Teluk — 152-153 F 9
Ladainha 102-103 LM 2
Ladākh 134-135 M 4
Ladākh Range 134-135 M 3-4
Ladan 126-127 F 1
Ladang, Ko — 150-151 B 9
La Danta 94-95 L 4
Ladário 102-103 D 3
Ladchhung 138-139 M 4
Ladder Creek 68-69 F 6
Laddonia, MO 70-71 E 6
Ladera Heights, CA 83 III b 2
La Desirade 88-89 Q 6
Lādhiqīyah, Al- 134-135 CD 3
Lādik 136-137 FG 2
Ladiqiya, El — = Al-Lādhiqīyah 134-135 CD 3
Ladismith 172 D 8
Ladner 66-67 B 1
Lādnun 138-139 E 4
Ladoga, IN 70-71 G 6
Ladoga, Lake — = Ladožskoje ozero 132-133 E 5
La Dorada 92-93 E 3
La Dormida 106-107 D 4
Ladožskoje ozero 132-133 E 5
Ladrillero, Golfo — 108-109 AB 7
Ladrillero, Monte — 108-109 CD 9
Ladrones Peak 76-77 A 5
Ladron Mountains 76-77 A 5
Ladue River 58-59 R 5
La Dulce 106-107 H 7
La Dulce, Laguna — 106-107 D 7
L'ady [SU, Gor'kovskaja Oblast'] 124-125 P 5
L'ady [SU, Pskovskaja Oblast'] 124-125 G 4
Lady Beatrix, Lac — 62 N 1
Ladybrand 172 E 7
Lady Evelyn Lake 72-73 F 1
Lady Franklinfjord 116-117 k 4
Lady Frere 174-175 G 6
Lady Grey 174-175 G 6
Lady Newnes Ice Shelf 53 B 18-17
Ladysmith, WI 70-71 E 3
Ladysmith [CDN] 66-67 AB 1
Ladysmith [ZA] 172 EF 7
Lae [PNG] 148-149 N 8
La Eduvigis 104-105 G 10
Laeken, Parc de — 128 II b 1
Laem, Khao — 150-151 C 5
Laem Ko Lamphuk = Laem Talumphuk 150-151 C 8
Laem Ngop 150-151 D 6
Laem Pho 148-149 D 5
Laem Pracham Hiang 150-151 B 7
Laem Si 150-151 B 8
Laem Sing 150-151 CD 6
Laem Talumphuk 150-151 C 8
La Encantada, Cerro de — 64-65 C 5
La Ensenada 108-109 H 3
Lærdalsøyri 116-117 BC 7
La Escondida 104-105 G 10
La Esmeralda [CO, Amazonas] 94-95 J 6
La Esmeralda [CO, Meta] 94-95 F 6
La Esmeralda [PY] 111 D 2
La Esmeralda [YV] 94-95 F 3
Læsø 116-117 D 9
La Esperanza [BOL] 104-105 EF 4
La Esperanza [C] 88-89 DE 3
La Esperanza [CO] 94-95 a 2
La Esperanza [Honduras] 88-89 BC 7
La Esperanza [RA, La Pampa] 106-107 D 6
La Esperanza [RA, Río Negro] 108-109 E 3
La Estrada 120-121 C 7
La Estrella 106-107 D 6
Lafagu 168-169 G 3
La Falda 106-107 E 3
Lafayette, AL 78-79 G 4
La Fayette, GA 78-79 G 3
Lafayette, IN 64-65 J 3
Lafayette, LA 64-65 H 5-6
Lafayette, TN 78-79 FG 2
Lafayette Hill, PA 84 III b 1
la Fère 120-121 J 4
Laferrere, La Matanza- 110 III b 2
Lafia 164-165 F 7
Lafiagi 164-165 EF 7
Laflamme, Rivière — 62 N 2
la Flèche 120-121 GH 5
Laflèche [CDN, Quebec] 82 I c 2
Laflèche [CDN, Saskatchewan] 61 E 6
La Florencia 104-105 EF 9
La Florida [CO, Cundinamarca] 91 III a 2
La Florida [CO, Nariño] 94-95 C 7
La Florida [PE] 96-97 F 3
La Florida, Parque — 91 III b 2
La Follette, TN 78-79 G 2
Lafontaine, Parc — 82 I b 1
Laforest 62 L 3
La Forestal 111 E 2
La Fragua 111 D 3
Lafreriere Park 85 I a 2
la Frette 129 I b 2
La Fría 92-93 E 3
La Fuente de San Esteban 120-121 DE 8
La Gallareta 106-107 G 2
Lagan 116-117 E 9
Lagan' = Kaspijskij 126-127 N 4
la Garenne-Colombes 129 I bc 2
Lagarfljót 116-117 f 2
La Garita Mountains 68-69 C 6-7
Lagarterito 64-65 b 2
Lagarto 100-101 F 6
Lagarto = Palmas Bellas 64-65 a 2
Lagbar 168-169 B 2
Lageadinho 102-103 G 7
Lågen 116-117 CD 7
Lager Döberitz 130 III a 1
Laghi Amari = Al-Buḥayrat al-Murrat al-Kubrā 173 C 2
Laghouat = Al-Aghwāt 164-165 E 2
Lagi = Ham Tân 150-151 FG 7
Lagič 126-127 O 6
Lāgin 141 F 2
La Gleta = Ḥalq al-Wad 166-167 M 1
La Gloria [CO] 92-93 E 3
La Gloria [RA] 106-107 F 6
Lågneset 116-117 j 6
Lagoa Açu 100-101 B 2
Lagoa Amaramba = Lagoa Chiuta 172 G 4
Lagoa Bonita 102-103 EF 5
Lagoa Carapebus 102-103 M 5
Lagoa Chiuta 172 G 4
Lagoa Chuali 174-175 K 3
Lagoa Clara 100-101 C 7
Lagoa da Conceição 102-103 H 7
Lagoa da Canoa 100-101 F 5
Lagoa da Rebeca 102-103 BC 1
Lagoa da Reserva 106-107 M 3
Lagoa da Tijuca 110 I ab 2
Lagoa de Araruama 102-103 L 5
Lagoa de Mostardas 106-107 M 3
Lagoa de Parnaguá 100-101 B 6
Lagoa de Prata 102-103 K 4
Lagoa do Caiuvá 106-107 LM 4
Lagoa do Capão do Poncho 106-107 MN 3
Lagoa do Pacheco 106-107 L 4
Lagoa do Peixe 106-107 M 3
Lagoa dos Barros 106-107 M 2
Lagoa dos Patos 111 F 4
Lagoa dos Quadros 106-107 MN 2
Lagoa Feia 92-93 L 9
Lagoa Gaíba 102-103 D 2
Lagoa Itapeva 106-107 MN 2
Lagoa Juparanã 100-101 DE 10
Lagoa Mangueira 111 F 4
Lagoa Maricá 102-103 L 5
Lagoa Marrângua 174-175 L 3
Lagoa Mirim 111 F 4
Lagoa Anibal Pinto 108-109 C 8-9
Lagoa Pequena 106-107 LM 3
Lagoa Piti 174-175 K 4
Lagoa Poelela 174-175 L 3
Lagoa Preta 100-101 D 8
Lagoa Rodrigo de Freitas 110 I b 2
Lagoa Santa 102-103 L 3
Lagoa Uberaba 102-103 D 2
Lago Auquinco 106-107 C 6
Lagoa Vermelha 106-107 M 2
Lago Badajos 92-93 G 5
Lago Banamana 174-175 KL 2
Lago Blanco [RA] 108-109 D 5
Lago Blanco [RCH] 108-109 E 10
Lago Brava 106-107 C 2
Lago Buenos Aires 111 B 7
Lago Buenos Aires, Meseta del — 108-109 D 6
Lago Calafquen 108-109 C 2
Lago Canacari 98-99 J 6
Lago Cardiel 111 B 7
Lago Cardiel [RA, place] 108-109 D 7
Lago Chepelmut 108-109 F 10
Lago Club de Los Lagortos 91 III bc 2
Lago Cochrane 108-109 C 6
Lago Colhué Huapí 111 C 7
Lago Colico 106-107 AB 7
Lago Comprida = Lagoa Nova 92-93 J 4
Lago da Pedra 100-101 B 3
Lago de Chapala 64-65 F 7
Lagodechi 126-127 MN 6
Lago de Chungara 104-105 B 6
Lago de Coipasa 104-105 C 6
Lago de Erepecu 92-93 H 5
Lago de Gatún 64-65 b 2
Lagodei, El- = Qardho 134-135 F 9
Lago de Ilopango 88-89 B 8
Lago de Izabal 64-65 HJ 8
Lago de Junin 96-97 C 7
Lago del Budi 106-107 A 7
Lago de los Arroyos 104-105 D 3
Lago del Toro 108-109 C 8
Lago de Managua 64-65 J 9
Lago de Maracaibo 92-93 E 2-3
Lago de Nicaragua 64-65 JK 9
Lago de Pátzcuaro 86-87 JK 8
Lago de Poopó 92-93 F 8
Lago de San Luis 104-105 D 3
Lago de Texcoco 91 I cd 1
Lago de Valencia 92-93 F 2
Lago de Vilama 104-105 C 8
Lago de Xochimilco 91 I c 3
Lago di Bolsena 122-123 DE 4
Lago di Bracciano 122-123 DE 4
Lago di Como 122-123 C 2-3
Lago di Garda 122-123 D 3
Lago do Coari 98-99 G 6-7
Lago do Junco 100-101 B 3
Lago dos Cajueiros 100-101 CD 2
Lago Dulce 108-109 E 6
Lago Enriquillo 88-89 L 5
Lago Fagnano 108-109 EF 10
Lago Fontana 108-109 D 5
Lago Futalaufquen 108-109 CD 4
Lago General Carrera 108-109 CD 6
Lago General Vintter 108-109 D 4-5
Lago Ghio 108-109 D 6
Lago Grande 113 III a 2
Lago Grande do Curuai 98-99 L 6
Lago Huachi 104-105 E 4
Lago Huechulafquén 108-109 D 2
Lago Lácar 108-109 D 3
Lago Lagunillas 96-97 F 9
Lagolândia 102-103 H 1
Lago La Plata 108-109 D 5
Lago Llanquihue 111 B 6
Lago Madden 64-65 b 2
Lago Madruba 98-99 J 6
Lago Maggiore 122-123 C 2-3
Lago Mapiripán 94-95 EF 6
Lago Menéndez 108-109 D 4
Lago Menzalé = Buḥayrat al-Manzilah 173 BC 2
Lago Musters 111 BC 7
Lago Nahuel Huapí 111 B 6
Lagonegro 122-123 FG 5
Lago Niassa = Lake Malawi 172 F 4
Lago Novo 92-93 J 4
Lago Ofhidro 108-109 E 9
Lago O'Higgins 108-109 C 7
Lago Paciba 94-95 H 6
Lago Panguipulli 108-109 CD 2
Lago Pastos Grandes 104-105 C 7
Lago Pellegrini 106-107 CD 7
Lago Petén Itzá 86-87 Q 9
Lago Piorini 92-93 G 5
Lago Pitari 104-105 F 3
Lago Posadas 108-109 D 6
Lago Pozuelos 104-105 CD 8
Lago Presidente Rios 108-109 B 6
Lago Pueyrredón 111 B 7
Lago Puyehue 108-109 C 3
Lago Quiroga 108-109 D 7
Lago Ranco 111 B 6
Lago Ranco [RCH, place] 108-109 C 3
Lago Rimachi 96-97 C 4
Lago Rogagua 92-93 F 7
Lago Rogoaguado 92-93 F 7
Lago Rupanco 108-109 CD 3
Lagos [P] 120-121 C 10
Lagos [WAN] 164-165 E 7
Lagos, Los — [RCH, administrative unit] 108-109 C 3-4
Lagos, Los — [RCH, place] 108-109 C 2
Lagosa 172 EF 3
Lago Salitroso 108-109 D 6
Lago San Martín 111 B 7
Lago San Nicolás 104-105 D 3
Lagos-Apapa 170 III b 2
Lagos-Apese 170 III b 2
Lagos de Moreno 64-65 F 7
Lagos-Ebute-Metta 170 III b 2
Lagos Harbour 170 III b 2
Lagos-Iddo 170 III b 2
Lagos-Iganmu 170 III b 2
Lagos-Ikoyi 170 III b 2
Lagos Island 170 III b 2

316 Kuzneck

Lagos Lagoon 170 III b 2
Lagos-New Lagos 170 III b 1
Lagos-Surulere 170 III b 1
Lagosta = Lastovo 122-123 G 4
Lagos Terminus 170 III b 2
Lago Strobel 108-109 D 7
Lagos-Yaba 170 III b 1
Lago Tábua 100-101 C 2
Lago Tar 108-109 D 7
Lago Titicaca 92-93 F 8
Lago Todos los Santos 108-109 CD 3
Lago Toronto 86-87 GH 4
Lago Traful 108-109 D 3
Lago Trasimeno 122-123 DE 4
Lago Tromen 108-109 D 2
La Goulette = Ḥalq al-Wad 166-167 M 1
la Goulette = Ḥalq al-Wad 166-167 M 1
Lago Varuá Ipana 94-95 EF 7
Lago Varvarco Campos 106-107 B 6
Lago Verde [BR] 100-101 B 2
Lago Verde [RA] 108-109 E 4
Lago Viedma 111 B 7
Lago Viedma [RA, place] 108-109 C 7
Lago Villarrica 108-109 C 2
Lagowa, El — = Al-Laqawah 164-165 K 6
Lago Xiriri 98-99 L 5
Lågøya 116-117 k 4
Lago Yehuin 108-109 EF 10
Lago Yelcho 108-109 C 4
Lago Ypoá 102-103 D 6
Lago Yulton 108-109 C 5
Lago Yusala 104-105 C 3
La Grande, OR 66-67 D 3
La Grange 158-159 D 3
La Grange, GA 64-65 JK 5
Lagrange, IN 70-71 H 5
La Grange, KY 70-71 H 6
La Grange, NC 80-81 H 3
La Grange, TX 76-77 F 7-8
Lagrange, WY 68-69 D 5
La Gran Sabana 92-93 G 3
La Grita 94-95 F 3
La Gruta 102-103 F 7
Lagua da Canabrava 100-101 D 6
La Guaira 94-95 H 2
La Guardia [BOL] 104-105 E 5
La Guardia [RA] 106-107 E 2
La Guardia [RCH] 106-107 C 1
La Guardia Airport 82 III c 2
Laguboti 150-151 B 11
Laguna, NM 76-77 A 5
Laguna [BR] 111 G 3
Laguna [PE] 96-97 B 5
Laguna, Ilha da — 98-99 N 5
Laguna, La — [PA ↑ Panamá] 64-65 b 2
Laguna, La — [PA ← Panamá] 64-65 b 3
Laguna, La — [RA] 106-107 F 4
Laguna 8 de Agosto 106-107 F 7
Laguna 8 de Agosto 108-109 H 2
Laguna Alsina 106-107 F 6
Laguna Arapa 96-97 FG 9
Laguna Ayarde 104-105 F 9
Laguna Beach, CA 74-75 DE 6
Laguna Blanca [RA, Formosa] 104-105 G 9
Laguna Blanca [RA, Neuquén] 106-107 B 7
Laguna Blanca [RA, Río Negro] 108-109 E 3
Laguna Blanca, Sierra — 104-105 C 10
Laguna Blanco 108-109 D 9
Laguna Caburgua 108-109 D 2
Laguna Cáceres 104-105 GH 6
Laguna Caimán 94-95 G 6
Laguna Campos 102-103 B 4
Laguna Cari Laufquen Grande 108-109 E 3
Laguna Castillos 106-107 KL 5
Laguna Chaira 94-95 D 7
Laguna Chasicó 106-107 F 7
Laguna Chichancanab 86-87 Q 8
Laguna Chicuaco 94-95 G 6
Laguna Concepción [BOL → Santa Cruz de la Sierra] 104-105 F 5
Laguna Concepción [BOL ↑ Santa Cruz de la Sierra] 104-105 E 4
Laguna Coronda 106-107 G 3-4
Laguna Curicó 108-109 G 3
Laguna Dam 74-75 FG 6
Laguna de Agua Brava 86-87 GH 6
Laguna de Babícora 86-87 FG 3
Laguna de Bacalar 86-87 Q 8
Laguna de Boyeruca 106-107 AB 5
Laguna de Caratasca 64-65 K 8
Laguna de Chiriquí 64-65 K 9-10
Laguna de Cuitzeo 86-87 K 8
Laguna de Fúquene 94-95 E 5
Laguna de Guavatayoc 104-105 CD 8
Laguna de Guzmán 86-87 G 2
Laguna de Jaco 76-77 C 9
Laguna del Abra 108-109 H 3
Laguna de la Laja 106-107 B 6
Laguna del Caimanero 86-87 G 6
Laguna del Carrizal 106-107 H 7
Laguna del Cisne 106-107 FG 2
Laguna del Maule 106-107 B 6
Laguna del Monte 106-107 H 5
Laguna de los Cisnes 108-109 D 6
Laguna de los Patos 106-107 F 3
Laguna de los Porongos 106-107 F 2-3
Laguna del Palmar 106-107 G 2
Laguna del Sauce 106-107 K 5
Laguna de Luna 106-107 J 2
Laguna de Monte 106-107 F 6
Laguna de Palo Parada 106-107 E 2
Laguna de Patos 86-87 GH 2
Laguna de Perlas 88-89 E 8
Laguna de Rocha 106-107 K 5
Laguna de Santiaguillo 86-87 H 5
Laguna de Tacarigua 94-95 J 2
Laguna de Tamiahua 64-65 G 7
Laguna de Términos 64-65 H 8
Laguna de Unare 94-95 J 2
Laguna de Vichuquén 106-107 AB 5
Laguna de Villarrica 106-107 AB 7
Laguna El Maestro 106-107 J 6
Laguna Epecuén 106-107 F 6
Laguna Escondida, Bajo de la — 108-109 F 2-G 3
Laguna Garzón 106-107 K 5
Laguna Grande [RA, Chubut] 108-109 F 4
Laguna Grande [RA, Santa Cruz lake] 108-109 E 6
Laguna Grande [RA, Santa Cruz place] 108-109 D 7
Laguna Guatraché 106-107 F 6
Laguna Huani 88-89 E 7
Laguna Huaunta 88-89 E 8
Laguna Iberá 106-107 J 2
Laguna La Amarga 106-107 DE 7
Laguna la Bella 102-103 B 6
Laguna La Brava 106-107 F 4
Laguna La Cocha 94-95 C 7
Laguna La Dulce 106-107 D 7
Laguna Larga 106-107 F 3
Laguna La Salada Grande 106-107 J 6
Laguna Limpia [RA ↖ Resistencia] 111 DE 3
Laguna Limpia [RA ↓ Resistencia] 106-107 H 1
Laguna Llancanelo 106-107 C 5
Laguna Lleulleu 106-107 A 7
Laguna Lorisccota 96-97 G 10
Laguna Los Chilenos 106-107 F 6
Laguna Madre 64-65 G 6-7
Laguna Mandioré 104-105 GH 6
Laguna Mar Chiquita 111 D 4
Laguna Melincué 106-107 G 4
Laguna Mountains 74-75 E 6
Laguna Negra [RA] 104-105 F 9
Laguna Negra [ROU] 106-107 L 4-5
Laguna Ocho de Agosto 106-107 F 7
Laguna Ojo de Liebre 86-87 CD 4
Laguna Paiva 106-107 G 3
Laguna Parinacochas 96-97 DE 9
Laguna Piranè 104-105 G 9
Lagunas [PE] 92-93 DE 6
Lagunas [RCH] 111 BC 2
Lagunas, Las — 106-107 E 5
Laguna Salada [MEX] 86-87 C 1
Laguna Salada [RA, Buenos Aires] 106-107 H 7
Laguna Salada [RA, Córdoba] 106-107 F 3
Laguna Salada [RA, La Pampa] 106-107 E 6
Laguna San Ignacio 86-87 D 4
Laguna Santa Catalina 110 III b 2
Laguna Saridú 94-95 GH 6
Laguna Atacavi 94-95 H 6
Lagunas de Gómez 106-107 G 5
Lagunas de Guanacache 106-107 CD 4
Lagunas Huatunas 104-105 C 3
Lagunas Sirven 108-109 E 6
Lagunas Las Tunas Grandes 106-107 F 5-6
Lagunas Saladas 106-107 F 2
Laguna Superior 64-65 H 8
Laguna Tarabillas 76-77 B 7
Laguna Trinidad 102-103 B 4
Laguna Tunaima 94-95 E 7
Laguna Tunas Chicas 106-107 F 6
Laguna Uinamarca 104-105 B 5
Laguna Urre Lauquen 106-107 E 7
Laguna Uvá 94-95 F 6
Laguna Verá 111 E 3
Laguna Yema 111 D 2
Laguna Ypacaraí 102-103 D 6
Lagundu, Tanjung — 152-153 N 10
Lagunetas 94-95 F 3
Lagunillas [BOL] 104-105 E 6
Lagunillas [RCH] 106-107 B 4
Lagunillas [YV, Mérida] 94-95 F 3
Lagunillas [YV, Zuila] 94-95 F 2
Lagunillas, Lago — 96-97 F 9
Lagunita Country Club, La — 91 II c 2
Lagunitas 94-95 F 2
La Habana 64-65 K 7
Lahad Datu 148-149 G 5-6
Lahaina, HI 78-79 d 2
Laham [RI] 148-149 G 6
Laham [RN] 168-169 G 2
Lahan, Nong — 150-151 E 4
Lahār 138-139 G 4
Lāharpur 138-139 H 4
Lahat 148-149 D 7
Lāhaur 134-135 L 4
La Have Bank 63 D 6
Lahe = Lahei 141 D 2
Lahei 141 D 2
La Hermosa 94-95 F 5
La Herradura 108-109 F 7
Lahewa 148-149 C 6
La Hierra 106-107 H 3
La Higuera 106-107 B 2
Laḥij 134-135 EF 8
Lāhījān 136-137 FG 3
Lahir 138-139 H 8
Lahn 118 D 3
Laholm 116-117 E 9
Laholms bukten 116-117 E 9
La Honda 94-95 C 4
Lahontan Reservoir 74-75 D 3
Lahore = Lāhaur 134-135 L 4
La Horqueta [YV, Bolívar] 94-95 L 4
La Horqueta [YV, Monagas] 94-95 K 3
Lahrī 138-139 AB 3
Lahti 116-117 LM 7
La Huacana 86-87 JK 8
La Huerta 106-107 AB 5
Laï 164-165 H 7
Lai, Mui — 150-151 F 4
Lai'an 146-147 G 5
Laibin 146-147 B 10
Lai Châu 148-149 D 2
Lai Chi Kok, Victoria- 155 I a 1
Lai-chou Wan = Laizhou Wan 146-147 G 3
Laidley 160 L 1
Laifeng 146-147 B 7
Lai Hka = Lechā 148-149 C 2
Laikot 141 C 3
Lailā = Laylā 134-135 F 6
Lailān = Laylān 136-137 L 5
Laim, München- 130 II ab 2
Lainé 168-169 C 3
Laingsburg 172 CD 8
Lainz, Wien- 113 I b 2
Lainzer Tiergarten 113 I ab 2
Lai-pin = Laibin 146-147 B 10
Laipo = Lipu 142-143 KL 7
Laird, CO 68-69 E 5
Lais [RI, Celebes] 152-153 O 5
Lais [RI, Sumatra] 152-153 DE 7
La Isabela 88-89 FG 3
Laisamis 171 D 2
Laiševo 124-125 RS 6
Laishui 146-147 E 2
La Islá [PE] 96-97 D 9
La Isla [RA] 106-107 DE 3
Laiwu 146-147 F 3
Laixi 146-147 H 3
Laiyang 146-147 H 3
Laiyuan 142-143 LM 4
Lai-yüan = Laiyuan 142-143 LM 4
Laizhou Wan 146-147 G 3
Laja 104-105 B 5
Lajā', Al- 136-137 G 6
Laja, Laguna de la — 106-107 B 6
Laja, Río de la — 106-107 AB 6
La Jagua 92-93 E 3
La Jalca 96-97 C 5
La Jara 120-121 E 9
La Jara, CO 68-69 CD 7
La Jarita 86-87 KL 4
Lajas, Las — 106-107 B 7
La Jaula 106-107 C 5
Laje [BR ↙ Salvador] 100-101 E 7
Laje [BR ↖ Senhor do Bonfim] 100-101 D 6
Laje, Cachoeira da — 98-99 L 5
Laje, Ilha da — 110 I c 2
Lajeado 106-107 LM 2
Lajeado, Cachoeira do — 98-99 H 10
Lajedo 100-101 F 5
Lajedo Alto 100-101 DE 7
Laje dos Santos 102-103 JK 6
Lajes [BR, Rio Grande do Norte] 92-93 M 6
Lajes [BR, Santa Catarina] 111 F 3
Lajinha 102-103 M 4
Lajitas, TX 76-77 C 8
Lajitas, Las — [RA] 104-105 DE 9
Lajitas, Las — [YV] 94-95 J 4
Lajkovac 122-123 HJ 3
La Jolla, CA 74-75 E 6
La Joya, NM 76-77 A 5
La Joya [BOL] 104-105 C 5
La Joya [PE] 96-97 F 10
Lajtamak 132-133 M 6
La Junta, CO 64-65 F 4
La Junta [BOL] 104-105 F 4
La Junta [MEX] 86-87 G 3
Lak Boggai 171 D 2
Lak Bor 172 G 1
Lak Dera 172 H 1
Lak Dima 171 E 2
Lake, WY 66-67 H 3
Lake, The — 88-89 K 4
Lake Abert 66-67 CD 4
Lake Abitibi 56-57 UV 8
Lake Acraman 158-159 FG 6
Lake Albert 158-159 GH 7
Lake Aleknagik 58-59 H 7
Lake Alexandrina 158-159 GH 7
Lake Alma 68-69 D 1
Lake Altus = Harlan County Reservoir 68-69 G 5-6
Lake Almanor 66-67 C 5
Lake Amadeus 158-159 F 4
Lake Amboseli 171 D 3
Lake Andes 68-69 G 4
Lake Andes, SD 68-69 G 4
Lake Arthur, LA 78-79 C 5
Lake Arthur, NM 76-77 B 6
Lake Ashtabula = Baldhill Reservoir 68-69 GH 2
Lake Athabasca 56-57 OP 6
Lake Auld 158-159 D 4
Lake Austin 158-159 C 5
Lake Avalon 76-77 BC 6
Lake Ballard 158-159 D 5
Lake Bangweulu 172 EF 4
Lake Baringo 171 D 2
Lake Barkley 78-79 EF 2
Lake Barlee 158-159 C 5
Lake Benmore 161 D 7
Lake Benton, MN 70-71 BC 3
Lake Berryessa 74-75 B 3
Lake Beverley 58-59 H 7
Lake Bistineau 78-79 C 4
Lake Blanche [AUS, South Australia] 158-159 GH 5
Lake Blanche [AUS, Western Australia] 158-159 D 4
Lake Bolac 160 F 6
Lake Borgne 78-79 E 5-6
Lake Bowdoin 68-69 C 1
Lake Brooks 58-59 K 7
Lake Butler, FL 80-81 b 1
Lake Cadibarrawirracanna 160 AB 2
Lake Callabonna 158-159 G 5
Lake Calumet 83 II b 2
Lake Carey 158-159 D 5
Lake Cargelligo 158-159 J 6
Lake Carnegie 158-159 D 5
Lake Cataouatche 85 I a 2
Lake Chamo = Tyamo 164-165 M 7
Lake Champlain 64-65 LM 3
Lake Charles, LA 64-65 H 5
Lake Charlevoix 70-71 H 3
Lake Chelan 66-67 C 1
Lake Chilwa 172 G 5
Lake Chiuta 172 G 4
Lake Chrissie = Chrissiesmeer 174-175 J 4
Lake City, CO 68-69 C 6
Lake City, FL 80-81 b 1
Lake City, IA 70-71 C 4
Lake City, MI 70-71 H 3
Lake City, MN 70-71 D 3
Lake City, SC 80-81 G 4
Lake City, SD 68-69 H 3
Lake Claire 56-57 O 6
Lake Clark 58-59 K 6
Lake Coleridge 161 D 6
Lake Cormorant, MS 78-79 DE 3
Lake Cowal 158-159 J 6
Lake Cowan 158-159 D 6
Lake Cowichan 66-67 AB 1
Lake Crescent 66-67 B 1
Lake Crowley 74-75 D 4
Lake Crystal, MN 70-71 C 3
Lake Cumberland 70-71 H 7
Lake C. W. MacConaughy 68-69 E 5
Lake Darling 68-69 F 1
Lake Dey Dey 158-159 F 5
Lake Diefenbaker 61 E 5
Lake Disappointment 158-159 DE 4
Lake Dora 158-159 D 4
Lake Dow 172 D 6
Lake Dundas 158-159 D 6
Lake Eaton 158-159 EF 4
Lake Echo 160 c 3
Lake Erie 64-65 KL 3
Lake Eucumbene 160 J 6
Lake Everard 158-159 F 6
Lake Eyasi 172 FG 2
Lake Eyre 158-159 G 5
Lake Eyre North 160 C 2
Lake Eyre South 160 C 2
Lakefield, MN 70-71 C 4
Lakefield [AUS] 158-159 H 2-3
Lakefield [ZA] 170 V c 2
Lake Forest, New Orleans-, LA 85 I c 1
Lake Francis Case 64-65 FG 3
Lake Frome 158-159 GH 6
Lake Gairdner 158-159 G 6
Lake Galilee 158-159 HJ 4
Lake Gem 85 II a 2
Lake Geneva, WI 70-71 F 4
Lake George, NY 72-73 JK 3
Lake George [AUS] 158-159 JK 7
Lake George [EAU] 172 F 2
Lake George [RWA] 171 B 3
Lake George [USA, Alaska] 58-59 PQ 5
Lake George [USA, Florida] 80-81 c 2
Lake George [USA, New York] 72-73 K 3
Lake Gillen 158-159 D 5
Lake Gilles 160 C 4
Lake Gogebic 70-71 F 2
Lake Gordon 160 bc 3
Lake Grace 158-159 C 6
Lake Granby 68-69 D 5
Lake Greeson 78-79 C 3
Lake Gregory 158-159 GH 5
Lake Grosvenor 58-59 K 7
Lake Harbour 56-57 WX 5
Lake Harris 160 B 3
Lake Havasu City, AZ 74-75 FG 5
Lake Hawea 161 C 7
Lake Hickory 80-81 F 3
Lake Hopkins 158-159 E 4
Lake Huron 64-65 K 2-3
Lake Indawgyi = Indaugyī Aing 141 E 3
Lake Itasca 64-65 G 2
Lake Jackson, TX 76-77 G 8
Lake Joseph 72-73 G 2
Lake Kampolombo 172 E 4
Lake Kariba 172 E 5
Lake Kemp 76-77 E 6
Lake King 158-159 CD 6
Lake Kissimmee 80-81 c 2-3
Lake Kosi = Kosimeer 174-175 K 4
Lake Kulik [USA ↑ Kuskokwim River] 58-59 G 6
Lake Kulik [USA ↓ Kuskokwim River] 58-59 H 7
Lake Kwania 171 C 2
Lake Kyoga 172 F 1
Lake Laberge 58-59 U 6
Lake Lanao 148-149 HJ 5
Lakeland, FL 64-65 K 6
Lakeland, GA 80-81 E 5
Lake Lefroy 158-159 D 6
Lake Louise 58-59 O 5
Lake Louise [CDN] 60 JK 4
Lakelse 60 C 2
Lake Macdonald [AUS] 158-159 E 4
Lake MacDonald [CDN] 66-67 FG 1
Lake Macfarlane 158-159 G 6
Lake Machattie 158-159 GH 4
Lake Mackay 158-159 E 4
Lake MacLeod 158-159 B 4
Lake MacMillan 76-77 BC 6
Lake Macquarie 160 KL 4
Lake Magadi 171 D 3
Lake Maitland 158-159 D 5
Lake Malawi 172 F 4
Lake Malombe 172 G 4
Lake Manapouri 158-159 N 9
Lake Manitoba 56-57 R 7
Lake Manyara 172 G 2
Lake Margherita = Abaya 164-165 M 7
Lake Marion 80-81 F 4
Lake Maurepas 78-79 D 5
Lake Maurice 158-159 EF 5
Lake Mead 64-65 D 4
Lake Mead National Recreation Area 74-75 FG 4
Lake Melville 56-57 YZ 7
Lake Meramangye 158-159 F 5
Lake Merced 83 I b 2
Lake Meridith 76-77 D 5
Lake Merrit 83 I c 2
Lake Michigan 64-65 J 2-3
Lake Mills, IA 70-71 D 4
Lake Mills, WI 70-71 F 4
Lake Minchumina 58-59 L 5
Lake Minchumina, AK 58-59 L 5
Lake Minigwal 158-159 D 5
Lake Minnewaska 70-71 C 3
Lake Minto 56-57 V 6
Lake Mistassini 56-57 W 7
Lake Monger 158-159 C 5
Lake Moore 158-159 C 5
Lake Moultrie 80-81 F 4
Lake Murray [PNG] 148-149 M 8
Lake Murray [USA] 80-81 F 3
Lake Muskoka 72-73 G 2
Lake Mweru 172 E 3
Lake Natron 172 G 2
Lake Neale 158-159 F 4
Lake Nerka 58-59 H 7
Lake Ngami 172 D 6
Lake Nipigon 56-57 ST 8
Lake Nipissing 56-57 UV 8
Lake Nunavaugaluk 58-59 H 7
Lake Oahe 64-65 F 2
Lake Odessa, MI 70-71 H 4
Lake of Bays 72-73 G 2
Lake of the Ozarks 64-65 H 4
Lake of the Woods 56-57 R 8
Lake Ohau 161 CD 7
Lake Okeechobee 64-65 K 6
Lake Ontario 64-65 L 3
Lake Oswego, OR 66-67 B 3
Lake O'The Cherokees 76-77 G 4
Lake Owyhee 66-67 E 4
Lake Panache 62 L 3
Lake Park, IA 70-71 C 4
Lake Pedder 160 bc 3
Lake Philippi 158-159 G 4
Lake Pine, NJ 84 III de 2
Lake Placid, FL 80-81 c 3
Lake Placid, NY 64-65 M 3
Lake Pleasant, NY 72-73 J 3
Lake Poinsett 68-69 H 3
Lake Pontchartrain 64-65 HJ 5
Lakeport, CA 74-75 B 3
Lake Powell 64-65 D 4
Lake Poygan 70-71 F 3
Lake Preston, SD 68-69 H 3
Lake Providence, LA 78-79 D 4
Lake Pukaki 161 D 7
Lake Quannapowitt 84 I b 1
Lake Range 66-67 D 5
Lake Rebecca 158-159 D 6
Lake Rukwa 172 F 3
Lake Saint Ann 60 K 3
Lake Saint Clair 56-57 U 9
Lake Saint John = Lac Saint Jean 56-57 W 8
Lake Saint Joseph 56-57 ST 7
Lake Saint Lucia = Sint Luciameer 172 F 7
Lake Saint Martin 61 JK 5
Lake Sakakawea 64-65 F 2
Lake Salisbury 172 FG 1
Lake Salvador 78-79 D 6
Lake Semiole 78-79 G 5
Lakes Entrance 160 HJ 6
Lake Sewell = Canyon Ferry Reservoir 66-67 H 2
Lakeshore, New Orleans-, LA 85 I b 1
Lake Sibayi = Sibayameer 174-175 K 4
Lakeside, AZ 74-75 J 5
Lakeside, NE 68-69 E 4
Lakeside, OR 66-67 A 4
Lakeside, UT 66-67 G 5
Lakeside, VA 80-81 H 2
Lakeside Estates, Houston-, TX 85 III a 2
Lakeside Forest, Houston-, TX 85 III a 1
Lake Sidney Lanier 80-81 DE 3
Lake Simcoe 56-57 V 9
Lake Sinclair 80-81 E 4
Lake Sorell 160 c 2
Lake Stephanie = Thew Bahir 164-165 M 8
Lake Summer 76-77 B 5
Lake Superior 64-65 HJ 2
Lake Superior Provincial Park 62 G 4
Lake Tahoe 64-65 BC 4
Lake Tanganyika 172 E 2-F 3
Lake Taupo 158-159 P 7
Lake Te Anau 158-159 N 9
Lake Telaquana 58-59 L 6
Lake Terrace, New Orleans-, LA 85 I b 1
Lake Texoma 64-65 G 5
Lake Tillery 80-81 FG 3
Lake Timagami 72-73 F 1
Lake Torrens 158-159 G 6
Lake Toxaway, NC 80-81 E 3
Lake Traverse 68-69 H 3
Lake Travis 76-77 EF 7
Lake Tschida 68-69 EF 2
Lake Turkana 172 G 1
Lake Tyrell 158-159 H 7
Lake Victor, TX 76-77 E 7
Lake Victoria [AUS] 160 E 4
Lake Victoria [lake] 172 F 2
Lakeview, MI 70-71 H 4
Lakeview, OR 66-67 C 4
Lakeview, Chicago-, IL 83 II ab 1
Lakeview, Houston-, TX 85 III a 1
Lakeview, New Orleans-, LA 85 I b 1-2
Lake Village, AR 78-79 D 4
Lake Vista, New Orleans-, LA 85 I b 1
Lake Volta 164-165 DE 7
Lake Waccamaw 80-81 G 3
Lake Waikaremoana 161 G 4
Lake Wakatipu 161 C 7
Lake Wales, FL 80-81 c 3
Lake Wanaka 161 C 7
Lake Waukarlycarly 158-159 D 4
Lake Way 158-159 D 5
Lake Wells 158-159 D 5
Lake White 158-159 E 4
Lake Winnebago 70-71 F 3-4
Lake Winnipeg 56-57 R 7
Lake Winnipegosis 56-57 R 7
Lake Winnipesaukee 72-73 L 3
Lakewood, CA 83 III d 2
Lakewood, CO 68-69 D 6
Lakewood, NJ 72-73 J 4
Lakewood, NM 76-77 B 6
Lakewood, NY 72-73 G 3
Lakewood, OH 72-73 EF 4
Lakewood East, New Orleans-, LA 85 I c 1
Lakewood Park 85 II b 2
Lake Woods 158-159 F 3
Lakewood Stadium 85 II b 2
Lake Worth, FL 64-65 KL 6
Lake Wright 158-159 EF 5
Lake Yamma Yamma 158-159 H 5
Lake Yeo 158-159 D 5
Lake Younghusband 160 BC 3
Lake Zwai = Ziway 164-165 M 7
Lakhadsweep 134-135 L 8
Lakhdar, Ouèd — = Wād al-Akhdar 166-167 C 4
Lakhdaria = Lakhḍarīyah 166-167 H 1
Lakhḍarīyah 166-167 H 1
Lakhī, Koh — 138-139 A 4-5
Lakhīmpur [IND, Assam] 141 D 2
Lakhīmpur [IND, Uttar Pradesh] 138-139 H 4
Lakhipur [IND ↘ Alīpur Duār] 138-139 N 4-5
Lakhipur [IND ← Imphāl] 141 C 3
Lakhnādaun = Lakhnādon 138-139 G 6
Lakhnādon 138-139 G 6
Lakhnaū = Lucknow 134-135 MN 5
Lakhpat 138-139 B 6
Lakhtar 138-139 CD 6
Lakin, KS 68-69 F 7
Lakin = Lāgin 141 F 2
Lakinskij 124-125 M 5
Lakkhīsarāy = Luckeesarai 138-139 KL 5
Lakonia, Gulf of — = Lakōnikòs Kólpos 122-123 K 7
Lakōnikòs Kólpos 122-123 K 7
Lakota 168-169 D 4
Lakota, IA 70-71 CD 4
Lakota, ND 68-69 G 1
Lak Sao 150-151 E 3
Laksar 138-139 G 3
Laksefjord 116-117 M 2
Lakselv 116-117 L 2
Lakṣhadvīp = Lakshadweep 134-135 L 8
Lākshām 141 B 4
Lakshettipet 140 D 1
Lakshmanpur 138-139 J 6
Lakshmeshwar 140 B 3
Lakshmikāntapur 138-139 M 6
Lakshmīpur [BD] 140 F 1
Lakshmīpūr [IND] 141 B 4
Lālāghāt 141 C 3
La Laguna [PA ↑ Panamá] 64-65 b 2
La Laguna [PA ← Panamá] 64-65 b 3
La Laguna [RA] 106-107 F 4
La Lagunita Country Club 91 II c 2
Lālapaṣa 136-137 B 2
La Lara 168-169 H 5
Lalaua 172 G 4
Lālbāg 138-139 M 5
Lalbagh = Lālbāg 138-139 M 5
La Leonesa 104-105 G 10
Lālganj [IND, Bihār] 138-139 K 5
Lālganj [IND, Uttar Pradesh] 138-139 J 5
Lālgolā = Krishnapur 138-139 M 5
Lālguḍi 140 D 5
Lālī 136-137 N 6
Lalībela 164-165 M 6
La Libertad [EC] 96-97 A 3
La Libertad [PE] 96-97 BC 5
La Ligua 111 B 4
La Lima 88-89 B 7
La Linea 120-121 E 10
Lalitpur 138-139 G 5
Lālmanīr Hāṭ 138-139 M 5
La Lobería 108-109 H 3
La Loche 56-57 P 6
La Loche West 61 CD 2
La Loma 104-105 D 7
Lālpur 138-139 BC 6
Lal'sk 124-125 QR 3
Lālsot 138-139 F 4
La Luisa 106-107 GH 5
La Luz, NM 76-77 AB 6
Lâm [VN] 150-151 F 2
La Macolla 94-95 F 1
La Madrid 104-105 D 10
Lamadrid [MEX] 76-77 D 9
La Magdalena Atlipac 91 I d 2
La Magdalena Contreras 91 I b 3
La Magdalena Puerto Nare 94-95 D 4
Lamaing 141 EF 8
Lama-Kara 168-169 F 3
la Malbaie 63 AB 4
Lamaline 63 J 4
La Mancha 120-121 F 9
Lamandau, Sungai — 152-153 J 6-7
Lamar, CO 68-69 E 6
Lamar, MO 70-71 C 7
La Mariposa, Embalse — 91 II b 2
La Mariscala 106-107 K 5
La Maroma 106-107 DE 5
Lamarque 106-107 E 7
La Marque, TX 76-77 G 8
La Marquesa 91 I a 3
La Maruja 106-107 E 5
Lamas 96-97 C 5
La Mata 94-95 E 3
La Matanza 110 III b 2
La Matanza-20 de Junio 110 III a 2
La Matanza-Aldo Bonzi 110 III b 2
La Matanza-Ciudad General Belgrano 110 III b 2
La Matanza-González Catán 110 III b 2
La Matanza-Isidro Casanova 110 III b 2
La Matanza-Laferrere 110 III b 2
La Matanza-Rafael Castillo 110 III b 2
La Matanza-Ramos Mejía 110 III b 1
La Matanza-San Justo 110 III a 1
La Matanza-Tablada 110 III b 2
La Matanza-Tapiales 110 III b 2
La Matanza-Villa Madero 110 III b 2
Lama Temple 155 II b 2
Lambaréné 172 B 2
Lambari 102-103 K 4
Lambasa 148-149 a 2
Lambayeque [PE, administrative unit] 96-97 AB 5
Lambayeque [PE, place] 92-93 CD 6
Lambert, MS 78-79 DE 3
Lambert, MT 68-69 D 2
Lambert Glacier 53 B 8
Lambertsbaai 174-175 BC 7
Lamberts Bay = Lambertsbaai 174-175 BC 7
Lambeth, London- 129 II b 2
Lambi Kyûn 148-149 C 4
Lambouti 168-169 F 3
Lambton, Cape — 56-57 M 3
L'amca 124-125 L 1
Lam Chi 150-151 D 5
Lam Chiang Krai 150-151 C 5
Lāmding = Lumding 134-135 P 5
Lam Dom Noi 150-151 E 5
Lam Dom Yai 150-151 E 5
Lamé 164-165 G 7
Lame Deer, MT 68-69 C 3
Lamego 120-121 D 8
Lameguapi, Punta — 108-109 BC 3
La Merced [PE] 96-97 D 7
La Merced [RA] 104-105 D 11
la Mère et l'Enfant = Nui Vong Phu 150-151 G 6
La Mesa, CA 74-75 E 6
La Mesa, NM 76-77 A 6
Lamesa, TX 76-77 D 6
Lamèzia Terme 122-123 FG 6
Lamía 122-123 K 6
La Miel 94-95 G 3
L'amin 132-133 N 5
La Mirada, CA 83 III d 2
La Misión 74-75 E 6
Lamma Island = Pok Liu Chau 155 I a 2
Lamni 138-139 H 6
Lamo = Lamu 172 H 2
Lamobagar Gola 138-139 L 4
Lamoille, NV 66-67 F 5
La Moine, CA 66-67 B 5
Lamona, WA 66-67 D 2
Lamon Bay 148-149 H 4
Lamond, Washington-, DC 82 II a 1
Lamoni, IA 70-71 CD 5
Lamont, CA 74-75 D 5
Lamont, ID 66-67 H 3-4
Lamont, WY 68-69 C 4
La Montaña [E] 120-121 DE 7
La Montaña [PE] 92-93 E 5-6
La Montañita [CO] 94-95 D 7
La Montañita [YV] 94-95 F 2
La Mora 106-107 D 5
Lamoriciere = Awlād Mīmūn 166-167 F 2
La Morita 76-77 B 8
Lamotrek 148-149 N 5
La Mott, PA 84 III c 1
La Moure, ND 68-69 GH 2
La Moyne 82 I c 1
Lampa [PE] 92-93 EF 8
Lampa [RCH] 106-107 B 4
Lampang 148-149 C 3
Lampasas, TX 76-77 E 7
Lampazos de Naranjo 86-87 K 4
Lampedusa 122-123 E 8
Lampedusa, Isola — 164-165 G 1
Lam Phao 150-151 D 4
Lamphun 150-151 B 3
Lampi Island = Lambi Kyûn 148-149 C 4
Lam Plai Mat 150-151 D 5
Lampman 68-69 E 1
Lampung 148-149 DE 7

Lampung 317

Lam Se Bai 150-151 E 4-5
Lamskoje 124-125 LM 7
Lamū [BUR] 141 D 6
Lamu [EAK] 172 H 2
Lamud 96-97 BC 5
La Mula 76-77 B 8
Lâm Viên, Cao Nguyên — 150-151 G 6-7
Lamy, NM 76-77 B 5
Lan' 124-125 F 7
Lan, Ko — 150-151 C 6
Lan, Lûy — 141 E 6
La Nacional 106-107 E 5
Lanai 148-149 e 3
Lanai City, HI 78-79 d 2
Lanao, Lake — 148-149 HJ 5
La Nava de Ricomalillo 120-121 E 9
Lancang Jiang 142-143 HJ 7
Lancaster 119 E 4
Lancaster, CA 74-75 DE 5
Lancaster, IA 70-71 D 5
Lancaster, KY 70-71 H 7
Lancaster, MN 68-69 H 1
Lancaster, NH 72-73 L 2
Lancaster, OH 72-73 E 5
Lancaster, PA 72-73 HJ 4
Lancaster, SC 80-81 F 3
Lancaster, WI 70-71 E 4
Lancaster Sound 56-57 TU 3
Lančchuti 126-127 K 5
Lancheu = Lanzhou 142-143 JK 4
Lan-ch'i = Lanxi [TJ, Hubei] 146-147 E 6
Lan-ch'i = Lanxi [TJ, Zhejiang] 146-147 G 7
Lanchou = Lanzhou 142-143 JK 4
Lanchow = Lanzhou 142-143 JK 4
Lancian = Lan Xian 146-147 C 2
Lanciano 122-123 F 4
Lanco 108-109 C 2
Lancun 142-143 N 4
Landa, ND 68-69 F 1
Lan Dao = Danhao Dao 146-147 DE 10
Landau 118 D 4
Landauk 141 E 2
Landeck 118 E 5
Landego 116-117 EF 4
Lander, WY 68-69 B 4
Landerneau 120-121 E 4
Lander River 158-159 F 4
Landeta 106-107 F 3-4
Landi 168-169 C 3
Landis 61 D 4
Landover Hills, MD 82 II b 1
Landri Sales 100-101 BC 4
Landrum, SC 80-81 E 3
Landsberg am Lech 118 E 4
Land's End [CDN] 56-57 LM 2
Land's End [GB] 119 CD 6
Landshut 118 F 4
Landskrona 116-117 E 10
Landsmeer 128 I ab 1
Lane Cove, Sydney- 161 I ab 1
Lane Cove National Park 161 I a 1
La Negra 106-107 H 6
Lanett, AL 78-79 G 4
La Nevada 106-107 FG 6
Lanfeng = Lankao 146-147 E 4
La Nga, Sông — 150-151 F 7
Langao 146-147 B 5
Langara 152-153 P 7-8
Langara Island 60 A 2
L'angasovo 124-125 RS 4
Langat, Sungei — 150-151 C 11
Langberge 174-175 E 4-5
Langbu Tsho 138-139 K 2
Lang Cây 150-151 E 2
Lang Chanh 150-151 E 2
Langchhen Khamba 142-143 DE 5
Lang-ch'i = Langxi 146-147 G 6
Langchung = Langzhong 142-143 JK 5
Langdon, ND 68-69 G 1
Langdon, Washington-, DC 82 II b 1
Langebaan 174-175 BC 7
Langeberge [ZA ← Hoë Karro] 174-175 C 6
Langeberge [ZA ↙ Klein Karro] 174-175 CD 7
Langeland 116-117 D 10
Langen = Langao 146-147 B 5
Langen, Staatsforst — 128 III b 2
Langenburg 61 GH 5
Langer See [DDR] 130 III c 2
Langerūd 136-137 O 4
Langer Wald 128 III b 1
Langford, SD 68-69 H 3
Langford, Seno — 108-109 C 9
Langjökull 116-117 cd 2
Lang Ka, Doi — 150-151 B 3
Langkawi, Pulau — 148-149 C 5
Langkha Tuk, Khao — 150-151 B 8
Langklip 174-175 D 5
Langkon 152-153 M 2
Langkrans 174-175 J 4
Langley, VA 82 II a 1
Langlois, OR 66-67 A 4
Langma Dsong 138-139 M 2
Langnau am Albis 128 IV b 2
Langngag Tsho = Rakasdal 138-139 H 2
Langon 120-121 G 6
Langøy 116-117 F 3
Lang Phô Rang 150-151 E 1
Langping 146-147 C 6
Langres 120-121 K 5
Langres, Plateau de — 120-121 K 5
Langruth 61 J 5
Langsa 148-149 C 6
Lang Shan = Char Narijn uul 142-143 K 3
Lang So'n 148-149 E 2
Lang Suan 150-151 B 8
Lang Tâm 150-151 F 4
Langtans udde 53 C 31
Langtao = Landauk 141 E 2
Langtry, TX 76-77 D 8
Lāngu [IND] 138-139 J 3
Langu [MAL] 150-151 B 9
Languedoc 120-121 J 7-K 6
Langueyú 106-107 H 6
Languna Jume 106-107 FG 4
Langwied, München- 130 II a 1
Langwieder See 130 II a 1
Langxi 146-147 G 6
Langzhong 142-143 JK 5
Lan Hsü 142-143 N 7
Laniel 72-73 G 1
Lanigan 61 F 5
Lanín, Parque Nacional — 108-109 D 2-3
Lanín, Volcán — 111 B 5
La Niña 106-107 G 5
Lānja 140 A 2
Lāñjēñ = Lānja 140 A 2
Lanji 138-139 H 7
Lankao 146-147 E 4
Lankou 146-147 E 10
Lankwitz, Berlin- 130 III b 2
Lannion 120-121 F 4
Lan Saka 150-151 B 8
Lansdale, PA 72-73 J 4
Lansdowne 138-139 G 3
Lansdowne, PA 84 III b 2
Lansdowne House 62 F 1
L'Anse, MI 70-71 F 2
Lansford, ND 68-69 F 1
Lanshan 146-147 D 9
Lansing, IA 70-71 E 4
Lansing, MI 64-65 K 3
Lanta, Ko — 150-151 B 9
Lan Tao = Danhao Dao 146-147 DE 10
Lantee, Gunung — 152-153 M 10
Lanteri 106-107 H 2
Lantian 146-147 B 4
Lantian = Lianyuan 146-147 C 8
Lantianchang 155 II a 2
Lantianchang, Beijing- 155 II a 2
Lan-t'ien = Lantian 146-147 B 4
Lan-ts'ang Chiang = Lancang Jiang 142-143 HJ 7
Lan-ts'un = Lancun 142-143 N 4
Lanús 110 III b 2
Lanús-Caraza 110 III b 2
Lanusei 122-123 C 6
Lanús-Monte Chingolo 110 III bc 2
Lanús-Remedios de Escalada 110 III b 2
Lanús-Villa Diamante 110 III b 2
Lanxi [TJ, Hubei] 146-147 E 6
Lanxi [TJ, Zhejiang] 146-147 G 7
Lan Xian 146-147 C 2
Lanzarote 164-165 B 3
Lanzhou 142-143 JK 4
Lao, Nam Mae — 150-151 B 3
Laoag 148-149 GH 3
Lao Bao 150-151 F 4
Lao-chung-chi = Laozhong 146-147 E 5
Laodicea = Al-Lādhiqīyah 134-135 CD 3
Laoha He 144-145 B 2
Lao-ha Ho = Laoha He 144-145 B 2
Laohekou = Guanghua 142-143 L 5
Laohokow = Guanghua 142-143 L 5
Lao-hu-k'ou = Hukou 146-147 H 9
Laohumiao, Beijing- 155 II b 2
Laohushan 144-145 BC 2
Lao Kay 148-149 D 2
Laolong = Longchuan 146-147 E 9
Laon 120-121 J 4
Laona, WI 70-71 F 3
Lao Pi 150-151 D 3
Laopukou 146-147 B 9
Laora 148-149 H 7
Laorīā-Nandangaṛh = Thori 138-139 K 4
La Oroya 92-93 D 7
Laos 148-149 D 2-3
Laoshan 142-143 N 4
Laoshan Wan 146-147 H 3
Lao-t'ieh-shan-hsi Chiao = Laotieshanxi Jiao 144-145 C 3
Laotieshanxi Jiao 146-147 H 2
Lāoū, Ouèd — = Wād Lāū 166-167 D 2
Laozhong 146-147 E 5
Lapa 111 FG 3
Lapa, Campos de — 102-103 GH 6
Lapa, Rio de Janeiro- 110 I b 2
Lapa, São Paulo- 110 II a 2
Lapachito 104-105 G 10
La Palca 104-105 D 6
La Palma, CA 83 III d 2
La Palma [CO] 94-95 D 5
La Palma [E] 164-165 A 3
La Palma [PA] 88-89 GH 10
La Paloma [RCH] 106-107 B 3
La Paloma [ROU, Durazno] 106-107 K 4
La Paloma [ROU, Rocha] 111 F 4
La Paloma, Cerro — 106-107 C 4
La Pampa 106-107 DE 6
La Panza Range 74-75 CD 5
La Para 106-107 F 3
La Paragua 92-93 G 3
Lapasset = Sīdī al-Akhḍar 166-167 FG 1
La Pastoril = Colonia La Pastoril 106-107 DE 6
la Patte-d'Oie 129 I b 1-2
La Paz [BOL, administrative unit] 104-105 B 3-C 5
La Paz [BOL, place] 92-93 F 8
La Paz [Honduras] 88-89 C 7
La Paz [MEX, Baja California Sur] 64-65 DE 7
La Paz [MEX, San Luis Potosí] 86-87 K 6
La Paz [RA, Entre Ríos] 111 DE 4
La Paz [RA, Mendoza] 111 C 4
La Paz [ROU] 106-107 J 5
La Paz [YV] 94-95 E 2
La Paz, Bahía de — 64-65 DE 7
La Pedrera 92-93 EF 5
Lapeer, MI 72-73 E 3
La Pelada 106-107 G 3
La Peña 106-107 AB 6
La Perla 86-87 HJ 3
La Perouse 61 K 3
La Pérouse, proliv — 132-133 b 8
La Perouse, Sydney- 161 I b 2
La Pérouse Strait = proliv la Pérouse 142-143 R 2
La Pesca 86-87 M 6
Lāpēthos 136-137 E 5
La Picada 106-107 G 3
La Piedad Cavadas 86-87 JK 7
Lapine, OR 66-67 C 4
Lapin lääni 116-117 L-N 4
Lapinlahti 116-117 MN 6
La Pintada 94-95 A 3
Lapithos = Lāpēthos 136-137 E 5
Laplace, LA 78-79 D 5
Laplacette 106-107 G 5
Laplae 150-151 BC 4
Laplan 96-97 C 5
Lapland 116-117 F 5-N 3
Laplandskij zapovednik 116-117 OP 4
La Plant, ND 68-69 F 3
La Plant, SD 68-69 F 3
La Plata, IA 70-71 D 5
La Plata, MD 72-73 H 5
La Plata, MO 70-71 D 5
La Plata [CO] 92-93 D 4
La Plata [RA] 111 E 5
La Plata, Lago — 108-109 D 5
La Playosa 106-107 F 4
La Pointe, WI 70-71 E 2
La Poma 111 C 2
La Porte, IN 70-71 G 5
Laporte, PA 72-73 H 4
La Porte, TX 76-77 G 8
La Porte City, IA 70-71 DE 4
La Porteña, Salinas — 106-107 EF 7
La Posta 106-107 F 3
Lapovo 122-123 J 3
Lappajärvi 116-117 KL 6
Lappeenranta 116-117 N 7
Lappi 116-117 L 5
La Prairie 82 I bc 2
Laprida [RA, Buenos Aires] 111 D 5
Laprida [RA, Santiago del Estero] 106-107 E 2
La Primavera 106-107 D 6
La Pryor, TX 76-77 DE 8
Lâpseki 136-137 B 2
Lapteva Strait = proliv Dmitrija Lapteva 132-133 a-c 3
Laptev Sea 132-133 V 2-Z 3
Lapua 116-117 K 6
La Puebla 120-121 J 9
La Puerta [RA, Catamarca] 104-105 D 11
La Puerta [RA, Córdoba] 106-107 F 3
La Puerta [YV] 94-95 F 3
La Puntilla 92-93 C 5
La Purísima 86-87 DE 4
Lapush, WA 66-67 A 2
Lâp Vo 150-151 E 7
Łapy 118 L 2
Laqawah, Al- 164-165 K 6
Lāqiyat al-Arba'īn 164-165 K 4
La Quemada 86-87 J 6
La Querencia 106-107 H 3
la Queue-en-Brie 129 I d 2
La Quiaca 111 CD 2
Lār 134-135 G 5
Lara 94-95 FG 2
Larache = Al-'Arā'ish 164-165 C 1
Laramie, WY 64-65 EF 3
Laramie Peak 68-69 D 4
Laramie Plains 68-69 D 4-5
Laramie Range 64-65 E 3
Laramie River 68-69 D 4-5
Laranjal 98-99 K 7
Laranjal Paulista 102-103 HJ 5
Laranjeiras 100-101 F 6
Laranjeiras, Rio de Janeiro- 110 I b 2
Laranjeiras do Sul 111 F 3
Larantuka 148-149 H 8
Larat, Pulau — 148-149 K 8
La Raya, Ciénage — 94-95 D 3
Lärbro 116-117 H 9
Larchmont, Houston-, TX 85 III b 2
Larch River 56-57 W 6
Larder Lake 62 M 2
Lare 171 D 2
Laredo, IA 70-71 D 5-6
Laredo, TX 64-65 G 6
La Reforma [RA, Buenos Aires] 106-107 H 5
La Reforma [RA, La Pampa] 106-107 DE 6
La Reforma [YV] 94-95 L 4
la Reine 62 M 2
la Réserve de Assinica 62 O 1
la Réserve de Chibougamau 62 OP 2
la Réserve de Kipawa 72-73 G 1
la Réserve de Mistassini 62 P 1
Lārestān 134-135 GH 5
Largeau = Faya-Largeau 164-165 H 5
Largō 138-139 L 3
Largo Remo, Isla — 64-65 b 2
Largo Remo Island 64-65 b 2
Lariang 148-149 G 7
Lariang, Sungai — 152-153 N 6
La Rica 106-107 H 5
Lari Larian, Pulau — 152-153 MN 7
Larimore, ND 68-69 GH 2
Larino 122-123 F 5
La Rioja [E] 120-121 F 7
La Rioja [RA, administrative unit] 106-107 D 2
La Rioja [RA, place] 111 C 3
Lárisa 122-123 K 6
Laristan = Lārestān 134-135 GH 5
Larjak 132-133 OP 5
Lārkāna 134-135 K 5
Larkspur, CO 68-69 D 6
Larnaka = Lárnax 134-135 C 4
Lárnax 134-135 C 4
Larne 119 D 4
Larned, KS 68-69 G 6
La Robla 120-121 E 7
la Rochelle 120-121 G 7
la Roche-sur-Yon 120-121 G 5
Larocque 62 L 2
la Roda 120-121 F 9
La Romana 64-65 J 8
la Ronge 56-57 P 6
La Rosita 86-87 K 3
Larrey Point 158-159 C 3
Larrimah 158-159 F 3
Larroque 106-107 H 4
Larry's River 63 F 5
Lars Christensen land 53 BC 7
Larsen Bay, AK 58-59 fg 1
Larsen is-shelf 53 C 30-31
Larslan, MT 68-69 CD 1
Larson 70-71 E 1
Larteh 168-169 EF 4
Lartigau 106-107 G 7
La Rubia 111 D 4
Larut, Pegunungan — 150-151 C 10
Larvik 116-117 D 8
Lasa = Lhasa 142-143 G 6
La Sabana [CO] 94-95 G 6
La Sábana [RA] 106-107 H 1
La Sabana [YV] 94-95 H 2
Las Acequias 106-107 EF 4
La Sagra 120-121 EF 8
La Sal, UT 74-75 J 3
La Salada Grande, Laguna — 106-107 J 6
Las Alicias 91 I a 3
La Salle, CO 68-69 D 5
La Salle, IL 70-71 F 5
La Salle [CDN, Montréal] 82 I b 2
La Salle [CDN, Windsor] 84 II b 3
La Salle College 84 III c 1
Las Animas 76-77 C 9
Las Animas, CO 68-69 E 6-7
Las Armas 106-107 HJ 6
la Sarre 56-57 V 8
Las Arrias 106-107 F 3
Las Aves, Islas — 92-93 F 2
Las Avispas 106-107 G 2
Las Bonitas 92-93 FG 3
Las Breñas 104-105 F 10
Las Cabras 106-107 B 5
Lascan, Volcán — 104-105 C 8
Las Cañas 104-105 D 11
Las Cañas, Bahía — 106-107 A 5
Lascano 106-107 KL 4
Lascar, CO 68-69 D 7
Las Cascadas 64-65 b 2
Las Casuarinas 106-107 CD 3
Las Catitas 106-107 CD 4
Las Catonas, Arroyo — 110 III a 1
Las Cejas 111 D 3
Las Chacras 106-107 BC 6
Las Chapas 108-109 F 4
Las Choapas 86-87 NO 9
la Scie 63 J 2
Las Conchas 104-105 G 5
Las Condes 106-107 B 4
Las Cruces 64-65 b 2
Las Cruces, NM 64-65 E 5
Las Cuevas 106-107 BC 4
Las Cuevas de los Guacharos 94-95 CD 7
la Selle 88-89 KL 5
La Seña 106-107 D 4
La Serena [E] 120-121 E 9
La Serena [RCH] 111 B 3
Las Esperanzas 76-77 D 9
la Seyne-sur-Mer 120-121 K 7
Las Flores [RA, Buenos Aires] 111 E 5
Las Flores [RA, Salta] 104-105 E 9
Las Flores [RA, San Juan] 106-107 C 3
Las Gamas 106-107 G 2
Lāsgird = Lāsjerd 134-135 G 3
Lashburn 61 D 4
Las Heras [RA, Mendoza] 106-107 C 4
Las Heras [RA, Santa Cruz] 111 C 7
Las Hermanas 106-107 G 6
Lashio = Lāshō 148-149 C 2
Lāsh Juwayn 134-135 J 4
Lashkar = Gwalior 134-135 M 5
Lashkar Satma 142-143 F 4
Lāshō 148-149 C 2
Las Horquetas 108-109 D 7
La Sierra [ROU] 106-107 K 5
La Sierrita 94-95 EF 2
La Sila 122-123 G 6
La Silveta, Cerro — 111 B 8
Lasíthion 122-123 L 8
Lāsjerd 134-135 G 3
Las Julianas, Presa — 91 I b 2
Las Junturas 106-107 F 3
L'askel'a 124-125 H 3
Las Lagunas 106-107 E 5
Las Lajas 106-107 B 7
Las Lajas, Cerro — 106-107 B 7
Las Lajitas [RA] 104-105 DE 9
Las Lajitas [YV] 94-95 J 4
Las Lomitas 111 D 2
Lašma 124-125 N 6
Las Majadas 94-95 J 4
la Smala des Souassi = Zamālat as-Suwāsī 166-167 M 2
Las Malvinas 106-107 C 5
Las Marianas 106-107 H 5
Las Marias 91 II bc 2
Las Marismas 120-121 D 10
Las Martinetas 106-107 G 6
Las Mercedes 92-93 F 3
Las Mesteñas 76-77 B 8
Las Minas, Bahía — 64-65 b 2
Las Nieves 76-77 B 9
Las Norias 76-77 C 8
Las Nutrias 106-107 H 7
La Sola, Isla — 94-95 K 2
La Solita 94-95 F 3
Lasolo 152-153 OP 7
Lasolo, Teluk — 148-149 H 7
Las Ortegas, Arroyo — 110 III b 2
La Sortija 106-107 G 7
Las Ovejas 106-107 B 6
Las Palmas 102-103 E 6
Las Palmas de Gran Canaria 164-165 AB 3
Las Palmeras 106-107 G 3
Las Palmitas 106-107 J 2
Las Palomas 86-87 FG 2
Las Palomas, NM 76-77 A 6
Las Parejas 106-107 G 4
Las Peñas 106-107 F 3
Las Perlas 88-89 E 8
Las Petacas 106-107 F 3
Las Petas 104-105 G 5
Las Petas, Río — 104-105 G 5
La Spèzia 122-123 C 3
Las Piedras [BOL] 104-105 C 2
Las Piedras [ROU] 106-107 J 5
Las Piedras [YV, Delta Amacuro] 94-95 L 3
Las Piedras [YV, Guárico] 94-95 H 3
Las Piedras [YV, Merida] 94-95 F 3
Las Playas 96-97 A 4
Las Plumas 111 C 6
Lasqueti Island 66-67 A 1
Las Rosanas 106-107 G 4
Las Salinas 96-97 C 7
Lassance 92-93 KL 8
Lassen Peak 64-65 B 3
Lassen Volcanic National Park 66-67 C 5
Las Tablas 88-89 FG 11
Lastarria 108-109 C 2
Lastarria, Volcán — 104-105 B 9
Last Chance, CO 68-69 DE 6
Las Termas 111 CD 3
Las Tinajas 102-103 A 7
Last Mountain Lake 61 F 5
Las Tortillas 76-77 E 9
Las Tórtolas, Cerro — 106-107 BC 2
Las Toscas 106-107 K 4
Las Totoras 106-107 E 4
Lastoursville 172 B 2
Lastovo 122-123 G 4
Lastra 106-107 G 6
Las Tres Matas 94-95 J 3
Las Tres Vírgenes 64-65 D 6
Las Trincheras 92-93 FG 3
Las Tunas [C] 88-89 H 4
Las Tunas [RA] 106-107 G 3
Las Tunas Grandes, Lagunas — 106-107 F 5-6
Las Varillas 111 D 4
Las Vegas 94-95 G 3
Las Vegas, NM 64-65 EF 4
Las Vegas, NV 64-65 C 4
Las Vegas Bombing and Gunnery Range 74-75 EF 4
Las Ventanas 94-95 H 4
Las Zorras 96-97 B 7
Lata 104-105 A 8
la Tabatière 63 G 2
Latacunga 92-93 D 5
Latady Island 53 BC 29
Lataghāt = Lālāghāt 141 C 3
La Tagua 94-95 D 8
Latakia = Al-Lādhiqīyah 134-135 CD 3
Latang, Ko — = Ko Ladang 150-151 B 9
la Tapa 106-107 F 1
Latchford 72-73 FG 1
Late 148-149 c 2
La Tebaida 94-95 D 5
Latehār 138-139 K 6
Laṭerī = Leteri 138-139 F 5
la Teste 120-121 G 6
La Teta 91 III bc 4
Lat Hane = Ban Lat Hane 150-151 CD 2
Lāthi 138-139 C 7
La Tina 96-97 B 4
Latina [I] 122-123 E 5
Latina, Madrid- 113 III a 2
Latinos, Ponta dos — 106-107 L 4
Latium = Lāzio 122-123 E 4-5
La Tola 92-93 D 4
La Toma 111 C 4
La Tordilla = Colonia La Tordilla 106-107 F 3
La Tortuga, Ila — 92-93 FG 2
Latouche, AK 58-59 N 7-O 6
Latouche Island 58-59 NO 7
La Tranca 106-107 D 4
La Trinidad 94-95 G 3
La Trinidad de Arauca 94-95 G 4
Latrobe 160 c 2
Latrobe, PA 72-73 G 4
Latsauk = Ratsauk 141 E 5
Latua 152-153 D 8
La Tunia 94-95 E 7
La Tuque 56-57 W 8
Lātūr 140 C 1
Latvia = Latvian Soviet Socialist Republic 124-125 C-F 5
Latvian Soviet Socialist Republic 124-125 C-F 5
Lat Yao 150-151 B 5
Lau 168-169 H 3
Lau Bangap 150-151 AB 11
Lauca, Río — 104-105 B 6
Lauder [CDN] 68-69 F 1
Lauderdale 160 c 3
Lauderdale, MS 78-79 E 4
Laudo, Cumbre del — 104-105 B 10
Lauenburg/Elbe 118 E 2
Laughing Fish Point 70-71 G 2
Laughlan Islands 148-149 h 6
Laughlin Peak 76-77 BC 4
Lau Group 148-149 b 2
La-un 150-151 B 7
Launceston [AUS] 158-159 J 8
Launceston [GB] 119 D 6
Launḍa = Londa 140 B 3
Launglôn 150-151 AB 6
Launglônbôk Kyûnzu 150-151 A 6
La Unión [BOL] 104-105 F 4
La Unión [CO, Nariño] 94-95 C 7
La Unión [CO, Valle del Cauca] 94-95 C 5
La Unión [E] 120-121 G 10
La Unión [ES] 64-65 J 9
La Unión [MEX] 86-87 K 9
La Unión [PE, Huánuco] 92-93 D 6-7
La Unión [PE, Piura] 96-97 A 4
La Unión [RCH] 111 B 6
La Unión [YV] 94-95 GH 3
Laupahoehoe, HI 78-79 e 3
Laura 158-159 H 3
Laura = Lavry 124-125 F 5
La Urbana 92-93 F 3
Laurel 152-153 M 8
Laurel, DE 72-73 J 5
Laurel, IN 70-71 H 6
Laurel, MD 72-73 H 5
Laurel, MS 64-65 J 5
Laurel, MT 68-69 B 3
Laurel, NE 68-69 H 4
Laurel, OH 72-73 D 5
Laurel, Mount — 84 III d 2
Laureles [PY] 102-103 D 7
Laureles [ROU] 106-107 JK 3
Laurel Hill 72-73 G 4-5
Laurel Hill, FL 78-79 F 5
Laurel Lake 85 II a 1
Laurel Springs, NJ 84 III c 3
Laurelton, New York-, NY 82 III d 3
Laurens, IA 70-71 C 4
Laurens, SC 80-81 EF 3
Laurentian Plateau 56-57 V 8-X 7
Laurentides, Parc provincial des — 56-57 W 8
Lauri 138-139 GH 5
La Uribe 91 III c 1
Laurie Island 53 C 32
Laurie River 61 H 2
Laurinburg, NC 80-81 G 3
Lauritsala 116-117 N 7
Laurium, MI 70-71 F 2
Lauro Müller 102-103 H 8
Lausanne 118 C 5
Lausitzer Gebirge 118 G 3
Laut, Pulau — [RI, Selat Makasar] 148-149 G 7
Laut, Pulau — [RI, South China Sea] 148-149 E 6
Lautan Hindia 148-149 B 6-D 8
Lautaro 106-107 A 7
Laut Halmahera 148-149 J 7
Laut Kecil, Pulau-pulau — 148-149 G 7-8
Lautoka 148-149 a 2
Laut Sulawesi 148-149 GH 6
Laut Tawar 152-153 B 3
Lauwater 174-175 C 2
Lauzon 63 A 4
Lava, NM 76-77 A 6
Lava Bads 74-75 JK 5
Lava Beds [USA, New Mexico ← Oscura Peak] 76-77 A 6
Lava Beds [USA, New Mexico ← Tularosa Basin] 76-77 AB 6
Lava Beds [USA, New Mexico ← United Pueblos Indian Reservation] 74-75 JK 5
Lava Beds [USA, Oregon ↘ Cedar Mountains] 66-67 E 4
Lava Beds [USA, Oregon ← Harney Basin] 66-67 C 4
Lava Beds [USA, Oregon ↘ Steens Mountain] 66-67 D 4
Lava Beds National Monument 66-67 C 5
Lavaisse 106-107 E 4
Laval [CDN] 56-57 VW 8
Laval [F] 120-121 G 4
La Valdesa 64-65 b 3
Laval-des-Rapides 82 I a 1
Lavalle [RA, Corrientes] 106-107 H 2
Lavalle [RA, Santiago del Estero] 106-107 E 2
Lavalleja [ROU, administrative unit] 106-107 K 4-5
Lavalleja [ROU, place] 106-107 J 4
Lavansaari = ostrov Moščnyj 124-125 FG 4
Lavapié, Punta — 111 AB 5
Laveaga Peak 74-75 C 4
La Vega [DOM] 64-65 MN 8
La Veguita 94-95 FG 3
La Vela de Coro 92-93 F 2
Lavelanet 120-121 HJ 7
La Venta 86-87 NO 8
La Ventana 86-87 KL 6
La Ventura 86-87 K 5
La Venturosa 94-95 G 4
La Vera 120-121 E 8
La Verde 106-107 E 5
La Verkin, UT 74-75 G 4
Laverlochère 72-73 G 1
Laverne, OK 76-77 DE 4
La Vernia, TX 76-77 EF 8
la Verrière 129 I a 3
Laverton 158-159 D 5
La Veta, CO 68-69 D 7
La Víbora 76-77 C 9
La Victoria [CO, Bogotá] 94-95 CD 5
La Victoria [CO, Valle del Cauca] 91 III a 3
La Victoria [YV] 94-95 H 2
Lavina, MT 68-69 B 2
La Viña [PE] 92-93 D 6
La Viña [RA] 111 C 3
Lavinia 102-103 G 4
La Violeta 106-107 GH 4
La Virginia 94-95 D 5
La Vista, GA 85 II c 1
La Viticola 106-107 F 7
Lavongai = New Hanover 148-149 gh 5
Lavonia, GA 80-81 E 3
Lavra = Monē Lávras 122-123 L 5
Lavrador = Labrador Peninsula 56-57 V 6-Y 7
Lavras 92-93 L 9
Lavras da Mangabeira 100-101 E 4
Lavras do Sul 106-107 L 3
Lavrentija 58-59 B 4
Lávrion 122-123 KL 7
Lavry 124-125 F 5
Lawa 92-93 J 4
La Ward, TX 76-77 F 8
Lawas 152-153 L 3
Lawashi River 62 H 1
Lawbida 141 E 6
Lawele 152-153 P 8
Lawen, OR 66-67 D 4
Lawers, Ben — 119 DE 3
Lawgi 158-159 K 4
Lawit, Gunung — [MAL] 150-151 D 10
Lawit, Gunung — [RI] 148-149 F 6
Lawn, TX 76-77 E 6
Lawndale, CA 83 III b 2
Lawndale, Chicago-, IL 83 II a 1
Lawndale, Philadelphia-, PA 84 III c 1
Lawnhill 60 B 3
Lawnside, NJ 84 III c 2
Lawnview Cemetery 84 III c 1
Lawowa 148-149 H 7
Lawqah 136-137 K 8
Lawra 164-165 D 6
Lawrence, KS 70-71 C 6
Lawrence, MA 72-73 L 3
Lawrence, NE 68-69 GH 5
Lawrence, NY 72-73 K 4
Lawrenceburg, IN 70-71 H 6
Lawrenceburg, KY 70-71 H 6-7
Lawrenceburg, OH 72-73 D 5
Lawrenceburg, TN 78-79 F 3
Lawrenceville, GA 80-81 DE 4
Lawrenceville, IL 70-71 G 6
Lawrenceville, VA 80-81 H 2
Laws, CA 74-75 D 4
Lawson, CO 68-69 CD 6
Lawton, OK 64-65 G 5
Lawz, Jabal al- 134-135 D 5
Laxå 116-117 F 8
Lay, CO 68-69 C 5
Laya 168-169 B 3
Lāyalpūr = Faisalābād 134-135 L 4
Layar, Tanjung — 148-149 DE 8
Laylā 134-135 F 6
Laylān 136-137 L 5
Layshi = Leshī 141 D 3
Layton, UT 66-67 G 5
Laž 124-125 R 5
La Zanja 106-107 F 6
Lazão, Ponta — 100-101 C 2
Lazarevo [SU, Chabarovskij kraj] 132-133 ab 7
Lazarevskoje, Soči- 126-127 J 5
Lázaro Cárdenas 86-87 C 2
Lazaro Cardenas, Presa — 86-87 H 5
Lazdijai 124-125 D 6
Lāzio 122-123 E 4-5
Lazzarino 106-107 H 6
Lbiščensk = Čapajevo 126-127 P 1
Lea Canal 129 II b 1
Léach, Phum — 150-151 DE 6
Leach Island 70-71 H 2
Leachville, AR 78-79 D 3
Lead, SD 64-65 F 3
Leader 61 D 5
Leadore, ID 66-67 G 3
Leadville, CO 68-69 C 6
Leaf Rapids 61 J 2
Leaf River [CDN, Manitoba] 62 A 1
Leaf River [CDN, Quebec] 56-57 W 6
Leakesville, MS 78-79 E 5
Leakey, TX 76-77 E 8
Leaksville, NC 80-81 G 2
Leal = Lihula 124-125 DE 4
Leamington 72-73 E 3-4
Leamington, UT 74-75 GH 3
Le'an 146-147 E 8
Leander, TX 76-77 EF 7
Leandro N. Alem [RA, Misiones] 106-107 K 1
Leandro N. Alem [RA, San Luis] 106-107 D 4
Le'an Jiang 146-147 F 7
Leavenworth, KS 70-71 C 6
Leavenworth, WA 66-67 C 2
Leavitt Peak 74-75 D 3
Łeba 118 H 1
Lebádeia 122-123 K 6
Lebam, WA 66-67 B 2

Lucerna 96-97 G 8
Lucerne, IA 70-71 D 5
Lucerne = Luzern 118 CD 5
Lucerne, Lake — = Vierwaldstätter See 118 D 5
Lucerne Lake 74-75 E 5
Lucerne Valley, CA 74-75 E 5
Lucero, El — [MEX] 76-77 C 10
Lucero, El — [YV] 94-95 G 4
Luch [SU, river] 124-125 O 5
Lu-chai = Luzhai 146-147 B 9
Lucheng 146-147 D 3
Lucheringo 171 CD 6
Lu-ch'i = Luxi 146-147 C 7
Luchiang 146-147 H 9
Lu-chiang = Lujiang 146-147 F 6
Lu-chou = Hefei 142-143 M 5
Luchow = Lu Xian 142-143 K 6
Luchthaven Schiphol 128 I a 2
Luchuan 142-143 KL 7
Luchwan = Luchuan 142-143 KL 7
Luci 152-153 J 7
Lucia, CA 74-75 C 4
Lucialva 104-105 G 4
Luciara 98-99 N 10
Lucie 98-99 K 3
Lucie, Lac — 62 M 1
Lucin, UT 66-67 G 5
Lucio V. Mansilla 106-107 E 2
Lucipara, Pulau-pulau — 148-149 J 8
Lucira 172 B 4
Luck, WI 70-71 D 3
Luck [SU] 126-127 B 1
Luckeesarai 138-139 KL 5
Luckenwalde 118 F 2
Luckhoff 174-175 F 5
Lucknow [CDN] 72-73 F 3
Lucknow [IND] 134-135 MN 5
Lucky Lake 61 E 5
Luc Nam 150-151 F 2
Lucrecia, Cabo — 88-89 J 4
Lucy, NM 76-77 B 5
Luda [SU] 124-125 M 1
Lüda [TJ] 142-143 N 4
Lüda-Dalian 142-143 N 4
Lüda-Lüshun 142-143 MN 4
Ludden, ND 68-69 G 2
Ludell, KS 68-69 F 6
Lüderitz [Namibia] 172 BC 7
Lüderitzbaai 172 BC 7
Ludgate 72-73 F 2
Ludhiāna 134-135 M 4
Ludhiyānā = Ludhiāna 134-135 M 4
Ludington, MI 70-71 G 4
L'udinovo 124-125 K 7
Ludlow, CA 74-75 EF 5
Ludlow, CO 68-69 D 7
Ludlow, SD 68-69 E 3
Ludogorie 122-123 M 4
Ludowici, GA 80-81 F 5
Luduş 122-123 KL 2
Ludvika 116-117 F 7
Ludwigsburg 118 D 4
Ludwigsfeld, München- 130 II ab 1
Ludwigshafen 118 CD 4
Ludwigslust 118 E 2
Ludza 124-125 F 5
Luebo 172 D 3
Lueders, TX 76-77 E 6
Luemba 171 B 3
Luembe, Rio — 172 D 3
Luena 172 D 4
Luena, Rio — 172 D 4
Luena Flats 172 D 4
Luepa 94-95 L 5
Lufeng 142-143 M 7
Lufingen 128 IV b 1
Lufira 172 E 3-4
Lufkin, TX 64-65 H 5
Lug 138-139 G 2
Luga [SU, place] 132-133 D 6
Luga [SU, river] 132-133 D 6
Lugana de Santa María 86-87 G 2
Lugano 118 D 5
Lugansk = Vorošilovgrad 126-127 JK 2
Luganville 158-159 N 3
Lugard's Falls 171 D 3
Lugela 172 G 5
Lugenda, Rio — 172 G 4
Lugh Ferrandi = Luuq 164-165 N 8
Luginino 124-125 K 5
Lugo [E] 120-121 D 7
Lugo [I] 122-123 D 3
Lugoj 122-123 JK 3
Lugones 106-107 F 2
Luḥayyah, Al- 134-135 E 7
Luhe [TJ] 146-147 G 5
Luhit 134-135 Q 5
Luhsien = Lu Xian 142-143 K 6
Lu Hu 146-147 E 6
Lu-i = Luyi 146-147 E 5
Luiana, Rio — 172 D 5
Luichow = Haikang 142-143 KL 7
Luichow Peninsula = Leizhou Bandao 142-143 L 7
Luik = Liège 120-121 K 3
Luilaka 172 D 2
Luimneach = Limerick 119 B 5
Luirojoki 116-117 M 4
Luisa, La — 106-107 GH 5
Luís Alves 102-103 H 7
Luís Correia 100-101 D 2
Luís Correira 92-93 L 5
Luís Domingues 100-101 AB 1
Luís Gomes 100-101 E 4
Luishia 172 E 4
Luisiânia 102-103 G 4
Luiza 172 D 3
Luizhou Jiang = Leizhou Wan 146-147 C 11
Luján [RA, Buenos Aires] 111 E 4
Luján [RA, Mendoza] 106-107 C 4
Luján [RA, San Luis] 106-107 DE 4
Lujenda = Rio Lugenda 172 G 4
Lujiang 146-147 F 6
Lujiang = Lu-chiang 146-147 H 9
Lujiapuzi 144-145 D 2
Lukanga 171 B 6
Lukanga Swamp 172 E 4
Lukašek 132-133 Z 7
Luk Chau [HK, island] 155 I a 2
Luk Chau [HK, place] 155 I a 2
Lukenie 172 C 2
Lukenie Supérieure, Plateau de la — 172 D 2
Lukfung = Lufeng 142-143 M 7
Lukiang = Lujiang 146-147 F 6
Lukimwa 171 D 5
Lukino 124-125 L 7
Lukmeshwar = Lakshmeshwar 140 B 3
Lukojanov 124-125 P 6
Lukolela 172 C 2
Lukou 146-147 D 8
Lukovit 122-123 L 4
Lukovnikovo 124-125 K 5
Łuków 118 L 3
L'uksemburg-Gruzinskij = Bolnisi 126-127 M 6
L'ukšudja 124-125 T 5
Lukuga 172 E 3
Lukuledi 171 D 5
Lukull, mys — 126-127 F 4
Lukulu 171 B 6
Lukunga 170 IV a 2
Lukusashi 171 B 6
Lūl, Nahr — 164-165 K 7
Lula, MS 78-79 D 3
Luleå 116-117 JK 5
Lule älv 116-117 J 4-5
Lülebargas = Lüleburgaz 136-137 B 2
Lüleburgaz 136-137 B 2
Luliani = Luliyānī 138-139 E 2
Luling, TX 76-77 F 8
Luliyānī 138-139 E 2
Lulong 146-147 G 2
Lulonga 172 C 1
Lulua 172 D 3
Luluabourg = Kananga 172 D 3
Lulung = Lulong 146-147 G 2
Luma 171 D 6
Lumajang 152-153 K 10
Lumb 106-107 H 7
Lumbala 172 D 4
Lumber River 80-81 G 3
Lumberton, MS 78-79 E 5
Lumberton, NC 64-65 L 5
Lumberton, NM 68-69 C 7
Lumbo 172 H 4-5
Lumby 60 H 4
Lumding 134-135 P 5
Lumege = Cameia 172 D 4
Lumeje 172 D 4
Lüm Fiord = Limfjorden 116-117 D 9
Lumpkin, GA 78-79 G 4
Lumsden 161 C 7
Lumu 148-149 G 7
Lumut 148-149 D 5
Lumut, Pulau — 150-151 C 11
Lumut, Tanjung — 152-153 FG 7
Lün 142-143 K 2
Lûn, Lûy — 141 F 5
Luna 138-139 B 6
Luna, NM 74-75 J 6
Luna, Laguna de — 106-107 J 2
Lūnāvāda 138-139 D 6
Lunawada = Lūnāvāda 138-139 D 6
Lund 116-117 E 10
Lund, NV 74-75 F 3
Lund, UT 74-75 G 3-4
Lunda 172 CD 3
Lunda, Kasongo- 172 C 3
Lundar 61 K 5
Lundazi [Z, place] 172 F 4
Lundazi [Z, river] 171 C 6
Lundi [ZW, place] 172 F 6
Lundi [ZW, river] 172 F 6
Lundy 119 D 6
Lüneburg 118 E 2
Lüneburger Heide 118 DE 2
Luneburg Heath = Lüneburger Heide 118 DE 2
Lunenburg 56-57 Y 9
Lunéville 120-121 L 4
Lung 138-139 N 3
Lunga [Z] 172 E 4
Lunga = Dugi Otok 122-123 F 4
Lunga Game Reserve 172 DE 4
Lungala N'Guimbo 172 CD 4
Lung-chên = Longzhen 142-143 O 2
Lung Chiang = Long Jiang 146-147 B 9
Lung-chiang = Qiqihar 142-143 N 2
Lung-ching-ts'un = Longjing 144-145 G 1
Lung-ch'uan = Longchuan 141 EF 3
Lungchuan = Longquan 146-147 G 7
Lung-chuan = Suichuan 142-143 L 6
Lung-ch'uang Chiang = Longchuang Jiang 141 F 3
Lung-hsi = Longxi 142-143 J 4-5
Lung-hua = Longhua 144-145 AB 2
Lung-hui = Longhui 146-147 C 8
Lungi 168-169 B 3
Lungkar Gangri 138-139 K 2-3
Lungkar Gonpa 138-139 JK 2
Lungkar La 138-139 JK 2
Lungki = Zhangzhou 142-143 M 7
Lung-k'ou = Longkou 146-147 GH 3
Lung-kuan Hu = Long Hu 146-147 F 7
Lunglê = Lungleh 134-135 P 6
Lungleh 134-135 P 6
Lungler = Lônlê 141 C 4
Lungling = Longling 142-143 H 7
Lungma Ri 138-139 L 2
Lungmen = Longmen 146-147 E 10
Lung-mêng-shih = Longmen 150-151 H 3
Lung-nan = Longnan 142-143 LM 7
Lungshan = Longshan 146-147 B 7
Lung-shêng = Longsheng [TJ ↖ Guilin] 146-147 BC 9
Lung-shêng = Longsheng [TJ ↙ Wuzhou] 146-147 C 10
Lung-shih = Ninggang 146-147 DE 8
Lungsi = Longxi 142-143 J 4-5
Lung-t'an = Longtan 146-147 C 8
Lung-t'ien = Longtian 146-147 G 9
Lungué-Bungo, Rio — 172 D 4
Lung-yen = Longyan 146-147 F 9
Lungyu = Longyou 142-143 M 6
Lūni [IND, place] 138-139 D 4
Lūni [IND, river] 134-135 L 5
Lūnī [PAK] 138-139 BC 2
Lūni Marusthal 138-139 CD 5
Luninec 124-125 F 7
Lunino 124-125 P 7
Lunjevka 124-125 V 4
Lūnkaransar 138-139 DE 3
Lunno 124-125 E 7
Lunsemfwa 172 EF 4
Lunsklip 174-175 H 3
Luntai = Buquq 142-143 E 3
Lunyuk 152-153 M 10
Luocheng = Lechang 146-147 D 9
Luocheng 146-147 B 9
Luochuan 146-147 B 4
Luoding 146-147 C 10
Luoding Jiang 146-147 C 10
Luodou Sha 150-151 H 2
Luofang 146-147 E 8
Luofu 171 B 3
Luohe [TJ, place] 146-147 E 5
Luo He [TJ, river ◁ Huang He] 146-147 CD 4
Luo He [TJ, river ◁ Wei He] 146-147 B 4
Luokou 146-147 E 8
Luombwa 171 B 6
Luonan 146-147 C 4
Luong, Pou — 150-151 E 2
Luongo 171 B 5
Luoning 146-147 C 4
Luoqing 146-147 BC 9
Luorong 142-143 K 7
Luoshan 146-147 E 5
Luotian 146-147 E 6
Luoyang 142-143 L 5
Luoyuan 146-147 G 8
Luozi 172 B 2
Lupa 171 C 5
Lupar, Sungei — 152-153 J 5
Lupilichi 171 C 5
Łupkowska, Przełęcz — 118 L 4
Lupolovo, Mogil'ov- 124-125 H 7
Lu-pu = Lubu 146-147 D 10
Luputa 172 D 3
Luque [PY] 102-103 D 6
Luray, VA 72-73 G 5
Luribay 104-105 C 5
Lurio 171 E 6
Lúrio, Rio — 172 GH 4
Luristan = Lorestān 134-135 F 4
Luro 106-107 F 6
Lurup, Hamburg 130 I a 1
Lusaka 172 E 5
Lusambo 172 D 2
Luscar 60 J 3
Lusenga Flats 172 E 3
Lushan [TJ, Henan] 146-147 D 5
Lu Shan [TJ, Jiangxi] 142-143 M 6
Lu Shan [TJ, Shandong] 146-147 FG 3
Lu Shan = Yi Shan 146-147 G 3
Lushi 146-147 C 4
Lu-shih = Lushi 146-147 C 4
Lushnjë 122-123 H 5
Lushoto 172 G 2
Lushui 141 F 2-3
Lüshun, Lüda- 142-143 MN 4
Lüsi 146-147 H 5
Lusien = Lu Xian 142-143 K 6
Lusikisiki 174-175 H 6
Lusk, WY 68-69 D 4
Luso = Moxico 172 CD 4
Lussanvira 102-103 G 4
Lussino = Lošinj 122-123 F 3
Lustheim 130 II b 1
Lustre, MT 68-69 D 1
Lü-szŭ = Lüsi 146-147 H 5
Lūţ, Dasht-e — 134-135 H 4
Lü-Tao = Huoshao Tao 146-147 H 10
Lutcher, LA 78-79 D 5-6
Lutembwe 171 C 6
Luther, MI 70-71 H 3
Luther, OK 76-77 F 5
Lutie, TX 76-77 D 5
Lutlhe 174-175 E 2
Luton 119 F 6
Lutong 148-149 F 6
Lutsk = Luck 126-127 B 1
Luttig 174-175 E 7
Lutunguru 171 B 3
Lützow-Holm bukt 53 C 4-5
Lutzputs 174-175 D 5
Luuq 164-165 N 8
Luverne, AL 78-79 F 5
Luverne, IA 70-71 CD 4
Luverne, MN 68-69 H 4
Luvua 172 E 3
Luwegu 172 G 3
Luwingu 172 F 4
Luwu 148-149 GH 7
Luwuk 148-149 H 7
Luxembourg [L, place] 120-121 KL 4
Luxembourg [L, state] 120-121 KL 4
Luxembourg, Jardin du — 129 I c 2
Luxi [TJ, Hunan] 146-147 C 7
Luxi [TJ, Yunnan] 141 F 3
Lu Xian 142-143 K 6
Luxico, Rio — 172 CD 3
Luxor = Al-Uqṣur 164-165 L 3
Luxora, AR 78-79 DE 3
Lu Xun Museum 155 II b 2
Lüyang 144-145 C 2
Luya Shan 146-147 CD 2
Lûy Hkaw 141 F 5
Lûy-Hoda 141 E 6
Lûy Hpālam 150-151 B 2
Lûy Hpālan 141 F 5
Lûy Hsan 141 E 5
Lûy Hsei 141 F 4
Luyi 146-147 E 5
Lûykau 148-149 C 3
Lûy Lan 141 E 6
Lûy Lin 141 EF 4
Lûylin 148-149 C 2
Lûy Lôn 141 E 5
Lûy Lûn 141 F 5
Lûylûn Taungdan 141 E 4
Lûy Maw [BUR, Kachin Pyinnei] 141 E 3
Lûy Maw [BUR, Shan Pyinnei] 141 E 5
Lûy Mû 141 F 4
Lûymwe 150-151 B 2
Lûy Myèbûm 141 E 3
Lûy Pan 141 E 4
Lûy Pannaung 150-151 C 2
Lûy Taunggyaw 141 E 4
Luz [BR] 92-93 K 8
Luz, Isla — 108-109 BC 5
Luza [SU, place] 132-133 H 5
Luza [SU, river] 124-125 Q 3
Luzern 118 CD 5
Luzhai 146-147 B 9
Luzhuba = Hetian 146-147 F 9
Luziânia 102-103 HJ 2
Luzilândia 100-101 C 2
Luzk = Luck 126-127 B 1
Lužma 124-125 H 2
Lužniki, Moskva- 113 V b 3
Luzon 148-149 H 3
Luzon Strait 148-149 H 2

L'vov 126-127 AB 2

Lwa = Mostva 124-125 F 8
Lwancheng = Luancheng 146-147 E 3
Lwanhsien = Luan Xian 142-143 M 4
Lweje = Lwīgyī 141 E 3
Lwela 171 B 5
Lwīgyī 141 E 3
Lwīthangalan 141 C 5
Lwow = L'vov 126-127 AB 2

Lyallpur = Faisalābād 134-135 L 4
Lyan Shan 141 F 3-4
Lyantonde 171 B 3
Lybrook, NM 76-77 A 4
Lyčkovo 124-125 J 5
Lycksele 116-117 H 5
Lydda = Lod 136-137 F 7
Lydell Wash 74-75 G 4
Lydenburg 172 EF 7
Lyell Island 60 B 3
Lyell Range 161 E 5
Lykabettós 113 IV ab 2
Lykwati 171 C 4
Lyle, MN 70-71 D 4
Lyle, WA 66-67 C 3
Lyles, TN 78-79 F 3
Lyleton 68-69 F 1
Lyme Bay 119 E 6
Lymva 124-125 T 2
Lynbrook, NY 82 III de 3
Lynch, KY 80-81 E 2
Lynch, NE 68-69 G 4
Lynchburg, VA 64-65 L 4
Lynches River 80-81 FG 3
Lynden, WA 66-67 B 1
Lyndhurst 160 D 3
Lyndon, KS 70-71 C 6
Lyndonville, VT 72-73 KL 2
Lyngenfjord 116-117 J 2-3
Lyngseiden 116-117 HJ 3
Lynhurst, NJ 82 III b 2
Lynn, IN 70-71 H 5
Lynn, MA 72-73 L 3
Lynn Canal 58-59 U 7
Lynndyl, UT 74-75 G 3
Lynnewood Gardens, PA 84 III bc 1
Lynn Harbor 84 I c 2
Lynn Haven, FL 78-79 G 5
Lynn Lake 56-57 Q 6
Lynn Woods Reservation 84 I c 1
Lynton 61 C 2
Lyntupy 124-125 F 6
Lynwood, CA 83 III c 2
Lyon 120-121 K 6
Lyon Park, Arlington-, VA 82 II a 2
Lyons, CO 68-69 D 5
Lyons, GA 80-81 E 4
Lyons, IL 83 II a 2
Lyons, KS 68-69 GH 6
Lyons, NE 68-69 H 5
Lyons, NY 72-73 H 3
Lyons = Lyon 120-121 K 6
Lyons River 158-159 C 4
Lysá hora 118 J 4
Lysekil 116-117 D 8
Lyserort = Lizerorta 124-125 C 5
Lysite, WY 68-69 C 4
Lyskovo 132-133 GH 6
Łysa gory 118 K 3
Ly So'n, Dao — = Cu Lao Rê 150-151 G 5
Lyster 63 A 4
Lys'va 132-133 K 6
Lyswa = Lys'va 132-133 K 6
Lyttelton [NZ] 161 E 6
Lyttelton [ZA] 174-175 H 3
Lytton [CDN, British Columbia] 60 G 4
Lytton [CDN, Quebec] 72-73 HJ 1

M

Ma, Sông — 150-151 E 2
Mā, Wād al- 164-165 C 4
Ma'abūs = Tazarbū 164-165 J 3
Ma'adī, Al-Qāhirah-al- 170 II b 2
Maādid, Djebel — = Jabal Ma'did 166-167 J 2
Maalaea, HI 78-79 d 2
Maalam 150-151 FG 7
Maalloûla = Ma'lūlā 136-137 G 6
Ma'ān [JOR] 134-135 D 4
Maan [TR] 136-137 H 4
Ma'anīyah, Al- 134-135 E 4
Ma'an Liedao 146-147 J 6
Ma-an Lieh-tao = Ma'an Liedao 146-147 J 6
Maanselkä 116-117 L 3-N 4
Maanshan 146-147 G 6
Maarianhamina = Mariehamn 116-117 HJ 7
Ma'ārīk, Wādī — 136-137 H 7
Ma'arrah, Al- 136-137 G 4
Ma'arrat an-Nu'mān 136-137 G 5
Maas 120-121 K 3
Maastricht 120-121 K 3
Ma'ātin 'Uwayqilah 136-137 C 7
Ma'azīz 166-167 CD 3
Ma'azzah, Jabal — 173 C 2
Mababe Depression 172 D 5
Mabalane 172 F 6
Mabana 171 B 2
Mabang Gangri 142-143 DE 5
Mabaruma 92-93 H 3
Mabein 141 E 4
Mabella 70-71 EF 1
Maben, MS 78-79 E 4
Mabi 146-147 D 4
Mabicun = Mabi 146-147 D 4
Mabogwe 171 B 4
Mabrouk 164-165 D 5
Mabrouk, El- = Al-Mabrūk 166-167 G 5
Mabruck = Mabrouk 164-165 D 5
Mabrūk, Al- 166-167 G 5
Mabton, WA 66-67 CD 2
Mabua Sefhubi 174-175 E 3
Mabudis Island 146-147 H 11
Mabuki 172 F 2
Mača 132-133 W 6
Macá, Monte — 111 B 7
Maçacará 100-101 E 6
Macachín 106-107 F 6
Macacos, Ilha dos — 98-99 N 5
Macacos, Rio — 100-101 A 8
MacAdam 63 C 5
Macaé 92-93 L 9
Macaé à Campos, Canal de — 102-103 M 4-5
Macagua, Presa — 94-95 K 3
Macaíba 100-101 G 3
Macajuba 100-101 D 7
MacAlester, OK 64-65 GH 5
MacAlister, NM 76-77 C 5
MacAllen, TX 64-65 G 6
Macalogne 171 C 6
MacAlpine Lake 56-57 PQ 4
Macambará 106-107 JK 2
Macamic 62 M 2
Macamic, Lac — 62 M 2
Macao = Macau 142-143 L 7
Macao, El — 88-89 M 5
Macapá [BR, Amapá] 92-93 J 4
Macapá [BR, Amazonas] 98-99 E 9
Macaparana 100-101 G 4
Macaquara, Cachoeira — 98-99 M 4
Macar 136-137 D 4
Macará 92-93 CD 5
Macaracuay, Petare- 91 II c 2
Maçaranduba, Cachoeira — 92-93 J 4-5
Macarani 92-93 LM 8
Macarena, Serranía de la — 94-95 DE 6
Macareo, Caño — 94-95 L 3
Macari 96-97 F 9
Maçaroca 100-101 D 5
MacArthur, OH 72-73 E 5
MacArthur Bridge 84 II c 2
MacArthur River 158-159 G 3
Macas 92-93 D 5
Macassar = Ujung Pandang 148-149 G 8
Macau [BR] 92-93 M 5-6
Macau [Macau] 142-143 L 7
Macauã, Rio — 98-99 D 9
Macaúba 92-93 J 7
Macaúbas 100-101 C 7
Macauley 208 J 6
Macayari 92-93 E 4
Macaza, Rivière — 72-73 J 1-2
MacBee, SC 80-81 F 3
MacBride 60 GH 3
MacCall, ID 66-67 EF 3
MacCamey, TX 76-77 C 7
MacCammon, ID 66-67 G 4
MacCarthy, AK 58-59 Q 6
Macchu Picchu 92-93 E 7
MacClellanville, SC 80-81 G 4
Macclenny, FL 80-81 b 1
Macclesfield Bank 148-149 FG 3
MacClintock, ostrov — 132-133 H-K 1
MacClintock Channel 56-57 Q 3
MacCloud, CA 66-67 BC 5
Maccluer, Teluk — = Teluk Berau 148-149 K 7
MacClure, PA 72-73 H 4
MacClure Strait 56-57 MN 2-3
MacClusky, ND 68-69 F 2
MacColl, SC 80-81 G 3
MacComb, MS 64-65 H 5
MacConnellsburg, PA 72-73 GH 5
MacConnelsville, OH 72-73 F 5
MacCook, NE 64-65 F 3
MacCormick, SC 80-81 EF 4
MacCormick Place 83 II b 1
MacCracken, KS 68-69 G 6
MacCreary 61 J 5
MacCullough, AL 78-79 F 5
MacCurtain, OK 76-77 G 5
MacDade, TX 76-77 F 7
MacDavid, FL 78-79 F 5
MacDermitt, NV 66-67 DE 5
Macdhui, Ben — [GB] 119 DE 3
Macdhui, Ben — [LS] 174-175 GH 6
Macdiarmid 70-71 FG 1
MacDonald 50-51 N 8
MacDonald, KS 68-69 F 6
Macdonald, Lake — [AUS] 158-159 E 4
MacDonald, Lake — [CDN] 66-67 FG 1
MacDonald Peak 66-67 G 2
Macdonnell Ranges 158-159 F 4
MacDonough, GA 80-81 DE 4
MacDouall Peak 158-159 F 5
MacDougall Sound 56-57 R 2-3
MacDowell Lake 62 C 1
MacDowell Peak 74-75 GH 6
Macedo 106-107 J 6
Macedonia 122-123 JK 5
Maceió 92-93 MN 6
Maceió, Ponta do — 100-101 F 3
Macenta 164-165 C 7
Macenta Maly 168-169 C 3
Macerata 122-123 E 4
Macfarlane, Lake — 158-159 G 6
MacGaffey, NM 74-75 J 5
MacGehee, AR 78-79 D 4
MacGill, NV 74-75 F 3
MacGillivray Falls 60 F 4
MacGill University 82 I b 1
MacGivney 63 C 4
MacGrath, AK 56-57 EF 5
MacGrath, MN 70-71 D 2
Macgregor 61 J 6
MacGregor, MN 70-71 D 2
MacGregor, TX 76-77 F 7
MacGregor Lake 61 B 5
Mac Gregor Park 85 III b 2
MacGuire, Mount — 66-67 F 3
Machacamarca 104-105 C 6
Machachi 92-93 D 5
Machačkala 126-127 NO 5
Machadinho, Rio — 104-105 E 1
Machado 102-103 K 4
Machado, Serra do — [BR, Amazonas] 98-99 H 8-9
Machado, Serra do — [BR, Ceará] 100-101 E 3
Machadodorp 174-175 J 3
Machagai 104-105 F 10
Machaila 172 F 6
Machakos 172 G 2
Machala 92-93 CD 5
Machambet 126-127 P 3
Ma-chan = Mazhan 146-147 G 3
Machaneng 172 E 6
Machang 150-151 D 10
Machanga 172 G 6
Machango 94-95 F 3
Macharadze 126-127 KL 6
Macharetí 104-105 E 7
Machattie, Lake — 158-159 GH 4
Machatuine 174-175 K 3
Machava 174-175 K 3
Machaze 172 F 6
Macheng 146-147 E 6
MacHenry, ND 68-69 G 2
Mācherla 140 D 2
Ma Chha 142-143 HJ 5
Machhalīpaṭṭaṇam = Bandar 134-135 N 7
Machhlīshar 138-139 HJ 5
Ma Chhu [Bhutan] 138-139 MN 4
Ma Chhu [TJ] 142-143 J 4
Ma-chiang = Majiang 146-147 C 10
Machias, ME 72-73 N 2
Machiche = Maxixe 174-175 L 2
Machiques 92-93 E 2-3
Ma-chi-t'ang = Majitang 146-147 C 7
Machunguel 174-175 L 2
Machupo, Río — 104-105 D 3
Machwe 174-175 E 2
Macia [Mozambique] 172 F 7
Maciá [RA] 106-107 H 4
Macias Nguema = Bioko 164-165 F 8
Maciel [PY] 102-103 D 7
Maciel [RA] 106-107 G 4
Mācin 122-123 N 3
Macina 164-165 CD 6
MacIntire, IA 70-71 D 4
MacIntosh 62 C 3
MacIntosh, SD 68-69 F 3
MacIntyre Bay 70-71 F 1
Macizo de las Guyanas 92-93 F 3-J 4
Mack, CO 74-75 J 3
Maçka = Cevizlik 136-137 H 2
MacKague 61 FG 4
Mackay 158-159 J 4
Mackay, ID 66-67 G 4
Mackay, Lake — 158-159 E 4
MacKay Lake [CDN, Northwest Territories] 56-57 O 5
MacKay Lake [CDN, Ontario] 70-71 G 1
MacKay River 61 BC 2
Mac Kean 208 J 3
MacKee, KY 72-73 DE 6
MacKeesport, PA 64-65 KL 3
MacKenzie, AL 78-79 F 5
MacKenzie, TN 78-79 E 2
Mackenzie [CDN, British Columbia] 60 F 2
MacKenzie [CDN, Ontario] 70-71 F 1
Mackenzie [GUY] 92-93 H 3
Mackenzie, District of — 56-57 L-P 5
Mackenzie Bay 56-57 J 4
MacKenzie Bridge, OR 66-67 BC 3
Mackenzie Highway 56-57 N 6
MacKenzie Island 62 BC 2
Mackenzie King Island 56-57 OP 2
Mackenzie Mountains 56-57 J 4-L 5
Mackenzie River 56-57 KL 4
Mackinac, Straits of — 70-71 H 3
Mackinaw City, MI 70-71 H 3
Mackinaw River 70-71 F 5
MacKinlay 158-159 H 4
MacKinley, Mount — 56-57 F 5
MacKinley Park, AK 58-59 N 5
MacKinney, TX 76-77 F 6
Mackinnon Road 172 GH 2
MacKirdy 70-71 FG 1
MacKittrick, CA 74-75 D 5
Macklin 61 D 4
Macksville 158-159 K 6
Maclaren River 58-59 O 5
MacLaughlin, SD 68-69 F 3
MacLean, TX 76-77 D 5
Maclean [AUS] 158-159 K 5
MacLean [USA] 82 II a 1
MacLeansboro, IL 70-71 F 6
Macleantown 174-175 GH 7
Maclear 172 E 8
Macleay River 160 L 3
MacLennan 56-57 N 6
MacLennan, Río — 108-109 F 9-10
Macleod 66-67 G 1
MacLeod, Lake — 158-159 B 4
MacLeod Bay 56-57 OP 5
MacLeod Lake 60 F 2
MacLeod River 60 J 3-K 2
MacLoughlin Peak 66-67 B 4
Maclovio Herrera 86-87 H 3
Mac-Mahon = 'Ayn Tūtah 166-167 J 2
MacMechen, WV 72-73 F 5
MacMillan, Lake — 76-77 BC 6
Macmillan River 58-59 U 5
MacMinnville, OR 66-67 B 3
MacMinnville, TN 78-79 FG 3
MacMorran 61 D 5
MacMunn 61 L 6
MacMurdo 53 B 16-17
MacMurdo Sound 53 B 17
MacNary, AZ 74-75 J 5
MacNary, TX 76-77 B 7
MacNeill, MS 78-79 E 5
Macoa, Serra — 98-99 JK 4
Macolla, La — 94-95 F 1
Macolla, Punta — 94-95 F 1
Macomb, IL 70-71 E 5
Macomb Mall 84 II c 1
Macomia 172 GH 4
Macon, GA 64-65 K 5
Macon, MO 70-71 D 6
Macon, MS 78-79 E 4
Mâcon [F] 120-121 K 5
Macondo 172 D 4
Macorís, San Francisco de — 64-65 MN 8
Macorís, San Pedro de — 64-65 N 8
Macoun 68-69 E 1
Macoun Lake 61 G 2
Macouria 98-99 M 2
MacPherson, KS 68-69 H 6
Macquarie 160 c 2-3
Macquarie, Lake — 160 KL 4
Macquarie Harbour 158-159 HJ 8
Macquarie Islands 53 D 16
Macquarie Ridge 50-51 Q 8
Macquarie River 158-159 J 6
MacRae 58-59 U 6
MacRae, GA 80-81 E 4
MacRitchie Reservoir 154 III ab 1
MacRoberts, KY 80-81 E 2
MacRobertson Land 53 BC 6-7
MacTavish Arm 56-57 N 4
MacTier 72-73 FG 2
Macuçaua 98-99 C 8
Macuco 102-103 L 4
Macuco, Cachoeira — 102-103 GH 4
Macujer 94-95 E 7
Macuma, Río — 96-97 C 3
Macumba 158-159 G 5
Macupari, Río — 104-105 C 3
Macuré 100-101 E 5
Macusani 92-93 E 7
Macuspana 86-87 O 9
Macuto 94-95 H 2
Macúzari, Presa — 86-87 F 4
MacVivar Arm 56-57 MN 4-5
Mā'dabā 136-137 F 7
Madadi 164-165 J 5
Madagascar 172 H 6-J 5
Madagascar Basin 50-51 M 7

322 Lucerna

Madagascar Ridge 50-51 M 7
Madā'in Şāliḥ 134-135 D 5
Maḍakalapūwa 134-135 N 9
Madakasira 140 C 4
Madakkan, Ḥāssī — 166-167 EF 5
Madale 168-169 H 4
Madalena 100-101 E 3
Madam 168-169 E 3-4
Madama 164-165 G 4
Mādampe 140 D 7
Madan 122-123 L 5
Madanapalle 140 D 4
Madang 148-149 N 8
Madania, Al-Jazā'ir-El — 170 I a 2
Madanīyīn 164-165 FG 2
Madanpur 138-139 G 5
Madaoua 164-165 F 6
Madāqin 166-167 H 3
Mādāri Hāt 138-139 M 4
Madārīpur 141 AB 4
Madauk 141 E 7
Madavā = Mandāwa 138-139 E 3
Madawaska [CDN, New Brunswick] 63 B 4
Madawaska [CDN, Ontario] 72-73 GH 2
Madawaska River 72-73 H 2
Madawrūsh 166-167 K 1
Madaya = Mattayā 141 E 4
Madaya River = Nam Bei 141 E 4
Maddagiri = Madhugiri 140 C 4
Maddalena 122-123 C 5
Madden, Lago — 64-65 b 2
Madden, Presa de — 64-65 b 2
Madden Dam = Presa de Madden 64-65 b 2
Madden Lake = Lago Madden 64-65 b 2
Maddikera 140 C 3
Maḍḍikĕrĕ = Maddikera 140 C 3
Maddox Park 85 II b 2
Maddūr 140 C 4
Maddūru = Maddūr 140 C 4
Madeira 164-165 A 2
Madeira = Arquipélago da Madeira 164-165 A 2
Madeira, Arquipélago da — 164-165 A 2
Madeira, Río — 92-93 G 6
Madeirinha, Rio — 98-99 H 9
M'adel' 124-125 F 6
Madeleine, Îles de la — 56-57 Y 8
Madelia, MN 70-71 C 3-4
Madeline, CA 66-67 C 5
Madeline Island 70-71 E 2
Madeline Plains 66-67 C 5
Maden 136-137 H 3
Maden = Madenhanları 136-137 J 2
Maden adası = Alibey adası 136-137 B 3
Maden dağları 136-137 H 3
Madenhanları 136-137 J 2
Madera 64-65 E 6
Madera, CA 74-75 CD 4
Madera, Sierra — 76-77 C 7
Madera, Sierra de la — 86-87 F 2-3
Madero, Ciudad — 64-65 G 7
Madgāṅv = Margao 140 A 3
Mādha 140 B 1
Māḍhēṅ = Mādha 140 B 1
Madhepura 138-139 L 5
Madhipura = Madhepura 138-139 L 5
Madhol = Mudhol 138-139 FG 8
Madhra 140 E 2
Madhubani 138-139 L 4
Madhugiri 140 C 4
Madhūmati 138-139 M 6
Madhupur 138-139 L 5
Madhūpūr Jangal 141 B 3
Madhupur Jungle = Madhūpūr Jangal 138-139 N 5
Madhya Andamān = Middle Andaman 134-135 P 8
Madhyama Palāna ◁ 140 E 7
Madhyamgram 154 II b 1
Madhya Pradesh 134-135 MN 6
Madi = Marsengdi 138-139 K 3
Madian 146-147 F 5
Madibira 171 C 5
Madibogo 174-175 F 4
Ma'dīd, Jabal — 166-167 J 2
Madidi, Río — 92-93 F 7
Madill, OK 76-77 F 5
Madimba 172 C 2-3
Madimele 174-175 D 2
Madina 168-169 C 2
Madina do Boé 164-165 B 6
Madīnah, Al- [IRQ] 136-137 M 7
Madīnah, Al- [Saudi Arabia] 134-135 DE 6
Madinani 168-169 D 3
Madīnat ash-Sha'ab 134-135 EF 8
Madingou 172 B 2
Madiq Jubal = Jazīrat Shadwan 164-165 LM 3
Mādirā = Madhra 140 E 2
Madison, FL 80-81 b 1
Madison, GA 80-81 E 4
Madison, IN 70-71 H 6
Madison, KS 68-69 H 6
Madison, ME 72-73 LM 2
Madison, MN 70-71 BC 3
Madison, NE 68-69 H 5
Madison, SD 68-69 H 3
Madison, WI 64-65 HJ 3
Madison, WV 72-73 F 5
Madison Heights, MI 84 II b 1
Madison Park 85 III b 2
Madison Range 66-67 H 3
Madison River 66-67 H 3
Madison Square Garden 82 III c 2
Madisonville, KY 70-71 FG 7
Madisonville, TX 76-77 G 7
Madiun 148-149 F 8
Madiyi 146-147 C 7
Mâdjen Bel'abbès = Māghin Bin al-'Abbās 166-167 L 2
Madjerda, Quèd — = Wad Majradah 164-165 F 1
Madjori 168-169 F 3
Madley, Mount — 158-159 D 4
Madoc 72-73 H 2
Mado Gashi 172 G 1
Madona 124-125 F 5
Madonela 174-175 H 6
Madonie 122-123 EF 7
Madou = Matou 146-147 H 10
Madra dağı 136-137 B 3
Madrakah, Rā's al- 134-135 H 7
Madras 134-135 N 8
Madras, OR 66-67 C 3
Madrās = Tamil Nadu 134-135 M 8-9
Madrasta = Madrās 134-135 N 8
Madre, Laguna — 64-65 G 6-7
Madre, Sierra — [MEX] 64-65 H 8
Madre, Sierra — [RP] 148-149 H 3
Madre de Dios [PE, administrative unit] 96-97 FG 7
Madre de Dios [PE, place] 92-93 EF 7
Madre de Dios, Isla — 111 A 8
Madre de Dios, Río — 92-93 F 7
Madrid, IA 70-71 D 5
Madrid, NE 68-69 F 5
Madrid, NM 76-77 AB 5
Madrid [CO] 94-95 D 5
Madrid [E] 120-121 EF 8
Madrid, La — 104-105 D 10
Madrid-Aravaca 113 III a 2
Madrid-Arganzuela 113 III a 2
Madrid-Barajas 113 III b 2
Madrid-Buenavista 113 III ab 2
Madrid-Campamento 113 III a 2
Madrid-Canillas 113 III b 2
Madrid-Canillejas 113 III b 2
Madrid-Carabanchel Alto 113 III a 2
Madrid-Centro 113 III a 2
Madrid-Chamartín 113 III ab 2
Madrid-Chamberí 113 III a 2
Madrid-Ciudad Lineal 113 III b 2
Madrid-Cuatro Vientos 113 III a 2
Madrid-Entrevías 113 III b 2
Madrid-Hortaleza 113 III b 2
Madrid-Latina 113 III a 2
Madrid-Moratalaz 113 III b 2
Madrid-Orcasitas 113 III a 2
Madrid-Palomeras 113 III b 2
Madrid-Peña Grande 113 III a 2
Madrid-Progresso 113 III ab 2
Madrid-Pueblo Nuevo 113 III b 2
Madrid-Puente Vallecas 113 III b 2
Madrid-Retiro 113 III ab 2
Madrid-San Fermín 113 III ab 2
Madrid-Tetuán 113 III a 2
Madrid-Usera 113 III a 2
Madrid-Valdebeba 113 III b 2
Madrid-Ventas 113 III ab 2
Madrid-Vicálvaro 113 III b 2
Madrid-Villaverde Bajo 113 III ab 2
Madrīsah 166-167 G 2
Mad River 66-67 B 5
Madrona, Sierra — 120-121 EF 9
Madruba, Lago — 98-99 J 6
Madu, Pulau — 152-153 OP 9
Madūbi 141 C 5
Madura 158-159 E 6
Madura = Madurai 134-135 M 9
Madura = Pulau Madura 148-149 F 8
Madura, Pulau — 148-149 F 8
Madura, Selat — 152-153 KL 9
Madurai 134-135 M 9
Madurai Malaikal 140 CD 5
Madurāntakam 140 DE 4
Maduranthakam = Madurāntakam 140 DE 4
Madureira, Rio de Janeiro- 110 I ab 2
Madūru Oya 140 E 7
Mádytos = Eceabat 136-137 AB 2
Madyūnah 166-167 C 3
Maé = Mahe 134-135 M 8
Mae Ai 150-151 B 2-3
Maebara, Funabashi- 155 III d 1
Maebashi 144-145 M 4
Mae Chaem 150-151 B 3
Mae Chan 150-151 B 2
Mae Hong Son 150-151 AB 3
Maekal = Maikala Range 138-139 H 6-7
Mae Khlong = Samut Songkhram 150-151 C 6
Mae Klong, Mae Nam - 141 F 7-8
Mae Klong = Mae Nam Klong 150-151 CD 3-4
Mae Klong = Samut Songkhram 150-151 C 6
Mae Klong, Mae Nam — 150-151 B 5-6
Mae La Noi 150-151 AB 3
Mae Nam Bang Pakong 150-151 C 6
Mae Nam Chao Phraya 148-149 CD 3-4
Mae Nam Khong 148-149 D 3
Mae Nam Khwae Noi 150-151 B 5-6
Mae Nam Kong 148-149 D 3
Mae Nam Mae Klong 150-151 B 5-6
Mae Nam Mai 141 EF 7
Mae Nam Mai = Mae Nam Moei 150-151 B 4
Mae Nam Moei 150-151 B 4
Mae Nam Mun 148-149 D 3
Mae Nam Nan 148-149 D 3
Mae Nam Pa Sak 150-151 C 4-5
Mae Nam Pattani 150-151 C 9
Mae Nam Ping 148-149 C 3
Mae Nam Sai Buri 150-151 C 9-10
Mae Nam Songkhram 150-151 DE 3-4
Mae Nam Suphan = Mae Nam Tha Chin 150-151 C 5-6
Mae Nam Tapi 150-151 B 8
Mae Nam Tha Chin 150-151 C 5-6
Mae Nam Wang 150-151 B 3
Mae Nam Yom 148-149 CD 3
Maengbu-san 144-145 F 2
Maeno, Tōkyō- 155 III b 1
Maenpurī = Mainpuri 138-139 G 4
Mae Phrik 150-151 B 4
Mae Ramat 150-151 B 4
Mae Rim 150-151 B 3
Mae Sai 148-149 CD 2
Mae Sariang 148-149 C 3
Mae Sot 150-151 B 4
Maestra, Sierra — 64-65 L 7-8
Mae Suai 150-151 B 3
Mae Taeng 150-151 B 3
Mae Tha 150-151 B 3
Mae Thot 150-151 B 4
Maevatanana 172 J 5
Maewo 158-159 N 3
Mae Yuam 150-151 A 3
Mafeking [CDN] 61 H 4
Mafeking = Mmabatho 172 DE 7
Mafeteng 174-175 G 5
Maffra 160 H 7
Mafia Channel 171 D 4-5
Mafia Island 172 GH 3
Mafra [BR] 111 FG 3
Mafraq, Al- 136-137 G 6
Mafrenso 100-101 D 5
Mafupa 172 E 4
Magadan 132-133 CD 6
Magadi 172 G 2
Magadi, Lake — 171 D 3
Magadoxo = Muqdiisho 164-165 O 8
Magalhães de Almeida 100-101 C 2
Magaliesberge 174-175 G 3
Magallanes, Caracas-Los — 91 II b 1
Magallanes, Estrecho de — 111 AB 8
Magallanes, Península — 108-109 C 8
Magallanes y Antártica Chilena 108-109 B 7-E 10
Magaļrēdēṅ = Mangalvedha 140 B 2
Magangué 92-93 E 3
Maǧara 136-137 EF 4
Maǧara = Höketçe 136-137 G 3
Magaria 164-165 F 6
Magariños 102-103 B 5
Magatoberge 174-175 J 2
Magato Mountains = Magatoberge 174-175 J 2
Magaw 141 E 2
Magazine Mountain 78-79 C 3
Magburaka 164-165 B 7
Magdagači 132-133 Y 7
Magdala [RA] 106-107 G 6
Magdalena, NM 76-77 A 5
Magdalena [BOL] 92-93 G 7
Magdalena [CO] 94-95 D 2
Magdalena [MEX, Baja California Sur] 86-87 DE 4
Magdalena [RA] 106-107 J 5
Magdalena, Bahía — 64-65 D 7
Magdalena, Bahía de — 94-95 C 5-6
Magdalena, Gunung — 152-153 M 3
Magdalena, Isla — 111 B 6
Magdalena, Llano de la — 64-65 D 6-7
Magdalena, Río — [CO] 92-93 E 2-3
Magdalena, Río — [MEX] 64-65 D 5
Magdalena, Río de la — 91 I b 3
Magdalena Atlipac, La — 91 I d 2
Magdalena Contreras, La — 91 I b 3
Magdalena Puerto Nare, La — 94-95 D 4
Magdalen Islands = Îles de la Madeleine 56-57 Y 8
Magdeburg 118 E 2
Magee, MS 78-79 DE 5
Mageik, Mount — 58-59 K 7
Magelang 148-149 EF 8
Magerøy 116-117 M 2
Magersfontein 174-175 F 5
Maggia Range 53 B 35-36
Maggiolo 106-107 FG 4
Maghāghah 173 B 3
Maghayrā', Al- 134-135 G 6
Māghin Bin al-'Abbās 166-167 L 2
Maghnia = Maghnīyah 166-167 F 2
Maghnīyah 166-167 F 2
Māghrah, Al- 136-137 C 7
Magi = Maji 164-165 M 7
Magic Reservoir 66-67 F 4
Magill, Islas — 108-109 C 10
Maginu, Kawasaki- 155 III a 2
Magliana 113 II a 2
Magliana, Roma- 113 II ab 2
Máglie 122-123 H 5
Magna, UT 66-67 GH 5
Magnesia = Manisa 134-135 B 3
Magness, AR 78-79 D 3
Magnetic Island 158-159 J 3
Magnitogorsk 132-133 KL 7
Magnolia, AR 78-79 C 4
Magnolia, MS 78-79 D 5
Magnolia, NJ 84 III c 2
Magnor 116-117 DE 7-8
Magny-les-Hameaux 129 I b 3
Magoè 172 F 5
Magog 72-73 KL 2
Magome, Tōkyō- 155 III b 2
M'agostrov 124-125 KL 1
Magoura = Maqūrah 166-167 F 2
Magpie 63 D 2
Magpie, Lac — 63 D 2
Magpie, Rivière — 63 D 2
Magpie River 70-71 H 1
Magrath 66-67 G 1
Magreb = Al-Maghrib 164-165 C 3-D 2
Magu, Rio — 100-101 C 2
Maguari, Cabo — 92-93 K 4-5
Magude 172 F 6-7
Maguí 94-95 B 7
Magumeri 168-169 J 2
Māgura 138-139 M 6
Magusheni 174-175 H 6
Magwe 148-149 BC 2
Magwe Taing 141 D 5-6
Mahābād 134-135 F 3
Mahābaleshwar 140 A 2
Mahābalipuram 140 E 4
Mahābhārat Lekh 134-135 NO 5
Mahabo 172 HJ 6
Mahabūbābād = Mahbūbābād 140 DE 2
Maha Chana Chai 148-149 DE 3
Mahād 140 A 1
Mahādeo Hills 138-139 G 6
Mahādeopur 140 DE 1
Mahadeo Range 140 B 1-2
Mahādēvapura = Mahādeopur 140 DE 1
Mahādēv Pahāṛiyāṅ = Mahādeo Hills 138-139 G 6
Mahagi 172 F 1
Mahaicony 92-93 H 3
Mahajamba, Helodranon'i — 172 J 4-5
Mahājan 138-139 D 3
Mahajanga 172 J 5
Mahakam, Sungai — 148-149 G 6-7
Mahalapye 172 E 6
Mahālchari 141 BC 4
Mahālingpur 140 B 2
Maḥallat al-Kubra, Al- 164-165 L 2
Maham 138-139 F 3
Maḥamīd, Al- 166-167 D 5
Mahānadi 134-135 N 6
Mahānadi Delta 134-135 O 7
Mahānanda 138-139 L 4-5
Mahanoro 172 J 5
Maha Nuwara 134-135 N 9
Maha Oya [CL, place] 140 E 7
Maha Oya [CL, river] 140 DE 7
Mahārājganj [IND ↗ Gorakhpoor] 138-139 J 4
Mahārājganj [IND ↘ Lucknow] 138-139 H 4
Mahārāshtra [IND, administrative unit] 138-139 D 8-G 7
Mahārāshtra [IND, landscape] 134-135 M 7
Maharatta = Mahārāshtra 138-139 D 8-G 7
Mahārī, Al- = Al-Muhārī 136-137 L 7
Mahārī, Sha'īb al- 136-137 KL 7
Maḥārīq, Al- 173 B 5
Maḥaris, Al- 166-167 M 2
Maharpur 138-139 M 6
Mahāsamand = Mahāsamund 138-139 J 7
Mahāsamund 138-139 J 7
Maha Sarakham 148-149 D 3
Mahato 171 E 5
Maḥaṭṭat 1 173 B 7
Maḥaṭṭat 2 173 BC 7
Maḥaṭṭat 3 173 BC 7
Maḥaṭṭat 4 173 C 7
Maḥaṭṭat al-Hilmīyah, Al-Qāhirah- 170 II bc 1
Mahawa 134-135 M 9
Mahawēli Ganga 140 E 7
Mahbūbābād 140 DE 2
Mahbūbnagar 140 CD 2
Mahd adh-Dhahab 134-135 E 6
Mahder, El- = 'Ayn al-Qasr 166-167 K 2
Mahdia 92-93 H 3
Mahdīyah 166-167 C 2
Mahdīyah, Al- 164-165 G 1
Mahe [IND] 134-135 M 8
Mahé [Seychelles] 204-205 N 9
Mahé Archipelago = Seychelles 50-51 MN 6
Mahebūbnagara = Mahbūbnagar 140 CD 2
Mahendragarh 138-139 EF 3
Mahendra Giri [IND, Orissa] 138-139 JK 8
Mahendra Giri [IND, Tamil Nadu] 140 C 6
Mahendranagar 138-139 H 3
Mahendra Parvata = Eastern Ghats 134-135 M 8-N 7
Mahenge 172 G 3
Maher 62 L 2
Mahēsāṇā = Mehsāna 134-135 L 6
Maheshtala 154 II a 3
Mahēshvar = Maheshwar 138-139 E 6
Maheshwar 138-139 E 6
Maheson Island 62 A 2
Mahi 138-139 D 6
Māhī = Mahe 134-135 M 8
Mahia, El — 164-165 D 4
Mahia Peninsula 158-159 P 7
Mahiāri 154 II a 2
Mahīdpur = Mehidpur 138-139 E 6
Māhīm 138-139 D 8
Mahina 168-169 C 2
Mahindi 171 D 5
Mahirija = Al-Ma'irījah 166-167 E 2-3
Mahlabatini 174-175 J 5
Mahlaing 141 D 5
Mahlsdorf-Süd, Berlin- 130 III c 2
Mahmedabad = Mĕhmadābād 138-139 D 6
Mahmel, Kef — = Jabal Mahmil 166-167 K 2
Mahmil, Jabal — 166-167 K 2
Maḥmūdīyah, Al- 136-137 L 6
Mahmudiye 136-137 D 3
Mahmut bendi 154 I a 1
Māhneshān 136-137 M 4
Mahnomen, MN 70-71 BC 2
Maho = Mahawa 134-135 M 9
Mahoba 138-139 GH 5
Mahogany Mountain 66-67 E 4
Mahón [F] 120-121 K 9
Mahon [HV] 168-169 D 3
Mahone Bay 63 DE 5
Mahrī 138-139 A 4
Mahroni 138-139 G 5
Mahtowa, MN 70-71 D 2
Mahu = Mhow 138-139 E 6
Mahuida, Campana — 108-109 E 4
Mahukona, HI 78-79 de 2
Mahuta 171 D 5
Mahuva 138-139 CD 7
Mahwah 138-139 F 4
Mai, Mae Nam — = Mae Nam Moei 150-151 B 4
Maïa, El — = Al-Māyah 166-167 G 3
Maï ad-Darwāwī, Ḥāssī — 166-167 K 3
Maiándros = Büyük Menderes nehri 136-137 B 4
Maiaú, Ponta — 98-99 P 5
Maicasagi, Lac — 62 N 1
Maicasagi, Rivière — 62 NO 1
Mai Chai 150-151 BC 3
Maichaila 172 F 6
Maichen 146-147 B 11
Maicoa 94-95 E 2
Maicuru, Rio — 92-93 J 5
Mā'idah, Ḍāya al- 166-167 D 4
Maidalpur 138-139 J 8
Maidālpura = Maidalpur 138-139 J 8
Maidān = Maydān 136-137 L 5
Maidan, Calcutta- 154 II ab 2
Maīdān Akbas = Maydān Ikbis 136-137 G 4
Maidī = Maydī 134-135 E 7
Maidstone [CDN] 61 D 4
Maidstone [GB] 119 G 6
Maidstone, Melbourne- 161 II b 1
Maiduguri 164-165 G 6
Maiella 122-123 F 4
Maigaiti = Marqat Bazar 142-143 D 4
Maigualida, Serranía de — 92-93 F 3-G 4
Maihar 138-139 H 5
Maijdī 134-135 P 6
Mai-kai-t'i = Marqat Bazar 142-143 D 4
Maikala Range 138-139 H 6-7
Maikal Mountains = Maikala Range 138-139 H 6-7
Maiko 172 E 1-2
Maiko, Parc national de — 172 E 2
Maikona 171 D 2
Maikoor, Pulau — 148-149 K 8
Mailan 138-139 J 6
Mailāni 138-139 H 3
Maillín, Arroyo de — 106-107 F 2
Mailsī 138-139 CD 3
Maimacheng = Altanbulag 142-143 K 1-2
Maimansingh 134-135 OP 5-6
Main [D] 118 D 4
Ma'īn [Y] 134-135 EF 7
Maināguri 138-139 M 4
Main Barrier Range 158-159 H 6
Main Centre 61 E 5
Main Channel 62 L 4
Maindargi 140 C 2
Mai Ndombe 172 C 2
Maine [F] 120-121 GH 4
Maine [USA] 64-65 MN 2
Maine, Gulf of — 64-65 N 3
Mainemĕnĕ = Menemen 136-137 B 3
Maïné-Soroa 164-165 G 6
Maingay Island = Zaraw Kyūn 150-151 AB 6
Mainggūn 141 E 2
Mainggwè 141 D 3
Maingy Island = Zaraw Kyūn 150-151 AB 6
Mainland [GB, Orkney] 119 DE 2
Mainland [GB, Shetland] 119 F 1
Main Pass 78-79 E 6
Mainpat Hills 138-139 J 6
Mainpur 138-139 J 7
Mainpuri 138-139 G 4
Main Saint Gardens, Houston-, TX 85 III ab 2
Main River 63 H 3
Maintirano 172 H 5
Mainz 118 D 3-4
Mainzer Berg 128 III b 2
Maio 204-205 E 7
Maioca 104-105 H 4
Maipo, Río — 106-107 B 4
Maipo, Volcán — 111 C 4
Maipú [RA, Buenos Aires] 111 E 5
Maipú [RA, Mendoza] 106-107 C 4
Maipú [RCH] 106-107 B 4
Maipures 92-93 F 3
Maiquetia 92-93 F 2
Maiquetía, Aeropuerto — 91 II b 1
Maiquinique 100-101 D 8
Mairabāri 141 C 2
Mairi 100-101 D 6
Ma'irījah, Al- 166-167 E 2-3
Mairipotaba 102-103 H 2
Mairta = Merta 138-139 DE 4
Maisarī, Al- = Al-Maysarī 136-137 H 7
Maisí, Cabo — 64-65 M 7
Maiskhāl Dīp 141 B 5
Maisome 171 C 3
Maison du Gouvernement 170 IV a 1
Maisonneuve, Parc de — 82 I b 1
Maisons-Alfort 129 I c 2
Maisons-Laffitte 129 I b 2
Maisūru = Mysore 134-135 M 8
Mait = Mayd 134-135 F 8
Maitén, El — 108-109 D 4
Maitencillo 106-107 B 3
Maitland 158-159 K 6
Maitland, Lake — 158-159 D 5
Maíz, Islas del — 64-65 K 9
Maizefield 174-175 H 4
Maizuru 142-143 Q 4
Maja 132-133 Za 6
Majadas, Las — 94-95 J 4
Majagual 92-93 E 3
Majal, Bi'r — 173 C 6
Majane 174-175 D 3
Majari, Rio — 98-99 H 3
Majarr al-Kabīr, Al- 136-137 M 7
Majdal = Ashqĕlōn 136-137 F 7
Majé 102-103 L 5
Majene 148-149 G 7
Majes, Río de — 96-97 F 10
Majevica 122-123 H 3
Mājhgāṅ = Mājhgaon 138-139 K 6
Mājhgaon 138-139 K 6
Maji 164-165 M 7
Majiadian = Madian 146-147 F 5
Majiang 146-147 C 10
Maji Moto 172 F 3
Majitang 146-147 C 7
Majja 132-133 Z 5
Majkain 132-133 O 7
Majkop 126-127 K 4
Majkor 124-125 U 4
Majma'ah 134-135 F 5
Majn 132-133 h 5
Majna 124-125 Q 6
Majngy-Pil'gyn = Mejnypil'gyno 132-133 j 5
Majoli 92-93 H 4
Majorca = Mallorca 120-121 J 9
Major Isidoro 100-101 F 5
Major Pablo Lagerenza 111 DE 1
Major Peak 76-77 C 7
Majradah, Jabal al- 166-167 KL 1
Majradah, Wad — 164-165 F 1
Majskij 126-127 M 5
Majunga = Mahajanga 172 J 5
Majuriã 98-99 F 8
Majuro 208 H 2
Mak, Ko — [T, Gulf of Thailand] 150-151 D 7
Mak, Ko — [T, Thale Luang] 150-151 C 9
Maka 168-169 AB 2
Makah Indian Reservation 66-67 A 1
Makala, Kinshasa- 170 IV a 2
Makale 152-153 N 7
Makale = Mekele 164-165 MN 7
Makallé 104-105 G 10
Makalle = Mekelē 164-165 M 6
Makālu 138-139 L 4
Makalut = Makālu 138-139 L 4
Makampi 171 C 5
Makanya 171 D 4
Makapuu Point 78-79 d 2
Makarfi 168-169 G 3
Makar-Ib 124-125 RS 2
Makarjev 124-125 OP 5
Makarjevo 124-125 P 5
Makarov 132-133 b 8
Makarska 122-123 G 4
Makasar = Ujung Pandang 148-149 G 8
Makasar, Selat — 148-149 G 6-7
Makassar = Ujung Pandang 148-149 G 8
Makassar Strait = Selat Makasar 148-149 G 6-7
Makat 132-133 J 8
Makatini Flats 174-175 K 4
Makedonía 122-123 JK 5
Makedonija 122-123 B-D 4
Makejevka 126-127 HJ 2
Make-jima 144-145 H 7
Makeni 164-165 B 7
Makeyevka = Makejevka 126-127 HJ 2
Makgadikgadi Salt Pan 172 DE 6
Makhachkala = Machačkala 126-127 NO 5
Makham 150-151 D 6
Makhatal = Makhtal 140 C 2
Makhfir al-Ḥammān 136-137 H 5
Makhiruq, Wādī el- = Wādī al-Makhrūq 136-137 G 7
Makhmūr 136-137 K 5
Makhrūq, Khashm al- 136-137 J 7
Makhrūq, Wādī al- 136-137 G 7
Makhtal 140 C 2
Makian, Pulau — 148-149 J 6
Makīlī, Al- 164-165 J 2
Makin 208 H 2
Makinsk 132-133 MN 7
Makinson Inlet 56-57 UV 2
M'akit 132-133 d 5
Makka = Makkah 134-135 DE 6
Makkah 134-135 DE 6
Makkaur 116-117 O 2
Maklakovo 132-133 R 6
Maklautsi 174-175 H 2
Maknāsī, Al- 166-167 L 2
Maknassi = Al-Maknāsī 166-167 L 2
Makó 118 K 5
Makokibatan Lake 62 F 2
Makoko 171 C 4
Makokou 172 B 1
Makomezawa 155 III cd 1
Makona 168-169 C 3
Makoop Lake 62 D 1
Makoua 172 BC 1-2
Makounda = Markounda 164-165 H 7
Makragéfyra = Uzunköprü 136-137 B 2
Makrai 138-139 F 6
Makran = Mokrān 134-135 HJ 5
Makrāna 134-135 L 5
Makrónēsos 122-123 L 7
M'aksa 124-125 M 4
Maks al-Baḥrī, Al- 173 AB 5
Maks al-Qiblī, Al- 164-165 L 4
Maksatikha 124-125 KL 5
Maks el-Baharî = Al-Maks al-Baḥrī 173 AB 5
Makteir = Maqṭayr 164-165 BC 4
Makthar 166-167 L 2
Mākū 136-137 L 3
Mākū Chāy 136-137 L 3
Makuhari 155 III d 2
Makumbako 171 C 5
Makumbi 172 CD 3
Makunudu 176 a 1
Makurazaki 144-145 GH 7
Makurdi 164-165 F 7
Makushin, AK 58-59 n 4
Makushin Bay 58-59 n 4
Makushin Volcano 58-59 n 4
Makuyuni 171 D 3
Makwassie 174-175 F 4
Makwie 168-169 BC 3
Māl 138-139 M 4
Māla [IND] 140 C 5
Mala [PE] 96-97 C 8
Mala = Malaita 148-149 k 6
Malabar Coast 134-135 L 8-M 9
Malabo 164-165 F 8
Malabriga 106-107 H 2
Mal Abrigo 106-107 J 5
Malacacheta [BR, Minas Gerais] 102-103 LM 2
Malacacheta [BR, Roraima] 94-95 L 6
Malacca = Malaiische Halbinsel 148-149 C 5-D 6
Malacca, Strait of — 148-149 C 5-D 6
Malad City, ID 66-67 G 4
Maladeta 120-121 H 7
Malaga, NM 76-77 B 6
Málaga [CO] 92-93 E 3
Málaga [E] 120-121 E 10
Malagarasi [EAT, place] 171 B 4
Malagarasi [EAT, river] 172 F 2
Malagas = Malgas 174-175 D 8
Malagueño 106-107 E 3
Malaḥ, Al- 166-167 F 2
Malah, Sabkhat al- 166-167 F 5
Malaija = Melayu 148-149 D 6
Malaita 148-149 k 6
Malaja Belozʼorka 126-127 G 3
Malaja Ob' 132-133 M 5-L 4
Malaja Sejdemincha = Kalininskoje 126-127 F 3
Malaja Serdoba 124-125 P 7
Malaja Višera 132-133 E 6
Malaja Viska 126-127 E 2
Malaja Znamenka = Kamenka-Dneprovskaja 126-127 G 3
Malaka, Selat — 152-153 A 3
Malakāl 164-165 L 7
Mālākaṇḍ 134-135 L 4
Malakoff 129 I c 2
Mala Krsna 122-123 J 3
Malalaling 172 D 7
Malam = Maalam 150-151 FG 7
Malamala 152-153 O 7
Mālanādu 140 B 3-4
Mālanchā 138-139 M 7
Malanchwane 174-175 D 3
Malang 148-149 F 8
Malange 172 C 3
Malangen 116-117 H 3
Malangowa = Malangwa 138-139 K 4
Malangwa 138-139 K 4
Malanzán 106-107 D 3
Mālaoṭ = Malaut 138-139 E 2
Malappuram 140 BC 5
Malapuram = Malappuram 140 C 5
Mälaren 116-117 G 8
Malargüe 111 C 5
Mälar Lake = Mälaren 116-117 G 8
Malartic 56-57 V 8
Malartic, Lac — 62 N 2
Malaspina 111 C 6-7
Malaspina Glacier 56-57 H 5-6
Malatia = Malatya 134-135 D 3
Malatosh Lake 61 F 3
Malatya 134-135 D 3
Malatya dağları 136-137 G 4-H 3
Malaut 138-139 E 2
Malavalli 140 C 4
Malāvī 136-137 MN 6
Malavi = Malawi 172 FG 4
Malawali, Pulau — 152-153 M 2
Malawi 172 FG 4
Malawi, Lake — 172 F 4
Malayagiri 134-135 O 6
Malayalam Coast = Malabar Coast 134-135 L 8-M 9
Malaya Parvata = Eastern Ghats 134-135 M 8-N 7
Malay Archipelago 50-51 O 5-Q 6
Malāyer 134-135 F 4
Malāyer, Rūdkhāneh-ye — 136-137 N 5
Malay Peninsula 148-149 C 5-D 6
Malaysia 148-149 D-F 6
Malayu = Melayu 148-149 D 6

Malayu 323

Malazgirt 136-137 K 3
Malbaie, la — 63 AB 4
Malbaza 168-169 G 2
Malbon 158-159 H 4
Malbooma 160 AB 3
Malbork 118 J 1-2
Malbrán 106-107 F 2
Malcanio, Cerro — 104-105 CD 9
Malcėsine 122-123 D 3
Malchow, Berlin- 130 III bc 1
Malcolm River 58-59 RS 2
Malden 156-157 K 5
Malden, MA 72-73 L 3
Malden, MO 78-79 DE 2
Malden River 84 I b 2
Maldive Islands 176 F 3
Maldives = Malediven 140 A 7
Maldonado [ROU, administrative unit] 106-107 K 5
Maldonado [ROU, place] 111 F 4
Maldonado, Punta — 64-65 FG 8
Maldonado-cué 102-103 D 5
Male [Maldive Is.] 178-179 N 5
Male, Lac du — 62 O 2
Maléas, Akrōtḗrion — 122-123 K 7
Male Atoll 176 a 2
Mālēgā̃v = Mālegaon 134-135 LM 6
Mālegaon 134-135 LM 6
Male Island 176 a 2
Maleize 128 II b 2
Male Karpaty 118 H 4
Malek Kandī 136-137 M 4
Malekula 158-159 N 3
Malela 172 E 2
Malelane 174-175 J 3
Malemo 172 G 4
Malena 106-107 E 4
Malen'ga 124-125 KL 2
Malepeque Bay 63 E 4
Māler Kotla 138-139 EF 2
Maleza 94-95 G 5
Malgas 174-175 D 8
Malghīr, Shaṭṭ — 164-165 F 2
Malgobek 126-127 M 5
Malgrat 120-121 J 8
Malhada 100-101 C 8
Malḥah 136-137 K 5
Malhār 138-139 J 7
Malhārgarh 138-139 E 5
Malheur Lake 66-67 D 4
Malheur River 66-67 E 4
Mali [Guinea] 168-169 B 2
Mali [RMM] 164-165 C 6-D 5
Mālia [IND] 138-139 C 7
Maliangping 146-147 C 6
Malian He 146-147 A 4
Ma-lien Ho = Malian He 146-147 A 4
Māliḥ, Sabkhat al- 166-167 M 3
Malihābād 138-139 H 4
Mali Hka 141 E 2
Malije Derbety 126-127 M 3
Malik, Wādī al- 164-165 KL 5
Malıköy 136-137 E 3
Mali Kyûn 148-149 C 4
Mali Mamou 168-169 BC 3
Malimba, Monts — 171 B 4
Malin, OR 66-67 C 4
Malin [SU] 126-127 D 1
Malinaltepec 86-87 L 9
Malinau 148-149 G 6
Malindi 172 H 2
Malines = Mechelen 120-121 K 3
Malingping 152-153 G 9
Malin Head 119 C 4
Malinké 168-169 B 2
Malino, Gunung — 152-153 O 5
Malinyi 171 CD 5
Malipo 142-143 J 7
Malita 148-149 HJ 5
Malītah 166-167 M 2
Maliwûn 150-151 B 7
Māliya 138-139 C 6
Māḷiyā = Mālia 138-139 C 7
Malizarathseik 150-151 AB 6
Malizayatseik = Malizarathseik 150-151 AB 6
Maljamar, NM 76-77 C 6
Malka 126-127 L 5
Malkangiri 140 EF 1
Malkāpur [IND ↘ Bhusāwal] 138-139 EF 7
Malkāpur [IND ↖ Kolhāpur] 140 A 2
Malkara 136-137 B 2
Małkinia Górna 118 L 2
Mallacoota Inlet 160 JK 6
Mallāg, Wād — 166-167 L 1-2
Mallāḥ, Wād al- 166-167 C 3
Mallaig 119 D 3
Mallakastër 122-123 HJ 5
Mallama 94-95 BC 7
Mallampalli 140 DE 1
Mallānvan = Mallānwān 138-139 H 4
Mallānwān 138-139 H 4
Mallapunyah 158-159 G 3
Mallawī 173 B 4
Malleco, Rio — 106-107 AB 7
Mallès Venosta 122-123 D 2
Mallet 102-103 G 6
Mallicolo = Malekula 158-159 N 3
Mallīt 164-165 K 6
Mallorca 120-121 J 9
Mallow 119 B 5
Malmberget 116-117 J 4
Malmedy 120-121 L 3
Malmesbury [ZA] 172 C 8
Malmö 116-117 E 10
Malmöhus 116-117 E 9-10
Malmyž 124-125 S 5
Malnad = Mālanādu 140 B 3-4
Maloarchangel'sk 124-125 L 7
Maloca 92-93 H 4
Maloca Macu 98-99 G 3
Malojaroslavec 124-125 KL 6
Maloje Karmakuly 132-133 HJ 3
Malole 171 B 5
Malombe, Lake — 172 G 4
Malone, NY 72-73 J 2
Maloney Reservoir 68-69 F 5
Malonga 172 D 4
Malosofijevka 126-127 G 2
Malošujka 124-125 L 2
Malova 154 I a 2
Malovata 126-127 D 3
Måløy 116-117 A 7
Mal Paso 106-107 E 1
Malpelo, Isla — 92-93 C 4
Malprabha 140 B 3
Mālpura 138-139 E 4
Mal'qat al-Widān 166-167 E 2
Māḷshiras = Mālsiras 140 B 2
Mālsiras 140 B 2
Malta, ID 66-67 G 4
Malta, MT 68-69 C 1
Malta [BR] 100-101 F 4
Malta [M] 122-123 EF 8
Malta [SU] 124-125 F 5
Maltahöhe 172 C 6
Maltepe 136-137 B 2
Malu 148-149 k 6
Maluku ◁ 148-149 J 7
Ma'lūlā 136-137 G 6
Malumba 172 E 2
Malumfashi 168-169 G 3
Malumteken 148-149 h 5
Malunda 152-153 N 7
Malung 116-117 E 7
Mālūr 140 CD 4
Mālūru = Mālūr 140 CD 4
Malūṭ 164-165 L 6
Maluti Mountains 174-175 GH 5
Mālvan 134-135 L 7
Malvern, AR 78-79 C 3
Malvern, IA 70-71 C 5
Malvern, Johannesburg- 170 V b 2
Malvern, Melbourne- 161 II c 2
Malvérnia 172 F 6
Malvinas 106-107 H 2
Malvinas, Las — 106-107 C 5
Mālwa 134-135 M 6
Malya 171 C 3
Malyj Irgiz 124-125 R 7
Malyj Jenisej 132-133 RS 7
Malyj Kavkaz 126-127 L 5-N 7
Malyj L'achovskij, ostrov — 132-133 bc 3
Malyj Tajmyr, ostrov — 132-133 UV 2
Malyj Uzen' 126-127 O 2
Mama 132-133 V 6
Mamadyš 124-125 S 6
Mamahatun 136-137 J 3
Mama Kassa 168-169 J 2
Mamanguape 100-101 G 4
Mamasa 148-149 G 7
Mamasa, Sungai — 152-153 N 7
Mambaí 100-101 A 8
Mambasa 172 E 1
Mamberamo 148-149 L 7
Mambere = Carnot 164-165 H 8
Mambirima Falls 171 B 6
Mambone = Nova Mambone 172 G 6
Mameigwess Lake 62 EF 1
Mamera, Caracas- 91 II b 2
Mamfe 164-165 F 7
Māmī, Rā's — 134-135 GH 8
Mamisonskij, pereval — 126-127 L 5
Mammamattawa 62 G 2
Màmmola 122-123 G 6
Mammoth, AZ 74-75 H 6
Mammoth Cave National Park 70-71 G 7
Mammoth Hot Springs, WY 66-67 H 3
Mamoi = Mawei 146-147 G 8-9
Mamoneiras, Serra das — 98-99 P 7-8
Mamonovo 118 JK 1
Mamoré, Río — 92-93 FG 7-8
Mamou 164-165 B 6
Mamou Macenta 168-169 BC 3
Mamoura, Hassi el — = Ḥāssī al-Mamūrah 166-167 F 4
Mamouroudougou 168-169 C 3
Mampang, Kali — 154 IV a 2
Mampang Prapatan, Jakarta- 154 IV a 2
Mampawah 148-149 E 6
Mampi = Sepopa 172 D 5
Mampong 164-165 D 7
Mamre 174-175 C 7
Mamry, Jezioro — 118 K 1
Mamuel Choique 108-109 DE 3
Mamuil Malal, Paso — 108-109 CD 2
Mamuíra, Cachoeira — 98-99 P 6
Mamuju 148-149 G 7
Mamūrah, Ḥāssī al- 166-167 F 4
Mamuru, Rio — 98-99 K 6
Man [CI] 164-165 C 7
Mān [IND] 140 B 2
Man, Isle of — 119 DE 4
Man, Nam ∼ 150-151 C 4
Mana, HI 78-79 c 1
Mana [French Guiana, place] 92-93 J 3
Mana [French Guiana, river] 98-99 M 2
Mana, Hassi — = Ḥāssī Manāh 166-167 E 5
Manaas 142-143 F 3
Manabí 96-97 AB 2
Manacacías, Río — 94-95 E 5-6
Manacapuru 92-93 G 5
Manacor 120-121 J 9
Manado 148-149 H 6
Managua 64-65 J 9
Managua, Lago de — 64-65 J 9
Manāh, Ḥāssī — 166-167 E 5
Manakara 172 J 6
Mana La 138-139 G 2
Manāli 138-139 F 1
Mānāmadurai 140 D 6
Manāmah, Al- 134-135 G 5
Manambaho 172 HJ 5
Manambolo 172 H 5
Manam Island 148-149 N 7
Manamo, Caño — 92-93 G 3
Mananara [RM, place] 172 J 5
Mananara [RM, river] 172 J 6
Mananjary 172 J 6
Manankoro 168-169 D 3
Manantenina 172 J 6
Manantiales 111 BC 8
Manapire, Río — 94-95 H 3
Manapouri, Lake — 158-159 N 9
Manappārai 140 D 5
Manāqil, Al- 164-165 L 6
Manar = Maner 138-139 K 5
Manār, Jabal al- 134-135 EF 8
Manās [IND] 141 B 2
Manás [PE] 96-97 C 7
Manas, gora — 132-133 N 9
Manāsa 138-139 E 5
Mānasārovar = Mapham Tsho 142-143 E 5
Manāṣif, Al- 136-137 J 5
Manasquan, NY 72-73 JK 4
Manastīr, Al- 166-167 M 2
Manatí [CO] 94-95 D 2
Manatí [Puerto Rico] 88-89 N 5
Manattala 140 BC 5
Manātu 138-139 K 5
Man'aung 141 C 6
Man'aung Reletkyā 141 CD 6
Manaure, Punta — 94-95 E 2
Manaus 92-93 H 5
Man'auung Kyûn 148-149 B 3
Mānāvadar 138-139 C 7
Manāvar = Manāwar 138-139 E 6
Manavgat 136-137 D 4
Mānavī = Mānvi 140 C 2-3
Manawan Lake 61 G 3
Manāwar [DZ] 166-167 E 4
Manāwar [IND] 138-139 E 6
Manayunk, Philadelphia-, PA 84 III b 1
Manbanbyet 141 EF 4
Mānbāzār 138-139 L 6
Manbij 136-137 G 4
Mancelona, MI 70-71 H 3
Mancha, La — 120-121 F 9
Mancha Khiri 150-151 D 4
Manchan 142-143 G 2
Manchar 138-139 DE 8
Mancherāl 140 D 1
Manchester, CT 72-73 K 4
Manchester, GA 78-79 G 4
Manchester, IA 70-71 E 4
Manchester, KS 68-69 H 6
Manchester, KY 72-73 DE 6
Manchester, MI 70-71 H 4
Manchester, NH 64-65 MN 3
Manchester, OK 76-77 EF 4
Manchester, TN 78-79 FG 3
Manchester, VT 72-73 K 3
Manchester [BOL] 104-105 BC 2
Manchester [GB] 119 EF 5
Manchhar, Jhīl — 138-139 A 4
Manchouli = Manzhouli 142-143 M 2
Manchuanguan 146-147 BC 5
Man-ch'uan-kuan = Manchuanguan 146-147 BC 5
Manchuria 142-143 N-P 2
Manchuria = Manzhou 142-143 N-P 2
Máncora 92-93 C 5
Máncora = Puerto Máncora 92-93 C 5
Mancos, CO 74-75 J 4
Mānd 138-139 J 6
Mand, Rūd-e- = Rūd-e Mond 134-135 G 5
Manda [BD] 138-139 M 5
Manda [EAT, Iringa] 172 FG 4
Manda [EAT, Mbeya] 171 C 4
Mandab, Bāb al- 134-135 E 8
Mandabe 172 H 6
Mandacaru 100-101 D 8
Mandaguari 102-103 G 5
Mandai 138-139 B 3
Mandai, Bukit — 154 III a 1
Mandal [Mongolia] 142-143 K 2
Mandal [N] 116-117 B 8-9
Mandalay = Mandale 148-149 C 2
Mandalay = Mandale Taing 141 DE 5
Mandale Taing 141 DE 5
Māndalgarh 138-139 E 5
Mandalgov' 142-143 JK 2
Mandalī 136-137 L 6
Mandalika = Pulau Mondoliko 152-153 J 9
Mandal Ovoo 142-143 JK 3
Mandalya körfezi 136-137 B 4
Mandalyat = Selimiye 136-137 B 4
Mandan, ND 68-69 F 2
Mandaon 148-149 H 4
Mandapeta 140 EF 2
Mandar 148-149 G 7
Mandar, Tanjung — 152-153 N 7
Mandar, Teluk — 148-149 G 7
Mandara, Monts — 164-165 G 6-7
Màndas 122-123 C 6
Mandasor 134-135 LM 6
Mandav Hills = Girnār Hills 138-139 C 7
Mānḍavī = Māndvi 134-135 K 6
Mandāwa 138-139 E 3
Mandeb, Bab al- = Bāb al-Mandab 134-135 E 8
Manderson, WY 68-69 BC 3
Mandeville 88-89 GH 5
Mandeville, LA 78-79 DE 5
Māndhātā = Godarpura 138-139 F 6
Mandi 134-135 M 4
Mandiana 168-169 C 3
Mandi Dabwāli 138-139 E 3
Mandidzudzure 172 F 5-6
Mandimba 172 G 4
Manding 164-165 C 6
Manding Plateau 168-169 C 3
Mandioli, Pulau — 148-149 J 7
Mandioré, Laguna — 104-105 GH 6
Mandiroba 100-101 C 8
Mandī Sādiqganj 138-139 D 2
Mandiyuti, Sierra de — 104-105 E 7
Mandla 134-135 N 6
Mandolegüe, Cordillera — 106-107 B 6
Mandor 152-153 H 5
Mandrael 138-139 F 4
Mandria 136-137 E 5
Mandritsara 172 J 5
Mandrūp 140 B 2
Mańdsaor 134-135 LM 6
Mandsaur = Mańdsaor 134-135 LM 6
Mandui = Māndvi 134-135 K 6
Mandurah 158-159 BC 6
Manduri 102-103 H 5
Mandùria 122-123 G 5
Māndvi [IND, Gujarāt ↙ Bhuj] 134-135 K 6
Māndvi [IND, Gujarāt → Surat] 138-139 D 7
Māndvi [IND, Mahārāshtra] 138-139 D 8
Mandya 140 C 4
Mané [HV] 168-169 E 2
Mane Grande 94-95 F 3
Manendragarh 138-139 HJ 6
Manenguba, Mount — 168-169 H 4
Maner [IND, place] 138-139 K 5
Māner [IND, river] 140 D 1
Māneru = Māner 140 D 1
Mānesht, Kūh-e — 136-137 M 6
Manevići 124-125 E 8
Manfalūṭ 173 B 4
Manfredònia 122-123 FG 5
Manfredònia, Golfo di — 122-123 FG 5
Manga [BR] 92-93 L 7
Manga [RN] 164-165 G 6
Mangabeiras, Chapada das — 92-93 K 6-L 7
Mangai 172 C 2
Mangalagiri 140 E 2
Mangaldai 141 BC 2
Mangaldēī = Mangaldai 141 BC 2
Mangalia 122-123 N 4
Mangalkot 138-139 LM 6
Mangalmé 164-165 HJ 6
Mangalore 134-135 L 8
Mangaḷūru = Mangalore 134-135 L 8
Mangalvedha 140 B 2
Manganore 174-175 E 5
Māṇgā̃v = Mángaon 140 A 1
Māngaon 140 A 1
Mangaratiba 102-103 K 5
Mangas, NM 74-75 J 5
Mangawān 138-139 H 5
Mangde Chhu 141 B 2
Mangeni, Hamada — 164-165 G 4
Manggar 148-149 E 7
Manggarai, Jakarta- 154 IV b 2
Manggyŏng-dong 144-145 GH 1
Mangham, LA 78-79 CD 4
Mangi 172 E 1
Mangkalihat, Tanjung — 148-149 GH 6
Mang Kung Uk 155 I b 2
Manglaralto 96-97 A 2
Manglares, Cabo — 92-93 CD 4
Mango 164-165 E 6
Mango, El — 94-95 H 7
Mangoche 172 G 4
Mangoky 172 H 6
Mangole, Pulau — 148-149 J 7
Mangoli = Pulau Mangole 148-149 J 7
Māngrol [IND, Gujarāt] 138-139 BC 7
Māngrol [IND, Rājasthān] 138-139 F 5
Mangrove, Punta — 64-65 F 8
Mangrullo, Cuchilla — 106-107 KL 4
Mangrūl Pīr 138-139 F 7
Mang-shih = Luxi 141 F 3
Mangšlaksij zaliv 126-127 P 4
Mangu 170 IV b 2
Manguari 98-99 D 5
Mangueigne 164-165 J 6
Mangueira, Lagoa — 111 F 4
Mangueirinha 102-103 F 6
Mangue Seco 100-101 F 6
Mangui 142-143 O 1
Manguinho, Ponta do — 92-93 M 7
Mangum, OK 76-77 E 5
Mangunça, Baía de — 100-101 B 1
Mangunça, Ilha — 100-101 B 1
Mangyai 142-143 G 4
Mang Yang, Đeo — 150-151 G 5
Mangyīchaung 141 C 5
Mangyšlak, plato — 134-135 G 2
Manhã 100-101 A 7
Manhasset, NY 82 III d 2
Manhattan, KS 64-65 G 4
Manhattan, MT 66-67 H 3
Manhattan, NV 74-75 E 3
Manhattan Beach, CA 74-75 D 6
Manhattan State Beach 83 III b 2
Manhatten, New York-, NY 82 III bc 2
Manhiça 174-175 K 3
Manhuaçu 92-93 L 9
Manhuaçu, Rio — 102-103 M 3
Manhumirim 102-103 LM 4
Maní [CO] 92-93 E 4
Mani [TJ] 142-143 F 5
Mani, Quebrada de — 104-105 B 7
Mānī', Wādī al- 136-137 J 5-6
Mania 172 J 6
Maniaçu 100-101 C 7
Maniamba 172 FG 4
Manibūra Myit 141 C 4
Manica [Mozambique, administrative unit] 172 5-6 F
Manica [Mozambique, place] 172 F 5
Manica e Sofala 172 F 5-6
Manicaland 172 F 5
Maniçauá-Miçu, Rio — 98-99 LM 10
Manicoré 92-93 G 6
Manicoré, Rio — 98-99 H 8
Manicouagan 63 B 2
Manicouagan, Lac — 63 BC 2
Manicouagan, Rivière — 56-57 X 7-8
Manicuaré 94-95 J 2
Maniema 171 AB 4
Manigotagan 62 AB 2
Manigotagan River 62 AB 2
Manihāri 138-139 L 5
Manihiki 156-157 JK 5
Manika, Plateau de la — 172 E 3-4
Māṇikganj 138-139 MN 6
Mānikhawa 138-139 B 2
Manila 148-149 H 3-4
Manila, UT 66-67 HJ 5
Manila Bay 148-149 GH 4
Manilla 160 K 3
Manilla, IA 70-71 C 5
Manimba, Masi- 172 C 2
Maninjau, Danau — 152-153 CD 6
Manipur [IND, administrative unit] 134-135 P 5-6
Manipur [IND, river] 141 C 3
Manipur = Imphāl 134-135 P 6
Manipur Hills 141 CD 3
Maniqui, Río — 104-105 C 4
Manisa 134-135 B 3
Manislee River 72-73 D 2
Manistee, MI 70-71 G 3
Manistee River 70-71 H 3
Manistique, MI 70-71 GH 2
Manistique Lake 70-71 H 2
Manitoba 56-57 Q-S 6
Manitoba, Lake — 56-57 R 7
Manito Lake 61 D 4
Manitou 68-69 G 1
Manitou, Rivière — 63 D 2
Manitou Island 70-71 G 2
Manitou Islands 70-71 G 3
Manitou Lake 62 L 4
Manitou Lakes 70-71 D 1
Manitou Lakes 62 C 3
Manitoulin Island 56-57 U 8
Manitou Springs, CO 68-69 D 6
Manitouwadge 56-57 T 8
Manitowoc, WI 64-65 J 3
Manîtsoq 56-57 Za 4
Maniwaki 56-57 V 8
Maniyāchchi 140 CD 6
Maṇiyāhū = Mariāhu 138-139 J 5
Manizales 92-93 D 3
Manja 172 H 6
Manjacaze 172 F 6-7
Manjarābād 140 B 4
Manjeri 140 BC 5
Manjeshwara 140 B 4
Manjhanpur 138-139 H 5
Manjīl 136-137 N 4
Manjimup 158-159 C 6
Mānjlēgā̃v = Manjlegaon 138-139 EF 8
Manjlegaon 138-139 EF 8
Mānjra 134-135 M 7
Manjuli Island 141 D 2
Mankāchar 138-139 MN 5
Mānkaḍnachā = Mānkarnācha 138-139 K 7
Mānkarnācha 138-139 K 7
Mankato, KS 68-69 GH 6
Mankato, MN 64-65 H 3
Mankayane 174-175 J 4
Mankeṛa 138-139 C 2
Mankono 164-165 C 7
Mankota 68-69 C 1
Mankoya 172 D 4
Mankūb 166-167 E 3
Mānkulam 140 E 6
Mānkur 138-139 L 6
Manley Hot Springs, AK 58-59 M 4
Manlu He 150-151 BC 2
Man-lu Ho = Manlu He 150-151 BC 2
Manly, IA 70-71 D 4
Manly, Sydney- 161 I b 1
Manly Warringah War Memorial Park 161 I b 1
Manmād 138-139 E 7
Manna 148-149 D 7
Mannahill 160 DE 4
Mannar = Mannārama [CL, island] 140 DE 6
Mannar = Mannārama [CL, place] 140 DE 6
Mannar, Gulf of — 134-135 M 9
Mannārama [CL, island] 140 DE 6
Mannārama [CL, place] 140 DE 6
Mannārgudi 140 D 5
Mannār Khāṛī = Gulf of Mannar 134-135 M 9
Manneken Pis 128 II ab 1
Manneru 140 D 3
Mannheim 118 D 4
Manning, AR 78-79 C 3
Manning, IA 70-71 C 5
Manning, ND 68-69 E 2
Manning, SC 80-81 FG 4
Manning Provincial Park 66-67 C 1
Mannington, WV 72-73 F 5
Man'niyah, Al — = Al-Ma'anīyah 134-135 E 4
Mannswörth 113 I bc 2
Mannville 61 C 4
Mano [WAL, place] 168-169 B 3-4
Mano [WAL, river] 168-169 C 4
Manoa [BR] 98-99 F 9
Manoa [YV] 94-95 L 3
Manoharpur 138-139 K 6
Manohar Thāna 138-139 F 5
Manokotak, AK 58-59 H 7
Manokwari 148-149 K 7
Manoli 140 B 3
Manombo 172 H 6
Manono 172 E 3
Manor, TX 76-77 F 7
Manorhaven, NY 82 III d 1
Mano River 168-169 C 4
Manouane, Lac — [CDN ↑ Québec] 63 A 2
Manouane, Lac — [CDN ← Québec] 72-73 J 1
Manouane, Rivière — 63 A 2-3
Manouanis, Lac — 63 AB 2
Manpaka 170 IV a 1
Manp'ojin 144-145 F 2
Manpur 138-139 H 7
Manqalah 164-165 L 7
Manresa 120-121 HJ 8
Mans, le — 120-121 H 4-5
Mānsa [IND, Gujarāt] 138-139 D 6
Mānsa [IND, Punjab] 138-139 E 3
Mansa [ZRE] 172 E 4
Mansa Konko 168-169 B 2
Mansalar = Pulau Musala 148-149 C 6
Mansar 138-139 G 7
Mansavillagra 106-107 K 4
Mansaya = Masaya 64-65 J 9
Mansel Island 56-57 U 5
Manseriche, Pongo de — 92-93 D 5
Mansfield, AR 76-77 G 5
Mansfield, LA 78-79 C 4
Mansfield, MO 78-79 C 2
Mansfield, OH 64-65 K 3
Mansfield, PA 72-73 H 4
Mansfield, WA 66-67 D 2
Mansfield [AUS] 160 H 6
Mansfield [GB] 119 F 5
Mansi = Manzī [BUR, Kachin Pyinnei] 141 E 3
Mansi = Manzī [BUR, Sitkaing Taing] 141 D 3
Manso, Rio — 92-93 J 7-8
Manson, IA 70-71 C 4
Manson Creek 60 E 2
Mansour, El- = Al-Manṣūr 166-167 F 6
Mansoura = Al-Manṣūrah 166-167 HJ 1
Manṣūr, Al- 166-167 F 6
Mansura, LA 78-79 C 5
Manṣūrābād = Mehrān 136-137 M 6
Manṣūrah, Al- [DZ] 166-167 HJ 1
Manṣūrah, Al- [ET] 164-165 L 2
Mańsūrī = Mussoorie 138-139 G 2
Manṣūrīyah, Al- 136-137 L 5
Manta 92-93 C 5
Manta, Bahía de — 92-93 C 5
Mantalingajan, Mount — 148-149 G 5
Mantanani, Pulau — 152-153 LM 2
Mantaro, Río — 92-93 E 7
Mante, Ciudad — 64-65 G 7
Manteca, CA 74-75 C 4
Mantecal [YV, Apure] 94-95 G 4
Mantecal [YV, Bolívar] 94-95 J 4
Manteco, El — 92-93 G 3
Mantena 102-103 M 3
Mantenópolis 100-101 D 10
Manteo, NC 80-81 J 3
Mantés 168-169 G 1
Mantes-la-Jolie 120-121 H 4
Man Tha = Manthī 141 E 3-4
Manthani 140 D 1
Manthī 141 E 3-4
Manti, UT 74-75 H 3
Mantiqueira, Serra da — 92-93 KL 9
Manto 88-89 C 7
Manton, MI 70-71 H 3
Mantova 122-123 D 3
Mantsinsari 124-125 H 3
Mänttä 116-117 L 6
Mantua = Mantova 122-123 D 3
Mantua Creek 84 III b 3
Mantua Terrace, NJ 84 III b 3
Mantung 160 E 5
Manturovo [SU, Kostromskaja Oblast'] 124-125 P 4
Manturovo [SU, Kurskaja Oblast'] 126-127 H 1
Mäntyharju 116-117 M 7
Mäntyluoto 116-117 J 7
Mantzikert = Malazgirt 136-137 K 3
Manú 92-93 E 7
Manú, Río — 96-97 F 7-8
Manua 208 K 4
Manuan 72-73 J 1
Manuel 86-87 LM 6
Manuel, Punta — 106-107 A 7
Manuel Alves, Rio — 98-99 OP 10
Manuel Benavides 86-87 HJ 3
Manuel Derqui 106-107 H 1
Manuelito, NM 74-75 J 5
Manuel Jorge, Cachoeira — 98-99 LM 7
Manuel Luís, Recife — 100-101 BC 1
Manuel Ribas 102-103 G 6
Manuel Rodriguez, Isla — 108-109 BC 9
Manuel Urbano 98-99 CD 9
Manuel Viana 106-107 K 2
Manuelzinho 92-93 HJ 6
Manui, Pulau — 152-153 P 7
Manuk, Pulau — 148-149 K 8
Mānūk, Tall — 136-137 H 6
Manukau 158-159 OP 7
Manukau Harbour 158-159 O 7
Manumukh 141 BC 3
Manurini, Río — 104-105 C 3
Manuripe, Río — 96-97 G 7
Manus 148-149 N 7
Manushūnash 166-167 K 2
Manvath = Mānwat 138-139 F 8
Mānvi 140 C 2-3
Manville, WY 68-69 D 4
Mānwat 138-139 F 8
Many, LA 78-79 C 5
Manyal Shīhah 170 II b 2
Manyara, Lake — 172 G 2
Manyas = Maltepe 136-137 B 2
Manyč 126-127 K 3
Manyč-Gudilo, ozero — 126-127 L 3
Manyčskaja vpadina, Kumo- 126-127 K 3-M 4
Manyonga 171 C 3-4
Manyoni 172 F 3
Manyunjie 141 E 3
Manzai 134-135 KL 4
Manzanares [E, place] 120-121 F 9
Manzanares [E, river] 120-121 F 8
Manzanares, Canal del — 113 III b 2-3
Manzanillo [C] 64-65 L 7
Manzanillo [MEX] 64-65 EF 8
Manzanillo, Punta — 64-65 L 9-10
Manzano, El — [RA] 106-107 E 3
Manzano, El — [RCH] 106-107 B 5
Manzano Mountains 76-77 A 5
Manzanza 171 B 4
Manzhouli 142-143 M 2
Manzī [BUR, Kachin Pyinnei] 141 E 3
Manzī [BUR, Sitkaing Taing] 141 D 3
Manzikert = Malazgirt 136-137 K 3
Manzilah, Al- 173 BC 2
Manzilah, Buḥayrat al- 173 BC 2
Manzil Būrgībah 166-167 L 1
Manzil Shākir 166-167 M 2
Manzil Tamīm 166-167 M 1
Manzini 172 F 7
Manzovka 132-133 Z 9
Mao 164-165 H 6
Mao, Nam — = Nam Wa 150-151 C 3
Maobi Tou = Maopi Tou 146-147 H 11
Maocifan 146-147 D 6
Maodahā = Maudaha 138-139 GH 5
Maoka = Cholmsk 132-133 b 8
Maoke, Pegunungan — 148-149 LM 7
Maoli 138-139 D 5
Maoming 142-143 L 7
Maoming = Gaozhou 146-147 C 11
Maoping = Xiangzikou 146-147 CD 7
Maopi Tou 146-147 H 11
Mao Songsang 141 D 3
Maotanchang 146-147 F 6
Maowei Hai = Qinzhou Wan 150-151 G 2
Mapaga 148-149 G 7
Mapai 172 F 6
Maparari 94-95 G 2
Maparuta 94-95 L 5
Mapastepec 86-87 O 10
Mapham Tsho 142-143 E 5
Mapham Yumtsho = Mapham Tsho 142-143 E 5
Mapi 148-149 L 8
Mapia, Kepulauan — 148-149 KL 6
Mapichí, Serranía de — 92-93 F 3-4
Mapimí 86-87 HJ 5
Mapimí, Bolsón de — 64-65 F 6
Maping 146-147 D 6
Ma-p'ing = Liuzhou 142-143 K 7
Mapinggang = Maping 146-147 D 6
Mapinhane 172 FG 6
Mapire 92-93 G 3
Mapireme 98-99 LM 4
Mapiri 104-105 B 4
Mapiri, Río — [BOL ◁ Río Abuña] 104-105 C 2
Mapiri, Río — [BOL ◁ Río Beni] 104-105 B 4
Mapiripán, Lago — 94-95 EF 6
Mapiripan, Salto — 92-93 E 4
Ma-pi-ts'un = Mabi 146-147 D 4
Maple Beach, PA 84 III d 1
Maple Creek 61 D 6
Maple Meadow Brook 84 I ab 1
Maple Shade, NJ 84 III cd 2
Maplesville, AL 78-79 F 4
Mapleton, IA 70-71 BC 4
Mapleton, MN 70-71 D 4
Mapleton, OR 66-67 AB 3
Mapoon 158-159 H 2
Mapor, Pulau — 152-153 F 5
Maporal 94-95 F 4
Maporillal 94-95 F 4
Mappi = Mapi 148-149 L 8
Maprik 148-149 M 7
Māpuca 140 A 3
Mapuera, Rio — 92-93 H 5
Mapula 171 D 6
Mapulanguene 174-175 K 3
Mapulau, Rio — 98-99 G 3-4

324 Malazgir

Maṭamūr, Al- 166-167 M 3
Matana, Danau — 152-153 O 7
Ma'tan as-Sarrah 164-165 J 4
Matancillas 111 B 4
Matandu 171 D 5
Matane 56-57 X 8
Matane, Parc provincial de — 63 C 3
Mata Negra 94-95 K 3
Matankari 168-169 FG 2
Ma'ṭan Oweiqila = Ma'ātin 'Uwayqilah 136-137 C 7
Ma'ṭan Shārib 136-137 C 7
Matanuska, AK 58-59 MN 6
Matanuska River 58-59 NO 6
Matanza [CO] 94-95 E 4
Matanza [RA] 106-107 H 5
Matanza, La — 110 III b 2
Matanza, Rio — 110 III b 2
Matanzas 64-65 K 7
Matanzilla, Pampa de la — 106-107 C 6
Matão 102-103 H 4
Matão, Serra do — 92-93 J 6
Matapalo, Cabo — 64-65 K 10
Matapédia, Rivière — 63 C 3
Mataporquera 120-121 E 7
Mataquito, Río — 106-107 B 5
Mātara [CL] 134-135 N 9
Matará [RA] 106-107 F 2
Mataraca 100-101 G 4
Mataram 148-149 G 8
Matarani 92-93 E 8
Mataranka [AUS] 158-159 F 2
Maṭarīyah, Al Qāhirah-al- 170 II bc 1
Matārkah 166-167 E 3
Mataró 120-121 J 8
Matas, Serra das — 100-101 DE 3
Matatiele 172 E 8
Mataura River 161 C 7-8
Mataven, Río — 94-95 G 5
Maṭāy 173 B 3
Mategua 92-93 G 7
Matehuala 64-65 F 7
Matelândia 102-103 EF 6
Matemo 171 E 6
Matera 122-123 G 5
Mátészalka 118 KL 4-5
Matetsi 172 E 5
Mâṭeur = Māṭir 164-165 FG 1
Mateus Leme 102-103 K 3
Mather, CA 74-75 D 4
Mātherān 138-139 D 8
Matheson 62 L 2
Matheson, CO 68-69 E 6
Mathews, VA 80-81 H 2
Mathis, TX 76-77 EF 8
Mathiston, MS 78-79 E 4
Mathon Tonbo = Htônbô 141 D 6
Mathura 134-135 M 5
Mati 148-149 J 5
Matiakouali 168-169 F 2
Mātiāli 138-139 M 4
Matiari = Matiyārī 138-139 B 5
Matias Barbosa 102-103 L 4
Matias Cardoso 100-101 C 8
Matías Hernández 64-65 bc 2
Matias Olimpio 100-101 C 2
Matías Romero 86-87 N 9
Matico, Río — 94-95 F 2
Ma-ti-i = Madiyi 146-147 C 7
Matilde 102-103 M 4
Matimana 171 D 5
Matimbuka 172 G 4
Matina 100-101 C 7
Matinenda Lake 62 K 3
Matinha 100-101 B 2
Matinicus Island 72-73 M 3
Māṭir 164-165 FG 1
Matiwane 174-175 HJ 5
Matiyārī 138-139 B 5
Matjesfontein = Matjiesfontein 174-175 D 7
Matjiesfontein 174-175 D 7
Mātla 138-139 M 7
Maṭlā', Al- 136-137 M 8
Matlabas [ZA, place] 174-175 G 3
Matlabas [ZA, river] 174-175 G 3
M'atlevo 124-125 K 6
Mātlī 138-139 B 5
Maṭlīl 166-167 H 3
Māṭlīn, Al- 166-167 M 1
Matlock 61 K 5
Matlock, WA 66-67 B 2
Maṭmāṭ, Ḥāssī — 166-167 K 3
Maṭmāṭah 166-167 L 3
Mato, Cerro — 94-95 J 4
Mato, Serranía de — 94-95 J 4
Matobe 152-153 D 7
Matochkin Shar = proliv Matočkin Šar 132-133 KL 3
Matočkin Šar 132-133 KL 3
Matočkin Šar, proliv — 132-133 KL 3
Matões 100-101 C 3
Mato Grosso [BR, Acre] 98-99 C 9
Mato Grosso [BR, Mato Grosso administrative unit] 92-93 HJ 7
Mato Grosso [BR, Mato Grosso place] 92-93 H 7-8
Mato Grosso, Planalto do — 92-93 HJ 7
Mato Grosso do Sul 92-93 HJ 8-9
Matola 174-175 K 3-4
Matombo 171 D 4
Matope 172 FG 5
Matopo Hills 172 E 6
Matorrales 106-107 F 3
Matos, Río — 104-105 CD 4
Matos Costa 102-103 G 7
Matosinhos [BR] 102-103 K 3
Matosinhos [P] 120-121 C 8
Matoso, Punta do — 110 I b 1
Matou 146-147 H 10
Matoury 98-99 M 2
Mato Verde 100-101 C 8
Mátra 118 JK 5
Matra = Mathurā 134-135 M 5
Maṭraḥ 134-135 H 6
Matraman, Jakarta- 154 IV b 2
Matraville, Sydney- 161 I b 2
Matrimonio, El — 76-77 C 9
Matriz de Camarajibe 100-101 G 6
Maṭroûḥ, Djezîrat el — = Jazīrat al-Maṭrūḥ 166-167 M 1
Maṭrûḥ = Marsā Maṭrūḥ 164-165 K 2
Maṭrūḥ, Jazīrat al- 166-167 M 1
Maṭrūḥ, Marsā — 164-165 K 2
Matsang Tsangpo 138-139 J 2-K 3
Matsap 174-175 E 5
Matsudo 155 III c 1
Matsudo-Kamihongo 155 III c 1
Matsudo-Yagiri 155 III c 1
Matsue 142-143 P 4
Matsugashima 155 III d 2
Ma-tsui Ling = Mazui Ling 150-151 G 3
Matsumae 144-145 ab 3
Matsumoto 144-145 LM 4
Matsunami = Suzu 144-145 L 4
Matsusaka 144-145 KL 5
Matsu Tao 142-143 MN 6
Matsuwa = Matua 206-207 T 5
Matsuyama 144-145 J 6
Mattagami River 56-57 U 7-8
Mattaldi 106-107 E 5
Mattamuskeet Lake 80-81 HJ 3
Mattapan, Boston-, MA 84 I b 3
Mattawa 72-73 G 1
Mattawamkeag, ME 72-73 MN 2
Mattawin, Rivière — 72-73 K 1
Mattayā 141 E 4
Matterhorn [USA] 66-67 F 5
Matthew, Île — 158-159 O 4
Matthews Peak 172 G 1
Matthew Town 88-89 JK 4
Maṭṭī, Sabkhat — 134-135 G 6
Mattice 62 H 3
Matto Grosso = Mato Grosso 92-93 HJ 7
Matu 152-153 J 4
Matua [RI] 148-149 F 7
Matua [SU] 206-207 T 5
Matucana 92-93 D 7
Matue = Matsue 142-143 P 4
Matugama 140 E 7
Matugusanos 106-107 C 3
Matuku 148-149 ab 2
Matumoto = Matsumoto 142-143 Q 4
Matūn 134-135 KL 4
Matundu 172 D 1
Matura = Mathurā 134-135 M 5
Maturin 92-93 G 2-3
Maturucá 98-99 H 2
Matuyama = Matsuyama 142-143 P 5
Matvejevka 124-125 TU 7
Matvejev Kurgan 126-127 J 3
Matvejevskoje, Moskva- 113 V b 3
Mau [IND ↗ Allahabad] 138-139 H 5
Mau [IND ↗ Vārānasi] 138-139 J 5
Maū = Mhow 138-139 E 6
Mauá [BR] 102-103 J 5
Maúa [Mozambique] 172 G 4
Mauá, Salto — 102-103 G 6
Maubeuge 120-121 JK 3
Mauchī 141 E 6
Maud, OK 76-77 F 5
Maud, TX 76-77 G 6
Maudaha 138-139 GH 5
Maude 160 G 5
Maudin Sûn 141 CD 8
Maudlow, MT 66-67 H 2
Maud Seamount 53 C 1
Mau-é-ele 174-175 L 3
Mauer, Wien- 113 I ab 2
Maués 92-93 H 5
Maués-Açu, Rio — 92-93 H 5
Mauganj 138-139 H 5
Mauhan 148-149 C 2
Maui 148-149 e 3
Maukmei 141 E 5
Maulaik 141 D 4
Maulamyaing 148-149 C 3
Maulamyainggyūn 141 D 7
Maule 106-107 AB 5
Maule, Laguna del — 106-107 B 6
Maule, Río — 106-107 AB 5
Maulin = Mol Len 141 D 3
Maullín 111 B 6
Maullín, Río — 108-109 C 3
Maulvī Bāzār 141 B 3
Maumee, OH 72-73 DE 4
Maumee River 70-71 H 5
Maumere 148-149 H 8
Maun [RB] 172 D 5
Mauna Kea 148-149 e 4
Mauna Loa 148-149 e 4
Mauna Loa, HI 78-79 d 2
Maunāth Bhanjan = Mau 138-139 J 5
Mauneluk River 58-59 K 3
Maungdaw 148-149 B 2
Maungmagan Kyūnzu 150-151 A 5
Mauni, Río — 96-97 G 10
Maunoir, Lac — 56-57 M 4
Maupertuis, Lac — 62 PQ 1
Maupin, OR 66-67 C 3
Maur 128 IV b 1
Mauralakitan 152-153 E 7
Mau Rānīpur 138-139 G 5
Maurepas, Lake — 78-79 D 5
Maurice, Lake — 158-159 EF 5
Mauriceville, TX 76-77 GH 7
Mauricie, Parc national — 62 P 3
Mauricio Mayer 106-107 E 6
Mauritania 164-165 BC 4
Mauriti 100-101 E 4
Mauritius 178-179 MN 7
Maury Mountains 66-67 C 3
Mausembi 152-153 O 10
Mauston, WI 70-71 EF 4
Mautong 148-149 H 6
Mava 148-149 M 8
Mavaca, Río — 94-95 J 6
Mavago 172 G 4
Mavānā = Mawāna 138-139 F 3
Mavaricani, Raudal — 94-95 G 6
Māvelikara 140 C 6
Mavinga 172 CD 5
Mavlāni = Mailāni 138-139 H 3
Māvlī = Maoli 138-139 D 5
Mavrobouni 113 IV b 2
Mavzolej V. I. Lenina 113 V c 2-3
Maw, Lûy — [BUR, Kachin Pyinnei] 141 E 3
Maw, Lûy — [BUR, Shan Pyinnei] 141 E 5
Mawa 172 E 1
Mawāgū 141 F 2
Mawai 150-151 DE 12
Mawāna 138-139 F 3
Mawasangka 152-153 OP 8
Mawei 146-147 G 8-9
Mawer 61 E 5
Mawhun = Mauhan 148-149 C 2
Mawk Mai = Maukmei 141 E 5
Mawlaik = Maulaik 141 D 4
Mawson 53 C 7
Max, ND 68-69 F 2
Maxacalis 100-101 D 3
Maxaranguape 100-101 G 3
Maxbass, ND 68-69 F 1
Maxcanú 86-87 P 7
Maxesibeni 174-175 H 6
Maxey Park 85 III c 1
Maximo 171 D 6
Máximo Paz 106-107 H 5
Maxixe 174-175 L 2
Maxstone 68-69 CD 1
Maxville 72-73 J 2
Maxville, MT 66-67 G 2
Maxwell, CA 74-75 B 3
May, ID 66-67 G 3
May, OK 76-77 E 4
Maya, Pulau — 148-149 E 7
Mayādīn 136-137 J 5
Mayaguana Island 64-65 M 7
Mayagüez 64-65 N 8
Māyah, Al- 166-167 G 3
Mayama 172 BC 2
Maya Maya = Aéroport de Brazzaville 170 IV a 1
Maya Mountains 64-65 J 8
Mayang 146-147 B 8
Mayang-do 144-145 G 2-3
Mayanja 171 BC 2
Mayapán 64-65 J 7
Mayari 88-89 HJ 4
Mayas, Caracas-Las — 91 II b 2
Māyavaram = Māyūram 140 D 5
Maybell, CO 68-69 B 5
Mayd 164-165 b 1
Maydān 136-137 L 5
Maydān Ikbis 136-137 G 4
Maydena 158-159 J 8
Maydī 134-135 E 7
Mayence = Mainz 118 D 3-4
Mayenne [F, place] 120-121 G 4
Mayenne [F, river] 120-121 G 4-5
Mayer, AZ 74-75 G 5
Mayerthorpe 60 K 3
Mayesville, SC 80-81 F 3-4
Mayfair 61 E 4
Mayfair, Houston-, TX 85 III b 2
Mayfair, Johannesburg- 170 V b 2
Mayfair, Philadelphia-, PA 84 III c 1
Mayfield, ID 66-67 F 4
Mayfield, KY 78-79 E 2
Mayhill, NM 76-77 B 6
Maymaneh 134-135 JK 3
Maymyo = Memyō 148-149 C 2
Maynard, WA 66-67 B 2
Maynas 92-93 DE 5
Māyni 140 B 2
Mayo 150-151 C 9
Mayo, FL 80-81 b 1-2
Mayo, Cerro — 108-109 D 5
Mayo, Río — [PE] 96-97 C 4
Mayo, Río — [RA] 108-109 D 5
Mayoco, El — 108-109 D 4
Mayo Landing 56-57 JK 5
Mayor, El — 74-75 F 6
Mayor Buratovich 106-107 F 7
Mayor Island 161 G 3
Mayotte 172 H 4
Mayoumba 172 AB 2
May Point, Cape — 72-73 J 5
Maypuco 96-97 D 4
Mayrhofen 118 EF 5
Maysarī, Al- 136-137 H 7
Maysville, KY 72-73 E 5
Maysville, MO 70-71 C 6
Maysville, NC 80-81 H 3
Maytown 158-159 HJ 3
Mayu, Pulau — 148-149 J 6
Mayū Myit 141 C 5
Mayunga 172 E 2
Mayurākshī 138-139 LM 6
Māyūram 140 D 5
Mayū Taungdan 141 C 5
Mayville, ND 68-69 H 2
Mayville, NY 72-73 G 3
Maywood, CA 83 III c 2
Maywood, NE 68-69 F 5
Maywood, NJ 82 III b 1
Mayyit, Baḥr al- 134-135 D 4
Maza 106-107 F 6
Mazabuka 172 E 5
Mazagan = Al-Jadīdah 164-165 C 2
Mazagão 92-93 J 5
Mazáka = Kayseri 134-135 D 3
Mazalet 168-169 H 1
Mazamet 120-121 J 7
Mazán 96-97 E 3
Mazan = Villa Mazán 111 C 3
Mazán, Río — 96-97 E 3
Māzandarān 134-135 GH 3
Mazār, Al- 136-137 F 7
Mazar, Oued — = Wādī Mazār 166-167 G 3
Mazār, Wādī — 166-167 G 3
Mazara del Vallo 122-123 DE 7
Mazār-i-Sharīf 134-135 K 3
Mazarredo 108-109 F 6
Mazarredo, Fondeadero — 108-109 F 6
Mazarrón 120-121 G 10
Mazarrón, Golfo de — 120-121 G 10
Mazar tagh 142-143 D 4
Mazaruni River 98-99 HJ 1
Mazatenango 64-65 H 9
Mazatlán 64-65 E 7
Mazatuni River 94-95 L 4
Mazatzal Peak 74-75 H 5
Mažeikiai 124-125 D 5
Mazeppabaai 174-175 H 7
Mazeppa Bay = Mazeppabaai 174-175 H 7
Mazgirt 136-137 H 3
Mazhafah, Jabal — = Jabal Buwārah 173 D 3
Mazhan 146-147 G 3
Mazi, Jabal — 166-167 F 3
Mazıdağı = Samrah 136-137 J 4
Mazimchopes, Rio — 174-175 K 3
Mazirbe 124-125 CD 5
Mazoco 171 C 5
Mazo Cruz 96-97 G 10
Mazomanie, WI 70-71 F 4
Mazr'a, Al- 136-137 F 7
Mazra'ah, Al- 166-167 K 2
Mazsalaca 124-125 E 5
Māzū 136-137 N 6
Mazui Ling 150-151 G 3
Mazūnzūt 141 E 2
Mazurskie, Pojezierze — 118 K 2-L 1
Mazzūnah, Al- 166-167 L 2

Mbabane 172 F 7
Mbacké 168-169 B 2
M'Baiki 164-165 H 8
Mbala 172 F 3
Mbalabala 172 EF 6
Mbale 172 F 1
M'Balmayo 164-165 G 8
Mbam 168-169 H 4
Mbam, Massif — 168-169 H 4
Mbamba Bay 171 C 5
Mbamou, Île — 170 IV b 1
Mbamou, Pointe — 170 IV a 1
Mbandaka 172 C 1-2
Mbanga 164-165 FG 8
Mbanza Congo 172 B 3
Mbanza Ngungu 172 B 2-3
Mbaracayú, Cordillera de — 102-103 E 5-6
Mbarangandu [EAT, place] 171 D 5
Mbarangandu [EAT, river] 171 D 5
Mbarara 172 F 2
Mbari 164-165 J 7
M'Bé 172 C 2
Mbemkuru 172 GH 3
Mbenkuru 171 D 5
Mbeya [EAT, mountain] 171 C 5
Mbeya [EAT, place] 172 F 3
M'Bigou 172 B 2
Mbin 164-165 F 8
M'Binda 172 B 2
Mbindera 171 D 5
Mbinga 171 C 5
Mbini [Equatorial Guinea, administrative unit] 164-165 G 8
Mbini [Equatorial Guinea, river] 168-169 H 5
Mbizi 172 F 6
Mbogo's 171 C 4
Mbomou 164-165 J 7-8
Mbonge 168-169 H 4
M'Boro 171 AB 2
M'Bour 164-165 A 6
Mbozi 171 C 5
Mbud 164-165 B 5
Mbuji-Mayi 172 D 3
Mbulu 171 C 3
Mburu 171 C 5
Mburucuyá 111 E 3
Mbuyapey 102-103 D 7

Mccheta 126-127 M 6
Mcensk 124-125 L 7
Mcherrah = Mashraḥ 166-167 DE 6
Mchinga 172 GH 3
Mchinji 172 F 4
M'Chouneche = Manushūnash 166-167 K 2
M'Clintok 58-59 U 6

Mdaina, Al- = Al-Madīnah 136-137 M 7
Mdakane, Hassi — = Ḥāssī Madakkan 166-167 EF 5
Mdandu 171 C 5
M'dīlah, Al- 166-167 L 2
M'Dourouch = Madawrūsh 166-167 K 1

Mê, Hon — 150-151 EF 3
Meacham, OR 66-67 D 3
Mead, WA 66-67 E 2
Mead, Lake — 64-65 D 4
Meade, KS 68-69 F 7
Meade Peak 66-67 H 4
Meade River 58-59 J 1
Meade River, AK 58-59 J 1
Meadow, TX 76-77 CD 6
Meadowbank Park 161 I a 1
Meadow Brook, Houston-, TX 85 III bc 2
Meadow Creek Village, Houston-, TX 85 III b 2
Meadow Lake 56-57 P 7
Meadow Lake Provincial Park 61 D 3
Meadowlands, Johannesburg- 170 V a 2
Meadows, The —, TX 85 III a 2
Meadow Valley Range 74-75 F 4
Meadow Valley Wash 74-75 F 4
Meadville, PA 72-73 FG 4
Meaford 72-73 F 2
Mealy Mountains 56-57 Z 7
Meander 152-153 N 1
Meandro = Büyük Menderes nehri 136-137 B 4
Mearim, Rio — 92-93 L 5
Meath Park 61 F 4
Meat Mount 58-59 G 2
Meaux 120-121 J 4
Mebote 172 F 6
Mebreije, Rio — = Rio M'Bridge 172 B 3
Mebridege, Rio — 172 B 3
Meca = Makkah 134-135 DE 6
Mecaya, Río — 94-95 D 7
Mecca, CA 74-75 EF 6
Mecca = Makkah 134-135 DE 6
Mechanicsburg, PA 72-73 H 4
Mechanicville, NY 72-73 K 3
Meched = Mashhad 134-135 HJ 3
Mechelen 120-121 K 3
Mechems = M'shams 166-167 BC 6
Mechéria = Mīshrīyah 164-165 DE 2
Méchins, les — 63 C 3
Mechlin = Mechelen 120-121 K 3
Mechongué 106-107 HJ 7
Mechraa Asfa = Mashra'a Aṣfā 166-167 G 2
Mechra' 'Ben 'Abou = Mashra' Bin Abū 166-167 C 3
Mechra' 'Ben el Qsīrī = Mashra' Bin al-Q'sīrī 166-167 CD 2
Mechren'ga 124-125 N 2
Meçitözü 136-137 F 2
Mecklenburg 118 EF 2
Mecklenburger Bucht 118 EF 1
Mecrihan 136-137 H 4
Mecsek 118 J 5
Mecúfi 172 H 4
Mecula 172 G 4
Meḍachala = Medchal 140 D 2
Medaguine = Madāqīn 166-167 H 3
Medak [IND] 140 D 1
Medan 148-149 C 6
Medanitos 104-105 C 10
Médano, Punta — 108-109 H 3
Médanos [RA, Buenos Aires landscape] 106-107 G 7-J 6
Médanos [RA, Buenos Aires place] 111 D 5
Médanos [RA, Entre Ríos] 106-107 H 4
Médanos, Istmo de — 94-95 G 2
Medanosa, Punta — 111 CD 7
Medaryville, IN 70-71 G 5
Medawachchiya 140 DE 6
Medchal 140 D 2
Médéa = Midyah 166-167 H 1
Medeiros Neto 100-101 D 3
Medellín [CO] 92-93 D 3
Medellín [RA] 111 D 3
Medelpad 116-117 FG 6
Medenîn = Madanīyīn 164-165 FG 2
Medetsiz 134-135 C 3
Medford, MA 72-73 L 3
Medford, OK 76-77 F 4
Medford, OR 64-65 B 3
Medford, WI 70-71 EF 3
Medford Hillside, MA 84 I b 2
Medfra, AK 58-59 K 5
Medgidia 122-123 N 3
Media, PA 84 III a 2
Médiadillet 168-169 E 1
Media Luna 106-107 D 5
Medianeira 102-103 E 6
Mediano 120-121 H 7
Mediapolis, IA 70-71 E 5
Mediaș 122-123 L 2
Medical Lake, WA 66-67 DE 2
Medicanceli 120-121 F 8
Medicine Bow, WY 68-69 C 5
Medicine Bow Mountains 68-69 CD 5
Medicine Bow Peak 64-65 EF 3
Medicine Bow River 68-69 CD 5
Medicine Hat 56-57 O 7
Medicine Lake 68-69 DE 1
Medicine Lake, MT 68-69 D 1
Medicine Lodge 60 J 3
Medicine Lodge, KS 76-77 EF 4
Medicine Mound, TX 76-77 E 5
Medina, ND 68-69 G 2
Medina, TX 76-77 E 8
Medina [BR] 102-103 M 2
Medina [CO] 94-95 E 5
Médina [WAG] 168-169 B 2
Medina = Al-Madīnah 134-135 DE 6
Medina del Campo 120-121 E 8
Medina de Rioseco 120-121 E 8
Medina River 76-77 E 8
Medinas, Río — 104-105 D 10
Medina-Sidonia 120-121 DE 10
Medininkai 124-125 E 6
Medinīpur = Midnapore 134-135 O 6
Medio, Arroyo del — 106-107 G 4
Mediodía 94-95 EF 8
Medioûna = Madyūnah 166-167 C 3
Mediterranean Sea 114-115 J 8-O 9
Medjdel, El — = Ashqĕlōn 136-137 F 7
Medjèz el Bâb = M'jaz al-Bāb 166-167 L 1
Mednogorsk 132-133 K 7
Mednoje 124-125 K 5
Mednyj, ostrov — 52 D 2
Médoc 120-121 G 6
Medora, KS 68-69 H 6
Medora, ND 68-69 E 2
Medstead 61 DE 4
Medur = Mettūr 140 C 5
Medvedica [SU ◁ Don] 124-125 P 7
Medvedkovo, Moskva- 113 V c 2
Medvedok 124-125 S 5
Medvedovskaja 126-127 J 4
Medvežij, ostrova — 132-133 f 3
Medvežjegorsk 132-133 EF 5
Medyn' 124-125 KL 6
Medžibož 126-127 C 2
Meekatharra 158-159 C 5
Meeker, CO 68-69 C 5
Meeker, OK 76-77 F 5
Meelpaeg Lake 63 H 3
Meerut 134-135 M 5
Mēga [ETH] 164-165 M 8
Mega [RI] 148-149 K 7
Mega, Pulau — 152-153 D 8
Megálē Préspa, Límnē — 122-123 J 5
Megalópolis 122-123 JK 7
Megálo Sofráno 122-123 M 7
Meganom, mys — 126-127 G 4
Mégantic 72-73 L 2
Mégara 122-123 K 6-7
Megāsini 138-139 L 7
Meghaier, El — = Al-Mighāīr 166-167 J 3
Meghalaya 134-135 P 5
Meghāsana = Megāsini 138-139 L 7
Meghnā 141 B 4
Megion 132-133 O 5
Mégiscane, Rivière — 62 NO 2
Megistē 136-137 C 4
Megler, WA 66-67 B 2
Megrega 132-133 E 5
Meguro 155 III b 2
Meguro, Tōkyō- 155 III b 2
Mehadia 122-123 K 3
Mehar 138-139 A 4
Mehdia = Mahdīyah 164-165 E 1
Mehepur = Maharpur 138-139 M 6
Meherrin River 80-81 H 2
Mehidpur 138-139 E 6
Me Hka 141 EF 3
Mehkar 138-139 F 7
Mehmadābād 138-139 D 6
Mehndāval = Mehndāwal 138-139 J 4
Mehndāwal 138-139 J 4
Mehrābān 136-137 M 3-4
Mehrān 136-137 M 6
Mehrow 130 III c 1
Mehsāna 134-135 L 6
Meia Ponte, Rio — 92-93 K 8
Meicheng 146-147 G 7
Mei-ch'i = Meixi 146-147 G 6
Mei-chou Wan = Meizhou Wan 146-147 G 9
Meidling, Wien- 113 I b 2
Meiendorf, Hamburg- 130 I b 1
Méier, Rio de Janeiro- 110 I b 2
Meighen Island 56-57 RS 1
Meihekou = Shanchengzhen 144-145 EF 1
Meihsien = Mei Xian 146-147 EF 9
Meiji Shrine 155 III b 1
Meikhtīlā 148-149 BC 2
Meiktila = Meikhtīlā 148-149 BC 2
Meiling Guan = Xiaomei Guan 142-143 LM 6
Meilin Jiang = Lian Jiang 146-147 E 9
Meilong 146-147 E 10
Meiningen 118 E 3
Meio, Ilha do — 110 I b 3
Meio, Rio do — 100-101 B 7
Meiqi = Meixi 146-147 G 6
Meissen 118 F 3
Meiten = Meitene 124-125 DE 5
Meitene 124-125 DE 5
Meixi 146-147 G 6
Mei Xian 142-143 M 7
Meizhou Wan 146-147 G 9
Meja 138-139 J 5
Mejicana, Cumbre de — 111 C 3
Mejillón, Punta — 108-109 G 3
Mejillones 111 B 2
Mejillones del Sur, Bahía de — 104-105 A 8
Mejnypil'gyno 132-133 j 5
Meka Galla 171 D 2
Mekambo 172 B 1
Mekelē 164-165 M 6
Mekerrhane, Sebkra — = Sabkhat Mukrān 164-165 E 3
Mekhar = Mehkar 138-139 F 7
Meḳhtar 138-139 B 2
Meknès = Miknās 164-165 C 2
Mê Kong 148-149 E 4
Mekong, Mouths of the — = Cu'a Sông Cu'u Long 148-149 E 5
Mekongga, Gunung — 148-149 H 7
Mekongga, Pegunungan — 152-153 O 7
Mekoryuk, AK 58-59 D 6
Mekran = Mokrān 134-135 HJ 5
Mékrou 164-165 E 6
Mel, Ilha do — 102-103 H 6
Mel, Serra do — 100-101 F 3
Melagénai 124-125 F 6
Melāgiri Hills 140 C 4
Mêlaḥ, Sebkhet el — = Sabkhat al-Māliḥ 166-167 M 3
Melah, Sebkra el — = Sabkhat al-Malah 166-167 F 5
Melaka [MAL, administrative unit] 150-151 D 11
Melaka [MAL, place] 148-149 D 6
Melaka, Selat — 148-149 CD 6
Melalap 152-153 LM 3
Melanesia 156-157 F 4-H 5
Melanieskop 174-175 H 5
Mēlas 122-123 L 7
Melawi, Sungai — 152-153 K 6
Melayu 148-149 D 6
Melba, ID 66-67 E 4
Melbourne, AR 78-79 D 2-3
Melbourne, FL 80-81 c 2
Melbourne [AUS] 158-159 H 7
Melbourne, University of — 161 II b 1
Melbourne-Airport West 161 II b 1
Melbourne-Albion 161 II b 1
Melbourne-Altona 161 II ab 2
Melbourne-Avondale Heights 161 II b 1
Melbourne-Balwyn 161 II c 1
Melbourne-Bentleigh 161 II c 2
Melbourne-Box Hill 161 II c 1-2
Melbourne-Braybrook 161 II b 1
Melbourne-Brighton 161 II bc 2
Melbourne-Brooklyn 161 II ab 1-2
Melbourne-Brunswick 161 II b 1
Melbourne-Camberwell 161 II c 2
Melbourne-Canterbury 161 II c 1
Melbourne-Caulfield 161 II c 2
Melbourne Cemetery 161 II b 1
Melbourne-Chadstone 161 II c 2
Melbourne-Coburg 161 II b 1
Melbourne-Collingwood 161 II bc 1
Melbourne-Doncaster 161 II c 1
Melbourne-Elsternwick 161 II bc 2
Melbourne-Elwood 161 II b 2
Melbourne-Essendon 161 II b 1
Melbourne-Fairfield 161 II c 1
Melbourne-Fawkner 161 II b 1
Melbourne-Fishermens Bend 161 II b 1
Melbourne-Fitzroy 161 II b 1
Melbourne-Flemington 161 II b 1
Melbourne-Footscray 161 II b 1
Melbourne-Gardenvale 161 II c 2
Melbourne-Hawthorn 161 II c 1
Melbourne-Heidelberg 161 II c 1
Melbourne-Homesglen 161 II c 2
Melbourne-Ivanhoe 161 II c 1
Melbourne-Keilor 161 II b 1
Melbourne-Kew 161 II c 1
Melbourne-Kingsville 161 II b 1
Melbourne-Lower Plenty 161 II c 1
Melbourne-Maidstone 161 II b 1
Melbourne-Malvern 161 II c 2
Melbourne-Moorabbin 161 II c 2
Melbourne-Mount Waverley 161 II c 2
Melbourne-Newport 161 II b 2
Melbourne-Northcote 161 II c 1
Melbourne-Notting Hill 161 II c 2
Melbourne-Nunawading 161 II c 1
Melbourne-Oakleigh 161 II c 2
Melbourne-Ormond 161 II c 2
Melbourne-Pascoe Vale 161 II b 1
Melbourne-Port Melbourne 161 II b 1-2
Melbourne-Prahran 161 II bc 2
Melbourne-Preston 161 II bc 1
Melbourne-Regent 161 II bc 1
Melbourne-Richmond 161 II bc 1
Melbourne-Rosanna 161 II c 1
Melbourne-Saint Kilda 161 II b 2
Melbourne-South Melbourne 161 II b 1-2
Melbourne-Spotswood 161 II b 1
Melbourne-Sunshine 161 II ab 1
Melbourne-Templestowe 161 II c 1
Melbourne-Thornbury 161 II bc 1
Melbourne-Toorak 161 II c 2
Melbourne-Werribee 160 FG 6
Melbourne-Williamstown 161 II b 2
Melbourne-Yarraville 161 II b 1
Melbu 116-117 F 3
Melchers, Kapp — 116-117 m 6
Melchor, Isla — 111 AB 7
Melchor de Mencos 86-87 Q 9
Melchor Múzquiz 64-65 F 6
Meldrim, GA 80-81 F 4
Meldrum Bay 62 K 3
Meleda = Mljet 122-123 G 4
Meleiro 106-107 N 2
Melekgon 174-175 D 4
Melendiz dağları 136-137 F 3
Melenki 124-125 N 6
Melero 106-107 F 2
Melfi [Chad] 164-165 H 6
Melfi [I] 122-123 F 5
Melfort 56-57 Q 7
Melgaço, Barão de — 104-105 F 3
Melik, Wadi el — = Wādī al-Malik 164-165 KL 5
Melili 171 CD 6
Melilla = Melilla 164-165 D 1
Melilla 164-165 D 1
Melimoyu, Monte — 111 B 6
Melinca 108-109 C 4
Melincué 106-107 G 4
Melincué, Laguna — 106-107 G 4
Melinde = Malindi 172 H 2
Melintang, Danau — 152-153 LM 6
Melipilla 111 B 4

326 Maṭamūr

Melita 68-69 F 1
Meliṭa = Malīṭah 166-167 M 2
Melitene = Malatya 134-135 D 3
Melito di Porto Salvo 122-123 FG 7
Melitopol' 126-127 G 3
Melk 118 G 4
Melkbosch Point = Melkbospunt 174-175 B 5
Melkbospunt 174-175 B 5
Mellâh, Ouèd el — = Wād al-Mallāḥ 166-167 C 3
Mellavāgu 140 D 2
Mellèg, Ouèd — = Wād Mallāg 166-167 L 1-2
Mellen, WI 70-71 E 2
Mellerud 116-117 E 8
Mellette, SD 68-69 G 3
Mellīt = Mallīt 164-165 K 6
Mellizo Sur, Cerro — 111 B 7
Mellwood, AR 78-79 D 3
Melmoth 174-175 J 5
Mel'nica-Podol'skaja 126-127 C 2
Mělník 118 G 3
Mel'nikovo [SU ← Tomsk] 132-133 P 6
Melo [RA] 106-107 F 5
Melo [ROU] 111 F 4
Melo, Cordillera de — 106-107 AB 7
Meloco 171 D 6
Melole 152-153 O 10
Meloupre y 150-151 E 6
Melovoje 126-127 JK 2
Melovoj Syrt 124-125 T 7
Melovskaja, gora — 124-125 NO 2
Melozitna River 58-59 KL 4
Melqa el Ouîdân = Mal'qat al-Wīdān 166-167 E 2
Melrhir, Chott — = Shaṭṭ Malghīr 164-165 F 2
Melrose, MA 84 I b 2
Melrose, MN 70-71 C 3
Melrose, MT 66-67 G 3
Melrose, NM 76-77 C 5
Melrose, New York-, Ny 82 III c 2
Melrose Highlands, MA 84 I b 2
Melrose Park 85 III b 1
Melrose Park, PA 84 III c 1
Melsetter = Mandidzudzure 172 F 5-6
Melstone, MT 68-69 BC 2
Melta, Gunung — 152-153 M 3
Meltaus 116-117 L 4
Melton Mowbray 119 F 5
Meluan 152-153 K 5
Meluco 171 D 6
Melun 120-121 J 4
Melunga 172 C 5
Melūr 140 D 5
Melūṭ = Malūṭ 164-165 L 6
Melville 61 G 5
Melville, LA 78-79 D 5
Melville, MT 66-67 HJ 2
Melville, Cape — 158-159 HJ 2
Melville, Johannesburg- 170 V ab 2
Melville, Lake — 56-57 YZ 7
Melville Bay 158-159 G 2
Melville Bugt 56-57 X-Z 2
Melville Hills 56-57 M 4
Melville Island [AUS] 158-159 F 2
Melville Island [CDN] 56-57 N-P 2
Melville Peninsula 56-57 U 4
Melville Sound = Viscount Melville Sound 56-57 O-Q 3
Memala 148-149 F 7
Memba 172 H 4
Memboro 148-149 G 8
Memel 174-175 H 4
Memmingen 118 DE 5
Memochhutshan 138-139 KL 3
Memorial Coliseum and Sports Arena 83 III c 1
Memorial Park 85 III b 1
Memorial Stadium 84 I b 2
Memphis 164-165 L 3
Memphis, IA 70-71 D 5
Memphis, TN 64-65 HJ 4
Memphis, TX 76-77 D 5
Memphremagog, Lac — 72-73 KL 2
Memuro 144-145 c 2
Memyŏ 148-149 C 2
Mena 126-127 F 1
Mena, AR 76-77 G 5
Menaa = Mana'ah 166-167 JK 2
Menado = Manado 148-149 H 6
Menafra 106-107 J 4
Ménaka 164-165 E 5
Menam = Mae Nam Chao Phraya 148-149 CD 3-4
Menan Khong 148-149 D 3
Me-nan-Kwa-noi = Mae Nam Khwae Noi 150-151 B 5-6
Menarandra 172 HJ 6-7
Menard, MT 66-67 H 3
Menard, TX 76-77 DE 7
Menasha, WI 70-71 F 3
Menaskwagama, Lac — 63 EF 2
Menbij = Manbij 136-137 G 4
Mencheong = Wenchang 150-151 H 3
Mencué 108-109 E 3
Mendawai, Sungai — 152-153 K 7
Mende 120-121 J 6
Mendenhall, MS 78-79 E 4-5
Mendenhall, Cape — 58-59 DE 7
Mendes Pimentel 100-101 D 10
Mendez [EC] 92-93 D 5
Méndez [MEX] 86-87 L 5
Mendī [ETH] 164-165 M 7
Mendi [PNG] 148-149 M 8
Mendocino, CA 74-75 AB 3
Mendocino, Cape — 64-65 AB 3
Mendocino Fracture Zone 156-157 KL 3
Mendocino Range 66-67 AB 5
Mendol, Pulau — 148-149 D 6
Mendong Gonpa 142-143 F 5
Mendota, CA 74-75 C 4
Mendota, IL 70-71 F 5
Mendoza [PA] 64-65 b 2
Mendoza [PE] 96-97 C 5
Mendoza [RA, administrative unit] 106-107 CD 5
Mendoza [RA, place] 111 C 4
Mendoza, Río — 106-107 C 4
Mendung 152-153 E 5
Mené 172 C 1
Mene de Mauroa 92-93 E 2
Menemen 136-137 B 3
Menéndez 106-107 J 4
Menéndez, Lago — 108-109 D 4
Menéndez, Paso de — 108-109 CD 4
Ménerville = Tinyah 166-167 H 1
Menetué 108-109 D 2
Mengalum, Pulau — 152-153 L 2
Mengcheng 146-147 F 5
Mêng-chia-lou = Mengjialou 146-147 CD 5
Mengdingjie 141 F 4
Mengen [TR] 136-137 E 2
Mengene dağı 136-137 KL 3
Menggala 148-149 E 7
Menggongshi 146-147 C 8
Menggudai 146-147 B 2
Mengjialou 146-147 CD 5
Mengjiang 146-147 C 10
Mengjin 146-147 D 4
Mêng-kung-shih = Menggongshi 146-147 C 8
Mengla 150-151 C 2
Menglian 141 F 4
Mêng-lien = Menglian 141 F 4
Mengoûb = Mankūb 166-167 E 3
Mengpeng 150-151 C 2
Meng Shan [TJ, mountains] 146-147 FG 4
Mengshan [TJ, place] 146-147 C 9
Mêng-ting = Mengdingjie 141 F 4
Mengtze = Mengzi 142-143 J 7
Mengulek, gora — 132-133 Q 7
Mengyin 146-147 FG 4
Mengzi 142-143 J 7
Menilmontant, Paris- 129 I c 2
Menindee 158-159 H 6
Menindee Lake 160 EF 4
Meninos, Ribeirão dos — 110 II b 2
Menjawak, Pulau — = Pulau Rakit 152-153 H 8
Menlo, KS 68-69 F 6
Menno, SD 68-69 H 4
Mennonietenbuurt 128 I a 2
Menominee, MI 70-71 G 3
Menominee Indian Reservation 70-71 F 3
Menominee River 70-71 FG 3
Menomonee Falls, WI 70-71 F 4
Menomonie, WI 70-71 DE 3
Menongue 172 C 4
Menorca 120-121 K 8
Menoreh, Pegunungan — 152-153 J 9
Menouarar = Manāwar 166-167 E 4
Mense = Misar 138-139 H 2
Menshikova, Cape — = mys Men'šikova 132-133 KL 3
Men'šikova, mys — 132-133 KL 3
Mentasta Mountains 58-59 Q 5
Mentawai, Kepulauan — 148-149 CD 7
Mentawai, Selat — 152-153 C 6-D 7
Mentawai Islands = Kepulauan Mentawai 148-149 CD 7
Mentekab 148-149 D 6
Menteng, Jakarta- 154 IV ab 2
Menterschwaige, München- 130 II b 2
Mentok = Muntok 148-149 DE 7
Mentolat, Monte — 108-109 C 5
Menton 120-121 L 7
Mentougou 146-147 E 2
Mên-t'ou-kou = Mentougou 146-147 E 2
Mentzdam 174-175 F 7
Menucos, Bajo de los — 108-109 F 2-3
Menucos, Los — 108-109 EF 3
Mĕnŭḥa, Bĕer- 136-137 F 7
Menyapa, Gunung — 152-153 M 5
Menzalé, Lago — = Buḥayrat al-Manzilah 173 BC 2
Menzel Boûrguîba = Manzil Būrgībah 166-167 L 1
Menzel Chaker = Manzil Shākir 166-167 M 2
Menzelinsk 124-125 T 6
Menzie, Mount — 58-59 V 6
Menzies 158-159 D 5
Menzies, Mount — 53 B 6-7
Meobbaai 174-175 A 3
Meob Bay = Meobbaai 174-175 A 3
Meoqui 64-65 E 6
Mepiskaro, gora — 126-127 L 6
Meponda 171 C 6
Meppel 120-121 KL 2
Meppen 118 C 2
Meqdâdiya, Al- = Al-Miqdādīyah 136-137 L 6
Mequinenza 120-121 GH 8
Mequinez = Miknās 166-167 D 3
Mera [EC] 96-97 BC 2
Merak 152-153 G 8
Meramangye, Lake — 158-159 F 5
Merang, Kuala — 148-149 D 5
Merano 122-123 D 2
Merapoh 148-149 D 6
Merasheen 63 J 4
Mēraṭh = Meerut 134-135 M 5
Meratus, Pegunungan — 148-149 G 7
Merauke 148-149 LM 8
Merbabu, Gunung — 152-153 J 9
Merbau 150-151 BC 11
Merbein 160 EF 5
Merca = Marka 172 HJ 1
Mercaderes 94-95 C 7
Mercāra 134-135 M 8
Merced, CA 64-65 BC 4
Merced, La — [PE] 96-97 D 7
Merced, La — [RA] 104-105 D 11
Merced, Lake — 83 I b 2
Mercedario, Cerro — 111 BC 4
Mercedes, TX 76-77 EF 9
Mercedes [RA, Buenos Aires] 111 DE 4
Mercedes [RA, Corrientes] 111 E 3
Mercedes [RA, San Luis] 111 C 4
Mercedes [ROU] 111 E 4
Mercedes [YV] 94-95 L 4
Mercedes, Las — 92-93 F 3
Mercedes, Punta — 108-109 FG 7
Merceditas 106-107 B 2
Merced River 74-75 C 4
Mercer, WI 70-71 EF 2
Mercês 102-103 L 4
Merchantville, NJ 84 III c 2
Mercier 104-105 BC 2
Mercier-Lacombe = Safīzaf 166-167 F 2
Mercimekkale = Sakavi 136-137 J 3
Mercoal 60 J 3
Mercury Islands 161 FG 3
Mercy, Cape — 56-57 Y 5
Merdeka Palace 154 IV a 1-2
Merdenik 136-137 K 2
Merdja, El — = Al-Marjah 166-167 H 2
Meredale, Johannesburg- 170 V a 2
Meredit, Cabo — = Cape Meredith 111 D 8
Meredith, Cape — 111 D 8
Meredosia, IL 70-71 E 6
Mère et l'Enfant, la — = Nui Vong Phu 150-151 G 6
Merefa 126-127 H 2
Meregh = Mareeg 172 J 1
Merena = Espíritu Santo 158-159 MN 3
Merga = Nukhaylah 164-165 K 5
Mergenevo 126-127 P 2
Mergezhung 138-139 K 2
Mergui = Myeik 148-149 C 4
Mergui Archipelago = Myeik Kyûnzu 148-149 C 4
Merhràoua = Mighrāwah 166-167 DE 3
Meriç = Büyük Doğanca 136-137 B 2
Meriç nehri 136-137 B 2
Merida [E] 120-121 D 9
Mérida [MEX] 64-65 J 7
Mérida [YV] 92-93 E 3
Mérida, Cordillera de — 92-93 EF 3
Meriden, CT 72-73 K 4
Meriden, WY 68-69 D 5
Meridian, ID 66-67 E 4
Meridian, MS 64-65 J 5
Meridian, TX 76-77 F 7
Meridith, Lake — 76-77 D 5
Mērikānam = Marakkānam 140 DE 4
Merimbula 160 JK 6
Meringur 158-159 H 6
Merino Jarpa, Isla — 108-109 BC 6
Merinos 106-107 J 4
Merion Station, PA 84 III b 2
Merir 148-149 K 6
Merissa = Madrīsah 166-167 G 2
Merka = Marka 164-165 ab 3
Merke [SU] 132-133 N 9
Merkel, TX 76-77 D 6
Merket Bazar = Marqat Bazar 142-143 D 4
Merla 126-127 G 1-2
Merlimau 150-151 D 11
Merlin, OR 66-67 B 4
Merlo [RA, Buenos Aires] 110 III a 1
Merlo [RA, San Luis] 106-107 E 4
Merlo Gómez 110 III b 2
Merlo-Libertad 110 III a 2
Merlo-Mariano Acosta 110 III a 2
Merlo-Pontevedra 110 III a 2
Merlo-San Antonio de Padua 110 III a 2
Merluna 158-159 H 2
Mermer = Alibardak 136-137 J 3
Merna, NE 68-69 G 5
Merna, WY 66-67 H 4
Meroua 168-169 F 2
Merouana = Marwānah 166-167 J 2
Merowē = Marawī 164-165 L 5
Merpatti 138-139 H 8
Merq, el- = Al-Marj 164-165 J 2
Merredin 158-159 C 6
Merrick 119 D 4
Merri Creek 161 II b 1
Merrill, IA 68-69 H 4
Merrill, MS 78-79 E 5
Merrill, OR 66-67 C 4
Merrill, WI 70-71 F 3
Merrillan, WI 70-71 E 3
Merrimack River 72-73 L 3
Merriman 174-175 E 6
Merriman, NE 68-69 EF 4
Merrionette Park, IL 83 II a 2
Merritt 56-57 M 7
Merritt, Lake — 83 I c 2
Merriwa 160 JK 4
Mer Rouge, LA 78-79 D 4
Merrymount Park 84 I bc 3
Merryville, LA 78-79 C 5
Merseburg 118 EF 3
Mers-el-Kébir = Mars al-Kabīr 166-167 F 1-2
Mersin [TR] 134-135 C 3
Mersing 148-149 D 6
Mers-les-Bains 120-121 H 3
Mĕrsrags 124-125 D 5
Merta 138-139 DE 4
Merṭān = Merta 138-139 DE 4
Merthyr Tydfil 119 DE 6
Merti 171 D 2
Merton, London- 129 II b 2
Mertz Glacier 53 C 15
Mertzon, TX 76-77 D 7
Meru [EAK] 172 G 1-2
Meru [EAT] 172 G 2
Meru = Gangrinpochhe 138-139 H 2
Merume Montains 98-99 H 1-J 2
Merume Mountains 94-95 L 4-5
Meru National Park 171 D 2
Merundung, Pulau — 152-153 H 4
Meruóca 100-101 D 2
Merv 134-135 J 3
Merv = Mary 134-135 J 3
Merwar = Mārwār 134-135 L 5
Merzifon 136-137 F 2
Merzouna = Al-Mazzūnah 166-167 L 2
Mesa, AZ 64-65 D 5
Mesa, NM 76-77 B 5-6
Mesa, Cerro — 108-109 D 7
Mesabi Range 64-65 H 2
Mesa Central = Mesa de Anáhuac 64-65 FG 7-8
Mesa Chupadera 76-77 A 5-6
Mesa de Anáhuac 64-65 FG 7-8
Mesa de Guanipa 94-95 J 3
Mesa del Rito Gaviel 76-77 C 6
Mesa de Mariapiri 94-95 FG 6
Mesa de San Carlos 86-87 C 3
Mesa de Yambí 92-93 E 4
Mesagne 122-123 GH 5
Mesa Montosa 76-77 B 5
Mesanak, Pulau — 152-153 F 5
Mesaniyeu, Sierra — 108-109 DE 3
Mesas de Iguaje 94-95 E 7
Mesa Verde National Park 74-75 J 4
Mescalero, NM 76-77 B 6
Mescalero Apache Indian Reservation 76-77 B 6
Mescalero Ridge 76-77 BC 6
Mescalero Valley 76-77 BC 6
Mescit dağı 136-137 J 2
Mescitli 136-137 JK 3
Meščʻora 124-125 MN 6
Meščʻorskij 113 V a 3
Meščovsk 124-125 K 6
Meščura 124-125 S 2
Meseied = Musā'id 166-167 A 5
Meseta de Jaua 94-95 J 5
Meseta de la Muerte 108-109 CD 7
Meseta de las Vizcachas 111 B 8
Meseta del Lago Buenos Aires 108-109 D 6
Meseta del Norte 64-65 F 6
Meseta del Viento 108-109 C 7
Meseta de Montemayor 111 C 6-7
Meseta de Somuncurá 111 C 6
Meseta de Zohlaguna 86-87 Q 8
Mesgouez, Lac — 62 O 1
Meshed = Mashhad 134-135 HJ 3
Meshhed = Mashhad 134-135 HJ 3
Meshkīn Shar 136-137 M 3
Meshra' er Req = Mashrā' ar-Raqq 164-165 K 7
Mesick, MI 70-71 H 3
Mesilinka River 60 E 1
Mesilla, NM 76-77 A 6
Meskanaw 61 F 4
Meskenê = Maskanah 136-137 GH 4-5
Meskiana = Miskyānah 166-167 K 2
Meškovskaja 126-127 K 2
Mesmiyé = Al-Mismīyah 136-137 G 6
Mesnil-Amelot, le — 129 I d 1
Mesnil-le-Roi, le — 129 I b 2
Mesolóngion 122-123 J 6
Mesopotamia [IRQ] 134-135 E 3-F 4
Mesopotamia [RA] 111 E 3-4
Mesquita 100-101 C 10
Mesquite, NV 74-75 F 4
Mesquite, TX 76-77 F 6
Messaad = Mis'ad 166-167 H 2
Messalo, Rio — 172 G 4
Messaoud, Oued — = Wādī Mas'ūd 166-167 F 5-6
Messaria 136-137 E 5
'Messeied = Musā'id 166-167 A 5
Messel 128 III b 2
Messeler Höhe 128 III b 2
Messênê [GR, place] 122-123 JK 7
Messênê [GR, ruins] 122-123 J 7
Messenhausen 128 III b 2
Messêniakós Kólpos 122-123 JK 7
Messier, Canal — 108-109 B 7
Messina [I] 122-123 F 6
Messina [ZA] 172 EF 6
Messina, Gulf of — = Messêniakós Kólpos 122-123 JK 7
Messina, Stretto di — 122-123 F 6-7
Messinge 171 C 5
Messojacha 132-133 O 4
Messeñas, Las — 76-77 B 8
Mestia 126-127 L 5
Mestour, Hassi — = Ḥāssī Mastūr 166-167 GH 4
Mestre, Venèzia- 122-123 E 3
Mesudiye 136-137 G 2
Mesuji, Wai — 152-153 F 7-8
Meta 94-95 E 6
Meta, Río — 92-93 E 3
Metagama 62 L 3
Meta Incognita Peninsula 56-57 X 5
Metairie, LA 64-65 H 5-6
Metairie Cemetery 85 I b 1
Metairie-East End, LA 85 I b 1
Metalici, Munţii — 122-123 K 2
Metaline Falls, WA 66-67 E 1
Metameur = Al-Maṭamūr 166-167 M 3
Metán 111 D 3
Metangula 172 FG 4
Metapan 88-89 B 7
Metaponto 122-123 G 5
Metarica 171 D 6
Metechi 126-127 M 6
Meteghan 63 CD 5
Metema 164-165 M 6
Metĕōra 122-123 J 6
Meteor Crater 74-75 H 5
Meteor Depth 50-51 HJ 8
Methouia = Al-Mithūyah 166-167 LM 3
Methow River 66-67 CD 1
Mê Thuôt = Ban Me Thuôt 148-149 E 4
Methy Lake 61 D 2
Mēthymna 122-123 LM 6
Methy River 61 D 2
Metileo 106-107 EF 5
Metili-Chaamba = Matlīlī 166-167 H 3
Metinic Island 72-73 M 3
Metković 122-123 GH 4
Metlakatla, AK 56-57 KL 6
Metlaouï, El — = Al-Mitlawī 164-165 F 2
Métlîn, El — = Al-Mātlīn 166-167 M 1
Metolius, OR 66-67 C 3
Metorica 171 D 6
Meṭouîa, El — = Al-Miṭūyah 166-167 LM 3
Metro 152-153 F 8
Metropolis, IL 70-71 F 7
Metropolitan Hospital Clinic 84 II b 2
Mētsobon 122-123 J 6
Metter, GA 80-81 E 4
Mettharaw 141 F 7
Mettuppālaiyam 140 C 5
Mettūr 140 C 5
Meṭṭur Kuḷam = Stanley Reservoir 134-135 M 8
Metuge 171 E 6
Metulla 136-137 F 6
Metundo 171 E 5
Metz 120-121 L 4
Meudon 129 I b 2
Meulaboh 148-149 C 6
Meulen, Isla van der — 108-109 B 7
Meureudu 148-149 C 5
Meuse 120-121 K 4
Meusegem 128 II a 1
Mevume 174-175 L 2
Mēwār 138-139 DE 5
Mexcala, Río — = Río Balsas 64-65 F 8
Mexia, TX 76-77 F 7
Mexicali 64-65 C 5
Mexican Hat, UT 74-75 J 4
Mexican Plateau = Altiplanicie Mexicana 64-65 E 5-F 7
Mexico, ME 72-73 L 2
Mexico, MO 70-71 DE 6
Mexico [MEX, administrative unit] 86-87 KL 8
México [MEX, place] 64-65 G 8
Mexico [MEX, state] 64-65 E 6-G 8
México, Bogotá- 91 III b 4
Mexico, Gulf of — 64-65 G-J 7
Mexico Basin 64-65 H-J 6
Mexico Bay 72-73 H 3
México City = México 64-65 G 8
Meyādīn = Mayādīn 136-137 J 5
Meyāndowab 136-137 M 4
Meyāneh 134-135 F 3
Meyāneh, Kūreh-ye — 136-137 M 5
Meydān Dāgh 136-137 MN 4
Meydān-e Naftūn 136-137 N 7
Mey ed Dahraoui, Hassi — = Ḥāssī Māï ad-Darwwī 166-167 K 3
Meyerland, Houston-, TX 85 III b 2
Meyersdale, PA 72-73 G 5
Meyronne 61 E 6
Mēzalīgōn 141 D 7
Mēzā Myit 141 E 3-4
Mezdra 122-123 KL 4
Meždurečenskij 132-133 LM 6
Meždušarskij, ostrov — 132-133 HJ 3
Mezen' [SU, place] 132-133 GH 4
Mezen' [SU, river] 132-133 H 5
Mézenc, Mont — 120-121 JK 6
Mezenskaja guba 132-133 G 4
Mezeraa, El — = Al-Mazra'ah 166-167 K 2
Mežgorje 126-127 A 2
Mezguiṭem = Mizgīṭim 166-167 E 2
Meziadin Lake 60 C 1
Mežirečje 126-127 B 2
Mezőkövesd 118 K 5
Mezoûna = Al-Mazzūnah 166-167 L 2
Mežpjanje 124-125 P 6
Mezquital 86-87 H 6
Mfongosi = Mfongozi 174-175 J 5
Mfongozi 174-175 J 5
Mfwanganu 171 C 3
Mga 124-125 H 4
M'ghîlah, Jabal — 166-167 L 2
Mglin 124-125 J 7
M. Gómez 110 III b 2
Mḥamīd, el — = Al-Maḥamīd 166-167 D 5
Mhāpasā = Māpuca 140 A 3
Mhasalān = Mhasla 140 A 1
Mhasla 140 A 1
Mhasvād 140 B 2
M. Heilman Memorial Field 84 II c 2
M. Hidalgo, Presa — 86-87 F 4
Mhlatuze 174-175 J 5
Mhow 138-139 E 6
Mia, Wed — = Wādī Miyāh 164-165 EF 2
Miajadas 120-121 E 9
Miājlar 134-135 KL 5
Miali = Miao-li 146-147 H 9
Miami, AZ 74-75 H 6
Miami, FL 64-65 K 6
Miami, OK 76-77 G 4
Miami, TX 76-77 D 5
Miami Beach, FL 64-65 KL 6
Miami Canal 64-65 K 6
Miami River 70-71 H 6
Miamisburg, OH 70-71 H 6
Miami Shores, FL 80-81 cd 4
Miamo, El — 94-95 L 4
Mianchi 146-147 CD 4
Miāndou Āb = Meyāndowab 136-137 M 4
Miandrivazo 172 J 5
Miangas, Pulau — 148-149 J 5
Mianwali = Miyānwālī 134-135 L 4
Mian Xian 142-143 K 5
Mianyang [TJ, Hubei] 146-147 D 6
Mianyang [TJ, Sichuan] 142-143 J 5
Miao Dao 146-147 H 3
Miaodao Qundao 142-143 N 4
Miaoli 146-147 H 9
Miao Liedao = Miaodao Qundao 142-143 N 4
Miao-tzŭ = Miaozi 146-147 CD 5
Miaozi 146-147 CD 5
Miass 132-133 L 7
Miastko 118 H 1-2
Miaws, Bi'r — 173 D 6
Mica 174-175 J 3
Mica Creek 60 H 3
Mica Dam 60 H 3
Micaela Cascallares 106-107 G 7
Micay 92-93 D 4
Micha Cchakaja 126-127 KL 5
Michaia Ivanoviča Kalinina 124-125 P 4-5
Michajliki 124-125 K 5
Michajlov 124-125 M 6
Michajlovka [SU, Rossijskaja SFSR Astrachanskaja Oblast'] 126-127 N 3
Michajlovka [SU, Rossijskaja SFSR Kurskaja Oblast'] 124-125 KL 7
Michajlovka [SU, Rossijskaja SFSR Volgogradskaja Oblast'] 126-127 L 1
Michajlovka [SU, Ukrainskaja SSR] 126-127 G 3
Michajlovskaja 124-125 PQ 3
Michajlovskij 132-133 OP 7
Michajlovskoje [SU, Moskva] 113 V b 3
Michalitsion = Karacabey 136-137 C 2
Michalovce 118 KL 4
Mī Chaung 141 C 5
Michel 66-67 F 1
Michel Peak 60 D 3
Michelson, Mont — 56-57 GH 4
Michigamme Reservoir 70-71 FG 2
Michigan 64-65 J 2-K 3
Michigan, ND 68-69 G 1-2
Michigan, Lake — 64-65 J 2-3
Michigan City, IN 70-71 G 5
Michigan State Fair Grounds 84 II b 2
Michikamau Lake 56-57 Y 7
Michikenis River 62 E 1
Michipicoten Bay 70-71 H 2
Michipicoten Harbour 70-71 H 1-2
Michipicoten Island 56-57 T 8
Michnevo 124-125 LM 6
Michoacán 64-65 F 8
Micronesia [archipelago] 156-157 G-H 4
Micronesia [Micronesia, state] 148-149 MN 5
Mičurin 122-123 MN 4
Mičurinsk 124-125 N 7
Mida 171 DE 3
Midáeion = Eskişehir 134-135 C 2-3
Midai, Pulau — 148-149 E 6
Midalt 166-167 D 3
Midār 166-167 E 2
Midas, NV 66-67 E 5
Mid Atlantic Ridge 50-51 H 3-J 8
Middelburg [ZA, Kaapland] 172 DE 8
Middelburg [ZA, Transvaal] 172 EF 7
Middelfart 116-117 CD 10
Middelpos 174-175 D 6
Middelpost = Middelpos 174-175 D 6
Middel Roggeveld 174-175 D 7
Middelsten Boskant 128 II a 1
Middelveld [ZA, Kaapland] 174-175 E 5
Middelveld [ZA, Transvaal] 174-175 FG 4
Middelwit 174-175 G 3
Middle Alkali Lake 66-67 CD 5
Middle America Trench 156-157 MN 4
Middle Andaman 134-135 P 8
Middle Atlas = Al-Aṭlas al-Mutawassiṭ 164-165 CD 2
Middle Bank 63 FG 5
Middlebro 70-71 C 1
Middlebury, VT 72-73 K 2
Middle Concho River 76-77 D 7
Middle East, The — 50-51 NO 4
Middle Fork Chandalar 58-59 O 2-3
Middle Fork Fortymile 58-59 Q 4
Middle Fork John Day River 66-67 D 3
Middle Fork Koyukuk 58-59 M 3
Middle Fork Salmon River 66-67 F 3
Middle Harbour 161 I b 1
Middle Head 161 I b 1
Middle Island = Ko Klang 150-151 AB 8
Middle Loup River 68-69 G 5
Middle Moscos = Maungmagan Kyûnzu 150-151 A 5
Middle Musquodoboit 63 E 5
Middleport, OH 72-73 E 5
Middle Rapids 61 BC 2
Middle Reservoir 84 I b 2
Middle Ridge 63 J 3
Middle River, MN 70-71 BC 1
Middle River Village 60 E 2
Middlesboro, KY 64-65 JK 4
Middlesbrough 119 F 4
Middlesex Fells Reservation 84 I b 2
Middleton, ID 66-67 E 4
Middleton, TN 78-79 E 3
Middleton [CDN] 63 D 5
Middleton [ZA] 174-175 F 7
Middleton, Mount — 62 N 1
Middleton Island 56-57 GH 6
Middleton Reef 158-159 L 5
Middletown, NJ 72-73 J 4
Middletown, NY 72-73 J 4
Middletown, OH 72-73 DE 5
Middle Water, TX 76-77 C 5
Middle West 64-65 F-J 3
Midelt = Midalt 166-167 D 3
Midhdharidhrah, Al- 164-165 A 5
Midhsandur 116-117 c 2
Midia = Midye 136-137 C 2
Mid-Illovo 174-175 J 5-6
Mid Indian Basin 50-51 NO 6
Midland 72-73 FG 2
Midland, CA 74-75 F 6
Midland, MI 70-71 H 4
Midland, SD 68-69 F 3
Midland, TX 64-65 F 5
Midland Beach, New York-, NY 82 III b 3
Midlandvale 61 B 5
Midlothian, TX 76-77 F 6
Mid Moscos = Maungmagan Kyûnzu 150-151 A 5
Midnapore 134-135 O 6
Midnapur = Midnapore 134-135 O 6
Midongy-atsimo 172 J 6
Midori, Yokohama- 155 III a 2
Mid Pacific Ridge 156-157 J 8-L 7
Midsayap 148-149 HJ 5
Midu 176 a 3
Midvale, ID 66-67 E 3
Midvale, UT 66-67 H 5
Midville, GA 80-81 E 4
Midway 156-157 J 3
Midway Islands 58-59 NO 1
Midway Range 60 H 5
Midwest, WY 68-69 CD 4
Midwest City, OK 76-77 F 5
Midyah 166-167 H 1
Midyān II 173 D 3
Midyat 136-137 J 4
Midye 136-137 C 2
Midžor 122-123 K 4
Mie 144-145 L 5
Miedo, El — 94-95 F 5
Międzyrzec Podlaski 118 L 3
Miel, La — 94-95 G 3
Mielec 118 K 3
Mien-ch'ih = Mianchi 146-147 CD 4
Mienhsien = Mian Xian 142-143 K 5
Mienyang = Mianyang [TJ, Hubei] 146-147 D 6
Mien-yang = Mianyang [TJ, Sichuan] 142-143 J 5
Miercurea-Ciuc 122-123 L 2
Mieres 120-121 DE 7
Miersdorf 130 III c 2
Mierzeja Helska 118 J 1
Mierzeja Wislana 118 J 1
Mīeso 164-165 N 7
Mifflintown, PA 72-73 H 4
Migamuwa 134-135 M 9
Migdal Ashqĕlōn = Ashqĕlon 136-137 F 7
Migdal Gad = Ashqĕlōn 136-137 F 7
Mighāir 166-167 J 3
Mighāir, Al- 166-167 J 3
Mighān, Kavīr-e — 136-137 N 5
Mighrāwah 166-167 DE 3
Migole 171 CD 4
Miguel Alemán, Presa — 86-87 M 8
Miguel Alves 92-93 L 5
Miguel Burnier 102-103 L 4
Miguel Calmon 92-93 LM 7
Miguel Cané 106-107 F 6
Miguel Hidalgo, Ciudad de México- 91 I b 2
Miguel Hidalgo, Parque Nacional — 91 I a 3
Miguel Riglos 106-107 F 6
Migues 106-107 K 5
Migulinskaja 126-127 K 2
Migyaungyè 141 D 6

Migyaung 327

Mihajlovgrad 122-123 K 4
Mihalıççık 136-137 D 3
Mihara 144-145 J 5
Mi He 146-147 G 3
Mi He = Ming He 146-147 E 3
Mihintalē 140 E 6
Mihmandar 136-137 F 4
Mi Ho = Mi He 146-147 G 3
Miho wan 144-145 J 5
Mi-hsien = Mi Xian 146-147 D 4
Mīīto = Moyto 164-165 H 6
Mijares 120-121 G 8-9
Mijnden 128 I b 2
Mijriyyah, Al- 164-165 B 5
Mikaševiči 124-125 F 7
Mikata 144-145 K 5
Mikawa wan 144-145 L 5
Miki 144-145 K 5
Mikindani 172 H 4
Mikir Hills 141 C 2
Mikkaichi = Kurobe 144-145 L 4
Mikkeli 116-117 M 7
Mikkwa River 61 A 2
Miknās 164-165 C 2
Mikojan-Šachar = Karačajevsk 126-127 KL 5
Mikumi 171 D 4
Mikumi National Park 171 D 4
Mikun' 132-133 HJ 5
Mikuni 144-145 KL 4
Mila = Mīlah 164-165 F 1
Milaca, MN 70-71 D 3
Miladummadulu Atoll 176 ab 1
Milagres 100-101 E 4
Milagro 96-97 B 3
Milagro, El — 111 C 4
Mīlah 164-165 F 1
Milāḥah, Wādī — 173 C 4
Milājerd 136-137 N 5
Milak 138-139 G 3
Milam 138-139 H 2
Milan 91 III c 2
Milan, IA 70-71 D 5
Milan, MI 72-73 E 3
Milan, TN 78-79 E 3
Milan, WA 66-67 E 2
Milan = Milano 122-123 C 3
Milano 122-123 C 3
Milano, TX 76-77 F 7
Milâs 136-137 B 4
Milazzo 122-123 F 6
Milbank, SD 68-69 H 3
Milbanke Sound 60 C 3
Milbertshofen, München- 130 II b 1
Milbridge, ME 72-73 N 2
Milden 61 E 5
Mildred, MT 68-69 D 2
Mildura 158-159 H 6
Mīleh, Kūh-e — 136-137 M 6
150 Mile House 60 G 3
100 Mile House 60 G 4
Milepa 171 D 5
Miles 158-159 JK 5
Miles, TX 76-77 DE 7
Miles, WA 66-67 D 2
Miles City, MT 64-65 E 2
Milesville, SD 68-69 EF 3
Milet = Miletos 136-137 B 4
Mileto = Miletos 134-135 B 3
Miletos 134-135 B 3
Miletus = Miletos 134-135 B 3
Milford, CA 66-67 C 5
Milford, DE 72-73 J 5
Milford, MA 72-73 L 3
Milford, NE 68-69 H 5
Milford, NH 72-73 L 3
Milford, PA 72-73 J 4
Milford, UT 74-75 G 3
Milford Sound [NZ, bay] 158-159 N 8
Milford Sound [NZ, place] 161 B 7
Milgis 171 D 2
Milḥ, Qurayyāt al- 136-137 G 7
Mili 208 H 2
Milia, El — = Al-Mīlīyah 166-167 JK 1
Miliân, Ouêd — = Wād Milyān 166-167 LM 1
Miliana = Milyānah 166-167 GH 1
Milicz 118 H 3
Miling 158-159 C 6
Military Museum 155 II a 2
Mīlīyah, Al- 166-167 JK 1
Milk, Wādī el — = Wādī al-Malik 164-165 KL 5
Mil'kovo 132-133 ef 7
Milk River [CDN] 66-67 GH 1
Milk River [USA] 64-65 E 2
Milk River Ridge 66-67 G 1
Millares 104-105 D 6
Millau 120-121 J 6
Mill City, OR 66-67 B 3
Mill Creek [USA, New Jersey] 84 III d 1
Mill Creek [USA, Pennsylvania] 84 III b 1
Milledgeville, GA 80-81 E 4
Millegan, MT 66-67 H 2
Mille Lacs Lake 64-65 H 2
Millen, GA 80-81 F 4
Miller 174-175 E 7
Miller, MO 76-77 GH 4
Miller, NE 68-69 G 5
Miller, SD 68-69 G 3
Miller, Mount — 58-59 QR 6
Millerovo 126-127 K 2
Miller Peak 74-75 H 7
Millersburg, OH 72-73 EF 4
Millersburg, PA 72-73 H 4
Millerton Lake 74-75 D 4
Millertown 63 H 3
Millevaches, Plateau de — 120-121 HJ 6
Mill Hill, London- 129 II b 1
Millican, OR 66-67 C 4
Millicent 158-159 GH 7
Millington, TN 78-79 E 3
Millinocket, ME 72-73 M 2
Mill Island [Antarctica] 53 C 11
Mill Island [CDN] 56-57 V 5
Millmerran 158-159 K 5
Millport, AL 78-79 EF 4
Millry, AL 78-79 E 5
Mills, NM 76-77 B 4
Millston, WI 70-71 E 3
Millville, NJ 72-73 J 5
Millwood Lake 76-77 G 6
Milmont Park, PA 84 III a 2
Milne Bay 148-149 h 7
Milnesand, NM 76-77 C 6
Milnet 72-73 F 1
Milnor, ND 68-69 H 2
Milo, IA 70-71 D 5
Milo, ME 72-73 M 2
Milo, OR 66-67 B 4
Milo [CDN] 61 B 5
Milo [Guinea] 164-165 C 7
Milolii, HI 78-79 de 3
Milparinka 158-159 H 5
Milton, FL 78-79 F 5
Milton, MA 84 I b 3
Milton, ND 68-69 GH 1
Milton, OR 66-67 D 3
Milton, PA 72-73 H 4
Milton, WI 70-71 F 4
Milton, WV 72-73 E 5
Milton [CDN] 63 D 5
Milton [NZ] 161 CD 8
Miltonvale, KS 68-69 H 6
Milton Village, MA 84 I b 3
Miluo 142-143 L 6
Miluo Jiang 146-147 D 7
Mil'utinskaja 126-127 KL 2
Milverton 72-73 F 3
Milwaukee, WI 64-65 J 3
Milwaukee Depth 64-65 N 8
Milwaukie, OR 66-67 B 3
Milyān, Wād — 166-167 LM 1
Milyānah 166-167 GH 1
Mim 168-169 E 4
Miminiska Lake 62 E 2
Mimitsu 144-145 H 6
Mimongo 172 B 2
Mimosa 100-101 A 7
Mimoso do Sul 102-103 M 4
Mimôt 150-151 EF 7
Mina, NV 74-75 DE 3
Mina, SD 68-69 G 3
Mina [MEX] 76-77 D 9
Mina [RI] 152-153 O 10-11
Mina, Ouêd — = Wādī Mīnā 166-167 G 2
Mīnā, Wādī — 166-167 G 2
Mīnā' al-Aḥmadī 136-137 N 8
Mīnā Bāzār 138-139 B 2
Mīn' 'Abd Allāh 136-137 N 8
Mina de São Domingos 120-121 D 10
Minago River 61 J 3
Minahasa 148-149 H 6
Minakami 144-145 M 4
Minaki 62 B 3
Minam, OR 66-67 E 3
Minamata 142-143 P 5
Minami, Yokohama- 155 III a 3
Minami Daitō-jima 142-143 P 6
Minami-Daitō zima = Minami-Daitō-jima 142-143 P 6
Minami-lo 206-207 S 7
Minami Iwo = Minami lo 206-207 S 7
Minami lo 206-207 S 7
Minamitane 144-145 H 7
Minami Tori 156-157 G 3
Minas 111 EF 4
Minas, Baruta-Las — 91 II b 2
Minas, Serra de — 102-103 L 3
Minas, Sierra de las — 86-87 PQ 10
Minas Basin 63 DE 5
Minas Cué 111 E 2
Minas de Corrales 106-107 K 3
Minas de Riotinto 120-121 DE 10
Minas do Mimoso 100-101 D 6
Minas Gerais 92-93 KL 8-9
Minas Novas 102-103 L 2
Minatare, NE 68-69 E 5
Minatitlán 64-65 H 8
Minato = Nakaminato 144-145 N 4
Minato, Tōkyō- 155 III b 2
Minbū 141 D 5
Minbyā 141 C 5
Mincha 106-107 B 3
Min Chiang = Min Jiang [TJ, Fujian] 146-147 G 8
Min Chiang = Min Jiang [TJ, Sichuan] 142-143 J 5-6
Min-ch'in = Minqin 142-143 J 4
Minchinābād 138-139 D 2
Min-ch'ing = Minqing 146-147 G 8
Minchinmávida, Volcán — 108-109 C 4
Min-ch'üan = Minquan 146-147 E 4
Minchumina, Lake — 58-59 L 5
Minco, OK 76-77 EF 5
Mindanao 148-149 J 5
Mindanao Sea 148-149 HJ 5
Mindanau = Mindanao 148-149 J 5
Mindat 141 C 5
Mindat Sakan = Mindat 141 C 5
Minden 118 D 2
Minden, IA 70-71 C 5
Minden, LA 78-79 C 4
Minden, NE 68-69 G 5
Minden, NV 74-75 D 3
Minderoo 158-159 C 4
Mindōn 141 D 6
Mindōn Myit 141 D 6
Mindoro 148-149 GH 4
Mindoro Strait 148-149 GH 4
Mindra, Vîrful — 122-123 KL 3
Mindživan 126-127 N 7
Mine 144-145 H 5
Mine Centre 62 C 3
Mineiga, Bîr — = Bi'r Munayjah 173 D 6
Mineiros 102-103 F 2
Mineola, NY 72-73 K 4
Mineola, TX 76-77 G 6
Miner, MT 66-67 H 3
Mineral, CA 66-67 C 5
Mineral, WA 66-67 B 2
Mineral Mountains 74-75 G 3
Mineral'nyje Vody 126-127 L 4
Mineral Point, WI 70-71 EF 4
Mineral Wells, TX 76-77 EF 6
Minersville, UT 74-75 G 3
Minerva, OH 72-73 F 4
Minervino Murge 122-123 FG 5
Mingan 63 DE 2
Mingan, Rivière — 63 E 2
Mingan Islands 63 DE 2
Mingan Passage = Jacques Cartier Passage 56-57 Y 7-8
Mingary 160 E 4
Mingečaur 126-127 N 6
Mingečaurskoje vodochranilišče 126-127 N 6
Mingenew 158-159 C 5
Mingfeng = Niya Bazar 142-143 E 4
Minggang 146-147 E 5
Ming He 146-147 E 3
Mingin 141 D 4
Mingjiang = Minggang 146-147 E 5
Mingo Junction, OH 72-73 F 4
Mingoya 171 D 5
Mingxi 146-147 F 8
Minhla [BUR, Magwe Taing] 141 D 6
Minhla [BUR, Pègū Taing] 141 D 7
Minh Long 150-151 G 5
Minho [P, landscape] 120-121 C 8
Minho [P, river] 120-121 C 7
Minhou 146-147 G 8
Minhow = Fuzhou 142-143 MN 6
Min-hsien = Min Xian 142-143 J 5
Minicoy Island 134-135 L 9
Minidoka, ID 66-67 G 4
Minier, IL 70-71 F 5
Minigwal, Lake — 158-159 D 5
Minikkōy Dvīp = Minicoy Island 134-135 L 9
Minilya River 158-159 BC 4
Mininco 106-107 A 6
Miniota 61 H 5
Ministro João Alberto 92-93 J 7
Minitonas 61 H 4
Min Jiang [TJ, Fujian] 142-143 M 6
Min Jiang [TJ, Sichuan] 142-143 J 5-6
Minkébé 172 B 1
Min'kovo 124-125 O 4
Minle 142-143 J 4
Min-lo = Minle 142-143 J 4
Minna 164-165 F 7
Minneapolis, KS 68-69 H 6
Minneapolis, MN 64-65 GH 2-3
Minnedosa 61 J 5
Minnekahta, SD 68-69 E 4
Minneola, KS 68-69 FG 7
Minneota, MN 70-71 BC 3
Minnesota 64-65 H 2-3
Minnesota River 64-65 H 3
Minnewaska, Lake — 70-71 C 3
Minnewaukan, ND 68-69 G 1
Minnipa 160 B 4
Minnitaki Lake 62 CD 3
Mino [J] 144-145 L 5
Miño [P] 120-121 D 7
Miño, Volcán — 104-105 B 7
Mino-Kamo 144-145 L 5
Minong, WI 70-71 DE 2
Minonk, IL 70-71 F 5
Minorca = Menorca 120-121 K 8
Minot, ND 64-65 F 2
Minqin 142-143 J 4
Minqing 146-147 G 8
Minquan 146-147 E 4
Min Shan 142-143 J 5
Minshāt al-Bakkārī 170 II a 1
Minshāt Dahshūr 173 B 3
Minsin 141 D 3
Minsk 124-125 FG 7
Minster, OH 70-71 H 5
Mintaqat al-Wajh 166-167 K 4
Minto, AK 58-59 N 4
Minto [CDN, Manitoba] 68-69 FG 1
Minto [CDN, New Brunswick] 63 C 4
Minto [CDN, Yukon Territory] 58-59 T 5
Minto, Lake — 56-57 V 6
Minto Inlet 56-57 N 3
Minton 68-69 D 1
Minturn, CO 68-69 C 6
Minūf 173 B 2
Minusinsk 132-133 R 7
Minuto de Dios, Bogotá- 91 III b 2
Min Xian 142-143 J 5
Minyā, Al- 164-165 KL 3
Mio, MI 70-71 H 3
Mios Num 148-149 KL 7
Mios Waar 148-149 KL 7
Miqdādīyah, Al- 136-137 L 6
Miquelon, Saint-Pierre et — 56-57 Za 8
Miquon, PA 84 III b 1
Mir 124-125 F 7
Mira 122-123 DE 3
Mira, Rio — [CO] 94-95 B 7
Mīrā', Wādī al- 136-137 HJ 7
Miracatu 102-103 J 6
Miracema 102-103 LM 4
Miracema do Norte 92-93 K 6
Miracle Mile, Los Angeles-, CA 83 III bc 1
Mirador [BR] 92-93 KL 6
Mirador [MEX] 91 I b 1
Mirador, El — 86-87 P 9
Miradouro 102-103 L 4
Miraflores [CO, Boyacá] 94-95 E 5
Miraflores [CO, Vaupés] 94-95 E 7
Miraflores [PA] 64-65 b 2
Miraflores [YV] 91 II b 1
Miraflores, Esclusas de — 64-65 b 3
Miraflores Locks = Esclusas de Miraflores 64-65 b 3
Miraí 102-103 L 4
Miraíma 100-101 DE 2
Miraj 140 B 2
Miralta 102-103 KL 2
Miramar 111 E 5
Miramichi Bay 63 D 4
Miramichi River 63 CD 4
Mirampéllu, Kólpos — 122-123 LM 8
Miranda [BR] 92-93 H 9
Miranda [RA] 106-107 H 6
Miranda [YV] 94-95 H 2
Miranda, Rio — 92-93 H 9
Miranda de Ebro 120-121 F 7
Miranda do Douro 120-121 D 8
Mirande 120-121 H 7
Mirandela 120-121 D 8
Mirandiba 100-101 E 5
Mirando City, TX 76-77 E 9
Mirándola 122-123 D 3
Mirangaba 100-101 D 6
Mirante, Serra do — 102-103 GH 5
Mirante do Paranapanema 102-103 FG 5
Mira Pampa 106-107 F 5
Mirapinima 92-93 G 5
Mirassol 102-103 H 4
Mir-Bašir 126-127 N 6
Mirbāṭ 134-135 GH 7
Mirear, Gezîret — = Jazīrat Marīr 173 DE 6
Mirebalais 88-89 KL 5
Mīrganj 138-139 K 4
Mirgorod 126-127 FG 1-2
Miri 148-149 F 6
Miriālguda 140 D 2
Miri Hills 141 CD 2
Mirim, Lagoa — 111 F 4
Mirimire 94-95 G 2
Miriñay, Esteros del — 106-107 J 2
Miriñay, Río — 106-107 J 2
Mirinzal 100-101 B 1-2
Miriti 92-93 H 6
Miriti, Cachoeira — 98-99 J 8
Miritiparaná, Río — 94-95 F 8
Mīrjāveh 134-135 J 5
Mirnyj [Antarctica] 53 C 10
Mirnyj [SU] 132-133 V 5
Mironovka 126-127 E 2
Mīrpūr Batoro 138-139 B 5
Mīrpūr Khāṣ 138-139 B 5
Mīrpūr Sākro 138-139 A 5
Mirror River 61 D 2
Mirslavl' 124-125 MN 5
Mirtağ 136-137 J 3
Miryang 144-145 G 5
Mirzaani 126-127 N 6
Mīrzāpur 134-135 N 5-6
Misāḥah, Bi'r — 164-165 K 4
Misaine Bank 63 G 5
Misaki 155 III d 1
Misān 136-137 M 6
Misantla 86-87 M 8
Misar 138-139 H 2
Misau [WAN, place] 168-169 H 3
Misau [WAN, river] 168-169 H 3
Miscouche 63 DE 4
Miscou Island 63 DE 4
Misgund 174-175 E 7
Mish'āb, Al- 134-135 F 5
Mishāb, Kūh-e — 136-137 L 3
Mishagomish, Lac — 62 NO 1
Mishagua, Río — 96-97 E 7
Mishan 142-143 P 2
Mishawaka, IN 70-71 GH 5
Mishawum Lake 84 I b 1
Mishbīḥ, Jabal — 164-165 L 4
Misheguk Mountain 58-59 G 2
Mi-shima 144-145 H 5
Mishomis 72-73 J 1
Mi Shui 146-147 D 8
Misima 148-149 h 7
Misión, La — 74-75 E 6
Misión del Divino Salvador 102-103 E 6
Misiones [PY] 102-103 D 7
Misiones [RA] 111 EF 3
Misiones, Sierra de — 102-103 EF 7
Misión Fagnano 108-109 F 10
Misión Franciscana Tacaaglé 104-105 G 9
Misión San Francisco de Guayo 94-95 L 3
Misis 136-137 F 4
Miskito, Cayos — 64-65 K 9
Miskito Cays = Cayos Miskitos 64-65 K 9
Miskolc 118 K 4
Miskyānah 166-167 K 2
Misli = Gölcük 136-137 F 3
Mismāḥ, Tall al — 136-137 G 6
Mismār 164-165 M 5
Mismīyah, Al- 136-137 G 6
Misoa 94-95 F 2
Misol = Pulau Misoöl 148-149 K 7
Misoöl, Pulau — 148-149 K 7
Misore = Mysore 134-135 M 8
Mişr, Al- 164-165 KL 3
Mişr al-Qadīmah, Al-Qāhirah- 170 II b 1
Misrātah 164-165 H 2
Mişr-Baḥrī 173 BC 2
Mişr el-Gedîda = Al-Qāhirah-Mişr al-Jadīdah 173 BC 2
Misınç 136-137 J 4
Misrikh 138-139 H 4
Missale 171 C 6
Missanabie 70-71 HJ 1
Missão 100-101 C 7
Missão Velha 100-101 E 4
Missinaibi Lake 70-71 J 1
Missinaibi River 56-57 U 7
Mission, SD 68-69 F 4
Mission, TX 76-77 E 9
Mission, San Francisco-, CA 83 I b 2
Mission City 66-67 B 1
Mission Dolores 83 I b 2
Mission San Gabriel Arcangel 83 III d 1
Missippinewa Lake 70-71 GH 5
Missisicabi, Rivière — 62 M 1
Mississauga 72-73 G 3
Mississippi 64-65 J 5
Mississippi River 64-65 H 3
Mississippi River Bridge 85 I b 2
Mississippi River Delta 64-65 J 6
Mississippi Sound 78-79 E 5
Missões, Serra das — 100-101 D 4
Missolonghi = Mesolóngion 122-123 J 6
Missoula, MT 64-65 D 2
Missouri 64-65 H 3-4
Missouri City, TX 85 III a 2
Missouri River 64-65 G 3
Missouri Valley, IA 70-71 BC 5
Missūr 166-167 DE 3
Mistassibi, Rivière — 62 P 2
Mistassini 62 PQ 2
Mistassini, Lake — 56-57 W 7
Mistassini, Lac — 62 P 1
Mistassini, Rivière — 62 P 2
Mistassini Post 62 OP 1
Mistelbach 118 H 4
Misti 96-97 F 10
Misumi 144-145 H 6
Misuráṭa = Misrātah 164-165 H 2
Mita, Punta de — 64-65 E 7
Mitai 144-145 H 6
Mitaka 155 III a 1
Mitare [CO] 94-95 F 6
Mitare [YV] 94-95 F 2
Mitcham, London- 129 II b 2
Mitchell, IN 70-71 G 6
Mitchell, NE 68-69 E 5
Mitchell, OR 66-67 CD 3
Mitchell, SD 64-65 G 3
Mitchell [AUS] 158-159 J 5
Mitchell [CDN] 72-73 F 3
Mitchell, Mount — 64-65 K 4
Mitchell Lake 78-79 F 4
Mitchell River [AUS, place] 158-159 H 3
Mitchell River [AUS, river] 158-159 H 3
Mitchinamecus, Lac — 72-73 J 1
Miteja 171 D 5
Miṭhankoṭ 138-139 BC 3
Miṭhī 138-139 B 5
Mithra 138-139 C 3
Mithrāu 134-135 KL 5
Miṭhūyah, Al- 166-167 LM 3
Mitidja = Mitīja 166-167 H 1
Mitīja 166-167 H 1
Mitilini = Mytilēnē 122-123 M 6
Mitino [SU, Moskovskaja Oblast'] 113 V a 2
Mi'tiq, Gebel — = Jabal Mu'tiq 173 C 4
Mitishto River 61 HJ 3
Mit Jamr 173 B 2
Mitla 86-87 M 9
Mitlā, Wādī al- 166-167 K 2
Mitlawī, Al- 164-165 F 2
Mitliktavik, AK 58-59 G 1
Mito 142-143 R 4
Mitowa 171 D 5
Mitra, Monte de la — 168-169 H 5
Mitre 158-159 O 2
Mitre, Peninsula — 111 CD 8
Mitrofania Island 58-59 d 2
Mitrofanovka 126-127 JK 2
Mitry-le-Neuf 129 I d 2
Mitry-Mory 129 I d 2
Mitsinjo 172 J 5
Mitsio, Nosy — 172 J 4
Mitšiwa 164-165 MN 5
Mitsuke 144-145 M 4
Mitsumata 144-145 c 2
Mitsushima 144-145 G 5
Mitta, Oued el — = Wādī al-Mitlā 166-167 K 2
Mittelberg [CH] 128 IV b 2
Mittellandkanal 118 CD 2
Mittersendling 130 II b 2
Mitū 92-93 EF 4
Mitumba, Chaîne des — 172 E 3-4
Mitumba, Monts — 172 E 2
Miṭūyah, Al- 166-167 LM 3
Mitwaba 172 E 3
Mityana 171 BC 2
Mitzic 172 B 1
Mitzusawa 142-143 QR 4
Mixcoac, Presa de — 91 I b 2
Mixcoac, Villa Obregón- 91 I b 2
Mi Xian 146-147 D 4
Miyagi 144-145 N 3
Miyāh, Wādī — 164-165 EF 2
Miyāh, Wadī al- 173 C 5
Miyāh, Wādī al- = Wādī Jarīr 134-135 E 5-6
Miya kawa 144-145 L 5
Miyake-jima 142-143 QR 5
Miyake zima = Miyake-jima 142-143 QR 5
Miyako 144-145 N 3
Miyako-jima 142-143 O 7
Miyakonojō 142-143 P 5
Miyakonozyō = Miyakonojō 142-143 P 5
Miyako wan 144-145 NO 3
Miyako zima = Miyako-jima 142-143 O 7
Mīyāneh = Meyāneh 134-135 F 3
Miyanoura = Kamiyaku 144-145 H 7
Miyānwālī 134-135 L 4
Miyazaki 142-143 P 5
Miyazu 144-145 K 5
Miyet, Baḥr el- = Baḥr al-Mayyit 134-135 D 4
Miyoshi 144-145 J 5
Mizā, Wādī — 166-167 J 3
Mizāb, Al- 166-167 J 3
Mizar 136-137 H 4
Mizdah 164-165 G 2
Mizen Head 119 AB 6
Mizgīṭim 166-167 E 2
Mizhi 146-147 C 3
Mizil 122-123 M 3
Mizoč 126-127 BC 1
Mizo Hills 141 C 4
Mizonokuchi, Kawasaki- 155 III a 2
Mizoram 134-135 P 6
Mizpah, MN 70-71 CD 2
Mizpah, MT 68-69 D 2
Mizque 92-93 FG 8
Mizque, Rio — 104-105 D 6
Mizue, Tōkyō- 155 III c 1
Mizur = Buron 126-127 M 5
Mizusawa 142-143 QR 4
Mjanyana 174-175 GH 6
Mja'ra, el- = Al-M'jarah 166-167 D 2
M'jārah, Al- 166-167 D 2
M'jaz al-Bāb 166-167 L 1
Mjölby 116-117 F 8
Mjøsa 116-117 D 7
Mkambati 174-175 HJ 6
Mkam-Sidi-Cheikh = Maqām Sīdī Shaykh 166-167 G 2
Mkata 171 D 4
Mkhili = Al-Makīlī 164-165 J 2
Mkobela 171 D 5
Mkokotoni 171 D 4
Mkondo 174-175 J 4
Mkondoa 171 D 4
Mkonga 171 CD 4
Mkulwe 171 C 5
Mkuranga 171 D 4
Mkushi 171 B 6
Mkusi = Mkuze 174-175 K 4
Mkuze [ZA, place] 174-175 JK 4
Mkuze [ZA, river] 174-175 K 4
Mkuze Game Reserve 174-175 K 4
Mkuzi = Mkuze 174-175 JK 4
Mladá Boleslav 118 G 3
Mladenovac 122-123 J 3
Mlangali 171 C 5
Mława 118 K 2
Mlayḥān, Bi'r — 136-137 H 4
Mlcusi Bay = Kosibaai 174-175 K 4
Mligazi 171 D 4
Mljet 122-123 G 4
Mmabatho 172 DE 7
Mnevniki, Moskva- 113 V b 2
Moa [C] 88-89 J 4
Moa [WAL] 168-169 C 4
Moa, Pulau — 148-149 J 8
Moa, Rio — 96-97 E 5
Moab, UT 74-75 J 3
Mōāb, Jabal — 136-137 F 7
Moaco, Rio — 96-97 G 6
Moak Lake 61 K 2-3
Moala 148-149 a 2
Moamba 172 F 7
Moapa, NV 74-75 F 4
Moba [WAN] 170 III b 2
Moba [ZRE] 172 E 3
Mobaye 164-165 J 8
Mobeetie, TX 76-77 D 5
Moberly, MO 64-65 H 4
Moberly Lake 60 FG 2
Mobert 70-71 H 1
Mobile, AL 64-65 J 5
Mobile Bay 64-65 J 5
Mobridge, SD 68-69 FG 3
Mobutu-Sese-Seko, Lac — 172 F 1
Moca = Al-Mukhā 134-135 E 8
Mocache 96-97 B 2
Mocajuba 92-93 K 5
Močališče 124-125 R 5
Moçambique [Mozambique, place] 172 H 4-5
Moçambique [Mozambique, state] 172 F 6-G 4
Moçambique, Canal de — 172 H 6-4
Moçâmedes 172 B 5
Mo Cay 150-151 F 7-8
Mocaya, Río — 94-95 E 7
Moccasin, MT 68-69 AB 2
Môc Châu 150-151 E 2
Mocha = Al-Mukhā 134-135 E 8
Mocha, Isla — 111 B 5
Mochara, Cordillera de — 104-105 D 7
Moche 96-97 B 6
Mochis, Los — 64-65 E 6
Môc Hoa 150-151 EF 7
Môch Sar'dag uul 142-143 HJ 1
Mochudi 172 E 6
Mocidade, Serra da — 98-99 GH 4
Mocidade, Sierra da — 94-95 KL 7
Mocímboa da Praia 172 GH 4
Mocksville, NC 80-81 F 3
Moclips, WA 66-67 A 2
Mocó, Rio — 98-99 E 6
Mocoa 92-93 D 4
Mococa 102-103 J 4
Mocoduene 174-175 L 2
Moções, Rio — 98-99 O 5
Mocoretá 106-107 HJ 3
Moçoró 92-93 M 6
Mocovi 106-107 H 2
Moctezuma 86-87 F 3
Moctezuma, Río — 86-87 F 2-3
Mocuba 172 G 5
Modane 120-121 L 6
Modāsa 138-139 D 6
Modderfontein [ZA, place] 170 V b 1
Modderfontein [ZA, river] 170 V b 1
Modderpoort 174-175 G 5
Modderrivier [ZA, place] 174-175 F 5
Modderrivier [ZA, river] 174-175 F 5
Moddi 168-169 F 2
Model, CO 68-69 DE 7
Modelia, Bogotá 91 III b 2
Mòdena 122-123 D 3
Modena, UT 74-75 FG 4
Modestino Pizarro 106-107 E 5
Modesto, CA 64-65 BC 4
Modhera 138-139 D 6
Mòdica 122-123 F 7
Modjamboli 172 D 1
Mödling [A, river] 113 I b 2
Modoc Lava Bed 66-67 C 5
Modriča 122-123 H 3
Mô Đu'c 150-151 G 5
Modur dağı 136-137 L 4
Moeda 102-103 K 4
Moeda, Serra da — 102-103 KL 4
Moedig 174-175 J 3
Moei, Mae Nam — 150-151 B 4
Moengo 92-93 J 3
Möen Island = Møn 116-117 E 10
Moenkopi Wash 74-75 H 4
Moe-Yallourn 158-159 J 7
Moffat, CO 68-69 D 6-7
Moffen 116-117 j 4
Moffett, Mount — 58-59 u 6-7
Moffit, ND 68-69 F 2
Mofolo, Johannesburg- 170 V a 2
Moga 138-139 E 2
Mogadiscio = Muqdiisho 164-165 O 8
Mogadishu = Muqdiisho 164-165 O 8
Mogador = Aş-Şawīrah 164-165 BC 2
Mogalakwenarivier 172 E 6
Mogami gawa 144-145 MN 3
Mōgaung [BUR, place] 141 E 3
Mōgaung [BUR, river] 141 E 3
Mogdy 132-133 Z 7
Mogees, PA 84 III b 1
Mogeiro 100-101 G 4
Moggar = Al-Muqqār 166-167 K 3
Moghān, Dasht-e — 134-135 F 3
Moghrane = Al-Mughrān 166-167 C 2
Moghrar = Mughrār 166-167 F 3
Mogila Bel'mak, gora — 126-127 H 3
Mogilev = Mogil'ov 124-125 GH 7
Mogil'ov 124-125 GH 7
Mogil'ov-Lupolovo 124-125 H 7
Mogil'ov-Podol'skij 126-127 CD 2
Mogincual 172 H 5
Mogna, Sierra de — 106-107 C 3
Mogoča [SU, place] 132-133 WX 7
Mogočin 132-133 P 6
Mogod = Muq'ud 166-167 L 1
Mōgōk 141 E 4
Mogol 174-175 G 2
Mogollon Mountains 74-75 J 6
Mogollon Rim 74-75 H 5
Mogororo = Mongororo 164-165 J 6
Mogotes, Cerro de los — 106-107 C 2
Mogotes, Punta — 106-107 J 7
Mogotes, Sierra de — 106-107 E 2
Mogotón, Cerro — 88-89 C 8
Moguer 120-121 D 10
Mogyichaung = Mangyichaung 141 C 5
Mogzon 132-133 V 7
Mohács 118 J 6
Mohājerān 136-137 N 5
Mohaka River 161 G 4
Mohaleshoek 174-175 G 6
Mohall, ND 68-69 F 1
Mohammadabad = Muhammadābād [IND ↓ Gorakhpoor] 138-139 J 4
Mohammadabad = Muhammadābād [IND ↗ Vārānasī] 138-139 J 5
Mohammadia = Muḥammadīyah 164-165 DE 1
Mohammed, Ras — = Râ's Muḥammad 164-165 LM 4
Moḥammedia = Al-Muḥammadīyah 166-167 C 3
Moḥammerah = Khorramshar 134-135 F 4
Mohana 138-139 K 8
Mohanganj 141 B 3
Mohania 138-139 J 5
Mohaniyā = Mohania 138-139 J 5
Mohanlālganj 138-139 H 4
Mohawk, AZ 74-75 G 6
Mohawk, MI 70-71 FG 2
Mohawk River 72-73 J 3
Mohe 142-143 N 1
Mohéli = Mwali 172 H 4
Mohenjodaro = Mūan-jo Daṛo 138-139 AB 4
Mohican, Cape — 56-57 C 5

328 Mihajlov

Mohilla = Mwali 172 H 4
Mohindergarh = Mahendragarh 138-139 EF 3
Mohine 174-175 K 3
Mohn, Kapp — 116-117 m 5
Moho 96-97 G 9
Mo-ho = Mohe 142-143 N 1
Mohol 140 B 2
Mohon Peak 74-75 G 5
Mohoro 172 G 3
Mō Ingyī 141 E 7
Mointy 132-133 N 8
Mo i Rana 116-117 F 4
Moira River 72-73 H 2
Mõisaküla 124-125 E 4
Moisés Ville 106-107 G 3
Moisie 63 CD 2
Moisie, Baie — 63 D 2
Moisie, Rivière — 56-57 X 7
Moissac 120-121 H 6
Moïssala 164-165 H 7
Moitaco 94-95 J 4
Mojave, CA 74-75 DE 5
Mojave Desert 64-65 C 4
Mojave River 74-75 E 5
Moji das Cruzes 92-93 KL 9
Mojiguaçu 102-103 J 5
Mojiguaçu, Rio — 102-103 HJ 4
Mojimirim 102-103 J 5
Mojiquiçaba 100-101 E 9
Mojjero 132-133 T 4
Mojo, Pulau — 148-149 G 8
Mojocaya 104-105 D 6
Mojokerto 148-149 F 8
Mojón, Cerro del — 106-107 CD 5
Mojotoro 104-105 D 6
Moju 98-99 L 6
Mŏka 144-145 MN 4
Mokai 158-159 P 7
Mŏkakchāng = Mokokchūng 141 D 2
Mokambo 172 E 4
Mokameh 138-139 K 5
Mokane, MO 70-71 DE 6
Mokatani 174-175 F 2
Mokau River 161 F 4
Mokeetsi = Mooketsi 174-175 J 2
Mokelumne Aqueduct River 74-75 C 3-4
Mokhāda 138-139 D 8
Mokhara = Mokhāda 138-139 D 8
Mokhotlong 174-175 H 5
Mokhrīşşêt = Mukhrişşat 166-167 D 2
Mokil 208 F 2
Moknīn, El — = Al-Muknīn 166-167 M 2
Mokochu, Khao — 150-151 B 5
Mokokchūng 141 D 2
Mokolo 164-165 G 6
Mŏkpalin 141 E 7
Mokp'o 142-143 O 5
Mokraja Ol'chovka 126-127 M 1
Mokrān 134-135 HJ 5
Mokrissêt = Mukhrişşat 166-167 D 2
Mokrous 124-125 Q 8
Mokša 124-125 P 7
Mokšan 124-125 P 7
Mŏktama 148-149 C 3
Mŏktama Kwe 148-149 C 3
Moktok-to = Kyŏngnyŏlbi-yŏlto 144-145 E 4
Mola di Bari 122-123 G 5
Mōļakālamuruvu = Hānagal 140 C 3
Molalla, OR 66-67 B 3
Molango 86-87 L 7
Molanosa 61 F 3
Molat 122-123 F 3
Moldary 132-133 O 7
Moldavia 122-123 M 2-3
Moldavian Soviet Socialist Republic 126-127 CD 3
Moldavskaja Sovetskaja Socialističeskaja Respublika = Moldavian Soviet Socialist Republic 126-127 CD 3
Molde 116-117 B 6
Moldes = Coronel Moldes 106-107 E 4
Moldova 122-123 M 2
Moldoviţa 122-123 L 2
Mole Creek 160 bc 2
Molenbeek 128 II a 1
Molepolole 172 DE 6
Molfetta 122-123 G 5
Molière = Burj Bū Na'amah 166-167 G 2
Molina 106-107 B 5
Molina de Segura 120-121 G 9
Moline, IL 64-65 HJ 3
Moline, KS 76-77 F 4
Molinito, El — 91 I b 2
Molino, FL 78-79 F 5
Molino, El — 91 III c 2
Molino do Rosas, Villa Obregón- 91 I b 2
Molinos 104-105 C 9
Moliro 172 EF 3
Molise 122-123 F 5
Mollāhāt 138-139 M 6
Mollakendi 136-137 H 3
Mollālar 136-137 M 4
Mollem 128 II a 1
Mol Len 141 D 3
Mollendo 92-93 E 8
Mollera, zaliv — 132-133 HJ 3
Molles 106-107 J 4
Molles, Los — 106-107 BC 5
Molles, Punta — 106-107 B 4
Mölndal 116-117 DE 9
Moločansk 126-127 GH 3
Moločnoje 124-125 M 4
Moločnoje, ozero — 126-127 G 3
Molócue 172 G 5
Molodečno 124-125 F 6
Molodežnaja 53 C 5
Molodogvardejcev 132-133 N 7
Molodoj Tud 124-125 JK 5
Mologa 124-125 L 5
Molokai 148-149 e 3
Molokovo 124-125 L 4
Moloma 124-125 R 4
Molong 158-159 J 6
Molopo 172 D 7
Molotovsk = Nolinsk 132-133 HJ 6
Molotovsk = Severodvinsk 132-133 FG 5
Moloundou 164-165 H 8
Molsgat 174-175 H 3
Molson 61 K 5
Molson Lake 61 K 3
Molt, MT 68-69 B 3
Molteno [ZA] 174-175 G 6
Molu, Pulau — 148-149 K 8
Moluccas 148-149 J 6-7
Molucca Sea 148-149 HJ 7
Molundu = Moloundou 164-165 H 8
Molvotícy 124-125 HJ 5
Moma [Mozambique] 172 G 5
Moma [SU] 132-133 bc 4
Momba 171 C 5
Mombaça 100-101 E 3
Mombasa 172 GH 2
Mombetsu 142-143 R 3
Mombongo 172 D 1
Momboyo 172 C 2
Mombuca, Serra da — 102-103 FG 3
Momčilgrad 122-123 L 5
Mŏmeik 141 E 4
Momence, IL 70-71 G 5
Mōminābād = Ambājogāi 134-135 M 7
Mompós 94-95 D 3
Momskij chrebet 132-133 b 4-c 5
Møn 116-117 E 10
Mona 64-65 N 8
Mona, UT 74-75 GH 3
Mona, Canal de la — 64-65 N 8
Móna, Punta — 88-89 E 10
Monaco [MC, place] 120-121 L 7
Monaco [MC, state] 120-121 L 7
Monagas 94-95 K 3
Monaghan 119 C 4
Monahans, TX 64-65 F 5
Monango, ND 68-69 G 2
Monapo 172 H 4-5
Monarāgala 140 E 7
Monarch, MT 66-67 H 2
Monarch Mount 60 E 4
Monashee Mountains 56-57 N 7
Monas National Monument 154 IV ab 2
Monasterio 106-107 J 5
Monasterio, El — 94-95 H 3
Monastir = Bitola 122-123 J 5
Monastir, El — = Al-Manastir 166-167 M 2
Monastyrščina 124-125 HJ 6
Monay 94-95 F 3
Monbetsu 144-145 bc 2
Monča Guba = Mončegorsk 132-133 DE 4
Monção [BR] 92-93 K 5
Mončegorsk 132-133 DE 4
Mönchaltorf 128 IV b 2
Mŏn Chaung 141 D 5
Mönchchaan 142-143 L 2
Mönch Chajrchan uul 142-143 FG 2
Mönchengladbach 118 BC 3
Monchique, Serra de — 120-121 C 10
Moncks Corner, SC 80-81 FG 4
Monclova 64-65 F 6
Moncton 56-57 XY 8
Mond, Rūd-e — 134-135 G 5
Mondaí 102-103 F 7
Mondamin, IA 70-71 BC 5
Monday, Río — 102-103 E 6
Mondego 120-121 CD 8
Mondego, Cabo — 120-121 C 8
Mondeodo 152-153 OP 7
Mondeor, Johannesburg- 170 V ab 2
Mondo 171 CD 4
Mondoliko, Pulau — 152-153 J 9
Mondoñedo 120-121 D 7
Mondovi 122-123 BC 3
Mondovi, WI 70-71 E 3
Mondragon 120-121 K 6
Monds Island 84 III b 2
Mondulkiri 150-151 F 6
Monē 141 EF 5
Monē Dafníon 113 IV a 1
Monē Kaisarian 113 IV b 2
Monē Lávras 122-123 L 5
Monembasia 122-123 K 7
Moneron, ostrov — 132-133 b 8
Mones Cazón 106-107 FG 6
Monessen, PA 72-73 G 4
Monet 62 O 2
Moneta, VA 80-81 G 2
Moneta, WY 68-69 C 4
Monett, MO 78-79 C 2
Monfalcone 122-123 E 3
Monfort 94-95 G 7
Monforte de Lemos 120-121 D 7
Monga [EAT] 171 D 5
Monga [ZRE] 172 D 1
Mongala 172 CD 1
Mongalla = Manqalah 164-165 L 7
Möngban 141 F 5
Möngbūn 141 E 5
Mongbwalu 171 B 2
Möngbyat 148-149 CD 2
Mong Cai 150-151 FG 2
Möngdôn 148-149 C 2
Monger, Lake — 158-159 C 5
Mönggan 150-151 C 2
Mönggôk 141 F 5
Mönggöng 141 E 5
Monggŭmp'o-ri 144-145 E 3
Mong Hkok = Mönggôk 141 F 5
Mong Hsat = Möngzat 141 F 5
Mong Hsu = Möngshū 141 F 5
Monghyr 134-135 O 5
Mongkol Borey, Stung — 150-151 D 6
Möng Kung = Monggöng 141 E 5
Möngman 141 F 4
Möng Nai = Mônē 141 EF 5
Möngnaung 141 EF 5
Möng Nawng = Möngnaung 141 EF 5
Möngnôn 141 F 5
Mongo [Chad] 164-165 H 6
Mongol Altajn Nuruu 142-143 F-H 2
Mongolia 142-143 H-L 2
Mongororo 164-165 J 6
Möng Pan = Möngban 141 F 5
Möng Pawn = Möngbûn 141 E 5
Möngshū 141 F 5
Möng Si = Möngzī 141 F 4
Möng Tun = Möngdôn 148-149 C 2
Mongu 172 D 5
Monguba 100-101 E 2
Möngwi 141 E 4
Möng Yai = Möngyei 141 F 4
Möngyan 150-151 B 2
Möngyaung 141 F 5
Möng Yawn = Möngyaung 141 F 5
Möngyei 141 F 4
Möngyu 150-151 C 2
Möngzat 141 F 5
Möngzī 141 F 4
Mo Nhai 150-151 F 2
Monhegan Island 72-73 M 3
Monico, WI 70-71 F 3
Monida Pass 66-67 GH 3
Monilla = Mwali 172 H 4
Monino 124-125 M 6
Moniquirá 94-95 E 5
Monitor 61 C 5
Monitor Range 74-75 E 3
Monkoto 172 D 2
Monmouth, IL 70-71 E 5
Monmouth, OR 66-67 B 3
Mônnaung 141 F 4
Mono 164-165 E 7
Mono, Punta del — 88-89 E 9
Monod = Sīdī 'Allāl al-Bahrāwī 166-167 CD 2
Mono Island 148-149 j 6
Mono Lake 64-65 C 4
Monomoy Point 72-73 M 4
Monon, IN 70-71 G 5
Monòpoli 122-123 G 5
Monor 118 J 5
Mŏnqalla = Manqalah 164-165 L 7
Monreale 122-123 E 6
Monroe 63 K 3
Monroe, GA 80-81 DE 4
Monroe, LA 64-65 H 5
Monroe, MI 72-73 E 3-4
Monroe, NC 80-81 F 3
Monroe, OR 66-67 B 3
Monroe, UT 74-75 GH 3
Monroe, VA 80-81 G 2
Monroe, WA 66-67 C 2
Monroe, WI 70-71 F 4
Monroe City, MO 70-71 DE 6
Monroeville, AL 78-79 F 5
Monroeville, IN 70-71 H 5
Monrovia 164-165 B 7
Mons 120-121 J 3
Monsalvo 106-107 J 6
Monsefú 96-97 AB 5
Monsélice 122-123 DE 3
Monsenhor Gil 100-101 C 3
Monsenhor Hipólito 100-101 D 4
Monsenhor Tabosa 100-101 DE 3
MOnserrate 91 III c 3
Monserrate, Isla — 86-87 E 5
Mönsterås 116-117 FG 9
Montagnac = Ramshi 166-167 F 2
Montagnana 122-123 D 3
Montagne Pelée 64-65 O 8
Montagnes, Lac des — 62 O 1
Montagnes de la Trinité 98-99 M 2
Montagne Tremblante, Parc provincial de la — 56-57 VW 8
Montagu 174-175 D 7
Montague, CA 66-67 B 5
Montague, MI 70-71 G 4
Montague, TX 76-77 EF 6
Montague Island 56-57 G 6
Montague Strait 58-59 N 7-M 6
Montain View, WY 66-67 HJ 5
Mont Ami 171 B 2
Montana 64-65 DE 2
Montana, AK 58-59 MN 5
Montaña, La — [E] 120-121 DE 7
Montaña, La — [PE] 92-93 E 5-6
Montañas de Convento 96-97 B 1-2
Montañas de Huapí 88-89 D 8
Montañas de Onzole 96-97 B 1
Montanha 100-101 D 10
Montañita, La — [CO] 94-95 D 7
Montañita, La — [YV] 94-95 F 2
Montargis 120-121 J 5
Montauban 120-121 H 6
Montauk, NY 72-73 L 4
Montauk Point 72-73 L 4
Mont aux Sources 172 E 7
Montbard 120-121 K 5
Montbéliard 120-121 L 5
Mont Blanc 120-121 L 6
Montbrison 120-121 K 6
Mont Cameroun 164-165 F 8
Mont Canigou 120-121 J 7
Montceau-les-Mines 120-121 K 5
Mont Cenis, Col du — 120-121 L 6
Montcevelles, Lac — 63 FG 2
Mont Cinto 122-123 C 4
Montclair, NJ 82 III a 2
Mont-de-Marsan 120-121 GH 7
Mont Dore 120-121 J 6
Monte, El — 104-105 D 7
Monte, Laguna de — 106-107 F 6
Monte, Laguna del — 106-107 H 5
Monte Adam = Mount Adam 111 DE 8
Monteagudo [BOL] 104-105 E 6
Monteagudo [RA] 111 F 3
Monte Águila 106-107 A 6
Monte Albán 64-65 G 8
Monte Alegre [BR, Pará] 92-93 J 5
Monte Alegre [BR, Rio Grande do Norte] 100-101 G 4
Monte Alegre de Goiás 100-101 A 7
Monte Alegre de Minas 102-103 H 3
Monte Alegro de Piauí 100-101 B 5
Monte Alegro 106-107 LM 2
Monte Alto [BR] 102-103 H 4
Monte Alto, Serra de — 100-101 C 8
Monte Amiata 122-123 D 4
Monte Antenne 113 II b 1
Monte Aprazível 102-103 GH 4
Monte Aymond 108-109 E 9
Monte Azul 92-93 L 8
Monte Azul Paulista 102-103 H 4
Montebello 72-73 J 2
Montebello, CA 83 III d 1
Montebello Islands 158-159 BC 4
Monte Belo 102-103 J 4
Montebu = Mombetsu 142-143 R 3
Monte Buey 106-107 F 4
Monte Burney 108-109 C 9
Monte Cabra 64-65 b 3
Montecarlo 102-103 E 7
Monte Carmelo 102-103 J 3
Monte Caseros 111 E 4
Monte Catedral 108-109 BC 6
Montecatini Terme 122-123 D 4
Monte Cervati 122-123 F 5
Monte Chingolo, Lanús- 110 III bc 2
Monte Cimone 122-123 D 3
Monte Circeo 122-123 E 5
Monte Comán 111 C 4
Montecoral 106-107 JK 4
Monte Creek 60 GH 4
Montecristi 96-97 A 2
Montecristo [I] 122-123 D 4
Monte Cristo [RA] 106-107 EF 3
Monte da Divisa 102-103 J 4
Monte das Araras 102-103 J 4
Monte de la Mitra 168-169 H 5
Monte de los Gauchos 106-107 F 4
Monte do Frado 102-103 K 5
Monte Etna 122-123 F 7
Monte Falterona 122-123 DE 4
Montefiascone 122-123 DE 4
Monte Fitz Roy 111 B 7
Montego Bay 64-65 L 8
Monte Grande 106-107 B 3
Monte Grande, Esteban Echeverría- 110 III b 2
Montegut, LA 78-79 D 6
Monte Hermaso 106-107 G 7
Monteiro 100-101 F 4
Monte Jervis 108-109 B 7
Montejinni 158-159 F 3
Monte Ladrillero 108-109 CD 9
Montelibano 94-95 D 3
Montélimar 120-121 K 6
Monte Lindo, Río — 102-103 CD 5
Monte Lindo Chico, Riacho — 104-105 G 9
Monte Lindo Grande, Río — 104-105 G 9
Monte Lirio 64-65 b 2
Montell, TX 76-77 D 8
Montello, NV 66-67 F 5
Montello, WI 70-71 F 4
Monte Macá 111 B 7
Monte Maíz 106-107 F 4
Monte María = Mount Maria 108-109 K 8
Monte Mario 113 II b 1
Montemayor, Meseta de — 111 C 6-7
Monte Melimoyu 111 B 6
Monte Mentolat 108-109 C 5
Montemorelos 64-65 G 6
Montenegro [BR] 106-107 M 2
Montenegro [CO] 94-95 CD 5
Montenegro [YU] 122-123 H 4
Monte Nievas 106-107 EF 5
Montenotte-au-Tênès = Sīdī 'Ukāskah 166-167 G 1
Monte Nuestra Señora 108-109 B 7
Monte Pascoal 100-101 E 9
Monte Pascoal, Parque National de — 100-101 E 9
Monte Pecoraro 122-123 FG 6
Monte Perdido 120-121 GH 7
Monte Pinón 64-65 b 2
Monte Pissis 106-107 C 1
Monte Plata 88-89 LM 5
Montepuez [Mozambique, place] 172 GH 4
Montepuez [Mozambique, river] 171 D 6
Montepulciano 122-123 D 4
Monte Quemado 111 D 3
Monte Rasu 122-123 C 5
Monterey, CA 64-65 B 4
Monterey, TN 78-79 G 2
Monterey, VA 72-73 G 5
Monterey Bay 64-65 B 4
Monterey Park, CA 83 III d 1
Montería 92-93 D 3
Montero 92-93 G 8
Monteros 104-105 D 10
Monte Rosa 122-123 BC 2-3
Monterrey [MEX] 64-65 FG 6
Montes, Punta — 108-109 E 8
Monte Saavedra 106-107 G 3
Monte Sacro, Roma- 113 II b 1
Montes Altos 100-101 A 3
Montesano, WA 66-67 B 2
Monte Sant'Angelo 122-123 FG 5
Monte Santo 92-93 M 7
Monte Santo de Minas 102-103 J 4
Monte Sarmiento 108-109 D 10
Montes Claros 92-93 KL 8
Montes de Leon 120-121 D 7
Montes de Oca 106-107 F 7
Montes de Toledo 120-121 E 9
Monte Sião 102-103 J 5
Montespaccato, Roma- 113 II a 2
Montesquieu = Madawrūsh 166-167 K 1
Monte Stokes 108-109 C 8
Monte Torres 111 D 4
Monte Tres Conos 108-109 D 9
Monte Tronador 111 B 6
Monte Vera 106-107 G 3
Montevideo 111 EF 4-5
Montevideo, MN 70-71 BC 3
Montevideo-Santiago Vázquez 106-107 J 5
Montevideo-Villa del Cerro 106-107 J 5
Montevidiu 102-103 G 2
Monte Viso 122-123 B 3
Monte Vista, CO 68-69 C 7
Monte Volturino 122-123 FG 5
Monte Vúlture 122-123 F 5
Monte Warton 108-109 C 9
Monte Yate 108-109 C 3
Monte Zeballos 108-109 D 6
Montezuma 102-103 L 1
Montezuma, GA 80-81 DE 4
Montezuma, IA 70-71 D 5
Montezuma, IN 70-71 G 6
Montezuma, KS 68-69 F 7
Montezuma Castle National Monument 74-75 H 5
Montfermeil 129 I d 2
Mont Forel 56-57 d 4
Montfort 120-121 FG 4
Montfort, WI 70-71 E 4
Montgeron 129 I c 3
Montgolfier = Raḥūyah 166-167 G 2
Montgomery, AL 64-65 J 5
Montgomery, LA 78-79 C 5
Montgomery, MN 70-71 D 3
Montgomery, WV 72-73 F 5
Montgomery = Sāhīwāl 134-135 L 4
Montgomery City, MO 70-71 E 6
Montgomery Pass 74-75 D 3
Mont Greboun 164-165 F 4-5
Monticello, AR 78-79 D 4
Monticello, FL 80-81 E 5
Monticello, GA 80-81 E 4
Monticello, IA 70-71 E 4
Monticello, IL 70-71 F 5
Monticello, IN 70-71 G 5
Monticello, KY 78-79 G 2
Monticello, MS 78-79 DE 5
Monticello, NM 76-77 A 6
Monticello, NY 72-73 J 4
Monticello, UT 64-65 DE 4
Monticello Reservoir = Lake Berryessa 74-75 B 3
Monti del Gennargentu 122-123 C 5-6
Montiel, Cuchilla de — 106-107 H 3
Montiel, Selva de — 106-107 H 3
Montigny-le-Bretonneux 129 I b 2
Montijo 120-121 D 9
Montijo, Golfo de — 88-89 F 11
Montilla 120-121 E 10
Monti Nebrodie 122-123 F 7
Monti Peloritani 122-123 F 6-7
Monti Sabini 122-123 E 4
Mont-Joli 63 B 3
Mont Karisimbi 172 E 2
Mont-Laurier 56-57 V 8
Montluçon 120-121 J 5
Montmagny [CDN] 63 AB 4
Montmagny [F] 129 I c 2
Montmartre 61 G 5
Montmartre, Paris- 129 I c 2
Mont Mézenc 120-121 JK 6
Mont Michelson 56-57 GH 4
Montmorency [CDN] 63 A 4
Montmorillon 120-121 H 5
Mont Nimba 164-165 C 7
Monto 158-159 K 4
Mont Opémisca 62 O 1-2
Montoro 120-121 E 9
Mont Oué 168-169 HJ 4
Montoya, NM 76-77 B 5
Montparnasse, Paris- 129 I c 2
Montpelier, ID 66-67 H 4
Montpelier, OH 70-71 H 5
Montpelier, VT 64-65 M 3
Montpellier 120-121 JK 7
Mont Perry 158-159 K 5
Montréal [CDN] 56-57 VW 8
Montréal, Île de — 82 I a 2-b 1
Montréal, Université de — 82 I b 1
Montréal-Ahuntsic 82 I b 1
Montréal-Bordeaux 82 I ab 1
Montréal-Cartierville 82 I a 1
Montréal-Côte-Visitation 82 I b 1
Montréal International Airport 82 I a 2
Montreal Island 70-71 H 2
Montreal Lake [CDN, lake] 61 F 3
Montreal Lake [CDN, place] 61 F 3
Montréal-Nord 82 I b 1
Montréal-Notre-Dame-des-Victoires 82 I b 1
Montréal-Ouest 82 I ab 2
Montreal River [CDN ◁ Lake Superior] 70-71 HJ 2
Montreal River [CDN ◁ North Saskatchewan River] 61 F 3
Montreal River [CDN ◁ Ottawa River] 72-73 FG 1
Montreal River Harbour 70-71 H 2
Montréal-Saint-Michel 82 I b 1
Montréal-Sault-au-Recollet 82 I b 1
Montréal-Tétreauville 82 I b 1
Montréal-Youville 82 I ab 1
Montreuil [F → Berck] 120-121 H 3
Montreuil [F → Paris] 120-121 J 4
Montreux 118 C 5
Montrose 119 EF 3
Montrose, AR 78-79 D 4
Montrose, CO 64-65 E 4
Montrose, PA 72-73 J 4
Montrose Harbor 83 II b 1
Montross, VA 72-73 H 5
Mont Rotondo 122-123 C 4
Montrouge-Gentilly 129 I c 2
Mont Royal [CDN, mountain] 82 I b 1
Mont-Royal [CDN, place] 82 I ab 1
Mont Royal, Parc du — 82 I b 1
Mont Royal Tunnel 82 I b 1
Mont-Saint-Michel, le — 120-121 FG 4
Mont-Saint-Pont 128 II b 2
Monts Baguezane 164-165 F 5
Monts Chic-Choqs 56-57 X 8
Monts de Daïa = Jabal aḍ-Ḍāyah 166-167 F 2
Monts de Droupolé 168-169 CD 4
Monts de la Margeride 120-121 J 6
Monts de Saïda = Jabal aş-Şāyda 166-167 G 2
Monts des Ksour = Jibāl al-Quşūr 166-167 FG 3
Monts des Nementcha = Jabal an-Namāmshah 166-167 K 2
Monts des Ouled Naïl = Jabal Awlād Nāīl 166-167 H 2
Monts de Tebessa = Jabal Tibissah 166-167 L 2
Monts de Tlemcen = Jabal Tilimsān 166-167 F 2
Monts de Zeugitane = Jabal az-Zūgitīn 166-167 L 1-2
Monts du Charolais 120-121 K 5
Monts du Forez 120-121 J 6
Monts du Hodna = Jibal al-Hudnah 166-167 J 1-2
Monts du Titeri = Jabal al-Titri 166-167 H 1-2
Monts du Toura 168-169 D 4
Monts du Vivarais 120-121 K 6
Monts du Zab = Jibal az-Zāb 166-167 J 2
Montseny 120-121 J 8
Montserrado 168-169 C 4
Montserrat [E] 120-121 H 8
Montserrat [West Indies] 64-65 O 8
Monts Faucilles 120-121 K 5-L 4
Montsinéry 92-93 J 4
Monts Malimba 171 B 4
Monts Mandara 164-165 G 6-7
Monts Mitumba 172 E 2
Monts Mugila 172 E 3
Monts Notre Dame 56-57 WX 8
Monts Shickshock = Monts Chic-Choqs 56-57 X 8
Mont Tamgak 164-165 F 5
Mont Tembo 168-169 H 5
Mont Tremblant Provincial Park = Parc provincial de la Montagne Tremblante 56-57 VW 8
Mont Valérien 129 I b 2
Mont Ventoux 120-121 K 6
Montverde Nuovo, Roma- 113 II b 2
Mont Wright 56-57 X 7
Monument, CO 68-69 D 6
Monument, NM 76-77 C 6
Monument, OR 66-67 D 3
Monumental Hill 68-69 D 3
Monument Mount 58-59 FG 4
Monumento a Los Proceres 91 II b 2
Monument Valley 74-75 H 4
Mŏnyin 141 E 3
Mŏnyŏ 141 D 7
Monyul 141 BC 2
Mŏnywā 141 D 4
Monza 122-123 C 3
Monze 172 E 5
Monzón [E] 120-121 H 8
Monzón [PE] 96-97 C 6
Mooca, Ribeirão da — 110 II b 2
Mooca, São Paulo- 110 II b 2
Moody, TX 76-77 F 7
Moody Park 85 III b 1
Mooi River = Mooirivier 174-175 HJ 5
Mooirivier [ZA, place] 174-175 HJ 5
Mooirivier [ZA, river] 174-175 J 5
Mookane 174-175 G 2
Mooketsi 174-175 J 2
Mookhorn 80-81 J 2
Moolawatana 160 DE 2-3
Moolman 174-175 J 4
Moomba 160 E 2
Moon, Altar of the — 155 II ab 2
Moonaree 160 B 3
Moonbeam 62 KL 2
Moonda Lake 158-159 H 5
Moonee Valley Racecourse 161 II b 1
Moonie 160 K 1
Moonie River 160 J 1
Moon Island 84 I c 3
Moon National Monument, Craters of the — 66-67 G 4
Moon Sound = Suur väin 124-125 D 4
Moonta 158-159 G 6
Moora 158-159 C 6
Moorabbin, Melbourne- 161 II c 2
Moorburg, Hamburg- 130 I a 2
Moorcroft, WY 68-69 D 3
Moore, ID 66-67 G 4
Moore, MT 68-69 B 2
Moore, OK 76-77 F 5
Moore, TX 76-77 E 8
Moore, Cape — 53 BC 17
Moore, Lake — 158-159 C 5
Moore Creek, AK 58-59 J 5
Mooreland, OK 76-77 E 4
Moore Park 161 I b 2
Moores 106-107 F 5
Moorestown, NJ 84 III d 2
Mooresville, IN 70-71 G 6
Mooresville, NC 80-81 F 3
Moorfleet, Hamburg- 130 I b 1
Moorhead, MN 64-65 G 2
Moorhead, MS 78-79 D 4
Moorhead, MT 68-69 CD 3
Moorreesburg 174-175 C 7
Moorwerder, Hamburg- 130 I b 2
Moorwettern 130 I a 2
Moose, WY 66-67 H 4
Moose Factory 62 LM 1
Moosehead Lake 72-73 M 2
Mooseheart Mount 58-59 M 4
Moose Jaw 56-57 P 7
Moosejaw Creek 61 F 6
Moose Lake, MN 70-71 D 2
Moose Lake [CDN, lake] 56-57 R 7
Moose Lake [CDN, place] 61 HJ 4
Mooselookmeguntic Lake 72-73 L 2
Moose Mountain Creek 61 G 6
Moose Mountain Provincial Park 61 G 6
Moose Pass, AK 58-59 N 6
Moose River [CDN, place] 62 L 1
Moose River [CDN, river] 56-57 U 7
Moosomin 61 H 5
Moosonee 56-57 U 7
Moosrivier = Mosesrivier 174-175 H 3
Mopane 174-175 HJ 2
Mopani = Mopane 174-175 HJ 2
Mopeia 172 G 5
Mopipi 172 DE 6
Mopoy 94-95 F 4
Moppo = Mokp'o 142-143 O 5
Mopti 164-165 D 6
Môq'od = Muq'ud 166-167 L 1
Moquegua [PE, administrative unit] 96-97 F 10
Moquegua [PE, place] 92-93 E 8
Moquegua, Río — 96-97 F 10
Moquehuá 106-107 H 5
Moqur 134-135 K 4
Mora, MN 70-71 D 3
Mora, NM 76-77 B 5
Mora [E] 120-121 EF 9
Mora [RFC] 164-165 G 6
Mora [S] 116-117 F 7
Mora, Cerro — 106-107 B 5
Mora, La — 106-107 D 5
Moraća 122-123 H 4
Morādābād 134-135 MN 5
Morada Nova 100-101 E 3
Morafenobe 172 H 5
Morais, Serra do — 100-101 E 4
Moral, El — 76-77 D 8
Moraleda, Canal de — 111 B 6-7
Morales [CO, Bolívar] 94-95 DE 3
Morales [CO, Cauca] 94-95 C 6
Morales, Arroyo — 110 III ab 2
Moram 140 C 2
Moramanga 172 J 5
Moran, KS 70-71 C 7
Moran, MI 70-71 H 2-3
Moran, TX 76-77 E 6
Moran, WY 66-67 H 4
Morānhāt 141 D 2
Morant Point 88-89 HJ 6
Morappur 140 D 4
Morás, Punta de — 120-121 D 6-7
Morass Point 61 J 4
Moratalaz, Madrid- 113 III b 2
Moratalla 120-121 FG 9
Moratuwa 140 D 7
Moraujana 94-95 L 4
Morava [CS] 118 H 4
Morava [YU] 122-123 J 3
Moravia, IA 70-71 D 5
Morawa 158-159 C 5
Morawhanna 92-93 H 3
Moray Firth 119 DE 3
Morbi = Morvi 138-139 C 6
Morcenx 120-121 G 6
Mordāb = Mordāb-e Pahlavī 136-137 N 4
Mordāb-e Pahlavī 136-137 N 4
Mordağı 136-137 L 4
Morden 68-69 GH 1
Morden, London- 129 II b 2
Mordino 124-125 S 3
Mordovian Autonomous Soviet Socialist Republic = 5 ◁ 132-133 H 7
Mordovo 124-125 N 7
Mordovskaja Avtonomnaja Sovetskaja Socialističeskaja Respublika = Mordovian Autonomous Soviet Socialist Republic 132-133 H 7
Mordovskij zapovednik 124-125 O 6
More, Ben — [GB, Mull] 119 C 3
More, Ben — [GB, Outer Hebrides] 119 C 3
Morea = Pelopónnēsos 122-123 JK 7
More Assynt, Ben — 119 DE 2

Moreau River 68-69 F 3
Moreau River, North Fork — 68-69 E 3
Moreau River, South Fork — 68-69 E 3
Morecambe Bay 119 E 4-5
Moree 158-159 J 5
Morehead, KY 72-73 E 5
Morehead City, NC 80-81 H 3
Morehouse, MO 78-79 E 2
Moreland, ID 66-67 G 4
Morelia 64-65 F 8
Morella [AUS] 158-159 H 4
Morella [E] 120-121 GH 8
Morelos [MEX, administrative unit] 64-65 G 8
Morelos [MEX, place Coahuila] 76-77 D 8
Morelos [MEX, place Zacatecas] 86-87 J 6
Morelos, Ciudad de México- 91 I c 2
Morena 138-139 G 4
Morenci, AZ 74-75 J 6
Morenci, MI 70-71 H 5
Moreno [BR] 92-93 M 6
Moreno [RA] 110 III a 1
Moreno, Bahía — 104-105 A 8
Moreno, Cerro — 106-107 K 1
Moreno, Sierra de — 104-105 B 7
Moreno-Mariano Moreno 110 III a 1
Moreno-Paso del Rey 110 III a 1
Møre og Romsdal 116-117 BC 6
Moreru, Rio — 98-99 J 10
Moresby Channel 176 a 1
Moresby Island 56-57 K 7
Moreses, Pulau — 152-153 L 8
Mores Isle 88-89 GH 1
Moreton 158-159 H 2
Moreton Bay 160 L 1
Moreton Island 158-159 K 5
Mörfelden, Staatsforst — 128 III a 1
Mórfu 136-137 E 5
Mórfu, Kólpos — 136-137 E 5
Morgan 158-159 GH 6
Morgan, TX 76-77 F 6
Morgan City, LA 78-79 D 6
Morganfield, KY 70-71 G 7
Morgan Hill, CA 74-75 C 4
Morgan Park, Chicago-, IL 83 II ab 2
Morganton, NC 80-81 F 3
Morgantown, IN 70-71 G 6
Morgantown, KY 70-71 G 7
Morgantown, WV 72-73 FG 5
Morgat 120-121 E 4
Morgenzon 174-175 HJ 4
Morguilla, Punta — 106-107 A 6
Morhân, el — = Al-Mughrān 166-167 C 2
Morhar 138-139 K 5
Mori [J] 144-145 b 2
Mori [RI] 148-149 H 7
Mori = Kusu 144-145 H 6
Moriah, Mount — 74-75 FG 3
Moriarty, NM 76-77 AB 5
Morib 150-151 C 11
Moribaya 168-169 C 3
Morice Lake 60 D 2
Morice River 60 D 2
Moricetown 60 D 2
Morichal 94-95 F 4
Moricha Largo, Río — 94-95 K 3
Morija 174-175 G 5
Moriki 168-169 G 2
Morillo 104-105 E 8
Morin Creek 61 D 3-4
Morinville 60 KL 3
Morioka 142-143 R 4
Morisset 160 K 4
Morita, La — 76-77 B 8
Morizane = Yamakuni 144-145 H 6
Morjärv 116-117 K 4
Morkoka 132-133 V 4
Morlaix 120-121 F 4
Morland, KS 68-69 FG 6
Morley 60 K 4
Mormon Range 74-75 F 4
Morningside 170 V b 1
Morningside, MD 82 II b 2
Morningside, Atlanta-, GA 85 II bc 2
Mornington, Isla — 111 A 7
Mornington Island 158-159 G 3
Morno 168-169 E 3
Moro, OR 66-67 C 3
Moro, El — 106-107 H 7
Morobe 148-149 N 8
Morocco 164-165 C 3-D 2
Morochata 104-105 C 5
Morococha 96-97 CD 7
Morogoro 172 G 3
Moro Gulf 148-149 H 5
Morokwen = Morokweng 172 D 7
Morokweng 172 D 7
Moroleón 86-87 K 7
Morombe 172 H 6
Morón [C] 64-65 L 7
Mörön [Mongolia] 142-143 J 2
Morón [RA] 111 E 4
Morón [YV] 94-95 G 2
Morona 96-97 C 3
Morona, Río — 92-93 D 5
Morona Santiago 96-97 BC 3
Morón-Castelar 110 III ab 1
Morondava 172 H 6
Morón de la Frontera 120-121 E 10
Morón-El Palomar 110 III b 1
Morón-Hurlingham 110 III b 1
Moroni 172 H 4
Moroni, UT 74-75 H 3
Morón-Ituzaingó 110 III b 1
Morón-Mariano J. Haedo 110 III b 1
Moróno, Arroyo — 110 III b 1
Mörönus 142-143 G 5
Morotai, Pulau — 148-149 J 6
Moroto [EAU, mountain] 171 C 2
Moroto [EAU, place] 172 F 1
Morozovsk 126-127 KL 2
Morpará 100-101 C 6
Morpeth 119 F 4
Morphou = Mórfu 136-137 E 5
Morphou Bay = Kólpos Mórfu 136-137 E 5
Morra, Djebel — = Jabal Murrah 166-167 L 2
Morra, Hassi — = Ḥassī Murrah 166-167 EF 4
Morrelganj 141 A 4
Morrestown Mall 84 III d 2
Morretes 102-103 H 6
Morrilton, AR 78-79 C 3
Morrinhos 100-101 DE 2
Morrinsville 158-159 OP 7
Morris 62 A 3
Morris, IL 70-71 F 5
Morris, MN 70-71 BC 3
Morris = Ban Mahdī 166-167 KL 1
Morris Brown College 85 II b 2
Morrisburg 72-73 J 2
Morris Jesup, Kap — 52 A 19-23
Morrison 106-107 F 4
Morrison, IL 70-71 EF 5
Morrison Canal 85 I bc 1
Morris Park 84 III a 2
Morristown, SD 68-69 EF 3
Morristown, TN 64-65 K 4
Morro, El — 106-107 E 4
Morroa 94-95 D 3
Morro Agudo 102-103 HJ 4
Morro Cacitúa 108-109 C 4
Morro da Boa Vista 102-103 K 5
Morro da Igreja 102-103 H 8
Morro d'Anta 100-101 DE 10
Morro das Flores 100-101 D 7
Morro da Taquara 110 I b 2
Morro de Puercos 88-89 FG 11
Morro do Caricó 110 I b 2
Morro do Chapéu 100-101 C 8
Morro do Chapéu [BR, place] 100-101 D 6
Morro do Cochrane 110 I b 2
Morro do Tabuleiro 102-103 H 7
Morro Grande 92-93 HJ 5
Morro Inácio Dias 110 I ab 2
Morro Iquiri 102-103 H 7
Mórrope 96-97 A 4-5
Morro Peñón 106-107 B 4
Morro Quatro Irmãos 104-105 F 5
Morros [BR, Bahia] 100-101 D 7
Morros [BR, Maranhão] 92-93 L 5
Morro Selado 102-103 JK 5
Morrosquillo, Golfo de — 92-93 D 2-3
Morrumbala 172 G 5
Morrumbene 172 G 6
Mors 116-117 C 9
Moršansk 124-125 NO 7
Mörsbacher Grund 128 III ab 2
Morse, TX 76-77 D 4
Mōrshī = Morsi 138-139 FG 7
Morsi 138-139 FG 7
Morsott = Mūrsuṭ 166-167 L 2
Mortandade, Cachoeira — 98-99 P 8
Mortara 122-123 C 3
Morteros 111 D 4
Mortes, Rio das — 102-103 K 4
Mortimer 174-175 F 7
Mortlake 160 F 7
Mortlock Islands 208 F 2
Morton, MN 70-71 C 3
Morton, PA 84 III b 2
Morton, TX 76-77 C 6
Mortugaba 100-101 C 8
Morumbi, São Paulo- 110 II a 2
Morundah 160 GH 5
Moruya 158-159 K 7
Morvan 120-121 K 5
Morven 158-159 J 5
Morvi 138-139 C 6
Morwell 158-159 J 7
Morzhovoi Bay 58-59 b 2
Moržovec, ostrov — 132-133 GH 4
Moša 124-125 N 2-3
Mosal'sk 124-125 K 6
Mosby, MT 68-69 C 2
Moschâton 113 IV a 2
Moščnyj, ostrov — 124-125 FG 4
Mosconi 106-107 G 5
Moscos, Mid — = Maungmagan Kyûnzu 150-151 A 5
Moscos, Southern — = Launglônbôk Kyûnzu 150-151 A 6
Moscovo = Moskva [SU, place] 132-133 F 6
Moscovo = Moskva [SU, river] 124-125 K 6
Moscow, ID 64-65 C 2
Moscow, KS 68-69 F 7
Moscow = Moskva 132-133 F 6
Mosēdis 124-125 CD 5
Mosel 118 C 4
Moselle 120-121 L 4
Mošenskoje 124-125 K 4
Mosera = Jazirat al-Maṣīrah 134-135 H 6
Mosera Bay = Khalīj al-Maṣīrah 134-135 H 6-7
Moses, NM 76-77 C 4
Moses Lake 66-67 D 2
Moses Lake, WA 66-67 D 2
Moses Point, AK 58-59 F 4
Mosesrivier 174-175 H 3
Mosetenes, Cordillera de — 104-105 C 5
Mosgiel 161 CD 7
Moshi [EAT] 172 G 2
Moshi [WAN] 168-169 G 3
Mosimane 174-175 D 3
Mosinee, WI 70-71 F 3
Mosi-Oa-Toenja 172 DE 5
Mosjøen 116-117 E 5
Moskal'vo 132-133 b 7
Moskenesøy 116-117 EF 4
Moskovskaja vozvyšennost 124-125 K-M 5-6
Moskva [SU, place] 132-133 F 6
Moskva [SU, river] 124-125 K 6
Moskva-Aminjevo 113 V b 3
Moskva-Babuškin 124-125 LM 5-6
Moskva-Bat'unino 113 V c 3
Moskva-Beskudnikovo 113 V bc 2
Moskva-Bir'ulovo 124-125 LM 6
Moskva-Bogorodskoje 113 V cd 2
Moskva-Borisovo 113 V cd 3
Moskva-Bratcevo 113 V ab 2
Moskva-Bratejevo 113 V cd 3
Moskva-Čerkizovo 113 V c 2
Moskva-Čer'omuski 113 V bc 3
Moskva-Čertanovo 113 V bc 3
Moskva-Chimki-Chovrino 113 V b 2
Moskva-Chorošovo 113 V b 2
Moskva-D'akovskoje 113 V c 3
Moskva-Davydkovo 113 V b 3
Moskva-Degunino 113 V b 2
Moskva-Derevlevo 113 V b 3
Moskva-Fili-Mazilovo 113 V b 3
Moskva-Goljanovo 113 V d 2
Moskva-Ivanovskoje 113 V d 2
Moskva-Izmajlovo 113 V d 2
Moskva-Jasenevo 113 V b 3
Moskva-Jugo-Zapad 113 V b 3
Moskva-Kapotn'a 113 V d 3
Moskva-Karačarovo 113 V cd 3
Moskva-Kolomenskoje 113 V c 3
Moskva-Kožuchovo 113 V c 3
Moskva-Krasnookt'abrskij 113 V b 2
Moskva-Krasnyj Stroitel 113 V c 3
Moskva-Krylatskoje 113 V ab 2
Moskva-Kuncevo 124-125 L 6
Moskva-Kuskovo 113 V d 3
Moskva-Kuz'minki 113 V cd 3
Moskva-Lenino 113 V c 3
Moskva-Lianozovo 113 V c 2
Moskva-L'ublino 113 V cd 3
Moskva-Lužniki 113 V b 3
Moskva-Matvejevskoje 113 V b 3
Moskva-Medvedkovo 113 V c 2
Moskva-Mnevniki 113 V b 3
Moskva-Nagatino 113 V c 3
Moskva-Nikol'skoje 113 V b 3
Moskva-Nikulino 113 V b 3
Moskva-Novochovrino 113 V b 2
Moskva-Novogirejevo 113 V cd 2
Moskva-Novyje Kuz'minki 113 V cd 3
Moskva-Očakovo 113 V b 3
Moskva-Ostankino 113 V c 2
Moskva-Perovo 124-125 LM 6
Moskva-Petrovsko-Razumovskoje 113 V b 2
Moskva-Pokrovskoje 113 V c 3
Moskva-Pokrovsko-Strešnevo 113 V b 2
Moskva-Ramenka 113 V b 3
Moskva-Rostokino 113 V c 2
Moskva-Saburovo 113 V c 3
Moskva-Sadovniki 113 V c 3
Moskva-Serebr'anyj Bor 113 V ab 2
Moskva-Strogino 113 V ab 2
Moskva-Tatarovo 113 V ab 2
Moskva-Tekstil'ščiki 113 V c 3
Moskva-Toplyj Stan 113 V b 3
Moskva-Troice-Lykovo 113 V a 2
Moskva-Tusino 113 V b 2
Moskva-Uzkoje 113 V b 3
Moskva-Vešn'ak 113 V d 3
Moskva-Vychino 113 V d 3
Moskva-Zil 113 V c 3
Moskva-Z'uzino 113 V b 3
Moskvy, kanal — 124-125 L 5
Moskvy, Kanal im. — 113 V b 2
Mosman, Sydney- 161 I b 1
Mosmota 106-107 D 4
Mosolovo 124-125 N 6
Mosonmagyaróvár 118 HJ 5
Mospino 126-127 HJ 3
Mosquera 92-93 D 4
Mosquero, NM 76-77 BC 5
Mosquitia 64-65 K 8
Mosquito, Rio — 102-103 M 1-2
Mosquito Lagoon 80-81 c 2
Mosquitos, Costa de — 64-65 K 9
Mosquitos, Golfe de los — 64-65 K 10
Moss 116-117 D 8
Mossaka 172 C 2
Mossâmedes 102-103 GH 2
Mossbank 61 EF 6
Mosselbaai 172 D 8
Mossendjo 172 B 2
Mossi 164-165 D 6
Mossleigh 61 B 5
Mossman 158-159 HJ 3
Moss Point, MS 78-79 E 5
Moss Town 88-89 J 2
Mossul = Al-Mūṣil 134-135 E 3
Moss Vale 158-159 JK 6
Mossy River 61 G 3
Most 118 F 3
Mostaganem = Mustaghānam 164-165 DE 1
Mostar 122-123 GH 4
Mostardas 111 D 4
Mostardas, Lagoa de — 106-107 M 3
Mostardas, Ponta de — 106-107 M 3
Mosteiro 110 I bc 2
Mostiska 126-127 A 2
Mostva 124-125 F 8
Mosty 124-125 E 7
Mosul = Al-Mūṣil 134-135 E 3
Mosŭlp'o 144-145 EF 6
Mota 164-165 M 6
Motaba 172 C 1
Motacucito 104-105 F 5
Motagua, Río — 86-87 Q 10
Motala 116-117 F 8
Motalerivier 174-175 J 2
Motatán, Río — 94-95 F 3
Moth 138-139 G 5
Mother and Child = Nui Vong Phu 150-151 G 6
Mother Brook 84 I ab 3
Mother Goose Lake 58-59 e 1
Motherwell and Wishaw 119 DE 4
Motīhāri 134-135 NO 5
Motley, MN 70-71 C 2
Motocuruña 94-95 J 5
Motoichiba = Fuji 144-145 M 5
Motol' 124-125 E 7
Motomachi, Yokohama- 155 III a 3
Motomiya 144-145 N 4
Motovskij zaliv 116-117 PQ 3
Motril 120-121 F 10
Mott, ND 68-69 E 2
Mottinger, WA 66-67 D 2-3
Mottingham, London- 129 II c 2
Motueka 161 E 5
Motul de Felipe Carillo Puerto 64-65 J 7
Mōṭuṅ Raṇ = Rann of Kutch 134-135 KL 6
Motupe 96-97 B 5
Motygino 132-133 RS 6
Motyklejka 132-133 c 6
Mouchalagane, Rivière — 63 B 2
Mouḩīṭ, Baḩr el — = Al-Baḩr al-Muḩīṭ 166-167 A 4-B 2
Mouila 172 B 2
Mouilah = Mwīlaḩ 166-167 C 5
Mouka 164-165 J 7
Moulamein 158-159 HJ 6-7
Moulamein Creek 158-159 HJ 7
Moulapamok 150-151 EF 5
Moûlây Boû Chtâ' = Mūlāy Bū Shtā' 166-167 D 2
Moûlây Boû Selhâm = Mūlāy Bū Salhām 166-167 C 2
Moûlây Idrîss = Mūlāy Idrīs Zarahūn 166-167 D 2-3
Moulay-Slissen = Mūlāy Salīsan 166-167 F 2
Mould Bay 56-57 MN 2
Moulins 120-121 J 5
Moulmein = Maulamyaing 148-149 C 3
Moulmeingyun = Maulamyainggyûn 141 D 7
Mouloûya, Oued — = Wād Mūlūyā 164-165 D 2
Moulton, AL 78-79 F 3
Moulton, IA 70-71 D 5
Moultrie, GA 64-65 K 5
Moultrie, Lake — 80-81 F 4
Mound City, IL 70-71 F 7
Mound City, KS 70-71 C 6
Mound City, MO 70-71 C 5
Mound City, SD 68-69 FG 3
Moundou 164-165 H 7
Moundsville, WV 72-73 F 5
Moundville, AL 78-79 F 4
Moung 148-149 D 4
Moungali, Brazzaville- 170 IV a 1
Mount, Cape — 168-169 C 4
Mount Adam 111 DE 8
Mount Adams 64-65 B 2
Mountain, WI 70-71 F 3
Mountainair, NM 76-77 A 5
Mountain City, NV 66-67 F 5
Mountain City, TN 80-81 EF 2
Mountain Grove, MO 78-79 C 2
Mountain Home, AR 78-79 C 2
Mountain Home, ID 66-67 F 4
Mountain Park 60 J 3
Mountain Park, OK 76-77 E 5
Mountain Pine, AR 78-79 C 3
Mountain View, AR 78-79 CD 3
Mountain View, GA 85 II b 3
Mountain View, HI 78-79 e 3
Mountain View, MO 78-79 D 2
Mountain View, OK 76-77 E 5
Mountain Village, AK 56-57 D 5
Mount Airy, NC 80-81 F 2
Mount Airy, Philadelphia-, PA 84 III b 1
Mount Albert Markham 53 AB 17-15
Mount Alida 174-175 J 5
Mount Allen 58-59 QR 5
Mount Aloysius 158-159 E 5
Mount Alverno, PA 84 III a 2
Mount Alverstone 58-59 S 6
Mount Ambition 58-59 W 8
Mount Amherst 158-159 E 3
Mount Amundsen 53 BC 11
Mount Apo 148-149 HJ 5
Mount Arkell 58-59 U 6
Mount Ashland 66-67 B 4
Mount Aspid 58-59 n 4
Mount Aspiring 158-159 N 8
Mount Assiniboine 56-57 NO 7
Mount Auburn Cemetery 84 I b 2
Mount Augustus 158-159 C 4
Mount Ayliff = Maxesibeni 174-175 H 6
Mount Ayr, IA 70-71 CD 5
Mount Baker 66-67 C 1
Mount Baldy 66-67 H 2
Mount Bamboulos 168-169 H 4
Mount Barker 158-159 C 6
Mount Barrington 158-159 K 6
Mount Batchawana 70-71 H 2
Mount Behn 158-159 E 3
Mount Benedict Cemetery 84 I a 3
Mount Berlin 53 B 23
Mount Binga 172 F 5
Mount Blackburn 56-57 H 5
Mount Bogong 158-159 J 7
Mount Bona 58-59 QR 6
Mount Bonaparte 66-67 D 1
Mount Brazeau 60 J 3
Mount Brockman 158-159 C 4
Mount Brooks 58-59 MN 5
Mount Brown 53 BC 9
Mount Bruce 158-159 C 4
Mount Brukkaros = Groot Brukkaros 172 C 7
Mount Buller 160 H 6
Mount Burgess 58-59 S 3
Mount Callahan 74-75 E 3
Mount Cameron 155 I ab 2
Mount Carleton 63 C 4
Mount Carmel, IL 70-71 FG 6
Mount Carmel, PA 72-73 H 4
Mount Carmel, UT 74-75 G 4
Mount Caroline Livermore 83 I b 1
Mount Caroll, IL 70-71 EF 4
Mount Chamberlin 58-59 P 2
Mount Chiginagak 58-59 e 1
Mount Cleveland 64-65 D 2
Mount Collins 62 L 3
Mount Collinson 155 I b 2
Mount Columbia 56-57 N 7
Mount Conner 158-159 F 5
Mount Cook [NZ] 158-159 NO 8
Mount Cook [USA] 58-59 RS 6
Mount Cowen 66-67 H 3
Mount Crillon 58-59 T 7
Mount Crysdale 60 F 2
Mount Dalgaranger 158-159 C 5
Mount Dall 58-59 LM 5
Mount Dalrymple 158-159 J 4
Mount Dana 74-75 D 4
Mount Darwin 172 F 5
Mount Deborah 58-59 O 5
Mount Deering 158-159 E 5
Mount Denison 58-59 KL 7
Mount Desert Island 72-73 MN 2
Mount Doonerak 56-57 FG 4
Mount Dora, FL 80-81 c 2
Mount Dora, NM 76-77 C 4
Mount Douglas 58-59 KL 7
Mount Douglas [AUS] 158-159 J 4
Mount Downton 60 E 3
Mount Draper 58-59 S 7
Mount Dutton 74-75 G 3-4
Mount Dutton [AUS] 160 BC 1
Mount Edgecumbe, AK 58-59 v 8
Mount Egmont 158-159 O 7
Mount Eisenhower 60 K 4
Mount Elbert 64-65 E 4
Mount Elgon 172 F 1
Mount Ellen 74-75 H 3
Mount Elliot = Selwyn 158-159 H 4
Mount Elliot Cemetery 84 II b 2
Mount Enid 158-159 C 4
Mount Ephraim, NJ 84 III c 2
Mount Erebus 53 B 17-18
Mount Essendon 158-159 D 4
Mount Etna = Mazui Ling 150-151 G 3
Mount Evans [CDN] 60 J 5
Mount Evans [USA, Colorado] 68-69 D 6
Mount Evans [USA, Montana] 66-67 G 2
Mount Everest = Sagarmatha 142-143 F 6
Mount Everett 72-73 K 3
Mount Faber 154 III a 2
Mount Fairweather 56-57 J 6
Mount Fletcher 174-175 H 6
Mount Floyd 74-75 G 5
Mount Foraker 56-57 F 5
Mount Forbes 60 J 4
Mount Forest 72-73 F 2-3
Mount Franklyn 161 E 6
Mount Frere = Kwabhaca 174-175 H 6
Mount Gambier 158-159 GH 7
Mount Garnet 158-159 HJ 3
Mount Gascoyne 158-159 C 4
Mount Gerdine 56-57 F 5
Mount Gilbert 58-59 o 3
Mount Gilead, OH 72-73 E 4
Mount Giluwe 148-149 M 8
Mount Godwin Austen = K2 134-135 M 3
Mount Goldsworthy 158-159 CD 4
Mount Graham 64-65 DE 5
Mount Grant [USA, Clan Alpine Mountains] 74-75 DE 3
Mount Grant [USA, Wassuk Range] 74-75 D 3
Mount Greenwood, Chicago-, IL 83 II a 2
Mount Greylock 72-73 K 3
Mount Hack 158-159 G 6
Mount Hagen 148-149 M 8
Mount Haig 66-67 F 1
Mount Hale 158-159 C 5
Mount Hamilton 74-75 F 3
Mount Hann 158-159 E 3
Mount Harper [CDN] 58-59 RS 4
Mount Harper [USA] 58-59 PQ 4
Mount Harvard 68-69 C 6
Mount Hawkes 53 A 32-33
Mount Hay 58-59 T 7
Mount Hayes 56-57 G 5
Mount Hebron, CA 66-67 BC 5
Mount Helen 74-75 E 4
Mount Henry 66-67 F 1
Mount Hickman 58-59 x 8
Mount Holly, NJ 72-73 J 4-5
Mount Holmes 66-67 H 3
Mount Hood 64-65 B 2
Mount Hope, WV 80-81 F 2
Mount Hope [AUS, New South Wales] 160 GH 4
Mount Hope [AUS, South Australia] 158-159 FG 6
Mount Hope Cemetery 84 I b 3
Mount Horeb, WI 70-71 F 4
Mount Houston, TX 85 III b 1
Mount Hubbard 56-57 J 5
Mount Humboldt 158-159 N 4
Mount Humphreys 74-75 D 4
Mount Huxley 58-59 R 6
Mount Intersection 60 G 3
Mount Isa 158-159 G 4
Mount Isto 58-59 Q 2
Mount Jacques Cartier 63 D 3
Mount Jāpvo 141 CD 3
Mount Jefferson [USA, Nevada] 74-75 E 3
Mount Jefferson [USA, Oregon] 66-67 C 3
Mount Joffre 60 K 4
Mount Judge Haway 66-67 BC 1
Mount Kalankpa 168-169 F 3
Mount Kaputar 160 JK 3
Mount Katahdin 64-65 MN 2
Mount Katmai 56-57 F 6
Mount Kelly 58-59 EF 2
Mount Kennedy 56-57 J 5
Mount Kenya 172 G 1-2
Mount Kenya National Park 171 D 3
Mount Kimball 58-59 PQ 5
Mount Klotz 58-59 R 4
Mount Kosciusko 158-159 J 7
Mount Laurel 84 III d 2
Mount Laurel, NJ 84 III d 2
Mount Lavinia, Dehiwala- 134-135 M 9
Mount Leisler 158-159 EF 4
Mount Lemmon 74-75 H 6
Mount Levick 53 B 16-17
Mount Lincoln 68-69 CD 6
Mount Linn 66-67 B 5
Mount Lister 53 B 17
Mount Livermore 64-65 F 5
Mount Lodge 58-59 T 7
Mount Lofty Range 158-159 G 6
Mount Logan [CDN, Quebec] 63 C 3
Mount Logan [CDN, Yukon Territory] 56-57 HJ 5
Mount Lola 74-75 C 3
Mount Lovenia 66-67 H 5
Mount Lucania 56-57 HJ 5
Mount Lyell 160 b 2
Mount MacGuire 66-67 F 3
Mount MacKinley 56-57 F 5
Mount MacKinley National Park 56-57 FG 5
Mount Madley 158-159 D 4
Mount Mageik 58-59 K 7
Mount Magnet 158-159 C 5
Mount Manara 158-159 H 6
Mount Manenguba 168-169 H 4
Mount Mantalingajan 148-149 G 5
Mount Marcus Baker 56-57 G 5
Mount Marcy 72-73 JK 2
Mount Maria 108-109 K 8
Mount Markham 53 A 15-16
Mount Marshall 72-73 G 5
Mount Marvine 74-75 H 3
Mount Maunganui 161 G 3
Mount Menzie 58-59 V 6
Mount Menzies 53 B 6-7
Mount Middleton 62 N 1
Mount Miller 58-59 QR 6
Mount Mitchell 64-65 K 4
Mount Moffett 58-59 u 6-7
Mount Morgan 158-159 K 4
Mount Moriah 74-75 FG 3
Mount Morris, MI 70-71 HJ 4
Mount Morris, NY 72-73 H 3
Mount Mulanje 172 G 5
Mount Mulligan 158-159 H 3
Mount Mumpu 171 B 6
Mount Mussali = Muṣa Ali 164-165 N 6
Mount Myenmoletkhat = Myinmöyletʼkhat Taung 150-151 B 6
Mount Napier 158-159 EF 3
Mount Nebo 74-75 H 3
Mount Needham 60 A 3
Mount Nesselrode 58-59 UV 7
Mount Nyiru 172 G 1
Mount Ogden 58-59 V 7
Mount Olga 158-159 EF 5
Mount Olive, NC 80-81 G 3
Mount Olivet Cemetery 84 II bc 2
Mount Olympus 66-67 B 2
Mount Ossa 158-159 J 8
Mount-Owen 161 E 5
Mount Paget 111 J 8
Mount Palgrave 158-159 C 4
Mount Panié 158-159 M 4
Mount Parker 155 I b 2
Mount Pattullo 60 C 1
Mount Peale 64-65 DE 4
Mount Picton 160 bc 3
Mount Pinos 74-75 D 5
Mount Pisgah 66-67 C 3
Mount Pleasant 80-81 G 2
Mount Pleasant, IA 70-71 E 5
Mount Pleasant, MI 70-71 H 4
Mount Pleasant, TN 78-79 F 3
Mount Pleasant, TX 76-77 G 6
Mount Pleasant, UT 74-75 H 3
Mount Plummer 58-59 GH 6
Mount Pulog 148-149 H 3
Mount Queen Bess 60 E 4
Mount Queen Mary 58-59 S 6
Mount Rainier 64-65 BC 2
Mount Rainier, MD 82 II b 1
Mount Rainier National Park 66-67 C 2
Mount Ratz 58-59 VW 8
Mount Remarkable 158-159 G 6
Mount Revelstoke National Park 60 HJ 4
Mount Rex 53 B 29
Mount Riley, NM 76-77 A 7
Mount Ritter 64-65 C 4
Mount Robe 160 E 3
Mount Robson 56-57 N 7
Mount Robson [CDN, place] 60 H 3
Mount Robson Provincial Park 60 H 3
Mount Roraima 92-93 G 3
Mount Rover 58-59 R 3
Mount Royal, NJ 84 III b 3
Mount Russell 58-59 LM 5
Mount Saint Elias 56-57 H 5
Mount Saint Helens 66-67 BC 2
Mount Salisbury 58-59 O 2
Mount Samuel 158-159 F 3
Mount Sanford 58-59 Q 5
Mount Scott [USA → Crater Lake] 64-65 B 3
Mount Scott [USA ↓ Pengra Pass] 66-67 BC 4
Mount Shasta 64-65 B 3
Mount Shasta, CA 66-67 B 5
Mount Shenton 158-159 D 5
Mount Sheridan 66-67 H 3
Mount Sidley 53 B 24
Mount Singleton 158-159 F 4
Mount Siple 53 B 24
Mount Sir Alexander 60 GH 2
Mount Sir James MacBrien 56-57 KL 5
Mount Sir Sanford 60 J 4
Mount Sir Thomas 158-159 EF 5
Mount Sir Wilfrid Laurier 60 GH 3
Mount Snowy 72-73 J 3
Mount Spranger 60 G 3
Mount Springer 62 O 2
Mount Spurr 58-59 LM 6
Mount Stanley 158-159 F 4
Mount Steele 58-59 RS 6
Mount Steller 58-59 Q 6
Mount Stenhouse 155 I a 2
Mount Sterling, IL 70-71 E 6
Mount Stewart 63 E 4
Mount Stimson 66-67 G 1
Mount Stokes 161 EF 5
Mount Sturt 158-159 H 5
Mount Swan 158-159 G 4
Mount Sylvester 63 J 3
Mount Takahe 53 B 25-26
Mount Talbot 158-159 E 5
Mount Tamboritha 160 H 6
Mount Tasman 161 CD 6
Mount Tatlow 60 F 4
Mount Taylor 76-77 A 5
Mount Tenabo 66-67 E 5
Mount Thielsen 66-67 BC 4
Mount Thynne 66-67 C 1
Mount Tipton 74-75 F 5
Mount Tobin 66-67 E 5
Mount Tom Price 158-159 C 4
Mount Tom White 58-59 PQ 6
Mount Torbert 58-59 LM 6
Mount Travers 161 E 5-6
Mount Trumbull 74-75 G 4
Mount Tutoko 161 BC 7
Mount Union 74-75 G 5
Mount Union, PA 72-73 H 4
Mount Usborne 111 E 8
Mount Vancouver 58-59 RS 6
Mount Veniaminof 58-59 d 1
Mount Vernon, GA 80-81 E 4
Mount Vernon, IA 70-71 E 5
Mount Vernon, IL 64-65 J 4
Mount Vernon, IN 70-71 FG 7
Mount Vernon, KY 70-71 H 7
Mount Vernon, NY 72-73 K 4
Mount Vernon, OH 72-73 E 4
Mount Vernon, OR 66-67 D 3
Mount Vernon, TX 76-77 G 6
Mount Vernon, WA 66-67 BC 1
Mount Victoria 148-149 N 8
Mount Victoria = Tomaniive 148-149 a 2
Mount Victory, OH 72-73 E 4
Mount Vinson 53 B 28
Mount Vsevidof 58-59 m 4
Mount Waddington 56-57 LM 7
Mount Washington 64-65 M 3
Mount Watt 158-159 E 5
Mount Waverley, Melbourne- 161 II c 2
Mount Weber 60 C 2
Mount Whaleback 158-159 CD 4
Mount Whewell 53 B 17-18
Mount Whipple 60 B 1
Mount Whitney 64-65 C 4
Mount Wilhelm 148-149 M 8
Mount Will 58-59 X 8
Mount Willibert 60 B 1
Mount Willoughby 158-159 F 5
Mount Wilson 68-69 BC 7
Mount Witherspoon 58-59 O 6
Mount Wood [CDN] 58-59 R 6
Mount Wood [USA] 66-67 J 3
Mount Woodroffe 158-159 F 5
Mount Wrangell 58-59 P 5
Mount Wrightson 74-75 H 7
Mount Wrottesley 66-67 B 1
Mount Yenlo 58-59 M 5
Mount Zeil 158-159 F 4
Mount Zirkel 68-69 C 5
Mouping = Muping 146-147 H 3
Moura [AUS] 158-159 JK 4
Moura [BR] 92-93 G 5
Moura [P] 120-121 D 9
Moura, Rio — 96-97 E 5-6
Mourão 120-121 D 9
Mourdi, Dépression du — 164-165 J 5
Mourdiah 164-165 C 6
Mouslimiyé = Muslimīyah 136-137 G 4
Moussoro 164-165 H 6
Moussy 106-107 H 2
Mouths of the Ganga 134-135 OP 6
Mouths of the River Niger 164-165 F 7-8

330 Moreau

Moutiers 120-121 L 6
Moutohora 158-159 P 7
Moutong = Mautong 148-149 H 6
Moutsamoudou = Mutsamudu 172 HJ 4
Mouydir = Jabal al-Mūḍīr 166-167 HJ 7
Mòvano 76-77 C 9
Moville, IA 70-71 BC 4
Mowasi 98-99 J 2
Moweaqua, IL 70-71 F 6
Mowich, OR 66-67 BC 4
Mowming = Maoming 142-143 L 7
Moxico 172 CD 4
Moxotó, Rio — 100-101 F 5
Moya [PE] 96-97 D 8
Moyale 172 G 1
Moyamba 164-165 B 7
Mo-yang Chiang = Moyang Jiang 146-147 C 10-11
Moyang Jiang 146-147 C 10-11
Moye Dao 146-147 J 3
Mo-yeh Tao = Moye Dao 146-147 J 3
Moyie 66-67 F 1
Moyie Springs, ID 66-67 E 1
Moylan, PA 84 III a 2
Moyne, La — 82 I c 1
Moyo [BOL] 104-105 D 7
Moyo [EAU] 171 B 2
Moyo = Pulau Moyo 148-149 G 8
Moyobamba 92-93 D 6
Moyock, NC 80-81 HJ 2
Moyowosi 171 B 3-4
Møysalen 116-117 FG 3
Moyto 164-165 H 6
M'oža [SU ◁ Unža] 124-125 P 4
M'oža [SU ◁ Zapadnaja Dvina] 124-125 J 5-6
Možajsk 124-125 KL 6
Mozambique 172 F 6-G 4
Mozambique = Moçambique [Mozambique, place] 172 H 4-5
Mozambique = Moçambique [Mozambique, state] 172 F 6-G 4
Mozambique Basin 172 H 4
Mozambique Channel 172 H 4-6
Možary 124-125 N 7
Mozdok 126-127 M 5
Možga 132-133 J 6
Mozuli 124-125 G 5
Mozyr' 124-125 G 7

Mpampáeski = Babaeski 136-137 B 2
Mpanda 172 F 3
Mpepo 172 F 4
Mpika 172 F 4
Mpila, Brazzaville- 170 IV a 1
Mporokoso 172 EF 3
M'Pouya 172 C 2
Mpulungu 172 F 3
Mpurakasese 172 G 4
Mpwapwa 171 D 4

M'rāītī, Al- 164-165 C 4
Mrayyah, Al- 164-165 C 5
Mreïti, El — = Al-M'rāītī 164-165 C 4
M. R. Gomez, Presa — 86-87 L 4
Mrhaïer = Al-Mighāīr 166-167 J 3
Mrīmīna = M'rīmīnah 166-167 C 5
M'rīmīnah 166-167 C 5

Msagali 172 G 3
Msaï'ida = Musā'idah 136-137 M 7
Msāken = Masākin 166-167 M 2
M'samrīr 166-167 D 4
Msasa 171 B 3
Mseleni 174-175 K 4
M'shams 166-167 BC 6
M'shīgīg, Sabkhat al- 166-167 L 2
Msid, Djebel — = Jabal Masīd 166-167 L 1
M'Sila = M'sīlah 166-167 J 2
M'sīlah 166-167 J 2
Msta [SU, place] 124-125 K 5
Msta [SU, river] 132-133 E 6
Mstinskij Most 124-125 J 4
Mstislavl' 124-125 HJ 6
Mswega 171 D 5

Mṭā el Rhèrra, Choṭṭ — = Shaṭṭ al-Ghurrah 166-167 M 2
Mtakuja 172 F 3
Mtama 171 D 5
Mtatarivier 174-175 H 6
Mtimbo 171 D 5
Mtito Andei 171 D 3
Mtowabaga 171 C 3
Mtubatuba 174-175 K 5
MTU im. Lomonosova 113 V b 3
Mtwalume 174-175 J 6
Mtwara 172 H 4

Mu'o'ng Boum 150-151 D 1
Mu'o'ng Khoua 148-149 D 2
Mu'o'ng Lam [VN, Sông Ca] 150-151 E 3
Mu'o'ng Lam [VN, Sông Ma] 150-151 D 2
Mu'o'ng Son 150-151 D 2
Mu'o'ng Soum 150-151 D 3
Mualama 172 G 5
Muan 144-145 F 5
Mu'ang Ba = Ban Mu'ang Ba 150-151 E 4
Muang Phichai = Phichai 150-151 C 4
Muang Phrae 150-151 C 4
Muang Pua = Pua 150-151 C 3
Muang Samsip 150-151 E 5
Mūan-jo Daṛo 138-139 AB 4
Muar 148-149 D 6
Muar, Sungei — 150-151 D 12
Muara 152-153 D 6
Muaraaman 148-149 D 7
Muaraancalung 148-149 G 6
Muarabenangin 152-153 LM 6
Muarabungo 152-153 E 6
Muaraenim 148-149 D 7
Muarajuloi 152-153 L 6
Muaralasan 148-149 G 6
Muarapangean 152-153 M 4
Muarapayang 152-153 LM 6
Muaras 152-153 N 5
Muarasabak 152-153 E 6
Muarasiberut 148-149 C 7
Muaratebo 148-149 D 7
Muaratembesi 148-149 D 7
Muarateweh 148-149 FG 7
Muaratunan 152-153 M 6
Muarawahau 152-153 M 5
Mū'askar 164-165 E 1
Mu'askar, Jabal — 166-167 D 3
Mubārak, Jabal — 136-137 F 8
Mubārakpur 138-139 J 4
Mubende 172 F 1
Mubi 164-165 G 6
Mubur, Pulau — 152-153 FG 4
Mucajaí, Rio — 92-93 G 4
Mucajaí, Serra do — 92-93 G 4
Mucambo 100-101 D 2
Muchanes 104-105 C 4
Muchinga Mountains 171 BC 5
Muchino 124-125 S 4
Muchiri 104-105 E 6
Muchorskij 126-127 P 2
Muchtolovo 124-125 O 6
Mučkapskij 124-125 O 8
Muco, Río — 94-95 F 5
Mucojo 172 H 4
Muconda 172 D 4
Mucoque 174-175 L 1
Mucuburi, Río — 171 D 6
Mucuchachí 94-95 F 3
Mucuchíes 94-95 F 3
Mucucuaú, Rio — 98-99 H 4
Mucuim, Rio — 98-99 F 8
Mucujê 100-101 D 7
Mucunambiba, Ilha — 100-101 C 1-2
Mucur 136-137 F 3
Mucuri 92-93 M 8
Mucuri, Rio — 92-93 L 8
Mucurici 100-101 D 10
Mucuripe, Ponta de — 92-93 M 5
Mucusso 172 D 5
Muda, Sungei — 150-151 C 10
Mudagērē = Mudigere 140 B 4
Mudanjiang 142-143 OP 3
Mudanya 136-137 C 2
Mudawwarah, Al- 134-135 D 5
Mudaysīsāt, Jabal — 136-137 G 7
Mud Butte, SD 68-69 E 3
Muddanūru 140 D 3
Muddebihāl 140 BC 2
Muḍḍēbihāla = Muddebihāl 140 BC 2
Muddo Gashi = Mado Gashi 172 G 1
Muddusnationalpark 116-117 J 4
Muddy Creek 74-75 H 3
Muddy Gap 68-69 C 4
Muddy Gap, WY 66-67 K 4
Muddy Peak 74-75 F 4
Mudgal 140 C 2
Mudgee 158-159 JK 6
Mudgere = Mudigere 140 B 4
Mudhol [IND, Karnataka] 140 B 2
Mudhol [IND, Mahārāshtra] 138-139 FG 8
Mudhola = Mudhol [IND, Karnataka] 140 B 2
Mudhola = Mudhol [IND, Mahārāshtra] 138-139 FG 8
Mudigere 140 B 4
Mūdīr, Jabal al- 166-167 HJ 7
Mudīriyat el Istwā'ya = Al-Istiwā'īyah 164-165 K-M 7
Mudīriyat esh Shimāliya = Ash-Shimālīyah 164-165 KL 5
Mudjuga 124-125 M 2
Mudkhed 138-139 F 8
Mud Lake 74-75 E 4
Mudôn 148-149 C 3
Mūdros 122-123 L 6
Mudug 164-165 b 2
Mudukulattūr 140 D 6
Mudūr 140 E 6
Mudurnu 136-137 D 2
Muecate 172 G 4
Mueda 172 G 4
Muendaze 171 E 6
Muermos, Los — 108-109 C 3
Muerte, Meseta de la — 108-109 CD 7
Muerto, Sierra del — 104-105 AB 9
Mufulira 172 E 4
Mufu Shan 146-147 E 7
Mugadok Taung 150-151 B 5
Muganskaja ravnina 126-127 O 7
Müggelberge 130 III c 2
Müggelheim, Berlin- 130 III c 2
Muggi Tsho 138-139 M 2
Mughal Bhīm = Jāti 138-139 B 5
Mughal Sarai 138-139 J 5
Mughayrā', Al- 136-137 G 8
Mughrān, Al- 166-167 C 2
Mughrār 166-167 F 3
Mugi 144-145 K 6
Mu' Gia, Deo — 150-151 E 4
Múgica 86-87 JK 8
Mugila, Monts — 172 E 3
Muğla 134-135 B 3
Mugodžary 132-133 K 8
Mugodzharskie Mountains = Mugodžary 132-133 K 8
Mugombazi 171 B 4
Mugrejevskij 124-125 O 5
Mūgu 138-139 J 3
Mūgu Karnāli 138-139 J 3
Muhamdī 138-139 GH 4
Muḥammad, Rā's — 164-165 LM 4
Muhammadābād [IND ↓ Gorakhpoor] 138-139 J 4
Muhammadābād [IND ↗ Vārānasī] 138-139 J 5
Muḥammadī, Wādī — 136-137 K 6
Muḥammadīyah, Al- 166-167 C 3
Muḥammad Ṭulayb 173 B 5
Muhammed, Ras — = Rā's Muḥammad 164-165 LM 4
Muhārī, Al- 136-137 L 7
Muhārī, Sha'īb al- 136-137 KL 7
Muhembo 172 D 5
Muhinga = Muyinga 172 EF 2
Mühlau 128 IV a 2
Mühlbach 128 III a 2
Mühldorf 118 F 4
Mühlenau 130 I a 1
Mühlenbecker See 130 III b 1
Mühlhausen 118 E 3
Mühlig-Hoffmann-Gebirge 53 B 1-2
Mühlleiten 113 I c 2
Muhu 124-125 D 4
Muhuwesi 171 D 5
Mui Bai Bung 148-149 D 5
Mui Ba Lang An = Mui Batangan 148-149 EF 3
Mui Batangan 148-149 EF 3
Mui Ca Mau = Mui Bai Bung 148-149 D 5
Mui Cho'n Mây 150-151 G 4
Mui Đa Du'ng 150-151 EF 3
Mui Đa Năng 150-151 G 4
Muiderberg 128 I b 2
Mui Diêu 148-149 EF 4
Mui Dinh 148-149 E 4
Mui En = Mui Yên 150-151 G 6
Mui Ke Ga 150-151 FG 7
Mui Lai 150-151 F 4
Muir Glacier 58-59 T 7
Muirite 171 D 6
Mui Ron Ma 148-149 E 3
Muisne 96-97 A 1
Mui Yên 150-151 G 6
Muizenberg 174-175 BC 8
Muja 132-133 W 6
Mujeres, Isla — 86-87 R 7
Mujezerskij 132-133 E 5
Mujlad, Al — 164-165 K 6
Mujnak 132-133 K 9
Muju 144-145 F 4-5
Mujunkum 132-133 MN 9
Muk, Ko — 150-151 B 9
Muka = Mouka 164-165 J 7
Mukačovo 126-127 A 2
Mukah 148-149 F 6
Mukallā, Al- 134-135 FG 8
Mukawa 144-145 b 2
Mukawwa', Jazīrat — 173 DE 6
Mukdahan 148-149 D 3
Mukden = Shenyang 142-143 NO 3
Mukebo 171 AB 4
Mukerīān 138-139 E 2
Mukhā, Al- 134-135 E 8
Mukhalid = Nětanya 136-137 F 6
Mukher 140 C 1
Mukhriṣṣat 166-167 D 2
Mukinbudin 158-159 C 6
Muknīn, Al- 166-167 M 2
Mukōjima, Tōkyō- 155 III bc 1
Mukoko 171 BC 3
Mukomuko 148-149 D 7
Mukrān, Sabkhat — 164-165 E 3
Mukry 134-135 K 3
Muktāgācha 138-139 MN 5
Mukthsar = Muktsar 138-139 E 2
Muktināth 138-139 J 3
Muktsar 138-139 E 2
Mukumbi = Makumbi 172 D 3
Mūküs 136-137 K 3
Mukutawa River 62 A 1
Mūl 138-139 G 7
Mula [IND] 138-139 E 8
Mula, La — 76-77 B 8
Mulainagiri 134-135 LM 8
Mulaku Atoll 176 a 2
Mulan 142-143 O 2
Mulanje 172 G 5
Mulanje, Mount — 172 G 5
Mulapamok = Moulapamok 150-151 EF 5
Mulata 98-99 LM 5
Mulatas, Archipiélago de las — 94-95 B 3
Mulativu 140 E 6
Mulatos 94-95 C 3
Mulatos, Punta — 91 II b 1
Mūlāy Bū Salhām 166-167 C 2
Mūlāy Bū Shtā' 166-167 D 2
Mūlāy Idrīs Zarahūn 166-167 D 2-3
Mūlayit Taung 148-149 C 3
Mūlāy Salīsan 166-167 F 2
Mulbāgal 140 D 4
Mulberry, KS 70-71 C 7
Mulchatna River 58-59 JK 6
Mulchén 106-107 A 6
Muldoon, ID 66-67 G 4
Muldrow, OK 76-77 G 5
Muleba 171 BC 3
Mule Creek, NM 74-75 J 6
Mule Creek, WY 68-69 D 4
Mulegé 86-87 DE 4
Mules, Pulau — 152-153 O 10
Muleshoe, TX 76-77 C 5
Mulgrave 63 F 5
Mulgrave Hills 58-59 F 3
Mulgrave Island 158-159 H 2
Mulgubi 144-145 G 2
Mulhacén 120-121 F 10
Mulhall, OK 76-77 F 4
Mulhouse 120-121 L 5
Muli = Vysokogornyj 132-133 ab 7
Mulka 160 D 2
Mülki 140 B 4
Mull 119 CD 3
Mullaitivu = Mulativu 140 E 6
Mullāmārī 140 C 2
Mullan, ID 66-67 EF 2
Mullan Pass 64-65 D 2
Mullen, NE 68-69 F 4
Mullens, WV 80-81 F 2
Müller, Pegunungan — 148-149 F 6
Müllerberg 116-117 l 6
Mullet Lake 70-71 H 3
Mullewa 158-159 C 5
Mulligan River 158-159 G 4-5
Mullin, TX 76-77 E 7
Mullingar 119 C 5
Mullins, SC 80-81 G 3
Mulobezi 172 DE 5
Mulshī = Waki 140 A 1
Mulshi Lake 140 A 1
Multai 138-139 G 7
Multān 134-135 L 4
Mulu, Gunung — 148-149 FG 6
Mulubāgala = Mulbāgal 140 D 4
Mulug 140 DE 1
Mulula, Wed — = Wād Mūlūyā 164-165 D 2
Mulungu 100-101 G 4
Mulungu do Morro 100-101 D 6
Mulūṣī, Bi'r al- 136-137 J 6
Mulūṣī, Shādir al- 136-137 HJ 6
Mūlūyā, Wād — 164-165 D 2
Muluzia 171 B 5
Mulvane, KS 68-69 H 7
Mulymja 132-133 LM 5
Mumbaī = Bombay 134-135 L 7
Mumbwa 172 E 5
Mumeng 148-149 N 8
Mumford, TX 76-77 F 7
Mumpu, Mount — 171 B 6
Mumra 126-127 N 4
Mumtrak = Coodnews, AK 58-59 FG 7
Mū Myit 141 D 4
Mun, Mae Nam — 148-149 D 3
Muna [MEX] 86-87 Q 7
Muna [SU] 132-133 W 4
Muna, Pulau — 148-149 H 8
Muñani 96-97 G 9
Munasarowar Lake = Mapham Tsho 142-143 E 5
Munayjah, Bi'r — 173 D 6
Münchehofe [DDR, Frankfurt] 130 III c 2
München 118 EF 4
München-Allach 130 II a 1
München-Au 130 II b 2
München-Aubing 130 II a 2
München-Berg am Laim 130 II b 2
München-Bogenhausen 130 II b 2
München-Daglfing 130 II bc 2
München-Denning 130 II bc 2
München-Englschalking 130 II bc 2
München-Fasanerie-Nord 130 II b 1
München-Fasangarten 130 II b 2
München-Forstenried 130 II ab 2
München-Freimann 130 II b 1
München-Gern 130 II b 2
München-Giesing 130 II b 2
München-Grosshadern 130 II a 2
München-Haidhausen 130 II b 2
München-Harlaching 130 II b 2
München-Hartmannshofen 130 II ab 2
München-Johanneskirchen 130 II bc 1
München-Kleinhadern 130 II a 2
München-Kolonie Lerchenau 130 II b 1
München-Laim 130 II ab 2
München-Langwied 130 II a 1
München-Lochham 130 II a 2
München-Lochhausen 130 II a 1
München-Ludwigsfeld 130 II ab 1
München-Menterschwaige 130 II b 2
München-Milbertshofen 130 II b 1
München-Neuhausen 130 II b 2
München-Nymphenburg 130 II ab 1
München-Oberföhring 130 II b 1
München-Obermenzing 130 II a 1
München-Obersendling 130 II b 2
München-Perlach 130 II b 2
München-Pipping 130 II a 2
München-Ramersdorf 130 II b 2
München-Riem, Flughafen — 130 II c 2
München-Siedlung Hasenbergl 130 II b 1
München-Siedlung Neuherberg 130 II b 1
München-Steinhausen 130 II b 2
München-Thalkirchen 130 II b 2
München-Trudering 130 II bc 2
München-Untermenzing 130 II a 1
München-Untersendling 130 II b 2
München-Waldperlach 130 II bc 2
München-Zamdorf 130 II b 2
Munchique, Cerro — 94-95 C 6
Munch'ŏn 144-145 F 3
Muncie, IN 64-65 JK 3
Mundal = Mūndalam 140 DE 7
Mūndalam 140 DE 7
Mundare 61 BC 4
Mundaú 100-101 E 2
Mundaú, Ponta de — 100-101 E 2
Munday, TX 76-77 E 6
Münden 118 D 3
Mundergi 140 BC 3
Mundgod 140 B 3
Mundiwindi 158-159 CD 4
Mundo, Río — 120-121 F 9
Mundo Novo [BR, Bahia ↖ Feira de Santana] 100-101 D 6
Mundo Novo [BR, Bahia ↓ Itabuna] 100-101 E 9
Mundo Novo [BR, Mato Grosso do Sul] 102-103 E 5
Mundra 138-139 B 6
Mundrabilla 158-159 E 6
Mundubbera 158-159 JK 5
Muṇḍugōḍa = Mundgod 140 B 3
Muṇḍugōḍe = Mundgod 140 B 3
Mundurucânia, Reserva Florestal — 98-99 JK 8
Muṇḍvā = Mūndwa 138-139 DE 4
Mūndwa 138-139 DE 4
Muneru 140 E 2
Munfordville, KY 70-71 H 7
Mungallala Creek 158-159 J 5
Mungana 158-159 H 3
Mungaoli 138-139 FG 5
Mungari 172 F 5
Mūṅgāvalī = Mungaoli 138-139 FG 5
Mungbere 172 E 1
Mungeli 138-139 H 6
Mungēr = Monghyr 134-135 O 5
Mungindi 158-159 J 5
Munhafaḍ al-Qaṭṭārah 164-165 K 2-3
Munhango 172 C 4
Munich = München 118 EF 4
Munim, Rio — 100-101 B 2
Munirābād 140 BC 3
Munising, MI 70-71 G 2
Muñiz, General Sarmiento- 110 III a 1
Munizaga 108-109 DE 9
Muniz Freire 102-103 M 4
Munk 61 L 3
Munkfors 116-117 EF 8
Munkhafad ath-Tharthār 134-135 E 4
Munksund 116-117 JK 5
Munnik 174-175 HJ 2
Muñoz 106-107 G 6
Muñoz Gamero, Península — 111 B 8
Munro, Vicente López- 110 III b 1
Munsan 144-145 F 4
Munsfjället 116-117 F 5
Munshiganj 141 B 4
Münster [D] 118 C 2-3
Münster [IRL] 119 B 5
Münsterer Wald 128 III b 2
Munte 148-149 G 6
Muntele Ceahlău 122-123 LM 2
Muntele Mare 122-123 K 2
Muntele Nemira 122-123 M 2
Munṭii Banatului 122-123 JK 3
Munṭii Bihor 122-123 K 2
Munṭii Călimai 122-123 L 2
Munṭii Metalici 122-123 K 2
Muntok 148-149 DE 7
Munyeru River = Manneru 140 D 3
Munyu 174-175 H 6
Munzur dağları 136-137 H 3
Muodoslompolo 116-117 K 4
Mu'one, Nam — 150-151 E 3
Mu'o'ng Beng 150-151 C 2
Mu'o'ng Bum = Mu'o'ng Boum 150-151 D 1
Mu'o'ng Hat Hin 150-151 D 1-2
Mu'o'ng Het 150-151 E 2
Mu'o'ng Hiem 150-151 D 2
Mu'o'ng Hong Sa 150-151 C 3
Mu'o'ng Houn 150-151 C 2
Mu'o'ng Hun = Mu'o'ng Houn 150-151 C 2
Mu'o'ng Hung 150-151 D 2
Mu'o'ng Hu'n Xiêng Hu'ng 150-151 D 2
Mu'o'ng Kau 150-151 E 5
Mu'o'ng Khay 150-151 CD 3
Muong Kwa = Mu'o'ng Khoua 148-149 D 2
Mu'o'ng Lat 150-151 E 2
Muong Mongne = Mu'o'ng Mu'gne 150-151 C 2
Mu'o'ng Mu'gne 150-151 C 2
Muong Ngeun 150-151 C 3
Mu'o'ng Ngoi 150-151 D 2
Mu'o'ng Nhie 150-151 D 1
Mu'o'ng Nông 150-151 F 4
Mu'o'ng Ou Neua 150-151 CD 1
Mu'o'ng Ou Tay 150-151 C 1
Mu'o'ng Pa 150-151 C 3
Mu'o'ng Pak Beng 148-149 D 2-3
Mu'o'ng Pak Tha 150-151 C 2
Mu'o'ng Phalane 150-151 E 4
Mu'o'ng Phieng 150-151 C 3
Mu'o'ng Phine 150-151 EF 4
Muong Plateau = Cao Nguyên Trung Phân 148-149 E 4
Mu'o'ng Sai 150-151 CD 2
Mu'o'ng Sen 150-151 E 3
Mu'o'ng Sen, Đeo — 148-149 DE 3
Mu'o'ng Sing 150-151 C 2
Mu'o'ng Song Khone 150-151 E 4
Mu'o'ng Soui 150-151 D 3
Muong Soum = Mu'o'ng Soum 150-151 D 3
Mu'o'ng Thadeua 150-151 C 3
Mu'o'ng Tourakom 150-151 D 3
Mu'o'ng Va 150-151 D 2
Mu'o'ng Wapi 150-151 EF 5
Mu'o'ng Yo 150-151 C 2
Muonio 116-117 KL 4
Muonio älv 116-117 K 4
Mupa 141 C 3
Mupa Upare Hill 168-169 GH 3
Muping 146-147 H 3
Mup'yŏng-ni = Chŏnch'ŏn 144-145 F 2
Muqattam, Jabal al- 170 II b 1-c 2
Muqayshit 134-135 G 6
Muqayyar, Al- = Ur 134-135 F 4
Muqqār, Al- 166-167 K 3
Muqsim, Jabal — 173 CD 6
Muq'ud 166-167 L 1
Muquém, Vereda do — 100-101 C 6
Muqui 102-103 M 4
Muqur = Moqur 134-135 K 4
Mur 118 FG 5
Mura 122-123 FG 2
Murādābād = Morādābād 134-135 MN 5
Muradiye [TR, Manisa] 136-137 B 3
Muradiye [TR, Van] 136-137 KL 3
Muraenā = Morena 138-139 G 4
Murafa 126-127 CD 2
Muraina = Morena 138-139 G 4
Murakami 144-145 M 3
Murallón, Cerro — 111 B 7
Mūrān [IR] 136-137 N 7
Murang'a 172 G 2
Mur'anyo 164-165 bc 1
Muraši 132-133 H 6
Murat dağı 134-135 B 3
Murat dağları = Serafettin dağları 136-137 J 3
Murathüyügü 136-137 G 4
Murat nehri 134-135 E 3
Murauaú, Rio — 98-99 H 4
Muravera 122-123 CD 6
Murav'anka [SU → RO] 124-125 N 7
Murayama 144-145 N 3
Muraywad, Al- 136-137 L 8
Murchison, Cape — 56-57 S 3
Murchisonberge 174-175 J 2
Murchison Falls = Kabelega Falls 172 F 1
Murchison Falls National Park = Kabelega Falls National Park 172 F 1
Murchisonfjord 116-117 k 4-5
Murchisonfjorden 116-117 kl 4
Murchison Island 62 EF 2
Murchison River 158-159 C 5
Murcia [E, landscape] 120-121 G 9-10
Murcia [E, place] 120-121 G 9-10
Murdale 60 G 1
Murdo, SD 68-69 F 4
Murdochville 56-57 XY 8
Murdock, FL 80-81 b 3
Mureș 122-123 K 2-3
Murfreesboro, AR 78-79 C 3
Murfreesboro, NC 80-81 H 2
Murfreesboro, TN 64-65 J 4
Murgab [SU, place] 134-135 L 3
Murgab [SU, river] 134-135 J 3
Murge 122-123 G 5
Murghābrōd 134-135 JK 3-4
Murghā Kibzai 138-139 B 2
Murgon 158-159 K 5
Muria = Gunung Muryo 152-153 J 9
Muriaé 92-93 L 9
Muriaé, Rio — 102-103 M 4
Murici 100-101 G 5
Muriel Lake 61 C 3
Mūrig, Jabal — 166-167 CD 3
Murikandi 140 E 6
Murindó 94-95 C 4
Müritz 118 F 2
Murkong Selek 141 D 2
Murliganj 138-139 L 5
Murmansk 132-133 EF 4
Murmansk Rise 132-133 EF 2
Murmaši 132-133 E 4
Murmino 124-125 N 6
Muro, Capo di — 122-123 C 5
Muro Lucano 122-123 FG 5
Murom 132-133 G 6
Muromcevo 132-133 O 6
Muroran 142-143 R 3
Muros 120-121 C 7
Muroto 144-145 JK 6
Muroto zaki 144-145 K 6
Murphy, ID 66-67 E 4
Murphy, NC 78-79 G 3
Murphy, TN 80-81 D 3
Murphy Canal 85 I b 2
Murphysboro, IL 70-71 F 7
Murr, Bi'r — 173 B 6
Murrah, Ḥāssī — 166-167 E 4
Murrah, Jabal — 166-167 L 2
Murrat al-Kubrá, Al-Buḥayrat al- 173 C 2
Murrat el-Kubrá, Buḥeiret el — = Al-Buḥayrat al-Murrat al-Kubrá 173 C 2
Murray, KY 78-79 E 2
Murray, Lake — [PNG] 148-149 M 8
Murray, Lake — [USA] 80-81 F 3
Murray Bridge 158-159 G 7
Murray Fracture Zone 156-157 KL 3
Murray Harbour 63 EF 5
Murray Lake 85 II b 3
Murray River [AUS] 158-159 H 6-7
Murray River [CDN] 60 G 2
Murraysburg 174-175 E 6
Murri, Río — 94-95 C 4
Murrumbidgee River 158-159 HJ 6
Murrumburrah 160 J 5
Murshidābād 138-139 M 5
Mürsut 166-167 L 2
Murtazāpur 138-139 F 7
Murtijāpur = Murtazāpur 138-139 F 7
Murtle Lake 60 H 3
Murtoa 160 F 6
Muru, Rio — 96-97 F 6
Murud 140 A 1
Murud, Gunung — 152-153 LM 4
Murumush 174-175 E 3
Murundu 102-103 M 4
Murung, Sungai — 152-153 L 7
Murunkan 140 E 6
Murupara 158-159 P 7
Murupu 92-93 G 4
Murvārā = Murwāra 134-135 N 6
Murwāra 134-135 N 6
Murwillumbah 158-159 K 5
Murygino 124-125 R 4
Muryo, Gunung — 152-153 J 9
Murzúq = Marzūq 164-165 G 3
Mürzzuschlag 118 G 5
Muş 134-135 E 3
Mūsā, Khūr-e — 136-137 N 7-8
Muşa Ali 164-165 N 6
Musabeyli = Murathüyügü 136-137 G 4
Musāfirkhāna 138-139 H 4
Musā'īd 166-167 A 5
Musā'idah 136-137 M 7
Mūsā Kḥel Bāzār 138-139 B 2
Musala 122-123 K 4
Musala, Pulau — 148-149 C 6
Musan 142-143 OP 3
Mūsa Qal'a 134-135 JK 4
Musashino 155 III a 1
Musashino-Kichijōji 155 III a 1
Musayīd 134-135 G 5-6
Musayyib, Al- 136-137 L 6
Musazade 136-137 J 2
Muscat = Masqaṭ 134-135 HJ 6
Muscatine, IA 70-71 E 5
Muscoda, WI 70-71 E 4
Muscongus Bay 72-73 M 3
Musées 128 II b 1
Museo 113 II b 2
Museo Arqueológico 113 III ab 2
Museo de Belles Artes 91 II b 1
Museo del Oro 91 III c 3
Museo del Prado 113 III a 2
Museo de Nariño 91 III b 3
Museo Nacional [BR] 110 I b 2
Museo Nacional [CO] 91 III c 3
Museo Nacional de Antropologia 91 I b 2
Museu do Ipiranga 110 II b 2
Museum of Fine Arts [USA, Boston] 84 I b 2
Museum of Fine Arts [USA, Houston] 85 III b 1
Museum of National History 155 II b 2
Museum of Natural Science 85 III b 2
Museum of Science and Industry 83 II b 2
Musgrave 158-159 H 2
Musgrave Ranges 158-159 F 5
Musgravetown 63 JK 3
Mūshā 173 B 4
Mushāsh, Bi'r — 136-137 G 7
Mushie 172 C 2
Mushin 168-169 F 4
Mushkābād = Ebrāhīmābād 136-137 O 5
Mushora = Mushūrah 136-137 K 4
Mushūrah 136-137 K 4
Mūsi 140 D 2
Musi, Sungai — 148-149 D 7
Mūṣīl, Al- 134-135 E 3
Musinia Peak 74-75 H 3
Musiri 140 D 5
Musisi 171 C 4
Musium Pusat Abri 154 IV a 2
Mūsīyān 136-137 M 6
Muskat = Masqaṭ 134-135 H 6
Muskeg Bay 70-71 C 1
Muskeg Lake 70-71 EF 1
Muskegon, MI 64-65 J 3
Muskegon Heights, MI 70-71 G 4
Muskegon River 70-71 GH 4
Muski, Al-Qāhirah-al- 170 II b 1
Muskingum River 72-73 EF 5
Muskogee, OK 64-65 GH 4
Muskoka, Lake — 72-73 G 2
Muslimīyah 136-137 G 4
Musl'umovo 124-125 T 6
Musmār = Mismār 164-165 M 5
Musoma 172 F 2
Musoshi 171 AB 5
Muş ovası 136-137 J 3
Musquaro, Lac — 63 F 2
Musquaro, Rivière — 63 F 2
Mussali, Mount — = Muşa Ali 164-165 N 6
Mussanāt, Al- 136-137 M 8
Mussau 148-149 N 7
Musselburgh 119 E 4
Musselshell River 64-65 E 2
Mussende 172 C 4
Mussoorie 138-139 G 2
Mussuma 172 D 4
Mustafābād 138-139 G 4
Mustafakemalpaşa 136-137 C 2-3
Mustaghānam 164-165 DE 1
Mustajevo 124-125 T 8
Mustāng 138-139 JK 3
Mustang, OK 76-77 EF 5
Mustang Island 76-77 F 9
Mustapha, Al-Jazā'ir- 170 I a 1
Musters, Lago — 111 BC 7
Mustique 88-89 Q 8
Mustla 124-125 EF 4
Mustvee 124-125 F 4
Mustwee = Mustvee 124-125 F 4
Mus'ūd, Wādī — 166-167 F 5-6
Musu-dan 144-145 GH 2
Muswellbrook 158-159 K 6
Mūt [ET] 164-165 K 3
Mut [TR] 136-137 E 4
Muta 171 A 3
Mutá, Ponta do — 100-101 E 7
Mutankiang = Mudanjiang 142-143 OP 3
Mutare 172 F 5
Mutãs 100-101 C 8
Mutatá 94-95 C 4
Muthanna, Al- 136-137 L 7

Mu'tiq, Jabal — 173 C 4
Mutis, Gunung — 148-149 H 8
Mutki = Mirtağ 136-137 J 3
Muṭlah = Al-Maṭlā' 136-137 M 8
Mutsamudu 172 HJ 4
Mutshatsha 172 D 4
Mutsu 144-145 N 2
Mutsu-wan 144-145 N 2
Mutton Bay 63 G 2
Muttra = Mathurā 134-135 M 5
Muttupet 140 D 5
Mutuípe 100-101 E 7
Mutum 102-103 M 3
Mutum, Rio — 98-99 D 7
Mutum Biyu 168-169 H 3
Mutumparaná 104-105 D 1
Mutuoca, Ilha de — 100-101 B 1
Mutuoca, Ponta da — 100-101 B 1
Mutur = Mudūr 140 E 6
Mututi, Ilha — 98-99 N 5
Mūvattupula 140 C 5-6
Mūvāt't'upuyḷa = Mūvattupula 140 C 5-6
Muwaffaqīyah, Al- 136-137 L 6
Muwayḥ, Al- 134-135 E 6
Muwayliḥ, Al- 173 D 4
Muxima 172 B 3
Muyeveld 128 I b 2
Muyinga 172 EF 2
Muyumanu, Río — 96-97 G 7
Muyumba 172 E 3
Muyuquira 104-105 D 7
Muẓaffarābād 134-135 LM 4
Muẓaffargaṛh 134-135 L 4-5
Muzaffarnagar 134-135 M 5
Muzaffarpur 134-135 NO 5
Muzambinho 102-103 J 4
Muži 132-133 L 4
Muzo 94-95 D 5
Muzon, Cape — 58-59 w 9
Muz tagh 142-143 E 4
Muz tagh ata 142-143 D 4

Mvōlō 164-165 KL 7
Mvuma 172 F 5

Mwali 172 H 4
Mwambwa 171 C 5
Mwanamundia 171 DE 3
Mwanza [EAT] 172 F 2
Mwanza [ZRE] 172 E 3
Mwatate 171 D 3
Mwaya 172 F 3
Mwazya 171 BC 5
Mweka 172 D 2
Mwene-Ditu 172 D 3
Mwenga 172 E 2
Mwenzo 171 C 5
Mweru, Lake — 172 E 3
Mweru Swamp 172 E 3
Mwīlah 166-167 C 5
Mwingi 171 D 3
Mwinilunga 172 DE 4
M'wīsāt, Bi'r al- 166-167 A 7
Mwitikira 171 C 4

Mya, Ouèd — = Wādī Miyāh 166-167 J 4
Myāchlār = Miājlar 138-139 C 4
Myaing 141 D 5
Myan'aung 148-149 BC 3
Myaung 141 D 5
Myaungmya 141 D 7
Myawadī 141 F 7
Myebôn 141 C 5
Myèbûm, Lûy — 141 E 3
Myeik 148-149 C 4
Myeik Kyûnzu 148-149 C 4
Myemûn 141 D 4
Myenmoletkhat, Mount — = Myinmôylet'hkat Taung 150-151 B 6
Myi Chhu 138-139 L 3
Myingyan 148-149 BC 2
Myinmoletkat Taung = Myinmôylet'hkat Taung 150-151 B 6
Myinmôylet'hkat Taung 150-151 B 6
Myinmū 141 D 5
Myinzaung 150-151 A 5
Myitkyīnā 148-149 C 1
Myitngei Myit 141 E 4-5
Myitthā 141 E 5
Myittha = Manibūra Myit 141 C 4
Myitthā Myit 141 D 4
Myjeldino 124-125 U 3
Mykénai 122-123 K 7
Mýkonos 122-123 L 7
Mymensingh = Maimansingh 134-135 OP 6
Mynämäki 116-117 JK 7
Mynaral 132-133 N 8
Mynfontein 174-175 EF 6
Myntobe 126-127 O 3
Myōgyī 141 E 5
Myôhaung 141 C 5
Myohyang-sanmaek 144-145 E 3-F 2
Myōkō-zan 144-145 LM 4
Myŏngch'ŏn 144-145 GH 2
Myothā 141 D 5
Myōthit 141 D 5
Myōzam 141 D 3
Mýra 116-117 c 2
Myrdal 116-117 B 7
Mýrdalsjökull 116-117 d 3
Mýrdalssandur 116-117 d 3
Myre 116-117 F 3
Mýrina 122-123 L 6
Myrnam 61 C 4
Myrthle 72-73 G 2
Myrtle Beach, SC 80-81 G 4
Myrtle Creek, OR 66-67 B 4
Myrtleford 160 H 6
Myrtle Point, OR 66-67 AB 4
mys Aleksandra 132-133 ab 7
mys Alevina 132-133 cd 6
mys Aniva 132-133 b 8
mys Barykova 132-133 jk 5
mys Bering 132-133 k 5
mys Blossom 132-133 jk 3
mys Borisova 132-133 a 6
mys Buor-Chaja 132-133 Z 3
mys Čel'uskin 132-133 T-V 2
mys Chersonesskij 126-127 F 4
mys Crillon 132-133 b 8
mys Čukotskij 132-133 l 5
mys Dežneva 132-133 lm 4
mys Duga-Zapadnaja 132-133 bc 6
mys Dzenzik 126-127 H 3
Myšega 124-125 L 6
Mysen 116-117 D 8
mys Enken 132-133 b 6
mys Gamova 144-145 H 1
mys Govena 132-133 g 6
mys Jakan 132-133 j 4
mys Jelizavety 132-133 b 7
mys Južnyj 132-133 e 6
mys Kazantip 126-127 G 4
mys Kiik-Atlama 126-127 GH 4
Myškino 124-125 LM 5
mys Kronockij 132-133 f 7
Myślenice 118 JK 4
mys Lopatka 52 D 3
mys Lukull 126-127 F 4
mys Meganom 126-127 G 4
mys Men'šikova 132-133 KL 3
mys Navarin 132-133 jk 5
mys Nizkij 132-133 hj 5
mys Ol'utorskij 132-133 h 6
mys Omgon 132-133 e 6
Mysore 140 C 4
Mysovsk = Babuškin 132-133 U 7
mys Ozernoj 132-133 fg 6
mys Peek 58-59 C 4
mys Pesčanyj 126-127 P 5
mys Picunda 126-127 K 5
mys Russkij Zavorot 132-133 JK 4
mys Sagyndyk 126-127 P 4
mys Saryč 126-127 F 4
mys Šelagskij 132-133 gh 3
mys Serdce Kamen' 58-59 BC 3
mys Sivučij 132-133 fg 6
mys Skuratova 132-133 LM 3
mys Sporyj Navolok 132-133 M-O 2
mys Šupunskij 132-133 f 7
mys Sv'atoj Nos 132-133 ab 3
mys Tajgonos 132-133 ef 5
mys Taran 118 JK 1
mys Tarchankut 126-127 EF 4
mys Terpenija 132-133 bc 8
Mystic, IA 70-71 D 5
Mystic, SD 68-69 E 3
Mystic River 84 I b 2
Mystic River Bridge 84 I b 2
mys Tolstoj 132-133 e 6
mys T'ub-Karagan 126-127 OP 4
mys Uengan 132-133 LM 3
mys Vchodnoj 132-133 QR 3
Mysy 124-125 TU 3
mys Želanija 132-133 MN 2
mys Z'uk 126-127 H 4
My Tho 148-149 E 4
Mytilēnē 122-123 M 6
Mytišči 124-125 LM 5-6
Myton, UT 66-67 HJ 5
Mývatn 116-117 e 2

Mzab = Al-Mizāb 166-167 HJ 3
Mzab, Ouèd — = Wādī Mizāb 166-167 J 3
Mzi, Djebel — = Jabal Mazī 166-167 F 3
Mziha 172 G 3
Mzimba 172 F 4
Mzuzu 171 C 5

N

Na, Nam — 150-151 D 1
Naab 118 F 4
Na'âg, Gebel — = Jabal Nī'āj 173 C 6
Naalehu, HI 78-79 e 3
Na'ām, Bi'r an- 136-137 G 7
Na'ām, Jabal Zarqat 173 D 6
Na'ām, Maqarr an- 136-137 HJ 7
Naama = Na'āmah 166-167 F 3
Na'āmah 166-167 F 3
Naantali 116-117 JK 7
Naas 119 C 5
Näätämöjoki 116-117 MN 3
Naauwpoort = Noupoort 172 DE 8
Naauwte, De — 174-175 DE 6
Nabā 141 E 3
Nababeep = Nababiep 174-175 B 5
Nababiep 174-175 B 5
Nabadwīp 138-139 LM 6
Nabāh, Bi'r — 173 C 7
Nabarangpura = Nowrangapur 138-139 J 8
Nābaw 141 E 3
Nabč 142-143 G 4
Naberežnyje Čelny 124-125 T 6
Nabesna, AK 58-59 Q 5
Nabesna Glacier 58-59 Q 5
Nâbeul = Nābul 164-165 G 1
Nābha 138-139 F 2
Nabiac 160 L 4
Nabīganj 141 B 3
Nabilatuk 171 C 2
Nabileque, Pantanal de — 102-103 D 3-4
Nabileque, Rio — 102-103 D 4
Nabīnagar 138-139 K 5
Nabire 148-149 L 7
Nabīsar 134-135 KL 5-6
Nabisipi, Rivière — 63 E 2
Nabk, An- [Saudi Arabia] 136-137 G 7
Nabk, An- [SYR] 134-135 D 4
Nāblus = Nābulus 136-137 F 6
Nabolo 168-169 E 3
Nabón 96-97 B 3
Naboomspruit 174-175 H 3
Nabordo 168-169 H 3
Nabou 168-169 C 3
Nabq 173 D 3
Nābul 164-165 G 1
Nābulus 136-137 F 6
Nabūn 141 C 4
Nabung = Nabūn 141 C 4
Nacaca 171 D 5
Naçala 172 H 4
Nacfa = Nakfa 164-165 M 5
Naches, WA 66-67 C 2
Nachičevan' 126-127 M 7
Nachingwea 172 GH 4
Nāchna 138-139 C 4
Nachodka 132-133 Z 9
Nachoi 138-139 M 5
Nachol = Nachoi 138-139 M 5
Nachrači = Kondirskoje 132-133 M 6
Nachtigal Falls 168-169 HJ 4
Nacimiento 106-107 A 6
Nacimiento Mountains 76-77 A 4-5
Nacional, La — 106-107 E 5
Naciria = Nāṣirīyah 166-167 HJ 1
Nacka 116-117 H 8
Naco 86-87 EF 2
Naco, AZ 74-75 HJ 7
Nacogdoches, TX 76-77 G 7
Nacololo 171 D 6
Nacozari de Gracia 64-65 DE 5
Ñacuñan 106-107 D 5
Ñacunday 102-103 E 7
Ñacunday, Río — 102-103 E 6
Nadadores 76-77 D 9
Nadbai 138-139 F 4
Nādendal = Naantali 116-117 JK 7
Nadeždinsk = Serov 132-133 L 6
Nadhatah, An- 136-137 J 6
Nadiād 134-135 L 6
Nadina River 60 D 3
Nadiyā = Kishnanagar 138-139 M 6
Nadjaf, An- = An-Najaf 134-135 E 4
Nadjd = Najd 134-135 E 5-6
Nādlac 122-123 J 2
Nadoa = Dan Xian 142-143 K 8
Nâdôr = An-Nāḍūr 166-167 E 2
Nadqān 134-135 G 6
Nāḍūr, An- 166-167 E 2
Nadvoicy 124-125 K 2
Nadvornaja 126-127 B 2
Naenpur = Nainpur 138-139 H 6
Naenwa 138-139 EF 5
Næstved 116-117 DE 10
Na Fac 150-151 E 1
Nafada 164-165 G 6
Nafīs, Wād — 166-167 B 4
Nafīshah 173 BC 2
Nafṭ, Āb-i — 136-137 L 6
Naftah 166-167 K 3
Naftalan 126-127 N 6
Naft-e Sefīd 136-137 N 7
Naft-e Shāh 136-137 L 5-6
Naft Hānah 136-137 L 5
Naft Khāna = Naft Hānah 136-137 L 5
Nafūd, An- 134-135 E 5
Nafūd ad-Daḥī 134-135 EF 6
Nafūd as-Sirr 134-135 E 5-F 6
Nafusah, Jabal — 164-165 G 2
Naga 148-149 H 4
Nagagami Lake 70-71 H 1
Nagahama [J, Ehime] 144-145 J 6
Nagahama [J, Shiga] 144-145 L 5
Naga Hills 141 D 2-3
Nagai 144-145 MN 3
Nagai Island 58-59 cd 2
Nāgāland 134-135 P 5
Nāgamāngala 140 C 4
Nagano 142-143 Q 4
Naganohara 144-145 M 4
Nagaoka 142-143 Q 4
Nāgaor = Nāgaur 134-135 L 5
Nāgapattinam 134-135 MN 8
Nagā Pradesh = Nāgāland 134-135 P 5
Nagar 138-139 F 4
Nāgar = Nāgore 140 DE 5
Nagara gawa 144-145 L 5
Nagar Aveli = Dādra and Nagar Haveli 134-135 L 6
Nagar Devla 138-139 E 7
Nagare Angū 141 CD 7
Nagar Haveli, Dadra and — 134-135 L 6
Nāgari 140 E 4
Nāgari Hills 140 D 4
Nāgārjuna Sāgar 140 D 2
Nagar Karnūl 140 D 2
Nāgarkōyil = Nāgercoil 134-135 M 9
Nagar Kurnool = Nāgar Karnūl 140 D 2
Nagar Pārkar 134-135 KL 6
Nagar Untāri 138-139 J 5
Nagasaki 142-143 O 5
Naga-shima [J, island] 144-145 GH 6
Nagashima [J, place] 144-145 L 5
Nagatino, Moskva- 113 V c 3
Nagato 144-145 H 5
Nagatsuda, Yokohama- 155 III a 2
Nāgaur 134-135 L 5
Nāgāvali 140 F 1
Nagayoshi 155 III d 3
Nāgbhīr 138-139 G 7
Nag Chhu 142-143 G 5
Nagchhu Dsong 142-143 G 5
Nagchhukha = Nagchhu Dsong 142-143 G 5
Nāgercoil 134-135 M 9
Nagīna 138-139 G 3
Nāginimara 141 D 2
Nāgīshōt = Nāqīshūt 164-165 L 8
Nāgod 138-139 H 5
Nagorje 124-125 M 5
Nagorno-Karabagh Autonomous Region 126-127 N 6
Nagornyj 132-133 Y 6
Nagorsk 124-125 S 4
Nagoudé 168-169 H 2
Nagoya 142-143 Q 4
Nāgpur 134-135 M 6
Nagtshang 138-139 LM 2
Nagura, Ras en — = Rā's an-Naqurah 136-137 F 6
Naguun Mörön 142-143 NO 1-2
Nagykanizsa 118 H 5
Nagykőrös 118 JK 5
Nagyvárad = Oradea 122-123 JK 2
Naha 142-143 O 6
Nahabuan 152-153 L 5
Nāhan 138-139 F 2
Nahanni National Park 56-57 LM 5
Nahant, MA 84 I c 2
Nahant Bay 84 I c 2
Nahari 144-145 JK 6
Nahariya 136-137 F 6
Nahariyya = Nahariya 136-137 F 6
Nahar Ouassel, Ouèd — = Wādī Wāsal 166-167 GH 2
Nahāvand 136-137 N 5
Nāhid, Bi'r — 136-137 C 7
Nahīlah, An- = An-Nakhīlah 166-167 E 2
Nahlin River 58-59 W 7
Nahr al-'Āṣī 136-137 G 5
Nahr al-Furāt 134-135 E 4
Nahr al-'Idhaim = Shaṭṭ al-'Uzaym 136-137 L 5
Nahr al-Jūr 164-165 K 7
Nahr al-Karākūrū 168-169 C 1-2
Nahr al-Khābūr 134-135 E 3
Nahr al-Khāzir 136-137 K 4
Nahr al-Liṭānī 136-137 F 6
Nahr ar-Rahad 164-165 L 6
Nahr ash-Sharī'ah 136-137 F 6-7
Nahr 'Aṭbarah 164-165 LM 5
Nahr Balīh 136-137 H 4
Nahr Begārī 138-139 B 3
Nahr Belīkh = Nahr Balīh 136-137 H 4
Nahr Dijlah 134-135 E 3
Nahr Diyālā 134-135 EF 4
Nahr el Jūr = Nahr al-Jūr 164-165 K 7
Nahr esh-Sherī'ah = Nahr ash-Sharī'ah 136-137 F 6-7
Nahr Lōl = Nahr Lūl 164-165 K 7
Nahr Lūl 164-165 K 7
Nahr Pībōr 164-165 L 7
Nahr Rohrī 138-139 B 4
Nahr Shalar 136-137 L 5
Nahr Sōbāṭ = As-Sūbāṭ 164-165 L 7
Nahr Sūī 164-165 K 7
Nahuelbuta, Cordillera de — 106-107 A 6-7
Nahuel Huapi 108-109 D 3
Nahuel Huapi, Lago — 111 B 6
Nahuel Huapi, Parque Nacional — 108-109 D 3
Nahuel Mapá 106-107 DE 5
Nahuel Niyue 108-109 F 3
Nahuel Rucá 106-107 J 6
Nahungo 171 D 5
Nahunta, GA 80-81 EF 5
Nāhyā 170 II a 1
Naica 76-77 B 9
Naicam 61 F 4
Naicó 106-107 E 6
Na'idah, 'Anu an- 166-167 K 6
Naiguatá 94-95 H 2
Naihāti 138-139 M 6
Nain [CDN] 56-57 Y 6
Nā'īn [IR] 134-135 G 4
Naindi 148-149 a 2
Naini Tal 134-135 M 5
Nainpur 138-139 H 6
Nain Singh Range = Nganglong Gangri 142-143 E 5
Nair = Ner 138-139 F 7
Nairn 119 E 3
Nairobi 172 G 2
Naissaar 124-125 E 4
Naivasha 172 G 2
Naiyyāttinkara = Neyyāttinkara 140 C 6
Najaf, An- 134-135 E 4
Najafābād 134-135 G 4
Najd 134-135 E 5-6
Naj' Ḥammādī 173 BC 4-5
Najībābād 138-139 G 3
Najin 142-143 P 3
Najran 134-135 E 7
Najstenjarvi 124-125 J 2
Naju 144-145 F 5
Naka 155 III c 1
Naka = Io 206-207 S 7
Naka, Yokohama- 155 III a 3
Nakadōri-shima 144-145 G 6
Na Kae 150-151 E 4
Naka gawa 144-145 K 6
Nakajima 155 III c 3
Nakajō 144-145 M 3
Nakakido 155 III d 1
Nakaminato 144-145 N 4
Nakamura 144-145 J 6
Nakamura = Sōma 144-145 N 4
Nakanbu, Tōkyō- 155 III b 2
Nakano 144-145 M 4
Nakano, Tōkyō- 155 III ab 1
Nakano-shima 144-145 J 4
Nakanoshima, Kawasaki- 155 III a 2
Nakano-umi 144-145 J 5
Nakasato 144-145 N 2
Naka-Shibetsu 144-145 d 2
Nakasongola 171 C 2
Nakatane 144-145 H 7
Nakatsu 144-145 H 6
Nakatsukawa 144-145 L 5
Nakatsukawa = Nakatsugawa 144-145 L 5
Nakatu 144-145 H 6
Nakayama, Yokohama- 155 III a 2
Nakchamik Island 58-59 e 1
Naked Island 58-59 O 6
Nakfa 164-165 M 5
Nakhichevan Autonomous Soviet Socialist Republic 126-127 M 7
Nakhīlah, An- 166-167 E 2
Nakhīl, Bi'r — 136-137 K 5
Nakhl 173 C 3
Nakhlāy, Bi'r — 173 B 6
Nakhon Lampang = Lampang 148-149 C 3
Nakhon Nayok 150-151 C 5
Nakhon Pathom 148-149 CD 4
Nakhon Phanom 148-149 D 3
Nakhon Ratchasima 148-149 D 3-4
Nakhon Rat Sima 150-151 DE 4-5
Nakhon Sawan 148-149 CD 3
Nakhon Si Thammarat 148-149 CD 5
Nakhon Tai 150-151 C 4
Nakhtarāna 138-139 B 6
Nakina 56-57 T 7
Nakło nad Notecią 118 H 2
Naknek, AK 56-57 E 6
Naknek Lake 58-59 JK 7
Nakodar 138-139 E 2
Nakonde 171 C 5
Nakop 174-175 CD 5
Nakou 146-147 F 8
Nakpanduri 168-169 EF 3
Nakskov 116-117 D 10
Nakta = Naqaṭah 166-167 M 2
Naktong-gang 144-145 G 5
Nakur 138-139 F 3
Nakuru 172 G 2
Nakusp 60 J 4
Nakwaby 168-169 E 3
Nāl 134-135 K 5
Nalagunḍa = Nalgonda 140 D 2
Nalajch 142-143 K 2
Nalazi 174-175 K 3
Nalbāri 141 B 2
Nalcayec, Isla — 108-109 C 6
Nal'čik 126-127 L 5
Na Le = Ban Na Le 150-151 C 3
Nalgonda 140 D 2
Nalhāti 138-139 L 5
Nali 150-151 G 2
Nalitābāṛī 141 AB 3
Nallamala Range 140 D 2-3
Nallıhan 136-137 D 2
Nalōn 141 E 3
Nālung 138-139 M 3
Na Lu'ong = Ban Na Lu'ong 150-151 E 4
Nālūt 164-165 G 2
Nama 174-175 BC 3
Namacurra 172 G 5
Na'mah, An- 164-165 C 5
Nam Ak 141 E 5
Namak, Daryācheh — 134-135 G 4
Nāmakkal 140 D 5
Namakwaland 172 C 7
Namakwaland = Klein Namakwaland 174-175 B 5
Namakwaland, Klein — 174-175 B 5
Namakzār-e Khwāf 134-135 HJ 4
Namakzār-e Shahdād 134-135 H 4
Namaland 172 C 7
Namamugi, Yokohama- 155 III b 3
Na'mān, Jazīrat an — = Jazīrat an-Nu'mān 173 D 4
Namanga 172 G 2
Namangan 134-135 L 2
Na'mānīyah, An- 136-137 L 6
Namanyere 172 F 3
Namapa 172 GH 4
Namaqua Land, Little — = Klein Namakwaland 174-175 B 5
Namarrói 172 G 5
Namasagali 172 F 1
Namasakata 171 D 5
Namāshah, Jabal an- 166-167 K 2
Namashu 138-139 J 3
Namatanai 148-149 h 5
Namatele 171 D 5
Namban 141 F 5
Nambanje 171 D 5
Nam Bei 141 E 4
Nam Beng 150-151 C 2
Nam Bô 148-149 DE 5
Nambour 158-159 K 5
Nam CaĐinh = Nam Theun 150-151 E 3
Năm Căn 148-149 D 5
Nāmche Bāzār 138-139 L 4
Namche Bazar = Nāmche Bāzār 138-139 L 4
Nam Chi 150-151 DE 5
Nam Choed Yai = Kra Buri 148-149 C 4
Nam Choen 150-151 CD 4
Namch'ŏnjŏm 144-145 F 3
Namcy 132-133 Y 5
Nam Đinh 148-149 E 2-3
Namerikawa 144-145 L 4
Nametil 172 GH 5
Namew Lake 61 G 3
Nam-gang 144-145 F 3
Namgôk 141 E 5
Namhae-do 144-145 G 5
Namhan-gang 144-145 F 4
Nam Hka 141 F 5
Namhkok = Namgôk 141 E 5
Namhoi = Foshan 142-143 L 7
Namhsan = Namzan 141 E 4
Nam Hsin 141 F 5
Nam Hu = Nam Ou 150-151 D 2
Nami 150-151 C 9
Namib = Namibwoestyn 172 B 5-C 7
Namib Desert = Namibwoestyn 172 B 5-C 7
Namibia 172 C 6
Namib-Naukluft Park 172 BC 6
Namibwoestyn 172 B 5-C 7
Namies 174-175 C 5
Namiziz 174-175 B 4
Namjabarba Ri 142-143 H 6
Nam Kam 150-151 E 4
Nam Khan 150-151 D 2-3
Nam Khan = Nangan 141 E 4
Nam Kok 150-151 B 2-3
Nam Kong 150-151 F 5
Namlan 141 E 4
Namlang River = Nam Ak 141 E 5
Namlāt, An- 166-167 KL 2
Namlea 148-149 J 7
Nam Lieau = Ea Hleo 150-151 F 6
Nam Lik 150-151 C 3
Namling Dsong 142-143 FG 6
Nam Luang 150-151 D 4
Nam Lwei 150-151 B 2
Nam Ma 150-151 D 1
Nammadū 141 E 4
Nam Madū Myit 141 EF 4
Nam Mae Chaem 150-151 B 3
Nam Mae Ing 150-151 C 2-3
Nam Mae Klong = Nam Mae Ngat 150-151 B 3
Nam Mae Lao 150-151 B 3
Nam Mae Ngat 150-151 B 3
Nam Mae Pai 150-151 B 3
Nam Mae Tun 150-151 B 4
Namman [BUR] 141 E 6
Nam Man [T, place] 150-151 C 4
Nam Man [T, river] 150-151 C 4
Nam Mao = Nam Wa 150-151 C 3
Nammeigôn 141 E 6
Nam Me Klong = Mae Nam Mae Klong 150-151 B 5-6
Nam-me Klong = Mae Nam Ma Klong 150-151 B 5-6
Nammokon = Nammeigôn 141 E 6
Nam Mu'one 150-151 E 3
Nam Na 150-151 D 1
Nam Ngum 150-151 D 3
Nam Nhiêp 150-151 D 3
Namoa = Nan'ao 146-147 F 10
Namoa = Nan'ao Dao 146-147 F 10
Namoi River 158-159 J 6
Namoluk 208 F 2
Namone = Ban Namone 150-151 D 3
Namorik 208 G 2
Nam Ou 150-151 D 1
Namous, Ouèd en — = Wādī an-Nāmus 164-165 D 2
Nampa 60 J 1
Nampa, ID 64-65 C 3
Nam Pak 150-151 D 2
Nampala 164-165 C 5
Nam Pat 150-151 C 4
Nam Phao = Ban Nam Phao 150-151 C 3
Nam Phong 150-151 CD 4
Nampo 142-143 NO 4
Namp'ot'ae-san 144-145 G 2
Nampula 172 GH 5
Nam Pūn 141 E 5-6
Nampung 138-139 M 4
Namru He = Ru He 146-147 E 5
Nam Sane 150-151 D 3
Namsen 116-117 E 5
Nam Seng 150-151 D 2
Namsi 144-145 E 3
Nam Si = Nam Chi 150-151 DE 5
Nam Soen = Nam Choen 150-151 CD 4
Nam Som 150-151 CD 4
Namsos 116-117 DE 5
Nam Suong = Nam Seng 150-151 D 2
Nam Tae = Ban Nam Tao 150-151 C 4
Nam Tan 141 F 5
Nam Teng = Nam Tan 141 F 5
Nam Tha 148-149 D 2
Nam Theun 150-151 E 3
Nam Tho'n = Nam Theun 150-151 E 3
Nam Tia = Ban Nam Tia 150-151 D 3
Nam Tīlū 141 E 5
Nam Tsho 142-143 G 5
Namtu = Nammadū 141 E 4
Namu [CDN] 60 D 4
Namu [Micronesia] 208 G 2
Nam U = Nam Ou 150-151 D 1
Namuli, Serra — 172 G 5
Namuling Zong = Namling Dsong 142-143 FG 6
Namulo 171 D 6
Namuno 171 D 6
Namur 120-121 K 3
Namur Lake 61 B 2
Nāmūs, Wādī an- 164-165 D 2
Nāmūs, Waw an- 164-165 H 4
Namutoni 172 C 5
Nam Wa 150-151 C 3
Namwala 172 E 5
Nam Wei 155 I b 1
Namwŏn 144-145 F 5
Nam Yao = Nam Madū Myit 141 EF 4
Namzan 141 E 4
Nan 148-149 D 3
Nan, Mae Nam — 148-149 D 3
Nana Candungo 172 D 4
Nanae 144-145 b 3
Nanafalia, AL 78-79 F 4
Nanaimo 56-57 M 8
N'an'ajol' 124-125 S 2
Nanam 144-145 GH 2
Nana-Mambéré 164-165 GH 7
Nan'an 146-147 G 9
Nanango 158-159 K 5
Nananib Plateau = Nananibplato 174-175 B 3
Nananibplato 174-175 B 3
Nanao [J] 144-145 L 4
Nan-ao [RC] 146-147 H 9
Nan'ao [TJ] 146-147 F 10
Nan'ao Dao 146-147 F 10
Nan-ao Tao = Nan'ao Dao 146-147 F 10
Nanao wan 144-145 L 4
Nanas Channel 154 III b 1
Nanau 171 E 1
Nanay 96-97 E 3
Nanay, Río — 92-93 E 5
Nanbē 141 E 6
Nancefield, Johannesburg- 170 V a 2
Nancha 142-143 O 2
Nanchang 142-143 LM 6
Nanchang = Nanchong 142-143 JK 5
Nan-chang = Nanzhang 146-147 CD 6
Nanchang He 155 II a 2
Nanchao = Nanzhao 146-147 D 5
Nancheng 142-143 M 6
Nan-ch'iao = Fengxian 146-147 H 6
Nan-ching = Nanjing [TJ, Fujian] 146-147 F 9
Nan-ching = Nanjing [TJ, Jiangsu] 142-143 M 5
Nanchino = Nanjing 142-143 M 5
Nan-chi Shan = Nanji Shan 146-147 H 8
Nanchong 142-143 JK 5
Nanchung = Nanchong 142-143 JK 5
Nancy 120-121 L 4
Nancy Creek 85 II b 1
Nanda Devi 134-135 MN 4
Nandalur 140 D 3
Nandan 144-145 K 5
Nandangarh, Lauriā- = Thori 138-139 K 4
Nandapur 140 F 1
Nandapura = Nandapur 140 F 1
Nānded 134-135 M 7
Nandeir = Nānded 134-135 M 7
Nāndgāṅv = Nāndgaon 138-139 E 7
Nāndgaon 138-139 E 7
Nandi [FJI] 148-149 a 2
Nandi [IND] 140 C 4
Nandigāma 140 E 2
Nandikotkūr 140 D 3
Nandikōṭṭakkūru = Nandikotkūr 140 D 3
N'andoma 132-133 G 5
Nanduan River 62 A 1
Ñandubay 106-107 GH 3
Ñanducita 106-107 G 3
Nandu He 150-151 H 3
Nāndūra 138-139 F 7
Nandurbār 134-135 L 6
Nandyāl 134-135 M 7
Nanfeng [TJ, Guangdong] 146-147 C 10
Nanfeng [TJ, Jiangxi] 146-147 F 8
Nangade 171 DE 5
Nanga-Eboko 164-165 G 8
Nangal 138-139 F 2
Nangan 141 E 4
Nan-gang = Nam-gang 144-145 F 3
Nangā Parbat 134-135 LM 3-4
Nangapinoh 148-149 F 7
Nangaraun 152-153 K 5
Nangaritza, Río — 96-97 B 4
Nangatayab 152-153 J 6
Nang'-ch'ien = Nangqian 142-143 H 5
Nanggûn Bûm 141 F 2
Nangkhartse Dsong 138-139 N 3
Nangnim-sanmaek 144-145 F 2
Nangong 146-147 E 3
Nangqian 142-143 H 5
Nang Rong 150-151 D 5
Nanguan 146-147 D 3
Nangugī 141 E 7
Nanguneri 140 C 6
Nan Hai 142-143 L 8-M 7
Nanhai = Foshan 142-143 L 7
Nanhe [TJ, place] 146-147 E 3
Nan He [TJ, river] 146-147 C 5
Nan-ho = Nanhe [TJ, place] 146-147 E 3
Nan Ho = Nan He [TJ, river] 146-147 C 5
Nanhsien = Nan Xian 146-147 D 7
Nan-hsiung = Nanxiong 142-143 LM 6
Nanhuatang 146-147 C 5
Nanhui 146-147 HJ 6
Nanika Lake 60 D 3
Nanikon 128 IV b 1
Nañjanagūḍu = Nanjangūd 140 C 4
Nanjangūd 140 C 4
Nanjiangqiao 146-147 DE 7

332 Mu'tiq

Nanjih Tao = Nanri Qundao 146-147 G 9
Nanjing [TJ, Fujian] 146-147 F 9
Nanjing [TJ, Jiangsu] 142-143 M 5
Nanji Shan 146-147 H 8
Nankana = Nankāna Sahib 138-139 DE 2
Nankāna Sahib 138-139 DE 2
Nankang [TJ, Guangdong] 146-147 B 11
Nankang [TJ, Jiangxi] 146-147 E 9
Nan-kang = Xingzi 146-147 F 7
Nankhu 142-143 G 3
Nanking = Nanjing 142-143 M 5
Nankoku 144-145 JK 6
Nan-kuan = Nanguan 146-147 D 3
Nankung = Nangong 146-147 E 3
Nanlaoye Ling 144-145 E 2-F 1
Nanle 146-147 E 3-4
Nan Ling [TJ, mountains] 142-143 L 6-7
Nanling [TJ, place] 142-143 M 5
Nan-liu Chiang = Nanliu Jiang 146-147 B 10-11
Nanliu Jiang 146-147 B 10-11
Nan-lo = Nanle 146-147 E 3-4
Nanma 146-147 H 7
Nanmofang, Beijing- 155 II b 2
Nanning 142-143 K 7
Nannup 158-159 C 6
Na Noi 150-151 C 3
Nanpan Jiang 142-143 JK 7
Nānpāra 138-139 H 4
Nanpi 146-147 F 2
Nanping [TJ, Fujian] 142-143 M 6
Nanping [TJ, Hubei] 142-143 L 6
Nan-p'u Ch'i = Nanpu Xi 146-147 G 8
Nanpu Xi 146-147 G 8
Nanqi = Youxikou 146-147 G 8
Nanripo 171 D 6
Nanri Qundao 146-147 G 9
Nansei Islands = Nansei-shotō 142-143 N 7-O 6
Nansei-shotō 142-143 NO 6-7
Nansei syotō = Nansei-shotō 142-143 NO 6-7
Nansen Sound 56-57 ST 1
Nan Shan 142-143 HJ 4
Nansio 172 F 2
Nantai-san 144-145 M 4
Nan-tch'ang = Nanchang 142-143 LM 6
Nan-tch'eng = Nancheng 142-143 M 6
Nan-tch'ong = Nanchong 142-143 JK 5
Nantes 120-121 G 5
Nantian 146-147 HJ 7
Nantian Dao 146-147 HJ 7
Nanticoke, PA 72-73 HJ 4
Nanton 60 L 4
Nantong 142-143 N 5
Nantongjao 152-153 K 2
Nantou [RC] 146-147 H 10
Nantou [TJ] 146-147 D 10
Nantsang = Nanchang 142-143 LM 6
Nantucket, MA 72-73 LM 4
Nantucket Island 64-65 N 3
Nantucket Sound 72-73 L 4
Nantung = Nantong 142-143 N 5
Nanty Glo, PA 72-73 G 4
Nanumanga 208 H 3
Nanumea 208 H 3
Nānun Ran = Little Rann 138-139 C 6
Nanuque 92-93 LM 8
Nanushuk River 58-59 M 2
Nan Xian 146-147 D 7
Nanxiong 142-143 LM 6
Nanyang 142-143 L 5
Nanyangchang 155 II b 3
Nanyang Hu 146-147 F 4
Nanyi = Nancha 142-143 O 2
Nanyuan, Beijing- 155 II b 3
Nanyuki 172 G 1
Nanzhang 146-147 CD 6
Nanzhao 146-147 D 5
Nanzheng = Hanzhong 142-143 K 5
Nao, Cabo de la — 120-121 H 9
Naochow Tao = Naozhou Dao 146-147 C 11
Naoconane Lake 56-57 W 7
Naoetsu 144-145 LM 4
Naogang = Nowgong 138-139 G 5
Naogāňv = Nowgong 141 C 2
Naogaon = Naugāon 138-139 M 5
Naōgata = Nōgata 144-145 H 6
Naoli He 142-143 P 2
Nao-li Ho = Naoli He 142-143 P 2
Naos 174-175 B 2
Naos, Isla — 64-65 bc 3
Naouá = Nawā 136-137 FG 6
Naozhou Dao 146-147 C 11
Napa, CA 74-75 B 3
Napabalana 152-153 P 8
Napaimiut, AK 58-59 H 6
Napakiak, AK 58-59 FG 6
Napaku 148-149 G 6
Napaleofú 106-107 H 6
Napan 148-149 L 7
Napanee 72-73 H 2
Napas 132-133 P 6
Napaseudut 52
Nape 148-149 DE 3
Napenay 104-105 F 10
Na Phao = Ban Na Phao 150-151 E 4
Napier [NZ] 158-159 P 7
Napier [ZA] 174-175 C 8
Napier, Mount — 158-159 EF 3
Napier Mountains 53 C 6
Napinka 68-69 F 1
Naples, FL 64-65 K 6
Naples, NY 72-73 H 3
Naples = Nápoli 122-123 EF 5
Naples, Gulf of — = Golfo di Nápoli 122-123 E 5
Napo 96-97 C 2
Napo, Río — 92-93 E 5
Napo, Serranía de — 96-97 C 2
Napoleon, ND 68-69 G 2
Napoleon, OH 70-71 HJ 5
Napoleonville, LA 78-79 D 5-6
Nápoli 122-123 E 5
Nápoli, Golfo di — 122-123 EF 5
Napostá 106-107 F 7
Nappanee, IN 70-71 GH 5
Napu 152-153 NO 10
Naqāda = Naqādah 173 C 5
Naqādah 173 C 5
Naqadeh 136-137 L 4
Naqaṭah 166-167 M 2
Nāqīshūt 164-165 L 8
Naqrīn 166-167 K 2
Naque 102-103 L 3
Naqūrah, Rā's an- 136-137 F 6
Nara [J] 144-145 KL 5
Nārā [PAK] 134-135 K 5
Nara [RMM] 164-165 C 5
Naracoorte 158-159 GH 7
Naradhan 160 GH 4
Naraingarh = Nārāyangarh 138-139 F 2
Nārāinpur 138-139 H 8
Narāl 138-139 M 6
Narala = Norla 138-139 J 7
Naramata 66-67 D 1
Naranjal 96-97 B 3
Naranjal, Río — 96-97 B 3
Naranjas, Punta — 92-93 C 3
Naranjito 96-97 B 3
Naranjo 94-95 C 6
Narasannapeta 140 G 1
Narasapur 140 E 2
Narasāpura = Narsāpur 140 D 2
Narasāpuram = Narasapur 140 E 2
Narasaraopet 140 E 2
Narasarāvpēṭa = Narasaraopet 140 E 2
Narashino 155 III d 1
Narasiṅhpur = Narsimhapur 138-139 G 6
Narasīpaṭṭaṇam = Narsīpatnam 140 F 2
Narasīpura = Tirumakūdal Narsipur 140 C 4
Narathiwat 148-149 DE 5
Nara Visa, NM 76-77 C 5
Nārāyaṇapēṭa = Nārāyanpet 140 C 2
Narāyanganj 134-135 OP 6
Nārāyangarh 138-139 F 2
Nārāyankher 140 CD 1-2
Nārāyanpet 140 C 2
Narbadā = Narmada 134-135 LM 6
Narberth, PA 84 III b 1
Narbonne 120-121 J 7
Narchhen 138-139 JK 3
Nardiganj 138-139 K 5
Nardò 122-123 GH 5
Naré 106-107 G 3
Narembeen 158-159 C 6
Naréna 168-169 C 2
Narendranagar 138-139 FG 2
Narew 118 K 2
Nargen = Naissaar 124-125 E 4
Nārgol 138-139 D 7
Nargund 140 B 3
Nargya 138-139 M 3
Nārī 134-135 K 5
Narib 174-175 B 3
Narimanabad 126-127 O 7
Narin 146-147 C 2
Narinda, Helodranon'i — 172 J 4
Narin Nur 146-147 AB 2
Nariño [CO, Antioquia] 94-95 D 5
Nariño [CO, Córdoba] 94-95 CD 3
Nariño [CO, Nariño] 94-95 BC 7
Nariño, Museo de — 91 III b 3
Narjan-Mar 132-133 JK 4
Narlı 136-137 G 4
Narmada 134-135 LM 6
Narman 136-137 J 2
Nārnaol = Nārnaul 138-139 F 3
Nārnaul 138-139 F 3
Naroč' 124-125 F 6
Narodnaja, gora — 132-133 L 5
Naro-Fominsk 124-125 KL 6
Narok 172 G 2
Narooma 158-159 JK 7
Narop 174-175 B 3
Narovl'a 124-125 G 8
Narōwāl 138-139 E 1
Narrabri 158-159 JK 6
Narragansett Bay 72-73 L 4
Narrandera 158-159 J 6
Narran Lake 160 H 2
Narran River 160 H 2
Narrogin 158-159 C 6
Narromine 158-159 J 6
Narrows, OR 66-67 D 4
Narrows, VA 80-81 F 2
Narrows, The — 82 III b 3
Narsampet 140 DE 2
Narsāpur 140 D 2
Narsimhapur 138-139 G 6
Narsingdī 141 B 3-4
Narsinghgarh 138-139 F 6
Narsinghpur 138-139 K 7
Narsīpatnam 140 F 2
Narsipur = Tirumakūdal Narsipur 140 C 4
Narssaq 56-57 bc 5
Narssarssuaq 56-57 bc 5
Narte de Santander 94-95 E 3-4
Nartkala 126-127 LM 5
Narubis 174-175 C 4
Narugas 174-175 C 5
Narugo 144-145 N 3
Narungombe 171 D 5
Naru-shima 144-145 G 6
Naruto 144-145 K 5
Narva [SU, place] 132-133 D 6
Narva [SU, river] 124-125 F 4
Narva Bay = Narva laht 124-125 F 4
Narváez 104-105 D 7
Narva-Jõesuu 124-125 FG 4
Narva laht 124-125 F 4
Narvānā = Narwāna 138-139 F 3
Narvik 116-117 G 3
Narvskoje vodochranilišče 124-125 G 4
Narwa = Narva 132-133 D 6
Narwāna 138-139 F 3
Narym 132-133 P 6
Naryn [SU, Kirgizskaja SSR place] 134-135 M 2
Naryn [SU, Kirgizskaja SSR river] 134-135 L 2
Naryn [SU, Rossijskaja SFSR] 132-133 S 7
Naryn = Taš-Kumyr 134-135 L 2
Narynkol 134-135 MN 2
Naryškino 124-125 K 7
Nasafjell 116-117 F 4
Nasaló 106-107 F 2
Na Sâm 150-151 F 1
Na San = Ban Na San 150-151 B 8
Nasarawa [WAN, Gongola] 168-169 J 3
Nasarawa [WAN, Plateau] 164-165 F 7
Nasaret = Nazērat 136-137 F 6
Năsăud 122-123 L 2
Nascente 100-101 D 4
Naschel 106-107 E 4
Naschitti, NM 74-75 J 4
Nash Harbor, AK 58-59 D 6
Nāshik = Nāsik 134-135 L 6-7
Nashiño, Río — 96-97 D 2
Nashū, Ḥāssī — 166-167 H 4
Nashua, MT 68-69 C 1
Nashua, NH 72-73 L 3
Nashu Bûm 141 E 3
Nashville, AR 76-77 GH 5
Nashville, GA 80-81 E 5
Nashville, IL 70-71 F 6
Nashville, KS 68-69 G 7
Nashville, MI 70-71 H 4
Nashville, TN 64-65 J 4
Nashville Basin 78-79 F 2
Nashwauk, MN 70-71 D 2
Nasia 168-169 E 3
Našice 122-123 H 3
Näsijärvi 116-117 KL 7
Nāsik 134-135 L 6-7
Nāṣir 164-165 L 7
Nasir, Jabal an- 164-165 F 4
Nasīrābād [IND] 138-139 E 4
Nasīrābād [PAK] 138-139 A 4
Nāsirīyah 166-167 HJ 1
Nāsirīyah, An- 134-135 F 4
Naṣir Muhammad 138-139 A 4
Nasīyah, Jabal — 173 C 6
Nas Nas Point = Melkbospunt 174-175 B 5
Nasondoye 172 DE 4
Na Song = Ban Na Song 150-151 E 4
Naṣr 173 B 4
Naṣr, An- 173 C 5
Naṣr, Hazzān an- 173 C 6
Naṣr, Khazzan an- 164-165 L 4
Nāṣrīyah 136-137 G 6
Nasrullāganj = Nāsrullāhganj 138-139 F 6
Nāsrullāhganj 138-139 F 6
Nassarawa = Nasarawa 164-165 F 7
Nassau [BS] 64-65 L 6
Nassau [island] 156-157 J 5
Nassau, Bahía — 111 C 9
Nassau Sound 80-81 c 1
Nass Basin 60 C 2
Nassenwil 128 IV a 1
Nässjö 116-117 F 9
Nass River 56-57 L 6-7
Nastapoka Islands 56-57 V 6
Nasva 124-125 GH 5
Nata 172 E 6
Na-ta = Dan Xian 142-143 K 8
Natagaima 92-93 DE 4
Natal [BR, Amazonas] 98-99 D 7
Natal [BR, Maranhão] 100-101 C 3
Natal [BR, Rio Grande do Norte] 92-93 MN 6
Natal [CDN] 66-67 F 1
Natal [RI] 148-149 C 6
Natal [ZA] 172 EF 7
Natal Basin 50-51 LM 7
Natalia, TX 76-77 E 8
Natalkuz Lake 60 E 3
Natal Ridge 172 G 8
Natanya = Nětanya 136-137 F 6
Natash, Wādī — 173 CD 5
Natashquan 63 EF 2
Natashquan River 56-57 Y 7
Natchez, MS 64-65 H 5
Natchitoches, LA 64-65 H 5
Na Thao 150-151 D 2
Na Thawi 150-151 C 9
Nāthdvāra = Nāthdwāra 138-139 DE 5
Nāthdwāra 138-139 DE 5
Na Thon = Ban Nathon 150-151 F 4
Nathorst land 116-117 jk 6
Nathrop, CO 68-69 C 6
Nathu La 138-139 M 4
Nation, AK 58-59 QR 4
Nation, Palais de la — 128 II b 1
National Arboretum 82 II b 2
National City, CA 74-75 E 6
National City, MI 70-71 HJ 3
National History, Museum of — 155 II b 2
Nationalities, Cultural Palace of — 155 II b 2
National Library 154 II b 2
National Library of Peking 155 II b 2
National Museum of Singapore 154 III b 2
National Park 80-81 E 3
National Park, NJ 84 III bc 2
National Park of Tōkyō 155 III b 2
National Reactor Testing Station 66-67 G 4
National Stadium 170 III b 2
National Stadium of Singapore 154 III b 2
National Stadium of Tōkyō 155 III b 1-2
National Zoological Park 82 II ab 1
Nation River [CDN] 60 F 2
Nation River [USA] 58-59 R 4
Natitingou 164-165 E 6
Natividade 92-93 K 7
Natívitas 91 I c 3
Natmauk 141 D 5
Natogyi = Nwādōgyī 141 D 5
Natoma, KS 68-69 G 6
Nātong Dsong 142-143 G 6
Nāṭor 138-139 M 5
Natron, Lake — 172 G 2
Natrun, Bir el — = Wāhāt al-'Aṭrūn 164-165 K 5
Naṭrūn, Wādī an- 173 AB 2
Natrun Lakes = Wādī an-Naṭrūn 173 AB 2
Nattalin 141 D 6
Nattam 140 D 5
Natuna Islands = Kepulauan Bunguran Utara 148-149 E 6
Natural Bridges National Monument 74-75 HJ 4
Naturaliste, Cape — 158-159 B 6
Natural Science, Museum of — 85 III b 2
Naturita, CO 74-75 J 3
Naṭuvangngāṭ = Nedumangād 140 C 6
Naucalpan de Juárez, Ciudad de — 91 I b 2
Nauchas = Naukhas 174-175 B 2
Na'u Chhu 138-139 J 2
Naufragados, Ponta — 102-103 HJ 7
Naugāon 138-139 M 5
Naugo Bûm 141 CD 4
Naugong = Nowgong 138-139 G 5
Nauja Vileika, Vilnius- 124-125 EF 6
Naukhas 174-175 B 2
Naulavaraa 116-117 N 6
Naulila 172 BC 5
Naunglôn 141 E 6
Nā'ūr 136-137 F 7
Nauru 156-157 H 5
Náusa 122-123 JK 5
Naushahro Fīroz 138-139 B 4
Nauški 132-133 U 7
Nauta 92-93 E 5
Nautanwā 138-139 J 4
Nautla 86-87 M 7
Nauvo 116-117 JK 7
Nava [MEX] 76-77 D 8
Navābganj = Nawābganj 138-139 H 4
Navādā = Nawāda 138-139 K 5
Nava de Ricomalillo, La — 120-121 E 9
Navajo, AZ 74-75 J 5
Navajo Indian Reservation 74-75 HJ 4
Navajo Mountain 74-75 H 4
Navajo Reservoir 68-69 C 7
Navākōṭ = Nawākot 138-139 K 4
Navalaguṇḍa = Navalgund 140 B 3
Naval Air Station [USA, New Orleans] 85 I b 2
Naval Air Station [USA, New York] 82 III c 3
Navalgaṛh = Nawalgarh 138-139 E 4
Navalgund 140 B 3
Naval Observatory 82 II a 1
Navan 119 C 5
Navangar = Jāmnagar 134-135 L 6
Navāṅshahar = Nawāshahr 138-139 F 2
Navāpur 138-139 DE 7
Navarin, mys — 132-133 jk 5
Navarino, Isla — 111 C 9
Navarra 120-121 G 7
Navarra, Bogotá- 91 III c 2
Navarre = Navarra 120-121 G 7
Navarro 106-107 H 5
Navašino 124-125 O 6
Navasota, TX 76-77 FG 7
Navasota River 76-77 F 7
Navassa Island 64-65 LM 8
Naver 119 D 2
Navia 120-121 D 7
Navidad 106-107 AB 4
Navio, Riacho do — 100-101 E 5
Navirai 102-103 E 5
Navl'a 124-125 K 7
Navlakhi = Nawlakhi 138-139 C 6
Navoi 132-133 M 9
Navoj 134-135 K 2
Navojoa 64-65 E 6
Navolato 64-65 E 7
Navoloki 124-125 NO 5
Návpaktos 122-123 JK 6
Návplion 122-123 K 7
Navrongo 164-165 D 6
Navṣar 136-137 L 4
Navsāri 138-139 D 7
Navy Board Inlet 56-57 U 3
Navy Town, AK 58-59 p 6
Nawā 136-137 FG 6
Nawa = Naha 142-143 O 6
Nawābganj [BD] 138-139 M 5
Nawābganj [IND ↗ Bareilly] 138-139 G 3
Nawābganj [IND ↗ Lucknow] 138-139 H 4
Nawābshāh 134-135 K 5
Nawāda 138-139 K 5
Nawādhību 164-165 A 4
Nawadwip = Nabadwip 138-139 LM 6
Nawai 138-139 EF 4
Nawākot [Nepal] 138-139 K 4
Nawa Koṭ [PAK] 138-139 C 3
Nawākshūt 164-165 A 5
Nawāl, Sabkhat an- 166-167 LM 2
Nāwalapitiya 140 E 7
Nawalgarh 138-139 E 4
Nawān Koṭ 138-139 C 2
Nawāpāra 138-139 J 7
Nawapur = Navāpur 138-139 DE 7
Nawari = Nahari 144-145 JK 6
Nawāshahr 138-139 F 2
Nawāṣīf, Ḥarrat — 134-135 E 6
Nawfalīyah, An- 164-165 H 2
Nawlakhi 138-139 C 6
Nawngchik = Nong Chik 150-151 C 9
Naws, Rā's — 134-135 H 7
Náxos [GR, island] 122-123 L 7
Náxos [GR, place] 122-123 L 7
Naxos [I] 122-123 F 7
Nayá, Río — 94-95 C 6
Naya Chor 138-139 B 5
Nayāgaḍa = Nayāgarh 138-139 K 7
Nayāgarh 138-139 K 7
Nayakot = Nawākot 138-139 K 4
Nayarit 64-65 EF 7
Nāy Band [IR, Banāder va Jazāyer-e Khalīj-e Fārs] 134-135 G 5
Nāy Band [IR, Khorāsān] 134-135 H 4
Nāy Band, Ra's-e — 134-135 G 5
Naylor, MO 78-79 D 2
Nayoro 144-145 c 1
Nayoro = Gornozavodsk 132-133 b 8
Nāyudupeta 140 DE 4
Nazacara 104-105 B 5
Nazan Bay 58-59 jk 4
Nazaré [BR, Amapá] 98-99 N 4
Nazaré [BR, Amazonas] 92-93 F 4
Nazaré [BR, Bahia] 92-93 M 7
Nazaré [BR, Pará] 98-99 M 8
Nazaré [P] 120-121 C 9
Nazaré = Nazērat 136-137 F 6
Nazaré da Mata 100-101 G 4
Nazaré do Piauí 100-101 C 4
Nazareno 104-105 D 7
Nazareth [PE] 96-97 B 4
Nazareth = Nazērat 136-137 F 6
Nazário 102-103 H 2
Nazarovka 124-125 N 6
Nazas, Río — 86-87 H 5
Nazca 92-93 DE 7
Nazca Ridge 156-157 N 6-O 5
Naze, The — = Lindesnes 116-117 B 9
Nazērat 136-137 F 6
Nazija 124-125 HJ 4
Nazilli 136-137 C 4
Nazimiye 136-137 HJ 3
Nazimovo 132-133 QR 6
Nazina 132-133 OP 5-6
Nāzira 141 D 2
Nažir Hāṭ 141 BC 4
Nazko 60 F 3
Nazko River 60 F 3
Nazlat as-Sammān 170 II ab 2
Nāzlū Rūd 136-137 L 4
Nazombe 171 D 5
Nazrēt 164-165 M 7
Nazwá 134-135 H 6
Nazyvajevsk 132-133 N 6
Nazzah 173 B 4
Nchanga 171 AB 6
Nchelenge 171 B 5
Ndabala 171 B 6
N'daghāmshah, Sabkhat — 164-165 AB 5
Ndai 148-149 k 6
Ndala 171 C 4
Ndalatando 172 BC 3
N'Dali 164-165 E 7
N'Dande 168-169 A 2
Ndélé 164-165 J 7
N'Dendé 172 B 2
Ndeni 148-149 l 7
Ndikiniméki 168-169 H 4
N'Dioum 168-169 B 1
N'djamena 164-165 GH 6
Ndjili 170 IV b 2
Ndjili, Grande Île de la — 170 IV b 1
Ndjolé [Gabon] 168-169 H 4
N'Djolé [RFC] 172 AB 2
Ndola 172 E 4
N'dolo = Aéroport de Kinshasa 170 IV a 1
N'dolo, Kinshasa- 170 IV b 1
Ndumu Game Reserve 174-175 K 4
Nduye 171 B 2
Ndwedwe 174-175 J 5
Ndye 171 B 2
Ndzuwani 172 HJ 4
Néa Filadélfeia 113 IV a 1
Neagh, Lough — 119 C 4
Neah Bay, WA 66-67 A 1
Néa Iōnía [GR, Athēnai] 113 IV b 1
Neale, Lake — 158-159 F 4
Neales 158-159 G 5
Néa Liósia 113 IV a 1
Neamati 141 D 2
Neápolis [GR, Grámmos] 122-123 J 5
Neápolis [GR, Pelopónnēsos] 122-123 K 7
Near Islands 52 D 1
Near North Side, Chicago-, IL 83 II b 1
Néa Smýrnē 113 IV a 2
Nebek, En — = An-Nabk 134-135 D 4
Nebeur = Nibr 166-167 L 1
Nebine Creek 158-159 J 5
Nebit-Dag 134-135 GH 3
Neblina, Pico da — 92-93 FG 4
Neblina, Pico de — 98-99 F 4
Neblina, Sierra de la — 94-95 HJ 7
Nebo 174-175 H 3
Nebo, Mount — 74-75 H 3
Nebolči 124-125 J 4
Nébou 168-169 E 3
Nebraska 64-65 FG 3
Nebraska City, NE 70-71 BC 5
Nebrodie, Monti — 122-123 F 7
Necadah, WI 70-71 E 3
Nechako Plateau 56-57 L 7
Neches, TX 76-77 G 7
Neches River 76-77 G 7
Nechi 94-95 D 3
Nechí, Río — 94-95 D 4
Nechou, Hassi — = Ḥāssī Nashū 166-167 H 4
Nechvorošča 126-127 G 2
Neckar 118 D 4
Necochea 111 E 5
Necoclí 94-95 C 3
Nederhorst den Berg 128 I b 2
Nederland, TX 76-77 G 8
Nederlandse Antillen 88-89 M 8
Nedlitz, Potsdam- 130 III a 2
Nédroma = Nidrūmā 166-167 F 2
Nedumangād 140 C 6
Neebish Island 70-71 H 2
Needham, Mount — 60 A 3
Needle Peak 74-75 E 5
Needles 60 HJ 4-5
Needles, CA 74-75 F 5
Ñeembucú 102-103 CD 7
Neem-ka-Thana = Nīm ka Thāna 138-139 EF 4
Neemuch = Nīmach 138-139 E 5
Neenah, WI 70-71 F 3
Neepawa 56-57 R 7
Neerach 128 IV a 1
Nee Soon 154 III ab 1
Nefoussa, Djebel — = Jabal Nafusah 164-165 G 2
Nefta = Naftah 166-167 K 3
Neftečala = 26 Bakinskij Komissarov 126-127 OP 7
Neftegorsk 126-127 J 4
Neftejugansk 132-133 NO 5
Neftekamsk 124-125 U 5
Neftekumsk 126-127 M 4
Nefud = An-Nafūd 134-135 E 5
Nefud, En — = An-Nafūd 134-135 E 5
Nefzāoua = Nifzāwah 166-167 L 3
Negade = Naqādah 173 C 5
Négansi 168-169 F 3
Negapatam = Nāgapattinam 134-135 MN 8
Negara 148-149 FG 8
Negara, Sungai — 152-153 L 7
Negaunee, MI 70-71 G 2
Negeb = Negev 136-137 F 7
Negelē 164-165 MN 7
Negenangira Palāna ◁ 140 E 7
Negeribatin 152-153 F 8
Negeri Sembilan 150-151 CD 11
Negerpynten 116-117 l 6
Negginan 61 K 4
Neggio = Nejo 164-165 M 7
Neghilli = Negelē 164-165 MN 7
Negoiu 122-123 L 3
Negomane 171 D 5
Negombo = Migamuwa 134-135 M 9
Negoreloje 124-125 F 7
Negotin 122-123 K 3
Negra, La — 106-107 H 6
Negrais, Cape — = Nagare Angū 141 CD 7
Negreiros 104-105 B 6
Negribreen 116-117 l 4
Negrillos 104-105 B 6
Négrine = Naqrīn 166-167 K 2
Negritos 96-97 A 4
Negro Muerto 108-109 G 2
Negros 148-149 H 5
Negru Vodă 122-123 N 4
Neguac 63 D 4
Negueve = Negev 136-137 F 7
Nehalem, OR 66-67 B 3
Nehbandān 134-135 HJ 4
Nehe 142-143 NO 2
Nehonsey Brook 84 III b 3
Neiafu 148-149 c 2
Neibbān 141 D 7
Nei-chiang = Neijiang 142-143 JK 6
Nei-ch'iu = Neiqiu 146-147 E 3
Neidpath 61 E 5
Neihart, MT 66-67 H 2
Nei-hsiang = Neixiang 146-147 C 5
Neihuang 146-147 E 4
Neijiang 142-143 JK 6
Neikiang = Neijiang 142-143 JK 6
Neilburg 61 D 4
Neilersdrif 174-175 D 5
Neillsville, WI 70-71 E 3
Neineva 136-137 JK 5
Neiqiu 146-147 E 3
Neisse 118 G 3
Neiva 92-93 DE 4
Neixiang 146-147 C 5
Neja 132-133 G 6
Nejd = Najd 134-135 E 5-6
Nejo 164-165 M 7
Nékaounté 168-169 D 4
Nekemtē 164-165 M 7
Nekhīla, en — = An-Nakhīlah 166-167 E 2
Nekl'udovo [SU, Gor'kovskaja Oblast'] 124-125 O 5
Nekmard 138-139 M 5
Nekoosa, WI 70-71 F 3
Nekrasovskoje 124-125 N 5
Nekropolis 173 C 5
Neksø 116-117 F 10
Nelahālu 140 C 4
Nelamangala 140 C 4
Nelidovo 124-125 J 5
Neligh, NE 68-69 GH 4
Nel'kan 132-133 Za 6
Nellāyi 140 C 5
Nellikkuppam 140 DE 5
Nellore 134-135 MN 8
Nellūru = Nellore 134-135 MN 8
Nel'ma 132-133 ab 8
Nelson, AZ 74-75 G 5
Nelson, CA 74-75 C 3
Nelson, NE 68-69 G 5
Nelson, WI 70-71 E 3
Nelson [CDN] 56-57 N 8
Nelson [NZ, administrative unit] 161 E 5
Nelson [NZ, place] 158-159 O 8
Nelson [RA] 111 DE 4
Nelson, Estrecho — 111 AB 8
Nelson Forks 56-57 M 6
Nelson House 61 J 3
Nelson Island 56-57 C 5
Nelson Reservoir 68-69 BC 1
Nelson River 56-57 RS 6
Nelsonville, OH 72-73 E 5
Nelspoort 174-175 E 7
Nelspruit 172 F 7
Nem 124-125 U 3
Nema 124-125 S 5
Nemah, WA 66-67 B 2
Neman [SU, river] 124-125 E 7
Ne'māniya, An — = An-Na'māniyah 136-137 L 6
Nemāwar 138-139 F 6
Nemenčine 124-125 E 6
Nementcha, Monts des — = Jabal an-Namāmshah 166-167 K 2
Nemira, Muntele — 122-123 M 2
Nemirov [SU, Vinnickaja Oblast'] 126-127 D 2
Nemiscau 62 N 1
Nemiscau, Lac — 62 N 1
Nemlét, El — = An-Namlāt 166-167 KL 2
Nemocón 94-95 DE 5
Nemours = Ghazawat 164-165 D 1
Nemrut dağı 136-137 JK 3
Nemunas = Neman 124-125 E 7
Nemuro 142-143 S 3
Nemuro-kaikyō 144-145 d 1-2
Nemuro wan 144-145 d 2
Nemurs = Ghazawāt 164-165 D 2
Nenagh 119 BC 5
Nenana, AK 56-57 FG 5
Nenana River 58-59 N 4-5
Nenasi 150-151 D 11
Neneo Rucá 108-109 D 3
Nenets Autonomous Area 132-133 J-L 4
Nenjiang [TJ, place] 142-143 O 2
Nen Jiang [TJ, river] 142-143 N 2
Nen Jiang = Naguun Mörön 142-143 NO 1-2
Nenusa, Pulau-pulau — 148-149 J 6
Neodesha, KS 70-71 BC 7
Neoga, IL 70-71 F 6
Neola, UT 66-67 H 5
Néon Fálēron 113 IV a 2
Neopit, WI 70-71 F 3
Neópolis 100-101 F 6
Neosho, MO 76-77 G 4
Neosho River 64-65 G 4
Nepa 132-133 U 6
Nepal 134-135 NO 5
Nepalganj 138-139 H 3
Nepeña 96-97 B 6
Nephi, UT 74-75 GH 3
Nephin 119 B 4
Nepisiguit River 63 CD 4
Nepoko 172 E 1
Neponset River 84 I b 3
Neponsit, New York-, NY 82 III c 3
Neptune 61 FG 6
Ner [IND] 138-139 F 7
Nérac 120-121 H 6
Neragon Island 58-59 D 6
Nerang, Kuala — 150-151 C 9
Nerbudda = Narmada 134-135 LM 6
Nerča 132-133 W 7
Nerčinsk 132-133 W 7
Nerčinskij Zavod 132-133 W 7
Nerdva 124-125 U 4
Nerechta 124-125 N 5
Nerecó, Valle — 106-107 E 6
Nereta 124-125 E 5
Neretva 122-123 H 4
Neri 138-139 G 7
Nerima, Tōkyō- 155 III a 1
Neringa 124-125 C 6
Neriquinha = N'Riquinha 172 D 5

Neriquin 333

Neris 124-125 E 6
Nerka, Lake — 58-59 H 7
Nerl' [SU, place] 124-125 LM 5
Nerl' [SU, river] 124-125 LM 5
Ñermete, Punta — 92-93 C 6
Nero, ozero — 124-125 M 5
Nerojka, gora — 132-133 KL 5
Nerópolis 102-103 H 2
Nerskoje ploskogorje 132-133 c 5
Nes aan de Amstel 128 I a 2
Nesebâr 122-123 MN 4
Neškan 58-59 A 3
Neskaupstadhur 116-117 fg 2
Nesna 116-117 E 4
Ness, Loch — 119 D 3
Ness City, KS 68-69 FG 6
Nesselrode, Mount — 58-59 UV 7
Nestaocano, Rivière — 62 P 1-2
Nesterov [SU, L'vovskaja Oblast'] 126-127 AB 1
Nestor Falls 70-71 D 1
Nestoria, MI 70-71 FG 2
Néstos 122-123 L 5
Nesttun, Bergen- 116-117 AB 7
Nesviž 124-125 F 7
Nětanya 136-137 F 7
Nethanya = Nětanya 136-137 F 7
Netherdale 158-159 J 4
Netherlands 120-121 J 3-L 2
Netrākonā 141 B 3
Netrāvati 140 B 4
Nettilling Lake 56-57 W 4
Nett Lake 70-71 D 1
Nett Lake Indian Reservation 70-71 D 1-2
Nettleton, MS 78-79 E 3
Netzahualcóyotl, Ciudad — 86-87 L 8
Netzahualcóyotl, Presa — 86-87 O 9
Neualbern, Wien- 113 I b 2
Neubeeren 130 III b 2
Neubrandenburg 118 F 2
Neuchâtel 118 C 5
Neuchâtel, Lac de — 118 C 5
Neuenfelde, Hamburg- 130 I a 1
Neuessling 113 I c 1
Neu Fahrland 130 III a 2
Neufchâteau [B] 120-121 K 4
Neufchateau [F] 120-121 KL 4
Neufchâtel-en-Bray 120-121 H 4
Neugraben, Hamburg- 130 I a 2
Neuhausen, München- 130 II b 2
Neuherberg 130 II b 1
Neu-Heusis 174-175 B 2
Neuhimmelreich 130 II a 1
Neuhönow, Kolonie — 130 III cd 1
Neuilly-sur-Marne 129 I d 2
Neuilly-sur-Seine 129 I bc 2
Neuland, Hamburg- 130 I ab 2
Neu Lindenberg 130 III c 1
Neumarkt 118 E 4
Neumünster 118 DE 1
Neunkirchen [A] 118 H 5
Neunkirchen [D] 118 C 4
Neuquén [RA, administrative unit] 106-107 BC 7
Neuquén [RA, place] 111 C 5
Neuquén, Río — 106-107 C 7
Neurara 104-105 B 9
Neuried [D, Bayern] 130 II a 2
Neurott 128 III a 1
Neuruppin 118 F 2
Neuschwabenland 53 B 36-2
Neuse River 80-81 H 3
Neusiedler See 118 H 5
Neustift am Walde, Wien- 113 I b 2
Neustrelitz 118 F 2
Neusüssenbrunn, Wien- 113 I bc 1
Neutral Zone 134-135 F 5
Neu-Ulm 118 E 4
Neu Vehlefanz 130 III a 1
Neuwaldegg, Wien- 113 I ab 2
Neuwied 118 CD 3
Neva [SU] 124-125 H 4
Nevada 64-65 CD 4
Nevada, IA 70-71 D 4-5
Nevada, MO 70-71 C 7
Nevada, La — 106-107 FG 6
Nevada City, CA 74-75 C 3
Nevada del Cocuy, Sierra — 94-95 E 4
Nevado, Cerro El — 92-93 E 4
Nevado, Sierra del — 111 C 5
Nevado Ancohuma 104-105 B 4
Nevado Cololo 92-93 F 7
Nevado de Acay 104-105 C 9
Nevado de Ampato 92-93 E 8
Nevado de Cachí 111 C 2
Nevado de Champara 96-97 C 6
Nevado de Colima 64-65 EF 8
Nevado de Cumbal 94-95 BC 7
Nevado de Illimani 92-93 F 8
Nevado del Huila 92-93 D 4
Nevado de los Palos 108-109 C 5
Nevado del Ruiz 92-93 DE 4
Nevado del Tolima 94-95 D 5
Nevado de Sajama 92-93 F 8
Nevado de Salcantay 96-97 E 8
Nevado de Toluca 64-65 FG 8
Nevado Huascaran 92-93 D 6
Nevado Illampu 92-93 F 8
Nevado Iluyana Potosí 104-105 B 5
Nevado Longaví 106-107 B 6
Nevado Ojos del Salado 111 C 3
Nevado Putre 104-105 B 6
Nevados de Chillán 106-107 B 6
Nevados de Condoroma 96-97 F 9
Nevados de Pomasi 96-97 F 9
Neve, Serra da — 172 B 4
Nevel' 124-125 G 5
Never 132-133 XY 7
Nevers 120-121 J 5
Nevinnomyssk 126-127 KL 4
Nevis 64-65 O 8
Nevis, MN 70-71 C 2
Nevis, Ben — 119 D 3
Nevjansk 132-133 KL 6
Nevşehir 134-135 C 3
Newala 172 G 4
New Albany, IN 64-65 J 4
New Albany, MS 78-79 E 3
New Alexandria, VA 82 II a 2
New Amalfi 174-175 H 6
New Amsterdam 92-93 H 3
Newark, DE 72-73 J 5
Newark, NJ 64-65 M 3
Newark, NY 72-73 H 3
Newark, OH 72-73 E 4
Newark [GB] 119 F 5
Newark Airport 82 III a 2
Newark Bay 82 III b 2
New Athens, IL 70-71 F 6
Newaygo, MI 70-71 H 4
New Bedford, MA 64-65 MN 3
Newberg, OR 66-67 B 3
New Bern, NC 64-65 L 4
Newbern, TN 78-79 E 2
Newberry, CA 74-75 E 5
Newberry, MI 70-71 H 2
Newberry, SC 80-81 F 3
New Bethesda = Nieu-Bethesda 174-175 F 6
New Boston, OH 72-73 E 5
New Boston, IL 70-71 E 5
New Boston, OH 72-73 E 5
New Boston, TX 76-77 G 6
New Braunfels, TX 64-65 G 6
New Brighton, New York-, NY 82 III b 3
New Britain 148-149 gh 6
New Britain, CT 72-73 K 4
New Britain Bougainville Trench 148-149 h 6
New Brunswick 56-57 X 8
New Brunswick, NJ 72-73 J 4
New Buffalo, MI 70-71 G 5
Newburg, MO 70-71 E 7
Newburgh, NY 72-73 J 4
Newburgh [CDN] 72-73 H 2
Newbury 119 F 6
Newburyport, MA 72-73 L 3
New Caledonia 158-159 MN 3
New Canada, Johannesburg- 170 V a 2
New Carlisle 63 D 3
New Carrollton, MD 82 II b 1
Newcastel 63 CD 4
Newcastel Creek 158-159 F 3
New Castile = Castilla la Nueva 120-121 E 9-F 8
New Castle, CO 68-69 C 6
New Castle, IN 70-71 H 5-6
New Castle, OH 72-73 D 5
New Castle, PA 72-73 F 4
Newcastle, TX 76-77 E 6
Newcastle, VA 80-81 F 2
Newcastle, WY 68-69 D 4
Newcastle [AUS] 158-159 K 6
Newcastle [GB] 119 D 4
Newcastle [ZA] 172 EF 7
Newcastle Bay 158-159 H 2
Newcastle upon Tyne 119 EF 4
Newcastle Waters 158-159 F 3
Newclare, Johannesburg- 170 V a 2
Newcomb, NM 74-75 J 4
Newcomerstown, OH 72-73 F 4
Newdale, ID 66-67 H 4
Newdegate 158-159 CD 6
New Delhi 134-135 M 5
New Dorp, New York-, NY 82 III b 3
Newell, SD 68-69 E 3
Newell Lake 61 BC 5
Newellton, LA 78-79 D 4
New England, ND 68-69 E 2
New England [USA] 64-65 M 3-N 2
New England [ZA] 174-175 G 6
New England Range 158-159 K 5-6
Newenham, Cape — 56-57 D 6
Newfane, VT 72-73 K 3
Newfolden, MN 70-71 BC 1
Newfoundland [CDN, administrative unit] 56-57 Y 6-Z 8
Newfoundland [CDN, island] 56-57 Za 8
Newfoundland Bank 50-51 G 3
Newfoundland Basin 50-51 GH 3
Newfoundland Ridge 50-51 G 3-H 4
New Georgia 148-149 j 6
New Georgia Group 148-149 j 6
New Georgia Sound = The Slot 148-149 j 6
New Germany 63 D 5
New Glasgow 56-57 Y 8
New Glatz, MD 82 II a 2
New Guinea 148-149 L 7-M 8
New Guinea Rise 148-149 M 5-6
Newgulf, TX 76-77 G 8
Newhalem, WA 66-67 C 1
Newhalen, AK 58-59 K 7
Newhall, CA 74-75 D 5
Newham, London- 129 II c 1
New Hamilton, AK 58-59 F 5
New Hampshire 64-65 M 3
New Hampton, IA 70-71 DE 4
New Hanover [PNG] 148-149 gh 5
New Hanover [ZA] 174-175 J 5
New Harmony, IN 70-71 G 6
New Haven, CT 64-65 M 3
New Haven, IN 70-71 H 5
New Haven, KY 70-71 H 7
Newhaven [GB] 119 G 6
New Hebrides 158-159 NO 2-3
New Hebrides Basin 158-159 MN 2
New Hebrides Trench 158-159 N 2-3
New Hyde Park, NY 82 III de 2
New Iberia, LA 64-65 H 5-6
Newington 174-175 J 3
New Ireland 148-149 h 5
New Island 108-109 J 8
New Jersey 64-65 M 3
New Kensington, PA 72-73 G 4
Newkirk, OK 76-77 F 4
New Knockhock, AK 58-59 E 5
New Kowloon 155 I b 1
New Lagos, Lagos- 170 III b 1
New Lexington, OH 72-73 EF 5
Newlin, TX 76-77 D 5
New Liskeard 56-57 UV 8
New London, CT 72-73 KL 4
New London, MN 70-71 C 3
New London, MO 70-71 E 6
New London, WI 70-71 F 3
New Madrid, MO 78-79 E 2
New Malden, London- 129 II ab 2
Newman, CA 74-75 C 4
Newman, NM 76-77 AB 6
Newman Grove, NE 68-69 GH 5
Newmarket [CDN] 72-73 G 2
Newmarket [ZA] 170 V b 2
Newmarket Race Course 170 V b 2
New Martinsville, WV 72-73 F 5
New Meadows, ID 66-67 E 3
New Mecklenburg = New Ireland 148-149 h 5
New Melbourne Cemetery 161 II b 1
New Mexico 64-65 EF 5
Newnan, GA 78-79 G 4
New Norfolk 158-159 J 8
New Orleans, LA 64-65 HJ 5-6
New Orleans, University of — 85 I b 1
New Orleans-Algiers, LA 85 I b 2
New Orleans-Aurora Gardens, LA 85 I c 2
New Orleans-Edgewood Park, LA 85 I b 2
New Orleans-Garden District, LA 85 I b 2
New Orleans-Gentilly, LA 85 I c 1
New Orleans-Gentilly Terrace, LA 85 I b 1
New Orleans-Gentilly Woods, LA 85 I b 1
New Orleans-Georgetown of New Orleans, LA 85 I bc 1
New Orleans International Airport 85 I c 2
New Orleans-Lake Forest, LA 85 I c 1
New Orleans Lakefront Airport 85 I b 1
New Orleans-Lakeshore, LA 85 I b 1
New Orleans-Lake Terrace, LA 85 I b 1
New Orleans-Lakeview, LA 85 I b 1-2
New Orleans-Lake Vista, LA 85 I b 1
New Orleans-Lakewood East, LA 85 I c 1
New Orleans Museum of Art 85 I b 2
New Orleans-Park Timbers, LA 85 I b 2
New Orleans-Pontchartrain Beach, LA 85 I b 1
New Orleans-Tall Timbers, LA 85 I c 2
New Orleans-Vieux Carré, LA 85 I b 2
New Philadelphia, OH 72-73 F 4
New Philippines = Caroline Islands 206-207 RS 9
New Pine Creek, OR 66-67 C 4
New Plymouth 158-159 O 7
New Pomerania = New Britain 148-149 gh 6
Newport, AR 78-79 D 3
Newport, KY 64-65 K 4
Newport, ME 72-73 M 2
Newport, NH 72-73 KL 3
Newport, OR 66-67 A 3
Newport, RI 72-73 L 4
Newport, TN 80-81 E 2-3
Newport, TX 76-77 EF 6
Newport, VT 72-73 KL 2
Newport, WA 66-67 E 1
Newport [GB, I. of Wight] 119 F 6
Newport [GB, Severn] 119 E 6
Newport, Melbourne- 161 II b 2
Newport News, VA 64-65 L 4
New Port Richey, FL 80-81 b 2
New Providence Island 64-65 L 6-7
Newquay 119 D 6
New Quebec 56-57 V-X 6
New Quebec Crater 56-57 VW 5
New Raymer, CO 68-69 E 5
New Redruth 170 V b 2
New Richmond 63 D 3
New Richmond, WI 70-71 DE 3
New River 98-99 JK 3
New Roads, LA 78-79 D 5
New Rochelle, NY 72-73 K 4
New Rockford, ND 68-69 G 2
Newry 119 CD 4
New Salem, ND 68-69 F 2
New Sharon, IA 70-71 D 5
New Sharon, NJ 84 III c 3
New Siberia = ostrov Novaja Sibir' 132-133 de 3
New Siberian Islands = Novosibirskije ostrova 132-133 Z-f 2
New Smyrna Beach, FL 80-81 c 2
New South Wales 158-159 H-K 6
New South Wales, University of — 161 I b 2
New Stuyahok, AK 58-59 J 7
New Territories 155 I a 1
Newton 106-107 H 5
Newton, AL 78-79 G 5
Newton, IA 70-71 D 5
Newton, IL 70-71 F 6
Newton, KS 64-65 G 4
Newton, MA 72-73 L 3
Newton, MS 78-79 E 4
Newton, NC 80-81 F 3
Newton, NJ 72-73 J 4
Newton, TX 78-79 C 5
Newton Falls, NY 72-73 J 2
Newtontoppen 116-117 k 5
New Town, ND 68-69 E 1-2
Newtown, Sydney- 161 I ab 2
Newtownards 119 D 4
Newtown Square, PA 84 III a 2
New Ulm, MN 70-71 C 3
New Ulm, TX 76-77 F 8
New Underwood, SD 68-69 E 3
New Waterford 63 FG 4
New Westminster 56-57 MN 8
New World Island 63 J 3
New York 64-65 LM 3
New York, NY 64-65 M 3-4
New York-Arverne, NY 82 III d 3
New York-Astoria, NY 82 III c 2
New York-Auburndale, NY 82 III d 2
New York-Baychester, NY 82 III cd 1
New York-Bay Ridge, NY 82 III b 3
New York-Bedford Park, NY 82 III c 1
New York-Bedford-Stuyvesant, NY 82 III c 2
New York-Bellerose, NY 82 III d 2
New York-Bergen Beach, NY 82 III c 3
New York-Bloomfield, NY 82 III ab 3
New York-Borough Park, NY 82 III bc 3
New York-Breezy Point, NY 82 III c 3
New York-Bronx, NY 82 III c 1
New York-Brooklyn, NY 82 III bc 3
New York-Canarsie, NY 82 III c 3
New York-Castleton Corners, NY 82 III b 3
New York-College Point, NY 82 III cd 2
New York-East Elmhurst, NY 82 III c 2
New York-East New York, NY 82 III c 2-3
New York-Eltingville, NY 82 III ab 3
New York-Faltbush, NY 82 III c 3
New York-Far Rockawa, NY 82 III d 3
New York-Financial District, NY 82 III bc 3
New York-Flushing, NY 82 III d 2
New York-Gravesend, NY 82 III c 3
New York-Great Kills, NY 82 III b 3
New York-Greenwich Village, NY 82 III b 2
New York-Grymes Hill, NY 82 III b 3
New York-Harlem, NY 82 III c 2
New York-Hollis, NY 82 III d 2
New York-Howard Beach, NY 82 III cd 3
New York-Jackson Heights, NY 82 III c 2
New York-Jamaica, NY 82 III d 2
New York-Kensington, NY 82 III c 3
New York-Laurelton, NY 82 III d 3
New York-Long Island City, NY 82 III c 2
New York-Manhatten, NY 82 III bc 2
New York-Mariners Harbor, NY 82 III ab 3
New York-Maspeth, NY 82 III c 2
New York-Melrose, Ny 82 III c 2
New York-Midland Beach, NY 82 III b 3
New York Mountains 74-75 F 5
New York-Neponsit, NY 82 III c 3
New York-New Brighton, NY 82 III b 3
New York-New Dorp, NY 82 III b 3
New York-Oakwood, NY 82 III b 3
New York-Port Richmond, NY 82 III b 3
New York-Princes Bay, NY 82 III a 3
New York-Queens, NY 82 III cd 2
New York-Richmond, NY 82 III ab 4
New York-Richmond Valley, NY 82 III a 3
New York-Ridgewood, NY 82 III c 2
New York-Riverdale, NY 82 III c 1
New York-Rockway Park, NY 82 III c 3
New York-Rossville, NY 82 III a 3
New York-Saint Albans, NY 82 III d 2
New York-Sheepshead Bay, NY 82 III c 3
New York-Soundview, NY 82 III c 2
New York-South Beach, NY 82 III b 3
New York-South Brooklyn, NY 82 III bc 2
New York-Springfield, NY 82 III d 2
New York-Tottenville, NY 82 III a 3
New York-Travis, NY 82 III a 3
New York-Utopia, NY 82 III d 2
New York-Wakefield, NY 82 III cd 1
New York-Westchester, NY 82 III d 1
New York-Whitestone, NY 82 III d 2
New York-Williams Bridge, NY 82 III c 1
New York-Williamsburg, NY 82 III c 2
New York-Woodhaven, NY 82 III cd 2
New York-Woodside, NY 82 III c 2
New Zealand 158-159 N 8-O 7
Neyed = Najd 134-135 E 5-6
Ney Rey Park 85 I a 1
Neyrīz 134-135 G 5
Neyshābūr 134-135 H 3
Neyveli 140 D 5
Neyyāttinkara 140 C 6
Nezametnyj = Aldan 132-133 XY 6
Nežin 126-127 E 1
Nezlobnaja 126-127 L 4
Nezperce, ID 66-67 EF 2
Nez Perce Indian Reservation 66-67 EF 2
Nfīḍa, En — = An-N'fīḍah 166-167 M 1
N'fīḍah, An- 166-167 M 1
Nfis, Ouèd — = Wād Nafīs 166-167 B 4

Ngaba, Kinshasa- 170 IV ab 2
Ngabang 148-149 EF 6
Ngabè 141 D 5
Ngabudaw 141 D 7
Ngaliema, Baie de — 170 IV a 1
Ngaliema, Kinshasa- 170 IV a 2
Ngamba, Brazzaville- 170 IV a 1
Ngambé [RFC → Douala] 168-169 H 4
N'Gambe [RFC → Foumban] 168-169 H 4
Ngamdo Tsonag Tsho 142-143 G 5
Ngami, Lake — 172 D 6
Ngamo Chhu 138-139 M 4
Ngamouéri 170 IV a 1
Ngan Chau 155 I ab 2
Ngang, Đeo — 150-151 F 3-4
Ngang Chhu = Shakad Chhu 138-139 M 2
Nganghouei = Anhui 142-143 M 5
Nganglaring Tso = Nganglha Ringtsho 142-143 EF 5
Nganglong Gangri 142-143 E 5
Ngangtha Ringtsho 142-143 EF 5
Ngangtse Tsho 142-143 F 5
Ngan-yang = Anyang 142-143 LM 4
Ngao 148-149 CD 3
Ngaoundéré 164-165 G 7
Ngape = Ngabè 141 D 5
Ngaputaw = Ngabudaw 141 D 7
Ngara 171 B 3
Ngari = Ngarikorsum 138-139 HJ 2
Ngarikorsum 138-139 HJ 2
Ngat, Nam Mae — 150-151 B 3
Ngatik 208 F 2
Ngau 148-149 a 2
Ngaumdere = Ngaoundéré 164-165 G 7
Ngau Mei Hoi = Port Shelter 155 I b 1
Ngaundere = Ngaoundéré 164-165 G 7
Ngauruhoe 161 FG 4
Ngawi 152-153 J 9
Ngayôk Au 141 CD 7
Ngazidja 172 H 4
Ngerengere 171 D 4
Nghia Lô 150-151 E 2
Ngiri-Ngiri, Kinshasa- 170 IV a 2
Ngiro, Ewaso — 172 G 2
Ngiva 172 C 5
Ngoc Diêm 150-151 EF 3
Ngoc Linh 148-149 E 3
Ngoko 172 C 1
Ngomba 171 C 5
Ngome 174-175 J 4
Ngong 172 G 2
Ngong Shun Chau 155 I a 2
Ngoring Tsho 142-143 H 4-5
Ngorongoro Crater 172 FG 2
Ngouma 168-169 E 2
N'Gounié 172 B 2
Ngoura 164-165 H 6
Ngouri 164-165 H 6
N'Gourti 164-165 G 5
Ngoywa 172 F 3
Ngozi 171 B 3
Ngqeleni 174-175 H 6
N'Guigmi 164-165 G 6
Ngulu 148-149 L 5
Ngum, Nam — 150-151 D 3
Ngumu 168-169 H 4
Ngunga 171 C 3
Ngunza 172 B 4
N'Guri = Ngouri 164-165 H 6
Nguru 164-165 G 6
Nguti 168-169 H 4
Ngwanedzi 174-175 J 2

Nha Bang = Tinh Biên 150-151 E 7
Nhachengue 174-175 L 2
Nhambiquara 98-99 J 11
Nhamundá 98-99 K 6
Nhamundá, Rio — 98-99 K 5
Nha Nam 150-151 EF 2
Nha Trang 148-149 EF 4
Nhecolândia 92-93 H 8
Nhiêp, Nam — 150-151 D 3
Nhi Ha, Sông — 148-149 D 2
Nhill 158-159 H 7
Nhommarath 150-151 E 4
Nhu Pora 106-107 JK 2

Niafounké 164-165 D 5
Niagara Falls 64-65 KL 3
Niagara Falls, NY 64-65 L 3
Niagara River 72-73 G 3
Niagassola 168-169 C 2
Niagui 168-169 D 4
Niah 148-149 F 6
Ni'āj, Jabal — 173 C 6
Niamey 164-165 E 6
Niamina 168-169 D 2
Niamtougou 168-169 F 3
Nian Chu = Nyang Chhu 138-139 M 3
Niandan-Koro 168-169 C 3
Niangara 172 E 1
Niangay, Lac — 168-169 E 2
Niangua River 70-71 D 7
Nia-Nia 172 E 1
Nianqingtanggula Shan = Nyanchhenthanglha 142-143 G 5-6
Niapa, Gunung — 152-153 M 5
Nias, Pulau — 148-149 C 6
Niassa 172 G 4
Niassa = Malawi 172 FG 4
Niassa, Lago — = Lake Malawi 172 F 4
Niausa 141 D 2
Nibāk 134-135 G 6
Nibe 116-117 C 9
Niblinto 111 B 5
Nibr 166-167 L 1
Nibria, Howrah- 154 II a 2
Nicaragua 64-65 JK 9
Nicaragua, Lago de — 64-65 JK 9
Nicaro 64-65 L 7
Nice 120-121 L 7
Niceville, FL 78-79 F 5
Nīcgale 124-125 F 5
Nichinan 144-145 H 7
Nicholasville, KY 70-71 H 7
Nichole = Nachoī 138-139 M 5
Nicholl's Town 88-89 GH 2
Nicholson [AUS] 158-159 E 3
Nicholson [CDN] 70-71 J 1-2
Nicholson River 158-159 G 3
Nickajack Creek 85 II a 1
Nickel Lake 62 C 3
Nickerie [GUY, administrative unit] 98-99 K 2-3
Nickerie [GUY, river] 98-99 K 2
Nickol Bay 158-159 C 4
Nicman 63 CD 2
Nicobar Islands 134-135 P 9
Nicolás, Canal — 64-65 KL 7
Nicolás Bruzone 106-107 EF 5
Nicolás Descalzi 106-107 G 7
Nicolet 72-73 K 1
Nicomedia = İzmit 134-135 BC 2
Nico Pérez 111 EF 4
Nicosia 122-123 F 7
Nicosia = Levkōsia 134-135 C 3
Nicoya 64-65 J 9
Nicoya, Golfo de — 64-65 J 9
Nicoya, Península de — 64-65 J 9-10
Nida 118 K 3
Nidadavole 140 E 2
Niḍḍavolu = Nidadavole 140 E 2
Nī Dillī = New Delhi 134-135 M 5
Nido, El — 148-149 G 4
Nidrūmā 166-167 F 2
Niebüll 118 D 1
Nied, Frankfurt am Main- 128 III a 1
Niederdorfelden 128 III b 1
Nieder Erlenbach, Frankfurt am Main- 128 III b 1
Niedere Tauern 118 FG 5
Niederglatt 128 IV b 1
Niederhasli 128 IV ab 1
Niederhöchstadt 128 III a 1
Nieder-Neuendorfer Kanal 130 III a 1
Niederösterreich 118 GH 4
Niederrad, Frankfurt am Main- 128 III a 1
Niedersachsen 118 C-E 2
Niederschöneweide, Berlin- 130 III b 2
Niederschönhausen, Berlin- 130 III b 1
Niedersteinmaur 128 IV a 1
Niederursel, Frankfurt am Main- 128 III a 1
Niederuster 128 IV b 1
Niederwaldpark 128 III a 2
Niederwil 128 IV a 2
Niekerkshoop 174-175 E 5
Niekerkshope = Niekerkshoop 174-175 E 5
Niéllé 168-169 D 3
Nieman = Neman 124-125 E 7
Niemba [ZRE, place] 171 B 4
Niemba [ZRE, river] 171 B 4
Niemen = Neman 124-125 E 7
Niena 168-169 D 3
Nienburg 118 D 2
Nienchentangla = Nyanchhenthanglha 142-143 F 6-G 5
Niendorf, Hamburg- 130 I a 1
Niendorfer Gehege 130 I a 1
Nienstedten, Hamburg- 130 I a 1
Nietverdiend 174-175 G 3
Nieu-Bethesda 174-175 F 6
Nieuw Amsterdam [SME] 92-93 HJ 3
Nieuw-Antwerpen = Nouvelle-Anvers 172 CD 1
Nieuwe Meer 128 I a 2
Nieuwe Meer, Het — 128 I a 1-2
Nieuwendam, Amsterdam- 128 I b 1
Nieuwenrode 128 II ab 1
Nieuwersluis 128 I b 2
Nieuwer ter Aa 128 I b 2
Nieuwerust = Nuwerus 174-175 C 6
Nieuw Nickerie 92-93 H 3
Nieuwoudtville 172 C 8
Nieuwveld Range = Nuweveldberge 174-175 DE 7
Nieve, Isla de la — 106-107 H 2
Nieves = Nevis 64-65 O 8
Nieves, Las — 76-77 B 9
Niffur = Nippur 136-137 L 6
Nifisha = Nafishah 173 C 2
Nifzāwah 166-167 L 3
Niğde 134-135 CD 3
Nigel 174-175 H 4
Niger [RN, administrative unit] 164-165 F 7
Niger [RN, river] 164-165 E 6
Niger [RN, state] 164-165 FG 5
Nīger = Niger 164-165 FG 5
Nigeria 164-165 E-G 7
Nigerian Museum 170 III b 2
Nighāsan 138-139 H 3
Nighthawk, WA 66-67 D 1
Nighthawk Lake 62 L 2
Nightingale 61 B 5
Nightingale, Île — = Đao Bach Long Vi 150-151 F 2
Nightingale Island = Đao Bach Long Vi 150-151 F 2
Nigisaktuvik River 58-59 H 1
Nigrita 122-123 K 5
Nigtevecht 128 I b 2
Nigtmute, AK 58-59 E 6
Nigu River 58-59 JK 2
Nihah 136-137 J 2
Nihoa 78-79 b 1
Nihonbashi, Tōkyō- 155 III b 1
Nihonmatsu = Nihommatsu 144-145 N 4
Nihuil, El — 106-107 C 5
Niigata 142-143 Q 4
Niihama 144-145 J 5-6
Niihau 148-149 de 3
Niimi 144-145 J 5
Nii-shima 144-145 M 5
Niitsu 144-145 M 4
Nijād al-'Alī 164-165 D 2-E 1
Nijamābād = Nizāmābād 134-135 M 7
Nijmegen 120-121 KL 3
Nikabuna Lakes 58-59 JK 6
Nikaia [GR, Athênai] 113 IV a 2
Nikawēratiya 140 DE 7
Nikel' 132-133 E 4
Nikēphorion = Ar-Raqqah 134-135 DE 3
Nikhaib, An- = Nukhayb 134-135 E 4
Nikishka Numero 2, AK 58-59 M 6
Nikito-Ivdel'skoje = Ivdel' 132-133 L 5
Nikki 164-165 E 6-7
Nikolai, AK 58-59 KL 5
Nikolajev 126-127 EF 3
Nikolajevka [SU, Rossijskaja SFSR] 124-125 Q 7
Nikolajevka [SU, Ukrainskaja SSR] 126-127 F 3
Nikolajevo 124-125 G 4
Nikolajevsk 126-127 MN 1
Nikolajevsk = Pugač'ov 132-133 HJ 7
Nikolajevsk-na-Amure 132-133 b 7
Nikolajevskoje = Bautino 126-127 OP 4
Nikolassee, Berlin- 130 III a 2
Nikolayev = Nikolajev 126-127 EF 3
Nikolo-Ber'ozovka 124-125 U 5
Nikol'sk [SU, Penzenskaja Oblast'] 124-125 PQ 7
Nikol'sk [SU, Severnyje uvaly] 132-133 H 6
Nikolski, AK 58-59 m 4
Nikol'skij 132-133 M 8
Nikol'skoje [SU, Komandorskije ostrova] 132-133 fg 6
Nikol'skoje [SU, Volgogradskaja Oblast'] 126-127 MN 3
Nikol'skoje, Moskva- 113 V b 3
Nikomēdeia = İzmit 134-135 BC 2
Nikonga 171 B 3-4
Nikopol [BG] 122-123 L 4
Nikopol' [SU] 126-127 G 3
Nikosia = Levkōsia 134-135 C 3
Nīk Pey 136-137 N 4
Niksar 136-137 G 2
Nikšić 122-123 H 4
Nikulino [SU, Perm'skaja Oblast'] 124-125 V 4
Nikulino, Moskva- 113 V b 3
Nīl, An- 164-165 L 5
Nīl, Bahr an- 164-165 L 3-4
Nila, Pulau — 148-149 JK 8
Nīlagiri = Nīlgiri Hills 134-135 M 8
Nilakkottai 140 C 5
Nīlakōṭṭai = Nilakkottai 140 C 5
Nīl al-Abyaḍ, An- 164-165 L 6
Nīl al-Azraq, An- [Sudan, administrative unit] 164-165 L 6
Nīl al-Azraq, An- [Sudan, river] 164-165 L 6
Nilambūr 140 C 5
Niland, CA 74-75 F 6
Nilandu Atoll 176 a 2
Nilanga 140 C 1
Nila Pahar = Blue Mountain 141 C 4
Nilarga = Nilanga 140 C 1
Nile = Bahr an-Nīl 164-165 L 3-4
Nile, Albert — 172 F 1
Niles, MI 70-71 G 5
Niles, OH 72-73 F 4
Nīleshwar 140 B 4
Nilgani 154 II b 1
Nīlgiri 138-139 L 7
Nīlgiri Hills 140 C 5
Nīlī Burewāla 138-139 D 2
Nilo 98-99 B 9
Nīlphāmārī 138-139 M 5
Nimach 138-139 E 5
Nimaikha River = Me Hka 141 EF 3
Nimaima 94-95 D 5
Nimāpaḍā = Nimapāra 138-139 KL 7-8
Nimapāra 138-139 KL 7-8
Nimār 138-139 EF 7
Nimāvar = Nemāwar 138-139 F 6
Nimba 168-169 C 4
Nimba, Mont — 164-165 C 7
Nimbahera 138-139 E 5
Nîmes 120-121 JK 7
Nimiuktuk River 58-59 H 2
Nim ka Thāna 138-139 EF 4
Nimmitabel 160 J 6
Nimnyrskij 132-133 Y 6
Nimrod, MT 66-67 G 2
Nimūlē 164-165 L 8
Niña, La — 106-107 G 5
Ninacaca 96-97 D 7
Ninawā = Ninive 136-137 K 4

334 Neris

Nindigully 160 J 2
Nine Degree Channel 134-135 L 9
Ninette 68-69 G 1
Nineve = Ninive 134-135 E 3
Ninfas, Punta — 111 D 6
Ning'an 142-143 OP 3
Ningbo 142-143 N 6
Ningcheng 144-145 B 2
Ning-chin = Ningjin [TJ ↗ Dezhou] 146-147 F 3
Ning-chin = Ningjin [TJ ↘ Shijiazhuang] 146-147 E 3
Ningde 142-143 M 6
Ningdu 142-143 M 6
Ninggang 146-147 DE 8
Ningguo 142-143 M 5
Ninghai 146-147 H 7
Ninghe 146-147 FG 2
Ning-ho = Ninghe 146-147 FG 2
Ninghsia, Autonomes Gebiet 142-143 H 3-K 4
Ning-hsiang = Ningxiang 142-143 L 6
Ninghsien = Ning Xian 142-143 K 4
Ninghua 142-143 M 6
Ninghwa = Ninghua 142-143 M 6
Ningjin [TJ ↗ Dezhou] 146-147 F 3
Ningjin [TJ ↘ Shijiazhuang] 146-147 E 3
Ning-kang = Ninggang 146-147 DE 8
Ningling 146-147 E 4
Ning-po = Ningbo 142-143 N 6
Ningshan 146-147 B 5
Ningsia = Ningxia 142-143 H 3-K 4
Ningsia Autonomous Region 142-143 JK 3-4
Ningteh = Ningde 142-143 M 6
Ningtsin = Ningjin 146-147 E 3
Ningtsing = Ningjin 146-147 F 3
Ninguta = Ning'an 142-143 OP 3
Ningwu 146-147 D 2
Ningxia 142-143 H 3-K 4
Ningxia Huizu Zizhiqu 142-143 JK 3-4
Ning Xian 142-143 K 4
Ningxiang 142-143 L 6
Ningyuan 146-147 CD 9
Ninh Binh 150-151 EF 2
Ninh Giang 148-149 E 2
Ninh Hoa [VN ↙ Chan Thô] 150-151 E 8
Ninh Hoa [VN ↑ Nha Trang] 148-149 EF 4
Ninigo Group 148-149 M 7
Ninilchik, AK 58-59 M 6
Ninive 134-135 E 3
Ninjintangla Shan = Nyanchhenthanglha 142-143 G 5-6
Nin Lan = Ban Nin Lan 150-151 E 3
Ninnis Glacier 53 C 16-15
Ninua = Ninive 134-135 E 3
Nioaque 102-103 E 4
Niobe, ND 68-69 E 1
Niobrara, NE 68-69 GH 4
Niobrara River 64-65 F 3
Niokolo-Koba, Parc National du — 164-165 B 6
Nioku 141 D 2
Niono 168-169 D 2
Nioro 168-169 C 2
Nioro-du-Rip 164-165 A 6
Nioro du Sahel 164-165 C 5
Niort 120-121 G 5
Niou 168-169 E 2
Nipani 140 B 2
Nipawin 56-57 Q 7
Nipawin Provincial Park 61 F 3
Nipe, Bahía de — 88-89 J 4
Nipepe 171 D 6
Nipigon 56-57 T 8
Nipigon, Lake — 56-57 ST 8
Nipigon Bay 70-71 FG 1
Nipigon-Onaman Game Reserve 62 F 2-3
Nipigon River 70-71 F 1
Nipissing, Lake — 56-57 UV 8
Nipisso 63 D 2
Nippers Harbour 63 J 3
Nippo, Yokohama- 155 III a 2
Nippur 136-137 L 6
Nipton, CA 74-75 F 5
Niquelândia 92-93 K 7
Niquero 88-89 GH 4
Niquivil 106-107 C 3
Nīr 136-137 N 3
Nira 140 B 1
Nirasaki 144-145 M 5
Ñire-Có 106-107 C 6
Ñireguco, Río — 108-109 CD 5
Nirgua 94-95 G 2
Niriz, Däryacheh i — = Daryācheh Bakhtegān 134-135 G 5
Nirka 124-125 J 3
Nirmal 138-139 G 8
Nirmala = Nirmal 138-139 G 8
Nirmāli 138-139 L 4
Nirsā 138-139 L 6
Niš 122-123 JK 4
Nisā', Wādī an- 166-167 J 3
Nisāb 134-135 E 5
Nişāb, An — = Anşāb 134-135 F 8
Nišava 122-123 K 4
Niscemi 122-123 F 7
Nischintapur 138-139 M 5
Nishi, Yokohama- 155 III a 3
Nishinomiya 144-145 K 5
Nishinoomote 144-145 H 7
Nishino shima 144-145 J 4
Nishio 144-145 L 5
Nishisonoki hantō 144-145 G 6
Nishiyama 144-145 M 4
Nishlik Lake 58-59 H 6
Nishtawn 134-135 G 7
Nishtūn = Nishtawn 134-135 G 7
Nísia-Floresta 92-93 MN 6
Nisibin = Nusaybin 134-135 E 3
Nisibis = Nusaybin 134-135 E 3
Niskey Lake 85 II a 2
Nisko 118 KL 3
Nisland, SD 68-69 E 3
Nisling Range 58-59 S 5-T 6
Nisling River 58-59 S 5
Nissan 116-117 E 9
Nisser 116-117 C 8
Nisutlin Plateau 56-57 K 5
Nísyros 122-123 M 7
Nitau = Nītaure 124-125 E 5
Nītaure 124-125 E 5
Niterói 92-93 L 9
Niterói-Armação 110 I c 2
Niterói-Centro 110 I c 2
Niterói-Gragoatá 110 I c 2
Nitra 118 J 4
Nitrito 106-107 B 7
Nitro, WV 72-73 F 5
Nitzgal = Nīcgale 124-125 F 5
Niuafo'ou 148-149 b 2
Niuatoputapu 148-149 c 2
Niue 156-157 J 5
Niulii, HI 78-79 e 2
Niut, Gunung — 148-149 E 6
Niutao 208 H 3
Niutou Shan = Nantian Dao 146-147 HJ 7
Niva 116-117 P 4
Nivāī = Nawai 138-139 EF 4
Nivās = Niwas 138-139 H 6
Nivernais 120-121 J 5
Niverville 61 K 6
Nivšera [SU, place] 124-125 T 2
Nivšera [SU, river] 124-125 T 2
Nivskij 132-133 E 4
Niwas 138-139 H 6
Nixon, TX 76-77 F 8
Niya Bazar 142-143 E 4
Nizāmābād 134-135 M 7
Nizamghāṭ 134-135 Q 5
Nizām Sāgar 134-135 M 7
Nižankoviči 126-127 A 2
Nizgal = Nīcgale 124-125 F 5
Nizhne Ilimsk = Nižne-Ilimsk 132-133 T 6
Nizhni Tagil = Nižnij Tagil 132-133 KL 6
Nizhniy Novgorod = Gor'kij 132-133 GH 6
Nizina, AK 58-59 Q 6
Nizina River 58-59 Q 6
Nizip 136-137 G 4
Nízke Tatry 118 JK 4
Nizki Island 58-59 pq 6
Nizkij, mys — 132-133 hj 5
Nižn'aja Omra 124-125 U 2
Nižn'aja Palomica 124-125 Q 4
Nižn'aja Peša 132-133 H 4
Nižn'aja Tojma 124-125 P 2
Nižn'aja Tunguska 132-133 TU 5
Nižn'aja Tura 132-133 K 6
Nižn'aja Voč' 124-125 TU 3
Nižneangarsk 132-133 UV 6
Nižne Čir 126-127 L 2
Nižnegorskij 126-127 G 4
Nižneilimsk 132-133 T 6
Nižneimbatskoje 132-133 QR 5
Nižneje Sančelejevo 124-125 RS 7
Nižnekamsk 132-133 J 7
Nižneleninskoje 132-133 Z 8
Nižnetroickij 124-125 TU 6
Nižneudinsk 132-133 S 7
Nižnevartovsk 132-133 O 5
Nižnij Baskunčak 126-127 N 2
Nižnije Serogozy 126-127 G 3
Nižnij Jenangsk 124-125 Q 4
Nižnij Karanlug = Martuni 126-127 M 6
Nižnij Lomov 124-125 OP 7
Nižnij Novgorod = Gor'kij 132-133 GH 6
Nižnij Oserednok, ostrov — 126-127 O 4
Nižnij Tagil 132-133 KL 6
Nizovaja 126-127 O 6
Nizy 126-127 G 1
Njala = Mono 164-165 E 7
Njardhvík 116-117 b 3
Njassa = Lake Malawi 172 F 4
Njeleli 174-175 J 2
Njemen = Neman 124-125 E 7
Njombe [EAT, place] 172 FG 3
Njombe [EAT, river] 172 F 3
Nkandhla = Nkandla 174-175 J 5
Nkandla 174-175 J 5
Nkata Bay = Nkhata Bay 172 F 4
Nkawkaw 168-169 E 4
Nkhata Bay 172 F 4
Nkióna 122-123 K 6
N'Kogo 168-169 H 6
Nkongsamba 164-165 FG 8
Nkréko, Ákra — = Akrōtḗrion Grḗko 136-137 F 5
Nkululu 171 C 4
Nkwalini 174-175 J 5
Noachabeb 174-175 C 4
Noa Dihing 141 E 2
Noākhāli 141 B 4
Noak Hill, London- 129 II c 1
Noanama 92-93 D 4
Noatak, AK 56-57 D 4
Noatak River 56-57 DE 4
Nobeoka 142-143 P 5
Noblesfontein 174-175 E 6
Noblesville, IN 70-71 GH 5
Noborito 155 III a 2
Nobsa 94-95 E 5
Nockatunga 160 F 1
Nodales, Bahía de los — 108-109 G 7
Nodaway River 70-71 C 5
Noel, MO 76-77 G 4
Noel Paul's River 63 H 3
Noetinger 106-107 F 4
Noe Valley, San Francisco-, CA 83 I b 2
Nófilia, en — = An-Nawfalīyah 164-165 H 2
Nogajsk = Primorskoje 126-127 H 3
Nogajskaja step' 126-127 MN 4
Nogal = Nugal 134-135 F 9
Nogales, AZ 64-65 D 5
Nogales [RCH] 106-107 B 4
Nogamut, AK 58-59 HJ 6
Nogat 118 J 1
Nōgata 144-145 H 6
Nogawa, Kawasaki- 155 III a 2
Nogent-sur-Marne 129 I cd 2
Noginsk 124-125 M 5-6
Nogoyá 111 DE 4
Noguchi 155 III d 1
Nogueira, Pampa — 108-109 E 2-3
Nohar 138-139 E 3
Nohaṭā = Nohta 138-139 G 6
Noheji 144-145 N 2
Nohta 138-139 G 6
Noi, Se — 150-151 E 4
Noir, Isla — 111 B 8
Noirmoutier, Île de — 120-121 F 5
Noiseau 129 I d 2
Noisy-le-Grand 129 I d 2
Noisy-le-Sec 129 I c 2
Nojima-saki 144-145 MN 5
Nojon 142-143 J 3
Nokha 138-139 D 4
Nokia 116-117 K 7
Nokilalaki 152-153 O 6
Nok Kuṇḍī 134-135 J 5
Nokomis 61 F 5
Nokomis, IL 70-71 F 6
Nokomis Lake 61 G 2
Nola [RCA] 164-165 H 8
No La [TJ] 138-139 K 3
Nolan, AK 58-59 M 3
Nolinsk 132-133 HJ 6
Nomamisaki 144-145 GH 7
Nome, AK 56-57 C 5
Nome, Cape — 58-59 E 4
No-min Ho = Nuomin He 142-143 N 2
Nõmme, Kilingi- 124-125 E 4
Nõmme, Reval- = Tallinn-Nõmme 124-125 E 4
Nõmme, Tallinn- 124-125 E 4
Nomo-saki 144-145 G 6
Nomtsas 174-175 B 3
Nomuka 208 J 5
Nonantum, MA 84 I ab 2
Nondalton, AK 58-59 K 6
Nondweni 174-175 J 5
Nong'an 142-143 NO 3
Nong Bua Lam Phu 150-151 D 4
Nong Chik 150-151 C 9
Nong Han 150-151 D 4
Nông Het 150-151 D 3
Nong Keun = Ban Nong Kheun 150-151 D 3
Nong Khae 150-151 C 5
Nong Khai 148-149 D 3
Nong Khayang 150-151 B 5
Nong Ko'n = Ban Nong Kheun 150-151 D 3
Nong Lahan 150-151 E 4
Nongoma 172 F 7
Nong Phai 150-151 C 5
Nôngpô = Nongpoh 141 BC 3
Nongpoh 141 BC 3
Nong Ri 150-151 B 5
Nong Rua 150-151 D 4
Nongstoin 141 B 3
Nonni = Nen Jiang 142-143 O 1-2
Nono 106-107 E 3
Nonoai 106-107 L 1
Nonoava 86-87 G 4
Nonogasta 106-107 D 2
Nonouti 208 H 3
Nonsan 144-145 F 4
Non Sang 150-151 D 4
Non Sung 150-151 D 5
Nonthaburi 150-151 C 6
Non Thai 150-151 CD 5
Nonvianuk Lake 58-59 K 7
Noordhollands kanaal 128 I b 1
Noordpunt 94-95 G 1
Noordzeekanaal 120-121 K 2
Noormarkku 116-117 JK 7
Noorvik, AK 56-57 DE 4
Nootka Island 56-57 L 8
Nootka Sound 60 D 5
Noqui 172 B 3
Nora [ETH] 164-165 MN 5
Nora [S] 116-117 F 8
Noranda 62 M 2
Norašen = Ilji'čovsk 126-127 M 7
Norbu 138-139 M 3
Norcatur, KS 68-69 F 6
Nòrcia 122-123 E 4
Norcross, GA 78-79 G 4
Nordaustlandet 116-117 k-m 5
Nordcross, GA 80-81 D 4
Nordegg = Brazeau 60 J 3
Norden 118 C 2
Nordenskiöld, archipelag — 132-133 RS 2
Nordenskiöld, zaliv — 132-133 JK 2
Nordenskiøldbreen 116-117 l 4
Nordenskiøld land 116-117 jk 6
Nordenskiold River 58-59 T 6
Norderelbe 130 I b 2
Nordfjord 116-117 AB 7
Nordfjorden 116-117 j 5
Nordfriesische Inseln 118 D 1
Nordhausen 118 E 3
Nordhorn 118 C 2
Nordhur-Ísafjardhar 116-117 b 1-2
Nordhur-Múla 116-117 f 2
Nordhur-Thingeyjar 116-117 ef 1-2
Nordkapp [N] 116-117 LM 2
Nordkapp [Svalbard] 116-117 k 4
Nordkinn 116-117 MN 2
Nordkjosbotn 116-117 HJ 3
Nordland 116-117 E 5-G 3
Nördlingen 118 E 4
Nord-Mossi, Plateaux du — 168-169 E 2
Nordos çayı 136-137 K 3
Nordostrundingen 52 A 18-20
Nord-Ostsee-Kanal 118 D 1-2
Nordre Kvaløy 116-117 H 2
Nordre Strømfjord 56-57 a 4
Nordrhein-Westfalen 118 CD 3
Nord-Trøndelag 116-117 DE 5
Nordvik 132-133 V 3
Nore 116-117 C 7
Norfolk, NE 64-65 G 3
Norfolk, VA 64-65 LM 4
Norfolk Island 158-159 N 5
Norfolk Lake 78-79 CD 2
Norfolk Ridge 158-159 N 6-O 7
Norheimsund 116-117 AB 7
Nori 132-133 N 4
Norias, TX 76-77 F 9
Norias, Las — 76-77 C 8
Norikura dake 144-145 L 4
Noril'sk 132-133 Q 4
Norische Alpen 118 FG 5
Norla 138-139 J 7
Norlina, NC 80-81 G 2
Normal, IL 70-71 F 5
Norman, AR 78-79 C 3
Norman, OK 64-65 G 4
Normanby 119 F 4
Normanby Island 148-149 h 7
Normandie 120-121 GH 4
Normandin 62 P 2
Normandy = Normandie 120-121 GH 4
Normangee, TX 76-77 F 7
Norman River 158-159 H 3
Normanton 158-159 H 3
Norman Wells 56-57 KL 4
Normetal 62 M 2
Nornalup 158-159 C 6-7
Noroeste, Brazo — 108-109 DE 10
Norquinco 111 B 6
Norra Bergnäs 116-117 H 4
Norra Storfjället 116-117 FG 5
Norrbotten [S, administrative unit] 116-117 G-K 4
Norrbotten [S, landscape] 116-117 J 5-K 4
Norrembega 62 L 2
Nørresundby, Ålborg- 116-117 CD 9
Norridge, IL 83 II a 1
Norris, MT 66-67 H 3
Norris Arm 63 J 3
Norris City, IL 70-71 F 7
Norris Lake 78-79 GH 2
Norristown, PA 72-73 J 4
Norrköping 116-117 G 8
Norrland 116-117 F-J 5
Norrtälje 116-117 H 8
Norseman 158-159 D 6
Norsk 132-133 Y 7
Norte, Brazo — 108-109 B 7
Norte, Cabo — 92-93 K 4
Norte, Canal do — 92-93 JK 4
Norte, Serra do — 92-93 H 7
North, SC 80-81 F 4
North, Cape — 56-57 YZ 8
North Adams, MA 72-73 K 3
North Albanian Alps = Alpet e Shiqërise 122-123 HJ 4
Northallerton 119 F 4
Northam [AUS] 158-159 C 6
Northam [ZA] 172 E 7
North America 50-51 DE 3
North American Basin 50-51 FG 4
Northampton, MA 72-73 K 3
Northampton [AUS] 158-159 B 5
Northampton [GB] 119 FG 5
North Andaman 134-135 P 8
North Arlington, NJ 82 III b 2
North Arm 56-57 NO 5
North Atlanta, GA 85 II b 2
North Augusta, SC 80-81 EF 4
North Australian Basin 50-51 P 6
North Balabac Strait 152-153 M 1
North Baltimore, OH 72-73 E 4
North Banda Basin 148-149 HJ 7
North Battleford 56-57 P 7
North Bay 56-57 UV 8
North Belcher Islands 56-57 U 6
North Bend, NE 68-69 H 5
North Bend, OR 66-67 A 4
North Bend, WA 66-67 C 2
North Bergen, NJ 82 III b 2
Northbrook, Houston-, TX 85 III b 2
Northbrook, ostrov — 132-133 GH 2
North Bruny 160 cd 3
North Caicos 88-89 L 4
North Canadian River 64-65 FG 4
North Cape [CDN] 63 E 4
North Cape [NZ] 158-159 O 6
North Cape [USA] 58-59 jk 4
North Cape = Nordkapp 116-117 LM 2
North Caribou Lake 56-57 ST 7
North Carolina 64-65 KL 4
North-Central Province = Uturė Mėda Palāna = 2 ◁ 140 E 6
North Channel [CDN] 56-57 U 8
North Channel [GB] 119 CD 4
North Charleston, SC 80-81 G 4
North Chicago, IL 70-71 G 4
Northcliff, Johannesburg- 170 V a 1
Northcliffe 158-159 C 6
Northcote, Melbourne- 161 II c 1
North Creek, NY 72-73 JK 3
North Dakota 64-65 FG 2
North Dum Dum 154 II b 2
North East, PA 72-73 FG 3
Northeast Branch 82 II b 1
Northeast Cape [USA] 58-59 CD 5
North East Carry, ME 72-73 LM 2
North Eastern 172 H 1-2
Northeastern University 84 I b 2
North-East Island = Nordaustlandet 116-117 k-m 5
Northeast Providence Channel 64-65 L 6
Northeim 118 DE 3
Northern [GH] 168-169 E 3
Northern [MW] 171 C 5-6
Northern [WAL] 168-169 BC 3
Northern [Z] 172 E 3-F 4
Northern Cheyenne Indian Reservation 68-69 C 3
Northern Indian Lake 61 K 2
Northern Ireland 119 C 4
Northern Light Lake 70-71 E 1
Northern Marianas 162 GH 2
Northern Pacific Railway 64-65 EF 2
Northern Province = Ash-Shimālīyah 164-165 KL 5
Northern Province = Uturė Palāna = 1 ◁ 140 E 6
Northern Sporades = Bóreioi Sporádes 122-123 KL 6
Northern Territory 158-159 FG 3-4
Northfield, MN 70-71 D 3
Northfield, VT 72-73 K 2
North Fiji Basin 158-159 O 2
North Foreland 119 GH 6
North Fork, CA 74-75 D 4
North Fork, ID 66-67 FG 3
North Fork Camp Creek 85 II a 3
North Fork Chandalar 58-59 N 2-3
North Fork Cimarron River 76-77 D 4
North Fork Clearwater River 66-67 F 2
North Fork Feather River 74-75 C 2-3
North Fork Fortymile 58-59 QR 4
North Fork Grand River 68-69 E 3
North Fork Humboldt River 66-67 F 5
North Fork John Day River 66-67 D 3
North Fork Koyukuk 58-59 M 3
North Fork Kuskokwim 58-59 KL 5
North Fork Moreau River 68-69 E 3
North Fork Mountain 72-73 G 5
North Fork Payette River 66-67 E 3
North Fork Peachtree Creek 85 II c 1
North Fork Powder River 68-69 C 4
North Fork Red River 76-77 E 5
North Fork Smoky Hill River 68-69 EF 6
North Fork Solomon River 68-69 FG 6
North Fox Island 70-71 H 3
North French River 62 L 1-2
North Frisian Islands = Nordfriesische Inseln 118 D 1
Northgate 68-69 EF 1
North Haycock 152-153 G 4
North Head [AUS] 161 I b 1
North Head [CDN] 63 C 5
North Horr 172 G 1
North Houston Heights, TX 85 III b 1
North Island [NZ] 158-159 P 7
North Island [USA] 80-81 G 4
North Islands 78-79 E 6
North Judson, IN 70-71 G 5
North Kamloops 60 GH 4
North Koel = Koel 138-139 J 5
North Korea 142-143 O 3-4
North Lakhimpur 141 CD 2
Northland 161 E 2
Northland, MI 70-71 G 2
North Land = Severnaja Zeml'a 132-133 ST 1-2
North Laramie River 68-69 D 4
North Las Vegas, NV 74-75 F 4
Northline Terrace, TX 85 III b 1
North Little Rock, AR 64-65 H 4-5
North Loup, NE 68-69 G 5
North Loup River 68-69 G 5
North Magnetic Pole 56-57 Q 3
North Magnetic Pole Area 52 B 29
North Malosmadulu Atoll 176 a 1
North Manchester, IN 70-71 H 5
Northmead 170 V c 2
North Miami, FL 80-81 cd 4
North Minch 119 C 3-D 2
North Moose Lake 61 HJ 3
North Natuna Islands = Kepulauan Bunguran Utara 148-149 E 6
North Negril Point 88-89 G 5
North New River Canal 80-81 c 3
Northolt, London- 129 II a 1
Northolt Aerodrome 129 II a 1
North Ossetian Autonomous Soviet Socialist Republic 126-127 LM 5
North Pacific Basin 156-157 H-K 2-3
North Pageh = Pulau Pagai Utara 148-149 C 7
North Palisade 64-65 C 4
North Park, Chicago-, IL 83 II a 1
North Pass 64-65 J 6
North Pease River 76-77 D 5
North Philadelphia, Philadelphia-, PA 84 III bc 2
North Philadelphia Airport 84 III c 1
North Platte, NE 64-65 F 3
North Platte River 64-65 F 3
North Point [AUS] 161 I b 1
North Point [USA] 72-73 E 2
North Point, Victoria- 155 I b 2
North Pole, AK 58-59 O 4
Northport, AL 78-79 F 4
Northport, MI 70-71 H 3
Northport, NE 68-69 E 5
Northport, WA 66-67 E 1
North Powder, OR 66-67 DE 3
North Quincy, MA 84 I bc 3
North Range 70-71 DE 2
North Reservoir 84 I b 2
North Rhine-Westphalia = Nordrhein-Westfalen 118 CD 3
North Richmond, CA 83 I b 1
North Riverside, IL 83 II a 1
North Rona 119 D 2
North Ronaldsay 119 EF 2
North Ryde, Sydney- 161 I a 1
North Sălmăra 141 B 2
North Santiam River 66-67 B 3
North Saskatchewan River 56-57 OP 7
North Sea 114-115 J 4
North Sea Channel = Noordzeekanaal 120-121 K 2
North Share Channel 83 II ab 1
North Shore Range 70-71 E 1-2
North Slape 58-59 G-N 2
North Star 60 HJ 1
North Stradbroke Island 158-159 K 5
North Stratford, NH 72-73 L 2
North Sydney 63 F 4
North Sydney, Sydney- 161 I b 1-2
North Taranaki Bight 158-159 O 7
North Thompson River 60 G 4-H 3
North Tonawanda, NY 72-73 G 3
North Truchas Peak 64-65 E 4
North Ubian Island 152-153 NO 2
North Uist 119 BC 3
Northumberland Islands 158-159 JK 4
Northumberland Strait 56-57 Y 8
North Umpqua River 66-67 B 4
North Utoy Creek 85 II b 2
North Valleystream, NY 82 III de 2
North Vancouver 66-67 B 1
North Vanlaiphai 141 C 4
North Vernon, IN 70-71 H 6
North Wabasca Lake 60 L 1
Northway, AK 58-59 QR 5
Northway Junction, AK 58-59 R 5
Northwest Australian Basin 50-51 OP 6
Northwest Branch 82 II b 1
North West Cape 158-159 B 4
North Western 172 DE 4
North-Western Province = Vayamba Palāna = 3 ◁ 140 E 7
Northwestern University 83 II b 1
North-West-Frontier 132-133 L 3-4
Northwest Highlands 119 D 2-3
Northwest Indian Ridge 50-51 N 5-6
Northwest Pacific Basin 156-157 G 3
Northwest Pacific Ridge 156-157 H 2-3
Northwest Passage 56-57 J-L 3
Northwest Territories 56-57 M-U 4
North Weymouth, MA 84 I c 3
North Wilkesboro, NC 80-81 F 2
Northwood, IA 70-71 D 4
Northwood, ND 68-69 H 2
Northwood, London- 129 II a 1
North York 72-73 G 3
Norton, KS 68-69 G 6
Norton, VA 80-81 E 2
Norton Bay 58-59 FG 4
Norton Point 82 III b 3
Norton Sound 56-57 D 5
Nortonville, ND 68-69 G 2
Norvegia, Kapp — 53 B 34-35
Norwalk, CA 83 III d 2
Norwalk, CT 72-73 K 4
Norwalk, MI 70-71 GH 3
Norwalk, OH 72-73 E 4
Norway 116-117 C 8-L 2
Norway, IA 70-71 DE 5
Norway, ME 72-73 L 2
Norway, MI 70-71 G 3
Norway House 56-57 R 7
Norwegian Basin 50-51 JK 2
Norwegian Bay 56-57 ST 2
Norwegian Sea 114-115 F-K 2
Norwegian Trench 114-115 K 4
Norwich, CT 72-73 KL 4
Norwich, NY 72-73 J 3
Norwich [CDN] 72-73 F 3
Norwich [GB] 119 G 5
Norwood, MN 70-71 CD 3
Norwood, NC 80-81 F 3
Norwood, NY 72-73 J 2
Norwood, OH 70-71 H 6
Norwood, PA 84 III b 2
Norwood, Johannesburg- 170 V b 1
Norwood Park, Chicago-, IL 83 II a 1
nos Emine 122-123 MN 4
Nosiro 142-143 QR 3
Nosiro = Noshiro 142-143 QR 3
nos Kaliakra 122-123 N 4
Nosovka 126-127 EF 1
Nosovščina 124-125 L 2
Nossa Senhora da Glória 100-101 F 6
Nossa Senhora das Dores 100-101 F 6
Nossa Senhora do Livramento 102-103 D 1
Nossa Senhora do Ó, São Paulo- 110 II ab 1
Nossa Senhora do Socorro 100-101 F 6
Nossegem 128 II b 1
Nossikon 128 IV b 2
Nossob 172 C 6
Nossombougou 168-169 D 2
Nošul' 124-125 R 3
Nosy-Bé 172 J 4
Nosy Boraha 172 K 5
Nosy Mitsio 172 J 4
Nosy Radama 172 J 4
Nosy-Varika 172 J 6
Notch Peak 74-75 G 3
Noteć 118 G 2
Noto [I] 122-123 F 7
Noto [J] 144-145 L 4
Notodden 116-117 C 8
Noto hantō 142-143 Q 4
Noto-jima 144-145 L 4
Notoro-ko 144-145 d 1
Notre Dame 129 I c 2
Notre-Dame, Bois — 129 I d 2
Notre Dame, Monts — 56-57 WX 8
Notre Dame Bay 56-57 Z 8-a 7
Notre-Dame-des-Lourdes 61 JK 6
Notre-Dame-des-Victoires, Montréal- 82 I b 1
Notre-Dame-du-Lac 63 BC 4
Notre-Dame-du-Laus 72-73 J 1
Notre Dame du Nord 62 M 3
Nottawasaga Bay 72-73 F 2
Nottaway River 56-57 V 7
Nottingham 119 F 5
Nottingham Island 56-57 VW 5
Nottingham Park, IL 83 II a 2
Nottinghamroad 174-175 HJ 5
Notting Hill, London- 129 II b 1
Notting Hill, Melbourne- 161 II c 2
Nottoway River 80-81 H 2
Notuken Creek 61 E 6
Notwani 174-175 FG 3
Nouadhibou = Nawādhību 164-165 A 4
Nouakchott = Nawākshūt 164-165 A 5
Nouâl, Choṭṭ en — = Sabkhat an-Nawāl 166-167 LM 2
Noukloofberge 174-175 AB 3
Noukloof Mountains = Noukloofberge 174-175 AB 3
Nouméa 158-159 N 4
Noun 168-169 H 4
Noupoort 172 DE 8
Nous 174-175 C 5
Nous West = Nous 174-175 C 5
Nouvelle Amsterdam 50-51 NO 7
Nouvelle-Anvers 172 CD 1
Nova Almeida 100-101 DE 11
Nova Andradina 102-103 F 5
Nova Aripuanã 98-99 H 9
Novabad 134-135 L 3
Nova Cachoeirinha, São Paulo- 110 II ab 1
Nova Chaves = Muconda 172 D 4
Nova Cruz 92-93 MN 6
Nova Era 102-103 L 3
Nova Esperança 102-103 FG 5
Nova Europa 102-103 H 4
Nova Floresta 100-101 E 3
Nova Freixo = Cuamba 172 G 4
Nova Friburgo 102-103 L 5
Nova Gaia 172 C 3-4
Nova Goa = Panjim 134-135 L 7
Nova Gradiška 122-123 GH 3
Nova Granada 102-103 H 4
Nova Iguaçu 92-93 L 9
Nova Iorque 100-101 B 4
Nova Itarana 100-101 DE 7
Novaja Basan' 126-127 E 1
Novaja Buchara = Kagan 134-135 J 3
Novaja Kachovka 126-127 F 3
Novaja Kalitva 126-127 K 1
Novaja Kazanka 126-127 O 2
Novaja Ladoga 124-125 HJ 3
Novaja Odessa 126-127 EF 3
Novaja Pis'm'anka = Leninogorsk 132-133 J 7
Novaja Sibir', ostrov — 132-133 de 3
Novaja Usman' 126-127 J 1
Novaja Zeml'a 132-133 J 3-L 2
Nova Lamego 164-165 B 6
Nova Lima 92-93 L 8-9
Nova Lisboa = Huambo 172 C 4
Nova Londrina 102-103 F 5
Nova Lusitânia 172 F 5
Nova Mambone 172 G 6
Nova Olímpia 104-105 H 4
Nova Olinda [BR, Ceará] 100-101 E 4
Nova Olinda [BR, Pará] 98-99 N 8
Nova Olinda do Norte 98-99 J 6
Nova Petropolis 106-107 M 2
Nova Ponte 102-103 J 3
Nova Prata 106-107 M 2
Novara 122-123 C 3
Nova Russas 100-101 D 3
Nova Scotia 56-57 X 9-Y 8
Nova Sofala 172 FG 6
Nova Soure 100-101 E 6
Novato, CA 74-75 B 3
Nova Trento 102-103 H 7
Nova Venécia 100-101 D 10
Nova Viçosa 100-101 E 9
Nova Vida 98-99 G 10
Novaya Zemlya = Novaja Zeml'a 132-133 J 3-L 2
Novaya Zemlya Trough 132-133 K 3-L 2
Nova Zagora 122-123 LM 4
Nové Zámky 118 J 4
Novgorod 132-133 E 6
Novgorod-Severskij 124-125 J 8
Novi Bečej 122-123 J 3
Noviembre, 28 de — 108-109 CD 8
Novigrad 122-123 E 3
Novije Basy 126-127 G 1
Novije Belokoroviči 126-127 C 1
Novillos, Los — 106-107 K 3-4
Novinka [SU ↓ Leningrad] 124-125 H 4
Novi Pazar [BG] 122-123 M 4

Orland, CA 74-75 B 3
Orlândia 102-103 J 4
Orlando, FL 64-65 K 6
Orlando, Johannesburg- 170 V a 2
Orleães 102-103 H 8
Orléanais 120-121 HJ 4-5
Orléans 120-121 HJ 5
Orleans, NE 68-69 G 5
Orléans, Île d' 63 A 4
Orléansville = Al-Asnām 164-165 E 1
Orlik 132-133 S 7
Orlinga 132-133 U 6
Orlov = Chalturin 132-133 H 6
Orlov Gaj 126-127 O 1
Orlovskij 126-127 L 3
Ormānjhi 138-139 K 6
Ormārā 134-135 JK 5
Ormesson-sur-Marne 129 I d 2
Ormoc 148-149 HJ 4
Ormond, Melbourne- 161 II c 2
Ormond, Point — 161 II b 2
Ormond Beach, FL 80-81 c 2
Órmos Faleru 113 IV a 2
Ormsby 72-73 GH 2
Ormsö = Vormsi 124-125 D 4
Ormuz, Strait of — = Tangeh Hormoz 134-135 H 5
Orne 120-121 G 4
Örnsköldsvik 116-117 H 6
Oro, El — [EC] 96-97 AB 3
Oro, El — [MEX, Coahuila] 76-77 C 9
Oro, El — [MEX, México] 86-87 K 8
Oro, Museo del — 91 III c 3
Oro, Río de — 104-105 G 10
Orobayaya 104-105 E 3
Orobó 100-101 G 4
Orobo, Serra do — 100-101 D 7
Oročen 132-133 Y 6
Orocó 100-101 E 5
Orocué 92-93 E 4
Orodara 164-165 CD 6
Orofino, ID 66-67 EF 2
Orogrande, NM 76-77 AB 6
Oro Ingenio 104-105 CD 7
Or'ol [SU] 124-125 L 7
Oroluk 208 F 2
Oromocto 63 C 5
Oron 168-169 H 4
Orongo 96-97 D 9
Orongo gol 142-143 F 2
Orono, ME 72-73 M 2
Oronoque 92-93 H 4
Oronoque River 98-99 K 3-4
Orontes = Nahr al-ʿĀṣī 136-137 G 5
Orope 92-93 E 3
Oroquieta 148-149 H 5
Oro-ri 144-145 F 2
Oros 92-93 M 6
Orós, Açude de — 100-101 E 4
Orosei 122-123 C 5
Orosháza 118 K 5
Orosi, Volcán — 64-65 JK 9
Orotukan 132-133 d 5
Orovada, NV 66-67 DE 5
Oroville, CA 74-75 C 3
Oroville, WA 66-67 D 1
Oroya 96-97 G 8
Oroya, La — 92-93 D 7
Orpha, WY 68-69 D 4
Orpington, London- 129 II c 2
Orpúa 94-95 C 5
Orr, MN 70-71 D 1
Orroroo 160 D 4
Orrville, OH 72-73 F 4
Orsa [S] 116-117 F 7
Orša [SU] 124-125 H 6
Orsha = Orša 124-125 H 6
Orsk 132-133 K 7
Orşova 122-123 K 3
Ørsta 116-117 AB 6
Ortaca 136-137 C 4
Ortahanak 136-137 K 2
Ortaköy [TR, Çorum] 136-137 F 2
Ortaköy [TR, Niğde ↑ Aksaray] 136-137 EF 3
Ortaköy [TR, Niğde ← Bor] 136-137 F 4
Ortega 94-95 D 6
Ortegal, Cabo — 120-121 CD 7
Orteguaza, Río — 94-95 D 7
Orthez 120-121 G 7
Ortiga, Cordillera de la — 106-107 BC 2
Ortigueira 120-121 CD 7
Orting, WA 66-67 BC 2
Ortiz [ROU] 106-107 K 5
Ortiz [YV] 94-95 H 3
Ortíz de Rozas 106-107 G 5
Ortler = Ortles 122-123 D 2
Ortlès 122-123 D 2
Ortón, Río — 104-105 C 2
Ortona 122-123 F 4
Ortonville, MN 68-69 H 3
Orumbo 174-175 BC 2
Orūmīyeh 134-135 E 3
Orūmīyeh, Daryācheh-ye — 134-135 E 3
Orumo 171 C 2
Oruro [BOL, administrative unit] 104-105 BC 6
Oruro [BOL, place] 92-93 F 8
Orust 116-117 D 8
Orvieto 122-123 DE 4
Orville Escarpment 53 B 29-30

Oš [SU] 134-135 L 2
Osa [SU] 124-125 U 5
Osa [ZRE] 171 AB 3
Osa, Peninsula de — 64-65 JK 10
Osaco 102-103 J 5
Osage, IA 70-71 D 4
Osage, NJ 84 III d 2
Osage, WY 68-69 D 4
Osage City, KS 70-71 BC 6
Osage Indian Reservation 76-77 F 4
Osage River 64-65 H 4
Ōsaka 142-143 Q 5
Ōsaka wan 144-145 K 5
Osakis, MN 70-71 C 3
Osām 122-123 L 4
Osan 144-145 F 4
Ošarovo 132-133 S 5
Osawatomie, KS 70-71 C 6
Osborne 61 K 6
Osborne, KS 68-69 G 6
Osborne, Cerro — = Mount Usborne 111 E 8
Osby 116-117 EF 9
Osceola, AR 78-79 DE 3
Osceola, IA 70-71 D 5
Osceola, MO 70-71 D 6
Osceola, NE 68-69 H 5
Osceola, WI 70-71 D 3
Oscoda, MI 72-73 E 2
Oscura, Sierra — 76-77 A 6
Oscura Peak 76-77 A 6
Osdorf [DDR] 130 III b 2
Osdorf, Hamburg- 130 I a 1
Osdorp, Amsterdam- 128 I a 1
Ösel = Saaremaa 124-125 CD 4
Ōse-zaki 144-145 G 6
Osgood, IN 70-71 H 6
Oshamambe 144-145 b 2
Oshawa 56-57 V 9
Ō-shima [J, Hokkaidō] 144-145 a 3
Ō-shima [J, Nagasaki] 144-145 G 6
Ō-shima [J, Sizuoka] 144-145 M 5
Ō-shima [J, Wakayama] 144-145 KL 6
Oshima hantō 142-143 Q 3
Oshin 168-169 G 3
Oshkosh, NE 68-69 E 5
Oshkosh, WI 64-65 HJ 3
Oshnavīyeh 136-137 L 4
Oshoek 174-175 J 4
Oshogbo 164-165 EF 7
Oshtorān Kūh 136-137 N 6
Oshtorīnān 136-137 N 5
Oshun 168-169 G 4
Oshwe 172 CD 2
Ošib 124-125 U 4
Osijek 122-123 H 3
Osima hantō = Oshima-hantō 142-143 QR 3
Osinniki 132-133 Q 7
Osintorf 124-125 H 6
Osipenko = Berd'ansk 126-127 H 3
Osipoviči 124-125 G 7
Oskaloosa, IA 64-65 H 3
Oskaloosa, KS 70-71 C 6
Oskar II land 116-117 j 5
Oskarshamn 116-117 G 9
Oskelaneo 62 O 2
Oslo 116-117 D 8
Oslo, MN 68-69 H 1
Oslofjord 116-117 D 8
Osmānābād 140 C 1
Osmancık 136-137 F 2
Osmaneli 136-137 C 2
Osmaniye 136-137 FG 4
Osmānnagar 140 D 1
Osm'any 124-125 EF 6
Os'mino 124-125 G 4
Osmussaar 124-125 D 4
Osnabrück 118 D 2
Osnaburgh House 62 D 2
Oso 171 B 3
Oso, WA 66-67 C 1
Oso, El — 94-95 J 5
Osogovski Planini 122-123 K 4
Osona 174-175 B 2
Ōsone 155 III d 3
Osório [RA] 106-107 M 2
Osorio [YV] 91 II b 1
Osório, Salto — 111 F 3
Osório Fonseca 98-99 JK 6
Osorno [RCH] 111 B 6
Osorno, Volcán — 111 B 6
Os'otr 124-125 M 6
Osowiec 118 L 2
Osoyoos 66-67 D 1
Osøyra 116-117 A 7
Ospika River 60 F 1
Ospino 94-95 G 3
Ossa 122-123 K 6
Ossa, Mount — 158-159 J 8
Ossabaw Island 80-81 F 5
Osse 168-169 G 4
Osseo, WI 70-71 E 3
Ossidinge = Mamfe 164-165 F 7
Ossineke, MI 70-71 J 3
Ossining, NY 72-73 K 4
Ossipee, NH 72-73 L 3
Ossipevsk = Berdičev 126-127 D 2
Ossora 132-133 f 6
Ostān-e Markazī 134-135 E 3-F 4
Ostankino, Moskva- 113 V c 2
Ostaškov 124-125 J 5
Ostbahnhof Berlin 130 III b 1
Oste 118 D 2
Ostend = Oostende 120-121 J 3
Ostende [RA] 106-107 J 6
Österbotten = Pohjanmaa 116-117 K 6-M 5
Österdalälven 116-117 E 7
Østerdalen 116-117 D 7
Östergötland 116-117 F 8-9
Osterley Park 129 II a 2
Östersund 116-117 F 6
Østfold 116-117 D 8
Ostfriedhof Ahrensfelde 130 III c 1
Ostfriesische Inseln 118 C 2
Östhammar 116-117 GH 7
Óstia Antica, Roma- 122-123 DE 5
Ost'or [SU, Rossijskaja SFSR place] 124-125 J 6
Ost'or [SU, Rossijskaja SFSR river] 124-125 J 7
Ost'or [SU, Ukrainskaja SSR place] 126-127 E 1
Ost'or [SU, Ukrainskaja SSR river] 126-127 F 1
Ostpark München 130 II b 2
Ostras 100-101 E 10
Ostrava 118 J 4
Ostróda 118 JK 2
Ostrog [SU] 126-127 C 1
Ostrogožsk 126-127 J 1
Ostrołęka 118 KL 2
Ostrov [CS] 118 H 4-5
Ostrov [SU] 124-125 G 5
ostrova Anjou 52 B 4-5
ostrova Arktičeskogo Instituta 132-133 OP 2
ostrova Belaja Zeml'a 132-133 L-N 1
ostrova de Long 132-133 c-e 2
ostrova Diomida 56-57 C 4-5
ostrova Dunaj 132-133 XY 3
ostrova Izvestij CIK 132-133 OP 2
ostrov Ajon 132-133 g 4
ostrova Komsomol'skoj Pravdy 132-133 U-W 2
ostrova Medvežij 132-133 f 3
ostrova Petra 132-133 VW 2
ostrov Arakamčečen 132-133 l 5
ostrov Arga-Muora-Sise 132-133 XY 3
ostrova Sergeja Kirova 132-133 QR 2
ostrov Askol'd 144-145 J 1
ostrov Atlasova 132-133 de 7
ostrova T'ulenji 126-127 OP 4
ostrov Barsakel mes 132-133 KL 8
ostrov Begičeva = ostrov Bol'šoj Begičev 132-133 VW 3
ostrov Bel'kovskij 132-133 Za 2
ostrov Belyj 132-133 MN 3
ostrov Bennett 132-133 cd 2
ostrov Bering 132-133 fg 7
ostrov Bol'ševik 132-133 T-V 2
ostrov Bol'šoj Klimeckij 124-125 KL 3
ostrov Bol'šoj Šantar 132-133 ab 7
ostrov Bol'šoj T'uters 124-125 FG 4
ostrov Bol'šoj Ver'ozovyj 124-125 FG 3
ostrov Bulla 126-127 O 6
ostrov Čečen' 126-127 N 4
ostrov Chiuma = Hiiumaa 124-125 CD 4
ostrov Dolgij 132-133 K 4
ostrov Džambajskij 126-127 OP 3
ostrov Džarylgač 126-127 F 3-4
ostrov Erge-Muora-Sisse = ostrov Arga-Muora-Sisse 132-133 XY 3
ostrov Faddejevskij 132-133 b-d 2
ostrov Gogland 124-125 F 3
ostrov Graham Bell 132-133 MN 1
ostrov Hall 132-133 KL 1
ostrov Henriette 132-133 ef 2
ostrov Herald 52 B 36
ostrov Iony 132-133 b 6
ostrov Iturup 132-133 c 8
ostrov Jackson 132-133 H-K 1
ostrov Jarok 132-133 a 3
ostrov Jeanette 132-133 ef 2
ostrov Karaginskij 132-133 fg 6
ostrov Karl Alexander 132-133 H-K 1
ostrov Kokaral 132-133 L 8
ostrov Kolgujev 132-133 GH 4
ostrov Komsomolec 132-133 P-R 1
ostrov Kotel'nyj 132-133 Za 2-3
ostrov Kulaly 126-127 O 4
ostrov Kunašir 132-133 c 9
ostrov MacClintock 132-133 H-K 1
ostrov Malyj L'achovskij 132-133 bc 3
ostrov Malyj Tajmyr 132-133 UV 2
ostrov Mednyj 52 D 2
ostrov Meždušarskij 132-133 HJ 3
ostrov Moneron 132-133 b 8
ostrov Moržovec 132-133 GH 4
ostrov Moščnyj 124-125 FG 4
ostrov Nižnij Oseredok 126-127 O 4
ostrov Northbrook 132-133 GH 2
ostrov Novaja Sibir' 132-133 de 3
ostrov Ogurčinskij 134-135 G 3
ostrov Okt'abr'skoj Revol'ucii 132-133 Q-S 2
ostrov Ol'chon 132-133 U 7
ostrov Olenij 132-133 O 3
ostrov Onekotan 132-133 de 8
ostrov Paramušir 132-133 de 7
ostrov Pesčanyj 132-133 WX 3
ostrov Petra I 53 C 27
ostrov Pioner 132-133 QR 2
ostrov Put'atina 144-145 J 1
ostrov Ratmanova 58-59 BC 4
ostrov Rikorda 144-145 H 1
ostrov Rudolf 132-133 JK 1
ostrov Russkij [SU, Japan Sea] 132-133 Z 9
ostrov Russkij [SU, Kara Sea] 132-133 RS 2
ostrov Salisbury 132-133 HJ 1
ostrov Salm 132-133 KL 2
ostrov Sengejskij 132-133 HJ 4
ostrov Sibir'akova 132-133 OP 3
ostrov Simušir 142-143 T 2
Ostrovskoje 124-125 NO 5
ostrov Šmidta 132-133 QR 1
ostrov Šokal'skogo 132-133 NO 3
ostrov Stolbovoj 132-133 Za 3
ostrov Sverdrup 132-133 O 3
ostrov T'ulenij 126-127 N 4
ostrov Ujedinenija 132-133 OP 2
ostrov Urup 132-133 cd 8
ostrov Ušakova 132-133 OP 1
ostrov Vajgač 132-133 KL 3
ostrov Valaam 124-125 H 3
ostrov Vil'kickogo [SU, East Siberian Sea] 132-133 de 2
ostrov Vil'kickogo [SU, Kara Sea] 132-133 NO 3
ostrov Vize 132-133 O 2
ostrov Vozroždenija 132-133 KL 9
ostrov Wrangel 132-133 hj 3
ostrov Žiloj 126-127 P 6
ostrov Žochova 132-133 de 2
ostrov Z'udev 126-127 O 4
Ostrowiec Świętokrzyski 118 KL 3
Ostrów Mazowiecka 118 KL 2
Ostrów Wielkopolski 118 HJ 3
Ostryna 124-125 E 7
Oststeinbek 130 I b 1
Osttirol 118 F 5
Ostuni 122-123 G 5
O'Sullivan Lake 62 F 2
O'Sullivan Reservoir = Potholes Reservoir 66-67 D 2
Osum 122-123 J 5
Osumi Channel = Ōsumi-kaikyō 142-143 P 5
Ōsumi-kaikyō 142-143 P 5
Ōsumi-shotō 142-143 OP 5
Ōsumisyotō = Ōsumi-shotō 142-143 OP 5
Osuna 120-121 E 10
Osvaldo Cruz 102-103 G 4
Osveja 124-125 G 5-6
Oswa = Ausa 140 C 1
Oswego, KS 76-77 G 4
Oswego, NY 64-65 L 3
Oswego = Lake Oswego, OR 66-67 B 3
Oświęcim 118 J 3-4

Ōta 144-145 M 4
Ōta = Mino-Kamo 144-145 L 5
Ōta, Tōkyō- 155 III b 2
Otadaonanis River 62 H 1
Otago 161 C 7
Otago Peninsula 158-159 O 9
Ōtahara = Ōtawara 144-145 N 4
Ōtake 144-145 HJ 5
Otaki 158-159 OP 8
Ōtakine yama 144-145 N 4
Otar 132-133 O 9
Otare, Cerro — 92-93 E 4
Otaru 142-143 QR 3
Otaru-wan = Ishikari-wan 144-145 b 2
Otatal, Cerro — 86-87 E 3
Otavalo 92-93 D 4
Otavi 172 C 5
Otawi = Otavi 172 C 5
Otepää 124-125 F 4
Oteros, Río — 86-87 F 4
Otgon Tenger uul 142-143 H 2
O'The Cherokees, Lake — 76-77 G 4
Othello, WA 66-67 D 2
Othmarschen, Hamburg- 130 I a 1
Othōnoí 122-123 H 6
Óthrys 122-123 K 6
Oti 164-165 E 7
Otimbingwe = Otjimbingue 174-175 B 2
Otis, CO 68-69 E 5
Otis, OR 66-67 B 3
Otish Mountains 56-57 W 7
Otjekondo 172 C 5
Otjimbingue 174-175 B 2
Otjiseva = Otjisewa 174-175 B 2
Otjisewa 174-175 B 2
Otjiwarongo 172 C 6
Otobe 144-145 b 2-3
Otofuke 144-145 c 2
Otog Qi 146-147 AB 2
Otoineppu 144-145 c 1
Otok = Otog Qi 146-147 AB 2
Otoskwin River 62 D 2
Otpor = Zabajkal'sk 132-133 W 8
Otra 116-117 B 8
Otradnaja 126-127 K 4
Otradnyj 124-125 S 7
Otranto 122-123 H 5
Otranto, Canale d' 122-123 H 5-6
Otsego, MI 70-71 GH 4
Ōtsu [J, Hokkaidō] 144-145 c 2
Ōtsu [J, Shiga] 144-145 KL 5
Ōtsuchi 144-145 NO 3
Otta 116-117 C 7
Ottakring, Wien- 113 I b 2
Ot't'apālam = Ottapallam 140 C 5
Ottapallam 140 C 5
Ottavia, Roma- 113 II a 1
Ottawa 56-57 V 8
Ottawa, IL 70-71 F 5
Ottawa, KS 70-71 C 6
Ottawa, OH 70-71 HJ 5
Ottawa Islands 56-57 U 6
Ottawa River 56-57 V 8
Ottenby 116-117 G 9
Ottensen, Hamburg- 130 I a 1
Otter 63 E 3
Otter, Peaks of — 80-81 G 2
Otter Creek 68-69 C 3
Otter Creek, FL 80-81 b 2
Otter Lake 72-73 G 2
Otter Lake, MI 72-73 E 3
Otter Passage 60 BC 3
Otter River 62 E 1
Ottikon 128 IV b 1
Ottosdal 174-175 F 4
Ottoshoop 174-175 FG 3
Ottumwa, IA 64-65 H 3
Otukamamoan Lake 62 C 3
Otumpa 104-105 EF 10
Otuquis, Bañados — 104-105 G 6
Otuquis, Río — 104-105 G 6
Oturkpo 164-165 F 7
Otuzco 92-93 D 6
Otway, Bahía — 111 AB 8
Otway, Cape — 158-159 H 7
Otway, Seno — 111 B 8
Otwock 118 K 2
Ötztaler Alpen 118 E 5

Ou, Nam — 150-151 D 1
Ouachita Mountains 64-65 GH 5
Ouachita River 64-65 H 5
Ouadaï 164-165 HJ 6
Ouadda 164-165 J 7
Ouâdî Jaghjagh = Wādī Jaghjagh 136-137 J 4
Ouagadougou 164-165 D 6
Ouahigouya 164-165 D 6
Ouahila = Wahilah 166-167 D 6
Ouahran = Wahrān 164-165 D 2
Ouahrân Sebkra d' = Khalīj Wahrān 166-167 F 2
Ouaka 164-165 J 7
Oualata = Walātah 164-165 C 5
Oualidia = Wālidīyah 166-167 B 3
Ouallam 168-169 F 2
Oua n'Ahaggar, Tassili — = Tāsīlī Wān al-Hajjār 164-165 E 5-F 4
Ouanary 98-99 MN 2
Ouanda Djallé 164-165 J 7
Ouango = Kouango 164-165 HJ 7
Ouangolodougou 164-165 C 7
Ouâouîzarht = Wāwīzaght 166-167 C 3
Ouareau, Rivière — 72-73 JK 1
Ouargla = Warqlā 164-165 F 2
Ouarsenis, Djebel — = Jabal al-Wārshanīs 166-167 GH 2
Ouarsenis, Massif de l' = Jabal al-Wārshanīs 166-167 GH 2
Ouarzāzāt = Warzazāt 166-167 C 4
Ouasiemsca, Rivière — 62 P 2
Ouassadou 168-169 B 2
Ouassel, Ouèd — = Wādī Wāsal 166-167 GH 2
Ouassou 168-169 B 3
Ouataouais, Rivière — 62 NO 3
Oubangui 172 C 1
Ou Chiang = Ou Jiang 146-147 H 7
Ouchougan Rapids 63 C 2
Oudeïka 168-169 E 1
Oude Kerk 128 I a 1
Oude Meer 128 I a 2
Oudenaken 128 II a 2
Ouder-Amstel 128 I ab 2
Oudergem = Auderghem 128 II b 2
Oudje, Région de l' = Minṭaqat al-Wajh 166-167 K 4
Oud-Loosdrecht 128 I b 2
Oud-Over 128 I b 2
Oûdref = Udrif 166-167 LM 2-3
Oudtshoorn 172 D 8
Oué, Mont — 168-169 HJ 4
Oued, El- = Al-Wād 164-165 F 2
Oued Akka = Wād ʿAqqah 166-167 B 5
Ouèd Asouf Mellene = Wādī Asūf Malān 166-167 H 7
Ouèd-Athmenia = Wādī Athmānīyah 166-167 JK 1
Ouèd Attar = Wādī ʿAṭṭār 166-167 J 3
Ouèd Beht = Wād Baḥt 166-167 D 3
Ouèd Chāref = Wād Shārīf 166-167 E 3
Oued Chélif = Shilif 166-167 G 1
Ouèd Chenachane = Wādī Shanāshīn 166-167 E 7
Ouèd Djafou = Wādī Jafū 166-167 H 4
Ouèd Djedi = Wādī Jaddī 166-167 JK 2
Ouèd Draa = Wād Dra'ah 166-167 C 5
Ouèd ed Daoura = Wādī ad-Dawrah 166-167 DE 5
Ouèd ed Drâ = Wad Dra'ah 164-165 BC 3
Oued el Abiod = Wādī al-Abyaḍ 166-167 JK 2
Ouèd-el-Abtal = Wādī al-Abṭāl 166-167 G 2
Ouèd el Djaret = Wādī al-Jarā' 166-167 H 6
Ouèd el Fahl = Wādī al-Faḥl 166-167 HJ 4
Ouèd el Hâi = Wād al-Ḥāy 166-167 E 2
Oued el Hamiz 170 I b 2
Oued el Hamra = Wād al-Ḥamrā' 166-167 B 6
Oued el Harrach 170 I b 2
Ouèd el Korima = Wādī al-Karīmah 166-167 F 3
Ouèd el Leham = Wādī al-Ham 166-167 HJ 2
Ouèd el Mellâh = Wād al-Mallāḥ 166-167 C 3
Ouèd el Mitta = Wādī al-Mitlā 166-167 K 2
Ouèd el Rharbi = Wādī al-Gharbī 166-167 G 3-4
Oued el Terro 170 I a 2
Ouèd en Namous = Wādī an-Nāmus 164-165 D 2
Ouèd en Nsa = Wādī an-Nisā' 166-167 J 3
Ouèd er Retem = Wādī ar-Ratam 166-167 J 3
Ouèd ez Zergoun = Wādī az-Zarqūn 166-167 H 3
Oued-Fodda = Wādī al-Fiḍḍah 166-167 GH 1
Oued Gheris = Wād Gharīs 166-167 D 3-4
Oued Hatâb = Wād al-Ḥatāb 166-167 L 2
Oued-Imbert = Ayn-al-Bard 166-167 F 2
Oued Imirhou = Wādī Īmirhu 166-167 L 7
Ouèd Inâouèn = Wād Īnāwīn 166-167 D 2
Ouèd Isser = Wādī Yassar 166-167 H 1
Ouèd Itel = Wādī Īṭal 166-167 J 2-3
Oued Kerma 170 I a 2
Ouèd Lakhdar = Wād al-Akhdar 166-167 C 4
Ouèd Lâoû' = Wād Lāū' 166-167 D 2
Oued-Marsa = Wādī Marsā 166-167 J 1
Ouèd Martin = Mārtīl 166-167 D 2
Ouèd Mazar = Wād Māzār 166-167 G 3
Ouèd Mellèg = Wād Mallāg 166-167 L 1-2
Oued Messaoud = Wādī Mas'ūd 166-167 F 5-6
Ouèd Miliân = Wād Milyān 166-167 LM 1
Ouèd Mina = Wādī Mīnā 166-167 G 2
Ouèd Mouloûya = Wād Mūlūyā 164-165 D 2
Ouèd Mya = Wādī Miyāh 166-167 J 4
Ouèd Mzab = Wādī Mīzāb 166-167 J 3
Ouèd Nahar Ouassel = Wādī Wāsal 166-167 GH 2
Ouèd Nfîs = Wād Nafīs 166-167 B 4
Oued Noûn = Wād Nūn 166-167 A 5
Ouèd Ouassel = Wādī Wāsal 166-167 GH 2
Ouèd Ouèrrha = Wād Warghah 166-167 D 2
Ouèd Oum er Rbia = Wād Umm ar-Rabīyah 164-165 C 2
Ouèd 'Rherîs = Wād Gharīs 166-167 D 3-4
Ouèd-Rhiou = Wādī Rāhīyu 166-167 G 2
Ouèd Saoura = Wādī as-Sāwrah 164-165 D 2-3
Ouèd Seboû = Wad S'bū' 166-167 D 2
Ouèd Seggueur = Wādī as-Sūqar 166-167 GH 3
Ouèd Sidi Moussa = Wādī Sīdī Mūsā 166-167 J 6
Ouèd Tafassasset = Wādī Tafāsasat 164-165 F 4
Ouèd Tarat = Wādī Tarāt 164-165 F 3
Ouèd Tekouiât = Wādī Tākwayat 164-165 E 4
Ouèd Tensîft = Wad Tansīft 164-165 C 2
Ouèd Tessâout = Wād Tissāut 166-167 C 4
Ouèd Tilia = Wādī Tīlayah 166-167 G 6
Oued Timedjerdane = Wādī Tamajirdayn 166-167 G 7
Oued Tim Mersoï 164-165 F 5
Ouèd-Tlelat = Wādī Thalāthah 166-167 F 2
Ouèd Todrha = Wād Tudghā' 166-167 D 4
Ouèd Touil = Wādī aṭ-Ṭawīl 166-167 H 2
Ouèd Zarga = Wādī az-Zargah 166-167 L 1
Ouèd Zarqa = Wādī az-Zargah 166-167 L 1
Ouèd Zegrir = Wādī Zāghrīr 166-167 J 3
Ouèd Zem = Wād Zam 164-165 C 2
Ouèd Zemoul = Wād Zimūl 166-167 C 5
Ouèd Zeroûd = Wād Zurūd 166-167 LM 2
Ouèd Zousfana = Wādī Zusfānah 166-167 EF 4
Oueïta 164-165 J 5
Ouelle 168-169 DE 4
Ouémé [DY, administrative unit] 168-169 F 4
Ouémé [DY, river] 164-165 E 7
Ouenkoro 168-169 E 2
Ouenza = Winzah 166-167 KL 1-2
Ouenzé, Brazzaville- 170 IV a 1
Ouèrrha, Ouèd — = Wād Warghah 166-167 D 2
Ouessa 168-169 E 3
Ouessant, Île d' 120-121 E 4
Ouesso 172 C 1
Ouezzān = Wazzān 164-165 C 2
Oufrane = Ūfran 166-167 G 5
Ougarta = Ūgharṭah 166-167 E 5
Ouham-Pendé 164-165 H 7
Ouidah 164-165 E 7
Ouina 164-165 G 7
Ouinarden 168-169 E 1
Ou Jiang 146-147 H 7
Ouke 168-169 F 3
Oukoop 128 I b 2
Oûlad Boû 'Alî = Walad Bū 'Alī 166-167 M 2
Oûlâd Saʿîd = Awlād Saʿīd 166-167 BC 3
Oulainen 116-117 L 5
Ouled-Djellal = Walad Ghalal 166-167 J 2
Ouled-Mimoun = Awlād Mīmūn 166-167 F 2
Ouled Naïl, Monts des — = Jabal Awlād Nāil 166-167 H 2
Ouled-Rahmoun = Awlād Raḥmūn 166-167 K 1
Ouled Smar 170 I b 2
Oûlmès = Ūlmās 166-167 CD 3
Oulu 116-117 LM 5
Oulujärvi 116-117 M 5
Oulujoki 116-117 M 5
Oumache = Ūm'āsh 166-167 J 2
Oum-Chalouba 164-165 J 5
Oum ed Drouss, Sebka — = Sabkhat Umm ad-Durūs 164-165 B 4
Oum el Achâr = Umm al-'Ashār 166-167 B 5
Oum-el-Bouaghi = Umm al-Bawāghī 166-167 K 2
Oum el Krialat, Sebkhet — = Sabkhat Umm al-Khiyālāt 166-167 M 3
Oum er Rbia, Ouèd — = Wād Umm ar-Rabīyah 164-165 C 2
Oum-Hadjer 164-165 H 6
Oumm el Drouss, Sebkha — = Sabkhat Umm ad-Durūs 164-165 B 4
Oum Semaa = Umm aṣ-Ṣam'ah 166-167 L 3
Ounarha = Unāghāh 166-167 B 4
Ounasjoki 116-117 L 4
Ounastunturi 116-117 KL 3
Ounasvaara 116-117 LM 4
Ou Neua = Mu'o'ng Ou Neua 150-151 C 1
Ounianga-Kebir 164-165 J 5
Ountivou 168-169 F 4
Ouolossébougou 168-169 D 2
Ouplaas 174-175 E 7
Oupu 142-143 O 1
Ouray, CO 68-69 C 6-7
Ouray, UT 66-67 J 5
Ourcq, Canal de l' 129 I d 2
Ourém 92-93 K 5
Ouri 164-165 H 4
Ouricana 100-101 E 8
Ouricana, Serra da — 100-101 DE 8
Ouricuri 100-101 D 4
Ouricuri, Serra — 100-101 FG 5
Ourinhos 92-93 K 9
Ourique 120-121 C 10
Ourlal = Urlāl 166-167 J 2
Ouro 100-101 A 5
Ouro, Rio do — 100-101 B 6
Ouro Fino 102-103 J 5
Ouro Preto [BR, Minas Gerais] 92-93 L 9
Ouro Preto [BR, Pará] 98-99 LM 7
Ouro Preto, Rio — 98-99 F 10
Oûroum eș Şoughrâ = Urūm aṣ-Ṣughrah 136-137 G 4
Ourou Rapids 168-169 G 3
Ourthe 120-121 K 3
Ōu sammyaku 144-145 N 2-4
Ouse 119 FG 5
Ouskir, Hassi — = Ḥāssī Uskir 166-167 F 4
Oûssel'tia, El — = Al-Ūssaltīyah 166-167 LM 2
Ousseukh, Al- = 'Ayn Dhahab 166-167 G 2
Oust 120-121 F 5
Oustaïa, El- = Al-Uṭāyah 166-167 J 2
Outaïa, El- = Al-Uṭāyah 166-167 J 2
Outaouais, Rivière — 72-73 G 2
Outardes, Rivière aux — 56-57 X 7-8
Outat Oûlad el Ḥâj = Awṭāt Awlād al-Ḥājj 166-167 E 3
Ou Tay = Mu'o'ng Ou Tay 150-151 C 1
Outenickwaberge = Outenikwaberge 174-175 E 7
Outenikwaberge 174-175 E 7
Outeniquas Mountains = Outenikwaberge 174-175 E 7
Outer Hebrides 119 B 3-C 2
Outer Island 70-71 E 2
Outer Mission, San Francisco-, CA 83 I b 2
Outjo 172 C 6
Outlook 61 E 5
Outremont 82 I b 1
Ouvéa, Île — 158-159 N 4
Ouyen 158-159 H 6-7
Ouzinkie, AK 58-59 L 8

Ovacık = Hacısaklı 136-137 E 4
Ovacık = Maraşalçakmak 136-137 H 3
Ovadnoje 126-127 B 1
Ovalau 148-149 a 2
Ovalle 111 B 4
Ovamboland 172 BC 5
Ovana, Cerro — 94-95 H 5
Ovando, MT 66-67 G 2
Ovar 120-121 C 8
Ovejas, Cerro de las — 106-107 E 4
Ovejas, Las — 106-107 B 6
Over 130 I b 2
Overbrook, Philadelphia-, PA 84 III b 2
Overdiemen 128 I b 1
Overflowing River 61 GH 4
Overflowing River = Dawson Creek 61 H 4
Överkalix 116-117 K 4
Overland Park, MO 70-71 C 6
Overo, Volcán — 106-107 BC 5
Overton, NV 74-75 F 4
Overton, TX 76-77 G 6
Övertorneå 116-117 K 4
Ovett, MS 78-79 E 5
Ovid, CO 68-69 E 5

338 Orland

Pampanua 152-153 O 8
Pampa Pelada 108-109 EF 5
Pampas [PE, Huancavelica] 92-93 DE 7
Pampas [PE, Lima] 96-97 D 8
Pampas [RA] 111 D 4-5
Pampas, Río — [PE, Apurímac] 96-97 E 8-9
Pampas, Río — [PE, Ayacucho] 96-97 D 8
Pampas de Corobamba 96-97 B 4-C 5
Pampas de Sihuas 96-97 EF 10
Pampa Seca 111 CD 4-5
Pampa Sierra Overa 104-105 AB 9
Pampayār = Pambiyar 140 C 6
Pampeiro 106-107 K 3
Pampero, El — 106-107 E 5
Pampilhosa 120-121 C 8
Pampitas 104-105 D 3
Pamplona [CO] 92-93 E 3
Pamplona [E] 120-121 G 7
Pampoenpoort 174-175 E 6
Pampus 128 I b 1
Pan, Lûy — 141 E 4
Pan, Tierra del — 120-121 DE 7-8
Pana, IL 70-71 F 6
Panaca, NV 74-75 F 4
Panache, Lake — 62 L 3
Panadero 102-103 E 5
Panadura = Pānaduraya 140 D 7
Pānaduraya 140 D 7
Panag'urište 122-123 KL 4
Panaitan, Pulau — 148-149 DE 8
Panaji = Panjim 134-135 L 7
Panama, OK 76-77 G 5
Panamá [BR] 102-103 H 3
Pānama [CL] 140 EF 7
Panamá [PA, administrative unit] 64-65 a 3-b 2
Panamá [PA, place] 64-65 bc 3
Panama [PA, state] 64-65 KL 10
Panamá, Bahía de — 64-65 bc 3
Panamá, Canal de — 64-65 b 2
Panamá, Golfo de — 64-65 L 10
Panama, Gulf of — = Golfo de Panamá 64-65 L 10
Panamá, Istmo de — 64-65 L 9-10
Panama Canal 88-89 FG 10
Panama City, FL 64-65 JK 5-6
Panamá Viejo 64-65 c 2
Panambí [BR, Misiones] 106-107 K 1
Panambi [BR, Rio Grande do Sul] 106-107 L 2
Pan-Americana, Rodovia — 102-103 H 5-6
Panamint Range 74-75 E 4
Panamint Valley 74-75 E 4-5
Panane = Ponnāni 140 B 5
Panao 92-93 D 6
Panaon Island 148-149 HJ 5
Panare 150-151 C 9
Panarukan 152-153 L 9
Panarūti = Panruti 140 D 5
Pana Tinani 148-149 h 7
Panay 148-149 H 4
Panbult 174-175 J 4
Pancake Range 74-75 EF 3
Panças 100-101 D 10
Pančevo 122-123 J 3
Pānchari Bāzār 141 BC 4
Panchet Pahār Bāndh 138-139 L 6
Pānchgani 140 AB 2
Panchh = Pench 138-139 G 7
Panch Mahāls 138-139 DE 6
Panchmahals = Panch Mahāls 138-139 DE 6
Panchmarhi = Pachmarhi 138-139 G 6
Panchor 150-151 D 11
Pānchur 154 II a 2
Pancoran, Jakarta- 154 IV ab 2
Panda 172 F 6
Pandale, TX 76-77 D 7
Pandan 152-153 K 4
Pandanau 141 D 7
Pandan Reservoir 154 III a 2
Pandaung 141 D 6
Pāndavapura 140 C 4
Pan de Azucar [CO] 92-93 D 4
Pan de Azúcar [ROU] 106-107 K 5
Pan de Azúcar, Quebrada — 104-105 A 10-B 9
Pandeiros, Rio — 102-103 K 1
Pandėlys 124-125 E 5
Pāndharkawada 138-139 G 7
Pandharpur 134-135 LM 7
Pāndhurna 138-139 G 7
Pandie Pandie 158-159 GH 5
Pando [BOL] 104-105 BC 2
Pando [ROU] 106-107 JK 5
Pandora 88-89 E 10
Pándormos = Bandırma 134-135 B 2
P'andž 134-135 K 3
Panelas 100-101 FG 5
Panepistēmion 113 IV a 2
Panevėžys 124-125 E 6
Panfilov 132-133 OP 9
Panfilovo [SU, Ivanovskaja Oblast'] 124-125 N 5
Pangaion 122-123 KL 5
Pangala 172 BC 2
Pangalanes, Canal des — 172 J 5-6
Pangandaran 152-153 H 9
Pangani [EAT, place Morogoro] 171 D 4
Pangani [EAT, place Tanga] 171 C 5
Pangani [EAT, river] 172 G 2
Pangbei = Erlian 142-143 L 3
Pangburn, AR 78-79 D 3
Pangeo 148-149 J 6
Pangi 172 E 2
Pangkajene 148-149 G 7
Pangkalanberandan 152-153 C 3
Pangkalanbuun 152-153 JK 7
Pangkalpinang 148-149 E 7
Pangkor, Pulau — 150-151 C 10
Pangnirtung 56-57 XY 4
Pangrango, Gunung — 152-153 G 9
Pāngri 140 C 1
Pangtara = Pindara 141 E 5
Panguipulli, Lago — 108-109 CD 2
Panguitch, UT 74-75 G 4
Panguruan 152-153 C 4
Pangutaran Group 148-149 GH 5
Pangutaran Island 152-153 NO 2
Pang Yang = Panyan 141 F 4
Panhāla 140 AB 2
Panhandle 56-57 JK 6
Panhandle, TX 76-77 D 5
Panī = Pauni 138-139 G 7
Panié, Mount — 158-159 M 4
Pānihāti 154 II b 1
Pānihāti-Sodpur 154 II b 1
Pānihāti-Sukchar 154 II b 1
Pānikota Island 138-139 C 7
Pānīpat 138-139 F 3
Pānj = P'andž 134-135 K 3
Panjāb = Punjab [IND] 134-135 LM 4
Panjāb = Punjab [PAK] 134-135 L 4
Panjalih 152-153 P 7
Panjang [RI, island] 150-151 G 11
Panjang [RI, place] 148-149 E 8
Panjang, Hon — 148-149 D 5
Panjang, Pulau — 152-153 H 4
Panjāw 134-135 K 4
Panjgūr 134-135 J 5
Pāñjharā = Pānjhra 138-139 E 7
Pānjhra 138-139 E 7
Panjim 134-135 L 7
Panjnad 138-139 C 3
Panjwīn 136-137 L 5
Pankeborn 130 III c 1
Pankof, Cape — 58-59 b 2
Pankop 174-175 H 3
Pankshin 164-165 FG 7
Panlı 136-137 E 3
Panlōn 141 F 4
P'anmunjŏm 144-145 F 3-4
Panna 134-135 N 6
Panna Hills 138-139 H 5
Pannaung, Lûy — 150-151 C 2
Paṇo Āqil 138-139 B 4
Panoche, CA 74-75 C 4
Panopah 152-153 J 6
Panorama 102-103 FG 4
Panruti 140 D 5
Panshan 144-145 D 2
Panshkuṛa = Pānskura 138-139 L 6
Pānskura 138-139 L 6
Pantanal de Nabileque 102-103 D 3-4
Pantanal de São Lourenço 102-103 D 3-E 2
Pantanal do Rio Negro 92-93 H 8
Pantanal do Taquari 102-103 DE 3
Pantanal Mato-Grossense 92-93 H 8
Pantanaw = Pandanau 141 D 7
Pantano, AZ 74-75 H 6-7
Pantar 152-153 LM 7
Pantar, Pulau — 148-149 H 8
P'anteg 124-125 UV 3
Pantelleria [I, island] 122-123 E 7
Pantelleria [I, place] 122-123 DE 7
Panthā 141 D 4
Pantin 129 I c 2
Pantjurbatu = Kuala 150-151 B 11
Pantoja 92-93 DE 5
Pantokrátōr 122-123 H 6
Pánuco 86-87 LM 6-7
Pánuco, Río — 64-65 G 7
Pan'utino 126-127 H 2
Panvel 138-139 D 8
Panwel = Panvel 138-139 D 8
Panyan 141 F 4
Panyu 146-147 D 10
Panyu = Guangzhou 142-143 LM 7
Panyusu, Tanjung — 152-153 FG 6
Panzan 141 F 4
Pão = Pahang 150-151 D 10-11
Pao, El — [YV, Anzoátegui] 94-95 J 3
Pao, El — [YV, Bolívar] 92-93 G 3
Pao, El — [YV, Cojedes] 94-95 GH 3
Pao, Río — [YV, Bolívar] 94-95 J 3
Pao, Río — [YV, Cojedes] 94-95 G 3
Paoan = Bao'an [TJ, Guangdong] 146-147 DE 10
Pao-an = Bao'an [TJ, Shaanxi] 146-147 BC 4
Pao-an = Zhuolu 146-147 E 1
Paochi = Baoji 142-143 K 5
Pao-ching = Baojing 142-143 K 6
Pao-ch'ing = Shaoyang 142-143 L 6
Pão de Açúcar 110 I c 2
Pão de Açúcar [BR, place] 100-101 F 5
Pao-fêng = Baofeng 146-147 D 5
Paokang = Baokang 146-147 C 6
Paoki = Baoji 142-143 K 5
Pàola 122-123 FG 6
Paola, KS 70-71 C 6
Paoli, IN 70-71 G 6
Paonia, CO 68-69 C 6
Paoning = Langzhong 142-143 JK 5
Paonta 138-139 F 2
Paoshan = Baoshan [TJ, Jiangsu] 146-147 H 6
Paoshan = Baoshan [TJ, Yunnan] 142-143 HJ 6
Paoteh = Baode 142-143 L 4
Paoti = Baodi 146-147 F 2
Pao-ting = Baoding 142-143 LM 4
Paotow = Baotou 142-143 KL 3
Paotsing = Baojing 142-143 K 6
Paotsing = Baoqing 142-143 P 2
Paoying = Baoying 142-143 M 5
Pápa 118 H 5
Papagaio, Rio — 98-99 J 11
Papagayo, Golfo del — 64-65 J 9
Papagayos, Río de los — 106-107 C 5
Pāpaghnī = Pāpāgni 140 D 3-4
Pāpāgni 140 D 3-4
Papago Indian Reservation 74-75 GH 6
Papaikou, HI 78-79 e 3
Papakura 161 F 3
Papalé 104-105 D 9
Pāpanāsam 140 C 6
Papanduva 102-103 G 7
Papantla de Olarte 64-65 G 7
Papatoetoe 158-159 OP 7
Papelón 94-95 G 3
Papelotte 128 II b 2
Papera 94-95 J 8
Paphos = Pâfos 136-137 E 5
Pa-pien Chiang = Babian Jiang 142-143 J 7
Papikion 122-123 L 5
Papilė 124-125 D 5
Papinau Labelle, Parc provincial de — 62 O 3-4
Paposo 104-105 A 9
Papua, Gulf of — 148-149 MN 8
Papua New Guinea 148-149 MN 7-8
Papudo 106-107 B 4
Papulovo 124-125 R 3
Papun = Hpāpûn 141 E 6-7
Papuri, Rio — 94-95 F 7
Paquica, Cabo — 104-105 A 7
Paquicama 98-99 N 6
Pará [BR] 92-93 J 5
Para [SME] 98-99 L 2
Para [SU] 124-125 N 6-7
Pará = Belém 92-93 K 5
Para, La — 106-107 F 3
Pará, Rio — 102-103 K 3
Pará, Rio do — 92-93 JK 5
Parabel' 132-133 P 6
Paraburdoo 158-159 C 4
Paracale 148-149 H 4
Paracas 96-97 CD 8
Paracas, Península — 92-93 D 7
Paracatu 92-93 K 8
Paracatu, Rio — [BR ↖ Rio São Francisco] 102-103 K 2
Paracatu, Rio — [BR ↙ Rio São Francisco] 102-103 K 2
Paracels, Îles — = Quần Đao Tây Sa 148-149 F 3
Parachilna 160 D 3
Parachute Jump Tower 155 II b 2
Paraćin 122-123 J 4
Paracuru 92-93 M 5
Parada, Punta — 92-93 D 8
Parada El Chacay = El Chacay 106-107 BC 5
Parade, SD 68-69 F 3
Pará de Minas 100-101 B 10
Pārādip 138-139 L 7
Paradise, CA 74-75 C 3
Paradise, MT 66-67 F 2
Paradise, NV 74-75 F 4
Paradise Hill 61 D 4
Paradise Hill, Johannesburg- 170 V b 2
Paradise Valley 61 C 4
Paradise Valley, NV 66-67 E 5
Parado 152-153 N 10
Parafijevka 126-127 F 1
Paragominas 98-99 P 6
Paragould, AR 64-65 H 4
Paragua, La — 92-93 G 3
Paraguá, Río — [BOL] 92-93 G 7
Paragua, Río — [YV] 92-93 G 3
Paraguaçu 102-103 K 4
Paraguaçu, Rio — 100-101 DE 7
Paraguaçu Paulista 102-103 G 5
Paraguai, Rio — 92-93 H 9
Paraguaipoa 92-93 E 2
Paraguaná, Península de — 92-93 F 2
Paraguari [PY, administrative unit] 102-103 D 6-7
Paraguarí [PY, place] 111 E 3
Paraguay 111 DE 2
Paraguay, Río — 111 E 2
Paraíba 92-93 M 6
Paraíba, Rio — 92-93 M 6
Paraíba do Sul 102-103 L 5
Paraíba do Sul, Rio — 102-103 L 4
Paraibano 100-101 B 4
Paraibuna 102-103 K 5
Paraim 100-101 B 6
Paraim, Rio — 100-101 A 8
Parainen = Pargas 116-117 K 7
Paraíso [BR, Mato Grosso do Sul] 102-103 F 3
Paraíso [BR, Rondônia] 104-105 E 2
Paraíso [MEX] 86-87 O 8
Paraíso [PA] 64-65 b 2
Paraíso [YV] 94-95 G 3
Paraíso, El — 106-107 GH 4
Paraisópolis 102-103 K 5
Parakou 164-165 E 7
Paralkote 138-139 H 8
Paramagudi 140 D 6
Paramānkuḍi = Paramagudi 140 D 6
Paramaribo 92-93 HJ 3
Parambu 100-101 D 4
Paramillo, Nudo de — 94-95 CD 4
Paramirim 92-93 L 7
Paramirim, Rio — 100-101 C 7
Páramo Cruz Verde 91 III c 4
Páramo Frontino 94-95 C 4
Paramonga 92-93 D 7
Paramoti 100-101 E 3
Paramount, CA 83 III d 2
Paramušir, ostrov — 132-133 de 7
Paraná [BR, administrative unit] 111 FG 2
Paranã [BR, place] 92-93 K 7
Paraná [RA] 111 DE 4
Paraná, Rio — [BR ◁ Rio de la Plata] 92-93 J 9
Paraná, Rio — [BR ◁ Rio Turiaçu] 100-101 B 2
Paranã, Rio — [BR ◁ Tocantins] 92-93 K 7
Paraná, Río — [RA] 111 E 3-4
Paranacito 106-107 H 4
Paranácity 102-103 F 5
Paraná Copea 98-99 G 6
Paraná de las Palmas, Río — 106-107 H 4-5
Paraná do Ouro, Rio — 96-97 F 6
Paranaguá 111 G 3
Paranaguá, Baía de — 102-103 HJ 6
Paraná Guazú, Río — 106-107 H 4-5
Paranaíba 92-93 J 8
Paranaíba, Rio — 92-93 JK 8
Paraná Ibicuy, Río — 106-107 H 4
Paranaita, Rio — 98-99 K 9-10
Paranam 98-99 L 2
Paraná Mirim Pirajauana 98-99 E 5
Paranapanema 102-103 H 5
Paranapanema, Rio — 92-93 J 9
Paranapiacaba, Serra do — 92-93 G 2-3
Paranapura, Río — 96-97 C 4
Paranaquara, Serra — 98-99 M 5
Paranari 98-99 EF 5
Paranatama 100-101 F 5
Paraná Urariá 98-99 JK 6
Paranavaí 111 F 2
Parandak, Īstgāh-e — 136-137 O 5
Paranggi Äru 140 E 6
Paraṅgippeṭṭai = Porto Novo 140 DE 5
Paranjang 144-145 F 4
Parāntij 138-139 D 6
Paraopeba 102-103 K 3
Paraopeba, Rio — 102-103 K 3
Parapeti, Río — 104-105 E 6
Parapol'skij dol 132-133 fg 5
Parapuã 102-103 G 4
Paraque, Cerro — 94-95 H 5
Pará Rise 50-51 GH 5
Parás [MEX] 76-77 E 9
Parás [PE] 96-97 D 8
Parasagaḍa = Manoli 140 B 3
Parasgaon 138-139 H 8
Parāsi 138-139 J 4
Parasnāth 138-139 L 6
Parasnath Jain Temple 154 II b 2
Parata, Pointe della — 122-123 BC 5
Parateca 100-101 C 7
Parati 102-103 K 5
Paratigi 100-101 E 7
Paratinga 92-93 L 7
Parauapebas, Rio — 98-99 NO 8
Paraúna 92-93 JK 8
Paravūr 140 C 6
Parayanālankulam 140 DE 6
Paraytepuy 94-95 L 5
Paray-Vieille-Poste 129 I c 3
Pārbati 134-135 M 5
Pārbatīpūr 134-135 O 5
Parbatsar 138-139 E 4
Parbhani 138-139 F 8
Parbig 132-133 P 6
Parc de Laeken 128 II b 1
Parc de Maisonneuve 82 I b 1
Parc du Mont Royal 82 I b 1
Parchim 118 EF 2
Parc Jarry 82 I b 1
Parc Lafontaine 82 I b 1
Parc national Albert = Parc national Virunga 172 E 1-2
Parc National de Kundelungu 171 AB 5
Parc national de la Bamingui 164-165 HJ 7
Parc National de la Boucle du Baoulé 168-169 C 2
Parc national de la Garamba 172 EF 1
Parc national de la Kagera 172 F 2
Parc National de la Marahué 168-169 D 4
Parc national de la Salonga Nord 172 D 2
Parc national de la Salonga Sud 172 D 2
Parc national de Maiko 172 E 2
Parc National de Taï 168-169 D 4
Parc National du Niokolo-Koba 164-165 B 6
Parc national Mauricie 62 P 3
Parc national Virunga 172 E 1-2
Parc procincial de la Montagne Tremblante 56-57 VW 8
Parc provincial de Causapscal 63 C 3
Parc provincial de Dunière 63 C 3
Parc provincial de Forestville 63 B 3
Parc provincial de James Bay 62 M 1
Parc provincial de Joliette 62 OP 3
Parc provincial de la Gaspésie 63 CD 3
Parc provincial de la Vérendrye 56-57 V 8
Parc provincial de Mastiogouche 62 P 3
Parc provincial de Matane 63 C 3
Parc provincial de Papinau Labelle 62 O 3-4
Parc provincial de Port-Cartier-Sept-Îles 63 C 2
Parc provincial des Laurentides 56-57 W 8
Parc provincial des Rimouski 63 BC 3-4
Parcs National du W 164-165 E 6
Parczew 118 L 3
Pārḍi 138-139 D 7
Pardo 106-107 H 6
Pardo, Rio — [BR ◁ Atlantic Ocean] 92-93 L 8
Pardo, Rio — [BR ◁ Rio Grande] 102-103 H 4
Pardo, Rio — [BR ◁ Rio Paraná] 92-93 J 9
Pardo, Rio — [BR ◁ Rio São Francisco] 102-103 K 1
Pardubice 118 GH 3
Pare 152-153 K 9
Parecis, Campos dos — 92-93 H 7
Parecis, Chapada dos — 92-93 GH 7
Pareditas 106-107 C 4-5
Paredón 86-87 K 4-5
Paredones 106-107 AB 5
Parejas, Las — 106-107 G 4
Parelhas 92-93 M 6
Pare Mountains 171 D 3-4
Parenda 140 B 1
Parent 62 O 3
Parent, Lac — 62 N 2
Parentis-en-Born 120-121 G 6
Parepare 148-149 G 7
Parera 106-107 E 5
Parfenjevo 124-125 O 4
Parfino 124-125 HJ 4-5
Parga 122-123 J 6
Pargas 116-117 K 7
Pargi 140 C 2
Pargolovo 124-125 H 3
Parguaza 94-95 H 4
Pari, São Paulo- 110 II b 2
Paria 104-105 C 5
Paria, Golfo de — 92-93 G 2
Paria, Península de — 92-93 G 2
Pariaguán 94-95 J 3
Pariaman 148-149 CD 7
Paria River 74-75 H 4
Pariaxá, Cachoeira — 98-99 N 6
Pariči 124-125 G 7
Paricutín, Volcán — 64-65 F 8
Parika 92-93 H 3
Parima, Reserva Florestal — 94-95 K 6
Parima, Rio — 98-99 FG 3
Parima, Sierra — 92-93 G 4
Parimé, Rio — 98-99 H 3
Parinacochas, Laguna — 96-97 DE 9
Pariñas, Punta — 92-93 C 5
Pariṇḍā = Parenda 140 B 1
Parintins 92-93 H 5
Paripārit Kyûn 148-149 B 4
Paris 120-121 J 4
Paris, AR 78-79 C 3
Paris, ID 66-67 H 4
Paris, IL 70-71 G 6
Paris, KY 70-71 H 6
Paris, MO 70-71 DE 6
Paris, TN 78-79 E 2
Paris, TX 64-65 GH 5
Paris-Auteuil 129 I c 2
Paris-Belleville 129 I c 2
Paris-Bercy 129 I c 2
Paris-Charonne 129 I c 2
Paris-Grenelle 129 I c 2
Parish [RA] 106-107 H 6
Parish [ROU] 106-107 J 4
Paris-la Villette 129 I c 2
Paris-les Batignolles 129 I c 2
Paris-Menilmontant 129 I c 2
Paris-Montmartre 129 I c 2
Paris-Montparnasse 129 I c 2
Paris-Passy 129 I c 2
Paris-Quartier-Latin 129 I c 2
Paris-Reuilly 129 I c 2
Paris-Vaugirard 129 I c 2
Parita, Golfo de — 88-89 FG 10
Parit Buntar 150-151 C 10
Parkāl 140 D 1
Parkano 116-117 K 6
Parkchester, New York, NY 82 III cd 2
Park City, KY 70-71 GH 7
Park City, UT 66-67 H 5
Parkdale, OR 66-67 C 3
Parkdene 170 V c 2
Parker, AZ 74-75 FG 5
Parker, KS 70-71 C 6
Parker, SD 68-69 H 4
Parker, Mount — 155 I b 2
Parker Dam, CA 74-75 F 5
Parkersburg, IA 70-71 D 4
Parkersburg, WV 64-65 K 4
Parkers Creek 84 III d 2
Parkerview 61 G 5
Parkes 158-159 J 6
Park Falls, WI 70-71 E 3
Park Hill [AUS] 161 I b 1
Park Hill [CDN] 72-73 F 3
Parkhurst 60 F 4
Parkin, AR 78-79 D 3
Parkland 60 KL 4
Parklawn, VA 82 II a 2
Parkman 61 H 6
Parkman, WY 68-69 C 3
Park Place, Houston-, TX 85 III b 2
Park Range 64-65 E 3-4
Park Rapids, MN 70-71 C 2
Park Ridge, IL 70-71 FG 4
Park River 68-69 H 1
Park River, ND 68-69 H 1
Park Royal, London- 129 II ab 1
Parkside 61 E 4
Parkside, PA 84 III a 2
Parkside, San Fransisco-, CA 83 I b 2
Park Station 170 V b 2
Parkston, SD 68-69 GH 4
Parksville 66-67 A 1
Park Timbers, New Orleans-, LA 85 I b 2
Park Town, Johannesburg- 170 V b 2
Park Valley, UT 66-67 G 5
Park View, NM 76-77 A 4
Parlākimidi 134-135 NO 7
Parlament 113 I b 2
Parlī = Purli 140 C 1
Parliament House [AUS, Melbourne] 161 II bc 1
Parliament House [AUS, Sydney] 161 I b 2
Parliament House [RI] 154 IV a 2
Parma 122-123 D 3
Parma, ID 66-67 E 4
Parma, MO 78-79 E 2
Parma, OH 72-73 F 4
Parmana 94-95 J 4
Parnaguá 92-93 L 7
Parnaguá, Lagoa de — 100-101 B 6
Parnaíba 92-93 L 5
Parnaíba, Rio — 92-93 L 5
Parnaibinha, Rio — 100-101 AB 5
Parnamirim [BR, Pernambuco] 100-101 E 5
Parnamirim [BR, Rio Grande do Norte] 100-101 G 3
Parnarama 100-101 C 3
Parnassós 122-123 K 6
Pārner 138-139 E 8
Párnēs 122-123 K 6
Párnōn 122-123 K 7
Pärnu 124-125 E 4
Pärnu jõgi 124-125 E 4
Pāro 138-139 K 4
Paro Dsong 138-139 M 4
Paro Jong = Paro Dsong 138-139 M 4
Pārola 138-139 E 7
Pāroḷēṅ = Pārola 138-139 E 7
Paromaj 132-133 b 7
Parona = Fındık 136-137 JK 4
Paroo Channel 158-159 H 6
Paroo River 160 G 2
Páros 122-123 L 7
Parowan, UT 74-75 G 4
Parque 3 de Febrero 110 III b 1
Parque Almirante Guillermo Brown 110 III b 1
Parque da Água Branca 110 II ab 2
Parque de Beisbol 91 I c 2
Parque del Retiro 113 III ab 2
Parque del Venado 91 I c 2
Parque Distrital de El Tunal 91 III b 4
Parque Distrital de Timiza 91 III ab 3
Parque do Estado 110 II b 2
Parque Jabaquara 110 II b 2
Parque Júlio Furtado 110 I b 2
Parque La Florida 91 III b 2
Parque Nacional Canaima 94-95 KL 5
Parque Nacional Cerro de la Estrella 91 I c 2-3
Parque Nacional de Aparados da Serra 106-107 MN 2
Parque Nacional de Este 91 II b 2
Parque Nacional de los Leones 91 I b 3
Parque Nacional de São Joaquim 106-107 MN 2
Parque Nacional de Ubajara 100-101 D 2
Parque Nacional do Araguaia 98-99 NO 10
Parque Nacional do Cachimbo 98-99 K 8-9
Parque Nacional do Iguaçu 102-103 EF 6
Parque Nacional do Xingu 98-99 M 10
Parque Nacional el Ávila 91 II bc 1
Parque Nacional El Pinar 91 II b 2
Parque Nacional Grão Pará 98-99 O 6
Parque Nacional Lanín 108-109 D 2-3
Parque Nacional Los Alerces 108-109 D 4
Parque Nacional Los Glaciares 108-109 C 7-8
Parque Nacional Miguel Hidalgo 91 I a 3
Parque Nacional Nahuel Huapi 108-109 D 3
Parque Nacional Paulo Afonso 100-101 E 5
Parque Nacional de Monte Pascoal 100-101 E 9
Parque Nacional de Porto Alexandre 172 B 5
Parque Popular de Diversiones 91 III bc 2-3
Parque Presidente Nicolás Avellaneda 110 III b 1
Parr, SC 80-81 F 3
Parral 111 B 5
Parral, Hidalgo del — 64-65 EF 6
Parramatta, Sydney- 161 I a 1
Parramatta River 161 I a 1-2
Parramore Island 80-81 J 2
Parras de la Fuente 64-65 F 6
Parravicini 106-107 HJ 6
Parrī = Pauri 138-139 G 2
Parrita 88-89 D 10
Parrsboro 63 D 5
Parry 61 F 6
Parry, Cape — 56-57 M 3
Parry Bay 56-57 U 4
Parry Island 72-73 F 2
Parry Islands 56-57 M-R 2
Parrøya 116-117 kl 4
Parry Sound 62 L 4
Parsa = Persepolis 134-135 G 5
Parsnip River 56-57 M 6-7
Parsons, KS 64-65 G 4
Parsons, TN 78-79 E 3
Parsons, WV 72-73 G 5
Parson's Pond 63 GH 2-3
Partābpur 138-139 J 6
Parṭa Jebel 122-123 J 3
Partāpgarh 138-139 E 5
Pårtefjället 116-117 GH 4
Parthenay 120-121 GH 5
Partinico 122-123 E 6
Partizansk 132-133 Z 9
Partol = Bandar 138-139 H 3
Partridge, KS 68-69 GH 7
Partridge River 62 L 1
Partūḍ = Partūr 138-139 F 8
Partūr 138-139 F 8
Pārū = Pāro 138-139 K 4
Paru, Rio — [BR] 92-93 J 5
Parú, Río — [YV] 94-95 H 5
Parú, Serranía — 94-95 J 5
Parucito, Río — 94-95 J 5
Paru de Este, Rio — 98-99 L 3-4
Paru de Oeste, Rio — 98-99 L 3-4
Parūr 140 C 5
Parur = Paravūr 140 C 6
Paruro 96-97 F 8
Parvān = Parwān 138-139 F 5
Pārvatī = Pārbati 134-135 M 5
Pārvatīpuram 134-135 N 7
Parwān 138-139 F 5
Parys 174-175 G 4
Paša 124-125 J 4
Paşabahce, İstanbul- 154 I b 2
Pasadena, CA 64-65 C 5
Pasadena, TX 64-65 GH 6
Pasadena Memorial Stadium 85 III c 2
Pasaje 92-93 D 5
Pasaje, Islas del — = Passage Islands 108-109 J 8
Pasaje, Río — 104-105 D 9
Pasajes de San Juan 120-121 FG 7
Pa Sak, Mae Nam — 150-151 C 4-5
Pa Sâm = Nam Ma 150-151 D 1
Pa Sang 150-151 B 3
Pasarbantal 152-153 D 7
Pasar Minggu, Jakarta- 154 IV ab 2
Pasarwajo 152-153 P 8
Pascagama, Rivière — 62 O 2
Pascagoula, MS 64-65 J 5
Pascagoula River 78-79 E 5
Paşcani 122-123 M 2
Pasco, WA 66-67 D 2
Pasco [PE] 96-97 CD 7
Pasco [RA] 110 III b 2
Pascoal, Monte — 100-101 E 9
Pascoe Vale, Melbourne- 161 II b 1
Pascuales 96-97 AB 3
Pas de Calais 120-121 HJ 3
Pasewalk 118 FG 2
Pasewalk = Pasvalys 124-125 E 5
Pashāwar 134-135 KL 4
Pashchimī Bangāl = West Bengal 134-135 O 6
Pashid Haihsia 142-143 N 7
Pasi, Pulau — 152-153 O 9
P'asina 132-133 QR 3
Pasinler = Hasankale 136-137 J 2-3
P'asino, ozero — 132-133 QR 4
P'asinskij zaliv 132-133 PQ 3
Pasión, Río — 86-87 PQ 9
Pasir 154 III b 1
Pasir Besar = Kampung Pasir Besar 148-149 D 6
Pasir Gudang 154 III b 1
Pasir Mas 150-151 CD 9
Pasir Panjang 150-151 C 11
Pasir Panjang, Singapore- 154 III a 2
Pasirpengarayan 152-153 D 5
Pasir Puteh 150-151 D 10
Pasir Ris 154 III b 1
Pasitanete, Pulau — 152-153 O 8
Paska 62 F 2
Paskenta, CA 74-75 B 3
Paškovo 124-125 O 7
Paškovskij 126-127 J 4
Pasley, Cape — 158-159 D 6
Pasman [RA] 106-107 F 6
Pašman [YU] 122-123 F 4
Pasnī 134-135 J 5
Paso, El — 92-93 E 3
Paso Ataques 106-107 K 3
Paso Caballos 86-87 PQ 9
Paso Chacabuco 108-109 D 3
Paso Codorníz 108-109 C 6
Paso Coihaique Alto 108-109 D 5
Paso Copahue 111 BC 5
Paso de Águila 108-109 D 6
Paso de Chonta 96-97 D 8
Paso de Chureo 106-107 B 6
Paso de Desecho 106-107 B 6
Paso de Indios 111 BC 6
Paso de la Cumbre 111 BC 4
Paso de la Fortaleza 96-97 C 7
Paso del Agua Negra 106-107 BC 3
Paso de la Patria 102-103 C 7
Paso del Arco 106-107 B 7
Paso de las Llareta 106-107 BC 4
Paso de los Algarrobos 106-107 D 6
Paso de los Indios 106-107 C 7
Paso de los Libres 111 E 3
Paso de los Toros 111 EF 4
Paso de los Vientos 64-65 M 7-8
Paso del Portillo 106-107 BC 3
Paso del Rey, Moreno- 110 III a 1
Paso del Sapo 108-109 E 4
Paso de Menéndez 108-109 CD 4
Paso de Peña Negra 106-107 C 2
Paso de Potrerillo 106-107 BC 2
Paso Limay 108-109 DE 3
Paso Mamuil Malal 108-109 CD 2

340 Pampanua

Paso Quichuapunta 96-97 C 6
Pasorapa 104-105 D 6
Paso Robles, CA 74-75 C 5
Pasos, Los — 94-95 D 7
Paso San Francisco 104-105 B 10
Paso Tranqueras 106-107 K 3
Paso Tromen 108-109 CD 2
Paspébiac 63 D 3
Pasquia Hills 61 G 4
Passage Islands 108-109 J 8
Passagem Franca 100-101 BC 4
Passaic, NJ 82 III b 1
Passa-Quatro 102-103 K 5
Passau 118 F 4
Passa Vinte 102-103 KL 5
Pass Cavallo 76-77 FG 8
Pàssero, Capo — 122-123 F 7
Passinho 106-107 M 3
Pašskij Perevoz 124-125 JK 3
Passo Borman 102-103 F 7
Passo dei Giovi 122-123 C 3
Passo della Cisa 122-123 CD 3
Passo do Sertão 106-107 N 2
Passo Fundo 111 F 3
Passo Fundo, Río — = Río Guarita 106-107 L 1
Passo Novo 106-107 K 2
Passos 92-93 K 9
Passy, Paris- 129 I c 2
Pastaza 96-97 C 2
Pastaza, Río — 92-93 D 5
Pasteur 106-107 FG 5
Pasto 92-93 D 4
Pastol Bay 58-59 F 5
Pastora Peak 74-75 J 4
Pastoril, La — = Colonia La Pastoril 106-107 DE 6
Pastos Blancos 108-109 D 5
Pastos Bons 100-101 B 4
Pastos Grandes, Lago — 104-105 C 7
Pastrana, Bogotá- 91 III ab 3
Pastura, NM 76-77 B 5
Pasul Turnu Roșu 122-123 KL 3
Pasuruan 152-153 K 9
Pasvalys 124-125 E 5
Pasvikelv 116-117 NO 3
Pata [BOL] 104-105 B 4
Pata [SN] 168-169 B 2
Patacamaya 104-105 BC 5
Patache, Punta — 104-105 A 7
Pata de Gallo, Cerro — 96-97 B 6
Patadkal 140 BC 3
Patagonia 111 B 8-C 6
Patagonia, AZ 74-75 H 7
Patagonian Cordillera = Cordillera Patagónica 111 B 8-5
Patagonian Shelf 50-51 FG 8
Patagónica, Cordillera — 111 B 8-5
Patamuté 100-101 E 5
Pātan [IND, Bihār] 138-139 K 5
Pātan [IND, Gujarāt] 138-139 D 6
Pātan [IND, Madhya Pradesh] 138-139 G 6
Pātan [IND, Mahārāshtra] 140 A 2
Pātan [Nepal] 134-135 NO 5
Pāṭan = Sōmnath 138-139 C 7
Patana = Pattani 148-149 D 5
Pātānapuram = Pāttānapuram 140 C 6
Patane = Pattani 148-149 D 5
Patang = Batang 142-143 H 6
Pataodī = Pataudi 138-139 F 3
Pātapatnam 140 G 1
Pāta Polavaram 140 F 2
Patara-Širaki 126-127 N 6
Patargān, Daqq-e — 134-135 J 4
Pātarghāṭa 138-139 MN 6
Paṭāshpur = Kasba Patāspur 138-139 L 6
Patauá, Cachoeira — 98-99 HJ 9
Pataudi 138-139 F 3
Patay Rondos 96-97 C 6
Patáz 96-97 C 5
Patchewollock 160 EF 5
Patchogue, NY 72-73 K 4
Pategi 168-169 G 3
Patensie 174-175 F 7
Paternal, Buenos Aires-La — 110 III b 1
Paternò 122-123 F 7
Pateros, WA 66-67 D 1-2
Paterson 174-175 FG 7
Paterson, NJ 72-73 J 4
Paterson, WA 66-67 D 2-3
Pathalgaon 138-139 J 6
Pathanapuram = Pāttānapuram 140 C 6
Pathānkōt 138-139 E 1
Pāthardi 138-139 E 8
Paṭhārgāñv = Pathalgaon 138-139 J 6
Paṭhārgāñv = Pathārgaon 138-139 JK 4
Pātharghāta 141 AB 4
Patherri = Pāthardi 138-139 E 8
Pathfinder Reservoir 68-69 C 4
Pathiu 150-151 B 7
Pāthri 138-139 F 8
Pathum Thani 148-149 CD 4
Pāti 138-139 E 7
Patía, Río — 92-93 D 4
Patiāla 134-135 M 4
P'atichatki 126-127 FG 2
Patience Well 158-159 E 4
P'atigorsk 126-127 L 4
P'atigory 124-125 U 3
P'atimar 126-127 P 2
Paṭiyāla = Patiāla 134-135 M 4
Pātkai Range 141 D 2
Pāṭkurā = Tirtol 138-139 L 7
Paṭlāvad = Petlāwad 138-139 E 6
Patlong 174-175 H 6
Pátmos 122-123 M 7
Patna 134-135 O 5
Pāṭnāgaḍa = Patnāgarh 138-139 J 7
Patnāgarh 138-139 J 7
Patnītola 138-139 M 5
Patnos 136-137 K 3
Pato Branco 102-103 F 7
Pātoda 140 B 1
Patomskoje nagorje 132-133 V 6-W 6
Patos [BR, Ceará] 100-101 E 2
Patos [BR, Paraíba] 92-93 M 6
Patos [BR, Piauí] 100-101 D 4
Patos, Lagoa dos — 111 F 4
Patos, Laguna de — 86-87 GH 2
Patos, Laguna de los — 106-107 F 3
Patos, Ponta dos — 100-101 E 2
Patos, Portillo de los — 104-105 B 10
Patos, Río de los — 106-107 C 3-4
Patos de Minas 102-103 J 3
Pa-tou = Badou 146-147 F 3
Patquía 111 C 4
Pátrai 122-123 J 6
Patraïkós Kólpos 122-123 J 6-7
Patras = Pátrai 122-123 JK 6
Patras, Gulf of — = Patraïkós Kólpos 122-123 J 6-7
Patreksfjördhur 116-117 ab 2
Patria, Cerro — 108-109 G 5
Patricia, SD 68-69 F 4
Patricia [CDN, landscape] 56-57 S-U 7
Patricia [CDN, place] 61 C 5
Patricinio do Muriaé 102-103 LM 4
Patricio Lynch, Isla — 111 A 7
Patricios 106-107 G 5
Patrimônio 102-103 H 3
Patrimônio União 102-103 E 5
Patrocínio 92-93 K 8
Paṭṭadakal = Patadkal 140 BC 3
Patta Island 172 H 2
Pat'ṭ'akkōṭṭai = Pudukkottai 140 D 5
Pāttānapuram 140 C 6
Pattani 148-149 D 5
Pattani, Mae Nam — 150-151 C 9
Patte-d'Oie, la — 129 I b 1-2
Patten, ME 72-73 M 2
Patterson, CA 74-75 C 4
Patterson, GA 80-81 E 5
Patti 122-123 F 6
Patti [IND, Punjab] 138-139 E 2
Patti [IND, Uttar Pradesh] 138-139 J 5
Pattiā 92-93 D 4
Pattikonda 140 C 3
Patton, PA 72-73 G 4
Pattonsburg, MO 70-71 CD 5
Pattukkottai 140 D 5
Pattullo, Mount — 60 C 1
Patu 92-93 M 6
Paṭūākhālī 141 B 4
Patuca, Punta — 64-65 K 8
Patuca, Río — 64-65 J 9-K 8
Patuha, Gunung — 152-153 G 9
Patung = Badong 142-143 KL 5
Pātūr 138-139 F 7
Pátzcuaro, Lago de — 86-87 JK 8
Pa-tzŭ = Bazai 146-147 E 9
Pau 120-121 G 7
Pau Brasil 100-101 E 8
Pauca 96-97 BC 5
Paucartambo 96-97 F 8
Pau d'Arco 92-93 K 6
Pau dos Ferros 100-101 E 4
Pau Ferro 100-101 D 5
Pauillac 120-121 G 6
Pauini 98-99 E 8
Pauini, Rio — [BR ◁ Rio Purus] 98-99 D 8-9
Pauini, Rio — [BR ◁ Rio Uniní] 98-99 G 5-6
Pauji, El — 91 II c 2
Pauk 141 D 5
Paukhkaung 141 D 6
Paukkaung = Paukhkaung 141 D 6
Pauksa Taung 141 D 6
Pauktaw 141 C 5
Paula 106-107 G 6
Paula Freitas 102-103 G 7
Paula Pereira 102-103 G 6-7
Paulding, MS 78-79 E 4
Paulding, OH 70-71 H 5
Paulicéia, Diadema- 110 II b 3
Paulina, OR 66-67 D 3
Paulina Mountains 66-67 C 4
Paulino Neves 100-101 C 2
Paulis = Isiro 172 E 1
Paul Island [USA] 58-59 d 2
Paulista [BR, Paraíba] 100-101 F 4
Paulista [BR, Pernambuco] 92-93 MN 6
Paulista [BR, Zona litigiosa] 92-93 L 8
Paulistana 92-93 L 6
Paulo Afonso 100-101 E 5
Paulo Afonso, Cachoeira de — 92-93 M 6
Paulo Afonso, Parque Nacional — 100-101 E 5
Paulo de Faria 102-103 H 4
Paulo Frontin 102-103 G 7
Paulpietersburg 174-175 J 4
Paul Roux 174-175 GH 5
Paulsboro, NJ 84 III b 3
Pauls Hafen = Pāvilosta 124-125 C 5
Paulshof 130 III c 1
Paulskirche 128 III b 1
Paulson 66-67 DE 1
Pauls Valley, OK 76-77 F 5
Paunero 106-107 E 4
Paung 141 E 7
Paungbyin = Hpaungbyin 141 D 3
Paungde = Paungdī 148-149 BC 3
Paungdī 148-149 BC 3
Paunglaung Myit 141 E 5-6
Pauni 138-139 G 7
Pauri [IND, Madhya Pradesh] 138-139 F 5
Pauri [IND, Uttar Pradesh] 138-139 G 2
Paurito 104-105 E 5
Pausin 130 III a 1
Pauto, Río — 94-95 EF 5
Pāvagada 140 C 3
Pavai = Pawai 138-139 H 5
Pavant Mountains 74-75 G 3
Pavěh 136-137 M 5
Pavelec 124-125 M 7
Pavia 122-123 C 3
Pavillon 60 G 4
Pavillons-sous-Bois, les — 129 I cd 2
Pāvilosta 124-125 C 5
Pavino 124-125 PQ 4
Pavle 96-97 B 3
Pavlodar 132-133 O 7
Pavlof Bay 58-59 c 2
Pavlof Harbor, AK 58-59 bc 2
Pavlof Islands 58-59 c 2
Pavlof Volcano 58-59 b 2
Pavlograd 126-127 GH 2
Pavlovac 122-123 G 3
Pavlovo 124-125 O 6
Pavlovsk [SU, Leningradskaja Oblast'] 124-125 H 4
Pavlovsk [SU, Voronežskaja Oblast'] 126-127 K 1
Pavlovskaja 126-127 JK 3
Pavlovskij 124-125 U 5
Pavlovskij Posad 124-125 M 6
Pavlyš 126-127 F 2
Pavo, GA 80-81 E 5
Pavte 96-97 B 3
Pavullo nel Frignano 122-123 D 3
Pavuvu = Russell Islands 148-149 j 6
Pavy 124-125 G 4
Pawahku = Mawāgū 141 F 2
Pawai 138-139 H 5
Pawan, Sungai — 152-153 J 6
Pawāyan 138-139 GH 3
Pawhuska, OK 76-77 F 4
Pawleys Island, SC 80-81 G 4
Pawnee, CO 68-69 E 5
Pawnee, OK 76-77 F 4
Pawnee City, NE 70-71 BC 5
Pawnee River 68-69 FG 6
Paw Paw, MI 70-71 GH 4
Pawtucket, RI 72-73 L 4
Páxoi 122-123 J 6
Paxson, AK 58-59 OP 5
Paxson Lake 58-59 OP 5
Paxton, IL 70-71 FG 5
Paxton, NE 68-69 F 5
Payakumbuh 148-149 D 7
Paya Lebar 154 III b 1
Paya Lebar Airport 154 III b 1
Payan 152-153 L 6
Payette, ID 66-67 E 3
Payette River 66-67 E 3-4
Payette River, North Fork — 66-67 E 3
Payinzet Kyūn 150-151 AB 6
Payḷani = Palni 140 C 5
Payne, OH 70-71 H 5
Payne Bay = Bellin 56-57 WX 5
Payne Lake 56-57 W 6
Payne River 56-57 W 6
Paynes Creek, CA 66-67 BC 5
Paynesville 168-169 C 4
Paynesville, MN 70-71 C 3
Payong, Tanjung — 152-153 K 4
Paysandú [ROU, administrative unit] 106-107 HJ 3-4
Paysandú [ROU, place] 111 E 4
Pays de Caux 120-121 H 4
Pays de León 120-121 E 4
Payson, AZ 74-75 H 5
Payson, UT 66-67 GH 5
Payún, Borde Alto del — 106-107 C 6
Payún, Cerro — 111 BC 5
Paz, La — [BOL, administrative unit] 104-105 B 3-C 5
Paz, La — [BOL, place] 92-93 F 8
Paz, La — [Honduras] 88-89 C 7
Paz, La — [MEX, Baja California Sur] 64-65 DE 7
Paz, La — [MEX, San Luis Potosí] 86-87 K 6
Paz, La — [RA, Entre Ríos] 111 DE 4
Paz, La — [RA, Mendoza] 111 C 4
Paz, La — [ROU] 106-107 J 5
Paz, La — [YV] 94-95 E 2
Paz, Río de la — 104-105 C 5
Paza, Ponta — 100-101 F 6
Pazagug 138-139 K 3
Pazar 136-137 J 2
Pazar = Şorba 136-137 E 2
Pazarcık [TR, Bilecik] 136-137 C 2-3
Pazarcık [TR, Maraş] 136-137 G 4
Pazardžik 122-123 KL 4
Pazaryeri = Pazarcık 136-137 C 2-3
Paz de Río 94-95 E 4
Pazña 104-105 C 6

Pčinja 122-123 J 4-5

Peabiru 102-103 F 5
Peabody, KS 68-69 H 6
Peabody, MA 84 I c 2
Peace River [CDN, place] 56-57 N 6
Peace River [CDN, river] 56-57 MN 6
Peach Island 84 II c 2
Peachland 66-67 CD 1
Peach Springs, AZ 74-75 G 5
Peachtree Creek 85 II b 1
Peachtree Creek, North Fork — 85 II c 1
Peachtree Creek, South Fork — 85 II c 2
Peachtree Hills, Atlanta-, GA 85 II b 1
Peacock Bay 53 B 26-27
Peaima Falls 98-99 H 1
Peake Creek 160 B 1-2
Peak Hill [AUS, New South Wales] 160 J 4
Peak Hill [AUS, Western Australia] 158-159 C 5
Peakhurst, Sydney- 161 I a 2
Peaks of Otter 80-81 G 2
Peale, Mount — 64-65 DE 4
Peam Chileang 150-151 EF 6
Peam Chor 150-151 E 7
Péam Prous = Phum Peam Prous 150-151 D 6
Pearce, AZ 74-75 J 7
Peard Bay 58-59 H 1
Pearl 70-71 F 1
Pearl Harbor 148-149 e 3
Pearl River 64-65 H 5
Pearl River, LA 78-79 DE 5
Pearsall, TX 76-77 E 8
Pearson 106-107 G 4
Pearson, GA 80-81 E 5
Pearston 174-175 F 7
Peary Channel 56-57 R 2
Peary Land 52 A 21-23
Peavine Creek 85 II c 2
Pebane 172 G 5
Pebas 92-93 E 5
Pebble Island 108-109 K 8
Peć 122-123 J 4
Peçanha 102-103 L 3
Pecan Island, LA 78-79 C 6
Peças, Ilha das — 111 G 3
Pecatonica River 70-71 F 4
Pečenežin 126-127 B 2
Pečenga [SU, place] 132-133 E 4
Pechabun = Phetchabun 148-149 CD 3
Pechawar = Pashāwar 134-135 KL 4
Pechincha, Rio de Janeiro- 110 I ab 2
Pech Nil, Deo — 150-151 E 7
Pechora Bay = Pečorskaja guba 132-133 JK 4
Pečora [SU, place] 132-133 K 4
Pečora [SU, river] 132-133 K 5
Pecoraro, Monte — 122-123 FG 6
Pečoro-Ilyčskij zapovednik 124-125 VW 2
Pečorskaja guba 132-133 JK 4
Pečorskaja magistral' 132-133 JK 5
Pečory 124-125 FG 5
Pecos, TX 64-65 F 5
Pecos River 64-65 F 5
Pécs 118 HJ 5
Peda Konda 140 E 2
Pedasí 88-89 FG 11
Peddapalli 140 D 1
Peddāpuram 140 F 2
Pedder, Lake — 160 bc 3
Peddie 174-175 G 7
Peddocks Island 84 I c 3
Pedee, OR 66-67 B 3
Pedernal, NM 76-77 B 5
Pedernal [PY] 102-103 D 5
Pedernal [RA] 106-107 H 3
Pedernales [DOM] 88-89 L 5-6
Pedernales [EC] 92-93 CD 4
Pedernales [RA] 106-107 GH 5
Pedernales [YV] 92-93 G 3
Pedernales, Salar de — 104-105 B 10
Pederneira, Cachoeira — 92-93 FG 6
Pederneiras 102-103 H 5
Pedernera 106-107 E 4
Pēḍgāñv = Pedgaon 140 B 1
Pedgaon 140 B 1
Pedra 100-101 F 5
Pedra Azul 92-93 L 8
Pedra Branca 100-101 E 3
Pedra Corrida 102-103 L 3
Pedra da Amolar, Cachoeira da — 100-101 B 5
Pedra de Amolar 98-99 P 10
Pedras, Rio das — 100-101 AB 7
Pedras Altas 106-107 L 3
Pedras Altas, Coxilha — 106-107 L 3
Pedras de Fogo 100-101 G 4
Pedras de Maria da Cruz 102-103 K 1
Pedra Sêca, Cachoeira da — 98-99 M 9
Pedras Negras 92-93 G 7
Pedras Negras, Reserva Florestal — 98-99 G 11
Pedregal [PA] 64-65 c 2
Pedregal [YU] 94-95 F 2
Pedregal, Caracas-El — 91 II b 1
Pedregulho 102-103 J 4
Pedreira 102-103 J 5
Pedreiras 92-93 KL 5
Pedreiras [ROU] 106-107 K 5
Pedrera, La — 92-93 EF 5
Pedro, Point — = Pēduru Tuḍuwa 134-135 N 9
Pedro Afonso 92-93 K 6
Pedro Avelino 100-101 F 3
Pedro Bay, AK 58-59 K 7
Pedro Cays 64-65 L 8
Pedro Chico 94-95 F 7
Pedro de Valdivia 111 BC 2
Pedro Díaz Colodrero 106-107 H 3
Pedro Dorado 94-95 F 7
Pedro E. Funes 106-107 F 4
Pedro Gomes 102-103 E 3
Pedro González 102-103 CD 7
Pedro González, Isla — 94-95 B 3
Pedro II 92-93 L 5
Pedro II, Ilha — 94-95 H 7
Pedro II, Serra de — 100-101 D 3
Pedro Juan Caballero 111 E 2
Pedro Leopoldo 102-103 K 3
Pedro Luro 106-107 F 7
Pedro Lustosa 102-103 FG 6
Pedro Miguel 64-65 b 2
Pedro Miguel, Esclusas de — 64-65 b 2
Pedro Miguel Locks = Esclusas de Pedro Miguel 64-65 b 2
Pedro P. Lasalle 106-107 G 6
Pedro Point = Pēduru Tuḍuwa 140 E 6
Pedro R. Fernández 111 E 3
Pedro Totolapan 86-87 MN 9
Pedro Vargas 106-107 C 5
Pedro Velho 100-101 G 4
Pedro Versiani 102-103 M 2
Pēduru Tuḍuwa [CL, cape] 134-135 N 9
Pēduru Tuḍuwa [CL, place] 140 E 6
Peebinga 158-159 H 6
Peebles, OH 72-73 E 5
Peebles [CDN] 61 G 5
Peebles [GB] 119 E 4
Pee Dee River 64-65 L 5
Peek, mys — 58-59 C 4
Peekskill, NY 72-73 K 4
Peel River 56-57 JK 4
Peel Sound 56-57 R 3
Peene 118 F 2
Peera Peera Poolanna Lake 158-159 G 5
Peerless, MT 68-69 D 1
Peerless Lake 60 K 1
Peetz, CO 68-69 E 5
Pegasano 106-107 E 5
Pegasus Bay 158-159 O 8
Pegram, ID 66-67 H 4
Pēgū 148-149 C 3
Pēgū Myit 141 E 7
Pegunungan Alas 152-153 B 4
Pegunungan Apo Duat 152-153 L 3-4
Pegunungan Barisan 152-153 D 6-E 8
Pegunungan Batui 152-153 OP 6
Pegunungan Iran 152-153 L 4-5
Pegunungan Iyang 152-153 K 9
Pegunungan Jayawijaya 148-149 LM 7
Pegunungan Kapuas Hulu 152-153 K 5
Pegunungan Kapur Utara 152-153 JK 9
Pegunungan Kendeng 152-153 JK 9
Pegunungan Kidul 152-153 J 9-K 10
Pegunungan Larut 150-151 C 10
Pegunungan Maoke 148-149 LM 7
Pegunungan Mekongga 152-153 O 7
Pegunungan Menoreh 152-153 J 9
Pegunungan Meratus 148-149 G 7
Pegunungan Müller 148-149 F 6
Pegunungan Pusat Gayo 152-153 B 3
Pegunungan Quarles 152-153 N 7
Pegunungan Schwaner 148-149 F 7
Pegunungan Serayu 152-153 H 9
Pegunungan Sewu 152-153 J 9-10
Pegunungan Sudirman 148-149 L 7
Pegunungan Takolekaju 152-153 N 6-O 7
Pegunungan Tamabo 152-153 L 4
Pegunungan Tanambo 152-153 L 4
Pegunungan Tengger 152-153 K 9-10
Pegunungan Tigapuluh 152-153 E 6
Pegunungan Tineba 152-153 O 6-7
Pēgū Taing 141 DE 6-7
Pēgū Yōma 141 DE 5-6
Pehpei = Beipei 142-143 K 6
Pehuajó 111 D 5
Pehuén-Có 106-107 G 7
Peian = Bei'an 142-143 O 2
Pei-chên = Beizhen 144-145 C 2
Peicheng 146-147 FG 4
Peichiang 146-147 H 10
Pei Chiang = Bei Jiang 146-147 D 10
Pei-chieh Ho = Beijie He 150-151 G 3
Pei-ch'uan Ho = Beichuan He 146-147 C 3
Pei-fei Ho = Beifei He 146-147 F 5
Peighambar Dāgh = Peyghambar Dāgh 136-137 N 4
Pei-hai = Beihai 142-143 K 7
P'ei-hsien = Pei Xian 142-143 M 5
Peikang = Peichiang 146-147 H 10
Pei-li = Beili 150-151 G 3
Pei-liu = Beiliu 146-147 C 10
Peinado, Cerro — 106-107 C 6
Peine 118 E 2
Pei-ngan = Bei'an 142-143 O 2
Peint 138-139 D 7
Peipei = Beipei 142-143 K 6
Pei-p'iao = Beipiao 144-145 C 2
Peiping = Beijing 142-143 LM 3-4
Peipsi Lake = Čudskoje ozero 132-133 D 6
Peiraiévs 122-123 K 7
Peirce, Cape — 58-59 FG 7
Peirce Reservoir 154 III a 1
Peisegem 128 II a 1
Pei Shan = Bei Shan 142-143 GH 3
Peitawu Shan 146-147 H 10
Peixe 92-93 K 7
Peixe, Lagoa do — 106-107 M 3
Peixe, Rio do — [BR, Bahia] 100-101 E 6
Peixe, Rio do — [BR, Goiás] 102-103 F 2
Peixe, Rio do — [BR, Minas Gerais ◁ Rio Preto] 102-103 L 4
Peixe, Rio do — [BR, Minas Gerais ◁ Rio Santo Antônio] 102-103 L 3
Peixe, Rio do — [BR, Santa Catarina] 102-103 G 7
Peixe, Rio do — [BR, São Paulo] 102-103 G 4
Peixes, Rio dos — 98-99 K 10
Pei Xian [TJ ↖ Xuzhou] 142-143 M 5
Pei Xian [TJ → Xuzhou] 146-147 FG 4
Peixoto, Represa do — 102-103 J 4
Pejagalan, Jakarta- 154 IV a 1
Pejantan, Pulau — 152-153 G 5
Pekalongan 148-149 EF 8
Pekan 148-149 D 6
Pe Kiang = Bei Jiang 146-147 D 10
Pekin, IL 70-71 F 5
Pekin, IN 70-71 GH 6
Pekin, ND 68-69 G 2
Peking = Beijing 142-143 LM 4
Peking University 155 II ab 2
Peking Workers' Stadium 155 II b 2
Peking Zoo 155 II ab 2
Pektubajevo 124-125 R 5
Pekul'nej, chrebet — 132-133 hj 4
Pelabuhanratu, Teluk — 152-153 FG 9
Pelada, La — 106-107 G 3
Pelada, Serra — 100-101 D 8
Pelado, Serra do — 100-101 F 4
Pelagosa = Palagruža 122-123 G 4
Pelahatchie, MS 78-79 E 4
Pelaihari 148-149 F 7
Pelalawan 152-153 E 5
Pelayo 94-95 K 3
Peleaga 122-123 K 3
Pelechuco, Río — 104-105 B 4
Peleduj 132-133 V 6
Pelée, Montagne — 64-65 O 8
Pelee Island 72-73 E 4
Pelee Point 72-73 E 4
Pelènaion 122-123 LM 6
Peleng, Pulau — 148-149 H 7
Peleng, Selat — 152-153 P 6
Pelgrimsrus 174-175 J 3
Pelham, GA 80-81 D 5
Pelham Bay Park 82 III d 1
Pelham Manor, NY 82 III d 1
Pelican, AK 58-59 TU 8
Pelicana 106-107 B 2-3
Pelican Lake, WI 70-71 F 3
Pelican Lake [CDN] 61 H 4
Pelican Lake [USA] 70-71 D 1
Pelican Mountains 60 KL 2
Pelican Narrows 61 G 3
Pelican Rapids [CDN, Alberta] 60 L 2
Pelican Rapids [CDN, Saskatchewan] 61 H 4
Pelicurá 106-107 F 7
Pelikan Rapids, MN 68-69 H 2
Pēlion 122-123 K 6
Pelješac 122-123 G 4
Pelkosenniemi 116-117 MN 4
Pella, IA 70-71 D 5
Pella [ZA] 174-175 C 5
Pellado, Cerro — 106-107 B 5
Pell City, AL 78-79 FG 4
Pellegrini 106-107 F 6
Pellegrini, Lago — 106-107 CD 7
Pellegrino, Cozzo — 106-107 HJ 5
Pellendorf 113 I b 2
Pello 116-117 L 4
Pellston, MI 70-71 H 3
Pelly Bay 56-57 S 4
Pelly Crossing 58-59 T 5
Pelly Mountains 56-57 K 5
Pelly River 56-57 K 5
Pelmaḍulla 140 E 7
Pelokang, Pulau — 152-153 N 9
Peloncillo Mountains 74-75 J 6
Pelopónnēsos 122-123 JK 7
Peloritani, Monti — 122-123 F 6-7
Pelotas 111 F 4
Pelotas, Rio — 111 F 3
Pelque, Río — 108-109 D 8
Pelusium 173 C 2
Pelusium, Bay of — = Khalīj aṭ-Ṭinah 173 C 2
Pelvoux 120-121 L 6
Pelym [SU, place] 132-133 L 6
Pelym [SU, river] 132-133 L 5
Pemadumcook Lake 72-73 M 2
Pemalang 148-149 EF 8
Pemanggil, Pulau — 150-151 E 11
Pematangsiantar 148-149 C 6
Pemba [EAT] 172 GH 3
Pemba [Mozambique] 172 H 4
Pemba [Z] 172 E 5
Pemberton [AUS] 158-159 C 6
Pemberton [CDN] 60 F 4
Pembina 56-57 NO 7
Pembina Forks 60 JK 3
Pembina Mountains 68-69 G 1
Pembina River 60 K 3
Pembine, WI 70-71 FG 3
Pembroke, GA 80-81 F 4
Pembroke [CDN] 64-65 L 2
Pembroke [GB] 119 D 6
Pembuang, Sungai — 152-153 K 6-7
Pemuco 106-107 AB 6
Pen 140 A 1
Peña, La — 106-107 AB 6
Peña, Sierra de la — 120-121 G 7
Peña Blanca 106-107 B 2
Peñablanca, NM 76-77 AB 5
Peñafiel 120-121 EF 8
Peñagolosa 120-121 G 8
Peña Grande, Madrid- 113 III a 2
Penalva 100-101 B 2
Penamar 100-101 C 7
Peña Negra, Paso de — 106-107 C 2
Peña Negra, Punta — 92-93 C 5
Peña Nevada, Cerro — 64-65 FG 7
Penang = George Town 148-149 CD 5
Penang = Pinang 150-151 C 10
Penang, Pulau — = Pulau Pinang 150-151 BC 10
Penanjung, Teluk — 152-153 H 9-10
Penápolis 102-103 GH 4
Peñarroya 120-121 G 8
Peñarroya-Pueblonuevo 120-121 E 9
Peñas, Cabo — 108-109 F 9
Peñas, Cabo de — 120-121 E 7
Penas, Golfo de — 111 AB 7
Peñas, Las — 106-107 F 3
Peñas, Punta — 92-93 G 2
Peña Ubiña 120-121 DE 7
Penawawa, WA 66-67 E 2
Pench 138-139 G 7
Penck, Cape — 53 C 9
Penco 106-107 A 6
Pendembu 164-165 B 7
Pendências 100-101 F 3
Pender, NE 68-69 H 4
Pender Bay 158-159 D 3
Pendjab = Punjab [IND] 134-135 LM 4
Pendjab = Punjab [PAK] 134-135 L 4
Pendjari 168-169 F 3
Pendleton, OR 64-65 C 2
Pend Oreille Lake 66-67 E 1-2
Pend Oreille River 66-67 E 1
Pendroy, MT 66-67 GH 1
Pendžikent 134-135 K 3
Pēneiós 122-123 K 6
Penembangan, Pulau — 152-153 H 6
Penetanguishene 72-73 FG 2
Pengalengan 152-153 G 9
Penganga 134-135 M 7
Peng Chau 155 I a 2
Pengchia Hsü 146-147 HJ 9
Pengcuo Ling = Phuntshog Ling 138-139 M 3
Penge [ZA] 174-175 J 3
Penge [ZRE, Haut-Zaïre] 171 AB 2
Penge [ZRE, Kasai-Oriental] 172 DE 3
Penge, London- 129 II b 2
P'eng-hu 146-147 G 10
Penghu Dao = Penghu Tao 146-147 G 10
Penghu Liedao = Penghu Lieh-tao 142-143 M 7
Penghu Lieh-tao 142-143 M 7
Penghu Shuitao 146-147 GH 10
Penghu Tao 146-147 G 10
P'êng-hu Tao = Penghu Tao 146-147 G 10
Pengibu, Pulau — 152-153 G 5
Pengjia Xu = Pengchia Hsü 146-147 HJ 9
Pengkou 146-147 F 9
Penglai 142-143 N 4
Peng Lem = Dak Hon 150-151 F 5
Pengra Pass 66-67 BC 4
Penguin Eilanden 174-175 A 3-5
Penguin Islands = Penguin Eilanden 174-175 A 3-5
Pengze 142-143 M 6
Penha, Rio de Janeiro- 110 I b 1
Penha, São Paulo- 102-103 J 5
Penha de França, São Paulo- 110 II b 2
Penhall 62 H 3
Penhurst 70-71 H 1
Penida, Nusa — 148-149 FG 8
Peninga 124-125 HJ 2
Península Antonio Varas 108-109 C 8
Península Brecknock 111 B 8-9
Península Brunswick 111 B 8
Península Córdova 108-109 C 9
Península de Araya 94-95 JK 2
Península de Azuero 64-65 K 10
Península de Ferrol 92-93 CD 6
Península de Guajira 92-93 E 2
Península de Guanahacabibes 88-89 D 4
Península de Nicoya 64-65 J 9-10
Península de Osa 64-65 JK 10
Península de Paraguaná 92-93 F 2
Península de Paria 92-93 G 2
Península de Taitao 111 AB 7
Península de Yucatán 64-65 HJ 8
Península de Zapata 88-89 F 3
Península Duende 108-109 B 6
Península Dumas 108-109 E 10
Península Hardy 111 BC 9
Península Huequi 108-109 C 4
Península Inhaca 174-175 K 4
Península Magallanes 108-109 C 8
Península Mitre 111 CD 8
Península Muñoz Gamero 111 B 8
Península Paracas 92-93 D 7
Península Sisquelan 108-109 BC 6
Península Skyring 108-109 B 5
Península Staines 108-109 C 8
Península Tres Montes 111 A 7
Península Valdés 111 D 6
Península Valiente 88-89 F 10
Península Verde 106-107 FG 7
Península Videau 108-109 C 7
Península Wilcock 108-109 BC 8
Peninsule de Gaspé 56-57 XY 8
Peñíscola 120-121 H 8
Penitente, Loma — 108-109 D 9

Penitent 341

Penitente, Río — 108-109 D 9
Penitente, Serra do — 92-93 K 6
Pénjamo 86-87 K 7
Penjaringan, Jakarta- 154 IV a 1
Penki = Benxi 142-143 N 3
Penmarch, Pointe de — 120-121 E 5
Penn 61 E 4
Pennandurchfahrt = Chong Phangan 150-151 BC 8
Pennāru = Penner 140 D 3
Pennask Mountain 66-67 C 1
Penne 122-123 EF 4
Penner 140 D 3
Penn Hills, PA 72-73 G 4
Pennine Chain 119 E 4-F 5
Pennsauken, NJ 84 III c 2
Pennsauken Creek North Branch 84 III d 2
Pennsauken Creek South Branch 84 III d 2
Pennsauken Merchandise Mart 84 III cd 2
Pennsylvania 64-65 KL 3
Pennsylvania, University of — 84 III b 2
Penn Valley, PA 84 III b 1
Penn Wynne, PA 84 III b 2
Penny 60 G 3
Penn Yan, NY 72-73 H 3
Penny Highland 56-57 X 4
Pennypack Creek 84 III c 1
Pennypack Park 84 III c 1
Penny Strait 56-57 R 2
Peno 124-125 J 5
Penobscot Bay 72-73 M 2
Penobscot River 72-73 M 2
Peñón 106-107 B 3
Peñon, Cerro — 91 I c 3
Peñón de Vélez de la Gomera 166-167 DE 2
Penong 158-159 F 6
Penonomé 88-89 F 10
Penrith 119 E 4
Pensa = Penza 132-133 GH 7
Pensacola, FL 64-65 J 5
Pensacola Bay 78-79 F 5
Pensacola Mountains 53 A 33-34
Pensamiento 104-105 F 4
Pensamiento, El — 106-107 G 7
Pensiangan 152-153 M 3
Pensilvania 94-95 D 5
Pentagon 82 II a 2
Pentakota 140 F 2
Pentecoste 100-101 E 2
Pentecoste, Açude — 100-101 E 2
Pentecost Island 158-159 N 3
Pēñṭh = Peint 138-139 D 7
Penthièvre = ʿAyn Bārdʿah 166-167 K 1
Penticton 56-57 N 8
Pentland Firth 119 E 2
Pentwater, MI 70-71 G 4
Penukonda 140 C 3
Penungah 152-153 M 3
Penunjok, Tanjung — 150-151 D 10
Penwegon = Pènweigôn 141 E 6
Pènweigôn 141 E 6
Penwell, TX 76-77 C 7
Penyu, Pulau-pulau — 148-149 J 8
Penza 132-133 GH 7
Penzance 119 CD 6
Penžina 132-133 g 5
Penzing, Wien- 113 I b 2
Penžinskaja guba 132-133 f 5
Peonias 91 II ab 1
Peoples Creek 68-69 B 1
Peoria, AZ 74-75 G 6
Peoria, IL 64-65 HJ 3
Peotillos 86-87 K 6
Peotone, IL 70-71 G 5
Pepani 174-175 E 3
Pepel 164-165 B 7
Peper Bay = Teluk Lada 152-153 F 9
Peperiguaçu, Rio — 102-103 F 7
Pepin, WI 70-71 D 3
Pepperdine University 83 III c 2
Peque 94-95 D 4
Pequeni, Río — 64-65 bc 2
Pequi 102-103 K 3
Pequiri, Rio — 102-103 E 2
Pequizeiro 98-99 O 9
Pequop Mountains 66-67 F 5
Pequot Lakes, MN 70-71 C 2
Perai 150-151 C 10
Perak 150-151 C 10-11
Perak, Sungei — 150-151 C 10
Perälä 116-117 JK 6
Peralillo 106-107 B 5
Peralta [ROU] 106-107 J 4
Perambalūr 140 D 5
Percas 106-107 F 2
Percé 63 DE 3
Perche 120-121 H 4
Percival Lakes 158-159 DE 4
Perdekop 174-175 H 4
Perdices 106-107 H 4
Perdido, Monte — 120-121 GH 7
Perdido Bay 78-79 F 5
Perdizes 102-103 J 3
Perdões 102-103 K 4
Perdue 61 E 4
Perdūru 140 B 4
Peredelkino 113 V a 3
Peregrino, El — 106-107 FG 5
Pereguete, Río — 64-65 b 3
Pereira 92-93 D 4
Pereira, Cachoeira — 98-99 KL 7
Pereira, Cachoeiro — 92-93 H 5
Pereira Barreto 102-103 G 4
Pereira d'Eça = N'Giva 172 C 5
Pereirinha 98-99 K 9
Pereiro 100-101 E 4
Perejaslav-Chmel'nickij 126-127 EF 1
Perekop 126-127 F 3
Perekop, Gulf of — = Karkinitskij zaliv 126-127 F 4
Perelazovskij 126-127 L 2
Perelik 122-123 L 5
Perel'ub 124-125 S 8
Peremul Par 134-135 L 8
Peremyšl' 124-125 L 6
Perené 96-97 D 7
Perené, Río — 96-97 D 7
Perenosa Bay 58-59 LM 7
Pereslavl'-Zalesskij 124-125 M 5
pereval Kluchorskij 126-127 K 5
pereval Kodorskij 126-127 MN 5
pereval Krestovyj 126-127 M 5
pereval Mamisonskij 126-127 L 5
Perevoz [SU ↗ Arzamas] 124-125 P 6
Perevoz [SU ↗ Bodajbo] 132-133 W 6
Pérez 106-107 G 4
Pérez, Isla — 86-87 PQ 6
Pergamino 111 D 4
Pergamon 136-137 B 3
Pergamos = Pergamon 136-137 B 3
Perham, MN 70-71 C 2
Perhentian, Kepulauan — 150-151 D 10
Perhonjoki 116-117 KL 6
Periá, Rio — 100-101 C 2
Peribonca, Lac — 63 A 2
Péribonca, Rivière — 56-57 W 7-8
Perico 111 CD 2
Perico, TX 76-77 C 4
Pericos 86-87 G 5
Pericumã, Rio — 100-101 B 2
Périgord 120-121 H 6
Perigoso, Canal — 92-93 K 4
Perigotville = ʿAyn al-Khabīrā 166-167 J 1
Périgueux 120-121 H 6
Perija, Sierra de — 92-93 E 2-3
Peril Strait 58-59 U 8
Perimetral Norte 94-95 J 7
Perim Island = Barīm 134-135 E 8
Perin = Colonia Perin 102-103 BC 6
Periperi de Poções 100-101 D 8
Periquito, Cachoeira do — 92-93 G 6
Peri suyu 136-137 J 3
Perito Moreno 111 BC 7
Peritoró 100-101 B 3
Peritos, Cachoeira — 98-99 GH 9
Periya 140 BC 5
Periyakuḷam 140 C 5
Periyāpaṭṭaṇa = Piriyāpatna 140 BC 4
Periyār 140 C 5
Periyar Lake 140 C 6
Perk 128 II b 1
Perkerson Park 85 II b 2
Perkins, OK 76-77 F 4-5
Perla, La — 86-87 HJ 3
Perlach, München- 130 II b 2
Perlas, Archipiélago de las — 64-65 KL 10
Perlas, Laguna de — 88-89 E 8
Perlas, Las — 88-89 E 8
Perlas, Punta de — 64-65 K 9
Perley, MN 68-69 H 2
Perlis 150-151 C 9
Perlis, Kuala — 148-149 CD 5
Perm' 132-133 K 6
Permas 124-125 P 4
Permé 88-89 H 10
Permskoje = Komsomol'sk-na-Amure 132-133 a 7
Perm-Zakamsk 124-125 UV 5
Perm-Zaozerje 124-125 UV 4
Pernambuco 92-93 LM 6
Pernambuco = Recife 92-93 N 6
Pernem 140 A 3
Pernik 122-123 K 4
Péronne 120-121 J 4
Peron Peninsula 158-159 B 5
Perouse, La — 61 K 3
Perovo, Moskva- 124-125 LM 6
Perovsk = Kzyl-Orda 132-133 M 9
Perow 60 D 2
Perpignan 120-121 J 7
Perrégaux = Muḥammadīyah 164-165 DE 1
Perreux-sur-Marne, le — 129 I d 2
Perrin, TX 76-77 EF 6
Perrine, FL 80-81 c 4
Perris, CA 74-75 E 6
Perry 70-71 H 2
Perry, FL 80-81 b 1
Perry, GA 80-81 E 4
Perry, IA 70-71 CD 5
Perry, NY 72-73 GH 3
Perry, OK 76-77 F 4
Perry Island 58-59 O 6
Perrysburg, OH 72-73 E 4
Perryton, TX 76-77 D 4
Perryvale 60 L 2
Perryville, AK 58-59 d 2
Perryville, AR 78-79 C 3
Perryville, MO 70-71 EF 7
Perşembe 136-137 G 2
Persepolis 134-135 G 5
Perseverancia 92-93 G 7
Persia = Iran 134-135 F-H 4
Persian Gulf 134-135 FG 5
Peršinskaja 124-125 N 3
Persip 174-175 C 3
Pertandangan, Tanjung — 152-153 D 4
Pertek 136-137 H 3
Perth [AUS, Tasmania] 160 c 2
Perth [AUS, Western Australia] 158-159 BC 6
Perth [CDN] 72-73 H 2
Perth [GB] 119 E 3
Perth Amboy, NJ 72-73 J 4
Perth-Andover 63 C 4
Perth-Fremantle 158-159 BC 6
Pertominsk 124-125 LM 1
Peru, IL 70-71 F 5
Peru, IN 70-71 GH 5
Peru [PE] 92-93 D 5-E 7
Perú [RA] 111 D 5
Perú, El — 104-105 C 3
Peru Basin 156-157 N 5
Peru Chile Trench 92-93 C 6-D 7
Perùgia 122-123 E 4
Perugorría 106-107 H 2
Peruíbe 111 G 2
Peṛundurai 140 C 5
Pervari = Hashır 136-137 K 4
Perveri 136-137 GH 4
Pervomajsk [SU, Rossijskaja SFSR] 124-125 OP 6
Pervomajsk [SU, Ukrainskaja SSR] 126-127 E 2
Pervomajskaja 124-125 T 3
Pervomajskij [SU, Rossijskaja SFSR Archangel'skaja Oblast'] 124-125 N 1
Pervomajskij [SU, Rossijskaja SFSR Tambovskaja Oblast'] 124-125 N 7
Pervoural'sk 132-133 KL 6
Pervyj Kuril'skij proliv 132-133 de 7
Perwenitz 130 III a 1
Perzhinsk, Gulf of — = zaliv Šelechova 132-133 e 5-6
Pesagi, Gunung — 152-153 F 8
Pesanggrahan, Kali — 154 IV a 2
Pèsaro 122-123 E 4
Pesca, La — 86-87 M 6
Pescada, Ponta da — 98-99 NO 3
Pescade, Pointe — 170 I a 1
Pescadero, CA 74-75 B 4
Pescador 100-101 D 10
Pescadores = Penghu Lieh-tao 142-143 M 7
Pescadores, Punta — 96-97 E 10
Pescadores Channel = Penghu Shuitao 146-147 GH 10
Pesčanaja 126-127 D 2
Pesčanoje 124-125 KL 2
Pesčanyj, mys — 126-127 P 5
Pesčanyj, ostrov — 132-133 WX 3
Pescara 122-123 F 4
Peschici 122-123 FG 5
Peshawar = Pashāwar 134-135 KL 4
Peshtigo, WI 70-71 G 3
Peshtigo River 70-71 F 3
Peshwar = Pashāwar 134-135 KL 4
Peski [SU, Rossijskaja SFSR Moskovskaja Oblast'] 124-125 M 6
Peski [SU, Rossijskaja SFSR Voronežskaja Oblast'] 126-127 L 1
Peski [SU, Ukrainskaja SSR] 126-127 F 1
Peskovka [SU, Rossijskaja SFSR] 124-125 ST 4
Peskovka [SU, Ukrainskaja SSR] 126-127 DE 1
Pešnoj, poluostrov — 126-127 P 3
Pesočnoje 124-125 M 5
Pesqueira 100-101 F 5
Pessene 174-175 K 3
Pessis-Bouchard, le — 129 I b 1-2
Peštera 122-123 KL 4
Pestovo 124-125 K 4
Pestravka 124-125 R 7
Petacalco, Bahía — 86-87 JK 9
Petacas, Las — 106-107 F 3
Petah Tiqwa = Petaḥ Tiqwa 136-137 F 6
Petaḥ Tiqwa 136-137 F 6
Petalíon, Kólpos — 122-123 L 7
Petaluma, CA 74-75 B 3
Petare 94-95 H 2
Petare-Caurimare 91 II bc 2
Petare-El Llanito 91 II c 2
Petare-El Marques 91 II c 2
Petare-Macaracuay 91 II c 2
Petare-Santa Ana 91 II bc 2
Petas, Las — 104-105 G 5
Petatlán 86-87 K 9
Petauke 172 F 4
Petawawa 72-73 H 2
Petén, El — 64-65 H 8
Petén Itzá, Lago — 86-87 Q 9
Petenwell Lake 70-71 F 3
Petenwell Reservoir = Petenwell Lake 70-71 F 3
Peterbell 70-71 J 1
Peterborough, NH 72-73 KL 3
Peterborough [AUS, South Australia] 158-159 GH 6
Peterborough [AUS, Victoria] 160 F 7
Peterborough [CDN] 56-57 V 9
Peterborough [GB] 119 FG 5
Peterhead 119 F 3
Peterhof = Petrodvorec 124-125 G 4
Peter Ist Island = ostrov Petra I 53 C 27
Petermann Ranges 158-159 E 4-F 5
Peter Pond Lake 56-57 P 6
Petersbach 113 I b 2
Petersburg, AK 56-57 K 6
Petersburg, IL 70-71 F 5
Petersburg, IN 70-71 G 6
Petersburg, TN 78-79 F 3
Petersburg, TX 76-77 D 6
Petersburg, VA 64-65 L 4
Petersburg, WV 72-73 G 5
Petersburg = Leningrad 132-133 E 5-6
Peters Creek, AK 58-59 M 5
Petersham, London- 129 II a 2
Peter's Mine 98-99 J 1
Petersville, AK 58-59 M 5
Petilia Policastro 122-123 G 6
Petit Bois Island 78-79 E 5-6
Petit-Cap 63 DE 3
Petit-Étang 63 F 4
Petit-Goâve 88-89 K 5
Petitjean = Sīdī Qāsim 164-165 CD 2
Petit Lac Manicouagan 63 C 2
Petit Manan Point 72-73 N 2
Petit Mécatina, Île du — 63 G 2
Petit Mécatina, Rivière du — 63 FG 2
Petitot River 56-57 M 5-6
Petit-Rocher 63 CD 4
Petlād 138-139 D 6
Petlāwad 138-139 E 6
Petnahor 154 I a 1
Peto 64-65 J 7
Peton Forest School Park 85 II b 2
Petorca 111 B 4
Petoskey, MI 70-71 H 3
Petra [JOR] 136-137 F 7
Petra, ostrova — 132-133 VW 2
Petra I, ostrov — 53 C 27
Petra Velikogo, zaliv — 132-133 Z 9
Petre, Point — 72-73 H 3
Petrel Bank 58-59 st 6
Petrerito de la Noria 104-105 G 6
Petrič 122-123 K 5
Petrified Forest National Monument 74-75 J 5
Petrikov 124-125 G 7
Petrikovka 126-127 G 2
Pétriou = Chachoengsao 148-149 D 4
Petriščevo 124-125 KL 6
Petroaleksandrovsk = Turtkul' 132-133 L 9
Petrodvorec 124-125 G 4
Petrograd = Leningrad 132-133 E 5-6
Petrolândia 92-93 M 6
Petrólea 92-93 E 3
Petroleum, TX 76-77 E 9
Petrolia 72-73 E 3
Petrolia, CA 66-67 A 5
Petrolina [BR, Amazonas] 98-99 E 6
Petrolina [BR, Pernambuco] 92-93 L 6
Petrolina de Goiás 102-103 H 2
Petronila 106-107 G 3
Petropavlovskoje = Sabirabad 126-127 O 6-7
Petropavlovka 132-133 TU 7
Petropavlovsk 132-133 MN 7
Petropavlovskij = Achtubinsk 126-127 MN 2
Petropavlovsk-Kamčatskij 132-133 ef 7
Petropavlovsk-Kamchatskiy = Petropavlovsk-Kamčatskij 132-133 ef 7
Petrópolis 92-93 L 9
Petroquímica Estación Comferpet 108-109 F 5
Petros, TN 78-79 G 2
Petrosa 113 II b 2
Petroṣeni 122-123 K 3
Petroskoi = Petrozavodsk 132-133 EF 5
Petrovaradin 122-123 HJ 3
Petrovka [SU, Kujbyševskaja Oblast'] 124-125 ST 7
Petrovka [SU, Vladivostok] 144-145 J 1
Petrovsk 124-125 P 7
Petrovskaja 126-127 HJ 4
Petrovskij Jam 124-125 KL 2
Petrovskij Zavod = Petrovsk-Zabajkal'skij 132-133 U 7
Petrovskoje [SU, Jaroslavskaja Oblast'] 124-125 M 5
Petrovskoje [SU, Moskva] 113 V d 4
Petrovskoje [SU, Tambovskaja Oblast'] 124-125 N 7
Petrovskoje = Balabino 126-127 G 3
Petrovsko-Razumovskoje, Moskva- 113 V b 2
Petrovsk-Port = Machačkala 126-127 NO 5
Petrovsk-Zabajkal'skij 132-133 U 7
Petrov Val 126-127 M 1
Petrozavodsk 132-133 EF 5
Petrúpolis 113 IV a 1
Petrusburg 174-175 F 5
Petrus Steyn 174-175 H 4
Petrusville 174-175 F 6
Petseri = Pečory 124-125 FG 5
Pettibone, ND 68-69 G 2
Pettigrew, AR 78-79 C 3
Pettus, TX 76-77 EF 8
Pettys Island 84 III c 2
Petuchovo 132-133 M 6
Peuetsagu, Gunung — 152-153 B 3
Peumo 111 B 4
Peureulak, Ujung — 152-153 BC 3
Peutie 128 II b 1
Pevek 132-133 gh 4
Peyghambar Dāgh 136-137 N 4
Peyrano 106-107 G 4
Peyton, CO 68-69 D 6
Pézenas 120-121 J 7
Pežma 124-125 N 3
Pezmog 124-125 ST 3
Pezones 104-105 G 5

Pfaffenhofen 118 E 4
Pfaffhausen 128 IV b 1
Pfannenstiel 128 IV b 2
Pfarrkirchen 118 F 4
Pfaueninsel 130 III a 2
Pforzheim 118 D 4
Pfungen 128 IV b 1
Phachi 150-151 C 5
Phāgi 138-139 E 4
Phagri Dsong 138-139 M 4
Phagwāṛā = Phagwāra 138-139 E 2
Phagwāra 138-139 E 2
Phai, Ko — 150-151 C 6
Phaisali 150-151 C 5
Phalaborwa 174-175 J 2
Pha Lai 150-151 F 2
Phalane = Mu'o'ng Phalane 150-151 E 4
Phalodi 134-135 L 5
Phaltan 134-135 LM 7
Pha Luat 150-151 C 4
Phālut Peak 138-139 LM 4
Pha Napo, Khao — 150-151 BC 4
Phanat Nikhom 150-151 C 6
Phangan, Chong — 150-151 BC 8
Pha-ngan, Chong — = Chong Phangan 150-151 BC 8
Phangan, Ko — 148-149 CD 5
Phanggong Tsho 142-143 DE 5
Phangnga 150-151 B 8
Phanna Nikhom 150-151 D 4
Phanom Bencha, Khao — 150-151 B 8
Phanom Dang Raek 148-149 DE 4
Phanom Phrai 150-151 DE 5
Phanom Sarakham 150-151 C 6
Phanom Thuan 150-151 B 5
Phan Rang 148-149 EF 4
Phan Ri = Hoa Đa 150-151 G 7
Phan Thiet 148-149 E 4
Phao, Lam — 150-151 D 4
Pha Pet, Phou — 150-151 E 3
Pharendā 138-139 J 4
Pharokha = Ferokh 140 B 5
Pharr, TX 76-77 E 9
Pharu Tsangpo 138-139 LM 2
Phat Diêm 150-151 F 2-3
Phatthalung 148-149 D 5
Phayam, Ko — 150-151 B 8
Phayao 150-151 BC 3
Phaykkhaphum Phisai 148-149 D 3
Phayuha Khiri 150-151 C 5
Phelps, WI 70-71 F 2-3
Phelps Corner, MD 82 II b 2
Phelps Lake 80-81 H 3
Phen 150-151 D 4
Phenix City, AL 64-65 J 5
Phetchabun 148-149 CD 3
Phetchaburi 148-149 CD 4
Phiafay 150-151 EF 5
Phia May 150-151 F 5
Phibun Mangsahan 150-151 E 5
Phichai 150-151 C 4
Phichit 150-151 C 4
Philadelphia, MS 78-79 E 4
Philadelphia, PA 64-65 LM 3-4
Philadelphia [ET] 173 B 3
Philadelphia [ZA] 174-175 C 7
Philadelphia-Bridesburg, PA 84 III c 2
Philadelphia-Burholme, PA 84 III c 1
Philadelphia-Bustleton, PA 84 III c 1
Philadelphia-Chestnut Hill, PA 84 III b 1
Philadelphia-Crescentville, PA 84 III c 1
Philadelphia-East Falls, PA 84 III b 1
Philadelphia-Eastwick, PA 84 III b 2
Philadelphia-Elmwood, PA 84 III b 2
Philadelphia-Fox Chase, PA 84 III c 1
Philadelphia-Frankford, PA 84 III c 1
Philadelphia-Germantown, PA 84 III b 1
Philadelphia-Holmesburg, PA 84 III c 1
Philadelphia International Airport 84 III b 2
Philadelphia-Juniata, PA 84 III c 1
Philadelphia-Kensington, PA 84 III c 2
Philadelphia-Lawndale, PA 84 III c 1
Philadelphia-Logan, PA 84 III c 1
Philadelphia-Manayunk, PA 84 III b 1
Philadelphia-Mayfair, PA 84 III c 1
Philadelphia-Mount Airy, PA 84 III b 1
Philadelphia Naval Shipyard 84 III bc 2
Philadelphia-North Philadelphia, PA 84 III bc 2
Philadelphia-Olney, PA 84 III c 1
Philadelphia-Overbrook, PA 84 III b 2
Philadelphia-Richmond, PA 84 III c 2
Philadelphia-Roxborough, PA 84 III b 1
Philadelphia-Somerton, PA 84 III c 1
Philadelphia-South Philadelphia, PA 84 III bc 2
Philadelphia-Tacony, PA 84 III c 1
Philadelphia-Tioga, PA 84 III bc 1
Philadelphia-Wissinoming, PA 84 III c 1
Philip, SD 68-69 F 3
Philip Island 158-159 N 5
Philipp, MS 78-79 DE 4
Philippe-Thomas = Al-Mittawī 164-165 F 2
Philippeville 120-121 K 3
Philippeville = Sakīkdah 164-165 F 1
Philippi, WV 72-73 FG 5
Philippi, Lake — 158-159 G 4
Philippiada = Filippiás 122-123 J 6
Philippines 148-149 H 3-J 5
Philippolis 174-175 F 6
Philippopolis = Plovdiv 122-123 L 4
Philippsthal 130 III a 2
Philipsburg, MT 66-67 G 2
Philipsburg, PA 72-73 G 4
Philip Smith Mountains 56-57 GH 4
Philipstown 174-175 F 6
Phillaor = Phillaur 138-139 EF 2
Phillaur 138-139 EF 2
Phillip Island 160 G 7
Phillips, ME 72-73 L 2
Phillips, WI 70-71 E 3
Phillipsburg, KS 68-69 G 6
Phillipsburg, MO 70-71 D 7
Phillipsburg, NJ 72-73 J 4
Phillips Mountains 53 B 22-23
Philo, CA 74-75 B 3
Phimai 150-151 D 5
Phinlaung 141 E 5
Phippsøya 116-117 kl 4
Phitsanulok 148-149 D 3
Phnom Damrei 150-151 DE 7
Phnom Dangraek = Phanom Dong Raek 148-149 DE 4
Phnom Kravanh 150-151 D 6-7
Phnom Kulên 150-151 DE 6
Phnom Penh 148-149 D 4
Phnom Samkos 150-151 D 6
Phnom Ta Det 150-151 D 6
Pho, Laem — 148-149 D 5
Phô Binh Gia 150-151 EF 2
Phoenix 208 JK 3
Phoenix, AZ 64-65 D 5
Phoenix Basin 162 KL 4
Phoenix Islands 156-157 J 5
Phoenix Trench 156-157 J 5
Phoenixville, PA 72-73 HJ 4
Phon 150-151 D 5
Phong, Nam — 150-151 CD 4
Phong Điên 150-151 F 4
Phong Lôc 150-151 F 4
Phong Phu 150-151 E 7
Phong Saly 148-149 D 2
Phong Thanh = Cao Lanh 150-151 E 7
Phong Thong 150-151 DE 4
Phon Phisai 150-151 D 3
Phopāgāñv = Phopāgaon 138-139 J 3
Phopāgaon 138-139 J 3
Pho Rang = Lang Phô Rang 150-151 E 1
Phorog Tsho 138-139 J 2
Phosphate Hill 158-159 GH 4
Photharam 150-151 B 6
Phou Bia 150-151 D 3
Phou Khao Khouai 150-151 D 3
Phou Loi 150-151 D 2
Phou Pha Pet 150-151 E 3
Phou Xai Lai Leng 150-151 DE 3
Phra Chedi Sam Ong 148-149 C 3-4
Phrae 150-151 C 3
Phra Nakhon Si Ayutthaya 148-149 D 4
Phran Kratai 150-151 B 4
Phra Thong, Ko — 150-151 AB 8
Phrom Buri 150-151 C 5
Phrom Phiram 150-151 C 4
Phsar Oudong 150-151 E 7
Phu Cat 150-151 G 5-6
Phu Cu'o'ng 150-151 F 7
Phu Diên Châu 148-149 E 3
Phu Ding Den 150-151 F 5
Phu Đoan 150-151 E 2
Phugsum 138-139 KL 3
Phuket 148-149 C 5
Phuket, Ko — 148-149 C 5
Phu Khieo 150-151 D 4
Phu Khu'o'ng 150-151 F 7
Phu Kradung 150-151 CD 4
Phūl 138-139 E 2
Phu Lang Thu'o'ng = Bǎc Giang 150-151 F 2
Phulbāni 138-139 JK 7
Phuljī 138-139 A 4
Phu Lôc 150-151 F 4
Phu Lôc = Thanh Tri 150-151 EF 8
Phūlpur 138-139 J 4
Phu Ly 148-149 E 2
Phum Damdek 150-151 DE 6
Phum Kompong Kdey 150-151 E 6
Phum Krasang 150-151 E 6
Phum Krek 150-151 E 7
Phum Léach 150-151 DE 6
Phum Peam Prous 150-151 D 6
Phum Rovieng 148-149 E 4
Phum Siembauk 150-151 E 6
Phum Treng 150-151 D 6
Phu My 150-151 G 5
Phunakha 134-135 OP 5
Phung Chhu 138-139 L 3
Phung Hiêp 150-151 E 8
Phungpo Tsho 138-139 L 2
Phu Nho Quan 150-151 EF 2
Phunphin 150-151 B 8
Phuntshog Ling 138-139 M 3
Phu'o'c Binh 150-151 F 7
Phu'o'c Lê 150-151 F 7
Phu'o'c Long 150-151 E 8
Phu'o'c Vinh 150-151 F 7
Phu Qui 150-151 E 3
Phu Quôc 150-151 D 7
Phu Quôc, Đao — 148-149 D 4
Phu Riêng 150-151 F 7
Phu Soai Dao 150-151 C 4
Phutha-Ditjhaba 174-175 H 5
Phu Tho 148-149 DE 2
Phu Tinh Gia 150-151 EF 3
Phutthaisong 150-151 D 5
Phu Wiang 150-151 CD 4
Phu Yên Binh 150-151 E 2
Phya Lat = Ban Phya Lat 150-151 D 2

Piacá 92-93 K 6
Piaçabuçu 100-101 F 6
Piacenza 122-123 C 3
Piacoá 94-95 K 3
Piacouadie, Lac — 63 A 2
Pialba 158-159 K 5
Piamonte 106-107 FG 4
Piancó 100-101 F 4
Piangil 158-159 H 7
Pianguan 146-147 C 2
Pianma 141 F 2
Pianosa, Ìsola — 122-123 D 4
Piara-Açu 98-99 M 9
Pias [PE] 96-97 C 5
Piaseczno 118 K 2
Piatã 100-101 D 7
Piatra 122-123 L 3
Piatra-Neamṭ 122-123 M 2
Piauí 92-93 L 6
Piauí, Rio — 92-93 L 6
Piauí, Serra do — 100-101 CD 5
Piave 122-123 E 2
Piaxtla, Punta — 86-87 G 6
Piaxtla, Río — 86-87 G 6
Piazza Armerina 122-123 F 7
Piazzi, Isla — 108-109 BC 8
Pībōr 164-165 L 7
Pībōr, Nahr — 164-165 L 7
Pica 104-105 B 7
Picabo, ID 66-67 F 4
Picacho, AZ 74-75 H 6
Picacho, CA 74-75 F 6
Picacho, NM 76-77 B 6
Picacho, Cerro del — 91 I c 1
Picacho del Centinela 64-65 F 6
Picada, La — 106-107 G 3
Picados, Cerro dos 86-87 CD 3
Pičajevo 124-125 O 7
Picardie 120-121 HJ 4
Picayune, MS 78-79 E 5
Pic Baumann 168-169 F 4
Pic Bette 164-165 HJ 4
Pic de Guéra 164-165 H 6
Pic de Tibé 168-169 C 3
Pichalo, Punta — 104-105 A 6
Pichamán 106-107 A 5
Pichanal 111 CD 2
Pichanes 106-107 E 3
Pichelsdorf 130 III a 1
Picher, OK 76-77 G 4
Pichhōr 138-139 G 5
Pichi Ciego 111 C 4
Pichieh = Bijie 142-143 K 6
Pichilemú 111 B 4
Pichi Mahuida 106-107 E 7
Pichi Mahuida, Sierra — 106-107 E 7
Pichincha [EC, administrative unit] 96-97 B 1-2
Pichincha [EC, mountain] 96-97 B 2
Pichirhua 96-97 E 9
Pichis, Río — 96-97 D 7
Pichon = Ḥaffūz 166-167 L 2
Pichor 138-139 G 5
Pichtovka 132-133 P 6
Pickens, MS 78-79 DE 4
Pickens, SC 80-81 E 3
Pickerel 72-73 F 2
Pickerel Lake 70-71 E 1
Pickle Crow 56-57 ST 7
Pickle Lake 62 D 2
Pico 204-205 E 5
Pico, El — 92-93 G 8
Pico, Río — 108-109 D 5
Pico Baú 102-103 K 5
Pico Bolívar 92-93 E 3
Pico Cristóbal Colón 94-95 E 2
Pico da Bandeira 92-93 L 9
Pico da Neblina 92-93 FG 4
Pico da Piedade 102-103 L 3
Pico das Almas 100-101 CD 7
Pico da Tijuca 110 I b 2
Pico de Aneto 120-121 H 7
Pico de Itambé 102-103 L 3
Pico de Johnson 86-87 DE 3
Pico de Neblina 98-99 F 4
Pico de Orizaba 86-87 M 8
Pico de Orizaba = Citlaltépetl 64-65 G 8
Pico de Salamanca 108-109 F 5
Pico de São Tomé 168-169 G 5
Pico de Tancítaro 64-65 F 8
Pico de Teide 164-165 A 3
Pico Duarte 64-65 M 8
Pico Francés 108-109 E 10
Pico Guaricana 102-103 H 6
Pico Itacambira 102-103 L 2
Pico Itacolomi 92-93 L 9
Pico Itapirapuã 102-103 H 6
Pico Kazer 108-109 F 10
Picola 160 G 5
Pico Negro 104-105 B 6
Pico Oriental 91 II bc 1
Pico Redondo 98-99 G 3
Pico Rivera, CA 83 III d 2
Pico Rondon 98-99 G 4
Pico Ruivo 164-165 A 2
Picos 92-93 L 6
Pico Salamanca 108-109 F 5
Picos de Europa 120-121 E 7
Picos de Urbión 120-121 F 8
Pico Sira 96-97 D 6
Pico Truncado 111 C 7
Pico Turquino 64-65 L 8
Pic River 70-71 G 1
Picton [CDN] 72-73 H 2-3
Picton [NZ] 158-159 O 8
Picton, Isla — 108-109 F 10
Picton, Mount — 160 bc 3
Pictou 63 E 5
Pic Toussidé 164-165 H 4
Picture Butte 66-67 G 1
Picuí 92-93 M 6
Picunda, mys — 126-127 K 5
Picún Leufú 111 BC 5
Picún Leufú, Arroyo — 106-107 BC 7
Picún Leufú, Cerro — 106-107 C 7
Pidurutalāgala 134-135 N 9
Piedad Cavadas, La — 86-87 JK 7
Piedade, Pico da — 102-103 L 3
Piedade, Rio de Janeiro- 110 I b 2
Piedade, Serra da — 100-101 F 4

342 Penitent

Pobeda 343

Pobedino 132-133 b 8
Pobedy, pik — 134-135 MN 2
Población 102-103 C 4
Pobohe = Pohe 146-147 E 6
Pocahontas 60 HJ 3
Pocahontas, AR 78-79 D 2
Pocahontas, IA 70-71 C 4
Poção, Salto — 98-99 L 5
Poção, Serra do — 100-101 F 4
Pocatello, ID 64-65 D 3
Poccha, Río — 96-97 C 6
Počep 124-125 J 7
Pocho, Sierra de — 106-107 E 3
P'och'ŏn 144-145 F 4
Pochutla 86-87 M 10
Pochval'nyj 132-133 cd 4
Pochvistnevo 124-125 ST 7
Pocillas 106-107 A 6
Pocinhos 100-101 FG 4
Počinki 124-125 P 6
Počinok [SU, Smolenskaja Oblast']
124-125 J 6
Pocito, El — 104-105 E 4
Pocitos, Salar — 104-105 C 9
Pocklington Reef 148-149 j 7
Pocoata 104-105 C 6
Poço Comprido, Riacho —
100-101 C 5-E 6
Poço Danta, Serra — 100-101 EF 6
Poço das Trincheiras 100-101 F 5
Poções 92-93 LM 7
Pocomoke City, MD 72-73 J 5
Pocomoke Sound 80-81 HJ 2
Poconé 92-93 H 8
Poço Redondo 100-101 F 5
Poços [BR ↗ Ibotirama]
100-101 C 7
Poços [BR ← Remanso]
100-101 C 5
Poços de Caldas 92-93 K 9
Poço Verde 100-101 E 6
Podberezje 124-125 H 5
Podborovje 124-125 K 4
Podčinnyj 126-127 M 1
Poddorje 124-125 H 5
Podgorenskij 126-127 J 1
Podgorica = Titograd 122-123 H 4
Podgornoje 132-133 P 6
Podgorodnoje † Dnepropetrovsk
126-127 G 2
Podile 140 D 3
Podkamennaja Tunguska
132-133 R 5
Podkova 122-123 L 5
Podol'sk 124-125 L 6
Podol'skaja vozvyšennost'
126-127 B 2-D 3
Podor 164-165 AB 5
Podosinovec 124-125 Q 3
Podporožje 132-133 EF 5
Podravska Slatina 122-123 GH 3
Podsosenje 124-125 NO 2
Podsvilje 124-125 FG 6
Podtesovo 132-133 R 6
Pod'uga 124-125 N 3
Podvoločisk 126-127 BC 2
Poelela, Lagoa — 174-175 L 3
Po-êrh-t'a-la Chou = Bortala
Monggol Zizhizhou 142-143 E 2-3
Pofadder 172 CD 7
Pogamasing 62 L 3
Pogar 124-125 J 7
Poggibonsi 122-123 D 4
Pogibi 132-133 b 7
Pogoreloje Gorodišče 124-125 KL 5
Pogrebišče 126-127 D 2
Pogromni Volcano 58-59 a 2
Pogyndeno 132-133 fg 4
Poh 152-153 P 6
Poh, Teluk — 152-153 P 6
P'oha-dong 144-145 GH 2
Po Hai = Bo Hai 142-143 M 4
Pohai, Gulf of — = Bohai Haixia
142-143 N 4
Po-hai Hai-hsia = Bohai Haixia
142-143 N 4
Po-hai Wan = Bohai Wan
146-147 FG 2
P'ohang 142-143 OP 4
Pohe 146-147 E 6
Pohjanmaa 116-117 K 6-M 5
Pohjois-Karjalan lääni 116-117 N 6
Pōhrī = Pauri 138-139 F 5
Pohsien = Bo Xian 142-143 LM 5
Pohue Bay 78-79 e 3
Pōide 124-125 D 4
Poinsett, Lake — 68-69 H 3
Point Abbaye 70-71 FG 2
Point Alexander 158-159 G 2
Point Arena 74-75 AB 3
Point Arena, CA 74-75 AB 3
Point Arguello 74-75 C 5
Point au Fer 78-79 D 6
Point Baker, AK 58-59 w 8
Point Barrow 56-57 EF 3
Point Blaze 158-159 EF 2
Point Bonita 83 I a 2
Point Brown 160 A 4
Point Buchon 74-75 C 5
Point Cabrillo 74-75 AB 3
Point Calimere 134-135 MN 8
Point Cloates 158-159 B 4
Point Conception 64-65 B 5
Point Culver 158-159 DE 6
Point Detour 70-71 G 3
Pointe-à-la-Fregate 63 D 3
Pointe a la Hache, LA 78-79 E 6
Pointe-à-Maurier 63 G 2
Pointe-à-Pitre 64-65 O 8
Pointe au Baril Station 72-73 F 2
Pointe Aux Barques 72-73 E 2
Pointe aux Pins 72-73 F 3
Pointe Behágue 92-93 J 3-4
Pointe de Barfleur 120-121 G 4
Pointe de la Gombe 170 IV a 1
Pointe della Parata 122-123 BC 5
Pointe de Penmarch 120-121 E 5
Pointe des Consuls 170 I a 1
Pointe-des-Monts 63 C 3
Pointe du Bois 62 B 2
Pointe du Raz 120-121 E 4
Pointe Isère 92-93 J 3
Pointe Mbamou 170 IV a 1
Pointe-Noire 172 B 2
Pointe Pescade 170 I a 1
Pointe Saint Mathieu 120-121 E 4
Point Europa 120-121 E 10
Point Franklin 58-59 H 1
Point Gellibrand 161 II b 2
Point Harbor, NC 80-81 J 2
Point Hibbs 160 b 3
Point Judith 72-73 L 4
Point Lake 56-57 O 4
Point Lay, AK 58-59 EF 2
Point Leamington 63 J 3
Point Lobos 83 I a 2
Point Marion, PA 72-73 G 5
Point of Ayre 119 DE 4
Point of Pines 84 I c 2
Point of Rocks, WY 68-69 B 5
Point Ormond 161 II b 2
Point Pedro = Pēduru Tuḍuwa
134-135 N 9
Point Petre 72-73 H 3
Point Pinos 74-75 BC 4
Point Pleasant, NJ 72-73 JK 4
Point Pleasant, WV 72-73 EF 5
Point Prawle 119 E 6
Point Reyes 74-75 B 3-4
Point Richmond 83 I b 1
Point Roberts, WA 66-67 B 1
Point Saint George 66-67 A 5
Point San Pablo 83 I b 1
Point San Pedro 83 I b 1
Point Spencer 58-59 D 4
Point Sur 74-75 BC 4
Point Vicente 74-75 D 6
Point Westall 160 AB 4
Point Weyland 160 AB 4
Point Whidbey 160 B 5
Poipet 150-151 D 6
Poisson Blanc, Lac — 72-73 J 1-2
Poitevin, Marais — 120-121 G 5
Poitiers 120-121 H 5
Poitou 120-121 GH 5
Poivre, Côte du — = Malabar Coast
134-135 L 8-M 9
Poix 120-121 HJ 4
Pojarkovo 132-133 Y 8
Pojezierze Chełmińskre 118 J 2
Pojezierze Mazurskie 118 K 2-L 1
Pojige, Río — 104-105 D 4
Pojo [BOL] 104-105 D 5
Pokaran 138-139 C 4
Pokataroo 160 J 2
Pokča 124-125 V 2
Pokegama Lake 70-71 CD 2
Pok Fu Lam 155 I a 2
Pokhara 134-135 N 5
Pok Liu Chau 155 I a 2
Poko 172 E 1
Poko Mount 58-59 F 2
Pokrovka [SU ↖ Abdulino]
124-125 T 7
Pokrovka [SU ↘ Buzuluk]
124-125 T 8
Pokrovsk 132-133 Y 5
Pokrovsk = Engels 124-125 Q 8
Pokrovskoje [SU, Archangel'skaja
Oblast'] 124-125 M 1
Pokrovskoje, Moskva- 113 V c 3
Pokrovsko-Strešnevo, Moskva-
113 V b 2
Pokrovsk-Ural'skij 132-133 K 5
Pokšen'ga 124-125 O 2
Pola [SU, place] 124-125 H 5
Pola [SU, river] 124-125 J 5
Polacca Wash 74-75 H 5
Pola de Siero 120-121 E 7
Polādpur 140 A 1-2
Polān [IR] 134-135 J 5
Poland 118 H-L 3
Pol'any [SU, Moskovskaja Oblast']
113 V b 4
Pol'arnyj [SU, Indigirka] 132-133 c 3
Pol'arnyj Ural 132-133 LM 4
Polar Plateau 53 A 31-6
Polathane 136-137 H 2
Polatlı 134-135 C 3
Polavaram 140 E 2
Polcirkeln 116-117 J 4
Polcura 106-107 B 6
Poldarsa 124-125 PQ 3
Polesje 124-125 E 8-H 7
Polessk 118 K 1
Polewali 152-153 N 7
Polgahawela 140 E 7
Pōlgyo 144-145 F 5
Poli 164-165 G 7
Poli = Boli 142-143 P 2
Policastro, Golfo di —
122-123 F 5-6
Police Headquarters 85 III b 1
Polillo Islands 148-149 H 3-4
Poliny Osipenko 132-133 a 7
Pólis 136-137 E 5
Polist' 124-125 H 5
Polk, PA 72-73 FG 4
Polḷāchchi = Pollāchi 140 C 5
Pollāchi 140 C 5
Polledo 106-107 E 5
Pollensa 120-121 J 9
Pollino 122-123 G 5-6
Pollock, ID 66-67 E 3
Pollock, LA 78-79 C 5
Pollock, SD 68-69 FG 3
Pollockville 61 C 5
Polmak 116-117 N 2
Polna [SU] 124-125 G 4
Polnovo-Seliger 124-125 J 5
Polo, IL 70-71 F 5
Polo = Boluo 146-147 E 10
Polock 124-125 G 6
Pologi 126-127 H 3
Polonio, Cabo — 111 F 4
Polonnaruwa 140 E 7
Polonnoje 126-127 C 1
Polotn'anyj 124-125 KL 6
Polousnyj kr'až 132-133 bc 4
Polovniki 124-125 S 2
Polovo 124-125 J 5
Polson, MT 66-67 FG 2
Poltava 126-127 G 2
Poltavakaja = Krasnoarmejskaja
126-127 J 4
Poltorack = Aščhabad
134-135 HJ 3
Põltsamaa 124-125 EF 4
Pol'udov Kamen' 124-125 V 3
Pol'udov kr'až 124-125 V 3
Poluj [SU, place] 132-133 MN 4
Poluj [SU, river] 132-133 M 4
Polunočnoje 132-133 L 5
poluostrov Gusinaja Zeml'a
132-133 HJ 3
poluostrov Jamal 132-133 MN 3
poluostrov Javaj 132-133 NO 3
poluostrov Kanin 132-133 GH 4
poluostrov Koni 132-133 d 6
poluostrov Pešnoj 126-127 P 3
poluostrov Pjagina 132-133 de 6
poluostrov Rybačij 132-133 EF 4
poluostrov Sara 126-127 O 7
poluostrov Tajgonos 132-133 f 5
poluostrov Tajmyr 132-133 R-U 2
poluostrov T'ub-Karagan
126-127 P 4
Polūr 140 D 4
Põlva 124-125 F 4
Polvaredas 106-107 C 4
Polvorines, General Sarmiento-los —
110 III ab 1
Polýaigos 122-123 L 7
Polýchnitos 122-123 LM 6
Polýgyros 122-123 K 5
Polynesia 156-157 J 4-5
Poma, La — 111 C 2
Pomabamba 96-97 C 6
Pomán 104-105 C 11
Pomarão 120-121 D 10
Pomasi, Cerro de — 92-93 E 8
Pomasi, Nevados de — 96-97 F 9
Pomba, Rio — 102-103 L 4
Pombal [BR] 92-93 M 6
Pombal [P] 120-121 C 9
Pombeba, Ilha da — 110 I b 2
Pombetsu = Honbetsu
144-145 cd 2
Pomerania 118 G 2-H 1
Pomeranian Bay = Pommersche
Bucht 118 FG 1
Pomeroy, OH 72-73 EF 5
Pomeroy, WA 66-67 E 2
Pomfret 174-175 E 3
Pomme de Terre River 70-71 C 2-3
Pommersche Bucht 118 FG 1
Pomona, CA 74-75 E 5-6
Pomona, KS 70-71 C 6
Pomona, MO 78-79 D 2
Pomona [Namibia] 174-175 A 4
Pomona [RA] 106-107 E 7
Pomorie 122-123 MN 4
Pomorskij bereg 124-125 K 1-L 2
Pomošnaja 126-127 E 2
Pomo Tsho 138-139 MN 3
Pomozdino 124-125 U 3
Pompano Beach, FL 80-81 cd 3
Pompeia 102-103 G 5
Pompeji 122-123 F 5
Pompeston Creek 84 III d 1-2
Pompéu 102-103 K 3
Pompeys Pillar, MT 66-67 JK 2
Ponape 208 F 2
Ponass Lake 61 F 4
Ponazyrevo 124-125 Q 4
Ponca, NE 68-69 H 4
Ponca City, OK 64-65 G 4
Ponca Creek 68-69 G 4
Ponce 64-65 N 8
Ponce de Leon, FL 78-79 FG 5
Ponce de Leon Bay 80-81 c 4
Poncha Springs, CO 68-69 C 6
Ponchatoula, LA 78-79 D 5
Ponda 140 B 3
Pondaung Range = Pônnyâ Taung
141 D 4-5
Pond Creek 68-69 E 6
Pond Creek, OK 76-77 F 4
Pondicheri = Pondicherry
134-135 MN 8
Pondicherry 134-135 MN 8
Pond Inlet [CDN, bay] 56-57 VW 3
Pond Inlet [CDN, place] 56-57 V 3
Pondo Dsong 142-143 G 5
Pondoland 174-175 H 6
Pondosa, CA 66-67 C 5
Pondosa, OR 66-67 E 3
Ponds Creek 161 II b 1
Ponedjel = Pandėlys 124-125 E 5
Ponferrada 120-121 D 7
Pong 148-149 CD 3
Pongba 138-139 K 2
Pong Klua 150-151 BC 3
Pongnim-ni = Pōlgyo 144-145 F 5
Pongo de Manseriche 92-93 D 5
Pongola [ZA, place] 174-175 J 4
Pongola [ZA, river] 172 F 7
Pongolapoortdam 174-175 JK 4
Ponizovje [SU, Smolenskaja Oblast']
124-125 H 6
Ponley 150-151 E 6
Pônnāgyūn 141 C 5
Ponnaiyār 140 DE 5
Ponnāni [IND, place] 140 B 5
Ponnāni [IND, river] 140 C 5
Ponneri 140 E 4
Ponnūru 140 E 2
Pônnyâ Taung 141 D 4-5
Ponoj 132-133 FG 4
Ponoka 60 L 3
Ponomar'ovka 124-125 TU 7
Ponorogo 152-153 J 9
Ponta Albina 172 B 5
Ponta Alta do Norte 98-99 P 10
Ponta Anastácio 106-107 M 3
Ponta Apaga Fogo 100-101 E 7
Ponta Bojuru 106-107 M 3
Ponta Cantagalo 102-103 H 7
Ponta Christóvão Pereira
106-107 M 3
Ponta Corumiquara 100-101 E 2
Ponta Curuçá 98-99 P 5
Ponta da Baleia 100-101 E 9
Ponta da Barra 174-175 L 2
Ponta da Barra Falsa 174-175 L 2
Ponta da Cancela 100-101 G 4
Ponta da Mutuoca 100-101 B 1
Ponta da Pescada 98-99 NO 3
Ponta das Palmeirinhas 172 B 3
Ponta da Taquara 102-103 HJ 7
Ponta de Atalaia 98-99 P 5
Ponta de Corumbaú 100-101 E 9
Ponta de Iguape 100-101 EF 2
Ponta Delgada 204-205 E 5
Ponta de Mostardas 106-107 M 3
Ponta de Mucuripe 92-93 M 5
Ponta de Mundaú 100-101 E 2
Ponta de Pedras 92-93 JK 5
Ponta de Regência 92-93 M 8
Ponta de Santa Rita 100-101 G 3
Ponta de Santo Antônio
100-101 GH 4
Ponta do Arpoador [BR, Rio de
Janeiro] 110 I bc 2
Ponta do Arpoador [BR, São Paulo]
102-103 J 6
Ponta do Aruacá 100-101 B 1
Ponta do Boi 102-103 K 6
Ponta do Calcanhar 92-93 M 6-N 5
Ponta do Coconho 100-101 G 3
Ponta do Conselho 100-101 E 7
Ponta do Coqueiros 100-101 G 4
Ponta do Flamengo 100-101 G 3
Ponta do Gameleira 100-101 G 3
Ponta do Juatinga 92-93 L 9
Ponta do Maceió 100-101 F 3
Ponta do Manguinho 92-93 M 7
Ponta do Morro, Serra da —
100-101 C 7
Ponta do Mutá 100-101 E 7
Ponta do Pinheiro 102-103 H 7
Ponta dos Cajuás 92-93 M 5
Ponta dos Latinos 106-107 L 4
Ponta dos Patos 100-101 E 2
Ponta do Tapes 106-107 M 3
Ponta do Tubarão 100-101 FG 3
Ponta do Zumui 100-101 B 1
Ponta Grande 100-101 E 9
Ponta Grossa [BR, Amapá] 92-93 K 4
Ponta Grossa [BR, Ceará]
100-101 F 3
Ponta Grossa [BR, Paraná] 111 F 3
Ponta Itacolomi 100-101 BC 1-2
Ponta Itaipu 102-103 J 6
Ponta Jeridoaquara 100-101 DE 2
Pontal 102-103 HJ 4
Pontal, Rio do — 100-101 D 5
Ponta Lazão 100-101 C 2
Pontal dos Ilhéus 100-101 E 8
Pontalina 102-103 H 2
Ponta Maiaú 98-99 P 5
Ponta Naufragados 102-103 HJ 7
Ponta Negra 100-101 G 3
Ponta Negra = Pointe-Noire
172 B 2
Ponta Paza 100-101 F 6
Ponta Porã 92-93 HJ 9
Ponta Rasa 106-107 LM 3
Ponta Redonda 92-93 M 5
Pontarlier 120-121 KL 5
Ponta São Sebastião 172 G 6
Ponta São Simão 106-107 M 3
Pontas dos Tres Irmãos
92-93 M 6-N 5
Ponta Tabajé 92-93 LM 5
Ponta Tropia 100-101 D 2
Pontault-Combault 129 I d 2
Ponta Verde 100-101 G 5
Pont Champlain 82 I b 2
Pontchartrain, Lake — 64-65 HJ 5
Pontchartrain Beach, New Orleans-,
LA 85 I b 1
Pontchartrain Park 85 I b 1
Pontchartrain Shores, LA 85 I a 1
Pont-du-Fahs = Al-Faḥṣ
166-167 LM 1
Ponte Alta do Bom Jesus
100-101 A 7
Ponte da Amizade 102-103 E 6
Ponte de Itabapoana 102-103 M 4
Ponte de Pedra [BR ↘ Cuiabá]
102-103 E 2
Ponte de Pedra [BR ↖ Diamantino]
92-93 H 7
Ponte Firme 102-103 JK 3
Ponteix 61 E 6
Ponte-Leccia 122-123 C 4
Ponte Nova 92-93 L 9
Ponte Presidente Costa e Silva
110 I bc 2
Pontes-e-Lacerda 92-93 H 8
Pontevedra 120-121 C 7
Pontevedra, Merlo- 110 III a 2
Ponthierville = Ubundu 172 DE 2
Pontiac, IL 70-71 F 5
Pontiac, MI 64-65 K 3
Pontianak 148-149 E 7
Pontic Mountains 134-135 C-E 2
Pontivy 120-121 F 4
Pont Jacques Cartier 82 I b 1
Ponto Galeria, Roma- 113 II a 2
Pontoise 120-121 HJ 4
Pontotoc, MS 78-79 E 3
Pontrémoli 122-123 CD 3
Pont-Viau 82 I a 1
Pont Victoria 82 I b 2
Pony, MT 66-67 GH 3
Ponza 122-123 E 5
Ponziane, Ìsole — 122-123 E 5
Poochera 160 B 4
Poole 119 E 6
Pool Malebo 172 C 2
Poona = Pune 134-135 L 7
Pooncarie 158-159 H 6
Poopó 92-93 F 8
Poopó, Lago de — 92-93 F 8
Poorman, AK 58-59 K 4
Poortje = Poortjie 174-175 E 6
Poortjie 174-175 E 6
Pōōsaspea 124-125 DE 4
Popa = Pôpkâ Taungdeik 141 D 5
Popa = Pulau Kofiau 148-149 JK 7
Po-pai = Bobai 146-147 BC 10
Popasnaja 126-127 J 2
Popayán 92-93 D 4
Popeljany = Papilė 124-125 D 5
Popeys Pillar, MT 68-69 BC 2
Popigaj 132-133 UV 3
Popihe = Pohe 146-147 E 6
Popilta Lake 160 E 4
Po-p'ing = Boping 146-147 F 3
Pôpkâ Taungdeik 141 D 5
Poplar, MT 68-69 D 1
Poplar, WI 70-71 E 2
Poplar, London- 129 II bc 1
Poplar Bluff, MO 64-65 H 4
Poplar Hill 62 B 1
Poplar River [CDN] 62 A 1
Poplar River [USA] 68-69 D 1
Poplar River, West Fork —
68-69 CD 1
Poplarville, MS 78-79 E 5
Popocatépetl 64-65 G 8
Popof Island 58-59 cd 2
Popoh 152-153 J 10
Popokabaka 172 C 3
Popondetta 148-149 N 8
Popovo 122-123 M 4
Poppenbüttel, Hamburg- 130 I b 1
Poprad [CS, place] 118 K 4
Poprad [CS, river] 118 K 4
Pōpsŏngp'o 144-145 F 5
Poptun 86-87 Q 9
Porādāha 138-139 M 6
Porāli 134-135 K 5
Porangatu 92-93 K 7
Porbandar 134-135 K 6
Porbunder = Porbandar
134-135 K 6
Porce, Río — 94-95 D 4
Porcher Island 60 B 3
Porchov 124-125 G 5
Porciúncula 102-103 LM 4
Porco 104-105 D 6
Porcos, Ilha dos — 102-103 K 5
Porcos, Rio dos — 100-101 B 7
Porcupine, AK 58-59 T 7
Porcupine Creek 68-69 C 1
Porcupine Creek, AK 58-59 M 3
Porcupine Hills 60 K 4-5
Porcupine Mountain 56-57 Q 7
Porcupine Plain 61 G 4
Porcupine River 56-57 H 4
Pordenone 122-123 E 2-3
Pore 92-93 E 3
Porecatu 102-103 G 5
Porečje [SU, Belorusskaja SSR]
124-125 E 7
Porez 124-125 S 5
Pórfido, Punta — 108-109 G 3
Pori 116-117 J 7
Porirua 161 F 5
Porjus 116-117 HJ 4
Porlamar 92-93 G 2
Pornic 120-121 F 5
Poroma [BOL, Chuquisaca]
104-105 D 6
Poroma [BOL, La Paz] 104-105 C 4
Poronajsk 132-133 b 8
Porong, Stung — 150-151 E 6
Porongo, Cerro — 106-107 D 3
Porongos 106-107 L 2
Porongos, Laguna de los —
106-107 F 2-3
Poroshiri-dake 144-145 c 2
Porosozero 124-125 J 2
Porotos, Punta — 106-107 B 2
Porpoise Bay 53 C 13
Porquis Junction 62 L 2
Porsangerfjord 116-117 LM 2
Porsangerhalvøya 116-117 L 2
Porsea 150-151 B 11
Porsgrunn 116-117 CD 8
Porsuk çayı 136-137 D 3
Portachuelo 92-93 G 8
Portadown 119 C 4
Portage, AK 58-59 N 6
Portage, UT 66-67 G 5
Portage, WI 70-71 F 4
Portage-la-Prairie 56-57 R 8
Portage Park, Chicago-, IL 83 II b 1
Portal, ND 68-69 E 1
Port Alberni 56-57 LM 8
Port Albert [AUS] 160 H 7
Port Albert [CDN] 72-73 EF 3
Portalegre 120-121 D 9
Portales, NM 64-65 F 5
Port Alexander, AK 58-59 v 8
Port Alfred 172 E 8
Port Alice 60 D 4
Port Allegany, PA 72-73 GH 4
Port Allen, LA 78-79 D 5
Port Angeles, WA 66-67 B 1
Port Antonio 64-65 L 8
Port Armstrong, AK 58-59 v 8
Port Arthur 160 cd 3
Port Arthur, TX 64-65 H 6
Port Arthur = Lüda-Lüshun
142-143 MN 4
Port Ashton, AK 58-59 N 6
Port Augusta 158-159 G 6
Port au Port 63 G 3
Port au Port Bay 63 G 3
Port au Port Peninsula 63 G 3
Port-au-Prince 64-65 M 8
Port Austin, MI 72-73 E 2
Port-Bergé 172 J 5
Port Blair 134-135 P 8
Port Blandford 63 J 3
Port Borden 63 E 4
Port-Bou 120-121 J 7
Port-Bouet 168-169 DE 4
Port Brega = Marsá al-Burayqah
164-165 H 2
Port Burwell [CDN, Ontario]
72-73 F 3
Port Burwell [CDN, Quebec]
56-57 XY 5
Port Canning 138-139 M 6
Port Cartier 56-57 X 7
Port-Cartier-Sept-Îles, Parc provincial
de — 63 C 2
Port Chalmers 158-159 O 9
Port Chilkoot 58-59 U 7
Port Clarence 58-59 D 4
Port Clements 60 AB 3
Port Clinton, OH 72-73 E 4
Port Colborne 72-73 G 3
Port Coquitlam 66-67 B 1
Port Curtis 158-159 K 4
Port Daniel 63 D 3
Port Darwin 111 E 8
Port Davey 158-159 HJ 8
Port de Ilheo Bay = Sandvisbai
174-175 A 2
Port de Kinshasa 170 IV a 1
Port-de-Paix 88-89 K 5
Port Dickson 150-151 C 11
Port Dunford = Buur Gaabo
172 H 2
Port Eads, LA 78-79 E 6
Porte d'Annam = Đeo Ngang
150-151 F 3-4
Porte des Morts 70-71 G 3
Port Edward [CDN] 60 B 2
Port Edward [ZA] 174-175 J 6
Porteira, Serra das — 100-101 F 5
Porteirinha 102-103 L 1
Portel [BR] 92-93 J 5
Portela 102-103 M 4
Port Elgin [CDN, New Brunswick]
63 DE 4-5
Port Elgin [CDN, Ontario] 72-73 F 2
Port Elizabeth 172 E 8
Porteña 106-107 FG 3
Porteño, Río — 104-105 G 9
Porterdale, GA 80-81 DE 4
Port Erin 119 D 4
Porterville 172 CD 8
Porterville, CA 74-75 D 4-5
Portes de l'Enfer 172 E 3
Port Essington 56-57 KL 7
Portete, Bahía de — 94-95 EF 1
Port-Étienne = Nawādhību
164-165 A 4
Portezuelo 106-107 B 1-2
Portezuelo Ascotán 104-105 BC 7
Portezuelo de Huaitiquina
104-105 C 8
Portezuelo de Socompa 104-105 B 9
Portezuelo Quilhuiri 104-105 B 6
Port Fairy 158-159 H 7
Port-Francqui = Ilebo 172 D 2
Port Fu'ad = Būr Sādāt 173 C 2
Port-Gentil 172 A 2
Port Gibson, MS 78-79 D 5
Port Graham, AK 58-59 M 7
Port-Gueydon = Azfūn 166-167 J 1
Port Harcourt 164-165 F 8
Port Hardy 56-57 L 7
Port Harrison = Inoucdjouac
56-57 V 6
Port Hawkesbury 63 F 5
Port Hedland 158-159 C 4
Port Heiden 58-59 d 1
Port Heiden, AK 58-59 de 1
Port Henry, NY 72-73 K 2-3
Port Herald = Nsanje 172 G 5
Porthill, ID 66-67 E 1
Port Hood 63 F 4
Port Hope 72-73 G 2-3
Port Hope, MI 72-73 E 3
Port Houston Turning, Houston-, TX
85 III b 1
Port Hudson, LA 78-79 D 5
Port Hueneme, CA 74-75 D 5
Port Huron, MI 64-65 K 3
Portile de Fier 122-123 K 3
Port Il'ič 126-127 O 7
Portillo 106-107 B 4
Portillo, Cordón de — 106-107 C 4
Portillo, Paso del — 106-107 BC 3
Portillo de los Patos 104-105 B 10
Portillo del Planchon 106-107 B 5
Portillo Puyehue 108-109 CD 3
Portimão 120-121 C 10
Port Isabel, TX 76-77 F 9
Port Jackson [AUS] 161 I b 2
Port Jackson [NZ] 161 F 3
Port Jefferson, NY 72-73 K 4
Port Jervis, NY 72-73 J 4
Port Keats 158-159 EF 2
Port Kembla, Wollongong-
158-159 K 6
Port Kennedy, PA 84 III a 1
Port Kenny 158-159 F 6
Port Klang 150-151 C 11
Port Lairge = Waterford 119 C 5
Portland, IN 70-71 H 5
Portland, ME 64-65 MN 3
Portland, MI 70-71 H 4
Portland, OR 64-65 B 2
Portland, TN 78-79 F 2
Portland, TX 76-77 F 9
Portland [AUS, New South Wales]
160 JK 4
Portland [AUS, Victoria] 158-159 H 7
Portland [CDN] 72-73 HJ 2
Portland = Dyrhólaey 116-117 d 3
Portland, Cape — 160 c 2
Portland Canal 58-59 x 9
Portland Inlet 58-59 xy 9
Portland Island 161 H 4
Portland Point 88-89 H 6
Portland Promontory 56-57 UV 6
Port Laoise 119 C 5
Port Lavaca, TX 76-77 F 8
Port Lincoln 158-159 FG 6
Port Lions, AK 58-59 KL 8
Port Loko 164-165 B 7
Port Louis [MS] 204-205 N 11
Port-Lyautey = Al-Q'nitrah
164-165 C 2
Port Mac Donell 160 DE 7
Port MacNeill 60 D 4
Port Macquarie 160 L 3
Port Maitland 63 C 5-6
Port Maria 88-89 H 5
Port Mayaca, FL 80-81 c 3
Port Melbourne, Melbourne-
161 II b 1-2
Port-Menier 63 D 3
Port Moller 58-59 c 1-2
Port Moller, AK 58-59 cd 1
Port Moody 66-67 B 1
Port Moresby 148-149 N 8
Port Mouton 63 D 6
Port Musgrave 158-159 H 2
Port Natal = Durban 172 F 7
Port Neches, TX 78-79 C 6
Port Neill 160 C 5
Port Nellie Juan, AK 58-59 NO 6
Port Nelson [BS] 88-89 J 3
Port Nelson [CDN, bay] 56-57 S 6
Port Nelson [CDN, place] 56-57 S 6
Portneuf, Rivière — 63 AB 3
Port Neville 60 DE 4
Port Nolloth 172 C 7
Port Norris, NJ 72-73 J 5
Porto [BR] 100-101 C 2
Porto [P] 120-121 C 8
Porto Acre 92-93 F 6
Porto Alegre [BR, Bahia]
100-101 D 7
Porto Alegre [BR, Pará] 98-99 M 7
Porto Alegre [BR, Rio Grande do Sul]
111 FG 4
Porto Alegre do Sul 102-103 F 4
Porto Alexandre 172 B 5
Porto Alexandre, Parque Nacional de
— 172 B 5
Porto Amazonas 102-103 GH 6
Porto Amboim 172 B 4
Porto Amélia = Pemba 172 H 4
Porto Artur 92-93 HJ 7
Porto Barra do Ivinheima
102-103 EF 5
Porto Belo [BR] 102-103 H 7
Portobelo [PA] 64-65 b 1
Porto Bicentenário 98-99 G 10
Port O'Brien, AK 58-59 KL 8
Porto Britânia 102-103 EF 6
Porto Calvo 100-101 G 6
Porto Camargo 102-103 F 5
Porto Caneco 92-93 HJ 7
Porto Conceição 92-93 H 8
Porto da Fôlha 100-101 F 5-6
Porto das Caixas 102-103 L 5
Porto de Más 92-93 H 8
Porto de Mós [BR] 92-93 J 5
Porto 15 de Novembro 102-103 F 4
Porto do Faval 100-101 B 1
Porto do Lontra 98-99 M 7
Porto dos Gaúchos 98-99 K 10
Porto Empédocle 122-123 E 7
Porto Esperança 104-105 F 3
Porto-Farina = Ghar al-Milḥ
166-167 M 1
Porto Feliz 102-103 J 5
Portoferráio 122-123 CD 4
Porto Ferreira 102-103 J 4
Porto Franco 92-93 K 6
Port of Spain 64-65 O 9
Porto Grande 98-99 N 4
Portogruaro 122-123 E 3
Porto Guareí 102-103 F 5
Port Okha = Okha 134-135 K 6
Portola, CA 74-75 C 3
Porto Lucena 106-107 K 1
Pörtom 116-117 J 6
Porto Mau 98-99 E 7
Porto Mendes 111 F 2
Porto Murtinho 102-103 D 4
Portonaccio, Roma- 113 II b 2
Porto Nacional 92-93 K 7
Porto Novo [DY] 164-165 E 7
Porto Novo [IND] 140 DE 5
Porto Novo Creek 170 III b 2
Porto Poet 98-99 F 4
Port Orchard, WA 66-67 B 2
Porto Real do Colégio 92-93 M 6-7
Port Orford, OR 66-67 A 4
Porto Rico 98-99 B 8
Porto Rubim 98-99 C 9
Porto Saide 96-97 E 6
Porto Santana 92-93 J 5
Porto Santo 164-165 AB 2
Porto São José 111 F 2

344 Pobedino

Porto Seguro 92-93 M 8
Porto Seguro, Cachoeira — 98-99 MN 8
Porto Tolle 122-123 E 3
Porto Tôrres 122-123 C 5
Porto União 111 F 3
Porto-Vecchio 122-123 C 5
Porto Velho 92-93 G 6
Porto Veloso 100-101 A 4
Portoviejo 92-93 C 5
Porto Villazón 104-105 F 3
Porto Walter 92-93 E 6
Portpatrik 119 D 4
Port Phillip Bay 158-159 H 7
Port Pirie 158-159 G 6
Port Radium 56-57 NO 4
Port Reading, NJ 82 III a 3
Port Renfrew 66-67 AB 1
Portrerillos 106-107 C 4
Port Rexton 63 K 3
Port Richmond, New York- , NY 82 III b 3
Port Rowan 72-73 F 3
Port Royal — Annapolis Royal 56-57 XY 9
Port Royal Sound 80-81 F 4
Port Safâga — Safâjah 164-165 L 3
Port Safety, AK 58-59 E 4
Port Said — Bûr Sa'îd 164-165 L 2
Port Saint Joe, FL 78-79 G 6
Port Saunders 63 H 2
Port-Say — Marsâ-Ban-Mahîdî 166-167 EF 2
Port Shelter 155 I b 1
Port Shepstone 172 F 8
Port Simpson 60 BC 2
Portsmouth, NH 64-65 MN 3
Portsmouth, OH 64-65 K 4
Portsmouth, VA 64-65 L 4
Portsmouth [GB] 119 F 6
Portsmouth [West Indies] 88-89 PQ 7
Port Stanley 72-73 F 3
Port Stanley — Stanley 111 E 8
Port Stephens 108-109 J 9
Port Sudân — Bûr Sûdân 164-165 M 5
Port Sulphur, LA 78-79 E 6
Port Swettenham — Port Klang 150-151 C 11
Port Talbot 119 DE 6
Port Tewfik — Bûr Tawfîq 173 C 3
Porttipahdan tekojärvi 116-117 LM 3-4
Port Townsend, WA 66-67 B 1
Portugal 120-121 C 10-D 8
Portugalete 120-121 F 7
Portugália — Luachimo 172 D 3
Portugues, El — 92-93 D 6
Portuguesa 94-95 G 3
Portuguesa, Río — 92-93 F 3
Port Union 63 K 3
Port-Vendres 120-121 J 7
Port Victoria [AUS] 160 C 5
Port Victoria [EUA] 172 F 1-2
Port Wakefield 160 CD 5
Port Washington, NY 82 III d 2
Port Washington, WI 70-71 G 4
Port Weld 148-149 CD 6
Port Wells 58-59 NO 6
Port Wing, WI 70-71 E 2
Porushottampur 138-139 K 8
Porvenir [RA] 106-107 FG 5
Porvenir [RCH] 108-109 DE 9
Porvenir [ROU] 106-107 HJ 4
Porvenir, El — [CO] 94-95 G 6
Porvenir, El — [MEX] 76-77 AB 7
Porvoo — Borgå 116-117 LM 7
Posadas [RA] 111 E 3
Posad-Pokrovskoje 126-127 F 3
Pošechonje-Volodarsk 124-125 MN 4
Posen, MI 70-71 J 3
Posesión, Bahía — 108-109 E 9
Poshan — Boshan 142-143 M 4
Posio 116-117 N 4
Posjet 132-133 Z 9
Poso 148-149 H 7
Poso, Danau — 152-153 O 6
Poso, Teluk — 152-153 O 6
Posof — Duğur 136-137 K 2
Posŏng 142-143 O 5
Posse 92-93 K 7
Possession Island — Possessions Eiland 174-175 A 4
Possessions Eiland 174-175 A 4
Possum Kingdom Reservoir 76-77 H 4
Post, OR 66-67 C 3
Post, TX 76-77 D 6
Posta, La — 106-107 F 3
Posta de San Martín 106-107 GH 4
Posta Lencinas 104-105 F 9
Postavy 124-125 F 6
Post Falls, ID 66-67 E 2
Postmasburg 172 D 7
Posto Fiscal Rolim de Moura 104-105 EF 3
Pôsto Indigena 98-99 H 5
Postojna 122-123 F 3
Poston, AZ 74-75 F 5
Postrervalle 104-105 E 6
Postville, IA 70-71 E 4
Poswol — Pasvalys 124-125 E 5
Poțângī — Pottangi 140 F 1
Potawatomi Indian Reservation 70-71 BC 6
Potchefstroom 172 E 7
Potčurk, gora — 124-125 T 2
Poté 102-103 M 2
Poteau, OK 76-77 G 5
Poteet, TX 76-77 E 8
Potenza 122-123 F 5
Potfontein 174-175 F 6
Potgietersrus 172 E 6

Pothea — Kálymnos 122-123 M 7
Potholes Reservoir 66-67 D 2
Poti [BR] 100-101 D 3
Poti [SU] 126-127 K 5
Poti, Rio — 100-101 CD 3
Potiraguá 100-101 E 8
Potiskum 164-165 G 6
Potlatch, ID 66-67 E 2
Potloer 174-175 D 6
Pot Mountain 66-67 F 2
Poto 152-153 O 10
Po To Au 155 I b 2
Po Toi Group 155 I b 2
Po Toi Island 155 I b 2
Potomac River 72-73 H 5
Potomac River, South Branch — 72-73 G 5
Potong Pasir, Singapore- 154 III b 1
Poto Poto, Brazzaville- 170 IV a 1
Potosí, MO 70-71 E 7
Potosí [BOL, administrative unit] 104-105 CD 7
Potosí [BOL, place] 92-93 F 8
Potosí [CO] 94-95 C 7
Potosí, El — 86-87 K 5
Potossí, El — 86-87 K 5
Potrerillos, Paso de — 106-107 BC 2
Potrerillos [Honduras] 86-87 R 10
Potrerillos [RCH] 111 C 3
Potrero, El — 76-77 B 8
Potrero, San Francisco-, CA 83 I b 2
Potsdam 118 F 2
Potsdam, NY 72-73 J 2
Potsdam-Bornim 130 III a 2
Potsdam-Bornstedt 130 III a 2
Potsdam-Cecilienhöhe 130 III a 2
Potsdam-Drewitz 130 III a 2
Potsdam-Nedlitz 130 III a 2
Pottangi 140 F 1
Pottˌoki 138-139 D 2
Potts Camps, MS 78-79 E 3
Potts Hill Reservoirs 161 I a 2
Pottstown, PA 72-73 J 4
Pottsville, PA 72-73 H 4
Pottuvil — Potuvil 134-135 N 7
Potuvil 134-135 N 7
Potzu 146-147 H 10
Pouce Coupe 60 GH 2
Poughkeepsie, NY 64-65 LM 3
Poulin de Courval, Lac — 63 AB 3
Poulo Condore — Côn Son 150-151 F 8
Poulo Gambir — Cu Lao Poulo Gambir 150-151 GH 6
Poulo Gambir, Cu Lao — 150-151 GH 6
Pou Luong 150-151 E 2
Poûn 144-145 F 4
Poung, Ban — 150-151 E 4
Poupan 174-175 EF 6
Pourtalè 106-107 G 6
Pouso 98-99 H 11
Pouso Alegre [BR, Mato Grosso] 92-93 H 7
Pouso Alegre [BR, Minas Gerais] 92-93 K 9
Poutè 168-169 B 2
Poutrincourt, Lac — 62 O 2
Povenec 124-125 K 2
Poveneckij zaliv 124-125 K 2
Pôvoa de Varzim 120-121 C 8
Povo Novo 106-107 L 3
Povorino 126-127 L 1
Povraz adasi — Alibey adasi 136-137 B 3
Povungnituk 56-57 V 6
Powassan 72-73 G 1
Powder River, WY 68-69 C 4
Powder River [USA, Montana] 64-65 E 2
Powder River [USA, Oregon] 66-67 E 3
Powder River, North Fork — 68-69 C 4
Powder River, South Fork — 68-69 C 4
Powder River Pass 68-69 C 3
Powderville, MT 68-69 D 3
Powell, WY 68-69 B 3
Powell Lake — 64-65 D 4
Powell Butte, OR 66-67 C 3
Powell Creek 158-159 FG 3
Powell Islands — South Orkneys 53 C 32
Powell River 56-57 M 8
Power, MT 66-67 H 2
Powers, MI 70-71 G 3
Powers, OR 66-67 AB 4
Powers Lake, ND 68-69 E 1
Powhatan, LA 78-79 C 5
Poxoréu 92-93 J 8
Poyang — Boyang 146-147 F 7
Poyang Hu 142-143 M 6
Poygan, Lake — 70-71 F 3
Poyraz 154 I b 1
Poyraz burnu 154 I b 1
Pozama 104-105 G 6
Pozantí 136-137 F 4
Požarevac 122-123 J 3
Poza Rica 64-65 G 7
Požeg 124-125 U 3
Poženkova 124-125 G 5
Poznań 118 H 2
Pozo, El — 86-87 F 2
Pozo Almonte 111 C 2
Pozo Anta 102-103 B 5
Pozoblanco 120-121 E 9
Pozo Borrado 106-107 G 2
Pozo Cercado 104-105 E 8
Pozo Colorado 102-103 D 6
Pozo del Molle 106-107 F 4
Pozo del Tigre 104-105 F 9
Pozo Dulce 106-107 F 2

Pozo Hondo [RA] 111 D 3
Pozos, Los — 106-107 E 3
Pozos, Punta — 108-109 G 6
Pozos Colorados 94-95 DE 2
Pozuelos 94-95 J 2
Pozuelos, Lago — 104-105 CD 8
Pozuzo 96-97 D 7
Požva 124-125 UV 4
Pozzallo 122-123 F 7
Pozzuoli 122-123 EF 5
Pra [WG] 164-165 D 7
Prabat Chean Chum 150-151 E 7
Praça Duque de Caxias 110 I bc 2
Praça Seca, Rio de Janeiro- 110 I a 2
Pracham Hiang, Laem — 150-151 B 7
Prachantakham 150-151 CD 5
Prachin Buri 150-151 C 5
Prachuap Khiri Khan 148-149 CD 4
Pradêd 118 H 3
Pradera 94-95 CD 6
Prades 120-121 J 7
Prades, Sierra de los — 106-107 HJ 6-7
Prades Thai — Muang Thai 148-149 CD 6
Prado [BR] 92-93 M 8
Prado [CO] 94-95 D 6
Prado, Bogotá-El — 91 III c 2
Prado, Museo del — 113 III a 2
Pradera, NE 68-69 H 5
Prague, OK 76-77 F 5
Prague — Praha 118 G 3
Praha 118 G 3
Prahran, Melbourne- 161 II bc 2
Praia 204-205 E 7
Praia da Juréia 102-103 J 6
Praia de Copacabana 110 I bc 2
Praia de Leste 102-103 H 6
Praia Grande 102-103 H 6
Praia Grande, Enseada da — 110 I c 2
Praião, Cachoeira do — 92-93 K 8
Praia Redonda 102-103 H 8
Prainha [BR, Amazonas] 92-93 G 6
Prainha [BR, Pará] 92-93 J 5
Prairie, ID 66-67 F 4
Prairie, La — 82 I bc 2
Prairie City, OR 66-67 D 3
Prairie Dog Creek 68-69 F 6
Prairie Dog Town Fork 76-77 DE 5
Prairie du Chien, WI 70-71 E 4
Prairie River 61 G 4
Prairies 56-57 Q 7-R 9
Prairies, Rivière des — 82 I ab 1
Prakhon Chai 150-151 D 5
Pran Buri 148-149 CD 4
Prangli 124-125 E 4
Prânhita 134-135 MN 7
Prânţij — Parântij 138-139 D 6
Prapat 150-151 B 11
Prasat 150-151 D 5
Praskoveja 126-127 M 4
Prasonnísi, Akrôtérion — 122-123 MN 8
Prat, Isla — 108-109 B 7
Prata [BR, Goiás] 100-101 A 6
Prata [BR, Minas Gerais] 102-103 H 3
Prata [BR, Pará] 92-93 K 5
Prata, Riacho de — 100-101 C 4
Prata, Rio — 98-99 P 9
Prata, Rio da — [BR ◁ Rio Paracatu] 102-103 J 2
Prata, Rio da — [BR ◁ Rio Paranaíba] 102-103 H 3
Pratâbgarh — Partâpgarh 138-139 E 5
Prata do Piauí 100-101 CD 3
Pratapgarh 138-139 H 5
Pratápolis 102-103 J 4
Pratas — Dongsha Qundao 142-143 LM 7
Prater 113 I b 2
Pratinha 102-103 J 3
Prato 122-123 D 4
Pratt 61 J 6
Pratt, KS 68-69 G 7
Prattville, AL 78-79 F 4
Pratudinho, Rio — 100-101 B 8
Pravara 138-139 E 8
Pravdinsk [SU, Volga] 124-125 O 5
Prawle, Point — 119 E 6
Praya 152-153 M 10
Pra'za 124-125 JK 3
Preah Vihear 150-151 E 5-6
Prêbeza 122-123 J 6
Prêvost-Paradol — Mashra'a Aşfâ 166-167 G 2
Precordillera 111 C 3-4
Predivinsk 132-133 R 6
Preeceville 61 G 4-5
Pregol'a 118 K 1
Pregonero 94-95 F 3
Pregradnaja 126-127 K 5
Preili 124-125 F 5
Preissac, Lac — 62 M 2
Prêk Chbar 150-151 F 6
Prêk Chhlong 150-151 F 6
Prêk Kak 150-151 E 6
Prêk Phnou 150-151 E 7
Prêk Sandek 150-151 E 7
Prêk Té 150-151 F 6
Prelate 61 D 5
Premier 58-59 y 8
Premier Mine 174-175 H 3
Premio 63 D 7
Premont, TX 76-77 EF 9
Premuda 122-123 F 3
Prentice, WI 70-71 EF 3
Prentiss, MS 78-79 E 5
Prenzlau 118 FG 2
Prenzlauer Berg, Berlin- 130 III b 1

Přerov 118 H 4
Presa Alvaro Obregón 86-87 F 4
Presa de Gatún 64-65 ab 2
Presa de la Amistad 86-87 JK 3
Presa de la Angostura 86-87 O 9-10
Presa de las Adjuntas 86-87 LM 6
Presa del Infiernillo 86-87 JK 8
Presa de Mixcoac 91 I b 2
Presa La Boquilla 86-87 GH 4
Presa Las Julianas 91 I b 2
Presa Las Jazmines 91 I b 2
Presa Lazaro Cardenas 86-87 H 5
Presa Macagua 94-95 K 3
Presa Macúzari 86-87 F 4
Presa M. Hidalgo 86-87 F 4
Presa Miguel Alemán 86-87 M 8
Presa M. R. Gomez 86-87 L 4
Presa Netzahualcóyotl 86-87 O 9
Presa Presidente Aleman 86-87 M 8
Presa Tarango 91 I b 2
Presa V. Carranza 86-87 KL 4
Prescott 72-73 J 2
Prescott, AR 78-79 C 4
Prescott, AZ 64-65 D 5
Prescott, WI 70-71 D 3
Presedio of San Francisco 83 I b 2
Presho, SD 68-69 FG 4
Présidence, Kinshasa- 170 IV a 1
Presidencia de la Plaza 104-105 G 10
Presidencia Roca 104-105 G 10
Presidencia Roque Sâenz Peña 111 D 3
Presidente Aleman, Presa — 86-87 M 8
Presidente Alves 102-103 GH 5
Presidente Bernardes 102-103 G 4-5
Presidente Costa e Silva, Ponte — 110 I bc 2
Presidente Dutra 92-93 L 6
Presidente Epitácio 92-93 J 9
Presidente Hayes 102-103 CD 5
Presidente Hermes 92-93 G 7
Presidente Murtinho 102-103 F 1
Presidente Nicolás Avellaneda, Parque — 110 III b 1
Presidente Olegário 102-103 J 3
Presidente Prudente 92-93 J 9
Presidente Rios, Lago — 108-109 B 6
Presidente Venceslau 102-103 FG 4
Presidio, TX 64-65 F 6
Presidof 122-123 J 5
Prešov 118 K 4
Prespa Lake — Prespansko jezero 122-123 J 5
Prespansko Ezero 122-123 J 5
Presque Isle, ME 64-65 N 2
Presque Isle Point 70-71 G 2
Press Lake 62 D 2
Prestea 164-165 D 7
Presto, El — 104-105 F 4
Preston, CA 74-75 B 3
Preston, ID 66-67 H 4
Preston, MN 70-71 DE 4
Preston, MO 70-71 D 7
Preston [AUS] 158-159 C 4
Preston [GB] 119 E 5
Preston, Melbourne- 161 II bc 1
Prestonburg, KY 80-81 E 2
Prestwick 119 DE 4
Preto, Rio — [BR ◁ Rio Grande] 92-93 K 7
Preto, Rio — [BR ◁ Rio Madeira] 98-99 G 9
Preto, Rio — [BR ◁ Rio Munim] 100-101 C 2
Preto, Rio — [BR ◁ Rio Negro] 98-99 F 4
Preto, Rio — [BR ◁ Rio Paracatu] 92-93 K 8
Preto, Rio — [BR ◁ Rio Paraíba] 102-103 L 5
Preto, Rio — [BR ◁ Rio Paranaíba] 102-103 G 3
Preto do Igapó-Açu, Rio — 98-99 H 7
Pretoria 172 E 7
Pretoriuskop 174-175 J 3
Pretos Forros, Serra dos — 110 I b 2
Pretty Prairie, KS 68-69 GH 7
Preungesheim, Frankfurt am Main- 128 III b 1
Preveza — Prêbeza 122-123 J 6
Préville 82 I c 2
Prey Lovea 150-151 E 7
Prey Nop 150-151 D 7
Prey Veng 148-149 E 4
Priargunsk 132-133 WX 7
Pribilof Islands 52 D 35-36
Příbram 118 G 4
Pribrežnyj chrebet 132-133 Za 6
Price 63 B 3
Price, UT 64-65 D 4
Price Island 60 C 3
Price River 64-65 D 4
Pricetown, LA 85 I a 2
Prichard, AL 64-65 J 5
Prichard, ID 66-67 EF 2
Prič`ornomorskaja nizmennost` 126-127 E-G 3
Pridneprovskaja nizmennost` 126-127 E-G 1-2
Pridneprovskaja vozvyšennost` 126-127 D-G 2
Priego de Córdoba 120-121 E 10
Priekulė 124-125 C 6
Prienai 124-125 DE 6
Prieska 172 D 7
Priest Lake 66-67 E 1

Priest Rapids Reservoir 66-67 CD 2
Priest River, ID 66-67 E 1
Prijedor 122-123 G 3
Prijutnoje 126-127 L 3
Prijutovo 124-125 T 7
Prikaspijskaja nizmennost 126-127 M 4-Q 2
Prikolotnoje 126-127 H 1
Prikubanskaja nizmennost 126-127 J 4
Prikumsk 126-127 LM 4
Prilep 122-123 J 5
Priluki [SU, Ukrainskaja SSR] 126-127 F 1
Prima Porta, Roma- 113 II b 1
Primavalle, Roma- 113 II ab 1
Primavera, La — 106-107 D 6
Primeira Cachoeira 98-99 J 5
Primeira Cruz 100-101 C 2
Primeiro de Maio 102-103 G 5
Primghar, IA 70-71 C 4
Primor 104-105 D 7
Primorsk [SU, Azerbajdžanskaja SSR] 126-127 O 6
Primorsk [SU, Rossijskaja SFSR] 124-125 G 3
Primorskij chrebet 132-133 TU 7
Primorsko-Achtarsk 126-127 HJ 3
Primorskoje [SU, Rossijskaja SFSR] 124-125 FG 3
Primorskoje [SU, Ukrainskaja SSR] 126-127 H 3
Primos, PA 84 III b 2
Primrose 170 V bc 2
Primrose Lake 61 D 3
Primrose River 58-59 U 6
Prince Albert 56-57 P 7
Prince Albert Mountains 53 B 16-17
Prince Albert National Park 56-57 P 7
Prince Albert Peninsula 56-57 NO 3
Prince Albert Road — Prins Albertweg 174-175 D 7
Prince Albert Sound 56-57 NO 3
Prince Alfred, Cape — 56-57 KL 3
Prince Alfred's Hamlet — Prins Alfred Hamlet 174-175 CD 7
Prince Charles Island 56-57 V 4
Prince Charles Range 53 B 7
Prince Edward Bay 72-73 H 2-3
Prince Edward Island 56-57 Y 8
Prince Edward Islands 53 E 4
Prince Edward Peninsula 72-73 H 2-3
Prince Frederick, MD 72-73 H 5
Prince George 56-57 M 7
Prince Gustav Adolf Sea 56-57 P 2
Prince Island — Pulau Panaitan 148-149 DE 8
Prince of Wales, Cape — 56-57 C 4-5
Prince of Wales Island [AUS] 158-159 H 2
Prince of Wales Island [CDN] 56-57 QR 3
Prince of Wales Island [USA] 56-57 JK 6
Prince of Wales Island — Pulau Pinang 150-151 BC 10
Prince of Wales Island — Wales Island 56-57 T 4
Prince of Wales Strait 56-57 N 3
Prince Patrick Island 56-57 M 2
Princes Island — Payinzet Kyûn 150-151 AB 6
Prince Regent Inlet 56-57 ST 3
Prince Regent Luitpold Land — Prinzregent-Luitpold-Land 53 B 33-34
Prince Rupert 56-57 KL 7
Princesa Isabel 100-101 F 4
Princes Bay, New York-, NY 82 III a 3
Princess Anne, MD 72-73 J 3
Princess Astrid Land — Princesse Astrid land 53 B 1-2
Princess Charlotte Bay 158-159 H 2
Princess Elizabeth Land 53 BC 8-9
Princess Royal Island 56-57 L 7
Princeton 66-67 C 1
Princeton, CA 74-75 BC 3
Princeton, IA 70-71 D 5
Princeton, IL 70-71 F 5
Princeton, IN 70-71 G 6
Princeton, KY 78-79 F 2
Princeton, MI 70-71 G 3
Princeton, MN 70-71 D 3
Princeton, NJ 72-73 J 4
Princeton, WI 70-71 F 4
Princeton, WV 80-81 F 2
Prince William Sound 56-57 G 5
Príncipe, Ilha do — 164-165 F 8
Príncipe da Beira 92-93 G 7
Prineville, OR 66-67 C 3
Pringle, SD 68-69 E 4
Pringle, Punta — 108-109 Ab 6
Prins Albert 174-175 E 7
Prins Albertweg 174-175 D 7
Prins Alfred Hamlet 174-175 CD 7
Prins Christian Sund 56-57 c 5-d 6
Prinsep Island — Payinzet Kyûn 150-151 AB 6
Prinsesse Astrid land 53 B 1-2
Prinsesse Ragnhild land 53 B 3
Prins Harald land 53 B 4-C 5
Prinzapolca [NIC, place] 88-89 E 8
Prinzapolca [NIC, river] 88-89 D 8
Prinzregent-Luitpold-Land 53 B 33-34
Priokskij 124-125 M 6
Prior, Cabo — 120-121 C 7
Priozernaja — Prioz`ersk 132-133 DE 6
Prioz`ersk 132-133 DE 6

Prip`at 124-125 G 8
Pripet — Prip`at 124-125 G 8
Pripoľarnyj Ural 132-133 KL 4-5
Prišib 126-127 O 7
Prišib — Leninsk 126-127 M 2
Pristen' 126-127 H 1
Priština 122-123 J 4
Pritchett, CO 68-69 E 7
Privas 120-121 K 6
Priverno 122-123 E 5
Privetnoje 126-127 G 4
Prividencia, Isla de — 92-93 C 2
Privodino 124-125 PQ 3
Privoľnoje 126-127 EF 3
Privolže 124-125 Q 7
Privolžsk 124-125 N 5
Privolžskaja vozvyšennost 124-125 P 8-Q 6
Privolžskij 126-127 NO 3
Privolžskoje 126-127 MN 1
Prizren 122-123 J 4
Probolinggo 148-149 F 8
Prochladnyj 126-127 LM 5
Procter 60 J 5
Proctor, TX 76-77 E 6-7
Proctor Creek 85 II b 2
Proddattûru — Proddatûr 134-135 M 8
Proddatûr 134-135 M 8
Professor Dr. Ir. W. J. van Blommesteinmeer 92-93 H 4
Progreso [MEX, Coahuila] 76-77 D 9
Progreso [MEX, Yucatán] 64-65 J 7
Progreso [RA] 111 D 4
Progreso, El — [GCA] 86-87 P 10
Progreso, El — [Honduras] 64-65 J 8
Progreso, El — [PE] 96-97 E 9
Progresso 106-107 L 2
Progresso, Madrid- 113 III ab 2
Prokopjevsk 132-133 Q 7
Prokopjevsk — Prokopjevsk 132-133 Q 7
Prokuplje 122-123 J 4
Proletarij 124-125 H 4
Proletarsk 126-127 KL 3
Proletarskij [SU, Belgorodskaja Oblast'] 126-127 GH 1
Proletarskij [SU, Moskovskaja Oblast'] 124-125 L 6
proliv de Long 132-133 j 3-4
proliv de Vries 142-143 S 2
proliv Dmitrija Lapteva 132-133 a-c 3
proliv Eterikan 132-133 ab 3
proliv Jugorskij Šar 132-133 L 4-M 3
proliv Karskije Vorota 132-133 J-L 3
proliv Krasnoj Armii 132-133 ST 1
proliv La Pérouse 142-143 S 2
proliv Matočkin Šar 132-133 KL 3
proliv Sannikova 132-133 ab 3
proliv Šokaľskogo 132-133 RS 2
proliv Viľkickogo 132-133 S-U 2
Prome — Pyin 148-149 C 3
Promissão 102-103 H 4
Promissao, Represa de — 102-103 H 4
Promyslovka 144-145 J 1
Pron`a [SU, ◁ Oka] 124-125 N 6
Pron`a [SU, river ◁ Sož] 124-125 H 7
Prončiščeva, bereg — 132-133 UV 2-3
Pronsk 124-125 MN 6
Propriá 92-93 M 7
Propriano 122-123 C 5
Pros`anaja 126-127 H 2
Proserpine 158-159 J 4
Proskurov — Chmeľnickij 126-127 C 2
Prosna 118 J 3
Prospect, OR 66-67 B 4
Prospector 61 H 4
Prospect Park, PA 84 III b 2
Prospect Point 82 III d 1
Prospekt Park 82 III c 3
Prosser, WA 66-67 D 2
Protem 174-175 D 8
Protva 124-125 L 6
Protection, KS 76-77 E 4
Provadija 122-123 M 4
Provence 120-121 K 7-L 6
Providence, KY 70-71 G 7
Providence, RI 64-65 MN 3
Providence, Cape — [NZ] 158-159 MN 9
Providence, Cape — [USA] 58-59 ef 1
Providence Island 172 JK 3
Providence Mountains 74-75 F 5
Providencia 64-65 KL 9
Providencia, Ilha — 94-95 J 8
Providencia, Serra da — 98-99 H 10
Providenciales Island 88-89 K 4
Providenija 132-133 kl 5
Provincetown, MA 72-73 LM 3
Provins 120-121 J 4
Provo, UT 64-65 D 4
Provo, UT 64-65 D 3
Provost 56-57 P 7
Prudentópolis 102-103 G 6
Prudenville, MI 70-71 H 3
Prudhoe Bay [CDN, bay] 58-59 NO 1
Prudhoe Bay [CDN, place] 56-57 G 3
Prudhoe Bay 56-57 XY 2
Prüm 118 C 3
Průnuši 152-153 J 9
Prupuk 152-153 J 9
Prus`a — Bursa 134-135 B 2-3
Pruszków 118 K 2
Prut [SU, place] 126-127 D 3
Prut [SU, river] 126-127 C 3
Pruth 122-123 N 3
Pružany 124-125 E 7

Pryor, OK 76-77 G 4
Pryor Creek 68-69 B 3
Pryor Mountains 68-69 B 3
Przełęcz Dukielska 118 KL 4
Przełęcz Łupkowska 118 L 4
Przemyśl 118 L 4
Prževal'sk 134-135 M 2
Prževal'skoje 124-125 HJ 6
Przeworsk 118 L 3
Przylądek Rozewie 118 J 1
Psará 122-123 L 6
Psérimos 122-123 M 7
Psiol — Ps'ol 126-127 F 2
Pskov 124-125 G 4
Pskovskoje ozero 124-125 FG 4-5
Ps'ol 126-127 F 2
Psychikón 113 IV b 1
Pszczyna 118 J 3-4
Ptič' 124-125 FG 7
Ptolemaïs 122-123 J 5
Ptuj 122-123 FG 2
Pu. Ko — 150-151 B 9
Púa [RCH] 106-107 A 7
Pua [T] 150-151 C 3
Puale Bay 58-59 K 8
Puán 106-107 G 6
Pubei 146-147 B 10
Pu Bia — Phou Bia 150-151 D 3
Pucacuro, Río — 96-97 D 3
Pucallpa 92-93 E 6
Pucapamba 96-97 B 4
Pucara [BOL] 104-105 DE 6
Pucará [PE] 96-97 F 9
Pucará, Río — 96-97 F 9
Pucarani 92-93 F 8
Pucatrihue 108-109 BC 3
Pučež 124-125 O 5
Puchang Hai — Lob nuur 142-143 G 3
Pucheng [TJ, Fujian] 142-143 M 6
Pucheng [TJ, Shaanxi] 142-143 KL 4-5
Pucheng [TJ, Shandong] 146-147 E 4
Puchi — Puqi 142-143 L 6
Pu-chiang — Pujiang 146-147 G 7
Puchuzún 106-107 C 3
Puck 118 J 1
Pucón 108-109 D 2
Pŭdāô 148-149 C 1
Pudasjärvi 116-117 M 5
Pudem 124-125 T 4
Pŭdimadaka 140 F 2
Pudimoe 174-175 F 4
Puding, Cape — Tanjung Puting 148-149 F 7
Pudino 132-133 OP 6
Pudož 132-133 F 5
Pudukkottai 140 D 5
Pudukkôttai — Pattukkottai 140 D 5
Puebla [MEX, administrative unit] 86-87 LM 8
Puebla [MEX, place] 64-65 G 8
Puebla, La — 120-121 J 9
Puebla de Sanabria 120-121 D 7
Puebla de Zaragoza 64-65 G 8
Pueblitos 106-107 GH 5
Pueblo, CO 64-65 F 4
Pueblo Bello 94-95 E 2
Pueblo Bonito, NM 74-75 JK 5
Pueblo Brugo 106-107 GH 3
Pueblo Hundido 111 BC 3
Pueblo Ledesma 104-105 D 8
Pueblo Libertador 106-107 H 4
Pueblo Moscas 106-107 H 4
Pueblonuevo [CO] 94-95 D 3
Pueblo Nuevo [PA] 64-65 b 2-3
Pueblo Nuevo [YV] 92-93 F 2
Pueblo Nuevo, Madrid- 113 III b 2
Pueblo Valley 74-75 HJ 6
Pueblo Viejo [CO] 92-93 F 4
Pueblo Viejo [EC] 96-97 B 2
Puelches 111 C 5
Puelén 106-107 D 6
Puelo, Río — 108-109 C 3
Puente, El — [BOL, Santa Cruz] 104-105 E 5
Puente, La — [BOL, Tarija] 104-105 D 7
Puente Alto 106-107 B 4
Puenteáreas 120-121 CD 7
Puente Batel 106-107 F 2
Puente de Ixtla 86-87 L 8
Puente del Inca 106-107 BC 4
Puente Vallecas, Madrid- 113 III b 2
Puerco, Río — 76-77 A 5
Puerto Alegre [BOL] 92-93 G 7
Puerto Alegre [PY] 102-103 D 5
Puerto Alfonso 92-93 E 5
Puerto Ángel 86-87 MN 10
Puerto Antequera 102-103 D 6
Puerto Argentina 92-93 E 4
Puerto Armuelles 64-65 K 10
Puerto Arrecife 102-103 D 5
Puerto Arturo 94-95 E 6
Puerto Asís 92-93 D 4
Puerto Ayacucho 92-93 F 3
Puerto Bajo Pisagua 108-109 C 6
Puerto Baquerizo 92-93 B 5

Puerto Barrios 64-65 HJ 8
Puerto Barros 96-97 D 2
Puerto Bermejo 104-105 G 10
Puerto Bermúdez 96-97 D 7
Puerto Berrío 92-93 E 3
Puerto Bertrand 108-109 C 6
Puerto Bolognesi 96-97 E 7
Puerto Boyaca 94-95 D 5
Puerto Caballas 92-93 D 7
Puerto Caballo 102-103 C 4
Puerto Cabello 92-93 F 2
Puerto Cabezas 64-65 K 9
Puerto Cahuinari 94-95 F 8
Puerto Capaz = Al-Jabhah 166-167 D 2
Puerto Carlos 94-95 F 8
Puerto Carranza 94-95 bc 2
Puerto Carreño 92-93 F 3
Puerto Casado 111 E 2
Puerto Castilla 88-89 CD 6
Puerto Catay 96-97 F 6
Puerto Ceticayo 96-97 F 7
Puerto Chacabuco 108-109 C 5
Puerto Chicama 92-93 CD 6
Puerto Cisnes 111 B 6-7
Puertocitos 86-87 C 2
Puerto Clemente 96-97 D 7
Puerto Coig 108-109 E 8
Puerto Colombia 94-95 D 2
Puerto Constanza 106-107 H 4
Puerto Cooper 102-103 CD 5
Puerto Cortés [CR] 88-89 DE 10
Puerto Cortés [Honduras] 64-65 J 8
Puerto Cumarebo 92-93 F 2
Puerto Dalmacia 102-103 CD 6
Puerto de Cayo 96-97 A 2
Puerto de Chorrera 64-65 b 3
Puerto de Despeñaperros 120-121 F 9
Puerto de Hierro 94-95 K 2
Puerto de Lobos 74-75 G 7
Puerto del Rosario 164-165 B 3
Puerto de Nutrias 92-93 EF 3
Puerto de Santa Maria, El — 120-121 D 10
Puerto Deseado 111 CD 7
Puerto Eduardo 96-97 D 6
Puerto Elvira 111 E 2
Puerto Escalante 96-97 C 4
Puerto Escondido [CO] 94-95 C 3
Puerto Escondido [MEX] 86-87 LM 10
Puerto Esperidião 92-93 H 8
Puerto Estrella 92-93 E 2
Puerto Ferreira 102-103 D 7
Puerto Fonciere 102-103 D 5
Puerto Francisco de Orellana 96-97 C 2
Puerto Frey 92-93 G 7
Puerto Gaboto = Gaboto 106-107 G 4
Puerto Galileo 102-103 CD 6
Puerto Gisela 106-107 K 1
Puerto Grether 92-93 FG 8
Puerto Guaraní 102-103 CD 4
Puerto Gulach 102-103 B 5
Puerto Harberton 111 C 8
Puerto Heath 92-93 F 7
Puerto Huitoto 94-95 D 7
Puerto Ibáñez 108-109 CD 6
Puerto Iguazú 111 EF 3
Puerto Inca 96-97 D 6
Puerto Inírida = Obando 94-95 H 6
Puerto Inuya 96-97 E 7
Puerto Irigoyen 102-103 AB 5
Puerto Isabel 92-93 H 8
Puerto Izozog 104-105 E 6
Puerto Juárez 64-65 J 7
Puerto La Cruz 92-93 G 2
Puerto La Paz 104-105 E 8
Puerto Leda 102-103 C 4
Puerto Leguízamo 92-93 E 5
Puerto Lempira 88-89 DE 7
Puerto Libertad 86-87 D 3
Puerto Libertador General San Martín = Libertador General San Martín 102-103 E 7
Puerto Libre 94-95 C 4
Puerto Limón [CO, Meta] 94-95 E 6
Puerto Limón [CO, Putumayo] 94-95 C 7
Puertollano 120-121 EF 9
Puerto Lobos [MEX] 86-87 D 2
Puerto Lobos [RA] 111 C 6
Puerto Lopez [CO, Guajira] 94-95 F 2
Puerto López [CO, Meta] 94-95 E 5
Puerto López [EC] 96-97 A 2
Puerto Madero 86-87 O 10
Puerto Madryn 111 C 6
Puerto Mainiqui 96-97 E 7
Puerto Maldonado 92-93 EF 7
Puerto Mamoré 104-105 D 5
Puerto Manatí 88-89 H 4
Puerto México = Coatzacoalcos 64-65 H 8
Puerto Mihanovich 102-103 CD 4
Puerto Miranda 94-95 L 4
Puerto Miranhas 94-95 F 8
Puerto Montt 111 B 6
Puerto Mosquito 94-95 E 3
Puerto Napo 96-97 BC 2
Puerto Nare 94-95 E 7
Puerto Nariño 94-95 GH 5
Puerto Natales 111 B 8
Puerto Navarino 108-109 EF 10
Puerto Nuevo [CO] 92-93 F 3
Puerto Nuevo [PY] 102-103 C 4
Puerto Ordaz, Ciudad Guayana- 92-93 G 3
Puerto Ospina 94-95 D 7
Puerto Padre 88-89 HJ 4
Puerto Páez 92-93 F 3
Puerto Palma Chica 102-103 CD 4
Puerto Palmares 102-103 BC 4
Puerto Pardo [PE, Loreto] 96-97 C 3
Puerto Pardo [PE, Madre de Dios] 96-97 G 8
Puerto Patillos 104-105 A 7
Puerto Peñasco 86-87 CD 2
Puerto Pilcomayo 104-105 GH 9
Puerto Pilón 64-65 b 2
Puerto Pinasco 111 E 2
Puerto Piracuacito 106-107 H 2
Puerto Pirámides 111 D 6
Puerto Píritu 92-93 FG 2-3
Puerto Pizarro 92-93 E 5
Puerto Plata 64-65 M 8
Puerto Portillo 92-93 E 6
Puerto Potrero 88-89 CD 9
Puerto Prado 92-93 DE 7
Puerto Princesa 148-149 G 5
Puerto Providencia 96-97 F 7
Puerto Puyuguapi 108-109 C 5
Puerto Quellón 111 B 6
Puerto Quellón = Quellón 111 B 6
Puerto Quijarro 104-105 GH 5
Puerto Ramírez 111 B 6
Puerto Rápido 94-95 CD 7
Puerto Real 120-121 DE 10
Puerto Rey 94-95 C 3
Puerto Rico [BOL] 92-93 F 7
Puerto Rico [CO, Caquetá] 94-95 D 6
Puerto Rico [CO, Meta] 94-95 D 7
Puerto Rico [Puerto Rico] 64-65 N 8
Puerto Rico [YV] 94-95 L 4
Puerto Rico = Libertador General San Martín 102-103 E 7
Puerto Rico Trench 50-51 FG 4
Puerto Río Negro 102-103 CD 5
Puerto Rondón 92-93 E 3
Puerto Ruiz 106-107 H 4
Puerto Saavedra 106-107 A 7
Puerto Sábalo 94-95 E 8
Puerto Salgar 94-95 D 5
Puerto San Agostino 94-95 b 2
Puerto San Augustín 96-97 F 3
Puerto San José 108-109 GH 4
Puerto San Julián 111 C 7
Puerto Santa Cruz 111 C 8
Puerto Santa Cruz = Santa Cruz 111 C 8
Puerto Santa Elena 102-103 D 6
Puerto Santa Rita 102-103 D 5
Puerto San Vicente 102-103 E 6
Puerto Sastre 111 E 2
Puerto Saucedo 104-105 E 3
Puerto Siles 104-105 D 3
Puerto Stigh 108-109 B 6
Puerto Suárez 92-93 H 8
Puerto Supe 92-93 D 7
Puerto Tejada 92-93 D 4
Puerto Tirol 104-105 G 10
Puerto Tirol = Tirol 106-107 H 1
Puerto Torno 104-105 D 5
Puerto Trinidad 64-65 b 3
Puerto Umbría 94-95 C 7
Puerto Unzué 106-107 H 4
Puerto Vallarta 86-87 H 7
Puerto Varas 108-109 C 3
Puerto Vassupe 96-97 D 7
Puerto Victoria [PE] 92-93 DE 6
Puerto Victoria [RA] 102-103 E 7
Puerto Viejo 106-107 B 1
Puerto Vilelas 104-105 G 10
Puerto Wilches 92-93 E 3
Puerto Williams 111 C 9
Puerto Yartou 108-109 DE 9
Puerto Ybapobó 102-103 D 5
Puerto Yeruá 106-107 H 3
Puesto, El — 104-105 C 10
Puesto de Castro 106-107 F 3
Pueyrredón, Lago — 111 B 7
Puga 102-103 D 3
Pugačov 132-133 HJ 7
Pūgal 134-135 L 5
Pugan 141 D 5
Puger 152-153 K 10
Puget Sound 66-67 B 2
Pùglia 122-123 FG 5
Pugwash 56-57 Y 8
Pūhalepa 124-125 D 4
P'u-hsi = Puxi 146-147 G 9
P'u-hsien = Pu Xian 146-147 C 3
Pui, Doi — = Doi Suthep 150-151 B 3
Pui Kau 155 I a 2
Puinahua, Canal de — 96-97 D 4
Puisoyé 106-107 HJ 1
Pujehun 164-165 B 7
Pujiang 146-147 G 7
Pujilí 96-97 B 2
Pujŏn-ho 144-145 FG 2
Pukaki, Lake — 161 D 7
Puka Puka 156-157 L 5
Pukatawagan 61 H 3
Pukchin 144-145 E 2
Pukch'ŏng 142-143 O 3
Puket = Ko Phuket 148-149 C 5
Pukhan-gang 144-145 F 3-4
Pukou 146-147 G 5
Puksa 124-125 N 2
Puksoozero 124-125 N 2
Puksubæk-san = Ch'ail-bong 144-145 F 2
Pula 122-123 E 3
Pulacayo 92-93 F 9
Pulador 106-107 L 2
Pulandian = Xinjin 144-145 CD 3
Pulangpisau 152-153 L 7
Pulantien = Xinjin 144-145 CD 3
Pulānto 138-139 HJ 3
Pulap 148-149 N 5
Pular, Volcán — 111 C 2
Pulaski, NY 72-73 HJ 3
Pulaski, TN 78-79 F 3
Pulaski, VA 80-81 F 2
Pulaski, WI 70-71 F 3
Pulau Adi 148-149 K 7
Pulau Adonara 148-149 H 8
Pulau Airabu 152-153 G 4
Pulau Alang Besar 150-151 C 11
Pulau Alor 148-149 HJ 8
Pulau Ambelau 148-149 J 7
Pulau Ambon 148-149 J 7
Pulau Aur 150-151 E 11
Pulau Babi 152-153 B 4
Pulau Bacan 148-149 J 7
Pulau Bahulu 152-153 P 7
Pulau Balambangan 148-149 G 5
Pulau Bali 148-149 FG 8
Pulau Banawaja 152-153 N 9
Pulau Banggai 148-149 H 7
Pulau Banggi 148-149 G 5
Pulau Bangka 148-149 E 7
Pulau Bangkaru 152-153 B 4-5
Pulau Bangkulu 152-153 P 6
Pulau Batam 148-149 D 6
Pulau Batanta 148-149 JK 7
Pulau Batuatu 152-153 P 8
Pulau Batudaka 152-153 O 6
Pulau Bawal 152-153 H 7
Pulau Bawean 148-149 F 8
Pulau Belitung 148-149 E 7
Pulau Bengkalis 148-149 D 6
Pulau Benua 152-153 G 5
Pulau Berhala 150-151 DE 11
Pulau Besar 152-153 P 10
Pulau Biak 148-149 L 7
Pulau Biaro 148-149 J 6
Pulau Binongko 152-153 Q 8
Pulau Bintan 148-149 DE 6
Pulau Bisa 148-149 J 7
Pulau Bonerate 152-153 O 9
Pulau Brani 154 III b 2
Pulau Breueh 148-149 B 5
Pulau Bruit 152-153 J 4
Pulau Bukum 154 III a 2
Pulau Bukum Kechil 154 III a 2
Pulau Bum Bum 152-153 N 3
Pulau Bunguran 148-149 E 6
Pulau Bunyu 148-149 G 6
Pulau Buru 148-149 J 7
Pulau Busing 154 III a 2
Pulau Butung 148-149 H 7-8
Pulau Damar 148-149 J 8
Pulau Dayang Bunting 148-149 C 5
Pulau Deli 148-149 DE 8
Pulau Dewakang Besar 152-153 N 8
Pulau Doangdoangan Besar 152-153 M 8
Pulau Dumdum 152-153 G 5
Pulau Enggano 148-149 D 8
Pulau Gam 148-149 JK 7
Pulau Gebe 148-149 J 7
Pulau Gelam 152-153 H 7
Pulau Gunungapi 148-149 J 8
Pulau Hantu 154 III a 2
Pulau Jamdena 148-149 K 8
Pulau Jemaja 148-149 DE 6
Pulau Jembongan 148-149 G 5
Pulau Kabaena 148-149 H 8
Pulau Kaburuang 148-149 J 6
Pulau Kai Besar 148-149 K 8
Pulau Kai Kecil 148-149 K 8
Pulau Kakaban 152-153 N 4
Pulau Kakabia 152-153 P 9
Pulau Kalambau 152-153 L 8
Pulau Kalao 152-153 O 9
Pulau Kalaotao 148-149 H 8
Pulau Kalukalukuang 152-153 MN 8
Pulau Kambing = Ilha de Ataúro 148-149 J 8
Pulau Kangean 148-149 G 8
Pulau Kapas 150-151 D 10
Pulau Karakelong 148-149 J 6
Pulau Karamian 148-149 F 8
Pulau Karas 148-149 K 7
Pulau Karompa 152-153 OP 9
Pulau Kasiruta 148-149 J 7
Pulau Katedupa 152-153 PQ 8
Pulau Kayoa 148-149 J 6
Pulau Kayuadi 152-153 O 9
Pulau Ketam 154 III b 1
Pulaukijang 152-153 E 6
Pulau Kisar 148-149 J 8
Pulau Klang 150-151 C 11
Pulau Kobroör 148-149 KL 8
Pulau Kofiau 148-149 JK 7
Pulau Kola 148-149 KL 8
Pulau Komba 152-153 P 9
Pulau Komodo 148-149 G 8
Pulau Komoran 148-149 L 8
Pulau Kundur 148-149 D 6
Pulau Labengke 152-153 P 7
Pulau Labuan 148-149 FG 5
Pulau Langkawi 148-149 C 5
Pulau Larat 148-149 K 8
Pulau Lari Larian 152-153 MN 7
Pulau Laut [RI, Selat Makasar] 148-149 G 7
Pulau Laut [RI, South China Sea] 148-149 E 6
Pulau Lemukutan 152-153 GH 5
Pulau Lepar 148-149 E 7
Pulau Liat 152-153 G 7
Pulau Lingga 148-149 DE 7
Pulau Lomblen 148-149 H 8
Pulau Lombok 148-149 G 8
Pulau Lumut 150-151 C 11
Pulau Madu 152-153 OP 9
Pulau Madura 148-149 F 8
Pulau Maikoor 148-149 K 8
Pulau Makian 148-149 J 6
Pulau Malawali 152-153 M 2
Pulau Mandioli 148-149 J 7
Pulau Mangole 148-149 J 7
Pulau Mantanani 152-153 LM 2
Pulau Manui 152-153 P 7
Pulau Manuk 148-149 K 8
Pulau Mapor 152-153 F 5
Pulau Maratua 148-149 G 6
Pulau Matak 150-151 F 11
Pulau Maya 148-149 E 7
Pulau Mayu 148-149 J 6
Pulau Mega 152-153 D 8
Pulau Mendol 148-149 D 6
Pulau Mengalum 152-153 L 2
Pulau Menjawak = Pulau Rakit 152-153 H 8
Pulau Merundung 152-153 H 4
Pulau Mesanak 152-153 F 5
Pulau Miangas 148-149 J 5
Pulau Midai 148-149 E 6
Pulau Misoöl 148-149 K 7
Pulau Moa 148-149 J 8
Pulau Mojo 148-149 G 8
Pulau Molu 148-149 K 8
Pulau Mondoliko 152-153 J 9
Pulau Moreses 152-153 L 8
Pulau Morotai 148-149 J 6
Pulau Mubur 152-153 FG 4
Pulau Mules 152-153 O 10
Pulau Muna 148-149 H 8
Pulau Musala 148-149 C 6
Pulau Nias 148-149 C 6
Pulau Nila 148-149 JK 8
Pulau Numfoor 148-149 KL 7
Pulau Obi 148-149 J 7
Pulau Padang 148-149 D 6
Pulau Padangtikar 148-149 E 7
Pulau Pagai Selatan 148-149 CD 7
Pulau Pagai Utara 148-149 C 7
Pulau Palu 152-153 O 10
Pulau Panaitan 148-149 DE 8
Pulau Pangkor 150-151 C 10
Pulau Panjang 152-153 H 4
Pulau Pantar 148-149 H 8
Pulau Pasi 152-153 O 9
Pulau Pasitanete 152-153 O 8
Pulau Pejantan 152-153 G 5
Pulau Peleng 148-149 H 7
Pulau Pelokang 152-153 N 9
Pulau Pemanggil 150-151 E 11
Pulau Penang = Pulau Pinang 150-151 BC 10
Pulau Penembangan 152-153 H 6
Pulau Pengibu 152-153 G 5
Pulau Pinang 150-151 BC 10
Pulau Pini 148-149 C 6
Pulau-pulau Badas 152-153 G 5
Pulau-pulau Balabalangan 148-149 G 7
Pulau-pulau Banyak 148-149 C 6
Pulau-pulau Bawah 152-153 G 4
Pulau-pulau Hinako 152-153 B 5
Pulau-pulau Karimata 148-149 E 7
Pulau-pulau Karimunjawa 148-149 EF 8
Pulau-pulau Kokos 152-153 A 4
Pulau-pulau Kumamba 148-149 LM 7
Pulau-pulau Laut Kecil 148-149 G 7-8
Pulau-pulau Lucipara 148-149 J 8
Pulau-pulau Nenusa 148-149 J 6
Pulau-pulau Pagai 148-149 CD 7
Pulau-pulau Penyu 148-149 J 8
Pulau-pulau Seribu 148-149 E 7-8
Pulau-pulau Tambelan 148-149 E 6
Pulau-pulau Watubela 148-149 K 7
Pulau Puteran 152-153 L 9
Pulau Raas 148-149 FG 8
Pulau Rakit 152-153 H 8
Pulau Rangsang 148-149 D 6
Pulau Redang 150-151 D 10
Pulau Repong 152-153 FG 4
Pulau Rinja 148-149 G 8
Pulau Romang 148-149 J 8
Pulau Roti 148-149 H 9
Pulau Rumberpon 148-149 KL 7
Pulau Rupat 148-149 D 6
Pulau Sabaru 152-153 N 9
Pulau Sakeng 154 III a 2
Pulau Sakijang Bendera 154 III ab 2
Pulau Sakijang Pelepah 154 III b 2
Pulau Salawati 148-149 K 7
Pulau Salayar 148-149 H 8
Pulau Salebabu 148-149 J 6
Pulau Salembu Besar 148-149 FG 8
Pulau Sambit 152-153 N 5
Pulau Samosir 148-149 C 6
Pulau Sanding 152-153 D 7
Pulau Sangeang 148-149 GH 8
Pulau Sangihe 148-149 J 6
Pulau Sapudi 148-149 FG 8
Pulau Sapuka Besar 152-153 N 9
Pulau Satengar 152-153 M 9
Pulau Sawu 148-149 H 9
Pulau Sebangka 148-149 DE 6
Pulau Sebarok 154 III a 2
Pulau Sebatik 148-149 G 6
Pulau Sebuku 148-149 G 7
Pulau Sedanau 150-151 F 11
Pulau Sekala 152-153 M 9
Pulau Selaru 148-149 K 8
Pulau Seletar 154 III b 1
Pulau Seluan 150-151 F 10
Pulau Selui 152-153 G 7
Pulau Semakau 154 III a 2
Pulau Semau 148-149 H 9
Pulau Sembilan 150-151 B 10
Pulau Semeuluë 148-149 BC 6
Pulau Semiun 150-151 F 10
Pulau Sempu 152-153 K 10
Pulau Senebui 150-151 C 11
Pulau Sentosa 154 III a 2
Pulau Sepenjang 148-149 G 8
Pulau Serangoon 154 III b 1
Pulau Serasan 150-151 G 11
Pulau Seraya 150-151 G 11
Pulau Sermata 148-149 J 8
Pulau Serua 148-149 K 8
Pulau Serutu 152-153 H 6
Pulau Siantan 150-151 EF 11
Pulau Siau 148-149 J 6
Pulau Siberut 148-149 C 7
Pulau Sibu 150-151 E 11
Pulau Simatang 152-153 NO 5
Pulau Singkep 148-149 DE 7
Pulau Sipora 148-149 C 7
Pulau Sipura = Pulau Sipora 148-149 C 7
Pulau Siumpu 152-153 P 8
Pulau Solor 148-149 H 8
Pulau Subar Luat 154 III ab 2
Pulau Subi 150-151 G 11
Pulau Subi Kecil 152-153 H 4
Pulau Sulabesi 148-149 J 7
Pulau Supiori 148-149 KL 7
Pulau Tahulandang 148-149 J 6
Pulau Taliabu 148-149 HJ 7
Pulau Tambelan 152-153 GH 5
Pulau Tambolongang 152-153 NO 9
Pulau Tanahbala 148-149 C 7
Pulau Tanahjampea 148-149 H 8
Pulau Tanahmasa 148-149 C 6-7
Pulau Tanakeke 148-149 G 8
Pulau Tanjungbuayabuaya 152-153 N 5
Pulau Tapat 148-149 J 7
Pulau Tarakan 152-153 MN 4
Pulau Tebingtinggi 148-149 D 6
Pulau Tekukor 154 III b 2
Pulau Tenggol 150-151 DE 10
Pulau Teun 148-149 J 8
Pulau Tidore 148-149 J 6
Pulau Tifore 148-149 J 6
Pulau Tiga 152-153 L 3
Pulau Timbun Mata 152-153 N 3
Pulau Tinggi 150-151 E 11
Pulau Tinjil 148-149 E 8
Pulau Tioman 148-149 DE 6
Pulau Tjendana = Sumba 148-149 G 9
Pulau Tobalai 148-149 J 7
Pulau Togian 152-153 O 6
Pulau Tomea 152-153 PQ 8
Pulau Trangan 148-149 K 8
Pulau Tuangku 152-153 B 4
Pulau Ubin 154 III b 1
Pulau Unauna 152-153 O 6
Pulau Waigeo 148-149 K 6
Pulau Wangiwangi 152-153 PQ 8
Pulau Weh 148-149 BC 5
Pulau Wetar 148-149 J 8
Pulau Wokam 148-149 KL 8
Pulau Wowoni 148-149 H 7
Pulau Wunga 152-153 B 5
Pulau Yapen 148-149 L 7
Puławy 118 L 3
Pulë 141 D 5
Pulga 138-139 F 1-2
Pūlgāṅv = Pulgaon 138-139 G 7
Pulgaon 138-139 G 7
Pulí [CO] 94-95 D 5
Puli [RC] 146-147 H 10
Puli = Tash Qurghan 142-143 D 4
Pulicat 140 E 4
Pulicat Lake 140 E 4
Pulikkaṭṭa = Pulicat 140 E 4
Pulivendla 140 D 3
Pulivēṇḍra = Pulivendla 140 D 3
Puliyangudi 140 C 6
Puliyankulama 140 E 6
Pullmann, WA 66-67 E 2
Pulo Anna 148-149 K 6
Pulog, Mount — 148-149 H 3
Pulo Gadung, Jakarta- 154 IV b 2
Pulozero 116-117 PQ 3
Púlpito, Punta — 86-87 E 4
Pułtusk 118 K 2
Pülümür 136-137 HJ 3
Pu-lun-t'o Hai = Ojorong nuur 142-143 F 2
Pulusuk 148-149 NO 5
Puluwat 148-149 NO 5
Pumasillo, Cerro — 96-97 E 8
Pumpkin Creek 68-69 D 3
Pumpville, TX 76-77 D 8
Pūn, Nam — 141 E 5-6
Puna [BOL] 104-105 D 6
Puná [EC] 92-93 CD 5
Puna [RA] 106-107 F 1
Puna = Pune 134-135 L 7
Puná, Isla — 92-93 C 5
Puna Argentina 111 C 2-3
Punākha = Phunakha 134-135 OP 5
Pūnalūr 140 C 6
Pūnalūra = Pūnalūr 140 C 6
Punan 152-153 L 5
Punata 92-93 F 8
Pūnbāgyin 141 F 6
Punchaw 60 F 3
Punchbowl, Sydney- 161 I a 2
Puncuri 96-97 B 6
Punda Milia 174-175 J 2
Pundaga 124-125 N 3
Pune 134-135 L 7
Puṇĕñ = Pune 134-135 L 7
Punganur = Punganūru 140 D 4
Punganūru 140 D 4
Pūngaya Būm 141 D 2
Punggol [SGP, place] 154 III b 1
Punggol [SGP, river] 154 III b 1
Punggol, Tanjong — 154 III b 1
P'ungnam-ni 144-145 F 5
P'ungnyu-ri 144-145 F 2
P'ungsan 144-145 FG 2
Punia 172 E 2
Punilla, Cordillera de la — 106-107 B 2
Punilla, Sierra de la — 106-107 C 2
Puning 146-147 F 10
Punitaqui 106-107 B 3
Punjab [IND] 134-135 LM 4
Punjab [PAK] 134-135 L 4
Punkuḍutivu 140 DE 6
Puno 96-97 FG 9
Puno = San Carlos de Puno 92-93 EF 8
Punta Abreojos 64-65 CD 6
Punta Achira 106-107 A 6
Punta Aguja 92-93 C 6
Punta Alcade 106-107 B 2
Punta Alice 122-123 G 6
Punta Alta 111 D 5
Punta Ameghino 108-109 G 4
Punta Angamos 111 B 2
Punta Animas 104-105 A 10
Punta Anton Lizardo 86-87 N 8
Punta Arena de las Ventas 86-87 F 5-6
Punta Arenas 104-105 A 7
Punta Arenas [RCH, place] 111 BC 8
Punta Arvejas 106-107 A 7
Punta Asunción 106-107 G 7
Punta Atalaya 106-107 J 5
Punta Atlas 108-109 G 5
Punta Baja [MEX, Baja California Norte] 64-65 C 5
Punta Baja [MEX, Sonora] 86-87 DE 3
Punta Baja [RCH] 108-109 AB 7
Punta Baja [YV] 92-93 G 3
Punta Ballena 106-107 K 5
Punta Banda 64-65 C 5
Punta Bermeja 108-109 H 3
Punta Blanca 106-107 J 5
Punta Brava 106-107 JK 5
Punta Buenos Aires 108-109 G 4-H 3
Punta Burica 64-65 K 10
Punta Cabeza de Vaca 104-105 A 10
Punta Cachos 111 B 3
Punta Canoas 94-95 D 2
Punta Caracoles 88-89 G 11
Punta Cardón 94-95 F 2
Punta Caribana 92-93 D 3
Punta Carnero 106-107 A 6
Punta Carretas 96-97 C 9
Punta Casacajal 94-95 B 6
Punta Castro 108-109 G 4
Punta Catalina 108-109 EF 9
Punta Cautén 106-107 A 7
Punta Cero 108-109 H 4
Punta Chala 96-97 D 9
Punta Chiguao 108-109 C 4
Punta Clara 108-109 G 4
Punta Cobija 104-105 A 8
Punta Coco 94-95 C 6
Punta Coicoi 106-107 A 6
Punta Cornejo 96-97 E 10
Punta Cosigüina 64-65 J 9
Punta Cruces 94-95 C 4
Punta Curaumilla 106-107 AB 4
Punta da Armação 110 I c 2
Punta de Araya 94-95 J 2
Punta de Arenas 111 C 8
Punta de Bombón 96-97 EF 10
Punta de Coles 92-93 E 8
Punta de Díaz 111 BC 3
Punta de Jurujuba 110 I c 2
Punta de la Baña 120-121 H 8
Punta de la Estaca de Bares 120-121 D 6-7
Punta del Agua 106-107 CD 5
Punta de las Entinas 120-121 F 10
Punta del Diablo 106-107 L 5
Punta del Este 106-107 K 5
Punta de Piaxtla 86-87 G 6
Punta Delgada [RA, cape] 108-109 H 4
Punta Delgada [RA, place] 111 D 6
Punta Delgada [RCH] 111 C 8
Punta del Lago, Hotel — 108-109 CD 7
Punta del Mono 88-89 E 9
Punta de Lobos 106-107 A 5
Punta de los Llanos 106-107 D 3
Punta del Palmar 106-107 L 5
Punta de Mata 94-95 K 3
Punta de Mita 64-65 E 7
Punta de Morás 120-121 D 6-7
Punta de Perlas 64-65 K 9
Punta de Salinas 92-93 D 7
Punta de San Bernardo 94-95 CD 3
Punta Descanso 86-87 B 1
Punta Desengaño 108-109 F 7
Punta Desnudez 106-107 H 7
Punta de Tarifa 120-121 DE 11
Punta de Tubiacanga 110 I b 1
Punta di Faro 122-123 F 6
Punta do Catalão 110 I b 2
Punta do Galeão 110 I b 2
Punta do Imbuí 110 I c 2
Punta do Marisco 110 I b 3
Punta do Matoso 110 I b 1
Punta Doña María 92-93 D 7
Punta Duao 106-107 A 5
Punta Dungeness 108-109 EF 9
Punta El Cojo 91 II b 1
Punta Entrada 108-109 EF 8
Punta Estrella 86-87 C 2
Punta Eugenia 64-65 C 6
Punta Falsa Chipana 104-105 A 7
Punta Foca 108-109 G 6
Punta Frontera 86-87 O 8
Punta Galera [CO] 94-95 D 2
Punta Galera [EC] 92-93 C 4
Punta Galera [RCH] 111 AB 6
Punta Gallinas 92-93 E 2
Punta Garachiné 94-95 B 3
Punta Gorda, FL 80-81 bc 3
Punta Gorda [BH] 64-65 J 8
Punta Gorda [NIC] 88-89 E 7
Punta Gorda [RCH] 104-105 A 6
Punta Gorda [YV, Distrito Federal] 91 II b 1
Punta Gorda [YV, Guajira] 94-95 F 1
Punta Gorda [YV, Zulia] 94-95 F 2
Punta Gravina 108-109 FG 5
Punta Grosa 120-121 H 9
Punta Grossa 110 I b 1
Punta Gruesa 104-105 A 7
Punta Guala 108-109 C 4
Punta Guarico 88-89 JK 4
Punta Guascama 92-93 D 4
Punta Guiones 88-89 CD 10
Punta Huechucuicui 108-109 B 3
Punta Indio 106-107 J 5
Punta Islay 96-97 E 10
Punta Judas 88-89 D 10
Punta Laberinto 106-107 FG 7
Punta Lameguapi 108-109 BC 3
Punta Lavapié 111 AB 5
Punta La Vieja 106-107 A 5
Punta Lengua de Vaca 111 B 4
Punta Licosa 122-123 F 5
Punta Lima 96-97 D 10
Punta Llorena = Punta San Pedro 64-65 K 10
Punta Lobería 106-107 AB 3
Punta Lobos [RA] 108-109 G 4
Punta Lobos [RCH, Atacama] 106-107 B 2
Punta Lobos [RCH, Tarapacá ↑ Iquique] 104-105 A 6
Punta Lobos [RCH, Tarapacá ↓ Iquique] 104-105 A 7
Punta Lora 106-107 A 5
Punta Loyola 108-109 E 8
Punta Lucas = Cape Meredith 111 D 8
Punta Macolla 94-95 F 1
Punta Mala 64-65 L 10
Punta Maldonado 64-65 FG 8
Punta Manaure 94-95 E 2
Punta Mangrove 64-65 F 8
Punta Manuel 106-107 A 7
Punta Manzanillo 64-65 L 9-10
Punta Médano 108-109 H 3
Punta Medanosa 111 CD 7
Punta Mejillón 108-109 G 3
Punta Mercedes 108-109 FG 7
Punta Mogotes 106-107 J 7
Punta Molles 106-107 B 4
Punta Móna 88-89 E 10
Punta Montes 108-109 E 8
Punta Morguilla 106-107 A 6
Punta Morro 111 B 3
Punta Mulatos 91 II b 1
Punta Naranjas 92-93 C 3
Punta Negra [PE] 92-93 C 6
Punta Negra [RA] 106-107 H 7
Punta Negra [ROU] 106-107 K 5
Punta Negra, Salar de — 104-105 B 9
Punta Ñermete 92-93 C 6
Punta Ninfas 111 D 6
Punta Norte 111 D 6
Punta Norte del Cabo San Antonio 111 E 5
Punta Nugurue 106-107 A 5
Punta Pájaros 111 B 3
Punta Paloma 104-105 A 6
Punta Parada 92-93 D 8
Punta Pariñas 92-93 C 5
Punta Patache 104-105 A 7
Punta Patuca 64-65 K 8
Punta Peña Negra 92-93 C 5
Punta Peñas 92-93 G 2
Punta Pequeña 86-87 D 4
Punta Pescadores 96-97 E 10
Punta Piaxtla 86-87 G 6
Punta Pichalo 104-105 A 6
Punta Piedras 106-107 J 5
Punta Piedras de Lobos 106-107 AB 3
Punta Pórfido 108-109 G 3
Punta Porotos 106-107 B 2
Punta Pozos 108-109 G 6
Punta Pringle 108-109 Ab 6
Punta Púlpito 86-87 E 4
Punta Quillagua 108-109 BC 3
Punta Quiroga 108-109 G 3-4
Punta Rasa 111 D 6
Puntarenas 64-65 K 9-10
Punta Rescue 108-109 B 6
Punta Reyes 94-95 B 6
Punta Rieles 102-103 C 5
Punta Roja 108-109 G 5
Punta Rosa 86-87 EF 4
Punta San Andrés 106-107 J 7
Punta San Blas 64-65 L 10
Punta San Carlos 86-87 C 3
Punta San Francisco Solano 92-93 D 3
Punta San Pablo 86-87 C 4
Punta San Pedro [CR] 64-65 K 10
Punta San Pedro [RCH] 104-105 A 9
Punta Santa Ana 96-97 D 9
Punta Santa María [MEX] 86-87 F 5
Punta Santa María [ROU] 106-107 KL 5
Punta San Telmo 86-87 HJ 8
Punta Scerpeddi 122-123 C 6
Punta Serpeddì 122-123 C 6
Punta Sierra 108-109 G 3
Puntas Negras, Cerro — 111 C 2
Punta Sur del Cabo San Antonio 111 E 5
Punta Talca 106-107 AB 4
Punta Taltal 104-105 A 9
Punta Tanaguarena 91 II c 1
Punta Tejada 106-107 G 7
Punta Tetas 111 B 2
Punta Tombo 108-109 G 5
Punta Topocalma 106-107 A 5
Punta Toro 106-107 AB 4
Punta Tucapel 106-107 A 6
Punta Tumbes 106-107 A 6
Punta Vacamonte 64-65 b 3
Punta Villa del Señor 106-107 AB 3
Punta Villarino 108-109 G 3
Punta Virgen 106-107 AB 3
Punta Weather 108-109 B 4
Punta Zamuro 94-95 G 2

346 Puerto

Puntijao 96-97 E 7
Puntilla, La — 92-93 C 5
Puntillas 104-105 B 7
Puntodo, Cerro — 106-107 E 7
Punuk Islands 58-59 C 5
Punxsutawney, PA 72-73 G 4
Punyu = Guangzhou 142-143 LM 7
Puolanka 116-117 MN 5
Pup'yŏng-dong 144-145 G 2
Puqi 142-143 L 6
Puqian 146-147 C 11
Puquio 92-93 E 7
Puquios [RCH ↗ Antofagasta] 104-105 B 7
Puquios [RCH ↗ Arica] 111 C 1
Puquios [RCH ↗ Copiapó] 106-107 C 1
Pur 132-133 O 4
Purace, Volcán — 94-95 C 6
Puraṅdar = Purandhar 140 AB 1
Purandhar 140 AB 1
Purang 138-139 H 2
Pūranpur 138-139 H 3
Purau 152-153 O 7
Purcell, OK 76-77 F 5
Purcell Mount 58-59 J 3
Purcell Mountains 56-57 N 7-8
Purcell Mountains Provincial Park 60 JK 4
Purén 106-107 A 6-7
Purgatoire River 68-69 DE 7
Purgatory, AK 58-59 N 3
Puri 134-135 O 7
Purificación 94-95 D 6
Purísima, La — 86-87 DE 4
Purley, London- 129 II b 2
Purli 140 C 1
Purma Gómez 96-97 E 6
Purmerbuurt 128 I b 1
Purmerland 128 I ab 1
Pūrna [IND, place] 138-139 F 8
Purna [IND, river ◁ Godāvari] 138-139 F 8
Pūrna [IND, river ◁ Tāpti] 138-139 F 7
Pūrnagad 140 A 2
Purnea 134-135 O 5
Purniyā = Purnea 134-135 O 5
Pursat 148-149 D 4
Pursat, Stung — 150-151 D 6
Purthi Ghāt 138-139 J 3
Purubi 104-105 F 6
Puruê, Rio — 96-97 G 3
Purukcau 148-149 F 7
Purūlia 134-135 O 6
Puruliyā = Purūlia 134-135 O 6
Purus, Rio — 92-93 F 6
Purvā = Purwa 138-139 H 4
Purvis, MS 78-79 E 5
Purwa 138-139 H 4
Purwa, Tanjung — 152-153 KL 10
Purwakarta 148-149 E 8
Purwaredja = Purworejo 148-149 EF 8
Purwokerto 148-149 EF 8
Purworejo 148-149 EF 8
Puryŏng 144-145 GH 1-2
Pusa 152-153 J 5
Pusad 138-139 F 8
Pusan 142-143 OP 4
Pusat Abri, Musium — 154 IV a 2
Pusat Gayo, Pegunungan — 152-153 B 3
Pushi 146-147 BC 7
P'u-shih = Pushi 146-147 BC 7
Pushkar 138-139 E 4
Pushpagiri [IND, mountain] 140 B 4
Pushpagiri [IND, place] 140 D 4
Pusi 96-97 G 9
Puškin 132-133 DE 6
Puškino [SU, Azerbajdžanskaja SSR] 126-127 O 7
Puškino [SU, Rossijskaja SFSR Moskovskaja Oblast'] 124-125 LM 5
Puškino [SU, Rossijskaja SFSR Saratovskaja Oblast'] 126-127 N 1
Puškinskije Gory 124-125 G 5
Puskitamika, Lac — 62 N 2
Pušlachta 124-125 L 1
Püspökladány 118 K 5
Pustoška 124-125 G 5
Pusur 138-139 M 6
Put, De — = Die Put 174-175 E 6
Put, Die — 174-175 E 6
Putaendo 106-107 B 4
Putai 146-147 GH 10
Putana, Volcán — 104-105 C 8
Putao = Pūdāō 148-149 C 1
Put'atina, ostrov — 144-145 J 1
Puteaux 129 I b 2
Puteran, Pulau — 152-153 L 9
Puthein 148-149 B 3
Puthein Myit 141 D 7
Puthimari 141 B 2
Putian 142-143 M 6
Putien = Putian 142-143 M 6
Putilovo 124-125 P 4
Putina 96-97 G 9
Puting, Tanjung — 148-149 F 7
Putivl' 126-127 F 1
Putla de Guerrero 86-87 M 9
Putnam 171 B 2
Putney, London- 129 II b 2
Putorana, plato — 132-133 RS 4
Putre 104-105 B 6
Putre, Nevado — 104-105 B 6
Putsonderwater 174-175 DE 5
Puttalam = Puttalama 134-135 M 9
Puttalama 134-135 M 9
Puttalam Kalapuwa 140 DE 6
Puttalam Lagoon = Puttalam Kalapuwa 140 DE 6
Puttgarden 118 E 1
Puttuchcheri = Pondicherry 134-135 MN 8
Puttūr [IND, Andhra Pradesh] 140 D 4
Puttūr [IND, Karnataka] 140 B 4
Puttūru = Puttūr [IND, Andhra Pradesh] 140 D 4
Puttūru = Puttūr [IND, Karnataka] 140 B 4
Putú 106-107 A 5
Putumayo [CO, administrative unit] 94-95 C 7-D 8
Putumayo [CO, place] 92-93 D 4-5
Putumayo, Río — 92-93 E 5
Pütürge = İmron 136-137 H 3
Putuskum = Potiskum 164-165 G 6
Putussibau 152-153 K 5
Putzbrunn 130 II c 2
Putzonderwater = Putsonderwater 174-175 DE 5
Pu-tzū = Potzu 146-147 H 10
Puulavesi 116-117 M 7
Puuwai, HI 78-79 b 2
Puvāṅyā = Pawāyan 138-139 GH 3
Pūvār 140 C 6
Puxi 146-147 G 9
Pu Xian 146-147 C 3
Puxico, MO 78-79 D 2
Puy, le — 120-121 J 6
Puyallup, WA 66-67 B 2
Puyang 146-147 E 4
P'u-yang Chiang = Puyang Jiang 146-147 H 7
Puyang Jiang 146-147 H 7
Puyango, Río — 96-97 A 4-B 3
Puy de Dôme 120-121 J 6
Puyehue [RCH, mountain] 108-109 C 3
Puyehue [RCH, place] 111 B 6
Puyehue, Lago — 108-109 C 3
Puyehue, Portillo — 108-109 CD 3
Puyo 92-93 D 5
Puyuguapi, Canal — 108-109 C 5
Puzla 124-125 U 2

Pwani 172 G 3
Pwehla 141 E 5
Pwela = Pwehla 141 E 5
Pweto 172 E 3
Pwllheli 119 D 5

Pyang 138-139 G 2
Pyanmalaw 141 D 8
Pyapon = Hpyābôn 141 D 7
Pyatigorsk = P'atigorsk 126-127 L 4
Pyaubwei 141 E 5
Pyawbwe = Pyaubwei 141 E 5
Pye Islands 58-59 MN 7
Pyelongyi = Pyilôngyī 141 C 5
Pyhäjärvi 116-117 L 6
Pyhäjoki 116-117 L 5-6
Pyhäranta 116-117 JK 7
Pyhätunturi 116-117 M 4
Pyilôngyī 141 C 5
Pyin 148-149 C 3
Pyingaing 141 D 4
Pyinmanā 148-149 C 3
Pyinshwā 141 D 7
Pyinzabu Kyūn 150-151 A 7
Pýlos 122-123 J 7
Pymatuning Reservoir 72-73 F 4
Pyŏktong 144-145 E 2
P'yŏngan-ni 144-145 F 5
P'yŏngan-namdo 144-145 EF 3
P'yŏngan-pukto 144-145 E 2-3
P'yŏngch'ang 144-145 G 4
P'yŏnggang 144-145 F 3
Pyŏnggok-tong 144-145 G 4
P'yŏnghae 144-145 G 4
P'yŏngnamjin 144-145 F 2
P'yŏngt'aek 144-145 F 4
P'yŏngyang 142-143 NO 4
Pyote, TX 76-77 C 7
Pyramid, NV 66-67 D 5
Pyramid Lake 64-65 C 3
Pyramid Lake Indian Reservation 74-75 D 3
Pyrenees 120-121 G-J 7
Pyre Peak 58-59 k 4
Pyrgion 122-123 LM 6
Pýrgos [GR, Pelopónnēsos] 122-123 J 7
Pýrgos [GR, Sámos] 122-123 M 7
Pyrzyce 118 G 2
Pyšak 124-125 R 4
Pyščug 124-125 P 4
Pytalovo 124-125 FG 5
Pyu = Hpyū 148-149 C 3
Pyuthān = Piuthān 138-139 J 3

Q

Qā'al 'Umarī 136-137 G 7
Qa'āmiyāt, Al- 134-135 F 7
Qa'ara, Al- = Al-Qa'rah 136-137 J 6
Qabāb, Al- 166-167 D 3
Qabāil, Al- 166-167 HJ 1
Qābes = Qābis 164-165 FG 2
Qabilī 166-167 L 3
Qābis 164-165 FG 2
Qābis, Khalīj al- 164-165 G 2
Qabīt, Wādī — = Wādī Qitbīt 134-135 G 7
Qabr Hūd 134-135 FG 7
Qabūdīyah, Rā's — 166-167 M 2
Qachasnek 174-175 H 6
Qaḍārif, Al- 164-165 M 6
Qadayal 166-167 F 2
Qaḍīmah, Al- 134-135 DE 6
Qādir Karam 136-137 L 5
Qādisiyah, Al- 136-137 L 7
Qā'en 134-135 H 4
Qaf, Bi'r al- 164-165 H 3
Qafṣah 164-165 F 2
Qa'fūr 166-167 L 1
Qāhirah, Al- 164-165 KL 2
Qāhirah-Miṣr al-Jadīdah, Al- 173 BC 2
Qā'im, Al- 136-137 J 5
Qairouân, El — = Al-Qayrawān 164-165 FG 1
Qairwan = Al-Qayrawān 164-165 FG 1
Qaisā = Qaysā' 134-135 G 8
'Qala 'et el Djerdâ' = Qal'at al-Jardah 166-167 L 2
Qala'et eṣ-Ṣenam = Qal'at Sinān 166-167 L 2
Qal'ah, Al- 164-165 F 1
Qal'āh-ye Shaharak = Shaharak 134-135 J 4
Qal'a-i-Bist 134-135 JK 4
Qal'a-i-Naw 134-135 J 3-4
Qal'a-i-Shahar 134-135 K 3
Qalāt 134-135 K 5
Qal'at al-'Azlam 173 D 4
Qal'at al-Jardah 166-167 L 2
Qal'at al-Kabīrah, Al- 166-167 M 2
Qal'at al-'Uwainid = Qal'at al-'Azlam 173 D 4
Qal'at as-S'rāghnah, Al- 166-167 C 3-4
Qal'at Bishah 134-135 E 6-7
Qal'at Dīzakh 136-137 L 4
Qal'at eḍ Ḍab'a = Ḍab'ah 136-137 G 7
Qal'at M'gūnā' 166-167 C 4
Qal'at Ṣāliḥ 136-137 M 7
Qal'at Sekar = Qal'at Sukkar 136-137 LM 7
Qal'at Sinān 166-167 L 2
Qal'at Sukkar 136-137 LM 7
Qal'at Tris 166-167 D 2
Qal'at 'Uneizah = 'Unayzah 136-137 FG 7
Qalb ar-Rīshāt 164-165 B 4
Qal'eh, Kūh-e — 136-137 N 6
Qal'eh Chāy 136-137 LM 4
Qal'eh Darreh 136-137 M 6
Qal'eh Sahar 136-137 N 7
Qalīb Bākūr 136-137 L 8
Qalībīyah 164-165 G 1
Qallābāt 164-165 M 6
Qalmah 164-165 F 1
Qalqīlyah 136-137 F 6
Qaltat Zammūr 164-165 B 3
Qalyūb 173 B 2
Qamār 166-167 K 3
Qamar, Ghubbat al- 134-135 G 7
Qamar, Jabal al- 134-135 G 7
Qamata 174-175 G 6
Qāmishlīyah, Al- 134-135 E 3
Qamqam 166-167 D 4
Qanādsah 166-167 E 4
Qanāṭir al-Ibrāhīmīyah 173 B 3
Qânâq 56-57 WX 2
Qanat as-Suways 166-167 L 2
Qanāt Djâliṭa = Qanāt Jalīṭah 166-167 L 1
Qanât es-Suweis = Qanat as-Suways 164-165 L 2
Qanāt Galīṭah = Qanāt Jalīṭah 166-167 L 1
Qanāt Jalīṭah 166-167 L 1
Qandahār = Kandahār 134-135 K 4
Qandala 164-165 b 1
Qandkoṭ 138-139 B 3
Qanṭarah, Al- [DZ, landscape] 166-167 J 3
Qanṭarah, Al- [DZ, place] 166-167 J 2
Qanṭarah, Al- [ET] 173 C 2
Qaqortoq 56-57 b 5
Qara Dāgh 136-137 L 5
Qara Dong 142-143 E 4
Qa'rah, Al- [IRQ] 136-137 J 6
Qa'rah, Al- [Saudi Arabia] 136-137 J 8
Qarah Dāgh 136-137 K 4
Qaramai 142-143 EF 2
Qaramurun davan 132-133 MN 3
Qarānqū, Rūd-e — 136-137 M 4
Qara Qash Darya 142-143 D 4
Qara Qorām = Karakoram 134-135 L 3-M 4
Qarārah, Al- 166-167 J 3
Qarārim 166-167 K 1
Qara Shahr 142-143 F 3
Qārat Ajnis 136-137 BC 8
Qārat al-Idad 136-137 C 8
Qārat al-Junūn 166-167 J 7
Qārat al-Mashrūkah 136-137 C 7
Qara Tappa 136-137 L 5
Qārat as-Sab'ah 164-165 H 3
Qar'at aṭ-Ṭarf 166-167 K 2
Qārat aṭ-Ṭarfāyah 136-137 BC 7
Qārat el Hireimis = Qārat Huraymis 136-137 B 7
Qārat Huraymis 136-137 B 7
Qar'at Jubab 136-137 J 5
Qardho 164-165 b 2
Qareh Āghāj 136-137 M 4
Qareh Būteh 136-137 M 4
Qareh Chāy 136-137 M 3
Qareh Dāgh 134-135 F 3
Qareh Ḍiyā' ad-Dīn 136-137 L 3
Qareh Sū [IR, Kermānshāhān] 136-137 M 5
Qareh Sū [IR, Tehrān] 136-137 N 5
Qāret el 'Ided = Qārat al-Idad 136-137 C 8
Qarghaliq 142-143 D 4
Qaria bā Moḥammed = Qaryat Bā Muḥammad 166-167 D 2
Qarliq Tagh 142-143 GH 3
Qarn at-Tays, Jabal — 173 C 6
Qarnayt, Jabal — 134-135 E 6
Qarqannah, Jazur — 164-165 G 2
Qārrāt Ṣaḥrā' al-Igīdi 164-165 C 4-D 3
Qārūn, Birkat — 164-165 KL 3
Qaryah 134-135 E 7
Qaryat al-'Ulyā 134-135 F 5
Qaryatayn, Al- 136-137 G 5
Qaryat Bā Muḥammad 166-167 D 2
Qarzīm 166-167 F 5
Qaṣab 136-137 K 4
Qaṣab = Al-Khaṣab 134-135 H 5
Qaṣab, Wādī — 173 C 4
Qaṣab, Wādī al- 136-137 K 4-5
Qaṣabah, Al- 136-137 B 7
Qaṣabeh 136-137 M 3
Qaṣābī, Al- 166-167 D 3
Qaṣba el Ouafīdia = Wālidīyah 166-167 B 3
Qaṣbah, Rā's — 173 D 3-4
Qaṣ'bat Tādlah 166-167 C 3
Qāshqār 142-143 CD 4
Qāshqār darya 142-143 CD 4
Qasigiánguit 56-57 ab 4
Qaṣīm, Al- 134-135 E 5
Qaṣr, Al- [DZ] 166-167 J 1
Qaṣr, Al- [ET] 164-165 K 3
Qaṣr al-Bukharī 166-167 H 1
Qaṣr al-Burqū 136-137 GH 6
Qaṣr al-Ḥayr 136-137 H 5
Qaṣr al-Khubbāz 136-137 JK 6
Qaṣr 'Amīj 136-137 J 6
Qaṣr as-Ṣabīyah 136-137 N 8
Qaṣrayn, Al- 164-165 F 1-2
Qaṣr Banī Walīd 164-165 G 2
Qaṣr Bilāl 136-137 M 8
Qaṣr-e Shīrīn 136-137 LM 5
Qaṣr Shillalah 166-167 H 2
Qaṣṣerīn, El — = Al-Qaṣrayn 164-165 F 1-2
Qastū 166-167 K 1
Qaṣūr 134-135 L 4
Qāsvīn = Qazvīn 134-135 FG 3
Qaṭanā 136-137 G 6
Qatar 134-135 G 5
Qaṭīf, Al- 134-135 F 5
Qaṭrānah, Al- 136-137 FG 7
Qaṭrānī, Jabal — 173 B 3
Qaṭrūn, Al- 164-165 GH 4
Qaṭṭār, Al- 166-167 J 2
Qaṭṭār, Ḥāssī al- 164-165 K 2-3
Qaṭṭār, Jabal — 173 C 4
Qaṭṭār, Shaṭṭ al- 166-167 L 2
Qattara Depression = Munhafaḍ al-Qaṭṭarah 164-165 K 2-3
Qaṭṭarah 166-167 E 4
Qaṭṭārah, Munhafaḍ al- 164-165 K 2-3
Qaṭṭārat ad-Duyūrah 136-137 C 7
Qaṭṭāret ad-Duyūrah 136-137 C 7
Qawām al-Ḥamzah 136-137 L 7
Qawz Rajab 164-165 M 5
Qay'īyah, Al- 134-135 E 6
Qayrawān, Al- 164-165 FG 1
Qaysā' 134-135 G 8
Qayṣūhmah, Al- 134-135 F 5
Qaysūm, Jazā'ir — 173 CD 4
Qayyārah 136-137 K 5
Qazvīn 134-135 FG 3

Qbâb, el — = Al-Qabāb 166-167 D 3

Qebilī = Qabilī 166-167 L 3
Qedhāref, El- = Al-Qaḍārif 164-165 M 6
Qeisari = Caesarea 136-137 F 6
Qeisūm, Gezir — = Jazā'ir Qaysūm 173 CD 4
Qela'a es 'Srarhnâ, el — = Al-Qal'at as-S'rāghnah 166-167 C 3-4
Qela'a Mgoûnâ = Qal'at M'gūnā' 166-167 C 4
Qelībia = Qalībīyah 164-165 G 1
Qenā = Qinā 164-165 L 3
Qenā, Wâdī — = Wādī Qinā 173 C 4
Qenaïṭra = Qunayṭirah 136-137 FG 6
Qenfoûda = Janfūdah 166-167 E 2
Qenîtra, el — = Al-Q'nitrah 164-165 C 2
Qeqertarssuatsiaq 56-57 a 5
Qeqertarssuq 56-57 Za 4
Qerqena, Djezîret — = Jazur Qarqannah 166-167 M 2
Qeshlāq 136-137 O 4-5
Qeshm 134-135 H 5
Qeshm = Jazīreh Qeshm 134-135 H 5
Qeshm, Jazīreh- 134-135 H 5
Qeṭaïfê = Al-Quṭayfah 136-137 G 6
Qeṭṭâr, Chott el — = Shaṭṭ al-Qaṭṭār 166-167 L 2
Qeydar 136-137 N 4
Qezel Owzan, Rūd-e — 134-135 F 3
Qēẓī'ōt 136-137 F 7

Qian'an 146-147 G 1
Qiancheng 146-147 BC 8
Qiandongnan Zizhizhou 142-143 K 6
Qianjiang [TJ, Guangxi Zhuangzu Zizhiqu] 146-147 B 10
Qianjiang [TJ, Hubei] 142-143 L 5
Qianjiang [TJ, Sichuan] 142-143 K 6
Qianligang 146-147 G 7
Qiannan Zizhizhou 142-143 K 6
Qian Shan [TJ, mountains] 144-145 D 2-3
Qianshan [TJ, place] 146-147 F 6
Qianwei 144-145 C 2
Qianxi 146-147 G 1
Qian Xian 146-147 B 4
Qianyang 146-147 C 8
Qianyou He 146-147 B 5
Qiblī Qamūlā, Al- 173 C 5
Qichun 146-147 E 6
Qichun = Qizhou 146-147 E 6-7
Qīdī Maghah 168-169 BC 2
Qidong [TJ, Hunan] 146-147 D 8
Qidong [TJ, Jiangsu] 146-147 H 6
Qidong [TJ, Shandong] 146-147 F 3
Qiduqou 142-143 GH 5
Qiemo = Chārchān 142-143 F 4
Qieshan = Yanshan 146-147 F 7
Qifṭ 173 C 4-5
Qigou = Xikou 146-147 C 7
Qihe 146-147 F 3
Qihu = Chihu 146-147 H 9-10
Qikou 146-147 F 2
Qil'a Safed 134-135 J 5
Qil'a Saif'ullāh 138-139 B 2
Qilātis, Rā's — 166-167 E 2
Qilian Shan 142-143 HJ 4
Qilingou 146-147 B 3
Qilin Hu = Seling Tsho 142-143 FG 5
Qilizhen 146-147 B 4
Qimen 146-147 F 7
Qinā 164-165 L 3
Qinā, Wādī — 173 C 4
Qin'an 142-143 K 5
Qing'an 142-143 O 2
Qingcheng = Qing'an 142-143 O 2
Qingdao 142-143 N 4
Qingduizi 144-145 D 3
Qingfeng 146-147 E 4
Qinghai 142-143 GH 4
Qing Hai = Chŏch nuur 142-143 H 4
Qinghe 146-147 E 3
Qinghecheng 144-145 E 2
Qinghemen 144-145 C 2
Qinghezhen 146-147 F 3
Qingjian 146-147 C 3
Qing Jiang [TJ, Hubei] 146-147 C 6
Qingjiang [TJ, Jiangsu] 142-143 M 5
Qingjiang [TJ, Jiangxi] 142-143 M 6
Qinglian 146-147 D 9
Qingliu 146-147 F 8
Qinglong 144-145 B 2
Qinglong He 144-145 B 2
Qingpu 146-147 H 6
Qingshuihe [TJ, place] 146-147 C 2
Qingshui He [TJ, river] 146-147 B 2
Qingshui Jiang 146-147 B 8
Qingshuitai 144-145 DE 1
Qingtian 146-147 H 7
Qing Xian 146-147 F 2
Qingxu 146-147 D 3
Qingyang [TJ, Anhui] 146-147 FG 6
Qingyang [TJ, Gansu] 142-143 K 4
Qingyuan [TJ, Fujian] 146-147 G 8
Qingyuan [TJ, Guangdong] 142-143 L 7
Qingyuan [TJ, Liaoning] 144-145 E 1
Qingyuan = Baoding 142-143 LM 4
Qingyun 146-147 F 3
Qingzhang Dongyuan 146-147 D 3
Qin He 142-143 L 4
Qinhuangdao 142-143 MN 3-4
Qin Ling 142-143 KL 5
Qinshui 146-147 D 4
Qin Xian 146-147 D 3
Qinyang 142-143 L 4
Qinyuan 146-147 D 3
Qinzhou 142-143 K 7
Qinzhou Wan 150-151 G 2
Qionghai 142-143 L 8
Qiongshan 142-143 L 8
Qiongzhong 150-151 GH 3
Qiongzhou Haixia 142-143 KL 7
Qiqihar 142-143 N 2
Qiraiya, Wādī — = Wādī Qurayyah 173 D 2
Qird'an, Bi'r al- 166-167 A 7
Qiryat Ātā' 136-137 F 6
Qiryat Shemona 136-137 F 6
Qisha 150-151 G 2
Qishan = Chishan 146-147 H 10
Qishm = Qeshm [IR, island] 134-135 H 5
Qishm = Qeshm [IR, place] 134-135 H 5
Qishn 134-135 G 7
Qishrān 134-135 D 6
Qishui 146-147 B 11
Qislah 136-137 N 8
Qitai 142-143 FG 3
Qitbīt, Wādī — 134-135 G 7
Qiu Xian 146-147 E 3
Qixia 146-147 H 3
Qi Xian [TJ, Henan ↘ Kaifeng] 146-147 E 4
Qi Xian [TJ, Henan ↗ Xinxiang] 146-147 DE 4
Qi Xian [TJ, Shanxi] 146-147 D 3
Qixing Dao 146-147 H 8
Qiyang 146-147 CD 8
Qiyi 146-147 D 5
Qizan = Jīzān 134-135 E 7
Qizhou 146-147 E 6-7
Qizhou Liedao 150-151 H 3
Qizil Uzun = Rūd-e Qezel Owzan 134-135 F 3

Q'nitrah, Al- 164-165 C 2

Qohord 136-137 N 5
Qojūr 136-137 N 5
Qom 134-135 G 4
Qom Rūd 136-137 O 6
Qomul = Hami 142-143 G 3
Qoqriāl = Qūqriāl 164-165 K 7
Qorātū = Qurraytū 136-137 L 5
Qorba = Qurbah 166-167 M 1
Qorbouṣ = Qurbūṣ 166-167 M 1
Qorveh 136-137 M 5
Qoseir, El- = Al-Quṣayr 164-165 L 3
Qōsh, Al- = Alqūsh 136-137 K 4
Qotbeh, Kūh-e — 136-137 M 6
Qoṭūr 134-135 E 3
Qoṭūr Chāy 136-137 L 3
Qoubayât, El- = Al-Qubayyāt 136-137 G 5
Q'oûr = Qu'ūr 166-167 L 3
Qoûriât, Djezir — = Jazā'ir Qūryāt 166-167 M 2
Qouṣaïr, El- = Al-Quṣayr 136-137 G 5
Qōz Regeb = Qawz Rajab 164-165 M 5

Q'runbālīyah 166-167 M 1

Qsâbī, El — = Al-Qaṣābī 166-167 D 3
Qṣar al-Kabīr, Al- 164-165 C 1
Qṣar aṣ-Ṣaghīr, Al- 166-167 D 2
Qṣar as-Sūq = Ar-Rashīdīyah 164-165 D 2
Qṣar Ben Khedâch = Banī Khaddāsh 166-167 LM 3
Q'ṣībah, Al- 166-167 CD 3
Qsour, El — = Al-Quṣūr 166-167 L 2
Qsoûr es Sâf = Quṣūr as-Sāf 166-167 M 2
Qṣoûr Sīdī 'Aïch = Quṣūr Sīdī 'Aysh 166-167 L 2
Qṣūr, Jabal al- 166-167 M 3

Quabbin Reservoir 72-73 K 3
Quadraro, Roma- 113 II bc 2
Quadros, Lagoa dos — 106-107 MN 2
Quakenbrück 118 CD 2
Quakertown, PA 72-73 J 4
Qual'at Īrīs 166-167 D 2
Quambatook 160 F 5
Quanah, TX 76-77 E 5
Quân Đao Hoang Sa 148-149 F 5
Quân Đao Tây Sa 148-149 EF 3
Quangbinh = Đồng Hơi 148-149 E 3
Quang Nam = Điện Ban 150-151 G 5
Quang Ngai 148-149 EF 3-4
Quang Tri 148-149 E 3
Quang Yên 148-149 E 2
Quan He 146-147 E 5
Quanjiao 146-147 FG 5
Quannan 146-147 E 9
Quannapowitt, Lake — 84 I b 1
Quantico, VA 72-73 H 5
Quanwan = Tsun Wan 155 I a 1
Quanxian = Quanzhou 142-143 KL 6
Quanxishi 146-147 D 8
Quanzhou [TJ, Fujian] 142-143 MN 6-7
Quanzhou [TJ, Guangxi Zhuangzu Zizhiqu] 142-143 KL 6
Quanzhou Gang 146-147 G 9
Qu'Appelle 61 G 5
Qu'Appelle River 56-57 Q 7
Quaraçu 100-101 D 8
Quarai 106-107 J 3
Quarles, Pegunungan — 152-153 N 7
Quarnaro, Gulf of — = Kvarner 122-123 F 3
Quartier-Latin, Paris- 129 I c 2
Quartu Sant'Elena 122-123 C 6
Quartzsite, AZ 74-75 FG 6
Quatá 102-103 G 5
Quatis 102-103 K 5
Quatre Chemins, les — 170 I b 2
Quatro Irmãos 106-107 L 1
Quatro Irmãos, Morro — 104-105 F 5
Quatsino 60 D 4
Quatsino Sound 60 CD 4
Quay, NM 76-77 C 5
Qubayyāt, Al- 136-137 G 5
Qubba, Al-Qāhirah-al- 170 II b 1
Qūchān 134-135 H 3
Quchaq Bai 142-143 D 4
Qūchghār 134-135 F 3
Quds, Al- 136-137 F 7
Quealy, WY 66-67 J 5
Queanbeyan 158-159 JK 7
Quebec [CDN, administrative unit] 56-57 V-Y 7
Québec [CDN, place] 56-57 W 8
Quebra-Anzol, Rio — 102-103 J 3
Quebrachal, El — 104-105 DE 9
Quebracho 111 E 4
Quebrachos 106-107 F 2
Quebrada Azapa 104-105 B 6
Quebrada Chugchug 104-105 B 8
Quebrada de Aroma 104-105 B 6
Quebrada de Chiza 104-105 AB 6
Quebrada del Salado 104-105 A 10
Quebrada de Mani 104-105 B 7
Quebrada de Soga 104-105 B 6
Quebrada de Taltal 104-105 AB 9
Quebrada Doña Inês Chica 104-105 B 10
Quebrada Grande 106-107 B 2
Quebrada Guamal 91 II b 1
Quebrada Pan de Azúcar 104-105 A 10-B 9
Quebrada San Julian 91 II b 1
Quebrado San Andrés 106-107 BC 1
Quebra Pote 98-99 K 5
Queçaba 102-103 H 7
Quedal, Cabo — 111 AB 6
Quèd er Remad = Wādī Ban ar-Ramād 166-167 F 3
Quèd Guîr = Wādī Gīr 166-167 E 4
Quedlinburg 118 E 3
Quèd Madjerda = Wad Majradah 164-165 F 1
Queen Alexandra Range 53 A 17-15
Queen Bess, Mount — 60 E 4
Queen Charlotte 56-57 K 7
Queen Charlotte Bay 108-109 J 8
Queen Charlotte Islands 56-57 K 7
Queen Charlotte Sound 56-57 KL 7
Queen Charlotte Strait 56-57 L 7
Queen Elizabeth II Reservoir 129 II a 2
Queen Elizabeth Islands 56-57 N-V 2
Queen Elizabeth National Park = Ruwenzori National Park 172 EF 2
Queen Mary, Mount — 58-59 S 6
Queen Mary Coast = Queen Mary Land 53 C 10
Queen Mary Land 53 C 10
Queen Mary Reservoir 129 II a 2
Queen Maud Gulf 56-57 Q 4
Queen Maud Land = Dronning Maud land 53 B 36-4
Queen Maud's Range = Dronning Maud fjellkjede 53 A
Queens, New York-, NY 82 III cd 2
Queen's Channel 158-159 E 2
Queenscliff 160 G 7
Queensland 158-159 G-J 4
Queen's Mercy 174-175 H 6
Queenstown [AUS] 158-159 HJ 8
Queenstown [NZ] 158-159 N 8
Queenstown [ZA] 172 E 8
Queens Town, Singapore- 154 III a 2
Queens Village, New-York, NY 82 III d 2
Queets, WA 66-67 A 2
Queguay 106-107 J 4
Queguay, Cuchilla de — 106-107 J 3
Queguay, Río — 106-107 J 4
Quehua 104-105 C 6
Quehué 106-107 E 6
Quehué, Valle de — 106-107 E 6
Queimada, Ilha — 98-99 N 5
Queimada, Serra — 102-103 J 5-6
Queimada Grande, Ilha — 102-103 J 6
Queimada Nova 100-101 D 5
Queimada Redonda, Serra — 100-101 E 4-5
Queimadas [BR, Bahia] 100-101 E 6
Queimadas [BR, Piauí] 100-101 C 5
Queimados, Serra dos — 104-105 E 1
Quela 172 C 3
Quelimane 172 G 5
Quella 106-107 AB 5-6
Quellen 108-109 C 4
Quelon 106-107 B 3
Quelpart = Cheju-do 142-143 NO 5
Queluz 102-103 K 5
Quemada, La — 86-87 J 6
Quemado, NM 74-75 J 5
Quemado, TX 76-77 D 8
Quemchi 108-109 C 4
Quemoy = Kinmen 146-147 G 9
Quemoy = Kinmen Dao 142-143 M 7
Quemú-Quemú 106-107 EF 6
Quenn City, IA 70-71 D 5
Quenuma 106-107 F 6
Quepem 140 B 3
Que Que = Kwekwe 172 E 5
Quequén 106-107 H 7
Quequeña 96-97 F 10
Quequén Grande, Río — 106-107 H 7
Queras, Rio — 64-65 a 3
Querco 96-97 D 8
Quercy 120-121 H 6
Querencia, La — 106-107 H 3
Querência do Norte 102-103 F 5
Querero, Cachoeira — 98-99 K 4-5
Querétaro 64-65 FG 7
Quero [EC] 96-97 B 2
Quesada 120-121 F 10
Queshan 142-143 L 5
Quesnel 56-57 M 7
Quesnel Lake 60 G 3
Questa, NM 76-77 B 4
Quetena 104-105 C 8
Quetico 70-71 E 1
Quetico Lake 62 CD 3
Quetico Provincial Park 70-71 E 1
Quetta = Kwatta 134-135 K 4
Queue-en-Brie, la — 129 I d 2
Queule 108-109 C 2
Quevedo 96-97 B 2
Quevedo, Río — 96-97 B 2
Quévillon, Lac — 62 N 2
Quezaltenango 64-65 H 9
Quezon City 148-149 H 4
Quffah, Wādī al- 173 C 6
Qufou = Qufu 146-147 F 4
Qufu 146-147 F 4
Quiaca, La — 111 CD 2
Quiansu = Jiangsu 142-143 LM 6
Quibala 172 BC 4
Quibaxe 172 B 3
Quibdó 92-93 D 3
Quibell 62 C 2-3
Quiberon 120-121 F 5
Quíbor 94-95 G 3
Quibray Bay 161 I b 3
Quichagua, Sierra de — 104-105 CD 8
Qui Châu 150-151 E 3
Quichuapunta, Paso — 96-97 C 6
Qui Dat 150-151 EF 4
Quidico 106-107 A 7
Quiindy 102-103 D 6
Quijingue 100-101 E 6
Quijotoa, AZ 74-75 GH 6
Quilán, Cabo — 108-109 B 4

Quilán 347

Quilán, Isla — 108-109 B 4
Quilāndi 140 B 5
Quilcene, WA 66-67 B 2
Quilcó 106-107 G 6
Quilengues 172 BC 4
Quilhuiri, Portezuelo — 104-105 B 6
Quilimarí 111 B 4
Quilingou 146-147 B 3
Quilino 106-107 E 3
Quillabamba 96-97 E 8
Quillacas 104-105 C 6
Quillacollo 92-93 F 8
Quillagua 111 BC 2
Quillagua, Punta — 108-109 BC 3
Quillaicillo 106-107 AB 3
Quillalauquén, Sierra de — 106-107 G 6
Quill Lakes 56-57 Q 7
Quillón 106-107 A 6
Quillota 111 B 4
Quilmes 106-107 HJ 5
Quilmes, Sierra de — 104-105 C 10
Quilmes-Bernal 110 III c 2
Quilmes-Don Bosco 110 III c 2
Quilmes-Ezpeleta 110 III c 2
Quilmes-San Francisco Solano 110 III c 2
Quilon 134-135 M 9
Quilpie 158-159 H 5
Quilpué 106-107 B 4
Quimal, Cerro — 104-105 B 8
Quimar, Alto de — 94-95 C 3
Quimbele 172 C 3
Quime 104-105 C 5
Quimet 70-71 F 1
Quimilí 111 D 3
Quiomone 104-105 F 5
Quimper 120-121 E 4-5
Quimperle 120-121 F 5
Quimpitirique 96-97 DE 8
Quimsachota, Cerro de — 104-105 B 5
Quimurcu, Cerros de — 104-105 AB 8
Quinault, WA 66-67 B 2
Quinault Indian Reservation 66-67 AB 2
Quince Mil 92-93 EF 7
Quinchao, Isla — 108-109 C 4
Quinchia 94-95 D 5
Quincy, CA 74-75 C 3
Quincy, FL 78-79 G 5
Quincy, IL 64-65 H 4
Quincy, MA 72-73 L 3
Quincy, WA 66-67 D 2
Quincy Bay 84 I c 3
Quindage 172 B 3
Quindío 94-95 D 5
Quines 111 C 4
Quinghua, Beijing- 155 II b 1
Quinghuayuan, Beijing- 155 II b 2
Quinhagak, AK 58-59 FG 7
Quinh Nhai 150-151 D 2
Qui Nho'n 148-149 EF 4
Quinigua, Serranía — 94-95 J 5
Quiñihual 106-107 G 6
Quinn, SD 68-69 EF 3
Quinn River 66-67 E 5
Quinn River Crossing, NV 66-67 DE 5
Quino 106-107 A 7
Quinta [BR] 106-107 L 4
Quinta [RCH] 106-107 B 5
Quintai 106-107 B 4
Quintanar de la Orden 120-121 F 9
Quintana Roo 64-65 J 7-8
Quinter, KS 68-69 FG 6
Quintero 106-107 B 4
Quinto, Río — 106-107 E 5
Quinton, OK 76-77 G 5
Quiongdong = Quionghai 142-143 L 8
Quipapá 100-101 FG 5
Quirigua 86-87 Q 10
Quiriguá, Bogotá- 91 III b 2
Quirihue 106-107 A 6
Quirima 172 C 4
Quirimba, Ilhas — 172 H 4
Quirindi 160 K 3
Quirinópolis 102-103 G 3
Quiriquina, Isla — 106-107 A 6
Quiriquire 94-95 K 3
Quiroga [BOL] 104-105 D 6
Quiroga, Lago — 108-109 D 7
Quiroga, Punta — 108-109 G 3-4
Quirquinchos, Los — 106-107 G 4
Quirusillas 104-105 DE 6
Quiruvilca 96-97 BC 6
Quisiro 94-95 F 2
Quissanga 172 H 4
Quissico 172 FG 6
Quitaque, TX 76-77 D 5
Quiterajo 171 E 5
Quitéria, Rio — 102-103 G 3
Quitilipi 104-105 F 10
Quitman, GA 80-81 E 5
Quitman, MS 78-79 E 4
Quitman, TX 76-77 G 6
Quitman Mountains 76-77 B 7
Quito 92-93 D 5
Quivilla 96-97 C 6
Quixaba 100-101 C 6
Quixadá [BR, Ceará] 92-93 M 5
Quixadá [BR, Rondônia] 98-99 G 10
Quixeramobim 92-93 M 5-6
Quixeré 100-101 EF 3
Qujiang 146-147 D 9
Qujiang = Shaoguan 142-143 L 6-7
Qujie 146-147 C 11
Qujing 142-143 J 6
Qūlāshgird = Golāshkerd 134-135 H 5
Qulay'ah, Ra's al- 136-137 N 8
Qulayb, Bi'r — 173 CD 5
Qulbān as-Sūfān 136-137 H 8
Qulbān aṭ-Ṭayyārāt 136-137 JK 5
Qulbān Layyah 136-137 M 8
Quleib, Bîr — = Bi'r Qulayb 173 CD 5
Qul'ah, Al- 166-167 H 1
Qulin, MO 78-79 D 2
Qull, Al- 166-167 K 1
Qūlonjī 136-137 L 4
Qum = Qom 134-135 G 4
Qumbu 174-175 H 6
Qum darya 142-143 F 3
Qum Köl 142-143 F 4
Qum tagh 142-143 G 4
Qumush 142-143 F 3
Qunāytirah 136-137 FG 6
Qundūz = Kunduz 134-135 K 3
Qunfudhah, Al- 134-135 DE 7
Qungur tagh 142-143 D 4
Qunluotuoyaozi = Zhangsanta 146-147 C 2
Quoin Point = Quoinpunt 174-175 C 8
Quoinpunt 174-175 C 8
Quoram = Korem 164-165 M 6
Quorn [AUS] 158-159 G 6
Quorn [CDN] 70-71 E 1
Qūqriāl 164-165 K 7
Quraynī, Al- 134-135 GH 6
Quraytū 136-137 L 5
Qurayyah, Al- 173 DE 3
Qurayyah, Wādī — 173 D 2
Qurayyāt al-Milḥ 136-137 G 7
Qurbah 164-165 M 1
Qurbūṣ 166-167 M 1
Qurdud 164-165 KL 6-7
Qûrénâ = Shaḥḥāt 164-165 J 2
Qurnah, Al- 136-137 M 7
Qurqul 168-169 B 2
Quruq Tagh 142-143 F 3
Qūryāt, Jazā'ir — 166-167 M 2
Qūṣ 173 C 5
Quṣaybah 136-137 J 5
Quṣay'ir 134-135 G 7-8
Quṣayr, Al- [ET] 164-165 L 3
Quṣayr, Al- [IRQ] 136-137 L 7
Quṣayr, Al- [SYR] 136-137 G 5
Qushrān 134-135 D 6
Qushui = Chhushul 142-143 FG 6
Qūṣīyah, Al- 173 B 4
Qustantīnah 164-165 F 1
Quṣūr, Al- 166-167 L 2
Quṣūr, Jibāl al- 166-167 FG 3
Quṣūr as-Sāf 166-167 M 2
Quṣūr Sīdī 'Aysh 166-167 L 2
Qutang 146-147 H 5
Quṭayfah, Al- 136-137 G 6
Quthing 174-175 G 6
Qu'ūr 166-167 L 3
Quwārib, Al- 164-165 A 5
Quwaymāt, Al- 136-137 GH 6
Quwayr, Al- 136-137 K 4
Quwayrah, Al- 136-137 F 8
Quwaysinā 173 B 2
Quwo 146-147 C 4
Qu Xian 142-143 M 6
Quyang [TJ, Hebei] 146-147 E 2
Quyang [TJ, Jiangxi] 146-147 E 8
Quynh Lu'u 150-151 EF 3
Quyon 72-73 H 2
Qūyūn, Jazīreh — 136-137 L 4
Quzhou 146-147 E 3
Quzi 146-147 A 3

Qytet Stalin 122-123 HJ 5

R

Raab 118 G 5
Raahe 116-117 L 5
Raakmoor 130 I b 1
Ra'an, Ar- 136-137 J 8
Raanes Peninsula 56-57 T 2
Raas, Pulau — 148-149 FG 8
Raas, Selat — 152-153 L 9
Raas Adado 164-165 b 1
Raasdorf 113 I c 2
Raas Haafuun 134-135 G 8
Raas Jumbo 172 H 2
Raas Khaanzuur 164-165 ab 1
Raas Sura 164-165 b 1
Rab 122-123 F 3
Raba [H] 118 H 5
Raba [RI] 148-149 G 8
Rabaçal 120-121 D 8
Rabat [M] 122-123 F 7
Rabat = Ar-Ribāṭ 164-165 C 2
Rabaul 148-149 h 5
Rabbit Ears Pass 68-69 C 5
R'abcevo 124-125 HJ 6
Rābigh 134-135 D 6
Rabindra Sarovar 154 II b 2
Rabnābād Dīpsamuh 141 B 5
Rabun Bald 80-81 E 3
Raccoon Island 84 III a 3
Raccoon Mountains = Sand Mountains 64-65 J 5
Raccoon River 70-71 C 4-5
Race, Cape — 56-57 a 8
Race Course of Calcutta 154 II ab 2
Race Course of Johor Baharu 154 III a 1
Race Course of Singapore 154 III a 1
Race Course of Tollygunge 154 II b 2
Raceland, LA 78-79 D 6
Râchayâ = Rāshayyā 136-137 FG 6
Rach Gia 148-149 DE 4-5
Rach Gia, Vung — 150-151 E 8
Rachgoun, Île — = Jazīrat Rāshqūn 166-167 EF 2
Rachnā Doāb 138-139 D 2
Rachov 126-127 B 2
Racht = Rasht 134-135 FG 3
Racibórz 118 J 3
Racine, WI 64-65 J 3
Radā' [Y] 134-135 EF 8
Rada de Ilo 92-93 E 8
Rada de Tumaco 92-93 CD 4
Radal 106-107 A 7
Radama, Nosy — 172 J 4
Rada Tilly 108-109 F 5
Rădăuṭi 122-123 L 2
Radebrück 130 III d 1
Radechov 126-127 B 1
Radford, VA 80-81 F 2
Rādhākishorepur 141 B 4
Rādhanpur 138-139 C 6
Rādhāpuram 140 CD 6
Radīsīyat Baḥrī, Ar- 173 C 5
Radisson 61 E 4
Radium 174-175 H 3
Radium Hot Springs 60 K 4
Radium Springs, NM 76-77 A 6
Radkersburg 118 GH 5
Radnor, PA 84 III a 1
Radom 118 K 3
Radomsko 118 JK 3
Radomyšl' 126-127 D 1
Radovicy 124-125 M 6
Radøy 116-117 A 7
Radul' 124-125 H 8
Radviliškis 124-125 DE 6
Radville 68-69 DE 1
Rae 56-57 NO 5
Rāe Bareli 134-135 N 5
Raeford, NC 80-81 G 3
Rae Isthmus 56-57 T 4
Rae Strait 56-57 RS 4
Rafael 106-107 A 6
Rafaela 111 D 4
Rafael Calzada, Almirante Brown- 110 III b 2
Rafael Castillo, La Matanza- 110 III b 1
Rafael del Encanto 92-93 E 5
Rafael Garcia 106-107 E 3
Rafael Obligado 106-107 G 5
Rafai 164-165 J 7-8
Rafḥah 134-135 E 5
Rafiganj 138-139 K 5
Rafsanjān 134-135 H 4
Rafter 61 H 3
Raft River 66-67 G 4
Raft River Mountains 66-67 G 5
Rāgā [Sudan] 164-165 K 7
Raga [TJ] 138-139 K 3
Ragaing Taing 141 C 5-D 7
Ragaing Yôma 148-149 B 2-3
Ragam 168-169 G 3
Rāgama 140 DE 7
Raga Tsangpo 138-139 L 3
Ragged Island 72-73 M 3
Ragged Island Range 88-89 J 3
Rāghugarh 138-139 F 5
Raghunāthpur [IND, Bihār] 138-139 K 4-5
Raghunāthpur [IND, West Bengal] 138-139 L 6
Ragland, AL 78-79 FG 4
Rago, KS 68-69 GH 7
Rago = Pag 122-123 F 3
Ragonvalia 94-95 E 4
Ragozino 132-133 O 6
Ragunda 116-117 FG 6
Ragusa 122-123 F 7
Ragusa = Dubrovnik 122-123 GH 4
Raguva 124-125 E 6
Raha 148-149 H 7
Rahāb, Ar- = Ar-Rihāb 136-137 L 7
Rahad, Ar- 164-165 L 6
Rahad, Nahr ar- 164-165 L 6
Rahad al-Bardī 164-165 J 6
Rahaeng = Tak 148-149 C 3
Rahaṭ, Ḥarrat — 134-135 DE 6
Rahel, Er — = Ḥāssī al-Ghallah 166-167 F 2
Raḥḥālīyah, Ar- 136-137 K 6
Rahimatpur 140 B 2
Rahīmyār Khān 138-139 C 3
Rāhjerd 136-137 O 5
Rahlī = Rehli 138-139 G 6
Rahlstedt, Hamburg- 130 I b 1
Raḥmat, Āb-e — 136-137 N 6
Rahnsdorf, Berlin- 130 III c 2
Rahouia = Raḥūyah 166-167 G 2
Rahue 106-107 B 7
Rāhuri 138-139 E 8
Raḥūyah 166-167 G 2
Rahway River 82 III a 3
Rai, Hon — 150-151 E 8
Raiada, Serra da — 100-101 EF 4
Raiāṭīt, Wādī — = Wādī Rayāyṭīt 173 D 6
Raices 106-107 H 3
Raichūr 134-135 M 7
RAI Congrescentrum 128 I ab 1
Raidāk 138-139 M 4
Raidat aṣ Ṣai'ar = Raydat aṣ-Ṣay'ar 134-135 F 7
Raidestós = Tekirdağ 134-135 B 2
Raiganj 138-139 M 5
Raigarh 134-135 N 6
Rāikot 138-139 E 2
Railroad Pass 74-75 E 3
Railroad Valley 74-75 F 3-4
Raimangal 138-139 M 7
Rāinagar 138-139 L 6
Rainbow 160 EF 5
Rainbow Bridge National Monument 74-75 H 4
Raincy, le — 129 I d 2
Rainham, London- 129 II c 1
Rainier, OR 66-67 B 2
Rainier, Mount — 64-65 BC 2
Rainsford Island 84 I c 3
Rainy Lake [CDN] 62 C 3
Rainy Lake [USA] 64-65 H 2
Rainy Pass Lodge, AK 58-59 L 5
Rainy River 62 B 3
Raippaluoto 116-117 J 6
Raipur [IND, Madhya Pradesh] 134-135 N 6
Raipur [IND, West Bengal] 138-139 L 6
Raipur = Rāypūr 141 B 4
Raipura 138-139 GH 6
Raisen 138-139 FG 6
Rāisinghnagar 138-139 D 3
Raith 70-71 F 1
Raivola = Roščino 124-125 G 3
Raiwind = Rāywind 138-139 DE 2
Raja, Kampung — 150-151 D 10
Raja, Ujung — 152-153 AB 4
Rajada 92-93 L 6
Rajado, Cerro — 106-107 C 2
Rajahmundry 134-135 N 7
Rājākhera 138-139 G 4
Rajakoski 116-117 N 3
Rājam = Rāzām 140 F 1
Rajamahēndri = Rajahmundry 134-135 N 7
Rājampet 140 D 3
Rājaṁpēṭa = Rājampet 140 D 3
Rajang [RI, place] 152-153 J 4
Rajang [RI, river] 148-149 F 6
Rājanpūr 138-139 C 3
Rājaoli = Rajauli 138-139 K 5
Rājapālaiyam 134-135 M 9
Rājapāḷayam = Rājapālaiyam 134-135 M 9
Rājāpur [IND] 140 A 2
Rājāpur [Nepal] 138-139 H 3
Rājasthān 134-135 LM 5
Rājasthān Canal 138-139 D 3
Rajauli 138-139 K 5
Rajbārī 138-139 M 6
Raj Bhawan Temple 154 II b 2
Rajčichinsk 132-133 YZ 8
Rajeputana = Rājasthān 134-135 LM 5
Rajevskij 124-125 U 6
Rājgarh [IND, Madhya Pradesh] 138-139 F 5
Rājgaṛh [IND, Rājasthān ← Bhiwāni] 138-139 E 3
Rājgarh [IND, Rājasthān ↗ Jaipur] 138-139 F 4
Rājgīr 138-139 K 5
Rajgorodok 126-127 Q 2
Rajik 152-153 FG 7
Rājim 138-139 HJ 7
Rājkot 134-135 L 6
Rājmahāl Hills 138-139 L 5
Rājnāndgāṅv = Rāj Nāndgaon 138-139 H 7
Rāj Nāndgaon 138-139 H 7
Rajnandgaon = Rāj Nāndgaon 138-139 H 7
Rājpīpla 138-139 D 7
Rājpur 138-139 E 7
Rājpura 138-139 F 2
Rajputana = Rājasthān 134-135 LM 5
Rājpūtāna = Rājasthān 134-135 LM 5
Rājshāhī 134-135 O 6
Rājula 138-139 C 7
Rajuña 94-95 J 5
Rājūra 138-139 G 8
Rakahanga 208 K 4
Rakaia 158-159 O 8
Rakaia River 161 D 6
Rakasdal 142-143 E 5
Rakata = Anak Krakatau 148-149 DE 8
Rakha La 138-139 L 4
Rakhni 138-139 B 2
Rakḥshān 134-135 JK 5
Rakit, Pulau — 152-153 H 8
Rakitnoje 126-127 GH 1
Rakiura = Stewart Island 158-159 N 9
Rakops 172 D 6
Rakovník 118 F 3
Rakšakiny 132-133 NO 5
Raksaul = Raxaul 138-139 K 4
Rakšino 124-125 U 4
Rakvere 124-125 F 4
Rakwāna 140 E 7
Raleigh 62 CD 3
Raleigh, NC 64-65 L 4
Raleigh, ND 68-69 F 2
Raleigh Bay 80-81 HJ 3
Raley 66-67 G 1
Ralik Chain 156-157 H 4
Ralls, TX 76-77 D 6
Ralos, Los — 104-105 D 10
Ralston, WY 68-69 B 3
Rām, Jabal — 136-137 F 8
Rama 88-89 D 8
Rāmachandrapuram 140 EF 2
Rāmachjāp = Rāmechhāp 138-139 KL 4
Ramādah 166-167 M 3
Ramadān Jamāl 166-167 K 1
Ramādī, Ar- 134-135 E 4
Ramaditas 104-105 B 7
Rāmadurga = Rāmdurg 140 B 2-3
Ramagiri 138-139 JK 8
Rāmagiri-Udayagiri = Udayagiri 138-139 K 8
Ramah 56-57 Y 6
Ramah, NM 74-75 J 5
Ramalho, Serra do — 92-93 KL 7
Rām Allāh 136-137 F 7
Ramallo 106-107 G 4
Raman [T] 150-151 C 9
Raman [TR] 136-137 J 4
Rāmanagaram 140 C 4
Rāmanapeta 140 D 2
Rāmanāthapuram 140 D 6
Rāmanguli 140 B 3
Ramansdrif 174-175 C 5
Rāmānuj Ganj 138-139 J 6
Ramapo Deep 142-143 R 5
Rāmapura = Rāmpur 140 E 1
Ramasucha 124-125 J 7
Ramathlabama 174-175 F 3
Ramayón 106-107 G 3
Rambha 138-139 K 8
Rambi 148-149 b 2
Rambler Channel 155 I a 1
Ramblón 106-107 C 4
Rambrè 148-149 B 3
Rambrè Kyûn 148-149 B 3
Rāmchandrapur 138-139 KL 7
Rāmchandrapura = Rāmchandrapur 138-139 KL 7
Ramḍā', Ar- 136-137 L 8
Ramdane-Djamal = Ramadān Jamāl 166-167 K 1
Rāmdurg 140 B 3
Rāmechhāp 138-139 KL 4
Ramenka, Moskva- 113 V b 3
Ramenskoje 124-125 M 6
Ramer, AL 78-79 F 4
Ramersdorf, München- 130 II b 2
Rāmēshvar = Rāmeshwar 138-139 F 5
Rāmēshvaram = Rāmeswaram 140 D 6
Rāmeshwar 138-139 F 5
Rameški 124-125 KL 5
Rāmeswaram 140 D 6
Ramganga 138-139 G 4
Rāmgaṛh [BD] 141 BC 4
Rāmgarh [IND, Bihār ↓ Bhāgalpur] 138-139 L 5
Rāmgarh [IND, Bihār ↗ Rānchi] 138-139 K 6
Rāmgarh [IND, Bihār → Vārānasi] 138-139 J 5
Rāmgaṛh [IND, Rājasthān → Bīkaner] 138-139 E 3
Rāmgarh [IND, Rājasthān ↖ Jaipur] 138-139 E 4
Rāmgarh [IND, Rājasthān ↖ Jodhpur] 138-139 C 4
Rāmhormoz 136-137 N 7
Ramīlas 166-167 D 5
Ramírez de Velazco 106-107 F 2
Ramis, Río — 96-97 FG 9
Ramitsogu 174-175 F 3
Ramiz Galvão 106-107 L 2
Ramla 136-137 F 7
Rammei 138-139 M 3
Ramnad = Rāmanāthapuram 140 D 6
Rāmnagar [IND ↗ Morādābād] 138-139 G 3
Rāmnagar [IND ↘ Vārānasi] 138-139 J 5
Ramon' 124-125 M 8
Ramon, NM 76-77 B 5
Ramona, CA 74-75 E 6
Ramón Lista 108-109 F 6
Ramón M. Castro 106-107 C 7
Ramón Santamarina 106-107 H 7
Ramón Trigo 106-107 K 4
Ramos 98-99 M 5
Ramos, Rio de Janeiro- 110 I b 2
Ramos Arizpe 86-87 K 5
Ramoshwani 174-175 D 2
Ramos Mejía, La Matanza- 110 III b 1
Ramos Otero 106-107 HJ 6
Ramoutsa 174-175 F 3
Rāmpāl 138-139 M 6
Rampart, AK 58-59 M 4
Rāmpur [IND, Andhra Pradesh] 140 E 1
Rāmpur [IND, Gujarāt] 138-139 DE 6
Rāmpur [IND, Himāchal Pradesh] 138-139 F 2
Rāmpur [IND, Orissa] 138-139 K 7
Rāmpur [IND, Uttar Pradesh → Morādābād] 134-135 MN 5
Rāmpur [IND, Uttar Pradesh ↓ Sahāranpur] 138-139 F 3
Rāmpura = Rāmpur 138-139 K 7
Rāmpur Hāt 138-139 L 5
Ramree = Rambrè 148-149 B 3
Ramree Island = Rambrè Kyûn 148-149 B 3
Rāmsanehīghāt 138-139 HJ 4
Ramsay 62 KL 3
Ramsay Lake 62 K 3
Ramseur, NC 80-81 G 3
Ramsey 119 DE 4
Ramsey, IL 70-71 F 6
Ramsgate 119 G 6
Ramsgate, Sydney- 161 I a 2
Ramshi 166-167 F 2
Rāmtek 138-139 G 7
Ramthā, Ar- 136-137 FG 6
Ram Tsho 138-139 M 3
Ramu River 148-149 N 8
Ramuro, Rio — 98-99 L 11
Raṇ, Mōṭuṇ — = Rann of Kutch 134-135 KL 6
Rānāghāt 138-139 M 6
Rānāhū 138-139 B 5
Rānāpur 138-139 D 5
Ranau 152-153 M 3
Ranau, Danau — 152-153 E 8
Rānāwa 138-139 B 7
Rancagua 111 BC 4
Rancharia 102-103 G 5
Rancheria 94-95 F 6
Ranchería, Río — 94-95 E 2
Ranchester, WY 68-69 C 3
Rānchi 134-135 O 6
Ranco, Lago — 111 B 6
Rancocas, NJ 84 III d 1
Rancocas Creek 84 III d 1
Rancocas Heights, NJ 84 III de 2
Rancocas Woods, NJ 84 III d 2
Rancul 106-107 E 5
Rand 160 H 5
Rand Airport 170 V b 2
Randazzo 122-123 F 7
Randberge [Namibia] 174-175 B 2
Randberge [ZA] 174-175 J 4
Randburg 170 V ab 1
Rānder 138-139 D 7
Randers 116-117 CD 9
Randijaur 116-117 HJ 4
Randolph, KS 68-69 H 6
Randolph, NE 68-69 H 4
Randolph, UT 66-67 H 5
Randolph, WI 70-71 F 4
Randon = Başbaş 166-167 KL 1
Randsburg, CA 74-75 DE 5
Randsfjord 116-117 D 7
Rand Stadium 170 V b 2
Randwick, Sydney- 161 I b 2
Randwick Racecourse 161 I b 2
Rāṇēbanūra = Rānībennur 134-135 M 8
Rāṇēbanūru = Rānībennur 134-135 M 8
Ranebennur = Rānībennur 134-135 M 8
Rāneswar 138-139 L 5
Ranfurly 61 C 4
Rangae 150-151 C 9
Rāngāmātī 141 C 4
Rangárvalla 116-117 cd 3
Rangasa, Tanjung — 152-153 N 7
Rangaunu Bay 161 EF 2
Rang Chhu 138-139 MN 3
Rangeley, ME 72-73 L 2
Rangely, CO 66-67 J 5
Ranger, TX 76-77 E 6
Ranger Lake = Saymo Lake 70-71 J 2
Rangia 141 B 2
Rangiora 158-159 O 8
Rangiya = Rangia 141 B 2
Rangkasbitung 152-153 FG 9
Rangôn 148-149 BC 3
Rangôn Myit 141 E 7
Rangoon = Rangôn 148-149 BC 3
Rangoon River = Rangôn Myit 141 E 7
Rangpūr [BD] 138-139 M 5
Rangpūr [PAK] 138-139 C 2
Rangsang, Pulau — 148-149 D 6
Rangun = Rangôn 148-149 BC 3
Rānībennur 134-135 M 8
Rānībirta 138-139 LM 4
Ranier, MN 70-71 D 1
Rānīganj [IND, Bihār] 138-139 L 4
Rānīganj [IND, West Bengal] 138-139 L 6
Rānīkhet 138-139 G 3
Rānīpeṭ 140 D 4
Rānīpūr 138-139 B 4
Rānīshvar = Rāneswar 138-139 L 5
Rānīvārā = Rānīwāra 138-139 CD 5
Rānīwāra 138-139 CD 5
Rānīyah 136-137 L 4
Rank, Ar- 164-165 L 6
Ranka 138-139 J 5-6
Rankin, TX 76-77 D 7
Rankins Springs 158-159 J 6
Rannersdorf 113 I b 2
Rann of Kutch 134-135 KL 6
Ranoke 62 L 1
Ranong 150-151 B 8
Ranot 150-151 C 9
Ranpur 138-139 K 7
Ranquelcó 106-107 E 5
Ransdorp 128 I b 1
Ransiki 148-149 K 7
Ransom, KS 68-69 FG 6
Rantau [MAL] 150-151 C 11
Rantau [RI] 152-153 L 7
Rantaupanjang 150-151 B 11
Rantauprapat 148-149 CD 6
Rantekombola, Gunung — 148-149 GH 7
Rantoul, IL 70-71 FG 5
Rānya = Rānīyah 136-137 L 4
Ranyah, Wādī — 134-135 E 6
Ranzī 141 D 2
Raobartsganj = Robertsganj 138-139 J 5
Rao Co 150-151 E 3
Raohe 142-143 P 2
Raoping 146-147 F 10
Raorī = Rori 138-139 E 3
Raoui, Erg er — = 'Irq ar-Rawī 164-165 D 3
Raoul 208 J 5
Raoyang 146-147 EF 2
Raoyang He 144-145 D 2
Rapa 156-157 K 6
Rāpaṛ = Rāpar 138-139 C 6
Rapallo 122-123 C 3
Rāpar 138-139 C 6
Rapel, Río — 106-107 B 4-5
Rapelje, MT 68-69 B 2-3
Rapelli 104-105 D 10
Raper, Cabo — 108-109 AB 6
Raper, Cape — 56-57 XY 4
Rapid City 61 H 5
Rapid City, SD 64-65 F 3
Rapide-Blanc 72-73 K 1
Rapides de Kintambo 170 IV a 1
Rapides de Lachine 82 I b 2
Rapides-des-Joachims 72-73 H 1
Rapides de Talanyené 168-169 E 3
Rapid River, MI 70-71 G 2-3
Rapid River [USA, Alaska] 58-59 R 3
Rapid River [USA, Minnesota] 70-71 C 1
Rapids 62 KL 1
Rāpina 124-125 F 4
Rapla 124-125 E 4
Rappahannock River 80-81 H 2
Rappang 152-153 NO 7
Rāpti [IND] 134-135 N 5
Rāpti [Nepal] 138-139 K 4
Rapulo, Río — 104-105 C 4
Rāpūr 140 D 3
Rāpūru = Rāpūr 140 D 3
Raqabat Zād 166-167 D 3
Raqqah, Ar- 134-135 DE 3
Rāqūbah 164-165 H 3
Raquette Lake 72-73 J 3
Raquette River 72-73 J 2
Rarotonga 156-157 J 6
Ra's, aḍ-Ḍab'ah 136-137 C 7
Ras, Riacho das — 100-101 C 7-8
Rasa [MAL] 150-151 C 11
Raša [YU] 122-123 EF 3
Rā's Abū Dārah 173 E 6
Rā's Abū Ğashwah 134-135 G 8
Rā's 'Adabīyah 173 C 3
Rā's ad-Dīmās 166-167 M 2
Rā's al-Abyaḍ 164-165 FG 1
Rā's 'Alam ar-Rūm 136-137 B 7
Rā's al-Arḍ 136-137 N 8
Rā's al-'Ayn 136-137 J 4
Rā's al-Baddūzzah 164-165 BC 2
Rā's al-Balā'im 173 C 3
Rā's al-Basīṭ 136-137 F 5
Rā's al Ḥadd 134-135 HJ 6
Rā's al-Ḥadīd 166-167 K 1
Rā's al-Ḥikmah 136-137 BC 7
Rā's al-Ḥirāsah 166-167 K 1
Ra's al-'Ishsh 166-167 KL 2
Rā's al-Jadīd 166-167 E 2
Rā's al-Kanā'is 136-137 BC 7
Rā's al-Khaymah 134-135 GH 5
Rasalkuṇḍā = Russelkanda 138-139 K 8
Rā's al-Mā' 166-167 F 2
Rā's al-Madrakah 134-135 H 7
Rā's al-Qulay'ah 136-137 N 8
Ra's al-Wād 164-165 E 1
Rā's al-Wardah 166-167 L 1
Rā's an-Naqb 134-135 D 4-5
Rā's an-Naqūrah 136-137 F 6
Rasappa = Riṣāfah 136-137 H 5
Rā's Ashaqār 166-167 CD 2
Rā's ash-Sharbithāt 134-135 H 7
Rā's ash-Shikk'ah 136-137 F 5
Rā's as-Sidr 173 C 3
Rā's at-Tannūrah 134-135 G 5
Râs Baghdâdî = Rā's Ḥunkurāb 173 D 5
Ras Ba'labakk 136-137 G 5
Ras Benas = Rā's Banās 164-165 M 4
Rā's Būjarun 166-167 JK 1
Rā's Bū Jaydūr 164-165 AB 3
Râs Chekkâ = Rā's ash-Shikk'ah 136-137 F 5
Ras Dashen 164-165 M 6
Rā's Duqm 134-135 H 7
Ra's-e Bahrgān 136-137 N 7-8
Rās-e Barkan = Ra's-e Bahrgān 136-137 N 7-8
Raseiniai 124-125 D 6
Râs el 'Aïn = Rā's al-'Ayn 136-137 J 4
Ras el-Auf = Rā's Banās 164-165 M 4
Ras el Ma 168-169 D 1
Ra's-e Nāy Band 134-135 G 5
Ras en Nagura = Rā's an-Naqurah 136-137 F 6
Rā's Falkun 166-167 F 2
Rā's Fartak 134-135 G 7
Rā's Fiqālu 166-167 F 2
Rā's Ghārib 173 C 3
Rā's Ghīr 166-167 AB 4
Râs Gihân = Rā's al-Balā'im 173 C 3
Rashad 164-165 L 6
Rā's Ḥadīd 166-167 AB 4
Rāshayyā 136-137 FG 6
Rashīd 173 B 2
Rashīd, Maṣabb — 173 B 2
Rāshidīyah, Ar- 164-165 D 2
Rashin = Najin 142-143 P 3
Rāshīpuram = Rāsipuram 140 D 5
Rāshqūn, Jazīrat — 166-167 EF 2
Rasht 134-135 FG 3
Rā's Ḥunkurāb 173 D 5
Rā's Ibn Hānī 136-137 F 5
Rāsipuram 140 D 5
Rasi Salai 150-151 E 5
Raška 122-123 J 4
Ras Kapoudia = Rā's Qabūdīyah 166-167 M 2
Ras Khânzûr = Raas Khaanzuur 164-165 ab 1
Rā's Māmī 134-135 GH 8
Rā's Masandam 134-135 H 5
Ras Mohammed = Rā's Muḥammad 164-165 LM 4
Rā's Muḥammad 164-165 LM 4
Ras Muhammed = Rā's Muḥammad 164-165 LM 4
Rā's News 134-135 H 7
Raso da Catarina 100-101 E 5
Rason Lake 158-159 D 5
Raspberry Island 58-59 KL 7
Rā's Qabūdīyah 166-167 M 2
Rā's Qaṣbah 173 D 3-4
Rā's Qilātis 166-167 E 2
Rasra 138-139 JK 5
Rass, Ar- 134-135 E 5
Râss Addâr = Rā's aṭ-Ṭīb 164-165 G 1
Rā's Sarrāṭ 166-167 L 1
Râss el Abiaḍ = Rā's al-Abyaḍ 164-165 FG 1

348 Quilán

Rass el Euch = Ra's al-'Ishsh 166-167 KL 2
Rass-el-Oued = Ra's al-Wād 164-165 E 1
Ras Shaka 171 E 3
Rā's Sīm 166-167 AB 4
Râss Kaboûdia = Ra's Qabūdiyah 166-167 M 2
Rasskazovo 124-125 NO 7
Râss Serrâṭ = Rā's Sarrāṭ 166-167 L 1
Rass Tourgueness = Rā's Turk an-Naṣṣ 166-167 M 3
Rā's Tafalnī 166-167 AB 4
Rā's Tarfāyah 164-165 B 3
Rastatt 118 D 4
Rastavica 126-127 D 2
Rastigaissa 116-117 LM 3
Rastreador, El — 106-107 F 4
Rastro 86-87 L 5
Rastro, El — 94-95 H 3
Rā's Turk an-Naṣṣ 166-167 M 3
Rasu, Monte — 122-123 C 5
Rāsvagarhī 138-139 K 3
Raswagarhi = Rāsvagarhī 138-139 K 3
Rā's Wūruq 164-165 D 1
Râs Za'farâna = Az-Za'farānah 173 C 3
Rata, Ilha — 92-93 N 5
Rata, Tanjung — 152-153 F 8
Ratak Chain 156-157 H 4
Ratam, Wādī ar- 166-167 J 3
Ratanakiri 150-151 F 5-6
Ratangarh [IND, Madhya Pradesh] 138-139 E 5
Ratangarh [IND, Rājasthān] 138-139 E 3
Ratanpur 138-139 HJ 6
Ratchaburi 148-149 C 4
Rāth 138-139 G 5
Rathedaung 141 C 5
Rathenow 118 F 2
Rathlin Island 119 C 4
Ratisbon = Regensburg 118 EF 4
Rätische Alpen 118 DE 5
Rat Island 58-59 s 7
Rat Islands 52 D 1
Ratka, Wādī ar- = Wādī ar-Ratqah 136-137 J 5-6
Ratlām 134-135 LM 6
Ratmanova, ostrov — 58-59 BC 4
Ratnagarh = Ratangarh 138-139 E 5
Ratnāgiri 134-135 L 7
Ratnapura = Ratnapūraya 140 E 7
Ratnapūraya 140 E 7
Ratno 124-125 E 8
Ratō = Lotung 146-147 HJ 9
Ratodero 138-139 B 4
Raton, NM 64-65 F 4
Ratqah, Wādī ar- 136-137 J 5-6
Rat Rapids 62 DE 2
Ratsauk 141 E 5
Rat Sima, Nakhon — 150-151 DE 4-5
Rattaphum 150-151 BC 9
Rattlesnake Creek 68-69 G 7
Rattlesnake Range 68-69 C 4
Rättvik 116-117 F 7
Ratua 138-139 LM 5
Ratz, Mount — 58-59 VW 8
Raualpindi = Rāwalpindī 134-135 L 4
Raub 150-151 C 11
Rauch 111 E 5
Rauchenwarth 113 I bc 2
Rauchfangswerder, Berlin- 130 III c 2
Raudal 94-95 D 4
Raudales 86-87 O 9
Raudal Itapinima 94-95 F 7
Raudal Jirijirimo 94-95 F 8
Raudal Mavaricani 94-95 G 6
Raudal Santa Rita 94-95 K 4
Raudal Yupurari 94-95 F 7
Raudhamelur 116-117 bc 2
Raudhatayn 136-137 M 8
Raufarhöfn 116-117 f 1
Raukumara Range 161 G 4-H 3
Raul Soares 102-103 L 4
Rauma 116-117 J 7
Raumo = Rauma 116-117 J 7
Raung Kalan 141 C 4
Raurkela 134-135 NO 6
Rausu 144-145 d 1-2
Ravalli, MT 66-67 F 2
Ravalpindi = Rāwalpindī 134-135 L 4
Ravānsar 136-137 M 5
Rāvar 134-135 H 4
Rava-Russkaja 126-127 AB 1
Ravendale, CA 66-67 CD 5
Ravenna 122-123 E 3
Ravenna, NE 68-69 G 5
Ravenna, OH 72-73 F 4
Ravensberg, Kleiner — 130 III a 2
Ravensburg 118 D 5
Ravenshoe 158-159 HJ 3
Ravensthorpe 158-159 D 6
Ravenswood 170 V c 2
Ravenswood, WV 72-73 F 5
Ravensworth 72-73 G 2
Ravensworth, VA 82 II a 2
Ravenwood, VA 82 II a 2
Rāver 138-139 EF 7
Rāvī 134-135 L 4
Rāwah 136-137 JK 5
Rāwalpindī 134-135 L 4
Rawamangun, Jakarta- 154 IV b 2
Rawa Mazowiecka 118 K 3
Rawāndūz 136-137 L 4
Rawḍah, Ar- 173 B 4
Rawd al-Faraj, Al-Qāhirah- 170 II b 1
Raw Hide Butte 68-69 D 4
Rawi 152-153 K 7
Rawī, 'Irq ar- 164-165 D 3
Rawi, Ko — 150-151 B 9
Rawicz 118 H 3
Rawlinna 158-159 E 6
Rawlins, WY 64-65 E 3
Rawlinson Range 158-159 E 4-5
Rawson [RA, Buenos Aires] 106-107 GH 5
Rawson [RA, Chubut] 111 CD 6
Rawwāfah, Ar- 173 E 4
Raxaul 138-139 K 4
Ray, MN 70-71 D 1
Ray, ND 68-69 E 1
Ray, Cape — 56-57 Z 8
Raya, Bukit — 148-149 F 7
Raya, Isla — 88-89 FG 11
Rāyabāga = Rāybāg 140 B 2
Rāyachoti 140 D 3
Rāyachūru = Raichūr 134-135 M 7
Rāyadrug 140 C 3
Rāyadurga = Rāyadrug 140 C 3
Rayāq 136-137 G 6
Rāyāt 136-137 L 4
Rayāytīt, Wādī — 173 D 6
Rāybāg 140 B 2
Rāy Barēlī = Rāe Bareli 134-135 N 5
Raydat aṣ-Ṣay'ar 134-135 F 7
Rāyganj = Raiganj 138-139 M 5
Rāygarh = Raigarh 134-135 N 6
Rāykōṭ = Rāikot 138-139 E 2
Rāymangal = Raimangal 138-139 M 7
Raymond 66-67 G 1
Raymond, CA 74-75 D 4
Raymond, IL 70-71 F 6
Raymond, MS 78-79 D 4
Raymond, MT 68-69 D 1
Raymond, WA 66-67 B 2
Raymond Terrace 160 KL 4
Raymondville, TX 64-65 G 6
Ray Mountains 56-57 F 4
Rāynagar = Rāinagar 138-139 L 6
Rayne, LA 78-79 C 5
Raynesford, MT 66-67 H 2
Rayo Cortado 106-107 F 3
Rayong 148-149 D 4
Rāypūr 141 B 4
Rāypur = Raipur [IND, Madhya Pradesh] 134-135 N 6
Rāypur = Raipur [IND, West Bengal] 138-139 L 6
Ray River 58-59 M 4
Rāysen = Raisen 138-139 FG 6
Rāysinhagar = Rāisinghnagar 138-139 D 3
Rayton 174-175 H 3
Rayville, LA 78-79 CD 4
Rāywind 138-139 DE 2
Raz, Pointe du — 120-121 E 4
Rāzām 140 F 1
Razampeta = Rājampet 140 D 3
Razān [IR, Kermānshāhan] 136-137 N 5
Razan [IR, Lorestān] 136-137 N 6
R'azan' [SU] 124-125 M 6
R'azancevo 124-125 M 5
Razazah, Hawr ar- 136-137 KL 6
Razdan 126-127 M 6
Razdel'naja 126-127 E 3
Razdolinsk 132-133 R 6
Razdol'noje 126-127 F 4
Razeh 136-137 N 6
Razelm, Lacul — 122-123 N 3
Razgrad 122-123 M 4
Razor Hill 155 I b 1
R'ažsk 124-125 N 7
R'bāṭah, Jabal — 166-167 L 2
Rbâṭ Tinezoûlîn = Tinzūlīn 166-167 CD 4
R'dayif, Ar- 164-165 F 2
Rê, Cu Lao — 150-151 G 5
Ré, Île de — 120-121 G 5
Reaburn 61 K 5
Reading, MA 84 I b 2
Reading, PA 64-65 L 3
Reading [GB] 119 F 6
Reading Terminal 84 III bc 2
Read Island 56-57 O 4
Readstown, WI 70-71 E 4
Readville, Boston-, MA 84 I b 3
Real, El — 88-89 H 10
Real, Rio — 96-97 G 6
Real del Castillo 74-75 E 6-7
Real del Padre 106-107 D 5
Realengo, Rio de Janeiro- 102-103 L 5
Realeza 102-103 L 4
Realicó 111 CD 4-5
Realitos, TX 76-77 E 9
Real Sayana 106-107 F 2
Rėam 148-149 D 4
Reamal = Riāmāl 138-139 K 7
Reartes, Los — 106-107 E 3
Reata 76-77 D 9
Reba'a, Er — = Ar-Rub'ah 166-167 L 1
Rebaa Ouled Yahia = Ar-Rub'ah 166-167 L 1
Rebbenesøy 116-117 GH 2
Rebbo 168-169 C 4
Rebeca, Lagoa da — 102-103 BC 1
Rebecca, Lake — 158-159 D 6
Rebel Hill, PA 84 III b 1
Rebia, Um er — = Wād Umm ar-Rabīyah 164-165 C 2
Rebiāna = Ribyānah 164-165 J 4
Rebiana Sand Sea = Ṣaḥrā Ribyānah 164-165 J 4
Rebojo, Cachoeira de — 98-99 J 9
Reboledo 111 EF 4
Reboly 124-125 H 2
Rebouças 102-103 G 6
Rebun-jima 142-143 QR 2
Recado, El — 106-107 FG 5
Recalde 111 D 5
Recherche, Archipelago of the — 158-159 D 6
Rechna Doab = Rachnā Doāb 138-139 D 2
Rechō Taung 148-149 C 4
Recht = Rasht 134-135 FG 3
Rečica 124-125 H 7
Recife 92-93 N 6
Recife, Cape — = Kaap Recife 174-175 FG 8
Recife, Kaap — 174-175 FG 8
Recife Manuel Luís 100-101 BC 1
Recinto 106-107 B 6
Recoleta, Buenos Aires- 110 III b 1
Reconquista 111 DE 3
Reconquista, Río — 110 III a 1
Recreio 102-103 L 4
Recreio, Serra do — 100-101 D 5
Recreo [RA, La Rioja] 111 CD 3
Recreo [RA, Santa Fe] 106-107 G 3
Recreo, Azcapotzalco-El — 91 I b 2
Rectificación del Riachuelo 110 III b 2
Rector, AR 78-79 D 2
Recuay 96-97 C 6
Reḏā'iyeh = Orūmīyeh 134-135 EF 3
Reḏā'iyeh, Daryācheh — = Daryācheh-ye Orūmīyeh 134-135 F 3
Redang, Pulau — 150-151 D 10
Red Bank, NJ 72-73 J 4
Red Bank Battle Monument 84 III b 2
Red Bay, TN 78-79 EF 3
Red Bay [CDN] 63 H 2
Reg Aftout = 'Irq Aflūt 166-167 DE 6
Redberry Lake 61 E 4
Red Bluff, CA 64-65 B 3
Red Bluff Lake 76-77 BC 7
Red Bluff Reservoir = Red Bluff Lake 76-77 BC 7
Redbridge, London- 129 II c 1
Red Bud, IL 70-71 EF 6
Red Butte 74-75 GH 5
Redby, MN 70-71 C 2
Redcliffe, Brisbane- 158-159 K 5
Red Cliffs 160 F 5
Red Cloud, NE 68-69 G 5
Redd City, MI 70-71 H 4
Red Deer 56-57 O 7
Red Deer Lake 61 H 4
Red Deer River 56-57 O 7
Reddersburg 174-175 G 5
Red Desert 68-69 B 4-5
Red Devil, AK 58-59 J 6
Reddick, FL 80-81 b 2
Redding, CA 64-65 B 3
Reddit 62 B 3
Redd Peak 68-69 D 4
Redelinghuis = Redelinghuys 174-175 C 7
Redelinghuys 174-175 C 7
Redenção 100-101 E 3
Redenção da Gurguéia 100-101 B 5
Redenção da Serra 102-103 K 5
Redeyef, Er — = Ar-R'dayif 164-165 F 2
Redfern, Sydney- 161 I b 2
Redfield, AR 78-79 C 3
Redfield, SD 68-69 G 3
Red Hill 158-159 HJ 7
Red Hills [USA, Alabama] 64-65 J 5
Red Hills [USA, Kansas] 68-69 G 7
Red House, NV 66-67 E 5
Redig, SD 68-69 E 3
Red Indian Lake 63 H 3
Redinha 100-101 G 3
Red Lake 61 GH 5
Red Lake [CDN, lake] 62 B 2
Red Lake [CDN, place] 56-57 S 7
Red Lake [USA] 64-65 G 2
Red Lake Falls, MN 70-71 BC 2
Red Lake Indian Reservation 70-71 C 1-2
Red Lake River 68-69 H 1-2
Redlands, CA 74-75 E 5-6
Red Lion, PA 72-73 H 5
Red Lodge, MT 68-69 B 3
Redmond, OR 66-67 C 3
Red Mountain, CA 74-75 E 5
Red Mountain [USA, California] 66-67 B 5
Red Mountain [USA, Montana] 66-67 G 2
Rednitz 118 E 4
Red Oak, IA 70-71 C 5
Redon 120-121 F 5
Redonda, Loma — 106-107 DE 6
Redonda, Ponta — 92-93 M 5
Redondela 120-121 C 7
Redondo [BR] 96-97 F 6
Redondo, Cerro — 106-107 C 4
Redondo, Pico — 98-99 G 3
Redondo Beach, CA 74-75 D 6
Redoubt Volcano 58-59 L 6
Red Pheasant 61 DE 4
Red River 64-65 H 5
Red River = Sông Nhi Ha 148-149 D 2
Red River, North Fork — 76-77 E 5
Red River, Salt Fork — 76-77 E 5
Red River of the North 64-65 G 2
Redrock, AZ 74-75 H 6
Redrock, NM 74-75 J 6
Red Rock, OK 76-77 F 4
Red Rock [CDN] 60 F 3
Red Rock [USA] 83 I b 1
Red Rock Point 158-159 E 6
Red Run 84 II b 1
Red Sandstone Desert = Ad-Dahnā' 134-135 E 5-F 6
Red Sea 134-135 D 5-E 7
Red Springs, NC 80-81 G 3
Redstone 60 F 3
Redstone, MT 68-69 D 1
Red Tank 64-65 b 2
Reduto 100-101 G 3
Reḏvandeh 136-137 N 4
Redvers 68-69 F 1
Red Volta 168-169 E 3
Redwater Creek 68-69 D 2
Red Willow Creek 68-69 F 5
Red Wing, MN 70-71 D 3
Redwood City, CA 74-75 B 4
Redwood Falls, MN 70-71 C 3
Redwood Valley, CA 74-75 B 3
Ree, Lough — 119 C 5
Reece, KS 68-69 H 7
Reed City, MI 72-73 D 3
Reeder, ND 68-69 E 2
Reed Lake 61 H 3
Reedley, CA 74-75 D 4
Reedpoint, MT 68-69 B 3
Reedsburg, WI 70-71 EF 4
Reedsport, OR 66-67 AB 4
Reedwoods, Houston-, TX 85 III b 2
Reefton 158-159 O 8
Reese, MI 70-71 J 4
Reese River 74-75 E 3
Refāī, Ar- = Ar-Rifāī 136-137 M 7
Refaniye 136-137 H 3
Reform, AL 78-79 EF 4
Reforma, La — [RA, Buenos Aires] 106-107 H 5
Reforma, La — [RA, La Pampa] 106-107 DE 6
Reforma, La — [YV] 94-95 L 4
Refugio, TX 76-77 F 8
Refugio, El — 94-95 E 6
Refugio, Isla — 108-109 C 4
Regattastrecke München-Feldmoching 130 II b 1
Regen 118 F 4
Regência 92-93 M 8
Regência, Ponta de — 92-93 M 8
Regeneração 100-101 C 4
Regensburg 128 IV a 1
Regensburg 118 EF 4
Regent, ND 68-69 E 2
Regent, Melbourne- 161 II bc 1
Regente Feijó 102-103 G 5
Regent's Park 129 II b 1
Regents Park, Johannesburg- 170 V b 2
Regents Park, Sydney- 161 I a 2
Reggane = Rijān 164-165 E 3
Règgio di Calàbria 122-123 FG 6
Règgio nell'Emìlia 122-123 D 3
Reggoû = Riggū 166-167 E 3
Regina, MT 68-69 C 2
Regina [CDN] 56-57 Q 7
Régina [French Guiana] 92-93 J 4
Regina Beach 61 F 5
Région de Hamada = Al-Hammadah 166-167 HJ 4
Région de la Chebka = Shabkah 166-167 H 3-4
Région des Daïa = Ḍāyah 166-167 HJ 3
Région des Guentras = Al-Qanṭarah 166-167 J 3
Registan = Rīgestān 134-135 JK 4
Registro 111 G 2
Registro do Araguaia 102-103 FG 1-2
Regocijo 86-87 H 6
Regresso, Cachoeira — 92-93 HJ 5
Regueïbat = Ar-Ruqaybah 166-167 AB 7
Reguengos de Monsaraz 120-121 D 9
Regyin 141 D 7
Reh 142-143 M 3
Rehār = Rihand 138-139 J 5
Rehberge, Volkspark — 130 III b 1
Rehbrücke, Bergholz- 130 III a 2
Rehli 138-139 G 6
Rehoboth 172 C 6
Rehoboth Beach, DE 72-73 J 5
Reḥōvōt 136-137 F 7
Rei = Rey 136-137 O 5
Reibell = Qaṣr Shillalah 166-167 H 2
Reichle, MT 66-67 G 3
Reid 158-159 E 6
Reidsville, NC 80-81 G 2
Reigate 119 FG 6
Reihoku 144-145 GH 6
Reims 120-121 JK 4
Reina Adelaida, Archipiélago — 111 AB 8
Reinbeck, IA 70-71 D 4
Reindeer Island 61 K 4
Reindeer Lake 56-57 Q 6
Reindeer Station, AK 58-59 GH 3
Reine, la — 62 M 2
Reinosa 120-121 E 7
Reinøy 116-117 H 2-3
Reisa 116-117 J 3
Reitbrook, Hamburg- 130 I b 2
Reitz 174-175 H 4
Rejaf 171 B 1
Relais, le — 63 A 4
Relalhuleu 86-87 OP 10
Relegem 128 II a 1
Relem, Cerro — 111 B 5
Reliance, SD 68-69 G 4
Reliance, WY 66-67 J 5
Relizane = Ghālizān 164-165 E 1
Rellano 76-77 B 9
Relmo 106-107 F 6
Reloj, Tlalpan-El — 91 I c 3
Reloncaví, Seno — 108-109 C 3
Remad, Ouèd er — = Wādī Ban ar-Ramād 166-167 F 3
Remada = Ramādah 166-167 M 3
Remansão 92-93 JK 5
Remanso 92-93 L 6
Remanso Grande 98-99 DE 10
Remarkable, Mount — 158-159 G 6
Rembang 152-153 J 9
Rembate = Lielvārde 124-125 E 5
Rembau 150-151 D 11
Rembrücken 128 III b 1
Remchi = Ramshi 166-167 F 2
Reme-Có 106-107 F 6
Remédios [BR, Bahia] 100-101 C 7
Remédios [BR, Fernando de Noronha] 92-93 N 5
Remedios [CO] 94-95 D 4
Remedios, Santuario de los — 91 I b 2
Remedios de Escalada, Lanús- 110 III b 2
Rementai 152-153 E 8
Remer, MN 70-71 D 2
Remeshk 134-135 H 5
Remiendos 104-105 A 9
Remígio 100-101 FG 4
Remington, IN 70-71 G 5
Remington, VA 72-73 H 5
Rémire 92-93 J 3-4
Remiremont 120-121 KL 4
Remolina 96-97 F 4
Remontnaja = Dubovskoje 126-127 L 3
Remontnoje 126-127 L 3
Remote, OR 66-67 B 4
Rems 118 D 4
Remscheid 118 C 3
Remsen, NY 72-73 J 3
Remus, MI 70-71 H 4
Rena 116-117 D 7
Renaico 106-107 A 6
Renāla Khurd 138-139 D 2
Renascença 92-93 F 5
Renault = Sīdī Muḥammad Ban 'Alī 166-167 G 1
Rencontre East 63 J 4
Rendova Island 148-149 j 6
Rendsburg 118 DE 1
Rênéia 122-123 L 7
Reneke, Schweizer- 174-175 F 4
Renfrew [CDN] 72-73 H 2
Rengam 150-151 D 12
Rengat 148-149 D 7
Rengo 106-107 B 5
Reng Tlāng 141 C 4-5
Ren He 146-147 B 5
Renhua 146-147 D 9
Reni 126-127 D 4
Renison 62 L 1
Renju 146-147 E 9
Renk = Al-Rank 164-165 L 6
Renmark 158-159 H 6
Rennell, Islas — 108-109 B 8-C 9
Rennell Island 148-149 k 7
Rennes 120-121 G 4
Rennick Glacier 53 C 16-17
Rennie 61 L 6
Rennie's Mill 155 I b 2
Rennplatz München-Daglfing 130 II c 2
Reno, ID 66-67 G 3
Reno, NV 64-65 C 4
Reno [I] 122-123 DE 3
Reno, El —, OK 64-65 G 4
Renohill, WY 68-69 C 4
Renosterkop [ZA, mountain] 174-175 H 3
Renosterkop [ZA, place] 174-175 E 7
Renosterrivier [ZA, river <] Groot Visrivier] 174-175 D 6
Renosterrivier [ZA, river <] Vaalrivier] 174-175 G 4
Renoville, CA 74-75 EF 5
Renovo, PA 72-73 H 4
Renqiu 142-143 M 4
Rensselaer, IN 70-71 G 5
Rensselaer, NY 72-73 JK 3
Renton, WA 66-67 B 2
Rentur, Houston-, TX 85 III a 2
Renville, MN 70-71 C 3
Renwer 61 H 4
Ren Xian 146-147 E 3
Reo 148-149 H 8
Repalle 140 E 2
Repartição 98-99 K 7
Repartimento 98-99 K 6
Repartimento, Rio — 98-99 E 7
Repartimento, Serra — 98-99 E 7
Repaupo, NJ 84 III b 3
Repelón 94-95 D 2
Repjevka 126-127 J 1
Repki 124-125 H 8
Repola = Reboly 124-125 H 2
Repong, Pulau — 152-153 FG 4
Reppisch 128 IV a 1-2
Represa da Boa Esperança 100-101 B 4
Represa de Água Vermelha 102-103 GH 3
Represa de Barra Bonita 102-103 HJ 5
Represa de Capivara 102-103 G 5
Represa de Estreito 102-103 J 4
Represa de Furnas 92-93 K 9
Represa de Itumbiara 102-103 H 3
Represa de Jaguara 102-103 J 3-4
Represa de Jupiá 92-93 J 9
Represa de Jurumirim 102-103 H 5
Represa de Promissao 102-103 H 4
Represa de São Simão 92-93 JK 8
Represa de Volta Grande 102-103 HJ 3-4
Represa de Xavantes 102-103 H 5
Represa do Limpopo 174-175 K 3
Represa do Peixoto 102-103 J 4
Reprêsa do Rio Grande 102-103 J 5
Represa Sobradinho 100-101 C 6-D 5
Represa Três Marias 102-103 K 3
Republic, MI 70-71 G 2
Republic, MO 78-79 C 2
Republic, WA 66-67 D 1
República 104-105 F 3
Republican River 64-65 G 3
Republican River, South Fork — 68-69 E 6
Republic Observatory 170 V b 2
Repulse Bay [AUS] 158-159 JK 4
Repulse Bay [CDN, bay] 56-57 T 4
Repulse Bay [CDN, place] 56-57 TU 4
Repunshiri = Rebun-jima 144-145 b 1
Reqba Zâd = Raqabat Zād 166-167 D 3
Reqi = Ruoxi 146-147 E 7
Reqiang = Charqiliq 142-143 F 4
Reque, Río de — 96-97 B 5
Requena [E] 120-121 G 9
Requena [PE] 92-93 E 6
Requeña [YV] 94-95 J 3-4
Reriutaba 100-101 D 3
Reşadiye [TR, Muğla] 136-137 B 4
Reşadiye [TR, Tokat] 136-137 G 2
Reşadiye yarımadası 136-137 BC 4
Reşāfé, Er- = Riṣāfah 136-137 H 5
Resa'iya = Orūmīyeh 134-135 EF 3
Resbaladero 96-97 E 6
Reschenpass 118 E 5
Rescue, Punta — 108-109 B 6
Resende [BR] 102-103 K 5
Resende Costa 102-103 K 4
Reserva 102-103 G 6
Reserva, Lagoa da — 106-107 M 3
Reserva Florestal Barotiré 98-99 MN 8
Reserva Florestal de Jaru 98-99 GH 9
Reserva Florestal do Rio Negro 94-95 G 7
Reserva Florestal Mundurucânia 98-99 JK 8
Reserva Florestal Parima 94-95 K 6
Reserva Florestal Pedras Negras 98-99 G 11
Reservatório de Guarapiranga 110 II a 3
Reserve 61 G 4
Reserve, NM 74-75 J 6
Réserve aux Éléfants 172 E 1
Réserve de Faune de Bouna 164-165 D 7
Réservoir Baskatong 72-73 J 1
Réservoir Cabonga 72-73 HJ 1
Réservoir Decelles 72-73 GH 1
Réservoir Dozois 72-73 H 1
Réservoir Pipmuacan 63 A 3
Rešetilovka 126-127 FG 2
Rešety 124-125 G 5
Resguardo 106-107 B 4
Resht = Rasht 134-135 FG 3
Reshteh Ālādāgh 134-135 H 3
Reshteh Kūhhā-ye Alborz 134-135 G 3
Resistencia 111 DE 3
Reşiţa 122-123 J 3
Resolana 106-107 C 5
Resolute 56-57 S 3
Resolution Island 56-57 Y 5
Resplandes 100-101 B 4
Resplendor 102-103 M 3
Restigouche River 63 C 4
Restinga da Marambaia 92-93 L 9
Restinga de Sefton 199 AB 7
Restinga Seca 106-107 L 2
Reston 68-69 F 1
Restrepo 94-95 E 5
Restrepo, Bogotá- 91 III b 3
Reta 106-107 GH 7
Retamito 106-107 C 4
Retamo, El — 106-107 D 3-4
Retamosa 106-107 K 4
Retem, Ouèd er — = Wādī ar-Ratam 166-167 J 3
Rethe 130 I a 1
Rethel 120-121 K 4
Réthymnon 122-123 L 8
Retimo = Réthymnon 122-123 L 8
Retiro 110 I b 2
Retiro, Buenos Aires- 110 III b 1
Retiro, Madrid- 113 III ab 2
Retiro, Parque del — 113 III ab 2
Retowo = Rietavas 124-125 C 6
Reuilly, Paris- 129 I c 2
Reus 120-121 H 8
Reuss 118 D 5
Reut 126-127 D 3
Reutersbron 174-175 A 3
Reutlingen 118 D 4
Reva, SD 68-69 E 3
Revā = Narmada 134-135 LM 6
Reval = Tallinn 124-125 E 4
Reval-Nõmme = Tallinn-Nõmme 124-125 E 4
Revāṛī = Rewāri 138-139 F 3
Revda [SU, Srednij Ural] 132-133 KL 6
Revelation Mountains 58-59 KL 6
Revelstoke 56-57 N 7
Reventador 96-97 C 1
Revenue 61 D 4
Revere, MA 84 I b 2
Revere Beach, MA 84 I c 2
Revesby, Sydney- 161 I a 2
Revillagigedo, Islas — 86-87 C-E 8
Revillagigedo, Islas de — 64-65 D 8
Revillagigedo Island 56-57 KL 6
Revillo, SD 68-69 H 3
Rĕvīvīm 136-137 F 7
Revoil-Beni-Ounif = Banī Wanīf 164-165 D 2
Rewa [IND] 138-139 H 5
Rewā = Narmada 134-135 LM 6
Rewāri 138-139 F 3
Rewa River 98-99 J 3
Rewda = Revda 132-133 KL 6
Rex, AK 58-59 N 4
Rex, Mount — 53 B 29
Rexburg, ID 66-67 H 4
Rexel Institute of Technology 84 III b 2
Rexford, MI 70-71 H 2
Rexford, MT 66-67 F 1
Rexton, MI 70-71 H 2
Rey, Arroyo del — 106-107 H 2
Rey, Isla del — 64-65 L 10
Reydon, OK 76-77 E 5
Reyên = Riyān 166-167 E 2
Reyes 104-105 C 4
Reyes, Ixtapalapa-Los — 91 I c 2
Reyes, Los — 91 I d 2
Reyes, Point — 74-75 B 3-4
Reyes, Punta — 94-95 B 6
Reyhanlı 136-137 G 4
Reykhólar 116-117 b 2
Reykholt 116-117 c 2
Reykjanes 116-117 b 3
Reykjanes Ridge 50-51 H 2-3
Reykjavík [CDN] 61 J 5
Reykjavík [IS] 116-117 bc 2
Reynaud 61 F 4
Reynolds, ID 66-67 E 4
Reynolds, IN 70-71 G 5
Reynolds Range 158-159 F 4
Reynoldsville, PA 72-73 G 4
Reynosa 64-65 G 6
Reynosa Tamaulipas, Azcapotzalco- 91 I b 2
Rezā'iyeh = Orūmīyeh 134-135 EF 3
Rēzekne 124-125 F 5
Rezina 126-127 D 3
R. Franco, Serra — 104-105 F 4
R'gâia = R'ghāyah 166-167 D 2
R'ghāyah 166-167 D 2
Rhaetian Alps = Rätische Alpen 118 DE 5
Rhafsâi = Ghafsāi 166-167 D 2
Rhar, In- = 'Ayn Ghar 166-167 G 6
Rharb, el — = Al-Gharb 166-167 C 2
Rharbi, Chott — = Ash-Shaṭṭ al-Gharbī 166-167 F 3
Rharbî, Djezîra el — = Jazīrat al-Gharbī 166-167 M 2
Rharbi, Ouèd el — = Wādī al-Gharbī 166-167 G 3-4
Rhâr ed Dimâ' = Ghār ad-Dimā' 166-167 L 1
Rhâr el Melḥ = Ghār al-Milḥ 166-167 M 1
Rhâr eş Şâllaḥ = Ghār aṣ-Ṣallaḥ 166-167 E 3
Rharis = Ghāris 166-167 J 7
Rharsa, Choṭṭ — = Shaṭṭ al-Jarsah 166-167 KL 2
Rheims = Reims 120-121 JK 4
Rhein 118 C 3
Rheine 118 C 2
Rheinland-Pfalz 118 CD 3-4
Rhemiles = Ramīlas 166-167 D 5
Rhenami, Hassi el — = Ḥāssī al-Ghanamī 166-167 JK 4
Rhenosterkop = Renosterkop 174-175 E 7
Rhenoster River = Renosterrivier 174-175 D 6
'Rheris = Gharis 166-167 D 4
'Rheris, Ouèd — = Wād Gharis 166-167 D 3-4
Rhine = Rhein 118 C 3
Rhinelander, WI 70-71 F 3
Rhineland-Palatinate = Rheinland-Pfalz 118 C 3-4
Rhino Camp 172 F 1
Rhîr, Berzekh — = Rā's Ghīr 166-167 AB 4
Rhode Island [USA, administrative unit] 64-65 MN 3
Rhode Island [USA, island] 72-73 L 4
Rhodes 174-175 G 6
Rhodes = Ródos 122-123 N 7
Rhodesdrif 174-175 H 2
Rhodes Memorial Hall 85 II b 2
Rhodes Park 170 V b 2
Rhodope Mountains 122-123 KL 5
Rhōn 118 DE 3
Rhondda 119 E 6
Rhone [CH] 118 C 5
Rhône [F] 120-121 K 6
Rhône au Rhin, Canal du — 120-121 L 4-5
Rhoumerâssen = Ghumrāssin 166-167 M 3
Rhourde-el-Baguel = Ghurd al-Baghl 166-167 K 4
Rhraïba, El — = Al-Ghraybah 166-167 LM 2
Rhu, Tanjong — 154 III b 2
Riachão 92-93 K 6
Riachão das Neves 100-101 B 6
Riachão do Dantas 100-101 F 6
Riachão do Jacuípe 100-101 E 6
Riachão São Pedro 102-103 J 2
Riacho 100-101 D 10
Riacho, Rio — 100-101 D 4
Riacho Cariús 100-101 E 4
Riacho Conceição 100-101 D 4
Riacho Corrente 100-101 B 4-5
Riacho da Estiva 100-101 B 4-5
Riacho das Almas 100-101 FG 5

Riacho 349

Riacho das Ras 100-101 C 7-8
Riacho da Vargem 100-101 E 5
Riacho da Vermelha 100-101 BC 4
Riacho de Prata 100-101 C 4
Riacho de Santana 100-101 C 7
Riacho do Brejo 100-101 C 5
Riacho do Navio 100-101 E 5
Riacho dos Cavalos 100-101 F 4
Riacho Eh-Eh 104-105 GH 9
Riacho Itaquatiara 100-101 D 5
Riacho Monte Lindo Chico 104-105 G 9
Riacho Pilagá 104-105 G 9
Riacho Poço Comprido 100-101 C 5-E 6
Riachos, Isla de los — 108-109 HJ 3
Riacho Salado 104-105 G 9
Riacho Santa Maria 100-101 C 7
Riacho São João 100-101 D 4
Riacho Yacaré Norte 102-103 C 5
Riachuelo 110 III b 1
Riachuelo, Rectificación del — 110 III b 2
Riad, Er — = Ar-Riyāḍ 134-135 F 6
Riāmāl 138-139 K 7
Riāng 134-135 P 5
Riau, Kepulauan — 148-149 DE 6
Ribadeo 120-121 D 7
Ribamar 100-101 BC 2
Ribas do Rio Pardo 92-93 J 9
Ribaṭ, Ar- 164-165 C 2
Ribatejo 120-121 C 9
Ribauè 172 G 4-5
Ribe 116-117 C 10
Ribeira [BR] 102-103 H 6
Ribeira [P] 120-121 C 7
Ribeira, Rio de Janeiro- 110 I c 1
Ribeira do Amparo 100-101 E 6
Ribeira do Iguape, Rio — 102-103 H 6
Ribeira do Pombal 100-101 E 6
Ribeirão [BR, Pernambuco] 92-93 MN 6
Ribeirão [BR, Rondônia] 92-93 FG 7
Ribeirão Aricanduva 110 II bc 2
Ribeirão Bonito 102-103 HJ 5
Ribeirão Branco 102-103 H 6
Ribeirão Claro 102-103 H 5
Ribeirão Cupecê 110 II b 2
Ribeirão da Mooca 110 II b 2
Ribeirão das Almas 102-103 JK 2
Ribeirão do Oratório 110 II bc 2
Ribeirão do Pinhal 102-103 G 5
Ribeirão do Salto 100-101 DE 8
Ribeirão dos Meninos 110 II b 2
Ribeirão Preto 92-93 K 9
Ribeirão Vermelho 102-103 K 4
Ribeira Taquaruçu 102-103 F 4
Ribeirinha, Rio — 102-103 H 6
Ribeiro Ariranha 102-103 F 2
Ribeiro Gonçalves 92-93 KL 6
Ribeirópolis 100-101 F 6
Ribeiro Tadarimana 102-103 E 2
Riberalta 92-93 F 7
Rib Lake 72-73 FG 1
Rib Lake, WI 70-71 EF 3
Ribo Parjul = Leo Pargial 138-139 G 1
Ribstone Creek 61 C 4
Ribyānah 164-165 J 4
Ribyānah, Ṣaḥrā' — 164-165 J 4
Rica, Cañada — 106-107 GH 1
Rica, La — 106-107 H 5
Ricardo Flores Magón 86-87 GH 2-3
Ricardo Franco, Rio — 104-105 E 2
Ricardo Gaviña 106-107 G 6
Ricaurte 94-95 C 7
Ricaurte, Bogotá- 91 III b 3
Riccione 122-123 E 3-4
Rice, CA 74-75 F 5
Riceboro, GA 80-81 F 5
Rice Lake 72-73 GH 2
Rice Lake, WI 70-71 E 3
Rice University 85 III b 2
Rīch = Ar-Rīsh 166-167 D 3
Richardsbaai 174-175 K 5
Richard's Bay 172 F 7
Richards Bay = Richardsbaai 174-175 K 5
Richardson, AK 58-59 OP 4
Richardson Bay 83 I ab 1
Richardson Mountains 56-57 J 4
Richardton, ND 68-69 EF 2
Richelieu, Rivière — 72-73 K 1-2
Richey, MT 68-69 D 2
Richfield, ID 66-67 FG 4
Richfield, KS 68-69 F 7
Richfield, MN 70-71 D 3
Richfield, UT 74-75 GH 3
Richford, VT 72-73 K 2
Richgrove, CA 74-75 D 5
Rich Hill, MO 70-71 C 6
Richland, GA 78-79 G 4
Richland, MO 70-71 D 7
Richland, MT 68-69 C 1
Richland, WA 64-65 C 2
Richland Balsam 80-81 E 3
Richland Center, WI 70-71 EF 4
Richlands, VA 80-81 F 2
Richland Springs, TX 76-77 E 7
Richmond, CA 64-65 B 4
Richmond, IN 64-65 JK 3-4
Richmond, KS 70-71 C 6
Richmond, KY 70-71 H 7
Richmond, MO 70-71 CD 6
Richmond, TX 76-77 FG 8
Richmond, VA 64-65 L 4
Richmond [AUS] 158-159 H 4
Richmond [CDN] 72-73 KL 2
Richmond [ZA, Kaapland] 172 D 8
Richmond [ZA, Natal] 172 F 7-8
Richmond, Melbourne- 161 II bc 1
Richmond, New York-, NY 82 III ab 4
Richmond, Philadelphia-, PA 84 III c 2
Richmond, Point — 83 I b 1
Richmond, San Francisco-, CA 83 I ab 2
Richmond Gulf 56-57 V 6
Richmond Hill, GA 80-81 F 5
Richmond Range 161 E 5
Richmond-San Rafael Bridge 83 I b 1
Richmond Valley, New York-, NY 82 III a 3
Rich Mountain 76-77 G 5
Richtberg 174-175 B 4
Richtersveld 174-175 B 5
Richterswil 128 IV b 2
Richton, MS 78-79 E 5
Richwood, OH 72-73 E 4
Richwood, WV 72-73 F 5
Rickmansworth 129 II a 1
Rico, CO 68-69 BC 7
Ricrān 96-97 D 7
Riddle, ID 66-67 EF 4
Riddle, OR 66-67 B 4
Rideau Lake 72-73 H 2
Ridgecrest, CA 74-75 E 5
Ridgecrest, Houston-, TX 85 III a 1
Ridgefield, NJ 82 III c 1-2
Ridgefield Park, NJ 82 III b 1
Ridgeland, SC 80-81 F 4
Ridgely, TN 78-79 E 2
Ridgetown 72-73 F 3
Ridgeway, SC 80-81 F 3
Ridgewood, New York-, NY 82 III c 2
Ridgway, CO 68-69 BC 6
Ridgway, PA 72-73 G 4
Riḍi Bāzār = Riri Bāzār 138-139 J 4
Riding Mountain 61 HJ 5
Riding Mountain National Park 56-57 Q 7
Riḍīsiya, Er- = Ar-Raḍīsīyat Baḥrī 173 C 5
Ridley Creek 84 III a 2
Ridley Park, PA 84 III b 2
Ridvan = Alenz 136-137 J 4
Riebeek-Wes 174-175 C 7
Riebeek West = Riebeek-Wes 174-175 C 7
Riecito 94-95 G 4
Riederwald, Frankfurt am Main- 128 III b 1
Riedikon 128 IV b 2
Riedt 128 IV a 1
Riekertsdam 174-175 G 3
Riemerling 130 II c 2
Riesa 118 F 3
Riesbach, Zürich- 128 IV b 1
Riesco, Cordillera — 108-109 D 9
Riesco, Isla — 111 B 8
Riesi 122-123 F 7
Rietavas 124-125 C 6
Rietbron 174-175 E 7
Rietfontein 172 D 7
Rieth, OR 66-67 D 3
Rieti 122-123 E 4
Rietkuil 174-175 H 4
Rietrivier 174-175 F 5
Rīf = Ar-Rīf 164-165 CD 1-2
Rīf, Ar- [MA, administrative unit] 166-167 DE 2
Rīf, Ar- [MA, mountains] 164-165 CD 1-2
Rīf, er — = Ar-Rīf 166-167 DE 2
Rifāʿī, Ar- 136-137 M 7
Rifferswil 128 IV ab 2
Rifle, CO 68-69 C 6
Rifstangi 116-117 ef 1
Rift Valley 172 G 1
Rīga 124-125 E 5
Rīga, Gulf of — = Rīgas Jūras Līcis 124-125 DE 5
Rīgas Jūras Līcis 124-125 DE 5
Rigby, ID 66-67 H 4
Rīgestān 134-135 JK 4
Riggins, ID 66-67 E 3
Riggū 166-167 E 3
Rigo 148-149 N 8
Rigolet 56-57 Z 7
Rihāb, Ar- 136-137 L 7
Rihand 138-139 J 5
Riihimäki 116-117 L 7
Riiser-Larsen halvøy 53 C 4-5
Rijān 164-165 E 3
Rijeka 122-123 F 3
Rijksmuseum 128 I a 1
Rijo, Ilha do — 110 I c 1
Rijpfjord 116-117 I 4
Rikers Island 82 III c 2
Rikeze = Zhigatse 142-143 F 6
Rikorda, ostrov — 144-145 H 1
Riksgränsen 116-117 GH 3
Rikubetsu 144-145 c 2
Rikugien Garden 155 III b 1
Rikuzen-Takada 144-145 NO 3
Rila 122-123 K 4-5
Riley, KS 68-69 H 6
Rimac, Río — 96-97 C 7
Rimachi, Lago — 96-97 C 4
Rimah, Wādī ar- 134-135 E 5
Rimāl, Ar- = Ar-Rubʿ al-Khālī 134-135 F 7-G 6
Rimāl al-Abyaḍ 166-167 L 4
Rimbey 60 K 3
Rimini 122-123 E 3
Rîmnicu Sărat 122-123 M 3
Rîmnicu Vîlcea 122-123 L 3
Rimouski 56-57 X 8
Rimouski, Parc provincial des — 63 BC 3-4
Rimouski, Rivière — 63 B 3
Rim Rocky Mountains 66-67 C 4
Rincão 102-103 HJ 4
Rincón 108-109 D 8
Rincon, NM 76-77 A 6
Rincon, El — 91 III b 2
Rincón, Salina del — 104-105 C 8-9
Rinconada 111 C 2
Rinconada, Caracas-La — 91 II b 2
Rinconada, Hipódromo de la — 91 II b 2
Rincón de Baygorria 106-107 J 4
Rincón del Bonete 106-107 JK 4
Rincón del Diamante 108-109 C 3
Rincón de Romos 86-87 J 6
Rincon Peak 76-77 B 5
Rin'gang = Riāng 134-135 P 5
Ringas = Rīngus 138-139 E 4
Ringerike-Hønefoss 116-117 CD 7
Ringgold, LA 78-79 C 4
Ringgold, TX 76-77 F 6
Ringim 168-169 H 2
Ringkøbing 116-117 BC 9
Ringling, MT 66-67 H 2
Ringling, OK 76-77 F 5
Ringold, OK 76-77 G 5
Rīngus 138-139 E 4
Ringvassøy 116-117 H 3
Ringwood, OK 76-77 E 4
Riñihue [RCH, mountain] 108-109 C 2
Riñihue [RCH, place] 111 B 5-6
Rinja, Pulau — 148-149 G 8
Rinjani, Gunung — 148-149 G 8
Rio Abacaxis 98-99 J 7
Rio Abaetê 102-103 K 3
Rio Abajo 64-65 bc 2
Río Abiseo 96-97 C 5
Rio Abunã 92-93 F 7
Rio Acaraú 100-101 D 2
Río Acaray 102-103 E 6
Rio Acari 98-99 J 7-8
Río Achuta 104-105 B 5
Rio Acima 102-103 L 4
Río Aconcagua 106-107 B 4
Rio Acre 92-93 F 6
Rio Açu 100-101 F 3
Rio Açú = Rio Piranhas 92-93 M 6
Río Acuruaá 96-97 F 6
Río Agrio 106-107 B 7
Río Agua Caliente 104-105 E 4
Río Aguán 64-65 J 8
Río Aguanaval 86-87 J 5
Rio Aguapeí [BR, Mato Grosso] 102-103 C 1
Rio Aguapeí [BR, São Paulo] 102-103 G 4
Río Aguapey 106-107 J 1-2
Río Aguaray Guazú 102-103 D 6
Río Aguarico 96-97 C 2
Río Aguaytía 96-97 D 6
Río Águeda 120-121 D 8
Río Aiari 96-97 G 1
Rio Aipena 96-97 CD 4
Río Ajajú 94-95 E 7
Rio Ajuana 94-95 J 8
Río Alalaú 92-93 G 5
Rio Alegre [BR, place] 102-103 D 2
Rio Alegre [BR, river] 102-103 C 1
Río Algodón 96-97 E 3
Río Alisos 86-87 E 2
Río Alonso 102-103 G 6
Río Alota 104-105 C 7
Río Alpercatas 92-93 KL 6
Río Altamachi 104-105 C 5
Río Altar 86-87 E 2
Río Alto Anapu 92-93 J 5
Río Aluminé 108-109 D 2
Río Amacuro 94-95 L 3
Río Amambaí 102-103 E 5
Rio Amapari 98-99 M 4
Rio Amazonas [BR] 92-93 HJ 5
Río Amazonas [PE] 92-93 E 5
Río Ameca 86-87 H 7
Río Amú 94-95 E 7
Río Anajás 98-99 N 5
Rio Anamu 98-99 K 4
Rio Anapali 96-97 E 7
Rio Anari 104-105 E 2
Rio Anauá 98-99 HJ 4
Rio Anhanduí-Guaçu 102-103 EF 4
Rio Anhanduízinho 102-103 EF 4
Rio Apa 111 E 2
Rio Apaporis 92-93 EF 5
Rio Apedia 98-99 H 11
Rio Apere 104-105 D 4
Rio Apiacá 98-99 K 9
Rio Apiaí 102-103 H 5
Rio Apiaú 94-95 L 6
Rio Aponguao 98-99 H 3
Rio Aporé 92-93 J 8
Rio Apure 92-93 F 3
Rio Apurimac 92-93 E 7
Rio Apurito 94-95 H 4
Río Aquidabán-mi 102-103 D 5
Rio Aquidauana 102-103 D 3
Rio Aquio 94-95 GH 6
Rio Arabela 96-97 D 2-3
Río Arabopó 94-95 L 5
Rio Araçá 98-99 G 4
Rio Araçuaí 102-103 L 2
Río Aragón 120-121 G 7
Rio Araguaia 92-93 J 7
Rio Araguari [BR, Amapá] 92-93 J 4
Rio Araguari [BR, Minas Gerais] 102-103 H 3
Rio Arantes 102-103 GH 3
Río Arapey Chico 106-107 J 3
Río Arapey Grande 106-107 J 3
Rio Arapiuns 98-99 L 6
Rio Arauá [BR ◁ Rio Madeiro] 98-99 H 8
Rio Arauã [BR ◁ Rio Purus] 98-99 F 9
Río Arauca 92-93 F 3
Rio Ariari 94-95 E 6
Rio Arinos 92-93 H 7
Río Ariporo 94-95 F 4
Rio Aripuanã 92-93 G 6
Río Armería 86-87 HJ 8
Río Aro 94-95 K 4
Río Aros 86-87 F 3
Rio Arraias [BR, Goiás] 100-101 A 7
Rio Arraias [BR, Mato Grosso] 98-99 L 10-11
Río Arrecifes 106-107 G 5-H 4
Rio Arrojado 100-101 B 7
Rio Atelchu 98-99 L 11
Rio Atibaia 102-103 J 5
Río Atoyac 86-87 L 8
Río Atrato 92-93 D 3
Río Atuel 106-107 D 5
Rio Auati Paraná 92-93 F 5
Río Ayambis 96-97 BC 3
Río Aycheyacu 96-97 C 4
Río Azero 104-105 D 6
Rio Azul [BR, Acre] 96-97 E 5
Rio Azul [BR, Paraná] 102-103 G 6
Rio Babahoyo 96-97 B 2-3
Rio Bacajá 98-99 N 7
Río Bacamuchi 86-87 EF 2-3
Río Balsas 64-65 F 8
Río Balsas ó Mezcala 86-87 KL 8-9
Riobamba 92-93 D 5
Rio Banabuiú 100-101 E 3
Rio Barima 94-95 L 3
Río Barrancas 106-107 BC 6
Río Baudó 94-95 C 5
Río Bavispe 86-87 F 2-3
Río Belén 104-105 C 10-11
Río Beni 92-93 F 7
Río Benicito 104-105 D 2-3
Rio Bento Gomes 102-103 D 2
Rio Berlengas 100-101 C 4-5
Río Bermejo [RA ◁ Río Desaguadero] 106-107 C 3
Río Bermejo [RA ◁ Río Paraguay] 111 D 2
Río Bermejo = Río Colorado 106-107 D 2
Río Bermejo, Antiguo Cauce del — 104-105 F 9
Río Bermejo, Valle del — 106-107 CD 3
Rio Bezerra 100-101 A 7
Rio Biá 98-99 E 7
Río Bío Bío 111 B 5
Rio Blanco [BR] 92-93 G 7
Río Blanco [CO, Magdalena] 94-95 D 3
Rioblanco [CO, Tolima] 94-95 D 6
Río Blanco [PE] 96-97 E 4
Río Blanco [RA] 106-107 C 2
Río Blanco [RCH] 106-107 BC 4
Río Blenque 96-97 B 2
Rio Boa Sorte 100-101 B 7
Rio Bobonaza 96-97 C 2
Río Boconó 94-95 G 3
Río Bogotá 91 III b 1
Rio Bonito 102-103 L 5
Río Boopi 104-105 C 5
Rio Boyuyumanu 104-105 B 2
Rio Braço do Norte 102-103 H 7-8
Rio Branco [BR, Acre] 98-99 D 9
Rio Branco [BR, Amazonas] 92-93 F 6
Rio Branco [BR, Bahia] 100-101 B 6-7
Rio Branco [BR, Mato Grosso] 104-105 F 2
Rio Branco [BR, Mato Grosso do Sul] 102-103 D 4
Rio Branco [BR, Rio Branco] 92-93 G 4-5
Rio Branco [BR, Rondônia] 98-99 F 9-G 10
Río Branco [ROU] 106-107 L 4
Rio Branco do Sul 102-103 H 6
Río Bravo 76-77 D 8
Río Bravo, Ciudad — 86-87 LM 5
Río Bravo del Norte 64-65 E 5-F 6
Rio Brilhante 102-103 E 4
Río Bueno [RCH, place] 108-109 C 3
Río Bueno [RCH, river] 108-109 C 3
Rio Buranhém 100-101 DE 9
Rio Buriti 104-105 G 3
Rio Buriticupu 100-101 A 3
Rio Caatinga 102-103 JK 2
Rio Cabaçal 102-103 CD 1
Río Cachapoal 106-107 B 5
Rio Cachoeira 100-101 E 8
Rio Caçiporé 92-93 J 4
Rio Caeté 98-99 D 9
Río Caguán 92-93 E 4
Río Cahuapanas 96-97 C 4
Río Cahuinari 94-95 EF 8
Rio Caiapó 102-103 G 2
Río Caimito 64-65 b 3
Rio Caine 104-105 D 6
Rio Cais 100-101 D 3
Rio Cal 104-105 G 6
Rio Calçoene 98-99 N 3-4
Río Caleufú 108-109 D 3
Río Calvas 96-97 B 4
Rio Camaquã 106-107 L 3
Rio Camararé 98-99 J 11
Río Camarones 104-105 AB 6
Río Camisea 96-97 E 7
Río Campuya 96-97 DE 2
Rio Candeias 98-99 G 9-10
Río Candelaria [BOL] 104-105 G 5
Río Candelaria [MEX] 86-87 P 8
Río Cañete 96-97 CD 8
Rio Canindé 100-101 C 4
Rio Canoas 102-103 G 7
Río Caño Quebrado [PA, Colón] 64-65 a 2
Río Caño Quebrado [PA, Panamá] 64-65 b 2-3
Río Cantu 102-103 F 6
Rio Canumã 98-99 J 7
Rio Canumã = Rio Sucunduri 92-93 H 6
Río Capahuari 96-97 C 3
Río Capanaparo 94-95 G 4
Rio Capanema 102-103 F 6-7
Rio Capim 92-93 K 5
Río Capitán Costa Pinheiro 104-105 GH 2
Rio Capitão Cardoso 98-99 HJ 10
Rio Caquetá 92-93 E 5
Río Carabaya 96-97 FG 9
Rio Carabinamí 98-99 G 6
Rio Caracol 100-101 A 5-6
Rio Caraná 104-105 G 3
Río Carapa 102-103 E 6
Río Cara-Paraná 94-95 E 8
Río Carapo 94-95 K 4
Río Carcarañá 106-107 FG 4
Río Caribe 86-87 P 8
Río Caribe [MEX] 86-87 P 8
Río Caribe [YV] 94-95 K 2
Rio Caris 94-95 K 3
Río Caroní 92-93 G 3
Río Carrao 94-95 K 4
Rio Caru 100-101 A 2
Río Casanare 92-93 E 3
Río Casas Grandes 64-65 E 5-6
Rio Casca 102-103 L 4
Río Casiquiare 92-93 F 4
Río Casireni 96-97 E 8
Río Casma 96-97 BC 6
Rio Cassai 172 CD 4
Río Catamayo 96-97 AB 4
Río Catatumbo 94-95 EF 3
Rio Catete 98-99 LM 8
Rio Catolé Grande 100-101 D 8
Rio Catrimani 92-93 G 4
Rio Cauaburi 98-99 E 4-F 5
Rio Cauamé 94-95 L 6
Rio Cauaxi 98-99 O 7
Río Cauca 92-93 E 3
Río Caura 92-93 G 3
Rio Caurés 98-99 G 5
Rio Cautário 98-99 FG 10
Rio Caveiras 102-103 G 7
Río Caxiabatay 96-97 D 5
Río Cebollatí 106-107 K 4
Río Cenepa 96-97 B 4
Río César 94-95 E 2
Río Chadileuvú 106-107 DE 6
Río Chagres 64-65 bc 2
Río Chalía 108-109 DE 7
Río Chama 76-77 A 4
Río Chamaya 96-97 B 4-5
Río Chambira 96-97 D 3
Río Chambira 96-97 D 4
Río Champotón 86-87 P 8
Río Chancay 96-97 C 7
Rio Chandless 98-99 C 9-10
Rio Changane 172 F 6
Río Chapare 104-105 D 5
Río Chaschuil 104-105 B 10
Río Chayanta 104-105 CD 6
Río Chevejecure 104-105 C 4
Río Chiapa = Río Grande 64-65 H 8
Río Chicama 96-97 B 5
Rio Chicapa 172 D 3
Rio Chichê 98-99 LM 9
Río Chico [RA, Chubut] 111 C 6
Río Chico [RA, Río Negro] 108-109 D 3
Río Chico [RA, Santa Cruz ◁ Bahía Grande] 111 C 7
Río Chico [RA, Santa Cruz ◁ Río Gallegos] 111 C 7
Río Chico [RA, Santa Cruz place] 111 C 7
Río Chico [YV] 92-93 F 2
Río Chico Carmen Silva 108-109 E 9
Río Chilete 96-97 B 5
Río Chillón 96-97 C 7
Río Chinchipe 96-97 B 4
Rio Chingovo 174-175 K 2
Río Chipillico 96-97 A 4
Río Chipiriri 104-105 D 5
Río Chira 96-97 A 4
Río Chirgua 94-95 H 3
Rio Chiulezi 171 D 5-6
Rio Chiumbe 172 D 3
Río Chixoy 64-65 H 8
Río Choapa 106-107 B 3
Rio Chopim 102-103 F 6-7
Río Choro [BOL] 104-105 D 5
Rio Choró [BR] 100-101 E 3
Río Chubut 111 C 6
Río Chucunaque 94-95 C 3
Río Cinaruco 94-95 G 4
Rio Cipó 102-103 L 3
Río Cirí 64-65 a 3
Río Cisnes 108-109 D 5
Río Cisnes [RCH, place] 108-109 D 5
Rio Citaré 98-99 L 4
Río Claro [BOL] 104-105 BC 3
Rio Claro [BR, Goiás ◁ Rio Araguaia] 92-93 J 8
Rio Claro [BR, Goiás ◁ Rio Paranaíba] 92-93 J 8
Rio Claro [BR, Mato Grosso] 102-103 D 2
Rio Claro [BR, São Paulo] 102-103 J 5
Rio Claro [TT] 64-65 O 9
Río Claro [YV] 94-95 G 3
Rio Claro, Serra do — 102-103 G 2
Rio Coari 92-93 G 5-6
Río Coca 96-97 C 2
Río Cocharcas 104-105 D 3-4
Río Coco 64-65 K 9
Rio Codózinho 100-101 B 3
Río Coengua 96-97 E 7
Rio Cofuini 98-99 K 4
Río Coig 108-109 D 8
Río Coig, Brazo Sur del — 108-109 D 8
Rio Coité 100-101 E 6
Río Cojedes 94-95 G 3
Río Colca 92-93 E 8
Río Collón Curá 108-109 D 3
Río Colorado [BOL] 98-99 GH 11
Río Colorado [MEX] 64-65 CD 5
Río Colorado [RA, La Pampa] 111 C 5
Río Colorado [RA, La Rioja] 106-107 D 2
Río Colorado [RA, Neuquén Río Negro] 111 D 5
Río Colorado [RA, Río Negro] 111 CD 5
Río Colorado, Delta del — 108-109 H 2
Rio Comprido, Rio de Janeiro 110 I b 2
Río Conambo 96-97 C 2
Rio Conceição 100-101 A 7
Río Conchos 64-65 EF 6
Río Confuso 102-103 C 6
Río Conlara 106-107 E 4
Río Cononaco 96-97 C 2
Río Conorochite 94-95 H 6
Río Consata 104-105 B 4
Río Copalyacu 96-97 D 3
Río Copiapó 106-107 B 1
Río Coralaque 96-97 F 10
Rio Corda 100-101 B 3-4
Rio Coreaú 100-101 D 2
Rio Corixa Grande 102-103 C 2
Rio Corrente [BR, Bahia] 92-93 L 7
Rio Corrente [BR, Bahia] 92-93 L 7
Rio Corrente [BR, Goiás ◁ Rio Paraná] 100-101 A 8
Rio Corrente [BR, Goiás ◁ Rio Paranaíba] 102-103 G 3
Rio Corrente [BR, Piauí] 100-101 D 3
Rio Correntes 102-103 E 2
Río Corrientes [EC] 96-97 C 3
Río Corrientes [RA] 106-107 H 2
Rio Corumbá 92-93 K 8
Rio Corumbataí 102-103 G 6
Río Cosapa 104-105 B 6
Río Cotacajes 104-105 C 5
Rio Cotegipe 102-103 F 6
Rio Cotia 104-105 D 1
Rio Coxim 102-103 E 3
Rio Cravari 104-105 GH 3
Río Cravo Norte 94-95 F 4
Río Cravo Sur 94-95 EF 5
Rio Crepori 98-99 K 7
Río Crisnejas 96-97 BC 5
Rio Cruxati 100-101 E 2
Río Cruzes 108-109 C 2
Rio Cuando 172 D 5
Rio Cuango 172 C 3
Río Cuao 94-95 H 5
Río Cuareim 106-107 J 3
Río Cuarto [RA, place] 111 D 4
Río Cuarto [RA, river] 106-107 EF 4
Rio Cubango 172 C 5
Rio Cuchi 172 C 4-5
Río Cuchivero 94-95 J 4
Río Cuemaní 94-95 E 7-8
Rio Cuiabá 92-93 H 8
Rio Cuieté 102-103 M 3
Rio Cuilo 172 C 3
Rio Cuito 172 CD 5
Rio Cuiuni 98-99 G 5
Río Cujar 96-97 E 7
Rio Culuene 92-93 J 7
Rio Cuminá 92-93 H 5
Rio Cuminapanema 98-99 L 4-5
Rio Cunene 172 B 5
Rio Curaçá 100-101 E 5
Río Curacó 106-107 E 7
Río Curanja 96-97 F 7
Río Curaray 92-93 D 5
Rio Curicuriari 98-99 DE 5
Rio Curimatá 100-101 B 5-6
Río Curiuja 96-97 E 7
Rio Curuá [BR ◁ Rio Amazonas] 98-99 L 4-5
Rio Curuá [BR ◁ Rio Iriri] 92-93 J 6
Rio Curuá do Sul 98-99 LM 6
Rio Curuaés 98-99 L 9
Rio Curuá Una 98-99 L 6
Rio Curuçá 98-99 C 7
Rio Curuguá 96-97 F 4
Rio Curucuinazá 104-105 GH 3
Rio Curupaí 102-103 EF 5
Rio Curuquetê 98-99 F 9
Rio Cururu-Açu 98-99 K 9
Río Cusiana 94-95 E 5
Río Cutzamala 86-87 K 8
Rio Cuvo 172 B 4
Rio da Areia 102-103 F 5-6
Rio da Cachoeira 110 I b 2
Rio da Conceição 100-101 A 6
Rio Dadache 174-175 K 2
Rio Dange 172 B 3
Rio da Prata [BR ◁ Rio Paracatu] 102-103 J 2
Rio da Prata [BR ◁ Rio Paranaíba] 102-103 H 3
Rio Daraá 94-95 J 7-8
Rio das Antas [BR, place] 102-103 G 7
Rio das Antas [BR, Rio Grande do Sul] 106-107 M 2
Rio das Antas [BR, Santa Catarina] 102-103 F 7
Rio das Arraias do Araguaia 98-99 N 9-O 8
Rio das Balsas 100-101 B 4
Rio das Éguas 100-101 B 7
Rio das Garças 102-103 F 1
Rio das Mortes 102-103 K 4
Rio das Ondas 100-101 B 7
Rio das Pedras 100-101 AB 7
Rio das Pedras [BR] 102-103 J 5
Rio das Pedras [Mozambique] 174-175 L 2
Rio das Velhas 92-93 L 8
Rio Daule 92-93 CD 5
Rio da Várzea [BR, Paraná] 102-103 H 6-7
Rio da Várzea [BR, Rio Grande do Sul] 106-107 L 1
Río de Bavispe 74-75 J 7
Rio de Contas 92-93 L 7
Rio de Contas, Serra do — 100-101 D 7-8
Rio de Geba 164-165 AB 6
Rio de Janeiro 100-101 B 6
Rio de Janeiro [BR, administrative unit] 92-93 LM 9
Rio de Janeiro [BR, place] 92-93 L 9
Rio de Janeiro-Acari 110 I a 1
Rio de Janeiro-Aldeia Campista 110 I b 2
Rio de Janeiro-Alto da Boa Vista 110 I b 2
Rio de Janeiro-Andaraí 110 I b 2
Rio de Janeiro-Anil 110 I a 2
Rio de Janeiro-Bangu 102-103 L 5
Rio de Janeiro-Barra da Tijuca 110 I ab 3
Rio de Janeiro-Bento 110 I a 2
Rio de Janeiro-Boca do Mato 110 I b 2
Rio de Janeiro-Bonsucesso 110 I b 2
Rio de Janeiro-Botafogo 110 I b 2
Rio de Janeiro-Caju 110 I b 2
Rio de Janeiro-Cascadura 110 I ab 2
Rio de Janeiro-Catete 110 I b 2
Rio de Janeiro-Cidade de Deus 110 I ab 2
Rio de Janeiro-Cocotá 110 I b 1
Rio de Janeiro-Copacabana 110 I bc 2
Rio de Janeiro-Cordovil 110 I b 1
Rio de Janeiro-Dende 110 I b 1
Rio de Janeiro-Encantado 110 I b 2
Rio de Janeiro-Engenho Nova 110 I b 2
Rio de Janeiro-Fáb. das Chitas 110 I b 2
Rio de Janeiro-Freguesia [BR ↑ Rio de Janeiro] 110 I bc 1
Rio de Janeiro-Freguesia [BR ↑ Rio de Janeiro] 110 I a 2
Rio de Janeiro-Furnas 110 I b 2
Rio de Janeiro-Galeão 110 I b 1
Rio de Janeiro-Gamboa 110 I b 2
Rio de Janeiro-Gávea 110 I b 2
Rio de Janeiro-Glória 110 I b 2
Rio de Janeiro-Grajaú 110 I b 2
Rio de Janeiro-Honório Gurgel 110 I a 2
Rio de Janeiro-Inhaúma 110 I b 2
Rio de Janeiro-Ipanema 110 I b 2
Rio de Janeiro-Irajá 110 I b 1
Rio de Janeiro-Jacarepaguá 110 I ab 2
Rio de Janeiro-Jardim Botânico 110 I b 2
Rio de Janeiro-Lapa 110 I b 2
Rio de Janeiro-Laranjeiras 110 I b 2
Rio de Janeiro-Leblon 110 I b 2
Rio de Janeiro-Leme 110 I bc 2
Rio de Janeiro-Madureira 110 I ab 2
Rio de Janeiro-Méier 110 I b 2
Rio de Janeiro-Olaria 110 I b 2
Rio de Janeiro-Pechincha 110 I ab 2
Rio de Janeiro-Penha 110 I b 1
Rio de Janeiro-Piedade 110 I b 2
Rio de Janeiro-Praça Seca 110 I a 2
Rio de Janeiro-Ramos 110 I b 2
Rio de Janeiro-Realengo 102-103 L 5
Rio de Janeiro-Ribeira 110 I c 1
Rio de Janeiro-Santa Cruz 102-103 L 5
Rio de Janeiro-São Conrado 110 I b 2
Rio de Janeiro-São Cristovão 110 I b 2
Rio de Janeiro-Tijuca 110 I b 2
Rio de Janeiro-Vigário Geral 110 I b 1
Rio de Janeiro-Vila Balneária 110 I b 3
Rio de Janeiro-Vila Pedro II 110 I a 1
Rio de Janeiro-Zumbi 110 I b 1
Río de la Cal 104-105 G 6
Río de la Fortaleza 96-97 C 7
Río de la Laja 106-107 AB 6
Río de la Magdalena 91 I b 3
Río de la Palca 106-107 C 2
Río de la Paz 104-105 C 5
Río de la Plata 111 EF 5
Río de las Piedras 92-93 E 7
Río de la Turba 108-109 E 9-10
Río del Carmen [MEX] 86-87 G 2-3
Río del Carmen [RCH] 106-107 B 2
Río del Ingenio 96-97 D 9
Río del Jagüé 111 C 3
Río de los Papagayos 106-107 C 5
Río de los Patos 106-107 C 3-4
Río de los Sauces 106-107 E 4
Río del Valle 104-105 D 11
Río del Valle del Cura 106-107 C 2
Río de Majes 96-97 F 10
Río de Mala 96-97 C 8
Rio Demini 92-93 G 4-5
Río de Ocoña 96-97 E 10
Río de Oro 104-105 G 10
Río de Oro [PY] 102-103 C 7
Río de Oro [YV] 94-95 E 3
Río de Reque 96-97 B 5
Río Desaguadero [BOL] 92-93 F 8
Río Desaguadero [RA] 106-107 D 4
Rio de São Pedro 100-101 DE 5
Río Deseado 111 BC 7
Río Deseado, Valle del — 108-109 E 6
Río Diamante 106-107 D 5
Rio Diamantino 102-103 F 2
Rio do Anil 110 I a 2
Rio do Antônio 100-101 C 8

350 Riacho

Rio do Cobre 102-103 FG 6
Rio do Côco 98-99 O 9
Rio do Meio 100-101 B 7
Rio do Ouro 100-101 B 6
Rio do Pará 92-93 JK 5
Rio do Peixe [BR, Bahia] 100-101 E 6
Rio do Peixe [BR, Goiás] 102-103 F 2
Rio do Peixe [BR, Minas Gerais ◁ Rio Preto] 102-103 L 4
Rio do Peixe [BR, Minas Gerais ◁ Rio Santo Antônio] 102-103 L 3
Rio do Peixe [BR, Santa Catarina] 102-103 G 7
Rio do Peixe [BR, São Paulo] 102-103 G 4
Rio do Pires 100-101 C 7
Rio do Pontal 100-101 D 5
Rio do Prado 100-101 D 3
Rio do Sangue 92-93 H 7
Rio dos Bois 102-103 G 3
Rio dos Elefantes 174-175 K 2-3
Rio dos Marmelos 92-93 G 6
Rio do Sono [BR, Goiás] 92-93 K 6-7
Rio do Sono [BR, Minas Gerais] 102-103 K 2
Rio dos Peixes 98-99 K 10
Rio dos Porcos 100-101 B 7
Rio do Sul 111 G 3
Rio Dourados [BR, Mato Grosso do Sul] 102-103 E 5
Rio Dourados [BR, Minas Gerais] 102-103 J 3
Río Duda 94-95 D 6
Rio Dueré 98-99 O 10
Río Dulce 111 D 3-4
Rio Eiru 96-97 F 5
Río Elquí 106-107 B 3
Río El Valle 91 II b 2
Rio Embari 94-95 H 8
Rio Embira 98-99 C 9
Rio Endimari 98-99 E 9
Rio Ene 92-93 E 7
Rio Erebato 94-95 J 5
Río Esmeraldas 92-93 D 4
Rio Farinha 100-101 A 4
Rio Fênix Grande 108-109 D 6
Rio Ferro 98-99 L 11
Río Fiambalá 104-105 C 10
Rio Fidalgo 100-101 C 4
Río Florido 76-77 B 8-9
Rio Formoso 100-101 B 7
Rio Formoso [BR, Goiás] 98-99 O 10
Rio Formoso [BR, Pernambuco] 100-101 G 5
Rio Fresco 98-99 N 8
Río Fucha 91 III b 3
Río Fuerte 64-65 E 6
Río Futaleufú 108-109 D 4
Río Galera 104-105 FG 4
Rio Galheirão 100-101 B 7
Río Gállego 120-121 G 7
Río Gallegos 111 BC 8
Río Gálvez 96-97 E 4
Río Gatún 64-65 b 2
Río Gatuncillo 64-65 b 2
Rio Gaviao 100-101 D 8
Rio Gongoji 100-101 DE 8
Rio Gorutuba 102-103 L 1
Rio Grajau [BR, Acre] 96-97 E 6
Rio Grajaú [BR, Maranhão] 92-93 K 5-6
Río Grande [BOL, place Potosí] 104-105 C 7
Río Grande [BOL, place Santa Cruz] 104-105 E 5
Río Grande [BOL, river] 92-93 G 8
Rio Grande [BR, Minas Gerais] 92-93 K 8-9
Rio Grande [BR, Rio Grande do Sul] 111 F 4
Río Grande [MEX] 64-65 H 8
Río Grande [NIC, place] 88-89 E 8
Río Grande [NIC, river] 64-65 JK 9
Río Grande [PE] 96-97 D 9
Río Grande [RA, Jujuy] 104-105 D 8
Río Grande [RA, La Rioja] 106-107 D 2
Río Grande [RA, Neuquén] 106-107 C 6
Río Grande [RA, Tierra de Fuego river] 108-109 E 9
Río Grande [RA, Tierra del Fuego place] 111 C 8
Rio Grande [USA, Colorado] 76-77 AB 4
Rio Grande [USA, Texas] 64-65 FG 6
Río Grande [YV, place] 91 II b 1
Río Grande [YV, river] 94-95 L 3
Rio Grande, Barragem do — 110 II a 3
Río Grande, Ciudad — 86-87 J 6
Rio Grande, Reprêsa do — 102-103 J 5
Río Grande, Salar de — 104-105 BC 9
Rio Grande City, TX 76-77 E 9
Rio Grande de Santiago 64-65 F 7
Rio Grande do Norte 92-93 M 6
Rio Grande do Norte = Natal 92-93 MN 6
Rio Grande do Piauí 100-101 C 4
Rio Grande do Sul 111 F 3-4
Rio Grande Rise 50-51 GH 7
Río Grandes de Lípez 104-105 C 7-8
Rio Gregório 98-99 C 8
Río Guachiria 94-95 F 5
Rio Guaçu 102-103 F 6
Rio Guaíba 106-107 M 3
Rio Guainia 92-93 F 4
Rio Guaire 91 II b 2
Río Gualeguay 106-107 H 4
Río Gualjaina 108-109 D 4
Rio Guamá 100-101 A 2
Río Guamués 94-95 C 7
Río Guanare 94-95 G 3
Río Guandacol 106-107 C 2
Río Guanipa 94-95 K 3
Río Guapay 104-105 E 5
Rio Guaporé [BR ◁ Rio Mamoré] 92-93 G 7
Rio Guaporé [BR ◁ Rio Taquari] 106-107 L 2
Rio Guará 100-101 B 7
Río Guárico 94-95 H 3
Río Guarita 106-107 L 1
Río Guarrojo 94-95 F 5
Río Guaviare 92-93 F 4
Río Guayabero 94-95 E 6
Río Guayapo 94-95 H 5
Río Guayas [CO] 94-95 D 7
Río Guayas [EC] 96-97 B 3
Rio Guaycurú 102-103 C 7
Río Guayllabamba 94-95 B 1
Río Guayquiraró 106-107 H 3
Río Guëjar 94-95 E 6
Río Guenguel 108-109 D 5-6
Río Güere 94-95 J 3
Río Güiza 94-95 BC 7
Rio Gurguéia 92-93 L 6
Rio Gurupi 92-93 K 5
Ríohacha 92-93 E 2
Río Hardy 74-75 F 6
Río Hato 88-89 FG 10
Rio Heath 96-97 G 8
Rio Hercilio 102-103 GH 7
Río Hondo [BOL] 104-105 BC 4
Río Hondo [MEX, place] 91 I b 2
Río Hondo [MEX, river] 91 I c 1
Rio Hondo [USA, California] 83 III cd 2
Rio Hondo [USA, New Mexico] 76-77 B 6
Río Hondo, Embalse — 106-107 E 1
Río Horcones 104-105 D 9
Río Huahua 88-89 DE 7
Río Huaiá-Miço 98-99 M 10
Río Huallabamba 96-97 C 5
Río Huallaga 92-93 D 6
Río Huarmey 96-97 B 7-C 6
Río Huasaga 96-97 C 3
Río Huasco 106-107 B 2
Río Huaura 96-97 C 7
Rio Iaco 92-93 EF 7
Rio Iapó 102-103 G 6
Rio Ibare 104-105 D 4
Río Ibicuí 111 E 3
Rio Ibirapuitã 106-107 K 2-3
Río Ibirizu 104-105 D 5
Rio Içá 92-93 F 5
Rio Icamaquã 106-107 K 2
Rio Içana 92-93 F 4
Rio Icatu 100-101 C 6
Río Ichoa 104-105 D 4
Rio Igara Paraná 94-95 E 8
Rio Iguaçu 111 F 3
Rio Iguará 100-101 C 3
Rio Iguatemi 102-103 E 5
Rio Ijuí 106-107 K 2
Rio Ilave 96-97 G 10
Rio Imabu 98-99 K 5
Rio Imperial 106-107 A 7
Rio Inajá 98-99 N 9
Rio Inauini 98-99 D 9
Rio Incomáti 174-175 K 3
Rio Indaia 102-103 K 3
Rio Indaiá Grande 102-103 F 3
Río Indio 64-65 c 2
Rio Inhambupe 100-101 E 6
Rio Inharrime 174-175 L 3
Río Inírida 92-93 F 4
Río Inuya 96-97 E 7
Rio Ipanema 100-101 F 5
Rio Ipixuna [BR ◁ Rio Juruá] 96-97 E 5
Rio Ipixuna [BR ◁ Rio Purus] 92-93 G 6
Rio Iquiri 98-99 E 9
Rio Irani 102-103 F 7
Rio Iriri 92-93 J 5
Rio Irivi Novo 98-99 M 9
Río Iruya 104-105 D 8
Río Isana 94-95 F 7
Rio Iscuandé 94-95 C 6
Río Isiboro 104-105 D 5
Rio Itabapoana 102-103 M 4
Rio Itacaiúnas 92-93 JK 6
Rio Itacambiruçu 102-103 L 2
Rio Itacuaí 96-97 F 5
Rio Itaguari 100-101 B 8
Rio Itaim 100-101 D 4
Rio Itaimbey 102-103 E 6
Rio Itajaí 102-103 H 7
Rio Itajaí do Sul 102-103 H 7
Rio Itajaí-Mirim 102-103 H 7
Rio Itala 106-107 A 6
Rio Itambacuri 102-103 M 3
Rio Itanhauã 98-99 F 7
Rio Itanhém 100-101 E 9
Rio Itaparaná 98-99 G 8
Rio Itapicuru [BR, Bahia] 92-93 M 7
Rio Itapicuru [BR, Maranhão] 92-93 L 5
Rio Itapicuru Açu 100-101 DE 6
Rio Itapicurumirim 100-101 DE 6
Rio Itapicuruzinho 100-101 C 3
Rio Itaquai 98-99 C 7
Rio Itararé 102-103 H 5
Rio Itaueira 100-101 C 4-5
Rio Itenes 104-105 E 3
Rio Itiquira 92-93 H 8
Rio Ituí 92-93 E 6
Rio Ituxi 92-93 F 6
Rio Ivaí 111 F 2
Rio Ivinheima 92-93 J 9
Rio Ivón 104-105 C 2
Rioja [PE] 92-93 D 6
Rioja [RCH] 104-105 B 8
Rioja, La — [E] 120-121 F 7
Rioja, La — [RA, administrative unit] 106-107 D 2
Rioja, La — [RA, place] 111 C 3
Rioja, Llanos de la — 106-107 DE 2
Rio Jacarai 100-101 D 2
Rio Jacaré [BR, Bahia] 92-93 L 6-7
Rio Jacaré [BR, Minas Gerais] 102-103 K 4
Río Jáchal 106-107 C 3
Rio Jaciparana 98-99 F 9-10
Rio Jacu 100-101 G 4
Rio Jacuí 106-107 L 2
Rio Jacuípe 92-93 LM 7
Rio Jacundá 98-99 N 6
Rio Jacurici 100-101 E 6
Rio Jaguari 106-107 K 2
Rio Jaguaribe 92-93 M 6
Rio Jalon 120-121 G 8
Rio Jamanxim 92-93 H 6
Rio Jamari 92-93 G 6
Rio Jaminaua 96-97 F 6
Rio Janaperi 92-93 G 4
Rio Jandiatuba 92-93 F 5-6
Rio Japurá 92-93 F 5
Rio Jarauçu 98-99 M 5-6
Rio Jari 92-93 J 5
Rio Jarina 98-99 M 10
Rio Jaru 98-99 G 10
Rio Jatapu 92-93 H 5
Rio Jaú 92-93 G 5
Rio Jauru [BR ◁ Rio Coxim] 102-103 EF 3
Rio Jauru [BR ◁ Rio Paraguai] 102-103 CD 2
Rio Javari 92-93 E 6
Río Jejuí Guazú 102-103 DE 6
Rio Jequitaí 102-103 K 2
Rio Jequitinhonha 92-93 L 8
Rio Jiparaná 92-93 G 6-7
Rio Jordão 102-103 G 6
Rio José Pedro 102-103 M 3-4
Rio Juçaral 100-101 C 2
Rio Jucurucu 100-101 DE 9
Río Juramento 104-105 D 9
Rio Juruá 92-93 F 6
Rio Juruázinho 96-97 FG 5
Rio Juruena 92-93 H 6-7
Rio Jurupari 96-97 F 5-G 6
Rio Jutaí 92-93 F 5
Rio Kwanza 172 B 3
Río Lagartos 86-87 QR 7
Rio Largo 92-93 MN 6
Río las Palmas 74-75 E 6
Río Las Petas 104-105 G 5
Río Lauca 104-105 B 6
Rio Lever 98-99 N 10
Rio Liberdade [BR, Acre] 96-97 E 5-6
Rio Liberdade [BR, Mato Grosso] 98-99 M 10
Rio Ligonha 172 G 5
Río Limarí 106-107 B 3
Río Limay 111 C 5
Rio Limpopo 174-175 K 3
Río Lluta 104-105 B 6
Río Loa 111 BC 2
Rio Loge 172 B 3
Río Lomas 96-97 D 9
Río Loncomilla 106-107 AB 5
Rio Longá 100-101 D 2
Rio Lontra 102-103 F 4
Río Lontué 106-107 B 5
Río Lora 94-95 E 3
Rio Losada 94-95 D 6
Rio Luando 172 C 4
Rio Luanginga 172 D 4
Rio Luangue 172 C 3
Rio Luatizi 171 D 6
Rio Luembe 172 D 3
Rio Luena 172 D 4
Rio Lugenda 172 G 4
Rio Luiana 172 D 5
Río Luján 106-107 H 5
Rio Lunguè-Bungo 172 D 4
Rio Lúrio 172 GH 4
Rio Luxico 172 CD 3
Rio Macacos 100-101 A 8
Rio Macauã 98-99 D 9
Rio Machadinho 104-105 E 1
Rio Machupo 104-105 D 3
Rio MacLennan 108-109 F 9-10
Rio Macuma 96-97 C 3
Rio Macupari 104-105 C 3
Rio Madeira 92-93 G 6
Rio Madeirinha 98-99 H 9
Rio Madidi 92-93 F 7
Río Madre de Dios 92-93 F 7
Río Magdalena [CO] 92-93 E 2-3
Río Magdalena [MEX] 64-65 D 5
Rio Magu 100-101 C 2
Rio Maicuru 92-93 J 5
Rio Maipo 106-107 B 4
Rio Majari 98-99 H 3
Río Malleco 106-107 AB 7
Rio Mamoré 92-93 FG 7-8
Rio Mamuru 98-99 K 6
Rio Manacacías 94-95 E 5-6
Rio Manapire 94-95 H 3
Rio Manhuaçu 102-103 M 3
Rio Manigaua-Miçu 98-99 LM 10
Rio Manicoré 98-99 H 8
Rio Maniqui 104-105 C 4
Rio Manso 92-93 J 7-8
Rio Mantaro 92-93 E 7
Rio Manú 96-97 F 7-8
Rio Manuel Alves 98-99 OP 10
Rio Manurini 104-105 C 3
Rio Manuripe 96-97 G 7
Rio Mapiri [BOL ◁ Río Abuñá] 104-105 C 2
Rio Mapiri [BOL ◁ Rio Beni] 104-105 B 4
Rio Mapuera 92-93 H 5
Rio Mapulau 98-99 G 3-4
Rio Maputo 174-175 K 4
Rio Maraca 98-99 N 5
Rio Maraçacumé 100-101 AB 1-2
Río Marañón 92-93 DE 5
Rio Marapi 98-99 K 4
Rio Marauiá 98-99 F 4-5
Rio Mariê 92-93 F 5
Rio Marine = Mārtīl 166-167 D 2
Rio Matacuni 94-95 J 6
Río Matanza 110 III b 2
Río Mataquito 106-107 B 5
Rio Mataven 94-95 G 5
Rio Maticora 94-95 F 2
Rio Matos 104-105 CD 4
Rio Maués-Açu 92-93 H 5
Rio Maule 106-107 AB 5
Rio Maullín 108-109 C 3
Rio Mauni 96-97 G 10
Rio Mavaca 94-95 J 6
Río Mayo [PE] 96-97 C 4
Río Mayo [RA] 108-109 D 5
Río Mayo [RA, place] 111 BC 7
Rio Mazán 96-97 E 3
Rio Mazimchopes 174-175 K 3
Rio Mearim 92-93 L 5
Rio Mebreije = Rio M'Bridge 172 B 3
Rio Mebridege 172 B 3
Rio Mecaya 94-95 D 7
Rio Medinas 104-105 D 10
Rio Meia Ponte 92-93 K 8
Rio Mendoza 106-107 C 4
Rio Messalo 172 G 4
Rio Meta 92-93 E 3
Rio Mexcala = Río Balsas 64-65 F 8
Rio Mira [CO] 94-95 B 7
Rio Miranda 92-93 H 9
Río Miriñay 106-107 J 2
Rio Miritiparaná 94-95 F 8
Rio Mishagua 96-97 E 7
Rio Mizque 104-105 D 6
Rio Moa 96-97 E 5
Rio Moaco 96-97 G 6
Rio Mocaya 94-95 E 7
Rio Mocó 98-99 E 6
Rio Moções 98-99 O 5
Rio Moctezuma 86-87 F 2-3
Rio Mojiguaçu 102-103 HJ 4
Rio Monday 102-103 E 6
Rio Monte Lindo 102-103 CD 5
Rio Monte Lindo Grande 104-105 G 9
Rio Moquegua 96-97 F 10
Rio Morerú 98-99 J 10
Rio Moricha Largo 94-95 K 3
Rio Morona 92-93 D 5
Rio Mosquito 102-103 M 1-2
Rio Motagua 86-87 Q 10
Rio Motatán 94-95 F 3
Rio Moura 96-97 E 5-6
Rio Moxotó 100-101 F 5
Rio Mucajaí 92-93 G 4
Rio Muco 94-95 F 5
Rio Mucuburi 171 D 6
Rio Mucucuaú 98-99 H 4
Rio Mucuim 98-99 F 8
Rio Mucuri 92-93 L 8
Rio Muerto 104-105 F 10
Rio Mulatos 92-93 F 8
Rio Mundo 120-121 F 9
Rio Muni = Mbini 164-165 G 8
Rio Munim 100-101 B 2
Rio Murauaú 98-99 H 4
Rio Muriaé 102-103 M 4
Rio Murri 94-95 C 4
Rio Muru 96-97 F 6
Rio Mutum 98-99 D 7
Rio Muyumanu 96-97 G 7
Rio Nabileque 102-103 D 4
Rio Ñacunday 102-103 E 6
Rio Nanay 92-93 E 5
Rio Nangariza 96-97 B 4
Rio Napo 92-93 E 5
Rio Naranjal 96-97 B 3
Rio Nashiño 96-97 D 2
Rio Nayá 94-95 C 6
Rio Nazas 86-87 H 5
Rio Nechí 94-95 D 4
Rio Negrinho 102-103 H 7
Rio Negro [BOL, place] 104-105 C 1
Rio Negro [BOL, river ◁ Laguna Concepción] 104-105 E 4
Rio Negro [BOL, river ◁ Rio Madeira] 104-105 C 2
Rio Negro [BR, Amazonas] 92-93 G 5
Rio Negro [BR, Mato Grosso] 92-93 H 8
Rio Negro [BR, Mato Grosso do Sul] 102-103 D 3
Rio Negro [BR, Paraná place] 111 F 3
Rio Negro [BR, Paraná river] 102-103 H 7
Rio Negro [BR, Rio de Janeiro] 102-103 L 4
Rionegro [CO, Antioquia] 94-95 D 4
Rionegro [CO, Santander] 94-95 E 4
Rio Negro [PY] 102-103 D 6
Rio Negro [RA, Chaco] 104-105 G 10
Rio Negro [RA, Rio Negro administrative unit] 111 C 6
Rio Negro [RA, Rio Negro river] 111 D 5-6
Rio Negro [RCH, place] 108-109 C 3
Rio Negro [RCH, river] 108-109 C 3
Rio Negro [ROU, administrative unit] 106-107 J 4
Rio Negro [ROU, river] 111 EF 4
Rio Negro [YV, Amazonas] 94-95 H 7
Rio Negro [YV, Zulia] 94-95 E 3
Rio Negro, Bogotá 91 III c 2
Rio Negro, Embalse del — 111 E 4
Rio Negro, Pantanal do — 92-93 H 8
Rio Negro, Reserva Florestal do — 94-95 G 7
Rio Neuquén 106-107 C 7
Rio Nhamundá 98-99 K 5
Rioni 126-127 KL 5
Río Ñireguco 108-109 CD 5
Rio Novo [BR, Amazonas] 96-97 F 4
Rio Novo [BR, Minas Gerais] 102-103 L 4
Rio Nuanetzi 174-175 J 2
Río Ñuble 106-107 B 6
Rio Nucuray 96-97 D 4
Río Ocamo 94-95 J 6
Rio Oiapoque 92-93 J 4
Río Olimar Grande 106-107 KL 4
Río Orinoco 92-93 F 3
Río Orituco 94-95 H 3
Río Orteguaza 94-95 D 7
Río Ortón 104-105 C 2
Río Oteros 86-87 F 4
Río Otuquis 104-105 G 6
Rio Ouro Preto 98-99 F 10
Rio Pacaás Novas 104-105 D 2
Rio Pacajá 98-99 N 6
Rio Pacaya 96-97 D 4
Río Pachitea 96-97 D 6
Rio Padauiri 92-93 G 4
Rio Paila 104-105 E 5
Rio Paituna 98-99 L 5-6
Rio Pajeú 100-101 E 5
Rio Pakuí 102-103 K 2
Río Palena 108-109 C 4-5
Rio Palma 98-99 P 11
Río Palmar [CO] 91 III c 4
Río Palmar [YV] 94-95 E 2
Rio Palmeiras 98-99 P 10-11
Rio Pampamarca 96-97 E 9
Río Pampas [PE, Apurímac] 96-97 E 8-9
Río Pampas [PE, Ayacucho] 96-97 D 8
Rio Pandeiros 102-103 K 1
Río Pánuco 64-65 G 7
Río Pao [YV, Bolívar] 94-95 J 3
Río Pao [YV, Cojedes] 94-95 G 3
Rio Papagaio 98-99 J 11
Rio Papuri 94-95 F 7
Rio Pará 102-103 K 3
Rio Paracatu [BR ↖ Rio São Francisco] 102-103 K 2
Rio Paracatu [BR ↙ Rio São Francisco] 102-103 K 2
Río Paraguá [BOL] 92-93 G 7
Río Paragua [YV] 92-93 G 3
Rio Paraguacu 100-101 DE 7
Rio Paraguai 92-93 H 9
Río Paraguay 111 E 2
Rio Paraíba 92-93 M 6
Rio Paraíba do Sul 102-103 L 4
Rio Paraim 100-101 A 8
Rio Paramirim 100-101 C 7
Rio Paraná [BR ◁ Río de la Plata] 92-93 J 9
Rio Paraná [BR ◁ Rio Turiaçu] 100-101 B 2
Rio Paranã [BR ◁ Tocantins] 92-93 K 7
Río Paraná [RA] 111 E 3-4
Río Paraná, Delta del — 106-107 H 4-5
Río Paraná de las Palmas 106-107 H 4-5
Rio Paraná do Ouro 96-97 F 6
Río Paraná Guazú 106-107 H 4-5
Rio Paranaíba 92-93 JK 8
Río Paraná Ibicuy 106-107 H 4
Rio Paranaita 98-99 K 9-10
Rio Paranapanema 92-93 J 9
Rio Paranapura 96-97 C 4
Rio Paraopeba 102-103 K 3
Rio Parapeti 104-105 E 6
Rio Parauapebas 98-99 NO 8
Rio Pardo [BR ◁ Atlantic Ocean] 92-93 L 8
Rio Pardo [BR ◁ Rio Grande] 102-103 H 4
Rio Pardo [BR ◁ Rio Paraná] 92-93 J 9
Rio Pardo [BR ◁ Rio São Francisco] 102-103 K 1
Rio Pardo [BR, Bahia] 92-93 L 8
Rio Pardo [BR, Mato Grosso] 92-93 J 9
Rio Pardo [BR, Minas Gerais] 102-103 K 1
Rio Pardo [BR, Rio Grande do Sul] 106-107 L 2-3
Rio Pardo [BR, São Paulo] 102-103 H 4
Rio Pardo de Minas 92-93 L 8
Rio Parima 98-99 FG 3
Rio Parimé 98-99 H 3
Rio Parnaíba 92-93 L 5
Rio Parnaibinha 100-101 AB 5
Rio Paru [BR] 92-93 J 5
Río Parú [YV] 94-95 H 5
Rio Parucito 94-95 J 5
Rio Paru de Este 98-99 L 3-4
Rio Paru de Oeste 98-99 L 3-4
Rio Pasaje 104-105 D 9
Rio Pasión 86-87 PQ 9
Rio Passo Fundo = Rio Guarita 106-107 L 1
Rio Pastaza 92-93 D 5
Rio Patía 92-93 D 4
Rio Patuca 64-65 J 9-K 8
Rio Pauini [BR ◁ Rio Purus] 98-99 D 8-9
Rio Pauini [BR ◁ Rio Unini] 98-99 G 5-6
Rio Pauto 94-95 EF 5
Rio Pelechuco 104-105 B 4
Rio Pelotas 111 F 3
Rio Pelque 108-109 D 8
Rio Penitente 108-109 D 9
Rio Peperiguaçu 102-103 F 7
Rio Pequeni 64-65 bc 2
Rio Pequiri 102-103 E 2
Rio Perdido [BR, Goiás] 98-99 P 9
Rio Perdido [BR, Mato Grosso do Sul] 102-103 D 4
Rio Pereguete 64-65 b 3
Rio Perené 96-97 D 7
Rio Periá 100-101 C 2
Rio Pericumã 100-101 B 2
Rio Pescado 104-105 D 8
Rio Piauí 92-93 L 6
Rio Piaxtla 86-87 G 6
Rio Pichis 96-97 D 7
Rio Pico 108-109 D 5
Rio Piedras 64-65 b 2
Rio Piedras [RA] 104-105 D 9
Rio Pilaya 104-105 D 7
Rio Pilcomayo [BR] 111 D 2
Rio Pilcomayo [PY] 102-103 C 6
Rio Pilmaiquén 108-109 C 3
Rio Pindaré 92-93 K 5
Rio Pindo 96-97 C 2
Rio Pinhuã 98-99 E 9
Rio Pinturas 108-109 D 6
Rio Piorini 92-93 G 5
Rio Piquiri 111 F 2
Rio Piracanjuba 102-103 H 2
Rio Piracicaba [BR, Minas Gerais] 102-103 L 4
Rio Piracicaba [BR, Minas Gerais, place] 102-103 L 3
Rio Piracicaba [BR, São Paulo] 102-103 J 5
Rio Piracuruca 100-101 C 2-D 3
Rio Piranhas [BR, Goiás ◁ Rio Caiapo] 102-103 G 2
Rio Piranhas [BR, Goiás ◁ Rio Grande do Norte] 98-99 O 9
Rio Piranhas [BR, Rio Grande do Norte] 92-93 M 6
Rio Piranji 100-101 E 3
Rio Pirapó [BR] 102-103 F 5
Rio Pirapó [PY] 102-103 D 7
Rio Piratini 106-107 K 2
Rio Piray 104-105 E 5
Rio Pisco 96-97 CD 8
Rio Pisqui 96-97 D 5
Rio Piura 96-97 A 4
Rio Pixuna 98-99 G 8
Rio Poccha 96-97 C 6
Rio Pojige 104-105 D 4
Rio Pomba 102-103 L 4
Rio Porce 94-95 D 4
Rio Porteño 104-105 G 9
Rio Portuguesa 92-93 F 3
Rio Poti 100-101 CD 3
Rio Prata 98-99 P 9
Rio Pratudinho 100-101 B 8
Rio Preto [BR ◁ Rio Grande] 92-93 K 7
Rio Preto [BR ◁ Rio Madeira] 98-99 G 9
Rio Preto [BR ◁ Rio Munim] 100-101 C 2
Rio Preto [BR ◁ Rio Negro] 98-99 F 4
Rio Preto [BR ◁ Rio Paracatu] 92-93 K 8
Rio Preto [BR ◁ Rio Paraíba] 102-103 L 5
Rio Preto [BR ◁ Rio Paranaíba] 102-103 G 3
Rio Preto, Serra do — 102-103 J 2
Rio Preto do Igapó-Açu 98-99 H 7
Rio Primero [RA, place] 111 D 4
Rio Primero [RA, river] 106-107 F 3
Rio Pucacuro 96-97 D 3
Rio Pucará 96-97 F 9
Rio Puelo 108-109 C 3
Rio Puerco 76-77 A 5
Rio Puruê 96-97 G 3
Rio Purus 92-93 F 6
Rio Putumayo 92-93 E 5
Rio Puyango 96-97 A 4-B 3
Rio Quebra-Anzol 102-103 J 3
Rio Queguay 106-107 J 4
Rio Quequén Grande 106-107 H 7
Rio Queras 64-65 a 3
Rio Quevedo 96-97 B 2
Rio Quinto 106-107 E 5
Rio Quitéria 102-103 G 3
Rio Ramis 96-97 FG 9
Rio Ramuro 98-99 L 11
Rio Ranchería 94-95 E 2
Rio Rapel 106-107 B 4-5
Rio Rapulo 104-105 C 4
Rio Real 96-97 G 6
Rio Real 92-93 M 7
Rio Reconquista 110 III a 1
Rio Repartimento 98-99 E 7
Rio Riacho 100-101 D 4
Rio Ribeira do Iguape 102-103 H 6
Rio Ribeirinha 102-103 H 6
Rio Ricardo Franco 104-105 E 2
Rio Rimac 96-97 C 7
Rio Rojas 106-107 G 5
Rio Roosevelt 92-93 G 6-7
Rio Rosario 104-105 D 9
Rio Rovuma 172 G 4
Rio Rubens 108-109 C 9-D 8
Rios, Los — 96-97 B 2
Rio Sabinas 86-87 JK 3
Rio Saladillo [RA, Córboda] 106-107 F 4
Rio Saladillo [RA, Santiago del Estero] 106-107 EF 2
Rio Saladillo = Río Cuarto 106-107 EF 4
Rio Saladillo, Bañado del — 106-107 F 4
Rio Salado [MEX] 86-87 L 4
Rio Salado [RA, Buenos Aires] 106-107 G 5
Rio Salado [RA, Catamarca ◁ Río Blanco] 106-107 C 2
Rio Salado [RA, Catamarca ◁ Rio Colorado] 104-105 C 11
Rio Salado [RA, Santa Fe] 111 D 3
Rio Salado [USA] 76-77 A 5
Rio-Salado = Al-Malaḥ 166-167 F 2
Rio Salí 104-105 D 10
Rio Salinas 102-103 L 2
Rio Salitre 100-101 D 6
Rio Sama 96-97 F 10
Rio Sambito 100-101 CD 4
Río Samborombón 106-107 J 5
Rio Samiria 96-97 D 4
Rio San Carlos 102-103 C 5
Río San Cristóbal 91 III b 3
Río San Fernando [BOL] 104-105 G 5
Río San Fernando [MEX] 86-87 LM 5
Río San Francisco 104-105 D 8
Rio Sangonera 120-121 G 10
Rio Sangrado 110 I b 2
Rio Sangutane 174-175 K 2-3
Rio San Javier 106-107 GH 3
Rio San Joaquín 104-105 E 3
Rio San Jorge 94-95 D 3
Rio San Juan [CO, Chocó] 94-95 C 5
Rio San Juan [CO, Nariño] 94-95 B 7
Rio San Juan [MEX] 86-87 L 5
Rio San Juan [NIC] 64-65 K 9
Rio San Juan [PE] 96-97 D 8
Rio San Juan [RA] 106-107 C 3
Río San Lorenzo 86-87 G 5
Río San Martín 92-93 G 8
Río San Miguel [BOL] 92-93 G 7-8
Río San Miguel [EC] 96-97 C 1
Río San Miguel [MEX, Chihuahua] 86-87 G 4
Río San Miguel [MEX, Sonora] 86-87 E 2
Río San Pablo 104-105 E 4
Río San Pedro [GCA] 86-87 P 9
Río San Pedro [MEX, river ◁ Pacific Ocean] 86-87 H 6
Río San Pedro [MEX, river ◁ Río Conchos] 86-87 GH 4
Río San Ramón 104-105 F 4
Río San Salvador 106-107 J 4
Rio Santa 96-97 B 6
Río Santa Cruz 108-109 E 7-F 8
Rio Santa Lucía 106-107 H 2
Rio Santa Maria [BR ◁ Rio Corrente] 100-101 A 8
Rio Santa Maria [BR ◁ Rio Ibicuí] 106-107 K 3
Río Santa María [MEX ◁ Laguna de Santa María] 86-87 G 2-3
Río Santa María [MEX ◁ Río Tamuín] 86-87 K 7
Río Santa María [RA] 104-105 D 10
Rio Santana 100-101 C 5
Río Santiago [EC] 96-97 B 1
Río Santiago [PE] 96-97 C 3
Rio Santo Antônio [BR ◁ Paraguaçu] 100-101 D 7
Rio Santo Antônio [BR ◁ Rio de Contas] 100-101 CD 8
Rio Santo Antônio [BR ◁ Rio Doce] 102-103 L 3
Rio Santo Antônio [BR ◁ Rio Iguaçu] 102-103 F 6
Río Santo Corazón 104-105 G 5
Río Santo Domingo [MEX] 64-65 G 8
Río Santo Domingo [YV] 94-95 G 3
Rio São Bartolomeu 102-103 J 2
Rio São Benedito 98-99 KL 9
Rio São Domingos [BR ◁ Rio Mamoré] 104-105 D 3-E 2
Rio São Domingos [BR ◁ Rio Paraná] 100-101 A 7
Rio São Domingos [BR ◁ Rio Paranaíba] 102-103 G 3
Rio São Domingos [BR ◁ Rio Verde] 102-103 F 3
Rio São Francisco [BR ◁ Atlantic Ocean] 92-93 LM 6
Rio São Francisco [BR ◁ Rio Paraná] 102-103 EF 6
Rio São João [BR ◁ Rio de Contas] 100-101 CD 8
Rio São João [BR ◁ Rio Paraná] 102-103 F 5
Rio São José dos Dourados 102-103 G 4
Rio São Lourenço 102-103 DE 2
Rio São Manuel 98-99 K 9
Rio São Marcos 102-103 J 2
Rio São Mateus 100-101 D 10
Rio São Miguel 102-103 J 1-2
Rio São Nicolau 100-101 D 3
Rio São Onofre 100-101 C 7
Rio Sapão 100-101 B 6
Rio Sapucaí 102-103 HJ 4
Rio Sarare 94-95 F 4
Rio Saturnina 98-99 J 11
Rio Sauce Chico 106-107 F 7
Rio Sauce Grande 106-107 G 7
Rio Saueuina 104-105 G 3
Rio Save 172 F 6
Rio Seco [MEX] 86-87 E 2
Rio Seco [RA] 104-105 E 8
Rio Seco, Bajo del — 108-109 EF 7
Rio Sécure 104-105 C 4
Rio Segovia = Río Coco 64-65 K 9
Rio Segre 120-121 H 8
Rio Segundo [RA, place] 106-107 F 3
Rio Segundo [RA, river] 106-107 F 3
Rio Segura 120-121 G 9
Rio Sepatini 98-99 E 9-F 8
Rio Sepotuba 102-103 D 1
Rio Sereno 98-99 P 8
Rio Sergipe 100-101 F 6
Rio Serreno 100-101 A 4
Rio Setúbal 102-103 L 2
Rio Shehuen 108-109 DE 7
Rio Sheshea 96-97 E 6
Rio Siapo 94-95 HJ 7

Río Sico 88-89 D 7
Río Siete Puntas 102-103 C 5
Río Simpson 108-109 C 5
Río Sinaloa 86-87 FG 4-5
Río Singuédzi 174-175 J 2
Río Sinú 94-95 CD 3
Río Sipapo 94-95 H 5
Río Soacha 91 III a 4
Río Sogamoso 94-95 E 4
Rio Solimões 92-93 G 5
Rio Solimões 92-93 F 5
Río Sonora 64-65 D 6
Rio Sotério 98-99 F 10
Rio Steinen 92-93 J 7
Rio Suaçuí Grande 102-103 L 3
Rio Suapure 94-95 H 4
Río Suches 104-105 B 4
Ríosucio 92-93 D 3
Río Sucio 94-95 C 4
Rio Sucunduri 92-93 H 6
Rio Sucuriú 92-93 J 8
Rio Suiá-Miçu 98-99 M 10-11
Río Suripá 94-95 F 4
Rio Surumú 98-99 H 2-3
Río Taboco 102-103 E 4
Río Tacuarembó 106-107 K 4
Rio Tacutú 98-99 HJ 3
Rio Tahuamanú 96-97 G 7
Río Tamaya 96-97 E 6
Río Tambo [PE ◁ Pacific Ocean] 96-97 F 10
Río Tambo [PE ◁ Río Ucayali] 92-93 E 7
Río Tambopata 96-97 G 8
Río Tamboryacu 96-97 D 2
Rio Tamuín 86-87 L 7
Rio Tapajós 92-93 H 5
Rio Tapauá 92-93 F 6
Rio Tapenaga 106-107 H 1-2
Rio Taperoá 100-101 F 4
Río Tapiche 96-97 D 5
Rio Tapuió 100-101 B 3-4
Rio Taquari [BR ◁ Rio Jacuí] 106-107 M 2
Rio Taquari [BR ◁ Rio Paranapanema] 102-103 H 5
Rio Taquari [BR ◁ Rio Taquari Novo] 102-103 F 3
Rio Taquari Novo 92-93 H 8
Rio Tarauacá 92-93 E 6
Río Tareni 104-105 C 3
Río Tarvo 104-105 F 4
Rio Tauini 98-99 J 4
Río Tayota 104-105 C 5-D 4
Río Tea [BR] 98-99 EF 5
Río Tebicuary 102-103 DE 7
Río Tebicuary-mi 102-103 D 6-7
Rio Tefé 92-93 F 5
Rio Teles Pires 92-93 H 6
Río Tembey 102-103 E 7
Rio Ten Lira 104-105 H 4
Río Tercero [RA, place] 111 D 4
Río Tercero [RA, river] 106-107 F 4
Río Tercero, Embalse del — 106-107 E 4
Río Teuco 111 D 2-3
Río Teuqito 104-105 F 9
Río Teusaca 91 III c 3
Río Thalnepantla 91 I b 1
Rio Tibaji 102-103 G 6
Rio Tietê 102-103 H 4
Rio Tietê, Canal do — 110 II b 2
Río Tigre [EC] 92-93 D 5
Río Tigre [YV] 94-95 K 3
Río Tijamuchi 104-105 D 4
Rio Tijucas 102-103 H 7
Rio Tijuco 102-103 H 3
Río Timane 102-103 B 4
Rio Timbó 102-103 G 7
Río Tinto 100-101 G 4
Río Tiputini 96-97 C 2
Rio Tiquié 94-95 G 7
Río Tiznados 94-95 H 3
Río Toachi 96-97 B 1-2
Rio Tocantins 92-93 K 5-6
Río Tocuco 94-95 E 3
Río Tocumen 64-65 c 2
Río Tocuyo 94-95 G 2
Rio Todos os Santos 102-103 M 2
Río Toltén 108-109 C 2
Río Tomo 92-93 F 3
Rio Traipu 100-101 F 5
Río Trinidad 64-65 b 3
Rio Trombetas 92-93 H 5
Río Trombudo 106-107 N 1
Río Truandó 94-95 C 4
Rio Tubarão 102-103 H 8
Río Tucavaca 104-105 G 6
Río Tucavaca [BOL, place] 104-105 G 6
Río Tuira 94-95 BC 3
Río Tulumayo 96-97 D 7
Río Tunjuelito 91 III a 3
Río Tunuyán 106-107 CD 4
Río Tuparro 94-95 G 5
Río Turbio [RA, place] 108-109 CD 8
Río Turbio [RA, river] 108-109 D 8
Rio Turiaçu 100-101 B 1-2
Rio Turvo [BR, Goiás] 102-103 G 2
Rio Turvo [BR, Rio Grande do Sul] 106-107 L 1-2
Rio Turvo [BR, São Paulo ◁ Rio Grande] 102-103 H 4
Rio Turvo [BR, São Paulo ◁ Rio Paranapanema] 102-103 H 5
Rio Uanetze 174-175 K 3
Rio Uatumã 92-93 H 5
Rio Uaupés 92-93 F 4
Río Ucayali 92-93 D 6
Río Ulúa 64-65 J 8
Rio Una 100-101 G 5
Rio Unare 94-95 J 3
Río Undumo 104-105 C 3
Rio Uneiuxi 92-93 F 5
Rio Unini 92-93 G 5
Río Upía 94-95 E 5
Rio Uraricaá 94-95 K 6
Rio Uraricoera 92-93 G 4
Río Uribante 94-95 F 4
Río Urique 86-87 G 4
Río Urituyacu 96-97 D 4
Rio Uriuaná 98-99 N 6
Rio Uruará 98-99 M 6
Río Urubamba 92-93 E 7
Rio Urubaxi 98-99 F 5
Rio Urubu 98-99 J 6
Rio Urucu 98-99 FG 7
Rio Urucuia 102-103 K 2
Rio Uruguí Preto 100-101 B 5
Rio Uruguí Vermelho 100-101 B 5
Rio Uruguai 111 F 3
Río Uruguay [RA ◁ Río de la Plata] 111 E 3
Río Uruguay [RA ◁ Río Paraná] 102-103 E 6
Rio Urupa 98-99 G 10
Río Usumacinta 64-65 H 8
Río Utcubamba 96-97 B 4
Río Uva 94-95 G 6
Riouw Archipel = Kepulauan Riau 148-149 DE 6
Rio Vacacaí 106-107 L 2-3
Rio Vacaria [BR, Mato Grosso do Sul] 102-103 E 4
Rio Vacaria [BR, Minas Gerais] 102-103 L 2
Río Vallevicioso 96-97 BC 2
Río Vasa Barris 100-101 E 6
Río Vaupés 92-93 E 4
Río Velille 96-97 F 9
Río Ventuari 92-93 F 3
Río Verde [BOL] 104-105 F 4
Rio Verde [BR, Bahia] 100-101 C 6
Rio Verde [BR, Goiás ◁ Chapada dos Pilões] 102-103 J 2
Rio Verde [BR, Goiás ◁ Rio Maranhão] 102-103 H 1
Rio Verde [BR, Goiás ◁ Rio Paranaíba] 92-93 J 8
Rio Verde [BR, Goiás ◁ Serra do Verdinho] 102-103 G 3
Rio Verde [BR, Goiás place] 92-93 J 8
Rio Verde [BR, Mato Grosso ◁ Rio Paraná] 92-93 J 9
Rio Verde [BR, Mato Grosso ◁ Rio Teles Pires] 92-93 H 7
Rio Verde [BR, Minas Gerais ◁ Represa de Furnas] 102-103 K 4
Rio Verde [BR, Minas Gerais ◁ Rio Grande] 102-103 H 3
Ríoverde [EC] 96-97 B 1
Río Verde [MEX, Oaxaca] 64-65 G 8
Ríoverde [MEX, San Luis Potosí place] 86-87 KL 7
Río Verde [MEX, San Luis Potosí river] 86-87 L 7
Río Verde [PY] 111 E 2
Río Verde [RCH] 111 B 8
Rio Verde de Mato Grosso 92-93 HJ 8
Rio Verde do Sul 102-103 E 5
Rio Verde Grande 100-101 C 8
Rio Vermelho [BR, Goiás] 98-99 P 8-9
Rio Vermelho [BR, Minas Gerais] 102-103 L 3
Rio Vermelho [BR, Pará] 98-99 O 7-8
Río Vichada 92-93 F 4
Río Viejo 106-107 F 2
Rio Vila Nova 98-99 MN 4
Río Vilcanota 96-97 F 8-9
Río Villegas 108-109 D 3
Río Vinchina 106-107 C 2
Río Virú 96-97 B 6
Río Vita 94-95 G 5
Río Vitor 96-97 F 10
Rio Xapecó 102-103 F 7
Rio Xapecózinho 102-103 FG 7
Rio Xaprui 98-99 D 10
Rio Xapuri 96-97 G 7
Rio Xeriuini 98-99 G 4
Rio Xié 98-99 E 4
Rio Xingu 92-93 J 6
Rio Xiruá 98-99 D 8
Río Yabebyry 102-103 D 7
Río Yacuma 104-105 C 4
Río Yaguarón 106-107 L 3-4
Río Yaguas 96-97 F 3
Río Yanatili 96-97 E 8
Río Yapacani 104-105 D 5
Río Yapella 94-95 E 7
Río Yaqui 64-65 E 6
Río Yaracuy 94-95 G 2
Río Yarí 92-93 E 4
Río Yasuní 96-97 C 2
Río Yata 104-105 D 3
Río Yatua 94-95 H 5
Río Yauca 96-97 E 9
Río Yauchari 96-97 C 3
Río Yavarí 92-93 E 5
Río Yavarí-Mirim 96-97 E 4
Río Yavero 96-97 E 8
Río Yguazú 102-103 E 6
Río Yí 106-107 J 4
Río Ypané 102-103 D 5
Río Yuruá 96-97 E 6
Río Zacatula 86-87 JK 8
Río Zambeze 172 F 5
Río Zamora 96-97 B 3
Río Zanjón Nuevo 106-107 CD 3
Riozinho [BR, Acre] 104-105 B 1
Riozinho [BR, Amazonas place] 98-99 E 9
Riozinho [BR, Amazonas river] 98-99 E 6
Río Zuata 94-95 J 3
Río Zutiua 100-101 B 3
Riparia, WA 66-67 DE 2
Ripley, CA 74-75 F 6
Ripley, MS 78-79 E 3
Ripley, NY 72-73 G 3
Ripley, TN 78-79 E 3
Ripley, WV 72-73 F 5
Ripoll 120-121 J 7
Ripon, WI 70-71 F 4
Ripon [CDN] 72-73 J 2
Ripple Mountain 66-67 E 1
Riri Bāzār 138-139 J 4
Riṣāfah 136-137 H 5
Rīsām 'Anayzah 173 C 2
Riṣānī, Ar- 164-165 D 2
Risaralda 94-95 CD 5
Risasi 172 E 2
Rīsh, Ar- 166-167 D 3
Rishīkesh 138-139 FG 2
Rishiri suidō 144-145 b 1
Rishiri tō 142-143 QR 2
Ri'shōn Lĕẕiyyōn 136-137 F 7
Rishra 154 II b 1
Rising Star, TX 76-77 E 6
Rising Sun, IN 70-71 H 6
Rising Sun, OH 72-73 D 5
Risiri 144-145 b 1
Risle 120-121 H 4
Rison, AR 78-79 CD 4
Risør 116-117 C 8
Rissen, Hamburg- 130 I a 1
Risso, Colonia — 102-103 D 5
Ristikent 116-117 O 3
Ristna neem 124-125 CD 4
Rithuggemphel Gonpa 138-139 M 3
Rito Gaviel, Mesa del — 76-77 C 6
Ritscherhochland 53 B 36
Ritter, Mount — 64-65 C 4
Rittman, OH 72-73 EF 4
Rittman,, OH 72-73 EF 4
Ritzville, WA 66-67 D 2
Riukiu = Ryūkyū 142-143 N 7-O 6
Riung 152-153 O 10
Riva [I] 122-123 D 3
Rīvā [IND] 138-139 GH 5
Rivadavia [RA, Buenos Aires] 111 D 5
Rivadavia [RA, Mendoza] 106-107 C 4
Rivadavia [RA, Salta] 111 D 2
Rivadavia [RA, San Juán] 106-107 C 3
Rivadavia [RCH] 111 B 3
Rivalensundet 116-117 mn 5
Rivaliza 98-99 B 8
Rīvān = Rewa 138-139 H 5
Rivas [NIC] 88-89 CD 9
Rivas [RA] 106-107 H 5
Rivasdale, Johannesburg- 170 V a 2
Rivera [RA] 111 D 5
Rivera [ROU, administrative unit] 106-107 K 3
Rivera [ROU, place] 111 E 4
River aux Sables 62 K 3
Riverbank, CA 74-75 C 4
River Cess 164-165 BC 7
Riverdale, CA 74-75 D 4
Riverdale, New York-, NY 82 III c 1
River Falls, WI 70-71 D 3
River Forest 83 II a 1
River Forest, Houston-, TX 85 III a 1
Riverhead, NY 72-73 K 4
Riverhurst 61 E 5
Riverina 158-159 HJ 6-7
Rivermeade Creek 85 II b 1
River Niger, Mouths of the — 164-165 F 7-8
Rivero, Isla — 108-109 B 5
Riveroaks, Houston-, TX 85 III b 2
River of Ponds 63 GH 2
River Ridge, LA 85 I a 2
River Rouge 84 II ab 3
River Rouge, MI 84 II b 3
Rivers 164-165 F 7-8
Riversdal 172 D 8
Riversdale = Riversdal 172 D 8
Riverside 84 II c 3
Riverside, CA 64-65 C 5
Riverside, IL 83 II a 1
Riverside, NJ 84 III d 1
Riverside, OR 66-67 DE 4
Riverside, Atlanta-, GA 85 II b 2
Rivers Inlet 60 D 4
Riverton, NJ 84 III cd 1
Riverton, WY 68-69 B 4
Riverton [AUS] 158-159 G 6
Riverton [CDN] 62 A 2
Riverton [NZ] 161 BC 8
Riviera, TX 76-77 EF 9
Riviera Beach, FL 80-81 cd 3
Rivière Aguanus 63 F 2
Rivière-à-Pierre 72-73 KL 1
Rivière Ashuapmuchuan 62 P 2
Rivière-au-Renard 63 DE 3
Rivière-au-Tonnerre 63 D 2-3
Rivière-aux-Graines 63 D 2
Rivière aux Outardes 56-57 X 7-8
Rivière aux Sables 63 A 3
Rivière Basin 62 O 3
Rivière Batiscan 72-73 K 1
Rivière Bell 62 N 2
Rivière Betsiamites 63 B 3
Rivière-Bleue 63 B 4
Rivière Broadback 62 MN 1
Rivière Caopacho 63 C 2
Rivière Capitachouane 62 N 2-3
Rivière Cascapédia 63 C 3
Rivière Chaudière 63 A 4-5
Rivière Claire = Sông Lô 150-151 E 2
Rivière Coulonge 72-73 H 1
Rivière des Prairies 82 I ab 1
Rivière du Chef 62 P 1-2
Rivière du Lièvre 72-73 J 1
Rivière-du-Loup 56-57 WX 8
Rivière Dumoine 72-73 H 1
Rivière du Petit Mécatina 63 FG 2
Rivière du Sault aux Cochons 63 B 3
Rivière Escoumins 63 B 3
Rivière Galineau 72-73 J 1
Rivière Gatineau 72-73 J 1-2
Rivière Hart-Jaune 63 BC 2
Rivière Jacques Cartier 63 A 4
Rivière Kitchigama 62 M 1
Rivière Laflamme 62 N 2
Rivière-la-Madelaine 63 D 3
Rivière Macaza 72-73 J 1-2
Rivière Magpie 63 D 2
Rivière Maicasagi 62 NO 1
Rivière Manicouagan 56-57 X 7-8
Rivière Manitou 63 D 2
Rivière Manouane 63 A 2-3
Rivière Marguerite 63 C 2
Rivière Marten 62 O 1
Rivière-Matane 63 C 3
Rivière Matapédia 63 C 3
Rivière Mattawin 72-73 K 1
Rivière Mégiscane 62 NO 2
Rivière Mingan 63 E 2
Rivière Missisicabi 62 M 1
Rivière Mistassibi 62 P 2
Rivière Mistassini 62 P 2
Rivière Moisie 56-57 X 7
Rivière Mouchalagane 63 B 2
Rivière Musquaro 63 F 2
Rivière Nabisipi 63 E 2
Rivière Nestaocano 62 P 1-2
Rivière Noire 72-73 H 1
Rivière Octave 62 M 2
Rivière Olomane 63 F 2
Rivière Opawica 62 O 2
Rivière Ouareau 72-73 JK 1
Rivière Ouasiemsca 62 P 2
Rivière Ouataouais 62 NO 3
Rivière Outaouais 72-73 G 1
Rivière Pascagama 62 O 2
Rivière-Pentecôte 63 C 3
Rivière Péribonca 56-57 W 7-8
Rivière-Pigou 63 D 2
Rivière Portneuf 63 AB 3
Rivière Richelieu 72-73 K 1-2
Rivière Rimouski 63 B 3
Rivière Romaine 56-57 Y 7
Rivière Saguenay 56-57 WX 8
Rivière Saint-Augustin 63 G 2
Rivière Saint-Augustin Nord-Ouest 63 G 2
Rivière Sainte Marguerite 63 A 3
Rivière Saint François 72-73 K 1-2
Rivière Saint-Jean [CDN, Pen. de Gaspé] 63 D 3
Rivière-Saint-Jean [CDN, place] 63 D 2-3
Rivière Saint-Jean [CDN, Quebec] 63 D 2
Rivière Saint-Maurice 56-57 W 8
Rivière Saint-Paul 63 H 2
Rivière Samaqua 62 P 1-2
Rivière Savane 63 A 2
Rivière Serpent 63 A 2-3
Rivière Shipshaw 63 A 3
Rivière Témiscamie 62 P 1
Rivière Turgeon 62 M 2
Rivière Vermillon 72-73 K 1
Rivière-Verte 63 BC 4
Rivière Wawagosic 62 M 2
Rivière Wetetnagani 62 N 2
Riviersonderend 174-175 CD 8
Rivoli 122-123 B 3
Rivungo 172 D 5
Riwan = Rewa 138-139 H 5
Riwa Pathar = Rīvā 138-139 GH 5
Riyad = Ar-Rīyāḍ 134-135 F 6
Rīyāḍ, Ar- 134-135 F 6
Riyadh = Ar-Rīyāḍ 134-135 F 6
Riyān 166-167 E 2
Rize 134-135 E 2
Rize dağları 136-137 J 2
Rizhao 146-147 G 4
Rizokárpason 136-137 EF 5
Rizzuto, Cabo — 122-123 G 6
Rjukan 116-117 C 8
R'kīz, Ar- 164-165 AB 5
R'kīz, Lac — = Ar-R'kīz 164-165 AB 5
Rmel el Abiod = Rimāl al-Abyaḍ 166-167 L 4
Roachdale, IN 70-71 G 6
Road Town 88-89 O 5
Roald Amundsen Sea = Amundsenhavet 53 BC 25-26
Roan Cliffs 74-75 J 3
Roan Creek 68-69 B 6
Roanne 120-121 K 5
Roanoke, AL 78-79 G 4
Roanoke, VA 64-65 KL 4
Roanoke Island 80-81 J 3
Roanoke Rapids, NC 80-81 H 2
Roanoke River 64-65 L 4
Roan Plateau 68-69 B 6
Roaring Fork 68-69 C 6
Roaring Springs, TX 76-77 D 6
Roatán, Isla de — 64-65 J 8
Roba el Khali = Ar-Rub' al-Hālī 134-135 F 7-G 6
Robalo 88-89 E 10
Robāṭ 136-137 M 5
Robb 60 J 3
Robbah = Rubbah 166-167 K 3
Robbeneiland 174-175 BC 7
Robben Island = Robbeneiland 174-175 BC 7
Robberson, TX 76-77 E 9
Robbinsdale, MN 70-71 D 3
Robbins Island 160 b 2
Robe [NZ] 160 D 6
Robe, Mount — 160 E 3
Robeline, LA 78-79 C 5
Robe Noir, Lac de la — 63 E 2
Roberta, GA 80-81 DE 4
Robert J. Palenscar Memorial Airport 84 III cd 2
Robert Lee, TX 76-77 D 7
Roberto Payan 94-95 B 7
Roberts 106-107 G 5
Roberts, ID 66-67 GH 4
Roberts Creek Mountain 74-75 E 3
Robertsfors 116-117 J 5
Robertsganj 138-139 J 5
Robertsham, Johannesburg- 170 V ab 2
Roberts Mount 58-59 E 7
Robertson 174-175 C 7
Robertson, WY 66-67 HJ 5
Robertson Bay 53 BC 17-18
Robertsons øy 53 C 31
Robertson Stadium 85 III b 2
Roberts Park, IL 83 II a 2
Robertsport 164-165 B 7
Robertstown 160 D 4
Roberval 56-57 W 8
Robinette, OR 66-67 E 3
Robinson 58-59 U 6
Robinson, IL 70-71 G 6
Robinson, TX 76-77 F 7
Robinson Crusoe 199 AB 7
Robinson Island 53 C 30
Robinson Mountains 58-59 QR 6
Robinson Ranges 158-159 C 5
Robinson River 158-159 G 3
Robinvale 158-159 H 6
Robla, La — 120-121 E 7
Robles 106-107 EF 2
Roblin 61 H 5
Robsart 68-69 B 1
Robson, Mount — 56-57 N 7
Robstown, TX 76-77 F 9
Roby, TX 76-77 D 6
Roca, Cabo da — 120-121 C 9
Roçadas = Xangongo 172 C 5
Rocafuerte 96-97 A 2
Roca Kong 150-151 E 7
Roçalgate = Rās al Ḥadd 134-135 HJ 6
Rocamadour 120-121 HJ 6
Roca Partida 86-87 D 8
Rocas, Atol das — 92-93 N 5
Rocas Alijos 86-87 C 5
Rocas Cormoranes = Shag Rocks 111 H 8
Rocas Negras = Black Rock 111 H 8
Roca Tarpeya, Helicoide de la — 91 II b 2
Ročegda 124-125 O 2
Rocha [ROU, administrative unit] 106-107 KL 4
Rocha [ROU, place] 111 F 4
Rocha, Laguna de — 106-107 K 5
Rochedo 102-103 E 3
Rochefort 120-121 G 5-6
Rochelle, IL 70-71 F 5
Rochelle, LA 78-79 C 5
Rochelle, TX 76-77 E 7
Rochelle, la — 120-121 G 7
Roche-Percée 68-69 E 1
Rocheport, MO 70-71 D 6
Rochester, IN 70-71 GH 5
Rochester, MI 72-73 E 3
Rochester, MN 64-65 H 3
Rochester, NH 72-73 L 3
Rochester, NY 64-65 L 3
Roche-sur-Yon, la — 120-121 G 5
Rocio, Bogotá-El — 91 III bc 3-4
Rock, MI 70-71 G 2
Rock, The — 160 H 5
Rockall 114-115 EF 4
Rockall Plateau 114-115 E 4
Rockaway Beach 82 III cd 3
Rockaway Inlet 82 III c 3
Rockaway Point 82 III c 3
Rock Bay 60 E 4
Rock Creek, OR 66-67 CD 3
Rock Creek [USA ◁ Clark Fork River] 66-67 G 2
Rock Creek [USA ◁ Milk River] 68-69 C 1
Rock Creek [USA ◁ Potomac River] 82 II a 1
Rock Creek Park 82 II a 1
Rockdale, TX 76-77 F 7
Rockdale, Sydney- 161 I a 2
Rockdale Park 85 II b 2
Rockdale Park, Atlanta-, GA 85 II b 2
Rockefeller Center 82 III c 2
Rockefeller Plateau 53 AB 23-24
Rock Falls, IL 70-71 F 5
Rockford, IA 70-71 D 4
Rockford, IL 64-65 HJ 3
Rockford, OH 70-71 H 5
Rockglen 68-69 CD 1
Rockham, SD 68-69 G 3
Rockhampton 158-159 JK 4
Rock Harbor, MI 70-71 FG 1
Rock Hill, SC 64-65 K 4-5
Rockingham 158-159 BC 6
Rockingham, NC 80-81 FG 3
Rockingham Bay 158-159 J 3
Rock Island, IL 64-65 HJ 3
Rock Island, WA 66-67 CD 2
Rock Lake 66-67 E 2
Rockland, ID 66-67 G 4
Rockland, ME 72-73 M 2-3
Rocklands Reservoir 158-159 H 7
Rockledge, PA 84 III c 1
Rockmart, GA 78-79 G 3
Rockport, IN 70-71 G 7
Rockport, MO 70-71 C 5
Rockport, TX 76-77 F 8
Rockport, WA 66-67 C 1
Rock Rapids, IA 70-71 BC 4
Rock River, WY 68-69 CD 5
Rock River [USA, Illinois] 70-71 F 4-5
Rock River [USA, Minnesota] 68-69 H 4
Rocksprings 86-87 KL 2-3
Rock Springs, AZ 74-75 GH 5
Rock Springs, MT 68-69 CD 2
Rocksprings, TX 76-77 D 7
Rock Springs, WY 64-65 E 3
Rockstone 92-93 H 3
Rockton, IL 70-71 F 4
Rock Valley, IA 70-71 BC 4
Rockville, IN 70-71 G 6
Rockville, MD 72-73 H 5
Rockville, OR 66-67 E 4
Rockwall, TX 76-77 F 6
Rockway Park, New York-, NY 82 III c 3
Rockwell City, IA 70-71 C 4
Rockwood, PA 72-73 G 5
Rockwood, TN 78-79 G 3
Rockwood Cemetery 161 I a 2
Rocky Boys Indian Reservation 68-69 B 1
Rocky Ford, CO 68-69 DE 6
Rockyford, SD 68-69 E 4
Rocky Island Lake 62 K 3
Rocky Mount, NC 80-81 H 2-3
Rocky Mount, VA 80-81 G 2
Rocky Mountain 66-67 G 2
Rocky Mountain House 60 K 3
Rocky Mountain National Park 64-65 EF 3
Rocky Mountains 56-57 L 5-P 9
Rocky Mountains Forest Reserve 60 JK 3-4
Rocky Mountain Trench 56-57 L 6-N 7
Rocky Point [USA, Alaska] 58-59 F 4
Rocky Point [USA, California] 66-67 A 5
Rocquencourt 129 I b 2
Rōḍā, Er- = Ar-Rawḍah 173 B 4
Roda, la — 120-121 F 9
Rodalquilar 120-121 FG 10
Rodaun, Wien- 113 I b 2
Rødberg 116-117 C 7
Rødby Havn 116-117 D 10
Roddickton 63 HJ 2
Rode 174-175 H 6
Rodeador 100-101 B 8
Rodeio 102-103 H 7
Rödelheim, Frankfurt am Main- 128 III a 1
Rodenpois = Ropaži 124-125 E 5
Rodeo 111 BC 4
Rodeo, NM 74-75 J 7
Rodeo, El — 94-95 J 3
Rodeo del Medio 106-107 C 4
Rodeo Viejo 106-107 E 4
Rodez 120-121 J 6
Roding [GB] 129 II c 1
Rodney 72-73 F 3
Rodney, Cape — 58-59 D 4
Rodniki 124-125 NO 5
Ródos [GR, island] 122-123 N 7
Ródos [GR, place] 122-123 N 7
Rodosto = Tekirdağ 134-135 B 2
Rodovia Pan-Americana 102-103 H 5-6
Rodovia Perimetral Norte 98-99 G 4
Rodovia Transamazônica 98-99 L 7
Rodrigo de Freitas, Lagoa — 110 I b 2
Rodrigues [BR] 98-99 B 8
Rodrigues [Mascarene Islands] 50-51 N 6-7
Rodriguez 76-77 D 9
Roebourne 158-159 C 4
Roebuck Bay 158-159 D 3
Roedtan 174-175 H 3
Roelofskamp 174-175 F 4
Roermond 120-121 K 3
Roeselare 120-121 J 3
Roe's Welcome Sound 56-57 T 4-5
Rogačov 124-125 H 7
Rogagua, Lago — 92-93 F 7
Rogaland 116-117 B 8
Rogers, AR 76-77 GH 4
Rogers, ND 68-69 G 2
Rogers, TX 76-77 F 7
Rogers City, MI 70-71 J 3
Rogerson, ID 66-67 F 4
Rogersville, TN 80-81 E 2
Roggeveld, Achter — = Agter Roggeveld 174-175 D 6
Roggeveld, Agter — 174-175 D 6
Roggeveld, Klein — 174-175 D 7
Roggeveld, Middel — 174-175 D 7
Roggeveldberge 174-175 C 6-D 7
Roggeveld Mountains = Roggeveldberge 174-175 C 6-D 7
Rognan 116-117 F 4
Rogoaguado, Lago — 92-93 F 7
Rogowo = Raguva 124-125 E 6
Rogue River 66-67 A 4
Rogue River Mountains 66-67 AB 4
Roha 140 A 1
Roha-Lalibela = Lalībela 164-165 M 6
Rohan 120-121 F 4
Rohanpūr 138-139 M 5
Rohault, Lac — 62 O 2
Rohil Khand 138-139 GH 3
Rohṛī 134-135 K 5
Rohṛī, Nahr — 138-139 B 4
Rohtak 134-135 M 5
Roi, Palais du — 128 II b 1
Roi Et 150-151 D 4
Roissy 129 I c 3
Roissy-en-France 129 I cd 1
Roja 124-125 D 5
Rojas 111 D 4
Rojas, Isla — 108-109 C 5
Rojas, Río — 106-107 G 5
Rojhān 138-139 BC 3
Rojhi Māta 138-139 BC 6
Rokan 152-153 D 5
Rokan, Sungai — 152-153 D 5
Rokel 168-169 B 3
Rokitnoje 124-125 F 8
Rokkasho 144-145 N 2
Rokugō, Tōkyō- 155 III b 2
Rokugō-saki = Suzu misaki 144-145 L 4
Roland 68-69 H 1
Roland, AR 78-79 C 3
Rolândia 102-103 G 5
Roldán 106-107 G 4
Roldanillo 94-95 C 5
Rolecha 108-109 C 3
Rolette, ND 68-69 FG 1
Rolfe, IA 70-71 C 4
Rolla 116-117 G 3
Rolla, KS 76-77 D 4
Rolla, MO 64-65 H 4
Rolla, ND 68-69 G 1
Rolleston 158-159 J 4
Rolleville 88-89 H 3
Rolling Fork, MS 78-79 D 4
Rolling Fork, TX 85 III a 1
Rollingwood, CA 83 I bc 1
Rollwald 128 III b 2
Roluos 150-151 D 6
Rolvsøy 116-117 K 2
Rom [EAU] 171 C 2
Rom [N] 116-117 B 8
Roma [AUS] 158-159 J 5
Roma [I] 122-123 E 5
Roma [LS] 174-175 G 5
Roma-Acilia 113 II a 2
Roma-Bufalotta 113 II b 1
Roma-Casaletti Mattei 113 II a 2
Roma-Casal Morena 113 II c 2
Roma-Casalotti 113 II a 2
Roma-Castel Giubileo 113 II b 1
Roma-Cecchignola 113 II b 2
Roma-Centocelle 113 II bc 2
Roma-Ciampino 113 II c 2
Roma-Cinecittà 113 II bc 2
Roma-Corviale 113 II ab 2
Roma-EUR 113 II b 2
Roma-Garbatella 113 II b 2
Romain, Cape — 80-81 G 4
Romaine, Rivière — 56-57 Y 7
Romainville 129 I c 2
Roma-La Giustiniana 113 II ab 1
Roma-Lido di Ostia 122-123 DE 5
Roma, Los Saenz, TX 76-77 E 9
Roma-Magliana 113 II ab 2
Roma-Monte Sacro 113 II b 1
Roma-Montespaccato 113 II a 2
Roma-Montverde Nuovo 113 II b 2
Roman 122-123 M 2
Romana, La — 64-65 J 8
Román Arreola 76-77 B 9
Romanche Deep 50-51 J 6
Romang 106-107 H 2
Romang, Pulau — 148-149 J 8
Romāni = Rummānah 173 C 2
Romania 122-123 K-M 2
Roman-Koš, gora — 126-127 FG 4
Romano, Cape — 80-81 bc 4
Romano, Cayo — 64-65 L 7
Romanov = Dzeržinsk 126-127 CD 1
Romanovka [SU, Bur'atskaja ASSR] 132-133 V 7
Romanovka [SU, Saratovskaja Oblast'] 124-125 O 8
Romanovka = Bessarabka 126-127 D 3
Romanovskij = Kropotkin 126-127 K 4
Romans-sur-Isère 120-121 K 6
Romanvloer 174-175 D 6
Roman Wall 119 E 4
Romanzof, Cape — 56-57 C 5
Romanzof Mountains 58-59 PQ 2
Roma-Ostia Antica 122-123 DE 5
Roma-Ottavia 113 II a 1
Roma-Ponto Galeria 113 II a 2
Roma-Portonaccio 113 II b 2
Roma-Prima Porta 113 II b 1
Roma-Primavalle 113 II ab 1
Roma-Quadraro 113 II b 2
Roma-San Basilio 113 II b c 1
Roma-Santa Maria del Soccorso 113 II bc 2
Roma-Sant'Onofrio 113 II b 1
Roma-Settecamini 113 II c 1
Roma-Spinaceto 113 II b 2
Roma-Spizzichino 113 II ab 1
Roma-Tomba di Nerone 113 II ab 1
Roma-Tor di Quinto 113 II b 1
Roma-Tor Marancia 113 II b 2
Roma-Tor Pignatara 113 II b 2
Roma-Torre Gaia 113 II c 2
Roma-Torre Lupara 113 II c 1
Roma-Torre Nova 113 II c 2
Roma-Torre Vècchia 113 II a 1
Roma-Tor Sapienza 113 II c 2
Roma-Tufello 113 II b 1
Roma-Valcanuta 113 II ab 2
Roma-Villini 113 II a 2
Roma-Vitinia 113 II ab 2
Romblon 148-149 H 4
Rome, GA 64-65 J 5
Rome, NY 64-65 LM 3
Rome, OR 66-67 E 4
Rome = Roma 122-123 E 5
Romeo = Romny 126-127 F 1
Romeo, MI 72-73 E 3
Römer 128 III ab 1
Romero, TX 76-77 C 5
Romford, London- 129 II c 1
Romilly-sur-Seine 120-121 J 4

Salar de Cauchari 104-105 C 8
Salar de Chalviri 104-105 C 8
Salar de Chiguana 104-105 C 7
Salar de Coipasa 92-93 F 8
Salar de Empexa 104-105 B 7
Salar de Huasco 104-105 B 7
Salar de la Isla 104-105 B 9
Salar del Hombre Muerto
104-105 C 9
Salar de Llamara 104-105 B 7
Salar de Maricunga 104-105 B 10
Salar de Pajonales 104-105 B 9
Salar de Pedernales 104-105 B 10
Salar de Pintados 104-105 B 7
Salar de Pipanaco 104-105 C 10-11
Salar de Punta Negra 104-105 B 9
Salar de Río Grande 104-105 BC 9
Salar de Tara 104-105 C 8
Salar de Uyuni 92-93 F 9
Salar Grande 104-105 AB 7
Salar Pocitos 104-105 C 9
Salatan, Cape — = Tanjung Selatan
148-149 F 7
Salatiga 148-149 F 8
Salavat [SU] 132-133 K 7
Salavat [TR] 136-137 F 2
Salaverry 92-93 D 6
Salavina 106-107 F 2
Salawati, Pulau — 148-149 K 7
Salāya 138-139 B 6
Salayar, Pulau — 148-149 H 8
Salayar, Selat — 152-153 N 9-O 8
Sala y Gómez 156-157 M 6
Salazar, NM 76-77 A 5
Salazar [CO] 94-95 E 4
Salazar = N'Dala Tando 172 BC 3
Sālbani 138-139 L 6
Salcantay, Nevado de — 96-97 E 8
Salcedo 94-95 B 8
Salcedo = San Miguel 96-97 B 2
Salcha River 58-59 P 4
Šalčininkai 124-125 E 6
Saldaña [CO] 94-95 D 5
Saldanha [BR] 100-101 C 6
Saldanha [ZA] 172 C 8
Saldungaray 106-107 G 7
Saldus 124-125 D 5
Sale [AUS] 158-159 J 7
Sale [BUR] 141 D 5
Salé = Slā' 164-165 C 2
Salebabu, Pulau — 148-149 J 6
Salechard 132-133 M 4
Saleh, Teluk — 148-149 G 8
Şāleḥābād [IR ↖ Hamadān]
136-137 N 5
Şāleḥābād [IR ↙ Īlām] 136-137 M 6
Salekhard = Salechard
132-133 M 4
Salem, AR 78-79 D 2
Salem, FL 80-81 b 2
Salem, IL 70-71 F 6
Salem, IN 70-71 GH 6
Salem, MA 72-73 L 3
Salem, MO 70-71 E 7
Salem, NJ 72-73 J 5
Salem, OH 72-73 F 4
Salem, OR 64-65 B 2
Salem, SD 68-69 H 4
Salem, VA 80-81 F 2
Salem, WV 72-73 F 5
Salem [IND] 134-135 M 8
Salem [ZA] 174-175 G 7
Salem, Winston-, NC 64-65 KL 4
Salembu Besar, Pulau —
148-149 FG 8
Salemi 122-123 E 7
Salempur 138-139 JK 4
Sälen 116-117 E 7
Salentina 122-123 GH 5
Salerno 122-123 F 5
Salerno, Golfo di — 122-123 F 5
Saleye 168-169 E 3
Salford 119 E 5
Salgir 126-127 G 4
Salgótarján 118 J 4
Salgueiro 92-93 M 6
Salhyr = Nižnegorskij 126-127 G 4
Sali [DZ] 166-167 F 6
Šali [SU] 126-127 MN 5
Salí, Río — 104-105 D 10
Salibabu Islands = Kepulauan
Talaud 148-149 J 6
Salida, CO 64-65 E 4
Şalīf, Aş- 134-135 E 7
Şāliḥīyah, Aş- [ET] 173 BC 2
Şāliḥīyah, Aş- [SYR] 136-137 J 5
Salihli 136-137 C 3
Salima 172 FG 4
Şalīmah, Wāḥāt — 164-165 K 4
Salin 141 D 5
Salina, KS 64-65 G 4
Salina, OK 76-77 G 4
Salina, UT 74-75 H 3
Salina, Isola — 122-123 F 6
Salina Cruz 64-65 G 8
Salina de Incahuasi 104-105 C 9
Salina de Jama 104-105 C 8
Salina del Bebedero 106-107 D 4
Salina del Gualicho 108-109 G 3
Salina del Pito 108-109 E 4
Salina del Rincón 104-105 C 8-9
Salina Grande 106-107 D 6
Salina Grandes 104-105 CD 8
Salina La Antigua 106-107 DE 2-3
Salina Llancanelo 106-107 C 5
Salinas, CA 64-65 B 4
Salinas [BOL] 104-105 D 7
Salinas [BR] 92-93 L 8
Salinas [EC] 92-93 C 5
Salinas [MEX] 86-87 H 8
Salinas [RCH] 104-105 B 8
Salinas, Cabo de — 120-121 J 9
Salinas, Las — 96-97 C 7
Salinas, Pampa de las —
106-107 D 3-4
Salinas, Punta de — 92-93 D 7
Salinas, Río — 102-103 L 2
Salinas de Garci Mendoza
104-105 C 6
Salinas de Hidalgo 86-87 JK 6
Salinas de Trapalcó 108-109 F 2
Salinas Grandes [RA ↖ Córdoba]
111 C 4-D 3
Salinas Grandes [RA, Península
Valdés] 108-109 GH 4
Salinas La Porteña 106-107 EF 7
Salinas Peak 76-77 A 6
Salinas River 74-75 C 4-5
Salinas Victoria 76-77 DE 9
Salin Chaung 141 D 5
Saline, LA 78-79 C 4
Saline River [USA, Arkansas]
78-79 CD 4
Saline River [USA, Kansas] 68-69 G 6
Saline Valley 74-75 E 4
Salingyī = Hsalingyī 141 D 4-5
Salinópolis 92-93 K 4-5
Sālīpur 138-139 L 7
Salisbury 119 EF 6
Salisbury, CT 72-73 K 3-4
Salisbury, MD 64-65 LM 4
Salisbury, MO 70-71 D 6
Salisbury, NC 64-65 KL 4
Salisbury = Harare 172 F 5
Salisbury, Lake — 172 FG 1
Salisbury, Mount — 58-59 O 2
Salisbury, ostrov — 132-133 HJ 1
Salisbury Island 56-57 VW 5
Salish Mountains 66-67 F 1-2
Salitre 96-97 B 2
Salitre, El — 91 III b 1
Salitre, Rio — 100-101 D 6
Salitre-cué 102-103 DE 7
Salitroso, Lago — 108-109 D 6
Saljany 126-127 O 7
Šalkar 126-127 PQ 1
Šalkar, ozero — 126-127 P 1
Şalkhad 136-137 G 6
Salkhia, Howrah- 154 II b 2
Salkum, WA 66-67 B 2
Salla 116-117 N 4
Salle, La — [CDN, Montréal] 82 I b 2
Salle, La — [CDN, Windsor] 84 II b 3
Salley, SC 80-81 F 4
Salliqueló 106-107 F 6
Sallisaw, OK 76-77 G 5
Sallyana 134-135 N 5
Salm, ostrov — 132-133 KL 2
Salmah, Jabal — 134-135 E 5
Salmān, As- 136-137 L 7
Salmanlı = Kayadibi 136-137 F 3
Salmanlı = Kaymas 136-137 D 2
Salmannsdorf, Wien- 113 I b 1
Salmān Pāk 136-137 L 6
Sālmāra, South — 138-139 N 5
Salmās 136-137 L 3
Salmi 132-133 E 5
Salmo 66-67 E 1
Salmon, ID 66-67 FG 3
Salmon Arm 60 H 4
Salmon Falls 66-67 F 4
Salmon Falls Creek 66-67 F 4
Salmon Falls Creek Lake 66-67 F 4
Salmon Fork 58-59 R 3
Salmon Gums 158-159 D 6
Salmon River [CDN, Acadie] 63 D 4
Salmon River [CDN, Anticosti I.]
63 E 3
Salmon River [USA, Alaska]
58-59 H 3
Salmon River [USA, Idaho]
64-65 CD 2
Salmon River, Middle Fork —
66-67 F 3
Salmon River, South Fork —
66-67 F 3
Salmon River Mountains
64-65 C 3-D 2
Salmon Village, AK 58-59 QR 3
Salo 116-117 K 7
Saloá 100-101 F 5
Salobel'ak 124-125 R 5
Salomé 100-101 F 5
Salon 138-139 H 4
Salonga 172 D 2
Salonga Nord, Parc national de la —
172 D 2
Salonga Sud, Parc national de la —
172 D 2
Salonika = Thessaloníkē
122-123 K 5
Salonika, Gulf of — = Thermaïkòs
Kólpos 122-123 K 5-6
Salonta 122-123 JK 2
Salor 120-121 D 9
Salor = Pulau Sedanau
150-151 F 11
Saloum, Îles — 168-169 A 2
Saloum, Vallée du — 168-169 B 2
Salpausselkä 116-117 L-O 7
Salsacate 111 CD 4
Sal'sk 126-127 K 3
Šal'skij 124-125 KL 3
Salso 122-123 E 7
Salsomaggiore Terme 122-123 C 3
Salt, As- 136-137 F 6
Salta [RA, administrative unit]
104-105 C 9-E 8
Salta [RA, place] 111 CD 2
Salta Ginete, Serra do —
102-103 K 3
Salt Basin 76-77 B 7
Salt Chaukī 138-139 B 5
Saltcoats 61 GH 5
Salt Creek 68-69 C 4
Salten 116-117 F 4-G 3
Saltfjord 116-117 EF 4
Salt Flat 76-77 B 7
Salt Flat, TX 64-65 EF 5
Salt Fork Brazos River 76-77 D 6
Salt Fork Red River 76-77 E 5
Saltillo 64-65 FG 6
Salt Lake, NM 74-75 J 5
Salt Lake City, UT 64-65 D 3
Salt Lakes 158-159 CD 5
Salt Lick, KY 72-73 E 5
Salt Marsh = Lake MacLeod
158-159 B 4
Salto [BR] 102-103 J 5
Salto [RA] 111 DE 4
Salto [ROU, administrative unit]
106-107 J 3
Salto [ROU, place] 111 E 4
Salto, El — 64-65 E 7
Salto Ariranha 102-103 G 6
Salto da Divisa 92-93 LM 8
Salto das Estrelas 104-105 G 4
Salto das Sete Quedas [BR, Paraná]
102-103 E 6
Salto das Sete Quedas [BR, Rio Teles
Pires] 92-93 H 6
Salto de Angostura I 92-93 E 4
Salto de Angostura II 92-93 E 4
Salto del Angel 92-93 G 3
Salto de las Rosas 106-107 CD 5
Salto del Erito 94-95 K 4
Salto de Pira 88-89 D 8
Salto do Aparado 102-103 G 6
Salto do Ubá 111 F 2
Salto Grande [BR] 102-103 H 5
Salto Grande [CO] 94-95 E 8
Salto Grande, Embalse — 111 E 4
Salto Grande del Uruguay 111 F 3
Saltoluokta 116-117 H 4
Salto Mapiripan 92-93 E 4
Salto Mauá 102-103 G 6
Salton, CA 74-75 F 6
Saltón, El — 111 B 7
Salton Sea 64-65 CD 5
Salto Osório 111 F 3
Salto Pocão 98-99 L 5
Sāltora 138-139 L 6
Salto Santiago 102-103 F 6
Salto Von Martius 92-93 J 7
Salt Pan Creek 161 I a 2
Salt River [USA, Arizona] 64-65 D 5
Salt River [USA, Kentucky]
70-71 H 6-7
Salt River [USA, Missouri] 70-71 E 6
Salt River = Soutrivier [ZA ◁ Atlantic
Ocean] 174-175 B 6
Salt River = Soutrivier [ZA ◁
Grootrivier] 174-175 E 7
Salt River Indian Reservation
74-75 H 6
Saltspring Island 66-67 B 1
Saltville, VA 80-81 F 2
Salt Water Lake 154 II b 2
Saltykovka 124-125 P 7
Saluda, SC 80-81 EF 3
Saluen 142-143 H 6
Salūm, As- 164-165 K 2
Salūmbar 138-139 DE 5
Salūr 140 F 1
Sālūru = Sālūr 140 F 1
Salus, AR 78-79 C 3
Salut, Îles du — 98-99 MN 2
Saluzzo 122-123 B 3
Salvación, Bahía — 108-109 B 8
Salvador 92-93 M 7
Salvador, El — [ES] 64-65 J 9
Salvador, El — [RCH] 104-105 B 10
Salvador, Lake — 78-79 D 6
Salvan = Salon 138-139 H 4
Salvatierra [MEX] 86-87 K 7
Salvation Army College 85 II b 2
Salvus 60 C 2
Salwā Baḥrī 173 C 5
Salween = Thanlwin Myit
148-149 C 2-3
Salyānā = Sallyana 134-135 N 5
Salyersville, KY 72-73 E 6
Salzach 118 F 4-5
Salzbrunn 172 C 6
Salzburg [A, administrative unit]
118 F 5
Salzburg [A, place] 118 F 5
Salzgitter 118 E 2-3
Salzwedel 118 E 2
Sama, Río — 96-97 F 10
Samacá 94-95 E 5
Sama de Langreo 120-121 E 7
Samae San, Ko — 150-151 C 6
Samaesan, Ko — = Ko Samae San
150-151 C 6
Sāmāguri 141 C 2
Samāh, Bi'r — 136-137 L 8
Samaipata 104-105 DE 6
Samalakōṭṭa = Sāmalkot 140 F 2
Samalayuca 76-77 A 7
Samales Group 152-153 O 3
Samalga Island 58-59 m 4
Sāmalkot 140 F 2
Samālūṭ 173 B 3
Samāna 138-139 F 2
Samaná, Bahía de — 64-65 N 8
Samaná, Cabo — 88-89 M 5
Samana Cay 88-89 K 3
Samānāḷakanda 134-135 N 9
Samanco, Bahía de — 96-97 B 6
Samandağ 136-137 F 4
Samán de Apure, El — 94-95 G 4
Samandéni 168-169 D 3
Samangān 134-135 K 3
Samani 142-143 R 3
Samaqua, Rivière — 62 P 1-2
Samar 148-149 J 4
Samara [SU, Rossijskaja SFSR]
132-133 J 7
Samara [SU, Ukrainskaja SSR]
126-127 G 2
Samara = Kujbyšev 132-133 HJ 7
Samarai 148-149 gh 7
Samarga 132-133 ab 8
Samariapo 94-95 H 5
Samarinda 148-149 G 7
Samarkand 134-135 K 3
Samarkand = Temirtau
132-133 N 7
Samaro 138-139 B 5
Sāmarrā' 134-135 E 4
Samāstipur 138-139 K 5
Samāwah, As- 134-135 EF 4
Sambaíba 100-101 B 4
Sambala 172 D 3
Sambaliung 148-149 G 6
Sambalpore = Sambalpur
134-135 N 6
Sambalpur [IND, Madhya Pradesh]
138-139 H 7
Sambalpur [IND, Orissa] 134-135 N 6
Sambar, Tanjung — 152-153 HJ 7
Sambas 148-149 E 6
Sambas, Sungai — 152-153 H 5
Sambava 172 K 4
Sambhal 134-135 M 5
Sāmbhar 138-139 E 4
Sāmbhar Salt Lake 138-139 E 4
Sambia 172 E 5-F 4
Sambit, Pulau — 152-153 N 5
Sambito, Rio — 100-101 CD 4
Sambo 168-169 E 3
Samboja 148-149 G 7
Sambongi = Towada 144-145 N 2
Sambor [K] 148-149 E 4
Sambor [SU] 126-127 A 2
Samborombón, Bahía — 111 E 5
Samborombón, Río — 106-107 J 5
Samborondón 96-97 AB 2
Sambre 120-121 K 3
Sambro Bank 63 E 6
Šamchal 126-127 N 5
Samch'ŏk 142-143 OP 4
Samch'ŏnp'o 144-145 FG 5
Šamchor 126-127 MN 6
Sam Creek, AK 58-59 Q 4
Samdŭng 144-145 F 3
Same [EAT] 172 G 2
Samet, Ko — 150-151 C 6
Samfya 171 B 5
Samḥah 134-135 G 8
Sam Houston Park 85 III b 1
Sami 138-139 C 6
Sami = Hsamī 141 C 5
Samia [RN] 168-169 H 2
Samia [WAN] 168-169 F 3
Samīm, Umm as- 134-135 H 6
Samiria, Río — 96-97 D 4
Sam Ka Tsun 155 I b 2
Samkos, Phnom — 150-151 D 6
Sammanturai = Sammantureyi
140 EF 7
Sammantureyi 140 EF 7
Sāmmār 166-167 E 2
Samnagjin 144-145 G 5
Sam Neua 148-149 D 2
Sam Ngam 150-151 BC 4
Sam Ngao 150-151 B 4
Samoa 148-149 c 1
Samoa, CA 66-67 A 5
Samoa Islands 148-149 c 1
Samoded 124-125 N 2
Samôn Chaung 141 DE 5
Samora = Zamora de Hidalgo
64-65 F 7-8
Sámos [GR, island] 122-123 M 7
Sámos [GR, place] 122-123 M 7
Samosir, Pulau — 148-149 C 6
Samothrákē 122-123 L 5
Šamovo 124-125 H 6
S'amozero 124-125 J 3
Sampacho 111 CD 4
Sampaga 152-153 N 7
Sampang 148-149 F 8
Samper de Calanda 120-121 G 8
Sampgāńv = Sampgaon 140 B 3
Sampgaon 140 B 3
Sampit 148-149 F 7
Sampit, Sungai — 152-153 K 7
Sampit, Teluk — 148-149 F 7
Sampués 94-95 D 3
Sampur 124-125 NO 7
Samrah 136-137 J 4
Samrāla 138-139 EF 2
Samran, Huai — 150-151 E 5
Sam Rayburn Lake 76-77 G 7
Samrong 148-149 D 4
Samshui = Sanshui 146-147 D 10
Samsø 116-117 D 10
Samson, AL 78-79 FG 5
Sâm Sơn [VN] 150-151 EF 3
Samstipur = Samāstipur
138-139 K 5
Samsu 144-145 G 2
Samsun 134-135 D 2
Sam Teu 150-151 E 2-3
Samtredia 126-127 L 5
Samuel, Cachoeira do — 98-99 G 9
Samuel, Mount — 158-159 F 3
Samuhú 106-107 G 1
Samui, Chong — 150-151 BC 8
Samui, Ko — 148-149 D 5
Samundarī 138-139 D 2
Samur 126-127 O 6
Samurskij chrebet 126-127 N 6
Samutlu 136-137 E 3
Samut Prakan 148-149 D 4
Samut Sakhon 150-151 BC 6
Samut Songkhram 150-151 C 6
Samyā La 138-139 K 2
Š'amža 124-125 N 3
San [PL] 118 L 3
San [RMM] 164-165 CD 6
San, Sê — 150-151 F 6
Sanā [ADN] 134-135 FG 7
Saña [PE] 96-97 B 5
Şan'ā' [Y] 134-135 EF 7
Sana [YU] 122-123 G 3
Sanaag 164-165 b 2
Sanābād 136-137 N 4
Şanabū 173 B 4
Sanad, As- 166-167 L 2
SANAE 53 b 36-1
Şanāfīr, Jazīrat — 173 D 4
Sanaga 164-165 G 8
San Agustín [BOL] 104-105 C 7
San Agustín [CO] 94-95 C 7
San Agustín [RA, Buenos Aires]
111 E 5
San Agustín [RA, Córdoba]
106-107 E 3
San Agustín, Arroyo —
104-105 CD 3
San Agustin, Cape — 148-149 J 5
San Agustín de Valle Fértil
106-107 D 3
Sanak Island 58-59 b 2
Sanām, As- 134-135 G 6
Sanām, Jabal — 136-137 M 7
San Ambrosio 199 B 6
Sanam Chai 150-151 C 6
Sanana = Pulau Sulabesi
148-149 J 7
Sānand 138-139 D 6
Sanandaj 134-135 F 3
Sanandita 104-105 E 7
Sanando 168-169 D 2
San Andreas, CA 74-75 C 3
San Andrés [BOL] 104-105 D 4
San Andrés [CO, island] 64-65 KL 9
San Andres [CO, place] 94-95 E 4
San Andrés, Punta — 106-107 J 7
San Andrés, Quebrado —
106-107 BC 1
San Andrés Atenco 91 I b 1
San Andrés de Giles 106-107 H 5
San Andres Mountains 64-65 E 5
San Andrés Tetepilco, Ixtacalco-
91 I c 2
San Andrés Totoltepec 91 I b 3
San Andres Tuxtla 64-65 GH 8
San Andrés y Providencia
88-89 F 8-9
Sananduva 106-107 M 1
San Angel 92-93 E 2-3
San Angelo, TX 64-65 FG 5
Sanangyi 146-147 BC 8
Sanankoroba 168-169 CD 2
San Anselmo, CA 74-75 B 4
San.Anton 96-97 F 9
San Antonio, NM 76-77 A 6
San Antonio, TX 64-65 G 6
San Antônio [BOL] 104-105 C 3
San Antonio [CO, Guajira] 94-95 E 2
San Antonio [CO, Tolima] 94-95 D 6
San Antonio [CO, Valle del Cauca]
94-95 C 6
San Antonio [PE] 96-97 EF 4
San Antonio [PY] 102-103 D 5
San Antonio [RA, Catamarca]
106-107 E 2
San Antonio [RA, Corrientes]
106-107 J 2
San Antonio [RA, Jujuy] 104-105 D 9
San Antonio [RA, La Rioja]
106-107 D 3
San Antonio [RA, San Luis]
106-107 D 4
San Antonio [RCH] 111 B 4
San Antonio [ROU] 106-107 J 3
San Antonio [YV, Amazonas]
94-95 H 6
San Antonio [YV, Barinas] 94-95 G 3
San Antonio [YV, Monagas]
94-95 K 2-3
San Antonio, Cabo — [C] 64-65 K 7
San Antonio, Cabo — [RA]
106-107 J 6
San Antonio, Sierra de —
86-87 E 2-3
San Antonio Bay 76-77 F 8
San Antonio de Areco 106-107 H 5
San Antonio de Caparo 92-93 E 3
San Antonio de Esmoraca
104-105 C 7-8
San Antonio de Galipán 91 II b 1
San Antonio de Lípez 104-105 C 7
San Antonio de Litín 106-107 F 4
San Antonio de los Cobres 111 C 2
San Antonio de Padua, Merlo-
110 III a 2
San Antonio de Táchira 94-95 E 4
San Antonio de Tamanaco
94-95 HJ 3
San Antonio Mountain 76-77 B 7
San Antonio Oeste 111 CD 6
San Antonio Peak 74-75 E 5
San Antonio River 76-77 F 8
San Antonio Zomeyucan 91 I b 2
San Ardo, CA 74-75 C 4
Sanare 94-95 G 3
Sanatorium, TX 76-77 D 7
San Augustine, TX 76-77 GH 7
Sanāwāḍ = Sanāwad 138-139 EF 6
Sanavirones 106-107 FG 2
Sanāw 134-135 G 7
Sanāwad 138-139 EF 6
Sanāwān 138-139 C 2
Sanbalpur = Sambalpur
134-135 N 6
San Bartolo [PE, Amazonas]
96-97 BC 4
San Bartolo [PE, Lima] 96-97 C 8
San Bartolo Ameyalco 91 I b 3
San Bartolomé, Cabo —
108-109 G 10
San Basilio 106-107 EF 4
San Basilio, Roma- 113 II b c 1
San Benedetto del Tronto
122-123 EF 4
San Benedicto, Isla — 64-65 DE 8
San Benedito 92-93 E 4
San Benito, TX 64-65 G 6
San Benito, Isla — 86-87 BC 3
San Benito Abad 94-95 D 3
San Benito Mountain 74-75 C 4
San Bernardino 91 III a 3
San Bernardino, CA 64-65 CD 5
San Bernardino, Caracas- 91 II b 1
San Bernardino Mountains 74-75 E 5
San Bernardo [CO] 94-95 CD 3
San Bernardo [RA, Buenos Aires]
106-107 G 6
San Bernardo [RA, Chaco]
104-105 F 10
San Bernardo [RCH] 111 BC 4
San Bernardo, Islas de —
94-95 CD 3
San Bernardo, Punta de —
94-95 CD 3
San Bernardo, Sierra de —
108-109 E 5
San Blas [MEX] 86-87 F 4
San Blas [RA] 106-107 D 2
San Blas, Archipiélago de —
88-89 GH 10
San Blas, Bahía de — 86-87 H 7
San Blas, Cape — 64-65 J 6
San Blas, Cordillera de —
64-65 L 10
San Blas, Punta — 64-65 L 10
San Borja 92-93 F 7
San Borja, Sierra de — 86-87 D 3
Sanborn, MN 70-71 C 3
Sanborn, ND 68-69 G 2
San Bruno Mountain 83 I b 2
San Buenaventura [BOL]
104-105 BC 4
San Buenaventura [MEX] 86-87 JK 4
San Buenaventura = Ventura, CA
74-75 D 5
San Buenaventura, Cordillera de —
104-105 BC 10
San Camilo 104-105 F 9
Sancang 146-147 H 5
San Carlos, AZ 74-75 H 6
San Carlos [CO, Antioquia Cord.
Central] 94-95 D 4
San Carlos [CO, Antioquia R. Nechí]
94-95 D 4
San Carlos [CO, Córdoba] 94-95 D 3
San Carlos [MEX, Baja California Sur]
86-87 DE 5
San Carlos [MEX, Tamaulipas]
86-87 L 5
San Carlos [NIC] 88-89 D 9
San Carlos [PY] 102-103 D 5
San Carlos [RA, Córdoba]
106-107 E 3
San Carlos [RA, Corrientes]
106-107 JK 1
San Carlos [RA, Mendoza]
106-107 C 4
San Carlos [RA, Salta] 104-105 CD 9
San Carlos [RCH] 111 B 5
San Carlos [ROU] 106-107 K 5
San Carlos [RP, Luzón]
148-149 GH 3
San Carlos [RP, Negros] 148-149 H 4
San Carlos [YV, Cojedes] 92-93 F 3
San Carlos [YV, Zulia] 94-95 F 2
San Carlos, Bahía — 86-87 D 3-4
San Carlos, Estrecho de — =
Falkland Sound 111 DE 8
San Carlos, Mesa de — 86-87 C 3
San Carlos, Punta — 86-87 C 3
San Carlos, Río — 102-103 C 5
San Carlos Bay 80-81 bc 3
San Carlos Centro 106-107 G 3
San Carlos de Bariloche 111 B 6
San Carlos de Bolívar 111 D 5
San Carlos del Meta 94-95 H 4
San Carlos de Puno 92-93 EF 8
San Carlos de Río Negro 92-93 F 4
San Carlos de Zulia 92-93 E 3
San Carlos Indian Reservation
74-75 HJ 6
San Carlos Lake 74-75 H 6
San Cayetano 106-107 H 7
San-ch'a = Sani 146-147 H 9
Sānchi 138-139 F 6
San-chiang = Sanjiang 146-147 B 9
Sānchor 138-139 C 5
Sanchore = Sānchor 138-139 C 5
San Clemente, CA 74-75 E 6
San Clemente [RCH] 106-107 AB 5
San Clemente del Tuyú
106-107 JK 6
San Clemente Island 64-65 BC 5
Sancos 96-97 E 8
San Cosme [PY] 102-103 D 7
San Cosme [RA] 106-107 H 1
San Cristóbal [BOL, Potosí]
104-105 C 7
San Cristóbal [BOL, Santa Cruz]
104-105 EF 3
San Cristóbal [CO, Amazonas]
92-93 E 5
San Cristóbal [CO, Bogotá] 91 III c 2
San Cristóbal [E] 113 III b 2
San Cristóbal [PA] 88-89 F 10
San Cristóbal [RA] 111 D 4
San Cristóbal [Solomon Is.]
148-149 k 7
San Cristóbal [YV] 92-93 E 3
San Cristóbal, Isla — 92-93 B 5
San Cristóbal, Río — 91 III b 3
San Cristóbal de las Casas
64-65 H 8
San Cristobal Wash 74-75 G 6
San Cristoval = San Cristóbal
148-149 k 7
Sancti Spíritu 106-107 F 5
Sancti-Spíritus [C] 64-65 L 7
Sančursk 124-125 Q 5
Sand 116-117 AB 8
Şandafā' 173 B 3
Sandai 148-149 F 7
Sandakan 148-149 G 5
Sandalwood Island = Sumba
148-149 G 9
Sandan 150-151 F 6
Sandane 116-117 AB 7
Sandanski 122-123 K 5
Sand Arroyo 68-69 E 7
Sanday 119 EF 2
Sandberg [ZA] 174-175 C 7
Sandbult 174-175 G 2
Sandefjord 116-117 D 8
Sanders, AZ 74-75 J 5
Sanderson, TX 76-77 C 7
Sanderstead, London- 129 II b 2
Sandersville, GA 80-81 E 4
Sandfish Bay = Sandvisbaai
174-175 A 2
Sandfontein [Namibia → Gobabis]
172 CD 6
Sandfontein [Namibia ↓ Karasburg]
174-175 C 5
Sandfontein [ZA] 174-175 H 2
Sandford Lake 70-71 E 1
Sandhornøy 116-117 EF 4
Sandia 92-93 F 7
Sandia Crest 76-77 AB 5
Sandiao Jiao = Santiao Chiao
146-147 HJ 9
Sandia Peak = Sandia Crest
76-77 AB 5
San Diego 76-77 B 8
San Diego, CA 64-65 C 5
San Diego, TX 76-77 E 9
San Diego, Cabo — 111 CD 8
San Diego Aqueduct 74-75 E 6
San Diego de Cabrutica 94-95 J 3
San Diego de la Unión 86-87 K 7
Sandıklı 136-137 CD 3
Sandıklı dağları 136-137 D 3
Sandīla 138-139 H 4
Sanding, Pulau — 152-153 D 7
Sandīp [BD, island] 141 B 4
Sandīp [BD, place] 141 B 4
Sandīp, Ābnāi — 141 B 4
Sand Island 70-71 E 2
Sand Islands 58-59 DE 5
Sandja, Îles — 170 I b 1
Sand Key 80-81 b 3
Sand Lake [CDN, lake] 62 B 2
Sand Lake [CDN, place] 70-71 H 2
Sand Mountains 64-65 J 5
Sandnes 116-117 A 8
Sandoa 172 D 3
Sandomierz 118 K 3
Sandonà 94-95 C 7
San Donà di Piave 122-123 E 3
Sandouping 146-147 C 6
Sandover River 158-159 FG 4
Sandovo 124-125 L 4
Sandoway = Thandwe 148-149 B 3
Sand Point, AK 58-59 c 2
Sandpoint, ID 66-67 E 1
Sandras dağı 136-137 C 4
Sandringham 158-159 G 4
Sandringham, Johannesburg-
170 V b 1
Sand River 61 C 3
Sandrivier [ZA ◁ Krokodilrivier]
174-175 G 3
Sandrivier [ZA ◁ Limpopo]
174-175 H 2
Sandrivier [ZA ◁ Vetrivier]
174-175 G 5
Sandspit 60 B 3
Sand Springs, MT 68-69 C 2
Sand Springs, OK 76-77 F 4
Sandspruit [ZA ↑ Johannesburg]
170 V b 1
Sandspruit [ZA ↑ Welkom]
174-175 G 4
Sandstone 158-159 C 5
Sandstone, MN 70-71 D 2
Sand Tank Mountains 74-75 G 6
Sandton 170 V b 1
Sandu 146-147 E 7
Sandu Ao 146-147 GH 8
Sandūr [IND] 140 C 3
Sandur [IS] 116-117 ab 2
Sāndūru = Sandūr 140 C 3
Sandusky, MI 72-73 E 3
Sandusky, OH 72-73 E 4
Sandusky Bay 72-73 E 4
Sandveld [Namibia] 172 CD 6
Sandveld [ZA] 174-175 C 6-7
Sandverhaar 174-175 B 4
Sandviken 116-117 G 7
Sandvisbaai 174-175 A 2
Sandwich, IL 70-71 F 5
Sandwich Bay = Sandvisbaai
174-175 A 2
Sandwip = Sandīp 141 B 4
Sandwip Channel = Ābnāi Sandīp
141 B 4
Sandwip Island = Sandīp 141 B 4
Sandwshin = Hsandaushin 141 C 6
Sandy, NV 74-75 F 5
Sandy Bay 61 G 3
Sandybeach Lake 62 CD 3
Sandy Cape [AUS, Queensland]
158-159 K 4
Sandy Cape [AUS, Tasmania]
160 ab 2
Sandy City, UT 64-65 D 3
Sandy Creek [USA, Georgia] 85 II a 2
Sandy Creek [USA, Wyoming]
66-67 J 4-5
Sandy Desert = Ar-Rub' al-Hālī
134-135 F 7-G 6

Sandy 355

Sandy Hills 64-65 GH 5
Sandy Hook 72-73 K 4
Sandy Hook, KY 72-73 E 5-6
Sandy Key 80-81 c 4
Sandy Lake [CDN, lake Newfoundland] 63 H 3
Sandy Lake [CDN, lake Ontario] 56-57 S 7
Sandy Lake [CDN, place Alberta] 60 L 2
Sandy Lake [CDN, place Ontario] 62 C 1
Sandy Lake [CDN, place Saskatchewan] 61 E 2
Sandy Narrows 61 G 3
Sandy Ridge 80-81 E 2
Sandy River 66-67 BC 3
Sandy Run 84 III c 1
Sane, Nam — 150-151 D 3
San Eduardo 106-107 F 4
San Emilio 106-107 G 5
San Enrique 106-107 G 5
San Estanislao 111 E 2
San Esteban, Golfo — 108-109 B 6
San Esteban de Gormaz 120-121 F 8
San Fabián de Alico 106-107 B 6
San Felipe, NM 76-77 A 5
San Felipe [CO] 92-93 F 4
San Felipe [MEX, Baja California Norte] 86-87 C 2
San Felipe [MEX, Guanajuato] 86-87 K 7
San Felipe [PE] 96-97 B 4
San Felipe [RCH] 111 B 4
San Felipe [YV] 92-93 F 2
San Felipe, Bahía — 108-109 DE 9
San Felipe de Jesús, Ciudad de México- 91 I c 2
San Felipe de Puerto Plata = Puerto Plata 64-65 M 8
San Felipe Terremotos, Ixtapalapa- 91 I c 2
San Feliu de Guixols 120-121 J 8
San Félix [RCH] 199 A 6
San Félix [YV] 94-95 E 3
San Fermín, Madrid- 113 III ab 2
San Fernando, CA 74-75 D 5
San Fernando [BOL] 104-105 G 5
San Fernando [E] 120-121 D 10
San Fernando [MEX] 86-87 LM 5
San Fernando [RA] 111 E 4
San Fernando [RCH] 111 B 4
San Fernando [RP ↖ Baguio] 148-149 GH 3
San Fernando [RP ↖ Manila] 148-149 H 3
San Fernando [TT] 64-65 L 9
San Fernando [YV] 92-93 F 3
San Fernando, Bogotá- 91 III c 2
San Fernando, Río — [BOL] 104-105 G 5
San Fernando, Río — [MEX] 86-87 LM 5
San Fernando de Atabapo 92-93 F 4
San Fernando del Valle de Catamarca 111 C 3
San Fernando-Victoria 110 III b 1
Sånfjället 116-117 E 6
Sanford 61 K 6
Sanford, FL 64-65 K 6
Sanford, ME 72-73 L 3
Sanford, NC 80-81 G 3
Sanford, Mount — 58-59 Q 5
San Francisco, CA 64-65 AB 4
San Francisco [BOL] 104-105 D 4
San Francisco [CO] 94-95 D 5
San Francisco [ES] 88-89 BC 8
San Francisco [MEX, Coahuila] 76-77 C 9
San Francisco [MEX, Sonora] 86-87 D 2
San Francisco [PE] 96-97 B 4
San Francisco [RA] 111 D 4
San Francisco [YV] 94-95 EF 2
San Francisco, Arroyo — 110 III bc 2
San Francisco, Paso — 104-105 B 10
San Francisco, Presedio of — 83 I b 2
San Francisco, Río — 104-105 D 8
San Francisco, University of — 83 I b 2
San Francisco Bay 74-75 B 4
San Francisco-Bayview, CA 83 I b 2
San Francisco Chimalpa 91 I a 2
San Francisco-Chinatown, CA 83 I b 2
San Francisco Culhuacán, Coyoacán- 91 I c 3
San Francisco de Bellocq 106-107 GH 7
San Francisco de Conchos 76-77 B 9
San Francisco de la Caleta 64-65 bc 3
San Francisco de Laishi 102-103 C 7
San Francisco del Chañar 106-107 EF 2
San Francisco del Monte de Oro 106-107 D 4
San Francisco del Oro 64-65 E 6
San Francisco del Parapetí 92-93 G 8-9
San Francisco del Rincón 86-87 JK 7
San Francisco de Macorís 64-65 MN 8
San Francisco de Naya 94-95 C 6
San Francisco de Paula, Bahía — = Byron Sound 108-109 J 8
San Francisco de Paula, Cabo — 108-109 F 7
San Francisco de Tiznados 94-95 GH 3
San Francisco-Ingleside, CA 83 I b 2
San Francisco-Marina North Beach, CA 83 I b 2
San Francisco Maritime State Historic Park 83 I b 2
San Francisco-Mission, CA 83 I b 2
San Francisco-Noe Valley, CA 83 I b 2
San Francisco-Oakland Bay Bridge 83 I bc 2
San Francisco-Outer Mission, CA 83 I b 2
San Francisco Peaks 74-75 GH 5
San Francisco Plateau 64-65 D 4-E 5
San Francisco-Potrero, CA 83 I b 2
San Francisco-Richmond, CA 83 I ab 2
San Francisco River 74-75 J 6
San Francisco Solano, Punta — 92-93 D 3
San Francisco Solano, Quilmes- 110 III c 2
San Francisco State University 83 I ab 2
San Francisco-Stonestown, CA 83 I b 2
San Francisco-Sunset, CA 83 I b 2
San Francisco Tlaltenco 91 I cd 3
San Fransisco-Parkside, CA 83 I b 2
Sangā 148-149 C 2
Sanga = Sangha 172 C 1-2
San Gabriel, CA 83 III d 1
San Gabriel [EC] 92-93 D 4
San Gabriel [RA] 106-107 J 2
San Gabriel Mountains 74-75 DE 5
Sangagchhö Ling 142-143 G 6
Šangaly 124-125 O 3
Sangam 140 D 3
Sangameshwar 140 A 2
Sangamner 138-139 E 8
Sangamon River 70-71 EF 5
Sangan [PAK] 138-139 A 3
Sangan [RI] 152-153 K 4
Sangar 132-133 Y 5
Sangareddigūdam = Zangareddigūdem 140 E 2
Sangareddipet 140 CD 2
Sangarh Nāla 138-139 C 2
Sangarios = Sakarya nehri 134-135 C 2
Sangasar 136-137 L 4
Sangay 92-93 D 5
Sangboy Islands 152-153 O 2
Sangchih = Sangzhi 146-147 C 7
Sangë = Sanguem 140 B 3
Sangeang, Pulau — 148-149 GH 8
Sangenjaya, Tōkyō- 155 III b 2
Sanger, CA 74-75 D 4
Sanger, TX 76-77 F 6
San Germán [Puerto Rico] 88-89 N 5-6
San Germán [RA] 106-107 F 7
Sanggabugdog 138-139 MN 3
Sanggan He 146-147 E 1
Sanggau 148-149 F 6
Sanggou Wan 146-147 J 3
Sangha 172 C 1-2
Sangihe, Kepulauan — 148-149 J 6
Sangihe, Pulau — 148-149 J 6
San Gil 94-95 E 4
Sang-i Māsha 134-135 K 4
San Giovanni in Laterano 113 II b 2
San Giovanni in Persiceto 122-123 D 3
Sangju 144-145 G 4
Sang-kan Ho = Sanggan He 146-147 E 1
Sangkapura 152-153 K 8
Sangkarang, Kepulauan — 152-153 N 8
Sangker, Stung — 150-151 D 6
Sangkha 150-151 DE 5
Sangkhla Buri 150-151 B 5
Sang-kou Wan = Sanggou Wan 146-147 J 3
Sangkulirang 148-149 G 6
Sangkulirang, Teluk — 148-149 G 6
Sāngli 134-135 LM 7
Sangmélima 164-165 G 8
Sangmobertheg La 138-139 K 2
Sangod 138-139 F 5
Sāngola 140 B 2
Sāngōlē = Sāngola 140 B 2
Sangolquí 96-97 B 2
Sangonera, Río — 120-121 G 10
San Gorgonio Mountain 74-75 E 5
Sangpo = Matsang Tsangpo 138-139 J 2-3
Sangrado, Rio — 110 I b 2
Sangre de Cristo Range 64-65 E 4
San Gregorio [PE] 96-97 D 7
San Gregorio [RA, Santa Fe] 106-107 FG 5
San Gregorio [RA, Santiago del Estero] 104-105 E 10
San Gregorio [RCH, Biobío] 106-107 B 6
San Gregorio [RCH, Magallanes y Antártica Chilena] 108-109 D 9
San Gregorio [ROU] 106-107 K 4
San Gregorio Atlapulco 91 I c 3
Sangre Grande 64-65 OP 9
Sangrūr 138-139 E 2
Sangsang 138-139 L 3
Sang Sôi, Se — 150-151 E 4
Sangsues, Lac aux — 72-73 GH 1
Sangū 141 C 5
Sangudo 60 K 3
Sangue, Cachoeira do — 98-99 L 7
Sangue, Rio do — 92-93 H 7
San Guillermo 106-107 FG 3
Sanguin River 168-169 C 4
San Gustavo 106-107 H 3
Sangutane, Rio — 174-175 K 2-3
Sangymgort 132-133 M 5
Sangzhi 146-147 C 7
Sanharó 100-101 F 5
San He [TJ, Anhui] 146-147 FG 5
Sanhe [TJ, Guangdong] 146-147 F 9
Sanhe [TJ, Hebei] 146-147 F 2
San Hilario 104-105 G 10
San Hipólito 86-87 CD 4
Sanho = Sanhe 146-147 F 2
San Hu 146-147 D 6
Sani 146-147 H 9
Sanibel Island 80-81 b 3
Sāni Bheri 138-139 J 3
San Ignacio, NM 76-77 B 5
San Ignacio [BOL ↗ La Paz] 92-93 F 7
San Ignacio [BOL ↗ Santa Cruz] 92-93 G 8
San Ignacio [MEX] 86-87 D 4
San Ignacio [PE] 96-97 B 4
San Ignacio [PY] 111 E 3
San Ignacio [RA, Buenos Aires] 106-107 HJ 6
San Ignacio [RA, Misiones] 106-107 K 1
San Ignacio, Laguna — 86-87 D 4
San Isidro [EC] 96-97 A 2
San Isidro [RA] 111 E 4
San Isidro, Catedral de — 113 III a 2
San Isidro-Acassuso 110 III b 1
San Isidro-Beccar 110 III b 1
San Isidro-Boulogne 110 III b 1
San Isidro-Juan Anchorena 110 III b 1
San Isidro-Martínez 110 III b 1
San Isidro-Villa Adelina 110 III b 1
Sanitatas 172 B 5
Saniyah, Hawr as- 136-137 M 7
San Jacinto, CA 74-75 E 6
San Jacinto [CO, Bolívar] 94-95 D 3
San Jacinto [CO, Magdalena] 94-95 D 3
San Jacinto, Serranía de — 94-95 D 3
San Jacinto Mountains 74-75 E 6
San Jacinto River 85 III c 1
San Javier [BOL, Beni] 104-105 D 4
San Javier [BOL, Santa Cruz] 92-93 G 8
San Javier [RA, Córdoba] 106-107 E 4
San Javier [RA, Misiones] 111 EF 3
San Javier [RA, Santa Fe] 106-107 GH 3
San Javier [RCH] 106-107 AB 5
San Javier [ROU] 106-107 HJ 4
San Javier, Río — 106-107 GH 3
San Jerónimo 106-107 D 4
San Jerónimo, Isla — 106-107 H 2
San Jerónimo, Serranía de — 92-93 D 3
San Jerónimo Lídice, Villa Obregón- 91 I b 3
Sanjiao 146-147 C 3
Sanjō 144-145 M 4
San Joaquín [BOL] 92-93 FG 7
San Joaquín [CO] 94-95 E 4
San Joaquín [PY, Boquerón] 102-103 B 4
San Joaquín [PY, Caaguazú] 102-103 D 6
San Joaquín [RA] 106-107 F 5
San Joaquín [YV] 94-95 J 3
San Joaquín, Río — 104-105 E 3
San Joaquin River 64-65 BC 4
San Joaquin Valley 64-65 BC 4
San Jon, NM 76-77 C 5
San Jorge [NIC] 88-89 CD 9
San Jorge [RA, Buenos Aires] 106-107 G 6
San Jorge [RA, Santa Fe] 106-107 FG 3
San Jorge [ROU] 106-107 JK 4
San Jorge, Bahía de — 86-87 D 2
San Jorge, Golfo — 111 CD 7
San Jorge, Golfo de — 120-121 H 8
San Jorge, Río — 94-95 D 3
San Jose, CA 64-65 B 4
San José [BOL] 104-105 F 6
San José [CO, Guainía] 94-95 G 6
San José [CO, Meta] 94-95 E 6
San José [CR] 64-65 K 9-10
San José [GCA] 64-65 H 9
San José [PA] 64-65 b 3
San José [PY, Caaguazú] 102-103 D 6
San José [PY, Itapúa] 102-103 E 7
San José [RA, Catamarca] 106-107 E 2
San José [RA, Mendoza ↗ Mendoza] 106-107 C 4
San José [RA, Mendoza ↙ Mendoza] 106-107 C 4
San José [RA, Misiones] 106-107 K 1
San José [RA, Santiago del Estero] 106-107 F 2
San José [ROU, administrative unit] 106-107 J 5
San José [ROU, place] 111 E 4
San José [RP] 148-149 H 3
San José [YV, Distrito Federal] 91 II b 1
San José [YV, Sucre] 94-95 K 2
San José [YV, Zulia] 94-95 E 2
San José, Golfo — 108-109 G 4
San José, Isla — [MEX] 64-65 DE 6
San José, Isla — [PA] 88-89 G 10
San José, Isla — = Weddell Island 111 D 8
San José, Serranía de — 104-105 F 5-6
San José de Buenavista 148-149 H 4
San José de Chiquitos 92-93 G 8
San José de Chupiamonas 104-105 B 4
San José de Feliciano 106-107 H 3
San José de Galipán 91 II b 1
San José de Guanipa 94-95 JK 3
San José de Guaribe 94-95 HJ 3
San José de Jáchal 111 C 4
San José de la Dormida 106-107 F 3
San José de la Esquina 106-107 FG 4
San José de la Mariquina 108-109 C 2
San Jose de las Raíces 86-87 KL 5
San José de las Salinas 111 CD 4
San José del Cabo 64-65 E 7
San José del Guaviare 92-93 E 4
San José de los Molinos 96-97 D 8
San José del Palmar 94-95 CD 5
San José del Rincon 106-107 G 3
San José de Maipo 106-107 BC 4
San José de Ocuné 92-93 E 4
San Josef Bay 60 C 4
San José-mi 102-103 D 7
San Jose River 74-75 JK 5
San Juan [BOL, Potosí] 104-105 C 7
San Juan [BOL, Santa Cruz] 104-105 FG 5
San Juan [DOM] 88-89 L 5
San Juan [MEX] 76-77 D 9
San Juan [PE] 92-93 DE 8
San Juan [Puerto Rico] 64-65 N 8
San Juan [RA, administrative unit] 106-107 CD 3
San Juan [RA, place] 111 C 4
San Juan, Cabo — [Equatorial Guinea] 164-165 F 8
San Juan, Cabo — [RA] 111 D 8
San Juan, Río — [CO, Chocó] 94-95 C 5
San Juan, Río — [CO, Nariño] 94-95 B 7
San Juan, Río — [MEX] 86-87 L 5
San Juan, Río — [NIC] 64-65 K 9
San Juan, Río — [PE] 96-97 D 8
San Juan, Río — [RA] 106-107 C 3
San Juan Archipelago 66-67 B 1
San Juan Bautista [E] 120-121 H 9
San Juan Bautista [PY] 111 E 3
San Juan Bautista = Villahermosa 64-65 H 8
San Juan Bautista Ñeembucú 102-103 D 7
San Juan Bautista Tuxtepec 86-87 M 9-10
San Juan Chimalhuacan 91 I d 2
San Juan de Aragón, Bosque — 91 I c 2
San Juan de Aragón, Ciudad de México- 91 I c 2
San Juan de Aragón, Zoológico de — 91 I c 2
San Juán de Arama 94-95 E 6
San Juan de Dios 91 II b 1
San Juan de Guadalupe 86-87 J 5
San Juan de Guía, Cabo de — 92-93 DE 2
San Juan del César 94-95 E 2
San Juan del Norte 88-89 E 9
San Juan del Norte = Bluefields 64-65 K 9
San Juan del Norte, Bahía de — 64-65 K 9
San Juan del Oro 96-97 G 8
San Juan de los Cayos 94-95 GH 2
San Juan de los Lagos 86-87 J 7
San Juan de los Morros 92-93 F 3
San Juan del Piray 104-105 DE 7
San Juan del Río 86-87 KL 7
San Juan del Sur 88-89 CD 9
San Juan de Manapiare 94-95 H 5
San Juan de Salvamento 108-109 H 10
San Juanico, Isla — 86-87 G 7
San Juan Ixtayopan 91 I d 3
San Juan Mountains 64-65 E 4
San Juan Nepomuceno [CO] 94-95 D 3
San Juan Nepomuceno [PY] 102-103 E 7
San Juan Quiotepec 86-87 MN 9
San Juan River 64-65 E 4
San Juan Toltoltepec 91 I b 2
San Julián, Bahía — = Queen Charlotte Bay 108-109 J 8
San Julián, Gran Bajo de — 108-109 E 7
San Julian, Quebrada — 91 II b 1
San Justo [RA, Buenos Aires] 110 III b 2
San Justo [RA, Santa Fe] 111 D 4
San Justo, Aeródromo — 110 III b 2
San Justo, La Matanza- 110 III a 1
Sankaranāyinarkovil 140 C 6
Sankarani 168-169 C 3
Sankaridrug 140 CD 5
Sankeng 146-147 D 10
Sankh 138-139 K 6
Sankheda 138-139 D 6
Sankisen 144-145 cd 2
Sankrāil 154 II a 2
Sankt Gallen 118 D 5
Sankt Georg, Hamburg- 130 I ab 1
Sankt Gotthard 118 D 5
Sankt Michel = Mikkeli 116-117 MN 7
Sankt Moritz 118 DE 5
Sankt Pauli, Hamburg- 130 I a 1
Sankt Pölten 118 G 4
Sankuru 172 D 2
San Lázaro 102-103 CD 5
San Lázaro, Cabo — 64-65 D 7
San Lázaro, Sierra — 86-87 EF 6
San Lázaro, Sierra de — 86-87 E 5-F 6
San Lorenzo [BOL ↙ Riberalta] 92-93 F 7
San Lorenzo [BOL ↑ Tarija] 92-93 FG 9
San Lorenzo [BOL, Beni] 104-105 D 4
San Lorenzo [CO, Nariño] 94-95 C 7
San Lorenzo [CO, Vaupés] 94-95 E 6
San Lorenzo [EC] 92-93 D 4
San Lorenzo [MEX, México] 91 I d 2
San Lorenzo [MEX, Veracruz] 86-87 N 9
San Lorenzo [PE] 96-97 C 4
San Lorenzo [PY] 102-103 D 6
San Lorenzo [RA, Corrientes] 106-107 H 2
San Lorenzo [RA, Santa Fe] 111 D 4
San Lorenzo [YV, Arauca] 94-95 F 4
San Lorenzo [YV, Falcón] 94-95 G 2
San Lorenzo [YV, Zulia] 92-93 E 3
San Lorenzo, Cabo de — 92-93 C 5
San Lorenzo, Cerro — 111 B 7
San Lorenzo, Isla — [MEX] 86-87 D 3
San Lorenzo, Isla — [PE] 92-93 D 7
San Lorenzo, Río — 86-87 G 5
San Lorenzo, Sierra de — 120-121 F 7
San Lorenzo Acopilco 91 I ab 3
San Lorenzo de Quinti 96-97 CD 8
San Lorenzo Tezonco 91 I c 3
Sanlúcar de Barrameda 120-121 D 10
San Lucas, CA 74-75 C 4
San Lucas [BOL] 104-105 D 7
San Lucas [EC] 96-97 B 3
San Lucas [MEX] 86-87 F 6
San Lucas [PE] 96-97 A 4
San Lucas, Cabo — 64-65 E 7
San Lucas, Serranía — 94-95 D 3-4
San Luis, CO 68-69 D 7
San Luis [C] 88-89 J 4
San Luis [CO, Bogotá] 91 III c 3
San Luis [CO, Tolima] 94-95 D 5
San Luis [GCA] 86-87 Q 9
San Luis [RA, administrative unit] 106-107 DE 4-5
San Luis [RA, place] 111 C 4
San Luis [RCH] 108-109 DE 9
San Luis [YV] 94-95 G 2
San Luis, Lago de — 104-105 D 3
San Luis, Sierra de — [RA] 106-107 DE 4
San Luis, Sierra de — [YV] 92-93 EF 2
San Luis de la Paz 86-87 KL 7
San Luis del Palmar 106-107 H 1
San Luis Gonzaga 86-87 C 3
San Luis Obispo, CA 64-65 B 4
San Luis Obispo Bay 74-75 C 5
San Luis Pass 76-77 G 8
San Luis Potosí 64-65 FG 7
San Luis Río Colorado 86-87 C 1
San Luis Valley 68-69 CD 7
San Manuel 106-107 H 6
San Manuel, AZ 74-75 H 6
San Marcial, NM 76-77 A 6
San Marco, Capo — 122-123 BC 6
San Marcos, TX 64-65 G 6
San Marcos [CO] 94-95 D 3
San Marcos [GCA] 86-87 OP 10
San Marcos [MEX] 86-87 L 9
San Marcos [RCH] 111 B 4
San Marcos, Isla — 86-87 DE 4
San Marcos, Sierra de — 76-77 CD 9
San Marino [RSM, place] 122-123 E 4
San Marino [RSM, state] 122-123 E 4
San Márquez 96-97 D 6
San Martín [BOL] 92-93 G 7-8
San Martín [CO] 94-95 E 6
San Martín [PE] 96-97 C 5
San Martín [RA, La Rioja] 111 C 3
San Martín [RA, Mendoza] 106-107 C 4
San Martín [RA, San Luis] 106-107 E 4
San Martín, Lago — 111 B 7
San Martín, Loma — 108-109 E 2
San Martín, Río — 92-93 G 8
San Martín de Alto Negro 106-107 DE 5
San Martín de los Andes 108-109 D 3
San Martín de Pangoa 96-97 D 7
San Mateo, CA 64-65 B 4
San Mateo [PE] 96-97 F 3
San Mateo [YV] 94-95 J 3
San Mateo Ixtatán 86-87 P 10
San Mateo Peak 64-65 E 5
San Mateo Tecoloapan 91 I b 1
San Mateo Tlaltenango 91 I b 2
San Matías 111 H 8
San Matías, Golfo — 111 D 6
Sanmaur 62 OP 3
San Mauricio 94-95 H 3
San Mayol 106-107 GH 7
Sanmen 146-147 H 7
San-mên-hsia = Sanmenxia 142-143 L 5
Sanmen Wan 146-147 HJ 7
Sanmenxia 142-143 L 5
San Miguel, AZ 74-75 H 7
San Miguel, CA 74-75 C 5
San Miguel, NM 76-77 B 5
San Miguel [BOL] 104-105 F 5
San Miguel [CO] 94-95 F 5
San Miguel [EC] 96-97 B 2
San Miguel [ES] 64-65 J 9
San Miguel [PA] 94-95 B 3
San Miguel [PE] 96-97 E 8
San Miguel [PY, Concepción] 102-103 D 5
San Miguel [PY, Misiones] 102-103 D 7
San Miguel [RA, Corrientes] 106-107 J 1
San Miguel [RA, Mendoza] 106-107 D 4
San Miguel [RA, Tucumán] 104-105 D 10
San Miguel [YV] 94-95 K 3
San Miguel, Cerro — 104-105 F 6
San Miguel, Golfo de — 88-89 G 10
San Miguel, Río — [BOL] 92-93 G 7-8
San Miguel, Río — [EC] 96-97 C 1
San Miguel, Río — [MEX, Chihuahua] 86-87 G 4
San Miguel, Río — [MEX, Sonora] 86-87 E 2
San Miguel, Sierra — 104-105 B 10
San Miguel de Allende 86-87 KL 7
San Miguel de Huachi 92-93 F 8
San Miguel del Monte 111 E 5
San Miguel de Pallaques 96-97 B 5
San Miguel de Tucumán 111 CD 3
San Miguel Island 74-75 C 5
San Miguelito [NIC] 88-89 D 9
San Miguelito [PA] 64-65 bc 3
San Miguel River 74-75 JK 3
Sanming 146-147 F 8
Sannār 164-165 L 6
San Narciso 148-149 GH 3
Sannaspos 174-175 G 5
Sannī 138-139 A 3
San Nicolás 96-97 D 9
San Nicolás, Bahía — 96-97 D 9
San Nicolás, Lago — 104-105 D 3
San Nicolás de los Arroyos 111 D 4
San Nicolas de los Garzas 86-87 KL 5
San Nicolas Island 64-65 BC 5
San Nicolás Totolapan 91 I b 3
San Nicolás Viejo 91 I ab 1
Sannikova, proliv — 132-133 ab 3
Sanniquellie 164-165 C 7
Sannohe 144-145 N 2
Sannois 129 I bc 2
Sannūr, Wādī — 173 B 3
Sañogasta 106-107 D 2
Sañogasta, Sierra de — 106-107 D 2
Sanok 118 L 4
San Onofre 94-95 D 3
San Pablito, Caracas- 91 II ab 2
San Pablo, CA 83 I bc 1
San Pablo [BOL, Potosí] 104-105 C 7
San Pablo [BOL, Santa Cruz] 104-105 E 4
San Pablo [RA] 108-109 F 10
San Pablo [RP] 148-149 H 4
San Pablo [YV] 94-95 J 3
San Pablo, Bogotá- 91 III a 2
San Pablo, Point — 83 I b 1
San Pablo, Punta — 86-87 C 4
San Pablo, Río — 104-105 E 4
San Pablo Bay 74-75 B 3
San Pablo Creek 83 I c 1
San Pablo de Balzar, Cordillera de — 96-97 AB 2
San Pablo Huitzo 86-87 M 9
San Pablo Reservoir 83 I c 1
San Pablo Ridge 83 I c 1
San Patricio 102-103 D 7
San Pedro [BOL, Chuquisaca] 104-105 D 6
San Pedro [BOL, Pando] 104-105 C 2
San Pedro [BOL, Potosí] 104-105 D 6
San Pedro [BOL, Santa Cruz ↗ Roboré] 104-105 G 5
San Pedro [BOL, Santa Cruz ↗ Santa Cruz] 92-93 G 8
San Pedro [BOL, Santa Cruz ↑ Trinidad] 92-93 G 7
San Pedro [CI] 168-169 D 4
San Pedro [EC] 96-97 B 3
San Pedro [MEX, Baja California Sur] 86-87 E 6
San Pedro [MEX, Chihuahua] 76-77 B 8
San Pedro [MEX, Durango] 76-77 AB 9
San Pedro [MEX, México] 91 I d 2
San Pedro [PE] 96-97 DE 4
San Pedro [PY, administrative unit] 102-103 D 5-6
San Pedro [PY, place] 111 E 2
San Pedro [RA, Buenos Aires] 111 E 4
San Pedro [RA, Misiones] 102-103 EF 7
San Pedro [RA, San Luis] 106-107 D 4
San Pedro [RA, Santiago del Estero] 111 C 3
San Pedro [RCH, O'Higgins] 106-107 B 4
San Pedro [RCH, Valparaíso] 106-107 B 4
San Pedro [YV, Anzoátegui] 94-95 K 3
San Pedro [YV, Bolívar] 94-95 K 4
San Pedro [YV, Caracas] 91 II c 1
San Pedro, Bahía de — 108-109 BC 3
San Pedro, Cerro — 108-109 C 4
San Pedro, Point — 83 I b 1
San Pedro, Punta — [CR] 64-65 K 10
San Pedro, Punta — [RCH] 104-105 A 9
San Pedro, Río — [GCA] 86-87 P 9
San Pedro, Río — [MEX, river <] Pacific Ocean] 86-87 H 6
San Pedro, Río — [MEX, river <] Río Conchos] 86-87 GH 4
San Pedro, Sierra de — 120-121 D 9
San Pedro, Volcán — 92-93 F 9
San Pedro Channel 74-75 D 6
San Pedro-cué 102-103 D 7
San Pedro de Arimena 94-95 F 5
San Pedro de Atacama 104-105 BC 8
San Pedro de Jujuy 104-105 D 9
San Pedro de la Cueva 86-87 F 3
San Pedro de las Colonias 64-65 F 6
San Pedro de Lloc 96-97 B 5
San Pedro del Paraná 102-103 DE 7
San Pedro de Macorís 64-65 N 8
San Pedro de Quemez 104-105 BC 7
San Pedro Mártir 91 I b 3
San Pedro Mártir, Sierra — 64-65 CD 5
San Pedro Mártir, Sierra de — 86-87 C 2
San Pedro Mountain 76-77 A 4
San Pedro Norte 106-107 E 3
San Pedro River 74-75 H 6
San Pedro Sula 64-65 J 8
San Pedro Taviche 86-87 M 9
San Pelayo 94-95 CD 3
San Perlita, TX 76-77 F 9
San Petro Xalostoc 91 I c 1
San Petro Zacatenco, Ciudad de México- 91 I c 1
San Pietro [I] 122-123 BC 6
San Pietro [V] 113 II b 2
San Quentin State Prison 83 I ab 1
San Quintín 86-87 BC 2
San Quintín, Bahía de — 86-87 BC 2
San Quintín, Cabo — 64-65 C 5
San Rafael, CA 64-65 B 4
San Rafael [BOL] 104-105 F 5
San Rafael [CO, Guainía] 94-95 G 6
San Rafael [CO, Vichada] 94-95 G 4-5
San Rafael [MEX] 91 I b 2
San Rafaél [PE] 96-97 CD 7
San Rafael [RA] 111 C 4
San Rafael [RCH] 106-107 B 5
San Rafael [YV] 94-95 EF 2
San Rafael, Bahía de — 86-87 D 3
San Rafael, Bogotá- 91 III b 4
San Rafael, Isla — = Beaver Island 108-109 J 8
San Rafael Bay 83 I b 1
San Rafael de Atamaica 94-95 H 4
San Rafael de Canaguá 94-95 F 3
San Rafael del Encanto 92-93 E 5
San Rafael Mountains 74-75 CD 5
San Rafael River 74-75 H 3
San Rafael Swell 74-75 H 3
San Ramón [BOL, Beni] 104-105 D 3
San Ramón [BOL, Santa Cruz] 104-105 E 5
San Ramón [NIC] 88-89 D 7
San Ramón [PE] 96-97 D 7
San Ramón [ROU] 106-107 K 5
San Ramón, Río — 104-105 F 4
San Ramón de la Nueva Orán 111 CD 2
Sanrao 146-147 F 10
San Remo 122-123 BC 4
San Román, Cabo — 92-93 EF 2
San Roque [RA] 106-107 H 2
San Rosendo 111 B 5
San Saba, TX 76-77 E 7
San Saba River 76-77 E 7
Sansalé 168-169 B 3
San Salvador [BS] 64-65 M 7
San Salvador [ES] 64-65 HJ 9
San Salvador [PY] 102-103 D 5
San Salvador [RA, Corrientes] 106-107 J 2
San Salvador [RA, Entre Ríos] 106-107 H 3
San Salvador, Cuchilla — 106-107 HJ 4
San Salvador, Isla — 92-93 A 5
San Salvador, Río — 106-107 J 4
San Salvador de Jujuy 111 CD 2
Sansanding 164-165 CD 6
Sansanding, Barrage — 168-169 D 2
Sansané Haoussa 168-169 F 2
Sansanné-Mango = Mango 164-165 E 6
San Sebastián [CO] 94-95 DE 8
San Sebastián [E] 120-121 FG 7
San Sebastián [RA] 111 C 8
San Sebastián [YV] 94-95 H 3
San Sebastián, Bahía — 108-109 EF 9
San Sebastian, Isla — 86-87 DE 3
San Sebastián de Buenavista 94-95 DE 3
San Sebastián de la Gomera 164-165 A 3
San Severo 122-123 F 5
Sansha Wan 146-147 GH 8
San Silvestre [BOL] 104-105 B 2
San Silvestre [YV] 92-93 EF 3
San Simeon, CA 74-75 C 5
San Simón 94-95 EF 3
San Simon, AZ 74-75 J 6
Sansing = Yilan 142-143 OP 2
San Solano 106-107 E 3
Sansuan Shan 146-147 H 7
Sansui 146-147 B 8
Santa, Río — 96-97 B 6
Santa Adélia 102-103 H 4
Santa Ana, CA 64-65 C 5
Santa Ana [BOL ↘ Roboré] 104-105 G 6
Santa Ana [BOL ↘ San Ignacio] 104-105 F 5

356 Sandy

Santa Ana [BOL ↖ Trinidad] 92-93 F 7
Santa Ana [CO, Guainía] 92-93 F 4
Santa Ana [CO, Magdalena] 94-95 D 3
Santa Ana [EC] 96-97 A 2
Santa Ana [ES] 64-65 HJ 9
Santa Ana [MEX] 64-65 D 5
Santa Ana [RA, Entre Ríos] 106-107 J 3
Santa Ana [RA, Misiones] 106-107 K 1
Santa Ana [YV, Anzoátegui] 94-95 J 3
Santa Ana [YV, Falcón] 94-95 FG 2
Santa Ana, Ilha — 102-103 M 5
Santa Ana, Petare- 91 II bc 2
Santa Ana, Punta — 96-97 D 9
Santa Ana Delicias 94-95 E 4
Santa Ana Jilotzingo 91 I a 1
Santa Ana Mountains 74-75 E 6
Santa Anna, TX 76-77 E 7
Santa Apolonia 94-95 F 3
Santa Barbara, CA 64-65 BC 5
Santa Bárbara [BR, Mato Grosso] 102-103 C 1
Santa Bárbara [BR, Minas Gerais] 102-103 L 3-4
Santa Barbara [CO] 94-95 D 5
Santa Bárbara [Honduras] 88-89 BC 7
Santa Bárbara [MEX] 64-65 E 6
Santa Bárbara [RCH] 111 B 5
Santa Bárbara [YV ↘ Ciudad Guayana] 94-95 K 4
Santa Bárbara [YV ↙ Maturín] 92-93 G 3
Santa Bárbara [YV → San Cristóbal] 92-93 E 3
Santa Bárbara [YV → San Fernando de Atabapo] 92-93 F 4
Santa Bárbara, Ilha de — 110 I b 2
Santa Bárbara, Serra de — 92-93 J 9
Santa Bárbara, Sierra de — 104-105 D 8-9
Santa Barbara Channel 74-75 CD 5
Santa Bárbara do Sul 106-107 L 2
Santa Barbara Island 74-75 D 6
Santa Catalina [RA, Córdoba] 106-107 E 4
Santa Catalina [RA, Jujuy] 111 C 2
Santa Catalina [RA, Santiago del Estero] 106-107 E 2
Santa Catalina = Catalina 111 C 3
Santa Catalina, Gulf of — 74-75 DE 6
Santa Catalina, Isla — 86-87 EF 5
Santa Catalina, Laguna — 110 III b 2
Santa Catalina Island 64-65 BC 5
Santa Catarina 111 FG 3
Santa Catarina, Ilha de — 111 G 3
Santa Catarina, Sierra de — 91 I cd 3
Santa Catarina, Valle de — 74-75 EF 7
Santa Catarina de Tepehuanes 86-87 H 5
Santa Catarina Yecahuizotl 91 I d 3
Santa Cecília 102-103 G 7
Santa Cecilia, Pirámide de — 91 I b 1
Santa Cecília do Pavão 102-103 G 5
Santa Clara, CA 64-65 B 4
Santa Clara [BOL] 104-105 C 3
Santa Clara [C] 64-65 KL 7
Santa Clara [CO] 92-93 EF 5
Santa Clara [MEX, Chihuahua] 76-77 B 8
Santa Clara [MEX, Durango] 86-87 J 5
Santa Clara [PE] 96-97 D 4
Santa Clara [RA] 104-105 D 9
Santa Clara [ROU] 106-107 K 4
Santa Clara Coatitla 91 I c 1
Santa Clara de Buena Vista 106-107 G 3
Santa Clara de Saguier 106-107 G 3
Santa Coloma 106-107 H 5
Santa Comba = Cela 172 C 4
Santa Cruz, CA 64-65 B 4
Santa Cruz [BOL, administrative unit] 104-105 E-G 5
Santa Cruz [BOL, place] 92-93 G 8
Santa Cruz [BR, Amazonas ↙ Benjamin Constant] 96-97 E 4
Santa Cruz [BR, Amazonas ↗ Benjamin Constant] 96-97 G 3
Santa Cruz [BR, Amazonas ↙ Benjamin Constant] 98-99 BC 7
Santa Cruz [BR, Amazonas ↗ Benjamin Constant] 98-99 D 6
Santa Cruz [BR, Espírito Santo] 100-101 DE 10
Santa Cruz [BR, Rio Grande do Norte] 92-93 M 6
Santa Cruz [BR, Rondônia ↖ Ariquemes] 104-105 E 1
Santa Cruz [BR, Rondônia ↘ Mategua] 104-105 E 3
Santa Cruz [CR] 88-89 CD 9
Santa Cruz [MEX] 86-87 E 2
Santa Cruz [PE, Cajamarca] 96-97 B 5
Santa Cruz [PE, Huánuco] 96-97 C 6
Santa Cruz [PE, Loreto] 96-97 D 4
Santa Cruz [RA, La Rioja] 106-107 D 2
Santa Cruz [RA, Santa Cruz] 111 BC 7
Santa Cruz [RCH] 106-107 B 5
Santa Cruz [YV, Anzoátegui] 94-95 J 3
Santa Cruz [YV, Barinas] 94-95 F 3
Santa Cruz [YV, Zulia] 94-95 F 2
Santa Cruz, Ilha de — 110 I c 2
Santa Cruz, Isla — [EC] 92-93 AB 5
Santa Cruz, Isla — [MEX] 86-87 E 5
Santa Cruz, Río — 108-109 E 7-F 8
Santa Cruz, Rio de Janeiro- 102-103 L 5
Santa Cruz, Sierra de — 104-105 E 5-6
Santa Cruz Alcapixca 91 I c 3
Santa Cruz Cabrália 92-93 M 8
Santa Cruz das Palmeiras 102-103 J 4
Santa Cruz de Barahona = Barahona 64-65 M 8
Santa Cruz de Bucaral 94-95 G 2
Santa Cruz de Goiás 102-103 H 2
Santa Cruz de la Palma 164-165 A 3
Santa Cruz del Quiché 86-87 P 10
Santa Cruz del Sur 88-89 GH 4
Santa Cruz de Tenerife 164-165 A 3
Santa Cruz do Capibaribe 100-101 F 4-5
Santa Cruz do Monte Castelo 102-103 F 5
Santa Cruz do Piauí 100-101 D 4
Santa Cruz do Rio Pardo 102-103 H 5
Santa Cruz dos Angolares 168-169 G 5
Santa Cruz do Sul 111 F 3
Santa Cruz Island 64-65 BC 5
Santa Cruz Islands 148-149 I 7
Santa Cruz Meyehualco, Ixtapalapa- 91 I c 2
Santa Cruz Mountains 74-75 BC 4
Santa Cruz River 74-75 H 6
Santa de la Ventana 106-107 G 7
Santa Efigênia, São Paulo- 110 II b 2
Santa Elena [BOL] 92-93 G 9
Santa Elena [EC] 96-97 A 3
Santa Elena [PE] 92-93 E 5
Santa Elena [RA, Buenos Aires] 106-107 G 6
Santa Elena [RA, Entre Ríos] 106-107 H 3
Santa Elena, Bahía de — 96-97 A 2-3
Santa Elena, Cabo — 64-65 J 9
Santa Elena, Cerro — 108-109 G 5
Santa Elena de Uairén 92-93 G 4
Santa Eleodora 106-107 F 5
Santa Eudóxia 102-103 J 4
Santa Fe, NM 64-65 E 4
Santa Fé [BOL] 104-105 E 6
Santa Fé [C] 88-89 E 4
Santa Fe [RA, administrative unit] 106-107 G 2-4
Santa Fe [RA, place] 111 D 4
Santa Fé [RCH] 106-107 A 6
Santa Fe [YV] 94-95 J 2
Santa Fe, Villa Obregón- 91 I b 2
Santa Fé des Minas 102-103 K 2
Santa Fé do Sul 92-93 J 9
Santa Fe Pacific Railway 64-65 F 4
Santa Fe Springs, CA 83 III d 2
Santa Filomena 92-93 K 6
Santa Genoveva = Cerro las Casitas 64-65 E 7
Sāntāhār 138-139 M 5
Santa Helena [BR, Maranhão] 92-93 K 5
Santa Helena [BR, Pará] 92-93 H 5-6
Santa Helena [BR, Paraná] 102-103 E 6
Santa Helena de Goiás 102-103 G 2
Santai 142-143 JK 5
Santa Inês [BR, Bahia] 92-93 LM 7
Santa Inês [BR, Maranhão] 100-101 B 2
Santa Inés [YV] 94-95 G 2
Santa Inés, Isla — 111 B 8
Santa Isabel [BR] 104-105 F 3
Santa Isabel [EC] 96-97 B 3
Santa Isabel [PE] 96-97 F 8
Santa Isabel [RA, La Pampa] 111 C 5
Santa Isabel [RA, Santa Fe] 106-107 G 4
Santa Isabel [Solomon Is.] 148-149 jk 6
Santa Isabel = Malabo 164-165 F 8
Santa Isabel, Cachoeira de — 98-99 OP 8
Santa Isabel, Ilha Grande de — 92-93 L 5
Santa Isabel do Araguaia 92-93 K 6
Santa Isabel do Morro 92-93 J 7
Santa Juana [RCH] 106-107 A 6
Santa Juana [YV] 94-95 H 4
Santa Juliana 102-103 J 3
Santa Justina 106-107 F 1
Santa Lidia 102-103 C 5
Santāl Parganas 138-139 L 5
Santa Lucía [RA, Buenos Aires] 106-107 GH 4
Santa Lucía [RA, Corrientes] 106-107 H 2
Santa Lucía [RA, San Juan] 106-107 C 3
Santa Lucía [RA, Santa Cruz] 108-109 E 8
Santa Lucía [ROU] 106-107 J 5
Santa Lucía, Esteros del — 106-107 HJ 1-2
Santa Lucía, Río — 106-107 H 2
Santa Lucía, Sierra de — 86-87 D 4
Santa Lucia Range 74-75 C 4-5
Santa Luísa, Serra de — 102-103 E 3
Santaluz [BR, Bahia] 92-93 M 7
Santa Luz [BR, Piauí] 100-101 C 5
Santa Luzia [BR, Maranhão] 100-101 B 2
Santa Luzia [BR, Minas Gerais] 102-103 L 3
Santa Luzia [BR, Rondônia] 98-99 G 9
Santa Magdalena 106-107 EF 5
Santa Magdalena, Isla — 86-87 D 5
Santa Margarida 102-103 LM 4
Santa Margarita, CA 74-75 C 5
Santa Margarita [RA] 106-107 G 2
Santa Margarita, Isla — 64-65 D 7
Santa Margherita Ligure 122-123 C 3
Santa Maria, CA 64-65 B 5
Santa Maria [Açores] 204-205 E 5
Santa María [BOL] 104-105 E 4
Santa Maria [BR, Amazonas] 92-93 H 5
Santa Maria [BR, Rio Grande do Sul] 111 EF 3
Santa María [CO] 94-95 G 6
Santa Maria [PE, Amazonas] 96-97 B 5
Santa María [PE, Loreto] 92-93 E 5
Santa Maria [RA] 111 C 3
Santa Maria [Vanuatu] 158-159 N 2
Santa María [YV, Apure] 94-95 H 4
Santa María [YV, Zulia] 94-95 F 3
Santa Maria [Z] 171 B 5
Santa María, Bahía de — 86-87 F 5
Santa María, Boca — 86-87 M 5
Santa Maria, Cabo de — 120-121 CD 10
Santa Maria, Cabo de — = Cap Sainte-Marie 172 J 7
Santa Maria, Isla — 106-107 A 6
Santa María, Laguna de — 86-87 G 2
Santa María, Punta — [MEX] 86-87 F 5
Santa María, Punta — [ROU] 106-107 KL 5
Santa María, Riacho — 100-101 C 5
Santa Maria, Rio — [BR ◁ Rio Corrente] 100-101 A 8
Santa Maria, Rio — [BR ◁ Rio Ibicuí] 106-107 K 3
Santa María, Río — [MEX ◁ Laguna de Santa María] 86-87 G 2-3
Santa María, Río — [MEX ◁ Río Tamuín] 86-87 K 7
Santa María, Río — [RA] 104-105 D 10
Santa María Asunción Tlaxiaco 64-65 G 8
Santa Maria da Boa Vista 100-101 E 5
Santa Maria das Barreiras 92-93 JK 6
Santa Maria da Vitória 100-101 BC 7
Santa Maria de Ipire 92-93 F 3
Santa Maria de Itabira 100-101 C 10
Santa María de la Mina 104-105 EF 5
Santa María del Oro 86-87 GH 5
Santa Maria del Soccorso, Roma- 113 II bc 2
Santa María de Nanay 96-97 E 3
Santa Maria di Leuca, Capo — 122-123 H 6
Santa Maria do Pará 98-99 P 5
Santa Maria do Suaçuí 102-103 L 3
Santa Maria Madalena 102-103 LM 4
Santa Maria Maggiore [I, Roma] 113 II b 2
Santa Mariana 102-103 G 5
Santa Marta Otaes 86-87 GH 5
Santa María Tulpetlac 91 I c 1
Santa Marta [CO] 92-93 DE 2
Santa Marta, Baruta- 91 II b 2
Santa Marta, Ciénaga Grande de — 94-95 DE 2
Santa Marta, Sierra Nevada de — 92-93 E 2
Santa Marta Grande, Cabo — 102-103 H 8
Santa Martha Acatitla, Ixtapalapa- 91 I cd 2
Santa Maura = Levkás 122-123 J 6
Santa Monica, CA 64-65 BC 5
Santa Monica, TX 76-77 F 9
Santa Mónica, Caracas- 91 II b 2
Santa Monica Bay 83 III ab 2
Santa Monica Mountains 83 III ab 1
Santa Monica Municipal Airport 83 III b 1
Santa Monica State Beach 83 III a 1
Santana 92-93 L 7
Santana, Coxilha da — 111 E 3-F 4
Santana, Ilha de — 92-93 L 5
Santana, Rio — 100-101 C 5
Santana, São Paulo- 110 II b 1
Santana, Serra de — [BR, Bahia] 100-101 C 7
Santana, Serra de — [BR, Rio Grande do Norte] 100-101 F 3-4
Santana da Boa Vista 106-107 L 3
Santana de Patos 102-103 J 3
Santana do Araguaia 98-99 NO 9
Santana do Cariri 100-101 E 4
Santana do Ipanema 100-101 F 5
Santana do Livramento 111 EF 4
Santana do Matos 100-101 F 3
Santana dos Garrotes 100-101 EF 4
Santander [CO, Cauca] 92-93 D 4
Santander [CO, Meta] 94-95 D 6
Santander [CO, Santander] 94-95 DE 4
Santander [E] 120-121 F 7
Santander Jiménez 86-87 LM 5
Santang 152-153 M 6
Sant'Angelo, Castel — 113 II b 2
Sant'Antioco [I, island] 122-123 BC 6
Sant'Antioco [I, place] 122-123 BC 6
Santañy 120-121 J 9
Santa Paula, CA 74-75 D 5
Santa Pola, Cabo de — 120-121 GH 9
Saṅtapura = Santpur 140 C 1
Santa Quitéria 100-101 DE 3
Santa Quitéria do Maranhão 100-101 C 2
Santa Regina 106-107 F 5
Santarém [BR] 92-93 J 5
Santarem [P] 120-121 C 9
Santaren Channel 64-65 L 7
Santa Rita, NM 74-75 J 6
Santa Rita [BR, Amazonas] 98-99 C 8
Santa Rita [BR, Paraíba] 92-93 MN 6
Santa Rita [YV, Guárica] 94-95 H 3
Santa Rita [YV, Zulia] 92-93 E 2
Santa Rita, Ponta de — 100-101 G 3
Santa Rita, Raudal — 94-95 K 4
Santa Rita, Serra de — 100-101 E 3
Santa Rita de Cássia 100-101 B 6
Santa Rita de Catuna 106-107 D 3
Santa Rita de Jacutinga 102-103 KL 5
Santa Rita do Araguaia 92-93 J 8
Santa Rita do Passa Quatro 102-103 J 4
Santa Rita do Sapucaí 102-103 K 5
Santa Rito do Weil 92-93 F 5
Santa Rosa, CA 64-65 B 4
Santa Rosa, NM 76-77 B 5
Santa Rosa [BOL, Beni ↘ Riberalta] 92-93 F 7
Santa Rosa [BOL, Beni ↙ Santa Ana] 104-105 C 4
Santa Rosa [BOL, Chuquisaca] 104-105 E 7
Santa Rosa [BOL, Pandó] 104-105 C 2
Santa Rosa [BOL, Santa Cruz] 104-105 E 5
Santa Rosa [BR, Acre] 92-93 EF 6
Santa Rosa [BR, Amazonas] 94-95 K 6
Santa Rosa [BR, Goiás] 100-101 A 8
Santa Rosa [BR, Rio Grande do Sul] 111 F 3
Santa Rosa [BR, Rondônia] 98-99 GH 10
Santa Rosa [CO, Cauca] 94-95 C 7
Santa Rosa [CO, Guainía] 92-93 EF 4
Santa Rosa [EC] 96-97 A 3
Santa Rosa [PE] 92-93 E 5
Santa Rosa [PY, Boquerón] 102-103 B 4
Santa Rosa [PY, Misiones] 102-103 D 7
Santa Rosa [RA, Corrientes] 106-107 HJ 2
Santa Rosa [RA, La Pampa] 111 CD 5
Santa Rosa [RA, Mendoza] 111 C 4
Santa Rosa [RA, Río Negro] 108-109 F 2
Santa Rosa [RA, San Luis] 111 C 4
Santa Rosa [RA, Santa Fe] 106-107 GH 3
Santa Rosa [RCH] 106-107 A 6-7
Santa Rosa [ROU] 106-107 JK 5
Santa Rosa [YV, Anzoátegui] 94-95 J 3
Santa Rosa [YV, Apure] 94-95 H 4
Santa Rosa [YV, Barinas] 94-95 G 3
Santa Rosa [YV, Lara] 94-95 F 2
Santa Rosa, Cordillera de — 106-107 C 2
Santa Rosa de Amanadona 94-95 H 7
Santa Rosa de Cabal 94-95 CD 5
Santa Rosa de Calamuchita 106-107 E 4
Santa Rosa de Copán 64-65 J 9
Santa Rosa de la Roca 104-105 F 5
Santa Rosa del Palmar 92-93 G 8
Santa Rosa de Osos 94-95 D 4
Santa Rosa de Río Primero 106-107 F 3
Santa Rosa de Viterbo 102-103 J 4
Santa Rosa Island [USA, California] 64-65 B 5
Santa Rosa Island [USA, Florida] 78-79 F 5
Santa Rosalía [MEX, Baja California Norte] 86-87 C 3
Santa Rosalía [MEX, Baja California Sur] 64-65 D 6
Santa Rosalía [YV] 94-95 J 4
Santa Rosalía de las Cuevas 86-87 G 3-4
Santa Rosalilia 86-87 C 3
Santa Rosa Range 66-67 E 5
Santa Rosa Wash 74-75 GH 6
Šantarskije ostrova 132-133 a 6-7
Santa Sylvina 111 DE 3
Santa Tecla = Nueva San Salvador 64-65 HJ 9
Santa Tecla, Serra de — 106-107 KL 3
Santa Teresa [BR] 102-103 M 3
Santa Teresa [MEX] 76-77 D 9
Santa Teresa [PE] 96-97 E 8
Santa Teresa [RA ↖ Rosario] 106-107 G 4
Santa Teresa [RA ↓ Rosario] 106-107 G 4
Santa Teresa [YV] 94-95 H 2
Santa Teresa, Cachoeira — 98-99 G 9-10
Santa Teresinha 100-101 DE 7
Santa Teresita 106-107 J 6
Santa União 98-99 O 10
Santa Victoria [RA ← Bermejo] 104-105 D 8
Santa Victoria [RA → Tartagal] 104-105 E 8
Santa Victoria, Sierra — 104-105 D 8
Santa Vitória 102-103 GH 3
Santa Vitória do Palmar 111 F 4
Santa Ynez, CA 74-75 CD 5
Santee River 80-81 G 4
San Telmo, Punta — 86-87 HJ 8
Sant'Eufêmia, Golfo di — 122-123 FG 6
Santiago [BR] 111 EF 3
Santiago [Cape Verde] 204-205 E 7
Santiago [DOM] 64-65 M 7
Santiago [EC] 96-97 BC 3
Santiago [MEX] 86-87 F 6
Santiago [PA] 64-65 K 10
Santiago [PY] 102-103 D 7
Santiago, Cabo — 108-109 AB 8
Santiago, Cerro — 88-89 EF 10
Santiago, Río — [EC] 96-97 B 1
Santiago, Río — [PE] 96-97 C 3
Santiago, Salto — 102-103 F 6
Santiago, Serranía de — 104-105 G 6
Santiago Acahualtepec, Ixtapalapa- 91 I c 2
Santiago de Chile 111 B 4
Santiago de Chocorvos 96-97 D 8
Santiago de Chuco 92-93 D 6
Santiago de Cuba 64-65 L 7-8
Santiago de Huata 104-105 B 5
Santiago de las Montañas 96-97 C 4
Santiago del Estero [RA, administrative unit] 102-103 AB 7
Santiago del Estero [RA, place] 111 CD 3
Santiago de Paracaguas 104-105 BC 3
Santiago di Compostela 120-121 CD 7
Santiago Ixcuintla 64-65 EF 7
Santiago Jamiltepec 86-87 LM 9
Santiagoma 92-93 H 8
Santiago Mountains 76-77 C 7-8
Santiago Papasquiaro 64-65 EF 6-7
Santiago Peak 76-77 C 8
Santiago Temple 106-107 F 3
Santiago Tepalcatlalpan 91 I c 3
Santiago Tepatlaxco 91 I ab 2
Santiago Vázquez, Montevideo- 106-107 J 5
Santiago Zapotitlán 91 I c 3
Santiaguillo, Laguna de — 86-87 H 5
Santiam Pass 66-67 BC 3
Santiao Chiao 146-147 HJ 9
San Tiburcio 86-87 K 5
Santigi 148-149 H 6
San Timoteo 94-95 F 3
Sāntipur 138-139 M 6
Santo, TX 76-77 E 6
Santo Agostinho, Cabo de — 100-101 G 5
Santo Amaro 92-93 M 7
Santo Amaro, Ilha de — 102-103 JK 6
Santo Amaro, São Paulo- 110 II a 2
Santo Amaro de Campos 102-103 M 5
Santo Anastácio 102-103 G 4
Santo André 92-93 K 9
Santo André = Isla de San Andrés 64-65 KL 9
Santo André-Utinga 110 II b 2
Santo André-Vila Bastos 110 II b 2
Santo Ângelo 111 EF 3
Santo Antão 204-205 E 7
Santo Antônio [BR, Pará] 98-99 O 6
Santo Antônio [BR, Rio Grande do Norte] 100-101 G 4
Santo Antônio [BR, Rio Grande do Sul] 106-107 MN 2
Santo Antônio [São Tomé and Príncipe] 164-165 F 8
Santo Antônio, Cachoeira — [BR, Rio Madeira] 92-93 FG 6
Santo Antônio, Cachoeira — [BR, Rio Roosevelt] 98-99 HJ 9
Santo Antônio, Ponta de — 100-101 GH 4
Santo Antônio, Rio — [BR ◁ Paraguaçu] 100-101 D 7
Santo Antônio, Rio — [BR ◁ Rio de Contas] 100-101 CD 8
Santo Antônio, Rio — [BR ◁ Rio Doce] 102-103 L 3
Santo Antônio, Rio — [BR ◁ Rio Iguaçu] 102-103 F 6
Santo Antônio da Platina 102-103 GH 5
Santo Antônio de Jesus 92-93 LM 7
Santo Antônio de Pádua 102-103 LM 4
Santo Antônio de Rio Verde 102-103 J 2
Santo Antônio do Içá 98-99 DE 6
Santo Antônio do Jacinto 100-101 DE 9
Santo Antônio do Leverger 102-103 DE 1
Santo Antônio do Monte 102-103 K 4
Santo Antônio do Sudoeste 102-103 F 7
Santo Antônio do Zaire = Soyo 172 B 3
Santo Corazón 92-93 H 8
Santo Corazón, Rio — 104-105 G 5
Santo Domingo [DOM] 64-65 MN 8
Santo Domingo [MEX, Baja California Norte] 86-87 CD 3
Santo Domingo [MEX, Baja California Sur] 86-87 DE 5
Santo Domingo [MEX, San Luis Potosí] 86-87 K 6
Santo Domingo [NIC] 88-89 D 8
Santo Domingo [PE, Junín] 96-97 D 7
Santo Domingo [PE, Loreto] 96-97 CD 3
Santo Domingo [RA] 106-107 J 6
Santo Domingo, Río — [MEX] 64-65 G 8
Santo Domingo, Río — [YV] 94-95 G 3
Santo Domingo de Guzmán = Santo Domingo 64-65 MN 8
Santo Domingo de los Colorados 96-97 B 2
Santo Domingo Tehuantepec 64-65 G 8
Santo Eduardo 102-103 M 4
Santo Estêvão 100-101 E 7
San Tomé 94-95 JK 3
Santoña 120-121 F 7
Sant'Onofrio, Roma- 113 II b 1
Santorinē = Thēra 122-123 L 7
Santos 92-93 K 9
Santos, Baía de — 102-103 JK 6
Santos, Laje dos — 102-103 JK 6
Santos, Los — 88-89 F 11
Santos Dumont [BR, Amazonas] 98-99 D 8
Santos Dumont [BR, Minas Gerais] 102-103 KL 4
Santos Dumont, Aeroporto — 110 I c 2
Santos Lugares 104-105 E 10
Santo Tomás [BOL] 104-105 G 5
Santo Tomás [CO] 94-95 D 2
Santo Tomás [MEX] 86-87 B 2
Santo Tomás [PE] 92-93 E 7
Santo Tomás de Castilla 88-89 B 7
Santo Tomé [RA, Corrientes] 111 E 3
Santo Tomé [RA, Santa Fe] 106-107 G 3
Santpur 140 C 1
San-tu = Sandu 146-147 E 7
San-tu Ao = Sandu Ao 146-147 GH 8
Santuario, El — 94-95 F 5
Santuario de los Remedios 91 I b 2
Sanup Plateau 74-75 G 5
San Valentín, Cerro — 111 B 7
San Vicente [BOL] 104-105 C 7
San Vicente [CO] 94-95 E 4
San Vicente [ES] 64-65 J 9
San Vicente [RA, Buenos Aires] 106-107 H 5
San Vicente [RA, Córdoba] 106-107 E 3
San Vicente [RA, Santiago del Estero] 106-107 E 2
San Vicente [RCH] 106-107 B 5
San Vicente, Bahía — 106-107 A 6
San Vicente, Cabo — 108-109 FG 10
San Vicente de Caguán 94-95 D 6
San Víctor 111 E 4
San Vito, Capo — 122-123 E 6
Sānwer 138-139 E 6
San Xavier Indian Reservation 74-75 H 6-7
Sanya = Ya Xian 142-143 KL 8
San Yanaro 92-93 EF 4
Sanyang 146-147 E 8
Sanya Wan 150-151 G 3
San Ygnacio, TX 76-77 E 9
San Ysidro, CA 74-75 E 6
Sanyuan 146-147 B 4
Sanzao Dao 146-147 D 11
Sanza Pombo 172 C 3
São Bartolomeu, Rio — 102-103 J 2
São Benedito 100-101 D 3
São Benedito, Rio — 98-99 KL 9
São Benedito do Rio Preto 100-101 C 2
São Bento [BR, Amazonas] 96-97 E 4
São Bento [BR, Maranhão] 100-101 B 2
São Bento [BR, Rio Grande do Sul] 106-107 L 2
São Bento do Norte 100-101 F 3
São Bento do Sapucaí 102-103 JK 5
São Bento do Una 100-101 F 5
São Bernardo 92-93 L 5
São Bernardo do Campo 102-103 J 5
São Bernardo do Campo-Rudge Ramos 110 II b 2-3
São Borja 111 EF 3
São Caetano 100-101 FG 5
São Caetano do Odivelas 98-99 OP 5
São Caetano do Sul 102-103 JK 5
São Carlos [BR, Rondônia] 98-99 G 9
São Carlos [BR, Santa Catarina] 102-103 F 7
São Carlos [BR, São Paulo] 92-93 K 9
São Conrado, Rio de Janeiro- 110 I b 2
São Cristóvão 100-101 F 6
São Cristovão, Rio de Janeiro- 110 I b 2
São Desidério 100-101 B 7
São Diogo 100-101 B 5
São Domingos [BR, Espírito Santo] 100-101 D 10
São Domingos [BR, Santa Catarina] 102-103 F 7
São Domingos [Guinea Bissau] 164-165 A 6
São Domingos, Rio — [BR ◁ Rio Mamoré] 104-105 D 3-E 2
São Domingos, Rio — [BR ◁ Rio Paranã] 100-101 A 7
São Domingos, Rio — [BR ◁ Rio Paranaíba] 102-103 G 3
São Domingos, Rio — [BR ◁ Rio Verde] 102-103 F 3
São Domingos, Serra — 100-101 D 3-E 4
São Domingos, Serra de — 100-101 A 7-8
São Domingos do Maranhão 100-101 BC 3
São Domingos do Prata 102-103 L 3
São Felipe 98-99 H 3
São Felix [BR, Mato Grosso] 98-99 N 10
São Félix [BR, Rondônia] 104-105 F 1
São Félix de Balsas 100-101 B 5
São Félix do Piauí 100-101 C 3
São Félix do Xingu 92-93 J 6
São Fernando 98-99 F 7
São Fidélis 102-103 M 4
São Filipe 92-93 M 7
São Francisco 102-103 K 1
São Francisco, Baía de — 102-103 HJ 7
São Francisco, Cachoeira — 98-99 LM 7
São Francisco, Ilha de — 102-103 HJ 7
São Francisco, Rio — [BR ◁ Atlantic Ocean] 92-93 LM 6
São Francisco, Rio — [BR ◁ Rio Paraná] 102-103 EF 6
São Francisco, Serra — 100-101 D 5-6
São Francisco de Assis 106-107 K 2
São Francisco de Paula 106-107 M 2
São Francisco de Sales 102-103 H 3
São Francisco do Conde 100-101 E 7
São Francisco do Maranhão 100-101 C 4
São Francisco do Sul 111 G 3
São Gabriel 111 EF 4
São Gabriel da Palha 100-101 D 10
São Gonçalo 102-103 L 5
São Gonçalo do Abaeté 102-103 K 3
São Gonçalo do Sapucaí 102-103 K 4
São Gonçalo dos Campos 100-101 E 7
São Gotardo 92-93 KL 8
Sao Hill 171 C 5
São Inácio 102-103 FG 5
São Jerônimo 106-107 M 2-3
São Jerônimo, Serra de — 92-93 J 8
São Jerônimo da Serra 102-103 G 5
São João [BR, Amazonas] 98-99 E 5
São João [BR, Rondônia] 104-105 E 2
Sao João, Ilhas de — 92-93 L 5
São João, Riacho — 100-101 D 4
São João, Rio — [BR ◁ Rio de Contas] 100-101 CD 8
São João, Rio — [BR ◁ Rio Paraná] 102-103 F 5
São João, Serra de — [BR, Amazonas] 98-99 GH 9
São João, Serra de — [BR, Paraná] 102-103 G 6
São João Batista 100-101 B 2
São João da Barra 102-103 M 4
São João da Boa Vista 102-103 J 4-5
São João da Ponte 102-103 L 1
São João de Araguaia 98-99 O 7
São João del Rei 102-103 K 4
São João de Meriti [BR, place] 102-103 L 5
São João de Meriti [BR, river] 110 I ab 1
São João do Ivaí 102-103 FG 5-6
São João do Paraíso 102-103 LM 1
São João do Piauí 92-93 L 6
São João dos Patos 100-101 C 4
São João do Triunfo 102-103 G 6
São João Evangelista 102-103 L 3
São João Nepomuceno 102-103 L 4
São Joaquim [BR, Amazonas] 98-99 E 4-5
São Joaquim [BR, Santa Catarina] 106-107 MN 2
São Joaquim, Parque Nacional de — 106-107 MN 2
São Joaquim da Barra 102-103 J 4
São Jorge 204-205 DE 5
São Jorge, Ilha — 100-101 B 1
São José [BR, Mato Grosso] 98-99 M 10
São José [BR, Paraíba] 100-101 E 4
São José [BR, Santa Catarina] 102-103 H 7
São José, Baía de — 100-101 BC 2
São José da Laje 100-101 FG 5
São José da Tapera 100-101 F 5
São José de Mipibu 100-101 G 4
São José do Anauá 98-99 H 4
São José do Belmonte 100-101 E 4
São José do Campestre 100-101 G 4
São José do Egito 100-101 F 4
São José do Gurupi 100-101 A 1
São José do Norte 106-107 LM 3-4
São José do Peixe 100-101 C 4
São José do Piriá 100-101 A 1
São José do Prado 100-101 E 9
São José do Rio Pardo 102-103 J 4
São José do Rio Preto [BR, Rio de Janeiro] 102-103 L 5
São José do Rio Preto [BR, São Paulo] 92-93 JK 9
São José dos Campos 92-93 KL 9
São José dos Dourados, Rio — 102-103 G 4
São José dos Pinhais 102-103 H 6
São Leopoldo 106-107 M 2

São Lourenço [BR, Mato Grosso] 102-103 E 2
São Lourenço [BR, Minas Gerais] 102-103 K 5
São Lourenço, Pantanal de — 102-103 D 3-E 2
São Lourenço, Rio — 102-103 DE 2
São Lourenço, Serra — 102-103 E 2
São Lourenço da Mata 100-101 G 4
São Lourenço do Sul 106-107 LM 3
São Lucas 106-107 K 2
São Lucas, Cachoeira de — 98-99 J 9
São Luís 92-93 L 5
São Luís, Ilha de — 100-101 BC 1-2
São Luís de Cacianã 98-99 F 8
São Luís do Curu 100-101 E 2
São Luís do Purunã 102-103 H 6
São Luís do Quitunde 100-101 G 5
São Luís Gonzaga 106-107 K 2
São Manuel 102-103 H 5
São Manuel, Rio — 98-99 K 9
São Marcelino 94-95 H 7
São Marcelo 100-101 B 6
São Marcos [BR, Rio Grande do Sul] 106-107 M 2
São Marcos [BR, Roraima] 94-95 L 6
São Marcos, Baía de — 92-93 L 5
São Marcos, Rio — 102-103 J 2
São Mateus [BR, Espírito Santo] 92-93 M 8
São Mateus [BR, Pará] 98-99 O 7
São Mateus, Rio — 100-101 D 10
São Mateus do Sul 102-103 GH 6
São Miguel [Açores] 204-205 E 5
São Miguel [BR, Maranhão] 100-101 C 3
São Miguel [BR, Rio Grande do Norte] 100-101 E 4
São Miguel, Rio — 102-103 J 1-2
São Miguel Arcanjo 102-103 HJ 5
São Miguel das Matas 100-101 E 7
São Miguel das Missões 106-107 K 2
São Miguel d'Oeste 102-103 F 7
São Miguel dos Campos 100-101 FG 5
São Miguel dos Macacos 98-99 N 5
São Miguel do Tapuio 92-93 L 6
Saona, Isla — 64-65 N 8
Saône 120-121 K 5
Saoner 138-139 G 7
São Nicolau 204-205 E 7
São Nicolau, Rio — 100-101 D 3
São Onofre, Rio — 100-101 C 7
São Paulo [BR, administrative unit] 92-93 JK 9
São Paulo [BR, island] 178-179 H 5
São Paulo [BR, place Acre] 98-99 BC 9
São Paulo [BR, place Amazonas] 98-99 B 8
São Paulo-Aclimação 110 II b 2
São Paulo Alto da Mooca 110 II b 2
São Paulo Americanópolis 110 II b 3
São Paulo-Barra Funda 110 II b 2
São Paulo-Bela Vista 110 II b 2
São Paulo-Bom Rétiro 110 II b 2
São Paulo-Brás 110 II b 2
São Paulo-Brasilândia 110 II a 1
São Paulo-Butantã 110 II a 2
São Paulo-Cambuci 110 II b 2
São Paulo-Cangaíba 110 II b 2
São Paulo-Cantareira 110 II b 1
São Paulo-Casa Verde 110 II b 1
São Paulo-Consolação 110 II ab 2
São Paulo de Olivença 92-93 F 5
São Paulo do Potenji 100-101 G 3
São Paulo-Ermelindo Matarazo 110 II bc 1
São Paulo-Ibirapuera 110 II ab 2
São Paulo-Indianópolis 110 II b 2
São Paulo-Interlagos 110 II a 3
São Paulo-Ipiranga 110 II b 2
São Paulo-Jabaquara 110 II b 2
São Paulo-Jaçanã 110 II b 1
São Paulo-Jaraguá 110 II a 1
São Paulo-Jardim América 110 II ab 2
São Paulo-Jardim Paulista 110 II ab 2
São Paulo-Lapa 110 II a 2
São Paulo-Liberdade 110 II b 2
São Paulo-Limão 110 II ab 1
São Paulo-Mooca 110 II b 2
São Paulo-Morumbi 110 II a 2
São Paulo-Nossa Senhora do Ó 110 II ab 1
São Paulo-Nova Cachoeirinha 110 II ab 1
São Paulo-Pari 110 II b 2
São Paulo-Penha 102-103 J 5
São Paulo-Penha de França 110 II b 2
São Paulo-Pinheiros 110 II a 2
São Paulo-Pirituba 110 II a 1
São Paulo-Santa Efigênia 110 II b 2
São Paulo-Santana 110 II b 1
São Paulo-Santo Amaro 110 II a 2
São Paulo-Saúde 110 II b 2
São Paulo-Sé 110 II b 2
São Paulo-Socorro 110 II a 2
São Paulo-Tatuapé 110 II b 2
São Paulo-Tremembé 110 II b 1
São Paulo-Tucuruvi 110 II b 1
São Paulo-Vila Boaçava 110 II a 1
São Paulo-Vila Formosa 110 II bc 2
São Paulo-Vila Guilherme 110 II b 2
São Paulo-Vila Jaguara 110 II a 2
São Paulo-Vila Madalena 110 II a 2
São Paulo-Vila Maria 110 II b 2
São Paulo-Vila Mariana 110 II b 2
São Paulo-Vila Matilde 110 II bc 2
São Paulo-Vila Prudente 110 II b 2
São Pedro [BR, Amazonas ↘ Benjamin Constant] 96-97 G 4
São Pedro [BR, Amazonas ↗ Benjamin Constant] 96-97 G 3
São Pedro [BR, Amazonas ↘ Benjamin Constant] 98-99 D 7
São Pedro [BR, Amazonas ↗ Benjamin Constant] 98-99 D 6
São Pedro [BR, Amazonas ↘ São Joaquim] 94-95 H 8
São Pedro [BR, Rio Grande do Sul] 106-107 LM 2
São Pedro [BR, Rondônia] 98-99 GH 9
São Pedro [BR, São Paulo] 102-103 J 5
São Pedro, Riachão — 102-103 J 2
São Pedro, Rio de — 100-101 DE 5
São Pedro, Serra de — 100-101 E 4
São Pedro da União 102-103 J 4
São Pedro de Ferros 102-103 L 4
São Pedro de Viseu 98-99 NO 6
São Pedro do Cipa 102-103 E 2
São Pedro do Ivaí 102-103 FG 5
São Pedro do Piauí 100-101 C 3
São Pedro do Sul [BR] 106-107 K 2
São Rafael 100-101 F 3
São Raimundo das Mangabeiras 100-101 B 4
São Raimundo de Codó 100-101 C 3
São Raimundo Nonato 92-93 L 6
São Romão [BR, Amazonas] 92-93 F 6
São Romão [BR, Minas Gerais] 92-93 KL 8
São Roque 102-103 J 5
São Roque, Cabo de — 92-93 MN 6
São Salvador [BR, Acre] 98-99 B 8
São Salvador [BR, Rio Grande do Sul] 106-107 M 2
São Sebastião [BR, Pará] 98-99 M 7
São Sebastião [BR, São Paulo] 102-103 K 5
São Sebastião, Canal de — 102-103 K 5-6
São Sebastião, Ilha de — 92-93 KL 9
São Sebastião, Ponta — 172 G 6
São Sebastião do Boa Vista 98-99 O 5
São Sebastião do Paraíso 102-103 J 4
São Sebastião do Passé 100-101 E 7
São Sebastião do Umbuzeiro 100-101 F 4-5
São Sepé 106-107 L 3
São Simão 102-103 J 4
São Simão, Ponta — 106-107 M 3
São Simão, Represa de — 92-93 JK 8
São Tiago 98-99 K 5
São Tomás de Aquino 102-103 J 4
São Tomé [BR] 100-101 F 3
São Tomé [São Tomé and Príncipe] 164-165 F 8
São Tomé, Cabo de — 92-93 LM 9
São Tomé, Ilha — 164-165 F 8-9
São Tomé, Pico de — 168-169 G 5
São Tomé and Principe 164-165 F 8
Saouîra, eṣ — = Aṣ-Ṣawīrah 164-165 BC 2
Saoula 170 I a 2
Saoura, Ouèd — = Wādī as-Sāwrah 164-165 D 2-3
São Vicente [BR, Goiás] 100-101 A 7
São Vicente [BR, São Paulo] 92-93 K 9
São Vicente [Cape Verde] 204-205 E 7
São Vicente, Cabo de — 120-121 C 10
São Vicente, Serra de — 104-105 G 4
São Vicente de Minas 102-103 K 4
São Vicente Ferrer 100-101 B 2
São Xavier, Serra de — 106-107 KL 2
Sāpai 122-123 L 5
Sapão, Rio — 100-101 B 6
Sapateiro, Cachoeira do — 92-93 H 5
Sapé [BR] 100-101 G 4
Sape [RI] 148-149 G 8
Sape, Selat — 152-153 N 10
Sapele 164-165 EF 7
Sapello, NM 76-77 B 5
Sapelo Island 80-81 F 5
Şaphane dağı 136-137 C 3
Sapiéntza 122-123 J 7
Sapinero, CO 68-69 C 6
Sapiranga 106-107 M 2
Şapki 124-125 H 4
Sapo, Serranía del — 94-95 B 4
Sapopema 102-103 G 5
Saposoa 92-93 D 6
Sa Pout = Ban Sa Pout 150-151 C 2
Sapožok 124-125 N 7
Sappa Creek 68-69 F 6
Sapphire Mountains 66-67 G 2-3
Sappho, WA 66-67 AB 1
Sapporo 142-143 QR 3
Sapri 122-123 F 5
Šapsucho, gora — 126-127 J 4
Sapt Kosi 134-135 O 5
Sapucaí, Rio — 102-103 HJ 4
Sapucaia 102-103 L 5
Sapucaia do Sul 106-107 M 2
Sapudi, Pulau — 148-149 FG 8
Sapudi, Selat — 152-153 L 9
Sapuka Besar, Pulau — 152-153 N 9
Sapulpa, OK 64-65 G 4
Sapulut 152-153 M 3
Sa Put = Ban Sa Pout 150-151 C 2
Sapwe 171 B 5
Saqasiq, Es- = Az-Zaqāzīq 164-165 KL 2
Sa Qi = Jin Jiang 146-147 FG 9
Saqīyat al-Ḥamrā' 164-165 B 3
Saqiyat Makki 170 II b 2
Sâqiyat Sîdî Yûsuf 166-167 L 1
Şaqqārah 173 B 3
Saqqez 134-135 F 3
Saquarema 102-103 L 5
Saquisilí 96-97 B 2
Sara, poluostrov — 126-127 O 7
Sarāb 136-137 M 4
Sarāb-e Gīlān 136-137 LM 5
Saraburi 148-149 D 4
Sarafutsu 144-145 c 1
Saragossa = Zaragoza 120-121 G 8
Saraguro 92-93 D 5
Sarai [SU] 124-125 N 7
Saraikelā 138-139 KL 6
Sarajevo 122-123 H 4
Sarala 132-133 Q 7
Saramabila 171 AB 4
Saramacca 98-99 KL 2
Saramaṭī 134-135 P 5
Sarampiuni 104-105 B 4
Saran' [SU, Kazachskaja SSR] 132-133 N 8
Šaran [SU, Rossijskaja SFSR] 124-125 U 6
Sāran = Chhaprā 134-135 N 5
Saran, Gunung — 152-153 J 6
Sarana Bay 58-59 p 6
Saranac Lake, NY 72-73 J 2
Saranda 171 C 4
Sarandë 122-123 HJ 6
Sarandi [BR] 106-107 L 1
Sarandí [ROU] 106-107 J 3
Sarandí, Arroyo — 106-107 H 2-3
Sarandí, Avellaneda- 110 III bc 2
Sarandí del Yí 111 EF 4
Sarandí Grande 106-107 J 4
Šaranga 124-125 Q 5
Sarangani Bay 148-149 HJ 5
Sarangani Islands 148-149 HJ 5
Sārangarh 138-139 J 7
Sārangpur 138-139 F 6
Saranlay 164-165 N 8
Saranpaul' 132-133 L 5
Saransk 132-133 GH 7
Sarânta Ekklēsies = Kırklareli 134-135 B 2
Saranzal, Cachoeira — 98-99 H 8
Sara-Ostrov = Narimanabad 126-127 O 7
Saraphi 150-151 B 3
Sarapuí 102-103 J 5
Sarapul 132-133 J 6
Sarapul'skaja vozvyšennost' 124-125 T 5-6
Sarapul'skoje 132-133 a 8
Sararāt Sayyāl, Bi'r — 173 D 6
Sararât Seiyit = Bi'r Sararāt Sayyāl 173 D 6
Sarare, Río — 94-95 F 4
Sarasa 106-107 G 4-5
Sarāskand = Hashtrūd 136-137 M 4
Sarasota, FL 64-65 K 6
Saraswati 138-139 C 6
Sarāt, Ḥāssī — 166-167 H 5
Saraoko 152-153 O 7
Sarata 126-127 D 3-4
Sarath 138-139 L 5
Saratoga, WY 68-69 C 5
Saratoga Springs, NY 64-65 M 3
Saratok 152-153 J 5
Saratov 124-125 PQ 8
Saratovskoje vodochranilišče 124-125 R 7
Sarāvān 134-135 J 5
Saravane 148-149 E 3
Saravatá, Ilha do — 110 I b 1
Saravena 94-95 E 4
Sarawak 148-149 F 6
Saray 136-137 B 2
Sarāyah 136-137 F 5
Saraykela = Saraikelā 138-139 KL 6
Saraykōy 136-137 C 4
Sarayū = Ghāghara 134-135 N 5
Sarbhōg = Sorbhog 141 B 2
Sarcelles 129 I c 2
Sār Cham 136-137 MN 4
Sarco 106-107 B 2
Sārda 138-139 H 3
Sardalas 164-165 GH 3
Sardarabad = Oktember'an 126-127 LM 6
Sardārpur 138-139 E 6
Sardārshahar = Sardārshahr 134-135 L 5
Sardārshahr 134-135 L 5
Sar Dasht [IR, Khūzestān] 136-137 N 6
Sar Dasht [IR, Kordestān] 136-137 L 4
Sardegna 122-123 C 5
Sardes 136-137 C 3
Sardhāna 138-139 F 3
Sardinata 94-95 E 3
Sardinia, OH 72-73 E 5
Sardinia = Sardegna 122-123 C 5
Sardis, GA 80-81 EF 4
Sardis, MS 78-79 E 3
Sardis Lake 78-79 E 3
Sardis Reservoir = Sardis Lake 78-79 E 3
Šardonem' 124-125 P 2
Sard Rūd 136-137 LM 3
Sare 171 C 3
Sarek nationalpark 116-117 GH 4
Sarektjåkko 116-117 G 4
Sarempaka, Gunung — 152-153 L 6
Sar-e Pol-e Dhahāb 136-137 LM 5
Sarepta = Krasnoarmejsk 126-127 M 2
Sarepul 134-135 K 3
Sargasso Sea 64-65 N-P 6
Sargent, NE 68-69 G 5
Sargent Icefield 58-59 N 6
Sargento Lores 96-97 D 3
Sargento Paixão, Serra do — 104-105 F 2
Sargento Valinotti 102-103 B 4
Sargents, CO 68-69 C 6
Sargho, Djebel — = Jabal Şaghrū' 164-165 C 2
Sargoda = Sargodhā 134-135 L 4
Sargodhā 134-135 L 4
Sargon, Dur — = Khorsabad 136-137 K 4
Šargorod 126-127 CD 2
Sargur 140 C 4-5
Sarh 164-165 H 7
Sarhade Wākhān 134-135 L 3
Şarhrō', Jbel — = Jabal Şaghrū' 164-165 C 2
Sārī 134-135 G 3
Sariá 122-123 M 8
Saridú, Laguna — 94-95 GH 6
Sarıgöl 136-137 C 3
Sarıkamış 136-137 K 2
Sarıkavak = Kumluca 136-137 D 4
Sarıkavak = Kürkcü 136-137 E 4
Sarıkaya = Gömele 136-137 D 2
Sarıkaya = Haman 136-137 F 3
Sarikei 148-149 F 6
Sarina 158-159 J 4
Sarıoğlan 136-137 FG 3
Sarir 164-165 J 3
Sarīr Tibastī 164-165 H 4
Sarīshābārī 138-139 M 5
Sarita 106-107 L 4
Sarita, TX 76-77 F 9
Sarī Tappah 136-137 KL 5
Sariwŏn 142-143 O 4
Sarıyar barajı 136-137 D 2
Sarıyer, İstanbul- 136-137 C 3
Sarız = Köyyeri 136-137 G 3
Sarj, Jabal as- 166-167 L 2
Šarja 132-133 H 6
Sarjāpur 140 C 4
Sarjāpura = Sarjāpur 140 C 4
Sarjū = Ghāghara 134-135 N 5
Sark 119 E 7
Šarkan 124-125 T 5
Şarkîkaraağaç 136-137 D 3
Sarkin Pawa 168-169 G 3
Şarkışla 136-137 G 3
Šarkovščina 124-125 FG 6
Sarlat 120-121 H 6
Sarles, ND 68-69 G 1
Sarmaor = Sirmūr 138-139 F 2
Şărmăsag 122-123 K 2
Sarmi 148-149 L 7
Sarmiento 111 BC 7
Sarmiento, Cordillera — 108-109 C 8-9
Sarmiento, Monte — 108-109 D 10
Sarmiento-José C. Paz 110 III a 1
Sār mörön 142-143 MN 3
Särna 116-117 E 7
Sarneh 136-137 M 6
Sarnia 56-57 U 9
Sarny 124-125 F 8
Saroako 152-153 O 7
Sarolangun 148-149 D 7
Saroma-ko 144-145 c 1
Saron 171 AB 5
Saronikós Kólpos 122-123 K 7
Saros körfezi 136-137 B 2
Šarpa 126-127 M 3
Sarpi 126-127 K 6
Sarpinskije oz'ora 126-127 M 2-3
Šar Planina 122-123 J 4-5
Sarpsborg 116-117 D 8
Sar Qal'ah 136-137 L 5
Sarrah, Ma'tan as- 164-165 J 4
Sarrāṭ, Rā's — 166-167 L 1
Sarre, la — 56-57 V 8
Sarrebourg 120-121 L 4
Sarreguemines 120-121 L 4
Sarria 120-121 D 7
Sarro, Djebel — = Jabal Şaghrū' 164-165 C 2
Sars, As- 166-167 L 1
Šar Süm = Altay 142-143 F 2
Sartana = Primorskoje 126-127 H 3
Sartang 132-133 Z 4
Sartène 122-123 C 5
Sarthe 120-121 G 5
Sartrouville 129 I b 2
Saruhan = Manisa 134-135 B 2
Saruhanlı 136-137 B 3
Sārūq Chāy 136-137 M 4
Saruyama-zaki 144-145 L 4
Sarvār = Sarwār 138-139 E 4
S'arve = Sõrve 124-125 D 5
Sarwār 138-139 E 4
Saryč, mys — 126-127 F 4
Sary-Išikotrau 132-133 O 8
Šaryngol 142-143 K 2
Saryozek 132-133 O 9
Saryšagan 132-133 N 8
Sarysu 132-133 M 8
Sarytaš [SU, Kazachskaja SSR] 126-127 P 4
Sary-Taš [SU, Tadžikskaja SSR] 134-135 L 3
S'as' 124-125 J 4
Sas, Het — 128 II b 1
Sāsabe 86-87 E 2
Sasaginnigak Lake 62 AB 2
Sasake, Yokohama- 155 III a 3
Sasar, Tanjung — 152-153 NO 10
Sasarām 138-139 JK 5
Sasardí Viejo 94-95 C 3
Sasebo 142-143 O 5
Sasel, Hamburg- 130 I b 1
Saskatchewan 56-57 PQ 6-7
Saskatchewan River 56-57 Q 7
Saskatoon 56-57 P 7
Saskylach 132-133 VW 3
Sasmik, Cape — 58-59 u 7
Sasolburg 174-175 G 4
Sason = Kabilcevaz 136-137 J 3
Sason dağları 136-137 J 3
Sasovo 124-125 NO 6
Saspamco, TX 76-77 E 8
Sassafras Mountain 80-81 E 3
Sassandra [CI, place] 164-165 C 7-8
Sassandra [CI, river] 164-165 C 7
Sássari 122-123 C 5
Sassnitz 118 FG 1
Sasstown 168-169 C 4
S'as'stroj 124-125 J 3
Sastobe 132-133 MN 9
Sastre 106-107 FG 3
Sāsvad 140 AB 1
Sasyk, ozero — [SU, Krymskaja Oblast'] 126-127 F 4
Sasyk, ozero — [SU, Odesskaja Oblast'] 126-127 DE 4
Sasykkol', ozero — 132-133 P 8
Sasyktau 126-127 O 3
Sata 144-145 H 7
Satadougou 164-165 B 6
Satakunta 116-117 JK 7
Sata-misaki 142-143 OP 5
Satāna 138-139 E 7
Satanov 126-127 C 2
Satanta, KS 68-69 F 7
Sātāra 134-135 L 7
Satawal 148-149 N 5
Satawan 208 F 2
Satelite, Ciudad — 91 I b 1
Satengar, Pulau — 152-153 M 9
Satevó 86-87 G 3-4
Sathing Phra 150-151 C 9
Satīḍera 138-139 C 5
Saṭīf 164-165 F 1
Saṭīl 166-167 J 2
Satilla River 80-81 F 5
Satipo 92-93 DE 7
Satiri 168-169 DE 3
Satırlar 136-137 C 4
Sátiro Dias 100-101 E 6
Satītan 166-167 G 3
Satka 132-133 KL 6
Satkania = Sātkāniya 141 BC 4
Sātkāniya 141 BC 4
Sātkhīrā 138-139 M 6
Satki 124-125 P 6
Satlaj 134-135 L 4
Satlaj = Langchhen Khamba 142-143 DE 5
Såtleg = Satlaj 134-135 L 4
Sātmāla Hills 138-139 DE 7
Satna 138-139 H 5
Sátoraljaújhely 118 K 4
Sātpura Range 134-135 L-N 6
Satsuma-hantō 144-145 GH 7
Satsuna, South Suburbs- 154 II a 3
Sattahip 148-149 D 4
Saṭṭāt 164-165 C 2
Sattenapalle 140 DE 2
Sattēnpalli = Sattenapalle 140 DE 2
Sāttūr 140 CD 6
Satuk 150-151 D 5
Satul = Satun 150-151 BC 9
Satu Mare 122-123 K 2
Satun 150-151 BC 9
Šatura 124-125 M 6
Saturnina, Rio — 98-99 J 11
Saturnino M. Laspiur 106-107 F 3
Satyamangalam 140 C 5
Sauce [RA] 111 E 3-4
Sauce [ROU] 106-107 JK 5
Sauce, El — 88-89 C 8
Sauce, Laguna del — 106-107 K 5
Sauce Chico, Río — 106-107 F 7
Sauce Corto, Arroyo — 106-107 G 6
Sauce de Luna 106-107 H 3
Sauce Grande, Río — 106-107 G 7
Sauces, Los — 106-107 A 6
Sauce Viejo 106-107 G 3
Saucier, MS 78-79 E 5
Saucillo 86-87 H 3-4
Saucito 86-87 E 2
Sauda 116-117 B 8
Sauda, Jebel el — = Jabal a Sawdā' 164-165 GH 3
Sauda, Jebel el — = Jabal as-Sawdā' 164-165 GH 3
Saudade, Cachoeira da — 98-99 M 8
Saudade, Serra da — 102-103 K 3
Saudável 100-101 CD 7
Saúde 92-93 L 7
Saúde, São Paulo- 110 II b 2
Saudhárkrókur 116-117 d 2
Saudi Arabia 134-135 D 5-F 6
Saudi Kingdom = Saudi Arabia 134-135 D 5-F 6
Saueuina, Rio — 104-105 G 3
Saugeen Peninsula = Bruce Peninsula 72-73 F 2
Saugeen River 72-73 F 2
Saugerties, NY 72-73 JK 3
Saugor = Sāgar 134-135 M 6
Saugus, MA 84 I bc 2
Saugus River 84 I c 2
Saūjbolāgh = Mahābād 134-135 F 3
Saujil 104-105 C 11
Sauk Centre, MN 70-71 C 3
Sauk City, WI 70-71 EF 4
Saukira Bay = Dawḥat as-Sawqirah 134-135 H 7
Sau Ki Wan, Victoria- 155 I b 2
Saukorem 148-149 K 7
Sauk Rapids, MN 70-71 CD 3
Saül 92-93 J 4
Šaul'der 132-133 M 9
Saulkrasti 124-125 DE 5
Saulspoort 174-175 G 3
Sault-au-Mouton 63 B 3
Sault-au-Recollet, Montréal- 82 I b 1
Sault aux Cochons, Rivière du — 63 B 3
Sault-Sainte-Marie 56-57 U 8
Sault Sainte Marie, MI 64-65 JK 2
Šaum'ani 126-127 M 6
Sau Mau Ping 155 I b 2
Saumlaki 148-149 K 8
Saumur 120-121 G 5
Saundatti 140 B 3
Şauqirah, Ghubbat — = Dawḥat as-Sawqirah 134-135 H 7
Saura, Wed — = Wādī as-Sāwrah 164-165 D 2-3
Saurāshtra 134-135 KL 6
Sauri Hill 168-169 G 3
Saurimo 172 D 3
Sausalito, CA 74-75 B 4
Sausar 138-139 G 7
Sausu 152-153 O 6
Sautar 172 C 4
Sautatá 94-95 C 4
Sauz, El — 86-87 G 3
Sauzal, El — 74-75 E 7
S'ava [SU] 124-125 Q 4
Sava [YU] 122-123 J 3
Savage, MT 68-69 D 2
Savage River 160 b 2
Savageton, WY 68-69 CD 4
Savai'i 148-149 c 1
Savāī Mādhōpur = Sawai Mādhopur 138-139 F 5
Savalou 164-165 E 7
Savane, Rivière — 63 A 2
Savanes 168-169 EF 3
Savanna, IL 70-71 E 4
Savannah, GA 64-65 KL 5
Savannah, MO 70-71 C 6
Savannah, TN 78-79 EF 3
Savannah Beach, GA 80-81 F 4
Savannah River 64-65 K 5
Savannakhet 148-149 DE 3
Savanna-la-Mar 88-89 G 5
Savanne 70-71 EF 1
Savant Lake [CDN, lake] 62 D 2
Savant Lake [CDN, place] 62 D 2
Sāvantvādi 140 AB 3
Savanūr 140 B 3
Savanūru = Savanūr 140 B 3
Sāvar = Sānwer 138-139 E 6
Savari = Sābarī 134-135 N 7
Savaştepe 136-137 B 3
Sāvda 138-139 E 7
Savé [DY] 164-165 E 7
Save [F] 120-121 H 7
Save, Rio — 172 F 6
Sāveh 134-135 G 3-4
Savery, WY 68-69 C 5
Savigliano 122-123 BC 3
Savin Hill, Boston-, MA 84 I b 3
Savinka 126-127 N 1
Savino [SU, Ivanovskaja Oblast'] 124-125 N 5
Savino-Borisovskaja 124-125 P 2
Sāvnēr = Saoner 138-139 G 7
Savo 116-117 M 6-7
Savoie 120-121 L 5-6
Sāvojbolāgh = Mahābād 134-135 F 3
Savona 122-123 C 3
Savonlinna 116-117 N 7
Savoy, MT 68-69 B 1
Savran' 126-127 DE 2
Şavşat = Yeniköy 136-137 K 2
Sävsjö 116-117 F 9
Savu = Pulau Sawu 148-149 H 9
Savukoski 116-117 N 4
Savur 136-137 J 4
Savu Sea 148-149 H 8
Saw = Hsaw 141 D 5
Şawāb, Wādī aş- 136-137 J 5
Sawa Besar, Jakarta- 154 IV ab 1
Sawahlunto 148-149 D 7
Sawai Mādhopur 138-139 F 5
Sawākīn 164-165 M 5
Sawang Daen Din 150-151 D 4
Sawankhalok 150-151 BC 4
Sawantwadi = Sāvantvādi 140 AB 3
Sawara 144-145 N 5
Sawata 144-145 M 3-4
Sawatch Mountains 64-65 E 4
Sawazaki-bana 144-145 LM 4
Sawbill 61 H 2
Sawdā', Jabal as- 164-165 GH 3
Sawdirī 164-165 K 6
Sawer = Sānwer 138-139 E 6
Sawi 150-151 B 7
Sawilo 168-169 C 4
Şawīrah, Aş- 164-165 BC 2
Sawknah 164-165 GH 3
Sawner = Saoner 138-139 G 7
Sawqirah 134-135 H 7
Sawqirah, Dawḥat as- 134-135 H 7
Şawrah, Aş- 173 D 4
Sāwrah, Wādī as- 164-165 D 2-3
Sawtooth Mount 58-59 MN 4
Sawtooth Mountains 66-67 FG 3
Sawtooth Range 66-67 C 1-2
Sawu, Pulau — 148-149 H 9
Şawwān, 'Arḍ aş- 136-137 G 7
Sawyer, KS 68-69 G 7
Saxon, WI 70-71 E 2
Saxony = Sachsen 118 F 3
Saxton, PA 72-73 GH 4
Say 164-165 E 6
Sayaboury 148-149 D 3
Sayalgudi = Sāyalkudi 140 D 6
Sāyalkudi 140 D 6
Sayán 96-97 C 7
Sayausí 96-97 B 3
Şayda' [DZ] 166-167 G 2
Şaydā [RL] 134-135 CD 4
Şāyda', Jabal aş- 166-167 G 2
Şayḥūt 134-135 G 7
Saykh, Jabal as- 136-137 FG 6
Sāyla 138-139 C 6
Saymo Lake 70-71 J 2
Sayn Shanda = Sajnšand 142-143 KL 3
Sayo = Dembī Dolo 164-165 LM 7
Şayq, Wādī — 134-135 F 8
Sayre, OK 76-77 E 5
Sayre, PA 72-73 H 4
Sayula 86-87 HJ 8
Say'ūn 134-135 F 7
Sazanit 122-123 H 5
Sāzīn 136-137 N 5
Sazonovo 124-125 K 4
Sba = Saba' 166-167 F 5
Sbartel, Berzekh — = Rā's Ashaqār 166-167 CD 2
Sbeïtla = S'bīṭlat 166-167 L 2
Sbība = Sabībah 166-167 L 2
Sbīkha = As-Sabīrah 166-167 M 2
Sbita, Oglat — = 'Uqlāt as-Sabīyah 166-167 D 7
S'bīṭlat 166-167 L 2
S'bū', Wād — 164-165 CD 2
Scafell Pike 119 E 4
Scalloway 119 F 1
Scammon Bay 58-59 E 5-6
Scammon Bay, AK 58-59 E 6
Scandia 61 BC 5
Scandia, KS 68-69 H 6
Scandinavia 114-115 K 4-N 1
Scània = Skåne 130 III b 1
Scapa 61 B 5
Scapa Flow 119 E 2
Scappoose, OR 66-67 B 3
Ščara 124-125 E 7
Scarborough [GB] 119 FG 4
Scarborough [TT] 64-65 OP 9
Scarpanto = Kárpathos 122-123 M 8
Scarsdale, LA 85 I c 2
Scarth 61 H 6
Sceaux 129 I c 2
Ščeglovsk = Kemerovo 132-133 PQ 6
Ščelejki 124-125 K 3
Scenic, SD 68-69 E 4
Scenic Woods, Houston-, TX 85 III b 1
Scerpeddi, Punta — 122-123 C 6
Schäferberg 130 III a 2
Schaffhausen 118 D 5
Schafflerhof 113 I c 2
Schafrivier 174-175 B 2
Schamelbeek 128 II a 2
Šchara, gora — 126-127 L 5
Schaumburg, IL 70-71 F 5
Schebschi Mountains 164-165 G 7
Schefferville 56-57 X 7
Schelde 120-121 J 3
Schell Creek Range 74-75 F 3
Schellingwoude 128 I b 1
Schenectady, NY 64-65 LM 3
Schenkenhorst 130 III a 2
Schepdaal 128 II a 1-2
Schildow 130 III b 1
Schiplaken 128 II b 1
Schiza 122-123 J 7
Schleinikon 128 IV a 1
Schleswig 118 DE 1
Schleswig-Holstein 118 D 1-E 2
Schloss Charlottenburg 130 III b 1
Schloss Fürstenried 130 II a 2
Schlosspark Nymphenburg 130 II ab 2
Schlüchtern 118 DE 3
Schmargendorf, Berlin- 130 III b 2
Schmidt Island = ostrov Šmidta 132-133 QR 1
Schnelsen, Hamburg- 130 I a 1
Schneppenhausen 128 III a 2
Schöfflisdorf 128 IV a 1
Scholle, NM 76-77 A 5
Schönberg [D, Hessen] 128 III a 1
Schöneck [D] 128 III b 1
Schönerlinde 130 III b 1
Schönfliess [DDR, Potsdam] 130 III b 1
Schönwalde [DDR, Potsdam] 130 III a 1
Schoombee 174-175 F 6
Schouten Island 160 d 3
Schouw, Het — 128 I b 1
Schouwen 120-121 J 3
Schrag, WA 66-67 D 2
Schreiber 70-71 G 1
Schuckmannsburg 172 D 5
Schuler 61 C 5
Schulpfontein Point = Skulpfonteinpunt 174-175 B 6
Schulzenhöhe 130 III cd 2
Schurz, NV 74-75 D 3
Schuyler, NE 68-69 H 5
Schuylkill River 84 III b 1
Schwabach 118 E 4
Schwabinger Bach 130 II bc 1
Schwäbische Alb 118 D 5-E 4
Schwäbisch Gmünd 118 DE 4
Schwäbisch Hall 118 DE 4
Schwamendingen, Zürich- 128 IV b 1
Schwandorf 118 F 4
Schwaner, Pegunungan — 148-149 F 7
Schwanheim, Frankfurt am Main- 128 III a 1
Schwänkelberg 128 IV a 1
Schwarzbach [D ◁ RO] 128 III a 2

Schwarze Elster 118 FG 3
Schwarzes Meer 126-127 E-J 5
Schwarzwald 118 D 4-5
Schwatka Mountains 56-57 EF 4
Schweinfurt 118 E 3
Schweinsand 130 I a 1
Schweitzergletscher 53 B 32-33
Schweizer Land 56-57 d 4
Schweizer-Reneke 174-175 F 4
Schwerin 118 E 2
Schwerzenbach 128 IV b 1
Schwyz 118 D 5
Sciacca 122-123 E 7
Scicli 122-123 F 7
Scie, la — 63 J 2
Science and Industry, Museum of — 83 II b 2
Ščigry [SU, Kurskaja Oblast'] 124-125 L 8
Scilly, Isles of — 119 C 7
Scioto River 72-73 E 5
Scipio, UT 74-75 G 3
Scobey, MT 68-69 D 1
Ščokino 124-125 M 6-7
Scone 160 K 4
Scoresby Land 52 B 21
Scoresby Sund [Greenland, bay] 52 B 20-21
Scoresbysund [Greenland, place] 52 B 20-21
Ščors 124-125 H 8
Scotia, CA 66-67 AB 5
Scotia Ridge 50-51 G 8
Scotland 119 D 3-E 4
Scotland, SD 68-69 GH 4
Scotland Neck, NC 80-81 H 2
Scotstown 72-73 L 2
Scott 53 B 17-18
Scott, Cape — 56-57 L 7
Scott, Mount — [USA → Crater Lake] 64-65 B 3
Scott, Mount — [USA ↓ Pengra Pass] 66-67 BC 4
Scottburgh 174-175 J 6
Scott Channel 60 C 4
Scott City, KS 68-69 F 6
Scottcrest Park 85 III b 2
Scott Glacier [Antarctica, Dronning Maud fjellkjede] 53 A 21-23
Scott Glacier [Antarctica, Knox Land] 53 C 11
Scottie Creek Lodge, AK 58-59 R 5
Scott Inlet 56-57 WX 3
Scott Island 53 C 19
Scott Islands 60 C 4
Scott Middle Ground 84 II c 2
Scott Mittle Ground 84 II bc 2
Scott Range 53 C 5-6
Scott Reef 158-159 D 2
Scott Run 82 II a 1
Scottsbluff, NE 64-65 F 3
Scottsboro, AL 78-79 FG 3
Scottsburg, IN 70-71 GH 6
Scottsburg = Scottburgh 174-175 J 6
Scottsdale 158-159 J 8
Scotts Head 88-89 Q 7
Scottsville, KY 78-79 F 2
Scottsville, VA 80-81 G 2
Scottville, MI 70-71 GH 4
Scranton, AR 78-79 C 3
Scranton, PA 64-65 LM 3
Scribner, NE 68-69 H 5
Ščučinsk 132-133 MN 7
Scunthorpe 119 FG 5
Scutari = İstanbul-Üsküdar 134-135 BC 2
Scutari = Shkodër 122-123 H 4
Scutari, Lake — = Skadarsko jezero 122-123 H 4
Scythopolis = Bet-Shĕan 136-137 F 6

Sé, São Paulo- 110 II b 2
Seabra 100-101 D 7
Seadrift, TX 76-77 F 8
Seaford, DE 72-73 J 5
Seagraves, TX 76-77 C 6
Seagull Lake 70-71 E 1
Seaham 119 F 4
Sea Islands 64-65 K 5
Seal, Cape — = Kaap Seal 174-175 E 8
Seal, Kaap — 174-175 E 8
Sea Lake 160 F 5
Seal Cape 58-59 d 1
Seale, AL 78-79 G 4
Sea Lion Islands 111 E 8
Seal Islands 58-59 d 1
Seal Point = Sealpunt 174-175 F 8
Sealpunt 174-175 F 8
Seal River 56-57 R 6
Sealy, TX 76-77 F 8
Sea of the Hebrides 119 C 3
Seara 102-103 F 7
Searchlight, NV 74-75 F 5
Searchmont 70-71 HJ 2
Searcy, AR 78-79 CD 3
Searles Lake 74-75 E 5
Searsport, ME 72-73 M 2
Sears Tower 83 II b 1
Seaside, CA 74-75 C 4
Seaside, OR 66-67 B 3
Seaside Park, NJ 72-73 JK 5
Seaton 60 D 2
Seat Plesant, MD 82 II b 2
Seattle, WA 64-65 B 2
Sebâ', Gebel es- = Qārat as-Sab'ah 164-165 H 3
Sebago Lake 72-73 L 3
Se Bai, Lam — 150-151 E 4-5
Sebangan, Teluk — 148-149 F 7
Se Bang Fai 150-151 E 4
Se Bang Hieng 150-151 E 4
Sebangka, Pulau — 148-149 DE 6
Sebarok, Pulau — 154 III a 2
Sebaru 152-153 M 10
Sebastian, FL 80-81 c 3
Sebastian, Cape — 66-67 A 4
Sebastián Elcano 106-107 F 3
Sebastián Vizcaíno, Bahía — 64-65 CD 6
Sebastopol, CA 74-75 B 3
Sebatik, Pulau — 148-149 G 6
Sebba 168-169 F 2
Sebbara = Al-Gārah 166-167 C 3
Sebdou = Sībdū 166-167 F 2
Sebeka, MN 70-71 C 2
Šebekino 126-127 H 1
Sébékoro 168-169 C 2
Seben 136-137 D 2
Seberi 106-107 L 1
Sebeş 122-123 K 2-3
Sebes Körös 118 K 5
Sebewaing, MI 72-73 E 3
Sebež 124-125 G 5
Sebḫa = Sabhah 164-165 G 3
Şebinkarahisar 136-137 H 2
Sebka Oum ed Drouss = Sabkhat Umm ad-Durūs 164-165 B 4
Sebkha el Adhibat = Sabkhat Tādit 166-167 M 3
Sebkha Oumm el Drouss = Sabkhat Umm ad-Durūs 164-165 B 4
Sebkhet el Mêlaḥ = Sabkhat al-Māliḥ 166-167 M 3
Sebkhet Kelbia = Sabkhat Kalbīyah 166-167 M 2
Sebkhet Oum el Krialat = Sabkhat Umm al-Khiyālāt 166-167 M 3
Sebkra Aïne Belbela = Sabkhat 'Ayn Balbālah 166-167 D 6
Sebkra Azzel Matti = Sabkhat 'Azmātī 164-165 DE 3
Sebkra de Timimoun = Sabkhat Tīmīmūn 166-167 G 5
Sebkra de Tindouf = Sabkhat Tindūf 164-165 C 3
Sebkra el Melah = Sabkhat al-Malah 166-167 F 5
Sebkra Mekerrhane = Sabkhat Mukrān 164-165 E 3
Sebkret Tadet = Sabkhat Tādit 166-167 M 3
Seboû, Ouèd — = Wad S'bū' 166-167 D 2
Sebree, KY 70-71 G 7
Sebring, FL 80-81 c 3
Sebseb = Sabsab 166-167 H 3
Sebta = Ceuta 164-165 CD 1
Sebt 'Imrhât = Sabt 'Imghāt 166-167 AB 4
Sebt Jzoûla = As-Sabt G'zūlah 166-167 B 3
Sebu = Wād Sbū' 166-167 D 2
Sebuku, Pulau — 148-149 G 7
Sebuku, Teluk — 148-149 G 6
Seburi-yama 144-145 H 6
Sebuyau 152-153 J 5
Secane, PA 84 III b 2
Secaucus, NJ 82 III b 2
Secen Chaan = Öndörchaan 142-143 L 2
Sečenovo 124-125 PQ 6
Sechelt 66-67 AB 1
Sechuan = Sichuan 142-143 J 5-6
Sechura 92-93 C 6
Sechura, Bahía de — 92-93 C 6
Sechura, Desierto de — 96-97 A 4-5
Seckbach, Frankfurt am Main- 128 III b 1
Secunderābād 134-135 M 7
Sécure, Río — 104-105 C 4
Sedalia 61 C 5
Sedalia, MO 70-71 D 6
Sedan, KS 76-77 F 4
Sedan [AUS] 158-159 G 6
Sedan [F] 120-121 K 4
Sedanau, Pulau — 150-151 F 11
Sedanka Island 58-59 no 4
Sedaw = Hsindau 141 E 4
Seddinsee 130 III c 2
Seddonville 158-159 O 8
Sedel'nikovo 132-133 O 6
Sedgwick, KS 68-69 H 7
Sédhiou 164-165 AB 6
Sedili Besar 150-151 E 12
Sedjenân = Sijnān 166-167 L 1
Šedok 126-127 K 4
Sedôktayâ 141 D 5
Sĕdôm 136-137 F 7
Sedona, AZ 74-75 H 5
Sedone 150-151 EF 5
Sedova, pik — 132-133 J 3
Sedrata = Ṣadrātah 166-167 K 1
Šeduva 124-125 DE 6
Seebach, Zürich- 128 IV b 1
Seeberg [DDR] 130 III c 1
Seeburg [DDR] 130 III a 1
Seechelt Peninsula 66-67 AB 1
Seefeld, Zürich- 128 IV b 1
Seeheim [Namibia] 172 C 7
Seehof 130 III b 2
Seeis 172 C 6
Seekoegat 174-175 E 7
Seekoerivier 174-175 F 6
Seeley Lake, MT 66-67 G 2
Şefaatli 136-137 F 3
Sefadu 164-165 B 7
Seferihisar 136-137 B 3
Séfeto 168-169 C 2
Sefīd, Kūh-e — 136-137 M 5-N 6
Sefīd Rūd 136-137 N 4
Sefkat 136-137 H 3
Şefroû = Şafrū 166-167 D 3
Segama, Sungei — 152-153 MN 3
Segamat 150-151 D 11
Segendy 126-127 P 5
Segesta 122-123 E 7
Segewold = Sigulda 124-125 E 5
Segeža 132-133 EF 5
Segguedim = Séguédine 164-165 G 4
Seggueur, Ouèd — = Wādī as-Sūqar 166-167 GH 3
Sego, UT 74-75 J 3
Segorbe 120-121 G 9
Ségou 164-165 C 6
Šegovary 124-125 O 2
Segovia, TX 76-77 E 7
Segovia [CO] 94-95 D 4
Segovia [E] 120-121 E 8
Segovia, Río — = Río Coco 64-65 K 9
Segozero 124-125 J 2
Segré 120-121 G 5
Segre, Río — 120-121 H 8
Segu = Ségou 164-165 C 6
Seguam Island 58-59 kl 4
Seguam Pass 58-59 k 4
Séguédine 164-165 G 4
Séguéla 164-165 C 7
Séguénéga 168-169 E 2
Seguí 106-107 GH 3
Seguin, TX 64-65 G 6
Seguine Point 82 III a 3
Segula Island 58-59 s 6
Seguntur 152-153 MN 5
Segura, Río — 120-121 G 9
Segura, Sierra de — 120-121 F 9-10
Şehirköy = Şarköy 136-137 B 2
Sehl Tamlélt = Sahl Tāmlilt 166-167 E 3
Sehore 138-139 F 6
Sehwan = Sihwān 138-139 AB 4
Şehzade Camiî 154 I a 2
Seibal 86-87 P 9
Seibert, CO 68-69 E 6
Seikpyu = Hseikhpyū 141 D 5
Seiland 116-117 K 2
Seiling, OK 76-77 E 4
Seinäjoki 116-117 K 6
Seine 120-121 H 4
Seine, Baie de la — 120-121 G 4
Seinlôngabâ 141 E 3
Seishin = Ch'ŏngjin 142-143 OP 3
Seishū = Ch'ŏngju 142-143 O 4
Seistan = Sīstān 134-135 J 4
Seitovka 126-127 O 3
Seival 106-107 L 3
Seiyit, Sararāt — = Bi'r Sararāt Sayyāl 173 D 6
Sejaka 152-153 G 7
Sejm 126-127 F 1
Sejmčan 132-133 d 5
Sejny 118 L 1
Sejrī, Bi'r — = Bi'r Sajarī 136-137 H 6
Sejtler = Nižnegorskij 126-127 G 4
Seka 150-151 DE 4
Sekala, Pulau — 152-153 M 9
Se Kamane 150-151 F 5
Sekayam, Sungai — 152-153 J 5
Sekayu 152-153 EF 7
Seke 172 F 2
Sekenke 172 F 2
Sekhuma 174-175 E 3
Sekiu, WA 66-67 A 1
Sekondi-Takoradi 164-165 D 7-8
Sê Kong [K] 150-151 F 5-6
Se Kong [LAO] 150-151 F 5
Sekretaris, Kali — 154 IV a 2
Šeksna [SU, place] 124-125 M 4
Šeksna [SU, river] 124-125 M 4
Selado, Morro — 102-103 JK 5
Šelagskij, mys — 132-133 gh 3
Selah, WA 66-67 C 2
Sêlam = Salem 134-135 M 8
Selama 150-151 C 10
Selangor 150-151 C 11
Selangor, Kuala — 148-149 D 6
Selaphum 150-151 DE 4
Selaru, Pulau — 148-149 K 8
Selat Alas 148-149 G 8
Selat Alor 152-153 PQ 10
Selatan, Tanjung — 148-149 F 7
Selat Bali 152-153 L 10
Selat Bangka 148-149 E 7
Selat Berhala 152-153 EF 6
Selat Bungalaut 152-153 C 6-7
Selat Butung 152-153 P 8
Selat Cempi 152-153 N 10
Selat Dampier 148-149 K 7
Selat Gaspar 148-149 E 7
Selat Kabaena 152-153 O 8
Selat Karimata 148-149 E 7
Selat Lombok 148-149 G 8
Selat Madura 152-153 KL 9
Selat Makasar 148-149 G 6-7
Selat Malaka 152-153 A 3
Selat Melaka 148-149 CD 6
Selat Mentawai 152-153 C 6-D 7
Selat Peleng 152-153 P 6
Selat Raas 152-153 L 9
Selat Salayar 152-153 N 9-O 8
Selat Sape 152-153 N 10
Selat Sapudi 152-153 L 9
Selat Sengkir 154 III ab 2
Selat Serasan 150-151 G 11
Selat Siberut 148-149 C 7
Selat Sipora 152-153 CD 7
Selat Sumba 148-149 GH 8
Selat Sunda 148-149 E 8
Selat Tioro 152-153 P 8
Selat Walea 152-153 P 6
Selat Wowotobi 152-153 P 10
Selat Yapen 148-149 L 7
Selawik, AK 56-57 DE 4
Selawik Lake 56-57 DE 4
Selawik River 58-59 H 3
Selbu 116-117 D 6
Selby 119 F 5
Selby, SD 68-69 FG 3
Selby, Johannesburg- 170 V b 2
Selchow [DDR, Potsdam] 130 III b 2
Selden, KS 68-69 F 6
Seldovia, AK 56-57 F 6
Selemdža 132-133 YZ 7
Selemiyé = Salamīyah 136-137 G 5
Selendi 136-137 C 3
Selenge [Mongolia, administrative unit = 11 ◁] 142-143 K 2
Selenge [Mongolia, place] 142-143 J 2
Selenge mörön 142-143 J 2
Selenn'ach 132-133 a 4
Selenodolsk = Zelenodol'sk 132-133 HJ 6
Sélestat 120-121 L 4
Seletar [SGP, place] 154 III b 1
Seletar [SGP, river] 154 III a 1
Seletar, Pulau — 154 III b 1
Seletar Reservoir 154 III a 1
Seletyteniz, ozero — 132-133 N 7
Seleucia = Silifke 134-135 C 3
Seleucia Pieria = Samandağ 136-137 F 4
Selêvkeia = Silifke 134-135 C 3
Selfoss 116-117 c 3
Selfridge, ND 68-69 F 2
Selhurst, London- 129 II b 2
Šelichova, zaliv — 132-133 e 5-6
Seliger, ozero — 124-125 J 5
Seligman, AZ 74-75 G 5
Seligman, MO 78-79 C 2
Selim 136-137 K 2
Selīma, Wāḥat es — = Wāḥāt Şalīmah 164-165 K 4
Selimiye 136-137 B 4
Selingdo 138-139 M 2
Seling Tsho 142-143 FG 5
Selinus 122-123 E 7
Seliphug Gonpa 142-143 E 5
Selišče [SU ↖ RO] 124-125 J 5
Seližarovo 124-125 JK 5
Seljord 116-117 C 8
Selkirk [CDN] 56-57 R 7
Selkirk Island 61 J 4
Selkirk Mountains 56-57 N 7-8
Selle, la — 88-89 KL 5
Selleck, WA 66-67 C 2
Sells, AZ 74-75 H 7
Selma, AL 64-65 J 5
Selma, CA 74-75 D 4
Selma, NC 80-81 G 3
Selmer, TN 78-79 E 3
Selong 152-153 M 10
Selous Game Reserve 172 G 3
Šeltozero 124-125 K 3
Selty 124-125 T 5
Seluan, Pulau — 150-151 F 10
Selui, Pulau — 152-153 G 7
Selukwe 172 F 5
Seluma 152-153 E 8
Selva 111 D 3
Selva de Montiel 106-107 H 3
Selvagens, Ilhas — 164-165 A 2
Selvas 90 DE 3
Selvas del Río de Oro 104-105 G 10
Selway River 66-67 F 2
Selwyn 158-159 H 4
Selwyn Mountains 56-57 KL 5
Selwyn Range 158-159 GH 4
Selz, ND 68-69 G 2
Šemacha 126-127 O 6
Semakau, Pulau — 154 III a 2
Seman 122-123 H 5
Semangka, Teluk — 152-153 F 8
Semans 61 F 5
Semarang 148-149 F 8
Se Mat = Ban Se Mat 150-151 F 6
Sematan 152-153 H 5
Semau, Pulau — 148-149 H 9
Sembakung, Sungai — 152-153 M 3-4
Sĕmbaliguḍā = Semiligūda 140 F 1
Sembawang [SGP, place] 154 III ab 1
Sembawang [SGP, river] 154 III a 1
Sembawang Hills 154 III ab 1
Sembien 140 E 4
Sembilan, Kepulauan — 150-151 C 10
Sembilan, Pulau — 150-151 B 10
Sembodja = Samboja 148-149 G 7
Şemdinli = Navşar 136-137 L 4
Semenanjung Blambangan 152-153 L 10
Semenivka = Sem'onovka [SU, Černigov] 124-125 J 7
Semenivka = Sem'onovka [SU, Poltavskaja Oblast'] 126-127 F 2
Semenovka = Sem'onovka [SU, Černigov] 124-125 J 7
Semenovka = Sem'onovka [SU, Poltavskaja Oblast'] 126-127 F 2
Semeru, Gunung — 148-149 F 8
Semeuluë, Pulau — 148-149 BC 6
Semeyen = Simēn 164-165 M 6
Semibratovo 124-125 M 5
Semibugry 126-127 O 3
Semidi Islands 58-59 e 1-2
Semikarakorskij 126-127 K 3
Semiligūda 140 F 1
Semiluki 124-125 M 8
Seminoe Dam, WY 68-69 C 4
Seminoe Mountains 68-69 C 4
Seminoe Reservoir 68-69 C 4
Seminole, OK 76-77 F 5
Seminole, TX 76-77 C 6
Seminole, Lake — 78-79 G 5
Semipalatinsk 132-133 OP 7
Semipolki 126-127 E 1
Semirara Islands 148-149 H 4
Semisopochnoi Island 58-59 st 6
Semitau 152-153 J 5
Semium 152-153 GH 3
Semiun, Pulau — 150-151 F 10
Semka = Sangā 148-149 C 2
Semmering 118 GH 5
Semnān 134-135 G 3
Semnan, Koll-e — 134-135 GH 3
Semois 120-121 K 4
Semonaicha 132-133 P 7
Sem'onov 124-125 P 5
Sem'onovka [SU, Černigovskaja Oblast'] 124-125 J 7
Sem'onovka [SU, Poltavskaja Oblast'] 126-127 F 2
Šemordan 124-125 S 5
Semporna 152-153 N 3
Sempu, Pulau — 152-153 K 10
Semu 171 C 3
Semuda 152-153 K 7
Šemyšejka 124-125 P 7
Sen, Mu'o'ng — 150-151 E 3
Sen, Stung — 150-151 E 6
Seña, La — 106-107 D 4
Sena Aisen 108-109 C 5
Senador Firmino 102-103 L 4
Senador Pompeu 92-93 LM 6
Senaisla = Sunaysilah 136-137 J 5
Senaja 152-153 M 2
Sena Madureira 92-93 F 6
Sēnānāyaka Samudraya 140 E 7
Senanga 172 D 5
Senate 68-69 B 1
Senatobia, MS 78-79 E 3
Senbei 132-133 M 8
Sendai [J, Kagoshima] 144-145 GH 7
Sendai [J, Miyagi] 142-143 R 4
Sendelingsdrif 174-175 B 5
Sĕndhavā = Sendhwa 138-139 E 7
Sendhwa 138-139 E 7
Sene 164-165 D 7
Senebui, Pulau — 150-151 C 11
Seneca, KS 68-69 H 6
Seneca, MO 76-77 G 4
Seneca, NE 68-69 F 4-5
Seneca, OR 66-67 D 3
Seneca, SC 80-81 E 3
Seneca, SD 68-69 G 3
Seneca Falls, NY 72-73 H 3
Seneca Lake 72-73 H 3
Sened, Es — = As-Sanad 166-167 L 2
Sénégal [SN, river] 164-165 B 5
Sénégal [SN, state] 164-165 AB 6
Senegal = Sénégal 164-165 AB 6
Sénégal-Oriental 168-169 AB 2
Sénégambia 168-169 AB 2
Senekal 174-175 G 5
Senen, Jakarta- 154 IV b 2
Seney, MI 70-71 H 2
Seng, Nam — 150-151 D 2
Sengejskij, ostrov — 132-133 HJ 4
Sengés 102-103 H 6
Sengge Khamba 142-143 DE 5
Senggetö 138-139 H 2
Sengilej 124-125 R 7
Sengkang 152-153 O 8
Sengkir, Selat — 154 III ab 2
Sengkuang 154 III a 1
Senguerr, Río 108-109 D 5
Sengwe 172 E 5
Senhor do Bonfim 92-93 L 7
Senibong 154 III a 1
Senigállia 122-123 E 4
Senījān 136-137 N 5
Senillosa 106-107 C 7
Senirkent 136-137 D 3
Senj 122-123 F 3
Senja 116-117 G 3
Senjū, Tōkyō- 155 III b 1
Senkaku-shotō 142-143 N 6
Senkaku syotō = Senkaku-shotō 142-143 N 6
Şenkaya 136-137 K 2
Šenkursk 132-133 G 5
Senlis 120-121 J 4
Senmonorom 148-149 E 4
Sennār = Sannār 164-165 L 6
Senneterre 62 N 2
Senno 124-125 G 6
Seno 148-149 DE 3
Seno Almirantazgo 108-109 DE 10
Seno Año Nuevo 108-109 E 10
Seno Choiseul = Choiseul Sound 108-109 KL 8
Seno Cornish 108-109 B 6
Seno Eyre 111 B 7
Se Noi 150-151 E 4
Senoia, GA 78-79 G 4
Senoka 154 III a 1
Seno Langford 108-109 C 9
Seno Otway 111 B 8
Seno Reloncaví 108-109 C 3
Seno Skyring 111 B 8
Sens 120-121 J 4
Sensfelder Tanne 128 III a 2
Senta 122-123 HJ 3
Šentala 124-125 S 6
Sentarum, Danau — 152-153 JK 5
Sentery 172 E 3
Sentinel, AZ 74-75 G 6
Sentinel Peak 60 G 2
Sentinel Range 53 B 28
Sentosa, Pulau — 154 III a 2
Sento-Sé 92-93 L 6
Senyavin Islands 208 F 2
Şenyurt = Derbisīye 136-137 J 4
Seo de Urgel 120-121 H 7
Seonāth 138-139 J 7
Seondha 138-139 G 4
Seoni 134-135 M 6
Seoni-Mālwa 138-139 F 6
Seorīnārāyan 138-139 J 7
Seoul = Sŏul 142-143 O 4
Separ, NM 74-75 J 6
Separation Well 158-159 D 4
Separ Shāhābād 136-137 MN 5
Sepasu 152-153 M 5
Sepatini, Rio — 98-99 E 9-F 8
Sepenjang, Pulau — 148-149 G 8
Sepetiba, Baía de — 102-103 KL 5
Šepetovka 126-127 C 1
Sepik River 148-149 M 7
Sepo La 138-139 M 3
Sepone 148-149 E 3
Sepopa 172 D 5
Sep'o-ri 144-145 F 3
Sepotuba, Rio — 102-103 D 1
Sept-Îles 56-57 X 7-8
Sept-Îles, Baie des — 63 CD 2-3
Sept Pagodes = Mahābalipuram 140 E 4
Sept Pagodes = Pha Lai 150-151 F 2
Sequim, WA 66-67 B 1
Sequoia National Park 64-65 C 4
Serachs 134-135 J 3
Şerafettin dağları 136-137 J 3
Serafimovič 126-127 L 2
Serafina, NM 76-77 B 5
Seram [IND] 140 C 2
Seram [RI] 148-149 JK 7
Seram-laut, Kepulauan — 148-149 K 7
Serampore 134-135 O 6
Seramsee 148-149 JK 7
Serang 148-149 E 8
Serang = Seram 148-149 JK 7
Serangoon 154 III b 1
Serangoon, Pulau — 154 III b 1
Serangoon Harbour 154 III b 1
Serasan, Pulau — 150-151 G 11
Serasan, Selat — 150-151 G 11
Serâyâ = Sarāyah 136-137 F 5
Seraya, Pulau — 150-151 G 11
Serayu, Pegunungan — 152-153 H 9
Serbia 122-123 H 3-J 4
Serbka 126-127 E 3
Serchhung 138-139 L 3
Serdar 136-137 G 4
Serdce Kamen', mys — 58-59 BC 3
Serdéles = Sardalas 164-165 G 3
Serdj, Djebel es — = Jabal as-Sarj 166-167 L 2
Serdobsk 124-125 P 7
Serebr'ansk 132-133 P 8
Serebr'anyj Bor, Moskva- 113 V ab 2
Serebr'anyje Prudy 124-125 M 6
Sereda [SU, Jaroslavskaja Oblast'] 124-125 N 4
Sereda [SU, Moskovskaja Oblast'] 124-125 K 6
Seredina-Buda 124-125 JK 7
Seredka 124-125 FG 4
Sered'anka 124-125 T 3
Serefiye = Dereköy 136-137 G 2
Şereflikoçhişar 136-137 E 3
Seregovo 124-125 S 2
Seremban 148-149 D 6
Šeremetjevka 124-125 S 6
Serena, La — [E] 120-121 E 9
Serena, La — [RCH] 111 B 3
Serengeti National Park 172 FG 2
Serengeti Plain 171 C 3
Serengka 152-153 J 6
Serenje 172 F 4
Serenli = Saranley 172 H 1
Sereno, Rio — 98-99 P 8
Seret 126-127 B 2
Ser'ga 124-125 V 5
Sergač 124-125 P 6
Sergeja Kirova, ostrova — 132-133 QR 2
Sergijev = Zagorsk 132-133 F 6
Serginy 132-133 LM 5
Sergiopolis = Riṣāfah 136-137 H 5
Sergipe 92-93 M 7
Sergipe, Rio — 100-101 F 6
Sergo = Kadijevka 126-127 J 2
Seria 148-149 F 6
Serian 152-153 J 5
Seribu, Pulau-pulau — 148-149 E 7-8
Seribudolok 150-151 B 11
Şerifali 154 I b 3
Sérifos 122-123 L 7
Serik 136-137 D 4
Seringa, Serra da — 92-93 J 6
Seringapatam = Srīrangapatnam 140 C 4
Seringapatap = Srīrangapatnam 140 C 4
Serīr Kalanshyū 164-165 J 3
Şerji Gonpa 138-139 L 2
Šerkaly 132-133 M 5
Šerlovaja gora 132-133 W 7
Sermādevi 140 C 6
Sermata, Pulau — 148-149 J 8
Sermilik 56-57 d 4
Serna, De la — 106-107 E 5
Sernovodsk 124-125 ST 7
Sernur 124-125 R 5
Serodino 106-107 G 4
Serón [RCH] 106-107 B 3
Serov 132-133 L 6
Serowe 172 E 6
Ser'oža 124-125 O 6
Serpa 120-121 D 10
Serpa Pinto = Menongue 172 C 4
Serpeddì, Punta — 122-123 C 6
Serpent, Rivière — 63 A 2-3
Serpentine Hot Springs, AK 58-59 EF 4
Serpiente, Boca de la — 92-93 G 2-3
Serpnevoje 126-127 D 3
Serpuchov 124-125 L 6
Serpukhov = Serpuchov 124-125 L 6
Serra 100-101 D 11
Serra Acaraí 92-93 H 4
Serra Azul [BR, mountains] 98-99 L 5
Serra Azul [BR, place] 102-103 J 4
Serra Barauanã 98-99 H 3-4
Serra Bodoquena 92-93 H 9
Serra Bom Jesus da Gurguéia 92-93 L 6-7
Serra Bom Sucesso 102-103 KL 1
Serra Bonita 100-101 A 8
Serra Botucaraí 106-107 L 2
Serra Branca [BR, Maranhão] 100-101 B 3-4
Serra Branca [BR, Paraíba] 100-101 F 4
Serra Branca [BR, Pernambuco] 100-101 DE 4
Serra Branca [BR, Rio Grande do Norte] 100-101 E 4
Serra Canelas 100-101 AB 4
Serra Central 100-101 C 8
Serra Curicuriari 98-99 E 5
Serra Curral Novo 100-101 EF 6
Serra da Araruna 100-101 G 4
Serra da Aurora 104-105 F 1-2
Serra da Balança 100-101 E 4
Serra da Boa Vista 100-101 EF 4
Serra da Bocaina 102-103 GH 7-8
Serra da Caatinga 100-101 EF 3
Serra da Canabrava [BR, Rio Jucuruçu] 100-101 DE 9
Serra da Cana Brava [BR, Rio São Onofre] 100-101 C 7
Serra da Canastra [BR, Bahia] 100-101 E 6
Serra da Canastra [BR, Minas Gerais] 92-93 K 9
Serra da Cangalha [BR, Goiás] 98-99 P 9
Serra da Cangalha [BR, Piauí] 100-101 D 3
Serra da Cantareira 110 II ab 1
Serra da Carioca 110 I b 2
Serra da Chela 172 B 5
Serra da Chibata 100-101 D 10-11
Serra da Cinta 92-93 K 6
Serra da Croeira 100-101 A 4
Serra da Cruz 100-101 A 5
Serra da Desordem 100-101 AB 2
Serra da Divisa 98-99 G 9
Serra da Esperança 102-103 G 6-7
Serra da Estrêla [BR] 100-101 D 4
Serra da Estrela [P] 120-121 CD 8
Serra da Farofa 106-107 MN 2
Serra da Fartura 102-103 FG 7
Serra da Flecheira 100-101 B 8
Serra da Gameleira 100-101 C 4
Serra da Garapa 100-101 C 7
Serra da Inveja 100-101 F 5
Serra da Joaninha 100-101 D 3
Serra da Mantiqueira 92-93 KL 9
Serra da Mata da Corda 92-93 K 8
Serra da Mocidade 98-99 GH 4
Serra da Moeda 102-103 KL 4
Serra da Mombuca 102-103 FG 3
Serra da Neve 172 B 4
Serra da Ouricana 100-101 DE 8
Serra da Piedade 100-101 F 4
Serra da Piranga 98-99 MN 6
Serra da Pitanga 102-103 G 6
Serra da Ponta do Morro 100-101 C 7
Serra da Providência 98-99 H 10
Serra da Raiada 100-101 EF 4
Serra das Almas 100-101 D 4
Serra das Alpercatas 100-101 B 3-4
Serra das Araras [BR, Maranhão] 98-99 P 8
Serra das Araras [BR, Mato Grosso] 92-93 J 8
Serra das Araras [BR, Minas Gerais] 102-103 K 1
Serra das Araras [BR, Paraná] 111 F 2-3
Serra da Saudade 102-103 K 3
Serra das Balanças 100-101 DE 3
Serra das Cordilheiras 98-99 OP 8
Serra das Divisões 92-93 JK 8
Serra das Encantadas 106-107 L 3
Serra da Seringa 92-93 J 6
Serra das Figuras 100-101 B 6
Serra das Mamoneiras 98-99 P 7-8
Serra das Marrecas 100-101 D 5
Serra das Matas 100-101 DE 3
Serra das Missões 100-101 D 4
Serra das Onças 98-99 H 9-10
Serra das Palmeiras 100-101 F 5
Serra das Porteira 100-101 F 5
Serra da Suçuarana 100-101 B 8
Serra das Umburanas 100-101 F 5-G 4
Serra das Vertentes 100-101 E 2-3
Serra da Tabatinga 100-101 B 6
Serra da Taquara 102-103 F 1
Serra da Vassouras 100-101 E 4-5
Serra de Amambaí 102-103 E 5
Serra de Apucarana 111 F 2
Serra de Araraquara 102-103 HJ 4
Serra de Caçapava 106-107 L 3
Serra de Carauna 98-99 H 3
Serra de Gorongosa 172 FG 5
Serra de Guampi 94-95 J 4-5
Serra de Maracaju 92-93 H 9-J 8
Serra de Minas 102-103 L 3
Serra de Monchique 120-121 C 10
Serra de Monte Alto 100-101 C 8
Serra de Pedro II 100-101 D 3
Serra de Santa Bárbara 92-93 J 9
Serra de Santa Luísa 102-103 E 3
Serra de Santana [BR, Bahia] 100-101 C 7
Serra de Santana [BR, Rio Grande do Norte] 100-101 F 3-4
Serra de Santa Rita 100-101 E 3
Serra de Santa Tecla 106-107 KL 3

Serra 359

Serra de São Domingos 100-101 A 7-8
Serra de São Jerônimo 92-93 J 8
Serra de São João [BR, Amazonas] 98-99 GH 9
Serra de São João [BR, Paraná] 102-103 G 6
Serra de São Pedro 100-101 E 4
Serra de São Vicente 104-105 G 4
Serra de São Xavier 106-107 KL 2
Serra de Saudade 102-103 K 3
Serra de Tiracambu 92-93 K 5
Serra de Uruburetama 100-101 DE 2
Serra do Acapuzal 98-99 MN 5
Serra do Açuruá 100-101 C 6
Serra do Almeirim 98-99 M 5
Serra do Alto Uruguai 106-107 L 1
Serra do Ambrósio 102-103 L 3
Serra do Angical 100-101 B 6
Serra do Apiaú 92-93 G 4
Serra do Arelão 98-99 M 5
Serra do Batista [BR, Bahia] 100-101 D 6
Serra do Batista [BR, Piauí] 100-101 D 4
Serra do Baturité 100-101 E 3
Serra do Boi Preto 102-103 F 6
Serra do Boqueirão [BR, Bahia] 92-93 L 7
Serra do Boqueirão [BR, Pernambuco] 100-101 F 5
Serra do Boqueirão [BR, Piauí] 100-101 C 4
Serra do Boqueirão [BR, Rio Grande do Sul] 106-107 K 2
Serra do Braga 100-101 E 4
Serra do Cabral 102-103 K 2
Serra do Cachimbo 92-93 HJ 6
Serra do Café 100-101 G 6
Serra do Caiapó 102-103 FG 2
Serra do Canguçu 106-107 L 3
Serra do Cantu 102-103 FG 6
Serra do Caparão 92-93 L 8-9
Serra do Capitão-Mór 100-101 F 4-5
Serra do Caracol 100-101 C 5
Serra do Castelo 100-101 D 11
Serra do Catramba 100-101 F 6
Serra do Catuni 102-103 L 2
Serra do Chifre 92-93 L 8
Serra do Cipó 102-103 L 3
Serra do Cocalzinho 102-103 H 1
Serra do Covil 100-101 BC 6
Serra do Cuité 100-101 F 4
Serra do Curunuri 98-99 MN 4
Serra do Diabo 102-103 F 5
Serra do Duro 98-99 P 10-11
Serra do Erval 106-107 LM 3
Serra do Espigão 102-103 G 7
Serra do Espinhaço 92-93 L 8
Serra do Espinilho 106-107 K 2
Serra do Estreito 100-101 C 6
Serra do Estrondo 92-93 K 6
Serra do Flamengo 100-101 E 4
Serra do Franco 100-101 E 3-4
Serra do Gado Bravo 100-101 A 4-5
Serra do Gomes 98-99 P 9
Serra do Gongoji 92-93 LM 7-8
Serra do Gurupi 92-93 K 5-6
Serra do Iguariaçá 106-107 K 2
Serra do Inajá 98-99 N 9
Serra do Inhaúma 100-101 B 3
Serra Dois Irmãos 92-93 L 6
Serra do Japão 100-101 F 5-6
Serra do Jaraguá 102-103 H 7
Serra do Jutaí 98-99 M 5
Serra do Machado [BR, Amazonas] 98-99 H 8-9
Serra do Machado [BR, Ceará] 100-101 E 3
Serra do Mar 111 G 2-3
Serra do Matão 92-93 J 6
Serra do Mel 100-101 F 3
Serra do Mirante 102-103 GH 5
Serra do Moa 96-97 E 5
Serra do Morais 100-101 E 4
Serra do Mucajaí 92-93 G 4
Serra do Navio 98-99 M 4
Serra do Norte 92-93 H 7
Serra do Orobo 100-101 D 7
Serra do Padre 100-101 E 4
Serra do Paranapiacaba 92-93 G 2-3
Serra do Pelado 100-101 F 4
Serra do Penitente 92-93 K 6
Serra do Piauí 100-101 CD 5
Serra do Pirapó 106-107 K 2
Serra do Poção 100-101 F 4
Serra do Ramalho 92-93 KL 7
Serra do Recreio 100-101 D 5
Serra do Rio Claro 102-103 G 2
Serra do Rio de Contas 100-101 D 7-8
Serra do Rio Preto 102-103 J 2
Serra do Roncador 92-93 J 7
Serra dos Aimorés 92-93 L 8
Serra do Salta Ginete 102-103 K 3
Serra dos Apiacás 92-93 H 6-7
Serra do Sargento Paixão 104-105 F 2
Serra dos Ausentes 106-107 M 1-2
Serra dos Bastiões 100-101 DE 4
Serra dos Baús 102-103 F 2-3
Serra dos Caiabis 92-93 H 7
Serra dos Carajás 92-93 J 5-6
Serra dos Cariris Novos 100-101 D 3-4
Serra dos Cristais 102-103 J 2
Serra dos Dourados 111 F 2
Serra dos Gradaús 92-93 JK 6
Serra dos Sincorá 100-101 D 7
Serra dos Itatina 102-103 J 6
Serra dos Javaés 98-99 O 10
Serra dos Órgãos 102-103 L 5
Serra dos Pacaás Novos 98-99 FG 10
Serra dos Pireneus 102-103 HJ 1
Serra dos Pretos Forros 110 I b 2
Serra dos Queimados 104-105 E 1
Serra dos Surucucus 98-99 G 3
Serra dos Três Rios 110 I b 2
Serra dos Tucuns 100-101 D 2
Serra do Surucucus 94-95 K 6
Serra dos Xavantes 92-93 K 7
Serra do Tapirapé 98-99 N 10
Serra do Taquaral 100-101 D 8
Serra do Tombador [BR, Bahia] 100-101 D 6
Serra do Tombador [BR, Mato Grosso] 92-93 H 7
Serra do Trucará 98-99 N 7-O 6
Serra do Tucano 94-95 LM 6
Serra do Tumucumaque 92-93 HJ 4
Serra do Uacamparique 104-105 E 2
Serra do Uopiane 104-105 E 2-3
Serra Dourada 92-93 K 7
Serra do Uruçuí 92-93 K 7-L 6
Serra do Valentim 92-93 L 6
Serra do Verdinho 102-103 F 2-G 3
Serra Formosa 92-93 HJ 7
Serra Gabriel Antunes Maciel 98-99 G 10-11
Serra Geral [BR, Bahia ↓ Caculé] 100-101 C 8
Serra Geral [BR, Bahia ↖ Jequié] 100-101 D 7
Serra Geral [BR, Goiás] 100-101 A 6
Serra Geral [BR, Rio Grande do Sul ↖ Porto Alegre] 111 F 3
Serra Geral [BR, Rio Grande do Sul ↑ Porto Alegre] 106-107 M 2
Serra Geral [BR, Santa Catarina] 111 F 3
Serra Geral = Serra Grande 98-99 P 10
Serra Geral de Goiás 92-93 K 7
Serra Grande [BR, Bahia] 100-101 D 5
Serra Grande [BR, Ceará] 100-101 D 3
Serra Grande [BR, Goiás] 98-99 OP 7
Serra Grande [BR, Piauí → Picos] 100-101 D 4
Serra Grande [BR, Piauí ↓ Ribeiro Gonçalves] 100-101 B 4-5
Serra Grande [BR, Rondônia] 98-99 H 9-10
Serra Grande [BR, Roraima] 94-95 L 6
Serra Grande ou de Carauna 98-99 H 3
Serra Iarauarune 98-99 HJ 4
Serra Imeri 92-93 F 4
Serra Iricoumé 98-99 K 4
Serra Itapicuru 92-93 KL 6
Serra Janquara 102-103 D 1
Serra J. Antunes 98-99 G 10-11
Serra Jauari 98-99 M 5
Serra João do Vale 100-101 F 3-4
Serra Linda 100-101 D 8
Serra Lombarda 92-93 J 4
Serra Macoa 98-99 JK 4
Serrán 96-97 B 4
Serrana 102-103 J 4
Serra Namuli 172 G 5
Serra Negra [BR, Goiás] 98-99 P 10
Serra Negra [BR, Maranhão] 100-101 A 4
Serra Negra [BR, Minas Gerais] 102-103 L 2-3
Serra Negra [BR, São Paulo] 102-103 J 5
Serra Negra [BR, Sergipe] 100-101 F 5-6
Serrania Chepite 104-105 BC 4
Serrania Chiru Choricha 104-105 BC 4
Serranía de Abibe 94-95 C 3-4
Serranía de Ayapel 94-95 D 4
Serranía de Baudó 94-95 C 4-5
Serranía de Cuenca 120-121 F 8-G 9
Serranía de Huanchaca 92-93 G 7
Serranía de Imataca 92-93 G 3
Serranía de la Cerbatana 92-93 F 3
Serranía de la Macarena 94-95 DE 6
Serranía del Beu 104-105 BC 4
Serranía del Darién 88-89 H 10
Serranía del Sapo 94-95 B 4
Serranía de Maigualida 92-93 F 3-G 4
Serranía de Mapichí 92-93 F 3-4
Serranía de Mataca 104-105 D 6
Serranía de Mato 94-95 J 4
Serranía de Napo 96-97 C 2
Serranía de San Jacinto 94-95 D 3
Serranía de San Jerónimo 92-93 D 3
Serranía de San José 104-105 F 5-6
Serranía de Santiago 104-105 G 6
Serranía de Sicasica 104-105 BC 5
Serranía de Sunsas 104-105 G 5-6
Serranía de Tabasará 88-89 EF 10
Serranía Parú 94-95 J 5
Serranía Quinigua 94-95 J 5
Serranía San Lucas 94-95 D 3-4
Serranías del Burro 64-65 F 6
Serranías Turagua 94-95 J 4
Serrano 106-107 F 5
Serrano, Isla — 108-109 B 7
Serra Nova 104-105 E 1
Serra Ôlho d'Água 100-101 E 5-F 4
Serra Ouricuri 100-101 FG 5
Serra Pacaraima 92-93 G 4
Serra Paranaquara 98-99 M 5
Serra Pelada 100-101 D 8
Serra Pintada 100-101 E 4
Serra Piranã 100-101 G 4
Serra Piranhinha 100-101 B 1-2
Serra Poço Danta 100-101 EF 6
Serra Preta 100-101 E 7
Serra Queimada 102-103 J 5-6
Serra Queimada Redonda 100-101 E 4-5
Serra Repartimento 98-99 E 7
Serra R. Franco 104-105 F 4
Serraria 100-101 G 4
Serra Saco Comprido 100-101 B 7
Serra São Domingos 100-101 D 3-E 4
Serra São Francisco 100-101 D 5-6
Serra São Lourenço 102-103 E 2
Serrâṭ, Râss — = Râ's Sarrâṭ 166-167 L 1
Serra Tabatinga 98-99 GH 4
Serra Taborda 100-101 F 5
Serra Talhada 92-93 M 6
Serra Tepequem 94-95 L 6
Serra Uaçari 92-93 H 4
Serra Upanda 172 BC 4
Serra Uscana 104-105 B 6
Serra Verde 100-101 F 3
Serra Verde, Chapada da — 100-101 FG 3
Serra Vermelha [BR ↑ Avelino Lopes] 100-101 BC 5
Serra Vermelha [BR ↓ Bertolínia] 100-101 BC 4-5
Serrezuela 111 C 4
Serrilhada 106-107 K 3
Serrinha [BR ↑ Feira de Santana] 92-93 M 7
Serrinha [BR ↑ Guaratinga] 100-101 E 9
Serrita 100-101 E 4
Serro 102-103 L 3
Serrolândia 100-101 D 6
Sers, Es — = As-Sars 166-167 L 1
Sertânia 92-93 M 6
Sertanópolis 102-103 G 5
Sertão 92-93 L 7-M 6
Sertão de Camapuã 92-93 J 8-9
Sertãozinho 102-103 HJ 4
Serua, Pulau — 148-149 K 8
Serule 172 E 6
Seruna 138-139 D 3
Serutu, Pulau — 152-153 H 6
Seruwai 150-151 B 10
Servilleta, NM 76-77 AB 4
Servon 129 I d 3
Serxü 142-143 H 5
Sê San 150-151 F 6
Sešan 58-59 B 3
Se Sang Sôi 150-151 E 4
Sesayap 152-153 M 4
Sesayap, Sungai — 152-153 M 4
Seščinskij 124-125 J 7
Sese Islands 172 F 2
Sesepe 148-149 J 7
Sesfontein 172 B 5
Seshachalam Hills 140 CD 3
Sesheke 172 DE 5
Sesimbra 120-121 C 9
Šešma 124-125 S 6
Sesquilé 94-95 E 5
Sessa Aurunca 122-123 EF 5
Šestakovo 124-125 RS 4
Šeštokaj 124-125 D 6
Sestroreck 132-133 DE 5
Setagaya, Tōkyō- 155 III a 2
Setana 142-143 Q 3
Sète 120-121 J 7
Sete Barras 102-103 HJ 6
Sete Cidades 100-101 D 3
Sētéia 122-123 M 8
Sete Lagoas 102-103 KL 3
Setenta, Pampa del — 108-109 E 6
Sete Quedas, Salto das — [BR, Paraná] 102-103 E 6
Sete Quedas, Salto das — [BR, Rio Teles Pires] 92-93 H 6
Setermoen 116-117 H 3
Setesdal 116-117 B 8
Seti 138-139 H 3
Setia Budi, Jakarta- 154 IV ab 2
Sétif = Saṭīf 164-165 F 1
Setiu, Kuala — = Setiu 150-151 D 10
Setlagodi 174-175 F 4
Seto 144-145 L 5
Seto-naikai 142-143 P 5
Seṭṭât = Saṭṭāt 164-165 C 2
Setté Cama 172 A 2
Settecamini, Roma- 113 II c 1
Sette-Daban, chrebet — 132-133 a 5
Settlers 174-175 H 3
Sētu Anaikkaṭṭ = Adam's Bridge 140 D 6
Setúbal 120-121 C 9
Setúbal, Baía de — 120-121 C 9
Setúbal, Rio — 102-103 L 2
Sētubandh = Adam's Bridge 140 D 6
Seul = Sŏul 142-143 O 4
Seul, Lac — 56-57 S 7
Sevan 126-127 M 6
Sevan, ozero — 126-127 M 6
Sevaruyo 104-105 C 6
Sevastopol' 126-127 F 4
Ševčenko 126-127 P 5
Ševčenkovo = Dolinskaja 126-127 F 2
Seven Emus 158-159 G 3
Seven Islands = Sept-Îles 56-57 X 7-8
Seven Pagodas = Mahābalipuram 140 E 4
Seven Pagodas = Pha Lai 150-151 F 2
Seventy Mile House 60 G 4
Severin 104-105 B 9
Severino Ribeiro 106-107 JK 3
Severn [GB] 119 E 6
Severn [ZA] 174-175 E 4
Severnaja 132-133 QR 4
Severnaja Dvina 132-133 G 5
Severnaja Kel'tma 124-125 U 3
Severnaja Semlja = Severnaja Zeml'a 132-133 ST 1-2
Severnaja Sos'va 132-133 L 5
Severnaja Zeml'a 132-133 ST 1-2
Severnaya Zemlya = Severnaja Zeml'a 132-133 ST 1-2
Severnoje [SU ↑ Kujbyšev] 132-133 O 6
Severnoje [SU, Orenburgskaja Oblast'] 124-125 T 6
Severn River 56-57 T 6-7
Severnyj 132-133 LM 4
Severnyj čink = Donyztau 132-133 K 8
Severnyj Donec 126-127 J 2
Severnyje uvaly 132-133 HJ 5-6
Severnyj Kommunar 124-125 TU 4
Severnyj Ledovityj okean 132-133 J-c 1
Severnyj Ural 132-133 K 5-6
Severo-Bajkal'skoje nagorje 132-133 UV 6
Severodoneck 126-127 J 2
Severodvinsk 132-133 FG 5
Severo-Jenisejsk 132-133 RS 5
Severo-Kuril'sk 132-133 de 7
Severo-Sibirskaja nizmennost' 132-133 P-X 3
Severo-Vostočnyj-Bank = Bank 126-127 O 7
Severo-Zanonsk 124-125 M 6-7
Severy, KS 68-69 H 7
Sevier Desert 74-75 G 3
Sevier Lake 74-75 G 3
Sevier River 64-65 D 4
Sevier River, East Fork — 74-75 GH 4
Sevierville 80-81 E 3
Sevierville, TN 80-81 E 3
Sevigné 106-107 HJ 6
Sevilla 120-121 E 10
Sevilla [CO] 94-95 D 5
Sevlievo 122-123 L 4
Sevran 129 I d 2
Sèvre 120-121 G 5
Sèvres 129 I b 2
Sevsib 132-133 M 6
Sevsk 124-125 K 7
Sewa 164-165 B 7
Seward, AK 56-57 G 5-6
Seward, KS 68-69 G 6
Seward, NE 68-69 H 5
Seward Glacier 58-59 R 6
Seward Peninsula 56-57 CD 4
Sewell, Lake — = Canyon Ferry Reservoir 66-67 H 2
Sewu, Pegunungan — 152-153 J 9-10
Sexsmith 60 H 2
Sey 104-105 C 8
Seya, Yokohama- 155 III a 3
Seybaplaya 86-87 P 8
Seychelles 172 J 3
Seydhisfjördhur 116-117 fg 2
Seydişehir 136-137 D 4
Seyhan = Adana 134-135 D 3
Seyhan nehri 134-135 D 3
Seyitgazi 136-137 D 3
Seyla' 164-165 N 6
Seymour, IA 70-71 D 5
Seymour, IN 64-65 JK 4
Seymour, MO 78-79 C 2
Seymour, TX 76-77 E 6
Seymour, WI 70-71 F 3
Seymour [AUS] 160 G 6
Seymour [ZA] 174-175 G 7
Seymour Arm 60 H 4
Seyne-sur-Mer, la — 120-121 K 7
Seytan 154 I b 2
Sezze 122-123 E 5

Sfax = Ṣafāqis 164-165 FG 2
Sfîntu Gheorghe 122-123 LM 3
Sfîntu Gheorghe, Braţul — 122-123 N 3
Sfîre = Safīrah 136-137 G 4
Sfissifa = Safīsifah 166-167 F 3
Sfizef = Safīzaf 166-167 F 2
Sfoûk = Sufūq 136-137 J 4

's-Graveland 128 I b 2
's-Gravenhage 120-121 JK 2

Sha Alam 148-149 D 6
Sha'ambah, Ḥāssī — 166-167 D 5
Shaanxi 142-143 K 4-5
Shaba 172 DE 3
Shābah, Ash- 166-167 M 2
Shabakah, Ash- [IRQ, landscape] 136-137 K 7
Shabakah, Ash- [IRQ, place] 136-137 K 7
Shabani = Zvishavane 172 F 6
Shabbona, IL 70-71 F 5
Shabeelle, Webi — 164-165 N 8
Shabellaha Dhexe = 5 ◁ 164-165 b 3
Shabellaha Hoose = 3 ◁ 164-165 N 8
Shabēlē, Webi — = Wabī Shebelē 164-165 N 7
Shabka 138-139 J 2
Shabkah 166-167 H 3-4
Shabunda 172 E 2
Shabūnīyah 166-167 H 2
Shabuskwia Lake 62 E 2
Shabwah 134-135 F 7
Sha Ch'i = Sha Xi 146-147 F 8
Shackleton Ice Shelf 53 C 10
Shackleton Inlet 53 A 19-17
Shackleton Range 53 A 35-1
Shacun 146-147 E 8
Shādegān 136-137 N 7
Shadehill Reservoir 68-69 E 3
Shadi 146-147 E 8
Shādir al-Mulūṣī 136-137 HJ 6
Shadow Oaks, Houston-, TX 85 III a 1
Shadūzût 141 E 3
Shady Acres, Houston-, TX 85 III b 1
Shady Lane Park 85 III b 1
Shafter, CA 74-75 D 5
Shafter, NV 66-67 F 5
Shafter, TX 76-77 B 8
Shagamu 168-169 F 4
Shageluk, AK 58-59 H 5
Shaglli 96-97 B 3
Shag Rocks 111 H 8
Shaguotun 144-145 C 2
Shāh, Godār-e — 136-137 MN 5
Shāhābād [IND, Andhra Pradesh] 140 CD 2
Shāhābād [IND, Maisūru] 134-135 M 7
Shāhābād [IND, Punjab] 138-139 F 2
Shāhābād [IND, Rājasthān] 138-139 F 5
Shāhābād [IND, Uttar Pradesh ↓ Rāmpur] 138-139 G 3
Shāhābād [IND, Uttar Pradesh ↓ Shāhjahāṅpur] 138-139 G 4
Shāhāda 138-139 E 7
Shaḥāmbī, Jabal — 164-165 F 1-2
Shaḥāmī 136-137 H 6
Shāhān, Kūh-e — 136-137 LM 5
Shahan, Wādī — = Wādī Shiḥan 134-135 G 7
Shāhāpur [IND, Karnataka] 140 B 3
Shāhāpur [IND, Mahārāshtra] 138-139 D 8
Shaharak 134-135 J 4
Shahbā 136-137 G 6
Shahbā', Ḥarrat ash- 136-137 G 6-7
Shāhbandar 138-139 AB 5
Shāhbāzpūr 141 B 4
Shāhdā = Shāhāda 138-139 E 7
Shahdād 134-135 H 4
Shahdād, Namakzār-e — 134-135 H 4
Shāhdadkoṭ 138-139 A 4
Shāhdadpūr 138-139 B 5
Shahdol 138-139 H 6
Shahe [TJ, Hebei place] 146-147 E 3
Sha He [TJ, Hebei river] 146-147 E 3
Shahe [TJ, Shandong] 146-147 G 3
Shahedian 146-147 D 5
Shāhganj 138-139 J 4-5
Shāhgarh 138-139 BC 4
Shāhī 134-135 G 3
Shahidulla Mazar 142-143 D 4
Shāhjahāṅpur 134-135 MN 5
Shaho = Shahe [TJ, Hebei place] 146-147 E 3
Sha Ho = Sha He [TJ, Hebei river] 146-147 E 5
Sha-ho = Shahe [TJ, Shandong] 146-147 G 3
Sha-ho-tien = Shahedian 146-147 D 5
Shāhpur [IND] 140 C 2
Shāhpūr [PAK] 138-139 B 3
Shāhpur = Shāhāpur 138-139 D 8
Shāhpura [IND, Madhya Pradesh ← Jabalpur] 138-139 G 6
Shāhpura [IND, Madhya Pradesh → Jabalpur] 138-139 H 6
Shāhpura [IND, Rājasthān] 134-135 L 5
Shāhpūrī Dīpsamuh 141 BC 5
Shahr-e Bābak 134-135 GH 4
Shahredā 134-135 G 4
Shahr-e Kord 134-135 G 4
Shahrestānbālā 136-137 NO 4
Shāhrig 138-139 A 2
Shāhrūd [IR, place] 134-135 GH 3
Shāh Rūd [IR, river] 136-137 NO 4
Shahsien = Sha Xian 146-147 F 8
Shahu 146-147 D 6
Shāhzand 136-137 N 6
Sha'īb Abū Marīs 136-137 L 7
Sha'īb al-'Aīf = Sha'īb al-'Aylī 136-137 H 7
Sha'īb al-'Aylī 136-137 H 7
Shā'ib al-Banāt, Jabal — 164-165 L 3
Sha'īb al-Judā' 136-137 L 8-M 7
Sha'īb al-Mahārī 136-137 KL 7
Sha'īb al-Muḥārī 136-137 KL 7
Sha'īb al-Wallij 136-137 H 6
Sha'īb Ḥasb 134-135 E 4
Sha'ib Hasib = Sha'īb Ḥasb 134-135 E 4
Shaikhpura 138-139 KL 5
Sha'īt, Wādī — 173 C 5
Shājāpur 138-139 F 6
Shajianzi 144-145 E 2
Shaka, Ras — 171 E 3
Shakad Chhu 138-139 M 2
Shakar Bolāghī = Qara Būteh 136-137 M 4
Shakespeare Island 70-71 F 1
Shakhty = Šachty 126-127 K 3
Shakh yar 142-143 E 3
Shaki 164-165 E 7
Shakir, Jazīrat — 164-165 LM 3
Shakopee, MN 70-71 D 3
Shakotan misaki 144-145 b 2
Shakou 146-147 D 9
Shaktī = Sakti 138-139 J 6
Shaktoolik, AK 58-59 G 4
Shaktoolik River 58-59 G 4
Shakujii 155 III a 1
Shāl 136-137 N 5
Shala 164-165 M 7
Shalanbod 164-165 N 8
Shalang 146-147 C 11
Shalar, Nahr — 136-137 L 5
Shalar Rūd = Nahr Shalar 136-137 L 5
Shallāl, Ash- [ET, place] 164-165 L 3
Shallāl, Ash- [ET, river] 164-165 L 3
Shallālāt Ḍahrānīyah 166-167 G 3
Shallop 63 E 3
Shallotte, NC 80-81 G 3-4
Shallowater, TX 76-77 CD 6
Shālmārā, Dakshiṇ — = South Sālmāra 138-139 N 5
Shāmah, Ash- = Al-Ḥarrah 136-137 GH 7
Shamā'īyah, Ash- 166-167 B 3
Shāmbah 164-165 L 7
Shamgong 138-139 N 4
Shāmguṛī = Sāmāguri 141 C 2
Shāmīyah, Ash- 136-137 L 7
Shāmli 138-139 F 3
Shammar, Jabal — 134-135 E 5
Shamo = Gobi 142-143 H-K 3
Shamokin, PA 72-73 H 4
Shamrock, FL 80-81 b 2
Shamrock, TX 76-77 DE 5
Shāmshīr = Pāveh 136-137 M 5
Sham Shui Po, Kowloon- 155 I a 2
Shamūrah 166-167 K 2
Shamva 172 F 5
Shamwam 141 E 2
Shanāshīn, Wādī — 166-167 E 7
Shanchengzhen 144-145 EF 1
Shan-ch'iu = Shenqiu 146-147 E 5
Shandan 142-143 J 4
Shandī 164-165 L 5
Shandish, MI 72-73 DE 3
Shandong 142-143 M 4
Shandong Bandao 142-143 MN 4
Shangani 172 E 5
Shangbahe 146-147 E 6
Shangbangcheng 144-145 B 2
Shangcai 146-147 E 5
Shangcheng 146-147 E 6
Shang-chia-ho = Shangjiahe 144-145 E 2
Shang-ch'iu = Shangqiu 142-143 LM 5
Shangchuan Dao 142-143 L 7
Shangchwan Tao = Shangchuan Dao 146-147 D 11
Shangcigang = Beijingzi 144-145 DE 3
Shangdachen Shan = Dachen Dao 146-147 HJ 7
Shangfu 146-147 E 7
Shanggang 146-147 H 5
Shanggao 146-147 E 7
Shanghai 142-143 N 5
Shanghang 142-143 M 6-7
Shanghe 146-147 F 3
Shangho = Shanghe 146-147 F 3
Shanghsien = Shang Xian 142-143 KL 5
Shangjao = Shangrao 142-143 M 6
Shangjiahe 144-145 E 2
Shangkan 146-147 C 6
Shang-kang = Shanggang 146-147 H 5
Shang-kao = Shanggao 146-147 E 7
Shangkiu = Shangqiu 142-143 LM 5
Shangnan 146-147 C 5
Shangqiu 142-143 LM 5
Shangrao 142-143 M 6
Shangshe 146-147 D 2
Shang Xian 142-143 KL 5
Shangyou 146-147 E 9
Shangyu 146-147 H 6-7
Shang-yu = Shangyou 146-147 E 9
Shang-yü = Shangyu 146-147 H 6-7
Shangzhi 142-143 O 2
Shanhaiguan 142-143 MN 3
Shan-hai-kuan = Shanhaiguan 144-145 BC 2
Shan-hsi = Shaanxi 142-143 L 4-5
Shaniko, OR 66-67 C 3
Shaṅkarīdurgam = Sankaridrug 140 CD 5
Shankh = Sankh 138-139 K 6
Shankiu = Shanqiu 142-143 LM 5
Shankou [TJ, Guangdong] 146-147 BC 11
Shankou [TJ, Hunan] 146-147 C 7
Shankou [TJ, Jiangxi] 146-147 E 7
Shānmalī = Shāmli 138-139 F 3
Shanngaw Taungdan 141 EF 2-3
Shannon [IRL] 119 B 5
Shannon [ZA] 174-175 G 5
Shannon Airport 119 B 5
Shannon Bay 60 A 3
Shannon Ø 52 B 20
Shannontown, SC 80-81 FG 4
Shan Pyinnei 148-149 C 2
Shanqiu 146-147 E 5
Shanshan 142-143 G 3
Shansi = Shanxi 142-143 L 4
Shan-tan = Shandan 142-143 J 4
Shantangyi 146-147 BC 8
Shantar Islands = Šantarskije ostrova 132-133 a 6
Shāntipur = Sāntipur 138-139 M 6
Shantou 142-143 M 7
Shantow = Shantou 142-143 M 7
Shantung = Shandong 142-143 M 4
Shan-tung Chiao = Chengshan Jiao 146-147 J 3
Shanwa 171 C 3
Shanwei 146-147 E 10
Shanxi 142-143 L 4
Shan Xian 146-147 EF 4
Shanyang 146-147 B 5
Shanyin 142-143 L 4
Shaobo 146-147 G 5
Shaodong 146-147 C 8
Shaoguan 142-143 L 6-7
Shaohsing = Shaoxing 142-143 N 5-6
Shao-kuan = Qujiang 146-147 D 9
Shaol Lake 70-71 C 1
Shao-po = Shaobo 146-147 G 5
Shaotze = Wan Xian 142-143 K 5
Shaowu 142-143 M 6
Shaoxing 142-143 N 5-6
Shaoyang 142-143 L 6
Shapaja 96-97 C 5
Ṣhapura = Shāhpur 140 C 2
Shaqlāwah 136-137 L 4
Shaqqah 166-167 JK 2
Shaqqāṭ, Ash- 164-165 C 3
Shaqrā' 134-135 F 5
Shār, Jabal — [Saudi Arabia] 173 D 4
Shā'r, Jabal — [SYR] 136-137 GH 5
Sharafkhāneh 136-137 LM 3
Sharāh, Ash- 136-137 F 7
Sharan Jogīzai 138-139 B 2
Sharavati 140 B 3
Sharbithāt, Rā's ash- 134-135 H 7
Sharbot Lake 72-73 H 2
Shārdā = Sārda 138-139 H 3
Shari 144-145 d 2
Shari = Chari 164-165 H 6
Sharī', Bahr ash- = Buhayrat Sharī 136-137 L 5
Sharī, Buhayrat — 136-137 L 5
Sharī'ah 166-167 H 1
Sharī'ah, Nahr ash- 136-137 F 6-7
Shārib, Ma'ṭan — 136-137 C 7
Shari-dake 144-145 d 2
Shārif 166-167 H 2
Shārif, Wād — 166-167 E 3
Shāriqah, Ash- 134-135 GH 5
Sharja = Ash-Shāriqah 134-135 GH 5
Shark Bay 158-159 B 5
Shark Point 161 I b 2
Sharmah, Ash- 173 D 3-4
Sharmah, Wādī ash- = Wādī Ṣadr 173 D 3
Sharm ash-Shaykh 173 D 4
Sharm Dumayj 173 DE 4
Sharm esh-Sheikh = Sharm ash-Shayḥ 173 D 4
Shar Mörön 146-147 C 1-2
Shar Mörön = Chatan gol 142-143 K 3
Sharon, KS 76-77 E 4
Sharon, PA 64-65 KL 3
Sharon Hill, PA 84 III b 2
Sharon Springs, KS 68-69 F 6
Sharps Run 84 III d 2
Sharpstown, Houston-, TX 85 III b 2
Sharpstown Country Club 85 III a 2
Sharq al-Istiwā'īyah 164-165 L 7-8
Sharqāṭ, Ash- 136-137 K 5
Sharqī, Ash-Shaṭṭ ash- 164-165 DE 2
Sharqī, Jazīrat ash- 166-167 M 2
Sharqī, Jebel esh — = Jabal Lubnān ash-Sharqī 136-137 G 5-6
Sharru 138-139 L 3
Sharrukīn, Dur — = Khorsabad 136-137 K 4
Sharshar 166-167 K 2
Sharuin = Shārwīn 166-167 F 5
Shārwīn 166-167 F 5
Shashamanna = Shashemene 164-165 M 7
Shashemenē 164-165 M 7
Shashi 142-143 L 5-6
Shasta, Mount — 64-65 B 3
Shasta Lake 66-67 B 5
Sha-ti = Shadi 146-147 E 8
Sha Tin 155 I b 1
Shaṭrah, Ash- 136-137 LM 7
Shaṭṭ al-'Arab 134-135 F 4
Shaṭṭ al-Fijāj 166-167 L 2-3
Shaṭṭ al-Furāt 136-137 LM 7
Shaṭṭ al-Gharbī, Ash- 166-167 F 3
Shaṭṭ al-Ghurrah 166-167 M 2
Shaṭṭ al-Jarīd 164-165 F 2
Shaṭṭ al-Jarsah 166-167 KL 2
Shaṭṭ al-Qaṭṭār 166-167 L 2
Shaṭṭ al-'Uzaym 136-137 L 5
Shaṭṭ Dijlah 134-135 F 4
Shaṭṭ Malghīr 164-165 F 2
Shaṭṭ Marwān 166-167 JK 2-3
Shattuck, OK 76-77 E 4
Shau = Wādī Huwār 164-165 K 5
Shaubak, Esh- = Ash-Shawbak 136-137 F 7
Shaukkôn 141 D 6
Shaunavon 66-67 J 1
Shaviovik River 58-59 O 2
Shavli = Šiauliai 124-125 D 6
Shaw 106-107 H 6
Shaw, MS 78-79 D 4
Shawan 146-147 G 8
Shawano, WI 70-71 F 3
Shawatun = Shaguotun 144-145 C 2
Shawbak, Ash- 136-137 F 7
Shawbridge 72-73 J 2
Shawinigan Sud 56-57 W 8
Shaw Island 58-59 L 7
Shāwīyah, Ash- 166-167 C 3
Shawnee, OK 64-65 G 4
Shawneetown, IL 70-71 F 7
Shawo 146-147 E 6
Shawocun, Beijing- 155 II a 2
Shaw River 158-159 C 4
Shawville 72-73 H 2
Sha Xi [TJ, Fujian] 146-147 F 8
Shaxi [TJ, Jiangxi] 146-147 G 7
Shaxi [TJ, Nanchang] 146-147 E 8
Sha Xian 142-143 M 6
Shayang 146-147 D 6

360 Serra

Shaykh, Ḥāssī — 166-167 G 4
Shaykh Aḥmad 136-137 J 4
Shaykh Hilāl 136-137 G 5
Shaykh Sa'd 136-137 M 6
Shaykh Ṣalāḥ 136-137 J 4
Shaykh 'Uthmān, Ash- 134-135 EF 8
Shayōg = Shyog 134-135 M 3-4
Shazhou 146-147 H 6
Shāẓī, Wādī ash- 136-137 J 7
Shcherbakov = Rybinsk 132-133 F 6
Shea 92-93 H 4
She'aiba, Ash- = Ash-Shu'aybah 136-137 M 7
Sheaville, OR 66-67 E 4
Shebelē, Wabī — 164-165 N 7
Sheboygan, WI 64-65 J 3
Shebu 146-147 C 10
Shediac 63 D 4
Shedin Peak 60 D 2
Sheduan Island = Jazirat Shadwān 164-165 LM 3
Sheenborough 72-73 H 1-2
Sheenjek River 56-57 H 4
Sheep Creek 68-69 CD 4
Sheep Mountain 68-69 D 3
Sheep Mountains 68-69 CD 2
Sheep Peak 74-75 F 4
Sheep Range 74-75 F 4
Sheepshead Bay, New York-, NY 82 III c 3
Sheerness 61 C 5
Sheet Harbour 63 EF 5
Sheffield, AL 78-79 EF 3
Sheffield, IA 70-71 D 4
Sheffield, TX 76-77 CD 7
Sheffield [AUS] 160 c 2
Sheffield [GB] 119 F 5
Sheffield Lake 63 H 3
Shefoo = Yantai 142-143 N 4
Shēgāňv = Shegaon 138-139 F 7
Shēgāňv = Shevgaon 141 B 2
Shegaon 138-139 F 7
Sheḥamī = Shaḥāmī 136-137 H 6
Sheho 61 G 5
Shehsien = She Xian 146-147 DE 3
Shê-hsien = She Xian [TJ, Anhui] 142-143 M 5-6
Shê-hsien = She Xian [TJ, Hebei] 146-147 DE 3
Shehuen, Río — 108-109 DE 7
Sheikh, Sharm esh- = Sharm ash-Shayh 173 D 4
Sheikh Othman = Ash-Shaykh 'Uthmān 134-135 F 8
Shekak River 70-71 H 1
Shekhar Dsong 142-143 F 6
Shekhpurā = Shaikhpura 138-139 KL 5
Sheki 126-127 N 6
Shekiak River 62 G 3
Shekki = Chixi 146-147 D 10-11
Shekkong = Shikang 146-147 B 11
Sheklukshuk Range 58-59 J 3
Sheklung = Shilong 146-147 DE 10
Shek O 155 I b 2
Shelār 136-137 N 6
Shelbina, MO 70-71 D 6
Shelburne [CDN, Nova Scotia] 63 D 6
Shelburne [CDN, Ontario] 72-73 FG 2
Shelburne Bay 158-159 H 2
Shelby, MI 70-71 G 4
Shelby, MS 78-79 D 4
Shelby, MT 66-67 H 1
Shelby, NC 64-65 K 4
Shelby, OH 72-73 E 4
Shelbyville, IL 70-71 F 6
Shelbyville, IN 70-71 H 6
Shelbyville, KY 70-71 H 6
Shelbyville, MO 70-71 DE 6
Shelbyville, TN 78-79 F 3
Sheldon 174-175 FG 7
Sheldon, IA 70-71 BC 4
Sheldon, MO 70-71 C 7
Sheldon, TX 85 III c 1
Sheldon, WI 70-71 E 3
Sheldon Reservoir 85 III c 1
Sheldons Point, AK 58-59 DE 5
Sheldrake 63 D 2
Shelikof Strait 56-57 EF 6
Shell, WY 68-69 C 3
Shell Beach, LA 78-79 E 6
Shellbrook 61 EF 4
Shell Creek [USA, Colorado] 66-67 J 5
Shell Creek [USA, Nebraska] 68-69 H 5
Shellem 168-169 J 3
Shelley, ID 66-67 GH 4
Shellharbour, Wollongong- 158-159 K 6
Shell Lake 61 E 4
Shell Lake, WI 70-71 E 3
Shellman, GA 78-79 G 5
Shell River 61 H 5
Shellrock River 70-71 D 4
Shelter, Port — 155 I b 1
Shelter Cove, CA 66-67 A 5
Shelter Island 155 I b 2
Shelton, WA 66-67 B 2
Shemankar 168-169 H 3
Shemichi Islands 58-59 pq 6
Shemya Island 58-59 q 6
Shenāfiya, Ash- = Ash-Shināfiyah 136-137 L 7
Shenandoah, IA 70-71 C 5
Shenandoah, PA 72-73 HJ 4
Shenandoah, VA 72-73 G 5
Shenandoah Mountains 72-73 G 5
Shenandoah National Park 72-73 GH 5
Shenandoah River 72-73 GH 5
Shenashan, Wed — = Wādī Shanāshīn 166-167 E 7
Shenchi 146-147 CD 2
Shenchih = Shenchi 146-147 CD 2
Shên-ching = Shenjing 146-147 D 10-11
Shendam 164-165 FG 7
Shendī = Shandī 164-165 L 5
Shendurni 138-139 E 7
Shengcai = Shangcai 146-147 E 5
Shenge 168-169 B 4
Sheng Xian 142-143 N 6
Shenhsien = Shen Xian 146-147 E 2
Shenhu 146-147 G 9
Shenhuguan 141 EF 3
Shenjing 146-147 D 10-11
Shenmu 142-143 L 4
Shennongjia 146-147 C 6
Sheno Hill 168-169 J 3
Shenpūchi Pass = Shipki La 138-139 G 2
Shenqiu 146-147 E 5
Shensa Dsong 142-143 FG 5
Shensi = Shaanxi 142-143 K 4-5
Shenton, Mount — 158-159 D 5
Shentseh = Shenze 146-147 E 2
Shentuan 146-147 G 4
Shen Xian 146-147 E 2
Shenyang 142-143 NO 3
Shenze 146-147 E 2
Shenzhen = Nantou 146-147 D 10
Sheo = Shiv 138-139 C 4
Sheopur 138-139 F 5
Sheopuri = Shivpuri 134-135 M 5
Shepahua 96-97 E 7
Shepard 60 KL 4
Shepherd, MT 68-69 B 2-3
Shepherd, TX 76-77 G 7
Shepparton 158-159 HJ 7
Sheptē 96-97 C 5
Sherborne [ZA] 174-175 F 6
Sherbro Island 164-165 B 7
Sherbrooke [CDN, Nova Scotia] 63 F 5
Sherbrooke [CDN, Quebec] 56-57 W 8
Sherburn, MN 70-71 C 4
Shereik = Ash-Shurayk 164-165 L 5
Shērgaṛh 138-139 CD 4
Sherghāti 138-139 K 5
Sherīʿah, Nahr esh- = Nahr ash-Sharīʿah 136-137 F 6-7
Sheridan, AR 78-79 C 3
Sheridan, MT 66-67 GH 3
Sheridan, OR 66-67 B 3
Sheridan, TX 76-77 F 8
Sheridan, WY 64-65 E 3
Sheridan, Mount — 66-67 H 3
Sheridan Lake, CO 68-69 E 6
Sherman, MS 78-79 E 3
Sherman, TX 64-65 G 5
Sherman Inlet 56-57 R 4
Sherman Mills, ME 72-73 MN 2
Sherman Mountain 66-67 EF 5
Sherpūr [BD ↗ Jamālpūr] 138-139 N 5
Sherpūr [BD ↙ Jamālpūr] 138-139 M 5
Sherridon 56-57 Q 6
Shertally 140 C 6
's-Hertogenbosch 120-121 KL 3
Sheru 138-139 L 3
Sherwood, ND 68-69 F 1
Sherwood Forest, CA 83 I c 1
Sherwood Forest, Atlanta-, GA 85 II bc 2
Sherwood Park 61 B 4
Sheshalik, AK 58-59 F 3
Sheshea, Río — 96-97 E 6
She Shui 146-147 E 6
Sheslay 58-59 W 7
Sheslay River 58-59 V 7
Shethātha = Shithāthah 136-137 K 6
Shetland 119 FG 1
Sheung Kwai Chung 155 I a 1
Shevaroy Hills 140 D 5
Shevgaon 138-139 E 8
Shewa 164-165 M 7
She Xian [TJ, Anhui] 142-143 M 5-6
She Xian [TJ, Hebei] 146-147 DE 3
Sheyang 146-147 H 5
Sheyang He 146-147 H 5
Sheyenne River 68-69 H 2
Sheykh Ḥoseyn 136-137 N 7
Shiādmā', Ash- 166-167 B 4
Shibām 134-135 F 7
Shibarghān 134-135 K 3
Shibata 144-145 M 4
Shibazaki, Chōfu- 155 III a 2
Shibecha 144-145 d 2
Shibei 146-147 G 8
Shibetsu [J ↑ Asahikawa] 144-145 c 1
Shibetsu [J ↖ Nemuro] 144-145 d 2
Shibetsu, Naka- 144-145 d 2
Shibicha, Ash- = Ash-Shabakah 136-137 K 7
Shībīgā 148-149 C 1
Shibīn al-Kawn 173 B 2
Shibīn al-Qanāṭir 173 B 2
Shib Kūh 134-135 G 5
Shibogama Lake 62 EF 1
Shibsāgar = Sibsāgar 141 D 2
Shibukawa 144-145 M 4
Shibushi 144-145 H 7
Shibushi-wan 144-145 H 7
Shibutami = Tamayama 144-145 N 3
Shibuya, Tōkyō- 155 III ab 2
Shicheng 146-147 F 8
Shicheng Dao 144-145 D 3
Shichuan Ding 146-147 CD 9
Shickshock, Monts — = Monts Chic-Choqs 56-57 X 8
Shidād, Umm ash- = Sabkhat Abā ar-Rūs 134-135 G-H 6
Shidao 146-147 J 3
Shiddādī, Ash- 136-137 J 4
Shideng 141 F 2
Shīdīyah, Ash- 136-137 FG 8
Shiḍlaghaṭṭā = Sidlaghatta 140 CD 4
Shields, ND 68-69 F 2
Shifshawn 164-165 CD 1
Shiga 144-145 KL 5
Shigatse = Zhigatse 142-143 F 6
Shiggāṇa = Shiggaon 140 B 3
Shiggāňv = Shiggaon 140 B 3
Shiggaon 140 B 3
Shiḥan, Wādī — 134-135 G 7
Shih-ch'êng = Shicheng 146-147 F 8
Shih-ch'êng Tao = Shicheng Dao 144-145 D 3
Shih-ch'ien = Shiqian 142-143 K 6
Shih-chiu-so = Shijiusuo 146-147 G 4
Shih-ch'ü = Serxü 142-143 H 5
Shihchuan = Shiquan 142-143 K 5
Shih-chuang = Shizhuang 146-147 H 5
Shih-hsing = Shixing 146-147 E 9
Shih-k'ang = Shikang 146-147 B 11
Shih-lou = Shilou 146-147 C 3
Shihlung = Shilong [TJ, Guangdong] 146-147 DE 10
Shih-lung = Shilong [TJ, Guangxi Zhuangzu Zizhiqu] 146-147 B 10
Shihmen = Shimen 146-147 C 7
Shihnan = Enshi 142-143 K 5
Shih-pei = Shibei 146-147 G 8
Shih-p'ing = Shiping 142-143 J 7
Shih-p'u = Shipu 146-147 HJ 7
Shiḥr, Ash- 134-135 F 8
Shih-shou = Shishou 146-147 D 7
Shihtai = Shitai 146-147 F 6
Shih-têng = Shideng 141 F 2
Shihtsien = Shiqian 142-143 K 6
Shih-wan-ta Shan = Shiwanda Shan 150-151 F 2
Shijiao 146-147 C 11
Shijiazhuang 142-143 L 4
Shijiu Hu 146-147 G 6
Shika 138-139 B 6
Shikang 146-147 B 11
Shikārpur [IND, Bihār] 138-139 K 4
Shikārpur [IND, Karnataka] 140 B 3
Shikārpūr [PAK] 134-135 K 5
Shikhartse = Zhigatse 142-143 F 6
Shikine-chima 144-145 M 5
Shikk'ah, Rā's ash- 136-137 F 5
Shikohābād 138-139 G 4
Shikoku 142-143 P 5
Shikoku sammyaku 144-145 JK 6
Shikotan-tō 142-143 S 3
Shikotsu-ko 144-145 b 2
Shikou 146-147 G 3
Shilaong = Shillong 134-135 P 5
Shilchar = Silchar 134-135 P 6
Shilif 164-165 E 1
Shilipu 146-147 CD 6
Shilka = Šilka 132-133 W 7
Shillington, PA 72-73 HJ 4
Shillong 134-135 P 5
Shilloguṛī = Siliguri 134-135 O 5
Shiloh National Military Park and Cemetery 78-79 EF 3
Shilong [TJ, Guangdong] 146-147 DE 10
Shilong [TJ, Guangxi Zhuangzu Zizhiqu] 146-147 B 10
Shilong = Shajianzi 144-145 E 2
Shilou 146-147 C 3
Shīlūṭ = Šilutė 124-125 C 6
Shīlyah, Jabal — 164-165 F 1
Shimabara 144-145 H 6
Shimabara hantō 144-145 H 6
Shimada 144-145 M 5
Shima-hantō 144-145 L 5
Shimālīyah, Ash- 164-165 KL 5
Shimane 144-145 HJ 5
Shimane, Tōkyō- 155 III b 1
Shimen 146-147 C 7
Shimen = Shijiazhuang 142-143 LM 4
Shimenjie 146-147 F 7
Shimizu 142-143 Q 4-5
Shimizu = Tosashimizu 144-145 J 6
Shimlā = Simla 134-135 M 4
Shimminato 144-145 L 4
Shimo = Kyūshū 142-143 P 5
Shimoda 144-145 M 5
Shimodate 144-145 MN 4
Shimoga 134-135 LM 8
Shimoigusa, Tōkyō- 155 III a 1
Shimoizumi 155 III d 3
Shimokita-hantō 142-143 R 3
Shimo-Koshiki-chima 144-145 G 7
Shimoni 172 GH 2
Shimonoseki 142-143 P 5
Shimono-shima 144-145 G 5
Shimoshakujii, Tōkyō- 155 III a 1
Shimoyaku = Yaku 144-145 H 7
Shimo-Yūbetsu 144-145 cd 1
Shimpi = Shinbī 141 C 4
Shimsha 140 C 4
Shimura, Tōkyō- 155 III b 1
Shimushiru = ostrov Simušir 132-133 d 8
Shimushu = ostrov Šumšu 132-133 e 7
Shin, Loch — 119 D 2
Shināfīyah, Ash- 136-137 L 7
Shinagawa, Tōkyō- 155 III b 2
Shinaibeidong 146-147 H 7
Shinaingbā 141 E 2
Shinano gawa 144-145 M 4
Shināṣ 134-135 H 6
Shināy, Bi'r — 173 D 6
Shinbī 141 C 4
Shinbwīyan 148-149 C 1
Shīndand 134-135 J 4
Shindidāy, Jabal — 173 E 6
Shiner, TX 76-77 F 8
Shingbwiyang = Shinbwīyan 148-149 C 1
Shingishu = Sinŭiju 142-143 NO 3
Shingleton, MI 70-71 G 2
Shingletown, CA 66-67 C 5
Shing Shi Mun 155 I b 2
Shingu 144-145 KL 6
Shingwedzi 174-175 J 2
Shingwidzi = Shingwedzi 174-175 J 2
Shing'ya 138-139 L 2
Shining Tree 62 L 3
Shiniu Shan 146-147 G 9
Shinjiang = Xinjiang Uyghur Zizhiqu 142-143 D-G 3
Shinji-ko 144-145 J 5
Shinjō 142-143 QR 4
Shinjō = Hsincheng 146-147 HJ 9
Shinjō, Kawasaki- 155 III a 2
Shinjuku, Tōkyō- 155 III b 1
Shinkafe 168-169 G 2
Shinko = Chinko 164-165 J 7
Shinkō = Hsincheng 146-147 HJ 9
Shinkolobwe 172 E 4
Shinmau Sûn 150-151 AB 6
Shin-nan = Enshi 142-143 K 5
Shinnston, WV 72-73 F 5
Shinohara, Yokohama- 155 III a 3
Shinqītī 164-165 B 4
Shinshān, Sabkhat — 164-165 B 4
Shinshū = Chinju 142-143 O 4
Shinyanga 172 F 2
Shinyukugyoen Garden 155 III b 1
Shiobara 144-145 MN 4
Shiogama 144-145 N 3
Shionomi, Cape — = Shiono-misaki 144-145 K 6
Shiono-misaki 144-145 K 6
Shioya-misaki 144-145 N 4
Shiping 142-143 J 7
Ship Island 78-79 E 5
Shipki 138-139 G 2
Shipki La 138-139 G 2
Shippegan 63 D 4
Shippegan Island 63 DE 4
Shippensburg, PA 72-73 GH 4
Shiprock, NW 74-75 J 4
Shipshaw, Rivière — 63 A 3
Shipu 146-147 HJ 7
Shiqian 142-143 K 6
Shiqiao 146-147 CD 6
Shiqq, Ḥāssī — 164-165 B 3
Shiquan 142-143 K 5
Shiquan He = Sengge Khamba 142-143 DE 5
Shirahama 144-145 K 6
Shirahaṭṭi = Shirhatti 140 B 3
Shirakami-saki 144-145 MN 2
Shirakawa 144-145 N 4
Shirāla 140 B 2
Shirane-san 144-145 LM 5
Shiranuka 144-145 cd 2
Shiraoi 144-145 b 2
Shirataka 144-145 MN 3
Shīrāz 134-135 G 5
Shiraze-hyōga 53 B 4-5
Shirbīn 173 B 2
Shire 172 FG 5
Shiretoko hantō 144-145 d 1-2
Shiretoko-misaki 144-145 d 1
Shirgaon 138-139 D 8
Shirhatti 140 B 3
Shīrīn Sū 136-137 N 5
Shiritoru = Makarov 132-133 b 8
Shiriya-saki 144-145 N 2
Shirley, AR 78-79 C 3
Shirley Basin 68-69 C 4
Shiro, TX 76-77 G 7
Shiroishi 144-145 N 3-4
Shirol 140 B 2
Shirotori 144-145 L 5
Shirpur 138-139 E 7
Shirqāṭ, Ash- = Ash-Sharqāṭ 136-137 K 5
Shirshāll 166-167 GH 1
Shirūr = Sirūr 140 B 1
Shishaldin Volcano 58-59 a 2
Shishāwah 166-167 B 4
Shishi 146-147 G 9
Shishihone, Tōkyō- 155 III c 1
Shishikui 144-145 K 6
Shishmaref, AK 56-57 CD 4
Shishmaref Inlet 58-59 DE 3
Shishou 146-147 D 7
Shitai 142-143 M 5
Shithāthah 136-137 K 6
Shitouzhai 141 F 4
Shiv 138-139 C 4
Shivagangā = Sivaganga [IND, mountain] 140 C 4
Shivagangā = Sivaganga [IND, place] 140 D 6
Shivakāshī = Sivakāsi 140 CD 6
Shivālak Pahāṛiyān = Siwālik Range 134-135 M 4-N 5
Shivamagga = Shimoga 134-135 LM 8
Shivarāya = Shevaroy Hills 140 D 4
Shivnārāyaṇ = Seorīnārāyan 138-139 J 7
Shivnāth = Seonāth 138-139 J 7
Shivpur = Sheopur 138-139 F 5
Shivpuri 134-135 M 5
Shivwits Indian Reservation 74-75 FG 4
Shivwits Plateau 74-75 G 4
Shiwanda Shan 150-151 F 2
Shiwa Ngandu 171 BC 5
Shixing 146-147 E 9
Shiyan 146-147 C 5
Shizhu 146-147 B 6
Shizhuang 146-147 H 5
Shizukawa 144-145 N 3
Shizunai 144-145 c 2
Shizuoka 144-145 LM 5
Shkodër 122-123 H 4
Shkumbin 122-123 H 5
Shmayṭīyah 136-137 H 5
Shmidt Island = ostrov Šmidta 132-133 QR 1
Shoa = Shewa 164-165 M 7
Shoal Lake [CDN, lake] 62 B 3
Shoal Lake [CDN, place] 61 H 5
Shoals, IN 70-71 G 6
Shōbara 144-145 J 5
Shobo Tsho 138-139 J 2
Shōdo-shima 144-145 K 5
Shodu 142-143 H 5
Shoe Cove 63 J 3
Shokā = Changhua 146-147 H 9
Shokalsky Strait = proliv Šokal'skogo 132-133 RS 2
Shokambetsu-dake 144-145 b 2
Shokotsu 144-145 c 1
Sholāpur 134-135 M 7
Sholavandan = Cholavandan 140 C 5
Shomolu 170 III b 1
Shooters Hill, London- 129 II c 2
Shōra, Ash- = Ash-Shūr'a 136-137 K 5
Shoranūr 140 C 5
Shorāpur 134-135 M 7
Shoreacres 66-67 E 1
Shoreditch, London- 129 II b 1
Shorewood, WI 70-71 G 4
Shorkoṭ 138-139 CD 2
Shorru Tsho 138-139 L 2
Shortland Island 148-149 hj 6
Shoshone, CA 74-75 EF 5
Shoshone, ID 66-67 F 4
Shoshone Falls 66-67 FG 4
Shoshone Mountain 74-75 E 4
Shoshone Mountains 64-65 C 3-4
Shoshone River 68-69 B 3
Shoshoni, WY 68-69 BC 4
Shō-Tombetsu 144-145 c 1
Shott el Jerid = Shaṭṭ al-Jarīd 164-165 F 2
Shotts, Plateau of the — = At-Tall 164-165 D 2-E 1
Shouchang 146-147 G 7
Shouguang 146-147 G 3
Shou-hsien = Shou Xian 146-147 F 5
Shou-kuang = Shouguang 146-147 G 3
Shoulder Mount 58-59 Q 3
Shouning 146-147 G 8
Shoup, ID 66-67 F 3
Shou Xian 146-147 F 5
Shouyang 146-147 D 3
Showak = Shuwak 164-165 M 6
Showhsien = Shou Xian 146-147 F 5
Showkwang = Shouguang 146-147 G 3
Show Low, AZ 74-75 H 5
Showning = Shouning 146-147 G 8
Showyang = Shouyang 146-147 D 3
Shrangavarapukoṭṭā = Srungavarapukota 140 F 1
Shreveport, LA 64-65 H 5
Shrewsbury 119 E 5
Shrīgonda 140 B 1
Shrīgōṅḍēṅ = Shrīgonda 140 B 1
Shrīharikoṭṭa Prāydvīp = Sriharikota Island 140 E 4
Shrīkākulam = Srīkākulam 134-135 N 7
Shrī Mādhōpur = Sri Mādhopur 138-139 E 4
Shrīmōhangaṛh = Sri Mohangarh 138-139 C 4
Shrimushanam = Srīmushnam 140 D 5
Shringēri = Sringeri 140 B 4
Shrīnivāsapura = Srīnivāspur 140 D 4
Shrīperambattūr = Srīperumbūdūr 140 DE 4
Shrīpūr 141 B 3
Shrīrāmpur = Serampore 134-135 O 6
Shrīrangam = Srīrangam 134-135 M 8
Shrīraṅgapaṭṭaṇa = Srīrangapatnam 140 C 4
Shrīshailam = Srīsailam 140 D 2
Shrīvaikuṇṭham = Srīvaikuntam 140 CD 6
Shrīvalliputtūr = Srīvilliputtūr 140 C 6
Shrīvardhan = Srīvardhan 134-135 L 7
Shuaiba = Ash-Shu'aybah 136-137 M 7
Shuaiba = As-Su'aybah 136-137 M 7
Shuangcheng 142-143 NO 2
Shuang-ch'êng = Shuangcheng 142-143 NO 2
Shuangfeng 146-147 D 8
Shuanggou [TJ, Hubei] 146-147 D 5
Shuanggou [TJ, Jiangsu ↓ Suqian] 146-147 G 5
Shuanggou [TJ, Jiangsu ↘ Xuzhou] 146-147 FG 4
Shuang-kou = Shuanggou [TJ, Hubei] 146-147 D 5
Shuang-kou = Shuanggou [TJ, Jiangsu ↓ Suqian] 146-147 G 5
Shuang-kou = Shuanggou [TJ, Jiangsu ↘ Xuzhou] 146-147 FG 4
Shuangliao 142-143 N 3
Shuangpai 146-147 C 8-9
Shu'aybah, Ash- 136-137 M 7
Shu'bah, Ash- 136-137 L 8
Shubert, NE 70-71 BC 5
Shublik Mountains 58-59 P 2
Shubrā, Al-Qāhirah- 170 II b 1
Shubrā al-Khaymah 170 II b 1
Shubuta, MS 78-79 E 5
Shucheng 146-147 F 6
Shufu = Qāshqār 142-143 CD 4
Shugra = Shuqrā 134-135 F 8
Shuguri Falls 171 D 5
Shuhekou 146-147 B 5
Shu-ho-k'ou = Shuhekou 146-147 B 5
Shuidong = Dianbai 146-147 C 11
Shuifeng Supong Hu = Supung Hu 144-145 E 2
Shuigoutou = Laixi 146-147 H 3
Shuiji 146-147 G 8
Shuikou 142-143 M 6
Shujā'ābad 138-139 C 3
Shujālpur 138-139 F 6
Shullsburg, WI 70-71 EF 4
Shulu 146-147 E 3
Shumagin Islands 56-57 DE 6
Shuman House, AK 58-59 PQ 3
Shumla 86-87 K 3
Shumla, TX 76-77 D 8
Shumlūl, Ash- = Ma'qalā' 134-135 F 5
Shūnāmganj 141 B 3
Shun'an = Chun'an 146-147 G 7
Shunchang 146-147 FG 8
Shunde 146-147 D 10
Shungnak, AK 56-57 EF 4
Shungnak River 58-59 J 3
Shunhua = Chunhua 146-147 B 4
Shunking = Nanchong 142-143 JK 5
Shunsen = Ch'unch'ŏn 142-143 O 4
Shuntak = Shunde 146-147 D 10
Shunteh = Shunde 146-147 D 10
Shunteh = Xingtai 142-143 L 4
Shuo-hsien = Shuo Xian 146-147 D 2
Shuo Xian 146-147 D 2
Shuqrā' 134-135 F 8
Shūr, Āb-e — 136-137 N 7
Shūr'a, Ash- 136-137 K 5
Shurayf 134-135 D 5
Shurayk, Ash- 164-165 L 5
Shurugwi 172 EF 5
Shūsh 136-137 N 6
Shushan = Susa 136-137 N 6
Shushartie 60 CD 4
Shushong 174-175 G 2
Shūshtar 134-135 F 4
Shuswap Lake 60 H 4
Shutō 138-139 MN 3
Shuwak 164-165 M 6
Shuwayyib, Ash- 136-137 MN 7
Shuyak Island 58-59 LM 7
Shuyak Strait 58-59 L 7
Shuyang 142-143 M 5
Shuzenji 144-145 M 5
Shwāmûn 141 D 5
Shwangcheng = Shuangcheng 142-143 NO 2
Shwangliao = Liaoyuan 142-143 NO 3
Shwebō 148-149 C 2
Shwedaung 141 D 6
Shwegū 141 E 3
Shwegûn 141 E 7
Shwegyin 141 E 7
Shwelī Myit 141 E 4
Shwemyō 141 E 5
Shyog 134-135 M 3-4
Shyopur = Shivpuri 134-135 M 5
Si, Laem — 150-151 B 8
Siabu 152-153 C 5
Siāh, Kūh-e — = Kūh-e Marzu 136-137 M 6
Siāhdehān = Tākestān 136-137 NO 4
Siak, Sungai — 152-153 DE 5
Siakiang = Xiajiang 146-147 E 8
Siak Sri Indrapura 152-153 DE 5
Siakwan = Xiaguan 142-143 J 6
Sialcote = Siyālkoṭ 134-135 LM 4
Sialkot = Siyālkoṭ 134-135 LM 4
Sialsūk 141 C 4
Siam = Thailand 148-149 CD 3
Si'an 146-147 G 6
Sian = Xi'an 142-143 K 5
Siangcheng = Xiangcheng 146-147 E 5
Siangfan = Fangcheng 142-143 L 5
Siangho = Xianghe 146-147 F 2
Siangning = Xiangning 146-147 C 3-4
Siangtan = Xiangtan 142-143 L 6
Siangyang = Xiangyang 142-143 L 5
Siangyin = Xiangyin 146-147 D 7
Siangyuan = Xiangyuan 146-147 D 3
Sianquião = Xiang Jiang 146-147 D 8
Siantan, Pulau — 150-151 EF 11
Siaofeng = Xiaofeng 146-147 G 6
Siao Hingan Ling = Xiao Hinggan Ling 142-143 O 1-P 2
Siaohsien = Xiao Xian 146-147 F 4
Siaokan = Xiaogan 146-147 D 6
Siaoyi = Xiaoyi 146-147 C 3
Siapa 94-95 H 6
Siapo, Río — 94-95 HJ 7
Siargao Island 148-149 J 4-5
Siau, Pulau — 148-149 J 6
Šiauliai 124-125 D 6
Siazan' 126-127 O 6
Sībah, As- 136-137 N 7
Sibā'ī, Jabal as- 173 CD 5
Sibā'īyah, As- 173 C 5
Sibaj 132-133 K 7
Sibasa 174-175 J 2
Sibayameer 174-175 K 4
Sibayi, Lake — = Sibayameer 174-175 K 4
Sibbald 61 C 5
Sībdū 166-167 F 2
Šibenik 122-123 FG 4
Siberia 132-133 O-X 5
Siberimanua 152-153 C 7
Siberut, Pulau — 148-149 C 7
Siberut, Selat — 148-149 C 7
Sibī 134-135 K 5
Sibigo 152-153 AB 4
Sibir'akova, ostrov — 132-133 OP 3
Sibirien 132-133 N-W 5
Sibiti [EAT] 171 C 3
Sibiti [RCA] 172 B 2
Sibiu 122-123 KL 3
Sibley, IA 70-71 BC 4
Sibley Provincial Park 70-71 F 1
Siboa 152-153 NO 5
Sibolga 148-149 C 6
Siborongborong 150-151 B 11
Sibpur, Howrah- 154 II a 2
Sibsāgar 141 D 2
Sibu 148-149 F 6
Sibu, Pulau — 150-151 E 11
Sibuatan, Gunung — 152-153 BC 4
Sibuco 152-153 OP 2
Sibū 'Gharb, As- 173 C 6
Sibuguey Bay 152-153 P 2
Sibuti 152-153 K 3
Sibutu Group 148-149 G 6
Sibutu Passage 152-153 N 3
Sibuyan Island 148-149 H 4
Sibuyan Sea 148-149 H 4
Siby 168-169 C 2
Sibyŏn-ni 144-145 F 3
Sica, Cascade de — 168-169 F 3
Sicamous 60 H 4
Sicasica 92-93 F 8
Sicasica, Serranía de — 104-105 BC 5
Sicasso = Sikasso 164-165 C 6
Sichang = Xichang 142-143 J 6
Sichang, Ko — 150-151 C 6
Šichany 124-125 Q 7
Sichem = Nābulus 136-137 F 6
Sichon 150-151 BC 8
Sichota-Alin = Sichote-Alin' 132-133 a 8-Z 9
Sichotė-Alin' 132-133 a 8-Z 9
Šichrany = Kanaš 132-133 H 6
Sichuan 142-143 J 5-6
Sichwan = Xichuan 142-143 L 5
Siclia 122-123 EF 7
Sicily = Sicilia 122-123 EF 7
Sico, Río — 88-89 D 7
Sicuani 92-93 E 7
Sīdamo 164-165 MN 8
Sīdamo-Borana = Sīdamo 164-165 MN 8
Sidao, Beijing- 155 II b 2
Sidaogou 144-145 F 2
Sidcup, London- 129 II c 2
Siddapur 140 B 3
Siddhapura = Siddapur 140 B 3
Siddipet 140 D 1
Siddipēṭa = Siddipet 140 D 1
Sideby 116-117 J 6
Sid-el-Hadj-Zaoui = Sīdī al-Ḥājj Zāwī 166-167 J 5
Sidéradougou 168-169 DE 3
Sidērókastron 122-123 K 5
Sideros, Akrōtērion — 122-123 M 8
Sidhaolī = Sidhauli 138-139 H 4
Sidhauli 138-139 H 4
Sidhi 138-139 H 5
Sidhout 140 D 3
Sidhpur 138-139 D 5-6
Sīdī 'Abd ar-Raḥmān 136-137 C 7
Sīdī-Aḥmadū 166-167 H 5
Sīdī-Aïch = Sīdī Aysh 166-167 J 1
Sīdī 'Āīsā 166-167 EF 2
Sīdī al-Akhḍar 166-167 FG 1
Sīdī al-Ḥājj ad-Dīn 166-167 G 3
Sīdī al-Ḥājj Zāwī 166-167 J 5
Sīdī al-Hānī, Sabkhat — 166-167 M 2
Sīdī-'Alī Ban Yūb 166-167 F 2
Sidi-Ali-Ben-Youb = Sīdī 'Alī Ban Yūb 166-167 F 2
Sīdī 'Alī Bin Naṣr Allah 166-167 LM 2
Sīdī 'Allāl al-Baḥrawī 166-167 CD 2
Sīdī al-Muhtār 166-167 B 4
Sīdī 'Amur Bū Ḥajalah 166-167 LM 2
Sīdī 'Aysā 166-167 H 2
Sīdī 'Aysh 166-167 J 1
Sīdī az-Zūīn 166-167 B 4
Sīdī Ban al-'Abbas 164-165 DE 1
Sīdī Barrānī 164-165 K 2
Sidi-bel-Abbès = Sīdī Ban al-'Abbas 164-165 DE 1
Sīdī Binnūr 166-167 B 3
Sīdī Boûbker = Abū Bakr 166-167 F 2
Sīdī Bū al-Anwār 166-167 B 4
Sīdī Bū Ghadrah 166-167 B 3
Sīdī Bū Zīd 166-167 L 2
Sīdī Chemākh = Sīdī Shammakh 166-167 M 3
Sidi Chemmakh = Sīdī Shammakh 166-167 M 3

Sīdī Chiger = Sīdī Shigar 166-167 B 4
Sidi-el-Hadj-ed-Dine = Sīdī al-Hājj ad-Dīn 166-167 G 3
Sīdī Īfnī 164-165 B 3
Sīdī Ismā'īl 166-167 B 3
Sidikalang 152-153 BC 4
Sidi-Lakhdar = Sīdī al-Akhḍar 166-167 FG 1
Sīdī Makhlūf 166-167 H 2
Sīdī Manṣūr 166-167 L 2
Sidi-Marūf 166-167 K 1
Sidi-Mérouane = Sīdī Mirwān 166-167 JK 1
Sidi-M'Hamed-Benali = Sīdī Muḥammad Ban Alī 166-167 G 1
Sīdī Mirwān 164-165 JK 1
Sīdī M'Mamed, Al-Jazā'ir- 170 I a 1
Sidi Mokhtar = Sīdī al-Muhthār 166-167 B 4
Sidi Moussa = Sīdī Mūsā 166-167 B 3
Sidi Moussa, Ouèd — = Wādī Sīdī Mūsā 166-167 J 6
Sīdī Muhammad Ban 'Alī 166-167 G 1
Sīdī Mūsā 166-167 B 3
Sīdī Mūsā, Wādī — 166-167 J 6
Sīdī Naṣīr 166-167 L 1
Sidinginan 152-153 D 5
Sīdī Nṣīr = Sīdī Naṣīr 166-167 L 1
Sīdī Omar Boû Hadjila = Sīdī 'Amur Bū Ḥajalah 166-167 LM 2
Sidi Ouada 170 I b 2
Sīdī Qāsim 164-165 CD 2
Sīdī Raḥḥāl 166-167 C 4
Sīdī Sālim 173 B 2
Sīdī Shammakh 166-167 M 3
Sīdī Shigar 166-167 B 4
Sīdī Slīmān = Sīdī Sulīmān 166-167 CD 2
Sidi Smaïl = Sidi Ismā'īl 166-167 B 3
Sīdī Sulīmān 166-167 CD 2
Sīdī Ṭla'a = Unāghāh 166-167 B 4
Sīdī 'Ukāskah 166-167 D 2
Sīdī Yaḥyā al-Gharb 166-167 CD 2
Sidi Youssef = Sāqīyat Sīdī Yusuf 166-167 L 1
Sidlaghatta 140 CD 4
Sidley, Mount — 53 B 24
Sidlī 138-139 N 4
Sidnaw, MI 70-71 F 2
Sidney 66-67 B 1
Sidney, IA 70-71 C 5
Sidney, MT 68-69 D 2
Sidney, NE 68-69 E 5
Sidney, NY 70-71 H 5
Sidney, OH 72-73 D 4
Sidobia 168-169 F 2
Sidoktaya = Sedôktayā 141 D 5
Sidorovo 124-125 N 4
Sidr, As- 164-165 H 2
Sidr, Wādī — 173 C 3
Sidra = As-Surt 164-165 H 2-3
Sidra, Khalīg — = Khalīj as-Surt 164-165 H 2
Sidrolândia 92-93 HJ 9
Siebenhirten, Wien- 113 I b 2
Siedlce 118 L 2
Siedlung Hasenbergl, München- 130 II b 1
Siedlung Neuherberg, München- 130 II b 1
Sieg 118 C 3
Siegen 118 D 3
Siegessäule 130 III b 1
Siembok = Phum Siembauk 150-151 E 6
Siemensstadt, Berlin- 130 III b 1
Siemiatycze 118 L 2
Siem Pang 150-151 F 5
Siem Reap 148-149 D 4
Siena 122-123 D 4
Sienfeng = Xianfeng 146-147 B 7
Sienku = Xianju 146-147 H 7
Sienning = Xianning 146-147 E 7
Sienyang = Xianyang 142-143 K 5
Sieradz 118 J 3
Sierpc 118 JK 2
Sierra, La — [ROU] 106-107 K 5
Sierra, Punta — 108-109 G 3
Sierra Ambargasta 106-107 EF 2
Sierra Añueque 108-109 E 3
Sierra Apas 108-109 F 3-4
Sierra Auca Mahuida 106-107 C 6
Sierra Azul 106-107 BC 5-6
Sierra Balmaceda 108-109 DE 9
Sierra Blanca, TX 76-77 B 7
Sierra Blanca de la Totora 108-109 E 3-F 2
Sierra Blanca Peak 64-65 E 5
Sierra Brava [RA, mountains] 106-107 E 2
Sierra Brava [RA, place] 106-107 E 2
Sierra Calcatapul 108-109 E 4
Sierra Cañadón Grande 108-109 E 5
Sierra Carapacha Grande 106-107 DE 6-7
Sierra Cavalonga 104-105 C 8
Sierra Chata 108-109 FG 4
Sierra Chauchaiñeu 108-109 E 3
Sierra Chica [RA, mountains] 106-107 E 3
Sierra Chica [RA, place] 106-107 G 6
Sierra Choique Mahuida 106-107 E 7
Sierra Colorada 111 C 6
Sierra Cuadrada 108-109 E 5
Sierra Cupupira 94-95 J 6-7
Sierra da Mocidade 94-95 KL 7
Sierra de Agalta 64-65 J 8-9
Sierra de Aguas Calientes 104-105 C 9
Sierra de Aguilar 104-105 D 8
Sierra de Ahogayegua 64-65 b 2-3
Sierra de Alcaraz 120-121 F 9
Sierra de Alférez 106-107 KL 4
Sierra de Ambato 104-105 C 11
Sierra de Ancasti 106-107 E 2
Sierra de Aracena 120-121 D 10
Sierra de Azul 106-107 GH 6
Sierra de Baraqua 94-95 FG 2
Sierra de Calalaste 111 C 2-3
Sierra de Cañazas 88-89 G 10
Sierra de Cantantal 106-107 D 3-4
Sierra de Carapé 106-107 K 5
Sierra de Carmen Silva 108-109 E 9
Sierra de Catán-Lil 106-107 B 7
Sierra de Chachahuen 106-107 C 6
Sierra de Chañi 104-105 D 8-9
Sierra de Chepes 106-107 D 3
Sierra de Chiribiquete 94-95 E 7
Sierra de Coalcomán 86-87 J 8
Sierra de Cochinoca 104-105 D 8
Sierra de Comechingones 106-107 E 4
Sierra de Córdoba [RA] 111 C 4-D 3
Sierra de Cura Mala 106-107 FG 6-7
Sierra de Divisor 92-93 E 6
Sierra de Famatina 106-107 D 2
Sierra de Gata 120-121 D 8
Sierra de Gredos 120-121 E 8
Sierra de Guadalupe [E] 120-121 E 9
Sierra de Guadalupe [MEX] 91 I c 1
Sierra de Guadarrama 120-121 EF 8
Sierra de Guasapampa 106-107 E 3
Sierra de Guasayán 104-105 D 10-11
Sierra de Huantraicó 106-107 C 6
Sierra de Juárez 64-65 C 5
Sierra del Aconquija 104-105 CD 10
Sierra de la Encantada 76-77 C 8
Sierra de la Encantanda 86-87 J 3-4
Sierra de la Giganta 64-65 D 6-7
Sierra de la Huerta 106-107 D 3
Sierra de la Iguana 76-77 D 9
Sierra de la Madera 86-87 F 2-3
Sierra de la Neblina 94-95 HJ 7
Sierra de la Palma 76-77 D 9-10
Sierra de la Peña 120-121 G 7
Sierra de la Punilla 106-107 C 2
Sierra de las Aguadas 106-107 BC 5
Sierra de las Minas 86-87 PQ 10
Sierra de las Tunas 106-107 G 6
Sierra de las Vacas 108-109 C 6-7
Sierra de la Ventana 111 D 5
Sierra del Carmen 86-87 J 3
Sierra del Centinela 104-105 D 8-9
Sierra del Cobre 104-105 C 8-9
Sierra de Lema 94-95 L 4
Sierra del Hueso 76-77 B 7
Sierra del Imán 106-107 K 1
Sierra de Lique 104-105 D 6-7
Sierra del Muerto 104-105 AB 9
Sierra del Nevado 111 C 5
Sierra del Norte 106-107 E 3
Sierra de los Alamitos 86-87 JK 4
Sierra de los Chacays 108-109 F 4
Sierra de los Cóndores 106-107 E 4
Sierra de los Filabres 120-121 F 10
Sierra de los Llanos 106-107 D 3
Sierra de los Prades 106-107 HJ 6-7
Sierra del Tandil 106-107 H 6
Sierra del Tigre 106-107 C 3
Sierra de Tlahualilo 76-77 C 9
Sierra del Volcán 106-107 H 6
Sierra del Zamura 94-95 K 5
Sierra de Mandiyutí 104-105 E 7
Sierra de Misiones 102-103 EF 7
Sierra de Mogna 106-107 C 3
Sierra de Mogotes 106-107 E 2
Sierra de Moreno 104-105 B 7
Sierra de Olte 108-109 E 4
Sierra de Outes 120-121 C 7
Sierra de Perija 92-93 E 2-3
Sierra de Pija 64-65 J 8
Sierra de Pillahuincó 106-107 G 7
Sierra de Pocho 106-107 E 3
Sierra de Quichagua 104-105 CD 8
Sierra de Quillalauquén 106-107 G 6
Sierra de Quilmes 104-105 C 10
Sierra de San Antonio 86-87 E 2-3
Sierra de San Bernardo 108-109 E 5
Sierra de San Borja 86-87 D 3
Sierra de San Lázaro 86-87 E 5-F 6
Sierra de San Lorenzo 120-121 F 7
Sierra de San Luís [RA] 106-107 DE 4
Sierra de San Luis [YV] 92-93 EF 2
Sierra de San Marcos 76-77 CD 9
Sierra de Sañogasta 106-107 D 2
Sierra de San Pedro 120-121 D 9
Sierra de San Pedro Mártir 86-87 C 2
Sierra de Santa Bárbara 104-105 D 8-9
Sierra de Santa Catarina 91 I cd 3
Sierra de Santa Cruz 104-105 E 5-6
Sierra de Santa Lucía 86-87 D 4
Sierra de Segura 120-121 F 9-10
Sierra de Tamaulipas 86-87 L 6
Sierra de Tartagal 104-105 E 8
Sierra de Tatul 106-107 B 2
Sierra de Tecka 108-109 D 4
Sierra de Tolox 120-121 E 10
Sierra de Tontal 106-107 C 3
Sierra de Tunuyan 111 C 4
Sierra de Ulapes 106-107 D 3
Sierra de Umango 106-107 C 2
Sierra de Unturán 94-95 J 7
Sierra de Uspallata 106-107 C 4
Sierra de Valle Fértil 106-107 CD 3
Sierra de Varas 104-105 B 9
Sierra de Velasco 106-107 D 2
Sierra de Vilgo 106-107 D 2-3
Sierra de Villicún 106-107 C 3
Sierra Diablo 76-77 B 7
Sierra Gorda 111 C 2
Sierra Gould 106-107 E 7
Sierra Grande [MEX] 86-87 H 3
Sierra Grande [RA, Córdoba] 106-107 E 3-4
Sierra Grande [RA, Río Negro mountains] 108-109 G 3
Sierra Grande [RA, Río Negro place] 111 C 6
Sierra Gulampaja 104-105 C 10
Sierra Huancache 108-109 DE 4
Sierra Laguna Blanca 104-105 C 10
Sierra Leone 164-165 B 7
Sierra Leone Basin 50-51 HJ 5
Sierra Leone Rise 50-51 HJ 5
Sierra Madera 76-77 C 7
Sierra Madre [MEX] 64-65 H 8
Sierra Madre [RP] 148-149 H 3
Sierra Madre [USA] 68-69 C 5
Sierra Madre del Sur 64-65 FG 8
Sierra Madre Mountains 74-75 CD 5
Sierra Madre Occidental 64-65 E 5-F 7
Sierra Madre Oriental 64-65 F 6-G 7
Sierra Madrona 120-121 EF 9
Sierra Maestra 64-65 L 7-8
Sierra Mariposa 104-105 B 8
Sierra Mesaniyeu 108-109 DE 3
Sierra Mochada 86-87 HJ 4
Sierra Mojada 86-87 J 4
Sierra Morena 120-121 D 10-E 9
Sierra Negra [RA ↘ Paso de Indios] 108-109 F 5
Sierra Negra [RA ↖ Paso de Indios] 108-109 DE 4
Sierra Negra [RA, Precordillera] 106-107 C 3
Sierra Nevada [E] 120-121 F 10
Sierra Nevada [RA] 108-109 E 4
Sierra Nevada [USA] 64-65 BC 4
Sierra Nevada [YV] 94-95 F 3
Sierra Nevada del Cocuy 94-95 E 4
Sierra Nevada de Santa Marta 92-93 E 2
Sierra Oscura 76-77 A 6
Sierra Pailemán 108-109 FG 3
Sierra Parima 92-93 G 4
Sierra Pereyra 106-107 G 3
Sierra Pichi Mahuida 106-107 E 7
Sierra Pie de Palo 106-107 C 3
Sierra Piedra Blanca 106-107 CD 7
Sierra Pinta 74-75 G 6
Sierra Rosada 108-109 E 4
Sierra Sabinas = Sierra de la Iguana 76-77 D 9
Sierra San Lázaro 86-87 EF 6
Sierra San Miguel 104-105 B 10
Sierra San Pedro Mártir 64-65 CD 5
Sierra Santa Victoria 104-105 D 8
Sierras Blancas 108-109 EF 2-3
Sierras de Zacatecas 86-87 JK 6
Sierras Pampeanas 111 C 3
Sierra Sumampa 106-107 F 2
Sierra Tapirapecó 92-93 FG 4
Sierra Taquetrén 108-109 E 4
Sierra Tarahumara 64-65 E 6
Sierra Telmo 104-105 D 8
Sierra Tepequem 98-99 GH 3
Sierra Valenzuela 104-105 A 8
Sierra Velluda 106-107 B 6
Sierra Vicuña Mackenna 104-105 AB 9
Sierra Vieja 76-77 B 7
Sierra Vizcaíno 64-65 D 6
Sierrita, La — 94-95 EF 2
Siesta Key 80-81 b 3
Siete Puntas, Río — 102-103 C 5
Sievering, Wien- 113 I b 1
Sifa, Cape — = Dahua Jiao 150-151 H 3
Sifa Point = Dahua Jiao 150-151 H 3
Sīf Fatimah, Bi'r — 166-167 L 4
Siffray 168-169 C 3
Sífnos 122-123 L 7
Sifton Pass 56-57 LM 6
Sig 166-167 F 2
Sigep 152-153 C 6
Sigep, Tanjung — 152-153 C 6
Sighetul Marmatiei 122-123 KL 2
Sighişoara 122-123 L 2
Sigiriya 140 E 7
Sigli 148-149 C 5
Siglufjördhur 116-117 d 1
Signai 62 N 2
Signal Hill 83 III cd 3
Signal Peak 74-75 FG 6
Signy 53 C 32
Sigoor 171 C 2
Sigourney, IA 70-71 DE 5
Sigsig 96-97 B 3
Sigtuna 116-117 GH 8
Siguiri 164-165 C 6
Sigulda 124-125 E 5
Si He 146-147 F 4
Sihlwald 128 IV b 2
Sihong 146-147 G 5
Sihōr = Sehore 138-139 F 6
Sihora 138-139 H 6
Sihsien = She Xian 142-143 M 5-6
Sihsien = Xi Xian [TJ, Henan] 146-147 E 5
Sihsien = Xi Xian [TJ, Shanxi] 142-143 L 4
Sihuas 96-97 C 6
Sihuas, Pampas de — 96-97 EF 10
Sihui 146-147 D 10
Sihwān 138-139 AB 4
Siilinjärvi 116-117 M 6
Siinai = Sīnā' 164-165 L 3
Siirt 134-135 E 3
Sijān 104-105 C 11
Sijerdijelach Jur'ach = Batamaj 132-133 YZ 5
Sijiao Shan 146-147 HJ 6
Sijiazi = Laohushan 144-145 BC 2
Sijnān 166-167 L 1
Sik 150-151 C 10
Sikandarābād 138-139 F 3
Sikandarābād = Secunderābād 134-135 M 7
Sikandrabad = Sikandarābād 138-139 F 3
Sikandra Rao 138-139 G 4
Sikao 148-149 C 5
Sīkar 138-139 E 4
Sikāripāra 138-139 L 5
Sikasso 164-165 C 6
Sikefti 136-137 KL 3
Sikeli 152-153 O 8
Sikem = Nābulus 136-137 F 6
Sikes, LA 78-79 C 4
Sikeston, MO 78-79 E 2
Sikhim = Sikkim 134-135 O 5
Sikhiu 148-149 D 4
Sikhoraphum 150-151 D 5
Sikhota Alin = Sichotė-Alin' 132-133 a 8-Z 9
Si Kiang = Xi Jiang 146-147 C 10
Siking = Xi'an 142-143 K 5
Síkinos 122-123 L 7
Sikirė 168-169 E 2
Šikirlykitaj = Suvorovo 126-127 D 4
Sikkim 134-135 O 5
Sikoku = Shikoku 142-143 P 5
Sikotan tō = Shikotan-tō 142-143 S 3
Sikt'ach 132-133 X 4
Siktyakh = Sikt'ach 132-133 X 4
Sikyôn 122-123 K 7
Sil 120-121 D 7
Sila, La — 122-123 G 6
Šilador 124-125 R 3
Šilalė 124-125 D 6
Silao 86-87 K 7
Silasjaure 116-117 G 3-4
Silcharī Bāzār 141 BC 4
Silcox 61 L 2
Şile 136-137 C 2
Silencio 86-87 K 3
Siler City, NC 80-81 G 3
Sileru 140 E 2
Silesia 118 GH 3
Silesia, MT 68-69 B 3
Silfke = Silifke 134-135 C 3
Silgarhi Doti 134-135 N 5
Silghāt 141 C 2
Silhaṭ 134-135 P 5-6
Silifke 134-135 C 3
Siligir 132-133 V 4
Silīguri 134-135 O 5
Silīpica 106-107 EF 2
Silistra 122-123 M 3
Silivri 136-137 C 2
Siljan 116-117 F 7
Šilka 132-133 W 7
Šilkan 132-133 c 6
Silkeborg 116-117 C 9
Sillajguai, Cordillera — 104-105 B 6
Silleiro, Cabo — 120-121 C 7
Silli 168-169 E 3
Sillyŏng 144-145 G 4
Šil'naja Balka 126-127 O 1
Siloam Springs, AR 76-77 G 4
Silondi 138-139 H 6
Silos 94-95 E 4
Šilovo [SU, R'azan'skaja Oblast'] 124-125 N 6
Šilovo [SU, Tul'skaja Oblast'] 124-125 M 7
Silsbee, TX 76-77 GH 7
Siltou 164-165 H 5
Siluas 152-153 H 5
Silumpur, Wai — 152-153 F 7
Siluria, AL 78-79 F 4
Šilutė 124-125 C 6
Silva 96-97 A 4
Silva, Ilha da — 98-99 F 5
Silva Jardim 102-103 LM 5
Silvan 136-137 J 3
Silvānī = Silwāni 138-139 G 6
Silvânia 102-103 H 2
Silva Porto = Bié 172 C 4
Silvāsa = Silvassa 138-139 D 7
Silvassa 138-139 D 7
Silverbell, AZ 74-75 H 6
Silverbow, MT 66-67 G 2-3
Silver City 64-65 b 2
Silver City, ID 66-67 E 4
Silver City, NM 64-65 E 5
Silver City, UT 74-75 G 3
Silver Creek 66-67 D 4
Silver Creek, MS 78-79 DE 5
Silver Creek, NE 68-69 H 5
Silver Creek, NY 72-73 G 3
Silver Lake, CA 74-75 EF 5
Silver Lake, OR 66-67 C 4
Silver Lake Reservoir 83 III c 1
Silver Mountain 70-71 EF 1
Silverpeak, NV 74-75 E 4
Silver Peak Range 74-75 E 4
Silverstreams 174-175 E 5
Silverthrone Mount 60 D 4
Silverton 158-159 H 6
Silverton, CO 68-69 C 7
Silverton, OR 66-67 B 3
Silverton, TX 76-77 D 5
Silvertown, London- 129 II c 2
Silves [BR] 98-99 J 6
Silves [P] 120-121 C 10
Silvia 94-95 C 6
Silvianópolis 102-103 K 5
Silvies River 66-67 D 4
Silwa Baḥarī = Salwá Baḥrī 173 C 5
Silwāni 138-139 G 6
Silyānah 166-167 L 1
Silyānah, Wād — 166-167 L 1-2
Sim, Rā's — 166-167 AB 4
Simandou 168-169 C 3
Šimanggang 148-149 F 6
Šimanovsk 132-133 Y 7
Simao 142-143 J 7
Simão Dias 100-101 F 6
Simard, Lac — 72-73 G 1
Simaria 138-139 K 5
Simatang, Pulau — 152-153 NO 5
Simav 136-137 C 3
Simav çayı 136-137 C 3
Simbillāwein, Es- = As-Sinbillāwayn 173 BC 2
Simbirsk = Ul'janovsk 132-133 H 7
Simcoe 72-73 FG 3
Simcoe, Lake — 56-57 V 9
Simēn 164-165 M 6
Simeonof Island 58-59 d 2
Simferopol' 126-127 G 4
Simhāchalam 140 F 2
Simḥām, Jabal as- 134-135 GH 7
Similkameen River 66-67 CD 1
Simingan = Samangān 134-135 K 3
Siming Shan 146-147 H 7
Simití 92-93 E 3
Simi Valley, CA 74-75 D 5
Simiyu 171 C 3
Simizu = Shimizu 142-143 Q 4-5
Sim Kolodiaziv = Lenino 126-127 G 4
Simla 134-135 M 4
Simla, Calcutta- 154 II b 2
Simmesport, LA 78-79 CD 5
Simmie 61 D 6
Simms, MT 66-67 GH 2
Simoca 104-105 D 10
Simões 100-101 D 4
Simokita hantō = Shimokita-hantō 142-143 R 3
Simola 116-117 MN 7
Simonette River 60 HJ 2
Simonhouse Lake 61 H 3
Simonicha 124-125 TU 5
Simonoseki = Shimonoseki 142-143 P 5
Simonstad 172 C 8
Simonstown = Simonstad 172 C 8
Simoom Sound 60 D 4
Šimozero 124-125 K 3
Simpang 152-153 F 6
Simpang Bedok 154 III b 1-2
Simpang-kanan, Sungai — 150-151 AB 11
Simpang-kiri, Sungai — 152-153 B 4
Simplício Mendes 92-93 L 6
Simplon 118 CD 5
Simpruk, Jakarta- 154 IV a 2
Simpson, Cape — 58-59 KL 1
Simpson, Isla — 108-109 C 5
Simpson, Río — 108-109 C 5
Simpson Desert 158-159 G 4-5
Simpson Island 70-71 G 1
Simpson Islands 56-57 O 5
Simpson Peninsula 56-57 T 4
Simpson Strait 56-57 R 4
Simra 138-139 K 4
Simrishamn 116-117 F 10
Sims Bayou 85 III b 2
Šimsk 124-125 H 4
Simular = Pulau Simeuluë 148-149 BC 6
Simunul Island 152-153 NO 3
Simušir, ostrov — 142-143 T 2
Sīnā' [ET] 164-165 L 3
Sina [IND] 140 B 1
Sinabang 148-149 C 6
Sinabung, Gunung — 152-153 C 4
Sinadhapo = Dhuusa Maareeb 164-165 b 2
Sinai = Sīnā' 164-165 L 3
Sinaloa 64-65 E 6-7
Sinaloa, Río — 86-87 FG 4-5
Sinamaica 94-95 F 2
Sinan 142-143 K 6
Sinanju 144-145 E 3
Sinanpaşa 136-137 CD 3
Sinaru, AK 58-59 HJ 1
Sinaûen = Sīnāwan 164-165 G 2
Sīnāwan 164-165 G 2
Sinbaungwe = Hsinbaungwè 141 D 6
Sinbillāwayn, As- 173 BC 2
Sincan 136-137 GH 3
Sincanlı = Sinanpaşa 136-137 CD 3
Sincé 94-95 D 3
Sincelejo 92-93 DE 3
Sinch'ang 144-145 G 2
Sinchang = Xinchang 146-147 H 7
Sinch'ang-ni 144-145 F 3
Sincheng = Xincheng 146-147 EF 2
Sincheng = Xingren 142-143 K 6
Sinch'ŏn 144-145 E 3
Sincik = Birimşe 136-137 H 3
Sinclair Mills 60 G 2
Sincorá, Serra do — 100-101 D 7
Sind 134-135 M 5
Sind = Sindh 134-135 K 5
Sinda = Sindh 134-135 K 5
Sindagi = Sindgi 140 C 2
Sindangbarang 148-149 E 8
Sindelfingen 118 D 4
Sindgi 140 C 2
Sindh 134-135 K 5
Sindhnūr 140 C 3
Sindh Sāgar Doāb 138-139 C 2-3
Sindhu = Sindh 134-135 L 4
Sindhūli Garhi 138-139 KL 4
Sindi 138-139 G 7
Sindi [SU] 124-125 E 4
Sındıran 136-137 E 3
Sındırgı 136-137 C 3
Sindkhed 138-139 F 7-8
Sindkhēḍ = Sindkheda 138-139 E 7
Sindkheda 138-139 E 7
Sindlingen, Frankfurt am Main- 128 III a 1
Sin-do 144-145 DE 3
Sindri 138-139 L 6
Sindy = Sajmak 134-135 L 3
Sinegorje 124-125 S 4
Sinegorskij 126-127 K 3
Sinel'nikovo 126-127 G 2
Sines 120-121 C 10
Sines, Cabo de — 120-121 C 10
Sine-Saloum 168-169 AB 2
Sinfra 168-169 D 4
Sing, Mu'o'ng — 150-151 C 2
Singah 164-165 L 6
Singaing 141 E 5
Si-ngan = Xi'an 142-143 K 5
Singapore 148-149 DE 6
Singapore, Strait of — 148-149 DE 6
Singapore-Alexandra 154 III ab 2
Singapore-Geylang 154 III b 2
Singapore-Holland 154 III a 2
Singapore-Katong 154 III b 2
Singapore-Pasir Panjang 154 III a 2
Singapore Polytechnic 154 III b 2
Singapore-Potong Pasir 154 III b 1
Singapore-Queens Town 154 III a 2
Singapore-Tanglin Hill 154 III ab 2
Singapore-Toa Payoh Town 154 III b 1
Singapore-Wayang Satu 154 III ab 2
Singapur 148-149 DE 6
Singaraja 148-149 G 8
Singatoka 148-149 a 2
Singaung = Hsindau 141 D 5
Singaung = Hsingaung 141 CD 6
Sing Buri 148-149 D 3-4
Singen 118 D 5
Singes, Île des — 170 IV a 1
Singhbhūm 138-139 K 6
Singhpur 138-139 HJ 7
Singia 138-139 KL 5
Singida 172 F 2
Singkarak, Danau — 152-153 CD 6
Singkawang 148-149 E 6
Singkep, Pulau — 148-149 DE 7
Singkil 148-149 C 6
Singleton 158-159 K 6
Singleton, Mount — 158-159 F 4
Singora = Songkhla 148-149 D 5
Sin'gosan 144-145 F 3
Singri 141 C 2
Singtai = Xingtai 142-143 L 4
Singtze = Xingzi 146-147 F 7
Singū 141 E 4
Singuédzi, Rio — 174-175 J 2
Sin'gye 144-145 F 3
Sinhbhūm = Singhbhūm 134-135 NO 6
Sin-hiang = Xinxiang 142-143 LM 4
Si Nho = Ban Si Nhô 150-151 E 4
Sinho = Xinhe 146-147 E 3
Sinhsien = Xin Xian 142-143 L 4
Sinickaja 124-125 P 3
Sining = Xining 142-143 J 4
Siniqal, Baḥr — 168-169 B 2
Siniscola 122-123 CD 5
Sinjai 148-149 GH 8
Sinjār 136-137 J 4
Sinjār, Jabal — 136-137 JK 4
Sin-kal'ajin 144-145 F 2
Sinkan = Xingan 146-147 E 8
Sinkāt 164-165 M 5
Sinkiang = Xinjiang 142-143 L 4
Sinkiang = Xinjiang Uygur Zizhiqu 142-143 G 3
Sinlo = Xinle 142-143 LM 4
Sinlungaba = Seinlôngabā 141 E 3
Sinmak 144-145 F 3
Sinmi-do 144-145 E 3
Sinmin = Xinmin 144-145 D 1-2
Sinn al-Kadhdhāb 173 BC 6
Sinnamary [French Guiana, place] 92-93 J 3
Sinnamary [French Guiana, river] 98-99 M 2
Sinnar 138-139 DE 8
Sinneh = Sanandaj 134-135 F 3
Sinnhabhūm = Singhbhūm 134-135 NO 6
Sin Nombre, Cerro — 108-109 C 5-6
Sinnūris 173 B 3
Sinnyŏng = Sillyŏng 144-145 G 4
Sinoe 168-169 C 4
Sinoe = Greenville 164-165 C 7-8
Sinola = Chinhoyi 172 EF 5
Sinop 134-135 D 2
Sinope = Sinop 134-135 D 2
Sinp'o 142-143 O 3-4
Sinquim = Xi'an 142-143 K 5
Sinqunyane 174-175 H 5
Sinsiang = Xinxiang 142-143 LM 4
Sint-Agatha-Berchem = Berchem-Sainte-Agathe 128 II a 1
Sintang 148-149 F 6
Sint-Anna-Pede 128 II a 2
Sint Blaize, Kaap — 174-175 E 8
Sint-Brixius-Rode 128 II ab 1
Sint Eustatius 64-65 O 8
Sint Francisbaai 174-175 F 8
Sint Franziskusbaai 174-175 A 3
Sint-Gertruide-Pede 128 II a 2
Sint Helenabaai 172 C 8
Sint-Lambrechts-Woluwe = Wolume-Saint-Lambert 128 II b 1
Sint Luciabaai 174-175 K 5
Sint Luciameer 172 F 7
Sint-Martens-Bodegem 128 II a 1
Sint Martin, Kaap — 174-175 B 7
Sint Nicolaas 94-95 G 1
Sinton, TX 76-77 F 8
Sint-Pieters-Woluwe = Woluwe-Saint-Pierre 128 II b 1
Sintra [BR] 92-93 G 6
Sintra [P] 120-121 C 9
Sintsai = Xincai 142-143 LM 5
Sint Sebastianbaai 174-175 D 8
Sint-Stevens-Woluwe 128 II b 1
Sint-Ulriks-Kapelle 128 II a 1
Sinú, Río — 94-95 CD 3
Sin'ucha 126-127 E 2
Sinuk, AK 58-59 D 4
Sinuk River 58-59 DE 4
Sinwŏn-ni 144-145 E 3
Sinyang = Xinyang 142-143 LM 5
Sinyu = Xinyu 146-147 E 8
Sinzyô = Shinjō 142-143 QR 4
Sió 118 J 5
Siocon 152-153 OP 2
Sioma 172 D 5
Sion [CH] 118 C 5
Sion [PE] 96-97 C 5
Sioux City, IA 64-65 GH 3
Sioux Falls, SD 64-65 G 3
Sioux Lookout 56-57 S 7
Sioux Rapids, IA 70-71 C 4
Sipaliwini 98-99 K 3
Sipang, Tanjung — 152-153 J 5
Sipapo, Río — 94-95 H 5
Siparia 94-95 L 2
Šipčenski prohod 122-123 LM 4
Siphageni 172 EF 8
Sipí 94-95 C 5
Šipicyno 124-125 PQ 3
Siping 142-143 N 3
Sipitang 148-149 G 5-6
Sipiwesk 61 K 3
Sipiwesk Lake 61 K 3
Siple, Mount — 53 B 24
Sipolilo = Chiporiro 172 F 5
Sipora, Pulau — 148-149 C 7
Sipora, Selat — 152-153 CD 7
Si Prachan 150-151 BC 5
Sip Sông Châu Thai 148-149 D 2
Sipura, Pulau — = Pulau Sipora 148-149 C 7
Siqueira Campos 102-103 GH 5
Siquijor Island 148-149 H 5
Siquisique 92-93 F 2
Sira [IND] 140 C 4
Sira [N, place] 116-117 B 8
Sira [N, river] 116-117 B 8
Šira [SU] 132-133 QR 7
Sira, Pico — 96-97 D 6
Si Racha 150-151 C 6
Siracuas 111 D 2
Siracusa 122-123 F 7
Siraguppa = Siruguppa 140 C 3
Šir'ajevo 126-127 E 3
Sirājganj 138-139 M 5
Sir Alexander, Mount — 60 GH 2
Sirama = Seram 140 C 2
Siran = Karaca 136-137 H 2
Sirasilla = Sirsilla 140 D 1
Sirāthu 138-139 H 5
Sirdar 66-67 E 1
Sir Edward Pellew Group 158-159 G 3
Siren, WI 70-71 D 3
Siret [RO, place] 122-123 M 2
Siret [RO, river] 122-123 M 3
Sirḥān, Wādī as — 134-135 D 4
Sirik, Tanjung — 152-153 J 4
Siringuši 124-125 O 7
Sirinhaém 100-101 G 5
Sirirskaja ravnina 132-133 L-P 5-6
Sir James MacBrien, Mount — 56-57 KL 5
Sirjān 134-135 H 5
Sir John Hayes Island = Kûnthī Kyûn 150-151 A 7
Sīrkāzhi 140 DE 5
Sırkıntı 136-137 F 4
Sirmaur 138-139 H 5
Sirmaur = Sirmūr 138-139 F 2
Sirmūr 138-139 F 2
Sirmūr = Sirmaur 138-139 H 5
Şırnak 136-137 K 4
Sirohi 138-139 D 5
Sironcha 140 DE 1
Sironj 138-139 F 5
Sirpur 138-139 J 7
Sirr, Nafūd as- 134-135 E 5-F 6
Sirsa 134-135 LM 5
Sir Sanford, Mount — 60 J 4
Sirsi 140 B 3
Sirsilla 140 D 1
Sirte = Khalīj as-Surt 164-165 H 2
Sirte, Gulf of — = Khalīj as-Surt 164-165 H 2
Sir Thomas, Mount — 158-159 EF 5
Sirtica = As-Surt 164-165 H 2-3
Siruguppa 140 C 3
Sirūr 140 B 1
Şirvan = Küfre 136-137 K 3
Sirvān, Rūd-e — 136-137 M 5
Sirvel 140 D 3
Sirvēlā = Sirvel 140 D 3
Sirven, Laguna — 108-109 E 6
Širvintos 124-125 E 6
Sirwah, Jabal — 166-167 C 4
Sirwān 136-137 LM 5
Sirwān, Ābi — 136-137 L 5
Sir Wilfrid Laurier, Mount — 60 GH 3
Sirya = Zeytinlik 136-137 JK 2
Sisak 122-123 G 3
Si Sa Ket 148-149 D 3-4
Sisal 86-87 P 7
Si Satchanalai 150-151 B 4
Si Sawat 150-151 B 5
Sishen 172 D 7
Sishuang Liedao 146-147 H 8
Sishui [TJ, Henan] 146-147 D 4
Sishui [TJ, Shandong] 146-147 F 4
Sisian 126-127 MN 7
Sisimiut 56-57 Za 4
Sisipuk Lake 61 H 3
Siskiyou, OR 66-67 B 4
Siskiyou Mountains 66-67 B 4-5

362 Sîdî

Si Songkhram 150-151 E 4
Sisophon 148-149 D 4
Sisquelan, Península — 108-109 BC 6
Sisseton, SD 68-69 H 3
Sisseton Indian Reservation 68-69 H 3
Sissili 168-169 E 3
Sīstān 134-135 J 4
Sīstān, Daryācheh — 134-135 HJ 4
Sīstān va Balūchestān 134-135 H 4-J 5
Sisteron 120-121 K 6
Sisters, OR 66-67 C 3
Siswa Bāzār 138-139 J 4
Sit' 124-125 L 4
Sita 168-169 B 3
Sitachwe 174-175 D 3
Sītāmarhi 138-139 K 4
Sītāmau 138-139 E 5-6
Sītāpur 138-139 H 4
Siteki 174-175 JK 4
Sithandone 150-151 EF 5
Sithōnia 122-123 K 5-6
Siting 146-147 D 3
Sítio da Abadia 92-93 K 7
Sítio do Mato 100-101 C 7
Sitio Grande 100-101 B 7
Sítio Novo [BR, Bahia] 100-101 E 7
Sítio Novo [BR, Maranhão] 100-101 A 3
Sítio Novo do Grajaú 100-101 A 3
Sitio Nuevo 94-95 D 2
Sitka, AK 56-57 J 6
Sitkaing 148-149 C 2
Sitkaing Taing 148-149 B 2-C 1
Sitkalidak Island 58-59 g 1
Sitkinak Island 58-59 g 1
Sitkinak Strait 58-59 fg 1
Šitkino 132-133 S 6
Sitn'aki 126-127 D 1
Sittang River = Sittaung Myit 141 E 6
Sittaung Myit 141 E 6
Sittwe 148-149 B 2
Siumbatu 152-153 P 7
Siumpu, Pulau — 152-153 P 8
Siunī = Seoni 134-135 M 6
Siunī-Mālvā = Seoni-Mālwa 138-139 F 6
Siurī = Sūri 138-139 L 6
Siushan = Xiushan 146-147 B 7
Siuslaw River 66-67 B 4
Siut = Asyūṭ 164-165 L 3
Siuxt = Džūkste 124-125 D 5
Siva [SU, place] 124-125 U 4
Siva [SU, river] 124-125 U 5
Sivaganga [IND, mountain] 140 C 4
Sivaganga [IND, place] 140 D 6
Sivakāsi 140 CD 6
Sivaki 132-133 Y 7
Sivān = Siwān 138-139 K 4
Sivānā = Siwāna 138-139 D 5
Sivand 134-135 G 4
Sivānī = Siwāni 138-139 E 3
Sivas 134-135 D 3
Sivaš, ozero — 126-127 FG 3-4
Sivaslı 136-137 C 3
Siverek 136-137 H 4
Siverskij 124-125 H 4
Siverst 124-125 H 5
Sivin' 124-125 P 6
Sivrice 136-137 H 3
Sivrihisar 136-137 D 3
Sivučij, mys — 132-133 fg 6
Siwa 152-153 O 7
Sīwah 164-165 K 3
Sīwah, Wāḥāt — 164-165 K 3
Siwālik Range 134-135 M 4-N 5
Siwān 138-139 K 4
Siwāna 138-139 D 5
Siwāni 138-139 E 3
Siwni = Seoni 134-135 M 6
Siwni-Malwa = Seoni-Mālwa 138-139 F 6
Si Xian 146-147 FG 5
Sixtymile 58-59 RS 4
Siyāh Chaman 136-137 M 4
Siyāl, Jazā'ir — 173 E 6
Siyālkoṭ 134-135 LM 4
Siyang 146-147 G 5
Siyang = Xiyang 146-147 D 3

Sjælland 116-117 DE 10
Sjöbo 116-117 EF 10
Sjøvegan 116-117 GH 3
Sjuøyane 116-117 l 4

Skadarsko jezero 122-123 H 4
Skadovsk 126-127 F 3
Skagafjardhar 116-117 d 2
Skagafjördhur 116-117 c 1-d 2
Skagen 116-117 D 9
Skagens Horn = Grenen 116-117 D 9
Skagerrak 116-117 B 9-D 8
Skagit River 66-67 C 1
Skagway, AK 56-57 JK 6
Skaland 116-117 G 3
Skalap, Bukit — 152-153 KL 4
Skala-Podol'skaja 126-127 C 2
Skálar 116-117 f 1
Skálholt 116-117 cd 2
Skalistyj Golec, gora — 132-133 WX 6
Skanderborg 116-117 CD 9
Skåne 116-117 E 10
Skanör 116-117 E 10
Skara 116-117 E 8
Skaraborg 116-117 EF 8
Skardū 134-135 M 3
Skarżysko-Kamienna 118 K 3
Skaudvilė 124-125 D 6
Skaw, The — = Grenen 116-117 D 9
Skead 72-73 F 1
Skeena 60 BC 2
Skeena Mountains 56-57 L 6
Skeena River 56-57 L 6
Skegness 119 G 5
Skeidharársandur 116-117 e 3
Skeldon 98-99 K 2
Skellefteå 116-117 J 5
Skellefte älv 116-117 H 5
Skelleftehamn 116-117 JK 5
Skene 116-117 E 9
Skhīrra, Es — = Aṣ-Ṣahīrah 166-167 M 2
Skhoûr, es — = Sukhūr ar-Rihāmnah 166-167 BC 3
Ski 116-117 D 8
Skíathos 122-123 K 6
Skidaway Island 80-81 F 5
Skidegate Inlet 60 AB 3
Skidel' 124-125 E 7
Skidmore, TX 76-77 EF 8
Skien 116-117 C 8
Skierniewice 118 K 3
Skiff 66-67 H 1
Skiftet 116-117 J 7
Skikda = Sakīkdah 164-165 F 1
Skilak Lake 58-59 M 6
Skipskjølen 116-117 NO 2
Skipskop 174-175 D 8
Skive 116-117 C 9
Skjalfandafljót 116-117 e 2
Skjálfandi 116-117 e 1
Skjervøy 116-117 J 2
Skjold 116-117 H 3
Sklad 132-133 X 3
Šklov 124-125 H 6
Skobelev = Fergana 134-135 L 2-3
Skógafoss 116-117 cd 3
Skokie, IL 70-71 FG 4
Skolpen Bank 114-115 OP 1
Skönvik 116-117 G 6
Skópelos 122-123 K 6
Skopin 124-125 M 7
Skopje 122-123 J 4-5
Skoplje = Skopje 122-123 J 4-5
Skorodnoje 126-127 H 1
Skoun 150-151 E 6
Skoûra = Ṣukhūrah 166-167 C 4
Skövde 116-117 EF 8
Skovorodino 132-133 XY 7
Skowhegan, ME 72-73 M 2
Skownan 61 J 5
Skrunda 124-125 CD 5
Skudeneshavn 116-117 A 8
Skuilte 170 V cd 1
Skukuza 172 F 7
Skul'any 126-127 C 3
Skull Valley, AZ 74-75 G 5
Skull Valley Indian Reservation 66-67 G 5
Skulpfonteinpunt 174-175 B 6
Skunk River 70-71 DE 5
Skuodas 124-125 CD 5
Skuratova, mys — 132-133 LM 3
Skutari, İstanbul- = İstanbul-Üsküdar 134-135 BC 2
Skutskär 116-117 GH 7
Skvira 126-127 D 2
Skwentna, AK 58-59 M 6
Skwentna River 58-59 LM 6
Skwierzyna 118 G 2
Skye 119 C 3
Skykomish, WA 66-67 C 2
Skyring, Península — 108-109 B 5
Skyring, Seno — 111 B 8
Skyrópula 122-123 KL 6
Skýros 122-123 L 6

Slā' 164-165 C 2
Slabberts 174-175 H 5
Slagelse 116-117 D 10
Slagnäs 116-117 H 5
Slamet, Gunung — 152-153 H 9
Slana, AK 58-59 PQ 5
Slancy 116-117 N 8
Slangberge 174-175 D 6
Slănic 122-123 L 3
Slate Islands 70-71 G 1
Slater, CO 68-69 C 5
Slater, MO 70-71 D 6
Slatina 122-123 L 3
Slaton, TX 76-77 D 6
Slatoust = Zlatoust 132-133 K 6
Slav'anka 144-145 H 1
Slav'ansk 126-127 HJ 2
Slav'ansk-na-Kubani 126-127 J 4
Slave Coast 164-165 E 7
Slave Lake 60 K 2
Slave River 56-57 O 5-6
Slavgorod [SU, Belorusskaja SSR] 124-125 H 7
Slavgorod [SU, Rossijskaja SFSR] 132-133 O 7
Slavgorod [SU, Ukrainskaja SSR] 126-127 G 2
Slavkov u Brna 118 H 4
Slavonija 122-123 GH 3
Slavonska Požega 122-123 GH 3
Slavonski Brod 122-123 GH 3
Slavskoje [SU, Ukrainskaja SSR] 126-127 A 2
Slavuta 126-127 C 1
Slavyansk = Slav'ansk 126-127 HJ 2
Sławno 118 H 1
Slayton, MN 70-71 BC 3
Sledge Island 58-59 D 4
Sleemanābād 138-139 H 6
Sleeping Bear Point 70-71 G 3
Sleepy Eye, MN 70-71 C 3
Sleetmute, AK 56-57 E 5
Slidell, LA 78-79 E 5
Slide Mountain 72-73 J 3
Sliema 122-123 F 8
Sligeach = Sligo 119 B 4
Sligo 119 B 4
Sligo Branch 82 II ab 1
Slīmanābād = Sleemanābād 138-139 H 6
Slim Buttes 68-69 E 3
Slipi, Jakarta- 154 IV a 2
Slipi Orchid Garden 154 IV a 2
Slissen = Mūlay-Salīsan 166-167 F 2
Slite 116-117 H 9
Sliten = Zlītan 164-165 GH 2
Sliven 122-123 M 4
Slivnica 122-123 K 4
Sloan, IA 68-69 H 4
Sloboda = Liski 126-127 J 1
Slobodčikovo 124-125 QR 3
Slobodka [SU, Ukrainskaja SSR] 126-127 D 3
Slobodskoj 132-133 HJ 6
Slobodzeja 126-127 D 3
Slobozia 122-123 M 3
Slocan 66-67 E 1
Slocan Lake 66-67 E 1
Sloko River 58-59 V 7
Slomichino = Furmanovo 126-127 OP 2
Slonim 124-125 E 7
Slot, The — 148-149 j 6
Sloter plas 128 I a 1
Slotervaar, Amsterdam- 128 I a 1
Slough 119 F 6
Sloûk = Sulūk 136-137 H 4
Slovenia 122-123 F 3-G 2
Slovenské rudohorie 118 JK 4
Slovinka 124-125 O 4
Sluč' 126-127 C 1
Sluck 124-125 F 7
Sl'ud'anka 132-133 T 7
Sludka 124-125 S 3
Slunj 122-123 F 3
Słupsk 118 H 1
Slurry 174-175 FG 3

Smach 150-151 D 7
Smackover, AR 78-79 C 4
Smala des Souassi, la — = Zamālat as-Suwāsī 166-167 M 2
Småland 116-117 EF 9
Smalininkai 124-125 D 6
Small, ID 66-67 G 3
Small Point 72-73 M 3
S'marah 164-165 B 3
Smederevo 122-123 J 3
Smela 126-127 E 2
Smeloje 126-127 FG 1
Smeru = Gunung Semeru 148-149 F 8
Smethport, PA 72-73 G 4
Šmidta, ostrov — 132-133 QR 1
Smiley 61 D 5
Smiley, Cape — 53 B 29
Smiltene 124-125 EF 5
Smith [CDN] 56-57 O 6-7
Smith [RA] 106-107 G 5
Smith Arm 56-57 M 4
Smith Bay 58-59 KL 1
Smith Center, KS 68-69 G 6
Smithers 56-57 L 7
Smithfield 174-175 G 6
Smithfield, NC 80-81 G 3
Smithfield, UT 66-67 H 5
Smithfield, VA 80-81 H 2
Smith Inlet 60 CD 4
Smith Island [CDN] 56-57 V 5
Smith Island [USA] 80-81 H 4
Smith River 66-67 H 2
Smith River, CA 66-67 A 5
Smiths Creek Valley 74-75 E 3
Smith's Falls 56-57 V 9
Smiths Ferry, ID 66-67 EF 3
Smiths Grove, KY 70-71 G 7
Smith Sound 56-57 W 2
Smithton 158-159 HJ 8
Smithtown 160 L 3
Smithville, GA 80-81 DE 5
Smithville, TN 78-79 G 2
Smithville, TX 76-77 F 7-8
Smjörfjöll 116-117 f 2
Smögen 116-117 D 8
Smoke Creek Desert 66-67 D 5
Smoky Bay 160 A 4
Smoky Cape 160 L 3
Smoky Falls 62 K 1
Smoky Hill River 64-65 FG 4
Smoky Hill River, North Fork — 68-69 EF 6
Smoky Hills 68-69 G 6
Smoky Lake 61 BC 3
Smoky Mountains 66-67 F 4
Smoky River 56-57 N 7
Smøla 116-117 B 6
Smol'an 122-123 L 5
Smolensk 124-125 J 6
Smolenskaja vozvyšennost 124-125 H-K 6
Smoleviči 124-125 G 6
Smōlikas 122-123 J 5
Smoot, WY 66-67 H 4
Smooth Rock Falls 62 L 2
Smoothrock Lake 62 DE 2
Smoothstone Lake 61 E 3
Smoothstone River 61 E 3
Smorgon' 124-125 F 6
Smotrič 126-127 C 2
Smyrna, GA 85 II a 1
Smyrna, TN 78-79 F 2-3
Smyrna = İzmir 134-135 B 3
Smyth, Canal — 108-109 B 8-C 9

Snaefell [GB] 119 D 4
Snæfell [IS] 116-117 f 2
Snæfellsjökull 116-117 ab 2
Snæfellsnes 116-117 b 2
Snag 56-57 HJ 5
Snaipol 150-151 E 7
Snake Creek [USA, Nebraska] 68-69 F 4
Snake Creek [USA, South Dakota] 68-69 G 3
Snake Range 74-75 F 3
Snake River [USA ◁ Columbia River] 64-65 C 2
Snake River [USA ◁ Croix River] 70-71 D 2-3
Snake River Canyon 66-67 E 3
Snake River Plains 64-65 D 3
Snake Valley 74-75 G 3
Snåsa 116-117 E 5
Sn'atyn 126-127 B 2
Sneeuberg 174-175 C 7
Sneeuberge 174-175 F 6
Sneeukop 174-175 C 7
Snežnoje 126-127 J 2
Śniardwy, Jezioro — 118 K 2
Sniežka 118 GH 3
Snigir'ovka 126-127 F 3
Snipe Lake 60 J 2
Snøhetta 116-117 C 6
Snohomish, WA 66-67 BC 2
Snoqualmie Pass 66-67 C 2
Snota 116-117 C 6
Snøtind 116-117 E 4
Snoul 150-151 F 6
Snov 124-125 H 8
Snowden, MT 68-69 D 1-2
Snowdon 119 DE 5
Snowdrift 56-57 OP 5
Snowflake, AZ 74-75 H 5
Snow Hill, MD 72-73 J 5
Snow Hill Island 53 C 31
Snow Lake 61 H 3
Snow Road 72-73 H 2
Snowshoe Peak 66-67 F 1
Snowtown 160 CD 4
Snowville, UT 66-67 G 5
Snowy Mountains 158-159 J 7
Snowy River 160 J 6
Snug Corner 88-89 K 3
Snyder, OK 76-77 E 5
Snyder, TX 64-65 F 5

Soacha 94-95 D 5
Soacha, Río — 91 III a 4
Soai Dao, Phu — 150-151 C 4
Soalala 172 HJ 5
Soanierana-Ivongo 172 JK 5
Soan-kundo 144-145 F 5
Soap Lake, WA 66-67 D 2
Soasiu 148-149 J 6
Soatá 94-95 E 4
Soavinandriana 172 J 5
Sobaek-sanmaek 144-145 F 5-G 4
Sôbâṭ, Nahr — = As-Sūbāṭ 164-165 L 7
Sobinka 124-125 N 6
Sobolev 124-125 S 8
Sobolevo 132-133 e 7
Sobo-zan 144-145 H 6
Sobozo 164-165 GH 4
Sobradinho [BR, Distrito Federal] 102-103 J 1
Sobradinho [BR, Pará] 98-99 K 7
Sobradinho [BR, Rio Grande do Sul] 106-107 L 2
Sobradinho, Represa — 100-101 C 6-D 5
Sobrado [BR] 92-93 J 6
Sobral [BR, Acre] 96-97 E 6
Sobral [BR, Ceará] 92-93 L 5
Soca [ROU] 106-107 K 5
Socavão 102-103 H 6
Socgorodok 126-127 J 1
Socha 92-93 E 3
Sochaczew 118 K 2
Soche = Yarkand 142-143 D 4
Sŏch'ŏn 144-145 F 4
Sochor, gora — 132-133 TU 7
Soči 126-127 J 5
Soči-Adler 126-127 J 5
Soči-Dagomys 126-127 J 5
Sociedade Hípica Paulista 110 II a 2
Society Islands 156-157 K 5
Soči-Lazarevskoje 126-127 J 5
Socompa, Portezuelo de — 104-105 B 9
Socompa, Volcán — 111 C 2
Socorro, NM 76-77 A 5-6
Socorro [BR] 102-103 J 5
Socorro [CO] 92-93 E 3
Socorro, El — [MEX] 76-77 C 9
Socorro, El — [RA] 106-107 G 4
Socorro, El — [YV] 94-95 J 3
Socorro, Isla — 64-65 DE 8
Socorro, São Paulo- 110 II a 2
Socoto = Sokoto 164-165 EF 6
Socotra = Suquṭrā' 134-135 G 8
Soc Trăng = Khanh Hu'ng 150-151 E 8
Socuéllamos 120-121 F 9
Sôdâ, Gebel es — = Jabal as-Sawdā' 164-165 GH 3
Soda Creek 60 F 3
Soda Lake 74-75 F 5
Sodankylä 116-117 LM 4
Soda Springs, ID 66-67 H 4
Soddu = Sodo 164-165 M 7
Soddy, TN 78-79 G 3
Sodegaura 155 III c 3
Söderhamn 116-117 G 7
Söderköping 116-117 G 8
Södermanland 116-117 G 8
Södertälje 116-117 GH 8
Sodīrī = Sawdirī 164-165 K 6
Sodium 174-175 E 6
Sodo 164-165 M 7
Sodom = Sĕdōm 136-137 F 7
Sodpur, Pānihāti- 154 II b 1
Sodus, NY 72-73 H 3
Soe 152-153 Q 10
Soekmekaar 172 E 6
Soela väin 124-125 D 4
Soen, Nam — = Nam Choen 150-151 CD 4
Soest 118 D 3
Sœurs, Île des — 82 I b 2
Sofala, Baía de — 172 FG 6
Sofala, Manica e — 172 F 5-6
Sofia 172 J 5
Sofia = Sofija 122-123 K 4
Sofija 122-123 K 4
Sofijevka = Červonoarmejskoje 126-127 GH 3
Sofijsk 132-133 Z 7
Sofporog 116-117 O 5
Soga 171 D 4
Soga, Quebrada de — 104-105 B 6
Sogakofe 168-169 F 4
Sogamoso 92-93 E 3
Sogamoso, Río — 94-95 E 4
Soğanlı çayı 136-137 E 2
Sogndalstrand 116-117 B 8
Sognefjord 116-117 AB 7
Sogn og Fjordane 116-117 AB 7
Söğüt 136-137 D 2-3
Söğütlü dere 136-137 G 3
Sogwip'o 144-145 F 6
Sōhâg = Sawhāj 164-165 L 3
Sohāgpur [IND → Jabalpur] 138-139 H 6
Sohāgpur [IND ↙ Jabalpur] 138-139 G 6
Sŏhan-man 142-143 NO 4
Sohano 148-149 h 6
Sohar = Ṣuḥār 134-135 H 6
Sohela 138-139 J 7
Sohella = Sohela 138-139 J 7
Sohna 138-139 F 3
Soho, London- 129 II b 1
So-hŭksan-do 144-145 E 5
Soi Dao, Khao — 150-151 B 9
Soi Dao Tai, Khao — 150-151 CD 6
Soignes, Fôret de — 128 II b 2
Soissons 120-121 J 4
Soitué 106-107 CD 5
Sōja 144-145 J 5
S'ojacha 132-133 N 3
Sojakpur 138-139 C 6
Sojat 138-139 D 5
Sojga 124-125 P 2
Sojiji Temple 155 III ab 2
Sojna [IND] 138-139 G 5
Šojna [SU] 132-133 G 4
Sŏjosŏn-man = Sŏhan-man 142-143 NO 4
Sok 124-125 S 6
Sokal' 126-127 B 1
Šokal'skogo, ostrov — 132-133 NO 3
Šokal'skogo, proliv — 132-133 RS 2
Söke 134-135 B 3
Sokhna = Sawkhah 164-165 GH 3
Sokku Wan 155 I a 2
Sokkloko 174-175 E 3
Sokodé 164-165 E 7
Sokol 132-133 G 5-6
Sokolji gory 124-125 S 7
Sokółka 118 L 2
Sokol'niki, PkiO — 113 V c 2
Sokolo 164-165 C 6
Sokołów Podlaski 118 L 2
Sokol'skoje 124-125 O 5
Sokotindji 168-169 F 3
Sokoto [WAN, administrative unit] 168-169 G 3
Sokoto [WAN, place] 164-165 EF 6
Sokoto [WAN, river] 164-165 E 6
Sokotra = Suquṭrā' 134-135 G 8
Sŏkpa 148-149 C 3
Sokskije jary 124-125 S 7-T 6
Sŏk-to 144-145 E 3
So Kun Tan 155 I a 1
Sol, Costa del — 120-121 EF 10
Sol, Isla del — 104-105 B 4-5
Solá [RA] 106-107 H 4
Sola de Vega 86-87 M 9
Solai 172 G 1-2
Solaklı 136-137 J 2
Solander, Cape — 161 I b 3
Solander Island 161 B 8
Solânea 100-101 G 4
Solanet 106-107 H 6
Sol'anka 124-125 RS 8
Solano, NM 76-77 BC 5
Solano, Bahía — 94-95 C 4
Solapur = Sholāpur 134-135 M 7
Sol'cy 124-125 H 4
Soldedad 92-93 DE 2
Sol de Julio 106-107 F 2
Soldier Fields 83 II b 1
Soldotna, AK 58-59 M 6
Soledad, CA 74-75 C 4
Soledad [MEX] 76-77 D 9
Soledad [RA] 106-107 G 3
Soledad [RCH] 104-105 B 7
Soledad [YV] 92-93 G 3
Soledad, Isla — = East Falkland 111 E 8
Soledad Díez Gutiérrez 86-87 K 6
Soledade [BR, Amazonas] 98-99 D 8
Soledade [BR, Rio Grande do Sul] 106-107 L 2
Soledade [BR, Roraima] 98-99 H 3
Soledade, Cachoeira — 98-99 LM 7
Solesmes 120-121 G 5
Soleure = Solothurn 118 C 5
Soleymān, Takht-e — 136-137 O 4
Solfonn 116-117 B 8
Solheim 170 V b 2
Soligalič 124-125 NO 4
Soligorsk 124-125 F 7
Solihull 119 F 5
Solikamsk 132-133 K 6
Sol'-Ileck 132-133 JK 7
Solīmān = Sulaymān 166-167 M 1
Solimões, Rio — 92-93 G 5
Solingen 118 C 3
Solís [RA] 106-107 H 5
Solís [ROU] 106-107 K 5
Solita, La — 94-95 F 3
Solitaire 174-175 AB 2
Sollefteå 116-117 G 6
Sóller 120-121 J 9
Sollum = As-Salūm 164-165 K 2
Sol-lun = Solon 142-143 N 2
Solna 116-117 GH 8
Solnceva 113 V a 3
Solnečnogorsk 124-125 L 5
Solo 168-169 D 3
Solo = Surakarta 148-149 F 8
Sologne 120-121 HJ 5
Šologoncy 132-133 VW 4
Solok 148-149 D 7
Sololá 86-87 P 10
Solomennoje 124-125 K 3
Solomon, AK 58-59 E 4
Solomon, KS 68-69 H 6
Solomondale 174-175 HJ 2
Solomon Islands [archipelago] 148-149 h 6-k 7
Solomon Islands [Solomon Is., state] 148-149 kl 7
Solomon River 68-69 GH 6
Solomon River, North Fork — 68-69 FG 6
Solomon River, South Fork — 68-69 F 6
Solomons Basin 148-149 h 6
Solomon Sea 148-149 hj 6
Solon, IA 70-71 E 5
Solončak Šalkarteniz 132-133 L 8
Solong Cheer = Sulan Cheer 142-143 K 3
Sol'onoje Ozero 126-127 G 4
Solonópole 100-101 E 3
Solon Springs, WI 70-71 DE 2
Solor, Kepulauan — 152-153 P 10
Solor, Pulau — 148-149 H 8
Solothurn 118 C 5
Soloveckije ostrova 132-133 F 4
Šolta 122-123 G 4
Solṭān, Bīr — = Bi'r Sulṭān 166-167 L 3
Solṭānābād = Arāk 134-135 F 4
Solṭānīyeh 136-137 N 4
Soltau 118 DE 2
Soluch = Sulūq 164-165 J 2
Solun 142-143 N 2
Soluq = Sulūq 164-165 J 2
Solvay, NY 72-73 H 3
Sölvesborg 116-117 F 9
Sol'vyčegodsk 132-133 H 5
Solway Firth 119 DE 4
Solwezi 172 E 4
Solza 124-125 M 1
Sōma [J] 144-145 N 4
Soma [TR] 136-137 B 3
Somabhula 172 E 5
Somalia 164-165 N 8-O 7
Somali Basin 50-51 M 5-6
Sōmapēṭa = Sompeta 138-139 K 8
Sōma Tsangpo 138-139 K 2
Sombor 122-123 H 3
Sombrerete 86-87 J 6
Sombrerito, El — 106-107 H 2
Sombrero 88-89 P 5
Sombrero, El — [RA] 106-107 H 1
Sombrero, El — [YV] 92-93 F 3
Sombrio 106-107 N 2
Sombye 138-139 M 4
Şomcuta Mare 122-123 K 2
Somerdale, NJ 84 III c 2
Somero 116-117 K 7
Somers, MT 66-67 F 1
Somerset, CO 68-69 C 6
Somerset, KY 70-71 H 7
Somerset, PA 72-73 G 4-5
Somerset [AUS] 158-159 H 2
Somerset [CDN] 68-69 G 1
Somerset East = Somerset-Oos 172 DE 8
Somerset Island 56-57 S 3
Somerset-Oos 172 DE 8
Somerset-Wes 174-175 C 8
Somersworth, NH 72-73 L 3
Somerton, AZ 74-75 F 6
Somerton, Philadelphia-, PA 84 III c 1
Somerville, MA 72-73 L 3
Somerville, NJ 72-73 J 4
Somerville, TN 78-79 E 3
Somerville, TX 76-77 F 7
Someş 122-123 K 2
Somesbar, CA 66-67 B 5
Somkele 174-175 K 5
Somme 120-121 H 3
Sommerset, MD 82 II a 1
Somnāth 138-139 C 7
Sompeta 138-139 K 8
Somuncurá, Meseta de — 111 C 6
Son [IND] 134-135 N 6
Son, Mu'o'ng — 150-151 D 2
Sona 88-89 F 11
Sonahula 138-139 L 5
Sonai 141 C 4
Sonaimuri = Sonāymurī 141 B 4
Sonāmukhī 138-139 L 6
Sonār 138-139 GH 5
Sonārī 141 D 2
Sonāymurī 141 B 4
Sonbarsa 138-139 K 4
Sonbarsa Raj 138-139 L 5
Sŏnch'ŏn 144-145 E 3
Sondagsrivier 174-175 F 7
Sønderborg 116-117 CD 10
Sondershausen 118 E 3
Sondheimer, LA 78-79 D 4
Søndre Kvaløy 116-117 GH 3
Søndre Strømfjord 56-57 a 4
Søndre Strømfjord = Kangerdlugssuaq 56-57 ab 4
Sondrio 122-123 CD 2
Sonduga 124-125 NO 3
Sonepat 138-139 F 3
Sonepur 138-139 J 7
Song [MAL] 152-153 K 4
Song [T] 150-151 C 3
Songarh 138-139 D 7
Songbai 146-147 D 8
Sông Be 150-151 F 7
Sông Boung 150-151 F 5
Songbu 146-147 E 6
Sông Bung = Sông Boung 150-151 F 5
Sông Ca 150-151 E 3
Sông Câu 150-151 E 2
Sông Chây 150-151 E 1
Songch'on 144-145 F 3
Sông Chu 150-151 E 3
Sông Đa 148-149 D 2
Songea 172 G 4
Songfou = Songbu 146-147 E 6
Sông Gâm 150-151 E 1
Songhua Hu 142-143 O 3
Songhua Jiang 142-143 O 2
Songhwan 144-145 F 4
Songjiang 142-143 N 5
Songjiangzhen 144-145 F 1
Songjin = Kim Chak 142-143 OP 3
Songjŏng-ni 144-145 F 5
Songkhla 148-149 D 5
Song Khôn = Ban Sông Khôn 150-151 E 3
Song Khone = Mu'o'ng Song Khone 150-151 E 4
Songkhram, Mae Nam — 150-151 DE 3-4
Songkla = Songkhla 148-149 D 5
Songkou 146-147 G 9
Sông La Nga 150-151 F 7
Sông Lô 150-151 E 2
Sông Ma 150-151 E 2
Songmen 146-147 H 7
Songnae-ri = Inhung-ni 144-145 F 3
Song Nhi Ha 148-149 D 2
Songnim 142-143 O 4
Songo 172 BC 3
Sông Ông Đốc 150-151 E 8
Songpan 142-143 J 5
Song Phi Nong 150-151 BC 5
Songrougrou 168-169 B 2
Song Shan 146-147 D 4
Songtao 146-147 B 7
Sông Tra 150-151 G 5
Songwe 171 C 5
Songwood, Houston-, TX 85 III bc 1
Songxi 146-147 G 8
Song Xian 146-147 CD 4
So'n Ha 150-151 G 5
Sonhaolā = Sonahula 138-139 L 5
Sonhāt 134-135 N 6
So'n Hoa 150-151 G 6
Sŏnkach 138-139 F 6
Sonkatch = Sŏnkach 138-139 F 6
Sonkovo 132-133 F 6
So'n La 150-151 D 2
Sonmiani = Sonmiyānī 134-135 K 5
Sonmiyānī 134-135 K 5
Sonmiyānī, Khalīj — 134-135 J 6-K 5
Sonneberg 118 E 3
Sono, Rio do — [BR, Goiás] 92-93 K 6-7
Sono, Rio do — [BR, Minas Gerais] 102-103 K 2
Sonoita 86-87 D 2
Sonoma, CA 74-75 B 3
Sonoma Range 66-67 E 5
Sonora 64-65 DE 6
Sonora, AZ 74-75 H 6
Sonora, CA 74-75 C 3-4
Sonora, TX 76-77 D 7
Sonora Peak 74-75 D 3
Sonqor 136-137 M 5
Sonsón 92-93 DE 3
Sonsonate 64-65 HJ 9
Sonsorol 148-149 K 5
Sonstraal 174-175 E 4
So'n Tây 150-151 E 2
Sopachuy 104-105 D 6
Soperton, GA 80-81 E 4
Sop Hao 150-151 E 2
Sop Khao 150-151 D 3
Sŏp'o-ri 144-145 FG 2
Sopot 118 J 1
Sop Prap 150-151 B 4
Sopron 118 H 5
Sop's Arm Provincial Park 63 H 3
Sor 120-121 C 9
Sora 122-123 E 5
Sorab 140 B 3
Sŏraba = Sorab 140 B 3
Sorada 138-139 K 8
Sorāh 138-139 B 4
Sŏrak-san 144-145 G 3
Soraon 138-139 H 5
Sorapa 96-97 G 10
Sorata 104-105 B 4
Sŏraṭh 138-139 BC 7
Sŏrath = Jūnāgaṛh 134-135 KL 6
Şorba 136-137 E 2
Sorbas 120-121 FG 10
Sorbhog 141 B 2
Sorbonne 129 I c 2
Sordwanabaai 174-175 K 4
Sorel 56-57 W 8
Sorell 160 cd 3
Sorell, Cape — 158-159 HJ 8

Sorell 363

Sorell, Lake — 160 c 2
Soren Arwa = Selat Yapen
148-149 L 7
Sørfonna 116-117 lm 5
Sòrgono 122-123 C 5
Sorgun = Büyük Köhne
136-137 F 3
Sörhäd = Sarhade Wākhān
134-135 L 3
Soria 120-121 F 8
Soriano [ROU, administrative unit]
106-107 HJ 4
Soriano [ROU, place] 106-107 H 4
Sorikmarapi, Gunung —
152-153 C 5
Sørkapp 116-117 k 6
Sørkapp land 116-117 k 6
Sørkjosen 116-117 J 3
Sorø [DK] 116-117 D 10
Soro [IND] 138-139 L 7
Soro [YV] 94-95 K 2
Sorocaba 111 G 2
Soročinka [SU, Kazachskaja SSR]
126-127 PQ 3
Soročinsk 132-133 J 7
Soroka = Belomorsk 132-133 EF 5
Soroki 126-127 CD 2
Sorokino = Krasnodon
126-127 JK 2
Sorol 148-149 M 5
Soron 138-139 G 4
Sorong 148-149 K 7
Soroti 172 F 1
Sørøy 116-117 K 2
Sørøysund 116-117 K 2
Sorraia 120-121 C 9
Sør-Randane 53 B 2-3
Sorrento 122-123 F 5
Sorsele 116-117 G 5
Sør-Shetland = South Shetlands
53 C 30
Sorsogon 148-149 HJ 4
Sortavala 132-133 E 5
Sorte Gobi = Char Gov'
142-143 GH 3
Sortija, La — 106-107 G 7
Sortland 116-117 F 3
Sør-Trøndelag 116-117 CD 6
Sørvågen 116-117 E 4
Sõrve 124-125 D 5
Sõrve säär 124-125 CD 5
Šorža 126-127 M 6
Sosa [PY] 102-103 D 7
Sōsan 144-145 F 4
Soscumica, Lac — 62 N 1
Sosedka 124-125 O 7
Sosenka 113 V ab 4
Sosenki 113 V b 3
Soshigaya, Tōkyō- 155 III a 2
Sosneado, El — 106-107 BC 5
Sosnica 126-127 F 1
Sosnogorsk 132-133 JK 5
Sosnovka [SU, Kirovskaja Oblast']
124-125 S 5
Sosnovka [SU, Tambovskaja Oblast']
124-125 N 7
Sosnovka, Čeboksary- 124-125 QR 5
Sosnovo 124-125 H 3
Sosnovoborsk 124-125 Q 7
Sosnovo-Oz'orskoje 132-133 V 7
Sosnovyj Solonec 124-125 RS 7
Sosnowiec 118 J 3
Sossenheim, Frankfurt am Main-
128 III a 1
Sossusvlei 174-175 A 3
Šostka 124-125 J 8
Sōsura 144-145 H 1
Sos'va [SU ↘ Serov] 132-133 L 6
Sos'va [SU, Chanty-Mansijskij NO]
132-133 L 5
Sosyka 126-127 J 3
Sota 168-169 F 3
Sotara 94-95 C 6
Sotará, Volcán — 94-95 C 6
So-tch'ê = Yarkand 142-143 D 4
Sotério, Rio — 98-99 F 10
Sotkamo 116-117 N 5
Soto 106-107 E 3
Soto, Cerro de — 106-107 B 3
Sotra 116-117 A 7
Souakria 170 I b 2
Souanké 172 B 1
Šoûâr = Aş-Şuwār 136-137 J 5
Soubré 164-165 C 7
Soudan 158-159 G 4
Soudana 168-169 H 1
Souf = Şūf 166-167 K 3
Souf, Aïn — = 'Ayn Şūf
166-167 H 5
Souf, Hassi — = Ḥāssī Şūf
166-167 F 5
Soufrière 64-65 O 9
Sougueur = Sūgar 166-167 G 2
Souillac 120-121 H 6
Souk-Ahras = Sūq Ahrās
164-165 F 1
Souk el Arba des Aït Baha = Sūq al-
Arba'ā' al-Aït Bāhā 166-167 B 4
Souk el Arba du Rhab = Sūq al-
Arb'ā' 166-167 CD 2
Souk el Khemis = Bū Sālām
166-167 L 1
Souk el Tleta = As-Sars
166-167 L 1
Soukhouma = Ban Sukhouma
150-151 E 5
Sǒul 142-143 O 4
Souloungou 168-169 F 2
Soum, Muong — = Mu'o'ng Soum
150-151 D 3
Sound, The — 161 I b 1
Sound, The — = Öresund
116-117 E 10
Sounders Island 108-109 J 8
Sounding Creek 61 C 5
Sound of Jura 119 D 4
Soundview, New York-, NY 82 III c 2
Soûq el Arb'â' = Jundūbah
166-167 L 1
Soûq el Arba = Sūq al-Arb'ā'
166-167 C 2
Soûq el Khemîs = Bū Sālām
166-167 L 1
Soûq Jema'â' Oûlâd 'Abou = Awlād
Abū 166-167 BC 3
Sources, Mont aux — 172 E 7
Soure [BR] 92-93 K 5
Sour-el-Ghozlane = Sūr al-Ghuzlān
166-167 HJ 1
Souris, ND 68-69 F 1
Souris [CDN, Manitoba] 61 H 6
Souris [CDN, Prince Edward I.] 63 E 4
Souris River 56-57 Q 8
Sourlake, TX 76-77 G 7
Sousa 92-93 M 6
Soûssâ = Sūsah 136-137 J 5
Sousse = Sūsah 164-165 G 1
Sout 174-175 C 6
Sout Doringrivier 174-175 C 6
South Africa 172 D-F 7
Southall, London- 129 II a 1
South Alligator River 158-159 F 2
South America 50-51 FG 6
Southampton, NY 72-73 KL 4
Southampton [CDN] 72-73 F 2
Southampton [GB] 119 F 6
Southampton Island 56-57 TU 5
South Andaman 134-135 P 8
South Auckland-Bay of Plenty
161 FG 3-4
South Aulatsivik Island 56-57 YZ 6
South Australia 158-159 E-G 5-6
South Australian Basin 50-51 PQ 8
South Baldy 76-77 A 5-6
South Banda Basin 148-149 J 8
South Baymouth 62 K 4
South Beach, New York-, NY
82 III b 3
South Bend, IN 64-65 JK 3
South Bend, WA 66-67 B 2
South Bend Park 85 II b 2
South Boston, VA 80-81 G 2
South Boston, Boston-, MA 84 I b 2
South Boston High School 84 I bc 2
South Branch Potomac River
72-73 G 5
South Brooklyn, New York-, NY
82 III bc 2
South Bruny 160 cd 3
South Carolina 64-65 K 5
South Charleston, OH 72-73 E 5
South Charleston, WV 72-73 EF 5
South Chicago, Chicago-, IL 83 II b 2
South China Basin 148-149 FG 3-4
South China Sea 142-143 L 8-M 7
South Dakota 64-65 FG 3
South Dum Dum 134-135 OP 6
South East Cape 158-159 J 8
Southeast Indian Basin 50-51 OP 7
Southeast Pacific Basin
156-157 MN 7-8
Southeast Pass 78-79 E 6
South East Point 160 H 7
South El Monte, CA 83 III d 1
Southend [CDN] 56-57 PQ 6
Southend-on-Sea 119 G 6
Southern [WAL] 168-169 BC 4
Southern [Z] 172 E 5
Southern Alps 158-159 NO 8
Southern California, University of —
83 III c 1
Southern Cross 158-159 CD 6
Southern Indian Lake 56-57 R 6
Southern Moscos = Launglônbôk
Kyûnzu 150-151 A 6
Southern Oaks, Houston-, TX
85 III b 2
Southern Pacific Railway 64-65 EF 5
Southern Pine Hills = Pine Hills
64-65 J 5
Southern Pines, NC 80-81 G 3
Southern Sierra Madre = Sierra
Madre del Sur 64-65 FG 8
Southern Uplands 119 DE 4
Southern Ute Indian Reservation
68-69 BC 7
Southeyville 174-175 G 6
South Fiji Basin 158-159 OP 4-5
South Fork, CO 68-69 C 7
South Fork Clearwater River
66-67 F 3
South Fork Flathead River 66-67 G 2
South Fork Grand River 68-69 E 3
South Fork John Day River
66-67 D 3
South Fork Koyukuk 58-59 M 3
South Fork Kuskokwim 58-59 KL 5
South Fork Moreau River 68-69 E 3
South Fork Mountains 66-67 B 5
South Fork Owyhee River
66-67 E 4-5
South Fork Peachtree Creek 85 II c 2
South Fork Powder River 68-69 C 4
South Fork Republican River
68-69 E 6
South Fork Salmon River 66-67 F 3
South Fork Solomon River 68-69 F 6
South Fork White River 68-69 F 4
South Fox Island 70-71 GH 3
South Gate, CA 74-75 DE 6
Southgate, London- 129 II b 1
South Georgia 111 J 8
South Georgia Ridge 50-51 H 8
South Grand River 70-71 CD 6
South Haven, KS 76-77 F 4
South Haven, MI 70-71 G 4
South Head 161 I b 1-2
South Henik Lake 56-57 R 5
South Hill, VA 80-81 G 2
South Hills, Johannesburg- 170 V b 2
South Honshu Ridge 142-143 R 5-6
South Horr 172 G 1
South Houston, TX 85 III c 2
South Indian Lake [CDN, place]
61 J 2
South Indian Ridge 50-51 OP 8
South Island 158-159 OP 8
South Junction 70-71 BC 1
South Koel 138-139 K 6
South Korea 142-143 OP 4
Southland 161 BC 7
South Lawn, MD 82 II b 2
South Loup River 68-69 FG 5
South Lynnfield, MA 84 I c 1
Southmag 72-73 FG 2
South Magnetic Pole Area
53 C 14-15
South Main Estates, Houston-, TX
85 III ab 2
South Male Atoll 176 ab 2
South Malosmadulu Atoll 176 a 1-2
South Mangsi Island 152-153 MN 2
South Media, PA 84 III a 2
South Melbourne, Melbourne-
161 II b 1-2
South Milwaukee, WI 70-71 G 4
South Moose Lake 61 H 4
South Mountain 72-73 H 4-5
South Nahanni River 56-57 LM 5
South Natuna Islands = Kepulauan
Bunguran Selatan 148-149 E 6
South Negril Point 88-89 G 5
South Ogden, UT 66-67 H 5
South Orkneys 53 C 32
South Ossetian Autonomous Region
126-127 LM 5
South Pacific Basin 156-157 KL 6-7
South Padre Island 76-77 F 9
South Pageh = Pulau Pagai Selatan
148-149 CD 7
South Paris, ME 72-73 L 2
South Pasadena, CA 83 III cd 1
South Pass [USA, Louisiana]
64-65 J 6
South Pass [USA, Wyoming]
64-65 E 3
South Philadelphia, Philadelphia-, PA
84 III bc 2
South Platte River 64-65 F 3
South Porcupine 62 L 2
Southport, NC 80-81 GH 3
Southport [AUS] 160 c 3
Southport, Gold Coast- 160 LM 1
South Portland, ME 72-73 LM 3
South Reservoir 84 I b 2
South River [CDN, place] 72-73 G 2
South River [CDN, river] 72-73 G 1-2
South River [USA] 85 II b 2
South Ronaldsay 119 EF 2
South Saint Paul, MN 70-71 D 3
South Sālmāra 138-139 N 5
South Sandwich Islands 53 CD 34
South Sandwich Trench 53 D 34
South San Gabriel, CA 83 III d 1
South Saskatchewan River
56-57 OP 7
South Seal River 61 J 2
South Shetlands 53 C 30
South Shields 119 F 4
South Shore, Chicago-, IL 83 II b 2
South Sioux City, NE 68-69 H 4
South Suburbs 138-139 LM 6
South Suburbs-Chakdaha 154 II ab 3
South Suburbs-Joka 154 II a 3
South Suburbs-Russa 154 II ab 3
South Suburbs-Satsuna 154 II a 3
South Suburbs-Thākurpukur
154 II a 3
South Sulphur River 76-77 G 6
South Taranaki Bight 158-159 O 7
South Tent 74-75 H 3
South Tyrol 122-123 D 2
South Uist 119 BC 3
South Umpqua River 66-67 B 4
Southview Cemetery 85 II bc 2
South Wabasca Lake 60 L 2
Southwark, London- 129 II b 2
South West Cape [AUS] 160 bc 3
Southwest Cape [NZ] 158-159 N 9
Southwest Cay 64-65 KL 9
Southwest Indian Basin 50-51 MN 7
Southwest Miramichi River 63 CD 4
Southwest Museum 83 III c 1
Southwest Pass [USA, Mississippi
River Delta] 64-65 J 6
Southwest Pass [USA, Vermillion Bay]
78-79 C 6
South Williamsport, PA 72-73 H 4
Soutpansberge 172 EF 6
Soutrivier [ZA ◁ Atlantic Ocean]
174-175 B 6
Soutrivier [ZA ◁ Grootrivier]
174-175 E 7
Souzel 92-93 J 5
Sovdozero 124-125 J 2
Soven 106-107 E 5
Sovetsk [SU, Kaliningradskaja Oblast']
118 K 1
Sovetsk [SU, Kirovskaja Oblast']
132-133 H 6
Sovetskaja 126-127 KL 2
Sovetskaja Gavan' 132-133 ab 8
Sovetskij [SU, Rossijskaja SFSR]
124-125 G 3
Sovetskij [SU, Ukrainskaja SSR]
126-127 G 4
Sovetskoje [SU, Čečeno-Ingušskaja
ASSR] 126-127 MN 5
Sovetskoje [SU, Saratovskaja Oblast']
124-125 Q 8
Soviet Union 132-133 E-b 5
Sowden Lake 70-71 E 1
Soweto, Johannesburg- 174-175 G 4
Sōya [J, Hokkaidō] 144-145 b 1
Sōya [J, Tōkyō] 155 III c 1
Sōya-kaikyō 142-143 R 2
Sōya misaki 144-145 bc 1
Söylemez = Mescitli 136-137 JK 3
Soyo 172 B 3
Soyopa 86-87 F 3
Sož 124-125 H 7
Sozing 138-139 M 4
Sozopol 122-123 MN 4
Spadenland, Hamburg- 130 I b 2
Spafarief Bay 58-59 FG 3
Spain 120-121 E 7-F 9
Špakovskoje 126-127 L 4
Spalato = Split 122-123 G 4
Spalding, ID 66-67 E 2
Spalding, NE 68-69 G 5
Spalding [AUS] 160 D 4
Spalding [GB] 119 FG 5
Spandauer Zitadelle 130 III a 1
Spangle, WA 66-67 E 2
Spanish Fork, UT 66-67 H 5
Spanish Head 119 D 4
Spanish Peak = West Spanish Peak
68-69 D 7
Spanish Town 64-65 L 8
Sparta, Akrōtērion — 122-123 KL 8
Sparbu 116-117 D 6
Spåre 124-125 D 5
Sparkman, AR 78-79 C 3-4
Sparks, GA 80-81 E 5
Sparks, NV 74-75 D 3
Sparta, GA 80-81 E 4
Sparta, IL 70-71 F 6
Sparta, MI 70-71 H 4
Sparta, NC 80-81 F 2
Sparta, TN 78-79 G 3
Sparta, WI 70-71 E 4
Sparta = Spártē 122-123 K 7
Spartanburg, SC 64-65 K 4-5
Spártē 122-123 K 7
Spartel, Cap — = Rā's Ashaqār
166-167 CD 2
Spartel, Cape — = Rā's Ashaqār
166-167 CD 2
Spartivento, Capo — [I, Calàbria]
122-123 G 7
Spartivento, Capo — [I, Sardegna]
122-123 G 6
Spasporub 124-125 R 3
Spassk = Kujbyšev 132-133 HJ 7
Spassk = Spassk-Dal'nij
132-133 Z 9
Spasskaja Guba 124-125 J 2
Spassk-Dal'nij 132-133 Z 9
Spasskoje [SU, Kostroma]
124-125 Q 4
Spassk-R'azanskij 124-125 N 6
Spatsizi River 58-59 X 8
Spearfish, SD 68-69 E 3
Spearhill 61 JK 5
Spearman, TX 76-77 D 4
Spearville, KS 68-69 G 7
Spectacle Island 84 I c 3
Spectrum 84 III bc 2
Speedwell Island 108-109 JK 9
Speising, Wien- 113 I b 2
Speke Gulf 172 F 2
Spelman College 85 II b 2
Speluzzi 106-107 EF 5
Spenard, AK 58-59 N 6
Spencer, IA 70-71 C 4
Spencer, ID 66-67 G 3
Spencer, IN 70-71 G 6
Spencer, NC 80-81 F 3
Spencer, SD 68-69 H 4
Spencer, WI 70-71 E 3
Spencer, WV 72-73 F 5
Spencer, Cape — [AUS]
158-159 G 7
Spencer, Cape — [USA] 58-59 T 7
Spencer, Point — 58-59 D 4
Spencerbaai 174-175 A 3
Spencer Bay = Spencerbaai
174-175 A 3
Spencer Gulf 158-159 G 6
Spencer Street Station 161 II b 1
Spencerville, OH 70-71 HJ 5
Spences Bridge 60 G 4
Spenser Mountains 161 E 6
Sperling 68-69 H 1
Spessart 118 D 3-4
Spétsai 122-123 K 7
Spey 119 E 3
Speyer 118 D 4
Spèzia, La — 122-123 C 3
Spezzano Albanese 122-123 G 6
Sphakia = Chốra Sfakiốn
122-123 L 8
Sphinx 170 II a 2
Spicer Islands 56-57 UV 4
Spike Mount 58-59 QR 3
Spilimbergo 122-123 E 2
Spillimacheen 60 J 4
Spinaceto, Roma- 113 II b 2
Spīn Bulgak 134-135 K 4
Spioenberg I 174-175 D 6
Spioenberg II 174-175 CD 6
Spirit Lake, IA 70-71 C 4
Spirit Lake, ID 66-67 E 1-2
Spirit Lake, WA 66-67 BC 2
Spirit River 60 H 2
Spiritwood 61 E 4
Spiro, OK 76-77 G 5
Spirovo 124-125 K 5
Spitak 126-127 LM 6
Spithamn = Pōōsaspea
124-125 DE 4
Spiti 138-139 FG 1
Spitsbergen 116-117 k 6-n 5
Spittal 118 F 5
Spizzichino, Roma- 113 II ab 1
Split 122-123 G 4
Split Lake [CDN, lake] 61 KL 2
Split Lake [CDN, place] 61 K 2
Split Rock, WY 68-69 C 4
Splügen 118 D 5
Spofford, TX 76-77 D 8
Spogi 124-125 F 5
Spokane, WA 64-65 C 2
Spokane Indian Reservation
66-67 DE 2
Spokane River 66-67 DE 2
Spokojnyj 132-133 YZ 6
Špola 126-127 E 2
Spoleto 122-123 E 4
Spong 150-151 E 6
Spooner, MN 70-71 C 1
Spooner, WI 70-71 E 3
Spoon River 70-71 E 5
Sporades 122-123 M 6-7
Sport, Palazzo dello — 113 II b 2
Sportsmans Park Race Track
83 II a 1
Sporyj Navolok, mys —
132-133 M-O 2
Spot Pond 84 I b 2
Spotswood, Melbourne- 161 II b 1
Spotted Horse, WY 68-69 D 3
Spotted Range 74-75 F 4
Sprague, WA 66-67 DE 2
Sprague River 66-67 C 4
Sprague River, OR 66-67 C 4
Spranger, Mount — 60 G 3
Spratly Islands = Quần Đao Hoang
Sa 148-149 F 5
Spray, OR 66-67 D 3
Spree 118 G 3
Spreewald 118 F 2-G 3
Spremberg 118 G 3
Sprengisandur 116-117 de 2
Spring, TX 76-77 G 7
Spring Bay 66-67 G 5
Springbok 172 C 7
Springbokvlakte 174-175 H 3
Spring City, TN 78-79 G 3
Spring Creek Park 82 III c 3
Springdale, AR 76-77 GH 4
Springdale, MT 66-67 HJ 3
Springdale, NV 74-75 E 4
Springdale, UT 74-75 G 4
Springdale, WA 66-67 DE 1
Springer, NM 76-77 B 4
Springer, Mount — 62 O 2
Springerville, AZ 74-75 J 5
Springfield, CO 68-69 E 7
Springfield, GA 80-81 F 4
Springfield, ID 66-67 G 4
Springfield, IL 64-65 HJ 4
Springfield, KY 70-71 H 7
Springfield, MA 64-65 M 3
Springfield, MN 70-71 C 3
Springfield, MO 64-65 H 4
Springfield, OH 64-65 K 3-4
Springfield, OR 66-67 B 3
Springfield, PA 84 III ab 2
Springfield, SD 68-69 GH 4
Springfield, TN 78-79 F 2
Springfield, VA 82 II a 2
Springfield, VT 72-73 K 3
Springfield, New York-, NY 82 III d 2
Springfontein 174-175 FG 6
Springhill, LA 78-79 C 4
Spring Hill, TN 78-79 F 3
Spring Hope, NC 80-81 GH 3
Springhouse 60 FG 4
Spring Mill, PA 84 III b 1
Spring Mountains 74-75 F 4
Spring Pond 84 I c 2
Springs 172 E 7
Springside, NJ 84 III de 1
Springsure 158-159 J 4
Springton Reservoir 84 III a 2
Spring Valley, IL 70-71 F 5
Spring Valley, MN 70-71 D 4
Spring Valley, TX 85 III a 1
Spring Valley [USA] 74-75 F 3
Spring Valley [ZA] 174-175 G 7
Springview, NE 68-69 G 4
Springville, AL 78-79 F 4
Springville, NJ 84 III d 2
Springville, NY 72-73 G 3
Springville, UT 66-67 H 5
Sproat Lake 66-67 A 1
Sprucedale 72-73 G 2
Spruce Grove 60 KL 3
Spruce Knob 64-65 KL 4
Spruce Mountain 66-67 F 5
Spruce Pine, NC 80-81 EF 2
Spry, UT 74-75 G 4
Spur, TX 76-77 D 6
Spur Lake, NM 74-75 J 5-6
Spurr, Mount — 58-59 LM 6
Sputendorf bei Grossbeeren
130 III a 2
Spy Pond 84 I a 2
Squamish 66-67 B 1
Squantum, MA 84 I bc 3
Squaw Harbor, AK 58-59 c 2
Squaw Rapids Dam 61 G 4
Squaw River 62 F 2
Squaw Valley, CA 64-65 BC 4
Squillace, Golfo di — 122-123 G 6
Squirrel River 58-59 G 3
Sralao = Kompong Sralao
150-151 E 5
Srê Antong = Phum Srê Antong
150-151 F 6
Srê Chis 150-151 F 6
Sredinnyj chrebet 132-133 f 6-e 7
Sredna gora 122-123 L 4
Sredn'aja Achtuba 126-127 M 2
Srednekolymsk 132-133 d 4
Srednerusskaja vozvyšennost'
124-125 L 6-8
Sredne-Sibirskoje ploskogorje
132-133 R-W 4-5
Srednij Ural 132-133 KL 6
Sredsib 132-133 L 7-P 7
Srê Koki 150-151 F 6
Srem 118 H 2
Sremot Kompong Som 150-151 D 7
Sremska Mitrovica 122-123 H 3
Sremska Rača 122-123 H 3
Sreng, Stung — 150-151 D 5-6
Srêpok 150-151 F 6
Sretensk 132-133 W 7
Srê Umbell 148-149 D 4
Sriharikota Island 140 E 4
Srīkākulam 134-135 M 7
Srī Lanka 134-135 N 9
Sri Mādhopur 138-139 E 4
Sri Mohangarh 138-139 C 4
Srīmushnam 140 D 5
Srīnagar 134-135 LM 4
Sringeri 140 B 4
Srīnivāspur 140 D 4
Srīperumbūdūr 140 DE 4
Sripur = Shrīpūr 138-139 N 5
Srīrangam 134-135 M 8
Srīrangapatnam 140 C 4
Srīsailam 140 D 2
Srīvaikuntam 140 CD 6
Srīvardhan 134-135 L 7
Srīvilliputtūr 140 C 6
Środa Wielkopolski 118 HJ 2
Srungavarapukota 140 F 1
Sseu-p'ing = Siping 142-143 N 3
Ssongea = Songea 172 G 4
Staaken, Berlin- 130 III a 1
Staaten River 158-159 H 3
Staatsforst Kranichstein 128 III b 2
Staatsforst Hamburg 128 III b 2
Staatsforst Mörfelden 128 III a 1
Stachanov 126-127 J 2
Stackpool 62 L 3
Stack Skerry 119 D 2
Stade [CDN] 82 I b 1
Stade [D] 118 D 2
Stade de Kinshasa 170 IV a 1
Stade Eboue 170 IV a 1
Städel 128 III b 1
Stádio 113 IV a 2
Stadion Dinamo 113 V b 2
Stadion im. Lenina 113 V b 3
Stadio Olimpio 113 II b 1
Stadium 82 II b 2
Stadium 200 85 III b 2
Städjan 116-117 E 7
Stadlandet 116-117 A 6
Stadlau, Wien- 113 I b 2
Stadtpark Hamburg 130 I b 1
Stafford 119 E 5
Stafford, KS 68-69 G 7
Stafford, NE 68-69 G 4
Stafford, TX 85 III a 2
Staicele 124-125 E 5
Staines 129 II a 2
Staines, Peninsula — 108-109 C 8
Staines Reservoir 129 II a 2
Staked Plain = Llano Estacado
64-65 F 5
Stalina, pik — = pik Kommunizma
134-135 L 3
Stalinabad = Dušanbe 134-135 K 3
Stalingrad = Volgograd
126-127 LM 2
Staliniri = Cchinvali 126-127 LM 5
Stalinka = Černovozavodskoje
126-127 FG 1
Stalino = Doneck 126-127 H 2-3
Stalino = Ošarovo 132-133 S 5
Stalinogorsk = Novomoskovsk
124-125 M 6
Stalinsk = Novokuzneck
132-133 Q 7
Stallikon 128 IV ab 2
Stallo, MS 78-79 E 4
Stalowa Wola 118 L 3
Stalwart 61 F 5
Stalwart Point = Stalwartpunt
174-175 G 7
Stalwartpunt 174-175 G 7
Stamboul 170 I b 1
Stambul = İstanbul 134-135 BC 2
Stamford 158-159 H 4
Stamford, CT 72-73 K 4
Stamford, TX 76-77 E 6
Stammersdorf, Wien- 113 I b 1
Stampriet 172 C 6
Stamps, AR 78-79 C 4
Stamsund 116-117 EF 3
Stanberry, MO 70-71 C 5
Stanbury Mountains 66-67 G 5
Stancy 124-125 G 4
Standerton 172 EF 7
Standing Rock Indian Reservation
68-69 F 2-3
Standish, MI 70-71 HJ 4
Stane = Stavnoje 126-127 A 2
Stanford, KY 70-71 H 7
Stanford, MT 66-67 H 2
Stanger 174-175 J 5
Stanislau = Ivano-Frankovsk
126-127 B 2
Stanislaus River 74-75 C 3-4
Stanke Dimitrov 122-123 K 4
Stanley, ID 66-67 F 3
Stanley, KY 70-71 G 7
Stanley, ND 68-69 E 1
Stanley, NM 76-77 AB 5
Stanley, WI 70-71 E 3
Stanley [AUS] 160 b 2
Stanley [CDN] 63 C 4
Stanley [Falkland Islands] 111 E 8
Stanley [HK] 155 I b 2
Stanley, Mount — 158-159 F 4
Stanley Mission 61 FG 3
Stanley Mound 155 I b 2
Stanley Pool = Pool Malebo
172 C 2
Stanley Reservoir 134-135 M 8
Stanleyville = Kisangani 172 E 1
Stanmore, London- 129 II a 1
Stann Creek 64-65 J 8
Stanovoj chrebet 132-133 X-Z 6
Stanovoje nagorje 132-133 VW 6
Stanthorpe 160 KL 2
Stanton, KY 72-73 E 6
Stanton, MI 70-71 H 4
Stanton, ND 68-69 F 2
Stanton, NE 68-69 H 5
Stanton, TX 76-77 CD 6
Stanwell 129 II a 2
Stanwick, NJ 84 III d 2
Stanwood, WA 66-67 B 1
Stapi 116-117 b 2
Stapleford Abbotts 129 II c 1
Staples, MN 70-71 C 2
Stapleton, NE 68-69 F 5
Star' 124-125 JK 7
Star, MS 78-79 DE 4
Star, NC 80-81 G 3
Starachowice 118 K 3
Staraja Buchara = Buchara
134-135 JK 3
Staraja Kulatka 124-125 Q 7
Staraja Ladoga 124-125 HJ 4
Staraja Majna 124-125 R 6
Staraja Matvejevka 124-125 T 6
Staraja Porubežka 124-125 RS 7
Staraja Račejka 124-125 QR 7
Staraja Russa 132-133 E 6
Staraja Toropa 124-125 HJ 5
Stara Pazova 122-123 J 3
Stara Zagora 122-123 L 4
Starbejevo 113 V b 1
Starbuck [CDN] 61 JK 6
Starbuck [island] 156-157 K 5
Star City, AR 78-79 D 4
Stargard Szczeciński 118 G 2
Starica 124-125 K 5
Starigrad 122-123 F 3
Starke, FL 80-81 bc 2
Starkey, ID 66-67 E 3
Starkville, CO 68-69 D 7
Starkville, MS 78-79 E 4
Starkweather, ND 68-69 G 1
Starnberg 118 E 4-5
Starnberger See 118 E 5
Starobel'sk 126-127 J 2
Starodub 124-125 J 7
Starogard Gdański 118 HJ 2
Staroizborsk 124-125 FG 5
Staroje 124-125 N 4
Starojurjevo 124-125 N 7
Starokonstantinov 126-127 C 2
Starominskaja 126-127 J 3
Staroščerbinovskaja 126-127 J 3
Starotimoškino 124-125 Q 7
Starotitarovskaja 126-127 H 4
Staroverčeskaja 124-125 QR 4
Staryj Bir'uz'ak 126-127 N 4
Staryje Dorogi 124-125 G 7
Staryj Krym 126-127 G 4
Staryj Oskol 126-127 HJ 1
Staryj Sambor 126-127 A 2
Staryj Terek 126-127 N 5
Stassfurt 118 E 3
Staszów 118 K 3
State Capitol 85 II bc 2
State College, PA 72-73 GH 4
State House [USA] 84 I b 2
State House [WAN] 170 III b 2
State Line, MS 78-79 E 5
Staten Island 72-73 JK 4
Staten Island = Isla de los Estados
111 D 8
Staten Island Airport 82 III b 3
Statenville, GA 80-81 E 5
Statesboro, GA 80-81 F 4
Statesville, NC 64-65 K 4
Statland = Stadland 116-117 A 6
Statue of Liberty 82 III b 2
Stauffer, OR 66-67 C 4
Staung, Stung — 150-151 E 6
Staunton, IL 70-71 F 6
Staunton, VA 64-65 KL 4
Stavanger 116-117 A 8
Stavely 60 KL 4
Stavern 116-117 CD 8
Stavka = Urda 126-127 N 2
Stavkoviči 124-125 G 5
Stavnoje 126-127 A 2
Stavropol' 126-127 KL 4
Stavropol' = Togliatti 132-133 H 7
Stavropol, Kraj — 202-203 R 6-7
Stavropol'skaja vozvyšennost'
126-127 K-M 4
Stavrós 122-123 K 5
Stawell 158-159 H 7
Stazione Termini 113 II b 2
Steamboat, NV 74-75 D 3
Steamboat Springs, CO 68-69 C 5
Stearns, KY 78-79 G 2
Stebbins, AK 58-59 F 5
Stedelijk Museum 128 I a 1
Steel Creek, AK 58-59 R 4
Steele, AL 78-79 F 4
Steele, MO 78-79 E 2
Steele, ND 68-69 FG 2
Steele, Mount — 58-59 RS 6
Steele Creek 161 II b 1
Steele Island 53 B 30-31
Steelpoort 172 EF 6
Steelpoortrivier 174-175 HJ 3
Steel River 70-71 G 1
Steelton, PA 72-73 H 4
Steelville, MO 70-71 E 7

364 Sorell

Steenkampsberge 174-175 HJ 3
Steenkool 148-149 K 7
Steenokkerzeel 128 II b 1
Steensby Inlet 56-57 V 3
Steens Mountain 66-67 D 4
Steenstrups Gletscher 56-57 Za 2
Steephill Lake 61 G 2-3
Steep Island 155 I b 2
Steep Point 158-159 B 5
Steep Rock 61 J 5
Steep Rock Lake 70-71 DE 1
Ştefăneşti 122-123 M 2
Stefansson Island 56-57 OP 3
Steffen, Cerro — 108-109 D 5
Stefleşti 122-123 K 3
Stege 116-117 E 10
Stéhoux, le — 128 II a 2
Steiermark 118 G 5
Steilloopbrug 174-175 H 2
Steilshoop, Hamburg- 130 I b 1
Steinbach 61 K 6
Steinbach (Taunus) 128 III a 1
Steinberg [D, Hessen] 128 III b 1
Steinen, Rio — 92-93 J 7
Steinhatchee, FL 80-81 b 2
Steinhausen, München- 130 II b 2
Steinhuser Wald 128 IV ab 2
Steinkjer 116-117 DE 5
Steinkopf 174-175 BC 5
Steinmaur 128 IV a 1
Steinneset 116-117 m 6
Steins, NM 74-75 J 6
Steinstücken, Berlin- 130 III a 2
Steinwerder, Hamburg- 130 I a 1
Stekľanka 124-125 N 4
Stella 174-175 F 4
Stella, LA 85 I c 2
Stellaland 172 D 7
Stellarton 63 E 5
Stellenbosch 172 CD 8
Steller, Mount — 58-59 Q 6
Stellingen, Hamburg- 130 I a 1
Stendal 118 E 2
Stende 124-125 D 5
Stenhouse, Mount — 155 I a 2
Stenòn Elafonêsu 122-123 K 7
Stenòn Kythêron 122-123 K 7-8
Stensele 116-117 G 5
Stepan' 124-125 F 8
Stepanakert 126-127 N 7
Stepana Razina 124-125 P 6
Stepanavan 126-127 LM 6
Stephanie, Lake — = Thew Bahir 164-165 M 8
Stephansdom 113 I b 2
Stephen, MN 68-69 H 1
Stephens, AR 78-79 C 4
Stephens, Cape — 161 EF 5
Stephens Island 60 B 2
Stephenson, MI 70-71 G 3
Stephens Passage 58-59 U 7-V 8
Stephenville 56-57 YZ 8
Stephenville, TX 76-77 EF 6
Stephenville Crossing 63 GH 3
Stepn'ak 132-133 N 7
Stepney, London- 129 II b 1
Stepovak Bay 58-59 cd 2
Štepovka 126-127 G 1
Sterkspruit 174-175 G 6
Sterkstroom 172 E 8
Sterkwater 174-175 H 3
Sterley, TX 76-77 D 5
Sterling, AK 58-59 M 6
Sterling, CO 64-65 F 3
Sterling, IL 70-71 F 5
Sterling, KS 68-69 GH 6
Sterling, ND 68-69 FG 2
Sterling City, TX 76-77 D 7
Sterling Heights, MI 72-73 E 3
Sterling Landing, AK 58-59 K 5
Sterling Park, CA 83 I b 2
Sterlitamak 132-133 K 7
Sterrebeek 128 II b 1
Stettler 61 B 4
Steuben, MI 70-71 G 2
Steubenville, OH 64-65 K 3
Stevenson, AL 78-79 FG 3
Stevenson, WA 66-67 BC 3
Stevenson Lake 62 A 1
Stevenson River 158-159 FG 5
Stevens Point, WI 70-71 F 3
Stevens Village, AK 58-59 N 3-4
Stevensville, MT 66-67 FG 2
Steveston 66-67 B 1
Stewart, AK 56-57 KL 6
Stewart, MN 70-71 C 3
Stewart, NV 74-75 D 3
Stewart, Isla — 111 B 8-9
Stewart Island 158-159 N 9
Stewart Islands 148-149 k 6
Stewart River [CDN, place] 56-57 J 5
Stewart River [CDN, river] 56-57 JK 5
Stewartsville, MO 70-71 CD 6
Stewart Valley 61 DE 5
Stewartville, MN 70-71 D 4
Steynsburg 174-175 F 6
Steynsrus 174-175 G 4
Steyr 118 G 4
Steytlerville 174-175 EF 7
Stickney, IL 83 II a 2
Stickney, SD 68-69 G 4
Stierstadt 128 III a 1
Stigler, OK 76-77 G 5
Stikine Mountains = Cassiar Mountains 56-57 KL 6
Stikine Plateau 56-57 K 6
Stikine River 56-57 KL 6
Stikine Strait 58-59 w 8
Stilbaai 174-175 D 8
Stiles, TX 76-77 D 7
Still Run 84 III b 3
Stillwater, MN 70-71 D 3
Stillwater, OK 76-77 F 4
Stillwater Mountains 74-75 DE 3
Stilwell, OK 76-77 G 5
Stimson 62 L 2
Stimson, Mount — 66-67 G 1
Stinear Nunataks 53 BC 7
Stinnett, TX 76-77 D 5
Stintonville 170 V c 2
Štip 122-123 K 5
Stirling [CDN] 66-67 G 1
Stirling City, CA 74-75 C 3
Stirling Range 158-159 C 6
Stites, ID 66-67 EF 2
Stitten = Saṭīṭan 166-167 G 3
Stjernøy 116-117 K 2
Stjørdalshalsen 116-117 D 6
Stobi 122-123 J 5
Stochod 124-125 E 8
Stockdale, TX 76-77 EF 8
Stockdorf 130 II a 2
Stockerau 118 H 4
Stockett, MT 66-67 H 2
Stockholm 116-117 GH 8
Stockholm, ME 72-73 MN 1
Stockholms län 116-117 GH 8
Stockport 119 E 5
Stocks Seamount 92-93 N 7
Stockton, CA 64-65 BC 4
Stockton, IL 70-71 EF 4
Stockton, KS 68-69 G 6
Stockton, MO 70-71 D 7
Stockton Island 70-71 E 2
Stockton Islands 58-59 OP 1
Stockton on Tees 119 F 4
Stockton Plateau 76-77 C 7
Stockville, NE 68-69 FG 5
Stodolišče 124-125 J 6
Stoffberg 174-175 H 3
Stoj, gora — 126-127 A 2
Stojba 132-133 Z 7
Stoke Newington, London- 129 II b 1
Stoke on Trend 119 EF 5
Stokes, Bahía — 108-109 C 10
Stokes, Monte — 108-109 C 8
Stokes, Mount — 161 EF 5
Stokes Point 160 ab 2
Stokkseyri 116-117 c 3
Stokksnes 116-117 f 2
Stolac 122-123 GH 4
Stolbcy 116-117 M 11
Stolbcy 124-125 F 7
Stolbovaja 124-125 L 6
Stolbovoj, ostrov — 132-133 Za 3
Stolin 124-125 F 8
Stolpe-Dorf 130 III b 1
Stolzenfels [Namibia] 174-175 C 5
Ston 122-123 G 4
Stone Canyon Reservoir 83 III b 1
Stone City, CO 68-69 D 6
Stonecutters Island 155 I a 2
Stoneham, MA 84 I b 2
Stonehaven 119 EF 3
Stonehenge [AUS] 158-159 H 4
Stonehenge [GB] 119 EF 6
Stone Mountains 80-81 F 2
Stoner, CO 74-75 J 4
Stonestown, San Francisco-, CA 83 I b 2
Stonewall 61 K 5
Stonewall, TX 76-77 E 7
Stonington 53 C 30
Stonington, ME 72-73 M 2-3
Stony Brook Reservation 84 I b 3
Stony Creek, VA 80-81 H 2
Stonyford, CA 74-75 B 3
Stony Point [CDN] 61 K 4-5
Stony Point [USA] 72-73 H 3
Stony River 56-57 EF 5
Stony River, AK 58-59 JK 6
Stony Tunguska = Podkamennaja Tunguska 132-133 R 5
Stopnica 118 K 3
Stora Lulevatten 116-117 HJ 4
Stora Sjöfallet 116-117 H 4
Stora-Sjöfallets nationalpark 116-117 GH 4
Storavan 116-117 H 5
Stord 116-117 A 8
Store Bælt 116-117 D 10
Støren 116-117 CD 6
Storfjord 116-117 B 6
Storfjordbotn 116-117 LM 2
Storfjorden 116-117 k 6
Storlien 116-117 E 6
Storm Bay 158-159 J 8
Stormberg 174-175 FG 6
Stormberge 174-175 G 6
Storm Lake, IA 70-71 C 4
Stormsrivier 174-175 E 7-F 8
Stormy Lake 62 CD 3
Stornorrfors 116-117 HJ 6
Stornoway 119 CD 2
Storøya 116-117 n 4
Storoževsk 132-133 J 5
Storsjön 116-117 E 6
Storuman [S, lake] 116-117 G 5
Storuman [S, place] 116-117 G 5
Story City, IA 70-71 D 4
Stosch, Isla — 111 A 7
Stoughton 61 G 6
Stoughton, WI 70-71 F 4
Stout Lake 62 B 1
Strabane 119 C 4
Strafford, PA 84 III a 1
Straight Cliffs 74-75 H 4
Strait of Belle Isle 56-57 Z 7
Strait of Canso 56-57 YZ 8
Strait of Dover 119 GH 6
Strait of Georgia 56-57 M 8
Strait of Juan de Fuca 56-57 LM 8
Strait of Singapore 148-149 DE 6
Straits of Florida 64-65 K 7-L 6
Straits of Mackinac 70-71 H 3
Strakonice 118 FG 4
Stralsund 118 F 1
Strand 172 C 8
Stranda 116-117 c 1-2
Stranraer 119 D 4
Strasbourg [CDN] 61 F 5
Strasbourg [F] 120-121 L 4
Strasburg, CO 68-69 D 6
Strasburg, ND 68-69 FG 2
Strašeny 126-127 D 3
Stratford, CA 74-75 D 4
Stratford, CT 72-73 K 4
Stratford, NJ 84 III c 3
Stratford, SD 68-69 GH 3
Stratford, TX 76-77 CD 4
Stratford, WI 70-71 EF 3
Stratford [AUS] 160 H 7
Stratford [CDN] 56-57 U 9
Stratford [NZ] 161 F 4
Stratford, London- 129 II c 1
Stratford on Avon 119 F 5
Strathcona Provincial Park 66-67 A 1
Strathcona Provincial Park 60 DE 5
Strathfield, Sydney- 161 I a 2
Strathgordon 160 bc 3
Strathmoor, Detroit-, MI 84 II a 2
Strathmore [CDN] 60 L 4
Strathmore [GB] 119 E 3
Strathnaver 60 FG 3
Strathroy 72-73 F 3
Stratonis Turris = Caesarea 136-137 F 6
Stratton, CO 68-69 E 6
Stratton, ME 72-73 L 2
Stratton, NE 68-69 F 5
Straubing 118 F 4
Straw, MT 68-69 AB 2
Strawberry Mountains 66-67 D 3
Strawberry Park 85 III c 2
Strawberry Point, CA 83 I ab 1
Strawberry Point, IA 70-71 E 4
Strawberry River 66-67 H 5
Strawbridge Lake 84 III d 2
Strawn, TX 76-77 E 6
Streaky Bay [AUS, bay] 158-159 F 6
Streaky Bay [AUS, place] 158-159 FG 6
Streatham, London- 129 II b 2
Streator, IL 70-71 F 5
Strebersdorf, Wien- 113 I b 1
69th Street Center 84 III b 2
Streeter, ND 68-69 G 2
Streetman, TX 76-77 FG 7
30th Street Station 84 III b 2
Streich Mound 158-159 D 6
Strelka-Čun'a 132-133 T 5
Strenči 124-125 E 5
Stresa 122-123 C 3
Strešen' = Strašeny 126-127 D 3
Stretto di Messina 122-123 F 6-7
Strevell, ID 66-67 G 4
Strickland River 148-149 M 8
Stringtown, OK 76-77 FG 5
Strižament, gora — 126-127 L 4
Striži 124-125 R 4
Strobel, Lago — 108-109 D 7
Stroeder 111 D 6
Strofádes 122-123 J 7
Strogino, Moskva- 113 V ab 2
Strómboli 122-123 F 6
Stromsburg, NE 68-69 H 5
Strömstad 116-117 D 8
Strömsund 116-117 F 6
Ströms Vattudal 116-117 F 5-6
Strong, AR 78-79 C 4
Strong City, KS 68-69 H 6
Stronsay 119 EF 2
Stroud 119 EF 6
Stroud, OK 76-77 F 5
Stroudsburg, PA 72-73 J 4
Struer 116-117 C 9
Strugi Krasnyje 124-125 G 4
Struisbaai 174-175 D 8
Struma 122-123 K 5
Strumica 122-123 K 5
Strunino 124-125 M 5
Struys Bay = Struisbaai 174-175 D 8
Strydenburg 174-175 E 5
Strydomsvlei 174-175 E 7
Strydpoortberge 174-175 H 3
Stryj [SU, place] 126-127 A 2
Stryj [SU, river] 126-127 A 2
Strymōn 122-123 K 5
Strzelecki Creek 160 E 2
Strzelno 118 HJ 2
Stuart, FL 80-81 c 3
Stuart, IA 70-71 C 5
Stuart, NE 68-69 G 4
Stuart, OK 76-77 FG 5
Stuart, VA 80-81 F 2
Stuart Island 56-57 D 5
Stuart Lake 56-57 M 7
Stuart Range 158-159 FG 5
Stubbenkammer 118 FG 1
Studenica 122-123 J 4
Studenka 124-125 G 6
Stumpy Point, NC 80-81 J 3
Stung Battambang = Stung Sangker 150-151 D 6
Stung Chikrang 150-151 E 6
Stung Chinit 150-151 E 6
Stung Daun Tri 150-151 D 6
Stung Mongkol Borey 150-151 D 6
Stung Porong 150-151 E 6
Stung Pursat 150-151 D 6
Stung Sangker 150-151 D 6
Stung Sen 150-151 E 6
Stung Sreng 150-151 D 5-6
Stung Staung 150-151 E 6
Stung Tanad 150-151 D 6
Stung Treng 148-149 E 4
Stupino 124-125 LM 6
Stura di Demonte 122-123 B 3
Sturge Island 53 C 17
Sturgeon Bay 61 JK 4
Sturgeon Bay, WI 70-71 G 3
Sturgeon Bay Canal 70-71 G 3
Sturgeon Falls [CDN, place] 72-73 FG 1
Sturgeon Falls [CDN, river] 62 L 2
Sturgeon Lake [CDN, Alberta] 60 J 2
Sturgeon Lake [CDN, Ontario] 62 D 3
Sturgeon Landing 61 H 3
Sturgeon River [CDN, Ontario] 72-73 F 1
Sturgeon River [CDN, Saskatchewan] 61 E 4
Sturgis, KY 70-71 G 7
Sturgis, MI 70-71 H 5
Sturgis, OK 76-77 C 4
Sturgis, SD 68-69 E 3
Sturt, Mount — 158-159 H 5
Sturt Creek 158-159 E 3
Sturt Desert 158-159 H 5
Sturt Plain 158-159 F 3
Stutterheim 172 E 8
Stuttgart 118 D 4
Stuttgart, AR 78-79 D 3
Stuurmen 174-175 CD 6
Stviga 124-125 F 8
Stykkisholm = Stykkishólmur 116-117 b 2
Stykkishólmur 116-117 b 2
Stylis 122-123 K 6
Styr' 126-127 B 1
Styria = Steiermark 118 G 5
Suaçuí Grande, Rio — 102-103 L 3
Suai 152-153 K 4
Suaita 94-95 E 4
Sūākin = Sawākin 164-165 M 5
Suan 144-145 F 3
Suancheng = Xuancheng 146-147 G 6
Suanen = Xuan'en 146-147 B 6-7
Süanhua = Xuanhua 142-143 LM 3
Suanhwa = Xuanhua 142-143 LM 3
Suan Phung 150-151 B 6
Suao 142-143 N 7
Su'ao = Suao 142-143 N 7
Suapi 104-105 C 4
Suapure, Río — 94-95 H 4
Suār 138-139 G 3
Suardi 106-107 G 3
Suárez [CO, Cauca] 94-95 C 6
Suárez [CO, Tolima] 94-95 D 5
Suárez [ROU] 106-107 J 5
Suaruro, Cordillera de — 104-105 DE 7
Suasúa 94-95 L 4
Suba 91 III b 2
Subansiri 141 D 2
Subarkuduk 132-133 K 8
Subar Luat, Pulau — 154 III ab 2
Subarnarekha 138-139 L 6
Sūbāṭ, As — 164-165 L 7
Subate 124-125 EF 5
Subayhah 136-137 H 7
Subbat = Subate 124-125 EF 5
Subi, Pulau — 150-151 G 11
Subiaco 122-123 E 5
Subi Kecil, Pulau — 152-153 H 4
Sublett, ID 66-67 G 4
Sublette, KS 68-69 F 7
Subotica 122-123 HJ 2
Subugo 171 C 3
Suburban Canal 85 I a 1-2
Success 61 D 5
Suceava 122-123 LM 2
Sucesso 100-101 D 3
Suchaj nuur 142-143 GH 4
Suchana 132-133 W 4
Suchbaatar [Mongolia, administrative unit = 17] 142-143 L 2
Süchbaatar [Mongolia, place] 142-143 JK 1
Sucheng = Su Xian 142-143 M 5
Suches, Río — 104-105 B 4
Su-chia-t'un = Sujiatun 144-145 D 2
Su-ch'ien = Suqian 142-143 M 5
Suchiniči 124-125 K 6
Suchobezvodnoje 124-125 P 5
Suchodn'a 113 V a 2
Suchoj Liman 126-127 E 3
Suchona 132-133 G 6
Suchou = Xuzhou 142-143 M 5
Su-chou = Yibin 142-143 JK 6
Suchow = Xuzhou 142-143 M 5
Suchow = Yibin 142-143 JK 6
Suchumi 126-127 K 5
Sucio, Río — 94-95 C 4
Suckling, Cape — 58-59 Q 7
Sucre [BOL] 92-93 FG 8
Sucre [CO, Caquetá] 94-95 D 7
Sucre [CO, Sucre administrative unit] 94-95 D 3
Sucre [CO, Sucre place] 94-95 D 3
Sucre [EC] 96-97 A 2
Sucre [PE] 96-97 C 6
Sucre [YV] 94-95 K 2
Sucúa 96-97 B 3
Suçuarana 100-101 D 8
Suçuarana, Serra da — 100-101 B 8
Sucuaro 92-93 F 4
Sucun 146-147 G 4
Sucunduri, Rio — 92-93 H 6
Sucupira 100-101 C 4
Sucuriú, Rio — 92-93 J 8
Sucy-en-Brie 129 I d 2
Sūd = As-Sudd 164-165 L 7
Suda [SU, river] 124-125 L 4
Sudaj 124-125 O 4
Sudak 126-127 G 4
Sudan, TX 76-77 C 5
Sudan [landscape] 164-165 C-K 6
Sudan [Sudan, state] 164-165 J-L 6
Sudau 152-153 N 3
Sudayr 134-135 EF 5
Sudbišči 124-125 L 7
Sudbury [CDN] 56-57 U 8
Sudbury, London- 129 II a 1
Sudd, As — 164-165 L 7
Suddie 92-93 H 3
Süderelbe 130 I a 2
Sudhāgarh 140 A 1
Súdhavík 116-117 b 1
Sudhur-Múla 116-117 f 2
Sudhur-Thingeyjar 116-117 ef 2
Sudirman, Pegunungan — 148-149 L 7
Sudislavl' 124-125 NO 5
Sudogda [SU, place] 124-125 N 6
Sudong-ni = Changhang 144-145 F 4-5
Sudost' 124-125 J 7
Sud-Ouest 168-169 E 3
Sudr = Rā's as-Sidr 173 C 3
Sudr, Wādī — = Wādī Sidr 173 C 3
Sudža 126-127 G 1
Sue = Nahr Sūī 164-165 K 7
Sueca 120-121 G 9
Sueco, El — 86-87 GH 3
Suemez Island 58-59 w 9
Suez = As-Suways 164-165 L 3
Suez, Gulf of — = Khalīj as-Suways 164-165 L 3
Sūf 166-167 K 3
Ṣūf, 'Ayn — 166-167 H 5
Ṣūf, Ḥāssī — 166-167 F 5
Sūfān, Qulbān as- 136-137 H 8
Sūfeyān 136-137 LM 3
Suffield 61 C 5
Suffolk, VA 80-81 H 2
Suffolk Downs Race Track 84 I c 2
Suflion 122-123 LM 5
Sufu = Qäshqär 142-143 CD 4
Sufūq 136-137 J 4
Šuga 132-133 N 4
Sugamo, Tōkyō- 155 III b 1
Sugano, Ichikawa- 155 III c 1
Sūgar 166-167 G 5
Sugar Creek 85 II b 2
Sugar Island 70-71 H 2
Sugarloaf Mountain 72-73 LM 2
Sugar Valley, Houston-, TX 85 III b 2
Suggi Lake 61 G 3
Suginami, Tōkyō- 155 III a 1
Sugita, Yokohama- 155 III a 3
Sugiyasu 144-145 H 6
Suğla gölü 136-137 DE 4
Šugozero 124-125 K 4
Sugut, Sungei — 152-153 M 2
Suguta 171 D 2
Sūhāj 164-165 L 3
Ṣuḥār 134-135 H 6
Suhelīpāḍ = Suheli Par 134-135 L 8
Suheli Par 134-135 L 8
Suhl 118 E 3
Su-hsien = Su Xian 142-143 M 5
Šuhūrah 166-167 C 4
Şuhut 136-137 D 3
Sūī 138-139 B 3
Sūī, Nahr — 164-165 K 7
Suiá-Miçu, Rio — 98-99 M 10-11
Sui'an 146-147 G 7
Suichang 146-147 G 7
Sui-ch'i = Suixi 146-147 C 11
Sui Chiang = Sui Jiang 146-147 D 10
Suichuan 142-143 L 6
Sui-chung = Suizhong 144-145 C 2
Suichwan = Suichuan 142-143 L 6
Suide 142-143 KL 4
Suifenhe 142-143 OP 3
Sui He 146-147 F 4-5
Sui Ho = Sui He 146-147 F 4-5
Suihsien = Sui Xian [TJ, Henan] 146-147 E 4
Suihsien = Sui Xian [TJ, Hubei] 142-143 L 5
Suihua 142-143 O 2
Suihwa = Suihua 142-143 O 2
Sui Jiang 146-147 D 10
Suilai = Manaas 142-143 F 3
Suining [TJ, Hunan] 146-147 BC 8
Suining [TJ, Jiangsu] 146-147 FG 5
Suipacha 106-107 H 5
Suiping 146-147 D 5
Suir 119 C 5
Suiteh = Suide 142-143 KL 4
Suitland, MD 82 II b 2
Suixi [TJ, Anhui] 146-147 F 5
Suixi [TJ, Guangdong] 146-147 C 11
Sui Xian [TJ, Henan] 146-147 E 4
Sui Xian [TJ, Hubei] 142-143 L 5
Suiyuan 142-143 K 4-L 3
Sui-yüan = Suiyuan 142-143 K 4-L 3
Suizhong 144-145 C 2
Šuja [SU, Ivanovo] 132-133 G 6
Šuja [SU, Karel'skaja ASSR] 124-125 J 3
Sūjāngarh 138-139 E 4
Sujāwal 138-139 B 5
Sujiatun 144-145 D 2
Šujostrov 124-125 K 1
Šujskoje 124-125 N 4
Sukabumi 148-149 E 8
Sukadana 148-149 EF 7
Sukadana, Teluk — 152-153 H 6
Sukagawa 144-145 MN 4
Sukaraja 148-149 F 7
Sukchar, Pānihāti- 154 II b 1
Sukch'ŏn 144-145 E 3
Sukhe Bator = Süchbaatar 142-143 JK 1
Şukhnah, Aş- 136-137 H 5
Sukhum = Suchumi 126-127 K 5
Sukhuma = Ban Soukhouma 150-151 E 5
Şukhūrah 166-167 C 4
Şukhūr ar-Rihāmnah 166-167 BC 3
Sūki, As- 164-165 L 6
Sukkertoppen = Maniitsoq 56-57 Za 4
Sukkothai 150-151 B 4
Sukkozero 124-125 J 2
Sukkur = Sukkhar 134-135 KL 5
Sūkīī = Sukri 138-139 D 5
Sukoharjo 152-153 J 9
Sukon, Ko — 150-151 B 9
Sukri 138-139 D 5
Sukromľa 124-125 K 5
Sukses 172 C 6
Sukulu 171 C 2
Sukumo 144-145 J 6
Sukumo wan 144-145 J 6
Sul, Canal do — 92-93 K 4-5
Sula, MT 66-67 FG 3
Sula [SU] 126-127 F 1
Sula, Kepulauan — 148-149 HJ 7
Sulabesi, Pulau — 148-149 J 7
Sulaimān, Kohistān — 134-135 KL 4-5
Sulak [SU, place] 126-127 N 5
Sulak [SU, river] 126-127 N 5
Sulakyurt 136-137 E 2
Sulan Cheer 142-143 K 3
Sula Sgeir 119 C 2
Sulatna Crossing, AK 58-59 JK 4
Sulatna River 58-59 K 4
Šulavery = Šaum'ani 126-127 M 6
Sulawesi 148-149 G 7-H 6
Sulawesi, Laut — 148-149 GH 6
Sulawesi Selatan = 21 ◁ 148-149 G 7
Sulawesi Tengah = 19 ◁ 148-149 H 6
Sulawesi Tenggara = 20 ◁ 148-149 H 7
Sulawesi Utara = 18 ◁ 148-149 H 6
Sulaymān 166-167 M 1
Sulaymānīyah 134-135 EF 3
Sulaymīyah, As- 134-135 F 6
Sulayyil, As- 134-135 F 6
Şulb, Aş- 134-135 F 5
Sul'ca 124-125 Q 2
Sule He 142-143 H 4
Sule Skerry 119 D 2
Sulet = Solta 122-123 G 4
Süleymanlı 136-137 G 4
Sullivan, IL 70-71 F 6
Sulima 164-165 B 7
Sulimov = Čerkessk 126-127 L 4
Sulina 122-123 N 3
Sulina, Braţul — 122-123 N 3
Sulitjelma [N, mountain] 116-117 G 4
Sulitjelma [N, place] 116-117 FG 4
Sullana 92-93 C 5
Süllberg 130 I a 1
Sülldorf, Hamburg- 130 I a 1
Sulligent, AL 78-79 E 4
Sullivan, IN 70-71 G 6
Sullivan, MO 70-71 E 6
Sullivan Bay 60 D 4
Sullivan Canyon 83 III a 1
Sullivan Island = Lambi Kyûn 148-149 C 4
Sullivan Lake 61 C 5
Šul'mak = Novabad 134-135 L 3
Sulmona 122-123 E 4-5
Su-lo Ho = Sule He 142-143 H 4
Sulphur, LA 78-79 C 5
Sulphur, NV 66-67 D 5
Sulphur, OK 76-77 F 5
Sulphurdale, UT 74-75 G 3
Sulphur River 76-77 GH 6
Sulphur Springs, TX 76-77 G 6
Sulţān, Bi'r — 166-167 L 3
Sultanabad = Arāk 134-135 F 4
Sultānābād = Osmānnagar 140 D 1
Sultan Ahmet Camiî 154 I a 3
Sultan dağları 136-137 D 3
Sultan Hamud 171 D 3
Sultanhisar 136-137 BC 4
Sultan Mosque 154 III b 2
Sultānpur 134-135 N 5
Şultus 124-125 M 3
Sulu Archipelago 148-149 H 5
Suluca 136-137 F 2
Sulūk 136-137 H 4
Sülüklü 136-137 E 3
Sulukna River 58-59 K 5
Sul'ukta 134-135 KL 3
Suluova = Suluca 136-137 F 2
Sulūq 164-165 J 2
Sūlūru 140 E 4
Sulu Sea 148-149 GH 5
Sulusee 148-149 GH 5
Sulwān 166-167 E 2
Sülz [D, river ◁ Mühlbach] 128 III b 2
Sulzbach (Taunus) 128 III a 1
Sulzberger Bay 53 B 21-22
Šumači 124-125 J 7
Sumaco, Volcán — 96-97 C 2
Šumadija 122-123 J 3-4
Sumalata 152-153 P 5
Sumampa 106-107 F 2
Sumampa, Sierra — 106-107 F 2
Sūmār 136-137 L 6
Sumas, WA 66-67 BC 1
Sumatera = Sumatra 148-149 C 6-D 7
Sumatera Barat = 3 ◁ 148-149 D 7
Sumatera Selatan = 6 ◁ 148-149 D 7
Sumatera Tengah = Riau = 4 ◁ 148-149 D 6
Sumatera Utara = 2 ◁ 148-149 C 6
Sumatra 148-149 C 6-D 7
Sumatra, FL 78-79 G 5
Sumatra, MT 68-69 C 2
Sumaúma 92-93 G 6
Sumba 148-149 G 9
Sumba, Selat — 148-149 GH 8
Sumbawa 148-149 G 8
Sumbawa, Teluk — 152-153 M 10
Sumbawa Besar 148-149 G 8
Sumbawanga 172 F 3
Sümber 142-143 K 2
Sumbu 171 B 5
Sumbu Game Reserve 171 B 5
Sumburgh Head 119 F 2
Šumbut 124-125 S 6
Sumé 100-101 F 4
Šumen 122-123 M 4
Sumenep 152-153 KL 9
Šumerľa 124-125 PQ 6
Sumgait [SU, place] 126-127 O 6
Sumgait [SU, river] 126-127 O 6
Šumicha 132-133 L 6
Sumida, Tōkyō- 155 III bc 1
Sumidouro 102-103 L 5
Šumilino 124-125 G 6
Šumina 124-125 T 3
Sumisu-jima 142-143 R 5
Sumisu zima = Sumisu-jima 142-143 R 5
Şummān, Aş- [Saudi Arabia ↑ Ar-Riyāḍ] 134-135 F 5
Şummān, Aş- [Saudi Arabia ↘ Ar-Riyāḍ] 134-135 F 6
Summer, Lake — 76-77 B 5
Summerfield, TX 76-77 C 5
Summer Island 70-71 G 3
Summer Lake 66-67 C 4
Summer Lake, OR 66-67 C 4
Summerland 66-67 CD 1
Summerside 62 E 4
Summertown, TN 78-79 F 3
Summerville, SC 80-81 FG 4
Summerville, WV 72-73 F 5
Summit 64-65 b 2
Summit, AK 58-59 N 5
Summit, CA 74-75 E 5
Summit, IL 83 II a 2
Summit, MS 78-79 D 5
Summit, OR 66-67 B 3
Summit, SD 68-69 H 3
Summit Lake [CDN] 60 FG 2
Summit Lake [USA] 58-59 P 5
Summit Lake Indian Reservation 66-67 D 5
Summit Mountain 74-75 E 3
Summit Peak 68-69 C 7
Summt 130 III b 1
Summter See 130 III b 1
Sumner, IA 70-71 D 4
Sumner, MO 70-71 D 6
Sumner Strait 58-59 w 8
Sumoto 144-145 K 5
Sumozero 124-125 K 1-2
Šumperk 118 H 3-4
Sumprabum = Hsûmbārabûm 148-149 C 1
Sumpter, OR 66-67 DE 3
Sumrall, MS 78-79 E 5
S'umsi 124-125 ST 5
Sumskij Posad 124-125 K 1
Sumter, SC 64-65 KL 5
Sumy 126-127 G 1
S'un' 124-125 T 6
Sun, Altar of the — 155 II b 2
Suna [EAT] 171 C 4
Suna [SU, place] 124-125 S 5
Suna [SU, river] 124-125 J 2
Sunagawa 144-145 b 2
Sunām 138-139 E 2
Sunamachi, Tōkyō- 155 III bc 1
Sunamganj = Shūnāmganj 141 B 3
Sunan 144-145 E 3
Sunato 171 DE 6
Sunaysilah 136-137 J 5
Sunburst, MT 66-67 H 1
Sunbury 129 II a 2
Sunbury, OH 72-73 E 4
Sunbury, PA 72-73 H 4
Sunchal, El — 106-107 D 2
Sunchales 106-107 G 3
Suncho Corral 111 D 3
Sunch'ŏn [North Korea] 144-145 E 3
Sunch'ŏn [ROK] 142-143 O 4-5
Sunchow = Guiping 142-143 KL 7
Suncook, NH 72-73 L 3
Sunda, Selat — 148-149 E 8
Sunda Kelapa, Jakarta- 154 IV ab 1
Sundance, WY 68-69 D 3
Sundar Ban = Sundarbans 134-135 OP 6
Sundarbans 134-135 OP 6
Sundargaḍa = Sundargarh 138-139 JK 6
Sundargarh 138-139 JK 6
Sunda Trench 50-51 P 6
Sunday Islands = Raoul 208 J 5
Sundays River = Sondagsrivier 174-175 F 7
Sunday Strait 158-159 D 3
Sundblad 106-107 F 5
Sundbyberg 116-117 G 8
Sunderbunds = Sundarbans 134-135 OP 6
Sunderland [CDN] 72-73 G 2
Sunderland [GB] 119 F 4
Sündiken dağlari 136-137 D 2-3
Sundown [AUS] 158-159 F 5
Sundown [CDN] 68-69 H 1
Sundre 60 K 4
Sundsvall 116-117 GH 6
Sun'ga 124-125 K 2
Sungaianyar 152-153 M 7
Sungai Arut 152-153 J 6-7
Sungai Asahan 152-153 C 4
Sungai Bahau 152-153 LM 4
Sungai Bampu 152-153 C 4
Sungai Barumun 152-153 CD 5
Sungai Belayan 152-153 L 5

Sungai 365

Sungai Berau 152-153 M 4
Sungaidareh 148-149 D 7
Sungaiguntung 152-153 E 5
Sungai Kahayan 148-149 F 7
Sungai Kampar 152-153 DE 5
Sungai Kapuas [RI, Kalimantan Barat] 148-149 F 6
Sungai Kapuas [RI, Kalimantan Tengah] 152-153 L 6
Sungai Karama 152-153 N 6-7
Sungai Kayan 152-153 M 4
Sungai Ketungau 152-153 J 5
Sungai Konaweha 152-153 O 7-P 8
Sungai Kualu 150-151 BC 11
Sungai Lamandau 152-153 J 6-7
Sungai Lariang 152-153 N 6
Sungailiat 152-153 G 6
Sungai Mahakam 148-149 G 6-7
Sungai Mamasa 152-153 N 7
Sungai Melawi 152-153 K 6
Sungai Mendawai 152-153 K 7
Sungai Murung 152-153 L 7
Sungai Musi 148-149 D 7
Sungai Negara 152-153 L 7
Sungai Pawan 152-153 J 6
Sungai Pembuang 152-153 K 6-7
Sungaipenuh 148-149 D 7
Sungaipinang 152-153 KL 6
Sungai Rokan 152-153 D 5
Sungai Rungan 152-153 K 6-7
Sungai Sambas 152-153 H 5
Sungai Sampit 152-153 K 7
Sungai Sekayam 152-153 J 5
Sungai Sembakung 152-153 M 3-4
Sungai Sesayap 152-153 M 4
Sungai Siak 152-153 DE 5
Sungai Simpang-kanan 150-151 AB 11
Sungai Simpang-kiri 152-153 B 4
Sungaisudah 152-153 K 5
Sungai Telen 152-153 M 5
Sungai Tembesi 152-153 E 6-7
Sungai Walahae 152-153 NO 8
Sungari 142-143 N 2-O 3
Sungari Reservoir = Songhua Hu 142-143 O 3
Sung-chiang = Songjiang 142-143 N 5
Sungei Baleh 152-153 K 5
Sungei Balui 152-153 KL 4
Sungei Dungun 150-151 D 10
Sungei Kelantan 150-151 CD 10
Sungei Kemena 152-153 K 4
Sungei Kinabatangan 152-153 M 3
Sungei Labuk 152-153 M 2-3
Sungei Langat 150-151 C 11
Sungei Lebir 150-151 D 10
Sungei Lupar 152-153 J 5
Sungei Muar 150-151 D 12
Sungei Muda 150-151 C 10
Sungei Nal = Kuala Nal 150-151 CD 10
Sungei Pahang 150-151 D 11
Sungei Patani 148-149 CD 5
Sungei Perak 150-151 C 10
Sungei Rompin 150-151 D 11
Sungei Segama 152-153 MN 3
Sungei Sugut 152-153 M 2
Sungei Terengganu 150-151 D 10
Sungguminasa 152-153 N 8
Sung-hsien = Song Xian 146-147 CD 4
Sung hua Chiang = Songhua Jiang 142-143 N 2-O 3
Sŭngjibaegam 144-145 G 2
Sungkai 150-151 C 11
Sungkiang = Songjiang 142-143 N 5
Sung Kong Island 155 I b 2
Sung-k'ou = Songkou 146-147 G 9
Sung Men 150-151 C 3
Sung-mên = Songmen 146-147 H 7
Sung Noen 150-151 CD 5
Sung-t'ao = Songtao 146-147 B 7
Sungu 172 C 2
Sungurlu 136-137 F 2
Sunhing = Xinxing 146-147 D 10
Sunhwa = Xunhua 142-143 J 4
Sunikon 128 IV a 1
Suning = Xiuning 146-147 FG 7
Súnion, Atrōtērion — 122-123 KL 7
Sunke = Xunke 142-143 O 2
Sūn Kosī 134-135 O 5
Sunnagyn, chrebet — 132-133 Y 6
Sunndalsøra 116-117 C 6
Sunniland, FL 80-81 c 3
Sunnūris = Sinnūris 173 B 3
Sunnyside, UT 74-75 H 3
Sunnyside, WA 66-67 CD 2
Sunnyside Park 85 III b 2
Sunnyvale, CA 74-75 B 4
Suno saki 144-145 M 5
Sunray, TX 76-77 D 4-5
Sunrise, AK 58-59 N 6
Sunrise, WY 68-69 D 4
Sun River 66-67 GH 2
Sunsas, Serranía de — 104-105 G 5-6
Sunset, San Francisco-, CA 83 I b 2
Sunset Country 160 E 5
Sunset Heights, Houston-, TX 85 III b 1
Sunset House 60 J 2
Sunset Prairie 60 G 2
Sunshine, Melbourne- 161 II ab 1
Sunstrum 62 C 2
Suntar 132-133 W 5
Suntar-Chajata, chrebet — 132-133 ab 5
Suntaug Lake 84 I b 1
Sûn Taung 141 D 5
Suntaži 124-125 E 5
Sunter, Jakarta- 154 IV b 1
Sunter, Kali — 154 IV b 1
Suntrana, AK 58-59 N 5
Suntsar 134-135 J 5
Sun Valley, ID 66-67 F 4
Sunyang = Xunyang 146-147 B 5
Sunyani 164-165 D 7
Suojarvi 132-133 E 5
Suojoki 124-125 J 2
Suokonmäki 116-117 KL 6
Suolahti 116-117 LM 6
Suomen selkä 116-117 K-N 6
Suomussalmi 116-117 N 5
Suō nada 144-145 H 6
Suonenjoki 116-117 M 6
Suong, Nam — = Nam Seng 150-151 D 2
Sūpa 140 B 3
Supai, AZ 74-75 G 4
Supaol = Supaul 138-139 L 4
Supaul 138-139 L 4
Supe 96-97 F 3
Superb 61 D 5
Superior, AZ 74-75 H 6
Superior, MT 66-67 F 2
Superior, NE 68-69 GH 5
Superior, WI 64-65 H 2
Superior, WY 68-69 B 5
Superior, Lake — 64-65 HJ 2
Superior, Valle — 108-109 FG 4
Suphan, Mae Nam — = Mae Nam Tha Chin 150-151 C 5-6
Suphan Buri 148-149 CD 4
Süphan dağı 136-137 K 3
Supiori, Pulau — 148-149 KL 7
Sup'ung-chŏsuji 144-145 E 2
Supung Hu 142-143 NO 3
Šupunskij, mys — 132-133 f 7
Sūq Ahrās 164-165 F 1
Sūq al-Arbiʻāʼ 166-167 C 2
Sūq al-Arbaʻāʼ al-Aït Bâhâ 166-167 B 4
Sūq al-Arbiʻāʼ 'Ayāshah 166-167 CD 2
Sūq al-Hamīs = Sūq al-Khamīs 166-167 B 4
Sūq al-Hamīs as-Sāḥil = Sūq al-Khamīs as-Sāḥil 166-167 C 2
Sūq al Hamīs Banī 'Arūs = Sūq al-Khamīs Banī 'Arūs 166-167 D 2
Sūq al-Khamīs 166-167 B 4
Sūq al-Khamīs as Sāḥil 166-167 C 2
Sūq al-Khamis Banī 'Arūs 166-167 D 2
Sūq ash-Shuyūkh 136-137 M 7
Sūq ath-Thalāthah 166-167 C 2
Sūq at-Talātah = Sūq ath-Thalāthah 166-167 C 2
Suqian 142-143 M 5
Suquṭrāʼ 134-135 G 8
Ṣūr [Oman] 134-135 H 6
Ṣūr [RL] 136-137 F 6
Sur, Point — 74-75 BC 4
Sura 124-125 Q 6
Sura, Calcutta- 154 II b 2
Sura, Raas — 164-165 b 1
Šurab 134-135 L 2
Surabaia = Surabaya 148-149 F 8
Surabaya 148-149 F 8
Surachany, Baku- 126-127 P 6
Surada = Sorada 138-139 K 8
Sūrajpur 138-139 J 6
Surakarta 148-149 F 8
Sūr al-Ghuzlān 166-167 HJ 1
Şūrān 136-137 G 5
Surat [AUS] 158-159 J 5
Surat [IND] 134-135 L 6
Surate = Surat 134-135 L 6
Sūratgaṛh 138-139 DE 3
Surat Thani 148-149 CD 5
Suraž [SU, Belorusskaja SSR] 124-125 H 6
Suraž [SU, Rossijskaja SFSR] 124-125 J 7
Surbiton, London- 129 II a 2
Surcubamba 96-97 D 8
Sūrdāsh 136-137 L 5
Surendranagar 138-139 C 6
Šuren'ga 124-125 M 2
Suresnes 129 I b 2
Surf, CA 74-75 C 5
Surf Inlet 60 C 3
Surgāna 138-139 D 7
Surgentes, Los — 106-107 FG 4
Surgut [SU, Chanty-Mansijskij NO] 132-133 N 5
Surgut [SU, Kujbyšev] 132-133 J 7
Surguticha 132-133 PQ 5
Sūri 138-139 L 6
Suriāpet 140 D 2
Surigao 148-149 J 5
Surin 148-149 D 4
Suriname [SME, administrative unit] 98-99 L 2
Suriname [SME, state] 92-93 HJ 4
Suring, WI 70-71 F 3
Suripá 94-95 G 4
Suripá, Río — 94-95 F 4
Surkhet 138-139 H 3
Šurma 124-125 RS 5
Sürmene = Hurmurgân 136-137 J 2
Surnadalsøra 116-117 C 6
Surovikino 126-127 L 2
Surprêsa 98-99 F 10
Surprise, Lac de la — 62 O 2
Surprise Valley 66-67 CD 5
Surrey, ND 68-69 F 1
Surrey Canal 129 II b 2
Sur-Sari = ostrov Gogland 124-125 F 3
Sursk 124-125 PQ 7
Surskoje 124-125 Q 6
Surt 164-165 H 2
Surt, As- 164-165 H 2-3
Surt, Khalīj as- 164-165 H 2
Surtanāhū 138-139 BC 4
Surtsey 116-117 c 3
Surubim 100-101 G 4
Sürüç 136-137 H 4
Surucucus, Serra dos — 98-99 G 3
Suruga wan 144-145 M 5
Surukom 168-169 E 4
Surulangun 148-149 D 7
Surulere, Lagos- 170 III b 1
Surumú, Río — 98-99 H 2-3
Surwāya 138-139 FG 5
Šuryškary 132-133 M 4
Sūs, As- 166-167 B 4
Sūs, Wād — 166-167 B 4
Susa [CO] 94-95 DE 5
Susa [I] 122-123 B 3
Susa [IR] 136-137 N 6
Susa [J] 144-145 H 5
Šuša [SU] 126-127 N 7
Susa = Sūsah 164-165 G 1
Sušac 122-123 G 4
Sūsah [LAR] 164-165 J 2
Sūsah [TN] 164-165 G 1
Susaki 144-145 J 6
Susami 144-145 K 6
Susan = Susa 136-137 N 6
Susang = Durgapūr 141 B 3
Susanino 124-125 N 4
Susanville, CA 64-65 B 3
Suščovo 124-125 GH 5
Suşehri 136-137 GH 2
Sushui = Xushui 146-147 E 2
Sušice 118 F 4
Susitna, AK 58-59 M 6
Susitna Lake 58-59 O 5
Susitna River 56-57 FG 5
Suslonger 124-125 R 5
Susner 138-139 F 6
Susong 146-147 F 6
Suspiro 106-107 K 3
Susquehanna, PA 72-73 HJ 4
Susquehanna River 72-73 H 5
Susques 111 C 2
Süssah 136-137 J 5
Süssenbrunn, Wien- 113 I bc 1
Sussex [CDN] 63 D 5
Sussey 119 FG 6
Sustut Peak 60 D 1
Susulatna River 58-59 K 5
Susuman 132-133 cd 5
Susung = Susong 146-147 F 6
Susurluk 136-137 C 3
Sütçüler 136-137 D 4
Suthep, Doi — 150-151 B 3
Sutherland, NE 68-69 F 5
Sutherland [CDN] 61 EF 4
Sutherland [ZA] 172 CD 8
Sutherland, Sydney- 161 I a 3
Sutherland Reservoir 68-69 F 5
Sutherlin, OR 66-67 B 4
Sutlej = Satlaj 134-135 L 4
Sutsien = Suqian 142-143 M 5
Su-ts'un = Sucun 146-147 G 4
Sutter Creek, CA 74-75 C 3
Sutton, NE 68-69 H 5
Sutton, WV 72-73 F 5
Sutton, London- 129 II b 2
Suttsu 144-145 ab 2
Sutvik Island 58-59 e 1
Suurberge [ZA ↑ Winterberge] 174-175 F 6
Suurberge [ZA ↙ Winterberge] 174-175 F 7
Suure-Jaani 124-125 E 4
Suur Manamägi 124-125 F 5
Suur väin 124-125 D 4
Suva 148-149 a 2
Suvadiva Atoll 176 ab 2
Suvainiškis 124-125 E 5
Suvorov [island] 156-157 JK 5
Suvorovo 126-127 D 4
Suwa 144-145 M 4
Suwa-ko 144-145 M 4-5
Suwałki 118 L 1
Suwalki = Vilkaviškis 124-125 D 6
Suwanna Phum 150-151 DE 5
Suwannee River 80-81 b 2
Suwannee Sound 80-81 b 2
Şuwār, Aş- 136-137 J 5
Suwaybit, As- 136-137 H 6
Suwaydāʼ, As- 134-135 D 4
Suwayḥ 134-135 HJ 6
Suwayqīyah, Hawr as- 136-137 LM 6
Şuwayr 136-137 J 7
Şuwayrah, Aş- 136-137 L 6
Suways, As- 164-165 L 2-3
Suways, Khalīj as- 164-165 L 3
Suways, Qanat as- 164-165 L 2
Suweis, Es- = As-Suways 164-165 L 2-3
Suweis, Khalīg es — = Khalīj as-Suways 164-165 L 3
Suweis, Qanât es- = Qanat as-Suways 164-165 L 2
Suwen = Xuwen 146-147 BC 11
Suwŏn 142-143 P 4
Şuwwān, 'Arḍ eş — = 'Arḍ aş-Şawwān 136-137 G 7
Su Xian 142-143 M 5
Suxima = Tsushima 144-145 G 5
Suyut 150-151 E 2
Suzaka 144-145 M 4
Suzdal' 124-125 N 5
Suzhou 142-143 N 5
Suzu 144-145 L 4
Suzuka 144-145 L 5
Suzu misaki 144-145 L 4
Svalbard = Spitsbergen 116-117 k 6-o 5
Svanetskij chrebet 126-127 L 5
Svapa 124-125 K 8
Svappavaara 116-117 J 4
Svār = Suār 138-139 G 3
Svartenhuk Halvø 56-57 Za 3
Svartisen 116-117 EF 4
Sv'atoj Krest' = Prikumsk 126-127 LM 4
Sv'atoj Nos, mys — 132-133 ab 3
Svatovo 126-127 J 2
Svay Chek 150-151 D 6
Svay Daun Keo 150-151 D 6
Svay Rieng 148-149 E 4
Sveagruva 116-117 k 6
Svealand 116-117 E-G 7
Sveča 124-125 Q 4
Svedala 116-117 E 10
Sveg 116-117 F 6
Svelvik 116-117 CD 8
Švenčionėliai 124-125 EF 6
Svendborg 116-117 D 10
Svenskøya 116-117 mn 5
Šventoji 124-125 E 6
Sverdlovo [SU, Vologodskaja Oblast'] 124-125 MN 4
Sverdlovsk [SU, Rossijskaja SFSR] 132-133 L 6
Sverdlovsk [SU, Ukrainskaja SSR] 126-127 JK 2
Sverdrup, ostrov — 132-133 O 3
Sverdrup Islands 56-57 P-T 2
Svessa 124-125 JK 8
Svetac 122-123 F 4
Svetlaja 132-133 a 8
Svetlogorsk [SU, Belorusskaja SSR] 124-125 GH 7
Svetlograd 126-127 L 4
Svetlyj [SU → Orsk] 132-133 L 7
Svetogorsk 124-125 G 3
Svetozarevo 122-123 J 3-4
Svijaga 124-125 R 6
Svilengrad 122-123 LM 5
Svir' [SU, place] 124-125 F 6
Svir [SU, river] 132-133 EF 5
Svirica 124-125 J 3
Svirsk 132-133 T 7
Svir'stroj 124-125 J 3
Svisloč' [SU, place] 124-125 E 7
Svisloč' [SU, river ◁ Berezina] 124-125 FG 7
Svištov 122-123 L 4
Svoboda [SU] 124-125 KL 8
Svobodnyj [SU ↑ Belogorsk] 132-133 YZ 7
Svobodnyj [SU, Saratovskaja Oblast'] 124-125 PQ 7
Svobodnyj = Svobodnyj 132-133 YZ 7
Svolvær 116-117 F 3
Swabian Alb = Schwäbische Alb 118 D 5-E 4
Swabue = Shanwei 146-147 E 10
Swaib, As — = Ash-Shuwayyib 136-137 MN 7
Swaibit, As — = As-Suwaybit 136-137 H 6
Swain Post 62 C 2
Swain Reefs 158-159 K 4
Swains 208 JK 4
Swainsboro, GA 80-81 E 4
Şwaira, Aş — = Aş-Şuwayrah 136-137 L 6
Swakop 174-175 B 2
Swakopmund 172 B 6
Swale 119 F 4
Swalferort = Sõrve säär 124-125 CD 5
Swallow Islands 148-149 l 7
Swāmihalli 140 C 3
Swampscott, MA 84 I c 2
Swanage 119 F 6
Swan Hill 158-159 H 7
Swan Hills 56-57 N 7
Swan Lake [CDN] 61 H 4
Swan Lake [USA] 68-69 FG 3
Swanley 129 II c 2
Swannell Ranges 60 E 1
Swan Range 66-67 G 2
Swan River [CDN, place] 56-57 Q 7
Swan River [CDN, river ◁ Little Slave Lake] 60 K 2
Swan River [CDN, river ◁ Swan Lake] 61 H 4-5
Swansea 119 DE 6
Swansea, SC 80-81 F 4
Swans Island 72-73 M 2-3
Swanton, VT 72-73 K 2
Swanville, MN 70-71 C 3
Swar = Suār 138-139 G 3
Swartberg 174-175 H 6
Swartberge 172 D 8
Swarthmore College 84 III ab 2
Swartkops 174-175 F 7
Swartmodder 174-175 D 5
Swart Nossob 174-175 C 2
Swartplaas 174-175 G 4
Swartrand 174-175 B 3-4
Swartruggens [ZA, Kaapland] 174-175 F 7
Swartruggens [ZA, Transvaal] 174-175 G 3
Swart Umfolozi 174-175 J 4-5
Swasiland 172 F 7
Swāt 134-135 L 3-4
Swatow = Shantou 142-143 M 7
Swaziland 172 F 7
Sweden 116-117 F 8-K 4
Swede Run 84 III d 1-2
Swedesburg, PA 84 III ab 1
Swedru 168-169 E 4
Sweeny, TX 76-77 G 8
Sweetgrass, MT 66-67 GH 1
Sweet Home, OR 66-67 B 3
Sweetwater, TX 64-65 FG 5
Sweetwater River 68-69 B 4
Swellendam 172 D 8
Swenyaung 141 E 5
Świdnica 118 H 3
Świdwin 118 GH 2
Świebodzin 118 G 2
Świecie 118 HJ 2
Swift Current 56-57 P 7-8
Swift River 58-59 K 6
Swinburne, Cape — 56-57 R 3
Swindon 119 F 6
Swinoujście 118 G 2
Swinton Islands = Hswindan Kyûnmyâ 150-151 AB 7
Switzerland 118 CD 5
Sybaris 122-123 G 6
Sycamore, IL 70-71 F 4-5
Sychem = Nābulus 136-137 F 6
Syčovka 124-125 JK 6
Sydney [AUS] 158-159 K 6
Sydney [CDN] 56-57 Y 8
Sydney [Phoenix Islands] 208 JK 3
Sydney, University of — 161 I ab 2
Sydney-Ashfield 161 I a 2
Sydney-Auburn 161 I a 2
Sydney-Balmain 161 I b 2
Sydney-Bankstown 161 I a 2
Sydney-Beverly Hills 161 I a 2
Sydney-Bexley 161 I a 2
Sydney-Botany 161 I b 2
Sydney-Brookvale 161 I b 1
Sydney-Burwood 161 I a 2
Sydney-Campsie 161 I a 2
Sydney-Canterbury 161 I a 2
Sydney-Carlingford 161 I a 1
Sydney-Chatswood 161 I b 1
Sydney-Chullora 161 I a 2
Sydney-Concord 161 I a 2
Sydney-Crows Nest 161 I b 1
Sydney-Drummoyne 161 I a 2
Sydney-Earlwood 161 I a 2
Sydney-Eastwood 161 I a 1
Sydney-Epping 161 I a 1
Sydney-Ermington 161 I a 1
Sydney-Gladesville 161 I a 1
Sydney Harbour Bridge 161 I b 2
Sydney-Hunters Hill 161 I ab 2
Sydney-Hurstville 161 I a 2
Sydney-Kogarah 161 I a 2
Sydney-Kurnell 161 I b 3
Sydney-Lane Cove 161 I ab 1
Sydney-La Perouse 161 I b 2
Sydney-Leichhardt 161 I ab 2
Sydney-Lidcombe 161 I a 2
Sydney-Lindfield 161 I ab 1
Sydney-Manly 161 I b 1
Sydney-Maroubra 161 I b 2
Sydney-Marrickville 161 I ab 2
Sydney-Matraville 161 I b 2
Sydney Mines 63 FG 4
Sydney-Mosman 161 I b 1
Sydney-Newtown 161 I ab 2
Sydney-North Ryde 161 I a 1
Sydney-North Sydney 161 I b 1-2
Sydney-Oatley 161 I a 2
Sydney-Parramatta 161 I a 1
Sydney-Peakhurst 161 I a 2
Sydney-Punchbowl 161 I a 2
Sydney-Ramsgate 161 I a 2
Sydney-Randwick 161 I b 2
Sydney-Redfern 161 I b 2
Sydney-Regents Park 161 I a 2
Sydney-Revesby 161 I a 2
Sydney-Rockdale 161 I a 2
Sydney-Rosebury 161 I b 2
Sydney-Rydalmere 161 I a 1
Sydney-Ryde 161 I a 1
Sydney-Strathfield 161 I a 2
Sydney-Sutherland 161 I a 3
Sydney-Sylvania 161 I a 3
Sydney-Vaucluse 161 I b 2
Sydney-Waverly 161 I b 2
Sydney-Willoughby 161 I b 1
Sydney-Woollahra 161 I b 2
Syene = Aswān 164-165 L 4
Syfergat 174-175 G 6
Syktyvkar 132-133 J 5
Sylacauga, AL 78-79 F 4
Sylarna 116-117 E 6
Sylhet = Silhaṭ 134-135 P 6
Sylt 118 D 1
Sylva 124-125 V 4
Sylva, NC 80-81 E 3
Sylvan Grove, KS 68-69 G 6
Sylvania, GA 80-81 F 4
Sylvania, Sydney- 161 I a 3
Sylvan Lake 60 K 3
Sylvan Pass 66-67 H 3
Sylvester, GA 80-81 E 5
Sylvester, TX 76-77 DE 6
Sylvester, Mount — 63 J 3
Sylvia, KS 68-69 G 7
Sylviaberg 174-175 A 3
Sylvia Hill = Sylviaberg 174-175 A 3
Sym 132-133 Q 5
Sýmē 122-123 M 7
Syndasko 132-133 UV 3
Syowa 53 C 4-5
Syracuse, KS 68-69 F 6-7
Syracuse, NY 64-65 LM 3
Syrdarja 132-133 M 9
Syria 134-135 D 4
Syriam = Thanlyin 148-149 C 3
Syrian Desert 134-135 DE 4
Sýrna 122-123 M 7
Sýros 122-123 L 7
Syrskij 124-125 M 7
Sysladobsis Lake 72-73 MN 2
Sysola 124-125 S 3
Sysran = Syzran' 132-133 N 7
Syt'kovo 124-125 K 5
Sytynja 132-133 YZ 4
Syzran' 132-133 H 7
Syzran'-Kašpirovka 124-125 R 7
Szamos 122-123 K 2
Szamotuły 118 H 2
Szczecin 118 G 2
Szczecinek 118 H 2
Szczytno 118 K 2
Szechuan = Sichuan 142-143 J 6-K 5
Szeged 118 JK 5
Szehsien = Si Xian 146-147 FG 5
Székesfehérvár 118 J 5
Szekszárd 118 J 5
Szemao = Simao 142-143 J 7
Szeming = Xiamen 142-143 M 7
Szentes 118 K 5
Szeping = Siping 142-143 N 3
Szeskie Wzgórza 118 KL 1
Szolnok 118 K 5
Szombathely 118 H 5
Szū-an = Si'an 146-147 G 6
Szū-mao = Simao 142-143 J 7
Szū-ming Shan = Siming Shan 146-147 H 7
Szū-nan = Sinan 146-147 B 8
Szū-p'ing = Siping 142-143 N 3
Szū-shui = Sishui [TJ, Henan] 146-147 D 4
Szū-shui = Sishui [TJ, Shandong] 146-147 F 4
Szū-tao-kou = Sidaogou 144-145 F 2
Szū-t'ing = Siting 146-147 D 3

T

Ta = Da Xian 142-143 K 5
Tababela 96-97 B 2
Tabacal 104-105 D 8
Tabaco 148-149 H 4
Tabacundo 96-97 B 1
Tābah, Bi'r — 173 D 3
Tabajé, Ponta — 92-93 LM 5
Tābalbalah 166-167 E 5
Tābalkūzah 166-167 G 5
Tabang Chhu 141 B 2
Tabankort 164-165 D 5
Tabankulu 174-175 H 6
Tabar Islands 148-149 h 5
Tabarka = Ṭabarqah 164-165 F 1
Ṭabarqah 164-165 F 1
Ṭabas 134-135 H 4
Tabasará, Serranía de — 88-89 EF 10
Tabasco 64-65 H 8
Tabašino 124-125 QR 5
Tabatière, la — 63 G 2
Tabatinga [BR, Amazonas] 92-93 F 5
Tabatinga [BR, São Paulo] 102-103 H 4
Tabatinga, Serra — 98-99 GH 4
Tabatinga, Serra da — 100-101 B 6
Tabayin = Dīpèyin 141 D 4
Tabelbala = Tābalbalah 166-167 E 5
Tabelkoza = Tābalkūzah 166-167 G 5
Taber 56-57 O 7
Taberdga = Sharshar 166-167 K 2
Taberg 116-117 EF 9
Tabiazo 96-97 B 1
Tabira 100-101 F 4
Tabiteuea 208 H 3
Tablada, La Matanza- 110 III b 2
Tablang Dsong = Tāplejung 138-139 L 4
Tablas, Cabo — 106-107 AB 3
Tablas, Las — 88-89 FG 11
Tablas Island 148-149 H 4
Tāblat 166-167 H 1
Tablazo, El — 94-95 F 2
Tablazo de Ica 96-97 CD 9
Table, Île de la — = Đao Cai Ban 148-149 E 2
Table Bay = Tafelbaai 174-175 C 7
Table Cape 161 H 4
Table Island 155 I b 2
Table Mount 58-59 Q 2
Table Mount = Tafelberg 174-175 BC 8
Table Mountain 66-67 G 3
Table Rock 68-69 G 4
Table Rock Lake 78-79 C 2
Tablón, El — [CO, Nariño] 94-95 C 7
Tablón, El — [CO, Sucre] 94-95 D 3
Taboada [RA] 106-107 F 1-2
Taboco, Rio — 102-103 E 4
Taboga 64-65 b 3
Taboga, Isla — 64-65 bc 3
Taboguilla, Isla — 64-65 bc 3
Taboleiro 100-101 E 5
Tábor 118 G 4
Tabora 172 F 3
Tabor City, NC 80-81 G 3
Taborda, Serra — 100-101 F 5
Tabou 164-165 C 8
Tabrīs = Tabrīz 134-135 F 3
Tabrīz 134-135 F 3
Tábua, Lago — 100-101 C 2
Tabu-dong 144-145 G 4
Tabūk 134-135 D 5
Tabuleirinho, Cachoeira 98-99 K 5
Tabuleiro 98-99 JK 7
Tabuleiro, Morro do — 102-103 H 7
Täby 116-117 GH 8
Tabyn-Bogdo-Ola = Tavan Bogd uul 142-143 F 2
Tacabamba 96-97 B 5
Tacagua 91 II a 1
Tacaimbó 100-101 F 5
Tacambaro de Codallos 86-87 K 8
Tacaná, Volcán de — 86-87 O 10
Tacañitas 106-107 F 2
Tacaratu 100-101 EF 5
Tacarcuna, Cerro — 94-95 C 3
Tacarigua [YV, Nueva Esparta] 94-95 JK 2
Tacarigua [YV, Valencia] 94-95 GH 2-3
Tacarigua, Laguna de — 94-95 J 2
Tacau = Kaohsiung 142-143 MN 7
Tačev 126-127 A 2
Ta-ch'ang-shan Tao = Dachangshan Dao 144-145 D 3
Tacheng = Chuguchak 142-143 E 2
Ta-ch'êng = Chuguchak 142-143 E 2
Tachi [RC ↘ Pingtung] 146-147 H 10
Tachi [RC ↙ Taipei] 146-147 H 9
Tachia 142-143 MN 7
Ta-ch'iao = Daqiao 146-147 E 7
Tachibana-wan 144-145 GH 6
Tachikawa 144-145 M 5
Tachin = Samut Sakhon 150-151 BC 6
Ta-ching = Dajing 146-147 H 7
Ta-ch'ing Shan = Daqing Shan 142-143 L 3
Táchira 94-95 EF 4
Tachiūmet = Takyūmit 166-167 LM 6
Ta-chou-Tao = Dazhou Dao 150-151 H 3
Tachrīrt, Djebel — = Jabal Tashrīrt 166-167 J 2
Tachta 132-133 a 7
Tachta-Bazar 134-135 J 3
Tachtabrod 132-133 M 7
Tachtojamsk 132-133 de 5
Ta-ch'üan = Daquan 142-143 H 3
Tacima 100-101 G 4
Tacloban 148-149 HJ 4
Tacna [PE, administrative unit] 96-97 F 10
Tacna [PE, place] 92-93 E 8
Tacoma, WA 64-65 B 2
Taconic Range 72-73 K 3-4
Tacony, Philadelphia-, PA 84 III c 1
Tacony Creek 84 III c 1
Tacony Creek Park 84 III c 1
Taco Pozo 104-105 E 9
Tacora, Volcán — 111 C 1
Tacuaras 102-103 CD 7
Tacuarembó [ROU, administrative unit] 106-107 JK 4
Tacuarembó [ROU, place] 111 EF 4
Tacuarembó, Río — 106-107 K 4
Tacuatí 102-103 D 5
Tacuato 94-95 G 2
Tacuba, Ciudad de México- 91 I b 2
Tacubaya, Ciudad de México- 91 I b 2
Tacural 106-107 G 3
Tacuru 102-103 E 5
Tacutú, Rio — 98-99 HJ 3
Tāda Kaṇḍera 138-139 C 3
Tadami gawa 144-145 M 4
Tadarimana, Ribeiro — 102-103 E 2
Tadau = Tandāʼū 141 D 5
Tadein 150-151 B 5
Tademaït, Plateau du — = Tādmaït 164-165 E 3
Tādepallegūdem 140 E 2
Ta Det, Phnom — 150-151 D 6
Tadet, Sebkret — = Sabkhat Tādit 166-167 M 3
Tāḍipatri = Tādpatri 134-135 M 7-8
Tādīsat, Ḥāssī — 166-167 K 6
Tādit, Sabkhat — 166-167 M 3
Tadjemout = Tajmūt 166-167 H 7
Tâdjerouïn = Tājarwīn 166-167 L 2
Tadjerouma = Tājrūmah 166-167 H 3
Tadjoura 164-165 N 6
Tadjoura, Golfe de — 164-165 N 6
Tādmāït 164-165 E
Tadmur 134-135 D 4
Tadnist, Hassi — = Ḥāssī Tādīsat 166-167 K 6
Tadó 94-95 C 5
Tadoussac 56-57 X 8
Tādpatri 134-135 M 7-8
Tadum = Tradum 142-143 E 6
Tadzhik Soviet Socialist Republic 134-135 KL 3
T'aean 144-145 F 4
T'aebaek-san 144-145 G 4
T'aebaek-sanmaek 142-143 O 4
Taebu-do 144-145 F 4
T'aech'ŏn 144-145 E 3
Taech'ŏng-do 144-145 E 4
Taedong-gang 144-145 EF 3
Taegu 142-143 O 4
Tae-hŭksan-do 144-145 E 5
Taehwa-do 144-145 E 3
Taejŏn 142-143 O 4
Taejŏng 144-145 EF 6
Tae-muŭi-do 144-145 EF 4
Ta-êrh Hu = Dalaj Nur 142-143 M 3
T'aet'an 144-145 E 3
Tae-yŏnp'yŏng-do 144-145 E 4
Tafalla 120-121 G 7
Tafalnī, Rāʼs — 166-167 AB 4
Ta-fan = Dafan 146-147 E 7
Tafaraut = Ṭarfāyah 164-165 B 3
Tafasasat, Wādī — 164-165 F 4
Tafassasset, Ouéd — = Wādī Tafāsasat 164-165 F 4
Tafassasset, Ténéré du — 164-165 FG 4
Tafdasat 164-165 F 3-4
Tafelbaai 174-175 C 7
Tafelberg [A] 113 I a 1
Tafelberg [SME] 98-99 K 3

366 Sungai

Tafelberg [ZA, mountain]
174-175 BC 8
Tafelberg [ZA, place] 174-175 F 6
Tafelney, Cap — = Rā's Tafalnī
166-167 AB 4
Tafesrit, Hassi — = Ḥāssī Tafzirt
166-167 K 7
Ṭafīlah, Aṭ- 136-137 F 7
Tāfīlāl't 166-167 DE 4
Tafinegoûlt = Tāfingūlt 166-167 B 4
Tāfingūlt 166-167 B 4
Tafí Viejo 111 C 3
Tafôrhalt = Tāfūghāh 166-167 E 2
Tafrannt = Tafrānt 166-167 D 2
Tafrānt 166-167 D 2
Tafrāūt 166-167 B 5
Tafresh 136-137 N 5
Tafresh, Kūh-e — 136-137 NO 5
Taft, CA 74-75 D 5
Taft, OK 76-77 G 5
Taft, TX 76-77 F 8-9
Taftān, Kūh-e — 134-135 J 5
Tāfūghāh 166-167 E 2
Tafzirt, Ḥāssī — 166-167 K 7
Tagagawik River 58-59 H 4
Tagalak Island 58-59 j 5
Tagalgan 142-143 H 4
Taganrog 126-127 J 3
Taganrogskij zaliv 126-127 HJ 3
Tāgau 148-149 C 2
Tagaung 141 E 4
Tagawa = Takawa 144-145 H 6
Tagbilaran 148-149 H 5
Tag-Dheer 164-165 b 2
Tagelswangen 128 IV b 1
Taghbālt 166-167 D 4
Taghbālt, Wād — 166-167 D 4
Taghghīsht 166-167 B 5
Tāghīt 164-165 D 2
Tagiúra = Tājūrā' 164-165 G 2
Tagla Khar 138-139 H 2
Tagmar 138-139 M 3
Tagna 94-95 b 2
Tagoûnît = Tāgūnīt 166-167 D 5
Tagrag Tsangpo 138-139 L 2
Tagsut = Ṭahār as-Sūq
166-167 DE 2
Tagtse 138-139 M 3
Tagu = Taegu 142-143 O 4
Tagua, La — 94-95 D 8
Taguatinga [BR, Distrito Federal]
92-93 K 8
Taguatinga [BR, Goiás] 92-93 K 7
Taguedoufat 168-169 H 1-2
Taguine = Tāḥīn 166-167 H 2
Tagula 148-149 h 7
Tagum 148-149 J 5
Tāgūnīt 166-167 D 5
Tagus = Tajo 120-121 F 8
Tahālah 166-167 D 2
Tahan, Gunung — 148-149 D 6
Tahara 144-145 L 5
Ṭahār as-Sūq 166-167 DE 2
Tahat 164-165 F 4
Tahaungdam 141 E 1
Tahawndam = Tahaungdam
141 E 1
Tāhīn 166-167 H 2
Tahiti 156-157 K 5
Tahlequah, OK 76-77 G 5
Tahltan 58-59 W 7
Tahoe, Lake — 64-65 BC 4
Tahoe City, CA 74-75 C 3
Tahoe Valley, CA 74-75 CD 3
Tahoka, TX 76-77 D 6
Tahola, WA 66-67 A 2
Tahoua 164-165 F 6
Taḥrīr, At- 173 AB 2
Ta-hsien = Da Xian 142-143 K 5
Ta-hsin-tien = Daxindian
146-147 H 3
Tahsis 60 D 5
Ta Hsü = Chimei Hsü 146-147 G 10
Ta-hsüeh Shan = Daxue Shan
142-143 J 5-6
Ṭaḥṭā 164-165 L 3
Tahtacı = Borlu 136-137 C 3
Tahtalı dağı 136-137 D 4
Tahtali dağlar 136-137 F 4-G 3
Tahtsa Peak 60 D 3
Ta-hu = Tachia 142-143 MN 7
Tahua 104-105 C 6
Ta-hua Chiao = Dahua Jiao
150-151 H 3
Tahulandang, Pulau — 148-149 J 6
Tahuna 148-149 HJ 6
Ta-hung Shan = Dahong Shan
146-147 D 6
Ta-hu-shan = Dahushan
144-145 D 2
Taï 164-165 C 7
Taï, Parc National de —
168-169 D 4
Tai'an [TJ, Liaoning] 144-145 D 2
Tai'an [TJ, Shandong] 142-143 M 4
Tai Au Mun 155 I b 2
Taiba 168-169 A 2
Taibai 146-147 B 3
Taibai Shan 142-143 K 5
Taibei = Taipei 142-143 N 6-7
Taïbet-el-Gueblia = Ṭāyabat al-
Janūbiyah 166-167 K 3
Taicang 146-147 H 6
Tai-chou Wan = Taizhou Wan
146-147 H 7
Taichū = Taichung 142-143 N 7
Taichung 142-143 MN 7
Tai-chung = Taichung
142-143 MN 7
Tai-chung-hsien = Fêngyüan
146-147 H 9
Tāīdālt 166-167 B 5
Taiden = Taejŏn 142-143 O 4
Taidong = Taitung 142-143 N 7
Taieri River 161 D 7
Ṭā'if, Aṭ- 134-135 E 6
Taigu 142-143 L 4
Tai Hang, Victoria- 155 I b 2
Taihang Shan 142-143 LM 4
Taihape 161 FG 4
Taihe [TJ, Anhui] 146-147 E 5
Taihe [TJ, Jiangxi] 142-143 L 6
Taihei yō 144-145 K 7-O 3
Taihing = Taixing 142-143 N 5
T'ai-ho = Taihe [TJ, Anhui]
146-147 E 5
Taiho = Taihe [TJ, Jiangxi]
142-143 L 6
Taihoku = Taipei 142-143 N 6-7
Taihsien = Dai Xian 146-147 D 2
Tai Hu [TJ, lake] 142-143 MN 5
Taihu [TJ, place] 146-147 F 6
Taikang 146-147 E 4
Taiki 144-145 c 2
Taikkyī 141 DE 7
Tai Koo Shing, Victoria- 155 I b 2
Taiku = Taigu 142-143 L 4
Taikyu = Taegu 142-143 O 4
Tailai 142-143 N 2
T'ai-lai = Tailai 142-143 N 2
Tailem Bend 158-159 GH 7
Tailie 146-147 B 8
Tai Long Head 155 I b 2
Taim 111 F 4
Tai Muang 152-153 BC 1
Taimyr Lake = ozero Tajmyr
132-133 TU 3
Taimyr Peninsula = Tajmyr
132-133 S-U 2
Tain [GB] 119 D 3
Tain [GH] 168-169 E 4
Tainan 142-143 MN 7
T'ai-nan = Tainan 142-143 MN 7
Tainão = Tainan 142-143 MN 7
Tainaron, Akrōtērion — 122-123 K 7
Taining 146-147 F 8
Tai No 155 I b 1
Taiō 102-103 GH 7
Taiobeiras 102-103 LM 1
T'ai-pai Shan = Taibai Shan
146-147 A 4-5
Taipale 116-117 N 6
Taipas 100-101 A 7
Taipeh = Taipei 142-143 N 6-7
Taipei 142-143 N 6-7
Taiping [MAL] 148-149 CD 5-6
Taiping [TJ, Anhui] 146-147 G 6
Taiping [TJ, Guangdong]
146-147 D 10
Taiping [TJ, Guangxi Zhuangzu
Zizhiqu] 146-147 C 10
Taipingshao 144-145 E 2
Taiping Wan 146-147 G 3
Taiping Yang 142-143 O 8-R 5
Taipinsan = Miyako-jima
142-143 O 7
Taipu 100-101 G 3
Taisei 144-145 ab 2
Tai Seng 154 III b 2
Taisha 144-145 J 5
Tai Shan [TJ, mountains]
146-147 F 3
Taishan [TJ, place] 146-147 D 10
Tai Shan = Dai Shan 146-147 HJ 6
Taishan Liedao 146-147 H 8
Taishun 142-143 MN 6
Taisien = Tai Xian 146-147 H 5
Ta'iss = Ta'izz 134-135 E 8
Tai Tam Bay 155 I b 2
Taitam Peninsula 155 I b 2
Tai Tam Reservoirs 155 I b 2
Taitao, Cabo — 111 A 7
Taitao, Peninsula de — 111 AB 7
T'ai-tchong = Taichung
142-143 MN 7
Taitō = Taitung 142-143 N 7
Taitō, Tōkyō- 155 III b 1
Taitsang = Taicang 146-147 H 6
Taitung 142-143 N 7
T'ai-tzŭ Ho = Taizi He 144-145 D 2
Taivalkoski 116-117 N 5
Taivassalo 116-117 JK 7
Taiwa 144-145 N 3
Tai Wai 155 I b 1
Tai Wan [HK] 155 I b 2
Taiwan [RC] 142-143 N 7
Taiwan Haihsia 142-143 M 7-N 6
Taiwan Haixia = Taiwan Haihsia
142-143 M 7-N 6
Taiwan Strait = Taiwan Haihsia
142-143 M 7-N 6
Tai Wan Tau 155 I b 2
Tai Xian 146-147 H 5
Taixing 142-143 N 5
Taiyanggong, Beijing- 155 II b 2
Taiyuan 142-143 L 4
T'ai-yüan = Taiyuan 142-143 L 4
Taiyue Shan 146-147 CD 3
Taizhong = Taichung
142-143 MN 7
Taizhou 142-143 MN 5
Taizhou Wan 146-147 H 7
Taizi He 144-145 D 2
Ta'izz 134-135 E 8
Tāj, At- 164-165 J 4
Taj, El — = At-Tāj 164-165 J 4
Tajan 148-149 F 7
Tajarḥī 164-165 G 4
Tājarwīn 166-167 L 2
Tajdžinar nuur 142-143 GH 4
Tajga 132-133 PQ 6
Tajgonos, mys — 132-133 ef 5
Tajgonos, poluostrov — 132-133 f 5
Tajīm, El — 86-87 M 7
Tajima 144-145 M 4
Tajique, NM 76-77 A 5
Tajis 134-135 G 8
Tajjal 138-139 B 4
Tajmura 132-133 ST 5
Tajmūt [DZ, Jabal 'Amūr]
166-167 H 7
Tājmūt [DZ, Sahara] 166-167 H 3
Tajmyr, ozero — 132-133 TU 3
Tajmyr, poluostrov — 132-133 R-U 2
Tajmyrskij Nacional'nyj Okrug =
Dolgano-Nenets Autonomous
Area 132-133 P-U 3
Tajo 120-121 F 8
Tajpur 154 II a 1
Tājrūmah 166-167 H 3
Tajsara, Cordillera de —
104-105 D 7
Tajšet 132-133 S 6
Tajsir 142-143 H 2
Tajumulco, Volcán de — 64-65 H 8
Tajuña 120-121 F 8
T'a-jung = Tarong 141 F 1-2
Tajūrā' 164-165 G 2
Tak 148-149 C 3
Takāb 136-137 M 4
Takaba 171 E 2
Takachiho = Mitai 144-145 H 6
Takachu 174-175 DE 2
Takada 142-143 Q 4
Takada = Bungotakada
144-145 H 6
Takada = Rikuzen-Takata
144-145 NO 3
Takahagi 144-145 N 4
Takahashi 144-145 J 5
Takahashi-gawa 144-145 J 5
Takahe, Mount — 53 B 25-26
Takaido, Tōkyō- 155 III a 1
Takaishi 155 III a 2
Takalar 148-149 G 8
Takamatsu 142-143 PQ 5
Takamatu = Takamatsu
142-143 PQ 5
Takamori 144-145 H 6
Takanabe 144-145 H 6
Takane 155 III d 1
Takao = Kaohsiung 142-143 MN 7
Takaoka 142-143 Q 4
Takapuna 158-159 O 7
Takasaki 142-143 Q 4
Takataka 148-149 k 6
Takawa 144-145 H 6
Takayama 144-145 L 4
Takayanagi 155 III c 3
Takefu 144-145 KL 5
Takemachi = Taketa 144-145 H 6
Takengon 148-149 C 6
Takenotsuka, Tōkyō- 155 III b 1
Takèo 148-149 D 4
Take-shima [J ↖ Oki] 144-145 HJ 4
Take-shima [J, Ōsumi shotō]
144-145 H 7
Tākestān 136-137 NO 4
Taketa 144-145 H 6
Takhini River 58-59 T 6
Takhli 150-151 C 5
Takhlīs, Bi'r — 173 AB 6
Takht-e Jāmshīd = Persepolis
134-135 G 4
Takht-e Soleymān 136-137 O 4
Taki 155 III d 1
Takieta 168-169 H 2
Takikawa 144-145 b 2
Takinogawa, Tōkyō- 155 III b 1
Takinoue 144-145 c 1
Takipy 61 H 3
Takiyuak Lake 56-57 O 4
Takkuna neem 124-125 CD 4
Takla Lake 56-57 LM 6
Takla Landing 60 DE 2
Takla Makan 142-143 D-F 4
Takla Makan Chŏli 142-143 D-F 4
Takla River 60 D 2
Tako-bana 144-145 J 5
Takolekaju, Pegunungan —
152-153 N 6-O 7
Takoradi = Sekondi-Takoradi
164-165 D 7-8
Takotna, AK 58-59 JK 5
Takslesluk Lake 58-59 F 6
Ta-ku = Dagu 146-147 F 2
Takua Pa 148-149 C 5
Takua Thung 150-151 B 8
Taku Glacier 58-59 U 7
Ta-ku Ho = Dagu He 146-147 H 3
Takum 168-169 H 4
Taku River 58-59 V 7
Tākwayat, Wādī — 164-165 E 4
Takyu = Taegu 142-143 O 4
Takyūmit 166-167 LM 6
Tala [ET] 173 B 2
Tala [MEX] 86-87 J 7
Tala [ROU] 106-107 K 5
Tāla = Tālah 166-167 L 2
Tala, El — [RA, San Luis]
106-107 D 4
Tala, El — [RA, Tucumán]
104-105 D 9-10
Talacasto 111 C 4
Talagante 106-107 B 4
Talagapa 108-109 E 4
Talagapa, Pampa de —
108-109 EF 4
Talāgh 166-167 F 2
Tālah 166-167 L 2
Talai [IND] 140 C 4
Ta Lai [VN] 150-151 F 7
Talaimannar = Taleimannārama
134-135 MN 9
Tālāinot = Tālāīnūt 166-167 D 2
Tālāīnūt 166-167 D 2
Talājā 138-139 CD 7
Talak 164-165 EF 5
Talakmau, Gunung —
152-153 CD 5-6
Talamanca, Cordillera de —
88-89 E 10
Talamba 138-139 D 2
Talampaya, Campo de —
106-107 CD 2-3
Talamuyuna 106-107 D 2
Talana 174-175 J 5
Talang, Gunung — 152-153 D 6
Tala Norte 106-107 F 3
Talanyené, Rapides de —
168-169 E 3
Tālaqān 136-137 O 4
Talar, Tigre-El — 110 III b 1
Talara 92-93 C 5
Talas 132-133 N 9
Talasea 148-149 gh 6
Talasherī = Tellicherry 140 B 5
Talasheri = Tellicherry 140 B 5
Talātā', At- = Ath-Thālātha' [MA,
Marrākush] 166-167 BC 3-4
Talātā', At- = Ath-Thālātha' [MA,
Miknās] 166-167 D 2
Talata Mafara 168-169 G 2
Talat Chum = Wang Thong
150-151 C 4
Talaud, Kepulauan — 148-149 J 6
Talaut Islands = Kepulauan Talaud
148-149 J 6
Talavera, Isla — 106-107 J 1
Talavera de la Reina 120-121 E 8-9
Talawdī 164-165 L 6
Talawgyi = Htālawgyī 141 E 3
Talberg 128 III b 1
Talbingo 160 J 5
Talbot, Cape — 158-159 E 2
Talbot, Mount — 158-159 E 5
Talbotton, GA 78-79 G 4
Talca 111 B 5
Talca, Punta — 106-107 AB 4
Talcan, Isla — 108-109 C 4
Tālcher 138-139 K 7
Talco, TX 76-77 G 6
Talcuhuano 111 AB 5
Taldykuduk 126-127 O 1
Taldy-Kurgan 132-133 OP 8
Talegaon Dābhāde 140 AB 1
Taleimannārama 134-135 MN 9
Tal-e Khosravī 134-135 G 4
Talembote = Tālāīnūt 166-167 D 2
Talemzane = Tālamzān
166-167 HJ 3
Talent, OR 66-67 B 4
Tālera 138-139 E 5
Tale Sap = Thale Luang
148-149 D 5
Talghemt, Tizi 'n — = Tizi 'N
Talrhemt 166-167 D 3
Talguppa 140 B 3
Tali = Dali [TJ, Shaanxi]
146-147 B 4
Tali = Dali [TJ, Yunnan]
142-143 HJ 6
Taliabu, Pulau — 148-149 HJ 7
Talibīyah, At- 170 II ab 2
Talica [SU, Kirov] 124-125 S 4
Talickij 124-125 Q 4
Talicnioc 96-97 D 7
Ta-lien = Lüda-Dalian 142-143 N 4
Ṭālīganj = Tollygunge 138-139 M 6
Talīghmah 166-167 K 1
Talihina, OK 76-77 G 5
Ta-li Ho = Dali He 146-147 B 3
Tālikota 140 C 2
Talimā 92-93 H 4
Talinay, Altos de — 106-107 B 3
Ta-ling Ho = Daling He
144-145 G 2
Talin Shan = Huaiyu Shan
146-147 F 7
Talīouîn = Talīwīn 166-167 C 4
Tāḷiparamb = Taliparamba 140 B 4
Taliparamba 140 B 4
Talita 106-107 E 4
Taliwang 148-149 G 8
Talīwīn 166-167 C 4
Talju, Jabal — 164-165 K 6
Talkeetna, AK 58-59 M 5
Talkeetna Mountains 56-57 G 5
Talkeetna River 58-59 N 5
Talkheh Rūd 136-137 M 3
Talkōt 138-139 H 3
Talladega, AL 64-65 J 5
Tall adh-Dhakwah 136-137 G 6
Tall 'Afar 136-137 K 4
Tallahassee, FL 64-65 K 5
Tall al-Abyaḍ 136-137 H 4
Tall al-'Amārinah 173 B 4
Tall al Mismāh 136-137 G 6
Tallapoosa, GA 78-79 G 4
Tall as-Samān 136-137 H 4
Tallassee, AL 78-79 G 4
Tall Bisah 136-137 G 5
Tallenga 96-97 C 6-7
Tall Ḥalaf 136-137 HJ 4
Tallī 138-139 B 3
Tallin = Tallinn 132-133 CD 6
Tallinn 132-133 CD 6
Tallinn-Nõmme 124-125 E 4
Tall Jāb 136-137 G 6
Tall Kalah 136-137 G 5
Tall Kayf 136-137 K 4
Tall Kujik 136-137 JK 4
Tall Mānūk 136-137 H 6
Tall Tāmir 136-137 J 4
Tall Timbers, New Orleans-, LA
85 I c 2
Tallulah, LA 78-79 D 4
Tall Umm Karār 136-137 H 6
Tall 'Uwaynāt 136-137 JK 4
Talmage 61 G 6
Tal'menka 132-133 PQ 7
Talmist 166-167 B 4
Talnach 132-133 QR 4
Tal'noje 126-127 E 2
Talo = Nantong 142-143 N 5
Taloda 138-139 DE 7
Talōdī = Talawdī 164-165 L 6
Taloga, OK 76-77 E 4
Talok 152-153 N 5
Talong Mai 150-151 F 6
Talovaja 126-127 K 1
Talpa, TX 76-77 E 7
Talpa de Allende 86-87 H 7
Talrhemt, Tīzī N — 166-167 D 3
Talsara 138-139 K 6
Talsi 124-125 D 5
Talsinnt = Talsīnt 166-167 E 3
Talsīnt 166-167 E 3
Taltal 111 B 3
Taltal, Punta — 104-105 A 9
Taltal, Quebrada de —
104-105 AB 9
Taltson River 56-57 O 5
Ta Luang, Ko — 150-151 B 8
Taludaa 152-153 P 5
Taluk 152-153 D 6
Talumphuk, Laem — 150-151 C 8
Talvār, Rūdkhāneh — 136-137 MN 5
Talvik 116-117 K 2
Talwat 166-167 C 4
Talwood 160 J 2
Talyawalka Creek 160 F 3-4
Talzazah 166-167 E 4
Tama, IA 70-71 D 5
Tama [J] 155 III b 2
Tama [RA] 106-107 D 3
Tamabo, Pegunungan —
152-153 L 4
Tamādah 164-165 E 4
Tamagawa, Tōkyō- 155 III ab 2
Tamaghzah 166-167 KL 2
Tamajirdayn, Wādī — 166-167 G 7
Tamala 124-125 O 7
Tamalameque 94-95 E 3
Tamale 164-165 D 7
Taman' [SU, Krasnodarskaja Oblast']
126-127 H 4
Taman [SU, Perm'skaja Oblast']
124-125 UV 4
Tamana [J] 144-145 H 6
Tamana [Kiribati] 208 H 3
Tamanā, Cerro — 94-95 CD 5
Ṭamanār 166-167 B 4
Tamanārt, Wād — 166-167 B 5
Tamanduateí 110 II b 2
Tamangueyú 106-107 H 7
Tamaniquá 98-99 F 6
Taman Kebangsaan 150-151 D 10
Taman Kebangsaan King George Vth
150-151 D 10
Tamano 144-145 JK 5
Tamanrāsat 164-165 EF 4
Tamanrāsat, Wādī — 164-165 E 4
Taman Sari, Jakarta- 154 IV a 1
Tamanthi = Tamanzī 141 D 3
Tamanzī 141 D 3
Tamaqua, PA 72-73 J 4
Tamaquari, Ilha — 98-99 F 5
Tamar 138-139 K 6
Tāmara 94-95 E 5
Tamarugal, Pampa del — 111 C 1-2
Tamasi 118 HJ 5
Tamāsīn 166-167 JK 3
Tamatama 94-95 HJ 6
Tamatave = Toamasina 172 JK 5
Tamaulipas 64-65 G 6-7
Tamaulipas, Sierra de — 86-87 L 6
Tamaya 106-107 B 3
Tamaya, Río — 96-97 E 6
Tamayama 144-145 N 3
Tamazula de Gordiano 86-87 J 8
Tamazunchale 86-87 KL 6-7
Tambach 171 CD 2
Tambacounda 164-165 B 6
Tambā Kosī 138-139 L 4
Tambaqui 92-93 G 6
Tambaram 140 E 4
Tambaú 102-103 J 4
També 100-101 G 4
Tambej 132-133 N 3
Tambelan, Pulau — 152-153 GH 5
Tambelan, Pulau-pulau —
148-149 E 6
Tamberia, Cerro — 106-107 C 2
Tamberías 106-107 C 3
Tambillo 96-97 B 5
Tambillos 106-107 B 3
Tambo [PE, Ayacucho] 96-97 DE 8
Tambo [PE, Cajamarca] 96-97 B 5
Tambo [PE, Loreto] 96-97 D 6
Tambo, El — [CO, Cauca] 92-93 D 4
Tambo, El — [CO, Nariño] 94-95 C 7
Tambo, El — [EC] 96-97 B 3
Tambo, Río — [PE ⊲ Pacific Ocean]
96-97 F 10
Tambo, Río — [PE ⊲ Río Ucayali]
92-93 E 7
Tambogrande, Pampa de —
96-97 DE 9
Tambo Gregoria 96-97 E 6
Tambohorano 172 H 5
Tambolongang, Pulau —
152-153 NO 9
Tambopata, Río — 96-97 G 8
Tambo Quemado 96-97 D 9
Tambora, Gunung — 148-149 G 8
Tambora, Jakarta- 154 IV a 1
Tambo Real 96-97 B 6
Tambores 106-107 JK 3
Tamboriaco 98-99 B 9
Tamboril 100-101 D 3
Tamboritha, Mount — 160 H 6
Tamboryacu, Río — 96-97 D 2
Tambov 124-125 N 7
Tāmbraparni 140 D 6
Tamburi 100-101 D 7
Tamč 142-143 G 2
Tam Cag Bulak = Tamsagbulag
142-143 M 2
Tam Cân = Câu Ke 150-151 EF 8
Tamchhog Khamba 138-139 J 2
Tamdah 166-167 B 3
Tam Đao 150-151 E 2
Tamdybulak 132-133 L 9
Tame 94-95 F 4
Tâmega 120-121 D 8
Tamel Aike 108-109 D 7
Tamerza = Tamaghzah
166-167 KL 2
Tamgak, Mont — 164-165 F 5
Tamgrūt 166-167 D 4
Tamiahua, Laguna de — 64-65 G 7
Tamiami Canal 80-81 c 4
Tamiḷnāḍ = Carnatic
134-135 M 8-9
Tamil Nadu 134-135 M 8-9
Tamin 152-153 K 4
Ta'mīn, At- 136-137 KL 5
Taming = Daming 146-147 E 3
Tāmir'z'qīd 164-165 AB 5
Tamīyah 173 B 3
Tamjūl 166-167 J 1
Tamiyanglayang 152-153 L 7
Tam Ky 148-149 E 3
Tamlelt, Plaine de — = Sahl Tāmlilt
166-167 E 3
Tāmlilt al-Gadīd 166-167 C 4
Tamlūk 138-139 L 6
Tammerfors = Tampere
116-117 K 7
Tammisaari = Ekenäs 116-117 K 7
Tampa, FL 64-65 K 6
Tampa Bay 64-65 K 6
Tampere 116-117 KL 7
Tampico 64-65 G 7
Tampico, MT 68-69 C 1
Tampin 148-149 D 6
Tampines 154 III b 1
Tampoketsa, Plateau du — =
Causse du Kelifely 172 HJ 5
Tampulonanjing, Gunung —
152-153 CD 5
Tāmralipti = Tāmluk 138-139 L 6
Tāmraparṇī = Tāmbraparni 140 D 6
Ṭamrīdah 134-135 G 8
Tamsagbulag 142-143 M 2
Tamsal = Tamsalu 124-125 F 4
Tamsalu 124-125 F 4
Tāmshikiṭ 164-165 BC 5
Tamshiyacu 96-97 E 3
Tamshiyacu 94-95 a 2-3
Tamū 141 D 3
Tamud = Thamūd 134-135 F 7
Tamuín, Río — 86-87 L 7
Tāmur 138-139 L 4
Tamworth [AUS] 158-159 K 6
Tamyang 144-145 F 5
Tan, Nam — 141 F 5
Tana [EAK] 172 GH 2
Tana [N, place] 116-117 N 2
Tana [N, river] 116-117 M 2-3
Tana [RCH] 104-105 B 6
Tana [Vanuatu] 158-159 N 3
Tana, Lake 164-165 M 6
Tanabe 144-145 K 6
Tanabi 102-103 H 4
Tanabu = Mutsu 144-145 N 2
Tanacross, AK 56-57 H 5
Tanad, Stung — 150-151 D 6
Tanadak Island 58-59 k 4
Tanada Lake 58-59 PQ 5
Ta n'Adar 164-165 F 5
Tanafjord 116-117 N 2
Tanaga Bay 58-59 t 7
Tanaga Island 52 D 36-1
Tanaga Pass 58-59 tu 7
Tanágra 122-123 K 6
Tanaguarena 91 II c 1
Tanaguarena, Punta — 91 II c 1
Tanah Abang, Jakarta- 154 IV a 2
Tanahbala, Pulau — 148-149 C 7
Tanahbato 148-149 C 6
Tanahgrogot 148-149 G 7
Tanahjampea, Pulau — 148-149 H 8
Tanahmasa, Pulau — 148-149 C 6-7
Tanah Merah 148-149 D 5
Tanahmerah 148-149 LM 8
Tanah-tinggi Cameron 148-149 D 6
Tanah Tinggi Idjen = Tanahtinggiljen
148-149 r 9-10
Tanahtinggiljen 152-153 L 9-10
Tanai Kha = Taning Hka 141 E 2-3
Tanak, Cape — 58-59 m 4
Tanakeke, Pulau — 148-149 G 8
Tanakpur 138-139 GH 3
Tanal 168-169 E 2
Taṇamalwila 140 E 7
Tanambo, Pegunungan —
152-153 L 4
Tanami 158-159 E 3
Tanami Desert 158-159 F 3
Tân An [VN ↓ Ca Mâu] 150-151 E 8
Tân An [VN ↙ Thành Phô Hô Chí
Minh] 150-151 F 7
Tân An = Hiêp Đưc 150-151 G 5
Tanana, AK 56-57 F 4
Tananarive = Antananarivo 172 J 5
Tanana River 56-57 G 5
Tanannt = Tānānt 166-167 C 4
Tānānt 166-167 C 4
Tân Âp 148-149 E 3
Tana River 58-59 Q 6
Tānaro 122-123 B 3
Tanārūt, Wādī — 166-167 M 4-5
Tanashi 155 III a 1
Ṭanburah 164-165 K 7
Tancacha 106-107 F 4
Tân Châu 150-151 E 7
Tanchavur = Thanjāvar
134-135 MN 8
Tancheng 146-147 G 4
Tan Chiang = Dan Jiang
146-147 C 5
Tanchoj 132-133 TU 7
Tanch'ŏn 144-145 G 2
Tanchow = Dan Xian 142-143 K 8
Tancítaro, Pico de — 64-65 F 8
Tānda [IND ↘ Faizābād]
138-139 J 4
Tānda [IND ↗ Morādābād]
138-139 G 3
Tandag 148-149 J 5
Tandaho = Tendaho 164-165 N 6
Ṭāndārei 122-123 M 3
Tandā'ū 141 D 5
Tandianwali = Ṭāndiyānwāla
138-139 D 2
Tandil 111 E 5
Tandil, Sierra del — 106-107 H 6
Ṭāndiyānwāla 138-139 D 2
Ṭaṇḍo Ādam 138-139 B 5
Ṭaṇḍo Allahyār 138-139 B 5
Ṭaṇḍo Bāgo 138-139 B 5
Ṭaṇḍo Jām 138-139 B 5
Ṭaṇḍo Muhammad Khān
138-139 B 5
Tandou Lake 160 EF 4
Tandrārah 166-167 EF 3
Tandulā Tāl = Tandula Tank
138-139 H 7
Tandula Tank 138-139 H 7
Tandun 152-153 D 5
Tāndūr 140 C 2
Tandūru = Tāndūr 140 C 2
Tanduy, Ci — 152-153 H 9
Tanega-shima 142-143 P 5
Tanega sima = Tanega-shima
142-143 P 5
Tanela 94-95 C 3
Tanen Taunggyi 150-151 B 3-5
Tanen Tong Dan 141 F 7
Tanew 118 L 3
Tanezrouft = Tānīzruft
164-165 DE 4
Ṭanezzûft, Uâdi — = Wādī Tanizzuft
166-167 M 7
Tanf, Jabal at- 136-137 H 6
Tan-fêng = Danfeng 146-147 C 5
Tang, Kâs — 150-151 D 7
Tanga 172 G 3
Tangail = Ṭangāyal 134-135 O 6
Tanga Islands 148-149 h 5
Tangale Peak 168-169 H 3
Tanganyika, Lake — 172 E 2-F 3
Tangar = Thangkar 142-143 J 4
Tangarā 111 F 3
Tangario National Park 161 F 4
Tangāyal 134-135 O 6
T'ang-chan = Tangshan
142-143 M 4
Tangdukou 146-147 C 8
Tangeh Hormoz 134-135 H 5
Tanger = Ṭanjah 164-165 C 1
Tangerang 152-153 G 9
Tanggalla 140 E 7-8
Tanggela Youmu Hu = Thangra
Yumtsho 142-143 EF 5
Tanggu 142-143 M 4
Tanghe [TJ, place] 146-147 D 5
Tang He [TJ, river ⊲ Bai He]
146-147 D 5
Tang He [TJ, river ⊲ Baiyang Dian]
146-147 E 2
T'ang-ho = Tanghe [TJ, place]
146-147 D 5
T'ang Ho = Tang He [TJ, river ⊲ Bai
He] 146-147 D 5
Tang Ho = Tang He [TJ, river ⊲
Baiyang Dian] 146-147 E 2
T'ang-hsien-chên = Tangxianzhen
146-147 D 6
Tāngi 138-139 K 8
Tangier 63 E 5
Tangiers = Ṭanjah 164-165 C 1
Tangier Sound 72-73 HJ 5
Tangjin 144-145 F 4
Tang Krasang 150-151 E 6
Tang La [TJ, Himalaya pass]
142-143 F 6
Tangla [TJ, Himalaya place]
138-139 K 3
Tang La [TJ, Tanglha] 142-143 G 5
Tangla = Tanglha 142-143 FG 5
Tanglewood, Houston-, TX 85 III b 1
Tanglha 142-143 FG 5
Tanglin Hill, Singapore- 154 III ab 2
Tang Phloch 150-151 DE 6-7
Tangshan 142-143 M 4
Tangshan = Dangshan 146-147 F 4
Tangshancheng 144-145 DE 2
Tangstedt 130 I a 1
Tangtou 146-147 G 4
Tangtu = Dangtu 146-147 G 6
T'ang-tu-k'ou = Tangdukou
146-147 C 8
Tangua 94-95 C 7
Tanguche 96-97 B 6
Tangueur, Bir — = Bi'r Tanqūr
166-167 L 4
Tanguieta 168-169 F 3
Tanguj 132-133 T 6
Tangung 152-153 LM 4
Tangutūru 140 E 3
Tangxi 146-147 G 7
Tang Xian 146-147 E 2
Tangxianzhen 146-147 D 6
Tangyiang = Dangyang
146-147 CD 6
Tangyin 146-147 E 4
Tangyuan 142-143 O 2
Tanhaçu 100-101 D 8
Tan Ho = Dan He 146-147 D 4
Tanhsien = Dan Xian 142-143 K 8
Tani 150-151 E 7
Tanimbar, Kepulauan —
148-149 K 8
Taning = Daning 146-147 C 3
Ta-ning = Wuxi 146-147 B 6

Taning Hka 141 E 2-3
Taninthārī 148-149 C 4
Taninthārī Kyūn 150-151 AB 6
Taninthārī Myitkyī 150-151 B 5-6
Taninthārī Taing 148-149 C 3-4
Taninthārī Taungdan 150-151 B 5-6
Tānīzruft 164-165 DE 4
Tanizzuft, Wādī — 166-167 M 7
Ṭanjah 164-165 C 1
Tanjay 148-149 H 5
Tanjong China 154 III ab 2
Tanjong Irau 154 III b 1
Tanjong Malim 148-149 D 6
Tanjong Pagar 154 III b 2
Tanjong Punggol 154 III b 1
Tanjong Rhu 154 III b 2
Tanjor = Thanjāvar 134-135 MN 8
Tanjung 148-149 G 7
Tanjung Api 152-153 O 6
Tanjung Aru 152-153 M 7
Tanjungbalai 148-149 CD 6
Tanjung Batikala 152-153 O 7
Tanjungbatu 152-153 MN 4
Tanjung Batubesar 152-153 N 10
Tanjung Batuk 152-153 P 10
Tanjung Beram 152-153 KL 3
Tanjung Berikat 152-153 G 7
Tanjung Besar 152-153 O 5
Tanjung Besi 152-153 O 10
Tanjungblitung 150-151 G 11
Tanjungbuayabuaya, Pulau — 152-153 N 5
Tanjung Bugel 152-153 J 9
Tanjung Cimiring 152-153 H 9-10
Tanjung Datu 148-149 E 6
Tanjung De Jong 148-149 L 8
Tanjung Fatagar 148-149 K 7
Tanjung Gelang 150-151 D 11
Tanjung Genteng 152-153 FG 9
Tanjung Genting 152-153 F 6
Tanjung Gertak Sanggui 150-151 BC 10
Tanjung Indramayu 152-153 H 9
Tanjung Jabung 148-149 DE 7
Tanjung Jambuair 152-153 BC 3
Tanjung Jamursba 148-149 K 7
Tanjung Kait 152-153 G 7
Tanjung Kandi 152-153 O 5
Tanjungkarang 148-149 DE 8
Tanjungkarang-Telukbetung 148-149 DE 8
Tanjung Kasossa 152-153 N 10
Tanjung Korowelang 152-153 H 9
Tanjung Krawang 152-153 G 8
Tanjung Lagundu 152-153 N 10
Tanjung Layar 148-149 DE 8
Tanjung Lokoloko 152-153 O 7
Tanjung Lumut 152-153 FG 7
Tanjung Mandar 152-153 N 7
Tanjung Mangkalihat 148-149 GH 6
Tanjung Pakar 152-153 O 8
Tanjungpandan 148-149 E 7
Tanjung Panyusu 152-153 FG 6
Tanjung Payong 152-153 K 4
Tanjung Penunjok 150-151 D 10
Tanjungperiuk 152-153 G 8-9
Tanjung Pertandangan 152-153 D 4
Tanjungpinang 148-149 DE 6
Tanjung Prick, Jakarta- 154 IV b 1
Tanjungpura 148-149 C 6
Tanjung Purwa 152-153 KL 10
Tanjungpusu 152-153 KL 5-6
Tanjung Puting 148-149 F 7
Tanjung Rangasa 152-153 N 7
Tanjung Rata 152-153 F 8
Tanjungredeb 148-149 G 6
Tanjung Sambar 152-153 HJ 7
Tanjung Sasar 152-153 NO 10
Tanjung Selatan 148-149 F 7
Tanjungselor 152-153 M 4
Tanjung Sigep 152-153 C 6
Tanjung Sipang 152-153 J 5
Tanjung Sirik 152-153 J 4
Tanjung Telukpunggur 152-153 DE 7-8
Tanjungtiram 150-151 B 11
Tanjung Unsang 152-153 N 3
Tanjung Vals 148-149 L 8
Tanjungwaringin 152-153 J 6
Tanjung Watupayung 152-153 P 10
Tankara 138-139 C 6
Tan Kena = Tān Kun 166-167 L 6
Tankersly, TX 76-77 D 7
Tankhala 138-139 DE 6-7
Tān Kol 150-151 F 5
Tankoro 168-169 F 2
Tān Kun 166-167 L 6
Tankwa 174-175 D 7
Tanlovo 132-133 NO 4
Tān My 150-151 G 7
Tännäs 116-117 E 6
Tannin 70-71 E 1
Tannūmah, At- 136-137 MN 7
Tannu-Ola 132-133 R 7
Tannu Tuva = Tuva Autonomous Soviet Socialist Republic 132-133 RS 7
Tano 164-165 D 7
Tanor = Ṭāŋūr 140 B 5
Tanoso 168-169 E 4
Tanot 138-139 C 4
Tanout 164-165 F 6
Tan Passage = Chong Tao 150-151 BC 8
Tanqua River = Tankwa 174-175 D 7
Tanque, AZ 74-75 J 6
Tanque Alvarez 76-77 C 9
Tanque Nova 100-101 C 7
Tanqūr, Bi'r — 166-167 L 4
Tanshui 142-143 N 6
Tan-shui = Danshui 146-147 E 10
Tanshui Chiang 146-147 H 9
Tansīft, Wad — 164-165 C 2
Tānsing 138-139 J 4
Ṭanṭā 164-165 KL 2
Tantabin = Htandabin [BUR, Bawlei Myit] 141 DE 7
Tantabin = Htandabin [BUR, Sittaung Myit] 141 E 6
Tantallon 61 GH 5
Ṭanṭan 166-167 A 5
Tantara 96-97 D 8
Tanti 106-107 E 3
Tantoyuca 86-87 LM 7
Tāntpur 138-139 F 4
Tanu 60 B 3
Tanuku 140 E 2
Tanunak, AK 58-59 E 6
Tānūr 140 B 5
Tanūshfī, Jabal — 166-167 F 2
Tanyan 141 F 4
Tan Yan = Kampung Jerangau 150-151 D 10
Tanyang 144-145 G 4
Tanyang = Danyang 146-147 G 6
Tanyeri 136-137 HJ 3
Tanzania 172 FG 3
Tanzī 141 D 4
Tanzilla River 58-59 W 7
Tao, Chong — 150-151 BC 8
Tao, Ko — 150-151 BC 7
Taoan 142-143 N 2
Tao'an = Baicheng 142-143 N 2
T'ao-chou = Lintan 142-143 J 5
Taocun 146-147 H 3
Tao-hsien = Dao Xian 146-147 C 9
Taohua Dao 146-147 J 7
Taojiang [TJ, place] 146-147 D 7
Tao Jiang [TJ, river] 146-147 E 9
Taole = Taoluo 146-147 G 4
Tao-li = Daoli 146-147 H 3
Taolihawa 138-139 J 4
Taoluo 146-147 G 4
Taoqi = Taoxi 146-147 F 6
Taormina 122-123 F 7
Taos, NM 64-65 E 4
Tao Shan = Peitawu Shan 146-147 H 10
Tao Shui = Dao Shui 146-147 E 6
T'ao-ts'un = Taocun 146-147 H 3
Taoudénni 164-165 D 4
Taouïala = Tāwaylah 166-167 G 3
Tāounāt = Tāwnāt 166-167 D 2
Taoura = Tawrah 166-167 KL 1
Taourirt = Tāwrīrt 164-165 D 2
Ṭāouz = Ṭāūz 166-167 D 4
Taoxi 146-147 F 6
T'ao-yüan [RC] 146-147 H 9
Taoyuan [TJ] 146-147 C 7
Tapa 124-125 E 4
Tapa, la — 106-107 F 1
Tapacaré 102-103 B 3
Tapacari 104-105 C 5
Tapachula 64-65 H 9
Tapah 150-151 C 10
Tapajós, Rio — 92-93 H 5
Tapaktuan 148-149 C 6
Tapal 96-97 B 4
Tapalquén 106-107 G 6
Tapanadsum 138-139 L 2
Tapanahony 98-99 L 3
Tapanatepec 86-87 NO 9
Tapanuli, Teluk — 152-153 C 5
Tapara, Ilha Grande do 98-99 L 6
Tapará, Serra do 98-99 M 6
Ta-pa Shan = Daba Shan 142-143 KL 5
Tapat, Pulau — 148-149 J 7
Tapauá 92-93 FG 6
Tapauá, Rio — 92-93 F 6
Tapebicuá 106-107 J 2
Tapejara 106-107 LM 2
Tapenaga, Río — 106-107 H 1-2
Ta-p'êng = Dapeng 146-147 E 10
Tapepo 171 B 4
Tapera [BR, Rio Grande dol Sul] 106-107 L 2
Tapera [BR, Rondônia] 104-105 F 3
Tapera Pesoe 102-103 B 1
Taperoá [BR, Bahia] 92-93 M 7
Taperoá [BR, Paraiba] 100-101 F 4
Taperoá, Rio — 100-101 F 4
Tapes 106-107 M 3
Tapes, Ponta do — 106-107 M 3
Tapeta = Tappita 164-165 C 7
Taphane = Ban Taphane 150-151 E 5
Taphan Hin 150-151 C 4
Tāpī = Tāpti 134-135 M 6
Tapi, Mae Nam — 150-151 B 8
Tapia 104-105 F 6
Tapiales, La Matanza- 110 III b 2
Tapiantana Group 152-153 P 2
Tapiche, Río — 96-97 D 5
Ta-pieh Shan = Dabie Shan 142-143 M 5
Ta-p'ing-tsu = Huitongqiao 141 F 3
Tapini 148-149 N 8
Tapiocanga, Chapada do — 102-103 J 2
Tapira 94-95 G 7
Tapirapé, Serra do — 98-99 N 10
Tapirapecó, Sierra — 92-93 FG 4
Tapirapua 104-105 GH 4
Tapita = Tappita 164-165 C 7
Tāplejung 138-139 L 4
Tapoa 168-169 F 2
Ta-p'o-ti = Dabaidi 146-147 E 8
Tappahannock, VA 72-73 H 5-6
Tappi-saki 144-145 MN 2
Tappita 164-165 C 7
Taps = Tapa 124-125 E 4
Tapsia, Calcutta- 154 II b 2
Tāpti 134-135 M 6
Tapuaenuku 158-159 O 8
Ta-pu-hsün Hu = Dabas nuur 142-143 H 4
Tapuió, Rio — 100-101 B 3-4
Tapul Group 152-153 O 3
Tapuruquara 92-93 FG 5
Taqānat, At- 168-169 C 1
Ṭaqṭaq 136-137 L 5
Taquara, Morro da — 110 I b 2
Taquara, Ponta da — 102-103 HJ 7
Taquara, Serra da — 102-103 F 1
Taquaral, Serra do — 100-101 D 8
Taquaras 100-101 D 10
Taquarembó 106-107 L 2
Taquari [BR, Mato Grosso] 102-103 F 2
Taquari [BR, Rio Grande do Sul] 106-107 M 2
Taquari, Pantanal do — 102-103 DE 3
Taquari, Rio — [BR ◁ Rio Jacuí] 106-107 M 2
Taquari, Rio — [BR ◁ Rio Paranapanena] 102-103 H 5
Taquari, Rio — [BR ◁ Rio Taquari Novo] 102-103 F 3
Taquari Novo, Rio — 92-93 H 8
Taquaritinga 102-103 H 4
Taquaritinga do Norte 100-101 FG 4-5
Taquarituba 102-103 H 5
Taquaruçu, Ribeira — 102-103 F 4
Taques, Los — 94-95 F 2
Taquetrén, Sierra — 108-109 E 4
Taquiará 100-101 E 3
Tar, Lago — 108-109 D 7
Tara [AUS] 158-159 K 5
Tara [SU, place] 132-133 N 6
Tara [SU, river] 132-133 O 6
Tara [YU] 122-123 H 4
Tara, Salar de — 104-105 C 8
Tarabganj 138-139 HJ 4
Tarabillas, Laguna — 76-77 B 7
Tarabuco 92-93 FG 8
Ṭarābulus 164-165 GH 2
Ṭarābulus al-Gharb 164-165 G 2
Ṭarābulus ash-Shām 134-135 CD 4
Tarādehi 138-139 G 6
Tarago 160 J 5
Tarahumar, Altos de — 86-87 G 4-5
Tarahumara, Sierra — 64-65 E 6
Tarai 138-139 F 5
Tarāī = Terāi 134-135 NO 5
Taraika Bay = zaliv Terpenija 132-133 b 8
Tarairí 104-105 E 7
Tarakan 148-149 G 6
Tarakan, Pulau — 152-153 MN 4
Taraklı 136-137 D 2
Taraklija 126-127 D 4
Taralga 160 JK 5
Taram Darya = Tarim darya 142-143 E 3
Taran, mys — 118 JK 1
Tarāna 138-139 EF 6
Taranaki 161 F 4
Taranaquis 104-105 G 5
Tarangire National Park 171 D 3-4
Tarango, Presa — 91 I b 2
Taran Tāran = Tarn Tāran 138-139 E 2
Tàranto 122-123 G 5
Tàranto, Golfo di — 122-123 G 5
Tarapacá [CO] 94-95 c 2
Tarapacá [RCH, administrative unit] 104-105 B 6-7
Tarapacá [RCH, place] 104-105 B 6
Tarapoto 92-93 D 6
Tarāpur 138-139 D 8
Taraquá 92-93 F 4
Tarārah, Ḥāssī — 166-167 GH 6
Tarare 120-121 K 6
Tararua Range 161 F 5
Tarās 138-139 M 5
Tarašča 126-127 E 2
Tarascon 120-121 K 7
Tarasovo [SU, Archangel'skaja Oblast'] 124-125 N 2
Tarasovskij 126-127 K 2
Tarat, Ouèd — = Wādī Tarāt 164-165 F 3
Tarāt, Wādī — 164-165 F 3
Tarata [BOL] 104-105 C 5
Tarata [PE] 96-97 F 10
Tarātmīn 166-167 H 7
Tarauacá 92-93 E 6
Tarauacá, Rio — 92-93 E 6
Tarāvganj = Tarabganj 138-139 HJ 4
Tarawa 208 H 2
Tarayfāwī 136-137 J 7
Tarazona 120-121 G 8
Tarbagataj, chrebet — 132-133 PQ 8
Tarbagatai 142-143 EF 2
Tarbaj 171 E 2
Tarbes 120-121 H 7
Tarboro, NC 80-81 H 3
Tarchankut, mys — 126-127 EF 4
Tarcoola 158-159 FG 6
Tarcoon 160 H 3
Tardoire 120-121 H 6
Tardoki-Jani, gora — 132-133 a 8
Taree 158-159 K 6
Tareja 132-133 R 3
Tarēndö 116-117 JK 4
Tareni, Río — 104-105 C 3
Tareraimbu, Cachoeira — 92-93 J 6
Tarf, Garaet et — = Qar'at at-Tarf 166-167 K 2
Ṭarfā', Wādī aṭ- 173 B 3
Ṭarfāia = Ṭarfāyah 166-167 AB 5-6
Ṭarfāwī, Bi'r — 136-137 K 5
Ṭarfāyah [MA, administrative unit] 166-167 AB 5-6
Ṭarfāyah [MA, place] 164-165 B 3
Ṭarfāyah, Qārat aṭ- 136-137 BC 7
Tarfāyah, Rā's — 164-165 B 3
Targane 168-169 G 1
Targhee Pass 66-67 H 3
Tārgīst 166-167 D 2
Tārgoviŝte 122-123 M 4
Targuīst = Tārgīst 166-167 D 2
Tarhbâlt = Taghbālt 166-167 D 4
Tarhit = Tāghīt 164-165 D 2
Tarhjîcht = Taghghīsht 166-167 B 5
Tarhūnah 164-165 G 2
Tariâga = Manzil Shākir 166-167 M 2
Tariana 94-95 G 7
Tarian Ganga = Dariganga 142-143 L 2
Tarian Gol 146-147 B 1
Táriba 94-95 EF 4
Tarīf 134-135 G 6
Tarifa 120-121 E 10
Tarifa, Punta de — 120-121 DE 11
Tarija [BOL, administrative unit] 104-105 DE 7
Tarija [BOL, place] 92-93 G 9
Tarikere 140 B 4
Tarīm 134-135 F 7
Tarim darya 142-143 E 3
Tarime 171 C 3
Tarka 174-175 FG 7
Tarkastad 174-175 G 7
Tarkhkan, Cape — = mys Tarchankut 126-127 EF 4
Tarkio, MO 70-71 C 5
Tarkio, MT 66-67 F 2
Tarkio River 70-71 C 5
Tarko-Sale 132-133 O 5
Tarkwa 164-165 D 7
Tarlac 148-149 H 3
Tarma [PE, Junín] 96-97 D 7
Tarma [PE, Loreto] 96-97 F 3
Ṭārmīyah, Aṭ- 136-137 KL 6
Tarn 120-121 H 7
Tärna 116-117 F 5
Tarnogskij Gorodok 124-125 O 3
Tarnopol' = Ternopol' 126-127 B 2
Tarnów 118 K 3
Tarn Tāran 138-139 E 2
Tarog Tsho 138-139 JK 2
Ṭārom 134-135 GH 5
Tarong 141 F 1-2
Taronga Zoological Park 161 I b 2
Taroom 158-159 JK 5
Ṭārūdānt = Tārūdānt 164-165 C 2
Tarpley, TX 76-77 E 8
Tarpon Springs, FL 80-81 b 2
Tarqui 96-97 B 2
Tarquinia 122-123 D 4
Tarragona 120-121 H 8
Tarrakoski 116-117 J 3
Tar River 80-81 H 3
Tarso = Tarsus 136-137 F 4
Tarso Emissi = Kégueur Terbi 164-165 H 4
Tarsus 136-137 F 4
Tarsusırmağı 136-137 F 4
Tartagal [RA, Salta] 111 D 2
Tartagal [RA, Santa Fe] 106-107 H 2
Tartagal, Sierra de — 104-105 E 8
Tartār, Wādī at- 136-137 K 5
Tartārat, Ḥāssī — 166-167 K 4
Tartas [SU] 132-133 O 6
Ṭarṭīn, Bi'r — 136-137 J 5
Tartu 124-125 F 4
Ṭarṭūs 134-135 D 4
Ṭārūdānt 164-165 C 2
Tarūfāwī, Bi'r — 136-137 K 6
Tarum, Ci — 152-153 G 9
Tarumirim 102-103 LM 3
Tarumizu 144-145 H 7
Tarusa [SU, place] 124-125 L 6
Tarutino 126-127 D 3
Tarutung 148-149 C 6
Tarvisio 122-123 E 2
Tarvita 104-105 D 6
Tarvo, Río — 104-105 F 4
Tasasah, Jabal — 166-167 F 2
Tašauz 132-133 K 9
Tasāwah 164-165 G 3
Taschereau 62 M 2
Taşçı 136-137 F 3
Tascosa, TX 76-77 C 5
Tasejevo 132-133 RS 6
Tasek Bera 150-151 D 11
Taseko River 60 F 4
Taşeli yaylâsı 136-137 E 4
Tasfaout = Tāsfāwat 166-167 F 5
Tāsfāwat 166-167 F 5
Tāsgāriv = Tāsgaon 140 B 2
Tasgaon 140 B 2
Ta Shan 146-147 D 8
Tashichhō Dsong = Thimbu 134-135 OP 5
Tashigong = Zhaxigang 142-143 DE 5
Tashigong Dsong 141 B 2
Tashi Gonpa 142-143 G 5
Ta-shih-ch'iao = Dashiqiao 144-145 D 2
Tashijong Dsong 134-135 P 5
Tashilhumpo = Zhaxilhünbo 142-143 F 6
Ṭashk, Daryācheh — 134-135 GH 5
Tashkent = Taškent 132-133 M 9
Tashota 62 F 2
Tash Qurghan 142-143 D 4
Tashrīt, Jabal — 166-167 J 2
Tasikmalaja 148-149 E 8
Tāsīlah 166-167 B 5
Tāsīlī Wān Ahjār 164-165 F 3
Tāsīlī Wān al-Hajjār 164-165 E 5-F 4
Taškent 132-133 M 9
Tasköprü [TR, Eskişehir] 136-137 D 3
Tasköprü [TR, Kastamonu] 136-137 F 2
Taš-Kumyr 134-135 L 2
Tas-Kystabyt 132-133 bc 5
Tašla 124-125 T 8
Taşlı 154 I b 2
Taşlıcay 136-137 K 3
Tasman, Mount — 161 CD 6
Tasman Bay 158-159 O 8
Tasman Head 160 cd 3
Tasmania 158-159 HJ 8
Tasman Land 158-159 D 3-E 2
Tasman Mountains 161 E 5
Tasman Peninsula 160 d 3
Tasman Rise 50-51 R 8
Tasman Sea 158-159 K-N 7
Tasmin 126-127 EF 2
Taşova = Yemişenbükü 136-137 G 2
Tassila 168-169 D 2
Tâssîla = Tāsīlah 166-167 B 5
Tassili n'Ajjer = Tāsīlī Wān Ahjār 164-165 F 3
Tassili Oua n'Ahaggar = Tāsīlī Wān al-Hajjār 164-165 E 5-F 4
Taštagol 132-133 Q 7
Tastūr 166-167 L 1
Taštyp 132-133 Q 7
Tasu 60 B 3
Tasūj 136-137 L 3
Tata 118 J 5
Tatabánya 118 HJ 5
Ṭāṭah 166-167 BC 5
Ṭāṭah, Wād — 166-167 B 5
Ta-t'ang = Datong 146-147 B 9
Tatar 152-153 M 10
Tatar Autonomous Soviet Socialist Republic = 6 ◁ 132-133 J 6
Tatarbunary 126-127 D 4
Tatarka 124-125 G 7
Tatarovo, Moskva- 113 V ab 2
Tatarsk 132-133 NO 6
Tatarskaja Avtonomnaja Sovetskaja Socialističeskaja Respublika = Tatar Autonomous Soviet Socialist Republic 132-133 J 6
Tatar Strait 132-133 b 7-a 8
Tatau 152-153 K 4
Tātā'ū, Rūd-e — 136-137 LM 4
Tataurovo 124-125 O 4
Taṭāwīn 164-165 G 2
Tate, Cabo — 108-109 BC 9
Tatenberg, Hamburg- 130 I b 2
Tateoka = Murayama 144-145 N 3
Tates Cairn 155 I b 1
Tateyama 144-145 M 5
Tateyamahōjō = Tateyama 144-145 M 5
Tathlina Lake 56-57 N 5
Tathlīth 134-135 E 7
Tathlīth, Wādī — 134-135 E 6-7
Tathong Channel 155 I b 2
Tathong Point 155 I b 2
Ta-tien = Dadian [TJ, Anhui] 146-147 F 5
Ta-tien = Dadian [TJ, Shandong] 146-147 G 4
Ta-t'ien = Datian 146-147 F 9
Tatiščevo 124-125 P 8
Tatitlek, AK 58-59 O 6
Tatla Lake 60 E 4
Tatlawiksuk River 58-59 K 5-6
Tatlayoko Lake 60 E 4
Tatfīt = Tathlīth 134-135 E 7
Tatlmain Lake 58-59 TU 5
Tatlow, Mount — 60 F 4
Tatman Mountain 68-69 B 3
Tatnam, Cape — 56-57 ST 6
Tatonduk River 58-59 R 4
Ta-t'ong = Datong 142-143 L 3
Tatos dağlar 136-137 J 2
Tatra = Tatry 118 JK 4
Tatran 142-143 EF 4
Tatry 118 JK 4
Tatsaitan = Tagalgan 142-143 H 4
Tatshenshini River 58-59 T 6-7
Tatsuno 144-145 K 5
Tatta = Ṭhaṭṭha 134-135 K 6
Tatuapé, São Paulo- 110 II b 2
Tatuí 102-103 J 5
Tatuk Lake 60 E 3
Ta-tu-k'ou = Dadukou 146-147 F 6
Tatul, Sierra de — 106-107 B 2
Tatum, NM 76-77 C 6
Tatum, TX 76-77 G 6
Tatums, OK 76-77 F 5
Tatung = Datong [TJ, Anhui] 146-147 F 6
Tatung = Datong [TJ, Shanxi] 142-143 L 3
Ta-t'ung Ho = Datong He 142-143 J 4
Tatvan 136-137 K 3
Tau 116-117 AB 8
Tauá 92-93 L 6
Taubaté 92-93 KL 9
Tauberbischofsheim 118 DE 4
Taučik 126-127 P 4
Tauene 174-175 K 3
Taufkirchen 130 II b 2
Tauini, Rio — 98-99 J 4
Taujskaja guba 132-133 cd 6
Taukum 132-133 O 9
Taumarunui 158-159 OP 7
Taumaturgo 92-93 E 6
Taum Sauk Mountain 70-71 E 7
Taunay 102-103 D 4
Taung 174-175 F 4
Taungdôngyī 141 E 6
Taungdwingyī 148-149 BC 2-3
Taunggôk 141 D 6
Taunggôk Taunggyā 141 D 6
Taunggyaw, Lûy — 141 E 4
Taunggyī 148-149 C 2
Taungma Taung 141 E 5
Taungmè 141 E 4
Taungngū 148-149 C 3
Taungnī 141 E 3
Taungs = Taung 174-175 F 4
Taungsūn 141 EF 8
Taungthā 141 D 5
Taungthônlôn 141 D 3
Taungup = Taunggôk 141 D 6
Taunsa 138-139 C 2
Taunton 119 E 6
Taunton, MA 72-73 L 4
Taunton Lake 84 III d 2
Taunton Lake, NJ 84 III de 2
Taunus 118 D 3
Taupo 158-159 P 7
Taupo, Lake — 158-159 P 7
Tauragė 124-125 D 6
Tauramena 94-95 E 5
Tauranga 158-159 P 7
Taureau, Lac — 72-73 K 1
Taurianova 122-123 G 6
Taurirt = Tāwrīrt 164-165 D 2
Taurovo 132-133 N 6
Taurus Mountains 134-135 C 3
Tausa [CO] 94-95 E 5
Taushqan Darya = Kök shal 142-143 D 3
Ṭāūz [MA] 166-167 D 4
Tauz [SU] 126-127 M 6
Tavai 102-103 E 7
Ṭavālesh, Kūhha-ye — 136-137 MN 3
Tavan Bogd uul 142-143 F 2
Tavares 100-101 F 4
Tavares, FL 80-81 c 2
Tavas = Yarangüme 136-137 C 4
Tavastehus = Hämeenlinna 116-117 L 7
Tavda [SU, place] 132-133 M 6
Tavda [SU, river] 132-133 L 6
Taveta 172 G 2
Taveuni 148-149 b 2
Ta Viang = Ban Ta Viang 150-151 D 3
Tavira 120-121 D 10
Tavistock, NJ 84 III c 2
Tavolara 122-123 CD 5
Tavoliere 122-123 F 5
Tavoy = Htāwei 148-149 C 4
Tavoy, Cape — = Shinmau Sūn 150-151 AB 6
Tavoy Island = Mali Kyūn 148-149 C 4
Tavoy Point = Shinmau Sūn 150-151 AB 6
Tavoy River = Htāwei Myit 150-151 B 5
Távros 113 IV a 2
Tavşanlı 136-137 C 3
Tavua 148-149 a 2
Ta-wa = Dawa 144-145 D 2
Tawake 168-169 D 4
Ta-wan = Dawan 146-147 B 10
Tawang = Tawan Hka 141 E 2
Ta-wang-chia Tao = Dawangjia Dao 144-145 D 3
Tawan Hka 141 E 2
Tawar, Laut — 152-153 B 3
Tāwargiri 140 C 3
Tawārij, Ḥāssī — 166-167 JK 4
Tawas City, MI 70-71 J 3
Tawau 148-149 G 6
Tāwaylah 166-167 G 3
Ta-wên-k'ou = Dawenkou 146-147 F 3-4
Ṭawīl, Bi'r — 164-165 L 4
Ṭawīl, Sabkhat aṭ- 136-137 J 5
Tawīl, Wādī at- 166-167 H 2
Ṭawīlah 166-167 C 7
Ṭawīlah, Juzur — 173 CD 4
Tawile Island = Juzur Ṭawīlah 173 CD 4
Tawitawi Group 152-153 NO 3
Tawi-tawi Island 148-149 GH 5
Ṭawkar 164-165 M 5
Tāwnāt 166-167 D 2
Tāwrīrt 164-165 D 2
Tawu 146-147 H 10
Tawūm Būm 141 E 2
Ṭāwūq 136-137 L 5
Ṭāwūq Chāy 136-137 L 5
Ṭāwurġā, Sabhat — 164-165 H 2
Tawzar 164-165 F 2
Taxco de Alarcón 64-65 FG 8
Tay 119 E 3
Tay, Firth of — 119 E 3
Tayabamba 92-93 D 6
Ṭāyabat al-Janūbiyah 166-167 K 3
T'a-ya Ch'ün-tao = Qizhou Liedao 150-151 H 3
Ta-yang Ho = Dayang He 144-145 D 2
Taya Qundao = Qizhou Lidao 150-151 H 3
Ta-ya Wan = Daya Wan 146-147 E 10
Ṭayb al-Fāl 136-137 J 5
Tayeegle 164-165 ab 3
Ta-yeh = Daye 146-147 E 6
Tayepharba La 138-139 J 2
Taÿgetos 122-123 K 7
Ta-ying Chiang = Daying Jiang 141 EF 3
Tayishan = Guanyun 142-143 MN 5
Taylor 60 G 1
Taylor, AK 58-59 E 4
Taylor, AR 78-79 C 4
Taylor, NE 68-69 G 5
Taylor, TX 76-77 F 7
Taylor, Mount — 76-77 A 5
Taylor Mountains 58-59 J 6
Taylor Ridge 78-79 G 3
Taylor River 60 C 1
Taylor Springs, NM 76-77 BC 4
Taylorsville, KY 70-71 H 6
Taylorsville, MS 78-79 E 5
Taylorsville, NC 80-81 F 2-3
Taylorville, IL 70-71 F 6
Taymā' 134-135 D 5
Tayna 171 B 3
Tây Ninh 148-149 E 4
Tāynīst 166-167 DE 2
Tayoltita 86-87 GH 5
Tayota, Río — 104-105 C 5-D 4
Ṭayr, Jabal aṭ- 134-135 E 7
Taytay 148-149 GH 4
Tayu 152-153 J 9
Ta-yü = Dayu 142-143 L 6
Ta-yü Ling = Dayu Ling 146-147 DE 9
Tayung = Dayong 142-143 L 6
Ta-yü Shan = Dayu Shan 146-147 H 6
Taz 132-133 OP 4
Tazādīt 164-165 B 4
Tāzāh 164-165 D 2
Tazarbū 164-165 J 3
Tāzārīn 164-165 CD 2
Tazarine = Tāzārīn 164-165 CD 2
Tazawako 144-145 N 3
Taze = Tanzī 141 D 4
Tazenâkht = Tāznākht 166-167 C 4
Tázerbó = Tazarbū 164-165 J 3
Tazewell, TN 80-81 E 2
Tazewell, VA 80-81 F 2
Tazimina Lakes 58-59 KL 6-7
Tazlina Lake 58-59 OP 6
Tazna 104-105 C 7
Tāznākht 166-167 C 4
Tazolé 168-169 H 1
Tazovskaja guba 132-133 NO 4
Tazovskij 132-133 OP 4
Tazovskij poluostrov 132-133 NO 4
Tazu = Tīgazū 141 D 3
Tazūndam 141 E 1
Tazungdam = Tazūndam 141 E 1
Tazzait, Aïn — = 'Ayn Tazārat 166-167 JK 6
Tazzeka, Jbel — = Jabal Tazzikā' 166-167 DE 2
Tazzikā', Jabal — 166-167 DE 2

Tbilisi 126-127 M 6
T'bursuq 166-167 L 1

Tchab, gora — 126-127 J 4
Tchabal Nbabo 168-169 HJ 4
Tchad, Lac — 164-165 G 6
Tch'ang-cha = Changsha 142-143 L 6
Tchang-kia-k'eou = Zhangjiakou 142-143 L 3
Tch'ang-tch'ouen = Changchun 142-143 NO 3
Tchan-kiang = Zhanjiang 142-143 L 7
Tchaourou 168-169 F 3
Tch'eng-tō = Chengde 142-143 M 3
Tch'eng-tou = Chengdu 142-143 J 5
Tchentlo Lake 60 E 2
Tchertchen = Chärchän 142-143 F 4
Tchibanga 172 B 2
Tchien 164-165 C 7
Tching Lan Xan, Đao — 150-151 FG 2
Tchin Tabaraden 164-165 F 5
Tchong King = Chongqing 142-143 K 6
Tchula, MS 78-79 D 4
Tczew 118 J 1

Tea, Rio — [BR] 98-99 EF 5
Teacapan 86-87 GH 6
Teague, TX 76-77 F 7
Tê-an = De'an 146-147 EF 7
Te Anau, Lake — 158-159 N 9
Teaneck, NJ 82 III bc 1
Teano 122-123 F 5
Teapa 86-87 O 9
Teapot Dome 68-69 CD 4
Tea Tree Well 158-159 F 4
Te Awamutu 158-159 OP 7
Tebaida, La — 94-95 D 5
Tebas = Thēbai [ET] 164-165 L 3
Tebedu 152-153 J 5
Teberda 126-127 K 5
Teberdinskij zapovednik 126-127 KL 5
Tebessa = Tibissah 164-165 F 1
Tebessa, Monts de — = Jabal Tibissah 166-167 L 2
Tebet, Jakarta- 154 IV b 2
Tebicuary, Río — 102-103 DE 7
Tebicuary-mí, Río — 102-103 D 6-7
Tebingtinggi [RI, Sumatera Selatan] 148-149 D 7
Tebingtinggi [RI, Sumatera Utara] 148-149 CD 6
Tebingtinggi, Pulau — 148-149 D 6
Tebleši 124-125 L 5
Ṭebourba = Ṭuburbah 166-167 L 1
Teboursouq = T'bursuq 166-167 L 1
Tebrau 154 III a 1
Tebulosmta, gora — 126-127 M 5
Tecate 64-65 C 5
Tecer dağları 136-137 G 3
Tê-ch'ing = Deqing 146-147 GH 6
Techis 142-143 E 3
Technical College of Kowloon 155 I b 2
Technische Universität Berlin 130 III b 1
Techo, Hipódromo de — 91 III b 3
Tecka 111 B 6
Tecka, Sierra de — 108-109 D 4
Teckla, WY 68-69 D 4

368 Taning

Tecolote, NM 76-77 B 5-6
Tecomán 64-65 F 8
Tecoripa 86-87 EF 3
Tecozautla 86-87 L 7
Tecuala 64-65 E 7
Tecuci 122-123 M 3
Tecumseh, MI 70-71 HJ 4
Tecumseh, NE 70-71 BC 5
Tedders = Tiddas 166-167 C 3
Teddington, London- 129 II a 2
Tedín Uriburu 106-107 H 6
Tedžen 134-135 J 3
Tees 119 EF 4
Teeswater 72-73 F 2-3
Tefariti = Atfāritī 166-167 A 7
Tefé 92-93 G 5
Tefé, Lago de 98-99 F 6
Tefé, Rio — 92-93 F 5
Tefedest = Tafdasat 164-165 F 3-4
Tefenni 136-137 C 4
Tegal 148-149 E 8
Tegeler See 130 III b 1
Tegelort, Berlin- 130 III ab 1
Tégerhi = Tajarhī 164-165 G 4
Tegernsee 118 EF 5
Tegheri, Bi'r — 166-167 M 6
Tegina 168-169 G 3
Tegineneng 152-153 F 8
Tegouma 168-169 H 2
Teguantepeque = Santo Domingo Tehuantepec 64-65 G 8
Tegucigalpa 64-65 J 9
Teguiddan Tessoum 168-169 G 1
Tegul'det 132-133 Q 6
Tehachapi, CA 74-75 D 5
Tehachapi Mountains 74-75 D 5
Tehachapi Pass 74-75 D 5
Tehama, CA 66-67 B 5
Tehata 138-139 M 6
Tehek Lake 56-57 R 4
Teheran = Tehrān 134-135 G 3
Téhini 168-169 E 3
Tehrān 134-135 G 3
Tehri 138-139 G 2
Tê-hsing = Dexing 146-147 F 7
Tê-hua = Dehua 146-147 G 9
Tehuacán 64-65 G 8
Tehuantepec, Golfo de — 64-65 GH 8
Tehuantepec, Istmo de — 64-65 GH 8
Tehuantepec, Santo Domingo — 64-65 G 8
Tehuelches 108-109 F 6
Teian = De'an 146-147 EF 7
Teide, Pico de — 164-165 A 3
Teixeira 100-101 F 4
Teixeira da Silva 172 C 4
Teixeiras 102-103 L 4
Tejada, Punta — 106-107 G 7
Tejar, El — 106-107 G 5
Tejkovo 124-125 N 5
Tejo 120-121 C 9
Tejon Pass 64-65 C 4-5
Teju 141 E 2
Tekağaç burun 136-137 B 4
Tekamah, NE 68-69 H 5
Te Kao 158-159 O 6
Tekāri 138-139 K 5
Tekax 86-87 Q 7
Teke [TR, landscape] 136-137 CD 4
Teke [TR, place] 136-137 C 2
Teke burnu [TR ↙ Çanakkale] 136-137 AB 2
Tekeli 132-133 O 9
Tekeli dağı 136-137 G 2
Tekirdağ 134-135 B 2
Tekkali 140 FG 1
Tekman 136-137 J 3
Tekna = Țarfāyah 166-167 AB 5-6
Țeknāf 141 C 5
Tekoa, WA 66-67 E 2
Tekouiât, Ouèd — = Wādī Tākwayat 164-165 E 4
Tekstil'ščiki, Moskva- 113 V c 3
Teku 152-153 P 6
Te Kuiti 158-159 OP 7
Tekukor, Pulau — 154 III b 2
Tel 134-135 N 6
Tela 64-65 J 8
Tēla = Tel 134-135 N 6
Telaga Papan = Nenasi 150-151 D 11
Telagh = Talāgh 166-167 F 2
Telanaipura = Jambi 148-149 D 7
Telaquana, Lake — 58-59 L 6
Telares, Los — 106-107 F 2
Telavi 126-127 M 5-6
Tel Avive Jafa = Tel Aviv-Yafō 134-135 C 4
Tel Aviv-Yafō 134-135 C 4
Telechany 124-125 EF 7
Teleférico 91 II b 1
Telefomin 148-149 M 8
Telegapulang 152-153 K 7
Telegino 124-125 P 7
Telegraph Bay 155 I a 2
Telegraph Creek 56-57 K 6
Telegraph Point 160 L 3
Telegraph Range 60 F 3
Tel el-'Amarina = Tall al-'Amārinah 173 B 4
Tel el-'Amarna = Tall al-'Amārinah 173 B 4
Telemark 116-117 BC 8
Telemsès = Tlemcès 164-165 EF 5
Telén 106-107 E 6
Telen, Sungai — 152-153 M 5
Telenešty 126-127 D 3
Teleno, El — 120-121 D 7
Teléphone, Île du — 170 IV a 1-2
Télergma = Talighmah 166-167 K 1
Telescope Peak 74-75 E 4
Teles Pires, Rio — 92-93 H 6
Teletaye 168-169 F 1
Telford 119 E 5
Telida, AK 58-59 L 5
Telig 164-165 D 4
Telijn nuur 142-143 F 2
Télimélé 164-165 B 6
Teljō, Jebel — = Jabal Talju 164-165 K 6
Telkwa 60 D 2
Tell, TX 76-77 D 5
Tell Abyad = Tall al-Abyaḍ 136-137 H 4
Tell Atlas 164-165 D 2-E 1
Tell Bīs = Tall Bisah 136-137 G 5
Tell City, IN 70-71 G 6-7
Tell Dekoûa = Tall adh-Dhakwah 136-137 G 6
Tell el-Amarna = Tall al-'Amārinah 173 B 4
Teller, AK 56-57 CD 4
Tell Ḥalaf = Tall Ḥalaf 136-137 HJ 4
Tellicherry 140 B 5
Tellico Plains, TN 78-79 G 3
Tellier 108-109 FG 6
Tellitcherri = Tellicherry 140 B 5
Tell Kalakh = Tall Kalah 136-137 G 5
Tell Kōttchak = Tall Kujik 136-137 JK 4
Tell Sem'ân = Tall as-Sam'ān 136-137 H 4
Telluride, CO 68-69 C 7
Tel'manovo 126-127 J 3
Tèlmèst = Talmist 166-167 B 4
Telmo, Sierra — 104-105 D 8
Telocaset, OR 66-67 E 3
Telok Anson 148-149 CD 6
Telok Betong = Tanjungkarang-Telukbetung 148-149 DE 8
Telok Datok 150-151 C 11
Teloloapan 64-65 FG 8
Tēlos 122-123 M 7
Telouet = Talwat 166-167 C 4
Tel'posiz, gora — 132-133 K 5
Telsen 111 C 6
Telšiai 124-125 D 6
Teltowkanal 130 III a 2
Teluk Adang 152-153 M 6
Teluk Airhitam 152-153 HJ 7
Teluk Anson = Telok Anson 148-149 CD 6
Teluk Apar 152-153 M 7
Teluk Banten 152-153 G 8
Telukbatang 152-153 HJ 6
Teluk Berau 148-149 K 7
Telukbetung = Tanjungkarang 148-149 DE 8
Teluk Bone 148-149 H 7
Teluk Brunei 152-153 L 3
Telukdalam 148-149 C 6
Teluk Darvel 152-153 N 3
Teluk Datu 148-149 EF 6
Teluk Endeh 152-153 O 10
Teluk Flamingo 148-149 L 8
Teluk Grajagan 152-153 KL 10
Teluk Irian 148-149 KL 7
Teluk Jakarta 152-153 G 8-9
Teluk Kau 148-149 J 6
Teluk Klumpang 152-153 M 7
Teluk Kotowana Watobo 152-153 P 9
Teluk Kuandang 152-153 P 5
Teluk Kumai 148-149 F 7
Teluk Labuk 152-153 M 2
Teluk Lada 152-153 F 9
Teluk Lasolo 148-149 H 7
Teluk Maccluer = Teluk Berau 148-149 K 7
Teluk Mandar 148-149 G 7
Telukmeranti 152-153 E 5
Teluk Palu 152-153 N 6
Teluk Pelabuhanratu 152-153 FG 9
Teluk Penanjung 152-153 H 9-10
Teluk Poh 152-153 P 6
Teluk Poso 152-153 O 6
Telukpunggur, Tanjung — 152-153 DE 7-8
Teluk Saleh 148-149 G 8
Teluk Sampit 148-149 F 7
Teluk Sangkulirang 148-149 G 6
Teluk Sebangan 148-149 F 7
Teluk Sebuku 148-149 G 6
Teluk Semangka 152-153 F 8
Teluk Sukadana 152-153 H 6
Teluk Sumbawa 152-153 M 10
Teluk Tapanuli 152-153 C 5
Teluk Tolo 148-149 H 7
Teluk Tomini 148-149 H 7
Teluk Tomori 148-149 H 7
Teluk Waingapu 152-153 O 10
Tema 164-165 DE 7
Témacine = Tamāsīn 166-167 JK 3
Temangan 150-151 D 10
Temassinine = Burj 'Umar Idrīs 164-165 EF 3
Temax 86-87 Q 7
Temazcal, El — 86-87 LM 5
Tembeling 150-151 D 10
Tembellaga = Timboulaga 164-165 F 5
Tembenči 132-133 S 4
Tembesi, Sungai — 152-153 E 6-7
Tembey, Río — 102-103 E 7
Tembilahan 148-149 D 7
Temblador 94-95 K 3
Temblor Range 74-75 D 5
Tembo 168-169 H 3
Tembo, Mont — 168-169 H 5
Temboeland 174-175 GH 6
Tembuland = Temboeland 174-175 GH 6
Temecula, CA 74-75 E 6
Temelli = Samutlu 136-137 E 3
Tementfoust 170 I b 1
Temerloh 150-151 D 11
Temescal Canyon 83 III a 1
Temesvár = Timișoara 122-123 J 3
Téminos, Laguna de — 64-65 H 8
Temir 132-133 K 8
Temir-Chan-Sura = Bujnaksk 126-127 N 5
Temirtau [SU, Kazachskaja SSR] 132-133 N 7-8
Temirtau [SU, Rossijskaja SFSR] 132-133 Q 7
Témiscamie, Lac — 62 PQ 1
Témiscamie, Rivière — 62 P 1
Témiscaming 56-57 V 8
Temiscouata, Lac — 63 BC 4
Temkino 124-125 K 6
Temnikov 132-133 G 7
Temora 158-159 J 6
Temosachic 86-87 G 3
Témpē 122-123 K 6
Tempe, AZ 74-75 GH 6
Tempe, Danau — 148-149 GH 7
Tempelfelde 130 III c 1
Tempelsee, Offenbach- 128 III b 1
Temperley, Lomas de Zamora- 110 III b 2
Tèmpio Pausània 122-123 C 5
Temple 129 I a 1
Temple, OK 76-77 E 5
Temple, TX 64-65 G 5
Temple Bay 158-159 H 2
Temple City, CA 83 III d 1
Temple Hills, MD 82 II b 2
Temple of Confucius 155 II b 2
Temple of Heaven 155 II b 2
Templestowe, Melbourne- 161 II c 1
Templeton, IN 70-71 G 5
Temple University 84 III bc 2
Tempoal de Sánchez 86-87 KL 6-7
Temporal, Cachoeira — 92-93 J 7
Temr'uk 126-127 H 4
Temr'ukskij zaliv 126-127 H 4
Temsiyas 136-137 H 3
Temuco 111 B 5
Tena [CO] 92-93 D 5
Tena [EC] 94-95 C 8
Tenabo 86-87 P 7-8
Tenabo, NV 66-67 E 5
Tenabo, Mount — 66-67 E 5
Tenafly, NJ 82 III c 1
Tenaha, TX 76-77 G 7
Tenakee Springs, AK 58-59 U 8
Tenāli 134-135 N 7
Tenancingo 86-87 L 8
Tenasserim = Taninthārī 148-149 C 4
Tenasserim = Taninthārī Taing 148-149 C 3-4
Tenasserim Island = Taninthārī Kyūn 150-151 AB 6
Tenasserim River = Taninthārī Myitkyī 150-151 B 5-6
Tenayuca, Pirámide de — 91 I b 1
Tenda, Colle di — 122-123 B 3
Tendaho 164-165 N 6
Tendega = Tendeka 174-175 J 4
Ten Degree Channel 134-135 P 8
Tendeka 174-175 J 4
Tendrovskaja kosa 126-127 EF 3
Tendūf 164-165 C 3
Tendürek dağı 136-137 KL 3
Tenedos = Bozca ada 136-137 AB 3
Ténenkou 168-169 D 2
Tenente Portela 106-107 L 1
Ténéré 164-165 FG 4-5
Ténéré du Tafassasset 164-165 FG 4
Tenerife [CO] 94-95 D 3
Tenerife [E] 164-165 A 3
Ténès = Tanas 164-165 E 1
Tenessi = Tennessee River 78-79 F 3
Tenf, Jebel — = Jabal at-Tanf 136-137 H 6
Teng, Nam — = Nam Tan 141 F 5
Tenga, Kepulauan — 148-149 G 8
Tengcheng = Chengcheng 146-147 BC 4
Têng-ch'iao = Tengqiao 150-151 G 3
Tengchong 142-143 H 6-7
Tengchow = Penglai 146-147 H 3
Tengchung = Tengchong 142-143 H 6-7
Tenggarong 148-149 G 7
Tenggeli Hai = Nam Tsho 142-143 G 5
Tengger, Pegunungan — 152-153 K 9-10
Tenggol, Pulau — 150-151 DE 10
Tenghai = Chenghai 146-147 F 10
Tenghsien = Deng Xiang 146-147 D 5
Tenghsien = Teng Xian 142-143 M 4
Tengiz, ozero — 132-133 M 7
Tengqiao 150-151 G 3
Tengréla = Tingréla 164-165 C 6
Tengri Nuur = Nam Tsho 142-143 G 5
Tengtian 146-147 E 8
Teng-t'ien-tsên = Tengtian 146-147 E 8
Teng Xian 142-143 M 4
Teng Xiang 146-147 C 10
Teniente, El — 111 BC 4
Teniente F. Delgado 102-103 B 5
Teniente Matienzo 53 C 30-31
Teniente Ochoa 102-103 B 4
Teniente Origone 106-107 F 7
Teniente Rueda 102-103 B 4
Teniet-el-Haad = Thanīyat al-Ḥad 166-167 GH 2
Tenimber Islands = Kepulauan Tanimbar 148-149 K 8
Tenino, WA 66-67 B 2
Tenkāshi = Tenkāsi 140 C 6
Tenkāsi 140 C 6
Tenke 172 E 4
Ten'ki 124-125 R 6
Tenkiller Ferry Lake 76-77 G 5
Tenkodogo 164-165 DE 6
Tenleytown, Washington-, DC 82 II a 1
Ten Lira, Rio — 104-105 H 4
Tennant, CA 66-67 C 5
Tennant Creek 158-159 FG 3
Tenndrâra = Tandrārah 166-167 EF 3
Tennessee 64-65 JK 4
Tennessee River 64-65 J 4-5
Tennille, GA 80-81 E 4
Teno 106-107 B 5
Tenom 152-153 LM 3
Tēnos 122-123 L 7
Tenosique de Pino Suárez 64-65 H 8
Tenouchfi, Djebel — = Jabal Tanūshfī 166-167 F 2
Tenquehuen, Isla — 108-109 B 5
Tensīft, Ouèd — = Wad Tansīft 164-165 C 2
Ten Sleep 66-67 K 3-4
Ten Sleep, WY 68-69 C 3-4
Tenstrike, MN 70-71 C 2
Tenterfield 158-159 K 5
Ten Thousand Islands 64-65 K 6
Tentolomatinan 152-153 OP 5
Tenyueh = Tengchong 142-143 H 6-7
Teocaltiche 64-65 F 7
Teodoro Sampaio 102-103 D 5
Teodor Sampaio 102-103 F 5
Teófilo Otoni 92-93 L 8
Teofipol' 126-127 C 2
Teonthar 138-139 H 5
Teotepec, Cerro — 64-65 FG 8
Teotihuacán 86-87 L 8
Teotitlán del Camino 86-87 M 8
Tepa 148-149 J 8
Tepalcates, Ixtapalapa- 91 I c 2
Tepasto 116-117 L 3-4
Tepatitlán de Morelos 64-65 F 7
Tepe 136-137 HJ 3
Tepeji del Río 86-87 L 8
Tepeköy [TR ↘ İzmir] 136-137 B 3
Tepepan, Tlalpan- 91 I c 3
Tepequem, Sierra — 98-99 GH 3
Tepic 64-65 EF 7
Tê-p'ing = Deping 146-147 F 3
Teplice 118 E 3
Teplovka 124-125 S 8
Teques, Los — 92-93 F 2
Tequila 86-87 J 7
Tēqūma 136-137 F 7
Ter 120-121 J 8
Tera [E] 120-121 D 8
Téra [RN] 164-165 E 6
Teradomari 144-145 M 4
Teraga, Hassi — = Ḥāssī Tarārah 166-167 GH 6
Terai 134-135 NO 5
Terang 160 F 7
Terangan = Pulau Trangan 148-149 K 8
Terayama, Yokohama- 155 III a 2
Terbuny 124-125 M 7
Tercan = Mamahatun 136-137 J 3
Terceira 204-205 E 5
Tercio, CO 68-69 D 7
Terechovka 124-125 HJ 7
Terek 126-127 N 5
Terek, Novyj — 126-127 N 5
Terek, Staryj — 126-127 N 5
Terek Autonomous Soviet Socialist Republic = Checheno-Ingush Autonomous Soviet Socialist Republic 126-127 MN 5
Terekli-Mekteb 126-127 M 4
Terekty = Karasaj 126-127 O 2
Terempa 150-151 EF 11
Terence 61 HJ 6
Teren'ga 124-125 R 7
Terengganu = Kuala Terengganu 148-149 DE 5
Terengganu, Sungei — 150-151 D 10
Terenos 102-103 E 4
Teresa, Isla — 108-109 C 5
Teresa Cristina 102-103 G 6
Teresina 92-93 L 6
Teresinha 92-93 J 4
Teresita 94-95 G 7
Tereška 124-125 Q 7
Teresópolis 102-103 L 5
Teressa Island 134-135 P 9
Terevinto 104-105 E 5
Terhazza [RMM, landscape] 164-165 CD 4
Terhazza [RMM, ruins] 164-165 CD 4
Teriberka [SU, place] 132-133 F 4
Terijoki = Zelenogorsk 124-125 G 3
Terlingua, TX 76-77 C 8
Termas, Las — 111 CD 3
Termas de Puyehue 108-109 C 3
Termas de Tolguaca 106-107 B 7
Terme 136-137 G 2
Terme di Caracalla 113 II b 2
Termet 164-165 G 5
Termez 134-135 K 3
Terminal 106-107 J 5
Tèrmini Imerese 122-123 E 7-F 6
Termit = Termet 164-165 G 5
Tèrmoli 122-123 F 4-5
Ternate 148-149 J 6
Ternej 132-133 a 8
Terni 122-123 E 4
Ternopol' 126-127 B 2
Ternovka 124-125 P 7
Terny 126-127 F 2
Terpenija, mys — 132-133 bc 8
Terpenija, zaliv — 132-133 b 8
Terra Boa 102-103 F 5
Terra Buena Island 83 I b 2
Terrace 56-57 L 7
Terracina 122-123 E 5
Terråk 116-117 E 5
Terra Nova 63 J 3
Terranova = Newfoundland 56-57 Za 8
Terranovo = Gela 122-123 F 7
Terra Roxa 102-103 H 4
Terra Roxa d'Oeste 102-103 EF 6
Terrassa 120-121 HJ 8
Terre Adélie 53 C 14-15
Terrebonne 72-73 K 2
Terrebonne, OR 66-67 C 3
Terrebonne Bay 78-79 D 6
Terre Clarie 53 C 14
Terre des Hommes 82 I b 1
Terre Haute, IN 64-65 J 4
Terrell, TX 64-65 G 5
Terrenceville 63 J 4
Terreros 91 III a 4
Terreton, ID 66-67 G 4
Territoire de Yukon = Yukon Territory 56-57 JK 4-5
Terro, Oued el — 170 I a 2
Terry, MT 68-69 D 2
Terrytown, LA 85 I b 2
Tersa 126-127 L 1
Tersizhan gölü 136-137 E 3
Terskej-Alatau, chrebet — 134-135 M 2
Terter 126-127 N 6
Terter = Mir-Bašir 126-127 N 6
Teruel [CO] 94-95 D 6
Teruel [E] 120-121 G 8
Terusan Banjir 154 IV a 1-2
Terutao, Ko — 148-149 C 5
Tesaua = Tasāwah 164-165 G 3
Tescott, KS 68-69 GH 6
Tesecav, Lac — 62 O 1
Teseney 164-165 M 5-6
Teshekpuk Lake 56-57 F 3
Teshikaga 144-145 d 2
Teshio 142-143 R 3
Teshio dake 144-145 c 2
Teshio-gawa 144-145 bc 1
Teshio-santi 144-145 bc 1
Tesijn gol 142-143 H 2
Tesio = Teshio 142-143 R 3
Teslin 56-57 K 5
Teslin Crossing 58-59 U 6
Teslin Lake 56-57 K 5
Teslin River 56-57 K 5
Tesouro 102-103 F 2
Tessala, Djebel — = Jabal Tasalah 166-167 F 2
Tessalit 164-165 E 4
Tessaoua 164-165 F 6
Tessâout, Ouèd — = Wād Tissāūt 166-167 C 4
Tessier 61 E 5
Tessolo 174-175 L 1
Test, Tīzī N — 166-167 B 4
Testa del Gargano 122-123 G 5
Teste, la — 120-121 G 6
Testoûr = Tastūr 166-167 L 1
Teta, La — 91 III bc 4
Tetagouche River 63 CD 4
Tetas, Punta — 111 B 2
Tete [Mozambique, administrative unit] 172 F 5
Tete [Mozambique, place] 172 F 5
Tête-à-la-Baleine 63 G 2
Teterboro Airport 82 III b 1
Tētērē 132-133 T 5
Teterev 126-127 D 1
Teteven 122-123 L 4
Tetlin, AK 58-59 Q 5
Tetlin Junction, AK 58-59 QR 5
Tetlin Lake 58-59 Q 5
Tetonia, ID 66-67 H 4
Teton Mountains 66-67 H 3-4
Teton River 66-67 H 2
Tetouan = Tițwān 164-165 CD 1
Tetovo 122-123 J 4-5
Tétreauville, Montréal- 82 I b 1
Tetuán = Tițwān 164-165 CD 1
Tetuán, Madrid- 113 III a 2
Tet'uche-Pristan' = Rudnaja Pristan' 132-133 a 9
Tet'uši 132-133 H 6-7
Teuco, Río — 111 D 2-3
Teufelsbach 174-175 B 2
Teufelsberg [D] 130 III ab 2
Teulada 122-123 C 6
Teul de González Ortega 86-87 J 7
Teulon 61 K 5
Teun, Pulau — 148-149 J 8
Teunom, Krueng — 152-153 AB 3
Teuquito, Río — 104-105 F 9
Teuri-tō 144-145 b 1
Teusaca, Río — 91 III c 3
Teutoburger Wald 118 C 2-D 3
Teutoburg Forest = Teutoburger Wald 118 C 2-D 3
Tèvere 122-123 E 4
Tĕverya 136-137 F 6
Teviot 174-175 F 6
Tevriz 132-133 N 6
Te Waewae Bay 161 B 8
Tewanthar = Teonthar 138-139 H 5
Tewksbury Heights, CA 83 I c 1
Texada Island 66-67 A 1
Texarkana, AR 64-65 H 5
Texarkana, TX 64-65 GH 5
Texas [AUS] 158-159 K 5
Texas [USA] 64-65 FG 5
Texas City, TX 64-65 GH 6
Texas Medical Center 85 III b 2
Texas Southern University 85 III b 2
Texcoco 86-87 L 8
Texcoco, Lago de — 91 I cd 1
Texel 120-121 K 2
Texhoma, OK 76-77 D 4
Texico, NM 76-77 C 5
Texline, TX 76-77 C 4
Texoma, Lake — 64-65 G 5
Teyateyaneng 174-175 G 5
Teza 124-125 N 5
Tezanos Pinto 104-105 F 10
Tezaua = Tasāwah 164-165 G 3
Teziutlán 64-65 G 7-8
Tezpur 134-135 P 5
Tezzeron Lake 60 EF 2

Tha, Nam — 148-149 D 2
Thabana Ntlenyana 174-175 H 5
Thaba Nchu 174-175 G 5
Thabantshongana = Thabana Ntlenyana 174-175 H 5
Thaba Putsoa [ZA, mountain] 174-175 GH 5
Thaba Putsoa [ZA, mountains] 174-175 G 5-6
Thābaung 141 D 7
Thabazimbi 172 E 6
Thabeikkyin 141 DE 4
Thablā La 138-139 K 3
Tha Bo 150-151 D 4
Thabt, Gebel eth — = Jabal ath-Thabt 173 CD 3
Thabt, Jabal ath- 173 CD 3
Thabye Tshākha Tsho 138-139 K 2
Thac Du'ot = Ban Thac Du'ot 150-151 F 5
Thachin = Samut Sakhon 150-151 BC 6
Tha Chin, Mae Nam — 150-151 C 5-6
Thach Xa Ha 150-151 F 4
Thadawleikkyī 150-151 B 6-7
Thadeua = Mu'o'ng Thadeua 150-151 C 3
Tha Do'a = Mu'o'ng Thadeua 150-151 C 3
Thadôn [BUR, Karin Pyinnei] 148-149 C 3
Thadôn [BUR, Shan Pyinnei] 141 E 5
Tha Dua 150-151 B 3-4
Thaerfelde 130 III c 1
Thagwebōlō 141 E 6
Thagyettaw 150-151 AB 6
Thai Binh 150-151 F 2
Thailand 148-149 CD 3
Thailand, Gulf of — 148-149 D 4-5
Thai Muang 150-151 AB 8
Thai Nguyên 150-151 EF 2
Thair 140 C 1
Thaj, Ath- 134-135 F 5
Tha Khanon = Khiri Ratthanikhom 150-151 B 8
Thakhek 148-149 DE 3
Thākuran 138-139 M 7
Thākurdwāra 138-139 G 3
Thākurgāon 134-135 O 5
Thākurmunda 138-139 L 7
Thākurpukur, South Suburbs- 154 II a 3
Thal [PAK] 134-135 L 4
Thala = Tālah 166-167 L 2
Thalabarivat 150-151 E 6
Thalang 150-151 B 8
Thalātha', Ath- [MA, Marrākush] 166-167 BC 3-4
Thalātha', Ath- [MA, Miknās] 166-167 D 2
Thale Luang 148-149 D 5
Tha Li 150-151 C 4
Thālith, Ash-Shallāl ath- 164-165 KL 5
Thalkirchen, München- 130 II b 2
Thallon 160 J 2
Thalmann, GA 80-81 F 5
Thalnepantla, Río — 91 I b 1
Thames [GB] 119 G 6
Thames [NZ] 158-159 P 7
Thames [RA] 106-107 F 6
Thames Ditton 129 II a 2
Thames River 72-73 F 3
Thamisatse 138-139 M 2
Tha Muang 150-151 BC 5-6
Thamūd 134-135 F 7
Tha Mun Ran 150-151 C 4
Thāna 138-139 D 8
Thanatpin 141 E 7
Thanbyūzayat 141 E 8
Thandaung 141 E 6
Thāndla 138-139 E 6
Thandwe 148-149 B 3
Thānēn = Thāna 138-139 D 8
Thānesar 138-139 F 2-3
Thăng Binh 150-151 G 5
Thangkar 142-143 J 4
Thangra Tsho = Thangra Yumtsho 142-143 EF 5
Thangra Yumtsho 142-143 EF 5
Thanh Hoa 148-149 E 3
Thanh Moi 150-151 F 2
Thành Phô Hô Chí Minh 148-149 E 4
Thành So'n 150-151 F 7
Thanh Tri 150-151 EF 8
Thanīyat al-Had 166-167 GH 2
Thanjāvar 140 D 5
Than Kyūn 150-151 A 8
Thanlwin Myit 148-149 C 2-3
Thanlyin 148-149 C 3
Thāno Bulla Khān 138-139 AB 5
Than Uyên 150-151 DE 2
Thanyaburi 150-151 C 5-6
Tha Phraya 150-151 D 5
Tha Pla 150-151 C 4
Thap Put 150-151 B 8
Thapsacus = Dibsah 136-137 GH 5
Thap Sakae 150-151 B 7
Thap Than 150-151 B 5
Thap Than, Huai — 150-151 D 5
Thar 134-135 L 5
Tharād 138-139 C 5
Tharawthèdangyī Kyūn 150-151 AB 6
Tharetkun 141 D 3
Thargo Gangri 138-139 L 2
Thargomindah 158-159 H 5
Thargo Tsangpo 138-139 L 2
Thārī 138-139 B 4
Tharrawaddy = Thāyāwadī 141 DE 7
Tharrawaw = Thāyawaw 141 D 7
Tharsis 120-121 D 10
Tharthār, Bahr ath — = Munkhafad ath-Tharthār 134-135 E 4
Tharthār, Munkhafad ath- 134-135 E 4
Tharthār, Wādī ath- 136-137 K 5
Tha Rua 150-151 C 5
Tharwāniyah = Ath-Tharwāniyah 134-135 GH 6
Tharwāniyah, Ath- 134-135 GH 6
Tha Sa-an = Bang Pakong 150-151 C 6
Tha Sae 150-151 B 7
Tha Sala 150-151 B 8
Tha Song Yang 150-151 B 4
Thásos [GR, island] 122-123 L 5
Thásos [GR, place] 122-123 L 5
Tha Tako 150-151 C 5
Thatcher, AZ 74-75 HJ 6
Thatcher, CO 68-69 DE 7
Tha Thom 150-151 D 3
Thāt Khê 150-151 F 1
Thaton = Thadôn 148-149 C 3
That Phanom 150-151 E 4
Thațțha 134-135 K 6
Tha Tum 150-151 D 5
Thaungdūt 141 D 3
Tha Uthen 150-151 E 4
Thauval = Thoubal 141 D 3
Tha Wang Pha 150-151 C 3
Thawatchaburi 150-151 D 4-5
Tha Yang 150-151 B 6
Thāyāwadī 141 DE 7
Thāyawaw 141 D 7
Thayer, KS 70-71 C 7
Thayer, MO 78-79 D 2
Thayetchaung 150-151 B 6
Thayetmyō 141 D 6
Thayne, WY 66-67 H 4
Thāzī 148-149 C 2
Thbeng 148-149 DE 4
Thbeng Meanchey 148-149 DE 4
Thēbai [ET] 164-165 L 3
Thēbai [GR] 122-123 K 6
Thebe = Thēbai 164-165 L 3
Thebes = Thēbai [ET] 164-165 L 3
Thebes = Thēbai [GR] 122-123 K 6
The Bluff 88-89 H 2
The Brothers = Jazā'ir al-Ikhwān 173 D 4
The Brothers = Samḥah, Darsah 134-135 G 8
The Capitol 82 II ab 2
Thèchaung 150-151 B 7
The Cheviot 119 EF 4
The Coorong 158-159 G 7
The Dallas, OR 66-67 C 3
The Dalles, OR 66-67 C 3
The Dangs = Dāngs 138-139 D 7
Thèdaw 141 E 5
Thedford, NE 68-69 F 4-5
Thègōn 141 D 6
The Granites 158-159 F 4
The Heads 66-67 A 4
Theimnī 141 EF 4
The Lake 88-89 K 4
Thelepte 166-167 L 2
Thelon Game Sanctuary 56-57 PQ 5
Thelon River 56-57 Q 5
The Meadows, TX 85 III a 2
The Narrows 82 III b 3
Thenia = Tinyah 166-167 H 1
Theodore 158-159 JK 4-5
Theodore, AL 78-79 E 5
Theodore Roosevelt Island 82 II a 2
Theodore Roosevelt Lake 74-75 H 6
Theodore Roosevelt National Memorial Park 68-69 E 2
The Pas 56-57 Q 7
Thepha 150-151 C 9
Thēra 122-123 L 7
Theresienwiese 130 II b 2
Thermaïkòs Kólpos 122-123 K 5-6
Thermopolis, WY 68-69 B 4
Thermopýlai 122-123 K 6
The Rock 160 H 5
Theron Range 53 AB 34-36
Theronsville = Pofadder 172 CD 7
Thèrūr = Thair 140 C 1
Thēseion 113 IV a 2
The Slot 148-149 j 6
The Sound 161 I b 1
Thessalía 122-123 JK 6
Thessalon 70-71 J 2
Thessaloníkē 122-123 K 5
Thessaly = Thessalía 122-123 JK 6
Thetford 119 G 5
Thetford Mines 56-57 W 8
Thethaitāngar 138-139 K 6
Thethiyanagar = Thethaitāngar 138-139 K 6
The Thumbs 161 D 6
The Twins 161 DE 5
The Two Rivers 61 G 3
Theun, Nam — 150-151 E 3

Theun 369

Theunissen 174-175 G 5
The Wash 119 G 5
Thiais 129 I c 2
Thībaw 141 E 4
Thibodaux, LA 78-79 D 6
Thicket Portage 61 K 3
Thickwood Hills 61 BC 2
Thief Lake 70-71 BC 1
Thief River Falls, MN 70-71 BC 1
Thiel 168-169 B 2
Thiel Mountains 53 A
Thielsen, Mount — 66-67 BC 4
Thieng, Ban — 150-151 CD 3
Thiers 120-121 J 6
Thiersville = Al-Gharīs 166-167 G 2
Thiès 164-165 A 6
Thiêu Hoa 150-151 E 3
Thieux 129 I d 1
Thika 171 D 3
Thikombia 148-149 b 2
Thillay, le — 129 I c 1
Thilogne 168-169 B 2
Thi Long 150-151 E 3
Thimbu 134-135 OP 5
Thinbôn Kyûn 141 C 5
Thingvallavatn 116-117 c 2
Thingvellir 116-117 c 2
Thio 158-159 N 4
Thionville 120-121 KL 4
Thirinam Tsho 138-139 K 2
Thiruvalla = Tiruvalla 140 C 6
Thisted 116-117 C 9
Thistilfjördhur 116-117 f 1
Thistle, UT 74-75 H 2-3
Thistle Creek 58-59 S 5
Thistle Island 158-159 G 7
Thjórsá 116-117 d 2
Thlèta Madârî, Berzekh — = Râ's Wūruq 164-165 D 1
Thlewiaza River 56-57 R 5
Thmail = Thumayl 136-137 K 6
Thmâr, Kompong — 150-151 E 6
Thnīn Rīāt, Ath- 166-167 B 3
Thoen 150-151 B 4
Thogchhen 138-139 HJ 2
Thogdoragpa 142-143 F 5
Thogjalung 142-143 E 5
Tho'i Binh 150-151 E 8
Thomas, OK 76-77 E 5
Thomas, WV 72-73 G 5
Thomaston, GA 80-81 DE 4
Thomaston, TX 76-77 F 8
Thomasville, AL 78-79 EF 5
Thomasville, GA 64-65 K 5
Thomasville, NC 80-81 F 3
Thomochabgo 138-139 L 2
Thompson 56-57 R 6
Thompson, UT 74-75 HJ 3
Thompson, Cape — 58-59 D 2
Thompson Falls, MT 66-67 F 2
Thompson Island 84 I bc 3
Thompson Pass 58-59 P 6
Thompson Peak [USA, Colorado] 66-67 B 5
Thompson Peak [USA, Montana] 66-67 F 2
Thompson River [CDN] 60 G 4
Thompson River [USA] 70-71 D 5-6
Thompson's Falls 171 D 2-3
Thompsonville, MI 70-71 GH 3
Thomson 154 III b 1
Thomson, GA 80-81 E 4
Thomson Deep 158-159 KL 6
Tho'n, Nam — = Nam Theun 150-151 E 3
Thon Buri 148-149 CD 4
Thong Pha Phum 148-149 C 4
Thongsa Chhu = Mangde Chhu 138-139 N 4
Thongsa Dsong 141 B 2
Thôngwa 141 E 7
Thonon-les-Bains 120-121 L 5
Thonpa 138-139 M 3
Thoreau, NM 74-75 JK 5
Thorez 126-127 J 3
Thori 138-139 K 4
Thørisvatn 116-117 de 2
Thornbury, Melbourne- 161 II bc 1
Thorndale, TX 76-77 F 7
Thornton, CO 68-69 D 6
Thornton, IA 70-71 D 4
Thornton, WA 66-67 E 2
Thornton Beach 83 I a 2
Thornton Heath, London- 129 II b 2
Thornville 174-175 HJ 5
Thorofare, PA 84 III b 2
Thorp, WA 66-67 C 2
Thorshafn = Tórshavn 114-115 G 3
Thórshöfn 116-117 f 1
Thôt Nôt 150-151 E 7
Thoubal 141 D 3
Thousand Islands 72-73 HJ 2
Thousand Islands = Pulau-pulau Seribu 148-149 E 7-8
Thousand Spring Creek 66-67 F 5
Thovala = Tovāla 140 C 6
Thowa 172 G 2
Thrākē 122-123 LM 5
Three Creek, ID 66-67 F 4
Three Creeks 60 J 1
Three Forks, MT 66-67 H 3
Three Hummock Island 160 bc 2
Three Kings Islands 158-159 O 6
Three Lakes, WI 70-71 F 3
Threemile Rapids 66-67 F 3
Three Pagodas Pass = Phra Chedi Sam Ong 148-149 C 3-4
Three Points, Cape — 164-165 D 8
Three Rivers, MI 70-71 H 5
Three Rivers, NM 76-77 A 6
Three Rivers, TX 76-77 EF 8
Three Rivers = Trois-Rivières 56-57 W 8
Three Sisters [USA] 66-67 C 3
Three Sisters [ZA] 174-175 E 6
Three Sisters Range 58-59 WX 7
Three Springs 158-159 BC 5
Three Valley 60 HJ 4
Throckmorton, TX 76-77 E 6
Throgs Neck 82 III d 2
Thu, Cu Lao — 148-149 EF 4
Thubby = Abū Ẓabī 134-135 G 6
Thu Bôn 150-151 G 5
Thu Dau Môt = Phu Cu'o'ng 150-151 F 7
Thugsum 138-139 J 2
Thul [PAK ↘ Dādū] 138-139 B 4
Thul [PAK ↑ Shikārpūr] 138-139 B 3
Thule = Qânâq 56-57 W-X 2
Thumayl 136-137 K 6
Thumb, WY 66-67 H 3
Thumbs, The — 161 D 6
Thun 118 C 5
Thunder Bay [CDN] 56-57 ST 8
Thunder Bay [USA] 72-73 E 2
Thunder Butte Creek 68-69 EF 3
Thunderhouse Falls 62 K 1-2
Thunder Mount 58-59 G 2
Thung Saliam 150-151 B 4
Thung Song 150-151 B 8
Thu'o'ng Đu'c 150-151 FG 5
Thuqb al-Ḥājj 136-137 L 8
Thüringen 118 E 3
Thüringer Wald 118 E 3
Thuringia = Thüringen 118 EF 3
Thuringian Forest = Thüringer Wald 118 E 3
Thurloo Downs 160 F 2
Thurso [CDN] 72-73 J 2
Thurso [GB] 119 E 2
Thurston Island 53 BC 26-27
Thutade Lake 60 D 1
Thyatera = Akhisar 136-137 BC 3
Thyatira = Akhisar 136-137 BC 3
Thykkvibær 116-117 c 3
Thynne, Mount — 66-67 C 1
Thysville = Mbanza-Ngungu 172 B 3

Tiahuanaco 92-93 F 8
Tía Juana 94-95 F 2
Tian'anmen 155 II b 2
Tianbao 146-147 F 9
Tianchang 146-147 G 5
Tiandu 150-151 G 3
Tianeti 126-127 M 5
Tiangol 168-169 B 2
Tianguá 92-93 L 5
Tianhe [TJ, Guangxi Zhuangzu Zizhiqu] 146-147 B 9
Tianhe [TJ, Hubei] 146-147 C 5
Tianjin 142-143 M 4
Tianmen 146-147 D 6
Tianmu Shan 146-147 G 6
Tianshui 142-143 JK 5
Tiantai 146-147 H 7
Tiantan Park 155 II b 2
Tianzhu 146-147 B 8
Tianzhuangtai 144-145 CD 2
Tiaofeng 150-151 H 2
Tiaraju 106-107 K 3
Tiaret = Tiyārat 164-165 E 1
Tiassalé 164-165 CD 7
Tīb 164-165 G 1
Tibaji 111 F 2
Tibaji, Rio — 102-103 G 6
Tibastī, Sarīr — 164-165 H 4
Tibati 164-165 G 7
Tibāzah 166-167 H 1
Tibé, Pic de — 168-169 C 3
Ṭīb el Fâl = Ṭayb al-Fāl 136-137 J 5
Tibell, Wādī — = Wādī at-Tubal 136-137 J 6
Tiberias = Ṭěvarya 173 D 1
Tibesti 164-165 H 4
Tibet, Plateau of — = Jang Thang 142-143 E-G 5
Tibetan Autonomous Region 142-143 E-G 5
Tibissah 164-165 F 1
Tibissah, Jabal — [DZ] 166-167 J 7
Tibissah, Jabal — [TN] 166-167 L 2
Tibnī 136-137 H 5
Tibooburra 158-159 H 5
Tibrikot 138-139 J 3
Tibú 94-95 E 3
Tibugá, Ensenada de — 92-93 D 3
Tiburon, CA 83 I b 1
Tiburón, Isla — 64-65 D 6
Tiburon Peninsula 83 I b 1
Tiburtina, Via — 113 II c 2
Tichao, Djebel — = Jabal Tīshāro 166-167 JK 2
Tichborne 72-73 H 2
Tichitt = Tīshīt 164-165 C 5
Tichka, Tīzī N — 166-167 C 4
Tichon'kaja Stancija = Birobidžan 132-133 Z 8
Tichoreck 126-127 JK 4
Tichvin 132-133 E 6
Tichvinka 124-125 JK 4
Tichvinskij kanal 124-125 K 4
Ticino [CH] 118 D 5
Ticino [RA] 106-107 F 4
Ticomán, Ciudad de México- 91 I c 1
Ticonderoga, NY 72-73 K 3
Ticul 64-65 J 7
Tidaholm 116-117 EF 8
Tidal Basin 82 II a 2
Tiddas 166-167 C 3
Tiddim = Tidein 141 C 4
Tidein 141 C 4
Tīdīghīn, Jabal — 166-167 D 2
Tidikelt = Tīdikilt 164-165 E 3
Tidioute, PA 72-73 G 4
Tidjikja = Tijiqjah 164-165 B 5
Tidore, Pulau — 148-149 J 6
Tidra, Île — 164-165 A 5
Tidwell Park 85 III b 1
Tiébissou 168-169 D 4
Tiechang 144-145 EF 2
Tiefwerder, Berlin- 130 III a 1
T'ieh-ling = Tieling 144-145 DE 1
Tiekel, AK 58-59 P 6
Tielinanmu Hu = Thirinam Tsho 138-139 K 2
Tieling 144-145 DE 1
T'ien-chia-an = Huainan 142-143 M 5
T'ien-chin = Tianjin 142-143 M 4
T'ien-chouei = Tianshui 142-143 JK 5
T'ien-chu = Tianzhu 146-147 B 8
T'ien-chuang-t'ai = Tianzhuangtai 144-145 CD 2
Tiên Giang 150-151 E 7
Tien-ho = Tianhe 146-147 B 9
Tienkiaan = Huainan 142-143 M 5
Tienko 168-169 D 3
Tienmen = Tianmen 146-147 D 6
Tien-pao = Tianbao 146-147 F 9
Tien Schan 142-143 C-G 3
Tien Shan 142-143 C-G 3
Tienshui = Tianshui 142-143 JK 5
Tientai = Tiantai 146-147 H 7
Tientsin = Tianjin 142-143 M 4
Tien-tu = Tiandu 150-151 G 3
Tiên Yên 148-149 E 2
Tierfontein 174-175 G 5
Tiergarten, Berlin- 130 III b 1
Tierp 116-117 G 7
Tierpark Berlin 130 III c 2
Tierpark Hellabrunn 130 II b 2
Tierpoortdam 174-175 G 5
Tierra Amarilla 106-107 BC 1
Tierra Amarilla, NM 76-77 A 4
Tierra Blanca [MEX, Chihuahua] 76-77 B 9
Tierra Blanca [MEX, Veracruz] 64-65 G 8
Tierra Blanca [PE] 96-97 D 5
Tierra Blanca Creek 76-77 CD 5
Tierra Colorada 86-87 L 9
Tierra Colorada, Bajo de los — 108-109 F 4
Tierra de Barros 120-121 D 9
Tierra de Campos 120-121 E 7-8
Tierra del Fuego [RA, administrative unit] 111 C 8
Tierra del Fuego [RA, landscape] 110 C 8
Tierra del Fuego, Isla Grande de — 108-109 D-F 9-10
Tierra del Pan 120-121 DE 7-8
Tierradentro 94-95 D 5
Tierralta 94-95 C 3
Tie Siding, WY 68-69 D 5
Tiétar 120-121 E 8
Tietê [BR, place] 102-103 J 5
Tietê [BR, river] 110 II a 2
Tietê, Rio — 102-103 H 4
Tieton, WA 66-67 C 2
Tiêu Cân 150-151 F 8
Tifariti = Atfārītī 164-165 B 3
Tiffany Mountain 66-67 CD 1
Tiffin, OH 72-73 E 4
Tifist, Bi'r — 166-167 M 4
Tiflat 166-167 C 3
Tiflis = Tbilisi 126-127 M 6
Tifore, Pulau — 148-149 J 6
Tifrīst 166-167 E 2
Tifton, GA 80-81 E 5
Tiga, Pulau — 152-153 L 3
Tigalda Island 58-59 o 3
Tigapuluh, Pegunungan — 152-153 E 6
Tigara = Point Hope, AK 58-59 D 2
Tigaras 150-151 B 11
Tigazū 141 D 3
Tiger Point 78-79 C 6
Tiger Ridge 85 I c 3
Tiger Stadium 84 II b 2
Tighennif = Tighinnif 166-167 G 2
Tighighīmīn 166-167 H 6
Tighina = Bendery 126-127 D 3
Tighinnif 166-167 G 2
Tighintūrīn 166-167 L 6
Tighintūrīn, Ḥāssī — 166-167 H 6
Tighzirt 166-167 J 1
Tigieglo = Tayeegle 172 H 1
Tigil' 132-133 e 6
Tiglīt 166-167 A 5
Tignish 63 DE 4
Tigra = Tigrē 164-165 MN 6
Tigra, Bajo de la — 106-107 E 7
Tigrē [ETH] 164-165 MN 6
Tigre [RCH] 104-105 B 8
Tigre, Cordillera del — 106-107 C 3-4
Tigre, Dent du — = Dông Voi Mêp 148-149 F 4
Tigre, El — [CO] 94-95 F 4
Tigre, El — [YV] 92-93 G 3
Tigre, Rio — [EC] 92-93 D 5
Tigre, Rio — [YV] 94-95 K 3
Tigre, Sierra del — 106-107 C 3
Tigre-Don Torcuato 110 III b 1
Tigre-El Talar 110 III b 1
Tigres, Loma de los — 106-107 DE 6
Tigris = Nahr-Dijlah 134-135 E 3
Tigris = Shaṭṭ Dijlah 134-135 E 4
Tiguelguemine = Tighighīmīn 166-167 H 6
Tiguentourine = Tighintūrīn 166-167 L 6
Tiguentourine, Hassi — = Ḥāssī Tighintūrīn 166-167 H 6
Tigui 164-165 H 5
Tiguidit, Falaise de — 168-169 GH 1
Tiguila 168-169 E 2
Tigur 138-139 K 3
Tigyaing = Htigyaing 141 E 4
Tīh, Jabal at- 164-165 L 3
Tīh, Ṣaḥrā' at- 164-165 L 2
Tiham = Tihāmah 134-135 D 6-E 8
Tihāmah 134-135 D 6-E 8
Tihodaïne, Erg — = 'Irq Tahūdawīn 166-167 K 7
Ṭīhrī = Tehri 138-139 G 2
Ti-hua = Ürümchi 142-143 F 3
Tihwa = Ürümchi 142-143 F 3
Tiirismaa 116-117 L 7
Tijamuchi, Río — 104-105 D 4
Tijāra 138-139 F 4
Tijeras, NM 76-77 A 5
Tijiqjah 164-165 B 5
Tijoca 92-93 K 5
Tijuana 64-65 C 5
Tijuca 100-101 B 5
Tijuca, Lagoa da — 110 I ab 2
Tijuca, Pico da — 110 I b 2
Tijuca, Rio de Janeiro- 110 I b 2
Tijucas 102-103 H 7
Tijucas, Baía de — 102-103 H 7
Tijucas, Rio — 102-103 H 7
Tijuco, Rio — 102-103 H 3
Tikal 64-65 J 8
Tikamgarh 138-139 G 5
Ṭikārī = Tekāri 138-139 K 5
Tikchik Lake 58-59 HJ 7
Tikhvin = Tichvin 132-133 E 6
Tikiklut, AK 58-59 J 1
Tikopia 158-159 N 2
Tikota 140 B 2
Tikrīt 136-137 K 5
Tiksi 132-133 Y 3
Tikšozero 116-117 OP 4
Tilādru 140 E 2
Tiladummati Atoll 176 a 1
Tilādūru = Tilādru 140 E 2
Tilaiya Reservoir 138-139 K 5
Tilama 106-107 B 4
Tilamuta 148-149 H 6
Tilayah, Wādī — 166-167 G 6
Tilbeşar ovası 136-137 G 4
Tilburg 120-121 K 3
Tilbury 72-73 E 3
Tilcara 111 CD 2
Tilden, NE 68-69 H 4-5
Tilden, TX 76-77 E 8
Tilemsi 164-165 E 5
Tilhar 138-139 G 4
Tilia, Ouèd — = Wādī Tilayah 166-167 G 6
Tiličiki 132-133 g 5
Tilimsān, Jabal — 166-167 F 2
Tilin = Htilin 141 D 5
Tilisarao 106-107 E 4
Tillabéri 164-165 E 6
Tillamook, OR 66-67 B 3
Tillamook Bay 66-67 AB 3
Tillery, Lake — 80-81 FG 3
Tilley 61 C 5
Tillia 164-165 E 5
Tillsonburg 72-73 F 3
Tilmās 166-167 C 7
Tilomonte 104-105 B 8
Tilos = Tēlos 122-123 M 7
Tilpa 158-159 H 6
Tilrahmat 166-167 H 3
Tilrhemt = Tilrahmat 166-167 H 3
Tilston 68-69 F 1
Tiltil 106-107 B 4
Tīlū, Nam — 141 E 5
Tilvāra = Tilwāra 138-139 CD 5
Tilwāra 138-139 CD 5
Tim 126-127 H 1
Ṭimā 173 B 4
Timagami 72-73 FG 1
Timagami, Lake — 72-73 F 1
Timah, Bukit — 154 III a 1
Timalūlīn 166-167 L 5
Timanā 92-93 D 4
Timane, Rio — 102-103 B 4
Timanskij kr'až 132-133 J 5-H 4
Timaru 158-159 O 8
Timaševo [SU, Kujbyševskaja Oblast'] 124-125 S 7
Timaševsk 126-127 J 4
Timasova Gora 124-125 Q 3
Timassah 164-165 H 3
Timassanin = Burj 'Umar Idrīs 164-165 EF 3
Timbalier Bay 78-79 D 6
Timbalier Island 78-79 D 6
Timbara 96-97 B 3
Timbaúba 100-101 G 4
Timbaúva 106-107 KL 2-3
Timbédra = Tinbadghah 164-165 C 5
Timber, OR 66-67 B 3
Timber Acres, Houston-, TX 85 III b 1
Timber Creek North Branch 84 III c 2
Timbergrove Manor, Houston-, TX 85 III b 1
Timber Lake, SD 68-69 F 3
Timber Mountain 74-75 F 3
Timbío 94-95 C 6
Timbiquí 94-95 C 6
Timbiras 100-101 C 3
Timbó [BR, Rio de Janeiro] 110 I b 2
Timbó [BR, Santa Catarina] 102-103 H 7
Timbo [Guinea] 164-165 B 6
Timbó, Rio — 102-103 G 7
Timboulaga 164-165 F 5
Timbun Mata, Pulau — 152-153 N 3
Timedjerdane, Ouèd — = Wādī Tamajirdayn 166-167 G 7
Timehri 98-99 JK 1
Timellouine = Timalūlīn 166-167 L 5
Timgad = Timkād 166-167 K 2
Timḥaḍīt 166-167 D 3
Timia 164-165 F 5
Timimoun = Tīmīmūn 164-165 E 3
Timimoun, Sebkra de — = Sabkhat Tīmīmūn 166-167 G 5
Tīmīmūn 164-165 E 3
Tīmīmūn, Sabkhat — 166-167 G 5
Timiş 122-123 J 3
Timişoara 122-123 J 3
Timiza, Parque Distrital de — 91 III ab 3
Timkād 166-167 K 2
Tim Mersoï, Oued — 164-165 F 5
Timmins 56-57 U 8
Timmonsville, SC 80-81 G 3
Timmoudi = Tīmmūdī 164-165 D 3
Timon 92-93 L 6
Timonha 100-101 D 2
Timor 148-149 H 9-J 8
Timorante 100-101 E 4
Timor Sea 158-159 E 2
Timor Timur = 23 ⊲ 148-149 J 8
Timor Trough 148-149 J 8
Timošino 124-125 L 3
Timote 106-107 F 5
Timotes 94-95 F 3
Timpahute Range 74-75 F 4
Timpas, CO 68-69 E 7
Timpson, TX 76-77 G 7
Timsāḥ, Buḥayrat at- 173 C 2
Timšer [SU, place] 124-125 U 3
Timšer [SU, river] 124-125 U 3
Tina 174-175 H 6
Tina, La — 96-97 B 4
Tinaco 94-95 G 3
Ṭinah, Khalīj aṭ- 173 C 2
Tinajas, Las — 102-103 A 7
Tinakula 148-149 kl 7
Tinaquillo 94-95 G 3
Tinbadghah 164-165 C 5
Tin City, AK 58-59 D 4
Tincopalca 96-97 F 9
Tindivanam 140 DE 4
Tindouf = Tindūf 164-165 C 3
Tindouf, Hamada de — = Hammadat Tindūf 166-167 B 6-C 5
Tindouf, Sebkha de — = Sabkhat Tindūf 164-165 C 3
Tindūf 164-165 C 3
Tindūf, Hammadat — 166-167 BC 5-6
Tindūf, Sabkhat — 164-165 C 3
Tineba, Pegunungan — 152-153 O 6-7
Tin Edrin 168-169 E 1
Tinejdād = Tinjdād 166-167 D 4
Tineo 120-121 D 7
Tin Essalak 164-165 E 5
Tinezoûlîn = Tinzūlīn 166-167 CD 4
Tin Fouchaye = Tin Fūshay 166-167 L 5
Tinfouchi = Tin Fūshī 166-167 D 5
Tin Fūshay 166-167 L 5
Tin Fūshī 166-167 D 5
Ting-an = Ding'an 150-151 H 3
Tingchei Dsong 138-139 LM 3
Tinggi, Pulau — 150-151 E 11
Tingha 160 K 2-3
Tinghing = Dingxing 146-147 E 2
Tinghīr 166-167 D 4
Tinghīrt, Hammadat — 164-165 FG 3
Ting-hsi = Dingxi 142-143 J 4
Tinghsien = Ding Xian 146-147 E 2
Ting-hsin = Dingxin 142-143 H 3
Ting-hsing = Dingxing 146-147 E 2
Ting Jiang 146-147 F 9
Ting Kau 155 I a 1
Tingling Shan = Qin Ling 142-143 KL 5
Tingmerkpuk Mount 58-59 FG 2
Ting-nan = Dingnan 146-147 E 9
Tingo 96-97 B 2
Tingo María 92-93 D 6
Tingpian = Dingbian 146-147 A 3
Tingréla 164-165 C 6
Tingri Dsong 142-143 F 6
Tingsiqiao 146-147 E 7
Tingsryd 116-117 F 9
T'ing-szŭ-ch'iao = Tingsiqiao 146-147 E 7
Tingtao = Dingtao 146-147 E 4
Tinguipaya 92-93 F 8
Tinguiririca, Volcán — 106-107 B 5
Tingvoll 116-117 BC 6
Tingwon 148-149 g 5
Ting-yüan = Dingyuan 146-147 F 5
Ting-yüan-ying = Bajan Choto 142-143 JK 4
Tinharé, Ilha de — 100-101 E 7
Tinh Biên 150-151 E 7
Tinhosa Island = Dazhou Dao 150-151 H 3
Tinicum Wildlife Preserve 84 III b 2
Tinjar, Batang — 152-153 L 4
Tinjdād 166-167 D 4
Tinjil, Pulau — 148-149 E 8
Tin Khéouné, Hassi — = Ḥāssī Tin Quwānīn 166-167 L 7
Tinkisso 164-165 BC 6
Tinnevelly = Tirunelveli 134-135 M 9
Tinogasta 111 C 3
Tinpak = Dianbai 146-147 C 11
Tin Quwānīn, Ḥāssī — 166-167 L 7
Tinrhert, Hamada de — = Hammadat Tinghīrt 164-165 FG 3
Tinsukia 134-135 Q 5
Tintah, MN 68-69 H 2-3
Tin Tarābīn, Wādī — 164-165 F 4
Tin Tehoun 168-169 E 1
Tintina 111 D 3
Tintinara 160 E 5
Tinyah 166-167 H 1
Tin Zakyū 166-167 JK 6-7
Tin Zekiou = Tin Zakyū 166-167 JK 6-7
Tinzūlīn 166-167 CD 4
Tío, El — 111 D 4
Tioga, CO 68-69 D 7
Tioga, LA 78-79 C 5
Tioga, ND 68-69 E 1
Tioga, TX 76-77 F 6
Tioga, Philadelphia-, PA 84 III bc 1
Tiogo 168-169 E 2
Tioman, Pulau — 148-149 DE 6
Tionesta, CA 66-67 C 5
Tionesta, PA 72-73 G 4
Tioro, Selat — 152-153 P 8
Tioukeline, Hassi — = Ḥāssī Tiyūkulīn 166-167 J 6
Tiourinine = Tiyūrīnīn 166-167 K 7
Tipaza = Tībāzah 166-167 H 1
Tipp City, OH 70-71 H 6
Tippecanoe River 70-71 GH 5
Tipperā 141 B 3-4
Tipperary 119 BC 5
Tipton, CA 74-75 D 4
Tipton, IA 70-71 E 5
Tipton, IN 70-71 G 5
Tipton, MO 70-71 D 6
Tipton, OK 76-77 E 5
Tipton, WY 68-69 B 5
Tipton, Mount — 74-75 F 5
Tiptonville, TN 78-79 E 2
Tip Top Hill 70-71 GH 1
Tiptūru = Tiptūr 140 C 4
Tiptūr 140 C 4
Tiputini, Río — 96-97 C 2
Tiquaruçu 100-101 E 6-7
Tiquié, Rio — 94-95 G 7
Tiquisate 86-87 P 10
Tiracambu, Serra de — 92-93 K 5
Tiradentes 102-103 KL 4
Tira Fogo 98-99 G 9
Tirān, Jazīrat — 173 D 4
Tirana = Tiranë 122-123 HJ 5
Tiranë 122-123 HJ 5
Tirāp 141 E 2
Tirapata 96-97 F 9
Tirap Frontier Division = Tirāp 141 E 2
Tirasdunes 174-175 B 4
Tiras Mountains = Tirasplato 174-175 B 3-4
Tirasplato 174-175 B 3-4
Tiraspol' 126-127 D 3
Tiratimine = Tarātmīn 166-167 H 7
Tirbande Turkestān 134-135 JK 3
Tire 136-137 B 3
Tirebolu 136-137 H 2
Tiree 119 C 3
Tiree Passage 119 C 3
Tîrgovişte 122-123 L 3
Tîrgu Cărbuneşti 122-123 KL 3
Tîrgu Jiu 122-123 K 3
Tîrgu Mureş 122-123 L 2
Tîrgu Neamţ 122-123 LM 2
Tirhatimine = Tarātmīn 166-167 H 7
Tirhut 138-139 K 4
Tirich Mīr 134-135 L 3
Tirikuṇāmalaya 134-135 N 9
Tírnabos 122-123 K 6
Tiro 168-169 C 3
Tirodi 138-139 G 7
Tirol 118 EF 5
Tirong Dsong 141 C 2
Tiros 102-103 K 3
Tirso 122-123 C 6
Tīrthahalli 140 B 4
Tirtol 138-139 L 7
Tirúa 106-107 A 7
Tiruchchendur 134-135 M 9
Tiruchchirāppalli = Tiruchirāpalli 134-135 M 8
Tiruchendur = Tiruchchendur 134-135 M 9
Tiruchengodu 140 CD 5
Tiruchinkōṭṭai = Tiruchengodu 140 CD 5
Tiruchirāpalli 134-135 M 8
Tirukkoyilūr 140 D 5
Tirukkunamalai = Tirikuṇāmalaya 134-135 N 9
Tirukoilur = Tirukkoyilūr 140 D 5
Tirumakūdal Narsipur 140 C 4
Tirumangalam 140 CD 6
Tirumayam 140 D 5
Tirunelveli 134-135 M 9
Tirupati 134-135 M 8
Tiruppattur = Tiruppattūr 140 D 5
Tiruppattūr [IND ↗ Madurai] 140 D 5
Tiruppattūr [IND ↗ Salem] 140 D 4
Tiruppundi 140 DE 5
Tiruppūr 140 C 5
Tirūr = Trikkandiyur 140 B 5
Tiruttani 140 D 4
Tirutturaippūndi 140 DE 5
Tiruvādānai 140 D 6
Tiruvalla 140 C 6
Tiruvallūr 140 DE 4
Tiruvālūr 140 D 5
Tiruvanatapurām = Trivandrum 134-135 M 9
Tiruvannāmalai 140 D 4
Tiruvarur = Tiruvālūr 140 D 5
Tiruvatāṅkūr = Travancore 140 C 6
Tiruvāyam = Tirumayam 140 D 5
Tiruvettipuram 140 D 4
Tiruvur = Tiruvūru 140 E 2
Tiruvūru 140 E 2
Tisa 122-123 J 3
Tisa = Tisza 118 K 5
Tisaiyanvilai 140 CD 6
Tīsamsīlt 166-167 G 2
Tisdale 56-57 Q 7
Tīshāro, Jabal — 166-167 JK 2
Tīshīt 164-165 C 5
Tīshlah 164-165 AB 4
Tishomingo, MS 78-79 E 3
Tishomingo, OK 76-77 F 5
Tīs Isat fwafwate 164-165 M 6
Tisiten, Jebel — = Jabal Tīdīghīn 166-167 D 2
Tiškovka 126-127 E 2
Tismana 122-123 K 3
Tissah 166-167 D 2
Tissamaharama = Tissamahārāmaya 140 E 7
Tissamahārāmaya 140 E 7
Tissāūt, Wād — 166-167 C 4
Tissemsilt = Tīsamsīlt 166-167 G 2
Tistā 138-139 M 5
Tisza 118 K 5
Tit 166-167 G 6
Ṭitabar 141 D 2
Ṭitagarh 138-139 M 6
Titaluk River 58-59 K 2
Titālya 138-139 M 4
Tit-Ary 132-133 Y 3
Titemsi 164-165 E 5
Titeri, Monts du — = Jabal al-Titrī 166-167 H 1-2
Titicaca, Lago — 92-93 F 8
Titlagarh 138-139 J 7
Titna River 58-59 L 4
Titograd 122-123 H 4
Titovo Užice 122-123 HJ 4
Titov Veles 122-123 JK 5
Titran 116-117 C 6
Tiṭrī, Jabal al- 166-167 H 1-2
Tittabawassee River 70-71 HJ 4
Titu [EAK] 171 D 2
Titule 172 DE 1
Titusville, FL 80-81 c 2
Titusville, PA 72-73 G 4
Tiṭwān 164-165 CD 1
Tiu Chung Chau 155 I b 1-2
Tiura Pipardih 138-139 JK 5
Tivaouane 164-165 A 5
Tiverton 119 E 6
Tivoli 122-123 E 5
Tixtla de Guerrero 86-87 L 9
Tiyāgai 140 D 5
Tiyārat 164-165 E 1
Tiyūkulīn, Ḥāssī — 166-167 J 6
Tiyūrīnīn 166-167 K 7
Tizapán, Villa Obregón- 91 I b 2
Tizimín 64-65 J 7
Tizi 'n Talghemt = Tizi 'N Talrhemt 166-167 D 3
Tīzī N Talrhemt 166-167 D 3
Tīzī N Test 166-167 B 4
Tīzī N Tichka 166-167 C 4
Tizi-Ouzou = Tīzī Wazū 164-165 E 1
Tīzī Wazū 164-165 E 1
Tiznados, Río — 94-95 H 3
Tīznīt 164-165 C 3
Tizoc 86-87 JK 5

Tjeggelvas 116-117 GH 4
Tjendana, Pulau — = Sumba 148-149 G 9
Tjertjen = Chārchān 142-143 F 4
Tjirebon = Cirebon 148-149 E 8
Tjörn [IS] 116-117 c 2
Tjörn [S] 116-117 D 8-9
Tjörnes 116-117 e 1
Tjøtta 116-117 E 5
Tjumen = T'umen' 132-133 M 6
Tjuvfjorden 116-117 l 6

Tkibuli 126-127 L 5
Tkvarčeli 126-127 K 5

Tlacotalpan 86-87 N 8
Tlahuac 91 I c 3
Tlahualilo, Sierra del — 76-77 C 9
Tlahualilo de Zaragoza 76-77 C 9
Tlalnepantla de Comonfort 86-87 L 8
Tlalpan 91 I b 3
Tlalpan-El Reloj 91 I c 3
Tlalpan-Huipulco 91 I c 3
Tlalpan-Tepepan 91 I c 3
Tlalpan-Villa Coapa 91 I c 3
Tlapa de Comonfort 86-87 LM 9
Tlaquepaque 64-65 F 7
Tl'arata 126-127 N 5
Tlaxcala 64-65 G 8
Tlaxcala de Xicoténcatl 64-65 G 8
Tlaxiaco, Santa María Asunción — 64-65 G 8
Tlell 60 B 3
Tlemcen = Tilimsān 164-165 D 2
Tlemcen, Monts de — = Jabal Tilimsān 166-167 F 2
Tlemcès 164-165 EF 5
Tleta = Sūq ath-Thalāthah 166-167 C 2
Tleta Beni Oulid = Ath-Thalātha 166-167 D 2
Tleta Ketama = Kitāmah 166-167 D 2
Tlumač 126-127 B 2
Tluste = Tolstoje 126-127 B 2

Tmessa = Timassah 164-165 H 3

Tnine Riat = Ath-Thnīn Rīāt 166-167 B 3

Toachi, Río — 96-97 B 1-2
Toamasina 172 JK 5
Toano, VA 80-81 H 2
Toano Range 66-67 F 5
Toa Payoh Town, Singapore- 154 III b 1
Toay 106-107 E 6
Toba [J] 144-145 L 5
Toba [RA] 106-107 G 2
Toba, Danau — 148-149 C 6
Tobago 64-65 OP 9

370 Theuniss

Tobago, Trinidad and — 64-65 O 9-10
Tobalai, Pulau — 148-149 J 7
Tobar, NV 66-67 F 5
Tobarra 120-121 G 9
Tobas 106-107 F 2
Ṭoba Ṭek Singh 138-139 CD 2
Tobatí 102-103 D 6
Tobelo 148-149 J 6
Tobelumbang 152-153 OP 6
Tobermorey 158-159 G 4
Tobermory 72-73 EF 2
Tobi 148-149 K 6
Tobias, NE 68-69 H 5
Tobias Barreto 100-101 EF 6
Tobin, Mount — 66-67 E 5
Tobin Lake [CDN, lake] 61 G 4
Tobin Lake [CDN, place] 61 G 4
Tobique River 63 C 4
Tobi-shima 144-145 M 3
Tobli 168-169 C 4
Tobo 148-149 JK 7
Toboali 148-149 E 7
Tobol [SU, place] 132-133 L 7
Tobol [SU, river] 132-133 M 6
Toboli 148-149 H 7
Tobol'sk 132-133 MN 6
Tô Bông 150-151 G 6
Toborochi 104-105 E 6
Tôbrang 138-139 K 3
Tobruch = Ṭubruq 164-165 J 2
Tobruk = Tubruq 164-165 J 2
Tobseda 132-133 J 4
T'ob'ulech 132-133 b 3
Tobys' 124-125 T 2
Tocache Nuevo 96-97 C 6
Tocaima 94-95 D 5
Tocantínia 92-93 K 6
Tocantinópolis 92-93 K 6
Tocantins, Rio — 92-93 K 5-6
Toccoa, GA 80-81 E 3
Tochigi 144-145 MN 4
Tochio 144-145 M 4
T'o-chi Tao = Tuoji Dao 146-147 H 2
Toch'o-do 144-145 E 5
Tochta 124-125 R 2
Tockoje 124-125 T 7
Toco [RCH] 111 C 2
Toco [TT] 94-95 L 2
Toco, El — 94-95 J 3
Tócome 91 II c 1
Toconao 104-105 C 8
Tocopilla 111 B 2
Tocorpuri, Cerro de — 92-93 F 9
Tocota 106-107 C 3
Tocqueville = Ra's al-Wād 164-165 E 1
Tocra = Tūkrah 164-165 HJ 2
Tocruyoc 96-97 F 9
Tocuco, Río — 94-95 E 3
Tocumen, Río — 64-65 c 2
Tocuyo, El — 92-93 F 3
Tocuyo, Río — 94-95 G 2
Tocuyo de La Costa 94-95 GH 2
Ṭoda Bhīm 138-139 F 4
Toda Rai Singh 138-139 E 4-5
Todatonten Lake 58-59 L 3
Todeli 148-149 H 7
Todenyang 171 C 1
Tödi [CH] 118 D 5
Todi [I] 122-123 E 4
Todmorden [AUS] 158-159 FG 5
Todness 92-93 H 3
To-dong 144-145 H 4
Todo-saki 144-145 O 3
Todos los Santos, Lago — 108-109 CD 3
Todos os Santos, Baía de — 92-93 M 7
Todos os Santos, Rio — 102-103 M 2
Todos Santos [BOL, Cochabamba] 92-93 F 8
Todos Santos [BOL, Pando] 104-105 C 3
Todos Santos [MEX] 64-65 D 7
Todos Santos, Bahía de — 86-87 B 2
Todrha, Ouèd — = Wād Tudghā' 166-167 D 4
Todro 171 B 2
Todupulai 140 C 6
Toei Yai, Khao — 150-151 B 7
Toejo 144-145 FG 3
Tōen = T'ao-yüan 146-147 H 9
Toeng 150-151 C 3
Toësse 168-169 E 3
Tóez 94-95 C 6
Tofino 60 E 5
Tofo, El — 106-107 B 2
Tofte, MN 70-71 E 2
Tofty, AK 58-59 M 4
Tofua 208 J 4
Togi 144-145 L 4
Togiak, AK 58-59 GH 7
Togiak Bay 58-59 G 7
Togiak Lake 58-59 GH 7
Togiak River 58-59 GH 7
Togian, Kepulauan — 148-149 H 7
Togian, Pulau — 152-153 O 6
Togliatti 132-133 H 7
Togo 164-165 E 7
Togochale = Togotyalē 164-165 N 7
Togotyalē 164-165 N 7
Togtoh = Tugt 142-143 L 3-4
Togye-dong 144-145 G 4
Tōgyu-sen 144-145 FG 5
Tohāna 138-139 EF 3
Tohatchi, NM 74-75 J 5
Tohma çayı 136-137 G 3
Tohma suyu 136-137 GH 3
T'o Ho = Tuo He 146-147 F 5
Tohoku 144-145 N 2-4
Toiama = Toyama 142-143 Q 4
Toijala 116-117 K 7
Toili 148-149 H 7
Toi-misaki 144-145 H 7
Toiserivier 174-175 G 7
Toivola, MI 70-71 F 2
Toiyabe Range 74-75 E 3
Tojo 152-153 D 6
Tok [SU] 124-125 U 7
Tokachi-dake 144-145 c 2
Tokachi-gawa 144-145 c 2
Tōkagi 155 III c 1
Tokai 144-145 LM 5
Tokaj 118 K 4
Tokala 152-153 O 6
Tokala, Gunung — 152-153 O 6
Tōkamachi 144-145 M 4
Ṭōkar = Ṭawkar 164-165 M 5
Tokara-kaikyō 142-143 O 5-P 6
Tokara-rettō 142-143 OP 6
Tokarevka 124-125 N 8
Tokat 134-135 D 2
Tōkchŏk-kundo 144-145 EF 4
Tōkch'ŏn 144-145 F 3
Tokelau Islands 156-157 J 5
Toki 144-145 L 5
Tokio, TX 76-77 C 6
Tokio = Tōkyō 142-143 QR 4
Tokitsu = Toki 144-145 L 5
Tok Junction, AK 58-59 Q 5
Tokko 132-133 WX 6
Tok-kol 144-145 GH 2
Toklat, AK 58-59 MN 4
Tokmak [SU, Kirgizskaja SSR] 132-133 O 9
Tokmak [SU, Ukrainskaja SSR] 126-127 GH 3
Tōkō = Tungchiang 146-147 H 10
Tokolimbu 148-149 H 7
Tokong Boro 152-153 G 3
Tokoro 144-145 cd 1
Tokosun = Toksun 142-143 F 3
Tokra = Tūkrah 164-165 HJ 2
Toksun 142-143 F 3
Toktat River 58-59 MN 4
Tokuno-shima 142-143 O 6
Tokuno sima = Tokuno-shima 142-143 O 6
Tokushima 142-143 PQ 5
Tokusima = Tokushima 142-143 PQ 5
Tokuyama 144-145 HJ 5
Tōkyō 142-143 QR 4
Tōkyō-Adachi 155 III b 1
Tōkyō-Akabane 155 III b 1
Tōkyō-Akasaka 155 III b 1
Tōkyō-Amanuma 155 III a 1
Tōkyō-Aoyama 155 III b 2
Tōkyō-Arakawa 155 III b 1
Tōkyō-Asagaya 155 III a 1
Tōkyō-Asakusa 155 III b 1
Tōkyō-Azabu 155 III b 2
Tōkyō-Bunkyō 155 III b 1
Tōkyō-Chiyoda 155 III b 1
Tōkyō-Chūō 155 III b 1
Tōkyō-Denenchōfu 155 III ab 2
Tōkyō-Ebara 155 III b 2
Tōkyō-Edogawa 155 III c 1
Tōkyō-Ekoda 155 III ab 1
Tōkyō-Fukagawa 155 III b 2
Tōkyō-Ginza 155 III b 1
Tōkyō-Haneda 155 III b 2
Tōkyō-Higashiōizumi 155 III a 1
Tōkyō-Hongō 155 III b 1
Tōkyō-Honjo 155 III b 1
Tōkyō-Horinouchi 155 III ab 1
Tōkyō-Ikegami 155 III b 2
Tōkyō-Inatsuke 155 III b 1
Tōkyō International Airport 155 III b 2
Tōkyō-Itabashi 155 III ab 1
Tōkyō-Kamata 155 III b 2
Tōkyō-Kameari 155 III c 1
Tōkyō-Kameido 155 III bc 1
Tōkyō-Kamiakatsuka 155 III ab 1
Tōkyō-Kamikitazawa 155 III a 2
Tōkyō-Kamishakujii 155 III a 1
Tōkyō-Kanamachi 155 III c 1
Tōkyō-Kanda 155 III b 1
Tōkyō-Kasai 155 III c 2
Tōkyō-Kashiwagi 155 III b 1
Tōkyō-Katsushika 155 III bc 1
Tōkyō-Kita 155 III b 1
Tōkyō-ko 155 III b 2
Tōkyō-Kōenji 155 III ab 1
Tōkyō-Koishikawa 155 III b 1
Tōkyō-Koiwa 155 III c 1
Tōkyō-Komagome 155 III b 1
Tōkyō-Komatsugawa 155 III c 1
Tōkyō-Kōto 155 III b 1
Tōkyō-Koyama 155 III b 2
Tōkyō-Maeno 155 III b 1
Tōkyō-Magome 155 III b 2
Tōkyō-Meguro 155 III b 2
Tōkyō-Minato 155 III b 2
Tōkyō-Mizue 155 III c 1
Tōkyō-Mukōjima 155 III bc 1
Tōkyō-Nakanbu 155 III b 2
Tōkyō-Nakano 155 III ab 1
Tōkyō National Museum 155 III b 1
Tōkyō-Nerima 155 III a 1
Tōkyō-Nihonbashi 155 III b 1
Tōkyō-Numata 155 III b 1
Tōkyō-Ochiai 155 III b 1
Tōkyō-Ōi 155 III b 2
Tōkyō-Okusawa 155 III ab 2
Tōkyō-Ōmori 155 III b 2
Tōkyō-Ōta 155 III b 2
Tōkyō-Ōyada 155 III bc 1
Tōkyō-Rokugō 155 III b 2
Tōkyō-Sangenjaya 155 III b 2
Tōkyō-Senjū 155 III b 1
Tōkyō-Setagaya 155 III a 2
Tōkyō-Shibuya 155 III ab 2
Tōkyō-Shimane 155 III b 1
Tōkyō-Shimoigusa 155 III a 1
Tōkyō-Shimoshakujii 155 III a 1
Tōkyō-Shimura 155 III b 1
Tōkyō-Shinagawa 155 III b 2
Tōkyō-Shinjuku 155 III b 1
Tōkyō-Shishihone 155 III c 1
Tōkyō-Soshigaya 155 III a 2
Tōkyō-Sugamo 155 III b 1
Tōkyō-Suginami 155 III a 1
Tōkyō-Sumida 155 III bc 1
Tōkyō-Sunamachi 155 III bc 1
Tōkyō-Taitō 155 III b 1
Tōkyō-Takaido 155 III a 1
Tōkyō-Takenotsuka 155 III b 1
Tōkyō-Takinogawa 155 III b 1
Tōkyō-Tamagawa 155 III ab 2
Tōkyō-Toshima 155 III b 1
Tōkyō Tower 155 III b 2
Tōkyō-Toyotama 155 III a 1
Tōkyō-Ueno 155 III b 1
Tōkyō-Ukita 155 III c 1
Tōkyō wan 144-145 M 5
Tōkyō-Yōga 155 III a 2
Tōkyō-Yukigaya 155 III b 2
Tola, La — 92-93 D 4
Tolageak, AK 58-59 FG 1-2
Tolar, NM 76-77 C 5
Tolar, Cerro — 104-105 C 10
Tolar Grande 111 C 2
Tolbuhin 122-123 MN 4
Tole 88-89 F 10
Toledo, OH 64-65 K 3
Toledo, OR 66-67 B 3
Toledo [BOL] 104-105 C 6
Toledo [BR, Amazonas] 96-97 E 4
Toledo [BR, Paraná] 102-103 F 6
Toledo [E] 120-121 EF 9
Toledo [PE] 98-99 B 7
Toledo [RCH] 106-107 B 1
Toledo, Alto de — 96-97 F 9
Toledo, Montes de — 120-121 E 9
Toledo Bend Reservoir 76-77 GH 7
Tolenay 94-95 F 6
Tolentino [MEX] 86-87 K 6
Tolga = Tūljā 164-165 EF 2
Toliary 172 H 6
Tolima 94-95 D 5-6
Tolima, Nevado del — 94-95 D 5
Töling 138-139 GH 2
Tolitoli 148-149 H 6
Toll'a, zaliv — 132-133 ST 2
Tolleson, AZ 74-75 G 6
Tolley, ND 68-69 EF 1
Tolloche 111 D 3
Tolly's Nullah 154 II b 3
Tolmač'ovo 124-125 G 4
Tolo, Teluk — 148-149 H 7
Toločin 124-125 G 6
Tolomosa 104-105 D 7
Tolono, IL 70-71 FG 6
Tolori 104-105 G 4
Tolosa 120-121 FG 7
Tolovana, AK 58-59 N 4
Tolovana River 58-59 N 4
Tolox, Sierra de — 120-121 E 10
Tolsan-do 144-145 FG 5
Tolstoj, mys — 132-133 e 6
Tolstoje 126-127 B 2
Toltén 111 B 5
Toltén, Río — 108-109 C 2
Tolú 94-95 D 3
Toluca, IL 70-71 F 5
Toluca, Nevado de — 64-65 FG 8
Toluca de Lerdo 64-65 FG 8
To-lun = Doloon Nuur 142-143 LM 3
Toma, La — 111 C 4
Tomah, WI 70-71 E 3-4
Tomahawk, WI 70-71 F 3
Tomakomai 142-143 R 3
Tomakovka 126-127 G 3
Tomamae 144-145 b 1
Tomaniive 148-149 a 2
Tomar [BR] 92-93 G 5
Tomar [P] 120-121 C 9
Tomar do Geru 100-101 F 6
Tomarovka 126-127 GH 1
Tomarrazón 94-95 E 2
Tomarza 136-137 F 3
Tomás Barrón 104-105 C 5
Tomaševka 124-125 DE 8
Tomás Gomensoro 106-107 J 3
Tomás Young 106-107 FG 2
Tomaszów Lubelski 118 L 3
Tomaszów Mazowiecki 118 K 3
Tomatlán 86-87 H 8
Tomave 104-105 C 7
Tomazina 102-103 H 5
Tomba di Nerone, Roma- 113 II ab 1
Tombador, Serra do — [BR, Bahia] 100-101 D 6
Tombador, Serra do — [BR, Mato Grosso] 92-93 H 7
Tomball, TX 76-77 G 7
Tombē 164-165 L 7
Tombes Royales = Lang Tâm 150-151 F 4
Tombetsu, Hama- 144-145 c 1
Tombetsu, Shō- 144-145 c 1
Tombigbee River 64-65 J 5
Tombo, Punta — 108-109 G 5
Tomboco 172 B 3
Tomboli 152-153 O 7
Tombos 102-103 L 4
Tombouctou 164-165 D 5
Tombstone, AZ 74-75 HJ 7
Tom Burke 174-175 G 2
Tomé 111 B 5
Tomea, Pulau — 152-153 PQ 8
Tomé-Açu 98-99 OP 6
Tömek = Aşağıpınarbaşı 136-137 E 3
Tomelilla 116-117 EF 10
Tomelloso 120-121 F 9
Tomiko 72-73 G 1
Tomini 148-149 H 6
Tomini, Teluk — 148-149 H 7
Tominian 168-169 D 2
Tomioka 144-145 N 4
Tomkinson Ranges 158-159 E 5
Tommot 132-133 Y 6
Tomo 92-93 F 4
Tomo, Río — 92-93 F 3
Tomolasta, Cerro — 106-107 DE 4
Tomori, Teluk — 148-149 H 7
Tompkins 61 D 5
Tompkinsville, KY 78-79 G 2
Tompo 132-133 a 5
Tomra 116-117 B 6
Tomsk 132-133 PQ 6
Toms River, NJ 72-73 JK 5
Tomtabakken 116-117 EF 9
Tom White, Mount — 58-59 PQ 6
Tō Myit 141 E 7
Tona [E] 94-95 E 4
Tonalá 64-65 H 8
Tonalea, AZ 74-75 H 4
Tonami 144-145 L 4
Tonantins 92-93 F 5
Tonasket, WA 66-67 D 1
Tonate 98-99 M 2
Tonbai Shan 142-143 L 5
Tonbridge 119 G 6
Tonda 148-149 M 8
Tønder 116-117 C 10
Tondern 70-71 H 1
Tondi 134-135 M 9
Tondibi 168-169 EF 1
Tone-gawa 144-145 N 5
Tonekābon 134-135 G 3
Tōngā [Sudan] 164-165 L 7
Tonga [Tonga] 148-149 bc 2
Tongaat 174-175 J 5
Tonga Islands 156-157 J 5-6
Tongaland 172 F 7
Tong'an 146-147 G 9
Tongatapu 208 J 5
Tonga Trench 148-149 c 2
Tongbai 146-147 D 5
Tongch'ang 144-145 EF 2
Tongcheng [TJ, Anhui] 146-147 F 6
Tongcheng [TJ, Hubei] 146-147 DE 7
Tongcheng [TJ, Jiangsu] 146-147 G 5
Tong Chhu 138-139 M 3
T'ongch'ŏn 144-145 FG 3
Tongchuan 142-143 K 4
Tongdao 146-147 B 8
Tonggu 146-147 E 7
Tongguan [TJ, Hunan] 146-147 D 7
Tongguan [TJ, Shaanxi] 142-143 L 5
Tonggu Jiao 150-151 H 3
Tonggu Zhang 146-147 F 10
Tonghan-man 142-143 O 4
Tonghua 142-143 O 3
Tonghui He 155 II bc 2
Tongjosŏn-man = Tonghan-man 142-143 O 4
Tongkil Island 152-153 O 2
Tong La 138-139 L 3
Tongliao 142-143 N 3
Tongling 142-143 M 5
Tonglu 142-143 M 5-6
Tongmun'gō-ri 144-145 F 2
Tongoy 111 B 4
Tongoy, Bahía — 106-107 B 3
Tongphu 142-143 H 5
Tongpu = Tongphu 142-143 H 5
Tongren 142-143 K 6
Ṭongsā Jong = Thongsa Dsong 138-139 N 4
Tongshan 146-147 E 7
Tongshan = Dongshan 146-147 F 10
Tongshan Dao = Dongshan Dao 146-147 F 10
Tongshannei Ao 146-147 F 10
Tongshi 146-147 F 4
Tongue River 68-69 CD 2
Tong Xian 142-143 M 3-4
Tongxiang 146-147 H 6
Tongxu 146-147 E 4
Tongyang 144-145 F 3
Tongyang = Dongyang 146-147 H 7
T'ŏngyŏng = Ch'ungmu 144-145 G 5
Tongyu 142-143 N 3
Tonhon 150-151 E 7
Tonk 134-135 M 5
Tonkawa, OK 76-77 F 4
Tonki Cape 58-59 M 7
Tonkin 148-149 DE 2
Tonkin = Bắc Bộ 148-149 D 2
Tonkin, Gulf of — 148-149 E 2-3
Tonlé Sap 148-149 D 4
Tonndorf, Hamburg- 130 I b 1
Tonneins 120-121 GH 6
Tonopah, NV 64-65 C 4
Tonosí 88-89 F 11
Tons 138-139 HJ 5
Tønsberg 116-117 CD 8
Tonsina, AK 58-59 P 6
Tonstad 116-117 B 8
Tontal, Sierra de — 106-107 C 3
Tontelbos 174-175 D 6
Tonya 136-137 H 2
Tōnzan 141 C 4
Tonzona River 58-59 L 5
Tooele, UT 66-67 D 3
Tooligie 160 B 4
Toolik River 58-59 N 2
Toompine 160 G 1
Toora 160 H 7
Toora-Chem 132-133 S 7
Toorak, Melbourne- 161 II c 2
Tooting Graveney, London- 129 II b 2
Toowoomba 158-159 K 5
Topagoruk River 58-59 JK 1
Topeka, KS 64-65 G 4
Topia 86-87 G 5
Topkapi 154 I a 2
Topkapı, İstanbul- 154 I a 2
Topki 132-133 PQ 6
Topko, gora — 132-133 a 6
Toplița 122-123 L 2
Toplyj Stan, Moskva- 113 V b 3
Topocalma, Punta — 106-107 A 5
Topock, AZ 74-75 F 5
Topoli 126-127 P 3
Topolobampo 64-65 E 6
Topolovgrad 122-123 M 4
Toponas, CO 68-69 C 5
Topozero 132-133 E 4
Toppenish, WA 66-67 C 2
Toprakkale 136-137 FG 4
Topsi 174-175 G 2
Ṭoqra = Tūkrah 164-165 HJ 2
Toqsun = Toksun 142-143 F 3
Toquepala 92-93 E 8
Toquerville, UT 74-75 G 4
Toquima Range 74-75 E 3
Tora [ZRE] 171 B 2
Torbalı = Tepeköy 136-137 B 3
Torbat-e Heydarīyeh 134-135 HJ 3-4
Torbat-e Jām 134-135 J 3
Torbat-e Sheikh Jām = Torbat-e Jām 134-135 J 3
Torbay 119 E 6
Torbert, Mount — 58-59 LM 6
Torbino 124-125 J 4
Torch Lake 70-71 H 3
Torch River 61 FG 4
Torčin 126-127 B 1
Torcy 129 I d 2
Tordesillas 120-121 E 8
Tordilla, La — = Colonia La Tordilla 106-107 F 3
Tor di Quinto, Roma- 113 II b 1
Töre 116-117 K 5
Torekov 116-117 E 9
Torellbreen 116-117 j 6
Torell land 116-117 k 6
Toreo Campo Militar 91 I b 2
Torgau 118 F 3
Tori 164-165 L 7
Toribulu 152-153 O 6
Toriñana, Cabo — 120-121 C 7
Torino 122-123 BC 3
Tōrīt = Tūrīt 164-165 L 8
Torixoréu 102-103 F 2
Torkamān 136-137 M 4
Torkoviči 124-125 H 4
Tor Marancia, Roma- 113 II b 2
Tormes 120-121 D 8
Tormosin 126-127 L 2
Tornado Peak 60 K 5
Torneå = Tornio 116-117 L 5
Torne älv 116-117 K 4
Torneträsk 116-117 H 3
Torngat Mountains 56-57 Y 6
Tornio 116-117 L 5
Torno Largo 98-99 G 9
Tornquist 111 D 5
Toro [CO] 94-95 C 5
Toro [E] 120-121 E 8
Toro [EAU] 171 B 2
Toro, Cerro del — 111 C 3
Toro, Lago del — 108-109 C 8
Toro, Punta — 106-107 AB 4
Torobuku 152-153 P 8
Torodi 164-165 E 6
Torodo 168-169 C 2
Torokina 148-149 hj 6
Toroku = Yünlin 146-147 H 10
Toronto 56-57 UV 9
Toronto, KS 70-71 C 7
Toronto, Lago — 86-87 GH 4
Toropalca 104-105 D 7
Toro Peak 74-75 E 6
Toropec 124-125 H 5
Tororo 172 F 1
Toros, Plaza de — 113 III b 2
Toros dağları 134-135 C 3
Torotoro 104-105 CD 6
Tor Pignatara, Roma- 113 II b 2
Torquato Severo 106-107 K 3
Torrance, CA 74-75 D 6
Torrance Municipal Airport 83 III b 3
Torre del Greco 122-123 F 5
Torre de Moncorvo 120-121 D 8
Torre Gaia, Roma- 113 II c 2
Torrelaguna 120-121 F 8
Torrelavega 120-121 E 7
Torre Lupara, Roma- 113 II c 1
Torre Nova, Roma- 113 II c 2
Torrens, Lake — 158-159 G 6
Torrens Creek 158-159 HJ 4
Torrent 106-107 J 2
Torrente 120-121 G 9
Torreón 64-65 F 6
Torreón de Cañas 76-77 B 9
Torres 111 G 3
Torres, Islas — 106-107 L 5
Torres de Alcalá = Qal'at Īrīs 166-167 D 2
Torres Islands 158-159 N 2
Torres Martinez Indian Reservation 74-75 E 6
Torres Strait 158-159 H 2
Torres Vedras 120-121 C 9
Torre Vecchia, Roma- 113 II a 1
Torrevieja 120-121 G 10
Torrijos 120-121 E 8-9
Torrington, CT 72-73 K 4
Torrington, WY 68-69 DE 4
Torrinha 102-103 HJ 5
Torsa 138-139 M 4
Tor Sapienza, Roma- 113 II c 2
Torsås 116-117 FG 9
Torsby 116-117 E 7
Tórshavn 114-115 G 3
Tortillas, Las — 76-77 E 9
Tortola 64-65 O 8
Tortolì 122-123 C 6
Tortona 122-123 C 3
Tortosa 120-121 H 8
Tortosa, Cabo de — 120-121 H 8
Tortue, Île de la — 64-65 M 7
Tortugas 106-107 FG 4
Tortuguero 88-89 E 9
Tortuguilla, Isla — 94-95 C 3
Tortuguitas, General Sarmiento- 110 III a 1
Tortum = Nihah 136-137 J 2
Ṭorūd 134-135 H 3
Torugart Davan 134-135 L 2
Torul = Ardasa 136-137 H 2
Toruń 118 J 2
Tõrva 124-125 E 4-5
Tory 119 B 4
Tory Hill 72-73 GH 2
Toržok 132-133 E 6
Torzym 118 G 2
Tosa [SU, place] 124-125 O 6
Tosa [SU, river] 124-125 O 6
Tosan = Chūbu 144-145 L 5-M 4
Tosashimizu 144-145 J 6
Tosa-wan 144-145 J 6
Toscana 122-123 D 4
Toscas, Las — 106-107 K 4
To-shima 144-145 M 5
Toshima, Tōkyō- 155 III b 1
Toshimaen Recreation Ground 155 III ab 1
Tosno 124-125 H 4
Tos nuur 142-143 H 4
T'o-so Hu = Tos nuur 142-143 H 4
Tosoncengel 142-143 H 2
T'osovo-Netyl'skij 124-125 H 4
Tosquita 106-107 E 4
Tossi 152-153 N 10
Tostado 111 D 3
Tõstamaa 124-125 D 4
Toston, MT 66-67 H 2
Tosu 144-145 H 6
Tosya 134-135 C 2
Totana 120-121 G 10
Toteng 172 D 6
Tothill 61 C 6
Tot'ma 132-133 G 5-6
Totogan Lake 62 E 1
Totonicapán 64-65 HJ 8-9
Totora [BOL, Cochabamba] 92-93 FG 8
Totora [BOL, Oruro] 104-105 BC 5
Totora, Cordillera de la — 106-107 BC 3
Totora, Sierra Blanca de la — 108-109 E 3-F 2
Totoral [RA] 106-107 D 3
Totoral [RCH] 106-107 B 1
Totoral [ROU] 106-107 J 4
Totoralejos 106-107 E 2
Totorapalca 104-105 D 6
Totoras, Las — 106-107 E 4
Totoya 148-149 ab 2
Totson Mount 58-59 J 4
Totsuka, Yokohama- 155 III a 3
Totta 132-133 a 6
Tottan Range 53 B 35-36
Totten Glacier 53 C 12
Tottenham [AUS] 158-159 J 6
Tottenham [CDN] 72-73 FG 2
Tottenham, London- 119 FG 6
Tottenville, New York-, NY 82 III a 3
Totteridge, London- 129 II b 1
Tottori 142-143 P 4
Totumal 94-95 E 3
Toṭupuyla = Todupulai 140 C 6
Tou 168-169 E 2
Ṭouâl 'Abâ = Ṭuwāl 'Abā' 136-137 H 4
Touareg, Hassi — = Ḥāssī Tawārij 166-167 JK 4
Touat = At-Tuwāt 164-165 DE 3
Touba [CI] 164-165 C 7
Touba [SN] 164-165 A 6
Toubqâl, Jbel — = Jabal Tubqāl 164-165 C 2
Toudao Jiang 144-145 F 1-2
Tougan 164-165 D 6
Touggourt = Tughghūrt 164-165 EF 2
Tougnifili 168-169 B 3
Tougouri 168-169 E 2
Tougue 168-169 C 3
Touho 158-159 N 4
Touil, Ouèd — = Wādī aṭ-Ṭawīl 166-167 H 2
Toukat = Hassī Tūkāt Nakhlah 166-167 A 6
Toukley 160 KL 4
Toukoto 164-165 BC 6
Tou-kou = Dougou 146-147 E 5
Toul 120-121 K 4
Toulépleu 164-165 C 7
Tou-lin = Yünlin 146-147 H 10
Toulon, IL 70-71 EF 5
Toulon [F] 120-121 KL 7
Toulon [ZA] 174-175 J 3
Touloûl, Dîret et — = Dīrat at-Tulūl 136-137 G 6
Touloûl eṣ Ṣafâ = Tulūl aṣ-Ṣafā 136-137 G 6
Toulouse 120-121 HJ 7
Toummo 164-165 G 4
Toumodi 164-165 CD 7
Toumotou, Îles — 156-157 K 5-L 6
Tounan 146-147 H 10
Tounassine, Hamada — = Hammadat Tūnasīn 166-167 D 5
Tounfit = Tūnfīt 166-167 D 3
Toungo 168-169 HJ 3
Toungoo = Taungngū 148-149 C 3
Toûnis = Tūnis 164-165 FG 1
Toûnis, Khalîdj — = Khalīj at-Tūnisī 166-167 M 1
Toura, Monts du — 168-169 D 4
Touraine 120-121 H 5
Tourakom = Mu'o'ng Tourakom 150-151 D 3
Tourane = Đa Nẵng 148-149 E 3
Tourane, Cap — = Mui Đa Nẵng 150-151 G 4
Tour Eiffel 129 I c 2
Tourgueness, Rass — = Rā's Turk an-Naṣṣ 166-167 M 3
Tournai 120-121 J 3
Tournavista 96-97 D 6
Tournon 120-121 K 6
Touro Passo 106-107 J 2
Touros 92-93 MN 5-6
Toûroûg = Tūrūg 166-167 D 4
Tours 120-121 H 5
Tourville 63 AB 4
Toussidé, Pic — 164-165 H 4
Toussus-le-Noble 129 I b 3
Tou-tao Chiang = Toudao Jiang 144-145 F 1-2
Touwsrivier [ZA, place] 174-175 D 7
Touwsrivier [ZA, river] 174-175 D 7
Tōv < 142-143 K 2
Tovāla 140 C 6
Tovar 94-95 F 3
Tovarkovskij 124-125 M 7
Tovmač = Tlumač 126-127 B 2
Tovqussaq 56-57 a 5
Tovste = Tolstoje 126-127 B 2
Towada 144-145 N 2
Towada-ko 144-145 N 2
Towanda, PA 72-73 H 4
Towani 174-175 G 2
Towari 152-153 O 8
Towdystan 60 E 3
Tower 129 II b 2
Tower, MN 70-71 D 2
Tower, London- 129 II b 1
Tower Bridge 129 II b 2
Towner, CO 68-69 E 6
Towner, ND 68-69 F 1
Townes Pass 74-75 E 4
Town Estates, NJ 84 III d 1
Town Hall 161 I b 1
Townley, NY 82 III a 2
Townley Place, Houston-, TX 85 III b 1
Townsend, GA 80-81 F 5
Townsend, MT 66-67 H 2
Townshend Island 158-159 K 4
Townsville 158-159 J 3
Towot 164-165 L 7
Towra Point 161 I b 3
Towson, MD 72-73 H 5
Towuti, Danau — 148-149 H 7
Toyah, TX 76-77 C 7
Toyahvale, TX 76-77 BC 7
Tōya-ko 144-145 b 2
Toyama 142-143 Q 4
Toyama-wan 142-143 Q 4
Toyohara = Južno-Sachalinsk 132-133 bc 8
Toyohashi 142-143 Q 5
Toyohasi = Toyohashi 142-143 Q 5
Toyoma 144-145 N 3
Toyonaka 144-145 K 5
Toyooka 144-145 K 5
Toyota 144-145 L 5
Toyotama 144-145 G 5
Toyotama, Tōkyō- 155 III a 1
Tôzeur = Tawzar 164-165 F 2
Tozitna River 58-59 LM 4
Tra, Sông — 150-151 G 5
Trabiju 102-103 H 5
Trabzon 134-135 DE 2
Tracadie 63 D 4
Trach, Kompong — [K, Kampot] 150-151 E 7
Trach, Kompong — [K, Svay Rieng] 150-151 E 7
Trachéia = Silifke 134-135 C 3
Tra Cu 148-149 E 5
Tracy 63 C 5
Tracy, CA 74-75 C 4
Trade Mart Tower 85 I b 2
Tradum 142-143 E 6
Træna 116-117 DE 4
Traer, IA 70-71 D 4
Trafalgar, Cabo de — 120-121 D 10
Trafāwī, Bi'r — 136-137 H 4
Traful, Lago — 108-109 D 3
Traição, Córrego — 110 II ab 2
Traiguén 106-107 A 7
Traiguén, Isla — 108-109 C 5
Trail 64-65 N 8
Trail, MN 70-71 C 2
Trail City, SD 68-69 F 3
Traill 106-107 G 3
Trainer, PA 84 III a 3
Traipu 100-101 F 5
Traipu, Rio — 100-101 F 5
Trairi 100-101 E 2
Trajanova vrata 122-123 L 4
Traka 174-175 E 7
Trakai 124-125 E 6
Trakan Phutphon 150-151 E 5
Trakya 136-137 AB 2
Tralach 150-151 E 7
Tralee 119 B 5
Trälleborg = Trelleborg 116-117 E 10
Tralung 138-139 GH 2
Tramandaí 106-107 MN 2
Tram Khnar 150-151 E 7
Tra Môn 150-151 F 7
Tra My = Hậu Đức 150-151 G 5
Tranås 116-117 F 8

Tranås 371

Tranca, La — 106-107 D 4
Trancas 111 CD 3
Trang 150-151 B 9
Trangan, Pulau — 148-149 K 8
Trang Bang 150-151 EF 7
Trani 122-123 G 5
Trañkabār = Tranquebar 140 DE 5
Trân Ninh, Cao Nguyên — 148-149 D 3
Tranquebar 140 DE 5
Tranqui, Isla — 108-109 C 4
Transamazônica, Rodovia — 98-99 L 7
Trans Canada Highway 56-57 P 7
Transcaucasia = Malyj Kavkaz 126-127 L 5-N 7
Transhimalaja = Transhimalaya 142-143 EF 5
Transhimalaya 142-143 EF 5
Transilvania 122-123 K-M 2
Transit istasyonu = Doğubayazıt 136-137 KL 3
Tránsito 106-107 F 3
Tránsito, El — 106-107 B 2
Transkasp 134-135 H 3
Transsib 132-133 L 6
Transturan 132-133 K 7
Transvaal 172 EF 6
Transylvanian Alps = Alpi Transilvaniei 122-123 KL 3
Tranum 150-151 CD 11
Tra Ôn 150-151 EF 7-8
Trapalcó 106-107 D 7
Trapalcó, Salinas de — 108-109 F 2
Trapandé, Baía de — 102-103 J 6
Trápani 122-123 E 6-7
Trapezûs = Trabzon 134-135 DE 2
Trappenfelde 130 III c 1
Trapper Peak 66-67 F 3
Trappes 129 I a 2
Traralgon 158-159 J 7
Trarza = At-Trārzah 164-165 AB 5
Trārzah, At- 164-165 AB 5
Trasimeno, Lago — 122-123 DE 4
Trás-os-Montes 120-121 D 8
Trás-os-Montes = Cucumbi 172 C 4
Trat 148-149 D 4
Traunstein 118 F 5
Trava, Cachoeira — 92-93 H 5
Travá, Cachoeiro 98-99 K 5
Travancore 140 C 6
Travers, Mount — 161 E 5-6
Traverse, Lake — 68-69 H 3
Traverse City, MI 64-65 JK 2-3
Traverse Peak 58-59 GH 4
Travesía del Tunuyán 106-107 D 4-5
Travesía Puntana 106-107 DE 5
Travessão do Urubu 98-99 M 8
Travessão Jacaré 98-99 O 10
Tra Vinh 148-149 E 5
Tra Vinh = Phu Vinh 148-149 E 5
Travis, Lake — 76-77 EF 7
Travis, New York-, NY 82 III a 3
Trbovle 122-123 F 2
Tre = Hon Tre 150-151 G 6
Tre, Hon — 150-151 G 6
Treasure Island 83 I b 2
Treasure Island Naval Station 83 I b 2
Treasury = Mono Island 148-149 j 6
Treat Island 58-59 JK 3
Třebíč 118 G 4
Trebinje 122-123 H 4
Trebisonda = Trabzon 134-135 DE 2
Trebol, El — 106-107 G 4
Trebolares 106-107 F 5
Trechado, NM 74-75 J 5
Trefâouî, Bîr — = Bi'r Trafāwī 136-137 H 4
Trego, MT 66-67 F 1
Trégorrois 120-121 F 4
Treherne 61 J 6
Treinta de Agosto 106-107 F 6
Treinta y Tres [ROU, administrative unit] 106-107 KL 4
Treinta y Tres [ROU, place] 111 F 4
Trekkopje 174-175 A 2
Trelew 111 C 6
Trelleborg 116-117 E 10
Tremadoc Bay 119 D 5
Tremblay, Hippodrome de — 129 I cd 2
Tremblay-lès-Gonesse 129 I d 2
Trembleur Lake 60 E 2
Tremedal 100-101 D 8
Tremembé 102-103 K 5
Tremembé, São Paulo- 110 II b 1
Trèmiti, Ìsole — 122-123 F 4
Tremonton, UT 66-67 G 5
Tremp 120-121 H 7
Trempealeau, WI 70-71 E 3-4
Trenary, MI 70-71 G 2
Trenčín 118 J 4
Trenel 106-107 E 5
Treng, Phum — 150-151 D 6
Trengganu 150-151 D 10
Trenque Lauquen 111 D 5
Trent = Trento 122-123 D 2
Trente et un Milles, Lac des — 72-73 HJ 1
Trentino-Alto Àdige 122-123 D 2
Trento 122-123 D 2
Trenton 72-73 H 2
Trenton, FL 80-81 b 2
Trenton, IA 70-71 D 5
Trenton, MI 72-73 E 3
Trenton, NE 68-69 F 5
Trenton, NJ 64-65 M 3-4
Trenton, TN 78-79 E 3
Trepassey 63 K 4
Tréport, le — 120-121 H 3
Treptow, Berlin- 130 III b 2
Treptower Park 130 III b 2
Tres Algarrobos 106-107 F 5
Tres Altitos, Cerro — 106-107 C 4
Tres Árboles 106-107 J 4
Tres Arroyos 111 DE 5
Três Barras 102-103 GH 7
Tres Bôcas [BR] 98-99 C 7
Tres Bocas [YV] 94-95 E 3
Tres Cerros [RA, mountain] 108-109 D 4
Tres Cerros [RA, place] 108-109 F 7
Tres Conos, Monte — 108-109 D 9
Três Corações 92-93 KL 9
Tres Cruces [RA] 104-105 D 8
Tres Cruces [RCH] 106-107 B 2
Tres Cruces [ROU] 106-107 J 3
Tres Cruces, Cerro — 106-107 C 1
Tres de Febrero 110 III b 1
Tres de Febrero-Ciudadela 110 III b 1
Tres de Maio 106-107 KL 1
Tres Esquinas 92-93 DE 4
Tres Forcas, Cap — = Rā's Wūruq 164-165 D 1
Tres Hermanas, Pampa de las — 108-109 F 6
Três Irmãos, Cachoeira 98-99 F 9
Três Irmãos, Ilhas — 102-103 H 7
Tres Irmãos, Pontas dos — 92-93 M 6-N 5
Três Rios, Serra dos 98-99 F 9
Três Isletas 104-105 F 10
Treska 122-123 J 5
Três Lagoas 92-93 J 9
Tres Lagos 111 B 7
Tres Lagunas 106-107 F 6
Três Marias 102-103 K 3
Três Marias, Represa — 102-103 K 3
Tres Matas, Las — 94-95 J 3
Tres Montes, Golfo — 108-109 B 6
Tres Montes, Península — 111 A 7
Tres Morros 104-105 D 8
Tres Ollas 102-103 D 5
Três Passos 106-107 KL 1
Tres Picos 106-107 F 7
Tres Picos, Cerro — 111 B 6
Tres Piedras, NM 76-77 B 4
Três Pontas 102-103 K 4
Tres Porteñas 106-107 CD 4
Tres Pozos 106-107 FG 2
Tres Puentes 106-107 BC 1
Tres Puntas, Cabo — 111 CD 7
Três Rios 92-93 L 9
Três Rios, Serra dos — 110 I b 2
Tres Unidos 96-97 D 4
Tres Vírgenes, Las — 64-65 D 6
Tret'akovskaja galereja 113 V c 3
Treuer River = Macumba 158-159 G 5
Treungen 116-117 C 8
Trêve, Lac la — 62 O 2
Treviglio 122-123 C 3
Treviño 120-121 F 7
Treviso 122-123 E 3
Trézel = Sūgar 166-167 G 2
Treze Quedas 92-93 H 4
Triabunna 160 c 3
Triang 150-151 D 11
Triangle, ID 66-67 E 4
Triangulos, Arrecifes — 86-87 OP 7
Trianons 129 I b 2
Tribugá 94-95 C 5
Tribune 68-69 DE 1
Tribune, KS 68-69 F 6
Tricacó 106-107 CD 7
Trichaty 126-127 E 3
Trichōnis, Límnē — 122-123 J 6
Trichūr 134-135 M 8
Trida 158-159 HJ 6
Tridell, UT 66-67 J 5
Trident Peak 66-67 D 5
Triel-sur-Seine 129 I b 2
Trier 118 C 4
Trieste 122-123 E 3
Trigo, El — 106-107 H 5
Tríkala 122-123 JK 6
Trikkandiyur 140 B 5
Trili 106-107 F 5
Trimān 138-139 B 3
Trinchera, CO 76-77 BC 4
Trincheras 86-87 E 2
Trincheras, Las — 92-93 FG 3
Trincomalee = Tirikuṇāmalaya 134-135 N 9
Trincomali = Tirikuṇāmalaya 134-135 N 9
Trindade [BR, Goiás] 102-103 H 2
Trindade [BR, Roraima] 98-99 H 4
Trindade = Trinidad [BOL] 92-93 G 7
Trindade = Trinidad [TT] 64-65 O 9
Trindade, Ilha da — 92-93 NO 9
Tring, Ban — = Buôn Hô 150-151 G 6
Trinidad, CA 66-67 A 5
Trinidad, CO 64-65 F 4
Trinidad, TX 76-77 FG 6
Trinidad, WA 66-67 CD 2
Trinidad [BOL, Beni] 92-93 G 7
Trinidad [BOL, Pando] 104-105 C 2
Trinidad [C] 64-65 KL 7
Trinidad [CO] 92-93 E 3
Trinidad [PY] 111 E 3
Trinidad [ROU] 111 E 4
Trinidad [TT] 64-65 O 9
Trinidad = Ilha da Trindade 92-93 NO 9
Trinidad, Bahía — 64-65 b 2
Trinidad, Baruta-La — 91 II b 2
Trinidad, Canal 108-109 B 7-8
Trinidad, Golfo — 108-109 B 7
Trinidad, Isla — 111 D 5
Trinidad, Isla — = Sounders Island 108-109 J 8
Trinidad, La — 94-95 G 3
Trinidad, Laguna — 102-103 B 4
Trinidad, Río — 64-65 b 3
Trinidad, Washington-, DC 82 II b 2
Trinidad and Tobago 64-65 O 9-10
Trinidad de Arauca, La — 94-95 G 4
Trinil 152-153 J 9
Trinité, Montagnes de la — 98-99 M 2
Trinity, TX 76-77 G 7
Trinity Bay 56-57 a 8
Trinity Center, CA 66-67 B 5
Trinity Gardens, Houston-, TX 85 III b 1
Trinity Islands 56-57 F 6
Trinity Mountains 66-67 B 5
Trinity Range 66-67 D 5
Trinity River [USA, California] 66-67 B 5
Trinity River [USA, Texas] 64-65 G 5
Trino, El — 94-95 E 6
Trio Island 155 I b 2
Trion, GA 78-79 G 3
Tripoli, WI 70-71 EF 3
Tripolis 122-123 K 7
Tripolis = Ṭarābulus al-Gharb 164-165 G 2
Tripolitania = Ṭarābulus 164-165 GH 2
Tripp, SD 68-69 GH 4
Tripps Run 82 II a 2
Tripura 134-135 P 6
Tripurāntakam 140 D 3
Trishshivaperūr = Trichūr 134-135 M 8
Trishūl = Trisūl 138-139 G 2
Trishūlī = Trisūlī 138-139 K 3-4
Tristan da Cunha 204-205 FG 12
Tristao, Îles — 168-169 B 3
Tristeza, Cuchilla de la — 106-107 C 5
Trisūl 138-139 G 2
Trisūlī 138-139 K 3-4
Tri Tôn 150-151 E 7
Triumph, MN 70-71 C 4
Triunfo [BOL] 98-99 E 9
Triunfo [BR] 100-101 E 4
Triunfo, El — 106-107 G 5
Triunfo, Pirámide el — 104-105 F 9
Trivandrum 134-135 M 9
Trnava 118 H 4
Trobriand Islands 148-149 h 6
Trochu 60 L 4
Trofors 116-117 E 5
Trogir 122-123 FG 4
Troglav 122-123 G 4
Tròia [I] 122-123 F 5
Troia [TR] 134-135 B 3
Troice-Lykovo, Moskva- 113 V a 2
Troick 132-133 L 7
Troickoje [SU, Rossijskaja SFSR] 132-133 a 8
Troickoje [SU, Ukrainskaja SSR] 126-127 HJ 2
Troicko-Pečorsk 132-133 K 5
Troickosavsk = K'achta 132-133 U 7
Trois-Pistoles 63 B 3
Trois-Rivières 56-57 W 8
Trojan 122-123 L 4
Trojanski prohod 122-123 L 4
Trojekurovo [SU, Lipeckaja Oblast'] 124-125 M 7
Trollhättan 116-117 E 8
Trolltindan 116-117 B 6
Tromba Grande, Cabo — 100-101 E 8
Trombetas, Rio — 92-93 H 5
Trombudo, Rio — 106-107 N 1
Trombudo Central 102-103 H 7
Tromelin 204-205 N 10
Tromen, Cerro del — 106-107 B 6
Tromen, Lago — 108-109 D 2
Tromen, Paso — 108-109 CD 2
Trompsburg 174-175 FG 6
Troms 116-117 G-J 3
Tromsø 116-117 H 3
Tron 116-117 D 6
Trona, CA 74-75 E 5
Tronador, Monte — 111 B 6
Tronco 100-101 B 4
Trondheim 116-117 D 6
Trondheimfjord 116-117 CD 6
Tronoh 150-151 C 10
Tróodos 134-135 C 4
Tropar'ovo, Moskva 113 V b 3
Tropêço Grande, Cachoeira de — 98-99 OP 11
Tropenmuseum 128 I b 1
Tropia, Ponta — 100-101 D 2
Tropic, UT 74-75 GH 4
Trosa 116-117 G 8
Trost'anec [SU, Sumskaja Oblast'] 126-127 G 1
Trost'anec [SU, Vinnickaja Oblast'] 126-127 D 2
Trotus 122-123 M 2
Troûmbâ = Turumbah 136-137 J 4
Troup, TX 76-77 G 6
Trout Creek 66-67 D 4
Trout Creek, MT 66-67 EF 2
Trout Creek, UT 74-75 G 3
Trout Lake, MI 70-71 H 2
Trout Lake [CDN, Alberta] 60 K 1
Trout Lake [CDN, Northwest Territories] 56-57 MN 5
Trout Lake [CDN, Ontario] 56-57 S 7
Trout Peak 68-69 B 3
Trout River 63 G 3
Trouwers Island = Pulau Tinjil 148-149 E 8
Trowbridge 119 EF 6
Troy, AL 64-65 J 5
Troy, ID 66-67 E 2
Troy, KS 70-71 C 6
Troy, MO 70-71 E 6
Troy, MT 66-67 F 1
Troy, NC 80-81 G 3
Troy, NY 64-65 M 3
Troy, OH 70-71 H 5
Troy, OR 66-67 E 3
Troy, PA 72-73 H 4
Troyes 120-121 K 4
Truandó, Río — 94-95 C 4
Trubčevsk 124-125 J 7
Trubetčino 124-125 M 7
Trucará, Serra do — 98-99 N 7-O 6
Truc Giang 150-151 F 7
Trucial Oman = United Arab Emirates 134-135 GH 6
Truckee, CA 74-75 CD 3
Truckee River 74-75 D 3
Trud [SU] 124-125 JK 5
Trudante = Tārūdānt 164-165 C 2
Trudering, München- 130 II bc 2
Trudfront 126-127 N 4
Trujillo [CO] 94-95 C 5
Trujillo [E] 120-121 DE 9
Trujillo [Honduras] 64-65 J 8
Trujillo [PE] 92-93 CD 6
Trujillo [YV] 92-93 EF 3
Trujillo, Ciudad — = Santo Domingo 64-65 MN 8
Truk 208 F 2
Trumann, AR 78-79 D 3
Trumbull, Mount — 74-75 G 4
Trung Bô 148-149 D 3-E 4
Trung Phân, Cao Nguyên — 148-149 E 4
Trung Phân, Plateau de — = Cao Nguyên Trung Phân 148-149 E 4
Truro, IA 70-71 D 5
Truro [CDN] 56-57 Y 8
Truro [GB] 119 D 6
Truscott, TX 76-77 E 6
Truskavec 126-127 A 2
Trus Madi, Gunung — 152-153 M 3
Truth or Consequences, NM 76-77 A 6
Trutnov 118 GH 3
Truxilho = Trujillo 64-65 J 8
Tryon, NE 68-69 F 5
Trysil 116-117 DE 7
Trysilelv 116-117 DE 7
Tsabong 172 D 7
Tsabrang 138-139 G 2
Tsaidam 142-143 GH 4
Tsai-Dam = Tsaidam 142-143 GH 4
Tsala Apopka Lake 80-81 bc 2
Tsamkong = Zhanjiang 142-143 L 7
Tsane 174-175 DE 3
Tsang 138-139 LM 3
Tsangpo 142-143 EF 6
Tsangwu = Wuzhou 142-143 L 7
Ts'ang-yüan = Cangyuan 141 F 4
Tsan-huang = Zanhuang 146-147 E 3
Tsaobis 174-175 A 2
Ts'ao-hsien = Cao Xian 146-147 E 4
Tsaoshui = Zhashui 146-147 B 5
Tsaratanana [RM, mountain] 172 J 4
Tsaratanana [RM, place] 172 J 5
Tsarskoye Selo = Puškin 132-133 DE 6
Tsau 172 D 6
Tsauchab 174-175 A 3
Tsau Tsau Flats 174-175 D 2
Tsavo [EAK, place] 172 G 2
Tsavo [EAK, river] 171 D 3
Tsavo National Park 172 G 2
Tschicoma Peak 76-77 AB 4
Tschida, Lake — 68-69 EF 2
Tsechang = Zichang 146-147 B 3
Tsekhung Tsho 138-139 L 2
Ts'ê-lo = Chira Bazar 142-143 DE 4
Tsengcheng = Zengcheng 146-147 D 10
Tseng Shue Tsai 155 I b 1
Tšerkassy = Čerkassy 126-127 EF 2
Tšernigov = Černigov 126-127 E 1
Tses 172 C 7
Tsesum 138-139 J 2
Tsethang 142-143 G 6
Tsetserlig = Cecerleg 142-143 J 2
Tseung Kwan 155 I b 2
Tshaidam 142-143 GH 4
Tshela 172 B 2-3
Tshikapa 172 CD 3
Tshimbo 171 B 4
Tshing Hai = Chöch nuur 142-143 H 4
Tshipa = Katakumba 172 D 3
Tshofa 172 DE 3
Tshomo Thritong 138-139 LM 3
Tsho Ngonpo = Chöch nuur 142-143 H 4
Tshopo 172 E 1
Tshuapa 172 D 2
Tshungu, Chutes — 172 DE 1
Tshwane 172 D 6
Tsiafajavona 172 J 5
Tsienkiang = Qianjiang 142-143 L 5
Tsihombe 172 HJ 7
Tsimlyanskaya = Cimľansk 126-127 KL 3
Tsimo = Jimo 146-147 H 3
Tsim Sha Tsui, Kowloon- 155 I a 2
Tsim Tsa Tsui 155 I ab 2
Tsinan = Jinan 142-143 M 4
Tsincheng = Jincheng 142-143 L 4
Tsinchow = Tianshui 142-143 JK 5
Tsineng 174-175 E 4
Tsinghai = Qinghai 142-143 GH 4
Tsingho = Qinghe 146-147 E 3
Tsinghu = Jinghe 142-143 E 3
Tsing Island 155 I a 1
Tsingkiang = Jingjiang 146-147 H 5-6
Tsingkiang = Qingjiang [TJ, Jiangsu] 142-143 M 5
Tsingkiang = Qingjiang [TJ, Jiangxi] 142-143 M 6
Tsinglo = Jingle 146-147 CD 2
Tsingpien = Jingbian 146-147 B 3
Tsingpu = Qingpu 146-147 H 6
Tsingtau = Qingdao 142-143 N 4
Tsingteh = Jingde 146-147 G 6
Tsingyuan = Baoding 142-143 LM 4
Tsingyun = Qingyuan 146-147 D 10
Tsinh Ho 150-151 D 1
Tsining = Jining 142-143 M 4
Tsining = Xining 142-143 J 4
Tsin Shui Wan 155 I b 2
Tsinsien = Jinxian 146-147 F 7
Tsinyang = Qinyang 142-143 L 4
Tsiroanomandidy 172 J 5
Tsitsa 174-175 H 6
Tsitsihar = Qiqihar 142-143 N 2
Tsitsikamaberge 174-175 EF 7
Tsivory 172 J 6
Tsiyang = Jiyang 146-147 F 3
Tsochuan = Zuoquan 146-147 D 3
Tsolo 174-175 H 6
Tsomo [ZA, place] 174-175 GH 7
Tsomo [ZA, river] 174-175 G 6-7
Tsôna 141 BC 2
Tsondab 174-175 A 2-3
Tsondabvlei 174-175 A 2
Tsorlū = Çorlu 136-137 B 2
Tsoshui = Zhashui 146-147 B 5
Tso Shui Wan 155 I b 2
Tsou-hsien = Zou Xian 146-147 F 4
Tsou-p'ing = Zouping 146-147 F 3
Tsou-shih = Zoushi 146-147 C 7
Tso-yün = Zuoyun 146-147 D 2
Tsu 142-143 Q 5
Tsubame 144-145 M 4
Tsuboi 155 III d 1
Tsuchiura 144-145 N 4
Tsudanuma, Funabashi- 155 III d 1
Tsugaru kaikyō 142-143 R 3
Tsū-hsing = Zixing 146-147 D 9
Tsukigata 144-145 b 2
Tsukumi 144-145 H 6
Tsuma = Saito 144-145 H 6
Tsumeb 172 C 5
Tsumis 174-175 B 2
Tsumispark 174-175 B 2
Tsunashima, Yokohama- 155 III a 2
Ts'ung-hua = Conghua 146-147 D 10
Tsung-hua = Zunhua 146-147 F 1
Tsunghwa = Conghua 146-147 D 10
Tsungjen = Chongren 146-147 EF 8
Tsungming = Chongming 142-143 N 5
Tsungteh = Chongde 146-147 H 6
Tsung-ts'un-hsü = Zongcun 146-147 D 8
Tsunhwa = Zunhua 146-147 F 1
Tsuno-shima 144-145 H 5
Tsun Wan 155 I a 1
Tsunyi = Zunyi 142-143 K 6
Tsuruga 144-145 KL 5
Tsurugi san 144-145 JK 6
Tsurumi 155 III ab 2
Tsurumi, Yokohama- 155 III a 2
Tsurumi-zaki 144-145 J 6
Tsuruoka 144-145 M 3
Tsurusaki 144-145 HJ 6
Tsushima 142-143 O 5
Tsushima-kaikyō 142-143 OP 5
Tsuyama 144-145 JK 5
Tsuyung = Chuxiong 142-143 J 7
Tswana 174-175 C 2
Tu = Tibesti 164-165 H 4
Tu = Tsu 142-143 Q 5
Tua 120-121 D 8
Tuamapu, Canal — 108-109 B 4-C 5
Tuamotu, Îles — 156-157 K 5-L 6
Tuamotu Basin 156-157 KL 6
Tuan, Ujung — 152-153 C 5
Tuân Giao 150-151 D 2
Tuangku, Pulau — 152-153 B 4
Tuan He 146-147 C 5
Tuan Ho = Tuan He 146-147 C 5
Tuan-shih = Duanshi 146-147 D 4
Tuapse 126-127 J 4
Tuaran 152-153 LM 2
Tubac, AZ 74-75 H 7
Tuba City, AZ 74-75 H 4
Tubal, Wādī at- 136-137 J 6
Tuban 148-149 F 8
Tubarão 111 G 3
Tubarão, Ponta do — 100-101 FG 3
Tubarão, Rio — 102-103 H 8
Tubau 148-149 F 6
Ṭubayq, Jabal aṭ- 134-135 D 5
Tubiacanga, Punta de — 110 I b 1
Tübingen 118 D 4
Tub-Karagan, mys — 126-127 OP 4
Tub-Karagan, poluostrov — 126-127 P 4
Tubqāl, Jabal — 164-165 C 2
Ṭubruq 164-165 J 2
Tubuai, Îles — 156-157 K 6
Ṭuburbah 166-167 L 1
Tucacas 92-93 F 2
Tucano 92-93 M 7
Tucano, Cachoeira — 94-95 G 7
Tucano, Serra do — 94-95 LM 6
Tucapel 106-107 AB 6
Tucapel, Punta — 106-107 A 6
Tucavaca 92-93 H 8
Tucavaca, Rio — 104-105 G 6
Tuchang 146-147 H 9
Tucholskie, Bory — 118 HJ 2
Tucho River 58-59 X 7
Tucker Bay 53 B 18
Tuckerman, AR 78-79 D 3
Tuckerton, NJ 72-73 JK 5
Tuckum = Tukums 124-125 D 5
Tucson, AZ 64-65 D 5
Tucson Mountains 74-75 H 6
Tucuman 104-105 D 10
Tucumán = San Miguel de Tucumán 111 CD 3
Tucumán, San Miguel de — 111 CD 3
Tucumcari, NM 64-65 F 4
Tucumcari Mountain 76-77 C 5
Tucume 96-97 AB 5
Tucunduva 106-107 K 1
Tucuns 100-101 B 5
Tucuns, Serra dos — 100-101 D 2
Tucunuco 111 C 4
Tucuparé 98-99 L 7
Tucupido 94-95 J 3
Tucupita 92-93 G 3
Tucupita, Caño — 94-95 L 3
Tucuruí 92-93 K 5
Tucuruvi, São Paulo- 110 II b 1
Tucu Tucu 108-109 D 7
Tuddo = Tudu 124-125 F 4
Tudela 120-121 G 7
Tudghā', Wād — 166-167 D 4
Tudu 124-125 F 4
Tuela 120-121 D 8
Tuensang [IND, landscape] 141 D 2-3
Tuensang [IND, place] 141 D 2
Tuensang Frontier Division = Tuensang 141 D 2-3
Tueré, Rio 98-99 N 6-7
Tufello, Roma- 113 II b 1
Tufi 148-149 N 8
Tufts University 84 I b 2
Tugaru kaikyō = Tsugaru-kaikyō 142-143 R 3
Tugela [ZA, place] 174-175 J 5
Tugela [ZA, river] 172 F 7
Tugela Ferry 174-175 J 5
Tuggurt = Tughghūrt 164-165 EF 2
Tugh Fafan = Fafen 164-165 N 7
Tughghūrt 164-165 EF 2
Tugidak Island 58-59 f 1
Tugt 142-143 L 3-4
Tuguegarao 148-149 H 3
Tugur 132-133 a 7
Tuhai He 146-147 FG 3
Tuht 136-137 E 2
Tuichang 141 C 4
Tuilianpui = Tūiliyanpūī 141 C 4
Tūiliyanpūī 141 C 4
Tuindorp, Amsterdam- 128 I ab 1
Tuinplaas 174-175 H 3
Tuira, Río — 94-95 BC 3
Tuito, El — 86-87 H 7
Tujmazy 132-133 JK 7
Tuka 150-151 B 11
Tukalinsk 132-133 N 6
T'u-kan = Shangkan 146-147 C 6
Tukangbesi, Kepulauan — 148-149 H 8
Tūkāt Nakhlah, Ḥāssī — 166-167 A 6
Tukayyid 136-137 L 8
Tukchor 150-151 D 6
Tuklung, AK 58-59 H 7
Tūkrah 164-165 HJ 2
Tuktoyaktuk 56-57 JK 4
Tukums 124-125 D 5
Tukung, Bukit — 152-153 JK 6
Tukuyu 172 F 3
Tula [EAK] 171 D 3
Tula [MEX] 86-87 L 6
Tula [SU] 124-125 L 6
Tul'ači 124-125 RS 6
Tula de Allende 86-87 KL 6-7
Tulagi 148-149 jk 6
Tulaguen, Cerro — 106-107 B 3
Tulameen 66-67 C 1
Tulancingo 64-65 G 7
Tulane University 85 I b 2
Tulangbawang, Wai — 152-153 F 8
Tulare, CA 64-65 C 4
Tulare, SD 68-69 G 3
Tulare Lake 64-65 C 4
Tulare Lake Area 74-75 D 5
Tularosa, NM 76-77 A 6
Tularosa Basin 76-77 A 6
Tularosa Mountains 74-75 J 6
Tūlasi 140 EF 1
Tulbagh [ZA, mountain] 174-175 D 6
Tulbagh [ZA, place] 174-175 C 7
Tulcán 92-93 D 4
Tulcea 122-123 N 3
Tul'čin 126-127 D 2
Tulcingo de Valle 86-87 LM 8-9
Tuléar = Toliary 172 H 6
Tulelake, CA 66-67 C 5
Tulenij, ostrov — 126-127 N 4
Tulenji, ostrova — 126-127 OP 4
Tule River 74-75 D 4
Tule River Indian Reservation 74-75 D 4-5
Tul'gan 132-133 K 7
Tuli 172 E 6
Tulia, TX 76-77 D 5
Tūljā 164-165 EF 2
Tuljāpur 140 C 1-
Tūl Karm 136-137 F 6
Tul'kino 124-125 V 4
Tullahoma, TN 78-79 FG 3
Tullamore 160 H 4
Tulle 120-121 HJ 6
Tullibigeal 160 GH 4
Tully 158-159 J 3
Tulos, ozero — 124-125 H 2
Tulpan 132-133 K 5
Tulsa, OK 64-65 G 4
Tulsa = La Barge, WY 66-67 HJ 4
Tulsequah 58-59 V 7
Tulsi 138-139 KL 4
Tūlsi = Tūlasi 140 EF 1
Tulsīpur 138-139 J 4
Tuluá 92-93 D 4
Tulufan = Turpan 142-143 F 3
Tuluga River 58-59 M 2
Tuluksak, AK 58-59 G 6
Tulūl, Dīrat at- 136-137 G 6
Tulūl al-Ashāqif 136-137 G 6
Tulūl ash-Shaḥm 136-137 FG 8
Tulūl aṣ-Ṣafā 136-137 G 6
Tulum 86-87 R 7
Tulumaya 106-107 C 4
Tulumayo, Río — 96-97 D 7
Tulun 132-133 ST 7
Tulungagung 152-153 J 10
Tulun Mosque 170 II b 1
Tulu Welel 164-165 LM 7
Tulyehualco 91 I c 3
Tuma [SU, Kazachskaja SSR] 126-127 P 2
Tuma [SU, Rossijskaja SFSR] 124-125 N 6
Tumacacori National Monument 74-75 H 7
Tumaco 92-93 D 4
Tumaco, Rada de — 92-93 CD 4
Tuman'an 126-127 M 6
Tuman-gang 144-145 G 1
Tumanovo 124-125 L 6
Tumany 132-133 e 5
Tumba, Lac — 172 C 2
Tumbarumba 158-159 J 7
Tumbaya 104-105 D 8
Tumbes [EC, administrative unit] 96-97 A 3-4
Tumbes [EC, place] 92-93 C 5
Tumbes, Punta — 106-107 A 6
Tumboni 172 G 2
Tumby Bay 160 C 5
Tumen' [SU] 132-133 M 6
Tumen [TJ] 142-143 O 3
Tumen Jiang 144-145 G 1
Tumeremo 94-95 L 4
Tumiritinga 102-103 M 3
Tumkūr 134-135 M 8
Tumkūru = Tumkūr 134-135 M 8
Ṭummō, Jabal — 164-165 G 4
Tumpat 148-149 D 5
Tumsar 138-139 G 7
Tumu 164-165 D 6
Tumucumaque, Reserva Florestal 98-99 L 3-4
Tumucumaque, Serra do — 92-93 HJ 4
Tumupasa 104-105 C 4
Tumureng 92-93 G 3
Tumusla 104-105 D 7
Tumut 160 J 5
Tun, Nam Mae — 150-151 B 4
Tunaima, Laguna — 94-95 E 7
Tunal, Bogotá-El — 91 III b 4
Tunal, El — 104-105 D 9
Tunas, Coxilha das — 106-107 L 3
Tunas, Las — [C] 88-89 H 4
Tunas, Las — [RA] 106-107 G 3
Tunas, Sierra de las — 106-107 G 6
Tunas, Victoria de las — 64-65 L 7
Tunas Chicas, Laguna — 106-107 F 6
Tūnasīn, Hammadat — 166-167 D 5
Tunceli 134-135 DE 3
Tunchang 150-151 GH 3
Tünchel 142-143 K 2
Tündla 138-139 G 4
Tundrino 132-133 N 5
Tunduma 172 F 3
Tunduru 172 G 4
Tundža 122-123 M 4
Túnel Boquerón 91 II ab 1
Tūnfit 166-167 D 3
T'ung 132-133 W 4
Tung-a = Dong'a 146-147 F 3
Tungabhadra 140 C 3
Tungabhadra Reservoir 140 C 3
Tung-an = Dong'an 146-147 C 8
Tungan = Tong'an 146-147 G 9
Tungaru = Tunqarū 164-165 L 6
Tung Chang 150-151 C 3
T'ung-ch'êng = Tongcheng [TJ, Anhui] 146-147 F 6
T'ung-ch'êng = Tongcheng [TJ, Hubei] 146-147 DE 7
T'ung-ch'êng = Tongcheng [TJ, Jiangsu] 146-147 G 5
Tungchiang 146-147 H 10
Tung Chiang = Dong Jiang 146-147 DE 10
Tung-chou = Dali 146-147 B 4
Tung-chou = Nantong 142-143 N 5
Tungchow = Nantong 142-143 N 5
T'ung-ch'uan = Tongchuan 142-143 K 4
Tungchwan = Huize 142-143 J 6
Tungchwan = Santai 142-143 JK 5
Tung-fang = Dongfang 142-143 K 8
Tung Hai = Dong Hai 142-143 NO 5-6
Tunghai Tao = Donghai Dao 146-147 C 11
Tunghiang = Tongxiang 146-147 H 6
Tung Ho = Dong He 146-147 A 3
Tung-hsiang = Dongxiang 146-147 F 7
T'ung-hsiang = Tongxiang 146-147 H 6
Tunghsien = Tong Xian 142-143 M 3-4

372 Tranca

Tung-hsi-lien Tao = Dongxi Lian Dao 146-147 GH 4
T'ung-hsü = Tongxu 146-147 E 4
Tunghua = Tonghua 142-143 O 3
Tunghwa = Tonghua 142-143 O 3
Ţungī 141 B 4
Tungjen = Tongren 142-143 K 6
Tung-k'ou = Dongkou 146-147 C 8
T'ung-ku = Tonggu 146-147 E 7
Tung-kuan = Dongguan 142-143 LM 7
Tungkuan = Dongguan 142-143 LM 7
T'ung-kuan = Tongguan 142-143 L 5
Tung-kuang = Dongguang 146-147 F 3
Tung Ku Chau 155 I b 2
T'ung-ku Chiao = Tonggu Jiao 150-151 H 3
T'ung-liao = Tongliao 142-143 N 3
Tung-liu = Dongliu 146-147 F 6
Tunglu = Tonglu 142-143 M 5-6
Tung Lung 155 I b 2
Tung-pai = Tongbai 146-147 D 5
Tungping = Dongping 146-147 F 4
Tung-p'ing Hu = Dongping Hu 146-147 F 3-4
T'ung-p'u = Tongphu 142-143 H 5
T'ung-shan = Tongshan 146-147 E 7
Tungshan = Xuzhou 142-143 M 5
Tung-shêng = Dongsheng 142-143 K 4
T'ung-shih = Tongshi 146-147 F 4
Tungsiang = Dongxiang 146-147 F 7
Tungtai = Dongtai 142-143 N 5
T'ung-tao = Tongdao 146-147 B 8
Tung-t'ing Hu = Dongting Hu 142-143 L 6
Tung-t'ou Shan = Dongtou Shan 146-147 H 8
Tungtuang = Tônzan 141 C 4
Tungurahua 96-97 B 2
Tung-wei-shê = Penghu 146-147 G 10
Tung-yang = Dongyang 146-147 H 7
Tun-hua = Dunhua 142-143 O 3
Tun-huang = Dunhuang 142-143 GH 3
Tunhwang = Dunhuang 142-143 GH 3
Tuni 140 F 2
Tunia, La — 94-95 E 7
Tunica, MS 78-79 D 3
Tūnis 164-165 FG 1
Tunis, Gulf of — = Khalīj at-Tūnisī 166-167 M 1
Tunisi, Canale di — 122-123 D 7
Tūnisī, Khalīj at- 166-167 M 1
Tunisia 164-165 F 1-2
Tunj 164-165 K 7
Tunja 92-93 E 3
Tunjuelito, Bogotá- 91 III b 4
Tunjuelito, Río — 91 III a 3
Tunkhannock, PA 72-73 HJ 4
Tunki 88-89 D 8
Tunliu 146-147 D 3
Tunnsjø 116-117 E 5
Tunqarū 164-165 L 6
Tuntum 100-101 B 3
Tuntutuliak, AK 58-59 F 6
Tunupa, Cerro — 104-105 C 6
Tunuyán 106-107 C 4
Tunuyán, Río — 106-107 CD 4
Tunuyan, Sierra de — 111 C 4
Tunuyán, Travesía del — 106-107 D 4-5
Tunxi 142-143 M 6
Tuo He 146-147 F 5
Tuoji Dao 146-147 H 2
Tuokeqin = Thogchhen 138-139 HJ 2
Tuoketuo = Tugt 142-143 L 3
Tuokexun = Toksun 142-143 F 3
Tuokezheng = Thogchhen 138-139 HJ 2
Tuolin = Tōling 138-139 GH 2
Tuolumne, CA 74-75 CD 4
Tuolumne River 74-75 CD 4
Tuoppajärvi = Topozero 132-133 E 4
Tuosuo Hu = Tos nuur 142-143 H 4
Tupã 92-93 JK 9
Tupaciguara 102-103 H 3
Tūp Āghāj 136-137 M 4
Tupambaé 106-107 K 4
Tupanatinga 100-101 F 5
Tupanciretã 111 F 3
Tu-p'ang Ling = Dupang Ling 146-147 C 9
Tuparai 106-107 JK 2
Tuparro, Río — 94-95 G 5
Tupelo, MS 64-65 J 5
Tupelo, OK 76-77 F 5
Tupi 94-95 G 2
Tupik [SU ↑ Mogoča] 132-133 WX 7
Tupik [SU ↗ Smolensk] 124-125 J 6
Tupim 100-101 D 7
Tupinambaranas, Ilha — 92-93 H 5
Tupirama 98-99 O 9
Tupiza 92-93 F 9
Tupper Lake, NY 72-73 J 2
Tupungato 106-107 C 4
Tupungato, Cerro — 111 BC 4
Tuque, la — 56-57 W 8
Túquerres 92-93 D 4
Ţūr, Aţ- 164-165 L 3
Tura [IND] 138-139 N 5
Tura [SU, place] 132-133 ST 5
Tura [SU, river] 132-133 L 6
Turā, Al-Qāhirah- 170 II b 2
Turabah 134-135 E 6
Turagua, Cerro — 94-95 J 4
Turagua, Serranías — 94-95 J 4
Turaiyūr 140 D 5
Turakom = Mu'o'ng Tourakom 150-151 D 3
Turan 132-133 R 7
Turan = Turanskaja nizmennosť 132-133 K 9-L 8
Turangi 161 FG 4
Turanian Plain = Turanskaja nizmennosť 132-133 K 9-L 8
Turanskaja nizmennosť 132-133 K 9-L 8
Tur'at al-Ismā'īlīyah 170 II b 1
Tur'at az-Zumar 170 II ab 1
Ţurayf 134-135 D 4
Turba, Río de la — 108-109 E 9-10
Turbaco 94-95 D 2
Turbat 134-135 J 5
Turbi 171 D 2
Turbio, El — 111 B 8
Turbo 92-93 D 3
Turbov 126-127 D 2
Turco 104-105 B 6
Turco, Cordillera de — 96-97 C 6
Turda 122-123 K 2
Turdera, Lomas de Zamora- 110 III b 2
Ţūreh 136-137 N 5
Turek 118 J 2
Turffontein, Johannesburg- 170 V b 2
Turffontein Race Course 170 V b 2
Turgaj [SU, place] 132-133 L 8
Turgaj [SU, river] 132-133 L 8
Turgajskaja ložbina 132-133 L 7
Turgel = Türi 124-125 E 4
Türgen Echin uul 142-143 FG 2
Turgeon, Lac — 62 M 2
Turgeon, Rivière — 62 M 2
Turgut 136-137 DE 3
Turgutlu 136-137 BC 3
Turhal 136-137 G 2
Türi 124-125 E 4
Turia 120-121 G 9
Turiaçu 92-93 K 5
Turiaçu, Baía de — 92-93 KL 5
Turiaçu, Rio — 100-101 B 1-2
Turiamo 94-95 GH 2
Turija 124-125 E 8
Turij Rog 132-133 Z 8
Turimiquire, Cerro — 94-95 JK 2
Turin 61 B 5-6
Turin = Torino 122-123 BC 3
Turinsk 132-133 L 6
Tūrīt 164-165 L 8
Turja 124-125 S 2
Turka 126-127 A 2
Turkana 171 C 2
Turkana, Lake — 172 G 1
Turk an-Naşş, Rā's — 166-167 M 3
Türkeli = Gemiyanı 136-137 F 2
Türkeli adası 136-137 B 2
Turkestan 134-135 K-O 3
Turkey 134-135 B-E 3
Turkey, TX 76-77 D 5
Turkey River 70-71 E 4
Turki 124-125 O 8
Türkmen dağı 136-137 D 3
Turkmen-Kala 134-135 J 3
Turkmen Soviet Socialist Republic 134-135 HJ 2-5
Turks and Caicos Islands 88-89 KL 4
Turksib 132-133 P 7
Turks Islands 64-65 M 7
Turku 116-117 K 7
Turkwel 172 G 1
Türler See 128 IV ab 2
Turlock, CA 74-75 C 4
Turmalina 102-103 L 2
Turmerito 91 II b 2
Turmero 94-95 H 2
Turnagain, Cape — 161 G 5
Turnberry 61 GH 4
Turneffe Islands 64-65 J 8
Turner, MT 68-69 B 1
Turner, WA 66-67 E 2
Turner Valley 60 K 4
Turnhout 120-121 K 3
Turning Basin 85 III b 2
Turnor Lake 61 D 2
Turnu Măgurele 122-123 L 4
Turnu Rosu, Pasul — 122-123 KL 3
Turo 171 DE 3
Turon, KS 68-69 G 7
Tuross Head 160 K 6
Turov 124-125 FG 7
Turpan 142-143 F 3
Turpicotay, Cordillera de — 96-97 D 8
Turqino, Pico — 64-65 L 8
Turquoise Lake 58-59 KL 6
Turrell, AR 78-79 D 3
Tursāq 136-137 L 6
Turtkuľ 132-133 L 9
Turtleford 61 D 4
Turtle Islands 168-169 B 4
Turtle Lake 61 D 4
Turtle Lake, ND 68-69 F 2
Turtle Lake, WI 70-71 D 3
Turtle Mountain 68-69 FG 1
Turtle Mountain Indian Reservation 68-69 G 1
Turton, SD 68-69 GH 3
Turuchansk 132-133 Q 4
Turuepano, Isla — 94-95 K 2
Turūg 166-167 D 4
Turugart = Torugart Davan 134-135 L 2
Turumbah 136-137 J 4
Turun ja Poorin lääni 116-117 K 6-7
Turut = Ţorūd 134-135 H 3
Turuvekere 140 C 4
Turuvēkkērē = Turuvekere 140 C 4
Turvo, Rio — [BR, Goiás] 102-103 G 2
Turvo, Rio — [BR, Rio Grande do Sul] 106-107 L 1-2
Turvo, Rio — [BR, São Paulo ◁ Rio Grande] 102-103 H 4
Turvo, Rio — [BR, São Paulo ◁ Rio Paranapanema] 102-103 H 5
Tuscaloosa, AL 64-65 J 5
Tuscany = Toscana 122-123 D 4
Tuscarora, NV 66-67 E 5
Tuscola, IL 70-71 F 6
Tuscola, TX 76-77 E 6
Tuscumbia, AL 78-79 EF 3
Tuscumbia, MO 70-71 D 6
Tusenøyane 116-117 I 6
Tu Shan = Du Shan [TJ, mountain] 144-145 B 2
Tu-shan = Dushan [TJ, place] 146-147 F 6
Tu-shêng-chên = Dusheng 146-147 F 2
Tuside = Pic Toussidé 164-165 H 4
Tusima = Tsushima 142-143 O 5
Tusima kaikyō = Tsushima-kaikyō 142-143 OP 5
Tuskegee, AL 78-79 G 4
Tussey Mountain 72-73 GH 4
Tustna 116-117 B 6
Tustumena Lake 58-59 MN 6
Tutajev 124-125 M 5
Tutak 136-137 K 3
Tutang 146-147 F 7
Tuti 96-97 F 9
Tuticorin 134-135 M 9
Tutna Lake 58-59 K 6
Tutóia 100-101 C 2
Tutoko, Mount — 161 BC 7
Tutončana 132-133 R 4
Tu-t'ou = Dutou 146-147 D 9
Tutrakan 122-123 M 3-4
Tuttle, ND 68-69 FG 2
Tuttle, OK 76-77 F 5
Tuttle Creek Lake 68-69 H 6
Tuttle Lake 70-71 C 4
Tuttlingen 118 D 4-5
Tūttukkudi = Tuticorin 134-135 M 9
Tutubu 171 C 4
Tutuila 148-149 c 1
Tutupaca, Volcán — 92-93 E 8
Tutwiler, MS 78-79 D 3-4
Tuul gol 142-143 JK 2
Tuva Autonomous Soviet Socialist Republic 132-133 RS 7
Tuvalu 208 HJ 3
Tu Vu 150-151 E 2
Ţuwāl 'Aba' 136-137 H 4
Ţuwat, At- 164-165 DE 3
Ţuwayq, Jabal — 134-135 F 6
Ţuwaysah, Aţ- 164-165 K 6
Tuxedni Bay 58-59 L 6
Tuxedo, MD 82 II b 2
Tuxford 61 EF 5
Tuxie He = Tuhai He 146-147 FG 3
Tuxpan [MEX, Jalisco] 86-87 J 8
Tuxpan [MEX, Nayarit] 64-65 E 7
Tuxpán de Rodríguez Cano 64-65 G 7
Tuxtepec 86-87 M 8
Tuxtla Gutiérrez 64-65 H 8
Túy 120-121 C 7
Tuy An 148-149 E 4
Tuya River 58-59 W 7
Tuyên Hoa 150-151 F 4
Tuyên Quang 150-151 E 2
Tuy Hoa 148-149 EF 4
Tuy Phong 150-151 G 7
Tüyserkān 136-137 N 5
Tuyun = Duyun 142-143 K 6
Tuzgölü 134-135 C 3
Ţuz Khurmātū 136-137 L 5
Tuzla [TR] 136-137 F 4
Tuzla [YU] 122-123 H 3
Tuzluca 136-137 K 2
Ţūzlū Gol = Kavīr-e Mīghān 136-137 N 5
Tuzly 126-127 E 4
Tvedestrand 116-117 C 8
Tver' = Kalinin 132-133 EF 6
Tverca 124-125 K 5
Twaingnu 141 C 4
Twande 141 DE 7
Twante = Twande 141 DE 7
Tweed [CDN] 72-73 H 2
Tweed [GB] 119 E 4
Tweedsmuir Provincial Park 56-57 L 7
Tweeling 174-175 H 4
Twee Rivieren 174-175 D 4
Twelvemile Summit 58-59 OP 4
Twentieth Century Fox Studios 83 III b 1
Twenty-four Parganas = 24-Parganas 138-139 M 6-7
Twentynine Palms, CA 74-75 EF 5
Twentytwo Mile Village, AK 58-59 PQ 3
Twickenham, London- 129 II a 2
Twilight Cove 158-159 E 6
Twin Bridges, MT 66-67 GH 3
Twin Buttes Reservoir 76-77 D 7
Twin Falls, ID 64-65 CD 3
Twin Heads 158-159 E 4
Twin Islands 56-57 UV 7
Twin Lakes 58-59 KL 6
Twin Oaks, PA 84 III a 2
Twin Peaks [USA, Idaho] 66-67 F 3
Twin Peaks [USA, San Francisco] 83 I b 2
Twins, The — 161 DE 5
Twin Valley, MN 70-71 BC 2
Two Butte Creek 68-69 E 7
Two Buttes, CO 68-69 E 7
Twodot, MT 66-67 HJ 2
Two Harbors, MN 64-65 HJ 2
Two Hills 61 C 4
Two Rivers, WI 70-71 G 3
Tyagadurgam = Tiyāgai 140 D 5
Tyamo 164-165 M 7
Tyārīt, Wādī — 166-167 LM 4
Tyborøn 116-117 BC 9
Tyencha 164-165 M 7
Tyew Bahir 164-165 M 8
Tygda 132-133 Y 7
Tygh Valley, OR 66-67 C 3
Tylden 174-175 G 7
Tyler, MN 68-69 H 3
Tyler, TX 64-65 GH 5
Tyler Park, VA 82 II a 2
Tylertown, MS 78-79 DE 5
Tylösand 116-117 E 9
Tylovaj 124-125 T 5
Tym 132-133 P 6
Tymfrēstós 122-123 JK 6
Tymovskoje 132-133 b 7
Tympákion 122-123 L 8
Tyndall, SD 68-69 H 4
Tyndinskij 132-133 XY 6
Tynemouth 119 F 4
Tynset 116-117 D 6
Tyonek, AK 58-59 M 6
Tyone River 58-59 O 5
Tyōnthar = Teonthar 138-139 H 5
Tyōsen kaikyō = Chōsen-kaikyō 142-143 O 5
Tyre = Şūr 136-137 F 6
Tyrell, Lake — 158-159 H 7
Tyrifjord 116-117 CD 7
Tyrma 132-133 Z 7
Tyrnyauz 126-127 L 5
Tyrol = Tirol 118 EF 5
Tyrone, OK 76-77 D 4
Tyrone, PA 72-73 G 4
Tyros = Şūr 136-137 F 6
Tyrrell, Lake — 160 F 5
Tyrrhenian Sea 114-115 L 7-8
Tyry = Mindživan 126-127 N 7
Tysnesøy 116-117 A 7-8
Tytuvėnai 124-125 D 6
Tyumen = Tumen' 132-133 M 6
Tyuo River = Twaingnu 141 C 4
Tzaneen 172 F 6
Tz-ch'iu = Ziqiu 146-147 C 6
Tzechung = Zizhong 142-143 JK 5-6
Tzekam = Zijin 146-147 E 10
Tzekung = Zigong 142-143 JK 6
Tzekwei = Zigui 146-147 C 6
Tzitzikama Mountains = Tsitsikamaberge 174-175 EF 7
Tzŭ-ch'ang = Zichang 146-147 B 3
Tzŭ-chin = Zijin 146-147 E 10
Tz'ŭ-hsien = Ci Xian 146-147 E 3
Tzŭ-hu = Bajan Choto 142-143 JK 4
Tzŭ-kuei = Zigui 146-147 C 6
Tzŭ-kung = Zigong 142-143 JK 6
Tz'ŭ-li = Cili 146-147 C 7
Tzŭ Shui = Zi Shui 146-147 C 7
Tzŭ-ya Ho = Ziya He 146-147 F 2
Tzŭ-yang = Ziyang 146-147 B 5
Tzŭ-yüan = Ziyuan 146-147 C 8

U

U, Nam — = Nam Ou 150-151 D 1
Uacamparique, Serra do — 104-105 E 2
Uaçari, Serra — 92-93 H 4
Uaco Cungo 172 C 4
Uacuru, Cachoeira — 98-99 HJ 10
Uaddán = Waddān 164-165 H 3
Uadi-Halfa = Wādī Ḥalfā 164-165 L 4
Uádi Ţanezzúft = Wādī Tanizzuft 166-167 M 7
Uádi Zemzen = Wādī Zamzam 164-165 G 2
Uagadugu = Ouagadougou 164-165 D 6
Uaianary, Cachoeira — 98-99 FG 4
Ualega = Welega 164-165 LM 7
Ualik Lake 58-59 H 7
Uanaraca 94-95 H 8
Uancheu = Wenzhou 142-143 N 6
Uanetze, Rio — 174-175 K 3
Uanle Uen = Wanleweeyn 172 H 1
Uarangal = Warangal 134-135 MN 7
Uari 98-99 K 8
Uaruma 94-95 G 7
Uaso Nyiro 171 D 2
Uatumã, Rio — 92-93 H 5
Uauá 92-93 M 6
Uáu el Chebii = Wādī Bay al-Kabīr 164-165 GH 2
Uáu en-Námús = Wāw an-Nāmūs 164-165 H 4
Uaupés 92-93 F 5
Uaupés, Rio — 92-93 F 4
Uaxactún 64-65 J 8
Uazzén = Wāzin 166-167 M 4
Ubá 92-93 L 9
Uba, Cachoeira do — 98-99 MN 9
Ubá, Salto do — 111 F 2
Ubaí 102-103 K 2
Ubaíra 100-101 E 7
Ubaitaba 92-93 M 7
Ubajara 100-101 D 2
Ubajara, Parque Nacional de — 100-101 D 2
Ubajay 106-107 H 3
Ubalá 94-95 E 5
Ubangi 172 C 1
Ubari = Awbārī 164-165 G 3
'Ubāri, Edeien- = Şaḩrā' Awbārī 164-165 G 3
Ubatã 100-101 E 8
Ubaté 94-95 E 5
Ubatuba 102-103 K 5
Ubauro 138-139 B 3
Ubaye 120-121 L 6
'Ubaylah, Al- 134-135 G 6
Ubayyiḍ, Al- 164-165 KL 6
Ubayyiḍ, Wādī al- 136-137 K 6
Ube 142-143 P 5
Úbeda 120-121 F 9
Ubekendt Ø 56-57 a 3
Uberaba 92-93 K 8
Uberaba, Lagoa — 102-103 D 2
Uberlândia 92-93 K 8
Ubiaja 168-169 G 4
Ubin, Pulau — 154 III b 1
Ubiña, Peña — 120-121 DE 7
Ubiraitá 100-101 D 7
Ubiritã 102-103 F 6
'Ubkayk, Jabal — 164-165 M 4
Ubombo 174-175 JK 4
Ubon Ratchathani 150-151 E 5
Uborť 124-125 FG 8
Ubsa Nur = Uvs nuur 142-143 G 1
Ubundu 172 DE 3
Ucacha 106-107 F 4
Učami 132-133 S 5
Ucayali 96-97 D 4
Ucayali, Río — 92-93 D 6
Uch = Uchh 138-139 C 3
Uchh 138-139 C 3
Uchiko 144-145 J 6
Uchi Lake 62 C 2
Uchinoko = Uchiko 144-145 J 6
Uchinoura 144-145 H 7
Uchiura-wan 144-145 b 2
Uchiza 96-97 C 6
Uchta [SU, Archangeľsk] 124-125 M 3
Uchta [SU, Komi ASSR] 132-133 J 5
Uchta = Kalevala 132-133 E 4
Üchturpan 142-143 DE 3
Ucluelet 60 E 5
Ucross, WY 68-69 C 3
Učur 132-133 Z 6
Uda [SU ◁ Čuna] 132-133 S 7
Uda [SU ◁ Selenga] 132-133 UV 7
Uda [SU ◁ Udskaja guba] 132-133 Z 7
Ūdah, Jabal — 164-165 M 4
Udaipur [IND ↗ Ahmadābād] 134-135 L 6
Udaipur [IND ↖ Jaipur] 138-139 E 4
Udaipur Garhi = Udaypur Gaṛhī 138-139 L 4
Udaj 126-127 F 1
Udala 138-139 L 7
Udalguri 141 C 2
Udamalpet 140 C 5
Udanguḍi = Udankudi 140 C 6
Udankudi 140 C 6
Udaquiola 106-107 H 6
Udayagiri [IND, Andhra Pradesh] 140 D 3
Udayagiri [IND, Orissa] 138-139 K 8
Udaypur Gaṛhī 138-139 L 4
'Udaysāt, Al- 173 C 5
Udbina 122-123 FG 3
Uddevalla 116-117 DE 8
Uddjaur 116-117 H 5
Udgīr 140 C 1
Udimskij 124-125 PQ 3
Údine 122-123 E 2
Udipi 134-135 L 8
Uḍīsā = Orissa 134-135 N 7-O 6
Udjidji = Ujiji 172 E 2-3
Udmurt Autonomous Soviet Socialist Republic = 2 ◁ 132-133 J 6
Udmurtskaja Avtonomnaja Sovetskaja Socialističeskaja Respublika = Udmurt Autonomous Soviet Socialist Republic 132-133 J 6
U-do 144-145 F 6
Udobnaja 126-127 K 4
Udomľa 124-125 K 5
Udon Thani 148-149 D 3
Udrif 166-167 LM 2-3
Udskaja guba 132-133 a 7
Uḍuppi = Udipi 134-135 L 8
Udža 132-133 W 3
Udžary 126-127 N 6
Uebonti 148-149 H 7
Ueda 144-145 M 4
Uedineniya Island = ostrov Ujedinenija 132-133 OP 2
Uegit = Wajid 172 H 1
Uele 172 D 1
Uelen 56-57 BC 4
Uelikon 128 IV b 2
Uelzen 118 E 2
Uengan, mys — 132-133 LM 3
Ueno 144-145 L 5
Ueno, Tōkyō- 155 III b 1
Ueno Parak 155 III b 1
Uere 172 E 1
Uerzlikon 128 IV ab 2
Uetikon 128 IV b 2
Uetliberg 128 IV ab 1
Ufa [SU, place] 132-133 K 7
Ufa [SU, river] 132-133 K 6
Ūfran 166-167 G 5
Uff'uga 124-125 Q 3
Ugak Bay 58-59 g 1
Ugak Island 58-59 gh 1
Ugāle 124-125 CD 5
Ugalen = Ugāle 124-125 CD 5
Ugalla 172 F 3
Ugamak Island 58-59 o 3
Ugamas 174-175 C 5
Uganda 172 F 1
Uganik Island 58-59 K 8
Ugarteche 106-107 C 4
Ugashik, AK 58-59 J 8
Ugashik Bay 58-59 HJ 8
Ugashik Lakes 58-59 J 8
Ugep 168-169 H 4
Ügharţah 166-167 E 5
Ugie 174-175 H 6
Ugleuralskij 124-125 V 4
Uglič 132-133 F 6
Ugljan 122-123 F 3
Uglovka 124-125 J 4
Ugogo 172 FG 3
Ugoľnyj = Beringovskij 132-133 j 5
Ugoma 171 B 3-4
Ugra [SU, place] 124-125 K 6
Ugra [SU, river] 124-125 K 6
Uguay 111 E 3
Uğurludağ = Kızılveran 136-137 F 2
Uha 172 F 2
Uha-dong 142-143 O 3
Uhlenhorst 174-175 B 2
Uhlenhorst, Hamburg- 130 I b 1
Uhrichsville, OH 72-73 F 4
Uibaí 100-101 C 6
Ui-do 144-145 E 5
Uíge 172 BC 3
Uijŏngbu 144-145 F 4
Uiju 144-145 E 2
Uil 132-133 J 8
Uilpata, gora — 126-127 L 5
Uinamarca, Laguna — 104-105 B 5
Uintah and Ouray Indian Reservation [USA ↓ East Tavaputs Plateau] 74-75 J 3
Uintah and Ouray Indian Reservation [USA ↓ Uinta Mountains] 66-67 HJ 5
Uinta Mountains 64-65 DE 3
Uiraponga 100-101 E 3
Uiraúna 100-101 E 4
Uisŏng 144-145 G 4
Uitdam 128 I b 1
Uitenhage 172 DE 8
Uitikon 128 IV a 1
Uj 132-133 L 7
Ujandina 132-133 b 4
Ujar 132-133 R 6
Ujda = Ujdah 164-165 D 2
Ujdah 164-165 D 2
Ujedinenija, ostrov — 132-133 OP 2
Ujhāni 138-139 G 3-4
Uji-guntō 144-145 G 7
Ujiji 172 E 2-3
Ujjaen = Ujjain 134-135 M 6
Ujjain 134-135 M 6
Ujunglamuru 152-153 NO 8
Ujung Pandang 148-149 G 8
Ujung Peureulak 152-153 BC 3
Ujung Raja 152-153 AB 4
Ujung Tuan 152-153 C 5
Ukamas = Ugamas 174-175 C 5
Ukara 171 C 3
'Ukāsh, Wādī — 136-137 J 5-6
Ukata 168-169 G 3
Ukerewe Island 172 F 2
Ukhrul 141 D 3
Ukiah, CA 64-65 B 4
Ukiah, OR 66-67 D 3
Ukimbu 172 F 3
Ukita, Tōkyō- 155 III c 1
Ukmergė 124-125 E 6
Ukonongo 172 F 3
Ukraina 126-127 F 3-J 2
Ukraine 114-115 O-Q 6
Ukrainian Soviet Socialist Republic 126-127 C-H 2
Ukrainskaja Sovetskaja Socialističeskaja Respublika = Ukrainian Soviet Socialist Republic 126-127 C-H 2
Uksora 124-125 NO 2
Ukumbi 172 F 3
Uku-shima 144-145 G 6
Ukwama 171 C 5
Ukwi 174-175 D 2
Ula 136-137 C 4
'Ulā', Al- 134-135 D 5
Ulaanbaatar 142-143 K 2
Ulaan Choto = Ulan Hot 142-143 N 2
Ulaangom 142-143 G 1-2
Ulaan mörön [TJ ◁ Dre Chhu] 142-143 G 5
Ulaan Mörön [TJ ◁ Kuye He] 146-147 BC 2
Ulaan uul 142-143 G 5
Ulak Island 58-59 t 7
Ulala = Gorno-Altajsk 132-133 Q 7
Ulamba 172 D 3
Ulan = Dulaan Chijd 142-143 H 4
Ulan Bator = Ulaanbaatar 142-143 K 2
Ulan Bator = Ulaan Bataar 142-143 K 2
Ulan-Burgasy, chrebet — 132-133 UV 7
Ulan-Erge 126-127 M 3
Ulan Gom = Ulaangom 142-143 G 1-2
Ulan Hot 142-143 N 2
Ulankom = Ulaangom 142-143 G 1-2
Ulan-Udė 132-133 U 7
Ulapes 111 C 4
Ulapes, Sierra de — 106-107 D 3
Ulaş 136-137 G 3
Ulastai = Uljastaj 142-143 H 2
Ulawa 148-149 k 6
Uľba 132-133 P 7
Ulchin 144-145 G 4
Ulcinj 122-123 H 5
Uldza = Bajan Uul 142-143 L 2
Üldzejt = Öldzijt 142-143 J 2
Uldz gol 142-143 L 2
Uleåborg = Oulu 116-117 L 5
Uleelheue 148-149 C 5
Ulen, MN 68-69 H 2
Ulete 172 G 3
Ulety 132-133 V 7
Ulge 172 BC 3
Ulhasnagar 134-135 L 7
Uliaga Island 58-59 m 4
Uliassutai = Uliastaj 142-143 H 2
Uliastaj 142-143 H 2
Ulijasutai = Uliastaj 142-143 H 2
Ulindi 172 E 2
Ulingan 148-149 N 7
Ulīpūr 138-139 M 5
Ulja 132-133 b 6
Uljanovka 126-127 E 2
Uljanovsk 132-133 H 7
Uljinskij chrebet 132-133 ab 6
Ulkatcho 60 E 3
Ulla 124-125 G 6
Ulladulla 158-159 K 7
Ullin, IL 70-71 F 7
Ulloma 104-105 B 5
Ullsfjord 116-117 HJ 3
Ullún 106-107 C 3
Ullŭng-do 142-143 P 4
Ullyul 144-145 E 3
Ulm 118 D 4
Ulm, AR 78-79 D 3
Ulm, MT 66-67 H 2
Ulm, WY 68-69 C 3
'Ulmah, Al- 166-167 J 1
Ulmarra 160 L 2
Ūlmās 166-167 CD 3
Uløy 116-117 J 3
Ulpad = Olpād 138-139 D 7
Ulsan 142-143 OP 4
Ulster 119 C 4
Ulster Canal 119 C 4
Ultadanga, Calcutta- 154 II b 2
Ulu 132-133 Y 5
Ulúa, Río — 64-65 J 8
Ulubat gölü = Apolyont gölü 136-137 C 2
Ulu Bedok 154 III b 2
Ulubey 136-137 C 3
Ulubey = Gündüzlü 136-137 G 2
Uluborlu 136-137 D 3
Uluçınar = Arsuz 136-137 F 4
Uludağ 136-137 C 2-3
Ulugh Muz tagh 142-143 F 4
Ulugurus Mountains 172 G 3
Ulukışla 136-137 F 4
Ulundi 174-175 J 5
Ulundurpettai = Kīranūr 140 D 5
Ulus 136-137 E 2
Ulutau 132-133 M 8
Ulutau, gora — 132-133 M 8
Ulverstone 160 bc 2
'Ulyā, Qaryat al- 134-135 F 5
Ulyastai = Uliastaj 142-143 H 2
Ulysses, KS 68-69 F 7
Ulysses, NE 68-69 H 5
Umala 92-93 F 8
Umal'tinskij 132-133 Z 7
Umán [MEX] 86-87 PQ 7
Uman' [SU] 126-127 DE 2
Umanak = Umánaq 56-57 ab 3
Umanak Fjord 56-57 Za 3
Umánaq 56-57 ab 3
Umango, Sierra de — 106-107 C 2
Umanskaja = Leningradskaja 126-127 J 3
Umarga 140 C 2
'Umarī, Qā'al — 136-137 G 7
Umaria 138-139 H 6
Umarkhed 138-139 F 8
Umarkher = Umarkhed 138-139 F 8
Umarkoţ 138-139 BC 5
Umarote 96-97 D 9
Ūm'āsh 166-167 J 2
Umatilla Indian Reservation 66-67 D 3
Umatilla River 66-67 D 3
Umba = Lesnoj 132-133 EF 4
Umbarger, TX 76-77 C 5
Umbarpāda 138-139 D 7
Umberto 1° 106-107 G 3
Umboi 148-149 N 8
Umbria 122-123 DE 4
Umbu [BR] 106-107 K 2
Umbu [TJ] 142-143 F 5
Umburanas 100-101 D 6
Umburanas, Serra das — 100-101 F 5-G 4
Umburatiba 100-101 D 3
Umbuzeiro 100-101 G 4
Umeå 116-117 HJ 6
Ume älv 116-117 H 5
Um er Rebia = Wād Umm ar-Rabīyah 164-165 C 2
Umet 124-125 O 7
Umfolozi 174-175 JK 5
Umfolozi Game Reserve 174-175 JK 5
Umgeni 174-175 J 5
Umhlatuzi = Mhlatuze 174-175 J 5
Umiat, AK 58-59 K 2
Umiris 98-99 J 7

Umiris 373

Umkomaas [ZA, place] 174-175 J 6
Umkomaas [ZA, river] 174-175 J 6
Umkomanzi = Umkomaas
174-175 J 6
Umm ad-Durūs, Sabkhat —
164-165 B 4
Umm al-'Abīd 164-165 H 3
Umm al-'Ashār 166-167 B 5
Umm al-Bawāghī 166-167 K 2
Umm al-Kataf, Khalīj — 173 D 6
Umm al-Khiyālāt, Sabkhat —
166-167 M 3
Umm al-Qaywayn 134-135 GH 5
Umm ar-Rabīyah, Wād —
164-165 C 2
Umm ash-Shidād = Sabkhat Abā ar-
Rūs 134-135 G-H 6
Umm aş-Şam'ah 166-167 L 3
Umm as-Samīm 134-135 H 6
Umm aţ-Ţuyūr al-Fawqānī, Jabal —
173 D 6
Umm aţ-Ţūz 136-137 K 5
Umm az-Zumūl 134-135 GH 6
Umm Badr 164-165 K 6
Umm Ball 164-165 K 6
Umm Bishtīt, Bi'r — 173 DE 6
Umm Bujmah 173 C 3
Umm Durmān 164-165 L 5
Umm el-'Abīd 164-165 H 3
Umm Hagar = Om Hajer
164-165 M 6
Umm Hajer = Om Hajer
164-165 M 6
Umm Ḥibāl, Bi'r — 173 C 6
Umm 'Inab, Jabal — 173 C 5
Umm Kaddādah 164-165 L 6
Umm Karār, Tall — 136-137 H 6
Umm Sa'īd, Bi'r — 173 CD 3
Umm Shāghir, Jabal — 173 B 6
Umnak Island 52 D 35-36
Umnak Pass 58-59 mn 4
Umniati 172 E 5
Umpqua River 66-67 AB 4
Umraniye 154 I b 2
Umrat 138-139 D 7
Umrēḍ = Umrer 138-139 G 7
Umrer 138-139 G 7
Umreth 138-139 D 6
'Umshaymin, Al- 136-137 H 6
Ůmsŏng 144-145 F 4
Umtali = Mutare 172 F 5
Umtata 172 E 8
Umtata River = Mtatarivier
174-175 H 6
Umtatarivier = Mtatarivier
174-175 H 6
Umtentweni 174-175 J 6
Umtwalumi = Mtwalume
174-175 J 6
Umuahia 168-169 G 4
Umuarama 102-103 F 5
Umuryeri, İstanbul- 154 I b 2
Umvoti 174-175 J 5
Umvuma = Mvuma 172 F 5
Umzimhlava 174-175 H 6
Umzimkulu [ZA, place] 174-175 H 6
Umzimkulu [ZA, river] 174-175 J 6
Umzimvubu 172 EF 8
Umzinto 174-175 J 6
Umzumbe 174-175 J 6
Umzumbi = Umzumbe 174-175 J 6

Una [BR] 92-93 M 8
Una [IND, Gujarāt] 138-139 C 7
Una [IND, Himāchal Pradesh]
138-139 F 2
Una [YU] 122-123 G 3
Una, Río — 100-101 G 5
'Unāb, Wādī el- = Wādī al-'Unnāb
136-137 G 7-8
Unac 122-123 G 3
Unadilla, GA 80-81 DE 4
Unāghah 166-167 B 4
Unaí 92-93 K 8
'Unaizah = 'Unayzah 134-135 E 5
Unaka Mountains 80-81 DE 3
Unalakleet, AK 56-57 D 5
Unalakleet River 58-59 GH 5
Unalaska Bay 58-59 n 3-4
Unalaska Island 52 D 35
Unalga Island [USA, Delarof Islands]
58-59 t 7
Unalga Island [USA, Unalaska Island]
58-59 no 4
Unango 171 C 6
Unare, Laguna de — 94-95 J 2
Unare, Río — 94-95 J 3
Unauna, Pulau — 152-153 O 6
'Unayzah [JOR] 136-137 FG 7
'Unayzah [Saudi Arabia] 134-135 E 5
'Unayzah, Jabal — 134-135 DE 4
Uncía 92-93 F 8
Uncompahgre Peak 64-65 E 4
Uncompahgre Plateau 74-75 JK 3
Underberg 174-175 H 5
Underbool 160 E 5
Underground 85 II b 2
Underwood, ND 68-69 F 2
Undory 124-125 QR 6
Undozero 124-125 M 2
Undurkhan = Öndörchaan
142-143 L 2

Uneča 124-125 J 7
Uneiuxi, Río — 92-93 F 5
UNESCO 129 I c 2
Unga, AK 58-59 c 2
Unga Island 56-57 D 6
Ungalik, AK 58-59 G 4
Ungalik River 58-59 GH 4
Ungava, AK 58-59 a 2
Ungava Bay 56-57 X 6
Ungava Crater = New Quebec
Crater 56-57 VW 5
Ungava Peninsula 56-57 VW 5
Ungeny 126-127 CD 3
Unggi 144-145 H 1
Uni 124-125 S 5
União 92-93 L 5
União da Vitória 102-103 G 7
União dos Palmares 92-93 MN 6
Unib, Khawr — 173 D 7
Unicorn Ridge 155 I b 1
Unidad Santa Fe, Villa Obregón-
91 I b 2
Unije 122-123 EF 3
Unimak, AK 58-59 a 2
Unimak Bight 58-59 ab 2
Unimak Island 52 D 35
Unimak Pass 58-59 o 3
Unini 96-97 E 7
Unini, Río — 92-93 G 5
Union, MO 70-71 E 6
Union, MS 78-79 E 4
Union, OR 66-67 E 3
Union, SC 80-81 F 3
Union, WV 80-81 F 2
Unión [PY] 102-103 D 6
Unión [RA] 111 C 5
Unión [Saint Vincent] 88-89 Q 8
Unión, La — [BOL] 104-105 F 4
Unión, La — [CO, Nariño] 94-95 C 7
Unión, La — [CO, Valle del Cauca]
94-95 C 5
Unión, La — [E] 120-121 G 10
Unión, La — [ES] 64-65 J 9
Unión, La — [MEX] 86-87 K 9
Unión, La — [PE, Huánuco]
92-93 D 6-7
Unión, La — [PE, Piura] 96-97 A 4
Unión, La — [RCH] 111 B 6
Unión, La — [YV] 94-95 M 3
Union, Mount — 74-75 G 5
Union City, IN 70-71 H 5
Union City, NJ 82 III b 2
Union City, PA 72-73 FG 4
Union City, TN 78-79 E 2
Union Creek, OR 66-67 B 4
Uniondale 174-175 E 7
Uniondale Road = Uniondaleweg
174-175 E 7
Uniondaleweg 174-175 E 7
Union Depot 84 II b 3
Union Pacific Railway 64-65 E 3
Union Point, GA 80-81 E 4
Union Springs, AL 78-79 G 4
Union Station [USA, Houston]
85 III b 1
Union Station [USA, Los Angeles]
83 III c 1
Uniontown, AL 78-79 F 4
Uniontown, KY 70-71 G 7
Uniontown, PA 72-73 G 5
Unionville, IA 70-71 D 5
Unionville, NV 66-67 DE 5
United Arab Emirates 134-135 GH 6
United Kingdom 119 G 4-5
United Nations-Headquarters
82 III c 2
United Provinces = Uttar Pradesh
134-135 MN 5
United Pueblos Indian Reservation
76-77 A 5
United States 64-65 C-K 4
United States Atomic Energy
Commission Reservation =
National Reactor Testing Station
66-67 G 4
United States Naval Annex 84 I b 1
Unity 61 D 4
Unity, ME 72-73 M 2
Universal City, TX 76-77 E 8
Universal City Mall 84 II b 2
Universidad Catolica Andrés Bello
91 II b 2
Universidad Militar Latino Americana
91 I b 2
Universidad Nacional 91 III bc 3
Universitas Katolik Indonesia
154 IV ab 2
Universität München 130 II b 2
Universität Wien 113 I b 2
Universität Zürich 128 IV b 1
Université de Al-Jazā'ir 170 I a 1
Université de Montréal 82 I b 1
Ùniversite İstanbul 154 I a 2
Universiteit van Amsterdam
128 I ab 1
University City, MO 70-71 E 6
University Gardens, NY 82 III d 2
University Heights, OH 72-73 F 4
University of Cairo 170 II b 1
University of Calcutta 154 II b 2
University of California [USA, Los
Angeles] 83 III b 1
University of California [USA, San
Francisco] 83 I b 1
University of Chicago 83 II b 2
University of Detroit 84 II b 2
University of Georgia at Atlanta
85 II bc 2
University of Hong Kong 155 I a 2
University of Houston 85 III b 2
University of Illinois 83 II ab 1
University of Indonesia 154 IV b 2

University of Lagos 170 III b 1
University of Massachusetts 84 I b 3
University of Melbourne 161 II b 1
University of New Orleans 85 I b 1
University of New South Wales
161 I b 2
University of Pennsylvania 84 III b 2
University of Saint Thomas 85 III b 2
University of San Francisco 83 I b 2
University of Singapore 154 III a 2
University of Southern California
83 III c 1
University of Sydney 161 I ab 2
University of the Americas 91 I b 2
University of Windsor 84 II b 3
University of Witwatersrand
170 V b 2
University Park, MD 82 II b 1
University Park, NM 76-77 A 6
Unja 124-125 W 3
Unjamwesi = Unyamwezi 172 F 2-3
'Unnāb, Wādī al- 136-137 G 7-8
Unnāo 138-139 H 4
Unnāv = Unnāo 138-139 H 4
U No'a = Mu'o'ng Ou Neua
150-151 CD 1
Unquillo 106-107 E 3
Unsan 144-145 E 2-3
Unsang, Tanjung — 152-153 N 3
Unsan-ni 144-145 EF 3
Unst 119 F 1
Unstrut 118 E 3
Unterbiberg 130 II b 2
Unterengstringen 128 IV a 1
Unterliederbach, Frankfurt am Main-
128 III a 1
Untermenzing, München- 130 II a 1
Untersendling, München- 130 II b 2
Unturán, Sierra de — 94-95 J 7
Unuk River 60 B 1
Unyamwezi 172 F 2-3
Ünye 136-137 G 2
Unža [SU < Gor'kovskoje
vodochranilišče] 124-125 P 4
Uolkitte = Welkītē 164-165 M 7
Uollega = Welega 164-165 LM 7
Uomán 94-95 K 5
Uopiane, Serra do — 104-105 E 2-3
Uoso Nyiro = Ewaso Ngiro 172 G 2
Uozu 144-145 L 4

Upanda, Serra — 172 BC 4
Upanema 100-101 F 3
Upardāng Garhī 138-139 K 4
Upata 94-95 K 3
Upemba, Lac — 172 E 3
Upemba, Parc national de l' 172 E 3
Upernavik 56-57 Z 3
Upham, ND 68-69 F 1
Upham, NM 76-77 A 6
Upi 152-153 PQ 2
Upía, Río — 94-95 E 5
Upington 172 D 7
Upland, PA 84 III a 2
Upleta 138-139 C 7
Upnuk Lake 58-59 H 6
Upolokša 116-117 O 4
Upolu 148-149 c 1
Upolu Point 78-79 de 2
Upper 168-169 E 3
Upper Arrow Lake 60 J 4
Upper Austria = Oberösterreich
118 F-H 4
Upper Bay 82 III b 2-3
Upper Darby, PA 72-73 J 4-5
Upper Egypt = Aş-Şa'īd
164-165 L 3
Upper Guinea 50-51 JK 5
Upper Humber River 63 H 3
Upper Hutt 161 F 5
Upper Klamath Lake 66-67 BC 4
Upper Laberge 58-59 U 6
Upper Lake 66-67 C 5
Upper Lake, CA 74-75 B 3
Upper Musquodoboit 63 E 5
Upper Mystic Lake 84 I ab 2
Upper Nile = Aali an-Nīl
164-165 KL 7
Upper Peninsula 64-65 J 2
Upper Red Lake 70-71 C 1
Upper Sandusky, OH 72-73 E 4
Upper Seal Lake = Lac d'Iberville
56-57 W 6
Upper Volta = Burkina Faso
164-165 D 6
Uppsala [S, administrative unit]
116-117 GH 7
Uppsala [S, place] 116-117 G 8
Upsala 70-71 E 1
Upsalquitch 63 C 4
Upstart Bay 158-159 J 3
Upton, KY 70-71 GH 7
Upton, WY 68-69 D 3
Uptown, Chicago-, IL 83 II ab 1
Uptown Business Park, Houston-, TX
85 III b 2
'Uqayah, Al- 164-165 H 2
Uqayr, Al- 134-135 FG 5
'Uqlah 166-167 AB 2
'Uqlat as-Sabīyah 166-167 D 7
'Uqlat Barābir 166-167 E 4
'Uqlat Ibn Ṣuqayh 136-137 M 8
'Uqlat Ṣudrā' 166-167 E 3
Uqṣur, Al- 164-165 L 3
Uquía 104-105 D 8

Ur 134-135 F 4
Ur, Wādī — 173 B 6-7
Urabá, Golfo de — 92-93 D 3
Urabá, Isla — 64-65 bc 3
Uracas = Farallon de Pajaros
206-207 S 1

Uracoa 94-95 K 3
Uraí = Oraí 138-139 G 5
Urakawa 144-145 c 2
Ural 132-133 J 8
Ural, MT 66-67 F 1
Ural, Pol'arnyj — 132-133 LM 4
Ural, Pripol'arnyj — 132-133 KL 4-5
Ural, Severnyj — 132-133 K 5-6
Uralla 160 K 3
Uralmed'stroj = Krasnoural'sk
132-133 L 6
Urals 132-133 K 5-7
Ural'sk 132-133 J 7
Uran 140 A 1
Urana 160 GH 5
Urandangi 158-159 G 4
Urandi 92-93 L 7
Urania, LA 78-79 C 5
Uranium City 56-57 P 6
Urat 134-135 MN 5 K 6
Uraricoera 98-99 H 3
Uraricoera, Rio — 92-93 G 4
Uraricuera 94-95 L 6
Ura-Tübe 134-135 K 3
Uravaćunda = Uravakonda 140 C 3
Uravan, CO 74-75 J 3
Urawa 142-143 QR 4
Urayasu 155 III a 2
'Uray'irah 134-135 F 5
'Urayyiḍah, Bi'r — 173 BC 3
Urazovo 126-127 J 1
Urbana, IL 70-71 FG 5
Urbana, OH 72-73 E 4
Urbana, La — 92-93 F 3
Urbano Santos 100-101 C 2
Urbe, Aeroporto dell' 113 I b 1
Urbino 122-123 E 4
Urbión, Picos de — 120-121 F 8
Urcos 92-93 E 7
Urda [SU] 126-127 N 2
Urdampilleta 106-107 G 6
Urdinarrain 106-107 H 4
Urdoma 124-125 R 3
Urdorf 128 IV a 1
Urdžar 132-133 P 8
Uren' 124-125 P 5
Ureparapara 158-159 N 2
Ure 64-65 DE 6
'Urf, Jabal al- 173 C 4
Urfa 134-135 D 3
Urfa Yaylası 136-137 H 4
'Urf Umm Rashīd 173 D 5
Urga 132-133 K 9
Urga = Ulaanbaatar 142-143 K 2
Urgenč 132-133 L 9
Ürgüp 136-137 F 3
Uria, Río — 94-95 F 4
Uribante, Río — 94-95 F 4
Uribe 92-93 E 4
Uribe, La — 91 III c 1
Uribelarrea 106-107 H 5
Uribia 92-93 E 2
Uriburu 106-107 EF 6
Urica 94-95 JK 3
Urickij 124-125 K 7
Urickoje 132-133 M 7
Urikura 155 III c 3
Urilia Bay 58-59 a 2
Urim = Ur 134-135 F 4
Uriondo 104-105 D 7
Urique, Río — 86-87 G 4
Urişă = Orissa 134-135 N 7-O 6
Urisino 160 F 2
Uritorco, Cerro — 106-107 E 3
Urituyacu, Río — 96-97 D 4
Uriuaná, Rio — 98-99 N 6
Urla 134-135 B 3
Urlāl 166-167 J 2
Urmannyj 132-133 M 5
Urmary 124-125 Q 6
Urmia = Daryācheh Orūmīyeh
134-135 F 3
Urmia, Daryācheh — = Daryācheh
Orūmīyeh 134-135 F 3
Uromi 168-169 G 4
Urrao 94-95 C 4
Urre Lauquen, Laguna —
106-107 E 7
Ursatjevskaja = Chavast
134-135 K 2
Ursine, NV 74-75 F 3-4
Urtigueira 102-103 G 6
Urt Mörön = Chadzaar 142-143 G 4
Uruaçu 92-93 K 7
Uruana 92-93 JK 7
Uruapan del Progreso 64-65 F 8
Uruará, Rio — 98-99 M 6
Urubamba 92-93 E 7
Urubamba, Río — 92-93 E 7
Urubaxi, Rio — 98-99 F 5
Urubicha 104-105 E 4
Urubici 102-103 H 7-8
Urubu, Cachoeira do —
98-99 OP 11
Urubu, Rio — 98-99 J 6
Urubu, Travessão do — 98-99 M 8
Uruburetama 100-101 E 2
Uruburetama, Serra de —
100-101 DE 2
Uruçanga 102-103 H 8
Urucu, Río — 98-99 FG 7
Urucuca 100-101 E 8
Urucuí, Serra do — 92-93 K 7-L 6
Urucuia 102-103 K 7
Urucuia, Rio — 102-103 K 3
Uruçuí Vermelho, Rio —
100-101 B 5
Urucurituba 92-93 H 5
Uruguai, Rio — 111 F 3

Uruguaiana 111 E 3
Uruguay 111 EF 4
Uruguay, Río — [RA < Río de la
Plata] 111 E 3
Uruguay, Río — [RA < Río Paraná]
102-103 E 6
Uruguay, Salto Grande del —
111 F 3
Urumacó 94-95 F 2
Urūm aş-Şughrā 136-137 G 4
Urumbi 92-93 F 4
Ürümchi 142-143 F 3
Urumchi = Ürümchi 142-143 F 3
Urundi = Burundi 172 EF 2
Urunga 160 L 3
Ur'ung-Chaja 132-133 VW 3
Urandi 92-93 L 7
Urun Islāmpur 140 B 2
Uruoca 100-101 D 2
Urup 126-127 K 4
Urup, ostrov — 132-133 cd 8
Urupa, Rio — 98-99 G 10
Urupês 102-103 H 4
Ur'upinsk 126-127 L 1
Uruppu = ostrov Urup
132-133 cd 8
Uruqué 100-101 E 3
Ururí, Jabal al- 100-101 A 8
Urutaí 102-103 HJ 3
Uruyén 92-93 G 3
Urville, Île d' 53 C 31
Urville, Mer d' 53 C 14-15
Urville, Tanjung d' 148-149 L 7
Urziceni 122-123 M 3
Uržum 132-133 HJ 6

Usa 132-133 K 4
Ušači 124-125 G 6
Usagara 172 G 3
Uşak 134-135 B 3
Usakos 172 BC 6
Ušakova, ostrov — 132-133 OP 1
Usambara Mountains 171 D 4
Usango 171 C 4
Usaquén 91 III c 2
Ušba, gora — 126-127 L 5
Usborne, Mount — 111 E 8
Uscana, Serra — 104-105 B 6
Usedom 118 F 1-G 2
Usengo 171 B 4
Usera, Madrid- 113 III a 2
Usetsu = Noto 144-145 L 4
Usevia 171 B 4
'Ushan 134-135 D 6
Ushagat Island 58-59 L 7
Ushakova Island = ostrov Ušakova
132-133 OP 2
Ushakov Island = ostrov Ušakova
132-133 OP 1
Ushero 171 BC 4
Usherville 61 G 4
Ushibaka 144-145 GH 6
Ushibukuro 155 III c 3
Ushirombo 171 BC 3
Ushuaia 111 C 8
Usk 66-67 C 2
Usk, WA 66-67 E 1
Uskir, Hāssi — 166-167 F 4
Üsküdar, İstanbul- 134-135 BC 2
Uskumruköy 154 I b 1
Üsküp = Skopje 122-123 J 4-5
Usman' 124-125 MN 7
Usme 94-95 DE 5
Usno 106-107 D 3
Usoke 171 C 4
Usolje [SU, Perm'skaja Oblast']
124-125 V 4
Usolje = Usolje-Sibirskoje
132-133 T 7
Usolje-Sibirskoje 132-133 T 7
Usolje-Solikamskoje = Berezniki
132-133 JK 6
Usolye Sibirskoye = Usolje-
Sibirskoje 132-133 T 7
Usoro 168-169 G 4
Usouil 96-97 C 5
Uspallata 106-107 C 4
Uspallata, Sierra de — 106-107 C 4
Uspara, Cerro — 106-107 E 4
Uspenka 126-127 J 2
Ussagara = Usagara 172 G 3
Üssaltýkh, Al- 166-167 LM 2
Ussuri = Wusuli Jiang 142-143 P 2
Ussurijsk 132-133 Z 9
Ussurijskij zaliv 144-145 HJ 1
Usta 124-125 PQ 5
Ust'-Abakanskoje = Abakan
132-133 R 7
Ust'-Barguzin 132-133 UV 7
Ust'-Bol'šereck 132-133 de 7
Ust'-Buzulukskaja 126-127 L 1
Ust'-Čaun 132-133 h 4
Ust'-Cil'ma 132-133 J 4
Ust'-Čižapka 132-133 OP 6
Ust'-Čorna 126-127 AB 2
Ust'-Čornaja 124-125 ST 3
Ust'-Dolgaja 124-125 V 4
Ust'-Doneckij 126-127 KL 2
Ust'-Džegutinskaja 126-127 KL 4
Ust'-Ilimsk 132-133 TU 7
Ust'-Ilych 126-127 S 3
Ust'-Ilyč 124-125 V 2
Ust'-Išim 132-133 N 6
Usta 124-125 P 3

Ustje [SU, Vologodskaja Oblast']
124-125 M 4
Ustje-Agapy = Agapa 132-133 Q 3
Ust'-Juribej 132-133 MN 4
Ustka 118 H 1
Ust'-Kamčatsk 132-133 f 6
Ust Kamchatsk = Ust'-Kamčatsk
132-133 f 6
Ust'-Kamenogorsk 132-133 OP 7-8
Ust'-Kan 132-133 PQ 7
Ust'-Karabula 132-133 S 6
Ust'-Karsk 132-133 W 7
Ust'-Kulom 132-133 JK 5
Ust'-Kut 132-133 U 6
Ust'-Labinsk 126-127 JK 4
Ust'-Luga 124-125 FG 4
Ust'-Maja 132-133 Z 5
Ust'-Nem 124-125 U 3
Ust'-Nera 132-133 b 5
Ust'-Orda = Ust'-Ordynskij
132-133 TU 7
Ust'-Ordynskij 132-133 TU 7
Ust'-Ordynsky-Buryat Autonomous
Area = 11 < 132-133 T 7
Ust'-Oz'ornoje 132-133 Q 6
Ust'-Pinega 124-125 NO 1
Ust'-Pinega 132-133 G 5
Ust'-Port 132-133 PQ 4
Ust'-Ša̧ugor 132-133 K 9
Ust'-Ša̧nosa 124-125 N 3
Ust'-Tatta 132-133 Za 5
Ust'-Tym 132-133 OP 6
Ust'-Ulagan 132-133 P 7
Ust'-Unja 124-125 V 3
Ust'-Ura 124-125 P 2
Ust'urt, plato — 132-133 K 9
Ust'-Usa 132-133 K 4
Ust'užna 124-125 L 4
Ust'-Vačerga 124-125 QR 2
Ust'-Vajen'ga 124-125 NO 1
Ust'-Vym' 124-125 S 2
Usu-dake 144-145 b 2
Usuki 144-145 HJ 6
Usuktuk River 58-59 J 1
Usule 171 C 4
Usulután 88-89 B 8
Usumacinta, Río — 64-65 H 8
Usumbura = Bujumbura 172 EF 2
Usun Apau Plateau 152-153 L 4
Usure 171 C 4
Usutu = Great Usutu 174-175 J 4
Usuŷǒng 144-145 EF 5
Usu zan 144-145 b 2
Usv'aty 124-125 H 6

Utah 64-65 DE 4
Utah Lake 64-65 D 3
Utasinai 144-145 c 2
U Tay = Mu'o'ng Ou Tay
150-151 C 1
Uṭāyah, Al- 166-167 J 2
Utcubamba, Río — 96-97 B 4
Ute, IA 70-71 C 4
Ute Creek 76-77 C 5
Utegi 171 C 3
Ute Mountain Indian Reservation
74-75 J 4
Utena 124-125 E 6
Utengule 171 C 5
Ute Peak 74-75 J 4
Utete 172 G 3
Utevka 124-125 S 7
Uthai Thani 150-151 C 5
'Uthmānīyah, Al- 173 BC 4
U Thong 148-149 C 4
Uthumphon Phisai 150-151 DE 5
Utiariti 92-93 H 7
Utica 166-167 M 1
Utica, KS 68-69 F 6
Utica, NY 64-65 LM 3
Utica, OH 72-73 E 4
Utik Lake 61 KL 3
Utikuma Lake 60 K 2
Utinga 100-101 D 7
Utinga, Santo André- 110 II b 2
Utique = Utica 166-167 M 1
Utiura-wan 142-143 R 3
Utnūr 138-139 G 8
Utopia, AK 58-59 J 3-4
Utopia, TX 76-77 E 8
Utopia, New York-, NY 82 III d 2
Utorgoš 124-125 H 4
Utoy Creek 85 II b 2
Utracán 106-107 E 6
Utracán, Valle de — 106-107 E 6
Utraula 138-139 J 4
Utrecht 120-121 K 2
Utrecht [ZA] 174-175 J 4
Utrera 120-121 E 10
Utrillas 120-121 G 8
Utsjoki 116-117 M 3
Utsunomiya 142-143 QR 4
Utta 126-127 M 3
Uttamapālaiyam 140 C 6
Uttamapālaiyam = Uttamapālaiyam
140 C 6
Uttaradit 148-149 D 3
Uttar Andamān = North Andaman
134-135 P 7
Uttar Pradesh 134-135 MN 5
Uttarākhāsi 138-139 G 2
Uttar Shālmāri = North Sālmāra
141 B 2
Uttar Lakhīmpur = North Lakhimpur
141 CD 2
Uttarpāra-Kotrung 154 II ab 2
Uttar Pradesh 134-135 MN 5
Uttar Shālmāri = North Sālmāra
141 B 2
'Uttī = Ootacamund 140 C 5
Uttnoor = Utnūr 138-139 G 8

Utukok River 58-59 GH 2
Utunomiya = Utsunomiya
142-143 QR 4
Utupua 148-149 I 7
Uture Mēda Palāna < 140 E 6
Uturē Palāna < 140 E 6
Utva 124-125 T 8

Uu = Wuhu 142-143 M 5
Uudenmaan lääni 116-117 K-M 7
Uusikaarlepyy = Nykarleby
116-117 K 6
Uusikaupunki 116-117 J 7
Uusimaa 116-117 KL 7

Üva [CL] 140 E 7
Uva [SU] 124-125 T 5
Uva̧, Laguna — 94-95 F 6
Uva, Río — 94-95 G 6
Uvaia 102-103 G 6
Uvalde, TX 64-65 G 6
Üva Palāna < 140 E 7
Uvarovo 124-125 NO 8
Uvat 132-133 M 6
Uvea 148-149 b 1
Uvea = Île Ouvéa 158-159 N 4
Uvinza 172 F 2-3
Uvira 172 E 2
Uvod' 124-125 N 5
Uvs 142-143 G 2
Uvs nuur 142-143 G 1

Uwajima 142-143 P 5
'Uwayjā', Al- 134-135 G 6
Uwayl 164-165 K 7
'Uwaynāt, Jabal al- 164-165 K 4
'Uwaynidhīyah, Jazīrat al- 173 DE 4
'Uwayqilah, Ma'ātin — 136-137 C 7
'Uwayriḍ, Ḥarrat al- 134-135 D 5
Uwaysit 136-137 GH 7
Uwazima = Uwajima 142-143 P 5
Uwimbi 172 FG 3
Uwinsa = Uvinza 172 F 2-3

Uxbridge 72-73 G 2
Uxbridge, London- 129 II a 1
Uxin Ju 146-147 B 2
Uxin Qi 146-147 B 2
Uxmal 64-65 J 7

Uyak Bay 58-59 KL 8
Uyere 168-169 G 4
Uyowa 171 BC 4
Uyu Myit 141 D 3
Uyuni 92-93 F 8
Uyuni, Salar de — 92-93 F 9

Už 126-127 D 1
Uza 124-125 P 7
'Uzaym, Shaṭṭ al- 136-137 L 5
'Uzayr, Al- 134-135 F 6
Uzbek Soviet Socialist Republic
134-135 J-K 2-3
Uzboj 134-135 H 2-3
Uzcudun 108-109 F 5
Uzda 124-125 F 7
Uzen', Bol'šoj — 126-127 O 2
Uzen', Malyj — 126-127 O 2
Uzès-le-Duc = Wādī-al-Abṭāl
166-167 G 2
Uzgorod 126-127 A 2
Užgorod 126-127 A 2
Uzinki = Ouzinkie, AK 58-59 LM 8
Uzkoje, Moskva- 113 V b 3
Uzlovaja 124-125 LM 7
Uzlovoje 126-127 A 2
Uzundere 154 I b 1
Uzunköprü 136-137 B 2
Uzun yaylā 136-137 G 3
Uzunye burnu 154 I b 1

Užur 132-133 QR 6

V

Vääkiö 116-117 N 5
Vaala 116-117 M 5
Vaalbrivier 174-175 EF 5
Vaaldam 172 E 7
Vaal-Harts-Weir 174-175 F 5
Vaal River = Vaalrivier 172 E 7
Vaalrivier 172 E 7
Vaalwater 172 E 6
Våäna 124-125 E 4
Vaasa 116-117 J 6
Vāc 118 J 5
Vača [SU] 124-125 O 6
Vacacaí 106-107 K 3
Vacacaí, Rio — 106-107 L 2-3
Vaca Cuá 106-107 HJ 2
Vacamonte, Punta — 64-65 b 3
Vacaria 111 F 3
Vacaria, Campos da — 106-107 M 2
Vacaria, Rio — [BR, Mato Grosso do
Sul] 102-103 E 4
Vacaria, Rio — [BR, Minas Gerais]
102-103 L 2
Vacas, Sierra de las —
Vacaville, CA 74-75 BC 3
Vach 132-133 O 5
Vachš 134-135 K 3
Vachtan 124-125 Q 5
Väckelsång 116-117 F 9
Vâda [IND] 138-139 D 8
Vadakara = Badagara 140 B 5
Vāḍēl = Vāḍa 138-139 D 8
Vader, WA 66-67 B 2
Vadheim 116-117 A 7
Vaḍhvan = Wadhwān 134-135 L 6
Vadnagar 138-139 D 6

Vestspitsbergen 116-117 j-l 5
Vestur-Bardhastrandar 116-117 ab 2
Vestur-Húnavatn 116-117 cd 2
Vestur-Ísafjardhar 116-117 b 1-2
Vestur-Skaftafell 116-117 de 3
Vestvågøy 116-117 EF 3
Vesúvio 122-123 F 5
Vesuvius = Vesúvio 122-123 F 5
Veszprem 118 HJ 5
Vetāpālem 140 E 3
Vetka 124-125 H 7
Vetlanda 116-117 F 9
Vetluga [SU, place] 124-125 P 5
Vetluga [SU, river] 124-125 P 5
Vetlužskij 124-125 P 5
Vetralla 122-123 DE 4
Vetrenyj Pojas, kr'až — 124-125 K-M 2
Vetrivier 174-175 F 4
Vevay, IN 70-71 H 6
Vevay, OH 72-73 D 5
Veynes 120-121 K 6
Veyo, UT 74-75 G 4
Veys 136-137 N 7
Vézère 120-121 H 6
Vezirköprü 136-137 F 2

V. Gómez 106-107 F 5

Via Appia 113 II b 2
Via Aurelia 113 II a 2
Via Cassia 113 II a 1
Viacha 92-93 F 8
Via Flaminia 113 II b 1
Vialar = Tīsamsīlt 166-167 G 2
Viale 106-107 GH 3
Viamão 106-107 M 3
Viamonte 106-107 F 4
Vian, OK 76-77 G 5
Viana [BR, Espírito Santo] 100-101 D 11
Viana [BR, Maranhão] 92-93 K 5
Viana, Ilha do — 110 I c 2
Viana del Bollo 120-121 D 7
Viana do Castelo 120-121 C 8
Vianópolis 92-93 K 8
Viarèggio 122-123 CD 4
Via Tiburtina 113 II c 2
Vibank 61 G 5
Víbora, La — 76-77 C 9
Viborg 116-117 C 9
Viborg, SD 68-69 H 4
Viborg = Vyborg 132-133 DE 5
Vibo Valentia 122-123 FG 6
Vic 120-121 J 8
Vicálvaro, Madrid- 113 III b 2
Vicência 100-101 G 4
Vicente, Point — 74-75 D 6
Vicente Guerrero [MEX, Baja California Norte] 86-87 BC 2
Vicente Guerrero [MEX, Durango] 86-87 HJ 6
Vicente López 106-107 H 5
Vicente López-Carapachay 110 III b 1
Vicente López-Florida 110 III b 1
Vicente López-Munro 110 III b 1
Vicentina 102-103 E 5
Vicenza 122-123 D 3
Viceroy 68-69 D 1
Vichada 94-95 FG 5
Vichada, Río — 92-93 F 4
Vichadero 106-107 K 3
Viche 96-97 B 1
Vichigasta 106-107 D 2
Vichuquén 106-107 A 5
Vichuquén, Laguna de — 106-107 AB 5
Vichy 120-121 J 5
Vici, OK 76-77 E 4
Vicksburg, AZ 74-75 FG 6
Vicksburg, MI 70-71 H 4
Vicksburg, MS 64-65 HJ 5
Viçosa [BR, Alagoas] 100-101 F 5
Viçosa [BR, Minas Gerais] 102-103 L 4
Viçosa do Ceará 100-101 D 2
Victor, CO 68-69 D 6
Victor, ID 66-67 H 4
Victor, MT 66-67 F 2
Victor Harbor 158-159 G 7
Victor-Hugo = Ḥamādīyah 166-167 GH 2
Victoria, KS 68-69 G 6
Victoria, TX 64-65 G 6
Victoria [AUS] 158-159 HJ 7
Victoria [BOL] 104-105 G 6
Victoria [CDN] 56-57 M 8
Victoria [HK] 142-143 LM 7
Victoria [MAL] 148-149 FG 5
Victoria [PE] 96-97 D 5
Victoria [RA] 111 DE 4
Victoria [RCH, Araucanía] 111 B 5
Victoria [RCH, Magallanes y Antártica Chilena] 108-109 E 9
Victoria [SY] 204-205 N 9
Victoria [WAN] 164-165 F 8
Victoria [ZW] 172 F 6
Victoria, Ciudad — 64-65 G 7
Victoria, Île — = Victoria Island 56-57 O-Q 3
Victoria, La — [CO, Bogotá] 94-95 CD 5
Victoria, La — [CO, Valle del Cauca] 91 III a 3
Victoria, La — [YV] 94-95 H 2
Victoria, Lake — [AUS] 160 E 4
Victoria, Lake — [lake] 172 F 2
Victoria, Mount — 148-149 N 8
Victoria, Mount — = Tomaniive 148-149 a 2
Victoria, Pont — 82 I b 2
Victoria, San Fernando- 110 III b 1
Victoria and Albert Mountains 56-57 VW 1-2
Victoria Beach [CDN] 62 A 2
Victoria Beach [WAN] 170 III b 2
Victoria Cove 63 J 3
Victoria de Durango 64-65 F 7
Victoria de las Tunas 64-65 L 7
Victoria Harbour 155 I ab 2
Victoria Hill 88-89 JK 2
Victoria Island [CDN] 56-57 O-Q 3
Victoria Island [WAN] 170 III b 2
Victoria-Kennedy Town 155 I a 2
Victoria-Lai Chi Kok 155 I a 1
Victoria Lake [CDN] 63 H 3
Victoria Lake [ZA] 170 V b 2
Victoria Land 53 B 17-15
Victoria Memorial 154 II b 2
Victoria-North Point 155 I b 2
Victoria Park [GB] 129 II b 1
Victoria Park [HK] 155 I b 2
Victoria Peak 60 DE 4
Victoria Peak [HK] 155 I a 2
Victoria Peak [USA] 76-77 B 7
Victoria Point = Kawthaung 148-149 C 4
Victoria River 158-159 EF 3
Victoria River Downs 158-159 F 3
Victoria-Sai Wan Ho 155 I b 2
Victoria-Sai Ying Poon 155 I a 2
Victoria-Sau Ki Wan 155 I b 2
Victoria Strait 56-57 QR 4
Victoria-Tai Hang 155 I b 2
Victoria-Tai Koo Shing 155 I b 2
Victoria Taungdeik 141 CD 5
Victoriaville 72-73 KL 1
Victoria-Wan Chai 155 I ab 2
Victoria-Wes 172 D 8
Victoria West = Victoria-Wes 172 D 8
Victorica 111 C 5
Victorino 92-93 F 4
Victorino de la Plaza 106-107 F 6
Victorville, CA 74-75 E 5
Vičuga 132-133 G 6
Vicuña 106-107 B 2-3
Vicuña Mackenna 106-107 EF 4
Vicuña Mackenna, Sierra — 104-105 AB 9
Vicus 96-97 AB 4
Vida, MT 68-69 D 2
Vidal, CA 74-75 F 5
Vidal Gormaz, Isla — 108-109 B 8-9
Vidalia, GA 80-81 E 4
Vidalia, LA 78-79 D 5
Videau, Península — 108-109 C 7
Videira 102-103 G 7
Videla 106-107 G 3
Vidim 132-133 T 6
Vidin 122-123 K 3-4
Vidio, Cabo — 120-121 DE 7
Vidisha 134-135 M 6
Vidlica 124-125 HJ 3
Vidor, TX 76-77 GH 7
Vidos 154 I a 2-3
Vidra 122-123 M 3
Vidzeme 124-125 EF 5
Vidzju 124-125 S 3
Vidzy 124-125 F 6
Viedma 111 D 6
Viedma, Lago — 111 B 7
Viena 96-97 D 7
Vienchan = Vientiane 148-149 D 3
Vienna, GA 80-81 E 4
Vienna, IL 70-71 F 7
Vienna, MO 70-71 E 6
Vienna, SD 68-69 H 3
Vienna, WV 72-73 F 5
Vienna = Wien 118 H 4
Vienne [F, place] 120-121 K 6
Vienne [F, river] 120-121 H 5
Vien Pou Kha 150-151 C 2
Vientiane 148-149 D 3
Viento, Cordillera del — 106-107 B 6
Viento, Meseta del — 108-109 C 7
Vientos, Los — 111 BC 2
Vientos, Paso de los — 64-65 M 7-8
Vientos, Planicie de los — 106-107 E 7
Vieques 64-65 N 8
Vierfontein 174-175 G 4
Vierwaldstätter See 118 D 5
Vierzon 120-121 J 5
Viesca 86-87 J 5
Viesīte 124-125 E 5
Vieste 122-123 G 5
Vietnam 148-149 D 2-E 4
Viêt Tri 148-149 E 2
Vieux Carré, New Orleans-, LA 85 I b 2
Vieux Fort 88-89 Q 8
Vievis 124-125 E 6
View, TX 76-77 E 6
View Park, CA 83 III bc 1
Vieytes 106-107 J 5
Viga 124-125 O 4
Viga, Cerro de la — 106-107 B 3
Vigan 148-149 GH 3
Vigário Geral, Rio de Janeiro- 110 I b 1
Vigia 92-93 K 5
Vigía, Cabo — 108-109 F 7
Vigía, El — 92-93 E 3
Vigia, Isla — = Keppel Island 108-109 K 8
Vigía Chico 86-87 R 8
Vigia de Curvaradó 94-95 C 4
Vignola 122-123 D 3
Vigo 120-121 C 7
Vigten Islands = Vikna 116-117 D 5
Vihāri 138-139 D 2
Vihowā 138-139 C 2
Vihren 122-123 K 5
Viipuri = Vyborg 132-133 DE 5
Viitasaari 116-117 LM 6
Vijāpur 138-139 D 6
Vijāpur = Bijāpur 134-135 LM 7
Vijayadurg 140 A 2
Vijayanagaram = Vizianagaram 134-135 NO 7
Vijayawāda 134-135 N 7
Vijaypur = Bijaipur 138-139 F 4
Vik 116-117 d 3
Vika 116-117 M 4
Vikārābād 140 C 2
Viking 56-57 O 7
Vikna 116-117 D 5
Vikøyri 116-117 B 7
Vila [RA] 106-107 G 3
Vil'a [SU] 124-125 O 6
Vila [Vanuatu] 158-159 N 3
Vila Arriaga = Bibala 172 B 4
Vila Artur de Paiva = Cubango 172 C 4
Vila Balneária, Rio de Janeiro- 110 I b 3
Vila Bastos, Santo André- 110 II b 2
Vila Bela 104-105 G 3
Vila Bittencourt 98-99 D 5
Vila Boaçava, São Paulo- 110 II a 1
Vila Cabral = Lichinga 172 G 4
Vila Cocaia, Guarulhos- 110 II b 1
Vila Conceição, Diadema- 110 II b 3
Vila Coutinho 172 F 4
Vila da Maganja 172 G 5
Vila de Aljustrel = Cangamba 172 C 4
Vila de Aviz = Oncócua 172 B 5
Vila de João Belo = Xai Xai 172 F 7
Vila de Manica = Manica 172 F 5
Vila de Sena 172 FG 5
Vila Fontes 172 G 5
Vila Fontes = Caia 172 G 5
Vila Formosa, São Paulo- 110 II bc 2
Vila Franca de Xira 120-121 C 9
Vila Galvão, Guarulhos- 110 II b 1
Vila General Machado = Coeli 172 C 4
Vila Gouveia = Catandica 172 F 5
Vila Guilherme, São Paulo- 110 II b 2
Vila Henrique de Carvalho = Saurimo 172 D 3
Vilaine 120-121 F 5
Vila Jaguara, São Paulo- 110 II a 2
Vila João de Almeida = Chibia 172 B 5
Vilaller 120-121 H 7
Vila Luísa 174-175 K 3
Vila Luso = Moxuco 172 CD 4
Vilama, Lago de — 104-105 C 8
Vila Macedo, Guarulhos- 110 II b 1
Vila Macedo do Cavaleiros = Andulo 172 C 4
Vila Madalena, São Paulo- 110 II a 2
Vila Marechal Carmona = Vige 172 C 3
Vila Maria, São Paulo- 110 II b 2
Vila Mariana, São Paulo- 110 II b 2
Vila Mariano Machado = Ganda 172 B 4
Vila Matilde, São Paulo- 110 II bc 2
Vilanculos 172 G 6
Viļāni 124-125 F 5
Vila Norton de Matos = Balombo 172 B 4
Vila Nova, Rio — 98-99 MN 4
Vila Nova do Seles 172 B 4
Vila Paiva Couceiro = Gambos 172 BC 4
Vila Pedro II, Rio de Janeiro- 110 I a 1
Vila Pereira d'Eça = N'Giva 172 C 5
Vila Pery = Manica 172 F 5
Vila Prudente, São Paulo- 110 II b 2
Vila Real 120-121 D 8
Vila Real de Santo Antônio 120-121 D 10
Vilar Formoso 120-121 D 8
Vila Roçadas = Roçadas 172 C 5
Vilas, SD 68-69 H 3
Vila Salazar = N'Dala Tando 172 BC 3
Vila Teixeira da Silva = Bailundo 172 C 4
Vila Teixeira de Sousa = Luau 172 CD 4
Vilāttikuļam 140 D 6
Vila Velha [BR, Amapá] 98-99 N 3
Vila Velha [BR, Espírito Santo] 92-93 LM 9
Vila Viçosa 120-121 D 9
Vilavila 104-105 C 7
Vilcabamba 96-97 E 8
Vilcabamba, Cordillera — 92-93 E 7
Vilcanota, Cordillera de — 96-97 E 8-F 9
Vilcanota, Río — 96-97 F 8-9
Vilcún 106-107 A 7
Viled' 124-125 R 3
Vilejka 124-125 F 6
Vilela 106-107 H 5
Vilelas 106-107 F 1
V. I. Lenina, Mavzolej — 113 V c 2-3
Vilgo, Sierra de — 106-107 D 2-3
Vil'gort [SU, Komi ASSR] 124-125 S 3
Vil'gort [SU, Perm'skaja Oblast'] 124-125 V 3
Vil'gort [SU, Syktyvkar] 132-133 HJ 5
Vilhelmina 116-117 G 5
Vilhena 92-93 G 7
Vilija 124-125 EF 6
Viljandi 124-125 E 4
Viljoenskroon 174-175 G 4
Vilkaviškis 124-125 D 6
Vil'kickogo, ostrov — [SU, East Siberian Sea] 132-133 de 2
Vil'kickogo, ostrov — [SU, Kara Sea] 132-133 NO 3
Vil'kickogo, proliv — 132-133 S-U 2
Vilkija 124-125 D 6
Vilkitsky Island = ostrov Vil'kickogo 132-133 NO 3
Vilkovo 126-127 D 4
Villa Abecia 92-93 FG 9
Villa Aberastain 106-107 C 3
Villa Acuña 76-77 D 8
Villa Acuña, GA 78-79 G 3
Villa Ada 113 II b 1
Villa Adelina, San Isidro- 110 III b 1
Villa Ahumada 86-87 G 2
Villa Aldama 86-87 K 4
Villa Ana 106-107 H 2
Villa Ángela 111 D 3
Villa Atamisqui 106-107 F 2
Villa Atuel 106-107 CD 5
Villa Ballester, General San Martín- 110 III b 1
Villa Barilari, Avellaneda- 110 III b 2
Villa Bella 92-93 F 7
Villa Berthet 104-105 F 10
Villablino 120-121 D 7
Villa Borghese 113 II b 1-2
Villa Bosch, General San Martín- 110 III b 1
Villa Brana 102-103 A 7
Villa Bruzual 94-95 G 3
Villa Bustos 106-107 D 2
Villacañas [E] 120-121 F 9
Villa Cañás [RA] 106-107 G 5
Villacarillo 120-121 F 9
Villa Carlos Paz 106-107 E 3
Villa Castelli 106-107 CD 2
Villach 118 F 5
Villacidro 122-123 C 6
Villa Cisneros = Ad-Dakhlah 164-165 A 4
Villa Clara = Clara 106-107 H 3
Villa Coapa, Tlalpan- 91 I c 3
Villa Colón 106-107 CD 3
Villa Constitución [MEX] 86-87 E 5
Villa Constitución [RA] 106-107 GH 4
Villa Coronado 86-87 H 4
Villa Cristóbal Colón, Avellaneda- 110 III b 2
Villa Cura Brochero 106-107 E 3
Villada 120-121 E 7
Villa de Cos 86-87 J 6
Villa de Cura 92-93 F 2-3
Villa de la Quebrada 106-107 DE 4
Villa del Cerro, Montevideo- 106-107 J 5
Villa del Rosario 106-107 F 3
Villa del Señor, Punta — 106-107 AB 3
Villa del Totoral 106-107 EF 3
Villa de María 111 D 3
Villa de Mayo, General Sarmiento- 110 III a 1
Villa de Praga 106-107 E 4
Villa de Ramos 86-87 K 6
Villa Devoto, Buenos Aires- 110 III b 1
Villa Diamante, Lanús- 110 III b 2
Villa Dolores 111 C 4
Villa Domínguez = Domínguez 106-107 H 3
Villa Dominico, Avellaneda- 110 III c 2
Villa Doria Pamphili 113 II b 2
Villa El Chocón 106-107 C 7
Villa Elisa 106-107 H 4
Villa Escolar 104-105 G 10
Villa Federal = Federal 111 E 4
Villa Flores 86-87 O 9
Villa Florida 102-103 D 7
Villa Franca [PY] 102-103 CD 7
Villafranca del Bierzo 120-121 D 7
Villafranca de los Barros 120-121 DE 9
Villafranca del Penedès 120-121 H 8
Villa Frontadó 94-95 K 2
Villa Frontera 64-65 F 6
Villagarcía de Arosa 120-121 C 7
Village Green, PA 84 III a 2
Villa General Roca 106-107 D 4
Villa Gesell 106-107 J 6
Village Square, LA 85 I c 2
Villágio Duca degli Abruzzi = Joowhar 172 J 1
Villa Grove, IL 70-71 FG 6
Villaguay 111 E 4
Villa Guillermina 106-107 H 2
Villa Gutiérrez 106-107 E 3
Villa Hayes 102-103 D 6
Villahermosa [MEX] 64-65 H 8
Villa Hernandarias 106-107 H 3
Villa Hidalgo 86-87 H 4
Villa Huidobro 106-107 E 5
Villa Industrial 104-105 B 5
Villa Iris 106-107 F 7
Villa Jiménez 106-107 E 1
Villa José L. Suárez, General San Martín- 110 III b 1
Villajoyosa 120-121 GH 9
Villa Krause 106-107 C 3
Villa La Angostura 108-109 D 3
Villa Larca 106-107 E 4
Villa Larroque = Larroque 106-107 H 4
Villaldama 76-77 D 9
Villa Lía 106-107 H 5
Villalonga 108-109 H 2
Villa López 76-77 B 9
Villa Lugano, Buenos Aires- 110 III b 2
Villa Luiza = Vila Luísa 174-175 K 3
Villa Lynch, General San Martín- 110 III b 1
Villa Madero, La Matanza- 110 III b 2
Villa Mantero 106-107 H 4
Villa María 111 D 4
Villa María Grande 106-107 H 3
Villa Maza = Maza 106-107 F 6
Villa Mazán 111 C 3
Villa Media Agua 106-107 CD 3
Villamil 92-93 A 5
Villa Minetti 106-107 G 2
Villa Moderna 106-107 E 5
Villa Montes 92-93 G 9
Villance, Cañada de — 106-107 D 4
Villa Nora 174-175 GH 2
Villanova, PA 84 III ab 1
Villanova i la Geltrú 120-121 HJ 8
Villanova University 84 III a 1
Villanueva, NM 76-77 B 5
Villanueva [CO, Bolívar] 94-95 D 2
Villanueva [CO, Guajira] 94-95 E 2
Villanueva [RA, Buenos Aires] 106-107 H 5
Villa Nueva [RA, Córdoba] 106-107 F 4
Villa Nueva [RA, Mendoza] 106-107 C 4
Villanueva de Córdoba 120-121 E 9
Villanueva de la Serena 120-121 E 9
Villanveva 86-87 J 6
Villa Obregón 91 I b 2
Villa Obregón-Alpes 91 I b 2
Villa Obregón-Mixcoac 91 I b 2
Villa Obregón-Molino do Rosas 91 I b 2
Villa Obregón-San Jerónimo Lídice 91 I b 3
Villa Obregón-Santa Fe 91 I b 2
Villa Obregón-Tizapán 91 I b 2
Villa Obregón-Unidad Santa Fe 91 I b 2
Villa Ocampo 111 DE 3
Villaodrid 120-121 D 7
Villa Ojo de Agua 111 D 3
Villa Oliva 102-103 D 6-7
Villapinzón 94-95 E 5
Villa Quesada 88-89 D 9
Villa Ramírez 106-107 GH 4
Villa Real, Buenos Aires- 110 III b 1
Villa Reducción 106-107 F 4
Villa Regina 106-107 D 7
Villa Rey 102-103 D 6
Villa Rica 104-105 C 2
Villarino, Punta — 108-109 G 3
Villa Rosario 94-95 E 4
Villarreal de los Infantes 120-121 GH 9
Villarrica [PY] 111 E 3
Villarrica [RCH] 108-109 C 2
Villarrica, Lago — 108-109 C 2
Villa Sáenz Peña, Buenos Aires- 110 III b 1
Villa San Isidro 106-107 CD 3
Villa San José 106-107 H 4
Villa San Martín 111 D 3
Villa Sarmiento 106-107 E 5
Villa Sauze 106-107 F 5
Villasboas 106-107 J 4
Villa Serrano 104-105 D 6
Villa Traful 108-109 D 3
Villa Trinidad 106-107 FG 3
Villa Tulumba 106-107 EF 3
Villa Unión [MEX, Coahuila] 76-77 D 8
Villa Unión [MEX, Sinaloa] 86-87 GH 6
Villa Unión [RA, La Rioja] 111 C 3
Villa Unión [RA, Santiago del Estero] 106-107 F 2
Villa Valeria 111 CD 4
Villaverde Bajo, Madrid- 113 III ab 2
Villavicencio [CO] 92-93 E 4
Villavicencio [RA] 106-107 C 4
Villaviciosa 120-121 E 7
Villa Victoria 86-87 J 8
Villavieja de Yeltes 120-121 D 8
Villa Viscara 104-105 D 6
Villazón [BOL, Chuquisaca] 104-105 E 7
Villazón [BOL, Potosí] 104-105 D 7-8
Villecresnes 129 I d 3
Villefranche-sur-Saône 120-121 K 5-6
Villejuif 129 I c 2
Ville-Marie 72-73 G 1
Villemomble 129 I cd 2
Villena 120-121 G 9
Villenes-sur-Seine 129 I a 2
Villeneuve-la-Garonne 129 I c 2
Villeneuve-le-Roi 129 I c 3
Villeneuve-Saint-Georges 120-121 J 4
Villeneuve-sur-Lot 120-121 H 6
Villeparisis 129 I d 2
Villepinte 129 I d 2
Ville Platte, LA 78-79 C 5
Villepreux 129 I b 2
Villers-le-Bel 129 I c 1
Villeta [CO] 94-95 D 5
Villeta [PY] 102-103 D 6
Villette, Paris-la — 129 I c 2
Villeurbanne 120-121 K 6
Villevaudé 129 I d 2
Villicún, Sierra de — 106-107 C 3
Villiers 174-175 H 4
Villiersdorp 174-175 C 7-8
Villiers-le-Bâcle 129 I b 3
Villiers-sur-Marne 129 I d 2
Villingen-Schwenningen 118 D 4
Villini, Roma- 113 II a 2
Villisca, IA 70-71 C 5
Villmanstrand = Lappeenranta 116-117 N 7
Villupuram 140 D 4-5
Vilnius 124-125 E 6
Vilnius-Nauja Vileika 124-125 EF 6
Vilos, Los — 111 B 4
Viloyo 104-105 C 6
Vilsandi 124-125 C 4
Vil'uj 132-133 W 5
Vil'ujsk 132-133 X 5
Vilyui = Vil'uj 132-133 X 5
Vimmerby 116-117 FG 9
Vimont 82 I a 1
Viña 106-107 G 4
Vina, CA 74-75 BC 3
Viña, La — [PE] 92-93 D 6
Viña, La — [RA] 111 C 3
Viña del Mar 111 B 4
Vinalhaven, ME 72-73 M 2-3
Viñalito, Bañados del — 104-105 E 9
Vinaroz 120-121 H 8
Vincennes 129 I c 2
Vincennes, IN 64-65 J 4
Vincennes Bay 53 C 11
Vinces 96-97 B 2
Vinchina 106-107 CD 2
Vinchina, Río — 106-107 C 2
Vinchos 96-97 D 8
Vinculo 91 III a 4
Vindelälven 116-117 H 5
Vindeln 116-117 HJ 5
Vindhya Achal = Panna Hills 138-139 H 5
Vindhya Range 134-135 L-N 6
Vineland, NJ 72-73 J 5
Vineyard Sound 72-73 L 4
Vinh = Xa-doai 148-149 E 3
Vinh Cam Ranh 150-151 G 7
Vinh Châu 150-151 EF 8
Vinh Ha Long 150-151 F 2
Vinh Hao = Tuy Phong 150-151 G 7
Vinh Linh 150-151 F 4
Vinh Lo'i 148-149 E 5
Vinh Long 148-149 E 4
Vinh Ninh = Ninh Giang 150-151 F 2
Vinho, País do — 120-121 CD 8
Vinh Phyên 150-151 EF 2
Vinh Thu'c, Đao — = Đao Kersaint 150-151 FG 2
Vinh Tuy 150-151 E 1
Vinh Yên 150-151 E 2
Vinings, GA 85 II b 1
Vinita, OK 76-77 G 4
Vinje 116-117 B 8
Vinjhān 138-139 B 6
Vinkekuil 174-175 D 7
Vinkeveen 128 I b 2
Vinkeveense plassen 128 I b 2
Vinkovci 122-123 H 3
Vinnica 126-127 D 2
Vinnitsa = Vinnica 126-127 D 2
Vinson, Mount — 53 B 28
Vinsulla 60 GH 4
Vinte de Setembro 98-99 J 11
Vinton, IA 70-71 DE 4
Vinton, LA 78-79 C 5
Vinton, VA 80-81 G 2
Vinuguṇḍa = Vinukonda 140 DE 2
Vinukonda 140 DE 2
Viola, KS 68-69 H 7
Violeta, La — 106-107 GH 4
Vioolsdrif 174-175 B 5
Vipos 104-105 D 10
Vipya Mountains 171 C 5
Virac 148-149 H 4
Viradouro 102-103 HJ 4
Virājapāṭā = Virarājendrapet 140 BC 4
Viramgām 134-135 L 6
Viramgaon = Viramgām 134-135 L 6
Virandozero 124-125 KL 1
Viranşehir 136-137 H 4
Virarājendrapet 140 BC 4
Viravaḷḷi 140 F 2
Virbalis 124-125 D 6
Virden 61 H 6
Virden, IL 70-71 F 6
Virden, NM 74-75 J 6
Vire 120-121 G 4
Virful Mindra 122-123 KL 3
Virgem da Lapa 102-103 L 2
Virgen, Punta — 106-107 AB 3
Vírgenes, Cabo — 111 C 8
Virgina Hills, VA 82 II a 2
Virgin Gorda 88-89 OP 5
Virginia, IL 70-71 EF 6
Virginia, MN 64-65 H 2
Virginia [USA] 64-65 KL 4
Virginia [ZA] 174-175 G 5
Virginia, La — 94-95 D 5
Virginia Beach, VA 80-81 HJ 2
Virginia City, MT 66-67 GH 3
Virginia City, NV 74-75 D 3
Virginia Highlands, Arlington-, VA 82 II a 2
Virginia Mountains 74-75 D 3
Virginiatown 62 M 2
Virgin Islands 64-65 NO 8
Virgin Mountains 74-75 FG 4
Virginópolis 102-103 L 3
Virgin River 74-75 FG 4
Virgolândia 102-103 LM 3
Virihaure 116-117 G 4
Virmond 102-103 FG 6
Viroflay 129 I b 2
Viroqua, WI 70-71 E 4
Virovitica 122-123 G 3
Virtaniemi 116-117 MN 3
Virtsu 124-125 D 4
Virú 96-97 B 6
Virú, Río — 96-97 B 6
Virudunagar 140 CD 6
Viruḍunagaram = Virudunagar 140 CD 6
Virunga, Parc national — 172 E 1-2
Vis 122-123 G 4
Visagapaṭāo = Vishākhapatnam 134-135 NO 7
Visakhapaṭṭaṇam = Vishākhapatnam 134-135 NO 7
Visalia, CA 74-75 D 4
Visapur 140 B 1
Visāvadar 138-139 C 7
Visayan Sea 148-149 H 4
Visby 116-117 GH 9
Visconde do Rio Branco 102-103 L 4
Viscount 61 F 4
Viscount Melville Sound 56-57 O-Q 3
Višegrad 122-123 H 4
Višera [SU, river ◁ Kama] 124-125 V 3
Višera [SU, river ◁ Vyčegda] 124-125 S 2
Višerskij kanal 124-125 HJ 4
Viseu [BR] 92-93 K 5
Viseu [P] 120-121 D 8
Vişeu-de-Sus 122-123 L 2
Vishākhapatnam 134-135 NO 7
Vishanpur = Bishenpur 134-135 P 6
Vishnupur = Bishnupur 138-139 L 6
Vishvanāth = Bishnāth 141 C 2
Visim 124-125 V 4
Visitation, Île de la — 82 I b 1
Visnagar 138-139 D 6
Višnevec 126-127 B 2
Viso, Monte — 122-123 B 3
Visrivier 174-175 B 4
Vissannapeta 140 E 2
Vista Alegre [BR, Rio Amazonas] 98-99 H 4
Vista Alegre [BR, Rio Içana] 98-99 DE 4
Vista Alegre [PE] 96-97 B 5
Vista Alegre [RA, La Pampa] 106-107 D 6
Vista Alegre [RA, Neuquén] 106-107 C 7
Vista Bella 91 I b 1
Vista Nova 100-101 D 8
Vista Reservoir 66-67 F 5
Vistula = Wisła 118 K 3
Vit 122-123 L 4
Vita [IND] 140 B 2
Vita, Río — 94-95 G 5
Vite = Vita 140 B 2
Vitebsk 124-125 H 6
Viterbo 122-123 DE 4
Vitiaz Strait 148-149 N 8
Vitichi 92-93 F 9
Vitícola, La — 106-107 F 7
Viti Levu 148-149 a 2
Vitim 132-133 V 6
Vitimskoje ploskogorje 132-133 V 7
Vitinia, Roma- 113 II ab 2
Vitjaz Deep 142-143 S 3
Vitor 96-97 F 10
Vitor, Río — 96-97 F 10
Vitoria [BR, Espírito Santo] 92-93 LM 9
Vitória [BR, Pará] 98-99 MN 6
Vitoria [E] 120-121 F 7
Vitória, Ilha da — 102-103 K 5
Vitória da Conquista 92-93 L 7
Vitória de Santo Antão 100-101 G 5
Vitória do Mearim 100-101 B 2
Vitorino Freire 100-101 B 3
Vitoša Planina 122-123 K 4
Vitré 120-121 G 4
Vitry-le-François 120-121 K 4
Vitshumbi 171 B 3
Vittangi 116-117 JK 4
Vit Thu Lu 150-151 F 4
Vittòrio d'Africa = Shalanbod 172 HJ 1
Vittòrio Vèneto 122-123 E 2
Vitu Islands 148-149 g 5
Vivarais, Monts du — 120-121 K 6
Vivario 122-123 C 4
Vivero 120-121 D 7
Vivi 132-133 S 4
Vivi, ozero — 132-133 R 4
Vivian 61 K 6
Vivian, LA 76-77 GH 6
Vivian, SD 68-69 F 4
Vivoratá 111 E 5
Vivsta 116-117 G 6
Viyḷupuram = Villupuram 140 D 4-5
Vižaj 124-125 VW 3
Vižajskij zavod = Krasnovišersk 132-133 K 5
Vizcachas, Meseta de las — 111 B 8
Vizcaíno, Desierto de — 86-87 CD 4
Vizcaíno, Sierra — 64-65 D 6
Vize 136-137 B 2
Vize, ostrov — 132-133 O 2
Vizianagaram 134-135 NO 7
Vizinga 132-133 HJ 5
Vižnica 126-127 B 2

Vjatka = Kirov 132-133 HJ 6
Vjosë 122-123 HJ 5

Vlaanderen 120-121 J 3
Vladikavkaz = Ordžonikidze 126-127 M 5
Vladimir 132-133 FG 6
Vladimir Iljič Lenina 124-125 Q 7
Vladimirovka [SU, Kazachskaja SSR] 126-127 P 1
Vladimirovka [SU, Rossijskaja SFSR] 126-127 MN 2
Vladimirovka [SU, Ukrainskaja SSR Doneckaja Oblast'] 126-127 H 3
Vladimirovka [SU, Ukrainskaja SSR Nikolajevskaja Oblast'] 126-127 F 3
Vladimir Volynskij 126-127 B 1
Vladislavovka 126-127 G 4
Vladivostok 132-133 Z 9
Vladyčnoje 124-125 M 4
Vlakfontein 174-175 F 4
Vlasenica 122-123 H 3
Vlasotince 122-123 K 4
Vleifontein 174-175 D 7

376 Vestspit

Vlezenbeek 128 II a 2
Vlissingen 120-121 J 3
Vlorë 122-123 H 5
Vltava 118 G 4

Vochma [SU, place] 124-125 Q 4
Vochma [SU, river] 124-125 Q 4
Vochtoga 124-125 N 4
Vodla 124-125 L 3
Vodlozero 124-125 L 2
Vodnyj 124-125 T 2
vodopad Girvas 124-125 J 2
vodopad Kivač 124-125 J 2
Voëleiland 174-175 G 7
Vœune Sai 148-149 E 4
Vogas 104-105 F 1
Vogel Creek 85 III c 1
Vogelkop = Candravasih 148-149 K 7
Vogel Peak 168-169 HJ 3
Vogelsang, Winterthur- 128 IV b 1
Vogelsberg [D, mountain] 118 D 3
Vogelsberg [D, place] 128 III b 2
Vogelsdorf [DDR, Frankfurt] 130 III c 1
Voghera 122-123 C 3
Vohémar = Vohimarina 172 K 4
Vohibinany 172 JK 5
Vohimarina 172 K 4
Vohipeno 172 J 6
Voi [EAK, place] 172 G 2
Voi [EAK, river] 171 D 3
Voinjama 164-165 BC 7
Voiron 120-121 K 6
Vojejkov šelfovyj lednik 53 C 12-13
Vojkovo 126-127 F 4
Vojvodina 122-123 HJ 3
Voj-Vož 124-125 U 2
Volborg, MT 68-69 D 3
Volcán, Cerro — 108-109 E 5
Volcán, Cerro del — 106-107 BC 3
Volcán, El — 106-107 BC 4
Volcán, Sierra del — 106-107 H 6
Volcán Antofalla 104-105 BC 9
Volcán Antuco 106-107 B 6
Volcán Apagado 104-105 BC 8
Volcán Atitlán 64-65 H 9
Volcán Barú 64-65 K 10
Volcán Calbuco 108-109 C 3
Volcán Callaquén 106-107 B 6
Volcán Copiapó 106-107 C 1
Volcán Corcovado 111 B 6
Volcán Cosigüina 64-65 J 9
Volcán Cutanga 94-95 C 7
Volcán de Fuego 64-65 H 9
Volcán Descabezado Grande 106-107 B 5
Volcán de Tacaná 86-87 O 10
Volcán de Tajumulco 64-65 H 8
Volcán Domuyo 111 BC 5
Volcán Guallatiri 104-105 B 6
Volcán Irazú 64-65 K 9
Volcán Irruputunco 104-105 B 7
Volcán Lanín 111 B 5
Volcán Lascan 104-105 C 8
Volcán Lastarria 104-105 B 9
Volcán Llaima 106-107 B 7
Volcán Llullaillaco 111 C 2-3
Volcán Maipo 111 C 4
Volcán Minchinmávida 108-109 C 4
Volcán Miño 104-105 B 7
Volcano Bay = Uchiura-wan 144-145 b 2
Volcano Islands 206-207 RS 7
Volcán Orosi 64-65 JK 9
Volcán Osorno 111 B 6
Volcán Overo 106-107 BC 5
Volcán Paricutín 64-65 F 8
Volcán Pihuel 106-107 C 6
Volcán Pular 111 C 2
Volcán Purace 94-95 C 6
Volcán Putana 104-105 C 8
Volcán San Pedro 92-93 F 9
Volcán Socompa 111 C 2
Volcán Sotará 94-95 C 6
Volcán Sumaco 96-97 C 2
Volcán Tacora 111 C 1
Volcán Tinguiririca 106-107 B 5
Volcán Tonorio 88-89 D 9
Volcán Tutupaca 92-93 E 8
Volcán Viejo 88-89 C 8
Volchov [SU, place] 132-133 E 5-6
Volchov [SU, river] 124-125 HJ 4
Volchovstroj = Volchov 132-133 E 5-6
Volčja 126-127 H 2
Volčki 124-125 N 7
Volda 116-117 B 6
Voľdino 124-125 U 2
Volga [SU, place] 124-125 M 5
Volga [SU, river] 132-133 F 6
Volgodonsk 126-127 L 3
Volgo-Donskoj kanal 126-127 LM 2
Volgograd 126-127 LM 2
Volgograd-Beketovka 126-127 M 2
Volgograd-Krasnoarmejsk 126-127 M 2
Volgogradskoje vodochranilišče 126-127 MN 1-2
Volgoverchovje 124-125 J 5
Volhynia and Podolia, Hills of — = Volynskaja vozvyšennosť 126-127 BC 1
Volin, SD 68-69 H 4
Volketswil 128 IV b 1
Volkovysk 124-125 DE 7
Volksdorfer Wald 130 I b 1
Volkspark Hamburg 130 I a 1
Volkspark Jungfernheide 130 III b 1
Volkspark Klein Glienicke 130 III a 2
Volkspark Rehberge 130 III b 1
Volkspark Wuhlheide 130 III c 2
Volksrust 174-175 H 4
Volnovacha 126-127 H 3

Voločanka 132-133 R 3
Voloč'ok 124-125 NO 2
Volodarsk 124-125 O 5
Volodarsk, Pošechonje- 124-125 MN 4
Volodarsk-Volynskij 126-127 D 1
Vologda 132-133 FG 6
Vologino 126-127 P 1
Volokolamsk 124-125 KL 5
Volokonovka 126-127 HJ 1
Voloma 124-125 P 3
Vološka [SU, place] 124-125 MN 3
Vološka [SU, river] 124-125 M 3
Volosovo 124-125 G 4
Volosskaja Balakleja 126-127 JK 2
Volot 124-125 H 5
Volovec 126-127 A 2
Volovo 124-125 LM 7
Vološin 124-125 F 6
Voľsk 132-133 H 7
Volta [BR] 100-101 E 5
Volta [GH] 164-165 E 7
Volta, Black — 164-165 D 7
Volta, Lake — 164-165 DE 7
Volta, White — 164-165 D 7
Volta Grande 102-103 L 4
Volta Noire [HV, administrative unit] 168-169 E 2
Volta Noire [HV, river] 164-165 D 6
Volta Redonda 102-103 KL 5
Voltera 122-123 D 4
Voltti 116-117 K 6
Volturino, Monte — 122-123 FG 5
Volturno 122-123 F 5
Volubilis 164-165 C 2
Voluntad 106-107 G 6
Volynskaja Oblasť 124-125 DE 8
Volynskaja vozvyšennosť 126-127 BC 1
Volžsk 132-133 H 6
Volžskij 126-127 M 2
Vôma 124-125 D 4
Vona = Perşembe 136-137 G 2
Von Frank Mount 58-59 K 5
Vong Phu, Nui — 150-151 G 6
Vonguda 124-125 M 2
Von Martius, Salto — 92-93 J 7
von Otterøya 116-117 I 5
Vop' 124-125 J 6
Vopnafjördhur [IS, bay] 116-117 fg 2
Vopnafjördhur [IS, place] 116-117 f 2
Vorarlberg 118 DE 5
Vorderrhein 118 D 5
Vordingborg 116-117 D 10
Vorenža 124-125 K 2
Vorga 124-125 J 7
Vorjapauľ 132-133 L 5
Vorkuta 132-133 L 4
Vormsi 124-125 D 4
Vorochta 126-127 B 2
Vorogovo 132-133 QR 5
Vorona 124-125 O 7
Voroncovo [SU, Dudinka] 132-133 PQ 3
Voroncovo [SU, Pskovskaja Oblasť] 124-125 G 5
Voronež [SU, Rossijskaja SFSR place] 124-125 M 8
Voronež [SU, Rossijskaja SFSR river] 124-125 MN 7
Voronež [SU, Ukrainskaja SSR] 124-125 J 8
Voronezh = Voronež 124-125 M 8
Voronežskij zapovednik 124-125 MN 8
Voronino 124-125 P 4
Voronje [SU, Kirovskaja Oblasť] 124-125 ST 4
Voronok 124-125 J 7
Voronovo 124-125 E 6
Voropajevo 124-125 F 6
Vorošilovgrad = Vorošilovgrad 126-127 JK 2
Vorošilov = Ussurijsk 132-133 Z 9
Vorošilovgrad 126-127 JK 2
Vorotan 126-127 M 7
Vorožba 126-127 FG 1
Vorpommern 118 F 1-2
Vorskla 126-127 G 2
Võrtsjärv 124-125 E 4
Võru 124-125 F 5
Vorzel' 126-127 E 1
Vosburg 174-175 E 6
Vösendorf 113 I b 2
Vosges 120-121 L 4-5
Voskapel 128 II b 1
Voskresensk 124-125 LM 6
Voskresenskoje [SU, Vologodskaja Oblasť ↑ Čerepovec] 124-125 LM 4
Voss 116-117 B 7
Vostočnyj 113 V d 2
Vostočnyje Karpaty 126-127 AB 2-3
Vostočnyj Sajan 132-133 R 6-T 7
Vostok [Antarctica] 53 B 11
Vostok [island] 156-157 K 5
Votchoj = Jegyrjach 132-133 M 5
Votice 118 G 4
Votkinsk 132-133 J 6
Votkinskoje vodochranilišče 132-133 JK 6
Votuporanga 102-103 H 4
Vouga 120-121 C 8
Vouonkoro Rapides 168-169 E 3
Vožajeľ 124-125 S 2
Voža'ol 124-125 RS 2
Vože, ozero — 124-125 M 3
Vožega 124-125 N 3
Vožgaly 124-125 S 4
Voznesenje 124-125 KL 3
Voznesensk 126-127 E 3
Voznesensk-Ivanovo = Ivanovo 132-133 FG 6

Voznesenskoje 124-125 O 6
Vozroždenija, ostrov — 132-133 KL 9
Vozvraščenija, gora — 132-133 b 8

Vraca 122-123 K 4
Vradijevka 126-127 E 3
Vranje 122-123 J 4
Vrbas [YU, place] 122-123 H 3
Vrbas [YU, river] 122-123 G 3
Vrede 174-175 H 4
Vredefort 174-175 G 4
Vredenburg 174-175 B 7
Vreed-en-Hoop 92-93 H 3
Vreeland 128 I b 2
Vriddachalam = Vriddhāchalam 140 D 5
Vriddhāchalam 140 D 5
Vrindāvan 138-139 F 4
Vrouwenakker 128 I a 2
Vrouwentroost 128 I a 2
Vršac 122-123 J 3
Vryburg 172 D 7
Vryheid 172 F 7

Vschody 124-125 JK 6
Vsetín 118 J 4
Vsevidof, Mount — 58-59 m 4
Vsevidof Island 58-59 m 4

Vu Ban 150-151 E 2
Vukovar 122-123 H 3
Vu Lao 150-151 DE 1
Vulcan 61 B 5
Vulcano, Ìsola — 122-123 F 6
Vu Liêt 150-151 E 3
Vulture, Monte — 122-123 F 5
Vũn = Wũn 138-139 G 7
Vundik Lake 58-59 Q 3
Vung Bên Goi = Vung Hon Khoi 150-151 G 6
Vung Hon Khoi 150-151 G 6
Vung Liêm 150-151 EF 7
Vung Rach Gia 150-151 E 8
Vung Tau 150-151 F 7
Vuotso 116-117 M 3
Vuria 171 D 3
Vurnary 124-125 Q 6
Vuyyūru 140 E 2

Vyāra 138-139 D 7
Vyatka = Kirov 132-133 HJ 6
Vyazma = V'az'ma 124-125 K 6
Vyborg 132-133 DE 5
Vyčegda 132-133 J 5
Vyčegodskij 124-125 Q 3
Vychegda = Vyčegda 132-133 J 5
Vychino, Moskva- 113 V d 3
Vyg 124-125 K 2
Vygoda 126-127 AB 2
Vygozero 124-125 K 2
Vyksa 132-133 G 6
Vym' 124-125 S 2
Vypolzovo 124-125 J 5
Vyrica 124-125 H 4
Vyša 124-125 O 7
Vyshniy Volochek = Vyšnij Voloček 132-133 EF 6
Vyšnij Voloč'ok 132-133 EF 6
Vysock 124-125 G 3
Vysokaja, gora — 132-133 a 8
Vysokogornyj 132-133 ab 7
Vysokoje [SU, Belorusskaja SSR] 124-125 D 7
Vysokoje [SU, Rossijskaja SFSR] 124-125 K 5
Vysokovsk 124-125 KL 5
Vytegra 132-133 F 5

W

W, Parcs National du — 164-165 E 6

Wa 164-165 D 6
Wa, Nam — 150-151 C 3
Waajid 164-165 a 3
Waal 120-121 K 3
Waar, Mios — 148-149 KL 7
Wababimiga Lake 62 FG 2
Wabag 148-149 M 8
Wabamun 60 K 3
Wabana 56-57 a 8
Wabasca 60 L 1
Wabasca River 56-57 NO 6
Wabash, IN 70-71 H 5
Wabasha, MN 70-71 D 3
Wabash River 64-65 J 3
Wabassi River 62 F 1-2
Wabasso, MN 70-71 C 3
Wabeno, WI 70-71 F 3
Wabigoon 62 C 3
Wabimeig Lake 62 G 2
Wabī Shebelē 164-165 N 7
Wabowden 61 J 3
Wabu Hu 146-147 F 5
Wabuska, NV 74-75 D 3
Waccamaw, Lake — 80-81 G 3
Waccasassa Bay 80-81 b 2
Wachan = Wākhān 134-135 L 3
Wachenbuchen 128 III b 1
Waco 63 D 2
Waco, TX 64-65 G 5
Wād, Al- 166-167 E 2
Wada = Vāda 138-139 D 8
Wād ad-Dawmah 166-167 D 4
Wadah, Al- 173 D 6
Wād Aīt 'Aysā 166-167 E 3
Wād al-'Abīd 166-167 CD 3-4
Wād al-Akhḍar 166-167 C 4
Wād al-Ḥamrā' 166-167 B 6
Wād al-Ḥaṭāb 166-167 L 2

Wād al-Ḥāy 166-167 E 2
Wād al-Khaṭṭ 164-165 B 3
Wād al-Mā 164-165 C 4
Wād al-Mallāḥ 166-167 C 3
Wād an-Nayl 164-165 LM 6
Wād 'Aqqah 166-167 B 5
Wād Atūwī 164-165 B 4
Wād Awlaytīs 164-165 B 3
Wadayama 144-145 K 5
Wād Ayn Bin Tīlī 166-167 B 6-7
Wād Baḥt 166-167 D 3
Wād Bandah 164-165 K 6
Wād Bū Raghragh 166-167 C 3
Wād Dādis 166-167 C 4
Waddān 164-165 H 3
Waddiāram 140 D 2
Waddington, Mount — 56-57 LM 7
Wād Dra'ah 164-165 BC 3
Wadena 61 G 5
Wadena, MN 70-71 C 2
Wadesboro, NC 80-81 F 3
Wād Gharīs 166-167 D 3-4
Wād Grū' 166-167 C 3
Wād Ḥāmid 164-165 L 5
Wadhwān 134-135 L 6
Wādī, Bi'r al — 136-137 K 6
Wādī Abā' al-Qūr 136-137 J 7
Wādī Abū Ḥādd 173 D 7
Wādī Abū Jaḥaf 136-137 K 6
Wādī Abū Jīr 136-137 K 6
Wādī Abū Khārga = Wādī Abū Kharjah 173 BC 3
Wādī Abū Kharjah 173 BC 3
Wādī Abū Marw 173 C 6
Wādī ad-Dawāsir 134-135 EF 6
Wādī ad-Dawrah 166-167 DE 5
Wādī Ajaj 136-137 J 5
Wādī 'Akāsh = Wādī 'Ukāsh 136-137 J 5-6
Wādī al-Abṭāl 166-167 G 2
Wādī al-Abyaḍ 166-167 JK 2
Wādī al-Afal = Wādī al-'Ifāl 173 D 3
Wādī al-'Ain = Wādī al-'Ayn 134-135 H 6
Wādī al-'Allāqī 173 C 6
Wādī al-'Aqabah 173 CD 2-3
Wādī al-'Arab 166-167 K 2
Wādī al-'Arabah 136-137 F 7
Wādī al-'Arīsh 173 C 2-3
Wādī al-Asyūṭī 173 B 4
Wādī al-Aṭrash 173 C 4
Wādī al-'Ayn 134-135 H 6
Wādī al-Bāṭin 134-135 F 5
Wādī al-Faḥl 166-167 HJ 4
Wādī al-Fārigh 164-165 HJ 2-3
Wādī al-Fiḍḍah 166-167 GH 1
Wādī al-Gharbī 166-167 G 3-4
Wādī al-Ghinah 136-137 G 7-8
Wādī al-Ham 166-167 HJ 2
Wādī al-Ḥamḍ 134-135 D 5
Wādī al Ḥammāl = Wādī 'Ajaj 136-137 J 5
Wādī al-Ḥasā [JOR, Al-Karak] 136-137 F 7
Wādī al-Ḥasā [JOR, Ma'ān] 136-137 G 7
Wādī al-Ḥaṭab 173 C 7
Wādī al-Ḥazimī 136-137 J 6
Wādī al-Hilālī 136-137 J 7
Wādī al-Hirr 136-137 K 7
Wādī al-Ḥzimī = Wādī al-Ḥazimī 136-137 J 6
Wādī al-'Ifāl 173 D 3
Wādī al-Jadaf 134-135 E 4
Wādī al-Jarā' 166-167 H 6
Wādī al-Jizl 134-135 D 5
Wādī al-Karīmah 166-167 F 3
Wādī al-Kharīṭ 173 CD 5
Wādī al-Khirr 134-135 E 4
Wādī al-Khurr = Wādī al-Khirr 136-137 K 7
Wādī al-Makhrūq 136-137 G 7
Wādī al-Malik 164-165 KL 5
Wādī al-Mānī' 136-137 J 5-6
Wādī al-Masīlah 134-135 F 7
Wādī al-Mirā' 136-137 HJ 7
Wādī al-Mitlā 166-167 K 2
Wādī al-Miyāh 173 C 5
Wādī al-Miyāh = Wādī Jarīr 134-135 E 5-6
Wādī al-Qaṣab 136-137 K 4-5
Wādī al-Quffah 173 C 6
Wādī al-Ubayyiḍ 136-137 K 6
Wādī al-'Unnāb 136-137 G 7-8
Wādī al-Wirāj 173 B 3
Wādī 'Āmīj 136-137 J 6
Wādī an-Nāmūs 164-165 D 2
Wādī an-Naṭrūn 173 AB 2
Wādī an-Nisā' 166-167 J 3
Wādī 'Arabah 173 C 3
Wādī 'Ar'ar 136-137 J 7
Wādī ar-Ratam 166-167 J 3
Wādī ar-Ratka = Wādī ar-Ratqah 136-137 J 5-6
Wādī ar-Ratqah 136-137 J 5-6
Wādī ar-Rimah 134-135 E 5
Wādī ar-Ru'ays 166-167 M 7
Wādī ash-Sharmah = Wādī Ṣadr 173 D 3
Wādī ash-Shāzī 136-137 J 7
Wādī aṣ-Ṣahbā' 134-135 F 6
Wādī aṣ-Ṣawāb 136-137 J 5
Wādī as-Sāwrah 164-165 D 2-3
Wādī as Sirḥān 134-135 D 4
Wādī Asūf Malān 166-167 H 7
Wādī Athmāniyah 166-167 JK 1
Wādī ath-Tharthār 136-137 K 5
Wādī 'Aṭṭār 166-167 J 3
Wādī aṭ-Ṭarfā' 173 B 3
Wādī at-Tartār 136-137 K 5
Wādī at-Tawīl 166-167 H 2
Wādī at-Tubal 136-137 J 6
Wādī Azawak = Azaouak 164-165 E 5
Wādī Azlam 173 DE 4

Wādī az-Zargah 166-167 L 1
Wādī az-Zarqūn 166-167 H 3
Wādī Bad' 173 C 3
Wādī Bā'ir 136-137 G 7
Wādī Ban ar-Ramād 166-167 F 3
Wādī Bay al-Kabīr 164-165 GH 2
Wādī Bayzaḥ 173 C 5
Wādī Beizaḥ = Wādī Bayzaḥ 173 C 5
Wādī Bīshah 134-135 E 6-7
Wādī Damā 173 DE 4
Wādī Dīrīb 173 DE 6-7
Wādī Dufayt 173 D 6
Wādī Elei = Wādī Ilay 173 D 7
Wādī el-Kharīṭ = Wādī al-Kharīṭ 173 CD 5
Wādī el-Makhiruq = Wādī al-Makhrūq 136-137 G 7
Wadi el Melik = Wādī al-Malik 164-165 KL 5
Wādī el Milk = Wādī al-Malik 164-165 KL 5
Wādī el-'Unāb = Wādī al-'Unnāb 136-137 G 7-8
Wādī Fajr 134-135 D 5
Wādī Ghadūn 134-135 G 7
Wādī Gīr 166-167 E 4
Wādī Ḥabīb 173 BC 4
Wādī Ḥaḍramaut = Wādī al-Musīlah 134-135 FG 7
Wādī Ḥalfā 164-165 L 4
Wādī Ḥalfīn 134-135 H 6
Wādī Hamār 136-137 H 4
Wādī Ḥamīr [IRQ] 136-137 JK 7
Wādī Ḥamīr [Saudi Arabia] 136-137 J 7
Wādī Ḥanīfah 134-135 F 6
Wādī Ḥawashīyah 173 C 3
Wādī Ḥawrān 134-135 E 4
Wādī Ḥaymūr 173 C 6
Wādī Ḥōḍein = Wādī Ḥuḍayn 173 D 6
Wādī Ḥōrān = Wādī Ḥawrān 134-135 E 4
Wādī Ḥubāra = Wādī al-Asyūṭī 173 B 4
Wādī Ḥuḍayn 173 D 6
Wādī Huwār 164-165 K 5
Wādī Ibib 173 D 6
Wādī Ilay 173 D 7
Wādī Īmirhu 166-167 L 7
Wādī Īṭal 166-167 J 2-3
Wādī Jabjabah 173 C 7
Wādī Jaddī 164-165 E 2
Wādī Jafū 166-167 H 3
Wādī Jaghjagh 136-137 J 4
Wādī Jarārah 173 D 6
Wādī Jarīr 134-135 E 5-6
Wadi Jemal Island = Jazirat Wādī Jimāl 173 D 5
Wādī Jimāl 173 D 5
Wādī Jimāl, Jazīrat — 173 D 5
Wādī Jurdī 173 C 4
Wādī Kuruskū 173 C 6
Wādī Ma'ārik 136-137 H 7
Wādī Marsā 166-167 J 1
Wādī Mazār 166-167 G 3
Wādī Milāḥah 173 C 4
Wādī Mīnā 166-167 G 2
Wādī Miyāh 164-165 EF 2
Wādī Mizā 166-167 J 3
Wādī Muḥammadī 136-137 K 6
Wādī Mus'ūd 166-167 F 5-6
Wādī Natash 173 CD 5
Wād Īnāwīn 166-167 D 2
Wādī 'Or = Wādī Ur 173 B 6-7
Wādī Qabīṭ = Wādī Qitbīt 134-135 G 7
Wādī Qaṣab 173 C 4
Wādī Qenā = Wādī Qinā 173 C 4
Wādī Qinā 173 C 4
Wādī Qiraiya = Wādī Qurayyah 173 D 2
Wādī Qitbīt 134-135 G 7
Wādī Qurayyah 173 D 2
Wādī Rāhiyu 166-167 G 2
Wādī Raiāitīt = Wādī Rayāytīt 173 D 6
Wādī Ranyah 134-135 E 6
Wādī Rayāytīt 173 D 6
Wādī Ṣadr 173 D 3
Wādī Sannūr 173 B 3
Wādī Ṣayq 134-135 F 8
Wādī Shaḥan = Wādī Shiḥan 134-135 G 7
Wādī Sha'īt 173 C 5
Wādī Shanāshin 166-167 E 7
Wādī Shiḥan 134-135 G 7
Wādī Sīdī Mūsā 166-167 J 6
Wādī Sidr 173 C 3
Wādī Sudr = Wādī Sidr 173 C 3
Wādī Tafāssast 164-165 F 4
Wādī Tākwayat 164-165 E 4
Wādī Tamajirdayn 166-167 G 7
Wādī Tamanrāsat 164-165 E 4
Wādī Tanārūt 166-167 M 4-5
Wādī Tanizzuft 166-167 M 7
Wādī Tarāt 164-165 F 3
Wādī Tathlīth 134-135 E 6-7
Wādī Thalāthah 166-167 F 2
Wādī Tibell = Wādī at-Tubal 136-137 J 6
Wādī Tilayah 166-167 G 6
Wādī Tīn Tarābīn 164-165 F 4
Wādī Tiyarīt 166-167 LM 4
Wādī 'Ukāsh 136-137 J 5-6
Wādī Ur 173 B 6-7
Wādī Wardān 173 C 3
Wādī Yassar 166-167 H 1
Wādī Zāghrīr 166-167 J 3
Wādī Zamzam 164-165 G 2
Wādī Zaydūn 173 C 5
Wādī Zeidūn = Wādī Zaydūn 173 C 5

Wādī Zusfānah 166-167 EF 4
Wadki 138-139 G 7
Wād Lāū' [MA, place] 166-167 D 2
Wadley, GA 80-81 E 4
Wad Madanī 164-165 L 6
Wad Majradah 164-165 F 1
Wād Mallāg 166-167 L 1-2
Wād Milyān 166-167 LM 1
Wād Mūlūyā 164-165 D 2
Wād Nafīs 166-167 B 4
Wād Nūn 166-167 A 5
Wād S'bū' 164-165 CD 2
Wād Shārīf 166-167 E 3
Wād Silyānah 166-167 L 1-2
Wād Sūs 166-167 B 4
Wadsworth, NV 74-75 D 3
Wād Taghbālt 166-167 D 4
Wād Tamanārt 166-167 B 5
Wād Tansīft 164-165 C 2
Wād Ṭāṭah 166-167 B 5
Wād Tissāūt 166-167 C 4
Wād Tudghā' 166-167 D 4
Wadu Channel 176 a 2
Wād Umm ar-Rabīyah 164-165 C 2
Wād Warghah 166-167 D 2
Wād Zam 164-165 C 2
Wād Zimūl 166-167 C 5
Wād Zīz 166-167 D 4
Wād Zurūd 166-167 LM 2
Waegwan 144-145 G 4-5
Waelder, TX 76-77 F 8
Wa-fang-tien = Fu Xian 142-143 N 4
Wagal-bong = Maengbu-san 144-145 F 2
Wāgeima 141 D 7
Wageningen [SME] 92-93 H 3
Wager Bay 56-57 T 4
Waggaman, LA 85 I a 2
Wagga Wagga 158-159 J 7
Wagin 158-159 C 6
Wagina 148-149 j 6
Wagner, SD 68-69 G 4
Wagoner, OK 76-77 G 5
Wagon Mound, NM 76-77 B 4
Wagontire, OR 66-67 D 4
Wągrowiec 118 H 2
Wāḥah 164-165 H 3
Wahai 148-149 J 7
Wāḥāt ad-Dākhilah 164-165 K 3
Wāḥāt al-'Aṭrūn 164-165 K 5
Wāḥāt al-Baḥarīyah 164-165 K 3
Wāḥāt al-Farāfirah 164-165 K 3
Wāḥāt al-Jufrah 164-165 GH 3
Wāḥāt al-Kufrah 164-165 J 4
Wāhāt el Cufra = Wāḥāt al-Kufrah 164-165 J 4
Wāḥāt el-Khārga = Al-Wāḥāt al-Khārījah 164-165 KL 3-4
Wāḥat es Selīma = Wāḥāt Ṣalīmah 164-165 K 4
Wāḥāt Jālū 164-165 J 3
Wāḥāt Ṣalīmah 164-165 K 4
Wāḥāt Sīwah 164-165 K 3
Wahilah 166-167 D 6
Wahlbergøya 116-117 k 5
Wahlenbergfjord 116-117 kl 5
Wahoo, NE 68-69 H 5
Wahpeton, ND 68-69 H 2
Wahrān 164-165 D 1
Wahrān, Khalīj — 166-167 F 2
Wah Wah Mountains 74-75 G 3
Wāi 140 A 1-2
Waialua, HI 78-79 c 2
Waianae, HI 78-79 c 2
Waiau 161 E 6
Waiau River 161 E 6
Waidhofen an der Thaya 118 G 4
Waidmannslust, Berlin- 130 III b 1
Waifang Shan 146-147 C 5-D 4
Waigama 148-149 JK 7
Waigeo, Pulau — 148-149 K 6
Waigev = Pulau Waigeo 148-149 K 6
Waiheke Island 161 F 3
Waihi Beach 161 FG 3
Waihou River 161 F 3-4
Waikabubak 148-149 G 8
Waikaremoana, Lake — 161 G 4
Waikawa 161 CD 8
Waikerie 158-159 GH 6
Waimate 158-159 O 8
Waimea, HI [USA, Hawaii] 78-79 e 2-3
Waimea, HI [USA, Kanai] 78-79 c 2
Wai Mesuji 152-153 F 7-8
Wainganga 134-135 MN 6-7
Waingapu 148-149 GH 8
Waingapu, Teluk — 152-153 O 10
Waingmau 141 E 3
Waingmaw = Waingmau 141 E 3
Waini Point 92-93 H 3
Wainwright 61 C 4
Wainwright, AK 56-57 DE 3
Waipahu, HI 78-79 c 2
Waipara 161 E 6
Waipukurau 161 G 4-5
Wairāgarh 138-139 H 7
Wairau River 161 E 5
Wairoa 158-159 P 7
Wai Silumpur 152-153 F 7
Waitaki River 158-159 O 8
Waitara 158-159 OP 7
Waitarini = Baitarani 138-139 KL 7
Waitsap = Huaiji 142-143 L 7
Waitsburg, WA 66-67 D 2
Wai Tulangbawang 152-153 F 8
Waiwerang 152-153 P 10
Waiyeung = Huiyang 142-143 LM 7
Wajh, Al- 134-135 D 5
Wajima 144-145 L 4
Wak, El — 172 H 1
Waka 172 D 2

Wakamatsu = Aizu-Wakamatsu 144-145 M 4
Wakamatsu-shima 144-145 G 6
Wakamiya, Ichikawa- 155 III c 1
Wakasa 144-145 K 5
Wakasa-wan 144-145 K 5
Wakatipu, Lake — 161 C 7
Wakaw 61 F 4
Wakayama 142-143 Q 5
Wake 156-157 H 4
Wa Keeney, KS 68-69 G 6
Wakefield, KS 68-69 H 6
Wakefield, MA 84 I b 1
Wakefield, MI 70-71 F 2
Wakefield, NE 68-69 H 4
Wakefield, New York-, NY 82 III cd 1
Wake Forest, NC 80-81 G 3
Wakeham = Maricourt 56-57 W 5
Wakema = Wāgeima 141 D 7
Wākhān 134-135 L 3
Wākhjīr, Koṭal — 134-135 LM 3
Waki 140 A 1
Wakinosawa 144-145 N 2
Wakkanai 142-143 R 2
Wakkerstroom 174-175 J 4
Wakō 155 III a 1
Wakomata Lake 70-71 J 2
Wakool 160 G 5
Wākṣa = Wāqiṣah 136-137 K 7
Wakunai 148-149 j 6
Wakwayowkastic River 62 L 1-2
Walad Bū 'Alī 166-167 M 2
Walad Ghalal 166-167 J 2
Walahae, Sungai — 152-153 NO 8
Wālājāpet 140 D 4
Walakpa, AK 58-59 HJ 1
Wa'lan 164-165 E 4
Walapai, AZ 74-75 G 5
Walasmula 140 E 7
Walātah 164-165 C 5
Walātah, Ḍhar — 164-165 C 5
Walawē Ganga 140 E 7
Wałbrzych 118 H 3
Walcha 160 KL 3
Walcheren 120-121 J 3
Walcott 60 D 2
Walcott, ND 68-69 H 2
Walcott, WY 68-69 C 5
Wałcz 118 H 2
Waldacker 128 III b 1
Waldegg [CH] 128 IV a 1
Walden, CO 68-69 CD 5
Waldenau-Datum 130 I a 1
Walden Pond 84 I c 2
Walden Ridge 78-79 G 3
Waldfriedhof München 130 II ab 2
Waldhofen an der Ybbs 118 G 5
Waldo, AR 78-79 C 4
Waldo, FL 80-81 bc 2
Waldpark Marienhöhe 130 I a 1
Waldperlach, München- 130 II bc 2
Waldport, OR 66-67 A 3
Waldron, AR 76-77 GH 5
Waldstadion 128 III ab 1
Walea, Selat — 152-153 P 6
Wales, AK 56-57 C 4
Wales, MN 70-71 E 2
Wales Island 56-57 T 4
Walfergem 128 II a 1
Walgaon 138-139 F 7
Walgett 158-159 J 6
Walgreen Coast 53 B 26
Walhalla, MI 70-71 GH 3
Walhalla, ND 68-69 H 1
Walhalla, SC 80-81 E 3
Wālidīyah 166-167 B 3
Waligiro 171 DE 3
Walikale 172 E 2
Walker, MN 70-71 C 2
Walker, SD 68-69 F 3
Walkerbaai 174-175 C 8
Walker Bay = Walkerbaai 174-175 C 8
Walker Cove 58-59 x 9
Walker Lake [CDN] 61 K 3
Walker Lake [USA] 64-65 C 4
Walker Mountain 80-81 F 2
Walker Mountains 53 B 26-27
Walker River Indian Reservation 74-75 D 3
Walkerton 72-73 F 2
Walkerton, IN 70-71 G 5
Walkerville, MT 66-67 G 2
Walkite = Welkītē 164-165 M 7
Wall, SD 68-69 E 3-4
Wallace 72-73 GH 2
Wallace, ID 66-67 EF 2
Wallace, MI 70-71 G 3
Wallace, NC 80-81 GH 3
Wallace, NE 68-69 F 5
Wallaceburg 72-73 E 3
Wallal Downs 158-159 D 3-4
Wallangarra 160 KL 2
Wallaroo 158-159 G 6
Wallasey 119 E 5
Walla Walla, WA 64-65 C 2
Wallekraal 174-175 B 6
Wallel = Tulu Welēl 164-165 LM 7
Wallīj, Sha'īb al- 136-137 H 6
Wallingford, CT 72-73 K 4
Wallingford, PA 84 III a 2
Wallington, NJ 82 III b 1
Wallington, London- 129 II b 2
Wallis, TX 76-77 F 8
Wallis, Îles — 148-149 b 1
Wall Lake, IA 70-71 C 4
Wallowa, OR 66-67 E 3
Wallowa Mountains 66-67 E 3
Wallowa River 66-67 E 3
Wallula, WA 66-67 D 2
Walmer 174-175 F 7
Walney 119 E 4
Walnut, IL 70-71 F 5
Walnut, KS 70-71 C 7

Walnut 377

Walnut, MS 78-79 E 3
Walnut Bend, Houston-, TX 85 III a 2
Walnut Canyon National Monument 74-75 H 5
Walnut Cove, NC 80-81 F 2
Walnut Creek 68-69 F 6
Walnut Grove, MO 70-71 D 7
Walnut Grove, MS 78-79 E 4
Walnut Park, CA 83 III c 2
Walnut Ridge, AR 78-79 D 2
Walod = Vālod 138-139 D 7
Walpole 158-159 NO 4
Walpole, NH 72-73 K 3
Walrus Islands 58-59 GH 7
Walsall 119 F 5
Walsenburg, CO 68-69 D 7
Walsh 158-159 H 3
Walsh, CO 68-69 E 7
Waltair 140 F 2
Walterboro, SC 80-81 F 4
Walter D. Stone Memorial Zoo 84 I b 2
Walter Reed Army Medical Center 82 II ab 1
Walters, OK 76-77 E 5
Waltersdorf [DDR] 130 III c 2
Waltershof, Hamburg- 130 I a 1
Waltham 72-73 H 2
Waltham Forest, London- 129 II bc 1
Walthamstow, London- 129 II b 1
Walthill, NE 68-69 H 4
Waltman, WY 68-69 C 4
Walton, IN 70-71 G 5
Walton, KY 70-71 H 6
Walton, NY 72-73 J 3
Walton-on-Thames 129 II a 2
Walton Run 84 III d 1
Walt Whiteman Homes, NJ 84 III bc 2
Walt Withman Bridge 84 III c 2
Walvisbaai [ZA, bay] 174-175 A 2
Walvisbaai [ZA, place] 172 B 6
Walvis Bay = Walvisbaai [ZA, bay] 174-175 A 2
Walvis Bay = Walvisbaai [ZA, place] 172 B 6
Walvis Ridge 50-51 K 7
Wamanfo 168-169 E 4
Wamba [EAK] 171 D 2
Wamba [WAN] 164-165 F 7
Wamba [ZRE, Bandundu] 172 C 3
Wamba [ZRE, Haut-Zaïre] 172 E 1
Wamego, KS 68-69 H 6
Wami 172 G 3
Wamlana 148-149 J 7
Wampú 88-89 D 7
Wanaaring 158-159 H 5
Wanaka, Lake — 161 C 7
Wan'an 146-147 E 8
Wanapiri 148-149 L 7
Wanapitei Lake 72-73 F 1
Wanapitei River 72-73 F 1
Wan Chai, Victoria- 155 I ab 2
Wanchuan = Zhangjiakou 142-143 L 3
Wanda 102-103 E 7
Wandarama 168-169 DE 3
Wanda Shan 142-143 P 2
Wandawasi = Wandiwāsh 140 D 4
Wandering River 60 L 2
Wandingzhen 141 EF 3
Wandiwāsh 140 D 4
Wandle 129 II b 2
Wan-do 144-145 F 5
Wandoan 158-159 JK 5
Wandse 130 I b 1
Wandsworth, London- 129 II b 2
Wanfu 144-145 D 2
Wanfu He 146-147 F 4
Wang, Mae Nam — 150-151 B 3
Wanganella 160 G 5
Wanganui 158-159 OP 7
Wanganui River 161 F 4
Wangaratta 158-159 J 7
Wangary 160 B 5
Wangasi 168-169 E 3
Wang-chia-ch'ang = Wangjiachang 146-147 C 7
Wang-chiang = Wangjiang 146-147 F 6
Wang Chin 150-151 B 4
Wangdu 146-147 E 2
Wangen [CH] 128 IV b 1
Wangen [D] 130 II a 2
Wangener Wald 128 IV b 1
Wanggamet, Gunung — 152-153 NO 10-11
Wangi 171 E 3
Wangiwangi, Pulau — 152-153 PQ 8
Wangjiachang 146-147 C 7
Wangjiang 146-147 F 6
Wangkiang = Wangjiang 146-147 F 6
Wang Lan 155 I b 2
Wangmudu 146-147 E 9
Wang Nua 150-151 B 3
Wangpang Yang 142-143 N 5
Wangpan Yang 146-147 H 6
Wang Saphung 150-151 CD 4
Wang Thong 150-151 C 4
Wangtu = Wangdu 146-147 E 2
Wangyemiao = Ulan Hot 142-143 N 2
Wanhsien = Wan Xian [TJ, Hebei] 146-147 E 2
Wanhsien = Wan Xian [TJ, Sichuan] 142-143 K 5
Wani, Gunung — 152-153 P 8
Wānkāner 138-139 C 6
Wankie = Hwange 172 E 5
Wankie National Park 172 E 5
Wanleweeyn 164-165 NO 8
Wannian 146-147 F 7
Wanning 142-143 L 8
Wannsee 130 III a 2
Wannsee, Berlin- 130 III a 2
Wanon Niwat 150-151 D 4
Wanparti 140 D 2
Wanshan Liehtao = Wanshan Qundao 146-147 DE 11
Wanshan Qundao 146-147 DE 11
Wanstead, London- 129 II c 1
Wantan 146-147 C 6
Wan-ta Shan-mo = Wanda Shan 142-143 P 2
Want'ing = Wandingzhen 141 EF 3
Wantsai = Wanzai 142-143 LM 6
Wan Xian [TJ, Hebei] 146-147 E 2
Wan Xian [TJ, Sichuan] 146-147 B 6
Wanyuan 146-147 B 5
Wanzai 142-143 LM 6
Wanzhi 146-147 G 6
Wapakoneta, OH 70-71 HJ 5
Wapanucka, OK 76-77 F 5
Wapato, WA 66-67 C 2
Wapawekka Lake 61 FG 3
Wapello, IA 70-71 E 5
Wapi = Mu'o'ng Wapi 150-151 EF 5
Wapikham Tong 150-151 E 5
Wapi Pathum 150-151 D 5
Wapiti, WY 68-69 B 3
Wapiti River 60 GH 2
Wapsipinicon River 70-71 E 5
Wa-pu He = Wabu Hu 146-147 F 5
Waqbá, Al- 136-137 L 8
Waqf, Al- 173 C 4
Wāqif, Jabal al- 173 B 6
Wāqiṣah 136-137 K 7
Waqooyi-Galbeed 164-165 a 1
War, WV 80-81 F 2
Wārāh 138-139 A 4
Warān 164-165 BC 4
Warangal 134-135 MN 7
Wārāseoni 138-139 H 7
Waratah 160 b 2
Waratah Bay 160 GH 7
Warba, MN 70-71 D 2
Warburton [AUS, place] 160 G 6
Warburton [AUS, river] 158-159 G 5
Wardah, Rā's al- 166-167 L 1
Wardān, Wādī — 173 C 3
Ward Cove, AK 58-59 x 9
Warden 174-175 H 4
Warden, WA 66-67 D 2
Wardere = Werdēr 164-165 O 7
Wardha [IND, place] 134-135 M 6
Wardha [IND, river] 134-135 M 6
Ward Hunt, Cape — 148-149 N 8
Wardlow 61 C 5
Ware 56-57 LM 6
Ware, MA 72-73 KL 3
Waren [DDR] 118 F 2
Waren [RI] 148-149 L 7
Warghah, Wād — 166-167 D 2
Wari'ah, Al- 134-135 F 5
Warialda 158-159 K 5
Warin Chamrap 148-149 DE 3
Waring Mountains 58-59 GH 3
Waritchaphum 150-151 D 4
Wāriyapola 140 E 7
Warland, MT 66-67 F 1
Warman 61 E 4
Warmbad [Namibia, administrative unit] 174-175 BC 5
Warmbad [Namibia, place] 172 C 7
Warmbad [ZA] 172 EF 6
Warmsprings, MT 66-67 G 2
Warm Springs, OR 66-67 C 3
Warm Springs, NV [USA ↓ Cherry Creek] 74-75 F 3
Warm Springs, NV [USA → Tonopah] 74-75 EF 3
Warm Springs Indian Reservation 66-67 C 3
Warm Springs Valley 66-67 C 5
Warnemünde, Rostock- 118 F 1
Warner 66-67 GH 1
Warner, SD 68-69 G 3
Warner Range 64-65 B 3
Warner Robins, GA 64-65 K 5
Warner Valley 66-67 CD 4
Warnes [BOL] 92-93 G 8
Warnes [RA] 106-107 G 5
Waropko 148-149 LM 8
Warora 138-139 G 7
Warpath River 61 J 4
Warqlā 164-165 F 2
Wārqzīz, Jabal — 164-165 C 3
Warra 158-159 K 5
Warracknabeal 160 F 6
Warragul 160 G 7
Warraq al-'Arab 170 II b 1
Warraq al-Hadar, Jazīrah — 170 II b 1
Warrego River 158-159 J 5
Warren, AR 78-79 CD 4
Warren, AZ 74-75 J 7
Warren, ID 66-67 F 3
Warren, IL 70-71 EF 4
Warren, IN 70-71 H 5
Warren, MI 72-73 E 3
Warren, MN 68-69 H 1
Warren, OH 64-65 K 3
Warren, PA 72-73 G 4
Warren, TX 76-77 G 7
Warren [AUS] 160 HJ 3
Warren [CDN] 72-73 F 1
Warren Landing 61 J 4
Warrensburg, MO 70-71 CD 6
Warrenton 172 DE 7
Warrenton, GA 80-81 E 4
Warrenton, MO 70-71 E 6
Warrenton, NC 80-81 GH 2
Warrenton, OR 66-67 AB 2
Warrenton, VA 72-73 H 5
Warri 164-165 F 7
Warriner Creek 160 BC 2
Warrington, FL 78-79 F 5
Warrior, AL 78-79 F 4
Warrnambool 158-159 H 7
Warroad, MN 70-71 C 1
Warsaw, IL 70-71 E 5
Warsaw, IN 70-71 H 5
Warsaw, KY 70-71 H 6
Warsaw, MO 70-71 D 6
Warsaw, NC 80-81 GH 3
Warsaw, NY 72-73 GH 3
Warsaw = Warszawa 118 K 2
Wārshanīs, Jabal al- [DZ, mountain] 166-167 G 1-2
Wārshanīs, Jabal al- [DZ, mountains] 166-167 GH 2
Warszawa 118 K 2
Warta 118 HJ 2
Wartenberg, Berlin- 130 III c 1
Warton, Monte — 108-109 C 9
Wartrace, TN 78-79 F 3
Warud 138-139 FG 7
Warwick, GA 80-81 DE 5
Warwick, RI 72-73 L 4
Warwick [AUS] 158-159 K 5
Warwick [GB] 119 EF 5
Warwisch, Hamburg- 130 I b 2
Warzazāt 166-167 C 4
Wasa 60 K 5
Wasatch, UT 66-67 H 5
Wasatch Range 64-65 D 3-4
Wasbank 174-175 J 5
Wascana Creek 61 F 5
Waschbank = Wasbank 174-175 J 5
Wasco, CA 74-75 D 5
Wasco, OR 66-67 C 3
Wase 168-169 H 3
Waseca, MN 70-71 D 3
Wash, The — 119 G 5
Washago 72-73 G 2
Washakie Needles 68-69 B 4
Wāshaung 141 E 3
Washburn, ND 68-69 F 2
Washburn, TX 76-77 D 5
Washburn, WI 70-71 E 2
Washburn Lake 56-57 PQ 3
Washington, AK 58-59 vw 8
Washington, AR 76-77 GH 6
Washington, DC 64-65 LM 4
Washington, GA 80-81 E 4
Washington, IA 70-71 DE 5
Washington, IN 70-71 G 6
Washington, KS 68-69 H 6
Washington, MO 70-71 E 6
Washington, NC 80-81 H 3
Washington, PA 72-73 F 4
Washington [RA] 106-107 E 4
Washington [USA] 64-65 BC 2
Washington, Mount — 64-65 M 3
Washington-Anacostia, DC 82 II b 2
Washington-Bellevue, DC 82 II a 2
Washington-Brightwood, DC 82 II a 1
Washington-Brookland, DC 82 II b 1
Washington-Burleith, DC 82 II a 1
Washington-Capitol Hill, DC 82 II ab 2
Washington Cemetery 85 III b 1
Washington-Cleveland Park, DC 82 II a 1
Washington-Columbia Heights, DC 82 II a 1
Washington-Congress Heights, DC 82 II b 2
Washington-Deanewood, DC 82 II b 2
Washington-Eckington, DC 82 II ab 1
Washington-Georgetown, DC 82 II a 1
Washington-Glendale, DC 82 II b 2
Washington-Good Hope, DC 82 II b 2
Washington Island 70-71 G 3
Washington-Kent, DC 82 II a 1
Washington-Lamond, DC 82 II a 1
Washington-Langdon, DC 82 II b 1
Washington Monument 82 II a 2
Washington National Airport 82 II a 2
Washington Naval Station 82 II ab 2
Washington Park [USA, Atlanta] 85 II b 2
Washington Park [USA, Chicago] 83 II b 2
Washington-Tenleytown, DC 82 II a 1
Washington-Trinidad, DC 82 II b 2
Washington Virginia Airport 82 II a 2
Washita River 64-65 G 4-5
Washm, Al- 134-135 EF 5-6
Washow Bay 62 A 2
Wash Shahri 142-143 F 4
Wasilla, AK 58-59 N 6
Wasior 148-149 KL 7
Wasipe 168-169 E 3
Wāsit 136-137 L 6
Wāsiṭah, Al- 164-165 L 3
Waskada 68-69 F 1
Waskaiowaka Lake 61 K 2
Waskatenau 60 L 2
Waskesiu Lake 61 F 4
Waskish, MN 70-71 C 1
Waskom, TX 76-77 G 6
Wassamu 144-145 c 1-2
Wassberg 128 IV b 1
Wasser 174-175 C 4
Wassmannsdorf 130 III bc 2
Wassuk Range 74-75 D 3
Wasta, SD 68-69 E 3
Wasum 148-149 g 6
Waswanipi 62 N 2
Waswanipi, Lac — 62 N 2
Watabeag Lake 62 L 2
Watampone 148-149 GH 7
Watansoppeng 148-149 G 7
Wataru Channel 176 a 2
Wat Bot 150-151 C 4
Watchung Mountain 82 III a 1
Watcomb 62 D 3
Waterberg 172 C 6
Waterberge 174-175 GH 3
Waterbury, CT 72-73 K 4
Wateree River 80-81 F 3
Waterfall, AK 58-59 w 9
Waterford, CA 74-75 C 4
Waterford [CDN] 72-73 F 3
Waterford [IRL] 119 C 5
Waterford [ZA] 174-175 F 7
Watergang 128 I b 1
Waterhen Lake [CDN, Manitoba] 61 J 4
Waterhen Lake [CDN, Saskatchewan] 61 DE 3
Waterhen River 61 D 3
Waterkloof 174-175 F 6
Waterloo, IA 64-65 H 3
Waterloo, IL 70-71 EF 6
Waterloo, MT 66-67 G 3
Waterloo, NY 72-73 H 3
Waterloo [AUS] 158-159 EF 3
Waterloo [B] 120-121 K 3
Waterloo [CDN, Ontario] 72-73 F 3
Waterloo [CDN, Quebec] 72-73 K 2
Waterloo [WAL] 168-169 B 3
Waterpoort 174-175 H 2
Waterproff, LA 78-79 D 5
Waters, MI 70-71 H 3
Watersmeet, MI 70-71 F 2
Waterton Lakes National Park 60 KL 5
Waterton Park 60 KL 5
Watertown, MA 84 I ab 2
Watertown, NY 64-65 LM 3
Watertown, SD 64-65 G 2
Watertown, WI 70-71 F 4
Waterval-Boven 174-175 J 3
Water Valley, MS 78-79 E 3
Water Valley, TX 76-77 D 7
Waterval-Onder 174-175 J 3
Waterville, KS 68-69 H 6
Waterville, ME 64-65 N 3
Waterville, MN 70-71 D 3
Waterville, WA 66-67 CD 2
Waterways 56-57 OP 6
Waterworks Park 84 II c 2
Watford City, ND 68-69 E 2
Watganj, Calcutta- 154 II a 2
Wathaman River 61 G 2
Watino 60 J 2
Watkins Glen, NY 72-73 H 3
Watkinsville, GA 80-81 E 4
Watlam = Yulin 142-143 L 7
Watling Island = San Salvador 64-65 M 7
Watonga, OK 76-77 E 5
Watrous 61 F 5
Watrous, NM 76-77 B 5
Watsa 172 E 1
Watseka, IL 70-71 G 5
Wat Sing 150-151 BC 5
Watson 61 F 4
Watson, AR 78-79 D 4
Watson, UT 74-75 J 3
Watson Lake 56-57 L 5
Watsonville, CA 74-75 BC 4
Watt 128 IV a 1
Watt, Mount — 158-159 E 5
Wattegama 140 E 7
Watthana Nakhon 150-151 D 6
Watts, Los Angeles-, CA 83 III c 2
Watts Bar Lake 78-79 G 3
Watubela, Pulau-pulau — 148-149 K 7
Watu Bella Islands = Pulau-pulau Watubela 148-149 K 7
Watupayung, Tanjung — 152-153 P 10
Wau 148-149 N 8
Waubay, SD 68-69 H 3
Wauchope 160 L 3
Wauchula, FL 80-81 bc 3
Wau el Kebir = Wāw al-Kabīr 164-165 H 3
Wau en Namus = Wāw an-Nāmūs 164-165 H 4
Waugh 62 B 3
Waukarlycarly, Lake — 158-159 D 4
Waukeenah, FL 80-81 DE 5
Waukegan, IL 70-71 G 4
Waukesha, WI 70-71 F 4
Waukon, IA 70-71 E 4
Wauneta, NE 68-69 F 5
Waupaca, WI 70-71 F 3
Waupun, WI 70-71 F 4
Waurika, OK 76-77 F 5
Wausa, NE 68-69 H 4
Wausau, WI 64-65 J 2-3
Wausaukee, WI 70-71 FG 3
Wausawng = Wāshaung 141 E 3
Wauseon, OH 70-71 HJ 5
Wauthier-Braine 128 II a 2
Wautoma, WI 70-71 F 3
Wauwatosa, WI 70-71 F 4
Wave = Vāv 138-139 C 5
Wave Hill 158-159 F 3
Waver 128 I a 2
Waverley 174-175 G 6
Waverly, IA 70-71 D 4
Waverly, NY 72-73 H 3
Waverly, OH 72-73 E 5
Waverly, SD 68-69 H 3
Waverly, TN 78-79 F 2
Waverly, VA 80-81 H 2
Waverly, Sydney- 161 I b 2
Waverly Hall, GA 78-79 G 4
Waverveen 128 I a 2
Wāw [BUR] 141 E 7
Wāw [Sudan] 164-165 K 7
Wawa 70-71 H 1-2
Wawagosic, Rivière — 62 M 2
Wawaitin Falls 62 L 2
Wāw al-Kabīr 164-165 H 3
Wāw an-Nāmūs 164-165 H 4
Wawina 88-89 D 7
Wāwīzaght 166-167 C 3
Wawota 61 GH 6
Waxahachie, TX 76-77 F 6
Waxell Ridge 56-57 H 5
Way, Hon — 150-151 D 8
Way, Lake — 158-159 D 5
Wayan, ID 66-67 H 4
Wayang Satu, Singapore- 154 III ab 2
Waycross, GA 64-65 K 5
Wayland, KY 80-81 E 2
Wayland, MI 70-71 H 4
Wayne, NE 68-69 H 4
Wayne, PA 84 III a 1
Wayne, WV 72-73 E 5
Waynesboro, GA 80-81 EF 4
Waynesboro, MS 78-79 E 5
Waynesboro, PA 72-73 H 5
Waynesboro, TN 78-79 F 3
Waynesboro, VA 72-73 G 5
Waynesburg, PA 72-73 FG 5
Wayne State University 84 II b 2
Waynesville, MO 70-71 DE 7
Waynesville, NC 80-81 E 3
Waynoka, OK 76-77 E 4
Wayside, TX 76-77 D 5
Waza 164-165 G 6
Wāza Khwā 134-135 K 4
Wāzin 166-167 M 4
Wāzīrābād = Balkh 134-135 K 3
Wazz, Al- 164-165 L 5
Wazzān 164-165 C 2

Wealdstone, London- 129 II a 1
Weapons Range 61 D 3
Weather, Punta — 108-109 B 4
Weatherford, OK 76-77 E 5
Weatherford, TX 76-77 F 6
Weaubleau, MO 70-71 D 7
Weaverville, CA 66-67 B 5
Webb 61 D 5
Webb, TX 76-77 E 9
Webbe Shibeli = Wābi Shebelē 164-165 N 7
Weber, Mount — 60 C 2
Webi Ganaane 164-165 N 8
Webi Jestro = Weyb 164-165 N 7
Webi Shabeelle 164-165 N 8
Webi Shabēlle = Wabī Shebelē 164-165 N 7
Webster 60 H 2
Webster, MA 72-73 KL 3
Webster, SD 68-69 H 3
Webster City, IA 70-71 D 4
Webster Reservoir 68-69 G 6
Webster Springs, WV 72-73 F 5
Weda 148-149 J 6
Weddell Island 111 D 8
Weddell Sea 156-157 PQ 8
Wedding, Berlin- 130 III b 1
Wed ed Daura = Wādī ad-Dawrah 166-167 DE 5
Wedel Jarlsberg land 116-117 j 6
Wedgeport 63 C 6
Wed Igharghar = Wādī Irhāran 166-167 J 6
Wed Mia = Wādī Miyāh 164-165 EF 2
Wed Mulula = Wād Mūlūyā 164-165 D 2
Wed Nun = Wād Nūn 166-167 A 5
Wedowee, AL 78-79 G 4
Wed Saura = Wādī as-Sāwrah 164-165 D 2-3
Wed Shenashan = Wādī Shanāshīn 166-167 E 7
Wed Zem = Wād Zam 164-165 C 2
Weed, CA 66-67 B 5
Weedon Centre 72-73 L 2
Weedville, PA 72-73 G 4
Weeks, LA 78-79 D 6
Weeksbury, KY 80-81 E 2
Weenen 174-175 J 5
Weenusk = Winisk 56-57 T 6
Weeping Water, NE 70-71 BC 5
Weerde 128 II b 1
Weesow 130 III c 1
Wee Waa 158-159 J 6
Wegendorf 130 III d 1
Wegener-Inlandeis 53 B 36-1
Weh, Pulau — 148-149 BC 5
Weichang 142-143 M 3
Weichou Tao = Weizhou Dao 146-147 B 11
Weiden 118 EF 4
Weidling 113 I b 1
Weifang 142-143 MN 4
Weigongcun, Beijing- 155 II ab 2
Weihai 142-143 N 4
Wei He [TJ ◁ Hai He] 142-143 M 4
Wei He [TJ ◁ Huang He] 142-143 K 5
Wei He [TJ ◁ Laizhou Wan] 146-147 G 3
Wei Ho = Wei He [TJ ◁ Hai He] 146-147 F 2
Wei Ho = Wei He [TJ ◁ Laizhou Wan] 146-147 G 3
Weihsien = Wei Xian 146-147 E 3
Wei-hsien = Yu Xian 146-147 E 2
Weilmoringle 160 H 2
Weimar 118 E 3
Weimar, TX 76-77 F 8
Weinan 146-147 B 4
Weiner, AR 78-79 D 3
Weining 142-143 JK 6
Weiningen 128 IV a 1
Weipa 158-159 H 2
Weir 138-139 F 4
Weir River 61 L 2
Weirton, WV 72-73 F 4
Weisburd 102-103 A 7
Weiser, ID 66-67 E 3
Weiser River 66-67 E 3
Weishan Hu 146-147 F 4
Weishi 146-147 E 4
Weisse Elster 118 F 3
Weissenfels 118 E 3
Weisskirchen [D] 128 III a 1
Weiss Knob 72-73 G 5
Weissrand Mountains = Witrandberge 174-175 C 3
Weitzel Lake 61 E 2
Weixi 141 F 2
Wei Xian [TJ, Hebei] 146-147 E 3
Wei Xian [TJ, Shandong] 146-147 G 3
Weiyang = Huiyang 142-143 LM 7
Weizhou Dao 146-147 B 11
Wejh = Al-Wajh 134-135 D 5
Wekusko 61 J 3
Wekusko Lake 61 J 3
Welaung 141 C 5
Welbourn Hill 158-159 F 5
Welch, TX 76-77 CD 6
Welch, WV 80-81 F 2
Welcome Monument 154 IV a 2
Weldon, NC 80-81 H 2
Weldona, CO 68-69 E 5
Weldon River 70-71 D 5
Weldya 164-165 M 6
Weleetka, OK 76-77 FG 5
Welega 164-165 LM 7
Welel, Tulu — 164-165 LM 7
Welgeleë 174-175 G 5
Welhe 140 A 1
Wèligama 140 E 7-8
Wèlimada 140 E 7
Welkītē 164-165 M 7
Welkom 172 E 7
Welland 72-73 G 3
Welland Canal 72-73 G 3
Wèllawāya 140 E 7
Wellesley Islands 158-159 GH 3
Wellesley Lake 56-57 J 5
Wellingsbüttel, Hamburg- 130 I b 1
Wellington, CO 68-69 D 5
Wellington, KS 76-77 F 4
Wellington, NV 74-75 D 3
Wellington, OH 72-73 E 4
Wellington, TX 76-77 D 5
Wellington [AUS] 158-159 JK 6
Wellington [CDN] 72-73 H 3
Wellington [NZ, administrative unit] 161 F 4-G 5
Wellington [NZ, place] 158-159 OP 8
Wellington [ZA] 174-175 C 7
Wellington, Isla — 111 AB 7
Wellington Channel 56-57 S 2-3
Wellman, IA 70-71 E 5
Wellman, TX 76-77 C 6
Wells 60 G 3
Wells, MN 70-71 D 4
Wells, NE 68-69 F 4
Wells, NV 64-65 C 3
Wells, TX 76-77 G 7
Wells, Lake — 158-159 D 5
Wellsboro, PA 72-73 H 4
Wellsford 158-159 OP 7
Wells Gray Provincial Park 56-57 MN 7
Wells next the Sea 119 G 5
Wellston, OH 72-73 E 5
Wellsville, KS 70-71 C 6
Wellsville, MO 70-71 E 6
Wellsville, NY 72-73 H 3
Wellton, AZ 74-75 FG 6
Welo 164-165 MN 6
Wels 118 FG 4
Welsford 63 C 5
Welshpool 119 E 5
Wembere 172 F 2-3
Wembley 60 H 2
Wembley, London- 129 II a 1
Wembley Stadium [GB] 129 II a 1
Wembley Stadium [ZA] 170 V b 2
Wen'an 146-147 F 2
Wenasaga River 62 C 2
Wenatchee, WA 64-65 BC 2
Wenatchee Mountains 66-67 C 2
Wenchang 150-151 H 3
Wên-ch'ang = Wenchang 150-151 H 3
Wenchi 168-169 E 4
Wên-chou Wan = Wenzhou Wan 146-147 H 8
Wenchow = Wenzhou 142-143 N 6
Wendel, CA 66-67 CD 5
Wendell, ID 66-67 F 4
Wendell, NC 80-81 G 3
Wenden, AZ 74-75 G 6
Wendeng 146-147 J 3
Wendenschloss, Berlin- 130 III c 2
Wendling, OR 66-67 B 3
Wendover, UT 66-67 FG 5
Wendover, WY 68-69 D 4
Wendte, SD 68-69 F 3
Wener Lake = Vänern 116-117 E 8
Wengyuan 146-147 DE 9
Wen He 146-147 G 4
Wên-hsi = Wenxi 146-147 C 4
Wenling 146-147 H 7
Wennington, London- 129 II c 2
Wenquan 146-147 B 6
Wenshan 142-143 JK 7
Wenshang 146-147 F 4
Wenshan Zhuangzu Miaozu Zizhizhou 142-143 JK 7
Wenshi 146-147 C 9
Wên-shih = Wenshi 146-147 C 9
Wenshui 146-147 CD 3
Wên-su = Aqsu 142-143 E 3
Wenteng = Wendeng 146-147 J 3
Wentworth 158-159 H 6
Wentworth, SD 68-69 H 3-4
Wentzville, MO 70-71 E 6
Wenxi 146-147 C 4
Wenzhou 142-143 N 6
Wenzhou Wan 146-147 H 8
Wepener 172 E 7
Werdēr [ETH] 164-165 O 7
Werftpfuhl 130 III cd 1
Wernecke Mountains 56-57 JK 5
Werner Lake 62 B 2
Wernigerode 118 E 3
Wernsdorf 130 III c 2
Wernsdorfer See 130 III c 2
Werra 118 D 3
Werribee, Melbourne- 160 FG 6
Werris Creek 158-159 K 6
Wesel 118 C 3
Weser 118 D 2
Weserbergland 118 D 2-3
Weser Hills = Weserbergland 118 D 2-3
Weskan, KS 68-69 F 6
Wesleyville 63 K 3
Wesleyville, PA 72-73 FG 3
Wessel, Cape — 158-159 G 2
Wessel Islands 158-159 G 2
Wesselsbron 174-175 G 4
Wessington, SD 68-69 G 3
Wessington Hills 68-69 G 3
Wessington Springs, SD 68-69 G 3-4
Wesson, MS 78-79 D 5
West, MS 78-79 E 4
West, TX 76-77 F 7
Westall, Point — 160 AB 4
West Allis, WI 70-71 FG 4
West Australian Basin 50-51 P 7
West Bank 136-137 F 6-7
West Bay 78-79 E 6
West Bend, IA 70-71 C 4
West Bend, WI 70-71 FG 4
West Bengal 134-135 O 6
West Berlin, NJ 84 III d 3
West Blocton, AL 78-79 F 4
Westboro, WI 70-71 E 3
Westbourne 61 J 5
West Branch, MI 70-71 HJ 3
Westbridge 66-67 D 1
West Bristol, PA 84 III d 1
Westbrook, ME 72-73 L 3
Westbrook, TX 76-77 D 6
Westbury, Houston-, TX 85 III b 2
West Butte 66-67 H 1
Westby, MT 68-69 D 1
Westby, WI 70-71 E 4
West Caicos Island 88-89 K 4
West Canal 85 III c 1
West Caroline Basin 156-157 FG 4
West Carson, CA 83 III c 2
Westchester, Los Angeles-, CA 83 III b 2
Westchester, New York-, NY 82 III d 1
Westcliffe, CO 68-69 D 6
West Collingswood, NJ 84 III c 2
West Collingswood Heights, NJ 84 III c 2
West Columbia, SC 80-81 F 4
West Columbia, TX 76-77 FG 8
West Conshohocken, PA 84 III b 1
Westcotville, NJ 84 III c 3
West Des Moines, IA 70-71 CD 5
West Drayton, London- 129 II a 2
West End 88-89 G 1
Westend, Atlanta-, GA 85 II b 2
Westerland 118 D 1
Westerly, RI 72-73 L 4
Western [EAK] 172 F 1
Western [GH] 168-169 E 4
Western [Z] 172 D 4
Western Area 168-169 B 3
Western Australia 158-159 C-E 4-5
Western Bank 63 E 6
Western Carpathians = Biele Karpaty 118 HJ 4
Western Ghats 134-135 L 6-M 8
Western Isles = Açores 204-205 E 5
Western Peninsula 62 B 3
Western Port 158-159 HJ 7
Westernport, MD 72-73 G 5
Western Sahara 164-165 A 4-B 3
Western Sayan Mountains = Zapadnyj Sajan 132-133 Q-S 7
Western Shoshone Indian Reservation 66-67 E 4-5
Western Sierra Madre = Sierra Madre Occidental 64-65 E 5-F 7
Westerschelde 120-121 J 3
Westerville, OH 72-73 E 4
Westerwald 118 CD 3
West European Basin 50-51 HJ 3
West Falkland 111 D 8
Westfall, OR 66-67 E 3-4
Westfield 63 C 5
Westfield, MA 72-73 K 3
Westfield, NY 72-73 G 3
Westfield, PA 72-73 H 4
West Fork, AR 76-77 GH 5
West Fork Des Moines River 70-71 C 4
West Fork Fortymile 58-59 Q 5
West Fork Poplar River 68-69 CD 1
West Fork White River 70-71 G 6
West Frankfort, IL 70-71 F 7
West Frisian Islands 120-121 KL 2
Westgate 158-159 J 5
Westham, London- 119 FG 6
Westhaven 128 I a 1
West Haven, CT 72-73 K 4
Westhoff, TX 76-77 F 8
West Hollywood, CA 83 III b 1
Westhope, ND 68-69 F 1
West Ice Shelf 53 C 9
Westindien 64-65 LM 7
West Indies 64-65 L-O 7
West Irian 148-149 K 7-L 8

378 Walnut

West Jefferson, NC 80-81 F 2
West Lafayette, IN 70-71 G 5
Westlake, LA 78-79 C 5
Westlake, OR 66-67 A 4
Westland [NZ] 161 CD 6
Westland National Park 161 D 6
West Lanham Hills, MD 82 II b 1
West Laurel Hill Cemetery 84 III b 1
Westleigh 174-175 G 4
West Liberty, IA 70-71 E 5
West Liberty, KY 72-73 E 6
Westlock 60 L 2
West Los Angeles, Los Angeles-, CA 83 III b 1
West Manayunk, PA 84 III b 1
West Medford, MA 84 I b 2
West Memphis, AR 64-65 H 4
Westminster 174-175 G 5
Westminster, CO 68-69 D 6
Westminster, MD 72-73 H 5
Westminster, London- 129 II b 2
Westminster Abbey 129 II b 2
Westminster School 85 II b 1
West Monroe, LA 78-79 C 4
Westmont, CA 83 III c 2
Westmont, NJ 84 III c 2
Westmoreland, KS 68-69 H 6
Westmorland, CA 74-75 F 6
Westmount 82 I b 2
West Mountain 72-73 JK 3
West New York, NJ 82 III b 2
West Nicholson 172 EF 6
Weston, CO 68-69 D 7
Weston, ID 66-67 GH 4
Weston, MO 70-71 C 6
Weston, OR 66-67 D 3
Weston, WV 72-73 F 5
Weston [CDN] 72-73 G 3
Weston [MAL] 148-149 G 5
Weston-super-Mare 119 E 6
Westover, TX 76-77 E 6
West Palm Beach, FL 64-65 KL 6
West Pass 78-79 G 6
West Plains, MO 78-79 CD 2
West Point, GA 78-79 G 4
West Point, KY 70-71 H 7
West Point, MS 78-79 E 4
West Point, NE 68-69 H 5
West Point, NY 72-73 K 4
West Point, VA 80-81 H 2
West Point [CDN] 63 D 3
West Point [USA] 58-59 P 4
Westport, CA 74-75 AB 3
Westport, OR 66-67 B 2
Westport [CDN] 63 C 5
Westport [IRL] 119 AB 5
Westport [NZ] 158-159 O 8
West Pullman, Chicago-, IL 83 II b 2
Westray [CDN] 61 H 4
Westray [GB] 119 E 2
Westree 62 L 3
West Road River 60 EF 3
Westrode 128 II a 1
West Roxbury, Boston-, MA 84 I b 3
West Scotia Basin 50-51 G 8
West Somerville, MA 84 I b 2
West Spanish Peak 68-69 D 7
West Spitsbergen = Vestspitsbergen 116-117 j-l 5
West Union, IA 70-71 DE 4
West Union, OH 72-73 E 5
West Union, WV 72-73 F 5
West Unity, OH 70-71 H 5
West University Place, TX 85 III b 2
Westview Cemetery 85 II b 2
Westville, IL 70-71 G 5-6
Westville, NJ 84 III c 2
Westville, OK 76-77 G 4-5
Westville Grove, NJ 84 III c 2
West Virginia 64-65 KL 4
Westwater, UT 74-75 J 3
Westwego, LA 78-79 DE 6
West Whittier, CA 83 III d 2
West Wickham, London- 129 II b 2
Westwood, CA 66-67 C 5
Westwood, Los Angeles-, CA 83 III b 1
West Wyalong 160 H 4
West Yellowstone, MT 66-67 H 3
Westzaan, Zaanstad- 128 I a 1
Westzaner Overtoom 128 I a 1
Wetar, Pulau — 148-149 J 8
Wetaskiwin 56-57 NO 7
Wete 172 GH 3
Wetetnagani, Rivière — 62 N 2
Weti = Wete 172 GH 3
Wetlet 141 D 4
Wetmore, OR 66-67 D 3
Wet Mountains 68-69 D 6-7
Wetonka, SD 68-69 G 3
Wetter = Pulau Wetar 148-149 J 8
Wetter Lake = Vättern 116-117 E 8
Wettswil 128 IV a 1-2
Wetumpka, AL 78-79 FG 4
Wevok, AK 58-59 DE 2
Wewahitchka, FL 78-79 G 5-6
Wewak 148-149 M 7
Wewela, SD 68-69 G 4
Wewoka, OK 76-77 F 5
Wexford 119 C 5
Weyanoke, VA 82 II a 2
Weyb 164-165 N 7
Weybridge 129 II a 2
Weyburn 56-57 Q 8
Weyland, Point — 160 AB 4
Weymouth, MA 84 I c 3
Weymouth [CDN] 63 CD 5
Weymouth [GB] 119 EF 6
Weymouth, Cape — 158-159 HJ 2
Weymouth Back River 84 I c 3
Weymouth Fore River 84 I c 3
Weyprecht, Kapp — 116-117 l 5
Wezembeek-Oppem 128 II b 1
Whakatane 158-159 P 7
Whaleback, Mount — 158-159 CD 4
Whale River 56-57 X 6
Whales, Bay of — 53 B 19-20
Whalsay 119 F 1
Whangarei 158-159 OP 7
Wharton, TX 76-77 FG 8
What Cheer, IA 70-71 D 5
Wheatland, CA 74-75 C 3
Wheatland, WY 68-69 D 4
Wheatley, AR 78-79 D 3
Wheaton, MN 68-69 H 3
Wheeler, OR 66-67 AB 3
Wheeler, TX 76-77 D 5
Wheeler Islands 138-139 L 7
Wheeler Lake 78-79 F 3
Wheeler Peak [USA, Nevada] 64-65 CD 4
Wheeler Peak [USA, New Mexico] 64-65 E 4
Wheeler Ridge, CA 74-75 D 5
Wheeler River 61 F 2
Wheeling, WV 64-65 KL 4-5
Whelan 61 D 3-4
Whewell, Mount — 53 B 17-18
Whichaway Nunataks 53 A 34-1
Whidbey, Point — 160 B 5
Whidbey Island 66-67 B 1
Whiporie 160 L 2
Whipple, Mount — 60 B 1
Whiskey Gap 66-67 G 1
Whitby [CDN] 72-73 G 3
Whitby, SD 68-69 H 3
White, Lake — 158-159 E 4
White Bay 56-57 Z 7
White Bear 61 DE 5
White Bear Lake, MN 70-71 D 3
White Bird, ID 66-67 EF 3
White Castle, LA 78-79 D 5
White City, FL 80-81 c 3
White City, KS 68-69 H 6
White Cliffs 158-159 H 6
White Cloud, MI 70-71 H 4
Whitecourt 60 K 2
White Deer, TX 76-77 D 5
White Earth, ND 68-69 E 1
White Earth Indian Reservation 70-71 C 2
White Eye, AK 58-59 O 3
Whiteface, TX 76-77 C 6
Whiteface Mountain 72-73 JK 2
Whitefish 62 L 3
Whitefish, MT 66-67 F 1
Whitefish Bay 70-71 H 2
Whitefish Bay, WI 70-71 G 4
Whitefish Falls 62 L 3
Whitefish Lake [CDN, Aleutian Range] 58-59 K 6
Whitefish Lake [CDN, Kilbuck Mts.] 58-59 GH 6
Whitefish Lake [CDN, Ontario] 70-71 F 1
Whitefish Lake [USA] 70-71 CD 2
Whitefish Point 70-71 H 2
Whitefish Point, MI 70-71 H 2
Whitefish Range 66-67 F 1
Whiteflat, TX 76-77 D 5
White Gull Lake 56-57 Y 6
White Hall, IL 70-71 EF 6
Whitehall, MI 70-71 G 4
Whitehall, MT 66-67 GH 3
Whitehall, NY 72-73 K 3
Whitehall, WI 70-71 E 3
Whitehaven 119 DE 4
White Hills 58-59 N 3
Whitehorse 56-57 JK 5
White Horse, CA 66-67 C 5
White Horse Pass 66-67 FG 5
White House 82 II a 2
White Island 161 G 3
White Island = Kvitøya 52 AB 15
White Lake, SD 68-69 G 4
White Lake, WI 70-71 F 3
White Lake [CDN] 70-71 H 1
White Lake [USA] 78-79 C 6
Whiteland, TX 76-77 E 7
Whitemark 160 cd 2
White Mountain, AK 56-57 D 5
White Mountains [USA, Alaska] 58-59 OP 4
White Mountains [USA, California] 74-75 D 4
White Mountains [USA, New Hampshire] 72-73 L 2
Whitemouth 61 KL 5-6
Whitemouth Lake 70-71 BC 1
White Nile = An-Nīl al-Abyaḍ 164-165 L 6
White Nossob = Wit Nossob 174-175 C 2
White Oak Acres, Houston-, TX 85 III b 1
White Oak Bayou 85 III ab 1
White Oak Park 85 III b 1
Whiteoak Swamp 80-81 H 3
White Otter Lake 62 CD 3
White Owl, SD 68-69 E 3
White Pass 58-59 U 7
White Pine, MT 66-67 F 2
White Pine Mountains 74-75 F 3
White Plains, NY 72-73 JK 4
White River, SD 68-69 F 4
White River [CDN, Ontario place] 70-71 H 1
White River [CDN, Ontario river] 70-71 GH 1
White River [CDN, Yukon Territory] 56-57 H 5
White River [USA, Alaska] 58-59 R 6
White River [USA, Arkansas] 64-65 H 4
White River [USA, California] 74-75 F 4
White River [USA, Colorado] 68-69 BC 5
White River [USA, Indiana] 70-71 G 6
White River [USA, South Dakota] 64-65 F 3
White River [USA, Texas] 76-77 D 6
White River = Witrivier 174-175 J 3
White River, East Fork — 70-71 GH 6
White River, South Fork — 68-69 F 4
White River, West Fork — 70-71 G 6
White River Plateau 68-69 C 6
White River Valley 74-75 F 3
White Rock, SD 68-69 H 3
White Russian Soviet Socialist Republic = Belorussian Soviet Socialist Republic 124-125 E-H 6-7
Whitesail Lake 60 D 3
White Salmon, WA 66-67 C 3
Whitesands = Witsand 174-175 D 8
White Sands National Monument 76-77 A 6
Whites Brook 63 C 4
White Sea 132-133 FG 4
Whiteshell Forest Reserve 61 KL 6
Whiteshell Provincial Park 62 B 2-3
Whiteside, Canal — 108-109 D 9-10
White Sox Park 83 II b 1-2
White Springs, FL 80-81 b 1
Whitestone, New York-, NY 82 III d 2
White Sulphur Springs, MT 66-67 H 2
White Swan, WA 66-67 C 2
Whitetail, MT 68-69 D 1
White Umfolozi = Wit Umfolozi 174-175 J 5
Whiteville, NC 80-81 G 3
Whiteville, TN 78-79 E 3
White Volta 164-165 D 7
Whitewater, CO 68-69 B 6
Whitewater, KS 68-69 H 7
Whitewater, MT 68-69 C 1
Whitewater, WI 70-71 F 4
Whitewater Baldy 64-65 E 5
Whitewater Lake 62 DE 2
Whitewood, SD 68-69 DE 3
Whitewright, TX 76-77 F 6
Whitfield 160 H 6
Whithorn 119 DE 4
Whiting, NJ 72-73 J 5
Whiting River 58-59 V 7
Whitla 61 C 6
Whitley City, KY 78-79 G 2
Whitman, ND 68-69 GH 1
Whitman, NE 68-69 F 4
Whitmire, SC 80-81 F 3
Whitmore Mountains 53 A
Whitney, NE 68-69 E 4
Whitney, OR 66-67 DE 3
Whitney, TX 76-77 F 7
Whitney, Mount — 64-65 C 4
Whitsett, TX 76-77 E 8
Whitsunday Island 158-159 JK 4
Whittier, AK 56-57 G 5
Whittier, CA 83 III d 2
Whittier College 83 III d 2
Whittier Narrows Dam 83 III d 1
Whittle, Cap de — 63 F 2
Whittlesea 160 G 6
Whitwell, TN 78-79 G 3
Wholdaia Lake 56-57 PQ 5
Whyalla 158-159 G 6

Wiang Pa Pao 150-151 B 3
Wiang Phran = Mae Sai 148-149 CD 2
Wiarton 72-73 F 2
Wibaux, MT 68-69 D 2
Wichian Buri 148-149 D 3
Wichita, KS 64-65 G 4
Wichita Falls, TX 64-65 FG 5
Wichita Mountains 76-77 E 5
Wick 119 E 2
Wickenburg, AZ 74-75 G 5-6
Wickersham, WA 66-67 BC 1
Wickes, AR 76-77 G 5
Wickham, Cape — 160 b 1
Wickliffe, KY 78-79 E 2
Wicklow 119 CD 5
Wicklow Mountains 119 C 5
Wide Bay 58-59 ef 1
Widen, WV 72-73 F 5
Widgiemooltha 158-159 D 6
Wi-do 144-145 F 5
Widŏn 141 C 5
Widyan, Al- 134-135 E 4
Więcbork 118 H 2
Wiegnaarspoort 174-175 E 7
Wieluń 118 J 3
Wien [A, place] 118 G 4
Wien [A, river] 113 I b 2
Wien-Altmannsdorf 113 I b 2
Wien-Azgersdorf 113 I b 2
Wien-Breitenlee 113 I bc 1
Wien-Donaufeld 113 I b 1
Wien-Donaustadt 113 I bc 2
Wien-Dornbach 113 I b 2
Wienerberg 113 I b 2
Wiener Neustadt 118 GH 5
Wienerwald 118 GH 4
Wien-Essling 113 I c 2
Wien-Favoriten 113 I b 2
Wien-Grinzing 113 I b 1
Wien-Grossjedlersdorf 113 I b 1
Wien-Hadersdorf 113 I ab 2
Wien-Hernals 113 I b 2
Wien-Hietzing 113 I b 2
Wien-Hirschstetten 113 I bc 2
Wien-Hütteldorf 113 I b 2
Wien-Inzersdorf 113 I b 2
Wien-Jedlesee 113 I b 1
Wien-Kagran 113 I b 2
Wien-Kaiserebersdorf 113 I b 2
Wien-Kalksburg 113 I ab 2
Wien-Lainz 113 I b 2
Wien Lake 58-59 M 4
Wien-Leopoldau 113 I b 1
Wien-Leopoldstadt 113 I b 2
Wien-Mauer 113 I ab 2
Wien-Meidling 113 I b 2
Wien-Neualbern 113 I b 2
Wien-Neustift am Walde 113 I b 2
Wien-Neusüssenbrunn 113 I bc 1
Wien-Neuwaldegg 113 I ab 2
Wien-Nussdorf 113 I b 1
Wien-Oberlaa 113 I b 2
Wien-Oberlisse 113 I b 1
Wien-Ottakring 113 I b 2
Wien-Penzing 113 I b 2
Wien-Rodaun 113 I b 2
Wien-Salmannsdorf 113 I b 1
Wien-Schwechat, Flughafen — 113 I c 2
Wien-Siebenhirten 113 I b 2
Wien-Sievering 113 I b 1
Wien-Speising 113 I b 2
Wien-Stadlau 113 I b 2
Wien-Stammersdorf 113 I b 1
Wien-Strebersdorf 113 I b 1
Wien-Süssenbrunn 113 I bc 1
Wieprz 118 L 3
Wierzbołowo = Virbalis 124-125 D 6
Wiesbaden 118 CD 3
Wiese Island = ostrov Vize 132-133 O 2
Wigadēn 164-165 NO 7
Wiga Hill 168-169 H 3
Wigan 119 E 5
Wiggins, CO 68-69 D 5
Wiggins, MS 78-79 E 5
Wight, Isle of — 119 F 6
Wijde Blik 128 I b 2
Wijdefjorden 116-117 j 5
Wilber, NE 68-69 H 5
Wilborn, MT 66-67 G 2
Wilbourn Hill 160 B 1
Wilbur, WA 66-67 D 2
Wilburton, OK 76-77 G 5
Wilcannia 158-159 H 6
Wilcock, Península — 108-109 BC 8
Wilcox, NE 68-69 G 5
Wilczek, zemľa — 132-133 L-N 1
Wilczek land = zemľa Wilczek 132-133 L-N 1
Wildcat Canyon Regional Park 83 I c 1
Wilde, Avellaneda- 110 III c 2
Wilderness = Wildernis 174-175 E 7-8
Wildernis 174-175 E 7-8
Wild Horse Reservoir 66-67 F 5
Wild Lake 58-59 M 3
Wildpark West 130 III a 2
Wild Rice River 70-71 BC 2
Wild River 58-59 M 3
Wildrose, ND 68-69 E 1
Wild Rose, WI 70-71 F 3
Wildwood, FL 80-81 bc 2
Wildwood, NJ 72-73 J 5
Wildwood Lake 85 II a 2
Wilge 174-175 H 4
Wilgena 160 B 3
Wilgespruit 170 V a 1
Wilhelm, Mount — 148-149 M 8
Wilhelmina Gebergte 92-93 H 4
Wilhelmøya 116-117 l 5
Wilhelmshaven 118 CD 2
Wilhelmshorst [DDR] 130 III a 2
Wilhelmstadt, Berlin- 130 III a 1
Wilhelmstal 174-175 B 1
Wilkes 53 C 12
Wilkes Barre, PA 64-65 L 3
Wilkes Land 53 BC 12-14
Wilkie 56-57 P 7
Wilkinsburg, PA 72-73 G 4
Wilkinson Lakes 158-159 F 5
Will, Mount — 58-59 X 8
Willacoochee, GA 80-81 E 5
Willamette River 64-65 B 3
Willandra Billabong Creek 160 G 4
Willapa Bay 66-67 AB 2
Willard, CO 68-69 E 5
Willard, MT 68-69 D 2
Willard, NM 76-77 AB 5
Willard, OH 72-73 E 4
Willard, UT 66-67 GH 5
Willcox, AZ 74-75 HJ 6
Willebroek, Kanaal van — 128 II b 1
Willemstad [NA] 64-65 N 9
Willeroo 158-159 F 3
Willesden, London- 129 II b 1
William B. Hartsfield Atlanta International Airport 85 II b 3
William Creek 158-159 G 5
William Girling Reservoir 129 II bc 1
William Lake 61 J 3-4
William P. Hobby Airport 85 III b 2
Williams, AZ 74-75 G 5
Williams, CA 74-75 B 3
Williams Bridge, New York-, NY 82 III c 1
Williamsburg, IA 70-71 DE 5
Williamsburg, KY 80-81 DE 2
Williamsburg, New York-, NY 82 III c 2
Williams Lake 56-57 M 7
Williamson, WV 80-81 E 2
Williamsport, IN 70-71 G 5
Williamsport, PA 64-65 L 3
Williamston, NC 80-81 H 2-3
Williamstown, KY 70-71 H 6
Williamstown, Melbourne- 161 II b 2
Williamsville, MO 78-79 D 2
Willibert, Mount — 60 B 1
Willimantic, CT 72-73 K 4
Willingboro, NJ 84 III d 1
Willingboro Plaza 84 III d 1
Willingdon 61 B 4
Willis, TX 76-77 G 7
Willis Group 158-159 K 3
Willis Island 63 K 3
Williston 172 D 8
Williston, FL 80-81 b 2
Williston, ND 64-65 F 2
Williston, SC 80-81 F 4
Williston Lake 60 F 1-2
Willits, CA 74-75 B 3
Willmar, MN 70-71 C 3
Willmar Station 68-69 E 1
Willmersdorf [DDR, Frankfurt] 130 III c 1
Willmore Wilderness Provincial Park 60 H 3
Willoughby, OH 72-73 F 4
Willoughby, Sydney- 161 I b 1
Willow 56-57 F 5
Willow Bend, Houston-, TX 85 III b 2
Willow Brook, CA 83 III c 2
Willow Brook, Houston-, TX 85 III b 2
Willow Bunch 68-69 D 1
Willow Creek, AK 58-59 P 6
Willow Creek [USA, California] 66-67 C 5
Willow Creek [USA, Oregon] 66-67 D 3
Willowdene, Johannesburg- 170 V a 2
Willow Lake, SD 68-69 H 3
Willowlake River 56-57 MN 5
Willowmore 172 D 8
Willow Ranch, CA 66-67 C 5
Willow River 60 F 2
Willow River, MN 70-71 D 2
Willow Run, MI 72-73 E 3
Willows, CA 74-75 B 3
Willow Springs, MO 78-79 CD 2
Willow Waterhole Bayou 85 III ab 2
Will Rogers State Historical Park 83 III a 1
Willsboro, NY 72-73 K 2
Wills Point, LA 85 I bc 3
Wills Point, TX 76-77 FG 6
Willswood, LA 85 I a 2
Willunga 160 D 5
Wilmer, AL 78-79 E 5
Wilmersdorf, Berlin- 130 III b 2
Wilmington, DE 64-65 LM 4
Wilmington, IL 70-71 FG 5
Wilmington, NC 64-65 L 5
Wilmington, OH 72-73 E 5
Wilmington [AUS] 160 D 4
Wilmington [GB] 129 II c 2
Wilmot, AR 78-79 D 4
Wilmot, SD 68-69 H 3
Wilpattu 140 DE 6
Wilsall, MT 66-67 H 3
Wilshire, Houston-, TX 85 III b 1
Wilson, AR 78-79 D 3
Wilson, NC 64-65 L 4
Wilson, NY 72-73 G 3
Wilson, OK 76-77 F 5
Wilson Bluff 158-159 EF 6
Wilson City 88-89 H 1
Wilson Creek, WA 66-67 D 2
Wilson Creek Range 74-75 F 3
Wilson Lake 78-79 F 3
Wilson River 158-159 H 5
Wilsons Promontory 158-159 J 7
Wilsonville, NE 68-69 FG 5
Wilstorf, Hamburg- 130 I a 2
Wilton, ND 68-69 F 2
Wilton, WI 70-71 E 4
Wilton River 158-159 F 2
Wiluna 158-159 D 5
Wimbledon, ND 68-69 G 2
Wimbledon, London- 119 F 6
Wimborne 60 L 4
Wimmera 158-159 H 7
Wina = Ouina 164-165 G 7
Winamac, IN 70-71 G 5
Winburg 172 E 7
Winchell, TX 76-77 E 7
Winchester, ID 66-67 E 2
Winchester, IL 70-71 EF 6
Winchester, IN 70-71 H 5
Winchester, KY 72-73 DE 5
Winchester, MA 84 I ab 2
Winchester, TN 78-79 F 3
Winchester, VA 64-65 L 4
Winchester, WY 68-69 BC 4
Winchester [CDN] 72-73 J 2
Winchester [GB] 119 F 6
Winchester Bay, OR 66-67 A 4
Windber, PA 72-73 G 4
Wind Cave National Park 68-69 E 4
Winder, GA 80-81 E 3-4
Windesi 148-149 K 7
Windfern Forest, TX 85 III a 1
Windham, AK 58-59 V 8
Windhoek 172 C 6
Windigo Lake 62 D 1
Windigo River 62 D 1
Windmill Point 84 II c 2
Windom, MN 70-71 C 4
Windorah 158-159 H 5
Wind River, WY 68-69 B 4
Wind River [USA, Alaska] 58-59 O 2-3
Wind River [USA, Wyoming] 68-69 B 4
Wind River Indian Reservation 66-67 J 4
Wind River Range 64-65 DE 3
Windsor, CO 68-69 D 5
Windsor, MO 70-71 D 6
Windsor, NC 80-81 H 2
Windsor, ND 68-69 G 2
Windsor, VT 72-73 K 3
Windsor [AUS] 160 K 4
Windsor [CDN, Newfoundland] 63 HJ 3
Windsor [CDN, Nova Scotia] 63 D 5
Windsor [CDN, Ontario] 56-57 U 9
Windsor [CDN, Quebec] 72-73 KL 2
Windsor [GB] 119 F 6
Windsor [ZA] 170 V a 1
Windsor, University of — 84 II b 3
Windsor Airport 84 II c 3
Windsor Hills, CA 83 III bc 2
Windsorton 174-175 F 5
Windsor Village, Houston-, TX 85 III b 2
Windward Islands [West Indies] 64-65 O 9
Windy, AK 58-59 N 5
Winefred Lake 61 C 3
Winfield, AL 78-79 F 3-4
Winfield, IA 70-71 E 5
Winfield, KS 64-65 G 4
Winfred, SD 68-69 H 3-4
Wing, ND 68-69 F 2
Wingham 72-73 F 3
Wingham Island 58-59 P 6
Wingo, KY 78-79 E 2
Winifred, MT 68-69 B 2
Winifreda 106-107 E 6
Winisk 56-57 T 6
Winisk Lake 56-57 T 7
Winisk River 56-57 T 7
Wink, TX 76-77 C 7
Winkel [CH] 128 IV b 1
Winkel [NL] 128 I b 2
Winkelman, AZ 74-75 H 6
Winkelpos 174-175 G 4
Winkler 68-69 H 1
Winlock, WA 66-67 B 2
Winneba 164-165 D 7
Winnebago, MN 70-71 CD 4
Winnebago, Lake — 70-71 F 3-4
Winnemucca, NV 64-65 C 3
Winnemucca Lake 66-67 D 5
Winner, SD 68-69 G 4
Winnetka, IL 70-71 G 4
Winnett, MT 68-69 B 2
Winnfield, LA 78-79 C 5
Winnibigoshish Lake 70-71 CD 2
Winnie, TX 76-77 G 8
Winning Pool 158-159 B 4
Winnipeg 56-57 R 7
Winnipeg, Lake — 56-57 R 7
Winnipeg Beach 62 A 2
Winnipegosis 61 HJ 5
Winnipegosis, Lake — 56-57 R 7
Winnipeg River 56-57 RS 7
Winnipesaukee, Lake — 72-73 L 3
Winnsboro, LA 78-79 D 4
Winnsboro, SC 80-81 F 3
Winnsboro, TX 76-77 G 6
Winona, AZ 74-75 H 5
Winona, KS 68-69 F 6
Winona, MI 70-71 F 2
Winona, MN 64-65 H 3
Winona, MO 78-79 D 2
Winona, MS 78-79 DE 4
Winona, TX 76-77 G 6
Winona, WA 66-67 DE 2
Winschoten 120-121 L 2
Winslow, AR 76-77 G 5
Winslow, AZ 64-65 DE 4
Winslow, IN 70-71 G 6
Winslow, ME 72-73 M 2
Winsted, CT 72-73 K 4
Winston, MT 66-67 GH 2
Winston, OR 66-67 B 4
Winston-Salem, NC 64-65 KL 4
Winterberg [CH] 128 IV b 1
Winterberg [D] 118 D 3
Winterberge 174-175 FG 7
Winter Garden, FL 80-81 c 2
Winter Harbour 60 C 4
Winterhaven, CA 74-75 F 6
Winter Haven, FL 80-81 c 2
Winter Hill, MA 84 I b 2
Winterhude, Hamburg- 130 I b 1
Winter Park, CO 68-69 CD 6
Winter Park, FL 80-81 c 2
Winters, CA 74-75 C 3
Winters, TX 76-77 E 7
Winterset, IA 70-71 CD 5
Winterthur 118 D 5
Winterthur-Vogelsang 128 IV b 1
Winterthur-Wülflingen 128 IV b 1
Winterton [ZA] 174-175 H 5
Winterveld 174-175 E 6
Winthrop, MA 84 I c 2
Winthrop, ME 72-73 LM 2
Winthrop, MN 70-71 C 3
Winthrop, WA 66-67 C 1
Winton, MN 70-71 E 2
Winton, WA 66-67 C 2
Winton, WY 66-67 J 5
Winton [AUS] 158-159 H 4
Winton [NZ] 158-159 N 9
Winyah Bay 80-81 G 4
Winzah 166-167 KL 1-2
Wipkingen, Zürich- 128 IV b 1
Wirāj, Wādī al- 173 B 3
Wirrulla 158-159 FG 6
Wiscasset, ME 72-73 M 2
Wisconsin 64-65 H 2-J 3
Wisconsin Dells, WI 70-71 F 4
Wisconsin Rapids, WI 70-71 EF 3
Wisconsin River 64-65 HJ 3
Wisdom, MT 66-67 G 3
Wiseman, AK 56-57 FG 4
Wishart 61 FG 5
Wishek, ND 68-69 G 2
Wisła 118 K 3
Wislana, Mierzeja — 118 J 1
Wislany, Zalew — 118 J 1
Wisłok 118 KL 4
Wisłoka 118 K 4
Wismar 118 E 2
Wisner, LA 78-79 D 4-5
Wisner, NE 68-69 H 4-5
Wissahickon Creek 84 III b 1
Wissel, Danau — 148-149 L 7
Wissembourg 120-121 LM 4
Wissinoming, Philadelphia-, PA 84 III c 1
Wissmann, Chutes — 172 CD 3
Wissous 129 I c 3
Wistaria 60 D 3
Wister, OK 76-77 G 5
Wiswila 171 AB 5
Witbank 172 EF 7
Witberge 174-175 G 6
Witchekan Lake 61 E 4
Witdraai 174-175 D 4
Witelsbos 174-175 F 8
Witfonteinrand 174-175 G 3
Withernsea 119 FG 5
Witherspoon, Mount — 58-59 O 6
Witikon, Zürich- 128 IV b 1
Witkop 174-175 D 4
Witkoppies 174-175 H 4
Wit Nossob 174-175 C 2
Witpoort 174-175 G 4
Witpoortje 170 V a 1
Witputs 172 C 7
Witrandberge 174-175 C 3
Witrivier 174-175 J 3
Witsand 174-175 D 8
Witteberge 174-175 D 7
Witte-Els-Bosch = Witelsbos 174-175 F 8
Witten, SD 68-69 FG 4
Wittenau, Berlin- 130 III b 1
Wittenberg 118 F 3
Wittenberg, WI 70-71 F 3
Wittenberge 118 EF 2
Wittenoom 158-159 C 4
Wittlich 118 C 4
Wittmann, AZ 74-75 G 6
Wittstock 118 F 2
Witu 172 GH 2
Wit Umfolozi 174-175 J 5
Witung = Widŏn 141 C 5
Witvlei 172 C 6
Witwatersrand 174-175 G 3-H 4
Wivenhoe 61 L 2
Wiwŏn 144-145 F 2

Wkra 118 JK 2

Włocławek 118 J 2
Włodawa 118 L 3

Woburn, MA 84 I ab 2
Wodonga 160 H 6
Woeonichi, Lac — 62 O 1
Wohlthatmassiv 53 B 2
Wokam, Pulau — 148-149 KL 8
Woking 60 H 2
Wolbach, NE 68-69 G 5
Wolcott, NY 72-73 H 3
Woleai 148-149 M 5
Wolf Creek, MT 66-67 G 2
Wolf Creek, OR 66-67 B 4
Wolf Creek Pass 68-69 C 7
Wolfe City, TX 76-77 F 6
Wolfenbüttel 118 E 2
Wolff, Chutes — 172 D 3
Wolfforth, TX 76-77 C 6
Wolf Mountains 68-69 C 3
Wolf Point, MT 68-69 D 1
Wolf River 70-71 F 3
Wolfsburg 118 E 2
Wolfsgarten, Berlin- 130 III c 2
Wolfville 63 DE 5
Wolhuterskop 174-175 G 3
Wolin 118 G 2
Wolkitte = Welkītē 164-165 M 7
Wollaston, MA 84 I b 3
Wollaston, Isla — 108-109 F 10
Wollaston, Islas — 111 C 9
Wollaston Lake 56-57 PQ 6
Wollaston Lake Post 61 FG 1
Wollaston Peninsula 56-57 NO 3-4
Wollega = Welega 164-165 LM 7
Wollishofen, Zürich- 128 IV b 1
Wollo = Welo 164-165 MN 6
Wollogorang 158-159 G 3
Wollongong 158-159 K 6
Wollongong-Port Kembla 158-159 K 6
Wollongong-Shellharbour 158-159 K 6
Wolmaransstad 174-175 F 4
Wolo 152-153 O 7
Wolok = Hele 150-151 H 3
Wołów 118 H 3
Wolseley [AUS] 158-159 GH 7
Wolseley [CDN] 61 G 5
Wolseley [ZA] 174-175 C 7
Wolsey, SD 68-69 G 3
Wolstenholme 56-57 VW 5
Wolstenholme, Cape — 56-57 VW 5
Wolsztyn 118 GH 2
Woluwe-Saint-Lambert 128 II b 1
Woluwe-Saint-Pierre 128 II b 1
Wolverhampton 119 E 5
Wolverine, MI 70-71 H 3
Woman River 62 K 3
Wonder, OR 66-67 B 4
Wonderfontein 174-175 HJ 3
Wonderkop 174-175 G 4
Wŏngsŏng-dong 144-145 DE 3
Wŏnju 142-143 O 4
Wonogiri 152-153 J 9
Wonosari 148-149 F 8
Wŏnsan 142-143 O 4
Wonthaggi 158-159 HJ 7
Woocalla 160 C 3
Wood, SD 68-69 F 4
Wood, Isla — 106-107 F 7
Wood, Islas — 108-109 E 10
Wood, Mount — [CDN] 58-59 R 6

Yanahuanca 96-97 C 7
Yanai 144-145 HJ 6
Yanaka 155 III d 3
Yanam 134-135 N 7
Yan'an 142-143 K 4
Yanaoca 92-93 E 7
Yanaon = Yanam 134-135 N 7
Yanatili, Río — 96-97 E 8
Yanbian 142-143 J 6
Yanbian Chaoxianzu Zizhizhou 142-143 OP 3
Yanbian Zizhizhou 144-145 GH 1
Yanbu' al-Baḥr 134-135 D 6
Yancapata 96-97 D 7
Yanchang 146-147 C 3
Yancheng [TJ, Henan] 146-147 E 5
Yancheng [TJ, Jiangsu] 142-143 N 5
Yan Chi 146-147 A 3
Yanchuan 142-143 KL 4
Yandama Creek 160 E 2
Yandoon = Nyaungdôn 141 D 7
Yane 106-107 A 6
Yanfolila 168-169 CD 3
Yangambi 172 DE 1
Yangang-do = Ryanggang-do 144-145 FG 2
Yangasso 168-169 D 2
Yangcheng 146-147 D 4
Yang-chiang = Yangjiang 142-143 L 7
Yang-chiao-kou = Yangjiaogou 146-147 G 3
Yangchuan = Yangquan 142-143 L 4
Yangchun 146-147 CD 10
Yangcun = Wuqing 146-147 F 2
Yangdog Tsho 138-139 N 3
Yangdŏk 144-145 F 3
Yangdong Tsho 142-143 G 6
Yanggu [ROK] 144-145 FG 3
Yanggu [TJ] 146-147 E 3
Yang-hsin = Yangsin 146-147 F 3
Yang-hsin = Yangxin 146-147 E 7
Yangi Hisar 142-143 CD 4
Yangjiang 142-143 L 7
Yangjiaogou 146-147 G 3
Yangjŏng-ni 144-145 F 4
Yangkiang = Yangjiang 142-143 L 7
Yangku = Taiyuan 142-143 L 4
Yangku = Yanggu 146-147 E 3
Yang-liu-ch'ing = Yangliuqing 146-147 F 2
Yangliuqing 146-147 F 2
Yangloudong 146-147 D 7
Yangmei 146-147 C 10
Yangping 146-147 C 6
Yangpu Gang 150-151 G 3
Yangp'yŏng 144-145 F 4
Yangqu 146-147 D 2
Yangquan 142-143 L 4
Yangsan 144-145 G 5
Yangshan 146-147 D 9
Yangshuling 144-145 B 2
Yangshuo 146-147 C 9
Yangsi 144-145 E 3
Yangsin = Yangxin 146-147 F 3
Yangso = Yangshuo 146-147 C 9
Yang Talat 150-151 D 4
Yangtze Kiang = Chang Jiang 142-143 K 5-6
Yangxi 146-147 E 8
Yangxin [TJ, Hubei] 146-147 E 7
Yangxin [TJ, Shandong] 146-147 F 3
Yangyang 142-143 O 4
Yangyuan 146-147 E 1
Yangzhong 146-147 GH 5
Yangzhou 142-143 M 5
Yangzhuoyong Hu = Yangdog Tsho 138-139 N 3
Yanhe [TJ, place] 146-147 B 7
Yan He [TJ, river] 146-147 BC 3
Yanina = Iōánnina 122-123 J 6
Yanji 142-143 O 3
Yanjin 146-147 DE 4
Yanjing 142-143 H 6
Yankee Stadium 82 III c 2
Yankton, SD 64-65 G 3
Yanku = Taiyuan 142-143 L 4
Yanling 146-147 DE 4
Yanna 158-159 J 5
Yanonge 172 D 1
Yān Oya 140 E 6
Yanping = Enping 146-147 D 10
Yanqi = Qara Shahr 142-143 F 3
Yanshan [TJ, Hebei] 146-147 F 2
Yanshan [TJ, Jiangxi] 146-147 F 7
Yanshi 146-147 D 4
Yanskoi Bay = Janskij zaliv 132-133 Za 3
Yantabulla 160 G 2
Yantai 142-143 N 4
Yanwa 141 F 2
Yanxi 142-143 L 6
Yanzhou 146-147 F 4
Yao 164-165 H 6
Yaoganhutun = Yaoqianhu 144-145 D 2
Yao-hsien = Yao Xian 146-147 B 4
Yao-kou = Yaowan 146-147 G 4
Yaolo 172 D 1
Yaoqianhu 144-145 D 2
Yaoundé 164-165 G 8
Yaowan 146-147 G 4
Yaowari 146-147 G 4
Yao Xian 146-147 B 4
Yao Yai, Ko — 150-151 B 9
Yap 206-207 R 9
Yapacana, Cerro — 94-95 H 6
Yapacani, Río — 104-105 D 5
Yāpanaya 134-135 MN 9
Yāpanē Kalapuwa 140 E 6
Yapehe 172 DE 2
Yapella, Río — 94-95 E 7
Yapen, Pulau — 148-149 L 7
Yapen, Selat — 148-149 L 7
Yapeyú 106-107 J 2
Yap Islands 148-149 L 5
Yapraklı = Tuht 136-137 E 2
Yaqui, Río — 64-65 E 6
Yaquina Head 66-67 A 3
Yaracuy 94-95 G 2
Yaracuy, Río — 94-95 G 2
Yaraka 158-159 H 4
Yaralıgoz dağı 136-137 EF 2
Yarang 150-151 C 9
Yarangüme 136-137 C 4
Yarani 168-169 D 3
Yari, Llanos de — 94-95 D 7
Yari, Río — 92-93 E 4
Yariga-take 142-143 Q 4
Yaring 150-151 C 9
Yaritagua 94-95 G 2
Yarkand 142-143 D 4
Yarkand darya 142-143 D 4-E 3
Yarmouth 56-57 X 9
Yarnell, AZ 74-75 G 5
Yāro Lunḍ 138-139 B 4
Yaroslavl = Jaroslavl' 132-133 FG 6
Yarra Bend National Park 161 II c 1
Yarram 158-159 J 7
Yarraman 158-159 K 5
Yarra River 161 II c 1
Yarras 160 L 3
Yarraville, Melbourne- 161 II b 1
Yarrawonga 160 GH 6
Yarumal 92-93 D 3
Yarvicoya, Cerro — 104-105 B 6-7
Yasanyama 164-165 J 8
Yasawa Group 148-149 a 2
Yashi 168-169 G 2
Yashima 144-145 N 3
Yashiro-jima 144-145 J 6
Yasothon 150-151 E 5
Yass 158-159 J 6
Yassar, Wādī — 166-167 H 1
Yasugi 144-145 J 5
Yasun burnu 136-137 GH 2
Yasuní 96-97 D 2
Yasuní, Río — 96-97 C 2
Yata 104-105 C 3
Yata, Río — 104-105 D 3
Yatağan 136-137 C 4
Yatakala 164-165 E 6
Yate, Monte — 108-109 C 3
Yates Center, KS 70-71 C 6-7
Yathkyed Lake 56-57 R 5
Yathung = Yadong 138-139 M 4
Yatina 104-105 D 7
Yatsu 155 III d 1
Yatsuga take 144-145 M 4-5
Yatsushiro 144-145 H 6
Yatsushiro-wan 144-145 H 6
Yatta Plateau 171 D 3
Yattī 166-167 B 7-C 6
Yatua, Río — 94-95 H 7
Yauca 96-97 D 9
Yauca, Río — 96-97 D 9
Yauchari, Río — 96-97 C 3
Yauco 88-89 N 6
Yau Mai Ti, Kowloon- 155 I a 2
Yaunde = Yaoundé 164-165 G 8
Yauri 96-97 F 9
Yautepec 86-87 L 8
Yau Tong 155 I b 2
Yau Ue Wan 155 I b 2
Yauyos 92-93 D 7
Yāval 138-139 E 7
Yavari, Río — 92-93 E 5
Yavari-Mirim, Río — 96-97 E 4
Yavatmāļ = Yeotmāl 138-139 FG 7
Yavello = Yabēlo 164-165 M 7-8
Yavero, Río — 96-97 E 8
Yavı [TR, Erzurum] 136-137 J 3
Yavı [TR, Sivas] 136-137 G 3
Yavi, Cerro — 92-93 F 3
Yaviza 94-95 C 3
Yavuzeli 136-137 G 4
Yawal = Yāval 138-139 E 7
Yawata, Ichikawa- 155 III c 1
Yawatahama 144-145 J 6
Yaw Chaung 141 D 5
Yawnghwe = Nyaungywe 141 E 5
Yaxchilán 64-65 H 8
Ya Xian 142-143 KL 8
Yayaköy = Palamut 136-137 B 3
Yayladağı 136-137 FG 5
Yayo 164-165 H 5
Yayuan 144-145 F 2
Yazd 134-135 G 4
Yazoo City, MS 78-79 D 4
Yazoo River 64-65 H 5
Ybytymí 102-103 D 6
Ycliff 62 D 2
Ye 148-149 C 3
Yeadon, PA 84 III b 2
Yebala = Jabalā 166-167 D 2
Ye-Buri midre Selate 164-165 N 5
Yebyū 150-151 B 5
Yecheng = Qarghaliq 142-143 D 4
Yech'ŏn 144-145 G 4
Yecla 120-121 G 9
Yécora 86-87 F 3
Yedashe = Yedāshī 141 E 6
Yedāshī 141 E 6
Yedikule, İstanbul- 154 I a 3
Yedo = Tōkyō 142-143 QR 4
Yegros 102-103 D 7
Yeh-ch'êng = Qarghaliq 142-143 D 4
Yeh-chih = Yanwa 141 F 2
Yeh-hsien = Ye Xian 146-147 D 5
Yeh Kyūn 141 C 6
Yehsien = Ye Xian 142-143 MN 4
Yehuin, Lago — 108-109 EF 10
Yei [Sudan, place] 164-165 L 8
Yei [Sudan, river] 171 B 1
Yeji [GH] 168-169 E 3
Yeji [TJ] 146-147 E 6
Yékia Sahal 164-165 H 5
Yelahanka 140 C 4
Yelandūr 140 C 4
Yelbārga 138-139 G 7
Yelbarga 140 BC 3
Yelcho, Lago — 108-109 C 4
Yele 168-169 BC 3
Yélimané 164-165 BC 5-6
Yelizavety, Cape — = mys Jelizavety 132-133 b 7
Yell 119 F 1
Yellamanchili = Elamanchili 140 F 2
Yellandu 140 E 2
Yellāpur 140 B 3
Yellāreḍḍi 140 CD 1
Yellareddy = Yellāreḍḍi 140 CD 1
Yellow Grass 61 FG 6
Yellowhead Highway 60 GH 3
Yellowhead Pass 56-57 N 7
Yellowknife 56-57 O 5
Yellow Medicine River 70-71 BC 3
Yellow Pine, ID 66-67 F 3
Yellow River 70-71 E 3
Yellow Sea 142-143 N 4
Yellowstone Lake 64-65 D 3
Yellowstone National Park 64-65 D 3
Yellowstone River 64-65 E 2
Yellowstone River, Clarks Fork — 68-69 B 3
Yellowtail Reservoir 66-67 JK 3
Yellville, AR 78-79 C 2
Yelwa 164-165 EF 6
Yemassee, SC 80-81 F 4
Yemen 134-135 E 7-8
Yemen, People's Democratic Republic of — 134-135 F 8-G 7
Yemişenbükü 136-137 G 2
Yemyet In 141 D 4
Yen 150-151 C 10
Yên, Mui — 150-151 G 6
Yenangyat 141 D 5
Yenangyaung 148-149 BC 2
Yenanma 141 D 6
Yên Bay 148-149 DE 2
Yên Binh Xa 150-151 E 1
Yenchang = Yanchang 146-147 C 3
Yên Châu 150-151 E 2
Yencheng = Yancheng [TJ, Henan] 146-147 E 5
Yencheng = Yancheng [TJ, Jiangsu] 142-143 N 5
Yen-ch'i = Qara Shahr 142-143 F 3
Yen-chi = Yanji 142-143 O 3
Yen-chin = Yanjin 146-147 DE 4
Yen-ching = Yanjing 142-143 H 6
Yen-ch'uan = Yanchuan 142-143 KL 4
Yendi 164-165 DE 7
Yengan 141 E 5
Yengejeh 136-137 N 4
Yengema 168-169 C 3
Yengī Kand 136-137 MN 4
Yen-hai = Hsincheng 146-147 HJ 9
Yenho = Yanhe 146-147 B 7
Yeniçağa 136-137 DE 2
Yenice [TR, Çanakkale] 136-137 B 3
Yenice [TR, Mersin] 136-137 F 4
Yenice = Sındıran 136-137 E 3
Yeniceırmağı 136-137 FG 3
Yenidoğan, Ankara- 136-137 E 2
Yenikapı, İstanbul- 154 I a 3
Yeniköy [TR, Artvin] 136-137 K 2
Yeniköy, İstanbul- 154 I b 2
Yenimahalle 136-137 E 2-3
Yenipazar 136-137 BC 4
Yenişehir 136-137 C 2
Yenişehir, Ankara- 136-137 E 3
Yenisei = Jenisej 132-133 Q 4
Yenisei Bay = Jenisejskij zaliv 132-133 OP 3
Yeniyol 136-137 JK 2
Yenki = Qara Shahr 142-143 F 3
Yenki = Yanji 142-143 O 3
Yên Lac 150-151 E 3
Yenling = Yanling 146-147 DE 4
Yenlo, Mount — 58-59 M 5
Yenpien = Yanbian 142-143 J 6
Yenping = Nanping 142-143 M 6
Yen-shan = Yanshan 146-147 F 2
Yen-shih = Yanshi 146-147 D 4
Yentai = Yantai 142-143 N 4
Yentna River 58-59 M 5
Yeo, Lake — 158-159 D 5
Yeola 138-139 E 7
Yeotmāl 138-139 FG 7
Yeovil 119 E 6
Yeoville, Johannesburg- 170 V b 2
Yeppoon 158-159 K 4
Yerbal Nuevo 106-107 K 1
Yerbas 106-107 GH 6
Yercaud 140 CD 5
Yerevan = Jerevan 126-127 M 6
Yerington, NV 74-75 D 3
Yerköy 136-137 F 3
Yerla 140 B 2
Yermo 76-77 B 9
Yerna Tsho 142-143 F 5
Yerqiang = Yarkand 142-143 D 4
Yerres [F, place] 129 I d 3
Yeruá 106-107 H 3
Yerupaja 92-93 D 7
Yĕrūshālayim 134-135 CD 4
Yesagyō 141 D 5
Yesan 144-145 F 4
Yeşilhisar 136-137 F 3
Yesilırmak 134-135 D 2
Yeşilova = Satırlar 136-137 C 4
Yeşilyurt = Ismetpaşa 136-137 H 3
Yeso, NM 76-77 B 5
Yesso = Hokkaidō 142-143 RS 3
Yeste 120-121 F 9
Yetman 160 K 2
Ye'ū 141 D 4
Yeu, Île de — 120-121 F 5
Yeungkong = Yangjiang 142-143 L 7
Yevpatoriya = Jevpatorija 126-127 F 4
Yewale = Yāval 138-139 E 7
Yew Mountain 72-73 F 5
Ye Xian [TJ, Henan] 146-147 D 5
Ye Xian [TJ, Shandong] 142-143 MN 4
Yezd = Yazd 134-135 G 4
Yezhi = Yanwa 141 F 2
Yezo = Hokkaidō 142-143 RS 3
Yezo Strait = Nemuro-kaikyō 144-145 d 1-2
Yguazú, Río — 102-103 E 6
Yhaty 102-103 D 6
Yhú 111 E 2
Yí, Río — 106-107 J 4
Yi'allaq, Gebel — = Jabal Yu'alliq 173 C 2
Yibin 142-143 JK 6
Yichang 142-143 L 5
Yicheng [TJ, Hubei] 142-143 L 5
Yicheng [TJ, Shanxi] 146-147 C 4
Yichuan [TJ, Henan] 146-147 D 4
Yichuan [TJ, Shaanxi] 146-147 BC 3
Yichun [TJ, Heilongjiang] 142-143 O 2
Yichun [TJ, Jiangxi] 142-143 LM 6
Yidda = Jiddah 134-135 D 6
Yidu [TJ, Hubei] 142-143 L 5
Yidu [TJ, Shandong] 142-143 M 4
Yiershi 142-143 MN 2
Yiewsley, London- 129 II a 1
Yifeng 146-147 E 7
Yiğılca = Cayırlıahmetçiler 136-137 D 2
Yi He [TJ, Henan] 146-147 D 4
Yi He [TJ, Shandong] 146-147 G 4
Yiheyuan Summer Palace 155 II a 1
Yihuang 146-147 F 8
Yijun 146-147 B 4
Yilan 142-143 OP 2
Yilan = Ilan 146-147 H 9
Yıldız dağı 136-137 G 2
Yıldızeli 136-137 G 3
Yilehuli Shan 142-143 NO 1
Yimen 146-147 F 5
Yinan 146-147 G 4
Yincheng 146-147 D 4
Yin-chiang = Yinjiang 146-147 B 7
Yinchuan 142-143 JK 4
Yindu He = Sengge Khamba 142-143 E 5
Yingcheng 146-147 D 6
Yingchuan 142-143 K 4
Yingde 142-143 L 7
Yingge Zui 150-151 G 3
Ying He 146-147 F 5
Ying Ho = Ying He 146-147 F 5
Yinghsien = Ying Xian 146-147 D 2
Yingjiang 146-147 C 9
Yingjing 141 E 3
Yingjisha = Yangi Hisar 142-143 CD 4
Ying-ko Tsui = Yingge Zui 150-151 G 3
Yingkou 142-143 N 3
Ying-k'ou = Yingkou 142-143 N 3
Yingkow = Yingkou 144-145 CD 2
Yingle Jiang = Anpu Gang 146-147 B 11
Yingpan 144-145 E 2
Yingshan [TJ → Nanchong] 142-143 K 5
Yingshan [TJ → Wuhan] 146-147 EF 6
Yingshan [TJ ↖ Wuhan] 146-147 D 6
Yingshang 146-147 EF 5
Yingtan 142-143 M 6
Ying-tê = Yingde 142-143 L 7
Ying Xian 146-147 D 2
Yining = Ghulja 142-143 E 3
Yining = Wutong 146-147 B 9
Yinjiang 146-147 B 7
Yinkeng 146-147 E 8
Yinkow = Yingkou 142-143 N 3
Yinmābin 141 D 4
Yin Xian 146-147 H 7
Yinxian = Ningbo 142-143 N 6
Yi-pin = Yibin 142-143 JK 6
Yirga-Alam = Yirga Alem 164-165 M 7
Yirga 'Alem 164-165 M 7
Yirōl 164-165 L 7
Yi Shan [TJ, mountains] 146-147 G 3
Yishan [TJ, place] 142-143 K 7
Yishi = Linyi 146-147 C 4
Yishui 146-147 G 4
Yi-tcheou = Linyi 142-143 M 4
Yitu = Yidu 142-143 M 4
Yiwu [TJ, Yunnan] 150-151 C 2
Yiwu [TJ, Zhejiang] 146-147 GH 7
Yi Xian [TJ, Anhui] 146-147 F 7
Yi Xian [TJ, Hebei] 146-147 E 2
Yi Xian [TJ, Liaoning] 142-143 N 3
Yixian = Ye Xian 142-143 LM 4
Yixing 146-147 GH 6
Yiyang [TJ, Henan] 146-147 D 4
Yiyang [TJ, Hunan] 142-143 L 6
Yiyang [TJ, Jiangxi] 146-147 F 7
Yiyang = Ruyang 146-147 D 4
Yiyuan 146-147 G 3
Yizhang 146-147 D 9
Yizheng 146-147 G 5
Yläne 116-117 K 7
Ylikita 116-117 N 4
Ylivieska 116-117 L 5
Yllästunturi 116-117 KL 4
Ymēttós [GR, mountains] 113 IV b 2
Ymēttós [GR, place] 113 IV ab 2
Yndin 124-125 U 3
Yo, Mu'o'ng — 150-151 C 2
Yoakum, TX 76-77 F 8
Yocalla 104-105 D 6
Yochow = Yueyang 142-143 L 6
Yoder, WY 68-69 D 5
Yodoe 144-145 J 5
Yōga, Tōkyō- 155 III a 2
Yogan, Cerro — 111 BC 8
Yōgīguphā = Jogīghopa 138-139 N 4
Yōgipēṭa = Jogipet 140 CD 2
Yogyakarta [RI, administrative unit = 13 ◁] 148-149 EF 8
Yogyakarta [RI, place] 148-149 EF 8
Yoho National Park 60 J 4
Yoichi 144-145 b 2
Yokadouma 164-165 H 8
Yōkaichiba 144-145 N 5
Yokchi-do 144-145 G 5
Yokkaichi 142-143 Q 5
Yokkaiti = Yokkaichi 142-143 Q 5
Yoko 164-165 G 7
Yokohama 142-143 QR 4
Yokohama-Asahi 155 III a 3
Yokohama-Eda 155 III a 2
Yokohama-Futamatagawa 155 III a 3
Yokohama-Futatsubashi 155 III a 3
Yokohama-Hino 155 III a 3
Yokohama-Hiyoshi 155 III a 2
Yokohama-Hodogaya 155 III a 3
Yokohama-Hommoku 155 III ab 3
Yokohama-Idogaya 155 III a 3
Yokohama-Imajuku 155 III a 3
Yokohama-Isogo 155 III a 3
Yokohama-Izumi 155 III a 3
Yokohama-Kamoshida 155 III a 2
Yokohama-Kanagawa 155 III a 3
Yokohama-Kashio 155 III a 3
Yokohama-Katsuta 155 III a 2
Yokohama-Kawashima 155 III a 3
Yokohama-Kawawa 155 III a 2
Yokohama-Kikuna 155 III a 2
Yokohama-ko 155 III ab 3
Yokohama-Kōhoku 155 III a 2
Yokohama-Kozukue 155 III a 2
Yokohama-Kumizawa 155 III a 3
Yokohama-Midori 155 III a 2
Yokohama-Minami 155 III a 3
Yokohama-Motomachi 155 III a 3
Yokohama-Nagatsuda 155 III a 2
Yokohama-Naka 155 III a 3
Yokohama-Nakayama 155 III a 2
Yokohama-Namamugi 155 III b 3
Yokohama National University 155 III a 3
Yokohama-Nippo 155 III a 2
Yokohama-Nishi 155 III a 3
Yokohama-Ōkubo 155 III a 3
Yokohama-Sasake 155 III a 3
Yokohama-Seya 155 III a 3
Yokohama-Shinohara 155 III a 3
Yokohama-Sugita 155 III a 3
Yokohama-Terayama 155 III a 2
Yokohama-Totsuka 155 III a 3
Yokohama-Tsunashima 155 III a 2
Yokohama-Tsurumi 155 III a 3
Yokohama-Yabe 155 III a 3
Yokohama-Yakō 155 III b 2
Yokosuka 142-143 QR 4
Yokote 142-143 QR 4
Yola 164-165 G 7
Yolaina, Cordillera de — 88-89 D 9
Yolo 170 IV a 2
Yolombo 172 D 2
Yom, Mae Nam — 148-149 CD 3
Yōmagyō 141 E 6
Yomoso 91 III b 4
Yomou 168-169 C 4
Yonago 144-145 J 5
Yŏnan 144-145 EF 4
Yoncalla, OR 66-67 B 4
Yŏnch'ŏn 144-145 F 3
Yonegasaki, Funabashi- 155 III d 1
Yoneshiro-gawa 144-145 N 2
Yonezawa 142-143 QR 4
Yŏngam 144-145 F 5
Yongamp'o 144-145 E 3
Yong'an 142-143 M 6
Yongcheng 146-147 F 5
Yŏngch'ŏn 144-145 G 5
Yongchun 146-147 G 9
Yongcong 146-147 B 8
Yongdeng 142-143 J 4
Yongdian 144-145 E 2
Yongding 146-147 F 9
Yongding He 146-147 F 2
Yongdingmen, Beijing- 155 II b 2
Yŏngdŏk 144-145 G 4
Yŏngdong 144-145 F 4
Yongfeng 146-147 E 8
Yongfeng = Shuangfeng 146-147 D 8
Yongfu 146-147 B 9
Yonggok-tang 144-145 E 2
Yŏnghae 144-145 G 4
Yongha-ri 144-145 F 3
Yonghe 146-147 C 3
Yonghŭng 144-145 F 3
Yŏnghŭng-do 144-145 EF 4
Yŏngil-man 144-145 G 4
Yongji 142-143 L 5
Yongjia 146-147 H 7
Yongjia = Wenzhou 142-143 N 6
Yŏngju 144-145 G 4
Yongkang 146-147 H 7
Yongling 144-145 E 2
Yonglonghe 146-147 D 6
Yongming = Jiangyong 146-147 C 9
Yongnian 146-147 E 3
Yongning 142-143 L 6
Yongning = Nanning 142-143 K 7
Yong Peng 150-151 D 11-12
Yongqing 146-147 F 2
Yŏngsan 144-145 G 5
Yongshou 146-147 AB 4
Yongshun 146-147 B 7
Yongsui = Huayuan 146-147 B 7
Yongtai 142-143 M 6
Yŏngwŏl 144-145 G 4
Yŏngwŏn 144-145 F 3
Yongxin 146-147 E 8
Yongxing 146-147 D 8
Yongxiu 142-143 LM 6
Yongyang 146-147 E 8
Yŏngyu 144-145 E 3
Yonker 61 CD 4
Yonkers, NY 64-65 M 3
Yonne 120-121 J 5
Yopal 94-95 E 5
York, AL 78-79 E 4
York, ND 68-69 G 1
York, NE 68-69 H 5
York, PA 64-65 L 3-4
York, SC 80-81 F 3
York [AUS] 158-159 C 6
York [GB] 119 F 5
York, Cape — 158-159 H 2
York, Kap — 56-57 X 2
Yorke Peninsula 158-159 G 6
Yorketown 158-159 G 6-7
York Factory 56-57 S 6
York Harbour 63 G 3
York River 80-81 H 2
Yorkshire 119 F 4
York Sound 158-159 DE 2
Yorkton 56-57 Q 7
Yorktown, TX 76-77 F 8
Yorktown, VA 80-81 H 2
Yoro 88-89 C 7
Yorosso 168-169 D 2
Yoruba 168-169 FG 3
Yosemite National Park 74-75 D 4
Yosemite National Park, CA 64-65 C 4
Yoshida 144-145 J 6
Yoshii-gawa 144-145 K 5
Yoshino-gawa 144-145 JK 5
Yoshioka = Taiwa 144-145 N 3
Yōsō-do 144-145 F 6
Yösön Bulag = Altaj 142-143 H 2
Yost, UT 66-67 G 5
Yŏsu 142-143 O 5
Yotala 104-105 D 6
Yotaú 92-93 G 8
Yōtei-dake 144-145 b 2
You'anmen, Beijing- 155 II ab 2
Youanmi 158-159 C 5
Youghal 119 C 6
Youkounkoun 164-165 B 6
Youks-les-Bains = Ḥammāmāt 166-167 K 2
Young, AZ 74-75 H 5
Young [AUS] 158-159 J 6
Young [CDN] 61 F 5
Young [ROU] 106-107 J 4
Younghusband, Lake — 160 BC 3
Younghusband Penisland 160 D 5-6
Young Island 53 C 16-17
Youngstown 61 C 5
Youngstown, FL 78-79 G 5
Youngstown, OH 64-65 KL 3
Younts Peak 66-67 J 4
You Shui 146-147 BC 7
Youshuwan = Huaihua 146-147 B 8
Youssoufia = Yūssufiyah 166-167 B 3
Youth Recreation Park 154 II a 2
Youville, Montréal- 82 I ab 1
Youxi [TJ, place] 146-147 G 8
You Xi [TJ, river] 146-147 G 8-9
You Xian 146-147 D 8
Youxikou 146-147 G 8
Youyang 146-147 B 7
Youyu 146-147 D 1
Yowl Islands = Kepulauan Aju 148-149 K 6
Yoyang = Yueyang 142-143 L 6
Yŏyu 144-145 F 4
Yozgat 134-135 CD 3
Ypacaraí 102-103 D 6
Ypacaraí, Laguna — 102-103 D 6
Ypané, Río — 102-103 D 5
Ypé Jhú 102-103 E 5
Ypoá, Lago — 102-103 D 6
Ypres = Ieper 120-121 J 3
Ypsilanti, MI 72-73 E 3
Ypsilanti, ND 68-69 G 2
Yreka, CA 66-67 B 5
Ysabel = Santa Isabel 148-149 jk 6
Ysabel Channel 148-149 NO 7
Ysleta, TX 76-77 A 7
Yssel Lake = IJsselmeer 120-121 K 2
Ystad 116-117 E 10
Yu'alliq, Jabal — 173 C 2
Yuam, Mae - 141 E 6
Yuam, Mae — 150-151 A 3
Yuan'an 142-143 L 5
Yüan-an = Yuan'an 142-143 L 5
Yüan Chiang = Hong He 142-143 J 7
Yüan Chiang = Yuan Jiang 142-143 L 6
Yüan-chou = Yichun 142-143 LM 6
Yuanchow = Zhijiang 142-143 KL 6
Yuanjiang [TJ, place] 146-147 D 7
Yuan Jiang [TJ, river] 142-143 L 6
Yuankiang = Yuanjiang 146-147 D 7
Yüanlin 146-147 H 9-10
Yuanling 142-143 L 6
Yüan-ling = Yuanling 142-143 L 6
Yuanmou 142-143 J 6
Yuanping 142-143 L 4
Yuanqu 146-147 C 4
Yuanshi 146-147 E 3
Yüan-shih = Yuanshi 146-147 E 3
Yuan Shui 146-147 E 8
Yuantan [TJ, Guangdong] 146-147 D 10
Yuantan [TJ, Henan] 146-147 D 5
Yuanyang 146-147 DE 4
Yuba City, CA 64-65 B 4
Yūbari 142-143 R 3
Yuba River 74-75 C 3
Yūbetsu 144-145 d 2
Yūbetsu, Shimo- 144-145 cd 1
Yūbetu ↖ Kusiro 144-145 d 2
Yubineto 96-97 D 2
Yubo = Lī Yūbū 164-165 K 7
Yucatán 64-65 J 7
Yucatán, Península de — 64-65 HJ 8
Yucatan Basin 64-65 JK 8
Yucatan Channel = Canal de Yucatán 64-65 J 7
Yucca, AZ 74-75 F 5
Yuchán 104-105 DE 8
Yucheng [TJ, Henan] 146-147 EF 4
Yucheng [TJ, Shandong] 146-147 F 3
Yu-ch'i = Youxi [TJ, place] 146-147 G 8
Yu Ch'i = You Xi [TJ, river] 146-147 G 8-9
Yü-chiang = Yujiang 146-147 F 7
Yuci 142-143 L 4
Yudian = Keriya 142-143 E 4
Yudu 146-147 E 9
Yuegezhuang, Beijing- 155 II a 2
Yüeh-k'ou-chên = Yuekou 146-147 D 6
Yüeh-yang = Yueyang 142-143 L 6
Yuekou 146-147 D 6
Yueqing 142-143 N 6
Yueqing Wan 146-147 H 7-8
Yuetan = Altar of the Moon 155 II ab 2
Yueyang 142-143 L 6
Yugan 146-147 F 7
Yugor Strait = proliv Jugorskij Šar 132-133 L 4-M 3
Yugoslavia 122-123 F 3-J 5
Yü-hang = Jiuyuhang 146-147 G 6
Yuheng = Yucheng 146-147 F 3
Yü-hsien = Yu Xian [TJ, Hebei] 146-147 E 2
Yuhsien = Yu Xian [TJ, Henan] 146-147 D 4
Yü-hsien = Yu Xian [TJ, Henan] 146-147 D 4
Yuhsien = Yu Xian [TJ, Shanxi] 146-147 D 2
Yü-hsien = Yu Xian [TJ, Shanxi] 146-147 D 2
Yuhuan 146-147 H 7
Yuhuan Dao 146-147 H 7-8
Yuhuang 142-143 M 4
Yuhuang Ding 142-143 M 4
Yujiang [TJ, place] 146-147 F 7
Yu Jiang [TJ, river] 146-147 B 10
Yü-kan = Yugan 146-147 F 7
Yukarı Doğancılar 136-137 D 2
Yukarı Hadım = Hadım 136-137 E 4
Yukarı ova 136-137 FG 4
Yuki = Yuxi 146-147 G 9
Yukiang = Yujiang 146-147 F 7
Yukigaya, Tōkyō- 155 III b 2
Yuki Mount 58-59 JK 4
Yuki River 58-59 J 4
Yukon, Territoire de — = Yukon Territory 56-57 JK 4-5
Yukon Crossing 58-59 T 5
Yukon Delta 58-59 EF 5
Yukon Plateau 56-57 J 5
Yukon River 56-57 H 4
Yukon Territory 56-57 JK 4-5
Yüksekkum 136-137 C 4
Yüksekova = Dize 136-137 L 4
Yukuduma = Yokadouma 164-165 H 8
Yukuhashi 144-145 H 6
Yulee, FL 80-81 c 1
Yule River 158-159 C 4
Yüli [RC] 146-147 H 10
Yuli [WAN] 168-169 H 3
Yulin [TJ, Guangdong] 150-151 G 3
Yulin [TJ, Guangxi Zhuangzu Zizhiqu] 142-143 L 7
Yulin [TJ, Shaanxi] 142-143 KL 4
Yü-lin = Yulin [TJ, Guangdong] 150-151 G 3
Yü-lin = Yulin [TJ, Guangxi Zhuangzu Zizhiqu] 142-143 L 7
Yü-lin = Yulin [TJ, Shaanxi] 142-143 KL 4
Yulongxue Shan 142-143 J 6
Yulton, Lago — 108-109 C 5
Yü-lung Shan = Yulongxue Shan 142-143 J 6
Yuma, AZ 64-65 D 5
Yuma, CO 68-69 E 5
Yuma Desert 74-75 F 6
Yuma Indian Reservation 74-75 F 6
Yumare 94-95 G 2
Yumari, Cerro — 92-93 F 4
Yumbel 106-107 A 6
Yumbo 94-95 C 6
Yumen 142-143 H 4
Yumu Yumu 106-107 B 7
Yuna 158-159 BC 5
Yunak 136-137 D 3

Yunak 381

Zlîtan 164-165 GH 2
Złobin 124-125 GH 7
Złoczew 118 J 3
Złotów 118 H 2
Zlynka 124-125 H 7

Zmeinogorsk 132-133 P 7
Zmeinyj ostrov 126-127 E 4
Zmejevy gory 124-125 Q 7-8
Žmerinka 126-127 D 2
Zmijev = Gottwaldov 126-127 H 2
Zmijovka 124-125 L 7

Znamenka [SU, Rossijskaja SFSR
　Smolenskaja Oblast'] 124-125 K 6
Znamenka [SU, Rossijskaja SFSR
　Tambovskaja Oblast'] 124-125 N 7
Znamenka [SU, Ukrainskaja SSR]
　126-127 F 2
Znamensk 118 K 1
Znamenskoje [SU, Orlovskaja Oblast']
　124-125 KL 7
Znojmo 118 GH 4

Zoar 174-175 D 7
Zóbuè 172 F 5
Žochova, ostrov — 132-133 de 2
Zogirma 168-169 FG 2
Zōgrafos 113 IV b 2
Zohlaguna, Meseta de — 86-87 Q 8
Zohreh, Rŭd-e — 136-137 N 7
Zok 136-137 J 3
Zola Chăy 136-137 L 3-4
Žolkev = Nesterov 126-127 AB 1
Žolkva = Nesterov 126-127 AB 1
Zollikerberg 128 IV b 1
Zollikon 128 IV b 1
Zoľnoje 124-125 RS 7
Zoločev [SU, Char'kovskaja Oblast']
　126-127 GH 1
Zoločev [SU, L'vovskaja Oblast']
　126-127 B 2
Zolotaja Gora 132-133 XY 7
Zolotar'ovka 124-125 P 7
Zolotonoša 126-127 F 2
Zomba 172 G 5
Zombi Nzoro 171 B 2
Zombo 172 F 5
Zonda 106-107 C 3
Zongcun 146-147 D 8
Zongo 172 C 1
Zonguldak 134-135 C 2
Zongwe 171 AB 4
Zoniënbos 128 II b 2
Zonūz 136-137 L 3
Zoo [SU] 113 V b 2
Zoo [USA, Chicago] 83 II b 1
Zoo [USA, New York] 82 III c 1
Zoo-Baba 168-169 J 1
Zoo Berlin 130 III b 1
Zoological Garden of Al-Qâhirah
　170 II b 1
Zoological Gardens [AUS] 161 II b 1
Zoological Gardens [IND] 154 II ab 2
Zoological Gardens [USA, Houston]
　85 III b 2
Zoological Gardens [USA, New
　Orleans] 85 I b 2
Zoological Gardens of Johannesburg
　170 V b 1-2
Zoological Gardens of Johor Baharu
　154 III a 1
Zoological Gardens of London
　129 II b 1
Zoológico de San Juan de Aragón
　91 I c 2
Zorgo 168-169 E 2
Zorra, Isla — 64-65 b 2
Zorras, Las — 96-97 B 7
Zorritos 96-97 A 3
Zortman, MT 68-69 B 2
Zorzor 164-165 C 7
Zou [DY, administrative unit]
　168-169 F 4
Zou [DY, river] 168-169 F 4
Zouar 164-165 H 4
Zouping 146-147 F 3
Zousfana, Ouèd — = Wâdî
　Zusfânah 166-167 EF 4
Zoushi 146-147 C 7
Zoutpansberge = Soutpansberge
　172 EF 6
Zou Xian 146-147 F 4
Žovkva = Nesterov 126-127 AB 1
Žovtnevoje 126-127 EF 3

Zrenjanin 122-123 J 3
Zribet-el-Oued = Zarîbat al-Wâd
　166-167 K 2

Zuar = Zouar 164-165 H 4
Zuata 94-95 J 3
Zuata, Río — 94-95 J 3
Zubaydîyah, Az- 136-137 L 6
Zubayr, Az- 136-137 M 7
Zubayr, Jabal — 173 C 4
Zubayr, Jazâ'ir az- 134-135 E 7-8
Zubayr, Khawr az- 136-137 MN 7
Zubcov 124-125 K 5
Zubova Poľana 124-125 O 6
Zubovo 124-125 L 3
Zubovskaja = Ali-Bajramly
　126-127 O 7
Zudañez 104-105 D 6
Z'udev, ostrov — 126-127 O 4
Zuénoula 164-165 C 7
Zuera 120-121 G 8
Žufār 134-135 G 7
Zug 118 D 5
Zugdidi 126-127 KL 5
Zug Island 84 II b 3
Zugspitze 118 E 5
Zuiderwoude 128 I b 1
Zuîla = Zawîlah 164-165 H 3
Zuishavane 172 F 6

Zújar 120-121 E 9
Zujevka 124-125 S 4
Zujevo, Orechovo- 132-133 FG 6
Zŭjîtîn, Jabal az- 166-167 L 1-2
Z'uk, mys — 126-127 H 4
Z'ukajka 124-125 U 4
Žukovka 124-125 J 7
Žukovskij 124-125 M 6
Zukur 164-165 N 6
Žuldyz 126-127 O 2
Zulia 94-95 EF 2
Zululand 174-175 J 5-K 4
Zumar, Tur'at az- 170 II ab 1
Zumba 92-93 D 5
Zumbi, Rio de Janeiro- 110 I b 1
Zumbrota, MN 70-71 D 3
Zumikon 128 IV b 2
Zumpango 86-87 L 8
Zumui, Ponta do — 100-101 B 1
Zumûl, Umm az- 134-135 GH 6
Zunderdorp 128 I b 1
Zungeru 164-165 F 7
Zunhua 146-147 F 1
Zuni, NM 74-75 J 5
Zuni Indian Reservation 74-75 J 5
Zuni Mountains 74-75 JK 5
Zunnebeek 128 II a 2
Zunyi 142-143 K 6
Zuo'an 146-147 E 8
Zuo'anmen, Beijing- 155 II b 2
Zuoquan 146-147 D 3
Zuoyun 146-147 D 2
Županja 122-123 H 3
Zûq, Ḥāssî — 164-165 B 4
Zuqar = Zukur 164-165 N 6
Zŭrâbâd 136-137 L 3
Zurak 168-169 H 3
Žuraviči 124-125 H 7
Zurbâṭîyah 136-137 LM 6
Zurdo, El — 108-109 D 8
Zürich 118 D 5
Zürich-Affoltern 128 IV ab 1
Zürich-Albisrieden 128 IV ab 1
Zürich-Altstetten 128 IV a 1
Zürich-Binz 128 IV b 1
Zürich-Enge 128 IV b 1
Zürich-Hirslanden 128 IV b 1
Zürich-Höngg 128 IV ab 1
Zürich-Hottingen 128 IV b 1
Zürich-Leimbach 128 IV ab 2
Zürich-Oerlikon 128 IV b 1
Zürich-Riesbach 128 IV b 1
Zürich-Schwamendingen 128 IV b 1
Zürichsee 118 D 5
Zürich-Seebach 128 IV b 1
Zürich-Seefeld 128 IV b 1
Zürich-Wipkingen 128 IV b 1
Zürich-Witikon 128 IV b 1
Zürich-Wollishofen 128 IV b 1
Zurmi 168-169 G 2
Zurnga Chhu 138-139 J 2
Zuru 164-165 F 6
Zurŭd, Wâd — 166-167 LM 2
Zurzuna 136-137 K 2
Zuša 124-125 L 7
Zusfânah, Wâdî — 166-167 EF 4
Zutiua, Rio — 100-101 B 3
Žutovo = Okt'abr'skij 126-127 L 3
Zuun 128 II a 2
Zuwârah 164-165 G 2
Zuwe 174-175 F 2
Z'uzino, Moskva- 113 V b 3

Zvenigorodka 126-127 E 2
Zvenigovo 124-125 QR 6
Zviaheľ = Novograd-Volynskij
　126-127 CD 1
Zvolen 118 J 4
Zvornik 122-123 H 3

Zwai, Lake — = Ziway
　164-165 M 7
Zwanenburg 128 I a 1
Zwartberg = Swartberg
　174-175 H 6
Zwartkops = Swartkops
　174-175 F 7
Zwartmodder = Swartmodder
　174-175 D 5
Zweibrücken 118 C 4
Zwelitsha 174-175 G 7
Zwettl 118 G 4
Zwickau 118 F 3
Zwiesel 118 F 4
Zwillikon 128 IV a 2
Zwölfaxing 113 I b 2
Zwolle 120-121 L 2
Zwolle, LA 78-79 C 5

Zyŏhana 144-145 L 4
Zyŏzankei 144-145 b 2
Zyr'anka 132-133 cd 4
Zyr'anovsk 132-133 PQ 8
Żyrardów 118 K 2